CYCLOPEDIA
OF
LITERARY
CHARACTERS

CYCLOPEDIA
OF
LITERARY
CHARACTERS

Edited by

FRANK N. MAGILL

HARPER & ROW, PUBLISHERS
New York, Evanston, and London

This work also appears under the title of
Masterplots Cyclopedia of Literary Characters

KEY TO PRONUNCIATION

â	pare, stair	ŏŏ	book, push
ă	man, rang	ōō	moor, move
ā	ale, fate	ou	loud, round
ä	calm, father	p	put, stop
b	bed, rub	r	red, try
ch	chin, reach	s	see, pass
d	day, bad	t	to, bit
ĕ	ten, ebb	th	thin, path
ē	equal, meat	ŧħ	then, mother
è	fern, bird	ŭ	up, dove
f	fill, off	ū	use, cube
g	go, rug	û	surge, burn
h	hot, hear	v	vast, above
ĭ	if, hit	w	will, away
ī	ice, right	y	yet, yam
j	joy, hedge	z	zest, amaze
k	keep, take	zh	azure, seizure
l	let, ball	ə	is a vowel occurring in an un-
m	man, him		accented syllable, as
n	now, ton	a *in*	above
ng	ring, English	e *in*	chapel
ŏ	lot, box	i *in*	veracity
ō	old, over	o *in*	connect
ô	order, shorn oi	u *in*	crocus
oi	boy, oil		

FOREIGN SOUNDS

à	pronounced as in the French *ami*
ll	usually pronounced like *y* in *yes* in Spanish America; in Spain like the *ll* in *million*
ṅ	a nasal *n* pronounced as in the French *bon*
ñ	pronounced like the *ny* in *canyon*
œ	pronounced as in the French *feu* or the German *böse*
r̂r	pronounced as in the Spanish *barranco*
ü	pronounced as in the French *du* or the German *grün*

PREFACE

IMAGINATION is the stock in trade of the storyteller. The characters he creates are the vehicles by means of which he transmits his imagination and insight to his audience. If he is a keen observer and a clever commentator on what he has observed, it is likely that his characters will seem lifelike and identifiable and will make a lasting impression on his readers.

It has been said that the greatest compliment an author can pay a predecessor is to try and emulate his characterizations. We have had innumerable *Milites Gloriosi* and Falstaffs down through the years. Shakespeare, and Dickens, too, supplied enough original character material to keep generations of authors hard at work for a lifetime trying to emulate them. Yet emulation is not always undesirable, for new insights cast new lights. And it is these new lights that make incisive fiction so rewarding. One excuse nonreaders of fiction give for avoiding the medium and devoting their reading time to nonfiction is that reading "make-believe" is a waste of time. Unfortunately for them, this group misses the whole point of character development, an artistic process that enables a wise and skillful author to probe a given "personality" with much greater accuracy and insight than would ever be possible with a complex living organism, including even himself. For example, Flem Snopes could not be any one particular individual in real life. But through him, Faulkner could give us a composite personality that followed a straight line to a sure end. Thus we could be instructed without being impeded by the unpredictable but realistic drawbacks of divergent human responses that are bound to occur in real life.

CYCLOPEDIA OF LITERARY CHARACTERS comprises a collection of more than sixteen thousand characters from some thirteen hundred novels, dramas, and epics drawn from world literature. Within this vast collection are the great names from fiction and drama, familiar characters whose exploits have entertained countless generations of readers. Though the cast of Aeschylus' THE SUPPLIANTS forms the oldest extant characters in European dramatic literature, tribal tales and Oriental literature had their well-developed fictional heroes and villains long before a Greek playwright formalized such figures for the stage.

In this book major characters receive a substantial writeup of perhaps one hundred or one hundred and fifty words in which an assessment of the character is given, a critical evaluation with regard to psychological motivation, development, possible flaws, and related matters. Lesser characters receive less space but they too are ana-

PREFACE

lyzed. Identification and relationships are given for even the most minor characters. Characters in each book appear together, in the order of diminishing importance. Book titles are arranged alphabetically in the text but a special character index of fifty pages will be found at the end of the text, in which characters are listed alphabetically. Thus, a character may be located readily regardless of whether the title of the book in which he appears is known. Following the alphabetical character index will be found an author index which lists all authors whose works are represented in CYCLOPEDIA OF LITERARY CHARACTERS.

The alphabetical character index is a massive collection of names containing 11,949 listings. To keep the index even within this limit certain abbreviations were employed. For example, *etc.,* following a name indicates that other characters of the same family name also appear in the article referred to. Thus, the listing *Babbitt, George F., etc., 72* means that other Babbitts (Myra, Verona, Ted) will also be found in the article on page 72 that includes George. Obviously, many names appear several times in a collection of this size. The name Antonio, for example, appears often in Shakespeare and more than a dozen times throughout this book. In such cases all page numbers on which the name appears are shown in the alphabetical character index.

Pronunciation is given for names likely to be mispronounced and for unfamiliar foreign names. A key to pronunciation with a guide for certain foreign sounds is included.

The preparation of this book has been a long and arduous task and as the project progressed it grew in complexity and scope. But despite the demands, it has been a pleasure to deal intimately for so long with the world's leading literary characters. The substantial writing staff and our tireless proofreaders join me in hoping that this collection will serve a useful purpose for those who are interested in studying the ways in which the master storytellers went about the job of making their characters compelling and timeless.

FRANK N. MAGILL

THE ABBÉ CONSTANTIN

Author: Ludovic Halévy (1834-1908)
Time of action: 1881
First published: 1882

PRINCIPAL CHARACTERS

The Abbé Constantin (à·bā′ kōn·stän-tǎń′), the elderly curé of the parish near the Château Longueval. He is a kindly, thoughtful man. Among his good works is the rearing of the son of an army friend who was killed in battle. The priest is saddened when the nearby chateau is sold to a wealthy American woman, for he is sure that the new owner will not be a Catholic and will not be interested in his work. He is delightfully surprised to find that he is wrong and that the new owners are a blessing to him and his village.

Mrs. Scott, the wealthy new owner of the chateau, an American. As a Catholic she is pleased to help the old curé. She tells the priest of a childhood spent in poverty and a lawsuit which made her a millionaire.

Bettina Percival (bĕ·tē′nà pĕr·sē·vàl′),

Mrs. Scott's young sister. She is a wealthy woman tired of proposals from men who want only her fortune. She falls in love with the curé's godson, Jean Reynaud. When he proves too bashful to ask her to marry him, she arranges, with the abbé's help, to tell the man of her love.

Jean Reynaud (zhäń′ rā·nō′), a brave, charitable, thoughtful young army officer, the abbé's godson. His bashfulness and his deep love for Bettina keep him from declaring himself as the young woman's suitor.

Paul de Lavardens (pôl′ dǝ là·vàr·däń′), a spendthrift young Frenchman from a well-to-do family. He brashly courts Bettina, but to no avail.

Mme. de Lavardens (dǝ là·vàr·däń′), Paul's mother. She is one of the abbé's parishioners and a good woman.

ABE LINCOLN IN ILLINOIS

Author: Robert E. Sherwood (1896-1955)
Time of action: 1831-1861
First presented: 1938

PRINCIPAL CHARACTERS

Abe Lincoln, at twenty-two, in 1831, an awkward, melancholy-minded young backwoodsman with no particular ambition, in 1861 a man of dedicated political principles whose personality and career have been shaped by friendship,

love, loss, marriage, his reactions to the Dred Scott Decision, and the great debates with Stephen A. Douglas.

Ann Rutledge, Lincoln's great love, who agrees to marry him after her engage-

1

ment to another man has been broken. She dies of a sudden fever.

McNeil, Ann's fiancé, who is unable to return from his home in New York State to marry Ann.

Mary Todd, an ambitious young woman who sees in Lincoln the means of fulfilling her own frustrated desires. After their marriage she bears Lincoln four children, but her jealousy and tantrums make his life so miserable that he is forced to shut her out of his election triumph.

Seth Gale, Lincoln's friend. When the possible death of his son Jimmie threatens the Gales' plans to move west, Lincoln, seeing in his friend's predicament a symbol of what could happen to his countrymen's hopes after the Dred Scott Decision, finds his political convictions shaped and strengthened.

Mentor Graham, the New Salem schoolmaster who taught Lincoln grammar and

encouraged his love of poetry and oratory.

Ninian Edwards, Lincoln's political mentor and Mary Todd's brother-in-law. Admiring Lincoln, he urges him to become a candidate for the Illinois State Assembly.

Judge Bowling Green, the New Salem justice of the peace.

Joshua Speed, a New Salem merchant.

Berry, Lincoln's whiskey-drinking partner in a general store. His whiskey drinking bankrupts the partnership and leaves Lincoln with a debt of fifteen hundred dollars.

Judge Stuart, with whom Lincoln opens a law office in Springfield.

William H. Herndon, Lincoln's law partner.

Stephen A. Douglas, Lincoln's political opponent.

Jimmie Gale, Seth's young son.

ABRAHAM AND ISAAC

Author: Unknown
Time of action: Biblical antiquity
First presented: Fifteenth century

PRINCIPAL CHARACTERS

Abraham, the willing servant of God. In spite of internal conflict, on the angel's command he prepares to sacrifice his beloved young son. His long speeches and prayers disclose his misery over losing his favorite child, but no complaint against God's command passes his lips. He is tender and frank in his explanation to Isaac about the necessity for the sacrifice.

Isaac, an appealing human child. He is terrified at the prospect of a violent death and asks if beating would not be suffi-

cient punishment for any unwitting misdemeanor he has committed. Finding that God has ordered the sacrifice, he accepts the situation meekly, but does say that God might have given him a better fate if it had been His will. He asks that his mother not be told about his death, for he hates to see her grieved. First pleading for delay, he changes his mind and requests prompt relief from the terrible suspense. After his reprieve by the angel, he blesses the sheep that is substituted for him, and prays thankfully to "the Holy Trinity(!)"; but during the

2

preparations for the sacrifice of the ram he still fears Abraham's sword and asks if he is not to be struck while his eyes are averted.

Deus, God, who commands the testing of Abraham and the saving of Isaac.

An Angel, the messenger of God. He brings the order to Abraham for the sacrifice of Isaac, and later furnishes the ram for the substitute sacrifice.

[**The Doctor,** who appears at the end to elaborate on the text and explain its meaning.]

ABSALOM, ABSALOM!

Author: William Faulkner (1897-1962)
Time of action: 1807-1910
First published: 1936

PRINCIPAL CHARACTERS

Thomas Sutpen, the owner of Sutpen's Hundred in Yoknapatawpha County, Mississippi. Born of a poor white family in the mountains of Western Virginia, he grows up to become an ambitious man of implacable will. After his arrival in Mississippi he thinks he can win his neighbors' respect by building a huge mansion and marrying the daughter of a respectable merchant. When he is not driving his wild African slaves and a kidnaped French architect to finish construction of his magnificent house, he seeks relaxation by fighting his most powerful slaves. Wishing to found a family dynasty, he wants, more than anything else, to have a male heir. When one son is killed and the other disappears, Sutpen, now aging, fathers a child by Milly, the granddaughter of Wash Jones, one of his tenants. After learning that the child is a girl, he rejects and insults Milly. Because of his callous rejection old Wash Jones kills him.

Ellen Coldfield, the wife chosen by Thomas Sutpen because he believes she is "adjunctive" to his design of founding a plantation family. A meek, helpless woman, she is completely dominated by her husband.

Henry Sutpen, the son born to Thomas and Ellen Sutpen. Unlike his sister Judith, he faints when he sees his father fighting with slaves. At first, not knowing that Charles Bon is also Sutpen's son, impressionable Henry idolizes and imitates that suave young man. Later he learns Bon's true identity and kills him, after their return from the Civil War, to keep Judith from marrying her half brother, who is part Negro.

Charles Bon, Thomas Sutpen's unacknowledged son by his earlier marriage in Haiti. A polished man of the world, he forms a close friendship with the more provincial Henry, whom he meets at college, and he becomes engaged to Judith Sutpen. When the two return from the Civil War, Bon's charming manner does not prevent his being killed by Henry, who has learned that his friend and sister's suitor is part Negro.

Judith Sutpen, Thomas Sutpen's daughter. After Charles Bon has been killed and Henry flees, she vows never to marry. She dies of smallpox contracted while nursing Charles Bon's colored wife.

Goodhue Coldfield, a middle-class storekeeper in the town of Jefferson, the father of Ellen and Rosa Coldfield. When the Civil War begins, he locks himself in his attic and disdainfully refuses to have any part in the conflict. Fed by Rosa, who sends him food that he pulls up in a basket, he dies alone in the attic.

3

Wash Jones, a squatter on Thomas Sutpen's land and, after the Civil War, his drinking companion. While his employer is away during the Civil War, Wash looks after the plantation. Ignorant, unwashed, but more vigorous than others of his type, he serves Sutpen well until the latter rejects Milly and her child by declaring that if she were a mare with a foal he could give her a stall in his stable. Picking up a scythe, a symbol of time and change, Wash beheads Sutpen.

Rosa Coldfield, Goodhue Coldfield's younger daughter. She is an old woman when she tells Quentin Compson that Sutpen, whom she calls a ruthless demon, brought terror and tragedy to all who had dealings with him. A strait-laced person, she recalls the abrupt, insulting fashion in which Sutpen had proposed to her in the hope that she would be able to bear him a son after his wife's death. Never married, she is obsessed by memories of her brother-in-law.

Clytemnestra Sutpen, called Clytie, Thomas Sutpen's former slave, who hides Henry Sutpen in the mansion when he returns, old and sick, years after the murder he committed. Fearing that he will be arrested, she sets fire to the house and burns herself and Henry in the conflagration which destroys that dilapidated monument to Thomas Sutpen's pride and folly.

Milly Jones, the granddaughter of Wash Jones. She and her child are killed by Wash after Sutpen's murder.

Charles Etienne de Saint Velery Bon, the son of Charles Bon and his octoroon mistress. He dies of smallpox at Sutpen's Hundred.

Jim Bond (Bon), the half-witted son of Charles Etienne de Saint Velery Bon and a full-blooded Negress. He is the only survivor of Sutpen's family.

Quentin Compson, the anguished son of a decaying Southern family. Moody and morose, he tells the story of the Sutpens to his uncomprehending roommate at Harvard. Driven by personal guilt, he is later to commit suicide. Before leaving for Harvard he learns about Thomas Sutpen from Rosa Coldfield.

Shrevlin McCannon, called Shreve, a Canadian student at Harvard and Quentin Compson's roommate. With great curiosity but without much understanding, he listens to Quentin's strange tale of Southern passions and tragedy leading to decay and ruin.

ABSALOM AND ACHITOPHEL

Author: John Dryden (1631-1700)
Time of action: Late seventeenth century
First published: 1681

PRINCIPAL CHARACTERS

David, the King of Israel, a poetic representation of Charles II, King of England. Many dissatisfied Jews (Whigs) wish to rebel against him and secure the succession of his illegitimate son, Absalom (the Duke of Monmouth), to the throne. The wiser Jews (Tories) see no cause for revolt against a just ruler.

Absalom, the illegitimate son of David, King of Israel, and a poetic representation of the Duke of Monmouth, illegitimate son of Charles II, King of England. The dissident Jews (Whigs) seek to make him heir to his father's throne.

Achitophel, chief of the rebellious Jews (Whigs) and a poetic representation of the Earl of Shaftesbury, who attempts to persuade Absalom (Duke of Monmouth) to seize his father's throne.

4

Zimri (Buckingham),
Shimei (Sheriff of London), and
Corah (Titus Oates), rebellious Israelite
(Whig) chieftains, whose characters are
sketched by the poet.

Barzillai (The Duke of Ormond),
Zadoc (The Archbishop of Canterbury),
The Sagan of Jerusalem (Bishop of London),

Adriel (The Earl of Mulgrave),
Jotham (The Marquis of Halifax),
Hushai (Laurence Hyde), and
Amiel (Edward Seymour), loyal Israelite
(Tory) chieftains, who convince King
David (Charles II) that his son Absalom
(the Duke of Monmouth) is being used
as a tool by Achitophel (the Earl of
Shaftesbury).

THE ABSENTEE

Author: Maria Edgeworth (1767-1849)
Time of action: Early nineteenth century
First published: 1812

PRINCIPAL CHARACTERS

Lord Clonbrony, owner of large estates in Ireland who absents himself to live in London. He is ignored in fashionable circles, travels with questionable associates, and gets into embarrassing financial circumstances.

Lady Clonbrony, an Irishwoman who apes English manners and speech. She makes herself ridiculous in London. Her chief desire is to see her son marry an heiress.

Sir Terence O'Fay, an impecunious sponger who attaches himself to Lord Clonbrony.

Lord Colambre, son of Lord Clonbrony, a student at Cambridge. He loves Grace Nugent, whom he marries. An honest, level-headed young man, he straightens out his father's financial affairs.

Grace Nugent, a distant relative of the Clonbronys. A beautiful, talented, and well-mannered girl, she eventually becomes Lord Colambre's wife.

Miss Broadhurst, a sensible young woman and an heiress whom Lady Clonbrony hopes to have as a daughter-in-law. Because she is not attracted to Lord

Colambre she eventually marries Arthur Berryl.

Arthur Berryl, a friend of Lord Clonbrony. He falls in love with and marries Miss Broadhurst.

Sir John Berryl, Arthur's father. He almost ends in debtors' prison because of money borrowed from Mr. Mordicai. He dies, leaving his family penniless.

Mr. Mordicai, a coachmaker and money lender.

Sir James Brooke, a British official in Dublin.

Nicholas Garraghty, Lord Clonbrony's agent. He is dishonest and hated by the nobleman's tenants. When he is found out he is dismissed.

Dennis Garraghty, Nicholas' dishonest brother.

Mrs. Raffarty, Nicholas' sister, a silly, affected woman.

Lady Dashfort, an Irish noblewoman who wants Lord Colambre as a son-in-law.

Lady Isabel, Lady Dashfort's daughter, a malicious flirt.

Lord and
Lady Killpatrick, examples of what is worst in the Irish nobility.

Count O'Halloran, Lord Colambre's friend. He loves his native Ireland.

Lord and
Lady Oranmore, examples of what is good in the Irish nobility.

Mr. Burke, an honest agent hired by Lord Clonbrony.

Mrs. O'Neill, one of Lord Clonbrony's tenants.

Brian O'Neill, Mrs. O'Neill's son.

Captain Reynolds, Grace Nugent's dead father. His papers reveal that his daughter is a legitimate child.

Mr. Reynolds, the Captain's father, Grace's grandfather. He is delighted to have the girl turn out to be his rightful heir.

THE ACHARNIANS

Author: Aristophanes (c. 448-c. 385 B.C.)
Time of action: The period of the Peloponnesian War, 431-404 B.C.
First presented: 425 B.C.

PRINCIPAL CHARACTERS

Dicaeopolis (dĭ'kē·ŏ'pō·lĭs), an Athenian farmer whose name means "honest citizen," a shrewd, earthy man who has had enough of deceptions wrought in the name of patriotism and who wants peace with the Spartans at practically any price. Although a loyal Athenian, he recognizes that the Spartans cannot be blamed for all the misfortunes of his homeland, and when the assembly refuses to discuss measures for ending the war, he concludes a separate peace and opens a market where all enemies of Athens may trade. Before a chorus of Acharnian charcoal burners, who wish to stone him as a traitor, he eloquently defends the cause of peace. His wisdom is shown even more plainly near the end of the play when he, in the company of two courtesans, makes ready for the Feast of the Cups, while the pompous militarist Lamachus dons his armor to march away to defend the border.

Lamachus (lă'mə·kəs), a general who is determined to fight the Spartans to the end. A mighty boaster, he at last receives his wounds, not at the hands of the enemy, but while leaping a ditch.

Euripides (ū·rĭ'pĭ·dēz), the tragic poet, who lends Dicaeopolis rags worn by Telephus, one of the most unfortunate of the playwright's heroes, so that Dicaeopolis will appeal to the pity of the Acharnians when he defends the cause of peace before them. Dicaeopolis takes not only the rags but also other accessories, such as a beggar's staff and a broken cup, until Euripides complains that he has parted with enough material for an entire tragedy.

Amphitheus (ăm·fī'thĭ·əs), a friend of Dicaeopolis. Though claiming immortality, he suffers from hunger because of the deprivations of war and arranges a truce with the Spartans for Dicaeopolis.

A Megarian (mĕ·gă'rĭ·ən), a resident of a city near Athens but allied to Sparta. Also suffering from hunger, he resolves to barter his daughters, disguised as pigs, to Dicaeopolis for garlic and salt. Dicaeopolis' examination of the wares leads to a bawdy exchange between the buyer and the seller.

A Boeotian (bē·ō'shĭ·ən), who gives his wares to Dicaeopolis in exchange for Nicharus, an Athenian informer.

6

A Husbandman and
A Bridesmaid, who try to obtain from
Dicaeopolis some of his precious balm of
peace. The former is refused, but when
the latter explains that she wants the substance so that the bride can keep her husband home from the war, Dicaeopolis
gives it to her, exclaiming that women
should not suffer as a result of the war.

The Chorus of Acharnian Elders (ă·kär′-
nĭ·ən), veterans who have fought at
Marathon, made angry when they hear
Dicaeopolis sacrificing to Bacchus after
his truce is concluded. They have suffered
from Spartan raids and are in no mood to
tolerate pacifists. Yet Dicaeopolis, dressed
in the costume he has obtained from
Euripides, speaks so tellingly for peace

that the chorus is divided in sentiment
and does not act against him.

An Ambassador, returned from a mission
sent to seek aid from the King of Persia.
He escorts Pseudartabas, a supposed
emissary from the Persian monarch, and
two disguised Athenian citizens posing
as eunuchs.

Pseudartabas (sōō·där′tə·bəs), the King's
Eye, who pretends to bring Dicaeopolis a
message from the King of Persia.

Theorus (thē·ō′rəs), an envoy sent on a
mission to Thrace. He returns with a
group of ragamuffins who, he announces
proudly, are the host of the Odomanti,
the most warlike soldiers in Thrace, sent
to aid the Athenians. Dicaeopolis is disgusted by his boasting and pretense.

ADAM BEDE

Author: George Eliot (Mary Ann Evans, 1819-1880)
Time of action: 1799
First published: 1859

PRINCIPAL CHARACTERS

Adam Bede, an intelligent young carpenter respected by everyone in the village of Hayslope. He is honored when
Arthur Donnithorne, the young heir to
Donnithorne Chase, has Adam put in
charge of managing the woods on the
estate. Three weeks later, however, he
sees Arthur kissing Hetty Sorrel, the
young woman Adam loves. Knowing
that Arthur will never marry Hetty,
Adam becomes angry and fights with
Arthur. As a result, Arthur leaves to
join his regiment and Hetty, deserted
and pregnant, promises to marry Adam.
When Hetty runs off, Adam is in despair. Later he stands by Hetty through
her trial for the murder of her child.
A man who has judged others—his
drunken father, Arthur, and Hetty—
harshly, Adam learns tolerance and forgiveness. Still later he falls in love with
Dinah Morris, a Methodist preacher, and
marries her.

Dinah Morris, a young Methodist
preacher, niece of Mrs. Poyser, a farmer's
wife in Hayslope. A compassionate
young woman, she aids those ill or in
trouble. When not needed by friends or
her family in Hayslope, she preaches at
Snowfield, a grimy industrial town
twenty miles away. Seth Bede, Adam's
younger brother, is in love with her
and proposes several times, but she says
that her religious dedication takes precedence over any private emotion. She
sympathizes with Hetty Sorrel and gets
Hetty to confess that she had abandoned
her illegitimate baby. Dinah later falls
in love with Adam Bede and recognizes
the claim of private emotions by marrying him.

Captain Arthur Donnithorne, the pleasant and impulsive young heir to Donnithorne Chase who tries to forward Adam
Bede's career. Attracted to Hetty Sorrel,

7

he does not intend to marry her. After he learns that she has given birth to and abandoned his baby, he recognizes that his acts can have fateful consequences for other people. In disgrace, he leaves Hayslope, not to return for seven years.

Hester Sorrel (Hetty), niece of Mr. Poyser, a dairy farmer. Fond of jewels and petty finery, Hetty is an easy prey for young Donnithorne. When she realizes Donnithorne will not marry her, she becomes engaged to Adam Bede; however, in the later stages of her pregnancy, she goes to Windsor to find Donnithorne, only to learn that his regiment has been shipped to Ireland. She then tries to find Dinah Morris, but on the way her baby is born. In confusion, she abandons the child, who is discovered dead. She is tried, found guilty, and sentenced to death, but Donnithorne, just back from Ireland, manages to have her sentence changed to deportation. She dies, a a few years later, while on her way back to Hayslope.

Mrs. Rachel Poyser, a bustling and efficient farmer's wife. Although meddling and talkative, Mrs. Poyser is generous and loyal. She also stands up for her rights and refuses to let old Squire Donnithorne impose a new farming arrangement on her and her husband. She is pleased when her niece Dinah marries Adam Bede.

Martin Poyser, her husband, the owner and manager of prosperous Hall Farm. A genial and understanding man, Poyser is regarded as the leader of the farmers and tradesmen in Hayslope. He is fond of Adam Bede and feels strongly about the deceit practiced by Hetty and Arthur Donnithorne.

Seth Bede, Adam's younger brother. Although more dreamy, less efficient, and less powerful than Adam, Seth is a fine and generous young man. A Methodist, he is in love with Dinah.

Jonathan Burge, Adam's employer, the owner of a firm of carpenters and builders. Burge makes Adam his partner.

Mrs. Lisbeth Bede, the cantankerous yet devoted mother of Adam and Seth. She is strongly partial to Adam and encourages him to marry Dinah Morris.

The Reverend Adolphus Irwine, the rector of Broxton and vicar of Hayslope. He is a genial Anglican clergyman, little interested in doctrine or conversion, who is friendly with both Arthur Donnithorne and Adam Bede. Shocked by Arthur's desertion of Hetty, he does all he can for her at the trial.

Bartle Massey, the intelligent, misogynous local schoolmaster. He values Adam as his prize pupil and teaches him mathematics in night school.

Matthias Bede, the father of Adam and Seth. Once a skillful carpenter, he has become an indolent drunkard. While drunk, he falls into a creek and drowns.

Squire Donnithorne, Arthur's aged and parsimonious grandfather, the owner of Donnithorne Chase. He dies just before Hetty's trial.

Joshua Rann, a shoemaker of Hayslope who also serves as parish clerk and strongly supports the Anglican Church.

Ben Cranage (Wiry Ben), a carpenter who works in Burge's firm. An iconoclastic man and a spirited dancer, he is the only villager who prefers Seth to Adam.

Jim Salt, another carpenter who works for Burge.

Mum Taft, a silent carpenter who works for Burge.

Chad Cranage, Ben's cousin, a blacksmith who is strongly opposed to Methodism.

Bess Cranage (Chad's Bess), his daughter, a young woman fond of wearing

8

finery. She is intermittently converted to Methodism.

Bess Salt (Timothy's Bess), her cousin, the wife of Jim Salt.

Will Maskery, the Hayslope wheelwright and one of the few local Methodists.

Mr. Casson, the rubicund landlord of the Donnithorne Arms.

Mary Burge, the daughter of Jonathan Burge. The townspeople expect her to marry Adam Bede.

Mrs. Irwine, Mr. Irwine's attractive and sophisticated mother.

Miss Lydia Donnithorne, Arthur's aunt and the daughter of old Squire Donnithorne. Adam's insistence on just payment for a screen he made for her causes the old Squire to become antagonistic to him.

Sarah Stone, a widow of Stoniton who takes in Hetty Sorrel and helps her when the baby is born.

John Olding, the farm laborer who discovers Hetty's dead child.

Marty Poyser, the Poysers' oldest, literal-minded son.

Tommy Poyser, the Poysers' second son, dependent and fond of his mother.

Charlotte Poyser (Totty), the Poysers' spoiled young daughter.

Martin Poyser Sr., the old father of Martin Poyser.

Alick, a shepherd on the Poyser farm.

Pym, Arthur Donnithorne's trusted servant.

Satchell, the Donnithorne steward; he suffers a stroke.

Mrs. Pomfret, a lady's maid at Donnithorne Chase who teaches Hetty to mend lace.

Mrs. Best, the housekeeper at Donnithorne Chase.

Mr. Craig, a gardener at Donnithorne Chase who is in love with Hetty.

Dolly, the Burge housekeeper.

Miss Kate Irwine, the older daughter of Mrs. Irwine.

Miss Anne Irwine, her younger sister, frequently subject to headaches.

Lisbeth Bede, the daughter of Dinah and Adam Bede.

Adam Bede, Jr., the son of Dinah and Adam Bede.

THE ADMIRABLE CRICHTON

Author: James M. Barrie (1860-1937)
Time of action: Early twentieth century
First presented: 1903

PRINCIPAL CHARACTERS

William Crichton (Bill), butler to the Earl of Loam. Stuffy, honest, efficient, Crichton has one complaint about his master: he is not contemptuous enough of his inferiors. While in England, Crichton believes that the established social order is absolutely correct. Stranded on an island, however, he believes in the natural selection of leaders. When every-

one realizes how efficient he is, Crichton takes command; he is stern, fair, almost regal in his deportment.

The Earl of Loam, a peer of the realm and Crichton's liberal master. In theory the Earl believes in the equality of all members of society. (Once a month he has his servants in for tea.) Actually, when he

9

has an opportunity to practice his theories in fact, he becomes an ardent believer in the supremacy of the aristocracy. When the yachting party of which he is host is cast away on a Pacific island, he proves completely ineffectual. For a time he is his pompous self until he realizes his utter incapability of leading the stranded party. After Crichton assumes command, the other castaways call him "Daddy," and he seems quite happy doing odd jobs around the camp.

The Hon. Ernest Woolley, nephew of the Earl of Loam and a maker of brilliant epigrams. Ernest is a cheerful, egotistical young man about town with enough shrewdness to avoid work entirely. In London he idles away his time making witty remarks. Soon after being stranded on the island, however, his talent for wit gets him into trouble with Crichton, now the leader of the party. With every epigram that Ernest makes, Crichton dips his head into a bucket of cold water, thus curing Ernest of a useless habit. Proving himself to be very adaptable, he becomes a diligent worker. Upon returning to England, however, he reverts to type, and between epigrams manages to write a book about his island experience, making himself the hero of the adventure. In the book the contributions of the rest of the party, including Crichton, are summarily dealt with.

Lady Mary, oldest daughter of the Earl of Loam. A part of a useless aristocracy, she is haughty, proud, and languorous. After the shipwreck she shows herself to be adaptable and courageous. Unlike her former self in England, she becomes a useful member of the island society. The hunter of the group, she has the opportunity to wait on the "Gov." (Crichton). If a rescue ship had not arrived, she would have been chosen to become Crichton's wife.

Agatha and Catherine, younger daughters of the Earl of Loam. After being on the island for a time, they also learn to do things for themselves and no longer do they depend on maids to answer their every whim. At first the lack of domestic help is trying to them.

Lord Brocklehurst, the man Mary has chosen to be her husband. He is a complete nonentity, a mother's boy, humorless, pompous, correct, cold, and useless.

Treherne, a pleasant and athletic young clergyman. He is the first to realize that Crichton is the natural leader of the group on the island.

Tweeny, in England the "between" maid. When the Earl of Loam decrees that the three sisters can have only one maid among them, she goes with them, mainly to be near Crichton. On the island she proves to be a useful helper.

Lady Brocklehurst, Lord Brocklehurst's formidable, domineering mother. After the return of the seafarers, she tries to learn what really happened on the island.

Rolleston, valet to the Earl of Loam.

Fisher, Lady Mary's maid, who refuses to go on the cruise.

ADOLPHE

Author: Benjamin Constant (1767-1830)
Time of action: Late eighteenth and early nineteenth centuries
First published: 1815

PRINCIPAL CHARACTERS

Adolphe (a·dôlf'), a precocious young man, the narrator. Influenced by his constrained relationship with his father and the strong, unconventional opinions of an older woman of whom he has been a protégé, he finds himself in conflict with himself and with the highly conventional, mediocre society of a small German principality. He sets about the conquest of Ellénore and finally succeeds in winning her away from Count P——. Even while basking in the joys of love, he is annoyed by its constraints. This conflict brings much unhappiness both to him and to Ellénore, and ends only when he is freed by her death, which leaves him desolate.

Ellénore (ĕ·lā·nôr'), the mistress of Count P—— and later of Adolphe. After sharing Count P——'s life for ten years, she gives in to Adolphe's suit and becomes his mistress. Although she is soon aware of his resentment over the constraints that such an affair inevitably places on its participants, she tries desperately to hold on to his love. Unable to prevent the final deterioration of their relationship, she becomes mortally ill.

Count P——, Ellénore's lover of ten years and the acknowledged father of her children. Even after her flight with Adolphe, he offers to settle her again in suitable circumstances, only to have his offer refused.

Baron T——, a friend of Adolphe's father who is asked to influence the young man to make a final break with Ellénore.

THE AENEID

Author: Publius Vergilius Maro (70-19 B.C.)
Time of action: The period immediately following the Trojan War
First transcribed: c. 17 B.C., by order of Augustus Caesar

PRINCIPAL CHARACTERS

Aeneas (ē·nē'əs), the legendary progenitor of the Roman rulers whose son Ascanius, in fulfillment of a prophecy, founded Alba Longa and whose later descendants, Romulus and Remus, founded Rome. The son of Venus and Anchises, King of Dardanus, Aeneas is somewhat more diffident than the warrior heroes of other ancient epics, and he displays the Latin virtues of moderation and filial devotion. Only occasionally does he indulge in righteous indignation. Twice during the siege of Troy he is saved from death by the intervention of his divine mother. After the fall of the city he flees, carrying his aged father on his shoulders and leading his son Ascanius by the hand. In the confusion his devoted wife Creusa is lost. Aeneas searches for her in vain until her shade appears to tell him that he will find his destiny in a distant land. After long wandering Aeneas and his small band of followers arrive in Italy. There he engages in warfare with the people of Latium and Rutuli. Eventually a truce is arranged and he marries Lavinia, the daughter of King Latinus. In her honor he founds the city of Lavinium.

Anchises (ăn·kī'sēz), the King of Dardanus, King Priam's ally in the Trojan War, and the father of Aeneas. A man of great wisdom, he guides his son through many dangers during the wanderings of Aeneas and his followers from Troy to Sicily, where Anchises dies. From the underworld he foretells the greatness of Rome and commands Aeneas to end his travels at the place where he will eat his tables. Though he appears only as a shade within the poem, the old man figures as a sage patriarch in the recital of earlier events.

Ascanius (ăs·kā'nĭ·əs), sometimes called Iulus, the son of Aeneas. He fulfills Anchises' prophecy of the place to settle when he declares, while the Trojans are eating food heaped on large pieces of

11

bread, that they are eating their tables. He takes part in one battle, in which he acquits himself with bravery befitting the future founder of a city and a kingdom.

Creusa (krē·ōō′sə), the wife of Aeneas. After she became separated from her husband and son during the flight from Troy, Aeneas searched for her despairingly until her shade appeared to tell him that she was lost to Troy forever and that in Italy an empire awaited him.

Dido (dī′dō), the Queen of Carthage, whose love for Aeneas causes her death. When Jupiter sends Mercury, the messenger of the gods, to remind Aeneas of his mission, the hero prepares to continue his wanderings, in spite of the vows he has sworn and Dido's pathetic pleas that he remain with her. On the pretext of burning the love tokens he gave her, Dido prepares a funeral pyre and, lamenting her betrayal, kills herself after the departure of Aeneas and his band. Considered one of the most wronged women in all literature, Dido has beauty, charm, and character, though the latter she sacrifices to the whims of Venus.

Anna (ăn′ə), Queen Dido's sister and confidante.

Latinus (lə·tī′nəs), the King of Latium. Because the oracles have foretold that a stranger will appear, marry his daughter, and rule his kingdom, Latinus befriends Aeneas and promises him the hand of Lavinia, the royal princess, in marriage. The prophecy is not immediately fulfilled, however, for Juno, the enemy of Aeneas, sends the Fury Alecto to turn Amata, the wife of Latinus, against Aeneas. Amata finds a confederate in Turnus, the leader of the Rutulians, her choice as a husband for Lavinia. Bewildered and grieved by this dissension, Latinus goes into retirement and Turnus takes command of the Latiums and Rutulians in the war with the Trojans and their allies.

Lavinia (lə·vĭ′nĭ·ə), the beautiful young daughter of King Latinus and his wife Amata. Loved by Turnus but betrothed to Aeneas, she becomes the prize for which the leaders contend in a bloody tribal war. She becomes the bride of Aeneas after the hero has killed Turnus in single combat and peace has been restored.

Turnus (tûr′nəs), the leader of the Rutulians and the enemy of Aeneas. A giant of a man, the favorite of Queen Amata for the hand of Lavinia, Turnus is a braggart warrior who makes good his boasts. Aided by Juno, he is almost successful in defeating the Trojan warriors led by Aeneas. When Turnus is decoyed away from the battle, Aeneas pursues and kills him. After the death of Turnus, according to the decision of the gods, Aeneas and his followers abandon Trojan ways and accept the customs of Latium.

Amata (ə·mä′tə), the wife of Latinus. Goaded by the Fury Alecto, she is moved to hate Aeneas and to plot against him.

Camilla (kə·mĭ′lə), a warrior maiden of the Rutulians brought up in the worship of Diana. She dies in battle, her exposed breast pierced by a Trojan spear, and her death incites Turnus to frenzied rage and even greater efforts against the warriors of Aeneas.

Aruns (ă′rəns), the slayer of Camilla.

Opis (ō′pĭs), the nymph charged by Diana to look over Camilla and protect her. Opis kills Aruns to avenge the death of the warrior maiden.

Evander (ə·văn′dēr), the leader of an Arcadian colony and the ruler of the city of Pallanteum, built on the site of later Rome. In a dream, Tiber, the stream-god, directs Aeneas to seek the help of Evander in the coming battle with the Latium and Rutulian forces under Turnus. The Arcadian leader welcomes Aeneas to his city and sends a band of warriors, under the leadership of his son Pallas, to aid the Trojans.

Pallas (păl′əs), the son of Evander. During a hard-fought battle, Pallas, while trying to rally his followers, meets Turnus in single combat and is killed by the Rutulian. His death causes great grief among the Trojans, and Evander is heart-broken. In the conflict between Aeneas and Turnus, Aeneas is about to spare his enemy's life when he sees that Turnus is wearing a gold-studded sword belt stripped from the body of Pallas. Proclaiming that Pallas really strikes the blow, Aeneas drives his sword through Turnus and kills the Rutulian leader.

Euryalus (ū·ri′ə·ləs) and
Nisus (nī′səs), valiant young Trojan warriors. During the absence of Aeneas, who has gone to Pallanteum to ask Evander for aid, the two leave the beleaguered Trojan camp and steal into the tents of the besieging enemy. There they kill a number of the Latin soldiers and collect trophies of their exploits before they are surrounded and killed. The followers of Turnus parade the heads of the dead heroes before the Trojan camp.

Anius (ă′nĭ·əs), the King of Ortygia, where Aeneas and his followers sail after the ghost of Polydorus has warned them

not to settle in Thrace. At Ortygia the priest of Apollo prophesies that the descendants of Aeneas will rule over a world empire if the wanderers will return to the ancient motherland of Troy. Anchises mistakenly declares that the Trojans had come from Crete.

Celaeno (sə·lē′nō), Queen of the Harpies. When the Trojans land in the Strophades, they unknowingly offend her and she threatens them with famine.

Acestes (ə·sĕs′tēz), the son of a Trojan maiden and a river-god. He rules over that part of Sicily where Aeneas and his followers go ashore to hold funeral games in observance of Anchises' death. Aeneas awards Acestes first prize in the archery contest because he is "the favorite of the gods."

Nautes (nô′tēz), the wisest of the Trojan band. He advises Aeneas to leave the aged and infirm behind with Acestes when the Trojans continue their wanderings.

Palinurus (pă·lĭ·nōō′rəs), the helmsman drowned shortly after the Trojans sail away from the kingdom of Acestes. Venus has offered his life as a sacrifice if Neptune will grant safe convoy to her son and his followers.

AGAINST THE GRAIN

Author: Joris Karl Huysmans (Charles Marie Georges Huysmans, 1848-1907)
Time of action: Nineteenth century
First published: 1884

PRINCIPAL CHARACTERS

M. Des Esseintes (dā·zĕ·săńt′), Jean Des Esseintes' father. He lives in Paris, visiting his wife and child but seldom. He dies while his son is still a young lad.

Mme. Des Esseintes (dā·zĕ·săńt′), Jean Des Esseintes' mother. She is a recluse who has a dread of light and spends her

life secluded in her darkened bedroom. She, like her husband, dies while her son is still quite young.

Jean Des Esseintes (zhäń′ dā·zĕ·săńt′), an effeminate descendant of rugged soldiers of France. As a child he is stubborn and undisciplined. After a series of mistresses

13

as a young man he loses his virility, although he seeks strenuously after sensual pleasure. He retires from the world at thirty and becomes an aesthete. He spends his time with his books and art treasures, excluding the world from his life. This existence almost kills him, and upon his doctor's advice he prepares to return to live a more normal existence in the world he really dislikes.

Miss Urania (ü·rá·nyá'), an American acrobat who is Jean's first mistress. He is attracted by her strength and repelled by a certain prudishness in her.

THE AGE OF INNOCENCE

Author: Edith Wharton (1862-1937)
Time of action: Late nineteenth century
First published: 1920

PRINCIPAL CHARACTERS

Newland Archer, a young lawyer who is a member of New York's high society. Married to May Welland, a girl from his own class, he falls in love with Ellen Olenska and for a time considers running away with her. He never does so because he is bound by his ties of marriage and convention.

Countess Ellen Olenska, A New York girl of good family who has married a Polish nobleman but now wishes a divorce from him. Intelligent and beautiful, she comes back to New York, where she tries to fit into the life she had known before her marriage. She falls in love with Newland Archer. When the young attorney, persuaded by her family, urges her not to seek a divorce, she leaves for Europe without him. Years later Archer's son visits Ellen in Paris.

May Welland Archer, Newland's wife, a typical New York socialite with all the restrictions and forms adopted by that class. She triumphs over Ellen Olenska and saves her marriage with the announcement that she is to become a mother.

Mr. Welland and
Mrs. Welland, May's parents. Rich, conservative, puritanical, they are somewhat shocked by the discovery that their relative, Ellen, plans to divorce her husband.

Clannishly, however, they give in her honor a party at which they announce the engagement of their daughter to Newland Archer.

Mrs. Catherine Mingott, May's grandmother, the mother of Mrs. Welland and a proud old aristocrat who dominates the clan.

Medora Mingott, May's aunt and Ellen's former chaperone. Flighty but goodnatured, she brings Ellen back to the family home in New York after Ellen and her husband have separated.

Mr. van der Luyden and
Mrs. van der Luyden, members of the old, conservative aristocracy. They generously offer to receive Ellen after she has been snubbed by others of her class.

Julius Beaufort, a successful New York businessman. Married, he carries on affairs on the side. Eventually he goes bankrupt.

Mrs. Beaufort, his wife, a fat, pleasant woman tolerant of her husband's philanderings.

Fanny Beaufort, the daughter of Julius by one of his mistresses. She marries Dallas Archer.

Dallas Archer, the son of May and Newland Archer. He manages to cut the ties

14

of formal society which have held his father captive for so long, marries Fanny Beaufort, and leads a more relaxed and happier life than his father's.

Ned Winsett, one of Newland Archer's friends, a journalist who tries to win Archer over to a less restrictive life.

Reggie and
Mrs. Chivers, Newland Archer's fashionable but understanding friends. They entertain him when he is trying to have a rendezvous with Ellen.

Jane Archer, Newland's wise and clever little sister. She has an ear for gossip and spends much time talking over tidbits of information with her mother.

Mrs. Archer, Newland's widowed mother. She intercedes for Ellen with the van der Luydens and manages to persuade them to give a dinner party for her after she has been snubbed by the rest of New York society.

Mrs. Lemuel Struthers, a lively, fat woman much interested in musicians and artists. She is considered quite vulgar by the "better" families.

Mr. Letterblau, the senior partner of the law firm for which Newland Archer works. He directs the young attorney to handle the Olenska divorce case.

Lawrence Lefferts, a society friend of the Archers and the Wellands.

AGNES GREY

Author: Anne Brontë (1820-1849)
Time of action: Mid-nineteenth century
First published: 1847

PRINCIPAL CHARACTERS

Agnes Grey, the pious, sheltered daughter of a clergyman. She takes employment as a governess when her family's financial situation becomes desperate.

Richard Grey, Agnes' father, a poor parson who loses his patrimony in a disastrous speculation.

Mrs. Grey, Agnes' mother.

Mary Grey, Agnes' sister.

Mrs. Bloomfield, mistress of Wellwood. Agnes' first employer, she is convinced that her incorrigible children, Agnes' charges, are angels.

Tom Bloomfield,
Mary Ann Bloomfield, and
Fanny Bloomfield, Agnes' arrogant, disobedient charges.

Mr. Bloomfield, the stern father of Tom, Mary Ann, and Fanny. He blames Agnes when the children misbehave.

Uncle Robson, Mrs. Bloomfield's brother. His encouragement of Tom's cruel behavior brings forth a protest from Agnes and causes her dismissal.

Mrs. Murray, mistress of Horton Lodge and Agnes' second employer.

Rosalie Murray, Agnes' pretty, flirtatious charge at Horton Lodge. At sixteen, she is interested only in making a good match.

Matilda Murray, Agnes' younger charge at Horton Lodge who is interested only in horses.

Edward Weston, the pious, sincere curate at Horton Lodge. He later becomes Agnes' husband.

Mr. Hatfield, the pompous rector of Horton and the rejected suitor of Rosalie Murray.

Harry Meltham and
Mr. Green, suitors of Rosalie.

15

Sir Thomas Ashby, the wealthy, boorish owner of Ashby Park with whom Rosalie makes an unhappy marriage.

Nancy Brown, an old widow at Horton visited by Agnes and Edward Weston during the development of their romance.

AJAX

Author: Sophocles (c. 496-406 or 405 B.C.)
Time of action: The Trojan War
First presented: After 441 B.C.

PRINCIPAL CHARACTERS

Ajax (ā′jăks), the son of Telamon and, excepting Achilles, the strongest and bravest of the Greeks who fought to win Troy. After Achilles was killed, his armor was claimed both by Ajax and by Odysseus; on the testimony of Trojan prisoners that Odysseus had been the more formidable foe, the Greeks awarded the coveted armor to him. Enraged and jealous, Ajax left his tent by night, stealthily, to kill not only Odysseus but Agamemnon and Menelaus as well. The goddess Athena cast a madness upon him so that, thinking them Greek leaders, he massacred the flocks and herds. Sophocles' play begins when Ajax is at the height of his delirium. After the fit has passed, he is seen to be immoderate and proud, but at the same time he commands sympathy not only because of his greatness of spirit but also because he has been, however deservedly, the victim of Athena's terrible wrath. His magnificent sense of personal honor demands that his scheme be eradicated by suicide, an action which he carries out in spite of the pleas of Tecmessa and the Chorus. He is a man of such colossal inner strength, nobility, and self-sufficiency that he is not only alienated from his fellow men but also brought into conflict with the gods themselves.

Odysseus (ō·dĭs′ūs), a resourceful leader of the Greeks at Troy. Ingenious in action and skillful in speech, he is a foil to Ajax. As Ajax is the type of the hero,

Odysseus is the type of the enlightened, reasonable man. Although he is an enemy of Ajax, he is horrified when Athena shows him the hero insanely torturing the animals. After the suicide of Ajax, Odysseus persuades Agamemnon to let Teucer give his corpse an honorable burial and, having befriended Teucer, nobly offers to assist at the funeral. While Ajax was alive, he and Odysseus had been at cross purposes; but after Ajax' death, Odysseus justly pays tribute of respect to the dead hero's greatness.

Teucer (tōō′sər), an archer, the son of Telamon and a captive princess, and a half brother of Ajax. He is absent on a raid during Ajax' madness and subsequent suicide. On his return to the Greek camp he is first taunted by enemies of Ajax because of his brother's shame and then warned by Calchas, the seer, that Ajax' safety depends upon his remaining within his tent for the rest of the day. But by the time Teucer reaches Ajax' tent, the hero has left for the scene where his suicide occurs. There is evidently a deep measure of trust and devotion between the brothers. Defying both Menelaus and Agamemnon, Teucer insists that Ajax be properly buried.

Tecmessa (těc·mēs′sà), a captive, the devoted concubine of Ajax and mother of his son Eurysaces.

Menelaus (měn·ə·lā′əs), King of Sparta and the deserted husband of Helen.

16

Sophocles pictures him as blustering and pusillanimous, eager to defame his dead enemy Ajax by forbidding burial and leaving his body to scavengers.

Agamemnon (ă·gə·mĕm'nŏn), commander in chief of the Greek forces and brother of Menelaus. When he also denies permission to bury Ajax, Teucer defies him. He at last permits the funeral, quite ungraciously, upon the intervention of Odysseus.

Eurysaces (ū·rĭ'sə·sēz), the young son of Ajax and Tecmessa, who receives his father's great shield from Ajax' own hand.

AL FILO DEL AGUA

Author: Agustín Yáñez (1904-   )
Time of action: Spring, 1909–Spring, 1910
First published: 1947

PRINCIPAL CHARACTERS

Don Dionisio (dōn dyō·nē'syō), a parish priest who gives unity to the separate chapters describing the people and festivals of the small Mexican town (of Yahualica?). He is stern and upright, yet understanding and compassionate. He can combine the best of the contrasting philosophies of his two priestly associates.

Padre Reyes (pä'drā r̄rā'yās), his liberal and progressive assistant. He enjoys seeing the parishioners marry and shocks Padre Islas by his earthy talk. He has advanced ideas about such things as the value of life insurance, though he cannot convince any of the town of its value.

Padre Islas (pä'drā ēs'läs), Don Dionisio's narrow-minded and unbelievably conservative associate. Unable to meet the townspeople on a personal basis, he scurries along the sunbaked streets with eyes averted. Yet as the sponsor of the church organization for unmarried girls, he exerts tremendous influence on the community by urging the girls to stay pure by remaining single, and he threatens them with damnation for even wholesome thoughts about the men of the town. After achieving a reputation for saintliness, he ends up in an epileptic fit on the church floor, after which he is separated from the priesthood.

María (mä·rē'ä), an orphan niece of Don Dionisio, who rebels against the drab life of the community and secretly reads newspapers from Mexico and the forbidden "The Three Musketeers." Her final rebellion takes the form of running away with the widow of Lucas González, a woman of doubtful reputation, to follow the revolutionary army fighting against Dictator Porfirio Díaz.

Marta (mär'tä), the other niece of Don Dionisio, twenty and unmarried, who follows the monotonous village pattern, working in the hospital, looking after children, and accepting the social and religious restrictions.

Damián Limón (dä·myän' lē·mōn'), who has returned from the United States "where Mexicans are treated like dogs." But he retorts that at least they get paid in money instead of promises, as in Mexico. Through the machinations of a political boss, he gets a light, six-year sentence after killing Micaela Rodríguez, following a scandalous love affair. Then, managing to escape while on his way to jail at the capital, he brazenly returns to María. She helps him escape again in order to join the revolutionary army.

Timoteo Limón (tē·mō·tā'ō lē·mōn'), a prosperous land owner and father of Damián. He dies of a heart attack following a violent quarrel with Damián over his will.

Micaela Rodríguez (mē·kä·ä'lä r̄ō·drē'gäs), a spoiled only child who learned about freedom while on a visit to Mexico City and tries to reproduce the gay life of the capital in her little town. She shocks it by her indecent dress and shameless flirtations. In the end, stabbed to death by jealous Damián, she dies forgiving him and putting the blame for her death on her own actions.

Gabriel (gä·brē·ĕl'), a young man reared by Don Dionisio. His religious life is upset by four talks with Victoria, a young widow from Guadalajara visiting the town.

Luis Gonzaga Pérez (lwēs gôn·sä'gä pä'räs), once a talented seminary student. Being convinced by Padre Islas of the evil of his natural desires toward the opposite sex, he ends up drawing pictures on the walls of his cell in an insane asylum.

Lucas Macías (lōō'käs mä·sē'äs), a fortuneteller whose prophecies concerning Halley's Comet upset his fellow villagers. Just before his death, receiving news of Madero's revolt, he declares in the words of the title: "The rains are coming. We'll have a fine clearing shower."

Mercedes Toledo (mėr·sä'dēs tō·lē'dō), a young girl of the town.

Victoria (vēk·tō'ryä), a young widow visiting from Guadalajara.

ALCESTIS

Author: Euripides (c. 485-c. 406 B.C.)
Time of action: Remote antiquity
First presented: 438 B.C.

PRINCIPAL CHARACTERS

Admetus (ăd·mē'tŭs), of Pherae, King of Thessaly. Because of his fair and friendly treatment of Apollo, placed at Admetus' mercy for punishment by Zeus, Admetus has been allowed to escape the appointed hour of his death if someone else will die in his place. His wife Alcestis has given her pledge to die for him, and the play opens on the day of her death. Admetus sincerely loves his wife, but he lacks the courage to die as he should instead of letting his wife die for him. Admetus is weak, but not a coward, and because he realizes his own baseness he gains in stature as the play proceeds. He advances from sincere but self-conscious lamentations to deeply moving and completely honest sorrow over his wife's sacrifice. He is saved by his one virtue: he is the best

of friends and hospitality is almost an obsession with him. He welcomes Herakles, hides the fact that his wife is dead, and insists that the great hero remain as a guest. When Herakles discovers the truth, he wrestles with Thanatos—Death —and saves Alcestis.

Alcestis (ăl·sĕs'tĭs), the wife of Admetus. Her offer to die for her husband when all others refuse glorifies the self-sacrificing devotion of a wife. She is also the devoted mother who dies to ensure her children's safety and to preserve the kingdom for her son. On stage she appears rather cold and reserves her passion for her children, but only because, though she does love her husband deeply, she has come to realize that his love is not of the same quality. After

18

Herakles rescues her from Death, she is led in veiled. She is forbidden to speak for three days until her obligations to the gods of the underworld have been fulfilled.

Herakles (hĕr'a·klēz), the son of Zeus and the Greek prototype of great physical strength. He stops at the house of Admetus on his way to capture the man-eating horses of Diomedes. Presented as a jovial, ingenuous boaster, he accepts Admetus' hospitality and drinks until he becomes quite merry. When told the truth about the death of Alcestis, he is stricken with remorse for his conduct and repays Admetus by rescuing Alcestis from Death. He provides comic relief when he is drinking and when, in the final scene of the play, he presents the veiled Alcestis to Admetus. He insists that Admetus take the woman into his household, even though Admetus has sworn to Alcestis that he will never remarry. Thus Admetus is made to refuse at first to take back Alcestis.

Pheres (fē'rēs), the aged father of Admetus. Presented as a horrible old man who refuses to sacrifice his life for his son, he is smug and complacent. He serves to make Admetus realize how ugly his conduct appears to others.

Apollo (a·pŏl'ō), the god befriended by Admetus. He speaks the prologue, and in his conversation with Death he foreshadows the victory of Herakles over Death.

Thanatos (thăn'a·tŏs), the god of death. Unrelenting in his right to take Alcestis, he is defeated by Herakles.

A Maid, an attendant of Alcestis. She describes Alcestis' preparations for death to the Chorus and helps to reveal Alcestis' love for Admetus.

Chorus of Men, citizens of Pherae. Loud in their praise of the devotion of Alcestis, they hold forth hope that Admetus' hospitality will prove a virtue to save him. Though they do not sympathize with Pheres, they realize that it is not in Admetus' place to condemn him and that Admetus breaks one of the most sacred of all rules, to honor one's parents. They rejoice at the rescue of Alcestis.

A Boy (Eumelus) (ū·mē'ləs), the son of Admetus and Alcestis. He breaks into lamentation as Alcestis dies and emphasizes vividly the child-motive in Alcestis. The characterization is not a happy one, for the boy is far too much a miniature adult.

A Servant to Admetus. He supposes Herakles to be fully aware of Alcestis' death and complains bitterly of the hero's unseemly conduct. He tells Herakles the truth. Later he declares that if there had been no death in the family Herakles' conduct would not have been objectionable.

THE ALCHEMIST

Author: Ben Jonson (1573?-1637)
Time of action: Early seventeenth century
First presented: 1610

PRINCIPAL CHARACTERS

Subtle, the Alchemist, a moldy, disreputable cheat. Joining forces with Jeremy Butler and Dol Common, he uses his fund of scientific and pseudo-scientific jargon to fleece the gullible. He promises large returns from transmutation of metals, astrological prophecies, physical nostrums, or whatever seems most likely to entrap his victims. When the master of the house returns, he is forced to take flight without his gains.

Face (Jeremy Butler), Subtle's contact man, who furnishes his master's house as the Alchemist's headquarters. He is a resourceful, quick-witted improviser. Disguised as a rough, blunt captain, he entices victims to the house. When his master, Lovewit, returns home unexpectedly, he arranges a marriage between Lovewit and the Widow Pliant, thereby escaping punishment.

Dol Common, the third of the tricksters, common mistress of the other two. Her dominant personality keeps her quarrelsome cohorts in line. She can act various roles, such as an exotic lady or the Queen of the Fairies to carry out Subtle's various schemes. Along with Subtle she is forced to flee with the jeers of Face following her.

Sir Epicure Mammon, a fantastic voluptuary. He is a veritable fountain of lust and imagined luxury, and he seeks the philosopher's stone to help him to unbounded self-indulgence. When his investment is wiped out by the explosion of the Alchemist's furnace, planned and well-timed by Subtle, Sir Epicure confesses that he has been justly punished for his voluptuous mind.

Abel Drugger, a small-time tobacconist ambitious for commercial success. Engaged to the Widow Pliant, he brings her and her brother Kastril to the Alchemist. He is tricked not only out of his money, but also of the widow.

Kastril, the angry boy, brother of the Widow Pliant. He has come up to London to learn to smoke and quarrel. Face

uses him to get rid of the skeptic, Surly. He is much taken with old Lovewit, who quarrels well, and consents to his sister's marriage with him.

Pertinax Surly, a sour skeptic who prides himself on being too astute to be tricked. First coming to the Alchemist's as a friend of Sir Epicure, he returns disguised as a Spanish don, planning to save the Widow Pliant from Subtle and Face and to marry her. He is driven away by Kastril and loses the widow to Lovewit.

Tribulation Wholesome, an oily Puritan hypocrite from Amsterdam. Himself quite willing to compromise his conscience for profit, he has difficulty restraining his uncompromising companion, Deacon Ananias.

Ananias, a deacon, a hot-tempered zealot who considers even the word Christmas a Papist abomination. Quarrelsome at first, he finally agrees that counterfeiting is lawful if it is for the benefit of the faithful. Along with Tribulation he is driven away by Lovewit.

Dame Pliant, an easy-going, attractive young widow, affianced to Drugger, but perfectly willing to accept another husband. Subtle and Face both hope to marry her, but the latter decides that it is safer to hand her over to Lovewit, his master.

Lovewit, the master of the house who has left London because of the plague. His absence sets up the plot; his return resolves it. He drives away Subtle, Dol, and their victims, but forgives Jeremy Butler (Face) when he arranges a marriage between his master and the rich young widow, Dame Pliant.

ALECK MAURY, SPORTSMAN

Author: Caroline Gordon (1895-   )
Time of action: Late nineteenth, early twentieth centuries
First published: 1934

Aleck Maury, a Southern sportsman. Trained in the classics in childhood by his father and his aunt and further educated classically at the University of Virginia, he becomes a teacher in several small schools and colleges. His principal loves, however, are fishing and hunting, which he cultivates as fine arts.

James Morris, his uncle, a Virginia planter who introduces Aleck to fox hunting.

Victoria (Aunt Vic) Morris, his aunt, a rigorous disciplinarian and learned woman who broadens and stimulates Aleck in his studies.

Julian Morris, his cousin, who hates studies and loves sports.

Doug Fayerlee, owner of Merry Point.

Sarah Fayerlee, his wife.

Molly Fayerlee, the Fayerlees' younger daughter, whom Aleck marries. She dies a number of years later after an operation.

Richard Maury, Aleck and Molly's son. He enjoys swimming and wrestling rather than hunting and fishing. He is accidentally drowned.

Sarah (Sally), Richard's younger sister.

Steve, Sarah's husband, a scholar and author.

Rafe, a handyman in the Maury home, a Negro giant who teaches young Aleck how to hunt coons.

Mr. Jones, a mill owner who takes young Aleck fishing and instills in him a lifelong love of the sport.

Harry Morrow, Aleck's assistant at the seminary and later his superior, president of Rodman College.

William Mason, Aleck's friend from whom he gets a pointer.

Colonel Wyndham, Aleck's friend, a fishing expert.

Jim Buford, a friend with whom Aleck lives for two years after Molly's death.

ALICE ADAMS

Author: Booth Tarkington (1869-1946)
Time of action: Early twentieth century
First published: 1921

PRINCIPAL CHARACTERS

Alice Adams, a dreamer whose family is not rich enough to send her to college. She tries to attract attenion by affected mannerisms. Disappointed in every ambition, she finally stops daydreaming and, reluctantly, enrolls in Frincke's Business College.

Virgil Adams, her father, an employee of the Lamb Wholesale Drug Company

and part discoverer of the formula for a special glue. The co-discoverer has died. The failure of Virgil's project to manufacture the glue is responsible for his having a stroke.

Mrs. Adams, Alice's socially ambitious mother, who nags her husband to make more money but ends up taking in boarders.

Walter Adams, their son, who has stolen three hundred dollars from his employer. He is more interested in gambling with waiters than in dancing with his sister at Mildred's party.

Mildred Palmer, Alice's best friend.

Frank Dowling, a fat, unpopular boy who is the only one attentive to Alice at the dance.

Arthur Russell, a distant relative of the Palmers who is momentarily interested in Alice, then finds her posing repulsive.

Mr. Lamb, who builds his own glue factory and destroys Virgil Adams' prospects.

Charley Lohr, who brings the Adamses news that the absconding Walter has left town.

ALICE IN WONDERLAND

Author: Lewis Carroll (Charles Lutwidge Dodgson, 1832-1898)
Time of action: Victorian England
First published: 1865

PRINCIPAL CHARACTERS

Alice, a curious, imaginative, strong-willed, and honest young English girl. She falls asleep by the side of a stream in a meadow and dreams that she follows a White Rabbit down his hole. She has many adventures in a Wonderland peopled by all kinds of strange characters and animals.

The White Rabbit, anxious, aristocratic, dandified. Alice follows him down his hole, which leads to an enchanted house and garden. The White Rabbit is a Prime Minister of sorts in this Wonderland, for he has close contact with the royalty there and carries out their orders, although he does not institute policy.

The Queen of Hearts, the ill-tempered Queen of Wonderland. She constantly demands that everyone who crosses her to be beheaded. Fond of croquet, she orders Alice to take part in a game in which flamingoes are used for mallets and hedgehogs for balls. She issues an order for Alice's execution at the end of the book, but this order is never carried out because Alice accuses the Queen and all her company of being only a pack of cards, an assertion that turns out to be true.

The King of Hearts, a timid, kindly man. Although he is completely under his wife's power because of her temper, he manages to pardon all her victims surreptitiously.

The Duchess, another member of royalty in Wonderland, a platitude-quoting, moralizing, ugly old woman who lives in a chaotic house. Deathly afraid of the Queen, she is ordered to be beheaded, but the sentence is never carried out.

The Cook, the Duchess' servant. She flavors everything with pepper, insults her mistress, and throws cooking pans at her.

The Cheshire Cat, the Duchess' grinning cat. Continually vanishing and reappearing, he is a great conversationalist, and he tells Alice much of the gossip in Wonderland.

The Duchess' Baby, a strange, howling, little infant. The baby turns into a pig when the Duchess entrusts it to Alice's care.

22

The Knave of Hearts, a timid, poetry-writing fellow accused of stealing some tarts that the Queen has made.

The March Hare, the rude host of a mad tea party to which Alice invites herself and then wishes that she had not.

The Mad Hatter, a riddle-making, blunt, outspoken guest at the tea party. He is a good friend of the March Hare, and at the party the two try to prove to Alice that she is stupid.

The Dormouse, another guest at the tea party. He is a sleepy creature, aroused long enough to recite for Alice and then pushed headfirst into the teapot.

The Gryphon, a mythical creature, half bird, half animal, who escorts Alice to the home of the Mock Turtle so that she may hear the recital of the Turtle's life story.

The Mock Turtle, an ever-sobbing animal. He recites his life's story to Alice and everyone else within earshot.

The Caterpillar, a hookah-smoking insect who perches on the top of a magic mushroom. Officious and easily offended, he tests Alice's intelligence with a series of ridiculous riddles.

Bill, The Lizard, an unfortunate fellow picked by the other animals to go down the chimney of the White Rabbit's house and try to force out Alice, who has assumed gigantic proportions after drinking a magic potion she found on the table.

The Mouse, who greets Alice in the pool of tears which she has made by crying while she was of gigantic size. Now of minute proportions, she is almost overwhelmed by the Mouse, a creature easily offended.

The Lorry,
The Duck,
The Dodo,
The Eaglet,
The Crab, and

The Baby Crab, all creatures whom Alice meets in the pool of her tears and who swim around with her.

Father William and
His Son, characters in a poem that Alice recites. The old man, a former athlete, can still balance an eel on his nose, much to the amazement of his curious and impertinent son. The poem is a parody of Robert Southey's "The Old Man's Comforts."

The Pigeon, a bird Alice meets after she has made herself tall by eating part of the Caterpillar's mushroom.

The Fish Footman, the bearer of a note from the Queen inviting the Duchess to play croquet.

The Frog Footman, the impolite servant of the Duchess; his wig becomes entangled with that of the Fish Footman when the two bow in greeting each other.

The Puppy, a playful animal Alice meets while she is in her small state.

The Flamingo, the bird Alice uses for a croquet mallet in the game with the Queen.

The Hedgehog, the animal that acts as the ball in the croquet game.

Five,
Two, and
Seven, three quarrelsome gardeners of the Queen. When Alice meets them, they are painting red all the white roses in the garden, to obliterate the mistake someone had made in ordering white ones.

Elsie,
Lacie, and
Tillie, three sisters in the Dormouse's story. They live at the bottom of a well and exist solely on treacle.

Dinah, Alice's pet cat in real life.

Alice's Sister, the wise older sister who is charmed by Alice's tales of her adventures in Wonderland.

ALL FOOLS

Author: George Chapman (c. 1559-1634)
Time of action: Sixteenth century
First presented: c. 1604

PRINCIPAL CHARACTERS

Gostanzo, a stern Florentine gentleman. He believes his son Valerio to be a shy, industrious farmer and contrasts his virtues with the supposed aberrations of Fortunio, counseling strong punishment for the filial ingratitude of the latter. He is unexpectedly won over by the elaborate schemes of the young people.

Valerio, his son, known to all but his father as a notorious gambler, drinker, and lover. He revels in schemes to gull Gostanzo and Cornelio, who once succeeded in duping him.

Marc Antonio, a mild-tempered gentleman who is ready to forgive his own son for his supposed secret marriage and is quick to intercede wherever he feels others are being too harsh or unjust.

Fortunio, his older son, a gallant who is enamored of Gostanzo's daughter Bellonora. He is party to all the schemes in the air, although he initiates none of them.

Rinaldo, Fortunio's cynical brother, the intriguer who arranges the elaborate deceptions which enable Fortunio and Valerio to be with their mistresses.

Cornelio, an upstart courtier who appears to be consumed with jealousy of his young wife.

Gratiana, Valerio's bride, a beautiful but penniless girl.

Bellonora, Fortunio's sweetheart. Her strict father, Gostanzo, keeps her under close watch, until he falls into Rinaldo's trap and gives her the much-desired opportunity to be with her lover.

Gazetta, Cornelio's wife. Chafing under her husband's jealousy, she confesses envy of the young women who have not yet settled down to married life; she entertains herself with Cornelio's friends.

ALL FOR LOVE

Author: John Dryden (1631-1700)
Time of action: First century B.C.
First presented: 1677

PRINCIPAL CHARACTERS

Mark Antony (märk ăn′tə·nē), a Roman triumvirate who, in his role of leader, is caught between concern for his people and his love for a woman. Antony shows various human traits as he tries to recapture his position of leadership against invading forces, as he accepts the friendship of his faithful officers, as he considers reconciliation with his wife and family, as he is duped by clever antagonistic individuals, and as he is shown incapable of adapting to these various relationships because of his devotion to Cleopatra, his mistress. Not strong enough or discerning enough to determine her motives, Antony dies a failure.

Cleopatra (klē·ō·pă′trə), Queen of Egypt

24

and mistress of Antony. Steadfast in her love, as she convinces him before his death, she is deluded by some of her servants and shows the vulnerability of the great at the hands of the crafty. Cleopatra is victorious over her peers, in that she averts Antony's return to his family, and she takes her life to avoid the celebration of victory over Antony's troops, a defeat that prompts Antony's suicide. Cleopatra glories in imminent death as the poison of the asp she has applied to her arm flows through her body.

Alexas (ə·lĕk′səs), Cleopatra's eunuch, opposed to his Queen's and Antony's love. Scheming Alexas uses flattery, chicanery, and lies to move people. Knowing that Antony's troops are about to be attacked, he encourages the troops to celebrate in honor of Antony's birthday; learning that Antony has been persuaded by his own officers to defend his position, Alexas connives to have Antony intercepted by Cleopatra as he leaves the city. Alexas also conspires to arouse Antony's jealousy and to cast doubt on Cleopatra's fidelity, and he lies when he tells Antony that Cleopatra has taken her life. Alexas is brought to justice for his perfidy.

Ventidius (vĕn·tĭ′dĭ·əs), Antony's general and faithful follower. Seeing through Alexas' devices, he is able to circumvent some of the disaster intended for his leader. Doubting Cleopatra's motives, Ventidius tries to divert Antony's attention from her. Although discerning, Ventidius becomes the tool of Alexas in one of his tricks. Feeling that he has unwittingly betrayed his leader, he tries to make amends too late. Ventidius takes his own life when he sees Antony dying.

Dolabella (dō′lə·bĕ′lə), Antony's friend who, although faithful, is banished because Antony fears that Cleopatra may fall in love with the handsome young Roman. Dolabella, dedicated to the Roman cause, attempts a reconciliation between Antony and his family. His affinity to Rome and Antony are reflected also in his willingness to see Cleopatra and to say farewell to her for Antony, who, realizing his lack of will, does not see his mistress before he attempts to renew his fight against the invaders. Dolabella's effort to serve is in vain; Antony believes, despite their denials, that Cleopatra and his young follower are in love.

Octavia (ŏk·tā′vĭ·ə), Antony's wife and sister to Octavius, another of the triumvirate. Although a woman of charm and determination, Octavia is no match for Cleopatra in the fight for Antony's love. Octavia's announcement that Octavius will withdraw his army if Octavia and Antony are reunited and the sight of his two daughters cause Antony to give serious consideration to a reconciliation. But his contemplation is relatively short-lived. Octavia accepts the failure of her mission and returns to the Roman camp.

Charmion (kär′mĭ·ən) and
Iras (ī′rəs), Cleopatra's maids. Loyal to their Queen, they are frequent emissaries to Antony in behalf of Cleopatra. Unwilling to face life without her, Charmion and Iras follow the Queen's example and allow themselves to be bitten by the asp that has already poisoned her.

Serapion (sĕ·rā′pĭ·ən), a priest of Isis. Although involved in the action of the play, he is principally a spokesman for the author. He opens the play with announcement of the ill omens and what they portend for Egypt; he also speaks last in pronouncing the valediction over Antony and Cleopatra.

Agrippina (ă′grĭ·pī′nə) and
Antonia (ăn·tō′nĭ·ə), Antony and Octavia's daughters. Their appearance before

25

their father and their delight in seeing him move him momentarily to consider returning to his family.

Myris (mī′rĭs), another priest. He discusses with Serapion the events that bode no good.

ALL MEN ARE BROTHERS

Author: Shih Nai-an (fl. fourteenth century)
Time of action: Thirteenth century or earlier
First transcribed: c. fifteenth century

PRINCIPAL CHARACTERS

Sung Chiang, The Opportune Rain, the greatest of the warrior chiefs and the principal instrument for uniting the many robber bands. A scribe and a poet, he receives divine inspiration and becomes the sworn leader of 107 other chieftains, in part for his brave exploits, his revolutionary poetry inscribed on walls, and his filial piety. While he avenges wrongs done him by warring chieftains, he is not as bloodthirsty or cannibalistic as are the pagan robbers.

Commander Kao and his **Son,** the chief antagonists of the robber chiefs, the evil dictatorial and lascivious usurpers in the name of the Emperor. The latter lusts for a magistrate's wife and because of this another is falsely accused, branded, and exiled. The wife commits suicide and her husband takes his revenge. Their soldiers often desert and go with the robbers. The bands finally unite to overthrow their military oppressors.

Wu Sung, The Hairy Priest, a giant of a man who kills a tiger in hand-to-hand combat and is a great hero. His brother's wife tries to seduce him. Later she takes a lover and the pair murder her husband. Wu Sung then kills the two lovers.

Ch'ai Chin, The Little Whirlwind, a lord of one of the four provinces who befriends the most valorous of the robber chiefs and protects them from Kao. When captured, he is saved by magic.

Li K'uei, The Black Whirlwind, a mixture of gentle and violent characteristics.

The most loyal of all the chieftains, as well as the most vengeful, he kills a false robber who is trying to spy. Gentle in some ways, he insists that his aged mother be brought to their lair, mourns her death from a tiger attack, and bravely kills all the tigers. He causes his commander a great deal of trouble because of his headstrong nature. He often rights wrongs and saves his friend Ch'ai Chin.

Lu Ta, who in protecting a girl is forced to become the priest Lu Chi Shen. This violent captain causes his abbot so much trouble that he is deported, largely because of his drunkenness, but the priest helps bring together the village lord and the robber chief, Li Chung. He opposes Kai and prevents the execution of a military instructor. Called The Tattooed Priest, he is much admired by village lords, robber chiefs, and military leaders.

Ch'ao Kai, The Heavenly King, one of the most resourceful and shifty of the robber chiefs, himself a lord. He starts his career by stealing birthday gifts from his governor, with the help of a teacher and a magician. He flees his territory and sets up as chief among robbers where he takes in refugees. When his band is attacked by the hated Chun family, Ch'ao Kai is killed. The robbers later conquer the Chun family and avenge his death. Sung Chiang follows Ch'ao Kai as chieftain.

Tai Chung, The Magic Messenger, the jailer who has the ability to walk three

26

hundred miles a day. He befriends the captured Sung Chiang and manages to forge release papers for the chieftain, although through a mixup he gets his own death papers and is freed by his friends the robbers, whom he promptly joins as a valuable scout.

Shi Wen Kung, a military instructor in the employ of the hated Chun family, chief antagonists after the death of Kao. It is he who steals a stolen horse intended for Sung Chiang and whose capture is to decide the successor to Ch'ao Kai. A braggart warrior, he nonetheless eludes the band and nearly succeeds in killing the robber leader; but he is finally captured by Lu Chün I.

Kung Sun Sheng, Dragon in the Clouds, a hermit magician twice called to aid in the bandit coalition. He joins in the conspiracy to rob Governor Liang, drugging the guard so that Ch'ao Kai can steal the treasure. Later, by countermagic, he enables Ch'ai Chin to escape a magic spell.

ALL QUIET ON THE WESTERN FRONT

Author: Erich Maria Remarque (1897-   )
Time of action: World War I
First published: 1928

PRINCIPAL CHARACTERS

Paul Bäumer (poul boi′mĕr), a nineteen-year-old soldier in the German army during World War I. Because he has been drafted so young he wonders what he will be able to do to earn a living if he ever becomes a civilian again. In a battle he stabs a French soldier and then, filled with remorse, tries to relieve the dying man's pain. When his conscience hurts him afterward his comrades tell him he has committed no crime. As the war drags on and more of his comrades fall, Paul becomes lonely and philosophical. But the meaning of the war still eludes him. One day in October, 1918, a quiet day on the Western front, he is killed by a stray bullet.

Albert Kropp (äl′bĕrt krŏp), a German soldier, one of Paul's comrades. He loses a leg and is jealous of Paul, who though wounded, loses no limbs.

Müller (mül′ér), a German soldier, a comrade of Paul. He gets Kemmerich's boots when the man is killed. Later, at his death, the boots go to Paul.

Leer (lär), a German soldier, one of Paul's comrades.

Stanislaus Katczinsky (stä′nĭs·lous′ kät-shĭns′kē), a German soldier nicknamed Kat. When he is wounded, Paul tries to rescue him, only to have Kat killed just before they reach safety.

Tjaden (tjä′dĕn), a German soldier. He is punished for insulting Corporal Himmelstoss but feels that the chance to insult the corporal was well worth the punishment.

Haie Westhus (hī′ă wăst′hōōs), a German soldier killed while Paul is on leave.

Detering (dä′tĕ·rĭng), one of Paul's comrades, a farmer before the war.

Kemmerich, one of Paul's comrades. He has a fine pair of boots which his friend Müller takes when he dies.

Corporal Himmelstoss (hĭm′măl·stŏss), a petty martinet who treats his soldiers cruelly.

Frau Bäumer, Paul's mother. She saves her son's favorite foods from her meager rations so that he can have them when he is on leave. She is dying of cancer.

Herr Bäumer, Paul's father.

Erna Bäumer, Paul's sister.

27

ALL THE KING'S MEN

Author: Robert Penn Warren (1905-   )
Time of action: Late 1920's and early 1930's
First published: 1946

PRINCIPAL CHARACTERS

Willie Stark (the Boss), the Governor of the state. A relentless, unyielding man, Willie has the capacity and the will to break anyone who opposes him. Often ruthless, he is not entirely bad, but his dictatorial powers grow until he is the leader of a powerful political machine. Nevertheless, he does more for the ordinary people of his state than did his more aristocratic predecessors. By improving schools, roads, and hospitals, he leaves these things behind him as monuments after his death. At last even Jack Burden realizes that there was a streak of greatness in Stark.

Jack Burden, the narrator and Willie Stark's factotum. Although a capable man, Burden has spells he calls the "Great Sleep." During these periods he becomes completely indifferent to what he is doing at the time. While finishing his Ph.D. dissertation, he went into the "Great Sleep"; as a result, the degree was never completed. A very cynical, sometimes negativistic person, he realizes after Willie's death the hidden greatness in the "Boss's" character. Somehow this realization makes Jack feel better about himself and the rest of mankind.

Anne Stanton, Jack Burden's former sweetheart and the daughter of an earlier governor. After meeting Willie Stark, Anne becomes his mistress, thus bringing destruction to him and to her brother Adam. After Stark's death she finally marries Jack Burden.

Adam Stanton, Anne's idealistic brother. A famous, dedicated surgeon, Adam represents, in many ways, the aristocratic past. His work is his life; money and fame mean little to him. Feeling that his sister has been ruined by a ruthless dictator, Adam shoots Willie and loses his own life in the process.

Judge Irwin (Monty), Jack Burden's real father. A hawk-visaged, still handsome old man, he has made one major error in his life. Through bribery, he managed to obtain a high-paying job. In this way he was able to pay off pressing debts, at the same time causing the death of the man whom he replaced. By doing so, he paved the way for his own downfall. When Jack discovers this indiscretion, the seemingly incorruptible old man commits suicide.

Sadie Burke, Governor Stark's hard-bitten, profane secretary. Feeling betrayed by Willie, the jealous woman has Tiny Duffy tell Adam Stanton about Stark's affair with Stanton's sister. No longer able to tolerate Willie's amorous dalliance with other women, she causes the death of two men—Adam and Willie.

Sugar-Boy O'Sheean (Robert), Willie Stark's devoted chauffeur and bodyguard. He causes Jack Burden many uneasy moments because of his fast, though expert, driving. He kills Adam Stanton after the latter shoots Willie.

Tiny Duffy, the shrewd Lieutenant Governor and Willie Stark's rotund foil. Biding his time, Tiny tells Adam that Anne Stanton is Willie's mistress. In this way the grossly fat Duffy gets revenge for years of ridicule. Although he becomes Governor after Stark's death, Tiny's political future is in doubt.

Sam MacMurfee, Willie Stark's slick political opponent.

28

Tom Stark, Willie's arrogant, football-playing son, who repays his father's pride with disdain.

Lucy Stark, Willie's long-suffering wife, a former schoolteacher.

Mrs. Ellis Burden, Jack's mother and Judge Irwin's mistress.

Miss Littlepaugh, the sister of the man whose job at the power company Judge Irwin got through bribery, thereby causing the man to commit suicide.

ALL'S WELL THAT ENDS WELL

Author: William Shakespeare (1564-1616)
Time of action: Sixteenth century
First presented: 1602-1604

PRINCIPAL CHARACTERS

Helena (hĕl'ə·nə), the orphaned daughter of Gerard de Narbon, a distinguished physician, and the ward of the Countess of Rousillon. She at first regards her love for Bertram, the Countess' son, as hopeless; then, with the independence characteristic of the heroines of Shakespeare's comedies, she resolves to try to win him with her father's one legacy to her, a cure for the ailing King's mysterious malady. Her charm and sincerity win the love and admiration of all who see her except Bertram himself. Hurt but undaunted by his flight from her on their wedding day, she mourns chiefly that she has sent him into danger in the Florentine war and deprived his mother of his presence. She leaves the Countess without farewell, hoping at least to free her husband to return to his home if she is not successful in fulfilling his seemingly impossible conditions for a reconciliation. She contrives through an ingenious trick, substituting herself for the Florentine girl he is trying to seduce, to obtain his ring and conceive his child. Thus she wins for herself a loving and repentant husband.

Bertram (bĕr'trəm), Count Rousillon (rōō·sĭl'yən, rōō·sē·yôn'), a rather arrogant, self-satisfied, impulsive young man. Proud of his noble blood, he feels degraded by the King's command that he marry Helena, and after the ceremony he flees with his dissolute companion Parol-les to the army of the Duke of Florence to escape such ignominy. He wins fame as a soldier, but he fares less well in his personal relationships. First Parolles' essential cowardice and disloyalty are exposed by his fellow soldiers to the young Count who had trusted him. Then his attempt to seduce Diana brings about the very end he is trying to escape, union with his own wife. His antagonism for Helena melts when he hears reports of her death and recognizes the depth of the love he has lost, and he is willingly reconciled to her when she is restored to him.

The Countess of Rousillon, Bertram's mother, a wise and gracious woman who is devoted to both Bertram and Helena and welcomes the idea of their marriage. Her son's calloused rejection of his virtuous wife appalls her and she grieves deeply for his folly, in spite of her protest to Helena that she looks upon her as her only remaining child. After Helena's reported death and Bertram's return, she begs the King to forgive her son's youthful rebelliousness.

Parolles (pā·rŏl'ĕs), Bertram's follower and fellow soldier, who has no illusions about his own character: "Simply the thing I am shall make me live . . . every braggart shall be found an ass." His romantic illusions are nonexistent; he en-

29

courages Bertram to be off to the wars with him, and he aids and abets the attempted seduction of Diana. The quality of his loyalty to his patron becomes all too obvious in the hilarious drum scene when he, blindfolded, insults and offers to betray all his countrymen to free himself from the enemies into whose hands he thinks he has fallen.

The King of France, a kindly old man who has almost resigned himself to the fact that his illness is incurable when Helena comes to court with her father's prescription, which heals him. He believes her the equal of any man in the kingdom and readily agrees to reward her service to him by letting her choose her husband from the noblemen of the kingdom. Only the pleas of Lafeu and the Countess and Bertram's late recognition of Helena's virtues prevent him from punishing the young man severely for his rebellious flight.

Lafeu (lä′fü′), an old lord, counselor to the King and the Countess' friend. He is as much captivated by Helena's grace as his King is, but he blames Parolles chiefly for Bertram's ungentle desertion of his wife. Out of friendship for the Countess

he arranges a marriage between Bertram and his own daughter in an attempt to assuage the King's anger against the Count.

Lavache (lä·väsh′), the Countess' servant, a witty clown who is expert in the nonsensical trains of logic spun by characters such as Touchstone and Feste.

Diana Capilet (dī·ăn′ə kăp′ĭ·lĕt), the attractive, virtuous daughter of a Florentine widow. She willingly agrees to help Helena win Bertram when she hears her story, and she wins a rich husband for herself as a reward from the King for her honesty.

A Widow, Diana's mother, who is concerned about the honor of her daughter and her house.

Violenta (vē·ō·lĕn′tȧ) and **Mariana** (mä·rē·ä′nȧ), the widow's honest neighbors.

The Duke of Florence, the general whose army Bertram joins.

Rinaldo (rĭ·näl′dō), the Countess' steward, who first tells her of Helena's love for Bertram.

ALMAYER'S FOLLY

Author: Joseph Conrad (Józef Teodor Konrad Korzeniowski, 1857-1924)
Time of action: Late nineteenth century
First published: 1895

PRINCIPAL CHARACTERS

Kaspar Almayer, an unsuccessful Dutch trader in Malaya. His ambition is to take a large profit from a secret gold mine and return with his daughter Nina to Amsterdam. He fails to find the mine, is deserted by his wife, and is disappointed by his daughter's elopement with a Malay. Friendless and an addict to opium, he lives out the last of his life in an unfinished house named Almayer's Folly.

Mrs. Almayer, a Malay. Her husband

loses the prospering business her adopted father had left her. She despises her husband and all white men. She wants her daughter to remain a Malay and wants to remain a Malay herself. After her daughter's marriage, Mrs. Almayer returns to her own people.

Captain Lingard, a prosperous trader who adopted Mrs. Almayer as a child and made her his heir.

Nina, the Almayers' daughter, educated

30

as a European despite her mixed blood. She returns to the little settlement of her girlhood because of her mistreatment by whites in Singapore. Although she is attractive to white men because of her beauty, she marries Dain Maroola, a Malay, with whom she is surer she can retain her dignity and self-respect.

Dain Maroola, a Malay. He and Nina fall in love with each other and are married. He is a great man among his own people, being the son of a rajah.

Lakamba, the Rajah of Sambir, Almayer's enemy. He befriends Dain when the young man runs afoul the Dutch authorities and he later becomes Mrs. Almayer's protector.

Babalatchi, Lakamba's chief aide.

AMADÍS DE GAUL

Author: Vasco de Lobeira (c. 1360-c. 1403)
Time of action: First century
First published: 1508

PRINCIPAL CHARACTERS

Amadís de Gaul, the natural son of King Perión of Gaul and Elisena, daughter of King Garinter of Lesser Britain. To be worthy of his beloved, Oriana, the daughter of the King of England, and to win her hand, he becomes a knight and passes through many brave adventures.

King Perión of Gaul, the father of Amadís de Gaul.

Princess Elisena, the mother of Amadís de Gaul.

Galaor, the brother of Amadís de Gaul.

Lisuarte, King of England and the father of Oriana.

Brisena, Queen of England and the mother of Oriana.

Oriana, the daughter of King Lisuarte and Queen Brisena. She is loved by Amadís de Gaul, who wins her hand after many knightly adventures.

Urganda, an enchantress and the protector of Amadís de Gaul.

Arcalaus, a wicked magician.

King Garinter, the grandfather of Amadís de Gaul.

Darioleta, Elisena's attendant. She hides the infant Amadís de Gaul, along with his father's ring, in an ark and sets him afloat.

Gandales, a knight who finds Amadís de Gaul in the sea and rears him.

Gandalín, the son of Gandales.

Languines, the King of Scotland, who takes Amadís de Gaul to his court.

Abies, the King of Ireland and the enemy of King Perión.

Galpano, a haughty robber who is overcome by Amadís de Gaul.

Barsinan, a traitor to King Lisuarte.

Apolidón, the son of the King of Greece.

King Aravigo, an enemy of King Lisuarte and Amadís de Gaul.

Gasquilán, the King of Sweden, who is overthrown in single combat by Amadís de Gaul.

Esplandián, a messenger.

31

THE AMBASSADORS

Author: Henry James (1843-1916)
Time of action: c. 1900
First published: 1903

PRINCIPAL CHARACTERS

Lambert Strether, the chief ambassador of Mrs. Newsome, his betrothed, sent to summon her son Chad back from Paris to the family business in Wollett, Massachusetts. A fifty-five-year-old editor of a review, Lambert Strether has all the tact and diplomacy necessary to accomplish his task, but his sensitivity will not allow him either to complete it or to take advantage of Chad's situation to gain his own ends. He sees Chad as immeasurably better off in Paris, himself as somehow changed and strengthened by his sojourn abroad, though he will not allow himself to stay in Europe after having failed his benefactress. His heady experiences renew his earlier impressions, and he forms friendships, visits cathedrals, and lives easily for the first time since his wife died while bearing their son, also dead. His delicacy—in approaching young Newsome and his mistress, Mme. de Vionnet; in handling Chadwick's sister, brother-in-law, and childhood sweetheart, and in breaking off from Maria Gostrey, who loves him—is the more remarkable when one considers that his own hopes of a rich marriage and great influence have been shattered by his actions.

Chadwick Newsome, called **Chad,** the handsome, twenty-eight-year-old successor to a family business on the one hand and the heir to a modest income from another source. Candid and open-hearted, the graying young man has been so improved by his years in Europe, largely under the tutelage of Mme. de Vionnet, that no thought of his return can really be habored by anyone who has seen him. Although he himself is willing to return for a visit and to con-sider taking over the advertising and sales promotion of the business he is well equipped to run, his proposed marriage to Mamie Pocock is unthinkable. His greatest triumph comes as the result of his mannerly presentation of his sister's group of ambassadors to his Parisian friends, while his saddest duty is to allow his good friend Lambert Strether to return to face the consequences of a diplomatic failure.

Maria Gostrey, a self-styled introducer and tour director and a chance acquaintance of Lambert Strether. A sensitive, genial, and understanding woman, she proves to be the agent through whom the ambassador discovers the irony of Chad Newsome's situation. Her generosity and devotion to her new friend first touch him and then move him deeply when he sees her loyalty and love unencumbered by desire for personal gain.

Mme. Marie de Vionnet (mȧ·rē′ də vē·ôn·nä′), the beautiful Comtesse whose religion and social position will not allow her to divorce an unloved and faithless husband. Gravely lovely and charming, she has educated young Chad Newsome in the social graces and has won his heart and soul. Called a virtuous connection by intimate friends, the arrangement seems shabby to Mr. Waymarsh and Mrs. Pocock, typically closed-minded Americans. Through the efforts of good friends, especially those of Lambert Strether, Mme. de Vionnet is allowed to retain her younger lover in spite of the fact that they have no future beyond their immediate happiness. Her daughter, who was believed by some to be in love with Chad Newsome, settles on a marriage more reasonable and agreeable to all.

John Little Bilham, called Little Bilham, an American expatriate artist and Chad Newsome's close friend. A perceptive, bright young man, little Bilham becomes the confidant of the ambassadors and, along with a friend, Miss Barrace, their interpreters of social and artistic life in Paris.

Miss Barrace, a shrewd, witty, understanding woman living in Paris. She asks Lambert Strether not to force the issue of Chad Newsome's return home.

Mr. Waymarsh, an American lawyer residing in England, Lambert Strether's friend. He accompanies Strether to Paris and directly involves himself in Chad Newsome's affairs when he writes a letter informing Mrs. Newsome that her ambassador is not fulfilling his mission.

Sarah Newsome Pocock, Chad Newsome's older sister. She, her husband, and her sister-in-law are also dispatched as Mrs. Newsome's ambassadors to make certain that Chad returns to America. She and Mr. Waymarsh join forces to separate Chad and Mme. de Vionnet.

James Pocock, Sarah's husband, who during Chad Newsome's absence is in control of the Newsome mills. He enjoys his trip to Paris, sympathizes with Chad, and becomes Lambert Strether's tacit ally.

Mamie Pocock, James Pocock's younger sister, the girl Mrs. Newsome has selected as a suitable wife for her son. Although she accompanies her brother and his wife on their mission to persuade Chad Newsome to return, she loses her personal interest in the young man after meeting John Little Bilham. Little Bilham's announced intention of marrying Mamie helps Chad solve his own problems of loyalty and love in his affair with Mme. de Vionnet.

Jeanne de Vionnet, Mme. de Vionnet's daughter. For a time society assumed that Chad Newsome might be in love with the daughter. Jeanne becomes engaged to M. de Montbron.

M. Gloriani, a sculptor, Mme. de Vionnet's friend, famous in the artistic and fashionable circles of Parisian society.

Mme. Gloriani, his lovely wife.

AMELIA

Author: Henry Fielding (1707-1754)
Time of action: The 1740's
First published: 1751

PRINCIPAL CHARACTERS

Amelia Harris Booth, a beautiful and virtuous young Englishwoman whose troubles begin when she marries William Booth, a young army officer, against her mother's wishes. After the Gibraltar campaign, when her husband is on half-pay in an inactive status, Amelia's life becomes a constant struggle against genteel poverty. Her beauty complicates matters, for several high-ranking men who might help her husband acquire a new command pursue her, in hopes that she will capitulate her charms in return for the help they can give. Amelia also faces the problem of her husband's gambling and philandering. She bears all her tribulations with patience and humility; finally her virtue is rewarded by the inheritance of her mother's estate.

William Booth, a British captain and Amelia's husband. Although he is a meritorious junior officer who served well at Gibraltar, incurring two wounds in the King's service, he has extreme difficulty in securing a new command because he is too poor to buy a commission and without sufficient political influence to gain one. He loves his wife deeply and fears their poverty for her sake. Captain Booth has other problems as well, his weaknesses for gambling and women.

Dr. Harrison, a benevolent Anglican clergyman who regards Amelia almost as a daughter. His kindness and help save Amelia and her family from disaster several times, for the good man lends them his house, advances them money, and is the person whose discoveries eventually place Amelia in possession of her inheritance.

Colonel Robert James, a fellow officer of William Booth during his active military duty. He, unlike Booth, remains in the military service, having the money and influence to rise in the military hierachy and become a member of Parliament. He extends help many times to the Booths through the years, but only because he is secretly desirous of having Amelia as his mistress.

Colonel Bath, another fellow officer. Always conscious of his honor and ready to fight a duel or encourage someone else to fight one, he forces a quarrel on Booth, who wounds the colonel.

Mrs. James, Colonel James's wife and Colonel Bath's sister. She is a great friend to Amelia until the latter's poverty causes that friendship to cool.

Betty Harris, Amelia's sister, a selfish, malicious woman who spreads lies about Amelia and enters into a complicated plot of forgery to deprive Amelia of her rightful inheritance.

Mr. Robinson, a shady character who is in and out of prison. On his deathbed his confession to Dr. Harrison reveals the plot to keep Amelia from her inheritance.

Mr. Murphy, a dishonest lawyer. He plots with Betty Harris to deprive Amelia of her fortune. Eventually apprehended by Dr. Harrison, he is tried, found guilty, and hanged at Tyburn.

Mrs. Ellison, the Booths' landlady in London. Although she seems an honest and well-meaning woman, she serves as bawd to an unnamed nobleman, procuring for him a whole series of women. Amelia's friends prevent her from being so victimized.

Mrs. Bennet, an unfortunate young widow who becomes Amelia's friend. Having been an earlier victim of Mrs. Ellison and the unnamed nobleman, she is able to help Amelia save herself from the plot against her virtue. Mrs. Bennet is loved by Sergeant Atkinson and becomes his wife.

Joseph Atkinson, the son of Amelia's nurse and, in a sense, her foster brother. He enlists in the army in order to be with William Booth and afterward remains in the service. Loyal to Amelia and her husband, he helps in every way he can to keep disaster from overtaking the Booths. He falls in love with Mrs. Bennet, marries her, and buys a commission with their pooled resources.

Fanny Matthews, a handsome, amoral woman who loves William Booth and tries to become his mistress. She is also Colonel James's mistress at the time. She and Booth renew their acquaintance while both are in prison.

THE AMERICAN

Author: Henry James (1843-1916)
Time of action: Mid-nineteenth century
First published: 1877

Christopher Newman, a young American millionaire who is looking for more in life than a business career. He goes to Paris to experience European culture, and he hopes to find a wife who can aid in developing his natural abilities. Both modest and astute, he has a depth of integrity that is recognized by both men and women. He is also generous in his response to the qualities of others. When he meets Claire de Cintré though his friend, Mrs. Tristram, he is drawn to her noble character and touched by her adverse situation. In his relationship with the Bellegarde family, Newman's innate decency stirs some of them to admiration and others to a desire to exploit Newman's naïveté. Newman is refused Claire, who retires to a convent; he is tempted to bargain for her because he has evidence showing that her father was put to death by his wife. But the family knows their man: his innate decency leads him to destroy the incriminating evidence. This action, as his friend Mrs. Tristram points out, was a part of the Bellegarde calculations.

Claire de Cintré, nee **Bellegarde,** a young French woman locked in the rigid confines of her mother's domination. When she was forced into marriage with a worldly old man, her invalid father could not save her; but a few years later her husband's death released her. This is the woman Newman meets and loves. Seeing in Newman a sensitive and reliable man, she responds to his goodness. She is just beginning to feel strength and freedom when the Bellegardes withdraw their permission for her marriage to Newman. She is further distressed when her amiable younger brother dies in a duel. She knows intuitively of her mother's crime of murder, but there seems no way out of her dilemma. She chooses the only path open to her—the convent—where she can at least escape her family. One senses that sorrow has taught her only to endure; she does not know the enormity of her sacrifice in giving up Newman.

Mr. Tristram, Newman's somewhat boisterous American friend.

Mrs. Tristram, a woman much more perceptive than her husband. Her warmth is a kind of sisterly affection for Newman to fall back upon.

Madame de Bellegarde (bĕl·gárd'), a French aristocrat by title but in actuality a hard woman with neither morality nor integrity.

The Marquis de Bellegarde (Urbain), the elder son in the family; he is like his mother in character.

Valentin de Bellegarde, the younger son. He is a man of wit and kindliness. He loves his sister and dies in Switzerland as the result of a duel motivated by his affair with Mlle. Nioche.

Mrs. Bread, the Bellegarde servant who is taken over by Newman after Valentin's dying words instruct her to reveal Madame de Bellegarde's secret.

M. Nioche, an elderly French shopkeeper whose age and experience permit him some philosophical observations.

Mlle. Nioche, his daughter. An indifferent artist, she is able to support herself by her physical charms. She is last seen in London escorted by Valentin's distant cousin, Lord Deepmere.

AN AMERICAN TRAGEDY

Author: Theodore Dreiser (1871-1945)
Time of action: Early twentieth century
First published: 1925

PRINCIPAL CHARACTERS

Clyde Griffiths, the tragic hero. The son of itinerant evangelists and raised in poverty and in an atmosphere of narrow-minded religiosity, he has always longed for the things that money can buy. At sixteen, he gets a job as a bellboy in a Kansas City hotel and uses his unexpectedly large earnings for his own pleasure rather than to help his family. When his sister is left penniless and pregnant, he contributes only a small sum; he is buying a coat for Hortense Briggs, a shopgirl whom he is trying to seduce. Because of a wreck in a stolen car, he has to leave Kansas City. In Chicago he meets his rich uncle, Samuel Griffiths, who gives him a job in his factory at Lycurgus, New York. The job is an unimportant one, and Clyde is resented by his cousins, particularly by Gilbert. Clyde is forbidden to associate with the factory girls, but out of loneliness he becomes friendly with one of them, Roberta Alden, whom he persuades to become his mistress. Meanwhile he is taken up by Sondra Finchley, the daughter of a wealthy family, who wishes to spite Gilbert. They fall in love, and Clyde dreams of a rich marriage. But Roberta becomes pregnant and demands that he marry her, thus shattering his hopes of having all that his life has lacked. When their attempts at abortion fail, Clyde, inspired by a newspaper account of a murder, plans to murder Roberta. Though he intends to kill her, her death is actually the result of an accident. A long trial ensues; but in spite of all efforts, Clyde is convicted, and the story ends with his electrocution.

Roberta Alden, Clyde's mistress. A factory girl and the daughter of poor parents, she falls in love with Clyde, whom she meets at the factory. In spite of her moral scruples, she becomes his mistress. When she finds herself pregnant, she tries to force him to marry her, though she knows that he no longer loves her.

This situation leads to her accidental death at Clyde's hands.

Titus Alden, Roberta's shiftless father.

Sondra Finchley, a wealthy girl who takes up Clyde to spite his cousin Gilbert. She falls in love with him and is planning to marry him when he is arrested for murder.

Asa Griffiths, Clyde's father, a poverty-stricken itinerant evangelist.

Elvira Griffiths, Clyde's mother, the strongest member of the family.

Hester (Esta) Griffiths, Clyde's sister, who is seduced and abandoned by an actor.

Samuel Griffiths, Clyde's uncle, a rich manufacturer who gives Clyde a job in his factory.

Elizabeth Griffiths, Samuel's wife.

Gilbert Griffiths, their son, a pompous young man who resents Clyde.

Myra Griffiths and
Bella Griffiths, daughters of Samuel and Elizabeth.

Hortense Briggs, a crude, mercenary shopgirl whom Clyde tries to seduce. She is interested only in what she can persuade him to spend on her.

Thomas Ratterer, a bellboy who works with Clyde and introduces him to fast life.

Willard Sparser, the boy who steals the car and causes the accident that drives Clyde from Kansas City.

Orville Mason, a ruthless and politically ambitious district attorney who prosecutes Clyde.

36

Burton Burleigh, Mason's assistant. In the morgue he threads some of Roberta's hair into Clyde's camera to provide the evidence necessary for conviction.

Alvin Belknap and
Reuben Jephson, defense attorneys.

Governor Waltham, of New York, who rejects Clyde's plea for commutation of sentence.

The Rev. Duncan McMillan, an evangelist. He brings Clyde spiritual comfort just before the execution.

AMPHITRYON

Author: Titus Maccius Plautus (c. 254-184 B.C.)
Time of action: The Heroic Age
First presented: c. 185 B.C.

PRINCIPAL CHARACTERS

Amphitryon (ăm·fĭt'rĭ·ən), a Theban general whose life becomes complicated when he goes off to fight the Teloboans. During his absence his wife gets with child by Jupiter, and Amphitryon, discovering the affair, is ordered by the god not to treat his wife harshly, for she acted unknowingly.

Alcmena (ălk·mē'nə), Amphitryon's wife who welcomes Jupiter, disguised as Amphitryon, to the marital bed. Pregnant with Amphitryon's child, she is able to bear Jupiter's also, because he makes time stand still until his child, Hercules, can be born.

Jupiter (jōō'pə·tər), a Roman god who,

having disrupted Amphitryon's life, apologizes for his chicanery and reconciles the husband and wife before he departs for other adventures.

Mercury (mêr'kyə·rĭ), the god who, to help his father Jupiter in his affair with Alcmena, assumes the guise of Sosia, Amphitryon's slave. Mercury, as Sosia, stands guard while Jupiter, as Amphitryon, woos Alcmena.

Sosia (sō'sĭ·ə), Amphitryon's slave, who becomes very much confused when Mercury, as Sosia, convinces the slave that he, Mercury, is actually Sosia. Sosia suddenly realizes that he has lost his identity.

AMPHITRYON 38

Author: Jean Giraudoux (1882-1944)
Time of action: The Heroic Age
First presented: 1929

PRINCIPAL CHARACTERS

Amphitryon (äṅ·fē·trē·ôṅ), a general of Thebes whose wife is seduced by Jupiter.

Alkmena (ălk·mē'nə), the wife of Amphitryon to whom she has promised to commit suicide if she ever knowingly deceives him. She is seduced by Jupiter, who comes to her in the guise of her

husband. The god saves her from self-destruction by convincing her that he has never visited her as a lover.

Jupiter (jōō'pə·tər), master of the gods, who plots the seduction of Alkmena. Disguised as Amphitryon, be begs to be admitted to her chamber as a lover. This

37

the logical, virtuous Alkmena refuses, but the god gains easy access to her bed as her husband.

Mercury (mér′kyə·rĭ), Jupiter's half son. He helps his father plan for the seduction of Alkmena. Disguised as Sosie, Amphitryon's servant, he sets the stage for the appearance of Jupiter in Alkmena's bedchamber.

Leda (lē′də), the Queen of Sparta. She has been seduced by Jupiter, who came to her disguised as a swan. Desiring another encounter with the god, she is persuaded to take Alkmena's place in the bedchamber to which he plans a second celestial visit.

Sosie (sŏ·zē′), the servant of Amphitryon and Alkmena.

AND QUIET FLOWS THE DON

Author: Mikhail Sholokhov (1905-   )
Time of action: 1913-1918
First published: 1928

PRINCIPAL CHARACTERS

Gregor Melekhov (grĭ·gō′rĭy mĕ·lĕ-khōf′), a native of the Don basin in Russia. He is married to one woman but openly goes about with another. His father whips him and he leaves home. He joins the army and distinguishes himself in action. When the Soviet Socialist Republic is established and civil war breaks out, Gregor joins the Red Army and is made an officer. When the Red Army is beaten, Gregor, after denouncing the cruelty of Podtielkov, his old revolutionary leader who is about to be executed, returns to his village.

Piotra Melekhov (pyō′trə mĕ·lĕ·khōf′), Gregor's elder brother, who is in the army with him. When the revolutionary troops advance on Tatarsk, their home village, Piotra is named commander of the villagers who are organized by a counterrevolutionary officer.

Natalia Melekhova (nä·tä′lĭ·yä mĕ·lĕ-khō′və), Gregor's wife. When she realizes that Gregor does not love her, she tries to commit suicide. After Gregor dis-

covers that his mistress has been unfaithful to him, Natalia and Gregor are reconciled and she bears him twins.

Aksinia Astakhova (äk·sĭ·nyä äs·tä′-khə·və), Gregor's mistress, married to Stepan Astakhov, who mistreats her. Her affair with Gregor becomes a village scandal. She goes away with him, and they become servants to a wealthy landowning family. When Gregor goes away to join the army, she is unfaithful to him with Eugene Listnitsky, the son of the family. The affair is broken off by Gregor, who whips her and goes home to his wife.

Ilia Bunchuk (ĭl·yä′ˌbŏŏn·chŏŏ′k), a revolutionary leader and the chief agitator in his company. He deserts the company before he can be handed over to the authorities. He joins the revolutionary troops as a machine gunner and is prominent in the administration of the local revolutionary government. He falls in love with Anna Poodko, a woman machine gunner who is killed.

ANDRIA

Author: Terence (Publius Terentius Afer, c. 190-159 B.C.)
Time of action: Second century B.C.
First presented: 166 B.C.

38

Simo (sī'mō), an aged Athenian. An outspoken, philosophical man, Simo has arranged a marriage between his son Pamphilus and Philumena, the daughter of his friend Chremes. Chremes breaks the engagement when it is discovered that Pamphilus is enamored of Glycerium, the sister of a courtesan. To test his son's fidelity, Simo goes ahead with preparations for the wedding. Advised of this ruse, Pamphilus pretends to agree to the marriage, but to his distress, Chremes renews the offer of his daughter's hand. Then Chremes discovers that Glycerium has borne Pamphilus' son and again breaks the engagement. Simo is berating his son for disgracing the family name when Crito, an Andrian, reveals that Glycerium is the long-lost daughter of Chremes. Overjoyed, Simo and Chremes order the marriage of Pamphilus and Glycerium to proceed.

Pamphilus (păm'fə·ləs), Simo's agreeable and moderate young son. He has fallen in love with Glycerium, made her pregnant, and promised to marry her. Simo's abrupt order that he marry Chremes' daughter leaves Pamphilus facing a dilemma: he must either disobey his father or betray his beloved Glycerium.

Davus (dā'vəs), Simo's servant. Deciding his love for Pamphilus is stronger than his fear of Simo, Davus, in spite of Simo's warnings, tries to disrupt the marriage plans. When Pamphilus, acting of Davus' advice, finds himself in a dilemma, Davus cleverly contrives to inform Chremes that Glycerium has borne Pamphilus' child. Simo has Davus imprisoned for his effrontery, but he is freed when all turns out well.

Sosia (sō'sĭ·ə), a former slave whom Simo had freed in appreciation of Sosia's faithfulness. Simo reveals to Sosia his plan to test his son's character.

Glycerium (glĭ·sē'rĭ·əm), Chremes' daughter, originally named Pasibula.

Shipwrecked with her uncle in Andros, Glycerium had grown up there as the daughter of an Andrian family.

Chremes (krā'mēz), a wealthy Athenian and Simo's friend. He is father of both Glycerium and Philumena.

Chrysis (krē'sĭs), a beautiful young Andrian who had become a courtesan after her arrival in Athens. Glycerium, reared as Chrysis' sister, had come to Athens with her. On her deathbed Chrysis had made Pamphilus swear to marry Glycerium.

Charinus (kă·rī'nəs), a young Athenian in love with Philumena. Pamphilus promises he will try to win Philumena for Charinus.

Crito (krī'tō), a native of Andros who comes to Athens to attend to the estate of his dead cousin, Chrysis. After a sharp exchange with Simo, who thinks Crito is a confidence man, Crito convinces Simo and Chremes that Glycerium is really Chremes' daughter.

Byrrhia (bĭ'rĭ·ə), Charinus' servant. Overhearing Pamphilus agree to marry Philumena, Byrrhia thinks his master is being betrayed.

Philumena (fĭ'lə·mē'nə), Chremes' daughter.

Mysis (mē'sĭs), Glycerium's maidservant. Davus stages an argument with Mysis to reveal to Chremes that Glycerium has borne Pamphilus' child.

Lesbia (les'bĭ·ə), the tippling midwife who is called to attend Glycerium.

Dromo (drō'mō), a servant called by Simo to carry off Davus.

Phania (fā'nĭ·ə), Chremes' brother. Pasibula, later named Glycerium, had been entrusted to Phania's care at the time of the shipwreck. He died in Andros.

39

ANDROMACHE

Author: Euripides (c. 485-c. 406 B.C.)
Time of action: About a decade after the Trojan War
First presented: c. 426 B.C.

PRINCIPAL CHARACTERS

Andromache (ăn·drŏ'mə·kē), the widow of Hector, allotted at the fall of Troy as a slave to Neoptolemus, son of Achilles. The prologue, spoken by Andromache, gives the necessary background. Andromache has borne a son, Molossus, to Neoptolemus; then he married a Spartan princess, Hermione, who blames her own sterility on the machinations of Andromache. For this reason Hermione wishes to kill both Andromache and her son and has called her father, King Menelaus, from Sparta to help her. Andromache has hidden her son and taken refuge at the altar of Thetis, for Neoptolemus has gone to Delphi to atone for his insolence to Apollo. The speech is restrained and dignified; Andromache, though a slave, is still the daughter of a great people. Hermione appears to see if her enemy will leave the sanctuary to face death. Andromache refuses and answers the accusations of Hermione directly, displaying the pride that at times gets the better of her discretion. Menelaus appears and reveals that he has found Andromache's son and that she must either surrender herself to be killed or sacrifice the child. In her pride she cannot resist insulting Menelaus as an example of undeserved reputation, but she does give a reasoned and effective plea for her life and that of her child. Menelaus then reveals that the son will be surrendered to Hermione to do with as she likes. Betrayed, Andromache delivers a violent tirade against Spartans and ends with a dignified statement that she will never flatter the Spartans with a plea for mercy. Peleus appears however, and saves both mother and child, who then disappear from the play.

Hermione (hûr·mī'ə·nē), the daughter of

Menelaus and Helen, wife of Neoptolemus. Proud of her Spartan heritage and independent of her husband, she attributes her sterility to Andromache. She states a major theme of the play, that a man who wishes to live happily should have only one wife, but this fact does not excuse the jealousy, cruelty, and impiety resulting from her sterility. Andromache rightfully accuses her of the lustfulness of her mother, Helen. When Menelaus leaves without her, she becomes hysterical and immodest and attempts suicide. Her fear of death is wild and none sympathizes with her. Orestes, Hermione's former suitor, appears. She leaves with him, feeling no remorse over the change of husbands.

Peleus (pē'lūs), the father of Achilles and grandfather of Neoptolemus. His rescue of Andromache is possible because of his rank as ruler of Pharsalia, but his attack on Menelaus as a general who has received far more credit than he deserved and on the Spartans and the causes of the Trojan War is an effective debasement of that "glorious war." He learns later of Orestes' plan to kill Neoptolemus, is too late to prevent the murder, but is assured by his former wife, the goddess Thetis, that Andromache's children will carry on the royal line and that she will take him to live with her eternally.

Menelaus (měn'ə·lā'əs) the King of Sparta and father of Hermione. Brutal, cynical, and self-satisfied, he appears glorious, Andromache points out, only because he has the power of wealth. He bases his interference in Hermione's struggle against Andromache on the fact that a woman must rely on her kinsman and on the sophists' argument that he has the right to dispose of what belongs to Neoptolemus, since they are friends.

Orestes (ō·rĕs'tēz), the son of Agamemnon and Clytemnestra, formerly betrothed to Hermione. Knowing that the murder of Andromache was attempted, he takes Hermione from Phthia. He reveals his plot to have Neoptolemus killed at Delphi because of Neoptolemus' refusal to give up his claim to Hermione.

Molossus (mŏ·lŏs'ŭs), the son of Andromache and Neoptolemus. Andromache's blessing in the person of a son emphasizes her contrast with the sterility of Hermione.

A Slave Woman, formerly the servingmaid of Andromache in Troy. She emphasizes the first impression of the dignity of Andromache.

A Nurse, the servant of Hermione. She reveals Hermione's reaction to the failure of her plan to kill Andromache.

Thetis, a goddess, chief of the Nereids and wife of Peleus. She commands that the body of Neoptolemus be buried at the Pythian temple and promises that Peleus will be transformed into a god.

Chorus of Phthian Women. They sympathize with Andromache, though they point out at times that she is hardly modest. They show only fear of Hermione and have not a word to say for her; they praise Peleus and disapprove of Menelaus because of his use of power to pervert justice. They speak of the disasters resulting from the Trojan War and wonder that the gods allowed that struggle.

ANDROMAQUE

Author: Jean Baptiste Racine (1639-1699)
Time of action: Shortly after the Trojan War
First presented: 1667

PRINCIPAL CHARACTERS

Andromaque (än·drô·màk'), the widow of Hector, the Trojan hero, and mother of his small son Astyanax. Andromaque, now a slave of the Greek hero Pyrrhus, spurns his advances; she has promised to be true to her dead husband. Pyrrhus does nothing to bring Andromaque to a real understanding of her situation as his slave. Frantic with love for her, Pyrrhus threatens to kill her son if she will not marry him, but he counters his extravagant threats against the boy's life with equally extravagant promises for the future of Andromaque and her son. Pyrrhus actually fosters Andromaque's capacity to live in a dream, in a world of words, of codes, of courtly manners, until her mind is filled with a view of her past estate so incurably romantic that she cannot comprehend her present condition. Pyrrhus finally abandons hope of

marrying Andromaque and repledges himself to Hermione, whereupon Andromaque begs Hermione to spare the life of Astyanax. Still jealous of Andromaque, Hermione rejects her plea. Andromaque, in order to save the life of her son, consents to marry Pyrrhus, but she remains full of unrealistic contrivance. Having obtained Pyrrhus' promises to guard her child forever, she plans to kill herself immediately after the wedding rites. Andromaque is still on this high note of idealistic foolhardiness when Pyrrhus is killed by the soldiers of Oreste.

Pyrrhus (pēr·rüs'), the King of Epirus, Achilles' son, betrothed to Hermione. He has come to regret his exploits in the Trojan War because they may have cost him Andromaque's love. He tries to move Andromaque by threatening to kill

41

her son. He is so wild with love that, like Oreste, he becomes unreasonable and unmanly. Aristocratic, demanding, he must have his way with Andromaque, whatever the cost, and despite his pledge to Hermione, who also must have her way. Caught in a situation designed to reveal the follies of a passion out of control and out of bounds, Pyrrhus is not so much a character as passion's ruin, although there are glimpses of the regal man he might be when rational.

Hermione (hĕr·myôn'), the daughter of Menelaus and Helen of Troy. Oreste loves her; she loves Pyrrhus; and Pyrrhus loves Andromaque, who has solemnly vowed to be true to her dead husband Hector. This situation brings out the worst in the four lovers. Each seeks his own satisfaction so that not a single altruistic action is born from the love of one for another, and tragedy ensues. While Pyrrhus vacillates between his promise to marry Hermione and his desire to wed his slave, the beautiful Andromaque, haughty Hermione vacillates between loving and hating Pyrrhus. Hermione rejects Oreste to accept the hand of Pyrrhus, encourages Oreste when Pyrrhus turns from her, rejects Oreste and triumphs over Andromaque when Pyrrhus returns to her, recalls Oreste to her side when Pyrrhus again rejects her, and arranges with Oreste the murder of Pyrrhus. After the death of Pyrrhus the proud and wretched Hermione spurns Oreste once again. She admits to him at last that she has always loved Pyrrhus, that she lied when she told Oreste she could not marry him because she was betrothed by her father and bound by her duty as a Greek princess to Pyrrhus. Though cruel and treacherous, Her-

mione is also pitiful in her plight. She commits suicide upon viewing Pyrrhus' body.

Oreste (ô·rĕst'), the son of Agamemnon, sent to Epirus to demand the death of Astyanax. Morbidly longing for his own death, melancholic, self-centered, adolescent, driven to frenzy whenever his passions are thwarted, Oreste believes himself born to be a living example of the wrath of the gods. For Hermione's sake he forsakes the course that his honor and his reason suggest to him. Careless of honor and duty, he arranges the murder of Pyrrhus on Pyrrhus' wedding day, only to have Hermione reject him because he has murdered the man she loves. Wild with disappointment, Oreste takes leave of his senses and in madness is borne from the stage.

Pylade (pē·làd'), Oreste's good friend. He provides the voice of reason to balance Oreste's passion, but his friendship leads him to conspire in the wild plot to kill Pyrrhus.

Cléone (klā·ôn'), Hermione's handmaiden. She counsels reason and self-control.

Céphise (sā·fēz'), Andromaque's good friend and counselor, another voice of practical good sense and duty in the midst of the emotional storms that agitate the characters in this drama.

Phoenix (fā·nēks'), the old man who counsels Pyrrhus. Phoenix' wise advice is ultimately an instrument for furthering the tragedy. The tides of passion cannot be stemmed in the young by the advice of the rational and the old.

ÁNGEL GUERRA

Author: Benito Pérez Galdós (1843-1920)
Time of action: Late nineteenth century
First published: 1890-1891

Ángel Guerra (än'hĕl gä'rrä), an idealistic widower of thirty whose unhappy childhood causes him to turn revolutionist. Defying his wealthy, domineering mother, he chooses the company of the violent, unsavory Babel family who, in spite of his later reformation, finally cause his death.

Doña Sales (dō'nyä sä'läs), Ángel Guerra's rich, overbearing mother. Her attempts to force her son into submission to her will drive him to take up with the criminal Babel family.

Encarnación (Ción) (än·kär·nä·thyōn'), Ángel Guerra's beloved little daughter.

Lorenza (Leré) (lō'rän'thä; lä·rä'), Encarnación's twenty-year-old tutor. On the death of her charge, she enters a convent in Toledo where, in his loneliness, Ángel Guerra follows her. Through her influence he seeks the comfort of the Church.

Arístides García Babel (ä·rēs'tē·ṭẖäs gär·thē'ä bä·bĕl') and
Fausto García Babel (fä'ōōs·tō gär·thē'ä bä·bĕl'), dishonest brothers, who, in an attempt to flee justice, demand money of Ángel Guerra. They stab him in a quarrel over his refusal to pay.

Dulcenombre (Dulce) Babel (dōōl·thä·nōm'brä bä·bĕl'), Ángel Guerra's mistress. She later enters a convent.

Padre Casado (pä'drē kä·sä'ṭẖō), a priest who is preparing Ángel Guerra for holy orders.

Captain Agapito Babel (ä·gä·pē'tō bä·bĕl'), an ex-slaver.

Matías Babel (mä·tē'äs bä·bĕl') and
Policarpo Babel (pō·lē·kär'pō bä·bĕl'), unsavory children of Captain Agapito Babel.

Dr. Maquis (mä'kēs), physician to Doña Sales.

ANNA CHRISTIE

Author: Eugene O'Neill (1888-1953)
Time of action: Early twentieth century
First presented: 1921

Anna Christopherson, a girl abandoned by her seagoing father and, after the death of her mother, raised by farmer relatives in Minnesota. She is a buxom, attractive girl who learns from farm boys the facts of life. In St. Louis she becomes a prostitute. She goes to New York to join her father, who now is skipper of a coal barge. When her father fights a man who has resolved to get Anna for his own, Anna realizes that men regard women as their property. At the end, Anna, her father, and her lover are reconciled, and Anna is to be married at last.

Chris Christopherson, Anna's father, a

man whose family has paid a dreadful toll in lives to the sea. Chris loves his daughter and sailing ships; he hates steam vessels and especially hates the men who stoke the furnaces in them. He opposes Anna's lover because he follows the sea in a steamship.

Mat Burke, Anna's lover, who is rescued from the sea one night when the "Simeon Winthrop" rides at anchor in the outer harbor of Provincetown, Massachusetts. Burke's Irish glibness both attracts Anna and makes her suspicious. When Burke, one night after a fight with Chris, learns Anna has been a prostitute, he calls her names and storms

43

out of her life. When he returns and talks with Anna, however, they realize they are in love.

Marthy Owen, an old prostitute who lives on the coal barge with Chris. When

Chris learns Anna is leaving St. Louis for New York, he asks Marthy to leave. She consents to move on to someone else because, as she says, Chris had always been good to her.

ANNA KARENINA

Author: Count Leo Tolstoy (1828-1910)
Time of action: Nineteenth century
First published: 1875-1877

PRINCIPAL CHARACTERS

Anna Karenina (än·nə′ kä·rĕ′nĭ·nə), Karenin's beautiful, wayward wife. After meeting the handsome officer, Count Vronsky, she falls completely in love with him, even though she realizes what the consequences of this act of infidelity may be. In spite of love for her child, she cannot give up Vronsky. Estranged from her husband, this unhappy woman, once so generous and respected, has an illegitimate child, runs off with Vronsky, and finally, when his love seems to wane, commits suicide by throwing herself in front of an approaching railway engine.

Count Alexey Kirilich Vronsky (ä·lĕk·sā′ kĭ·rĭ′lĭch vrōn′skĭy), a wealthy army officer who eagerly returns Anna Karenina's love. He is not a bad man; in fact, he is thoughtful and generous in many ways, as he proved when he gave part of his inheritance to his brother. But he thinks nothing of taking Anna away from her husband. Actually, such behavior is part of his code, which includes patronizing his inferiors. After Anna's death he becomes a gloomy seeker after death.

Alexei Karenin (ä·lĕk·sā′ kä·rĕ′nĭn), a public official and a cold-blooded, ambitious man whose main desire is to rise in government service. Seemingly incapable of jealousy or love (except self-love), he allows Anna to see Vronsky away from home. He is afraid only that

his reputation will be blemished by his wife's infidelity. In spite of his cold temperament he is a good official who knows how to cut red tape and bureaucratic inefficiency.

Sergey Alexeyich Karenin (sĕr·gā′ ä·lĕk-sā′ĭch kä·rĕ′nĭn), called **Serezha** (sĕ-rĕ′zhə), Anna Karenina's bewildered young son. Recognizing the schism between his father and mother, he is often distraught by what he senses but does not understand.

Konstantine Levin (kôn·stän·tĭn′ lĕ′vĭn), a prosperous landowner. A fine, decent man, he intensely dislikes all forms of chicanery and hypocrisy. With his generous spirit and democratic outlook, he wants to help his peasants by giving them larger profits from their work on his estate. In return he believes they will work better in his behalf. Forgetting his pride, he finally marries Kitty Shtcherbatskaya, and together they work hard to make his agricultural theories succeed.

Prince Stepan Oblonsky (stĕ·pän′ ôb-lōn′skĭy), a high government official and Anna's brother. With his strong well-fed body, he is the very picture of robust energy. A kind, often guilt-ridden man, he has a bachelor's temperament, and he finds it practically impossible to be true to his unattractive, jealous wife. After each affair he strongly feels his guilt and tries to make amends, only to be smitten by the next pretty face he sees. He is so cheerful and happy that people like to be around him.

Princess Darya Oblonskaya (dä'ryə ôb-lōn'skə·yə), called **Dolly**, Oblonsky's long-suffering and unattractive wife. Faced with her husband's infidelity, she finds solace in her six children. Although she often threatens to leave him, she never does, and she becomes partly reconciled to his philandering.

Princess Catharine Shtcherbatskaya (shchĕr·bät'skə·yə), called **Kitty**, Dolly's younger sister who cannot choose between sober, generous Konstantine Levin and the more dashing Count Vronsky. When she learns that Vronsky obviously is not interested in marriage, she knows she has made an error in refusing Levin's proposal. After a short period of despondency she, naturally buoyant and happy, realizes that the future is not completely gloomy, and she marries Levin.

Prince Alexander Shtcherbatsky (ä·lĕk-sän'dĕr shchĕr·bät'skĭy), a bluff, hardy man, the father of Kitty and Dolly. He likes Levin as Kitty's suitor because he is often suspicious of Vronsky's intentions toward his daughter. His cheerfulness lifts the spirits of his associates.

Princess Shtcherbatskaya (shchĕr·bät'-skə·yə), Dolly and Kitty's ambitious mother. At first she hopes Kitty will marry handsome Count Vronsky. Later she is willing to accept Levin as Kitty's husband.

Nicholas Levin (nĭ·kô·lĭ' lĕ'vĭn), Konstantine's brother. A rather pitiful figure, he is aware of his approaching death from tuberculosis. Dreading his fate, he is a somber man, subject to violent rages and childish behavior.

Sergius Ivanich Koznyshev (sĕr'jĭ·ŭs ĭ·vän'ich kŏz'nĭy·shĕf), Konstantine Levin's half brother, a noted novelist and philosopher whose favorite pastime is debating the issues of the day. Although he

has many convincing arguments, it is doubtful that he understands the peasants as much as his more inarticulate brother.

Countess Vronskaya (vrōn'skə·yə), Count Vronsky's mother. An emaciated old woman, she tries to keep her favorite son under close watch. Failing in this effort, she withholds his allowance.

Mary Nikolavna (mä'ryə nĭ·kō'ləv·nə), called **Masha** (mä'shə), Nicholas Levin's mistress. She looks after the sick man as she would a child, even though he does not seem to appreciate her attempts to help him.

Tanya Oblonskaya (tän'yə ôb·lōn'-skə·yə), Prince Oblonsky's daughter.

Grisha (grĭ'shə), Oblonsky's son.

Princess Elizabeth Fëdorovna Tvershaya (fyō'dərəv·nə tvĕr·shä'yə), called **Betsy**, who acts as a go-between for Vronsky and Anna. Like many women in her social set, Betsy has a lover.

Agatha Mikhaylovna (mĭ·hī'lə·vnə), Levin's trusted housekeeper and confidante.

Princess Myagkaya (myäg·kä'yə), who likes to gossip and has a sharp, vituperative tongue.

Lieutenant Petritsky (pĕt·rĭt'skĭy), Count Vronsky's friend, a hard-drinking gambler. His commanding officer often threatens to expel him from the regiment.

Prince Yashvin (yä'shvĭn), Vronsky's friend. Like Petritsky, he is a hard drinker and an inveterate gambler.

Kuzma (kōōz·mä'), Levin's manservant.

Mikhail (mĭ·hä·ĭl') and **Piotr** (pyō'tr), Vronsky's servants.

Piotr Ivanovich (pyō'tr ĭ·vä'nə·vich), a professor.

Petrov (pĕt·rōf'), an invalid artist dying

45

of tuberculosis. He is infatuated with Kitty.

Anna Pavlovna (än'nə päv'ləv·nə), Petrov's jealous wife.

Sappho Stolz, a full-blown actress.

Lisa Merkalova (lĭ'sə mĕr·kä'lə·və), Betsy Tvershaya's friend. A beautiful, charming girl, she always has a number of ardent admirers following her.

Nicholas Ivanich Sviyazhsky (nĭ·kô·lĭ' ĭ·vä'nĭch svĭ·yä'zh·skĭy), a wealthy landowner and a marshal of the nobility.

Mlle. Varenka (vä·rĕn'kə), Kitty's friend. She is wholesome and pure, and her greatest pleasure is caring for the sick.

Mme. Stahl, Mlle. Varenka's malingering foster mother. According to one person, she never gets up because she has short legs and a bad figure.

Annushka (än·nūsh'kə), Anna Karenina's maid.

ANNA OF THE FIVE TOWNS

Author: Arnold Bennett (1867-1931)
Time of action: Late nineteenth century
First published: 1902

PRINCIPAL CHARACTERS

Anna Tellwright, deprived of love and money in childhood. She inherits fifty thousand pounds from her mother's estate upon reaching twenty-one. The money makes little difference in her life, for she turns it over to her father and, later, her fiancé to manage for her. She discovers she really loves Willie Price, but she is already engaged and refuses to break her betrothal to Henry Mynors.

Henry Mynors, Anna's fiancé. A sound businessman, he knows the value of money and teaches in the Sunday School, thus acquiring the approval of Anna's father. He dominates Anna as her father does.

Ephraim Tellwright, Anna's father, a wealthy, miserly ex-preacher. A stern Wesleyan, he rears his daughters most frugally. He gives his children little love.

Beatrice Sutton, Anna's friend. She brings Anna out a little into society and shows her that a little money well spent can make life far pleasanter. When Beatrice is seriously ill, Anna nurses her competently and lovingly.

Willie Price, a young man in love with Anna. After his father's business failure, he decides to start afresh in Australia. But when he discovers the extent of his love for Anna, and its hopelessness, and also learns that his father was a thief, he commits suicide by throwing himself into the shaft of an abandoned mine.

Agnes Tellwright, Anna's half sister. She is the daughter of Ephraim and his second wife, also dead.

Titus Price, Willie's father and one-time tenant of Anna. His factory is one property owned by the young woman. His business fails and he is proved a thief. He hangs himself.

Mrs. Sutton, Beatrice's mother, a social leader.

ANNALS OF THE PARISH

Author: John Galt (1779-1839)
Time of action: 1760-1810
First published: 1821

PRINCIPAL CHARACTERS

The Reverend Micah Balwhidder, appointed to the Presbyterian church in the village of Dalmailing in western Scotland, in the 1760's. Appointed without the approval of the congregation, he is harshly rebuffed at first but the resentment soon dies and he is accepted. He fights earnestly against smuggling and drinking. He also fights a losing battle against the appearance of other church groups in his parish. He serves his congregation for fifty years, from 1760 to 1810. He decides to retire when he finds himself deaf and forgetful.

Betty Lanshaw, a distant cousin of Mr. Balwhidder. He marries her because he feels that a minister can best serve his people when he is married. She dies a few years after their marriage.

Lord Eaglesham, a nearby nobleman who becomes Mr. Balwhidder's close friend and helps him in his good works.

Thomas Thorl, a dour Scot. He is the most outspoken of the people who resent the appointment of Mr. Balwhidder. He is, however, the first to relent.

Mrs. Malcolm, a widow with five children. Mr. Balwhidder does a great deal to help her and her family.

Charles Malcolm, one of the Widow Malcolm's sons. He becomes a successful officer in the merchant marine. His death in a naval battle saddens Mr. Balwhidder, who has come to regard him almost as a son.

Lizy Kibbock, Mr. Balwhidder's second wife, who gives the congregation a good example by her industry and thrift, making her family independent of her husband's salary.

Mr. Cayenne, an American Tory who sets up a weaving mill in Dalmailing.

Mrs. Nugent, a widow of good reputation who becomes Mr. Balwhidder's third wife.

Mr. Heckletext, a visiting minister who embarrasses Mr. Balwhidder by turning out to be the parent of an illegitimate child in Dalmailing.

Lady MacAdam, a domineering woman of the parish who is sometimes a problem for Mr. Balwhidder.

ANTHONY ADVERSE

Author: Hervey Allen (1889-1949)
Time of action: Late eighteenth and early nineteenth centuries
First published: 1933

PRINCIPAL CHARACTERS

Anthony Adverse, the illegitimate son of Denis Moore and Maria; grandson and heir of John Bonnyfeather, under whom he serves as an apprentice. Anthony becomes a slave trader in Africa and a banker, businessman, and plantation owner in New Orleans. Successively captured by Indians and by soldiers, he is imprisoned in Mexico, and later bleeds to death after an accident there. Anthony

47

is more a romantic, daring man of action than an intellectual. In the variety of his adventures he resembles the heroes of picaresque fiction, but he has neither their low-caste background nor their roguish character.

Don Luis, Marquis da Vincitata, the arrogant husband of Anthony's mother and landlord of Casa Bonnyfeather. He fails in an attempt to murder Anthony and Vincent Nolte. Later governor at Santa Fé, Don Luis dies of a stroke after sentencing Anthony to prison.

Maria Bonnyfeather, daughter of John Bonnyfeather, mother of Anthony, and wife of Don Luis. She dies in childbirth.

John Bonnyfeather (secretly the Jacobite Marquis of Aberfoyle), Anthony's grandfather, a prominent merchant of Leghorn.

Faith Paleologus, Mr. Bonnyfeather's lustful housekeeper who seduces young Anthony. She becomes Don Luis' mistress and afterward his wife.

Angela Guiseppe, Faith's daughter and Anthony's mistress and mother of his son. She is later a mistress to Napoleon.

Florence Udney, Anthony's first wife. She is burned to death with Maria, her young daughter by Anthony.

Dolores de la Fuente, Anthony's second wife, a relative of Don Luis de la Casas. She bears Anthony two children.

Vincent Nolte, Anthony's friend, a banker.

Sandy McNab, Mr. Bonnyfeather's chief clerk.

Denis Moore, an Irish-French nobleman, Maria's gallant lover, who is killed by her husband.

Captain Jorham, skipper of the American ship "Wampanoag."

Father Xavier, a Jesuit priest, Anthony's childhood guardian, who tells him of his origin and of his being Mr. Bonnyfeather's heir.

Gallego, a slave trader who owes money to Mr. Bonnyfeather. He dies in Africa.

Don Luis de la Casas, captain-general in Havana.

Father François, a compassionate monk shipped from Cuba to Africa for aiding and comforting slaves.

Ferdinando, Gallego's factor in Africa, crucified by Mnombibi.

Mnombibi, an African witch doctor.

Neleta, Ferdinando's half-breed sister; Anthony's mistress, whom he deserted.

Captain Bittern, skipper of the "Unicorn."

M. Ouvrard, a French financier.

David Parish, husband of Florence Udney, whom Anthony marries after David's death.

Anna Frank, the cousin of Vincent Nolte and guardian of Anthony's son.

Mary Jorham, the young niece of Captain Jorham.

ANTIGONE

Author: Sophocles (c. 496-406 or 405 B.C.)
Time of action: Remote antiquity
First presented: 441 B.C.

PRINCIPAL CHARACTERS

Antigone (ăn·tĭg′ə·nē), the daughter of Oedipus, sister of Eteocles, defender of Thebes, and Polynices, an exile from the city and one of its attackers. After Eteocles and Polynices have killed each other in battle, Creon, Antigone's uncle and now King of Thebes, decrees that Eteocles' body shall be buried with honors befitting a national hero but that Polynices' body shall be left unburied, a prey to scavengers. Divine law, Greek custom, and simple humanity demand, however, that Antigone see her brother buried; she must choose, therefore, between obedience to the temporal rule of Creon and the duty she owes to a brother she had loved. Although she knows that her fate will be death, she chooses to bury the body of her brother. She is undoubtedly strong-willed and defiant; having been apprehended by the guards posted to prevent the burial, she replies to Creon's wrathful accusations of treason with an equal ferocity. Yet she emerges as immensely heroic, for she alone seems clearly to understand that the King's law is inferior to divine law and that if sacrifice is required to follow the right, such sacrifice must be made. She is always aware of the glory of her deed and dies for love in the largest sense of the word, but her concurrent awareness of her youth and her loss of earthly love humanizes her and makes her a profoundly tragic figure.

Creon (krē'ŏn), King of Thebes. Although he gives lip service to the necessity for order and for obedience to the law, he is a tyrant who has identified the welfare of the state with his own self-interest and self-will. He commits hybris through his violent misuse of his temporal power; he too has a duty to bury the dead, and his unjust condemnation of Antigone to death is murder of a near relative, although he changes her sentence from stoning to burial alive in order to avoid the formal pollution which would accompany such a deed. He has a regard for the external forms of religion but no understanding of its essential meaning. When Tiresias brings the gods' curse on his actions, he relents, but too late to save Antigone or his son.

Haemon (hē'mŏn), Creon's son, engaged to wed Antigone. He attempts to placate his father. Failing, he declares his fidelity to Antigone. When Creon comes to release Antigone from the cave in which she has been entombed, he finds that she has hanged herself and that Haemon is embracing her suspended body. Haemon attempts to kill his father, then falls on his own sword.

Ismene (ĭs·mē'nē), Antigone's sister, as gentle and timid as Antigone is high-minded and strong. She pleads a woman's weakness when Antigone asks her to help with Polynices' burial, yet her love for her sister makes her willing to share the blame when Antigone is accused.

Eurydice (ū·rĭd'ĭ·sē), Creon's wife. She kills herself when she is informed of Haemon's death.

Tiresias (tī·rē'sĭ·ɔs), a prophet who brings to Creon a warning and a curse that cause him belatedly to revoke his decision to execute Antigone. He is the human in closest affinity with the divine; his intercession is therefore equivalent to divine sanction for Antigone's deeds.

THE ANTIQUARY

Author: Sir Walter Scott (1771-1832)
Time of action: Late eighteenth century
First published: 1816

49

Lovel (Major Neville), a wealthy young man of undetermined background who is forced to fight a duel and then go into hiding because he thinks he has mortally wounded his opponent. By a stroke of luck, he overhears a conversation that helps him act to save the fortune of the nobleman whose daughter, Isabella, he wishes to marry. Because of his uncertain parentage, she gives him no encouragement. Eventually, however, he is proved to be an aristocrat. His proper background established, he and Isabella are married.

Edie Ochiltree, a beggar and Lovel's friend. It is Ochiltree who is instrumental in helping Lovel save Sir Arthur from financial ruin. Ochiltree leads Sir Arthur to a cave on his property where Lovel, supposedly abroad, has hidden a chest of money. When Ochiltree "discovers" the money, the aristocrat's financial troubles are ended.

Jonathan Oldbuck of Monkbarns, an antiquarian and a friend of Lovel and Sir Arthur. It is through his good offices that Sir Arthur discovers the chest of money in the cave and Lovel and Isabella finally can marry.

Dousterswivel, a charlatan who extorts money from innocent people by asking a fee for which he promises to favor them by finding minerals or treasure, for example, on their property. Dousterswivel meets his match in Ochiltree, for the latter embarrasses the magician and also gives him a good scare.

The Earl of Glenallan, who is told by a spiteful mother that his wife is his sister. Thus, when his wife bears a son, he is distraught. The boy's mother takes her own life. It is learned that the baby, whisked away by a servant, is actually Lovel, whose benefactor had been the Earl's brother.

Captain Hector M'Intyre, Oldbuck's nephew, who forces Lovel to duel. Because Lovel thinks he has killed Hector, he goes into hiding. Hector recovers, but Lovel does not learn the truth until much later.

Sir Arthur Wardour, a nobleman whose daughter is loved by Lovel. Restored to financial security by Lovel's efforts, Sir Arthur blesses the marriage of Isabella to Lovel.

Miss Isabella Wardour, Sir Arthur's daughter, who eventually becomes Lovel's wife.

ANTONY AND CLEOPATRA

Author: William Shakespeare (1564-1616)
Time of action: c. 30 B.C.
First presented: 1606-1607

PRINCIPAL CHARACTERS

Mark Antony (märk ăn'tə·nē), also Marcus Antonius, the majestic ruin of a great general and political leader, a Triumvir of Rome. Enthralled by Cleopatra, he sometimes seems about to desert her for her real and dangerous rival: Rome. He marries Caesar's sister Octavia for political reasons, but returns to Cleopatra. His greatness is shown as much by his effect on others as by his own actions. His cynical, realistic follower Enobarbus is deeply moved by him; his soldier's adore him even in defeat; his armorbearer remains with him to the death; even his enemy Octavius Caesar praises him in life and is shocked into heightened eulogy when he hears of his death. Antony is capable of jealous fury and reckless indiscretion; but he bears the aura of greatness. He dies by his own hand after hearing the false report of Cleopatra's death, but lives long enough to see her once more and bid her farewell.

Cleopatra (klē·ō·pā′trə), Queen of Egypt. Considered by many critics Shakespeare's greatest feminine creation, she has the complexity and inconsistency of real life. Like Antony, she is displayed much through the eyes of others. Even the hard-bitten realist Enobarbus is moved to lavish poetic splendor by her charm and beauty. Only Octavius Caesar, of all those who come in contact with her, is impervious to her charms, but the nobility of her death moves even him. She is mercurial and self-centered, and there is some ambiguity in her love of Antony. It is difficult to be certain that her tragic death would have taken place had cold Octavius Caesar been susceptible to her fascination. She is most queenly in her death, which she chooses to bring about in "the high Roman fashion," calling the dead Antony "husband" just before she applies the asp to her bosom.

Octavius Caesar, Triumvir of Rome, Antony's great rival. His youthfulness is set off against Antony's age; his coldness against Antony's passion; his prudence against Antony's recklessness. The result, from a dramatic point of view, is heavily in Antony's favor. Caesar's affection for his sister Octavia is almost the only warm note in his character; but his comments on the deaths of Antony and Cleopatra show unexpected generosity and magnanimity.

Domitius Enobarbus (dō·mĭsh′yŭs ē·nō-bär′bŭs), Antony's friend and follower. Of the family of Shakespeare's loyal Horatio and Kent, he is a strong individual within the type. Though given to the disillusioned cynicism of the veteran soldier, he has a splendid poetic vein which is stimulated by Cleopatra. He knows his master well and leaves him only when

Antony seems to have left himself. Miserable as a deserter, Enobarbus is moved so deeply by Antony's generosity that he dies of grief. He serves as a keen, critical chorus for about three-fourths of the play.

Marcus Aemilius Lepidus (mär′kŭs ē-mĭl′ĭ·ŭs lĕp′ĭ·dŭs), the third Triumvir, a "poor third," as Enobarbus calls him. He tries to bring together Antony and Octavius and to quell the thunderstorms which their rivalry frequently engenders. He is the butt of some teasing by Antony when they are both drinking heavily on Pompey's galley. After the defeat of Pompey, Octavius Caesar destroys Lepidus, leaving himself and Antony to fight for control of the world.

Sextus Pompeius (Pompey) (sĕks′tŭs pŏm·pē′yŭs; pŏm′pĭ), the son of Pompey the Great. Ambitious and power-hungry, he has a vein of chivalric honor which prevents his consenting to the murder of his guests, the Triumvirs, aboard his galley. He makes a peace with the Triumvirs, largely because of Antony, but is later attacked and defeated by Caesar and loses not only his power but his life as well.

Octavia, sister of Octavius Caesar. A virtuous widow, fond of her brother and strangely fond of Antony after their marriage, she serves as a foil to Cleopatra. She is not necessarily as dull as Cleopatra thinks her. There is pathos in her situation, but she lacks tragic stature.

Charmian, a pert, charming girl attending Cleopatra. Gay, witty, and risqué, she rises under the stress of the death of her Queen to tragic dignity. She tends Cleopatra's body, closes the eyes, delivers a touching eulogy, and then joins her mistress in death.

Iras, another of Cleopatra's charming attendants. Much like Charmian, but not quite so fully drawn, she dies just before Cleopatra.

51

Mardian, a eunuch, servant of Cleopatra. He bears the false message of Cleopatra's death to Antony, which leads Antony to kill himself.

Alexas, an attendant to Cleopatra. He jests wittily with Charmian, Iras, and the Soothsayer. Deserting Cleopatra and joining Caesar, he is hanged by Caesar's orders.

A Soothsayer. He serves two functions: one to make satirical prophecies to Charmian and Iras, which turn out to be literally true; the other to warn Antony against remaining near Caesar, whose fortune will always predominate. The second helps Antony to make firm his decision to leave Octavia and return to Egypt.

Seleucus (sĕ·lōō′kŭs), Cleopatra's treasurer. He betrays to Caesar the information that Cleopatra is holding back the greater part of her treasure. She indulges in a public temper tantrum when he discloses this; but since the information apparently lulls Caesar into thinking that the Queen is not planning suicide, perhaps Seleucus is really aiding, not betraying her.

A Clown, who brings a basket of figs to the captured Queen. In the basket are concealed the poisonous asps. The clown's language is a mixture of simple-minded philosophy and mistaken meanings. The juxtaposition of his unconscious humor and Cleopatra's tragic death is reminiscent of the scene between Hamlet and the gravedigger.

Ventidius (vĕn·tĭd′ĭ·ŭs), one of Antony's able subordinates. A practical soldier, he realizes that it is best to be reasonably effective, but not spectacular enough to arouse the envy of his superiors; therefore, he does not push his victory to the extreme.

Eros (ē′rŏs), Antony's loyal bodyguard and armorbearer. He remains with his leader to final defeat. Rather than carry out Antony's command to deliver him a death stroke, he kills himself.

Scarus (skä′rŭs, skā′rŭs), one of Antony's tough veterans. Fighting heroically against Caesar's forces in spite of severe wounds, he rouses Antony's admiration. In partial payment, Antony requests the Queen to offer him her hand to kiss.

Canidius (că·nĭd′ĭ·ŭs), Antony's lieutenant general. When Antony refuses his advice and indiscreetly chooses to fight Caesar's forces on sea rather than on land, and consequently meets defeat, Canidius deserts to Caesar.

Dercetas (dėr′cĕ·tɔs), a loyal follower of Antony. He takes the sword stained with Antony's blood to Caesar, announces his leader's death, and offers either to serve Caesar or die.

Demetrius (dɔ·mē′trĭ·ŭs) and
Philo (fī′lō), followers of Antony. They open the play with comments on Antony's "dotage" on the Queen of Egypt.

Euphronius (ū·frō′nĭ·ŭs), Antony's old schoolmaster. He is Antony's emissary to Caesar asking for generous terms of surrender. Caesar refuses his requests.

Silius (sĭl′yŭs), an officer in Ventidius' army.

Menas (mē′năs), a pirate in the service of Pompey. He remains sober at the drinking bout on board Pompey's galley and offers Pompey the world. He intends to cut the cable of the galley and then cut the throats of the Triumvirs and their followers. Angered at Pompey's rejection of his proposal, he joins Enobarbus in drunken revelry and withdraws his support from Pompey.

Menecrates (mĕn·ĕk′rɔ·tēz) and
Varrius (vă′rĭ·ŭs), followers of Pompey.

Maecenas (mē·sē′nɔs), Caesar's friend and follower. He supports Agrippa and Lepidus in arranging the alliance between Caesar and Antony.

52

Agrippa (ə·grĭp′ə), Caesar's follower. He is responsible for the proposal that Antony and Octavia be married to cement the alliance. His curiosity about Cleopatra leads to Enobarbus' magnificent description of her on her royal barge.

Dolabella (dŏl·ə·bĕl′ə), one of Caesar's emissaries to Cleopatra. Enchanted by her, he reveals Caesar's plan to display her in a Roman triumph. This information strengthens her resolution to take her own life.

Proculeius (prō·kū·lē′ŭs), the only one of Caesar's followers whom Antony advises Cleopatra to trust. She wisely withholds the trust, for Proculeius is sent by Caesar to lull her into a false sense of security.

Thyreus (thĭ′rē·ŭs), an emissary of Caesar. Antony catches him kissing Cleopatra's hand and has him whipped and sent back to Caesar with insulting messages.

Gallus (găl′ŭs), another of Caesar's followers. He captures Cleopatra and her maids in the monument and leaves them guarded.

Taurus (tô′rŭs), Caesar's lieutenant general.

THE APOSTLE

Author: Sholem Asch (1880-1957)
Time of action: Shortly after the Crucifixion
First published: 1943

PRINCIPAL CHARACTERS

Saul of Tarshish, or Tarsus, afterward known as Paul. A devout Jew but intellectually a searcher, he at first resents the Messianist followers of Yeshua and he becomes a zealous spy and a persecutor of them. Troubled by Istephan's dying prayer of forgiveness of his slayers, Paul has on the road to Damascus a mystic vision which causes him to become an apostle of the Messiah, who appears to him several times, so that he believes himself divinely appointed to bring the word of Yeshua to the gentiles. As Paul he establishes several churches. Arrested for accepting gentiles, he demands a trial as a Roman before Caesar and is finally beheaded.

Simon bar Jonah, called Peter. Imprisoned for healing in Yeshua's name, he is miraculously released. Imprisoned again, he is freed after eloquently defending his doctrine. He founds the church at Antioch, where he accepts gentiles as members. After working with Paul in Rome, he is crucified.

Joseph bar Naba of Cyprus, or Barnabas, Saul's friend, an early convert who had known Yeshua before his crucifixion.

Reb Istephan, or Stephen, a famous Jewish preacher.

Reb Jacob, a strict Jew, son of Joseph and younger brother of Yeshua, who leads the Messianist cult in Jerusalem after Yeshua's disappearance.

Yeshua of Nazareth, Jesus.

Nehemiah, a cripple healed by Simon in the name of Yeshua.

Jochanan, or John, Simon's follower imprisoned with him and, like him, miraculously released.

Titus, Saul's first convert, a Greek.

Lukas, or Luke, a Greek physician, minister, and scholar who writes the life of Yeshua.

Nero, Roman Emperor, who imprisons Paul. Nero burns Rome and blames the Christians, many of whom die forgiving their persecutors.

Seneca, a Roman through whose intervention Nero frees Paul.

Gabelus, a gladiator who becomes a Christian.

THE APPLE OF THE EYE

Author: Glenway Wescott (1901-   )
Time of action: Twentieth century
First published: 1924

PRINCIPAL CHARACTERS

Hannah Madoc, a natural, primitive young woman. Orphaned and penniless after her drunken father dies from a fall occasioned by Hannah's pushing him off a porch in self-defense, Hannah goes to work in a store. Falling in love with Jule Bier, she rejects the attentions of others; but Jule's father wants him to marry someone else, and the grief-stricken Hannah goes away and becomes a prostitute. Jule goes to bring her home at last. The prematurely broken and bitter Hannah dies as the result of a fall.

Jule Bier, a young farm hand. In love with Hannah, he nevertheless follows his father's orders and marries a wealthy girl. He acquires a wonderful understanding of life, and as an old man advises his wife's nephew to accept the simple values, like Hannah's, rather than the warped, false values of people whose religion masks a fear of life.

Selma Duncan, Jule's wife, daughter of a wealthy farmer. She brings up her daughter to fear love and sex, with disastrous results. When the daughter's body is found, the news is kept from the ailing Selma.

Rosalia Bier, the daughter of Jule and Selma. Seduced, she is tormented by feelings of guilt, though she hides her fear from her lover. After her lover leaves, she is convinced that a baby is her inevitable punishment. She runs away in a snowstorm; her body is found the following spring in a swamp, and quietly buried there by Jule, his nephew, and a neighbor.

Mike Byron, a robust, zestful young man who works on Jule's farm. He loves Rosalia and becomes her lover. Jule tells him that he would not object to the marriage, but Mike feels trapped and leaves.

Dan Strane, Selma's nephew. A frustrated adolescent brought up in ignorance of sex by his tight-lipped mother, he is torn between curiosity and feelings of shame. Mike instructs Dan, telling him that life's processes are not obscene but wonderful. Mike is Dan's idol, but after Rosalia's desertion and death, Dan hates the memory of Mike. A talk with the understanding Jule reconciles the conflicts Dan feels. At the story's close, Dan is preparing to enter the state university.

Mrs. Strane, Selma's sister, Dan's straitlaced mother.

Mr. Bier, Jule's father, cold and calculating. He orders his son to court Selma.

Mrs. Boyle, in whose store the orphaned Hannah works.

Mr. Boyle, her husband. Hannah leaves the store to go to work on a farm near Jule's home after Mr. Boyle tries to make love to her.

APPOINTMENT IN SAMARRA

Author: John O'Hara (1905-   )
Time of action: 1930
First published: 1934

PRINCIPAL CHARACTERS

Julian English, an automobile dealer who drinks too much. He picks fights with his friends and benefactors, gets publicly drunk, drives his wife to seek a divorce, and chases after a bootlegger's woman. When his acts add up and life becomes too complicated for him, he commits suicide.

Caroline English, a woman as superficial as her husband. When she decides to seek a divorce from her husband she acts like a heroine in melodrama, even to cancelling a big party on short notice.

Harry Reilly, a wealthy Irish Catholic who has a highball thrown in his face by a bored Julian English at a party, despite the fact that it is Reilly who has befriended Julian and lent him the money needed to keep his Cadillac agency solvent. Julian seems a bit surprised when Reilly holds a grudge.

Helene Holman, a night-club singer and a bootlegger's woman. She and Julian get together while drunk at a Christmas celebration. Helene is, as her bootlegger-lover knows, a woman of easy virtue.

Ed Charney, a bootlegger. Though a family man, he keeps Helene as his mistress and is resentful of the favors she shows other men. He becomes angry at his aide, Al Grecco, for letting Helene become involved with Julian.

Al Grecco, a small-time gangster who becomes angry at his boss's insults and vows to kill Ed Charney.

Froggy Ogden, Caroline English's one-armed cousin, who tries to goad Julian into a fight after reproaching him for his conduct.

Dr. English, Julian's father, who looks for moral weakness in his son because his own father was an embezzler and a suicide.

Father Creedon, a priest who agrees with Julian that Harry Reilly is a bore and refuses to take the incident of Julian's insulting Reilly seriously.

THE ARABIAN NIGHTS' ENTERTAINMENTS
(SELECTIONS)

Author: Unknown
Time of action: The legendary past
First published: Fifteenth century

PRINCIPAL CHARACTERS

Shahriar, Emperor of Persia and India. Convinced of the unfaithfulness of all women, he vows to marry a new woman every day and have her executed the next morning.

Scheherazade, his wise and beautiful bride. On the night of their wedding, she begins to tell him a tale which so fascinates him that he stays her execution for a day so that he can learn the end of the story. The stories are continued for a thousand and one nights. Then, convinced of her worthiness, he bids her

55

live and makes her his consort. The following are characters in some of her stories:

The King of the Black Isles. He nearly kills the lover of his unfaithful Queen, who gets revenge by turning her husband's lower half into marble, and his town and all its people into a lake of fish. A neighboring Sultan kills the lover and deceives the Queen into undoing all her enchantments; then she too is killed.

Sindbad the Sailor, who, in the course of his voyages, visits an island that is really the back of a sea monster, a valley of diamonds, an island inhabited by cannibal dwarfs and black one-eyed giants, and an underground river.

The Caliph Harun-al-Rashid of Baghdad, Sindbad's ruler.

Houssain,
Ali, and
Ahmed, sons of the Sultan of India. They compete for the hand of their father's ward; after an archery contest Ali is proclaimed the winner, though Ahmed's arrow has gone so far that no one can find it.

Periebanou, a fairy living in a mountain, at whose door Ahmed finds his arrow.

He marries her and with her help performs unreasonable tasks for his father, who has been persuaded by courtiers to be suspicious of his son, now secretive about his life and apparently rich and powerful. The Sultan is killed by Periebanou's annoyed brother, and Ahmed succeeds him as Sultan.

Princess Nouronnihar, the ward of the Sultan. She is sought in marriage by the brothers. Ali wins her.

Ali Baba, a Persian woodcutter who happens upon a thieves' cave filled with riches.

Cassim, his greedy brother, who forgets the password, "Open Sesame," and so cannot get out of the cave. The thieves kill him.

Morgiana, Ali Baba's beautiful slave. She discovers that the thieves are hiding in oil jars brought by their disguised Captain to Ali Baba's house. Morgiana kills the robbers, is rewarded with her freedom, and becomes Ali Baba's son's wife.

Aladdin, a young vagabond in China who gets possession of a magic lamp, and through the power of its genie, gains incredible wealth and wins the Sultan's daughter as his wife.

THE ARBITRATION

Author: Menander (342-291 B.C.)
Time of action: Fourth century B.C.
First presented: c. 310 B.C.

PRINCIPAL CHARACTERS

Pamphila (păm'fĭ·lə), Smicrines' daughter. She is ravished by an unknown, drunken young man who leaves his signet ring at the scene. She later marries her ravisher, Charisius, and bears his child. The baby is exposed in the hills along with the signet ring. Found by peasants, the baby is identified by the ring and returned to its rightful parents.

Charisius (kà·rĭ'sĭ·əs), an upright young Athenian. During a drunken revel he ravishes Pamphila, whom he later marries without remembering her as his victim. Disavowing the child he learned was born to his wife during his absence, he leaves home and spends his substance on the slave girl, Habrotonon. He is reunited with his wife after Habrotonon identifies Pamphila as his companion at the revel of a year before.

Smicrines (smĭ'krĭ·nēz), Pamphila's father.

56

Habrotonon (hă·brō'tə·nŏn), a pretty slave girl who turns out to be Smicrines' long-lost daughter. Companion of Charisius after he learns that his wife has born a child whom he disclaims, she brings about the reunion of the husband and wife by identifying Pamphila as Charisius' victim on the night of the revel. She marries Chaerestratus.

Onesimus (ō·nē'sĭ·məs), Charisius' slave.

Chaerestratus (kē·rĕs'trə·təs), Charisius' friend, who marries Habrotonon.

Sophrona (sō'frə·nà), Pamphila's nurse.

Davus (dă'vəs), a goatherd who discovers Pamphila's baby in the hills.

Syriscus (sĭ·rĭs'kəs), a charcoal burner who adopts Pamphila's baby.

Carion (kâ'rĭ·ən), a vain, prying cook.

ARCADIA

Author: Sir Philip Sidney (1554-1586)
Time of action: Classical antiquity
First published: 1590

PRINCIPAL CHARACTERS

Pyrocles (pī'rōk·lēz), Prince of Macedon. Journeying with his cousin Musidorus, he fights on the side of justice in many countries before he reaches Arcadia and falls in love with a picture of the Princess Philoclea. He disguises himself as an Amazon, Zelmane, to be near his lady, only to find himself tormented by the passion of both her parents.

Musidorus (mōō'sĭ·dō'rəs), his cousin and loyal friend, Prince of Thessalia. He masquerades as Dorus, a shepherd, and pretends to court the homely Mopsa in order to win the hand of the noble Princess Pamela, who is finally persuaded to run away with him.

Basilius (bə·sĭ'lĭ·əs), the ruler of Arcadia, who takes his Queen and their daughters into the country to prevent the fulfillment of an oracle's prophecy which he fears portends disaster for him. He betrays both his age and his dignity in his passion for his daughter's companion, Zelmane.

Gynecia (jĭ·nē'shĭ·ə), his young wife, who suffers agonies of conscience for the desire and jealousy she feels for Pyrocles, whose disguise she has penetrated. Re-

senting his attentions to Philoclea, she is freed from her passion only after she has almost killed her husband with a love potion intended for Zelmane.

Pamela (pă'mə·lə), their stately, reserved older daughter, who is wooed and, after much resistance, won by Musidorus.

Philoclea (fĭ'lōk·lē'ə), her sweeter, more submissive sister. She responds quickly to Pyrocles' love, but she lacks the strength with which Pamela meets difficulties.

Amphialus (ăm·fĭ'ə·ləs), Basilius' warrior nephew, who is spurred on by his ambitious mother and by his love for Philoclea to kidnap the princesses and take over the kingdom. Although he deeply regrets the deaths he causes, he cannot restrain his desire for fighting.

Cecropia (sēk·rō'pĭ·ə), Amphialus' ruthless mother, who spurs him on his ambitious path to overthrow her hated brother Basilius.

Philanax (fĭ·lă'năks), regent of Arcadia, a man of intelligence and integrity.

Dametas (dā·mē'təs), a foolish, arrogant shepherd, Pamela's guardian.

57

Miso (mī'sō), the sharp-tongued, jealous wife of Dametas.

Mopsa (mŏp'sə), their homely daughter. Her stupidity makes her a useful cover for the blossoming romance between Musidorus and Pamela.

Argalus (är'gə·ləs), a worthy young lord and a devoted lover and husband. He dies defending the rights of his cousins, Pamela and Philoclea, against Amphialus.

Parthenia (pär·thē'nĭ·ə), Argalus' gracious wife. Grief-stricken at his death, she arms herself and fights a fatal duel with Amphialus, unwilling to live without her husband.

Demagoras (dĕ·mä'gə·rȧs), her vengeful rejected suitor.

Evarchus (ə·vär'kəs), King of Macedon, who is judge in the trial after Basilius' apparent death. He is deeply grieved to learn that he has condemned his son Pyrocles and his nephew Musidorus, but he insists that he must endure his own suffering and uphold law and order.

Helen (hĕ'lən), Queen of Corinth. Enamored of Amphialus, she pursues him over the countryside while adoring his picture. She comes to heal his wounds after his combat with Musidorus.

Philoxenus (fĭ'lək·zē'nəs), a suitor of Helen. Jealous of her attentions to his foster brother, Amphialus, he challenges his rival and dies in the ensuing duel.

Timotheus (tĭ·mō'thĭ·əs), the father of Philoxenus.

Kalander (kə·lăn'dėr), an Arcadian gentleman who shelters Musidorus after he has been shipwrecked.

Clitophon (klī'tə·fŏn), his son.

Ismenus (ĭs·mē'·nəs), Amphialus' devoted squire, killed in a battle with Philanax.

Phalantus (fə·lăn'təs), a Corinthian knight who is persuaded by his selfish lady to defend the supremacy of her beauty against all challengers.

Artesia (är·tē'shĭ·ə), Phatantus' disdainful lady, who spurns him after he loses a battle. Cecropia makes her a tool in her plot against Basilius and finally has her beheaded.

The King of Paphlagonia (pă'flə·gō'nĭ·ə), the model for Gloucester in Shakespeare's "King Lear"; a ruler blinded and exiled by his bastard son and aided by his more loyal child.

Leonatus (lē'ə·nā'təs), his devoted son.

Plexirtus (plĕk·sėr'təs), the bastard usurper, who tries to kill his virtuous brother.

Tydeus (tī'dĭ·əs) and
Telenor (tə·lē'nėr), allies of Plexirtus.

Erona (ə·rō'nə), a Lydian princess who defies her father to marry the son of her nurse.

Antiphilus (ăn·tĭ'fĭ·ləs), her selfish, treacherous husband.

Tiridates (tī'rĭ·dā'tēz), the cruel King of Armenia, rejected by Erona.

Artaxia (är·tăk'sĭ·ə), his sister and successor.

Plangus (plăn'gəs), the son of the King of Iberia. He joins Telenor's army after an unfortunate affair with a married woman. When he returns, he finds her wedded to his father. He later takes refuge in Arcadia.

Andromana (ăn·drō'mə·nə), his wanton stepmother.

Pamphilus (păm'fə·ləs), a knight despised for his inhuman treatment of women.

Dido (dī'dō), one of his victims.

Chremes (krā'mēz), her miserly father.

Palladius (pə·lă'dĭ·əs), Plangus' half

brother, the unlucky lover from whom Musidorus took his pseudonym.

Zelmane (zĕl·mä′nē), his sweetheart, who adored Pyrocles and followed him, in the disguise of a page, until her death.

Clinias (klī′nĭ·əs), a smooth-tongued, crafty shepherd in Cecropia's service.

Anaxius (ə·năk′shĭ·əs), a powerful, gigantic knight who fought with Amphialus' army.

Zoilus (zoi′ləs) and

Lycurgus (lī·kûr′gəs), his brothers, leaders of Amphialus' army after he is wounded.

Timautus (tĭ·mô′təs), an ambitious nobleman who attempts to oust Philanax.

Sympathus (sĭm′pə·thəs), Philanax's articulate supporter.

Kalodulus (kə·lŏ′jŏŏ·ləs), a devoted friend of Musidorus.

Dorilaus (dō′rĭ·lā′əs), Musidorus' father, killed in battle.

ARGENIS

Author: John Barclay (1582-1621)
Time of action: The Hellenistic Era
First published: 1621

PRINCIPAL CHARACTERS

Argenis (är·jē′nĭs), a beautiful, resourceful priestess of Pallas Athena and the daughter of Meleander, King of Sicily; she also symbolizes the throne of France. Having met Poliarchus, a hero in the Sicilian rebellion, she can never return the love of Archombrotus, a suitor favored by her father, or that of Radirobanes, King of Sardinia, who insists on pressing his suit and attempts to blackmail her for meeting her beloved in secret. She thwarts Radirobanes' designs, appeases her father's wrath, discovers that Archombrotus is her half brother, and marries the man of her choice.

Poliarchus (pŏ·lĭ·är′kəs), in reality Prince Astioristes of France, allegorically King Henry IV of Navarre, a warrior-hero in chivalric disguise. As a daring fighter for King Meleander, the young knight insists on a firm peace rather than a truce, and he thereby alienates his loved one's father and makes an enemy of the rebel leader, Lycogenes. An outcast, Poliarchus assumes female disguise and calls himself Theocrine in order to enter the heavily guarded castle where Argenis and her maidens have been sent by Meleander

after Lycogenes has threatened to abduct the Princess; Poliarchus' purpose is to see for himself whether Argenis is as beautiful as she is reported. The two meet and fall deeply in love. The adventures of Poliarchus include routing pirates, slaying a Sardinian interloper in single combat, and succeeding to the throne of France, as well as marrying Argenis. He is a character cast in the mold of the great legendary heroes whose bravery and virtue are inevitably rewarded.

Archombrotus (är·kŏm·brō′təs), Poliarchus' good friend, in reality Hyempsal, Prince of Mauritania and King Meleander's favorite warrior. The first to know of his friend's deep love for Argenis, he too is smitten and presses his suit for the lovely Princess. He is above reproach, however, in his attentions, and he truly merits her hand after he kills Lycogenes, the rebel leader, in single combat, thereby ending the revolt. His bravery is rewarded when his friend Poliarchus helps to defend Mauritania and aids Queen Hyanisbe in successfully routing the invaders. In the end Archombrotus is revealed as the royal son of King Meleander by his first

59

wife, the sister of the Queen of Mauritania.

Meleander (mĕ·lē·ăn'dėr), King of Sicily, the father of Argenis and Archombrotus. A cautious, often mistaken, but always generous man, he is unable to subdue an insurrection until two foreign knights, Poliarchus and Archombrotus, come to his aid. His friendship for the latter, who rescues him from drowning and defeats the rebel leader, and his antagonism toward the other complicate the plot. When it looks as if his kingdom will be lost, he finally takes the initiative. By leading his ships to victory and his daughter to the altar, he rights wrongs and rewards the deserving.

Radirobanes (ră·dĭ·rō·bā'nēz), the King of Sardinia, at first the ally of King Meleander but later his antagonist for the hand of his daughter. Though brave in war, Radirobanes is a dastard in love. He bribes a maid in order to learn of a rendezvous of the hero and heroine, attempts blackmail to win the hand of the Princess, and schemes to abduct her. Thwarted in both love and war, he falls victim to Astioristes, the new King of France.

Lycogenes (lī·kō'jē·nēz), a traitorous nobleman who almost succeeds in unseating King Meleander but whose breaking of a truce brings about his deserved death at the hands of Archombrotus.

Timoclea (tĭ·mō·klē'ȧ), a wise and loyal matron of Sicily who becomes the chief lady of King Meleander's household after she uncovers Selenissa's part in the plot to abduct Argenis. The devoted friend of Poliarchus as well, she hides him after his banishment, acts as his agent, and consoles Argenis.

Arsidas (är'sĭ·dȧs), the Governor of Messana, a Sicilian nobleman loyal to the crown. He acts as a comforter to Argenis when rumors of her beloved's death are received, as an arbiter to the King, and as the confidant of the two lovers.

Selenissa (sē·lē·nĭs'ȧ), Argenis' nurse and companion, who commits suicide after the failure of the plan to have her mistress abducted by Radirobanes.

Gobrias (gō'brē·ȧs), the commander of the war fleet sent by the King of France to invade Sicily. He rescues shipwrecked Arsidas and tells him the story of King Astioristes' adventures in Sicily while disguised as Poliarchus. Overjoyed to learn that the knight he knew as Poliarchus still lives, Arsidas offers his aid in reuniting the lovers.

Gelanorus (jē·lȧ·nō'rȧs), the French nobleman who attends Poliarchus in Sicily and acts as his servant.

Nicopompus (nĭk·ȧ·pŏm'pȧs), the court poet who composes the epithalamium for the wedding of Argenis and Poliarchus, now revealed as Astioristes, the King of France.

Hyanisbe, Queen of Mauritania.

DER ARME HEINRICH

Author: Hartmann von Aue (c. 1170-between 1210 and 1220)
Time of action: Late twelfth century
First transcribed: Between 1192 and 1202

PRINCIPAL CHARACTERS

Heinrich von Aue (hīn'rĭsh fŏn ou'ȧ), a Swabian knight. Wealthy, handsome, and of noble birth, purity and honor are the marks of his life; fulfillment of the obligations of knighthood is his goal. Suddenly, all is changed by the terrible knowledge that he is a leper. In search of a remedy, he finally learns that his only cure lies in finding a virgin who, out of love, will yield her heart's blood. When a peasant girl begs Heinrich to allow her to make the sacrifice, he gives in to her pleas, but at the moment before the operation, he cannot accept her offering. On the way home, God's healing grace restores Heinrich to health, and he and the girl are wed amid the rejoicings of his people.

A Peasant Girl, the daughter of the family with whom Heinrich von Aue lives as a leper. Deeply moved by Heinrich's suffering, and for the eternal life that will be her reward, she willingly offers her heart's blood for his cure. After the knight's refusal of her sacrifice and his miraculous cure, she and Heinrich are married.

ARNE

Author: Björnstjerne Björnson (1832-1910)
Time of action: Early nineteenth century
First published: 1858

PRINCIPAL CHARACTERS

Arne, the illegitimate son of Margit and Nils. As he grows up, Arne is weaned away from his mother by his father. After the father's death, he takes up drinking, as had the father. He becomes a carpenter and also interests himself in Norwegian folklore and music. Falling in love with Eli, the daughter of his father's enemy, he marries her, thus ending a feud of many years' standing.

Nils, a tailor who fiddles for country dances. He is also a drunkard. He suffers a broken back in a fight with Baard Böen and is nursed by Arne's mother, whom he later marries. A gloomy, frustrated, morose man, he finally dies in drunken violence.

Margit, Arne's thrifty, solid, peasant mother. She hopes her son will not turn out like his father. She is pleased when the young man marries Eli Böen. Before

the marriage she shows the girl the treasures she has accumulated for her son and his bride. She believes Eli can save Arne from a dissolute and wasted life.

Eli Böen, daughter of Baard Böen, Nils' enemy. She falls in love with Arne and marries him.

Baard Böen, Nils' enemy, with whom Nils has the fight in which his back is broken. Years later Baard tries to explain what happened. He finds, trying to tell Arne, that he cannot clearly recollect the cause of the quarrel which resulted in lifelong enmity.

Kristian, Arne's friend who has gone to America. He writes to Arne in hopes that Arne can be persuaded, as his mother feels he may, to join Kristian in America.

ARROWSMITH

Author: Sinclair Lewis (1885-1951)
Time of action: Early twentieth century
First published: 1924

PRINCIPAL CHARACTERS

Martin Arrowsmith, a doctor, chiefly interested in bacteriological research. As

a medical student he falls under the influence of Dr. Gottlieb, who gives him

61

an inkling of the excitement of pure science as opposed to the practical aspect of medicine. After a brief engagement to Madeline Fox, a graduate student in English, Martin marries Leora Tozer, and his marriage forces him to give up his bacteriological research for general medicine study. After graduation, he established himself as a general practitioner in Leora's home town of Wheatsylvania, North Dakota. He becomes acting head of the Department of Public Health there, but his honesty makes him unpopular and he joins the staff of Dr. Pickerbaugh at Nautilus, Iowa. Pickerbaugh is a fake; the job leaves Martin no time for research, and again his honesty makes enemies. He next moves to Chicago, as a pathologist in the Rouncefield Clinic. Through his old teacher, Gottlieb, he next joins the McGurk Institute in New York, an organization more interested in publicity than in pure science. He works on a cure for bubonic plague; and, when a plague is reported on an island in the West Indies, he goes there with Leora and Dr. Sondelius. With scientific detachment, he promises Gottlieb to test the antitoxin by giving it to only half the population, using the others as controls. After Sondelius and Leora both die of the plague, Martin, in his grief, gives the antitoxin to everyone, thus ruining the value of his experiment. On his return to the McGurk Institute, Martin marries Joyce Lanyon. a wealthy and fashionable widow. The marriage is unhappy because he cannot enter her social world and she will not leave him time for his research. Resigning from the Institute and leaving Joyce, he joins Terry Wickett in the Vermont woods, where, in a crude laboratory, they begin the work that they both want to do.

Madeline Fox, Martin's first fiancée, a graduate student in English. She is pretentiously intellectual but fascinating to the crude Martin.

Leora Tozer, Martin's first wife, whom he marries while a student. Though not very intelligent, she is warm-hearted and kind and adores Martin. She dies in the West Indies of the plague.

Joyce Lanyon, a wealthy widow, Martin's second wife. The marriage fails because she finds Martin crude and uncultivated and can never understand his devotion to research.

Professor Max Gottlieb, German-born scientist, Professor of Immunology at the University of Winnemac. He represents pure science, unconcerned with practical results. But his intellectual arrogance and uncompromising honesty make it difficult for him to hold a position, and his career is a failure. He gives Martin the ideal of the scientist: a man dedicated to truth.

Terry Wickett, a scientist. As rough and uncouth as Martin, he is devoted to his work. He and Martin finally establish a laboratory in the Vermont woods.

Gustaf Sondelius, a dynamic Swedish fighter against diseases all over the world. He goes to the West Indies with Martin to combat the plague, is infected, and dies.

Cliff Clawson, a vulgar, clowning, but generous fraternity brother at the university. He reappears later when Martin is married to Joyce. He has become a slick salesman of fake oil stock.

Dr. Almus Pickerbaugh, in the Public Health Service. He is a complete fake, a high-pressure salesman rather than a doctor, interested only in publicity. He likes to be compared with Billy Sunday. Martin tries to work under him but is much too honest to succeed. Pickerbaugh eventually becomes a Congressman.

Orchid Pickerbaugh, his nineteen-year-old daughter, who has a brief flirtation with Martin.

Dr. Rippleton Holabird, Head of the Department of Physiology at the McGurk

Institute and later Director. He is an example of the pseudo-scientist, interested only in personal advancement.

Angus Duer, a mercenary classmate un-

der whom Martin later works at the fashionable Rouncefield Clinic.

Dean Silva, who exerts a good influence on Martin at medical school.

ARTAMÈNE

Author: Madeleine de Scudéry (1607-1701)
Time of action: 500 B.C.
First published: 1646-1653

PRINCIPAL CHARACTERS

Artamène, in reality **Cyrus the Great,** the son of the King of Persia. Given as a child to a shepherd to be destroyed because of an ill omen, the boy is reared by the shepherd and, as Artamène, becomes a great general. He falls in love with Mandane, a beautiful Princess, and, along with numerous others, pursues her endlessly and against great odds throughout the ten volumes that make up this novel. After conquering many of the kingdoms of Asia while in pursuit of Mandane, Artamène finds his Princess still alive and safe, and they are wed.

Cyaxares, King of Cappadocia and Media. Artamène becomes his best general and falls in love with his daughter Mandane.

Mandane, the daughter of King Cyaxares. Her hand is sought by numerous kings and princes but she loves only Artamène. She is the object of the Queen of Scythia's jealousy and when captured by the Queen, she is marked for murder; by mistake, a maid of honor is killed in her place. Rescued by Artamène, she marries him at last.

Philidaspes, King of Assyria, who is in love with Mandane. He abducts her and takes her to Babylon but there loses her to a rival.

Mazare, the Prince of Sacia, who also loves Mandane. While Philidaspes is locked in a tower, Mazare takes Mandane away.

The King of Pontus, also in love with

Mandane. He captures her when she and Mazare are shipwrecked near his fortress. When his fortress is threatened by Artamène, he carries Mandane away.

Anaxoris, in reality **Aryante,** Prince of the Massagetae and Queen Thomyris' brother. Anaxoris also loves Mandane. Entrusted with Mandane's safety by his friend Philidaspes, he turns her over to Thomyris to keep her away from Artamène.

Thomyris, the powerful Queen of Scythia. In love with Artamène, her jealousy causes her to order Mandane's death. A maid of honor is killed by mistake and before Thomyris can act again, Mandane is rescued by Artamène.

Spargapises, Thomyris' son, who commits suicide in disgrace because he is not recognized when captured in battle.

Araminta, the sister of the Queen of Pontus. Mandane is jealous of her because she mistakenly thinks Artamène is enamored of Araminta.

Spithridates, Araminta's suitor, who resembles Artamène and thus causes Mandane to think it is Artamène who is pursuing Araminta. He is killed in battle and, still being mistaken for Artamène, his head is presented to Thomyris.

Prince Phraortes, who abducts Araminta, leaving Spithridates desperate.

Panthea, the wife of Abradantes, who,

along with Araminta, is taken as a hostage by Artamène at Sardis.

Abradantes, one of the rulers whom Artamène fights in his siege of Sardis.

Martésie, Mandane's maid of honor.

The Queen of Corinth, who forms a platonic attachment for Artamène and sends her fleet to help him capture Cumae, to which the King of Pontus has fled with Mandane.

Metrobate, a traitor.

THE ARTAMONOV BUSINESS

Author: Maxim Gorky (Aleksei Maksimovich Peshkov, 1868-1936)
Time of action: c. 1862-1918
First published: 1925

PRINCIPAL CHARACTERS

Ilia Artamonov (ĭ·lyä′ är·tä′mə·nəf), a dictatorial stranger who builds a factory in Dromov. His business and power continue to grow despite increased resentment against him.

Peter Artamonov (pyō′tr är·tä′mə·nəf), Ilia Artamonov's eldest son and the heir to his business. Blind to the changes time has made in the attitude of his workers, he ends his days as a prisoner of the revolutionists.

Nikita Artamonov (nĭ·kĭ′tə är·tä′mə·nəf), Ilia Artamonov's hunchbacked son. Failing in his efforts to become a good monk, he leaves the religious life and is seen frequently in the company of the revolutionary, Vialov.

Alexey Artamonov (ä·lĕk·sā′ är·tä′mə·nəf), Ilia Artamonov's adopted son and business representative.

Ilia (ĭ·lyä), Peter Artamonov's elder son. Indifferent to the affairs of the factory, he leaves home to become a historian and, later, a revolutionary.

Yakov (yä′kəf), Peter Artamonov's

younger son and the heir to his father's place in the factory. Fearing for his life among the increasingly restless workers, he flees, only to be killed by robbers on the train to Moscow.

Tikhon Vialov (tĭ′hən vyä′ləf), a worker-philosopher in the Artamonov factory. Finally, as a soldier of the revolution, he becomes Peter Artamonov's gaoler.

Natalia Baimakov (nä·tä′lĭ·yə bī·mä′kəf), Peter Artamonov's wife.

Uliana Baimakov (ū·lĭ·ä′nə bī·mä′kəf), the wife of Evgeny Baimakov, and, as his widow, the mistress of Ilia Artamonov.

Evgeny Baimakov (ĕv·gĕ′nĭy bī·mä′kəf), the mayor of Dromov.

Elena (ĕ·lĕ′nə), the daughter of Peter Artamonov.

Miron (mĭ′rən), Alexey Artamonov's son.

Pauline, the mistress of Yakov Artamonov.

AS I LAY DYING

Author: William Faulkner (1897-1962)
Time of action: Early twentieth century
First published: 1930

64

Anse Bundren, an ignorant poor white. When Addie, his wife, dies, he is determined to take her body to Jefferson, as he had promised, even though the town is forty miles away. In a rickety old wagon he and his sons must get across a flooding river which has destroyed most of the nearby bridges. Ostensibly, the shiftless and unlucky man is burying Addie there because of the promise. After a long trip with her unembalmed corpse, now dead more than a week, he arrives in Jefferson, pursued by a flock of buzzards which, like a grim chorus, hang apparently motionless against a sultry Mississippi sky. On reaching Jefferson, his family learns Anse's true reason for the trip: a set of false teeth and the "duck-shaped woman" whom he marries, to the surprise of his children.

Addie Bundren, Anse's overworked wife. Though dying, she wants to see her coffin finished. Anse does not know it, but she has always thought him to be only a man of words; and words, she thinks, are useless. Feeling isolated from him and her children, she has always tried to break through the wall of isolation surrounding her, but despairing, she never finds any meaning in her grinding existence. To her, sexual relationship means only violation, whereas, to Anse, it means love. Before her death she knows her father's words to be true: "The reason for living was to get ready to stay dead a long time."

Darl Bundren, Addie's strange son, thought by his family to be feeble-minded. Unlike the others, he seems to have the gift of second sight. Knowing the true reasons why Anse and the others are going to Jefferson, he tries to burn the barn housing his mother's body. For this act of attempted purification, his family declares him insane, and he is taken to the asylum at Jackson.

Jewel Bundren, Preacher Whitfield's illegitimate son. A violent young man, he loves only his horse, which cost him many long hours of labor at night. Although devoted to the animal, he allows Anse to trade it to Snopes for a badly needed team of mules. Like the rest of the Bundrens, he tenaciously hauls his mother on the long eventful trip, all the while cursing and raging at his brothers. When Darl tries to burn the corpse, it is Jewel who manages to save her body for burial.

Cash Bundren, Anse's son, a carpenter. While his mother is dying, he busily saws and hammers away at her coffin, just outside her window. Carefully beveling the wood (he hates shoddy work) and showing his mother each board before nailing it in place, he finishes the job shortly after Addie's death. At the flooded river he desperately tries to save his treasured tools when the wagon overturns. His leg broken on the trip, he stoically endures the pain, even after his father uses cement to plaster the swollen and infected leg.

Vardaman Bundren, Anse's son. Constantly, he repeats to himself, "My mother is a fish."

Dewey Dell Bundren, Anse's daughter. A well-developed girl of seventeen, she has a reason for going to Jefferson. She is pregnant and wants to buy drugs which she hopes will cause a miscarriage.

Dr. Peabody, a fat, seventy-year-old country doctor. During his long practice he has ministered to many poor-white families like the Bundrens. When his unpaid bills reach fifty thousand dollars, he intends to retire.

Vernon Tull, Anse's helpful neighbor. He does what he can to help Bundren on his ghoulish journey.

Cora Tull, Vernon's fundamentalist wife. Constantly praying and singing hymns, she tries to make Addie repent.

Preacher Whitfield, Addie's former lover, the father of Jewel. Hearing of her sickness, this wordy man goes to confess his sin to Anse. On the way he decides that his fight against the elements, as he crosses the flooding river, helps to expiate his sins. After she dies, he does not feel that a public confession is necessary.

Lafe, a field hand, the father of Dewey Dell's unborn child.

Mr. Gillespie, in whose barn Addie's coffin lies when Darl attempts to burn it.

AS YOU LIKE IT

Author: William Shakespeare (1564-1616)
Time of action: The Middle Ages
First presented: 1599-1600

PRINCIPAL CHARACTERS

Rosalind (rŏz′ə·lĭnd)—disguised as Ganymede (găn′ə·mēd) in the forest scenes—the daughter of the banished Duke Senior. A witty, self-possessed young woman, she accepts whatever fortune brings, be it love or exile, with gaiety and good sense. She is amused by the ironic situations arising from her disguise as a youth, and she wryly recognizes the humorous aspects of her growing love for Orlando, whose passion she pretends to be curing. Her central place in the lives of her companions is epitomized in the final scene where she sorts out the tangled skeins of romance and, with Orlando, joins three other couples before Hymen, the god of marriage.

Orlando (ôr·lăn′dō), youngest son of Sir Rowland de Boys, the late ally of Rosalind's father. Although his elder brother mistreats him and neglects his education, he reveals his gentle birth in his manner and appearance. His love for Rosalind provokes extravagantly romantic gestures, but the deeper feeling of which he is capable is evident in his concern for his faithful old servant Adam, as well as in his fidelity to his sweetheart.

Celia (sē′lĭ·ə), Rosalind's gentle cousin, who refuses to let her depart alone for the Forest of Arden. She, too, is gay and witty, ready to exchange quips with Touchstone and tease Rosalind about her love for Orlando. When she meets Orlando's brother Oliver, however, she succumbs to Cupid even more rapidly than did her cousin.

Touchstone, Duke Frederick's clever fool, who accompanies his master's daughter Celia and Rosalind into the Forest of Arden, much to the amusement of Jaques and to the consternation of the old shepherd Corin, who finds himself damned for never having been at court, according to Touchstone's logic. The fool, more than any of the other characters, remains at heart a courtier, even in Arcadia, but he returns from the forest with a country wench as his bride.

Jaques (jā′kwēz), a hanger-on of Duke Senior's court in Arden, a professional man of melancholy who philosophizes on the "seven ages of man." He is fascinated by the presence in the forest of a "motley fool," and he delights in Touchstone's explanations of court formalities. He remains in the forest when his lord recovers his dukedom, and he goes off to observe and comment on the unexpected conversion of Duke Frederick.

Oliver (ŏl′ĭ·vər), Orlando's greedy, tyrannical brother, who tries to deprive him of both wealth and life. Sent by Duke Frederick to find his brother or forfeit all his lands, he is rescued by Orlando from a lioness. This kindness

66

from his mistreated brother gives him new humanity, and he becomes a worthy husband for Celia.

Duke Frederick, Celia's strong, self-centered father, the usurper. Fearing her popularity with the people, he arbitrarily sends Rosalind away to her exiled father. Later, equally unreasonably, he banishes Orlando for being the son of an old enemy and then sets Oliver wandering in search of the brother he despises. He is reported at the end of the play to have retired from the world with an old hermit.

Duke Senior, Rosalind's genial father, banished by his brother Duke Frederick, who holds court under the greenwood trees, drawing amusement from hunting, singing, and listening to Jaques' melancholy philosophy in the golden world of Arden.

Silvius (sĭl'vĭ·ŭs), a lovesick young shepherd. He asks "Ganymede" to help him win his scornful sweetheart Phebe.

Phebe (fē'bē), a disdainful shepherdess. Rebuked by "Ganymede" for her cruelty to Silvius, she promptly becomes enamored of the youth. She promises, however, to wed Silvius if she refuses Ganymede, and, of course, she does so once Rosalind reveals her identity.

Audrey (ô'drĭ), Touchstone's homely, stupid, good-hearted country wench.

William, Audrey's equally simple-minded rustic suitor.

Corin (kŏr'ĭn), a wise, well-meaning old shepherd. He gives good counsel to William and expresses the virtues of the simple life in his cross-purposes discussion of court and country with Touchstone.

Adam, a faithful old servant of Orlando's family. He accompanies his young master into the forest.

Jaques (jā'kwēz, jăk), the brother of Orlando and Oliver. He brings the news of Duke Frederick's retirement to the forest.

Sir Oliver Martext, a "hedge-priest" hired by Touchstone to marry him to Audrey in somewhat dubious rites.

Le Beau (lə bō), Duke Frederick's pompous attendant.

Charles, a champion wrestler challenged and defeated by Orlando.

Amiens (ā'mĭ·ĕnz), one of Duke Senior's lords.

Dennis, Oliver's servant.

Hymen (hī'mən), the god of marriage.

ASHES

Author: Stefan Żeromski (1864-1925)
Time of action: 1796-1812
First published: 1904

PRINCIPAL CHARACTERS

Raphael Olbromski, adventurous son of an aristocratic Polish landowner. As a boy he is thrown out of school for an escapade and then is cast out of the family by his strict father for bringing disgrace upon his name. Befriended by a nobleman, Raphael settles down and spends some time in school. After working four years as a laborer on his father's land he serves for a time as secretary to his benefactor, Prince Gintult. Following a tragic escapade with the girl he loves, Raphael joins the forces of Napoleon and fights bravely with the French armies.

Prince Gintult, a Polish nobleman who

befriends Raphael. He treats the young man almost as a member of his family, pays for the youth's education, and makes him his private secretary. Raphael later saves the Prince's life in battle.

Elizabeth, the Prince's sister. A haughty young woman, she strikes Raphael with her riding crop when he kisses her after rescuing her from a runaway horse. Later she helps him escape from Austrian-held Poland to join the French forces led by Napoleon.

Helen, a beautiful young woman who loves Raphael and is loved by him for many years. Meeting after years of separation, she and Raphael flee to the country, but the lovers are set upon by bandits, who bind Raphael and rape Helen. To escape her tormentors, Helen jumps off a cliff and is killed.

Christopher Cedro, a long-time friend of Raphael. The two are schoolmates and later serve together under Napoleon. Like Raphael, Christopher is an adventurous boy and, later, a brave soldier.

Nardzevski, Raphael's uncle, a landowner who fiercely adheres to the old ways and mistreats his peasants as they were mistreated in feudal times. He will not acknowledge the Austrian occupation of Poland and refuses to pay the taxes levied by Austria.

Casper, a huntsman who is Nardzevski's only loyal friend.

Peter Olbromski, Raphael's older brother. He, too, is cast out of the family by the boys' stern father. He befriends Raphael until his untimely death.

AT THE SIGN OF THE REINE PÉDAUQUE

Author: Anatole France (Jacques Anatole Thibault, 1844-1924)
Time of action: Eighteenth century
First published: 1893

PRINCIPAL CHARACTERS

Jacques Ménétrier (zhàk′ mā·nā·trē·yā′), a carefree young scholar and lover who becomes a respectable citizen. Born of poor parents, he is educated by clerics and philosophers, loved by tavern bawds and a Jewess who had fled Spain to live in France with her elderly lover. Having lived a dissolute life, Jacques finally settles down as a bookseller who supports comfortably his kindly mother and father in their declining years.

Jael (zhà·ĕl′), an attractive young Jewess who abandons her elderly lover, an uncle, to accept Jacques, only to abandon him to accept another who entices her with a gift of silver plate. Jael, however, is not peevish or vindictive. While she loves one, she likes the other man for whom she has once had the grand passion.

Catherine (kà·tə·rēn′), a young lace maker turned courtesan. She moves in and out of Jacques' life with predictable consistency. Though she accepts the gifts of wealthy men, her love for Jacques is constant.

Maître Jérôme Coignard (mĕtr′ zhà-rôm′ kwàn·yàr′), an abbé, a Greek and Latin scholar who is Jacques' tutor and who appreciates the joys of the flesh. He is killed by Jael's outraged lover, Mosaïde, who mistakenly believes that the abbé has stolen Jael's affections.

Hercule d'Astarac (ĕr·kül′ dà·stà·ràk′), a wealthy philosopher, a student of the occult, who maintains a broken-down estate where scholars are free to pursue metaphysical delights. He comes to an

68

unfortunate end when his home catches fire and he dies in the flames.

Brother Ange (änzh'), a secular member of a begging order who teaches Jacques the alphabet, spends some time in jail for engaging in drunken brawls, and secretly sighs for Catherine. He eventually runs away with her.

Maurice d'Anquetil (mō·rēs' dänk·tēl'), a nobleman who loves Catherine and also steals Jael from Jacques. He is carefree, takes chances, lives by his wits. He and Jacques are good friends.

De la Guéritaude (də lä gä·rē·tōd'), a prosperous tax collector who keeps Catherine in a fine house. He is in a perpetual fit of rage because Catherine treats him

outrageously with other men. He is finally seriously injured when, locked out of his own house, he causes a disturbance and is set upon by the revelers Catherine is entertaining.

Mosaïde (mō·zà·ēd'), a Jewish banker who fled Spain, taking his niece Jael with him as his mistress, after killing a Christian. He pretends to be a student of Hebraic texts and lives at d'Astarac's estate to do scholarly work. When d'Astarac's estate burns, Mosaïde, running from the holocaust, stumbles into a swamp and drowns.

Jeannette (zhà·nĕt'), a tavern hurdy-gurdy woman who initiates Jacques in the rites of love.

ATALA

Author: François René de Chateaubriand (1768-1848)
Time of action: Early eighteenth century
First published: 1801

PRINCIPAL CHARACTERS

René, a young Frenchman who wishes to become a member of the Natchez Indian tribe. He is accepted and is told the story of Chactas by the Indian chief himself.

Chactas, a Natchez chief. He is loyal to his people and their religion. He risks death to remain with his beloved Atala, a beautiful Indian girl. After the girl's death, under her influence, he eventually becomes a Christian. He is killed when an old man by a hostile tribe.

Lopez, a kindly Spaniard at St. Augustine who treats Chactas as his own son, until the young Indian returns to his

own people. He turns out to be Atala's father.

Atala, a beautiful Indian princess. She is a Christian and will not marry Chactas because he is a pagan and because of her vow to her dying mother to remain a virgin. Her mother had been Lopez' mistress. Because she thinks she cannot be released from her vow of chastity to marry Chactas, she commits suicide by taking poison.

Father Aubry, a dedicated missionary to the Indians. He befriends Chactas and Atala. He eventually sees his faith supported by Chactas' conversion to Christianity. He dies at the hands of hostile Indians.

ATALANTA IN CALYDON

Author: Algernon Charles Swinburne (1837-1909)
Time of action: Remote antiquity
First published: 1865

69

Œneus (ē'nōōs), King of Calydon. He has neglected his sacrifice to Artemis, goddess of the hunt. The wild boar sent by Artemis into Calydon, in punishment, is the object of the fateful hunt. Finally, after much tragedy, Œneus rules alone in Calydon.

Althæa (ăl·thē'ə), his wife, a woman of strong will. To avert a prophecy that her new-born son would live and prosper until the brand on the hearth was consumed, she extinguished the brand and hid it. Years later, after her son has slain her brothers, she returns the brand to the fire to be consumed. After her son's death, she dies of sorrow.

Meleager (mə·lē'gėr), the son of Œneus and Althæa. Strong and valiant, he is afflicted with great pride and lacks a proper submission to fate. He slays the boar and gives the spoils of the hunt to Atalanta. This results in a fight in which

Meleager, protecting Atalanta, kills his uncles. He dies hoping his name will live among men.

Atalanta (ă·tə·lăn'tə), an Arcadian maiden of great beauty and a priestess of Artemis. She joins the hunt, and Meleager, though strongly warned against an infatuation, falls in love with her. Her laugh of pleasure on being given the spoils of the hunt is misinterpreted as a taunt by the Calydonians, who attack her. At last, hailing Meleager's greatness, she returns to Arcadia.

Toxeus (tŏk'sōōs) and Plexippus (plĕk·sĭ'pəs), Althæa's brothers, who are slain by Meleager.

Leda (lē'də), Althæa's sister.

The Chorus, whose philosophizing on life and love, and comments on the action, illuminate the poem.

AUCASSIN AND NICOLETTE

Author: Unknown
Time of action: Twelfth century
First transcribed: Fourteenth century

PRINCIPAL CHARACTERS

Aucassin (ō·kả·săṅ'), the son of Count Garin de Beaucaire. He loves Nicolette, a slave girl bought from the Saracens by a captain who has reared her as his own daughter. Aucassin's father is relentlessly opposed to the marriage, and both Aucassin and Nicolette are imprisoned in the course of the proceedings. At last they run away together and live happily for a time, until they are captured by Saracens. A storm scatters the ships, and the one on which Aucassin is a prisoner drives ashore at Beaucaire, of which he is now Count, his parents having died.

Nicolette (nē·kô·lĕt'). After the lovers are separated by the Saracens, she reaches

Carthage and there learns that she is the daughter of the King of Carthage. He wants her to marry a king of the Saracens, but she remains true to Aucassin. She makes her way to Beaucaire, where they are married at last.

Count Garin de Beaucaire (gả·răṅ' də bō·kėr'), father of Aucassin and opposed to Nicolette as a daughter-in-law.

Count Bougars de Valence (bōō·gả̇r' də vȧ·läṅs'), at war with Count Garin. Having his father's promise to let him see Nicolette on his return from battle, Aucassin fights so fiercely that he captures Count Bougars. When his father refuses to keep the bargain, Aucassin releases

Count Bougars and is cast temporarily into a dungeon.

The King of Carthage, who proves to be Nicolette's father.

THE AWAKENING OF SPRING

Author: Frank Wedekind (1864-1918)
Time of action: Nineteenth century
First presented: 1891

PRINCIPAL CHARACTERS

Melchior Gabor (měl'shē·ŏr gä·bōr'), a promising high school student. He is beginning to feel the effects of sexual phenomena. In a note he imparts his knowledge of sex to his friend, Moritz Stiefel. When Moritz commits suicide and the note is found, Melchior is condemned for moral corruption. His mother upholds him until she is confronted with the fact of his classmate Wendla Bergmann's pregnancy, for which he is responsible.

Moritz Stiefel (mō'rĭts stē'fel), a friend of Melchior Gabor. Plagued by sexual urges and fear of failure in his studies, he commits suicide.

Wendla Bergmann (vän'dlä bĕrg'män), a schoolgirl of fourteen who conceives a child by Melchior Gabor. She dies during an attempted abortion.

Mrs. Bergmann (bĕrg'män), Wendla's mother. She evades the truth in answering her daughter's questions on love and sex.

Mr. and Mrs. Gabor (gä·bōr'), Melchior's parents.

Martha (mär'tä) and
Thea (tä'ä), friends of Wendla, with whom she exchanges confidences on love and sex.

Ilse (ĭl'sě), a prostitute who attempts to seduce Moritz Stiefel.

Mr. Stiefel (stē'fel), Moritz Stiefel's father, a pensioner.

Dr. Von Brausepulver (dôk·tōr' fôn brou'sĕ·pŏŏl'fĕr) and
Mother Schmidt (shmĭt), abortionists whose concoctions cause Wendla Bergmann's death.

A Muffled Gentleman, who appears to the ghost of Moritz Stiefel and the living Melchior Gabor as they converse among the graves. He upbraids Moritz for his attempt to lure Melchior into the land of the dead. He and Melchior withdraw together.

THE AXE

Author: Sigrid Undset (1882-1949)
Time of action: Late thirteenth century
First published: 1925

PRINCIPAL CHARACTERS

Olav Audunsson, the master of Hestviken, who is betrothed to Ingunn Steinfinnsdatter from infancy. After slaying a kinsman of hers in a quarrel, Olav is proclaimed an outlaw, and thus is unable to marry Ingunn, though he has been sleeping with her. Returning home much

later, he finds her with child by another man. He kills the man in secret—a deed he can never confess, lest disclosure of his motive result in Ingunn's shame.

Steinfinn Toresson, the father of Ingunn and foster father of Olav. In love with a woman promised to another, he steals her away. They live together until everyone is reconciled to their wedding —at which time their daughter Ingunn is three years old.

Ingebjörg Jonsdatter, Steinfinn's wife. Her rejected suitor comes years afterwards to take revenge on Steinfinn, whom he shames before his household. Steinnfinn swears not to sleep with his wife until he gets vengeance; the first opportunity comes years later, and Steinfinn kills his rival in combat. Ingebjörg dies in her sleep that very night, and later Steinfinn dies of his wounds.

Ingunn Steinfinnsdatter, betrothed to Olav. Her child by another man is given to a forester's wife at birth, and at last Ingunn and Olav are married.

Arnvid Finnsson, Steinfinn's kinsman. He gives much help to the romance between Ingunn and Olav.

Kolbein Toresson, Steinfinn's gloomy half brother. He is relentlessly opposed to Ingunn's marrying Olav.

Einar Kolbeinsson, who is killed by Olav in a quarrel between the Kolbeinssons and Arnvid and Olav. As a result, Olav is outlawed and must leave Ingunn.

Teit, an Icelander and a merry, pert clerk. Ingunn succumbs to him during Olav's absence. He fathers her child and is killed by Olav.

Eirik, the illegitimate son of Teit and Ingunn.

Tore Toresson, the father of Steinfinn. He sends his son to the royal bodyguard at Bergen, where Steinfinn first sees Ingebjörg.

Queen Ingebjörg, with whom Ingebjörg Jonsdatter came from Denmark.

King Magnus, who has promised Ingebjörg to Mattias.

Mattias Haraldsson, Ingebjörg's rejected promised bridegroom. He takes revenge by shaming Steinfinn, who later kills him in combat.

Tora Steinfinnsdatter, Ingunn's sister.

Hallvard Steinfinnsson and Jon Steinfinnsson, younger brothers of Ingunn.

Audun Ingolfsson, of Hestviken, the father of Olav. Told he is soon to die, he holds Steinfinn to an agreement made during a drinking bout that Olav and Ingunn shall marry. The orphaned Olav is then reared by Steinfinn.

Haakon Gautsson, the husband of Tora.

Bishop Thorfinn, a stern but just man. But for Olav's slaying of Einar, the Bishop might have succeeded in helping Olav and Ingunn to marry, despite her kinsmen's opposition.

Earl Alf Erlingsson, Queen Ingebjörg's liegeman, in whose train Olav returns briefly, to make peace with the Kolbeinssons. Upon the Queen's death, her son proclaims Alf and his men outlaws.

Lady Magnhild, who gives Ingunn's child to a foster mother.

BABBITT

Author: Sinclair Lewis (1885-1951)
Time of action: The 1920's
First published: 1922

PRINCIPAL CHARACTERS

George F. Babbitt, a satirically-portrayed prosperous real estate dealer in Zenith, a typical American city. He is the standardized product of modern American civilization, a member of the Boosters' Club, hypnotized by all the slogans of success, enthralled by material possessions, envious of those who have more, patronizing towards those who have less, yet dimly aware that his life is unsatisfactory. His high moment comes when, after delivering a speech at a real estate convention, he is asked to take part in a political campaign against Seneca Doane, a liberal lawyer who is running for mayor. As a result of his campaign efforts, Babbitt is elected vice-president of the Boosters. His self-satisfaction is shattered when his one real friend, Paul Riesling, shoots his nagging wife and is sent to prison. For the first time Babbitt begins to doubt the values of American middle-class life. He has a love affair with a client, Mrs. Judique, and becomes involved with her somewhat bohemian friends; he publicly questions some of the tenets of Boosterism; he refuses to join the Good Citizens' League. But the pressure of public opinion becomes too much for him; when his wife is taken ill, his brief revolt collapses, and he returns to the standardized world of the Boosters' Club.

Myra Babbitt, his colorless wife, whom he married because he could not bear to hurt her feelings. She lives only for him and the children.

Verona Babbitt, their dumpy daughter. Just out of college, she is a timid intellectual whose mild unconventionality angers her father. He is relieved when she marries Kenneth Escott.

Theodore (Ted) Babbitt, their son. A typical product of the American school system, he hates study and the thought of college. He elopes with Eunice Littlefield, thus winning his father's secret admiration, for he has at least dared to do what he wanted.

Paul Riesling, Babbitt's most intimate friend since college days. With the soul of a musician, he has been trapped into a lifetime of manufacturing tar-roofing

and is burdened with a shrewish wife. Goaded to desperation, he shoots her and, though she lives, is sent to prison.

Zilla Riesling, Paul's nagging wife. With a vicious disposition that is made worse by having too much time on her hands, she finally drives Paul to the point of shooting her.

Mrs. Daniel (Tanis) Judique, a widow with whom Babbitt has a brief affair as a part of his revolt against conventionality.

Seneca Doane, a liberal lawyer, the anathema of all the solid businessmen of Zenith.

William Washington Eathorne, a rich conservative banker. He represents the real power behind the scene in Zenith.

**Charles and
Lucille McKelvey,** wealthy members of Zenith's smart set. The Babbitts are hopeful of being accepted socially by the McKelveys but do not succeed.

**Ed and
Mrs. Overbrook,** a down-at-heels couple. They are hopeful of being accepted socially by the Babbitts but do not succeed.

The Rev. Dr. John Jennison Drew, the efficient, high-powered pastor of Babbitt's church.

Vergil Gunch, a successful coal dealer. He is prominent in all the civic organizations to which Babbitt belongs.

T. Cholmondeley (Chum) Frink, a member of Babbitt's social group. He is a popular poet whose work is syndicated throughout the country.

Howard Littlefield, Babbitt's next-door neighbor. An economist for the Zenith Street Traction Company, he can prove to everyone's satisfaction that Zenith is the best of all possible worlds.

Eunice Littlefield, his flapper daughter.

73

She elopes with Ted Babbitt to the public surprise and indignation of both families but to Babbitt's secret delight.

Kenneth Escott, a newspaper resporter. After a tepid courtship, he finally marries Verona Babbitt.

THE BACCHAE

Author: Euripides (c. 485-c. 406 B.C.)
Time of action: Remote antiquity
First presented: 405 B.C.

PRINCIPAL CHARACTERS

Dionysus (dī'ə·nī'sûs), also called Bromius, Evius, and Bacchus. He is a god of the general fertility of nature and especially of wine. He has been traveling through the world spreading his teachings but has met with opposition at Thebes, where he appears disguised as his own prophet to take measures on the human level to overcome his opponents. He has driven his mother's sisters (he was the son of Semele by Zeus) to frenzy because they refused to recognize him as a god, and they now revel as thyrsus-bearing Bacchantes with the other women of Thebes on the slopes of Mount Cithaeron. Chief of the god's foemen was young King Pentheus, who refuses to recognize Dionysus as a god. Appearing at first as the friend of mortals, he is joyful and willing to reason with the young King, even when Pentheus imprisons him in the royal stables. He frees himself and makes one last attempt to convince Pentheus that he must acknowledge Dionysus' divinity and power. Only when Pentheus determines to drive the Bacchantes from the hills by force does Dionysus reveal the opposite aspect of his character. Becoming cruel, ruthless, and cunning, he establishes control over the mind of Pentheus and leads him, disguised as a woman, through the streets of Thebes to Cithaeron, where he is torn apart by the maddened women of his own city, led by Pentheus' mother, Agave. At the end of the play, after Agave has returned and has realized what she has done, Dionysus appears to pass the sentence of exile on the family of Pentheus. The most terrible aspect of his character emerges as he extends Pentheus' fate to include the suffering of the old and the innocent.

Pentheus (pĕn'thūs), the young, still beardless King of Thebes. He is a puritan with something in his own mind which prevents his seeing any but the extreme aspects, the supposed sexual excesses, of the worship of Dionysus. His opposition to the god is adamant; he imprisons some of the women who follow Dionysus and even the disguised Dionysus himself. When the imprisoned women are miraculously released he remains angry and scornful. After he determines to move with armed force against the Bacchantes, Dionysus exerts control over him and the young King appears beastly drunk, losing all self-control and self-respect. Disguised as a woman, he is led off by Dionysus to spy, as he thinks, on the Bacchantes. The maddened women fall on him and tear him to pieces.

Agave (ə·gā'vē), the mother of Pentheus. In a frenzy she leads the Bacchantes as they tear her son limb from limb under the delusion that he is a lion. Still under her delusion, she first appears carrying her son's mangled head affixed to her thyrsus like a trophy. She praises the gods for guiding her in the deed, inquires after her father, Cadmus, and calls out to Pentheus to come and receive the trophy she has brought. When Cadmus slowly and painfully brings her back to

74

sanity, dazed and perplexed, she realizes what she has done. She is condemned to exile by Dionysus.

Cadmus (kăd'mŭs), the father of Agave. He first appears on his way to worship Dionysus, whom he has conventionally accepted as a god for the good of the family, since Dionysus is reputed to be the cousin of Pentheus. He urges his grandson to do the same but is refuted. He next appears, after gathering the mangled remains of his grandson from the slopes of Cithaeron, to bring Agave back to sanity. He is condemned to exile by Dionysus, even though he protests that such action is too severe.

Tiresias (tī·rē'sĭ·əs), the blind prophet of Thebes. He appears with Cadmus as they prepare to worship Dionysus. He has cleverly accepted Dionysus while retaining his old beliefs. He is proud of his good sense; he has not reasoned dangerously. He urges Pentheus to do the same.

[Ino (ī'nō) and Autonoë (ô·tōn'ō·ĭ), Agave's sisters who help her tear apart Pentheus' body.]

Chorus of Asian Bacchae, followers of Dionysus. Their odes in praise of Dionysus present a picture of Dionysus worship in its purer form and contrast with Pentheus' warped ideas.

BACK TO METHUSELAH

Author: Bernard Shaw (1856-1950)
Time of action: The past and the future
First published: 1921; *first presented:* 1922

PRINCIPAL CHARACTERS

["Back to Methuselah" is really five plays in one. It is starkly didactic, and most of the characters are either Shavian types or allegorical figures. The theme is Creative Evolution, the idea that "the power that produced Man when the monkey was not up to the mark, can produce a higher creature than Man if Man does not come up to the mark." Man, further, can "will" the change. The five plays which make up "Back to Methuselah" are explorations of this theme. It will be most convenient to consider the characters, a few of whom shall reappear, in five groups, one for each play.]

PART I
"In the Beginning: B.C. 4004"

Adam, the first man, created by the splitting of Lilith into male and female. Adam is dull and plodding, the tradition-bound agrarian who adheres to conventional morality solely from a lack of curiosity.

Eve, who eagerly eats the Forbidden Fruit in order to trade the agonies of individual immortality for racial immortality. Eve, the eternally curious, has a compulsion to create. Dissatisfied by both Adam's passivity and Cain's senseless hunger for glory, she yearns for something better.

The Serpent, a wise and beneficent female serpent. She frees Adam and Eve from the burden of immortality and tells them their wills have the power to create anything they desire.

Cain, the archetype of the ruling-class man: the destroying man and the exploiting man. Cain demonstrates that it is "the Voice of God" that makes him kill, while it is "the Voice of the Devil" that tells Adam, "Thou shall not kill."

Enoch, the intellectual who, while young, manufactures doctrines to justify Cain's rapacity. Fortunately, Enoch lives long enough to understand "the Voice"

75

more clearly and to repudiate Cain. Unfortunately, Shaw intimates, our intellectuals do not live so long.

Lua, Eve's daughter and Cain's wife. For her own greedy ends, she encourages Cain's conquests.

PART II

"The Gospel of the Brothers Barnabas: A.D. 1920"

Franklyn Barnabas, a clerical English gentleman of about fifty.

Conrad, Franklyn's brother, a professor of biology. He and Franklyn are preparing to publish their proposal that human life be extended to three hundred years. Their belief is that this change is necessary if Man is not to destroy himself.

Mr. Joyce Burge, a fifty-year-old former Liberal Prime Minister.

Lubin, a patriarch of seventy, Prime Minister before Burge. Lubin and Burge are obvious demonstrations that short-lived men are too inexperienced to rule rationally. Both dismiss the Barnabas' scheme when they cannot see how it can win votes in the next election.

Cynthia, Franklyn's eighteen-year-old daughter. Because she has grown up without bourgeois manners, she is known as "Savvy," short for "Savage."

William Haslam, a boyish clergyman who is to marry Cynthia. He is one of those destined to live three hundred years.

A Parlor Maid, who is leaving Franklyn's employ to marry the village woodsman. Although she speaks ironically of only one life to live, she too is to live three hundred years.

PART III
"The Thing Happens: A.D. 2170"

The Archbishop, actually William Haslam of Part II. Now 283 years old, he still looks forty-five. His longevity, which he had concealed by faking drowning accidents, is accidentally discovered.

Mrs. Lutestring, the Domestic Minister. She is actually the parlor maid, now aged 274. She and the Archbishop discuss the difficulty of living in a world without grownups in it. They agree to marry and have long-lived children.

Burge-Lubin, the President of England, a composite of the two politicians in Part II, but hardly an improvement on either of them.

Barnabas, the Accountant-General, a younger and more commonplace version of Conrad Barnabas. He threatens the long-lived ones with extinction because he fears them and because they upset his actuarial tables.

Confucius, one of the Chinese civil servants who govern England in 2170. He takes stoically the fact that long-livedness is confined to the English race.

The Negress, Minister of Health, with whom Burge-Lubin has been carrying on a flirtation via television. The chance that he, too, may be long-lived makes him turn down a rendezvous with her.

PART IV
"Tragedy of an Elderly Gentleman, A.D. 3,000"

Joseph Popham Bolge Bluebin Barlow, O.M., the Elderly Gentleman, a descendant of Burge-Lubin. The British Isles are now reserved for the long-livers. Visitors from the Empire, which now has its capital in Baghdad, visit the British Isles to consult with them. The Elderly Gentleman is at Galway with a party come to consult the Oracle. His tragedy is his realization of the infinite foolishness of his own society. Unable to bear returning to his own world and too immature to remain in Britain, he is at last put mercifully to death by the Oracle.

76

Zoo, a "girl of fifty" who resembles Savvy of Part II. Acting as Barlow's nurse, she is so enraged at his manner that she announces her conversion to the party of Colonizers, who wish to exterminate the short-livers.

Napoleon I, Cain Adamson Charles, "the man of destiny." He is a great general who fights because he has no other talents. He asks the Oracle how he can stop being a general without losing his glory. The Oracle quite logically takes his pistol from him and tries to shoot him.

The British Envoy,
His Wife, and
Their Daughter, conventional and uncomprehending Britishers who act as chorus. The Envoy is Badger Bluebin, son-in-law of the Elderly Gentleman.

The Pythoness, 170 years old. She is so advanced beyond the "mortals," although only half-grown herself, that her gaze is enough to cow Napoleon and to kill the Elderly Gentleman.

Zozim, a very young "adult." His bored and mocking manner and Zoo's, as they attend the Oracle, offend the visitors.

PART V

"As Far As Thought Can Reach: A.D. 31,920"

[Children, in 31,920, are born from eggs at the age of twenty, skipping the painful years of childhood and adolescence. In the next four years of compressed aging, they reach the maturity of seventy years. Thereafter they live on until killed by inevitable accident.]

Strephon and
Acis, two youths, and
Chloe and
Ecrasia, two nymphs. The four frolic in a glade before a temple in the style of Greece in the Fifth Century B.C. They watch the birth of a nymph and also the tragedy that grows out of the sculptors' competition.

Amaryllis, a beautiful nymph delivered from her egg while the children watch.

A She-Ancient, who delivers Amaryllis from her egg.

Arjillax and
Martellus, two sculptors. Martellus claims that he has discovered the greatest of artists, Pygmalion.

Pygmalion, squarish, benevolent, somewhat pedantic; he has captured the Life Force and sculptured a living man and woman. When Pygmalion tries to keep the female figure from killing the male, she bites him. Her being is so gross in comparison to Pygmalion's that he dies on the spot.

Ozymandias and
Cleopatra-Semiramis, the male and female figures. As primitive as humans of today, they pompously proclaim mystical claptrap and, after Pygmalion dies, plead human nature and beg for mercy.

A He-Ancient, called to decide the creatures' fate. He humanizes them to the point of wishing to die for each other, then allows them to die. The Ancients' evolutionary goal, he tells the young people, is complete freedom from the flesh, existence as a state of pure intelligence.

The Ghost of Adam,
The Ghost of Eve,
The Ghost of the Serpent, and
The Ghost of Cain, who all appear as the children drift off. They puzzle over the meaning of all that has happened.

Lilith, the Universal Mother. She appears to pronounce a benediction over Man's history. He has redeemed himself from sin and violence. Best of all, he is not yet satisfied.

BAMBI

Author: Felix Salten (1869-1945)
Time of action: Indefinite
First published: 1929

PRINCIPAL CHARACTERS

Bambi, a deer who as a fawn longs to be with his mother and his cousins, who asks many questions of his forest friends and learns much through their answers and his own observation, and who at last in maturity learns to stay by himself.

The Old Prince, a wise old stag who befriends Bambi, gives him much sage advice, saves him once from Man, and later instructs him about herbs which will heal him after Bambi has been wounded by a hunter.

Bambi's Mother. She lovingly cares for young Bambi and teaches him forest lore and how to protect himself from Man. Before Bambi grows his new antlers she disappears forever.

Faline, Bambi's lovely cousin with whom he plays when they are fawns and whom he later loves.

Gobo, her small, delicate brother who is caught by Men, kept as a pet until full-grown, and then released. Foolishly trusting all Men, he is killed when he goes to talk with a hunter.

Ena, mother of Faline and Gobo.

Man, a puzzling and dangerous creature with a black stick that sends out thunder, fire, and death, even to his own kind.

Ronno, a stately stag who escaped after a hunter wounded him in the foot. The following year he ceases his pursuit of Faline when Bambi challenges and defeats him in battle before the admiring Faline.

Karus, an older stag who attempts to interfere with Bambi when he wishes to play with Faline as he did when they were fawns. Karus flees when attacked by Bambi.

Nettla, an old doe, self-sufficient and with her own ideas about everything. She regards Man with disgust.

Marena, a young, half-grown doe who predicts that Man will some day be as gentle as the deer themselves.

BARABBAS

Author: Pär Lagerkvist (1891-   )
Time of action: First century
First published: 1949

PRINCIPAL CHARACTERS

Barabbas, a convicted robber freed that Christ might be crucified in his stead. Puzzled by the events of the Crucifixion, he wanders about the earth and is finally enslaved in a Roman mine. Concealing the true nature of his relationship with the crucified Jesus, Barabbas poses as a Christian, but when confronted by the Roman governor, he readily renounces his "faith" and is taken to Rome. One night, seeing flames, he imagines that Christ has returned to save the world and destroy the city. He seizes a burning brand, and is arrested and imprisoned with the Christians, who tell him that it is Caesar, not Christ, who has set the fires. Barabbas is crucified for his "crime," saying, ambiguously, as he dies, that he delivers his soul "to thee."

A Girl, Barabbas' mistress, the mother of his dead child. She becomes a Christian and is stoned to death for her beliefs.

Eliahu, Barabbas' father, the leader of a robber band. Barabbas kills him in order to take over leadership of the robbers.

Sahak, Barabbas' fellow slave in the

Roman mines, crucified for his faith in Christ.

Mary, the Mother of Jesus, who disturbs Barrabbas with her look of silent reproach as he leaves the Crucifixion.

Peter, the Apostle, of whom Barabbas asks questions about Christ. They are imprisoned and crucified together after the fire in Rome.

Lazarus, raised from the dead; he tells Barabbas that, once one has died, life and death are nothing.

THE BARBER OF SEVILLE

Author: Pierre Augustin Caron de Beaumarchais (1732-1799)
Time of action: Eighteenth century
First presented: 1775

PRINCIPAL CHARACTERS

Figaro (fē′gə·rō), the barber of Seville. Figaro is a gay and not overscrupulous barber and apothecary who does not hesitate to be of help to Count Almaviva in his pursuit of marriage with Rosine. Full of stratagems, he multiplies false identities, to the confusion of everyone. His own vein of comment reveals that he is the foe of the old and their heavy, unjustified wielding of authority. His malice, however, is only skin-deep.

Count Almaviva (äl·mä·vē′vä), a Spanish grandee from Madrid. The conventional ardent lover, he is thoroughly determined to reach his goal, marriage with the beautiful Rosine. Lacking the intelligence and guile to achieve his purposes, he enlists the aid of Figaro. At Figaro's suggestion he assumes two other indentities. He pretends to be Lindor, a soldier enamored of Rosine; when this plan fails, he becomes Alonzo, a pretended music teacher and a substitute for Don Bazile, Rosine's real music teacher. Almaviva finally quiets outraged local authority by an appeal to his rank.

Doctor Bartholo (bär′tô·lō), Rosine's elderly guardian, a man suspicious of all young persons and new ideas. Fearful of losing his ward and the money she represents, he keeps her locked away from all suitors and allows her only the company of an elderly music teacher, Don Bazile. Because of increasing suspicion, he plans to marry Rosine himself and thus keep control of her property. He is foiled, however, by the strategies of Figaro and the revealed prestige of Count Almaviva.

Don Bazile (dōn bá·zēl′), a slanderous music teacher and Doctor Bartholo's tool. It is he who makes arrangements for the secret marriage between Rosine and Doctor Bartholo. Although he has brought the notary to Bartholo's house, he accepts a bribe from Almaviva and deserts his former patron.

Rosine (rō·zēn′), the object of Almaviva's love, an innocent, oppressed young woman. She is, however, capable of prudent suspicion about the pretended music

79

teacher Alonzo and can be persuaded that Alonzo is preparing to sell her to the Count. When the identity of Alonzo as the Count is revealed, Rosine faints, but she recovers in time for a happy marriage and the frustration of her guardian.

The Notary, the performer of the marriage between Almaviva and Rosine. Although he is brought to the house to perform a marriage that will link Rosine and Bartholo forever, Figaro is able to persuade him that it is Count Almaviva and Rosine who should be married.

BARCHESTER TOWERS

Author: Anthony Trollope (1815-1882)
Time of action: Mid-nineteenth century
First published: 1857

PRINCIPAL CHARACTERS

Eleanor Bold, younger daughter of the Reverend Septimius Harding, the "Warden," and wealthy widow of John Bold. She lives with her baby son and her sister-in-law, Mary Bold. Much of the novel revolves around Eleanor's choice of one of her three suitors: Mr. Slope, Bertie Stanhope, and Mr. Arabin. Throughout a large portion of the novel, most of her ecclesiastical friends and relatives assume that she will choose Mr. Slope.

Dr. Proudie, the clergyman who becomes Bishop of Barchester after the death of Archdeacon Grantly's father. Dr. Proudie is a vain but weak man, dominated by his wife and by Mr. Slope. Although all Barchester expects him to offer the wardenship of Hiram's Hospital to Mr. Harding, Dr. Proudie allows Mr. Slope's chicanery to gain the appointment for Mr. Quiverful.

Mrs. Proudie, the aggressive and domineering wife of the Bishop of Barchester. She attempts to control Barchester by championing evangelical and Low Church causes, awarding church patronage, and manipulating people through the offices of Mr. Slope. She antagonizes the established ecclesiastical society in Barchester.

The Rev. Obadiah Slope, the Bishop's chaplain. An evangelical clergyman, Mr.

Slope antagonizes most of the chapter with his initial fiery sermon at Barchester Cathedral. He first acts as Mrs. Proudie's agent, but, after he supports the claims of Mr. Harding in an attempt to gain favor with Eleanor Bold, Mrs. Proudie scorns him. Unable to win favor or Eleanor or the post of Dean of Barchester, he returns to London.

The Rev. Theophilus Grantly, the Archdeacon of Barchester and rector of Plumstead Episcopi. He strongly supports the claims of Harding, his father-in-law, to be reinstated as warden of Hiram's Hospital. When the nearby living of St. Ewold's becomes vacant, he goes to Oxford to obtain the post for the Reverend Francis Arabin. He also fears that his sister-in-law, Eleanor Bold, will marry the Low Churchman, Slope.

Susan Grantly, wife of Archdeacon Grantly and the elder daughter of Mr. Harding. She generally follows her husband, but attempts to mitigate his anger at her sister.

The Rev. Septimus Harding, former Warden of Hiram's Hospital. He desires his former charge but is denied it through the machinations of Mr. Slope and Mrs. Proudie, who make his appointment conditional on his assuming extra duties and administering evangelical Sunday Schools. Later he is offered the Deanship of Barchester Cathedral, but he refuses the post because of his advanced age.

The Rev. Francis Arabin, a scholarly High Church clergyman from Oxford who is brought into the living at St. Ewold's to strengthen forces against Bishop Proudie and Mr. Slope. He eventually becomes Dean of Barchester and marries Eleanor Bold.

Dr. Vesey Stanhope, holder of several livings in the Barchester area who has spent the preceding twelve years in Italy. He is summoned to Barchester by Dr. Proudie, through Slope, but has little interest in the political or ecclesiastical affairs of Barchester.

Mrs. Stanhope, his wife, interested chiefly in dress.

Charlotte Stanhope, the oldest daughter of the Stanhopes, who manages the house and the rest of the family with efficiency and intelligence. She, a friend of Eleanor Bold, urges her brother to propose to Eleanor.

La Signora Madeline Vesey Neroni, nee Stanhope, the great beauty of the Stanhope family who has been crippled in a short, disastrous marriage to a brutal Italian. Although confined to her sofa, she attracts men easily. One of her victims is Mr. Slope, whose hypocrisy she exposes, but she is sufficiently generous to encourage Eleanor to marry Mr. Arabin.

Ethelbert Stanhope (Bertie), the amiable son of the Stanhopes, who has dabbled in law, art, and numerous religions. His family wishes to settle him with Eleanor and her money, but Bertie's proposal fails and he is sent back to Carrara by his father.

Mr. Quiverful, the genial clergyman and father who is persuaded to accept the preferment at Hiram's Hospital in addition to his living at Puddingdale.

Mrs. Letty Quiverful, his wife and the mother of fourteen children, who begs Mrs. Proudie to bestow the preferment at Hiram's Hospital on her husband.

Miss Thorne of Ullathorne, the member of an old family at St. Ewold's who gives a large party at which both Mr. Slope and Bertie Stanhope propose to Eleanor. Miss Thorne, however, favors Arabin and invites both Arabin and Eleanor to stay until the engagement is settled.

Wilfred Thorne, Esq., of Ullathorne, the younger brother of Miss Thorne, a bachelor, and an authority on tradition and geneology.

Dr. Gwynne, Master of Lazarus College, Oxford, the man instrumental in securing the Deanship for Mr. Arabin.

Olivia Proudie, the daughter of the Proudies, briefly thought to be engaged to Mr. Slope.

Mary Bold, the sister-in-law and confidante of Eleanor Bold.

Johnny Bold, the infant son of Eleanor and the late John Bold.

Griselda Grantly, the pretty daughter of Archdeacon Grantly.

Dr. Trefoil, Dean of Barchester Cathedral, who dies of apoplexy.

The Bishop of Barchester, the father of Archdeacon Grantly. He dies at the very beginning of the novel.

Dr. Omicron Pi, a famous doctor from London.

BARNABY RUDGE

Author: Charles Dickens (1812-1870)
Time of action: 1775-1780
First published: 1841

Barnaby Rudge, the title character but a figure of lesser importance than a number of other personages in this semi-historical novel which has for its background the "No Popery" or Gordon riots of 1780. Born on the night of his father's supposed murder, he is, in his twenties, half-witted, physically strong, and grotesque, almost unearthly, in appearance because of his shock of red hair. At the same time his sensitivity to beauty, his near idolatry of Hugh, the hostler at the Maypole Inn, and his devotion to Grip, his tame, talking raven, reveal his simple, good nature. Pardoned after being arrested and condemned to death for taking part in the rioting, he becomes his mother's stay and comfort in later years.

Mrs. Rudge, his mother, whose life has been one of hardship and sorrow. Her efforts to support her mentally disordered son and to protect him from the tribulations that befall the weak-minded are rewarded after the riots, when she and Barnaby go to live at the restored Maypole Inn under the protection of kind-hearted Joe Willet and his wife Dolly.

Rudge, a savage, violent man, the former steward at The Warren, a fugitive from justice after murdering his employer, Reuben Haredale, and a gardener whose mutilated body was mistaken for Rudge's. Returning twenty-two years later, he lives a life of skulking and crime, his identity known only to his wife. Recognized while taking part in the "No Popery" riots, he is sentenced to death and hanged. Before his death his wife makes futile efforts to get him to repent.

Emma Haredale, the daughter of the murdered Reuben Haredale. She is the victim of an agreement between her guardian-uncle and her fiancé's father that she shall not marry Edward Chester because of their different religious beliefs and because John Chester desires a grander alliance for his son. Eventually she and Edward are married, and he rebuilds The Warren, looted and burned by "No Popery" rioters.

Geoffrey Haredale, a Roman Catholic country squire, Emma Haredale's uncle and guardian, and a victim of mob violence during the riots. A kind-hearted man, he is especially solicitous for the welfare of Barnaby Rudge and his mother. Planning to leave England, he revisits the ruins of The Warren. There he encounters Sir John Chester and kills him in a duel. Haredale dies several years later in a religious establishment in Italy.

Edward Chester, Emma Haredale's fiancé, who defies his father's wishes for the son's marriage to a Protestant heiress. Disowned, he goes to the Indies. He returns to become a hero at the time of the riots, saves Emma from her abductors, and marries her after her uncle withdraws his objection to the match.

John Chester, later Sir John, an egocentric man completely lacking in compassion and concerned only with his own importance and advancement. His career of selfish intrigue is ended when Geoffrey Haredale kills him in a duel. His character is modeled after that of Philip Dormer Stanhope, Lord Chesterfield.

John Willet, the landlord of the Maypole Inn, near Epping Forest. An obstinate, domineering man, he treats his grown son Joe as if he were still a boy. He never fully recovers from the mob's abuse when the inn was plundered during the rioting, but he spends his last days peacefully in a cottage where he entertains his cronies in a miniature replica of the Maypole bar.

Joe Willet, the landlord's son. Bullied by his father and unhappily in love with Dolly Varden, he runs away and joins the army. After losing an arm while fighting in the American Revolution, he returns to England at the time of the "No Popery" riots and with Edward Haredale displays great heroism during that time of violence. For his services he receives a silver snuffbox from the King. He and Dolly, whom he rescues after she and Emma Haredale have been abducted, are comfortably married and settled at the restored Maypole Inn, where old soldiers are always treated well by the landlord and his plump, cheerful wife.

Gabriel Varden, an honest, good-hearted locksmith, abducted by the rioters and ordered to open the great lock when the mob storms Newgate Prison. His defiance of the mob is only one instance of his goodness, a trait recognized and respected by all who know him.

Dolly Varden, his daughter, loved by Joe Willet. Plump, naïve, garrulous, she is the antithesis of Emma Haredale, with whom she is abducted during the riots. Rescued by Joe, she leaves no doubt as to her love for him.

Mrs. Varden, a woman of uncertain temper and changeable moods.

Hugh, the hostler at the Maypole Inn and a leader in the riots. A paradoxical character, he is a mixture of kindness and bitterness. His better side shows in his kindness to Barnaby Rudge and in his loyalty to those he trusts. Embittered by the execution of his mother, a gipsy hanged at Tyburn, he is vituperative in his attitude toward society. Condemned to die, he attributes his contempt for society and his indifference to death to his parentage—a gipsy mother and an aristocratic father. Before his execution he divulges the fact that Sir John Chester is his father. Informed by Gabriel Varden, Sir John refuses to acknowledge the relationship and abandons Hugh to his fate.

Simon Tappertit, also called **Sim** and **Simmun,** Gabriel Varden's apprentice, Joe Willet's rival for the love of Dolly Varden, and a leader of the rioters. During the confusion he and Dennis, a hangman, abduct Dolly and Emma Haredale.

Shot, with both legs crushed, he is eventually freed. His former master helps to set him up in business as a bootblack, and he is so successful that he is able to marry the widow of a rag collector. On occasion he beats his wife. She retaliates by removing his wooden legs, exposing him to the derision of street urchins.

Miss Miggs, a servant in the Varden household, in love with Simon Tappertit. During the riots she forsakes the Vardens to follow and look after the apprentice. She always insists that her own virtue makes her a soul-saver, and she eventually finds her proper place as a female turnkey at the County Bridwell, where for more than thirty years she shows no mercy to women prisoners who have proved themselves weak in virtue.

Ned Dennis, a former hangman and one of the ringleaders of the "No Popery" riots. He is a composite of undesirable traits. Sadistic, he treats prisoners with violence; audacious, he is also traitorous; cowardly, he snivels when he is faced with his own execution.

Lord George Gordon, the fanatical instigator of the "No Popery" riots. Arrested on a charge of treason, he is imprisoned in the Tower. He is later acquitted when the offense with which he is charged cannot be proved.

Gashford, Lord George Gordon's toadying secretary. He deserts his employer when the nobleman is arrested.

John Grueby, Lord George Gordon's servant.

Solomon Daisy, a parish clerk and sexton, **Tom Cobb,** a chandler and post-office keeper, and
Phil Parkes, a ranger, John Willet's cronies who frequent the Maypole Inn.

Mr. Langdale, a vintner. He hides Geoffrey Haredale in his house during the riots. Joe Willet and Edward Chester save him and the squire when the mob storms the house.

BARON MÜNCHAUSEN'S NARRATIVE

Author: Rudolph Erich Raspe (1737-1794)
Time of action: Eighteenth century
First published: 1785

PRINCIPAL CHARACTERS

Baron Münchausen (mün'chou·zən), a famous traveler who was in real life Baron Karl Friedrich Hieronymus von Münchhausen (1720-1797). His tales, "with nothing but simple additions to the truth," have been augmented by subsequent compilers.

Sinbad,
Ananias,
Aladdin, and
Gulliver, who are appealed to as witnesses to the Baron's veracity.

BARREN GROUND

Author: Ellen Glasgow (1874-1945)
Time of action: Late nineteenth and early twentieth centuries
First published: 1925

PRINCIPAL CHARACTERS

Dorinda Oakley, the daughter of a poor white Virginia farmer. Tall, dark-haired, radiant-eyed, she is not pretty, but when she smiles her eyes and mouth reveal an inner warmth. A vein of iron in her enables her to survive Jason's desertion of her, his marriage to Geneva Ellgood, her own attempt to kill him, the loss of her baby in a New York accident, the deaths of her parents and of Nathan, and the years of hard work necessary to maintain and improve her dairy farm. Dorinda, one of Ellen Glasgow's self-admitted favorite characters, is among the most impressive rural heroines in modern American fiction. She may be compared with Willa Cather's Alexandra Bergson and Ántonia Shimerda.

Josiah Oakley, her brother, a personification of futility who seems to Dorinda to ooze failure from the pores of his skin.

Rufus Oakley, another brother who, accused of murdering a neighboring farmer, is saved by his mother's lying statement that he was at home when the shooting occurred.

Jason Greylock, the last member of an old Virginia family. Red-haired, chinkapin-eyed, and slightly freckled, he is charming when he smiles; and young Dorinda is charmed. An inner weakness leads him to desert the pregnant Dorinda and marry Geneva. The same weakness takes him on the road his father has followed, a road to death through drink.

Geneva Ellgood, later Jason's wife. She ages rapidly from living with Jason, her mind begins to fail, and she eventually drowns herself.

Nathan Pedlar, a country farmer and merchant. A tall, lank, homely man of unimpressive personality, Nathan has an instinctive knowledge of intelligent farm practices which conserve land instead of wearing it out. He wisely advises Dorinda in the development of her dairy farm and later marries her. He is killed while trying to save the lives of passengers in a train wreck and is given a hero's funeral.

Dr. Greylock, Jason's father. Formerly a

man of prominence and owner of a fine farm, he has been for some years drinking his life away and letting the farm go to ruin.

Eudora Abernethy Oakley, Dorinda's mother, who after her husband's death reveals a suppressed religious mania. After her lie saves Rufus, her conscience drives her insane. She dies in her sleep.

Dr. Faraday, a physician who saves Dorinda's life after an accident in New York. He later hires her to look after his office and his children.

Aunt Mehitable Green, an old Negro conjure woman and midwife in whose home Dorinda becomes ill and learns she is pregnant.

Elvira Oakley, Josiah's wife, a scold who is as much a failure as her husband.

John Abner Pedlar, Nathan's crippled son, who helps Dorinda farm and toward whom she feels almost as close as if he were her own son.

Matthew Fairlamb, a retired carpenter, a still vigorous and talkative old man.

James Ellgood, the owner of Green Acres, a flourishing stock farm.

Joshua Oakley, Dorinda's father, a good and industrious but ineffectual man.

Rose Milford, Nathan's sick wife, a former schoolteacher who faces death by pretending it is not near.

BARRY LYNDON

Author: William Makepeace Thackeray (1811-1863)
Time of action: Eighteenth century
First published: 1843

PRINCIPAL CHARACTERS

Redmond Barry, later **Redmond Barry Lyndon,** after his marriage. The boastful and petulant narrator of this picaresque novel set in the eighteenth century, he is a corrupt bully. Throughout his many adventures, he behaves with consistent dishonor. Suffering from delirium tremens, he dies in the Fleet Prison.

The Widow Barry, his mother, who was deprived of wealth and estates by relatives. She devotes herself to the rearing of her son until his Uncle Brady persuades her to let him take the boy to Brady Castle. Much later, after Barry's marriage, Widow Barry lives with her son and aids him in his nearly successful attempt to drive his wife mad.

Lady Honoria Lyndon, who holds the former Barry lands. Immediately upon learning of her husband's death, Barry begins an underhanded and relentless courtship which at last wears down her

resistance. So brutal a husband is he that Lady Lyndon's natural haughtiness is thoroughly subdued. Kept virtually a prisoner by Barry and his mother, she is almost driven mad before her former suitor and her indignant relatives contrive to free her from Barry's custody.

Lord Bullingdon, Lady Lyndon's son and heir. Barry does his best to deplete Lord Bullingdon's future property in order to live in style and to provide for his own son, who will have no rights of inheritance. Lord Bullingdon is driven by his stepfather to run off to fight the rebels in America. He is reported killed but shows up again just in time to keep his weak-willed mother from succumbing once more to her now estranged husband.

Bryan Lyndon, the son of Lady Lyndon and Barry, a boy overindulged by his father. Thrown from his horse, he is killed. His mother's anguish over his death causes a report that she is mad.

Uncle Brady, who invites the young Barry to Castle Brady and treats him kindly.

Nora Brady, Barry's cousin. He falls in love with her when he is fifteen and she twenty-four. In a fit of jealousy, and with characteristic selfishness, Barry fights a duel with the man she loves and whom her family wants her to marry.

Captain John Quinn, loved by Nora. Believing he has wounded Quinn, Barry flees to Ireland. Later he finds that the dueling pistols were loaded with tow and that Captain Quinn, far from dead, is married to Nora.

Mrs. Fitzsimons, a highway robbery victim whom Barry befriends on the road to Dublin. Visiting at her castle, he attempts to make a lavish impression. When his money is gone, his host and hostess are glad to see him leave.

Chevalier Balibari, suspected of being an Austrian agent by the Prussians. Having deserted from the British Army to the Prussians, Barry, now in Berlin, is sent to spy on Balibari, whom he discovers to be his own father's brother, Barry of Ballybarry, now an elderly gambler. Barry, in disguise, leaves the Prussian service and goes to Dresden with this uncle.

Countess Ida, a wealthy heiress whom Barry dislikes but courts.

Chevalier De Magny, the fiancé of Countess Ida. Barry wins from him, in gambling, all his possessions, including his claim to the hand of Countess Ida. Involvement in a court intrigue, however, foils the matrimonial scheme when Barry is forced to leave the duchy.

Lord Charles Lyndon, the husband of Lady Honoria Lyndon. Barry becomes acquainted with them at a spa and resolves to marry Lady Lyndon as soon as the sickly Lord Lyndon is dead.

Lord George Poynings, Lady Lyndon's former suitor, who helps in freeing her from Barry's custody.

Mick Brady, Barry's cousin. He persecutes young Barry during the latter's stay in Brady Castle.

Mrs. Brady, the wife of Uncle Brady. She hates Barry.

Frederick the Great, of Prussia. He sends Barry to spy on the Chevalier Balibari.

The Duke of X——, at whose court Barry pursues the Countess Ida.

BARTHOLOMEW FAIR

Author: Ben Jonson (1573?-1637)
Time of action: Early seventeenth century
First presented: 1614

PRINCIPAL CHARACTERS

Bartholomew Cokes, a foolish, prodigal young gentleman of Harrow. He is made of the stuff without which fairs and carnivals cannot succeed; fortunately for them, his kind is supposed to be born at the rate of one a minute. A trinket-buyer, he is carried away by the trifles in the booths, and he is an easy victim for pickpockets and confidence men. Blessed with a lovely, well-to-do fiancée, he neglects and loses her.

John Littlewit, a petty official with a pretty wife and a mother-in-law with Puritan leanings. He takes great pride in the fair, especially in the puppet show, for which he has written the script. He and his wife have some difficulty in persuading the mother-in-law to go to the fair, but they finally succeed.

Win-the-Fight Littlewit, John's wife, Dame Purecraft's daughter. As simple-minded as her husband, she falls in with his plans to go to the fair, convinces her mother and Zeal-of-the-Land Busy that she should go to satisfy her longing for pork. She is deceived by Captain Whit into putting on a green gown (a badge of harlotry) and letting him offer her favors to a gentleman at the fair; however, she escapes the fate her foolishness has almost brought on her.

Dame Purecraft, John Littlewit's mother-in-law. Hesitating between two suitors, Rabbi Busy and Ned Winwife, she is troubled by a prophecy that she is to marry a madman. When she meets the insane Troubleall at the fair, she pursues him, thinking it is her fate to marry him. She finally consents to marry Tom Quarlous, in disguise, believing him to be Troubleall.

Zeal-of-the-Land Busy, a Puritan divine. Filled with thunderous rhetoric against the foul fair, papistry, and other abominations, he is a gluttonous hypocrite. He manages to get himself into the stocks for disturbing the peace and at the fair is bested in an argument with a puppet.

Ned Winwife, first the suitor of Dame Purecraft, then the successful suitor of Grace Wellborn. He is a sensible foil to many of the foolish characters.

Tom Quarlous, Winwife's friend. He is the chief mover of the action, employing Edgeworth to steal Cokes' license, disguising himself as Troubleall to marry Dame Purecraft, and showing up Justice Overdo to prevent a cloud of punishments on all the inhabitants of the fair.

Humphrey Waspe (Numps), Cokes' servant and tutor. A small man of demonic fury and with a foul and stinging tongue which he uses freely, he constantly rebukes his young master for irresponsibility. He himself is discomfited by losing the strongbox with the wedding agreement and by being put in the stocks.

Adam Overdo, a meddling justice of the peace, the guardian of Grace Wellborn. Thinking himself a sort of English Haroun al-Raschid, he disguises himself to seek out evil and good at the fair, in hopes of righting wrongs and punishing "enormities." His reforming zeal, misdirected by poor judgment, leads him to beatings and to the stocks. Completely discountenanced when he finds his wife in the green gown of a prostitute squired by a pimp, he gives up his crusade of stern justice and treats the motley horde to a supper.

Dame Overdo, Adam's foolish wife. She becomes intoxicated, threatens to commit a riotous group to prison in the King's name and her husband's, and is persuaded, like Win Littlewit, to put on a green gown and wear it to the puppet play, where she gets sick.

Grace Wellborn, Cokes' fiancée. An attractive and intelligent girl, she is so much annoyed with Cokes' behavior that she offers to marry either Winwife or Quarlous. Each is to choose a fictitious name and show it to the mad beggar Troubleall, his pick to determine her husband. He chooses Winwife's pseudonym.

Lanthorn Leatherhead, a versatile operator in the fair. He runs a booth selling hobby-horses and doubles as a puppet master. Speaking through one of his puppets, he successfully confutes Busy's blasts at the theater.

Joan Trash, a gingerbread woman. She runs a booth near Leatherhead's. When Busy turns over her booth with all the gingerbread (the gingerbread figures were idols in his opinion), she has him arrested and put in the stocks.

Troubleall, a madman. He has an obsession that nothing is legal or suitable without a warrant from Justice Overdo.

His violence at the stocks allows Busy, Numps, and the disguised Overdo to escape. Dame Purecraft wishes to marry him so that she can have a real madman for a husband according to the prophecy; but she mistakes Quarlous for him and marries Quarlous.

Ezekiel Edgeworth, a proficient cutpurse. A handsome young man, he draws the attention of Justice Overdo, who seeks to give him advice on the danger of bad companions and to rescue him before he goes wrong. To save himself from disclosure, he steals the strongbox from Numps and turns it over to Quarlous.

Nightingale, a ballad singer. He and Edgeworth work together; Nightingale attracts a crowd and distracts their attention while Edgeworth picks their pockets. They customarily squander their gains at Ursula's at the end of the day.

Ursula, a pig-woman. She sells pork and ale and has some less savory sidelines. An enormous, greasy, bawdy, quarrelsome woman, she is something of a she-Falstaff, lacking his essential wit.

Alice, a harlot. Angry at the competition professionals receive from amateurs, she quarrels savagely with Dame Overdo, whom she suspects of being a rival.

Dan Jordan Knockem, a horse trader,
Val Cutting, a roaring bully,
Captain Whit, a male bawd,
Puppy, a wrestler, and
Northern, a clothier, members of the noisy crew that hangs around Ursula's booth.

Mooncalf, Ursula's tapster.

Solomon, Littlewit's man.

Haggis and
Bristle, members of the watch.

Pocher, a beadle.

Filcher and
Sharkwell, doorkeepers at Leatherhead's puppet show.

BATOUALA

Author: René Maran (1887-   )
Time of action: c. 1910
First published: 1921

PRINCIPAL CHARACTERS

Batouala, a chief of many villages in French Equatorial Africa. Vigorous and strong of limb, his prowess in the hunt, in love, and in war is a legend across his domain. He is a jealous, violent, and vengeful man. He honors Bissibingui with particular esteem until he becomes aware of the young man's desire for his favorite wife, Yassiguindja. From then on he uses his friendship as a cloak for his jealousy and quietly plans revenge on his rival. At the hunt, he hurls a javelin at Bissibingui but misses his target and is, himself, ripped open by a panther's paw. As he lies dying, Yassiguindja yields to Bissibingui's desire, and the two flee into the night.

Bissibingui, a desirable young man. Having received from eight of Batouala's nine wives proofs of their admiration and affection, he now desires his chief's ninth and favorite wife, Yassiguindja. He finally possesses her as Batouala lies dying of a wound received from a panther as he himself was in the act of trying to kill his young rival.

Yassiguindja, the favorite among Batouala's nine wives. Though she desires

Bissibingui, she is aware of Batouala's jealousy and violence and she will not give herself to his rival until she feels safe from discovery. She finally becomes Bissibingui's as Batouala lies dying from the panther wound.

Indouvoura, another of Batouala's wives.

THE BAY OF SILENCE

Author: Eduardo Mallea (1903-   )
Time of action: 1926-1940
First published: 1940

PRINCIPAL CHARACTERS

Martín Tregua, a young ex-law student, the narrator. Disgusted with the unscientific and spiritless faculty and their unproductive teaching methods, he leaves the law school and takes up writing. In his first venture, "The Forty Nights of Juan Argentino," he attempts to give meaning to the life and suffering of the average Argentine. "The Bay of Silence" then grows out of the inspiration of a young woman to whom he writes telling the story of his life. In three parts he takes his correspondent from the uncertainties of his younger days ("Youth"), through his travels about Europe ("The Islands"), and into the disillusioned wisdom of his middle years ("The Defeated").

Gloria Bambil, a librarian in whom Martín Tregua vainly seeks to instill self-confidence. His failure in this effort makes him one of the defeated in the final section of "The Bay of Silence."

Anselmi, a fellow law student.

Jiménez, an office employee.

César Acevedo, a wealthy Argentine.

Blagoda, an associate on the student magazine "Enough."

Mercedes Miró, a companion of Martín Tregua.

THE BEACH OF FALESÁ

Author: Robert Louis Stevenson (1850-1894)
Time of action: Nineteenth century
First published: 1892

PRINCIPAL CHARACTERS

Wiltshire, a rough, uneducated, but courageous trader who has just come to Falesá. His predecessors having been killed or driven away by Case, a rival trader, Wiltshire immediately finds himself the object of Case's villainy. Pretending friendship, Case persuades him to marry a native girl who is under a taboo. As a result, not a single native will trade with Wiltshire.

Case, a rival who plays on the superstitions of the natives. In order to control the island he pretends to be in league with a powerful devil. When discovered, he shoots and wounds both Wiltshire and Uma; Wiltshire then kills him with a knife.

Uma, a modest islander married in a false ceremony to Wiltshire. Because she is under a taboo, the natives will not trade with Wiltshire. Her mother is a producer of copra.

Tarleton, the missionary who marries Wiltshire and Uma properly.

89

Captain Randall, the supposed owner of a trading post and a friend of Case.

Black Jack, Case's colored confederate.

Maea, the most powerful chief of Falesá, who eventually gives his trade to Wilt-

shire in order to break Case's hold on the natives.

Vigours, an earlier trader frightened away by Case.

John Adams, another trader, who died insane.

BEAUCHAMP'S CAREER

Author: George Meredith (1828-1909)
Time of action: Nineteenth century
First published: 1874-1875

PRINCIPAL CHARACTERS

Nevil Beauchamp, a young man who is eager to reform the world. He starts out as a naval officer but later decides to run for Parliament as a Liberal candidate. He falls in love with the sister of a French officer whose life he has saved, but she marries a man her father has chosen for her. Nevil loses the election, but during his campaign the daughter of a Tory friend has fallen in love with him. When he proposes and she refuses him because of her father's demands, he falls ill. He marries Jenny Denham, who has nursed him during his illness. His death by drowning while trying to rescue a child ends his reformer's career.

Renée Rouaillout (rĕ·nyā′ rōŏ·ĕ·yōŏ′), nee de Croisnel, a rather fickle young Frenchwoman with whom Beauchamp falls in love. She refuses to marry him because she has promised her father that she will marry Rouaillout. After her marriage she sends for Nevil because she has wagered with a friend that he will come if she sends for him. Renée leaves her husband and goes to Nevil, but he is no longer in love with her and effects a reconciliation between her and her husband.

Colonel Halkett, a friend of Beauchamp who is also a Tory and deplores Beauchamp's political views.

Cecelia Halkett, the daughter of the

Colonel, who falls in love with Beauchamp because she admires his courage and thinks he is a man of high honor, in spite of his politics. She remains loyal to him through his various difficulties with Renée, but she finally bows to her father's wishes and marries a more stable young man.

Dr. Shrapnel, a wild political radical who is supposed to be helping Beauchamp with his campaign for Parliament, but who is really ruining his chances by giving him unstable ideas and advice. He is horsewhipped by Beauchamp's Uncle Everard when the uncle reads a letter that Shrapnel has written to Beauchamp and which is full of radical advice.

Jenny Denham, Shrapnel's ward, who nurses Beauchamp back to health after his illness and finally marries him. She is loyal and steadfast through all of his troubles.

Everard Romfrey, Beauchamp's uncle, who is a good conservative Englishman. He approves of an alliance between Cecelia and Beauchamp and hates Dr. Shrapnel. Romfrey's beating of Shrapnel causes a break between him and Beauchamp, but they are reconciled when Romfrey apologizes to Shrapnel.

Mrs. Rosamund Culling, Romfrey's housekeeper, whom he finally marries.

90

THE BEAUX' STRATAGEM

Author: George Farquhar (1678-1707)
Time of action: Early eighteenth century
First presented: 1707

PRINCIPAL CHARACTERS

Charles, Viscount Aimwell, a gentleman who, being low in funds, is traveling in disguise, hoping to attract a country heiress. He finds her in the person of Dorinda, but consummating the union takes considerable doing. Being a second son, he is at first without the title which, upon his brother's death, comes to him shortly before he marries the heiress. In their pretended commonness, Aimwell and Archer are a source of perpetual amusement.

Francis Archer, Esq., also a gentleman out of funds, masquerading as Aimwell's servant. The men take turns, by the month, at being master and servant. Archer's initial idle flirtation with Cherry develops into true love. Because of their secretive behavior—the result of their assumed roles—Archer and Aimwell are falsely suspected of being highwaymen, adding to the havoc created by their pursuits of wealthy ladies.

Cherry, the vivacious daughter of Boniface, an innkeeper. She is privy to the highwaymen's activities and her father's alliance with them. Prompted by her father, she spies on Aimwell and Archer, but she falls in love with Archer and he with her. Cherry contributes greatly to the comic spirit and humor of the play.

Dorinda, the modest, reserved daughter of Lady Bountiful. Hearing Dorinda spoken of as the finest woman in the country and a prospective heiress, the calculating Aimwell sets out to win her for her money. When he gains his title and wealth, he marries her for love.

Bonniface, an innkeeper, Cherry's father. About fifty-eight years old, he has, according to his word, subsisted mainly on ale his entire life. An unscrupulous rogue, he does not hesitate to offer his daughter to an unworthy suitor when he thinks the arrangement might aid his purposes. It is finally revealed that he has run away in fear of reprisal from the other rogues.

Sullen, Dorinda's brother, a country blockhead. He is rude, stupid, and frequently drunk. He speaks little and thinks and acts even less. Although he is a man of property and idolized by his influential mother, he is generally disliked and disregarded.

Mrs. Sullen, his wife. Unhappy in her marriage, she is frank to say so. Paradoxically, she admits she would endure the rude Sullen if only his manner were tempered with a little kindness. Sarcastic and abusive, she is really gentler than she sounds. With romantic scheming, she rids herself of one husband and gets another.

Scrub, Sullen's crude, comical servant. He carries the secrets of the ladies and the beaux as circumstances require.

Lady Bountiful, the mother of Sullen and Dorinda. She is reputed to be the wisest and kindest nurse in Litchfield, and to have cured more people—although by strange methods—in ten years than the doctors have killed in twenty.

Count Bellair, a French officer held prisoner in Litchfield, with whom Mrs. Sullen begins a flirtation to arouse Sullen's jealousy. The scheme merely increases Sullen's indifference; the Sullens are divorced by mutual agreement, and Mrs. Sullen will marry the Count.

Sir Charles Freeman, a gentleman from

91

London. Arriving to rescue Mrs. Sullen, his sister, from her unfortunate marriage, he brings news of Aimwell's newly granted title.

Foigard (fwä·gär'), an Irishman pretending to be the priest and chaplain of the French officers. He provides comedy with his lack of understanding and poor command of spoken English. Finally he is unmasked.

Gibbet, a highwayman, an emissary between Bonniface and the gang.

Hounslow and

Bagshot, highwaymen who contribute to the development of the subplot.

THE BEAVER COAT

Author: Gerhart Hauptmann (1862-1946)
Time of action: Nineteenth century
First presented: 1893

PRINCIPAL CHARACTERS

Frau Wolff (frou vôlf), a washerwoman and the ringleader of a gang of dealers in stolen goods. Protected by her reputation as an honest woman, she sets about stealing from her daughter's employer, Krüger, a load of wood and a beaver coat for delivery to the fence, Wulkow. By virtue of her own wit, the false testimony of other witnesses, and the incompetence of the Justice of the Peace, von Wehrhahn, the innocent in the affair are made to appear guilty, and Frau Wolff emerges as the soul of honor.

Julius Wolff (jöl'yus vôlf), Frau Wolff's husband, a shipwright and ferry captain who uses his nautical activities as a front for his real business in life, the illegal snaring of game.

Leontine (lā'ōn·tē·nə), the elder daughter of Julius and Frau Wolff. She is hired out to Krüger but returns home complaining that he sends her after wood late at night. Her flight is used by Frau Wolff as an opportunity for stealing the wood.

Udelheid (ŏŏ'dĕl·hīd), Julius and Frau Wolff's younger daughter. She is used by her family as a verifier of invented evidence.

Wulkow (vŏŏl'kō), a boatman and a receiver of stolen goods. When he makes known his desire for a fur, his request is cheerfully filled by Frau Wolff, who delivers to him, for a price, Krüger's beaver coat.

Krüger (krü'gər), Leontine's well-to-do employer, who is relieved by her thieving family of his load of wood and his beaver coat.

Von Wehrhahn (fŏn vär'hän), the Justice of the Peace. He is so taken up with rigging evidence against Dr. Fleischer for a supposed slight that he cannot see to it that justice is done in his court.

Doctor Fleischer (flī'shər), Krüger's friend, a liberal democrat who incurs the wrath of von Wehrhahn and, unwittingly, blocks the path of justice.

Motes, an informer and the giver of false evidence.

THE BEGGARS' BUSH

Authors: John Fletcher (1579-1625) and Philip Massinger (1583-1640)
Time of action: The Renaissance
First presented: c. 1622

Florez, also called **Goswin,** the rightful heir, through his mother, to the earldom of Flanders. When Wolfort took over the government of the country, Florez' father entrusted his young son to the care of a wealthy merchant, and the boy grew up ignorant of his real identity. He is widely known as a talented, fortunate merchant and a generous benefactor to all who need help. He often bestows gifts on Clause, an old beggar to whom he feels drawn by a peculiar bond. Ever conscious of his honor, he is distressed at the prospect of falling prey to his debtors when his ships, like Antonio's in "The Merchant of Venice," fail to appear. Even his love cannot withstand the strength of his sense of obligation to Clause, who has relieved him of his financial burdens, and he agrees to forsake his promised bride at the beggar's request.

Gerrard, his father, who disguises himself as **Clause,** king of the beggars, to escape death at the hands of Wolfort. He is a leader in the tradition of Robin Hood, cozening rich fools and protecting honest men in difficulties, while he keeps a watchful eye on the affairs of his son. He reluctantly halts Florez' proposed marriage, for he feels that the girl's lineage is too humble to make her a suitable wife for a duke.

Hubert, a bold, honest young courtier who bravely accuses Wolfort of crime and treason before he flees the usurper to search for his lost sweetheart, Gerrard's daughter Jacqueline. He joins the beggars' band as a hunter and plans the elaborate trap, set for Wolfort and his men, to restore Florez to his earldom.

Wolfort, the proud usurping Earl. When Hubert confronts him with his guilt, he feigns a reformation, hoping to persuade the young man to reveal the whereabouts of Gerrard and his supporters, but he continues his wicked course until his fall.

He refuses to repent, even after he has been captured, and chooses rather to laugh at the clever plot by which he was betrayed.

Captain Hempskirke, Wolfort's henchman. Unaware of Florez' identity, he is indignant at the young man's presumptuous courtship of the girl whom he claims as his niece. Without any of Florez' honorable scruples, he callously accepts his rival's challenge, then hires ruffians to capture him at the appointed meeting place. Taken prisoner by the beggars, he falls blindly into Hubert's trap, leading himself and his master, Wolfort, into the hands of Gerrard's men and the loyal burghers.

Vandunke, a good-hearted, practical burgher who makes no secret, among his friends, of his opposition to the usurper and brings forces to aid in deposing him. A jovial romantic, he looks with favor upon the love of Florez and his ward Bertha, and he prepares elaborate festivities to celebrate their wedding.

Margaret, his dutiful, quiet wife.

Frances, their daughter, a gracious young woman who is obviously a favorite with her father's friends.

Bertha, the daughter of the Duke of Brabant. Kidnaped by Wolfort, she has been placed in Vandunke's care as Hempskirke's niece. A sensible, forthright girl, she reassures her cowardly guide when he trembles with terror at sights and sounds in the forest, and she accepts Florez' puzzling decisions with a minimum of feminine hysteria.

Jacqueline (Jaculin), Gerrard's daughter, who wanders with him in the beggar band, calling herself **Minche.** She is delighted to be reunited with Hubert, her fiancé, but she insists that he help her conceal her identity.

93

Herman, a courtier, sympathetic to Florez and Gerrard's cause.

Higgen,
Ferret,
Prig, and
Snaps, merry beggars who revel in their vagabond existence. The prospect of honest work, offered by Gerrard, so ap-

palls them that they flee to England to continue practicing their trades, juggling, singing, peddling, and stealing.

Lord Arnold and
Lord Costin, loyal nobles who joined the beggars with Gerrard.

Vanlock, an old Flemish merchant who comes to celebrate Florez' wedding.

THE BEGGAR'S OPERA

Author: John Gay (1685-1732)
Time of action: Early eighteenth century
First presented: 1728

PRINCIPAL CHARACTERS

Captain Macheath (măk·hēth'), the swashbuckling leader of a band of highwaymen. A great lover of the ladies, he wins Polly Peachum with protestations of sincere and virtuous affection, privately commenting, "What a fool is a fond wench," as he prepares to entertain his favorite group of London prostitutes. Thrown into prison by Peachum and Lockit, he plays upon the feelings of another "fond wench," Lucy Lockit, the jailer's daughter. He soon finds himself in the midst of a stormy quarrel between Lucy and Polly, who both believe themselves his wife. In the farcical conclusion, when he is forced to pick a spouse from the large group of ladies who claim the role, he dances away with Polly.

Polly Peachum, the gay, buxom daughter of one of Macheath's colleagues. She disgraces her family by marrying and thus ruining her prospects for wealth and advancement. She stanchly defends her rights as Macheath's wife against Lucy with tirades and malicious sweetness, not at all deceived by her rival's proffered friendship.

Peachum, her father. He dispenses the stolen goods of the robber band and increases his fortune by betraying members of the troop to the police. Deter-

mined to leave his daughter free and to prevent her from revealing his double-dealing to her husband, he has Macheath arrested as soon as he hears of Polly's marriage.

Mrs. Peachum, his wife, who assists him in his shady dealings. She, too, is distressed at the prospect of Polly's single-minded devotion to Macheath and laments her daughter's inability to be as fickle as the rest of her sex.

Lucy Lockit, the jailer's daughter, who, like Polly, falls victim to Macheath's charms and helps him escape from prison. She is violently jealous of Polly and even tries to poison her, but the two are reconciled by the realization that they have both been duped.

Lockit, her father, who shares with Peachum the profits which come from the arrest of the highwaymen.

Filch, Mrs. Peachum's favorite, a skillful pickpocket and errand boy for Peachum.

Diana Trapes, one of Peachum's customers, a bawd who buys stolen finery to adorn her "ladies."

Jemmy Twitcher,
Crook-Fingered Jack,
Wat Dreary,

94

Robin of Bagshot,
Nimming Ned,
Harry Padington,
Matt of the Mint, and
Ben Budge, members of Macheath's gang.

Mrs. Coaxer,
Dolly Trull,

Mrs. Vixen,
Betty Doxy,
Jenny Diver,
Mrs. Slammekin,
Suky Tawdry, and
Molly Brazen, Macheath's favorite "ladies of easy virtue," who betray him for Peachum.

BEL-AMI

Author: Guy de Maupassant (1850-1893)
Time of action: c. 1885
First published: 1885

PRINCIPAL CHARACTERS

Georges Duroy (zhôrzh′ dü·rwä′), also called **Bel-Ami,** an ambitious young reporter and M. Walter's employee. A complete rascal, Duroy, who later assumes the more aristocratic name of **Georges du Roy de Cantel,** shrewdly manipulates his acquaintances as he continues to rise in prominent social circles. With the help of Madeleine Forestier, whom he marries after her husband's death, he receives an editorial position. Luckily for him, most women find the dashing ex-army officer irresistible; even the somewhat aloof Madame Walter is unable to resist his charms. At the opportune moment Duroy accuses his wife of infidelity and wins a divorce, thus leaving him free to marry Suzanne, M. Walter's lovely and wealthy young daughter.

Madeleine Forestier (mȧd·lēn′ fô·rĕs·tyā′), Duroy's wife after the death of her husband. A rather cool and calculating woman, she has the ability to evaluate accurately ambitious young men like Duroy. Knowing many prominent people, she shows him how to advance professionally and socially. But in him she finds her match. Before their divorce he manages to assuage his "grief" with five hundred thousand francs from her fortune. Not one to look back in regret,

Madeleine quickly discovers an ambitious young man to take Duroy's place.

Clotilde de Marelle (klô·tēld′ də mȧ·rĕl′), Duroy's mistress. She, like most women, immediately falls under his hypnotic spell. Even when he neglects her, she is unable to stay away from him. After Suzanne's marriage to Duroy, Clotilde presses his hand warmly to indicate her continuing love for him.

Charles Forestier (shärl′ fô·rĕs·tyā′), Duroy's former brother officer and the editor who befriends him. Blessed with an intelligent wife and doomed by weak lungs, Forestier helps Duroy get a job as a reporter for M. Walter's newspaper. After the former's death and before his body is cold, Duroy proposes marriage to the dead man's wife.

M. Walter (vȧl·târ′), the owner of the newspaper for which Duroy works. Using his powerful connections, this shrewd, avaricious man has become one of the wealthiest men in France, but he is unaware that he is a cuckold. When he learns of Duroy's intentions to marry his daughter, he dissents violently. Later, being a practical man, he realizes that Duroy has enough information to ruin him, and he consents readily to the marriage.

Basile Walter (bá·zēl′ vàl·târ′), M. Walter's wife. Falling desperately in love with Duroy, she offers him anything in her power. All she desires is a little affection in return, even though she knows that he is increasingly bored with her. When she learns of Duroy's plans to marry her daughter, she almost goes insane from jealousy. As the marriage approaches, she is still unable to reconcile herself to losing her lover. Seeing her inconsolable grief, one is almost tempted to warn Duroy: "Beware of the jealous and vindictive woman."

Suzanne Walter (sü·zàn′ vàl·târ′), Basile Walter's daughter. After Duroy wins his divorce from Madeleine, the naïve young girl is quite prepared to elope with him, even over the strenuous objections of her mother. She remains completely unaware of her husband's numerous intrigues with other women, including Basile.

A BELL FOR ADANO

Author: John Hersey (1914-   )
Time of action: 1943
First published: 1944

PRINCIPAL CHARACTERS

Major Victor Joppolo, the first military governor of Adano after the Americans have retaken Italy in World War II. He is sincerely interested in restoring the dignity of the people there, and consequently he is willing to suffer what many military men would consider a lack of respect for their position. He succeeds in replacing the bell, the town's most prized possession, which the Fascists had taken.

Sergeant Borth, an outspoken aide to Major Joppolo. He is in complete sympathy with what the Major is trying to do in the town, if not with the methods he uses.

Captain Purvis, Officer-in-Charge of the Military Police in Adano. Adhering rigidly to military regulations, he is careful to report any infractions of orders, including the Major's countermand of General Marvin's order to keep all carts out of Adano.

General Marvin, the overbearing Commander-in-Chief of the American forces in Italy. He cares nothing about the Italian people or their needs and is far too conscious of his own position and the respect he feels is due him.

Giuseppe, Major Joppolo's interpreter, who is quite proud of his position close to the Major.

Tomasino, a fisherman. He distrusts all authority and firmly believes in the dignity of the individual.

Gargano, an ex-Fascist policeman whom Joppolo restores to a position of authority.

Lieutenant Trapani, Captain Purvis's subordinate. He is not afraid of the military and is willing to take some liberty with regulations when the outcome may be helpful.

Colonel Middleton, General Marvin's aide.

BEN HUR: A TALE OF THE CHRIST

Author: Lewis (Lew) Wallace (1827-1905)
Time of action: At the time of Christ
First published: 1880

Ben Hur (běn hěr'), the son of a Jew honored by Rome. He breaks with his old friend, Messala, now arrogant, and defeats him in a chariot race in Antioch. While escaping his enemy's treachery, he cripples Messala for life. Following meetings with the Nazarene, Ben Hur becomes a Christian.

Messala (mə·să'lə), a Roman who turns enemy of the Hur family. He is instrumental in having their property confiscated, and in having Ben Hur made a galley slave. Later he has Ben Hur's sister Tirzah and her mother put in prison, where they contract leprosy.

Simonides (sĭ·mŏ'nĭ·dēz), a Jewish merchant who preserves some of the Hur fortune.

Esther (ěs'thēr), Simonides' daughter, whom Ben Hur marries.

Balthasar (bôl·thă'sēr), an Egyptian, one of the original Magi.

Iras (ī'rəs), his daughter, who kills Messala.

Tirzah (tĭr'zə), Ben Hur's beautiful sister.

Quintus Arrius (kwĭn'təs â'rĭ·əs), who adopts Ben Hur for saving his life during a naval battle.

Jesus the Nazarene (jē'səs the nă'zə·rēn). He cures Tirzah and her mother of leprosy, and inspires Ben Hur to follow Him.

Pilate (pī'lət), the Procurator of Judea.

BENITO CERENO

Author: Herman Melville (1819-1891)
Time of action: 1799
First published: 1856

Amasa Delano (ä·mä'sä děl'ə·nō), an American sea captain. Off the coast of Chile he sees a ship in distress and sets out with food and water for her company. He finds a Spanish merchantman carrying slaves. Ship and crew are in deplorable condition, and their captain suffers from what appear to be severe mental disorders. A series of strange and sinister events lead Captain Delano to the knowledge that the Spanish Captain is a prisoner of the slaves. He is able to rescue the captive and take him ashore.

Don Benito Cereno (dōn bā·nē'tō thā·rā'nō), the Captain of a Spanish slave ship. His human cargo mutinies and makes him a prisoner, forced to witness horrible atrocities on and murders

of the Spanish crew. After his rescue by Captain Delano, he gives testimony concerning the mutiny and dies broken in mind and spirit.

Babo (bä'bō), a mutinous slave. He poses as the devoted servant of Captain Cereno and attempts to deceive Captain Delano concerning his master's true condition. Failing in this attempt, he is captured and hanged on Captain Cereno's testimony.

Don Alexandro Aranda (dōn ä·lä·ksän'drō ä·rän'dä), owner of the cargo of the Spanish slave ship. He is murdered and mutilated by the mutinous slaves.

Raneds (rä'nādz), the slave ship's mate, murdered by the mutinous slaves.

BEOWULF

Author: Unknown
Time of action: c. Sixth century
First transcribed: c. 1,000 or earlier

PRINCIPAL CHARACTERS

Beowulf (bā·ə·wōōlf), the nephew and thane of King Hygelac of the Geats. A warrior who proves his superhuman strength and endurance in his struggle with the monster Grendel, he exemplifies the ideal lord and vassal, rewarding his own men generously and accomplishing glorious deeds to honor his king, while he fulfills all the forms of courtesy at Hrothgar's court.

Hrothgar (hrōth'gär), the aging lord of the Danes, a good and generous ruler deeply distressed by Grendel's ravaging visits to Heorot, his great hall. He adopts his savior, Beowulf, as his son and parts with him tearfully in a moving scene, for he knows that he will not see the young warrior again.

Wealhtheow (wē'äl·thā·ō), his Queen, a gracious, dignified hostess to the visiting Geats. She, too, grows fond of Beowulf and commends the welfare of her young sons into his hands.

Unferth (ōōn'fârth), Hrothgar's adviser, typical of the wicked counselors of folklore. Jealous of Beowulf and heated with wine, he taunts the Geat with his failure to defeat Breca in a youthful swimming match. He is won over by Beowulf's victory against Grendel and lends the hero his sword, Hrunting, for the undersea battle against Grendel's mother.

Grendel (grĕn'dəl), one of the monstrous descendants of Cain, condemned to wander alone in the wastelands of the world. Given pain by the light and merriment in Hrothgar's hall, he visits it and regularly carries off warriors to devour until he is mortally maimed in a struggle with Beowulf.

Grendel's Dam, another monster. She invades Heorot to avenge her dead son, and is herself killed by Beowulf after a long and difficult combat in her underwater cave.

Hygelac (hē'gə·läk), Beowulf's lord, the wise ruler of the Geats. He is killed while leading a raid in the Rhineland.

Hygd (hĭj), his young, accomplished, intelligent Queen. She offers the throne of her young son to Beowulf after Hygelac's death.

Hrothmund (hrōth'mōōnd) and **Hrethric** (hrāth'rēk), the sons of Hrothgar and Wealhtheow.

Hrothulf (hrōth'ōōlf), Hrothgar's nephew and ward. Although Wealhtheow professes trust in his care of her children, there are hints of his subsequent treachery to them.

Freawaru (frā'ä·wä·rōō), Hrothgar's daughter, about to be betrothed to Ingeld of the Heathobards as a political pawn. Beowulf prophesies that only unhappiness will arise from this alliance.

Wiglaf (wēg'läf), the last of Beowulf's kinsmen and his heir. He alone helps the old hero in his last fight against a ravaging dragon, and he later berates his companions for their cowardice.

Heardred (hē'ärd·rād), Hygelac's son, who succeeds his father as King of the Geats. Beowulf serves as his regent until the boy reaches maturity and replaces him after Heardred is killed in battle with the Swedes.

Ongentheow (ŏn'yən·thē·ō), the Swedish King, slain by the Geats at the battle of Ravenswood.

98

Onela (ôn′ĕ·lə),
Ohthere (ōht′ĕr·ə),
Eanmund (ā′än·mōŏnd), and
Eadgils (ā′äd·gĭls), members of the
Swedish royal family.

Wulfgar (wōŏlf′gär), Hrothgar's messenger, famous for wisdom and courtesy.

Hrethel (hrāth′əl), Hygelac's father, who
trained his grandson Beowulf.

Haethcynn (hăth′kĭn) and
Herebeald (hĕr′ə·bā·äld), his sons, who
brought tragedy to their father by Herebeald's accidental killing of Haethcynn.

Eofor (ā′ə·fôr), a warrior of the Geats,
the slayer of Ongentheow.

Aeschere (ĕsh′hĕr·ə), Hrothgar's thane,
a victim of Grendel and his mother.

Scyld (shēld) and
Beowulf (bā′·ə·wōŏlf), legendary Danish
kings.

Breca (brĕk′ə) a prince of the Brondings,
Beowulf's companion in a swimming
marathon.

Daeghraefn (dāy′rāf·ən), a Frankish warrior whom Beowulf crushes in his powerful grip.

Finn (fĭn), the Frisian ruler in a minstrel's legend.

Hildeburh (hĭl′də·bōōr), his Queen.

Sigemund (sĭg′ə·mōōnd) and
Fitela (fĭt′ə·lə), the legendary Volsungs,
uncle and nephew, whose valor is compared to Beowulf's.

Heremod (hĕr′ə·mōd), the minstrel's example of an evil, oppressive ruler.

Offa (ôf′fə), King of the Angles, another
figure from an illustrative legend.

BÉRÉNICE

Author: Jean Baptiste Racine (1639-1699)
Time of action: First century
First presented: 1670

PRINCIPAL CHARACTERS

Bérénice (bā·rā·nēs′), the beautiful Queen
of Palestine, deeply in love with Titus,
who has succeeded Vespasian, his father,
as Emperor of Rome. This love obliterates
everything about her and makes her neglectful and unfair in her treatment of Antiochus, King of Commagene, who also
loves her and who seems better fated
than Titus to answer her passion. When
Titus learns that Bérénice, as Empress,
would be unacceptable to the people of
Rome, he realizes that he cannot tell her
the truth. Blaming his father's death for
the delay in announcing his plan to
marry her, he asks Antiochus to explain
to Bérénice that the Emperor is preparing to sacrifice his love out of duty to his
people. At first Bérénice refuses to believe
Antiochus, and she accuses him of speak-

ing and acting because of jealousy. In a
last interview with Titus she expresses
her anger and despair; but when she is
certain that the Emperor still loves her,
she finds strength enough in her own
love to give up all thought of happiness.
She asks Antiochus to renounce the love
he feels for her as well, and she leaves behind her in Rome the two men whose
love she can, in her difficult situation,
neither accept nor return.

Titus (tē·tüs′), Emperor of Rome. As a
monarch he is majestic, conscientious,
even clever, but as a man he suffers because of the unhappiness he must inflict
upon himself and others. In order to
overcome his understandable weakness of
will because of his love for Bérénice and

his friendship with Antiochus, he must look constantly to the great examples of history as models for his own conduct. In parting with Bérénice he must lose the person who has given him most help in discovering his own virtues as a man and as a prince.

Antiochus (ăn·tī′ə·kŭs), King of Commagene. A considerate friend and war companion of Titus and a chivalrous lover of Bérénice, he becomes the devoted and tortured confidant of the two lovers. He suffers to see Bérénice unhappy because of a rival who is also his friend. In this difficult position he reveals an impulsive and anxious nature; he is easily blinded by the smallest hint of hope and depressed by any disgrace, and he would gladly sacrifice himself if he could be sure of the happiness of the woman he loves without hope. He contemplates suicide until Bérénice strengthens him by her own nobility of deed and firmness of will.

Paulin (pō′lăn′), the confidant of Titus. He represents the point of view of Rome, both the Senate and its people, when he explains that Titus cannot make Bérénice his wife without arousing public protest. Paulin's belief is that a hero should be able to master his passions.

Arsace (är·sàs′), the confidant of Antiochus. He tries to remain optimistic and to comfort Antiochus in his distress. Although Arsace's arguments are logical, Antiochus, deeply in love with Bérénice, knows that love has no logic.

Phénice (fā·nēs′), the confidante of Bérénice. She tries to plead the cause of Antiochus.

Rutile (rü·tēl′), a Roman citizen, representing on stage the people of Rome.

THE BETROTHED

Author: Alessandro Manzoni (1785-1873)
Time of action: Seventeenth century
First published: 1825-1826

PRINCIPAL CHARACTERS

Lorenzo, a young Italian peasant whose wedding is interrupted by the whim of a wicked nobleman, Don Rodrigo. Lorenzo and his betrothed seek safety by separating temporarily. He goes to Milan but is banished from the city for taking part in a famine riot. After a year, he returns to Milan and there finds Lucia ill of the plague. At last she recovers and they are married.

Lucia, Lorenzo's betrothed. The object of Don Rodrigo's lust, she is kidnaped by his henchmen. She vows to enter a convent if rescued from her kidnapers. Fra Cristoforo tells her that her betrothal vow takes precedence over her vow to the Church, and so Don Abbondio marries them.

Don Rodrigo, an arrogant seventeenth century noble who, on a bet, plans to seduce Lucia. He dies of the plague while searching for her.

Don Abbondio, the cowardly parish priest ordered by Don Rodrigo not to marry Lorenzo and Lucia.

Fra Cristoforo, a saintly Capuchin who provides sanctuary for Lucia.

A Nun, who is blackmailed into sending Lucia out of the sanctuary.

The Un-named, a powerful outlaw nobleman indebted to Don Rodrigo. His men kidnap Lucia, but her innocence persuades the noble outlaw to protect her from Don Rodrigo.

Cardinal Federigo, another protector of Lucia.

BETWEEN THE ACTS

Author: Virginia Woolf (1882-1941)
Time of action: June, 1939
First published: 1941

PRINCIPAL CHARACTERS

Bartholomew Oliver, retired from civil service and the disgruntled owner of Pointz Hall where a historical pageant is being held.

Giles Oliver, Bartholomew's son, a stockbroker who has longed to be a farmer. Recently on rather chilly terms with his wife, he is engaged in an affair with Mrs. Manresa.

Isa Oliver, Giles's wife, secretly a writer of poetry. She suspects her husband's unfaithfulness and fancies herself in love with Rupert Haines.

Mrs. Lucy Swithin, Bartholomew's widowed sister. In her imagination she lives in England's historic past.

Mrs. Manresa, a cheerful, vulgar, and uninvited guest of the Olivers. She is carrying on an affair with Giles.

William Dodge, an uninvited and unwanted guest brought to the Olivers by Mrs. Manresa. Talking with Isa, he finds solace in his rejection and loneliness, as does she in hers.

Miss La Trobe, the lonely, frustrated writer and director of the historical pageant being presented at Pointz Hall.

Rupert Haines, a married gentleman farmer with whom Isa fancies herself in love.

George and
Caro, grandchildren of Bartholomew.

Eliza Clark,
Albert,
Mrs. Otter, and
Mr. Budge, villagers who act in the pageant.

BEVIS OF HAMPTON

Author: Unknown
Time of action: c. Tenth century
First transcribed: c. 1200-1250

PRINCIPAL CHARACTERS

Bevis, a knight and the heir to the estate of Hampton. When the child was seven years old, his father was murdered by his mother's lover. The assassin was beaten into senselessness by the child, whose mother, fearing further disturbances, sold him to slave merchants who took him to a Saracen court. Favorably impressing the Saracen King, he received many honors. As a knight he passed through a series of remarkable exploits before he married the King's daughter, won several king-

doms, and regained his rightful inheritance.

Josyan, the daughter of Bevis' Saracen master. She marries Bevis after his many brave knightly adventures.

Ermyn, a Saracen King, Josyan's father, into whose court Bevis goes as a slave.

Sir Murdour, the murderer of Bevis' father and usurper of Hampton.

Ascapard, the giant who becomes Bevis'

page boy after the knight has subdued him.

Saber, a knight, the uncle and ally of Bevis.

Inor and
Bradmond, Saracen Kings and enemies of Bevis.

Guy and
Mile, sons of Bevis of Hampton and Josyan.

King Edgar, the enemy of Bevis and Saber. To end a savage war, he agrees to give his daughter in marriage to Bevis' son, Mile.

BEYOND HUMAN POWER, II

Author: Björnstjerne Björnson (1832-1910)
Time of action: Late nineteenth century
First presented: 1895

PRINCIPAL CHARACTERS

Rachel Sang, a wealthy young Norwegian liberal who tries to spread social enlightenment by using a fortune inherited from an American aunt. She establishes a hospital and a newspaper. She cannot understand why the workingmen resort to violence.

Elias Sang, Rachel's brother, also a liberal. Under the influence of the demagogic Bratt he comes to believe in sensational means to achieve the workers' ends. He tells his sister death is the only way to a new life. He commits suicide by staying in Holger's castle when he knows it will be blown up.

Bratt, an extremist union leader and an ex-preacher. The workers led by him plant explosives under Holger's castle and blow it up during a meeting of industrialists there.

Pastor Falk, an idealist who preaches that social conditions can best be improved by exercising Christian patience and forbearance. He is ineffectual as an influence among the working people.

Holger, an industrialist and something of a philanthropist. He turns his mansion over to Rachel to be made into a workers' convalescent hospital.

Credo Holger, Holger's nephew, the son of Summer, Holger's liberal brother, now dead. Guided by Rachel, he dedicates his life to inventions that may make life easier and pleasanter.

Spera Holger, Holger's niece, Credo's sister. Under Rachel's influence she decides to spend her life bringing greater freedom to women.

Maren Haug, a worker's wife who, while drunk, kills her two children and herself as an expression of the futility of life for the workers.

Halden, a young architect. Sympathizing with the workers, he helps them plant the explosives under Holger's castle, even though, as it is later discovered, he is Holger's son.

THE BIG SKY

Author: A. B. Guthrie, Jr. (1901-   )
Time of action: 1830-1843
First published: 1947

Boone Caudill, a young mountain man, strong, reticent, moody, quick to anger, and savage when crossed. Like an Indian, he wears his long hair braided. He loves the open country and the independent life of a hunter, and he resents the settlement of the West by eastern immigrants. Stubborn and brave, he is less a thinker than a doer. Having set his mind on marrying Teal Eye, he is unceasing in his search until he finds her. Once the suspicion about the source of his blind son's red hair has been put into his mind, he broods on it until he finds the suspicion apparently confirmed, and he kills innocent Jim Deakins, whom he had once saved. After learning that his son could have inherited his red hair through Boone himself, he is deeply troubled. Yet he appears to regard the shooting of Jim not as a crime but only as a grave injustice to his best friend.

Teal Eye, his Indian wife, the young daughter of a Blackfoot chief. As a child she was captured by Crows, escaped, was rescued, and was taken to St. Louis. While being returned to her people so that she may be used as a basis for a friendship to be established between Jourdonnais and the Blackfoot Indians, she escapes in Blackfoot territory. Found long afterward with her people by Boone, she happily accepts him as her husband, and she bears his son. Though he deserts her when he suspects the baby's paternity, he is at the story's end on his way back to Teal Eye, in whose faithful love he now believes.

Jim Deakins, Boone's red-haired, talkative friend who enjoys companionship, joking, drinking, and bedding down with women. Restless, he never likes to stay anywhere for long, especially away from the communities where he can enjoy associating with men and women. He is shot to death by Boone, who suspects him of having fathered Teal Eye's reddish-haired son.

Dick Summers, an old hunter, long-chinned, and with a lined, lean, and humorous face. He lives much in the past. Realizing that he is too old to continue the life of a mountain man, he returns east, marries, and becomes a farmer.

Jourdonnais, a French keelboat captain ambitious to build a trading post and establish his own company to compete with the American Fur Company. He is killed in an Indian attack on his new fort.

Poordevil, a half-witted Blackfoot, ugly, tousle-haired, long-nosed, and gap-toothed. He loves whiskey and is often amusing with his rough trapper-talk English.

Elisha Peabody, a Yankee speculator who envisons hordes of Americans pushing westward and himself or his agents profiting from their passage.

McKenzie, an American Fur Company trader, cold-eyed, broad-faced, something of a dandy, and a deceitful bargainer. He loses his job because of whiskey-making.

Uncle Zeb Calloway, an old-time mountain man, brother of Serena Caudill. He is grizzled, long-nosed, and bushy-browed; he drinks heavily.

John and
Serena Caudill, Boone's parents.

Red Horn, brother of Teal Eye. He succeeds his father, Heavy Otter, as chief after smallpox kills most of the Piegans, a tribe of Blackfoot Indians.

Jonathan Bedwell, a thief who steals Boone's rifle.

Streak, a hunter killed by Boone in a fight after Streak had threatened to kill Poordevil because he was a Blackfoot.

Nancy Litsey, a foolish and forward young girl whom Boone takes sexually on one occasion on his return home.

Dan, Boone's younger brother.

Cora, Boone's sister-in-law.

Punk and
Andy Caudill, Boone's two young nephews.

BILLY BUDD, FORETOPMAN

Author: Herman Melville (1819-1891)
Time of action: 1797
First published: 1924

PRINCIPAL CHARACTERS

Billy Budd, a youthful member of the crew of the merchantman "Rights-of-Man," who is impressed into service aboard H.M.S. "Indomitable" during the last decade of the eighteenth century. Billy is twenty-one, "welkin-eyed," and possessed of great masculine beauty; he has no idea who his father and mother were, having been left a foundling in a basket on the doorstep of a "good man" in Bristol, England. Billy was a cheerful, stabilizing influence on the rough crew of the merchantman; when he is taken aboard the "Indomitable," he is popular with all the officers and crew except John Claggart, the master-at-arms, who is envious of Billy's almost perfect physique and personality. Claggart falsely accuses Billy of fomenting a mutiny aboard the ship. When he repeats the charges in the Captain's quarters while Billy is present, the young man (who stutters under stress and sometimes suffers a total speech block) can say nothing in his own defense and hits Claggart on the forehead with his fist. Claggart falls and dies. In the subsequent trial at which the Captain is the sole witness, there can be no leniency because of the recent Great Mutiny in the fleet. Billy is sentenced to hang. At the execution his last words are, "God bless Captain Vere!" Honest, refreshing, ingenuous, uncomplaining—these adjectives may be applied to Billy Budd, who represents an innocent youth trapped by the brutality of fleet regulations or, perhaps, who represents truth and beauty trapped by the wickedness of the world.

Captain the Honourable Edward Fairfax

Vere, of the "Indomitable." He is known in the fleet as "Starry" Vere to distinguish him from a kinsman and officer of like rank in the navy. The nickname is a misnomer, however, for Captain Vere, a bachelor of about forty, is a quiet, brooding intellectual who reads a great deal. He is also a fine commander, but he lacks the flamboyance of the more famous Nelson. He suffers greatly at having to testify before the three-man court against Billy Budd, whom he recognizes as an efficient, attractive, impulsive seaman. He, too, seems trapped by regulations (tightened during the Great Mutiny) which state that striking an officer is a capital offense. When Claggart comes to Captain Vere with his foggy, unsubstantiated charges that Billy is mutinous, the Captain summons Billy to his quarters only to prove that Claggart is a false witness.

John Claggart, the master-at-arms of the ship. Since guns have replaced the many small arms used in naval fighting, his duties are mainly to oversee the crew and its work. When Claggart observes Billy Budd, he quickly becomes envious of the personal beauty of the young man. In this respect he is like Iago in "Othello"; Iago hates Cassio partly because he is an open, honest, handsome man. So with the Claggart-Budd relationship. The only basis for the charges Claggart makes against Billy is that an afterguardsman, a troublemaker, tries to be friendly and confidential with the foretopman. Because he joined the navy for no apparent reason and because he never makes any reference to his previous life ashore, Claggart is a man of mystery about whom many rumors are circulated on the ship.

The Dansker, an old veteran who serves as mainmast-man in his watch. He likes Billy from the start and is the one who nicknames him "Baby." When Billy comes to him for counsel and to ask why his petty mistakes are getting him into trouble, the Dansker astutely remarks that "Jimmy Legs" (meaning the master-at-arms) is down on him.

The Afterguardsman, a troublemaking sailor. He approaches Billy and tries to tempt him to join an incipient mutiny. Billy angrily rebuffs him but does not report the incident to any officer.

Lieutenant Ratcliffe, the officer who goes aboard the "Rights-of-Man" and selects Billy to be impressed into his majesty's service.

THE BIRDS

Author: Aristophanes (c. 448-c. 385 B.C.)
Time of action: Second Peloponnesian War
First presented: 414 B.C.

PRINCIPAL CHARACTERS

Pisthetærus (pĭs'thĕ·tī'rəs), an old man of Athens who has left his native city in disapproval because of the corruption, especially the litigiousness, of his countrymen. High-spirited, comically fantastic, and sometimes even vulgar, he nevertheless has an underlying vein of hardheaded good sense which makes him despise hypocrites and frauds. His oratorical skill convinces the birds that they are the superiors of the gods, and he proposes the creation of Nephelococcygia (nĕ'fə·lō·kō·sĭ'jĭ·ə), or "Cloud Cuckoo Land," the strategic location of which will give the birds power over both gods and men. For his pains he is awarded wings and a position of respect in the land of the birds. He adopts a very casual attitude toward the gods who come to negotiate a peace, and through shrewd dealing wins not only the scepter of Zeus for the birds but the hand of Basileia (bă·sĭ·lē'yə), or "Sovereignty," and celestial bounty for himself.

Euelpides (ū·ĕl'pĭ·dēz), another old Athenian, Pisthetærus' companion and foil. Not as sharply individualized, he is, like Pisthetærus, disgusted with Athenian life and ready to coöperate in his friend's schemes. He too has a broadly comic wit and a keen eye for a pretty courtesan.

Epops (ĕ'pŏps), the hoopoe. Now King of the Birds, he was once Terus, a King of Thrace and the son of Ares, who, after his marriage to Procne, violated her sister Philomela and cut out her tongue so that she could not tell of the deed. All three were transformed by the gods: Tereus became a hoopoe (in the version of the myth followed by Aristophanes), Procne a nightingale, and Philomela a swallow. Epops is reunited with Procne in the land of the birds, where he has special status because he has human as well as bird knowledge. He is delighted with Pisthetærus' suggestion regarding the foundation of Nephelococcygia.

Trochilus (trō'kĭ·ləs), the wren, a servant to Epops.

Phoenicopterus (fē'nĭ·kŏp'tĕ·rəs), the flamingo, who attends the council of birds which votes to establish Nephelococcygia.

105

A Priest. After the establishment of Nephelococcygia he sacrifices to all the bird gods and goddesses.

A Poet, who addresses some rather bad verses to the new city.

A Prophet,
Meton (mē'tŏn), a geometrician and astronomer,
An Inspector of Tributary Towns, and
A Dealer in Decrees, who also arrive for the inaugural ceremonies but are driven away by Pisthetærus, who knows them for frauds.

Iris (ī'rĭs), the messenger of Zeus who wanders into Nephelococcygia on her way to command mankind to offer sacrifices to the gods. She is denied passage and treated impolitely because she has failed to get a safe conduct from the birds. She carries the news to Olympus that communication between gods and men has been cut off.

A Parricide,
Cinesias (sĭ·nē'sĭ·əs), a dithyrambic poet, and
An Informer, who come to Nephelococcygia seeking wings to aid them in attaining their various objectives. The first is sent to Thrace to fight; the second and third are beaten.

Prometheus (prō·mē'thĭ·əs), the Titan, who tells Pisthetærus that the gods are ready to come to terms with the birds for the smoke of sacrifices has been cut off and the Olympians are starving.

Poseidon (pō·sī'dən), the god of the sea, Herakles (hĕ'rə·klēz), the demi-god, and Triballus (trĭ·bă'ləs), a barbarian god, who negotiate a truce with the birds by bargaining away the power of Zeus to Pisthetærus.

THE BLACK ARROW

Author: Robert Louis Stevenson (1850-1894)
Time of action: Fifteenth century
First published: 1888

PRINCIPAL CHARACTERS

Sir Daniel Brackley, a villainous knight who fights on both sides during the fifteenth century Wars of the Roses. He adds to his own lands by becoming the guardian of children orphaned by war. He is killed by Ellis Duckworth.

Richard Shelton, called Dick, the orphaned son of Sir Harry Shelton of the Moat House estates. Sir Daniel is suspected of murdering Sir Harry in order to become the boy's guardian. After many difficulties, Dick marries Joanna Sedley.

Joanna Sedley, the orphaned heiress of Kettley, intended by Sir Daniel as a wife for Dick. She first meets Dick while disguised in boy's clothes and calling herself John Matcham. Held prisoner by Sir Daniel, she is almost forced into marriage with Lord Shoreby, but at the church he is slain by a black arrow.

Lord Foxham, the enemy of Sir Daniel and Joanna's legal guardian, who promises her to Dick if they can rescue her.

Alicia Risingham, the niece of a powerful Lancastrian lord and Joanna's friend.

Lord Shoreby, who tries to force Joanna to marry him.

Richard of York, the Duke of Gloucester. He is saved from bandits by Dick, whom he knights after the Battle of Shoreby, in which the Lancastrians are defeated.

The Earl of Risingham, the judge of Dick and Lawless when they are denounced by Sir Oliver Oates.

106

Nick Appleyard, a veteran of Agincourt, killed at Moat House by a black arrow.

Bennet Hatch, Sir Daniel's bailiff at Moat House.

Sir Oliver Oates, Sir Daniel's clerk, who is accused by the outlaws of the death of Sir Harry Shelton.

Ellis Duckworth, who was ruined by Sir Daniel and is now the leader of a band of outlaws. He calls himself John (Jon) Amend-All, and uses only black arrows for weapons. Eventually he kills his enemy, Sir Daniel.

Will Lawless, one of the outlaws and a friend of Dick. He finally takes orders and dies a friar.

BLACK VALLEY

Author: Hugo Wast (Gustavo Martínez Zuviría, 1883-   )
Time of action: Early twentieth century
First published: 1918

PRINCIPAL CHARACTERS

Gracián Palma (grä·syän' päl'mä), the ward of Don Jesús de Viscarra, to whose estate, Black Valley, he is taken for the summer. He becomes a member of and learns the secrets of Don Jesús' turbulent family and his equally turbulent neighbors.

Don Jesús de Viscarra (dōn hä·sōōs' dä bēs·kä'r̄rä), the guardian of Gracián Palma and owner of Black Valley. Engaged in a life-long boundary dispute with a neighboring landowner, Don Pablo Camargo, he is shot and killed by his adversary after a lawsuit is decided in Don Jesús' favor.

Mirra (mē'r̄rä), Don Jesús de Viscarra's daughter, who is in love with Gracián Palma.

Flavia (flä'byä), the sister of Don Jesús. She is the mistress of Don Pablo Ca-

margo and the mother of his daughter, Victoria.

Don Pablo Camargo (dōn pä'blō kämär'gō), a neighbor of Don Jesús de Viscarra and his sworn enemy. He kills Don Jesús as the result of a boundary dispute. He is the lover of Don Jesús' sister, Flavia, and the father of her daughter Victoria.

Victoria (bēk-tō'ryä), the natural daughter of Flavia and Don Pablo. She marries Gracián Palma.

Lazarus (lä-sä'rōōs), the overseer of Black Valley, who is in love with Flavia and the possessor of the secret of her affair with Don Pablo.

Amoroso (ä-mō-rō'sō), the devoted servant of Flavia.

Pichana (pē-chä'nä), an old beggar woman.

BLEAK HOUSE

Author: Charles Dickens (1812-1870)
Time of action: Mid-nineteenth century
First published: 1852-1853

John Jarndyce, the unmarried, aging owner of Bleak House and a party in the famous and protracted Chancery suit of Jarndyce vs. Jarndyce. Generous to a fault, he makes two young cousins, Ada Clare and Richard Carstone, his wards, in the hope that they will fall in love and fill his ancestral home with renewed life. He also takes into his home an orphan, Esther Summerson, as a companion to Ada. He himself falls in love with Esther, but when he learns that she is in love with Allan Woodcourt, a young surgeon, he releases her from her promise to him and gives the couple a new Bleak House of their own. He is loyal to his old friend and is always scrupulously fair, even though he calls his library "The Growlery" and retreats there when the winds of adversity blow on him. Admirable in every way, the head of the Jarndyce family creates rather than preserves a family dignity.

Esther Summerson, the orphan whom John Jarndyce takes into his home and later into his heart. In reality she is the natural daughter of Lady Dedlock and a gallant named Captain Hawdon (who dies and is buried under the name of Nemo). Though part of the story is told by Esther, her ingenuousness makes of her less of a heroine and more of a companion and comforter who goes under various motherly terms of endearment. Although she respects and admires her benefactor, she truly loves the compassionate doctor, Allan Woodcourt, who woos her in spite of her disease-ravaged face, the result of a serious illness incurred while nursing Charley, her maid. Her immediate sympathies are aroused by any homeless beings and by those, as in the case of Caddy Jellyby, whose homes are friendless and loveless. She finally finds happiness with her husband and two daughters.

Ada Clare, John Jarndyce's cousin and ward. She secretly marries Richard Carstone, her cousin, to protect him from the

grinding poverty that lawyers and the courts bring upon him. She manages to keep her loyalties and sympathies divided by remaining with her benefactor while extending her love to Carstone. Beautiful and tractable, she displays evenness of disposition and generous motives which make her a tearful heroine.

Richard Carstone, Ada's cousin and husband. Anything suits this young man who has already sold his soul to the case of Jarndyce vs. Jarndyce. He tries medicine, the law, and the army, only to die of disappointment after the suit in Chancery has been settled and he learns that legal costs have eaten up the whole of his inheritance. John Jarndyce provides for Ada and her infant son.

Lady Honoria Dedlock, secretly the mother of Esther Summerson by Captain Hawdon, a rake to whom she was once engaged. When Tulkinghorn, her husband's legal adviser, threatens to inform her husband of her past, she flees from her home and dies, a victim of shame and exposure, at the gate of the cemetery where her lover has been buried under the name of Nemo. Her body is discovered by Esther Summerson.

Sir Leicester Dedlock, an honorable gentleman of prejudice and pride of family, completely unaware of his wife's guilty secret.

Mr. Tulkinghorn, a conniving solicitor who threatens to expose the secret in Lady Dedlock's past. He is murdered by Lady Dedlock's French maid when he refuses to pay her blackmailing demands and threatens her with imprisonment.

Allan Woodcourt, the surgeon who attends Captain Hawdon at the time of his death and who extends his help to Esther Summerson and Richard Carstone as well. He marries Esther after John Jarndyce releases her from her promise to him.

Mrs. **Woodcourt,** his handsome mother, proud of her Welsh ancestry.

William Guppy, a lawyer's clerk in the firm of Kenge and Carboy, John Jarndyce's solicitors. Attracted to Esther Summerson, he "files a declaration" of his love. Later, discovering that she has lost her beauty as a result of illness, he regrets his proposal and asks her to make a statement, before a witness, that there was never any formal engagement between them. He also meddles, though in a cowardly and humorous fashion, in Tulkinghorn's intrigue to discover Lady Dedlock's connection with the dead Nemo.

Miss Flite, a Jarndyce relative, half-crazed by the frustrations and delays of the suit in Chancery. Bright, friendly, perceptive of the crushing power of the law, she raises birds for release when the case is settled, and she tries to keep others from her own sad fate.

Miss Barbary, Lady Dedlock's sister and Esther Summerson's aunt and godmother, a good, austere woman.

Mademoiselle Hortense, Lady Dedlock's French maid. She murders Tulkinghorn when he resists her attempt at blackmail.

Inspector Bucket, the police detective who solves the mystery of Tulkinghorn's murder.

Rosa, a village girl also employed as a maid by Lady Dedlock. She is engaged to marry Watt Rouncewell.

Mrs. Rouncewell, the Dedlock housekeeper.

Mr. Rouncewell, her son, the father of Watt Rouncewell.

George Rouncewell, another son, a soldier and later the owner of a shooting gallery in London. He is falsely arrested for the murder of Tulkinghorn.

Watt Rouncewell, the young man engaged to Rosa.

Mrs. Rachael, later **Mrs. Chadband,** a servant to Miss Barbary.

The Reverend Mr. Chadband, her husband, a self-conscious clergyman given to flowery speech.

Mrs. Snagsby, one of his parishioners, a shrew.

Mr. Snagsby, a law-stationer, her mild, hen-pecked husband.

Captain Hawdon, now calling himself **Nemo,** a law writer, the former lover of Lady Dedlock. Dying in a garret over Krook's dingy shop, he is buried in the Potter's Field.

Jo, also called **Toughey,** a street sweeper, befriended by Nemo. Lady Dedlock pays him two half-crowns to point out Nemo's grave.

Krook, the owner of a rag-and-bottle shop and the landlord of Miss Flite and Nemo. He has in his possession a packet of papers belonging to the former Captain Hawdon. This fact has been ferreted out by Tony Jobling, who calls himself Weevle while lodging with Krook, and William Guppy has agreed to reclaim the papers for Lady Dedlock. On the night that the papers are to change hands, Krook, a habitual drunkard, perishes of spontaneous combustion. Apparently the papers are destroyed in the fire.

Mrs. Smallweed, Krook's sister.

Mr. Smallweed, her husband, a superannuated man of unimpaired and irascible mind.

Bartholomew Smallweed, also called **Chickweed,** their grandson, a sponging friend of William Guppy.

Judy Smallweed, Bartholomew's twin sister.

Tony Jobling, a law writer for Mr.

Snagsby and a friend of William Guppy. Calling himself **Weevle,** he takes lodgings in Krook's establishment and learns that Krook has in his possession a bundle of Captain Hawdon's papers.

Mrs. Jellyby, a plump, strong-minded woman who neglects her house and family while interesting herself in philanthropic projects, one of which is to settle a colony of English poor in Boorioboola-Gha, on the Niger River in Africa.

Caroline Jellyby, also called **Caddy,** Mrs. Jellyby's oldest daughter. Tired of her mother's endless projects, she marries Prince Turveydrop. A close friend of Esther Summerson, Caddy names her first daughter Esther.

Mr. Jellyby, a mild, miserable man who goes bankrupt.

"Peepy" Jellyby, the Jellybys' weak and neglected son.

Prince Turveydrop, named in honor of the Prince Regent. He marries Caddy Jellyby.

Mr. Turveydrop, Prince Turveydrop's father, a model of deportment and a monster of selfishness.

Harold Skimpole, the sentimental, unworldly recipient of John Jarndyce's bounty, a character thought to have been modeled after Leigh Hunt.

Mrs. Skimpole, his sickly wife.

Arethusa, the "Beauty" daughter, **Laura,** the "Sentiment" daughter, and

Kitty, the "Comedy" daughter, the Skimpole children.

Lawrence Boythorn, John Jarndyce's friend. His character is modeled on that of Walter Savage Landor.

Mr. Gridley, also called **"The Man from Shropshire,"** a farmer's son ruined by a suit in Chancery, frequently jailed for contempt of court. While hiding from the law, he dies in a London shooting gallery.

Bayham Badger, a medical practitioner to whom Richard Carstone is articled for a time. He is proud of his wife's two former husbands.

Mrs. Badger, his wife, who brings glory to her present married state because she is the widow of Captain Swosser, an officer of the Royal Navy, and Professor Dingo, a scientist.

Charlotte Neckett, also called **Charley,** Esther Summerson's devoted maid.

Mr. Kenge, nicknamed **"Conversation" Kenge,** a member of the law firm of Kenge and Carboy. Through him John Jarndyce first meets Esther Summerson.

Mr. Vholes, Richard Carstone's solicitor. He helps to bring about the young man's ruin.

Mr. Quale, Mrs. Jellyby's partner in her impractical philanthropic schemes.

Miss Wisk, betrothed to Mr. Quale.

Mr. Tangle, a legal authority on the case of Jarndyce vs. Jarndyce.

THE BLITHEDALE ROMANCE

Author: Nathaniel Hawthorne (1804-1864)
Time of action: Mid-nineteenth century
First published: 1852

PRINCIPAL CHARACTERS

Miles Coverdale, a young New England poet and the narrator of the story. He is a highly sensitive young man and an eager observer of the persons he meets at Blithedale Farm, an experiment in communal living which he joins for a time. Three of his fellow experimenters particularly attract his attention: Zenobia Fauntleroy, Priscilla Moodie, and a man named Hollingsworth. As an observer of their lives, Miles is intrigued, caught by his interest in them as human souls and, as well, by his love for Priscilla Moodie, a love he never reveals to her.

Hollingsworth, a dark, powerful man who was once a blacksmith. He has fastened himself to a single project in obsessive fashion: he desires to set up a philanthropic institution for the reform of criminals and thus to reduce the amount of evil in the world. This project is Hollingsworth's ruling passion, and all else in his life must be subservient to it. He joins the experiment at Blithedale Farm because he sees in the farm a place to erect the buildings to house his reformatory and because he sees in Zenobia, a wealthy young woman of the group, a person who can help his project with her money and influence. Unfortunately for Hollingsworth's project, he falls in love with Priscilla Moodie and thus alienates Zenobia, who is Priscilla's half sister. Zenobia's later suicide weighs heavily on Hollingsworth's conscience, for she left him with a curse. He gives up his idea of reforming other persons until he can assure himself that he is not guilty of crime. His tragedy is that of conscience, for he believes he is responsible for Zenobia's death; he believes he has driven the girl to suicide and so regards himself as her murderer. With this thought weighing upon him he can no longer consider trying to reform others guilty of crime. Though he marries Priscilla Moodie, he is a broken man.

Zenobia Fauntleroy, a wealthy young woman from another part of the United States. She is attractive both in personality and in appearance. Her vivid presence is always accentuated by her habit of wearing a flamboyant flower in her hair. She is unhappy with woman's lot in life, and her mission is to remake society so that she and her fellow women can take what she regards as their rightful places in the affairs of the world. She falls in love with Hollingsworth and offers her fortune to help him in the establishment of his reformatory, as well as her personal aid in the project. As the months pass, however, she learns that Hollingsworth loves her half sister, Priscilla Moodie. Unhappy Zenobia suffers other shocks. She loses all her wealth in a strange way, apparently to her half sister, and learns for the first time the girl's identity as a relative. These blows unnerve Zenobia, who drowns herself. Her real name is Fauntleroy, although the narrator avoids using any other than her Biblical pseudonym.

Mr. Moodie, an extremely shy and retiring man, a peddler of sorts. He reveals to Miles Coverdale that he was once wealthy and came of good family. He has given up his family name of Faunterloy, however, and assumed that of Moodie. He has been driven from home by crime and his wealth has passed to his daughter, the Zenobia of the story, inasmuch as he is supposedly dead. In New England he has remarried, and the daughter of that marriage is Priscilla Moodie, actually Zenobia's half sister. Mr. Moodie puts Priscilla under the protection of Hollingsworth and thus precipitates the tragic chain of events.

Priscilla Moodie, Zenobia's ethereal half sister, who has supported herself and her father for many years by sewing little articles for her peddler father to sell. Though she enters the story as a poor, shadowy excuse for a girl, she develops a personality through her love for Hollingsworth and his affection for her. After Zenobia's suicide Priscilla marries Hollingsworth and becomes his psychological support in his battle against feelings of guilt.

111

Mr. Westervelt, a fine-appearing but shallow man who is a promoter and rascal. He has a vague connection with Zenobia, as if they had known each other well at one time. Westervelt comes to dominate Zenobia and uses her in an act on the lyceum circuit, in which she figures as the Veiled Lady. He uses her, perhaps under hypnosis, to make people believe that he can forecast the future. His exploitation of the girl ends when she runs to Hollingsworth for protection during a performance.

BLOOD WEDDING

Author: Federico García Lorca (1899-1936)
Time of action: Probably early 1900's
First presented: 1933

PRINCIPAL CHARACTERS

The Bridegroom, whose father and brother have been killed by the Félix family.

The Bridegroom's Mother, who is opposed to the marriage.

The Bride, aged twenty-two, once courted by her cousin Leonardo, and uncertain about this marriage.

The Bride's Father, the possessor of valuable vineyards.

Leonardo Félix, who still loves the bride; after the ceremony he persuades her to run away with him.

Leonardo's Wife, who has to force her husband to accompany her to the ceremony.

A Servant, who accuses the bride of having seen Leonardo secretly late at night.

Death, disguised as a beggar, who directs the Bridegroom to the fleeing couple. He and Leonardo kill each other.

A BLOT IN THE 'SCUTCHEON

Author: Robert Browning (1812-1889)
Time of action: Eighteenth century
First presented: 1843

PRINCIPAL CHARACTERS

Thorold, Earl Tresham, a proud English nobleman who is resolved to keep his family's reputation untarnished. Horrified when he discovers that his sister has taken a lover, he traps the man and kills him in a duel. He poisons himself, hoping that his death, his sister's, and her lover's will erase the blot on the family escutcheon.

Henry, Earl Mertoun, suitor of Mildred, Earl Tresham's sister. He wants to cover up their affair by marrying the girl, whom he truly loves. He is found sneak-

ing into the castle one night, challenged to a duel, and killed by Earl Tresham, against whom he does not try to defend himself.

Mildred, Earl Tresham's fourteen-year-old sister, led by her innocence into taking Earl Mertoun as her lover. When he offers marriage she feels she cannot in honor accept his suit to marry her as though she were truly a virgin. She dies of grief on hearing that her lover is dead.

Guendolen, cousin to Earl Tresham and

Mildred. She tries to help the young girl by convincing Earl Tresham that Earl Mertoun's suit is honorable.

Austin Tresham, Earl Tresham's brother and Guendolen's fiancé. He tries, with Guendolen's help, to save Earl Mertoun's life after he has been wounded. Austin and his bride Guendolen inherit the title and estates after Earl Tresham's death.

Gerald, the retainer who informs Earl Tresham of Mildred's affair.

THE BOHEMIANS OF THE LATIN QUARTER

Author: Henri Murger (1822-1861)
Time of action: Early nineteenth century
First published: 1848

PRINCIPAL CHARACTERS

Rodolphe (rô·dôlf'), an impoverished poet who takes up with Mimi and later writes a successful book, but who is not lucky in love.

Mimi (mē·mē'), "**La Bohème**" (là bô-ĕm'), who becomes the mistress of Rodolphe, and briefly of Paul. She dies grieving for Rodolphe.

Alexander Schaunard (á·lĕk·sän'dr shō-när'), a composer and portrait painter, ejected from his studio in the Latin Quarter.

Marcel (màr·sĕl'), a painter who takes over Schaunard's studio.

Mother Cadet (ká·dä'), whose rabbit stew attracts the penniless Bohemians.

Colline (kô·lēn'), a philosopher who shares his stew with Schaunard.

The Uncle of Rodolphe, who wants him to write a manual on stove-making.

Mlle. Musette (mü·zĕt'), the mistress of Marcel, and others, who gives a party for the artists.

The Councilor of State, who jilts Musette.

M. Benoit (bə·nwá'), the landlord of Rodolphe, whose room he rents to Mimi.

Momus (mô·müs'), the owner of Café Momus. He is generous to artists.

Barbemuche (bàrb·müsh'), who pays for the artists' Christmas Eve in the Café Momus.

M. Maurice (mō·rēs'), a temporary lover of Musette.

Viscount Paul (pōl'), a lover of Mimi.

Phémie (fä·mē'), the mistress of Schaunard.

THE BONDMAN

Author: Philip Massinger (1583-1640)
Time of action: Fourth century B.C.
First presented: c. 1623

PRINCIPAL CHARACTERS

Pisander (pǐ·săn'dẽr), a Theban nobleman disguised as Marullo, a bondsman. He is diverted by his love of Cleora from taking revenge on Leosthenes, who has jilted his sister. He instigates a revolt of the slaves in the absence of the Syra-

113

cusan army, his purpose being to obtain Cleora's love. His gracious and generous behavior while he is in power in the city and his fortitude in adversity win her heart. He is much given to verbal heroics.

Cleora (klǝ·ō'rǝ), the daughter of Archidamus, beloved by Leosthenes and Pisander. Filled with noble sentiments and rhetoric, she is angered by Leosthenes' distrust of her and vows to remain blindfolded and speechless until he returns from the war with Carthage. She becomes further angered when, after fulfilling her vow, she is still distrusted. Finally she accepts Pisander.

Leosthenes (lǝ·ŏs'thǝ·nēz), formerly contracted to Statilia. His lack of faith in Cleora and his persecution of Pisander-Marullo alienate her. When confronted with Statilia in the trial scene, he shamefacedly acknowledges her claim and gives up Cleora to Pisander.

Statilia (stǝ·tī'lǐ·ǝ), Pisander's sister in disguise as Timandra, Cleora's slave. She loves Leosthenes and helps her brother win Cleora for both selfish and unselfish reasons.

Archidamus (är'chǐ·dǎ'mǝs), Praetor of Syracuse, a just and noble-hearted ruler. He dislikes Leosthenes and, after protecting his supposed slave Marullo in the trial, finally welcomes him as a son-in-law in the person of Pisander.

Timagoras (tǐ·mǎ'gō·rǝs), Cleora's hot-tempered brother, the friend of Leosthenes. His snobbish, arrogant behavior toward Pisander-Marullo and his angry abuse of his sister for favoring a slave help to strengthen Cleora's growing love.

Timoleon (tǐ·mō'lǝ·ŏn), a Corinthian general aiding the Syracusans against the Carthaginians. He admires Cleora for her inspirational speeches to the soldiers. Undismayed by the slaves who hold

Syracuse when he returns from the war, he puts down their rebellion.

Cleon (klē'ŏn), a foolish, impotent old man.

Corisca (kô·rǐs'kǝ), his wanton second wife. When the army takes away the presentable male citizens, she is too snobbish to take a lover from among the slaves but too lustful to be without a lover; therefore she attempts to seduce her stepson. During the temporarily successful revolt of the slaves, in her suffering and sorrow as a slave of slaves, she gains self-knowledge and redemption.

Asotus (ǝ·sō'tǝs), Cleon's stupid, cowardly son. Left behind when the able warriors go out to battle, he mistreats the slaves and becomes enamored of his stepmother. When the slaves rebel, he is forced to play the ape with a chain around his neck.

Olympia (ō·lǐm'pǐ·ǝ), a wanton rich widow, the friend of Corisca. So man-crazy that she has love affairs with her own slaves, when other men are not available, she marries Poliphron while the slaves are in power.

Poliphron (pŏ'lǐ·frŏn), a slave, the friend and confidant of Marullo.

Cimbrio (sǐm'brǐ·ō), a slave. He becomes drunken and rowdy while the slaves have control, but is terrified into submission on the return of the masters.

Gracculo (grǎ'kǝ·lō), a satirical slave. He makes comical remarks on Cleon, Corisca, and Asotus in asides to the audience. During the rule of the slaves, he leads Asotus around on his chain and makes him do tricks. He is a spokesman for the repentant slaves.

Zanthia (zǎn'thǐ·ǝ), Corisca's slave. She takes part in the play-acting scene which Corisca plans for the seduction of Asotus.

114

THE BONDS OF INTEREST

Author: Jacinto Benavente y Martínez (1866-1954)
Time of action: Early seventeenth century
First presented: 1907

PRINCIPAL CHARACTERS

Leander (lä·än·dår'), a rogue with gentlemanly qualities who impersonates a rich, mysterious nobleman. Though in love with Silvia, he does not want to marry her under false pretenses.

Crispín (krēs·pēn'), Leander's accomplice, who pretends to be his servant. He arranges Leander's marriage by playing the self-interest of one creditor against another.

Silvia Polichinelle (sēl'vyä pō·lē·chē-nĕ'lyĕ), a rich girl who convinces Leander that they are united by the greatest bond of interest, love.

Signor Polichinelle (sē·nyôr' pō·lē·chē-nĕ'lyĕ), Silvia's miserly father, who is forced to agree to the marriage and dowry.

Signora Polichinelle (sē·nyō'rä pō·lē·chē-nĕ'lyĕ), Silvia's mother, who despises her husband as a vulgar tradesman.

Doña Sirena (dō'·nyä sē·rä'nä), an aristocratic but penniless widow who foresees money for arranging Silvia's marriage.

Columbine (kō·loom·bē'nĕ), the maid and confidante of Doña Sirena, who is won over by Crispín.

An Innkeeper, deceived by Crispín's rudeness into thinking Leander is an important noble.

Harlequin (är·lä·kēn'), an impoverished poet in love with Columbine and befriended by Crispín in the name of Leander.

A Captain, a down-at-the-heels rogue, also befriended by Crispín.

BORIS GODUNOV

Author: Alexander Pushkin (1799-1837)
Time of action: 1598-1605
First published: 1831

PRINCIPAL CHARACTERS

Boris Godunov (bô·rĭs' gô·dŏŏ·nôf'), a privy counselor who manages to have Tsarevitch Dimitry assassinated without having to take the blame for the murder. As the new Tsar, Godunov exacts strict obedience from his subordinates, treats the masses cruelly, and puts down ruthlessly any attempt to unseat him. While engaged in a war against a pretender, he is suddenly taken ill and dies, naming his son the new Tsar.

Grigory Otrepyev (grĭ·gō'rĭy ôt·rĕ'pyĕf),

a young monk turned rebel who pretends he is the late Dimitry. He marshals armies in Poland and, eventually, marches against Godunov. The struggle is bitter, and Grigory, finally triumphant, is disturbed because the populace stand silent when asked to acclaim him.

Basmanov (bäs·mä'nŏf), a general interested in military victory, not political complexities. First he supports Godunov's son as Tsar; then, persuaded by Pushkin, a Grigory supporter, he leads his troops

115

over to the other side. It is Basanov's defection that spells victory for Grigory.

Maryna (mä·rǐ'nə), a girl who holds Grigory's army idle in Poland because Grigory, having fallen in love with her, is loathe to give the order to advance against Godunov. Maryna, although repelled because Grigory is only an unfrocked priest and not Dimitry, as he claims to be, still consents to become Grigory's wife if his armies overthrow Godunov.

Feodor (fě·o'dôr), Godunov's son, who is Tsar for a short time before, according to the Grigory followers who last saw him, he takes poison.

Pushkin (pŏŏsh'kĭn), a Grigory supporter who persuades Basanov to defect to the pretender's side and who, making a violent speech in the great square, inflames the people against Godunov.

Father Pimen, an old monk, formerly a soldier, who counsels Grigory to put worldly ambitions out of his thoughts.

THE BOURGEOIS GENTLEMAN

Author: Molière (Jean Baptiste Poquelin, 1622-1673)
Time of action: Seventeenth century
First presented: 1670

PRINCIPAL CHARACTERS

Monsieur Jourdain (mə·syœ' zhôr·däṅ'), a rich, forty-year-old tradesman. Ashamed of and denying his father's occupation, he tries to pass as a gentleman by elaborate spending of his wealth. He has a "sweet income and visions of nobility and grandeur," says his Music Master, "though he is an ignorant cit." In addition to his Music Master, he has also in attendance a Dancing Master, a Fencing Master, and a Philosophy Master, and through their instructions he hopes to ape persons of quality. He wants concerts every week, but would add a marine trumpet to the chamber music strings. He stages elaborate serenades and fireworks to impress a Marchioness, sends her his diamond ring through a Count who uses the ring and money borrowed from Jourdain to court the Marchioness for himself. He is vain and childish about his fine clothes, even though he is uncomfortable in them, and he has two lackeys in attendance whom he keeps busy putting on and taking off his gown so that he may show off his new breeches and vest underneath. He is completely befuddled by the Philosophy Master's explanation of—and rejects instruction in—

logic (he wants something prettier), morality (he wants passion whenever he wants it), and Latin; but he is entranced to learn of the placing of tongue and lips in the pronunciation of vowels and consonants, and is delighted to hear he has been speaking prose all his life. After he has heard some speech supposed to be Turkish, he apes the flowery Oriental manner in his own discourse, to the amusement of all. Because his wife realizes how ridiculous he is, he calls her names and damns her impertinence.

Madame Jourdain, his wife, a woman of rare good sense who knows that her husband is making a fool of himself and scolds him accordingly. She dislikes his parties and his guests. Her ideas concerning her daughter's marriage to Cléonte are sensible; she does not want her son-in-law to be able to reproach his wife for her parents or grandchildren to be ashamed to call her grandmother. By taking literally the statements of the Count, and replying to them, she shows a keen sense of humor. The Marchioness she holds in scorn and scolds her for making a fool of Jourdain. She makes

116

her maid her confidante and partner in her efforts to bring sense into the house.

Nicole (nē·kô·là′), the maid, also a sensible woman and trusted by her mistress. She ridicules and laughs at Jourdain's clothes; when she cannot stop laughing, despite his commands, she requests a beating rather than choke herself trying to stop. Her bold, frank comments on Jourdain's guests earn her blows and evil epithets from her master. Her witty gaiety is her fine quality.

Dorante (dô·ränt′), a Count who flatters Jourdain, and calls him his friend, and offers to gain him admittance to court entertainments. These attentions enable him to borrow money from Jourdain, pay his numerous bills, and make gifts to the Marchioness he is wooing, even to the point of using Jourdain's diamond ring as a gift to the lady from himself. He is a clever trickster who avails himself of every opportunity Jourdain's foolishness provides.

Cléonte (klā·ônt′), a young man in love with Jourdain's daughter but despised by her father because of his ordinary birth, though favored by her mother as a sensible fellow eminently suitable as a son-in-law. With noble frankness he admits his army service and his working parents, and he says that he neither is nor pretends to be a gentleman. He is sincere in his love, and after a lovers' misunderstanding is upset until both he and his servant, with whom he is friendly, are reconciled with their loves.

Covielle (kô·vyĕl′), servant to Cléonte, in love with and loved by Nicole. When he and Cléonte make up an amusing inventory of their beloveds' qualities and shortcomings, Covielle speaks out boldly to his master on the subject. It is Covielle who plans and stages the farcical "Son of the Great Turke" masquerade which unites the lovers. Even Dorante is impressed by his cleverness and subtlety.

Lucile (lü·sē·lyà), the daughter of the Jourdains. Because of her love for Cléonte, she refuses to marry her father's choice of a husband, a real gentleman. Her happy turn of wit is shown in her clever play with Nicole about their feelings for Cléonte and Covielle.

Dorimène (dô·rē·mĕn′), a Marchioness and a widow, loved by Dorante. Though she has accompanied him to Jourdain's house, she does not favor going because she knows nobody there. Though Madame Jourdain, on her surprise entrance at a dinner Monsieur Jourdain is giving to impress the nobility, rails at her, she blames Dorante for the unpleasantness. She finally and sensibly decides to marry Dorante before he ruins himself with the many gifts he brings her.

A Music Master,
A Dancing Master,
A Fencing Master, and
A Philosophy Master, Jourdain's tutors, who rail at and ridicule one another. At the same time they ridicule Jourdain and similar dupes. All are vain of their own arts.

A Master Tailor, clever at turning aside Jourdain's complaints about the clothes made for him by saying that those colors and patterns and tight shoes are the fashion among gentlemen.

A Journeyman Tailor, clever at getting money from Jourdain by raising him in rank with each remark addressed to him.

BOUVARD AND PÉCUCHET

Author: Gustave Flaubert (1821-1880)
Time of action: Nineteenth century
First published: 1881

117

Bouvard (bōō·vár'), a middle-class clerk, the protagonist of Flaubert's unfinished, posthumously published novel. He meets Pécuchet beside the Canal Saint Martin one summer afternoon and finds they have many common interests and traits. Upon receiving a bequest from a man he had thought his uncle, but who turns out to be his natural father, he decides, after consultation with his friend, to buy a house and farm far from the desk where he has toiled, and forget his plebeian occupation. In this way, circumstances that have prevented his extraordinary mind from achieving success, will be changed. After a round of unsuccessful endeavors and undertakings, he returns to his desk.

Pécuchet (pā·kü·shā'), his fat friend, who comes to help Bouvard run his farm. Consulting their neighbors, buying all the books and magazines available, they vainly try to make the farm pay, but the live stock runs away or dies on the wire fences. After the wheat field burns, Pécuchet persuades his friend to give up most of the farm in order to concentrate on a beautiful formal garden.

Madame Bordin (bôr·dăn'), who attends the official banquet and opening of the formal garden and finds the dinner a failure and the garden impossible to see in the late evening. However, when Bouvard begins reading historical romances, as a way of understanding psychology, she is his romantic interest until she suggests that he give her part of his land. Then she is abruptly dropped.

M. Vaucorbeil (vō·kôr·bĕy'), the local doctor. When the experiments of the partners to preserve food results in an explosion, and their study of chemistry leads them to an interest in medicine, Dr. Vaucorbeil protests their attempts to cure some of his own patients. However, he is avenged when their reading about medical symptoms convinces them that they are suffering from many ailments.

Abbé Jeufroy (zhœ·frwá'), the village priest, who comes into conflict with the pair after their interest in the study of life and the universe turns up geologic findings that contradict the teachings of the Church.

M. Foureau (fōō·rō'), the village mayor, who follows the partners' interest in archaeology that turns their farmhouse into a museum, a situation which in time leads to a study of psychology, then to an interest in historical romances.

Mélie (mā·lē'), the servant of the partners. Pécuchet's romantic interest in her leaves him with an attack of venereal disease.

Victorine (vēk·tô·rēn'), a girl about to be sent to an orphan asylum. She is adopted by the partners, but she will not learn obedience and is eventually sent away. She is one more of their failures.

Victor (vēk·tôr'), whom the partners think they can salvage from a reformatory. He proves to be an incorrigible delinquent.

Gorju (gôr·zhü'), a veteran of seven years of African fighting who turns up in the town and stays on.

[Other characters were to appear, according to the novelist's notes, in complications that reveal his distrust of the middle class. Bouvard and Pécuchet were to explore other fields, always becoming disgusted or frustrated until finally they were to realize how foolish they had been since coming to the country. Deciding to return to being clerks, they would order a desk and writing materials and prepare to go to work.]

THE BRACKNELS

Author: Forrest Reid (1876-1946)
Time of action: Early twentieth century
First published: 1911

PRINCIPAL CHARACTERS

Mr. Bracknel, an Irish businessman who prides himself on his practicality. He is a tyrannical husband and father, although he believes his family defies him only to displease him. He is disappointed in his wife because she is sickly, in his son Denis because he thinks the boy mad. He also tries to keep his daughters from meeting young men. He dies of a heart attack brought on by an argument with his eldest son, Alfred, a ne'er-do-well.

Mrs. Bracknel, a sickly woman who seems much older than her forty-six years.

Alfred Bracknel, the eldest son, who has a job in his father's business but prefers to devote himself to pleasure. Though he is incompetent, he inherits his father's business, a fact which makes him glad of his father's death.

Denis Bracknel, seventeen years old. He is interested in the mystical and occult. He finds the world too much to bear and commits suicide beside a pagan altar he discovers near his home.

May Bracknel, a healthy normal person, eldest of the Bracknel daughters.

Amy Bracknel, a man-crazy, sensual girl who is infatuated with Mr. Rusk. She annoys the tutor, who is oblivious to her, by disturbing his charge's lessons. She even tries to announce her engagement to Mr. Rusk.

Hubert Rusk, Denis Bracknel's tutor, an easy and affable young man hired because he can understand Denis' mental condition. He comes to fear that the boy's mental aberrations are bad for his own mental health, but he stays on the job, in deference to the wishes of the Bracknels' doctor, until the boy commits suicide.

THE BRAGGART SOLDIER

Author: Titus Maccius Plautus (c. 255-184 B.C.)
Time of action: Third century B.C.
First presented: c. 206 B.C.

PRINCIPAL CHARACTERS

Pyrgopolinices (pĭr'gō·pŏl·ĭ·nī'sēs), a vain and stupid braggart and professional soldier. Convinced that all women find him irresistible, he seizes a young Athenian girl, Philocomasium, and carries her off to his house in Ephesus. The slave of the girl's sweetheart is, by coincidence, also in the braggart's household. Pleusicles, the girl's lover, takes up residence in the house of an old man next door to Pyrgopolinices. Pleusicles and his slave, Palaestrio, plot to free the girl. Pyrgopolinices is persuaded that the wife of his neighbor is in love with him. A courtesan, playing the part of the wife, tempts Pyrgopolinices and asks him to make room for her in his house. Philocomasium pretends, when Pyrgopolinices tries to send her away, that she is overcome with grief at having to leave him. To get rid of her, the braggart presents her with rich gifts and allows Palaestrio to accompany her. That night Pyrgopolinices is escorted into the house

119

next door, where he expects to meet his latest conquest. Instead, he is soundly beaten by the servants of the house, who have been lying in wait for him.

Palaestrio (pă·lēs′trĭ·ō), Pleusicles' faithful slave. Hurrying by sea to inform his master that Philocomasium had been abducted, Palaestrio had been captured by pirates. His captors presented him to Pyrgopolinices. When Pleusicles arrives in Ephesus, Palaestrio contrives to dig a tunnel between the two houses so that the two lovers can meet. It is Palaestrio who takes the major part in directing the complicated scheme which frees Philocomasium and disgraces Pyrgopolinices.

Pleusicles (plōō′sĭ·klēz), a young gentleman of Athens. After Pyrgopolinices has been persuaded that the wife of his neighbor is in love with him, Pleusicles appears at the braggart's house in the disguise of a sailor. He introduces himself as an agent of Philocomasium's mother and escorts away both the girl and Palaestrio.

Periplecomenus (pĕr′ĭ·plĕ·kō′mĕ·nəs), the old gentleman who owns the house next to Pyrgopolinices. A bachelor who likes to discourse wittily on the joys of celibacy, Periplecomenus enthusiastically cooperates with the plot to reunite the two lovers.

Philocomasium (fĭl′ə·kō·mā′sĭ·əm), the girl kidnaped by Pyrgopolinices. A type of the good courtesan. Philocomasium is faithful to Pleusicles.

Sceledrus (skĕ′lə·drəs), the braggart's drunken slave. He accidentally sees Pleusicles and Philocomasium embracing. Before he can report this irregularity to Pyrgopolinices, Sceledrus is intercepted by Palaestrio, who convinces the latter that Philocomasium's twin sister is the girl he saw.

Acroteleutium (ăk′rə·tĕ·lōō′tĭ·əm), a clever courtesan who impersonates Periplecomenus' wife. She is impudent and quite frank about her depravity.

Milphidippa (mĭl′fĭ·dĭ′pə), Acroteleutium's maid, who conducts the braggart into the trap set for him in Periplecomenus' house.

Artotrogus (ärt′ō·trō′gəs), Pyrogopolinices' parasite, to whom the braggart displays his vanity and stupidity.

Cario (kă′rĭ·ō), Periplecomenus' cook, who threatens to torture the braggart after he has been taken in the wrong house.

Lurcio (lŭr′kĭ·ō), Pyrgopolinices' impudent slave boy.

BRAND

Author: Henrik Ibsen (1828-1906)
Time of action: Nineteenth century
First published: 1866

PRINCIPAL CHARACTERS

Brand, an uncompromising young priest who vows to bring about the cure of the world's triple sickness, as exemplified in the faint-hearted, the light-hearted, and the uncontrolled. Demanding of his followers all or nothing, he is faced with the same choice for himself when he is confronted with the possible death of his son and, later, of his wife, Agnes. He makes the sacrifices he feels are required of him and calls on the people to go up the mountain with him to a new life, where every day is dedicated to God. When the way becomes too hard for his followers, they drop by the wayside, and he goes on alone except for Gerd, who sees that his hands are pierced and his brow marked with thorns.

Agnes, Brand's wife, who challenges her husband to make the choice he demands of others: all or nothing—his duty or her life. She rejoices when he chooses his holy work, and soon afterward she dies.

A Peasant, symbol of the faint-hearted. He will not give his own life for his daughter's.

Einar, a painter, symbol of the lighthearted. Engaged to Agnes, he becomes a fanatical missionary after her marriage to Brand.

Gerd, a gypsy girl, symbol of the uncontrolled. She follows the forsaken Brand up the mountain, where she sees him as Lord and Redeemer.

The Mother. She refuses her son Brand's request that she relinquish all her earthly possessions, and she dies unrepentant.

The Doctor. He reminds Brand that an attempt to save his son's life will require him to belie his demand of all or nothing from his followers.

The Mayor,
The Dean,
The Sexton, and
The Schoolmaster, other members of Brand's flock.

BRAVE NEW WORLD

Author: Aldous Huxley (1894-   )
Time of action: 632 A.F. (After Ford)
First published: 1932

PRINCIPAL CHARACTERS

Bernard Marx, a citizen of the world in the year 632 A.F., a world dominated by science in which individuality has long been forgotten, a world dehumanized and organized around the motto, "Community, Identity, Stability." Marx, born of a "prenatal bottle" instead of woman, is an anomaly in the community because too much alcohol got into his blood surrogate while he was incubating before birth. He has sensibilities, therefore, similar to those of people living during the time of Henry Ford. Marx conducts an experiment that fails: by studying a savage named John, whom he brings to the new culture, he learns that human emotions produce only tragedy in the brave new world.

Lenina Crowne, an Alpha worker in The Central London Hatchery and Conditioning Center, who is interested in Marx. She was predestined to her class, as were all citizens of the community, for, depending upon the community work to be done, citizens may come from the bottles as Alpha Plus Intellectuals all the way down through Epsilon Minus Morons. Lenina helps Marx with the experiment, falls in love with the savage, and is whipped to death by him when he attacks her in a fit of passion.

Thomakin, the Director of Hatcheries, who years before had abandoned a woman he had taken with him on vacation to the Savage Reservation, a wild tract in New Mexico preserved by the state to advance the study of primitive societies. When it is discovered that Thomakin is the father of the savage whom Marx brings back to London, Thomakin resigns his directorship of the Hatcheries.

John, the Savage who is the subject of Marx's experiment and is Thomakin's son. John received his only education by reading an old copy of Shakespeare's plays he found at the Savage Reservation.

121

While beside himself with passion, he whips Lenina to death and, in a fit of remorse, hangs himself.

Mustapha Mond, a World Controller responsible in the main for the conditioning of the young to the ways of the brave new world.

Linda, John's mother, the woman abandoned by Thomakin at the Savage Reservation.

BREAD AND WINE

Author: Ignazio Silone (1900-   )
Time of action: The 1930's
First published: 1937

PRINCIPAL CHARACTERS

Pietro Spina, a former favorite pupil of Don Benedetto. Despite physical hardships and intellectual disappointments, Spina remains faithful to his concept of justice and thus demonstrates that good men will fight, even if unsuccessful, as long as they exist. He ages his features with iodine and as a priest, "Don Paolo Spada," becomes an anti-war agitator among the mountaineers.

Doctor Nunzio Sacca, an old friend who finds and helps Spina.

Matelena Ricotta, owner of the mountain inn where Spina hides.

Bianchina Girasole, who considers Spina a saint because he consoled her following an abortion. She seduces Alberto, the brother of her friend Cristina, and becomes a prostitute when sent to Rome by Spina to agitate against the Abyssinian War frenzy.

Cristina Colamartini, whose devotion to God goes beyond reason. She sacrifices herself to cold and the wolves to carry food to the hidden Spina.

Alberto Colamartini, the brother of Cristina, and socially above any Girasole.

Pompeo, the son of a Fossa chemist. Once a reformer, he catches the war frenzy and nearly denounces Spina for writing anti-war slogans on walls.

Romeo, head of the anti-war movement in Rome until captured.

Uliva, a disillusioned Italian killed by the bomb he was making to blow up a church filled with government officials.

Murica, a potential ally in Spina's struggle to put God back in the affairs of man. He is killed by government authorities.

Don Benedetto, an old Catholic teacher and Spina's intellectual mentor.

Marta, his faithful sister.

THE BRIDE OF LAMMERMOOR

Author: Sir Walter Scott (1771-1832)
Time of action: Late seventeenth century
First published: 1819

PRINCIPAL CHARACTERS

Edgar, popularly called the Master of Ravenswood, even though the Ravenswood estate has passed into the hands of his family's enemy, Sir William Ashton. Edgar and Lucy Ashton fall in love, but tragedy and death prevent the resurgence of the Ravenswood fortunes and the marriage of the lovers.

Sir William Ashton, Lord Keeper of Scotland. He is the new master of the Ravenswood estate and the long-time enemy of the late Lord Ravenswood. He is prevented by his wife from befriending Edgar and bringing about a marriage between him and Lucy, his daughter.

Lucy Ashton, daughter of Sir William and secretly betrothed to Edgar, Master of Ravenswood. Forced to marry Frank Hayston of Bucklaw, she loses her mind and dies the day after the wedding.

Lady Ashton, wife of Sir William. Her cruel persecution and virtual imprisonment of her daughter Lucy drive the girl to madness and, finally, to her death.

Frank Hayston of Bucklaw, a wealthy young nobleman and Lady Ashton's favored contender for the hand of Lucy, who dies the morning after being married to him.

Caleb Balderstone, Edgar's faithful old servant who tries to keep alive the ancient glories of the Ravenswood family.

The Marquis of A—, Edgar's powerful kinsman.

Alice, a blind tenant on the Ravenswood estate who prophesies tragedy will result from the union of a Ravenswood and an Ashton. Her ghost warns Edgar of the danger of such an alliance.

Captain Craigengelt, an adventurer-soldier, companion of Frank Hayston.

Young Ashton, Lucy's brother. Believing that Edgar is responsible for his sister's death, he challenges Edgar to a duel. On the way to this duel Edgar is trapped in quicksand and perishes.

BRIDESHEAD REVISITED

Author: Evelyn Waugh (1903-   )
Time of action: Twentieth century
First published: 1945

PRINCIPAL CHARACTERS

Charles Ryder, a young man who in his days at Oxford meets Sebastian Marchmain and is gradually introduced to the Marchmain family of Brideshead. He becomes an architectural painter and marries the sister of another Oxford friend; but his ties to the Marchmain family persist, and later he falls in love with Sebastian's sister Julia, who is also married. They plan to divorce their spouses and marry each other, and for a while they live together; but Julia's Catholic faith claims her at last, and she gives up Charles.

Lady Marchmain, the stanchly Catholic mother of Sebastian and Julia, who are in revolt from her as well as from their religion. After her death, her rebellious husband and children are drawn back to the values of the Church.

The Marquis of Marchmain, Lady Marchmain's husband and the owner of Brideshead. For many years he has lived with his mistress in Italy. After the death of his wife, he returns to Brideshead with his mistress to spend his last days. Although he is in failing health, he refuses to see a priest; but as he is dying the priest is brought in, and Lord Marchmain makes the sign of the cross.

Brideshead (Bridey) Marchmain, the oldest of their children. A pompous man, he marries a self-righteous widow with three children.

Sebastian Marchmain, Charles Ryder's

123

friend, an ineffectual though clever and charming young man. His rebellion takes the form of severe alcoholism. After years of aimless wandering, he tries to enter a monastery in Carthage and is refused. Unconscious from drink, he is carried into the monastery by the monks. He plans to stay there as an under-porter for the rest of his life.

Julia Marchmain, whose form of rebellion is to marry a rich but socially inferior Protestant of whom her mother disapproves. Though he is willing to be converted, it is discovered that he is divorced, and they are forced to marry in a Protestant ceremony. Later Julia falls in love with Charles and has an affair with him, but, believing that to marry him would only magnify the sin, she gives him up.

Cordelia Marchmain, the youngest of the four children. On returning from Spain, where she worked with an ambulance corps, she tells her family about Sebastian, whom she visited.

Cara, Lord Marchmain's lifelong mistress.

Rex Mottram, Julia's vital and ambitious but ill-bred husband.

Boy Mulcaster and

Anthony Blanche, Oxford friends of Sebastian and Charles.

Celia Ryder, Boy Mulcaster's sister and Charles' wife.

Beryl Muspratt, a widow with three children. Engaged to Bridey, she refuses to come to Brideshead because Charles and Julia are living there in sin. Traveling with Bridey in Italy after their marriage, she meets Lord Marchmain, who dislikes her.

Kurt, Sebastian's roommate and companion in Fez. Kurt is seized by Germans and taken back to Germany. Sebastian follows him, but after Kurt hangs himself in a concentration camp, Sebastian returns to Morocco.

Mr. Samgrass, who is employed in doing some literary work for Lady Marchmain. She hires him also to keep Sebastian away from alcohol, but the plan is doomed to failure.

Father Mackay, the priest whom the Marchmain children and Cara bring to the bedside of the dying Lord Marchmain.

Johnjohn Ryder and
Caroline Ryder, children of Charles and Celia.

THE BRIDGE OF SAN LUIS REY

Author: Thornton Wilder (1897-   )
Time of action: Early eighteenth century
First published: 1927

PRINCIPAL CHARACTERS

Brother Juniper, a Spanish friar who tries to prove that the collapse of the bridge of San Luis Rey in Peru is an act showing the wisdom of God, who properly sent five persons to their deaths in the accident. For his book, which is condemned by the Church, the friar is burned at the stake.

The Narrator, who finds a copy of

Brother Juniper's eighteenth century book and reconstructs for the reader the lives of the five persons who died when the bridge collapsed.

The Marquesa de Montemayor, an ugly woman with a beautiful daughter. She is highly possessive and selfish, first to her daughter and then to Pepita, her maid. By reading a letter from Pepita to an abbess the Marquesa learns her own nature, becomes contrite, and resolves to be a better woman, only to die the next day when the bridge collapses.

Pepita, maid for the Marquesa de Montemayor, who dies also when the bridge collapses. She is unhappy when she is sent from her convent by the Abbess Madre María del Pilar, whom she loves, to serve the noblewoman. Her letter confessing her unhappiness reveals to the Marquesa the noblewoman's thoughtless and self-centered life.

Uncle Pio, an actor who discovers La Périchole singing in a tavern. He makes a great actress and singer of her, and comes to love her. He is disappointed by the girl, who becomes the mistress of the viceroy and soon is too proud for her own good. Uncle Pio takes her illegitimate child to rear, but the next day he and the child are victims of the collapse of the bridge.

Jaime, illegitimate son of La Périchole and the viceroy. He dies when the bridge collapses.

Esteban, a young man whose twin brother gives up his love for La Périchole because of the affection between the two brothers, foundlings reared by the Abbess Madre María del Pilar. Manuel dies, and his brother, who becomes a victim of the bridge's collapse, is inconsolable.

La Périchole, an actress who is overly proud, especially after becoming the viceroy's mistress. Her pride diminishes when smallpox destroys her beauty. She puts her son in the care of Uncle Pio the day before both of them die.

Manuel, twin brother of Esteban. He hides his love for La Périchole so he will not hurt his brother's feelings, but in a delirium, close to death, he reveals his secret passion.

The Abbess Madre María del Pilar, who befriends the twin brothers, Esteban and Manuel, as well as Pepita, the girl who becomes the Marquesa de Montemayor's maid. The Abbess is a wise and kindly woman.

Doña Clara, cynical daughter of the Marquesa de Montemayor. She learns too late of her mother's change of heart and inner goodness.

BRITANNICUS

Author: Jean Baptiste Racine (1639-1699)
Time of action: A.D. 55
First presented: 1669

PRINCIPAL CHARACTERS

Britannicus, the son of the dead Emperor Claudius. Used as the proving ground in the contest for power between the Emperor Néron and Agrippine, he is finally poisoned in the struggle. His murder sets the pattern for the remainder of Néron's reign.

Agrippine (à·grē·pēn'), the widow of the Emperor Claudius and mother of the Emperor Néron. She wins the throne for her son; then, dominated by her lust for power, she attempts to continue her dominion over him. Fearing the diminution of her influence, she plots to replace Néron with Britannicus. Néron's violent reaction against her causes his first crime, the poisoning of Britannicus, and sets the direction of his destiny.

Néron (nā·rōn'), Agrippine's son and the Emperor of Rome. Impatient under the yoke of his mother's domination, he learns of her plan to place Britannicus on

125

the throne in his stead and commits the first of his many crimes, the murder of the would-be usurper.

Junie (zhü·nē'), Britannicus' betrothed, abducted by Néron, who falls in love with her and plans to divorce his wife in her favor. Junie remains faithful to Britannicus and becomes a priestess of Vesta after his death.

Narcisse (när·sēs'), Britannicus' tutor, an

opportunist who works on Néron's baser instincts.

Burrhus (bû'rəs), Néron's tutor, who tries to emphasize the better elements in the Emperor's character.

Albina (àl·bē·nà'), a confidante of Agrippine.

Pallas, a freedman, a friend and adviser to Agrippine.

Octavia (ôk·tà·vyà'), Néron's wife.

BROAD AND ALIEN IS THE WORLD

Author: Ciro Alegría (1909-   )
Time of action: 1912-1926
First published: 1941

PRINCIPAL CHARACTERS

Rosendo Maquis (r̄ō·sän'dō mä'kēs), mayor of the Peruvian Indian village of Rumi. He fights a losing battle to keep his people from losing their ancestral lands. He is a peaceful man who seeks only justice from the white men. Seeking to recover the village's prize bull, he is imprisoned as a thief. He dies in prison, victim of a brutal beating administered when he is erroneously thought to be responsible for helping another prisoner, Fiero Vasquez, escape.

Bismarck Ruiz (bēs·märk' r̄wēs'), an unethical lawyer. He is retained by the Indians to help them in court to keep their lands from falling into the hands of Don Amenabar, a white rancher. Ruiz is but half-hearted in his efforts, as he is also in the employ of Don Amenabar.

Don Amenabar (dōn ä·mä·nä·bär'), a greedy, ruthless rancher. He treats the Indians as an inferior people and robs them of their cattle and lands. He tries,

too, to make slaves of them for his mines.

Correa Zavala (kō·r̄ä'ä sä·bä'lä), a zealous young lawyer. He, filled with indignation, undertakes to help the Indians, but his well-meant efforts are unsuccessful.

Fiero Vásquez (fyä'rō bäs'käs), a notorious Peruvian bandit. Implored by an Indian woman from Rosendo's village who loves him, he offers to help the Indians fight eviction by force. The peaceful villagers, knowing violence will not bring them any lasting peace, reject his offer.

Benito Castro (bä·nē'tō käs'trō), successor to Rosendo as the leader of the Indians of the village of Rumi. He is killed by soldiers who evict the poor people from their lands.

La Castelaña (lä käs·tä·lä'nyä), a notorious woman, mistress of the lawyer Bismarck Ruiz.

126

THE BROKEN JUG

Author: Heinrich von Kleist (1777-1811)
Time of action: Late eighteenth century
First presented: 1808

PRINCIPAL CHARACTERS

Adam (ä'däm), the village judge. In an attempted seduction of Eve, a village girl, he is surprised by her betrothed, beaten up by him, and forced to jump out of her window to escape recognition by his attacker. In spite of his invention of a series of unlikely stories designed to conceal his identity from the townsfolk and explain away the scars of battle, he is eventually found out, exposed before his court, and forced to flee the village to escape another beating.

Martha Rull (mär'tĕ rōōl), a village woman. She is in Adam's court carrying a broken jug and furiously demanding justice.

Ruprecht (rōōp'räsht), Eve's suitor, who is accused by Martha Rull of breaking her pitcher. Under duress he finally testifies that he had broken the jug during

an altercation with Eve's would-be seducer.

Eve (āfă), Martha Rull's daughter, engaged to Ruprecht and the object of Adam's attempted seduction.

Brigitte (brē'gǐ'tĕ), Ruprecht's aunt and a witness to the would-be seducer's hasty retreat from Eve's house. Her appearance in court with a wig dropped by the fleeing lover establishes Adam's identity as the culprit.

Walter (väl'tĕr), Counselor of the High Court, who is on a tour of inspection, during which he finds Adam's court in a state of chaos.

Licht (lǐsht), the clerk of the court.

Veit Tümpel (fīt tüm'pel), Ruprecht's father.

THE BROTHERS

Author: Terence (Publius Terentius Afer, c. 190-159 B.C.)
Time of action: Second century B.C.
First presented: 160 B.C.

PRINCIPAL CHARACTERS

Micio (mē'shǐ·ō), an easy-going Athenian bachelor. Adopting Aeschinus, son of his austere brother Demea, he becomes an indulgent, permissive parent. His wise handling of Aeschinus' escapades finally convinces his brother of the wisdom of ruling by kindness rather than fear.

Demea (dē'mǐ·ə), Micio's unyielding brother, who is dedicated to strict discipline in the upbringing of children. Father of Ctesipho, his severity makes the boy fearful of his parent. Learning through experience the folly of trying to rule by fear, he tries leniency and gen-

erosity, to the gratification of all concerned.

Aeschinus (ĕs'kǐ·nəs), the son of Demea adopted by Micio. A report that Aeschinus has entered a house and abducted a woman causes the distressed foster father to be accused of parental overindulgence. When the break-in is finally and satisfactorily explained, the foster father's leniency is justified and Aeschinus is permitted to marry Pamphila.

Ctesipho (tĕ'sǐ·fō), Demea's son. He is

127

in love with a slave girl he cannot afford to buy. Angered by his father's severity, he, with the help of his brother Aeschinus, abducts the girl in defiance of parental restraint. His father, finally realizing the error of his disciplinary methods, gives his approval to Ctesipho's passion.

Sostrata (sōs′trə·tə), Pamphila's mother.

Pamphila (păm′fĭ·lə), Sostrata's daughter, loved by Aeschinus.

Sannio (să′nĭ·ō), a slave dealer.

Hegio (hē′jĭ·ō), an old Athenian and a friend of Demea.

Syrus (sĭ′rəs) and
Phrygia (frĭ′jĭ·ə), slaves freed by Micio.

THE BROTHERS ASHKENAZI

Author: Israel Joshua Singer (1893-1944)
Time of action: Late nineteenth and early twentieth centuries
First published: 1936

PRINCIPAL CHARACTERS

Simcha Meyer Ashkenazi, the elder of twin brothers. A shrewd schemer, he advances in affluence through successive marriages and unscrupulous dealings. Later, though his fortune is not always spared, he does manage to survive various historical disasters: the trade-union movement, a pogrom against the Jews, World War I, the Russian revolution.

Jacob Bunim Ashkenazi, his brother, who is popular and extroverted. His rise in the world results from his ebullience and popularity, and parallels Simcha's. At last, returning to Poland from Russia with Simcha, whom he has freed from jail by bribery, he is shot by anti-Jewish border guards because, unlike Simcha, he refuses to grovel and repudiate his religion.

Abraham Ashkenazi, their father, greatly respected in his town of Lodz in Poland. After Simcha connives succesfully to take over his father's position, Abraham counts Simcha among the dead.

Dinah Ashkenazi, Simcha's wife. In love with Jacob, she is betrothed to Simcha at thirteen. He divorces her to marry a rich widow.

Pearl Ashkenazi, Jacob's wife, who is too sickly to keep up with her vigorous husband. She divorces him.

Nissan, the son and pupil of a famous rabbi, and Simcha's fellow student. A reader of secular books, he is betrayed by Simcha and cast out by his father. He becomes a weaver and a revolutionary. Beaten in his capacity as strike leader by Simcha, he avenges himself in Russia after the revolution; his party confiscates Simcha's property.

Tevyeh, a weaver and a fanatical revolutionary. Simcha has him arrested and exiled along with Nissan.

Gertrude Ashkenazi, the daughter of Dinah and Simcha, and Jacob's second wife. He marries her because she reminds him of Dinah.

Ignatz Ashkenazi, Simcha's longforgotten son. Simcha, returned from Russia and rebuilding his factory, induces Ignatz to come back from France. Simcha suspects darkly that Ignatz' French wife is not Jewish.

Huntze, the German owner of the biggest steam mill in Lodz. Abraham is Huntze's general agent until Huntze's death, after which Huntze's sons dismiss Abraham and appoint Simcha in his place, to repay a favor.

THE BROTHERS KARAMAZOV

Author: Fyodor Mikhailovich Dostoevski (1821-1881)
Time of action: Nineteenth century
First published: 1880

PRINCIPAL CHARACTERS

Fyodor Pavlovitch Karamazov (fyō'dər päv'lô·vĭch kä·rä·mä'zəf), a crude buffoon of a father and the extremist, sensual, materialistic progenitor of a line of doomed sons. As an aging libertine he is brought in competition with his sons over a woman, money, and status, and also by a sheer determination to live and control his destiny without interference. His manners are as threatening as his brooding appearance, and as a sensual his debauchery is extreme, unabated even in his dwindling years. He is crafty, greedy, close-fisted, exhibiting a low cunning which speaks of a special kind of intelligence. His pose is artful; his lust for life and his voluptuousness are phenomenal. Obscene as he is, a malignant joker of low order, he has about him an air of magnificence gone to seed in an aging domestic tyrant.

Dmitri (dmĭ'trĭy), often called **Mitya,** his oldest son, who most resembles his father and most despises him for the wrong done the dead mother and himself. Morbidly fearful of his heredity, Dmitri reviles his father not so much for what he has done as a man who has cheated his son of both birthright and lover, but for what he is, a cruel, crafty despoiler of all that is decent. Like his father, he is muscular, though slender, sallow, with large dark eyes. He is a kind of scapegoat, the one on whom the curse of sensuousness falls most heavily, given as he is to strong feelings and actions. He has a brooding Russian personality, an excitability, a violent nature capable of deep emotions and lasting love and antagonisms, though he has also simplicity, natural goodness, an open heart, directness, and awareness.

Ivan (ĭ·vän'), his half brother, an intellectual, poet, and atheist, given to visions and flights of fancy, secretiveness, remote aloofness. Five years younger than Mitya, he seems older, more mature, better poised. He has a subtle mind, both skeptical and idealistic, mercurial and unrealistic. Although none of the boys, having been cared for by relatives, is close to their tempestuous father, Ivan is the least known to Fyodor Karamazov and the one he most fears for qualities so remote from his own. Though he wills his father's death, he is greatly shocked at the deed and his part in it, and he suffers a guilt complex so great that it unhinges his dualistic mind. He serves as the author's mouthpiece in the long Grand Inquisitor scene and the account of his private devil. Ivan is loved distantly and respected by his brothers for this very lucidity and clairvoyance. He inherits the lust, the extremism, the egocentricity of his father, but in a refined, inward, though almost as compulsive a way.

Alyosha (ä·lyō'shə), or **Alexey** (ä·lĕk·sā'), Ivan's brother and Dmitri's half brother, the spiritual son who is the peacemaker, the sympathizer, the trusted and beloved brother if not son. Nineteen, healthy, bright, personable, good-looking, Alyosha, out of goodness and love, forms a bond with his unregenerate father and his distrustful brothers. His devotion to the good Father Zossima, his acceptance of his own worldliness at war with his spirituality, and his sheer love of life make him an attractive character, a natural, human person among grotesques.

Grushenka (grōō'shĕn·kə), beloved by father and son, an intemperate temptress, an earthy type who realizes more than

129

she can communicate. She appears a hussy with all tricks of her kind, but she is also devoted, loyal in her own way, and loving. Primitive, independent, free of the petty vindictiveness that plagues her lovers, Grushenka enlivens the story with a wholesome, womanly, even motherly quality.

Katerina Ivanovna (kä·těr·ĭn′ə ĭ·vä′-nôv·nə), beloved by Ivan but engaged to Dmitri, an aristocrat and compulsive lover of great force of character. Willing to beg for love, to buy her beloved, she also has a fierce pride that flames up in revenge. Though she is attractive in a more austere way than Grushenka, they share many eternally feminine traits.

Smerdyakov (směr·dyä′kəf), a half-witted servant, perhaps a natural son of Karamazov, and his murderer. He is scornful and sadistic. As the murderer who cannot live with his guilt, he is seen as more sinned against than sinning, the victim more than the antagonist. He hates his master and Dmitri, but he is curiously

drawn to Ivan and in reality dies for him. Smerdyakov hangs himself.

Father Zossima (zō′sě·mə), a devout religious ascetic, Aloysha's teacher in the monastery to which the boy retires for a time. Aware of the sensual nature of the Karamazovs, the old priest advises the boy to go back to the world. Because of his holy example, his followers expect a miracle to occur when Father Zossima dies. Instead, his body decomposes rapidly, a circumstance viewed by other monks as proof that the aged man's teachings have been false.

Marfa (mär′fə), a servant in the Karamazov household and Smerdyakov's foster mother.

Grigory (grĭ·gô′rē), Marfa's husband.

Lizaveta (lyē·zä·vě′tə), the half-witted girl who was Smerdyakov's mother. Many people in the village believed that Fyodor Karamazov was the father of her child.

THE BRUSHWOOD BOY

Author: Rudyard Kipling (1865-1936)
Time of action: Nineteenth century
First published: 1895

PRINCIPAL CHARACTERS

Georgie Cottar, the character to whom the book's title refers. The Brushwood Boy is a highly imaginative young man of the upper middle class who, alone among his nurse, his father and mother, and a houseful of domestics, dreams dreams. His dreams always begin the same way. There is a pile of brushwood on a beach; there are people, sometimes a policeman; and there is always an adventure, usually a pleasant one. The story takes Georgie from his third year, through public school, to Sandhurst, to the Indian service as an officer in charge of many soldiers, and back to England as a young adult. Each stage of his life

is productive of the dream that begins at the brushwood pile. A girl moves in and out of the dreams, but, as he gets older, Georgie notices that the girl becomes more consistently the same person. She finally materializes as the girl Georgie hopes to marry and live with in real life.

Miriam Lacy, the young girl Georgie meets when he returns to England on a year's furlough from his regiment. She, like the girl in his dreams, has her black hair fixed in a widow's peak, and she speaks with a slight lisp. Strangely, she seems to know all about Georgie's dream, because she sings songs that are summaries of the stories he has dreamed.

Annieanlouise, the name formed by running together Georgie's two favorite female names, Anna and Louise. In the dreams of his childhood, Georgie called the girl he dreamed about by this name. Annieanlouise becomes, of course, the Miriam of Georgie's real world.

THE BRUT

Author: Layamon (fl. twelfth century)
Time of action: From the fall of Troy to the seventh century
First transcribed: c. 1205

PRINCIPAL CHARACTERS

Aeneas (ē·nē′əs), the Trojan hero, legendary ancestor of the ancient rulers of Britain.

Ascanius (ăs·kā′nĭ·əs), his son.

Brutus (brōō′təs), his grandson, who colonizes Britain with a group of Trojan descendants. Brave and generous to his followers, he is an ideal leader in the tradition of Beowulf.

Assaracus, the heir of a Greek knight and his Trojan concubine, Brutus' companion and military aide.

Corineus, the ruler of a Trojan colony in Spain and, later, of Cornwall; a man of violent temper and great bravery.

Geomagog, the giant who rules Logice, the island where Brutus lands.

Locrin, Brutus' successor, who brings chaos upon his country by repudiating his wife, Corineus' daughter, for his mistress, a maiden of his enemies, the Huns.

Camber and
Albanact, his brothers, rulers of Wales and Scotland.

Humber, King of the Huns, defeated by Locrin and Camber.

Aestrild, Locrin's mistress.

Guendoline, Locrin's rejected Queen, who raises an army to defeat her husband and kill her rival.

Leil, a monarch who dies of sorrow at the uprising of his barons.

Ruhhudibras, the founder of Winchester and Canterbury.

Bladud, his heir, whose discovery of hot springs is considered evidence of his consultation with devils.

Leir, the legendary original of Shakespeare's Lear. He divides his kingdom between two of his daughters but rejects the third for her refusal to flatter him. After suffering persecution from the elder two, he is happily reunited with his youngest child.

Gornuille,
Ragun, and
Cordoille, his daughters.

Aganippus, King of France, Cordoille's husband.

Gorbodiago, a good king, the model of the title figure in "Gorboduc."

Fereus and
Poreus, his sons, murdered and murderer.

Jadon, their mother, who takes Poreus' life to avenge his killing of Fereus.

Cloten, Duke of Cornwall, the man with the greatest right to Gorboduc's throne. He lacks wealth and power to claim it.

Donwallo Molinus, his son, the fairest

131

king of England, who brings peace, quiet, and good laws to his people.

Belen and
Brennes, brothers and joint rulers. They conduct successful campaigns against Scandinavian and Roman forces.

Julius Caesar and
Claudius, Roman emperors and rulers of Britain.

Luces, the just monarch in whose reign Christianity reaches England.

Asclepidiot, the ruler who expels the Romans.

Helen, the daughter of Coel, King of Britain, and Constantine's mother, who discovers the Cross of Christ in Jerusalem.

Constantine, her son, who reigns in Britain and expels the tyrant Maxenz from Rome.

Vortiger, a powerful earl, controller of half of Wales. To acquire power, he instigates a plot to place on the throne his King's son Constance, a monk, who is therefore ineligible to rule.

Constance, a weak king.

Uther, his brother, a fine warrior who, before he becomes king, defeats both the Irish and the invading heathens under Hengest.

Hengest, the leader of the Germanic tribes who joins Vortiger's court at his own request.

Vortimer, Vortiger's son and heir, a Christian ruler who tries to expel Hengest.

Merlin, a magician, "son of no man," counselor to Uther and Arthur.

Ygærne, the wife of Gorlois, Earl of Cornwall, desired by Uther.

Arthur, the son of Uther and Ygærne, recalled from his home in Brittany to be a wise and generous King of England and sworn enemy to the Saxon invaders. A fierce warrior, he extends his conquests to Rome itself. Mortally wounded in battle against his treacherous nephew, Modred, he departs for Avalon to be healed by the fairy queen, promising to return.

Wenhavere (Guinevere), his queen. She betrays him with Modred and retreats to a nunnery after her lover's defeat.

Walwain (Gawain), Arthur's nephew, a noble, virtuous knight, prototype of the hero of "Sir Gawain and the Green Knight," who is debased in Malory's "Le Morte d'Arthur."

Kay, one of Arthur's trusted knights.

Beduer (Bedivere), Arthur's steward and another of his favorite knights.

Modred, Walwain's treacherous brother.

Luces, the Roman emperor killed by Arthur after he had demanded tribute from the British.

Austin, a priest sent, years later, to introduce Christianity into Britain a second time.

Æthelbert, his royal convert.

Aeluric, his enemy, a Northumbrian king.

Penda, the King of Marcia, who treacherously murders the son of his ally, King Edwine.

Cadwalader, last of the British kings, beset by plague and famine.

Athelstan, the first English king of all England.

132

BUDDENBROOKS

Author: Thomas Mann (1875-1955)
Time of action: Nineteenth century
First published: 1901

PRINCIPAL CHARACTERS

Johann Buddenbrook (yō'hän bōō'dĕn-brōk), the stout, rosy-faced, benevolent-looking patriarch of the Buddenbrook family. He is the wealthy, successful senior partner of a grain-trading firm inherited from his father.

Johann (yō'hän) **Buddenbrook, Jr. (Jean, The Consul),** his serious-looking, aquiline-nosed, blond-bearded first son by his second wife. Jean combines the sentimentalist and the businessman. He rejoices over a happy family gathering, worries about the alienation of his half brother, Gotthold, from the family, and then advises coolly that Gotthold's request for money be denied because of likely future results to both family and firm. Jean's pietism seems foreign to the other Buddenbrooks, whose religion is superficial and confined to conventional sentiments proper to people of their class.

Antonie (än'tō·nē), **(Tony) Buddenbrook,** later **Frau Grünlich** and **Frau Permaneder,** Jean's oldest child. She has ash-blonde hair, gray-blue eyes, and finely shaped but stumpy hands. Impetuous in youth, she becomes conventional in maturity, but to her brother Tom she always remains a child in her reactions to the incidents in her life. She easily adapts herself to any situation; she is not humiliated by the dissolution of her marriage to Grünlich and is proud of the fact that she becomes a person of importance in the family. She adapts as readily to the breaking up of her marriage to Permaneder. As she develops a closer intimacy with her father following her first divorce, she recognizes and establishes closer ties with Tom after the death of their father. She sees the two of them as true Buddenbrooks, for

their brother Christian does not really seem one of the family and young Clara remains an unimportant sister. The retention of dignity for both herself and the family becomes almost a religion with Tony.

Tom Buddenbrook, Jean's older son (modeled upon Thomas Mann's father). A quick-witted, intelligent, even-tempered boy, he becomes a strong, sturdy youth resembling his grandfather Johann. As he matures, he develops a stocky, broad-shouldered figure and a military air. His excessive clothes consciousness seems out of character for a Buddenbrook. An earnest, responsible businessman, he is proud of his burgher ancestry, and he contrasts his own desire to preserve the family name with the lack of imagination and idealism shown by Gotthold, his half brother. He is increasingly disgusted with Christian's business irresponsibility and his reputation as a strange kind of clown. He cannot forgive Christian's joking observation in company that all businessmen are swindlers. In his prime Tom is more aggressive than the earlier Buddenbrooks, but occasionally a little less scrupulous. His participation in public affairs and his interest in culture set him somewhat apart from his ancestors and his business associates. Early in his forties, he becomes increasingly aware that he has grown prematurely old, and he thinks more and more of death. At forty-eight he feels that death is stalking him. He dies not many months later following a fall in a snowy street after the partial extraction of a rotted tooth.

Christian (krĭs'tē·än) **Buddenbrook,** Jean's younger son. A born mimic, he is

133

a moody, whimsical, sometimes extravagantly silly boy. As a youth he first betrays his weakness for pretty women and his deep interest in the theater. During an eight-year absence from home, principally in South America, he becomes lean and pallid, his large humped nose more prominent, his neck thinner, his hair sparse. Through association with Englishmen abroad he himself has grown to look like an Englishman. His self-absorption and his lack of dignity in his social manners disturb Tom Buddenbrook's sense of propriety. Christian becomes more and more a neurotic and a hypochondriac as he ages. After Tom's death Christian marries his mistress, who not long afterward has to put him in a mental institution. Like Tom's son Hanno, he symbolizes the decay of the Buddenbrook family.

Frau Consul Elizabeth Kröger (frou kŏn·sōōl' ā·lē'sä·băt krœ'gèr) **Buddenbrook,** the wife of Jean Buddenbrook. A woman of the world and a lover of life, she becomes well known in her later years for her piety and her numerous charities. After a long life with her family she dies of pneumonia.

Clara (clä'rä) **Buddenbrook,** the fourth and youngest child of Jean and Elizabeth. Hawk-nosed, dark-haired, and firm-mouthed, she is at times haughty. She marries Pastor Tiburtius, a minister from Riga, and dies childless a few years later.

Gotthold (gŏt'hôld) **Buddenbrook,** the elder Johann's unambitious son by his first wife. Having angered his father by a disapproved marriage and by becoming a shopkeeper, he is thereafter shunned by the family. He resents the favored treatment accorded his half brother Jean. After his father's death Gotthold retires and lives on the income from his inheritance and the sale of his shop. He dies at sixty of a heart attack.

Gerda Arnoldsen (gär'dä är'nŏld·sĕn) **Buddenbrook,** an aristocratic Dutch heiress who attends school with Tony. Her immense dowry later influences Tom's decision to marry her, though he declares to his mother at the time that he loves Gerda. The marriage is a happy one, but Gerda (perhaps modeled in part on Thomas Mann's mother), with her high degree of refinement, her detached nature, and her intense interest in music, remains somewhat a stranger among the Buddenbrooks.

Little Johann, or **Hanno** (hän'nō), **Buddenbrook,** the pathetic, sickly son of Tom and Gerda. He shares his mother's love of music and she thinks him a precocious genius. He dies in his teens of typhoid fever. Like his Uncle Christian, Hanno symbolizes the decadence of the family, and with his death the family itself comes to an end, for no male is left to carry on the Buddenbrook name.

Bendix Grünlich (bĕn'dĭks grün'lĭsh), Tony's first husband, a well-to-do Hamburg merchant and a pink-faced, blue-eyed, golden-whiskered, obsequious flatterer and rascal. His bogus charm takes in Jean, who urges Tony to marry him despite her disgust for him. When his impending bankruptcy later leads him to seek money from Jean, Buddenbrook angrily discovers that Grünlich, even before marrying Tony, had unscrupulously capitalized on his supposed connection with the family. A divorce follows shortly after Tony's return to her parents' home with her daughter.

Morten Schartzkopf (mōr'tĕn schärts'-kŏpf), a charming, serious-minded, liberal-thinking but naïve medical student whose brief romance with Tony is broken up when Grünlich reports to Morten's father a prior claim on Tony.

Alois Permaneder (ä'lō·ĕs pĕr'mä·nä·dèr), Tony's second husband, a bullet-headed, walrus-like, fat-cheeked, man of forty, a Munich brewer. Vulgar in speech and desirous of an easy life, he gets no sympathy from Tony regarding his decision to retire from the brewing business to live on his income from rents and investments. After Tony finds him one night drunkenly forcing his attentions on Babette, the cook, she leaves him. When she seeks a divorce, he willingly agrees to it and returns her dowry because he has no need of it.

Erica Grünlich (ä′rĭ·kä grün′lĭsh), the daughter of Tony and her first husband. Tall, fresh-colored, pretty, healthy, and strong, she is occasionally inclined to melancholy moods. Her marriage, after the birth of a daughter, ends in disaster.

Hugo Weinschenk (hoo′gō wīn′shănk), Erica's husband, a crude, pompous, self-made man, the middle-aged Silesian director of a fire insurance company. Convicted of unscrupulous business practices, he goes to prison. Upon his release and after a brief visit with the Buddenbrooks, he disappears.

Friederick Wilhelm Marcus (frē′dĕ·rĭk wĭl′hĕlm mär′kŏs), Jean's confidential clerk. After Jean's death he becomes a junior partner in the Buddenbrook firm. His conservatism counteracts Tom's occasional tendency to overstretch himself.

THE BULWARK

Author: Theodore Dreiser (1871-1945)
Time of action: 1890 to the mid-1920's
First published: 1946

PRINCIPAL CHARACTERS

Solon Barnes, an upright, severe Quaker businessman who raises his children in strict accordance with Quaker moral principles. A family tragedy brings him to the realization that over-concern for business and strict standards has obscured for him the central "Inner Light" of the Quaker faith. With the help of his daughter Etta, he regains his serenity during his last days.

Rufus Barnes, Solon's respected Quaker father and the founder of the family fortune.

Hannah Barnes, Solon's upright Quaker mother and the sister of Phoebe Kimber.

Benecia Wallin Barnes, Solon's quiet, religious wife.

Isobel Barnes, Solon's studious, unattractive oldest daughter.

Orville Barnes, Solon's severe, respectable elder son.

Dorothea Barnes, Solon's beautiful second daughter.

Etta Barnes, Solon's sensitive, intelligent youngest daughter. An individualist, she becomes the mistress of an artist, Willard Kane. She leaves her lover when Solon needs her and becomes her father's mainstay in his last days.

Stewart Barnes, Solon's spoiled, unprincipled younger son. Interested only in the pursuit of lower-class girls, he becomes involved in the death of Psyche Tanzer. Charged with rape and murder, he commits suicide in his jail cell.

Phoebe Kimber, Hannah Barnes' sister.

Cynthia Barnes, Solon's sister.

Volida La Porte, Etta Barnes' unconventional friend.

Victor Bruge and
Lester Jennings, reckless friends of Stewart Barnes charged, with him, with the rape and murder of Psyche Tanzer.

Psyche Tanzer, a young girl killed by "drops" administered by Victor Bruge.

Rhoda Kimber and

Laura Kimber, Phoebe's daughters.

Justus Wallin, Benecia Barnes' father.

Hester Wallin, Justus' sister.

Willard Kane, Etta Barnes' artist lover.

BUSSY D'AMBOIS

Author: George Chapman (c. 1559-1634)
Time of action: Sixteenth century
First presented: 1604

PRINCIPAL CHARACTERS

Bussy d'Ambois (bü·sē′ dän·bwä′), an ambitious, unscrupulous commoner. He is brought by Monsieur to court, where he quickly insinuates himself into the King's favor, seduces the woman his patron desires, and wins the enmity of most of his fellow courtiers by his insolence. His quick tongue saves him more than once from hanging; but he disregards the warning of devils that he conjures up, and he dies propped on his sword, shot by Monsieur and the Duc du Guise.

Henry III (än·rē′), King of France. He is essentially both just and honorable, but he is too susceptible to Bussy's flattery.

Monsieur (mə·syœ′), the Duc d'Alençon, who so desperately desires his brother's throne that he is willing to do almost anything except murder to win it.

Maffé (mà·fā′), his servant, concerned more to serve himself than his master.

Tamyra (tà·mē·rà′), the Countess of Montsurry. She scorns Monsieur's advances but arranges, through her friar, secret meetings with Bussy. She betrays her husband with few qualms. When caught, she finally succumbs to torture and writes the letter which brings Bussy to his death. Torn by conflicting loyalties to her husband and her lover, she finally begs Montsurry's forgiveness and vows to wander alone until her death.

Montsurry (mōn·sü·rē′), her devoted husband, who is made almost mad by the knowledge of her infidelity. He, too, is distressed by conflicting emotions of love and honor.

The Duc du Guise (dük′ də gēz′), the King's second brother, Bussy's sworn enemy.

Elenor (ā·lä·nôr′), his Duchess, to whom Bussy first pays court.

Barrisor (bà·rē·zôr′),
l'Anou (là·nōō′), and
Pyrrhot (pē·rō′), courtiers who, enraged by Bussy's presumption, challenge him to a duel and die in the ensuing combat.

A Friar, the go-between for Tamyra and Bussy. His ghost warns them of their danger.

Pero (pā·rō′), Tamyra's maid, who betrays her mistress to Monsieur.

THE CABALA

Author: Thornton Wilder (1897-   )
Time of action: c. 1920
First published: 1926

PRINCIPAL CHARACTERS

Samuele, a young American writer and student introduced to the members of the

Cabala, a group of wealthy, clever, esoterics in Rome. He becomes involved in many of their varied activities and learns that the Cabalists are the pagan gods who have become victims of their human-like frailties.

James Blair, a bookish man and friend of Samuele, who introduces his friend to the Cabala. Blair is upset when one of the Cabalists, Alix d'Espoli, falls in love with him and haunts his presence.

The Duchess d'Aquilanera, an Italian noblewoman and a Cabalist. She is a loving mother and is disturbed by the wildness of her teen-age son, Marcantonio.

Marcantonio d'Aquilanera, son of the Duchess. He is a youth of sixteen who already has had a series of love affairs, conduct that threatens to spoil his chances of a good marriage. He loves to drive his expensive cars at high speed, just as he drives himself. Denounced for his immorality by Samuele, Marcantonio commits suicide.

Cardinal Vaini, a former missionary to China. Though a Cardinal, he speaks derisively of prayer. After having been shot at by a religious fanatic, he resolves to return to China, only to die of a fever en route.

Astrée-Luce de Morfontaine, a religious fanatic whose faith is shaken by Cardinal Vaini's comments. She accuses him of being the devil and tries to kill him with a pistol.

Alix d'Espoli, an Italian princess, a Cabalist. She falls in love with Blair and makes him miserable by pursuing him. Though unintelligent, she appeals to many people by her charm and beauty.

Elizabeth Grier, an American girl who is a member of the Cabala. She reveals to Samuele that the Cabalists are really ancient gods and goddesses. She disturbs Samuele by saying that he is the pagan Mercury.

THE CABIN

Author: Vicente Blasco Ibáñez (1867-1928)
Time of action: Nineteenth century
First published: 1898

PRINCIPAL CHARACTERS

Batiste Borrull (bä·tēs'tä bō·r̄rōōl'), a tenant farmer near Valencia, Spain, who vainly fights public opinion.

Roseta (r̄rō·sä'tä), his daughter, a worker in a Valencia silk mill.

The Bishop, his chubby youngest son, who dies from exposure after being beaten and thrown into a water-filled ditch by his schoolmates.

Pimentó (pē·mān·tō'), the community bully, fatally wounded by Borrull.

Pepeta (pā·pā'tä), Pimentó's anemic but hard-working wife.

Barret, the previous occupant of the

Cabin, evicted for nonpayment of rent. He murders his landlord, Don Salvador.

Rosario (r̄rō·sä'ryō), one of Barret's three daughters, all of whom end up as prostitutes.

Don Salvador (dōn säl·bä·t̄hôr), a greedy landowner and usurer.

The Sons of Salvador, who continue their father's evil practices.

Joaquín (hōä·kēn'), a schoolteacher.

Tonet (tō·nĕt'), in love with Rosario.

Old Tomba (tōm'bä), a blind shepherd and prophet of doom.

CADMUS

Author: Unknown
Time of action: Remote antiquity
First transcribed: Unknown

PRINCIPAL CHARACTERS

Cadmus (kăd′məs), the founder of Thebes. Told by his father not to return to Phenicia without Europa, his kidnaped sister, he goes off to found the Greek city of Thebes, aided by five warriors who spring from a dragon's teeth. Harassed by Mars for killing the dragon, he leaves Thebes for the land of the Enchelians. But he finds no peace and is finally changed into a serpent by the gods.

Agenor (à·jē′nėr), Cadmus' father, King of Phenicia. He commands his son to bring back Europa when she is stolen by Jupiter.

Europa (ū·rō′pə), Cadmus' sister. When Jupiter, in the form of a bull, kidnaps her, her brother is sent to find her and bring her back to her father.

Jupiter (jōō′pĭ·tėr), king of the gods.

Enamored of Europa, he steals her from her family.

Minerva (mĭ·nėr′və), the goddess of wisdom, daughter of Jupiter. She tells Cadmus to sow the teeth of a dragon he has slain, from which spring a host of warriors. All but five kill one another in battle; the remaining warriors become Cadmus' servants and help him build the city of Thebes.

Harmonia (här·mō′nĭ·ə), the daughter of Mars and Venus. She is given by Jupiter to Cadmus to be his wife. Because she loves her husband she begs to be turned into a serpent when he is transformed into one. The gods grant her request.

Mars (märs), god of war. He seeks revenge for Cadmus' slaying of a dragon and puts a curse on the man and his children. He causes the children to die and harasses Cadmus so relentlessly that he asks to be turned into a serpent.

CAESAR AND CLEOPATRA

Author: Bernard Shaw (1856-1950)
Time of action: Autumn 48—Spring 47 B.C.
First presented: 1901

PRINCIPAL CHARACTERS

Julius Caesar, dictator of Rome and conqueror of the world. A middle-aged, rather prosaic man, he meets the childish Cleopatra on a moonlit night in the desert. Though fascinated and rather amused by the beautiful child, he is too practical and detached to be enthralled by her charms. He forces her out of her childishness and teaches her statecraft that makes her truly Queen of Egypt.

Cleopatra, the sixteen-year-old Queen of Egypt. An excitable schoolgirl, she is at war with her husband-brother, Ptolemy Dionysus, for the crown. She believes herself to be in love with the elderly Caesar, who forces her to assume her dignity as queen, but she really loves only herself. At the end of the play, she is looking forward to the arrival of the young and handsome Antony.

138

Ptolemy Dionysus, Cleopatra's brother, husband, and rival for her crown, killed in battle against Caesar.

Ftatateeta, Cleopatra's bullying and savage nurse, against whom the Queen finally revolts, at Caesar's instigation. She is killed by Rufio.

Britannus, Caesar's secretary. The eternal Englishman, conventional and easily shocked, he is doggedly faithful to Caesar.

Rufio, a Roman officer and the slayer of Ftatateeta.

Pothinus, Ptolemy Dionysus' guardian. He plots against Caesar and, at Cleopatra's instigation, is killed by Ftatateeta.

Apollodorus, a Sicilian.

CAESAR OR NOTHING

Author: Pío Baroja (1872-1956)
Time of action: Early twentieth century
First published: 1919

PRINCIPAL CHARACTERS

Caesar Moncada (thä'sär mōn·kä'dä), who has a highwayman and a cardinal among his ancestors. He turns his back on the Church to become a financial dictator. He adopts the Borgia motto: "Caesar or Nothing." He turns out to be nothing.

Cardinal Fort, formerly Father Vicente de Valencia. He is Caesar's uncle.

Laura (lä'ōō·rä), Caesar's sister, who becomes the Marchesa of Vaccarone and a social leader of Rome.

The Abbé Preciozi (prä·thyo'thē), who is sent as Caesar's adviser by Cardinal Fort.

Father Miró (mē·rō') and
Father Herreros (ā·r̄rä'rōs), two priests who might have helped Caesar's scheming if Cardinal Fort had not stopped them.

Archibald Marchmont, who is in love with Laura.

Susanna Marchmont, his wife, who takes a trip with Caesar as Caesar's wife.

Kennedy, an Englishman who tells Caesar about Roman history and the Borgias.

Countess Brenda, an important member of Roman society with whom Caesar has an affair.

Senator Calixto (kä·lēs'tō), a political leader of Zamora who offers to put Caesar's name on the ballot whenever he returns to Spain. Don Calixto is Amparo's uncle.

Don Platón Peribáñez (dōn plä·tōn' pä·rē·bä'nyäth) and
Antonio San Román (än·tō'nyō sän r̄rō·män'), political figures in the district of Castro Duro.

Father Martín Lafuerza (mär·tēn' lä·fwâr'thä), another local vote-getter and an opponent of Caesar.

Ignacio Alzugaray (ēg·nä'thyō äl·thōō·gä·rä'ē), Caesar's school friend.

Carlos Yarza (kär'lōs yär'thä), a Paris bank employee who interests Caesar in speculation.

García Padilla (gär·thē'ä pä·dē'lyä), a political opponent beaten by Caesar in the first campaign. By fraudulent practices he defeats Caesar in the next election.

"Driveller," a ruffian hired by Father Martín to browbeat Caesar's followers.

"The Cub-Slut," a female member of the local underworld who warns Caesar of an attempt on his life.

"Lengthy," the son of "The Cub-Slut." He is killed by "Driveller" in a political row.

"Gaffer," one of Caesar's followers, attacked by "Driveller."

Amparo (äm·pä′rō), the niece of Don Calixto; she marries Caesar, after some uncertainty.

CAIN

Author: George Gordon, Lord Byron (1788-1824)
Time of action: The period of Genesis
First published: 1821

PRINCIPAL CHARACTERS

Adam, the first man. He orders Cain to leave the family after the murder of Abel.

Eve, Adam's wife, the first woman. Because she was bitter at the expulsion from Eden, Cain blames her for his undying bitterness against God and death and claims this bitterness was transmitted to him before birth.

Cain, Adam's elder son. He refuses to pray because of the expulsion from Eden and is sullen at the loss of immortality. He hates work and doubts God's goodness. Tempted, he follows Lucifer and expresses a wish to remain in Hades. Jealous of his brother Abel, Cain strikes him a blow, killing him. Marked by an angel, Cain leaves his family. Destined to grow no living thing, he is a bitter man.

Abel, Cain's young brother and victim. He is a good man who worships God sincerely. He is killed for telling Cain that he loves God more than life.

Adah, Cain's wife. She tries to keep her husband from following Lucifer to Hades. When her husband is banished from the family, she accompanies him, taking their children. She is a faithful wife.

Zillah, Abel's wife, a good woman.

Lucifer, the fallen angel. He says he did not appear as a snake to tempt Eve. He exults that Cain shares his misery.

Enoch, the son of Cain and Adah.

CAKES AND ALE

Author: W. Somerset Maugham (1874-   )
Time of action: Early twentieth century
First published: 1930

PRINCIPAL CHARACTERS

Ashenden, a writer who is asked by Alroy Kear, another writer and a friend, to contribute his reminiscences of the younger days of still another writer, Edward Driffield, about whom Kear is planning to write a biography. Ashenden

was a friend of Driffield and his first wife when they lived in the Kentish town where Ashenden lived, as a boy, with his uncle. Ashenden met the Driffields again in London when he was a medical student and became Driffield's wife's lover. Driffield's wife, Rosie, ran off with another man, however, and Driffield divorced her. Ashenden was hurt that she would run away with someone else.

Alroy Kear, a novelist who is writing the official biography of an eminent Victorian author, Edward Driffield. He invites his friend Ashenden to lunch in order to get Ashenden's impressions of Driffield in his younger days. Kear is not satisfied with Ashenden's material, since it would tend to embarrass Driffield's widow.

Rosie Driffield, Edward Driffield's first wife, a former barmaid. She had a great love of life and could not deny love to anyone. Ashenden became her lover and for a time she visited his rooms regularly. But her great love was George Kemp. When she ran away with him to New York, Driffield divorced her. Years later Ashenden saw her again, a wealthy widow in New York. She confided that of all her lovers Kemp had been her favorite because he was always the perfect gentleman.

Edward Driffield, a famous English writer of the Victorian era. He became more and more famous and then his health failed. When Rosie ran away, he divorced her and married his nurse.

George Kemp, a contractor with whom Rosie was unfaithful to Driffield and with whom she finally ran away. She went with him to New York and they were married.

Amy Driffield, Driffield's nurse during his convalescence from pneumonia. She became his second wife.

CALEB WILLIAMS

Author: William Godwin (1756-1836)
Time of action: Eighteenth century
First published: 1794

PRINCIPAL CHARACTERS

Caleb Williams, a naïve, bookish, courageous, and incurably inquisitive secretary puzzled by his employer's black moods and determined to trace them to their source. Having received Falkland's confession, Caleb becomes Falkland's prisoner until he escapes. Accused on a false charge of theft and jailed, he escapes, joins a thieves' gang, leaves it, is rearrested on a theft charge, but is released when Falkland drops the charge. Relentlessly followed by Gines, Caleb finally makes a public charge of murder against Falkland who, touched by Caleb's recital of his own miseries, confesses. The remorseful Caleb, feeling that he has saved his own good name only through contributing to Falkland's death, resolves to live a better life.

Ferdinando Falkland, Caleb's employer, a wealthy and highly respected squire intensely desirous of keeping his reputation. He is a considerate employer but is subject to uncharacteristic fits of distemper. Formerly a man of graceful manners and warm intelligence, he is secretly embittered by his difficulties with Tyrrel and troubled by his guilt over Tyrrel's murder. Caleb's nemesis until his better nature triumphs, Falkland confesses publicly and dies shortly afterward from his long inward torture.

Barnabas Tyrrel, Falkland's enemy, a proud, jealous, combative man finally murdered by Falkland out of resentment for his cruelties.

Gines, a member of a thieves' gang and Caleb's enemy, responsible for his second arrest and the repeated exposure of his imprisonment.

Captain Raymond, the philosophical leader of the thieves' gang.

Emily Melvile, Tyrrel's cousin, saved by Falkland from death by fire and later from a forced marriage to Grimes. She finally dies as a result of Tyrrel's continued cruelties.

Thomas, a servant of Falkland and a

former neighbor of Caleb's father. He helps Caleb escape from prison.

Collins, another of Falkland's servants. He tells Caleb the story of Falkland's early life.

Grimes, a clumsy, loutish tenant whom Tyrrel intends as Emily's husband. When Grimes attempts to seduce Emily, Falkland saves her.

THE CALL OF THE WILD

Author: Jack London (1876-1916)
Time of action: 1897
First published: 1903

PRINCIPAL CHARACTERS

Buck, a cross between a St. Bernard and an intelligent Scotch shepherd. He is the leader of all the dogs on Judge Miller's estate in California until stolen and carted off to the Alaska gold rush. Passed from one owner to another, he finally breaks away to run with a wolf pack.

A Spitz, the bloodthirsty enemy of Buck

and lead dog on the sled, until killed by Buck.

John Thornton, a prospector who protects Buck from stupid gold seekers. After John is killed by Indians, his body is left at the river, to which once a year Buck returns and utters the call of the wild, the howl of a savage beast for his human friend.

CAMILLE

Author: Alexandre Dumas, *fils* (1824-1895)
Time of action: Nineteenth century
First presented: 1852

PRINCIPAL CHARACTERS

Camille Gautier (kà·mēy gō·tyā′), a poor needleworker who becomes a notorious courtesan. She passes up a chance to become mistress to Count de Varville because she loves a younger man, Armand Duval, for whom she leaves the gaiety of Paris to live in the country. For her lover's sake she finally leaves him because her liaison is hurting his family. He believes until she is dying that she has left him because she is fickle. Her symbol is a camellia.

Count de Varville (dǝ vàr·vēl′), a French

nobleman in love with Camille. He offers to pay all her debts if she becomes his mistress. He becomes her lover after she leaves Armand Duval. He and Armand fight a duel, in which the Count is wounded.

Armand Duval (àr·mäń′ dü·vàl′), a young man who has nothing but love to offer Camille. They become lovers. He thinks she has deserted him, until on her deathbed she tells him she left him for his own good and that of his family.

M. Duval (dü·vál'), Armand's father. He pleads with Camille to leave his son so that Armand and his family will not suffer in their reputations.

Mme. Prudence (prü·däns'), a milliner,

Camille's friend. She introduces Armand to Camille.

Nanine (nà·nēn'), Camille's faithful maid.

CAMPASPE

Author: John Lyly (c. 1554-1606)
Time of action: c. 325 B.C.
First presented: 1584

PRINCIPAL CHARACTERS

Alexander, King of Macedon, eager for conquest and glory, but generous and merciful when victorious. Passionately enamored of his captive, Campaspe, he asks Apelles, his court painter, to paint her portrait. He becomes suspicious of Apelles and angrily jealous; but finally he is moved to allow the lovers to marry because, as he says, a man who cannot command himself is unworthy to command the world.

Hephestion (hē·fĕs'tĭ·ən), Alexander's chief general. Worried about the softening influence of love on the great warrior, he rejoices when Alexander conquers his desire for Campaspe and returns to military conquest.

Diogenes (dī·ŏj'ə·nēz), the crusty independent philosopher. Scorning luxury and emotion, he lives in a tub. Even Alexander's glories do not impress him.

Alexander is forced to admit that if he were not Alexander he would like to be Diogenes, who has neither wants nor fears.

Apelles (ə·pel'ēz), Alexander's painter. He loves Campaspe, he thinks hopelessly, for he knows that Alexander loves her also; but he wins her love while painting her portrait and finally receives her at Alexander's hands.

Campaspe (kăm·păs'pē), Alexander's beautiful and virtuous Theban captive. At first skeptical of Apelles' love, she later accepts and returns it.

Sylvius (sil'vĭ·əs), an Athenian citizen who wishes the unwilling Diogenes to instruct his sons.

Manes (mā'nēz), the discontented servant of Diogenes.

CANDIDA

Author: Bernard Shaw (1856-1950)
Time of action: 1894
First presented: 1897

PRINCIPAL CHARACTERS

Eugene Marchbanks, an eighteen-year-old poet, the nephew of an earl. Having left Oxford, Marchbanks is found sleeping outdoors by Morell, who brings him home. Marchbanks proceeds to fall in love with Morell's lovely wife, Candida.

Marchbanks is slight, effeminate, frightened, and painfully sensitive; but he has the genuine poet's insight into human motivations. He is sure that his own helplessness and inadequacy will prove irresistible to a woman so purely femi-

143

nine as Candida. He is horrified that Candida must dirty her hands working around the house. Unable to understand what a woman could find to love in Morell, Marchbanks demands that Candida be given a chance to choose between them. When confronted with the choice, Candida says she chooses "the weakest." Marchbanks at once understands why Candida loves Morell: he is even more in need of maternal care and pampering than is Marchbanks. Suddenly a man, Marchbanks leaves to get about his work, after thanking Morell for giving Candida so much opportunity to love.

Candida, the wife of the Reverend James Morell. Attractive enough to charm men into doing her will, her use of the feminine advantages is ennobled by dignity and intelligence. Taught by her husband to think for herself, Candida does so, to her husband's distress. She suggests to him that perhaps she should make love to Marchbanks lest some bad woman do it and damage his spirit, but the occasion never arrives. When Morell leaves Candida alone with Marchbanks, the latter is afraid to speak and reads poetry to her.

The Reverend James Mavor Morell, a Christian Socialist clergyman of the Church of England. Vigorous and handsome, Morell is immensely in demand as a speaker for progressive causes. He is admired by men and adored by women. He himself is proud of his strength and competence and, until the end of the play, unaware of his absolute dependence on his wife. At last he realizes that it is Candida, the personification of feminine urges, who is his protector and supporter. Becoming conscious of the true nature of her love for him, Morell avows that he is the product of her love.

Mr. Burgess, Candida's father. A vulgar and ignorant man who has grown rich in commerce, Burgess is instinctively respectful to people of rank. He frightens Marchbanks into near-hysterics by trying to be friendly with him. Morell, a good Socialist, detests his father-in-law. Burgess thinks Morell is mad, but Morell's political influence is useful to him and he is patronizingly polite to his son-in-law.

Miss Proserpine Garnett, Morell's secretary. Efficient and affectionate, Proserpine is in love with Morell. Marchbanks unnerves her by trying to discover what a woman could find to love in a man like Morell. She causes the sensitive Marchbanks to break into tears. When Burgess reprimands her for annoying an earl's nephew, Proserpine calls Burgess a fathead.

The Rev. Alexander Mill (Lexy), Morell's enthusiastic young curate, newly out of Oxford, who follows Morell about with doglike devotion. He and Proserpine, both teetotalers, get drunk on Burgess' champagne after one of Morell's speeches.

[Jimmy and Fluffy, the Morells' children, who do not appear.]

CANDIDE

Author: Voltaire (François Marie Arouet, 1694-1778)
Time of action: Eighteenth century
First published: 1759

PRINCIPAL CHARACTERS

Candide (kän·dēd'), a gentle, honest, and pleasant young man, reputed to be the illegitimate son of the sister of Baron Thunder-ten-tronckh and a decent man she was too proud to accept as a husband. Expelled from the Baron's

144

castle after exploring the mysteries and pleasures of love with Cunegonde, the Baron's daughter, Candide travels all over the world. A dutiful young man who has been taught that this is the best of all possible worlds, Candide searches the globe for proof, meeting old friends and acquaintances in unexpected places and unusual circumstances. During his travels he has many misadventures and endures many hardships and pains. Impressed into the Bulgarian army, he discovers the horrors of war. He lives through the Lisbon Earthquake and is ordered flogged by officers of the Inquisition. He finds and loses his sweetheart Cunegonde. He discovers wealth and loses it. He kills men when he does not mean to do so. All of these experiences slowly convince Candide that this is really not the best of all possible worlds. After years of wandering he retires to a little farm where he lives with a small group of friends and his wife, Cunegonde, now old and far from pretty.

Cunegonde (kü·nā·gōńd′), the beautiful daughter of the Baron Thunder-ten-tronckh. With Candide she explores love, only to have her young lover dismissed violently from the castle. After his dismissal she endures much pain and many adventures. She is captured by the Bulgarians, raped, and wounded. She makes her way to Portugal, where she becomes the mistress of two men, a Jew and an officer of the Inquisition. She is reunited with Candide, only to be separated from him by another series of unhappy adventures. At last she and Candide are reunited. Married, they settle down on a small farm. By that time his ardor for her has been cooled by the adventures she has undergone and the effect they have had upon her. She becomes adept as a pastry cook, happy in that humble occupation.

Pangloss (päń·glôs′), Candide's tutor, a professor of metaphysico-theologo-cosmo-lonigology—in other words, abstract non-sense. Despite the terrible adventures that befall Candide and Pangloss' other friends, he is unwilling to forego theorizing or to admit that this is not the best of all possible worlds. He settles down with Candide on the latter's farm after undergoing many misadventures, including being hanged unsuccessfully by the Inquisition.

Baron Thunder-Ten-Tronckh (tün·dâr-tĕn·trōńk′), Cunegonde's brother, who inherits his father's title. He is a proud young man, even in adversity and poverty, and he refuses again and again to give his consent to a marriage between his sister and Candide. Tired at last of the Baron's refusals, uttered with no regard for what Candide has endured on behalf of Cunegonde or the girl's changed condition, Candide causes the proud Baron to be shipped as a galley slave.

Jacques (zhäk′), a kindly Anabaptist who befriends Candide in Holland and travels with him to Portugal, only to be drowned at the time of the Lisbon Earthquake.

Martin (mȧr·tăń), a friend Candide meets in Surinam. Martin, accused by the Church of being a Socinian heretic, admits to Candide that he is a Manichee, though none are supposed to be left in the world. Martin travels with Candide on the latter portion of Candide's wanderings and settles down with Candide on the young man's little farm.

Paquette (pȧ·kĕt′), a maid to the Baroness Thunder-ten-tronckh. Loved by Pangloss, she gives him venereal disease. After many misadventures of her own she turns up again in Candide's life and becomes a member of the little colony on his farm, where she earns her living by doing embroidery.

Friar Giroflée (jē·rô·flā′), a discontented friar who falls in love with Paquette during her travels and leaves his order for her sake. Befriended by Candide, he

145

joins the colony on Candide's farm and turns carpenter.

The Old Woman, Cunegonde's servant. She relates that she was once a beautiful princess, the daughter of the Princess Palestrina and a fictional pope, Urban X. The splendid life she expects is lost when she is captured by Moroccan pirates and condemned to a hard life as a slave. She clings to Cunegonde and Candide and settles with them on Candide's farm.

Cacambo (kä·käm′bō), Candide's servant. Separated from Candide in South America, he turns up later in Venice as a slave belonging to the deposed Sultan Achmet III. Through Cacambo's intercession Candide and his party are allowed to visit Turkey.

A Contented Old Man, who has learned that hard work and minding one's own business are the best means to happiness. He avoids boredom, vice, and need by working a twenty-acre farm. Following his advice, Candide settles with his friends on a farm of his own.

THE CANTERBURY TALES

Author: Geoffrey Chaucer (1340?-1400)
Time of action: Remote antiquity to fourteenth century
First transcribed: 1380-1390

PRINCIPAL CHARACTERS

The Knight, a courtly medieval fighting man who has served king and religion all over the known world. Modest in dress and speech, though the highest in rank of the pilgrims to Canterbury, he rides with only his son and a yeoman in attendance. He tells a metrical romance, the first of the stories in the series related by the various pilgrims. His is a tale of courtly love, the story of the love two young Theban noblemen, Palamon and Arcite, have for Emily, beautiful sister-in-law of Duke Theseus of Athens. The young men compete in a tourney for the girl's hand; Palamon wins but is killed in an accident, so that Arcite eventually has his love rewarded.

The Squire, the Knight's son. A young man of twenty, he has fought in several battles. Like his father, he is full of knightly courtesy, but he also enjoys a good time. He tells a story of adventure and enchantment in a distant land. The story he leaves unfinished tells of three gifts sent to Canacee, daughter of King Cambuscan. Each of the gifts has magic powers: a ring that enables the bearer to talk to birds, a brass horse that will take its rider anywhere, and a mirror that shows the truth and the future. The ring enables Canacee to learn the story of a lovelorn hawk for the mate who has deserted her.

The Yeoman, the Knight's attendant, a forester who takes excellent care of his gear. He wears a St. Christopher medal on his breast. Chaucer assigned no story to his telling.

The Prioress (Madame Eglentyn), who travels with another nun and three priests as her attendants to the shrine of St. Thomas Becket at Canterbury. A woman of conscience and sympathy, she wears a curious brooch upon which appears the ambiguous statement, in Latin, "Love conquers all." Her story is that of a little schoolboy murdered for his religion by Jews. The child's death is discovered by a miracle of Our Lady. Like most of the stories told in the collection of tales, this one fits the personality of its narrator.

The Second Nun, who accompanies the

146

Prioress. She also tells a Christian legend of the martyrdom of St. Cecilia, a story typical of medieval hagiography.

The Nun's Priest, whose name is **John.** He tells the beast epic relating the adventures of the cock, Chauntecleer, and the fox. It is a didactic yet humorous story suitable for the Prioress' father confessor.

The Monk, a fat hedonist who prefers to be out of his cloister. No lover of books and learning, he prefers to hunt and eat. He cites tragedy as being the story of a man fallen from high degree and then offers many examples, including anecdotes of Lucifer, Adam, Samson, Hercules, Balthasar, Ugolino of Pisa, Julius Caesar, and Croesus. His lugubrious recital is interrupted by the Knight.

The Friar, named **Huberd.** He is a merry chap who knows barmaids better than the sick. Having the reputation of being the best beggar in his house, he appears to be a venal, worldly man. His story is a fabliau telling about a summoner who loses his soul to the devil; the story arouses the discomfiture of the Summoner in the group of pilgrims.

The Merchant, a tight-lipped man of business. Unhappily married, he tells a story of the evils of marriage between old men and young women. A variation of an old "Märchen," it relates how a superannuated husband named January is deceived by his young and hearty spouse named May.

The Clerk of Oxford, a serious young scholar who heeds philosophy and prefers books to worldly pleasures. His tale is an answer to the Wife of Bath's idea that in marriage the woman ought to have dominion. The Clerk's tale is of an infinitely patient wife named Griselda, who endures all manner of ill-treatment from her husband.

The Sergeant of Law, a busy man who seems busier than he really is. He makes a great show of his learning, citing cases all the way back to William the Conqueror.

The Franklin, a rich landlord who loves to eat and keeps a ready table of dainties. In his time he has been sheriff of his county. His story is an old Breton lay, a tale of chivalry and the supernatural. He apologizes for his story and its telling, saying he is an uneducated man.

The Haberdasher,
The Carpenter,
The Weaver,
The Dyer, and
The Tapestry Maker, all members of a guild, each one rich and wise enough to be an alderman. None has been assigned a tale by Chaucer.

The Cook, named **Roger,** hired by the master workmen to serve them during their journey. He is a rollicking fellow. Pleased by the bawdy tales of the Miller and the Reeve, he insists upon telling a bawdy story of his own, one left unfinished by Chaucer.

The Shipman, captain of the "Maudelayne," of Dartmouth. He is a good skipper and a smuggler. Like others of the company, he tells a fabliau, a bawdy tale. He relates the misadventures of a merchant of St. Denis, in Belgium, who is cheated of his wife's favors and his money by a sly monk named John.

The Doctor of Physick, a materialistic man greatly interested in money. He knows all the great medical authorities, as well as his astrology, though he seldom reads the Bible. His story, which he attributes to Livy, is the old tale of Appius and Virginia.

The Wife of Bath, named **Alice,** a clothmaker and five times a widow. Apparently wealthy from her marriages, she has traveled a great deal, including three trips to Jerusalem. She is well-versed in marriage and love making. Her theory is that the woman must dominate in mar-

147

riage and to make her point tells a tale of a loathly lady who, when her husband is obedient, becomes fair.

The Parson, a poor but loyal churchman who teaches his parishioners by his good example. Refusing to tell an idle tale to his fellow pilgrims, he tells what he terms a merry tale about the Seven Deadly Sins.

The Plowman, an honest man, the Parson's brother. He tells no tale.

The Miller, a jolly drunken reveler who leads the company playing on his bagpipes. He tells a bawdy story about a carpenter named John who is cuckolded by his young wife, Alison, and her witty lover, Nicholas.

The Reeve, a slender, choleric man, named **Oswald.** Having been a carpenter, he is incensed by Miller's tale. In retribution he tells a story about a miller cuckolded by two lusty students who sleep with the miller's wife and daughter.

The Manciple, an uneducated man who is shrewd enough to steal a great deal from the learned lawyers who hire him to look after their establishments. He relates the old folk tale of the tattling bird.

The Summoner, a lecherous, drunken fellow who loves food and strong drink. Angered by the Friar's tale about a sum-

moner, he tells a tale about a friar who becomes the butt of coarse humor.

The Pardoner, a womanish man with long, blond hair. He tells a tale of three young men who seek death and find it. His story is actually a sermon on the evils of unnatural love of money. He follows up the sermon with an attempt to sell phony relics to his fellow pilgrims.

Harry Bailey, the host at the Tabard Inn in Southwark. He organizes the storytelling among the pilgrims, with the winner to have a meal at his fellows' cost upon the company's return. He is a natural leader, as his words and actions show.

Geoffrey Chaucer, the author, who put himself into his poem as a retiring, mildmannered person. He tries to recite the Rime of Sir Thopas, a dreary tale which is interrupted as dull, whereupon he tells the story of Melibee and Dame Prudence.

The Canon, a traveler who joins the pilgrims briefly on the road to Canterbury. He leaves when it is hinted that he is a cheating alchemist.

The Canon's Yeoman, who remains with the pilgrim company and tells an anecdote about an alchemist, a canon like his master, who swindles a priest.

CAPTAIN HORATIO HORNBLOWER

Author: C. S. Forester (1899-   )
Time of action: Early nineteenth century
First published: 1937, 1938, 1939

PRINCIPAL CHARACTERS

Captain Horatio Hornblower, the tall, well-muscled commander of H.M.S. "Lydia" and H.M.S. "Sutherland"; a capable, brave, skillful but nervous, shy, and diffident veteran of twenty years' naval service who rigorously disciplines himself against a natural talkativeness with his officers and men. He sinks the "Natividad," captures the "Amelie,"

loses the "Sutherland," is captured, is reported dead, escapes, seizes an English prize ship in Nantes, sails to England, is knighted, and is reunited with the now widowed Lady Barbara, who will apparently become Mrs. Hornblower.

Bush, Hornblower's stern, swarthy-faced, capable, fearless first lieutenant. Captured with Hornblower after losing a foot in battle, he is awarded a captaincy on his return to England.

Brown, Hornblower's simple, uneducated, cheerfully willing coxswain, a man of strength, common sense, and adaptability to any situation.

Don Julian Alvarado (El Supremo), a rich plantation owner of Central America; a small, swarthy, restless, tyrannical megalomaniac. After the sinking of the "Natividad" he is captured by the Spanish and executed.

Maria, Hornblower's short, dumpy wife, whom he does not love; a sickly woman who dies in childbirth.

Lady Barbara Wellesley, the Duke of Wellington's accomplished, self-possessed sister. Sailing toward England aboard the "Lydia," she falls in love with Hornblower. She later marries Admiral Leighton, is widowed, and adopts Hornblower's son after Maria's death.

Admiral Sir Percy Leighton, Hornblower's immediate commander and Lady Barbara's husband. He is injured in the destruction of a French squadron, and he later dies of wounds sustained at Gibraltar.

Colonel Jean-Baptiste Caillard, an officious aide to Napoleon. He is knocked out by Brown and left bound in a snow-stalled stagecoach.

Comte de Graçay, the kindly French host of Hornblower, Bush, and Brown, who helps them escape from France.

Vicomtesse de Graçay, his stout but attractive, dark-eyed, auburn-haired, widowed daughter-in-law, a peasant's daughter who becomes Hornblower's mistress.

Polwheal, Hornblower's steward.

Napoleon.

Ferdinand, King of Spain.

CAPTAIN SINGLETON

Author: Daniel Defoe (1660-1731)
Time of action: Eighteenth century
First published: 1720

PRINCIPAL CHARACTERS

Captain Bob Singleton, sailor, explorer, and pirate. Early in life he becomes accomplished in the arts of navigation and thievery, talents which are to stand him in good stead in his subsequent careers as explorer and pirate. Driven by storm, shipwreck, and mutiny to a trek across Africa, he makes explorations that yield a considerable treasure which he recklessly spends on his return to England. To recover his losses he sets sail again, joins a mutinous crew, and becomes a pirate. The pirate crew is joined by a Quaker surgeon, William Walters, under whose influence Singleton begins to feel qualms of conscience about his crimes. Finally,

his moral regeneration complete, he marries William's widowed sister and lives the remainder of his life in quiet contentment.

William Walters, a Quaker surgeon. A member of the crew of a captured ship, he joins the pirate, Bob Singleton, and gradually gains a considerable moral influence over him. When the two men decide to abandon piracy, Williams takes command of their ventures and dissuades the conscience-stricken Singleton from suicide so that, together, they may put their illegal fortune to a worthy use.

Captain Wilmot and
Captain Avery, masters of ships in the

pirate fleet commanded by Captain Singleton.

CAPTAINS COURAGEOUS

Author: Rudyard Kipling (1865-1936)
Time of action: The 1890's
First published: 1897

PRINCIPAL CHARACTERS

Harvey Cheyne, the fifteen-year-old son of an American millionaire. Washed overboard from the liner he is taking from America to Europe, he is picked up by the "We're Here," a schooner out of Gloucester bound for the Grand Banks. Young Harvey is forced to live from May until the following September aboard the fishing schooner. He is arrogant and peevish at first, but by the time the ship returns to Gloucester he has changed. He is now a self-reliant young man who has proved himself in a rigorous environment.

Dan Troop, the son of the schooner's skipper and a boy of about Harvey's age. Dan believes Harvey's account of the family's wealth and influence, but he and the cook are the only people aboard who do accept the story as true. Later in life, Dan becomes mate on one of the fast freighters Harvey owns.

Disko Troop, the owner and skipper of the "We're Here." He resents Harvey's presence aboard his schooner and meets the youth's insolence with hard discipline. As the voyage continues, Troop learns to respect the boy's quick grasp of the principles of navigation and his good work generally aboard the schooner. When the "We're Here" is first back to Gloucester with a full ship, Troop's respect for Harvey is complete.

Mr. Cheyne, Harvey's father, a wealthy ship owner who has risen from poverty to wealth through sea trade. Mr. Cheyne is delighted to see the change the tour at sea has effected in his son.

Long Jack,
Manuel,
Salters,
Pennsylvania, and
The Cook, crew members aboard the "We're Here."

THE CAPTAIN'S DAUGHTER

Author: Alexander Pushkin (1799-1837)
Time of action: c. 1774
First published: 1836

PRINCIPAL CHARACTERS

Piotr Andreitch Grineff (pyō′tr än·drĕ′-ĭch grĭ·nĕf′), a young officer in a Russian regiment. A kindly and generous young man who falls in love with the commandant's daughter, he goes to great lengths to protect her from harm and fights a duel when a fellow officer criticizes a love poem he has written to her. At first

his parents do not approve of the girl, but they later give their consent to the marriage.

Maria Ivanovna (mä′ryə ĭ·vä′nəv·nə), the Captain's daughter, a lovely girl very much in love with Piotr. When he sends her to his parents for her protection, she so impresses them that they change their minds about not allowing their son to marry her. She saves her lover from exile in Siberia by appealing to the Empress.

Alexey Ivanitch Shvabrin (ä·lĕk·sā′ ĭ·vän′ĭch shvä′brĭn), an officer in the same regiment with Piotr. A suitor rejected by Maria, he is jealous of her love for Piotr. When the rebel Pougatcheff takes the Bailogorsk fortress, Shvabrin deserts to the rebel side. He does everything in his power to separate Maria and Piotr. He accuses Piotr of being a spy for the rebels and is responsible for his rival's sentence of exile.

Emelyan Pougatcheff (ĕ·mĕ·lyän′ pōō·gä′chəf), a Cossack rebel leader who claims to be the dead Emperor Peter III. He is cruel and ruthless, but after the capture of the Bailogorsk fortress he spares Piotr's life and sends him away under safe conduct because the young officer had sometime before given the rebel, disguised as a traveler, a sheepskin coat to protect him during a snowstorm.

Savelitch (sä·vĕ′lĭch), Piotr's old servant, whose intervention saves his master from several predicaments. He is faithful, loyal, and shrewd.

Vassilissa Egorovna (vä·sĭ′lĭ·sə ĕ·gō′-rəv·nə), the Captain's wife, a very capable woman who runs her household and her husband's regiment with great efficiency. When she protests against her husband's murder by the Cossack rebels, she is killed.

Captain Ivan Mironoff, the commanding officer at the Bailogorsk fortress and Piotr's superior. Captured when Cossacks under Emelyan Pougatcheff seize the fortress, he and his aides are hanged by order of the rebel chief.

Captain Zourin, who rescues Piotr, his family, and Maria from death at the hands of the renegade Shvabrin.

THE CAPTIVES

Author: Titus Maccius Plautus (c. 255-184 B.C.)
Time of action: During war between Aetolia and Elis
First presented: c. 210 B.C.

PRINCIPAL CHARACTERS

Hegio (hē′jĭ·ō), a rich Aetolian who spends his time negotiating for the return of a son, Philopolemus, captured in war by the Elians. Hegio mourns another son, Tyndarus, kidnaped when he was four years old. Prisoner exchanges take place, confessions are made, false identities are put straight, and Hegio's sons are at last reunited with their father.

Tyndarus (tĭn′də·rəs), the son who, kidnaped when four years old, is returned to his father because the slave who had stolen the boy is caught and confesses the deed, thus identifying to Hegio the now adult Tyndarus.

Philopolemus (fĭ′lə·pŏ′lə·məs), the captive son who is returned to Hegio in ex-

change for Philocrates, the wealthy Elian whom Hegio held captive.

Ergasilus (ėr′gə·sī′ləs), a parasite who, fearing the loss of favors from his host Hegio, works diligently to straighten out the confusion attendant upon the prisoner exchange. Hegio rewards Ergasilus' good work by promising him board for the rest of his life.

Philocrates (fĭ·lŏ′krə·tēz), a very rich Elian prisoner of war and Tyndarus' master. He is bought in a lot of prisoners by Hegio when the father is looking for an Elian to exchange for Philopolemus.

Aristophontes (ə·rĭs′tō·fŏn′tēz), a pris-

151

oner of war who knows Philocrates. It is Aristophontes who explains to Hegio that a hostage he holds, Tyndarus, is not Philocrates. Ironically, Hegio, not knowing that Tyndarus, posing as Aristophontes, is his son, sends Tyndarus to work in the quarries.

Stalagmus (stə·lăg'məs), Hegio's onetime slave, who kidnaped Tyndarus and sold him to the Elians. When he confesses his crime, Tyndarus is brought home to his father's house and Stalagmus, in Tyndarus' chains, takes the son's place in the quarries.

CARMEN

Author: Prosper Mérimée (1803-1870)
Time of action: Early nineteenth century
First published: 1847

PRINCIPAL CHARACTERS

Carmen (cär'mən), the chief character in this novelette that inspired Bizet's opera; she is a quick-tempered gipsy employee in a Seville cigarette factory. For amusement, she distracts Don José from his duty as a soldier. Later, when he has to flee, she takes him to the bandit band for which she is a spy. Finally she tells him she no longer loves him, although she realizes that he will kill her as a result.

Don José (dōn hō·sā'), a dashing cavalryman from Navarre who is both loved and ridiculed by fickle Carmen. He kills his lieutenant in a quarrel over Carmen and has to flee and become a bandit.

Finally he kills Carmen in a jealous rage and then surrenders to the constabulary.

García (gär·thē'ä), the one-eyed leader of an outlaw band and Carmen's husband. He is killed by Don José.

Lucas (lö'käs), a bullfighter who loves Carmen in Granada and is gored when distracted by her in a Cordoba bull ring.

Dancaire (dän·kĕr'), a smuggler who tries with Don José to organize another outlaw band.

A Monk, begged by Don José to say a mass for Carmen's soul.

THE CASE OF SERGEANT GRISCHA

Author: Arnold Zweig (1887-   )
Time of action: 1917
First published: 1927

PRINCIPAL CHARACTERS

Sergeant Grischa Iljitsch Paprotkin, a Russian soldier held as a prisoner by the Germans in 1917. Though not ill-treated by his captors, he wishes to return to his family, and so he contrives an escape. During his lonely wanderings he begins to lose his humanity but recovers it when he becomes the lover of Babka, a woman leading a band of refugees who take

him into their midst. Sergeant Grischa assumes the identity of Sergeant Pavlovitsch Bjuscheff, a Russian deserter, so that he can avoid punishment as an escaped prisoner. He is recaptured and, under his assumed identity, sentenced to death as a spy. While his case is fought over by German generals after he has revealed the truth about himself, Grischa remains in prison, hoping the war will end. When his sentence is not revoked he behaves like a brave soldier, even when forced to dig his own grave before being killed.

Babka, a strong-minded, vigorous Russian woman, known affectionately as "Grandmother," who leads a band of homeless refugees. She finds Grischa wandering across the countryside and makes him a member of her band and her lover. When he is sentenced to death, she bravely goes to him, walking many miles to do so. She hopes to free her lover by poisoning his guards, but he prevents her carrying out the plan, believing he must meet his fate. After Grischa's death Babka bears his child.

General von Lychow, a Prussian officer of the military caste who is a commander of combat troops. He is jealous of upstart administrative officers who question his authority and authorizes his aide to work on the case of Grischa to save the life of the condemned man.

Ponsanski, General von Lychow's aide, a Jewish lawyer who is interested in the case primarily from the view that it is an interesting instance of legal jurisdiction.

General Schieffenzahn, an administrative officer who usurps the authority of General von Lychow. He wishes to execute Grischa to demonstrate his power. Although he is persuaded to send a reprieve for the sergeant, a snowstorm prevents delivery of the message.

Lieutenant Winfried, a German officer and friend of Ponsanski.

Lieutenant Wilhelmi, General Schieffenzahn's aide, who recommends the death of Grischa.

CASS TIMBERLANE

Author: Sinclair Lewis (1885-1951)
Time of action: The 1940's
First published: 1945

PRINCIPAL CHARACTERS

Cass Timberlane, district judge in Grand Republic, Minnesota. A good man, he lives a lonely life after his divorce, until he is stirred in his forty-first year by a young girl, Jinny Marshland, who is from the lower classes. He marries the girl, despite the objections of his friends and hers. The marriage is not entirely a happy one, but thanks to the judge's patience and love the marriage succeeds.

Blanche Timberlane, the judge's ex-wife.

Jinny Marshland, a young girl who marries Judge Timberlane. She finds difficulty in adjusting to her new life. She has an affair with Bradd Criley and, wanting to live in New York, almost breaks up her marriage. When she falls ill and realizes she needs her husband, she goes back to him and the small town in which they live.

Bradd Criley, one of Judge Timberlane's friends. He makes love to the judge's wife, as he does to every attractive woman, and becomes her lover.

Dr. Roy Drover, one of the judge's friends, a philanderer.

Boone and
Queenie Havock, wealthy but vulgar friends of Judge Timberlane.

Jay Laverick, the rich, drunkard friend of Judge Timberlane. His attentions to Jinny cause gossip.

Chris Grau, a well-to-do, attractive

153

woman in love with Judge Timberlane. She sympathizes with his problems.

Mrs. Higbee, Judge Timberlane's understanding housekeeper.

CASTE

Author: Thomas William Robertson (1829-1871)
Time of action: Nineteenth century
First presented: 1867

PRINCIPAL CHARACTERS

The Marquise de St. Maur, an Englishwoman married to a French nobleman. She is a proud person, conscious of rank and family. Only her son's return from supposed death enables her to accept her lower-class daughter-in-law without reservation.

Capt. George D'Alroy, the son of the Marquise de St. Maur, who falls in love with a beautiful dancer from the lower classes and marries her despite her origins. He insists that he would rather die or lose his commission than lose her love. His faith in his wife is rewarded, for when he returns from India after having been presumed dead he finds that she has proved sincere and capable.

Capt. Hawtree, D'Alroy's friend, who tries realistically to point out the social chasm between the dancer and his friend,

and the difficulties which a successful marriage between them must overcome.

Esther Eccles, the pretty young dancer who marries D'Alroy. When her husband is thought to be dead in India, she successfully cares for herself and her child, refusing to be patronized by her proud mother-in-law.

Polly Eccles, Esther's sister, who is satisfied to marry a tradesman. Even when her sister is accepted in aristocratic circles, Polly believes that she is happier than Esther.

Mr. Eccles, father of Esther and Polly, a ne'er-do-well drunkard. He even squanders money left by D'Alroy to take care of Esther.

Sam Gerridge, Polly's fiancé. He is a good man who contributes to Esther's support when she needs help.

THE CASTLE

Author: Franz Kafka (1883-1924)
Time of action: Any time
First published: 1926

PRINCIPAL CHARACTERS

K., a young man seeking entrance to the Castle. He is both puzzled and irritated by his inability to get to the Castle where he had thought himself needed as a Land Surveyor. He never reaches the Castle. Kafka intended, in a chapter planned but never written, to relate that K. was to be given permission to live and work in the village though not to

enter the Castle itself. K.'s efforts to reach the Castle resemble Christian's struggle in "The Pilgrim's Progress" to reach the Celestial City. Christian succeeded but K. did not.

Frieda, a little fair-haired, sad-eyed, hollow-cheeked young barmaid; Klamm's mistress. She becomes K.'s fiancée and stays with him at the Bridge Inn and later at the schoolhouse. Jealous of his apparent interest in Olga and Amalia, she rejects K. for Jeremiah.

Barnabas, a white-clad young messenger who brings K. a letter from Klamm and introduces him to Barnabas' family. He is a servant at the Castle.

Olga, his yellow-haired sister, a strapping girl with a hard-looking face. She shows kindness to K. and tells him much about the organization of the Castle and about the village people.

Amalia, another sister who closely resembles both Olga and Barnabas.

Arthur, K.'s assistant, a slim, brown-skinned, jolly young man with a little pointed black beard. He and Jeremiah keep an almost constant watch on K.

Jeremiah, another assistant who looks so like Arthur that K., who says they are as alike as two snakes, calls him Arthur also.

Klamm, a chief at the Castle who is often seen at the Herrenhof. He is plump, ponderous, flabby-cheeked, and wears a pointed black mustache and a pince-nez.

Schwarzer, a young man who telephones the Castle to check on K. He is in love with Gisa.

The Superintendent, a kindly, stout, clean-shaven man suffering from gout. He tries to explain to K. the intricacies of the management of the Castle.

Gardana, the landlady at the Bridge Inn. She was once, briefly, Klamm's mistress.

Momus, the village secretary, a deputy of Klamm.

Gisa, the lady schoolteacher.

Sortini, a great official at the Castle who once wrote an obscene letter to Amalia.

THE CASTLE OF FRATTA

Author: Ippolito Nievo (1831-1861)
Time of action: 1775-1852
First published: 1867

PRINCIPAL CHARACTERS

Carlo Altoviti, a poor relation in the feudal Fratta family and the narrator. He becomes an honored member of the family and a patriot who lives to see the Castle of Fratta reduced to rubble and the Frattas dispersed. In his old age he returns to Fratta to write his memoirs.

Giovanni, the Count of Fratta, the austere head of the Fratta family.

Cleonice the Countess of Fratta, Count Giovanni's haughty wife.

Clara, Count Giovanni's grave, beautiful daughter, who finally enters a convent.

Pisana, Count Giovanni's fascinating younger daughter, loved by Carlo Altoviti. She eventually becomes his mistress.

Aquilina Provedoni, Carlo Altoviti's wife.

Todero Altoviti, Carlo's father. Deserted by Carlo's mother, he disappears. When he has grown wealthy in trade he returns, hoping to establish a prominent family. His hopes are dashed with the capitulation of Venice to the French.

Monsignor Orlando, a stupid, gluttonous priest, Count Giovanni's brother.

Lucilio Vianello, a young doctor. He is in love with Clara Fratta. After the fall

155

of the patricians, she refuses to return from the convent and marry him.

Leopardo Provedoni, Carlo Altoviti's friend.

Antonio Provedoni, Leopardo's father, the mayor of the Commune.

Doretta, the daughter of the chancellor of Venchieredo, Leopardi Provedoni's wife.

Raimondo di Venchieredo, Doretta's lover.

The Count of Venchieredo, Raimondo's father, sentenced to prison for laying siege to Fratta.

Alberto Partistagno, a young nobleman, Clara Fratta's suitor.

Giulio del Ponte, a young poet, another of Clara's suitors, later in love with Pisana Fratta.

Aglaura, Carlo Altoviti's half sister.

Spiro Apostulos, Aglaura's husband.

Mauro Navagero, an aged Fratta kinsman, Pisana Fratta's husband.

Almoro Frumier, a Venetian senator, a Fratta kinsman.

The Spaccafumo, a bandit.

Father Pendola, a Jesuit priest and a political intriguer in the Venetian Republic.

Lady Badoer, Clara and Pisana Fratta's grandmother, who dies of atrocities committed by the soldiers of Napoleon.

Captain Sandracca, captain of the militia at Fratta.

Amilcare Dossi, a young political liberal who influences Carlo Altoviti.

Ettore Carafa, a lover of Pisana Fratta.

Napoleon Bonaparte.

THE CASTLE OF OTRANTO

Author: Horace Walpole (1717-1797)
Time of action: Twelfth century
First published: 1764

PRINCIPAL CHARACTERS

Manfred, Prince of Otranto, a usurper. After Manfred's son is mysteriously killed on his wedding day, Manfred plans to divorce his wife and marry the promised bride himself, in order to have a male heir. After much frightening supernatural intervention, Manfred surrenders his claims to Otranto; he and his wife then enter neighboring convents.

Conrad, the fifteen-year-old son of Manfred. On his wedding day he is found crushed to death beneath a gigantic helmet.

Isabella, the daughter of the Marquis of Vicenza and the fiancée of Conrad. Manfred plans to marry her after Conrad's death, but she escapes him with the aid of the true heir to Otranto, whom she marries after Manfred's abdication.

Theodore, a young peasant and the true heir to Otranto. He is imprisoned and nearly executed by Manfred's order, but with both human and supernatural aid he triumphs, marrying Isabella and becoming the new Prince of Otranto.

Matilda, Manfred's daughter. She gives aid to Theodore. Learning that Theodore is in the chapel with a woman, the jealous Manfred goes there and stabs the woman, only to learn that he has killed his daughter Matilda.

Father Jerome, formerly Prince of Falconara, now a priest. Called to give absolution to the condemned Theodore, he discovers that Theodore is his own son, born before he entered the Church.

The Marquis of Vicenza, Isabella's father. Disguised as the **Knight of the Gigantic Sabre,** he comes to Otranto, bringing with him a huge sword carried by a hundred men. On its blade is written that only Manfred's blood can atone for the wrongs done to the family of the true heir. By betrothing the Marquis to Matilda, Manfred gets his consent to his own marriage with Isabella; but terrifying omens and warnings cause the Marquis to renounce Matilda.

Prince Alfonso the Good, formerly the ruler of Otranto. It was the helmet of his statue which crushed Conrad. His giant form appears to proclaim Theodore, the son of his daughter, heir to Otranto. He then ascends to Heaven.

St. Nicholas, who receives Prince Alfonso into Heaven.

CASTLE RACKRENT

Author: Maria Edgeworth (1767-1849)
Time of action: Eighteenth century
First published: 1800

PRINCIPAL CHARACTERS

Thady Quirk, known as **Honest Thady, Old Thady,** and finally **Poor Thady,** the narrator of the story and a lifelong attendant to a procession of masters of Rackrent Castle in Ireland. Loyal and steadfast, he embodies all the qualities of the true Irish servant. Clothed in his heavy great cloak, he observes the world as he experiences it in terms of the differing characters of his several masters.

Sir Patrick Rackrent, a lusty, generous landowner whose original family name was O'Shaughlin. He is convivial to a fault and friendly to all, and he dies singing while Thady himself is still a lad.

Sir Murtagh Rackrent, the heir. He is a close-fisted lawyer married to a widow of the Skinflint family. The two live on the tenants' "duty" fowls and services so that the castle is almost free of expense on the part of Sir Murtagh. As Thady notes, it is lamentable that knowledge of the law permits Sir Murtagh to take land and property from other people. Sir Murtagh dies fittingly after hearing the cry of a banshee; actually, his death is a result of overstraining his voice in the law courts and in arguments with his wife, who strips the house after the death of her husband.

Sir Kit, Sir Murtagh's younger brother. A warm and friendly person, he is kind to the tenants, yet he turns all Rackrent affairs over to an agent, an Irish "middleman" who is all servility to his master and tyrannical to every wretch beneath him. Sir Kit orders the castle renovated before he brings a Jewish bride from England, an heiress reputed to own many diamonds. She hates Castle Rackrent and the bog in front of it. Because she insists on her own dietary restrictions and refuses to give up any of her money, Sir Kit imprisons her in her room, where she remains for seven years. Rackrent is heavily mortgaged because of Sir Kit's gambling debts, and he is finally killed in a duel after philandering extensively. His wife returns to England.

Sir Conally (Sir Condy), a member of a remote branch of the family and Sir Kit's successor. Educated at a college in Dublin, he had sat as a child at Old Thady's knee and heard many family stories. He had also attended grammar school with Jason, old Thady's son, who had helped him with his book learning. Sir Condy marries Isabella Moneygawl of Mount Juliet's Town; her father cuts her off without money because he disapproves of her marriage. Head over heels in debt, Sir Condy wins a seat in Parliament and so keeps from going to jail. His debts mount, and he leaves Castle Rackrent for the Lodge, Old Thady accompanying him. Here he holds his own wake with the friendly townspeople. His wife leaves him for her father's home, but word comes that she has had a runaway accident and is not expected to live. Poor Sir Condy dies bereft of everything.

Jason Quirk, Old Thady's son, a lawyer who contrives to take over the Rackrent property by assuming its debts. He aspires to own all that has belonged to Sir Condy, especially when Lady Isabella Rackrent is expected to die also.

Isabella Rackrent, the attractive wife of Sir Condy. She leaves her husband when Castle Rackrent is up for auction. Badly injured in a carriage accident, she recovers and fights for her widow's rights against Jason Quirk.

Judy Quirk, old Thady's grandniece, admired by Sir Condy. Remaining loyal to the Rackrent family, she scorns Jason and his maneuvers and, as the wife of a huntsman, lives on at the Lodge in a manner proper to her station in life. Thady respects and loves her, partly because his own son now travels a different road from that followed by the loyal old retainer.

CASUALS OF THE SEA

Author: William McFee (1881-   )
Time of action: Early twentieth century
First published: 1916

PRINCIPAL CHARACTERS

Bert Gooderich, a stolid machinist who falls off a bridge and is drowned.

Mary, his wife, thankful to marry Bert after having been deserted by her lover, a baker's boy, the father of Minnie.

Young Bert, their son, big, strong, and pugnacious, with an ambition to be a soldier. Shortly after his enlistment he is killed at Pretoria.

Hannibal, another son, a big, inarticulate, bungling lout; a factory worker, a ship's mess boy, and finally a trimmer on the S.S. "Caryatid." He dies of lobar pneumonia caused partly by inhalation of coal dust and partly by the cough syrup for which Minnie had written advertisements.

Minnie, Mary's daughter, a stubborn, difficult girl, thin and reserved, engaged for a time to a coal clerk. She becomes Captain Briscoe's mistress, later his wife. She is jailed for engaging in a suffragette demonstration. She is also a writer of advertisements for cough syrup.

Captain Briscoe, a ship's captain, Minnie's lover and later her husband.

Nellie, Hannibal's wife, a plump, merry girl. She works in her uncle's tavern and later manages it.

Mrs. Gaynor, an American woman, next-door neighbor of the Gooderich family.

Hiram, her son, a sailor.

Mrs. Wilfley, a greedy woman who organizes a benefit musicale for the Gooderich family and pockets most of the receipts.

Anthony Gilfillan, a middle-aged man who befriends Minnie at a party and later takes her to the Continent with him.

CATILINE

Author: Ben Jonson (1573?-1637)
Time of action: 62 B.C.
First presented: 1611

PRINCIPAL CHARACTERS

Catiline (kă′tə·lĭn), also Lucius Sergius Catilina (lōō′shĭ·əs sėr′jĭ·əs kă′tə·lī′nə), a patrician traitor. Power-mad, blood-thirsty, venomous, given to monstrous crime, he corrupts others and draws them to his party, with which he hopes to control Rome. His inhumanity is disclosed in his sacrifice of a slave and a hideous, perverted communion of the conspirators in which they drink the slave's blood. He is, fortunately for Rome, indiscreet and hasty. Failing to win a consulate by election, he hastens his attempted revolution before his preparations are complete. His death demonstrates his reckless courage.

Marcus Tullius Cicero (mär′kəs tŭ′lĭ·əs sĭ′sə·rō), a "new man," not an established aristocrat. Able and self-confident, he wins a consulate and uses his governmental position and oratorical powers to save Rome from Catiline's conspiracy. He is willing to use dubious characters as spies, and with information furnished by them he forces Catiline into premature action and consequent defeat. A cautious politician, he does not force the hands of sympathizers with the subversives, and he sends to execution only those active in the conspiracy; hence Caesar and Crassus survive as threats to Rome's future.

Caius Julius Caesar (gā′yəs jōō′lĭ·əs sē′zėr), potentially more dangerous to Rome than any of the active conspirators. He is too shrewd to make an open break with the Republic until he sees how matters are likely to turn out. When Catiline is goaded into premature action by Cicero, Caesar refrains from joining the conspirators openly. He pleads in vain for moderation in punishing the arrested conspirators and prophetically warns Cicero of his future fate.

Publius Lentulus (pŭb′lĭ·əs lĕn′chōō·ləs), a Senator formerly ejected from the Senate for infamous behavior, but later restored. He is filled with family pride and delusions of grandeur. Catiline flatters him with prophecies that a third member of the family Cornelii is to rule Rome, and Lentulus is easily convinced that he is the man intended. He remains in Rome, is arrested, and is executed.

Caius Cethegus (gā′yəs sə·thē′gəs), a savage, fire-eating conspirator. Indiscreet and tactless, he requires considerable care by Catiline to keep him from disrupting the revolutionary forces. He is hasty, reckless, and chronically angry. He is executed with the rest of the rebels who remain in Rome when Catiline leaves.

Quintus Curius (kwin′təs kōō′rĭ·əs), a former Senator also ejected from the Senate for infamous behavior. Enslaved by his passion for Fulvia, he rashly betrays himself and the other conspirators to her. Under her influence, combined with fear and greed, he becomes a spy for Cicero. His information enables Cicero to avoid assassination and to expose Catiline's machinations to the Senate. Caesar prevents his receiving official reward after Rome is saved.

Fulvia (fŭl′vĭ·ə), an expensive and extravagant courtesan. She gives her favors where the return is greatest; but suspecting some major plot, she takes back the degraded Curius in order to wheedle his secret from him. Unwilling to take second place to another woman, she chooses to go over to Cicero rather than to Catiline. Although Cicero feels shame at having to depend on such tools, he skillfully uses Fulvia and Curius to thwart Catiline and thus save Rome.

Sempronia (sĕm·prō'nĭ·ə), the snobbish wife of Decius Brutus. She is an intellectual feminist, past her prime, but still hungry for masculine attention, for which she pays lavishly. She is active in Catilinarian politics but escapes punishment, for Cicero says a government should not show its anger against fools or women.

Marcus Porcius Cato (mär'kəs pôr'shĭ·əs kā'tō), **Cato the Younger,** called "the voice of Rome." A stanch, loyal Roman citizen, he is a strong supporter of Cicero, whom he considers sometimes too mild; however, in general he gives him complete approbation.

Caius Antonius (gā'yəs ăn·to'nĭ·əs), a candidate for consul in the same election as Cicero and Catiline. He and Cicero win, and Cicero buys his support with a province.

Marcus Crassus (mär'kəs kră'səs), a cautious Roman. Like Caesar, he is sympathetic to Catiline, but unwilling to risk open commitment.

Petreius (pə·trē'yəs), leader of the Roman forces against Catiline's army. He gives a vivid and poetic account of the defeat and death of Catiline.

Quintus Fabius Sanga (kwĭn'təs fā'bĭ·əs săn'gə), Cicero's emissary to the ambassadors from the Allobroges. From them he gets documentary evidence of the conspiracy for the Senate.

Aurelia Orestilla (ô·rē'lĭ·ə ō·rĕs·tĭ'lə), Catiline's wife, for whom he murdered his former wife and son. She aids him in his conspiracy by holding a meeting of the feminine auxiliary of the conspirators.

Volturtius (vŏl·tĕr'shĭ·əs), a conspirator captured with the Allobroges. He gives evidence to the Senate against the other conspirators.

Quintus Cicero (kwĭn'təs sĭ'sə·rō), brother of the consul. He gathers help to prevent Vargunteius and Cornelius from assassinating his brother.

Sylla's Ghost (sĭl'ə), the Prologue. He narrates Catiline's inhuman crimes and invokes terror on Rome comparable to what he himself had brought in the past.

Flaccus (flă'kəs) and
Pomtinius (pŏm·tī'nĭ·əs), praetors. Cicero trusts them and calls them in to help prevent his assassination.

Syllanus (sĭ·lā'nəs), a Senator. He favors death for the arrested conspirators.

Autronius (ô·trō'nĭ·əs),
Vargunteius (vär·gŭn·tē'yəs),
Lucius Cassius Longinus (loo'shĭ·əs kă'sĭ·əs lŏn·jī'nəs),
Portius Lecca (pōr'shĭ·əs lĕ'kə),
Fulvius (fŭl'vĭ·əs),
Lucius Bestia (loo'shĭ·əs bĕs'tĭ·ə),
Gabinius Cimber (gə·bĭ'nĭ·əs sĭm'bĕr),
Statilius (stə·tĭ'lĭ·əs),
Ceparius (sē·pâ'rĭ·əs), and
Caius Cornelius (gā'yəs kôr·nē'lĭ·əs), conspirators.

CAVALLERIA RUSTICANA

Author: Giovanni Verga (1840-1922)
Time of action: Mid-nineteenth century
First published: 1880

PRINCIPAL CHARACTERS

Turiddu Macca, a swaggering Sicilian ex-soldier with more glamor than cash.

Lola, Turiddu's former sweetheart who, though married to Alfio, is still attracted by Turiddu and meets him during her husband's absence.

Alfio, a wealthy carter who kills Turiddu in a duel over Lola.

Mistress Nunzia, Turiddu's widowed and impoverished mother.

Master Angelo, Lola's father.

Master Cola, who gives Turiddu work in his vineyard across the street from Alfio's house.

Santa, Cola's pretty daughter, with whom Turiddu flirts to make Lola jealous.

CAWDOR

Author: Robinson Jeffers (1887-1962)
Time of action: 1900
First published: 1928

PRINCIPAL CHARACTERS

Cawdor, a farmer of fifty, hard and strong. Drawn to worship Fera's youthful beauty and contrarily to possess her sexually, he bargains to let her father stay in his home if Fera will marry him. Rightly suspecting Fera's later passion for Hood but mistaken in believing Hood guilty, Cawdor seeks confirmation of his suspicions. Burning with jealousy, he believes Fera's lie that she was raped in the laurels; enraged, he meets Hood at the high Rock and knocks him over the adjacent cliff. When he learns from Fera of Hood's innocence, he blinds himself like Oedipus of old, who put out the eyes that could not see the truth.

Hood Cawdor, his second son, a strong young hunter who has been separated from his father because of a quarrel. Loyal to his father after his return, Hood resists Fera's attempts at seduction by the seashore, in his room, and in the laurels. He is killed anyway by gulled Cawdor.

Fera, Martial's daughter, an intense, bold girl who admires strength and who expects hardness and pride in Cawdor's treatment of her as a wife. She begins a sexual pursuit of Hood almost upon his return home. Inflamed with desire and angry at being rebuffed when she tries repeatedly to seduce him, she goads Cawdor with the lie that Hood violated her in the laurels. Thus, through her dupe, she accomplishes her revenge for being spurned. Having failed at seduction, she also fails in attempting suicide and still again in her cruel urging that Cawdor kill himself. Though Fera speaks often of longing for death and of death as a blessing, it is difficult to decide how sincere she is since she lies with such ease. Like Jeffers' Tamar, Fera is destructive by nature.

George Cawdor, Hood's brother, a farmer, in contrast to Hood the hunter.

Michal Cawdor, younger sister of George and Hood. She traps ground squirrels and watches her caged, crippled eagle kill and eat them. At Fera's suggestion she finally has George shoot the eagle.

Martial, an ex-schoolmaster, a dreamer, and an abject alcoholic failure; a former enemy of Cawdor blinded in the explosion of an oil drum during a sweeping brush fire. A pitiful remnant of a man,

161

he slowly declines and dies as the result of his burns and is buried near the graves of Cawdor's wife and child.

Concha Rosas, Cawdor's Indian servant and mistress.

Jesus Acanna, Cawdor's Indian farm hand.

Dante Vitello, a new Swiss farm hand.

Romano, Concha Rosas' young son.

CECILIA

Author: Fanny Burney (Madame d'Arblay, 1752-1840)
Time of action: Eighteenth century
First published: 1782

PRINCIPAL CHARACTERS

Cecilia Beverley, a charming, benevolent heiress. To retain the fortune left her by an eccentric uncle, she must marry a man who will take the name of Beverley. During her minority, Cecilia is the ward of three distinct types of men named by her uncle. Her extended love affair with the son of one of the guardians brings her insult, near-poverty, temporary insanity, and finally happiness. Cecilia is the model heroine who reciprocates to those who befriend her, has compassion for those who would harm her, and is benevolent to those who need help.

Mortimer Delvile, her lover and husband. He is a violent admixture of submission to his parents, devotion to Cecilia, and jealousy of others attending to her. Sensitive and unworldly, Mortimer is always in need of a protector.

Compton Delvile, his father and one of Cecilia's guardians, whose chief objective in life is preservation of the family name. His pride is odious because it is tainted with meanness and incapacity.

Augusta Delvile, his high-spirited and fastidious wife. She loves Cecilia, but accepts her as a daughter-in-law with great misgivings because she fears unhappiness for her son in marriage. Her pride is coupled with dignity and generosity of mind.

Mr. Monckton, the self-appointed protector of Cecilia. In love with her, he lies, pries, and spies to avert any attachment between her and any man.

Mr. Harrel, one of Cecilia's guardians. Using her as a perpetual go-between with moneylenders, he draws heavily on Cecilia's funds. His gay, fashionable, splendid way of life leads to his suicide while preparing to leave England to escape his creditors.

Priscilla Harrel, his helpmate in lavish living. Cecilia provides for her after Harrel's suicide.

Mr. Albany, "the old man in the corner" at various functions. He is silent in groups but articulate with Cecilia in pronouncing his philosophy of benevolence. Through Albany, she provides pensions for the indigent of the countryside.

Mr. Briggs, the third legally appointed guardian, who manages Cecilia's finances during her minority. Rich, eccentric, uncouth, and miserly, Briggs would have Cecilia live in his comfortless home, to conserve her money.

Mr. Arnot, Priscilla Harrel's brother. Mild, serious, and comfortable financially, he tries to discipline Priscilla in her spending.

Mr. Belfield, an animated, intelligent young man, who gives his time to company, his income to his whims, and his heart to the Muses. Injured in a duel,

162

he is helped secretly by Cecilia, whose kindness to him arouses Mortimer's jealousy.

Henrietta Belfield, his sister, befriended by Cecilia and in love with Mortimer. Through Cecilia, she becomes friendly with Arnot.

Sir Robert Floyer, a vain, supercilious man about town. A contender for Cecilia's affection, he involves Belfield in the duel.

Mrs. Charlton, Cecilia's long-time friend and confidante.

Lady Margaret Monckton, Monckton's cold, irascible wife, considerably older than her husband and jealous of Cecilia. Ill most of her life, she dies of apoplexy.

Miss Bennet, Lady Monckton's submissive companion, an accessory to Monckton's schemes to keep Cecilia unmarried.

Mrs. Matt, one of Cecilia's pensioners, hired by Miss Bennet to disrupt Cecilia's wedding.

Mr. Morrice, an officious young lawyer. He keeps Monckton's friendship by spying on Cecilia.

Lady Honoria Pemberton, Compton Delvile's cousin. Volatile and high-spirited, she belies her fashionable education.

Lord Derford, a young nobleman whom Compton Delvile, in his effort to separate Cecilia and his son, urges upon Cecilia.

Lord Ernolf, Derford's father, willing to accept Cecilia as a daughter-in-law because of her income.

Mrs. Wyers, the landlady of the house where Cecilia goes looking for Mortimer. She keeps Cecilia confined, thinking her mentally unsound.

Mrs. Hill, the wife of an injured carpenter, one of Cecilia's pensioners. Her rooming house becomes a rendezvous for Mortimer and Cecilia.

Dr. Lyster, the Delvile family physician, who philosophizes, in describing Delvile, Sr., that people make themselves miserable by seeing only one road to contentment, when fifty other channels would serve equally as well.

Mr. Biddulph, Mortimer's former schoolmate, who convinces him of Cecilia's devotion.

CELESTINA

Author: Fernando de Rojas (1475?-1538?)
Time of action: Fifteenth century
First published: Burgos edition, 1499; longer Seville edition, 1502

PRINCIPAL CHARACTERS

Calisto (kä·lēs′tō), a nobleman who sees and falls in love with Melibea. He hires Celestina to arrange a meeting. He is killed by falling from a ladder while leaving Melibea's garden.

Melibea (mā·lē·bā′ä), a beautiful girl who lets herself be talked into a rendezvous with Calisto and who commits suicide after his death by leaping from her roof.

Celestina (thā·lĕs·tē′nä), an elderly go-

between and seller of love charms whose greediness over payment brings about her death.

Lucrecia (lōō·krā′thyä), Melibea's maid. She warns Melibea's mother against the evil Celestina but to no avail.

Pármeno (pär′mā·nō) and
Sempronio (sām·prō′nyō), servants of Calisto, who promote Celestina's arrangement with their master and murder her when she refuses them a reward. Appre-

163

hended by the police, they are beheaded on the spot for their crime.

Sosia (sō'syä), another servant of Calisto who helps to plot his master's death.

Areusa (ä·rä'oo·sä) and
Elicia (ä·lē'thyä), prostitutes in Celestina's house. Areusa loves Pármeno;

Elicia loves Sempronio. The girls hire Centurio to avenge the servants' deaths.

Pleberio (plä·bä'ryō), the father of Melibea.

Alisa (ä·lē'sä), the mother of Melibea.

Centurio (thän·too'ryō), a scoundrelly soldier hired to kill Calisto.

THE CENCI

Author: Percy Bysshe Shelley (1792-1822)
Time of action: 1599
First published: 1819

PRINCIPAL CHARACTERS

Count Francesco Cenci (frän·chäs'kō chěn'chē), a Roman nobleman who lives to make people suffer. His special target for punishment is his family. He persecutes his sons—two of whom are sent to Salamanca to die—his wife, and his daughter Beatrice, against whom he commits unmentionable crimes. Finally, he is assassinated; but even in death his baleful influence continues, for his wife and daughter, though literally innocent, die for his murder.

Count Orsino (ôr·sē'nō), a nobleman turned priest who is responsible for much of the scheming that takes place in the play. He loves Beatrice but betrays her when she is tried for her father's murder. He hires assassins to kill Cenci and abandons them when they are caught. He betrays Beatrice's brother, Giacomo, to the Roman police. Orsino escapes punishment by disguising himself and fleeing the scene when the officials close in.

Lucretia (lö·krē'shyä), Cenci's wife and Beatrice's stepmother. She helps the assassins by giving Cenci a sleeping potion. After languishing a long time in prison,

she is executed for her part in her husband's assassination.

Beatrice (bä·ä·trē'chä), Cenci's daughter, the chief object of his persecution, who loves Count Orsino and who is executed along with her stepmother.

Giacomo (jä'kō·mō), Cenci's son, whose wife's dowry the father takes. After the assassination, Orsino tricks Giacomo, and the son is caught by the police.

Bernardo (běr·när'dō), Cenci's youngest son, who pleads at the papal court for the lives of his sister and stepmother. His petition is rejected.

Olimpio (ō·lēm'pyō) and
Marzio (mär'tsyō), assassins hired by Orsino to murder Cenci. After some hesitation, they strangle the sleeping nobleman.

Savella (sä·věl'lä), an official of the papal court who comes to arrest Cenci for his crimes. Finding the Count dead, Savella launches the investigation that exposes the Cenci family and the assassins as participants in Cenci's murder.

164

CÉSAR BIROTTEAU

Author: Honoré de Balzac (1799-1850)
Time of action: Early nineteenth century
First published: 1837

PRINCIPAL CHARACTERS

César Birotteau (sā·zàr' bē·rô·tō'), a self-made man who at the peak of his success mistook it for the beginning, and whose downfall resulted from his lack of judgment of the jackals in the business world. A peasant in appearance and manners, of straightforward honesty and perseverance, César Birotteau is a man in love with his own wife, devoted to his lovely daughter, loyal to his good friends, and gentle even to those who despise and misuse him. His noble character is revealed through adversity, and he dies following his exoneration from the debts of his bankruptcy. As a manufacturer of perfume and as a manager of a business he is canny, even ingenious, but in dealing with the world of finance he is an infant sustained finally by his brave wife and daughter.

Constance Birotteau (kōn·stäns'), his beautiful and devoted wife, who is not only wiser than her husband but more resourceful as well. Endowed with a fine physique and constitution, Mme. Birotteau manages all of the business for the family and even has a presentiment concerning their over-extended credit. As kind and honest as her husband but with more will power and intelligence, she never succumbs to pride of possession or the desire for prestige in social life. She never fails to back her bungling husband, however, and she works and saves toward this end. In spite of attempts on her honor, she is a heroine of dimensions only hinted at in her husband.

Césarine (sā·zà·rēn'), their beautiful daughter, who combines in her person all the good traits of her parents. Robbed of her dowry by an ironic blow of fortune,

she refuses to be humbled. Instead, she uses adversity as a means to attain her deepest ambitions: the love of a devoted and fine young man, a home free from social pretense, and an independence from all that a large dowry implies of social position and prestige. Her touching sacrifices for her parents, her loving attention to their needs and wishes, and her sincerity in all catastrophes make of her a strange contrast to most of Balzac's wealthy daughters who repay devotion with ingratitude.

Anselm Popinot (än·sĕlm' pô·pē·nō'), Birotteau's son-in-law, a young peasant with a club foot who in a few years elevates himself from the humble position of apprentice to the rank of perfumer by honesty and hard work, plus imagination and daring. He has a remarkable character and evenness of disposition which will not allow him to make sentimental errors of such proportions as would have made the Birotteau fortunes irretrievable. At the risk of seeming ingratitude, he refuses to add his small profits to the sinking capital of his benefactor. Instead, he builds a new business into an enterprise which saves both family fortune and honor, and makes him its master and the husband of Césarine.

Ferdinand du Tillet (fĕr·dē·nän' dü tē·yā'), a reprobate who as apprentice to César Birotteau makes advances to Constance and steals three thousand francs from the firm. Not content to repay good with evil, he makes it his life's work to ruin the man who so generously forgives him his offenses. A real villain, du Tillet uses his experience in knavery, learned at Birotteau's expense, to seduce and

165

abduct, and parlay sin into a fortune and a secure position in corrupt society.

M. Pillerault (mə·syœ′ pē·yə·rō′), an ironmonger, the uncle and benefactor of Constance as well as the firm friend and financial adviser of Birotteau. A noble and self-effacing gentleman of the old order, the elderly tradesman remains true to his nephew and other friends who have been ruined by a thieving notary. Admirable in his business principles, he firmly sustains his family.

Roguin (rô·găn′), a dishonest notary, du

Tillet's tool in his scheme to ruin César Birotteau. Persuaded to invest in a land speculation venture, Birotteau turns three hundred thousand francs over to Roguin, but gets no receipt for his money.

Claparon (klä·pà·rōn′), a dummy banker also involved in du Tillet's plot.

La Belle Hollandaise (lä běl ô·län·děz′), a courtesan loved by Roguin.

Vauquelin (và·kə·lăn), a chemist who aids Birotteau in the expansion of his business in the days of his prosperity.

THE CHAINBEARER

Author: James Fenimore Cooper (1789-1851)
Time of action: c. 1785
First published: 1845

PRINCIPAL CHARACTERS

Mordaunt Littlepage, a young landowner and the narrator of "The Chainbearer." On a visit to his wilderness tract, Ravensnest, he has a run-in with lawless squatters, who imprison him; but he is finally rescued by a posse after a battle with his captors. He marries Chainbearer's niece, Dus Malbone.

Andries Coejemans (Chainbearer), an old woodsman and surveyor, Mordaunt Littlepage's devoted friend from Revolutionary War days when they were both captains. In his attempt to rescue Mordaunt from the squatter outlaws, he is imprisoned with his friend and mortally wounded by his captors. Feeling deeply indebted to Chainbearer for their happiness, the Littlepage family erects a monument in his honor and reveres his memory all of their lives.

Ursula Malbone (Dus), Chainbearer's orphaned niece who marries Mordaunt.

Jaap, Mordaunt's loyal Negro servant.

Aaron Timberman (Thousandacres), a

squatter and illegal operator of a sawmill on Mordaunt's land. He imprisons Mordaunt and is later slain by the rescuing posse.

Tobit and
Zephanaiah Timberman, Aaron's lawless sons.

Lowiny Timberman, Aaron's daughter. She tries to help the imprisoned Mordaunt, and, after his marriage to Dus, becomes their maid.

Jason Newcome, the untrustworthy squire at Ravensnest village.

Frank Malbone, Dus' half brother and Mordaunt's agent at Ravensnest.

Susquesus (Trackless), an Indian hunter, loyal friend of Mordaunt and Chainbearer.

Cornelius Littlepage and
Anneke Littlepage, Mordaunt's parents.

Kate Littlepage, Mordaunt's sister.

166

Tom Bayard, betrothed to Kate.

Priscilla Bayard, Tom's sister.

Dirck Follock, Cornelius Littlepage's friend.

THE CHANGELING

Authors: Thomas Middleton (1580-1627) with William Rowley (1585?-1642?)
Time of action: Early seventeenth century
First presented: 1622

PRINCIPAL CHARACTERS

Beatrice-Joanna (bā·ä·trēth′ hō·ä′nyä), the beautiful daughter of Vermandero, a wealthy government official. Her sudden infatuation for the handsome Spaniard, Alsemero, precipitates her rapid moral degeneration, which culminates in the grotesque irony of her wedding night; she spends it with De Flores, a man whom she loathes, while her servant enjoys the husband for whom she entered upon her career of deceit and murder. She proceeds boldly in her villainy and professes love she does not feel to procure De Flores' help in the murder of her fiancé, Alonzo. Yet she is so completely unaware of the implications of what she is doing that she is almost stunned when De Flores demands the fruits of this feigned love as his payment. Dying of the wounds he has inflicted on her, she wonders at the evil influence this strange lover has exerted over her, drawing her into his power in spite of her intense loathing of him.

De Flores (dā flō′räs), her strange partner in crime, Vermandero's servant. His life revolves around a single obsession, his passion for this young woman who shows him nothing but scorn and loathing. Although he is not convinced of the sincerity of Beatrice-Joanna's blandishments, he sees in her request for help the means to satisfy his desire. Her wishes are, for him, sufficient justification for all his crimes, and he dies defying the hell into which he has brought himself, satisfied by the few moments when he possessed her.

Vermandero (bâr·män·dä′rō), Beatrice-

Joanna's father, governor of the castle of Alicante. Although he seeks the best possible marriage for his daughter, he sternly expects her to follow his wishes. Struck by the full horror of the crimes of his daughter and De Flores, he sees himself and his companions circumscribed within the hell the guilty pair have created.

Alsemero (äl·sä·mä′rō), a Spanish nobleman who falls in love with Beatrice-Joanna at first sight, wins her father's favor, and quickly weds her after Alonzo's strange disappearance. He dabbles in magic and produces a liquid to test the virtue of his betrothed, for he is determined not to marry her unless she can be proved chaste. He, too, is appalled by his wife's villainy and sees only justice in her death. His sympathy is reserved for his father-in-law, to whom he offers himself as a son to replace his lost daughter.

Alonzo de Piracquo (ä·lōn′thō ᵺä pē·rä′kwō), Beatrice-Joanna's husband, a trusting man who is insensitive to his bride's lack of feeling for him. He goes blindly to his death, completely unaware of De Flores' villainous intentions.

Tomaso (tō·mäs′ō), Alonzo's brother, who perceives at a glance that Beatrice-Joanna is indifferent to Alonzo and warns him of the danger of a loveless marriage. Certain that his brother was murdered, he presses the investigation of Alonzo's death. His instinctive impressions of individuals are invariably accurate; he is overwhelmed with a sense

167

of evil and corruption when he meets De Flores.

Jasperino (häs·pā·rē'nō), Alsemero's servant, sensitive to his master's moods and watchful over his affairs. It is he who discovers the bizarre liaison between De Flores and Beatrice-Joanna and brings about their deaths.

Diaphanta (dyä·fän'ta), Beatrice-Joanna's waiting woman, who is virtuous in spite of her witty, worldly-wise conversation. Ignorant of the fate which De Flores has in store for her, she agrees to substitute for her mistress on her wedding night.

Alibius (ä·lē'byōōs), a jealous old doctor who keeps his lovely young wife confined at home with his patients, a crew of fools and madmen.

Lollio (lō'lyō), his servant, who is responsible for keeping order among the inmates of the house, watching his mistress as well as the doctor's patients. His sharp eyes quickly see through the disguises of Antonio and Franciscus, but he disregards his master's orders to seek money from the "changeling" and the madman and to try to win a share of his mistress' favors.

Isabella (ē·sä·bě'lyä), Alibius' young wife. She chafes under her virtual imprisonment and welcomes Antonio's profession of love as a happy diversion.

Antonio (än·tō'nyō) and
Franciscus (frän'thēs'kōōs), Vermandero's men, who disguise themselves as fool and madman to gain access to Isabella.

Pedro (pā'drō), Antonio's friend, who takes him to Alibius, pretending to be his cousin.

CHARLES DEMAILLY

Authors: Edmond (1822-1896) and Jules (1830-1870) de Goncourt
Time of action: Mid-nineteenth century
First published: 1860

PRINCIPAL CHARACTERS

Charles Demailly (shȧrl' də·má·yē'), a writer. Burdened with a loneliness and a super-sensitivity that make it difficult, if not impossible, for him to find satisfaction in real life, he falls in love with an ingénue, Marthe Mance, and endows her with the perfection of which he has always dreamed. When, by her shallowness, insincerity, and cruel treatment, she finally destroys his image of her, his creativity is also destroyed, and he sinks into apathy and, finally, into madness.

Marthe Mance (mȧrt' mäns'), an actress and Charles Demailly's wife, who is endowed by her husband with qualities of perfection which, in reality, she has never possessed. Enchanted at first by her husband's play in which she is the idealized heroine, she begins to show her shallowness and insincerity when the play is unfavorably criticized and she fears for her own success as its leading lady. Step by step, she then destroys Charles' image of her until she has destroyed the man himself.

Nachette (nȧ·shět') and
Couturat (kōō·tü·rȧ'), writers for "Scandal," a journal that thrives on gossip, superficial aesthetic criticism, and sensationalism.

Chavannes (shȧ·vȧn'), Charles Demailly's boyhood friend, who encourages him in his efforts at serious writing.

Remonville (rə·mōn·vēl'), a writer and Charles Demailly's friend.

Boisroger (bwȧ·rô·zhä'), a poet who introduces Charles Demailly to a circle of serious artists.

168

CHARLES O'MALLEY

Author: Charles Lever (1806-1872)
Time of action: 1808-1812
First published: 1841

PRINCIPAL CHARACTERS

Charles O'Malley, an Irish dragoon. He is a big man, an excellent shot and horseman. He goes to Dublin to study law but indulges in too many escapades. He then enters the army as an ensign, serving gallantly in the war against Napoleon in Spain. He returns to Ireland to look after his estates after the death of his uncle but returns to war when Napoleon leaves Elba. He wins the hand of Lucy Dashwood by rescuing her father from execution by the French.

Lucy Dashwood, daughter of General Dashwood, an English girl. She marries Charles after he saves her father from execution.

General Dashwood, an Englishman. When he tries to buy estates in Ireland, he is challenged to a duel by Charles' Uncle Godfrey and Billy Considine. When the general is captured by the French and condemned to death, he is rescued by Charles.

Godfrey O'Malley, Charles' uncle, master of O'Malley Castle in Galway. He is a hard-drinking, hard-riding man who is good to his tenants and to his nephew.

Blake, a distant cousin of Godfrey who refuses to support him when he stands for Parliament. Charles first meets Lucy at Blake's home.

Billy Considine, Charles' good friend and his second in a duel.

Captain Hammersley, General Dashwood's aide and Charles' rival for the hand of Lucy.

St. Croix, a French officer befriended by Charles in Spain. Later he helps Charles rescue General Dashwood from the French.

Donna Inez, a Spanish girl who becomes a friend of Charles after he rescues her.

Captain Powers, who prevents a duel between Charles and Hammersley. He marries Donna Inez.

Frank Webber, Charles' roommate at college in Dublin and the ringleader in their escapades.

Michael Free, Charles' faithful servant.

THE CHARTERHOUSE OF PARMA

Author: Stendhal (Marie-Henri Beyle, 1783-1842)
Time of action: Early ninetenth century
First published: 1839

PRINCIPAL CHARACTERS

Fabrizio del Dongo, an Italian nobleman destined to become an archbishop in the family tradition. A romantic youth, devotedly attached to Napoleonic ideals, the sixteen-year-old adventurer abandons the security of wealth and position to engage in the Battle of Waterloo under an assumed name, with the papers and uniform of a deceased hussar, and in complete ignorance of the ways of war and the world. This episode leads him gradually into deceptions of a higher

169

order, an education he does not want, and an ecclesiastical post for which he is unfitted. Gentle and considerate in private friendships, and devoted to humanitarian principles, he nevertheless resorts to intrigue and even murder to attain his ends in the Italian court at Parma. Never really in love until the romantic hopelessness of an affair makes him act in an unorthodox way, Fabrizio gains and loses patronage and affection. He spends his declining years in quiet meditation in the Charterhouse of Parma, a monastery.

Clelia Conti, the beautiful daughter of a traitor count. As a girl, Clelia sets her heart on the handsome and chivalrous young soldier lately home from France. Although she takes a vow never to set eyes on the man who becomes her father's prisoner after his arrest for murder, she finally takes him as her lover in spite of her marriage vows to a marchese whom she cannot love. Clelia is one of the two great beauties of the Parmese court, both enamoured of the young monsignor. She dies soon after the death of the child fathered by Fabrizio, now an archbishop.

Gina Pietranera, the Duchess of Sanseverina, the mistress and later wife of Count Mosca, and the aunt and benefactress of Fabrizio del Dongo. Widowed before she is thirty, the unorthodox and spirited beauty becomes the chief ornament of the court of the Prince of Parma. Taking part in political intrigue, Gina effects the escape of her nephew, the discomfiture of the Prince, and the devotion of her lover. Though greatly attracted to her nephew, she never pleads the cause of what the whole court assumes to be an established fact, a ménage. Capable of acting under the whim of a moment, Gina is also able to act with cool precision and great foresight.

Count Mosca, Gina's lover, a prime minister under two heads of state, and the jealous friend of Fabrizio. The Count,

against all reason, successfully wooes the penniless Gina, finds her a husband who needs a court accomplice and preferment, and then gives up his portfolio in order to live as her husband in penury. He is an inspired Machiavelli, a generous nobleman, and a clear-headed cynic.

Father Blanès, a priest-astrologer and a friend of Fabrizio. This ghostly cleric, the surrogate father of the impressionable young mystic whose real father early disowned him, proves to be the awakener of spiritual qualities as well as churchly ambitions in his protégé.

Ludovico, the trusted servant of the Duchess and the great friend and protector of Fabrizio. Valorous and canny, Ludovico protects the headstrong and amorous young man from many intrigues and aids the imaginative poet, Ferrante, who supervised his eventual escape from prison.

Marietta Valsera, the young actress whose jealous lover is killed by Fabrizio. A young and not very talented performer, Marietta unconsciously leads her admirer into an ambush. She redeems herself by protecting her lover's identity even at her own peril. For Fabrizio she personifies conquest and no more.

Fausta, a beautiful and famous soprano who inspires Fabrizio to imaginative and romantic heights.

Count Conti, the treacherous militia officer and keeper of the prison where Fabrizio is confined. He acquiesces in a plot on the life of his political prisoner.

Rassi, a plebian but brilliant lawyer of the Parmese court who sells preferment among the nobility to his best advantage.

Giletti, Marietta Valsera's rascally protector and lover. Jealous of Fabrizio, he attacks the young man and is killed during the scuffle. His death creates a scandal which leads to Fabrizio's arrest when the young cleric returns to Parma.

A CHASTE MAID IN CHEAPSIDE

Author: Thomas Middleton (1580-1627)
Time of action: Early seventeenth century
First presented: 1611

PRINCIPAL CHARACTERS

Yellowhammer, a goldsmith. Anxious to see his children rise in the world, he betroths his daughter to Sir Walter Whorehound, giving heed to the man's title but not to his reputation, and arranges for his son to wed the nobleman's supposed niece, who proves to be a Welsh prostitute and Sir Walter's mistress. His harsh refusal to allow Moll to marry her sweetheart, Touchwood Junior, nearly brings tragedy upon his family.

Maudlin, his loquacious wife. She scolds her daughter for her sluggishness, regaling the girl with tales of her own gay youth, and she embarrasses her university-trained son by fussing over him before his tutor and many of her friends. She is as distressed as her husband when she learns that her stern treatment of Moll has apparently caused her death.

Moll, their daughter, whose languid attitude is simply a cloak for her love for young Touchwood. She is never quite successful in her attempts to elude her parents long enough to marry until her clever maid arranges for her feigned death and reunion with her lover.

Timothy, her learned, self-confident brother. He comes home from Cambridge with his tutor to impress his family and friends with his knowledge of Latin. Tricked by Sir Walter into marriage with a prostitute, he is consoled by her wit and physical attractions for the loss of the nineteen Welsh mountains he hoped to gain as her dowry.

Sir Walter Whorehound, a loose-living gentleman who tries unsuccessfully to bring about at one time his own marriage with Moll, Timothy's with his Welsh mistress, and the christening of his son by Allwit's wife, without having his duplicity discovered. His plans are thwarted. Wounded in a duel with young Touchwood, he learns that he will not be Sir Oliver Kix's heir, and he is promptly deserted by the Allwits.

Allwit, a contented cuckold who allows Sir Walter to possess his wife, father the children who bear his name, and maintain his entire household. Unwilling to lose all his worldly comforts, he judiciously spreads gossip about his patron's character whenever he suspects Sir Walter of considering marriage. Once the knight's fortunes change, Allwit leaves him to his late fate without a qualm, planning with his wife to live comfortably off the possessions Sir Walter has given them over the years.

Mistress Allwit, his wife. She is happy to bear Sir Walter's children and accept the compliments of her friends on their looks and accomplishments, but, like her husband, she has no qualms about deserting her lover when he falls into difficulties.

Sir Oliver Kix and
Lady Kix, a devoted couple who spend much of their time quarreling and making up their disagreements. Their great source of trouble is their unfulfilled desire for a child. They are completely taken in by the scheme of Touchwood Senior, who ensures that an heir to the Kix fortune is conceived.

Touchwood Senior, a poor but prolific gentleman who is forced to separate from his wife to limit the size of their ever-increasing brood. His good services for Sir Oliver and Lady Kix enable him to

171

be reunited with his family, for Sir Oliver promises to support them.

Mistress Touchwood, his wife, who obligingly agrees to live apart from him, in spite of her fondness for her husband.

A Country Girl, the mother of one of Touchwood's many children.

Touchwood Junior, Moll's husband-to-be, a brother of the older Touchwood. He plans his elopement and thoroughly enjoys having his bride's father make the ring with which his daughter intends to deceive him. After his marriage plans have been twice thwarted he is severely wounded by Sir Walter in a duel and writes to Moll as if he were dying. He is, however, miraculously revived, and, at the third try, his wedding takes place, much to the delight of all concerned.

Davy Dahanna, Sir Walter's servant, a "poor relation" from Wales.

Susan, Moll's maid, who plans the counterfeit death and marriage of her mistress and Touchwood Junior.

A Welsh Girl, Sir Walter's mistress, who becomes Timothy's bride. She counters her husband's philosophy with her own wit, arguing that her past is blotted out; her marriage makes her honest.

CHÉRI

Author: Colette (Sidonie Gabrielle Claudine Colette, 1873-1954)
Time of action: c. 1910
First published: 1910

PRINCIPAL CHARACTERS

Fred Peloux (frĕd' pə·lōō'), called **Chéri** (shā·rē'), a handsome, moody young man. To remove him from his dissipated life in Paris, he has been taken, in late adolescence, to Normandy by a friend of his mother, Léa de Lonval, an aging but still beautiful courtesan. He and Léa become lovers. After his marriage to Edmée, he still wants Léa, who loves him, but he finally realizes that his only course is to return to his family.

Léonie Vallon (lā·ô·nē' và·lōn'), called **Léa de Lonval** (lā·à də lōn·vàl'), a passionate, aging, and still beautiful courtesan who is in love with and the mistress of young Chéri. When her lover is unable to assume the responsibilities of marriage, she realizes that her pampering has caused him to remain a child. Suffering from the loss of a "great love," she flees from Paris to return a year later much aged but still in love with Chéri, who fancies himself still in love with her. Inevitably, as she has known it would be from the beginning, their fate is to part, and she is left alone.

Madame Peloux (pə·lōō'), Chéri's miserly, gossipy, and inquisitive mother.

Edmée (ĕd·mā'), Chéri's wife. Miserable in her marriage with the erratic, heartless Chéri and convinced of his love for Léa, she suggests divorce. Her suggestion is rejected by her husband as no real solution to the problem. Chéri returns to her when he realizes that he must part from Léa.

Marie-Laure (mà·rē' lōr'), Edmée's elegant mother.

172

THE CHERRY ORCHARD

Author: Anton Chekhov (1860-1904)
Time of action: Early twentieth century
First presented: 1904

PRINCIPAL CHARACTERS

Madame Lubov Andreyevna Ranevskaya (lū·bōf' än·dre'ĕv·nə rä·nĕf'skä·yä), a middle-aged woman and the owner of a large estate which has become impossible to maintain because of debts. Madame Ranevskaya is a remnant of the old order of Russian feudal aristocracy being pushed aside by social change. Her estate, her mansion, and especially the cherry orchard exist for her as symbols of her past, her innocent youth, her carefree life. She cannot reconcile herself to giving them up; she cannot change with the times; she cannot assume the financial and emotional responsibility demanded of her. The forces that molded her are disappearing from Russian life.

Anya (än'yä), Madame Ranevskaya's seventeen-year-old daughter. Although she loves the estate and the cherry orchard, her youth makes it possible for her to bend with the social tide. She reconciles herself to loss and change, to a new Russia of which she will be a part. Her love for Peter Trofimov, a student representative of the intellectual liberal in the new order, influences her to confidence and hope for the future.

Varya (vä'ryä), the adopted daughter of Madame Ranevskaya. Having managed the estate for years, she is exhausted by concern for debts, for the servants, for the future. Her efforts have come to nothing. In love with Lopakhin, a wealthy merchant who is so busy making money that he cannot bring himself to propose to her, Varya's illusions of happiness and peace tempt her to run away in order to enter a convent. Neither of the aristocracy nor of the rising middle class, but caught between both, she finds

that only work can ease her frustration and unhappiness.

Leonid Andreyevitch Gaev (lĕ·ô·nĭd' än·dre'yĕ·vich gä·ef'), Madame Ranevskaya's brother, a restless, garrulous, impractical dreamer. Bound to the old ways, he tries vainly to save the estate by borrowing or begging the necessary money. Like his sister, he is unwilling to sell off the cherry orchard for a housing subdivision. Until the last, he cherishes his illusions that they will be saved by a stroke of good fortune.

Ermolai Alexeyevitch Lopakhin (ĕr·mô·lī' ä·lĕk·sĕ'yĕ·vich lô·pä'khĭn), a wealthy merchant whose father was a peasant. Without sentiment for the past, he lives in the present and for commercial opportunism, except that he redeems the past, literally, when he buys the Ranevsky estate, where his father and grandfather had been serfs. His feelings are calculated in terms of profit and loss; his love for Varya cannot compete with his commercial zeal.

Peter Sergeyevitch Trofimov (pyō'tr sĕr·gĕ'yĕ·vich trô·fī'məf), an idealistic young student willing to work for the future betterment of mankind. He claims his mission is freedom and happiness, escape from the petty and deceptive elements of life. His love for Anya is confused with social zeal, and his understanding of people is slight.

Boris Borisovitch Simeonov-Pishchik (bô·rĭs' bô·rĭs'ə·vich sĭ·mĕ'ən·əf pĭ'·shchik), a landowner constantly in debt, always trying to borrow money. Unlike the Ranevskys, he has no feeling for the land or his heritage; he eventually

173

leases his land to be torn up for the valuable deposits of clay.

Charlotta Ivanova (shär·lōt′tə ĭ·vä′nə·və), governess to the Ranevskys, a young woman who does not know her parentage. She is classless, ready to be swept by any tide.

Simeon Panteleyevitch Epikhodov (sĕ-myōn′ pän·tĕ·lĕ′yĕ·vich ĕ·pĭ·khōd′əf), a clerk in the Ranevsky household, in love with Dunyasha, a maid, who does not return his love.

Dunyasha (dōō·nyä′shə), in love with the brash young footman, Yasha. She dresses well, pretends to be a lady.

Fiers (fĭrs), an old footman, faithful to the Ranevsky family for generations. Concerned only with the well-being of his employers, he is inadvertently left to die in the abandoned house, a symbol of the dying past.

Yasha (yä′shə), an insolent young footman, Fiers' grandson. Caring nothing for his family, Yasha thrives on cruelty and opportunism. He knowingly leaves his grandfather to die alone.

THE CHEVALIER OF THE MAISON ROUGE

Author: Alexandre Dumas, *père* (1802-1870)
Time of action: 1793
First published: 1846

PRINCIPAL CHARACTERS

Maurice Lindey (mō·rēs′ lăn·dā′), a lieutenant in the Civil Guard of France. He rescues a beautiful, unknown woman from a group of drunken volunteers and falls in love with her before she vanishes into the night. Searching for her, he falls into the hands of a group of loyalists disguised as tanners and learns the identity of his beloved. She is Geneviève Dixmer. Maurice is used by the loyalist tanners to further their plot to rescue Marie Antoinette, and, finally, along with Geneviève and Louis Lorin, he dies on the scaffold.

Geneviève Dixmer (zhən·vyĕv′ dĕks-mĕr′), a beautiful aristocrat and loyalist conspirator loved by Maurice Lindey. Arrested as a suspect in the futile attempts to rescue Marie Antoinette, she dies with Maurice on the scaffold.

Monsieur Dixmer (dĕks·mĕr′), the husband of Geneviève Dixmer and manager of a tannery business used as a front for loyalist activities. He is killed by Maurice during a quarrel.

Morand (mō·rän′), the Chevalier of the Maison Rouge. He is Monsieur Dixmer's business partner in the tannery, which is used as a cover for Morand's real identity as the Chevalier of the Maison Rouge. He is dedicated to the rescue of Marie Antoinette.

Louis Lorin (lwē′ lô·rän′), the faithful friend of Maurice Lindey, with whom he dies on the scaffold as a loyalist suspect.

Héloïse Tison (ā·lô·ēz′ tē·zôn′), a young girl who is executed for her aid to the loyalist conspirators.

Simon (sē·môn′), a shoemaker and the cruel guardian of the Dauphin.

Marie Antoinette (mȧ·rē′ än·twȧ·nĕt′), Queen of France.

CHILDREN OF GOD

Author: Vardis Fisher (1895-   )
Time of action: 1820-1890
First published: 1939

PRINCIPAL CHARACTERS

Joseph Smith, a visionary and mystic, founder of the Church of Latter-day Saints; a poor, handsome, humorless giant who believes himself a prophet of God and who reports the finding of some golden plates which he translates into a bible for his followers. Persecuted in New York, Ohio, and Missouri, he is finally killed by a mob in Illinois.

Brigham Young, the strong, able leader of the Church after Smith's death. Unsentimental, hardheaded, and unceasingly devoted to the Church, he leads his saints to Utah and becomes governor until the territory is made a state. After withstanding many onslaughts he dies just before being tried for his reputed crimes.

John Taylor, leader of the Church after Young's death.

Oliver Cowdery, a schoolteacher, Joseph's first convert, who records Joseph's dictated translation of the Book of Mormon and later becomes a missionary to the Indians.

Heber Kimball, Brigham's close friend and one of his chief aides. He dies of pneumonia after falling from a carriage.

Emma Hale Smith, Joseph's first wife who complains, among many other things, of Joseph's many wives.

Newel Knight, a convert who introduces Joseph to conditions among his Ohio followers.

Ulysses S. Grant, disgusted President of the United States, who plans to wipe out the Mormon empire.

Bill Hickman, an adventurous former Methodist who becomes a volunteer avenger, scout, and Indian fighter for the Mormons until he finally sours on Mormonism.

Sidney Rigdon, an unpredictable, strong-voiced prophet who, after Joseph's death, is ambitious to head the Church; excommunicated by the Twelve.

John Bennett, a handsome, sensual adventurer and jack-of-all-trades attracted to Mormonism by Joseph's plural marriage policy.

Jedediah Grant, a zealous preacher, the firebrand of the Church who pleads with Brigham for a casting out of the sinners.

Moroni and
Nephi McBride, grandfather and grandson, leaders of a group of dissident Mormons who leave Salt Lake City after the abolition of plural marriages.

Alfred Cumming, enormously fat United States governor of Utah.

Horace Greeley,
Artemus Ward, and
Richard Burton, three visitors to Salt Lake City who later write about the Mormons and their activities.

Wilford Woodruff, Mormon leader after John Taylor. He abolishes plural marriages in an attempt to save the Church from destruction.

The Whitmers, a family of early converts.

[**Moroni**, an angel who tells Joseph where to find the golden plates and commands him to translate them.]

175

THE CHILDREN OF HERACLES

Author: Euripides (c. 485-c. 406 B.C.)
Time of action: The age of legend
First presented: c. 430 B.C.

PRINCIPAL CHARACTERS

Iolaus (ī·ō·lā'ŭs), an aged warrior, the former companion and friend of Heracles and the guardian of Heracles' children in their attempt to escape the efforts of Eurystheus, King of Argos, to destroy them. At the opening of the play, after long wandering, Iolaus has sought refuge with the children before the altar of the temple of Zeus at Marathon. He pleads successfully for their sanctuary before Demophon, King of Athens, against the arguments of Copreus, the messenger of Eurystheus. The protection offered by the Athenians means inevitable attack from Eurystheus, and the oracles tell Demophon that for him to be victorious a maiden of a noble house must be sacrificed to Persephone. As Demophon will not offer up his own child and cannot expect any other citizen to do so, Iolaus offers to give himself up to Eurystheus if the children can be saved. Though made in vain, the suggestion is sincere. The question is resolved by the sacrifice of Macaria, a daughter of Heracles. When a messenger appears with news of the preparation for battle with the Argive host, Iolaus, whose feebleness has been repeatedly emphasized, suddenly insists that he go with him, and he is led off, stumbling in his weakness. In the course of the battle, however, he is rejuvenated temporarily by special gift of the gods and, with the help of Hyllus, a son of Heracles, he captures Eurystheus. Iolaus' character is strangely uneven and he does not develop into the great and tragic figure he might easily have been.

Demophon (dē'mə·phŏn), the son of Theseus and King of Athens. A personification of the spirit of Athens, he exhibits all the qualities attributed to the

city, for he is noble, brave, dignified, and kind. He offers sanctuary to the children not only because he is a kinsman to Heracles, but also because his city is free. He is democratic as a ruler; he will not compel the sacrifice of any citizen and is careful to accept that of Macaria only after she has indignantly rejected any substitution.

Alcmene (ălk·mē'nē), the mother of Heracles. She appears late in the play when she mistakes a messenger, bringing news of the arrival of Hyllus, for an Argive and repels him furiously. She earnestly begs Iolaus not to go into battle; however, when Eurystheus is brought captive before her, the violence of her character is given full play. Although the chorus forbids the murder of a prisoner, she thirsts for the death of her enemy and offers to take the blood-guilt upon herself. She has her way after agreeing to surrender the body to his friends after death. The scene is abrupt and horrible because the reader has not been made to feel the suffering which would lead Alcmene to such violence.

Eurystheus (ū·rĕs'thūs), King of Argos and Mycenae. Though spoken of throughout the play, he appears only at the end and then is not villain enough to fit the impression that has been built up. He has been spoken of as proud, a bully, and a coward; but he is calm, dignified, and brave before Alcmene and the threat of death. Refusing to plead for his life, he assures the Athenians that because they tried to save him, his spirit will help them against the descendants of the children of Heracles who will later invade Attica.

176

Macaria (mə·kär′ē·ə), the daughter of Heracles who gives her life as a sacrifice for the safety of her brothers and sisters. She has pride of blood but is nonetheless restrained and modest. She is the ideal type of the young virgin.

Copreus (kŏp′rē·ŭs), the herald of Eurystheus. He attempts to drag the children from the temple of Zeus and attacks Iolaus. Because he is a messenger of Eurystheus, his action accounts largely for the impression of insolent pride which the chorus has of the King.

Children of Heracles. Though silent, they are on the stage from beginning to end and the play is named for them.

CHILDREN OF THE GHETTO

Author: Israel Zangwill (1864-1926)
Time of action: Nineteenth century
First published: 1892

PRINCIPAL CHARACTERS

Esther Ansell, a poor Jewish girl adopted and educated by a rich woman. Esther, sensitive and very intelligent, graduates from London University. She writes a novel of Jewish life entitled "Mordecai Josephs." A shy girl, she hides behind the pen name, Edward Armitage. Despite her success Esther returns to the ghetto. Later she migrates to New York, drawn by her love for her family, who are already in the United States.

Mrs. Henry Goldsmith, a wealthy Jewess who adopts Esther Ansell and educates her, even sending Esther's family to America to free the girl from ghetto life. Mrs. Goldsmith is a woman who likes intellectuals and is generous to them.

Moses Ansell, a pious, orthodox, unworldly Jew. He is Esther's father. He spends too much time praying and too little time earning a living.

Benjamin Ansell, Esther's young brother, who is placed in an orphanage at his mother's death.

Becky Belcovitch, a kindly neighbor of the Ansells in the ghetto.

Malka Birnbaum, cousin of Moses Ansell's dead wife. She tries to help her cousin's family.

Sam Levine, a commercial traveler who through ignorance of the ancient Jewish traditions marries the wrong girl.

Leah Birnbaum, loved by Sam Levine. She gives up her beloved because he is not an orthodox Jew.

Hannah Jacobs, Sam Levine's accidental and temporary wife. She loves David Brandon, who has left the orthodox customs of his people.

David Brandon, Hannah's suitor, whom she loves but finally rejects because of his unorthodxy.

Reb Shemuel Jacobs, Hannah's indulgent father. He is a rabbi.

Melchitsekek Pinchas, a young, poor Jewish poet and scholar. He becomes editor of a newspaper sponsored by the Goldsmiths.

Raphael Leon, a young journalist of strong moral principles. He loves Esther Ansell and promises to follow her to America.

Sugarman, a marriage broker in the London ghetto.

Wolf, a Jewish labor leader who wants to be sent to Parliament.

Shosshi Shmendrik, a street hawker who marries for money.

177

Widow Finkelstein, a storekeeper who marries Shosshi.

Bear Belcovitch, a neighbor of Moses Ansell. He wants his daughter to marry Shosshi Shmendrik.

Debby, a poor young seamstress, Esther Ansell's friend.

Leonard James, Hannah Jacob's brother. He is a snobbish, vulgar young Jew who deserts his name and religion.

Rabbi Joseph Strelitski, a clergyman at a fashionable synagogue in London. He sees himself as a hypocrite and leaves his church to start a new life in New York.

CHITA

Author: Lafcadio Hearn (1850-1904)
Time of action: Nineteenth century
First published: 1889

PRINCIPAL CHARACTERS

Chita, a child rescued from the sea during a storm off the Louisiana coast. She is so young that all she can tell her rescuers on Last Island is that her real name is Lili, her Creole name is Zouzoune, and her mother and father are named Adele and Julien. Called by her new friends Chita, the little girl grows up on the island without knowing any more of her earlier existence.

Dr. Julien La Brierre, a physician from New Orleans who comes to see a patient on Last Island. He falls ill himself, and in his delirium he is reminded of his dead wife by Chita's startling resemblance to the drowned woman. He dies without realizing that the girl is really his daughter.

Feliu Viosca, a fisherman who lives on Last Island. He rescues Chita from the sea and takes her into his home.

Carmen Viosca, the fisherman's wife.

She treats the foundling from the sea as though she were her own child.

Laroussel, a Creole who was Dr. La Brierre's rival for his dead wife's hand years before. At one time the doctor and Laroussel fought a duel over Adele, who became the doctor's wife. He questions Chita on Viosca's island and gives her a trinket but does not discover that she is Dr. La Brierre's child.

Captain Harris, a sea captain who checks for survivors after the storm. He decides it is best for Chita to remain with the fisherman and his wife who have given the girl a home.

Captain Abraham Smith, a sea captain who tries to rescue as many people as he can from the hurricane.

Mr. Edwards, the patient whose illness summons Dr. La Brierre to Last Island.

THE CHOUANS

Author: Honoré de Balzac (1799-1850)
Time of action: 1799
First published: 1829

PRINCIPAL CHARACTERS

The Marquis de Montauran (mȯṅ·tō-räṅ'), fiery leader of the Chouans, rebels against the French Republic. His nickname is **Gars,** and he is the son of Mme.

178

du Gua. He loves Marie de Verneuil, although he is warned that she is a spy. He goes to her home to marry her after she herself has told him she has been hired to betray him. The morning after the marriage he is shot, captured, and later dies in prison, after he tries to escape from her house in Fougères.

Marie de Verneuil (mā·rē′ də vĕr·nœ′yə), in love with Montauran. She is the natural daughter of the Duke de Verneuil and the former wife of Danton. When Montauran's jealous mother tries to shoot her, Marie seeks revenge, but her love eventually conquers her hate. She marries Montauran hoping they can escape from intrigues and leave France. Her plans fail, and she is shot wearing her husband's uniform while acting as a decoy to help him escape.

Hulot (ü·lō′), an officer in the French Republican Army, sent to put down the rebellious Chouans, an aggregation of aristocrats, smugglers, and Breton peasants. He is utterly disgusted by the cap-

ture and death of Montauran and Marie de Verneuil.

Mme. du Gua Saint-Cyr (dü gwä′ săn′-sēr′), jealous mother of Montauran. She knows of her son's rebellious activities and supports him in them. When she discovers Marie's love for her son, she tries to shoot Marie with a rifle as her son looks on.

Corentin (kô·rän·tän′), a spy for the French Republic. It is he who employs Marie as a lure to trap Montauran and bring the Chouan leader to his death.

Francine (frän·sēn′), former sweetheart of Marche-à-Terre. She is Marie's maid.

Marche-à-Terre (mär-shä-tĕr′), one of the rebellious Chouans. A fierce and rapacious villain, he leads the rebels in forays of thievery and violence.

Galpe-Chopine (gälp′-shô·pēn′), a peasant who helps Marie in many ways.

Barbette (bär·bĕt′), the wife of Galpe-Chopine.

A CHRISTMAS CAROL

Author: Charles Dickens (1812-1870)
Time of action: Nineteenth century
First published: 1843

PRINCIPAL CHARACTERS

Ebenezer Scrooge, a grasping, covetous, flinty old pinchpenny. With his pointed nose, shriveled cheeks, and stiff gait, he is repulsive to all his acquaintances. Drop by drop he has squeezed all vestiges of humanity from his shriveled soul.

Bob Cratchit, Scrooge's destitute clerk. Although overworked and underpaid by Scrooge, Cratchit still retains his goodness and generosity.

Tiny Tim, Bob Cratchit's youngest son. Tiny Tim, crippled and frail, seems doomed to an early death unless there are improvements in the family fortunes.

Weak in body but not in spirit, he does not die; instead he lives to enjoy the generosity of a regenerated Ebenezer Scrooge.

The Ghost of Christmas Past. With a strong beam of light streaming from his head, this is the first of three phantoms who are to attempt the difficult task of converting Scrooge.

The Ghost of Christmas Present. A huge, jolly figure, this specter, bearing a glowing torch, takes Scrooge to many homes, among them Bob Cratchit's.

The Ghost of Christmas Yet to Come. This is the most fearful sight of all. Shrouded in black, this ghost conducts Scrooge to many cheerless scenes, including a view of his own neglected grave.

Jacob Marley's Ghost. The specter of Scrooge's former business partner. In life he had been just as ruthless as Ebenezer; in death he is compelled to wander far and wide, searching for spiritual salvation.

Fred, Scrooge's jovial nephew.

THE CID

Author: Pierre Corneille (1606-1684)
Time of action: Eleventh century
First presented: 1636

PRINCIPAL CHARACTERS

Don Rodrigue (rô·drēg′), the Cid, son of aged Don Diègue. As his father's champion, he kills Don Gomès, mightiest swordsman of Castile. It appears he may eventually marry Chimène.

Don Diègue (dyĕg′), once Spain's greatest warrior.

Chimène (shē·mĕn′), the daughter of the slain Don Gomès, who demands Rodrigue's death in punishment. Later, when he determines to let Sanche kill him, she begs Rodrigue to defend himself.

Don Gomès (gô·mĕs′), the father of

Chimène, who quarrels with Diègue over tutoring the King's son and is slain by Rodrigue.

Don Fernand (fĕr·nän′), King of Castile, who names Rodrigue "The Cid" (Lord) after his victory over the Moors in Seville.

Don Sanche (sänsh), a suitor of Chimène who challenges Rodrigue to avenge Gomès' death. The Cid magnanimously spares his life.

Doña Urraque (ü·räk′), the daughter of Fernand, who loves Rodrigue but yields to Chimène's prior claims.

CINNA

Author: Pierre Corneille (1606-1684)
Time of action: c. A.D. 10
First presented: c. 1640

PRINCIPAL CHARACTERS

Cinna (sĭ′nə), the grandson of Pompey. In love with Amelia, he seeks to win her hand by avenging her father's death through the murder of the Emperor Augustus, whom he regards as a tyrant. He is finally led to remorse for his evil intentions by the Emperor's display of forgiveness, mercy, and generosity.

Amelia (ə·mē′lĭ·ə), who is loved by Cinna. She asks, as a provision of their

marriage, that he avenge her father by murdering the Emperor Augustus. Long remorseless in her demands for revenge, she is finally won by the Emperor's nobility and clemency, takes blame for the plot on herself, and gives her friendship to Augustus.

Augustus (ô·gŭs′təs), Emperor of Rome. Discovering, among those he loves and trusts, a plot to take his life, the Em-

180

peror, through his mercy and forgiveness, causes remorse among the conspirators and wins their admiration and friendship.

Livia (lǐ'vǐ·ə), Empress of Rome. She commends her husband's generosity and mercy to all future rulers.

Maximus (măk'sǐ·məs), Cinna's friend and fellow conspirator.

Fulvia (fŏŏl'vǐ·ə), Amelia's friend and confidante.

Evander (ĕ·văn'dẽr), Cinna's freedman.

Euphorbus (ū·fôr'bəs), Maximus' freedman and fellow conspirator.

Polyclitus (pŏl·ĭ·klī'təs), Augustus' freedman.

CINQ-MARS

Author: Alfred Victor de Vigny (1797-1863)
Time of action: Seventeenth century
First published: 1826

PRINCIPAL CHARACTERS

Henri d'Effiat (äṅ·rē' dĕf·fyä'), Marquis of Cinq-Mars (săṅk-màrs'), a real-life character in France's first historical novel. He serves the King through hatred of Richelieu and desire for permission to marry Marie de Gonzaga. As a conspirator he signs a secret treaty providing for help from Spain, then tells Marie about it in the presence of the spy-priest who affiances them. He is beheaded.

Cardinal Richelieu (kar·dē·nàl' rē·shə·lyœ'), who, to maintain power with the King, has the messenger with Cinq-Mars' treaty killed at the Spanish frontier. He resigns as Minister of State in order to force the helpless King Louis XIII to increase his power.

King Louis XIII (lwē' trĕz'), who makes Cinq-Mars an officer in his guards. After Richelieu's resignation he is unable to handle the affairs of the kingdom alone and he reappoints Richelieu, giving him permission to kill the conspirators.

Marie de Gonzaga (mà·rē' də gôṅ·zà'·gə), Duchess of Mantua, who loves Cinq-Mars, though she is destined to become Queen of Poland.

Anne of Austria, who tries to protect the King and their son, the future Louis XIV, from the ambitious Richelieu.

François August de Thou (frän·swà' ō·güst' də tōō'), a friend of Cinq-Mars, beheaded as a conspirator.

The Duke de Bouillon (də bōō·yôṅ'), estranged from the King by Richelieu.

Gaston d'Orléans (gàs·tôṅ' dôr·lä·äṅ'), brother of the King, banished by Richelieu.

Marshal Bassompierre (bà·sôṅ·pyĕr'), an enemy of Richelieu arrested at the home of Cinq-Mars in Touraine in 1639.

Urbain Grandier (ür·băṅ' grän·dyä'), a monk of Loudun, executed as a magician by order of Richelieu.

The Abbé Quillet (à·bā' kē·yā'), Cinq-Mars' former tutor, who defends Grandier.

A Judge, Richelieu's agent at the trial of Grandier. Cinq-Mars strikes him in the face with a red-hot cross that had been given to Grandier to kiss.

THE CIRCLE OF CHALK

Author: Unknown; sometimes attributed to Li Hsing-Tao (n.d.)
Time of action: Before the thirteenth century
First presented: Thirteenth or fourteenth century

PRINCIPAL CHARACTERS

Chang-hi-tang, a beautiful sixteen-year-old girl who has been sold to a house of ill repute in order to keep her family from starving. Immediately befriended by a wealthy man, the delicate and talented young girl is brought as second wife into a childless household. Her sweet demeanor as well as her ability to bring forth a son causes the first wife to vow revenge. Hi-tang, above reproach, follows her mentor's directions in all things, even to serving the tea with which the elder wife poisons her husband. Hi-tang is accused of the murder by the elder wife, who also claims that Hi-tang's son is really her own. The wise Emperor devises a test. He orders the child placed in a chalk circle, from which each wife may try to pull the child and claim him. Because of her true mother love, Hi-tang refuses to try pulling her son away from the other woman across a chalk circle, for fear of hurting him. She thus proves her innocence. She is made Empress when it is revealed that the new Emperor is the true father of her child. Hi-tang had always thought that the Prince had come to her only in a dream.

Ma Chun-shing, the duped husband whose first wife is unfaithful and treacherous while his second is always loving and trustworthy. He elevates in his heart the beautiful young wife and thereby brings down the wrath of the barren Mrs. Ma. On one occasion, the victim of jealousy, he believes his young wife has given away jewels and robes to a lover but he discovers that the man is her unfortunate brother. When Mr. Ma considers divorcing his first wife in order that he may elevate Hi-tang to the position of first wife, Mrs. Ma poisons him.

Mrs. Ma, the vindictive first wife of Ma Chun-shing, who claims Hi-tang's son as her own and contrives with a lover to poison her generous husband. Unable to find fault or complain against the model second wife for many years, a plot of revenge finally reaches fruition. With bribery and mendacity, the evil woman wins the trial, has Hi-tang imprisoned, and thus keeps the young son and the fortune of the family. When she is called to a high tribunal by the new Emperor, her evil deeds are revealed and her fate is sealed.

Chang-ling, Hi-tang's brother, a young scholar embittered by the duplicity and oppression of the government's representatives. Arrested for expressing doubts that the new Emperor will improve the lot of the common people, he is taken before the same high tribunal as his sister. The new Emperor is in sympathy with his ideas of reform, however, and he is not only pardoned but also made a judge in place of the evil Chu-chu.

Chow, the lover and accomplice of Mrs. Ma, a clerk in the local court. This despicable man cruelly watches virtue suffer and vice triumph as he carries on him the poison his mistress finally asks of him. Calculating and brutal, he conspires to rig the trial and bribe witnesses until he at last is brought to justice.

Chu-chu, a judge of the local court who accepts a bribe to find Mrs. Ma innocent and Hi-tang guilty. He sentences Hi-tang to death, but before the sentence is carried out, all involved are called before the new Emperor for an investigation. Chu-chu's decision is then overruled and he loses his judgeship to Chang-ling.

182

Prince Po, one of the old Emperor's sons and later the new Emperor. As a dashing young Prince he had fallen in love with Hi-tang and on her wedding night he had stolen through her window and made love to her as she slept. Thus, her child is actually his, not Mr. Ma's. When Hi-tang is brought before him he recognizes her, and after learning the truth in the case he metes out justice to the evildoers and makes Hi-tang Empress.

CLARISSA HARLOWE

Author: Samuel Richardson (1689-1761)
Time of action: Early eighteenth century
First published: 1747-1748

PRINCIPAL CHARACTERS

Mr. Harlowe, a domineering man who cannot understand how his children can disobey him. He arranges a loveless marriage for his daughter Clarissa. When she refuses to obey his commands, he locks her in her room with only an insolent servant allowed to see her. After her elopement with Robert Lovelace, another suitor, her father disowns her and will not let her have clothes or money. Not until she is dying does he lift his ban and seek a reconciliation.

Clarissa Harlowe, his young and beautiful daughter, who accepts Lovelace's attentions as a way of escaping from her father's demands. Thinking that he is taking her to the home of Lord M—, his kinsman, she flees with Lovelace, only to be put into a house of ill repute where, for fear of being tracked down by her father, she claims to be Lovelace's wife. Once she escapes, only to be dragged back, drugged, and raped. Escaping again, she is caught and jailed for debt. She is freed but goes into a physical decline and buys her casket, inscribed with her death date, the day she left the Harlowe home. Though the repentant Lovelace now wants to marry her, she refuses him. Despite letters from her contrite family—for the whole novel is told in letters—she dies, to the grief and remorse of all.

Arabella, the older Harlowe daughter.

She hates Clarissa for attracting her own suitor, Robert Lovelace.

James Harlowe, Clarissa's older brother, selfish and domineering, like his father. Having known and disliked Lovelace at Oxford University, he starts rumors that Lovelace is a profligate. He is also jealous of Clarissa because she is the heiress of their wealthy grandfather.

Robert Lovelace, a young Englishman of noble family. Brought by an uncle to the Harlowe home as suitor of Arabella, he falls in love with Clarissa. Because of his choice he is spurned by the whole family. In revenge for their insults, he determines to seduce Clarissa and gets her to run away with him under promises of marriage, only to break his word. Finally, when he discovers he really loves her, he vainly offers her marriage. After her death he goes to France, where he fights a duel by Clarissa's cousin, Colonel Morden, and is killed. He dies repentant of his crimes.

John Belford, a friend of Lovelace, who frees Clarissa from jail by proving that the charges of debt against her are false. He receives from Lovelace letters that narrate the course of his courtship and his perfidy.

Roger Solmes, a rich, elderly, but uncouth man chosen as Clarissa's husband by her father. When Clarissa writes him,

183

begging him to end their relationship, he refuses.

Mrs. Sinclair, the keeper of the London bawdy house where Clarissa is kept prisoner.

Colonel William Morden, Clarissa's cousin, who tries first to reconcile Clarissa and her family and then to persuade her to marry Lovelace. He finally avenges her death when he kills Lovelace in a duel fought in France.

Miss Anna Howe, the friend and confidante of Clarissa; through their interchange of letters most of the story is told.

Aunt Hervey, who wants Lovelace to marry Arabella.

Uncle Harlowe, who brings Lovelace to the house.

Mr. Mennell, who manages the affairs of Mrs. Fretchville and wants to rent her apartment to Clarissa.

Hannah, Clarissa's faithful servant.

Mr. Diggs, the surgeon who looks after James Harlowe's wound after he and Lovelace duel.

Elizabeth Lawrence, Lovelace's aunt, who wants to meet his "wife."

Charlotte Montague, a cousin of Lovelace.

Dorcas Martindale, who tries to help Clarissa escape.

F. J. de la Tour, who writes the final letter describing the duel and death of the Chevalier Lovelace.

CLAUDIUS THE GOD

Author: Robert Graves (1895-   )
Time of action: A.D. 41-54
First published: 1934

PRINCIPAL CHARACTERS

Tiberius Claudius Drusus Nero Germanicus (tĭ·bĭ′rĭ·əs klô′dĭ·əs drōō′səs nē̌′rō jėr·mă′nĭ·kəs), Emperor of Rome; popularly supposed at the beginning of his rule to be a cripple, a stammerer, and an idiot; in reality a planner of governmental, financial, and social reforms, including abolition of many of Caligula's cruel decrees. Busy with state affairs, he is long ignorant of Messalina's depravities. He is deified as a result of his planning of the great Roman victory in Britain at Brentwood Hill. After a wholesale execution of Messalina's immoral associates and following his marriage to Agrippinilla, he takes little interest in governmental affairs and is finally poisoned by his wife.

Messalina (mĕ·sə·lī′nə), his third wife.

Though Director of Public Morals, she herself pursues a life of debauchery, licentiousness, political intrigue, bribery, cheating, and murder. After her divorce from Claudius, her remarriage to Silius, and Claudius' discovery of her debaucheries, she is killed by the colonel of the palace guard.

Calpurnia (kăl·pûr′nĭ·ə), Claudius' mistress, who finally reveals to Claudius the truth about Messalina.

Agrippina (ăg′rĭ·pī′nə), called **Agrippinilla**, Claudius' fourth wife, whom he marries for political reasons. She poisons him so that Nero may succeed him. She is killed by soldiers sent by Nero to murder her.

Lucius Domitius (lōō′shĭ·əs dō·mĭ′-

184

shĭ·əs), later called **Nero,** Agrippinilla's son and Claudius' grandnephew. Adopted by Claudius and appointed joint heir with Brittanicus, he becomes Emperor through his mother's plotting. After a reign marked by debauchery and murder he is killed at his own request by a servant.

Herod Agrippa (hĕ'rəd ə·grĭ'pə), Claudius' friend since his youthful days; imprisoned by Tiberius for treasonous sentiments but released by Caligula and made Tetrarch of Bashan; given control of Judea, Samaria, and Edom by Claudius. His plan to set up a Jewish kingdom with himself as Messiah collapses with his death.

Brittanicus (brĭ·tă'nĭ·kəs), Claudius' son whom Claudius suspects of having been fathered by Caligula; poisoned in A.D. 55.

Octavia (ŏk·tā'vĭ·ə), Claudius' supposed daughter, believed by Claudius to have been fathered by the Commander of the Germans under Caligula. Married to Nero, she dies violently.

Varus (vâ'rəs), a general who lost an eagle standard in Germany.

Caractacus (kə·răk'tă·kəs) and **Togodumnus** (tō'gə·dŭm'nəs), brothers and joint rulers of Britain. Togodumnus is slain in battle; Caractacus is captured, brought to Rome, and then generously freed by Claudius.

Aulus Plautius (ô'ləs plô'shĭ·əs), leader of Claudius' invasion forces against Britain.

Barbillus (bär·bĭ'ləs), an astrologer who predicts Claudius' death.

Silius (sĭ'lĭ·əs), Messalina's former husband whom she remarries.

Antonia (ăn·tō'nĭ·ə), Claudius' daughter, married to Pompey. After his death she marries Faustus.

Pompey (pŏm'pĭ), a homosexual murdered, by Claudius' orders, in bed with his slave Lycidas.

THE CLAYHANGER TRILOGY

Author: Arnold Bennett (1867-1931)
Time of action: 1872-1895
First published: 1910, 1911, 1915

PRINCIPAL CHARACTERS

Edwin Clayhanger, in 1872 a gawky sixteen-year-old boy about to finish school. His dream of studying architecture is quashed by his father, Darius Clayhanger, a Bursley printer, who forces his son to leave school and begin work in the family print shop. Friendship with an older man, an architect and a student of the arts, comforts Edwin over the years. The association rankles Edwin's father and makes for misunderstanding between father and son. An unrequited love also warps Edwin's already strange bachelorhood. Some of his love is spent on the small son of the unresponding woman,

Hilda Lessways, and he finds gratification in aiding Hilda financially. His own odd circumstances blind Edwin to the fact that he is loved by Janet Orgreave, who would marry him, and whom the entire town expects him to marry. After his father's illness and death, Edwin becomes master in name of the business he has actually conducted for many years. After knowing each other for ten years, he and Hilda Lessways are married and Edwin adopts Hilda's son by George Cannon. Both parties are set in their ways and the marriage is not a smooth one. Hilda interferes with Edwin's busi-

185

ness affairs and tries to dominate his life completely. Edwin's success in the printing business enables him to dabble in politics and eventually to buy a country house which he does not want but which is forced on him by Hilda. At first enraged over her pressure about buying the house, Edwin slowly comes to realize that his marriage means a great deal to him and that by accepting Hilda's domination, he can have peace.

Darius Clayhanger, Edwin's father. He is the proprietor of the Clayhanger printing establishment, a business that grew, haphazardly, faster than the character of its owner. Stern, domineering, and niggardly, he privately admires and respects Edwin. His final illness, softening of the brain, is the more pathetic because of the marked contrast of the senile shell to the commanding character once contained in that shell.

Maggie Clayhanger, Darius' daughter. Four years older than Edwin, she early becomes the old-maid member of the family. She is trapped, partly by volition and partly through necessity, into giving her life to the domestic care of her sick father and bachelor brother. She is adroit in handling her two subjects.

Clara Clayhanger, the youngest of the Clayhanger children. Fair and fragile as a young woman, she becomes the untidy and uninteresting mother of four after her marriage to Albert Benbow.

Hilda Lessways, Edwin Clayhanger's love. Though homely, arrogant, and acrimonious, Hilda excites Edwin to make a proposal of marriage. Erratic and unstable, she disappears, to marry George Cannon. Although he knows the story of Hilda's son and her unhappy marriage, Edwin finds himself still in love with her when she returns to Bursley. Some ten years after their first meeting they are married and Edwin adopts young George Edwin Cannon, who actually is illegitimate because his father already had a wife at the time he married

Hilda. The poverty and hardships of her life as Cannon's wife leave their mark on Hilda. As Edwin's wife she is selfish, aggressive, and domineering. She complains bitterly when Edwin's aunt leaves her entire estate to Clara's needy children instead of leaving a share to Edwin, who has no real need of the money. Hilda almost overreaches herself when, by trickery, she forces Edwin into the position of having to buy a country house he does not really want. After an outburst of righteous rage, however, he decides that for all her faults Hilda Lessways is the woman for him.

George Cannon, who marries Hilda and serves two years in prison when his undivorced first wife tracks him down. He leaves Hilda and his small son destitute when he is imprisoned again for a ten-year term on a charge of forgery. Eventually found innocent of the forgery and released from prison, he goes to America on money obtained from Edwin Clayhanger. His repayment of this loan from America is a pleasant surprise to Edwin and is one of the things that helps to re-establish Edwin's faith in human nature.

George Edwin Cannon Clayhanger, the son of George and Hilda, who is adopted by Edwin Clayhanger. His presence is an asset to the family life of Edwin and Hilda, for Edwin is very fond of the boy. He especially enjoys seeing his adopted son turn to architecture, as he himself had wanted to do.

Clara Hamps, the dead Mrs. Clayhanger's widowed sister. In times of indecision and crisis, Aunt Clara Hamps helps manage the Clayhanger household. Her religious pretentions and tedious moralizing are wearying and wearing. Darius turns to her for solace, in his senility.

Mr. Shushion, superintendent of the Sunday school. He symbolizes the miserable might-have-been life of Darius, whom Shushion saved, as a poverty-stricken child, from the workhouse. Through a tragic twist, which haunts Darius' plagued mind, Shushion dies in the workhouse.

Osmond Orgreave, an architect. Edwin's hunger for culture attracts him to the architect. Their friendship makes Edwin's life as a businessman more bearable.

Janet Orgreave, his daughter, the beautiful, brilliant member of the Orgreave family. Because of his love for Hilda, Edwin never realizes that Janet loves him devotedly.

Charlie Orgreave, her brother, nicknamed **The Sunday.** He and Edwin were close friends as schoolmates, but in maturity they, in their different interests, are virtually strangers to each other.

Mrs. Nixon, the Clayhangers' thin, grayhaired, dreamy-eyed housekeeper. Shriveled and deaf by the time of her death, she had been an influential figure in the family's development.

James Yarlett, called **Big James,** the foreman and compositor at the print shop. Devoted to his employer, he is the symbol of the model employee.

Miss Ingamells, another employee. Personable but sexless, she is the indispen-sable woman employee. Her devotion to her career makes her a boon to Darius.

Albert Benbow, Clara Clayhanger's husband. Decent but dull and undistinguished, he is the perfect partner for commonplace Clara.

Enoch Peake, the apoplectic chairman of the Bursley Mutual Burial Club. He represents a phase of the political atmosphere of the times.

Florence Simcox, a pretty dancer at "The Dragon." Her performance and attentions awaken young Edwin's awareness of women.

Mr. Lovatt, the banker who authorizes Edwin to handle the business after Darius becomes ill, an act dealing the last blow to the old man's dominance.

Mr. Ingpen, Edwin Clayhanger's business friend, whose mistress is married to an insane man, a situation Ingpen likes, for it prevents his being trapped into marriage.

Florrie, Hilda's seduced maid.

John Orgreave, the neighbor who aids young George Clayhanger in the study of architecture.

CLIGÉS

Author: Chrétien de Troyes (c. 1150-c. 1190)
Time of action: Sixth century
First transcribed: Before 1164

PRINCIPAL CHARACTERS

Alexander, a Prince of Greece. Ardently desiring knighthood in King Arthur's court, he goes to Britain. After many brave deeds in Arthur's service, he is knighted by the King. He marries Soredamors, and they become the parents of Cligés.

Cligés, the son of Alexander and Soredamors. He fulfills his father's wish that he be knighted by King Arthur. In love with Fenice, he engages, with her, in an elaborate scheme to deceive her husband Alis. On Alis' death, the lovers succeed, as husband and wife, to the throne of Greece.

Soredamors, Alexander's wife and the mother of Cligés. She is the sister of Sir Gawain and the niece of King Arthur.

187

Fenice, Alis' wife. With her lover Cligés, she deceives her husband. On his death she marries Cligés and becomes Empress of Greece.

Alis, Alexander's brother and the regent for Cligés. He breaks his vow never to marry, weds Fenice, and is deceived by her and her lover Cligés, who assumes the throne on his uncle's death.

Thessala, a sorceress whose potions assist Fenice in deceiving her husband.

John, a stonecutter who provides a trysting place for the lovers Cligés and Fenice.

Arthur, King of Britain.

Guinevere, King Arthur's Queen.

Sir Gawain, a knight of the Round Table and Cligés' uncle.

Count Angrès, a traitor to King Arthur.

Sagremore,
Lancelot of the Lake, and
Perceval of Wales, knights of the Round Table who are defeated in tournaments by Cligés.

The Duke of Saxony, a contender for the hand of Fenice.

THE CLOISTER AND THE HEARTH

Author: Charles Reade (1814-1884)
Time of action: Fifteenth century
First published: 1861

PRINCIPAL CHARACTERS

Gerard Eliason, an artist. He goes to Rome, where he becomes a Dominican monk named Brother Clement. Believing his fiancée is dead, he returns to his homeland to find she is alive and has borne him a son. After becoming a parson at Gouda, he lives apart from Margaret, his beloved, but allows her to help him in his religious work.

Elias, Gerard's father, a Dutch cloth and leather merchant. He does not want his artist son to marry Margaret Brandt and has him imprisoned to prevent the suit. However, he is finally reconciled to her.

Katherine, Elias' wife. Like her husband, she does not want her son to marry Margaret.

Margaret Van Eyck, sister of the famous painter Jan. She is Gerard's teacher.

Reicht Heynes, Margaret Van Eyck's servant, who encourages Gerard as an artist.

Peter Brandt, an old man befriended by Gerard.

Margaret Brandt, Peter's daughter. She is betrothed to Gerard and bears him a son. When he returns to Holland as a monk she helps him in his religious work.

Gerard, son of Gerard and Margaret Brandt, who grows up to be Erasmus, the famous scholar.

Ghysbrecht Van Swieten, burgomaster of Gerard's village. He is an evil man who cheats his people and makes life difficult for Gerard and Margaret.

Giles, Gerard's dwarf brother, who helps Gerard escape from prison.

Kate, Gerard's crippled sister, who helps Gerard escape from prison.

Denys, a Burgundian soldier who befriends Gerard on his way to Italy. Denys is a worldly but loyal man. He finds Margaret Brandt and befriends her for Gerard's sake.

Martin, an old retired soldier who procures a pardon for Gerard after the young man's escape from prison.

188

Hans Memling, a messenger who takes false word to Gerard that Margaret has died.

Pietro, a young artist in Rome with whom Gerard works for a time.

Fra Colonna, a classical scholar for whom Gerard works in decorating manuscripts.

Luke Peterson, a suitor for Margaret Brandt's hand in marriage.

THE CLOSED GARDEN

Author: Julian Green (1900-   )
Time of action: 1908
First published: 1927

PRINCIPAL CHARACTERS

Adrienne Mesurat (à·dryĕn′ mə·zü·rä′), a highly impressionable French girl of sixteen. She falls in love with Dr. Maurecourt when he tips his hat to her. Her peculiar actions, including stealing out of the house to watch Maurecourt's house, arouse suspicions in her sister and even the neighbors. After her sister has left home for a hospital, Adrienne accidentally kills her father by knocking him down a flight of stairs. Alone in the world, robbed by Mme. Legras, Adrienne goes mad.

Germaine Mesurat (zhĕr·mĕn′ mə·zü·rä′), Adrienne's older sister, an invalid. She suspects Adrienne of having a lover. When Germaine's father refuses to acknowledge her illness, she leaves for a hospital after taking some of her sister's dower money.

M. Antoine Mesurat (än·twän′ mĕ·zü·rä′), a retired teacher living with his two daughters in the placid little French town of La Tour l'Evêque, leading a

quiet life. He never thinks that his two daughters may be unhappy sharing his tranquil existence. Thinking the girls superior to any proposals they have, he repulses their suitors. He is accidentally killed when Adrienne knocks him down a flight of stairs.

Dr. Denis Maurecourt (də·nē′ mō·rə·kōōr′), a physician. He tips his hat to Adrienne, by that action unknowingly causing her to fall in love with him. When she tells him of her infatuation, he informs her that he is ill and has only a short time to live.

Mme. Legras (lə·grä′), a temporary neighbor to the Mesurats. She is a prying woman who tries to find out if Adrienne has a lover and if M. Mesurat's death was truly accidental. She assumes the role of protectress to Adrienne in order to pry into the girl's life. When she has a chance, she steals all of Adrienne's valuables and disappears.

THE CLOUDS

Author: Aristophanes (c. 488-c. 385 B.C.)
Time of action: Fifth century B.C.
First presented: 423 B.C.

PRINCIPAL CHARACTERS

Strepsiades (strĕp·sī′ə·dēs), an old, plodding, stolid citizen of Athens who is

hounded by creditors and burdened with debts incurred partly through the excesses

189

of his horse-loving son, Phidippides. Resolving to cure his financial troubles, he sends his son to study the new science, taught by Socrates in the Thoughtery, a plan Strepsiades believes will guarantee the confutation of his creditors and the preservation of his fortune. His son refusing to be tutored, Strepsiades resolves to attend the Thoughtery himself, but he proves himself a bumbling pupil, exhausting the patience of Socrates. Strepsiades then convinces his son to sit under Socrates. Socrates calls up the Just and Unjust Discourses to instruct Phidippides. In a violent dialogue, the Unjust Discourse wins and converts Phidippides to a modern position. Upon returning home, Phidippides demonstrates that he has been an apt pupil of the Sophists; he beats his father unmercifully, justifying himself by his new learning. Outraged at Socrates and his disciples, Strepsiades, with the help of a servant, burns down the Thoughtery.

Phidippides (fĭd·dĭp'ə·dēs), the son of Strepsiades, converted from his lethargic, spendthrift ways by the Sophists into a man who discovers the joys of defying established laws. By subtle reasoning, he justifies beating his father and declares that he intends to beat his mother as well.

Socrates (sŏk'rə·tēs), a philosopher and teacher of the new science, owner of the house called Thoughtery. Approached by Strepsiades to teach Strepsiades the new ways, he is found suspended in a basket "contemplating the sun." Socrates, attempting to teach Strepsiades that the clouds are the genii of the universe; invokes them with prayers and praises. The clouds, he says, control human thought,

speech, trickery, roguery, boasting, lies, and sagacity. In this play Aristophanes lampoons the new science, yet in choosing Socrates as a caricature of the new scientist he perverts Socrates' true convictions. Socrates had rejected the natural sciences, had refused to organize a school of philosophy, had rejected the Sophists, never took pay for his teaching, and affected not omniscience, but ignorance.

Disciples of Socrates. They relate to the newly arrived Strepsiades examples of the new science, which Aristophanes ridicules through the examples and through them.

Just Discourse, a defender of the old ways: silence as a rule for children, respect for elders, physical fitness, modesty. He is defeated by Unjust Discourse in the debate.

Unjust Discourse, a critic of the old ways. He celebrates deception, disrespect, slovenliness, immorality, sexual promiscuity. His students become accomplished Sophists.

Pasias (păs·ī'əs) and
Amynias (ə·mĭn·ī'əs), moneylenders who visit Strepsiades to collect their due. The little that Strepsiades learned in the Thoughtery enables him to confute them and drive them away empty-handed.

A Chorus of Clouds. Singing praises to the Sophists for their acumen, they advise Socrates to take advantage of the ignorant and the stupid and extol the power of the clouds over the lives of men. In the parabasis, the Chorus berates the Athenians for having treated Aristophanes' play scornfully and recommends highest awards for the play.

THE COCKTAIL PARTY

Author: T.S. Eliot (1888-   )
Time of action: Mid-twentieth century
First presented: 1949

Edward Chamberlayne, a middle-aged lawyer. Faced with the prospect of having to meet people without the aid of his wife, who has just left him, he discovers that he cares nothing for the young woman with whom he has been having an affair and that he definitely wants his wife to return. Later, after he thinks he has had a nervous breakdown, he sees a psychiatrist and comes to realize and accept the fact that he is a mediocre man who is afraid that he is incapable of really loving anyone. From this point he begins to build a happy life.

Lavinia Chamberlayne, his wife. Having put herself under the care of a psychiatrist, Lavinia is allowed to believe that she has been to a sanitarium and been cured. After she has returned to her husband, the psychiatrist unexpectedly brings them together in a new and revealing relationship. Lavinia finally realizes that she has always been afraid that she is completely unlovable. She, too, can then adjust and build a satisfactory life with Edward.

Julia Shuttlethwaite, a friend of the Chamberlaynes. Although she gives the impression of being a meddlesome old woman with only a few of her wits about her, it is really Julia who contrives to have the Chamberlaynes take the action that they do.

Celia Coplestone, a sensitive young poet. Having fancied herself in love with Edward Chamberlayne, she is somewhat shocked when she realizes what he is really like. She is also led by Julia and Alex to the psychiatrist and finds her purpose in life through him. After a short period of training she enters a religious order and becomes a nurse on an island in the East, where she is killed by the natives.

Peter Quilpe, a shy young man in love with Celia. He also has had an affair with Lavinia. When he realizes that Celia does not care for him he goes to California and makes a success of himself in the film industry.

Alexander (Alex) MacColgie Gibbs, another friend of the Chamberlaynes who, like Julia, gives the impression of being meddlesome. He is also a part of the conspiracy between Julia and the psychiatrist which ultimately straightens out the lives of the Chamberlaynes and Celia.

Sir Henry Harcourt-Reilly, at first known only as an unidentified guest at a cocktail party in the Chamberlaynes' flat. He is later revealed to all as the psychiatrist who helps them to solve their problems. He sets up, with Julia and Alex, the conspiracy involving the Chamberlaynes.

THE COLLEGIANS

Author: Gerald Griffin (1803-1840)
Time of action: Late eighteenth century
First published: 1828

PRINCIPAL CHARACTERS

Hardress Cregan, a wealthy, spirited young man of the upper classes. He lives for sports and a good time. Though a courageous man, he is shy around women. Disdainful of the lower classes, he nevertheless marries Eily O'Connor, a lower-class girl. He is afraid to let his family know of the alliance. He regrets his marriage when he comes to love his cousin, Ann Chute. His servant murders Eily and then Hardress plans to marry Ann, but the servant confesses to his crime, implicates Hardress, and Hardress is sent into exile as a criminal.

Kyrle Daly, a middle-class young man, a friend of Hardress during and after their college days. He loves Ann Chute and marries her after Hardress is exiled.

Eily O'Connor, a ropemaker's daughter, secretly married to Hardress. She is a beautiful girl. When her husband falls in love with Ann Chute, Eily is willing to go to Canada to be out of the way, but she is murdered by her husband's servant.

Ann Chute, a beautiful upper-class girl, Hardress' cousin. She loves Hardress and wants to marry him. After his crime is discovered, however, she marries Kyrle, realizing at last that he is much the better man.

Mrs. Cregan, Hardress' mother. Not knowing her son is already married, she throws him and Ann together and tries to make a match between them.

Danny Mann, Hardress' devoted servant, a cruel hunchback. He kills Eily to get her out of her husband's way. When he confesses his crime to avenge a beating by Hardress, he is found guilty and hanged.

COLOMBA

Author: Prosper Mérimée (1803-1870)
Time of action: Early nineteenth century
First published: 1840

PRINCIPAL CHARACTERS

Colomba della Rebbia, who demands the death of her family's blood enemy, Barricini, for the murder of her father. She considers the evidence of his innocence faked. She vainly tries to rouse her brother to murder him. Later she learns from the broken Barricini that he had indeed faked the proof of his innocence. She feels no sympathy for him in his adversity; instead, she finds satisfaction in the belief that her father's blood is thus avenged.

Lieutenant Orso della Rebbia, of Napoleon's army, Colomba's brother. He refuses to murder Barricini as his sister demands. He is accused of murdering two sons of Barricini, but is cleared when Colonel Nevil testifies that the sons first ambushed Orso. He marries Lydia.

Lawyer Barricini, mayor of the village and the suspected murderer of Orso's father.

Two Sons of Barricini, who ambush Orso but are shot by him.

Colonel Sir Thomas Nevil, an Irish officer who has come to Corsica to hunt. He testifies that Orso's shooting of Barricini's sons was in self-defense.

Lydia Nevil, his daughter, who wants to leave the settlement of crime to the law.

THE COMEDY OF ERRORS

Author: William Shakespeare (1564-1616)
Time of action: First century B.C.
First presented: 1592-1594

Antipholus of Syracuse (ăn·tĭf'ō·lŭs of sĭr'ə·kūs), the son of Aegeon and Aemilia. Separated from his twin brother in his childhood, he meets him again under the most baffling circumstances. Shortly after he and his servant, Dromio of Syracuse, land in Ephesus, the whole series of comic errors begins. Antipholus meets his servant's lost twin brother, who is also bewildered by the ensuing conversation. Thinking this Dromio to be his own servant, Antipholus belabors the mystified man about his pate with great vigor. Finally, at the end, this puzzle is solved when he recognizes that he has found his identical twin.

Antipholus of Ephesus (ĕf'ē·sŭs), the identical twin brother of Antipholus of Syracuse. Equally bewildered by his mishaps, he is disgruntled when his wife locks him out of his house; she is blissfully unaware of the truth—that the man at her house is not her husband. In addition, a purse of money is received by the wrong man. Never having seen his own father, or at least not aware of the relationship, he is even more amazed when the old man calls him son. By this time the entire town believes him to be mad, and he, like his twin, is beginning to think that he is bewitched. It is with great relief that he finally learns the true situation and is reunited with his family.

Dromio of Syracuse (drō'mĭ·ō), the twin brother to Dromio of Ephesus and attendant to Antipholus of Syracuse. He is as much bewildered as his master, who, in the mix-up, belabors both Dromios. To add to his misery, a serving wench takes him for *her* Dromio and makes unwanted advances. Much to his chagrin she is "all o'er embellished with, rubies, carbuncles, sapphires"; also she is "no longer from head to foot than from hip to hip. She is spherical, like a globe. . . ."

Dromio of Ephesus. When the two Antipholuses were separated during a shipwreck, he, too, was separated from his identical twin. As is his brother, he is often belabored by his master. In this case, if his master does not pummel him, his mistress will perform the same office. During all this time he is involved in many cases of mistaken identity. Sent for a piece of rope, he is amazed when his supposed master knows nothing of the transaction.

Aegeon (ē·jē'ŏn), a merchant of Syracuse. Many years before, he had lost his beloved wife and one son. Since then his other son has left home to find his twin brother. Now Aegeon is searching for all his family. Landing in Ephesus, he finds that merchants from Syracuse are not allowed there on penalty of death or payment of a large ransom. When Aegeon is unable to raise the ransom, the Duke gives the old man a one-day reprieve. He finds his sons just in time, the ransom is paid, and the family reunited.

Adriana (ā·drĭ·ā'nə), the wife of Antipholus of Ephesus. When her husband denies his relationship to her, she (unaware he is the wrong man) thinks he is insane. Already suspicious of her husband because of supposed infidelities, she suspects him even more.

Aemilia (ē·mĭl'ĭ·ə), the wife to Aegeon, and abbess at Ephesus. In the recognition scene she finds her husband, who has been separated from her for many years.

Solinus (sō·lī'nŭs), Duke of Ephesus.

Luciana (lōō·shē·ä'nə), Adriana's sister, wooed by Antipholus of Syracuse.

Angelo (ăn'jě·lō), a goldsmith.

Pinch, a schoolmaster and "a hungry lean-fac'd villain, a mere anatomy."

COMRADES

Author: August Strindberg (1849-1912)
Time of action: Late nineteenth century
First presented: 1888

PRINCIPAL CHARACTERS

Axel, an established artist. Married to the feminist, Bertha, he has agreed to live with her not as a husband but as a comrade, each partner with equal rights and freedom to achieve artistic expression in his own way. Finally, disgusted by Bertha's demanding self-assertiveness and conniving, he leaves her for a "womanly woman."

Bertha, an aspiring artist and ardent feminist married to Axel, with whom she lives as a comrade with equal rights. Less gifted than her husband and jealous of his talent, she attempts to assert herself and humiliate him. She finally succeeds in losing him to a more feminine woman.

Dr. Östermark, Axel's friend and the divorced husband of Mrs. Hall.

Mrs. Hall, Dr. Östermark's divorced wife. She seeks the help of the feminist, Bertha, in planning revenge on her former husband.

Abel, Bertha's mannish woman friend. An ardent feminist, Abel is in league with Bertha to humiliate Axel.

Willmer, Bertha's effeminate author friend.

Carl Starck, Axel's happily married friend, an army officer.

COMUS

Author: John Milton (1608-1674)
Time of action: The age of myth
First presented: 1634

PRINCIPAL CHARACTERS

Comus (kō′məs), the sorcerer son of Bacchus and Circe, who transforms men into animals shapes with a magic potion and leads this herd of beasts in nightly revels and rites of Hecate. He captures the Lady and tries to lure her into his control by persuasively and eloquently urging her to emulate the generous, unstinting bounty of nature by permitting the enjoyment of her beauty while she is young.

The Lady, a young noblewoman. Separated from her brothers in a wood, she is frightened by the sounds of Comus' revels, by "beckn'ing shadows dire, and airy tongues that syllable men's names on Sands and Shores and desert Wilder-

nesses"; but she places her trust in Providence and in her own virtue. She counters Comus' plea that she make the most of her beauty while it lasts with her own view of nature as a power which bestows its blessings according to "sober laws and holy dictate of spare Temperance." She finds her strongest defense in "the sublime notion and high mystery that must be utter'd to unfold the sage and serious doctrine of Virginity."

The Elder Brother, her companion, who is, like his sister, convinced of the supernatural power of Virtue and Wisdom as defenses against all evils. Explaining his inclination to be hopeful, rather than afraid, after the Lady's disappearance, he

194

speaks rhapsodically of the divine nature of Chastity, which purifies the mind and brings it to the refined state of the immortal soul. He is ready for action as well as philosophy, and he valiantly attacks Comus and breaks his magic glass.

The Second Brother, a far more fearful young man. He sees his sister's beauty as a great temptation to every evil creature and finds but little comfort in his brother's "divine philosophy." Following the advice of the Attendant Spirit, he joins the attack on Comus to free the Lady.

The Attendant Spirit, a being dedicated to the preservation of the true servants of Virtue. He disguises himself as Thyrsis, a shepherd, to warn the brothers of Comus' presence in the wood and to lead them to the place where their sister is fastened motionless in the sorcerer's enchanted chair. He calls up the nymph Sabrina to free the Lady, powerless himself when Comus' magic glass has been broken.

Sabrina (sȧ·bri'nȧ), the nymph who lives in the Severn River, the legendary King Locrine's daughter, who drowned herself to escape her stepmother's fury. Called up from her underwater home, she sprinkles the Lady with clear water from her stream and releases her from enchantment.

CONFESSIONS OF FELIX KRULL, CONFIDENCE MAN

Author: Thomas Mann (1875-1955)
Time of action: Early twentieth century
First published: 1954

PRINCIPAL CHARACTERS

Felix Krull (fā'lĭks krōōl), alias **Armand,** a hotel employee; alias the **Marquis de Venosta.** Impressed at a theatrical performance by the ease with which the actors create various impressions, Felix himself becomes an actor. From that time on he plays whatever role his situation calls for. As Armand, the waiter in a hotel, he leads a double life on the proceeds from the sale of jewels he steals from a guest, Mme. Houpflé; impersonating the Marquis de Venosta, he sets out on a trip around the world.

Müller Rose (mü'lér rō'sė), an actor whose performance inspires Felix Krull himself to become an actor.

Madame Houpflé (mä·däm hōōpf·lā'), a guest at the hotel where Felix Krull, alias Armand, is employed. She becomes Armand's mistress, and, to complete her humiliation, she begs him to rob her of all her valuables.

The Marquis de Venosta (mär·kēs' dä vä·nō'stä), a nobleman. In despair because his parents plan to send him around the world, thus separating him from his mistress Zaza, he engages Armand (Felix Krull) to impersonate him and make the journey in his stead.

Dom Antonio José Kuckuck (dōm än·tō'nyō hō·sā' kōō'kōōk), a Portuguese museum director whom Felix Krull, alias the Marquis de Venosta, visits in Lisbon.

Dona Maria Pia Kuckuck (dō'nya mä·rē'ä pē'ä kōō'kōōk), the wife of Dom Antonio José Kuckuck. She falls in love with Felix Krull, alias the Marquis de Venosta, while he is attempting to seduce her daughter.

Susanna Kuckuck (Zouzou) (sōō·sä'nä kōō'kōōk), Dom Antonio's daughter.

Engelbert Krull (ăng·gel'bért krōōl) and **Frau Krull** (frou krōōl), Felix Krull's parents.

Olympia Krull (ō·lǐm'pē·ä krōōl), Felix Krull's sister.

Herr Schimmelpreester (hâr shǐ'mǎl'prä·stèr), Felix Krull's godfather.

Lord Strathbogie, a guest at the hotel where Felix Krull, alias Armand, works.

Zaza (sä·sä), the Marquis de Venosta's mistress.

THE CONFIDENCE MAN

Author: Herman Melville (1819-1891)
Time of action: Nineteenth century
First published: 1857

PRINCIPAL CHARACTERS

The Confidence Man, masquerading, in turn, as a deaf-mute beggar; as a crippled Negro beggar named Black Guinea; as John Ringman; as a solicitor of funds for the Seminole Widow and Orphan Society; as Mr. Truman, president of the Black Rapids Coal Company; as an herb doctor; as a representative of the Philosophical Intelligence Office; and as Francis Goodman, world traveler. By means of his glib tongue and show of sympathetic camaraderie, he succeeds in duping the passengers on board the "Fidele" even as a placard offering a reward for the impostor is posted on the steamship's deck.

Mr. Roberts, a kindly, gullible merchant swindled by the confidence man.

An Episcopal Clergyman, an officious demander of references who is blandly gulled out of alms for "Black Guinea" as well as a contribution to the Seminole Widow and Orphan Society.

Pitch, a misanthropic frontiersman inspired by the confidence man's glib tongue to hire a boy through the impostor's "employment agency."

Charles Noble, a garrulous passenger who succeeds in evading the confidence man's appeals for a loan.

Mark Winsome, a mystic philosopher who accuses Charles Noble of being the confidence man.

Egbert, a disciple of Mark Winsome. He disgusts the confidence man by relating a long story concerning the folly of making loans between friends.

CONINGSBY

Author: Benjamin Disraeli (1804-1881)
Time of action: 1832-1840
First published: 1844

PRINCIPAL CHARACTERS

The Marquis of Monmouth, a British nobleman opposed to reform, especially the Reform Bill of 1832.

Harry Coningsby, a liberal-minded young English nobleman, grandson of the Marquis of Monmouth. Disinherited

for defying his grandfather on political grounds, he is eventually elected to Parliament. He marries Edith Millbank and after the death of his grandfather he inherits the Marquis' fortune indirectly.

Edith Millbank, the beautiful but shy

196

daughter of a wealthy industrialist. Harry Coningsby falls in love with her, but her father refuses at first to permit the marriage. Later he relents and she is married to Coningsby.

Oswald Millbank, Edith's father. A wealthy manufacturer, he thinks England should be governed by an aristocracy of talent, rather than a hereditary aristocracy. He was at one time the fiancé of Coningsby's mother.

Oswald Millbank, the son of the industrialist of the same name. He is one of Coningsby's close friends and Edith's brother.

Lucretia, a young Italian noblewoman. She tries to attract Coningsby and his friend Sidonia. Failing in these attempts, she settles for marriage with the Marquis of Monmouth for his wealth. Her husband sends her away when she proves to be unfaithful.

Princess Colonna, Lucretia's stepmother.

She is a strong supporter of young Coningsby in his early relations with his grandfather.

Sidonia, a wealthy young Jew, a friend of Coningsby. He is also a friend of the Millbank family. He is suspected, wrongly, by Coningsby of being a rival for Edith's hand in marriage.

Flora, a young actress befriended by Coningsby. She turns out to be the natural daughter of the Marquis of Monmouth. The marquis leaves her his fortune, but she in turn wills it to Coningsby when she dies.

Mr. Rigby, a member of Parliament who is supported by the Marquis of Monmouth. He is young Coningsby's caretaker.

Lord and
Lady Wallinger, relatives of Edith who take her to Paris, where Coningsby renews his acquaintance with Edith and falls in love with her.

THE CONJURE WOMAN

Author: Charles Waddell Chesnutt (1858-1932)
Time of action: Post-Civil War
First published: 1899

PRINCIPAL CHARACTERS

The Narrator, a grape farmer from Ohio who settles in North Carolina because of his wife's ill health, buying a dilapidated plantation which has an old vineyard. He hires Uncle Julius, an elderly Negro, and is regaled by the old man with pointed stories of witchcraft many times. The narrator learns by experience that the stories are usually told for a purpose, most often to the benefit of the old servant.

Annie, the narrator's wife, whose ill health causes her husband's removal from Ohio to North Carolina.

Uncle Julius, an elderly Negro who tries

to prevent the narrator from buying the plantation because he has been selling the grapes from the untended vineyard. He becomes the narrator's coachman and loyal employee, but he often tells stories of witchcraft to amuse his employers or to prevent them from taking some action detrimental to his own well-being.

Aunt Peggy, the Negro conjure woman of Uncle Julius' stories. Her generally beneficent supernatural powers are used to place "goophers," or spells, on people, places, or things.

Mabel, the narrator's sister-in-law, who is persuaded by one of Uncle Julius' stories to cease being jealous of a rival and to marry her fiancé.

Becky, a slave in one of Uncle Julius' stories. She is helped by the powers of the conjure woman when her infant is traded by her owner for a horse.

Sandy, a slave in one of Uncle Julius' stories who is turned into a tree by the conjure woman. She turns him into a tree so that their owner cannot take Sandy, whom she loves, away from her.

A CONNECTICUT YANKEE AT KING ARTHUR'S COURT

Author: Mark Twain (Samuel L. Clemens, 1835-1910)
Time of action: Sixth century
First published: 1889

PRINCIPAL CHARACTERS

The Connecticut Yankee, an ingenious man struck on the head during a quarrel in a New England arms factory. He awakes in Merrie England, in June, 528. About to be burned at the stake on the twenty-first of June, he remembers that history has recorded a solar eclipse for that day. By prophesying the eclipse, he saves his life and discredits Merlin. He gets the name of "The Boss" and determines to raise the status of the common people. He sets up public schools, installs a telephone system, introduces gunpowder, points out to Arthur the grave injustices of the feudal system while accompanying the King on a tour of his realm. He marries Alisande and when their little daughter becomes ill, he takes her to the seashore to recuperate. While he is away, the Church orders all his improvements in Camelot destroyed. When he returns, Merlin casts a spell on him that will cause him to sleep for thirteen hundred years.

Clarence, a foppish page who becomes "The Boss's" chief assistant in his efforts to modernize the land and improve the lot of the common people.

King Arthur, a kind and courageous ruler who does not realize the inequities that exist in the social structure of his kingdom. He is killed in a battle with Sir Lancelot over Queen Guinevere. His death is the signal for the Church to move against and destroy the social progress brought about by the Yankee's democratic innovations.

Sir Kay, who first captures the Yankee.

Sir Sagramor, who challenges the Yankee to a joust and is aided by Merlin.

Merlin, the sorcerer whose magic power cannot match the Yankee's nineteenth century knowledge.

Alisande (Sandy), a damsel in distress whom the Yankee helps and whom he finally marries.

Hello-Central, their daughter, whose illness gives Merlin a chance to unite feudal power and destroy "The Boss."

THE CONSCIOUS LOVERS

Author: Sir Richard Steele (1672-1729)
Time of action: Early eighteenth century
First presented: 1722

Young Bevil, a gentleman of means who is in love with one girl but engaged to another, who in turn loves another man. After many complications of plot, the lovers are properly paired off.

Lucinda Sealand, engaged to young Bevil, who has sent her a letter permitting her to break the engagement. Her thankful letter of reply raises a misunderstanding and almost results in a duel between young Bevil and his friend Mr. Myrtle, whom Lucinda plans to marry.

Indiana Danvers, a girl whom young Bevil has befriended and whom he wishes to marry. She is the daughter of a British merchant who disappeared in the Indies some time before.

Mr. Sealand, Lucinda's father. Learning that young Bevil is paying Indiana's bills, he wrongly suspects that she is his mistress. Going to investigate before breaking off Lucinda's engagement to Bevil, he finds that Indiana is his long-lost

daughter and he agrees to her marriage with Bevil.

Mr. Myrtle, young Bevil's friend, who is in love with Lucinda. Hoping to frustrate Mrs. Sealand's plan to marry Lucinda to Mr. Cimberton, Myrtle goes in disguise to the Sealand house; finally, when all is cleared up, he reveals his identity and claims his bride.

Sir John Bevil, young Bevil's father, at whose request young Bevil is engaged to Lucinda. Later, finding that Indiana is also Mr. Sealand's daughter, he is pleased that she will marry his son.

Mrs. Sealand, Lucinda's mother, a foolish woman who is anxious to marry Lucinda to a rich man.

Mr. Cimberton, a peculiar and wealthy suitor for Lucinda's hand, favored by Mrs. Sealand. He looks over Lucinda as if he were buying a prize mare. Learning that Lucinda will have only half her father's fortune, he leaves in a huff.

Tom, young Bevil's artful servant.

CONSUELO

Author: George Sand (Mme. Aurore Dudevant, 1804-1876)
Time of action: Eighteenth century
First published: 1842

PRINCIPAL CHARACTERS

Consuelo, a gifted singer, who, before her mother dies, promises to marry a young musician named Anzoleto. Consuelo is a charming and beautiful woman, in addition to being a fine artist. After she finds that her betrothed is untrue to her, she becomes a companion to Amelia, the niece of Count Rudolstadt. The Count's son Albert falls in love with her and tells her that she is the only person who can save him from insanity. She helps her rival, Corilla, give birth to an illegitimate child the girl has by Anzoleto. Just before Albert dies, she marries

him, but she refuses any of the fortune that comes to her as a result. She goes to Berlin and becomes the idol of Frederick the Great.

Porpora, Consuelo's music teacher and godfather. He is determined to make a great artist out of her and, by his duplicity, manages to keep her away from Albert until it is too late for her to help him.

Count Albert Rudolstadt, the son of a nobleman, who calls Consuelo by name the first time he hears her sing, although no one has told him her true name. He is convinced that Consuelo is his salvation and that no one else can save him from the curse of insanity. When Porpora writes to tell Albert that he will never consent to Consuelo's marriage to the young nobleman, Albert weakens and dies, after begging Consuelo to marry him so that his soul can find peace.

Anzoleto, the poor young musician whom Consuelo has promised to marry. When Consuelo's success becomes greater than his, he tries to assure his position in the theater by pretending to be in love with her rival, Corilla. Porpora dislikes Anzoleto, and he contrives to have Consuelo find Anzoleto and Corilla together. Anzoleto fathers Corilla's child and is never heard from again.

Count Rudolstadt, a Bohemian nobleman, Albert's father. He is willing to consent to Consuelo's marriage to Albert in order to save his son.

Corilla, a singer and Consuelo's rival, both in the theater and in Anzoleto's affections. Corilla does not know that Consuelo, who was disguised as a boy at the time, had helped her with the birth of her child.

Joseph Haydn, the composer whom Consuelo meets on the road to Vienna. She takes him along to be a pupil of Porpora.

Amelia, the niece of Count Rudolstadt. Betrothed to Albert, she fears him because he is thought to be mad.

THE COPPERHEAD

Author: Harold Frederic (1856-1898)
Time of action: The 1860's
First published: 1893

PRINCIPAL CHARACTERS

Abner Beech, a farmer and a violent Anti-Abolitionist in the equally violent Abolitionist community of Dearborn County, New York. His political sentiments earn for him the name "Copperhead" (a Northerner with Southern sympathies) and the enmity of his neighbors, who plan to tar and feather him. When Abner's house is ignited and burned by the bonfire for the tarring, the neighbors recover their senses, ask his forgiveness, and offer to restore his property. Goodwill reigns again among the folk of Dearborn County.

Jee Hagadorn, Abner Beech's Abolitionist neighbor and enemy.

Jeff Beech, Abner Beech's son, a Union soldier in love with Esther Hagadorn.

Esther Hagadorn, Jee Hagadorn's daughter and the sweetheart of Jeff Beech.

Ni Hagadorn, Jee Hagadorn's son.

Jimmy, an orphan boy who lives with Abner Beech.

Hurley, Abner Beech's Anti-Abolitionist hired man.

Warner Pitts, Abner Beech's former hired man, now an officer in the Union Army.

Byron Truax, a fellow soldier of Jeff Beech.

M'rye, Abner Beech's wife.

Janey, a hired girl.

Avery, the local squire.

CORIOLANUS

Author: William Shakespeare (1564-1616)
Time of action: Third century
First presented: 1607-1608

PRINCIPAL CHARACTERS

Caius Marcius, afterward **Caius Marcius Coriolanus** (kā′yŭs mär′shŭs kôr′ĭ·ō·lā′-nŭs), a great warrior of the Roman Republic, a man of immense valor and equally great pride. He does not desire public acclaim for his achievements; his own knowledge of their worth is sufficient. He violently resents having to beg for the voices of the common people, whom he has watched flee from the battlefield in fear, and he is ultimately unable to stifle his contempt long enough to win the consulship. For his arrogance he is banished from Rome. His alliance with Aufidius to avenge the wrongs he has received from Rome is a manifestation of his fierce pride. The dominant force in his life is the personality of his mother, who has shaped him into the confident, arrogant, single-minded man he is. Although he cannot obey her injunction to betray himself in order to win the favor of the people, he is ultimately broken by her will and agrees to make peace between the Volscians and the Romans. There is, after this submission, no course for him but death, and he perishes, branded a traitor by both nations and taunted as "boy" by the Volscians.

Volumnia (vōl·lŭm′nĭ·ə), his mother, a noble Roman matron, who has instilled in her son a strong sense of personal pride, integrity, and a streak of brutality. She dominates both Coriolanus and his wife and speaks proudly of the ruthlessness of her young grandson. Apparently oblivious to the effects of her pressure on her son, she rejoices in having saved Rome from a bloody destruction.

Menenius Agrippa (mĕ·nē′nĭ·ŭs ə·grĭp′ə), a witty Roman Senator who uses his reputation as something of a buffoon to communicate with the people and their tribunes. He loves Coriolanus like a son, and the younger man almost breaks his heart when he sends him unheeded from the Volscian camp.

Tullus Aufidius (tŭl′ŭs ô·fĭd′ĭ·ŭs), the Volscian general and Coriolanus' great rival, who welcomes him as an ally when he appears at the Volscian camp. He comes to regret his decision when he finds the allegiance of his army transferred to the Roman who had defeated him each time they met on the battlefield. Coriolanus' submission to his mother enrages him, for he had hoped to march victorious through Rome. He conspires to have Coriolanus killed as a traitor to the Volscians; however, he pays tribute to the nobility of his adversary as he stands over his body at the end of the play.

Cominius (kŏ·mĭn′ĭ·ŭs), a general of the Roman army, a man of dignity and wisdom who recognizes and praises the great gifts of Coriolanus, to whom he is devoted. He mourns his banishment and offers to accompany him into exile.

Virgilia (vĕr·jĭl′ĭ·ə), Coriolanus' gentle wife, whom he calls "my gracious silence." She avoids her husband's public triumphs when she can, but she joins her mother-in-law at the Volscian camp to seek the salvation of Rome.

Sicinius Velutus (sĭ·sĭn′ĭ·ŭs vĕ·lū′tŭs) and
Junius Brutus (jōō′n′yŭs brōō′tŭs), the tribunes of the people, jealous of their prerogative and fearful of the effects of Coriolanus' pride and power on those they represent. Disregarding the advice

and the pleas of Menenius and Cominius, they initiate the popular uprising which results in the great soldier's banishment.

Titus Lartius (tī′tŭs lär′shŭs), another of the Roman generals.

Young Marcius, Coriolanus and Virgilia's son, who has inherited his father's intense, amoral valor.

Valeria (vă·lĭr′ĭ·ə), a noble lady, Virgilia's sympathetic friend.

Nicanor (nī·kā′nôr) and **Adrian** (ā′drĭ·ən), representatives, respectively, of the Romans and the Volscians. They meet between Rome and Antium and discuss the probable results of Coriolanus' banishment.

THE CORSICAN BROTHERS

Author: Alexandre Dumas, *père* (1802-1870)
Time of action: 1841
First published: 1845

PRINCIPAL CHARACTERS

Madame Savilia de Franchi, the kind, indomitable, aristocratic Corsican hostess of the narrator. Although widowed and reduced to lesser means from former affluence, Madame de Franchi takes great pride in hospitality at her Sullacaro estate and is honored to have as a guest an eminent novelist. The mother of Siamese twins who had been separated successfully, she learns of her absent son's health through the report of the psychic twin at home. As a family, she explains, the de Franchis have had an interesting history; she and her husband, with guns kept prominently on display, managed to settle an ancient vendetta by killing simultaneously two enemy brothers. One son received from her his ability to fight and manage; the other was more scholarly and introspective. Gracious and dignified, she impressed the author with epitomized Corsican traits.

Lucien de Franchi, her outgoing, sportsman son who has remained with his mother to manage the family estate and provide for her welfare. Something of a diplomat, the hardy and handsome Lucien succeeds in settling another vendetta carried on for years between rival families living nearby. As the host of the author, Lucien takes his guest along to witness the truce, discusses his love of

his native mountains, and displays his skill in hunting. He explains also that he and his brother Louis are completely devoted to each other in spite of their sharp differences in tastes, abilities, interests and appearances, strange differences for identical twins who seem to share in part their nervous systems. Some months later in Paris, the loyal brother avenges the death of his scholarly twin. No vendetta results, but his vengeance is complete when he kills his antagonist in a duel, just as Louis had been killed. Only then is the young Corsican able to give vent to his grief for the loss of a part of himself.

Louis de Franchi, the scholarly twin, a somewhat effete young man who nevertheless possesses the feelings of pride and honor of his illustrious family. He also plays host to the narrator in Paris and reveals that he is distraught over a love affair, the reason why his brother Lucien has recently felt depressed. His deep love for Emelie, concealed from his good friend, her husband, forces him to defend her honor even though he knows the result will be his death. Hoping to conceal the truth from his mother and brother, he entrusts to his new friend a letter in which he says that he is suffering from a brain fever. The narrator acts as Louis' second in the duel. As he feared, Louis is killed. Lucien learns of the tragedy by intuition, for Louis died of a bullet wound below his sixth rib and Lucien carries the stigmata. In spite of the fact that Louis wished no more Corsican violence, his death is courageously avenged.

Emelie, the beautiful but unfaithful wife of a sea captain and the friend of Louis, in whose trust she is placed. Herself in love with a married man and beloved by her loyal friend, she resents the young man's intrusion into her intrigue. Being made the sport of the lover, she turns to Louis in order to save face.

M. de Chateau-Renaud, Emelie's lover, who humiliates her at a supper party attended by the narrator and his Corsican friend. Having compelled Emelie to accompany him on a wager, he challenges her defender to a duel. He responds just as bravely to the challenge from the murdered man's brother, who kills him.

The Narrator, Alexandre Dumas, the Corsican traveler. With all the romantic flamboyance of his nature, Dumas reveals himself as an admirer of the Corsican spirit, the pride of birth, family, country as well as independence, bravery, and loyalty. Purportedly recounting a historic tragedy, the narrator really embellishes a legend.

Orlandi, a Corsican bandit, and
Colonna, the heads of two families whose vendetta was caused by a quarrel over a chicken. Lucien de Franchi is the mediator in settling the feud.

Griffo, the servant of Lucien de Franchi.

D——, the narrator's friend, the host at the supper party at which M. de Chateau-Renaud appears with Emelie.

THE COSSACKS

Author: Count Leo Tolstoy (1828-1910)
Time of action: Nineteenth century
First published: 1863

PRINCIPAL CHARACTERS

Dmitri Andreyevitch Olyenin (dĭ·mĭt'-rĭy änd·rā'ĕv·ĭch ôl·yĕn'ĭn), a young man of noble birth attached to a Russian military company. Stationed in a Cossack village, Olyenin feels a strong sympathy for these wild and happy people so different from the effete, useless society that he knew at home. An idealistic young man, he lives in the home of a beautiful Cossack girl who is alternately affectionate and disdainful toward him. In his somewhat confused idealism he, at first, believes that "happiness consists in living for others." He decides to renounce self and find happiness in the love of beautiful, proud Maryanka. Later, realizing the vast cultural gulf between them, he rides sadly out of the village, his going barely noticed by the young girl.

Maryanka (mä·rĭ·än'kə), the attractive daughter of a Cossack ensign, a man of property and position in the village. The girl has no objection to a temporary connection with Olyenin, but he is unable to hold her affections for long because she loves Lukashka, a vigorous warrior. At the last she drives Olyenin off with loathing and scorn. She is not to be won by a lover who is not a Cossack.

Lukashka (lŏŏ·käsh'kə), the young Cossack who is to marry Maryanka if he can quit carousing long enough for the ceremony. During his infrequent leaves from guard duty, the brave Lukashka makes love to his mistress, pursues Maryanka intermittently, drinks vast quantities of wine in the village streets, and

203

still manages to keep a clear head. He becomes a leader in his Cossack company when he kills the savage captain of a raiding mountaineer band. His reputation is enhanced after Olyenin generously gives him a horse, a real status symbol for the aspiring Cossack. As the novel ends, Lukashka lies badly wounded. Perhaps, unlike Uncle Yeroshka, he will not live to enjoy his fame as a bravo.

Uncle Yeroshka (yĕ·rōsh'kə), an aged but still powerful Cossack. From Yeroshka's own lips Olyenin learns of the hardy old man's feats as a warrior and a hunter. Like most of his countrymen, Uncle Yeroshka can drink great quantities of wine and vodka and is still able to hunt game all day after a night of drunkenness. Now about seventy, he becomes a good friend to young Olyenin and teaches him much about hunting wild game and ferocious mountaineers who come out of the Caucasus to rob and kill.

Dame Ulitka (ŏŏ·lĭt'kə), Maryanka's virago of a mother. At first she is rude to Olyenin, who is boarding in her home. She thinks of him as another Russian outsider until she learns that he is a wealthy nobleman.

Prince Byeletsky (bĕ·lĕt'skĭy), "who believes in taking all the good the gods may give, and thus in a week's time becomes hail fellow well met with everyone in the stanitsa." A merry young man, this friend of Olyenin soon enjoys great popularity in the village.

Ensign Ilya Vasilyevitch (ĭl·yä' vä·sĭ'lĕ·vĭch), Maryanka's father. A man of forty, he is passionately interested in acquiring money and property, even if he must use his brother to get them.

Vanyusha, (vä·nū'shə), Olyenin's friend and servant. He never quite approves of the drunken Cossack life.

THE COUNT OF MONTE-CRISTO

Author: Alexandre Dumas, *père* (1802-1870)
Time of action: Nineteenth century
First published: 1844

PRINCIPAL CHARACTERS

Edmond Dantès (ĕd·mōn' dän·tĕs'), a young man unjustly imprisoned in the grim Château D'If. He escapes fourteen years later, after he has learned where a vast fortune is amassed. He secures the fortune and assumes the title of Count of Monte-Cristo. He then sets about avenging himself on those who were instrumental in having him imprisoned.

M. Morrel (mə·syœ' mô·rĕl'), a merchant and shipowner, the friend of young Dantès and the benefactor of Edmond's father. He is later saved by Monte-Cristo from bankruptcy and suicide.

M. Danglars (mə·syœ' dän·glär'), an employee of M. Morrel. He helps to betray Edmond Dantès to the authorities because of professional jealousy. He later amasses a fortune which Monte-Cristo causes him to lose. He is further punished by being allowed to starve almost to death as he had allowed Edmond's father to starve.

Mercédès (mĕr·sä·dĕz'), the betrothed of young Edmond Dantès. Believing him to be dead, she marries his rival, Fernand Mondego. In the end she leaves her husband's house, gives his fortune to charity, and lives on the dowry Edmond had saved for her in her youth.

Louis Dantès (lwē' dän·tĕs'), Edmond's father. He dies of starvation after his son is imprisoned.

Gaspard Caderousse (gàs·pàr' ka·də·rōōs'), a tailor, innkeeper, and thief. One of Edmond's betrayers, he is killed while robbing Monte-Cristo's house.

Fernand Mondego, Count de Morcerf (fĕr·nän' mōn·də·gō', kōnt' də môr·sĕr'), a fisherman in love with Mercédès. He mails the letter which betrays Edmond to the authorities. He later marries Mercédès, becomes a soldier and a count. Monte-Cristo later brings about the revelation that Fernand got his fortune by selling out the Pasha of Janina to the enemy. His wife and son leave him and he commits suicide.

The Marquis and Marchioness de Saint-Méran (də săn'mā·rän'), the father and mother of M. Villefort's first wife, poisoned by his second wife.

Renée (rə·nā'), the daughter of the Marquis and Marchioness de Saint-Méran. She marries Villefort.

M. Villefort (mə·syœ' vēl·fôr'), a deputy prosecutor, later attorney general, and a royalist. He causes Edmond to be imprisoned because he fears involvement in a Napoleonic plot. Monte-Cristo later discovers an attempted infanticide on the part of Villefort and causes this secret to be revealed publicly at a trial Villefort is conducting. After this public denunciation and the discovery that his second wife has poisoned several members of his household, then her son and herself, Villefort goes mad.

The Abbé Faria (à·bā' fà'ryà), Edmond's fellow prisoner, who dies of a stroke after educating Edmond and revealing to him the whereabouts of the vast lost fortune of the extinct family of Spada in the caverns of the isle of Monte-Cristo.

Emmanuel Herbaut (ā·mà·nü·ĕl' ĕr·bō'), a clerk in Morrel's business establishment. He marries Julie Morrel.

Julie Morrel (zhü·lē' mô·rĕl'), the daughter of the merchant Morrel. She finds the purse in which Monte-Cristo had put money to repay the loan that Morrel had given his father, old Dantès, and thus saves her own father from bankruptcy. She later marries Emmanuel Herbaut.

Maximilian Morrel (màk·sē·mēl·yän' mô·rĕl'), the son of the merchant, a soldier and a loyal friend of Monte-Cristo. He marries Valentine de Villefort.

Viscount Albert de Morcerf (àl·bĕr' də môr·sĕr'), the son of Fernand and Mercédès. He leaves his disgraced father's house, gives his fortune to charity, and seeks his own fortune as a soldier.

Baron Franz d'Épinay (fräns dā·pē·nā'), the friend of Albert, about to be betrothed to Valentine de Villefort when the betrothal is called off after Franz discovers that her grandfather had killed his father.

Luigi Vampa (lwē'jē vàm'pà), a Roman bandit and friend of Monte-Cristo. He kidnaps Albert but frees him at Monte-Cristo's order. Later he also kidnaps Danglars, robs, and almost starves him.

Peppino (pā·pē'nō), also known as **Rocca Priori** (rō'kà prē·ō·rē'), one of Vampa's band. Monte-Cristo saves him from being beheaded.

Countess Guiccioli (gwēt'chō·lē), the friend of Franz and Albert in Rome and later in Paris.

Giovanni Bertuccio (jō·vän'nē bĕr·tōōt'chyō), the steward of Monte-Cristo, who reveals to his master Villefort's attempted infanticide. Unknown to Villefort, he saves the child's life.

Lucien Debray (lü·syän' də·brē'), a friend of Albert, secretary to the Internal Department, and the lover of Mme. Danglars.

M. Beauchamp (mə·syœ' bō·shän'), Albert's friend, a newspaper editor.

Count Château-Renaud (shà·tō′ rə·nō′), another of Albert's friends.

Eugénie Danglars (œ·zhā·nē′ däṅ·glár′), the daughter of Danglars, about to be betrothed, first to Albert, then to Andrea Cavalcanti. She later runs away with her governess to go on the stage.

Assunta (à·sün′tà), Bertuccio's sister-in-law. She claims Villefort's child from the foundling home where Bertuccio had placed it.

Benedetto (bā·nā·dā′tō), also Andrea Cavalcanti (äṅ·drā·à′ kà·vàl·käṅ′tē), the illegitimate son of Villefort and Mme. Danglars. He does not know who his parents are, and they believe him to be dead. He is a forger, a thief escaped from the galleys, and the murderer of Caderousse. He discovers that Villefort is his father and reveals this fact at the trial. It is implied that the court will find "extenuating circumstances" in his new trial.

Haidée (ĕ·dā′), the daughter of Ali Tebelen, Pasha of Janina and Basiliki, captured and sold as a slave by Fernand Mondego after he betrays her father. She is bought by Monte-Cristo, and they fall in love with each other.

Baptistin (bà·tēs·tăṅ′), the servant of Monte-Cristo.

Hermine Danglars (ĕr·mēn′ däṅ·glár′), Danglars' wife and the mother of Benedetto and Eugénie.

Héloïse de Villefort (ā·lô·ēz′ də vēl·fôr′), the second wife of Villefort. She poisons the Saint-Mérans and tries to poison Noirtier and Valentine so that her son may inherit their vast wealth. Her guilt discovered, she kills her son and herself.

Edouard de Villefort (ā·dwár′ də vēl-fôr′), the spoiled, irresponsible son of Héloïse and Villefort. He is killed by his mother.

Valentine de Villefort (và·län·tēn′ də vēl·fôr′), the daughter of Villefort and Renée Saint-Méran Villefort. She is poisoned by the second Mme. Villefort but is saved by Noirtier and Monte-Cristo after being given a sleeping potion that makes her appear dead. After her rescue she marries Maximilian Morrel.

Noirtier de Villefort (nwár·tyā′ də vēl-fôr′), the father of Villefort and a fiery Jacobin of the French Revolution. Completely paralyzed by a stroke, he communicates with his eyes.

The Marquis Bartolomeo Cavalcanti (bár·tō·lō·mā·ō′ kà·vàl·käṅ′tē), the name assumed by a man pretending to be Andrea Cavalcanti's father.

Barrois (bà·rwà′), a faithful servant of old Noirtier, poisoned by drinking some lemonade intended for Noirtier.

Ali Tebelen (à·lē tāb·lăṅ′), the father of Haidée, betrayed by Fernand.

Louise d'Armilly (lwēz′ dár·mē·yē′), the governess to Eugénie Danglars. Together they run away in hopes they can go on the stage as singers.

Lord Wilmore and
Abbé Busoni (à·bā′ bü·zō′·nē), aliases used by the Count of Monte-Cristo.

THE COUNTERFEITERS

Author: André Gide (1869-1951)
Time of action: Early 1920's
First published: 1925

PRINCIPAL CHARACTERS

Edouard (ā·dwár′), a novelist who resembles André Gide. He is a close observer of and a commentator on the other characters and their actions, and he is a connecting link in their stories. He believes it is a person's duty to be himself regardless of consequences, though the difference between the real and the counterfeit self may sometimes be hard to discern. His interest in Olivier is homosexual but on a higher level than Passavant's.

Olivier Molinier (ô·lē·vyā′ mô·lē·nyā′), his thoughtful, reserved nephew, jealous of Edouard's interest in Bernard, which he thinks is erotic. He temporarily falls under Passavant's malign influence but escapes. He attempts suicide but is revived by Edouard.

George Molinier (zhôrzh′ mô·lē·nyā′), Olivier's younger brother, a passer of counterfeit coins. The coins are symbolic of the false selves which people reveal in society. Boris's shocking death has a sobering effect on him.

Vincent Molinier (văn·sän′ mô·lē·nyā′), Olivier's tall, handsome older brother, a friend of Passavant; Laura's lover and father of her child. He becomes insane after Lady Griffith's death which he may have brought about.

Bernard Profitendieu (bĕr·när′ prô·fē-tän·dyœ′), Olivier's friend and Edouard's bold, unscrupulous, impudent secretary and disciple; an illegitimate son. He resembles Gide's Lafcadio ("Lafcadio's Adventures").

Laura Douviers (lō·rä′ dōō·vyā′), Edouard's friend and Vincent's discarded pregnant mistress whom he met while both were patients in a sanatorium.

Felix Douviers (fa·lēks′ dōō·vyā′), Laura's generous husband, willing to forgive her and accept the child as his own.

Comte Robert de Passavant (rô·bĕr′ də pä·sä·vän′), a cynical libertine, homosexual, and dilettante writer. He symbolizes aristocratic decadence.

Armand Vedel (är·män′ və·dĕl′), Laura's younger brother and Olivier's friend; he succeeds Olivier as editor of Passavant's journal and apparently as sexual partner also.

Rachel (rä·shĕl′), Laura's older sister, manager of the Vedel School.

Sarah (sä·rä′), Armand's submissive sister in whom Bernard is briefly interested sexually.

Lady Lillian Griffith, a friend of Passavant. She and Vincent elope to Africa where she is drowned.

Albéric Profitendieu (äl·bä·rēk′ prô·fē-tän·dyœ′), Bernard's foster father, a magistrate who is concerned about the counterfeiters' operations. He is disliked by Bernard, who runs away after discovering his illegitimacy.

La Pérouse (lä pā·rōōz′), an old music teacher, a friend of Edouard.

Boris (bô·rēs′), his young grandson. In a school initiation into boys' secret society he shoots himself after a real pistol bullet has been substituted for a dummy.

The Vedels (və·dĕl′), Laura's family, close friends of Edouard's. They are symbols of bourgeois decadence.

Oscar Molinier (ôs·kär′ mô·lē·nyā′), Edouard's brother-in-law, a magistrate.

Pauline (pô·lēn′), his wife, Edouard's unhappy half-sister.

THE COUNTESS DE CHARNY

Author: Alexandre Dumas, *père* (1802-1870)
Time of action: 1791
First published: 1853-1855

Countess Andrée de Charny (än·drä' də shär·nē'), the wife of Count Olivier de Charny. Forced, as a young girl, by a peasant later to become Dr. Gilbert, she bore a son, Sebastian. Fearful lest her early misfortune become known to her beloved husband, she maintains a distant marriage relationship which mystifies him. When her secret is finally revealed by Dr. Gilbert himself, husband and wife are happily united.

Dr. Gilbert (zhēl·bĕr'), Louis XVI's physician and trusted friend. As a humble peasant, years before, he had attacked a young woman, later to become the Countess Andrée de Charny, who bore his son Sebastian. As Dr. Gilbert, he seeks to expiate his crime by deeds of charity.

Count Olivier de Charny (ō·lē·vyā' də shär·nē'), an aide to King Louis XVI and devoted to the cause of the monarchy. He is the husband of Countess Andrée de Charny.

Sebastian, the illegitimate son of the Countess Andrée de Charny and Dr. Gilbert.

Louis XVI (lwē'), King of France.

Marie Antoinette (mà·rē' än·twà·nĕt'), Queen of France.

The Marquis de Favras (mär·kē' də fà·vrä'), a trusted aide of Louis XVI.

Count Alessandro di Cagliostro (ä·lĕ·sań'drō dē kà·glē·ō'strō), or Joseph Balsamo (zhō·zĕf' bàl·sà·mō'), an Italian adventurer involved in the intrigues surrounding Louis XVI and Marie Antoinette.

Gamain (gà·măń'), locksmith to Louis XVI.

Honoré Mirabeau (ô·nô·rä' mē·rà·bō'), a French statesman and man of the hour with revolutionary sympathies with whom Dr. Gilbert advises Louis XVI to join forces.

The Marquis de Bouille (mär·kē' də boo'yə), a French general involved in the abortive plan for the escape of Louis XVI.

M. de Malden (də màl·dän') and The Marquis de Choiseul (mär·kē' də shwà·zœl'), a trusted nobleman in the cause of Louis XVI.

Jean Drouet (zhäń' droo·ä'), a revolutionary patriot who informs the nationalist troops of the attempted escape of Louis XVI.

A COUNTRY DOCTOR

Author: Sarah Orne Jewett (1849-1909)
Time of action: Mid-nineteenth century
First published: 1884

Nan Prince, a young girl who, in the nineteenth century, wants to become a medical doctor. As a child she is mischievous, but likes to care for animals. She assists the local doctor, who rears her after her mother's and grandmother's deaths. The girl attends medical school, despite pressure from her relatives and her suitor. Upon receiving her medical education she returns to the town to assist the doctor and eventually to take over his practice.

Adeline Thacher Prince, Nan's mother. She returns home to Oldfields to die, bringing her infant daughter. She is a wild, rebellious woman who reputedly is addicted to drink. She resents her husband's family because they opposed her marriage.

Mrs. Thacher, Nan's maternal grandmother, who cares for the child until her own death.

Dr. Leslie, the doctor in Oldfields. He looks after Nan and rears her in his own home after her grandmother's death. He encourages her study of medicine.

Miss Nancy Prince, a wealthy spinster, Nan's aunt. She is shocked at Nan's seemingly unladylike ambition to be a doctor and tries to dissuade the girl from studying medicine. She also tries to interest Nan in a young man, George Gerry, in hopes that Nan will marry and abandon her ambition to practice medicine.

George Gerry, a young friend of Miss Nancy Prince. He and Nan fall in love, as Nan's aunt hopes, but George cannot persuade Nan to marry him and abandon medicine.

THE COUNTRY DOCTOR

Author: Honoré de Balzac (1799-1850)
Time of action: Early nineteenth century
First published: 1833

PRINCIPAL CHARACTERS

Dr. Benassis (bə·nȧ·sē′), the self-appointed godfather to a remote and dying mountain village where he revitalizes the economy and administers to its physical and spiritual needs. A hundred years ahead of his time, the benevolent despot removes a dying line of cretins, imposes a regimen of self-sacrifice and good works on village officials, and surrounds himself with vital workers who in eight years carry out a reform program of health and welfare. He devotes his life to anonymous good works because of heavy burdens on his conscience: a lost fortune, the betrayal of a loved one who died, and the loss of his son by his mistress. As a doctor he practices psychology and even recognizes the psychosomatic bases of many illnesses. As a mayor he genially dispenses the village's wealth as well as his own in order to make the helpless self-sufficient. His death leaves the populace devastated but inspired.

Colonel Pierre Joseph Genestas (pyěr zhō·zěf′ zhə·něs·tás′), one of Napoleon's finest soldiers, who has seen the political tide go against him and who comes to see the doctor for a purpose. Posing as a Captain Bluteau, the Colonel observes the physician on his rounds of mercy and administration before asking him to care for his foster child, a sixteen-year-old weakling. Knowing the old man to be sublime, he vows to return to the village and carry on the doctor's good works in appreciation of his son's recovery.

Adrien (ȧ·dryăṅ′), his adopted son, the child of an army officer and a Polish Jewess, who has ruined his health through his intensive study and lack of exercise. A very sensitive, even beautiful, child, Adrien responds splendidly to the doctor's prescriptions: a milk diet and hardy exercise in hunting and mountain climbing. More fortunate than a young consumptive, Jacques of the beautiful voice, Adrien recovers fully, but the other boy dies shortly after his benefactor's death. Adrien, deeply appreciating the efforts of his foster father and the doctor, returns kindness for kindness.

La Fosseuse (là fô·sœz′), the ward of the doctor, who has been despised and rejected by society for her inability to work or produce. The beautiful young girl, a kind of poetess of nature, after a very sad childhood is cared for by the aging doctor.

Jacquotte (zhà·kôt'), the doctor's faithful servant and housekeeper.

Curé Janvier (kü·rā' zhän·vyā'), the enlightened village priest.

THE COUNTRY HOUSE

Author: John Galsworthy (1867-1933)
Time of action: Early twentieth century
First published: 1907

PRINCIPAL CHARACTERS

Horace Pendyce, a British landholder of the late nineteenth century whose conservative opinions represent promulgation of traditional social attitudes and actions. When his son seeks his fortune at race tracks and, furthermore, is named corespondent in a divorce action, Pendyce feels his world slipping away from him. His efficient but unobtrusive wife takes the situation in hand, however, and after extricating her son from his involvement with a married woman, she persuades the injured husband to drop his divorce suit naming young Pendyce. Aristocratic tradition is again secure and life at the country estate of Worsted Skeynes becomes serene once more.

Margery Pendyce, Horace's wife. She takes prompt action when her husband threatens to disinherit their son for not arranging his social affairs to his father's liking. She leaves Horace, takes her son George in hand in London, and persuades a husband not to press proceedings in a divorce action in which the husband has named her son.

George Pendyce, the irresponsible heir to Worsted Skeynes, the Pendyce country estate. Unconventional, he refuses to conform to the sort of behavior society expects of him. Helen Bellew and his gambling indebtedness create problems that distress his conservative father.

Mrs. Helen Bellew, a rash young woman, judged by the standards of late nine-

teenth century English country society. She falls in love with George Pendyce when she is not divorced from her husband, of whom she has grown tired. She tires of George, too, and tells his mother so. Her conduct, generally, is a portent, Galsworthy implies, of the role English women of the future will assume.

The Reverend Hussell Barter, a typical parish rector of the era. His views are ultra-conservative, and his opinions influence appreciably the direction society takes. When he discovers George and Helen kissing at a social affair, he considers it his duty to inform the husband. He is a stanch defender of traditional morality.

Captain Jaspar Bellew, Helen's husband, who does not love her. He initiates divorce proceedings because his pride has been injured, but he is persuaded by Mrs. Pendyce to drop the action.

Gregory Vigil, Helen's cousin and guardian, who himself is in love with her. Despite advice to the contrary, he attempts to start divorce action on behalf of his ward. Captain Bellew, at last aware of his wife's flirtatious ways, begins proceedings before Vigil can act.

Edmund Paramor, Vigil's lawyer, who advises him not to start the divorce action, primarily because it always causes social embarrassment.

THE COUNTRY OF THE POINTED FIRS

Author: Sarah Orne Jewett (1849-1909)
Time of action: Late nineteenth century
First published: 1896

PRINCIPAL CHARACTERS

The Boarder, a woman writer who comes to Dunnet Landing, Maine, to work in seclusion. Here she meets many people and finds friendly, interesting characters.

Mrs. Almira Todd, a friendly widow who accepts the writer as a boarder. She is also an herb doctor, growing herbs in her garden and searching out others in the fields.

Captain Littlepage, an elderly, retired sea captain who tells the writer a yarn about his own shipwreck and a town of ghosts near the North Pole, where souls await their passage to the next world.

Mrs. Blackett, Mrs. Todd's aged mother. She lives on an island with her son William and does her own housework.

William Blackett, Mrs. Todd's brother, a bashful man. He loves Esther Hight and finally is able to marry her when he is in his fifties.

Mrs. Fosdick, a friend of Mrs. Todd. She comes often to visit with her friend and to tell stories about the local folk.

Mr. Tilley, an old fisherman. He is reserved with strangers, but he accepts the writer as a friend and shows her the house he has kept for eight years the same as it was when his wife died.

Esther Hight, a woman loved by William Blackett. She supports herself and her elderly mother by tending sheep. After her mother's death she is free to marry William.

THE COUNTRY WIFE

Author: WilliamWycherley (1640?-1716)
Time of action: Seventeenth century
First presented: 1673

PRINCIPAL CHARACTERS

Mr. Horner, a man with a reputation for lewdness. Newly returned from France, he finds an excellent method of duping unsuspecting husbands. With the aid of a quack, he spreads the fictitious information that he is no longer sexually potent. Foolish husbands, needing someone to escort and amuse their wives, invite the clever Mr. Horner to their homes. In this way he finds his way to the bedchambers of many high-born ladies who no longer have to fear the tarnishing of their reputations if they associate with an "impotent" man.

Mr. Pinchwife. Like Sparkish and Sir

Jasper Fidget, he is a cuckold who helps to bring about the very thing he fears most, the seduction of his naïve wife. He is right when he says that cuckolds are generally the makers of their own misfortune. Dour, humorless, and exceedingly jealous, he takes every precaution to keep his wife from falling into the predatory hands of Horner. Foolishly, he is the very instrument which brings about this event.

Mrs. Margery Pinchwife, his country wife. She is little aware of London's pleasures until she is inadvertently informed of them by her husband. Little

211

by little she loses some of her innocence until, finally, she meets Horner. After this brief interlude she learns what a dullard her husband is. Cleverly, she manages to send a love letter, carried by her unsuspecting husband, to Horner. man of considerable parts. Only when he

Mr. Sparkish, a boring idiot who desires, more than anything else, to be a wit, a is called "a bubble, a coward, a senseless idiot" is he outraged. Credulously, he is duped by all he meets, always feeling, however, that he is a wit, even to the very end.

Sir Jasper Fidget, the husband of Lady Fidget. Almost the equal of Sparkish in stupidity, he unsuspectingly begs Horner to be an escort for Lady Fidget. Even when he is in the next room from the lovers, he is unaware that his wife and Horner are doing anything other than looking for china plates.

Lady Fidget, a woman who wants to protect her reputation for virtue at all costs. In public she raves about her chastity; in private, however, she tells bawdy jokes, drinks wine, and, in her boudoir, finds the indefatigable Horner a delightful and stimulating companion.

Alithea, a comely young woman, the sister of Pinchwife and the mistress of Sparkish. At first she remains true to her

witless lover. Later, however, she finds Harcourt a much more interesting person.

Mr. Harcourt, a friend of Horner. Clever and somewhat unscrupulous, he gulls the would-be-wit, Sparkish, by pretending to be a good and faithful friend.

Lucy, Alithea's maid. Although a serving girl, she is clever enough to help Mrs. Pinchwife meet Horner. At the end of the play, she convinces Pinchwife and Sir Jasper that there has been no intrigue between their wives and Horner.

Mrs. Dainty Fidget. Like Lady Fidget, she is infatuated with Horner, particularly when she can associate with him without endangering her reputation.

Mrs. Squeamish, another of the many women surrounding Horner. In the end she learns, as do the others, that she must share him with several women.

A Quack, through whose professional status Horner is able to convince the gulls of his impotency. Quack helps him by spreading this information through the city. He is amazed when the scheme works so well.

Mr. Dorilant, Horner's friend and a man about town. During Horner's dalliance with Mrs. Pinchwife, Dorilant shows considerable interest in Lucy.

THE COURTESAN

Author: Pietro Aretino (1492-1556)
Time of action: Early sixteenth century
First presented: 1534

PRINCIPAL CHARACTERS

Messer Maco (mä′kō), a wealthy fool who is in Rome to become a cardinal. He is deluded into the notion that he must first become a courtier.

Maestro Andrea (än·drä′ä), a charlatan. Hoping to fleece Messer Maco, he promises to transform him into a courtier and

gives him lessons in blaspheming, gambling, slandering, and related arts.

Signor Parabolano (pä·rä·bō·lä′nō), a nobleman enamoured of the virtuous matron Livia.

Valerio (vä·lä′ryō), Parabolano's loyal

chamberlain, who defends his master against the jeers of the groom Rosso.

Rosso (rôs'sō), Parabolano's groom, a rascal and the sworn enemy of Valerio. He plots to pander to his master's lust, win his favor, and be revenged on Valerio.

Alvigia (äl·vē'jē·ä), a procuress in league with Rosso to secure Livia for Parabolano.

Togna (tō'nyä), a baker's wife substituted for the inaccessible Livia in a nocturnal assignation with Parabolano. She

steals away to the tryst in her husband's clothes.

Arcolano (är·kō·lä'nō), a baker, the husband of Togna. He catches his wife in her disguise and follows her, dressed in her clothes, to the house of the procuress, where Parabolano discovers the ruse.

Livia (lē'vē·ä), a virtuous matron and the object of Parabolano's lust.

Camilla (kä·mēl'lə), a courtean beloved by Messer Maco and used by Andrea to make a fool of him.

THE COURTSHIP OF MILES STANDISH

Author: Henry Wadsworth Longfellow (1807-1882)
Time of action: 1621
First published: 1858

PRINCIPAL CHARACTERS

Miles Standish, a gruff captain of the Pilgrim colony in Massachusetts in 1623. His wife has died the year before, and Standish suddenly decides he will ask Priscilla to marry him. Diffident about his courting ability, he begs Alden to plead his cause and is angry at Alden's lack of success. Later, returning after his supposed death during an expedition against unfriendly Indians, Standish gives his blessing to Alden and Priscilla, now married.

John Alden, a young scholar who shares a cabin with Captain Standish and who

is himself in love with Priscilla. He cannot refuse the favor asked in the name of friendship. Dejected, he determines to return to England on the "Mayflower" the next day. But the thought of leaving Priscilla causes him to reconsider, and he remains in Massachusetts.

Priscilla, an orphan who feels insulted that Standish will not bother to do his own proposing. She asks John why he does not speak for himself. When news of Standish's supposed death reaches the colony, she marries John.

COUSIN BETTE

Author: Honoré de Balzac (1799-1850)
Time of action: Early nineteenth century
First published: 1847

PRINCIPAL CHARACTERS

Baron Hector Hulot d'Ervy (ĕk·tôr' ü·lō' dĕr·vē'), a Councilor of State, an officer of the Legion of Honor, and a hopeless profligate whose rise in government cir-

cles has been accompanied by a series of scandals bringing distress to members of his family. After some years of happy married life he turned from his beauti-

213

ful, devoted wife and began to associate with the most notorious courtesans in Paris; now he is incorrigible. Not only does he dissipate the family fortune in his gradual degradation, but he also sullies the family honor and causes the deaths of his honorable brother and his wife's uncle as the result of unwise speculations and the misappropriation of state funds. His great charm, wit, and good manners go for nothing finally, and when he returns to his family he seduces a kitchen maid and marries her after his wife's sudden death on learning of this final outrage. Within the course of the novel his conquests number six—an actress, a singer, the wife of a vile traducer, two young girls, and the peasant wench whom he finally marries.

Baroness Adeline Hulot, nee **Adeline Fischer** (ȧd·lēn′ fē·shĕr′), Baron Hulot's devoted, long-suffering wife. In spite of her husband's many offenses, she trusts in God and the mystery of His ways. She maintains her dignity under compromising circumstances, even to the extent of enlisting the aid of one of her husband's mistresses at a time of crisis. Her final blow is her discovery that her husband has promised to make a kitchen servant a baroness as soon as his ailing wife dies. The shock kills her.

Lisbeth Fischer (lēz·bĕt′ fē·shĕr′), called **Cousin Bette,** the cousin of Baroness Hulot and the family old maid. Although envious of her cousin's place in the world, she hides her peasant avariciousness and resentment so well that the Hulots often turn to her for comfort in times of trouble. Although she insists that she is proud of her independence and financial security as an employee of a firm of embroiderers, she is nevertheless a lonely person, and she takes as her protégé-lover a talented young Polish sculptor, Count Wenceslas Steinbock, whom she has saved from suicide. When Steinbock falls in love with Adeline's daughter, charming Hortense Hulot, and marries her, Cousin Bette plans a subtle revenge.

Her malice leads her to introduce Steinbock and Baron Hulot to her friend Madame Valérie Marneffe. Her plan succeeds when both men become infatuated with that beautiful but heartless woman. Though her spite and scheming are undone in the end, Adeline and Hortense are never aware of the plot she has set in motion to destroy their happiness, and she remains good-hearted Cousin Bette, the family eccentric.

Victorin Hulot (vēk·tô·rȧn′ ü·lō), the son of Baron Hulot and his wife His father's escapades and disgrace turn Victorin into a man of responsibility and integrity, and he rebuilds the family fortune.

Célestin Hulot (sə·lĕs·tȧn′ ü·lō′), the wife of Victorin Hulot and the daughter of Monsieur Crével, a wealthy retired perfumer.

Monsieur Crével (krā·vĕl′), a wealthy man who admires and imitates the manners of Napoleon. Smarting because Baron Hulot has stolen his mistress, he attempts to seduce Adeline Hulot but is repulsed. Later he disrupts the marriage that has been arranged between Hortense Hulot and Counselor Lebas, when he reports that Baron Hulot will not be able to give his daughter a proper dowry. Through Cousin Bette he also meets Valérie Marneffe and becomes the Baron's rival for the coquette's charms. He marries Valérie after her husband's death, but his happiness as the husband of so charming a woman is short-lived. He and his wife die a short time later of a mysterious disease.

Valérie Marneffe (vȧ·lā·rē′ mȧr·nĕf′), the illegitimate daughter of a Marshal of France and the wife of an obscure government clerk. Unfaithful to her husband, she is as famous for her infidelities as she is for her beauty. At first a pawn in Cousin Bette's scheme to be revenged on the Hulot family, she soon takes matters into her own hands and cleverly plays one lover against another, as when she informs Baron Hulot, Steinbock, Crével, and her cuckold husband that each is the father of the unborn child whose real father is the dashing Baron Montès Montejanos. After the deaths of her stillborn child and her husband she marries Crével; her scheme is to inherit the retired perfumer's fortune and then marry Montejanos. Not aware of her intentions and wildly jealous, Montejanos apparently causes the death of the Crévels by infecting them with a loathsome and incurable tropical disease.

Monsieur Marneffe (mȧr·nĕf'), a minor government clerk. An acquiescent cuckold, he never interferes in his wife's affairs, but he is not above using her infidelities to advance himself in his work. His death leaves her free to marry a wealthy widower.

Baron Montès Montejanos (mōn̄·tĕs' mōn̄·tə·zhȧ·nō), a gallant Brazilian nobleman, the only man Valérie Marneffe truly loves. Not knowing that she hopes to secure a fortune by marrying Crével, he is greatly disconcerted on hearing the news and swears revenge against Valérie for her supposed infidelity to him.

Le Maréchal Hulot (lə mȧ·rā·shȧl ü·lō'), Baron Hulot's older brother, a man of distinguished military service and great personal honor. Cousin Bette gains his confidence and becomes his housekeeper. A short time later the banns for their marriage are published. Although the government scandal involving his brother is hushed up, the old man insists on making restitution by paying his entire

fortune into the state treasury. He then takes to his bed and dies three days later. His death is a blow to Cousin Bette, for it is the indirect result of her own intrigue involving Baron Hulot and Valérie Marneffe, and it ends her hope of outranking through marriage her Cousin Adeline's position in society.

Johann Fischer (zhō·ȧn' fē·shĕr'), Adeline Hulot's uncle and her husband's accomplice in his scheme to defraud the government. Arrested for his dishonest activities, Fischer commits suicide.

Josepha (zhō·zə·fȧ'), a singer at the Opera and at one time Crével's mistress. When Baron Hulot takes the beautiful young Jewess away from him, Crével tries to seduce the Baron's wife.

Dr. Bianchon (byän̄·shōn'), the physician who attends the Crévels during their fatal illness.

Agathe Piquetard (ȧ·gȧt' pē·kə·tȧr'), the kitchen maid whom Baron Hulot marries after his wife's death.

Counselor Lebas (lə·bȧ'), a lawyer at one time betrothed to Hortense Hulot. To get revenge on the Hulots, Crével causes the engagement to be broken off when he tells Lebas that the Baron cannot supply an adequate marriage portion for his daughter.

Carabine (kȧ·rȧ·bēn'), the demimondaine at whose intimate supper party Baron Montès Montejanos learns that Valérie Marneffe is to marry Crével.

COUSIN PONS

Author: Honoré de Balzac (1799-1850)
Time of action: The 1840's
First published: 1847

PRINCIPAL CHARACTERS

Sylvain Pons (sēl·văn̄' pōn̄s), usually called **Cousin Pons** but sometimes referred to as "The Parasite," an elderly musician whose twin passions are art

215

and food. Born ugly, with a massive head and a huge nose, he was at one time a composer of popular songs and several operas; he now makes a modest living as an orchestra conductor and music teacher. He dresses shabbily and constantly dines out at the tables of his distant relatives in order to save money for the purchase of new objects for his valuable art collection. Naïve, greedy in his love of food, perfectly harmless, and shyly affectionate, he plans to leave his collection to Cécile Camusot, the daughter of a cousin-in-law once removed. Denied his relatives' house after he proposes an unfortunate match for his favorite, he takes to his bed, never to recover. While dying, he learns the ways of the world. He tries to thwart his selfish relatives and grasping housekeeper by making a false will leaving his entire collection to the state with a provision that Schmucke, his only true friend, will receive from the government a lifetime pension. His plans fail because Schmucke, who by another will is his only heir, innocently allows himself to be defrauded of his inheritance. A brilliant collector and amateur art connoisseur, Cousin Pons is the victim of a campaign carried on by his doctor, a rascally lawyer, his relatives, his housekeeper, and a rival art collector.

Herr Schmucke (shmük), a pianist, the only close friend of Cousin Pons. Unselfish in his devotion, he becomes the victim of the greedy Camusots, who, bringing a suit to break their relative's will, break the old musician's spirit also and put him in his grave. Schmucke possesses such delicacy of manner and personal integrity that he will not fight to claim the fortune that is rightfully his.

Monsieur Camusot de Marville (kȧ-mü·zō′ dǝ mȧr·vēl′), Cousin Pons' cousin-in-law and one of the presiding judges of the Royal Court of Justice in Paris, who has added the name of the family estate to his own in order to distinguish him from his father. A just man, he is ungenerous in his treatment of his distant relative only because his wife, who detests Cousin Pons, blames the old musician for their daughter's loss of a suitor. He willingly joins in the plan to get possession of Pons' estate because it will provide a handsome dowry for the daughter and add considerably to the family fortune. He is one of the few who understand the true nature of Cousin Pons, and on one occasion he attempts to effect a reconciliation after his wife, daughter, and servant have insulted the elderly musician.

Madame Amélie Camusot de Marville (ȧ·mā·lē′ kȧ·mü·zō′ dǝ mȧr·vēl′), an ambitious, socially proud woman who receives Cousin Pons at her table with great reluctance. During one of his calls she and her daughter plead a previous engagement and insultingly tell him that he will be compelled to dine alone. Her attitude toward the old man softens somewhat when Cousin Pons introduces to the household a wealthy German banker, Frédéric Brunner, whom he has proposed as a possible match for Cécile Camusot. But the banker, who considers Cécile a nonentity and her mother a dry stick, is not impressed by the Camusots and refuses to consider an alliance with them. Mme. Camusot, convinced that Cousin Pons has planned the whole affair to humiliate his relatives, becomes more virulent than ever in her attitude toward him and forbids him her house.

Cécile Camusot (sā·sēl′ kȧ·mü·zō′), the red-haired, plain-spoken, but not unattractive daughter of the Camusots, still unmarried, to her mother's distress, at the age of twenty-three. In an attempt to please his relatives, Cousin Pons suggests a match between her and Frédéric Brunner, a young millionaire banker of German descent, but Brunner is cautious and critical and refuses to consider Cécile as his wife. After all legal entanglements have been resolved, she inherits the fortune represented by Cousin Pons' art collection. She marries Vicomte Popinot.

216

Madame Cibot (sē·bō'), the portress at Cousin Pons' lodgings and his housekeeper. Called in to nurse Cousin Pons during his last illness, and inspired by tales of legacies left by bachelor lodgers to deserving housekeepers, she plans to secure a part of Pons' art collection for herself after she has heard a report of its value. Her scheming involves her with Monsieur Frasier, a rascally lawyer; Dr. Poulain, Pons' physician; Remonencq, an unscrupulous dealer in bric-a-brac, and Elie Magus, a famous art collector who buys some of Pons' most valuable paintings at ridiculously low prices after she is able to convince innocent Schmucke that funds are needed to provide for his sick friend. When Pons rallies sufficiently to realize what has happened, he makes two wills in an effort to outwit Madame Cibot. In the first she is mentioned as one of his heirs. In the other the collection is left to his friend Schmucke without reservation. Offered one hundred thousand francs to destroy the first will, Madame Cibot tries unsuccessfully to do so. Remonencq, also eager to share in Pons' estate, helps to poison Cibot as a step toward marrying the widow. The dealer also dies after drinking a glass of vitriol intended for his wife, and Madame Remonencq becomes the sole proprietress of an art shop on the Boulevard de la Madeleine.

Monsieur Remonencq (rə·mō·năṅk'), a rascally dealer in curios and cheap art objects. Taken into Madame Cibot's confidence, he helps Elie Magus, a celebrated art dealer, swindle Schmucke in the purchase of eight paintings from Pons' art collection. Hoping to carry his partnership with Madame Cibot a step farther, he poisons her invalid husband's barley water and marries the widow. He himself dies after drinking a glass of vitriol he intended for his wife.

Monsieur Frasier (frĕ·zyā'), the shyster lawyer who directs the legal wrangle that follows the death of Cousin Pons. A cadaverous, ailing, unscrupulous man,

he makes Madame Cibot his tool while working in the interest of the Camusot family. He persuades Madame Camusot de Marville to contest the will on the ground that Schmucke had exercised undue influence over his sick friend. Brokenhearted by this accusation, Schmucke lets the estate go unchallenged to the Camusots and dies a short time later. Frasier is appointed to the post of justice of the peace as his reward for handling the legal battle with shrewdness and dispatch.

Dr. Poulain (pōō·lăṅ), the physician who attends Cousin Pons during his last illness. Having heard that the sick man's art collection is extremely valuable, he repeats this information to Madame Cibot and advises her to feather her nest while there is time. He sends her to consult his legal friend, Monsieur Frasier, and thus draws the conniving lawyer into the affair. Frasier tells him that he will be made the head of a hospital if Pons dies intestate.

Elie Magus (ā·lē' mȧ·güs'), an impassioned amateur art collector covetous of Cousin Pons' art treasures. His desire to corner the art market causes him to join in the plot to swindle Schmucke and buy some of Pons' best pictures at a low cost.

Comte Popinot (kōṅt' pô·pē·nō'), a prominent figure in political circles. He treats Cousin Pons kindly, and the old musician frequently dines at his house.

Vicomte Popinot (vē·kōṅt' pô·pē·nō'), a hero of the July Revolution. Though not enchanted by Cécile Camusot's charms, he eventually marries her and shares in Cousin Pons' legacy.

Frédéric Brunner (frā·dā·rēk' brŭn'ĕr), called **Fritz**, a wealthy young German banker. Cousin Pons proposes him as a possible husband for Cécile Camusot, but nothing except the resentment of the girl's mother results from his attempt at matchmaking.

217

Gaudissart (gō·dē·sȧr'), the proprietor of the theater where Cousin Pons conducts the orchestra. He tries without success to protect Schmucke's interests in the matter of the contested will.

Topinard (tô·pē·nȧr'), a supernumerary at the theater to whom Cousin Pons had given five francs every month. He takes Schmucke into his own poor lodgings, after Frasier has evicted Cousin Pons'

friend, and nurses the German until his death.

Madeleine Vivet (mȧ·də·lĕn' vē·vā'), a scrawny spinster, lady's maid and housekeeper to Madame Camusot. Ambitious to become Madame Pons, she is disappointed when he pays no attention to her charms or her savings. She never misses an opportunity to ridicule the old man or play malicious tricks on him.

THE COXCOMB

Authors: Francis Beaumont (1585?-1616) and John Fletcher (1579-1625)
Time of action: Early seventeenth century
First presented: 1608-1610

PRINCIPAL CHARACTERS

Antonio, the coxcomb, a ridiculous parody of the conventional friend. He insists that his traveling companion, Mercury, visit his home. Finding that Mercury is infatuated with his wife, he decides to become immortal as a famous friend. He appears in various disguises attempting to persuade Maria to commit adultery with Mercury.

Maria, Antonio's beautiful but heartless wife. She sees through Antonio's disguises and thwarts him several times, finally having the disguised Antonio accused of murdering the real Antonio. At last she becomes so irritated with him that she commits adultery with Mercury.

Mercury, Antonio's traveling companion. Overwhelmed with Antonio's fatuous friendship and horrified at his own passion for Maria, he strives to avoid temptation; but Maria breaks down his

resistance. After the adulterous affair he loses interest in her.

Viola, a lovely and virtuous young girl. Running away from home to marry Ricardo, she finds him drunk, rowdy, and dangerous. Fleeing from him, she suffers various perils and hardships. Moved to tenderness by his repentance, she forgives him and consents to marry him.

Ricardo, Viola's sweetheart. Becoming drunk on his proposed wedding night, he mistakes Viola for a harlot, terrifying her into flight. Repentant, he devotes himself to finding her. When he does find her as a servant of Mercury's mother, he confesses his unworthiness and begs forgiveness.

Valerio, a married man who befriends Viola, but attempts to make her his mistress. Ricardo persuades him to help in her discovery.

THE CRADLE SONG

Author: Gregorio Martínez Sierra (1881-1947)
Time of action: Early twentieth century
First presented: 1911

218

PRINCIPAL CHARACTERS

The Prioress, whose fortieth birthday occasions a celebration.

Teresa (tä·rä′sä), left as a baby at the convent, and cared for by the nuns. Her departure at the age of eighteen concludes the play.

Sister Joanna of the Cross (hō·ä′nyä), who is eighteen when Teresa is left at the convent. As the child grows, she looks upon Sister Joanna as her mother.

Sister Marcella (mär·thä′lyä),
Sister María Jesús (mä·rē′ä hä·sōōs′), and
Sister Sagrario (sä·grä′ryō), young nuns.

The Mistress of Novices.

The Old Prioress.

Sister Tornera (tor·nä′rä) and
Sister Inez (ē·näth′), older nuns at the time of Teresa's arrival.

The Doctor, the convent physician. He legally adopts baby Teresa and leaves her in the care of the nuns.

Antonio (än·tō′nyō), who loves Teresa and plans to marry her and take her to America.

CRANFORD

Author: Mrs. Elizabeth Gaskell (1810-1865)
Time of action: Early nineteenth century
First published: 1853

PRINCIPAL CHARACTERS

Mary Smith, a young Englishwoman who narrates the little affairs of the spinsters living in the village of Cranford.

Miss Deborah Jenkyns, a domineering spinster. She makes all the decisions for herself and her fifty-five-year-old unmarried sister Matilda, called Matty. They are the daughters of a rector. When Deborah dies, her sister finds it difficult to make decisions for herself.

Miss Matilda (Matty) Jenkyns, who, though she has a better mind than Deborah, allows herself to be dominated by her sister. As a young woman she had rejected a suitor in order to remain with her mother. When her financial situation becomes grave her greatest concern is that she will be too poor to be included in the society of the village spinsters. She sets up a small shop and sells tea.

Thomas Holbrook, Matty's rejected suitor.

Lady Glenmire, Mrs. Jamieson's sister-in-law. She upsets the little community by marrying a doctor, whom many regard as no better than a tradesman.

Mrs. Jamieson, a friend of Matty. She becomes the social leader of Cranford's spinster population upon the death of Deborah. She upsets her friends by not including them among the people she invites to meet her sister-in-law, Lady Glenmire. She later drops her sister-in-law when Lady Glenmire marries a doctor.

Mr. Hoggins, the doctor whom Lady Glenmire marries.

Miss Pole and
Mrs. Forrester, friends of Matty.

Peter Jenkyns, the long-lost brother of Matty and Deborah. He returns to the village to care for Matilda when she is in financial straits.

Martha, Matty's faithful maid.

Captain Brown, a semi-retired man who

219

is crude but whom the spinsters learn to accept because he is kind and considerate to them, and because he has two unmarried daughters.

Mary Brown, Captain Brown's older daughter, who is dying of an incurable illness.

Jessie Brown, Captain Brown's younger

daughter. After the death of her father and sister, she marries a suitor of long standing.

Major Gordon, who marries Jessie.

Mr. Smith, the narrator's kindly father. He becomes Matty's adviser.

Betsy Barker, the owner of a famous cow.

THE CREAM OF THE JEST

Author: James Branch Cabell (1879-1958)
Time of action: Twentieth century
First published: 1917

PRINCIPAL CHARACTERS

Felix Kennaston, a successful, highly romantic author. He is writing a novel about Ettarre, the ageless woman, and his plot centers around a broken round medallion with mysterious symbols, which he calls the sigil of Scoteia. In his dreams he talks with Ettarre and accompanies her to historical places and times; but when he tries to touch her, the dream invariably ends. One day in his garden he finds a shiny broken disc which, giving full play to his romantic imagination, he chooses to believe is the real sigil of Scoteia. He finds the other half of the disc in his wife's bathroom and wonders about her relation to Ettarre. After his wife dies, he shows his two magic pieces to his neighbor Harrowby, who readily identifies them as the broken top of a cosmetic jar. Disillusioned at last, Felix prepares to face the realities of middle age.

Kathleen Kennaston, his wife (nee Eppes). She is thin and capable and she treats her husband with polite boredom. Though she is a good wife, Kennaston finds her unexciting and a dull conversationalist. She dies in her sleep.

Richard Harrowby, Felix' neighbor, who admits he cares little for Kennaston, whose story he tells. Harrowby manu-

factures toilet preparations and for a hobby studies the occult. He is both entertained and sometimes annoyed by Kennaston's romanticism.

Ettarre, a woman in Kennaston's novel and in his dreams. His ideal (and the ideal of all men), she is similar to, and the younger sister of, Dorothy la Désirée in Cabell's "Jurgen." Ettarre accompanies Kennaston in his nightly dreams in which the two are present on important dates in many widely separated ages. When he is about to touch her, however, his dream always ends.

Horvendile, a clerk, a character in Kennaston's novel with whom the author identifies himself. The names Horvendile and Kennaston are often used interchangeably to suggest that they are two sides of one personality.

Muriel Allardyce, one of Kennaston's former loves.

Characters in Kennaston's novel:

Count Emmerick, brother of La Beale Ettarre.

Dame Melicent, his elder sister.

Comte Perion de la Forêt, Melicent's husband.

220

Maugis d'Aigremont, a master villain, a brigand slain by Horvendile in Ettarre's bedroom.

Sir Guiron des Rocques, Ettarre's betrothed.

CRIME AND PUNISHMENT

Author: Fyodor Mikhailovich Dostoevski (1821-1881)
Time of action: Mid-nineteenth century
First published: 1866

PRINCIPAL CHARACTERS

Rodion Romanovitch Raskolnikov (rô-dǐ·ōn rô·mä′nə·vǐch räs·kōl′y·nǐ·kəf), called **Rodya,** a psychologically complex young law student who murders not for wealth but as an experiment, to see if he is one of those who can circumvent society's restrictions. Impoverished and weakened by illness and hunger, he decides to rid society of a worthless person in order to preserve his genius for posterity, to relieve his devoted mother and sister from compromising themselves, and to prove that he is above conscience. He kills Alonya Ivanovna, a miserly old crone, and her sister. Later, in his loss of illusions, of peace of mind, and of the wealth he sought, he learns through suffering. Important changes result from acceptance of his inward punishment. His humanitarian instincts are brought out; his deep love of family and friends is revealed, and his belief that life must be lived is renewed. The study of his psychoses from the time he conceives his mad theory to his attempt at expiation in Siberia is masterly in Dostoevski's characterization of a tormented mind and shattered body. The study is one of contrasts, of good and evil, within all mankind.

Pulcheria Alexandrovna (pooly·chě′rǐ·yə ä·lĕk·sän′drəv·nə), his long-suffering mother whose faith in her son sustains her but whose mind gives way under the strain of his deed and guilt. A handsome, middle-aged woman of distinction, a widow who has supported her family and urged her son to make his

way in life, Pulcheria is a study of motherhood thwarted, a woman tortured by her inability to fathom her favorite's depravity.

Avdotya Romanovna (äv·dōt′yə rô·mä′-nəv·nə), called **Dounia** (doo′nyə), her daughter and the younger sister who has aided in her mother's effort to make something of the brother through working and skimping. A mirror of her mother's fortitude and faith, Dounia is the beautiful, impoverished, clear-sighted savior of her family. In spite of attempted seductions, the devoted sister continues her efforts to sustain her beloved brother in his reversals and suffering.

Dmitri Prokofitch Razumihin (dmǐ′trǐ prô·kō′fĭch rä·zoo′mǐ·hǐn), Raskolnikov's devoted friend. Enamored of Dounia, he is the savior of the family honor. Like Dounia, he has all the normal responses of a generous nature and works unceasingly to discover and repair the tragic situation of his friend. Affianced to the beautiful Dounia, he founds a publishing company to aid the hapless girl, mother, and brother. He is one of the few characters with a sense of humor; his good deeds lighten a psychologically gloomy and depth-insighted plot.

Piotr Petrovitch Luzhin (pyō′tr pět·rō′-vǐch lyooz′hǐn), a minor government official betrothed to Dounia, a man filled with a sense of his own importance. Raskolnikov objects to his suit. Dounia herself loses interest in him after she meets Razumihin, whom she later marries.

Sofya Semyonovna Marmeladov (sō'fyə sĕ·myō'nəv·nə mär·mĕ'lä·dəf), called **Sonia,** the daughter of a drunken clerk and stepdaughter of the high-strung Katerina Ivanovna. It is her father who brings the luckless prostitute to Rodya's attention and whose funeral the unstable student finances. From gratitude the benevolent though soiled child of the streets comforts the murderer and supports him in his transgressions so that he finally will confess. Forced to support her father, her stepmother, and their three children, she remains unsullied and her spirit transcends these morbid conditions. With great depth of character and faith, Sonia follows the criminal to Siberia, where she inspires the entire prison colony with her devotion and goodness.

Marmeladov (mär·mĕ'lä·dəf), an impoverished ex-clerk and drunkard, Sonia's father. He is killed when struck by a carriage. Raskolnikov, who witnesses the accident, gives Marmeladov's wife some money to help pay for his friend's funeral expenses.

Katerina Ivanovna (kä·tĕr·in'ə ĭ·vä'nôv·nə), Marmeladov's wife, slowly dying of tuberculosis. She collapses in the street and dies a short time later.

Arkady Ivanovitch Svidrigaïlov (är·kä'dĭy ĭ·vä'nə·vĭch svĭ·drĭg'ĭ·ləf), the sensualist in whose house Dounia had been a governess. He is both the would-be seducer and savior of Dounia, and through her of Sonia's orphaned half sisters and brother, when he gives her money as atonement for his conduct. A complicated character, sometimes considered, with Raskolnikov, one of the alter egos of the writer, he is obsessed by guilt and driven by libido.

Porfiry Petrovitch (pôr·fĭ'rĭy pĕt·ro'vĭch), a brilliant detective more interested in the rehabilitation than the prosecution of the murderer. Somewhat disturbed and neurotic himself, Porfiry seconds Sonia's influence and causes Raskolnikov to confess his crime and thus begin his redemption.

Alonya Ivanovna (ä·lyō'nyə ĭ·vä'nôv·nə), a miserly old pawnbroker and usurer, murdered by Raskolnikov.

Lizaveta Ivanovna (lyē·zä·vĕ'tə ĭ·vä'nôv·nə), a seller of old clothes and Alonya Ivanovna's sister, also killed by Raskolnikov.

THE CRIME OF SYLVESTRE BONNARD

Author: Anatole France (Jacques Anatole Thibault, 1844-1924)
Time of action: Nineteenth century
First published: 1881

PRINCIPAL CHARACTERS

Sylvestre Bonnard (sēl·vĕs'tr bô·när'), a shy philologist who has a penchant for getting involved in other people's lives. A bachelor, Bonnard befriends a poor widow and, later, an orphan girl who is the daughter of Clementine, Bonnard's love in his youth. He lives a good life among books and is happy in his late years because a young couple he has helped return his affection.

M. Coccoz (mə·syœ' kō·kōz'), a poverty-stricken bookseller from whom Bonnard buys no books. Out of compassion for the poor man and his wife and child, he sends logs to their attic room to keep them warm. Coccoz soon dies, leaving his wife and child to face the world alone. His beautiful widow eventually marries Prince Trépof, a wealthy Russian.

Prince Trépof (trä·pôf') and **Princess Trépof** (trä·pôf'), who had married after M. Coccoz' death. The Prince, inordinately wealthy, travels the world expanding his match box collection. Princess Trépof, remembering the kindness Bonnard had shown her and her first husband, obtains for Bonnard the "Golden Legend," a manuscript he had given up hope of ever owning.

Jeanne Alexandre (zhän' à·lĕk·sän'dr), the shy daughter of Clementine, Bonnard's early love. She is befriended by Bonnard, and when she marries he sells his library, except for a single volume, to provide money to give the young couple a start in life.

Signor Polizzi (pô·lē·zē'), a slippery jack-of-all-trades who owns the manuscript of the "Golden Legend." Polizzi allows Bonnard to travel from Paris to the Polizzi place in Sicily to read the manuscript. Arriving there, Bonnard discovers that the manuscript had already been sent to the Paris bookstore of Polizzi's son.

M. and Mme. de Gabry (də gà·brē'), a couple who invite Bonnard to their country estate to catalog de Gabry's ex-tensive library. While there, Bonnard discovers Jeanne and learns that she is the de Gabrys' ward.

Henri Gélis (än·rē' zhä·lēs'), a student who, while receiving help for his thesis from Bonnard, falls in love with Jeanne, who is now Bonnard's ward. They marry and have a baby, Sylvestre, who dies. Bonnard knows, however, that since they are young, they will eventually raise a family.

Maître Mouche (mĕ'tr mōōsh'), Jeanne's guardian while she is the de Gabrys' ward. When Mouche disappears after embezzling some money, Bonnard becomes Jeanne's legal guardian.

Mlle. Préfère (prā·fĕr'), Jeanne's teacher in the select school the girl attends. At first Mlle. Préfère has hopes of marrying Bonnard. When her affection is not returned, however, she grows hostile toward him.

Thérèse (tā·rĕz'), Bonnard's maid, whose firm hand keeps her master's domestic affairs in order.

THE CRISIS

Author: Winston Churchill (1871-1947)
Time of action: Civil War period
First published: 1901

PRINCIPAL CHARACTERS

Stephen Brice, a young Boston lawyer who migrates to St. Louis in 1858. He falls in love with Virginia Carvel and, influenced by Lincoln, becomes an active Republican. Enlisting in the Union Army, he serves in the Civil War. His saving of Clarence Colfax's life and his outstanding qualities enable him to marry Virginia despite the fact that she is an ardent Southerner.

Judge Whipple, Stephen's friend. He helps the young man get started in a political career.

Mrs. Brice, Stephen's widowed mother, who migrates with him to St. Louis.

Virginia Carvel, an ardent Southerner. Though her partisan loyalties conflict with Stephen's, she comes to love him and, eventually, marries him.

Colonel Carvel, Virginia's father. He serves in the Confederate forces.

Abraham Lincoln, who is an influence in Stephen's life. He makes Stephen and Virginia realize they must forgive and forget their sectional loyalties.

Clarence Colfax, a young Southerner, a rival for Virginia's love. His life is twice saved by the intervention of Stephen.

Ulysses S. Grant, the famous Union general. Stephen meets him at the outbreak of the war before Grant gets a command. Near the end of the war Stephen, now a major, is sent to Virginia to report to General Grant on Sherman's campaigns.

William T. Sherman, famous Union general. Stephen meets him early in the Civil War and later serves as a member of the General's staff.

Eliphalit Hopper, an unscrupulous carpetbagger.

THE CRITIC

Author: Richard Brinsley Sheridan (1751-1816)
Time of action: Eighteenth century
First presented: 1779

PRINCIPAL CHARACTERS

Mr. Dangle, a wealthy Londoner who is stage-struck and brings into his house a constant parade of musicians, actors, critics, and other theatrical types. He is one of the witnesses to the rehearsal of Mr. Puff's new play.

Mrs. Dangle, Dangle's wife, who objects to the stream of theatrical callers that clutter up her house. She discusses the theater and drama with Mr. Sneer, who comes to call, and also rescues her husband from some musicians who cannot speak English but want him to get them jobs.

Mr. Puff, a playwright as well as an eighteenth century press agent who praises things for a price. He has several categories of "puffs" which he writes in praise of anyone or anything when he is well paid. His play is the one being rehearsed, and he quarrels with the actors and the under-prompter because they have cut his lines and scenes and because the scenery has not been made. Puff is very proud of his playwriting ability.

Mr. Sneer, Dangle's friend, with whom he discusses the theater. He is one of the group who watch the rehearsal of Puff's play.

Sir Fretful Plagiary, a dramatist who cannot stand any kind of criticism of his work. He brushes aside any critical remarks about his new play and holds forth at great length against those who say anything unflattering about his playwriting.

THE CROCK OF GOLD

Author: James Stephens (1882-1950)
Time of action: Any time
First published: 1912

PRINCIPAL CHARACTERS

The Old Philosopher, living in the center of a pine wood. Many come to seek his advice.

Another Old Philosopher, who lives with the first Philosopher. When he decides that he has learned all he is capable of learning, he spins around in the room until he falls dead.

The Grey Woman, the wife of the second Philosopher. She spins herself to death

224

because of her grief over her husband's demise. These two bodies are buried under the hearthstone by the Thin Woman. The finding of them later results in the first Philosopher's arrest.

The Thin Woman, the wife of the first Philosopher. After his arrest, she goes to seek help from Angus Óg, who with all the other gods comes to bring happiness to the people. The charges against the Philosopher are forgotten and he is freed.

Seumas, the son of the first couple.

Brigid, the daughter of the second couple. For a while they are lured away by the vengeful and troublemaking leprechauns, but are freed because the leprechauns fear the Thin Woman.

Meehawl MacMurrachu, who, in following the Philosopher's advice to steal the leprechauns' crock of gold because they stole his wife's washboard, rouses the ire of the leprechauns.

Caitilin, Meehawl's daughter. The leprechauns send Pan to steal her away.

The Great God Pan, god of the beast which is in every man. He lures Caitilin away and teaches her the meaning of hunger and pain.

Angus Óg, an early Irish god. Petitioned by the Philosopher, he forces Caitilin to choose between Pan and him. He is Divine Inspiration. She chooses Angus Óg and so is saved from the beast in man. At the story's end, the birth of Angus Óg's and Caitilin's child is awaited.

**The Most Beautiful Man,
The Strongest Man,** and
The Ugliest Man, "the Three Absolutes," gods whose questions the Thin Woman must answer on her way to seek Angus Óg's aid for her husband.

CROME YELLOW

Author: Aldous Huxley (1894-   )
Time of action: The 1920's
First published: 1922

PRINCIPAL CHARACTERS

Henry Wimbush, the owner of Crome, a country house in England. He is the host for the house party that brings together the unusual group of people who are characters in the novel. Wimbush is so interested in Crome that he has been writing its history for thirty years. He frequently calls his guests together to read to them choice portions of his account.

Denis Stone, a young poet, almost a symbol in the novel for artistic ineffectuality, who loves Anne Wimbush, old Henry's niece. Stone is disturbed by the other guests at the party, particularly by Scogan, a very rational man. Stone's suit is never realized, though Anne has decided she will accept him if he proposes.

The indecisive Stone makes one decision in the novel: he arranges to have sent a fake telegram recalling him to London. Ironically, his one decisive action separates him from Anne.

Anne Wimbush, a young woman, four years Stone's senior, who looks on his suit for her affection first with scorn, finally with sympathy. She, unlike Stone, thinks life should be accepted as it unfolds; Stone attempts to carry personally all the troubles of the world on his shoulders.

Mr. Scogan, Stone's opposite. Scogan is rational to the degree that Stone is sentimental. Scogan's cold-blooded intelligence annoys Stone.

225

Mrs. Priscilla Wimbush, a rather scatter-brained woman, Henry's wife, who studies the stars. She is enthusiastic because she has picked a winner at a horse race with information she divined from the movements of the celestial bodies.

Gombauld, an artist who is invited to Crome to paint Anne's picture. He expresses his love for Anne and is repulsed.

Jenny Mullion, a young deaf woman who makes up for her lack of hearing by observing very accurately the people at the party. She draws sketches of them in a book she carries, and she writes her impressions of life primarily for her own amusement.

Mary Bracegirdle, a woman remembered for her repressions and Freudian dreams. She is anxious most of the time and given to discussing her psychological ills with anyone who will listen. She decides first to pursue Stone and then Gombauld, and manages to talk with each man at the wrong time, when he is occupied with other interests. She does attract a painter of ghosts and spirits, Ivor Lombard, but after visiting her once, Lombard leaves Crome and sends back to Mary only a postcard with a terse message. She becomes convinced her life is a ruin.

CROTCHET CASTLE

Author: Thomas Love Peacock (1785-1866)
Time of action: Nineteenth century
First published: 1831

PRINCIPAL CHARACTERS

Ebenezer Mac Crotchet, the elderly squire of Crochet Castle, whose ability to make money and translate it into a fake family background is his chief attribute. He fancies himself to be a guardian of ideas and holds long sessions with pseudo-intellectuals discussing science and philosophy.

Young Crotchet, Ebenezer's son, who inherits his father's talent for making money. Young Crotchet's business ethics, however, are shady, and his personal relationships are founded primarily on monetary considerations. When he loses his money, he goes to America to join a banker who, having absconded with a bank's funds, has set up business across the Atlantic.

Susannah Touchandgo, the girl whom Young Crotchet abandoned when her father took the bank's money and went to America, leaving her penniless. She keeps body and soul together by teaching a farmer's children, but finally she marries a gentleman of some means.

Lady Clarinda Bossnowl, a girl betrothed to Young Crotchet because she has a title. When Crotchet goes bankrupt and leaves the country, she is happy to marry a young army officer who has a small but stable fortune.

Mr. Chainmail, an antiquarian who yearns for the olden days of iron clothing. When he discovers that Susannah Touchandgo was gently reared, he happily marries her.

Captain Fitzchrome, a young man who pines for Lady Bossnowl and who finally has the good fortune to win her.

Lemma Crotchet, Ebenezer's daughter, who marries Lady Bossnowl's brother.

THE CRUISE OF THE CACHALOT

Author: Frank T. Bullen (1857-1915)
Time of action: Late nineteenth century
First published: 1898

PRINCIPAL CHARACTERS

Frank T. Bullen, who recounts his whaling adventures aboard the "Cachalot," out of New Bedford, Massachusetts.

Captain Slocum, a hard driver and a foul talker. He is dragged overboard to his death by his deranged fourth mate.

Mr. Count, the first mate and the only decent officer aboard the "Cachalot." When he becomes captain following Slocum's death, he appoints Bullen as the fourth mate.

Mr. Jones, the fourth mate, a gigantic and cruel Negro. Crazed by a dream, he pulls Captain Slocum into the ocean with him.

Abner Cushing, one of the twelve white sailors aboard. He is beheaded by a whaling line.

Louis, the harpooner.

CRY, THE BELOVED COUNTRY

Author: Alan Paton (1903-   )
Time of action: Mid-twentieth century
First published: 1948

PRINCIPAL CHARACTERS

The Reverend Stephen Kumalo, a Zulu who is an educated man and an Anglican priest. He lives in the country and is unused to the ways of the city and its people. Even so, he goes to Johannesburg to help his sister and find his son. He does his best, which is not enough, to help his relatives. When his son is executed he cries out for help, for his land and his people, as well as his son.

Gertrude, the clergyman's sister. She has become a prostitute and dealer in illegal liquor in Johannesburg.

John, the clergyman's brother in Johannesburg, a practical man and a successful merchant. As a native politician he is disturbed by the police and kept under their surveillance. He is a selfish man; he has also abandoned the Christian faith.

Absalom, the clergyman's son. He is a country boy ruined by the white man's ways in the city. He drinks, commits adultery, and steals, at last killing a man who is an avid worker for the natives, trying to help them improve their condition. Found guilty of the crime, Absalom is sentenced to hang. His one act of goodness is to marry the woman who carries his unborn child.

Arthur Jarvis, Absalom's victim, a young white man who works very hard to help the natives improve their lot in Africa. There is irony in his death at the hands of one of the natives he wants to spend his life helping.

Msimangu, a native Anglican clergyman in Johannesburg. He is a good man who tries to help Stephen Kumalo find his people and understand them.

Mr. Jarvis, Arthur Jarvis' father. He carries on his son's work for the natives

227

by bringing milk for their children, farm machinery, an agricultural demonstrator, good seed, and a dam to provide water for irrigation. He even becomes Kumalo's friend after they have both lost their sons, one a murderer and the other his victim.

CUDJO'S CAVE

Author: John Townsend Trowbridge (1827-1916)
Time of action: 1861
First published: 1863

PRINCIPAL CHARACTERS

Penn Hapgood, a young Quaker schoolmaster in a Tennessee town. It is 1861, and Penn's anti-slavery convictions make him unpopular among the Secessionists. He steadfastly defends his convictions and aids others with anti-slavery and Unionist leanings, though his reversals include being tarred and feathered, having to hide out in a secret cave, undergoing capture and just missing hanging, and being captured again and almost bayoneted. At last his chief enemy is taken and forced to sign a safe-conduct pass for Penn and his party. Reaching Pennsylvania by way of Ohio, Penn enlists in the Union Army; his heroism earns him the name, "The Fighting Quaker."

Mr. Villars, a blind clergyman who shelters Penn and thus incurs the enmity of the Secessionists. His trials include imprisonment. He escapes and is guided to the cave, where he hides with the others. The safe-conduct pass gets him to Ohio.

Salina Sprowl, Mr. Villars' older daughter. Her vacillating attitude toward her estranged Secessionist husband constantly puts her friends in jeopardy.

Lysander Sprowl, Salina's worthless husband. Her weakness informs him that the anti-slavery group is safe in hiding. In order to undo her mischief, she has to set fire to her father's house to create confusion. Later she makes it possible for Sprowl to escape from the cave, where he is held prisoner. Returning with an attacking force, he is shot by his wife. She is bayoneted by Confederate soldiers.

Virginia Villars, the younger daughter of Mr. Villars and loved by a Secessionist planter whom she rejects. She too hides in the cave; in the end she reaches Ohio with her father.

Augustus Blythewood, a planter in love with Virginia. He is the relentless leader of the Secessionists. In the attack on the cave he captures Virginia and takes advantage of the opportunity to plead his suit again. She spurns him and, captured in turn, he signs a safe-conduct pass for all of Penn's group.

Carl, a German boy and a friend of Penn. He is accepted in the Confederate Army in place of Penn, who was faced with the choice of volunteering or hanging. As a Confederate soldier, Carl has many opportunities to help his friends in escaping. He goes with them to Ohio and thence with Penn to Pennsylvania, where they enlist in the same regiment.

Farmer Stackridge, a stanch Unionist. He befriends Penn and later brings a band of Unionists to the cave, which they fortify and help to defend.

Toby, a freed slave in the minister's household and a loyal friend to Penn and his fellow Unionists.

Pomp, a magnificent and heroic slave, owned by Blythewood. Reaching the North with the others, he serves the Union as a scout.

Cudjo, a fellow runaway slave. He and

228

Pomp hide and befriend Penn in a cave previously known only to escaping slaves. Cudjo's body is left in the cave.

Silas Ropes, a bully and the leader of a Secessionist mob. He causes much trouble before the attack on the cave in which he and Cudjo kill each other.

Dan Pepperill, a poor white man who befriends a slave and is flogged in consequence. Penn's aiding him is instrumental in making Penn unpopular.

Mrs. Sprowl, Penn's landlady and Lysander's mother.

CUPID AND PSYCHE

Author: Unknown
Time of action: The Golden Age
First transcribed: Unknown

PRINCIPAL CHARACTERS

Cupid, a god, Venus' son. He falls in love with Psyche and becomes her lover. When Psyche tries to see him, against his command, he kills her sisters, who had encouraged her action. He also abandons Psyche to the world. His love conquers his will, however, and he takes Psyche back again, petitioning Jove, king of the gods, to let her become immortal.

Psyche, a Greek princess. An oracle tells her father to leave her exposed upon a mountain to prevent the destruction of his people. Psyche, because of her beauty, arouses the jealousy of Venus. After being abandoned by Cupid, her lover, Psyche wanders the earth and finally becomes Venus' slave. With supernatural help she completes the otherwise insurmountable tasks assigned by Venus and wins back Cupid's love. Upon drinking ambrosia given her by Jove, Psyche becomes immortal.

Venus, goddess of love. Jealous of Psyche, she makes the girl her slave and assigns her four tasks: to separate an immense pile of mixed seeds, to gather the golden fleece of Venus' sheep, to fill a jug with water from a stream which feeds the rivers Styx and Cocytus, and to collect some of Proserpine's beauty in a box.

Zephyrus, god of the south wind. He carries Psyche to Cupid's palace. He also delivers Psyche's sisters there when Cupid grants Psyche their company in her loneliness.

Mercury, the messenger god who conducts Psyche to the presence of Jove.

Jove (Jupiter), king of the gods. He grants immortality to Psyche so that she and Cupid can be together forever.

THE CUSTOM OF THE COUNTRY

Author: Edith Wharton (1862-1937)
Time of action: Late nineteenth century
First published: 1913

PRINCIPAL CHARACTERS

Undine Spragg, an insatiably ambitious young woman whose beauty gains for

her a place in society, four marriages, each more materially profitable than the

229

last, and, finally, a desire for a fifth marriage to which she cannot attain because of her divorces.

Elmer Moffatt, Undine's vulgar, outspoken first husband. Forced by Undine's parents to get a divorce early in his marriage, Moffatt goes to New York where he becomes a significant financial figure. Later, as one of the richest men in the city, he remarries Undine and becomes her fourth husband.

Ralph Marvell, Undine's second husband. Disillusioned by his wife's ruthless desire for money and her insatiable social ambitions, he takes his own life.

Raymond de Chelles, a French *comte* and Undine's third husband. When he begins to neglect her, she divorces him and remarries the now wealthy Moffatt.

Jim Driscoll, American ambassador to England and an old society acquaintance of Undine. She aspires to become his wife.

Peter Van Degen, Undine's lover, who deserts her in Paris when he learns of her callous treatment of Ralph.

Paul Marvell, son of Undine and Ralph.

Laura Fairford, Ralph's sister.

Clare Dagonet, Ralph's cousin and the wife of Peter Van Degen.

Mr. Spragg, Undine's father. He is forced by Moffatt to invest money to further Moffatt's early financial career.

THE CYCLOPS

Author: Euripides (c. 485-c. 406 B.C.)
Time of action: Remote antiquity
First presented: Fifth century B.C.

PRINCIPAL CHARACTERS

Odysseus (ō·dĭs'ūs), the crafty King of Ithaca. On his way home from the sack of Troy he lands at Etna, in Sicily, the home of the Cyclops. Seeking food, he is captured by the Cyclops Polyphemus but manages to escape by blinding the giant after giving him wine. The story is taken from Book Nine of the "Odyssey," but Euripides has changed both some details of the original story and the character of Odysseus. Odysseus and his men do not escape by clinging to a ram's belly nor does the Cyclops block the entrance to his cave with a boulder. The change in the character of Odysseus is more important. He is not the son of Laertes, but of Sisyphus, the famous sinner of Corinth, a cheat and a thief. Odysseus becomes in the play a representative of civilized brutality. His speech for mercy before the Cyclops is filled with sophistry, and the sympathy which he arouses at the beginning of the play,

when he is weak and oppressed, is reversed by the brutality of his blinding of the Cyclops who, drunk, becomes a decadent but rather likable buffoon.

The Cyclops (sī'klŏps), called **Polyphemus** (pŏl·ĭ·fē'məs), the son of Poseidon. The one-eyed giant of the Homeric legend, he is the exponent of egoism and immoral application of might and right. To Odysseus' argument that the Cyclops should spare him and his men because the Greeks have preserved the temples of his father Poseidon and saved Hellas, the giant replies that he has no respect for the gods; his religion is his belly and his desires. He disregards morality through an appeal to nature and believes mercy a mere convention of the weak. The gory description of his cannibalism (he has two of Odysseus' men for his meal) does much to justify Odysseus' revenge, but he changes as he drinks.

230

Then he becomes the decadent buffoon who loathes war and tries to rape Silenus. Blinded, he is comic because of his repeated assertion that "Nobody," the name Odysseus has used, has done him in. As Odysseus leaves, having revealed his true identity, the Cyclops prophesies that Odysseus will be forced to wander the seas before returning to his home.

Silenus (sī·lē'nŭs), a follower of Dionysus. Shipwrecked on Etna while searching for Dionysus, who had been captured by Lydian pirates, he was taken by the Cyclops and has remained his slave. He is the "father" of the satyric chorus and a standard part of satyric convention. A lewd, fat, bald, boastful, cowardly, and drunken old man, he freely offers to trade Odysseus food for wine; however, when the Cyclops appear, he says that Odysseus has stolen the wine. He continues to drink throughout the play and is given in mock marriage to the Cyclops.

The Chorus of Satyrs. They are also a standard part of satyric convention. They are "horse-men," lewd in appearance, speech, and action. They exhibit a strong streak of cowardice. They offer to aid Odysseus in blinding the Cyclops, but when the time for action arrives they excuse themselves on the grounds that they have become lame while standing still. Their only real interest is in resuming the worship of Bacchus.

Coryphaeus (cŏ·rĭf'ē·ûs), the leader of the Chorus.

The Companions of Odysseus, members of his crew. They remain silent throughout the play. They help Odysseus blind the Cyclops.

CYMBELINE

Author: William Shakespeare (1564-1616)
Time of action: First century B.C.
First presented: 1609

PRINCIPAL CHARACTERS

Cymbeline (sĭm'bĕ·lēn), King of Britain. On the whole, he is more a conventional figure made to help the plot than a complex human being comparable to Shakespeare's greater creations. Quick-tempered, arbitrary, and unreasonable, he is naturally well-meaning and generous. His second wife influences him far more than he realizes. His forgiveness of his enemies and his son-in-law at the end of the play is an example of his essential goodness.

Imogen (ĭm'ō·jĕn)—disguised for part of the play as **Fidele** (fĭ·dē·lē, fĭ·dāl), a boy—Cymbeline's daughter by his former queen. She is the most admired character in the play, so much so that many critics feel it has small excuse for being except as a vehicle for her. She is a faithful wife, independent and courageous.

She escapes her father's court, her husband's plot to have her murdered, her wicked stepbrother's attempt to violate her, and her evil stepmother's plot to poison her. Disguised as a boy, she finds her unknown brothers in the forest. She forgives her husband for his lack of trust.

Posthumus Leonatus (pŏs'tū·mŭs lē·ō·nā'tŭs), Imogen's husband. A gentleman of good lineage but poor fortune, he is unacceptable to Cymbeline as a son-in-law. Banished for marrying Imogen, he goes to Italy. There, carried away while praising his wife, he makes an unwise wager with the evil Iachimo that his wife's chastity will withstand any temptation. She lives up to his faith, but Iachimo presents such strong circumstantial evidence that she has been unfaithful that Posthumus sends orders to

231

his servant to kill her. He receives undeserved forgiveness from her and is reunited with her.

Cloten (klŏ′tən), the Queen's repulsive son. Ignorant and stupid as well as vicious, he clothes himself in Leonatus' garments and follows Imogen, intending to violate her. He meets and threatens Guiderius, who promptly chops off his head. Finding his headless corpse in the familiar garments, Imogen thinks that her husband is dead.

The Queen, second wife of Cymbeline, whom she deceives and manages. The typical stepmother of folk tales, she endeavors to destroy Imogen with a supposed restorative which she has poisoned. She is largely responsible for the strife between Rome and England. She dies before her villainies are discovered, but they are exposed after her death.

Iachimo or **Jachimo** (yä′kĭ·mō, jä′kĭ·mō), an Italian villain. Irritated by Posthumus' praise of Imogen, he wagers that he can seduce her. When he fails in his attempt he hides in a trunk which is conveyed into her room, observes her sleeping, steals a bracelet from her, and memorizes her bedroom furnishings. With this circumstantial evidence and sworn lies he deceives Posthumus. He becomes remorseful, and when captured by Cymbeline's forces and questioned by Fidele-Imogen, he confesses all, repents, and is included in the general forgiveness.

Belarius (bĕ·lā′rĭ·ŭs), a banished lord, disguised as **Morgan.** Having been unjustly accused of treason, he has kidnaped the sons of Cymbeline and has reared them in a Welsh forest as his own sons. When Rome sends forces against England, he and the two youths come to the aid of the English forces. He discloses the identity of the young men to Cymbeline and receives forgiveness in the general rejoicing.

Guiderius (gwĭ·dē′rĭ·ŭs, jĭ·dē′rĭ·ŭs), living in the forest as **Polydore** (pŏl′ĭ·dōr), the elder son of Cymbeline. Though rough and untutored, he has a bold and royal nature. After his heroic deeds in the battle, he confesses to Cymbeline that he has killed Cloten and that he would be delighted to do so again if Cloten were still alive. He is condemned to death by Cymbeline, but is pardoned when his true identity is revealed.

Arviragus (är·vĭ·rā′gŭs), living in the forest as **Cadwal** (kăd′wôl), the younger son of Cymbeline. He and his brother welcome the homeless "Fidele" as a brother and grieve deeply at his supposed death. They rejoice when they learn that their supposed brother is actually their sister and that her apparent death was only a drugged sleep.

Caius Lucius (kā′yŭs lū′shĭ·ŭs), general of the Roman forces. He finds Fidele mourning over the body of the supposed Posthumus and offers his protection as a father rather than as a master. After the battle he is spared by Cymbeline's generosity.

Pisanio (pē·zä′nē·ō), Posthumus' loyal, intelligent servant. He disobeys his master's command to kill Imogen and falsely reports her death, but both disobedience and falsehood are higher level loyalty than literal obedience would have been. He confuses Cloten with false information, which happily leads to the violent death of the villainous prince. He gives the Queen's drug to Imogen, thinking it a restorative.

Cornelius (kôr·nē′lĭ·ŭs), a physician. Mistrusting the Queen, he gives her not the poison she asks for, but a harmless drug which gives a temporary appearance of death. The drug deceives Belarius and the brothers into thinking Fidele dead. At the play's end, Cornelius exposes the Queen's evil plot to Cymbeline.

Philario (fĭ·lä′rē·ō), an Italian friend of Posthumus. He introduces Posthumus to

Iachimo, thereby making the wager plot possible.

Helen (hĕl'ən), a lady attending Imogen.

Sicilius Leonatus (sĭ·sĭl'ĭ·ŭs lē·ō·nā'tŭs), the father of Posthumus. His ghost, along with those of his wife and two dead sons, appears in the masque-like vision of Posthumus in prison.

Jupiter (jōō'pə·tər). He also appears in the vision and promises a happy outcome for Posthumus.

CYRANO DE BERGERAC

Author: Edmond Rostand (1868-1918)
Time of action: Seventeenth century
First presented: 1897

PRINCIPAL CHARACTERS

Cyrano de Bergerac (sē·rà·nô' də bĕr-zhə·ràk'), a historical poet-playwright-soldier who as a contemporary of the three famous musketeers creates an image of romance considerably heightened by his lines in the play. Although the possessor of an enormous nose, which its owner declared was a symbol of generosity and independence, Cyrano has a romantic heart and a gifted tongue as well as a spirit of fierce independence. He chooses as his symbol, too, his white plume of unsullied integrity, never lowered for expediency's sake. While appearing boastful in the braggart warrior tradition, he actually is shy and diffident, especially when confronting beauty in any form. As the accomplice in a love plot, he never speaks for himself until wounded mortally. His name stands not only for an ugly handicap for which compensation must be made but for all that is good, true, loyal, and fine in human nature. Such integrity is in the great tradition of Don Quixote, whom Cyrano admires because tilting at the windmills of pomposity and philistinism, while it may throw the challenger down, more often elevates.

Christian de Neuvillette (krēs·t'yän' də nœ·vē·yĕt'), Cyrano's protégé in love, who never learns the language of sentiment. Often mistaken for a silent lover, the young soldier has greater depths of feeling and finer sensibilities than he can express. Undoubtedly handsome and generous, his valor in battle is offset by this morbid shyness in love, and while he acts the dupe of his mentor he resents very much his own inadequacies. He dies bravely, knowing that another man has won his wife, but realizing also that he will not be betrayed by his beloved friend and poet.

Roxane (rôk·sàn'), or **Madeleine Robin**, who as "précieuse" seems the prototype of thoughtless love, but who as suffering widow becomes the ideal of womanhood. Bright and beautiful, gay and youthful, Roxane is the symbol of beauty that all men desire. She insists that the amenities and conventions of love come before the character of the lover, only to learn that there is no substitute for sincerity of feeling and expression. She is also a romantic and somewhat silly heroine who becomes wise and thoughtful only after revelation.

Ragueneau (rà·gə·nō'), a pastry cook-poet who as a bard of the oven befriends the hero and holds a salon for destitute artists. While obviously the Silenus of the plot, this tippling pretender suffers the scorn of his wife and the appetite of his poets. He is loyal to an ideal and constant in his loyalties.

Le Bret (lə brā'), the friend and counselor of Cyrano and the author's commentator who interprets the brave soldier's heart. Steadfast in his regard for the hero, Le

233

Bret is the only one permitted to speak directly to him of his inconsistencies. He proves loyal and devoted always.

Montfleury (mōn̂·flœ·rē′), a famous actor whom Cyrano will not permit to play because of his lack of refinement and sensitivity to language. As the pompous idol of his day, the actor represents popular tastes, a symbol of decadence that Cyrano cannot tolerate.

The Comte de Guiche (kōn̂t′ də gēsh′), who woos Roxane without success and who has his revenge when he sends Christian, her husband, into battle and to his death. Though a representative of civil and military power, he displays some redeeming features even while he plays the villain of the play. He is a step above the fops and dandies, and he admires the bravery of Cyrano against the odds of life.

DAISY MILLER

Author: Henry James (1843-1916)
Time of action: Mid-nineteenth century
First published: 1878

PRINCIPAL CHARACTERS

Daisy Miller, the charming and unconforming American tourist whose inattention to decorum (she walks unchaperoned with an Italian suitor in the daytime) results in her ostracism by the Europeanized Americans in Rome. In defiance, she visits the Colosseum at night with the same young man and later dies of a fever contracted there.

Frederick Winterbourne, an American expatriate from whose point of view the story is told. At first puzzled by Daisy, he soon becomes convinced that she is immoral. However, after her death, he realizes that her manners indicated only a native American freedom, and that he loved her.

Giovanelli, the young Italian whose companionship causes the scandal involving Daisy. An adventurer interested primarily

in Daisy's money, he admits to Winterbourne after her death that she never would have consented to marry him.

Mrs. Walker, an American expatriate. Because Daisy rejects Mrs. Walker's efforts to preserve her from scandal, Mrs. Walker cuts her at a party, thus beginning Daisy's complete ostracism.

Randolph Miller, Daisy's young and spoiled brother. His impudence also shocks the American expatriates.

Mrs. Costello, Winterbourne's aunt. She refuses to meet Daisy because she is convinced that the Millers are common.

Eugenio, the Millers' courier and servant. That the Millers treat him almost as a member of the family also causes talk among the American expatriates.

DAME CARE

Author: Hermann Sudermann (1857-1928)
Time of action: Nineteenth century
First published: 1887

PRINCIPAL CHARACTERS

Max Meyerhofer (mäx mī′ér·hō′fér), a violent and brutal man, given to grandi-

ose but unsuccessful schemes for making money. He loses the family estate through forced sale and sinks constantly deeper into poverty. He finally dies of a stroke as he is about to fire the Douglas barn.

Frau Elsbeth Meyerhofer (frou ĕls'băt mī'ĕr·hō'fĕr), his long-suffering wife; after years of patience her spirit is broken and she dies a lingering death.

Paul Meyerhofer (poul mī'ĕr·hō'fĕr), their third son, born at the time the estate is lost and reared in poverty. His father ridicules him but his mother is loving. After his father attacks a servant wildly, Paul overpowers him and from that day takes over. By hard work he becomes a man of substance but, suspecting his father's intention to burn Douglas' barn, he attempts to distract him by setting fire to his own house and barn. Seriously burned, Paul recovers and spends two years in prison. Having lost everything, he feels free from his nemesis, Dame Care.

Mr. Douglas (dŭg'lăs), the new owner of the Meyerhofer estate. Sympathy for Paul causes him to agree to join in one of Meyerhofer's schemes. Meyerhofer becomes violent when Douglas objects to having his name used in borrowing money—but Douglas remains steadfast in his friendship to Paul.

Mrs. Douglas (dŭg'lăs), his wife, a kind-hearted woman, fond of Frau Elsbeth. She acts as godmother for Paul.

Elsbeth Douglas (ĕls'băt dŭg'lăs), their daughter. Engaged to marry her cousin, she loves Paul. After he is burned she stays by his bed, and her wedding is called off. When he is released from prison, Elsbeth and the family estate are to be his.

Katie (kä'tē) and
Greta (grā'tä), Paul's younger twin sisters. Learning that they have been dishonored by his old tormentors the Erdmann boys, Paul forces the Erdmanns at pistol point to swear they will marry the sisters.

Levy (lā'fē), a sharp trader who dupes Meyerhofer in a money-making scheme.

Michel (mē'shăl), a servant. Attacked by Meyerhofer, he gets revenge by burning the Meyerhofer barn.

THE DAMNATION OF THERON WARE

Author: Harold Frederic (1856-1898)
Time of action: The 1890's
First published: 1896

PRINCIPAL CHARACTERS

Theron Ware, a young Methodist minister whose religious training and faith are too frail to support the stresses of his life. Unhappy as a small-town minister, he decides to write a book about Abraham, only to find his learning is too slight on this or any intellectual subject. He learns that his Catholic acquaintances have a great deal more culture than he. As his faith totters he becomes suspicious of people and alienates his friends and his wife. He proves unfit for the ministry and becomes a real estate agent.

Alice Ware, a friendly, cheerful young woman, Theron's wife. Though she is accused by her husband of being unfaithful, she is loyal to her husband. When he falls ill, she nurses him back to health and helps him prepare for a new career.

Celia Madden, a pretty Irish-Catholic girl who becomes friendly with Theron and helps him discover that his prejudices are groundless. Her cultural interests also show him how thin the culture of his own people is. She is wrongly and

235

outrageously accused by Theron of being in love with Father Forbes. For a time Theron thinks he is in love with her, but he alienates her by saying that he is afraid of scandal if he is seen talking to her.

Father Forbes, a Catholic priest who becomes Theron's friend until Theron alienates him by talking slightingly about Dr. Ledsmar, the priest's friend, and by following the priest and Celia to New York.

Dr. Ledsmar, a friend of Father Forbes and Theron. He is alienated when Theron suggests that there is a scandalous relationship between Father Forbes and Celia.

Mr. Soulsby, a professional revivalist. He tries to convince the young minister that his sales approach to religion is not hypocritical. When Theron falls ill and leaves the ministry, Mr. Soulsby proves to be a true friend.

Mrs. Soulsby, Mr. Soulsby's wife, a practical woman who with her husband helps Theron make a new start in life as a real estate agent.

Mr. Gorringe, a trustee of Theron's church. He is the man whom Theron suspects of having an affair with his wife.

Michael Madden, Celia's brother. He, taking a dying man's privilege, tells Theron the truth about himself, as others see the young minister.

THE DANCE OF DEATH

Author: August Strindberg (1849-1912)
Time of action: Late nineteenth century
First presented: 1901

PRINCIPAL CHARACTERS

Edgar, a captain in the Swedish coast artillery. A man who regards all the world with contempt, he is a thorough domestic tyrant. His deliberate destruction of the happiness of his nearest family connections finally is ended by his death.

Alice, his wife. Virtually a prisoner and tyrannized for twenty-five years, she can only hope that her husband, who is ill and may die at any moment, will do so. She takes some vengeance in thwarting his plans occasionally and in taunting him on his deathbed. She feels reconciled to him after his death.

Curt, Alice's cousin. Edgar, jealous of his relations with Alice and hating him, succeeds in undermining Curt's career thoroughly, but Curt remains stoical.

Judith, the daughter of Edgar and Alice. The parents do not realize the seriousness of her love for Curt's son. Edgar's plan to marry her to a colonel forty years older than herself is ended when she reveals her true love for Allan, insults the colonel, and breaks the engagement. With her mother's help, she goes to the military post to which Edgar has sent Allan.

Allan, the son of Curt and therefore hated by Edgar. He is a young cadet in love with Judith.

DANGEROUS ACQUAINTANCES

Author: Pierre Choderlos de Laclos (1741-1803)
Time of action: Mid-eighteenth century
First published: 1782

The Marquise de Merteuil (már·kēz' də měr·tœ'y), a fashionable and unscrupulous matron. Abandoned by the Comte de Gercourt, she seeks vengeance for her wounded vanity by a series of manipulations that bring disaster or death to all who become involved with this dangerous acquaintance.

The Comte de Gercourt (kônt' də zhěr·kōōr'), betrothed to Cécile de Volanges. After he deserts the Marquise de Merteuil in favor of Madame de Tourvel, his humiliation becomes the object of the malicious Marquise's ruinous machinations.

Cécile de Volanges (sā·sēl' də vô·länzh'), a young girl betrothed by her mother to the Comte de Gercourt. She becomes a pawn in the Marquise de Merteuil's scheme of revenge on Gercourt.

The Vicomte de Valmont (vē·kônt' də vál·môn'), an unscrupulous libertine and ally of the Marquise de Merteuil in her scheme to humiliate the Comte de Gercourt.

The Chevalier Danceny (shə·vá·lyā' däns·nē'), a tool of the Marquise de Merteuil and the Vicomte de Valmont. Encouraged by them to form a liaison with Cécile de Volanges, Danceny is to make a laughing stock of the Comte de Gercourt.

Madame de Tourvel (də tōōr·vel'), a judge's wife for whom the Comte de Gercourt deserts the Marquise de Merteuil. She becomes the mistress of the Vicomte de Valmont.

Madame de Volanges (də vô·länzh'), the mother of Cécile de Volanges.

Madame de Rosemonde (də rōz·môñd'), the aunt of the Vicomte de Valmont.

Sophie Carnay (sō·fē' kár·nē'), Cécile de Volanges' friend and confidante.

DANIEL DERONDA

Author: George Eliot (Mary Ann Evans, 1819-1880)
Time of action: Mid-nineteenth century
First published: 1876

PRINCIPAL CHARACTERS

Daniel Deronda, the ward of Sir Hugo Mallinger and a noble, well-educated gentleman. At Cambridge University he helps a poor student, Hans Meyrick, to pass a scholarship examination. He rescues a young Jewish girl, Mirah Lapidoth, from drowning in the Thames, helps to start her on a singing career, and later marries her. He spends a great deal of time wondering about his parentage and searching for some knowledge of his past in the Jewish East End of London. At the end of the novel, before his marriage, he is pleased to learn that he is Jewish.

Gwendolen Harleth, an impoverished beauty who feels that she must marry a wealthy man in order to live the elegant life she desires. After rejecting several dull suitors, she marries Henleigh Mallinger Grandcourt, a wealthy heir, despite the fact that she knows Grandcourt has deserted the mistress who has borne him four children. She marries him after her widowed mother has lost all their money in a stock failure. The marriage is unhappy because Gwendolen is secretly in love with Daniel Deronda. After Grandcourt drowns in a yachting accident, Gwendolen feels guilty because she might have done much more to save him and had previously wished him dead. She confesses as much to Daniel, who has always disapproved of her gambling, recklessness, and love of finery.

237

Hoping to marry Daniel, she is disappointed when he tells her about Mirah. She resolves to reform and to live for others.

Mirah Lapidoth, the young Jewess whom Daniel saves from suicide and later marries. Because she has been abandoned, Daniel takes her to the home of some friends. She recovers, has a successful singing career, and is reunited with her brother Morecai before marrying Daniel.

Henleigh Mallinger Grandcourt, the nephew and heir of Sir Hugo Mallinger. He deserts his mistress after nine years and marries Gwendolen Harleth. A cold, supercilious man, he succeeds in breaking Gwendolen's spirit. After he drowns, his will reveals that he has left his property to his illegitimate son and has provided for his mistress better than he has for Gwendolen.

Sir Hugo Mallinger, the intelligent and benevolent owner of Diplow Hall. He has brought up Daniel Deronda and is enormously fond of him. He feels that Daniel is an English gentleman and objects when Daniel wishes to acknowledge the fact that he is Jewish; however, the two remain close friends.

Lady Mallinger, his wife, whom he did not marry until after he had adopted Daniel.

Ezra Lapidoth (Mordecai), Mirah's brother, a consumptive, learned young Jew who lives with the Cohens and gives lessons to Cohen's son. He also works in a bookshop. Abandoned by his father, he has known poverty and hardship. Daniel finds him, discovers his relationship to Mirah, and reunites the two. Much of Daniel's feeling of identification with Jews comes through his conversations with Mordecai. Mordecai dies at the end of the novel.

Ezra Cohen, a crafty but generous East End shopkeeper with whom Mordecai

boards. He first introduces Daniel to life in the Jewish section of London.

Mrs. Lydia Glasher, an attractive woman who had left her husband, an Irish officer, and son to become Grandcourt's mistress. She has four illegitimate children by him. She tells her story to Gwendolen because she believes that Gwendolen should morally refuse Grandcourt's offer of marriage.

Hans Meyrick, a Cambridge student. Daniel Deronda helps him win a scholarship when Hans' eyes are temporarily useless as the result of an accident. Hans falls in love with Mirah, but she rejects him. He becomes an artist and something of a dilettante.

Mrs. Fanny Davilow, Gwendolen's widowed mother. She is constantly ruled by headstrong Gwendolen.

The Reverend Henry Gascoigne, formerly Captain Gaskin, the rector of Pennicote, near Offendene.

Mrs. Nancy Gascoigne, his wife, Mrs. Davilow's sister. She tries to help Fanny, her less fortunate sister, and she introduces Gwendolen to eligible young men, but she cannot resist letting everyone know of her generosity.

Rex Gascoigne, their son, reading for the law. He is in love with his cousin Gwendolen.

Anna Gascoigne, his rather plain and meek sister who tries to help Gwendolen.

Warham Gascoigne, her brother, who goes to India.

Herr Julius Klesmer, a German-Jewish musician who is hired as a tutor at Quetcham Hall, the home of the Arrowpoints. He helps to launch Mirah's singing career and becomes important in the London musical world.

Catherine Arrowpoint, a talented and attractive young woman, Gwendolen's only rival in the social world near Pennicote. She falls in love with her tutor, Julius Klesmer, and marries him despite her parents' objections.

Mrs. Arrowpoint, of Quetcham Hall, Catherine's mother. She had hoped her daughter would make a more socially acceptable match.

Mr. Arrowpoint, her husband, a hospitable gentleman.

Thomas Lush, Grandcourt's scheming follower and companion.

Mrs. Meyrick, Hans' mother, who takes in and nurses Mirah when Daniel brings her to the Meyrick home. A poor and kind woman, she dotes on Daniel.

Kate Meyrick, her oldest daughter, who sews and embroiders.

Amy Meyrick, the second daughter.

Mab Meyrick, the youngest daughter, talented musically.

Alice Davilow, Gwendolen's half sister, a rather plain girl.

Bertha Davilow and **Fanny Davilow,** also half sisters, both "whisperers."

Isabel Davilow, another half sister, a listening child.

Miss Merry, governess to the four Davilow girls.

Mr. Middleton, the curate at Pennicote, in love with Gwendolen.

Lady Brackenshaw, the social leader of Pennicote.

Lord Brackenshaw, her husband.

Mrs. Vulcany, a Pennicote gossip.

Princess Leonora Halm-Eberstein, Daniel's mother, a singer and actress who had deliberately given Daniel to Sir Hugo Mallinger in order that her son might be brought up a gentleman and not be aware of his Jewish origin. Sir Hugo, in love with her at the time, had agreed. She reveals herself to Daniel in Genoa.

Joseph Kalonymos, a Mainz banker and a friend of Daniel's grandfather. Daniel visits him to learn more about his heritage.

Mr. Lapidoth, Mirah's father, an unsuccessful actor and singer who had deserted his children and absconded with their money. He reappears eventually and his children forgive him.

Mrs. Addy Cohen, Ezra Cohen's wife.

Mrs. Cohen, Ezra's mother, who helps in the shop.

Jacob Alexander Cohen, Ezra's very precocious son whom Mordecai tutors.

Adelaide Rebekah Cohen, Ezra's pretty, dark-eyed daughter.

Eugenie Esther Cohen, a baby.

Mr. Ram, owner of the East End bookshop where Mordecai works during the lunch hour. Mordecai and Daniel meet there.

Baroness von Langen, Gwendolen's hostess when she is gambling at the Casino in Leubronn.

Baron von Langen, her husband.

Mr. Vandernoodt, a wealthy and social gentleman staying at Leubronn.

DAPHNIS AND CHLOË

Author: Attributed to Longus (third century)
Time of action: Indefinite
First transcribed: Third century manuscript

Daphnis (dăf'nĭs), found as a baby by Lamo and reared by him. Though finally discovering that he loves Chloë, Daphnis is unable to ask for her in marriage until he finds a purse of silver. He is discovered to be Philopoemen, lost son of Dionysophanes.

Chloë (klō'ē), found as an infant girl by Dryas in the Cave of the Nymphs, on Lesbos. She is discovered to be Agéle, the daughter of Megacles.

Lamo (lă'mō), a goatherd of Lesbos and the foster father of Daphnis.

Myrtale (mĭr'tə·lē'), his wife, who hides the purple cloak and ivory dagger found with Daphnis.

Dryas (drī'əs), a shepherd and the foster father of Chloë.

Nape (nă'pē), his wife, who brings up Chloë.

Dorco (dôr'kō), a fisherman who wants to marry Chloë and tries to kidnap her. He later saves Daphnis after he has been captured by pirates.

Lampis (lăm'pĭs), another suitor of Chloë, who steals her.

Gnatho (nă'thō), Astylus' parasite, who rescues Chloë.

The Methymneans (mə·thĭm'nĭ·əns), who carry off Chloë but, frightened by Pan, return her.

Lycaenium (lī·sē'nĭ·əm), who teaches love to Daphnis.

Megacles (mĕ'gək·lēz), of Mitylene, the father of Chloë.

Dionysophanes (dī'ō·nĭ·sŏ'fə·nēz), owner of Lamo and the father of Daphnis.

Astylus (ăs·tī'ləs), the son of Dionysophanes and the young master of Lamo.

Eudromus (ū·drō'məs), Astylus' page.

THE DARK JOURNEY

Author: Julian Green (1900-   )
Time of action: Early twentieth century
First published: 1929

PRINCIPAL CHARACTERS

Paul Guéret (pôl' gā·rē'), an incompetent, prematurely aged tutor. Tired of his wife, he tries to take up an affair with Angèle, a young laundress who is also a prostitute. Disturbed when he learns that Angèle is a prostitute, he beats the girl and disfigures her for life. Still in a passion, he shortly after kills a feeble old man. Guéret is trapped by his employer's wife, who locks both of them in a room and then shoots herself, dooming Guéret to capture.

M. Grosgeorge (grō·zhôrzh'), Guéret's employer. Realizing Guéret's frustrations, he suggests a mistress and, not knowing of Guéret's infatuation with Angèle, reveals his own relationships with her.

Mme. Grosgeorge (grō·zhôrzh'), M. Grosgeorge's wife. She is a woman of twisted emotions who nags her husband, beats her son, and humiliates her son's tutor. She seems only to rejoice when Guéret disfigures his and her husband's mistress. She finds Guéret, takes him home, and hides him, though she despises him. When he wants to leave, she locks both of them in a room and calmly shoots herself.

Angèle (än·zhĕl'), a little laundress forced by her aunt, Mme. Londe, to be a prostitute. She is loved by Guéret, who both attracts and repels her. She is beaten and disfigured by Guéret when he learns that she is a prostitute.

Mme. Londe (lōnd'), Angèle's aunt, a restaurant owner who seeks power over other people through the knowledge of their guilt and vices learned from Angèle.

Fernande (fĕr·nänd'), a twelve-year-old girl turned into a prostitute by Mme. Londe when Angèle refuses to continue her practices.

André Grosgeorge (än·drä' grō·zhôrzh'), the boy whom Guéret is hired to tutor. He is a backward lad.

DARK LAUGHTER

Author: Sherwood Anderson (1876-1941)
Time of action: The 1920's
First published: 1925

PRINCIPAL CHARACTERS

Bruce Dudley, born **John Stockton,** who revolts against the sort of rational sterility that characterizes modern technological society. Dudley wanders around the country taking various jobs. He travels from Chicago to New Orleans, and from there to Old Harbor, Indiana, the town where he grew up. He is a reporter, an auto worker, a gardener. His love affair with Aline Grey, his employer's wife, which results in her pregnancy, as well as his flight with Aline towards an unknown destination, are for Anderson facets of the conduct to be expected of two people who love each other but who are unable to reconcile their values with a society dedicated only to material manipulation and acquisition.

Aline Grey, the unhappy wife of an automobile wheel factory owner. She is attracted to Dudley and encourages his love, though she knows her behavior is likely to cause comment in the small Indiana town where she lives. Her affair with Dudley ruins her husband's life.

Fred Grey, practically an Anderson symbol for blind devotion to technology. Grey is incapable of dealing with any situation that depends for its resolution on a knowledge of human nature. When Dudley and Aline leave, Grey becomes completely confused. Not knowing whether to use a revolver on himself, on Dudley and Aline, or simply on Dudley, he fires a wild shot into the river. Confused, desperate, ineffectual in the knowledge of his wife's desertion, Grey is scorned by the easy laughter of some uneducated Negro domestics for whom his problem is childishly simple.

Sponge Martin, a worker in the Grey factory. He loves the simple things: fishing, sipping moonshine whiskey, making love to his carefree wife. Martin is used in the novel to lend authority to Dudley and Aline's love affair.

Rose Frank, an acquaintance of Aline. It was at Rose's apartment in Paris, just after World War I, that Aline met a man she wanted in much the same way she was to want Dudley years later in Old Harbor.

241

DARKNESS AT NOON

Author: Arthur Koestler (1905-   )
Time of action: The 1930's
First published: 1941

PRINCIPAL CHARACTERS

Nikolai Rubashov (nĭ·kô·lī′ rōō·bä′shəf), a political prisoner, an ex-Commissar of the People once politically powerful but now in disfavor and accused of crimes he did not commit. He broods over his actual deeds for the Party and attempts to rationalize them. After publicly denouncing his supposed errors, he is executed. He resembles such Old Bolsheviks as Trotsky and Bukharin, who wielded ruthless power for supposedly good ends in the early years of the Russian Soviet and who were then liquidated by an even more ruthless dictator, Stalin.

Ivanov (ĭ·vä′nəf), a prison official, Rubashov's old college friend and former battalion commander. After interrogating Rubashov on two occasions and persuading him to renounce his opposition to Party policies and to acknowledge his errors, Ivanov is executed for negligence in conducting Rubashov's case. Like Rubashov, Ivanov resembles the Old Bolsheviks whom Stalin regarded as dangerous enemies. Ivanov may also be compared to Dostoevski's Stepan Verhovensky.

Gletkin (glĕt′kĭn), another official who represents the new Party policy of practical application of theoretical principles. He believes in the power of brute force and the instilling of fear to maintain control and order in the state. He is reminiscent of Stalin's police-state aides, of Dostoevski's Pyotr Verhovensky and of George Orwell's O'Brien.

Mikhail Bogrov (mĭ·hä·ĭl′ bôg·rôf′), another prisoner, long a close friend of Rubashov. Frightened, beaten, and whimpering, Bogrov is dragged past Rubashov's cell and shot.

Kieffer, called **Hare-Lip**, an informer, the son of a former friend and associate of Rubashov. After being tortured in a steam bath and later used to testify that Rubashov plotted to have him poison Number 1, Hare-Lip is executed.

Number 402, an anonymous prisoner with whom Rubashov exchanges many tapped-out conversations through the wall which separates their cells.

Number 1, the Party dictator who resembles Joseph Stalin and George Orwell's Big Brother.

Richard, a young man arrested in Germany while Rubashov headed the Party Intelligence and Control Department.

Arlova (är·lō′və), Rubashov's former secretary and mistress, who was executed after Rubashov shifted a charge of treasonable activities from himself to her.

Little Loewy, a Party worker who hanged himself after being denounced as an agent provocateur.

Rip Van Winkle, a little old man, the inmate of cell 406 and a veteran of twenty years' imprisonment.

DAVID COPPERFIELD

Author: Charles Dickens (1812-1870)
Time of action: Early nineteenth century
First published: 1849-1850

David Copperfield, the orphaned hero-narrator whose story of his early years and growing maturity comprises one of the best-known works of fiction in the English language. A posthumous child, extremely sensitive in retrospect, he first experiences cruelty and tyranny when his young widowed mother marries stern Mr. Murdstone, and he quickly forms emotional alliances with the underprivileged and the victimized. His loyalties are sometimes misplaced, as in the case of Steerforth, his school friend who seduces Little Em'ly, but his heart remains sound and generous toward even the erring. As he passes from childhood to disillusioned adolescence, his perceptions increase, though he often misses the truth because he misreads the evidence before him. His trust is all the more remarkable when one considers the recurrence of error which leads him from false friends to false love and on to near catastrophe. Finally, unlike his creator, David finds balance and completion in his literary career, his abiding friendships, and his happy second marriage.

Clara Copperfield, David's childlike but understanding and beautiful mother, destined to an early death because of her inability to cope with life. Strong in her own attachments, she attributes to everyone motives as good and generous as her own. Misled into a second marriage to an unloving husband, she is torn between son and husband and dies soon after giving birth to another child. Mother and child are buried in the same coffin.

Edward Murdstone, Clara Copperfield's second husband and David's irascible stepfather, who cruelly mistreats the sensitive young boy. Self-seeking to an extreme degree, Murdstone has become a synonym for the mean and low, the calculating and untrustworthy. His cruelty is touched with sadism, and his egoism borders on the messianic.

Jane Murdstone, Edward Murdstone's sister. Like her brother, she is harsh and unbending. Her severe nature is symbolized by the somber colors and metallic beads she wears. Her suspicious mind is shown by her belief that the maids have a man hidden somewhere in the house.

Clara Peggotty, Mrs. Copperfield's devoted servant and David's nurse and friend. Cheerful and plump, she always seems about to burst out of her clothing, and when she moves buttons pop and fly in all directions. Discharged after the death of her mistress, she marries Barkis, a carrier.

Daniel Peggotty, Clara Peggotty's brother, a Yarmouth fisherman whose home is a boat beached on the sands. A generous, kind-hearted man, he has made himself the protector of a niece and a nephew, Little Em'ly and Ham, and of Mrs. Gummidge, the forlorn widow of his former partner. His charity consists of thoughtful devotion as much as material support.

Ham Peggotty, Daniel Peggotty's stalwart nephew. He grows up to fall in love with his cousin, Little Em'ly, but on the eve of their wedding she elopes with James Steerforth, her seducer. Some years later, during a great storm, Ham is drowned while trying to rescue Steerforth from a ship in distress off Yarmouth beach.

Little Em'ly, Daniel Peggotty's niece and adopted daughter, a girl of great beauty and charm and David's first love. Though engaged to marry her cousin Ham, she runs away with James Steerforth. After he discards her, Daniel Peggotty saves her from a life of further shame, and she and her uncle join a party emigrating to Australia.

Barkis, the carrier between Blunderstone and Yarmouth. A bashful suitor, he woos Peggotty by having David tell her that "Barkis is willin'!" This tag-line, frequently repeated, reveals the carter's good and simple nature.

Mrs. Gummidge, the widow of Daniel Peggotty's fishing partner. After he takes her into his home she spends most of her time by the fire, meanwhile complaining sadly that she is a "lone, lorn creetur."

Miss Betsey Trotwood, David Copperfield's great-aunt, eccentric, sharp-spoken, but essentially kind-hearted. Present on the night of David's birth, she has already made up her mind as to his sex and his name, her own. When she learns that the child is a boy, she leaves the house in great indignation. Eventually she becomes the benefactress of destitute and desolate David, educates him, and lives to see him happily married to Agnes Wickfield and established in his literary career.

Richard Babley, called **Mr. Dick,** a mildly mad and seemingly irresponsible man befriended by Miss Trotwood. He has great difficulty in keeping the subject of King Charles the First out of his conversation and the memorial he is writing. Miss Trotwood, who refuses to admit that he is mad, always defers to him as a shrewd judge of character and situation.

Dora Spenlow, the ornamental but helpless "child-wife" whom David loves protectively, marries, and loses when she dies young. Her helplessness in dealing with the ordinary situations of life is both amusing and touching.

Agnes Wickfield, the daughter of Miss Trotwood's solicitor and David's stanch friend for many years. Though David at first admires the father, his admiration is soon transferred to the sensible, generous daughter. She nurses Dora Copperfield at the time of her fatal illness, and Dora on her deathbed advises David to marry Agnes. The delicacy with which Agnes contains her love for many years makes her an appealing figure. Eventually she and David are married, to Miss Trotwood's great delight.

Uriah Heep, the hypocritical villain who, beginning as a clerk in Mr. Wickfield's law office, worms his way into the confidence of his employer, becomes a partner in the firm, ruins Mr. Wickfield, and embezzles Miss Trotwood's fortune. His insistence that he is a very humble person provides the clue to his sly, conniving nature. His villainy is finally uncovered by Wilkins Micawber, whom he has used as a tool, and he is forced to make restitution. After Mr. Wickfield and Miss Trotwood refuse to charge him with fraud, he continues his sharp practices in another section of the country until he is arrested for forgery and imprisoned.

Wilkins Micawber, an impecunious man who is "always waiting for something to turn up" while spending himself into debtors' prison, writing grandiloquent letters, indulging in flowery rhetoric, and eking out a shabbily genteel existence on the brink of disaster. David Copperfield lodges with the Micawbers for a time in London, and to him Mr. Micawber confides the sum of his worldly philosophy: "Annual income twenty pounds; annual expenditure nineteen, nineteen, six—result happiness. Annual income twenty pounds; annual expenditure twenty pounds nought six—result misery." He tries a variety of occupations in the course of the novel and is for a time employed by Uriah Heep, whose villainy he contemptuously unmasks. Miss Trotwood aids him and his family to emigrate to Australia, where he becomes a magistrate. A figure of improvidence, alternating between high spirits and low, well-meaning but without understanding of the ways of the worldly, Mr. Micawber is one of Dickens' great comic creations.

Mrs. Emma Micawber, a woman genteelly born (as she frequently insists) and as mercurial in temperament as her husband, capable of fainting over the prospect of financial ruin at three o'clock and of eating with relish breaded lamb chops and drinking ale, bought with

244

money from two pawned teaspoons, at four. Loyal in nature, she says in every crisis that she will never desert Mr. Micawber.

Master Wilkins and
Miss Emma, the Micawber children.

James Steerforth, David Copperfield's fellow student at Salem House. The handsome, spoiled son of a wealthy widow, he hides his true nature behind pleasing manners and a seemingly engaging disposition. Introduced by David into the Peggotty household at Yarmouth, he succeeds in seducing Little Em'ly and persuading her to elope with him on the eve of her marriage to Ham. Later he tires of her and plans to marry her off to Littimer, the servant who aids him in his amorous conquests. He is drowned when his ship breaks up during a storm off Yarmouth.

Mrs. Steerforth, James Steerforth's mother, a proud, austere woman, at first devoted to her handsome, wayward son but eventually estranged from him.

Rosa Dartle, Mrs. Steerforth's companion. Older than Steerforth but deeply in love with him, she endures humiliation and many indignities because of her unreasoning passion. Her lip is scarred, the result of a wound suffered when Steerforth, in a childish fit of anger, threw a hammer at her.

Littimer, Steerforth's valet, a complete scoundrel. Tired of Little Em'ly, Steerforth plans to marry her to his servant, but the girl runs away in order to escape this degradation.

Miss Mowcher, a pursy dwarf. A hairdresser, she makes herself "useful" to a number of people in a variety of ways. Steerforth avails himself of her services.

Markham and
Grainger, Steerforth's lively, amusing friends.

Francis Spenlow, a partner in the London firm of Spenlow and Jorkins, proctors, in which David Copperfield becomes an articled clerk. During a visit at the Spenlow country place David meets Dora, Mr. Spenlow's lovely but childlike daughter and falls in love with her, but her father opposes David's suit after Miss Trotwood loses her fortune. Mr. Spenlow dies suddenly after a fall from his carriage and Dora is taken in charge by two maiden aunts. Following the discovery that Mr. Spenlow's business affairs were in great confusion and that he died almost penniless, David marries Dora.

Miss Clarissa and
Miss Lavinia Spenlow, Mr. Spenlow's sisters, who take Dora into their home after her father's death.

Mr. Jorkins, Mr. Spenlow's business partner.

Mary Anne Paragon, a servant to David and Dora during their brief married life.

Mr. Tiffey, an elderly, withered-looking clerk employed by Spenlow and Jorkins.

Mr. Wickfield, a solicitor of Canterbury and Miss Trotwood's man of business, brought to ruin by Uriah Heep's scheming and adroit mismanagement of the firm's accounts. He is saved from disaster when Wilkins Micawber exposes Heep's machinations. Mr. Wickfield is a weak, foolish, but high-principled man victimized by a scoundrel who exploits his weaknesses.

Mr. Creakle, the master of Salem House, the wretched school to which Mr. Murdstone sends David Copperfield. Lacking in scholarly qualities, he prides himself on his strict discipline. Years later he becomes interested in a model prison where Uriah Heep and Littimer are among the inmates.

Mrs. Creakle, his wife, the victim of her husband's tyranny.

Miss Creakle, their daughter, reported to be in love with Steerforth.

Charles Mell, a junior master at Salem House, discharged when Mr. Creakle learns that the teacher's mother lives in an almshouse. Emigrating to Australia, he eventually becomes the head of the Colonial Salem-House Grammar-School.

Mr. Sharp, the senior master at Salem House.

George Demple, one of David Copperfield's schoolmates at Salem House.

Thomas Traddles, another student at Salem House. As an unhappy schoolboy he consoles himself by drawing skeletons. He studies law, marries the daughter of a clergyman, and eventually becomes a judge. He, with David Copperfield, acts for Miss Trotwood after Uriah Heep's villainy has been revealed.

Miss Sophy Crewler, the fourth daughter of a clergyman's family, a pleasant, cheerful girl who marries Thomas Traddles. Her husband always refers to her as "the dearest girl in the world."

The Reverend Horace Crewler, a poor clergyman and the father of a large family of daughters.

Mrs. Crewler, his wife, a chronic invalid whose condition mends or grows worse according to the pleasing or displeasing circumstances of her life.

Caroline,
Sarah,
Louisa,
Lucy, and
Margaret, the other Crewler daughters. They and their husbands form part of the family circle surrounding happy, generous Traddles.

Dr. Strong, the master of the school at Canterbury where Miss Trotwood sends her great-nephew to be educated. After Miss Trotwood loses her money, Dr.

Strong hires David to help in compiling a classical dictionary.

Mrs. Strong, a woman much younger than her husband.

Mrs. Markleham, the mother of Mrs. Strong. The boys at the Canterbury school call her the "Old Soldier."

Mr. Quinion, the manager of the warehouse of Murdstone and Grinby, where David Copperfield is sent to do menial work after his mother's death. Miserable in these surroundings, David finally resolves to run away and look for his only relative, Miss Betsey Trotwood, in Dover.

Tipp, a workman in the Murdstone and Grinby warehouse.

Mealy Potatoes and
Mick Walker, two rough slum boys who work with David at the warehouse of Murdstone and Grinby.

Miss Larkins, a dark-eyed, statuesque beauty with whom David Copperfield falls in love when he is seventeen. She disappoints him by marrying Mr. Chestle, a grower of hops.

Miss Shepherd, a student at Miss Nettingall's Establishment for Young Ladies and another of David Copperfield's youthful loves.

Mrs. Crupp, David Copperfield's landlady while he is an articled clerk in the firm of Spenlow and Jorkins. She suffers from "the spazzums" and takes quantities of peppermint for this strange disorder.

Martha Endell, the unfortunate young woman who helps to restore Little Em'ly to her uncle.

Janet, Miss Betsey Trotwood's servant.

Jack Maldon, Mrs. Strong's cousin, a libertine for whom her kind-hearted husband finds employment.

DAVID HARUM

Author: Edward Noyes Westcott (1846-1898)
Time of action: Late nineteenth century
First published: 1898

PRINCIPAL CHARACTERS

David Harum, a dry, quaint, semi-literate banker and horse trader through whom the author presents a picture of Upstate New York life. Harum acquires a reputation for being tight-fisted, but only to cover his secret philanthropic deeds. He tests John's character to make sure the young man is worthy to take over the Harum bank in Homeville.

John Lenox, the twenty-six-year-old son of a once well-to-do New York City businessman, educated for no special job, who enters Harum's bank as an assistant and withstands all of Harum's traps and temptations.

Mary Blake, an heiress whom John, now penniless, will not court until he has proved that he can succeed in business. He meets Mary in Europe but does not ask her to marry him. Several years later, on their second meeting, while John is traveling in Europe to recover from an illness, they declare their love and are married.

Polly Bixbee, Harum's widowed sister and housekeeper.

DEAD FIRES

Author: José Lins do Rêgo (1901-   )
Time of action: 1848-1900
First published: 1943

PRINCIPAL CHARACTERS

José Amaro (zhōō·zā' ä·mä'rōō), a crippled saddlemaker. Embittered by his failures, he hides his sense of inferiority and his cowardice under a cloak of scorn, especially for the district's wealthy plantation owners. Finally, disillusioned in his fight against the aristocrats, deserted by his family, and friendless, he commits suicide.

Antonio Silvino (än·tō'nyōō sēl·vē'nōō), a bandit who inspires the admiration, and, finally, the disillusionment of José Amaro.

Captain Victorino Carneiro da Cunha (vēk·tō·rē'nōō kär·nä'rōō də kōōn'yə), a penniless lawyer connected with the best families but censuring their misuse of power. Regardless of the cost to himself, he fights courageously against cruelty and injustice.

Colonel Lula César de Holanda Chacón (lōō'lə sē·zər' də ō·län'də shä·kōn'), the owner of Santa Fe sugar plantation. Deserted by his emancipated Negro slaves because of his cruel treatment in the past, Lula's sugar refinery is doomed to become a place of dead fires.

Colonel José Paulino (zhōō·zā' pou·lē'nōō), the owner of Santa Clara plantation. José's humane treatment of his field hands causes Santa Clara to prosper in contrast to doomed Santa Fe.

Leandro (lā·än'drōō), a kindly Negro hunter and friend of José Amaro.

Sinha (sē'nyə), José Amaro's wife.

247

Lieutenant Mauricio (mou·rē′syōō), a cruel army officer.

Captain Tomás Cabral de Malo (tō-mäs kə·bräl′ də mä′lōō), the father-in-law of Colonel Lula César de Holanda Chacón.

Quinca Napoleon (kēń′kə), the prefect of Pilar, victim of Antonio Silvino.

Laurentino (lou-rän′tē·nōō), a house painter, neighbor of José Amaro.

Floripes (flō·rē′pəs), Negro overseer of Santa Fe plantation and enemy of José Amaro.

Torcuato (tôr·kwä′tōō), a blind man accused as a spy and beaten by Lt. Mauricio.

DEAD SOULS

Author: Nikolai V. Gogol (1809-1852)
Time of action: Early nineteenth century
First published: 1842

PRINCIPAL CHARACTERS

Pavel Ivanovitch Tchitchikov (pä′vĕl ĭ·vä′nə·vĭch chēt′chē·kəf), an adventurer of early nineteenth century Russia. He buys "dead souls," that is, the names of serfs who have died since the last census but who still continue to cost their owners taxes until they can be written off in the next census. Using their names, he plans to get from his uncle's estate the money, refused him in the old man's will, by mortgaging his own "estate," with its dead souls, to the Trustee Committee. To find dead souls, he rides from village to village visiting landowners and exerting his charm to obtain the names of dead serfs. But the villagers begin to talk and, not able to guess what he is up to, accuse him of all sorts of crimes. He has an encounter with the law and is arrested. He is finally released by an unscrupulous lawyer who brings to light all the local scandals, so that the villagers are glad to get Tchitchikov out of town.

Selifan (sĕ′lĭ·vən), Pavel's coachman, through whose mistake about roads he visits Madame Korobotchkina. They are put onto the right road by her twelve-year-old maid, Pelageya.

Nastasya Petrovna Korobotchkina (näs-tä′syə pĕt·rov′nə kô·rō·bach′kēnə), an overnight hostess who sells Pavel eighteen of her dead souls for fifteen rubles each.

Petrushka (pĕt·rōōsh′kə), Pavel's valet, who shares his adventures.

Nozdryov (nōz′dryəf), a gambler and liar who meets Pavel at an inn and finally denounces him to the police as a spy and forger. He himself is arrested for assaulting a friend, Maximov.

Manilov (mä·nĭ·lōf′), a genial landowner who offers hospitality to Pavel and gives him his first dead souls.

Lizanka (lĭ·zän′kə), the wife of Manilov.

Themistoclus (tĕ·mĭs′tə·kləs), one of Manilov's two children.

Mihail Semyonovitch Sobakevitch (mĭ-hä·ĭl′ sĕ·myō′nə·vĭch sô·bä′kĕ·vĭch), a landowner who at first demands a hundred rubles apiece for his dead souls but finally settles for two and a half.

Plyushkin (plūsh′kĭn), a miser who haggles fiercely over 120 dead souls and seventy-eight fugitives. He finally gives Pavel a letter to the town president.

Ivan Grigoryevitch (ĭ·vän′ grĭ·gō′ryĕ-vĭch), the town president, who transfers Pavel's purchased dead souls to the adventurer's imaginary estate in the Kherson province and makes the transactions legal.

248

Ivan Antonovitch (ĭ·vän' än·tō'nə·vĭch), a minor clerk who must be bribed to record the purchases.

The Governor, who entertains at a big ball.

The Governor's Daughter, with whom Pavel is supposed to be eloping. His coach had previously collided with hers.

Captain Kopeykin (kô·pā'kĭn), a legendary soldier of the War of 1812, turned bandit. Some think he has returned disguised as Pavel.

Andrey Ivanovitch Tyentyelnikov (än-drā' ĭ·vä'nə·vĭch tyĕn·tyĕl'nĭ·kəf), a thirty-three-year-old bachelor who plays host to the adventurer. Pavel aids him in his suit for a neighbor's daughter.

General Betrishtchev (bĕt·rĭsh'chĕf), a neighbor of Tyentyelnikov, who gives the young landowner his daughter in marriage and sells more dead souls to Pavel.

Ulinka (ōō·lĭn'kə), the general's daughter, in love with Tyentyelnikov.

Vishnepokromov (vĭsh·nyĕ·pōk'rə·məf), who tries to prevent Ulinka's engagement.

Pyetukh (pĕ'tūk), a generous glutton who entertains Pavel.

Platonov (plä'tə·nəf), a young friend who accompanies Pavel on his travels and introduces him to his sister and his brother-in-law.

Konstantin Skudronzhoglo (kôn·stän·tĭn' skōō·drôn·zhō'glə), a prosperous landowner and the brother-in-law of Platonov. He lends Pavel ten thousand rubles to buy an estate.

Hlobuev (hlô·bōō'ĕf), a spendthrift whose land Pavel wants to buy. By forging a will Pavel tries to help him claim an inheritance from a rich aunt, but he forgets to cancel in it all earlier documents.

Alexy Ivanovitch Lyenitzyn (ä·lĕk·sā' ĭ·vä'nə·vĭch lĕ·nĭ'tsōōn), a public official who discovers two wills of the old woman, one contradicting the other. He has Pavel jailed on a charge of forgery.

Ivan Andreitch (ĭ·vän' än·drā'ĭch), the postmaster of "N."

Samosvitov (sä·mōs'vĭ·təf), who offers to get Pavel out of jail for thirty thousand rubles.

Murazov (mōō·rä·zōf'), the shrewd, unscrupulous lawyer who gets Pavel freed by raking up scandals against all those who have accused his client.

DEAR BRUTUS

Author: James M. Barrie (1860-1937)
Time of action: Midsummer Eve
First presented: 1917

PRINCIPAL CHARACTERS

[In this fantasy the characters are seen as themselves in a drawing room, then in the woods as the people they might have been, and finally as themselves again. Thus there are triple characterizations.]

Will Dearth, in the drawing room a

shaky, watery-eyed relic of what was once a good man. An artist at one time, he and Alice Dearth had loved madly. In the woods he is a successful artist and the father of a daughter named Margaret. He claims credit for all his daughter's charm, except her baby laugh; this she lost when he allowed her to lose perfect faith in him. Back in the drawing room he grants he is not the man he thought he was. However, the Dearths, probably the only ones to gain by their revelation, may be able to breast their way into the light.

Mrs. Alice Dearth, Will's wife. In the drawing room she is a woman of fierce, smoldering desires. Hers is a dark but brave spirit, a kiss-or-kill personality. In the woods she becomes a vagrant woman, a whimperer who warns Dearth to take good care of Margaret, for her kind is easily lost. Returned to the drawing room, she lies about what happened in the woods. Although she resents losing her might-have-been station as "the Honorable Mrs. Finch-Fallowe" and her husband's contentment with a might-have-been daughter, Mrs. Dearth shares his present interest in painting. She will try for compatibility, despite her avowal that her husband will not get much help from her.

Margaret, in the woods a beautiful and bewitching young girl. Her knowledge that "they" will take Dearth away stands between her and Dearth, to cloud their joy.

Mrs. Mabel Purdie, in the drawing room a good companion for her philandering husband. Feigning other interests, she is apparently indifferent to his affair with a woman of their set. In the woods she becomes a charmer who carries on passionately with her husband. Again in the drawing room, she sees her husband for what he is, a rotter. Indifferent, she pledges to stay by him as long as she cares to bother.

Jack Purdie, in the drawing room a brilliant, intellectual man accepted—in fact, liked—despite his unfaithfulness to his wife. In the woods he walks alone. No woman can plumb the well of his emotions. Once more in the drawing room, he sees himself objectively; he is a phi-

landerer with no prospect of change in store for himself.

Joanna Trout, in the drawing room a woman attractive in face and figure, but dull and humorless in love. She imagines herself the natural mate for the strong-hearted male, Purdie. In the woods, married to Purdie, she is drab and complaining because he is unfaithful. Back to the here and now of the drawing room, she recalls the might-have-been experience sufficiently to realize that she and Jack are hardly worth sorrowing about.

Matey, in the drawing room the perfect butler, a general favorite among those who know him, despite his being a pilferer. In the woods he becomes James Matey, a dishonest business tycoon, and the husband of the disdainful Lady Caroline. Among his real satisfactions is being called "Jim" by Lady Caroline. Back in the drawing room, although he returns reluctantly to normality, he makes the full change quickly. Confronted by a coffee tray, he picks it up and goes to the pantry.

Lady Caroline Laney, in the drawing room a snobbish aristocrat, not so taken as others are by the thieving Matey. In the woods she cavorts, uninhibited, with her handsome, brawny husband, Matey, answering gladly to his "Caroliny." In the drawing room, like Matey, she retains her role into the return and is shocked when her Jim picks up the coffee tray. She then assumes her former manner.

Mrs. Emma Coade, an elderly, rounded woman called "Coady," as is her husband. She is the most congenial of the ladies gathered at the scene. Mrs. Coade did not go to the woods, but she knows that the others did. She senses that Lob, their host, is back of these fantastic happenings. The fact that she is Mr. Coade's second wife adds to her sadness when she learns of her husband's second-chance experience.

Mr. Coade, in the drawing room a gracious, older man with a gentle smile. Comfortably well-to-do, he has always meant to write a book but is always conveniently distracted. In the woods he becomes a jolly, ne'er-do-well old bachelor. Later, in the drawing room, he is still gentle with Mrs. Coade in the same empty way; he sees himself as a genial, lazy old man who gained nothing by his second chance.

Mr. Lob, the wizened, ageless host to his guests, all of whom want a second chance. He is Puck from "A Midsummer Night's Dream," in disguise, and he introduces his guests to the Midsummer Eve of what-might-have-been.

DEATH COMES FOR THE ARCHBISHOP

Author: Willa Cather (1873-1947)
Time of action: 1851-1889
First published: 1927

PRINCIPAL CHARACTERS

Father Jean Marie Latour, a devout French priest consecrated Vicar Apostolic of New Mexico and Bishop of Agathonica in partibus in 1850. With Father Vaillant, his friend and fellow seminarian, he journeys from his old parish on the shores of Lake Ontario to Santa Fé, seat of the new diocese in territory recently acquired from Mexico. In those troubled times he finds many of the old missions in ruins or abandoned, the Mexican clergy lax and unlearned, the sacraments corrupted by native superstitions. The travels of these two dedicated missionary priests over a desert region of sand, arroyos, towering mesas, and bleak red hills, the accounts of the labors they perform and the hardships they endure to establish the order and authority of the Church in a wild land, make up the story of this beautifully told chronicle. Father Latour is an aristocrat by nature and tradition. Intellectual, fastidious, reserved, he finds the loneliness of his mission redeemed by the cheerfulness and simple-hearted warmth of his old friend and by the simple piety he often encounters among the humblest of his people; from them, as in the case of old Sada, he learns lessons of humility and grace. For years he dreams of building a cathedral in Santa Fé, and in time his ambition is realized. By then he is an Archbishop and an old man. In the end he decides not to return to his native Auvergne, the wet, green country of his youth that he had often remembered with yearning during his years in the hot desert country. He retires to a small farm outside Santa Fé, and when he dies his body rests in state before the altar in the cathedral he had built. Father Latour's story is based on the life of a historical figure, Jean Baptiste Lamy, the first Archbishop of Santa Fé.

Father Joseph Vaillant, Father Latour's friend and vicar. The son of hardy peasant stock, he is tireless in his missionary labors. If Father Latour is an intellectual aristocrat, Father Vaillant is his opposite, the hearty man of feeling, able to mix with all kinds of people and to move them as much by his good humor and physical vitality as by his eloquence. Doctrine, he holds, is good enough in its place, but he prefers to put his trust in miracles and the working of faith. When the gold rush begins in Colorado, he is sent to Camp Denver to work among the miners. There he continues his missionary labors, traveling from camp to camp in a covered carriage that is both his sleeping quarters and an improvised

251

chapel. Borrowing and begging wherever he can, he builds for the Church and for the future. When he dies, the first Bishop of Denver, there is not a building in the city large enough to hold the thousands who come to his funeral. Like Father Latour, Father Vaillant is modeled after a real person, Father Joseph P. Machebeuf.

Padre Antonio José Martinez, the vigorous but arrogant priest at Taos credited with having instigated the revolt of the Taos Indians. A man of violence and sensual passions, he has lived like a dictator too long to accept the authority of Father Latour with meekness or reason. When Father Latour visits him in Taos, he challenges his Bishop on the subject of celibacy. After the Bishop announces his intention to reform lax practices throughout his diocese, Padre Martinez tells him blandly that he will found his own church if interfered with. As good as his promise, he and Padre Lucero defy Father Latour and Rome and try to establish a schism called the Old Holy Catholic Church of Mexico. Until his death a short time later Padre Martinez carries on his personal and ecclesiastical feud with Father Taladrid, appointed by Father Latour to succeed the old tyrant of Taos.

Padre Marino Lucero, the priest of Arroyo Hondo, who joins Padre Martinez in defying Father Latour's authority. Padre Lucero is said to have a fortune hidden away. After he repents of his heresy and dies reconciled to Rome, buckskin bags containing gold and silver coins valued at almost twenty thousand dollars are found buried under the floor of his house.

Padre Gallegos, the genial, worldly priest at Albuquerque, a lover of whiskey, fandangos, and poker. Although Father Latour likes him as a man, he finds him scandalous and impossible as a priest. As soon as possible he suspends Padre Gallegos and puts Father Vaillant in charge of the Albuquerque parish.

Manuel Lujon, a wealthy Mexican. During a visit at his rancho Father Vaillant sees and admires a matched pair of white mules, Contento and Angelica. The priest praises the animals so highly that Lujon, a generous, pious man, decides to give him one of them. But Father Vaillant refuses to accept the gift, saying that it would not be fitting for him to ride on a fine white mule while his Bishop rides a common hack. Resigned, Lujon sends the second mule to Father Latour.

Buck Scales, a gaunt, surly American at whose house Father Latour and his vicar stop on one of their missionary journeys. Warned away by the gestures of his frightened wife, they continue on to the next town. The woman follows them to tell that in the past six years her husband has murdered four travelers as well as the three children she has borne. Scales is arrested and hanged.

Magdalena, the Mexican wife of Buck Scales, a devout woman who reveals her husband's crimes. After her husband's hanging she lives for a time in the home of Kit Carson. Later Father Latour makes her the housekeeper in the establishment of the Sisters of Loretto in Santa Fé. She attends the old Archbishop in his last days.

Kit Carson, the American trapper and scout. He and Father Latour become friends when they meet after the arrest of Buck Scales.

Jacinto, an intelligent young Indian from the Pecos pueblo, often employed as Father Latour's guide on the priest's missionary journeys. On one of these trips the travelers are overtaken by a sudden snowstorm. Jacinto leads Father Latour into a cave which has obviously been used for ceremonial purposes. Before he builds a fire Jacinto walls up an opening in the cave. Waking later in the night, Father Latour sees his guide standing guard over the sealed opening. He realizes that he has been close to some secret ceremonial mystery of the Pecos, possibly connected with snake worship, but he respects Jacinto's confidence and never mentions the matter.

Don Antonio Olivares, a wealthy ranchero who has promised to make a large contribution to Father Latour's cathedral fund. He dies suddenly before he can make good his promise, leaving his estate to his wife and daughter for life, after which his property is to go to the Church. Two of his brothers contest the will.

Doña Isabella Olivares, the American wife of Father Latour's friend and benefactor. After her husband's death two of his brothers contest the will on the grounds that Doña Isabella is not old enough to have a daughter of the age of Señorita Inez and that the girl is the child of one of Don Antonio's indiscreet youthful romances, adopted by Doña Isabella for the purpose of defrauding the brothers. Father Vaillant convinces the vain woman that it is her duty to tell the truth about her age in order for her and her daughter to win the case. Much against her will Doña Isabella confesses in court that she is fifty-two years old and not forty-two, as she has claimed. Later she tells Father Vaillant and Father Latour that she will never forgive them for having made her tell a lie about a matter as serious as a woman's age.

Señorita Inez, the daughter of Doña Isabella and Don Antonio Olivares. Her age and her mother's are questioned when the Olivares brothers try to break Don Antonio's will.

Boyd O'Reilly, a young American lawyer, the manager of Don Antonio Olivares' affairs.

Sada, the wretched slave of a Protestant American family. One December night she escapes from the stable where she sleeps and takes refuge in the church. Father Latour finds her there, hears her confession, blesses her, and gives her a holy relic and his own warm cloak.

Eusabio, a man of influence among the Navajos. Though he is younger than Father Latour, the priest respects him greatly for his intelligence and sense of honor. Father Latour grieves when the Navajos are forced to leave their country and rejoices that he has been able to live long enough to see them restored to their lands. When the old Archbishop dies, Eusabio carries word of his death to the Indians.

Bernard Ducrot, the young priest who looks after Father Latour in his last years. He becomes like a son to the gentle old man.

Padre Jesus de Baca, the white-haired, almost blind priest at Isleta. An old man of great innocence and piety, he lives surrounded by his tame parrots.

Trinidad Lucero, a slovenly young monk in training for the priesthood whom Father Latour meets in the house of Padre Martinez. He passes as Padre Lucero's nephew, but some say he is the son of Padre Martinez. When Padre Martinez and Padre Lucero proclaim their schism, Trinidad acts as a curate for both.

Padre Taladrid, the young Spanish priest whom Father Latour appoints to succeed Padre Martinez at Taos.

DEATH IN VENICE

Author: Thomas Mann (1875-1955)
Time of action: Early twentieth century
First published: 1912

253

Gustave von Aschenbach (gōō′stäf fŏn ä′shĕn·bäch′), a middle-aged German writer. Small, dark, his bushy gray hair (thinning on top) is brushed back on his overlarge head. His mouth is large, his cheeks lean and furrowed, and his prominent chin slightly cleft. He wears rimless gold glasses on his thick, aristocratically hooked nose, and his eyes are weary and sunken. A widower, he has one child, a married daughter. Precocious, Aschenbach early longed for fame, which he has achieved through several works acclaimed by the general public and the critics as well. He is not a born artist but has made himself one through rigorous discipline and unwavering dedication. A solitary man, he has only a superficial, limited knowledge of the real world. In cultivating his intellect he has denied his feelings. His passion for Tadzio is symbolic of his narcissism, which first degrades and then destroys him. Aschenbach is a symbol of the artist in modern society.

Tadzio (täd′tsĭ·ō), a Polish boy of fourteen who possesses a perfect Greek classic beauty of face and form. To Aschenbach his beautiful head seems that of Eros and the boy himself the essence of beauty. When Aschenbach almost touches Tadzio and then draws back in panic, the action symbolizes the artist's fear of giving way to an emotion. Sometimes the artist sees in Tadzio the youth Hyacinth, who died the victim of the rivalry of two gods. When after many days Tadzio finally smiles at Aschenbach, the smile is that of Narcissus looking in the pool, and the artist whispers his love. Tadzio's is the last face the artist sees before he dies.

A Stranger. Thin, beardless, snub-nosed, red-haired, freckled, and exotic-looking, he seems to Aschenbach to be bold, domineering, even ruthless.

Another Stranger, an old man masquerading as a youth on an old, dingy Italian ship. He is flashily dressed, his face and eyes are wrinkled, his cheeks rouged, his brown hair and yellow teeth false, and his turned-up mustaches and imperial are dyed. He becomes disgustingly drunk before the ship reaches Venice. When Aschenbach's desperate passion for Tadzio consumes him he, like the painted stranger, tries foolishly to hide his age.

A Strolling Player, a pale, thin-faced, snub-nosed, red-haired man of slight build whose singing is entertaining but obscene and who carries with him an odor of carbolic acid.

A Gondolier. Undersized, brutish-looking, an expert boatman, he is gruff and rude, and he disappears before Aschenbach returns with change to pay him. The gondolier represents Charon, and the artist's ride in the gondola portends his death in Venice.

DEATH OF A HERO

Author: Richard Aldington (1892-   )
Time of action: World War I
First published: 1929

PRINCIPAL CHARACTERS

George Winterbourne, a young Englishman for whom the world goes awry. After an unhappy childhood he turns to dabbling in writing, painting, and sex.

Becoming an officer in World War I, he finds himself regarded as a failure by his superiors. Discouraged by opinion, as well as by the lives and characters of his father, mother, wife, and mistress, he stands erect during shelling by German guns and is killed.

Elizabeth Winterbourne, young George's promiscuous wife. She is a would-be intellectual who as a young woman is infatuated by the idea of free love. When she thinks she is with child, however, she forces a marriage with George. Although she remains promiscuous afterward, she is angered by her best friend's becoming her husband's mistress.

Fanny Welford, Elizabeth's best friend and George's mistress. A blasé creature, she spends George's last night in England with him, but she is not interested enough to arise from bed, or even awaken fully, when he leaves her the following morning.

Mr. George Winterbourne, young George's father. He marries to escape a domineering mother, only to find that he hates his promiscuous wife. Being a sentimental man, he prays for his wife's soul and awaits her pleasure when sent to a hotel while she entertains one or another of a string of lovers.

Mrs. George Winterbourne, young George's mother. She is an elderly wanton who is proud of having had in her life a series of twenty-two lovers. She lavishes a kind of love upon her son and, when he dies, plays a role as the mother bereft of a hero son.

DEATH OF A SALESMAN

Author: Arthur Miller (1915-   )
Time of action: Mid-twentieth century
First published: 1949

PRINCIPAL CHARACTERS

Willy Loman, a sixty-three-year-old traveling salesman who has begun to dwell on the past and not to know where he is. In the last two days of his life his past rolls before him. He is a father who loves his sons and wants them to have worldly success, although he does not know how to help them achieve it. His last gesture for his son Biff is to commit suicide so that the son can have the insurance money.

Biff Loman, Willy's thirty-four-year-old son, who is still trying to find himself. A high-school athlete, he gets nowhere after graduation. When he is refused a loan to start a business, he steals a cheap fountain pen. Angry and defeated, he curses his father as a fool and a dreamer, though he loves the man.

Happy Loman, Willy's younger son, modestly successful in life as a clerk in a store. He is a woman chaser and a seeker after pleasure.

Charley, Willy Loman's friend and neighbor. He lends Willy money and offers him a job.

Bernard, Charley's son, a successful lawyer whose own success is an accusation to Willy's sons.

Linda Loman, Willy's wife, a fearful but patient woman who loves her husband despite his failures.

Howard Wagner, Willy's boss's son, who lets Willy know he is finished as a salesman.

Uncle Ben, Willy's brother. He goes out into the jungle and in a few years returns from the diamond mines a rich man. His success is an accusation to Willy.

The Woman, an unnamed character whom Biff, as a teen-ager, finds in a hotel room with his father.

255

THE DEATH OF IVAN ILYICH

Author: Count Leo Tolstoy (1828-1910)
Time of action: The 1880's
First published: 1884

PRINCIPAL CHARACTERS

Ivan Ilyich Golovin (ĭ·vän' ĭl·yĭch' gô-lō'vĭn), a prominent judge. A genial and conscientious lawyer, the popular Ivan Ilyich hides from reality under a cloak of decorum. Obtaining an excellent appointment in St. Petersburg, he finds there a house and an ordered routine exactly to his taste. He feels that life is, at last, just as it should be. Then he learns that he is the victim of a fatal disease. Facing death, he is forced to look, for the first time, at the truth about his life. Only as he becomes aware of the real meaning of his past decisions does he free himself from the fear of death.

Praskovya Fedorovna Golovina (präs-kō'vyä fyō'də·rəv·nə gô·lō'vĭnə), Ivan Ilyich Golovin's wife. Dissatisfied with the role her husband has chosen for her, she becomes demanding and quarrelsome and, finally, isolated from him. Only in death does her husband become aware of her as a person deserving pity and forgiveness.

Gerasim (gě·rä'sĭm), Ivan Ilyich Golovin's peasant servant boy. In his candid admission of the reality and naturalness of death, and with his honesty and clean young strength, Gerasim comforts and cares for his master through his last illness.

Peter Ivanovitch (pyō'tr ĭ·vä'nə·vĭch), Ivan Ilyich Golovin's colleague. Under a show of observing the proper protocol, Peter hides his true feelings about the dying and dead Ivan Ilyich.

THE DEATH OF THE GODS

Author: Dmitri Merejkowski (1865-1941)
Time of action: Fourth century
First published: 1896

PRINCIPAL CHARACTERS

Caesar Constantius (sē'zėr kŏn·stăn'-shĭ·əs), Emperor of Rome, who rose to power through assassination.

Julian Flavius (jōō'lĭ·ən flā'vĭ·əs), cousin of Constantius, a young man learned in the pagan philosophies. At twenty he travels to Asia Minor as a Christian monk. Secretly he is won over to paganism. Later he fights a successful campaign as a general in Gaul and is hailed as emperor. He becomes embittered when his wife leaves him to become a nun, and he denounces Christianity and reinstates paganism in the Roman Empire. He is ridiculed for his scholarly studies and undertakes a campaign against Persia, believing a victory will win respect for him and for paganism. He is mortally wounded in battle and dies saying Christ defeated him.

Gallus Flavius (gă'ləs flā'vĭ·əs), Julian's younger brother, a girlish young man. He is made co-regent with Constantius for a brief time before he is assassinated.

Arsinoë (är·sĭ'nō·ē), a young woman who delights in paganism. She tells Julian he must believe in himself, rather than any gods. Later she disappoints Julian by becoming a Christian. Although he wants to make her his empress, she refuses Julian's offer of love and marriage. Just before Julian dies Arsinoë visits him and tries unsuccessfully to win him back to Christianity.

Publius Porphyrius (pū′blĭ·əs pôr·fĭ′-rĭ·əs), who takes Julian to a wrestling arena to watch the ancient Greek games. There he sees Arsinoë, a young pagan, for the first time.

THE DEATH OF THE HEART

Author: Elizabeth Bowen (1899-   )
Time of action: After World War I
First published: 1938

PRINCIPAL CHARACTERS

Portia Quayne, a sixteen-year-old girl. She lives with her stepbrother and is confused and demanding. Through affection for Eddie she loses some of her childish idealism and sense of the simplicity of human affairs.

Thomas Quayne, Portia's stepbrother, a partner in a London advertising firm. He takes his stepsister into his home, though he scarcely knows her. Because he and his wife have no children of their own, Portia is disturbing to them.

Anna Quayne, Thomas' wife. Her friendship for Eddie arouses a confused jealousy in Portia. Anna becomes upset when she learns, by reading the girl's diary, that Portia is unhappy in her home.

Eddie, a callow, self-assured twenty-three-year-old employee at Thomas Quayne's office. He is both demanding and disdainful of Portia's affection for him. He upsets her by showing fondness for Daphne Heccomb.

Mrs. Heccomb. Anna's old governess, who takes over Portia when the Quaynes go to Capri for an extended holiday.

Daphne Heccomb, Mrs. Heccomb's stepdaughter who is friendly to Portia.

Major Brutt, a retired officer. Portia runs away from home to him, offering to marry him and polish his boots. The major tactfully sends her back to her stepbrother.

St. Quentin Miller, an author and close friend of the Quaynes. He is Anna's confidant, to whom she pours out her problems with respect to young Portia.

Matchett, the Quaynes' housekeeper; a possessive person, she resents Portia's affection for Eddie.

Miss Paullie, one of Portia's teachers.

Lilian, an inquisitive school friend of Portia.

THE DEATH OF VIRGIL

Author: Hermann Broch (1886-1951)
Time of action: 19 B.C.
First published: 1945

PRINCIPAL CHARACTERS

Virgil (Publius Vergilius Maro) (vêr′gəl; pŏŏb′lĭ·əs vêr·jĭ′lĭ·əs mâ·ro), the dying

Roman poet who, returning to Rome with Augustus Caesar, takes a long look into

257

his own soul and sees his life as hypocrisy. In his devotion to poetry he feels that he has denied love and has thus served death rather than life. He insists that his "Aeneid," because it lacks this perception, should be destroyed, but finally agrees to preserve the poem at Augustus' bidding. Knowing, at the last, the salvation that is self-knowledge, the poet dies.

Plotia Hieria (plō'shĭ·ə hĭ·é'rĭ·ə), a woman whose love Virgil had renounced long ago. She appears to the dying poet in the visionary world of his hallucinations and beckons him on to the renunciation of poetry for love.

Augustus Caesar (ô·gŭs'təs sē'zér), Emperor of Rome, whose glory is revealed to the dying Virgil as a hollow majesty. The Emperor persuades the poet not to destroy the "Aeneid" since the poem's true owner is the Roman people.

Lysanias (lĭ·sā'nĭ·əs), a young boy who attends the dying Virgil, sometimes in reality, sometimes in the poet's hallucinations.

DEBIT AND CREDIT

Author: Gustav Freytag (1816-1895)
Time of action: Early nineteenth century
First published: 1855

PRINCIPAL CHARACTERS

Anton Wohlfart (än'tōn vōl'färt), a young middle-class German. Intelligent and attractive, he wins the esteem of his employer, T. O. Schröter, whom he later antagonizes by becoming the agent of Baron von Rothsattel. After bringing order out of the chaos of the Baron's affairs, he marries Sabine Schröter and becomes a partner in T. O. Schröter's firm.

T. O. Schröter (shrœ'tér), an honorable German businessman and the employer of Anton Wohlfart.

Sabine Schröter (sä·bē'nä shrœ'tér), T. O. Schröter's sister who marries Anton Wohlfart.

Baron von Rothsattel (ba·rōn' fôn rōt'-sä·täl), a German nobleman. His chaotic business affairs are put in order by Anton Wohlfart, whom the Baron insults and finally dismisses because of a misplaced sense of rank.

Lenore von Rothsattel (lä·nō'rä fôn rōt'-sä·täl), Baron von Rothsattel's beautiful daughter, who persuades Anton Wohlfart to become her father's agent and retrieve the Baron's ruined estates. She marries Fritz von Fink.

Hirsch Ehrenthal (hĭrsh â'ren·täl), an unscrupulous usurer who plots the financial ruin of Baron von Rothsattel.

Veitel Itzig (fī'tĕl ĭt'sĭg), an employee of Hirsch Ehrenthal. With his knowledge of Ehrenthal's affairs and by means of a dishonest manipulation of documents, he plots to acquire Baron von Rothsattel's estates. He is drowned in his attempt to escape arrest.

Fritz von Fink (frĭts fôn fĭnk), an Americanized German nobleman and friend of Anton Wohlfart. He is instrumental in saving Baron von Rothsattel's Polish estates and marries Lenore von Rothsattel.

Eugen von Rothsattel (oi'gĕn), Baron von Rothsattel's gallant but impractical son.

258

DECLINE AND FALL

Author: Evelyn Waugh (1903-   )
Time of action: Twentieth century
First published: 1928

PRINCIPAL CHARACTERS

Paul Pennyfeather, an inoffensive divinity student at Oxford. The victim of a prank, he is sent down for indecent exposure when debagged by some riotous students. He teaches at a school in Wales, and is hired as vacation tutor for one of his pupils. He becomes engaged to the boy's mother, Margot Beste-Chetwynde, but just before the wedding he is arrested and later is convicted of operating the international white-slave trade she runs. After she has arranged for his successful escape from prison, Paul is officially declared dead. Disguised by a heavy mustache, he returns to his college at Oxford to continue his interrupted study for the Church.

Sir Alastair Digby-Vaine-Trumpington, whose prank results in Paul's dismissal from Oxford. Later, as Paul's former fiancée's young man, he assists in Paul's escape from prison.

Dr. Augustus Fagan, the head of the inadequate Llanabba Castle school where Paul teaches. Fagan forsakes education for medicine and becomes the owner of the nursing home where Paul's death certificate is signed by a drunken doctor.

Peter Beste-Chetwynde, one of Paul's pupils.

Margot Beste-Chetwynde, his mother and Paul's fiancée. Paul is convicted of her crimes. He spends the interval between his prison escape and his return to Oxford resting up at her villa on Corfu.

Mr. Prendergast, a master at Llanabba Castle school. Later he turns up as chaplain at Blackstone Gaol, where Paul is a prisoner. Prendergast is killed by a crazed inmate.

Captain Grimes, a scoundrel who is periodically in difficulties. To get out of trouble he marries one of Fagan's daughters, and later fakes a drowning. He appears as Paul's fellow prisoner. He is subsequently believed to have perished in the swamp while trying to escape, but Paul believes that the escape was successful.

Arthur Potts, whom Paul knew at Oxford. Working for the League of Nations, he shows an interest in Margot's business affairs. He is chief witness for the prosecution at Paul's trial.

Flossie Fagan, one of Fagan's daughters, a vulgar young woman who wants to be married and is consequently useful to Grimes in getting out of trouble.

Diana Fagan, another of Fagan's daughters, who economizes in sugar and soap.

Philbrick, the butler at Llanabba Castle and a confidence man. He tells varying stories about himself, claiming, among other things, that he is really Sir Solomon Philbrick, a millionaire shipowner. He flees Llanabba as he is about to be arrested on charges of false pretenses. At Blackstone Gaol Paul finds Philbrick a trusty.

Lord Tangent, a pupil at Llanabba. Acting as starter during an annual field sports meet, Prendergast accidentally shoots Lord Tangent in the heel. Lord Tangent dies of the infection.

Lady Circumference, Lord Tangent's rude mother.

Lord Pastmaster, Margot's impoverished brother-in-law, from whom she buys her country house, King's Thursday.

Otto Silenus, an eccentric designer who changes King's Thursday from the finest example of Tudor domestic architecture in England into a structure of concrete, glass, and aluminum.

Sir Humphrey Maltravers, Minister of Transport; later Lord Metroland and the Home Secretary. He is Paul's rival for Margot's hand. First refused because Margot's son Peter prefers Paul, he is accepted after Paul's conviction. He is involved in the arranging of Paul's escape from prison.

DEEPHAVEN

Author: Sarah Orne Jewett (1849-1909)
Time of action: Nineteenth century
First published: 1877

PRINCIPAL CHARACTERS

Helen Denis, the narrator.

Kate Lancaster, the narrator's friend, who asks Helen Denis to spend a summer at Deephaven with her in the house left to her mother by her great-aunt Katherine Brandon. She and Helen are made welcome by those who have known the Lancaster family through several generations.

Dick Carew, a retired East India merchant, one of Deephaven's leading citizens.

Mrs. Carew, his wife, a social leader in Deephaven.

Mr. Lorimer, a minister in Deephaven.

Mrs. Lorimer, the minister's wife.

Mrs. Kew, wife of the keeper of a light-house near Deephaven. She becomes a great friend to Kate Lancaster and Helen Denis.

Captain Lant, a retired sailor who tells the girls about Peletiah Daw and Peletiah's wild nephew Ben.

Danny, a silent, weather-beaten sailor who tells the girls about his pet cat.

Captain Sands, another old seafarer who befriends Helen and Kate.

Mrs. Bonny, an unconventional woman who lives near Deephaven. She reminds the girls of a friendly Indian.

Miss Chauncey, an aristocratic old lady who lives, mildly insane, in an unfurnished old mansion.

THE DEERSLAYER

Author: James Fenimore Cooper (1789-1851)
Time of action: 1740
First published: 1841

PRINCIPAL CHARACTERS

Natty Bumppo, called Deerslayer. A skilled, modest, honorable, brave young hunter, he has been brought up by Delaware Indians and taught by Moravian pietists; he embodies a natural innocence and nobility. Arriving at Lake Glimmerglass, he allies himself with Hurry Harry March and the Hutter family, at the same time trying to help his Indian friend Chingachgook rescue his betrothed from hostile Iroquois. He is soon forced to kill his first man, an

260

Indian. He ransoms the captured Harry and Hutter after their capture during a raid on an Iroquois camp, but he himself is caught while assisting Chingachgook. The Iroquois respect his word and give him leave to offer his friends terms of surrender. When these are rejected, he goes back to be tortured. He escapes but is recaptured. His torture is stopped only by the timely arrival of Chingachgook and Hurry Harry with British troops. Unresponsive to Judith Hutter's charms, he leaves to join the Delaware tribe.

Hurry Harry March, a ferocious, greedy, swaggering frontiersman. Captured with Hutter during a raid for Indian scalps, he is released only by Deerslayer's bargaining. His impulsive shooting of an Indian girl endangers his companions. Large and handsome, he is nevertheless refused by Judith Hutter, who favors Deerslayer. He redeems himself by leading the British soldiers to the Indian camp, thus saving Deerslayer's life.

Chingachgook (chĭn·găch′gŏŏk), the Great Serpent, a Delaware chief. A noble savage, he is as adept in woodcraft and warfare as his friend Deerslayer. He manages to escape with his beloved,Wahta!-Wah, when Deerslayer is captured. Later he saves Hurry Harry in an ambush at Hutter's "castle," and he cuts Deerslayer's bonds just before the British rout the Iroquois. Years later he revisits Lake Glimmerglass with his son Uncas and his friend Deerslayer.

Tom Hutter, a predatory former pirate who became a trapper in order to escape the law. Living with his two adopted daughters in Muskrat Castle, a hut built on a shoal, he makes his trapping rounds of the lake in a houseboat. As avaricious as Hurry Harry, he joins him on an ill-fated raid, when both are made prisoners by hostile Indians. After being ransomed he joins Harry on another raid. Returning to his hut, he is scalped in an ambush and buried in the lake by his daughters.

Judith Hutter, his gay, coquettish, shrewd young daughter, who prides herself on her clothes and appearance. Having been seduced by Captain Warley, she is cautious about men and refuses Hurry Harry. Deerslayer, however, resists her attractions and declines her offer of marriage. Having no relatives left when her sister dies, she goes to the British fort, possibly to become Warley's mistress later on.

Hetty Hutter, Judith's simple-minded sister. She embodies a pure Christian simplicity unalloyed by a sense of expediency. The Indians are in awe of her and allow her to pass unmolested as she serves as a kind of messenger between the captured and uncaptured. Her naïve love for Hurry Harry remains unrequited when she is accidentally shot in the final battle with the Indians.

Wah-ta!-Wah, Chingachgook's beloved, a Delaware maiden captured by Iroquois. A practical child of nature, she condones scalping but deplores Hurry Harry's wanton killing. Although she escapes with Chingachgook, she returns to the enemy camp with Judith and Hetty in an effort to save Deerslayer.

Captain Warley, head of the troop that saves Deerslayer and routs the Indians. A man of the world, his interest in Judith revives when he sees her in the camp in a stunning gown.

Rivenoak, the enemy Iroquois chief, a fierce foe but honorable in character. He offers to let Deerslayer live if he will marry the widow of the brave he killed.

Le Loup Cervier (lə lōō sâr·vyā′), an Indian, the first person Deerslayer ever killed. In dying he names Deerslayer "Hawkeye."

Sumach, his wife, whom Deerslayer refuses.

The Panther, an Indian who attempts to

kill the captured Deerslayer but is himself killed instead.

Catamount, the brave who unsuccessfully taunts captured Deerslayer.

DEIRDRE

Author: James Stephens (1882-1950)
Time of action: The Heroic Age
First published: 1923

PRINCIPAL CHARACTERS

Conachúr mac Nessa, King of Ulster, strong and willful, beloved by his people. Pride forces him to ignore a prophecy that the infant Deirdre will bring destruction upon Ulster. She is brought up as his ward. Seeing her, at sixteen, he determines to make her his Queen. After her escape to Scotland he resorts to treachery in an attempt to lure her back.

Nessa, the Ungentle, the mother of Conachúr. Daughter of a King of Ulster, she was called Assa, the Gentle, until she set forth to seek vengeance on the murderer of her tutors.

Cathfa, a magician, Conachúr's father. He forces Nessa to marry him as an alternative to death, but she later leaves him. It is he who makes the direful prophecy about Deirdre.

Fergus mac Roy, King of Ulster, who is so in love, at eighteen, with the still-beautiful Nessa that, to get her to marry him, he temporarily abdicates his throne to the sixteen-year-old Conachúr. The abdication proves permanent, and Fergus becomes one of Conachúr's most trusted followers.

Clothru, the daughter of the High King of Connacht, and Conachúr's first wife. She is killed by her sister Maeve.

Maeve, the sister of Clothru. Claiming to avenge Clothru's death, Conachúr instead falls in love with Maeve and marries her against her wishes. Much later, when she leaves him, her unforgiveness is such that she goes to great lengths to take back every bit of the riches she brought with her.

Deirdre, Conachúr's ward, brought up to see only women servants and the ugliest guards in Ulster. Evading them, however, she finds three youths around a campfire. She falls in love with the eldest and, to escape Conachúr, persuades them to take her away. Brought back from Scotland by Conachúr's pretense of friendship and promise of safety, she escapes him again in death.

Lavarcham, Conachúr's conversation-woman. In charge of Deirdre's upbringing, she decides to groom her to be Queen. She reports on Deirdre to Conachúr and in turn tells Deirdre all she needs to know about the King, but she cannot succeed in making Deirdre want him as a husband.

Naoise, who is a brave and handsome youth of nineteen when first seen by Deirdre. She loves him and lives six years with him and his brothers in Scotland. Tricked into returning with her, he is killed.

Ainnle and
Ardan, Naoise's brothers, also killed as a result of Conachúr's treachery.

Felimid mac Dall, Conachúr's storyteller and Deirdre's father.

Uisneac, Conachúr's brother-in-law and father of Naoise, Ainnle, and Ardan.

mac Roth, Maeve's spy, who makes possible her secret preparations to leave Conachúr.

262

DEIRDRE OF THE SORROWS

Author: John Millington Synge (1871-1909)
Time of action: The legendary past
First presented: 1910

PRINCIPAL CHARACTERS

Deirdre (dâr'drä), a Gaelic legendary heroine foretold to bring trouble into the world. Loved by King Conchubor, she, in turn, loves Naisi, with whom she flees. After seven years of happiness, the lovers are lured back to the King's castle, where Naisi is slain. In her sorrow, Deirdre kills herself in order to join her lover in another world.

Naisi (nä'shē), a Gaelic legendary hero. Winning Deirdre's love, he takes her from King Conchubor. After seven happy years with his bride, he is tricked into a meeting with the King and slain.

Conchubor, the lonely King of Ulster. In love with Deirdre, whom he has resolved to marry in spite of the prophecy that she is born for trouble, he loses her to Naisi.

Eventually he tricks the lovers into a meeting at which Naisi is slain. When Deirdre commits suicide in her grief, the King is led away, old and broken.

Lavarcham, Deirdre's nurse.

Fergus, King Conchubor's friend. In good faith he brings King Conchubor's peace offering to Deirdre and Naisi. When he learns of the lovers' betrayal, he burns the King's castle.

Owen, King Conchubor's friend and spy. In despair over his hopeless love for Deirdre, he destroys himself.

Ainnle and
Ardan, Naisi's brothers, slain with him by King Conchubor's warriors.

DELPHINE

Author: Madame de Staël (Baronne de Staël-Holstein, 1766-1817)
Time of action: Late eighteenth century
First published: 1802

PRINCIPAL CHARACTERS

Delphine d'Albemar (dĕl·fēn' dàl·bə-màr'), the tragic heroine of this sentimental epistolary novel. Intellectually and financially independent upon her widowhood at twenty, she gives away part of her fortune to enable Matilda de Vernon, the daughter of a friend, to marry a yet unseen Spanish nobleman. When Delphine herself falls in love with the young nobleman, she is maligned and deceived by Matilda's mother in order that the proposed marriage may take place. Always virtuous but never an adherent to convention, Delphine constantly finds her reputation in jeopardy. Deceived into

taking vows as a nun, she renounces them to marry her lover, now a widower. But because public opinion is against her, she refuses to marry him, not wishing to make his life miserable. Ultimately she takes poison and dies on his execution ground. The lovers, kept apart in life, are buried side by side.

Madame de Vernon (də vĕr·nôn'), her close friend, a treacherous woman. On her deathbed she confesses that she lied about Delphine.

Matilda de Vernon (mà·tēl'dà də vĕr-nôn'), Madame de Vernon's daughter.

263

Her marriage to the man who loves Delphine is doomed to unhappiness. When her death frees her husband, he and Delphine are still unable to find happiness.

Léonce Mondeville (lā·ŏns′ mŏn·də·vēl′), a Spanish nobleman, Matilda's fiancé. In love with and loved by Delphine, he is tricked by Matilda's mother into going ahead with the marriage to Matilda. After Madame de Vernon, on her deathbed, clears Delphine's name, he and Delphine decide to continue seeing each other. Their affair is not immoral, but is assumed to be so. At last, having joined the royalist forces, he is captured and sentenced to death by the republican French government. After Delphine's suicide at the spot where he is to be executed, the soldiers refuse to shoot him; but he taunts them until they do so.

Madame d'Ervin (dĕr·văn′), a friend of Delphine, at whose house she meets her lover. In keeping Madame d'Ervin's presence in the house a secret, Delphine finds that she herself is believed to be the object of the lover's nocturnal visits. Madame de Vernon, informed of the truth, lies about it to Mondeville.

Monsieur de Serbellane (də sĕr·bĕ·làn′), Madame d'Ervin's lover. He kills her husband in a duel.

Monsieur de Valorbe (də và·lôrb′), a friend of Delphine's late husband. His pursuit of Delphine results in repeated scandal. Distracted because she still refuses to marry him, he causes his own death.

Mademoiselle d'Albemar (dàl·bə·màr′), Delphine's sister-in-law. She vainly warns Delphine against Madame de Vernon.

DELTA WEDDING

Author: Eudora Welty (1909-   )
Time of action: Early 1920's
First published: 1946

PRINCIPAL CHARACTERS

Laura McRaven, a cousin to the Fairchilds, a remarkable and close-knit Delta family. At nine, Laura makes her first journey alone. She is going to the Delta to visit her dead mother's people; her cousin Dabney is being married. Laura's chief regret is that she is not to be in the wedding party, but at the last minute, when one of the children falls sick, this wish is granted. After the wedding Laura's aunt asks her to live with them. Being wanted by the Fairchild's seems wonderful beyond belief; but Laura knows that she must go back to her father.

Dabney Fairchild, Laura's cousin, a bride-to-be. Dabney is marrying the plantation manager, whose social position is inferior. Dabney, before her marriage,

feels ambivalent—loving her fiancé, but at the same time afraid of being at all outside her family. After the honeymoon, the couple returns to live at Marmion, an estate owned by the family. Everything now seems right to Dabney.

Battle Fairchild, her father, the owner of Shellmound plantation. The Fairchilds seldom talk as a family, but always act as one. Characteristically, Battle is reluctant to let Dabney go, but cannot even say that he will miss her.

Ellen Fairchild, Dabney's mother. Sharing the Fairchild reticence, which is in fact family loyalty, she expresses only to her husband her anger against her brother-in-law's wife Robbie, who is making George unhappy.

George Fairchild, Battle's brother, the best loved of all. He married beneath him and his wife, resentful of George's family, especially after George risked his life to save a feeble-minded cousin, has deserted him. But she comes to the Fairchild place and at last, though not in words, George makes her see his love for her.

Robbie Fairchild, George's wife. She believes that the Fairchilds love one another because in doing so they are really loving themselves. Defeated by the family feeling, she wants George to show that he loves her above them.

Shelley Fairchild, the eldest Fairchild daughter. The family disapproves of her plan to become a nun, but characteristically does not try to get her to change her mind. Shelley, understanding the family best, knows that George is the best loved because he alone seems to love them all as individuals, not collectively.

Troy Flavin, the manager of Shellmound plantation and Dabney's husband-to-be. His mother sends some beautiful hand-made quilts from her mountain shack. Troy is proud, but the Fairchilds are even more ashamed of his background, though unwillingly.

DESIRE UNDER THE ELMS

Author: Eugene O'Neill (1888-1953)
Time of action: 1850
First presented: 1924

PRINCIPAL CHARACTERS

Ephraim Cabot, a greedy, harsh old New England widower. He has taken over his second wife's farm and worked her to death. He has brutalized his three sons, working them like animals on the farm until they hate him bitterly. At the age of seventy-six he marries thirty-five-year-old Abbie Putnam, a deed intended to cheat his sons of their inheritance. The two older sons have left the farm but Eben, the youngest, remains. Abbie, whom Eben hates, cleverly seduces him and he fathers a child that Ephraim, duped by flattery, believes is his own. Taunted by his father, Eben threatens to kill Abbie for tricking him. But by this time she has fallen in love with Eben and, as her way of proving this love, she murders the baby. When Abbie is about to be arrested, Eben realizes that he now loves her and he insists on accepting part of the blame for her crime. As the sheriff takes them away, Ephraim is left alone to contemplate his empty victory over his sons.

Eben Cabot, Ephraim's son by his second wife. He hates Ephraim for the way the self-righteous old hypocrite treated his mother. Believing that the farm is really his, Eben buys out the potential claim of his brothers by giving each three hundred dollars from a hoard of gold his mother had hidden. He bitterly resents the arrival of a young stepmother and he still hates her even after she seduces him and he fathers her child. But her final act of love toward him changes his hatred of her to love, and he willingly goes away with her to share her punishment.

Abbie Putnam, Ephraim's third wife who, though half his age, marries him to get a home. Her appearance heightens the hostility that exists between Ephraim and Eben. Abbie seduces Eben in order to get a child who will be Ephraim's heir and who will deprive Eben of his expected inheritance. Though Eben tells her he hates her, Abbie has fallen in

265

love with him and to prove this love she smothers the baby she has tricked him into fathering. Shocked by this crime Eben goes for the sheriff, but when he begins to realize that he really loves Abbie, he tells the sheriff that he is an accomplice in the crime and is taken away with her.

Simeon and
Peter Cabot, Ephraim's sons and Eben's half brothers. Hating their father and wanting desperately to join the gold rush to California, they accept Eben's offer of three hundred dollars each and renounce all claims to the farm.

DESTINY BAY

Author: Donn Byrne (Brian Oswald Donn-Byrne, 1889-1928)
Time of action: Early twentieth century
First published: 1928

PRINCIPAL CHARACTERS

Kerry MacFarlane, heir to Destiny Bay. He is the narrator.

Jenepher MacFarlane, Kerry's blind but beautiful aunt. She has a deep perception of human goodness. She is Sir Valentine's sister.

Sir Valentine MacFarlane, Kerry's red-headed, red-bearded uncle, the lord of Destiny Bay. He is courtly and hospitable. Loving people, he does all he can to help them.

The Duke of la Mentera, a Spanish nobleman. A relatively poor man, he comes to Destiny Bay in search of a treasure chest lost from the Spanish Armada by an ancestor.

Don Anthony (Ann-Dolly), the Duke of la Mentera's grandson, who turns out to be a beautiful girl, known then as Ann-Dolly. She falls in love with and marries Jenico Hamilton.

James Carabine, Sir Valentine's faithful valet. A great prizefighter, he fell on evil ways in New York City. He was rescued from drunkenness and failure by Sir Val-

entine, who went to America to bring him back to Ireland.

Jenico Hamilton, Kerry's cousin who lives near Destiny Bay. He marries Ann-Dolly.

Patrick Herne, Jenepher's husband. He looks like Digory Pascoe, Jenepher's dead fiancé, who, though killed in a fight, is kept alive for Jenepher for twelve years by Sir Valentine through letters written as though from Digory to Jenepher. Sir Valentine brings Patrick home as Digory. He and Jenepher fall in love and are married, after Jenepher learns he is not truly her supposed first fiancé.

The Fair Maid of Wu, a Chinese girl whom Cosimo MacFarlane saw three times and came to love.

Cosimo MacFarlane, Sir Valentine's brother. He is a great, happy, joyous man. A heavy drinker who reforms, he works to reform other drunkards and ends up as the Bishop of Borneo.

Anselo Loveridge, Cosimo's friend. He is a gipsy rescued from the hangman's noose by Cosimo. He finds the Fair Maid of Wu for his benefactor.

266

THE DEVIL'S ELIXIR

Author: Ernst Theodor Amadeus Hoffman (1776-1822)
Time of action: Eighteenth century
First published: 1815-1816

PRINCIPAL CHARACTERS

Medardus, a monk. He is put in charge of the relics of his order, which include among them an elixir reputed to cause any who drink of it to belong to the devil. Also, if two should taste of the potion, they would be as one in thought and desire while secretly wishing to destroy each other. Medardus drinks of the elixir and is then confronted with all the devices of the powers of darkness which weave about him a web of falsehoods, murders, mistaken indentities, and madness until he recovers and is purged of his guilt. He is then asked by Father Spiridion, the monastery librarian, to put his life story in writing.

Count Victorin, Medardus' brother, who has also drunk of the devil's elixir. Unknown to each other as brothers, the two resemble each other and have the same desires, but in one guise or another, each tries continually to destroy the other.

Aurelia, a young noblewoman loved by Medardus but claimed by Victorin as his intended bride. She is killed by Victorin as she is taking her vows as a nun.

Hermogen, Aurelia's brother, killed by Medardus.

Baron von F——, the father of Aurelia and Hermogen.

Euphemia, Baron von F——'s sinister wife engaged in an affair with Victorin.

Pietro Belcampo, a hairdresser and Medardus' benefactor.

Francesco, a painter revealed as Medardus' father.

Leonardus, a prior, Medardus' spiritual adviser, from whom he receives forgiveness for his crimes.

Reinhold, an old man at Baron von F——'s castle.

Prince von Rosenthurm, at whose castle Medardus learns that Francesco is his father.

The Duke of Neuenburg, the Prince's brother, murdered on his wedding night.

Father Spiridion, the librarian of the Capuchin monastery at Königswald.

THE DEVOTION OF THE CROSS

Author: Pedro Calderón de la Barca (1600-1681)
Time of action: Seventeenth century
First presented: c. 1633

PRINCIPAL CHARACTERS

Eusebio (ā·ōō·sā′byō), one of two infants abandoned by a wayside cross. Surviving several disasters in which the sign of the cross is miraculously manifested, he feels himself ennobled by his devotion to the cross and worthy of Julia, whom he loves.

When he kills her brother, Lisardo, in a duel, and she orders him out of her life, he turns bandit and spares only victims who mention the cross. During ensuing adventures he learns his identity, that of his father, Curcio, and that of his brother

267

and sister, Lisardo and Julia. Fatally wounded, he wins redemption because of his devotion to the cross.

Julia (hōō'lyä), who is loved by Eusebio. Later, by the sign of the cross on her breast, she is revealed as Eusebio's sister, the other infant abandoned at the wayside cross.

Lisardo (lē·sär'dō), Julia's brother, killed in a duel by Eusebio and later revealed as Eusebio's brother.

Curcio (kōōr'thyō), the father of Eusebio, Julia, and Lisardo. A baseless suspicion of his wife's unfaithfulness causes him to abandon the twins, Eusebio and Julia, by a wayside cross. When he fatally wounds Eusebio in a fight, his son's identity is established by the cross on his body.

Father Alberto (äl·bâr'tō), a priest whose life is saved by the bandit Eusebio. In thankfulness for being spared, he hears the outlaw's last confession.

Gil (hēl) and
Menga (měn'gä), peasant witnesses to the duel between Eusebio and Lisardo.

LE DIABLE BOITEUX

Author: Alain René Le Sage (1668-1747)
Time of action: Early eighteenth century
First published: 1707

PRINCIPAL CHARACTERS

Don Cleophas Leandro Perez Zambullo, a student. At the home of his inamorata, Donna Thomasa, he finds himself worsted in a fight with hired ruffians. He flees to the rooftops and enters a garret where he finds the demon Asmodeus and frees him from a bottle in which he is imprisoned. In return for this favor, the demon takes Don Cleophas on a flight over Madrid, during which he gives the student glimpses into the varied life of the city. He provides explanations of the sights they see, wreaks vengeance for Don Cleophas on the treacherous Donna Thomasa, rescues the beautiful Donna Seraphina from imminent death, and bequeathes her to the young man as a bride.

Asmodeus, the Devil on Two Sticks, the friend of hapless lovers. Imprisoned in a bottle by a magician, he is freed from his captivity by Don Cleophas Leandro Perez Zambullo, whom he takes on a flying trip over Madrid.

Donna Thomasa, Don Cleophas' treacherous inamorata.

Donna Seraphina, a beautiful lady rescued from a fire by Asmodeus disguised as Don Cleophas Leandro Perez Zambullo, whom she later marries.

Don Pedro de Escolano, Donna Seraphina's father.

The Count de Belflor, a court gallant,
Leonora de Cespedes, loved by the Count de Belflor,
Marcella, Leonora de Cespedes' treacherous duenna,
Don Luis de Cespedes, Leonora's father,
Don Pedro, Leonora's brother, in love with Donna Eugenia, and
Donna Eugenia, the Count de Belflor's sister, characters in a story told to Don Cleophas Leandro Perez Zambullo by Asmodeus as they watch a wedding festival through a window.

Don Juan de Zarata and
Don Fabricio de Mendoza, devoted friends in love with Donna Theodora de Cifuentes,
Don Alvaro Ponza, the rejected suitor of Donna Theodora de Cifuentes,

268

Donna Theodora de Cifuentes, a beautiful widow in love with Don Juan de Zarata, and

The Dey of Algiers, characters in a story of true friendship and love told by Asmodeus.

DIANA OF THE CROSSWAYS

Author: George Meredith (1828-1909)
Time of action: Nineteenth century
First published: 1885

PRINCIPAL CHARACTERS

Diana Merion Warwick, a witty, charming, and beautiful woman. She is a person who makes mistakes because she does not believe that the conventional thing is always the right thing. She learns from her experiences, however, and becomes a wiser woman. She marries Augustus Warwick primarily as a matter of convenience. When she becomes friendly with the elderly Lord Dannisburgh, her husband accuses her of infidelity. She is found not guilty of this charge by a court, but she refuses to return to her husband. She becomes a novelist, but her initial success does not last and she finds herself reduced to poverty. In these circumstances, she sells some information told to her by Sir Percy Dacier, who is in love with her, thus betraying his confidence. She finally consents to become the wife of a man who has loved her for many years. Diana makes many enemies, but she is also the sort of woman who is loved and admired by many men.

Augustus Warwick, the politician whom Diana marries when she is a young woman. He is calculating and ambitious and is completely incapable of understanding his wife's innocence of the demands of conventionality. He tries to force Diana to return to him, but she will not. He is finally struck down and killed by a cab in the street.

Sir Percy Dacier, a young politician who falls in love with Diana after she has

refused to return to her husband. He spends a great deal of time following her about and, in a moment of indiscretion, tells her a very important political secret. Diana sends him away. Needing money desperately, she sells his information to a newspaper. Feeling betrayed, he turns from her and marries an heiress.

Thomas Redworth, a brilliant member of Parliament who falls in love with Diana. He announces his love too late, after she is engaged to Warwick. He is steadfast, however, and, when Diana is forced to sell her family home and all of her belongings, he buys them, expecting that some day she will consent to become his wife. His loyalty is rewarded when Diana marries him.

Lady Emma Dunstane, a friend of Diana who introduces her to Redworth. She remains faithful to Diana through all of her troubles and unpopularity.

Lord Dannisburgh, the older man with whom Diana is friendly and with whom she appears, rather indiscreetly, while her husband is away on a government mission. He is Sir Percy Dacier's uncle. When he dies, he leaves Diana a sum of money in his will.

Sullivan Smith, a hot-tempered Irishman who challenges Redworth to a duel because he objects to Redworth's attentions to Diana. He proposes to Diana, but she refuses him.

THE DIARY OF A COUNTRY PRIEST

Author: Georges Bernanos (1888-1948)
Time of action: The 1920's
First published: 1937

PRINCIPAL CHARACTERS

A Priest, the thirty-year-old cleric of Ambricourt Parish, in France, who strives to be frank with himself. Lonely and sympathetic, a child of poverty, he tries to help his people materially, as well as spiritually. He believes the rich have a duty to the poor. His efforts to help his people undermine his health and bring scorn upon him. He fails again and again; only in death does he find peace, believing in God.

Dr. Maxence Delbende (màk·säns′ dĕl-bänd′), a thwarted, bitter man. He helps frustrate the priest's efforts to aid the parish materially. When disappointed at not receiving an expected legacy, he commits suicide.

The Curé de Torcy (də tôr·sē′), the priest's superior and ideal. He thwarts the priest's efforts to raise living standards and ridicules the priest for his spiritual and worldly failures.

Seraphita Dumouchel (sā·rà·fē·tà′ dü-mōō·shĕl′), a sensual girl in the priest's catechism class. She thrusts unsavory attentions on the priest and spreads the word that he is addicted to drink.

The Count, a local aristocrat. He carries on an affair with the family governess and embitters his family by a series of infidelities over the years.

Mlle. Chantal (shäṅ·tàl′), daughter of the Count and Countess. Upset and filled with hatred, she threatens to kill either herself or the governess with whom her father is having an affair.

The Countess, a woman of atheistic tendencies. With the priest's help she dies in spiritual peace, though consumed by physical agony.

Mlle. Louise (lwēz′), the governess who is the Count's mistress.

M. Dufrety (dü·frə·tē′), the priest's seminary friend. He is with the priest at his death.

Dr. Laville (lə·vēl′), a drug addict. He bluntly tells the priest he is dying of stomach cancer. The priest was supposed to go to Dr. Lavigne, but consults the wrong physician.

DIGBY GRAND

Author: George J. Whyte-Melville (1821-1878)
Time of action: Early nineteenth century
First published: 1853

PRINCIPAL CHARACTERS

Digby Grand, a spirited young Englishman, perfectly willing to follow his father's wish that he be a man of fashion. Leaving Eton, he is commissioned as an ensign in a regiment of infantry. After being stationed first in Scotland and then in Canada, Digby finds that his father has purchased him a lieutenancy in the most social brigade in the service, the Life Guards, stationed in London. Digby is popular in the best society, but he goes heavily into debt. He falls in love with a penniless girl whom his father forbids him to marry. Prevented by creditors from leaving England to go to India as his general's aide, he sells everything he owns, including his commission and, upon his father's death, his estate. Left only his title, he is taken into business by a friend who has become a wine merchant. Business prospers, and Digby, settling down at last, makes plans to marry his old sweetheart.

Sir Peregrine Grand, of Haverley Hall, Digby's father, who wants his son to be a man of great social position and to marry a wealthy heiress.

Tom Spencer, Digby's boyhood chum. Studying for holy orders at Oxford, Tom co-signs moneylenders' notes for Digby. Later he is arrested as a result and consequently cannot finish his degree at Oxford. He then becomes a successful wine merchant and takes Digby into the business with him.

Flora Belmont, the fortuneless daughter of a retired colonel. Digby falls in love with her, but his father opposes the marriage. Well off at last and ready to settle down, Digby finds her still single and they make plans to marry.

Coralie de Rivolte, a famous dancer with whom Digby has an affair.

Colonel Cartouch, Digby's commanding officer, who likes him and who intervenes to prevent the teen-age ensign from marrying the young French-Canadian girl with whom he has an affair in Canada. Later, prosecuting a man forging checks in his name, Colonel Cartouch

finds out that the forger is married to Coralie de Rivolte, and that Coralie is his own daughter by a Spanish woman who left him after killing her sister, whom she believed to be in love with Cartouch.

Shadrach, a moneylender who lends Digby money at high interest rates. To satisfy him and other creditors, Digby gives up everything he owns.

Captain Levanter, one of Digby's fellow officers. He introduces Digby to Shadrach.

General Sir Benjamin Burgonet, who likes Digby and makes it possible for him to secure his original commission. He later makes Digby his aide, but Digby is prevented from leaving for India by his creditors.

Lady Burgonet, a woman in her thirties who, while Digby is stationed in Scotland, almost succeeds in tricking him into marriage. Instead, she becomes the wife of the regimental drum major. When he is preparing to go with the General to India, Digby is aghast to find that the woman is now Lady Burgonet.

Dubbs, the regimental drum major, Lady Burgonet's husband before her marriage to General Burgonet.

St. Heliers, a young peer with whom Digby is friendly in London.

Mrs. Mantrap, a woman who basks in the attentions of young men. She is one of Digby's London friends.

Zoë, a French-Canadian girl with whom Digby has an affair in Canada.

THE DISCIPLE

Author: Paul Bourget (1852-1935)
Time of action: Late nineteenth century
First published: 1889

Adrien Sixte (à·drē·ăn' sĕkst'), a brilliant philosopher, teacher, and writer who develops a deterministic theory that each effect comes from a cause, and that if all causes are known, results can be predicted accurately in all forms of human activity. The strict regularity of his life is interrupted by Robert's arrest, and his reading of Robert's confessional manuscript makes him feel morally responsible for Robert's acts. Again, at Robert's funeral, Adrien feels a moral guilt in the death of his disciple.

Robert Greslou (rô·bĕr' grĕs·lōō'), his disciple, a precocious student of philosophy who tests his master's theory by seducing Charlotte through providing causes which produce the result he wishes to achieve. Pretending to enter a suicide pact, he spends a night with her, then repudiates the pact and leaves. Arrested on suspicion of murder, he is willing to die to keep Charlotte's suicide a secret, but he is acquitted after André's testimony. As they reach the street after the trial, André shoots Robert in the head.

M. de Jussat (zhü·sȧ'), a hypochondriac and a boorish nobleman.

Charlotte (shȧr·lôt'), his beautiful young daughter who, suffering from discovery of Robert's duplicity, drinks strychnine after writing a suicide note to André.

André (än·drȧ'), her older brother, an army officer fond of hunting and riding. Influenced by Adrien to free Robert from the murder charge, he then avenges his sister's seduction and death.

Lucien (lü·sē·ȧn'), Charlotte's younger brother, a fat, simple boy of thirteen who is tutored by Robert.

THE DIVINE COMEDY

Author: Dante Alighieri (1265-1321)
Time of action: The Friday before Easter, 1300
First transcribed: completed c. 1320

Dante (dän'tä), the exile Florentine poet, who is halted in his path of error through the grace of the Virgin, St. Lucy, and Beatrice, and is redeemed by his journey through Hell, Purgatory, and Paradise. He learns to submerge his instinctive pity for some sinners in his recognition of the justice of God, and he frees himself of the faults of wrath and misdirected love by participating in the penance for these sins in Purgatory. He is then ready to grow in understanding and love as he moves with Beatrice nearer and nearer the presence of God.

Beatrice (bĕ'ȧ·trē'chä), his beloved, who is transformed into an angel, one of Mary's handmaids. Through her intercession, her compassion, and her teaching, Dante's passion is transmuted into divine love, which brings him to a state of indescribable blessedness.

Virgil, Dante's master, the great Roman poet who guides him through Hell and Purgatory. The most favored of the noble pagans who dwell in Limbo without hope of heavenly bliss, he represents the highest achievements of human reason and classical learning.

St. Lucy, Dante's patron saint. She sends him aid and conveys him through a part of Purgatory.

Charon, traditionally the ferryman of damned souls.

Minos, the monstrous judge who dooms sinners to their alloted torments.

Paolo and
Francesca, devoted lovers, murdered by Paolo's brother, who was Francesca's husband. Together even in hell, they arouse Dante's pity by their tale of growing affection.

Ciacco, a Florentine damned for gluttony, who prophesies the civil disputes which engulfed his native city after his death.

Plutus, the bloated, clucking creature who guards the entrance of the fourth circle of Hell.

Phlegyas, the boatman of the wrathful.

Filippo Argenti, another Florentine noble, damned to welter in mud for his uncontrollable temper.

Megaera,
Alecto, and
Tisiphone, the Furies, tower warders of the City of Dis.

Farinata Degli Uberti, leader of the Ghibelline party of Florence, condemned to rest in an indestructible sepulchre for his heresy. He remains concerned primarily for the fate of his city.

Cavalcante, a Guelph leader, the father of Dante's friend Guido. He rises from his tomb to ask about his son.

Nessus,
Chiron, and
Pholus, the courteous archer centaurs who guard the river of boiling blood which holds the violent against men.

Piero Delle Vigne, the loyal adviser to the Emperor Frederick, imprisoned, with others who committed suicide, in a thornbush.

Capaneus, a proud, blasphemous tyrant, one of the Seven against Thebes.

Brunetto Latini, Dante's old teacher, whom the poet treats with great respect;

he laments the sin of sodomy which placed him deep in Hell.

Guido Guerra,
Tegghiaio Aldobrandi,
Jacopo Rusticucci, and
Guglielmo Borsiere, Florentine citizens who gave in to unnatural lust.

Geryon, a beast with human face and scorpion's tail, symbolic of fraud.

Venedico Caccianemico, a Bolognese pander.

Jason, a classical hero, damned as a seducer.

Alessio Interminei, a flatterer.

Nicholas III, one of the popes, damned to burn in a rocky cave for using the resources of the Church for worldly advancement.

Amphiaraus,
Tiresias,
Aruns,
Manto,
Eurypylus,
Michael Scot, and
Guido Bonatti, astrologers and diviners whose grotesquely twisted shapes reflect their distortion of divine counsel.

Malacoda, chief of the devils who torment corrupt political officials.

Ciampolo, one of his charges, who converses with Dante and Virgil while he plans to outwit the devils.

Catalano and
Loderingo, jovial Bolognese friars, who wear the gilded leaden mantles decreed eternally for hypocrites.

Caiphas, the high priest who had Christ condemned. He lies naked in the path of the heavily laden hypocrites.

Vanni Fucci, a bestial, wrathful thief, the damned spirit most arrogant against God.

Agnello,
Francisco,

273

Cianfa,
Buoso, and
Puccio, malicious thieves and oppressors, who are metamorphosed from men to serpents, then from serpents to men, before the eyes of the poet.

Ulysses and
Diomed, Greek heroes transformed into tongues of flame as types of the evil counselor. Ulysses retains the splendid passion for knowledge which led him beyond the limits set for men.

Guido de Montefeltro, another of the evil counselors, who became involved in the fraud and sacrilege of Pope Boniface.

Mahomet,
Piero da Medicina, and
Bertran de Born, sowers of schism and discord, whose bodies are cleft and mutilated.

Capocchio and
Griffolino, alchemists afflicted with leprosy.

Gianni Schicchi and
Myrrha, sinners who disguised themselves because of lust and greed, fittingly transformed into swine.

Master Adam, a counterfeiter.

Sinon and
Potiphar's Wife, damned for malicious lying and treachery.

Nimrod,
Antaeus, and
Briareus, giants who rebelled against God.

Camincion de' Pazzi,
Count Ugolino,
Fra Alberigo,
Judas Iscariot,
Brutus, and
Cassius, traitors to family, country, and their masters. They dwell forever in ice, hard and cold as their own hearts.

Cato, the aged Roman sage who was, for the Middle Ages, a symbol of pagan virtue. He meets Dante and Virgil at the base of Mount Purgatory and sends them on their way upward.

Casella, a Florentine composer who charms his hearers with a song as they enter Purgatory.

Manfred, a Ghibelline leader,
Belacqua,
La Pia,
Cassero, and
Buonconte da Montefeltro, souls who must wait many years at the foot of Mount Purgatory because they delayed their repentance until the time of their death.

Sordello, the Mantuan poet, who reverently greets Virgil and accompanies him and his companion for part of their journey.

Nino Visconti and
Conrad Malaspina, men too preoccupied with their political life to repent early.

Omberto Aldobrandesco,
Oderisi, and
Provenzan Salvani, sinners who walk twisted and bent over in penance for their pride in ancestry, artistry, and power.

Sapia, one of the envious, a woman who rejoiced at the defeat of her townspeople.

Guido del Duca, another doing penance for envy. He laments the dissensions which tear apart the Italian states.

Marco Lombardo, Dante's companion through the smoky way trodden by the wrathful.

Pope Adrian, one of those being purged of avarice.

Hugh Capet, the founder of the French ruling dynasty, which he castigates for its crimes and brutality. He atones for his own ambition and greed.

Statius, the author of the "Thebaid." One of Virgil's disciples, he has just completed his penance for prodigality. He tells Dante and Virgil of the liberation of the truly repentant soul.

Forese Donati, Dante's friend, and **Bonagiunta,** Florentines guilty of gluttony.

Guido Guinicelli and **Arnaut,** love poets who submit to the flames which purify them of lust.

Matilda, a heavenly lady who meets Dante in the earthly paradise at the top of Mount Purgatory and takes him to Beatrice.

Piccarda, a Florentine nun, a fragile, almost transparent spirit who dwells in the moon's sphere, the outermost circle of heaven, since her faith wavered, making her incapable of receiving greater bliss than this.

Justinian, the great Roman Emperor and law-giver, one of the champions of the Christian faith.

Charles Martel, the heir to Charles II, King of Naples, whose early death precipitated strife and injustice.

Cunizza, Sordello's mistress, the sister of an Italian tyrant.

Falco, a troubadour who was, after his conversion, made a bishop.

Rahab, the harlot who aided Joshua to enter Jerusalem, another of the many whose human passions were transformed into love of God.

Thomas Aquinas, the Scholastic philosopher. He tells Dante of St. Francis when he comes to the sphere of the sun, the home of those who have reached heaven through their knowledge of God.

St. Bonaventura, his companion, who praises St. Dominic.

Cacciaguida, Dante's great-great-grandfather, placed in the sphere of Mars as a warrior for the Church.

Peter Damian, a hermit, an inhabitant of the sphere of Saturn, the place allotted to spirits blessed for their temperance and contemplative life.

St. Peter,
St. James, and
St. John, representatives, for Dante, of the virtues of Faith, Hope, and Love. The three great disciples examine the poet to assure his understanding of these three qualities.

Adam, the prototype of fallen man, who is, through Christ, given the greatest redemption; he is the companion of the three apostles and sits enthroned at the left hand of the Virgin.

St. Bernard, Dante's guide during the last stage of his journey, when he comes before the throne of the Queen of Heaven.

THE DIVINE FIRE

Author: May Sinclair (1870?-1946)
Time of action: The 1890's
First published: 1904

PRINCIPAL CHARACTERS

Savage Keith Rickman, a young unknown poet, a genius, who for all his warring personality traits is always honorable. Disillusioned over dishonorable dealings between his bookseller father and a financier, and kept from success by the indecisiveness of a literary editor, he spends years slaving and starving himself to redeem what he considers a debt of honor. At last his genius is acknowledged and success enables him to go to the woman for whom he has loved and slaved.

Horace Jewdwine, the literary editor who believes he has discovered a genius but who fears to jeopardize his reputation by proclaiming it. He encourages Rickman privately, but fails him in every important matter and finally loses the credit for his "discovery."

Lucia Harden, a baronet's daughter, Jewdwine's cousin and Rickman's inspiration. Rickman's aim in life is to redeem and to return to Lucia her father's library, which his own father cheated her of and then lost to an unscrupulous financier. When she finally receives Rickman's gift, Lucia is ill and unable to walk. However, realizing that her malady is only heartbreak, she recovers.

Mr. Pilkington, an unethical financier. He holds the Harden library mortgage and enjoys the spectacle of the young genius' apparently doomed struggle to redeem it.

Flossie Walker, a conventional young woman and Rickman's fellow boarder. Her goal is a house in the suburbs, and with this in mind she traps Rickman into a proposal of marriage. But she refuses to wait the years necessary for the paying off of his "debt of honor"; to his relief, she marries another.

DOCTOR FAUSTUS

Author: Thomas Mann (1875-1955)
Time of action: 1885-1945
First published: 1947

PRINCIPAL CHARACTERS

Adrian Leverkühn (ä'drē·än lā'vėr·kün), or **Adri** (ä'drē), a gifted musical composer who is convinced that he has entered into a twenty-four-year compact with Satan in which he has pledged his soul for an extended period of creativity. Like his Faustian predecessor in legend, he masters various academic goals while studying at Kaiseraschern, Halle, and Leipzig. At first he intends to become a student of theology, but while at Halle he deserts this field as arid and unchallenging. As a composer he is influenced greatly by the technique of Schönberg. His most significant works are "Apocalypsis cum figuris" and the monumental "The Lamentation of Dr. Faustus," for both of which he feels he has received unearthly inspiration at the expense of his salvation. Affable and spirited in his early years, he becomes literally and emotionally darker and more reclusive as his obsession intensifies. At the conclusion of the twenty-four years, in which time he has become internationally respected for his genius, he calls his friends to him and in anguish describes the imminent payment he must make of his soul. As he strikes the opening chords of "The Lamentation of Dr. Faustus," he suddenly collapses over the keyboard, a victim of a paralytic stroke from which he never recovers in either mind or body. The novel, narrated by Leverkühn's warmest and most sympathetic friend, Serenus Zeitblom, is presented as the biography of this afflicted genius.

Serenus Zeitblom (sâ'rā'n oos tsīt'blōm), or **Seren** (sâ·rān'), a Doctor of Philosophy, the narrator of the novel. A retired professor of classical languages, sixty years of age at the time he is writing, he describes the creative life and the hideous transformation of Leverkühn, whom he has known since childhood and with whom he studied at Halle and Leipzig. Through Zeitblom, Mann creates a double chronology which achieves a rich, symbolic pattern. While the pro-

276

fessor describes the life and death of his friend in a symbolic form that shows evil meeting its inevitable reward in chaos and destruction, he constantly refers to the current global struggle motivated by Hitler and his fanatic dreams for the German Fatherland. The description of Leverkühn's destruction (1930) prefigures the collapse of the perverted Nazi power (1945); hence, the symbolic motif is present in both an individual and national pattern.

Wendell Kretschmar (věn'dǎl krätsh'-mär), a cathedral organist who is Leverkühn's first music teacher. A short, bullet-headed man with a little clipped mustache and prone to stutter, this instructor gains over his student an uncanny power which he exercises throughout his life. He directs Leverkühn for several years and introduces him to new concepts of scale and harmony. Largely responsible for Leverkühn's decision to devote his life to music rather than to theology, Kretschmar is Mann's symbolic Mephistopheles.

Rüdiger Schildknapp (rü'dĭ·gėr shĭld'-knäp), a frequent companion of Leverkühn, an author who is forced by necessity to perform the hack work of translation. Having inherited his father's anguish of unfulfilled ambition, he is a parasitic admirer of Leverkühn's creative genius.

Rudolf Schwerdtfeger (rōō'dōlf shwârt'-fā'gėr), a gifted young violinist, a member of the Zapfenstösser Orchestra. He persuades Leverkühn to compose a violin sonata for him.

Sammael (sä'mä·äl) (**Dicis et non Facis**), the name which Satan assumes when he visits Leverkühn and discusses the terms of the twenty-four-year agreement.

Nepomuk (nä'pō·mŏŏk), also called **Nepo** and **Echo** (nä'pō, ä'shō), Leverkühn's young nephew, who brings new joy and hope into his uncle's life as the contract nears its fulfillment. But when young Schneidewein is fatally stricken

with cerebro-spinal meningitis, Leverkühn is convinced that Satan is ruthlessly destroying his last hope and joy.

Clarissa Rodde (klä'rē'sä rô'dě), an aspiring actress who commits suicide rather than face the truth concerning her lack of talent.

Inez Rodde Institoris (ē·näs' rô'dě ĭn'stĭ·tō'rēs), her sister who, although married, can find satisfaction only in an adulterous relationship with Rudolf Schwerdtfeger. When he tires of her love, in fanatic desperation she shoots him.

Jonathan (yō'nä·tän) and **Elsbeth Leverkühn** (ěls'bět lā'vėr·kün), Adrian's parents living in Kaiseraschern. Jonathan, an apothecary by trade, possesses a passion to investigate the mysteries of nature, even at the expense of negating various religious beliefs of his society.

Max (mäks) and **Else Scheigestill** (el'sė shī'gě·stĭl), the owners of the home in which Leverkühn lives in Pfeiffering during much of his adult life.

Ehrenfried Kumpf (ā'rėn·frēd kŏŏmpf) and **Eberhard Schleppfus** (ā'bėr·härd shlěp'-fōōs), professors of theology, Leverkühn's teachers at the University of Halle.

Marie Godeau (mä·rē' gō·dō'), a beautiful woman loved by Leverkühn. Hesitant to woo her forthrightly, he entrusts the courtship to his friend, Schwerdtfeger. The violinist falls in love with her, however, and woos her for himself.

Madame de Tolna (mä·däm' de tōl'nä), a wealthy Hungarian widow, Leverkühn's benefactress.

Jeanette Scheurl (shä·ně'tė shoirl), a novelist, a friend of Leverkühn.

Esmerelda (äs·mė·räl'dä), the prostitute from whom Leverkühn contracts a venereal infection.

DOCTOR FAUSTUS

Author: Christopher Marlowe (1564-1593)
Time of action: Sixteenth century
First presented: 1592?

PRINCIPAL CHARACTERS

Faustus (fous′tŭs, fôs′tŭs), a learned scholar and theologian. Ambitious for boundless knowledge, he abandons the accepted professions for black magic and sells his soul for knowledge and power. Though haunted by remorse, he is unrepentant. After he gains power his character deteriorates, and he adds cruelty to cowardice in asking tortures for an old man who tries to save his soul. He shows a final flash of nobility in sending his friends away before the expected arrival of the devils, and he delivers a poignant soliloquy while awaiting his death and damnation.

Mephistophilis (mĕf′ĭ·stof′ĭ·lĭs), a tormented devil aware of the horror of being an outcast from the sight of God. He speaks frankly to Faustus before the signing of the bond; after that, he is not concerned with fair play, being sometimes tricky, sometimes savage. At the expired time, he carries Faustus off to Hell.

Lucifer (lū′sĭ·fər), the commander of the fallen spirits. Eager for human souls to join him in misery, he puts forth great efforts to keep Faustus from escaping by repentance.

Belzebub (bĕl′zē·bŭb), the third evil spirit of the perverted trinity.

An Old Man, a godly elder concerned with saving Faustus' soul. Rejected by Faustus and made the physical prey of devils, he escapes them and rises to God by means of his great faith.

Alexander The Great,
Alexander's Paramour, and
Helen of Troy, spirits raised by Mephistophilis and Faustus. The beauty of Helen, "the face that launched a thou-

sand ships," further entangles Faustus in evil and confirms his damnation.

Valdes (väl′dās) and
Cornelius, learned magicians to whom Faustus turns for counsel when he decides to engage in black magic.

Wagner (väg′nər), the comical and impudent servant of Faustus. He follows his master in conjuring and furnishes a ridiculous contrast to the tragic Faustus.

Three Scholars, friends of Faustus for whom he produces the apparition of Helen and to whom he makes his confession just before his death.

The Pope, a victim of Faustus' playful trickery.

The Cardinal of Lorrain, an attendant to the Pope.

Charles V, Emperor of Germany. Faustus and Mephistophilis entertain him with magical tricks.

A Knight, a scornful skeptic whom Faustus abuses and infuriates by making stag horns grow on his head. He is restored to his normal state at the request of the Emperor.

The Duke of Vanholt and
The Duchess of Vanholt, patrons of Faustus whom he gratefully entertains.

The Good Angel and
The Evil Angel, who contend for Faustus' soul, each urging him to choose his way of life.

Robin, an ostler, and
Ralph, a servingman, comical characters who find Faustus' books and raise Mephistophilis, to their great terror.

A **Vintner,** the victim of Robin's and Ralph's pranks.

A **Horse Courser,** a trader deceived and abused by Faustus.

A **Clown,** the gullible victim of Wagner's conjuring.

Baliol (bā'lĭ-ŏl) and
Belcher, evil spirits raised by Wagner to terrify the Clown.

Pride,
Covetousness,
Wrath,
Envy,
Gluttony,
Sloth, and
Lechery, the Seven Deadly Sins, who appear in a pageant for Faustus.

The Chorus, who serves as prologue, commentator, and epilogue to the play.

THE DOCTOR IN SPITE OF HIMSELF

Author: Molière (Jean Baptiste Poquelin, 1622-1673)
Time of action: Seventeenth century
First presented: 1666

PRINCIPAL CHARACTERS

Sganarelle (zgȧ·nȧ·rĕl'), a faggot-gatherer whose wife accuses him of drunkenness, gambling, and lechery. Though he admits that she is a good wife, he intends to be the boss of the household. Because he believes that beatings increase affection, he whips her. When he is mistaken for a doctor, through his wife's trickery to have him beaten in turn, he displays, though he has had no education beyond the lowest class in school, wit, quick thinking, and convincing inventiveness by his use of garbled Latin, jumbled up anatomical terms, and quotations from Cicero and Hippocrates. Learning that his patient suffers dumbness only because of thwarted love, he prescribes a remedy known to make parrots talk, bread soaked in wine. He displays avarice when he gets what money he can from Géronte to cure his daughter, from Léandre to enable him to see Lucinde, and from Perrin to help his mother. At the happy ending to this farce, Sganarelle forgives his wife the beatings he has received; but he reminds her that she must hereafter show greater respect for him, for he is now a doctor and not a wood-gatherer.

Martine (mȧr·tēn'), Sganarelle's wife, who nags her husband for his drinking

and gambling, and for selling their household possessions for these purposes. She seeks revenge for his frequent beatings by claiming that Sganarelle is an eccentric doctor who amuses himself by cutting wood and who must be beaten before he will admit to being a physician. After her husband has successfully cured his patient, she overtakes him just as he is about to be hanged for helping in an elopement; she decides to witness the hanging in order to give him courage. When he is not hanged after all, she demands thanks for making him a doctor.

Géronte (zhā·rōṅt'), the father of a daughter feigning loss of speech because he objects to her marriage to anyone other than the wealthy man he himself has chosen. A great quoter of maxims, he is deceived by Sganarelle's garbled Latin and anatomical jargon. When he learns that his daughter's lover has inherited his uncle's wealth, he finds virtue in the young man and gives the couple his blessing.

Lucinde (lü·sănd'), Géronte's daughter, who stubbornly refuses to marry any of her father's selected suitors and feigns illness and loss of speech. Her clever

279

pretense allows her to elope with Léandre.

Léandre (lā·äṅdr′), Lucinde's lover. Disguised as an apothecary working with the physician, he is able to elope with Lucinde. He soon returns to ask Géronte's permission for their marriage, a request readily granted when he tells of his inheritance from his uncle.

Valère (vȧ·lĕr′), Géronte's simple, credulous servant, who tries to reason with Sganarelle before beating him, in order to make the wood-gatherer admit that he is a doctor.

Lucas (lü·kȧ′), another servant to Géronte, foster father to Valère, and the husband of Géronte's nurse. He is an ill-tempered man who jealously prevents Sganarelle from embracing and fondling his wife Jacqueline.

Jacqueline (zhäk·lēn′), Lucas' wife and nurse to Lucinde. She is a sensible, realistic woman who sees that Lucinde is feigning an illness that love will cure.

M. Robert (mɔ·syœ′ rô·bĕr′), Sganarelle's neighbor, a busybody who objects to wifebeating. He is forced to admit his meddling in order to avoid a similar drubbing.

Thibaut (tē·bō′), a peasant who, hearing of Sganarelle's fame as a physician, comes to the wood-gatherer. Trying to tell about his wife's illness, he talks in garbled medical terms.

Perrin (pĕr·rȧṅ′), Thibaut's son.

DR. JEKYLL AND MR. HYDE

Author: Robert Louis Stevenson (1850-1894)
Time of action: Nineteenth century
First published: 1886

PRINCIPAL CHARACTERS

Dr. Henry Jekyll, a London physician who leads a double life. He concocts a drug to change his personality at times to conform to his evil side. To protect himself, he then makes a will leaving his money to the incarnation of his other personality, Edward Hyde. Finally, after the medicine to restore his original personality has run out, he kills himself while in the person of Hyde.

Edward Hyde, the evil side of Dr. Jekyll, a trampler of children and the murderer of Sir Danvers Carew.

Dr. Hastie Lanyon, an intimate friend of Jekyll, who was once present at one of the transformations and who leaves a written description of it, to be opened after Jekyll's death.

Sir Danvers Carew, a kindly old man murdered by Hyde for the joy of doing evil.

Poole, Dr. Jekyll's servant, who vainly seeks the rare drug for the restorative needed by his master.

Mr. Utterson, Jekyll's lawyer, who holds, unopened, Lanyon's letter.

Richard Enfield, who has witnessed Hyde's cruelty and wants an investigation to learn why Hyde is Jekyll's heir.

DOCTOR PASCAL

Author: Émile Zola (1840-1902)
Time of action: Late nineteenth century
First published: 1893

280

Pascal Rougon (pȧs·kȧl′ rōō·gōn′), a dedicated and selfless doctor interested in heredity. Using experimental methods, he is, to his mother's dismay, using the members of his family as the field for his investigations. Feeling betrayed by the family's efforts to destroy his files, Dr. Pascal fails in health. He is temporarily restored by a love affair with Clotilde but later suffers a heart attack and dies, after which the records of his research are destroyed.

Clotilde (klō·tēld′), Pascal Rougon's niece. Living in quiet happiness with Dr. Pascal and Martine, a growing religious conviction causes her to try to persuade Pascal to destroy his files on heredity. Urged by Dr. Ramond to marry him, she realizes that Pascal is the one she loves and she becomes his mistress. She bears his child after his death.

Félicité Rougon (fā·lē·sē·tā′ rōō·gōn′), Dr. Pascal's mother. Ashamed because her son is not the kind of successful physician she wishes him to be, and terrified lest his papers on heredity fall into the hands of strangers, she continually seeks ways to destroy his files. She succeeds in this design immediately after Dr. Pascal's death.

Martine (mȧr·tēn′), Dr. Pascal's devoted housekeeper.

Dr. Ramond (rĕ·mōn′), Dr. Pascal's friend and Clotilde's suitor.

Maxime (måk·sēm′), Clotilde's dissolute brother.

DOCTOR THORNE

Author: Anthony Trollope (1815-1882)
Time of action: Mid-nineteenth century
First published: 1858

Dr. Thomas Thorne, the benevolent physician of Greshamsbury in East Barsetshire. He had adopted Mary, the illegimate child of his brother and Mary Scatcherd, a village girl, after his brother was killed by Roger Scatcherd, Mary's brother, Dr. Thorne conceals Mary's identity until after she has inherited Roger Scatcherd's fortune. A humane man, Dr. Thorne is friendly with both the Scatcherds and with the aristocratic Greshams of Greshamsbury Park.

Mary Thorne, the niece of Dr. Thorne, unaware, until the end of the novel, of her illegitimate origin. She was brought up with the young Greshams at Greshamsbury Park and is in love with Frank Gresham, the heir. Although banished from Greshamsbury Park because Frank must marry money, Mary remains true to Frank. When she learns of her origin and her inheritance, she is able to marry Frank.

Frank Gresham, the young heir to Greshamsbury Park. Although his mother constantly insists on his need to marry a wealthy heiress, Frank never wavers in his devotion to Mary. Sent to win wealthy Miss Dunstable, Frank cannot overcome his innate honesty, despite family pressure.

Francis Newbold Gresham, the father of Frank and Squire of Greshamsbury. He has dissipated his family fortune in an unsuccessful attempt to regain his father's seat in Parliament. He has also sired ten children and watched his land gradually sold in order to pay his bills.

Although kindly, he recognizes that his son must marry money in order to rebuild the family's holdings.

Lady Arabella De Courcy Gresham, wife of Squire Gresham and mother of Frank. A proud member of the De Courcy clan, she is ambitious for her son and eager to assert her lineage. She insists that Frank marry money and banishes Mary Thorne from her house.

Sir Roger Scatcherd, the poor stonemason who served six months in jail for killing Dr. Thorne's brother after he betrayed Mary Scatcherd. Through intelligence and industry, he becomes a wealthy railroad manufacturer. He is elected to Parliament, but later is unseated when an election fraud of which he is innocent is uncovered. Always fond of alcohol, he then drinks himself to death. His will leaves all his property to his son, and, in the event of his son's death, to his sister's child.

Lady Scatcherd, Sir Roger's loyal and patient wife. She is a good friend to Dr. Thorne and was once wet nurse to young Frank Gresham.

Louis Philippe Scatcherd, Sir Roger's only son and a drunkard. He is in love with Mary Thorne; rejected, he drinks himself to death. His early death brings the family fortune to Mary Thorne.

Countess Rosina De Courcy, sister-in-law of Lady Arabella, equally ambitious both politically and socially. She invites young Frank to Courcy Castle to give him his chance at an heiress.

Earl De Courcy, the owner of Courcy Castle and one of the principal Whig aristocrats of Barsetshire. He is completely overshadowed by his wife.

Lord Porlock, the oldest son and heir to Courcy Castle.

The Honourable George De Courcy, the second son, neither honorable nor wise.

The Honourable John De Courcy, the third son, a spendthrift.

Martha Dunstable, the wealthy heiress to a patent medicine fortune, accustomed to refusing importunate young men. Frank Gresham is expected to win her at Courcy Castle, and she is rather charmed by his naïve inability to be dishonest (she is ten years older than he). They become good friends and she gives him advice about Mary Thorne. The Honourable George proposes to her but is not accepted.

Augusta Gresham, the dutiful eldest daughter of the Squire of Greshamsbury, jilted by her fiancée, Mr. Moffat.

Mr. Moffat, a local member of Parliament, defeated by Sir Roger Scatcherd. He jilts Augusta Gresham when he realizes that the Greshams have less money than he has assumed.

Beatrice Gresham, the second daughter of the Squire of Greshamsbury and particular friend of Mary Thorne, later married to the Reverend Caleb Oriel.

The Reverend Caleb Oriel, the young rector of Greshamsbury, an adherent of High Church doctrine.

Patience Oriel, his sister, a close friend to Mary Thorne.

Lady Amelia De Courcy, eldest daughter of the De Courcys. She maintains rigorous standards of propriety and social caste.

Mortimer Gazebee, a hard-working and opportunistic young attorney of no family. He proposes to Augusta Gresham, who, on the advice of her cousin, Lady Amelia, rejects him. He later marries Lady Amelia.

Dr. Fillgrave, the Barchester physician who sometimes attends Sir Roger Scatcherd.

Harry Baker, a friend of Frank Gresham.

Mr. Nearthewinde, a Parliamentary agent.

Mr. Closerstil, another Parliamentary agent.

Mr. Romer, a barrister who manages Sir Roger Scratcherd's campaign for Parliament.

Mrs. Proudie, the aggressive wife of the Bishop of Barchester.

Mr. Reddypalm, a publican interested in politics.

The Duke of Omnium, owner of Gathe-rum Castle and the leading Whig aristocrat in the vicinity.

Fothergill, the Duke's agent.

Miss Gushing, a young lady in love with the Reverend Caleb Oriel; she later marries Mr. Rantaway.

Jonah (Joe), a brutal servant to Louis Philippe Scatcherd.

Mr. Bideawhile, a London attorney.

Lady Rosina De Courcy,
Lady Margaretta De Courcy, and
Lady Alexandrina De Courcy, younger daughters of the De Courcys.

DODSWORTH

Author: Sinclair Lewis (1885-1951)
Time of action: The 1920's
First published: 1929

PRINCIPAL CHARACTERS

Sam Dodsworth, a wealthy automobile manufacturer from Zenith. Retired from business, with ample money and leisure, he takes his wife Fran on what is planned as a long trip to Europe. He is eager to see the places he has read so much about, but he finds it difficult to adjust to European life and impossible to please his wife, whose restlessness and social climbing, as well as her endless criticism of him, get more and more on his nerves. No sooner does he begin to enjoy one country than she wants to move on to another. She begins to consider herself a European and constantly reminds him that he is an uncultivated American businessman who cannot appreciate what he sees. The climax comes in Germany, when she announces that she wants a divorce so that she can marry Count von Obersdorf, an impecunious Austrian nobleman. Sam leaves her in Berlin to arrange for the divorce. In Paris he is so lonely that he drifts into a brief affair with Fernande Azerede. Tiring of this affair, he goes to Venice and there meets a Mrs. Cortright, an attractive widow whom he had met casually before. They become interested in each other and are considering marriage when Fran writes that Obersdorf has declined to marry her. Out of a sense of duty Sam returns to his temporarily penitent wife, but on the voyage to America he realizes that he can no longer endure her continual criticism. He finally breaks with her, to return to Italy and Mrs. Cortright, with whom he can find happiness. He is a portrait of the American trying desperately to understand the older culture of Europe, which he both admires and dislikes.

Frances (Fran) Dodsworth, Sam's wife, the daughter of a rich brewer. She is spoiled, selfish, and superficial, and constantly critical of her husband, whose good qualities she can never see. She demands attention and yet is insulted when the attention becomes serious. Thus, she encourages Major Lockert, then is furious when he makes love to her. In Ger-

283

many she meets the aristocratic Count von Obersdorf, whom she wants to marry. Sam agrees to a divorce, but Fran finds that Obersdorf's mother considers her "déclassée" and the Count is eager to escape from the marriage. She appeals to Sam to forgive her, but during the trip home she resumes her nagging criticisms, thus driving him away forever. She is last seen in New York, a lonely and pathetic figure. She is Lewis' bitter portrait of the American woman.

Brent Dodsworth, their son, a student at Yale and a future go-getter.

Emily Dodsworth, their daughter. Married, she no longer needs her father.

Edith Cortright, the widow of an Englishman. She is sincere and dependable, the exact opposite of Fran. She and Sam plan to marry.

Major Clyde Lockert, an Englishman whom the Dodsworths meet on shipboard and who introduces them to English social life. Attentive to Fran, he infuriates her by making love to her.

Count Kurt von Obersdorf, an impoverished Austrian, head of one of the greatest families in Europe. Fran wants to divorce Sam to marry Obersdorf, but the Count ends the affair when his mother objects to the marriage.

Renée de Pénable, a mysterious international character who lives on rich Americans. She completely fools Fran.

Fernande Azerede, a Parisian wanton with whom Sam has a brief affair.

Tub Pearson, Sam's best friend, a typical Babbitt.

Matey Pearson, his wife. Crude but warm-hearted and intelligent, she sees through Fran perfectly.

Ross Ireland, a journalist, whose function is to speak the author's scathing comments on America.

Lord and
Lady Herndon, Lockert's cousins in London who give a dinner party at which Fran revels in the snobbery while Sam feels completely out of place.

Hurd, London manager of Sam's former company who educates him concerning the pleasures of living abroad.

Arnold Israel, a Jewish playboy with whom Fran has an affair.

The Biedners, Fran's cousins in Berlin through whom she meets Count von Obersdorf.

A DOLL'S HOUSE

Author: Henrik Ibsen (1828-1906)
Time of action: Nineteenth century
First presented: 1879

PRINCIPAL CHARACTERS

Nora, the "doll-wife" of Torvald Helmer. Seeking to charm her husband always, Nora is his "singing lark," his pretty "little squirrel," his "little spendthrift." She seems to be a spendthrift because secretly she is paying off a debt which she incurred to finance a year in Italy for the sake of Torvald's health. To get the money, she had forged her dying father's name to a bond at the bank. Now Krogstad, a bookkeeper at the bank where Torvald has recently been appointed manager, aware that the bond was signed after Nora's father's death, is putting pressure on Nora to persuade Torvald to promote him. Frightened, Nora agrees to help him. When her friend Christine Linde, a widow and

284

formerly Krogstad's sweetheart, also asks for help, Nora easily persuades Torvald to give Christine an appointment at the bank. The position, unfortunately, is Krogstad's. Torvald, finding Krogstad's presumption unbearable, plans to discharge him. While Christine helps Nora prepare a costume for a fancy dress ball in which she will dance the tarantella, Krogstad writes a letter, following his dismissal, telling Torvald of Nora's forgery. Nora desperately keeps Torvald from the mailbox until after the dance. She decides to kill herself so that all will know that she alone is guilty and not Torvald. After the dance Torvald reads the letter and tells Nora in anger that she is a criminal and can no longer be his wife, although she may continue to live in his house to keep up appearances. When Krogstad, softened by Christine's promise to marry him and care for his motherless children, returns the bond, Torvald destroys it and is willing to take back his little singing bird. Nora, realizing the shallow basis of his love for her as a "doll-wife," leaves Torvald to find her own personality away from him. She leaves him with the faint hope that their marriage might be resumed if it could be a "real wedlock."

Torvald Helmer, the newly promoted manager of a bank. Concerned with business, he is unaware that his wife Nora, whom he regards as a plaything, is capable of making serious decisions. When he discovers her forgery, he is horrified and convinced that he will be blamed as the instigator, and he plans to try to appease Krogstad in order to forestall his own disgrace. As soon as the bond is returned, Torvald becomes himself again, wants his pet reinstated, and is eager to forget the whole affair. He is baffled when Nora says that she no longer loves him and is leaving him. At the end, he has a sudden hope that what Nora has called "the most wonderful thing of all" might really happen, the "real wedlock" which she wanted. But Nora has gone.

Nils Krogstad, a bookkeeper at the bank, dissatisfied with his appointment and with life in general. At first Krogstad appears as a sinister blackmailer threatening Nora with disaster if she does not help him gain a promotion at the bank. Later, when he finds the love of Christine Linde, whose loss had embittered him in the first place, he becomes a changed man and returns the bond.

Christine Linde, a widow and Nora's old schoolfriend. When Mrs. Linde first appears, she is quite worn and desperate for work. She had married for money which she needed to support her mother and two young brothers. Now husband and mother are dead and the brothers grown. In the end, when she and Krogstad have decided to marry, she is happy because she will have someone to care for. She decides that Nora cannot continue to deceive Torvald and that Krogstad should not retrieve his letter. Presumably Krogstad will retain his position at the bank.

Doctor Rank, a family friend, in love with Nora. Suffering bodily for his father's sins, Dr. Rank is marked by death. Nora starts to ask Dr. Rank to help her pay off the debt, but after he reveals his love for her, she will not ask this favor of him. He tells Nora that he is soon to die and that when death has begun, he will send her his card with a black cross on it. The card appears in the mailbox with Krogstad's letter. Dr. Rank serves no purpose in the play except to show Nora's fidelity to Torvald when she refuses Rank's offer of help after she knows that he loves her.

DOMBEY AND SON

Author: Charles Dickens (1812-1870)
Time of action: Early nineteenth century
First published: 1846-1848

PRINCIPAL CHARACTERS

Paul Dombey, a London merchant, referred to as Mr. Dombey throughout the novel. Twenty successful years in the firm of Dombey and Son have brought wealth to the stern and pompous Mr. Dombey. Ten years of marriage finally bring a son and happiness (despite his wife's death) to the unemotional, dignified, glossy businessman, for the son will occupy his rightful place in the firm. Jealous and possessive, Mr. Dombey resents his son's affection for Florence, the older Dombey daughter. Later he sends Walter Gay, a young clerk attentive to the daughter, on an extended trip to the West Indies, and he loses his second wife because he approaches personal relationships as if they were business transactions in his office. Through reversals in both personal and business affairs, Mr. Dombey senses that his shortcomings lie in what he has always considered his strength: a belief in his indomitability. This realization results in a modicum of happiness for him as he accepts his daughter's love after spurning her all her life.

Paul Dombey, his son and heir, who is the essence of Dombey's life. Before the child was born, Mr. Dombey had yearned for a son; during Paul's life, he is jealous of his attentions to others, over-solicitous for his health, and unrealistic in treating the child as his longed-for business partner; after Paul's death, at six years, Mr. Dombey in his disillusionment considers the death a personal injustice to himself. Paul, a weak, precocious child, is uncommonly preoccupied with death, an interest which seems, in the Dickensian manner, to portend his early demise.

Florence Dombey, six years older than Paul. Until she is grown, Florence is the brunt of her father's unreasonable animosity. Courageous and compassionate, she withstands her father's affronts and ill-temper. Of strong faith, she does not despair at failures or rebuffs. Devoted and appreciative of love, she is a good wife to Walter Gay. Ultimately, Florence's altruism comes full circle when she has a son, Paul, who aids in her father's realization of his daughter's long-standing love.

Walter Gay, her childhood friend and later her husband. The model of good upbringing and training, he is instrumental in her safety and well-being. The last instance of his protectorship is as her husband and father of their children, when the Gays return to London to save Dombey from self-destruction and to give him renewed interest in life when he sees his grandchildren in the light in which he should have viewed his own daughter and son.

Mrs. Fanny Dombey, Mr. Dombey's first wife, the mother of Florence and Paul.

Mrs. Edith Granger, Dombey's second wife and his female counterpart in stubbornness and pride. Thwarted in her role as wife, she strikes back by pretending to elope with James Carker, Dombey's head clerk. Her wounded pride continues through the years; she finally declares her innocence of an affair with Carker, but she refuses to see Dombey to ask his forgiveness.

James Carker, Dombey's trusted head clerk and manager, whose villainy brings about his employer's professional and personal ruin. Deserted by Mrs. Dombey in the hour of their elopement, he is killed by a train while trying to avoid a meeting with Dombey.

Solomon Gills, a maker of nautical instruments and Walter Gay's uncle. With his loyal friend and partner, Captain Cuttle, he produces instruments that make his name a byword in safe navigation.

Edward Cuttle, an old sailor generally known as **Captain Cuttle** or **Captain Ned.** Adding much to the story with his salty mariner jargon, he becomes Florence Dombey's protector when she is rejected by her father.

Miss Lucretia Tox, a friend of Dombey's sister, who finds the wet nurse for the infant Paul. In her attentions to the child, she obviously has designs on Dombey, her devotion to him being sustained in a platonic manner throughout his life.

Major Joseph Bagstock, a retired army officer, a neighbor and an admirer of Miss Tox. The typically proud old officer is introduced to point up the transition in Miss Tox's affections. It is he who introduces Mr. Dombey to Edith Granger.

Mrs. Polly Toodle, the wet nurse, renamed Richards, a more respectable appellation for the atmosphere of the Dombey house. Summarily dismissed for negligence after Florence strays and suffers a traumatic experience with a derelict woman, Mrs. Toodle remains in the story in connection with Miss Tox and lesser characters.

Mr. Toodle, Polly Toodle's husband, a stoker and engine-driver.

Robin Toodle, their son, also called **Biler** and **Rob the Grinder.** Mr. Dombey secures him a place in the establishment of "The Honorable Grinders," but he meets with so much ridicule and abuse that he runs away. Later he acts as a spy for James Carker. Still later he enters the employ of Miss Tox in his attempt to regain respectability.

Dr. Blimber, the owner of a select private school attended by Paul Dombey.

Mrs. Blimber, his wife, a silly, stupid woman.

Cornelia Blimber, their daughter, a bluestocking and a lover of dead languages.

John Carker, James Carker's brother and an under-clerk in the employ of Dombey and Son. Years before he had stolen money from the firm, but, because he had been led astray by bad companions, he had not been discharged. He repays this trust by years of faithful service. Dismissed after his brother's elopement with Mrs. Dombey and death, he inherits his brother's fortune and is able to live quietly but comfortably. After Mr. Dombey goes bankrupt he turns the interest of his fortune over to his former employer and pretends that he is repaying an old, forgotten debt.

Harriet Carker, the sister of James and John Carker. She marries Mr. Morfin.

Mr. Morfin, the cheerful head clerk at Dombey and Son. He befriends John Carker and marries his sister Harriet.

Susan Nipper, Florence Dombey's maid and companion. Discharged after she reproves Mr. Dombey for his treatment of his daughter, she marries Mr. Toots.

Mr. P. Toots, a pupil at Doctor Blimber's school for young gentlemen. Rich and eccentric, he spends much of his time writing letters to himself and signing them with the names of famous personages, and his most commonplace remarks are filled with biblical and literary allusions. He falls in love with Florence Dombey, but when she discourages his attentions he marries Susan Nipper instead and fathers a large brood of children.

Captain Jack Bunsby, Captain Cuttle's close friend. Innocently unaware of the wiles of women, he marries Mrs. MacStinger, his landlady.

Mrs. MacStinger, a domineering, designing widow, as quick with her hand as with her tongue. She marries Captain Bunsby.

Alexander,
Charles (Chowley), and
Juliana, Mrs. MacStinger's children by her first marriage.

Mrs. Pipchin, an ill-favored widow with whom Paul and Florence Dombey are sent to board at Brighton, later Mr. Dombey's housekeeper.

Berinthia, also called **Berry,** Mrs. Pipchin's spinster niece and servant.

Alice Brown, also called **Alice Marwood,** James Carker's former mistress, transported for felony. She returns, filled with hate and defiance, to England.

Mrs. Brown, her mother.

Mrs. Louisa Chick, Mr. Dombey's sister, a good-natured but smug woman.

John Chick, her husband, who constantly hums or whistles tunes.

Mr. Feeder, B.A., an assistant at Doctor Blimber's school and later his son-in-law.

The Reverend Alfred Feeder, M.A., his brother.

The Hon. Mrs. Skewton, also called **Cleopatra,** an aged beauty and Edith Dombey's mother, who puts her daughter up for the highest bidder in the marriage market. She dies soon after her daughter's marriage to Mr. Dombey.

Lord Feenix, Mrs. Skewton's superannuated nephew, a man about town.

The Game Chicken, a professional prize fighter and Mr. Toot's boxing instructor.

The Reverend Melchisedech Howler, a ranting clergyman who predicts the end of the world.

Sir Barnet Skettles, a time-serving, self-seeking member of the House of Commons.

Lady Skettles, his wife.

Barnet Skettles, a pupil at Doctor Blimber's school.

Tozer and
Briggs, Paul Dombey's roommates at Doctor Blimber's school.

Anne, a housemaid,
Thomas Towlinson, a footman, and
Mary Daws, a kitchen maid, servants in the Dombey household.

Mr. Clark, a clerk, and
Mr. Perch, a messenger, employees of Dombey and Son.

Mrs. Perch, the messenger's wife, usually in an interesting condition.

Dr. Parker Peps, the attending physician at the birth of Paul Dombey because of his reputation as an obstetrician.

Dr. Pilkins, Mr. Dombey's family doctor.

DOMINIQUE

Author: Eugène Fromentin (1820-1876)
Time of action: Nineteenth century
First published: 1862

PRINCIPAL CHARACTERS

Dominique de Bray (dô·mē·nēk′ də brē′), a gentleman who tells the narrator the story of his life up to his early retirement to a quiet, happy life with his wife and children. Attracted to Madeleine de Nièvres during his schooldays, his love for her, after she marries another, fills his life with conflicts between the emotions and the disciplines of the mind. Finally realizing the mediocrity of his

288

talents as a writer and the hopelessness of his and Madeleine's love, he retires to the Château des Trembles to become the unpretentious and beloved friend of all in the community.

Olivier d'Orsel (ô·lē·vyä′ dôr·sĕl′), Dominique's friend. A wealthy, luxury-loving man of engaging manner, he comes to hate the world and himself and suddenly retires from social life. Hearing of Olivier's attempted suicide, Dominique is led to tell the narrator the story of his own life.

Augustin (ō·gü·stăń′), Dominique's practical, disciplined tutor. He attempts to help his pupil solve his emotional problems by encouraging him in the pursuits of the mind.

Madeleine de Nièvres (måd·lĕn′ də nyĕ′vrə), beloved of Dominique. A married woman, her love for Dominique brings her the conflicts of a troubled conscience which causes her to send her lover away.

Monsieur de Nièvres (də nyĕ′vrə), the husband of Madeleine.

Madame Ceyssac (sĕ·såk′), Dominique's aunt.

Julie (zhü·lē′), Madeleine de Nièvres' sister, in love with Olivier d'Orsel.

DON CARLOS

Author: Johann Christoph Friedrich von Schiller (1759-1805)
Time of action: Sixteenth century
First presented: 1787

PRINCIPAL CHARACTERS

Don Carlos, the sensitive, twenty-three-year-old heir to the throne of Spain. His life is a constant battle with his father, neither holding any love for the other. Resenting his father's second marriage— Don Carlos had been in love with the bride, Elizabeth de Valois—the Prince wants to leave Madrid. He hopes to free himself of the constant reminder of his continuing love for his father's wife and, as heir to the throne, establish his stature as an emissary to Flanders. Despite the unstinted efforts of his close friend for Don Carlos' happiness, Carlos' implied lot is commitment by his father to a monastery.

Philip the Second, King of Spain. An austere monarch lacking in compassion, he knows no love either as the loved or as the lover. In only one instance is he forgiving, toward an admiral who lost a fleet in rough seas. The King's goodness, much acclaimed by his court, is motivated more by self-gain than by altruism. Jealous and insecure, Philip is easily duped by any talebearer. He blames the Church for not protecting him by warning him of forces working against him. He is rebuked, in turn, for not asking the help of the Church. Philip's character is quickly reflected in the question put to him: "When you whine for sympathy, is not the world your equal?"

The Marquis de Posa, the friend of Don Carlos, who calls him Roderigo. Posa swore lifelong allegiance to Don Carlos for his defense of Posa in a childhood mishap. A hero in every sense of the word, Posa shows military prowess, is beneficent in his role as confidant to the major personages, is studious, and is forthright with and unmoved by those who seek to injure their fellow men. His marked influence reaches its height when he secures Philip's approval to move about the court at will. This permission follows Posa's fervent, unselfish plea to Philip for better conditions for mankind. Posa, it is learned after his death, is a

289

peripatetic member of a monastic group, roaming to spread his philosophy of brotherly love.

The Duke of Alva, the trusted agent of Philip, who works to alienate the King against Don Carlos. His duplicity is abetted by other members of the court, a group resenting the King's ready acceptance of Posa.

Elizabeth de Valois, Queen of Spain, Philip's second wife. The Queen's love for Don Carlos intensifies her hatred for the King and motivates her to contemplated intrigue to further Don Carlos' ambition for the throne. Immediately before her death of grief, the love she and Carlos have for each other is purified of selfish passion as he goes forth to fight, in Posa's memory, for oppressed mankind.

The Princess de Eboli, an attendant on the Queen, whose letters to Don Carlos are mistaken for the Queen's writing. The Princess' affair with Philip makes her a likely accomplice to aid Alva in his conspiracy against Don Carlos. Her treacheries are abhorred by Posa, who, as confidant to Philip, would banish her from the court.

The Grand Inquisitor of Spain, the blind cardinal who identifies Posa as a member of a religious order. Rebuked for his indifference to the Church, Philip delivers Don Carlos to the Inquisitor to serve in place of murdered Posa.

Domingo, confessor to the King. He works with Alva in his plots. Because of Don Carlos' religious beliefs, Domingo deplores the thought of Carlos becoming king.

Count Lerma, the colonel of the royal bodyguard. Lerma's chief role is talebearer to Don Carlos. Much of the news he brings is half reports that distort facts and bring anguish to Don Carlos.

The Marchioness de Mondecar, an attendant to the Queen. Sacrificing herself to the Queen's happiness, she is dismissed by Philip when she reports that it was she, not the Queen, in the garden with Don Carlos.

Don Raimond de Taxis, the postmaster general, who reveals Posa's letters in which Posa pictures himself as the Queen's lover, in order to vindicate Don Carlos and allow him to escape from Spain. The letters lead to Posa's murder.

Don Louis Mercado, physician to the Queen. The accomplice of Don Carlos in arranging the final meeting between the Prince and the Queen, Mercado prepares the monkish disguise which allows Don Carlos to pass into the Queen's chambers.

The Duke of Medina Sidonia, admiral of the King's fleet, whose negligence is forgiven, making the King appear humane in the eyes of the court.

THE DON FLOWS HOME TO THE SEA

Author: Mikhail Sholokhov (1905-   )
Time of action: 1918-1920
First published: 1933, 1938

PRINCIPAL CHARACTERS

Gregor Melekhov (grĭ·gō′rĭy mĕ·lĕ-khōf′), a soldier in the White Army fighting the Reds. He returns home to his wife, but when he discovers that the Red government of his village intends to arrest him, he escapes. He joins a Cossack rebellion against the Reds and becomes a cold and ruthless fighter after his brother is killed in cold blood. He has a reputation for not keeping live prisoners. He comes home on furlough and takes up his affair with Aksinia, his former mistress. Finally, tired of fighting, Gregor throws away his arms and returns to his house and his son.

Piotra Melekhov (pyō'trə mĕ·lĕ·khōf'), Gregor's elder brother, also a soldier in the White Army. Once saved through his friendship with Fomin, a Red commander, he is eventually killed by Koshevoi. He has none of Gregor's ambivalence of mind and is decidedly anti-Red.

Aksinia Astakhova (äk·sĭ·nyä äs·tä'khō·və), Gregor's mistress, who, scorning her husband, Stepan Astakhov, tries to escape with Gregor to the south. She falls ill of typhus and has to be left behind. She is killed by a Red patrol. She was once the mistress of a rich Cossack officer, Eugene Listnitsky, but she was cast aside after Eugene married Olga, the widow of a fellow officer.

Natalia Melekhova (nä·tä'lĭ·yä mĕ·lĕkhō'və), Gregor's wife, who becomes very cold toward him when she finds that he has taken up with his former mistress. She refuses to bear him another child and tries to have an abortion, but it is clumsily done and she bleeds to death.

Mikhail Koshevoi (mĭ·hä·ĭl' kô·shĕ·vōy'), a Communist sympathizer who is put in charge of the government in Gregor's village, Tatarsk, in which job he is assisted by a professional Red named Stockman. After becoming a full-fledged Communist, he kills Piotra outright. Koshevoi's family disappears and his father's house is destroyed; he then takes great joy in firing the wealthy landowners' houses in revenge. After he becomes commissar of Tatarsk he brazenly marries Dunia, the sister of Gregor and Piotra.

Daria Melekhova (dä'ryä mĕ·lĕ·khō'və), Piotra's wife, who kills the man she thinks is responsible for her husband's death. She soon recovers from her grief and begins to have various affairs. She catches syphilis and drowns herself.

DON JUAN

Author: George Gordon, Lord Byron (1788-1824)
Time of action: Late eighteenth century
First published: 1819-1824

PRINCIPAL CHARACTERS

Don Juan, the young son of Donna Inez and Don José, a hidalgo of Seville. He is a handsome, mischief-making boy whose education, after his father's death, is carefully supervised by his mother, who insists that he read only classics expurgated in the text but with all the obscenities collected in an appendix. He is allowed to associate only with old or ugly women. At the age of sixteen he learns the art of love from Donna Julia, a young matron. The ensuing scandal causes Donna Inez to send her son to Cadiz, there to take ship for a trip abroad. The vessel on which he is a passenger sinks after a storm; he experiences a romantic interlude with the daughter of a Greek pirate and slave trader; he is sold to the Turks; he takes part in the siege of Ismail, a Turkish fort on the Danube River; he becomes the favorite of the Empress Catherine of Russia; and he is sent on a diplomatic mission to England, where he becomes a critical observer of English society.

Donna Inez, Don Juan's mother, a domineering and short-sighted woman who first tries to protect her son from the facts of life but later rejoices in his good

291

fortune and advancement when he becomes the favorite of Empress Catherine of Russia.

Don José, Don Juan's father, a gallant man often unfaithful to his wife, with whom he quarrels constantly. He dies while his son is still a small boy.

Donna Julia, Don Juan's first love, a woman of twenty-three married to a fifty-year-old husband, Don Alfonso. She is forced to enter a convent after her irate husband discovers his wife and her young lover in her bedchamber. In a long letter, written on the eve of Don Juan's departure from Spain, she professes her undying love for him.

Don Alfonso, the cuckold husband who discovers Don Juan hiding in a closet in his wife's bedroom.

Haidée, the second love of Don Juan. A tall, lovely child of nature and passion, she finds him unconscious on the seashore following the sinking of the ship on which he had sailed from Spain. Filled with love and sympathy, she hides and protects him. This idyllic island romance ends when Lambro, her pirate father, returns from one of his expeditions and finds the two sleeping together after a great feast which Lambro has watched from a distance. Don Juan, wounded in a scuffle with Lambro's men, is bound and put aboard one of the pirate's ships. Shortly afterward Haidée dies lamenting her vanished lover, and his child dies with her.

Lambro, Haidée's father, "the mildest-manner'd man that ever scuttled ship or cut a throat." Returning from one of his piratical expeditions, he surprises the young lovers and sends Don Juan, wounded in a fight with Lambro's men, away on a slave ship. Later he regrets his hasty action when he watches his only child die of illness and grief.

Gulbeyaz, the Sultana of Turkey. Having seen Don Juan in the slave market where he is offered for sale, along with an Ital-

ian opera troupe sold into captivity by their disgusted impresario, she orders one of the palace eunuchs to buy the young man. She has him taken to the palace and dressed in women's clothes. Even though she brings her strongest weapon, her tears, to bear, she is unable to make Don Juan her lover.

The Sultan of Turkey, the father of fifty daughters and four dozen sons. Seeing the disguised Don Juan in his wife's apartments, he orders the supposed female slave to be taken to the palace harem.

Baba, the African eunuch who buys Don Juan at the Sultana's command. He later flees with Don Juan and John Johnson from Constantinople.

Lolah,

Katinka, and

Dudú, three girls in the Sultan's harem. Dudú, lovely and languishing, has the disguised Don Juan for her bed fellow. Late in the night she awakes screaming after a dream in which she reached for a golden apple and was stung by a bee. The next morning jealous Gulbeyaz orders Dudú and Don Juan executed, but they escape in the company of Johnson and Baba.

John Johnson, a worldly Englishman fighting with the Russians in the war against the Turks. Captured, he is bought in the slave market along with Don Juan. The two escape and make their way to the Turkish lines before Ismail. Johnson is recognized by General Suwarrow, who welcomes him and Don Juan as allies in the attack on Ismail.

Leila, a ten-year-old Moslem girl whose life Don Juan saves during the capture of Ismail. He becomes her protector.

General Suwarrow (Souvaroff), the leader of the Russian forces at the siege and taking of Ismail.

Catherine, Empress of Russia, to whose court Don Juan is sent with news of the

292

Turkish victory at Ismail. Voluptuous and rapacious in love, she receives the young man with great favor and he becomes her favorite. After he becomes ill she reluctantly decides to send him on a diplomatic mission to England.

Lord Henry Amundeville, an English politician and the owner of Norman Abbey. Don Juan meets the nobleman in London and the two become friends.

Lady Adeline Amundeville, his wife, who also becomes Don Juan's friend and mentor. She advises him to marry because she is afraid that he will become seriously involved with the notorious Duchess of Fitz-Fulke. During a house party at Norman Abbey she sings a song telling of the Black Friar, a ghost often seen wandering the halls of the Abbey.

The Duchess of Fitz-Fulke, a woman of fashion notorious for her amorous intrigues. She pursues Don Juan after his

arrival in England and finally, disguised as the ghostly Black Friar of Norman Abbey, succeeds in making him her lover.

Miss Aurora Raby, a young English-woman with whom Don Juan contemplates matrimony. Although she seems completely unimpressed by his attentions, he is piqued by her lack of interest.

Pedrillo, Don Juan's tutor. When the ship on which he and his master sail from Cadiz sinks after a storm, they are among those set adrift in a longboat. When the food runs out, the unlucky pedagogue is eaten by his famished companions. Although Don Juan considers the man an ass, he is unable to help eat the hapless fellow.

Zoe, Haidée's maid.

Lady Pinchbeck, a woman of fashion who, after Don Juan's arrival in London, takes Leila under her protection.

DON JUAN

Author: Molière (Jean Baptiste Poquelin, 1622-1673)
Time of action: Seventeenth century
First presented: 1665

PRINCIPAL CHARACTERS

Don Juan (dōn̄ zhü·än̄'), a philanderer and scoundrel. A seducer of women of whom he soon tires, a neglector of debts, a dishonorer of friends, Don Juan is called on to repent. He replies by becoming a greater hypocrite than ever, continuing his evil ways until he finally offends heaven itself and is destroyed.

Sganarelle (zgà·nà·rĕl'), Don Juan's valet, who hates his master's evil acts but remains loyal to him through fear.

Elvire (ĕl·vēr'), Don Juan's betrayed wife. Finally free of her passion for her husband, she agrees to return to the convent from which he had abducted her.

She begs him to reform and escape the wrath of heaven.

Don Carlos (kàr·lōs') and
Don Alonse (à·lōn̄s'), Elvire's brothers, seeking vengeance on Don Juan for his betrayal of their sister.

The Statue of the Commander, part of the tomb of one of Don Juan's victims. Don Juan and Sganarelle ask the statue to dine with them. It accepts, thus causing Don Juan to pretend conversion and repentance. The statue reappears threatening a terrible death for the really unrepentant sinner.

293

Don Louis (lwē'), Don Juan's distressed father.

Monsieur Dimanche (dē·mänsh'), Don Juan's creditor hypocritically put off by his debtor.

Charlotte (shár·lôt') and **Mathurine** (má·tü·rēn'), country girls each deceived by Don Juan into thinking she is his only love.

Pierrot (pyĕ·rō'), a country lad.

DON JUAN TENORIO

Author: José Zorrilla y Moral (1817-1893)
Time of action: c. 1545
First presented: 1844

PRINCIPAL CHARACTERS

Don Juan Tenorio (dōn hwän tā·nō'ryō), a wild young gallant whose life is so devoted to vice he wagers his friend Mejía that he can perform more evil deeds than Mejía in a year's time. Don Juan wins the wager but in doing so he ravishes his fiancée, Inés, kills her father, ravishes Mejía's fiancée, and kills Mejía. Inés dies of grief. Don Juan's saddened father establishes a cemetery containing statues of his son's victims. Years later, when Don Juan visits the cemetery, Inés' statue pleads with him to repent. He hesitates, but her love is so strong that she saves him just as he is about to be dragged off to Hell.

Marcos Ciutti (mär'kōs thyōō'tē), Don Juan's villainous servant. He bribes Ana's duenna to admit his master, and Brígida to carry a note to Inés.

Inés de Ulloa (ē·nās' ṭ͟hā ōō·lyō'ä), a novice in a convent, whom Don Juan hopes to marry. Her appearance to Don Juan after her death persuades him to repent, so that at the end she can save him from Hell's eternal fire.

Don Luis Mejía (dōn lwēs mā·hē'ä), a gallant of Seville, engaged to Ana and killed seeking revenge for her wrongs from Don Juan.

Don Gonzalo de Ulloa (dōn gōn·thä'lō ṭ͟hā ōō·lyō'ä), Comendador (Knight Commander) of Calatrava. His attempt to rescue Inés brings him death.

Don Diego Tenorio (dōn dyā'gō tā·nō'ryō), who visits a Seville inn to check on his son's bad reputation. He later establishes a cemetery containing statues of Don Juan's victims.

Ana de Pantoja (ä'nä ṭ͟hā pän·tō'hä), the fiancée of Mejía.

The Duenna of Ana.

Brígida (brē·gē'ṭ͟hä), the duenna of Inés.

Two Officers, who witness the discussion of the wager and five years later explain to Don Juan the significance of the cemetery. He invites them and the statue of the Comendador to come to dinner.

DON QUIXOTE DE LA MANCHA

Author: Miguel de Cervantes Saavedra (1547-1616)
Time of action: Late sixteenth century
First published: Part I, 1605; Part II, 1615

Don Quixote (dōn kǐ·hō'tā), possibly a gentle but impoverished man named Alonso Quijano (or perhaps Quixana) of Argamasilla, in the Spanish province of La Mancha. Driven mad by reading many romances of chivalry, he determines to deck himself out in rusty armor and a cardboard helmet and to become a knight-errant. Under the name of "Don Quixote" he will roam the world, righting wrongs. His squire calls him "The Knight of the Sorrowful Countenance." He has moments of lucidity, especially at the end of the novel when a victorious enemy forces him to give up his questing. He returns home, repents of his folly, and dies.

Sancho Panza (sän'chō pän'thä), a paunchy rustic at first described as "long-legged." He is persuaded by promises of governorship of an island to become squire and attendant of the knight. He is the best drawn of the 669 characters in this 461,000 word novel. He does get his island, but he abdicates upon news of the approach of a hostile army.

Rocinante (r̄rō·thē·nän'tā), the nag that carries Don Quixote on his journeying. His companion is Dapple, the donkey of Sancho Panza.

Aldonza Lorenzo (äl·dōn'thä lō·rän'thō), a sweaty peasant girl of Toboso, whom Don Quixote idealizes under the name of **Dulcinea del Toboso;** he chooses her to be his Queen of Love and Beauty, the inspiration of his knightly questing.

Antonia Quixana (än·tō'nyä kē·hä'nä), Don Quixote's niece, who by the terms of his dying will can marry only a man who is not given to reading books of chivalry.

Teresa Cascajo (tā·rä'sä käs·kä'hō), also called **Juana Gutiérrez** (hwä'nä gōō-tyä'r̄rāth), the wife of Sancho Panza.

An Innkeeper, the fat master of a roadside inn which Don Quixote mistakes

for a fortress. He dubs Don Quixote a knight.

Andrés (än·drās'), an unpaid servant, temporarily saved from a beating in Don Quixote's first attempt at righting wrongs.

Pedro Pérez (pä'drō pä'rāth), the curate who burns the knight's library of chivalric romances in an attempt to cure him of his madness.

Master Nicolás (nē·kō·läs'), the village barber, who assists in burning the books. Dressed in woman's clothes, he impersonates Dulcinea in an effort to persuade Don Quixote to leave the Sierra Morena.

Cardenio (kär·dä'nyō), who meets Don Quixote in the Sierra Morena and tells his sad story.

Dorotea (dō·rō·tā'ä), another ill-starred wanderer with a melancholic tale. She pretends to be a damsel in distress in order to persuade the knight to go home.

Ginés de Pasamonte (hē·nās' dä pä·sä-mōn'tā), a criminal condemned to the galleys. Don Quixote rescues him and a dozen more from the chain gang, only to be stoned by them.

Two Friars, acting as escort for a noble lady in a coach. The knight believes they are abducting her and attacks the Biscayan squire and the retinue. They beat up Sancho Panza.

Roque Guinart (rō'kä gē·närt'), a man driven to banditry by bad luck. He captures Don Quixote and Sancho. Refusing to be persuaded by them to turn knight-errant, he sends his prisoners to a neighboring bandit and recommends them as entertaining persons.

Master Pedro (pä'drō), the owner of a divining ape and a puppet show whose characters the knight mistakes for real people. He tries to rescue the leading lady.

A **Barber,** whose shaving basin Don Quixote mistakes for Mambrino's golden helmet.

A **Carter,** taking caged lions from the Governor of Oran to King Philip. In outfacing one of them, Don Quixote achieves his only successful adventure in the novel.

A **Duke and his Duchess,** who invite Don Quixote and Sancho Panza to their palace and play jokes on them, such as a supposed ride through space on a magic wooden horse, Clavijero. They make Sancho governor of an island, a village owned by the Duke.

Samson Carrasco (säm'sōn kä·rräs'kō), a neighbor who disguises himself as the Knight of the Mirrors and the Knight of the White Moon. He eventually overcomes Don Quixote and sentences him to abandon knight-errantry and return home. There Don Quixote dies after denouncing knight-errantry as nonsense, never realizing that he himself has been a true knight and a gallant gentleman.

DON SEGUNDO SOMBRA

Author: Ricardo Güiraldes (1882-1927)
Time of action: Late nineteenth century
First published: 1926

PRINCIPAL CHARACTERS

Don Segundo Sombra (dōn sā·gōōn'dō sōm'brä), an elderly Argentina gaucho who for five years allows Fabio to accompany him in his wanderings and instructs him in the life and the culture of the pampas. He then persuades Fabio to accept the responsibility of the ranch he has inherited and stays with him until he gets established.

Fabio (fä'byō), a waif who turns to Sombra for understanding, and in many adventures with him learns courage and self-reliance.

Two Aunts, who bring up Fabio without interest or affection.

Don Fabio Cáceres (dōn fä'byō kä'sä-räs), Fabio's father, who ignores him as a child but later wills him a ranch and a fortune.

Pedro Barrales (pä'drō bä·rrä'läs), a one-time gaucho companion who brings Fabio news of his inheritance.

Don Leandro Galván (dōn lā·än'drō gäl·bän'), a rancher and later Fabio's guardian.

Paula (pä'ōō·lä), a fickle country girl over whom Fabio duels with a rancher's son.

DOÑA BÁRBARA

Author: Rómulo Gallegos (1884-   )
Time of action: Early twentieth century
First published: 1929

PRINCIPAL CHARACTERS

Doña Bárbara (dō'nyä bär'bä·rä), a beautiful but unscrupulous mestiza, once wronged by a white man and now taking her revenge on all men. She is superstitious and given to witchcraft. For a time she was the mistress of Lorenzo

Barquero, heir to half the Altamira ranch, and by him had a daughter, Marisela. Then she ran him off his land and took possession. With the help of her cowboys, she is acquiring the rest of the ranch by moving the boundary fences and stealing the cattle. She has won over the local authorities. Unfortunately, she falls in love with Santos Luzardo, heir to the other half of the estate. When she goes soft, her followers desert her. Finally she rides to Altamira to shoot her daughter, whom she considers her rival, only to soften at the sight of Santos' display of affection for Marisela. She draws up papers leaving the Barquero land to Marisela and restoring what she has been stealing, then rides off, never to be heard of again.

Dr. Santos Luzardo (dŏk·tôr′ sän′tōs lōō·sär′dō), a descendant of owners of the other half of the ranch. Taken to Caracas as a child, he studies law, then returns to his ancestral property in the wildest section of the Arauca River basin of Venezuela, in order to get the land ready for sale. Seeing its deterioration under irresponsible overseers, he determines to restore the ranch to productivity. To end the long feud between the Luzardos and the Barqueros, he brings the dying Lorenzo Barquero and his daughter Marisela from their swamp cabin to live at the Altamira ranch house. From his knowledge of law, he is able to force the magistrate to call for a round-up to separate the cattle. He also sends some of his cowboys to collect heron feathers, from whose sale he will get money to repair his fences. They are murdered and the feathers stolen. When the local magistrate does nothing, Santos decides to follow the law of the jungle and match violence with violence. Hunting the feathers, on a tip from Bárbara, he finds the Wizard, her most trusted henchman, and leaves him dead.

Lorenzo Barquero (lô·ren′zo bär·kä′rō), the weak-willed heir to half the Altamira ranch. Doña Bárbara becomes his mistress

and gives him a daughter, Marisela. Tiring of him, Bárbara drives him off his land and begins to take over the ranch.

Marisela (mä·rē·sä′lä), a young girl, beautiful under her dirt, the daughter of Lorenzo Barquero. Her mother Bárbara abandons her, and her father sells her to William Danger for five bottles of whiskey. But Santos determines to civilize her. She falls so deeply in love with him that she is willing to challenge her mother's witchcraft in order to get him for herself. Finally they marry and the two halves of the estate are reunited.

Señora Luzardo (sĕ·nyō′rä lōō·sär′dō), the mother of Santos, whose life has been tragic. Not only has she seen the constant feuding between the two branches of the family, but her husband killed her oldest son in a quarrel and in remorse starved himself to death. She takes Santos back to the civilization of Caracas to study, but cannot keep him there.

William Danger, a North American squatter who enjoys demoralizing Lorenzo Barquero by giving him liquor. He is compelled by Santos to build fences, since his herd is too small to run wild.

Antonio Sandoval (än·tō′nyō sän·dō·bäl′), a cowboy faithful to Santos who helps him rebuild the ranch.

Balbino Paiba (bäl·bē′nō pä′ē·bä), the Luzardo overseer, whose love for Doña Bárbara makes him unfaithful to his emloyers. To make money, he steals feathers and kills Santos' cowboys. He is killed at Bárbara's orders when she tires of him and prefers Santos Luzardo.

Carmelito López (kär·mä·lē′to lō′päs), one of Santos' cowboys, killed by Balbino.

Pajarote (pä·hä·rō′tä), a cowboy who helps Santos.

Ambrosio (äm·brō′syō), a one-eyed cowboy musician.

297

Melquíades Gamarra (měl·kē'ä·t̃hās gä-mä'r̃rä), called **The Wizard**, Bárbara's trigger man.

Juan Primito (hwän' prē·mē'tō), a demented cowboy who feeds the birds of ill omen and prophesies evil.

Ño Pernalete (nyō' pâr·nä·lä'tä), the local magistrate, partial at first to Doña Bárbara, but compelled by Santos to administer justice.

Mujiquita (mōō·hē·kē'tä), the clerk of the court.

DOÑA PERFECTA

Author: Benito Pérez Galdós (1843-1920)
Time of action: Late nineteenth century
First published: 1876

PRINCIPAL CHARACTERS

José Rey (hō·sä' r̃rä'ē), called **Pepe,** whose father was impoverished by legal battles with Perfecta's husband. Pepe's unorthodox views earn him the hatred of the religious city of Orbajosa, whose citizens refer to him as "the heretic."

Doña Perfecta Rey (dō'nyä pâr·fäk'tä r̃rä'ē), Pepe's very religious aunt and the city's leading citizen. She orders her nephew shot when he enters her garden to see Rosario.

Rosario (r̃ro·sä'ryō), Perfecta's daughter, who is too dominated to assert her love

for Pepe. When he is killed, she goes insane.

Don Inocencio (dōn ē·nō·thän'thyō), canon of the cathedral, who tries to get Rosario to marry Jacinto. Though unsuccessful, he wins a victory for "The Faith."

María Remedios (mä·rē'ä r̃rä·mä'thyōs), his sister, who notifies Perfecta that "the heretic" is coming to elope with Rosario.

Jacinto (hä·thēn'tō), the nephew of Don Inocencio.

THE DOUBLE-DEALER

Author: William Congreve (1670-1729)
Time of action: Seventeenth century
First presented: 1694

PRINCIPAL CHARACTERS

Jack Maskwell, the double-dealer, whose villainy can only be admired because of its audacity. A pensioner of Lord Touchwood, he plots to become his benefactor's heir and marry an heiress. To this end he pretends to be a friend of Mellefont, Lord Touchwood's nephew and heir. He also becomes Lady Touchwood's lover, both for his sensual delight and for an opportunity to put her in a position where she will be a willing tool against

the innocent Mellefont. All of Maskwell's evil machinations appear to be so well planned as to bear fruit, but his success causes him to overreach himself, so that he is unmasked as a traitorous friend and as a cuckold-maker. He is motivated only by selfishness and sensuality in his wicked schemes against his friends.

Mellefont, the chief victim of Maskwell's plots. He is a mannerly, virtuous young

298

man who is his uncle's heir and about to marry Cynthia, a rich heiress. He trusts Maskwell, for his own honesty blinds him to the dishonesty in his enemy, to the point that he makes Maskwell his confidant and tells him all his thoughts and plans.

Lady Touchwood, Mellefont's aunt by marriage. She is a passionate woman who falls in love with Mellefont, even to offering herself to him in his bedroom. When she is repulsed by the honest young man her love-turned-hate puts her in league with Maskwell to ruin Mellefont. She then becomes Maskwell's mistress. But her zeal to enter Mellefont's bed, even after being repulsed, proves her undoing, and her husband catches her and reveals her as an adulteress. Sensuality, driven by passions, dominates her nature.

Lord Touchwood, an honest man who, like his nephew, is deceived by dishonest people. When he is misled by Lady Touchwood and Maskwell, he casts off his nephew, believing that Mellefont has tried to seduce Lady Touchwood. He then vows he will make Maskwell his heir and help that young man marry the rich heiress, Cynthia. But with Cynthia's help he discovers the treachery of Maskwell and his wife in time to reconsider his actions and reinstate his nephew.

Cynthia, a beautiful young heiress in love with Mellefont. She refuses to consider Maskwell as a husband because she is sincerely in love with the man she wants to marry. She helps unmask the plot against Mellefont.

Lady Plyant, Cynthia's stepmother, the second wife of Sir Paul Plyant. She pretends to great piety and virtue, even to the point of letting her husband enter the marriage bed only once a year, on their wedding anniversary. She dominates her husband, reading all his mail and issuing him pocket money as one would give an allowance to a child. Her hypocrisy becomes manifest, however, when Careless, Mallefont's friend, courts her and easily turns her from her virtuous path, revealing her piety to be mere silliness and hypocrisy. That she wishes to be of easy virtue is also indicated by her too ready belief that Mellefont, under cover of marrying Cynthia, will attempt to seduce her. Like her sister-in-law, Lady Touchwood, she is dominated by sensuality.

Sir Paul Plyant, Cynthia's father. A good man but stupid, he accepts his wife's dominance and her supposed piety, not wanting to admit that she fails him as a wife. He wishes his daughter to marry in order to provide him with a grandson, since his wife appears unlikely to produce a son and heir. He is Lady Touchwood's brother.

Ned Careless, a happy, witty young man, Mellefont's good friend. He distrusts Maskwell and tries to warn Mellefont against him. Careless, almost as a joke, undertakes to sue for Lady Plyant's love, in hopes of leading that woman to provide a son for her husband.

Lord Froth, a solemn, stupid nobleman. He tries to appear a bit better than everyone else. He fears especially to demean himself by laughing at other people's jokes.

Lady Froth, a vain, silly woman. She wants to appear as a scholar and poet, but poetical efforts merely show she has neither taste nor talent.

Mr. Brisk, a would-be wit who succeeds only in being a coxcomb. He strives desperately to be a brilliant conversationalist, only to prove himself a bore.

The Rev. Mr. Saygrace, an absurd clergyman who is Maskwell's willing tool. He would like to be considered a great writer of sermons, as well as a scholar and a wit.

DOWN THERE

Author: Joris Karl Huysmans (Charles Marie Georges Huysmans, 1848-1907)
Time of action: Late nineteenth century
First published: 1891

PRINCIPAL CHARACTERS

Durtal (dür·tàl'), a writer. Speaking through Durtal, Huysmans himself is the hero of "Down There," the first in a series of four novels tracing the author's spiritual journey through skepticism and despair to the final goal of faith. While engaged in compiling the history of Gilles de Rais, Durtal becomes interested in church history and especially in Satanism. He is taken to witness a Black Mass by his mistress, Hyacinthe Chantelouve, who afterwards tricks him into committing sacrilege. In disgust, he breaks off their relationship, thus ending this novel, the first of the four.

Gilles de Rais (zhēl' dɔ rĕ'), (1404-1440), Marshal of France, murderer, sadist, and Satanist. Durtal's readings from his history of the infamous marshal, youthful companion-in-arms to Jeanne d'Arc, comprise large sections of "Down There." Research into the details of his subject's progress from early religious exaltation, through unspeakable perversion, arrest, trial, and repentance, leads Durtal into his interest in Satanism and from there to the Black Mass and sacrilege.

Hyacinthe Chantelouve (yà·sănt' shänt·lōōv'), Durtal's mistress, who takes him to a Black Mass and afterwards betrays him into committing sacrilege.

Des Hermies (dà·zĕr·mē), Durtal's friend, whose function in the novel is to listen to the writer talk.

Carhaix (kà·rĕ'), the bell ringer of Saint-Suspice, with whom Durtal discusses church history and Satanism.

Canon Docre (kà·nŏṅ' dôkr'), a renegade priest and a Satanist.

Chantelouve (shänt·lōōv'), a Catholic historian and the husband of Hyacinthe Chantelouve.

THE DOWNFALL

Author: Émile Zola (1840-1902)
Time of action: 1870-1871
First published: 1892

PRINCIPAL CHARACTERS

Corporal Jean Macquart, a French peasant serving in the army during the Franco-Prussian War. He is a veteran of many battles who manages to survive honorably during the devastating fighting at Sedan. Captured by the Germans, he escapes with one of his men and bravely makes his way back to join the French Army of the North. In the civil war which breaks out against the Second Republic he bayonets one of his friends fighting for the other side and is heartbroken.

Private Maurice Levasseur, a middle-class Frenchman who joins the French Army to escape debts and is assigned to Corporal Macquart's squad. Levasseur, who believes in the evolutionary necessity of war, at first despises the corporal but comes to admire Macquart for his bravery and common sense. In the fight-

300

ing at Sedan, Levasseur saves the corporal's life; later the corporal helps him to escape the Germans after capture. In the civil war against the Second Republic Levasseur is killed in night street fighting by his friend Macquart.

Honoré Fouchard, a French artilleryman who is helped by Macquart and Levasseur in saving his father from pillaging German soldiers. He is a gallant man who offers to marry his father's servant-girl, who is pregnant by a man suspected of being a German spy. Honoré is killed during the fighting around Sedan.

M. Fouchard, Honoré's father, a farmer. He works with the French partisans against the Germans.

Silvine, M. Fouchard's servant-girl, pregnant by one of the hired men. She finds the body of Honoré, who has offered to marry her, on the battlefield and brings it home for burial.

Goliath, M. Fouchard's servant, who seduces Silvine. Goliath becomes a spy for the Germans. When he returns to the farm to renew his affair with Silvine, he is killed by French partisans.

Henriette Weiss, Maurice Levasseur's twin sister. Her husband's death at the hands of German soldiers almost unhinges her mind. She finds her brother in Paris dying of a wound inflicted by Corporal Macquart.

M. Weiss, Henriette's husband, who organizes a band of soldiers and other civilians to fight the Germans. When captured, he is stood against a wall and executed, despite the entreaties of his wife, who sees him shot in cold blood.

M. Delaherche, M. Weiss's employer, a textile manufacturer who finds collaboration with the Germans enables him to reëstablish his business.

Capt. von Gartlauben, a Prussian officer billeted in M. Delaherche's home. He helps his host collaborate with the conquerors.

Gunther, Maurice Levasseur's cousin, an officer commanding a company of Prussian Guards.

DRACULA

Author: Bram Stoker (1847-1912)
Time of action: Nineteenth century
First published: 1897

PRINCIPAL CHARACTERS

Count Dracula, a vampire. A corpse during the day, he comes to life at night. He has lived for centuries by sucking blood from living people. He pursues his victims in many harrowing episodes, and is pursued in turn from England to Rumania. There his body, in transport home to his castle, is overtaken and a stake driven through the heart, making it permanently dead.

Jonathan Harker, an English solicitor. He goes to Castle Dracula to transact business with the Count, whose nocturnal habits and total absence of servants puzzle Harker. Harker finds himself a prisoner in the castle, comes one day upon Dracula's corpse, and is occasionally victimized by the vampire. Then the coffin-like boxes are carried away and Harker finds himself left alone, still a prisoner. Later, after he has escaped, he is able to throw light on certain strange happenings in England.

Mina Murray, Harker's fiancée. She joins

301

in the pursuit of Dracula; in a trance, she is able to tell the others that Dracula is at sea, on his return voyage.

Lucy Westenra, a lovely friend whom Mina visits at the time of Harker's trip to Rumania. She is the repeated victim of Dracula, now in England, who appears sometimes in werewolf guise. Finally she dies and becomes a vampire also.

Dr. Van Helsing, a specialist from Amsterdam called to aid the failing Lucy. His remedies are effective, but a fatal attack comes after he leaves; he then returns to England to still her corpse as well as to hunt Dracula.

Dr. Seward, Lucy's former suitor, who attends her during her illness. Until he makes a midnight visit to her empty tomb, he does not believe Van Helsing's advice that the dead girl's soul can be saved only if a stake is driven through her heart.

Arthur Holmwood, a young nobleman and Lucy's fiancée. As he kisses the dying Lucy, her teeth seem about to fasten on his throat. He goes with Seward and Van Helsing to the empty tomb and joins them in tracking down Dracula.

DRAGON SEED

Author: Pearl S. Buck (1892-   )
Time of action: World War II
First published: 1942

PRINCIPAL CHARACTERS

Ling Tan, a Chinese farmer during World War II.

Ling Sao, his industrious and efficient wife.

Lao Ta, their oldest son, whose children and wife died during the Japanese occupation.

Orchid, the wife of Lao Ta. She is murdered by Japanese soldiers.

Lao Er, Ling Tan's second son, who flees from the Japanese with his wife Jade. He returns as messenger to the guerrilla fighters. He gets word of help coming from England and the United States.

Jade, the wife of Lao Er. She is a rebel against traditional rules for wives. She helps fight the Japanese. Her twin sons are "dragon seed" to defend their country.

Lao San, Ling Tan's youngest son, who is turned into a killer by Japanese attacks on him.

Pansiao, his sister in the mission school, who looks for a wife for him.

Mayli, a mission teacher who becomes curious about Lao San and has a love affair with him.

Wu Lien, a merchant and the husband of Ling Tan's oldest daughter. Though the Japanese killed his mother, he collaborates with them profitably.

DREAM OF THE RED CHAMBER

Author: Tsao Hsueh-chin (c. 1715-1763), with a continuation by Kao Ou
Time of action: c. 1729-1737
First published: 1792

302

Madame Shih, called **the Matriarch,** the widow of Chia Tai-shan and the oldest living ancestress of the family Chia. In her eighties, she rules with authority and grace her large families in two palace compounds. Although she shows favoritism to her favorite grandson, she is fair in her judgments and unselfish in her actions. She sacrifices her personal wealth to aid her decadent descendants, but she herself never compromises her integrity.

Chia Cheng, her younger son. A man of strict Confucian principles, he manages to keep his integrity in spite of calumnious actions against him. Extremely autocratic and strong-willed, he is puritanic as well. Although he loves his talented son, Chia Cheng cannot condone his frivolous ways or his lack of purpose; hence he disciplines the delicate boy too severely.

Madame Wang, Chia Cheng's wife.

Pao-yu, Chia Cheng's son by Madame Wang and the favorite of the Matriarch. Born with a jade tablet of immortality in his mouth, the boy is thought by all to be favored by the gods and distinguished among mortals. He is extremely handsome, sensitive, and perceptive, though delicate in health. He is also lazy, self-indulgent, effeminate—in short all the things his father does not want him to be—and he lives surrounded by faithful maidservants whose loving care is most touching. His character develops as he associates with his beloved cousin, Black Jade, and her cousin, Precious Virtue. His loss of the jade amulet causes him great pain and trouble, especially when his parents and grandmother decide on the wrong wife for him. When Black Jade dies of a broken heart, he turns to scholarship and distinguishes himself and his family, renewing their fortune before he disappears in the company of a Buddhist monk and a lame Taoist priest. His filial piety in redeeming the reputation and fortune of the Chias atones for all the trouble he caused his family. Precious Virtue, his wife, bears him a son to carry on the family line.

Tai-yu, called **Black Jade,** another of the Matriarch's grandchildren, a girl born into mortality from the form of a beautiful flower. Delicate in health and gravely sensitive, the beautiful and brilliant child comes to live in the Matriarch's home after her mother dies. Immediately she and Pao-yu sense their intertwined destinies, and their mutual love and respect develop to uncanny depths, to the point that manifestation of her dream appears as stigmata on Pao-yu's body. Given to jealousy and melancholy, she finally wastes away to the point that the Matriarch will not allow Pao-yu to have her in marriage. Black Jade dies in consequence, at the time when Pao-yu marries Precious Virtue, disguised as Black Jade.

Pao-chai, called **Precious Virtue,** the demure and reserved niece of Black Jade's mother, brought into the Matriarch's pavilion as a companion to her favored grandchildren. Obedient to her benefactress' wishes, devoted to the handsome Pao-yu, loyal to Black Jade, and generous to all the many Chia relatives, Pao-chai well fits her name. Her virtues are the more remarkable in the face of the many trials placed before her, especially in giving herself in marriage to one who loves another. She is the model Chinese wife and companion, a great contrast to her brother Hsueh Pan, a reckless libertine.

Hsi-feng, called **Phoenix,** the efficient but treacherous wife of Chia Lien. At first a careful manager of the estate, she eventually indulges her greedy nature, lends money at high interest, and finally brings disgrace upon the Chia family. Her jealous nature causes tragedy and unhappiness among the loving members of the household, but she dies repentant.

Chia Lien, the husband of Phoenix and the son of Chia Sheh by an unnamed concubine, an idle, lecherous man unfaithful to his wife. After the death of Phoenix he marries Ping-er, called Patience, a devoted maid of the household.

Chia-chieh, the young daughter of Phoenix and Chia Lien.

Chia Sheh, the Matriarch's older son and master of the Yungkuofu, one of the two great palace compounds of the Chia family. He is a man of very ordinary talents, holds no important official post, and takes little part in the affair of his household.

Madame Hsing, the wife of Chia Sheh.

Ying-chun, called **Welcome Spring,** the daughter of Chia Sheh by an unnamed concubine. Although the Matriarch and Chia Cheng oppose the match, Chia Sheh marries her to Sun Shao-tsu. Her husband beats her and she is miserable in her marriage.

Chia Gen, master of the Ningkuofu. A man of no moral scruples, he carries on an intrigue with his daughter-in-law, Chin-shih. He helps to bring disgrace on the Chia family when he is accused of corrupting the sons of noble families and of turning the Ningkuofu into a gambling resort.

Chia Ging, Chia Gen's aged father. He has renounced the world and retired to a Taoist temple.

Yu-shih, the wife of Chia Gen.

Chia Jung, Chia Gen's son. He involves himself in several family intrigues.

Chin-shih, the wife of Chia Jung. She dies after a long illness, possibly a suicide. Before her death she carries on an affair with her father-in-law.

Hsi-chun, called **Compassion Spring,** the daughter of Chia Ging.

Chia Chiang, the Matriarch's greatgrandson. An orphan, he grows up in the household of Chia Gen and is a close friend of Chia Jung.

Chin Chung, the brother of Chin-shih. He and Pao-yu become good friends. He dies while still a schoolboy.

Chih-neng, a young nun at Iron Sill Temple, in love with Chin Chung.

Cardinal Spring, the daughter of Chia Cheng and Madame Wang. She brings great honor to the Chia family when she becomes an Imperial Concubine.

Chao Yi-niang, Chia Cheng's concubine. Jealous of Pao-yu and hating Phoenix, she secretly pays to have a spell put on them. Both become desperately ill and their coffins are prepared. Then a Buddhist monk and a lame Taoist priest miraculously appear and restore the power of Pao-yu's jade tablet. Pao-yu and Phoenix recover.

Chia Huan, Chia Cheng's son by Chao Yi-niang. Like his mother, he resents the favoritism shown to Pao-yu.

Tan-chun, called **Quest Spring,** Chia Cheng's daughter by Chao Yi-niang. She marries the son of an important frontier official.

Hsueh Yi-ma, a widow, the sister of Madame Wang. After her husband's death she goes with her son and daughter to live with the Chia family in the Yungkuofu. Precious Virtue, her daughter, becomes the bride of Pao-yu.

Hsueh Pan, a drunkard and libertine always in pursuit of girls and young men. His purchase of a maid, Lotus, involves him in controversy and a law suit. Eventually he marries Cassia, a shrew, and is unfaithful to her. Cassia dies, accidentally poisoned, while he is living in exile on the frontier. After his return he makes Lotus his chief wife.

Cassia, Hsueh Pan's selfish, quarrelsome, disobedient wife. While her husband is exiled she tries to seduce his cousin, Hsueh Kuo, but he repulses her. She then tries to poison Lotus, her husband's maid, but drinks the poison by mistake and dies.

Hsueh Kuo, Hsueh Pan's cousin. Incapable of disloyalty, he spurns Cassia's attempts to make him her lover.

Lotus, Hsueh Pan's maid. Stolen from her family while a child, she later attracts the attention of Hsueh Pan, who buys her but soon becomes indifferent to her beauty and grace. Married to her master after his wife's death and his return from exile, Lotus dies in childbirth.

Chen Shih-yin, the father of Lotus. After his daughter has been stolen and he has lost all his possessions in a fire, he and his wife go to live with her family. One day he disappears in the company of a lame Taoist priest and is never seen again.

Feng-shih, Cheng Shih-yin's wife and the mother of Lotus. After her husband's disappearance she supports herself as a seamstress.

Lin Ju-hai, the well-born descendant of an ancient family of Soochow, the Matriarch's son-in-law and the father of Black Jade. A widower without a male heir, he decides to give his daughter the education that in those times only sons of noble families received.

Chia Yu-tsun, a scholar befriended by Chen Shih-yin. He becomes Black Jade's tutor in the household of Lin Ju-hai. Later he is appointed to the post of provincial prefect.

Hsiang-yun, called **River Mist,** a grandniece of the Matriarch. She lives with her Chia relatives for a time, but after Black Jade dies and Pao-yu and Precious Virtue are married she returns to her own family.

Yu Lao-niang, the stepmother of Yushih.

Er-chieh, the daughter of Yu Lao-niang by a previous marriage. Chia Lien, enamored of the girl, makes her his secret

concubine and installs her with her sister, San-chieh, in a separate house. Phoenix, learning of her husband's second establishment, pretends to be reasonable and without jealousy. Secretly hating her rival, she finds an accomplice in a maid from the other household. The maid insults her mistress and treats her with such abuse that Er-chieh commits suicide by swallowing gold.

San-chieh, the sister of Er-chieh. When Chia Gen and Chia Lien decide to find a husband for her, she announces that the only man she will marry is Liu Hsiang-lien, a handsome young actor. He changes his mind, however, after a formal engagement has been arranged. San-chieh, grief-stricken, kills herself with his sword.

Liu Hsiang-lien, a handsome young actor. Although a female impersonator, he is not effeminate in mind or habits, and he rejects Hsueh Pan's suit when that licentious young nobleman pursues him. He breaks his betrothal to San-chieh after hearing gossip about her, and the girl commits suicide. Conscience-stricken, he cuts off his hair and goes away with a lame Taoist priest.

Hsi-jen, called **Pervading Fragrance,** Pao-yu's devoted maid and concubine. After the disappearance of her master she wishes only to remain faithful to his memory, but her brother arranges her marriage to a son of the Chiang family. To her surprise, her bridegroom is Chiang Yu-han, once called Chi-kuan, an actor who had been Pao-yu's close friend.

Chiang Yu-han, a young actor whose professional name is Chi-kuan, a friend of Pao-yu. Accused of seducing the handsome player, Pao-yu is beaten severely by his stern father. Chiang Yu-han later marries Pervading Fragrance, his friend's loyal maid.

Golden Bracelet, a maid accused of attempting to seduce Pao-yu. Sent back to her family, she drowns herself.

305

Liu Lao-lao, a poor relation of Madame Wang. Visiting the Yungkuofu from time to time, she grows prosperous from gifts that the Chias give her.

Pan-er, her grandson, a shy boy.

Exquisite Jade, a pious, fastidious nun living in the Yungkuofu. Bandits who break into the compound seize her and take her away beyond the frontier.

Chia Lan, Pao-yu's young kinsman who also distinguishes himself in the Imperial Examinations.

Chia Jui, an oaf who tries to force his attentions on Phoenix.

A Buddhist Monk and
A Taoist Priest, lame in one leg, mysterious figures, possibly messengers of the Immortals, who appear suddenly and mysteriously in times of revelation or crisis.

Faith,
Ching-wen, called Bright Design,
Sheh-yueh, called Musk Moon,
Oriole,
Tzu-chuan, called Purple Cuckoo,
Autumn Sky, and
Snow Duck, maids in the Yungkuofu.

Chiao Ta, a privileged old family servant.

DRINK

Author: Émile Zola (1840-1902)
Time of action: Second half of the nineteenth century
First published: 1877

PRINCIPAL CHARACTERS

Gervaise (zhĕr·vĕz′), a laundress. Deserted by her lover, Lantier, she marries Coupeau, with whom she prospers until her husband is disabled by an accident and takes to drink. When Lantier returns, she begins to degenerate until, worn out by the hardships of her life, she dies alone.

Lantier (län·tyā′), Gervaise's lover, who deserts her and their two children only to return later and complete the ruin of her life.

Coupeau (kōō·pō′), Gervaise's husband. A roofer, he works hard to support his family until, idled by an accident, he takes to drink.

Adèle (à·dĕl′), the prostitute for whom Lantier deserts Gervaise.

Virginie (vēr·zhē·nē′), Adèle's sister and the enemy of Gervaise, over whom she

finally triumphs by acquiring Gervaise's shop and the favors of Lantier.

Nana (nà·nà′), the daughter of Gervaise and Coupeau. Her decision to leave home for the streets causes Gervaise to lose all interest in life and hastens her complete degeneracy and death.

Goujet (gōō·zhā′), a neighbor secretly in love with Gervaise, whom he tries in vain to help.

Claude (klōd′) and
Étienne (ā·tyĕn′), the children of Gervaise and Lantier.

Madame Boche (bôsh′), an older friend of Gervaise.

Madame Fauconnier (fō·kô·nyā′), the proprietress of a laundry, who gives Gervaise work after her desertion by Lantier.

DRUMS

Author: James Boyd (1888-1944)
Time of action: American Revolution
First published: 1925

PRINCIPAL CHARACTERS

Squire John Fraser, a North Carolina planter, a strict but kind Scotsman determined to educate his son as a gentleman.

Caroline Fraser, his wife.

John Fraser, their son. Educated in Edenton, he returns to his inland farm home when British authority is overthrown in the coastal town. Sent to England on business by his father, he becomes a clerk for an importing firm. He does a favor for Paul Jones (whom he had met at Wylie Jones's home) and later signs as a sailor on Jones's ship when he raids the Scottish coast. On the "Bonhomme Richard," a later and larger command of Jones's, John is wounded in a sea battle and, still feverish, he sails for home on a Dutch ship. At first rejected for the militia, he is later accepted and is wounded in a skirmish. No longer a fighter, John rejoices to learn that the British have been defeated.

Sir Nat Dukinfield, a young sportsman and John's friend. He is killed in a tavern brawl while visiting John in a French port.

Captain Tennant, Collector of the Port at Edenton.

Eve Tennant, his daughter, a coquette who becomes interested in John.

Wylie Jones, a plantation owner who promotes the North Carolina rebellion against the British.

Paul Jones, an adventurous Scottish sailor who takes Wylie Jones's last name and becomes a raiding captain in the American Navy.

Sally Merrillee, John's childhood playmate, a neighbor of the Frasers. She and John fall in love.

James Merrillee, Sally's father, killed in the war. For a time John manages the Merrillee farm.

Dr. Clapton, an English clergyman who tutors John in Edenton.

Captain Flood, John's friend, a river boat skipper who takes him up river to Halifax.

Plain Clothes Hewes, a shipbuilder.

Teague Battle, a young lawyer.

Master Hal Cherry, a repulsive rich boy.

General Nathanael Greene, a victorious American commander.

DRUMS ALONG THE MOHAWK

Author: Walter D. Edmonds (1903-   )
Time of action: 1775-1783
First published: 1936

PRINCIPAL CHARACTERS

Gilbert (Gil) Martin, a young pioneer, a hard worker ambitious to have a place of his own at Deerfield and willing to continue fighting after each defeat. Senecas burn his first home and he is wounded in the ambushing of General

Herkimer's militia. He works on the land and fights when needed until the valley is at last safe and he is able to return with his family to Deerfield.

Magdelana (Lana) Borst Martin, his pretty wife. She loses her first baby after the flight from Deerfield to Fort Schuyler but bears a boy, Gilly, the following spring and another boy, Joey, in August of the next year. Recovery from this birth is prolonged, but by the end of the war she has a baby girl to take to Deerfield with her husband and boys.

Mark Demooth, a captain of the militia, a small, slightly built man rather proud of himself.

John Wolff, a Tory convicted of aiding the British and sent to prison; he later escapes to Canada.

Blue Back, a friendly old Oneida Indian, dirty and paunchy, who likes Gil. He warns the Deerfield residents of a planned raid and later serves as scout and guide for the militia. His young Indian wife is proud of his fertility despite his age.

Mrs. Sarah McKlennar, Captain Barnabas McKlennar's widow for whom Gil works as a hired hand. Her home is burned by two drunken Indians who take her bed out for her while the fire is burning.

Joseph Brant, an Indian chief who refuses to pledge neutrality in the war.

General Benedict Arnold, General Herkimer's successor appointed to reorganize the patriot army and lead it against St. Leger's camp.

Jurry McLonis, a Tory who seduces Nancy Schuyler.

Nancy Schuyler, Mrs. Demooth's maid, who bears Jurry's child and is taken by an Indian as his wife.

Hon Yost, Nancy's brother, another Tory who, when arrested, promises to spread in the British camp false reports of American strength.

Clem Coppernol,
The Weavers, and
The Realls, neighbors who help with the Deerfield log-rolling that is interrupted by the Seneca raid.

Mrs. Wolff, John's wife, reported missing after the Seneca raid.

General Nicholas Herkimer, commander of the Mohawk Valley patriots; he is mortally wounded when his men are ambushed and routed.

General Barry St. Leger, British general who leads a combined force of British and Indians against the patriots.

General Butler, British leader of a group of raiding and pillaging parties; he is finally killed and his army routed.

Mrs. Demooth, a snobbish woman who so torments and frightens Nancy about her pregnancy that she leaves; Mrs. Demooth later loses her mind.

Colonel Van Schaick, leader of an attack against the Onondaga towns.

Adam Helmer and
Joe Boleo, two scouts who help Gil build a cabin after Mrs. McKlennar's house is burned.

Lt. Colonel Marinus Willett, leader of an army which pursues and attacks Butler's army, killing him and scattering his men in the wilderness.

THE DUCHESS OF MALFI

Author: John Webster (?-Before 1635)
Time of action: Sixteenth century
First presented: c. 1613

The Duchess of Malfi, sister of Duke Ferdinand and the Cardinal. She is a woman of strong character and deep feeling. Capable of gaiety and affectionate teasing, she is also able to bear danger, grief, and terror with fortitude. Her brothers' attempt to drive her mad fails; her dignified nobility at her death transforms the character of her murderer.

Ferdinand, Duke of Calabra, the cruel twin brother of the Duchess. Arrogant, domineering, and cruel, he forbids his widowed sister to marry again and sets a master spy to watch over her. Finding that she is in love and secretly married, he uses every form of inhuman torture that he can devise to break her mind, then has her murdered. Remorse drives him to madness. In his frenzy he wounds his brother, mortally wounds Bosola, and receives his death wound from the latter.

The Cardinal, a worldly and evil churchman. Lacking the demon which drives his brother mad, he is completely unscrupulous, killing his mistresss dispassionately when she worms from him his secret guilt in the murder of the Duchess and her children. His death is a grisly irony, for he has forbidden his followers to enter his room, and they think his howls for help are tests of their obedience.

Daniel de Bosola (bŏ·sō'lă), an embittered, satirical villain. A complex character, intelligent and witty, but ruthless, he acts as a spy for the evil brothers and betrays the Duchess to them. The fortitude and loveliness of the Duchess pierce his heart; and after murdering her, he has a strange devotion for her and avenges her. He bears a strong kinship to Iago: his language is violent, sometimes filthy, but emanates a savage poetry.

Antonio Bologna (än·tō'nyō bô·lô'nyä), the Duchess' steward. Although deeply in love with the Duchess, he does not declare himself until she subtly proposes to him. He is a good man, intelligent and loyal, and shrewd enough not to trust Bosola. He is accidentally killed by Bosola after the death of the Duchess.

Delio (dĕl'yō), Antonio's faithful friend. After the deaths of Antonio and the Duchess he protects their only surviving child.

Cariola (kä·rē·ō'lä), the faithful waiting woman of the Duchess, who shares the secret of the Duchess' and Antonio's clandestine marriage. Fear makes her plead vainly for life in notable contrast to the dignity of the Duchess in facing death.

Julia (yōōl'yä), the wanton wife of Castruccio and mistress of the Cardinal. She is fascinated by Bosola and entices him into an affair. Her curiosity leads to her death by poisoning at the hands of the Cardinal.

The Marquis of Pescara (pās·kä'rä), a nobleman of integrity and sensitivity, endowed with a superior ethical sense.

A Doctor, employed to treat Duke Ferdinand in his madness. His extreme self-confidence leads him to a beating by the madman.

Castruccio (käs·trōō't·chyō), an aged, impotent fool, husband of Julia.

Count Malateste (mä·lä·tĕs'tä), a worthy nobleman, proposed by Duke Ferdinand and as a second husband for the Duchess.

Silvio (sēl'vyō), a lord.

Roderigo (rŏd·ə·rē'gō) and Grisolan (grē·sō'län), attendants to Duke Ferdinand who refuse to answer his cries for help because they are sure that he is testing them.

An Old Lady, the butt of Bosola's gruesome jesting.

Several Madmen, sent to the Duchess by Duke Ferdinand in hopes of driving her mad.

Three Children, the offspring of Antonio and the Duchess. Two are murdered; one survives.

THE DYNASTS

Author: Thomas Hardy (1840-1928)
Time of action: 1806-1815
First published: 1903-1908

PRINCIPAL CHARACTERS

Napoleon Bonaparte, portrayed by Hardy as a man driven by an inscrutable fate and conscious of his ability to master Europe. He is a great leader, at times impatient with his subordinates' abilities. Above all, he wants to found a new dynasty to rank with the established royal families of Europe. Disappointed in his negotiations with Tsar Alexander for the hand of a Russian princess, he turns to the defeated Emperor Francis of Austria, who gives him the hand of Marie Louise for his second wife after Napoleon has divorced the unfortunate Empress Josephine because of her failure to provide an heir. Even though defeated by the Austrians and Prussians at Leipzig, Napoleon does not lose his sense of destiny. Exiled to Elba, he returns for the famous Hundred Days, only to be defeated a second time at Waterloo. His efforts are finally compared by the Spirit of Years, who sees all of history, to the struggles of an insect upon a leaf. Napoleon fluttered many lives and caused great slaughter, all for nothing.

Josephine, Napoleon's first wife, who cannot believe it is truly her fault that she bears no children, even though Napoleon points to bastard children as proof of his own potency in the marriage bed. Despite her protests and tears, for she truly loves her husband, Josephine is forced to consent to make way for Marie Louise.

Marie Louise, Princess of Austria and a pawn of circumstances and politics. She is married to Napoleon to help save Austria from conquest. Eventually she bears a son to Napoleon, though almost at the sacrifice of her own life. When Napoleon is defeated and exiled to Elba, Marie Louise and her small son, styled the King of Rome, go to her native Austria for asylum.

George III, King of England. He is shown first, in 1805, as a robust monarch watching preparations being made along the English coast to meet the expected French invasion. Later King George is shown at the age of seventy-two, shortly before his death, at the mercy of his physicians, who bleed him, drug him, and give him cold-water treatments in cruel, though well-meaning, fashion. From the state of a monarch he is reduced to the condition of a pathetic mental case who stands as a living symbol between the Prince Regent and the British throne.

Tsar Alexander of Russia, portrayed as a self-seeking monarch who looks down on Napoleon as an upstart, despite the friendship he expresses for Napoleon and the French at the famous meeting between Alexander and Napoleon on a raft in the middle of the River Niemen.

The Emperor Francis of Austria, a monarch forced, against his judgment as a father, to deliver up Marie Louise as Napoleon's second wife. This alliance is concluded after Napoleon has dictated bitter terms following the defeat of the Austrian and Russian forces at Austerlitz.

Sir William Pitt, the energetic Prime Minister of England, who struggles to save his country and Europe from Napoleon. In 1805, Pitt works manfully against isolationist members of the Parliament to provide for the defense of England. Later he works even harder to enlist the Continent against Napoleon. Weakened in health, he continues his political struggles, even though George III refuses to permit a coalition government.

Charles James Fox, Prime Minister after Sir William Pitt. Fox tries to negotiate with Napoleon, even to warning Bonaparte of an attempt at assassination. Unfortunately for Fox, his sincere efforts at negotiation are used by Napoleon to screen his plotting against Prussia.

Lord Horatio Nelson, the famous British Admiral who defeated the naval forces of Napoleon at the Battle of Trafalgar and thus saved his country from invasion. A man of great courage and hardihood, he paces the deck of his flagship in a bright uniform until cut down by a musket shot during the battle.

Admiral Villeneuve, Napoleon's naval planner, who works against the odds of poor ships and equipment to forge a fighting navy for his master. When his best efforts meet defeat at Trafalgar, he stabs himself to death at an inn.

The Immanent Will, the force Thomas Hardy saw as the power or energy behind the workings of the universe. Because it is blind and uncreative in any rational sense, Hardy terms the force It, rather than He.

The Spirit of Years, the oldest of the allegorical spirits introduced by Hardy to give "The Dynasts" a sense of panorama and perspective. The Spirit of Years is the leader among the other spirits, chastening them and dampening their enthusiasms when necessary.

The Spirit of Pities, a spirit of the universal spirit of human nature. This allegorical figure is an idealized human spectator, the chief commentator for the author on the events described.

The Spirit Sinister, a savage allegorical spirit who rejoices in the carnage and the evil displayed during the Napoleonic era.

The Spirit Ironic, an allegorical spirit who comments on the irony, sometimes tragic, sometimes humorous, as the events of the drama unfold.

EARTH

Author: Émile Zola (1840-1902)
Time of action: The 1860's
First published: 1887

PRINCIPAL CHARACTERS

Fouan (fwäṅ), a proud, tough, suspicious old peasant whose waning powers lead him, like King Lear, to divide his land among his children. Without land he loses their fear and respect, and they strip him of the rest of his possessions until he is powerless. Humiliated everywhere, he moves from home to home. Finally his youngest son, fearing Fouan will report him for murder, smothers and burns him.

Rose (rōz), his simple, submissive wife, who dies after being hit by the youngest son, leaving Fouan in solitude.

Hyacinthe (yà·sănt'), called Jésus-Christ, their older son, the amiable village loafer who loves drinking and poaching. He

311

offers Fouan the irregular life of his home, but his father leaves when he learns that Hyacinthe is after his bonds.

Fanny (fả·nē′), the daughter, a self-righteous, competent housekeeper whose insults and restrictions on her father drive him to leave for good.

Buteau (bü·tō′), the younger son, a brutal, greedy, lustful man. After rejecting his land inheritance out of pride, he accepts it and marries his cousin for her land, vowing never to lose any of it. He tries to keep his sister-in-law from claiming her share and makes violent attempts to rape her. When she does claim her land, he and his wife are evicted, but they return, rape, and kill her. The land reverts to them. In the end Buteau's vicious greed has caused the death of his parents and sister-in-law.

Delhomme (də·lôm′), Fanny's husband, a man whose avarice is checked by a crude sense of justice but who supports his wife's policy with regard to her father.

Lise (lēz), a cheerful girl who marries Buteau after bearing his child and then becomes coarse, sullen, and greedy. She makes an enemy of her sister, helps Buteau rape her, and then accidentally kills her in a fight.

Françoise (frän·swäz′), Lise's sister, a sensitive, attractive girl disgusted by Buteau to the point where she moves to her aunt's house, accepts a husband whom she does not love, and claims her land. When Buteau finally ravishes her, she realizes she loves him. Dying, she wills him her land.

Jean Macquart (zhän mả·kảr′), an ex-soldier, tradesman, and farmhand. A manly, kind person, attracted to Françoise, he finds himself drawn into a violent feud with Buteau and a loveless marriage. When his wife wills her land

to Buteau, he decides to become a soldier again.

Hourdequin (ōōr·də·kăn′), a gentleman farmer, Macquart's employer and friend, a man oppressed by ill-used farm equipment and a promiscuous mistress. In the end his misfortunes overcome him.

Jacqueline (zhảk·lēn′), his loose mistress, an illegitimate girl who sleeps with all the farmhands.

La Frimat (lả frē·mả′), an old woman gardener who takes in Buteau and Lise when they are evicted.

La Grande (lả gränd′), Fouan's sister, a vicious old woman who commands fear, delights in family feuds, and takes in Françoise for a short time.

Old Mouche (mōōsh), Lise's father and Fouan's brother, an old peasant who dies and leaves his land to his daughters.

La Truille (lả trwē′yə), Hyacinthe's lively, promiscuous illegitimate daughter and housekeeper.

Jules (zhül) and
Laure (lōr), the children of Buteau and Lise. They mistreat Fouan.

Maître Baillehache (mĕtr bảy·ảsh′), the notary who supervises the division of Fouan's land.

Grosbois (grō·bwả′), a fat, drunken surveyor.

M. Charles (shảrl′), a sentimental, retired brothel-keeper.

The Abbé Godard (ả·bā′gô·dảr′), the local priest, invariably angry at the peasants but generous to the poor.

Bécu (bā·kü′), the local constable and Hyacinthe's drinking companion.

Lequeu (lə·kœ′), the local schoolmaster, an anarchist who advocates total destruction when, finally, he breaks out of his reserved manner.

312

Canon (kà·nōn'), a Communist tramp whom Hyacinthe takes home with him.

Palmyre (pàl·mēr'), an old farm woman who dies while working for Buteau.

Hilarion (ē·là·ryōn'), her idiot, crippled

brother, killed while trying to rape La Grande.

Macqueron (mà·kə·rōn'), the local inn keeper and merchant who is elected mayor.

EAST OF EDEN

Author: John Steinbeck (1902-   )
Time of action: 1865-1918
First published: 1952

PRINCIPAL CHARACTERS

Adam Trask, a settler in the Salinas Valley. He marries Cathy Ames in Connecticut and moves west where he and their twin sons, Caleb and Aron, are deserted by her.

Cathy Ames, Adam Trask's innocent appearing but evil wife. Deserting Adam and their twin sons, Caleb and Aron, she becomes the proprietress of a notorious brothel.

Aron Trask, smugly religious, idealistic twin son of Adam Trask and Cathy Ames. Unable to face the knowledge of his parents' past, he joins the army and is killed in France.

Caleb Trask, impulsive twin son of Adam Trask and Cathy. Rejected in an effort to help his father, he takes revenge by revealing to his brother Aron the secret of their mother's identity. He later accepts responsibility for the disillusioned Aron's death.

Abra Bacon, Aron Trask's fiancée. Disturbed because she feels unable to live up to Aron's idealistic image of her, she finally turns to the more realistic Caleb Trask.

Charles Trask, Adam Trask's half brother.

Samuel Hamilton, an early settler in the Salinas Valley.

Liza Hamilton, Samuel Hamilton's wife.

Lee, Adam Trask's wise and good Chinese servant.

Faye, proprietress of a Salinas brothel. Her death is engineered by Cathy Ames as she seeks to gain full control of Faye's establishment.

Will Hamilton, business partner of Caleb Trask.

EASTWARD HO!

Authors: George Chapman (c. 1559-1634), Ben Jonson (1573?-1637), and John Marston (1576-1634)
Time of action: c. 1605
First presented: 1605

PRINCIPAL CHARACTERS

Touchstone, a blunt, honest goldsmith. The pretensions of his daughter Gertrude

and his wild apprentice, Quicksilver, irritate him, while the duty and devotion of

313

his daughter Mildred and his steady apprentice, Golding, gratify him. Though stern, he is too good-hearted to deny mercy to the repentant sinners at the last.

Mistress Touchstone, his somewhat simple wife. Dazzled by her social-climbing daughter and her knighted son-in-law, she too irritates Touchstone. When Gertrude comes to grief, Mistress Touchstone urges her to beg her father's forgiveness.

Gertrude, Touchstone's haughty and ambitious daughter. She scorns her father and patronizes her mother and sister. When her husband runs off with another woman and is jailed, her pride has a fall; but even in her plea for her father's pardon, she cannot completely avoid impudence.

Mildred, Touchstone's dutiful daughter. She is kind and friendly even to her contemptuous, self-centered sister. With her father's support, she marries Golding.

Francis Quicksilver, Touchstone's idle and prodigal apprentice. He keeps a mistress, gambles, and wastes his little substance in riotous living. He joins Sir Petronel in a plan for a Virginia voyage. When shipwreck ends the voyage almost

at its very beginning, he is imprisoned for theft and sentenced to death. He becomes sincerely repentant, and Touchstone forgives him and secures his release.

Golding, Touchstone's diligent apprentice. Good without being self-righteous or priggish, he rises rapidly in the world and becomes an alderman's deputy. He persuades Touchstone to visit the prison and manipulates the angry old man into forgiving his prodigal son-in-law and his prodigal apprentice.

Sir Petronel Flash, a new-made knight. He dazzles Mistress Touchstone and Gertrude, whom he marries and deserts for Winifred. Imprisoned with Quicksilver, he also repents and receives forgiveness, returning to his own wife.

Security, an old usurer, also imprisoned, but released by Touchstone's bounty.

Winifred, Security's attractive young wife, who runs off with Sir Petronel but returns to Security.

Sindefy, Quicksilver's mistress, Gertrude's maid. At Golding's urging, Quicksilver agrees to marry her.

THE ECCLESIAZUSAE

Author: Aristophanes (c. 448-c. 385 B.C.)
Time of action: Early fourth century B.C.
First presented: 392 B.C.

PRINCIPAL CHARACTERS

Praxagora (prăk·să'gō·rə), a housewife of Athens who has become disgusted with the dishonesty of public officers, the fickleness and greed of the people, and the mismanagement of domestic and foreign affairs. She has encouraged a number of her female friends to disguise themselves as men, pack the assembly, and vote for her proposal that the government of the state be turned over to the women. Although not above occasional vulgarity, she is quick-witted

and courageous. An accomplished orator, she carries her plan to success and finds herself designated dictator. She quickly institutes a program of reform, evidently based on Aristophanes' knowledge of an early version of Plato's "Republic." In her utopian society crime will become impossible because property will be held in common; meals will be taken in communal dining halls, marital restrictions will be abolished (with the proviso that the old and ugly have first claims on de-

314

sirable sexual partners), and courtesans will be done away with so that honest women may have their choice of the young men. Praxagora fears that her reforms are too extreme for adoption, but she is assured that "love of novelty and disdain for the past" among the Athenians will secure the coöperation of the people.

Blepyrus (blĕ·pī′rəs), Praxagora's husband, some years her senior. He, like his neighbors, dabbles in thievery, lechery, and bearing false witness, but he is reasonably good-natured, if a little dense. Pleased that his wife has been elevated to the dictatorship, he plans to bask in her reflected glory.

Chremes (krā′mēz), a friend of Blepyrus who brings him the news that the assembly has voted to turn the rule of Athens over to the women.

A Man, a neighbor of Blepyrus who also awakens to find that his wife and his clothing, in which she went disguised to the assembly, are missing from his house.

Two Citizens, one of whom hastens to deliver his property to the common store, as has been decreed; the other of whom wishs to retain his property but still to get his part of the common feast.

A Young Girl, who desires her lover.

A Young Man, the lover, who, because of the new law, must be relinquished to

The First Old Woman, who is ugly, but who must relinquish him to

The Second Old Woman, who is even uglier, but who must share him with

The Third Old Woman, who is as ugly as it is possible to be.

A Group of Women who go disguised as men with Praxagora to the assembly. Each is prepared to speak in favor of women's sovereignty, but each betrays herself in a practice session, one by bringing wool to card, another by calling for neat wine to drink, another by swearing by the two goddesses. Praxagora is finally chosen as their spokesman.

A Chorus of Women.

EDWARD THE SECOND

Author: Christopher Marlowe (1564-1593)
Time of action: Fourteenth century
First presented: c. 1590

PRINCIPAL CHARACTERS

Edward the Second, the headstrong, dissolute King of England. In his attempts to please his sycophantic favorites, Gaveston and Spencer, he neglects his responsibilities to the state, alienates Queen Isabella, and provokes rebellion among his nobles, who deprive him of his crown and eventually of his life. He responds to his dethronement with histrionic protests which are echoed by Shakespeare's Richard II and, like him, expresses a longing for a quiet life of contemplation.

Piers Gaveston (pǐrz găv′əs·tən), Edward's ambitious favorite. He deliber-

ately plans to corrupt his weak monarch with music, poetry, and "Italian masks," and to enrich himself at the expense of the English lords, whom he views with unceasing scorn. He overestimates Edward's power to protect his friends and falls into the hands of his bitter enemies, Mortimer and Warwick, who have him killed.

Hugh Spencer, Gaveston's protégé and successor in Edward's favor. He urges the King to stand firm against the seditious barons and sends messengers to thwart Isabella's pleas for aid from the French

315

king. Loyal to Edward to the end, he flees with him to Ireland, where he is captured, returned to England, and hanged.

Queen Isabella, Edward's neglected wife. She remains loyal to her husband during his first infatuation with Gaveston, although it grieves and repels her, and to please Edward she even appeals to Mortimer to allow Piers to return from exile. However, the King's continual rejection of her and her failure to win help from the King of France, her brother, drive her into the arms of Mortimer. She becomes a far less sympathetic figure as Mortimer's mistress and accomplice in his rise to power, and her imprisonment by her son for conspiring in her husband's murder seems just and inevitable.

Edmund Mortimer, leader of the forces arrayed against Edward. He is enraged by the King's submission to the flattery of Gaveston, whom he hates bitterly, and he insists upon the use of force to rid the realm of his enemy. Although he begins his campaign to free his country from evil influences, he becomes trapped by his own ambition and resorts to regicide in order to secure the regency for himself and Isabella. He retains a certain grandeur in his death, boasting that Fortune raised him to the heights before she hurled him down.

The Duke of Kent, Edward's brother Edmund. He participates temporarily in Mortimer's campaign against Gaveston after his advice and service have been rejected by Edward, but he comes to regret his disloyalty and tries unsuccessfully to rescue his brother from his murderers. He is beheaded by order of Mortimer, who fears his influence with young Prince Edward.

Prince Edward, later King Edward III, the precocious young heir to the throne. He is pathetically eager to win his father's love and offers to help win aid from France to do so. Although he is not strong enough to prevent Kent's execu-

tion, he musters a group of loyal lords to assist him in condemning Mortimer for his father's death.

Old Spencer, father of the King's favorite. He supplies military aid for Edward's defense and meets defeat with his son and the King.

Baldock, Hugh Spencer's tutor, who rises and falls with his pupil. He accepts his fate philosophically, telling Spencer, "All live to die, and rise to fall."

Sir John of Hainault, the kindly nobleman who aids Isabella and Prince Edward after the French king has rejected their suit.

Gurney and
Matrevis, Mortimer's henchmen, Edward's prison guards and murderers.

Lightborn, a hired assassin who devises the means of Edward's death.

Lancaster,
Warwick,
Pembroke,
Elder Mortimer,
The Archbishop of Canterbury, and
The Bishop of Winchester, leaders of the rebellion against Gaveston and Spencer.

The Bishop of Coventry, an outspoken prelate who is sent to the tower for voicing his opposition to Gaveston.

Arundel, a nobleman loyal to Edward.

Beaumont,
Levune, and
Trussel, messengers.

Rice ap Howell, Old Spencer's Welsh captor.

Leicester and
Berkeley, Edward's guardians, relieved of their charge by Mortimer, who finds them too lenient.

Edward's Niece, daughter of the Duke of Gloucester, married by her uncle to Gaveston.

316

EFFI BRIEST

Author: Theodor Fontane (1819-1898)
Time of action: Second half of the nineteenth century
First published: 1895

PRINCIPAL CHARACTERS

Effi von Briest (ăfē fôn brēst), only child of Ritterschaftsrat von Briest and his wife. Married at sixteen to Baron von Innstetten, she goes with her husband to a small town on the Baltic Sea. Bored and depressed by the formal stiffness of her new home, she is attracted to Major von Crampas. With this relationship a burden on her conscience, she is happy to move to Berlin, her husband's new post. There old letters from von Crampas come to light. She is divorced by her husband, socially ostracized, and dies at her parents' home believing that her husband, in divorcing her, has done the right thing for his honor.

Baron von Innstetten (bä·rōn' fôn ĭn'stă·ten), Effi's formal, disciplined husband. Discovering a packet of love letters

written six years before by Major von Crampas to Effi, he avenges his honor by killing von Crampas in a duel and divorcing his wife.

Major von Crampas (mä·yōr' fôn kräm'-päs), Effi's carefree, witty admirer, who is killed in a duel by Baron von Innstetten.

Annie von Innstetten (ä'nē fôn ĭn'stă-ten), the daughter of Baron von Innstetten and Effi.

Roswitha (rŏs·vē'tä), Effi's maid and faithful friend.

Ritterschaftsrat von Briest (rĭtér'shäfts·rät fôn brēst) and Frau von Briest (frou fôn brēst), Effi's parents.

EGMONT

Author: Johann Wolfgang von Goethe (1749-1832)
Time of action: Sixteenth century
First presented: 1788

PRINCIPAL CHARACTERS

Count Lamoral Egmont, who was born in Flanders and who serves the Spanish as a capable general and an excellent statesman. When Philip II, main instrument of the Inquisition, sends the Duke of Alva to The Netherlands to prevent disorders that have arisen as a consequence of Dutch displeasure with Spanish rule, Egmont freely speaks his mind in spite of warnings given by trusted friends such as Count Oliva. He urges Alva to use patience and tact in his affairs with the burghers. Alva, however, accuses

Egmont of treason and orders his execution.

William of Orange, founder of the Dutch Republic, who is an intelligent, cautious man admired by Charles V but hated by Philip. There is outward harmony between Egmont and William, and Alva tries to trap them both. William, however, keeps his distance, is not so outspoken as is Egmont, and escapes the latter's fate.

Margaret of Parma, Philip's half sister,

named by him Regent of The Netherlands. She is firm but not cruel toward the Protestants. She does what she can to keep order, but she knows that she is only the titular head of Holland and that Alva will actually rule.

The Duke of Alva, the cruel emissary of Philip II. He has no patience with the Dutch commoners' claims for their rights and believes that force has to be used in order to keep them in line. He garrisons an army and turns Holland into a police state.

Clärchen, a commoner of lowly station who loves and is loved by Egmont. When he is arrested, she attempts to rally the people to rescue him. When she fails, she goes to her house and drinks poison.

Fritz Brackenburg, a citizen who loves Clärchen. Clärchen's mother supports his suit, but the young woman has eyes only for Egmont.

Machiavel, Margaret's shrewd, wise, and capable secretary.

Ferdinand, Alva's natural son, who is given a small part to play in the plan to trap William and Egmont. He actually sympathizes with Egmont.

Silva, the official who reads Egmont's sentence to him in the prison.

THE EGOIST

Author: George Meredith (1828-1909)
Time of action: Nineteenth century
First published: 1879

PRINCIPAL CHARACTERS

Sir Willoughby Patterne, a nobleman whose pattern of egocentricities includes duplicity, austerity, snobbery, and sententiousness. Though he has played on the heartstrings of his most devoted Laetitia Dale, he learns through two broken engagements that all his barren heart can hope for is the solace of the good woman whom he has converted to egoism. Finally, Sir Willoughby is forced to abandon double dealing, to come down from the pedestal where he has viewed himself only in a favorable light, to bend his pride for the sake of a young cousin and a former servant whom he has wronged, and to accommodate himself to the understanding that his wife sees through him and cannot therefore love him. He will, of course, continue to be an egoist, though a more enlightened and flexible one.

Laetitia Dale, his silent admirer for many years and finally his public scourger. A long-time tenant of Sir Willoughby's in a cottage where she nursed her invalid father and wrote for a living, she finally sickens of Patterne's self-centered ways, particularly toward his kinsman and her student, young Crossjay Patterne, whose life is being forced into the wrong mold. Always gentle, amenable, trustworthy, Laetitia finally tires of being a confidante and becomes defiant in her refusal of the nobleman's hand after all others have failed him. Her warmth of admiration has been chilled by observation; her youth has gone in yearning; her health has suffered from literary drudgery. She makes her own terms for becoming Lady Patterne, to which Sir Willoughby agrees.

Clara Middleton, the betrothed of Sir Willoughby and his severest critic. At first attracted by the force of his personality, she soon discovers in him the tendency to manipulate lives and to order life. Feeling stifled and caged, she begs for her release, which the egoist cannot

318

grant since he has only recently been jilted by Constantia Durham. Despairing of gaining her father's permission to break the engagement, she tries to escape to the home of her best friend and maid of honor. In this desperate but abortive effort she is aided by the sensitive scholar-cousin of Sir Willoughby, Vernon Whitford, whom she will later marry. She, too, defends young Crossjay against the benevolent tyranny of the egotistical nobleman.

The Rev. Dr. Middleton, Clara's father, a retired clergyman, learned scholar, and warm-hearted wit. Dr. Middleton becomes more enamored of Sir Willoughby's fine wine and library than his daughter feels necessary, but he humorously involves himself in the plot to remake the egoist after he learns that the two-faced lover wishes to abandon his spirited daughter for the more complacent Laetitia.

Vernon Whitford, a poor relation of the Patternes and a writer who has taken in young Crossjay Patterne out of sympathy when his wealthy cousin refuses to aid the boy. Almost morbidly shy with women, and the more pitied by his bene-

factor, Vernon finally asserts himself in league with Clara and Laetitia to save his young charge from education as a "gentleman" when it is service with the Marines that the boy wants.

Colonel Horace De Craye, the Irish cousin and best man at a wedding which does not come off, partly because of his machinations. The best friend of Sir Willoughby, Colonel De Craye has long been suspicious of the nobleman's lack of nobility. He finds it easy to side with Clara, with whom he is in love, and all the others who wish to thwart the egoist.

Crossjay Patterne, the penniless son of a Marine hero who is not welcomed at Patterne Place. Though not scholarly by nature, the youth is irrepressibly happy and loving, strangely in contrast to his distant, rich relative. He loves most his guardian, Vernon Whitford, and Clara Middleton, his benefactress.

Constantia Durham, Sir Willoughby's betrothed, who jilts him ten days before their wedding date.

Harry Oxford, a military man with whom Constantia elopes.

ELECTIVE AFFINITIES

Author: Johann Wolfgang von Goethe (1749-1832)
Time of action: Eighteenth century
First published: 1808

PRINCIPAL CHARACTERS

Edward (ăd'värd), a wealthy nobleman. He lives an idyllic life on his estate with his wife, Charlotte, until the arrival of Ottilie, for whom he develops a passion which, in his immaturity, he does little to control. He and Ottilie are finally united in death.

Charlotte (shär·lŏ'tĕ), Edward's wife. She lives happily with her husband until his friend, the Captain, comes to live with them, and she and the Captain fall

in love. A mature person, she controls her passion and resolves to adhere to the moral code. She is united with the Captain after Edward's death.

Ottilie (ō·tē'lē·ă), Charlotte's young protégée, who comes to live on Edward's estate. She develops for her host a passion which he encourages. Finally, in despair over her situation, she dies of self-imposed starvation. She is soon followed by Edward, and the lovers are united in death.

319

The Captain, Edward's friend. Living on Edward's estate, he and Charlotte fall in love. Controlling his emotions, he plays an honorable role and is finally united with Charlotte after Edward's death.

Otto (ōtō), the infant son of Edward and Charlotte.

Herr Mittler (hâr mǐt'lĕr), a self-appointed marriage counselor who tries and fails to bring about a reconciliation between Edward and Charlotte.

Luciana (lōō'zē·ä'nä), Charlotte's daughter by a former marriage.

Nanny (nä'nē), Ottilie's young friend.

ELECTRA

Author: Euripides (c. 485-c. 406 B.C.)
Time of action: After the fall of Troy
First presented: 413 B.C.

PRINCIPAL CHARACTERS

Electra (ē·lek'trə), the daughter of Agamemnon and Clytemnestra. On his return from the Trojan War, Agamemnon was slain by Clytemnestra and Aegisthus, her lover, who now rules in Argos. For his own safety Orestes, Electra's brother, was smuggled out of the kingdom; Electra remained, was saved from death at the hands of Aegisthus by Clytemnestra, and was married to a poor farmer by Aegisthus. The farmer, out of respect for the house of Agamemnon, has never asserted his marital rights. In her first appearance Electra is thus the slave princess, unwashed and in rags, longing for attention and some emotional outlet, morbidly attached to her dead father and powerfully jealous of Clytemnestra. Orestes appears and, posing as a friend of the exiled brother, discusses with Electra the conduct of their mother and Aegisthus. In her speech to him she betrays herself as a woman whose desire for revenge has through continuous brooding become a self-centered obsession; her motive for the murder of Clytemnestra has now become hatred for her mother rather than love for her father, and she is an ugly and perverted being. Her expression of joy in the thought of murdering her mother causes Orestes not to reveal his identity until an old servant recognizes him. Electra takes no part in plotting vengeance on Aegisthus but arranges the

murder of her mother. She sends a message that she has been delivered of a son and needs Clytemnestra to aid in the sacrifices attending the birth. When the body of Aegisthus is brought in, Electra condemns him. The language in her speech is artificial and stilted; it contrasts sharply with her passionate condemnation of Clytemnestra shortly after. Electra never realizes that she is committing exactly the same atrocity for which she wishes to punish her mother. She leads her mother into the house and guides Orestes' sword when he hesitates. It is only after the deed is committed that she feels the burden of what she has done. At the end of the play she is given by the gods in marriage to Pylades. The characterization of Electra is ugly, but it represents Euripides at his most brilliant and convincing.

Orestes (ō·rĕs'tēz), Electra's brother. He returns secretly from exile under compulsion from Apollo to kill Aegisthus and his mother. Guided by the oracle, he does not share Electra's extreme lust for revenge. He kills Aegisthus by striking him in the back as he is preparing a sacrifice to the Nymphs and then, driven on by Electra, stabs his mother when she enters the house of Electra. The gods reveal that he will be pursued by the Furies of blood-guilt for his actions, but

320

that he will find release at Athens before the tribunal of the Areopagus, where Apollo will accept responsibility for the matricide.

Clytemnestra (klī′təm·nĕs′trə), the regal mother of Electra, who took Aegisthus as her lover before Agamemnon returned from Troy. Together the pair plotted the murder of the husband. Her attempt to justify the murder on the grounds that Agamemnon had sacrificed her daughter Iphigenia is unsuccessful. Her cruelty, vanity, and sordid private affairs alienate her from any great sympathy, but she has saved the life of Electra and has enough affection to answer Electra's request that she help in the sacrifice to celebrate the birth of her daughter's son. She is murdered by Orestes, at his sister's urging.

A Farmer, a Mycenaean to whom Aegis-

thus has given Electra in marriage. He understands and accepts his station in life with nobility. Electra acknowledges her gratitude for his understanding behavior.

Pylades (pĭl′ə·dēz), a mute character. He is the faithful friend who accompanies Orestes during his exile and is given Electra as a wife by the gods.

An Old Man, a former servant in the house of Agamemnon who is still faithful to Electra. Summoned by her, he recognizes Orestes and helps to devise a plan for the murder of Aegisthus.

Castor (kăs′tər) and **Polydeuces** (pŏl′ĭ·dū′sēz), the Dioscuri, brothers of Clytemnestra. They appear at the end of the play to give Electra in marriage and to foretell the future of Orestes.

THE EMIGRANTS

Author: Johan Bojer (1872-1959)
Time of action: Late nineteenth century
First published: 1925

PRINCIPAL CHARACTERS

Erik Foss, an emigrant to the United States. He returns to Norway to lead a band of his people to a new start in America, even helping them with money. His feet are frosbitten while he searches for cattle in a prairie blizzard, and he dies as a result.

Morten Kvidal, one of the emigrants. He assumes the leadership of the group after the death of Erik Foss and leads them for many years. He returns briefly to Norway to bring a wife, Bergitta, to Dakota. He becomes a railroad agent, helps his people become Americans, and shows them how to prosper in their adopted land. Blinded by an exploding lamp, he returns as an old man to Norway. He feels that he is still a Norwegian, though his children are Americans.

Ola Vatne, a Norwegian laborer in love with his employer's daughter. After serving a term in prison for burning his employer's barn, he migrates to America with Erik, taking his wife Else with him. A drunkard and gambler, he cannot succeed without help from his friends.

Else Vatne, Ola's wife. She marries him against her father's wishes after he is released from prison.

The Colonel, Else's father, who dismisses Ola when he discovers the love between his daughter and the man.

Per Föll, a big, hardworking emigrant. He is jealous of his wife, knowing her too well. His jealousy drives him mad and he is placed in an institution.

321

Anne Föll, Per's wife, admired by Morten Kvidal's young brother. She is pregnant by another man when Per marries her.

Bergitta Kvidal, Anne's sister and Morten's wife.

Kal Skaret, a hardworking, efficient emigrant who succeeds well in the Dakotas.

Karen Skaret, Kal's hardworking, efficient wife.

THE EMIGRANTS OF AHADARRA

Author: William Carleton (1794-1869)
Time of action: The 1840's
First published: 1848

PRINCIPAL CHARACTERS

Hycy (Hyacinth) Burke, a well-to-do, dissolute young man. Determined to seduce Kathleen Cavanagh, he is publicly snubbed; he resolves to have revenge on her and on Bryan M'Mahon, who loves her. A series of maneuvers designed to bring about Bryan's financial ruin finally causes Hycy, himself, to be exposed as a robber, an accomplice of whiskey smugglers, a counterfeiter, and a plotter against Bryan and his family. He is given two hundred pounds by his father with orders to leave the country and stay away.

Bryan M'Mahon, an honest farmer. In love with Kathleen Cavanagh, he is the object of Hycy's plan of revenge for Kathleen's snub. When, as a result of Hycy's plottings, Bryan is near financial ruin and dishonored in the sight of Kathleen and his neighbors, his friends manage to expose Hycy and restore Bryan to his rightful place in the community.

Kathleen Cavanagh, a young girl in love with Bryan. Scorning the blandishments of Hycy, she is, inadvertently, the cause of his attempts to ruin Bryan. When evidence against Bryan seems overwhelming, she reluctantly believes him guilty but regains her trust and affection when he is cleared.

Nanny Peety, a beggar girl who lives with the Burkes and who resents Hycy's attempts to seduce her.

Kate Hogan, Nanny's aunt. She is the wife of one of Hycy's smuggling associates.

Patrick O'Finigan, master of a hedge-school. He and Nanny and Kate are friends of Bryan and Kathleen. They bring in evidence against Hycy that clears Bryan of the charges against him.

Jemmy Burke, Hycy's father. When he discovers his son's true nature, he forces Hycy to leave the country.

ÉMILE

Author: Jean Jacques Rousseau (1712-1778)
Time of action: Eighteenth century
First published: 1762

PRINCIPAL CHARACTERS

Jean Jacques Rousseau (zhän' zhàk' rōō·sō'), the author himself, who assumes the role of a tutor in this work, which is hardly a novel at all but a treatise on education. With the imaginary Émile as a pupil, he illustrates his theories of education as he tries them out on his student. The tutor prescribes for the child's surroundings, diet, and hygiene, and gives him the freedom to learn the natural limits of his powers. For the adolescent Émile, he provides an education of the intellect, and for his maturing pupil, a moral education and the study of human relationships. The tutor, all through the life of the pupil, follows a philosophy of learning designed primarily to create neither a noble savage nor a cultivated gentlemen but a man living freely and fearlessly according to his nature.

Émile (ā·mēl'), an imaginary French orphan who is used as a child-symbol in the illustrations of Jean Jacques Rousseau's theories of education. Fulfilling Rousseau's requirements for an ideal subject for experimentation, he grows to manhood under his teacher's guidance. As a prospective father, he announces his determination to educate his child according to the theories of his beloved tutor.

Sophie (sō·fē'), a woman-symbol used by the tutor, Jean Jacques Rousseau, to enable him to discuss marriage problems with his pupil Émile.

EMILIA GALOTTI

Author: Gotthold Ephraim Lessing (1729-1781)
Time of action: Early eighteenth century
First presented: 1771

PRINCIPAL CHARACTERS

Emilia Galotti, the beautiful daughter of a soldier. She is betrothed to Count Appiani. Lecherous Prince Hettore Gonzaga, though engaged to marry the Princess of Massa, and in love with his mistress, the Countess Orsina, desires Emilia. The Prince's wily chamberlain, the Marquis Marinelli, suggests to the Prince that Count Appiani be sent on a mission to another province, thus leaving Emilia unprotected from the designs of the Prince. When Count Appiani refuses to go on the mission, he is assassinated; Emilia is abducted and taken to the Prince's palace. When her father sees that his daughter's chastity is about to be violated, he stabs her and presents her body to the lustful Prince.

Prince Hettore Gonzaga, the lascivious ruler of Sabionetta and Guastalla, who covets Count Appiani's betrothed. Led on by his wicked chamberlain, the Prince agrees to Marinelli's treacherous plot to kill Count Appiani and take Emilia by force. In the end, however, he loses the love of his mistress, Countess Orsina, and is left with only Emilia's dead body at his feet.

Odoardo Galotti, Emilia's father. Unable to protect his daughter from the machinations of Marinelli, he takes her life rather than have her violated by the carnal Prince. After stabbing his daughter he throws the dagger at the Prince's feet and gives himself up to the guards.

Claudia Galotti, Emilia's mother. Frantic when she and her daughter are abducted while on the way to Emilia's wedding, she accuses Marinelli of plotting Count Appiani's murder.

The Marquis Marinelli, Prince Gonzaga's evil chamberlain. It is he who contrives the treacherous plan to remove Count Appiani so that the Prince can seduce Emilia.

Count Appiani, Emilia's betrothed. When he refuses to be beguiled into leaving

323

Emilia on the day of their wedding, he is assassinated.

The Countess Orsina, the Prince's mistress. When he spurns her she first plans to stab him; instead, she gives the dagger to Odoardo Galotti. It is this knife with which Galotti stabs his daughter.

EMMA

Author: Jane Austen (1775-1817)
Time of action: Early nineteenth century
First published: 1816

PRINCIPAL CHARACTERS

Emma Woodhouse, the younger daughter of the wealthy owner of Hartfield and the most important young woman in the village of Highbury. Good-hearted, intelligent, but spoiled, she takes under her protection Harriet Smith, a seventeen-year-old girl of unknown parentage, who is at school in the village. Given to matchmaking, Emma breaks up the love affair between Harriet and Robert Martin, a worthy farmer, because she thinks Harriet deserves better, and persuades her to fall in love with the vicar, Mr. Elton. To her dismay, Elton proposes to her rather than to Harriet and is indignant when she refuses him. Next, Emma becomes interested in Frank Churchill, an attractive young man who visits his father in Highbury, and thinks him in love with her; but it develops that he is secretly engaged to Jane Fairfax. Emma had never really cared for Churchill, but she thinks him a possible match for Harriet. She becomes really concerned when she discovers that Harriet's new interest is in Mr. Knightley, an old friend of the Woodhouse family. She now realizes that Knightley is the man she has always loved and happily accepts his proposal. Harriet marries her old lover, Martin, and the matrimonial problems are solved.

George Knightley, a landowner of the neighborhood, sixteen years Emma's senior, and an old family friend. Honorable, intelligent, and frank, he has always told Emma the truth about herself. When she thinks that he may marry someone else,

she realizes that she has always loved him and accepts his proposal.

John Knightley, George's brother, married to Emma's older sister.

Isabella Knightley, nee Woodhouse, John Knightley's wife and Emma's sister, a gentle creature absorbed in her children.

Henry Woodhouse, father of Emma and Isabella, kindly and hospitable but an incurable hypochondriac.

Mr. Weston, a citizen of Highbury who has married Anne Taylor, Emma's former governess.

Anne Weston, nee Taylor, Emma's former governess, a sensible woman whom Emma regards highly.

Frank Churchill, Mr. Weston's son by a former marriage. He has been adopted by and taken the name of his mother's family. His charm attracts Emma briefly, but she is not seriously interested. He is secretly engaged to Jane Fairfax.

Jane Fairfax, a beautiful and accomplished orphan who visits her family in Highbury. Emma admires but cannot like her, finding her too reserved. The mystery of her personality is solved when it is learned that she is engaged to Churchill.

Mrs. Bates and
Miss Bates, grandmother and aunt of Jane Fairfax. Poor but worthy women, they are intolerably loquacious and boring.

Harriet Smith, the illegitimate daughter of a tradesman. Young, pretty, and impressionable, she is taken up by Emma Woodhouse, rather to her disadvantage, for Emma gives her ideas above her station. She is persuaded to refuse the proposal of Robert Martin and to believe that Mr. Elton, the vicar, is in love with her. When Elton proves to be interested in Emma, Harriet is deeply chagrined. After considering the possibility of Harriet as a match for Churchill, Emma finds to her dismay that Harriet is thinking of Knightley. This discovery makes Emma realize how much she has always loved him. After Emma and Knightley are engaged, Harriet is again proposed to by Robert Martin; she happily marries him.

Robert Martin, the honest young farmer who marries Harriet Smith.

The Rev. Philip Elton, vicar of the parish. A conceited, silly man, he proposes to Emma Woodhouse, who has thought him in love with Harriet Smith. Emma's refusal makes him her enemy.

Augusta Elton, nee Hawkins, the woman Elton marries after being refused by Emma. She is vulgar, pretentious, and officious.

THE EMPEROR JONES

Author: Eugene O'Neill (1888-1953)
Time of action: Early twentieth century
First presented: 1920

PRINCIPAL CHARACTERS

Brutus Jones, an American Negro who has gained control of a group of superstitious natives on a West Indian island. He flees for his life when he discovers that the natives have finally rebelled against his cruel regime. He runs in circles in the jungle all night. As he runs, he encounters apparitions that reveal his story and the history of his race. Jeff, a Pullman porter whom Jones thought he had killed with a razor, is the first wraith. A chain gang, followed by a slave auction, then by the hold of a slave ship, and then by an altar-like arrangement of boulders at which Jones is selected to be a human sacrifice, form the subjects that complete the series of ghostly scenes. The natives finally shoot Jones with a silver bullet, the only missile they believe capable of killing him, but the audience understands that Jones actually dies of fear.

Lem, the leader of the rebel force that hunts down Jones.

Henry Smithers, a cockney trader who first suspects that the natives are rebelling. Though he is contemptuous of Jones, he warns him of the danger he faces.

ENDYMION

Author: John Lyly (c. 1554-1606)
Time of action: Remote antiquity
First presented: 1588

PRINCIPAL CHARACTERS

Endymion (ĕn·dĭm'ĭ·ən), who is hopelessly in love with the goddess Cynthia.

To keep his true love secret, he pretends to be in love with Tellus. Being put into

325

an enchanted sleep at the instigation of his jealous deceived sweetheart, he is awakened by Cynthia. He vows to spend his life in platonic devotion to her.

Cynthia (sĭn'thĭ·ə), the Goddess of the Moon. Chastely above mortal passion, she is moved to pity by Endymion's enchanted sleep, awakens him, and accepts his platonic worship. She has been interpreted as an idealized portrait of Queen Elizabeth I.

Tellus (tĕ'lŭs), the Goddess of the Earth. Loving Endymion, she is angered at what she considers his treachery to her. Imprisoned by Cynthia, she learns to love her jailer, Corsites, and releases Endymion to his moon-worship. She has been interpreted as a portrait of Mary, Queen of Scots.

Eumenides (ū·mĕ'nĭ·dēz), Endymion's faithful friend and confidant. He is able to learn the secret of Endymion's enchantment because he is a faithful lover. Unselfishly he asks for the secret to save his friend instead of for his own success in love.

Semele (sĕ'mə·lē'), a witty, sharp-tongued girl, delighted with flouting her lover, Eumenides. She is finally moved by Cynthia's request and Eumenides' faithfulness to accept him.

Corsites (kôr·sī'tēz), Tellus' jailer, in love with his prisoner.

Sir Thopas (tō'pəs), a fantastical braggart of the literary family which contains Falstaff among many others. Scornful of love and bloodthirsty in language only, he strangely falls in love with Dipsas, the hideous, elderly enchantress. Disappointed in his expectations there, he accepts Bagoa.

Dares (dă·rēz),
Samias (să'mĭ·əs), and
Epiton (ĕ'pĭ·tŏn), witty and mischievous pages who delight in making sport of Sir Thopas.

Dipsas (dĭp'səs), a malicious old enchantress, the estranged wife of Geron. She aids Tellus by casting Endymion into an enchanted sleep for forty years. Cynthia's benign influence reforms her and restores her to her husband.

Bagoa (bə·gō'ə), Dipsas' assistant. She pities Endymion and confesses her part in the spell. When she is turned into a tree by Dipsas, Cynthia restores her.

Geron (jĕ'rŏn), Dipsas' aged husband, who helps Eumenides find out that the cure for the spell on Endymion is a kiss from Cynthia.

Floscula (flŏs'kə·lə), Tellus' friend, who warns her against love inspired by witchcraft.

AN ENEMY OF THE PEOPLE

Author: Henrik Ibsen (1828-1906)
Time of action: Late nineteenth century
First presented: 1883

PRINCIPAL CHARACTERS

Dr. Thomas Stockmann, the medical officer of the Municipal Baths, a conscientious man of science and the enemy of illness and deceit. Because Stockmann discovers that the healing waters, the principal source of income for the town, are polluted, causing typhoid fever and gastric illnesses to the users, he incurs the censure of the town and is proclaimed an "Enemy of the People." Stockmann is the one honest man in public life in the town. When he realizes that all his associates would prefer concealing the fact that the baths are polluted, he is at first amazed and then infuriated. Denied all means of spreading his information through the press or in public meeting, he at last calls a meeting in the home of a ship captain, Captain Horster. Before Stockmann can speak, however, the group elects a chairman, Aslaksen, who permits Stockmann's brother, Peter, mayor of the town, to make a motion forbidding the doctor to speak on the matter of the baths because unreliable and exaggerated reports might go abroad. Aslaksen seconds the motion. Stockmann then speaks on the moral corruption of the town and manages to offend everyone, including his wife's adoptive father, Morten Kiil, a tanner whose works are one of the worst sources of water pollution. Morten Kiil buys up the bath stock the next day and proposes that the doctor call off the drive because he has bought it with money which Kiil had planned to leave Mrs. Stockmann and the children. Stockmann rejects the suggestion. He thinks of leaving the town and going to America; but when Captain Horster is discharged for permitting Stockmann to speak in his house, he cannot sail on Horster's ship and he decides to remain in the town, educate the street urchins, and bring up his own sons to be honest men. He says that only the middle class opposes him and that the poor people will continue to call on him. In his decision, he is cheered by his young schoolteacher daughter, Petra, and by Mrs. Stockmann and one of the boys. Although Stockmann is not an especially personable character, he is an excellent representation of the frustrations which confront the reformer.

Peter Stockmann, the mayor of the town and brother of Dr. Stockmann. Peter Stockmann is a typical, willfully blind public official who would rather poison the visitors of his town than cut its income. Under the pretense of concern for the town he is able to win others to his side. He ruins his brother, but suggests that he will reinstate him if he recants.

Hovstad, the editor of the "People's Messenger." At first Hovstad supports Dr. Stockmann and plans to print his article about the baths. However, when he learns that public opinion is against Stockmann, he deserts him until he hears that Morten Kiil has bought up the bath stock. Then he offers to support Stockmann again because he thinks that Stockmann will cash in on the baths and he wants to be in on the deal. Because Hovstad starts off as a forthright newspaper man, he is a disappointment when he abruptly changes character and sides.

Aslaksen, a printer. Aslaksen starts out as a volunteer supporter of Stockmann's proposal to clean up the baths. As chairman of the Householder's Association, he promises the support of the majority in the town, but as soon as matters become difficult, and when Dr. Stockmann grows more emotional than Aslaksen thinks is in keeping with his idea of moderation, he turns against the doctor. He comes with Hovstad to try to cash in on the profits which they think Stockmann expects to make with Morten Kiil.

Petra, the daughter of Dr. and Mrs. Stockmann. An earnest young woman, a teacher, Petra is the first to discover Hovstad's insincerity. Petra refused to translate an English story for Hovstad to print because its theme is that a supernatural power looks after the so-called good people in the world and that everything happens for the best, while all the evil are punished; she has no such belief. When Hovstad tells her that he is giving his readers exactly the kind of story they want, Petra is distressed. When he blurts out a few minutes later that the reason he is supporting Dr. Stockmann is that he is Petra's father, Petra tells him that he has betrayed himself, that she will never trust him again. Because she supports her father, she loses her job. Her employer tells her that a former guest in the Stockmann home has revealed Petra's emancipated views. Petra is her father's true child.

Mrs. Stockmann, the doctor's wife and his loyal supporter. At first she does not want her husband to go against the wishes of his brother, but she soon gives her full approval. She is not presented as a woman of strong personality.

Morten Kiil, a tanner, Mrs. Stockmann's adoptive father. Although described by other characters as an "old badger," a man of wealth whose influence and money Dr. Stockmann hates to lose because of his wife and children, Morten Kiil seems to live more by reputation than by representation in the play. He goes against Dr. Stockmann and buys up all the bath stock with money he had intended leaving to Mrs. Stockmann.

Captain Horster, a ship's captain who befriends Dr. Stockmann, the only person outside the Stockmann family who remains loyal to the doctor. He allows Stockmann to attempt his public speech about the baths to an audience assembled in his house.

Ejlif and
Morten, the two young sons of the Stockmanns.

Billing, a sub-editor. He agrees with Aslaksen and Hovstad.

ENOCH ARDEN

Author: Alfred, Lord Tennyson (1809-1892)
Time of action: Late eighteenth century
First published: 1864

PRINCIPAL CHARACTERS

Enoch Arden, a fisherman. He marries his childhood playmate Annie and has seven happy years of marriage with her. Then he is injured and their prosperity vanishes in his months of recuperation. He sells his fishing boat to set Annie up as a trader to support their three children in his absence, and sails on a merchantman. Shipwrecked on a desert island, he worries constantly about his family. Years later he gets back to England. There, learning that Annie is happily married and again the mother of a new baby, he does not reveal his identity until he is on his deathbed.

Annie Lee, his wife. A poor businesswoman and burdened by grief, her difficulties continue until, more than ten years after Enoch's disappearance, another former childhood playmate asks her to marry him. She insists that they wait another year and a half, and even then she is not thoroughly happy and at peace until her child is born.

Philip Ray, Enoch's friend and himself secretly in love with Annie since childhood. Only well after Enoch's presumed death does he disclose his love. A miller's son, he is well-to-do.

Miriam Lane, a widowed tavernkeeper. Enoch takes lodgings with her on his return. It is she who tells him of Annie and Philip, and to whom he relates his story on his deathbed.

THE ENORMOUS ROOM

Author: E. E. Cummings (1894-1962)
Time of action: 1917
First published: 1922

E. E. Cummings, an American ambulance driver. Arrested on suspicion because of his close friendship with W. S. B. but never charged with any specific offense, he is imprisoned at La Ferté for three months. Naturally observant and interested in people, he sees in his fellow prisoners varied traits ranging from humanity's best to its most animalistic and depraved. Gifted with a satiric sense of humor, he endures the imprisonment without going insane, as do many of the unfortunates.

W. S. B. (B.), his American friend. He is arrested by French military police because he wrote some letters suspected by the censor. He is transferred from La Ferté to another prison before Cummings is released. W. S. B. is actually William Slater Brown.

Apollyon, head of the French prison, a gross, fiendish man who reminds Cummings of Ichabod Crane and who questions him about why he is in prison, though Cummings himself does not know. Apollyon is despised by the prisoners.

Rockyfeller, a livid, unpleasant-looking, impeccably dressed Rumanian who causes an uproar the night he arrives at La Ferté.

The Fighting Sheeney, Rockyfeller's revolting bully-boy, a former pimp.

Joseph Demestre (The Wanderer), a strong man of simple emotions whose wife (or possibly mistress) and three small children are in the women's ward of the prison. Toward his six-year-old son who sleeps with him he shows deep love and understanding. Until sent away he is Cummings's best friend.

Zoo-Loo, a Polish farmer who, ignorant of French and English, communicates by signs. He is a wizard at hiding money from the guards and he is kind to Cummings and B.

Surplice, a friendly, inquisitive little man who finds everything astonishing and whose talk makes even small things seem important and interesting.

Jean le Nègre, a gigantic, simple-minded Negro given to practical jokes and tall tales. Arrested for impersonating an English officer, he becomes a favorite with the women prisoners. After a fight over Lulu's handkerchief and the resultant punishment, Jean becomes quiet and shy. When B. is sent away, Jean attempts, with scant success, to cheer Cummings with funny stories and whopping lies.

Count F. A. de Bragard, a Belgian painter of horses, a neat, suave gentleman with whom Cummings discusses painting and the arts. Before Cummings leaves, the Count has withdrawn from the other prisoners, his mind finally breaking under the strain of the sordid prison life.

Lulu, Jean's favorite among the women prisoners; she sends him money and a lace handkerchief.

Judas, a corpulent, blond, large-headed, mop-haired, weak-chinned prisoner who nauseates Cummings.

M. le Gestionnaire, a very fat, stupid man with an enormous nose and a Germanic or Dutch face; he reminds Cummings of a hippopotamus.

THE EPIC OF GILGAMESH

Author: Unknown
Time of action: Remote antiquity
First transcribed: c. 2000 B.C.

Gilgamesh, King of Uruk, a demigod. He is the wisest, strongest, and handsomest of mortals. In earth-shaking combat he overcomes Engidu, who has been fashioned by Aruru to be his rival. After the battle the heroes become inseparable friends and companions through a series of heroic exploits. When Engidu dies, the grieving Gilgamesh seeks for and finds his friend in the land of the dead.

Engidu, a demigod formed by Aruru to be a rival to Gilgamesh. Vanquished by Gilgamesh, he becomes the hero's inseparable companion and goes with him to conquer Khumbaba. Accidentally touching the portal of the gate to Khumbaba's lair, he receives a curse from which he eventually dies. Allowed to meet the grief-stricken Gilgamesh in the underworld, he reveals to his friend the terrors of death.

Utnapishtim, a mortal possessing the secret of life. After Engidu's death Gilgamesh receives from Utnapishtim the secret—a magic plant—only to lose it on his homeward journey.

Aruru, a goddess who fashions Engidu from clay.

Anu, chief of the gods.

Ninsun, a goddess and adviser to Gilgamesh.

Ishtar, a fertility goddess in love with Gilgamesh.

Siduri, the divine cupbearer.

Ur-Shanabi, the boatman on the waters of death.

Ea, lord of the depths of the waters, who grants to Gilgamesh a meeting with the dead Engidu.

Khumbaba, a fearful monster.

EPITAPH OF A SMALL WINNER

Author: Joaquim Maria Machado de Assis (1839-1908)
Time of action: 1805-1869
First published: 1880

PRINCIPAL CHARACTERS

Braz Cubas, a wealthy Brazilian who writes his autobiography after his death at sixty-five, in order to while away a part of eternity. He has had several mistresses but no wife, since his fiancée died in an epidemic. He decides that in the game of life he has been a small winner, for he has brought no one into this world of misery.

Marcella, a courtesan and Braz's first mistress. She will not accompany him to Spain for study. Before his return, she is disfigured by smallpox.

Virgilia, a lame heiress chosen by Papa Cubas as Braz's wife. She prefers Neves, though later becoming Braz's mistress. Their child dies at birth.

Lobo Neves, Virgilia's ambitious husband, who is blind to the infidelity of his wife.

Doña Placida, Virgilia's servant, at whose house Virgilia and Braz have their meetings.

Quincas Borba, Braz's down-at-the-heels schoolmate, who is reduced to begging and thievery. With improved economic status, he becomes a philosopher.

EREC AND ENIDE

Author: Chrétien de Troyes (c. 1140-c. 1190)
Time of action: Sixth century
First transcribed: Before 1164

Erec, a fair and brave knight of the Round Table. In a town where he is lodging, he meets his host's daughter, the beautiful damsel Enide. He returns with her to King Arthur's court and makes her his bride. So enamored is he of the fair lady that he neglects all knightly pursuits in favor of dalliance with her. When the report reaches him that the people think him a coward, he sets out with Enide on a journey of knight-errantry during which he bears himself with such bravery that he returns to King Arthur's court with honor, and, on his father's death, becomes king of his own land.

Enide, the most beautiful damsel in Christendom, Erec's bride. After she hears reports that Erec's dalliance with her has caused him to be suspected of cowardice, she taunts him about the change that love has made in him. When he angrily sets forth on a journey to prove his valor and her love, she accompanies him, bravely shares his adventures, and returns triumphant with him to King Arthur's court.

Guivret the Little, a knight who challenges Erec to combat and, after a brave fight on both sides, becomes his friend and benefactor.

Count Galoin, a nobleman so smitten by Enide's beauty that he desires to make her mistress of all his lands. His plot to take Erec's life is thwarted by Enide, for which the defeated Count gallantly praises the lady's prudence and virtue.

Evrain, a King whose land is delivered from thralldom by Erec.

King Arthur, of the Round Table.

Guinevere, his Queen.

King Lac, Erec's father.

Sir Gawain and
Sir Kay, knights of the Round Table.

Yder, a haughty knight challenged and defeated by Erec.

Cadoc of Tabriol, a knight rescued from giants by Erec.

EREWHON

Author: Samuel Butler (1835-1902)
Time of action: The 1870's
First published: 1872

Strong, a blond young sheep farm worker who journeys into Erewhon; he discovers there a civilization partly the reverse of and partly similar to that of England. Somewhat like Swift's Gulliver, Strong seems a thoughtful, observant, inquiring, and sometimes rather naïve traveler. He

should not be identified with the author, since Butler used him only as a convenient mouthpiece to convey the satire in the novel.

Kahabuka (Chowbok), an old native, a sort of chief with a little knowledge of

English and a great thirst for grog, with which Strong bribes him for information about the land beyond the mountains. In England, upon his return, Strong finds Chowbok posing as a missionary, the Reverend William Habakkuk.

Senoj Nosnibor (anagram for Jones Robinson), a citizen and leading merchant of Erewhon recovering, as if from sickness, from a serious case of embezzlement. He is assigned to instruct Strong in Erewhonian customs.

Arowhena, his beautiful younger daughter, with whom Strong falls in love. She helps him to escape from Erewhon, after which they marry and she is baptized into the Anglican Church, though she retains some of her former beliefs in Erewhonian deities who personify hope, fear, love, and the like.

Ydgrun (anagram of Grundy), Erewhon's main goddess, both an abstract concept and a silly, cruel woman. A law of Ydgrun enforces conformity to the point of intolerability. Her devotees, including priests, worship her in heart and deed rather than in words.

Zulora, the handsome older daughter of Nosnibor. She wishes to marry Strong, who develops a dislike for her.

Yram (anagram for Mary), the jailor's pretty daughter, who is attracted to Strong. She teaches him the Erewhonian language and explains to him some of the customs of the land.

The Straighteners, specialists who treat Erewhonians suffering from ailments such as petty theft and embezzlement. They resemble twentieth century psychiatrists.

Mahaina, a homely woman, reputedly a drunkard, whose supposed drinking may perhaps be what would today be called a compensation for an inferiority complex.

Thims (anagram for Smith), a cashier at a musical bank; a friend of Strong.

Giovanni Gianni, captain of the ship which rescues Strong and Arowhena.

ESTHER WATERS

Author: George Moore (1852-1933)
Time of action: Late nineteenth century
First published: 1894

PRINCIPAL CHARACTERS

Esther Waters, an uneducated servant girl, sturdily built but graceful; rather sullen-looking except when she smiles. As she grows older she becomes stout but retains a natural dignity despite her unhappy life. Her devoutness, though it causes mockery among the Barfield servants, brings her comfort. Pregnant and disgraced, Esther loses her job and is later left alone when her mother dies and her stepfather moves to Australia. She experiences hard times until Miss Rice employs her before her marriage to the reckless William Latch. Her love for and pride in Jackie provide some joy in an otherwise sad life.

William Latch, son of the cook at Woodview. He is strong but shallow-chested. His forehead is low and narrow, his nose long, chin pointed, cheeks hollow and bloodless, and eyes lusterless. He is an inveterate gambler. Taking advantage of Esther's innocence, he seduces her by promising to marry her. Annoyed by Esther's sulking, he elopes with Peggy, who later leaves him. Chancing upon Esther several years later, he persuades her to marry him instead of Fred. Though he prospers for a while, gambling ruins him and tuberculosis finally kills him.

Mrs. Barfield, Esther's mistress at Woodview, a deeply religious woman who is Esther's friend as well as her employer. Though she dismisses Esther after her pregnancy is discovered, it is to Mrs. Barfield that Esther returns after William's death, and she proudly introduces Jackie to her before he leaves for army service.

Sarah Tucker, another servant at Woodview who is jealous of William's attentions to Esther.

Jackie, Esther's son whom she loves deeply and of whom she is very proud when he becomes a soldier.

Fred Parsons, Esther's betrothed, color-less but honest, dependable, and religious. Against her good judgment Esther turns from a planned marriage to Fred to the uncertainty of one to William because Jackie prefers him.

Miss Rice, a writer and a later employer of Esther who is sympathetic regarding her plight before her marriage to William.

Mrs. Latch, William's ill-tempered mother who makes working conditions unpleasant for Esther at Woodview.

Peggy Barfield, Mr. Barfield's cousin with whom William elopes.

Mr. Barfield, master of Woodview, formerly a famous steeplechase rider, now a portly and well-to-do owner of a stable of racehorses. When Esther returns to Woodview years later, Barfield has died after losing most of his money because of racing debts.

ETHAN FROME

Author: Edith Wharton (1862-1937)
Time of action: Late nineteenth century
First published: 1911

PRINCIPAL CHARACTERS

Ethan Frome, a farmer frustrated in his ambition to become an engineer or a chemist, and in his marriage to a nagging, sour, sickly wife. He falls in love with his wife's good and lovely cousin, Mattie Silver, who comes to live with them. When his wife finally drives the girl away, Ethan insists on taking her to the station. Ethan and Mattie decide to take a sleigh ride they have promised themselves and, in mutual despair over the impending separation, they resolve to kill themselves by running the sled against a tree. But they are not killed, only permanently injured, and Ethan's wife is to look after them for the rest of their lives.

Zenobia Pierce Frome (Zeena), Ethan's wife, a distant cousin who nursed his mother during a long illness. The marriage is loveless, and Zeena is sickly and nagging.

Mattie Silver, Zeena's cousin, who comes to live with the Fromes. She returns Ethan's love, and once when Zeena spends a night away from home, she and Ethan spend a happy evening together, not making love but sitting quietly before the fire, as Ethan imagines happily married couples do. Mattie feels that she would rather die than leave Ethan, but in the crash she suffers not death, but a permanent spine injury, and must submit thereafter to being nursed by Zeena.

Ruth Varnum and
Ned Hale, a young engaged couple

whom Ethan observes stealing a kiss, On his night alone with Mattie he tells her wistfully about it; it is as close as he comes to making advances.

EUGENE ARAM

Author: Edward George Earle Bulwer-Lytton (1803-1873)
Time of action: Mid-eighteenth century
First published: 1832

PRINCIPAL CHARACTERS

Eugene Aram, a character based on a real-life scholar and scientist. He is in love with Madeline Lester. In his confession, opened after his execution, he explains that he robbed for money to continue experiments of value to the world. He claimed that his killing of Geoffrey had been an accident.

Geoffrey Lester, a dissipated wanderer who abandons his family, later receives a legacy from a friend in India, and becomes Mr. Clark. His disappearance starts a search. When his grave is discovered, Aram is revealed as his murderer.

Rowland Lester, an English gentleman who adopts his brother's forsaken family.

Madeline Lester, the daughter of Rowland. Because of her love for Aram, she dies of grief when his crime is discovered.

Ellinor Lester, another daughter of Rowland. She is in love with her cousin, Walter.

Walter Lester, the son of Geoffrey, who tracks down his father's murderer. Though originally in love with Madeline, he marries Ellinor.

Houseman, a rogue and the accomplice of Aram. He blackmails Aram for the support of his daughter, whose eventual death nearly drives him mad.

Bunting, Walter's servant, who helps in the search for Geoffrey.

EUGENE ONEGIN

Author: Alexander Pushkin (1799-1837)
Time of action: Early nineteenth century
First published: 1833

PRINCIPAL CHARACTERS

Tatyana Larin (tä·tyä′nə lä′rĭn), also called **Tanya Larina** (tän′yä lä′rĭn·ə), the reserved and withdrawn older daughter of the well-to-do, upper middle class Larin family, of whose marriage her parents despair. But she falls in love at first sight with Eugene Onegin and, unable to write grammatical Russian, sends him a passionate letter written in French. Although he fails to encourage her, she turns down several other proposals of

marriage. When her family takes her to Moscow, she picks up beauty hints at a ball and attracts the attentions of a retired general who persuades her to marry him. Years later she again sees Onegin, who falls in love with her and writes her passionate letters. She reads them and preserves them to read again, but she gives him no encouragement and remains faithful to her general to the end of her life.

334

Eugene Onegin (ĕu·gĕ'nĭy ô·nĕ'gĭn), the hero of this narrative poem, with many resemblances to its author. Brought up in the aristocratic tradition, he is a brilliant, witty man of the world. Successful in many light love affairs, he is bored with living. City life, with its opera and ballet, has lost its appeal. A stay on the country estate willed to him by his uncle wearies him after several days. He is finally persuaded by his friend, Vladimir Lensky, to accompany him on a visit to the Larin family. There he finds the conversation dull, the refreshment too simple and too abundant, and Tatyana unattractive. Visiting her later, after receiving her passionate love letter, he tells her frankly that he would make her a very poor husband because he has had too many disillusioning experiences with women. He returns to the lonely estate and the life of an anchorite. When Vladimir takes him under false pretenses to Tatyana's birthday party, he gets revenge by flirting with her sister Olga, engaged to Vladimir. His jealous friend challenges him to a duel. Onegin shoots Vladimir through the heart.

Olga Larin (ōly'gə lä'rĭn), also called **Olenka** (ô·lĕn'kə), the pretty and popular younger daughter of the Larin family, betrothed to Vladimir Lensky. At a ball she dances so often with Onegin that her

fiancé gets angry. Though she assures him that she means nothing by her innocent flirtation, he challenges Onegin to a duel and is killed. Later she marries an army officer.

Vladimir Lensky (vlä·dĭ'mĭr lĕn'skĭy), a German-Russian friend of Onegin, brought up in Germany and influenced by romantic illusions of life and love. Although his reading of Schiller and Kant sets him apart from most other young Russians, he and Onegin have much in common. He tries to get his friend interested in Tatyana Larin, even to inviting him to her big birthday party, which he describes as an intimate family affair. In resentment Onegin avoids Tatyana and devotes himself to Olga. After the challenge is given, he is too proud to acknowledge his misjudgment and is killed.

M. Guillot (gĭl·yō'), Onegin's second in the duel.

Zaretsky (zä·rĕt'skĭy), Lensky's second.

The Prince (called **Gremin** in the operatic version), a fat, retired general and Onegin's friend. Seeing Tatyana at a ball in Moscow, he falls in love with her and proposes. She accepts. Later he invites Onegin to his house, and Onegin meets Tatyana again.

EUGÉNIE GRANDET

Author: Honoré de Balzac (1799-1850)
Time of action: Early nineteenth century
First published: 1833

PRINCIPAL CHARACTERS

Eugénie Grandet (œ·zhā·nē' grän·dā'), the young heiress to a fortune, who lives in the world but is not of it. Reared without a childhood in the penurious surroundings of Saumur, a provincial French town, Eugénie for a brief period lives in the love of her cousin, newly orphaned and a guest in the Grandet

home. Strong of character and handsome in appearance, she pledges herself to young Charles Grandet and remains true to him throughout her life. As an obedient daughter of parents and Church, she tries to live righteously but defies her father in the matter of love. Her kind ministrations to both her dying parents, her lifelong devotion to her one loyal friend, and her constancy of memory make her one of the most steadfast and pitiable of heroines. Her good deeds and her loving devotion to the poor whom she serves give her life tragic beauty.

Monsieur Grandet (mǝ·syœ′ grän·dä′), her father, one of the most miserly figures in all literature. The author of the family tragedy, Goodman Grandet, as Balzac satirically calls him, is unyielding in his niggardliness without seeming to realize his great fault. He appears to be trying to clear his brother's good name by not allowing him to fall into bankruptcy, but in reality he profits from the delaying action. His towering angers at the least "extravagance" finally put his devoted wife on her deathbed, and his unrelenting love of gold destroys the loving confidence of his daughter. Shrewd and grasping in his business deals, he has no redeeming features. Ironically enough, his fortune is finally put to good purposes through his daughter, who makes restitution for his wrongs.

Madame Grandet, his long-suffering wife, whose piety is taxed by the burden of her husband's stinginess. Accustomed to her hard lot and strengthened by her religion, Madame Grandet bows under her heavy yoke of work and harsh treatment until she takes up the cause of her daughter's right to love and devotes herself to the memory of that love. Still she prays for reconciliation, and when it comes she dies happy, without knowing her dowry is the reason for the deathbed forgiveness.

Charles Grandet (shärl), the dandified cousin of the heroine, who loses his for-tune through his father's suicide but who regains a fortune through unscrupulous dealings financed, ironically, by Eugénie's gift of money to him. Heroic only in his unselfish grief for his father and generous only once in bestowing his love, Charles reveals a twisted mind tutored by a corrupt society. Outwardly prepossessing, inwardly vacillating, he chooses to disregard the one fine thing that was given him, a dowry of unselfish love, and bases his life on treachery, lechery, and adultery.

Nanon (nà·nōṅ′), the faithful servant who loyally defends the indefensible in her master because it was he who raised her a full step in the social order. Large and mannish, Nanon manages the entire Grandet household with such efficiency as to cause admiration from the master, himself efficient and desperately saving. Her devotion to him, however, does not preclude rushing to the defense of his wife and daughter, the victims of his spite. Finally she marries the gamekeeper and together they rule the Grandet holdings for their mistress Eugénie.

Monsieur Cruchot (mǝ·syœ′ krü·shō′), a notary and petty government official who becomes husband in name only to Eugénie. He feels that by marrying the name and inheriting the fortune his own name will become illustrious. His untimely death ends the reign of self-seeking misers.

Monsieur de Grassins (mǝ·syœ′ dǝ grà·săṅ′), the provincial banker sent to Paris to act for M. Grandet at the time of his brother's bankruptcy. Attracted to the gay life in the capital, he fails to return to Saumur.

THE EUNUCH

Author: Terence (Publius Terentius Afer, c. 190-159 B.C.)
Time of action: Fourth century B.C.
First presented: 161 B.C.

Thaïs (thā'ĭs), a Rhodian courtesan living in Athens. She is wooed by Phaedria, whom she loves, and by Thraso, a braggart captain. Thaïs encourages Thraso's love because she wishes him to make her a present of a young slave girl. This girl, Pamphila, had been reared as Thaïs' sister. In fact, she is an Athenian citizen. Thaïs wants to restore the girl to Chremes, her brother. After Thraso gives her Pamphila, Thaïs goes to Thraso's house. She quarrels with him and returns home to find that Pamphila has been ravished by Chaerea, who entered Thaïs' house disguised as a eunuch. Pamphila is restored to Chremes and promised in marriage to Chaerea, who loves her. Thaïs reaffirms her love for Phaedria.

Phaedria (fēd'rĭ·ə), the son of Laches, who loves Thaïs. Hurt because Thaïs excludes him from her house while admitting Thraso, Phaedria listens to her explanation and agrees to leave Athens for two days until Thraso has given Pamphila to the courtesan. Unable to stay away so long, Phaedria returns to find that his brother Chaerea has disgraced him by attacking Pamphila.

Thraso (thrā'sō), a rich, pompous, and conceited soldier, a foreigner who had formerly been in the service of an Asiatic king. He is used by both Thaïs and his parasite Gnatho for their own ends. When, after being deserted by Thaïs, he asks that Pamphila be returned to him, his demand is refused. When he brings a gang of thugs to storm Thaïs' house and recover Pamphila, he is thwarted by the revelation that Pamphila is an Athenian citizen and, therefore, cannot be held as a slave.

Chaerea (kē'rē·ə), Phaedria's younger brother, sixteen years old. Seeing Pamphila on the street as she is being taken to Thaïs' house, he falls in love with her. With the aid of Parmeno, he impetuously enters Thaïs' house in the garb of a eunuch and ravishes Pamphila. When Pamphila's identity is revealed, Chaerea receives his father's permission to marry her.

Parmeno (pär'mĕ·nō), Phaedria's outspoken and intelligent servant. Having been sent by Phaedria to deliver to Thaïs a eunuch and an Ethiopian girl, Parmeno meets Chaerea. He sympathizes with Chaerea's infatuation with Pamphila and agrees to introduce him into Thaïs' house disguised as the eunuch.

Gnatho (nă'thō), Thraso's parasite. Gnatho is a scheming cynic who detests his patron. At the end, with a view to his continuing prosperity, Gnatho asks Thaïs and Phaedria not to have Thraso banished for his effrontery in besieging Thaïs' house. He persuades them to allow Thraso to continue to pay court to Thaïs, for Thraso's money can supply luxuries that Phaedria could not otherwise afford.

Chremes (krā'mēz), a young Athenian, the brother of Pamphila.

Dorus (dō'rŭs), an old eunuch. Phaedria had bought Dorus to present to Thaïs. Chaerea enters Thaïs' house in Dorus' clothes.

Laches (lă'kēz), an old Athenian, the father of Phaedria and Chaerea. When Laches learns that Pamphila is an Athenian citizen, he approves his son's marriage to her because he is glad to save the family from disgrace.

Antipho (ăn'tĭ·fō), the young man to whom Chaerea relates what he had done in Thaïs' house.

Pamphila (păm'fĭl·ə), a sixteen-year-old girl. The sister of Chremes, Pamphila had been kidnaped while a child and sold into slavery in Rhodes. She had been reared there as Thaïs' sister.

Sophrona (sŏ·frō·nə), an old nurse in Thaïs' household.

337

Pythias (pǐ'thǐ·əs) and Dorias (dō'rǐ·əs), Thaïs' female attendants.

Sanga (săn'gə), Thraso's cook.

Donax (dō'năks), Simalio (sǐ·mă'lǐ·ō), and Syriscus (sǐ·rǐs'kəs), servants of Thraso. Thraso brings them with him to storm Thaïs' house.

EUPHUES AND HIS ENGLAND

Author: John Lyly (c. 1554-1606)
Time of action: 1579-1580
First published: 1580

PRINCIPAL CHARACTERS

Euphues (ū'fū·ēz), the hero of "Euphues, the Anatomy of Wit," grown older and wiser, who travels to observe customs in England.

Philautus (fǐ·lô'təs), his friend. He suffers torments for the love of Camilla, but he soon turns to Frances, who is readier to return his affection.

Camilla (kă·mǐ'lə), a gay, modest Englishwoman. She answers Philautus' amorous epistles with elegant, firm refusals and devotes her own energies to secret adoration of Surius.

Lady Flavia (flā'vǐ·ə), her friend, a gracious woman who uses her greater maturity to put her young guests at ease. It is at her suggestion that the witty young people debate the nature of love, in the manner of the noble ladies and gentlemen in Castiglione's "The Courtier."

Frances (frăn·sĕs), her niece, Philautus' "violet," whose gaiety and quick wit console him for Camilla's hard-heartedness.

Surius (sū'rǐ·əs), an exemplary young Englishman, brave, eloquent, and witty, whose gifts make him the object of Camilla's love.

Fidus (fē'dəs), a wise innkeeper who welcomes Euphues and Philautus in Canterbury, apologizing profusely for the poverty of his house and bristling when they presume to praise his queen. He lectures them on the nature of government, drawing examples from his bee hives, then describes his experiences as courtier to Henry VIII.

EUPHUES, THE ANATOMY OF WIT

Author: John Lyly (c. 1554-1606)
Time of action: Sixteenth century
First published: 1579

PRINCIPAL CHARACTERS

Euphues (ū'fū·ēz), a witty, well-born young man. He disregards Eubulus' good advice about the traps which lie in the path of an indiscreet youth, and finds himself betraying his friend Philautus for the favors of a fickle young woman. He recognizes the value of the wisdom of age when she casts him off for another gallant.

Philautus (fǐ·lô'təs), his friend, a clever, courteous young gentleman. He trusts Euphues at first and is furious to learn that his "friend" has stolen the affections of his bride-to-be.

Lucilla (loo·sǐ'lə), a bright, attractive girl whose interest shifts quickly from one young man to another. She debates

338

her motives before she turns from Philautus to Euphues, but she forsakes the latter with no qualms.

Don Ferardo (fĕ·rär'dō), her father, a wealthy nobleman of Naples. He tries to deal wisely with his willful child, but he is so heartbroken by her fickleness that he dies, leaving his estate to be squandered by Lucilla and the foolish Curio.

Curio (kū'rĭ·ō), a Neapolitan gentleman "of little wealth and less wit," who draws Lucilla's attentions from Euphues to himself.

Eubulus (ū'bə·ləs), a wise old man. He laments the waste of Euphues' natural gifts and advises him to govern his wit with wisdom.

Livia (lĭ'vĭ·ə), Lucilla's companion, a young woman of more character and virtue than her friend.

EVAN HARRINGTON

Author: George Meredith (1828-1909)
Time of action: Nineteenth century
First published: 1861

PRINCIPAL CHARACTERS

Evan Harrington, the son of a tailor, who proves his character in upper-class society. He is a young man who accepts the responsibility of doing good for those he loves, though the gesture on occasion works against his own interest. Apprenticed to Mr. Goren, a tailor, Evan Harrington eventually marries a woman of the upper class and manages to provide abundantly for her.

Rose Jocelyn, the heiress who finally becomes Harrington's wife. She is genuinely kind and fair; but she is set against Harrington on one occasion when he lies to her for her own good. When Harrington can tell her the truth, all things between them are put right again.

Ferdinand Laxley, a young man of the upper class who dislikes Harrington for two reasons: he is the son of a common tradesman, and he loves Rose, the girl Laxley is trying to win. Laxley is pugnacious; persistently he challenges Harrington to a duel. In the end he is, ironically, disgraced for revealing a secret of which he has no knowledge.

Louisa, the Countess de Saldar, Harrington's sister, who has married a titled man. She works energetically to find a good marriage for her brother. It is she who brings about Laxley's downfall by writing an anonymous letter she knows will be attributed to Laxley.

Juliana Bonner, Rose's plain, crippled cousin, who loves and defends Harrington until her death. She leaves him Beckley Court, the Jocelyn estate; but he refuses the bequest and returns Beckley Court to Lady Jocelyn, Rose's mother.

Harriet Cogglesby, Harrington's sister, who is married to Andrew Cogglesby, a brewer whose fortunes are up and down.

Caroline Strike, another of Harrington's sisters; she is married to Major Strike. Harriet and Caroline play less important roles in the novel than does Louisa, the third sister.

Jack Raikes, Harrington's old school friend.

Tom Cogglesby, Andrew's brother.

Harry Jocelyn, Rose's brother.

George Uploft, a man who, allegedly, ran away sometime before with Louisa. Harrington's father, Old Mel, supposedly

339

caught the pair and stopped the elopement.

Mrs. Melchisedek Harrington, the mother of Evan, Caroline, Louisa, and Harriet.

She ends her days as Tom Cogglesby's housekeeper.

Mr. Goren, a London tailor to whom Harrington is apprenticed.

EVANGELINE

Author: Henry Wadsworth Longfellow (1807-1882)
Time of action: Mid-eighteenth century
First published: 1847

PRINCIPAL CHARACTERS

Benedict Bellefontaine (bā·nä·dĕkt′ bĕl-fŏṅ·tĕn′), a farmer of Grand-Pré, in French Canada, who dies after the British fleet captures and burns his village.

Evangeline Bellefontaine (ā·vän·zhē·lēn′ bĕl·fŏṅ·tĕn′), his lovely daughter, betrothed to Gabriel Lajeunesse. After he is exiled by the British, she roams the United States from Louisiana to the Ozark Mountains and Michigan in search of him. Finally she becomes a Sister of Mercy in Philadelphia, and there she finds him dying. Soon afterward she dies and is buried beside him.

Gabriel Lajeunesse (gȧ·brē·ĕl′ lȧ·zhœ-nĕs′), Evangeline's sweetheart, deported from Acadia by the British. After years of hunting and trapping he ends up in Philadelphia. There he is struck down by yellow fever and dies in an almshouse where Evangeline at last finds him in time to comfort him in his dying moments.

Basil Lajeunesse (bȧ·zēl′ lȧ·zhœ·nĕs′), Gabriel's father, a blacksmith who becomes prosperous in his new home, but is unable to keep track of Gabriel.

Father Felician (fȧ·lē·syäṅ′), the priest at Grand-Pré who buries Benedict and comforts Evangeline.

Baptiste Leblanc (bȧ·tēst′ lə·bläṅ′), the son of a notary. Unable to persuade Evangeline to marry him, he loyally follows her in her search for Gabriel.

A Shawnee Indian Woman, who tells tribal legends to Evangeline.

Mowis, a legendary Indian bridegroom made of snow who is dissolved in the sunshine.

Lilinau, another legendary Indian, who follows her phantom sweetheart into the woods and disappears forever.

THE EVE OF ST. AGNES

Author: John Keats (1795-1821)
Time of action: The Middle Ages
First published: 1820

PRINCIPAL CHARACTERS

Madeline, a young virgin, first shown preoccupied at a ball given in the castle of her noble father. Eager to carry out the ritual of St. Agnes' Eve and thereby

see her future husband in a dream, she leaves the revelry and retires to her room where, falling asleep, she dreams of Porphyro, the son of an enemy house. Awak-

340

ing to find him beside her bed, she is at first frightened; but after he tells her, "This is no dream, my bride," she steals with him out of the castle, past the sleeping, drunken wassailers, and away into the stormy night.

Porphyro (pôr'fĭ·rō), her gallant young knight, who comes from his home across the moors, slips into the castle full of his enemies, and with the aid of Angela, an understanding old nurse, goes to Madeline's chamber before she prepares for bed. After she is asleep he emerges from the closet where he has hidden himself, sets a table loaded with exotic foods, and wakes his beloved with a song, "La belle dame sans mercy," to the accompaniment of Madeline's lute. He persuades his beloved to leave her home of hate and flee with him.

Angela, an old beldame, Madeline's nurse and Porphyro's friend. Convinced, after Porphyro has revealed his plan, that the young lover's intentions are honorable, she hides him in Madeline's bedchamber and provides the dainties for a feast. She dies "palsy-twitched."

The Beadsman, an aged supplicant who at the beginning of the poem is telling his rosary with cold-numbed fingers in the castle chapel. He closes the story by sleeping forever unsought for "among his ashes cold."

EVELINA

Author: Fanny Burney (Madame d'Arblay, 1752-1840)
Time of action: Eighteenth century
First published: 1778

PRINCIPAL CHARACTERS

Evelina Anville, a pretty, unaffected seventeen-year-old girl whose letters, principally to The Rev. Arthur Villars, her guardian, comprise the book. They tell of her party-going, her love affairs, and her many admirers in the London and Bristol social sets. Evelina's mother was Caroline Evelyn, who died shortly after Evelina's birth; her father, Sir John Belmont, a profligate young man, had deserted Caroline, his wife, when he was disappointed in the fortune he expected to receive from his marriage. After much maneuvering to avoid the advances of unwelcome suitors and upon being legally identified as Miss Belmont, Evelina finally marries Lord Orville.

The Rev. Arthur Villars, Evelina's devoted guardian since her mother's death. He guides and counsels her by letter, in answer to her voluminous messages to him at his Dorsetshire home. At first Mr. Villars advises Evelina against being taken in by Lord Orville, only to give his blessing when he learns of his charge's happiness.

Lord Orville, a young nobleman of good family. He is the quintessence of the well-bred young man and the ardent, jealous lover.

Sir Clement Willoughby, an obnoxious admirer of Evelina, always persisting in his effort to win her. He writes letters to Evelina and Lord Orville, signing their respective names, trying to alter their affections for each other.

Mme. Duval, Evelina's maternal grandmother. She instigates Evelina's visit to London, where she has come after twenty years of residence in Paris. Given to double superlative, she attributes her double negative and speech habits to the French influence. Blunt, indelicate, and severe, she is a vulgar old woman. Annoyed by Evelina's independence, she declares she will not leave Evelina an inheritance.

Macartney, a young, indolent poet whom Evelina meets early in her London visit. She befriends him, saving him from suicide on one occasion. Macartney is a source of jealousy on the part of Lord Orville. He learns that he is the illegitimate son of Sir John Belmont and marries Polly Green, the daughter of a designing nurse who substituted her own infant for Sir John's child.

Sir John Belmont, Evelina's father. He repents for his many years of unkindness to his legitimate daughter when he reads the deathbed letter written by Evelina's mother and delivered to him by Evelina. He bequeaths Evelina 30,000 pounds.

Captain Mirvan, a coarse practical joker. Surly and officious, he never smiles except at another's expense. He and Mme. Duval, in their grossness, turn many a genteel function into a brawl with their uncouthness and fighting.

Mrs. Mirvan, his wife. An amiable, well-bred woman, she introduces Evelina to many social affairs.

Maria, their daughter, Evelina's only close friend. They confide in each other, sharing happiness and heartaches.

Lady M. Howard, Mrs. Mirvan's mother and the mistress of Howard Grove, the scene of Evelina's first visit away from home. She intercedes for Mme. Duval with Mr. Villars so that Evelina may visit London.

M. Du Bois, Mme. Duval's friend from Paris. Insipid, he is the brunt of many of Captain Mirvan's practical jokes.

Polly Green, the supposed daughter of Sir John Belmont. Her mother, overhearing Rev. Mr. Villars' pledge that he would not part with the infant Evelina, delivered her own child to Sir John, as his daughter. Polly marries Macartney.

Mr. Branghton, Mme. Duval's nephew, the keeper of a shop and rooming house where Macartney lives. The Branghtons are a gauche, quarrelsome family, ignorant in entertaining.

Tom, his son, and admirer of Evelina.

Biddy and Polly, Branghton's daughters. Proud and conceited, they cause Evelina and Maria Mirvan many anxious, unpleasant moments.

Mrs. Selwyn, a wealthy neighbor of Mr. Villars. She takes Evelina on a visit to Bristol Hot Wells.

Mrs. Beaumont, the hostess of Clifton Hill, where Mrs. Selwyn and Evelina are entertained. Mrs. Beaumont would have Evelina believe that good qualities originate from pride rather than from principles.

Lady Louisa Larpent, Lord Orville's sister. Sullen and arrogant, she tries to divert her brother's attentions from Evelina. She attends the wedding willingly after Evelina's heritage has been established.

Lord Merton, a nobleman of recent title and Lady Louisa's fiancé. At Mrs. Beaumont's party Merton becomes drunk and offends Evelina with his attentions.

Mr. Lovel, a fop who demeans Evelina by constant references to her background. His reckless driving in his phaeton makes for much conversation at social functions.

Mr. Smith, a neighbor of Branghton. Verbose, he irks Evelina with his prolonged speeches on her beauty and his devotion to her.

Jack Coverley, a gay young man who adds humor to the long philosophical conversations engaged in by party guests. His droll wit is seldom aimed at others and is never malicious.

Mrs. Clinton, Mr. Villars' housekeeper. She attends Evelina on her first visit away from Berry Hill, Dorsetshire.

EVERY MAN IN HIS HUMOUR

Author: Ben Jonson (1573?-1637)
Time of action: Late sixteenth century
First presented: 1598; rewritten before 1616

PRINCIPAL CHARACTERS

Knowell, an old gentleman. A kind and
generous father, he is somewhat inclined
to formality and overstrictness in governing his son. After being tricked into a
ridiculous situation by Young Knowell,
Wellbred, and Brainworm, he good-
humoredly forgives them and confesses
that he has brought on his discomfiture
by his own meddlesomeness.

Edward Knowell, Old Knowell's son. A
bright young student, he troubles his
father by too much attention to poetry,
"that fruitless and unprofitable art."
With his friend Wellbred he finds enjoyment in the foibles of his associates.
He is much taken with Kitely's lovely
sister Bridget; and with Wellbred's and
Brainworm's help, he marries her.

Brainworm, Knowell's witty, mischievous servant. A literary descendant of the
witty slave of Roman comedy, he is the
prime mover of the dramatic action.
Having, as he says, "a nimble soul," he
appears in various disguises, aids his
young master, and befools his old one.
His wit arouses Justice Clement's admiration and earns his pardon.

Wellbred, Dame Kitely's younger
brother. A gay, somewhat impish young
bachelor, he writes to Edward Knowell
an uninhibited letter which is intercepted and read by Old Knowell, who
is shocked at its flippant disrespect.
When the old gentleman endeavors to
separate this baneful influence from his
son, Wellbred, aided by Brainworm,
tricks the old man. He also arranges Edward's marriage.

Captain Bobadill, a braggart captain. Of
the family of the Latin "Miles Gloriosus"
and the English Falstaff, he is still an
individual in his own right. He is fond
of quoting snatches of Elizabethan plays,
particularly from "The Spanish Tragedy." His fund of anecdotes of his pretended military career is boundless. He is
foolish and cowardly, but not vicious.
One of the distinctions of the role is that
Charles Dickens acted it in a nineteenth
century performance of the play.

Master Matthew, a poetaster. A suitor of
Mistress Bridget, he pours out plagi-
arized verse at the slightest excuse, pretending that it is extemporaneous. He is
a great admirer of Captain Bobadill, who
condescends to show him fencing skills
and delivers critical comments on current
plays.

Master Stephen, a country gull, nephew
of Old Knowell. A foolish, self-important
youth, he admires Bobadill's bluster and
far-fetched oaths and tries to imitate him.
He provides much amusement for his
Cousin Edward and Wellbred. His stupidity and dishonesty lead him into difficulties with Downright and the law.

Kitely, a pathologically jealous husband.
Comically obsessed with the mistaken
idea that his wife is faithless, he is ridiculous in his efforts to have her spied on
and to guard her. His jealousy makes
him an easy dupe for his brother-in-law
Wellbred, who sends him on a wild-
goose chase while Edward Knowell and
Bridget are married. He is apparently
cured of his jealousy by Justice Clement.

Dame Kitely, an attractive young woman who enjoys company. Her brother Well-bred sends her and her husband separately to Cob's house to catch each other in supposed unfaithful conduct.

Downright, a blunt country squire, Wellbred's half brother. Humorless and fiery-tempered, he irritates and insults many people, including Captain Bobadill, who threatens him and gets a beating in exchange for threats.

Justice Clement, an ebullient, jovial eccentric. Shrewd enough to see through the plots that have confused Old Knowell and Kitely, he is so much amused by Brainworm's pranks and so pleased with the young married couple that he asks forgiveness for them and obtains it. Although he is disgusted with the sham soldier, the sham poet, and the country gull, he indicates that they shall have clemency—in harmony with his name.

Oliver Cob, a water bearer, Captain Bobadill's landlord. He is a mixture of stupidity and native wit. Beaten by Captain Bobadill, he sets the law on him. Discovering the quarrelsome gathering at his hovel, he believes Kitely's accusation that his wife is the bawd for Dame Kitely and Old Knowell and gives her a beating.

Tib, Cob's foolish wife. Angry and sullen after her undeserved beating, she finally allows Justice Clement to pacify her and accepts Cob again as her loving and obedient husband.

Mistress Bridget, Kitely's charming sister. A romantic heroine without sharply individualized traits, she is attracted to Edward Knowell and consents to her brother-in-law's plan for her to become Knowell's wife.

Thomas Cash, a foundling, Kitely's protégé and employee. He is caught in the middle of the mutual jealousies of Kitely and Dame Kitely, but escapes damage.

Roger Formal, Justice Clement's gullible clerk, who allows Brainworm to get him drunk and steal his gown and his identity.

EVERY MAN OUT OF HIS HUMOUR

Author: Ben Jonson (1573?-1637)
Time of action: Early seventeenth century
First presented: 1599

PRINCIPAL CHARACTERS

Macilente, a malcontent. Morbidly envious of his fellows, he rages at the flourishing folly of the times and plays malicious tricks on his associates. When they have all been discomfited, he is cured of his envy.

Carlo Buffone, a foul-mouthed jester. His indiscriminate verbal assaults lead to his having his mouth sealed by hot sealing wax in his beard.

Deliro, a wealthy, doting husband. He is finally driven out of his uxoriousness by suspicion that his wife is unfaithful.

Fallace, Deliro's wife, Sordido's daughter. Enamored of Fastidious Brisk, she behaves so foolishly that she loses her husband's love.

Sordido, a miserly farmer. He consults the almanac, hoards grain, and hopes for bad weather. A good harvest by his neighbors causes him to attempt suicide.

Sogliardo, Sordido's social-climbing brother. He pays Carlo to teach him to be a gentleman, the lessons being unsuccessful.

Fungoso, Sordido's foolish son. He tries

hopelessly to keep up with Fastidious Brisk's fashionableness.

Fastidious Brisk, an affected courtier. He changes the style of his clothes so rapidly that an imitator is always at least an hour out of fashion. He lands in a debtors' prison.

Puntarvolo, an old-fashioned knight. He acts romantic scenes with his wife and wagers a sum at five-to-one that he, his wife, and his dog will return safely from a Continental tour. He loses when Macilente poisons his dog. He angrily seals Carlo's lips to silence his taunts.

Shift, a cheap rascal who pretends to be a criminal. He is too cowardly for real crime.

Saviolina, an affected court lady, Fastidious' mistress.

EVERYMAN

Author: Unknown
Time of action: Any time
Earliest extant version: 1508

PRINCIPAL CHARACTERS

God, who has decided to have a reckoning of all men.

Death, summoned to receive God's instructions to search out Everyman. Death agrees to give Everyman some time to gather together companions to make the journey with him.

Everyman, whom Death approaches and orders to make the long journey to Paradise in order to give an accounting for his life.

Good-Deeds, the one companion who can and will make the entire journey with Everyman. Everyman finds Good-Deeds too weak to stir, but after Everyman accepts penance, Good-Deeds is fit for the journey.

Knowledge, the sister of Good-Deeds. Knowledge offers to guide Everyman, but cannot go with him into the presence of his Maker.

Confession, who lives in the house of salvation. Confession gives penance to Everyman.

Discretion,
Strength,
Beauty, and
The Five Wits, companions who go part of the way with Everyman.

Fellowship,
Kindred, and
Goods, to whom Everyman turns for companions. All offer to help, but refuse when they learn the nature of the journey.

A Messenger, who appears in prologue to announce a moral play to the audience. He warns that man should look to the end of his life.

A Doctor, who appears at the end to remind the audience that only Good-Deeds will avail at the final judgment.

EXILES

Author: James Joyce (1882-1941)
Time of action: 1912
First published: 1918

Richard Rowan, an intellectually independent and emotionally self-reliant Irish writer. In his desire not to bind or be bound, even in love, he refuses ever to advise his common-law wife Bertha, or to ask anything of her. When she accuses him of neglect, he is faced with a conflict between personal integrity and love with its consequent feelings of guilt. His conflict is resolved when he can accept Bertha's desire to revive her relationship with Robert Hand, and Bertha is able to accept her lover's friendship with Beatrice Justice.

Bertha, Richard Rowan's common-law wife. Feeling neglected by her lover's refusal to influence her or to bind her in any way, and mistaking his friendship for Beatrice Justice for a love affair, she turns to Robert Hand, who has loved her in the past. Finally, she realizes that she can never betray Richard, but her expressed desire to meet Robert freely helps her to accept Richard's account of his objective relationship with Beatrice.

Robert Hand, a newspaper editor. He is dominated by the ideas and personality of Richard Rowan. Formerly in love with Bertha, he woos her again when she feels neglected by Richard; but he falters when he faces the demand to accept moral responsibility.

Beatrice Justice, Richard Rowan's devoted and admiring friend.

Archie, the young son of Bertha and Richard Rowan.

A FABLE

Author: William Faulkner (1897-1962)
Time of action: 1918
First published: 1954

The Corporal, a Christ-like soldier. Accompanied by his twelve squad members, the Corporal brings about a cease fire along the entire Western front by preaching peace on earth. His story bears a strong, yet often subtle resemblance to the life of Christ, the Passion, and the Crucifixion as events unfold which correspond in some degree to the birth, the betrayal, the denial, the Last Supper, and the death of Christ. Refusing an offer of freedom, the Corporal is executed between two murderers and buried at his sister's farm. Shellfire destroys the grave, but ironically his body is recovered and placed in the Unknown Soldier's tomb. These events suggest resurrection and immortality of a sort.

The Marshal, Commander-in-Chief of the Allied Armies in France. As a young man stationed in the Middle East he had seduced a woman and fathered a son who turns out to be the Corporal who instigated the mutiny. The old man never seems surprised by the turn of events and apparently is omniscient. He offers the Corporal an opportunity to escape, but must order his execution when he refuses.

General Gragnon, the French Division Commander. When his regiment refuses to attack the German line, he arrests the entire three thousand and insists upon his own arrest. While in prison he is executed by a brutal American soldier named Buchwald.

The Quartermaster General, the Marshal's former fellow student. After the Corporal's execution, he loses faith in the cause for which the Marshal stands.

346

The Runner, a former officer. Sympathizing with the Corporal's aims, he is crippled in a surprise barrage while fraternizing with the Germans. At the Marshal's funeral he throws a medal obtained at the Corporal's grave at the caisson and shouts his derision and defiance.

Marthe, the Corporal's younger half sister.

Marya, the Corporal's feeble-minded half sister.

Polchek, the soldier in the Corporal's squad who betrays him.

Pierre Bouc, the soldier in the Corporal's squad who denies him.

The Corporal's Wife, a former prostitute.

Buchwald, the American soldier who executes General Gragnon.

The Reverend Tobe Sutterfield, an American Negro preacher.

David Levine, a British flight officer who commits suicide.

THE FAERIE QUEENE

Author: Edmund Spenser (c. 1522-1599)
Time of action: The Age of Chivalry
First published: Books I-III, 1590; Books IV-VI, 1596

PRINCIPAL CHARACTERS

Gloriana, the Faerie Queene, an idealized portrait of Queen Elizabeth. Although she does not appear in the extant portion of the poem, many of the knights set out upon their quests from her court, and they often praise her virtue and splendor.

Prince Arthur, the legendary British hero, who represents Magnificence, the perfection of all virtues. He rides in search of Gloriana, who had appeared to him in a vision, and, on his way, aids knights in distress.

The Red Cross Knight, the hero of Book I, where he represents both England's patron, Saint George, and Christian man in search of Holiness. He sets out confidently to rescue Una's parents from the dragon of evil, but he is attacked by forces of sin and error which drive him to the point of suicide. He is restored in the House of Holiness by the teachings and offices of the Church and, refreshed by a fountain and a tree, symbolizing the sacraments of baptism and communion, he triumphs in his three-day combat with the dragon.

Una, the daughter of the King and Queen of the West, Adam and Eve; she personifies Truth and the Church. She advises her knight wisely, but she cannot protect him from himself. Deserted, she is aided by a lion and a troop of satyrs, and is finally restored to the Red Cross Knight, who is betrothed to her after his victory over the dragon.

The Dwarf, her companion, Common Sense.

Error, the Red Cross Knight's first adversary, a monster who lives in the wandering wood.

Archimago, a satanic figure who uses many disguises in his attempts to lure the knights and ladies of the poem into sin and disaster.

Duessa, his accomplice, whose attractive appearance hides her real hideousness. She represents variously Falsehood, the Roman Catholic Church, and Mary, Queen of Scots.

Sans Foy,
Sans Loy, and
Sans Joy, Saracen knights, who attack Una and her knight.

Fradubio, a knight betrayed by Duessa and transformed into a tree.

Kirkrapine, a church robber, slain by Una's lion when he tries to enter the cottage where she has taken refuge.

Abessa, his mistress.

Corceca, her blind mother.

Lucifera, mistress of the House of Pride.

Malvenu, her porter.

Vanity, her usher.

Night, the mother of falsehood, to whom Duessa appeals for help.

Aesculapius, the physician of the gods.

Sylvanus, the leader of the satyrs who rescue Una from Sans Loy.

Satyrane, a valiant, gentle knight who is half nobleman, half satyr.

Despair, an emaciated creature who drives warriors to suicide with his sophistic recitals of their sins.

Trevisan, one of his intended victims.

Dame Coelia, a virtuous matron who lives in the House of Holiness.

Fidelia,
Speranza, and
Charissa, her daughters, Faith, Hope, and Charity.

Contemplation, a holy hermit who gives the Red Cross Knight a vision of the City of God, then sends him back into the world to complete his quest.

Guyon, the Knight of Temperance, the sternest of the Spenserian heroes, who must violently destroy Acrasia's power and all its temptations that lead men to intemperance.

Palmer, his faithful companion, who stands for Reason or Prudence.

Acrasia, the Circe-like mistress of the Bower of Bliss. She lures men to their ruin in her world of debilitating luxuriance and turns them into animals.

Amavia, the desolate widow of one of her victims.

Ruddymane, her baby, whose hands cannot be cleansed of his dying mother's blood.

Medina,
Perissa, and
Elissa, sisters who personify the mean, the deficiency, and the excess of temperance.

Sir Huddibras, a malcontent, Elissa's lover.

Braggadocio, a vain-glorious braggart who masquerades as a knight on Guyon's stolen horse.

Trompart, his miserly companion.

Belphoebe, a virgin huntress, reared by the goddess Diana, who cannot respond to the devotion offered by Prince Arthur's squire, Timias. She is another of the figures conceived as a compliment to Elizabeth.

Furor, a churlish fellow whom Guyon finds furiously beating a helpless squire.

Occasion, his mother, a hag.

Phedon, the maltreated squire, who falls into Furor's hands through his jealousy of his lady, Pryene, and his friend Philemon.

Pyrochles and
Cymochles, intemperate knights defeated by Guyon.

Atin, Pyrochles' servant.

Phaedria, a coquette who lures knights to her island, where she lulls them into forgetfulness of their quests.

Mammon, the god of riches, who sits in rusty armor surveying his hoard of gold.

Philotime, his daughter, who holds the golden chain of ambition.

348

Alma, the soul, mistress of the castle of the body where Guyon and Prince Arthur take refuge.

Phantastes and **Eumnestes,** guardians, respectively, of fantasy and of memory.

Maleger, the captain of the shadowy forces who attacked the bulwarks of the House of Alma.

Verdant, a knight released by Guyon from Acrasia's clutches.

Grille, one of Acrasia's victims. He reviles Guyon and the Palmer for restoring his human form.

Britomart, the maiden knight, heroine of the book of Chastity. She subdues the forces of lust as she travels in search of Artegall, with whom she fell in love when she saw him in a magic mirror. Her union with him represents the alliance of justice and mercy as well as Spenser's ideal of married chastity, which surpasses the austere virginity of Belphoebe.

Malecasta, the lady of delight, beautiful and wanton, who entertains Britomart in Castle Joyous.

Glauce, Britomart's nurse, who accompanies her as her squire.

Merlin, the famous magician, whom Glauce and Britomart consult to learn the identity of the knight in the mirror.

Marinell, the timid son of a sea nymph and Florimell's lover.

Cymoent, his mother.

Florimell, the loveliest and gentlest of the ladies in Faerie Land. She is pursued by many evil beings, men and gods, before she is wed to Marinell.

Timias, Prince Arthur's squire, who is healed of severe wounds by Belphoebe. Although he falls in love with her, he can never win more than kindness as a response.

Crysogene, the mother of Belphoebe and Amoret, who were conceived by the sun.

Argante, a giantess, one of the figures of lust.

Ollyphant, her brother and lover.

A Squire of Dames, Argante's prisoner.

Snowy Florimell, Braggadocio's lady, a creature made by a witch with whom Florimell had stayed.

Proteus, the shepherd of the sea, who rescues Florimell from a lecherous fisherman.

Panope, an old nymph, his housekeeper.

Paridell, a vain, lascivious knight.

Malbecco, a miserly, jealous old man.

Hellenore, his young wife, who runs away with Paridell.

Scudamour, the knight most skilled in the art of courtly love. He wins Amoret at the court of Venus, but she is taken from him almost immediately.

Amoret, his beautiful bride, who is taken prisoner at her own wedding by Busirane, who represents her own passions and the confining forces of the rigid code of love in which she has grown up.

Busirane, her captor.

Venus, the goddess of love and a personification of the creative force in nature, Amoret's foster mother.

Adonis, her lover.

Diana, the divine huntress, the virgin goddess who raises Belphoebe.

Ate, Discord, a malicious old woman who stirs up strife.

Blandamour, a fickle knight.

Sir Ferraugh, one of the suitors of Snowy Florimell.

Cambello, one of the knights of friendship.

349

Canacee, his sister, a wise and beautiful lady who is won by Triamond.

Cambina, Cambello's wife.

Priamond,
Diamond, and
Triamond, brothers who fight for the hand of Canacee. The first two are killed, but their strength passes into their victorious surviving brother.

Artegall, the knight of Justice, Britomart's beloved.

Talus, the iron man, his implacable attendant, who upholds justice untempered by mercy.

Aemylia, a lady imprisoned with Amoret by a villainous churl and rescued by Belphoebe.

Corflambo, a mighty pagan who corrupts his enemies by filling them with lust.

Poeana, his rude, tyrannical daughter.

Amyas, the Squire of Low Degree, Aemylia's suitor.

Placidas, another squire loved by Poeana. Encouraged by Prince Arthur, Placidas marries Poeana and reforms her.

Druon and
Claribell, pugnacious companions of Blandamour and Paridell.

Thames and
Medway, the river god and goddess whose marriage is attended by the famous waterways of the world.

Neptune, the sea god to whom Marinell's mother pleads for Florimell's release from Proteus.

Grantorto, a tyrant who holds Irena's country in his power. He is the emblem of the political strength of the Roman Catholic church.

Irena, his victim, who appeals to the Faerie Queene for help.

Sir Sanglier, a cruel lord, chastened by Talus.

Pollente, a Saracen warrior who extorts money from travelers.

Munera, his daughter, the keeper of his treasury.

Giant Communism, Artegall's foe. He tries to weigh everything in his scales, but he learns, before Talus hurls him into the sea, that truth and falsehood, right and wrong, cannot be balanced.

Amidas and
Bracidas, brothers whose dispute over a treasure chest is settled by Artegall.

Philtera, Bracidas' betrothed, who weds his wealthy brother.

Lucy, Amidas' deserted sweetheart, Bracidas' wife.

Sir Turpine, a knight whom Artegall discovers bound and tormented by Amazon warriors.

Radigund, Queen of the Amazons. She captures Artegall and dresses him in woman's clothes to humiliate him, then falls in love with him and tries unsuccessfully to win him.

Clarinda, her attendant, who comes to love Artegall as she woos him for her mistress.

Dolon, Deceit, a knight who tries to entrap Britomart.

Mercilla, a just and merciful maiden queen whose realm is threatened by a mighty warrior.

The Souldan, her enemy, thought to represent Philip of Spain. He is destroyed by the brilliant light of Prince Arthur's diamond shield.

Malengin, an ingenious villain who transforms himself into different shapes at will. Talus crushes him with his iron flail.

Belgae, a mother who loses twelve of her

seventeen children to the tyrant Geryoneo and appeals to Mercilla for help.

Geryoneo, her enemy, the power of Spain, who is slain by Artegall.

Burbon, a knight rescued by Artegall as he fights Grantorto's men to rescue his lady, Flourdelis, France.

Sir Sergis, Irena's faithful adviser.

Calidore, the knight of Courtesy, sent to destroy the Blatant Beast, malicious gossip.

Briana, a proud lady who abuses the laws of hospitality by demanding the hair and beards of ladies and gentlemen who pass her castle.

Crudor, the disdainful knight for whom she weaves a mantle of hair.

Tristram, a young prince reared in the forest, who impresses Prince Arthur by his instinctive courtesy.

Aldus, a worthy old knight.

Aladine, his son.

Priscilla, Aladine's lady.

Serena, a noble lady, severely wounded by the Blatant Beast.

Calepine, her knight.

Sir Turpine, a discourteous gentleman who refuses aid to Calepine and Serena.

Blandina, his wife, who tries to assuage his cruelty.

The Salvage Man, a "noble savage," another untaught practitioner of courtesy.

Matilde, a childless noblewoman who adopts a baby rescued by Calidore from a bear.

Mirabella, a proud, insolent lady.

Disdaine and
Scorne, her tormentors.

Pastorella, a nobleman's daughter who grows up with shepherds. Calidore falls in love with her and with her rustic life.

Meliboee, her wise foster father, who warns Calidore that happiness is not to be found in one place or another but in oneself.

Coridon, Pastorella's shepherd admirer.

Colin Clout, a shepherd poet who pipes to the graces on Mount Acidale.

Sir Bellamour, Calidore's friend, Pastorella's father.

Claribell, his wife.

Melissa, her maid, who discovers Pastorella's true identity.

Mutability, a proud Titaness who challenges the power of Cynthia, the moon goddess.

Cynthia, her rival.

Mercury, the messenger of the gods.

Jove, the king of the gods.

Mollana, a nymph and an Irish river.

Faunus, a satyr who pursues her.

Dame Nature, a great veiled figure who hears Mutability's arguments and judges, finally, that order reigns in all change.

THE FAIR MAID OF PERTH

Author: Sir Walter Scott (1771-1832)
Time of action: 1396
First published: 1828

PRINCIPAL CHARACTERS

Catharine Glover, the Fair Maid of Perth. Agreeing to be Henry Gow's Val- entine, she nonetheless refuses to agree to marry him because of his propensity for

351

quarreling. Finally, becoming reconciled to the brave Henry's warlike impulses, she does marry him, and he vows to take up arms again only in defense of his country.

Simon Glover, her father.

Henry Gow, an armorer of Perth. He is in love with Catharine Glover. Of a fiery spirit, his offer of marriage is refused by Catharine because of his quarrelsomeness. Involved bravely in the Highland wars between the clans Quhele and Chattan, he finally wins her hand.

Conachar (Eachin MacIan), the son of the chief of Clan Quhele and an apprentice to Simon Glover. In love with Catharine Glover, he flees when he meets his rival for her hand, Henry Gow, in battle. Ashamed of his cowardice, he takes his own life.

Robert III, King of Scotland.

The Duke of Albany, King Robert's brother James,

The Earl of March, and

The Earl of Douglas, called **The Black Douglas,** noblemen involved in a strug-gle for power over Robert III and Scotland.

The Duke of Rothsay, heir to the Scottish throne. He is starved to death by Sir John Ramorny and Henbane Dwining.

Sir John Ramorny, the Duke of Rothsay's Master of Horse and, later, his murderer.

Henbane Dwining, an apothecary and physician to Sir John Ramorny, with whom he kills the Duke of Rothsay.

Oliver Proudfute, a Perth burgher and friend of Henry Gow. He is murdered while masquerading in Henry's clothes to frighten away assailants.

Father Clement, confessor to Catharine Glover.

Bonthron, the murderer of Oliver Proudfute, whom he mistakes for Henry Gow.

Louise, a glee-maiden.

Lady Marjory, the Duchess of Rothsay.

Sir Patrick Charteris, the provost of Perth.

THE FAITHFUL SHEPHERDESS

Author: John Fletcher (1579-1625)
Time of action: Remote antiquity
First presented: c. 1609

PRINCIPAL CHARACTERS

Clorin (klō'rēn), the faithful shepherdess. She lives in a sacred grove beside the tomb of her dead lover, mourning him and cultivating herbs to heal injured shepherds. Like the Lady of Milton's "Comus," she finds her chastity a magical defense against all evils of the wood, and her healing arts are effective only when she has purged her patients of lust.

Thenot (tā·nō'), a disillusioned shepherd who loves Clorin for the virtue and constancy which he finds in her alone. He languishes in this passion which by its very nature cannot be satisfied, until Clorin mercifully decides to free him from it by offering to return his love and forsake her dead sweetheart. His illusions shattered, he leaves her, resolving to choose a lady for her beauty and convinced that no woman can be loved for her merit.

Perigot (pā·rē·gō'), a virtuous young shepherd who gives extravagant assurances of his undying love for Amoret. Deceived by Amaryllis' transformation, he is horrified to hear her offer herself

352

to him, and he twice wounds the real Amoret, who appears soon afterward, for deceiving him. Clorin restores his faith in his beloved, and they are happily reconciled.

Amoret (ăm′ô·rĕt), Perigot's sweetheart, whose beauty and innocence win the devotion of a river god and a satyr as well as the love of her shepherd swain. Although she cannot understand Perigot's treatment of her, she quickly forgives him and again promises him her hand and heart.

Amaryllis (ăm′ə·rĭl′ĭs), a passionate shepherdess who desires Perigot and has herself magically disguised as Amoret to win him for herself. However, his misery awakens her sympathy and she tells him the truth before she flees the Sullen Shepherd, whose help she had enlisted by promising him her love. She is rescued and cleansed by the Priest of Pan.

Cloe (klō′ĭ), another lustful shepherdess who makes assignations with both Daphnis and Alexis, hoping to compensate for the shyness of the one by the boldness of the other. She, like Perigot, is purified by Clorin's teaching.

Daphnis (dăf′nĭs), her shy, modest admirer. Blind to her desires, he assures her of his virtuous affection.

Alexis (ə·lĕk′sĭs), Cloe's more passionate suitor. Wounded by the Sullen Shepherd, he is healed of both his injury and his lust by Clorin.

The Sullen Shepherd, almost the personification of blind desire. He professes love to Amaryllis and aids her to separate Perigot and Amoret, but he confesses secretly that any woman satisfies him and that he is willing to use any trick to win one.

A Satyr, a gentle creature of nature who worships Clorin and brings her gifts of fruit from the wood. He searches the forest to bring to her those who need her help and carries out the mystic rites which purify her grove.

The Priest of Pan, the guardian of all the shepherds. He rescues Amaryllis, then goes to Clorin's grove to find the rest of his flock, bless them, and send them to their homes with a hymn to Pan.

An Old Shepherd, his companion, who notes disapprovingly the disappearance of the young shepherds and shepherdesses into the wood.

The God of the River, Amoret's protector, who raises her from the fountain where the Sullen Shepherd has dropped her. He begs her to leave her mortal life and join him in his crystal streams.

THE FALL OF THE HOUSE OF USHER

Author: Edgar Allan Poe (1809-1849)
Time of action: Nineteenth century
First published: 1839

PRINCIPAL CHARACTERS

Roderick Usher, a madman. Excessively reserved in childhood and thereafter, Usher is the victim not only of his own introversion but also of the dry rot in his family, which because of inbreeding has long lacked the healthy infusion of vigorous blood from other families. His complexion is cadaverous, his eyes are lustrous, his nose is "of a delicate Hebrew model," his chin is small and weak though finely molded, his forehead broad, and his hair soft and weblike. (The detailed description of Usher's face and head in the story should be compared with the well-known portraits of Poe himself.) In manner Usher is inconsistent, shifting from excited or frantic vivacity to sullenness marked by dull, guttural talk like that of a drunkard or opium addict. It is evident to his visitor, both through his own observation and through what Usher tells him, that the wretched man is struggling desperately but vainly to conquer his fear of fear itself. His wide reading in his extensive library, his interest in many art objects, his playing the guitar and singing to its accompaniment, his attempts at conversation and friendly communication with his guest—all seem piteous efforts to hold on to his sanity. The battle is finally lost when Madeline, risen from her grave and entering through the doors of the guest's apartment, falls upon Usher and bears him to the floor "a corpse, and a victim to the terrors he had anticipated."

Madeline, his twin sister, a tall, white-robed, wraithlike woman who succumbs to catalepsy, is buried alive, escapes from her tomb, confronts her brother in her bloodstained cerements, and joins him in death.

The Narrator, Usher's visitor and only personal friend, who has been summoned to try to cheer up Usher but who himself is made fearful and nervously excited by the gloomy, portentous atmosphere of the Usher home. Having witnessed the double deaths of Usher and Madeline, the narrator flees in terror and, looking back, sees the broken mansion fall into the tarn below.

THE FAMILY AT GILJE

Author: Jonas Lie (1833-1908)
Time of action: Nineteenth century
First published: 1883

PRINCIPAL CHARACTERS

Captain Jäger, a Norwegian army officer in command of the mountain post near Gilje. He wants his favorite daughter, Inger-Johanna, to be a society woman and sends her to live with his sister in the city. He is bitterly disappointed when the girl refuses a good marriage because she loves a radical student. The captain's health fails rapidly after this disappointment, and he dies.

Inger-Johanna Jäger, the captain's charming and favorite daughter. She falls in love with a radical student, Arent Grip, who teaches her to look beneath the symbols of success to the inner human nature. Because she loves the young man she refuses to marry Captain Rönnow and becomes instead a schoolteacher. When her beloved is fatally ill, she goes to nurse him.

Mrs. Jäger, the captain's wife.

Thinka Jäger, a pliant girl who marries Sheriff Glücke as her father wishes. She makes a considerate wife, but she is a sad woman. She really loves a young clerk her father will not consider as a husband for her.

Jörgen Jäger, the captain's son. He has aptitude as a mechanic and migrates to America, where he does well for himself.

Captain Rönnow, a suitor for Inger-Johanna's hand in marriage. She refuses to marry him, though the captain has her father's approval, because she does not love him.

Arent Grip, a radical student who loves Inger-Johanna and is loved by her. He is a failure in the world, becoming by turns a drunkard and an ascetic, always wan-

354

dering about the country. After twenty years of aimless roving he returns and is nursed during his final illness by Inger-Johanna.

Gülcke, the sheriff, a widower who marries Thinka, though she loves a younger man her father will not allow her to marry.

THE FAMILY REUNION

Author: T. S. Eliot (1888-   )
Time of action: Twentieth century
First published: 1939

PRINCIPAL CHARACTERS

Amy, Dowager Lady Monchensey. As an old member of the English aristocracy, she is determined to preserve the family estate, Wishwood, as it has always been and use it as a means for keeping the family together. Like most people who are used to giving orders, she believes that her desires will eventually be fulfilled, in this case her wish that her oldest son will return to take over the estate and marry her ward. As she dies she begins to see that she has been living in an unreal world; some of the things happening around her then begin to make sense.

Harry, Lord Monchensey, Amy's son. Having returned home for the first time in eight years, he finds his family still trying to deny any change in the world. While he was gone he had murdered his wife, and he is currently searching for some satisfactory way of life. In the few hours that he spends at Wishwood he finds that the ghosts which have been following him are not his at all, but his father's, and that he is really pursuing them. He soon leaves to seek out the deeper reality that he has just glimpsed.

Agatha, Amy's sister. Many years prior to the action of the play, Agatha fell in love with her sister's husband but convinced him he must not murder Amy because of her pregnancy. At the time of the play, Agatha is making her first visit to Wishwood in thirty years. She is the only one of the older members of the

family who has any sense of reality or who is aware of the changes that have taken place around them. She helps Harry to glimpse reality and advises him to leave immediately.

Downing, Harry's servant and chauffeur. Although he has seen the Eumenides, he realizes they have nothing to do with him and is therefore able to treat the subject with equanimity. He has complete faith in his master's ability to cope with the situation.

Mary, Amy's niece and ward. Although aware of Lady Monchensey's plans for her marriage to Harry, she knows that it will not do. Upon Harry's return she finally gains courage to leave the estate and enlists the aid of Agatha in carrying out her plans.

Ivy and
Violet, Amy's other two sisters. They understand nothing of what is going on around them, not even that they are old and no longer a part of a moving world. Their chief interest in life is Amy's will.

Col. the Hon. Gerald and
The Hon. Charles Piper, brothers of Amy's deceased husband. Much like Amy's sisters, they are living in the past; but they retain their confidence that they can meet the challenges of a changing world.

Dr. Warburton, an old friend of the family who is called in to try to diagnose Harry's trouble.

355

The Eumenides, the evil spirits that Harry feels are following him. They are seen by him and Dowling, and by Agatha and Mary.

Denman, a parlormaid.

Sergeant Winchell, a policeman in the local village.

FAR FROM THE MADDING CROWD

Author: Thomas Hardy (1840-1928)
Time of action: 1869-1873
First published: 1874

PRINCIPAL CHARACTERS

Gabriel Oak, a sturdy young English farmer. Refused as a husband by Bathsheba Everdene, he also loses his farm through ill luck. Disheartened by these events, he becomes a shepherd and is taken on at the farm just inherited by his beloved. Although the girl proposes to manage the farm herself, she soon puts more and more of its affairs into the hands of Gabriel Oak, whose skill and loyalty she can trust. Saying no more of love or marriage, Gabriel watches the courtship of Bathsheba by Mr. Boldwood, a well-to-do farmer of the neighborhood. He also watches when the girl is courted by Sergeant Francis Troy and becomes the latter's wife. During this time, although disappointed in love, Gabriel is so successful at managing his beloved's farm that he becomes the manager of Mr. Boldwood's farm as well. When Bathsheba's marriage ends tragically for her, and Mr. Boldwood is imprisoned for murder, Gabriel still loyally serves both. He finally decides to leave England. When he informs Bathsheba of his intention, she suddenly realizes that she loves the loyal young farmer. She reveals her love for him and they are married.

Bathsheba Everdene, a vain and unpredictable young woman of great beauty, loved for many years by Gabriel Oak. Despite her personal weaknesses she is a practical woman after taking over the farm inherited from her uncle. She hires Gabriel as a shepherd but soon makes him the bailiff in all but name. She rejects the proposal of Mr. Boldwood, a well-to-do neighbor, but she readily falls to the audacious lovemaking of Sergeant Troy. Though she loves him, she distrusts his character; she travels to Bath to break the engagement with him, but her trip results in their marriage. The marriage is unfortunate, for her husband is a wasteful, disloyal man who has married her without love, attracted by her beauty and her money. After being revealed as the seducer of one of the farm girls he disappears and is presumed dead. His wife gradually admits Mr. Boldwood as a suitor once again because she pities the man. But Troy suddenly reappears to claim his wife and her fortune. His effort is cut short by a blast from a shotgun in the hands of Mr. Boldwood. For Bathsheba, who loved her wastrel husband despite his faults, the shock is deep, but as the months go by her emotional wounds heal. Given an opportunity, she recognizes the worth of Gabriel Oak, whom she marries. She has learned by bitter experience what to value in a man.

Francis Troy, an arrogant, selfish man. Reared as the son of a doctor and his French wife, Troy is reputedly the son of the doctor's wife and a nobleman who was her lover. Though given a good education, Troy enlists in a regiment of dragoons and becomes a sergeant. A handsome man and a pleasant one when he wants to be, he has many successes

356

with women, including Bathsheba Everdene, who becomes his wife; he is attracted by her beauty, wealth, and position. With her money he buys himself out of the army, leads a pleasant, wasteful life, and almost ruins his wife's farm. One of his earlier victims appears and with her infant dies. For Troy, who really loved the girl, the shock is great. After a violent scene with his wife he disappears and is presumed dead, although he actually lives a hand-to-mouth existence as an actor in a cheap company. Tiring of that life, he returns to claim his wife. His brutal and surprising reappearance is cut short when he is killed by Mr. Boldwood, his wife's suitor.

Mr. Boldwood, a confirmed bachelor of middle age who falls in love with Bathsheba Everdene and courts her, only to lose her to another man. His love endures and, after her husband's disappearance, he courts her again. His patient courtship, about to succeed, is ended by the reappearance of Francis Troy, who brutally tries to force his wife to go to her home with him from a Christmas party at Mr. Boldwood's house. Boldwood, outraged by Troy's behavior, shoots Troy and kills him. Mr. Boldwood is convicted of murder and sentenced to hang, but his sentence is commuted to imprisonment when evidence is brought forward that he is mentally deranged.

Fanny Robin, a pretty servant in the Everdene household. She foolishly allows herself to be seduced by Francis Troy while he is in the army. Though he promises to marry her, she finds herself deserted and expecting a child. She returns to her home community just in time to have her baby, only to die along with the infant. Their deaths, caused in part by Troy's refusal to help the girl when he finds her on the road in need, reveal him for what he is.

Jan Coggan, a worker on the Everdene farm, a good friend to Gabriel Oak.

Lydia (Liddy) Smallbury, Bathsheba's loyal and trusted maid.

A FAREWELL TO ARMS

Author: Ernest Hemingway (1899-1961)
Time of action: World War I
First published: 1929

PRINCIPAL CHARACTERS

Lieutenant Frederic Henry, an American who has volunteered to serve with an Italian ambulance unit during World War I. Like his Italian companions, he enjoys drinking, trying to treat the war as a joke, and (it is implied) visiting brothels. Before the beginning of a big offensive he meets Catherine Barkley, one of a group of British nurses assigned to staff a hospital unit. Henry begins the prelude to an affair with her but is interrupted by having to go to the front during the offensive; he is wounded, has an operation on his knee, and is sent to recuperate in Milan, where he again meets Miss Barkley, falls in love with her, and sleeps with her in his hospital room. When Henry returns to the front, he knows Catherine is pregnant. In the retreat from Caporetto, Henry is seized at a bridge across the Tagliamento River and realizes he is about to be executed for deserting his troops. He escapes by swimming the river. At Stresa he rejoins Catherine and, before he can be arrested for desertion, the two lovers row across Lake Como to Switzerland. For a few months they live happily at an inn near Montreux—hiking, reading, and discussing American sights (such as Niagara Falls, the stockyards, and the Golden Gate) that Catherine must see after the war. Catherine is to have her baby in a hospital. Her stillborn son is delivered by Caesarian section and that same night Catherine dies. Lieutenant Henry walks back to his hotel through darkness and rain. As developed by Hemingway, Henry is a protagonist who is sensitive to the horrors and beauties of life and war. Many of his reactions are subtly left for the reader to supply. At the end of the novel, for instance, Henry feels sorrow and pity for the dead baby strangled by the umbilical cord, but the full, unbearable weight of Catherine's death falls upon the reader.

Catherine Barkley, the nurse whom Frederic Henry nicknames "Cat." She had been engaged to a childhood sweetheart killed at the Somme. When she falls in love with Henry she gives herself freely to him. Although they both want to be married, she decides the ceremony would not be a proper one while she is pregnant; she feels they are already married. Catherine seems neither a deep thinker nor a very complex person; but she enjoys life, especially good food, drink, and love. She has a premonition that she will die in the rain; the premonition is tragically fulfilled at the hospital in Lausanne.

Lieutenant Rinaldi, Frederick Henry's jokingly cynical friend. Over many bottles they share their experiences and feelings. Although he denies it, Rinaldi is a master of the art of priest-baiting. He is very fond of girls, but he teases Henry about Catherine, calling her a "cool goddess."

The Priest, a young man who blushes easily but manages to survive the oaths and obscenities of the soldiers. He hates the war and its horrors.

Piani, a big Italian soldier who sticks by Henry in the retreat from Caporetto after the others in the unit have been killed or have deserted. With other Italian soldiers he can be tough but with Henry he is gentle and tolerant of what men suffer in wartime.

Helen Ferguson, a Scottish nurse who is Catherine Barkley's companion when Frederic Henry arrives in Stresa. She is harsh with him because of his affair with Catherine.

Count Greffi, ninety-four years old, a contemporary of Metternich and a former diplomat with whom Frederic Henry plays billiards at Stresa. A gentle cynic, he says that men do not become wise as they grow old; they merely become more careful.

Ettore Moretti, an Italian from San Francisco serving in the Italian army. Much decorated, he is a professional hero whom Frederic Henry dislikes and finds boring.

THE FATHER

Author: August Strindberg (1849-1912)
Time of action: Mid-nineteenth century
First presented: 1887

PRINCIPAL CHARACTERS

The Captain, a Captain of Cavalry who is the chief sufferer in this domestic tragedy. He was rejected by his mother and consequently sought a mother-wife in marriage. Driven to raving madness by his wife, he is strait-jacketed and suffers a stroke.

Laura, his wife. Accepting the maternal side of her relationship with her husband, she loathes her role as wife and takes vengeance on her husband by destroying him. In her efforts to prove him mad, she resorts to forgery and to misrepresentation of his scientific interests, which in fact she does not understand. She also exploits a suspicion she has planted in his mind that their daughter is not his.

Bertha, their daughter and a chief object of conflict.

Margaret, the Captain's old nurse. She tries to reassure him periodically; it is she who at last calms him enough to slip a strait jacket on him.

Dr. Östermark, the new village doctor, to whom Laura goes with her "evidence" of her husband's insanity.

Auditor Säfberg, a freethinker with

whom the Captain intends to board Bertha so that she will be educated away from the influence of her mother and of her grandmother, who is bent on teaching her spiritualism.

Nöjd, a trooper in difficulties because he got a servant girl in trouble. His relatively trivial problem suggests to Laura the weapon she successfully uses against her husband.

Emma, the servant girl in trouble.

Ludwig, who Nöjd claims may well be the father of Emma's child.

The Pastor, Laura's brother, before whom Nöjd is called. His sympathy for Nöjd is greater than the Captain's. Later, when the Pastor sees through Laura's scheme, she dares him to accuse her.

FATHER GORIOT

Author: Honoré de Balzac (1799-1850)
Time of action: 1819
First published: 1835

PRINCIPAL CHARACTERS

Father Goriot (gô·ryō′), a lonely old lodger at the pension of Madame Vauquer in Paris. Known to the other boarders as Old Goriot, he is a retired manufacturer of vermicelli who sold his prosperous business in order to provide handsome dowries for his two daughters. During his first year at the Maison Vauquer he occupied the best rooms in the house; in the second year he asked for less expensive quarters on the floor above, and at the end of the third year he moved into a cheap, dingy room on the third story. Because two fashionably dressed young women have visited him from time to time in the past, the old man has become an object of curiosity and suspicion; the belief is that he has ruined himself by keeping two mistresses. Actually Old Goriot is a man in whom parental love has become an obsession, a

love unappreciated and misused by his two selfish, heartless daughters, who make constant demands on his meager resources. After a life of hard work, careful saving, and fond indulgence of his children, he has outlived his usefulness and is now in his dotage. Happy in the friendship of Eugène de Rastignac, the law student who becomes the lover of one of the daughters, he uses the last of his money to provide an apartment for the young man, a place where Old Goriot will also have his own room. But before the change can be made the daughters drive their father to desperation by fresh demands for money to pay their bills. He dies attended only by Eugène and Bianchon, a poor medical student, and in his last moments he speaks lovingly of the daughters who have ruined him and made him the victim of their

359

ingratitude. The daughters send their empty carriages to follow his coffin to the grave.

Countess Anastasie de Restaud (à·nà·stà·zē′ də rĕs·tō′), the more fashionable of Old Goriot's daughters, constantly in need of money to indulge her extravagant tastes and to provide for her lover. Meeting her at a ball given by his distant relative, Madame de Beauséant, Eugène de Rastignac immediately falls in love with Anastasie. When he calls on her he finds Old Goriot just leaving. His mention of his fellow lodger causes Anastasie and her husband to treat the young law student with great coldness, and he realizes that he is no longer welcome in their house. Later Madame de Beauséant explains the mystery, saying that Anastasie is ashamed of her humble origins and her tradesman father.

Baroness Delphine de Nucingen (dĕl·fēn′ də nü·săn·zhäṅ′), Old Goriot's second daughter, the wife of a German banker. Like her sister Anastasie, she married for position and money, but her place in society is not as exalted as that of the Countess de Restaud, who has been received at court. As a result, the sisters are not on speaking terms. Madame de Beauséant, amused by Eugène de Rastignac's youthful ardor, suggests that he introduce her to the Baroness de Nucingen in order to win Delphine's gratitude and a place for himself in Parisian society. Delphine accepts the young man as her lover. Though self-centered and snobbish, she is less demanding than her sister; she has asked for less, given more of herself, and brought more happiness to her father. When Old Goriot is dying she goes to the Maison Vauquer at Eugène's insistence, but she arrives too late to receive her father's blessing.

Eugène de Rastignac (œ·zhĕn′ də rás·tē·nyák′), an impoverished law student, the son of a landed provincial family. As ambitious as he is handsome, he is determined to conquer Paris. At first his lack of sophistication makes him almost irresistible to his relative, Madame de Beauséant, and Delphine de Nucingen, whose lover he becomes. He learns cynicism without losing his warm feelings; he never wavers in his regard for Old Goriot, and while he does not attend seriously to the law studies for which his family is making a great sacrifice, he manages to get on in fashionable society, where friendships and influence are important. The revelation of the ways of the world that he gains through the patronage of Madame de Beauséant, his love affair with Delphine, and his regard for Old Goriot, as well as the shabby activities in which he engages in order to maintain himself in the world of fashion, make him all the more ambitious and eager to succeed.

Madame Vauquer (vō·kā′), the sly, shabby, penurious owner of the Maison Vauquer, the perfect embodiment of the atmosphere that prevails in the pension. When Old Goriot first moves into her establishment, she sees him as a possible suitor, but after he fails to respond to her coy attentions she makes him an object of gossip and ridicule.

Monsieur Vautrin (vō·trăṅ′), a man who claims to be a former tradesman living at the Maison Vauquer. Reserved, sharp-tongued, secretive, he observes everything that goes on about him and is aware of Old Goriot's efforts to provide money for his daughters. Knowing that Eugène de Rastignac desperately needs money in order to maintain himself in society, he suggests that the young man court Victorine Taillefer, another lodger, an appealing young girl whose father has disinherited her in favor of her brother. Vautrin says that he will arrange to have the brother killed in a duel, a death that will make Victorine an heiress. He gives Eugène two weeks to consider his proposition. Eugène considers Vautrin a devil, but in the end, driven to desperation by his mistress, he begins to court Victorine. True to Vau-

360

trin's word, Victorine's brother is fatally wounded in a duel. Vautrin's scheme fails when he is arrested and revealed as a notorious criminal, Jacques Collin, nicknamed Trompe-la-Mort. Though his identity has been betrayed within the pension, he swears that he will return and continue his climb to good fortune by the same unscrupulous means used by those who call themselves respectable.

Victorine Taillefer (vēk·tô·rēn' tà·yə·fĕr'), a young girl cast off by her harsh father, who has decided to make his son his only heir. She lives with Madame Couture at the Maison Vauquer.

Madame Couture (kōō·tür'), the widow of a public official and a lodger at the Maison Vauquer. A kind-hearted woman, she fills the place of a mother in the lonely life of Victorine Taillefer.

Monsieur Poiret (pwà·rā'), a lodger at the Maison Vauquer. To him Gondureau, a detective, confides his suspicion that Monsieur Vautrin is in reality the famous criminal, Trompe-la-Mort.

Mademoiselle Michonneau (mē·shô·nō'), an elderly spinster living at the Maison Vauquer. Disliking Monsieur Vautrin, her fellow boarder, she agrees to put a drug in his coffee. While Vautrin is asleep, she discovers the brand of a criminal on his shoulder. Acting on this information, the police appear and arrest Vautrin.

Gondureau (gōṅ·dü·rō'), the detective who is trying to track down Jacques Col-

lin, called Trompe-la-Mort, a criminal who lives at the Maison Vauquer under the name of Vautrin. Gondureau arranges with Monsieur Poiret and Mademoiselle Michonneau to have Vautrin drugged in order to learn whether he bears a criminal brand on his shoulder.

Count Maxime de Trailles (màk·sēm' də trà'yə), an arrogant but impecunious young nobleman, the lover of Anastasie de Restaud. For his sake she helps to impoverish her father.

Madame de Beauséant (də bō·sā·yän'), a relative of Eugène de Rastignac. Aristocratic and high-minded, she is the ideal of inherited culture and good manners—kind, reserved, warm-hearted, beautiful. Though saddened by the loss of her lover, she treats Eugène with great kindness, receives Delphine de Nucingen for his sake, and introduces the young man into fashionable Parisian society.

Bianchon (byän·shōn'), a poor medical student living at the Maison Vauquer. Like Eugène de Rastignac, he befriends Old Goriot and attends him when the old man is dying. Bianchon extends friendship easily and allows warm human feelings to influence his relations with other people.

Sylvie (sēl·vē'), the plump cook at the Maison Vauquer.

Christophe (krēs·tôf'), Madame Vauquer's man of all work.

FATHERS AND SONS

Author: Ivan Turgenev (1818-1883)
Time of action: 1859
First published: 1862

PRINCIPAL CHARACTERS

Yevgeny Vassilyitch Bazarov (ĕv·gĕ'nĭy vä·sĭ'lĭch bä·zä'rəf), a nihilistic young medical school graduate and Arkady's closest friend. Arrogant and ruthless, Bazarov believes only in the power of the intellect and science. As a revolutionary, he feels himself far superior to Nikolai Kirsanov and his brother. To him, they are hopelessly antiquated humanitarians. He tells them: "You won't fight—and yet you fancy yourselves gallant chaps—but we mean to fight. . . . We want to smash other people."

Arkady Kirsanov (är·kä′dĭy kĭr·sä′nəf), Nikolai's son and Bazarov's naïve young disciple. For a time he worships his leader and echoes everything that Bazarov says; however, Arkady lacks the necessary ruthlessness required for a revolutionary spirit. He is unable to believe, as Bazarov does, that a good chemist "is twenty times as useful as any poet." After Bazarov's death he marries Katya and settles down to a prosaic life on the family estate.

Nikolai Petrovitch Kirsanov (nĭ′kô·lĭ pĕt·rŏ′vĭch kĭr·sä′nəf), Arkady's gentle music-loving father. Possessing a liberal, well-meaning spirit, he is happy to free his serfs and to rent them farm land. In his ineffectual way he attempts to run the estate profitably. Unfortunately, the newly freed serfs take every opportunity to cheat him out of his rent.

Pavel Kirsanov (pä′vĕl kĭr·sä′nəf), Nikolai's brother. A dandified patrician, he has little liking for Bazarov or his revolutionary ideals. Believing strongly in the aristocratic way of life, he considers Bazarov a charlatan and a boor. In his own heart, however, Pavel knows that the new must supplant the old. Finally, dissatisfied with provincial life, he moves to Dresden, where he is much sought after by the aristocrats.

Katya Loktiv (kä′tyä lôk·tĭf′), Anna Odintsov's attractive young sister. Although she is shy and somewhat afraid of her sister, Katya becomes interested in Arkady. When he asks her to marry him, she readily accepts his proposal and shortly afterward becomes his wife.

Anna Odintsov (än′nä ô·dĭn′tsəf), a haughty young aristocrat, a widow. Because of her beauty even the unsentimental Bazarov falls in love with her. At first he interests her, but he is never able to pierce her cold exterior for long. She does show some feeling for him as he is dying and even brings a doctor to his deathbed. Unable to help him, she unbends enough to kiss his forehead before he dies.

Vasily Bazarov (vä·sĭ′·lĭy bä·zä′rəf), a village doctor, the father of young Bazarov. Like the other fathers, he is unable to bridge the gulf between his generation and his son's; in fact, he has no desire to do so. Doting on his son, the old man thinks Yevgeny to be beyond reproach.

Arina Bazarov (ä·rĭ′·nə bä·zä′rəf), Yevgeny Bazarov's aging mother. In her way the old woman, although quite superstitious, is clever and interesting. She also loves her son deeply. When he dies, she becomes, like her husband, a pathetic, broken figure.

Fenitchka Savishna (fĕ·nĭ·ch′kə sä·vĭsh′nə), Nikolai's young mistress. At Pavel's urging, Nikolai finally marries her and thereafter lives a happy life with the gentle, quiet girl.

FAUST

Author: Johann Wolfgang von Goethe (1749-1832)
Time of action: Timeless
First published: 1790-1831

PRINCIPAL CHARACTERS

Faust (foust), a perpetual scholar with an insatiable mind and a questing spirit. The middle-aged Faust, in spite of his enthusiasm for a newly discovered source of power in the sign of the macrocosm, finds his intellectual searches unsatisfactory and longs for a life of experiences in the world of man. On the brink of despair and a projected suicide, he makes a wager with the Devil that if he ever lies on his bed of slothfulness or says of any moment in life, "Stay thou art so fair," at that moment will he cease to be. He can not be lured by the supernatural, the sensual, the disembodied spiritual, but he does weaken in the presence of pure beauty and capitulates to humanitarian action. He displays himself as a sensual man in his deep love for Gretchen (Margarete), only to be goaded to murder by her brother, who sees not selfless love in their actions, but only sin. Faust aspires to the love of Helen of Troy, but he is finally disconsolate when she appears. As an old man he returns to his early vision of being a man among men, working and preparing for a better world to be lived here on earth. His death is not capitulation, though he thinks at this point man can cry "stay," and he has never taken his ease or been tempted by a life of sloth. His death is his victory and his everlasting life is to be lived resourcefully among the creators.

Mephistopheles (měf·ĭ·stŏf′ə·lēz), the Devil incarnate and Lucifer in disguise of dog and man. Portrayed here as a sophisticate, cynic, and wit, he is most persuasive and resourceful. He works magic, manages miracles, creates spirits and situations for Faust's perusal and delectation. His persistence is the more remarkable for the ability of Faust to withstand and refute, though Mephistopheles often expresses resentment. Somehow more attractive than God and the archangels, he powerfully represents the positive force of evil in its many and attractive guises.

Gretchen, sometimes called **Margarete,** an innocent, beautiful young maiden. A foil for the Devil, Gretchen remarkably personifies womanly love without blemish or fear. She gives herself to Faust, who swears he cannot molest her, with an earthy abandon and remains for a time unearthly innocent in her raptures, until the forces for morality convince her she has sinned deeply and that she must pay first by destroying her child and then by being sacrificed to the state, suffering death for her transgressions. Brooding over her brother's death, she refuses solace from her lover.

Valentin, a soldier and Gretchen's brother, killed by Faust with the aid of Mephistopheles.

Wagner (väg′nər), Faust's attendant, an unimaginative pedant. Serving as a foil for Faust, Wagner expresses himself in scholarly platitudes and learns only surface things. He aspires not to know all things but to know a few things well, or at least understandably; the unobtainable he leaves to Faust. He serves as the Devil's advocate, however, in the temptation of Faust by helping Mephistopheles create Homunculus.

Homunculus (hō·mŭng′kyōō·ləs), a disembodied spirit of learning. This symbol of man's learning, mind separated from reality, interprets for Mephistopheles, and accurately, what Faust is thinking. The spirit discloses Faust's near obsession with ideal beauty, and thus Faust was given the temptress, Helen of Troy.

Helen of Troy, who appears as a wraith at first and then with form. Representing the classical concept of eternal or ideal beauty, aesthetic, complete, Helen very nearly succeeds where Gretchen failed. She finally seems to Faust only transitory beauty, no matter how mythological and idealized. After this final experience Faust denounces such hypothetical pursuits and returns to deeds.

Dame Marthe Schwerdtlein, Gretchen's neighbor and friend, an unwitting tool in the girl's seduction.

363

FELIX HOLT, RADICAL

Author: George Eliot (Mary Ann Evans, 1819-1880)
Time of action: 1832-1833
First published: 1866

PRINCIPAL CHARACTERS

Felix Holt, the radical, an energetic and intelligent young man who objects to his mother's business, selling patent medicines, as fraudulent. Formerly apprenticed to an apothecary, he now works as a watchmaker in order to feel himself closer to the people. A political radical, Felix supports Harold Transome in the first Parliamentary election after the passage of the 1832 Reform Bill, but he objects to the bribery and rabble-rousing that others indulge in. As he fears, the workers riot on Election Day. Trying to disperse the riot, Felix inadvertently kills a constable. He is tried, convicted, sentenced to four years in prison; but a petition to Parliament secures his release. He marries Esther Lyon.

Harold Transome, the younger son of Mrs. Transome and apparently the heir to Transome Court. Harold has been away in Smyrna for fifteen years, building up a fortune as a merchant and banker. He returns and decides to run for Parliament as a Radical, an allegiance that shocks his Tory mother. He is honest and committed but loses the election. When he discovers that his mother's lawyer, Matthew Jermyn, has been cheating the estate for years, he decides to sue Jermyn. Jermyn attempts to avoid the suit by uncovering the fact, through an old will, that Esther Lyon is really the heiress of Transome Court. Harold invites Esther to his home and falls in love with her, but she rejects his suit and gives up her rights to the property. He abandons his plans to sue Jermyn when he learns that the latter is his father. At first crushed and furious, he is reconciled to his mother by Esther.

Rufus Lyon, another radical, the Dissent-ing minister of the Independent Chapel in Treby Magna (the Chapel is referred to as "Malthouse Yard"). He had found a destitute Frenchwoman, Annette Ledru, on the street with her infant daughter. He brought them home, later married Annette, and cared for Esther, the daughter, as his own after Annette died. Some papers that Felix finds in the woods lead to Lyon's discovery of the identity of Esther's father. Lyon regards Felix as an exceptional young man.

Esther Lyon, the sensitive and poetic daughter of Annette Ledru and Maurice Christian Bycliffe, brought up by the Dissenting minister, Rufus Lyon. Educated in France, she teaches French in Treby Magna. At first she and Felix argue about the relative importance of the aesthetic and the political, but she finds him entirely honest and vital. She soon falls in love with him and remains entirely loyal through his trial and short prison sentence.

Mrs. Arabella Transome, Harold's mother, who has long held Transome Court together despite legal and financial problems, an incompetent husband, and an idiot older son. She places all her faith in Harold, her illegitimate son by Matthew Jermyn. Despite her disapproval of her son's politics and his disapproval of Jermyn, the two value and appreciate each other.

Matthew Jermyn, the florid and insinuating lawyer who has mismanaged the estate, for his own benefit. He also handles Harold's political campaign and is not above offering bribes.

Mr. Johnson, a London lawyer hired by

364

Jermyn to stir up rabble-rousing activity among the new electorate. He also helps Jermyn in various shady financial operations. Johnson accuses Felix of leading the riot.

Philip Debarry, the successful Conservative candidate in the election. An honorable man, he intercedes on Felix's behalf after the trial.

Henry Scaddon, alias **Maurice Christian Bycliffe (Christian),** the servant to Philip Debarry, an unsavory character who had, in order to escape the law, changed identities with Maurice Christian Bycliffe, Esther's father, just before Bycliffe's death. Papers in Christian's purse, tossed away as a practical joke and discovered by Felix, reveal the assumed identity.

Mrs. Holt, a poor widow who makes a living selling patent medicines. Later her son Felix cheerfully supports her. She is a member of Mr. Lyon's Chapel.

The Reverend John Lingon, rector of Little Treby and Mrs. Transome's brother. He is very fond of his nephew Harold and supports his political campaign.

Sir Maximus Debarry, the owner of Treby Manor and Philip's father. Although Sir Maximus is an arch-Tory, he helps petition Parliament to gain Felix's release from prison.

The Reverend Augustus Debarry, his brother and a strong Tory.

Peter Garstin, a mine owner and a Liberal candidate for Parliament.

Sir James Clement, a poor baronet and a Liberal candidate for Parliament.

Mr. Chubb, the politically interested publican of the Sugar Loaf at Sproxton.

Tucker, the constable Felix inadvertently kills during the riot.

Mr. Spratt, a local Tory whose life Felix saves in the riot.

The Reverend Theodore Sherlock, a diffident young rector put to writing political speeches.

Thomas Transome (Tommy Trounsem), an old and alcoholic bill-paster trampled in the election riot.

Lady Debarry, the wife of Sir Maximus.

Mrs. Jermyn, Matthew's socially pretentious wife, who hates tobacco.

Miss Louisa Jermyn, her daughter, who takes French lessons from Esther Lyon.

Mr. Scales, the butler to the Debarrys, who tosses away the sleeping Christian's purse as a practical joke.

Denner, Mrs. Transome's faithful maid and confidant.

Hickes, Denner's husband, Mrs. Transome's butler.

Dominic, Harold Transome's servant, whom he brings back from Smyrna.

Lyddy, Rufus Lyon's trusted maid.

Mr. Transome, Mrs. Transome's old, paralyzed husband.

Durfey Transome, Mrs. Transome's imbecile older son, who dies at an early age.

Harry Transome, Harold Transome's attractive young son, whose mother, a native of Smyrna, is dead.

Mr. Sircome, a local miller and businessman.

Mr. Crowder, a local citizen.

Miss Harriet Debarry, the oldest daughter of the Debarrys.

Miss Selina Debarry, the Debarrys' "radiant" daughter.

Job Tudge, an independent child in Treby Magna, friendly with Esther and Felix.

Felix Holt, Jr., the oldest child of Esther and Felix.

365

THE FIELDS

Author: Conrad Richter (1890-   )
Time of action: Early nineteenth century
First published: 1946

PRINCIPAL CHARACTERS

Sayward Wheeler, called **Saird,** a strong pioneer woman who wants many children; but after having eight, she decides that seven living and one dead are enough, and she leaves her husband's bed. She lives through a period when the forest disappears as the pioneer settlement grows. She contributes her share to this growth and donates land for a meeting house. She realizes that she has neglected her husband and that he has been sleeping with the schoolteacher in the community. When the schoolteacher must quickly marry another man because she is going to have Portius' baby, Sayward is very much ashamed and is reconciled with her husband.

Portius Wheeler, a backwoods lawyer and schoolteacher, Sayward's husband. He has a hand in making Ohio a state and in making his community thrive and grow. Having no desire to return to his family in Boston, he tells them so. Portius wants to move his family into the new town, but Sayward refuses to be parted from the country. Portius has an affair with the schoolmistress but later returns to Sayward.

Genny Scurrah, Sayward's sister, who is a fine singer and who helps Sayward deliver her first child.

Wyitt Luckett, Sayward's brother, who realizes that he is a woodsman, as was his father. When he finds that all the game is gone from the woods, he moves on west.

Resolve Wheeler, Sayward's eldest son. He breaks his leg on a trip with his father and, while recuperating, he discovers that he has a great love of learning and books. When he returns home, he again breaks his leg in order to have time to read.

Sulie Wheeler, Sayward's daughter, who is named after Sayward's lost sister. The young Sulie is burned to death.

Mistress Bartram, a schoolteacher, to whom Portius turns when Sayward refuses to sleep with him. Because she is pregnant with Portius' child, she is married rather hurriedly to Jake Tench.

Jake Tench, the man who builds the first keelboat in the township.

Judah MacWhirter, a neighbor of the Wheelers who is bitten by a dog and dies of rabies.

Guerdon,
Kinzie,
Huldah,
Sooth,
Libby,
Dezia, and
Mercy Wheeler, Sayward and Portius' other children.

FILE NO. 113

Author: Émile Gaboriau (1835-1873)
Time of action: 1866
First published: 1867

Monsieur Lecoq (mə·syœ′ lə·kôk′), a brilliant detective and master of disguise. He clears Prosper chiefly to shame Gypsy, who was formerly his mistress.

Prosper Bertomy (prôs·pĕr′ bĕr·tô·mē′), a trusted bank clerk who has one of the two bank keys, and is therefore suspected of a robbery there. After being cleared he marries Madeleine.

M. André Fauvel (än·drā′ fō·vĕl′), a Paris banker who possesses the other key to his bank.

Valentine (vȧ·läṅ·tēn′), Fauvel's wife. As a young girl, she had an affair with a young neighbor, Gaston de Clameran, and secretly bore him a son in England. The child is now dead. Her husband is unaware of her indiscretion.

Louis de Clameran (lwē′ də klȧ·mə·räṅ′), Gaston's younger brother. He coaches Raoul to impersonate Valentine's dead son. He goes mad in prison.

Raoul de Lagors (rȧ·ōōl′ də lȧ·gôr′), an impostor claiming to be Valentine's son and now living with her as her "nephew." He forces her to provide Fauvel's key. Lecoq unmasks him by means of a scratch on the bank safe.

Madeleine (mȧd·lĕn′), Fauvel's niece, who is in love with Prosper but is willing to marry de Clameran in order to silence him about Valentine's indiscretion.

Chocareille (shô·kȧ·rĕ′y), called Gypsy, an ex-criminal and now the mistress of Prosper.

Fanferlot (fäṅ·fĕr·lō′), a detective secretly married to Mme. Alexandre.

Mme. Alexandre (ȧ·lĕk·säṅ′dr), the manager of the Archangel Hotel, where Gypsy is hidden.

Cavaillon (kȧ·vä·yōṅ′), a friend of Prosper who carries Prosper's warning note that puts the police on Gypsy's trail.

THE FINANCIER

Author: Theodore Dreiser (1871-1945)
Time of action: About 1871 to 1874
First published: 1912

Frank Algernon Cowperwood, the "financier," primarily interested in acquiring a fortune. Energetic and skillful, he begins by dealing successfully in soap when he is about thirteen years old. His uncle gets him a job in a grain commission house. Cowperwood's skill leads him into the brokerage business. He then marries Lillian Semple, the attractive widow of a business associate, five years older than he. Branching out into city railways and loans, he becomes involved with local politicians in Philadelphia. The daughter of a contractor, friendly with politicians, becomes Frank's mistress. When his speculations in municipal

railways and city loans are brought to light in the turmoil following the Chicago fire of 1871, he is apprehended and sent to jail. Released in thirteen months, he rebuilds his fortune during the panic of 1873. He then decides to move to Chicago.

Lillian Semple Cowperwood, his wife. A beautiful, passive woman, she becomes inadequate for Cowperwood. She knows of his affair with Aileen Butler but tolerates it until he decides to go to Chicago. Then she divorces him.

Henry Worthington Cowperwood, Frank's father, who began as a bank

367

clerk, later becoming teller, head cashier, and finally president. He is forced to resign when his son becomes involved in the City Treasury scandal.

Edward Malia Butler, a Philadelphia contractor. For a time Cowperwood is his financial adviser, thereby meeting his daughter Aileen. When Butler discovers, through an anonymous letter, that his daughter is Frank's mistress, he hires detectives to trail his daughter but he is unable to break up the affair. Through powerful political friends, he helps to ruin Cowperwood and send him to jail.

Aileen Butler, his daughter, strongly attracted by Cowperwood's personal and financial magnetism. She remains loyal to him despite her awareness of her father's objections. She visits him in jail and goes to Chicago as his mistress.

George W. Stener, the City Treasurer, appointed because he could easily serve as a dupe for the politicians. Through weakness and fear, he refuses to lend Cowperwood the additional city money necessary to cover his speculations.

Nancy Arabella Cowperwood, Frank's mother, happy with the elegant house he builds for her.

Seneca Davis, her wealthy brother, a former planter in Cuba. He encourages his nephew early in his career.

Anna Adelaide Cowperwood, Frank's sister. She becomes a clerk in the City Water Office.

Joseph Cowperwood, Frank's brother, whom he hires to work in the brokerage business.

Edward Cowperwood, another brother and a faithful employee.

Frank Cowperwood, Jr., Frank's son.

Lillian Cowperwood, Frank's daughter and favorite child.

Mrs. Edward Butler, Aileen's religious mother who never knows of her daughter's affair.

Nora Butler, Aileen's younger sister.

Owen Butler, the older brother of Aileen, a hard, cruel man who is a member of the State Legislature.

Callum Butler, his younger brother, a clerk in the City Water Office and an assistant to his father.

Harper Steger, Frank's friend and defense counsel.

Alfred Semple, Lillian's first husband.

Henry A. Mollenhauer, a rich coal dealer, the most vicious politician in Philadelphia. A city profiteer, he opposes Cowperwood bitterly during the scandal in order to get his railway shares.

Edward Strobik, president of the Philadelphia City Council, a henchman of Mollenhauer.

Senator Mark Simpson, a State Senator who joins Mollenhauer and Strobik in their financial dealings.

Albert Stires, Stener's secretary, the city clerk who issues the check that later gets Frank in legal trouble.

Van Nostrand, the State Treasurer.

Senator Terence Relihan, another crooked politician.

Judge Wilbur Payderson, the judge at Cowperwood's trial. To please the politicians, he hands down the maximum sentence.

Dennis Shannon, the district attorney who prosecutes Frank.

Mary Calligan (Mamie), Aileen's school friend, now a teacher, with whom Aileen lives when she leaves her family.

Mrs. Katherine Calligan, Mary's mother, a widow and a dressmaker.

Alderson, the Pinkerton detective who uncovers Aileen's and Frank's trysting place.

Judge Rafalsky, the jurist who writes the dissenting opinion, in Frank's favor, at the appeal.

Judge Marvin, another dissenting judge.

Stephen Wingate, who acts financially for Frank while the latter is in prison.

Warden Desmas, warden at the Philadelphia prison in which Frank is kept. He treats Frank very well.

THE FINN CYCLE

Author: Unknown
Time of action: Third century
First transcribed: Reputed eleventh century manuscript

PRINCIPAL CHARACTERS

Finn (fĭn), an Irish legendary hero, the leader of the King's warriors known as the Fianna Erinn. "The Finn Cycle" is composed of a series of ballads celebrating the brave exploits of this third century hero and his band of warriors; their virtues and their weaknesses; the eventual diminution of their powers; the dissolution of the band, and the waning of a heroic age.

Cumhal, the former leader of the Fianna Erinn and Finn's father.

Murna, Finn's mother.

Goll Mac Morna, the leader of the rival clan and, later, Finn's strong and loyal warrior.

The Lord of Luachar, a chieftain slain by Finn in his first heroic exploit.

Finegas, a sage from whom Finn learns wisdom and the art of poetry.

Conn, the ruler of Ireland, who makes Finn captain of his band of warriors known as the Fianna Erinn.

Oisin (ŭ·shēn'), Finn's son. He is a warrior poet. After his father's death, he is taken to an enchanted land where none grows old. After more than two

hundred years, homesick for Ireland, he returns and finds the land populated by weaklings, and the heroic age long since passed.

Oscar, Finn's grandson, the fiercest fighter of the Fianna Erinn.

Dermot, the ladies man,
Keelta, the warrior poet,
Conan the Bald, the gluttonous and slothful trickster, and
Mac Luga, the one skilled in courtesy, Finn's men.

The Dark Druid, a sorcerer who changes his beloved into a deer. She is released from the spell by Finn and becomes his wife. When Finn is called away to war, the Dark Druid recaptures the girl and takes her away, this time forever.

Vivionn, a giantess.

Fergus, a minstrel whose music restores peace between quarreling clans.

Grania, the daughter of the King of Ireland. She is married to Finn in his old age.

Niam, a fairy Princess who takes Oisin to an enchanted land where none grows old.

369

FINNEGANS WAKE

Author: James Joyce (1882-1941)
Time of action: A cycle of history
First published: 1939

PRINCIPAL CHARACTERS

Finnegan, the title character, whose name is derived from Finn MacCool, for two hundred years the legendary captain of Ireland's warrior heroes; the name change is coined in a Joycean pun ". . . Mister Finn, you're going to be Mister Finnagain." Finnegan, a hod carrier, has fallen from a ladder and is apparently dead. The fall is symbolic of the various falls (with implied corresponding resurrections) of mankind. At the wake, Finnegan's friends become noisy and unrestrained, and in the course of the festivities, at the mention of the Irish word for "whiskey" (usqueadbaugham!), Finnegan sits up, threatening to rise. The mourners soothe him back. With Finnegan's demise, a new day is structured, and the hod carrier is supplanted by a man who has arrived to start life as Finnegan's successor.

Humphrey Chimpden Earwicker, also **Here Comes Everybody** and **Haveth Childer Everywhere.** HCE, the newcomer, is a tavern keeper. In keeping with the metamorphosis, his initials are a carry over from Finnegan's vocation of "hod, cement, and edifice." Another connection between the two men lies in Earwicker's emerging from Howth Castle and Environs, to which locale Finnegan's interment fades in the story. HCE has wandered widely, leaving his progeny along the way, from Troy and Asia Minor, through the lands of the Goths, the Franks, the Norsemen; he has traveled in Britain and Eire; he has Germanic and Celtic manifestations; up through history he becomes Cromwell. In short, he is Here Comes Everybody and Haveth Childer Everywhere, representing civilization. At present, he is

Earwicker, HCE, a sympathetic character, harrowed by relentless fate. In Phoenix Park (the Garden of Eden) he is caught exhibiting himself to several girls. This impropriety and the Dubliners' resentment of HCE as an intruder give rise to rumors that plague Earwicker, as the scandal takes on aspects of troubled times throughout history. The tumult in Earwicker's soul is consistent with the struggles of all battles in the past. The trials and tribulations of HCE continue until ultimately, after a description of the shadows on a windowblind of him and his wife in copulation, HCE turns from his wife. He is now the broken shell of Humpty Dumpty. The hopes of the parents are in the children. The cycle of man is ready to start anew.

Ann, also **Anna Livia Plurabelle,** HCE's wife. Just as Earwicker becomes Adam, Noah, Lord Nelson, a mountain, or a tree, so is ALP (as Ann is referred to generally throughout the book) metamorphosed into Eve, Isis, Iseult, the widow who serves at the wake, a passing cloud, a flowing stream. In this last transformation, as the River Liffey (which flows through Dublin), Ann plays her most important role. At the source, as a brooklet, she is a gay, young girl. Passing her husband's tavern, she is comely, matronly. Flowing on through Dublin, she becomes the haggard cleaning woman, carrying away the filth of the city. She finally moves on to the ocean, from which she rises again in mist to become rain and start again as a mountain stream. As Earwicker's wife, Ann plays the part of the motivator of her husband's energies. She is the housekeeper. She is the mother of his children.

370

Among the various polarities spelled out in the book, Ann is love, opposed to war as depicted by Earwicker.

Kevin, also **Shaun the Postman, Chuff, Jaun,** and **Yawn,** one of their sons. In his domestic role as Kevin, he is the extrovert, the man of action. He is the political orator, the favorite of the people, policeman of the planet, bearer of the white man's burdens. He is the aggressor and the despoiler. As the symbolic Shaun, he is the Postman delivering to mankind the great message discovered and penned by his brother Jerry. Shaun, whose advice is "Collide with man, collude with money," enjoys the rewards of the carrier of good tidings. Shaun is one of the opposites in another polarity stressed by Joyce, the opposites being the principals in the Brother Battle.

Jerry, also **Shem the Penman, Dolph,** and **Glugg,** Kevin's twin brother. As the polar extreme of his brother, Jerry acts on inturned energy. The books he writes are mortifying in that they lose the lines of good and evil; they are rejected by the decent. Erratic in his introversion, he vacillates between vehement action and unselfish forgiveness. His uncontrolled love is as dangerous as his wanton hate. Among the domestic scenes, the personalities of the two boys are shown as Glugg (Shem) loses to Chuff (Shaun) in their fights for the approval of girls. Also, as Dolph and Kevin working at their lessons, Dolph, the studious one, helps his brother with a problem; Kevin indignantly strikes Dolph, who forgives.

Isobel, HCE and ALP's daughter and sister of the twins. In the domestic scene she behaves as the child of an average family—playing, studying, and brooding on love. Symbolically, Isobel figures in episodes involving Swift and Vanessa, Mark and Iseult. Identifying her with Tristram's Iseult, HCE has illicit desires for Isobel; also, he envisions her as the reincarnation of the wife. These thoughts keep him young.

Among the myriad other characters—local and historical—that are intermingled in this poetic, convoluted account of birth, conflict, death, and resurrection are two significant groups:

Twelve Stately Citizens, who are variously a jury sitting in judgment on HCE, constant customers of Earwicker's tavern, leading mourners at Finnegan's wake, and the twelve signs of the zodiac.

Four Old Men, who are intermittently four senile judges, the four winds, the four recorders of Irish annals, the four phases of the Viconian cycle: theocratic, aristocratic, democratic, and chaotic. This last phase, marked by individualism and sterility, represents the nadir of man's fall. But mankind will rise again in response to the thunderclap, which polysyllabic sound Joyce uses to introduce his story of mankind.

THE FISHER MAIDEN

Author: Björnstjerne Björnson (1832-1910)
Time of action: Early nineteenth century
First published: 1868

PRINCIPAL CHARACTERS

Petra, known as the fisher maiden. She is the illegitimate child of Pedro Ohlsen and Gunlaug. As a child she is brought back to her home village by her mother. When she grows up she acquires three suitors who fight over her. She leaves the village for Bergen because she is attracted to the stage. She is later forgiven by Hans Ödegaard, who has felt that she ruined his life when he was her suitor.

Hans Ödegaard, the village pastor's son. He teaches Petra to read and falls in love with her. To his father's sorrow he is indifferent to a career as a clergyman. Though he feels his life is ruined by Petra's having other suitors, he gets over his despair and marries a girl named Signe, daughter of a clergyman.

Pedro Ohlsen, a dreamer and a flute player. He has an affair with Gunlaug which results in Petra's birth. His father and grandfather leave him a fortune which he in his turn wills to Petra upon his death.

Gunlaug, an audacious and bewitching woman, the mother of Petra. She helps her daughter escape from the village in the disguise of a sailor, after the village is aroused by the girl's having three suitors.

Gunnar, a poor sailor. He is one of Petra's three suitors.

Yngve Vold, a rich shipowner, one of Petra's three suitors. When he announces that he plans to marry Petra, he is beaten by both Gunnar and Hans.

Signe, a friend of Petra. She loves Hans and plans to marry him. She is a suitable wife because she is a pastor's daughter of unimpeachable reputation.

FIVE WOMEN WHO LOVED LOVE

Author: Ibara Saikaku (c. 1642-1693)
Time of action: Seventeenth century
First published: c. 1685

PRINCIPAL CHARACTERS

THE FIRST STORY

Seijûrô, a handsome young man apprenticed to a shopkeeper. Reluctantly, he returns the love of his master's sister. They elope and are discovered. Wrongly convicted of stealing money (actually mislaid), Seijûrô is executed.

Onatsu, the shopkeeper's sister, who is in love with Seijûrô. After his execution she goes mad for a time and later enters a nunnery.

THE SECOND STORY

Osen, the young wife of a cooper. Wrongly accused of adultery by Chôzaemon's wife, she takes impulsive revenge by actually giving herself to him. Discovered by her husband, she commits suicide.

Chôzaemon, a yeast maker and Osen's partner in adultery, suspected and real. When his guilt is discovered, he is executed.

THE THIRD STORY

Osan, a wife whose scheme to punish her maid's reluctant lover by taking the maid's place in bed runs counter to plan. She falls in love with him herself; after a period of hiding together in a distant village, they are found and executed.

Rin, Osan's maid. She is a party to the scheme by which her lover is supposed to be punished.

Moemon, a clerk and Rin's reluctant lover, who is the victim of the substitution. He falls in love with Osan. When caught, they are executed.

THE FOURTH STORY

Oshichi, a young girl. Having taken refuge in a temple after her house burned down, she falls in love with a man she meets there. Later, unable to see him, she decides to arrange another meeting by setting a fire. Discovered, she is burned at the stake.

Onogawa Kichisaburô, a young samurai whom Oshichi loves. Learning of her death, he contemplates suicide but finally becomes a monk.

THE FIFTH STORY

Gengobei, a Buddhist monk and a former pederast.

[Hachijûrô, now dead, a boy whom Gengobei loved.]

Oman, a young girl in love with Gengobei. Disguising herself as a boy, she wins Gengobei's love. He leaves the priesthood to live with her and later to marry her.

FOMA GORDYEEFF

Author: Maxim Gorky (Aleksei Maksimovich Peshkov, 1868-1936)
Time of action: Late nineteenth century
First published: 1899

PRINCIPAL CHARACTERS

Foma Gordyeeff (fō'mə gôr·dĕ'yĕf), the son of a tough trader who owns barges and tugs and speculates on the exchange. Foma, wishing to know the meaning of life, has trouble accepting capitalistic views and, at the end, he denounces local moneyed dignitaries by shouting reminders of their unsavory pasts for all to hear at a ship launching. He is hustled off to an insane asylum. Released, he is a drunken, broken man who wanders about the town, out of his mind and in rags. He is befriended only by his godfather's daughter, a childhood friend, who gives him a small room to live in.

Mayakin (mä·yä'kĭn), Foma Gordyeeff's godfather, in whose house Foma lived until he was six years old. Mayakin takes a personal interest in his godson's life and fortune. He advises, intervenes, finally takes a power of attorney over Gordyeeff's holdings and sends Foma to a mental hospital when he makes his outraged speech exposing the lives of respectable townsmen.

Liuboff (lū'bəf), Mayakin's daughter, Foma's friend from childhood. She never understands him but tries to do so by discussing ideas with him. She gives him sanctuary after his release from the asylum.

Ignat Gordyeeff (ĭg·nät'), Foma's father,

a ruthless, thoroughgoing trader who makes his fortune by hard work and cunning. He falls under the influence of a woman who persuades him to give much of his wealth to charity. He dies a foolish, confused man.

Smolin (smô·lĭn') and
Ezhoff (ĕzh·ôf'), Foma's school friends. Ezhoff was poor but intelligent; Smolin, fat, rich, undistinguished. Ezhoff becomes a quick-witted journalist who makes revolutionary speeches to laborers. Foma and Ezhoff do not argue about politics; they simply drink together. Smolin becomes a sharp trader, the betrothed of Liuboff.

Sasha (sä'shə), a river girl who, along with her sister, fascinates Foma. He has a wild, carousing affair with her, but she abandons him because his philosophical speculations bore her.

Madame Medynsky (mĕ·dĭn'skĭy), the guiding hand in Ignat's philanthropic ventures. She is cosmopolitan and sophisticated, and willing to bestow her favors where they will do the most good. Foma, deeply attracted to her, is disappointed when he thinks she does not take him seriously.

Natalya (nä·tä'lyä), a handsome young

373

woman, Ignat's second wife and Foma's mother. She dies soon after his birth.

Aunt Anfisa (än·fi′sə), the relative who cares for Foma after he leaves Mayakin's house. Her fantastic adventure stories greatly impressed him when he was young.

THE FOOL OF QUALITY

Author: Henry Brooke (c. 1703-1783)
Time of action: Eighteenth century
First published: 1766-1770

PRINCIPAL CHARACTERS

Henry (Harry) Clinton, the second son of the Earl of Moreland, put out to nurse when an infant. Educated to be perfect, he is liberal and friendly, impressing even the King and the court. At his father's death, his older brother being already dead, he becomes the Earl of Moreland and uses his fortune and position to help many people.

Mr. Fenton, a wealthy elderly gentleman who becomes young Harry Clinton's benefactor. He, too, is a Harry Clinton, the uncle of the hero. After he makes himself known to his brother the Earl, he is known as Mr. Clinton.

Ned, a beggar lad who becomes Harry's companion as a boy. He turns out to be of good family and is returned to his parents, from whom he had been stolen as a baby.

Lady Maitland (Fanny Goodall), Mr. Fenton's cousin. Years before, they had been in love. She is married to Louisa d'Aubigny's brother, and is thus Mr. Fenton's sister-in-law.

The Earl of Moreland, Harry's father. He is remorseful for his treatment of his son and brother and is happy when they are restored to him.

Louisa d'Aubigny, Mr. Fenton's second wife. She dies after a fall.

Eloisa, daughter of Mr. Fenton and Louisa d'Aubigny. Thought lost at sea, she is rescued and becomes the wife of the Emperor of Morocco.

Abenaide, daughter of the Emperor of Morocco and Eloisa Fenton. She appears in England disguised as a page. Later she appears in her true form and marries Harry, now the Earl of Moreland.

FOR WHOM THE BELL TOLLS

Author: Ernest Hemingway (1899-1961)
Time of action: 1937
First published: 1940

PRINCIPAL CHARACTERS

Robert Jordan, an American expatriate school teacher who has joined the Loyalist forces in Spain. Disillusioned with the world and dissatisfied with his own country, Jordan has come to Spain to fight and die, if necessary, for a cause he knows is vital and worth while, that of the native, peasant, free soul against the totalitarian cruelty of Franco and his Fascists. He is, however, aware of the contrast between his ideals and the realities he has found among narrow, self-important, selfish, bloodthirsty men capable of betrayal and cruelty as well as

374

courage. He also finds love, devotion, generosity, selflessness in the persons of Anselmo, Pilar, and especially Maria. The latter he loves with the first true selflessness of his life, and he wishes to avenge her cruel suffering and someday make her his wife in a land free of oppression and cruelty. With bravery, almost bravado, he carries out his mission of blowing up a bridge and remains behind to die with the sure knowledge that in Maria and Pilar his person and ideals will survive. Successful for the first time in his life, in love and war, he awaits death as an old friend.

Maria, a young and innocent Spanish girl cruelly ravaged by war and men's brutality. Befriended by Pilar, a revolutionary, Maria finds a kind of security in the guerrilla band and love in her brief affair with Robert Jordan. As his common-law wife almost all memory of her rape and indignities disappear, and at a moment of triumph for their forces it looks as if they will live to see their dreams of the future fulfilled. Elemental in her passions and completely devoted to her lover, she refuses to leave him and must be forced to go on living. The embodiment of Jordan's ideals, she must live.

Pilar, the strong, almost masculine leader of the guerrilla group with whom Jordan plans to blow up the bridge. Although a peasant and uneducated, Pilar has not only deep feeling but also a brilliant military mind; she is somewhat a Madame Defarge of the Spanish Civil War. Her great trial is her murderous, traitorous husband whom she loves but could kill. Without fear for herself, she has sensitive feelings for Maria, who is suffering from her traumatic experiences as the victim of Fascist lust and cruelty behind the lines. Greatly incensed by inhumanities, Pilar valorously carries out her mission in destroying the bridge, the symbol of her vindictiveness.

Pablo, Pilar's dissolute, drunken, treach-erous husband, a type of murderous peasant for whom nothing can be done but without whom the mission cannot be successfully carried out. A hill bandit, Pablo feels loyalty only to himself, kills and despoils at random, is given to drinking and whoring at will. Nevertheless he displays a kind of generosity, even after he has stolen the detonators and peddled them to the enemy, when he comes back to face almost certain death and to go on living with the wife whom he loves and fears. This admixture of cunning, cruelty, and bravado finally leads the band to safety. Pablo represents that irony of ways and means which war constantly confuses.

Anselmo, the representative of peasant wisdom, devotion to duty, high-minded, selfless love for humanity, and compassion for the human condition. Hating to kill but not fearing to die, Anselmo performs his duty by killing when necessary, but without rancor and with a kind of benediction, and dies as he lived, generously and pityingly. While the others of the guerrilla band are more of Pablo's persuasion, brutally shrewd and vindictive in loyalty, Anselmo tempers his devotion to a cause with a larger view. Aligned with Pilar and Jordan in this larger vision, he displays disinterested and kindly loyalty that is almost pure idealism, all the more remarkable for his age, background, and experience. The benignant, almost Christ-like Anselmo dies that others may live and that Robert Jordan may know how to die.

El Sordo, a Loyalist guerrilla leader killed in a Fascist assault on his mountain hideout.

General Golz, the Russian officer commanding the Thirty-fifth Division of the Loyalist forces.

Karkov, a Russian journalist.

Andrés, a guerrilla sent by Robert Jordan with a dispatch for General Golz.

André Marty, the commissar who prevents prompt delivery of the dispatch
intended for General Golz.

Rafael, a gipsy,

Agustín,
Fernando,
Primitivo, and
Eladio, other members of the guerrilla
band led by Pablo and Pilar.

THE FORSYTE SAGA

Author: John Galsworthy (1867-1933)
Time of action: 1886-1920
First published: "The Man of Property," 1906; "In Chancery," 1920; "To Let,"
1921

PRINCIPAL CHARACTERS

Soames Forsyte (fôr'sīt), the head of an
upper middle-class English family. He
has been at odds with his wife Irene but
hopes to bring about a reconciliation by
building a large country house at Robin
Hill. His tragedy is that he is unlovable
and knows it.

Old Jolyon Forsyte, formerly a tea merchant, who gives a party in 1886 to
celebrate the engagement of his granddaughter June to Philip Bosinney. He
buys the house built by his nephew
Soames and moves to Robin Hill, where
he dies.

Young Jolyon Forsyte, his son, the
father of June. He is estranged from the
rest of the Forsyte family because he had
run away with a governess and married
her after the death of June's mother. He
has become an underwriter for Lloyd's
and paints watercolors in his leisure
time.

June Forsyte, Young Jolyon's daughter,
whose fiancé, Philip Bosinney, is attracted to Irene. He is killed by an omnibus while wandering, distraught, in a
fog.

Holly Forsyte, the daughter of Young
Jolyon's second marriage, and a friend of
Fleur. She falls in love with her cousin
Val Dartie. When he goes to fight in the
Boer War, she becomes a Red Cross
nurse.

Jolly Forsyte, the son of Young Jolyon's
second marriage, Holly's twin. He enlists as a yeoman to fight in the Boer
War and dies of enteric fever, in Africa,
in 1900.

Philip Bosinney, a young architect engaged to June Forsyte. He is hired by
Soames to build his country home at
Robin Hill. Seeing Irene, he falls in love
with her and spends an afternoon with
her. Soames brings suit against him for
exceeding the original building estimate,
and Philip loses. He is run over by an
omnibus in the fog and is killed.

James Forsyte, the brother of Old Jolyon
and father of Soames. He believes Bosinney's death a suicide.

Irene Forsyte, a lovely woman presented
as a symbol of the beauty all men desire.
Unhappily married to possessive Soames,
she falls in love with Bosinney, but his
death forces her to return to her husband. At last she arranges a separation,
aided by a fifteen-thousand-pound legacy
from Old Jolyon. She falls in love with
Young Jolyon, who administers her inheritance, and they go to France to live.
Soames divorces her.

Jon Forsyte, the son of Irene and Young
Jolyon. His decision to study farming
and visit the Darties leads to his meeting
with Fleur and their romance. A letter
from his father, telling the story of

Soames, Irene, and Young Jolyon, causes him to give up all hope of marrying Fleur.

Annette Lamotte, a French girl selected by Soames to give him an heir. When the child is about to be born, Soames is willing to sacrifice Annette for the sake of the child, but she lives anyway. When accused by Soames of having an affair with Prosper Profond, she acknowledges it, but insists she is avoiding any scandal.

Fleur Forsyte, the daughter of Soames and Annette, badly spoiled by her father. Meeting Jon, she falls in love with him, but the family feud prevents the marriage. She eventually marries Michael Mont.

Swithin Forsyte, an uncle of Soames who takes Irene to see the Robin Hill house and is therefore responsible for the meeting between her and Bosinney.

Winifred Forsyte Dartie, the sister of Soames. Though deserted by her husband when he eloped with a dancer, she takes him back when he returns repentant.

Montague (Monty) Dartie, married to Winifred. He steals her pearls and runs away to South America with a Spanish dancer but returns to Winifred when the girl leaves him after his money runs out.

Val Dartie, the son of Monty and Winifred, in love with Holly. On a dare he enlists to fight in the Boer War. After the war he marries Holly, to the discomfiture of both branches of the Forsyte family. He and Holly make their living training race horses.

Michael Mont, a young man brought by Soames to the Forsyte house to look at a collection of paintings. He falls in love with Fleur.

Prosper Profond, with whom Annette has an affair. His account to Fleur of the Forsyte feud makes her scheme for a hasty marriage to Jon.

Timothy Forsyte, an uncle of Soames and the last of the older generation of the family. His death ends the age of the Forsytes.

Mr. Belby, Soames' lawyer and a partner of Dream, Q.C.

Boris Strumolowski, an advanced sculptor, and a friend of June Forsyte.

FORTITUDE

Author: Hugh Walpole (1884-1941)
Time of action: Late nineteenth century
First published: 1913

PRINCIPAL CHARACTERS

Peter Westcott, the son of a harsh father and an invalid mother. Having been sent for a time to school, and now reading law in an office, he finds his home life intolerable after the death of his mother, and he leaves Cornwall to accept a job in an acquaintance's London bookshop. In London he writes a novel which proves successful, and he marries; but his subsequent books are failures, his small son dies, and his wife leaves him. At last, ready to give up the struggle, he returns to Cornwall. There he meets an old friend who is dying and from her he learns fortitude.

Clare Elizabeth Rossiter, whom Peter marries. He blames her for the death of their son. In spite of Peter's efforts to preserve their marriage, Clare leaves him for another man.

Stephen Brant, a farmer with whom Peter becomes friendly as a boy, and from whom Peter learns much about life. It is through Stephen that Peter meets the bookseller who employs him. When the political activities going on in the bookshop prove dangerous, Stephen comes to take Peter away. Clare disapproves of Stephen.

Nora Monogue, whom Peter meets in London. She encourages him to write. Much later, the dying Nora admits that she has always loved him; her dying request is that he go back to London and continue writing. Through her he learns fortitude.

Jerry Cardillac (Cards), Peter's idol at school. After Peter's marriage, Clare becomes interested in Cardillac; later she leaves Peter to join Cardillac in France.

Emilio Zanti, a London bookseller who gives Peter a job. Clare disapproves of him.

Bobby Galleon, the son of a famous writer and Peter's schoolfriend. After Peter has been instrumental in the expelling of the school's best bowler, Bobby alone does not join in hissing him.

Jerrard, the best bowler in school. On the eve of a big game, Peter finds him forcing whiskey down the throat of a small boy and reports him. Jerrard is expelled, the game is lost, and Peter is hissed in school.

Zachary Tan, the operator of a curiosity shop to which Stephen Brant takes young Peter. There he meets Emilio Zanti.

Mr. Aitchinson, in whose office Peter reads law for a time.

Gottfried Hanz, an employee in Mr. Zanti's bookshop. Peter works as Hanz' assistant.

Mrs. Brockett, in whose lodging house Peter lives while working in the bookshop and while writing his first novel.

Mrs. Launce, whom Peter meets after his introduction to literary circles. She is instrumental in bringing Peter and Clare together.

Stephen Westcott, the son of Peter and Clare. His early death is a final blow to Peter's happiness.

THE FORTRESS

Author: Hugh Walpole (1884-1941)
Time of action: Nineteenth century
First published: 1932

PRINCIPAL CHARACTERS

Judith Paris (also see "Judith Paris"), who has returned with her illegitimate son to live with her nephew's widow. She continues to resist the persecution of another nephew's son.

Jennifer Herries, the widow of Judith's nephew Francis (also see "Judith Paris"). A principal in an old quarrel, she is now its victim. The strain of her nephew's persecution is too much for her, and she dies.

Walter Herries (also see "Judith Paris"), the son of Judith's nephew William. De-

termined to drive Jennifer and Judith out of their home, he offers first to buy it. When they refuse, he does his best to drive them away by persecution. To this end, he builds a great mansion, called the Fortress, on a hill overlooking their house.

Elizabeth Herries, Walter's beautiful and kind daughter. She loves Jennifer's son John, but agrees not to see him because of family hatred. She goes to live with London relatives until her father's command that she marry a detested suitor drives her to take employment as a governess. There her employer's pursuit causes her to marry John. They are happy until John is killed by Elizabeth's brother. Learning that her father, who has resisted all her overtures, is seriously ill, Elizabeth storms the Fortress, nurses him back to health, and even succeeds in effecting a semblance of reconciliation between him and Judith on Judith's hundredth birthday.

John Herries (also see "Judith Paris"), the son of Jennifer. A parliamentary secretary, his future seems bright; but he is dogged by his wife's brother, whose hatred makes John feel powerless. At last he confronts Uhland, who shoots him.

Uhland Herries, Walter's lame, pampered, and rancorous son. After shooting John, he kills himself.

Adam Paris, Judith's illegitimate son (also see "Judith Paris"). Robust and rebellious, he leaves for London at twenty-two and becomes involved in the Chartist movement. He marries and returns to his mother's house to live.

Caesar Kraft, Adam's guide in London. He urges moderation on the Chartists, is blamed for the failure of a procession, and is killed in a riot.

Margaret Kraft, his daughter. She marries Adam and at first, with him and his mother, feels herself an outsider. But Adam comes to understand her needs and gives her first place over Judith.

Benjie Herries, the son of Elizabeth and John.

Mr. Temple, a fat and rich lawyer who is Elizabeth's suitor. He is favored by her father and brother.

Christabel Herries, Walter's weak mother. (Also see "Judith Paris.")

Reuben Sunwood (also see "Judith Paris"), whose death is an addition to the trouble between Judith and Walter.

FORTUNATA AND JACINTA

Author: Benito Pérez Galdós (1845-1920)
Time of action: 1869-1875
First published: 1886-1887

PRINCIPAL CHARACTERS

Juanito Santa Cruz (hwä·nē'tō sän'tä krōōth), the protagonist in a realistic four-volume novel of bourgeois life in Madrid in the 1870's. He is without morals or scruples.

Bárbara Santa Cruz (bär'bä·rä sän'tä krōōth), Juanito's mother and the proprietor of a dry goods store established by the family in the previous century. She spoils her son.

Plácido Estupiñá (plä'thē·ʈħō ĕs·tōō-pē·nyä'), a part-time smuggler and her adviser.

Fortunata (fôr·tōō·nä'tä), a lively, attractive lower-class woman who becomes Juanito's mistress. Later she marries Maximiliano. She dies of exposure while seeking revenge for Jacinta and herself.

Petusin (pä·tōō'sēn), the illegitimate son of Juanito and Fortunata.

Jacinta (hä·thēn'tä), Juanito's placid, beautiful cousin, chosen by his mother to be his wife. She cannot have children.

Maximiliano Rubín (mä·sē·mē·lyä'nō ɍōō·bēn'), the ugly schizophrenic orphan son of a goldsmith. He marries Fortunata.

Lupe (lōō'pä), Maximiliano's aunt, who warns Fortunata against the marriage.

379

Juan Pablo Rubín (hwän pä'blō r̄roo-bēn'), one of Maximiliano's brothers and a loafer.

Colonel Evaristo Feijóo (ā·bä·rēs'tō fā·ē-hō'ō), an elderly protector of Fortunata.

Guillermina Pancheco (gē·lyâr·mē'nä pän·chā'kō), at whose house Jacinta learns of her husband's infidelity.

The Widow Samaniego (sä·mä·nyē'gō), the owner of a drugstore, who employs Maximiliano.

Aurora (äoo·rō'rä), her flashy daughter, who attracts Juanito. They become lovers.

Moreno Isla (mō·rē'nō ēs'lä), whose proposition is refused by the faithful Jacinta.

THE FORTUNES OF NIGEL

Author: Sir Walter Scott (1771-1832)
Time of action: Early seventeenth century
First published: 1822

PRINCIPAL CHARACTERS

Nigel Olifaunt, Lord of Glenvarloch, a gallant young Scotsman who comes to England to collect payment for injustices committed against his noble family. Naïve and impressionable, he becomes involved in gambling and ribaldry in the ordinaries and gaming houses of the town. This experience leads to his association with ruffians and life in Alsatia, the haunt of bully-boys, thieves, and murderers. A brave youth, he kills a robber in his rooming house and saves the life of Martha Trapbois, his landlord's daughter. Imprisoned for carrying arms in the presence of King James, he languishes while his faithful servant negotiates for the money owed the Glenvarlochides, as the King calls them. On his return to Scotland, he is accompanied by his bride, Margaret Ramsay, an English commoner now known to be of noble Scottish descent.

James I, King of England, whose conduct makes him a portentous clown among the Stuarts. His folly, insensibilities, and erudition are interwoven to make him a comedic character, to the detriment of the suspense of the story.

Richard (Richie) Moniplies, Nigel's faithful page. His capabilities and fortitude make Nigel's expedition a success. Richie's impudence is offset by better qualities, to justify his winning the wealthiest woman, although of low birth, in the story. Money becomes Richie more than rank or station.

Lord Dalgarno, a gay, spendthrift Scotsman who knows the ways of London. Befriending the newly arrived Nigel, Dalgarno introduces him to the seamy side of life, only to desert him in time of reverses and to report Nigel's unbecoming behavior to court circles. The villain, Dalgarno marries Martha Trapbois, a usurer's daughter, for her large sum of money, but deserts her and takes another man's wife with him when he starts back to Scotland. Richie murders him.

Master George Heriot, an old goldsmith and confidant of the King who is involved in most of the political intrigue surrounding Nigel's efforts to regain family property and Dalgarno's rascality to prevent Nigel's success.

Reginald Lowestoffe, a young, profligate law student who befriends Nigel in Alsatia. He aids Richie in avenging Nigel against Dalgarno.

Margaret Ramsay, the beautiful young daughter of a London clockmaker. Enamored of Nigel because of his handsome appearance and his ill fortune at the hands of Dalgarno, she goes before the King in the disguise of a page to plead for Nigel's release from the Tower. Through Heriot's efforts, Margaret and Nigel are married, Margaret's noble heritage having been established to save the union from that of nobleman and commoner.

Martha Trapbois, the uneducated but wise daughter of a moneylender in Alsatia, in whose house Nigel lives in his exile from society. Nigel saves her life during a robbery and flees with her when she takes her father's great money chest. She is intercepted on her way to John Christie's rooming house by Dalgarno, who marries her for her wealth. After Dalgarno's murder she marries Richie Moniplies.

Lady Hermione, a descendant of the House of Glenvarloch and long an isolate in the house of George Heriot, after her criminal abduction from her Spanish husband. Approached for counsel by Margaret Ramsay, Lady Hermione encourages the young woman to leave no stone unturned in winning and keeping her lover, Nigel.

Andrew Skurliewhitter, the scrivener who handles all court papers. An accomplice to Dalgarno, he lacks courage to complete the thefts that will accomplish Dalgarno's purposes, and he disappears from the scene and the story when Dalgarno is murdered.

Dame Nelly Christie, the housewife who elopes with Dalgarno when he flees with money and papers to Scotland. A simpering woman, she pleads to become Dalgarno's loving wife rather than his loving lady. She is apprehended by her husband at the scene of Dalgarno's murder.

John Christie, her husband, a ship chandler who acts as a news carrier from his rooming house.

Sir Mungo Malagrowther, a confidant of the King. As Nigel's adversary, he adds considerably to the young nobleman's difficulties.

Dame Ursula Suddlechop, a barber's wife who acts as a matchmaker, her activity bordering on sorcery. She predicts marriage between Margaret Ramsay and Jenkin Vincent, as well as other unfulfilled prophecies. Dame Suddlechop ends her career in a "Rasp-haus" in Amsterdam.

Jenkin Vincent, a young apprentice to the clockmaker. Thwarted in his desire for Margaret, he is sent, through the efforts of George Heriot, on an important business mission to Paris. It is assumed that he returns to London and establishes a prosperous business with his fellow apprentice.

Frank Tunstall, another apprentice to the clockmaker, introduced into the plot only as a possible suitor to Margaret.

David Ramsay, Margaret's father. An ingenious, whimsical mechanic, he becomes a successful horologist.

The Duke of Buckingham, a favorite of King James, at odds with Nigel when he appears at court to sue for money due his family.

Prince Charles, the son of King James. His chief function seems to be to point up the foolish behavior of the King.

Lord Huntinglen, Dalgarno's father. A righteous man, he would have the Glenvarlochs compensated. In the manner of the old nobility, he deplores his son's villainy.

Trapbois, Martha's father, a usurer, murdered by accomplices of the scrivener, who thinks that Trapbois was able to steal Nigel's mortgage papers while Nigel lived in the Trapbois house in Alsatia.

Captain Colepepper, a cowardly criminal who flees any danger but may be talked into any villainy. He and the scrivener plot against Dalgarno as Dalgarno plots against Nigel.

De Beaujeu, a gaming-house keeper whose establishment, as a rendezvous, is a focal point for much of the action in the novel.

THE FORTUNES OF RICHARD MAHONY

Author: Henry Handel Richardson (Mrs. Henrietta Richardson Robertson, 1870-1946)
Time of action: Nineteenth century
First published: 1917, 1925, 1929

PRINCIPAL CHARACTERS

Richard Mahony, a sincere young Irish doctor who leaves a practice in England to become a prospector in the Australian gold fields. After failures as a prospector and storekeeper he returns to medical practice. Suddenly finding himself a rich man through gold stocks he bought, he goes to England only to be snubbed; returning to Australia, he becomes a snob and a recluse, giving up his friends and a normal life for an interest in spiritualism. He loses his fortune, and his mind deteriorates. He has to be confined as a madman until shortly before his death.

Polly Turnham, who becomes Richard Mahony's wife. She is a stalwart woman who can take life's trials. Unlike her husband, she never becomes a snob, no matter how rich she is. When her husband goes mad she does her best to support her children and provide the costs of her husband's illness.

John Turnham, Polly's brother. He is a successful businessman and politician. He helps Mahony with both advice and money. He becomes a bitter man after the deaths of his two wives and comes to depend emotionally upon his sister. When he dies of cancer, the Mahonys move back to England.

Purdy Smith, an old schoolmate of Mahony. He introduces Mahony to the girl who becomes his wife. Smith is a coarse man, quite the opposite of the fastidious Mahony.

Henry Ocock, a long-time friend of the Mahonys. He is a lawyer and helps them arrange their affairs. Through his advice Mahony buys the gold mine stocks that make him rich. When the Mahonys are poor again, Henry Ocock helps them out.

Lallie Mahony, one of the Mahony children. She dies tragically while still a child. Afer her death her father's mental health deteriorates rapidly.

THE FORTY DAYS OF MUSA DAGH

Author: Franz Werfel (1890-1945)
Time of action: 1915
First published: 1934

PRINCIPAL CHARACTERS

Gabriel Bagradian, a loyal Armenian, although he is an officer in the Ottoman reserves. Married to a Frenchwoman and long a resident of Paris, he has returned to his native village, Yoghonoluk, in order to settle some business affairs managed by his older brother Avetis, who has just died. Gabriel has never

382

been able to forget his Armenian home and ancestry. The mountain, Musa Dagh, is as dear to him as if it were a relative. War is imminent, and the Turkish plan is to exile all the Armenians of the district. After Gabriel assumes leadership of the community, the Armenians vote to defend Musa Dagh and take their position on that natural fortress. Their bravery is unmatched, but they have little food and insufficient ammunition for a siege. After forty days, the last attack is planned by Gabriel, and they have set fire to the mountainside. Three days of starvation have weakened the people, and they fly the flag of distress which the French boat in the harbor sees. Immediately it fires a protective barrage, which stops the Turks from their planned advance. After the survivors have been placed aboard the French ship, Gabriel climbs the mountain for one last farewell beside his son's grave. A Turkish sniper shoots him, and he falls across the grave of his son; the last of the Bagradians lies on the bosom of Musa Dagh.

Juliette, Gabriel's French wife. A woman with strong love for her own country, she finds her husband's patriotism difficult to share. However, she falls in love with the country home in Yoghonoluk, and she enjoys its gardens and the refurbishing of the house. She also makes smart costumes for the servants, who enjoy her devoted care of the home. As Gabriel is drawn into political problems and has less time for his family, Juliette allows herself to respond to the charms

of an adventurer. After the terrors of the defense of Musa Dagh and after she is consumed by fever, she is carried, a raving madwoman calling only for her son, to the French ship.

Gonsague Maris, a Greek adventurer with an American passport, a one-time journalist who seduces Juliette. In the hue and cry aroused by his perfidy, he escapes down the mountainside.

Stephan Bagradian, Gabriel's adolescent son, deeply aware of his Armenian heritage and admiring of his father. Stephan tries to accompany his friend Haik, a hardy young scout, on a trip to ask aid of the American consul. He turns back, ill, and is shot by the Turks.

Samuel Avakian, Stephan's competent tutor. He has the long, narrow face of an intellectual but the guarded look of the Armenian patriot.

Ter Haigasun, the Gregorian priest of the village and one of the three members of the council that plans the defense of Musa Dagh.

Sarkis Kilikian, a deserter from the Turkish army, an Armenian patriot.

Iskuhi Tomasian, the sister of a pastor, deeply in love with Gabriel Bagradian.

Agha Rifaat Bereket, an old Turkish friend of Avetis Bagradian; a religious mystic.

Dr. Johannes Lepsius, a German pastor in charge of rescue work.

FRAMLEY PARSONAGE

Author: Anthony Trollope (1815-1882)
Time of action: The 1850's
First published: 1861

PRINCIPAL CHARACTERS

Mark Robarts, vicar of Framley in Barsetshire, a living he gained at the age of twenty-five through his friendship with

the Lufton family. At a house party given by Sowerby, a man Lady Lufton disapproves of, he foolishly signs a note for four hundred pounds. When the note falls due, Sowerby has him sign another note he cannot pay. Sowerby is able, through political connections, to get Robarts a prebendal stall at Barchester. His friends feel that he has become too worldly. Events finally reach the point where Robarts is subjected to a sheriff's inventory because he is unable to meet his financial obligations. At the last moment Lord Lufton appears and assumes responsibility for the debt.

Fanny Robarts, Mark's wife. She remains loyal to her husband through all his financial difficulties.

Lucy Robarts, the sister of Mark Robarts, who comes to live at Framley Parsonage when her father, a doctor, dies. Although quiet and shy, Lucy soon gains the love of the highly eligible young Lord Lufton, but his mother disapproves of the "insignificant" match. Although Lord Lufton proposes, Lucy honorably refuses until such time as his mother may approve. Lucy then goes to nurse Mrs. Crawley, the wife of a neighboring clergyman, stricken with typhoid fever. At the end of her stay at Hogglestock, Lady Lufton relents and Lucy marries Lord Lufton.

Lady Lufton, the matriarchal ruler of Framley Court. Although she has made a pact with the mother of Griselda Grantly, an agreement that their children will wed, she does not force her point of view once she sees that her son is not in love with Griselda. She pays her son's gambling debts and forgives Mark Robarts' folly in money matters.

Lord Ludovic Lufton, a close friend of Mark Robarts and a persistent suitor for Lucy's hand.

Nicholas Sowerby, the squire of Chaldicotes, an improvident and parasitical young man greatly in debt to the Duke of Omnium. He uses both Mark Robarts and Lord Lufton in his financial dealings. At the suggestion of his sister, he proposes to Miss Dunstable, a very wealthy woman, in an effort to regain his fortune. Miss Dunstable wisely refuses the offer of marriage but buys Chaldicotes and allows Sowerby to live there.

Harold Smith, the brother-in-law of Sowerby and a member of Parliament who becomes Petty Bag when Lord Brock is made Prime Minister. His influence secures the prebendal stall for Mark Robarts.

Mrs. Harold Smith, the sister of Sowerby and good friend of Miss Dunstable.

Martha Dunstable, the wealthy heiress to a patent medicine fortune, humorously accustomed to refusing young men who seek her for her money. She admires Dr. Thorne, whom she marries, and they later live at Chaldicotes.

Dr. Thomas Thorne, a bachelor physician at Greshamsbury. Without worldly interests, he marries Miss Dunstable but not for her money.

Mary Gresham, Dr. Thorne's niece, married to Frank Gresham, master of the hunt in Greshamsbury.

Lady Scatcherd, the widow of Sir Roger Scatcherd, a poor stonemason who became wealthy. She is friendly with Dr. Thorne.

Susan Grantly, the wife of Archdeacon Grantly of Barchester. Eager to get her daughter Griselda married, she defeats her arch-adversary, Mrs. Proudie, because Griselda marries Lord Dumbello, while young Olivia Proudie makes an unsuitable marriage.

Mrs. Proudie, the aggressive wife of the Bishop of Barchester whose efforts toward social position and elegance are constantly foiled.

Olivia Proudie, the oldest daughter of the Bishop of Barchester; she marries a widower with three children.

The Rev. Tobias Tickler, the widower who marries Olivia Proudie.

Griselda Grantly, the attractive daughter of Archdeacon Grantly. Her marriage to Lord Dumbello makes her the future Marchioness of Hartletop.

The Duke of Omnium, the wealthiest landowner in Barsetshire. Although usually indifferent to politics, he exercises himself to remove Sowerby from Parliament.

Lord Brock, briefly Prime Minister of England.

Lord Supplehouse, an opportunistic politician who writes letters to the newspaper against Harold Smith.

Lord Dumbello, an unprepossessing nobleman who wins Sowerby's seat in Parliament with the help of the Duke of Omnium.

Mr. Fothergill, agent of the Duke of Omnium and a man of business instrumental in Sowerby's defeat.

Tom Tozer, a shady moneylender who holds Mark Robarts' notes.

The Rev. Josiah Crawley, the clergyman at Hogglestock parish. He lectures Mark Robarts concerning the danger of worldliness in a parson.

Mrs. Crawley, his wife, who becomes ill with typhoid fever and is nursed back to health by Lucy Robarts.

Grace Crawley, the bright and charming oldest daughter of the Crawleys.

The Rev. Francis Arabin, Dean of Barchester and an old school fellow of austere Mr. Crawley.

FRANKENSTEIN

Author: Mary Godwin Shelley (1797-1851)
Time of action: Eighteenth century
First published: 1817

PRINCIPAL CHARACTERS

Victor Frankenstein, a native of Geneva who early evinces a talent in natural science. Having concluded his training at the university at Ingolstadt, he works until he discovers the secret of creating life. He makes a monster from human and animal organs found in dissecting rooms and butcher shops. The Monster brings only anguish and death to Victor and his friends and relatives. Having told his story, he dies before his search for the Monster is complete.

The Monster, an eight-foot-tall synthetic man endowed by its creator with human sensibilities. Rebuffed by man, it turns its hate against him. Its program of revenge accounts for the lives of Frankenstein's bride, his brother, his good friend, and a family servant. Just after Victor dies, the Monster appears and tells the explorer that Frankenstein's was the great crime, for he had created a man devoid of friend, love, or soul.

Robert Walton, an English explorer who, on his ship frozen in a northland sea of ice, hears the dying Frankenstein's story and also listens to the Monster's account of, and reason for, its actions.

Elizabeth Lavenza, Victor's foster sister and later his bride, who is strangled by the Monster on her wedding night.

William, Victor's brother, who is killed by the Monster while seeking revenge on its creator.

Henry Clerval, Victor's friend and a man of science who is killed by the Monster to torment Frankenstein.

Justine Moritz, a family servant tried and condemned for William's murder.

FRATERNITY

Author: John Galsworthy (1867-1933)
Time of action: Early twentieth century
First published: 1909

PRINCIPAL CHARACTERS

Ivy Barton, the girl around whom the story revolves. She is a lower-class country girl who is transported to the city to serve as a model for an artist, Bianca Dallison. Through no fault of her own she causes trouble because she is pursued by the husband of the Dallisons' seamstress and befriended by Bianca's husband. Ivy Barton is finally abandoned by Hilary Dallison, who throws a handful of money on her bed in a rented London room and leaves her forever.

Hilary Dallison, a prosperous writer who found Ivy and brought her to London to pose for a painting by his wife, Bianca. His emotions for Ivy are a mixture of pity and love, but at the end he chooses his own way by refusing to befriend Ivy and by deciding not to return to Bianca, a woman with whom he has not lived as a husband for several years.

Bianca Dallison, Hilary's artist wife who, though she refuses Hilary his marital prerogatives, still becomes extremely jealous when another woman attracts his attention, as Ivy does.

Mr. Hughs, a lecherous, suspicious ne'er-do-well who pursues Ivy, spies on her, and spreads gossip about her and Hilary. Finally, for beating his wife and wound-

ing her with a bayonet, he is sent off to prison for a short time.

Mrs. Hughs, the Dallisons' seamstress, who lives a hellish existence with her husband. Nevertheless, she is still jealous of him; and when she sees that he is enamored of Ivy, she tells the story to Bianca's sister, who makes the news known to the whole family. While her husband is in prison, Mrs. Hughs loses her baby because she is too nervous to nurse him.

Stephen Dallison, Hilary's brother, who tries to make Hilary see what his attentions to Ivy are doing to his reputation.

Mr. Sylvanus Stone, Hilary's father-in-law, who is writing a book on the brotherhood of man. His subject leads him to make philosophical remarks intended to instruct the reader on the subject of the classes in British society. Ivy works as a copyist for Mr. Stone.

Cecilia Dallison, Hilary's rather bland sister-in-law, whose chief concern seems to be the Dallison reputation in the community.

Thyme Dallison, Stephen and Cecilia's daughter, who helps the plot along by guessing that her uncle Hilary has bought the new clothes she sees Ivy wearing.

FRIAR BACON AND FRIAR BUNGAY

Author: Robert Greene (1558-1592)
Time of action: Thirteenth century
First presented: c. 1589

Edward, the pleasure-loving Prince of Wales. Delighted by the charms of the milkmaid, Margaret, he sends his friend Lacy to woo her. He is filled with jealousy when he learns that the courtier has won her for himself, but he quickly overcomes his anger and has their marriage solemnized with his own.

Lacy, the Earl of Lincoln, a gracious young courtier who disguises himself as a farmer to visit Margaret. He feels no disloyalty in winning her love for himself, for he wishes to marry her, and he knows that Edward's attentions would be fleeting.

Margaret, the fair maid of Fressingfield, whose youth and charm win the love of both the Prince and Lacy. She is notable chiefly as one of the first romantic heroines in English drama.

King Henry III, Edward's father, who follows the Prince to Oxford with his court.

Ralph Simnell, the King's rotund fool, Edward's companion. He revels in his opportunity to masquerade as the Prince in Oxford.

Friar Bacon, the wise necromancer of Brasenose College, the only man capable of defeating Vandermast in a battle of wits. He breaks his magic mirror and renounces his studies when he sees the tragedies brought about by his skills.

Miles, his servant, a poor scholar. Notoriously stupid, he lets the Friar sleep through his one chance to master his art, when the Brazen Head speaks. For his negligence he is carried off to Hell on a devil's back, bragging about his mount.

Friar Bungay, another necromancer, inferior to Bacon, who magically prevents him from marrying Margaret and Lacy.

Jaques Vandermast, a learned doctor, brought by the Emperor of Germany to dispute with Oxford's wisest men.

Elinor of Castile, the attractive young princess who is betrothed to Edward.

Burden, a spokesman for a group of learned doctors who visit Friar Bacon at Oxford to inquire about his proposed Brazen Head.

FRITHIOF'S SAGA

Author: Esaias Tegnér (1782-1846)
Time of action: Eleventh century
First published: 1825

PRINCIPAL CHARACTERS

Frithiof, the Viking hero of this nineteenth century reshaping of a tale of ancient Scandinavia. After the death of his father and of the King his father served, Frithiof is humiliated by the new brother-Kings, who refuse him their sister's hand in marriage. Frithiof is at last outlawed but gains riches and glory as a sea fighter. He goes in disguise to the kingdom of the man now married to the woman he has consistently loved. He

saves the lives of both King and Queen, and the good King gives up his Queen to Frithiof and makes him war-guardian of the kingdom. Frithiof succeeds to the throne after the King dies and later defeats his old enemies the brother-Kings in battle.

Helge, one of the brother-Kings. When Frithiof returns from a difficult journey to collect tribute money, he finds Helge's

387

wife wearing the ring of gold he once gave to Ingeborg. In the resultant struggle the temple is burned and Frithiof is outlawed. After Frithiof himself becomes King, the brother-Kings wage war on him and Helge is slain.

Halfdan, the brother of Helge and co-ruler of the kingdom. At last he is made to swear fealty to Frithiof.

Ingeborg, the sister of Helge and Halfdan and loved by Frithiof. Though she and Frithiof exchange vows and gold rings, she is forced to marry King Hring. But she remains in love with Frithiof and, as a result of Hring's generosity, is at last united to him.

Hring, a Scandinavian King. Victorious

in battle against the brothers, he extracts their promise to give him Ingeborg as a wife. Much later, when Frithiof appears disguised in the kingdom, Hring recognizes him but pretends not to until Frithiof has proved himself.

King Bele, the father of Helge and Halfdan. Dying, he warns them against losing Frithiof's friendship.

Thorsten Vikingsson, Frithiof's father. He has greatly helped King Bele in the past. Dying, he requests his son to help the brother-Kings.

Yarl Angantyr, the ruler of the Faroe Islands. The brother-Kings send Frithiof to collect tribute-money from him.

THE FROGS

Author: Aristophanes (c. 448-c. 385 B.C.)
Time of action: Fifth century B.C.
First presented: 405 B.C.

PRINCIPAL CHARACTERS

Dionysus (dī·ō·nī′səs), the god of wine and revelry, who combines in a farcical fashion many of the defects which Aristophanes ridiculed in his fellow Athenians—cowardice, egoism, lechery, effeminacy, and laziness—but is, nevertheless, the patron god of the drama. Inspired by a reading of Euripides' "Andromeda," he resolves to journey to Hades to bring the tragic poet back to Athens. To facilitate his entry to the Underworld, he disguises himself as his kinsman Herakles, who had earlier made the dangerous trip. This is a ludicrous idea, for the two are of totally different natures, and Dionysus is terrified of the monsters he sees, or thinks he sees, along the way. Eventually, with the aid of a chorus of initiates into the Mysteries of Dionysus and Demeter, souls who enjoy a favored place in Hades, he gains the realm of Pluto. There he learns that the chair of tragedy, which Sophocles had

refused to take from Aeschylus, the elder poet, has been usurped by Euripides, who, upon his arrival in the Underworld, gained the support of the rabble. Aeschylus has challenged Euripides, and Dionysus finds that he has been chosen to judge between them. He has each poet recite lines from his dramas, a situation which allows Aristophanes ample opportunity to parody the defects of each and to have Dionysus make critical comments, some incisive, some obtuse. At last scales are produced. Because Aeschylus' verses are the weightier and because he has displaced Euripides in the affections of the god, Dionysus chooses Aeschylus to accompany him to the upper world. The chair of tragedy is left to Sophocles, and Euripides is contemptuously dismissed.

Xanthias (zăn′thĭ·əs), Dionysus' slave, who has been compared with Sancho Panza. He has a highly comical sense of the many wrongs his master visits upon him, but too broad a humor to take them very seriously. He is not above taking mild revenge when the opportunity offers itself, and on several occasions he exhibits a shrewdness which makes Dionysus appear all the more foolish.

Euripides (ū·rǐ′pǐ·dēz), the tragic poet, presented in a very unfavorable light as a debaser of poetry and the drama, a purveyor of corrupt ideas and empty rhetoric, a sentimentalist, a weakener of the public morality, and a self-seeking pleaser of the mob. He is allowed, however, to make some telling criticism of Aeschylus' tragedies before he is defeated.

Aeschylus (ĕs′kǐ·ləs), a tragic poet considerably more dignified than Euripides, but not above shrewdness in argument against his opponent. He takes credit for stiffening the moral fibre of his countrymen, but he must bear charges of deficiency in dramatic action and the use of pompous language. His style at its best, however, is deemed far superior to anything Euripides can offer.

Herakles (hĕ′rə·klēz), the demi-god, who

advises Dionysus on his journey to Hades.

Charon (kā′rən), the ferryman of the dead, who makes Dionysus row across Acheron. He will not admit Xanthias to the ferry, however, and the slave, loaded with baggage, is forced to walk around the lake.

Pluto (plōō′tō), the god of Hades.

Aeacus (ē′ə·kəs), usually one of the judges of the Underworld, here presented as Pluto's porter.

A Landlady of Hades and **Plathané** (plǎ·thǎ·nā′), her servant, who attack Dionysus. They mistake him for Herakles, a great glutton, who had robbed them of food.

A Chorus of Frogs. They mock noisy spectators at the theater. At the entrance to Hades they sing of the rain and the marshes.

A Chorus of Initiates. They praise the gods of the Mysteries, advise the citizens of Athens, and sing a farewell when Dionysus and Aeschylus return to the upper world.

THE FRUIT OF THE TREE

Author: Edith Wharton (1862-1937)
Time of action: Late nineteenth century
First published: 1907

PRINCIPAL CHARACTERS

John Amherst, an assistant mill manager. Concerned with the low standard of working conditions at the mill, he endeavors to convince Bessy Westmore, the owner, of the necessity for improvement. Impressed by her apparent interest in the project, he marries her, only to be disillusioned by her unwillingness to make any sacrifice in the cause. On her death, he marries Justine Brent.

Bessy Westmore, a mill owner and John Amherst's first wife. Selfish and self-

indulgent, she disillusions her husband by her lack of interest in the working conditions at the mill. She is paralyzed by an injury and dies of an overdose of morphine she has begged from her nurse, Justine Brent.

Justine Brent, the nurse who becomes John Amherst's second wife. As a companion to Bessy Westmore, she nurses Bessy after she is paralyzed by an accident. She gives in to her patient's pleading for release from pain and administers an overdose of morphine, an act that is to plague her life as John Amherst's wife.

Dr. Wyant, Bessy Westmore's physician, who guesses the truth about her death and uses the knowledge to blackmail Justine Brent.

Mr. Langhope, Bessy Westmore's father.

Cicely Westmore, Bessy Westmore's daughter.

Dillon, a millhand whose injury brings to the fore the miserable working conditions at the mill.

Mrs. Harry Dressel, a friend of Justine Brent.

THE FUNERAL

Author: Sir Richard Steele (1672-1729)
Time of action: Early eighteenth century
First presented: 1701

PRINCIPAL CHARACTERS

The Earl of Brumpton, a British nobleman. Believed dead, he recovers immediately after the funeral but is persuaded by his faithful servant to remain "dead" until his survivors reveal their true characters.

Lady Brumpton, his young wife by a second marriage. Having gotten him to disown his only son, she is delighted with her presumed widowhood and large fortune. She plots to ruin the Earl's two young wards, but counterplots are successful. Even after the Earl's reappearance, she hopes to regain his favor, but when it is revealed that she has a still-living first husband, she loses everything.

Lord Hardy, the Earl's son by a first marriage. An officer in the army, he remains steadfast in his loyalty to his father even after his disinheritance. In love with one

of his father's wards, he is at last united with her and reinstated as his father's heir.

Mr. Campley, Lord Hardy's friend and junior officer. He is in love with the Earl's other ward, whom he helps to escape in disguise from the Brumpton mansion.

Lady Sharlot, loved by Lord Hardy. She hides in the Earl's empty coffin, which Lord Hardy's soldiers take by force from the Brumpton mansion.

Lady Harriot, Lady Sharlot's sister and the Earl's other ward. He gives his blessing to her marriage with Mr. Campley.

Trusty, Lord Brumpton's faithful servant and the only person present at the Earl's recovery. He recognizes the opportunity to prove Lady Brumpton's falsity.

THE GAMBLER

Author: Fyodor Mikhailovich Dostoevski (1821-1881)
Time of action: Mid-nineteenth century
First published: 1866

PRINCIPAL CHARACTERS

Alexey Ivanovitch (ä·lĕk·sā ĭ·vä′nə·vĭch), a young, impoverished nobleman, the tutor in a decadent, aristocratic Russian

household where he falls in love with the stepdaughter of the family. Boorish and insolent, in response to the patronizing impoliteness of his sponsor, he causes his own dismissal but remains in the German gambling resort town to be near his beloved Polina, who makes use of his devotion to send him on errands and to win for her at the roulette tables. Although perceptive and cultured, Alexey is addicted to the tables, so much so that he wins a fortune in order to relieve Polina of financial worries. When she refuses to accept his gift she leaves him so despondent that he takes up with a French adventuress who impoverishes and then discards him. Even after he hears Polina, ill at the time, really loves him and wishes him to return, he goes again and again to the salons, for by this time his gambling has become compulsive.

Polina Alexandrovna (pô·lĭ′nə ä·lĕk·sän′drəv·nə), the stepdaughter of a Russian general. Beautiful in a strange way, Polina is the mistress of a false Marquis, an adventurer who practices usury and who is ruining the General by attaching his real estate in order to keep the Russian in gambling money. Her influence on Alexey is so great that he not only gambles for her, literally and figuratively, but obeys her slightest whim. She in turn is under the spell of the false Marquis. Mr. Astley, who is also in love with Polina, finally takes her to Switzerland for her health.

The General, the son-in-law of a wealthy old lady and the stepfather to Polina. Formerly a colonel, he had bought his preferment upon retirement. In desperate straits financially and madly in love with Mlle. Blanche, a French adventuress, he sees health and prospects grow dimmer each day that his aged aunt lives. A mixture of suspicion and haughtiness, his whole life is built on pretense. Although he never finishes a sentence, his ideas are so simple and self-centered that no one misunderstands him. His two children mean no more to him than the dim memory of Victoria, his dead wife. After years of anticipation while waiting for his inheritance, he lives only a few months

longer than the dowager, who has gambled away most of her fortune in the meantime.

Antonida Vassilievna Tarasevitcheva (än·tô·nĭ′də väs·sĭ′lyĕv·nə tä·räs·sĕ′vĭ·chə·və), the General's aunt, a sprightly seventy-five-year-old aristocrat and autocrat who rules her family with wicked glee. Called Grandmother by her family and, derisively, "La Baboulenka" by the Frenchman, she is confined to her chair, where she sits like a ramrod and issues orders in a stentorian voice. Fond of Polina, she loathes the General and threatens to cut him off for his chicanery. Suddenly possessed, almost overwhelmed, by gambling fever, she loses a fortune at the gaming tables. Her keen wit and cunning intuition make her a delightful eccentric, tender to those she loves, a terror to the others.

Mr. Astley, an English businessman with an inherent nobility of nature and an actual title which he conceals because of almost morbid shyness and diffidence. Desperately in love with Polina, he aids the young tutor out of a generous nature and takes in the despondent girl when she is abandoned by the gambler and her family. His shyness is offset by a fierce sense of independence. An observer of human foibles, he also declares himself on the side of the genuine, those of strong character and the finer motives.

Mlle. de Cominges, called **Mlle. Blanche,** a woman with many invented names, an adventuress on the grand order and of shady dealings. In spite of her outward appearances, she has a sense of loyalty, even generosity, toward those she loves or pities. The false Marquis is her accomplice and a thoroughly despicable one.

The Marquis de Grieux (də grē·œ′), a self-styled French nobleman and an alleged kinsman of Mlle. Blanche. He lends the General money with which to gamble and in the end succeeds in ruining the reckless nobleman. Polina is in love with him, much to Alexey Ivanovitch's distress.

THE GARDEN

Author: L. A. G. Strong (1896-   )
Time of action: Early twentieth century
First published: 1931

PRINCIPAL CHARACTERS

Dermot Gray, an Anglo-Irish boy who spends his holidays with his maternal grandparents in Ireland. To him, his grandparents' cottage at Sandycove is home, beloved as his home in England is not. After a happy childhood and a comparatively painless adolescence, Dermot is killed in World War I.

Mrs. Gray, his mother; to her also the cottage in Ireland is home.

Mr. Gray, his father. He confuses Dermot, who does not know whether he will react to something with patience or anger. Dermot is afraid of his father, who is sickly, and is also afraid for him.

Eithne, Dermot's younger sister. As she grows older she shares in his pleasures and excursions; when Dermot and her beloved cousin are killed in the war, she feels torn apart but comforts herself with the belief that the young men are together and surely happy.

Granny, Dermot's grandmother. As a very young child he has her garden confused with the Garden of Eden.

Grandpapa, his grandfather, a wise and loving man.

Ben McManus, Dermot's uncle, a boisterous retired mariner who is also a strict Puritan.

Aunt Patricia McManus, Ben's wife. They live a happy-go-lucky life in a seaside house containing such wonders as a telescope and the dried jaws of a whale.

Con McManus, one of their four children. Much older than Dermot, he is boyish and exuberant. When Eithne is fourteen he falls in love with her. He and Dermot are killed only a day apart.

Eileen McManus, Con's sister, a lovely and lively girl whom Dermot adores.

Paddy Kennedy, a crippled lad hired by Granny to teach Dermot to fish.

Long Mike Hogan and **Peg-leg O'Shea,** Paddy's pals. From these three Dermot learns a great tolerance for poor people.

THE GARDENER'S DOG

Author: Lope de Vega (Lope Félix de Vega Carpio, 1562-1635)
Time of action: Late sixteenth century
First presented: c. 1615

PRINCIPAL CHARACTERS

Diana (dyä'nä), Countess of Belflor, who is like the gardener's dog that will not eat the food or let anyone else enjoy it. Investigating the story of a man seen escaping from the top story of her palace, she discovers that her secretary, Teodoro, has been seeing Marcela, one of her ladies in waiting. At first she gives permission for their wedding; then she changes her mind and in a letter dictated to Teodoro hints at her affection for him, though his blood is not noble. Meanwhile she is courted by two nobles and consents to marry Ricardo, even while alternately encouraging and rejecting Teodoro. At last, angered by Teodoro, she wounds him with a knife. His announcement that he is leaving Naples for Madrid makes her decide to marry him; also, his servant has concocted a plan to make him one of the nobility. Though assured by Teodoro that the scheme is false, Diana decides that happiness is found in a union of souls, not of social classes, especially if they conceal the truth of his lowly status; so they marry.

Teodoro (tā·ō·t̸hō′rō), the secretary of Countess Diana. He loves Marcela, one of her ladies in waiting, but he turns to Diana, then back to Marcela, and again to his employer when her jealousy is aroused by seeing him embrace Marcela. At last he tells Marcela to marry Fabio, but at his next rebuff by Diana, because of his lowly birth, he announces his departure for Spain. Too honorable to make false claims about noble blood, he refuses to let his servant Tristán persuade Count Ludovico to claim him as a long-lost son. Nevertheless, Diana now takes him for her husband.

Tristán (trēs·tän′), the shrewd, picaresque servant of Teodoro. He protects his master by hurling his cap at a candle when Teodoro is almost discovered leaving Marcela's chamber at night. Reluctantly he advises his master to marry her; however, when Teodoro yearns for the Countess, Tristán invents a noble lineage for him. On another occasion, when the nobles, Federico and Ricardo, want Teodoro killed, Tristán accepts their gold for the murder, then confesses the plot to his master. At the end, when everybody is getting married, he is paired off with Dorotea, of the Countess' household.

Marcela (mär·thä′lä), a good-hearted girl who is looking, like most girls in Spanish comedies, for a husband. After her off-and-on engagement to Teodoro, she is satisfied to get Fabio instead.

Count Federico (fä·t̸hä·rē′kō), a mercenary noble who knows Diana's wealth and comes wooing her. When he learns of Teodoro's wound, he decides the man must have offended her, and he pays to have the secretary assassinated.

The Marquis Ricardo (r̄ē·kär′dō), a money-seeking suitor whom Diana at one time decides to marry as the lesser of two evils.

Fabio (fä′byō), a gentleman of Naples, tossed from Anarda to Marcela as a possible husband, and ending in Marcela's possession.

Anarda (ä·när′dä), one of Diana's ladies in waiting. She accuses Marcela of harboring a man in her room and hints the man is Teodoro, in revenge for Marcela's encouragement of Fabio, who is courting Anarda.

Dorotea (dō·rō·tā′ä), another of the Countess' household, who at the end becomes a consolation prize for Tristán.

Count Ludovico (lōō·t̸hō·bē′kō), an elderly nobleman who, having lost a son named Teodoro twenty years before, is easily persuaded by Tristán that his master is the missing boy.

Octavio (ōk·tä′byō), Diana's squire.

Celio (thä′lyō), a servant of the Marquis Ricardo.

Leonardo (lä·ō·när′t̸hō), a servant of Count Federico.

GARGANTUA AND PANTAGRUEL

Author: François Rabelais (1490?-1553)
Time of action: The Renaissance
First published: Begun 1533; first complete edition, 1567

Gargantua, an affable prince, a giant—as an infant over 2,000 ells of cloth are required to clothe him—who has many adventures. He travels over Europe and other parts of the world fighting wars from which all prisoners are set free, straightening out disputes in other kingdoms, and helping his friends achieve their goals.

Pantagruel, Gargantua's giant son, who once got an arm out of his swaddling clothes and ate the cow that was nursing him. Pantagruel was born when his father was 400 years old. Accepting with good nature the responsibility of aiding the oppressed, he spends a good deal of his time traveling the earth with his companion Panurge. In their travels they visit a land where all citizens have noses shaped like the ace of clubs and a country in which the people eat and drink nothing but air.

Panurge, a beggar and Pantagruel's companion, who knows sixty-three ways to make money and two hundred fourteen ways to spend it. He speaks twelve known and unknown tongues, but he does not know whether he should marry. Finally, he decides to consult the Oracle of the Sacred Bottle to find the answer to his question. The trip to the island of the Sacred Bottle is filled with adventures for Panurge and Pantagruel. The Oracle, when finally consulted, utters one word, "trinc." Panurge takes this pronouncement, translated as "drink," to mean that he should marry.

Friar John of the Funnels, a lecherous, lusty monk who fights well for Gargantua when the latter finds himself at war with King Picrochole of Lerné. To reward the friar for his gallantry, Gargantua orders workers to build the Abbey of Thélème, which has been Friar John's dream. Here men and women live together and work to accumulate wealth.

Grandgousier, the giant king who is Gargantua's father.

Gargamelle, Gargantua's mother who, taken suddenly in labor, bears Gargantua from her left ear.

Picrochole, King of Lerné, who invades Grandgousier's country. His army is repulsed by Gargantua, with the aid of Friar John and other loyal helpers. The prisoners captured are all allowed to go free.

Anarchus, King of Dipsody, who invades the land of the Amaurots. His army is overcome by Pantagruel, who makes the King a crier of green sauce.

Bacbuc, the priestess who conducts Panurge to the Sacred Bottle and translates the Oracle's message for him.

Ponocrates, Gargantua's teacher in Paris.

Holofernes and **Joberlin Bridé,** Gargantua's first teachers.

THE GAUCHO: MARTÍN FIERRO

Author: José Hernández (1834-1886)
Time of action: Nineteenth century
First published: Part I, 1872; Part II, 1879

PRINCIPAL CHARACTERS

Martín Fierro (mär·tēn' fyä'rro), an Argentine gaucho who tells in verse the story of his life, to the accompaniment of his guitar. Drafted to fight Indians because he did not vote for the local judge, he returns to find his home destroyed and his family scattered. Finally he is reunited with his sons, whom he sends on their way with advice, after which he lays down his guitar forever.

Cruz (krōōs), another gaucho who joins Fierro to fight off the police, who are pursuing him following a cowboy fight. They are comrades during their Indian captivity. Cruz dies while nursing a friendly Indian through a smallpox epidemic.

Fierro's Older Son, who, victimized, tells his father his story of government injustice.

Fierro's Younger Son, who is robbed of his inheritance by his tutor and sent into the army.

Vizcacha (bēs·kä'chä), the crooked tutor who robs Fierro's younger son.

Picardia (pē·kär'dyä), the son of Cruz, another victim of wicked officials.

A Negro, killed by Fierro in a fair fight.

His Brother, who competes with Fierro in a singing match, then tries to kill him to avenge his brother's death.

THE "GENIUS"

Author: Theodore Dreiser (1871-1945)
Time of action: 1889-1914
First published: 1915

PRINCIPAL CHARACTERS

Eugene Witla, a sensitive young man with vaguely artistic aspirations. Haunted by an ideal of beauty, he is led to become an artist and to fall in love with many women. Finding no enduring peace in his search for beauty, he seeks it in social and financial success with the same negative results. After years of dryness, his impulse toward beauty is reawakened by his infant daughter, around whom he begins to weave impossible dreams for their future together.

Angela Blue, a young schoolteacher seduced by and later married to Eugene. In an attempt to save their marriage, she has a baby against all medical advice, and dies in childbirth, leaving her husband with a daughter who revives his interest in artistic endeavor.

Angela Witla, the daughter of Eugene and Angela. She becomes her father's inspiration for a renewed interest in his artistic life.

Stella Appleton, Eugene's first love.

Margaret Duff, Eugene's first mistress.

Ruby Kenny, an artist's model and mistress of Eugene.

Miriam Finch, a sculptress Eugene meets in New York.

Christina Channing, a singer. She and Miriam become friends of Eugene and help educate him in the ways of the New York artistic world. Christina becomes Eugene's mistress briefly.

Anatole Charles, an art dealer and exhibitor of Eugene's paintings.

Frieda Roth, a young girl attractive to Eugene.

Carlotta Wilson, a gambler's wife with whom Eugene has a passionate affair.

Daniel Summerfield,
Obadiah Kalvin,
Marshall P. Colfax, and
Florence J. White, Eugene's associates in the publishing and advertising businesses. White is jealous of Eugene's rise in the company and cheerfully helps Mrs. Dale get him fired.

395

Suzanne Dale, a young girl with whom Eugene falls in love. Her influential mother takes her away and has Eugene fired from his job.

Mrs. Emily Dale, a wealthy socialite, mother of Suzanne.

Thomas Witla, Eugene's father.

Sylvia and
Myrtle Witla, Eugene's sisters.

Mrs. Johns, a Christian Science practitioner.

THE GENTLEMAN DANCING MASTER

Author: William Wycherley (1640-1716)
Time of action: Seventeenth century
First presented: 1672

PRINCIPAL CHARACTERS

Mr. James Formal (Don Diego), the father of Hippolita. Engaged in trade with the Spaniards, he is so enamored of their gallantry and pride that he attempts to imitate their manners and confines his daughter to her house in true Spanish fashion. Blinded by his pride, he allows himself to be duped by Hippolita and her allies to the point where, in order to save face, he must pretend to have been a willing collaborator in her plans to wed Mr. Gerrard.

Hippolita, the daughter of Mr. Formal. Though engaged to her cousin, Mr. Paris, and confined to her home by her father, she manages to become enamored of Mr. Gerrard, whom she sees from her balcony. By a series of ruses, she, Mr. Gerrard, and her maid, Prue, contrive to deceive her father and her fiancé and bring about a wedding between her and her beloved.

Mr. Paris (Monsieur de Paris), the nephew of Mr. Formal and the ap-

proved suitor of Hippolita. Fresh from Paris, he affects French manners to the point of absurdity and his silliness causes him to be the willing dupe of Hippolita in her love affair with Mr. Gerrard.

Mr. Gerrard, a young gentleman about town who courts Hippolita while disguised as a dancing master. His suit is aided by Mr. Formal's fierce Spanish pride in his ability to protect his daughter under his own roof. Mr. Gerrard marries the lady under the deceived parent's nose.

Mrs. Caution, Mr. James Formal's sister and Hippolita's duenna.

Prue, Hippolita's resourceful maid and ally.

Mistress Flirt, a prostitute by whom Mr. Paris is undone.

Mr. Martin, Mr. Gerrard's friend and ally.

THE GENTLEMAN USHER

Author: George Chapman (c. 1559-1634)
Time of action: Seventeenth century
First presented: c. 1602

PRINCIPAL CHARACTERS

Duke Alphonso, an elderly widower in love with Margaret. Under the influence

of a sinister favorite who calls himself Medice, he banishes his son for attempting to marry Margaret. Though hot-tempered, the Duke is generous-hearted and finally forgives the young couple.

Prince Vincentio, the Duke's son. Rather than lose Margaret, he makes a private marriage contract with her, gaining access to her by flattering her father's gentleman usher. Seriously wounded by Medice, he recovers, receives his father's forgiveness, and is united with Margaret.

Margaret, Count Lasso's daughter. Thinking Vincentio slain by his father's orders, she disfigures her face and denounces the Duke for his tyranny, bringing about his repentance and reformation.

Count Lasso, Margaret's tyrannical father, who wishes her to marry the Duke.

Cortezza, Lasso's sister, who steals a letter from Margaret's jewel box and betrays the young lovers to the Count and Duke.

Bassiolo, the Count's pompous gentleman usher. Susceptible to flattery, he aids Vincentio in sending a letter to Margaret and in bringing the lovers together. He also is forgiven by his angry master.

Count Strozza, Vincentio's friend. Medice has him treacherously shot with an arrow, but he recovers to unmask Medice and furnishes a physician to heal Vincentio and Margaret.

Medice, the Duke's malicious parasite, an impostor. Responsible for most of the misfortune befalling the other characters, he is terrorized into confessing his crimes and his real identity and is banished by the Duke.

GERMINAL

Author: Émile Zola (1840-1902)
Time of action: Nineteenth century
First published: 1885

PRINCIPAL CHARACTERS

Étienne Lantier, a French laboring man who becomes a miner and falls under the influence of Marxism, which he believes is the workers' only hope. He organizes the miners, only to lose his popularity when a strike is settled and the people go back to work. His suffering, even the loss of his lover in a mine accident, only persuades him that he must continue his revolutionary work. He is the illegitimate son of Gervaise Macquart.

Catherine Maheu, a girl who works as a miner. She is loved by Lantier, even though she takes another man as her lover. She eventually becomes Lantier's mistress, sharing his miserable, lonely life until she dies of suffocation after an accident in the mine where she and Lantier work.

Vincent Maheu, an elderly miner nick-named Bonnemort because of his many escapes from accidental death in the mines.

Maheu, Vincent's son, the father of seven children. He becomes Lantier's friend and works with him in the mine. He is killed by soldiers during a strike at the mine.

Maheude, Maheu's wife.

Zacharie Maheu, a young miner who marries his mistress after she presents him with two children.

Philomène Levaque, Zacharie's mistress and, later, his wife.

Souvarine, a misogynist who becomes Lantier's friend.

M. Hennebeau, one of the mine owners.

He refuses to make any concessions to the miners and imports strikebreakers to operate the closed mines.

Négrel Hennebeau, nephew of M. Hennebeau. He feels compassion for the miners and leads a rescue party to save them after an accident traps Lantier and others below the surface of the ground.

Chaval, a miner who seduces Catherine Maheu. He is jealous of his rival, Lantier, and their mutual animosity ends in a fight below the surface of the ground in which Chaval is killed.

Dansaert, head captain of the mine in which Lantier works.

Cécile Grégoire, daughter of a mine owner, fiancée of Négrel Hennebeau.

Maigrat, a rapacious storekeeper who lends money to the women who grant him amorous favors.

M. Grégoire, a mine owner who justifies low pay for the workers by believing they spend their money only for drink and vice.

Jeanlin Maheu, an eleven-year-old child who works in a mine until he is crippled in an accident. He murders a mine guard, but his crime is hidden by Lantier.

Alzire Maheu, a sister of Catherine. The little girl dies of starvation during the strike.

Pluchart, a mechanic who persuades Lantier to become a Marxist.

GERMINIE LACERTEUX

Authors: Edmond (1822-1896) and Jules (1830-1870) de Goncourt
Time of action: Nineteenth century
First published: 1865

PRINCIPAL CHARACTERS

Germinie Lacerteux (zhĕr·mē·nē' lȧ·sĕr-tœ'), an orphan reared by her sisters. Set to work as a waitress at the age of fourteen, she is soon seduced and bears a stillborn child. After a series of jobs she becomes the maid of Mlle. de Varandeuil. Because she is naïve, people take advantage of her, even members of her family. She has a desperate need for love, physically and psychologically, which proves her undoing many times. She becomes an alcoholic. She dies of pleurisy after standing hours in the rain in hopes of seeing Jupillon, her former lover.

Mlle. de Varandeuil (dǝ vȧ·rän·dœy'), an old maid with few friends or acquaintances and little money. She becomes Germinie's employer. She does not see Germinie's weaknesses, even her drunkenness, for she is too old to want to hire a new servant. She learns of the frustra-

tions in Germinie's life only after the girl's death.

M. Jupillon (zhü·pē·yōṅ'), loved by Germinie, though he is ten years her junior. He, like everyone else, takes advantage of her and becomes her lover. They have a son who lives but a few months. Though he leaves Germinie for another woman, he still takes her hard-earned money to buy his way out of military service.

Mme. Jupillon (zhü·pē·yōṅ'), M. Jupillon's mother. She owns a dairy store near where Germinie is employed by Mlle de Varandeuil. She takes advantage of Germinie's willingness to help in the store.

M. Gautruche (gō·trüsh'), another of Germinie's lovers. She wants him only as an object for her affections. To his surprise she refuses to marry him when he proposes marriage, and they part forever.

GHOSTS

Author: Henrik Ibsen (1828-1906)
Time of action: Nineteenth century
First presented: 1881

PRINCIPAL CHARACTERS

Mrs. Helen Alving, a widow, the mother of an ailing only son. Although she reads liberal books and has extraordinarily liberal views concerning the possible marriage of her son and his illegitimate half sister, whose identity is known only to Mrs. Alving, she is an outwardly severe woman whose life has been governed by duty. As a young wife she had fled from her profligate husband, whom she had married for his money, to seek refuge with the parish pastor, Mr. Manders, with whom she had fallen in love. Mr. Manders righteously had sent her back to her husband and they maintain the appearance of a home for the remainder of his life. With her husband's money, which she now loathes, Mrs. Alving has built an orphanage in memory of her husband. On the advice of Mr. Manders she decides not to insure the building because to do so would be to show lack of faith. When the building burns, Mrs. Alving is indifferent. Although Mrs. Alving promises her son Oswald that she will administer some fatal pills to him when his mind goes, she is unable to do so at the conclusion of the play. Her revulsion and terror are unrelieved.

Oswald Alving, an art student, afflicted with a disease, apparently syphilis, contracted or inherited from his father. He reveals to his mother that his mind is being blotted out by the disease, which doctors have told him was acquired almost from birth. Since Mrs. Alving had sent Oswald away from home at seven years of age so that he would not realize his father's true nature, he believes he has brought the disease on himself. In addition, he has inherited his father's joy of life, now left behind with his art and his free-living companions abroad. Faced

with mental oblivion, he comes home but finds no solace except in the contemplation of a possible marriage and departure with Regina, a young servant, in whom he recognizes the joy of life they have both inherited from their father. Incapacitated by the knowledge of his destiny, Oswald can no longer paint. He tries drink but gets little relief. After he tells his mother of his condition and his hope of marrying Regina, Mrs. Alving decides that she must tell them that they have the same father. This knowledge devastates Oswald. Shortly after he has shown his mother the pills, which he says Regina would have been willing to give him, his mind goes, and he plaintively asks his mother to give him the sun.

Regina Engstrand, a servant, ostensibly the daughter of a carpenter. Her mother, Joanna, now dead, had been a maid in the Alving household. Mr. Alving was Regina's father. Unaware of her identity, Regina feels that she is above Engstrand, who wants her to return to him and help him run a "home for homeless sailors." Regina, ambitious to marry Oswald and improve her station even before the idea has occurred to Oswald, detests Engstrand, who drinks and accuses her mother of immoral behavior. When Regina finds that she is Oswald's half sister, she leaves for the "Alving Home," the sailors' refuge Engstrand will finance with money from the Alving estate which Mr. Manders has secured for him. When Mrs. Alving tells her that she is going to her ruin, Regina shows no concern.

Mr. Manders, the pastor of the parish. When Mr. Manders reproves Mrs. Alving for deserting her husband and for

399

sending her young son away to become a free-thinking artist, she reveals the true nature of Mr. Alving, her reason for sending Oswald away, and the identity of Regina. After young Helen Alving's flight to him, Mr. Manders, fearful of his reputation, had never come again to the Alving house. He is present now only to advise her about the business of the orphanage, but he proves a poor counselor. When the orphanage burns as the result of his carelessly snuffing a candle at prayer services and throwing it on a heap of shavings, his remorseful cry is, "And no insurance!" Manders, a self-righteous man, reproves Mrs. Alving for her liberal reading and unwise behavior and Oswald for his unconventional views, but is completely taken in by the rascal Engstrand, who, Manders thinks, wants to reform. He pays Engstrand to assume blame for the orphanage fire.

Jacob Engstrand, a carpenter paid to marry Joanna, Regina's mother. Engstrand is a drinking man of no consequence, a rascal. Regina thinks at first that it would be improper for her to live in his home, even though at the time she thinks of him as her father. Engstrand suggests the fatal prayer service at the orphanage and later claims to have seen the candle fall in the shavings. Since he uses the occasion to get the Alving money from Manders, he may be lying. For the sake of the money paid him, he gladly assumes responsibility for the fire.

GIANTS IN THE EARTH

Author: O(le) E(dvart) Rölvaag (1876-1931)
Time of action: Late nineteenth century
First published: 1924-1925; first American edition, 1927

PRINCIPAL CHARACTERS

Per Hansa, as his friends call him, born **Peder Hansen** and later renamed **Peder Holm** to fit his new life in the Dakota Territory. A strong, self-reliant man who came to America to be near his best friend and great hero, Per Hansa saves his small Norwegian pioneer community by his ingenuity and perseverance in the face of great odds. Though beset by family problems, the powerful man turns his wilderness tract into the finest farmland, superior to all the other farms in the region. He is loving, cheerful, and even-tempered, except for a few black and angry moods caused mostly by his wife's piety on the one hand and her lack of wifely respect on the other. He goes to his certain death in a blizzard for the spiritual comfort of his best friend.

Beret, his beautiful, pious, superstitious wife, who sees the giants or trolls of destruction come out of the untamed prairie. She often confounds her enterprising husband with sharp criticism of his seemingly dishonest acts, such as removing claim jumpers' stakes from their land. She suffers from a mental disorder brought on by childbirth and depression over their hard life, but after a traveling preacher sets her mind at ease she becomes the loving wife of former years, with only her dark piety causing discord. It is she who persuades the dying friend that he needs the ministrations of the preacher; thus she sends her husband out into the blizzard that claims his life.

Ole Haldor,
Hans Kristian,
Anna Marie, and
Peder Seier, their four children, the latter born on Christmas day of their first year in the wilderness. Ole and Hans are useful to their father and mother, while the younger sister And-Ongen (Happy

400

Duckling) keeps them all cheered by her sunny looks and disposition. The new arrival, christened Per Victorious in a touching frontier ceremony, is born with a caul or helmet, a sign of future greatness which the mother hopes will mean he will become a minister.

Hans Olsa, born Hans Olsen, who later changes his name to Hans Vaag, after his wife's birthplace. Hans Olsa, the leader of the community and the great friend of Per Hansa, is as steady as he is strong. Only once is he roused to anger when an Irish claimjumper curses him; and then one sledge-hammer blow with his great fist fells the man and a great swoop of the Norwegian's arms throws the poor fellow into his own wagon. Hans performs christening ceremonies, fills out the legal papers, opens up new lands, and generally manages the pioneering community's business. His wife Sörine cares for the Hansa child while Beret is ill, looks after the bachelor Solum brothers when they are teaching the neighborhood youngsters, and ministers gently to the needy immigrants. Their daughter is a favorite among Per Hansa's boys. Hans Olsa loses his life as the result of exposure and frostbite, and he dies waiting for the preacher he knows his friend Per will bring safely through the blizzard.

Sorïne, Hans Olsa's devoted wife.

Sofie, their daughter.

Syvert Tönseten, the foolish, garrulous justice of the peace of the community. Although his wife Kjersti is a favorite of the group, Tönseten is embittered because he has no children and because he is never consulted on matters of importance. While Kjersti is beloved for her secret generosity, Syvert is laughed at for his pompous ways. He keeps the Solum brothers from leaving the community, but he offsets the value of keeping them on as schoolteachers by displaying his own authority in the classroom.

Henry and
Sam Solum, the Norwegian-American brothers who come with the wagon train from Minnesota. Both good boys, Henry shows goods sense and courage at all times, though Sam develops these pioneer qualifications as he grows to manhood. Since they speak English, they interpret for the group.

GIL BLAS OF SANTILLANE

Author: Alain René Le Sage (1668-1747)
Time of action: Seventeenth century
First published: 1715, 1724, 1735

PRINCIPAL CHARACTERS

Gil Blas of Santillane (zhēl bläs sän·tē-lyän'), a rogue who serves a series of masters and finally ends up a country gentleman.

Blas of Santillane, his father, married to an elderly chambermaid.

Gil Pérez (zhēl pā'rāth), Gil's uncle, a fat canon who gives Gil forty pistoles and a donkey and sends him to the University of Salamanca.

Antonia (än·tō'nyä), a farmer's daughter who becomes Gil's wife. She and their baby daughter die.

Dorothea (dō·rō·tā'ä), Gil's second wife, with whom he spends his remaining days in Lirias on an estate given him by Don Alfonso.

Scipio (sē'·pyō), Gil's servant, who tries to arrange a marriage with the rich daughter of a goldsmith, an effort ruined by Gil's arrest.

Captain Rolando (rō·län'dō), a leader of robbers who captures Gil on his way to Salamanca.

Donna Mencia (dō'nyä mān'thyä), a prisoner of the robbers who is rescued by Gil.

Fabricio (fä·brē'thyō), Gil's schoolmate, who advises him to go into service.

Doctor Sangrado (dōk·tôr' sän·grä'thō), one of Gil's masters, whose universal remedy is bleedings.

Don Matthias (mä·tē'äs), another master, whose fashionable clothes Gil borrows to impress a "fine lady." She turns out to be a serving maid.

Arsenia (är·sā'nyä), an actress who em-ploys Gil for a short time after Don Matthias is killed in a duel.

Aurora (äōō·rō'rä), a virtuous girl whose love affair with Lewis is furthered by Gil.

Lewis, a college student desired by Aurora. They eventually marry.

Don Alphonso (dōn äl·fōn'sō), whom Gil gets appointed Governor of Valencia.

The Archbishop, who angrily discharges Gil for criticizing his sermons.

The Duke of Lerma (lâr'mä), the Prime Minister, whom Gil serves as a confidential agent.

Count Olivarez (ō·lē·bä'räth), the new Prime Minister, who tries unsuccessfully to keep Gil at court.

THE GILDED AGE

Authors: Mark Twain (Samuel L. Clemens, 1835-1910) and Charles Dudley Warner (1829-1900)
Time of action: Nineteenth century
First published: 1873

PRINCIPAL CHARACTERS

Colonel Beriah Sellers, an improvident opportunist of Missouri and an operator on a grand scale.

Squire Hawkins, of Obedstown, Tennessee, persuaded by Sellers to move to Missouri, where his affairs fail to prosper.

Nancy Hawkins, his wife.

Emily, their daughter.

George Washington, their son.

Henry Clay, an orphan adopted by Hawkins during his journey.

Laura, the survivor of a steamboat accident, who is also adopted by Hawkins. She is fraudulently married by Colonel Selby, who already has a wife. When she sees him later, she shoots him. At the trial she pleads insanity and is acquitted, only to die of grief.

Colonel Selby, of the Union Army.

Major Lackland, who boasts of knowing about Laura's missing father.

General Boswell, a real estate man who employs Washington Hawkins.

Louise Boswell, the general's daughter, in love with Washington.

Philip Sterling, a young New York engineer who is building the railroad in Missouri.

Harry Brierly, his friend, in love with Laura.

402

Ruth Bolton, who is in love with Philip and eventually becomes his wife. She wants to study medicine.

Eli Bolton and Margaret Bolton, Ruth's Quaker parents of Philadelphia. They are shocked by her modern ways.

Alice Montague, whom Ruth visits in New York.

Senator Dilworthy, who investigates Seller's request for Congressional funds to improve the area. The Senator's bill to establish a Negro university on Hawkins' land is defeated when his attempt to buy votes is exposed.

THE GLASS KEY

Author: Dashiell Hammett (1894-1961)
Time of action: The 1930's
First published: 1931

PRINCIPAL CHARACTERS

Ned Beaumont, a tall, lean, narrow-eyed, mustached, cigar-smoking, tough gambler and amateur detective. He finds Taylor Henry's body, collects the money Bernie owes him, is tortured by O'Rory, disbelieves Madvig's confession, witnesses O'Rory's murder, receives Senator Henry's confession, and gets the girl Janet.

Paul Madvig, his blond, heavy-set, ruddily handsome friend and the city's political boss, in love with Janet. Though innocent, he confesses to Taylor's murder.

Senator Henry, Madvig's distinguished, patrician-faced candidate for reëlection; the real murderer of his son Taylor during a violent quarrel.

Janet Henry, his brown-eyed daughter who hates Madvig and falls in love with Ned.

Shad O'Rory, Madvig's rival, a gangster and ward boss who has Ned brutally beaten for refusing to help frame Paul. He is killed by Jeff.

Opal Madvig, Madvig's blue-eyed, pink-skinned daughter who had been meeting Taylor secretly. She attempts suicide.

Bernie Despain, a gambler Ned suspects of having murdered Taylor. He owes Ned money which he finally pays.

Taylor Henry, Senator Henry's son, found dead in the street.

Jack Rumsen, a private detective hired by Ned to trail Bernie.

Michael Joseph Farr, the district attorney, stout, florid, pugnacious.

Jeff, O'Rory's apish bodyguard who beats Ned and later strangles O'Rory.

THE GLASS MENAGERIE

Author: Tennessee Williams (1914-   )
Time of action: The 1930's
First presented: 1945

PRINCIPAL CHARACTERS

Amanda Wingfield, a middle-aged woman and an incurable romantic. Deserted by her husband and forced to live in dreary lower middle-class surroundings, she retreats from reality into the illusory world of her youth. Living for her children, whom she fiercely loves, she nevertheless, by her constant nagging, her endless retelling of romantic stories of her girlhood, and her inability to face life as it is, stifles her daughter Laura, and drives away her son Tom.

Tom Wingfield, Amanda's son, through whose memory the story of "The Glass Menagerie" is seen. Professing to literary ambitions, he is trapped by his dreary surroundings, the care of a nagging mother and a crippled sister, and the stifling monotony of a job in a warehouse. He finally rebels and makes his escape.

Laura Wingfield, the crippled daughter of Amanda Wingfield. So shy that she finds ordinary human relationships almost unbearable, she is totally unequipped for the romantic role in which her mother has cast her. She takes refuge among her glass figurines, the "glass menagerie" that is the symbol of her fragility and her retreat from reality.

Jim O'Connor, a former high school hero whom Laura Wingfield has admired from afar. Working with Tom Wingfield, he is invited to dinner and brings Laura her one moment of confident happiness before the crude but honest Jim tells her that he is engaged to be married.

GOAT SONG

Author: Franz Werfel (1890-1945)
Time of action: Late eighteenth century
First presented: 1921

PRINCIPAL CHARACTERS

Gospodar Stevan Milic, a farmer and the father of two sons, both grown. One is a monster, hidden since birth. He crawls on all fours like a goat and screams terribly. A physician wants Stevan to have him placed in a home, but Stevan refuses because this will mean revealing his secret. The monster's escape worries Stevan so much that people think him mad. In a struggle between the villagers and nearby vagabonds, the monster, now bound and hidden behind the church altar, is regarded as a saint. The vagabonds murder and plunder, thinking that they are appeasing the monster. At last Stevan is forced to claim the monster as his son before everyone. Later, with both sons dead, Stevan feels young. Their guilty secret disclosed, he and his wife find each other again.

Mirko Milic, his normal son. When he attacks the leader of the vagabonds, he is killed by a guard.

Stanja Vesilic, who is betrothed to Mirko. The marriage has been arranged by the parents, and Stanja comes to stay in the Milic house for a month, as is the custom. Because the vagabond leader says that the monster is to be released only to Stanja, she takes a knife to go into the sanctuary to cut the monster's bonds. After Mirko's death she insists on staying with Stevan and his wife. At the end of the drama she reveals that she is carrying the monster's child.

Mirko's Mother, Stevan's wife. She always yearns secretly for the misshapen son she has not seen since birth. When Mirko is killed she is happy, though she does not understand why she wants her good son dead.

Juvan, a student and the leader of the vagabonds. Knowing the truth about the monster, he uses his knowledge to work the vagabonds into a frenzy, thus forcing the landowners to bargain. He sends Stanja in to release the monster. Later, condemned to hang, Juvan tells Stanja that he loves her; her sacrifice to the monster has changed him from an animal knowing only lust to a man capable of love. Though she wants to die with him, Juvan insists that she live.

The Monster, Stevan's malformed son. Hidden in a hut since birth and now grown, the human monster is released by a physician who visits him in the interest of science. He is captured by vagabonds, who are in the area demanding land from the farmers, and they install him as a god behind the church altar. The vagabonds force Stevan to acknowledge his afflicted son and then sacrifice Stanja to him before they are dispersed by soldiers. The monster escapes from the church and is later found burned to death in the woods.

THE GODS ARE ATHIRST

Author: Anatole France (Jacques Anatole Thibault, 1844-1924)
Time of action: 1793-1794
First published: 1912

PRINCIPAL CHARACTERS

Évariste Gamelin (ā·và·rēst′ gàm·lăǹ′), a young painter. Convinced that the success of the Jacobin cause will bring about a new day for France, he becomes an ardent revolutionary genuinely desiring justice for all. Blinded by his passion for the cause, he gradually assumes the role of self-righteous reformer, and finally, as a member of the Grand Tribunal, orders the execution of men in lots without trial. Among them is his closest friend, Maurice Brotteaux. He thus becomes a symbol of the romantic whose devotion to a cause corrupts his humanity.

Maurice Brotteaux (mō·rēs′ brô·tō′), Évariste Gamelin's friend, an atheist and intellectual who lacks Gamelin's faith in the goodness of the masses. Executed without trial by the Tribunal of which Évariste is a member, he becomes the symbol of the intellectual who will not abandon his integrity for a cause in which he does not believe.

Élodie Blaise (ā·lô·dē′ blĕz′), the seducer of Évariste Gamelin. Purely physical, without ideals or fidelity to any cause, she survives the Reign of Terror to become the mistress of the non-political Philippe Desmahis.

Jean Blaise (zhäǹ′ blĕz′), a printseller and Élodie Blaise's father.

Jacques David (zhàk′ dà·vēd′), a painter and young Évariste Gamelin's teacher.

Père Longuemare (pĕr′ lôǹ·gɘ·màr′), a monk falsely accused as a thief and given refuge by Maurice Brotteaux, with whom he is finally convicted without trial and executed.

Madame de Rochemaure (dɘ rôsh·mōr′), a revolutionary opportunist.

Henry (äǹ·rē′), a dragoon who is the lover of Madame de Rochemaure and Élodie Blaise.

Marat (mà·rà′) and
Robespierre (rô·bĕs·pyĕr′), French revolutionaries.

Athenaïs (à·tā·nà·ēs′), a prostitute once befriended by Maurice Brotteaux and executed with him.

Madame Gamelin (gàm·lăǹ′), Évariste Gamelin's mother.

Julie Gamelin (zhü·lē′ gàm·lăǹ′), Évariste's sister.

Jacques Maubel (zhàk′ mō·bĕl′), a young man convicted by Évariste Gamelin for lack of faith in the people and executed.

Philippe Desmahis (fē·lēp′ dā·mà·ēs′), a non-political engraver who survives the Reign of Terror to become the lover of Élodie Blaise.

THE GOLD BUG

Author: Edgar Allan Poe (1809-1849)
Time of action: Early nineteenth century
First published: 1843

PRINCIPAL CHARACTERS

The Narrator, who relates the story of William Legrand's discovery of Captain Kidd's treasure. He fears for a time that his friend is going out of his mind because of Legrand's peculiar behavior when he finds a piece of parchment that eventually leads to his locating a fortune of more than a million and a half dollars in gold and jewels.

William Legrand, a young man of good family from New Orleans who has taken up residence in a hut on Sullivan's Island, near Charleston, South Carolina, because his family fortune is gone. He spends his time fishing, hunting, and searching for specimens of shells and insects to add to his collection. One day he finds a peculiar new beetle, gold in color, and a piece of old parchment. His behavior becomes very peculiar for about a month. Later, helped in his digging by Jupiter, his servant, and the narrator, he uncovers a rich buried treasure. Le-grand then reveals that he has played a joke on the narrator and Jupiter: realizing that they thought he was going crazy, he led them on by acting peculiarly. Legrand's solving of the cryptograph on the parchment shows that he has rare intelligence as well as a sense of humor.

Jupiter, a manumitted slave who once belonged to the Legrand family. After being freed he stays as a servant and has followed William Legrand to Sullivan's Island. He is devoted and loyal to his master, as much a trusted associate as a servant. Like the narrator, Jupiter is fearful that Legrand is losing his mind.

Lt. G——, an army officer stationed at Fort Moultrie. He is a friend of Legrand and very much interested in entomology. He is fascinated by the gold bug or beetle discovered on Sullivan's Island by Legrand.

THE GOLDEN ASS OF LUCIUS APULEIUS

Author: Lucius Apuleius (125?-?)
Time of action: Early second century
First transcribed: Second century manuscript

PRINCIPAL CHARACTERS

Lucius (lōō'shǐ·əs), a traveler who is turned into an ass, in which form he has several adventures before becoming a man again.

Charites (kâ'rə·tēz), a Greek lady abducted from her wedding by the thieves who stole Milo's gold.

Lepolemus (lə·pŏ'lə·məs), her resourceful husband. He joins the robbers who stole his wife, makes them drunk and chains them, rescues his wife, and causes the robbers to be killed.

Thrasillus (thrə·sǐ'ləs), Lepolemus' friend, in love with Charites, who blinds him with a pin while he is drunk.

Milo (mī'lō), a rich usurer robbed by thieves who use Lucius (now an ass) to carry their stolen gold.

Pamphile (păm'fə·lē), his wife, a witch who turns herself into an eagle.

406

Fotis (fō'tĭs), her buxom and lusty maid who grants her favors to Lucius and then turns him into an ass.

Aristomenes (ă'rĭs·tŏ'mə·nēz), a merchant who tells Lucius of Socrates' misfortune.

Socrates (sŏk'rə·tēz), Aristomenes' good friend. Beaten and robbed, he is cared for by Aristomenes. At midnight two hags cut his throat and substitute a sponge for his heart, which they steal. The next day he dies when the sponge drops out of his severed throat.

Byrrhaena (bĭ·rē'nə), Lucius' cousin, a rich gentlewoman.

Cupid (kū'pĭd), a young good, the son of Venus, who, envious of Psyche's beauty, sends Cupid to make her fall in love with a monster. Instead he takes Psyche for his wife.

Psyche (sī'kē), beauteous young wife of Cupid. Urged by her jealous sisters, she looks upon her sleeping husband's face and he, influenced by Venus, deserts her. Pitied by Jupiter, the pregnant girl becomes immortal, united to Cupid forever.

Queen Isis (ī'sĭs). Through a priest she provides for Lucius to eat roses so that he may return to human form.

THE GOLDEN BOWL

Author: Henry James (1843-1916)
Time of action: c. 1900
First published: 1904

PRINCIPAL CHARACTERS

Maggie Verver, the motherless daughter of an American millionaire. For a number of years the Ververs have spent much of their time abroad, where Mr. Verver has devoted himself to acquiring a magnificent art collection for the museum he plans to build in American City. Sharing her father's quiet tastes and aesthetic interests, Maggie has become his faithful companion, and they have created for themselves a separate, enclosed world of ease, grace, and discriminating appreciation, a connoisseurship of life as well as of art. Even Maggie's marriage to Prince Amerigo, an Italian of ancient family, does not change greatly the pattern of their lives, a pattern that she believes complete when Mr. Verver marries her best friend, Charlotte Stant. What Maggie does not know is the fact that before her marriage the Prince and Charlotte, both moneyless and therefore unable to marry, had been lovers. Several years later the Prince, bored by his position as another item in the Verver collection, and Charlotte, restless because she takes second place beside her elderly husband's

interest in art, resume their former intimacy. Maggie finds her happiness threatened when her purchase of a flawed gold-and-crystal bowl leads indirectly to her discovery of the true situation. Her problem is whether to disclose or conceal her knowledge. Deeply in love with her husband and devoted to her father, she decides to remain silent. Her passivity becomes an act of drama because it involves a sense of ethical responsibility and a moral decision; her predicament is the familiar Jamesian spectacle of the innocent American confronting the evil of European morality, in this case complicated by Maggie's realization that she and her father are not without guilt, that they have lived too much for themselves. In the end her generosity, tact, and love resolve all difficulties. Mr. Verver and his wife leave for America and Maggie regains her husband's love, now unselfishly offered.

Prince Amerigo, a young Italian nobleman, handsome, gallant, sensual, living in England with his American wife. A man of politely easy manners, he is able to mask his real feelings under an appearance of courteous reserve. Though he has loved many women, he has little capacity for lies or deception in his dealings with them; he objects when Charlotte Stant, his former mistress, wishes to purchase a flawed golden bowl as a wedding gift to his wife, for he wants nothing but perfection in his marriage. He and Charlotte are often thrown together after she marries his father-in-law, and they become lovers once more. When his wife learns, through purchase of the same flawed bowl, the secret of his infidelity, he tries to be loyal to all parties concerned, and he so beautifully preserves the delicate harmony of family relationships that no outsiders except their mutual friends, the Assinghams, know of the situation. Maggie, his wife, is able to save her marriage because his delicacy in the matter of purchased and purchasable partners makes tense situations easier. After Mr. Verver and his wife return to America, the Prince shows relief as unselfish as it is sincere; their departure allows him to be a husband and a father in his own right.

Charlotte Stant, the beautiful but impecunious American girl who needs a wealthy husband to provide the fine clothes and beautiful things she believes necessary for her happiness. Because Prince Amerigo is poor, she becomes his mistress but never considers marrying him. After his marriage to Maggie Verver, her best friend, Mr. Verver proposes to Charlotte. She accepts him and, though Mr. Verver cannot understand her claim of unworthiness, declares herself prepared to be as devoted as possible, both as a wife and as a stepmother to her good friend. Often left in the Prince's company while Maggie and her father pursue their interest in art, she resumes her affair with her former lover. When the truth is finally revealed, Charlotte, determined to prove her loyalties to all concerned, persuades Mr. Verver to return with her to America. Her poised and gracious farewell to Maggie and the Prince is more than a demonstration of her ability to keep up appearances; it shows the code of responsibility she has assumed toward her lover, her friend, and her husband.

Adam Verver, a rich American who has given over the pursuit of money in order to achieve the good life for himself and his daughter Maggie. In his innocence he believes that this end may be attained by seeing and collecting the beautiful art objects of Europe. A perfect father, he cannot realize that there is anything selfish in the close tie that exists between himself and his daughter, and he tries to stand in the same relationship with his son-in-law, Prince Amerigo, and Charlotte Stant, his daughter's friend, whom he marries. All he really lives for is to provide for Maggie and his grandson the life of happiness and plenty he envisions for them. When he finally realizes that the pattern of his life has been a form of make-believe, he sacrifices his own peace of mind and agrees to return with his wife to make the United States his permanent home.

Fanny Assingham, the friend of Maggie and Adam Verver, Prince Amerigo, and Charlotte Stant, and the guardian angel of their secret lives. As one who senses the rightness of things, she helps to bring about both marriages with a sensitive understanding of the needs of all, a delicacy she will not allow to be disrupted by Maggie's discovery of her husband's infidelity. Her belief is that even wickedness is more to be condoned than wrongness of heart. She helps to resolve the situation between Maggie and Prince Amerigo when she hurls the golden bowl, symbol of Maggie's flawed marriage and the Prince's guilt, to the floor and smashes it.

Colonel Robert Assingham, called **Bob,** a retired army officer who understands his wife's motives in the interest she takes in the Verver family but who manages

to keep himself detached from her complicated dealings with the lives of others.

The Principino, the small son of Prince
Amerigo and his wife Maggie.

GOLDEN BOY

Author: Clifford Odets (1906-1963)
Time of action: The 1930's
First presented: 1937

PRINCIPAL CHARACTERS

Joe Bonaparte, a young violinist who becomes a prize fighter. At heart a musician, he has been laughed at and hurt by
people against whom he longs to fight
back. The fame and money gained in
the ring make retaliation possible but
brutalize Joe and change his personality. He falls in love with Lorna Moon,
who finally persuades him to give up the
ring. That night they are both killed in
an automobile accident.

Tom Moody, Joe Bonaparte's fight manager and part owner.

Lorna Moon, Tom Moody's mistress.
Asked by Joe Bonaparte's father to help
the fighter find himself, she falls in love
with him but feels that she cannot give
up Tom Moody, whose wife has at last

consented to a divorce so that he can
marry her. Finally, in Joe's dressing
room after a triumphant fight, she tells
him again that she loves him and persuades him to leave the ring. She is killed
with him that night in an automobile accident.

Mr. Bonaparte, Joe Bonaparte's father.
Hoping that Joe will give up fighting
and return to music, he refuses the parental blessing on Joe's career until he sorrowfully sees that his son is totally committed to the ring. When Joe is killed, he
claims the body and brings the boy home
where he belongs.

Eddie Fuseli, a gambler and part owner
of Joe Bonaparte.

THE GONDOLIERS

Author: W. S. Gilbert (1836-1911)
Time of action: 1750
First presented: 1889

PRINCIPAL CHARACTERS

The Duke of Plaza-Toro, a Grandee of
Spain. The Duke, who always led his
regiment from behind, except when it
retreated, is eager to place his daughter
on the throne of Barataria and to feather
his own nest as much as possible.

The Duchess of Plaza-Toro, his formidable wife.

Casilda, their daughter, married in infancy to the royal heir of Barataria. She
is in love with Luiz.

Don Alhambra del Bolero, the Grand
Inquisitor of Spain. He is searching for
the royal heir, whom he had stolen in
infancy and left with a tippling gondolier to rear with his own son. The
gondolier could not remember which of
the two boys was his own son and which
the Prince; hence the Inquisitor decides
to torture their former nurse to find out
which is which.

Marco Palmieri and
Giuseppi Palmieri, gondoliers with re

publican principles. Each being half a king until the truth could be discovered, they promote everybody in the kingdom to a lord high something-or-other, to the Inquisitor's disgust. They are separated from their recent brides and told that one is an unconscious bigamist.

Giannetta and
Tessa, flower girls, wives of Marco and Giuseppi.

Luiz, Casilda's lover and the Duke's attendant, who carries a drum to beat before the Duke. He turns out to be the real King of Barataria.

Inez, an elderly nurse. She is readily persuaded by torture to confess that Luiz is the King of Barataria, for whom she had substituted her own son, actually the child stolen by the Grand Inquisitor. Her testimony reunites Luiz and Casilda and the gondoliers and their brides.

GONE WITH THE WIND

Author: Margaret Mitchell (1900-1949)
Time of action: 1861-1873
First published: 1936

PRINCIPAL CHARACTERS

Scarlett O'Hara, a Georgia belle. Gently bred on Tara plantation and the wife of Charles Hamilton, she finds herself, through the fortunes of war, a widow and the mistress of a ruined plantation with a family to feed. With an indomitable will to survive and an unquenchable determination to keep Tara, she improves her fortunes with the aid of her own native abilities and opportunistic marriages to Frank Kennedy and Rhett Butler.

Ashley Wilkes, Scarlett O'Hara's sensitive, sophisticated neighbor, with whom she fancies herself in love until, through adversity, he is shorn of the aura of romance with which she has endowed him and shows himself for the weakling that he is.

Rhett Butler, a cynical, wealthy blockade runner, Scarlett O'Hara's third husband. Knowing Scarlett for the unscrupulous materialist that she is, he nevertheless

admires her will to survive and is plagued with a love for her which he finally overcomes just as she discovers that it is he and not Ashley Wilkes that she loves.

Charles Hamilton, Scarlett's first husband, whom she marries for spite.

Frank Kennedy, Scarlett's second husband, whom she marries for money.

Melanie (Hamilton) Wilkes, Ashley Wilkes' reticent, ladylike wife.

Gerald O'Hara and
Ellen O'Hara, Scarlett's parents.

Bonnie Blue Butler, the daughter of Scarlett O'Hara and Rhett Butler.

Suellen O'Hara, Scarlett's sister.

Miss Pittypat, Melanie Wilkes' aunt.

India Wilkes, Ashley Wilkes' sister.

Mammy, Scarlett's nurse.

THE GOOD COMPANIONS

Author: J. B. Priestley (1894-   )
Time of action: The 1920's
First published: 1929

Jess Oakroyd, a Yorshireman. A stolid, seemingly dull man, he proves that he is no fool. He sets off, tired of home, to see England. Meeting Elizabeth Trant, he befriends her and joins her, becoming the handyman of The Good Companions. He keeps the group united when they are dispirited. His adventures with the traveling company convince him he wants to go on traveling.

Elizabeth Trant, an old maid at thirty-five. She inherits a little money and sets out to see England. She falls in with a traveling vaudeville company, takes them over, and enjoys life for the first time. She meets a doctor who had been her suitor years before and marries.

Inigo Jollifant, a teacher who leaves his job because he is unhappy. He begins to travel; meeting The Good Companions, he joins them as their songwriter. He falls in love with Susie Dean, the comedienne.

Morton Mitcham, a banjo-playing profes-

sional who becomes one of The Good Companions.

Susie Dean, a pretty young comedienne who wants to become a star on the London stage. She cannot understand why Inigo Jollifant prefers writing for the literary journals to his success as a writer of popular tunes.

Jerry Jerningham, a male dancer with The Good Companions. He marries a wealthy woman and uses his influence to get Susie a chance to play in London. He gets places, too, for the other members of the troupe.

Jimmy Nunn and **Elsie Longstaff,** members of The Good Companions.

Dr. Hugh McFarlane, Elizabeth's former suitor whom she meets again and marries.

Mrs. Oakroyd, whose nagging causes Jess to leave home. When she becomes seriously ill he returns to her; but when she dies he again takes to the open road.

THE GOOD EARTH

Author: Pearl S. Buck (1892-   )
Time of action: Early twentieth century
First published: 1931

Wang Lung, an ambitious farmer who sees in the land the only sure source of livelihood. But at the end of his life his third son has left the land to be a soldier and his first and second sons callously plan to sell the land and go to the city as soon as Wang dies.

O-Lan, a slave bought by Wang's father to marry Wang. She works hard in their small field with Wang, and during civil war violence she loots in order to get money to buy more land. She dies in middle age of a stomach illness.

Nung En, their oldest son, who, when he covets his father's concubine, Lotus Blossom, is married to the grain merchant Liu's daughter.

Nung Wen, their second son, apprenticed to Liu.

The Fool, their feeble-minded daughter.

Liu, a grain merchant in the town.

The Uncle, who brings his wife and shiftless son to live on Wang's farm. Secretly a lieutenant of a robber band, he also brings protection.

Lotus Blossom, Wang Lung's concubine, who is refused entrance into the house by O-Lan.

Ching, a neighbor hired by Wang Lung as overseer, as the farm is extended.

Pear Blossom, a pretty slave taken by Wang after the death of his wife.

GOODBYE, MR. CHIPS

Author: James Hilton (1900-1954)
Time of action: 1870-1933
First published: 1933

PRINCIPAL CHARACTERS

Mr. Chipping (Chips), a retired schoolmaster, white-haired, semi-bald, fairly active for his age. Unprofound, he prefers detective novels to the Greek and Latin works which he taught for so long. His mind is filled with memories of his dead wife, the many boys he taught at Brookfield, and the many experiences he had there. He is a legend at the school and is remembered with affection. He dies dreaming of the thousands of boys he had taught.

Mrs. Wickett, his landlady.

Wetherby, the head of Brookfield when Mr. Chips came there.

Colley, a Brookfield boy whom Mr. Chips disciplined on his first day at the school. Colley's son and grandson later become pupils of Mr. Chips.

Katherine (Kathie) Bridges Chipping, Mr. Chips' young wife, whom he marries at forty-eight. She is very popular with the boys. She dies in childbirth and her son with her.

Dr. Merivale, Mr. Chips' physician.

Collingwood, a Brookfield boy who becomes a major and is killed in the war.

Ralston, a young headmaster at Brookfield whom Mr. Chips never likes.

Chatteris, Ralston's successor as headmaster; he and Mr. Chips get on well.

Max Staefel, a former German master at Brookfield, drafted while visiting in Germany and later killed on the Western Front.

Linford, a Brookfield boy, the last to say, "Goodbye, Mr. Chips," the night before the old man dies.

GORBODUC

Authors: Thomas Norton (1532-1584) and Thomas Sackville (1536-1608)
Time of action: Before the Saxon invasion of Britain
First presented: 1562

PRINCIPAL CHARACTERS

Gorboduc (gôr·bō′dŭk), King of ancient Britain. After ruling his land wisely for many years he disregards the advice of his sage counselors, divides the realm between his two sons, and thus brings

tragedy upon his family and his country. He recognizes the folly of his decision too late, when he learns of the unnatural deaths of his sons. Filled with remorse, he learns that as a human being, he must grieve; the patience prescribed by his advisers is an attribute of gods alone. He is finally murdered by his people, who have fallen into anarchy as a result of the overturning of the natural order of succession and government.

Videna (vē·dā′nă), his Queen. She is partial to her older son and disapproves from the beginning the King's resolution to deprive Ferrex of half his rightful inheritance, for she foresees in Porrex the envy and pride which later erupt in his brother's murder. Horrified by Ferrex' death, she curses and disowns her younger child, then wreaks her unnatural revenge on him.

Ferrex (fĕr′ĕks), Gorboduc's older son, his mother's favorite. Although he is less malleable than Porrex, he listens to the counselors who encourage him to build up an army as protection against the jealous ambition of his brother, thus provoking Porrex' attack.

Porrex (pôr′ĕks), Ferrex' brother. Easily persuaded by flatterers that Ferrex intends to rob him of his realm, he is enraged to learn that his brother is armed and retaliates by invading his territory and murdering him. Returning grief-stricken to his parents, he finds that Gorboduc will not accept his explanation that he killed Ferrex to save his own life. Banished from his father's sight, he is slain by his own mother.

Arostus, Gorboduc's counselor. He praises the King's decision to give the kingdom to his sons, for he believes that the young men can learn to rule wisely under their father's guidance. After the death of the princes he moralizes to the King about the uncertainty of man's life, but his words give no comfort to his master.

Philander, another of the King's advisers, who later attempts to control Porrex' ambition and anger. Although he does not foresee the inevitable strife which is to arise from the division of the realm, he argues that the princes should learn to govern well from their father's example and suggests that to disrupt the natural order by handing down the crown before the death of the King is to "corrupt the state of minds and things."

Eubulus, Gorboduc's secretary. He pleads with the King to preserve the kingdom intact for the sake of its citizens, for he knows that "divided reigns do make divided hearts." He prophesies the dissatisfactions which arise in both princes. After the death of the King and Queen he counsels the immediate quelling of the popular revolt and argues that no subject has a right to rebel against his prince for any cause whatever. When he hears of Fergus' rebellion he laments the fate of his country, which will be torn by civil wars until the legitimate heir can be restored to the throne.

Dordan, Ferrex' wise counselor, who attempts to mollify the Prince's resentment at being deprived of half his kingdom.

Hermon and
Tyndar, parasites of the two princes. They play upon their masters' feelings of resentment and ambition, inciting them on to their disastrous combat.

Fergus, Duke of Albany. Leagued with other noblemen to put down the popular revolt, he decides to try to win the crown for himself by force; his ambition begins a long series of civil wars.

Clotyn, Duke of Cornwall,
Mandud, Duke of Loegris, and
Gwenard, Duke of Cumberland, lords allied to put down rebellion and later to overcome Fergus' army.

Marcella, Videna's lady in waiting, who relates with grief and horror the Queen's murder of her remaining son.

GRAND HOTEL

Author: Vicki Baum (1896-1960)
Time of action: The 1920's
First published: 1930

PRINCIPAL CHARACTERS

Baron Gaigern (bä·rōn′ gī′gėrn), one of the guests at Berlin's Grand Hotel who, while seeming rich, is actually a gambler and a thief. He tries unsuccessfully to steal from the other guests in the hotel and, for various reasons, fails in each case. As a result of trying to steal jewelry from Elisaveta Grusinskaya, a ballerina, he becomes her lover. While he is trying to steal Herr Preysing's wallet, he is killed, felled by a blow inflicted with a bronze inkstand.

Herr Preysing (hâr prī′sĭng), general manager of the Saxonia Cotton Company and a guest at the hotel. He tries to reëstablish his company's financial position by a merger with another company. He hires Miss Flamm as a stenographer and then offers to make her his mistress. He murders Gaigern when he discovers the Baron trying to steal his wallet. Because the Baron is unarmed at the time, Preysing is held for murder.

Otto Kringelein (ō′tō krĭng′gä·līn), a forty-six-year-old junior clerk in Preysing's company and a guest at the hotel. Having been told that he is dying, he is out for one last frolic in the world, inasmuch as he has been a meek, downtrodden man all his life. His personality changes when Miss Flamm flees to him for help when Baron Gaigern is killed.

Her friendship and interest in him give Kringelein some purpose in life. He decides to go to England with her.

Miss Flamm (fläm), nicknamed Flaemmchen by Herr Preysing. She is a beautiful stenographer who works as a part-time photographer's model. When Herr Preysing kills Baron Gaigern, she flees from her employer to ask Kringelein's help and becomes interested in her protector.

Elisaveta Alexandrovna Grusinskaya (ĕ·lĕ′sä·vä′tä älex·änd′drôv′nä grōō·sĭns′kä·yä), an aging ballerina. She finds Baron Gaigern in her room. He denies trying to steal from her and becomes her lover, giving her the admiration and self-confidence she desperately needs.

Dr. Otternschlag (dôc′tôr ō·tėrn′shläg), a retired doctor staying at the hotel. Having been disfigured in World War I, he has no real interest in life. When he tries to commit suicide, he finds, however, he really wants to live.

The Grand Duke Sergei (sâr′yī), an aristocrat who gave expensive pearls to Elisaveta Grusinskaya.

[Anna Kringelein (änä krĭng′gä·līn), Kringelein's wife he left at home in Fredersdorf.]

THE GRANDISSIMES

Author: George W. Cable (1844-1925)
Time of action: 1804
First published: 1880

Honoré Grandissime, a merchant, head of the Grandissimes. Extremely handsome and well-dressed, he is an impressive figure, the flower of the family. His egalitarian views and his opposition to slavery are viewed with suspicion and distaste by other Grandissimes. He represents the peacemaking element as his uncle, Agricola, represents the strifemaking element in the family. Conscience-stricken over his possession of and profit from Aurora's property (given him by Agricola), he returns it and thereby angers his family. He further alienates them by going into partnership with another Honoré Grandissime, a free man of color.

The Darker Honoré Grandissime, his older quadroon half brother, a rentier. (To prevent confusion, he is usually distinguished from the white Honoré by the initials f. m. c.—free man of color—after his name.) He has strong feelings about the lot of the Louisianians of mixed blood, but he is feeble of will about fighting the caste system. He hates Agricola and loves Palmyre. After going with Palmyre to Bordeaux following Agricola's death, he vainly courts her and then drowns himself.

Agricola Fusilier, Honoré's uncle, a sturdy, bearded old lion careless of his dress. Loving all things French, he scorns Americans and their jargon. He is proud of his Creole blood, contemptuous of all people of color, and fearful of Palmyre. He is mortally stabbed by Honoré f. m. c., whom he has attacked. Dying, he affects to forgive all enemies of the Creole aristocracy, but he dies with his prejudices.

Aurora Nancanou (nee De Grapion), a beautiful young widow whose husband died in a duel after accusing Agricola of cheating at cards. She is poor but proud, and she superstitiously believes in Palmyre's spellmaking powers. In love with Honoré, she is mindful of the enmity of the Grandissimes toward her own family, the De Grapions. After Agricola, dying, admits to having, years before, promised a marriage between Honoré and Aurora, she still resists, but finally accepts her formerly diffident adorer.

Clotilde Nancanou, her lovely daughter, who appears to be a younger sister rather than the daughter of the youthful-looking Aurora. Loved by Joseph, she finally accepts his suit.

Joseph Frowenfeld, a handsome young American immigrant of German ancestry whose family all die of yellow fever, which Joseph survives. He becomes a proprietor of an apothecary shop. A serious student, he has liberal views which are resented by the Creoles. He cannot understand why the caste system for people of varied colors is permitted to continue in Louisiana. Wounded mistakenly while attending Palmyre after she is shot, he recovers and becomes a partner in an expanded drug business supported by capital from Aurora. He falls in love with Clotilde and apparently will marry her.

Dr. Charlie Keene, Joseph's physician and friend, red-haired and freckled. Intelligent and perceptive, he acquaints Joseph with the Creole-dominated society of New Orleans.

Palmyre Philosophe, a freed quadroon slave, formerly Aurora's maid, who hates Agricola and who is wounded after stabbing him. Loved by Honoré f. m. c., she ignores him and hates all men except the white Honoré and Bras Coupé, to whom she was married before he ran away. She passionately desires the love of Honoré, but in vain.

Bras Coupé, a giant African prince captured by slavers and brought to Louisiana. After marrying Palmyre, he strikes his master in a drunken fit and escapes. Returning to get Palmyre, he is captured, imprisoned, and mutilated, and

415

he dies in prison after removing the curse he had put upon Don José's family and land. Bras Coupé is a symbol of the dignity, the native worth, and the tragedy of his race.

Don José Martinez, Honoré's brother-in-law and Bras Coupé's master.

Governor Claiborne, a young Virginian, governor-general of Louisiana.

Numa Grandissime, father of the two Honorés.

Raul Innerarity, an amateur artist, a cousin of Honoré. He becomes Joseph's clerk.

Achille,
Valentine,
Jean-Baptiste,
Hippolyte,
Sylvestre, and
Agamemnon, kinsmen of Honoré.

Clemence, Palmyre's voodoo accomplice, shot to death by an unknown marksman after her lynching is interrupted.

THE GRANDMOTHERS

Author: Glenway Wescott (1901-   )
Time of action: 1830-1925
First published: 1927

PRINCIPAL CHARACTERS

Alwyn Tower, a young boy deeply interested in the history of his family. He pours over the family albums and pieces together his relatives' stories.

Henry Tower, Alwyn's grandfather. He came to Wisconsin from New York planning, but failing, to become rich. His first and dearly loved wife dies, leaving a baby boy. He marries again to give the child a mother. After the boy dies, Henry loses interest in life, though he has many other children. In his old age his chief interest is his new garden. He lives to be eighty-two, but to Alwyn he never seems completely alive.

Serena Cannon, Henry's first wife, who dies of a fever.

Rose Hamilton, Henry's second wife, Alwyn's grandmother. Jilted by Henry's brother, her one true love, she marries Henry and gives him many children. She too never seems completely alive to Alwyn, though she appears resigned and not unhappy.

Leander Tower, Henry's brother. Returning from the Civil War, he no longer wants to marry Rose, and goes to Cali-

fornia. Later he returns to Wisconsin. Rose, though she still loves him, remains true to Henry.

Hilary Tower, the younger brother of Leander and Henry. He disappeared in the war, and Leander seems always to be looking for a substitute for him. Old Leander seems happy only when helping a young boy.

Nancy Tower, Alwyn's great-aunt, insane for part of her life.

Mary Harris, another great-aunt whose first husband was killed by Southerners because he was a Northern sympathizer. Her second husband was a drunken sot; often she had to beg for food to stay alive. With her third husband, one of the Tower men, she knows happiness and prosperity for the first time.

Jim Tower, Alwyn's uncle, the son of Henry and Rose. A minister who married a rich woman, he lives in Chicago and has been persuaded by his wife to give up preaching. Living with him and his wife in Chicago, Alwyn gets his only chance for a good education. After his wife's death, Jim goes on living with

416

and humoring the whims of his mother-in-law and his sisters-in-law. Alwyn likes but does not admire Jim.

Evan Tower, Alwyn's uncle, another son of Henry and Rose. He was a deserter from the Spanish-American War who went west under a different name. He comes home sometimes to see his father, but relations between them are so strained that on his last visit the old man refuses to enter the house while Evan is there.

Flora Tower, Alwyn's aunt, the daughter of Henry and Rose. Afraid of being awakened to love, she refuses to marry. Having nothing to fear from her young nephew, she loves him whole-heartedly.

She dies at twenty-nine, appearing to Alwyn happy as she draws her last breath.

Ralph Tower, Alwyn's father, another son of Henry and Rose. He wanted to be a veterinarian, but Jim was the one chosen to be educated. Ralph, resigned rather than bitter, takes over his father's farm.

Marianne Tower, Ralph's wife and Alwyn's mother. Her parents hated each other, and Marianne was lonely until she met Ralph. Their marriage is completely happy; they love each other so much that Alwyn is sometimes embarrassed to see them together.

THE GRAPES OF WRATH

Author: John Steinbeck (1902-   )
Time of action: The 1930's
First published: 1939

PRINCIPAL CHARACTERS

Tom Joad, Jr., an ex-convict. Returning to his home in Oklahoma after serving time in the penitentiary for killing a man in self-defense, he finds the house deserted, the family having been pushed off the land because of dust bowl conditions and in order to make way for more productive mechanization. With Casy, the preacher, he finds his family and makes the trek to California in search of work. During labor difficulties Tom kills another man when his friend Casy, who is trying to help the migrant workers in their labor problems, is brutally killed by deputies representing the law and the owners. He leaves his family because, as a "wanted" man, he is a danger to them, but he leaves with a new understanding which he has learned from Casy: it is no longer the individual that counts but the group. Tom promises to carry on Casy's work of helping the downtrodden.

Tom Joad, Sr., called **Pa,** an Oklahoma

farmer who finds it difficult to adjust to new conditions while moving his family to California.

Ma Joad, a large, heavy woman, full of determination and hope, who fights to hold her family together. On the journey to California she gradually becomes the staying power of the family.

Rose of Sharon Rivers, called **Rosasharn,** the married, teen-age daughter of the Joads. Her husband leaves her, and she bears a stillborn baby because of the hardships she endures. As the story ends she gives her own milk to save the life of a starving man.

Noah, the slow-witted second son of the Joads. He finally wanders off down a river when the pressures of the journey and his hunger become too much.

Al, the third son of the Joads. In his

teens, he is interested in girls and automobiles. He idolizes his brother Tom.

Ruthie, the pre-teen-age daughter of the Joads.

Winfield, the youngest of the Joads.

Uncle John, the brother of Tom Joad, Sr. He is a lost soul who periodically is flooded with guilt because he let his young wife die by ignoring her illness.

Grampa Joad, who does not want to leave Oklahoma and dies on the way to California. He is buried with little ceremony by the roadside.

Granma Joad, also old and childish. She dies while crossing the desert and receives a pauper burial.

Jim Casy, the country preacher who has given up the ministry because he no longer believes. He makes the trek to California with the Joads. He assumes the blame and goes to jail for the "crime" of a migrant worker who has a family to support. He is killed as a "red" while trying to help the migrant workers organize and strike for a living wage.

Connie Rivers, Rosasharn's young husband, who deserts her after arriving in California.

Floyd Knowles, a young migrant worker with a family, called a "red" because he asks a contractor to guarantee a job and the wages to be paid. He escapes from a deputy sheriff who is attempting to intimidate the workers. Tom Joad trips

the deputy and Jim Casy kicks him in the back of the head.

Muley Graves, a farmer who refuses to leave the land, although his family has gone. He remains, abstracted and lonely, forced to hide, hunted and haunted.

Jim Rawley, the kind, patient manager of a government camp for the migrant workers.

Willy Feeley, a former small farmer like the Joads; he takes a job driving a tractor over the land the Joads farmed.

Ivy Wilson, a migrant who has car trouble on the way to California with his sick wife Sairy. The Joads help them and the two families stay together until Sairy becomes too ill to travel.

Sairy Wilson, Ivy's wife. When the Wilsons are forced to stay behind because of her illness, she asks Casy to pray for her.

Timothy Wallace, a migrant who helps Tom Joad find work in California.

Wilkie Wallace, his son.

Aggie Wainwright, the daughter of a family living in a box car with the Joads while they work in a cotton field. Al Joad plans to marry her.

Jessie Bullitt,
Ella Summers, and
Annie Littlefield, the ladies' committee for Sanitary Unit Number Four of the government camp for migrant workers.

GREAT EXPECTATIONS

Author: Charles Dickens (1812-1870)
Time of action: Nineteenth century
First published: 1860-1861

PRINCIPAL CHARACTERS

Philip Pirrip, called **Pip,** an orphan and the unwanted ward of his harsh sister, Mrs. Joe. Although seemingly destined

for the blacksmith shop, he sees his fortunes improve after he meets a convict hiding in a graveyard. Afterward,

418

through Miss Havisham, he meets Estella, the eccentric old woman's lovely young ward. Thinking Miss Havisham is his benefactor, he goes to London to become a gentleman. Unfortunately for his peace of mind, he forgets who his true friends are. Finally, after Magwitch dies and the Crown confiscates his fortune, Pip understands that good clothes, well-spoken English, and a generous allowance do not make one a gentleman.

Miss Havisham, a lonely, embittered old spinster. When her lover jilted her at the altar, she refused ever to leave her gloomy chambers. Instead, she has devoted her life to vengeance. With careful indoctrination she teaches Estella how to break men's hearts. Just before her death she begs Pip to forgive her cruelty.

Estella, Miss Havisham's ward. Cold, aloof, unfeeling, she tries to warn Pip not to love her, for she is incapable of loving anyone; Miss Havisham has taught her too well. But years later Pip meets her in the garden near the ruins of Satis House, Miss Havisham's former home. She has lost her cool aloofness and found maturity. Pip realizes that they will never part again.

Joe Gargery, Pip's brother-in-law. Even though he is married to the worst of shrews, Mrs. Joe, he manages to retain his gentle simplicity and his selfless love for Pip. After he marries Biddy, he finds the domestic bliss which he so richly deserves.

Mrs. Georgiana Maria Gargery, commonly called **Mrs. Joe,** Pip's vituperative sister, who berates and misuses him and Joe with impunity. When she verbally assails Joe's helper, Orlick, she makes a mortal enemy who causes her death with the blow of a hammer. Later he tries to do the same for Pip.

Abel Magwitch, alias **Mr. Provis,** Pip's benefactor. When Pip helps him, an escaped convict, Magwitch promises to repay the debt. Transported to New South Wales, he eventually makes a large fortune as a sheep farmer. When he returns illegally to England years later, the escaped felon reveals himself as Pip's real patron. Casting off his distaste, Pip finds a real affection for the rough old man and attempts to get him safely out of England before the law apprehends him once more. Recaptured, Magwitch dies in prison.

Mr. Jaggers, a criminal lawyer employed by Magwitch to provide for Pip's future. He is a shrewd man with the ability to size up a person at a glance. To him, personal feelings are unimportant; facts are the only trustworthy things. Although completely unemotional, he deals with Pip and Magwitch honestly throughout their long association.

Herbert Pocket, Miss Havisham's young relative and Pip's roommate in London. Almost always cheerful and uncomplaining, he is constantly looking for ways to improve his prospects. With Pip's aid he is able to establish himself in a profitable business.

John Wemmick, Mr. Jaggers' efficient law clerk. Dry and businesslike in the office, he keeps his social and business life completely separate. As a friend, he proves himself completely loyal to Pip.

Biddy, Joe Gargery's wife after the death of Mrs. Joe. A gentle, loving girl, she is a good wife to him.

Compeyson, a complete villain, the man who jilted Miss Havisham and betrayed Magwitch. He is killed by Magwitch as the two struggle desperately just before the ex-convict is recaptured.

The Aged, John Wemmick's deaf old father. In their neat little home, his chief pleasures are reading the newspaper aloud and listening to his son's nightly firing of a small cannon.

Dolge Orlick, Joe Gargery's surly helper in the blacksmith shop. After an altercation with Mrs. Joe, he attacks her with

419

a hammer. Later he plots to kill Pip, his hated enemy. Only the timely arrival of Herbert Pocket and Startop prevents the crime.

Molly, Mr. Jaggers' housekeeper, a woman of strange, silent habits, with extraordinarily strong hands. A murderess, she is also revealed as Magwitch's former mistress and Estella's mother.

Matthew Pocket, Miss Havisham's distant relative and Pip's tutor during his early years in London. He is also Herbert Pocket's father.

Mrs. Belinda Pocket, a fluttery, helpless woman, the daughter of a knight who had expected his daughter to marry a title.

Alick,
Joe,
Fanny, and
Jane, other children of the Pockets.

Sarah Pocket, another relative of Miss Havisham, a withered-appearing, sharp-tongued woman.

Uncle Pumblechook, a prosperous corn chandler and Joe Gargery's relative. During Pip's childhood he constantly discusses the boy's conduct and offers much platitudinous advice.

Clara Barley, a pretty, winning girl engaged to Herbert Pocket. Magwitch is hidden in the Barley house while Pip is trying to smuggle the former convict out of England.

Old Bill Barley, Clara's father. A former

purser, he is afflicted by gout and bedridden.

Mr. Wopsle, a parish clerk who later becomes an actor under the name of Mr. Waldengarver. Pip and Herbert Pocket go to see his performance as Hamlet.

Bentley Drummle, called **The Spider,** a sulky, rich boy notable for his bad manners. He is Pip's rival for Estella's love. After marrying her, he treats her cruelly. Pip meets him while Drummle is being tutored by Mr. Pocket.

Startop, a lively young man tutored by Mr. Pocket.

Mr. Trabb, a village tailor and undertaker.

Trabb's Boy, a young apprentice whose independence is a source of irritation to Pip.

Mr. John (Raymond) Camilla, a toady.

Mrs. Camilla, his wife, Mr. Pocket's sister. She and her husband hope to inherit a share of Miss Havisham's fortune.

Miss Skiffins, a woman of no certain age but the owner of "portable property," who marries John Wemmick.

Clarriker, a young shipping broker in whose firm, Clarriker & Company, Pip secretly buys Herbert Pocket a partnership.

Pepper, also called **The Avenger,** Pip's servant in the days of his great expectations.

THE GREAT GALEOTO

Author: José Echegaray y Eizaguirre (1832-1916)
Time of action: Nineteenth century
First presented: 1881

PRINCIPAL CHARACTERS

Ernesto (âr·näs′tō), a young playwright taken into the home of his father's close friend Don Julián as secretary. Don

Julián has a young and beautiful wife, Teodora, and the presence of the handsome young secretary in the household

420

causes gossip. When Don Julián's brother Severo voices his suspicions, Ernesto, though entirely innocent, moves from Don Julián's house into a garret. The Viscount Nebreda repeats the malicious slander publicly in Ernesto's presence and is challenged to a duel. But before they can fight, Don Julián finds Nebreda, fights him, and is gravely wounded. He is taken to Ernesto's room where he finds Teodora, who has innocently come to say goodbye before Ernesto leaves Spain the following day. The circumstantial evidence now seems overwhelming and before he dies, Don Julián slaps Ernesto's face and threatens to kill him in a duel. After his death, Severo claims his brother's house and orders Teodora banished from the premises. When she faints, Ernesto denounces Severo and all gossiping society as no better than an evil panderer determined to bring two innocent people to ruin with vague innuendoes and vicious rumors. The title of the play is derived from Galeoto, the go-between for Lancelot and Guinevere, as referred to in Dante's story of Paolo and Francesca.

Don Julián (dōn hōō·lyän'), a wealthy businessman who befriends Ernesto. He is then led by slander to suspect an affair between Ernesto and Teodora.

Teodora (tā·ō·t́hō'rä), Julián's young and faithful wife, wrongly suspected by society of being in love with Ernesto. Severo bars her from her dying husband's room and later tries to put her out of the house. When she faints, Ernesto lifts her up and tells Severo that he will take her away.

Severo (sā·bā'rō), the brother of Julián, who voices the rumors of Madrid. He is forced by Ernesto to apologize on his knees to Teodora.

Mercedes (mår·thā't́häs), Severo's gossiping wife, who passes on the rumors of scandal to Teodora.

Pepito (pā·pē'tō), the son of Severo and Mercedes, who carries the news of Julián's duel.

The Viscount Nebreda (nä·brä·t́hä), challenged to a duel by Ernesto for slandering Teodora. Julián, taking up the challenge, is fatally wounded by Nebreda, who, in turn, is killed by Ernesto.

THE GREAT GATSBY

Author: F. Scott Fitzgerald (1896-1940)
Time of action: The 1920's
First published: 1925

PRINCIPAL CHARACTERS

Nick Carraway, the narrator. A young Midwesterner who was dissatisfied with his life at home, he was attracted to New York and now sells bonds there. He is the most honest character of the novel and because of this trait fails to become deeply fascinated by his rich friends on Long Island. He helps Daisy and Jay Gatsby to renew a love they had known before Daisy's marriage, and he is probably the only person in the novel to have any genuine affection for Gatsby.

Jay Gatsby, a fabulously rich racketeer whose connections outside of the law are only guessed at. He is the son of poor parents from the Middle West. He has changed his name from James Gatz and becomes obsessed with a need for making more and more money. Much of his time is spent in trying to impress, and become accepted by, other rich people. He gives lavish parties for people he knows nothing about and most of whom he never meets. He is genuinely in love

421

with Daisy Buchanan and becomes a sympathetic character when he assumes the blame for her hit-and-run accident. At his death he has been deserted by everyone except his father and Nick.

Daisy Buchanan, Nick's second cousin. Unhappy in her marriage because of Tom Buchanan's deliberate unfaithfulness, she has the character of a "poor little rich girl." She renews an old love for Jay Gatsby and considers leaving her husband, but she is finally reconciled to him. She kills Tom's mistress in a hit-and-run accident after a quarrel in which she defends both men as Tom accuses Gatsby of trying to steal her from him; but she allows Gatsby to take the blame for the accident and suffers no remorse when he is murdered by the woman's husband.

Tom Buchanan, Daisy's husband. The son of rich Midwestern parents, he reached the heights of his career as a college football player. Completely without taste, culture, or sensitivity, he carries on a rather sordid affair with Myrtle Wilson. He pretends to help George Wilson, her husband, but allows him to think that Gatsby was not only her murderer but also her lover.

Myrtle Wilson, Tom Buchanan's mistress. She is a fat, unpleasant woman who is so highly appreciative of the fact that her lover is a rich man that she will suffer almost any degradation for him. While she is with Tom, her pretense that she is rich and highly sophisticated becomes ludicrous.

George Wilson, Myrtle's husband, and a rather pathetic figure. He runs an auto repair shop and believes Tom Buchanan is really interested in helping him. Aware that his wife has a lover, he never suspects who he really is. His faith in Tom makes him believe what Buchanan says, which, in turn, causes him to murder Gatsby and then commit suicide.

Jordan Baker, a friend of the Buchanans, a golfer. Daisy introduces Jordan to Nick and tries to throw them together, but when Nick realizes that she is a cheat who refuses to assume the elementary responsibility of the individual, he loses all interest in her.

Meyer Wolfshiem, a gambler and underworld associate of Gatsby.

Catherine, Myrtle Wilson's sister, who is obviously proud of Myrtle's rich connection and unconcerned with the immorality involved.

Mr. and Mrs. McKee, a photographer and his wife who try to use Nick and Tom to get a start among the rich people of Long Island.

Mr. Gatz, Jay Gatsby's father who, being unaware of the facts of Jay's life, thought his son had been a great man.

THE GREAT MEADOW

Author: Elizabeth Madox Roberts (1886-1941)
Time of action: 1775-1783
First published: 1930

PRINCIPAL CHARACTERS

Diony Hall Jarvis, a pioneer wife and a lover of books and learning who is by nature introspective and is often philosophical and poetic in her thoughts. She frequently muses over her own identity and the part she is playing in the settling of a new land. She sees herself and the others creating order out of disorder. Combining the idealist and the practical woman, she trains herself carefully for her mission by learning the homely arts which will be needed to establish enduring order. When, after Berk's return, she is faced with the problem of choosing between her two husbands, she is loyal to the one to whom she first gave herself.

Berk Jarvis, her husband, a strong, adventurous, restless fighting man experienced in enduring the many hardships of pioneer life and the dangers of Indian warfare. Intent on avenging his mother's murder and bringing back her hair, he leaves his wife and child in order to achieve his goal. He represents the early pioneers who opened the wilderness for white American occupancy and who fought the Indians and the British who tried to drive them out.

Evan Muir, married to Diony after Berk's supposed death. Patient, industrious, and capable, he is a symbol of the men who followed the wilderness trail blazers and conquerors. Such men as Evan were needed to establish the settlements and homesteads on a permanent basis.

Thomas Hall, Diony's father, a wilderness surveyor who accepted land as pay for surveying a great tract for a Maryland company. A cultured man, he has encouraged Diony's studies in the arts and philosophy. Though disappointed in Diony's choice of Berk, he permits their marriage.

Elvira Jarvis, mother of Will, Berk, and Jack Jarvis. She is scalped by an Indian.

Betty Hall, Diony's younger sister. In contrast to Diony, who is excited by the prospect of a pioneer life in newly settled country, Betty loves the seaboard towns and the settled life there, and she romantically dreams of going east to live.

Polly Hall, wife of Thomas Hall. A pious Methodist, she opposes Berk and Diony's going into the wilderness because they will be taking land that belongs to the Indians.

James (Jim) Harrod, valorous founder of Harrod's Fort and Harrodstown.

George Rogers Clark, the commander at Harrod's Fort.

Daniel Boone, the famed wilderness pioneer who helped build Harrodstown.

THE GREAT VALLEY

Author: Mary Johnston (1870-1936)
Time of action: 1735-1760
First published: 1926

PRINCIPAL CHARACTERS

John Selkirk, a Scottish Presbyterian minister. Considered too liberal by his Scottish congregation, he emigrates, with his family, to Virginia's Shenando Valley. After establishing a new home and a new church, he decides to move a day's journey west in spite of rumors of sporadic Indian uprisings. Shortly after the move he is killed by an Indian.

Jean Selkirk, John Selkirk's wife.

Andrew Selkirk, John Selkirk's son and fellow settler in the Shenando Valley.

Colonel Matthew Burke, a wealthy landowner and developer of the Shenando Valley, from whom John and Andrew Selkirk buy their tract.

Conan Burke, Colonel Matthew Burke's son, who has settled on his father's land. His homestead is attacked by a band of Indians and his family taken captive. He is later reunited with his wife and daughter after their escape from captivity.

Elizabeth Selkirk, John Selkirk's daughter and the wife of Conan Burke. Kidnaped by Indians, she is made the squaw of Long Thunder. She finally escapes with her daughter and, after a long trek through the wilderness, is reunited with her husband.

Eileen Burke, the daughter of Elizabeth Selkirk Burke, with whom she escapes from the Indians.

423

Andrew Burke, Elizabeth Selkirk Burke's infant son, killed by an Indian.

Stephen Trabue, a driver and guide.

Nancy Milliken Selkirk, Andrew Selkirk's wife.

Mother Dick, an old woman captured by Indians along with Elizabeth Selkirk Burke.

Ajax and
Barb, servants captured along with Elizabeth Selkirk Burke by Indians.

Robin and
Tam Selkirk, Elizabeth Selkirk's brothers.

George Washington, a young surveyor.

THE GREEN BAY TREE

Author: Louis Bromfield (1896-1956)
Time of action: Early twentieth century
First published: 1924

PRINCIPAL CHARACTERS

Julia Shane, a wealthy widow, a cynical, proud, stubborn woman who feels separated from both her worldly older daughter and her neurotically religious younger daughter. A Scotch Presbyterian, she scorns Irene's piousness and her desire to be a nun, though in her will she leaves Irene free to make her own choice. In her declining years Julia spends much of her time recalling the past and reading French novels.

Lily Shane, her older daughter, tall and lovely, with honey-colored hair. She refuses the Governor despite his offer to marry her to prevent a scandal and she later rejects Willie. Lily lives in Paris for ten years before her mother's death, which occurs while Lily is back home on a visit. She returns to Paris, takes a lover, and finally marries a French diplomat, M. de Cyon.

Irene Shane, Julia's frail blonde younger daughter, a pious, introverted teacher of mill hands. After her mother's death she becomes a Carmelite nun named Sister Monica.

The Governor, a vulgar politician twenty years older than Lily and the father of her son. After Lily's rejection of him he marries the plain, sturdy daughter of a Middle-Western manufacturer.

Hattie Tolliver, Julia's niece, who cares for Julia during the long illness which ends in her death.

Ellen Tolliver, Hattie's daughter, a talented pianist who marries a traveling salesman, studies music in Paris, and becomes a noted pianist under the name of Lilli Barr.

M. de Cyon, Lily's husband, a dignified French diplomat several years her senior.

William (Willie) Harrison, a millionaire steel mill owner, a mother-dominated young man who wishes to marry Lily. He increasingly resents his mother's bullying and after her stroke longs for her death.

Mrs. Julis Harrison, Willie's dictatorial mother who suspects the reason for Lily's leaving her home town.

Madame Gigon, a widow with whom Lily lives in Paris; she dies during the war.

Judge Weissman, a political boss whose Jewishness revolts Julia.

John Shane, Julia's husband, a wealthy man of unknown background who was a political boss until he died of apoplexy.

Jean, the son of Lily and the Governor; he is wounded in the war.

424

Stepan Krylenko, a big, burly young Ukrainian strike leader. He is befriended by Irene. After he is shot by a mill guard at a strikers' meeting, he is hidden by Lily. He later becomes an international labor leader and dies of typhus in Moscow.

The Baron, Lily's lover, a cousin of Madame Gigon. He is killed in the war.

GREEN GROW THE LILACS

Author: Lynn Riggs (1899-1954)
Time of action: 1900
First presented: 1931

PRINCIPAL CHARACTERS

Curly McClain, a cowboy. In love with Laurey Williams, he wins her hand only to win, also, the fierce enmity of her hired man, Jeeter Fry. At a shivaree on Curly and Laurey's wedding night, a fight ensues in which Jeeter is killed. Curly is arrested and put in jail to await trial.

Laurey Williams, a young farm owner desired by her hired man, Jeeter Fry, and loved by Curly McClain, whom she marries.

Jeeter Fry, Laurey Williams' hired man. Fond of reading lurid crime stories and obsessed by sex, he desires Laurey. When he attempts to embrace her, she fires

him. He slinks away, a sworn enemy. On the night of Laurey's wedding to Curly McClain, he appears at the shivaree, and in an attack on the bridegroom falls on his own knife and dies.

Aunt Eller Murphy, Laurey Williams' aunt, whose strength and good sense give her niece the courage to face her troubles.

Ado Annie Carnes, Laurey Williams' friend.

Old Man Peck and
Cord Elam, neighbors of Laurey Williams and Curly McClain.

GREEN MANSIONS

Author: W. H. Hudson (1841-1922)
Time of action: Nineteenth century
First published: 1904

PRINCIPAL CHARACTERS

Abel Guevez de Argensola (Abel), a Venezuelan living in Georgetown, British Guiana. Uninterested in politics, sport, or commerce, he loves the world of nature and the spirit. As a youth he was involved in an abortive Caracas political conspiracy. Fleeing for his life, he disappeared into the Guayana wilderness and lived for some months among the Indians and with Nuflo and Rima.

Loving Rima with an etherealized but passionate love, he (with Nuflo) accompanied her in a fruitless search for her mother's people. Maddened and grief-stricken upon learning of Rima's murder, he fled from Runi's village, returned after it was sacked by Managa, gathered Rima's ashes in an urn, and, half-dead, finally reached Georgetown, where he has since lived. Having loved and lost

425

Rima, he understands the loneliness she felt when she longed for her mother's people.

Riolama (Rima), a girl of the Venezuelan forest. Daughter of an unknown father and a mysterious girl whose life Nuflo saved about seventeen years earlier, she has been brought up by the old man who pretends that he is her grandfather. Slim, less than five feet tall, with delicately small hands and feet, she is like the wood nymphs of ancient legend or like the spirit of nature itself in its beautiful, mysterious aspects. Her abundant, dark, iridescent hair is cloudlike, her pale skin seems at times almost transparent, and her dark eyes are lustrous. In the forest she is like a wild creature but one that fears no harm and will permit no harm to other creatures. Here she utters a beautiful, birdlike language in a lovely, warbling voice. In Nuflo's lodge she is shy and reticent and speaks Spanish, in which she also converses with Abel. When occasionally angered, she reminds Abel of a beautiful wasp as stinging words issue from her. After the trip to Riolama and the final realization that it was a vain illusion that she would find her mother's people, she confesses her love for Abel. Return-ing to Nuflo's lodge ahead of Nuflo and Abel, she is found in a tree by Runi's men and is burned to death.

Nuflo, a white-bearded, brown-skinned old hunter with whom Rima lives. To avoid offending her he sneaks away to kill forest animals and cook them for himself and his two foul-smelling dogs. A frequent critic of the state of the world, he superstitiously believes that Rima has supernatural powers which she might use to make things better, especially for an old man with many sins on his conscience. He is killed by Indians.

Runi, a Guayana Indian chief, a friend and later an enemy of Abel.

Kua-Kó, nephew of Runi and friend of Abel, whom he teaches to use a blowpipe in the hope that he will kill Rima, for the Indians regard her as an evil spirit, a daughter of the Didi. After telling Abel of the burning of Rima, he pursues when Abel flees, and is stabbed to death.

Cla-Cla, a talkative, wrinkled old woman, grandmother of Kua-kó.

Managa, chief of an Indian tribe at enmity with Runi. Abel flees to Managa after killing Kua-kó and incites him to kill Runi and the murderers of Rima.

THE GREEN MOUNTAIN BOYS

Author: Daniel Pierce Thompson (1795-1868)
Time of action: 1775-1776
First published: 1839

PRINCIPAL CHARACTERS

Captain Charles Warrington, a fictional disguise for the Vermont patriot, Seth Warner, who is the protagonist of a homespun American novel that achieved widespread popularity. Owner of land in dispute between New York and New Hampshire, Warrington is an outlaw, who sometimes travels as "Mr. Howard."

Lieutenant Selden (later identified as Edward Hendee), Warrington's friend, who is in love with Jessy Reed.

Colonel Reed, who, after buying a land title in Albany, has expelled the settlers and fortified the region.

Jessy Reed, his daughter who is captured at her father's fort by Selden. She eventually marries him.

426

Sergeant Donald McIntosh, who is in charge of the Reed fort's garrison.

Zilpah, Jessy Reed's half-Indian servant, who marries Neshobee.

Munroe, a New York sheriff in pursuit of Warrington.

Neshobee, a friendly Indian who brings Warrington a warning from Mrs. Story that a band of New Yorkers is planning an attack.

Ann Story, a widow who is resisting eviction from her farm. She has built an underground shelter for her family.

Jacob Sherwood, Munroe's guide and a Tory turncoat in the pay of New York. He loves Alma Hendee but does not win her.

Pete Jones, a Green Mountain Boy who captures and beats Sherwood.

Colonel Skene, with whose daughters Jessy Reed takes refuge.

Alma Hendee, whose family farms land on Lake Champlain. She marries Warrington.

Captain Hendee, her father, whose estate had been squandered by Sherwood's father.

Gilbert Hendee, the Captain's brother, who is persuaded by Sherwood's father to will Jacob the estate if little Edward Hendee fails to reach maturity.

Ruth, Alma's maid, who marries Pete Jones in a quadruple wedding.

Bill Darrow, the partner of Sherwood, who, when dying, confesses to the kidnaping of Edward Hendee, and identifies Selden as the son of Captain Hendee.

Ethan Allen, the leader of the Green Mountain Boys. He sometimes travels as "Mr. Smith." He brings the news of Lexington and Concord to the Green Mountain Boys.

Squire Prouty, a York Justice of the Peace captured by the Green Mountain Boys.

Benedict Arnold, who helps capture Fort Ticonderoga.

GRETTIR THE STRONG

Author: Unknown
Time of action: Eleventh century
First transcribed: Thirteenth century manuscript

PRINCIPAL CHARACTERS

Grettir the Strong, a folk hero of Iceland. Outlawed at fourteen after killing a man, he goes to Norway where he routs a party of berserk raiders. Acclaimed as a hero, he becomes increasingly involved in murderous feuds, particularly after his return to Iceland. At last, able to trust no one because of the price on his head yet tormented by a growing fear of the dark which makes it impossible for him to live alone, he settles with a brother and a servant on an island accessible only by rope ladders.

Several years later he is overcome by witchcraft and killed.

Onund, his ancestor, a Viking who fled Norway to escape injustice and settled in Iceland.

Aesa, the wife of Onund.

Ofeig, the father of Aesa.

Thrand, a great hero who accompanied Onund to Iceland.

Asmund Longhair, the father of Grettir.

427

During Grettir's youth father and son quarreled constantly.

Skeggi, whom Grettir kills in the course of a quarrel. Thus begins Grettir's long outlawry.

Thorfinn, a Norwegian landman with whom Grettir makes a home after being shipwrecked.

Thorir and **Ogmund,** the leaders of a band of raiders who come to lay waste to Thorfinn's district during his absence. Grettir kills both.

Karr-the-Old, the long-dead father of Thorfinn. After Grettir kills the raiders, Thorfinn gives him an ancient sword from the treasure hoard of Karr-the-Old.

Bjorn, who is jealous of Grettir's strength and bravery. Grettir kills him.

Jarl Sveinn, before whom Grettir is summoned after killing Bjorn.

Thorgils Maksson, Asmund's kinsman, slain in a quarrel. Asmund takes up the feud against the murderers.

Glam, a shepherd possessed by a fiend. Grettir fights him and kills him, but before his death Glam predicts that Grettir will come to fear the dark.

Thorbjorn Slowcoach, an enemy killed by Grettir.

Thorbjorn Oxmain, a kinsman of Slowcoach. He gets revenge for Slowcoach's death by killing Grettir's brother. Grettir then kills Oxmain and his son.

Atli, Grettir's brother, who is killed by Oxmain.

Thorir of Gard, whose sons are having a drunken feast in an inn to which Grettir has swum for coals to make a fire. In the ensuing fight, the inn and Thorir's sons are burned. Thorir later puts a price on Grettir's head.

Thorodd, a kinsman of Thorbjorn Oxmain. He also puts a price on Grettir's head.

Einar, on whose lonely farm Grettir lives for a time. Grettir falls in love with Einar's daughter, but he knows that his suit is hopeless because of his reputation.

Snaekoll, a wild, lawless man who comes to Einar's farm. Grettir kills him.

Thorsteinn Dromund, the half brother of Grettir. Grettir goes to stay with him after giving up his suit for Einar's daughter. Thorsteinn swears to avenge Grettir if he should be slain. Years later, after Grettir's death, Thorsteinn pursues the murderer to Constantinople, where he kills him with the sword of Karr-the-Old.

Thorbjorg, a wise woman who releases Grettir after he is captured by some farmers.

Grim, an outlaw whom Grettir kills because Grim is intending to kill him for the reward money.

Redbeard, an outlaw hired by Thorir of Gard to kill Grettir, but who is killed by Grettir.

Hallmund, Grettir's friend. He prevents Grettir's capture by helping him against a force of eighty men led by Thorir of Gard. Later, Hallmund is treacherously slain for the aid he gave to Grettir.

Steinvor of Sandhauger, who gives birth to a boy whom many call Grettir's son. The boy dies at seventeen.

Illugi, Grettir's youngest brother, who lives with him in an almost inaccessible island. He dies with Grettir when they are attacked.

Thorbjorn Angle, who overcomes Grettir with the aid of witchcraft and kills him. Outlawed, Thorbjorn goes to Constantinople, where he is pursued and killed by Grettir's half brother, Thorsteinn Dromund.

Steinn the Lawman, who decrees that Thorbjorn Angle cannot collect the reward because of his use of witchcraft.

428

LA GRINGA

Author: Florencio Sánchez (1875-1910)
Time of action: Early twentieth century
First presented: 1904

PRINCIPAL CHARACTERS

Victoria (bēk·tō'ryä), "La Gringa," the daughter of Italian immigrants and in love with Próspero, the son of a creole (native-born) farmer.

Don Nicola (dōn' nē·kō'lä), her ambitious immigrant father. He takes over Cantalicio's land when its owner runs into debt.

María (mä·rē'ä), her mother, who distrusts Próspero's attentions to Victoria.

Horacio (ō·rä'syō), Victoria's modern brother, who has studied engineering in the city.

Don Cantalicio (dōn kän·tä·lē'syō), typical of the easy-going land owners with Spanish blood. He is content to continue to raise cattle unprofitably rather than change over to wheat and make a profit. He is crippled when his horse is frightened by an automobile.

Próspero (prōs'pä·rō), his son, who sees the need for work to improve the land. He takes a job on the farm that was once in the possession of his family. Don Nicola discharges him when he is caught kissing Victoria.

Mr. Daples, an agent for farm machinery and later the employer of Próspero.

GROWTH OF THE SOIL

Author: Knut Hamsun (Knut Pedersen Hamsund, 1859-1952)
Time of action: Late nineteenth century
First published: 1917

PRINCIPAL CHARACTERS

Isak, a sturdy Norwegian peasant, the rough-hewn, monumental hero of the novel. Starting out on his own, he clears some isolated forest land and builds a sod hut. He sends out word by way of some Lapps that he is looking for a woman, and eventually a robust, harelipped woman comes to live with him. Together they acquire livestock, better living quarters, sufficient crops, and a happy life blessed with four children. Then she is sent to jail for killing her newborn, harelipped baby, and Isak is unhappily forced to live without her for five years. After her release he is forced to make some adjustments to her new ideas, but things tend to go on as productively as before. He sells some orebearing property; he builds a saw-mill and a grain mill; he buys farming machinery; his children, for the most part, thrive; and he is made a Margrave—all the result of his fidelity to the soil and a fruitful way of life.

Inger, Isak's hardy, loving, spirited wife. She admires her husband a great deal and lives contentedly with him, bearing his children and helping with the work. A rather primitive person but a woman of deep feeling, she gains some refinement in prison and has an operation that mends her harelip. After her return to Isak she finds that their coarse way of life is hard on her, but because their relationship is based on mutual love and respect, they continue to live and prosper together.

Eleseus, Isak and Inger's first child, a relatively weak man who becomes a village clerk. After an abortive romance he goes from job to job, always with a taste for luxury and a penchant for failure. In the end he leaves for America.

Sivert, the second child, a high-spirited, active boy. He takes naturally to the rough pioneering life of his parents and at last is fit to take his father's place.

Leopoldine, the third child, a girl born in prison. She grows up on the farm and becomes an attractive, marriageable young woman.

Rebecca, the last child, born in Inger and Isak's middle age, a likable, affectionate little girl.

Oline, a relative of Inger, a malicious and thieving old woman. Her gossip leads to Inger's arrest for child murder; and because Isak has no one else to help him she is given the management of the household while Inger is in jail. An expert on domestic intrigue, she steals and lies. Later her gossip leads to the arrest of another girl on the same charge. She dies when she is no longer wanted by anyone.

Geissler, a good friend of Isak and Inger, a mysterious, powerful man with a deep respect for men of sense and worth. He manages the sale of Isak's mining property, secures a pardon for Inger, helps Isak irrigate his land, and always turns up to offer assistance. A lonely person, he has no real roots of his own.

Axel Ström, Isak's nearest neighbor, a hard-working and sensible man who nevertheless has hard luck. After Barbro, his servant, murders her child by him and goes away to Bergen, Oline saves his life and forces him to take her on as his housekeeper. Finally Barbro, whom he really cares for, comes back and they marry.

Barbro, Axel Ström's servant, a shallow, frivolous girl who dislikes responsibility. Arrested for child murder, she is acquitted and placed with Fru Heyerdahl, the wife of the sheriff's officer. After a time Barbro decides that life with Axel will be better than her present position.

Brede Olsen, Barbro's father, a shiftless man unable to manage his jobs, his farm, or his boarding house.

Aronson, a well-to-do shopkeeper whose store fails when the mines close down. He buys it back when the mines reopen.

Os-Anders, a Lapp tramp who spreads Oline's rumors.

Heyerdahl, a rather feckless man who takes over Geissler's job as sheriff's officer when he is fired.

Fru Heyerdahl, his outspoken wife; she defends Barbro at her trial and then tries to take her in hand.

Gustaf, a light-hearted miner with whom Inger has a slight romance in her middle age.

Uncle Sivert, Inger's supposedly rich uncle; he has almost nothing to leave to anyone when he dies.

Jensine, Inger's maid, a girl to whom Sivert takes a liking.

DER GRÜNE HEINRICH

Author: Gottfried Keller (1819-1890)
Time of action: Mid-nineteenth century
First published: 1854-1855; revised 1879

Heinrich Lee (hīn'rĭsh lā), a painter. Losing his father in early childhood and, later, finding it impossible to finish his studies, he sets out to fulfill his dreams of becoming a painter. Studying in Switzerland and then in Munich, and after many discouragements and hardships, he becomes a successful artist and a moderately rich man. He returns to his native town, is elected a county official, and, finally, writes the story of his life.

Frau Lee (frou lā), Heinrich Lee's devoted, self-sacrificing mother. Having used her slender inheritance to further her son's career, she is all but forgotten by the successful Heinrich and dies just as he finally returns home.

Anna (ä'nä), Heinrich Lee's frail cousin and first love, who dies as a young girl.

Judith (yōō'dĭt), a widow who loves Heinrich Lee. When Heinrich tells her he wishes to be faithful to Anna's memory, she emigrates to America, but returns in Heinrich's later years to be near him.

Roemer (rœ'măr), an unstable painter who is Heinrich Lee's teacher.

Ericson (ä'rĭk·sôn) and Lys (lüs), painters who introduce Heinrich Lee to favorable contacts in the artistic world of Munich.

Schmalhoefer (shmäl'hœ·fĕr), a secondhand dealer who sells some of the indigent Heinrich Lee's pictures and offers him a job as a flagpole painter. The young man accepts the work and so impresses his employer with his willingness that Schmalhoefer later leaves him a considerable sum of money in his will.

Count Dietrich zu W . . . berg (dē'trikh zö v . . . bĕrg), the purchaser of Heinrich Lee's paintings and the sponsor of his successful exhibit.

Dorothea (dō'rō·tā'ä), Count W . . . berg's adopted daughter, who is loved by Heinrich Lee. Doubting his love because he delays so long in speaking of it, she marries another.

GUARD OF HONOR

Author: James Gould Cozzens (1903-   )
Time of action: Three days during World War II
First published: 1948

Major General Ira N. (Bus) Beal, Commanding General of Ocanara Air Force Base. Brooding unhappily over troubles of his own, he appears unaware of the seriousness of certain tensions that have developed on the huge base until an accident occurs during a parachute jump. General Beal immediately arouses himself from his melancholy and directs rescue operations with all his old skill and resourcefulness.

Colonel Norman Ross, Major General

Ira Beal's Air Inspector and resourceful assistant in the complicated running of huge Ocanara Air Force Base.

Lieutenant Willis, a Negro pilot who violates the right of way and nearly collides with a plane piloted by Major General Beal. He is struck and hospitalized by Lieutenant Colonel Benny Carricker.

Lieutenant Colonel Benny Carricker, Major General Beal's co-pilot, who strikes and hospitalizes Lieutenant Willis, thus

431

triggering a series of problems and tensions, including a near riot, at Ocanara Air Force Base.

Brigadier General Nichols, assistant to the Commanding General of the Air Force. A sympathetic and tolerant man, he understands the problems of Ocanara Air Force Base at a glance.

Mr. Willis, Lieutenant Willis' father.

Sal Beal, Major General Beal's wife.

Cora Ross, Colonel Norman Ross' wife.

Lieutenant Edsell, a writer assigned to Special Projects.

Lieutenant Lippa, a WAC in love with Lieutenant Edsell.

Captain Nathaniel Hicks, an officer in Special Projects.

Second Lieutenant Amanda Turck, a WAC.

Colonel Mowbray, an officer on Ocanara Air Force Base.

Chief Warrant Officer Botwinick, Colonel Mowbray's assistant.

GUEST THE ONE-EYED

Author: Gunnar Gunnarsson (1889-   )
Time of action: c. 1900
First published: Af Borgslaegtens Historie, 1912-1914; abridged in translation as *Guest the One-Eyed*, 1920

PRINCIPAL CHARACTERS

Ketill Ørlygsson, the devious, blasphemous, and dishonest son of Ørlygur à Borg. As a parish priest eager for the family property at Borg, he seeks to destroy his father's good name by accusing him of being the father of Runa's child. After Ketill himself is revealed as the father, he repents of his sins and becomes a homeless and compassionate wanderer. Regarding himself as a guest on earth, and losing an eye while saving the life of a child, he becomes "Guest the one-eyed." Finally, the old self of Ketill destroyed, he returns to Borg as Guest and is forgiven by his family.

Ormarr Ørlygsson, Ketill Ørlygsson's honest, intelligent, and artistic brother,

who sacrifices his own concerns to marry Runa.

Ørlygur à Borg, a well-to-do landowner and the father of Ketill and Ormarr. Falsely and publicly accused by his son Ketill of the crime of lust, he is killed by the knowledge of his son's depravity.

Gudrun (Runa), the daughter of a poor farmer and the mother of Ketill's son, Ørlygur the Younger.

Pall à Seyru, Runa's father.

Ørlygur the Younger, the son of Ketill and Runa.

Snebiorg (Bagga), an illegitimate girl engaged to marry Ørlygur the Younger.

GULLIVER'S TRAVELS

Author: Jonathan Swift (1667-1745)
Time of action: 1699-1713
First published: 1726-1727

Lemuel Gulliver, a surgeon, sea captain, traveler and the narrator of these travel accounts, the purpose of which is to satirize the pretentions and follies of man. Gulliver is an ordinary man, capable of close observation; his deceptively matter-of-fact reportage and a great accumulation of detail make believable and readable a scathing political and social satire. On his first voyage he is shipwrecked at Lilliput, a country inhabited by people no more than six inches tall, where pretentiousness, individual as well as political, is ridiculed. The second voyage ends in Brobdingnag, a land of giants. Human grossness is a target here. Moreover, Gulliver does not find it easy to make sense of English customs and politics in explaining them to a king sixty feet high. On Gulliver's third voyage pirates attack the ship and set him adrift in a small boat. One day he sees and goes aboard Laputa, a flying island inhabited by incredibly abstract and absent-minded people. From Laputa he visits Balnibari,

where wildly impractical experiments in construction and agriculture are in progress. Then he goes to Glubbdubdrib, the island of sorcerers, where he is shown apparitions of such historical figures as Alexander and Caesar, who decry the inaccuracies of history books. Visiting Luggnagg, Gulliver, after describing an imaginary immortality of constant learning and growing wisdom, is shown a group of immortals called Struldbrugs, who are grotesque, pitiable creatures, senile for centuries, but destined never to die. Gulliver's last journey is to the land of the Houyhnhnms, horse-like creatures in appearance, possessed of great intelligence, rationality, restraint, and courtesy. Dreadful human-like creatures, called Yahoos, impart to Gulliver such a loathing of the human form that, forced to return at last to England, he cannot bear the sight of even his own family and feels at home only in the stables.

GUY MANNERING

Author: Sir Walter Scott (1771-1832)
Time of action: Eighteenth century
First published: 1815

PRINCIPAL CHARACTERS

Captain Brown (Harry Bertram), a young Scottish aristocrat whose life took a turn when he was kidnaped in his sixth year. He becomes an officer and, while stationed in India, falls in love with Julia Mannering. The Mannerings, old friends of the Bertrams, do not recognize Brown as young Harry Bertram. Through a chain of events—an interview with a Dutch smuggler and a secret revealed by an old gipsy—Bertram has his identity and inheritance restored and becomes eligible to marry Julia.

Colonel Guy Mannering, a British gentleman and a friend of the Bertrams who,

being a student of astrology, predicts dire events for Harry Bertram: the boy's fifth, tenth, and twenty-first years will be especially dangerous, he says. His predictions are more or less accurate. Mannering, finally, is happy to see his friend's son, Harry Bertram, whom he has known as Captain Brown, restored to his inheritance, and he blesses his daughter Julia's alliance with Bertram.

Gilbert Glossin, a crooked lawyer who sets in motion the machinery of the novel. It is he who arranges to have Harry Bertram kidnaped; for with Harry out of the way, the lawyer is able to buy inexpensively the Bertram estate, Ellangowan. He is finally unmasked and, while in prison awaiting trial, is killed by one of his partners in crime.

Charles Hazlewood, a young gentleman who loves Lucy Bertram, Harry's sister. Once mistaking Captain Brown for a bandit, he tries to shoot him. He himself is wounded, however, when, as he and Brown wrestle for the weapon, it is discharged. Glossin, in order to gain favor with gentlemen, offers to capture Brown. This move on Glossin's part precipitates the unraveling of the plot, including the identification of Brown as Bertram. Hazlewood, when everything is put straight, marries Lucy Bertram.

Meg Merrilies, an old gipsy woman who played a serious role in the kidnaping. When young Bertram is twenty-one, she confesses her part, thus disclosing a smuggler and Glossin as her confederates. The smuggler kills Meg before he is taken to prison.

Dirk Hatteraick, a Dutch smuggler and murderer who killed the revenue officer with whom young Bertram was riding the day Dirk and Meg kidnaped him. Later, he shoots Meg and, while Glossin's cellmate, kills him. Before the law can send him to the scaffold, Hatteraick hangs himself.

Julia Mannering, Guy Mannering's daughter, who finally becomes Harry Bertram's wife.

Lucy Bertram, Harry Bertram's sister, who marries Charles Hazlewood.

Godfrey Bertram, Laird of Ellangowan, who is Lucy and Harry's father. He dies seventeen years after Harry's kidnaping, leaving Lucy an orphan.

Sir Robert Hazlewood, Charles' father.

Dominie Sampson, the faithful tutor to the Bertram children.

GUY OF WARWICK

Author: Unknown
Time of action: Tenth century
First transcribed: Thirteenth century

PRINCIPAL CHARACTERS

Guy, a knight of Warwick. Son of the steward of Rohaud, the Earl of Warwick, and principal cupbearer to the Earl, Guy falls in love with his master's daughter, Felice la Belle. To satisfy his lady's demand that he become the foremost knight in the world, he enters into adventures which bring about the deaths of many brave knights. He marries Felice only to become beset with qualms of conscience over the mischief he has caused to satisfy a lady's whims. He ends his life as a penitent pilgrim.

Rohaud, Earl of Warwick, Guy of Warwick's master, and the father of Felice la Belle.

Felice la Belle, the daughter of Rohaud, Earl of Warwick. Loved by Guy of Warwick, she demands, as the price of her hand, that he become the greatest knight in the world.

Herhaud of Ardern, Guy of Warwick's mentor and companion in knight-errantry.

Otous, Duke of Pavia, defeated by Guy of Warwick.

Segyn, Duke of Louvain, assisted in battle by Guy of Warwick.

Reignier, Emperor of Germany. In an unlawful attempt to take the lands of

434

Segyn, he is captured by Guy of Warwick, who brings about a rapprochement between the enemies.

Ernis, Emperor of Greece, assisted by Guy of Warwick against the Soudan of the Saracens.

Loret, Ernis' daughter, promised to Guy of Warwick for his services in battle.

Morgadour, a knight enamored of Loret and a traitor to Guy of Warwick.

Tirri, a knight and friend of Guy of Warwick. He is rescued by Guy from his persecutor, Otous, Duke of Pavia.

Athelstan, King of England.

Anlaf, King of Denmark.

Colbrand, a Danish giant slain by Guy of Warwick.

The Soudan of the Saracens.

GUZMÁN DE ALFARACHE

Author: Mateo Alemán (1547-1613?)
Time of action: Sixteenth century
First published: Part I, 1599; Part II, 1604

PRINCIPAL CHARACTERS

Guzmán de Alfarache (gōōth·män' dä äl·fä·rä'chä), a rogue who early learns he must trick or be tricked. He lives by his wits in Spain and Italy until caught and sentenced to life imprisonment as a galley slave. Winning a pardon by revealing the slaves' conspiracy to seize the vessel, he determines to lead an exemplary life.

Don Guzmán, his father. Cheated by a partner in Genoa, he recovers most of his money in Seville. When he becomes rich, he buys an estate in San Juan de Alfarache and takes a mistress, whom he eventually marries. Addicted to gambling and high living, he dies penniless.

A Muleteer, who teaches Guzmán the world's crookedness.

Two Friars, who hire animals from the muleteer.

A Constable, who arrests and severely beats Guzmán, thinking he is a thieving page.

An Innkeeper, who hires Guzmán and teaches him to cheat travelers.

A Captain of Soldiers, with whom Guzmán plans to travel to Italy.

Don Beltrán (dōn bĕl·trän'), Guzmán's uncle in Genoa, who orders the servants to beat his nephew. The boy gets revenge by tricking him out of jewelry.

A Cardinal, who thinks the fake sores on Guzmán's legs are real, and who gives him money and a job. He soon discharges Guzmán for stealing.

The French Ambassador, who hires Guzmán for intrigues

Sayavedra (sä·yä·bä'drä), a supposed friend who rifles Guzmán's possessions, but later helps him cheat the rich of Florence.

Alexandro Bentivoglio (ä·lä·ksän'drō bän·tē·bō'glyō), a thieves' fence.

Guzmán's First Wife, who is not the heiress she pretends to be.

Guzmán's Second Wife, who helps him rob wealthy men and then deserts him for an Italian sea captain.

Soto (sō'tō), a fellow galley slave of Guzmán who plots the seizure of the ship. In revenge for a previous wrong

435

committed against him by Soto, Guzmán reports the plot and Soto is executed. The grateful ship's captain frees Guzmán from the oars.

HAJJI BABA OF ISPAHAN

Author: James Morier (1780-1849)
Time of action: Early nineteenth century
First published: 1824

PRINCIPAL CHARACTERS

Hajji Baba, the son of a barber of Ispahan, who learns his father's trade and many Persian tales and quotations. He becomes an early nineteenth century Persian picaro whose training in thievery and trickery eventually prepares him admirably for a career in diplomatic intrigue at the Shah's court.

Osman Agha, a wealthy Turkish merchant who invites Hajji to entertain him on a buying trip to Meshed. They are captured by Turcoman robbers. Later they combine in a profitable enterprise in Constantinople.

Dervish Sefer, who buys Hajji's adulterated tobacco, then admiringly invites him to become a dervish. Before he can do so, however, Hajji is arrested and beaten

until unconscious for selling adulterated tobacco.

The Court Physician, who is persuaded by stolen credentials to give Hajji a position of confidence.

Zeenab, a slave of the physician who gives her favors to Hajji and is condemned to death when the Shah discovers she is pregnant.

Mollah Bashi, whose accidental drowning gives Hajji a chance to put on the priest's clothing and collect money owed to the priest.

Mollah Nadan, a priest who gets Hajji's help in an illegal marriage market. When he forces Hajji to give him the clothes stolen from the dead Mollah Bashi, he is himself accused of Bashi's murder.

THE HAMLET

Author: William Faulkner (1897-1962)
Time of action: Late nineteenth century
First published: 1940

PRINCIPAL CHARACTERS

Flem Snopes, a character who epitomizes an economic force that moved into the South shortly after hostilities between the states ceased. Snopes is cunning, ruthless, cruel, devoted to self-aggrandizement through the power that comes with owning property. His business ethics are an abomination; his contempt for the ignorant townspeople he cheats is complete. Flem Snopes, along with his many relatives, is a symbol of economic rape

that Faulkner presents throughout the stories and novels he has written about a mythological Mississippi county.

Eula Varner, a sexually precocious rural beauty who becomes Mrs. Flem Snopes after she becomes pregnant by one of three suitors who leave the region when her condition becomes known. Flem marries Eula, not out of compassion but because she is the daughter of the hamlet's

436

wealthiest man, and Snopes is anxious to get established in the community.

Will Varner, Eula's father, who is the leading citizen of Frenchman's Bend and the town's largest property owner.

Henry Armstid, a local farmer distinguished by his stupidity and bull-headedness. He is twice duped by Flem Snopes. He buys a worthless horse from him and later, with two other men, a piece of property on which Snopes has led them to believe buried treasure will be found. Armstid's blind pride prevents him from learning anything from the crooked transactions. At last, disappointed because he finds no treasure on the property, he loses his mind.

V. K. Ratliff, the sewing machine salesman who knows everything about everybody in the countryside. Flem Snopes bilks him out of some money by selling him and Armstid a worthless piece of property.

Ab Snopes, Flem's father, a newcomer to the hamlet, who rents a farm from Will Varner. He is suspected of being an arsonist, and he is known to be an unscrupulous horse trader. Poetic justice is served when he, trying to cheat a horse trader, is himself roundly cheated.

Jody Varner, Will Varner's son and heir.

Isaac Snopes, a mentally deficient boy whose peculiar erotic behavior toward a cow causes a town scandal.

Mink Snopes, one of the Snopes clan convicted of murder and sent to prison for life.

Jack Houston, the citizen who impounds Mink Snopes' stray cow and is murdered following a dispute over the cost of feeding the animal.

Labove, a schoolteacher who attempts to seduce Eula Varner, fails, and leaves Frenchman's Bend forever.

Mrs. Henry Armstid, a shy, uneducated woman who lives in abject poverty with Armstid and their four children.

Pat Stamper, an extremely shrewd horse trader who buys a worthless horse from Ab Snopes, paints it and fattens it with a bicycle pump, then sells it back to him.

Buck Hipps, a Texan who, in collusion with Flem Snopes, sells a group of wild spotted horses to the credulous farmers of the Frenchman's Bend area.

Hoake McCarron, one of Eula Varner's more gallant suitors and the father of her unborn child.

Eckrum (Eck) Snopes, a member of the Snopes tribe who receives a wild horse as a gift from Buck Hipps.

Vernon Tull, a townsman who is injured when Eck Snopes's wild horse collides with his wagon.

Odum Bookwright, a naïve citizen who, along with Ratliff and Armstid, is taken in by Flem Snopes on a property deal.

HAMLET, PRINCE OF DENMARK

Author: William Shakespeare (1564-1616)
Time of action: c. 1200
First presented: 1600-1601

PRINCIPAL CHARACTERS

Hamlet (hăm′lət), Prince of Denmark. Generally agreed to be Shakespeare's most fascinating hero, Hamlet has been buried under volumes of interpretation, much of it conflicting. No brief sketch can satisfy his host of admirers nor take into account more than a minute fraction of the commentary now in print. The

437

character is a mysterious combination of a series of literary sources and the phenomenal genius of Shakespeare. Orestes in Greek tragedy is probably his ultimate progenitor, not Oedipus, as some critics have suggested. The Greek original has been altered and augmented by medieval saga and Renaissance romance; perhaps an earlier "Hamlet," written by Thomas Kyd, furnished important material; however, the existence of such a play has been disputed. A mixture of tenderness and violence, a scholar, lover, friend, athlete, philosopher, satirist, and deadly enemy, Hamlet is larger than life itself. Torn by grief for his dead father and disappointment in the conduct of his beloved mother, Hamlet desires a revenge so complete that it will reach the soul as well as the body of his villainous uncle. His attempt to usurp God's prerogative of judgment leads to all the deaths in the play. Before his death he reaches a state of resignation and acceptance of God's will. He gains his revenge but loses his life.

Claudius (klô'dĭ·ŭs), King of Denmark, husband of his brother's widow, Hamlet's uncle. A shrewd and capable politician and administrator, he is courageous and self-confident; but he is tainted by mortal sin. He has murdered his brother and married his queen very soon thereafter. Although his conscience torments him with remorse, he is unable to repent or to give up the throne or the woman that his murderous act brought him. He has unusual self-knowledge and recognizes his unrepentant state. He is a worthy and mighty antagonist for Hamlet, and they destroy each other.

Gertrude, Queen of Denmark, Hamlet's mother. Warm-hearted but weak, she shows deep affection for Hamlet and tenderness for Ophelia. There are strong indications that she and Claudius have been engaged in an adulterous affair before the death of the older Hamlet. She loves Claudius, but she respects Hamlet's confidence and does not betray him to his uncle when he tells her of the mur-

der, of which she has been obviously innocent and ignorant. Her death occurs after she drinks the poison prepared by Claudius for Hamlet.

Polonius (pə·lō'nĭ·ŭs), Lord Chamberlain under Claudius, whom he has apparently helped to the throne. An affectionate but meddlesome father to Laertes and Ophelia, he tries to control their lives, He is garrulous and self-important, always seeking the devious rather than the direct method in politics or family relationships. Hamlet jestingly baits him but he apparently has some affection for the officious old man and shows real regret at killing him. Polonius' deviousness and eavesdropping bring on his death; Hamlet stabs him through the tapestry in the mistaken belief that Claudius is concealed there.

Ophelia, Polonius' daughter and Hamlet's love. A sweet, docile girl, she is easily dominated by her father. She loves Hamlet but never seems to realize that she is imperiling his life by helping her father spy on him. Her gentle nature being unable to stand the shock of her father's death at her lover's hands, she loses her mind and is drowned.

Laertes (lā·ûr'tēz), Polonius' son. He is in many ways a foil to Hamlet. He also hungers for revenge for a slain father. Loving his dead father and sister, he succumbs to Claudius' temptation to use fraud in gaining his revenge. This plotting brings about his own death but also destroys Hamlet.

Horatio (hō·rā'shĭ·ō), Hamlet's former schoolmate and loyal friend. Well balanced, having a quiet sense of humor, he is thoroughly reliable. Hamlet trusts him implicitly and confides in him freely. At Hamlet's death, he wishes to play the antique Roman and die by his own hand; but he yields to Hamlet's entreaty and consents to remain alive to tell Hamlet's story and to clear his name.

Ghost of King Hamlet. Appearing first

438

to the watch, he later appears to Horatio and to Hamlet. He leads Hamlet away from the others and tells him of Claudius' foul crime. His second appearance to Hamlet occurs during the, interview with the Queen, to whom he remains invisible, causing her to think that Hamlet is having hallucinations. In spite of Gertrude's betrayal of him, the ghost of murdered Hamlet shows great tenderness for her in both of his appearances.

Fortinbras (fôr′tĭn·brăs), Prince of Norway, son of old Fortinbras, the former King of Norway, nephew of the present regent. Another foil to Hamlet, he is resentful of his father's death at old Hamlet's hands and the consequent loss of territory. He plans an attack on Denmark, which is averted by his uncle after diplomatic negotiations between him and Claudius. He is much more the man of action than the man of thought. Hamlet chooses him as the next King of Denmark and expresses the hope and belief that he will be chosen. Fortinbras delivers a brief but emphatic eulogy over Hamlet's body.

Rosencrantz (rō·zĕn′krănz) and **Guildenstern** (gĭl′dən·stẽrn), the schoolmates of Hamlet summoned to Denmark by Claudius to act as spies on Hamlet. Though hypocritical and treacherous, they are no match for him, and in trying to betray him they go to their own deaths.

[**Old Norway**, uncle of Fortinbras. Although he never appears on the stage, he is important in that he diverts young Fortinbras from his planned attack on Denmark.]

[**Yorick** (yŏr′ĭk), King Hamlet's jester. Dead some years before the action of the play begins, he makes his brief appearance in the final act when his skull is thrown up by a sexton digging Ophelia's grave. Prince Hamlet reminisces and moralizes while holding the skull in his hands. At the time he is ignorant of whose grave the sexton is digging.]

Reynaldo (rā·nôl′dō), Polonius' servant. Polonius sends him to Paris on businesss, incidentally to spy on Laertes. He illustrates Polonius' deviousness and unwillingness to make a direct approach to anything.

First Clown, a gravedigger. Having been sexton for many years, he knows personally the skulls of those he has buried. He greets with particular affection the skull of Yorick, which he identifies for Hamlet. He is an earthy humorist, quick with a witty reply.

Second Clown, a stupid straight man for the wit of the First Clown.

Osric (ŏz′rĭk), a mincing courtier. Hamlet baits him in much the same manner as he does Polonius, but without the concealed affection he has for the old man. He brings Hamlet word of the fencing match arranged between him and Laertes and serves as a referee of the match.

Marcellus (mär·sĕl′ŭs) and **Bernardo** (bər·när′dō), officers of the watch who first see the Ghost of King Hamlet and report it to Horatio, who shares a watch with them. After the appearance of the Ghost to them and Horatio, they all agree to report the matter to Prince Hamlet, who then shares a watch with the three.

Francisco (frăn·sĭs′kō), a soldier on watch at the play's opening. He sets the tone of the play by imparting a feeling of suspense and heartsickness.

First Player, the leader of a troop of actors. He produces "The Murder of Gonzago" with certain alterations furnished by Hamlet to trap King Claudius into displaying his guilty conscience.

A Priest, who officiates at Ophelia's abbreviated funeral. He refuses Laertes' request for more ceremony, since he believes Ophelia has committed suicide.

Voltimand (vŏl′tĭ·mänd) and **Cornelius** (kôr·nēl′yŭs), ambassadors sent to Norway by Claudius.

A HANDFUL OF DUST

Author: Evelyn Waugh (1903-   )
Time of action: Twentieth century
First published: 1934

PRINCIPAL CHARACTERS

Anthony Last, called **Tony,** a young Englishman whose dream is to restore his Hetton Abbey to its feudal glory. He does not suspect his wife's infidelity until she informs him of it and asks for a divorce. Agreeing at first, he becomes angry at her family's greed for alimony and refuses to give her a divorce. To get away, he goes on an expedition to the jungles of South America. There he contracts a fever and is nursed back to health by a trader who keeps Tony a permanent prisoner, forcing him to read and reread aloud the works of Dickens interminably. Finally Tony is declared officially dead. His abbey passes on to a cousin; his wife moves on to a new husband.

Brenda Last, Tony's wife. Bored with their life, she takes a room in London and has an affair with a selfish young man who loses interest when Brenda can obtain neither money nor a divorce. After Tony is declared dead, she marries another of his bachelor friends.

John Beaver, a worthless young bachelor whose social success consists chiefly in his availability as an extra man. He has an affair with Brenda, but later discards her.

Mrs. Beaver, his mother, an interior decorator. She rents Brenda the one-room flat from which Brenda conducts her affair with John; but after Tony's disappearance, with Brenda unable to get his money, she refuses Brenda's application for a job.

John Andrew Last, Brenda and Tony's son. He is killed while fox hunting, when his mount is struck by a runaway horse. Receiving the news of his death, Brenda at first thinks that John Beaver is being spoken of. Learning that her son is the one who is killed, she is relieved and, thus realizing how much she cares for Beaver, she resolves to get a divorce.

Jock Grant-Menzies, Tony's friend, whom Brenda marries after Tony's disappearance.

Dr. Messinger, the explorer with whom Tony sets out on his travels. Deserted by their Indian guides, he and Tony venture down a jungle river in hopes it will lead them out. Dr. Messinger leaves the delirious Tony on shore and goes on for help; but the boat capsizes and he drowns.

Todd, a half-cast, illiterate trader who loves Dickens' novels. After finding Tony and nursing him back to health, Todd keeps him a prisoner so that he can spend his life hearing Tony read Dickens over and over.

HANDLEY CROSS

Author: Robert Smith Surtees (1803-1864)
Time of action: Nineteenth century
First published: 1843; enlarged, 1854

Michael Hardy, who before his death had been leader of the hunt in Sheepwash Vale.

John Jorrocks, a wealthy but lower-class grocer and a lover of fox hunting. He is invited to come to Handley Cross to revive fox hunting.

Julia Jorrocks, his wife.

Belinda Jorrocks, his pretty niece, who adds to his popularity.

Pigg, a Scot of puny appearance but enormous appetite, hired by Jorrocks as a huntsman.

Dr. Swizzle, whose discovery of the curative powers of a local spring makes Handley Cross a fashionable watering place.

Dr. Mello, another shady doctor who nightly pours Epsom salts into his own spring.

Captain Doleful, a lean, hypocritical soldier on half pay, who thinks Handley Cross should have social life and a hunt club. It is he who invites Jorrocks to Handley Cross.

Mrs. Barnington, the leader of the social set in Handley Cross.

Fleeceall, a social secretary who helps Doleful select Jorrocks.

The Earl of Bramber, the owner of Ongar Castle, where Jorrocks mistakenly becomes an overnight guest and ends up sleeping in the bathhouse.

HANDY ANDY

Author: Samuel Lover (1797-1868)
Time of action: Nineteenth century
First published: 1842

Andy Rooney, a naïve, mischievous Irish boy who figures in twelve stories serialized in a magazine. Eventually Andy inherits the estate and the title of his father and goes to Parliament.

Mrs. Rooney, his mother.

Oonah, a cousin of Andy whom he marries.

Squire Edward Egan of Merryvale Hall, who hires Andy as a stable boy.

Mrs. Egan, his wife.

Murtough Murphy, an attorney and political boss.

Sir Timothy Trimmer, the aging holder of a political office.

The Honorable Sackville Scatterbrain, a candidate for Trimmer's post.

Lord Scatterbrain, Sackville's uncle, the secret father of Andy, who finally acknowledges him.

Squire O'Grady, of Neck-or-Nothing Hall, a supporter of Scatterbrain.

Gustavus O'Grady, his son and heir.

M'Garry, an apothecary who becomes involved in one of Andy's mistakes and almost causes a duel.

Edward O'Connor, a poet and a brave gentleman. He fatally wounds Squire O'Grady in a duel.

Fanny Dawson, who is in love with O'Connor.

Major Dawson, Fanny's father, who dislikes O'Connor.

Mr. Furlong, who is on O'Grady's side. He is forced to marry Augusta.

Augusta, the daughter of Squire O'Grady, innocently involved with Furlong.

Larry Hogan, who tries to blackmail Squire Egan.

Father Phil, Andy's confessor.

James Casey, who fails to turn up for his wedding.

Matty Dwyer, who is in love with Casey.

Jack Dwyer, her father, who will settle for Andy as a son-in-law.

Shan More, to whose cave the kidnaped Andy, disguised as Oonah, is taken.

Bridget, Shan's sister, who takes Andy, disguised as Oonah, to bed with her. The next morning, lamenting her lost honor, she forces Andy to marry her. He is later freed by the discovery that she is already married to a convict. Thus, Andy at last can marry Oonah.

HANGMAN'S HOUSE

Author: Donn Byrne (Brian Oswald Donn-Byrne, 1889-1928)
Time of action: Early twentieth century
First published: 1925

PRINCIPAL CHARACTERS

James O'Brien, Lord Glenmalure, called Jimmy the Hangman for his record as a judge. He marries his daughter to John D'Arcy and dies the same night.

John D'Arcy, an ambitious, tricky man of little character. Lord Glenmalure hopes he will become a great politician, but he does not. He is a weak character who takes to gambling. Challenged to a duel by The Citizen for deserting The Citizen's sister, D'Arcy cheats by shooting before the signal. He burns down his wife's house and dies when he jumps from a window to escape the flames.

Dermot McDermot, a serious young Irishman, D'Arcy's cousin. He mistrusts the loyalties of D'Arcy. He falls in love with Connaught and tries to prevent The Citizen from killing D'Arcy, Connaught's husband. When Hangman's House is burned by D'Arcy, McDermot builds a cottage on the site, hoping Connaught will return.

Connaught, Lord Glenmalure's daugh-

ter, who marries D'Arcy. After her husband's weak character becomes apparent, she falls in love with McDermot. She leaves Ireland for England but returns to live after her husband's death in the cottage built for her by McDermot.

The Citizen, an Irishman who is an officer in the French army. He returns to try to prevent civil war in Ireland. He seeks revenge for his sister Maeve, deserted by D'Arcy. He fights a duel with D'Arcy and is wounded. After D'Arcy's death he returns to France and his regiment.

Tricky Mick, D'Arcy's father, an old friend of Lord Glenmalure.

Maeve, The Citizen's sister. She married D'Arcy, who deserted her. After the desertion she and her little son die.

The Bard of Armagh, Connaught's famous race horse. D'Arcy kills the horse after he bet heavily against the animal in a race and lost a small fortune.

HARD TIMES

Author: Charles Dickens (1812-1870)
Time of action: Mid-nineteenth century
First published: 1854

PRINCIPAL CHARACTERS

Thomas Gradgrind, a retired hardware merchant and the founder of an experimental school where only facts and proved scientific laws are taught. A firm believer that "two and two are four, and nothing over," he is the father of five unhappy fact-finders and the husband of an ailing dispirited woman quite worn out from the facts of life. While he is essentially a kind and good man, his excessive attention to the scientific and the practical and his total neglect of the imaginative and the speculative make him a kind of bumbling ogre. Through Gradgrind's theories and activities Dickens projects his sharp criticism of nineteenth century industry and culture.

Louisa Gradgrind, his older daughter, called **Loo** by her husband, a wealthy, elderly industrialist to whom she was married according to her father's calculated mathematical theories. A sensible young woman, trained to have respect for hard facts by Mr. M'Choakumchild, master of the model school, she has no nonsense about her and therefore makes a proper wife for unsentimental and callous Josiah Bounderby. She cannot wonder, speculate, or love. Her two thwarted rebellions, an attempt in her girlhood to see a circus and a planned elopement from her unhappy marriage, fail because she lacks courage. Resisting the temptation to run away with another man, she returns to her father's house and stays there when she cannot bring herself to return to her husband's bed and board within the time limit he sets.

Thomas Gradgrind, the younger son. Although trained in the same school of hard facts, he is filled with melancholy and a lack of ambition which lead him to a determination to sample life's vices. Loved and protected by his sister, he becomes a drunkard, a sensualist, and finally a thief, stealing one hundred and fifty pounds from his brother-in-law's bank, where he is employed as a clerk. For a time he is able to throw suspicion on an innocent man, but eventually his guilt is revealed. Easily led, he accepts the overtures of cynical James Harthouse, who uses the relationship of weak brother and protective sister as a wedge in his attempted seduction of Louisa. Tom is given another chance to face the facts, something he has rebelled against, when his sister and Sissy Jupe give him an opportunity to flee the country, away from Bounderby's wrath and the law's long arm.

Malthus,
Adam Smith, and
Jane, the other Gradgrind children, all victims of their father's harsh training.

Josiah Bounderby, a wealthy industrialist, the friend of Thomas Gradgrind and Louisa's husband. The owner of a Coketown (Manchester) factory, he is exceedingly proud of the fact that he is a self-made man. He advises Mr. Gradgrind against taking Sissy Jupe into his home or allowing her to attend the experimental school. In the end he loses his wife and the respect of his friends—everything but his money.

Cecilia Jupe, called **Sissy,** the daughter of a circus clown. Deserted by her father, she grows up in the Gradgrind home, a companion to Louisa. Unsuccessful in learning facts, she is constantly forced to face them and is turned from her foster home to work in Bounderby's factory. A sensitive, loving girl, she is convinced that her father has not abandoned her, that the Gradgrinds have been generous, that people are generally trustworthy. She proves her own trust by supporting confused Louisa, persuading Harthouse to leave the neighborhood, and helping Tom Gradgrind escape from the law.

James Harthouse, a cynical political aspirant and a shrewd observer of human nature and behavior. Handsome, smooth-spoken, he attempts the seduction of lonely, unloved Louisa. Sissy Jupe saves her friend from folly when she visits the young politician and persuades him the planned elopement would bring unhappiness to all concerned, including himself.

Mrs. Sparsit, born **Powler,** a woman of aristocratic pretensions and closed mind, formerly Bounderby's housekeeper. Deposed from her position of authority after his marriage, she embarrasses the self-made industrialist by producing his respectable mother and thus proving that his story of his rise from rags to riches is a hoax.

Mrs. Pegler, the mother of Josiah Bounderby, a figure of mystery after her appearance in Coketown. The truth, finally revealed, is that she had reared her son in modest but comfortable circumstances and given him an education. Ashamed of his real background, the son has paid her a pension to stay away from him so that she cannot disprove his story that he lifted himself from the gutter.

Stephen Blackpool, a poor, honest weaver in Bounderby's factory. The victim of a drunken wife and the factory system, his life is a hard one. During a labor disturbance at the factory he refuses to join the rebellious workers or to side with his employer. Discharged, he leaves Coketown to look for work elsewhere. During his absence he is accused of the robbery committed by Tom Gradgrind. Louisa and Sissy find the miner in an abandoned mine shaft into which he had fallen while returning to prove his innocence. He is brought to the surface alive but severely injured, and he dies soon afterward.

Mrs. Blackpool, his wife, a confirmed drunkard.

Rachel, a worker in Bounderby's factory, hopelessly in love with Stephen Blackpool.

Bitzer, a typical product of Mr. Gradgrind's school. Acting as Bounderby's agent, he tracks down Tom Gradgrind and arrests him, only to lose the culprit when Tom makes his escape with the aid of a circus owner, a performer, a trained dog, and a dancing horse.

Mr. M'Choakumchild, the master of Mr. Gradgrind's model school, also a believer that facts are facts.

Mr. Sleary, the proprietor of a circus troupe. A friend of Sissy Jupe, he helps Tom Gradgrind to flee the country.

E. W. B. Childers, a circus performer billed as "The Wild Huntsman of the North American Prairies." He aids Mr. Sleary in the plan for Tom Gradgrind's escape from Bitzer.

Emma Gordon, Sissy Jupe's friend and a member of the circus troupe.

Master Kidderminster, a young boy with a strangely aged face, the member of the circus troupe who assists E. W. B. Childers in his high-vaulting act.

Josephine Sleary, the lovely daughter of the circus proprietor.

Slackbridge, a trade union organizer.

Lady Scadgers, the eccentric, incredibly fat, bedridden aunt of Mrs. Sparsit.

Signor Jupe, the circus clown who deserts his daughter.

444

HARP OF A THOUSAND STRINGS

Author: H. L. Davis (1896-1960)
Time of action: Late eighteenth and early nineteenth centuries
First published: 1947

PRINCIPAL CHARACTERS

Melancthon Crawford, an American trader and one of the men who names a Western town. A slave of the Tripolitan pirates, he escapes with two companions, returns to America, founds a trading post, and makes a small fortune. Because of his eccentricities, his relatives return him to Pennsylvania as an old man, thus making sure he will not give away the money they hope to inherit from him.

Commodore Robinette, a former slave with Crawford. He turns out to be a philanderer and ends up as a fugitive from the authorities for participation in the Gutiérrez insurrection.

Apeyahola, called **Indian Jory.** A Creek Indian, he is Crawford's other companion in the escape from Tripoli. He ends up as a fugitive from the law after killing a man in Georgia.

Jean-Lambert Tallien (zhän'-län·běr' tá-lyän'), a man who tells his story to the three escaping Americans in Tripoli as they hide in a warehouse. He was once a leader in the French Revolution but has fallen because of a woman.

The Marquis de Bercy (már·kē' də běr-sē'), benefactor of Tallien while the latter is a young man.

Anne-Joseph Théroigne (án'-zhō·zěf' tá-rwán'·yə), a woman in love with René de Bercy. She later becomes a revolutionist and is stripped, beaten, and driven

insane by a mob for helping the man she loves. She is exposed as a traitor to the mob by Tallien.

René de Bercy (rə·nā' də běr·sē'), son of the Marquis de Bercy. He is Tallien's rival for the love of Countess Thérèse de Fontenay. He scorns Tallien's offer of escape to England and is among a group of pursuers killed by Tallien's order during the French Revolution.

Father Jarnatt (zhár·nát'), a priest who befriends and protects Tallien when he is sought by a mob of peasants for injuring the son of the Marquis.

Countess Thérèse de Fontenay (tā·rěz' də fōn·tə·nā), loved by Tallien, who marries her and protects her during the French Revolution. While Tallien tells his story to the Americans in the warehouse, she enters with another man. She identifies herself to the Americans but not to Tallien.

Captain Belleval (běl·vál'), an officer who incurs Tallien's jealousy by befriending Thérèse de Fontenay.

M. de Chimay (də shē·mā'), a wealthy French aristocrat and merchant. He comes to the warehouse accompanied by Thérèse de Fontenay to transact business with Tallien.

M. Ouvrard (ōō·vrár'), Thérèse de Fontenay's one-time lover, a wealthy, influential banker.

HAVELOK THE DANE

Author: Unknown
Time of action: Tenth century
First transcribed: c. 1350

445

Havelok, the son and heir of the King of Denmark. Exiled and raised in England by an old fisherman, he is a typical hero of the popular romances, renowned rather for his strength, his athletic prowess, his size, and his gentle nature than for his intellectual acumen.

Goldeboru, his wife, the lovely heiress to the English throne. Unwillingly married to an unknown kitchen boy, she rejoices to find him in reality a king, and she supports him in his successful attempts to regain his own throne and hers.

Athelwold, Goldeboru's father, the brave, just, and devout King of England. He entrusts his young daughter to his noblemen on his deathbed.

Godrich, a treacherous lord, named regent and Goldeboru's guardian by Athelwold. He marries the rightful Queen to Havelok in order to secure the throne for himself and is ultimately burned at the stake for this act of treason.

Birkabeyn, the good King of Denmark, whose only fault is his lack of judgment in leaving his three children in Godard's hands at his untimely death.

Godard, the Danish regent, who murders two of his charges and sends the third, Havelok, to be drowned. His tyrannical reign is brought to a close by Havelok's return.

Grim, Havelok's loyal guardian, an old fisherman who raises the Prince as one of his own children.

Ubbe, a powerful Danish lord. He protects Havelok and Goldeboru when they arrive in his country, and he rallies the gentry and nobility to the cause of their rightful ruler.

A HAZARD OF NEW FORTUNES

Author: William Dean Howells (1837-1920)
Time of action: The 1880's
First published: 1890

PRINCIPAL CHARACTERS

Basil March, an unsuccessful Boston insurance man who accepts the editorship of a literary magazine in New York. His adventures with the magazine's promoters, financial backers, and staff members constitute the story. Though March has little self-confidence, the magazine thrives. Eventually he has a chance to buy the publication, in partnership with the promoter, a happy circumstance which will make him not only financially successful but also spiritually fulfilled.

Mr. Dryfoos, a rustic who had made a fortune from his natural gas holdings. It is he who finances the magazine March edits. He lives a harassed existence: his womenfolk are socially ambitious, he cannot approve his daughter's choice in suitors, his son, determined to be a minister, makes a bad businessman, and a socialist on the magazine's staff plagues him on political issues. Dryfoos finally solves his problems by selling the magazine to March and the promoter, Fulkerson, and taking his family on an extended trip to Europe.

Henry Lindau, March's tutor, a German socialist who becomes the magazine's foreign editor and reviewer. His clash with Dryfoos results in Lindau's dismissal from "Every Other Week," Dryfoos' periodical. While demonstrating with the workers in a streetcar strike, Lindau is set upon by the police and beaten so severely that he eventually dies. He receives a proper funeral by a contrite Dryfoos.

Conrad Dryfoos, Dryfoos' son and the ostensible publisher of "Every Other Week." While defending the one-armed Lindau from the police who are beating him, he is struck by a stray bullet and killed.

Mr. Fulkerson, the promoter who invites March to accept the editorship of the magazine. He is happy when he and March buy the magazine because in this act he sees a secure future for himself and the girl he wants to marry, a Southern belle whose Virginia colonel father loves to extol the merits of slavery.

Christine Dryfoos, Dryfoos' daughter,

who is bent on entering society and who finally has her way. First, however, she loves a young man to whom her father objects, but whom she rejects when her father later approves of him. In Europe her fondest dreams come true when she becomes engaged to a penniless French nobleman.

Mrs. March, March's wife, who, though reluctant to leave Boston, persuades her husband to take the editorship in New York.

Angus Beaton, the art director of "Every Other Week," who loves Christine and is paid for his trouble when, despite her love for him, she scratches his face and forcibly ejects him from her father's house.

HEADLONG HALL

Author: Thomas Love Peacock (1785-1866)
Time of action: Early nineteenth century
First published: 1816

PRINCIPAL CHARACTERS

Mr. Foster, an intellectual devoted to the proposition that the world is constantly improving man's lot and that advances in technology, government, and sociology will eventually produce human perfection. He is, in short, a confirmed optimist.

Mr. Escot, a pessimist who deplores change and predicts that the world, taking its present course, will soon enslave man. He believes that only the earliest, primitive civilizations were happy and morally straight.

Mr. Jenkinson, a defender of the "status

quo." He listens to Foster and Escot on a number of subjects and then, invariably, announces that much can be said for both sides.

Squire Harry Headlong, the Welshman responsible for the debates. He invites Foster, Escot, Jenkinson, a landscape gardener, and several ladies to Headlong Hall for the Christmas holidays. He hears the discussions and, when his guests take a respite from talk, picks a wife for himself, for Escot, and for Foster.

Caprioletta Headlong, the Squire's sister, who is lovely and agreeable.

THE HEART IS A LONELY HUNTER

Author: Carson McCullers (1917-   )
Time of action: The 1930's
First published: 1940

John Singer, a tall, immaculate, soberly dressed mute who mysteriously attracts troubled people to him. He considers Mick pitiful, Jake crazy, Dr. Copeland noble, and Biff thoughtful; and they are all welcome to visit or talk to him. Ironically, he himself longs to talk manually to his insane mute friend Spiros in the asylum but cannot penetrate Spiros' apathy and craving for food. Singer shoots himself, leaving his other four friends variously affected by his death.

Mick Kelly, a gangling adolescent girl always dressed in shorts, a shirt, and tennis shoes until she gets a job in a five-and-ten-cent store. A passionate lover of music, she finds relief from her loneliness by talking to Mr. Singer and listening to his radio. After his death the loneliness returns, along with a feeling that she has been cheated, but by whom she does not know.

Biff Brannon, a café proprietor, a stolid man with a weakness for cripples and sick people and an interest in human relationships. Having watched Mr. Singer with Jake and Mick, he is left after Singer's death puzzled and wondering whether love is the answer to the problem of the human struggle.

Jake Blount, a frustrated, idealistic workingman who tries to rouse his fellow workers; a squat man with long, powerful arms. He believes that Mr. Singer is the only one who understands him. After

Singer's death Jake joins a free-for-all and later, evading the police, leaves town.

Dr. Benedict Mady Copeland, the only Negro physician in town; an idealistic man devoted to raising the standards of his race. Trying to see the judge about Willie, he is severely beaten by white men and jailed but is released on bail. Still sick from the beating, he broods over Singer's death.

Portia, his daughter, the Kellys' maid, a devout Presbyterian who worries over her father's and Mick's lack of religious belief.

Willie, Portia's brother, sentenced to hard labor for knifing a man. After brutal punishment for an attempted escape, he loses both feet from gangrene.

Spiros Antonapoulos, Mr. Singer's mute Greek friend, a fat, dreamy, slovenly man who works for his cousin. Spiros is interested in food, sleep, and drink, and sometimes in prayer before sleeping. Becoming insane and a public nuisance as well as a petty thief, he is put into an asylum.

Charles Parker, Spiros' cousin, a fruit store owner, who has taken an American name. Finally fed up with Spiros' insane actions, he has him committed to the asylum.

Alice, Biff's complaining wife, with whom he has little communication.

Highboy, Portia's husband.

HEART OF DARKNESS

Author: Joseph Conrad (Józef Teodor Konrad Korzeniowski, 1857-1924)
Time of action: Late nineteenth century
First published: 1902

Marlow, the narrator and impartial observer of the action, who becomes the

central figure when the story is interpreted psychologically. He makes a trip into the center of Africa which becomes, symbolically, a journey toward the essential meaning of life. After talking with Kurtz, with whom he identifies himself, he is able to see deeply into his own being.

Mr. Kurtz, manager of an inland trading station in the Belgian Congo. After having arrived in the Congo with high ideals and a self-imposed mission to civilize the natives, he is instead converted by them to savagery. His awareness of his downfall and his conviction that evil is at the heart of everything is revealed in a long talk which he has with Marlow.

The District Manager, an avowed enemy of Mr. Kurtz. His only interest is in collecting as much ivory as possible, and he is totally unaware of the central darkness.

A Russian Traveler, an admirer and disciple of Mr. Kurtz, but one who thought Kurtz lived before his time.

Kurtz's Fiancée, whom Marlow allows to retain her belief in Kurtz's goodness and power.

THE HEART OF MIDLOTHIAN

Author: Sir Walter Scott (1771-1832)
Time of action: Early eighteenth century
First published: 1818

PRINCIPAL CHARACTERS

David Deans, a moderately prosperous Scottish farmer in the early 1700's. A vigorous, stern Presbyterian, he is hurt and stunned when his younger daughter is charged with child murder, and he finds comfort only in the devotion of his older daughter Jeanie, who indirectly gets him a more fertile farm while obtaining a pardon for her sister. Although David cannot wholly approve of Jeanie's fiancé, he is reconciled to the marriage.

Jeanie Deans, a rather plain and simple girl who shows much moral earnestness and courage when she refuses to lie to save her sister from a death sentence and then goes to London at great risk to present her case before the Queen. Her force and warmth impress the Duke of Argyle and the Queen, who obtain a pardon for her sister, give her father a better farm, and give her betrothed a good clerical position. As a result, she is able to marry, and eventually she bears three children.

Effie Deans, Jeanie's spoiled, pretty younger sister. When Effie's illegitimate child disappears, she is arrested and sentenced to hang for child murder. Released through the steadfast efforts of Jeanie, she marries her betrayer, the criminal known as Geordie Robertson, and when he later acquires a title under his rightful name of George Staunton, she becomes a court beauty. Years after, she and her husband return to Scotland, where he is killed by a young outlaw who is really his long-lost son. Effie then retires to a convent.

Reuben Butler, Jeanie's betrothed, a sensible, educated, somewhat pedantic young minister. Unable to marry because of his impoverishment, his difficulties are cleared away when he gives Jeanie a hereditary claim on the Duke, is given a church on one of the Duke's estates, and earns the respect of David.

Geordie Robertson, in reality George Staunton, a reckless, profligate young man who seduces two girls but tries to redeem his past by offering to turn himself in as the leader of the Porteous riot in return for Effie's freedom. Jeanie, however, makes this offer unnecessary. After Effie has been pardoned he marries her and achieves a respectable life, first in the West Indies, later in the English court. When he willfully returns to seek his illegitimate son, the outlaw son kills him in a robbery attempt.

Meg Murdockson, a vicious old woman who serves as Effie's midwife, tries to destroy the child, and testifies that Effie killed the baby. Motivated by her desire for revenge because Robertson loves Effie instead of her own daughter, whom he had also seduced, she tries everything in her power to destroy Effie, including a murder attempt on Jeanie. Finally, after confessing her evil deeds, she is hanged as a witch.

John, Duke of Argyle, a skilled, honorable Scottish statesman in the court of King George II. He shows his generosity by giving Jeanie a hearing with the Queen and by aiding her father and Reuben Butler. He becomes a family friend.

The Laird of Dumbiedikes, a member of the gentry and Jeanie's clumsy suitor. He pays for Effie's defense and Jeanie's trip to London.

Madge Wildfire, Meg Murdockson's daughter, crazed after Robertson betrays her. She helps Jeanie escape Meg and is later harried to death by a mob.

Ratcliffe, the ex-criminal keeper of the Edinburgh jail. He treats Effie well and suggests to Jeanie that she seek a pardon from the Queen.

Queen Caroline, the touchy, powerful Queen who, affected by Jeanie's simplicity, secures her sister's pardon and gives Jeanie fifty pounds.

The Reverend Mr. Staunton, Robertson's righteous father. He shelters Jeanie after her escape from Meg Murdockson and gives her an escort to London.

The Whistler, Effie and Robertson's illegitimate son. After killing his father he escapes to the wilds of America.

Bartoline Saddletree, a friend of the Deanses, a stupid, pompous, meddlesome lawyer who tries to take over Effie's case.

Mrs. Saddletree, his generous, motherly wife, who employs Effie as a servant during her pregnancy.

John Porteous, an officer who needlessly fired into a crowd of citizens at a hanging and was afterwards killed by a mob led by Robertson.

Andrew Wilson, Robertson's partner in crime, a smuggler hanged by Porteous.

Archibald, the Duke's groom of chambers, who escorts Jeanie back to Scotland.

Duncan of Knock, the brusque, lively protector of the Duke's estate on which David Deans is placed.

David,
Donald, and
Euphemia, Jeanie and Reuben Butler's three spirited children.

THE HEART OF THE MATTER

Author: Graham Greene (1904-   )
Time of action: World War II
First published: 1948

PRINCIPAL CHARACTERS

Major Scobie, "Ticki" to his wife, a police chief in a British-controlled West African colony. He is a man whose merit is frequently overlooked and whose ca-

pacities for sensitive reaction are underestimated. Thus, when he learns he is not to be chosen district commissioner, he feels the slight more for his wife than

450

for himself. He is scrupulous in his dealings, and he has a reputation for honesty which he has earned in fifteen years of hard work. His scrupulousness is a result of religious convictions that force him to view every problem as a moral conflict; the tendency also diminishes his powers of decision. Compromising with his principles under the hysterical pressure of his wife, who feels that she must leave the colony, he borrows money from Yusef, a suspected Syrian smuggler. Another threat of compromise arises when, during his wife's absence, he meets Helen Rolt, a young widow who is among the survivors of a torpedoed British ship. Greatly in need of friendship and encouragement, she becomes Scobie's mistress. But it is desperation as much as love that binds him to Helen. An honest man, he cannot conceal from himself the fact that he is an adulterer. The same honesty forces him to recognize that he has profaned the act of communion by sharing the rite with his returned wife; this act is another step toward damnation. He reaches the end of his rope when he discovers that he is under official surveillance because of his relationship with Yusef. He commits suicide after fabricating the hoax of a serious heart condition, even though he knows that his act points toward complete damnation.

Louise Scobie, the Major's wife, essentially a weak woman whose pretenses and lack of perspective set her apart from the colony. She is ambitious for her husband, and she has suffered the loss of her only child. Her lack of perception appears after her husband's suicide; she remarks to the priest that her husband was a "bad Catholic" and speaks of Scobie's defects. She has no sense of the utter despair that her husband had reached before his act.

Helen Rolt, a young woman rescued after a British ship has been torpedoed by a German submarine. She becomes Scobie's mistress and cannot understand why his religion prevents divorce and remarriage. Her recent widowhood makes her seek the security of a second marriage—if not to Scobie, then to a young officer who is attracted to her.

Wilson, a counter-intelligence agent sent to investigate the smuggling of industrial diamonds to Nazi Germany. He sees in Scobie a man who neglects his wife, deals with Yusef, a patently suspicious character, and is in love with another woman. He hates Major Scobie because he has himself fallen in love with Louise Scobie.

Yusef, a wily Syrian merchant. He loves Scobie as a fellow human being beset with problems, but he hates Scobie because he is honest and perhaps because he recognizes Scobie's tarnished but still superior moral strength.

Father Rank, a priest of less than saintly demeanor, who sees more deeply than the colony knows. He has compassion for Scobie and sees in him the lonely man forced by his conscience to choose among the evils that face him. It would not have shocked him to know that Scobie's angina was feigned and that his suicide was the surrender of a soul endlessly tormented. As he says, a priest knows only sins; a man does not confess his virtues.

Tallit, a Syrian involved with Yusef. He is capable of great double-dealing.

Ali, Scobie's favorite "boy," who loses his life.

HEARTBREAK HOUSE

Author: Bernard Shaw (1856-1950)
Time of action: 1913
First published: 1919; *first presented:* 1920

451

Captain Shotover, the white-bearded retired sea captain who is master of Heartbreak House. An eighty-eight-year-old eccentric, he symbolizes England's past glory; his house, built to resemble a ship, represents "cultured, leisured Europe before the war." Shotover, who presides over an anarchic household full of semi-allegorical characters, has two goals: to learn how to explode dynamite with his mental forces, so as to blow up all profiteers and exploiters; and to attain to the perfect state of tranquillity he calls "the seventh degree of concentration." He achieves tranquillity by staying half-drunk on rum. England, he says, is a ship with a drunken captain and a negligent crew; the crew must learn to navigate if the ship is not to go on the rocks. But the crew, the play suggests, is too ignorant and unperceptive to learn navigation. At the end of the play the bombers come, the war begins, and the society of Heartbreak House collapses.

Lady Ariadne Utterword (Addy), Captain Shotover's younger daughter, age forty-two. Very handsome, blonde, and seemingly scatterbrained, Lady Utterword is really quite competent. She is married to a man who has been Governor of all the colonies in turn. Returning to Heartbreak House for the first time in twenty-three years, she finds it as disorganized as ever. Ariadne can visualize, as an alternative to the confusion of Heartbreak House, only a conservative squirearchy concerned only with horses and hunting.

Mrs. Hesione Hushabye (Hessy), Ariadne's sister, perhaps two years her elder. Even better looking than Ariadne, but dark haired and statuesque, Hesione has invited Ellie Dunn to Heartbreak House in order to discourage her from marrying Boss Mangan. Although Hesione seems to represent the homely virtues, her boredom leads her, when the bombers come at the end of the play, to exult in the excitement and destruction and to hope it will continue.

Hector Hushabye, Hesione's husband. Hector, fiftyish and dandified, is an extremely heroic but very shy man. Rather than boast of heroic deeds he actually has done, he makes up tales of high adventure. People, he reasons, need to hear such tales and to believe in heroes. When the bombers come over, Hector defiantly turns on all the lights in the house.

Ellie Dunn, a young singer in love with a mysterious Marcus Darnley, who turns out to be Hector Hushabye. Disillusionments like this destroy Ellie's romantic picture of the world and turn her into a "modern girl." She becomes aware of her power over men but cannot find values or a wisdom she can respect. Unhappy, Ellie also welcomes the coming of the bombers.

Mazzini Dunn, Ellie's father, a little, elderly, earnest man. Poverty-stricken, Mazzini had spent his life quietly fighting for liberty. Now seedy and a little pathetic, Mazzini is the type of the nineteenth century Liberal, the ineffectual good man.

Alfred (Boss) Mangan, the capitalist to whom Ellie is engaged. Fifty-five, careworn, suspicious, completely commonplace, Mangan contributes to Ellie's disillusionment by revealing he is not rich, but in fact only an agent for rich men. Mangan is killed when a bomb drops where he is hiding in the cave which holds the dynamite Shotover uses in his experiments.

Billy Dunn, an ex-pirate turned burglar, no relation to Ellie or Mazzini. Captured when he tries to rob Heartbreak House, Billy, terrified of the Captain, whom he had robbed years earlier, demands to be turned over to the law. Instead, his captors give him a servant's job. Mangan and Billy are referred to as either "the

452

two burglars" or "the two practical men of business." Billy is killed with Mangan.

Nurse Guiness, Captain Shotover's elderly servant and, secretly, Billy Dunn's wife. She is casual and impudent and in the habit of calling titled guests "lovey."

Randall Utterword, the younger brother of Ariadne's husband. Gentlemanly-looking and mannered, Randall is also untalented, peevish, and generally childish.

He represents foolish aristocratic pride. Ariadne, with whom he is in love, treats him as she would a small boy.

[**Sir Hastings Utterword,** Ariadne's husband; he is referred to in the play but does not appear. A governor of colonies, he has an insatiable appetite for routine administrative work. He encourages Ariadne's flirtations because they keep her in good humor.]

THE HEAT OF THE DAY

Author: Elizabeth Bowen (1899-   )
Time of action: 1942-1944
First published: 1949

PRINCIPAL CHARACTERS

Stella Rodney, an attractive English widow. She is unbelieving when told that her lover is a Nazi sympathizer. Because she cannot keep her knowledge to herself in fairness, she tells her lover the accusations. He shocks her by revealing that the accusations are true. Even after this revelation, she still tries to shield him from the authorities.

Robert Kelway, Stella's lover and, although a veteran of Dunkirk, a Nazi sympathizer. After he reveals his nature to Stella, he climbs out to her roof, from which he jumps and falls to his death.

Harrison, an intelligence agent. He informs Stella of her lover's Nazi pro-

pensities. At first he seems affectionate, but after the war he seems relieved she is planning to marry someone else.

Roderick Rodney, Stella's son, a soldier in the British army. He is an enthusiastic young man. His mother looks after his estate, inherited from a cousin in Ireland, while he is in the service during World War II.

Louie Lewis, a soldier's wife. A clumsy, cowlike person, she on impulse tries to make a pickup with Harrison. Later she intrudes herself upon Stella and Harrison while they are dining out.

Francis Morris, Stella's relative who bequeathed his Irish estate to Stella's son.

HEAVEN'S MY DESTINATION

Author: Thornton Wilder (1897-   )
Time of action: 1930-1931
First published: 1935

PRINCIPAL CHARACTERS

George Marvin Brush, a traveling salesman for a textbook company. He tries hard to live a clean, Christian life. Having undergone a religious conversion, he

tries to live up to unattainable ideals, often irritating people by his priggishness and his insistence that other persons ought to live better lives. He is a believer

453

in "ahimsa," a theory requiring that he react in the exact opposite to what others expect in a given situation. This belief and its practice often plunge him into trouble.

Roberta, a farmer's daughter seduced at one time by George Brush. He marries her to salve his conscience, even though she really wants nothing more to do with him. Exasperated by the conditions of their marriage, she finally leaves her husband, whom she heartily dislikes, and returns to her parents' farm.

Doremus Blodgett, a traveling salesman for a hosiery company. He is infuriated by George's righteousness and idealism until he learns that George has not lived entirely untouched by sin.

Mrs. Margie McCoy, Blodgett's mistress, who travels with him posing as a cousin.

Herb, a newspaper reporter in Kansas City who becomes George's friend. Herb tries to help George see that he must let other people live in their own ways. At Herb's death he leaves a child for George to care for.

Elizabeth, Herb's daughter. She is adopted by George and complicates her

foster parents' married life, as both of them compete for her affection.

George Burkin, a movie director. He and George meet in jail. Burkin is in jail for being a peeping Tom and George for graciously helping a robber hold up a store. Burkin tries to convince George that he has never grown up.

Lottie, Roberta's sister, who tries to persuade George that the answer to his problem with Roberta is a marriage and an immediate divorce.

Morrie,
Bat, and
Louie, three of George's friends in Kansas City. They play enormous practical jokes on George. Once, angered by his priggishness, they almost beat him to death.

Mrs. Crofut, keeper of a brothel. She is passed off to George as a genteel society matron. When her identity is told, George refuses to believe the truth about her and her bevy of beautiful "daughters."

Mrs. Efrim, the owner of the store George helps a man rob.

HEDDA GABLER

Author: Henrik Ibsen (1828-1906)
Time of action: Late nineteenth century
First presented: 1890

PRINCIPAL CHARACTERS

Hedda Gabler Tessman, the exciting but unenthusiastic bride of George Tessman, who holds a scholarship for research into the history of civilization. Back from a six-month wedding trip during which George studied civilization, Hedda is dangerously bored. The daughter of General Gabler, she keeps as her prize possession her father's pistols, with which she plays on occasion. She also plays with people: with George's Aunt Julia, whose

new bonnet Hedda pretends to think belongs to the servant; with George, who has bought her a villa which she pretended to want and who now must buy her a piano because her old one does not suit her new home; with an old school acquaintance, Mrs. Elvsted, who has rescued Hedda's talented former lover, Eilert Lovberg, from drink; with Eilert Lovberg, whom she cannot bear to see rescued by Mrs. Elvsted; with

454

Judge Brack, who outmaneuvers her and pushes her over the brink of endurance to her death. Hedda is a complete egocentric, caring for no one, careless of life for herself and for others. Badly spoiled, she seems to gain her only pleasure from making everyone miserable. Eilert Lovberg she finds more amusing than anyone else, even though she had dismissed him when she was free. When she realizes that he has destroyed his career, she gives him a pistol and tells him to use it—beautifully. When the pistol discharges accidentally and injures him fatally in the boudoir of Mademoiselle Diana, and when Judge Brack convinces her that he knows where Eilert got the pistol, Hedda takes its mate, goes to her room, and shoots herself in the temple, but not before she has seen Mrs. Elvsted quietly gain a hold on George Tessman.

George Tessman, Hedda's husband, a sincere, plodding young man dazzled by his bride but devoted to his work. When Hedda burns Eilert's manuscript, which George has found, she tells George that she did so to keep Eilert from surpassing him; but in reality she burned it because Eilert wrote it with Mrs. Elvsted and they call it their "child." George's surprised horror at her deed turns to warm delight when he thinks that Hedda loves him enough to destroy the manuscript for his sake. When Mrs. Elvsted says that she has notes for the manuscript, George says that he is just the man to work on someone else's manuscript and that they can put the book together again. Sincerely delighted that he can help restore the lost valuable book, he plans to work evenings with Mrs. Elvsted, to the disgust of Hedda, who in cold, calm rage and despair shoots herself.

Eilert Lovberg, a former suitor of Hedda who has written a book in the same field as Tessman's. He could easily win the appointment which Tessman expects, but he decides not to compete with him. Since Hedda broke up their association after it threatened to become serious, he has been living with the family of Sheriff Elvsted, teaching the Elvsted children and writing another book. His manuscript completed, he comes to town. In his writing and in his reform from his old wild ways, he has been inspired by Mrs. Elvsted. Eilert shows the effects of hard living. As soon as Hedda has an opportunity, she reasserts her control over him, destroying his confidence in Mrs. Elvsted and persuading him to resume his drinking. Hedda says that he will return "with vine leaves in his hair—flushed and fearless." Instead, he returns defeated, having lost his manuscript. He tells Thea Elvsted that all is over between them, because he has destroyed the manuscript, but he has merely lost it and is ashamed to tell her so. After leaving Judge Brack's party he had gone to the rooms of Mademoiselle Diana, a red-haired entertainer whom he had known in his riotous days. There, missing his manuscript, he had accused Diana and her friends of robbing him. When the police appeared, he struck a constable and was carried off to the police station. Released the next day, he goes in despair to Mademoiselle Diana's rooms to look for his lost manuscript. Here the gun discharges, killing him. Wanting the manuscript desperately because he claimed it contained his "true self" and dealt with the future, he had planned to deliver lectures on it after Tessman's appointment had gone through.

Judge Brack, a friend of the family, a sly man whom Tessman trusts. Hedda agrees to the apparently harmless arrangement to keep her entertained. After Eilert Lovberg's death, Judge Brack tells Hedda that he knows the true story, but there is no danger if he says nothing. When Hedda protests that she will now be his slave, a thought which she cannot bear, he replies that he will not abuse the advantage he now holds. He is incredulous when he hears that Hedda has killed herself.

Thea Elvsted, the wife of Sheriff Elvsted, a sweet-faced woman with blonde hair, born to inspire men, although, unfortunately, not her husband. She rescues Eilert, works with him, preserves his notes, seeks to preserve him, and after his death and Hedda's will no doubt inspire Tessman. When Eilert comes to town, Mrs. Elvsted, who is in love with him, follows him because she is afraid that he will relapse into his old ways. Because she and Hedda had known each other in school, she comes to see Hedda. Mrs. Elvsted had been afraid of her when they were girls because Hedda sometimes pulled her hair and threatened to burn it off. However, she confides to Hedda the story of her love for Eilert and thus helps to bring about his death and Hedda's.

Miss Juliana Tessman (Aunt Julia), Tessman's aunt, who is eternally hoping for an offspring for Hedda and George. Her constant, veiled remarks about sewing and the use for the two empty rooms are lost on George and ignored by Hedda. With her sister, Rina, now dying, Aunt Julia had reared George. She serves in the play to remind George of his past and to irritate Hedda. She is a sweet, good woman who loves her nephew and wants to help the helpless.

THE HEIMSKRINGLA

Author: Snorri Sturluson (1179-1241)
Time of action: Legendary times to twelfth century
First transcribed: Thirteenth century

PRINCIPAL CHARACTERS

Odin, an Asian conqueror who finally settles in the Scadinavian peninsula. From him later rulers of the northland claim descent.

Mime, Odin's friend, a spy, killed by a neighboring people. Receiving the head, Odin preserves it with herbs and sings incantations over it; thereafter, it speaks and discovers secrets for him.

On Jorundsson, King of Sweden. He extends his life by sacrificing a son to Odin every ten years. His people refuse to permit his tenth son to be sacrificed, and he dies of extreme old age.

Halfdan the Black (born about 820), King of Norway. A good King, he dies young. His quartered body is sent to separate provinces to spread his good influence.

Harald the Fairhaired, Halfdan's son. Challenged by a girl who refuses his advances because of the smallness of his territory, he conquers all of Norway and marries her.

Aethelstan, King of England. He and Harald constantly try to trap each other into acknowledging the other's mastery, but each rules his own kingdom until death.

Hakon the Good, Harald's son. Sent by Harald as foster son to Aethelstan (foster fathers being subject to real fathers), Hakon returns to Norway at Harald's death, and becomes King of Norway. A Christian, he does not force Christianity on his followers, but many are converted.

Eric Blood-Ax, Hakon's brother. Slayer of at least four other brothers, he is killed in England.

Tryggve Olafsson, a petty King slain by Eric's sons, who rule Norway after Hakon is killed in battle.

Olaf Tryggvesson, the son of Tryggve, who becomes a Viking chieftain when twelve. Converted to Christianity after his raids on England, he in turn converts all of Norway to Christianity. He dies at the hands of Danish kings in 1000.

Aethelred, King of England. Olaf makes and keeps peace with him.

Olaf Haraldsson the Saint, a descendant of Harald the Fairhaired. He extends the influence of Christianity and persistently tries to establish independence and national union. Slain in 1030 by petty chieftains whose traditional powers he is trying to reduce, he has long-lasting influence. After his death, many miracles are attributed to him.

Magnus the Good, the stepson of Olaf the Saint. He becomes King of Norway; later he is also King of Denmark.

Hardacanute, King of Denmark and King of England. According to peace terms with Magnus, the survivor is to rule the other's country.

Edward the Good, King of England. So sensible and courageous is his reply to Magnus' claim to the English throne after Hardacanute's death, that Magnus is content to let him rule in England.

Harald Sigurdsson the Stern, the brother of Olaf the Saint. He collects great wealth in his plundering travels. Returning to Norway, he is troublesome to his nephew Magnus, who finally gives him half of Norway in return for half his booty.

Ellisiv, the daughter of the Russian King and the wife of Harald the Stern.

Harald Godwinsson, successor to Edward the Good of England. Trying to unthrone him, Harald the Stern meets his death in England.

Magnus, a son of Harald the Stern. Co-ruler of Norway with his brother, he dies young of sickness.

Olaf the Quiet, another son of Harald the Stern. He is a successful ruler of Norway for twenty-six years.

Magnus Barefoot, so called after his return from Scotland in Scottish national costume. The son of Olaf the Quiet, he greatly extends the power of the central government during his ten-year rule of Norway. Not yet thirty, he is killed in Ireland in 1103.

Hakon Magnusson, the nephew of Olaf the Quiet. He shares with Magnus Barefoot in the rule of Norway until his early death from sickness.

Olaf, the youngest son of Magnus Barefoot. He dies young.

Eystein, another son of Magnus Barefoot. Co-ruler of Norway, he is jealous of his brother Sigurd.

Sigurd the Crusader, another son of Magnus Barefoot. He travels for three years to the Holy Land and elsewhere while Eystein rules at home. Surviving his brother, he greatly improves the legal system of his country.

Magnus the Blind, the son of Sigurd and a foolish king. Captured and blinded by Harald Gille, he retires to a monastery.

Harald Gille, from Ireland. Claiming to be Sigurd's half brother, he proves his paternity in an ordeal by hot iron. Proclaimed ruler over part of Norway, he is a cruel sovereign.

Sigurd Slembedegn, a pretender to the throne, by whose order and treachery Harald Gille is killed.

Sigurd and
Eystein, sons of Harald Gille. Constant unrest results from their leadership of separate factions.

Crippled Inge, Harald Gille's most popular son. Surviving his brothers, he rules alone for a time and dies at twenty-six.

Cardinal Nicholas, who comes from Rome in 1152 to establish an archbishopric at Nidaros, shrine of Olaf the Great. Well-loved, he later becomes Pope Adrian IV.

Hakon Sigurdsson the Broad-Shouldered, an untrustworthy claimant to Eystein's part of Norway. He kills Inge and is defeated in battle at fifteen in 1162.

Erling Skakke, a power behind Inge's throne. He gives up power to archbishops and to Denmark and becomes a tyrant in order to secure the Norwegian throne for his son.

Valdemar, King of Denmark. Erling Skakke gives him part of Norway as a fief under the Danish crown in exchange for peace.

Magnus Erlingsson, the son of Erling Skakke. Son of a daughter of Sigurd the Crusader, he is a legitimate candidate for the throne of Norway. He is five years old when his father's supporters make him King.

HELEN

Author: Euripides (c. 485-c. 406 B.C.)
Time of action: Seven years after the fall of Troy
First presented: 412 B.C.

PRINCIPAL CHARACTERS

Helen, wife of King Menelaus of Sparta. Promised by Aphrodite to Paris for his judgment, Helen was rescued by Hermes and supernaturally transported to Egypt. A phantom-image was given to Paris and Helen was promised that she would return to Sparta to be with her husband, who should know that she did not elope to Troy. She has been protected in Egypt by King Proteus, but he is now dead and his son Theoclymenus wishes to marry her. She has taken refuge at the tomb of Proteus and, at the beginning of the play, laments her misfortunes. When a Greek, Teucer, appears with the news that Menelaus is reported dead, Helen takes the report as fact. She goes to consult Theonoe, a prophetess who is the sister of Theoclymenus, and learns that Menelaus is alive and will arrive in Egypt. When she returns, Menelaus has appeared. He cannot believe, because he has been wandering for seven years with the phantom-image, that Helen is really in Egypt until one of his men comes to report that the phantom-image has returned to the skies. He and Helen then retell their separate stories, convince the all-knowing Theonoe not to reveal their presence to Theoclymenus, and devise a plan to escape. Helen has Menelaus, ragged and dirty after his wanderings, report his own death to Theoclymenus. She agrees to marry the young King if he will allow her to perform burial rites at sea for dead Menelaus. Once at sea, Helen and Menelaus make their escape. Helen is a romantic figure; she has charm, wit, self-importance, and self-pity combined with loveliness and virtue.

Menelaus (mĕ′nə·lā′əs), King of Sparta. Shipwrecked on the coast of Egypt, he hides his men and the phantom-image of Helen and sets out in search of aid. He appears, shabbily clothed, and is faced down and treated as a beggar by an old portress at the house of Theoclymenus; she tells him of Helen's presence in the house and of her master's hostility toward all Greeks. Helen enters and, after Menelaus learns that the gods had substituted a phantom-image for his wife, they are reconciled and seek the aid of Theonoe. In his plea before her, Menelaus is the "miles gloriosus," the braggart soldier; he threatens, is highly rhetorical, and even congratulates himself during his speech. After he makes several useless suggestions for their escape, he accepts Helen's plan and carries out his role bravely.

Theoclymenus (thē·ɔ·klīm'ɔ·nûs), King of Egypt, a pious and kindly man whose love for Helen has caused him to attempt to make her his wife in spite of his father's oath of protection. He dislikes Greeks because he is afraid they may come to steal Helen. Eager to believe the reports of Menelaus' death and overjoyed because Helen now seems willing to accept his suit, he is easily duped into agreeing to any funeral arrangements she wishes to make. He is kept from pursuit by the intervention of the gods, whose advice he gladly follows.

Theonoe (thē·ŏn'ō·ē), a prophetess and the sister of Theoclymenus. Helen consults her, off stage, and learns that Menelaus is not dead. The seeress makes a spectacular entrance and reveals that the final decision in the fate of Menelaus is hers. After hearing from both Helen and Menelaus, she decides, out of self-respect and piety, for Menelaus.

Castor (kăs'tər) and
Polydeuces (pŏl·i·dū'sēz), the twin

brothers of Helen. They appear at the end of the play to keep Theoclymenus from pursuing Helen and to prevent his punishment of Theonoe for deceiving him.

Teucer (tōō'sər), the famous archer. Traveling to Rhodes because his father, Telamon, has banished him for failing to protect his brother Ajax at Troy, he gives Helen news of the fall of Troy and of the wanderings and reported death of Menelaus.

The Portress, a guardian of the house of Theoclymenus. A manly woman, typical of Egypt, she faces Menelaus down when he attempts to beg.

A Servant, a simple-minded but faithful servant of Menelaus who brings news of the disappearance of the phantom Helen and who has some bitter things to say against soothsayers.

The Chorus. Captive Greek women, sympathetic to Helen, they render the odes which lift the play above the level of mere comedy.

HENRY ESMOND

Author: William Makepeace Thackeray (1811-1863)
Time of action: Late seventeenth and early eighteenth centuries
First published: 1852

PRINCIPAL CHARACTERS

Henry Esmond, an orphan believed to be the illegitimate son of the late Thomas Esmond, Lord Castlewood. He is seen first as a grave, observant boy and later as an intelligent, level-headed young man. The novel, though narrated in the third person, takes the form of his memoirs, beginning when he is twelve years old and continuing until his early manhood and marriage. A lonely boy under the guardianship of his kinsman, Francis

Esmond, Viscount Castlewood, Henry spends his adolescence at the Castlewood estate. The untimely death of Viscount Castlewood, fatally wounded in a duel, leads to Henry's discovery that he is the true heir to the Castlewood title. This secret he continues to keep out of affection for his kinsman's widow and her children. For years he believes himself in love with his beautiful cousin, Beatrix Esmond, and for her sake he becomes involved in a Jacobite plot to secure the English throne for James, the young Stuart Pretender, at the time of Queen Anne's death. When events prove that he has been deceived in both Beatrix and the Stuart exile, he realizes that the real object of his affection is Rachel Esmond, the youthful mother of Beatrix. With her he emigrates to America, leaving her son Frank in possession of the title and the Castlewood estate.

Francis Esmond, Viscount Castlewood, a hard-living, pleasure-seeking nobleman, the amiable, though hardly devoted, guardian of young Henry Esmond. Having aided in concealing the secret of Henry's birth, he repents the injustice done the boy and on his deathbed reveals that Henry is the true heir to the Castlewood title.

Rachel Esmond, the Viscount's much younger wife, a quiet, attractive woman whose loyalty to her husband never fails, even when he begins to neglect her for drinking and gambling with his reckless, pleasure-loving London friends. Her chief fault, a tendency to possessiveness, is displayed first toward the Viscount and later toward Henry Esmond, whom she marries after the plot to put James Stuart on the throne of England has failed.

Beatrix Esmond, the beautiful and lively daughter of Francis and Rachel Castlewood. As fickle and unstable as she is fascinating, lovely but ambitious and scheming, she accepts Henry Esmond's attentions when no more suitable admirer is at hand. Her affair with James,

the Stuart Pretender, finally reveals to Henry her true nature.

Frank Esmond, the sturdy, unimaginative younger brother of Beatrix Esmond. He is, by virtue of Henry Esmond's sacrifice, the eventual successor to the lands and title wrongly held by his father, the former Viscount.

Father Holt, Henry Esmond's tutor in boyhood. The priest secretly acts as a Jacobite spy, helping to prepare the way for the return of the Stuart Pretender.

Lord Mohun, a London rake with designs on Rachel Esmond. He kills her husband in a duel.

The Duke of Hamilton, an impetuous young nobleman engaged to marry Beatrix Esmond. He is killed in a duel in which he fatally wounds Lord Mohun.

The Duke of Marlborough, the famous military commander-in-chief. During his campaigns of 1702-1704 Henry Esmond sees service as a soldier in France and Spain.

General John Webb, the officer to whom Henry Esmond serves as aide-de-camp. Webb becomes involved in a bitter controversy with the Duke of Marlborough.

Richard Steele, an early friend of Henry Esmond. Steele is presented as a henpecked husband and lovable scapegrace; his status as a literary man is only lightly accented.

Joseph Addison, a leading Whig of the period as well as a prominent man of letters.

HENRY THE EIGHTH

Author: William Shakespeare (1564-1616); with John Fletcher? (1579-1625)
Time of action: 1520-1533
First presented: 1612-1613

PRINCIPAL CHARACTERS

King Henry the Eighth, King of England. Possibly because he may be a com-

posite portrait by two authors, possibly because of the difficulty of writing about

460

a controversial political figure so nearly contemporary, King Henry is not one of the more successful creations in Shakespeare's gallery. At times he seems to be an allegorical figure of Royalty, like Magnificence in John Skelton's morality play of that title. The injustice of his treatment of Queen Katharine is partly offset by his generous protection of Cranmer against the Council's attack.

Thomas Cardinal Wolsey (wŏŏl′zĭ), Cardinal of York and Lord Chancellor of England. A far better dramatic creation than the King, he is drawn as arrogant and stubborn when he is in power and ruthless in hounding the Duke of Buckingham to his death and in attempting to force Queen Katharine to submit the decision on her divorce to Henry and Wolsey. He falls through pride, but accepts his fall with dignity. His death is reported to Queen Katharine as a good death, and she speaks of him with forgiveness.

Queen Katharine (kăth′ə·rĭn), called **Katharine of Aragon**, the first wife of Henry VIII. Characterized by dignity, firmness, and compassion, she never allows her adversity and her material losses to shake her integrity or reduce her to bitterness. Even her successful rival for the King's affections, Anne Bullen, speaks of her with pity and admiration. The King himself has nothing to say in dispraise of her character or conduct, either before or after the divorce.

Thomas Cranmer (krăn′mər), Archbishop of Canterbury, a loyal friend and supporter of King Henry. He is considered a heretic by Wolsey. Saved from the plots of the Council by the King, and chosen godfather for the infant Elizabeth, he delivers a glowing prophecy of the future of his tiny goddaughter. This supposed prophecy, actual eulogy of the late Queen, is the true end of the play, followed only by the concluding speech of King Henry, in keeping with the con-

temporary convention of giving royalty the last word on stage.

Anne Bullen (bŏŏl′ən), also **Anne Boleyn**, Queen Katharine's Maid of Honor. She becomes the King's second wife and the mother of Elizabeth. Although she has sympathy for the Queen and says that she would not be a queen for all the riches under heaven, she readily consents to be Queen Katharine's successor.

The Duke of Buckingham, Edward Bohun, son of the Duke of Buckingham beheaded under Richard III, He is the bitter enemy and victim of Cardinal Wolsey. His role in Act One is a large one, but it ends early in Act Two as he goes to his death with great dignity and nobility.

The Duke of Norfolk, Thomas Howard, son of "Jockey of Norfolk," who appears in Shakespeare's "Richard the Third." A moderate nobleman, an admirer of Queen Katharine and supporter of her plea for relief of the hardship of the commons, he has no love for Cardinal Wolsey. He bears the King's command that Wolsey give up the seal of the Lord Chancellor.

The Earl of Surrey, son of Norfolk and son-in-law of Buckingham. He shares in Wolsey's downfall and heaps recriminations on him.

The Duke of Suffolk, Charles Brandon, another enemy of Wolsey. He also shares in the overthrow of the Cardinal and taunts him in his adversity.

Brandon (perhaps this otherwise unidentified character could be Suffolk). He supervises the arrest of Buckingham and escorts him to the Tower of London.

The Lord Chamberlain, Charles Somerset, Earl of Worcester. He is present at the Cardinal's party, which is attended by the King and Anne Bullen. He informs the King who Anne is.

Lord Sands, Sir William Sands, a coltish old gentleman, given to flirting. He also attends the Cardinal's party.

461

Sir Thomas Lovell, another guest at the Cardinal's party. He is in charge of Buckingham's execution and asks forgiveness from the Duke, which is granted.

Cardinal Campeius (kăm·pā'ŭs), an emissary sent from Rome to hear the case for the divorce between King Henry and Queen Katharine. He endeavors in vain to persuade the Queen to submit to the judgment of the King and Wolsey in the matter of her divorce.

Capucius (kă·pū'shŭs, kà·pū'sē·ŭs), the ambassador from Charles V (Queen Katharine's nephew) to Henry VIII. He visits Queen Katharine just before her death and tries to console her.

The Lord Chancellor, Sir Thomas More, the successor to Cardinal Wolsey. He presides at Cranmer's hearing before the Council.

Stephen Gardiner, Bishop of Winchester, a follower of Wolsey and an enemy of Cranmer. He becomes reconciled with Cranmer on the King's command.

An Old Lady, a friend of Anne Bullen. She and Anne discuss Queen Katharine's case. She may be the officious old lady who announces to the King the birth of his daughter Elizabeth.

Griffith, Gentleman Usher to Queen Katharine. He remains faithful to her in her retirement and ill health to her death.

Doctor Butts, Sir William Butts, the King's physician. He is friendly to Cranmer and informs the King of the Council's hostility toward him.

The Surveyor to the Duke of Buckingham, who sells out his master to the Cardinal and aids in bringing about the execution.

Thomas Cromwell, Wolsey's loyal servant, to whom he speaks the famous and much-quoted passage on ambition.

Sir Henry Guildford (gĭl'fərd), who welcomes the guests at the Cardinal's party.

The Duchess of Norfolk, godmother of Elizabeth. She carries the infant in the ceremonial procession.

The Marchioness of Dorset, the second godmother of Elizabeth.

Sir Nicholas Vaux (vôks), who is responsible for conducting the Duke of Buckingham to execution.

Lord Abergavenny (ăb'ər·gĕn'ĭ), a friend of Buckingham and Norfolk.

The Bishops of Lincoln,
Ely,
Rochester, and
Saint Asaph (ā'săf), present at the hearing of the divorce proceedings.

HENRY THE FIFTH

Author: William Shakespeare (1564-1616)
Time of action: Early part of the fifteenth century
First presented: 1598-1599

PRINCIPAL CHARACTERS

Henry the Fifth, King of England from 1413 to 1422, the wild "Prince Hal" of the "Henry IV" plays. Since his accession to the throne, he has grown into a capable monarch whose sagacity astonishes his advisers. The question of state that most concerns him is that of his right, through his grandfather, Edward III, to certain French duchies and ultimately to the French crown. His claim to the duchies is haughtily answered by the Dauphin of France, who sends Henry a barrel of tennis balls, a jibe at the English King's misspent youth. Having crushed at home a plot against his life fomented by his cousin, the Earl of Cambridge, abetted by Lord Scroop and Sir Thomas Gray, and having been assured by the Archbishop of Canterbury that his claim to the French crown is valid, Henry invades France. After the capture of Harfleur, at which victory he shows mercy to the inhabitants of the town, the King meets the French at Agincourt in Picardy. The French take the impending battle very lightly, since they outnumber the English. Henry spends the night wandering in disguise around his camp, talking to the soldiers to test their feelings and to muse on the responsibilities of kingship. In the battle on the following day, the English win a great victory. The peace is concluded by the betrothal of Henry to the Princess Katharine, daughter of the French king, and the recognition of his claim to the French throne. To Shakespeare, as to most of his contemporaries, Henry was a great national hero, whose exploits of two centuries earlier fitted in well with the patriotic fervor of a generation that had seen the defeat of the Spanish Armada.

Charles the Sixth, the weak-minded King of France.

Queen Isabel, his wife.

Lewis, the Dauphin of France, whose pride is humbled at Agincourt.

Katharine of France, daughter of Charles VI. As part of the treaty of peace, she is betrothed to Henry V, who woos her in a mixture of blunt English and mangled French.

Edward, Duke of York, the cousin of the King, though called "uncle" in the play. He dies a hero's death at Agincourt.

Richard, Earl of Cambridge, the younger brother of York. Corrupted by French gold, he plots against the life of Henry and is executed for treason.

Lord Scroop and **Sir Thomas Gray,** fellow conspirators of Cambridge.

Philip, Duke of Burgundy, the intermediary between Charles VI and Henry V. He draws up the treaty of peace and forces it on Charles.

Montjoy, the French herald who carries the haughty messages from the French to Henry.

Pistol, a soldier, addicted to high-flown language and married to Mistress Quickly, once hostess of a tavern in Eastcheap. Later, Fluellen proves him a coward. When he learns of his wife's death, he resolves to return to England to become a cutpurse.

Nell Quickly, once hostess of the Boar's Head Tavern in Eastcheap and now married to Pistol. It is she who gives the famous account of the death of Falstaff. She dies while Pistol is in France.

Bardolph, now a soldier, formerly one of Henry's companions in his wild youth. In France, he is sentenced to be hanged for stealing a pax.

Fluellen, a Welsh soldier, tedious and long-winded. By a trick, the King forces him into a fight with Williams.

Michael Williams, a soldier who quarrels with Henry while the King is wandering incognito through the camp. They exchange gages to guarantee a duel when they next meet. When the meeting occurs, the King forgives Williams for the quarrel.

John, Duke of Bedford, the "John of Lancaster" of the "Henry IV" plays and the younger brother of Henry V.

Humphrey, Duke of Gloucester, youngest brother of Henry V.

HENRY THE FOURTH, PARTS ONE AND TWO

Author: William Shakespeare (1564-1616)
Time of action: 1400-1413
First presented: 1597-1598

PRINCIPAL CHARACTERS

King Henry the Fourth, England's troubled ruler. Haunted by his action in the deposition and indirectly in the death of his predecessor and kinsman, Richard II, and deeply disturbed by the apparent unworthiness of his irresponsible eldest son, he also faces the external problem of rebellion. He wishes to join a crusade to clear his conscience and to carry out a prophecy that he is to die in Jerusalem; it turns out that he dies in the Jerusalem chamber in Westminster.

Henry, Prince of Wales (Prince Hal, Harry Monmouth), later King Henry V. A boisterous youth surrounded by bad companions, he matures rapidly with responsibility, saves his father's life in battle, and kills the dangerous rebel, Hotspur. When he comes to the throne, he repudiates his wild companions.

Sir John Falstaff, a comical, down-at-the-heels follower of Prince Hal. Considered by many to be one of Shakespeare's finest creations, by some to be his greatest, Falstaff is a plump fruit from the stem of the "Miles Gloriosus" of Plautus. He is the typical braggart soldier with many individualizing traits. As he says, he is not only witty himself, but the cause of wit in other men. Innumerable pages have been written on whether or not he is a coward. He is a cynical realist, a fantastic liar, a persuasive rascal. Also, he is apparently a successful combat soldier. His colossal body, which "lards the lean earth as he walks along," appropriately houses his colossal personality. In the second part of the play, there is some decline of his character, perhaps to prepare the way for Prince Hal, as King Henry V, to cast him off.

Prince John of Lancaster, another of King Henry's sons, who also bears himself well in battle at Shrewsbury. He commands part of his father's forces in Yorkshire and arranges a false peace with the Archbishop of York and other rebels. When their troops are dismissed, he has them arrested and executed.

Humphrey of Gloucester and **Thomas of Clarence,** other sons of Henry IV, brothers of Henry V.

Thomas Percy, Earl of Worcester, a leading rebel against King Henry IV. He conceals the King's offer of generous terms from his nephew Hotspur, thereby causing the young warrior's death. He is executed for treason.

Henry Percy, Earl of Northumberland, Worcester's brother. Having had an important share in the deposition of Richard II and the enthronement of Henry IV, he feels that he and his family are entitled to more power and wealth than they receive. He is also influenced to rebellion by his crafty brother and his fiery son. He fails his cause by falling ill or feigning illness before the Battle of Shrewsbury, and he does not appear there. Later he disconcerts Mowbray by withdrawing to Scotland, where he is defeated.

Hotspur (Henry Percy), son of Northumberland. A courageous, hot-tempered youth, he seeks to pluck glory from the moon. He is a loving, teasing husband, but his heart is more on the battlefield than in the boudoir. He rages helplessly at the absence of his father and Glendower from the Battle of Shrewsbury. In the battle he falls by Prince Henry's hand.

Edmund Mortimer, Earl of March, Hotspur's brother-in-law, designated heir to the English throne by Richard II. Captured while fighting against Glendower, he marries his captor's daughter. King Henry's refusal to ransom him leads to the rebellion of the Percys. He too fails to join Hotspur at Shrewsbury.

Owen Glendower, the Welsh leader. Hotspur finds his mystical self-importance irritating and almost precipitates internal strife among King Henry's opponents. Glendower also fails Hotspur at Shrewsbury. Some time later, Warwick reports Glendower's death to the ailing King.

Sir Richard Vernon, another rebel. He is with the Earl of Worcester when King Henry offers his terms for peace, and with great reluctance he agrees to conceal the terms from Hotspur.

Archibald, Earl of Douglas, a noble Scottish rebel. After killing Sir Walter Blunt and two others whom he mistakes for King Henry at Shrewsbury, he is prevented from killing the King by Prince Hal. After the battle, Prince Hal generously releases him without ransom.

Richard Scroop, Archbishop of York, a principal rebel. He thinks to make peace with King Henry and take later advantage of his weakness, but is tricked by Prince John and executed.

Sir Walter Blunt, a heroic follower of the King. At the Battle of Shrewsbury he pretends to Douglas that he is the King, thus bringing death on himself.

Mistress Quickly, hostess of the Boar's Head Tavern in Eastcheap. She is a silly, voluble woman with a stupendous fund of malapropisms. Easily angered, but gullible, she is a frequent victim of Falstaff's chicanery.

Bardolph, the red-nosed right-hand man of Falstaff. His fiery nose makes him the butt of many witticisms. Like Falstaff, he is capable of sudden and violent action.

Poins, Prince Hal's confidant. Masked, he and the Prince rob Falstaff and the other robbers at Gadshill and endeavor to discountenance Falstaff at the Boar's Head Tavern afterward.

Gadshill and Peto, other members of the Prince's scapegrace following.

Pistol, a cowardly, loud-mouthed soldier with the mannerism of quoting or misquoting snatches of drama. He swaggers and roars until Falstaff is forced to pink him in the shoulder, and Bardolph ejects him from the inn.

Page, a tiny and witty boy given to Falstaff, apparently to make a ridiculous contrast. He makes impudent and spicy remarks on several of the characters.

Doll Tearsheet, a frowsy companion of Sir John Falstaff. She flatters and caresses the old knight, but cannot abide Pistol.

The Sheriff, who seeks Falstaff after the robbery. Prince Hal sends him away with the promise that Sir John will answer for his behavior.

The Lord Chief Justice, a stern man who has dared even to commit the Prince. After Mistress Quickly's complaints, he rebukes Falstaff and demands that he make restitution. Because Falstaff's reputation has increased since the Battle of Shrewsbury, the justice is more lenient than expected.

Justice Shallow, a garrulous old man. Before furnishing Falstaff with a roll of soldiers from his district, he pours out a flood of reminiscences about their wild youth.

Justice Silence, Shallow's cousin.

Davy, Shallow's servant.

Fang and Snare, two sergeants called in by the hostess to arrest Falstaff.

**Ralph Mouldy,
Simon Shadow,
Thomas Wart,**

Francis Feeble, and Peter Bullcalf, country soldiers furnished to Falstaff's company.

Rumour, an abstraction who presents exposition at the beginning of the Second Part of "King Henry the Fourth."

Lady Northumberland, Hotspur's mother, Northumberland's troubled wife.

Lady Percy, Hotspur's wife, Mortimer's sister. A charming and playful girl, she is deeply in love with her fiery husband and tragically moved by his death.

Lady Mortimer, daughter of Glendower. Speaking only Welsh, she is unable to understand her husband, to whom she is married as a political pawn.

Sir Michael, a follower of the Archbishop of York, for whom he delivers secret messages to important rebels.

Sir John Colville (Colville of the Dale), Lord Mowbray, Lord Hastings, Lord Bardolph, Travers, and Morton, rebels against King Henry IV.

The Earl of Westmoreland, The Earl of Warwick, The Earl of Surrey, Gower, and Harcourt, followers of King Henry IV.

HENRY THE SIXTH, PARTS ONE, TWO, AND THREE

Author: William Shakespeare (1564-1616)
Time of action: 1422-1471
First presented: 1589-1591

PRINCIPAL CHARACTERS

King Henry the Sixth, a simple, peace-loving, almost saintly monarch. He becomes the pawn of his Queen and his powerful noblemen. Although he is aware of their evil, he remains incapable of action against them.

Margaret of Anjou, his strong-minded, articulate Queen. She despises Henry for his weakness and allies herself with the Duke of Suffolk to become, in effect, the ruler of England.

William de la Pole, Earl of Suffolk, later Duke, her lover. A stanch Lancastrian, he tries to govern the kingdom by his influence over the Queen.

Humphrey, Duke of Gloucester, the Lord Protector. A violent, uncontrollable foe to Cardinal Beaufort in Part I, he becomes in Part II the idol of the people, almost alone in his devotion to righteousness and the King.

Henry Beaufort, Cardinal of Winchester,

his power-hungry uncle and bitter enemy.

Lord Talbot, later Earl of Shrewsbury, the English military hero who leads his nation to victory over France and Joan of Arc.

John Talbot, his valiant son.

Joan la Pucelle (jŏn lä pōō·sel'), commonly called Joan of Arc, the French shepherdess who becomes the leader of the Dauphin's army. She is presented by Shakespeare as a witch, possessed by devils.

Charles, the Dauphin of France, who readily accepts Joan's aid and offers himself as her lover.

Richard Plantagenet, Duke of York, the ambitious leader of the Yorkist party. He proclaims his title to the English throne and forces Henry to make him his heir. Future glory does not satisfy him, however, and he attacks the Lancastrians again. He loses his own life but leaves a crown for his son Edward.

Edmund Mortimer, Earl of March, the elderly Yorkist heir, who bequeathes his cause to Richard.

The Earl of Salisbury and **The Earl of Warwick,** the powerful Nevilles, father and son, who bring Edward IV to the throne. They turn their allegiance to the Lancastrians after Edward's marriage to Elizabeth Woodville.

The Duke of Bedford, Henry VI's uncle, regent of France.

Thomas Beaufort (bō'fərt), Duke of Exeter, Henry's great-uncle.

The Duke of Burgundy, a powerful ruler who is persuaded by Joan to forsake his English allies and come to France's aid.

The Bastard of Orleans (ôr'lā'än') and **The Duke of Alençon** (ä·län·sôn'), French courtiers.

Reignier (rā'nyā'), the Duke of Anjou, Queen Margaret's father.

The Countess of Auvergne (ō·vĕrn'y), a patriotic Frenchwoman who tries unsuccessfully to capture Talbot by trickery.

Sir John Fastolfe (făst'olf), a cowardly English knight.

The Duke of Somerset, leader of the Lancastrian nobles.

Added in Part Two

Edward, heir to Richard, Duke of York, a stanch supporter of his father's cause. He becomes Edward IV, a rather self-indulgent monarch who throws away the support of his most powerful nobles by sending them to arrange a French marriage while he falls in love with Elizabeth Woodville and weds her, against the advice of his brothers and friends.

Richard, Duke of Gloucester, his brother, who confesses his own desire for the crown and begins scheming to acquire it, even before Edward becomes king.

George, Duke of Clarence, Richard's third son, who temporarily joins the Lancastrians.

Eleanor, Duchess of Gloucester, who falls into the hands of dabblers in magic when she tries to further her husband's political career, much against his will.

Sir John Hume, her priest, who encourages her folly, hoping that it will cause her husband's fall.

Margery Jourdain (jĕr·dān', zhōōr·dān') and **Roger Bolingbroke,** practitioners of magic.

Sir John Stanley, the sheriff who has custody of the Duchess of Gloucester.

The Duke of Buckingham, Somerset's ally against Duke Humphrey and Cardinal Beaufort.

Lord Clifford, killed at the first battle of St. Alban's,
Lord Say,
Sir Humphrey Stafford,
William Stafford, and
Lord Scales, noblemen who defend Henry against Jack Cade's rebellion.

Young Clifford, the son of Lord Clifford.

Jack Cade, the Kentish clothier who, pretending to be a Yorkist claimant to the throne, leads a rebellion against the King.

Bevis,
Holland,
Dick the Butcher,
Smith the Weaver, and
Michael, his fellow rebels.

Peter, an apprentice.

Thomas Horner, Richard Plantagenet's servant, accused by Peter of treasonously asserting his master's right to the throne.

Saunder Simpcox, a "miraculously cured" citizen of St. Alban's, an impostor.

Walter Whitmore, a sailor, the "Water" prophesied to cause Suffolk's death.

Vaux (vôks), a messenger.

Added in Part Three

Lord Clifford, also called Young Clifford and "the Butcher," the Lancastrian nobleman who cold-bloodedly kills Edmund, Earl of Rutland, to avenge his father's death at the hand of Richard, Duke of York.

Edmund, Earl of Rutland, the second son of the Duke of York. The young Prince's death is greatly mourned by his father, Duke Richard.

Edward, Prince of Wales, a well-spoken boy who early comprehends his royal rights and responsibilities.

Elizabeth Woodville, Lady Grey, the attractive widow who becomes Edward IV's queen.

Louis XI, King of France, Queen Margaret's ally after Edward marries Lady Grey while his ambassadors ask for the hand of Bona for him.

Bona, sister to the Queen of France.

Lord Rivers, Lady Grey's brother.

Henry, Earl of Richmond, the young man recognized by King Henry VI as heir to the Lancastrian hopes, later King Henry VII.

The Marquess of Montague, Warwick's brother, who switches allegiance after the fiasco of Edward's marriage.

Vernon,
The Duke of Norfolk,
Sir John Mortimer,
Sir Hugh Mortimer,
Lord Hastings, and
Sir John Montgomery, Yorkist nobles.

Sir William Lucy,
Basset,
The Earl of Northumberland,
The Earl of Westmoreland,
The Duke of Exeter, and
The Earl of Oxford, Lancastrian noblemen.

HERAKLES MAD

Author: Euripides (c.485-c. 406 B.C.)
Time of action: Remote antiquity
First presented: c. 420 B.C.

PRINCIPAL CHARACTERS

Herakles (hĕr'ə·klēz), the Greek hero who passes, through suffering, from the courage of outward physical strength to internal courage raised against intolerable necessity and based on true friendship. During the first third of the play he does not appear, but Amphitryon, his father, his wife Megara, his small sons, and the Chorus attest to his heroism and to the increasing fear that he is dead; he has gone to Hades to capture Cerberus, the last of his labors to be performed. He appears suddenly, just before Lycus, usurper of the throne of Thebes, returns to kill Herakles' father, children, and wife. He determines, sure of his physical strength, to march against Lycus and his forces, but Amphitryon persuades him to enter his house and wait for Lycus. He does so. Lycus returns, enters the house to drag out Megara and the children, and is killed by Herakles. Suddenly Iris and Madness appear to carry out the will of Hera, queen of the gods and persecutor of Herakles, to make him murder his children in a fit of in-

468

sanity. The murders, described by a messenger, are terrible. Herakles believes his own children to be those of Eurystheus, and he kills them and Megara. When he turns on his father, however, the goddess Athena appears and knocks him unconscious with a rock. As he awakens, Theseus, the King of Athens, rescued from Hades by Herakles, appears. He has come to aid Herakles against Lycus. Herakles speaks of suicide, but Theseus' taunt that it is a "boorish folly" worthy only of cowards causes him to renounce self-death and to accept Theseus' offer of refuge and honor in Athens. Herakles' last words are that it is a sad error to seek "wealth or strength" rather than fine friends.

Amphitryon (ăm·fĭt'rĭ·ən), the father of Herakles. His opening monologue provides the background and states the plight of Herakles' kin. His defense of his son before Lycus is vigorous and overshadows his plea for exile rather than death. He curses the gods because the plea is not granted, but he then prays to them for deliverance. He tempers Herakles' desire for wholesale vengeance against Lycus and his followers. At the end of the play he is left to bury Megara and her children.

Megara (mĕg'á·rá), the wife of Herakles. Driven to hasty refuge by Lycus, she still has hope that her husband is alive and accepts Amphitryon's plea for a delay of death. But when Lycus threatens to burn the suppliants, she reveals her true dignity as Herakles' wife; they must accept death, now inevitable, willingly and not beg from Lycus. She requests that she be allowed to enter the house of Herakles and clothe herself and her children for death. When Herakles appears, Megara reveals the circumstances and enters the house with him. She is killed by Herakles in his madness.

Theseus (thē'sōōs, thē'sĭ·əs), King of Athens. He appears at the close of the play with an army to help Herakles against Lycus. He is the model of what a friend should be. Since he cannot fight for Herakles, he offers, unafraid of the pollution that contact with a murderer was thought to bring upon an innocent person, to share his sufferings. He warns Herakles against suicide and offers him refuge, wealth, and honor in Athens. The two leave together.

Lycus (lĭ'kəs), the usurper of the throne of Thebes. He had killed Creon, father of Megara, and taken the throne. A tyrant, he feels it necessary to destroy the family of Herakles. His belief that Herakles is dead contrasts with the remaining hope of Megara and Amphitryon. He is killed by Herakles when he enters the latter's house to drag Megara from the altar.

Iris (ī'rĭs), the messenger of Hera, queen of the gods. She is sent to carry out Hera's wrath against Herakles as well as her own, and she sees to it that Madness does not rebel against her task.

Madness, who rebels against divine vindictiveness, but to no avail. Though she must obey the goddess' command, she calls upon the sun to witness her reluctance. In carrying out her task she is madness incarnate.

The Chorus of Old Men of Thebes. Friends who are sympathetic to the plight of Megara, they are helpless because of age. In spite of their weakness they threaten Lycus and attempt to intervene, but his show of force makes them realize there is nothing they can do.

A Messenger. He reports Herakles' madness and the murder of Megara and the children.

HERCULES AND HIS TWELVE LABORS

Author: Unknown
Time of action: Remote antiquity
First transcribed: Unknown

PRINCIPAL CHARACTERS

Hercules (hûr′kyə·lēz), the son of Jupiter and Alcmena. He is a mortal. As a child he is the object of Juno's jealousy. Through her influence he is commanded to carry out twelve labors, in hopes that he will be killed in accomplishing one of them: (1) he must strangle the Nemean lion; (2) he must kill the nine-headed hydra; (3) he must capture the dread Erymanthian boar; (4) he must capture a stag with golden antlers and brazen feet; (5) he must get rid of the carnivorous Stymphalian birds; (6) he must cleanse the stables of Augeas; (7) he must capture the sacred bull of Minos; (8) he must drive away the carnivorous mares of Diomedes; (9) he must secure the girdle of Hippolyta, Queen of the Amazons; (10) he must bring back the oxen belonging to the monster Geryoneus; (11) he must bring back the golden apples of the Hesperides; and

(12) he must bring back Cerberus, the three-headed dog of the Underworld.

Jupiter (jōō′pə·tər), king of the gods, Hercules' father.

Alcmena (ălk·mē′nē), a mortal woman, Hercules' mother.

Juno (jōō′nō), Jupiter's wife. Jealous of mortal Alcmena, she hopes to cause Hercules' death and thus be avenged.

Eurystheus (yōō·rĭs′thōōs), Hercules' cousin. Acting for Juno, he assigns the twelve labors.

Rhadamanthus (răd′ə·măn′thəs), Hercules' tutor, killed by Hercules when he punishes the boy.

Amphitryon (ăm·fĭt′rĭ·ən), Hercules' foster father. He rears the boy as a shepherd, high in the mountains.

HEREWARD THE WAKE

Author: Charles Kingsley (1819-1875)
Time of action: Eleventh century
First published: 1866

PRINCIPAL CHARACTERS

Hereward Leofricsson (Hereward the Wake), a handsome, bold, adventurous Saxon thane and outlaw; a high-spirited, rebellious, irreligious youth who later becomes a great knight and leader of the English against the Normans. After his marriage to Alftruda he again becomes what he was before Torfrida inspired him to heroic stature—a toper and an idle boaster. Though he makes his peace with William, he has many Norman enemies who cause his imprisonment and finally bring about his murder.

Lady Godiva, his mother, who causes him to be declared an outlaw, an action for which she later asks his pardon.

Leofric, Lord of Bourne, a Saxon nobleman, father of Hereward, whom he outlaws at Lady Godiva's request.

Torfrida, Hereward's blue-eyed, ravenhaired first wife and mother of his daughter, also named Torfrida. She falsely declares herself a sorceress to gain annulment of her marriage to Hereward. Though he had betrayed her with Alftruda, Torfrida loyally claims his butchered body and buries it. She herself later is put in the same grave.

Alftruda, Hereward's second wife with whom he committed adultery before marrying her.

Martin Lightfoot, a faithful companion in Hereward's wanderings. He goes mad with grief after Hereward's murder.

William the Conqueror, Duke of Normandy and King of England.

Gilbert of Ghent, the stout, hearty guardian of Alftruda and sometime friend of Hereward; the leader of a group of men who arrest Hereward on various charges of enmity to William.

Harold, King of England, killed in the Battle of Hastings.

Abbot Brand, aged, infirm uncle of Hereward. He dies after warning Hereward of English drunkenness, French cleverness, and the doom of those who live by the sword.

Baldwin of Flanders, a powerful ruler of the Lowlands of Western Europe for whom Hereward performs valiant services.

Sir Ascelin, a knight who plots against Hereward and severs his head after his murder.

Ivo Taillebois and

Hugh of Evermue, two Normans who attack Hereward from behind and run him through with lances.

A HERO OF OUR TIME

Author: Mikhail Yurievich Lermontov (1814-1841)
Time of action: 1830-1838
First published: 1839

PRINCIPAL CHARACTERS

The First Narrator, the "I" of the novel, who is supposedly the author himself. On a trip he meets Maksim Maksimich (the second narrator), who tells him of his friendship with Grigoriy Aleksandrovich Pechorin (the third narrator). The first narrator comes into possession of Pechorin's journal and, on the diarist's death, publishes from it three tales just as they were written.

Maksim Maksimich (mäk·sǐm′ mäk·sǐm′-ǐch), the second narrator. He tells to the first narrator the story of his friendship with Grigoriy Aleksandrovich Pechorin (the third narrator). Later, scorned by Pechorin, he angrily throws away his friend's diary, which he had been saving, and the journal falls into the hands of the first narrator.

Grigoriy Aleksandrovich Pechorin (grǐ-gō′rǐy ä·lěk·sän′drə·vǐch pě·chō′rǐn), the third narrator, the "Hero of Our Time."

A companion of Maksim Maksimich at a frontier post in the Caucasus, he later scorns his old friend, who throws away his journal. The diary is rescued by the first narrator who publishes excerpts from it, thus making Pechorin the third narrator in the novel.

Bela (bě′lə), a beautiful Princess,
Azamat (ä·zä·mät′), Bela's younger brother, and
Kazbich (käz·bǐch′), a bandit, three characters in Maksim Maksimich's tale of his friendship with Grigoriy Aleksandrovich Pechorin.

Yanko (yän′kə), a smuggler. He is a character in the first tale from the journal of Grigoriy Aleksandrovich Pechorin.

Princess Mary, the daughter of Princess Ligovskoy,
Grushnitski (grŏŏsh·nǐts′kǐy), Princess Mary's suitor, and

Vera (vĕ·rə), a former sweetheart of Grigoriy Aleksandrovich Pechorin, three characters from the second tale of Pechorin's journal.

Lieutenant Vulich (vōō'lĭch), a Cossack officer in the third tale from the journal of Grigoriy Aleksandrovich Pechorin.

HERSELF SURPRISED

Author: Joyce Cary (1888-1957)
Time of action: First quarter of the twentieth century
First published: 1941

PRINCIPAL CHARACTERS

Sara Monday, an open-hearted, self-indulgent cook whose thoughtless behavior has a way of getting her in trouble. Finally, landing in jail, she looks at herself, examines her weaknesses, and resolves, with the help of her newly found self-knowledge, to regain her "character" and keep it when her sentence is over.

Matthew (Matt) Monday, Sara Monday's husband. An ineffectual man dominated by his family, his marriage to Sara emancipates him until his jealousy of Gulley Jimson destroys the self-confidence he has achieved.

Gulley Jimson, an artist who persuades the widowed Sara Monday to live with him after she learns that he has a legal wife and cannot marry her. He mistreats Sara, who leaves him, but he never loses his hold over her, and eventually he is the cause of her arrest and imprisonment for the indiscretions she commits to support him.

Mr. Hickson, an art collector and a friend of Sara and Matt Monday.

Mr. Wilcher, the employer and, later, the lover of Sara Monday. His plans to marry Sara are interrupted by her arrest and imprisonment.

Nina, the supposed wife of Gulley Jimson.

Blanche Wilcher, Mr. Wilcher's niece by marriage.

Clarissa Hipper, Blanche Wilcher's sister.

A HIGH WIND RISING

Author: Elsie Singmaster (Mrs. E. S. Lewars, 1879-1958)
Time of action: 1728-1755
First published: 1942

PRINCIPAL CHARACTERS

Johann Sebastian Schantz (jō'hän sē-bäs'tĭ·än shänts), called **Bastian** or **Owkwari-owira** (Young Bear), a white boy freed from the Mohawk Indians by Weiser.

Ottilia Zimmer (o'tē'lyä tsĭm'mėr), an orphan who is first seen by Bastian among the immigrants in Philadelphia. He locates her later in Lancaster and marries her. She is attacked by Indians and left for dead but recovers and returns to safety.

Margaretta (mär'gä·rä'tä) and **Gertraud** (gėrt'roud), their twin daughters who are later stolen by Indians.

Conrad Weiser (kŏn'räd vī'sėr), an Indian Agent and interpreter who helps keep the Six Nations loyal to the British.

Anna Eve Weiser (än·nä ā'fä vī'sèr), Conrad's wife, who brings up Bastian until he can be taken to Anna Sabilla Schantz.

Anna Maria (än·nä mä·rē'ä), Weiser's daughter, in love with Bastian.

Anna Sabilla Schantz (än·nä sä·bǐ'lä shänts), a pioneer matriarch and the grandmother of Bastian.

Margaretta (mär'gä·rā'tä), her daughter, who runs away with an English trader.

Nicholas (ni'kō·läs), Anna Sabilla's paralyzed brother.

Skelet (skĕ·lĕt'), a sickly, humpbacked Delaware Indian, befriended by Anna, who teaches woodlore to Bastian. Chiefly moved by greed, he repays Anna by rescuing her and the twins during an In-dian massacre, and he returns with them to the settlement.

The Rev. Henry Melchior Muhlenburg (hăn'rē mĕl'shē·ôr mōō'lĕn·bŏŏrg), who eventually marries Anna Weiser.

Sibby Heil (sǐ'bē hīl), who is in love with Bastian.

Israel Fitch (ēs'rä·āl fĭtsh), a trader who buys Anna Sabilla's carved puppets.

General Edward Braddock, who tries to drive the French out of Ohio.

Shekellimy, a Delaware chief friendly to Weiser.

Sassoonan, another Delaware chief.

Tanacharison and
Scarouady, Indian war leaders when the winds of violence rise in the West.

THE HILL OF DREAMS

Author: Arthur Machen (1863-1947)
Time of action: Late nineteenth century
First published: 1907

PRINCIPAL CHARACTERS

The Reverend Mr. Taylor, an Anglican rector of a rural parish. He becomes unpopular in his parish as his fortunes decline. Because of his misfortunes he is unable to send his son to Oxford. He becomes a moody man.

Lucian Taylor, the rector's son, a studious, reflective lad who is introverted. When he cannot go to Oxford because his father lacks the necessary money, he wanders about the countryside or studies in his father's library the things he likes: ancient history, the medieval church, and works on magic. Because of his introversion and because he refuses to take a job, he becomes something of an outcast. When he tries to become a writer, his attempts are regarded as foolish, es-pecially when he cannot find a publisher. He makes up an imaginary world from his study of Britain in Roman times, and there he lives. He escapes from his imaginary world when he receives a small legacy, only to become an opium addict. His addiction causes his death.

Mrs. Taylor, the rector's wife. She dies while her son is still in his youth.

Annie Morgan, a farmer's daughter who loves Lucian. She shows him how to escape into a world of imagination. She succeeds so well in showing him that he thinks only of himself and his dream world, even when she is about to go away.

473

HILLINGDON HALL

Author: Robert Smith Surtees (1803-1864)
Time of action: Nineteenth century
First published: 1845

PRINCIPAL CHARACTERS

John Jorrocks, "the Cockney Squire," a wealthy London grocer turned sportsman, who buys Hillingdon Hall. He whole-heartedly takes part in the community life. He wins election to Parliament against a marquis and leaves Pigg in charge of Hillingdon Hall when he returns to London for sessions of Parliament.

Julia Jorrocks, his shrewish wife who, as patroness of the local school, forces the girls to wear flashy, tasteless uniforms.

Mr. Westbury, the former owner of Hillingdon Hall.

Joshua Sneakington, called Sneak, the manager of Jorrocks' estate until jailed for cheating his master.

James Pigg, the new manager.

The Duke of Donkeyton, who wants

Jorrocks' political help. He invites the family to dinner and appoints Jorrocks a magistrate.

The Marquis of Bray, the Duke's effeminate son, who finds Emma attractive. He coöperates with Jorrocks in an agricultural society and runs for Parliament.

Bill Bowker, who runs against Bray for Parliament until bought off by the Duke. The farmers then put up Jorrocks to replace him and Jorrocks wins the election by two votes.

Emma Flather, a country girl in search of a husband.

Mrs. Flather, her mother.

James Blake, Emma's favorite until she can do better.

Mrs. Trotter, the neighborhood gossip.

HIPPOLYTUS

Author: Euripides (c. 485-c. 406 B.C.)
Time of action: Remote antiquity
First presented: 428 B.C.

PRINCIPAL CHARACTERS

Hippolytus (hĭ·pŏl'ĭ·tŭs), the son of Theseus by Hippolyta, Queen of the Amazons. Because he pays exclusive worship to the virgin goddess Artemis, Aphrodite, the goddess of sexual love, determines to punish him by making Phaedra, the wife of Theseus, fall in love with her stepson. Phaedra is dying of her guilty passion; when her nurse reveals her state to Hippolytus, after swearing him to secrecy, he is horrified. Phaedra kills herself for shame, but because Hippolytus has shown no pity

for her plight she leaves a tablet saying that she has killed herself because Hippolytus had raped her. Theseus, calling down on his son one of the infallible curses granted him by Poseidon, asks that Hippolytus be killed that day; in addition, he pronounces a sentence of exile against him. In the subsequent interview with his father, Hippolytus reveals the same inability to show the affection, understanding, and tact that he had exhibited earlier in the interview with the nurse. He cannot reveal the truth and his de-

474

fense becomes an unpleasant exhibition of ostentatious purity, a long catalogue of all his virtues: his piety, his seriousness, his modesty, and his chastity. His aloofness and self-satisfaction can be related to his illegitimacy, which is repeatedly emphasized; abandoned by his father and ashamed of his mother, he has cultivated his aloofness, revolted against the passion of love, and cut himself off from life itself. Hippolytus is mortally wounded as he prepares to leave the country; a tidal wave delivers a miraculous bull to frighten the horses which draw his chariot, and he is dragged behind the panic-stricken animals. When he is brought before his father, Artemis reveals his innocence. Hippolytus releases Theseus from blood-guilt and the two are reconciled.

Phaedra (fē'drə), Theseus' wife and the means of Aphrodite's vengeance on her stepson Hippolytus. She is introduced in the last stages of voluntary starvation, weak and delirious, and the nurse is able to wring a confession of her passion for Hippolytus from her; but she fails to forbid absolutely any action on the part of the nurse. After Hippolytus refuses the nurse's plea for help, Phaedra feels she must kill herself to preserve the honor of her children. It is Hippolytus' shocked brutality that leads her to a desire for personal vengeance. She is not entirely guiltless and hopes that Hippolytus will learn true modesty.

Theseus (thē'sōōs, thē'si·əs), King of Athens. His hasty temperament causes passion and jealousy to blind him to anything but Phaedra's accusation; he fails to understand, or to make any real effort to understand, his son. In fact, his attack on Hippolytus' virtues is brutal and unfair. His undue haste is his chief weakness.

Aphrodite (ă·frō·dī'tē), the goddess of beauty and patroness of love. She speaks the prologue and reveals her plan to punish Hippolytus. Her presence is felt throughout the drama as a personification of one of the forces in conflict which give the play universal significance.

Artemis (är'tə·mĭs), the virgin goddess and goddess of the chase. She is worshiped by Hippolytus, reveals his innocence to Theseus at the close of the play, and vows revenge on Aphrodite. She is not so clear-cut a representation of one quality as Aphrodite, but she is presented as a form of beauty. Hippolytus' prayers to her reveal his ability to put into words those feelings he cannot express for Theseus or Phaedra.

The Nurse, Phaedra's devoted servant. Although cynical by nature, she is at first shocked by Phaedra's confession of passion for Hippolytus. Later she deliberately tries to persuade her mistress to give way to her passion and abandon her plan of suicide. She reveals Phaedra's passion to Hippolytus but does so in the hope of preventing Phaedra's death.

The Chorus. They are palace women who announce the arrival of various characters.

A Servant of Hippolytus. In his attempt to rebuke his master for failing to acknowledge properly the powers of Aphrodite, he reveals Hippolytus' insolence to her.

THE HISTORY OF COLONEL JACQUE

Author: Daniel Defoe (1660-1731)
Time of action: Late seventeenth century
First published: 1722

Colonel Jacque, called Colonel Jack, an adventurer who commits many misdeeds. An illegitimate child, he is given to a nurse who dies when Jack is but ten years old. Having to fend for himself, Jack the waif becomes a successful though sometimes conscience-stricken pickpocket. He is tossed by fate into the American Colonies and becomes an indentured servant on a plantation, where he becomes a successful and kindly overseer of Negro slaves. When freed from his period of indenture, he becomes a landowner in Virginia. Leaving his plantation in the hands of his faithful overseer, he returns to England and marries. Unfortunate in love, he attacks his wife's lover and flees to France to become a professional soldier, fighting with the French against his countrymen. After another sojourn in Virginia and many adventures, he finally repents of his life of crime and violence, seeks a pardon from the English crown, and settles down in England, persuaded that only the goodness of God has saved him. He hopes that his life story will make other persons repent of their sins and become good Christians.

Captain Jack, Colonel Jack's thoroughly evil foster brother. He is a witty, intelligent rogue who introduces Jack to the picking of pockets. Captain Jack rebels against indentured servitude, flees to England to resume his criminal life, and is at last hanged as a common criminal.

Will, a pickpocket and a partner in crime of Colonel Jack. Will is a vicious man who murders as well as robs. Will's hanging at Newgate Prison saddens Colonel Jack, even though he knows the punishment is deserved.

Jack's First Wife, an unfaithful woman, as well as a gambler and spendthrift. She turns up years later as an indentured servant and a repentant woman. She and Colonel Jack are remarried and live happily for many years in their old age.

Jack's Second Wife, the daughter of an Italian innkeeper, who is unfaithful to her husband.

Jack's Third Wife, a beautiful and virtuous woman who becomes a drunkard and finally commits suicide. By her Colonel Jack has three children.

Jack's Fourth Wife, an older woman who provides Jack with a pleasant home and is good to his children. She dies after a fall.

THE HISTORY OF MR. POLLY

Author: H. G. Wells (1866-1946)
Time of action: Early twentieth century
First published: 1909

The "Historian," an anonymous first-person narrator, brisk, pleasantly jocular, and rather Dickensian. Although he has no part in the action, he provides humorous commentary on it.

Mr. Alfred Polly, a sensitive, dyspeptic petty tradesman, given to romantic dreams, mispronunciation, and pungent phrases. After starting as a draper's assistant, he was left some money by his father, and acquired a shop and a wife. Fifteen years later Mr. Polly is bald and chubby, and imagination and good will have been stifled by his neighbors and his wife. He bungles a suicide attempt but unexpectedly becomes a hero when he saves an old woman from the fire he has started. A short time later he runs away. He wanders until he finds a wayside inn kept by a plump woman who is threatened by her worthless nephew, called Uncle Jim. Mr. Polly shows his pluck by standing up, rather quakingly, to Jim and defeating him in a series of comic fights. Five years later he returns home, finds himself unneeded, and goes back to the inn for good.

Mrs. Miriam Polly, his dowdy, unimaginative wife, a poor housekeeper and a worse cook, whom Mr. Polly married on the rebound from an abortive romance. Under the illusion that she would be tidy and affectionate, he soon learns otherwise. After he disappears and his supposd corpse is found, she and her sister start a tea shop with the insurance money. She is horrified when her husband returns to the village and is glad to see him go away again.

The Plump Woman, the proprietress of the Potwell Inn, a warm, easy-going, motherly person. Mr. Polly immediately likes her and takes a job as a handyman at the inn. She gives him permission to leave when Uncle Jim shows up, but the devotion she inspires induces Mr. Polly to defend her.

Uncle Jim, a short, tough, mean ex-convict. A comic villain, he teaches the plump woman's granddaughter to swear, goes after Mr. Polly with beer bottles, an axe, and a gun, but complains that Mr. Polly does not fight fair when he finds himself dumped in the river. Eventually he runs off, drowns, and gets mistaken for Mr. Polly.

Polly, the plump woman's granddaughter, a sprightly nine-year-old who at first worships Uncle Jim and then comes to admire Mr. Polly.

Aunt Larkins, the mother of Mrs. Polly. She misrepresents her daughters and cries vulgarly at the wedding.

Annie Larkins, her daughter and Mrs. Polly's sister. One of Mr. Polly's kissing cousins, she enjoys vigorous embraces and laughs loudly at all his jokes. Then, as a middle-aged frump, she becomes Miriam's partner in the tea shop venture.

Minnie Larkins, another sister of Miriam. Though ill-bred and common, she almost won Mr. Polly for a husband.

Christabel, a coy, pretty schoolgirl, Mr. Polly's only romantic interest. For ten days he courts her as she sits on the schoolyard wall, but at last her teen-age schoolmates giggle and she runs off, shattering Mr. Polly's dream.

Parsons, Mr. Polly's best friend when he was a draper's assistant. Chubby, imaginative, a lover of poetry, Parsons gets in a battle with the store manager over a window display, is fired, and leaves.

Platt, the third member of the Parsons, Polly, Platt trio, also a clerk.

Mr. Howard Johnson, the cousin who puts Mr. Polly up for a while, urges him to buy a shop, and becomes sullen at the loss of rent when Mr. Polly marries.

Mrs. Johnson, his optimistic, vulgar wife.

Mr. Garvace, the store manager who fired Parsons.

Rusper, a shopkeeper, ignorant but with pretense to knowledge, whose quarrel with middle-aged Mr. Polly ends in a law court.

Rumbold, another obnoxious, mulish neighbor.

Mrs. Rumbold, his mother, the old woman Mr. Polly saves in a fire.

Hicks, a grumpy, gossipy, low-bred neighbor.

Mr. Voules, a fat, stupid man who takes charge of Mr. Polly's wedding.

Uncle Pentstemon, an old, crotchety, offensive relative.

Mrs. Amy Punt, another odious relative.

477

HIZA-KURIGE

Author: Jippensha Ikku (1765-1831)
Time of action: Late eighteenth and early nineteenth centuries
First published: 1802-1814

PRINCIPAL CHARACTERS

Yajirobei, or Yaji for short. Born into a well-to-do merchant family but now in greatly reduced circumstances as a result of his dissipations, he travels about Japan and becomes involved in a variety of broadly humorous episodes. More quick-witted than virtuous, he is a recognizable type of picaresque traveler. His creation was, however, an innovation and a popular one; previous Japanese travel accounts did not make use of this kind of robust and realistic traveler.

Hana-no-suke, an actor, later renamed **Kitahachi, or Kita** for short. Exuberant and shrewd, Kita is Yaji's traveling companion and shares in his adventures.

H.M.S. PINAFORE

Author: W. S. Gilbert (1836-1911)
Time of action: Latter half of the nineteenth century
First presented: 1878

PRINCIPAL CHARACTERS

Sir Joseph Porter, First Lord of the Admiralty, the pompous ruler of the Queen's Navy. He has reached his exalted station by sticking to his desk and never going to sea. Wherever he goes, he is accompanied by a host of admiring female relatives. A great equalitarian, he believes a British tar the equal of every man except himself. He intends to condescend to marry Josephine, and makes an official pronouncement that love levels all ranks, but in practice finds some limitations in this dogma.

Captain Corcoran, the well-bred Captain of the "Pinafore." He is hardly ever sick at sea and seldom uses profanity. When his daughter is discovered eloping with a common seaman, he allows a "damme" to slip, greatly shocking Sir Joseph. When he loses his exalted station, he takes his former nurse, Little Buttercup, to be his wife and promises that he will hardly ever be untrue to her.

Mrs. Cripps (Little Buttercup), a Portsmouth Bumboat Woman. She confesses that many years ago when she practiced baby-farming she mixed up Captain Corcoran and Ralph Rackstraw in their cradles, causing a great social upheaval in later years. Her plump and pleasing presence captivates the Captain, who proposes to her when he loses his social standing.

Ralph Rackstraw, the smartest lad in all the fleet. He loves the Captain's daughter, though painfully conscious of their difference in social station. When he and the Captain are discovered to be victims of mistaken identity, he, being the rightful captain, joyfully marries Josephine.

Josephine, the Captain's daughter. She would gladly laugh her rank to scorn for love if Ralph were more highly born or she more lowly. Sir Joseph's pronouncement about the leveling power of love convinces her that she should accept Ralph.

478

Dick Deadeye, a hideously ugly and deformed able seaman. Even the kindhearted Buttercup admits that he is a plain man. Finding that even sweet sentiments cause horror from his lips, Dick becomes embittered, deserts his shipmates, and betrays Ralph and Josephine to the Captain. He takes malicious pleasure in the foiling of the young lovers, but fades into insignificance in the general rejoicing at the end.

The Boatswain, a British tar who takes pride in being an Englishman. Along with Buttercup and most of his shipmates he supports the young lovers in their plans to elope.

Cousin Hebe, the leader of Sir Joseph's numerous sisters, cousins, and aunts who follow him adoringly. When Sir Joseph feels that Josephine's social decline is too great for even love to level her rank with his, Cousin Hebe decides that they should make a triple wedding along with Ralph and Josephine and the now-seaman Corcoran and Buttercup. After the wedding it will be farewell to the sisters and the cousin and the aunts, for Hebe will brook no rivals.

THE HOLY TERRORS

Author: Jean Cocteau (1891-   )
Time of action: The present
First published: 1929

PRINCIPAL CHARACTERS

Paul (pōl'), a sensitive, imaginative adolescent living insulated from the real world. With his sister Elisabeth he inhabits the Room, the one material reality of their two lives, and with her plays the Game—a willful withdrawing into the world of the imagination. With the appearance of outsiders this world is threatened, and in the fight to recapture it, Paul is destroyed.

Elisabeth (ä·lē·zá·bĕt'), Paul's older sister. Utterly absorbed in her brother and their life together in the dream world of the Room and the Game, she is terrified by, and retaliates against, any threat to their isolation. Finally, in a successful effort to separate Paul from Agatha, whom he loves, she brings about her brother's destruction and her own.

Agatha (à·gà·tä'), Elisabeth's friend, whose devotion to Paul threatens the dream world of the brother and sister and finally brings about its destruction.

Gérard (zhā·rár'), a friend of Paul and Elisabeth. He is persuaded by Elisabeth to marry Agatha, whose devotion to Paul threatens Elisabeth's domination of her brother.

Dargelos (dár·zhə·lō'), the school hero, worshiped by the fragile Paul for his strength and beauty.

Mariette (mà·ryĕt'), the nurse who loves and cares for Paul and Elisabeth.

Michael, an American to whom Elisabeth transfers her dream world when her dominance over Paul is threatened. He marries Elisabeth, only to be killed a few hours after the wedding.

THE HONEST WHORE, PARTS ONE AND TWO

Author: Thomas Dekker (c. 1572-1632?) (Part One with Thomas Middleton, 1580-1627)
Time of action: Sixteenth century
First presented: Part One, 1604; Part Two, c. 1605

Gasparo Trebazzi (gäs'pä·rō trĕ·bä'tsē), the Duke of Milan, a just ruler but a somewhat tyrannical father.

Infelice (ēn·fä·lē'chä), his daughter who, despite his opposition, marries her beloved Hippolito. Years later she is furious to find evidence of his infidelity to her, and she urges severe punishment for her rival, Bellafront.

Count Hippolito (ē·pō'lē·tō), Infelice's husband. A paragon of virtue in his youth, he converts Bellafront to an honest life. He later finds her irresistible and tries to make her his mistress, betraying the wife to whom he had been so devoted.

Bellafront (bĕl'ə·frŭnt), a courtesan who is redeemed by her love for Hippolito. She bears her husband's cruelties patiently and remains faithful to him, refusing Hippolito's offers of affection.

Matheo (mä·tä·ō), a dissolute courtier who unwillingly marries Bellafront and forces her to lead a wretched existence

while spending their meager funds on luxuries for himself.

Candido (kän'dē·dō), the patient linen draper whom no insults or vexations can move to anger.

Viola (vē·ō'lä), Candido's shrewish first wife, who is determined to vex him. Her death leaves Candido free to marry a young bride.

Fustigo (fŭs'tē·gō), Candido's brother, a bawdy sailor.

Orlando Friscobaldo, (ôr·län'dō frēs'kō-bäl·dō), Bellafront's father, a man of strong temper and deep affection. He pretends to scorn his daughter, but he cares for her, disguised as an old servant, even though he despises her husband.

Candido's Bride, a woman potentially as shrewish as her predecessor. She is tamed by her husband's first show of firmness.

Mrs. Horseleech, an old bawd.

Botts, her colleague, an equally corrupt procurer.

HONEY IN THE HORN

Author: H. L. Davis (1896-1960)
Time of action: 1906-1908
First published: 1935

PRINCIPAL CHARACTERS

Wade Shiveley, suspected of robbery and murder, though he declares himself innocent. He is hated by his father because he has previously killed his own brother in a fight over an Indian woman. Later he is framed by his relative, Clay Calvert, and hanged by a posse for another murder he did not commit. After his death he is proved innocent of the murder and robbery for which he was originally jailed.

Uncle Press Shiveley, Wade's father. He sends his son, whom he hates and has

vowed to kill, a gun loaded with blank cartridges; he hopes Wade will be killed while trying to break out of jail.

Clay Calvert, who is either Wade's son or Wade's brother's son. Nobody ever knew which. He hates Wade but believes him innocent. Sought by the authorities as an accomplice in Wade's escape from jail, he becomes a migratory worker and takes up with a horse trader's daughter. He drifts about Oregon, always seeking and never finding a place where he and his woman can make a real home.

The Horse Trader, a wanderer who ekes out a living trading horses and having his family pick hops in season. He is a weak man who loses most of the family's money by gambling. He dies of natural causes. He is suspected by Clay of having committed the crimes for which Wade is blamed.

Luce, the horse trader's daughter. She takes up with Clay and lives with him. She claims to have shot the man whose murder is blamed on Wade, but her lover believes she is only trying to shield her father, even after his death. She never completely trusts Clay because she is afraid that he may leave her.

Clark Burdon, leader of a band of settlers in eastern Oregon. He befriends Clay.

THE HOOSIER SCHOOLMASTER

Author: Edward Eggleston (1837-1902)
Time of action: c. 1850
First published: 1871

PRINCIPAL CHARACTERS

Ralph Hartsook, the schoolmaster at Flat Creek, Indiana. He makes a place for himself in the community until his enemies accuse him of being a thief. He escapes a mob and gives himself up to the authorities. He is tried and found innocent. Being a friendly and democratic man, he tries to help everyone. He falls in love with Hannah, a hired girl, and marries her.

Hannah Thomson, the "bound girl" at the Means home. She defeats the schoolmaster in a spelling bee. He falls in love with her and marries her.

Bud Means, one of the older pupils in Ralph's school. He becomes the schoolmaster's friend. Chagrined when he is ignored by Martha Hawkins, he falls in with evil companions, but he saves himself and tries to help the schoolmaster.

Martha Hawkins, daughter of the local squire. She is in love with bashful Bud.

Dr. Small, a thief. He is Ralph's enemy and tries to lay his crime upon the schoolmaster's head. At Ralph's trial he incriminates himself and is later hanged for his misdeeds.

Pete Jones, Dr. Small's accomplice. He tries to lay the blame for the robbery on

Mr. Pearson, an honest man. He and his brother are sent to prison as punishment for their part in the robbery.

Walter Johnson, another of Dr. Small's accomplices. He is Ralph's cousin. He turns out to be a religious man who cannot keep his crime hidden. He turns state's evidence and goes unpunished.

Shocky Thomson, Hannah's young brother.

Bill Means, Bud's brother, one of Ralph's pupils.

Granny Sander, a gossipy woman who spreads evil rumors about Ralph.

Mirandy Means, sister of Bud and Bill. Infatuated with the schoolmaster, she tries to come between Ralph and Hannah.

Mrs. Means, mother of Mirandy, Bud, and Bill. She testifies against Ralph at the robbery trial to spite him for spurning Mirandy.

Mr. Pearson, a basketmaker who took in Shocky when his blind mother went to the poorhouse. He is an honest man wrongly accused of the theft.

Mrs. Matilda White, Ralph Hartsook's

aunt. She refuses to take in the unfortunate Mrs. Thomson.

Miss Nancy Sawyer, Ralph's home-town friend who takes in Shocky to prevent his being bound out.

Mrs. Thomson, Hannah and Shocky's mother, a poor but honest widow who is blind and who is finally forced to go to the poorhouse. Later she is able to make a home for Shocky again through the kindness of Nancy Sawyer.

HORACE

Author: Pierre Corneille (1606-1684)
Time of action: Remote antiquity
First presented: 1640

PRINCIPAL CHARACTERS

Horace (ô·ràs'), a Roman warrior. With the cities of Rome and Alba at war, the battle is to be decided by armed combat between three heroes from each side. Horace and his two brothers, the Roman combatants, are victorious over their prospective Alban brother-in-law, Curiace, and his two brothers. All for honor and country, Horace taunts his sister Camille with the glory of Rome, and he kills her when she declares that his deed is not patriotism but murder. He defends this act as one of justice, but he is aware that his glory is dimmed because of it, and he wishes to die. The King decrees that Horace's fate shall rest with the gods.

Sabine (sà·bēn'), Horace's Alban wife and the sister of the Alban brothers killed by Horace in combat. Torn between her loyalty to the city of her birth and the city of her husband, she pleads

in vain the cause of home and family against that of honor and patriotism. In despair over her husband's killing of her brothers and the murder of his sister, she wishes only to die.

Camille (kà·mē'y), Horace's sister and the prospective wife of Curiace. She is killed by Horace when she reviles Rome in her grief over the death of Curiace.

Curiace (kü·ryàs'), Sabine's brother and the prospective husband of Camille. He is killed in combat with Horace.

Old Horace, Horace's father, an ardent patriot and a former warrior.

Julie (zhü·lē'), the confidante of Sabine and Camille.

Valère (và·lēr'), a Roman warrior.

Tulle (tül'), the ruler of Rome.

THE HORSE'S MOUTH

Author: Joyce Cary (1888-1957)
Time of action: The 1930's
First published: 1944

PRINCIPAL CHARACTERS

Gulley Jimson, an aging unconventional artist, ex-jailbird, and occasional thief who has sudden grandiose inspirations for big paintings on such subjects as the Fall and the Creation but who,

dogged by ill luck, cannot manage to finish them. His only paintings anyone wants are nudes he did years ago of Sara Monday and which he cannot get from her or from Hickson, who ob-

482

tained most of them. After Gulley accidentally kills Sara, he returns home and paints furiously, trying to finish the Creation before his arrest. In a fall from his scaffold he suffers a stroke from which he awakes in an ambulance taking him to jail.

Sara Monday, Gulley's one-time model and former mistress, now a fat, frowzy old woman. Visited by Gulley and Coker, she signs a statement that she let Hickson have the paintings she stole from Gulley and she vainly tries to reawaken Gulley's old interest in her. She refuses to give up a few of the nudes which she kept and which she likes to look at, wistfully remembering her former beauty. The last time Gulley attempts to get a painting from her, he angrily pushes her down the cellar stairs and breaks her back.

Coker, a barmaid, a short, stout, homely woman to whom Gulley owes money and who makes repeated efforts to get it by buying paints for his pictures and urging him to get some of Sara's pictures from Hickson. When she becomes pregnant and loses her job, she moves into Gulley's shed with her mother.

Nosy, a young aspiring artist, green-eyed, hay-haired, and flat-nosed; a stammerer. He worships art and Gulley and he helps Gulley with his painting of the Creation.

Mr. Hickson, an elderly art collector who obtained from Sara a number of beautiful nudes which she had stolen when she and Gulley broke up. Though he obtained them legitimately, he is willing to pay Gulley a small sum when Gulley visits him about them. On Hickson's death the Sara nudes are given to the nation and Gulley becomes famous.

Professor Alabaster, a critic who plans a biography of Gulley.

Sir William Beeder, Gulley's benefactor, a wealthy art collector whose London apartment (during Sir William's absence) Gulley appropriates and ransacks for pawnable items in order to buy canvas and paints.

HORSESHOE ROBINSON

Author: John P. Kennedy (1795-1870)
Time of action: 1780
First published: 1835

PRINCIPAL CHARACTERS

Sgt. Galbraith (Horseshoe) Robinson, a shrewd, rustic, good-natured colonial patriot. Tall, broad, brawny, and erect, he is brave, scornful of the British and their Tory supporters, and ingenious in aiding Butler and others among the patriots. A somewhat idealized version of the pioneer, he may be compared with such historical ones as Daniel Boone and David Crockett and with a fictional one like Leatherstocking.

Major Arthur Butler, his handsome, gentlemanly friend who is captured along with Horseshoe by Tories, escapes with the aid of John Ramsay and Mary Musgrove, is captured again by British troops, and is rescued this time by Horseshoe. With the end of the Tory ascendancy in South Carolina, Butler and his wife Mildred are free to live a long and happy life together.

Philip Lindsay, a Loyalist because of financial interests in England but sympathetic with Mildred over her distress at Butler's capture. He is fatally wounded while accompanying Tyrrel in a search for Mildred, who had gone to seek clemency for Butler from Cornwallis.

Before dying, Lindsay forgives Mildred and Henry for their support of the patriot cause.

Mildred, Lindsay's daughter, secretly married to Butler for a year but forbidden by her father to see him because of his colonial army connections. In her determination to save Butler from harm she is reminiscent of one or two of Cooper's intrepid heroines—even to her fainting when she greets her dear rescued husband.

Henry, Lindsay's son, sympathetic to the American cause. He fights at King's Mountain and discovers Tyrrel's body after the battle.

Wat Adair, a Tory woodman and deceitful former friend of Butler, who thinks him a patriot. He is captured at King's Mountain and punished for his treachery.

Tyrrel, a disguised English officer who visits the Lindsay home supposedly to enlist aid for the Loyalists but actually to court Mildred, who despises him. He is killed at King's Mountain.

Mary Musgrove, a patriot, Wat Adair's

pretty relative who warns Butler of Wat's treachery and who later informs the captured Butler of rescue plans for him.

John Ramsay, Mary's sweetheart, a trooper who aids in Butler's first escape but is killed shortly afterward.

James Curry, a rascally Tory spy masquerading as Tyrrel's servant. At King's Mountain he is captured by rebel forces.

General Gates, commander of the patriot forces.

Lord Cornwallis, gentlemanly commander of the British forces.

Allen Musgrove, Mary's elderly father.

Stephen Foster, a woodman and lieutenant of mounted patriot riflemen.

Michael Lynch, a friend of the Adairs. An opportunist willing to support either side, he submits to Wat's conviction that Tory support is more profitable because the Tories will win.

Hugh Habershaw, captain of a gang of ruffians, including Curry, who capture Butler and Horseshoe.

THE HOUSE BY THE CHURCHYARD

Author: Joseph Sheridan Le Fanu (1814-1873)
Time of action: Late eighteenth century
First published: 1863

PRINCIPAL CHARACTERS

Mr. Mervyn, the son of Lord Dunoran, who was an Irish nobleman wrongly convicted and executed for the murder of a man named Beauclerc and whose estates and title were taken from his family because of his conviction. Mervyn takes a house in Chapelizod, a Dublin suburb, in order to find the real murderer and clear his father's name. With the help of Zekiel Irons he aids in proving Paul Dangerfield guilty of Beauclerc's murder, and thus his father's innocence.

He regains his family's good name, and by official action the title and estates are returned to him as his father's heir. As the new Lord Dunoran, he marries the daughter of the commanding general of the Royal Irish Artillery.

Paul Dangerfield (Charles Archer), a stranger who comes to Chapelizod about the same time as Mr. Mervyn. He is rich and liberal, qualities which quickly make him popular. He is really Charles

Archer, the murderer of Beauclerc. He beats Dr. Sturk and later arranges for an operation for the doctor, hoping he will die, as the doctor was a witness to the murder of Beauclerc. Dangerfield's good works make it difficult for the authorities to believe he is really Charles Archer and a murderer. His guilt is ascertained; however, he cheats the gallows by dying in jail while awaiting trial.

Zekiel Irons, Archer's accomplice in the murder of Beauclerc. He lives in Chapelizod and becomes alarmed when Archer appears as Paul Dangerfield. Irons goes to Mervyn and gives him information about the murder of Beauclerc and a later murder committed by Archer.

Dr. Barnaby Sturk, a surgeon at the local garrison and a witness to Beauclerc's murder. He threatens Dangerfield, who then beats him terribly. Dr. Sturk regains consciousness long enough to give depositions revealing Archer-Dangerfield as his own assailant and the murderer of Beauclerc.

Charles Nutter, a man suspected of being Dr. Sturk's assailant. He finally proves that he is innocent.

Mrs. Sturk, the doctor's wife.

THE HOUSE BY THE MEDLAR TREE

Author: Giovanni Verga (1840-1922)
Time of action: Mid-nineteenth century
First published: 1881

PRINCIPAL CHARACTERS

Padron 'Ntoni Malavoglia, head of the once-prosperous family that lives by the medlar tree.

Bastianazzo, his son. His ambition to take black beans to Riposto to sell at a huge profit ruins the family when his boat, the "Provvidenza," is wrecked.

La Longa, Bastianazzo's wife, who distrusts Uncle Crucifix, the moneylender, but signs over to his assignee her rights to the house when he repeatedly demands payment for his loan on the lost beans. She dies of cholera.

'Ntoni, their oldest son, who returns from military service and becomes a smuggler. Caught, he is sentenced to the galleys for five years.

Luca, their second son, who is conscripted and killed in battle.

Alessio, their youngest son, who earns the money to regain his house by the medlar tree.

Mena, their oldest daughter.

Lia, their youngest daughter, loved by Don Michele.

Uncle Crucifix Dumbbell, a local usurer who takes over the house after his loan to buy beans is not repaid.

Goosefoot, his assistant. Uncle Crucifix pretends to assign his loan to Goosefoot, hoping collection will thus be easier.

Don Michele, commander of the coast guard, who is stabbed by 'Ntoni.

Alfio Mosca, a carter who loves Mena.

485

THE HOUSE IN PARIS

Author: Elizabeth Bowen (1899-   )
Time of action: After World War I
First published: 1936

PRINCIPAL CHARACTERS

Miss Naomi Fisher, Karen Michaelis' friend. She helps Karen when the latter becomes pregnant and has a child by Max Ebhart, Naomi's fiancé. Her home is the setting for the story.

Leopold Moody, a nine-year-old boy. He has come to Naomi's house to see the mother he has never met, Karen Michaelis. When he learns she will not come he tries to be indifferent, but his stoic attitude dissolves into tears. Only Mme. Fisher can console him. He seems pleased when his mother's husband, Ray Forrestier, encourages him to go to his mother with him.

Henrietta Mountjoy, a sympathetic eleven-year-old girl, who tries to console Leopold that day at Naomi's house.

Mme. Fisher, Naomi's invalid mother. She helps young Leopold accept, even if he cannot understand, the world in which he finds himself.

Karen Michaelis, Leopold's mother. After her child's birth she gives up the child and her fiancé, who is not the boy's father. She finally marries her fiancé, Ray Forrestier, and allows him to overrule her resolve not to have her son in their home.

Max Ebhart, once Naomi's fiancé, he is the father of Leopold, the result of a one-night love affair with Karen. Brilliant and sensitive, he is driven by his predicament into suicide. He kills himself by slashing his wrists.

Ray Forrestier, Karen's fiancé at the time of her brief affair with Max. He eventually marries Karen and it is he who insists that Leopold join the family, despite Karen's doubts.

THE HOUSE OF ATREUS

Author: Aeschylus (c. 525-c. 456 B.C.)
Time of action: After the fall of Troy
First presented: 458 B.C.

PRINCIPAL CHARACTERS

Agamemnon (ăʹgə·mĕmʹnŏn), of the doomed House of Atreus, King of Argos and leader of the Greek expedition against Troy. When the Greeks were detained at Aulis, he had been commanded by the gods to sacrifice his daughter Iphigenia, so that the fleet might sail. This deed brought him the hatred of his wife Clytemnestra, who plots his death. On his return to Argos after the fall of Troy, she persuades him to commit the sin of pride by walking on purple car-

pets to enter his palace. Once within the palace, he is murdered in his bath by Clytemnestra and her lover Aegisthus.

Clytemnestra (klīʹtəm·nĕsʹtrə), daughter of Leda and wife of Agamemnon. Infuriated by his sacrifice of their daughter Iphigenia, she murders him and rules Argos with her lover, Aegisthus, until she is killed by her son Orestes.

Cassandra (kă·sănʹdrə), the daughter of

486

King Priam of Troy. She is fated always to prophesy truth but never to be believed. Captured by Agamemnon and brought to Argos, she foretells the King's death and is then killed by Clytemnestra.

Aegisthus (ē·jĭs'thəs), cousin of Agamemnon and the lover of Clytemnestra. After Agamemnon's death he rules Argos with her until he is slain by Orestes.

Orestes (ō·rĕs'tez), the son of Agamemnon and Clytemnestra. After his father's murder, he is driven by his mother and her lover from his heritage of Argos. Returning from exile, he meets his sister Electra at their father's tomb and tells her that he has been commanded by the oracle of Apollo to avenge Agamemnon by killing his murderers. This revenge he carries out, but he is driven mad by the Furies, who pursue him to the Delphi, where he takes refuge in the temple of Apollo. Athena, the goddess of wisdom, appears. Unable to decide the case, she calls in twelve Athenian citizens to act as judges. It is argued against Orestes that Clytemnestra, in killing Agamemnon, had not slain a blood-member of her family and thus did not deserve death. Apollo argues that Clytemnestra, having only nourished the father's seed in her womb, was no blood relation of Orestes, and therefore the latter was innocent. The judges vote six to six, and Orestes is declared free of blood-guilt.

Electra (ē·lĕk'trə), the daughter of Agamemnon and Clytemnestra and sister of Orestes. After the murder of her father and the exile of her brother, she is left alone to mourn Agamemnon's death and to perform the rites at his tomb. There she meets Orestes, who has returned to Argos, but at first does not recognize him. Convinced at last of his identity, she urges him to avenge their father by killing their mother and her lover.

The Furies or **Eumenides** (ū·men'ĭ·dēz), children of Night, whose duty it is to dog the footsteps of murderers and to drive them mad. They pursue Orestes but are balked of their prey by the judges' decision that he is innocent. They rail against the younger gods who have deprived them of their ancient power. They are pacified by Athena, who promises them great honor and reverence if they will remain at Athens as beneficent deities.

Athena (ə·thē'nə), the goddess of wisdom and patron of Athens, she is always on the side of mercy. She defends the new law against the old in the case of Orestes, pacifies the Furies, and changes them into the Eumenides or "gracious ones."

Apollo (ə·pŏl'ō), the god of poetry, music, oracles, and healing. It is he who commands Orestes to avenge his father's death by killing his guilty mother. He then appears at Orestes' trial and defends the accused with the argument that, by killing his mother, Orestes was not guilty of shedding family blood, for the mother, being only the nourisher of the seed, is no relation to her child. Family relationship comes only through the father.

A HOUSE OF GENTLEFOLK

Author: Ivan Turgenev (1818-1883)
Time of action: Nineteenth century
First published: 1858

PRINCIPAL CHARACTERS

Marya Dmitrievna Kalitin (mä'ryə dmĭt'-rĭ·ĕv·nə kä·lĭ'tĭn), a well-to-do widow, about fifty, fadingly pretty, sentimental, self-indulgent, tearful when crossed but

487

sweet otherwise. She is easily taken in by Panshin's blandishments and she succumbs also to Varvara's sly hypocrisy.

Fedor Ivanitch Lavretsky (fyō'dər ĭ·vä'-nĭch läv·rĕt'skĭy), called **Fedya** (fĕ'dyə), her cousin, rosy-cheeked, thick-nosed, curly-haired, well-built. As a boy he was reared according to a Rousseauistic system rigorously applied by his father. After his father's death he attempted to get, in Moscow, a university education to supplement his eccentric, secluded, narrow training. Following his marriage to Varvara he gave up his formal schooling but continued to educate himself through private study. Naïvely trusting his wife to seek her own social entertainment, he was shocked to learn of her infidelity, and he immediately left her. Although he still broods bitterly on Varvara at times, he finds himself falling in love with Lisa. Having learned of Varvara's rumored death, he longs to marry Lisa despite the age difference between them. But his happiness over Lisa's acceptance of his suit is destroyed by Varvara's reappearance. For Lisa's sake and at Marya's insistence he agrees to live with Varvara but only on a formal basis. But he stays with her only briefly. He is finally left with memories of the happy time when he thought Lisa could be his, the only happy moments in his whole life. Lavretsky symbolizes the liberal Russian of Turgenev's day. He has attained a Westernized culture; he loves his country; and he wishes to apply democratic ideas in his relationship with the peasants who till his land according to the agricultural principles he has learned abroad. He resembles in appearance, character, and ideas the hero of "Virgin Soil," Solomin, who feels toward the factory workers as Lavretsky does toward the peasants.

Elisaveta Mihailovna Kalitin, (e·lĭ·zä'vě'tə mĭ·hä'ləv·nə), called **Lisa,** Marya's slender, dark-haired daughter. Thoughtful and deeply religious, she is troubled because Lavretsky had left Varvara and has never seen their daughter. Despite

Varvara's adultery, Lisa believes she should be forgiven and taken back. When it appears that Varvara has died, Lisa at first gently rejects Lavretsky's attentions. Later, recognizing his goodness and deep sincerity, and feeling a spiritual kinship with him despite his indifference to religion, she accepts him. Their happiness is destroyed by Varvara's return. Lisa says goodbye not only to Lavretsky but also to her family and the world, and she becomes a nun. As Lavretsky symbolizes one kind of Russian, Lisa represents another. Her education is limited; she has the standard learning and attainments of a girl of her class; she is traditionalist and conservative in her views. Religion, her comfort and stay from childhood on, offers a retreat in her sorrow.

Varvara Pavlovna (vär·rä'rə päv'ləv·nə), Lavretsky's wife, a lovely, intelligent, charming, and gregarious woman who deceived her husband with a young French lover while giving Lavretsky the impression of being a devoted wife. Taking advantage of the rumor of her death, she leaves Paris and comes with her daughter to Vassilyevskoe to seek a reconciliation. Her attempts to win Lavretsky's pity fail, but he agrees to let her stay at Lavriky, where he had taken her as a bride. Because of Lisa and Marya he lives with her briefly. When he leaves, Panshin becomes Varvara's lover. She soon moves to St. Petersburg and later to Paris, where she resumes her former life, somewhat subdued by age.

Vladimir Nikolaitch Panshin (vlä·dĭ'mĭr nĭ·kô·lä'ich pän'shĭn), a government official, a handsome, self-confident, socially accomplished, multilingual, dissipated, cold, and false dilettante. Marya thinks him an eligible prospective son-in-law, but Marfa sees through him, as do Lemm and Lavretsky. After Lisa rejects his offer of marriage he begins an affair with Varvara, who is later succeeded by a number of other women. He remains a bachelor.

488

Marfa Timofyevna Pestov (mär'fə tĭ-mô·fyĕv'nə pĕs·tôf'), the eccentric, independent, bluntly truthful, and sharply critical sister of Marya's father.

Sergei Petrovitch Gedeonovsky (sĕr·gā' pĕt·rō'vĭch gĕ·dĕ·on·of'skĭ), a bachelor, a councilor, and an inveterate gossip and liar.

Christophor Fedoritch Lemm (chrĭs·tô-fôr' fyō'də·rĭch lĕm), an old German music teacher who detests Russia but is too poor to leave it. He idolizes Lisa and becomes a sympathetic friend of Lavretsky.

Ivan Petrovitch (ĭ·vän' pĕt·rō'vĭch), Lavretsky's father. Irresponsible when young and even after his marriage, he returns to Russia from France after his father's death with plans to bring some order and system into Russian life, starting with his own estate and his son. A combination of Anglomaniac, French liberal, and domestic despot, he dominates Fedya, even after his health breaks and he goes blind, until the son is freed by his father's death when Fedya is twenty-three. Turgenev uses Ivan to satirize the foolish efforts of some eighteenth and early nineteenth century Russian liberals to Westernize Russia hurriedly and by force.

Malanya Sergyevna (mä·lä'nyə sĕr·gĕy'-ĕv·nə), a former servant, Lavretsky's mother. Uneducated, submissive, timid, ailing, she dies when Fedya is a child.

Pavel Petrovitch Korobyin (pä'vĕl pĕt-rō'vĭch kô·rō'bĭn), Varvara's vain, greedy father, a retired general who left the army after an embezzlement scandal. He becomes the overseer of Lavretsky's estate until he is dismissed following Lavretsky's separation from Varvara.

Mihalevitch (mĭ·hä·lĕ'vĭch), Lavretsky's university friend who introduced him to Varvara. During a brief visit at Vasilyevskoe he is noisy, brusque, agrumentative, and critical of what he calls Lavretsky's loafing, which he considers a primary Russian fault.

Glafira Petrovna (glä·fī'rə pĕt·rōv'nə), Ivan's harsh-voiced, haughty, dictatorial sister.

Elena Mihalovna (ĕ·lĕ'nə mĭ·hä'ləv·nə), called Lenotchka (lĕ·nōt'chkə), Marya's younger daughter.

Nastasya Karpovna Ogarkov (näs·tä'syə kär·pōv'nə ô·gär'kəf), an elderly, childless widow, the cheerful, devoted companion of Marfa Timofyevna.

Agafya Vlasyevna (ä·gä'fyə vlä'sĕv·nə), Lisa's nurse, a peasant who was formerly the mistress of Lisa's maternal grandfather. She is responsible for Lisa's early interest in religion.

Shurotchka (shoō·rōt'chkə), a young orphan girl given to Marfa Timofyevna by the child's drunken, brutal uncle.

THE HOUSE OF MIRTH

Author: Edith Wharton (1862-1937)
Time of action: Early twentieth century
First published: 1905

PRINCIPAL CHARACTERS

Lily Bart, a fascinating, beautiful young woman sacrificed to the false ideals of New York social life, the belief that a "good" marriage is preferable to a happy one and that appearances must be maintained, regardless of the expense. Through the machinations of a jealous wife whose husband has fallen in love with Lily, the hapless girl is eventually brought to social disgrace, poverty, and death.

Lawrence Selden, an intellectual young bachelor lawyer in love with Lily. Although he prefers to remain on the outskirts of New York high society, he is popular and invited into many fashionable homes. Always in the background, he tries to steer Lily's life for her, but he is too weak to marry her.

Gertrude Farish, called **Gerty,** Selden's cousin, who lives alone in a modest apartment and is much taken up with philanthropy. In desperation, Lily goes to her for help, but Gertrude can offer her little solace.

Mr. Rosedale, a young Jewish financier who is trying to enter the upper brackets of New York society. At the beginning of the story, when Lily retains her position in society, he wants to marry her. Later, after her conduct has been questioned and she is willing to marry him, he is no longer interested.

Percy Gryce, a shy young man protected from designing women by his strong-minded, possessive mother. He is much taken with Lily Bart because she shows great interest in his collection of Americana. Eventually he is frightened off because of Lily's popularity with other men, and he ends up marrying Gwen Van Osburgh.

Mrs. Gryce, Percy's mother, a monumental woman with the voice of a public orator and a mind divided between concern for her son and the iniquities of her servants.

George Dorset, a mournful dyspeptic, unhappily married. He falls in love with Lily and thus arouses his wife's jealousy and resentment, bringing about the scandal which contributes to Lily's downfall.

Bertha Dorset, George Dorset's garrulous, pretty wife, who is vicious in her treatment of Lily Bart after she has

learned that her husband has grown fond of the girl. Mrs. Dorset behaves indiscreetly with Ned Silverton, carries on a clandestine correspondence with Lawrence Selden, and has several other affairs, but she cannot tolerate her husband's affection for Lily.

Ned Silverton, a handsome, weak young "poet of passion." Spoiled by wealthy patronesses, he develops too expensive a taste for bridge and incurs many gambling debts.

Mrs. Carrie Fisher, a striking divorcee. She takes pity on Lily in the midst of that young woman's poverty and tries to establish for her connections that will help her out of her predicament.

Mrs. Peniston, Lily's aunt, the widowed sister of Hudson Bart, who takes charge of her niece after the death of Lily's parents. Mrs. Peniston gives Lily little affection; however, she leaves her ten thousand dollars when she dies, with instructions that Lily is to use the money in payment of her debts.

Charles Augustus Trenor, called **Gus,** an investment broker, and
Judy Trenor, prominent New York society people. Lily is invited to many parties and cruises on their yacht. Mrs. Trenor seems to exist solely as a hostess, while Mr. Trenor is in Wall Street and deeply interested in his business affairs. He invests for Lily some money she has won at bridge and gets large returns from the small sum. Later Lily finds out that the returns have been from Trenor's pocket and that she owes him ten thousand dollars. This debt and its implications horrify Lily and her attempt to repay it precipitates the cause of her breakdown and subsequent death from an overdose of chloral.

Jack Stepney and
Grace Stepney, Lily Bart's cousins. Typical in their conforming attitudes, they obey all the social forms and are shocked by Lily's behavior.

Gwen Van Osburgh, the girl, "reliable as roast mutton," whom Percy Gryce marries. She has a deep affinity with Gryce; they share the same prejudices and ideals and have the same ability to make other standards nonexistent by ignoring them.

Mr. Wetherall and Mrs. Wetherall, guests at Bellemont, the Dorset estate. They belong to the vast group of people who go through life without neglecting to perform a single one of the gestures executed by the social puppets that surround them.

THE HOUSE OF THE SEVEN GABLES

Author: Nathaniel Hawthorne (1804-1864)
Time of action: 1850
First published: 1851

PRINCIPAL CHARACTERS

Colonel Pyncheon, a stern Massachusetts magistrate who, during the famous witchcraft trials of the seventeenth century, sent to his death a man whose property he coveted for himself. Cursed by his innocent victim, the Colonel died on the day his big new house, the House of the Seven Gables, built on his victim's land, was officially opened to guests.

Matthew Maule, Colonel Pyncheon's victim, who swore that his unjust accuser should drink blood, as Colonel Pyncheon did when he died.

Thomas Maule, the son of Matthew Maule. As the head carpenter building the House of the Seven Gables, young Maule took an opportunity to build a secret recess in which was hidden the deed by which the Pyncheons hoped to claim a vast domain in Maine.

Jaffrey Pyncheon, one of Colonel Pyncheon's nineteenth century descendants and a man like his ancestor in many ways. A judge, a member of Congress at one time, a member of many boards of directors, and an aspirant to the governorship of his state, he is a rich man who through his own efforts has multiplied the fortune he inherited from his uncle. Although he tries to present himself in a good light, Jaffrey Pyncheon is a hard man and not entirely honest. He

destroys one of his uncle's wills, which names his cousin Clifford as heir, and he stands by while his cousin is wrongly sent to prison for a murder he did not commit. Convinced that his wronged cousin knows of additional family wealth hidden by their uncle, Jaffrey threatens the broken man with confinement in an insane asylum if the hiding place of the remaining wealth is not revealed. Fortunately for his cousin, Jaffrey dies of natural causes induced by emotion while making his threats.

Clifford Pyncheon, Jaffrey's unfortunate cousin, who serves a thirty-year prison term for allegedly murdering his uncle, who really died of natural causes. A handsome, carefree, beauty-loving man at one time, he emerges from prison three decades later a broken, pale, and emaciated wreck of a human being, content to hide away in the House of the Seven Gables, where he is looked after by his sister Hepzibah and their young cousin Phoebe. Clifford's mind is weakened and his spirit so broken by misfortune that he actually does strange, if harmless, acts, so that Jaffrey's threat to force Clifford into an asylum could be made good. At Jaffrey's unexpected death Clifford feels a great release after having been oppressed by his cousin for so long. Clifford, his sister, and Phoebe Pyncheon inherit Jaffrey's fortune and have the

491

promise of a comfortable life in the future.

Hepzibah Pyncheon, Clifford's spinster sister, who lives alone for many years in shabby gentility in the House of the Seven Gables while her brother is in prison. She has few friends, for she seldom leaves the house, and she is so near-sighted that she always wears a frown, making people think she is a cross and angry woman. After the return of her brother from prison, she sets up a little shop in her house to try to provide for herself and Clifford, to whom she is devoted. Opening the shop is very difficult for her, as she dislikes meeting people and believes that entering trade is unladylike for a member of the Pyncheon family.

Phoebe Pyncheon, a young, pretty, and lively girl from the country. She comes to live with Hepzibah when her mother, a widow, remarries. Phoebe takes over the little cent-shop and makes it a profitable venture for Hepzibah. Phoebe also brings new life to the House of the Seven Gables by cheering it with her

beauty and song, as well as by tending the neglected flowers and doing other homely tasks. She is highly considerate of her elderly cousins and spends much of her time entertaining Clifford.

Mr. Holgrave, a liberal-minded young daguerreotypist who rents a portion of the House of the Seven Gables from Hepzibah. An eager, energetic young man of twenty-two, he falls in love with Phoebe Pyncheon, and they are engaged to be married. When Phoebe inherits a third of Jaffrey's large fortune, Holgrave decides to become more conservative in his thinking. It is he who reveals the secret recess hiding the now useless deed to the vast tract of land in Maine. He knows the secret because he is a descendant of Thomas Maule. In fact, his name is Maule, but he hides his true identity by assuming for a time the name of Holgrave.

Uncle Venner, an old handy man befriended by the Pyncheons. He is one of the few persons of the town to accept Hepzibah and Clifford as friends when they are in unfortunate circumstances.

THE HOUSE WITH THE GREEN SHUTTERS

Author: George Douglas (George Douglas Brown, 1869-1902)
Time of action: Late nineteenth century
First published: 1901

PRINCIPAL CHARACTERS

John Gourlay, a Scots merchant. He works hard to become rich and is proud of his house with the green shutters and his other possessions. His pride is insolent; he simply wants more than other people and to be acknowledged as superior. While he works hard, he is also mean, stingy, boastful, and evil. He is ashamed of his weakling son and his slovenly wife. He goes mad and, in his madness, goads his son into murdering him. He dies with no friends and with his wealth all but gone.

Mrs. Gourlay, Gourlay's wife. She was

once a pretty woman, but she has become slatternly, having been denied love by her husband. She lavishes all her affection upon her son, who is her only reason for living. She is both a slattern and a bore. After her son's death she commits suicide, knowing she is consumed by cancer.

Janet Gourlay, their daughter. She also commits suicide after her brother's death.

Young John Gourlay, Gourlay's weak, cowardly, but boastful son. He is unambitious, and only his father's influence keeps him in school. His father wants him to become a minister, but he cannot do the required work at college and is finally expelled for drunkenness and insubordination. Tortured at home by his father, he finally kills him with a poker. After the murder he commits suicide by taking poison.

James Wilson, a man who returns to Gourlay's village with sufficient money to become the merchant's competitor. By honest, friendly dealing with his customers he expands his business and drives Gourlay into financial ruin.

HOW GREEN WAS MY VALLEY

Author: Richard Llewellyn (Richard D. V. Llewellyn Lloyd, 1907-   )
Time of action: Nineteenth century
First published: 1940

PRINCIPAL CHARACTERS

Gwilym Morgan, a Welsh miner. At first sympathetic with union agitators, he is later opposed to strikers and quarrels with his sons over their views. As mine superintendent he is disliked by many of the workers. He dies in the cave-in of a flooded mine.

Beth Morgan, his wife, whose life is saved by young Huw just before Angharad's birth.

Huw, their son and the narrator, who many years afterward sadly recalls the days of his childhood and young manhood. He remembers the strike troubles that divided the family, his illness from exposure suffered in saving his mother's life, his fights at school and his expulsion for beating the schoolmaster, his joining his brothers in the pits, his leaving to become a carpenter, and finally his entering the mine to find his father and stay with him until he died.

Ivor, the oldest son, sympathetic with his father's views. He is killed in a mine cave-in.

Davy, another son, the last one to leave the mines. He migrates to New Zealand.

Owen and Gwilym, two sons who (with Davy) move away from home for a time because of their union views. They later leave the valley for London and then America.

Ianto, a son who marries a village girl and leaves the valley. He returns after her death and works in the mines until he leaves for similar work in Germany.

Angharad, the Morgan daughter who loves Mr. Gruffydd but marries Iestyn.

Bronwen, Ivor's wife, whom Huw loves from the moment he sees her as a child. He goes to stay with her after Ivor is killed.

Marged, Gwilym's wife, who goes mad from love of Owen and burns herself to death.

Iestyn Evans, son of the mine owner and husband of Angharad.

Mr. Gruffydd, the new minister who becomes Huw's best friend. He loves Angharad but is too poor to marry her.

Ceinwen Phillips, Huw's sweetheart.

HOWARDS END

Author: E. M. Forster (1879-   )
Time of action: Early twentieth century
First published: 1910

Henry Wilcox, a prosperous British businessman who has his fair share of domestic bliss and trouble. He owns Howards End, a country home near London, and it is here that the climactic scenes in the novel take place. At the end of his life he wills Howards End to his second wife with the understanding that after her death it is to go to the illegitimate child of his second wife's daughter.

Ruth Wilcox, Wilcox's first wife and Margaret Schlegel's good friend. She becomes ill and dies suddenly after writing a note that leaves Howards End to Margaret. Because the note was not part of the formal will, Wilcox and the rest of the family disregard it.

Helen Schlegel, the sister of Wilcox's second wife, who provides much of the continuity of the novel's narrative line. She at one time loved Wilcox's younger son. She has a child by a man Wilcox caused to lose his job. It is her baby that Wilcox learns to love just before his death.

Margaret Schlegel, Wilcox's second wife. She is cool, sensible, cautious. She is a good friend to Wilcox's first wife; it was, in fact, to Margaret that Wilcox's first wife willed Howards End just before she died. Margaret is a faithful wife to Wilcox and a good sister to Helen.

Leonard Bast, a poor, reasonably intelligent, rather neurasthenic worker who loses his job by acting on information Wilcox purposefully provides. His life, by accident, becomes woven into the lives of the Wilcox and Schlegel households. Helen has an illegitimate child by him. He dies of a heart attack caused by the shock of unexpectedly seeing Helen and the trauma of a beating administered to him by Wilcox's older son.

Paul Wilcox, Wilcox's younger son, who loved Helen but had been unable to marry her because both families disapproved of the union.

Charles Wilcox, Wilcox's older son, who is sent to prison for beating Leonard Bast. Though Bast dies of a heart attack and not of the injury sustained in the beating, Charles Wilcox is convicted of manslaughter and sent to prison for three years. His son's trial and conviction break Henry Wilcox's health.

Jacky Bast, Leonard's wife, an older woman who tricks Bast into an unpleasant marriage. She has an unsavory reputation caused as much as anything by the fact that she drinks too much.

Theobald Schlegel, Helen and Margaret's brother.

HUASIPUNGO

Author: Jorge Icaza (1902-   )
Time of action: Twentieth century
First published: 1934

Andrés Chiliquinga (än·dräs′ chē·lē-kēn′gä), an Indian who dies defending his "huasipungo" (a small plot of ground given workers on an estate) against the greedy whites.

Cunshi (kōōn′shē), his wife, wronged by Pereira.

Alfonso Pereira (äl·fōn′sō pā·rä′ē·rä), a debt-ridden Ecuadorian landowner who cheats the Indians and sells timber rights on his estate.

Blanca (blän′kä), his wife, who uses Cunshi as wet nurse for their baby.

494

Lolita (lō·lē′tä), their seventeen-year-old daughter, in love with a mestizo.

Don Julio (dōn hōō′lyō), Pereira's uncle, who demands repayment for a ten-thousand-sucre loan.

Policarpio (pō·lē·kär′pyō), Pereira's overseer, who is somewhat sympathetic toward the Indian tenants.

Padre Lomas (pä′drä lō′mäs), the avaricious, lustful village priest who overcharges for masses and burials and tricks the Indians into building a road to open their territory.

Mr. Chapy, a North American promoter interested in timber and oil.

Jacinto Quintana (hä·sēn′tō kēn·tä′nä), proprietor of the village store and saloon.

Juana (hwä′nä), his wife, who is forced to accept the attentions of Pereira and the priest.

Juancho Cabascango (hwän′chō kä·bäs·kän′gō), a prosperous Indian, cursed by the priest and killed by the Indians.

A Captain, who burns out and machine-guns the rebellious Indians.

HUCKLEBERRY FINN

Author: Mark Twain (Samuel L. Clemens, 1835-1910)
Time of action: Mid-nineteenth century
First published: 1885

PRINCIPAL CHARACTERS

Huckleberry Finn, a small-town boy living along the banks of the Mississippi in the 1800's before the American Civil War. Perhaps the best-known youthful character in world fiction, Huck has become the prototype of the boy who lives a life that all boys would like to live; he also helped to shape such diverse characters as Hemingway's Nick Adams and Salinger's Holden Caulfield. His adventurous voyage with the Negro slave Jim, when they drift down the Mississippi on a raft, is the trip every boy dreams of making, on his own, living by his adaptable wits and his unerring ingenuity. When he contrasts himself with his flamboyant and wildly imaginative friend, Tom Sawyer, Huck feels somewhat inadequate, but deep inside he has a triumphant reliance on the power of common sense. Thus the world of Huck's reality—his capture by and escape from old drunken Pap; the macabre pageant of his townsfolk searching the Mississippi for his supposedly drowned body; his encounters with the King and the Duke, two preposterous swindlers; his stay among the feuding Grangerfords and

Shepherdsons; and his defense of the pure, benighted Wilks sisters—is proved to be far more imaginative than Tom Sawyer's imagination. Yet Huck is not some irresponsible wanderer through adolescence. He has a conscience. He knows it is wrong to be harboring a runaway slave, but his friendship with Jim makes him defy the law. His appreciation of the ridiculous allows him to go along with the lies and swindles of the King and the Duke until they seem ready to bring real harm to the Wilks sisters, and he himself will fib and steal to get food and comfort; but his code of boyhood rebels at oppression, injustice, hypocrisy. Mark Twain has created in Huckleberry Finn a magnificent American example of the romanticism that rolled like a great wave across the Atlantic in the nineteenth century.

Jim, the Negro slave of Miss Watson. Believing that he is about to be sold down the river for eight hundred dollars, he runs away and hides on Jackson's Island, where Huck also takes refuge after faking his own murder in order to

495

escape from Pap. Jim has all the charm and the many inconsistencies of the Southern Negro. Ignorant, superstitious, gullible, Jim is nevertheless, in Huck's words, "most always right; he had an uncommon level head, for a nigger." He will laugh at everything comical, but he suffers poignantly when he thinks of the family he has left in bondage. He protects Huck physically and emotionally, feeling that the boy is the one white person he can trust, never suspecting that Huck is struggling with his conscience about whether to turn Jim in. When the two companions encounter the King and the Duke, Jim is completely taken in by their fakery, though at one point he asks, "Don't it 'sprise you, de way dem kings carries on, Huck?" Typically, Jim is subservient to and patient with the white man. Even when Tom Sawyer arrives at the Phelpses, where Jim has been caught and held, the Negro goes through Tom's complicated and romantic ritual of escape with grumbling good nature. Jim is a sensitive, sincere man who seems to play his half-comic, half-tragic role in life because he is supposed to play it that way.

Tom Sawyer, Huck's friend, who can, with a lively imagination stimulated by excessive reading, turn a raid by his gang on a Sunday-School picnic into the highway robbery of "a whole parcel of Spanish merchants and rich A-rabs . . . with two hundred elephants, and six hundred camels, and over a thousand 'sumter' mules, all loaded down with di'monds. . . ." He is a foil to the practicality of Huck; he is the universal boy-leader in any small town who can sway his gang or his pal into any act of fancy, despite all grumbling and disbelief. His ritual for the rescue of the captured Jim (who he knows has already been set free by Miss Watson's last will) is a masterful selection of details from all the romantic rescues of fact and fiction.

Pap, Huck's father and the town drunkard. When he learns that Huck has been awarded in trust a share of the money derived from the box of gold found in the robber's cave, he shows up one night at Huck's room at the Widow Douglas's. He takes the pledge and stays in the widow's spare room. Finding that Huck's share of the money is legally beyond his reach, he breaks the pledge and creates such havoc in the room that "they had to take soundings before they could navigate it." Pap kidnaps his son, keeping him prisoner in an old cabin. He then proceeds to go on a classic drunk, followed by a monumental case of delirium tremens. Snakes in abundance crawl all over him and one bites his cheek, though Huck, of course, can see nothing. The boy finally makes his escape from Pap by killing a pig and leaving bloody evidence of a most convincing murder. Pap's end in life is discovered by Jim: a dead body in a flooded boat on the Mississippi.

The King and
The Duke, two rapscallions and confidence men with whom Huck and Jim join up on their trip down the Mississippi. Their so-called play, "The Royal Nonesuch," finally leads to their just deserts: tarring, feathering, riding out of town on a rail.

The Widow Douglas and
Miss Watson, unsuccessful reformers of Huck after he comes into his fortune.

Aunt Polly, Tom Sawyer's relative who at the end of the story sets straight the by-now complicated identities of Huck and Tom.

The Grangerfords and
The Shepherdsons, two feuding families. Huck spends some time with the Grangerfords, who renew the feud when a Grangerford daughter elopes with a young Shepherdson.

Mr. and Mrs. Phelps, at whose farm the captured Jim is confined until Tom arrives to effect his "rescue."

Mary Jane,
Susan, and
Joanna Wilks, three sisters whom the

496

King and the Duke set out to bilk; Huck thwarts the connivers.

Judge Thatcher, "the law" who protects Huck's interests.

HUDIBRAS

Author: Samuel Butler (1612-1680)
Time of action: 1640-1660
First published: 1663-1678

PRINCIPAL CHARACTERS

Sir Hudibras (hū'dĭ·brăs), a Presbyterian knight and the hero of a poem intended to ridicule the Presbyterians, the religious Independents, and the pretensions of false learning in seventeenth century England. Full of learned conversation liberally sprinkled with Latin, Greek, and Hebrew, and riding a skinny nag, Sir Hudibras sallies forth with his squire Ralpho, intent on putting to right the sinners of the world. The reforming knight and his squire, obnoxious nuisances both, get the worst of every encounter with sin. In a final humiliation, their ardor is cooled when they are forced to make an undignified exit through the Widow's window and escape on their saddleless horses.

Ralpho, Sir Hudibras' squire. A religious Independent full of high-flown arguments on matters of faith, he accompanies his master on his crusade against sin.

Crowdero, a fiddler captured and put in the stocks by Sir Hudibras and Ralpho.

Trulla, an Amazon who subdues Sir Hudibras and puts him in the stocks in place of Crowdero.

Sidrophel, an astrologer consulted by Sir Hudibras and Ralpho.

Whachum, Sidrophel's apprentice.

The Widow, a wealthy woman who agrees to have Sir Hudibras freed from the stocks if he will consent to a whipping. When he lies to her, she causes his final humiliation and the end of his reforming career.

Orsin, a bear keeper whose escaped bear causes the melee that finally lands Sir Hudibras and Ralpho in the stocks.

Talgol, a butcher.

HUGH WYNNE, FREE QUAKER

Author: Silas Weir Mitchell (1829-1914)
Time of action: 1753-1783
First published: 1897

PRINCIPAL CHARACTERS

Hugh Wynne, a young man in Revolutionary War times who is torn between his father's Quakerism and more worldly views. The rigors of his father's religion prove too much, and he leaves the Quakers to become a valiant soldier in the Continental Army fighting for colonial independence. He receives praise from General Washington, wins a captaincy, and after the war marries Darthea Peniston, the girl he loves. A loyal American, he gives up the title to estates in Wales.

John Wynne, Hugh's father, an orthodox Quaker. Bitter when his son leaves his faith, John tries to disinherit Hugh. He fails, however, because his clouded mind

497

causes him to mistake Hugh for Hugh's cousin Arthur. The poor man dies insane.

Gainor Wynne, Hugh's aunt, his father's sister. She is not a Quaker and surrounds herself with worldly friends, including British officers. She wants her nephew to leave the Quaker faith to take part in the patriot cause to free the American colonies. She befriends Hugh when he is cut off by his father.

Jack Warder, Hugh's schoolmate and friend. With Hugh he becomes a patriot in the American Revolution and serves valiantly in the Continental Army.

Arthur Wynne, Hugh's cousin. He is a deceitful and cruel young man who is a Tory sympathizer and becomes an officer in the British forces during the American Revolution. On one occasion he leaves his cousin Hugh to die in a filthy prison. He is Hugh's unsuccessful rival for the hand of Darthea Peniston. A sly villain, he wheedles the family estate in Wales from Hugh's hoodwinked father.

Marie Wynne, Hugh's mother, a loving and understanding woman. She dies while Hugh is still a young man.

Darthea Peniston, a childhood sweetheart of Hugh. She is at one time engaged to Arthur, Hugh's cousin, but she discovers he is a deceitful man and breaks the engagement. Later she marries Hugh.

THE HUMAN COMEDY

Author: William Saroyan (1908-   )
Time of action: Twentieth century
First published: 1943

PRINCIPAL CHARACTERS

Katey Macauley, a widow who is trying to bring up her family alone. She has imaginary talks with her dead husband, in which she discusses family problems with him. She feels that her husband is not dead as long as he lives in the lives of his children. She accepts Tobey into the family after Marcus is killed.

Homer Macauley, Katey's second oldest son, who takes a night job at the telegraph office. He gets up early every day and exercises so that he will be in shape to run the hurdles at the high school. He finds the telegram that Mr. Grogan has typed out telling Katey that Marcus has been killed.

Marcus Macauley, Katey's oldest son, who goes into the army and makes friends with Tobey George. Tobey has no family of his own, and so Marcus shares stories of his family with Tobey. Marcus wants Tobey to go to his home and marry his sister, Bess, after the war. Marcus is killed in action.

Mary Arena, Marcus' sweetheart.

Tobey George, an orphan whom Marcus befriends in the army. Tobey is lonely and lives vicariously through Marcus' family. He returns to Marcus' home after the war and, in a sense, takes Marcus' place as a son.

Mr. Grogan, Spangler's assistant in the telegraph office, with whom Homer has long talks concerning the efficacy of war. Mr. Grogan has a weak heart and gets drunk every night. One of Homer's duties is to see that he stays awake. He dies after typing out the message that Marcus has been killed in action.

Thomas Spangler, the manager of the telegraph office.

498

Bess Macauley and Ulysses Macauley, Katey's two other children.

Lionel, Ulysses' friend, who takes him to the library and shows him the many books.

HUMPHRY CLINKER

Author: Tobias Smollett (1721-1771)
Time of action: Mid-eighteenth century
First published: 1771

PRINCIPAL CHARACTERS

Matthew Bramble, a Welsh bachelor who, while traveling in England and Scotland, keeps track of his affairs at Brambleton Hall through correspondence with Dr. Richard Lewis, his physician and adviser. Bramble, an eccentric and a valetudinarian, writes at great length of his ailments—the most pronounced being gout and rheumatism—and gives detailed accounts of his various attacks. With the same fervor that he discusses personal matters—health and finances— he launches into tirades on laws, art, mores, funeral customs, and the social amenities of the various communities he and his party pass through on their travels. As various members of the entourage become attracted to one another and are married, and the group plans to return to Brambleton Hall, Bramble senses that his existence has been sedentary. In his new-found interest of hunting, he changes from an officious, cantankerous attitude toward the affairs of others. He writes Lewis that had he always had something to occupy his time (as he has in hunting), he would not have inflicted such long, tedious letters on his friend and adviser.

Tabitha Bramble, his sister. A fussy old maid, she is the female counterpart of her brother in telling her correspondents of the annoyances of everyday life. Hers is a more personal world than her brother's, people being of more importance than ideas and things. With little likelihood of a change in interests, Tabitha does return home a married woman.

Jerry Melford, the nephew of Matthew and Tabitha, whose letters to a classmate at Cambridge, where Jerry is regularly a student, give a more objective account of incidents of travel and family. With the articulateness of the scholar and the verve of youth, Jerry describes the lighter side of everyday happenings. In his final correspondence, he admits to his friend that in the midst of matrimonial goings-on he has almost succumbed to Cupid. However, fearing that the girl's qualities—frankness, good humor, handsomeness, and a genteel fortune—may not be permanent, he passes off his thought as idle reflections.

Lydia Melford, his sister. The recipient of her letters, Miss Letitia Willis, is the object of Jerry's "idle reflections." Lydia, just out of boarding school, is concerned in her letters with the styles and movement of the young in various stops the party makes. Her primary concern, however, is with the presence or absence of young men. Lydia, it is learned, is carrying on a correspondence with a young actor, with Miss Willis acting as a go-between. A duel between the young man and Jerry is averted, but he continues to show up at various stages of the journey in various disguises. Lydia marries him after he has proved himself a young man of rank and wealth.

Winifred (Win) Jenkins, the maid, and the fifth of the letter writers whose correspondence makes up the story. Her correspondent is another servant at Brambleton Hall. Winifred's spelling exceeds all other known distortions of the English language. She sees people riding in "coxes," visits a zoo where she sees "hillyfents," looks forward to getting back "huom," and closes her letters with "Yours with true infection." But such ineptness does not hamper her personal achievements; able to make herself attractive, she is won by the natural son of Matthew Bramble. In the last letter in the book, Win makes her position clear to her former fellow servant, for she plans to return home as a member of the family rather than as a domestic. She reminds her correspondent that "Being, by God's blessing, removed to a higher spear, you'll excuse my being familiar with the lower servants of the family; but as I trust you'll behave respectful, and keep a proper distance, you may always depend upon the good will and purtection of Yours W. Loyd."

Humphry Clinker, the country youth later revealed as Matthew Loyd, the illegitimate son of Matthew Bramble. Clinker, a poor, ragged ostler, is taken on the trip by Bramble after a clumsy coachman has been dismissed. Clinker proves to be the soul of good breeding, a devout lay preacher, and a hero in saving Bramble from drowning. Quite by accident he hears Bramble addressed as Matthew Loyd, at which time Clinker produces a snuff box containing proof of his parentage. Bramble explains his having used the name Loyd as a young man for financial reasons and accepts Clinker as his son when "the sins of my youth rise up in judgment against me." Clinker, under his legal name, marries Winifred Jenkins.

George Dennison, the young actor who successfully follows the party in pursuit of Lydia's hand. George has masqueraded as an actor, Wilson, to avoid an unwelcome marriage being forced on him by his parents. His status in rank and wealth are proved by his father's and Bramble's recognition of each other as former classmates at Oxford.

Lieutenant Obadiah Lismahago, a Scottish soldier who joins the party at Durham. Lismahago's shocking stories of the atrocities he suffered as a captive of the American Indians entertain the party and win the devotion of Miss Tabitha. Lismahago's manner of doing things is best illustrated by his wedding present to Tabitha: a fur cloak of American sables, valued at eighty guineas.

Mr. and Mrs. Dennison, country gentry and George Dennison's parents.

THE HUNCHBACK OF NOTRE DAME

Author: Victor Hugo (1802-1885)
Time of action: Fifteenth century
First published: 1831

PRINCIPAL CHARACTERS

Quasimodo (kä·zē·mô′do), a bellringer abandoned in infancy at Notre Dame Cathedral on Quasimodo Sunday, 1476, and now deaf from the din of the bells he rings. He is also unspeakably ugly, with tusk-like teeth and a wen over one eye, bristling red hair and eyebrows, and a snoutlike nose. Because of his horrible appearance, the Paris crowd selects him King of Fools for the Epiphany cele-brations of 1482. During the carnival he sees Esmeralda, the gipsy who dances before him. When he is later pilloried and beaten, she brings him a drink. From then on he is her devoted slave and on several occasions saves her from Archdeacon Frollo, his benefactor. When she is hanged, through Frollo's scheming, he hurls the priest from the bell tower, then weeps at the death of the only two people he has ever loved. Years later, when the vault of Montfaucon, burial place of criminals, is opened, a skeleton of a woman in white is found in the arms of a misshapen man with a crooked spine. The bones disintegrate into dust when touched.

Esmeralda (ĕz·mā·räl′dä), a lovely and kind-hearted gipsy who possesses an amulet by which she hopes to find her family. She and her goat Djali dance to earn their living. Attracted to Captain Phoebus after he saves her from kidnaping, she agrees to a rendezvous in a house on the Pont St. Michel. There the officer is stabbed by Frollo, but Esmeralda is accused of the crime. Under torture, she confesses to everything and is sentenced to be hanged. With Quasimodo's help, however, she escapes while confessing to Frollo and takes sanctuary in the church. Gringoire deceives her into leaving when the mob attacks Notre Dame. For a time she hides in the cell of a madwoman, in reality her mother from whom the gipsies had stolen her. Soldiers of Captain Phoebus' company find her there. Clothed in white, she is hanged at dawn.

Pierre Gringoire (pyâr′ grăn·gwär′), a penniless and stupid Parisian poet who falls in love with Esmeralda. He writes a play to entertain the Flemish ambassadors at the Palace of Justice. Captured later by thugs and threatened with hanging, he is freed when Esmeralda promises to marry him, but the marriage is never consummated. At Frollo's bidding, Gringoire tempts the girl from her sanctuary and she is captured.

Captain Phoebus de Châteaupers (fā·büs′ də shá·tō·pĕrs′), loved by Esmeralda. He reveals to Frollo his rendezvous with her and is stabbed by the jealous priest. When Esmeralda is accused of the crime, Phoebus allows her be tried for his murder because he is fearful for his reputa-tion if he appears. Soon he forgets the gipsy and marries his cousin, Fleur-de-Lys.

Claude Frollo (klōd frô·yō′), the arch-deacon of Notre Dame, once an upright priest but now a student of alchemy and necromancy as well as a pursuer of women. Determined to possess Esmeralda, he sends Quasimodo in disguise to seize her. Her rescue by Captain Phoebus makes him try to kill the officer. When Esmeralda is accused of the crime, he offers to save her if she will give herself to him. Failing to possess her, he shakes with evil laughter as he looks down from Notre Dame at her hanging in the Place de Gréve. Here he is found by Quasimodo and hurled to his death on the pavement below.

The Dauphin Charles (dō·fän′ shärl), of France, whose marriage to Margaret of Flanders occasions the celebration at the beginning of the novel.

Charles, Cardinal de Bourbon (shärl′, kár·dē·nál′ də bōōr·bôn′), who provides the dramatic entertainment for the visiting Flemish guests.

Tristan (trēs·tän′), who directs Captain Phoebus' soldiers in search of Esmeralda.

Jacques Charmolue (zhäk shär·mô·lü′), the King's Attorney in the Ecclesiastical Court that tries Esmeralda for witch-craft.

Philippe Lheulier (fē·lēp′ lû·lyā′), the King's Advocate Extraordinary, who accuses her.

Gudule (gü·dül′), an ex-prostitute whose daughter Agnes had been stolen by gipsies. She has gone mad and for fifteen years has lived in a cell. She fondles constantly a shoe that her baby had worn. When Esmeralda takes refuge there, she produces its companion, and mother and daughter are briefly reunited.

HUNGER

Author: Knut Hamsun (Knut Pedersen Hamsund, 1859-1952)
Time of action: Late nineteenth century
First published: 1890

PRINCIPAL CHARACTERS

The Narrator, a young man down on his luck who writes articles and plays. He is paid so little for his work, however, that he is desperately hungry most of the time. He tells his story in the feverish state of mind that hunger produces. It is a story of his encounters in the town with girls, beggars, pawnbrokers, old friends, policemen, editors, potential employers. Sick with hunger, he is eventually turned out of his room and, finally and violently, out of the house itself. His story ends when he throws into his landlady's face a crumpled envelope containing a half sovereign and a letter from a woman.

An Old Cripple, a penniless beggar to whom the narrator gives a halfpenny after he has pawned his waistcoat to get the money.

Two Women, who are strolling about the town. They take the narrator for a madman because he tells the younger one that she is losing her book, when the fact of the matter is that she carries no book with her. Later, the younger woman—now **The Lady in Black**—befriends the narrator because she is an adventuresome girl who is intrigued with the idea of odd experiences, including those madmen might provide for her.

A Company Manager, an employer who refuses to give the narrator a job as a bookkeeper because he had carelessly dated his letter of application several years before he was born.

A Policeman, an officer who sends the narrator to the police barracks as a homeless man.

A Pawnbroker, a merchant who laughs at the narrator when he appears at the pawnshop to sell the buttons from his coat.

An Editor, a kindly gentleman who likes the narrator's work, but cannot accept his sketch on Correggio. He offers the narrator money, certain that the narrator can repay the obligation with his writing, but the narrator refuses the advance.

A Young Clerk, a boy who gives the narrator change for a crown when he has given the boy only a florin with which to buy a candle. The narrator profits by the clerk's mistake by renting a room in a hotel and buying two full meals.

A Landlady, a woman with a family who patiently waits for the narrator to pay his rent. She finally rents his room to a sailor but allows the narrator to sleep in the house. She throws him out of the house, however, when he protests the children's cruel game of sticking straws into the nose of the paralyzed grandfather who lies in a bed before the fire.

A Beautiful Girl, dressed in silk, who appears to the narrator in a dream. She offers him erotic pleasure.

HUON DE BORDEAUX

Author: Unknown
Time of action: Ninth century
First transcribed: First half of the thirteenth century

Huon de Bordeaux (ü·ōn' də bôr·dō'), the older son of the dead Duke of Guienne. On his way with his brother Gerard to pay homage to King Charlemagne, he is ambushed by the King's son, Charlot, whom he kills in self-defense. He is then sent, by the angry Charlemagne, on a pilgrimage to Jerusalem. After many adventures, through which he is assisted by Oberon, the fairy king, he returns to court to claim the rights usurped during his absence by his brother.

Gerard (zhā·rár'), the younger brother of Huon de Bordeaux and the usurper of his rights.

King Charlemagne (shár·lə·màn'y), who bears little resemblance to the great king of legend. Here he is pictured as in his dotage, petulant, violent, and unreasonable. Unjustly angry with Huon de Bordeaux, he sends him on a dangerous pilgrimage to Jerusalem.

Charlot (shár·lō'), King Charlemagne's son, who ambushes Huon de Bordeaux and is killed by him in self-defense.

Oberon (ô·bā·rōn'), the dwarf King of the Otherworld, who aids Huon de Bordeaux in his adventures. Granting Huon the right to summon him in the time of danger, Oberon finally brings about the restoration of Huon's rights and promises him the inheritance of his fairy kingdom.

Gawdis (gô·dēs'), the Amir of Babylon.

Claramond (klá·rà·mōn'), Gawdis' lovely daughter, won by Huon de Bordeaux.

Gerames (zhā·rám'), a hermit and loyal follower of Huon de Bordeaux.

The Abbot of Cluny (klü·nē'), the uncle of Huon de Bordeaux.

Earl Amaury (á·mō·rē'), the evil adviser to Charlot and the cause of his own and Charlot's death at the hand of Huon de Bordeaux.

Duke Naymes (nĕm'), the wise adviser to King Charlemagne and a well-wisher of Huon de Bordeaux.

HYDE PARK

Author: James Shirley (1596-1666)
Time of action: Early seventeenth century
First presented: 1632

Mistress Bonavent, a wife who believes herself a widow. Her husband having been missing for seven years, she considers marriage to her persistent suitor, Lacy. After the marriage, but before its consummation, she learns of her husband's return.

Lacy, her suitor.

Bonavent, a merchant and the husband of Mistress Bonavent. Held captive by Turkish pirates and recently ransomed after seven years' absence, he returns to the sound of his wife's wedding festivi-

ties. He makes himself known to her before the second marriage is consummated.

Mistress Carol, Mistress Bonavent's cousin and companion. She flirts with Rider and Venture and plays one against the other while, all along, Fairfield is the favored suitor. Turning coquette to test the favorite's affection, she nearly loses him before she is forced to abandon her pride and propose to him. He accepts immediately.

Fairfield, the favored suitor of Mistress

Carol. In despair over his lady's off-again, on-again coquettishness, he threatens to become a gelding and free himself from all such concerns. The threat wins her hand on the spot.

Rider and Venture, Mistress Carol's rejected suitors.

Lord Bonvile, a sporting peer. Under the delusion that Julietta is a lady of easy virtue, he is in hot pursuit of her. When he goes too far in his suit, he receives from the lady a lecture on good breed-ing, takes it to heart, and finally wins her hand.

Julietta, Fairfield's sister, who is pursued by Lord Bonvile under the mistaken impression that she is a prostitute. She accepts him as a suitor after his thoughts become as lofty as his rank.

Jack Trier, Julietta's betrothed. To test his lady's chastity, the jealous lover leaves her with Lord Bonvile, whom he has told that she is a prostitute. He loses her to Bonvile for his pains.

HYPATIA

Author: Charles Kingsley (1819-1875)
Time of action: Fifth century
First published: 1853

PRINCIPAL CHARACTERS

Philammon (fĭ·lă'mən), a young monk who leaves the monastic life to see the rich, varied society of Alexandria. Excited by a Christian attack on the city's Jews, he joins the despoilers. Accused of heresy because of his interest in Hypatia, he almost loses his life. After Hypatia's death he returns to his monastery and later becomes abbot there.

Hypatia (hī·pā'shĭ·ə), a beautiful Greek philosopher and teacher, one of the last to champion the Greek gods. She agrees to marry Orestes if he will renounce his Christian faith and aid her in restoring the Greek gods. Her gods, which exist only in her own mind, fail her, and she is torn to pieces by some of Cyril's monks.

Raphael Aben-Ezra (rä'fə·ĕl ä·bĕn-ēz'rə), a wealthy young Jew, Miriam's son, though he does not know it. He becomes Hypatia's pupil but turns from the Greek gods to Christianity.

Miriam (mĭ'rĭ·əm), an old Jewish crone formerly converted to Christianity until she renounced it and developed a hatred of everyone except Jews. She tells Philammon of his slave status, sends Orestes

the false report of Heraclian's victory, and informs Raphael that she is his mother. She dies of wounds received during an attack by the Goths.

Amal (ă'məl), a young Gothic chief who travels up the Nile searching for Asgard, home of the old Gothic gods. In a fight with Philammon he falls from a tower and dies.

Pelagia (pə·lā'jĭ·ə), Amal's mistress and (though he does not at first know it) sister of Philammon; a beautiful courtesan to whose home Philammon flees to avoid being forced to return to his monastery. After Amal's death she becomes a solitary penitent in the desert. At her death she is buried with Philammon.

Orestes (ō·rĕs'tēz), the Roman prefect of Alexandria who envisions a rise in his own fortunes and power if Heraclian succeeds in overthrowing the Goths.

Aufugus (ô'fə·gəs), a monk who warns Philammon not to go to Alexandria and later attempts to rescue him from Hypatia's influence. Though Philammon does not know it until informed by

504

Miriam, he is Aufugus' slave bought many years earlier.

Cyril (sī'rĭl), the Christian Patriarch of Alexandria who reports to Orestes a Jewish plot to slaughter Alexandria's Christians. By the death of Hypatia he gains a temporary victory over the Greek religion.

Heraclian (hē·rā'klĭ·ən), a Roman leader who plans to destroy the Gothic conquerors of Rome and make himself emperor. He is defeated.

Victoria (vĭc·tō'rĭ·ə), the beautiful blonde daughter of Majoricus, saved from two barbarian soldiers by Raphael, who later marries her.

Majoricus (mə·jō'rĭ·cəs), a Roman prefect rescued from a heap of rubble by Raphael and Victoria. He is later killed in battle.

Augustine (ô·gŭs'tĭn), the famous philosopher-monk. He persuades Raphael to turn Christian.

THE HYPOCHONDRIAC

Author: Molière (Jean Baptiste Poquelin, 1622-1673)
Time of action: Seventeenth century
First presented: 1673

PRINCIPAL CHARACTERS

Argan (àr·gäṅ'), the hypochrondriac, though without the melancholia frequently associated with his state; his associates keep things too lively in his house to permit it, and he revels in his poor health. He gauges his health by the number of purges and clysters he has had this month compared to last. If the number is fewer, it is obvious that his condition is worse. He is glad he has only two children; more would leave him with no time for his illnesses. Though he enjoys the attention of two physicians and an apothecary, he is suspicious of their bills and checks them carefully, cutting the amount he intends to pay because "20 sous in the language of an apothecary is as much as to say 10 sous." To have a physician in the family to attend to him at all times is his wish; therefore, he refuses to consider any other as a son-in-law. His temper is revealed in his shouting at his servant when she is not prompt in answering the bell, and he calls her names, "jade," "carrion," and "impudent." That he is extremely foolish is shown by his worry about orders of the physician to walk in his room: should it be the long or the broad

way? When his brother orders the physician out of the house, Argan is convinced that without his doctor's attention he will die. He is completely taken in by his second wife and her affectionate manner until her true feelings for him are revealed by the maid's trick. This also shows him his daughter's real love, and he permits the marriage to Cléante, provided he will become a physician, or at least an apothecary.

Toinette (twà·nĕt'), Argan's servant, a sensible, amusing, clever girl. She loves Argan's daughter Angélique, shares her confidences, and aids her love affair. She is also aware of Argan's wife's true feelings toward her hypochrondriac husband, and she proposes a test which convinces Argan that his wife is interested only in his money. Toinette gets along with her master very well, though she speaks up against his plan to marry Angélique to a physician and argues with him. She ridicules the young physician Argan has chosen as Angélique's husband, and then apes the young man's speeches for those who missed hearing them. In an attempt to cure the hypo-

505

chondriac of his fear of and respect for physicians, she disguises herself as a physician and ridicules the profession by absurd diagnoses and diet suggestions. Her final clever plan for Argan to feign death to test the true feelings of his wife and daughter results in a happy close to the play.

Béline (bā·lēn'), Argan's second wife. Her relations with her husband seem calm and affectionate, but her true nature is revealed when she begs Argan not to talk about making his will, though she has the notary at hand to consult with him on this matter. She says she is not interested in his money, then checks on where he has hidden it and on the amount due on notes he has mentioned. She tries to persuade Argan to place both daughters in a convent so that she will get the entire property. Her real nature is revealed by Toinette's trap. On hearing of Argan's supposed death, she states her relief at his demise. She quickly leaves when he is proved alive.

Angélique (än·zhā·lēk'), Argan's older daughter. Although an obedient girl, she objects to her betrothal to the young physician, but when Toinette argues with Argan against his marriage plans for Angélique and the physician, she merely listens. Toinette is her real confidante, especially in questions of her love for Cléante; Toinette says that their conversation for six days was only about him. Part of this conversation is a witty catechism. Despite Angélique's differences with her father, she objects to the trick her uncle plans to play on him, but agrees when assured it is only a giving in to his fancies and not really a trick on him. When Argan is supposed dead, Angélique's expression of her love and her sense of loss convinces Argan that she should not be forced into an unwelcome marriage.

Cléante (klā·änt'), the young man in love with Angélique. Because of Argan's objection to him as a suitor, Cléante dis-

guises himself as a music master in order to see his beloved. He cleverly states the plot of an opera he will sing with her; it is a statement of their own circumstances, but Argan sees through the story and calls it an impertinence. Cléante returns at the time of Argan's pretended death, to pay his respects and to try once again for the hypochrondriac's good will. After Argan agrees to the marriage if he will become a physician, Cléante promises to become even an apothecary.

Béralde (bā·rȧld'), Argan's brother, opposed to physicians because he believes that nature will cure all ills. He recommends Molière's comedies exposing the ridiculousness of physics, if not of physicians. After he forbids the apothecary to administer the clyster ordered by the physician, and drives him from the house, he calls his brother a simpleton. He also sees through Béline's plan to have the daughters placed in a convent and warns his brother. Argan, he suggests, should become a physician himself rather than ask Cléante to become one; he could learn all by merely putting on a gown and cap. Finally he plans an Interlude of a doctor's mission in which Argan will play the principal character.

Thomas Diafoirus (tô·mä' dyȧ·fwȧ·rüs'), the son of Dr. Diafoirus, a stupid young physician favored by Argan as his son-in-law. Though he takes his cues from his father, he forgets parts of his memorized speeches to Angélique and Béline and mistakes one for the other. In medicine he sticks to the ancients, not believing in any of the experiments of the day. He invites Angélique to witness the dissection of a woman.

Dr. Diafoirus (dyȧ·fwȧ·rüs'), the father of Thomas, a physician who admits that his son is somewhat of a blockhead. Father and son, after an amusing examination of Argan, tie their diagnosis to Dr. Purgon's, which Argan repeats for them.

Dr. Purgon (pür·gön'), Argan's regular

506

physician. Angry at the rejection, by Béralde's order, of the clyster ordered, he leaves, prophesying Argan's decline in health in four days, from "a bradypepsia to dyspepsia to apepsia to lienteria to dissenteria to dropsy to death."

Bonnefoy (bôn'fwȧ'), a notary. In league with Béline, he tells Argan he cannot will his wife anything because only gifts given now or secretly to friends, for return to his wife later on, are legally permitted.

Fleurant (flœ·rän'), an apothecary working with Dr. Purgon. Argan says he is "extremely civil," but feels his charges ought to be more reasonable.

Louison (lwē·zōn'), the younger daughter of Argan. She sides with her sister, though her father does learn from her that Cléante is disguised as the music master. When her father threatens to beat her for not readily volunteering the information, she feigns death.

I, CLAUDIUS

Author: Robert Graves (1895-   )
Time of action: 10 B.C.-A.D. 41
First published: 1934

PRINCIPAL CHARACTERS

Tiberius Claudius Drusus Nero Germanicus (tī·bĭ'rĭ·əs klô'dĭ·əs drōō'səs nē'rō jėr·mȧ'nĭ·kəs), Emperor of Rome after Caligula; a scholarly author of dull, sententious state histories; lame and a stammerer from childhood. His scholarship and stability bring him into favor with Augustus and Livia, who make him a priest of Mars. Having fainted at a bloody public sword fight, he is barred by Livia from public view. Forced by Livia to marry Urgulanilla, he later divorces her to marry Aelia, whom Tiberius orders him still later to divorce. He is afterward forced by Caligula to marry Messalina, though he loves Calpurnia.

Augustus Caesar (ô·gŭs'təs sē'zėr), first Emperor of Rome. He suffers stomach disorders and dies, possibly poisoned by Livia.

Livia (lĭ'vĭ·ə), his wife, Claudius' grandmother, a power-mad woman who divorces her boring husband, arranges her marriage to Augustus, and poisons those who interfere with her plans; suspected by Claudius of having poisoned Augustus. She is suspicious of Claudius and Germanicus as plotters against Tiberius,

suspected by Claudius of having poisoned Claudius' young son, and set aside by Tiberius, who later refuses to return from Capri for her funeral.

Tiberius (tī·bĭ'rĭ·əs), Claudius' uncle, successor to Augustus, son of Livia by an early marriage and husband of Julia. A successful commander against the barbarians but unpopular in Rome, he is responsible for the torture and murder of Postumus, jealous of Germanicus' successes against the Germans, instigator of a reign of terror against Livia's faction, and responsible for the deaths of Sejanus and his children.

Germanicus (jėr·mȧ'nĭ·kəs), Claudius' brother, a successful commander poisoned by Livia and Tiberius because of fear that his popularity would grow too great.

Caligula (kə·lĭg'ū·lə), successor to Tiberius, Germanicus' depraved son who with Macro takes command of the army and smothers the insane Tiberius. Having declared himself both Emperor and a god, Caligula is at last murdered because of his excesses.

507

Julia (jōōl'yə), daughter of Livia and Augustus and wife of Tiberius. Banished with Tiberius, she is slowly starved to death by Livia.

Urgulanilla (ûr'gū·lə·nĭ'lə), Claudius' gigantic young first wife forced on him by Livia. Claudius and Urgulanilla detest each other.

Postumus (pŏs'tū·mŭs), son of Augustus; banished by his father, restored in Augustus' will, reported killed, later tortured and killed on Tiberius' orders.

Agrippina (ăg'rĭ·pī·nə), wife of Germanicus.

Sejanus (sə·jā'nəs), the friend of Tiberius who arranges Claudius' divorce from

Urgulanilla in order for him to marry Aelia. Later he is killed along with his children on Tiberius' orders.

Aelia (ē'lĭ·ə), sister of Sejanus by adoption, the second wife of Claudius.

Macro (măk'rō), commander of the guards, relieved by Caligula and later forced to kill himself.

Messalina (mĕ·sə·lī·nə), Claudius' third wife, forced on him by Caligula.

Calpurnia (kăl·pûr'nĭ·ə), Claudius' only true friend, a prostitute banished by Caligula.

Urgulania (ûr'gū·lā'nĭ·ə), the monstrous-looking grandmother of Urgulanilla.

AN ICELAND FISHERMAN

Author: Pierre Loti (Julien Viaud, 1850-1923)
Time of action: Nineteenth century
First published: 1886

PRINCIPAL CHARACTERS

Jean-Marie-Sylvestre Moan, a strongly built, good-looking young Breton with dark beard and gray-blue eyes; innocent and devout. He vainly tries to interest Yann in marrying Gaud. Serving with the French Navy in Indo-China, he is shot by a Chinese soldier. He dies of his wound while returning to France aboard a transport ship and is buried at Singapore.

Yvonne Moan, his grandmother, toothless but rosy-cheeked, fresh, and pretty despite her age. She is desolated by Sylvestre's death and becomes increasingly enfeebled in mind and body.

Marguerite (Gaud) Mevel, his charming and wealthy cousin, flaxen-haired, hazel-eyed, with a Grecian profile and a body like a lovely statue; tall, serious, virtuous, quietly poised, and low-voiced. In love with Yann, she longs desperately for him but, ladylike, will not thrust her-

self upon him. After her father's death the now poor Gaud becomes a seamstress and goes to live with the bereft Yvonne. Supremely happy when she is finally married to Yann, she bears the grief of his loss with quiet dignity.

Jean (Yann) Gaos, a fisherman and ex-gunner in the French Navy, a giant of a man, clean-shaven, with a curling blond mustache. Kindhearted, he is occasionally rough and almost brutal without intending harm, and now and then given to bursts of temper. Not seriously interested in women, he loves the sea. He is grieved to learn of Sylvestre's death and his burial far from home. Urged by his relatives and Yvonne, he finally proposes to a joyously surprised Gaud and they are married six days before he leaves again with the fishing fleet. But his ship does not return; the sea he loved has married him at last.

508

Marie Gaos, Sylvestre's fiancée, sister of Yann.

Captain Guermeur, skipper of the "Marie."

M. Mevel, Gaud's father, a wealthy,

semi-piratical speculator who dies after losing his fortune.

Mme. Tressoleur, a portly, mustached, blunt, coquettish tavern operator.

Guillaume, a fisherman on the "Marie."

THE IDES OF MARCH

Author: Thornton Wilder (1897-   )
Time of action: 45 B.C.
First published: 1948

PRINCIPAL CHARACTERS

Julius Caesar, who expects to be assassinated because many individuals and groups would like to see him dead and his career ended. All he hopes is that his assassins will be true lovers of Rome, not selfish men and women. He believes he has been right in taking over the government of the Roman Empire, for he believes that the masses of people want a strong leader who will make their decisions for them, even though they resent a concurrent loss of freedom. As for himself, Caesar wonders about life, being unsure of the gods and their influence upon human affairs. But though he sometimes feels intuitively that there are no gods, he guides himself by the advice of soothsayers and their omens.

Pompeia, Caesar's wife, who is embittered because she is ordered to receive Cleopatra, the Queen of Egypt, even though Cleopatra is notorious for her immorality, including an affair with Caesar himself. Pompeia is divorced by Caesar when rumor has it that she gave help to Clodia Pulcher in profaning a religious ceremony devoted to the Good Goddess. Caesar says his wife must be above rumor.

Calpurnia, whom Caesar marries after divorcing Pompeia. When Caesar is about to leave Rome, he entrusts Calpur-

nia's welfare to Brutus, not knowing Brutus himself will be one of his murderers.

Marcus Brutus, one of Caesar's slayers. Once loyal to Caesar, he is persuaded by his mother, who hates Caesar and is ambitious for her own son, to become an assassin. Brutus is rumored to be an illegitimate son of Caesar.

Clodia Pulcher, a beautiful woman of great wealth and patrician birth. She blames the gods for her immorality. In defiance of law and tradition she introduces her disguised brother into ceremonies open only to women. Caesar's pardon for her blasphemous action only makes her resentful of him.

Cleopatra, the Queen of Egypt, who is making an official visit to Rome. Because of her reputation for intrigue, Caesar believes she may be a conspirator against him.

Catullus, a young poet in love with Clodia Pulcher. For her sake Catullus writes scurrilous poems and tracts about Caesar. Catullus' death saddens Caesar.

Lady Julia Marcia, Caesar's aunt and a directress of the mysteries of the Good Goddess. She is renowned for her dignity and moral virtue.

THE IDIOT

Author: Fyodor Mikhailovich Dostoevski (1821-1881)
Time of action: Mid-nineteenth century
First published: 1868-1869

PRINCIPAL CHARACTERS

Prince Lef Nicolaievitch Myshkin (lĕv nĭ·kô·lĭ'ĕ·vĭch mōōsh'kĭn), a noble man whose behavior at first is only strange and unconventional but who later shows a deterioration of mind. Short, slight, with light hair and moustaches, nearly white beard, and searching blue eyes, he arrests all who see him. His naïve, unblemished goodness, in part the result of his long epilepsy, causes men to doubt him and women to love him. Toward the end of his life he is wholly compassionate, selfless, and pitying toward those forced into tragedy about him. In his weakened, susceptible condition he degenerates until he is unable to cope with life, decisions, hatreds, worldliness. Able to see human foibles without malice, to reverence the human condition without judgment, to love without the thought of attainment, he is a Christus figure set in a corrupt society where the facile, dishonest, worldly, and unconscionable prevail in absolute terms of money and position. His deterioration under heavy pressures of murder, disloyalty, vituperation, and vindictiveness is saintly, a martyrdom to unheroic life. A tragic figure, he is destroyed by those whom he loves most, and he is sent to a sanitarium in Switzerland.

Nastasya Filipovna, (näs·tä'syə fĭ·lĭpōv'nə), the tragic figure of despair and vindictiveness with whom the Prince identifies himself. Beautiful in a dark, sulky way, Nastasya is the victim of a man's lust. From this degradation she rises to a sense of power over many men, the power that leads her to her death at the hands of the pathologically jealous Rogozhin. Drawn mysteriously to the benign young invalid, she also helps to determine his fate. A magnificent talker,

a kind of actress of many parts, a moody dreamer, a defiant lover, she is a woman of great talents and deep motives.

Madame Lizaveta Prokofyevna Epanchin (lĭ·zä·vĕ'tə prô·kō'fyĕv·nə ĕ·pän'chĭn), a simple woman of great moodiness, honorable, sensitive, and inherently good. Beneath her outlandish speeches, even insults, she hides hurt feelings and a sensitive nature. Her husband, who loves and honors her, only increases her tensions because of his worldliness and business mind. She understands the very goodness of Prince Myshkin, but she finally withdraws her daughter from marriage with him for purely conventional and genetic reasons. She is deeply devoted to her family, proud of her own heritage and position, and very Russian.

General Epanchin, her husband.

Aglaya Ivanovna (äg·lä'yə ĭ·vä'nəv·nə), the Epanchins' youngest and most beautiful daughter, betrothed to Prince Myshkin. On her the family had set a price, the best match to the finest man in all St. Petersburg, and for this reason the pampered beauty is a mass of contradictions with the saving grace of feminine, intuitive insights. She is virginal, capricious, reticent, yet loving, devoted and understanding. Her intense nature will not allow her to think of Nastasya and Myshkin as innocent; her jealousy is sombre and unrelenting, a cause of deep personal tragedy.

Parfen Rogozhin (pär'fĕn rô·gō'zhĭn), a chance acquaintance of Prince Myshkin. A sensitive but impassioned sensualist who becomes deeply involved in the Prince's life, Rogozhin has higher traits

510

than appear in his rough, dark, uncouth, and powerful exterior. His tragic nature, irascible yet contrite, turns him after the violent murder of Nastasya into a blubbering repentant. The world has perverted him through a niggardly father and jealous, vindictive relatives.

Ganya Ardalionovitch (gä′nyə är·dä·lĭ-ōn′ə·vĭch), General Epanchin's secretary. Belying his appearance and manners, he is inwardly a thorough scoundrel. He hopes to marry Aglaya because of her money. He is also involved with Nastasya.

THE IDYLLS OF THE KING

Author: Alfred, Lord Tennyson (1809-1892)
Time of action: Fifth century
First published: Separately, 1859-1885

PRINCIPAL CHARACTERS

King Arthur, of Camelot. His birth is shrouded in great mystery, and he is reared by Merlin the magician. He receives his magic sword Excalibur from the Lady of the Lake, and marries Guinevere. With his Round Table knights he drives out the enemy and unifies his kingdom. He rules wisely and is successful until his Round Table fellowship diminishes in the knights' quest for the Holy Grail. Exposure of Guinevere's infidelity with Lancelot proves thoroughly demoralizing, and in a traitorous revolt Arthur is mortally wounded. After his last remaining faithful knight returns Excalibur to the Lady of the Lake, three maidens come in a barge to the shore to carry Arthur away as mysteriously as he had come.

Guinevere, Arthur's beloved Queen and his inspiration. She falls in love with the courtly, gay Lancelot, whom Arthur had sent to bring her from her father's home. Much later, when her guilty love is exposed, she goes to a nunnery, where she remains until her death.

Lancelot, a knight of the Round Table. His lifelong love for Guinevere is a source of great misery. He is loved by another woman, whom he cannot love in return. At last, the scandal with Guinevere revealed, he leaves Camelot and dies a monk.

Gareth, a knight of the Round Table

and Arthur's sister's youngest son. His first quest is on behalf of a lady who is disdainful of her untried knight. Victorious in his quest, he wins her approval and her hand.

Geraint, a knight of the Round Table. Married to Enid, he jealously keeps her away from the court and as a result of his absence from Camelot his valor is doubted. Enid's reticence on this subject convinces him that she loves another knight, but at last she is able to prove her love. They go to Camelot, where Guinevere welcomes Enid to the court.

Balan, a knight of the Round Table. Returning from a mission for Arthur, he hears mad shrieks and rushes against the knight making them, who is in fact his unrecognized brother.

Balin, Balan's mad brother and a knight of the Round Table. Disillusioned on discovering the intimacy of Guinevere and his idol Lancelot, he leaves hanging on a tree the shield Guinevere had given him. Without the shield he is unrecognized by his brother, and in the struggle between them Balin kills Balan and is crushed by his own horse.

Gawain, a knight of the Round Table. He falls in love with Elaine of Astolat, who rejects him because she loves Lancelot. Later he promises to help Pelleas with Ettarre, who has rejected Pelleas'

511

love. At her castle he tells her he has killed Pelleas, and he becomes intimate with her.

Pelleas, a knight of the Round Table. Suspicious on hearing nothing from Gawain, he steals into Ettarre's castle and finds the lovers in bed together. He places his naked sword across their throats and rushes madly away. After hearing about the scandal of Lancelot and Guinevere, he returns to Camelot, where his rudeness to the Queen foreshadows the ruin of the Round Table.

Galahad, the youngest and purest of the knights of the Round Table. To him the Holy Grail appears in all its splendor, but the experience proves fatal to him.

Percivale, the only other knight of the Round Table pure enough, according to Arthur's gloomy prediction, to see the Holy Grail.

Bors, a knight of the Round Table. He reports back to Arthur that he has seen the Holy Grail.

Tristram, a knight of the Round Table. He and Lancelot, equally guilty in loving other men's wives, fight in a tournament which Tristram wins. He then goes to Isolt of Cornwall, whom he loves. Her husband finds the lovers together and kills Tristram.

Modred, the real Judas among the knights of the Round Table. Malevolent and opportunistic, he traps Lancelot and Guinevere. He heads the revolt which ends in Arthur's death.

Bedivere, Arthur's last remaining knight of the Round Table. Reluctant to throw Excalibur into the lake, he falsely reports to Arthur that he has done so, but is sent back again. When he finally brings the report that an arm reached from the lake to take the sword, Arthur knows that Bedivere has truly done his bidding.

Merlin, the magician who reared Arthur. Tricked by the wanton Vivien into teaching her his magic powers, he is enchanted by her and left forever a prisoner in a hollow tree.

Kay, a surly knight and Arthur's seneschal.

Lynette, the disdainful lady won by Gareth.

Enid, the faithful wife of Geraint.

Vivien, a vain and coquettish woman of the court. Unsuccessful in her efforts to seduce Arthur, she goes to work on Merlin.

Elaine, the lily maid of Astolat. In love with but rejected by Lancelot, she is loved by Gawain, whom she rejects. At last she dies of grief and, according to her dying wish, is sent floating in a boat to Camelot, where Arthur and Lancelot find her. There she is buried.

Ettarre, loved by Pelleas, whom she rejects, and by Gawain, to whom she succumbs.

Isolt of the White Hands, Tristram's bride, whom he leaves.

Isolt of Cornwall, the wife of King Mark and loved by Tristram.

King Mark of Cornwall, the husband of Isolt of Cornwall and the slayer of Tristram.

Ygerne, the mother of Arthur.

Gorloïs, the first husband of Ygerne and possibly Arthur's father.

King Uther. He overcomes Gorloïs in battle and immediately forces the widow Ygerne to marry him. Thus he is possibly Arthur's father.

Bellicent, the daughter of Gorloïs and Ygerne and the mother of Gareth.

Morning Star, the first knight overcome by Gareth on Lynette's behalf.

Death, Gareth's fourth opponent in his quest. Death proves to be a mere boy, forced by his brothers to assume a fearful disguise.

512

Earl Yniol, the impoverished father of Enid.

King Pellam, whose refusal to pay his yearly tribute to Arthur is the occasion

for Balan's leaving the court, thus neglecting the care of his mad brother.

Lavaine, the brother of Elaine of Astolat.

IF WINTER COMES

Author: A. S. M. Hutchinson (1879-   )
Time of action: 1912-1919
First published: 1920

PRINCIPAL CHARACTERS

Mark Sabre, an idealistic man whose love for humanity results in his persecution and betrayal by unsympathetic people. Suspected of fathering the child of a girl he befriends and later of having been responsible for her suicide, he loses his wife, his job, and his reputation. After discovering the identity of the illegitimate child's father, he generously refrains from disclosing it.

Mabel Sabre, his wife, a totally conventional and unsympathetic woman. Never able to understand her husband, she construes his willingness to help an unwed mother as guilt, and she divorces him.

Effie Bright, the daughter of an employee at Sabre's office. Cast off after the birth of her baby by everyone, including her father, Effie appeals for help to Sabre. Later, horrified by the trouble she has caused him, she kills her child and herself.

Lady Nona Tybar, Sabre's former sweetheart and his one understanding friend.

She believes in him throughout his troubles and finally marries him.

Mr. Twyning, Sabre's business associate. His misunderstanding and persecution of Sabre are largely responsible for Sabre's ruin.

Harold Twyning, the son of Mr. Twyning. Effie's suicide letter names him as her child's father. Sabre, going to Twyning's office with the letter, finds him grieving over the news that Harold has been killed in battle. Sabre then destroys the letter.

Mr. Fortune, Sabre's employer, concerned that scandal will hurt his business.

Lord Tybar, Nona's charming and unfaithful husband. He is killed in the war.

Mrs. Perch, an old woman whose son wishes to enlist in the army. Sabre's first act of benevolence to Effie, before her troubles begin, is to arrange for her to be Mrs. Perch's companion. The news of young Perch's death kills Mrs. Perch.

Mr. Fargus, Sabre's neighbor and friend.

THE ILIAD

Author: Homer (c. Ninth century B.C.)
Time of action: The Trojan War
First transcribed: Sixth century B.C.

513

Achilles (ə·kǐ'lēz), the son of Peleus and the Nereid Thetis, Prince of the Myrmidons, and mightiest of the Achaian warriors at the siege of Troy. At his birth his mother had dipped him in the Styx so that all parts of his body are invulnerable to hurt except the heel by which she held him. A young man of great beauty, strength, courage, and skill in battle, he nevertheless possesses two tragic flaws, an imperious will and a strong sense of vanity. Enraged because King Agamemnon orders him to surrender the maid Briseis, whom Achilles had taken as his own prize of war, he quarrels bitterly with the commander of the Greek forces and withdraws from the battlefield. When the Trojan host attacks, driving the Greeks back toward their ships, Achilles remains sulking in his tent. So great is his wrath that he refuses to heed all entreaties that he come to the aid of the hard-pressed Greeks. When the Trojans begin to burn the Greek ships he allows his friend Patroclus, dressed in the armor of Achilles, to lead the warlike Myrmidons against the attackers. Patroclus is killed by Hector, the Trojan leader, under the walls of the city. Seeing in the death of his friend the enormity of his own inaction, Achilles puts on a new suit of armor made for him by Hephaestus and engages the Trojans in fierce combat. Merciless in his anger and grief, he kills Hector and on successive days drags the body of the vanquished hero behind his chariot, while King Priam, Hector's father, looks on from the walls of the city. When the sorrowing King visits the tent of Achilles at night and begs for the body of his son, Achilles relents and permits Priam to conduct funeral rites for Hector for a period of nine days. In a later battle before the walls of Troy an arrow shot by Paris, King Priam's son, strikes Achilles in the heel and causes his death.

Hector (hek'tèr), the son of King Priam and Queen Hecuba. As the commander of the Trojan forces he is the greatest and most human of the heroes, an ideal figure in every respect: a skilled horseman, a brave soldier, an able leader, a man devoted to his family and his city, and the master of his emotions under every circumstance. His courage in battle, his courtesy in conference, his submission to the gods, and his sad fate at the hands of revengeful Achilles provide an admirable contrast to the actions of the blustering, cunning, cruel, rapacious Greeks.

Andromache (ăn·drŏm'ə·kē), the devoted wife of Hector and the mother of Astyanax. After the fall of Troy she was taken into captivity by Neoptolemus, the son of Achilles. Still later, according to the "Aeneid," she married Helenus, the brother of Hector, and ruled with him in Pyrrhus.

[**Astyanax** (ăs·tī'ə·năks), the young son of Hector and Andromache. During the sack of Troy Neoptolemus killed the child by hurling him over the city wall.]

Agamemnon (ăg'ə·měm'nŏn), King of Mycenae and the older brother of King Menelaus, husband of the lovely Helen whose infidelity brought about the Trojan War. Courageous and cunning, but often rash and arrogant, as in his treatment of Achilles, he is the commander of the Greeks in the war. He stands as a symbol of the capable leader, without the heroic qualities of the more dramatic warriors who fight under his command. He is killed by his wife Clytemnestra after his return from Troy.

Menelaus (mě'nə·lā'əs), King of Sparta and husband of beautiful but faithless Helen, seduced and abducted by Paris, Prince of Troy, in fulfillment of a promise made by Aphrodite. He stands more as a symbol than as a man, a victim of the gods and an outraged husband who avenges with brave deeds the wrong done to his honor. At the end of the war he takes Helen back to Sparta with him, and in the "Odyssey" she is shown presiding over his royal palace.

Helen (hě'lən), the wife of King Menelaus of Sparta and for nineteen years after her abduction the consort of Paris. Being confined within the walls of Troy, in the company of doting elders, she plays a minor part in the story; and because she is the victim of Aphrodite's promise to Paris, she does not suffer greatly for her actions. Her attempts at reconciliation unwittingly aid the Greek cause in the capture of Troy.

Paris, (pă'rĭs), the son of King Priam and Queen Hecuba. Called to judge a dispute between Aphrodite, Hera, and Athena, he awarded the prize, the golden apple of discord, to Aphrodite, who in turn promised him the most beautiful woman in the world as his wife. Although his love for Helen, the bride he stole from her husband, has become proud devotion to a principle, Paris nevertheless places himself in jeopardy as a champion of the Trojan cause and offers to meet King Menelaus, the injured husband, in single combat. Aphrodite, fearful for the safety of her favorite, watches over him and saves him from harm. An arrow from his bow strikes Achilles in the heel and kills the Achaian warrior. One story says that Paris was slain by a poisoned arrow from the bow of Philoctetes.

Priam (prī'ăm), King of Troy and the beneficent father of a large family. While not a ruler of Agamemnon's stature, he is a man of shrewdness and quiet strength who suffers much at the hands of fate and the rivalry of the gods. Although he does not condone the abduction of Helen by Paris, he is fair in his judgment of both because he knows that they are victims of Aphrodite's whims. His devotion to his son Hector and his pity for all who suffer in the war elevate him to noble stature.

Hecuba (hě'kū·bə), the wife of King Priam. Her fate is tragic. She witnesses the death of her sons, the enslavement of her daughter Cassandra, carried into captivity by Agamemnon, and the sacrifice of her daughter Polyxena to appease the shade of Achilles.

Calchas (kăl'kəs), the seer and prophet of the Greeks. After many animals and men have been slain by the arrows of Apollo, Calchas declares that the destruction is a divine visitation because of Agamemnon's rape of Chryseis, the daughter of Chryses, a priest of Apollo. He counsels that the maid be returned to her father without ransom.

Chryseis (krī'sĭ·əs), a maiden seized by the Greeks during the plundering of Chrysa and given to Agamemnon as a prize of war. Forced by the intervention of Apollo to send the girl back to Chryses, her father, Agamemnon announces that he will in turn take any other maid he desires. His choice is Briseis, the slave of Achilles. Agamemnon's demand leads to a quarrel between the two Greeks.

Briseis (brī'sĭ·əs), a captive slave taken by Achilles as a prize of war. Agamemnon's announcement that he intends to take the girl into his own tent leads to a quarrel between the two men. Forced to surrender Briseis, Achilles and his followers retire from the battlefield and refuse to engage in the fierce fighting that follows. Agamemnon returns the girl to Achilles shortly before the sulking warrior undergoes a change of mood and returns to the fighting in order to avenge the death of his friend Patroclus.

Patroclus (pă·trō'kləs), the noble squire and loyal friend of Achilles. His death at the hands of Hector is mercilessly and horribly revenged when Achilles and Hector meet in hand-to-hand combat and the Greek warrior kills his Trojan rival. Reasonable in argument and courageous in the face of great odds, Patroclus distinguishes himself in battle and is sublime in his willingness to die for a cause and a friend.

515

Odysseus (ō·dĭs′ūs), the crafty, middle-aged warrior who with Diomedes scouts the Trojan camp, captures a Trojan spy, Dolon, and kills Rhesus, a Thracian ally of the Trojans. Although a minor figure in the story, he serves as a foil to haughty Agamemnon and sulking Achilles. He and Nestor are the counselors who interpret rightly the will of the gods.

Diomedes (dī′ō·mē′dēz), a valiant Argive warrior who dashes so often and fearlessly between the Greek and Trojan lines that it is difficult to tell on which side he is fighting. He is the companion of Odysseus on a night-scouting expedition in the Trojan camp, and he is the slayer of Pandarus. In hand-to-hand fighting he attacks Aeneas so fiercely that the gods wrap the Trojan in a veil of mist to protect him from Diomedes' onslaught.

Dolon (dō′lən), a Trojan spy captured and put to death by Odysseus and Diomedes.

Nestor (nĕs′tẽr), the hoary-headed King of Pylos and a wise counselor of the Greeks. Though the oldest of the Greek leaders, he survives the ten years of war and returns to his own land, where Telemachus, the son of Odysseus, visits him.

Machaon (mə·kā′ən), the son of Asclepius, the famous physician of the ancient world. He is the chief surgeon in the Greek forces. He heals Menelaus after the King of Sparta has been wounded by an arrow from the bow of Pandarus.

Ajax (ā′jăks), the son of Telamon of Salamis and half brother of Teucer. A warrior of great physical size and strength, he uses his mighty spear to hold off the Trojans attempting to burn the Greek ships after breaching the rampart around the vessels. According to a later story he goes mad when Agamemnon, acting on the advice of Athena, awards the armor of dead Achilles to Odysseus.

Teucer (tōō′sẽr), the half brother of Ajax and a mighty bowman. He helps Ajax defend the Greek ships from the attacking Greeks. During one of the Trojan onslaughts he kills the charioteer of Hector.

Glaucus (glô′kəs), a Lycian ally of the Trojans. Meeting him in battle, Diomedes recognizes the Lycian as a guest-friend by inheritance. To seal a covenant between them, they exchange armor, Glaucus giving up his gold armor, worth a hundred oxen, for the brass armor of Diomedes, worthy only nine oxen.

Sarpedon (sär·pē′dən), leader of the Lycian allies fighting with the Trojans. He is killed by Patroclus.

Aeneas (ē·nē′əs), the son of Anchises and Aphrodite. A warrior descended from a younger branch of the royal house of Troy, he commands the Trojan forces after the death of Hector. Earlier, while trying to protect the fallen body of his friend Pandarus, Aeneas is struck down by Diomedes, who would have slain him if the gods had not hidden the Trojan in a misty cloud. The wounds of Aeneas are miraculously healed in the temple of Apollo and he returns to the battle.

Pandarus (păn′də·rəs), a Lycian ally of the Trojans and a skilled archer. After Paris has been spirited away from his contest with Menelaus, Pandarus aims at the King of Sparta and would have pierced him with an arrow if Athena had not turned the shaft aside. Diomedes kills Pandarus.

Cassandra (kă·săn′drə), the daughter of King Priam and Queen Hecuba. Gifted with second sight, she is never to have her prophecies believed because she has rejected the advances of Apollo. She becomes Agamemnon's captive after the fall of Troy.

Helenus (hĕ′lə·nəs), the son of King Priam and Queen Hecuba. Like his sister Cassandra, he possesses the gift of second sight. He eventually marries Andromache, the wife of his brother Hector.

516

Deïphobus (dē·ï′fə·bəs), the son of King Priam and Queen Hecuba. He becomes the husband of Helen after the death of Paris and is killed during the sack of Troy.

Antenor (ăn·tē′nər), the Trojan elder who advises that Helen be returned to the Greeks in order to avoid bloodshed.

Polydamus (pŏ·lĭ·dă′məs), a shrewd, clear-headed leader of the Trojans.

Aphrodite (ă·frō·dī′tē), the goddess of Love. Because Paris had awarded her the fated golden apple and Aeneas is her son, she aids the Trojans during the war.

Apollo (ə·pŏ′lō), the god of Poetry, Music, and Prophecy, as well as the protector of flocks and the patron of bowmen. He fights on the side of the Trojans.

Athena (ə·thē·nə), also called **Pallas**

Athena, the goddess of Wisdom. She aids the Achaians.

Poseidon (pō·sī′dən), the god of the Sea and Earthquakes. The enemy of the Trojans, he aids the Achaians.

Ares (ā′rēz), the god of War. Because of Aphrodite, he fights on the side of the Trojans.

Hera (hĭr′ə), the consort of Zeus and the enemy of the Trojans.

Zeus (zōōs), the supreme deity. He remains for the most part neutral during the war.

Thetis (thē′tĭs), a Nereid, the mother of Achilles, whom she aids in his quarrel with Agamemnon.

Hephaestus (hē·fĕs′təs), the artificer of the gods. At the request of Thetis he makes the suit of armor which Achilles is wearing when he slays Hector.

THE IMPORTANCE OF BEING EARNEST

Author: Oscar Wilde (1856-1900)
Time of action: Late nineteenth century
First presented: 1895

PRINCIPAL CHARACTERS

Algernon Moncrief, called **Algy,** a young man of fashion, considerable worldly charm, and a confirmed Bunburyist; that is, he uses an imaginary sick friend's name and condition as an excuse to leave London when he finds his aristocratic aunt, Lady Bracknell, too domineering or her dinner parties too dull. He delights in the artificial, the trivial, the faddish, and he employs them for his own amusement, the only thing about which, as he insists, he is ever serious. Out for a jape, he poses as John Worthing's fictitious brother Ernest in order to court his friend's ward, Cecily Cardew. Though genuinely in love, he never abandons his pose of reckless pretense or his cynically amusing observations on coun-

try and city life, manners, fashions, and relatives.

John Worthing, J.P., called **Jack,** Algernon Moncrief's friend, who poses as Ernest in order to win the hand of Algy's cousin, the Hon. Gwendolen Fairfax, Lady Bracknell's daughter. Also a Bunburyist, he has invented a fictitious brother Ernest, a reprobate who is always getting into scrapes, as an excuse for his frequent visits to London. Jack is serious about most things, especially love. He was a foundling, brought up by a wealthy man who made Jack the guardian of his benefactor's granddaughter, Cecily Cardew. When Jack proposes to Gwendolyn he arouses Lady Bracknell's dis-

517

pleasure because he cannot trace his family tree. All he knows is that he had been found abandoned in a leather bag left at Victoria Station. Finally his parentage is traced, and he learns that he is the long-lost son of Lady Bracknell's sister, that Algy is his younger brother, and that his Christian name really is Ernest. This last fact is the most pleasing, for Gwendolyn could not possibly love him under any other name.

Lady Augusta Bracknell, Algernon Moncrief's aunt, a strong-willed woman of fashion who lives only by society's dictates. The hostess at numerous dinner parties to which her nephew is always invited but which he seldom attends, she dominates the lives of all about her in the same compulsive fashion that makes her move only in the best circles. Although Jack Worthing is an eligible young bachelor of means, she rejects his suit of Gwendolyn and advises him to find some acceptable relatives as quickly as possible. Although witty in her pronouncements, she never deviates into good sense about the artificial world she inhabits with other snobs and pretenders, but her sense of social superiority is punctured when she learns that her daughter's rejected suitor is her own nephew.

The Hon. Gwendolyn Fairfax, Lady Bracknell's daughter, in love with Jack Worthing, whose name she believes to be Ernest. Although she moves in the same conventional snobbish social world with her mother, her outlook is whimsical and rebellious. Determined to marry the man of her choice, she is pleased to discover that Worthing, his parentage revealed, can offer her not only the right name and devotion but also family connections and wealth. She accommodates herself to her good fortune.

Cecily Cardew, an eighteen-year-old girl given to romantic dreams and a diary of fictitious events. She is the ward of Jack Worthing, who had been adopted by her eccentric grandfather. Lovely, determined, rusticated, she is seemingly without guile, but she is in reality as poised as her newly discovered friend, Gwendolyn Fairfax. The dupe of her guardian's story that he has a wicked brother named Ernest in the city, she is charmed and won when that supposed roué, as impersonated by Algy Moncrief, appears in the country. She is also pleased that the man she intends to marry is named Ernest. After learning the truth, she decides that she still loves him, in spite of his having such a name as Algernon.

Miss Letitia Prism, the forgetful authoress of a sentimental three-volume romance, the governess of Cecily Cardew and, earlier, of Jack Worthing. Bent on marriage herself, she contrives to keep her charge's mind on the serious business of learning inconsequentials. In the end she is revealed as the absent-minded nurse who twenty-eight years before had placed the infant Ernest Moncrief in a leather handbag deposited in the cloakroom at Victoria station and the manuscript of her novel in a perambulator.

The Rev. Frederick Chasuble, D.D., an Anglican clergyman who is amenable to performing any rite for anyone at any time, in much the same way that he fits one sermon into many contexts. Delightful in his metaphorical allusions, he meets his match in Miss Prism, whose allusions contain direct revelation of matrimonial intent.

IN DUBIOUS BATTLE

Author: John Steinbeck (1902-   )
Time of action: The 1930's
First published: 1936

Mac, a Communist labor organizer who organizes a fruit pickers' strike. After many hardships, in the face of starvation and imminent eviction, the strike seems doomed. Then Mac rallies the strikers with a stirring speech over the body of his friend and co-organizer, Jim Nolan, who is shot when he and Mac are enticed into a trap.

Jim Nolan, the friend and co-organizer who is finally killed. The son of a workingman whose death was caused by policemen's blows, he has come to communism by way of starvation and early ill-treatment.

London, the leader of the fruit pickers.

Doc Burton, a philosopher and skeptic. He does much to maintain the sanitation of the camp and the strikers' health during the strike. Things worsen after his disappearance. It is in response to a report that he is lying wounded in a field that Jim and Mac rush out into the trap in which Jim is killed.

Al Townsend, the owner of a lunch cart. He gives handouts to the strikers, for whom he feels sympathy. His father permits the strikers to camp on his farm.

Lisa London, the daughter of the camp leader. Mac's influence around the camp greatly increases after he, giving the impression he is a doctor, delivers Lisa of a baby.

Joy, an old and crippled comrade who is killed in an early conflict. Mac's speech on this occasion does much to unify the workers.

Dick, a handsome comrade who uses his charms on women in order to get food for the strikers.

IN THE WILDERNESS

Author: Sigrid Undset (1882-1949)
Time of action: Early fourteenth century
First published: 1927

Olav Audunsson (also see "The Axe" and "The Snake Pit"), the master of Hestviken. When his wife dies, he goes to England. There he is tempted by the pleasures of the flesh and of violence, part of his redemption, he believes, for his unconfessed crime of murder. He returns to Hestviken, where there is conflict between him and his supposed son Eirik. Wounded while fighting the invading Swedes, Olav recovers but feels that he has become an old man.

Eirik, the son of Olav's late wife Ingunn (also see "The Axe" and "The Snake Pit") and falsely claimed by Olav. After much conflict, he leaves Hestviken and is reported to be among the men-at-arms at Oslo. Olav goes there to provide Eirik with money and a squire's gear, and the two part amiably.

Cecilia Olavsdatter (also see "The Snake Pit"), the daughter of Olav and Ingunn. A healthy, spirited girl, on one occasion she slashes a man who, after a drinking party, tries to seize her. Olav feels that she should be the boy of the house.

Asger Magnusson, an old friend of Olav. Dying, he asks Olav to foster his daughter.

Bothild Asgersdatter, who, after her father's death, goes to Hestviken, where she and Cecilia live as sisters.

Mærta Birgersdatter, the mother-in-law of Asger. She comes with her granddaughter Bothild to Hestviken. Grim, gaunt, but capable, she runs the house well but does not get along with Eirik.

Torhild Björnsdatter (also see "The Snake Pit"), the mother of a child by Olav; she lives at Rundmyr, the farm he gave her and carries on for her. After she marries, Olav asks her to send their son to live with him, but she refuses.

Ketil, a young man on the farm. Torhild marries him.

Björn (also see "The Snake Pit"), the son of Torhild and Olav.

Liv, a slatternly serving-woman at Hestviken. Returning from England, Olav marries her to his house-carl and sends the pair to live at Rundmyr, so that she will not corrupt his daughter.

Arnketil, Olav's house-carl, married to Liv. After their move, Rundmyr gets a bad name as a place of gaming and wenching and as a thieves' den.

Sira Hallbjörn, a priest who loves falconry and hunting. Olav is often in his company. Sira is killed fighting the invading Swedes.

Sir Ragnvald Torvaldsson, a skillful and courtly knight whom Eirik serves in Oslo.

Duke Eirik, the leader of the invading Swedish troops.

King Haakon, Duke Eirik's father-in-law, against whom the Duke is directing his troops.

INAZUMA-BYÔSHI

Author: Santô Kyôden (1761-1816)
Time of action: Fifteenth century
First published: 1806

PRINCIPAL CHARACTERS

Sasaki Katsura, a young man, the elder son of a feudal lord and his late first wife. After a period of dissipation, Katsura, with the help of loyal friends and retainers, successfully foils a plot to prevent him from being named as his father's heir.

Sasaki Sadakuni, Katsura's father, a feudal lord of Yamato Province. For a time he is deceived by the plot against Katsura. But when the plot is revealed he forgives Katsura and makes him his heir.

Kumode no Kata (Lady Spider), the present wife of Sadakuni and a plotter against Katsura. She wants her own son to be Sadakuni's heir.

Sasaki Hanagata, the twelve-year-old son of Lady Spider and Sadakuni.

Ichô no Mae (Lady Ginkgo), Katsura's wife. Persecuted and abducted by her husband's enemies, she is rescued and finally reunited with her husband.

Tsukiwaka (Young-moon), the young son of Katsura and Lady Ginkgo. He is saved from attempted kidnaping and at last is restored to his parents.

Fuwa Dôken (Road-dog), steward to the House of Sasaki. He is the chief villain, Lady Spider's co-plotter. Foiled in his attempts to discredit Katsura and to murder Lady Ginkgo and Young-moon, his plot is exposed and he is imprisoned.

Fuwa Banzaemon, Katsura's retainer and the son of Road-dog. He promotes Katsura's infatuation with a dancing girl whom he himself loves. Discharged, he

520

commits a murder and hides out in the brothels of Kyoto.

Fujinami (Wisteria-wave), the dancing girl loved by Katsura and Banzaemon. She is killed by a loyal retainer of Katsura.

Sasara Sampachirô, Katsura's loyal retainer. Having killed Wisteria-wave, he rescues Young-moon and goes into hiding under the name of Namuemon. Later he saves Young-moon's life by beheading his own blind son and identifying the head as that of Young-moon.

Kuritaro (Chestnut-son), Sampachirô's blind son, sacrificed by his father in order to save the life of Young-moon.

Kaede (Maple), Sampachirô's daughter, who is haunted by serpents. Having sold herself for a treasured painting previously stolen by a disloyal retainer of the House of Sasaki, she is cured of her affliction by the magical power of the painting.

Hasebe Unroku, a disloyal retainer. He steals the magic painting and disappears. Later he is recognized as the perpetrator of a six-year-old robbery. Sampachirô forces him to commit suicide to expiate his sins.

Nagoya Sansaburô, a loyal retainer. Unsuccessful in his early efforts to reform Katsura, he engineers Young-moon's

escape. It is he who finally locates Banzaemon and his gang.

Nagoya Saburozaemon, Sansaburô's father, killed by Banzaemon.

Yuasa Matahei, a painter, the brother of Wisteria-wave. Impressed by Sampachirô's loyalty and learning that Sampachirô aided his wife when she was robbed six years before, he takes only symbolic revenge for the killing of Wisteria-wave: he assaults Sampachirô's hat instead of his head.

Umezu Kamon (Good-gate), a hero-recluse. He rescues Lady Ginkgo from death at the hands of Road-dog. He is instrumental in restoring Katsura to his father's favor.

Sarujiro (Monkey-son), a street preacher and Sansaburô's son. He saves Katsura's life at a temple festival.

Shikazô (Deer), Sansaburô's faithful servant, who helps him search for Banzaemon.

Ashikaga Yoshimasa, under whose shogunship Sadakuni lives.

Hamana, the Governor General with whose connivance Road-dog plans to take over his lord's domain.

Katsumoto, the new Governor General, who backs Katsura in his attempts to return to paternal favor.

INDEPENDENT PEOPLE

Author: Halldór Laxness (1902-   )
Time of action: Twentieth century
First published: 1934-1935

PRINCIPAL CHARACTERS

Gudbjartur Jonsson (Bjartur), a stubborn, roughly poetic, often cruel, fiercely independent crofter. He loses two wives, one quickly, the other after years of his harshness. He rears Asta, knowing of her illegitimacy. He loses several children in their infancy, Helgi as a child, and Nonni to a home in America. Only Gvendur remains after the ejection of the pregnant Asta. But even Gvendur longs to join Nonni in America and later to join the political radicals opposed to

521

the Icelandic government. At last, reunited with Asta after the loss of his big, unfinished home by foreclosure, Bjartur takes her and her children to live with him and Hallbera in the old woman's sod home. Bjartur appears to be a symbol not only of the Icelandic peasant but perhaps of land-loving, independent farmers the world over.

Rosa, Bjartur's first wife, a small, sturdy girl with a cast in one eye; pregnant with Asta when she marries Bjartur. A believer in tradition and folk superstition, she opposes Bjartur's scorn of these things. She dies when Asta is born.

Finna, Bjartur's second wife, a pauper sent by Madam Myri to care for Asta. She dies after several years of poor diet, rapid childbearing, and unfeeling scorn and neglect, climaxed by Bjartur's slaughter of her beloved cow.

Asta Sollilja (Sola), Rosa's romantic, imaginative daughter, doomed to unhappiness. Pale-faced and dark-haired, she has, like her mother, a cast in one eye. Pregnant by a drunken, tubercular tutor, she is thrown out by Bjartur, has another child by another father, and is carrying a third when Bjartur comes for her. Independent like Bjartur, she has rejected the offer of Ingolfur, her father, to help her. Consumptive when she is reunited with Bjartur, she has only a short time to live but finds joy in the anticipation of being again with the first man she ever loved. It is ironic that, having lost all his own children, Bjartur should seek out the daughter he had scorned as having none of his blood in her. Symbolically, the two strong independents are drawn to each other.

Gvendur, Bjartur's son who plans to join Nonni in America but who decides to remain at home after falling in love with Ingolfur's only daughter, who later shuns him as an inferior.

Jon (Nonni), Bjartur's younger son, who goes to America to join an uncle just before World War I.

Ingolfur Arnarson Jonsson, Asta's father, manager of a Co-operative Society.

Helgi, Bjartur and Finna's first son, lost on the moor.

Bailiff Jon of Myri, Bjartur's employer for eighteen years. Slovenly, like a tramp in appearance, he is nevertheless more forceful and complex than the men over whom he exerts authority. Bjartur dislikes him.

Madam Myri, poetess wife of Bailiff Jon and mother of Ingolfur Arnarson. She has an aristocratic consciousness of her superiority to people like Bjartur and Rosa.

Thorthur of Nitherkot, Rosa's father, a serenely stoical old man.

Pastor Gudmundur, the parish minister, who is also an able farmer and breeder of fine sheep. Blunt and gruff in speech, he combines superficial Christian views with his apparent unconcern for unfortunate people whom he regards as contemptible sinners.

Hallbera, aged mother of Rosa.

Audur Jonsdottir, ladylike daughter of Bailiff Jon. When she leaves for Reykjavik, Bjartur suspects it is because she is pregnant by a man who camped on his land some time earlier.

Fritha, a talkative, complaining old woman who works one summer for Bjartur.

INDIAN SUMMER

Author: William Dean Howells (1837-1920)
Time of action: Shortly after the American Civil War
First published: 1886

522

Theodore Colville, a middle-aged American architect who leaves Italy for the United States when a young woman rejects his suit. In America he runs a newspaper for a time and then enters Indiana politics. Defeated at the polls, he returns to Italy to resume his study of architecture. He learns to love two American women, one a middle-aged widow, the other a girl half his age. He almost marries the girl but complications and misunderstandings prevent him from doing so. Finally, he marries the widow.

Imogene Graham, a young girl who falls in love with Colville, though he is old enough to be her father. She finally understands, chiefly through the influence of her mother and the appearance of a young minister, that her love is actually infatuation. She returns to America from Italy and marries the minister, who is now established in a prosperous church near Buffalo.

Lina Bowen, a widow who has known Colville for some time. She acts as Imogene's chaperone while Imogene and

Colville see each other. She tries to act properly toward the Colville-Imogene affair by not allowing her personal bias to enter her discussions with Imogene about the problems that her marriage with Colville may produce. When Imogene at last rejects Colville, Mrs. Bowen accepts Colville's suit.

Effie Bowen, Mrs. Bowen's thirteen-year-old daughter, who is very fond of Colville. It is largely through Effie's efforts that Colville and Mrs. Bowen finally decide to marry.

Mr. Morton, a young minister who loves Imogene and comes to Italy to court her. Both return to the United States and the Colvilles suspect that they will marry.

Mrs. Graham, Imogene's mother, who comes to Italy when she learns that her daughter is thinking seriously of marrying Colville. Her influence on her daughter is instrumental in causing the girl to see that her love for Colville is only infatuation.

INDIANA

Author: George Sand (Mme. Aurore Dudevant, 1804-1876)
Time of action: Early nineteenth century
First published: 1832

PRINCIPAL CHARACTERS

Indiana Delmare (ăṅ·dyȧ·nȧ′ dĕl·mȧr′), a young woman who lives a bored and frustrated existence. She is faithful to her husband but is very friendly with her cousin, Sir Ralph Brown. When Raymon de Ramière begins paying her attentions, she reciprocates, but when she decides to leave her husband to go to de Ramière, she finds, much to her dismay, that he has married someone else. She finally retires to a life of seclusion with Sir Ralph.

Monsieur Delmare (mȧ·syœ′ dĕl·mȧr′),

Indiana's husband. He is very suspicious and jealous but never hears of his wife's affairs with de Ramière. He is a businessman, financially ruined, who retires to the Isle of Bourbon. It is at this point that Indiana leaves him.

Rodolphe Brown (Sir Ralph) (rô·dôlf′), Indiana's faithful admirer and cousin. He is a frequent guest in the Delmare house and a trusted friend, and he is very fond of Indiana. After Indiana runs away from her husband and finds that de Ramière is married, she meets Sir Ralph and they decide on a suicide pact. They change their minds, however, and go away to live together as recluses.

Raymon de Ramière (rā·mōń' də rȧmyĕr'), Indiana's lover. He is a scoundrel who is found climbing over the Delmare's wall one night. He has actually come to visit Indiana's maid; but once he has met Indiana, he tires of the maid and begins to pursue her mistress. He is fickle, and when Indiana leaves with her husband for the Isle of Bourbon, he marries someone else.

Noun (nōōn'), Indiana's maid. She has been de Ramière's mistress for some time before he meets Indiana. She finds that she is pregnant and commits suicide because de Ramière refuses to marry her.

INÊS DE CASTRO

Author: António Ferreira (1528?-1569)
Time of action: 1354-1360
First presented: c. 1558

PRINCIPAL CHARACTERS

Inês de Castro, the illegitimate daughter of a nobleman, who is beloved by Prince Pedro, the son and heir of King Alfonso. On the death, in childbirth, of Prince Pedro's wife, Inês de Castro hopes that, now that her lover is provided with a legitimate heir, their love may be made public, their marriage solemnized, and their four children recognized by their grandfather. Before her hopes can be realized, however, she is murdered by the King's advisers.

Prince Pedro, heir of Alfonso IV and the lover of Inês de Castro. Compelled by his father to marry a Princess of Castile, he feels free at her death in childbirth to proclaim his love for Inês de Castro. He pleads with the King for a state wedding and the recognition of their four children. The King refuses, and when Inês is killed by the royal advisers, Prince Pedro swears vengeance on all involved in the murder, including his father.

Alfonso IV, King of Portugal and the father of Prince Pedro. In an attempt to put an end to the love of Prince Pedro for the illegitimate Inês de Castro, he compels his son to marry a Princess of Castile, who dies at the birth of a legitimate heir. When his son then begs for a state wedding to Inês and the recognition of their four children, King Alfonso refuses, and permits the murder of Inês.

Diogo Lopes Pacheco,
Pero Coelho, and
Gonzalves, advisers to King Alfonso and the murderers of Inês de Castro.

THE INFORMER

Author: Liam O'Flaherty (1896-   )
Time of action: The 1920's
First published: 1925

PRINCIPAL CHARACTERS

Francis Joseph McPhillip, an Irish revolutionary. Having killed a man, he is disavowed by the rebel organization and is a lonely fugitive. In his great loneli-

524

ness he tries to see his family. Because he is betrayed the police find him at his parents' home, and he commits suicide.

Gypo Nolan, the informer, a stupid man and an Irish revolutionary. Because he is penniless he tells the police where to find Francis. He does not really know what he is doing or why. Later he goes to the McPhillip home and gives Mrs. McPhillip part of his blood money. The rebel organization condemns him for his act, and he is shot as he flees his executioners. He runs into a church to die. There Mrs. McPhillip forgives his treachery to her son.

Katie Fox, a prostitute who occasionally befriends Gypo out of pity. When he seeks refuge from his organization after having turned informer, Katie discloses his whereabouts, hoping by this act in some way to expiate her own sins.

Bartly, a revolutionary sent to shadow Gypo.

Dan Gallagher, an intelligent revolutionary leader, though he tends to be terrified in an emergency. He loves Mary McPhillip, Francis' sister, and takes action against the man who informed against her brother.

Mr. McPhillip, Francis' father.

Mrs. McPhillip, Francis' mother, who forgives Gypo for informing the police of her son's whereabouts as he lies dying at her feet in church.

Mary McPhillip, Francis' sister, loved by Dan.

Rat Mulligan, a man falsely accused by Gypo of having betrayed Francis.

Maggie, a prostitute patronized by Gypo.

THE INNOCENT VOYAGE

Author: Richard Hughes (1900-)
Time of action: Early nineteenth century
First published: 1929

PRINCIPAL CHARACTERS

Mr. Bas-Thornton, a plantation owner in Jamaica who sends his children to school in England. On the way the children, with two of their friends, are taken aboard a pirate ship. Though the children are returned within a few months, their father and mother never realize what the experience has done to them psychologically.

Mrs. Bas-Thornton, his wife.

John, oldest of the Bas-Thornton children. He is killed in a fall from a warehouse when his pirate captors, who have taken the children accidentally and treated them well, are selling their booty at a Cuban port.

Emily, John's sister, an excitable ten-year-old child. She and the pirate captain

achieve a strange psychological relationship, though a stormy one. While emotionally upset, Emily slashes one of the pirates' prisoners, a Dutch sea captain, to death with a knife. Months later she allows the pirate captain to go to his death by hanging for her own crime, without apparently suffering any qualms of conscience.

Edward,
Rachael, and
Laura, other children of the Bas-Thorntons.

Margaret Fernandez, Emily's friend and fellow captive. Margaret voluntarily goes to the captain's cabin to live, being an older girl. She knows that Emily actually killed the prisoner but does nothing to

525

change what happens to the innocent man. She appears to suffer from shock and loss of memory when she finally reaches England.

Harry Fernandez, Margaret's young brother.

Captain Jonsen, the pirate captain. He is not a bad man, so far as the children are concerned. He sees that they are left alone by his men and treated well. He did not intend to keep the children and gives them up voluntarily to a passing ship. Later he is condemned to hang for the murder Emily committed.

Captain James Marpole, from whose raided ship pirates remove the children for their supper. Thinking the children killed, he sails away, leaving them aboard the pirate ship.

THE INSPECTOR GENERAL

Author: Nikolai V. Gogol (1809-1852)
Time of action: Early nineteenth century
First presented: 1836

PRINCIPAL CHARACTERS

Anton Antonovich Skvoznik-Dmokhanovsky (än·tōn′ än·tō′nə·vĭch skvōz′nĭk-dmōō·hän·ōf′skĭ), the Prefect of a small provincial town in early nineteenth century Russia. He has received a warning letter from a friend that an Inspector General is coming, traveling incognito, to visit the district in an attempt to find evidence of bribery and injudicial acts. The prefect calls a meeting of the citizens and orders them to mend their ways. However, he does not take kindly to their criticism that he has been taking bribes and recently had the wife of a non-commissioned officer beaten.

Ivan Alexandrovich Hlestakov (ĭ·vän′ ä·lĕk·sän′drə·vĭch hlĕs·tä·kōf′), a smartly dressed traveler who, taking lodgings at the local inn, is mistaken for the Inspector. A shrewd opportunist, he accepts money and gifts, goes to stay at the Prefect's house, and accepts an invitation to an official dinner at the hospital. He gets drunk and goes to sleep. When he awakens, he makes love to the Prefect's daughter and asks to marry her. Then he requests five hundred rubles from complaining shopkeepers, borrows a coach, and, after writing to a friend an account of his hoax, rides off with promises to return the next day.

Osip (ō′sĭp) or **Yosif** (yō′sĭf), Ivan Alexandrovich's elderly and philosophic servant, who considers all gentlefolk queer. He is shrewd enough to capitalize on his master's mistaken identity and adds to the hoax by allowing himself to be bribed into revealing all sorts of imaginary details of his Ivan's high place in society. Then he advises his master to skip town.

Anna Andreyevna (än′nə än·drā′əv·nə), the Prefect's wife, given to arguing about clothes. She enjoys having Ivan Alexandrovich ogle her and delightedly agrees to his proposal of marriage to her daughter.

Marya Antonovna (mä′ryə än·tō′nəv·nə), the Prefect's daughter.

Mishka (mĭsh′kə), a servant of the mayor.

Piotr Ivanovich Bobchinsky (pyō′tr ĭ·vä′nə·vĭch bôb·chĭn′skĭy) and
Piotr Ivanovich Dobchinsky (pyō′tr ĭ·vä′nə·vĭch dôb·chĭn′skĭy), two squireens of the town who discover a mysterious stranger at the inn and declare him the expected Inspector General.

Artemy Filippovitch Zemlyanika (är·tĕ′-

526

mĭy fĭ·lĭp′pə·vĭch zĕm·lyä·nĭ′kə), the manager of the hospital. He believes that if a patient is going to die, he will die. To prepare for the arrival of the Inspector General he provides clean nightcaps for his patients and puts over each bed a Latin sign stating the patient's illness.

Ammos Fyodorovitch Lyapkin-Tyapkin (äm′məs fyō′də·rə·vĭch lyäp′kin-tyäp′-kĭn), the local judge, a dedicated huntsman who keeps his guns and his whip in the courtroom.

Stepan Ilyitch Uhovyortov (stĕ·pän′ ĭ·lyĭch ōō·hôv·yôr·tôf′), the Police Inspector.

Luka Lukich Hlopov (lōō′kə lōō′kĭch hlô·pôf′), the head of the local school. He is ordered to curb the unprofessional actions of some of his teachers, like the history teacher who leaps on his desk to describe the Macedonian Wars and the fat one who grimaces and pulls his beard under his necktie.

Shpyokin (shpyō′kĭn), the postmaster, who reads all the mail. Told to be on the lookout for details about the visit of the Inspector General, he opens Ivan Alexandrovich's letter and reads the rogue's description of the muddle-headed town officials and the hoax played on them.

The Inspector General, who, at the end of the play, arrives at the inn and sends a policeman to summon the town officials to wait upon him immediately.

INTRUDER IN THE DUST

Author: William Faulkner (1897-1962)
Time of action: Early 1930's
First published: 1948

PRINCIPAL CHARACTERS

Charles (Chick) Mallison, a sixteen-year-old boy. While hunting with two Negro companions, he falls through the ice and is taken home by an old Negro, Lucas Beauchamp, to dry out and have some food. All offers of payment are refused by Lucas, leaving Chick with an unpaid obligation on his conscience. When Lucas is accused of murder, Chick goes to the old man's assistance and helps to prove his innocence. He feels himself free of his debt until Lucas appears and insists on paying for services rendered.

Lucas Beauchamp, an old Negro. When he takes Chick Mallison home after an accident, he proudly refuses payment for his hospitality and puts the boy in his debt. Later, when Lucas is falsely accused of murder, he is assisted by Chick, who believes he has evened the score until the old Negro comes to pay for services rendered. When Lucas' two dollars are accepted for "expenses," he demands a receipt.

Gavin Stevens, Chick Mallison's uncle and the lawyer for Lucas Beauchamp.

Aleck Sander, Chick Mallison's young colored friend and companion in his efforts to prove Lucas Beauchamp's innocence.

Miss Habersham, an old woman of good family who assists Chick Mallison and Aleck Sander in their efforts on behalf of Lucas Beauchamp.

Hope Hampton, the sheriff.

Crawford Gowrie, the murderer, the proof of whose guilt saves the falsely accused Lucas Beauchamp from the violence of a mob.

527

THE INVISIBLE MAN

Author: H. G. Wells (1866-1946)
Time of action: Late nineteenth century
First published: 1897

PRINCIPAL CHARACTERS

Griffin, the Invisible Man. He arrives at a village inn and takes a room. Wearing dark glasses and bushy side whiskers, and having a completely bandaged head, he causes much curiosity in the village. Later it develops that these are a disguise for his invisibility. Getting into trouble over an unpaid bill, he escapes and begins to terrify the people with his mysterious thefts. Wounded, he flees to a former acquaintance's rooms. He reveals that to get money for his experiments in invisibility he robbed his father of money belonging to someone else, and as a result his father committed suicide. Going thoroughly mad, he sends his former friend a note announcing that he plans to kill a man each day; his friend is to be the first victim. After a grotesque struggle, the Invisible Man is held by two men and struck with a spade by another man. As he is dying, his body slowly becomes visible.

Dr. Kemp, a physician. Griffin knew him when both were university students. To Kemp, Griffin reveals his story. Later he says that he plans to use Kemp's rooms as a base for his reign of terror,

and he threatens Kemp's life. Kemp goes to the police, with whose aid he finally succeeds in destroying Griffin.

Mr. Hall, the landlord of the Coach and Horses Inn, where Griffin takes a room.

Mrs. Hall, his wife. The Halls are the first to be puzzled by unexplainable activities on the part of their guest. Unintimidated, however, Mr. Hall swears out a warrant for Griffin's arrest after the lodger becomes abusive because of ill feeling over an unpaid bill. After a struggle, Griffin at last unmasks and escapes in the ensuing horror and confusion.

Colonel Ayde, chief of the Burdock police. Kemp goes to him with his information about Griffin. Ayde is wounded by his own revolver, which Griffin has snatched from his pocket.

Marvel, a tramp whom Griffin frightens into aiding him. Griffin's turning on Marvel is the occasion for some eerie scenes of pursuit.

[**Mr. Wicksteed,** who is found murdered. A weird manhunt for Griffin follows.]

IOLANTHE

Author: W. S. Gilbert (1836-1911)
Time of action: Nineteenth century
First presented: 1882

PRINCIPAL CHARACTERS

The Lord Chancellor, the husband of the supposedly dead Iolanthe. Highly susceptible to feminine charm, he hates to

give away his lovely wards in Chancery in marriage. He is sometimes jocular, sometimes severe, and quite jealous of

Strephon, who he does not know is his son. The return of Iolanthe keeps him from marrying Phyllis.

Iolanthe (ī·ō·lăn'thē), a loving, gentlehearted fairy, condemned to banishment instead of death by the kindness of the Queen of the Fairies. She has violated the fairy law by marrying a mortal. After her release by the Queen, she risks death a second time to save the happiness of her son.

Strephon (strĕ'fŏn), an Arcadian shepherd, the son of the Chancellor and Iolanthe. He is a fairy down to the waist, but human and material in the legs; therefore, he can accomplish none of the fairy tricks such as going through a keyhole or becoming completely invisible. He loves Phyllis, but in his anger at her jealousy, he takes revenge by going into Parliament and thwarting the will of the lords.

Phyllis (fĭ'lĭs), a beautiful shepherdess loved by the House of Peers to a man, as well as by the Lord Chancellor and Strephon. Finding Strephon kissing a beautiful girl of apparently seventeen (Iolanthe), she refuses to believe the girl is his mother. Finally she becomes convinced that he is truthful, and she consents to marry him.

The Queen of the Fairies, a noble-hearted monarch in whom severity and mercy struggle for mastery. She forgives Iolanthe; but angered at the Peers, she sends Strephon into Parliament to destroy their privileges. When Iolanthe reveals herself to the Chancellor, the Queen sentences her to death; but she again relents on finding that all the other fairies have fallen in love with mortals. She is captivated by the manly charms of Private Willis, but controls her passion until the fairy constitution is changed to make it a mortal crime "not" to marry a mortal.

Private Willis, a philosophical sentry who is willing to inconvenience himself to save a female in distress.

The Earl of Mountararat (mount·â'rə·răt) and
Earl Tolloler, suitors of Phyllis.

ION

Author: Euripides (c. 485-c. 406 B.C.)
Time of action: Remote antiquity
First presented: Fifth century B.C.

PRINCIPAL CHARACTERS

Ion (ī'ŏn), the son of Apollo and Creusa, a princess of Athens. At his birth he was, by Apollo's command, hidden in a cave from which, unknown to Creusa, Hermes carried the infant to Delphi. There he was nurtured in the temple. As keeper of the temple he leads a happy life, marred only by his ignorance of his origin. At the beginning of the play Creusa and Xuthus, to whom she has been given in marriage because of his military aid to Athens, come to the temple to seek Apollo's aid because they are childless. Ion and Creusa meet outside the temple and an immediate sympathy is born between them: Creusa is childless and Ion lacks knowledge of his background. Creusa tells him her own story, alleging it to be that of another woman on whose behalf she wants to question Apollo. Ion, in his sheltered innocence, is shocked that Apollo could have behaved as he did to Creusa and tries to make excuses for him. This is the first contact of Ion's cloistered virtue with worldliness; it is continued through the play and he quickly gains self-confidence and strength of will. Apollo gives Ion to Xuthus as his own son and the two, as father and son, leave to celebrate this gift of the god. Creusa, thinking that an alien will come to rule Athens, plots to kill Ion. He learns of her attempts and leads the Delphians to stone her, but she takes refuge at the altar of Apollo. A priestess of Apollo appears with the cradle in which she found Ion, and Creusa recognizes it. Ion suspects a trick to save her life but, after she describes certain tokens left in the cradle, he acknowledges that she is his mother. Athena appears to assure Ion that Apollo is his father (though the fact is to be kept from Xuthus), that he will rule Athens, and that his four sons will sire the tribes that will dwell on the coasts and on the isles of the Aegean Sea.

Creusa (krē·ōō′sə), the daughter of E-rechtheus, King of Athens. Seduced by Apollo and forced to abandon her child to die, as she believes, she is introduced as a tragic character. In her first interview with Ion she is able for the most part to keep her sorrow and feeling of rebellion without bounds, but she ends by criticizing Apollo directly and by name for compelling her to abandon his child. She also reveals that she has not married Xuthus by choice, so that when Ion is revealed as his son she, out of fear that foreigners will rule Athens, plans to kill Ion. The dynastic theme is important in this play and Creusa's national loyalty is the major aspect of it. Her belief that Apollo has given Xuthus a son while she will have no other makes the loss of her own son and the treachery of Apollo seemingly more intolerable and

emphasizes her role as a tragic figure. When the true facts are revealed, she accepts her triumph, her house is saved, and the stigma of childlessness is removed without any of the moral questionings about the actions of the gods which bother Ion.

Xuthus (zū′thûs), Creusa's husband. He consults the oracle and is told that the first man he meets on leaving the temple will be his son. Meeting Ion, he is so overjoyed that he does not worry over the identity of the mother or the problems of accepting a foreigner as heir to the throne of Athens.

The Chorus of Creusa's Attendants. They mirror the point of view of Creusa entirely and it is their function to amplify her feeling and lend support to what she represents in the play.

An Old Man, an aged slave to Creusa. He represents the pride of the house he has served; he is devoted, but foolish and irresponsible. His questioning of Creusa leads to her account of her relations with Apollo. He suggests and attempts to carry out the poisoning of Ion.

The Priestess of Apollo. At the god's direction she reveals the cradle she has kept hidden.

Athena (ə·thē′nə), the goddess of wisdom. She appears as "dea ex machina" sent by Apollo to assure Ion that the god is his father.

Hermes (hûr′mēz), the messenger of the gods, who speaks the prologue. He is not directly concerned in the action, except that he had taken Ion to the shrine at Delphi at Apollo's request. His tone is not emotional or dramatic.

IPHIGENIA IN AULIS

Author: Euripides (c.485-c. 406 B.C.)
Time of action: The beginning of the Trojan War
First presented: c. 405 B.C.

Iphigenia (ĭf′ə·jĭ·nī′ə), the older daughter of King Agamemnon. The Greek prophet Calchas has revealed that Iphigenia must be sacrificed to the goddess Artemis in order to secure a favorable wind for the Greek ships becalmed on their way to conquer Troy. Agamemnon has summoned his daughter to Aulis, where the ships have been delayed, under pretext that she is to be married to Achilles. She appears as a very young and delicate girl, completely devoted to her father. She greets him with affection and gaiety, but the scene is pathetic and filled with tragic irony. When she reappears she has learned that she is to be sacrificed, and she pleads with her father for her life; her appeal is entirely in terms of pity and love, for at this point she sees the sacrifice as entirely a matter between her and her father. Agamemnon replies that he does not serve his personal desires but Greece and that Iphigenia must be sacrificed for the good of the Greek cause. He leaves and Achilles enters. Unaware at first of the use of his name to bring Iphigenia to Aulis, he has since learned of the truth and he has promised Clytemnestra, Iphigenia's mother, to defend the girl; he appears to keep the promise. Iphigenia intervenes, however, for she has resolved to die. She is now the arbiter of the fate of Greece, and she will give her life to obey the will of the gods and to punish the barbarians who took Helen away. With a plea to her mother not to hate Agamemnon or to mourn her death, she leaves to go willingly to her sacrifice. She is the only person in the play who is blind to the weakness of Agamemnon; to her he is a great man, sacrificing her for the sake of Greece.

Agamemnon (ă′gə·mĕm′nŏn), commander-in-chief of the Greek army. He is an ambitious politician, but unsure of his own motives and in some respects a coward. At the beginning of the play he writes a second letter to Iphigenia telling her not to come to Aulis, but his message is intercepted by Menelaus, husband of Helen and brother of Agamemnon. In the interview between the two brothers Agamemnon's true character is revealed; he is ambitious to control the Greek forces and, though he sincerely loves his daughter, he agrees to sacrifice her of his own free will. It is clear that he will do so, for a refusal now may mean opposing the whole army. He lies to Iphigenia and Clytemnestra when they appear. After they have learned the truth, he argues that the sacrifice is necessary for the good of Greece.

Clytemnestra (klī′təm·nĕs′trə), a commanding and efficient woman who treats her weak husband Agamemnon with scant respect. Refusing to return home, as he suggests, she discovers through a servant his true intention of sacrificing his daughter. By appealing to Achilles' injured pride she elicits his promise to defend Iphigenia, but she agrees first to appeal to Agamemnon herself. Her speech to her husband is a strong one containing reproach for his past and threats for the future. To Iphigenia's last request that she should not hate her husband, Clytemnestra replies that he acted by guile and in a manner unworthy of a son of Atreus and that for his deeds "he must needs run a fearful course."

Achilles (ə·kĭ′lēz), the noble Greek warrior whose name is used, without his knowledge, to bring Iphigenia, who expects to become his bride, to Aulis. He comes to speak with Agamemnon and is greeted warmly by Clytemnestra. His amazement causes them to realize the deceit that has been practiced upon them. He is angry at the indignity such usage brings to his name and he promises Clytemnestra, who plays on the insult to his pride, that he will protect Iphigenia. He is self-centered, for he reveals that had his permission been sought he would not have refused it for the sake of Greece. After the appeal to Agamemnon has failed, he reappears; the army is clamoring for the sacrifice and his opposition to it has almost cost him his life. But he is true to his promise. Even after Iphigenia's decision to accept her sacrifice, he offers to wait at the altar to defend her if she should change her mind.

Menelaus (mĕ′nɔ·lā′ɔs), the husband of ravished Helen and brother of Agamemnon. Eager for the sacrifice of Iphigenia, he intercepts Agamemnon's second letter. Although his interpretation of Agamemnon's motives is prejudiced, it corrects and completes Agamemnon's own.

When he is sure that Agamemnon will carry out the sacrifice he insincerely protests affection and pity; he says he has changed his mind and will not demand the sacrifice.

An Old Man, servant of Agamemnon. He sets out with the second message for Iphigenia but is intercepted. Later he reveals Agamemnon's plan to Clytemnestra and Achilles.

The Chorus of Women of Chalcis. They have come to Aulis to see the Greek ships and warriors. Their description of the Greek fleet and army emphasizes the importance of the war to follow.

IPHIGENIA IN TAURIS

Author: Euripides (c. 485-c. 406 B.C.)
Time of action: Several years after the Trojan War
First presented: c. 420 B.C.

PRINCIPAL CHARACTERS

Iphigenia (ĭf′ɔ·jĭ·nī′ɔ), the daughter of King Agamemnon, sister of Orestes and Electra, and a priestess of Artemis in Tauris. According to her opening monologue, Artemis took pity on her just as she was about to be sacrificed at Aulis, snatched her away from the priest's knife, and left a deer in her place. Transported to the land of the barbarian Taurians, she became the priestess of Artemis; it is her duty to preside over the sacrificial murder of all strangers captured by the Taurians. She dislikes both her duties and the country, and her longing for Greece is one of the major themes of the play. After she has spoken the opening monologue, a herdsman brings news that two Greeks have been captured and that Iphigenia must make preparations for their sacrifice. They are Orestes, the brother Iphigenia believes dead, and his friend Pylades. After much questioning in which each is careful not to reveal his identity, brother and sister recognize each other. Orestes, seeking

release from the Furies for the murder of his mother, has been ordered to bring the statue of Artemis and Tauris to Attica. Iphigenia devises a plan for escape and Thoas, King of Tauris, accepts it: she will take Orestes, unfit for sacrifice because of his crime of matricide, and the statue, defiled by his presence, to be cleansed in the sea. The plan succeeds until a storm prevents the Greek ship from leaving the harbor. Just as Thoas is about to send soldiers to kill the Greeks, the goddess Athena appears, orders Thoas to desist from his pursuit, and instructs Iphigenia to establish a new temple to Artemis in Attica; Iphigenia will be its priestess. The characterization of Iphigenia is effective but does not reach great depths; her bitterness against those who would have sacrificed her at Aulis is easily overcome by her longing for Greece and her dislike of the barbarian sacrifices.

Orestes (ō·rĕs′tēz), the brother of Iphigenia. He arrives at Tauris to steal the statue of Artemis and thus gain release from the pursuit of the Furies. Their pursuit drives him to fits of temporary madness, and during one of these he is captured by the Taurians. When Iphigenia offers, before the recognition scene, to save one of the men if he will deliver a letter to Argos for her, Orestes insists that Pylades be saved. After the recognition he follows Iphigenia's plan of escape and Athena promises that he will be released from the Furies.

Pylades (pĭl'ə·dēz), the faithful friend of Orestes and husband of Electra, sister of Iphigenia and Orestes. He is the apostle of common sense, in sharp contrast to Orestes' restlessness. He saves Orestes from despair over the difficulty of his task when they arrive at Tauris, and he fights to defend his companion when they are attacked by the Taurians. He offers to die with Orestes rather than save himself by delivering Iphigenia's letter; he still has hope that Apollo will save them.

Thoas (thô'əs), King of Tauris. A foil to Greek cleverness, he is the simple-minded barbarian. Iphigenia has no difficulty in deceiving him, for he is convinced that Iphigenia hates all things Greek. He is consistently courteous and kind, and rather too gentle and pious to be the ruler of a people whose barbarity is so strongly emphasized.

Athena (ə·thē'nə), the goddess of wisdom. At the end of the play she orders Thoas to give up his pursuit of the Greeks and to send the Chorus home. She has already asked Poseidon to still the waves. She also instructs Iphigenia in the construction of a new temple to Artemis.

The Chorus of Temple Maidens. Exiles from Greece who long to return home, they agree to aid in Iphigenia's escape by not revealing the plan to deceive Thoas. Athena instructs Thoas to send them back to Greece.

A Herdsman. He brings news of the capture of Orestes and Pylades and tells the story of Orestes' madness.

ISRAEL POTTER

Author: Herman Melville (1819-1891)
Time of action: 1774-1826
First published: 1855

PRINCIPAL CHARACTERS

Israel Potter, a wanderer. Brought up in the rugged New England hills and immersed in their austere virtues, he quarrels with his father and leaves home. He wanders about, the innocent American, for fifty years, and in the course of his many adventures, he becomes the spokesman through whom the author satirizes various ideas and institutions, among them war, patriotism, and so-called civilized behavior.

King George III, whom Israel Potter meets in London. The mad King, realizing that Israel is an American, is ineffectually kind to him after the many snubs Israel has received because of his nationality.

Squire Woodcock, a secret friend of America who befriends Israel Potter and sends him on a mission to Benjamin Franklin.

Benjamin Franklin, who gives Israel Potter lessons in proper behavior based on maxims from "Poor Richard's Almanack." The lessons, carefully learned, are quickly forgotten.

John Paul Jones, with whom Israel Potter engages in piracy and in the sea fight between the "Bon Homme Richard" and the "Serapis."

The Earl of Selkirk, whose home is plundered by the pirate companions of Israel

Potter and John Paul Jones. After receiving a large sum of money from another exploit, the two Captains buy back and return the Earl's possessions.

Ethan Allen, whom Israel Potter tries unsuccessfully to help escape from England.

IT IS BETTER THAN IT WAS

Author: Pedro Calderón de la Barca (1600-1681)
Time of action: Seventeenth century
First presented: 1631

PRINCIPAL CHARACTERS

Carlos Colona (kär′lōs kō·lō′nä), the son of the Governor of Brandenburg. Attracted to a veiled lady, Flora, his efforts to speak to her cause a quarrel with her fiancé, Licio, whom Don Carlos kills in the ensuing duel. He seeks asylum in the house of his father's friend, Don César, the father of the veiled Flora. After a series of adventures involving disguises, recognitions, escapes, pursuits, fights, and problems of honor, Don Carlos wins Flora's hand.

Don César (dōn thä′sär), Flora's father and an old friend of Carlos Colona's father. When Don Carlos, after killing Licio in a duel, seeks asylum in his house, Don César faces the dilemma of having to choose between the obligations of friendship, which demand that he aid the young man, and the obligations of a magistrate, which require that he arrest and execute him.

Flora (flō′rä), Don César's daughter. Veiled, she attracts the attention of Carlos Colona, who kills her fiancé Licio, in a duel. When Don Carlos arrives at her house as a fugitive seeking asylum, she hides him. After many complications her identity becomes known, everyone's honor is satisfied, and she and Don Carlos are married.

Laura (lä′ōō·rä), Flora's friend, who is loved by Arnaldo.

Arnaldo (är-näl′dō), Laura's suitor.

Dinero (dē-nā′rō), Carlos Colona's servant.

Fabio (fä′byō), Laura's brother.

Silvia (sēl′byä), Flora's servant.

IT IS WORSE THAN IT WAS

Author: Pedro Calderón de la Barca (1600-1681)
Time of action: Seventeenth century
First presented: 1630

PRINCIPAL CHARACTERS

César Ursino (thä′sär ōor-sē′nō), a fugitive from justice. Preparing to marry Flérida Colona, he is also having assignations with a veiled lady who has fired

his imagination. She is Lisarda. A series of adventures involving mistaken identities follows and ends in César's marriage to Flérida.

Lisarda (lē·sär'dä), the daughter of Juan de Aragón. Veiled, she has been meeting César Ursino, fiancé of Flérida Colona. Finally, following a succession of adventures during which a mistaken identity threatens her reputation, she is compelled, in order to save her honor, to give up César to Flérida and to marry Don Juan.

Flérida Colona (flā'rē·t͡hä kō·lō'nä), loved by César Ursino and finally his bride after a series of complications brought about by his attraction to the veiled Lisarda.

Don Juan (dōn hwän'), César Ursino's friend and the suitor with whom Lisarda must be satisfied when César is paired off with Flérida Colona.

Camacho (kä-mä'chō), César Ursino's servant, who marries Celia.

Celia (thā'lyä), Lisarda's servant and Camacho's bride.

Juan de Aragón (hwän' dä ä·rä·gōn'), Governor of Gaeta.

THE ITALIAN

Author: Mrs. Ann Radcliffe (1764-1823)
Time of action: 1758
First published: 1797

PRINCIPAL CHARACTERS

Vincentio di Vivaldi, a young nobleman of Naples. Impressed by the grace and voice of the veiled Ellena di Rosalba, he is warned by a ghostly stranger not to seek her identity. Disregarding the warning, he succeeds in learning the young woman's name, falls in love with her, and determines to marry her in spite of his parents' strenuous objections because of her apparent lowly station. His mother's plottings to prevent the alliance set up a train of sinister events through which the young man passes before he is finally united with his beloved.

Ellena di Rosalba, a young girl of supposed humble origin, loved by Vincentio di Vivaldi. Before her wedding, she is abducted and carried off to a strange religious establishment, the first of a series of violent and sinister adventures which end in the revelation of her identity as the daughter of Sister Olivia and the dead Count di Bruno, and at last in her marriage to Vincentio.

The Marchesa di Vivaldi, the haughty and vindictive mother of Vincentio di Vivaldi. She plots, with the monk Schedoni, to do away with Ellena di Rosalba in order to prevent the girl's marriage to her son.

The Marchese di Vivaldi, Vincentio di Vivaldi's father.

Schedoni, the Marchesa di Vivaldi's confessor and her chief ally in the plot to murder Ellena di Rosalba. He is finally revealed as the second Count di Bruno, murderer of the first Count, his brother, and as a fugitive in the disguise of a monk.

Sister Olivia, a nun who befriends Ellena di Rosalba and is finally revealed as the former Countess di Bruno, Ellena's mother.

Signora Bianchi, Ellena di Rosalba's aunt and guardian, later revealed as the sister of the Sister Olivia.

Paulo Mendrico, Vincentio di Vivaldi's faithful servant.

Bonorma, Vincentio di Vivaldi's friend.

535

Beatrice, the servant of Signora Bianchi and Ellena di Rosalba.

Ansaldo di Rovalli, the grand penitentiary.

Brother Jeronimo, a monk.

Spalatro, an assassin in the pay of Schedoni.

Father Nicola, a monk who turns against the sinister Schedoni and gathers evidence against him for the Inquisition.

THE ITCHING PARROT

Author: José Joaquín Fernández de Lizardi (1776-1827)
Time of action: The 1770's to 1820's
First published: 1816

PRINCIPAL CHARACTERS

Pedro Sarmiento (pä′drō sär·myĕn′tō), nicknamed Periquillo (The Itching Parrot, or Poll), the young rogue protagonist of Spanish America's first novel. As the son of upper middle-class people of Mexico City, he seeks the easiest way of earning a living. A monk's life is too exhausting. He tries other professions: barber, physician, apothecary, beggar, and finally secretary to a colonel in Manila. Finally, a schoolmate, now a priest, turns him to a prosperous, honest life, resulting in Poll's marriage and respectability.

Señor Sarmiento (sä·nyôr′ sär·myĕn′tō), Pedro's father, who wants Pedro to become a tradesman.

Señora Sarmiento (sĕ·nyō′rä sär·myĕn′to), who, wanting her son to be a priest, dies of grief at his many vices.

Januario (hä·nwä′ryō), a schoolmate who makes a fool of Pedro for his attentions to Januario's cousin, with whom Januario himself is infatuated.

Don Antonio (dōn än·tō′nyō), a good man, unjustly jailed, who helps Pedro. Later Pedro finds him destitute and aids him.

The Daughter of Don Antonio, who becomes the wife of the reformed Pedro.

A Scrivener, who arranges Pedro's release from jail so that he may serve as the scrivener's secretary.

IVANHOE

Author: Sir Walter Scott (1771-1832)
Time of action: 1194
First published: 1820

PRINCIPAL CHARACTERS

Cedric the Saxon, the rude, warlike master of Rotherwood, a small landholder during the reign of Richard I. Obstinately hoping for Saxon independence, he wishes his ward, Lady Rowena, to marry Athelstane of Coningsburgh, a descendant of the ancient Saxon kings, and he disinherits his son, Wilfred of Ivanhoe, for learning Norman customs.

When Ivanhoe returns from the Crusades and falls wounded after winning the tournament at Ashby-de-la-Zouche, Cedric allows him to be cared for by strangers. Captured by Normans, Cedric is taken to Torquilstone Castle, but he escapes and helps the besiegers take the castle. In the end he becomes somewhat reconciled to the marriage of Ivanhoe and Rowena and with Norman rule under King Richard I.

Wilfred of Ivanhoe, the chivalrous, disowned hero, a Crusader. Returning home disguised as a pilgrim, he befriends a Jew, Isaac of York, and his daughter Rebecca on the way to the tournament at Ashby. After defeating his opponents in the tourney he reveals his true identity and faints from loss of blood while accepting the prize from Rowena. Captured with the Jew, along with Cedric and his party, he is cared for by Rebecca at Torquilstone and is rescued by the disguised King Richard. He repays Rebecca's kindness by defending her when she is accused of witchcraft. After Athelstane relinquishes his claim to Rowena, Ivanhoe marries her and enjoys prosperity under Richard's rule.

Lady Rowena, Cedric's beautiful ward. At Rotherwood she inquires of Ivanhoe's exploits from the disguised knight himself, becomes the tournament queen at his request, and learns his identity after he is declared victor. Seized by Norman knights, she is saved from the advances of a captor and the Torquilstone fire by the timely intervention of Richard, Cedric, and Robin Hood. Happy when Athelstane disclaims her, she weds Ivanhoe.

Isaac of York, an avaricious but kindly Jew. He supplies Ivanhoe with a horse and armor for the tournament and takes him off to be cared for after the knight has been wounded. Isaac is taken prisoner and about to be tortured for his gold when rescuers lay siege to the castle. He is set free but forced to pay a ransom. Learning of his daughter's abduction at the hands of haughty Sir Brian de Bois-Guilbert, he sends for Ivanhoe to rescue her. Sick of England, he and his daughter move to Spain.

Rebecca, the generous, lovely Jewess who returns Ivanhoe's payment for the horse and armor and nurses his wound. She is carried off by an enamoured Templar during the siege. Accused of witchcraft at Templar headquarters, she is rescued from burning by the exhausted Ivanhoe's defense.

Sir Brian de Bois-Guilbert (brē·än′ də bwä′-gēl·bĕr′), the fierce and passionate Templar who kidnaps Rebecca, deserts her because of Templar politics, and fights a fatal battle against her defender, Ivanhoe.

Richard the Lion-Hearted, an audacious, hardy king. Secretly returning to England, he saves Ivanhoe's life at the tournament and leads the siege of Torquilstone. After thwarting an ambush, he throws off his disguise of the "Black Sluggard" and claims his rightful throne.

Robin Hood (Locksley), the famed outlaw. He wins an archery contest, supports Richard during the siege of Torquilstone, and becomes a loyal subject of the restored King.

Athelstane of Coningsburgh (ath′əl-stān), the sluggish Saxon knight who half-heartedly woos Rowena and loses fights with Richard and Bois-Guilbert.

Maurice de Bracy, an ambitious Norman who captures Rowena; however, he possesses too much honor to pursue his designs on her.

Reginald Front de Boeuf (rĕ·zhē·nál′ frôn′ də bĕf′), the savage Norman who seizes Isaac for his gold. He dies of a wound inflicted by Richard amid the flames of Torquilstone.

Prince John, Richard's haughty, unscrupulous brother, who has tried to usurp the throne with the aid of the Norman nobles.

Lucas de Beaumanoir (lü·kä′ də bō·má·nwàr′), the bigoted, ascetic head of the Templars who presides over Rebecca's trial on a charge of witchcraft. His Order is disbanded by Richard because of treasonous activities and plotting against the King and the realm.

Philip and
Albert Malvoisin (ăl·bĕr' măl·vwà·zăn'),
Templars executed by King Richard for
treason.

Waldemar Fitzurse (văl·də·màr' fĭts·êrs'),
Prince John's wily, aspiring follower, who
is banished by Richard.

Aymer (ā'mêr), the comfort-loving Prior
of Jorvaulx, who is captured by Robin
Hood and forced to pay a ransom.

Ulrica (ōōl·rē'kə), the Saxon hag who

burns Torquilstone in order to be re
venged on the Normans.

Gurth, Cedric's swineherd and Ivanhoe's
loyal servant, who is given his freedom.

Wamba, Cedric's quick-witted jester; he
helps Cedric escape Torquilstone by
dressing him in a priest's robe.

Friar Tuck, Robin Hood's hefty, hearty
follower, a hedge priest who treats Richard to a meal.

JACK OF NEWBERRY

Author: Thomas Deloney (1543?-1607?)
Time of action: Reign of Henry VIII
First published: 1597

PRINCIPAL CHARACTERS

Jack Winchcomb, known as Jack of
Newberry, a young weaver. Wild as a
young man, he settles down, marries his
master's widow, and becomes a solid
businessman. He patriotically raises a
company of men to fight for Henry VIII
against the Scots. He is offered knighthood by that sovereign but declines,
saying he knows his place in the world.

Jack's Master's Widow. She trusts the
young man, putting her business and
then herself in his hands. She dies, leaving Jack all her business and wealth.

Jack's Second Wife, a younger woman.
She is a foolish gossip who makes difficulties for her husband.

Henry VIII, King of England. Pleased
with Jack for being a witty and loyal
subject, he offers the weaver knighthood.

Queen Catherine, Henry VIII's queen.
She thanks Jack for bringing a company
of men to help fight against the Scots.

Cardinal Wolsey, Henry VIII's chancellor. He has Jack and other weavers
thrown into prison when they attempt
to petition the King.

The Duke of Somerset, who intervenes
on Jack's behalf when he is in prison
and convinces Cardinal Wolsey that the
weavers mean no harm.

Benedick, an Italian merchant. He has
an amorous adventure in Newberry and
is punished by being put to bed with a
pig.

Joan, a pretty girl employed by Jack. She
disdains Benedick when he makes advances to her.

Sir George Rigley, a knight who seduces
one of Jack's women employees. He is
tricked by Jack into marrying the girl.
Angry at first, he comes to see the justice
of Jack's action and becomes the weaver's
friend.

JACK SHEPPARD

Author: William Harrison Ainsworth (1805-1882)
Time of action: 1702-1724
First published: 1839

Jack Sheppard, a housebreaker and popular jailbreaker. After many crimes and several escapes, he is seized at his mother's funeral and executed at Tyburn.

Joan Sheppard, his mother, widow of Tom Sheppard (executed for theft). Insane from worry over Jack's dissolute, criminal life, she is put in Bedlam hospital; recovering her senses, she is released. Wild reveals that she is Sir Rowland's long-lost sister Constance, stolen in childhood by a gipsy. She kills herself rather than marry Wild after his brutal murder of Sir Rowland.

Owen Wood, a London carpenter who becomes wealthy.

Mrs. Wood, his wife, murdered by Blueskin.

Winifred, their daughter who marries Thames Darrell.

Sir Rowland Trenchard, an aristocrat plotting to inherit his sister Alvira's estates. He is arrested for treason on Wild's accusation; after his release from prison he is murdered by Wild.

Thames Darrell, Sir Rowland's nephew and foster son of Owen Wood. He is rescued from drowning as a baby. In youth he is arrested as a thief and sent to sea after escaping prison with Sheppard. Thrown overboard, he is rescued and taken to France, where he serves under Philip of Orleans. Returning to England to visit the Woods, he learns through letters that he is of noble birth, and he inherits the Trenchard estates.

Darrell, a fugitive drowned while being pursued by a mob led by Sir Rowland; in reality, the French Marquis de Chatillon and father of Thames Darrell.

Lady Alvira, mother of Thames and widow of Chatillon; later wed by force to her cousin, Sir Cecil Trafford.

Jonathan Wild, a thief-taker. Pretending to aid Sir Rowland's plot, he counterplots to get the Trenchard fortune for himself. Eventually found out, he dies on the same gallows to which he had sent Tom and Jack Sheppard.

Blueskin, the devoted henchman of Jack Sheppard.

Van Galgebrok, a Dutch seaman and conjurer who attempts to drown Thames.

Sir Montacute Trenchard, grandfather of Thames.

JALNA

Author: Mazo de la Roche (1885-1961)
Time of action: The 1920's
First published: 1927

PRINCIPAL CHARACTERS

Grandma Whiteoak, the ninety-nine-year-old matriarch of the family. She tyrannizes over her grandchildren, even to giving them physical blows to enforce her whims.

Renny Whiteoak, eldest of Grandma's grandchildren. A bachelor, he holds the family together and supervises their farms. While he has power and position, he does not delight in them. He falls in love with his sister-in-law, Alayne, Eden's wife.

Meg Whiteoak, Renny's sister. She is a spinster because she broke her engagement to Maurice Vaughan after he had fathered an illegitimate child. Many years later she forgives and marries him.

Maurice Vaughan, Renny's friend and former fiancé of Meg. He is the father of the girl known as Pheasant. He eventually marries Meg.

Eden Whiteoak, Renny and Meg's half brother. He is a dreamer and poet. He marries Alayne Archer, a publisher's reader from New York. He accuses her of nagging when she tries to encourage his writing. He falls in love with Pheasant and deserts Alayne.

Alayne Archer, Eden's wife. She is a gentle, helpful woman. She falls in love with Renny but returns to New York to prevent scandal and divorce.

Piers Whiteoak, half brother to Renny and Meg. He is a plodding man who marries Pheasant. He resents Alayne because the family accepts her more readily than they do his wife.

Finch Whiteoak, half brother to Renny and Meg. He is an unambitious young man who finally is encouraged to be a musician by Alayne.

Wakefield Whiteoak, half brother to Renny and Meg. He is a badly spoiled eight-year-old.

Pheasant Vaughan, the illegitimate daughter of Maurice, and Piers' wife. She makes a play for Eden's attentions.

JANE EYRE

Author: Charlotte Brontë (1816-1855)
Time of action: 1800
First published: 1847

PRINCIPAL CHARACTERS

Jane Eyre, a plain child with a vivid imagination, intelligence, and great talent in art and music. Left an orphan in childhood, she is forced to live with her aunt Reed, who was the sister-in-law of her father. At the Reed home she is mistreated and spurned, and is finally sent to a charity home for girls. Her education completed, she teaches at the school for several years and then takes a position as a private governess to the ward of Mr. Rochester. After a strange, tempestuous courtship she and Mr. Rochester are to be married, but the revelation that his insane first wife still lives prevents the wedding. After each has suffered many hardships, Jane and Mr. Rochester are eventually married.

Edward Fairfax Rochester, a gentleman of thirty-five, the proud, sardonic, moody master of Thornfield. Before Jane Eyre's arrival to become a governess in his household he visits Thornfield only occasionally. After he falls in love with Jane, much of his moroseness disappears.

When they are separated because the presence of his insane wife becomes known, Mr. Rochester remains at Thornfield. His wife sets fire to the house and Mr. Rochester loses his eyesight and the use of an arm during the conflagration, in which his wife dies. Summoned, she believes, by his call, Jane Eyre returns a short time later and the two are married.

Adele Varens, the illegitimate daughter of Mr. Rochester and a French opera singer, his ward upon her mother's death. She is pale, small-featured, extremely feminine, and not especially talented.

Mrs. Fairfax, the elderly housekeeper at Thornfield. She has been extremely kind to Jane and is delighted that she and Mr. Rochester are to be married.

Grace Poole, a stern woman with a hard, plain face, supposedly a seamstress at Thornfield but actually the keeper of mad Mrs. Rochester. Occasionally she tipples too much and neglects her post.

Bertha Mason Rochester, Mr. Rochester's insane wife, kept in secret on an upper floor at Thornfield. She had lied and her family had lied when Mr. Rochester met her in Jamaica while traveling, for she was even then demented. During Jane's stay at Thornfield Mrs. Rochester tries to burn her husband in bed. Finally she burns the whole house and herself, and seriously injures her husband.

Mrs. Reed, an exact, clever, managing woman, the guardian of Jane Eyre. She hates her charge, however, misuses her, and locks her in dark rooms for punishment. At her death she repents of her actions. Her children turn out badly.

Eliza Reed, her older daughter, a penurious, serious girl who eventually becomes a nun.

John Reed, the son, a wicked child who torments Jane Eyre and then blames her for his own bad deeds. He ends up as a drunk in London and dies in disgrace.

Georgiana Reed, the younger daughter, a pretty, spoiled child who later becomes very fat. She makes a poor marriage.

Bessie Leaven, Mrs. Reed's governess, pretty, capricious, hasty-tempered. Before Jane Eyre leaves the Reed house, Bessie has become fond of her.

Robert Leaven, Bessie's husband and Mrs. Reed's coachman.

Abbot, the Reed's bad-tempered maid.

Mr. Lloyd, an apothecary called in when Jane Eyre becomes sick and feverish after having been locked in a dark room. He suggests that she be sent off to school.

Mr. Brocklehurst, a strict clergyman and the master of Lowood School. He forces the girls to wear short, uncurled hair and plain wrappers, and he feeds them on a starvation diet.

Maria Temple, the supervisor of Lowood School, a pretty, kind woman who tries against tremendous odds to make her pupils' lot as easy and pleasant as possible. She is interested in Jane Eyre's talents and is responsible for her getting a teaching position later at Lowood.

Miss Smith,
Miss Scratcherd, and
Miss Miller, teachers at Lowood School.

Helen Burns, a clever thirteen-year-old pupil at Lowood School, constantly ridiculed and punished by her teachers because she is not neat and prompt. She dies during a fever epidemic.

Miss Gryce, a fat teacher at Lowood School and Jane Eyre's roommate when they both teach there.

Mary Ann Wilson, one of Jane Eyre's fellow students, a witty and original girl.

John and
Leah, the house servants at Thornfield Hall.

Sophie, the French maid.

Mrs. Eshton, a guest at a house party given by Mr. Rochester. Once a handsome woman, she still has a well-preserved style.

Mr. Eshton, her husband, a magistrate of the district.

Amy Eshton, their older daughter, rather small, naïve, and childlike in manner.

Louisa Eshton, the younger daughter, a taller and more elegant young woman.

Lady Lynn, another woman whose family is invited to the Thornfield house party; she is large, stout, haughty-looking, and richly dressed.

Mrs. Dent, another guest, less showy than the others, with a slight figure and a pale, gentle face.

Colonel Dent, her husband, a soldierly gentleman.

The Dowager Lady Ingram, another

guest, a proud, handsome woman with hard, fierce eyes.

Blanche Ingram, her daughter, a young woman with an elegant manner and a loud, satirical laugh, to whom Mr. Rochester is reported engaged.

Mary Ingram, her sister.

Henry Lynn and
Frederick Lynn, gentlemen at the party, two dashing sparks.

Lord Ingram, Blanche's brother, a tall, handsome young man of listless appearance and manner.

Mr. Mason, Mr. Rochester's brother-in-law. During a visit to see his sister, she wounds him severely. He halts the marriage of Jane Eyre and Mr. Rochester.

Diana Rivers and
Mary Rivers, daughters of the family with which Jane Eyre takes refuge after running away from Thornfield. They turn out to be her cousins, their mother having been Jane's aunt. At first they do not know that Jane is a relative because she calls herself Jane Eliot.

St. John Rivers, their brother, a complex religious-minded man who wishes to marry Jane but plans to live with her in platonic fashion while they devote their lives to missionary work in India.

Hannah, the Rivers' housekeeper, a suspicious but kind woman.

Rosamund Oliver, a beautiful, kind heiress, the sponsor of the school in which St. John Rivers finds Jane a post. Miss Oliver is coquettish and vain, but she holds real affection for Rivers.

Mr. Oliver, her father, a tall, massive-featured man.

Alice Wood, an orphan, one of Jane's pupils in the school where she teaches after leaving Thornfield.

JASON AND THE GOLDEN FLEECE

Author: Unknown
Time of action: Remote antiquity
First transcribed: Unknown

PRINCIPAL CHARACTERS

Jason (jā'sən), a Greek prince whose father has been driven from his throne. Jason is commanded to regain the throne, but to do so he must bring back the Golden Fleece for the usurper, his uncle Pelias. Jason bravely sets out and brings back the Golden Fleece. Although Pelias refuses to keep his promise, he dies that same night, leaving the throne to Jason.

Pelias (pē'lǐ·əs), Jason's cruel uncle, who usurps his brother's throne and plots to kill Jason. When Jason brings back the Golden Fleece to Iolcus, Pelias does not want to fulfill his bargain and give up the throne, but death takes him the same night.

Chiron (kī'rŏn), a centaur. He is Jason's foster father and tutor.

Herakles (hĕr'ə·klēz) and
Orpheus (ôr'fí·əs), Jason's companions on the quest for the Golden Fleece.

Argus (är'gəs), another of Jason's companions on the quest for the Golden Fleece. He builds the ship "Argo" for Jason.

Zetes (zē'tēz) and
Calais (kă'lā·əs), sons of the North Wind, companions of Jason.

Phineus (fĭ'nē·əs), the blind King of Salmydessa, saved from the Harpies by Jason.

542

Æëtes (ē·ē'tēz), King of Colchis, who agrees to give up the Golden Fleece if Jason can accomplish deeds beyond mortal skill and strength.

Medea (mĭ·dē·ə), a princess of Colchis. She falls in love with Jason, aids him in gaining the Golden Fleece, and returns with him to become his queen in Iolcus.

JAVA HEAD

Author: Joseph Hergesheimer (1880-1954)
Time of action: The 1840's
First published: 1919

PRINCIPAL CHARACTERS

Gerrit Ammidon, a Yankee sea captain, his father's favorite son; a romantic man with an arresting, blue-eyed gaze. He is critical of the hypocrisy, the pious pretense, and the scandalmongering of his home town. Conscious of having done Nettie an injustice in dropping her because of anger at her grandfather, he confesses his love for her, and after Taou Yuen's death he marries her and takes her with him away from Salem.

Taou Yuen, Gerrit's Chinese bride, a Manchu noblewoman who seems completely out of place in Salem. Gerrit thinks of her as the perfection of aristocratic beauty, charm, and refinement; but she represents the Orient, not America. To save herself from Edward she commits suicide.

Nettie Vollar, the illegitimate daughter of Kate Dunsack and a seaman who drowned; Gerrit's black-haired, dimpled, pert-nosed former sweetheart and later his wife.

Edward Dunsack, Nettie's weak-willed, drug-addicted uncle who is resentful of Gerrit's possessing Taou Yuen. Failing to seduce her, he gives her a distorted account of the love affair of Nettie and Gerrit. Drug-crazed, he threatens to strangle Taou Yuen and causes her to commit suicide with opium pills. Edward goes mad.

Captain Jeremy Ammidon, Gerrit's father, senior partner in the firm of Ammidon, Ammidon, and Saltonstone. He dies of a heart attack upon discovering that two of the firm's schooners are transporting opium.

William Ammidon, Gerrit's handsome brother, a money-minded tradesman who disagrees with his father on many trade and shipping matters and who sees no objection to trading in opium if it brings in money. He is sharply critical of Gerrit's marriage. He symbolizes nineteenth century New England commercialism and business ethics.

Rhoda Ammidon, William's cheerful and sensible wife, a large, handsome woman.

Barzil Dunsack, father of Edward and Kate; once a friend but afterward an enemy of Jeremy.

Kate Dunsack Vollar, Nettie's mother.

James Saltonstone, partner of the Ammidons.

Laurel Ammidon, William and Rhoda's young daughter.

JEAN-CHRISTOPHE

Author: Romain Rolland (1866-1944)
Time of action: Late nineteenth and early twentieth centuries
First published: 1904-1912

Jean-Christophe Krafft (zhäṅ-krēs·tôf′ krȧft′), a musical genius in a ten-volume, seven-thousand-page Nobel Prize novel, who is uneducated in most phases of life. He has temporary love affairs and gets involved in the syndicalist political movement. He dies alone in Paris, recognized as the world's greatest composer of modern music.

Melchior Krafft (mĕl·kyôr′ krȧft′), his virtuoso father.

Louisa (lwēz′ə), his lower-class mother.

Jean Michel (zhäṅ′ mē·shĕl′), a famous orchestra conductor and Jean-Christophe's grandfather.

Ada (ȧ·dä′), a vulgar shop girl who becomes Jean-Christophe's first mistress.

Lorchen (lôr·shäṅ′), a young farm girl in whose defense Jean-Christophe kills a soldier and has to leave Germany.

Colette Stevens (kô·lĕt′ stā·vĕn′), a coquette to whom Jean-Christophe gives music lessons.

Grazia (grȧ·zyȧ′), Colette's cousin, who secretly helps build Jean-Christophe's reputation. After her husband's death, she encourages Jean-Christophe in Switzerland.

Antoinette (äṅ·twȧ·nĕt′), who dies of consumption while educating her brother Olivier.

Olivier (ô·lē·vyā′), a writer who admires Jean-Christophe's work. He is killed while with Jean-Christophe in a May Day political riot.

Jacqueline (zhȧk·lēn′), a shallow girl and Olivier's wife.

Anna (ȧ·nä′), a married woman with whom Jean-Christophe has an affair during his Swiss exile.

JENNIE GERHARDT

Author: Theodore Dreiser (1871-1945)
Time of action: Late nineteenth century
First published: 1911

Genevieve Gerhardt (Jennie), the oldest of six children of a poor, hard-working glass blower in Columbus, Ohio. Both beautiful and innocent, Jennie is forced to work at a local hotel when her father becomes ill; there she attracts Senator Brander, who stays at the hotel. When Brander helps her family and keeps her brother out of jail for stealing coal from the railroad, Jennie, in gratitude, sleeps with him. At his sudden death she is left pregnant. She later moves to Cleveland, where she meets Lester Kane. With her family in need again, she goes on a trip to New York with him in return for his help: In Chicago Lester finds out about Jennie's daughter and agrees to allow the child to live with them. Jen-

nie realizes that his family's disapproval of their relationship is harming Lester both financially and socially, and she influences him to leave her. He later marries an old childhood sweetheart. Jennie's daughter dies and she adopts two orphan children. Some years later, while his wife is in Europe, Lester has a heart attack and sends for Jennie, who nurses him until his death.

Lester Kane, the son of a wealthy carriage manufacturer. A weak man, Lester is torn between his desire for social and financial affluence and his feeling for Jennie. He neither marries her nor leaves her, until his father's will demands that he act within three years. Pursued by

Mrs. Gerald, a widow, he finally follows his family's wishes and leaves Jennie with a generous settlement.

William Gerhardt, Jennie's father, a poor glass blower. After his wife dies and his family grows up he lives with Jennie, the daughter he disapproved of but who is ultimately kindest to him. He dies in Chicago.

George Sylvester Brander, a Senator from Ohio. A bachelor, he intends to marry Jennie but dies of a heart attack.

Wilhelmina Vesta, Jennie's daughter by Senator Brander; she dies of typhoid fever at the age of fourteen.

Mrs. Letty Pace Gerald, a wealthy widow and childhood sweetheart of Lester Kane. Lester finally marries her but is not happy.

Mrs. Gerhardt, Jennie's mother, hard-working and sympathetic. She dies in Cleveland before Jennie moves to Chicago.

Robert Kane, Lester's older brother, vice president of the carriage company. A ruthless financier, interested only in power, he influences his father to make the will that cripples Lester.

Archibald Kane, Lester's father. According to his will, Lester must abandon Jennie to get his share in the business. If he marries Jennie, he is to receive ten thousand dollars a year for life; if he con-

tinues to live with her without marriage, he gets nothing after three years.

Sebastian Gerhardt (Bass), Jennie's oldest brother and the closest to her.

George Gerhardt, another brother.

Martha Gerhardt, a sister; she becomes a teacher.

William Gerhardt, Jr., a brother who becomes an electrical engineer.

Veronica Gerhardt, a sister who marries a wholesale druggist in Cleveland.

Louise Kane, Lester's youngest sister, a cold, social woman who discovers that Lester is living with Jennie in a Chicago hotel.

Amy and
Imogene Kane, other sisters.

Mrs. Kane, Lester's mother.

Mrs. Henry Bracebridge, Jennie's Cleveland employer at whose home she meets Lester Kane.

Mr. O'Brien, a lawyer, the executor of Archibald Kane's estate; he suggests that Jennie influence Lester to leave her.

Rose Perpetua and
Henry Stover, orphans adopted by Jennie.

Samuel E. Ross, a real estate promoter through whom Lester loses money in Chicago.

JERUSALEM DELIVERED

Author: Torquato Tasso (1544-1595)
Time of action: The Middle Ages
First published: 1580-1581

PRINCIPAL CHARACTERS

God, on the side of the Christians.

The Archangel Gabriel, sent by God in the seventh year of the Crusade to encourage the Crusaders in beginning their march on Jerusalem.

The Archangel Michael, sent by God to inspire the Christians during the final stages of the capture of the city.

Satan, on the side of the Pagans.

545

Godfrey de Bouillon, the leader of the Crusaders and victorious after many setbacks.

King Aladine, the pagan King from whom the Crusaders finally take Jerusalem.

Clorinda, a beautiful pagan warrior who scorns female dress. She is instrumental in preventing pagan tyrannies as well as in holding off the Christians for a time. At last she is killed in combat.

Tancred, a mighty Christian noble in love with Clorinda. He wounds her mortally in combat, and then realizes who she is. He has time to ask her pardon and to baptize her before her death.

Erminia of Antioch, in love with Tancred. She goes in Clorinda's armor to Tancred's camp when he is wounded, but she is frightened at the last minute and takes refuge with a shepherd.

Argantes, sent by the King of Egypt to parley with Godfrey, who haughtily rejects his overtures. He and his army aid Jerusalem, and Argantes is finally killed in single combat by Tancred.

Rinaldo, an Italian Crusader and the most valorous of all. Banished temporarily after a jousting duel, he is later summoned back and is with the Crusaders when Jerusalem is taken.

Armida, an enchantress in Satan's employ. She treacherously lures fifty Christians to her castle and changes them into fishes; later she imprisons Tancred. All are liberated by Rinaldo, who then dallies with Armida until summoned back to duty. At last, the pagans defeated, she surrenders herself to Rinaldo.

Hugh, the former commander of the French forces. He appears to Godfrey in a vision and orders him to recall Rinaldo.

Otho, Tancred's companion, who is defeated by Argantes and taken prisoner.

Gernando, a rival of Rinaldo for a certain post. They quarrel and in the resultant joust Gernando is killed.

Peter the Hermit, who adds his exhortations to Godfrey's in reminding the Crusaders of their vows to take Jerusalem.

Ismeno, a sorcerer. He advises King Aladine to steal a statue of the Virgin Mary, which later disappears.

Sophronia, a beautiful Christian subject of King Aladine. To save the rest of the Christians from massacre she confesses to the theft of the statue and is condemned to be burned.

Olindo, in love with Sophronia. He hopes to save her by confessing to the theft, but is only condemned as well. Clorinda rescues both.

Sweno, Prince of Denmark. He is killed with his followers during his occupation of Palestine. The Crusaders are spurred on by thoughts of vengeance for this deed.

THE JEW OF MALTA

Author: Christopher Marlowe (1564-1593)
Time of action: Fifteenth century
First presented: 1589

PRINCIPAL CHARACTERS

Barabas (bə·răb′əs), the wealthy, miserly Jew of Malta who guides his actions by Machiavellian policy which transcends all human ties of affection and loyalty. With considerable reason he resents the Christian rulers of Malta, who arbitrarily deprive him of his fortune, and he chooses a particularly cruel form of revenge, setting the young man his daughter loves against the Governor's son in a duel fatal to both combatants. Rejected by the two people for whom he has any feeling, his daughter and his servant Ithamore, he contrives the murder of each and finally betrays Malta to her Turkish enemies. He is caught in the trap which he lays for Selim Calymath and dies cursing mankind.

Abigail (ăb'ĭ·gāl), his daughter. She lies and professes her conversion to Christianity in order to retrieve her father's hidden treasure, but the death of Mathias so disillusions her that she enters a nunnery to escape Barabas' evil.

Ithamore (ēth·ɔ·mō'rē), Barabas' slave, who is as ruthless as his master. He carries out the murder of Abigail, the friars, and the nuns, and delivers the fraudulent challenges to Mathias and Lodowick as the Jew wishes; but he readily betrays his master to Bellamira, hoping to make her his mistress with his own eloquence and Barabas' money.

Ferneze (fĕr·nā'zā), Governor of Malta. He considers the need of his state to meet the demands of the Turks ample justification for his confiscation of the wealth of the Jewish merchants. He grieves deeply for the death of his son and vows vengeance on those who caused his slaying. It is his craftiness which finally brings Barabas to destruction.

Don Mathias (dōn ma·tē'ɔs), a good young man who wins Abigail's love and tries to gain her father's favor. He is, in a sense, the innocent victim of Barabas' vendetta against Malta, although he is too ready to be jealous of Lodowick's attentions to Abigail.

Lodowick (lŏd'ō·wĭk), Ferneze's son. Knowing of his friend Mathias' love for Abigail, he visits Barabas' house to catch a glimpse of her and is himself captivated by her beauty. His jealousy, too, is aroused by Barabas' carefully planted suggestions of Mathias' claims on his daughter, and he is ready to accept the false challenge.

Selim Calymath (sē'lĭm kăl'ĭ·măth), the leader of the Turkish embassy which demands ten years' tribute from Ferneze. He takes Malta by Barabas' treachery, but he finds himself betrayed by his accomplice and is held as hostage by Ferneze after Barabas' death.

Bellamira (bĕl'ɔ·mē·rɔ), an ambitious courtesan who uses Ithamore's susceptibility to her charms as a means for acquiring some of Barabas' money.

Pilia-Borsa (pēl'ē·ɔ·bŏr'sä), her accomplice, a greedy, resourceful rascal.

Katherine, Mathias' devoted mother. She joins Ferneze in his vow to take vengeance on those who set their sons against each other.

Barnardine (bär·när'dēn) and **Jacomo** (yä·kō'mō), lecherous, avaricious friars who are murdered after they try to blackmail Barabas with information revealed by Abigail in her dying confession.

Martin Del Bosco (mär·tēn' dĕl bŏs'kō), Vice-Admiral of the King of Spain. He promises to help Malta resist the Turks.

THE JEWESS OF TOLEDO

Author: Franz Grillparzer (1791-1872)
Time of action: c. 1195
First presented: 1872

PRINCIPAL CHARACTERS

Alfonso VIII (äl·fōn'sō), King of Castile. Made ruler of Castile as a child after the deposition of his tyrant predecessor, Alfonso has been a wise and just ruler of

547

his people. Attracted to the beautiful and vain young Jewess Rachel, he lets his passion cause him to neglect his obligations in the face of an imminent war. He finally realizes and acknowledges his weakness, forgives those who have plotted Rachel's destruction, and reaffirms his duty to the people.

Rachel (rä·chĕl'), a Jewess of Toledo. Walking in the royal garden where Jews are forbidden during the King's outing, she is pursued by guards and runs to Alfonso for protection. Attracting the monarch, she arouses in him a passion for her that leads to his shame and remorse and to her death.

Isaac (ē·säk'), Rachel's mercenary father, who is more concerned for his profits than for his daughter's death.

Esther (ĕs·tĕr), Rachel's gentle sister. Ashamed of her sister's wantoness and her father's greed, she blames them equally with Alfonso for Rachel's tragic death.

Eleanor of England, Queen of Castile. Realizing that Alfonso's infatuation for Rachel is causing him to neglect his responsibilities, she plots the death of the Jewess, for which she is forgiven when the King finally acknowledges the foolishness of his passion.

Manrique (män·rē'kä), Count of Lara and the ally of Queen Eleanor.

Don Garceran (dōn gär·thä'rän), Manrique's son, who is loyal to Alfonso.

Doña Clara (dō'nyä klä'rä), Lady in waiting to Eleanor and betrothed of Don Garceran.

JOANNA GODDEN

Author: Sheila Kaye-Smith (1888-1956)
Time of action: Early twentieth century
First published: 1921

PRINCIPAL CHARACTERS

Joanna Godden, a strong woman who upon the death of her father takes firm control of the family farm, Little Ansdore, and her sister Ellen. Her neighbors consider her a foolish, stubborn woman, but she thinks she can operate a farm better than anyone else, and she proves she can. But her life seems empty of a man after the man she loves, Martin Trevor, dies. After some years she takes a casual lover and becomes pregnant. She decides to sell the farm and start life anew with her child, though she will not marry the father because she does not really love him.

Martin Trevor, the man who makes Joanna feel for the first time that she is a woman before she is a farmer. He falls ill, however, and dies before he and Joanna can be married.

Squire Trevor, Martin's father. Ellen Godden becomes infatuated with him after her marriage and follows him to Dover.

Albert Hill, a man thirteen years younger than Joanna, whom she meets on a trip. Though he fathers her child, she will not marry him.

Arthur Alce, who loves Joanna deeply. He loves her so much that at her request he marries her sister. His wife thinks, however, that she has stolen the man from Joanna. When Ellen follows Squire Trevor to Dover, Arthur Alce moves away but refuses to give his wife a divorce. He dies accidentally, leaving his farm not to his wife, but to Joanna.

Ellen Godden, Joanna's young sister,

dominated by Joanna. She marries Arthur thinking she has taken him from Joanna. Later she becomes infatuated with Squire Trevor. After following him to Dover she returns to live with her sister.

JOHN BROWN'S BODY

Author: Stephen Vincent Benét (1898-1943)
Time of action: 1859-1865
First published: 1928

PRINCIPAL CHARACTERS

Jack Ellyat, a Connecticut boy symbolic of the Northern soldier during the American Civil War. He is an ambitious young man whose favorite dream role is that of Phaëton driving his chariot across the sky, proudly displaying the trophy-sun; but Jack, member of an Abolitionist family, is troubled by signs of approaching war. He joins the Connecticut volunteers, is mustered out after the Northern defeat at Bull Run, later joins the Illinois volunteers in Chicago, acquires the opprobrious nickname of "Bull Run Jack," is captured after running away at Pittsburg Landing, escapes, finds refuge at John Vilas' farm, falls in love with John's daughter Melora, gets her pregnant, and is reunited with her at the end of the war. Like most soldiers, Jack bears as best he can the buffetings of fate.

Clay Wingate, Jack Ellyat's opposite in the South. He is the son of a plantation owner, lives at white-pillared Wingate Hall. Clay feels himself become a man as war approaches. He and Sally Dupré are drawn to each other before Clay joins the Black Horse Troop and rides away to the battle of Bull Run. When he returns to his Georgia home on leave, he falls in love with Lucy Weatherby, a Virginia girl, but at the end of the war when he returns to an accidentally burned and ruined Wingate Hall, the weary and wounded soldier finds Sally Dupré waiting for him. Clay Wingate is the Southerner who, though used to a soft-living, fox-hunting life, hardens himself into a fierce, efficient soldier.

Luke Breckinridge, a gangling mountain boy who joins up to fight the Yankees simply because the Kelceys, an enemy family, have shown they are not afraid to fight. Luke becomes infatuated with Sophy, a chambermaid at Pollet's Hotel in Richmond; he is delighted when his patrol catches, searches, and finds incriminating evidence in the boots of one Shippy, a Union spy in the guise of a peddler and Luke's chief rival for Sophy's affections.

Melora Vilas, the girl who shelters Jack Ellyat and falls in love with him; she is straight and slim, with grave, brown eyes. After the war, with her father and Jack's son, born in Tennessee, she searches for the father of her baby. As she drives her cart up a hill in Connecticut, Jack, who was wounded at Gettysburg, is standing under some elms, waiting.

Lucy Weatherby, a fickle Virginia beauty who is more concerned with the men in her life than with the outcome of the war. Although she has an interlude with Clay Wingate in Pollet's Hotel in Richmond, Lucy seems deeply in love not with Clay or any other suitor but with herself.

Sally Dupré, the daughter of "French" Dupré, a dancing master. Although temporarily displaced by Lucy in Clay's

549

affections, she is the faithful lover who waits for her man to come back.

Spade, a slave on the Zachary plantation, near Wingate Hall. He escapes, makes his way to freedom in the "promised land" of the North and is immediately forced into a labor gang. He later joins the Union army, is wounded in the crater at Petersburg, and after the war is hired by Jake Diefer as a field hand on his Pennsylvania farm.

Sophy, the hotel maid whom Luke Breckinridge takes with him when he decides to "leave" the war. Hungry and scared, she willingly goes with him back to his mountains when he announces his intention of putting in a crop and butchering a hog—because there were always hogs in the mountains.

Jake Diefer, "the barrel-chested Pennsylvanian" who volunteers for the Union forces but does not really get his fighting dander up until he discovers that the Johnnie Rebs are fighting on his farm at Gettysburg.

Shippy, the sharp peddler-spy for the Union who is to bring Sophy some perfume from the North but who is caught by a Confederate patrol and accused by jealous Luke Breckinridge. He is hanged after papers proving him a spy are found sewed in his boots.

John Vilas, Melora's father. He is a lover of the classics and a lonely, restless man who has made his life a Faustian search for the wilderness stone. During the war, having little sympathy for either side, he becomes a hider in the woods in order to protect his son Bent from recruiters. Later he accompanies Melora and her child on her search for Jack Ellyat.

JOHN HALIFAX, GENTLEMAN

Author: Dinah Maria Mulock (Mrs. George Craik, 1826-1887)
Time of action: Turn of the nineteenth century
First published: 1857

PRINCIPAL CHARACTERS

John Halifax, an orphan who has an honest face and wants only to be given a chance to prove himself. He is given a chance by Abel Fletcher and proceeds to rise in the world by his efforts, honest dealings, and gentlemanly behavior. He wins the hand of a wealthy heiress, becomes a behind-the-scenes political power and a wealthy manufacturer. He is a good husband and father, rearing a fine family before he dies peacefully in his sleep.

Abel Fletcher, a wealthy Quaker, owner of a tannery and mill. He gives John Halifax a chance to prove himself and for many years is the young man's benefactor.

Phineas Fletcher, invalid son of John's benefactor. He and John become fast friends. He sees John's good qualities before anyone else does so.

Ursula March, who becomes John's wife. She loves him even though he is from a lower class and marries him despite opposition from her family and friends. Her love for her husband is so great that when he dies she dies too, as if she cannot bear to be separated from him.

Guy Halifax, the Halifaxes' eldest son and his mother's favorite child. He leaves home after a quarrel with his brother. Later he almost kills a man in France and flees to America, where he does well. He returns eventually to be reunited joyfully with his family.

Maud Halifax, the Halifaxes' youngest daughter and her father's favorite child. Because she loves a man of whom her father disapproves, she remains a spinster many years. Her patience and love are rewarded when the man, Lord Ravenel, proves his worth and is able to marry her.

Lord (William) Ravenel, a worldly and wild young man. He wants to marry Maud, but her father refuses to permit the marriage. Ravenel goes to America, proves his worth, returns to England with Guy, and marries Maud with her father's blessing.

JOHN INGLESANT

Author: Joseph Henry Shorthouse (1834-1903)
Time of action: Seventeenth century
First published: 1881

PRINCIPAL CHARACTERS

John Inglesant, the hero of this historical novel set in the seventeenth century. The younger of twin sons, he is educated in philosophy and the classics. After a series of adventures in the service of Charles I of England, and later in Italy, he is sent back to England, where he leads a life of contemplation.

Eustace Inglesant. A few minutes older than his brother John, he is given a worldly education. He is murdered by an Italian enemy. Years later John finds the murderer, who is now a blind monk, and spares his life.

Father St. Clare, a Jesuit and John's tutor. His dream is to return England to the domination of Rome, and with this in mind he aids the crown against the Puritans.

Charles I, King of England. Guided by Father St. Clare, John is employed on secret missions by the King. Imprisoned, John refuses to give evidence against the King. After Charles' execution, Father St. Clare arranges John's release.

Lord Glamorgan, an Irish lord attempting to raise an army on Charles' behalf. He sends John to the besieged royal garrison at Chester, with promises of aid.

Lord Biron, commander of the garrison at Chester. After weeks of waiting, he finds that the King has denied plans for the Irish invasion because of a popular outcry. The garrison is lost to the Puritans.

Lauretta Capece, with whom John falls in love in Florence. He marries her and lives with her for several years in Umbria until, returning from a personal mission, he finds the family wiped out by the plague.

Cardinal Chigi, later elected Pope. He is John's Italian patron.

The Duke of Umbria, to whom John is sent on a successful mission by the Jesuits.

JONATHAN WILD

Author: Henry Fielding (1707-1754)
Time of action: Late seventeenth century
First published: 1743

Jonathan Wild, a descendant of many men hanged for thievery and treason. He becomes a notorious criminal, beginning as a pickpocket while still a schoolboy. He becomes a criminal leader and gathers about him a gang of thieves who do his bidding. He shows his "greatness" as a criminal by being dishonest even to his friends and companions. His highest aim is to send his honest friend, Heartfree, to the gallows. Instead, he himself dies on the gallows, cursing mankind.

Count La Ruse, a fellow criminal with Jonathan Wild. He is a pickpocket befriended by Jonathan while in debtors' prison. He has a long career in crime which ends when he is executed by being broken on the wheel in France.

Laetitia Snap, who becomes Jonathan's wife. She keeps him at a distance for a time in order to keep her lover a secret.

She is a fitting wife for Jonathan, being herself a pickpocket and a cheat at cards. She ends up on the gallows.

Mr. Heartfree, a good man who loves his family and is honest in his dealings. He is a former schoolmate of Jonathan. He is a jeweler by trade and is ruined by Jonathan and his gang, who steal his stock, beat him terribly, and say at the same time they are his friends.

Mrs. Heartfree, an honest woman. Jonathan convinces her that her husband wants her to go with Jonathan to Holland. Jonathan mistreats her, but she returns from her extensive travels in time to save her husband from hanging, after he has been framed by Jonathan. When she returns she has a fabulous jewel, the gift of a savage chief, which restores the family's prosperity.

JORROCKS' JAUNTS AND JOLLITIES

Author: Robert Smith Surtees (1803-1864)
Time of action: The 1830's
First published: 1838

John Jorrocks, a fat, pretentious Cockney grocer who apes his aristocratic betters. In this series of tales he provides unity for amusing episodes satirizing sporting life and customs.

Julia Jorrocks, his wife, who can be sure her husband will not be late for a meal.

Mr. Stubbs, a footloose Yorkshireman, keen for sport if someone else will pay the bills.

A Swell, a mysterious, daring horseman who shames the riders with his riding

until his horse goes lame. He is rumored to be a Russian diplomat.

Nosey Browne, the bankrupt owner of a small hunting place.

Squire Cheatum, who fines Jorrocks for shooting on his land.

Countess Benvolio, "Benwolio" to Jorrocks, whom she encourages to write a book on France. She skips with the money he wins in a race.

Betsy, the Jorrocks' cook.

JOSEPH ANDREWS

Author: Henry Fielding (1707-1754)
Time of action: Early eighteenth century
First published: 1742

Joseph Andrews, a simple, handsome young man of great virtue who, because of his looks and purity, becomes the erotic prey of various women. Discharged from his post as Lady Booby's footman when he fails to respond to her advances, he leaves London to return to his native Somersetshire and his true love, Fanny Goodwill. On the way he is robbed, beaten, made fun of, and nearly raped. At an inn he meets his old tutor, Parson Adams, and together they travel home. On the way Parson Adams rescues Fanny from a brutal ruffian. At home, however, Joseph's marriage to Fanny is thwarted by a jail term on charges brought by revengeful Lady Booby, the objections of his relatives, and the discovery that Fanny is supposedly his sister. When it turns out that he is really a son of a family named Wilson—the children had been exchanged by gipsies—the marriage takes place.

Fanny Goodwill, Joseph Andrews' attractive, virtuous sweetheart. Traveling to meet Joseph in London, after hearing that Lady Booby has dismissed him, she accompanies her lover and Parson Adams back to Somersetshire. Her adventures consist mainly of hairbreadth escapes from attackers until she is married.

Parson Abraham Adams, an earthy man who loves food, drink, and tobacco. At the same time he is idealistic and charitable. An absent-minded tutor and the friend of Joseph and Fanny, he accompanies them home, protecting them with his fists and sharing their troubles, and at last marries them.

Lady Booby, a noblewoman torn between her pride of class and her love for her handsome young footman. After dismissing him, she returns to her Somersetshire estate and uses all her influence to prevent his marriage to Fanny.

Mrs. Slipslop, Lady Booby's housekeeper, an aggressive, misshapen woman who almost rapes Joseph and tries continually to win him over.

Pamela Booby, Joseph's sister, who tries to prevent his marriage to Fanny. Adapted from Richardson's novel "Pamela," she exemplifies virtue based on vanity rather than, as in Fanny's case, on natural goodness.

Squire Booby, Pamela's husband, a good man who frees Joseph from jail and accepts him as an equal, but because of class pride he objects to Joseph's marriage to Fanny.

Peter Pounce, Lady Booby's steward, a stingy, uncharitable man who, on one occasion, saves Fanny from rape but plans to enjoy her himself.

Mr. Wilson, a kindly, intelligent man who serves as host to the penniless Joseph, Fanny, and Parson Adams. He later turns out to be Joseph's true father.

Mrs. Wilson, his wife.

The Pedlar, a good-hearted person who pays a debt for Parson Adams, saves his son from drowning, and explains the mystery of Fanny's parentage.

Mrs. Adams, the Parson's good but practical wife. She objects to Joseph's marriage because she thinks it will interfere with her children's advancement.

Beau Didapper, a London fop who visits Lady Booby and tries to seduce Fanny.

Gammer and
Gaffer Andrews, Joseph and Pamela's rather fatuous parents.

A Lecherous Squire. He sets his hounds on Parson Adams, humiliates him at dinner, and tries to gain Fanny first by cunning and then by force.

A Captain, his agent, who captures Fanny at the inn, takes her off to the Squire, but is stopped in time by Peter Pounce.

A Gentleman. He promises food and lodging to Joseph, Fanny, and Parson Adams, but fails to make good.

A Generous Innkeeper. He promises nothing but lets the group stay at his inn without payment.

Parson Trulliber, a gluttonous, bad-tempered minister who refuses charity to Parson Adams.

Mr. Tow-Wouse, an innkeeper who is meek and stingy.

Mrs. Tow-Wouse, his vixenish wife.

Betty, their servant, who nearly ravishes Joseph while nursing him.

Mr. Scout, Lady Booby's lawyer, who throws Joseph and Fanny into jail on trumped up charges.

JOSEPH VANCE

Author: William De Morgan (1839-1917)
Time of action: Mid-nineteenth century
First published: 1906

PRINCIPAL CHARACTERS

Joseph Vance, an honest Englishman who helps his friends and suffers sometimes for his goodness. Even his love is denied because he refuses to hurt the woman he loves by telling her that her own brother's rascality is what has put Joseph himself in a bad light.

Mr. Christopher Vance, Joseph's prodigal father. A drunkard, he is one of his son's greatest problems. He almost bankrupts himself because, while drunk, he causes a fire in the building housing his business.

Mrs. Vance, Christopher's first wife, Joseph's mother. She dies shortly after Joseph graduates from Oxford.

Dr. Randall Thorpe, Joseph's benefactor. It is he who sends Joseph to Oxford.

Lossie Thorpe, Dr. Thorpe's oldest child, loved by Joseph. Eventually she and Joseph spend their last days together in Italy.

Joe (Beppino) Thorpe, Dr. Thorpe's son. He is a bigamist, in one marriage using Joseph Vance's name. His son by that marriage is adopted by Joseph, whose action causes Lossie to turn against him, for she thinks he is the child's real father. Beppino is a would-be poet. He dies of typhoid fever.

Violet Thorpe, Lossie's sister.

Nolly Thorpe, Lossie's other brother.

General Desprez, a wealthy army officer, Lossie's husband. He dies before he can clear Joseph of the charges of which his wife thinks Joseph guilty.

Pheener, the Christopher Vances' maid. After her mistress' death she marries Christopher.

Bony Macallister, Joseph's school friend. Later he and Joseph become business partners in an engineering firm.

Janey Spencer, Joseph's wife. She loves him dearly and is drowned when she refuses to go into a lifeboat from a sinking ship after choosing to try to swim to shore with her husband.

Sibyl Perceval, an heiress who marries Beppino shortly before his death.

JOURNEY TO THE END OF NIGHT

Author: Louis-Ferdinand Céline (Louis Ferdinand Destouches, 1894-1961)
Time of action: World War I and following years
First published: 1932

PRINCIPAL CHARACTERS

Ferdinand Bardamu (fĕr·dē·nän' bär·dà·mü'), a war-wounded, disillusioned, cynical neurotic and a rogue. Successively a medical student, soldier, mental patient, pimp, flea expert, Ford worker, doctor, music hall supernumerary, and administrator of a madhouse, he undergoes experiences which would tax the strongest constitution and the sanest mind. In his restless shifting from one job to another and from one locale to another, he resembles not only the rogues of picaresque fiction but also his creator, Ferdinand Céline.

Léon Robinson (lā·ōń' rô·bäń·sōń'), his friend, an unscrupulous cynic who turns up, like a personal demon, everywhere Ferdinand goes. The planner of the bombing of old Madame Henrouille, he is temporarily blinded by his own bomb. He is later killed by Madelon.

Madelon (màd·lōń'), an attractive young girl of easy morals. Engaged to Léon, she becomes insanely jealous when he attempts to get rid of her; and after threatening to inform the police of his murder of Madame Henrouille, she shoots him in a rage and flees.

Lola, an American Red Cross worker who becomes Ferdinand's mistress in France and who later permits him to live with her for a time after he comes to New York.

Musyne (mü·zēn'), a dancer and prostitute, another of Ferdinand's mistresses.

Madame Hérote (ā·rôt'), a Parisian lingerie-glove-bookshop keeper and a prostitute.

Doctor Bestombes (bā·tōńb'), a psychiatrist in a mental hospital.

Roger Puta (rô·zhā' pü·tä'), a jeweler for whom Ferdinand works before the war; during the war he is a driver for a cabinet minister.

Lieutenant Grappa (grà·pà'), a brutal officer in charge of Topo station in Africa.

Molly, an American prostitute in Detroit; Ferdinand is briefly in love with her.

The Abbé Protiste (à·bā' prô·tēst'), a priest who arranges for Léon and Madame Henrouille to set up a little business in Toulouse, showing mummies in a crypt to tourists.

Tania (tà·nyà'), a Polish friend of Ferdinand whose lover dies in Berlin.

Doctor Baryton (bà·rē·tōń'), a psychiatrist who operates a madhouse, becomes mad about English (which he learns from Ferdinand and from reading Macaulay), and rushes off to England and other lands, leaving the madhouse in Ferdinand's charge.

Doctor Serge Parapine (sĕrzh' pà·rà·pēn'), a medical researcher later employed as a staff physician at Baryton's asylum; a friend of Ferdinand.

The Henrouilles (än·rōō'yə), a Parisian family for whom Ferdinand performs various medical services.

Bébert (bā·bĕr'), a young boy, a patient of Ferdinand, who dies of typhoid fever.

Gustave Mandamour (gü·stàv' mäń·dà·mōōr'), a traffic policeman, a friend of Ferdinand and Léon.

Sophie (sô·fē'), a voluptuous Slovak nurse hired by Ferdinand; he is fascinated by her.

555

JOURNEY'S END

Author: Robert C. Sherriff (1896-)
Time of action: March, 1918
First presented: 1929

PRINCIPAL CHARACTERS

Captain Dennis Stanhope, a British officer whose three years in the front lines have made him a hard, cynical, and heavy-drinking man. Stanhope is first and foremost a soldier, however, and, when his young friend is fatally wounded, he returns immediately to his duties as commanding officer.

Lieutenant Osborne, Stanhope's second in command. He is a middle-aged man who was a schoolteacher in civilian life. Osborne is anxious to keep peace in the company. He is killed, along with several other members of a raiding party sent out to capture some prisoners from whom the colonel of the regiment hopes to obtain information.

Lieutenant Raleigh, a school friend of Stanhope and the brother of Stanhope's fiancée. Raleigh is a hero worshiper of Stanhope and can hardly recognize his old friend when he meets him in the front lines. Raleigh is a callow youth, full of vitality, who soon makes friends with Osborne. He cannot understand how the other men in the company can celebrate after Osborne and several others are killed in the raiding party. Raleigh is fatally wounded in a German attack.

2nd Lieutenant Hibbert, an officer in Stanhope's company who is a malingerer and a coward. Stanhope bullies Hibbert into staying on duty when Hibbert tries to get a doctor to give him a medical excuse for being relieved from duty.

A JOVIAL CREW

Author: Richard Brome (?-1652 or 1653)
Time of action: Seventeenth century
First presented: 1641

PRINCIPAL CHARACTERS

Oldrents, a kindly country squire. Troubled by a fortuneteller's prediction that his daughters will become beggars, he becomes so melancholy and unlike his usual self that he drives them to run away with a troop of wandering beggars. At their return, his happy nature is restored.

Springlove, Oldrents' good-hearted and reliable steward. His only fault is an annual restlessness which makes him turn over his accounts to an assistant and take to the open road. He aids the Squire's daughters in their runaway plan and looks after their safety. He is finally

revealed as their half brother, an illegitimate son of Oldrents and the nephew of the Patrico of the beggars.

Rachel and
Meriel, the Squire's romantic daughters, who find begging in reality less pleasant than their imaginings.

Amie, niece of Justice Clack. He tries to force her to marry Talboy. She runs away with Martin, joins the beggars, falls in love with Springlove, and is united with him in marriage when he is discovered to be Oldrents' son.

Master Talboy, Amie's jilted bridegroom.

Justice Clack, a talkative and officious country justice. His examination of the beggars in the presence of Oldrents leads to the needful disclosures and the happy ending.

The Patrico, the priest of the beggars. He reveals to Oldrents that Springlove is his son.

Hearty, a decayed gentleman, Oldrents' friend and parasite.

Martin, Hearty's cowardly nephew, a second potential bridegroom disappointed in his hopes of winning Amie.

Oliver, the lecherous son of Justice Clack. He fails in his attempt to attack Rachel.

Vincent and
Hilliard, the lovers of the Squire's daughters, who accompany them on their adventure.

JUDE THE OBSCURE

Author: Thomas Hardy (1840-1928)
Time of action: Nineteenth century
First published: 1894

PRINCIPAL CHARACTERS

Jude Fawley, a village stonemason who is thwarted in every attempt to find success and happiness. His chief desire from the time of his youth is to become a religious scholar, but because of his sensuous temperament he is forced into an early marriage. After his first wife leaves him he falls in love with his cousin and lives with her illegally for several years. The weight of social disapproval forces them downhill. After the tragic death of their children his cousin leaves him also, and Jude, having turned to drink, dies a miserable death.

Arabella Donn, a country girl who tricks Jude into his first marriage. She has nothing in common with Jude and soon leaves him to go to Australia. She later returns but makes no immediate demands on him, preferring to marry another and advance her station in life. After the death of her second husband and the separation of Jude and his cousin, she tricks him into marrying her a second time. But instead of helping to brighten the last of his life she increases his misery and is planning her next marriage even before his death.

Sue Bridehead, Jude's cousin. Although priding herself on being a free-thinker,

she marries a much older man out of a sense of obligation and leaves him shortly afterward because of her revulsion toward him. She lives with Jude for several years and bears him three children. She is a strong influence on him and through her unorthodox thought becomes the primary reason for his giving up his attempts to enter the ministry. After the tragic death of her children, she undergoes a complete change in personality; now wanting to conform, she returns to her first husband.

Richard Phillotson, a village schoolmaster who instills in Jude his first desires to learn. He falls in love with Sue after she becomes his assistant and marries her in spite of obvious differences in age, thought, and belief. When she expresses her desire to live with Jude, he allows her a divorce, although it causes his own downfall. He gladly remarries her when she wants to come back to him, even though he is fully aware that she does not love him.

Little Father Time, the son of Jude and Arabella. He is a precocious child who seems to feel the weight of the world on his shoulders. Having been sent to Jude by Arabella when she married the second

557

time, he is bothered by a sense of being unwanted and feels that he is a source of anxiety for his elders. This feeling becomes so intensified that he hangs himself and the two younger children.

Drusilla Fawley, Jude's great-aunt, who raises him after the death of his parents. During his youth she constantly warns him against ever marrying because the Fawleys have never had successful marriages.

Anny and
Sarah, friends of Arabella. They give her the idea of tricking Jude into marriage.

Mr. Donn, Arabella's father. Although he has nothing to do with the first trick on Jude, he helps Arabella carry out the second one.

Gillingham, a friend and confidant of Phillotson, whose advice Phillotson never takes.

Mrs. Edlin, a neighbor of Drusilla Fawley; she is always ready to help Jude and Sue when they need her.

Vilbert, a quack doctor. He serves as Jude's first source of disillusionment about life.

Cartlett, Arabella's second husband.

JUDITH PARIS

Author: Hugh Walpole (1884-1941)
Time of action: Nineteenth century
First published: 1931

PRINCIPAL CHARACTERS

Judith Herries, later **Judith Paris,** the daughter of Francis Herries and Mirabell (also see "Rogue Herries"), both of whom die on the night of her birth. After a stormy girlhood in the home of her half brother, she marries for love at seventeen. Her husband is a smuggler, a gambler, and an intriguer by turns. After his violent death, Judith goes to live in the home of a nephew and his wife. Out of pity she gives herself to a neighbor. Now nearly forty, she finds that she is with child, and goes to Paris. The expected child's father follows her, but dies shortly after finding her. It is just after Waterloo, and a café shooting of a Prussian so unnerves Judith that she gives birth to a son at once, behind a screen. The nephew with whom she lived has committed suicide, and Judith, taking her son, goes back to live with his widow.

David Herries (also see "Rogue Herries"), who is fifty-five years older than

his half sister Judith. Her girlhood is spent in his home.

William Herries, David's son. A women's quarrel sets him relentlessly against his brother.

Francis Herries, William's brother, with whom Judith lives after her widowhood. He shuts his eyes to his wife's infidelity, but malicious interference on the part of his nephew, acting as agent of the old feud, forces the discovery upon him. When his wife's lover escapes, Francis kills himself in futile despair.

Christabel Herries, William's wife.

Jennifer Cards, a beautiful belle. The great Herries feud begins with a quarrel between her and Christabel at a ball given by William. When Francis marries Jennifer, he becomes involved in the quarrel. Jennifer never loves her husband, and her infidelity results in Francis' suicide.

558

Fernyhirst, Jennifer's lover.

Walter Herries, the son of William. Intent on destroying Jennifer, he succeeds in destroying Francis.

Georges Paris, Judith's husband, with whom she leads a lonely life.

Stane, who is involved with Georges in mysterious business. After Stane causes the failure of Georges' prospects, Georges kills him and is in turn killed by Stane's father.

Warren Forster, a tiny, kindly man who has long admired Judith. She gives herself to him out of pity. He follows her to Paris and dies there.

Squire Gauntry, a tough and taciturn man. He finds the orphaned infant Judith unattended, the midwife being drunk, and takes her to his home until her half brother comes for her. She visits his place frequently as a child and is under no restrictions there. On one of her visits she meets Georges.

Emma, Squire Gauntry's mistress and Judith's long-time friend. Judith lives with Emma, now on the stage, in Paris.

Madame Paris, the beautiful mother of Georges. Judith meets her at Squire Gauntry's place.

Reuben Sunwood, Judith's kinsman and friend, killed in a riot incited by Walter Herries.

Adam Paris, the illegitimate son of Judith and Warren Forster.

John and
Dorothy Herries, the children of Jennifer and Francis.

JULIUS CAESAR

Author: William Shakespeare (1564-1616)
Time of action: 44 B.C.
First presented: 1599-1600

PRINCIPAL CHARACTERS

Marcus Brutus (mär′kŭs brōō′tŭs), one of the leading conspirators who intend to kill Julius Caesar. Although defeated in the end, Brutus is idealistic and honorable, for he hopes to do what is best for Rome. Under Caesar, he fears, the Empire will have merely a tyrant. Something of a dreamer, he, unlike the more practical Cassius, makes a number of tactical errors, such as allowing Marcus Antonius to speak to the citizens of Rome. Finally, defeated by the forces under young Octavius and Antonius, Brutus commits suicide. He would rather accept death than be driven, caged, through the streets of Rome.

Caius Cassius (kā′yŭs kǎs′ĭ·ŭs), another leading conspirator, one of the prime movers in the scheme. A practical man, and a jealous one, he is a lean and ambitious person. Some of his advice to Brutus is good. He tells Brutus to have Antonius killed. When this is not done, the conspirators are doomed to defeat. Like Brutus, Cassius commits suicide when his forces are routed at Philippi. To the last a brave man, he has fought well and courageously.

Julius Caesar (jōōl′yŭs sē′zər), the mighty ruler of Rome, who hopes to gain even more power. As portrayed in the play, he is a somewhat bombastic and arrogant man, possibly even a cowardly one. From the first he mistrusts men who, like Cassius, have "a lean and hungry look." Finally reaching for too much power, he is stabbed by a large number of conspirators led by Brutus and Cassius.

Marcus Antonius (mär'kŭs ăn·tō'nĭ·ŭs), also **Mark Antony**, the close friend of Caesar. Although he denies it, he has a great ability to sway a mob and rouse them to a feverish pitch. As a result of his oratorical abilities, he, with the help of a mob, forces the conspirators to ride for their lives to escape the maddened crowd. Later, along with Octavius and Lepidus, he is to rule Rome.

Calpurnia (kăl·pėr'nĭ·ə), the wife of Caesar. Afraid because she has had frightful dreams about yawning graveyards and lions whelping in the streets, she begs her arrogant husband not to go to the Capitol on the day of the assassination.

Portia (pôr'shə), wife of Brutus. When she learns that her husband has been forced to flee for his life, she becomes frightened for his safety. As matters worsen, she swallows hot coals and dies.

Decius Brutus (dē'shŭs broō'tŭs), one of the conspirators against Julius Caesar. When the others are doubtful that the superstitious Caesar will not come to the Capitol, Decius volunteers to bring him to the slaughter; for he knows Caesar's vanities and will play upon them until he leaves the security of his house.

Publius (pŭb'lĭ·ŭs),
Cicero (sĭs'ə·rō), and
Popilius Lena (pō·pĭl'ĭ·ŭs lē'nə), Senators.

A Soothsayer. At the beginning of the play, he warns Caesar to beware the Ides of March. For his trouble he is called a dreamer.

Artemidorus of Cnidos (är'tə·mĭ·dō'rus of nĭ'dŏs), a teacher of rhetoric who tries to warn Caesar to beware of the conspirators led by Brutus and Cassius. Like the soothsayer, he is ignored.

Casca (kăs'kə),
Caius Ligarius (kā'yŭs lĭ·gā'rĭ·ŭs),
Cinna (sĭn'ə), and
Metellus Cimber (mē·tĕl'ŭs sĭm'bər), the other conspirators.

Flavius (flā'vĭ·ŭs) and
Marullus (mă·rŭl'ŭs), tribunes who speak to the crowd at the beginning of the play.

Pindarus (pĭn'dà·rŭs), Cassius' servant. At his master's orders he runs Cassius through with a sword.

Strato (strā'tō), servant and friend to Brutus. He holds Brutus' sword so that the latter could run upon it and commit suicide.

Marcus Aemilius Lepidus (mär'kŭs ē·mĭl'ĭ·ŭs lĕp'ĭ·dŭs), the weakest member of the triumvirate after the deaths of Brutus and Cassius.

Lucius (loō'shĭ·ŭs), Brutus' servant.

Young Cato,
Messala (mē·sā'lə), and
Titinius (tĭ·tĭn'ĭ·ŭs), friends of Brutus and Cassius.

THE JUNGLE

Author: Upton Sinclair (1878-   )
Time of action: Early twentieth century
First published: 1906

PRINCIPAL CHARACTERS

Jurgis Rudkus, a Lithuanian peasant immigrant who works in the Chicago stockyards. Victimized, hurt at the plant, and jailed for attacking a man who takes his wife to a house of prostitution, he finally hears a Socialist speaker and joins the party because of the rebirth of hope and faith it offers.

560

Ona, Jurgis' wife, who sells herself to her boss for money for the family. She dies in childbirth.

Connor, a stockyards boss attracted by Ona.

Antanas, Jurgis' baby, who drowns when left unattended.

Elzbieta, Ona's stepmother, and the mother of six.

Stanislovas, the oldest son of Elzbieta, who lies about his age to get a job.

Antanas Rudkus, Jurgis' aged father, who kicks back part of his wages in order to keep his job. He dies of tuberculosis.

Jonas, Elzbieta's brother, who works at the stockyards.

Jack Duane, a Chicago safe-cracker who shows Jurgis how to get quick money.

Marija, Ona's orphan cousin, who loses her job at the stockyards and becomes a prostitute.

THE JUNGLE BOOKS

Author: Rudyard Kipling (1865-1936)
Time of action: Nineteenth century
First published: 1894, 1895

PRINCIPAL CHARACTERS

Mowgli, the boy-hero who strays away from a village in India when he is a very small child. He is pursued by Shere Khan, the tiger, but escapes when the beast misses a leap at the boy. Mowgli is reared by Mother Wolf with her own cubs and becomes a member of the jungle wolf pack. He has many adventures among the jungle animals but finally, when he is about seventeen years old, he realizes that he must return to the Man-pack to stay.

Messua, the woman who adopted Mowgli for a time. She finally tells Mowgli that she believes he is her son who was lost in the jungle many years before.

Shere Khan, the tiger who pursues Mowgli when he is first lost in the jungle. Shere Khan shocks the other animals when he announces that he has killed a man from choice and not for food. Then follows the story of how the tiger first killed Man and was condemned to wear stripes.

Mother Wolf and
Father Wolf, who find Mowgli, give him his name, and rear him with their own cubs in the jungle.

Baloo, the bear who becomes Mowgli's teacher and instructs him in jungle lore.

Bagheera, the black panther who speaks for Mowgli's acceptance into the wolf pack and advises Mowgli to get fire to protect himself against his enemies.

Akela, the leader of the wolf pack and Mowgli's friend in many adventures.

The Bandar-Log, the monkey people, who are despised by the other jungle dwellers. They carry Mowgli off when he climbs a tree and tries to make friends with them.

KAA, the rock python who helps to rescue Mowgli when he is carried off by the monkeys.

Gray Brother, Mowgli's brother in the wolf pack, who helps Mowgli rescue Messua and her husband when they are confined by the other villagers.

Buldeo, a village hunter, who follows Mowgli's trail when he returns to the jungle after living with Messua in the human village.

Hathi, the wise elephant, who tells the story of why the tiger has stripes.

JUNO AND THE PAYCOCK

Author: Sean O'Casey (1884-   )
Time of action: 1922
First presented: 1924

PRINCIPAL CHARACTERS

"Captain" Jack Boyle, called the "paycock" by his wife because of his slow, consequential strut. The quintessence of impracticality, Jack needs only enough money for his daily consumption of ale or whiskey. News of an inheritance of two thousand pounds from a distant relative and the subsequent reversal, because of a legal technicality in the will, make little difference in the Paycock's life. His few fleeting dreams of better conditions for the Boyle family are no discouragement to the "Captain" when he learns that the money will not be forthcoming; he is drunk, he has sixpence in his pocket, and he is with "Joxer" Daley, long-time drinking pal. That they are in an almost empty room while they discuss their devotion to Ireland and the wretched state of the world, the unpaid-for furniture having been reclaimed, is inconsequential.

Juno Boyle, his wife. Once a pretty woman, she has now a look of listless and harassed anxiety. This appearance results from a life as Jack Boyle's wife and the mother of their two children. Under more favorable conditions, she would probably be handsome, active, and clever. Her lot in life is to achieve some semblance of practicality in order to balance her husband's insensibility.

Mary, their twenty-two-year-old daughter who, like her mother, would be an attractive woman under better circumstances. Looking for improved circumstances leads Mary to an affair, ultimately to pregnancy; and her would-be benefactor abandons her. Despite her active mind, shown in her reading and her imagination, life will probably continue

to pull her back as she works futilely to go forward.

Johnny, the Boyle's son, who is as dissatisfied with family conditions as is Mary. Rebellious, Johnny fights more actively than does his sister. He has lost one arm and sustained a crippling hip injury in an Irish political demonstration. The information he gives against a member of his group shows his lack of standards and strength. When he is sought out for his informing, his cowardliness is evident as he is led out to be shot by two armed Irish Irregulars.

"Joxer" Daly, Boyle's carousing crony. His evasion of work surpasses Boyle's indifference to responsibility. His constant grinning and the twinkle in his eyes make him more amiable but no more respectable than Boyle.

Charlie Bentham, a schoolteacher, who brings news of Boyle's legacy. Bentham's studiousness and wide knowledge are attractive to Mary, for she sees him as the means of escaping life in the tenement. Bentham's misinterpretation of the will, depriving the Boyles of the expected money, is secondary to his abandonment of pregnant Mary.

Jerry Devine, a tenement-dweller and an active member of the Irish youth movement. Long in love with Mary, Devine would still have her after Bentham deserts her, until she tells him she is pregnant. Mary's candor is repugnant to Johnny, who berates his sister for losing an opportunity to escape to a higher scale of living.

Mrs. Maisie Madigan, a tenement-dweller and the female counterpart of

562

Boyle and "Joxer." She is as abusive of Boyle, when he cannot repay loans she made him on the strength of the inheritance, as she is exuberant in celebrating with "Joxer" and Boyle the news of the legacy.

"Needle" Nugent, a tailor in the tenement. To reclaim the suit Boyle orders, to be paid for when he collects his legacy, "Needle" snatches the suit from beside Boyle's bed.

Mrs. Tancred, a tenement neighbor of the Boyles and the mother of the boy shot after Johnny informed against him.

Mrs. Tancred's lament as she goes to her son's funeral is the forecast of Juno's cry when Johnny is shot.

Irregular Mobilizers, who come for Johnny when he is to be shot.

A Coal-Block Vendor, A Sewing-Machine Man, and Furniture Removal Men, in the activity of their various trades, along with the mobilizers, add to the general confusion of the final scenes of the play. Their activity spells disintegration of the Boyle household and family.

JURGEN

Author: James Branch Cabell (1879-1958)
Time of action: The Middle Ages
First published: 1919

PRINCIPAL CHARACTERS

Jurgen, a middle-aged pawnbroker who, searching for his lost wife, returns twenty years to the days of his youth, in which he thought himself a very clever fellow. After a year, during which he becomes a duke, a prince, a king, an emperor, and a pope, he asks to be returned to plain, practical, and moderately peaceful middle age with his wife, who is rather well suited, after all, to a man like him.

Adelais (Dame Lisa), his shrewish wife who, contemptuous of poetry and romance, converted a poet into a pawnbroker.

Dorothy la Désirée, his childhood sweetheart, second sister of Count Emmerick. She is Jurgen's Heart's Desire who married Heitman Michael. She also appears for a time to be Helen of Troy.

Mother Sereda (also Aesred and Res Dea), an old woman, Jurgen's godmother, who takes the color out of things and who controls Wednesdays. Her shadow follows Jurgen everywhere after

she has restored to him a year of his youth, following which time she makes him the middle-aged man he is.

Queen Guenevere. Jurgen has a love affair with her before her marriage to King Arthur. She does not recognize him after he has returned to middle age.

King Gogyrvan Gawr, her father, to whom Jurgen returns her after murdering King Thragnar.

Dame Anaïtis (The Lady of the Lake and Queen of Cocaigne), a myth woman of lunar legend who instructs Jurgen in many varieties of pleasure and to whom he becomes for a while Prince Consort. Like Guenevere, she does not recognize the older Jurgen.

Chloris, a plump Hamadryad to whom Jurgen is husband for a time.

Queen Helen of Troy, the legendary Swan's daughter, Jurgen's (and man's) vision of supreme beauty.

Queen Dolores, Philistine ruler to whom

563

Jurgen explains Praxagorean mathematics.

Grandfather Satan, Hell's horned and bushytailed magistrate with whom Jurgen discusses Hell as a democracy.

St. Peter, Heaven's gatekeeper, with whom Jurgen talks over pseudo-Christian beliefs.

Koshchei the Deathless (also **The Prince of Darkness**), the maker of things as they are. Because Jurgen once spoke a good word for him, Koshchei disencumbers him of Dame Lisa; but after a year he restores her at Jurgen's request.

Nessus, a centaur who gives Jurgen a glittering shirt and takes him to the garden between dawn and sunrise.

Azra, Jurgen's mother, loved briefly by Coth.

Coth, Jurgen's father, whom he meets and quarrels with in Hell.

Heitman Michael, the man who married Dorothy, over whom he and Jurgen duel with swords.

Felise de Puysange, one of many women loved by Jurgen, who fathered her son.

King Thragnar, the Troll King who captured and imprisoned Guenevere. He disguises himself as Dame Lisa and Jurgen slays him.

Dame Yolande. Jurgen kills a giant for her and with her he spends a most agreeable night after he blows out the candles.

King Smoit and **Queen Sylvia Tereu,** ghosts of King Gogyrvan's grandfather and his ninth wife. According to King Smoit's story, he is also secretly the father of Coth and therefore Jurgen's grandfather.

Merlin Ambrosius, a sorcerer sent with Dame Anaïtis to fetch Guenevere for King Arthur.

Florimel, a seductive and humorously talkative vampire whom Jurgen meets and marries in Hell.

Steinvor, Jurgen's grandmother, an old woman with illusions about her children and grandchildren.

The God of Steinvor, created by Koshchei to satisfy the old woman.

JUSTICE

Author: John Galsworthy (1867-1933)
Time of action: 1910
First presented: 1910

PRINCIPAL CHARACTERS

William Falder, a junior clerk in a law firm who raises a company check from nine to ninety pounds and is sent to prison for three years. When he is released on parole, he is apprehended by the police for not reporting to the parole authorities. He breaks away from the arresting officer and kills himself by jumping from an office window.

Ruth Honeywell, the woman for whom Falder altered the check. He had intended to take Ruth and her two children from her brutish husband, and he needed the money for the expenses they would incur when they left London.

Robert Cokeson, a senior clerk in the firm who supports Falder through the trial, while he is in prison, and after his release.

James and **Walter How,** partners in a law firm and Falder's employers. They cause Falder's arrest, but after his release from prison they are also willing to discuss taking him back into their employ.

Davis, a junior clerk first suspected of altering the check.

Hector Frome, Falder's attorney during the trial.

Harold Cleaver, the counselor for the prosecution at Falder's trial.

THE KALEVALA

Author: Elias Lönnrot (1802-1884)
Time of action: Mythological antiquity
First published: 1835

PRINCIPAL CHARACTERS

Kaleva, the ancestor of all heroes. Although he, himself, never appears in "The Kalevala," he is one of the unifying principles of this epic, which is put together from the Finnish folk tales of many generations.

Väinämöinen, the singer-hero, who is the Son of the Wind and the Virgin of the Air. Seeking a daughter of Louhi, the witch, for his wife, Väinämöinen is required to furnish the mother with a magic Sampo which grinds out riches. He provides the Sampo, but the daughter chooses another for a husband. A large part of Väinämöinen's story is then concerned with his efforts to recover the Sampo and the catastrophic results of his theft.

Ilmarinen, the smith-hero and forger of the sky and of the Sampo required of Väinämöinen by Louhi. He is in love with Louhi's daughter and is chosen by her over Väinämöinen.

Lemminkäinen, the warrior-hero, who seeks as a wife a daughter of Louhi.

Joukahäinen, a young man defeated by Väinämöinen in a duel of magic songs.

Aino, Joukahäinen's sister, who is won in a song duel by Väinämöinen. She drowns herself rather than marry him.

Louhi, a witch, ruler of Pohjola, and the mother of beautiful daughters sought as wives by Väinämöinen, Ilmarinen, and Lemminkäinen.

Kyllikki, the flower of Saari, who is abducted by Lemminkäinen.

Vipunen, a giant who swallows and disgorges Väinämöinen.

Tiera, Lemminkäinen's warrior companion.

Kullervo, a sullen, powerful slave who kills Ilmarinen's wife and ravishes his own sister. At last, in despair, he falls on his sword.

Untamöinen, Kullervo's uncle, who carries off Kullervo's mother. When Kullervo grows up, he kills Untamöinen.

Kalervo, Kullervo's father.

Ukko, the supreme god.

Marjatta, a holy woman and virgin who gives birth to a son in a stable.

The King of Carelia, Marjatta's wise son.

KATE FENNIGATE

Author: Booth Tarkington (1869-1946)
Time of action: Twentieth century
First published: 1943

565

Kate Fennigate, a managing woman who knows what she wants in life and usually gets it, sometimes against great odds.

Mrs. Fennigate, her mother, interested only in eating. She dies after Kate's graduation from high school.

Mr. Fennigate, her father, interested in women and drinking. He dies during a trip to Europe with Kate.

Aunt Daisy, who takes Kate in as a household drudge. She loses her money in the stock market and later loses her mind.

Mary, Daisy's delicate daughter, whose death desolates her mother.

Ames Lanning, Mary's husband, whom Kate loves and tries to spur to success as a lawyer. After Mary's death, he marries her.

Celia, the daughter of Mary and Ames, in love with Miley Stuart.

Miley Stuart, a young engineer at the Roe Metals factory.

Mr. Roe, who employs both Kate and Ames.

Mr. Bortshleff, a lawyer who invites Ames to work with him.

Laila Capper, Kate's rich and beautiful classmate, who tries to break up Kate's marriage to Ames.

Tuke Speer, interested in Kate but persuaded by Laila to elope with her. Kate arranges for Tuke to be sent to manage Roe's New York office, thus removing the predatory Laila from Ames's presence.

KENILWORTH

Author: Sir Walter Scott (1771-1832)
Time of action: 1575
First published: 1821

Edmund Tressilian, an impoverished young gentleman, a friend of the Earl of Sussex and an unsuccessful suitor for Amy Robsart's hand. Generous, intelligent and honorable, he seeks to free Amy from Richard Varney, whom he believes to be her paramour. When Amy, secretly the wife of the Earl of Leicester, refuses to leave Cumnor Place, he tries to put his case before Queen Elizabeth. Supported by Amy's father and Sussex, he nonetheless makes a poor showing because of Varney's cleverness and his own desire to protect Amy. Accused later of cuckolding the Earl of Leicester, Tressilian is forced to duel with the Earl but is saved by the timely intervention of two friends. He clears himself before the

Queen, though too late to save Amy from Varney's treachery.

Robert Dudley, the Earl of Leicester and master of Kenilworth Castle. Rivaled only by Sussex in Elizabeth's esteem, he has the advantage of appealing to her femininity. Knowing his marriage to Amy would spoil his chance for advancement, he keeps her at Cumnor Place under Varney's supervision. Basically noble, he is also quite gullible. When he tries to tell Elizabeth of his marriage, Varney convinces him Amy has been unfaithful. In a rage he orders Varney to kill her and fights a duel with Tressilian. On learning the truth he reveals his marriage and tries in vain to save

Amy. He suffers the loss of his wife and temporary court disfavor.

Amy Robsart, Leicester's unfortunate wife. Deeply in love with him, she wants recognition as his lawful wife but hesitates to ruin his life at court. Imprisoned at Cumnor Place, she escapes with Tressilian's servant, Wayland Smith, to Kenilworth after Varney gives her a mild dose of poison. There she tries to see her husband and reveal her true identity, but she is deemed insane by Queen Elizabeth. Through Varney's scheme she is sent back to Cumnor Place and tricked into falling to her death. Lovely and honorable, she is also willful and tragic.

Richard Varney, Leicester's courtier and right-hand man, a cautious, charming, clever, imaginative person who is also ambitious and unscrupulous. He is instrumental in poisoning Sussex. Facing failure in his plans to keep Amy from interfering with Leicester's advance in royal favor, he persuades his master of her infidelity. He is captured after Amy's death and commits suicide in prison.

Michael Lambourne, a swashbuckling, unprincipled man of action in Varney's service and a participant in the plans to dispose of Amy. Varney's pupil in rascality, he tries to surpass his master and is killed for his efforts.

Queen Elizabeth, an extremely shrewd and skillful ruler, adept at playing court factions against one another but still capricious and feminine. Hot-tempered, vain, and jealous, she loses her self-control when Leicester reveals his marriage, and she threatens him with execution. She eventually forgives him and restores him to royal favor.

Wayland Smith, Tressilian's hardy friend and servant. A skilled smith and alchemist, he saves Sussex from poison, assists Amy to go to Kenilworth, and prevents Leicester from killing Tressilian in a duel.

Dickie Sludge (Flibbertigibbet), Wayland's swift, ugly, clever, elfish friend.

He almost causes Tressilian's death by mischievously withholding Amy's letter to Leicester, but he redeems himself by delivering it in time.

Thomas Ratcliffe, the Earl of Sussex, the soldierly court opponent of Leicester. Poisoned under Varney's direction, he recovers and supports Tressilian.

Walter Raleigh, a Sussex courtier who wins Elizabeth's favor and is knighted. A friend of Tressilian, he assists at Varney's arrest.

Nicholas Blount, a soldierly, middle-aged courtier who becomes a court fool when knighted.

Dr. Demetrius Doboobie (Alasco), a villainous alchemist and astrologer serving Leicester. Used by Varney as a poisoner, he also dies accidentally of his own poison.

Anthony Foster, the keeper of Cumnor Place, a vulgar, ugly, puritanical and miserly person who serves as Amy's jailer. After her death he dies hiding in his gold room, unable to get out.

Janet Foster, his good-hearted daughter and Amy's maid. She aids Amy in her escape.

Sir Hugh Robsart, Amy's poor, senile father who encourages Tressilian to free her.

Master Michael Mumblazen, Sir Hugh's overseer, a rustic, generous person who supplies Tressilian with money for the purpose of thwarting Varney.

Giles Gosling, the Cumnor innkeeper who suggests that Tressilian put his case before Queen Elizabeth but then refuses to help Wayland.

Laurence Goldthred, a customer at Gosling's inn who wagers with Lambourne and later has his horse "borrowed" by Wayland.

Erasmus Holiday, a pretentious, pedantic schoolmaster who directs Tressilian to Wayland.

KIDNAPPED

Author: Robert Louis Stevenson (1850-1894)
Time of action: 1751
First published: 1886

PRINCIPAL CHARACTERS

David Balfour, who tries to claim the inheritance of his dead father. He partially succeeds after many adventures, beginning with his kidnaping aboard the "Covenant" at the behest of his wicked uncle.

Ebenezer Balfour, of Shaws, David's uncle, an unscrupulous man hated by his neighbors. He holds the Balfour possessions.

Captain Hoseason, master of the "Covenant," who shanghaies David to prevent his claiming his inheritance.

Alan Breck Stewart, a Jacobite rescued when the "Covenant" sinks his small ship. He becomes friendly with David.

Mr. Riach, the second mate of the "Covenant," David's only friend aboard.

Mr. Shuan, the first mate of the "Covenant," who while drunk beats to death the cabin boy, Ransome. David inherits Ransome's job aboard ship.

Mr. Rankeillor, the family lawyer, who reveals Ebenezer's treachery to David.

Mr. Campbell, the minister of Essendean, who carries a letter to David from his dead father.

Colin of Glenure, called **The Red Fox,** who hunts Alan for conspiracy against King George. His death is blamed on Alan.

KIM

Author: Rudyard Kipling (1865-1936)
Time of action: Late nineteenth century
First published: 1901

PRINCIPAL CHARACTERS

Kimball O'Hara (Kim), the son of an Irish mother, who died in India when he was born, and an Irish father, who was color sergeant of the regiment called the Mavericks and who died and left Kim in the care of a half-caste woman. Kim grows up on the streets of Lahore and his skin becomes so dark that no one can tell he is white. He attaches himself to a Tibetan lama as a chela. Kim is caught by the chaplain of the Maverick regiment, who discovers his real identity. The lama pays for Kim's education, and Kim finally distinguishes himself as a member of the British Secret Service.

A Tibetan Lama, who becomes Kim's instructor and whose ambition it is to find the holy River of the Arrow that would wash away all sin. The lama pays for Kim's schooling. After Kim's education is complete, he accompanies the lama in his wanderings, though he is really a member of the Secret Service. In the end, the lama finds his holy river, a brook on the estate of an old woman who befriends him and Kim.

Mahbub Ali, a horse trader who is really a member of the British Secret Service. Mahbub Ali is largely responsible for Kim's becoming a member of the Secret Service.

Colonel Creighton, the director of the British Secret Service, who permits Kim

568

to resume the dress of a street boy and do Secret Service work.

Hurree Chunder Mookerjee, a babu, and also a member of the Secret Service. He is Kim's confederate in securing some valuable documents brought into India by spies for the Russians.

A KING AND NO KING

Authors: Francis Beaumont (1585?-1616) and John Fletcher (1579-1625)
Time of action: Indefinite
First presented: 1611

PRINCIPAL CHARACTERS

Arbaces (är′bə·sēz), King of Iberia. He proudly proclaims his own humility and bravery after his victory over the Armenians, but he finds his self-confidence shaken by his passion for the girl he believes to be his sister. His melodramatic inner torments are relieved when he discovers that he is not the son of the previous King and is therefore free to marry Panthea.

Tigranes (tĭ·grā′nēz), King of Armenia, who is conquered and taken prisoner by Arbaces. He succumbs briefly to the charms of Panthea, but recognizes the virtues of the faithful Spaconia and resolves to be constant to her.

Arane (ə·rā′nē), the Queen Mother, who attempts to murder her foster son in order to make her daughter Queen.

Gobrias (gō′brĭ·əs), the Lord Protector, Arbaces' father. He is forced to thwart Arane's plots until he can reveal the truth at the time when his son most welcomes it.

Panthea (pǎn′thē·ə), Arane's daughter. She is distressed by her unsisterly feelings for Arbaces and accepts imprisonment to save them both from sin.

Spaconia (spǎ·kō′nĭ·ə), an Armenian lady who follows her beloved Tigranes to Iberia. She readily forgives his brief infatuation with Panthea and agrees to become his wife.

Lygones (lĭ′gō·nēz), her father, whose anger with his runaway daughter is mollified when he learns that she is to be Tigranes' Queen.

Mardonius (mär·dō′nĭ·əs), Arbaces' captain, the one person who dares to criticize the King to his face.

Bessus (bĕ′səs), another captain, a notorious cowardly braggart, one in the long tradition of the "milites gloriosi."

Bacarius (bǎ·kâ′rĭ·əs), an Iberian lord who plans a trap to deflate Bessus' pride.

KING JOHN

Author: John Bale (1495-1563)
Time of action: Early thirteenth century
First presented: c. 1548

PRINCIPAL CHARACTERS

England, a poor widow, persecuted by agents of the Church of Rome. She is sorely distressed at her own hardships and those of her King, which end with his defeat and ultimate death by poisoning. She is saved from her wretchedness when Verity brings in Imperial Majesty to overthrow her enemies.

King John, champion of the oppressed widow, enemy of the Church of Rome. He lays aside his anger at the corrupt clergy and domination from overseas in compassion for his people. In order to spare them the horrors of war, he surrenders his crown to Usurped Power (Pope Innocent III) and receives it from him as a vassal of the Church. Too trusting, he shares a poisoned cup with Dissimulation and dies, lamenting the fate of his poor people.

Nobility, the King's shaky supporter. Fearful of the power of Rome, he deserts his rightful ruler. After John's death, Nobility is brought back into the fold by Verity.

Clergy, the King's corrupt, unwilling follower. He swears loyalty with reluctance, breaks his oath with joy. He too reforms and serves Imperial Majesty.

Civil Order, another unreliable follower. He too deserts the King in the crisis. He returns when Imperial Majesty becomes ruler.

Commonalty, the poor, blind, ignorant child of the Widow England. His goods taken by the Church, deprived of the Holy Scripture by the clergy, he too is found wanting and abandons his ruler.

Sedition (Stephen Langton), the corrupt, wittily foul-mouthed agent of the Church

of Rome. Sometimes appearing as the Vice itself, he also assumes the person of Stephen Langton, Archbishop of Canterbury. He is an active villain throughout the play and is finally hanged by command of Imperial Majesty.

Dissimulation (Simon of Swinsett), another agent of the Church, also part vice and part man. Willing to accept martyrdom in order to remove an enemy of the Church and expecting canonization for committing murder, he shares a cup of poison with King John, joining his victim in death.

Private Wealth (Cardinal Pandulphus), a strong supporter of Usurped Power and a harsh oppressor of England and tormentor of King John.

Usurped Power (Pope Innocent III), most powerful of John's enemies.

Treason, a criminal protected by benefit of clergy.

Verity, supporter and restorer of historical truth. He rebukes the defecters and gives England a savior, Imperial Majesty.

Imperial Majesty (perhaps Henry VIII), destroyer of the usurping powers in England. He hangs Sedition and redeems the country.

KING JOHN

Author: William Shakespeare (1564-1616)
Time of action: Early thirteenth century
First presented: 1596-1597

PRINCIPAL CHARACTERS

King John, who, as one witty scholar has put it, was "every other inch a king." As a champion of opposition to the Church of Rome, he is treated with a sympathy rare in English literature. This sympathetic treatment appears in John Bale's "King John" and the anonymous

"Troublesome Reign of John King of England," from which Shakespeare no doubt borrowed it. John is not a clearly characterized or consistent figure. His conscience or his sense of expediency torments him when he hears that his nephew Arthur is dead by his command.

Cordelia (kôr·dēl′yə), Lear's youngest daughter. Endowed with her father's stubbornness, she refuses to flatter him as her sisters have done. In his adversity she returns to him with love and forgiveness, restoring his sanity and redeeming him from bitterness. Her untimely death brings about Lear's death.

The Earl of Kent, Lear's frank and loyal follower. Risking Lear's anger to avert his impetuous unreason, he accepts banishment as payment for truth. Like Cordelia, but even before her, he returns to aid Lear—necessarily in disguise —as the servant Caius. The impudence of Oswald arouses violent anger in him. For his master no service is too menial or too perilous.

The Earl of Gloucester, another father with good and evil children, parallel to Lear and his daughters. Having had a gay past, about which he speaks frankly and with some pride, he believes himself a man of the world and a practical politician. He is gullible and superstitious and, deceived by Edmund, he casts off his loyal, legitimate son Edgar. His loyalty to the persecuted King leads to the loss of his eyes; but his inner sight is made whole by his blinding. He dies happily reconciled to Edgar.

Edgar (in disguise, **Tom o' Bedlam**), Gloucester's legitimate son. He is forced into hiding by his credulous father and the machinations of his evil half brother. As Tom o' Bedlam he is with the King during the tempest, and later he cares for his eyeless father both physically and spiritually. Finally he reveals himself to Gloucester just before engaging in mortal combat with Edmund, who dies as a result of Edgar's wounding him.

Edmund, Gloucester's illegitimate younger son. A Machiavellian villain governed by insatiable ambition, he attempts to destroy his half brother and his father for his own advancement. Without passion himself, he rejoices in his ability to arouse it in others, particu-

larly Lear's two evil daughters. He has a grim and cynical sense of humor. His heartlessness is demonstrated by his plotting the murders of Lear and Cordelia, in which he is only half successful. He shows signs of repentence at the time of his death, but hardly enough to color his villainy.

The Duke of Cornwall, Regan's husband. An inhuman monster, he aids in heaping hardships on the aged King and tears out Gloucester's eyes when the Earl is discovered aiding the distressed monarch. His death, brought on by his cruelty, leaves Regan free to pursue Edmund as a potential husband.

The Duke of Albany, Goneril's husband. Noble and kind, he is revolted by Goneril's behavior toward her father, by Gloucester's blinding, and by the murder of Cordelia. He repudiates Goneril and Regan and restores order to the kingdom.

The Fool, Lear's jester, "not altogether a fool." A mixture of cleverness, bitterness, and touching loyalty, he remains with the old King in his terrible adversity. His suffering rouses Lear's pity and leads to the major change from selfish arrogance to unselfish love in the old King. The Fool's end is obscure; he simply vanishes from the play. The line which says "My poor fool is hanged" may refer to Cordelia.

Oswald, Goneril's doglike servant. Insolent, cowardly, and evil, he is still devoted to his mistress, whom ironically he destroys. His last act of devotion to her is to urge his slayer to deliver a letter from her to Edmund. Since the slayer is Edgar, the letter goes to the Duke of Albany as evidence of Goneril's and Edmund's falsehood.

The King of France, a suitor of Cordelia. Captivated by her character and loveliness, he marries her with only her father's curse for dowry. He sets up an invasion of England to restore the old

King but is called back to France before the decisive battle, leaving the responsibility on his young queen.

The Duke of Burgundy, a suitor of Cordelia. Cautious and selfish, he rejects Cordelia when he finds out that she has been cast off by her father.

First Servant of Cornwall. Moved by Cornwall's inhuman cruelty, he endeavors to save Gloucester from being blinded. Although his appearance is brief, he makes a profound impression as a character, and his action in mortally wounding Cornwall alters the course of events and leads to the overthrow of the evil forces.

An Old Man, Gloucester's tenant. Helping the blinded man, he delivers him to the care of the supposed mad beggar, actually Edgar.

A Captain, employed by Edmund to murder Lear and Cordelia in prison. He hangs Cordelia but later is killed by the aged King, who is too late to save his beloved daughter.

A Doctor, employed by Cordelia to treat her father in his illness and madness. He aids in restoring Lear to partial health.

Curan, a courtier.

THE KING OF THE GOLDEN RIVER

Author: John Ruskin (1819-1900)
Time of action: The legendary past
First published: 1851

PRINCIPAL CHARACTERS

Gluck, a good youth who, with his two brothers, owns and farms Treasure Valley, in the ancient kingdom of Stiria. His brothers make Gluck work hard at the worst tasks but give him nothing. After his brothers' failures to change the Golden River into gold, he tries. He succeeds because he is kind and he earns the help of the King of the Golden River, who had in turn tested each brother's mercy toward a thirsty child, an old man, and a dog. Only Gluck shared his water. All his life Gluck proves he is charitable and thoughtful, even after he becomes a rich man.

Schwartz and
Hans, nicknamed the **Black Brothers.** They are stingy and mean, mistreating Gluck, killing anything that brings in no money, cheating their servants, and giving nothing to charity, although they are very rich. Both the brothers, because they are evil men, fail to turn the Golden River into gold and are themselves metamorphosed into black stones.

The South-West Wind, a strange little old man befriended by Gluck when he appears at the brothers' house. Gluck gives the man shelter and offers him his own meager portion of food. When Hans and Schwartz try to throw the little man out of the house, he causes a storm to ruin the entire valley and permits no more rain to fall, so that the valley becomes a wasteland.

The King of the Golden River, who is imprisoned in a gold mug until released by Gluck. He tells Gluck how to turn the Golden River into gold by dropping holy water into it. When Gluck succeeds, the river irrigates Treasure Valley for him, making it fertile and a source of wealth.

574

THE KING OF THE MOUNTAINS

Author: Edmond François About (1828-1885)
Time of action: Mid-nineteenth century
First published: 1856

PRINCIPAL CHARACTERS

Hadgi-Stavros (häd′jī stäv′rôs), "King of the Mountains," a cruel Greek brigand. He holds people for ransom, killing them if the ransom is not paid. He shows his cruelty by torturing Hermann Schultz, even trying to roast the young German alive.

Hermann Schultz, a young German botanist doing research in the Greek mountains. Captured by the brigands, he daringly dupes them of their hostages and their ransom. He poisons the brigands, too, with arsenic from his specimen box.

Mrs. Simons, a wealthy, arrogant Englishwoman captured by Hadgi-Stavros. She encourages Hermann with her daughter until rescued. After their rescue she is but icily polite to the young man.

John Harris, Hermann's American friend. He keeps Photini as a hostage until the young German is released by the bandits.

Photini (fô·tē′nē), a homely Greek girl in love with John Harris. She turns out to be the daughter of the King of the Mountains.

Dmitri (dmē′trē), a young Greek in love with Photini. He acts as Mrs. Simons' guide while on her tour of the Greek countryside, during which she is captured by the brigands.

Mary Ann Simons, the daughter of Mrs. Simons. She is loved by Hermann, although he realizes her mother will not let them marry.

Captain Pericles (pĕr′ĭ·klēz), a soldier in league with the brigands.

KING PARADOX

Author: Pío Baroja (1872-1956)
Time of action: Early twentieth century
First published: 1906

PRINCIPAL CHARACTERS

Abraham Wolf, a wealthy British banker who is sailing his yacht, the "Cornucopia," to found a Jewish colony in Africa.

Dr. Silvestre Paradox (sēl·vĕs′trə pä·rä-dôks′), who is invited to accompany Wolf. In Africa he becomes king of a native tribe. He voices the author's philosophic ideas throughout the book.

Avelino Diz (ä·bä·lē′nō dēth), Paradox's companion and skeptical friend.

Pelayo (pä·lä′yō), a scoundrel who was once Paradox's secretary.

Arthur Sipsom, an English needle manufacturer and another guest aboard the "Cornucopia."

Eichthal Thonelgeben, a scientist guest.

Miss Pich (pēsh′), an ex-ballet dancer and guest.

"The Cheese Kid," an ex-cancan dancer and guest.

575

General Pérez (hä·nä·räl′ pä′räth), another guest.

Dora Pérez, his daughter.

Mingote (mēn·gō′tä), a revolutionist aboard the "Cornucopia."

Hardibrás (är·dē·bräs′), a soldier with a hook in place of his hand.

Monsieur Chabouly (mə·syœ′ shä-bōō·lē′), a French chocolate maker and Emperor of Western Nigritia, the location of his plantations.

Goizueta (gôē·thwä′tä), who is made

Captain of the "Cornucopia" when the original Captain is lost in a storm.

King Kiri (kē′rē), who enjoys killing those subjects he dislikes. When rebels kill him, Paradox is made king.

Funangué (fōō·nän·gä′), Prime Minister of King Kiri.

Princess Mahu (mä′ōō), the King's daughter, who ends up as a nude night club dancer.

Bagú (bä·gōō′), a jealous medicine man who hates Paradox, but loves Mahu.

Ugú (ōō·gōō′), a friendly Negro.

KING SOLOMON'S MINES

Author: H. Rider Haggard (1856-1925)
Time of action: Nineteenth century
First published: 1886

PRINCIPAL CHARACTERS

Allan Quatermain, an English explorer and sportsman. He agrees to help Sir Henry Curtis find the latter's lost brother. He is the leader of the expedition to find the brother and, also, Solomon's treasure.

Sir Henry Curtis, Quatermain's friend and companion on the expedition.

Captain John Good, a retired army officer, Quatermain's friend and companion on the expedition.

George Neville, Sir Henry Curtis' brother, who has changed his name. Lost while hunting for King Solomon's mines, he is found and given one-third of the treasure the expedition discovers.

José Silvestre, a Portuguese explorer who, as he was dying, gave Quatermain a map showing the location of King Solomon's mines.

Ventvögel, a Hottentot hired by Quatermain for the safari. He freezes to death in the mountains during the expedition.

Umbopa, a Zulu hired by Quatermain. He is really Ignosi, hereditary chief of the Kukuana tribe. He regains his rightful place and befriends the white men.

Khiva, a Zulu hired by Quatermain. He dies saving Captain Good from an enraged elephant.

Infadoos, a native sub-chieftain among the Kukuanas who helps Ignosi regain his kingship of the tribe.

Twala, a hideous one-eyed giant who has usurped the kingship of the Kukuanas. He is killed by Sir Henry during a battle between his forces and the Kukuanas loyal to Ignosi.

Scragga, Twala's cruel son. He is killed with his own spear by Quatermain.

Gagool, a native sorceress who murders many of her tribesmen in a witch hunt and tries to kill the white men.

Foulata, a beautiful native girl. Saved once by the white men, she is later stabbed to death by Gagool.

THE KING, THE GREATEST ALCALDE

Author: Lope de Vega (Lope Félix de Vega Carpio, 1562-1635)
Time of action: Sixteenth century
First presented: c. 1623

PRINCIPAL CHARACTERS

Sancho (sän'chō), a poor peasant of Spain who loves an equally poor girl, Elvira. Before he can marry her, she is abducted by the feudal lord, Don Tello. Sancho goes with Nuño, her father, to the castle to say they could not believe a nobleman guilty of such a crime. They witness the lord's evidence of outrage at such rumors; then Elvira appears to reveal his villainy. Sancho and Nuño flee to escape being beaten to death. Sancho gives in to despair in spite of Nuño's certainty that his daughter would die rather than lose her honor.

Elvira (äl·bē'rä), the daughter of Nuño, a poor farmer. Because she loves Sancho deeply, when their wedding is delayed she agrees to let him visit her room, for they have already taken their vows before the priest. When she opens her door, she sees that the man waiting there is Tello, not her lover. Firm in her reverence for virtue and honor, she will not yield to him, but he later forces her. Then, with her honor lost, she declares that never again will she know joy.

Don Tello de Neira (dōn tä'lyō thä nä'ē·rä), the feudal lord whose consent must be obtained before the marriage of his peasants. In the case of Sancho and Elvira, he agrees to the wedding before he sees the beauty of the girl; then he lusts after her. He decrees the postponement of the wedding because he plans to force her to spend the night with him and then go to Sancho the next day. That night he and his servants go masked to her home and take her to his castle. He is unable to force her to come willingly to him, though he keeps her prisoner for a long time. Finally, enraged, he takes her to the woods and ravishes her there.

Feliciana (fä·lē·thyä'nä), the noble sister of Tello, who pleads with her brother to remember his good name and honor and not to stain them through lust. Though she cannot persuade Tello, the King later respects her efforts and at the end promises her his protection and help in finding a worthy husband.

Nuño (nōō'nyō), the peasant father of Elvira, who knows that his daughter is virtuous and proud. His pleas for her release have no effect on his evil overlord.

Pelayo (pä·lä'yō), a swineherd who provides much of the humor of this play. He is preëminent among Spain's "graciosos" or clowns. He accompanies Sancho to the court of King Alfonso of Castile and takes back the King's letter ordering Tello to release Elvira. He carries news of the nobleman's disobedience and refusal back to the King and persuades him to go personally to force the lord to return the girl to her father and her sweetheart.

Alfonso VII (äl·fōn'sō), King of Leon and Castile, well-known for his justice to high and low and therefore the "best alcalde" or governor. When Tello disobeys his written order, he goes in disguise to the castle, uncovers the truth, and reveals his identity to his rebellious subject. Then he delivers his sentence: Because Tello has dishonored Elvira, he must marry her. Following the ceremony, he will be beheaded. As his widow, Elvira will inherit half his lands

577

and gold for her dowry when she marries Sancho. The repentant Tello finds the decision just, as he has sinned against both his own honor and the King. The peasants, in this early social drama, bless the King's wisdom as well as his actions in righting the wrongs done by the nobility to the lower class.

THE KINGDOM OF GOD

Author: Gregorio Martínez Sierra (1881-1947)
Time of action: Early twentieth century
First presented: 1915

PRINCIPAL CHARACTERS

Sister Gracia (grä'thyä), a member of the benevolent order of St. Vincent de Paul. In the play Sister Gracia is shown in three stages of her devotion to the alleviation of suffering to which she has pledged herself. At nineteen she is assigned to a home for poverty-stricken old men. At twenty-nine she is assisting in a home for unwed mothers where the confusion and heartbreak bring her to the verge of collapse and Dr. Enrique, who loves her, asks her to marry him. She refuses, asks for a transfer, and is last seen at seventy when she is Mother Superior in charge of an orphanage.

Gabriel (gä·brē'ĕl), formerly valet to Sister Gracia's grandfather,
Liborio (lē·bō·rē'ō), a half-wit Cuban, and
Trajano (trä·hä'nō), a superannuated anarchist, three pensioners at the home for poverty-stricken old men, Sister Gracia's first assignment.

Sister Manuela (mä·nwĕl'ä), Mother Superior of the old men's home.

Quica (kē'kä), a perennial and casual offender,
Candelas (kän·dä'läs), a fundamentally good, fiercely independent girl, and
Margarita (mär·gä·rē'tä), a bitter aristocrat, three inmates of the home for unwed mothers, Sister Gracia's second assignment.

Doctor Enrique (ĕn·rē'kä), a physician at the home for unwed mothers. He loves Sister Gracia and tries to persuade her to marry him.

Sister Cristina (krēs·tē'nä), Mother Superior at the home for unwed mothers.

Sister Dionisia (dyō·nē'sē·ä), an assistant at the orphanage, Sister Gracia's last assignment.

Juan de Dios (hwän dä dyōs), an aspiring bullfighter and former inmate of the orphanage. He returns to honor Sister Gracia with a souvenir of his first triumph in the ring.

Felipe (fä·lē'pä), a mutinous inmate of the orphanage, to whom Sister Gracia gives counsel and assurance.

Don Lorenzo (dōn lō·rĕn'thō) and
María Isabela (mä·rē'ä ē·sä·bĕl'ä), Sister Gracia's parents.

KINGS IN EXILE

Author: Alphonse Daudet (1840-1897)
Time of action: Nineteenth century
First published: 1879

Christian II (krēs·tyäṅ'), a rather foolish, vapid, and childish monarch who rules Illyria until he is deposed after a revolution and forced to flee to Paris with Frédérique, his Queen, and Léopold, his son. He spends his exile waiting for his restoration, frequenting Parisian theaters and cafés, and selecting and rejecting mistresses. A faction working for financial gain is at the point of securing his abdication when Frédérique, in a burst of hysterical melodramatics, dissuades him. At last he does abdicate, after an invasion of Illyria launched to restore him fails, in favor of his son, who becomes King Léopold V of Illyria and Dalmatia.

Frédérique (frā·dā·rēk'), Queen of Illyria, who actively runs the affairs of the kingdom during the period of exile. It is she who attends to financial problems, selects a tutor for the Prince, and prevents the King's irrational behavior from destroying the royal family. Her platonic affair with her son's tutor, Méraut, is dignified and poignant.

Élysée Méraut (ā·lē·zā' mā·rō'), the Prince's tutor and a man of good taste and discretion. The warm friendship with the Queen that Méraut enjoys is broken when an unfortunate accident occurs while the tutor and the Prince are target shooting. The Prince loses the sight of one eye and the Queen, holding Méraut responsible for the incident, discharges him. Later the Queen, learning Méraut is dying, visits him, with the Prince, in time to reconcile all their differences.

The Duke of Rosen, a former Illyrian minister who is deposed by Christian. The Duke welcomes the royal family when they arrive in Paris, uses his own funds to see that they want for nothing, and remains loyal to the monarch, even though the Duke's daughter-in-law becomes Christian's mistress.

Prince Léopold (lā·ô·pôl'), Christian's not particularly intelligent young son, who is Méraut's pupil.

Séphora Lévis (sā·fō·rä' lā·vē'), the wife of a commoner. Christian is enamored of her and she promises to become his mistress if he abdicates. She is never in love with Christian, but his abdication would be financially profitable to her and her husband.

Tom Lévis (lā·vē'), Séphora's husband, an impostor who has made a fortune catering to the whims of exiled aristocrats.

KING'S ROW

Author: Henry Bellamann (1882-1945)
Time of action: Late nineteenth century
First published: 1940

Parris Mitchell, an orphan who lives in King's Row with his German-born grandmother. He studies medicine in Vienna and becomes a staff physician in the King's Row insane asylum. Through Louise he discovers the tragedy caused in King's Row by Dr. Gordon's needless operations. During an absence in Europe he is accused of profiting from the sale of land to the hospital, but nothing comes of the charges. He broods over the many tragedies of his home town.

Drake McHugh, Parris' friend, another orphan, an idler obsessed with women.

After his guardian absconds with his money inherited from his aunt and uncle, Drake gets a railroad job through Randy's father. Following an accident, Dr. Gordon amputates Drake's legs. Randy marries Drake, Parris gives them the Tower property which he had inherited, and they start a real estate business in which Parris is a silent partner. Drake dies from illness which Parris attributes to the unnecessary amputation performed by Dr. Gordon.

Randy Monaghan, a railroad employee's daughter who marries Drake after he loses his legs. Following Drake's death she cares for her brother Tod.

Cassandra Tower (Cassie), Parris' friend who gives herself to him. She is shot to death by her father, who afterward kills himself.

Dr. Tower, Cassie's father, a strange physician who commits suicide after incest with Cassie and who wills his money and property to Parris.

Elise Sandor, a newcomer to King's Row, Parris' friend whose father buys Madame von Eln's home. Parris falls in love with her.

Jamie Wakefield, Parris' friend.

Renée, Parris' first love, who moves away from King's Row.

Madame von Eln, Parris' grandmother.

Dr. Perdorff, Parris' piano teacher.

Dr. Gordon, a physician who amputates Drake's legs; a medical butcher, obsessed with performing surgery.

Louise Gordon, his daughter, who reveals to Parris her father's butcheries.

Dr. Nolan, Parris' superior at the asylum.

Tod Monaghan, Randy's mentally incompetent brother.

KIPPS

Author: H. G. Wells (1866-1946)
Time of action: Early twentieth century
First published: 1905

PRINCIPAL CHARACTERS

Arthur Kipps, a simple soul. He knows that there was something mysterious about his birth. Reared by an aunt and uncle, he spends a bleak childhood. After seven years of apprenticeship to a draper, he is given a position in the firm at twenty pounds a year. As a boy, he falls in love with Ann Pornick, a poor girl who goes into domestic service; later he is enamored of a lady who teaches woodcarving in a class he attends for self-improvement. His life is radically changed when he is left a legacy of a handsome house and twelve hundred pounds a year by his paternal grandfather, who relented before his death, though he had forbidden his son to marry Kipps' mother. At once the bewildered Kipps is petitioned by everyone for money. He buys an interest in a friend's play and is maneuvered into becoming engaged to the woodcarving teacher, who tries to change him completely and gets him to give her brother control of his money. Kipps meets his childhood sweetheart again and begins to yearn for a simpler life. They marry, and his wife is at first made unhappy by their pretentions to grandeur. But his former fiancée's brother loses most of his money, and Kipps' now comfortable but necessarily simple life is thoroughly happy. Even after he becomes almost as rich as before, with the success of his friend's play, he continues to live simply and happily.

Ann Pornick, Kipps' first love and later his wife. Seeing her as a servant in a house where he is a guest, Kipps proposes, and in spite of her apprehension over the difference in their social positions, he is accepted.

Helen Walsingham, a lady of whom Kipps becomes enamored. Engaged to him after his acquisition of wealth, she attempts to change his speech, dress, manners, and attitudes. Grateful at first, he becomes gloomy. Her solicitor brother speculates with Kipps' money and loses most of it.

Mr. Chitterlow, Kipps' friend, a would-be playwright. Because of Chitterlow's influence, Kipps gets drunk and stays out all night, for which he loses his job; but shortly afterward Kipps gets his fortune. He buys a quarter interest in Chitterlow's play, which later restores his fortune almost to its original amount.

Pornick, Ann's brother. A socialist, he is both contemptuous and jealous of Kipps' new wealth, and so he does not tell Ann of Kipps' fortune. Therefore, when Ann first sees Kipps again, her naturalness and simplicity make him yearn for the old, uncomplicated life.

THE KNIGHT OF THE BURNING PESTLE

Author: Francis Beaumont (1585?-1616)
Time of action: Early seventeenth century
First presented: c. 1607

PRINCIPAL CHARACTERS

A Citizen (George), a London grocer. He brings his wife and servant to the theater and insists that the actors include in their play the exploits of some member of his profession. He frequently comments upon the progress of the action, reassures his wife, and suggests at intervals additional adventures for his hero.

Nell, his naïve wife, who is given to malapropisms. Deeply concerned for the welfare of the characters in the play, she alternately advises them, sympathizes with them, and discusses their difficulties with her devoted husband.

Ralph (Rafe), their servant, well-known for his histrionic talents. Encouraged by his mistress, he steps into the play within the play as George's grocer-hero, the Knight of the Burning Pestle. The Knight is, like Don Quixote, an avid reader of romances, and he resolves to win honor and the favor of his lady, Susan, "the cobbler's maid in Milk Street," by rescuing distressed damsels.

His heroic efforts to aid Mistress Merrythought and Humphrey are doomed to failure, but he wins, in his own view, a signal victory over the giant Barbaroso, the village barber.

Tim and
George, the Knight's witty apprentices. They accompany him on his adventures, acting as his squire and his dwarf, and take great delight in using the courtly phrases their master teaches them.

Venturewell, a strong-minded, quick-tempered London merchant. He is continually infuriated by his apprentice Jasper and his daughter, who thwart his plan to marry the girl to a foolish but wealthy tradesman. Cowardly at heart, he is gulled by Jasper, who appears to him as a ghost, and he agrees at last to allow the marriage of the young couple.

Luce, his daughter. She speaks to Jasper in the extravagant language of a romantic heroine, but she participates in his

581

schemes to deceive her father with a resourcefulness which marks her as the pert tradesman's daughter she is.

Jasper, her sweetheart, Venturewell's brash young apprentice. He, too, plays the romantic figure, especially when he threatens Luce with death in order to test her constancy. However, he readily dispenses with his heroics when he beats Ralph and, later, plays dead to trick his master.

Humphrey, Luce's well-meaning, rather unintelligent suitor, who inevitably finds himself at the wrong end of a cudgel, outwitted by Jasper. Even Venturewell, his staunch supporter, is turned against him in the end. He speaks in rhymed couplets which heighten the effect of his stupidity.

Merrythought, Jasper's impecunious father. He lives convinced that there will be food and drink on his table in time for his next meal and meets every experience, good or bad, with a song.

Mistress Merrythought, his shrewish wife. She refuses her blessing to Jasper and, to spite him, leaves home with her favored younger son and the money she has saved for the child. Her husband rejoices at her departure and forces her,

much to her chagrin, to sing to him before he will let her return.

Michael, her young son.

Tapster and
Host, attendants at the Bell Inn, where Ralph visits. They refuse to enter so fully into the spirit of chivalry that they will overlook the twelve shillings the Knight owes them, but they gleefully propose a quest for him, an attack on the giant, "ycleped Barbaroso."

Nick, the barber, who willingly participates in the Host's game with Ralph.

The First Knight and
The Second Knight (Sir Pockhole), the barber's patients, "prisoners" freed by Ralph and his squire.

Pompiona, the Princess of Moldavia, who appears in one of the scenes suggested by George the grocer. The Knight, loyal to his Susan, refuses her offer of her hand.

William Hammerton, a pewterer.

George Greengoose, a poulterer. He and Hammerton are members of a troop of soldiers whom Ralph leads through the city, following another of George the grocer's requests.

THE KNIGHTS

Author: Aristophanes (c. 448-385 B.C.)
Time of action: Fifth century B.C.
First presented: 424 B.C.

PRINCIPAL CHARACTERS

Demos (dē'mŏs), a personification of the Athenian people to whom all citizens owe obeisance. He is represented as a selfish, testy, sometimes foolish old man who seems to ignore the corruption in the officials and politicians who minister to him. The play opens with Cleon, his favorite (i.e., his "servant" or his "slave"), firmly entrenched in power, ostensibly by virtue of his whining, ob-

sequious, insolent, arrogant, and cunning qualities. Before the play is concluded, however, Demos displays his strength and craftiness (the strength and craftiness of the people themselves) in that he tolerates such knavish managers as Cleon because he can control them, because he can raise them up and dash them down at will. The farcical relations of Demos and those who govern him (Cleon, succeeded by the Sausage-Seller) generate the major dramatic action of the play.

Cleon (klē'ŏn), the Tanner, so-called because of his ownership of a leather-processing factory, or the Paphlagonian, a nickname given him to ridicule his mode of speaking ("paphlazo," to foam). He assumes that his political power over Demos is secure, and he is the terror of his fellow officials. A secret oracle, however, has predicted that he will lose his position and power to one even more base than himself. Accordingly, the Sausage-Seller challenges him. They engage in vigorous debate, eventually wrestle, and Cleon loses. Each displays, through the long harangue and dialogue, those mean qualities of self-interest which Aristophanes suggests are at the root of the political mind and which Aristophanes exposes by their degradation of public oratory, infected with vulgar jargon and low metaphor.

A Sausage-Seller, Agoracritus (ăg·ô·răk'-rĭ·tŭs), named for the area in which he plies his trade. He is favored by the Oracle to supersede Cleon because he is a villain and trickster whose abilities (loud shrieks) make him, in Aristophanes' ironic view, more suitable to hold public office. After a long struggle against Cleon, his overwhelming vulgarity is crowned with success when he is installed as the governor of Demos.

Nicias (nĭsh'ĭ·əs) and Demosthenes (dĭ·mŏs'thə·nēz), two able and successful Athenian generals of opposite characters. Nicias is cautious and superstitious, Demosthenes blunt, hearty, resolute, a lover of good wine, and a religious skeptic. They appear in the opening scenes of the play, having been mistreated by Cleon, who is at the height of his power. Because of their grievances against him, they set the machinery in motion to have him deposed when they consult the Oracle as to a successor.

The Chorus, the "knights" of the title. Representing the middle order of the State, they are hostile to Cleon. They consistently ridicule the Senate and government of Athens, jeer at Cleon, and applaud the Sausage-Seller. Their emotional envelopment and lack of perception, their endorsement of change in government for the sake of change alone, define Aristophanes' most pointed thrust at the weakness in these citizens, a weakness which promotes corruption and dishonor in the State.

THE KREUTZER SONATA

Author: Count Leo Tolstoy (1828-1910)
Time of action: Late nineteenth century
First published: 1889

PRINCIPAL CHARACTERS

Vasyla Pozdnishef (väs'lyä pŏz·dnĭ'shĕf), a phrenetic Russian landed proprietor who describes the horror of marriage and the murder of his wife. The only character in the novel developed to any extent, Pozdnishef relates his macabre story to a fellow traveler on the train, who in turn relates it to the reader. The hero-villain has been brought up to avoid all moral responsibility. As a wealthy young man he looked on women merely as the instruments of his sensual gratification. At thirty he married and settled down to what he supposed would be an ideal and pure relationship, but instead of bliss he found only misery or "swinish carnality." From sex satiation and boredom on their honeymoon, husband and wife move to quarreling in an increasingly violent manner, to threats of separation and attempts at suicide. A new lover for Madame Pozdnishef furnishes the final

583

straw. By this time Pozdnishef has come to view marriage as a sham, a married woman as functionless unless she is bearing children. Trukhashevsky, the wooer, plays the violin, and Madame Pozdnishef frequently accompanies him on the piano; their music infuriates Pozdnishef. One evening he becomes frantic while listening to the first movement of Beethoven's "Kreutzer Sonata"; on another occasion, finding them together, he stabs his wife with a curved Damascus dagger, while her cowardly lover flees in desperation. The entire novel is a psychological study of the effects of domestic misery, and certainly the effects are devastating. Pozdnishef himself remarks, "I'm supposed to be more or less insane." Shown in this morbid light, he is a consummate villain. But he is also a hero figure in that he is the vehicle for Tolstoy's views that the physical nature of man is vile and that the ills of the world stem from his failure to triumph over the desires of his body. For many pages Pozdnishef's conversation to his unidentified listener reads more like a formal disquisition on morality and ethics than a work of fiction. Pozdnishef remains a curious paradox. His message is straight from Tolstoy's heart, but his fanaticism and curious mannerisms estrange the reader from both him and his ideas. It is only as a tormented soul impelled to a dreadful act that Pozdnishef becomes tragically human.

Madame Pozdnishef, the beautiful daughter of an impoverished landowner.

Although the reader sees her merely as a puppet manipulated for Pozdnishef's narrative, it is obvious that for several years she was a faithful and dutiful wife who bore him five children. After their relationship becomes strained, she grows peevish and moody, given to wild accusations against her husband and occasional attempts on her own life. She is moderately talented at the piano, and through a common interest in music she becomes intimate with Trukhashevsky. After she is stabbed, she is haughty until the very end, swearing that her husband is but completing the murder begun years ago.

Trukhashevsky, (trōō·khä·shĕf′skĭy), a semi-professional violinist with some standing in society, the illicit lover of Madame Pozdnishef. Moist eyes, smiling red lips, a waxed mustache make him the type of man most women call handsome. He presents himself as a gallant and talented gentleman; however, his failure to defend Madame Pozdnishef against the fury of her husband depicts his true nature.

A Merchant,
A Lady,
A Lawyer, and
A Clerk, people on the train at the beginning of the novel who discuss marriage and the place of women in society. This conversation draws Pozdnishef into his narrative.

Ivan Zakharich (ĭ·vän′ zä·khä′rĭch), the doctor in attendance on Madame Pozdnishef.

KRISTIN LAVRANSDATTER

Author: Sigrid Undset (1882-1949)
Time of action: Fourteenth century
First published: "The Bridal Wreath," 1920; "The Mistress of Husaby," 1921; "The Cross," 1922

PRINCIPAL CHARACTERS

Lavrans Björgulfssön, the knightly landholder of a medieval manor named Jörundgaard, in Norway. A good and gentle man who strives to live his life

584

by strict Christian standards, he particularly loves Kristin, his oldest daughter, and allows her great freedom of speech and action.

Ragnfrid Ivarsdatter, Lavrans' wife, who had inherited Jörundgaard from her father. She is a good woman who does her best to be a loving wife and mother, although she suffers pangs of conscience all her life for loving another man before her marriage to Lavrans.

Kristin Lavransdatter, their beautiful but headstrong daughter, who is used to having her own way. When she falls in love with Erlend Nikulaussön she breaks her troth to Simon Andressön, a neighbor, much to her father's embarrassment. She has an affair with Erlend and later, during their betrothal, becomes pregnant. Though she begins married life under untoward circumstances, she becomes a good wife, looking after her husband's lands and other property as well as giving him many sons. She and her husband have a stormy married life, however, for the husband is as vehement and proud as his wife. Always in the background, too, is the fact that Kristin dishonored her father by her premarital behavior. Kristin works hard to provide an inheritance for her sons, especially after her husband loses his lands through treason to the crown and his family takes refuge on the manor at Jörundgaard, inherited by Kristin. After her husband's death, when her sons are old enough to fend for themselves, Kristin enters a convent. She dies there a few years later, during an epidemic of the Black Plague in 1349.

Erlend Nikulaussön, a young nobleman who falls in love with Kristin and woos her away from her betrothed. He is a handsome, violent, and contumacious man, always in some sort of scrape because he acts without thinking of the consequences. His greatest mistake is seeking to separate Norway from Sweden in the days of King Magnus VII.

Charged with treason, he is found guilty and loses his lands and almost his life. Retirement to his wife's manor is galling, and so he separates from his wife to lead a lonely life on a small farm once owned by a relative, Lady Aashild. He returns to vindicate Kristin's honor when she is accused of adultery but is killed in a brawl upon his arrival.

Nikulaus Erlendssön (Naakve), the eldest son of Kristin and Erlend, a handsome, quiet person. Affected by the bickering and antagonism between his parents, he becomes a monk when he reaches manhood.

Björgulf Erlendssön, Kristin and Erlend's second son. He is an unfortunate child who early begins to become blind. He enters a monastery with Nikulaus, his older brother, who cares for him tenderly. Björgulf and Nikulaus also die of the Black Plague.

Gaute Erlendssön, the third son of Kristin and Erlend, a lover of the land and farming. He is the son who takes over Kristin's manor of Jörundgaard when he grows up.

Skule and
Ivar Erlendssön, the twin sons of Kristin and Erlend, adventurous boys who grow up to take service under distant kinsmen and seek their careers far from their native land. Ivar finally settles down and marries Signe Gamalsdatter, a rich young widow.

Lavrans Erlendssön, the sixth son of Kristin and Erlend. He migrates to Iceland in the service of a bishop when he grows up.

Munan Erlendssön, the seventh son of Kristin and Erlend, who dies during an epidemic while still a boy.

Erlend Erlendssön, the eighth son of Kristin and Erlend, conceived during a secret visit made by Kristin to see her husband after he had left Jörundgaard. The birth of this child, who lives but three months, causes Kristin to be wrongly accused of adultery.

Simon Andressön of Dyfrin, the young nobleman jilted by Kristin Lavransdatter when she falls in love with Erlend Nikulaussön. Simon continues to love Kristin and works on her behalf many times, even saving the life of Erlend when the latter is sentenced to die for treason. He marries Kristin's younger sister, Ramborg.

Sigrid, Simon Andressön's sister.

Arngjerd, the illegitimate daughter of Simon Andressön.

Simon Simonssön, the son of Ramborg and Simon Andressön, born after his father dies of a wound suffered while separating some brawlers.

Ramborg, the sister of Kristin. She falls in love with Simon Andressön after he has been jilted by Kristin, and marries him. She is always hostile to Kristin and jealous of her.

Ulvhild, another sister of Kristin. She is crippled by a falling timber at the age of three and dies while still a young girl.

Lady Aashild, Erlend Nikulaussön's aunt and the mistress of Hangen, supposedly a witch-wife. She befriends Erlend and Kristin at the time of their marriage.

Sir Björn, Lady Aashild's husband, a strange, secretive man.

Arne Gyrdssön, a childhood playmate of Kristin who falls in love with her as he grows up. He and Kristin are falsely accused of loose sexual conduct when they are in their teens.

Bentein, a licentious young man who tries to rape Kristin and, not succeeding, spreads the false tale that she and Arne Gyrdssön have been lovers.

Sira Eirik, Bentein's grandfather, a priest.

Eline Ormsdatter, a married woman who takes Erlend Nikulaussön as her lover before he meets Kristin. Eline and Erlend have two illegitimate children. The woman, jealous of Kristin, tries to make a leper of the girl. She fails and then stabs herself to death.

Ulf Haldorssön, Erlend Nikulaussön's loyal henchman for thirty-five years and a distant kinsman. Wrongly accused of fathering Kristin's eighth son, he kills a man in defense of her good name.

Jardtrud, Ulf's wife, a hate-filled and jealous woman who wrongly accuses her husband of being Kristin's lover.

Ingebjörg Filippusdatter, Kristin's friend and bed-partner during the time she spends in a convent in Oslo.

THE LADY FROM THE SEA

Author: Henrik Ibsen (1828-1906)
Time of action: Nineteenth century
First presented: 1889

PRINCIPAL CHARACTERS

Ellida Wangel, a woman dominated by the sea. She feels stifled in her new home when she marries and goes away from the sea to live in the mountains. She feels strangely drawn to a sailor who had known and loved her years before. When he appears again she feels his hold over her, as she feels the conflicting hold her husband has, too. Left to her own choice, she stays with her husband. She feels that she has retained her sanity by being able to make a choice for herself.

Dr. Wangel, Elida's husband, a physician. He tries to understand the strains on his wife's mind and gives her a verbal release from her vows so that she can decide for herself whether to go with her former suitor or remain with her husband.

Boletta and
Hilda Wangel, Dr. Wangel's daughters by his first wife. They find their stepmother a difficult person to make friends with.

Arnholm, Boletta's former tutor and another early sweetheart of Ellida. She refused in the past to marry Arnholm because, she said, she was already betrothed.

The Stranger, a sailor who has a powerful psychological hold over Ellida because he makes her think she has been betrothed to him in a strange ceremony by the sea. He has murdered a man and is a fugitive from justice. Ellida finally decides to stay with her husband and breaks the hold the stranger has over her mind.

Lyngstrand, a traveling sculptor who stops at the Wangel's house. His story of a sailor and his wife reawakens in Ellida's mind memory of the sailor who had betrothed himself to her years before.

LADY INTO FOX

Author: David Garnett (1892-   )
Time of action: 1880
First published: 1923

PRINCIPAL CHARACTERS

Mr. Richard Tebrick, a young Englishman who finds he has married a vixen. His worry over her and her cubs and his jealousy of her mate make him seem a madman not only to his neighbors but even occasionally to himself. When he and his wife are attacked by dogs who kill her, Mr. Tebrick does lose his reason. He recovers, however, and lives many years.

Silvia Fox Tebrick, his wife, a beautiful country girl with hazel eyes, reddish-brown hair, and brownish, freckled skin, who, in her twenty-third year, turns into a small, bright-red fox. Though she can no longer speak, she communicates by looks and signs, and she understands her husband as she did before. At first retaining in part her womanly nature, she gradually becomes more foxlike in eating and in other habits. When released, she disappears, mates with a dog-fox, and later lets her cubs play with their godfather, Mr. Tebrick.

Nanny Cork, Silvia's old nurse who becomes the Tebricks' housekeeper. She accepts Silvia's transformation as if it were nothing unusual and continues her interest in Silvia's welfare.

Askew, a jockey hired by Mr. Tebrick to follow the fox hunts and report on the animals killed.

Sorel,
Kaspar,
Selwyn,
Esther, and
Angelica, Silvia's cubs. Angelica, who greatly resembles her mother, is Mr. Tebrick's favorite.

The Reverend Canon Fox, Silvia's uncle, a clergyman who visits Mr. Tebrick and thinks him insane.

James, the Tebrick gardener or groom.

Polly, Mrs. Cork's grandaughter, who enjoys playing with Mrs. Tebrick until the vixen leaves to seek a mate.

Simon, Mrs. Cork's son.

THE LADY OF THE LAKE

Author: Sir Walter Scott (1771-1832)
Time of action: Sixteenth century
First published: 1810

PRINCIPAL CHARACTERS

Ellen Douglas, who, with her rebel father, hides from the King near Loch Katrine in the Highlands. Befriended by James Fitz-James, a powerful nobleman, she is instrumental in bringing the rebel clans and the King's forces together. In the end, her marriage to Malcolm Graeme is blessed by the monarch.

James of Douglas, Ellen's father, who once was a powerful nobleman but who now is in rebellion against the King. Finally, because he can no longer agree with one of his powerful leaders, he gives himself up to the royal court. He finally is restored to favor.

Roderick Dhu, a rebel Highland chief who befriends Ellen and her father, but whose ruthless military tactics Ellen abhors. Dhu, in the guise of a guard, fights a duel with James Fitz-James and is overcome. The rebel and loyal forces do not fight, but Dhu, in prison, dies

thinking his clans fought a glorious battle.

James Fitz-James, a nobleman, friendly to Ellen, who at the poem's end is discovered to be the King.

Allan-Bane, a minstrel in the service of James of Douglas who is faithful to that nobleman even while he hides with his forces in the Highlands. The minstrel is also a prophet and seer of sorts, and he knows everything between the clans and the King will end well. It is Allan-Bane who, as a kindly gesture, gives the dying Roderick Dhu the impression that the clans fought bravely against the King.

Malcolm Graeme, a young rebel nobleman who was once the object of an attack by Dhu's forces after Ellen had refused Dhu's suit because she and Malcolm were in love. Finally, with the King's blessing, he marries Ellen.

LADY WINDERMERE'S FAN

Author: Oscar Wilde (1856-1900)
Time of action: Nineteenth century
First presented: 1892

PRINCIPAL CHARACTERS

Lady Margaret Windermere, a proper woman. Discovering that her husband is giving money to a Mrs. Erlynne, she doubts his assertions that the relationship is honorable. Angry that he insists on inviting Mrs. Erlynne to their ball, Lady Windermere threatens to strike Mrs. Erlynne with her fan if she appears, but Lady Windermere loses her nerve and drops the fan instead. Put in a reckless mood, Lady Windermere accepts the attentions of a man about town

and agrees to run off with him. Mrs. Erlynne intercepts Lady Windermere's letter to her husband and follows her. At the expense of her own reputation, Mrs. Erlynne saves that of Lady Windermere. From that time on, Lady Windermere defends Mrs. Erlynne and calls her a good woman, though she does not understand Mrs. Erlynne's motives.

Mrs. Erlynne, who years ago left her husband and daughter to run away with another man. Her daughter is Lady Windermere, whom she saves from similar ignominy. She does not reveal the relationship to Lady Windermere, not wishing to destroy her illusions.

Lord Windermere, the husband of Lady Windermere. He is helping Mrs. Erlynne, whom he admires, to regain the approval of society, and hence he insists that she be invited to the ball. After she takes the blame when Lady Windermere's fan is found in Lord Darlington's rooms, he is furious and thinks she has betrayed his confidence.

The Duchess of Berwick, who informs Lady Windermere of a rumored affair between Mrs. Erlynne and Lord Windermere.

Lord Augustus Lorton, the disreputable brother of the Duchess of Berwick. He breaks his engagement with Mrs. Erlynne when she takes Lady Windermere's blame. But later he accepts her explanation that his own interests took her to Lord Darlington's rooms, and the engagement is renewed.

Lord Darlington, a man about town. He persuades Lady Windermere to run away with him. Mrs. Erlynne pursues Lady Windermere to his rooms and, reminding her of her duty to her child, persuades her to go back to her husband.

THE LADY'S NOT FOR BURNING

Author: Christopher Fry (1907-)
Time of action: c. 1400
First presented: 1948

PRINCIPAL CHARACTERS

Thomas Mendip, a discharged soldier who wants to be hanged. He is part egoist and part misanthrope. In order to be hanged he claims to have killed old Skipps. After being tortured to make him stop confessing he falls in love with Jennet Jourdemayne, and his love for her makes him decide to escape from jail and go on living.

Jennet Jourdemayne, a beautiful girl accused of being a witch so that her property can be confiscated by the town. She is accused of turning old Skipps into a dog. When her supposed victim turns up, she is allowed to escape with Thomas, leaving her property confiscate. She learns that love and fancy have a place in life.

Old Skipps, an old rag and bone man, supposedly turned into a dog by Jennet Jourdemayne. Thomas claims to have killed him, too. He turns up hale and hearty.

Hebble Tyson, the mayor of Cool Clary.

He wants to confiscate Jennet's property and is bothered by Thomas' attempts to be hanged. His problem is solved when Jennet and Thomas fall in love and escape from jail.

Richard, an orphan and the mayor's clerk. He loves Alizon Eliot and is married to her.

Alizon Eliot, a handsome young girl betrothed to Humphrey Devize. She loves Richard and on the night of her betrothal party elopes with him.

Humphrey Devize, the mayor's nephew. He decides he does not really want to marry Alizon, though he and his brothers had fought over her. He tries to seduce Janet by offering to help her escape. She refuses him.

Nicholas Devize, Humphrey's brother. He thinks for a while that the stars have decreed he shall marry Alizon. When his brother decides he does not

589

want to marry the girl, Nicholas does not want to marry her either.

Margaret Devize, the sister of the mayor. She is Humphrey and Nicholas' mother.

L'AIGLON

Author: Edmond Rostand (1868-1918)
Time of action: 1830-1832
First presented: 1900

PRINCIPAL CHARACTERS

Franz, Duke of Reichstadt, called **L'Aiglon,** Napoleon's son, a weak and idealistic youth. He dreams of returning to France as emperor, but he is in delicate health. He plans an escape from his ever-present guards, but his plot is discovered, and he is stopped while trying to get away. He realizes that he is not strong enough or brave enough to make the sacrifices necessary to become another Napoleon. Death from pulmonary tuberculosis soon overcomes him.

Prince Metternich, the Austrian statesman who is Franz's official jailer. He makes it his business to keep Franz closely guarded at all times and discovers his plan to escape. He provides tutors for Franz who never speak Napoleon's name in any of their lessons. He taunts Franz by pointing out to him how unlike his father he is.

Seraphin Flambeau (sā·rá·făn' flän·bō'), an old soldier in Napoleon's army. He encourages Franz in his dreams of returning to France and helps him in his plan to escape. When the plan is discovered, he kills himself rather than face a firing squad.

Marie-Louise (mà·rē'-lwēz'), the mother of Franz and daughter of the Austrian Emperor. She does not greatly regret her husband's death and would be very happy in the Austrian court if Franz were not so grief-stricken.

Countess Camerata, Franz's cousin, who appears in Austria as a fitter from Paris. She is an accomplice in the plot for Franz's escape. She wears a uniform exactly like his to a fancy dress ball and, when she and Franz exchange cloaks, the guards follow her instead of him, temporarily allowing him to escape.

The Archduchess, Franz's aunt, who makes Franz promise that he will ask the Emperor to allow him to go back to France before he makes any plans with his friends.

The Emperor Franz, Franz's grandfather, who, when Franz appears in a disguise at court and asks permission to go to France, grants it to him without realizing who Franz is.

Thérèse de Lorget (tā·rĕz' də lôr·zhā'), Franz's beloved and a French exile.

Fanny Elssler, a dancer who helps in Franz's escape plot.

Count Sedlinsky, who is in charge of the police guard that spies on Franz.

LALLA ROOKH

Author: Thomas Moore (1779-1852)
Time of action: c. 1700
First published: 1817

Lalla Rookh (Tulip Cheek), Emperor Aurungzebe's daughter. Promised to King Aliris, she sets forth by caravan for Cashmere, where she is to meet and marry her betrothed. Among the servants in the bridal entourage is the poet Feramorz, with whom Lalla Rookh falls in love. Wishing to present her heart undefiled to her bridegroom, she banishes the poet from her presence, only to learn to her joy on her arrival in Cashmere that Feramorz is Aliris disguised for the purpose of winning her love.

Aliris, the young King of Bucharia. To win the love of his betrothed, Lalla Rookh, he disguises himself as the poet Feramorz and accompanies the bridal caravan to Cashmere. With his beauty and the charms of his music and poetry, Feramorz wins the love of the bride-to-be. When the caravan arrives in Cash-mere, he reveals himself as King Aliris, disguised.

Fadladeen, the chamberlain of the harem and a bumptious know-all. As protector of Lalla Rookh in the bridal caravan, he delivers himself of opinions on all subjects and persons, and especially on the poet Feramorz, whose beautiful love poems he attacks with a particular vehemence as he analyzes them from every possible angle. When he finally learns Feramorz' true identity as King Aliris, he recants and proclaims the King the greatest poet of all time.

Aurungzebe, the Emperor of Delhi and Lalla Rookh's father.

Abdalla, the recently abdicated King of Lesser Bucharia and the father of young King Aliris.

L'AMOROSA FIAMMETTA

Author: Giovanni Boccaccio (1313-1375)
Time of action: Fourteenth century
First transcribed: 1340-1345

Fiammetta, a passionate, intelligent, and sensitive lady of Naples. In reality Maria d'Aquino, reported to be the daughter of King Robert of Anjou, she is pictured by Boccaccio telling the story of her betrayal as a warning to others of the tribulations of love. Married and universally admired, she catches the eye of Panfilo (Boccaccio), and, overcome by love, she is obsessed by his image and finally admits him to her bedroom. Completely absorbed in her lover, she imagines that no other gentlewoman has known the true meaning of passion. Finally betrayed by him, she is sure that no other has been so unfortunate.

Panfilo, a poet, in reality Boccaccio, who is writing the story of his pursuit of Maria d'Aquino to show that it was not she who left him, but, indeed, he who deserted her. At a church festival, Panfilo catches the eye of Fiammetta and, later, at a series of meetings in society, instructs her in the subtle art of revealing love to one while conversing with many. He finally gains access to her bedroom. After they have spent many passionate nights together, he wearies of Fiammetta. To extricate himself, he tells her that he must make a four-month journey to visit his dying father. Despite her protests and entreaties, he leaves her forever.

THE LAST ATHENIAN

Author: Viktor Rydberg (1829-1895)
Time of action: Fourth century
First published: 1859

PRINCIPAL CHARACTERS

Chrysanteus (krĭ·săn'tĭ·əs), an archon of Athens and its richest citizen. A pagan, he believes in Plato's philosophy of moderation and reason, as opposed to the Christian philosophy. He is forced to flee to the mountains and there is killed by the forces of Domitius.

Hermione (hėr·mī'ō·nē), Chrysanteus' daughter and also a believer in the pagan philosophy. She is captured by Domitius' forces and is forcibly baptized a Christian. Rather than live under these conditions, she kills herself.

Peter (pē'tėr), Bishop of Athens. He is a sworn enemy of Chrysanteus and also of the Athanasian Christians. He connives to obtain Chrysanteus' wealth in order to buy the bishopric of Rome. He is poisoned by his fellow priests on orders of the Athanasians.

Charmides (kär'mĭ·dēz), Hermione's betrothed. He is used by Bishop Peter in his fight against paganism and Chrysanteus. He is killed by a young Jew who discovers that Charmides has seduced his betrothed, the daughter of a Jew to whom Charmides owed a large amount of money.

Clemens (klē'mĕns), Chrysanteus' long-lost son, who was reared as a Christian. He is returned to his father's pagan household but is so fanatic a Christian that he leaves and becomes a hermit, living in a cave outside Athens.

Annaeus Domitius (ă·nē'əs dō·mĭ'shĭ·əs), the Roman proconsul in Athens, who tries to keep to a middle of the road policy and not sympathize with any of the religious factions in the city.

THE LAST CHRONICLE OF BARSET

Author: Anthony Trollope (1815-1882)
Time of action: Mid-nineteenth century
First published: 1867

PRINCIPAL CHARACTERS

The Rev. Josiah Crawley, "perpetual curate of Hogglestock," a poor parish. He is frequently unable to pay his bills from his meager living and Dean Arabin often gives him money he is shy about taking. On one occasion he pays a butcher's bill with a stolen check and is brought before a magistrate's court. The court decides on a full trial, for Crawley's explanation is vague and contradictory. In addition, Mrs. Proudie attempts to have him removed from his living. Finally, John Eames reaches Mrs. Arabin,

traveling in Europe, who completely exonerates Crawley and explains the stolen check. Crawley later receives the more profitable living of St. Ewold's.

Grace Crawley, his daughter, in love with Major Henry Grantly. When Mr. Crawley is accused, Henry Grantly feels he must stick by Grace and, despite the fierce objection of his father, he proposes to her. Grace nobly refuses, but, after her father is cleared, she marries Henry.

Mrs. Mary Crawley, the self-sacrificing

592

wife of Mr. Crawley who copes extremely well with his intransigence and eccentricity.

Bishop Thomas Proudie, Bishop of Barchester, a weak man who is harassed by his wife until he agrees to bring Mr. Crawley before a clerical commission.

Mrs. Proudie, wife of the Bishop, who believes it her mission to uphold the honor of the Church. She persecutes Crawley and shames her husband by insisting on attending all his conferences. She dies of a heart attack.

Major Henry Grantly, a retired officer and a widower with a small daughter. When his father opposes his plans to marry Grace Crawley, he is ready to sell his lodge and move to France.

Archdeacon Theophilus Grantly, Archdeacon and wealthy ecclesiastical power in Barchester. He opposes his son's marriage to Grace Crawley.

Susan Grantly, his wife, who tries to keep peace between her husband and son.

Francis Arabin, Dean of Barchester Cathedral, who has always befriended the Crawleys.

Eleanor Arabin, his wife, whose generosity in stuffing an additional twenty pounds into the envelope for Mr. Crawley inadvertently precipitates the events of the novel. When she hears of the trouble, she immediately returns to give evidence.

Lilian Dale (Lily), a friend of Grace Crawley previously jilted by Adolphus Crosbie. Although Crosbie's wife, Lady Alexandrina has died, Lily still refuses to allow Crosbie to court her again.

John Eames, now private secretary to Sir Raffle Buffle and the cousin of Grace Crawley. At his own expense, he goes to Italy to find Mrs. Arabin. Although in love with Lily, he barely extricates himself from the clutches of Madalina Demolines.

Bernard Dale, the heir of the Squire of Allington, Lily's cousin, who becomes engaged to Emily Dunstable.

Emily Dunstable, cousin of Mrs. Martha Dunstable Thorne, a wealthy heiress.

Mrs. Martha Dunstable Thorne, a jolly social woman who tries to give Henry Grantly the courage to remain loyal to Grace.

Dr. Thomas Thorne, her husband, who sides with the Crawleys.

Christopher Dale, the Squire of Allington, who is extremely fond of Grace Crawley.

Mrs. Mary Dale, Lily's mother, who invites Grace to stay at Allington after the magistrate's hearing.

Lady Julia de Guest, the constant benefactress of John Eames.

Lady Lufton, an aristocrat who constantly opposes Mrs. Proudie and befriends the Crawleys.

Lord Ludovic Lufton, a friend of the Crawleys whose check was originally stolen.

Lady Lucy Robarts Lufton, his wife, a friend of the Crawleys.

Mr. Soames, Lord Lufton's business agent who thought he had dropped the check at Hogglestock parsonage.

Adolphus Crosbie, now a widower, in debt to Gagebee, who would like to marry Lily Dale.

Lady Dumbello, the Marchioness of Hartletop, Griselda Grantly, daughter of the Archdeacon, who sides with her father in objecting to Henry's marriage to Grace.

The Rev. Septimus Harding, the aged father of Eleanor Arabin, with whom he

593

lives, and Susan Grantly. A warm old man, he requests, on his deathbed, that Crawley be given the living at St. Ewold's.

Edith Grantly, daughter of Major Henry Grantly.

Mr. Thomas Toogood, the lawyer who defends Mr. Crawley.

The Rev. Caleb Trumble, the clergyman Mrs. Proudie sends to take over Mr. Crawley's parish.

The Rev. Dr. Mortimer Tempest, a rural dean and vicar of Silverbridge. He leads the clerical commission investigating the case and thinks that Crawley should be judged by the court before the Church decides about his living.

Miss Madalina Demolines, a young London lady who plots to marry John Eames and writes an anonymous note to Lily Dale.

Lady Demolines, willingly a partner in her daughter's schemes.

Sir Raffle Buffle, the pompous chairman of the Income Tax Office.

Mr. Fletcher, the butcher who received the stolen check.

Mr. Quiverful, a member of the clerical commission and warden of Hiram's Hospital. Mrs. Proudie appoints him to the commission.

The Rev. Caleb Oriel, rector of Greshamsbury and a member of the clerical commission at Mrs. Proudie's suggestion.

The Rev. Mark Robarts, vicar of Framley, a member of the clerical commission.

Mr. Kissing, a silly secretary in the Income Tax Office.

Mr. Peter Bangles, a wine merchant who finally marries Madalina Demolines.

THE LAST DAYS OF POMPEII

Author: Edward George Earle Bulwer-Lytton (1803-1878)
Time of action: A.D. 79
First published: 1834

PRINCIPAL CHARACTERS

Glaucus (glô'kəs), a handsome and popular Greek. He is saved from death in the arena by the eruption of Vesuvius; he is saved from death after the eruption by the blind flower girl Nydia.

Clodius (klō'dǐ·əs), a foppish Roman of Pompeii and a friend of Glaucus.

Nydia (nǐ'dǐ·ə), a blind flower girl from Greece who is hopelessly in love with Glaucus. Through her ability to move in the darkness, she is able to guide Glaucus and Ione to safety aboard a small ship. Then she drowns herself.

Burbo (bûr'bō), a wine seller and the owner of Nydia.

Arbaces (är'bə·sēz), priest of Isis, who

prays for the return of Egypt's power. Meanwhile he tries to turn his ward Apaecides into a priest and to marry the boy's sister, Ione. He stabs Apaecides and puts the blame on Glaucus, who is then condemned to the arena.

Apaecides (ə·pē'sǐ·dēz), the ward of Arbaces, converted to Christianity by an earthquake.

Ione (ī·ō'nē), a lovely Neapolitan girl, seen and loved by Glaucus.

Diomed (dī'ō·měd), a wealthy freedman.

Julia (jōōl'yə), his daughter, in love with Glaucus.

A Priest, a witness to the innocence of Glaucus but held prisoner by Arbaces.

594

Sallust (să'ləst), a friend of Glaucus, but too drunk to answer Nydia's letter for help. Finally his appeal to the praetor at the arena causes the crowd to demand that Arbaces be thrown to the lion; but before this can take place the fatal earthquake begins.

THE LAST OF SUMMER

Author: Kate O'Brien (1897-1954)
Time of action: 1939
First published: 1943

PRINCIPAL CHARACTERS

Hannah Kernahans, a strong-willed Irishwoman who seeks to order the world to suit herself. She binds her eldest son to her and, refusing to let him go, uses whatever means she must to hold him. As a young woman she had been jilted by a suitor who discovered her iron will. She married the suitor's brother but always claimed that it was she who changed her mind.

Tom Kernahans, Hannah's son who is tied to her. He believes she is always right, always unselfish, and always serving his best interests. He fails to realize, when he breaks off with the girl he loves, that he is doing what his mother planned for him to do for her own selfish interests. Nor does he realize that his mother will not let him marry anyone else. Tom is weak, rather than stupid.

Angèle Maury, Hannah's niece, in love with Tom. She is the daughter of the man who jilted Hannah, and the woman fiercely resents the girl. Angèle is torn between her love for Tom, which keeps her in Ireland, and her love for her mother's country, France, a love which urges her to return to France, threatened by war with Nazi Germany. Tom makes the decision for her and she returns to France. Angèle is an actress by profession.

Martin Kernahans, Tom's brother, a self-reliant, widely traveled student. He is also in love with Angèle, who goes to France with him after Tom, thinking Angèle loves his brother, has released her from their engagement. Martin goes to France because he feels a duty to help protect Europe from the Nazis.

Norrie O'Byrne, a girl who loves Tom deeply. She is used by Tom's mother as bait in getting Tom to break his engagement with Angèle.

THE LAST OF THE BARONS

Author: Edward George Earle Bulwer-Lytton (1803-1873)
Time of action: 1467-1471
First published: 1843

PRINCIPAL CHARACTERS

Marmaduke Nevile, a noble whose father fought for Lancaster. He comes to London to seek service with Warwick.

Nicholas Alwyn, a younger son of a good family, who fights to restore King Edward. He captures Nevile in battle.

Lord Montagu, Warwick's brother, who, as a Yorkist, refuses help to Nevile.

The Earl of Warwick, the King Maker, who takes Nevile into his household. Insulted by Edward IV, he puts Henry VI on the throne. He is killed at the battle of Barnet.

Isabella, Warwick's haughty older daughter.

Anne, his gentle younger daughter. When lecherous King Edward comes to her bedroom, Warner and Nevile save her.

Edward IV, King of England, deposed by the insulted Warwick.

Henry VI, put on the throne by Warwick but removed by a coalition of the rich merchants and the Yorkists.

William de Hastings, a royal Chamber-

lain to Edward IV and in love with Sibyll.

Adam Warner, an alchemist who is working on a model of a steam engine. He and Sibyll are killed during the Wars of the Roses.

Sibyll Warner, his daughter, rescued by Nevile from a crowd. Later, when he is wounded by robbers, she cures him.

The Duchess of Bedford, a patroness of science and of Warner.

Katherine de Bonville, Warwick's sister, who secretly marries Hastings after her husband's death.

THE LAST OF THE MOHICANS

Author: James Fenimore Cooper (1789-1851)
Time of action: 1757
First published: 1826

PRINCIPAL CHARACTERS

Natty Bumppo, called **Hawkeye,** the hardy, noble frontier scout in his prime during the French and Indian Wars. Traveling with his Indian companions, Chingachgook and his son Uncas, in Upper New York, he befriends an English soldier, a Connecticut singing master, and their two female charges. When the travelers are ambushed by hostile Huron warriors, he leaves the party to get help, in turn ambushes their captors with the aid of Chingachgook and Uncas, and leads the group to Fort William Henry, besieged by the French. In the massacre of English that takes place after the garrison is forced to surrender, the girls are captured again by Indians. Hawkeye assists once more in the escape of one of the girls; however, a renegade Huron chief, Magua, claims the other as his reluctant wife. In the ensuing fighting the girl and Hawkeye's friend, the noble young Uncas, are killed. Hawkeye shoots Magua in return. In the end he and Chingachgook return sorrowfully to the wilderness.

Chingachgook (chĭn·gäch'gŏok), a courageous, loyal Mohican Chief, Hawkeye's inseparable friend. An implacable enemy of the Hurons, he is decorated like a figure of Death. Left to protect the English Colonel after the massacre, he joins the final battle with intense ferocity, only to see his son die. His grief is relieved somewhat by Hawkeye's companionship.

Uncas (ŭn'kəs), Chingachgook's stalwart son, the last of the Mohicans. A young and handsome chieftain, he falls in love with Cora Munro while protecting her and proves invaluable in tracking her after she has been captured. When a Delaware chief awards her to Uncas' rival, Magua, he follows them and is killed avenging her murder.

Major Duncan Heyward, the young English officer in charge of escorting the Munro girls from Fort Edward to Fort William Henry. Brave, good-looking and clever, he falls in love with Alice Munro and eventually succeeds in rescuing her from the Hurons. He finally marries her with Colonel Munro's blessing.

Magua (mă′gū·ə), "Le Renard Subtil," the handsome, renegade Huron chief. Both cunning and malicious, he seeks to avenge himself on Colonel Munro by turning his spirited daughter Cora into a servile squaw. Twice thwarted by Hawkeye and his companions, he wins Cora by putting his case before Tamenund, a Delaware chieftain. This victory, however, is short-lived. Cora is killed by another Huron and Magua, after killing Uncas, is shot by Hawkeye.

Cora Munro, the Colonel's beautiful older daughter. She is independent, equal to every situation, and bears up well under the strain of a capture, a massacre, and the threat of marrying Magua. Her love for Uncas, however, remains unrequited when she is carried off by Magua and then stabbed.

Alice Munro, the Colonel's younger daughter, a pale, immature, but lovely half sister of Cora. Frail and clinging, she excites Heyward's protective feelings during their adventures, and he marries her.

Colonel Munro, the able but unsuccessful defender of Fort William Henry and the affectionate father of Cora and Alice.

After surrendering to the French he is forced to watch helplessly the slaughter of the men, women, and children from the fort. His sorrow is doubled when Cora is killed.

David Gamut, a mild, ungainly singing master who accompanies Heyward and the Munro girls. His schoolbook piety contrasts with Hawkeye's natural pantheism. A rather ineffective person, he is nevertheless useful to Hawkeye, for the Hurons believe him insane and let him pass without trouble.

The Marquis de Montcalm, the skilled, enterprising general who captures Fort William Henry and then allows the defeated English to be massacred by savage Hurons.

Tamenund (tă·mə·nŭnd′), the old Delaware chief who foolishly decides to give Cora to Magua.

Hard Heart, the Delaware chief whom Magua flatters to gain Cora.

General Webb, the incompetent commander of Fort Edward. He refused to aid Colonel Munro against the French.

A Huron Chief. He calls on Heyward, who is impersonating a witch doctor, to cure a relative, and he is duped when his captives are released.

THE LAST OF THE VIKINGS

Author: Johan Bojer (1872-1959)
Time of action: Early nineteenth century
First published: 1921

PRINCIPAL CHARACTERS

Khristàver Myran, a Lofoten fisherman, owner of the "Seal." He goes into debt to buy his boat, but brings her through a difficult fishing season with success. His career makes him feel a veritable son of the Vikings of old.

Lars, Kristàver's son. He dreams of being a Viking. On his first trip to the fishing grounds he proves himself a man at work and play.

Elezeus Hylla, a crew member of the

"Seal," brother-in-law to Kristàver. He dies of exposure on the fishing expedition.

Kaneles Gomon, a boyish member of the crew of the "Seal." He is vain of his yellow mustache. When the vessel overturns he is the only man lost.

Arnt Awson, a landlubber who makes his first trip to sea as a fisherman on the "Seal."

Henry Rabben, a crewman aboard the "Seal," very vain of his beard.

Peter Suzansa, owner and captain of the "Sea-fire."

Andreas Ekra, owner and captain of the "Storm-bird."

Jacob Damnit-all-with-a-limp, owner and captain of the "Sea-bird." He rescues the crew of the "Seal" when their vessel overturns.

The Inspector, a government official who enforces the fishing regulations at the fishing grounds.

THE LAST PURITAN

Author: George Santayana (1863-1952)
Time of action: Early twentieth century
First published: 1936

PRINCIPAL CHARACTERS

Oliver Alden, a young man who despises human weakness. He is a puritan in spite of himself. He is not prudish or a prig; he simply and truly believes that one must do one's duty, whether it is pleasant or unpleasant. He does not really believe in love because it is illogical and unreasonable at times, and for this reason he is rejected by the two women to whom he proposes out of a sense of duty. At the end of his life, he provides in his will for all of the people to whom he feels responsible, but he leaves the largest sum to his mother because he feels it is his duty to do so.

Peter Alden, Oliver's father, who spends most of his life wandering about the world. He marries the daughter of a psychiatrist because the psychiatrist tells him that what he needs to cure his mostly imaginary ills are a home and a wife. He commits suicide in order to free Oliver of, at least, a sense of duty toward him.

Harriet Alden, Oliver's mother. She does not allow Oliver to play with other children because they might be vulgar or dirty, and she allows Oliver no exposure to the frivolities of life.

Fraulein Irma Schlote, Oliver's governess, who gives Oliver a love of nature and a love of the German language, and brings a little light into his childhood.

Jim Darnley, Oliver's closest friend, who is very worldly and sophisticated and who has no sense of duty whatever. He is killed in the war, adding his wife and child to Oliver's list of responsibilities.

Rose Darnley, Jim's sister. She is one of the women to whom Oliver proposes. She refuses him because she knows that he is proposing because he feels it is his duty to marry and have children.

Mario Van de Weyer, Oliver's cousin, a romantic young man who lives off his rich relatives. Oliver is greatly puzzled by the fact that Mario does not mind sponging off others. Mario is a happy-go-lucky fellow who immediately enlists when the war breaks out.

Edith Van de Weyer, also Oliver's cousin, to whom he proposes marriage. She refuses him because Oliver forgets to say anything about loving her in his pro-

598

posal, and she wants more than mere duty in marriage.

Bobby, Jim's illegitimate son, for whom Oliver provides in his will.

THE LAST TYCOON

Author: F. Scott Fitzgerald (1896-1940)
Time of action: The 1930's
First published: 1941

PRINCIPAL CHARACTERS

Monroe Stahr, a brilliant, young film producer, as much interested in the artistic value of motion pictures as in making money. Having lost his wife whom he had loved deeply, he now courts death through overwork. He is extremely interested in the welfare of his employees, although he is not always appreciated by them. His short but passionate affair with Kathleen seems to be at the center of this unfinished novel.

Kathleen Moore, Stahr's mistress, who reminds him of his dead wife. She later marries another man out of a sense of obligation but continues her affair with Stahr.

Pat Brady, Stahr's partner. Interested only in making money, Brady is a cold and calculating man. He often opposes Stahr's policies although he understands almost

nothing of the technical end of the industry.

Cecilia Brady, Pat's daughter and the narrator of the story. She falls in love with Stahr but he pays no attention to her. After an affair with another man she suffers a complete breakdown and relates the story from a tuberculosis sanitarium.

Wylie Whyte, a screenwriter who tries to marry Cecilia and thus gain her father's influence.

Pete Zavras, a cameraman whom Stahr helps to find work. He later helps Stahr when Kathleen's husband finds out she is having an affair.

Schwartz, a ruined producer who commits suicide.

THE LATE GEORGE APLEY

Author: John P. Marquand (1893-1960)
Time of action: Late nineteenth and early twentieth centuries
First published: 1937

PRINCIPAL CHARACTERS

George William Apley, a proper Bostonian carefully trained since childhood to be a respectable member of Boston Brahmin society. Though as a college student he belittled the Brahmin pride of family, he acquired it himself as he matured, and later he attempted to pass it on to his children. Undistinguished academically at Harvard, he had been active in campus affairs and a member of a select club. Unfit for active business,

he derived his income from investments and from his father's substantial legacy. Though he admired Emerson's writings he never became an Emersonian nonconformist; in fact, he believed that the individual in society must submit to the common will. Like his father and his Uncle William, he was a generous giver to worthy causes.

John Apley, his son, who stirred George's

heart with pride over his war service, including a wound, and who later married a girl of good family. It was John who requested the writing of his father's life story.

Eleanor Apley, his daughter. She greatly disappointed George by marrying a journalist.

Catharine Bosworth Apley, his wife, whose marriage to George was unexciting but successful. According to his sister Amelia, George simply let Catherine and her family dominate him.

Mr. Willing, George Apley's biographer, staid, polished, and politely dull. Like George himself, Mr. Willing is snobbish, for he is also a Brahmin. In accordance with John's request, he includes along with George's commendable characteristics and actions some derogatory and unsavory details in his life; but he attempts to excuse these as minor aberrations in an essentially admirable man.

Mary Monahan, an attractive girl whose love affair with George ended when George's parents removed him from such a lower-class association.

William Apley, George's uncle, a wealthy businessman who spent little on himself and scorned ostentation but who was secretly a generous philanthropist. He controlled the Apley mills and opposed labor unions. When over eighty he shocked the family by marrying his nurse.

Amelia Apley, George's sister. She was more independent and forceful than George.

O'Reilly, a lawyer who tricked George into a scandal.

Horatio Apley, holder of a diplomatic post in Rome.

Thomas and **Elizabeth Hancock Apley,** George's parents.

Miss Prentiss, the young nurse whom Uncle William married.

Newcomb Simmings, Amelia Apley's husband.

Louise Hogarth Apley, John's wife. She is a divorcee but when George learns that she is from a fine family, he is satisfied.

William Budd, Eleanor's husband.

THE LATE MATTIA PASCAL

Author: Luigi Pirandello (1867-1936)
Time of action: Early twentieth century
First published: 1904

PRINCIPAL CHARACTERS

Mattia Pascal, a young Italian who undergoes the experience of living two different lives. Forced into an unhappy marriage with Romilda Pescatore, he flees on impulse and in Monte Carlo makes a sizable coup at the gaming tables. On his way home he hears that the body of a dead man has been identified by his wife as his own. Thus he is free to become another man, and he decides that this man will be called

Adriano Meis. A large portion of the novel concerns the failure of "Adriano" to achieve a sense of identity. As "Adriano," Mattia is both a legal and psychological nonentity, but his anomalous position can be corrected only by assuming the hardly more real identity of the "late Mattia Pascal." Returning to his village after staging a fake suicide, he learns that Romilda has married again. Not wishing to create new problems in this domestic situation, he settles down to a quiet, retiring life. Mattia's chief quality as the teller of his own story is ironical detachment from both of his identities.

Batty Malagna, the cheating steward of Mattia's widowed mother. He is chiefly responsible for thrusting Mattia into his unhappy marriage.

Signora Marianna Dondi-Pescatore, the old harridan who becomes Mattia's mother-in-law. Having driven Mattia away on his adventures, she is dismayed and alarmed by his return after he has been presumed dead.

Romilda Pescatore, Mattia's wife and after his supposed death the wife of his best friend, Gerolamo Pomino. She is a beautiful woman of no moral integrity, and in spite of the law and her marriage vows she has no desire to take up with Mattia after his reappearance.

Don Eligio Pellegrinotto, an aged priest and librarian who encourages Mattia to write the account of his startling adventures.

Roberto Pascal, Mattia's brother. He marries well and has no desire to help either his widowed mother or Mattia. After Mattia's reappearance he underlines the legal problems facing a man who has been legally declared dead.

The Cavaliere Tito Lenzi, a chance acquaintance of "Adriano." The fantasies of the older man and his useless learning warn Mattia of the emptiness of a rootless life.

Adriana Paleari, a virtuous and devout Roman girl. She is attracted to Mattia but cannot understand the ambiguousness of his position. Not knowing that it is impossible for Mattia to go to the police because of his false identity, she is dumbfounded when he refuses to prosecute her brother-in-law for theft.

Anselmo Paleari, Adriana's father and Mattia Pascal's landlord. A confirmed spiritualist, he is behind the séances that lead to Mattia's final catastrophe in his life as "Adriano Meis."

Terenzio Papiano, Adriana's scoundrelly brother-in-law. He robs Mattia to get the money he needs to repay the dowry of his dead wife.

Silvia Caporale, a middle-aged Roman music teacher. She is the confidante of Adriana and tries, by persuasion and séance, to bring Mattia to the point of proposing marriage. In appearance Silvia is ugly and cannot hope for attention from men.

The Marquis Giglio d'Auletta, Terenzio Papiano's employer. He hopes to refound the Kingdom of the Two Sicilies.

Pepita Pantagoda, the granddaughter of the Marquis Giglio d'Auletta. Her vanity almost involves Mattia in a duel.

Manual Bernaldez, a Spanish painter. He paints a portrait of Pepita's dog and threatens to fight a duel with Mattia.

Francesco Meis, a supposed relative of "Adriano Meis." Meeting him frightens Mattia Pascal.

LAVENGRO

Author: George Henry Borrow (1803-1881)
Time of action: Nineteenth century
First published: 1851

PRINCIPAL CHARACTERS

George, the narrator, who is called "Lavengro," the Zingary gipsy word for "word master," or "philologist." In this romance of circumstantial incidents and

601

philosophical conversations, George is in search of something to believe in. As a child, he moves about with his family. Apprenticed to a lawyer, he is convinced that authorship is his calling. Always mindful of his surroundings—nature, people, things—George goes through the strain of establishing himself in London, getting some of his writing accepted, and leaving the city to become a gipsy. His circumstantial relationships with various associates constitute the theme that no man is an island. A pickpocket leaves his bit of economic philosophy with George; George, a searcher for truth for himself, brightens the outlook of an evangelist who sees himself hopelessly lost to God; George comes to know his physical acumen through a fight with a gipsy friend who must avenge a suicidal death, brought on by George's not dying when the suicide had tried to poison him earlier. George passes through the stages of scholar, writer, and tinker.

Lavengro's Father, an army officer. His influence on his son is manifest in two ways. The father's gift of books, including "Robinson Crusoe," to his young son turns George's interest to reading. George's escapade in fighting can be traced to his early recollection of his father's having fought for an hour with a swarthy individual, Big Ben Brain. Typical of the barrier between father and his sensitive child is the father's lack of understanding of his second son's interests and his preference for George's older brother.

John, George's older brother, an artist.

Jasper Petulengro, George's gipsy friend. From childhood, George and Mr. Petulengro meet intermittently. Their first meeting is in a gipsy camp near George's home, when he attracts the young Jasper with a de-fanged viper George plays with. At successive meetings Mr. Petulengro offers George a home with the gipsies, avenges his mother-in-law's death by fighting with George, and teaches George to make horseshoes, that he may sustain himself on the road.

Isopel Berners, George's companion in the gipsy camp when he turns tinker. The handsome young woman, called Belle, is the illegitimate child of a gipsy mother and a noble father. At their first meeting Belle instructs George in defending himself against a gipsy with whom she is roaming and who wants to steal George's tinker supplies. George and Belle's platonic relationship is the essence of beauty as they sustain themselves by peddling George's wares. She is also in search of something beyond her present condition. They live fully as they converse in the dingle with the various passers-by who stop to discuss religions, nationalities, words, and dreams of far-off places.

Mrs. Herne, also **Hearne,** Petulengro's mother-in-law, who takes a violent dislike to George, the gorgio, or outsider. Biding her time, some years later Mrs. Herne gives him poisoned food. Seeing that he is not going to die, the old crone jabs at his face, attempting to blind him. Unsuccessful, she commits suicide because of her loss of face resulting from her failing attempts at murder.

Peter Williams, a Welsh evangelist. He happens by at the time of George's poisoning and sees George restored to health. Hearing Peter's harangue of self-condemnation for having sinned against the Holy Ghost, George gives his benefactor a new view of himself and his evangelistic work. Believing in his own goodness, Peter goes back to Wales to continue preaching the gospel.

Winifred, his wife, whose compassion toward her husband and his guilt-feelings is supported by George's attitudes. The Williamses try to get George to travel and work with them in their evangelism, but the young tinker declines their offer in order to continue his own search for truth.

Francis Ardry, George's associate in London. A young man of means, being groomed for Parliament, he shows George, in his period as a writer, the night spots of London: public houses, theaters, and inns.

Glorious John, a wealthy Armenian publisher in London and George's friend. After a long period of conversations on writing, translating, and relationships among peoples, George loses his friend through philosophizing that had he the Armenian's wealth, he would fight the Persians in their oppression of the Armenians. This chance remark provokes Glorious John's unceremonious departure for his home country.

The Apple Woman, an old vendor at London Bridge. The rare volume of "Mary Flanders," owned by the apple woman, plays a big part in this romance. Given to George, who will exchange the book for a Bible, the book is stolen. The theft and the grand price the thief unwittingly receives for the rare volume is a lesson, from the thief, to George in his subsequent bartering. Intertwined relations among people are implied as George

meets a sailor returned from a long sea voyage and looking for his old mother, the implication being that the sailor is the apple woman's son and that her and George's association has left a real impression on the scholar-writer.

The Flaming Tinman, a tinker who accosts George to take his tinker supplies from him. Called "the Blazing Bosville" by Belle, the Tinman, a bully of the roads, has driven other tinkers out of business. George's defiance of the Tinman is abetted by Belle, who leaves the company of the Tinman and Moll, his wife, to stay with George.

Jack Slingsby, the tinker whom George bought out as he starts on the last stage of his search. Slingsby has been forced out of business by the threats of the Tinman.

The Man in Black, a patron of the public house near George and Belle's dingle, who comes to the camp at night to talk. It was Borrow's tales of Catholicism and of the conduct of priests that aroused criticism of "Lavengro" when the book was first published.

THE LAY OF THE LAST MINSTREL

Author: Sir Walter Scott (1771-1832)
Time of action: Mid-sixteenth century
First published: 1805

PRINCIPAL CHARACTERS

Sir William of Deloraine, a knight who has served the Lord of Branksome. When Branksome is killed in a battle against the English, Deloraine remains faithful to the memory of his leader and stays on to serve Lady Buccleuch, Branksome's widow. Returning from a mission to get a magic book, Deloraine fights Lord Cranstoun, Branksome's former enemy who is in love with Branksome's daughter—and Deloraine falls wounded. Fortunately, he recovers and lives to see

harmony restored between the Scots and the English.

Lady Buccleuch, Lord Branksome's widow, the daughter of a magician. Spirits tell her that Branksome Castle is doomed unless pride dies and frees love. Lady Buccleuch does not heed the spirits at first. Finally, however, when Deloraine's life may be lost, and when her son may be taken from her, she relents. Her change of heart, shown by the bless-

603

ing she gives to the love of her daughter Margaret for Lord Cranstoun, the late Lord Branksome's enemy, brings peace to Branksome Castle and the Scottish border.

Lord Cranstoun, a knight who fought against Lord Branksome, but who loves Margaret, Branksome's daughter. Cranstoun, having wounded Deloraine, makes amends by donning Deloraine's armor and fighting, as that knight, against an English champion. When he wins, the English forces retire, Lady Buccleuch blesses his suit for Margaret's hand, and Deloraine has leisure for his wounds to heal.

The Dwarf, an evil magician devoted to Lord Cranstoun. The Dwarf causes mis-

chief at Branksome Castle by posing as the Master of Buccleuch. At a banquet, the Dwarf is killed by a thunderbolt, and in the eerie light Deloraine sees the form of the dead wizard, Michael Scott, whose book Lady Buccleuch had sent Deloraine to bring from Melrose Abbey.

The Ghost of Michael Scott, a wraith whose activities complicate the lives of those who live at Branksome Castle. At the end, Branksome's knights make pilgrimages to pray for rest for Michael Scott's soul.

Margaret, Lady Buccleuch's daughter and Cranstoun's beloved.

The Master of Buccleuch, Lady Buccleuch's son, a small boy.

LAZARILLO DE TORMES

Author: Unknown
Time of action: Sixteenth century
First published: 1553

PRINCIPAL CHARACTERS

Lazarillo de Tormes (lä·thä·rē′lyō t̸hä tôr′mäs), so named because he was born in a mill over the River Tormes. Bereaved at an early age by the death of his father, Lazarillo is given by his impoverished mother to his first master, a blind beggar whose cruelty is precisely the kind of education the unfortunate lad needs to remove his naïveté and prepare him to exist in a cruel world which promises only hardships for him. Treated cruelly, Lazarillo learns all the tricks of providing himself with food and drink. Becoming sharp and witty, although keeping his good nature, he develops the ability to please people and impress them. He is a kind-hearted, generous lad, though his environment might well train him in the opposite direction. He is what may be best described as one of nature's gentlemen. Given an opportunity by a

kindly chaplain, Lazarillo settles down to a respectable career as a water carrier. A diligent worker, he saves enough money to become respectable. Another friend, the Archpriest of St. Savior's Church, in Toledo, provides Lazarillo with an opportunity to marry an honest and hardworking woman who gives her husband no trouble, though gossip, until silenced by Lazarillo, tries to make out that the young woman is the Archpriest's mistress. By his wit, competence, and industry Lazarillo thrives and becomes a government inspector of wines at Toledo, a post which provides him with comfort and self-respect, if not affluence or great honor.

Antonia Pérez Goncales (än·tō′nyä pā′-räth gōn·thä′läs), Lazarillo's mother. A good but poor woman, she faces adversity following the death of her husband. To help her keep alive and provide for her small son, she takes a Moorish lover, by whom she has a dark-skinned child. After her lover's conviction of theft she is thrown upon her own meager resources, at which time she tries to provide for Lazarillo by putting him in the service of a blind beggar.

Thome Goncales (tō'mä gōn·thä'läs), Lazarillo's father, a miller. Convicted of fraud and theft, he enters military service and is killed shortly thereafter, in a battle with the Moors, while Lazarillo is a small child.

The Zayde (thä'ē·t̸hä), a stable master for the Comendador de la Magdalena. He is a Moor who becomes the lover of Lazarillo's mother. Being a poor man, the Zayde steals to provide for his mistress and the two children, Lazarillo and his half brother. His thievery discovered, the unhappy man is punished brutally and forbidden to see his adopted family.

The Blind Beggar, Lazarillo's first master. He treats Lazarillo cruelly from the first, beating the boy and starving him. He is a clever man who imparts his knowledge of human nature to the boy. No better master could have been found to acquaint Lazarillo with the rigors of life for a poor boy in sixteenth century Spain, though Lazarillo realizes this fact only later in life. As a boy he becomes bitter toward the man because of brutality and starvation.

The Penurious Priest, Lazarillo's second master, who also starves the lad and

keeps up a battle for months to prevent his acolyte from stealing either food or money; he has little success against the ingenious Lazarillo.

The Proud Squire, Lazarillo's third master. A man of honor, he starves himself rather than admit he is without money. Lazarillo joins him in the expectation of finding a rich master, only to learn he must beg on behalf of his master as well as for himself. Eventually the Squire, besieged by creditors, disappears.

The Friar, Lazarillo's fourth master, who is so busy and walks so far each day that Lazarillo leaves him after a few days.

The Seller of Papal Indulgences, a hypocritical pardoner who knows, like Chaucer's famous Pardoner, all the tricks to part poor Christians from their money. He is a fraud in every way, but he has little effect on the quite honest Lazarillo.

The Chaplain, Lazarillo's sixth master and first real benefactor. He gives Lazarillo work as his water carrier, enters into a partnership with the lad, and provides Lazarillo with a mule and the other necessities of his work.

The Archpriest of St. Savior's Church, a good and benevolent clergyman who helps Lazarillo to preferment and becomes his friend. He introduces Lazarillo to his future wife.

Lazarillo's Wife, a former servant of the Archpriest. She gives birth to Lazarillo's child, a daughter.

THE LEGEND OF GOOD WOMEN

Author: Goeffrey Chaucer (c. 1343-1400)
First transcribed: 1380-1386

PRINCIPAL CHARACTERS

Chaucer, a dreamer. In a vision he is denounced by Cupid for heresy against the laws of love for writing and translating disparaging remarks about womankind.

605

Cupid, the god of love. In a dream he accuses Chaucer, the dreamer, of heresy against love's laws.

Alceste, the wife of Admetus and the companion of Cupid in Chaucer's dream. She suggests that Chaucer win Cupid's forgiveness by writing a legend of wives and maidens forever true in love.

Cleopatra, Queen of Egypt, whose love of Antony is so great that, on his death, she causes herself to be bitten by a poisonous serpent.

Antony, Cleopatra's beloved.

Thisbe, the daughter of a lord of Babylon. She is loved by Pyramus, who, mistakenly thinking her dead, commits suicide. She finds his body and, in her grief, joins him in death.

Pyramus, the son of a lord of Babylon, Thisbe's beloved.

Dido, Queen of Carthage. According to Chaucer, Aeneas wins Dido's love, seduces her, and when he has grown weary of her, invents a vision which gives him an excuse to leave her. In her grief, she stabs herself.

Aeneas, Dido's betrayer.

Hypsipyle, Queen of Lemnos. She marries Jason and dies of a broken heart when he leaves her.

Medea, a princess of Colchis. She marries Jason, who leaves her for Creüsa.

Jason, the betrayer of Hypsipyle and Medea.

Creüsa, the daughter of Kreon, King of Corinth, for whom Jason betrays Medea.

Lucretia, the chaste, devoted wife of Colatyne (Collatinus). When she is ravished by Tarquinius (Tarquin), she takes her own life so that her husband will not have to bear the shame.

Colatyne (Collatinus), Lucretia's husband.

Tarquinius (Tarquin), Lucretia's ravisher.

Ariadne, the daughter of King Minos. Taken from Crete by Theseus, she is deserted on their way to Athens.

Theseus, a prince of Athens, Ariadne's betrayer.

Philomela, a princess of Athens ravished by her brother-in-law, Tereus.

Tereus, a lord of Thrace, Philomela's ravisher.

Progne, Tereus' wife, Philomela's sister.

Phyllis, a Greek maiden betrayed by Demophon, who promises marriage and instead sails away.

Demophon, Theseus' son, Phyllis' betrayer.

Ypermistra (Hypermnestra), one of the fifty daughters of Danao (Danaüs), King of Egypt. She is urged by her father to kill her bridegroom, Lino, but, for pity, she cannot, and warns him to escape, which he forthwith does, leaving her to her fate.

Lino, Ypermistra's bridegroom.

Danao, Ypermistra's father.

THE LEGEND OF SLEEPY HOLLOW

Author: Washington Irving (1783-1859)
Time of action: Eighteenth century
First published: 1819-1820

606

PRINCIPAL CHARACTERS

Ichabod Crane, a schoolmaster of Sleepy Hollow, near Tarry Town on the Hudson. He dreams of a comfortable marriage to Katrina. Because of his belief in ghosts, he is frightened from the area by a ghostly rider.

Gunpowder, Ichabod's gaunt horse.

Katrina Van Tassel, a rosy-cheeked student in Ichabod's singing classes.

Mynheer Van Tassel, her wealthy farmer father.

The Headless Horseman, a legendary apparition, supposedly a Hessian cavalryman whose head was shot off by a cannonball.

Abraham Van Brunt, called **Brom Bones,** who is in love with Katrina. Disguised as the Headless Horseman, he pursues Ichabod and throws a pumpkin at him. Ichabod leaves Sleepy Hollow permanently.

LEGEND OF THE MOOR'S LEGACY

Author: Washington Irving (1783-1859)
Time of action: Seventeenth century
First published: 1832

PRINCIPAL CHARACTERS

Pedro Gil (pā'drō hēl), called **Peregil,** a hardworking water carrier whose charitable impulse brings him riches.

His Wife, a nagging spendthrift who keeps Peregil from prospering.

A Traveler, too ill to travel, whom Peregil shelters in his house until the man's death. He leaves a parchment scroll that tells of great treasure hidden under the Alhambra.

Pedrillo Pedrugo (pā·drē'lyō pā·drōō'gō),

a spying barber who carries tales to the Alcalde, and dies amid the treasure he covets.

A Moorish Shopkeeper, who translates the magic incantation that opens a treasure vault under the Alhambra.

The Alcalde, a greedy governor who sells justice, and dies entombed in the treasure vault.

The Constable, also brought to his death by his greed.

THE LEGEND OF TYL ULENSPIEGEL

Author: Charles Théodore Henri de Coster (1827-1879)
Time of action: Sixteenth century
First published: 1867

PRINCIPAL CHARACTERS

Tyl Ulenspiegel (tēl ōō'lén·spē·gĕl), a young Fleming who seeks revenge upon the Spanish for the mistreatment of his parents. He wanders far, fighting the Spanish and looking for the Seven, who will save his land. He finds the Seven

in a vision. He appears dead and is buried, but later rises from his grave to be the spirit of the new Flanders freed from the grip of the Spanish.

Katheline (kä'·té·lē'né), a midwife who

607

brings Tyl Ulenspiegel into the world. She is the first to see him, in a vision, as the spirit of his native Flanders. Tortured as a witch, she goes mad. A later witch's trial by water causes her death.

Nele (nä′lĕ), Katheline's illegitimate daughter. She is Ulenspiegel's childhood playmate and, later, his wife. She goes in search of her wandering lover, saves him from the gallows, and marries him. She becomes the spirit of the heart of Flanders after it is freed from Spanish domination.

Claes (klās), Ulenspiegel's father. He is tortured and put to death by the Inquisition.

Soetkin (sœt′kĭn), Ulenspiegel's mother. She dies of grief over her husband's death and the tortures inflicted upon her by the Inquisition.

Hans Dudzeele (häns dōōd′sä′lĕ), Katheline's lover. He steals Claes' money from Soetkin and kills his accomplice. Denounced as a witch by mad Katheline,

who did not realize what she was doing, he is tortured and put to slow death by fire.

Lamme Goedzak (lä′me goed′säk), Ulenspiegel's companion in his wanderings. He is a fat buffoon seeking his wife, who has become a nun. He drowns in food and drink his sorrow over losing her. Eventually they are reunited.

The Seven, the Seven Deadly Sins, seen in a vision by Ulenspiegel. With the freeing of Flanders from the Spanish they become seven virtues: Pride, Gluttony, Idleness, Avarice, Anger, Envy, and Lust become Noble Spirit, Appetite, Reverie, Economy, Vivacity, Emulation, and Love, respectively.

Philip (fĭ′lĭp), King of Spain and symbol to Ulenspiegel of the Spanish domination of Flanders.

Prince William of Orange (wil′ē·äm), with whose forces Ulenspiegel fights against King Philip and the Inquisition.

LETTERS FROM THE UNDERWORLD

Author: Fyodor Mikhailovich Dostoevski (1821-1881)
Time of action: Mid-nineteenth century
First published: 1864

PRINCIPAL CHARACTERS

The Narrator, the "I" of the treatise, a man convinced of his own depravity. A theorist addressing imaginary listeners, his readers, he declares he will tell only the truth. Ugly in face and misshapen in body, though with an intelligent, even practiced alertness, he was for many years morbidly shy and grotesque in his vices. A government clerk of a mean and vindictive disposition, he declares that he would devote his life to idleness and the creation of beauty could he live again. As it is, he will continue in the same vein, acutely conscious of his intellectual prowess, aware of the pleasure he finds in humiliating himself painfully. He knows

himself a pretender (even this autobiographical sketch is in jest), but he is now incapable of feeling. He describes incidents which show his lack of acumen, his inability to love or take action, his despicable indulgence in self-pity, and his consciously depraved behavior. His bookishness, his intense self-consciousness, his inability to follow a line of action, his masochistic-sadistic impulses he presents as examples of man's perverse nature, which refuses the attainment of perfection or even the striving.

Liza (lĭ′zə), a peasant girl come to St. Petersburg, an inexperienced prostitute.

608

As the victim of the Narrator's determined debauch, the rather handsome, strong, contemplative Liza finds in the man's drunken meanderings a kind of solace. Accepting his admonitions as to the life she is beginning, she goes to see him because she believes that he offers her hope and love. Although his own surroundings are even more distasteful than hers, she insists on unburdening her feeling of love for him. Taking advantage of her tender feelings, he makes love to her and then tells her spitefully that he has no feelings except the desire to wield power, to hold another soul in his hands. Humiliated, she throws back the money he disdainfully gives her and leaves him.

Anton Antonitch Syetotchkin (än·tōn' än·tōn'ĭch sĕ·tōch'kĭn), the Narrator's immediate superior in a government office, a kind man with a pleasant family and a generous disposition and the one person the Narrator seems to respect. Anton lends the young clerk advances on his salary and welcomes the lonely and bookish young man into his home. Evenings spent listening to discussions of conservative politics and mundane af-fairs cause the young man to postpone his burning desire to embrace mankind, a desire which is as false as his other emotions.

Simonov (sĭ·myō'nəf), the Narrator's school friend, a pleasant person who lends him money and occasionally entertains the self-conscious clerk. Simonov allows the Narrator to come with other student friends to a farewell party for a mutual friend. Later he becomes embarrassed at the fellow's boorish behavior but lends him money to continue the debauch at a brothel.

Zverkov (zvĕr·kōf'), an army officer who owns two hundred serfs and is much respected in consequence. Because he is a hale fellow, an amusing storyteller, and a man about town, the Narrator resents him. Zverkov, instead of taking offense at the insulting manner of his former schoolmate, declares that such a low person cannot insult him. This haughtiness, coupled with his bragging stories of conquest, infuriates but tantalizes the Narrator, who abases and humiliates himself purposely before his old friends.

LIBER AMORIS

Author: William Hazlitt (1778-1830)
Time of action: 1820-1822
First published: 1823

PRINCIPAL CHARACTERS

H. (William Hazlitt), a writer and lover. The author is here writing an account of his own foolish passion for a young girl, S. (Sarah Walker), whom he meets in a boarding house owned by her father, M.W. (Micaiah Walker). Aware, in his heart, that the girl allows him more liberties than her show of demureness would justify, he is, nonetheless, romantic enough to endow her with an innocence and good intent that cause him to keep trying to persuade her to marry him. As he inevitably must, he finally learns that reality and one's own image of it are not necessarily the same.

S. (Sarah Walker), a young girl loved by H. (William Hazlitt). In her late teens when she meets the writer, she sits on his lap day after day exchanging kisses with him. She fails, however, to appreciate his elaborate protestations of love and can answer only that her regard can go no further than friendship. When she

609

is caught playing the same game with another, her lover is forced to realize that his love is not what she seems.

C.P. (Peter George Patmore), William Hazlitt's friend, to whom he writes about his love for Sarah Walker.

J.S.K. (James Sheridan Knowles), William Hazlitt's friend, to whom the closing letters of "Liber Amoris" are addressed.

M.W. (Micaiah Walker), William Hazlitt's landlord, the father of Sarah Walker.

THE LIFE AND DEATH OF MR. BADMAN

Author: John Bunyan (1628-1688)
Time of action: Anytime
First published: 1680

PRINCIPAL CHARACTERS

Mr. Badman, a sinner lately dead and the subject of a dialogue that makes up this story which is, in a sense, a companion piece to the author's "The Pilgrim's Progress." The very epitome of evil, Mr. Badman is used, in a conversation between Mr. Wiseman and Mr. Attentive, as a model of what happens to the unrepentent sinner as he makes his heedless way through life. Bearing the seeds of corruption within himself, his evil doing begins while he is yet a child and the inventor of, and example in, bad actions. One sin begets another until the sinner's corruption is complete. The author expects his reader to rejoice in the punishment Mr. Badman so richly deserves.

Mr. Wiseman, the author's spokesman, who relates to Mr. Attentive the story of the late Mr. Badman's evil life. Each sinful episode related by Mr. Wiseman brings forth from him or his listener a kind of sermon or the recitation of a series of edifying examples designed to prove the author's point to his readers.

Mr. Attentive, the listener to, and commentator on, Mr. Wiseman's account of Mr. Badman's wicked career.

Courteous Reader, who is addressed by the author as a probable sinner. He is asked seriously to consider Mr. Badman's life and to decide whether or not he is following him on the road to destruction.

LIFE IN LONDON

Author: Pierce Egan (1772-1849)
Time of action: Early nineteenth century
First published: 1821

PRINCIPAL CHARACTERS

Corinthian Tom, the scion of a wealthy British family. He is a young chap anxious to experience life. Under the tutelage of Bob Logic he explores all the facets of London life by getting into scrapes and out of them. He is accompanied part of the time by his cousin, Jerry Hawthorn.

Bob Logic, a one-time law student in London. He is a merry chap who always has a joke. He is Corinthian Tom's mentor after Tom's parents die. He ends up in debtor's prison.

Corinthian Kate (Catherine), a beautiful and talented courtesan, one of the most desired in London. She becomes Corinthian Tom's mistress.

Jerry Hawthorn, Tom's country cousin. He comes down to London to learn about life in the city. He is a likable young chap. He has to leave the life of London when he falls ill.

Doctor Pleas'em, favorite doctor of the gay young blades of London.

Mr. Primefit, a most accomplished tailor. He is popular because he does not press his customers for payment.

Miss Satire, a fashionable woman attracted to Jerry.

Lady Wanton, Miss Satire's sister, a lively woman who first embarrasses Jerry and then, disguised as a nun, flirts with him.

The Duchess of Hearts, a fashionable, beautiful woman who strikes Jerry dumb with her beauty.

Trifle, the skinniest dandy in the city.

Sue, a friend of Corinthian Kate. She is attracted to Jerry.

LIFE IS A DREAM

Author: Pedro Calderón de la Barca (1600-1681)
Time of action: Sixteenth century
First presented: 1635

PRINCIPAL CHARACTERS

Segismundo (sä·hēs·mōōn'dō), heir to the throne of Poland, who has been imprisoned in a tower on the Russian frontier because horrible portents at his birth and later predictions by astrologers have convinced his father, King Basilio, that the boy will grow up into a monster who will destroy the land. Finally because the King sees his land split over the matter of succession, Segismundo is drugged and transported from his prison to the Court of Warsaw. There, uncouth and inexperienced, he behaves boorishly. He accuses the Court of wronging him and scorns his father's explanations thus: "What man is so foolish as to lay on the disinterested stars the responsibility for his own actions?" Impossible as a king, he is again drugged and returned to his tower, where he is told it was all a dream. Later liberated by an army recruited by Rosaura, in revenge on the ambitious Astolfo, he thinks he is still dreaming. So why should he strive in a dream for something that disappears upon awaking? On that account he will not accept the throne when his followers overthrow King Ba-

silio. He treats everybody kindly and generously, marries Estrella, and forces Astolfo to keep his promise and marry Rosaura.

Rosaura (r̄o·sä'ōō·rä), a Russian woman traveling with her servant Fife to the Court of Warsaw to seek the Pole who had promised to marry her. Crossing the Russian-Polish boundary, disguised as a man for protection against bandits, she loses her horse and her way. She finds and sympathizes with a young man, chained to the doorway of a tower and bemoaning his fate. He warns her to flee, which she does, after giving him the sword she has been carrying.

Clotaldo (klō·täl'dō), a Polish general and guardian of the imprisoned Segismundo. He captures Rosaura and Fife but sends them on their way. He recognizes the sword as one he had left in Russia with a noblewoman with whom he had been in love, and he supposes the disguised Rosaura is his own son. However, duty to his King seals his lips. When Segismundo returns to his tower prison from his unfortunate experiences

611

in Warsaw, Clotaldo assures the Prince that life is a dream and that in dreams men's evil thoughts and ambitions are unchecked. Awake, one can control his passions and behave like a sane individual. Later, when Segismundo gets a second chance, Clotaldo is unharmed because of his earlier advice.

King Basilio (bä·sē·lyō), the father of Segismundo, faced by the problem of succession to the Polish throne. Claimants are Astolfo, his nephew, and Estrella, his niece; their rival supporters form political factions that will disrupt the country in civil war. Calling an assembly, King Basilio announces that his son, who supposedly died with his mother, is really alive. With the consent of the claimants, he will send for the Prince and see what sort of king he might make.

Astolfo (äs·tōl'fō), one claimant for the Polish throne. While in Russia, he had contracted matrimony with Rosaura, but now he wants to marry Estrella so that he can be sure of becoming King of Poland. When Segismundo awakes from his drugged sleep, he manhandles Astolfo for daring to touch the attractive Estrella.

Estrella (ĕs·trä'lyä), a Princess whom Segismundo embraces, to the consternation of the courtiers. Eventually, after his second visit to the court, where he acts with proper dignity because of his conviction that life is a dream, Estrella becomes his Queen.

Fife (fē'fä), the "gracioso", or comic servant of Rosaura, who adds humor and philosophy to the comedy.

LIFE WITH FATHER

Author: Clarence Day, Jr. (1874-1935)
Time of action: Late nineteenth century
First published: 1935

PRINCIPAL CHARACTERS

Clarence Day, Sr., a domestic tyrant, critical, quick-tempered, and eccentric, who dominates his family, but not completely. Father (Clare to his wife) is a loud groaner when he himself is ill, but he has little sympathy with others' illnesses. Since he is a systematic businessman, he cannot understand his wife's dislike of figures and the keeping of household accounts. Companionable and popular with his chosen friends, he is dictatorial toward people he does not care for. He enjoys his family despite all the complaints he makes about them.

Mrs. Clarence (Vinnie) Day, his wife, who puts up with Father's tantrums, sometimes ignoring them, at other times countering with feminine scorn and illogic to exasperate and often defeat her noisy mate.

Clarence Day, Jr., the narrator, the near-sighted oldest son who as a child suffers the misfortune of the name Clarence, vainly tries to play the violin, and is alternately entertained and frightened by Father's many explosions.

Margaret, cook in the Day household for twenty-six years.

George and
Julian, younger brothers of Clarence, Jr.

Herr M., Clarence, Jr.'s violin teacher.

Cousin Julie, Mrs. Day's favorite niece who lives with the Days after finishing school.

Miss Edna Gulick, conductor of a current events class attended by Mrs. Day.

Delia, a temporary cook who is quickly dismissed after Father's complaint about her.

612

LIGEIA

Author: Edgar Allan Poe (1809-1849)
Time of action: Early nineteenth century
First published: 1838

PRINCIPAL CHARACTERS

The Narrator, a learned man enslaved to the memory of a woman whose powerful will once triumphed over death itself to return to him whom she so passionately loved. Half insane through grief after Ligeia's death, and addicted to opium, he nevertheless remarries. Forgetful of Ligeia for a month, he abandons himself to Lady Rowena; but memory returns, and love turns to hatred and loathing. He witnesses (or so he believes) the dropping of poison into some wine he gives Rowena when she is ill. After Rowena's death he is awed by the rising of her corpse which he recognizes not as that of Rowena but of his lost Ligeia.

Ligeia, his first wife, a beautiful woman of rare learning and musically eloquent voice. Tall and slender, she is quietly majestic whether in repose or walking with "incomprehensible lightness and elasticity." Her features are "strange" rather than clasically regular: the skin pale, forehead broad, luxuriously curly hair glossy and black. Her nose is slightly aquiline; and when her short upper lip and her voluptuous under one part in a radiant smile, her teeth gleam brilliantly. Her eyes are most notable: unusually large and luminously black, with long and jetty lashes and slightly irregular black brows. Though Ligeia is outwardly calm and speaks in a low, distinct, and melodious voice, a passionately intense will shows in the fierce energy of her wild words. Her knowledge of classical and modern European languages leads her (and her worshiping husband) into extensive metaphysical investigations. When Ligeia falls ill her wild eyes blaze, her skin turns waxen, and the veins in her forehead swell and sink. Though her voice drops lower, she struggles fiercely against the Shadow. Moments before her death she shrieks and fiercely protests against the Conquering Worm in her poem which her husband has read to her. With her dying breath she murmurs that man submits to death only through feebleness of will. When Lady Rowena later dies, Ligeia, through the power of her will, returns from death and enters the body of her successor.

Lady Rowena Trevanion, the second wife, fair-haired and blue-eyed. She falls ill and slowly dies, wasting away while she becomes increasingly irritable and fearful, her fear being increased by mysterious sounds and sights she is aware of. (Her illness may be compared to that which for five years tortured and finally killed Virginia Poe, the author's young wife.)

LIGHT IN AUGUST

Author: William Faulkner (1897-1962)
Time of action: 1930
First published: 1932

PRINCIPAL CHARACTERS

Joe Christmas, a mulatto. Placed in an orphan home by his demented grandfather, he is to lead a tortured life of social isolation, as he belongs neither to the white nor to the colored race; in fact, he prefers this kind of existence.

613

After staying with the fanatical Calvin McEachern during his boyhood, Joe knocks his foster father unconscious and strikes out on his own, rejecting any friendly overtures. At last, he is driven to his final desperate act: he kills his benefactress, Joanna Burden, and faces death at the hands of merciless Percy Grimm.

Joanna Burden, Joe Christmas' mistress, the descendant of a New England family. Rejected by many of her neighbors, she is the friend of Negroes and interested in improving their lot. In her efforts to make Joe useful to the world, she also tries to possess and dominate him sexually, and so meets her death.

Calvin McEachern, Joe's foster father. A ruthless, unrelenting religious fundamentalist, McEachern, without real animosity, often beats the boy savagely for trifling misdemeanors and tells him to repent. He demands that "the Almighty be as magnanimous as himself."

Eupheus Hines (Doc), Joe Christmas' grandfather. Always a hot-tempered little man, he is often in fights. When he learns that his daughter Milly has a mulatto lover, the fiery old man kills him. Later he allows Milly to die in childbirth, unaided by a doctor. Soon after her death he places the baby in an orphanage. Years later, learning of Joe's imprisonment, Doc Hines demands that his grandson be lynched. Prior to this time, the old man has devoted much effort to preaching to bemused Negroes about white supremacy.

Gail Hightower, a minister. Most of Hightower's life has been devoted to a dream. Long before, his grandfather had died while serving with a troop of Confederate cavalry. Because of his grandfather he becomes obsessed with the Civil War. Now an outcast, he has driven his wife to her death because of this obsession; in the process he is forced from his church by his outraged congregation.

Joe Brown (Lucas Burch), Lena Grove's lover and the unwilling father of her child. A loudmouthed, weak man, he deserts Lena and finds work in another town. After meeting Joe Christmas, he becomes a bootlegger and lives with Joe in a cabin behind Joanna Burden's house. When Christmas is captured, Brown, hoping for a large reward, tells the sheriff that Joe has murdered Miss Burden. Unable to face responsibilities, he hops a freight train in order to avoid Lena.

Lena Grove, a country girl seduced and deserted by Joe Brown. Ostensibly, this simple-hearted, fecund young woman pursues her lover because he is the father of her child; actually, she continues looking for him so that she can see different parts of the South.

Milly Hines, Doc Hines' daughter. She dies in childbirth because her enraged father refuses to let a doctor deliver a mulatto child.

Byron Bunch, a worker at the sawmill. Although he loves Lena, this good man helps her look for Joe Brown.

Mrs. Hines, Joe Christmas' grandmother. Always loving Joe, she tries to get Hightower to say that Joe was elsewhere when the murder was committed.

Mrs. McEachern, Calvin McEachern's long-suffering, patient wife. Like the other women, she is rebuffed when she tries to help Joe Christmas.

Percy Grimm, a brutal National Guard captain. He hunts Joe down after the latter escapes from a deputy. Not satisfied with shooting Christmas, Grimm also mutilates the injured man.

LILIOM

Author: Ferenc Molnar (1878-1952)
Time of action: Early twentieth century
First presented: 1909

PRINCIPAL CHARACTERS

Mrs. Muskat, the owner of a merry-go-round in Budapest.

Liliom, her successful barker, discharged for flirting with Julie, whom he eventually marries. He refuses to go back to Mrs. Muskat because he has plans to rob a factory paymaster. When caught, he stabs himself and dies. In a vision, after sixteen years of purification by fire, he returns to earth to find himself idealized by his wife and his daughter.

Julie, a country girl who marries Liliom.

Louise, their daughter. She has been taught by Julie to idolize her father. When he returns from death for a day after sixteen years and strikes Louise in irritation, she says the blow felt tender, like a caress.

Marie, Julie's friend, who is lured by Wolf's uniform and marries him.

Wolf, a porter.

Mrs. Hollunder, Julie's aunt, who runs a photograph gallery.

Ficsur, who encourages Liliom to steal a knife from the Hollunder kitchen and hold up the cashier.

Linzman, the factory paymaster whom Liliom plans to rob. Having already paid off the workers, he has no money when Liliom accosts him.

Two Policemen, who carry the dying Liliom to the photographer's shop and later figure as heavenly police in his vision.

THE LINK

Author: August Strindberg (1849-1912)
Time of action: Late nineteenth century
First presented: 1893

PRINCIPAL CHARACTERS

Baron Sprengel and
Baroness Sprengel, principals in a divorce case. Having agreed between themselves on terms for an amicable settlement of their difficulties, the Baron and Baroness go to court confident that they will divide between them the care of their child and that the details of their quarrel will not be aired in public. When the husband and wife find that it is the court and not themselves who will decide on the disposition of the child, their fears of losing him, and the goading of the court, cause them

to become overt enemies hurling charges and countercharges at each other. When the jury places the child in the custody of a peasant couple for a year, the Baron suggests that their anguish is a judgment of God.

The Judge, a young man taking the bench for the first time. Observing the bitter quarreling of the Baron and Baroness Sprengel, he adjourns the court in despair of doing justice. He seeks help from the Pastor, who advises him always to stick to the letter of the law and avoid personal involvements if he wants to keep his sanity.

The Pastor, the spiritual adviser to the Judge.

Alexandersson, a farmer who loses a case

in which it is agreed that he is actually right but technically guilty. He later appears as a witness (probably false) against Baroness Sprengel.

Alma Jonsson, Alexandersson's servant, whom he accuses of theft. He loses the case.

THE LION OF FLANDERS

Author: Hendrik Conscience (1812-1883)
Time of action: 1298-1305
First published: 1838

PRINCIPAL CHARACTERS

Philip the Fair, King of France. With his treasury almost depleted, he eyes the rich cities of Flanders for possible revenue. When the Flemish burghers refuse to pay the taxes levied by the King, he brings his armies against them. He encounters such stubborn resistance that he finally is forced to give up his efforts to subdue the fiercely independent people of Flanders.

Joanna of Navarre, Queen of France, whose hatred of the Flemings causes King Philip to dishonor himself and to make an enemy of his brother, Charles de Valois.

Count Guy of Flanders, a vassal of Philip the Fair. A victim of Philip's displeasure, he finds himself the King's prisoner and, at the same time, the rallying point of the party supporting Flemish independence. He dies in prison before the peace treaty with France is signed.

Count Robert de Bethune, called **The Lion of Flanders.** He is the son of Count Guy of Flanders. Imprisoned with his father by Philip the Fair, he is released for a time when Adolf of Niewland takes his place. During his freedom, he rallies the forces of Flanders and finally leads them to victory against the French. Returning to prison, he is freed after the signing of the peace treaty and becomes the ruler of Flanders.

Adolf of Niewland, a Flemish knight who goes to prison as a hostage for Count Robert de Bethune. He is the protector and, later, the husband of Lady Matilda.

Peter Deconinck, the dean of the cloth-workers' guild at Bruges, and
Jan Breydel, the dean of the butchers' guild, who are knighted by Count Robert de Bethune for their services in the cause of Flemish independence.

Lady Matilda, Count Robert de Bethune's daughter and later the bride of Adolf of Niewland.

Philippa, Count Guy of Flander's daughter, who is imprisoned and poisoned by the French.

Sir Diederik die Vos, called **The Fox,** a Flemish noble who has escaped from prison in France. Disguised as a friar, he brings word from Count Robert de Bethune that Count Robert's jailer would free him temporarily if someone would take his place.

Lord Guy, the younger brother of Count Robert de Bethune.

Count Robert d'Artois, leader of the French forces defeated at Courtrai.

Charles de Valois, King Philip's brother, who is betrayed by the King when he tries to effect a reconciliation between the Flemish nobles and King Philip.

THE LITTLE CLAY CART

Author: Shudraka (fl. 100 B.C.)
Time of action: Fifth century B.C.
First presented: Unknown

PRINCIPAL CHARACTERS

Chārudatta, a wise and honorable young Brāhmana left impoverished after spending his fortune for the welfare of others. In love with and loved by Vasantasenā, he is falsely accused of her murder and condemned to die. As he is being prepared for execution, Vasantasenā appears just in time to identify the true murderer and save her lover's life. Chārudatta's fortune is restored, and he is made an official at court by the new and just King, Āryaka.

Vasantasenā, a wealthy courtesan who is in love with Chārudatta. When she goes to the park to meet her lover, she is set upon by Samsthānaka, who chokes her and leaves her for dead. She is rescued by a Buddhist monk. While Chārudatta is being falsely accused and tried for her murder, she is being nursed back to health. She appears at the place of execution in time to save her lover's life.

Samsthānaka, King Pālaka's brother-in-law. Enamored of Vasantasenā and madly jealous of her attentions to Chārudatta,

he chokes her, leaves her for dead, and accuses his rival of the murder.

Āryaka, a captive Prince freed through the efforts of Sarvilaka and Chārudatta. He later deposes King Pālaka and restores to Chārudatta his fortune and his rightful place in the world.

Sarvilaka, a thieving Brāhmana, Prince Āryaka's friend and liberator. He steals the jewels left by Vasantasenā in Chārudatta's care and buys his bride, Madanikā, with them.

Madanikā, Vasantasenā's slave and confidante, whom Sarvilaka purchases as his bride.

Rohasena, Chārudatta's son, to whom Vasantasenā gives a little gold cart to replace a clay one, which is all his father is able to afford.

Maitreya, a poor Brāhmana, Chārudatta's friend and confidant.

Pālaka, the unjust King deposed by Prince Āryaka.

LITTLE DORRIT

Author: Charles Dickens (1812-1870)
Time of action: Early nineteenth century
First published: 1855-1857

PRINCIPAL CHARACTERS

William Dorrit, a quiet, shy, self-contained man so long imprisoned for debt that he has become known to all as the "Father of the Marshalsea." Never able to understand the complexity of business details that reduced him to bankruptcy, he accepts his fate and "testimonials," as he calls small gifts of money given him by visitors to the prison, with the same equanimity. His wife and two children had joined him in prison, where a third child, their daughter Amy, had been born; and Mrs. Dorrit had died there. Over the Dorrit family hangs the shadow of some great but mysterious wrong. When it is discovered that Mr. Dorrit is the heir at law to an unclaimed fortune, he leaves the prison and begins a life of extravagance and display on the fringes of society. His mind, weakened by twenty-five years of imprisonment, slowly deteriorates. He dies, in a palace in Rome, believing he is back in the Marshalsea.

Amy Dorrit, called **Little Dorrit** because she is the youngest child of the family, born in the Marshalsea Prison. After her mother's death she becomes the stay and protector of the family, ministering to the needs of her gentle father, her sister Fanny, and her brother Tip. A seamstress, she sews for Mrs. Clennam, who has suppressed the codicil to a will which gave Little Dorrit an inheritance of two thousand guineas. Little Dorrit is never at ease surrounded by the splendor and wealth of the Dorrits once they are freed from the Marshalsea, and she returns to the prison to nurse Arthur Clennam after his confinement there. The wrongs done to both are eventually righted, and they marry.

Fanny Dorrit, Mr. Dorrit's older daughter. A ballet dancer, she is able to make her way into society, and she marries Edmund Sparkler.

Edward Dorrit, nicknamed **Tip,** a ne'er-do-well and spendthrift for whom, before their restoration to affluence, Little Dorrit secures a variety of jobs, none of which he holds very long.

Frederick Dorrit, Mr. Dorrit's brother, also a bankrupt. After losing his money he gave up washing and supported himself by playing a clarinet in a theater orchestra. He had taken in and cared for Arthur Clennam's real mother. He remains simple in tastes and heart.

Mrs. Clennam, a stern, implacable, cold-hearted woman, an invalid who for years has managed from her sickbed the English branch of her husband's business. She has kept from Arthur Clennam the knowledge that he is the son of a woman whom his father had loved but never married, and she has withheld Little Dorrit's rightful inheritance. Threatened with exposure by M. Blandois, who is trying to blackmail her, she confesses the wrong to Little Dorrit and is forgiven.

Arthur Clennam, the son of the woman his father put aside when he married Mrs. Clennam. For twenty years he has lived with his father in China. After Mr. Clennam's death he returns to England, bringing with him his father's last bequest, an old watch inscribed with the letters DNF (Do Not Forget). On his arrival he is attracted to Little Dorrit, who is partly a servant and partly a friend in the Clennam household. Arthur incurs Mrs. Clennam's displeasure when he withdraws from the family business and goes into partnership with Daniel Doyce, an engineer and inventor. Ruined when Mr. Merdle's involved financial structure collapses, he is imprisoned in the Marshalsea. There, during an illness, he is nursed by Little Dorrit. They marry after his release.

M. Blandois (blän·dwä′), alias **Rigaud** (rē·gō′), "a cruel gentleman with slender white hands." Condemned to death for the murder of his wife, he escapes from the prison in Marseilles and makes his way to England, where, having gained knowledge of Mrs. Clennam's deceptions and frauds, he attempts to blackmail her. He is killed when the rickety Clennam house collapses, burying him in the ruins.

Daniel Doyce, the engineer who becomes Arthur Clennam's partner. Because he has been successful during a business trip abroad he is able to free Arthur from the Marshalsea and to assure the future prosperity of the firm of Doyce and Clennam.

Mrs. Flora Finching, Arthur Clennam's first love. Now widowed, she is still artless, sentimental, and gushingly foolish in her conversation. She lives with her father, Christopher Casby.

Christopher Casby, the miserly landlord of Bleeding Heart Yard and Flora Finching's father. A complete hypocrite, he poses as a benefactor and philanthropist while his agent forces his tenants into greater poverty. To those unaware of his true nature he is known as "The Last of the Patriarchs."

Mr. Pancks, Mr. Casby's agent and rent collector, who finally rebels against his skinflint employer and publicly humiliates him. He advises Arthur Clennam to invest in Mr. Merdle's financial enterprises and thus helps to bring about Arthur's bankruptcy.

Mr. Merdle, a financial wizard. His bankruptcy ruins many investors, and he commits suicide by bleeding himself with a penknife.

Mrs. Merdle, his wife, Edmund Sparkler's mother.

Edmund Sparkler, the son of Mrs. Merdle and her first husband, an army officer stationed for a time in North America. It is reported that Edmund's brains were frozen when he was born, during a great Canadian frost. Claiming that Fanny Dorrit is a "doosed fine gal," he marries her.

Mr. Meagles, a benevolent, sentimental retired banker who mistakenly prides himself on the fact that he is a practical man.

Mrs. Meagles, his homely but cheerful wife, a perfect partner in the marriage.

Minnie Meagles, their daughter, familiarly called **Pet.** Fair and mild of temper, like her parents, she marries Henry Gowan.

Henry Gowan, a young artist who marries Minnie Meagles. He is a distant connection of the Barnacle family.

Mrs. Gowan, his mother, somewhat aloof in manner because she is proud of her family connections.

Mrs. General, a wealthy widow who becomes the social mentor of the Dorrit family after they have become wealthy. Mr. Dorrit proposes to her shortly before his death.

Jeremiah Flintwinch, at one time Mrs. Clennam's servant, later her rascally partner in her deceptions and acts of fraud.

Affery Flintwinch, Mrs. Clennam's maid, whom Flintwinch married against her will. She is gentle and submissive to Mrs. Clennam, abused by her husband.

Ephraim Flintwinch, Jeremiah's brother and confederate.

Harriet Beadle (Tattycoram), a foundling taken in by Mr. Meagles. She is called Tattycoram because Harriet has been shortened Hatty and then changed to Tatty and because the name Beadle, being disliked, was changed to Coram. A headstrong girl, she runs away from her benefactors and seeks the protection of Miss Wade. Later she recovers the papers which gave M. Blandois his hold over Mrs. Clennam and returns to service with the Meagles family.

Miss Wade, a strange, tormented, unhappy woman who persuades Tattycoram to desert Mr. and Mrs. Meagles. She gains possession of the documents with which Mr. Blandois is trying to blackmail Mrs. Clennam.

Lord Decimus Tite Barnacle, a pompous official high in the Circumlocution Office of the government.

Tite Barnacle, an official of the Circumlocution Office, involved in the circumstances of Mr. Dorrit's bankruptcy. Arthur Clennam interviews him while trying to secure Mr. Dorrit's release from the Marshalsea Prison.

Clarence Barnacle, called **Barnacle, Junior,** Tite Barnacle's son, a fatuous clerk in the Circumlocution Office.

Ferdinand Barnacle, Lord Barnacle's

private secretary, an airy, sprightly young man.

John Baptist Cavalletto, an Italian smuggler imprisoned with M. Blandois, then called Rigaud, in Marseilles. He later enters the employ of Arthur Clennam and is instrumental in tracking down Blandois.

John Chivery, the turnkey of the Marshalsea Prison.

John Chivery, his son, in love with Little Dorrit.

Bob, another turnkey of the Marshalsea, Little Dorrit's godfather.

Mr. Cripples, a schoolmaster who offers instruction to children of the prisoners confined in the Marshalsea.

Dr. Haggage, the brandy-drinking debtor who officiates at the birth of Little Dorrit.

Mrs. Bangham, a charwoman, nurse, and messenger between the outer world and prisoners in the Marshalsea.

Mr. Plornish, a plasterer, one of Mr. Casby's tenants in Bleeding Heart Yard.

Mrs. Plornish, his wife, a friend of Little Dorrit.

John Nandy, Mrs. Plornish's father, considered by his daughter a "sweet singer."

Maggy, Mrs. Bangham's granddaughter, Little Dorrit's friend. "Never to be older than ten," she is blind in one eye and partly bald as the result of fever. She helps to care for the Plornish children.

Mrs. Tickit, housekeeper to the Meagles family.

Lord Lancaster Stiltstalking, an austere superannuated politician maintained by the Circumlocution Office in diplomatic posts abroad.

Mr. Rugg, Mr. Pancks's landlord, an accountant and debt collector.

Anastasia Rugg, his daughter, the owner of a modest property acquired through a breach of promise suit.

THE LITTLE FOXES

Author: Lillian Hellman (1905-   )
Time of action: 1900
First presented: 1939

PRINCIPAL CHARACTERS

Regina Giddens, a conniving and grasping woman. Eager for her share in the profits of a proposed cotton mill, she contrives to get her fatally ill husband, Horace, home from the hospital to be worked on by her family to supply her share of the needed investment. When he refuses to have anything to do with the project, she cruelly taunts him with her contempt and refuses him his medicine when he feels a fatal attack coming on.

Benjamin and
Oscar Hubbard, Regina Giddens' con-

niving and grasping brothers. Lacking Regina's share of the investment needed for the construction of the cotton mill, they descend on the fatally ill Horace Giddens in an attempt to persuade him to put up the money. When he refuses to have anything to do with the venture, they "borrow" his bonds and go off to complete the deal.

Horace Giddens, Regina Giddens' honest, fatally ill husband. Sick of his scheming wife and her grasping family, he refuses to invest in the projected cotton mill. When he learns of the theft of his bonds by Benjamin and Oscar Hubbard, he ties Regina's hands by planning a will that makes her the beneficiary of the bonds. He dies when she deprives him of his medicine as an attack is imminent.

Alexandra, the daughter of Regina and Horace Giddens. Sickened by the treatment given her father by her mother and her uncles, she leaves Regina and the Hubbards after Horace's death.

Birdie Hubbard, Oscar Hubbard's wife, who longs for a return to the refinements of a bygone day.

Leo Hubbard, Oscar Hubbard's son and ally in the theft of Horace Giddens' bonds.

THE LITTLE MINISTER

Author: James M. Barrie (1860-1937)
Time of action: Mid-nineteenth century
First published: 1891

PRINCIPAL CHARACTERS

Gavin Dishart, the little minister of Auld Licht Parish, in Thrums. He falls in love with Babbie, a girl he believes to be a gipsy but who is actually the ward of Lord Rintoul. Their path of love is strewn with difficulties, but the sincere and able young minister wins out and marries Babbie, at first in a gipsy camp and, later, in a church. He and his wife live happily afterward, parents of a little daughter who learns their story from her grandfather.

Mr. Gavin Ogilvy, a schoolmaster. He is really Gavin Dishart's father. When his wife's first husband returns, Mr. Ogilvy disappears from her life, thinking he can thus make happy the woman he loves. Eventually he tells Gavin the story, but never lets his identity be known to Gavin's mother.

Babbie, a girl whom Lord Rintoul was expected to marry. In an attempt to help rebellious weavers escape the law, she disguises herself as a gipsy. While disguised she claims to be the little minister's wife at one time. Although at first she laughs at the minister, she falls in love with him eventually. After some harrowing adventures she and Gavin are married.

Margaret Dishart, Gavin's mother. She marries Mr. Ogilvy, thinking her first husband has been lost at sea. When the first husband returns, Mr. Ogilvy disappears to save her embarrassment and she never sees him again.

Lord Rintoul, a local aristocrat. Planning to marry Babbie himself, he tries unsuccessfully to prevent her marriage to the little minister at the gipsy camp.

Rob Dow, a man rescued from drink by the minister. He tries to protect the minister from Babbie, whom he believes to be a witch. He leaps to his death to save the minister from drowning during a flood.

Nanny Webster, a penniless old woman in Gavin's parish. Babbie thwarts the minister's attempt to send the old lady to the poorhouse.

Dr. McQueen, who helps Gavin in his attempt to send Nanny to the poorhouse.

Micah, Rob's little son.

Adam Dishart, Margaret's first husband, for a time believed lost at sea. He eventually returns home to claim his wife.

LITTLE WOMEN

Author: Louisa May Alcott (1832-1888)
Time of action: Nineteenth century
First published: 1868

PRINCIPAL CHARACTERS

Meg, the oldest of the March girls, a plump governess to unruly neighborhood children. She marries John Brooke.

Jo, a tall, awkward, tomboyish girl who likes to write and to devise plays and entertainments for her sisters. In character and personality she corresponds to the author. She resents Meg's interest in John but later is happy to have him as a brother-in-law. She writes and sells stories and becomes a governess for Mrs. Kirke in New York. Proposed to by Laurie, she rejects him. She later marries Professor Bhaer with whom she establishes a boys' school at Plumfield, Aunt March's old home.

Beth, a gentle homebody helpful to Mrs. March in keeping house. She contracts scarlet fever from which she never fully recovers. She dies during the spring after Jo's return from New York.

Amy, a curly-haired dreamer who aspires to be a famous artist. She is a companion of Aunt Carrol on a European trip. She marries Laurie.

Mrs. March (Marmee), the kindly, understanding, lovable mother of the four March girls.

Mr. March, her husband, an army chaplain in the Civil War who becomes ill while away but who later returns well and happy.

Theodore Lawrence (Laurie), a young neighbor who joins the March family circle. He falls in love with Jo, but after his rejection by her he transfers his feelings to Amy, whom he marries.

Professor Bhaer, a tutor in love with Jo, whom he marries.

Mr. Lawrence, the wealthy, indulgent grandfather of Laurie.

Aunt March, a wealthy, irascible relative who wills her home to Jo.

John Brooke, Laurie's tutor, who falls in love with and marries Meg.

Aunt Carrol, a relative of the Marches.

Mrs. Kirke, a New York boarding-house keeper.

Daisy and **Demi,** Meg's children.

LIZA OF LAMBETH

Author: W. Somerset Maugham (1874-   )
Time of action: Late nineteenth century
First published: 1897

PRINCIPAL CHARACTERS

Liza Kemp, a working girl of Lambeth who lives a brutal life in that depressing borough. She works in a factory and gives most of her wages to a drunken mother who never speaks civilly to anyone. Spurning a faithful lover, Liza accepts a married man who has five children. After many unpleasant events, such as a thorough beating at the hands of her lover's wife, Liza dies of a miscarriage for which her lover is responsible.

Jim Blakeston, Liza's married lover, who is typical of the brutish lower class husband. He beats his wife, drinks too much, and is fond of but neglectful of his children. Liza's death depresses him, but no one doubts that his shoddy life will go on about as usual without her.

Tom, a young man of Liza's class whose love for her is honest. When her neighbors turn against Liza, Tom remains

faithful. Though knowing she is to bear Jim's child, he wants to marry her. His concern for her is the one genuinely kind emotion in the novel.

Sally, Liza's friend, who is typical of the lower class young girl who marries a brutish husband but has too much pride to disclose that he abuses her.

Mrs. Blakeston, Jim's wife, who gives Liza a fatal beating for stealing her husband.

THE LONG JOURNEY

Author: Johannes V. Jensen (1873-1950)
Time of action: The Age of Man
First published: 1923-1924

PRINCIPAL CHARACTERS

Fyr, a man living before the glacial age. He brings fire from a volcano and learns to use it for personal warmth, for cooking, and as a god. A band of human beings gathers about him, and he teaches them many primitive arts. Fyr is made a sacrifice to the fire god he created, and he is cooked and eaten by his people.

Carl, a typical man of the glacial age. An outcast for letting his tribe's fire go out, he flees to the north and learns to live with the cold, protecting himself against the elements in the early Stone Age.

Mam, Carl's mate, who brings new ideas, such as using vegetables for food and keeping a permanent home.

White Bear, a late Stone Age man. He becomes an outcast after killing a priest in a dispute over a woman. Becoming a builder of boats, he travels over the seas. He also learns to tame horses and use them with a chariot.

May, White Bear's mate. While her husband and son are at sea she and her

daughters take care of the crops and animals.

Wolf, White Bear's son. He learns how to sit astride a horse and becomes a nomad.

Norna Gest, a strange mortal who lives so long as he keeps a partially burned candle. He brings techniques of smelting and forging metals. He also becomes a wandering skald. He helps create a bronze bull to serve as an idol for the Jutlanders.

Gro, Norna Gest's mother.

Tole, a leader in Jutland who, with Norna Gest's help, casts a bronze idol.

Christopher Columbus, who is portrayed as carrying man's long journey from Europe to the West Indies.

Cortés, the European who defeats the Stone Age people of Mexico and thus extends man's journey from Europe to the American continent.

Charles Darwin, a modern man whose new weapon is science.

623

THE LONG NIGHT

Author: Andrew Lytle (1902-   )
Time of action: 1857-1862
First published: 1936

PRINCIPAL CHARACTERS

Lawrence McIvor, the narrator of Part 1; William McIvor's son to whom Pleasant McIvor, his uncle, tells a strange story of revenge and war.

Cameron (Cam) McIvor, his grandfather, an Alabama planter; good-natured except when drunk or angry, when he is dangerous and fearless. Having discovered Tyson Lovell's unscrupulous operations, he is murdered on Lovell's orders.

Pleasant, Cameron's favorite son; powerfully built, daring, wily, and determined avenger of his father's death. He kills off Lovell's gang one after another, first with aid, then by himself, until in the war he gives up his vengeance-seeking. He will kill no more—privately or as a soldier—and he deserts.

William, Pleasant's older brother. Tall, spare, quiet, and scholarly, he is different from the other McIvors. He dies of gangrene from war wounds.

Levi, Pleasant's younger brother and close companion. He dies after attending William in his illness.

Eli McIvor, Pleasant's uncle, killed at Shiloh.

Tyson Lovell, a wealthy landowner and leader of a gang of slave speculators and mule stealers. To get rid of Cameron he gets him declared an outlaw and then arranges his murder. Found by Pleasant two years later, he is knocked out with a pistol butt before Pleasant flees Lovell's trap.

Lieutenant Roswell Ellis, Pleasant's friend. He dies of wounds received in an action the danger of which had not

been reported by Pleasant, who had been busy seeking his private vengeance.

Albert Sydney Johnston, Confederate general killed at Shiloh.

Job Caruthers, a young bully shot to death by Cameron.

Mebane Caruthers, Job's twin, who helps him get revenge for a well-deserved beating by Cameron. Mebane is wounded by Cameron, brings suit, and almost ruins him financially.

Penter and
Jeems Wilton, brothers who, after a quarrel with Cameron, hold him in bed while he is killed. Penter is later dragged to death by his horse and Jeems is shot to death.

Fox, the murderer of Cameron.

Bob Pritchard, a McIvor kinsman and avenger trapped and killed by Botterall's posse.

Sheriff Lem Botterall, an enemy who is trampled to death by a wild stallion lashed by Pleasant.

Judge Lawson Wilton, a district attorney, Lovell's tool, killed after telling of the plot that resulted in Cameron's murder.

Armistead McIvor, Judge Wilton's killer. Armistead is later a Confederate colonel.

Dee Day and
Damon, two gang members stabbed to death by Pleasant.

Awsumb, a gang member stalked but not attacked by Pleasant, who decides he has had enough of vengeance.

624

THE LONGEST JOURNEY

Author: E. M. Forster (1879-   )
Time of action: Early twentieth century
First published: 1907

PRINCIPAL CHARACTERS

Frederick (Rickie) Elliot, a sensitive young man. After a childhood made lonely and unhappy by his lameness and the loveless relationship between his father and mother, he finds a certain contentment as a student at Cambridge. During his engagement to Agnes Pembroke he learns that Stephen Wonham is his half brother. When Rickie's marriage turns out to be an empty gesture, his flight with Stephen marks the beginning of his soul's regeneration, until he is killed in an effort to save Stephen's life.

Agnes Pembroke, Rickie Elliot's old friend, who marries him after the death of her fiancé, Gerald Dawes. She forces him into a dull and conventional life, but, finally, in her effort to alienate him from his half brother, Stephen Wonham, she loses him when he and Stephen go away together.

Herbert Pembroke, Agnes Pembroke's brother, with whom she and Rickie Elliot live after their marriage.

Stephen Wonham, Rickie Elliot's half brother. When he learns of his relationship to Rickie, he comes to him and Agnes hoping for love and a home, but he is refused both. Later he persuades Rickie to turn his back on Agnes' domination and go away with him.

Stewart Ansell, Rickie Elliot's Cambridge friend, who opposes his marriage to Agnes Pembroke and later persuades him to accept Stephen Wonham.

Mrs. Emily Failing, Rickie Elliot's domineering aunt.

Gerald Dawes, Agnes Pembroke's fiancé, who is killed before their marriage.

LOOK HOMEWARD, ANGEL

Author: Thomas Wolfe (1900-1938)
Time of action: 1900-early 1920's
First published: 1929

PRINCIPAL CHARACTERS

Eugene Gant, a shy, imaginative, awkward boy. The youngest child in a tumultuous family, with a wastrel father and a penny-pinching mother, he passes through childhood alone and misunderstood, for there is no family affection. He is precocious, with an insatiable appetite for books. He hates his mother's penuriousness, the family jealousies, and the waste of all their lives, yet is fascinated by the drunken magniloquence of his father. His salvation is the private school he is allowed to attend, for the Leonards, who operate it, develop and shape his mania for reading. At fifteen he enters the state university, where he is considered a freak although he does brilliantly in his studies. He has his first bitter love affair with Laura James during that summer. In his sophomore year he becomes something of a campus personality. The great tragedy of these years is the death of his brother Ben, who had loved him in his own strange abrupt fashion. Just before he leaves for Harvard for graduate study, his brother Luke asks him to sign a release of his future inheritance on the excuse that he has had his share of their parents' estate in extra schooling. Knowing that he is being tricked by his grasping and jealous family, he signs so that he can break away from them forever.

Oliver Gant, his father, a stonecutter from Pennsylvania who has wandered to North Carolina and married there. Hating his wife and her miserly attitude, he is drunken and promiscuous, yet fascinating to his children because of his wild generosities and his alcoholic rhetoric. He is the exact opposite of his wife: she has an overpowering urge to acquire property and he wants none of it. He will not go with her when she moves to another house so that she can take in boarders. Their entire marriage has been an unending war, but she wins at last, for his failing health forces him to live with her.

Eliza Gant, Oliver's wife and Eugene's mother, the daughter of a family named Pentland from the mountains. They have all grown prosperous through financial acumen and native thrift. Eliza has an instinctive feeling for the future value of real estate and an almost insane penuriousness; she acquires land until she is a wealthy woman. She alienates Eugene by the stinginess which will never allow her to enjoy the money that she has accumulated. She is rock-like in her immobility, absorbed in her passion for money and her endless, involved reminiscences.

Ben Gant, their son, silent and withdrawn, yet capable of deep affection for Eugene. He dies of pneumonia because his mother will not call a reliable doctor in time. His is a wasted life, for he was endowed with potentialities that were never realized.

Steve Gant, another son. He is a braggart and wastrel, with all of his father's worst qualities but none of his charm.

Luke Gant, another son. He is a comic figure, stuttering, generous, and ineffectual.

Helen Gant, a daughter. She has her father's expansive nature and takes his side against her mother. She is the only member of the family who can handle Gant when he is drunk.

Daisy Gant, another daughter. She is a pretty but colorless girl who plays little part in the family drama.

Margaret Leonard, wife of the principal of the private school that Eugene attends. She directs his haphazard reading so as to develop the best in his mind; she really takes the place of the mother who has had no time for him.

Laura James, a young girl five years older than Eugene, who is spending the summer at Eliza's boarding house. Eugene falls in love with her and she with him. But when she returns home, she writes that she is to marry a man to whom she has been engaged for a year.

LOOKING BACKWARD

Author: Edward Bellamy (1850-1898)
Time of action: A.D. 2000
First published: 1888

PRINCIPAL CHARACTERS

Julian West, a young Bostonian who, sleeping under hypnosis in his sound-proofed cellar, goes forward into the year 2000 to find himself in a socialistic United States where government controls everything and everyone is happy, healthy, and well-off. Julian is delighted with this new world and falls in love with a young woman of the time. They marry and plan a secure, happy life in the twenty-first century.

Dr. Leete, Julian's host in the year 2000. He is a doctor who, like everyone else at the time, has retired at forty-five. He likes Julian and enjoys telling him of and showing him the brave new world of the year 2000.

Edith Leete, the great-granddaughter of Julian's nineteenth century sweetheart. She falls in love with Julian through the love letters he wrote to his sweetheart in the 1880's. She readily agrees to marry

Julian, who has found security as a college lecturer in history.

Edith Bartlett, Julian's sweetheart in the nineteenth century. She saved his letters and passed them on to posterity after his mysterious disappearance.

Dr. Pillsbury, a quack who performs the hypnosis that allows Julian to sleep from 1887 to 2000. He administers the treatment to relieve the young man's chronic insomnia.

Mr. Bartlett, Edith Bartlett's father and Julian's host during his last evening spent in the year 1887.

LORD JIM

Author: Joseph Conrad (Józef Teodor Konrad Korzeniowski, 1857-1924)
Time of action: Late nineteenth century
First published: 1900

PRINCIPAL CHARACTERS

Jim, a British seaman and chief mate of the "Patna." When the ship seems sinking, after striking a submerged derelict, he jumps at the call of the officers who have already abandoned the ship and her pilgrim passengers. The "Patna" does not sink but is discovered by a French gunboat and towed to port. Jim and his three companions are sighted and brought to port separately. After the investigation Jim spends the remainder of his life trying to regain his heroic conception of himself and to prove to men that it was not "he" who jumped. Finally, on the island of Patusan, he earns from the natives the title of Lord Jim and faces up to his death in a heroic manner.

Marlow, an intelligent sea captain and "insatiably curious psychological observer" who sympathizes with Jim and aids him. Narrating most of the story, he says Jim is "one of us," meaning, per-

haps, that he is neither maliciously evil nor moderately good.

Captain Brierly, the "unimpeachable professional seaman" and a nautical assessor at the inquiry into the desertion of the "Patna." He identifies himself with Jim in some strange way. Awakened to man's vulnerability, perhaps, he commits suicide on his next voyage.

The French Lieutenant, an unimaginatively brave man who stays aboard the "Patna" for thirty hours while she is being towed to port. He never thinks that he has been heroic.

Stein, a trader who is also a naturalist and a moral philosopher. He gives Jim a chance to have his dream of rehabilitation come true by making him the agent for his enterprises on the island of Patusan.

Chester, a loathsome creature who has

627

been everything but a pirate. He offers Jim a job which would exile him on a guano island for life because, as he says, Jim "is no earthly good for anything else." He mistakes Jim for one of his own kind.

Cornelius, the former unsuccessful agent for Stein on Patusan. He resents Jim and finally aids Brown in causing Jim's destruction.

Gentleman Brown, a renegade who with a cutthroat crew lands on Patusan to get supplies, but remains to rob and plunder. In sympathy, not understanding Brown's deceit, Jim makes a pact with him. Brown's deception results in Jim's death.

Doramin, the leader of Patusan natives with whom Jim makes friends, earning the title of Lord Jim. When Doramin's son is killed because of Jim's misjudgment, Doramin is bound by honor to kill Jim.

Dain Waris, Doramin's son and Jim's friend, killed treacherously by Brown. By his error in judgment Jim is responsible for his friend's death.

The Rajah, the ruler of the natives on Patusan; he unsuccessfully opposes Jim.

Tamb' Itam, the faithful servant of Jim on Patusan.

Kossim, the confidant of the Rajah.

Sherif Ali, a wandering stranger, an Arab half-breed, who invites tribes from the interior to form a third force on Patusan.

The Captain, the German skipper of the "Patna," who abandoned his ship and its load of passengers without remorse.

The Chief Engineer, who swears that he saw the ship go down.

The Second Engineer, who also seems to have no remorse for abandoning the ship.

Captain O'Brien, a large, noisy old man who says that abandoning the "Patna" was a disgrace.

Captain Jones, the first mate serving under Captain Brierly. He finds it hard to explain Brierly's suicide, all the more because he did not like Brierly while the man was alive.

Captain Robinson, an old renegade who has done almost everything from opium smuggling to stealing. Chester takes him in on the guano deal because Robinson has some money.

Jewel, Jim's native wife on Patusan. She finds it difficult to understand his ideals.

LORNA DOONE

Author: R. D. Blackmore (1825-1900)
Time of action: Late seventeenth century
First published: 1869

PRINCIPAL CHARACTERS

John Ridd, the narrator and courageous hero of this novel set in seventeenth century England. His hatred of the outlaw Doone clan is at variance with his love for beautiful Lorna Doone. At last, after many adventures, including the vanquishing of the Doones, he marries Lorna.

Sir Ensor Doone, the head of the Doone clan, loved by Lorna. Dying, he gives his blessing to her and John Ridd.

Lorna Doone, Sir Ensor's ward. Captured by the Doones when a small child, she turns out to be an heiress, Lady Dugal. In love with John Ridd and hating the savage members of the Doone clan, she bravely resists the Doones' tyrannical efforts to marry her to Carver Doone.

Carver Doone, Sir Ensor's son and the most villainous of the Doones. The actual murderer of John Ridd's father, he is finally slain by John.

Annie Ridd, John's sister.

Tom Faggus, a highwayman and John Ridd's cousin. Annie's love for Tom involves John in his concerns, almost resulting in John's execution.

Jeremy Stickles, the King's messenger. Saved by John Ridd from death at the hands of the Doones, he is later able to rescue John from execution.

Reuben Huckaback, John Ridd's great-uncle, who is also a victim of robbery by the Doones.

Ruth, the granddaughter of Huckaback, who wants John Ridd to marry her.

John Fry, who, at the start of the novel, is sent to bring John Ridd home from school. Returning, they discover that the Doones have murdered John Ridd's father.

Lord Alan Brandir, Lorna's relative, whose brutal murder by Carver Doone is instrumental in causing her to hate the clan.

LOST HORIZON

Author: James Hilton (1900-1954)
Time of action: 1931
First published: 1933

PRINCIPAL CHARACTERS

Hugh Conway, a charming, brilliant man—tall, bronzed, with short brown hair and blue eyes—who is a veteran of ten years of unspectacular work in the British Consular Service. He is found by his friend Rutherford in a mission hospital suffering from fatigue. He relates how he was kidnaped and flown to Shangri-La, a peaceful lamasery in the high Himalayas, where the ancient and wise High Lama hoped to preserve a record of the culture of Western civilization against the total destruction of modern warfare. When the aged High Lama knew he was about to die, he asked Conway to succeed him as High Lama. Though tempted to accept, Conway decided it was his duty to accompany his kidnaped companions back to civilization when the opportunity to leave arose. Before Rutherford hears the rest of the story, Conway disappears from the hospital, apparently drawn back to the tranquility of Shangri-La.

Rutherford, his friend and former schoolmate who finds Conway suffering from fatigue and amnesia in a mission hospital in China.

Henry Barnard, a large, fleshy man with a hard-bitten face who is wanted for fraud and embezzlement in the United States. He is satisfied to stay in Shangri-La and enjoy the pleasant life there.

Miss Roberta Brinklow, a missionary, neither young nor pretty, who plans to convert the lamas and the tribesmen in the valley of Shangri-La.

Captain Mallison, another British consul, young, pink-cheeked, intelligent, excitable. He is anxious to leave Shangri-La and turn Barnard over to British authorities, and is later insistent upon taking Lo-Tsen with him. Rutherford is unable to learn what happened to Mallison.

Chang, a Chinese lama who meets Conway and his friends near their wrecked plane and conducts them to Shangri-La.

Father Perrault, the High Lama, a very intelligent, scholarly man two hundred and fifty years old. Formerly a Capuchin friar, he adopts the Buddhist faith and establishes the lamasery of Shangri-La. He adds guests from time to time but permits none to leave.

Lo-Tsen, a beautiful Chinese girl with whom Mallison falls in love and who accompanies Conway and Mallison when they leave Shangri-La. In reality sixty-five years old, she quickly loses her youth and beauty outside the charmed lamasery and becomes a bent, withered old woman. She brings Conway to the mission hospital.

Briac, a Frenchman who was once a pupil of Chopin and who plays for Conway some unpublished music of Chopin.

LOST ILLUSIONS

Author: Honoré de Balzac (1799-1850)
Time of action: Early nineteenth century
First published: 1837-1843

PRINCIPAL CHARACTERS

David Séchard (dȧ·vēd′ sā·shȧr′), a naïve printer who is the victim of knavery throughout his life. Even his avaricious father cheats him when he sells the son his business. David's friendship for Lucien Chardon, his brother-in-law, also costs him a great deal. David spends his time working on a new process for making paper and eventually loses his business. All turns out well in the end, as Lucien Chardon sends him a large sum of money and David's father dies leaving him well off.

Lucien Chardon (lü·syěn′ shȧr·dōn′), an unscrupulous but attractive poet, David's brother-in-law. His escapades help to disgrace his sister and her husband and to ruin them financially for a time. After an affair with an aristocratic woman, which ends in his being found in her bedroom, he goes to Paris to lead a dissolute life as a journalist and man about town, living at the expense of David and Eve and an actress who is his mistress.

Eve Chardon (ěv shȧr·dōn′), Lucien's sister, who marries David Séchard. She lavishes love and money on her scapegrace brother. After her husband becomes involved with his paper process, she tries vainly to save his printing business by taking over its management.

Mme. de Bargeton (də bȧr·zhə·tōn′), Lucien's first mistress. When her affair with him is discovered, she takes him to Paris, where later she leaves him penniless. She becomes eventually the wife of the Comte du Châtelet.

M. de Bargeton (bȧr·zhə·tōn′), elderly first husband of Mme. Bargeton. Despite his age, he fights a duel in defense of his wife's honor.

M. Petit-Claud (pə·tē′-klō′), an unscrupulous lawyer who helps David's business rivals, even though David is his client.

The Cointet Brothers (kwěn·tā′), David's business rivals in the printing business. They cheat him out of his paper-making invention and his print shop.

Coralie, an actress who becomes Lucien's mistress.

M. Séchard (sā·shȧr′), David's avaricious

630

father. He refuses to help his son financially to keep him out of debtors' prison.

A Spanish Priest, who hires Lucien to act
as a front in his unscrupulous dealings.

A LOST LADY

Author: Willa Cather (1873-1947)
Time of action: Late nineteenth and early twentieth centuries
First published: 1923

PRINCIPAL CHARACTERS

Marian Forrester, the charming, lovely
wife of Captain Daniel Forrester, a contractor during the great railroad-building
period in the West. She is shown first in
her home in Sweet Water, Colorado,
where she sheds the warm radiance of
her personality on all about her, from
the railway and mining aristocracy who
come visiting in their private cars to the
village boys who go fishing in the creek
running through the Forrester property.
One of these is Niel Herbert, an impressionable adolescent through whose eyes,
as he grows in years and understanding,
the story of her decline is presented. The
flaw in Mrs. Forrester's character is the
fact that she possesses no inner resources
of her own. As long as she can draw on
her husband's quiet strength, she is her
gay, gracious self. But when a series of
misfortunes strike the old railroader—a
fall from a horse, a bank failure, a crippling stroke—she finds herself tied to a
semi-invalid, trapped in a dwindling
community no longer important on the
Burlington line, and she becomes desperate. Unable to face neglect or hardship, she finds escape in love affairs and
drink, and in the end surrenders herself
as well as her business affairs to Ivy
Peters, an unscrupulous shyster lawyer of
the new generation in the West. Eventually Niel Herbert hears that she has
died in the Argentine as the wife of an
English rancher named Henry Collins.
Mrs. Forrester is one of Willa Cather's
most complex characters, a figure requiring great insight and skill to reveal clearly
the reasons for her degradation and the
contradictory, ambiguous elements in her
nature that make her both a woman of
grace and poise and a person capable
of coarseness and lust in her pursuit of
virile younger men. The picture of her
deterioration is linked subtly with the
declining importance of Sweet Water as
a frontier town and the passing of the
old West into a newer and less heroic
age.

Captain Daniel Forrester, a builder whose
great dream had been to see the railroads
spanning the continent. A reserved, silent
man, he has been a doer rather than a
sayer, as unimpeachable in his honor as
he is punctilious in courtesy. After a fall
from his horse he retires to his Sweet
Water home with his younger wife.
When a Denver bank fails, he assumes
a moral obligation and uses his private
fortune to satisfy its depositors. A short
time later he suffers a stroke from which
he never fully recovers. Courteous, considerate, honorable, he never reveals his
knowledge of his wife's infidelities. His
death leaves her finally lost without his
patience and strength to sustain her
bright but brittle charm. The passing of
Captain Forrester shows a way of life
that was once great and spacious giving
place to a new way that is tawdry, petty,
and crude.

Niel Herbert, the sensitive, perceptive
young man from whose point of view
much of Mrs. Forrester's story is presented. His attitude toward her is one of
boyish adoration until he accidentally
learns of her affair with Frank Ellinger.
As he grows older he thinks of her more

631

and more in relation to her husband, the dignified, noble old man whom he sees as the embodiment of the imagination and enterprise that went into the building of the West. After reading law for a time in his uncle's office, Niel eventually goes East to study architecture at the Massachusetts Institute of Technology.

Francis Bosworth Ellinger, called **Frank,** a bachelor of forty with a reputation for being fast and dangerous; he had on one occasion driven publicly through Denver with a pretty prostitute. He is a frequent visitor at the Forrester home. During one of these visits, while Captain Forrester is in Denver, Niel Herbert goes out early in the morning to pick a bunch of wild roses for Mrs. Forrester. As he is about to put them outside the French window of her bedroom, he hears Frank's voice inside. Niel's discovery that she has a lover ends his admiration for Mrs. Forrester and his loyalty to an ideal, though she continues to fascinate and puzzle him. Mrs. Forrester becomes hysterical when she reads the account of Frank's marriage to Constance Ogden, and she creates a town scandal by attempting to telephone him while he is on his honeymoon.

Ivy Peters, so nicknamed because of his red, puffy skin, a shrewd, ruthless young man who gets ahead in the world by carrying on a tricky law practice. He becomes Mrs. Forrester's lover and persuades her to turn her business affairs over to him; and he eventually comes into possession of the Forrester home. He represents the new generation, taking the profits without any of the risks, despised by Judge Pommeroy.

Judge Pommeroy, Niel Herbert's uncle. When Niel's father decides to leave Sweet Water for work in Denver, the boy remains behind to read law in his uncle's office. The Judge has been Captain Forrester's friend for twenty years and has attended to all his business affairs, since the Captain's illness without a fee. After her husband's death Mrs. Forrester sends an order asking him to turn all money and securities over to Ivy Peters and to give an account of his transactions. Judge Pommeroy is hurt and offended.

Constance Ogden, a rather pretty but spoiled and determined young woman who wants to marry Frank Ellinger and does so, with her mother's clever assistance.

Orville Ogden, a businessman from Denver and Captain Forrester's friend. After the Captain's death he is concerned for Mrs. Forrester's future when he stops over in Sweet Water and learns that she is no longer Judge Pommeroy's client.

Mrs. Ogden, his homely, affected, but shrewd wife. Her concern is to get her daughter Constance married.

THE LOST WEEKEND

Author: Charles Jackson (1903-   )
Time of action: Twentieth century
First published: 1944

PRINCIPAL CHARACTERS

Don Birnam, an unsuccessful writer who becomes an alcoholic. Even though his friends and relatives try to help him, he has no wish to overcome his alcoholism. When sent to a rest farm for a cure he manages to find liquor there. He is left alone one weekend and to get liquor he takes the housekeeper's money, tries to steal a purse in a restaurant, and finally manages to borrow some money. He is hospitalized for a few hours; upon his release he immediately goes to get more whiskey to satisfy his need.

Wick Birnam, Don's brother. He tries to help Don break away from alcohol in every way he can. Wick is spending a weekend in the country when his brother has his nightmarish experiences.

Helen, Don's friend, who tries with Wick to help the alcoholic. She even takes Don to her apartment. When she does, he steals her fur coat and pawns it for a few dollars for whiskey.

Gloria, a hostess at Sam's Bar. She agrees to go on a date with Don after he tells her a fiction about having a frigid wife and several children. He forgets the appointment.

Bim, a male nurse in the alcoholic ward of a hospital where Don is taken after he loses consciousness.

LOVE FOR LOVE

Author: William Congreve (1670-1729)
Time of action: Seventeenth century
First presented: 1695

PRINCIPAL CHARACTERS

Valentine Legend, a young would-be playwright. He loves Angelica. He is also in debt, having wasted his money in high living. Though he falls into disfavor with his father, Sir Sampson Legend, he redeems himself and eventually marries Angelica.

Sir Sampson Legend, who decides to disinherit his son Valentine, a wastrel. His plan fails when Valentine feigns madness.

Angelica, a beautiful young woman loved by Valentine. She is both wealthy and clever. Loving Valentine, she puts up with his temporary faults and finally marries him.

Jeremy, Valentine's clever but knavish servant.

Trapland, a lecherous elderly scrivener, one of Valentine's creditors.

Scandal, Valentine's friend. He plays upon Foresight's belief in astrology to prevent a marriage between Ben Legend and Prue Foresight. He also flirts with Mrs. Foresight, a young woman married to an old man.

Ben Legend, Valentine's young brother, who stands to inherit Sir Sampson's estate if Valentine is cut off.

Foresight, a foolish old man who believes in astrology and has a young wife. He is Angelica's uncle. He finds at last that he is really an old fool and admits it.

Prue, Foresight's countrified daughter. She dislikes Ben, whom her father wants her to marry. Though she is fascinated by Tattle, who almost succeeds in seducing her, she ends up by wanting to marry Robin, a butler.

Mrs. Foresight, Foresight's young, flirtatious wife.

Mistress Frail, Mrs. Foresight's sister. She wants to marry a rich man, but she is finally tricked into marrying Tattle.

Tattle, a talkative young dandy. He is tricked into marrying Mistress Frail.

Buckram, a lawyer working for Sir Sampson.

Robin, a butler, in love with Prue.

633

LOVE IN A WOOD

Author: William Wycherley (1640-1716)
Time of action: Seventeenth century
First presented: 1671

PRINCIPAL CHARACTERS

Lady Flippant, a widow in search of a husband. Though temporarily enamored of Mr. Dapperwit, to whom she makes advances, she has her eye on Sir Simon Addleplot, whom she intends all along to marry and finally does.

Alderman Gripe, an elderly usurer, Lady Flippant's brother. Enamored of Lucy, he is brought to her by Mrs. Joyner. He frightens the girl with his hasty attentions and is forced to pay five hundred pounds in hush money to her mother, Mrs. Crossbite. He later marries Lucy to get even with his son-in-law, Dapperwit.

Mr. Dapperwit, a witless fop. Enamored of Lucy, he is tricked into marrying the six-months-pregnant Mistress Martha.

Mistress Martha, Alderman Gripe's daughter. Finding herself six-months pregnant, she succeeds in marrying Dapperwit.

Lucy, Mrs. Crossbite's daughter, who is in love with Dapperwit. She is married to Alderman Gripe in revenge for Dapperwit's marriage to his daughter, Mistress Martha.

Sir Simon Addleplot, a fortune hunter. In pursuit of Mistress Martha, he must finally be satisfied with Lady Flippant.

Mrs. Crossbite, a procuress and Lucy's mother. She blackmails Alderman Gripe and maneuvers him into marrying her daughter.

Mrs. Joyner, a matchmaker and procuress engaged in finding a husband for Mrs. Flippant, in finding a wife for Sir Simon Addleplot, and in procuring Lucy for Alderman Gripe.

Mr. Ranger, a young man about town engaged to Lydia.

Mr. Vincent, Mr. Ranger's friend and confidant.

Lydia, Mr. Ranger's cousin and his betrothed.

Mr. Valentine, a young gallant betrothed to Christina.

Christina, a young woman in love with Mr. Valentine.

LOVE'S LABOUR'S LOST

Author: William Shakespeare (1564-1616)
Time of action: Sixteenth century
First presented: 1595

PRINCIPAL CHARACTERS

Berowne (bĕ·rōōn), a witty, sophisticated young lord in the court of King Ferdinand of Navarre. Although he joins his monarch's idealistic academy, he warns his companions of the folly of study for its own sake and advises them to seek

wisdom in the contemplation of feminine beauty. He delights in words, exchanging puns and rhymes with his friends and waxing rhapsodic when he falls in love. He meets his match in Rosaline and swears that he will henceforth woo with "rustic yeas and honest kersey noes." She orders him to temper his ironic wit with sympathy; he must spend the next year jesting in hospitals.

Rosaline (rŏz'ə·lĭn), one of the charming ladies in waiting to the Princess of France. Clever and sparkling, she whets her mind in verbal battles with Boyet and spars endlessly with Berowne, who is continually overcome by her wit. She is the first of Shakespeare's bright, confident heroines, the prototype for Beatrice, Viola, Portia, and Rosalind.

Ferdinand, King of Navarre, an idealistic young ruler who intends to win everlasting fame by establishing a Platonic academy devoted to study and ascetic living. The appearance of the Princess of France on a diplomatic mission quickly disperses his noble goals as he and his lords promptly fall in love and turn their attention to sonnets, masques, and gifts. Brought suddenly to earth by the news of the death of the Princess' father, he affirms the seriousness of his love and promises to spend a year in a hermitage, as his lady requests, to prove the depth of his affection.

The Princess of France, a dignified young woman who remains aware of her serious responsibilities while she delights in jesting with Boyet, her ladies, and the hunters, and in teasing the lovesick lords.

Longaville (lŏng'gə·vĭl) and
Dumaine (dū·mān'), Ferdinand's courtiers. They fall in love with Katharine and Maria when their king succumbs to the charms of the girls' mistress, the Princess. Both are quick-witted young men and eloquently poetic lovers, a little bewildered by the wit and independence of their ladies.

Katharine (kăth'ə·rĭn) and
Maria (mä·rē'ə), the Princess' ladies, who gleefully torment their lovers with endless repartee, although they admit their romantic inclinations within their own circle.

Boyet (boi·ĕt'), a sharp-tongued courtier who accompanies the Princess to Navarre and passes his time exchanging bawdy quips with her ladies.

Don Adriano de Armado (ä·drē·ä'nō dä är·mä'dō), a boastful Spanish soldier, a descendant of the braggart of the "commedia dell'arte" productions. He fancies himself a gallant courtier and amuses the lords and ladies with his fantastic phraseology and his elaborate dress which only temporarily hides the fact that he is too poor to own a shirt. He embroiders his affair with the country wench, Jaquenetta, and almost convinces himself that it is a "grande amour" in the tradition of King Cophetua and the Beggar Maid of the old ballads.

Costard (kŏs'tərd), a rustic clown. He is fascinated by all the extravagant language he hears and takes great pleasure in using the long words of Armado and Berowne and the Latinisms of Holofernes and Sir Nathaniel.

Moth (mŏth), Don Adriano's impudent page, who impishly taunts his master.

Holofernes (hŏl·ə·fûr'nēz), the village schoolmaster, an incurable pedant. He prides himself on the excellence of his Latin and the precison of his pronunciation.

Sir Nathaniel, the curate, who admires Holofernes and joins him in snubbing their less learned fellow citizens, such as Costard and Dull, for their ignorance.

Dull, the constable, a worthy predecessor of Dogberry and Verges. He can make no sense of the Latinate effusions of Holofernes and Sir Nathaniel and clings to his facts: " 'Twas not a 'haud credo,' 'twas a pricket."

Jaquenetta (jăk'ə·nĕt'ə), a country girl who is much admired by Don Adriano.

LOVING

Author: Henry Green (Henry Vincent York, 1905-   )
Time of action: World War II
First published: 1945

PRINCIPAL CHARACTERS

Mrs. Tennant, the owner of a mansion in Eire. She is a vague woman. Though she loses a valuable ring, she does not blame her servants, for she realizes she is forgetful.

Charley Raunce, Mrs. Tennant's English footman who aspires to be the butler. Immediately upon the death of old Eldon, the long-time butler, Raunce acquires the household account book, secures Mrs. Tennant's agreement, and assumes the butler's authority in the servants' quarters. He loves Edith, one of the maids, and finds that she loves him too. He is content to remain in Eire, safe from service in World War II, until he realizes he is missing out on the excitement and satisfaction of aiding in the war effort by staying in Ireland. He decides to return to England, and he and Edith elope.

Edith, an upstairs maid in love with Raunce. It is she who twice finds Mrs. Tennant's ring and sees to its return. She elopes with Raunce to England.

Kate, another upstairs maid.

Mrs. Burch, the caustic housekeeper, in charge of Edith and Kate.

Mrs. Jack Tennant, Mrs. Tennant's daughter-in-law. Her love affair with Captain Davenport scandalizes the servants' quarters.

Captain Davenport, one of Mrs. Tennant's neighbors. He is found one morning by Edith in bed with Mrs. Jack Tennant.

Albert, Raunce's assistant. He leaves Mrs. Tennant's service because he thinks his employer suspects he might have stolen the ring that disappears. He returns to England and becomes an aerial gunner.

Jack Tennant, Mrs. Tennant's son on military duty in England. When his mother and wife leave Ireland to visit him, the servants are upset at being left on their own in the mansion and almost desert their duties.

THE LOWER DEPTHS

Author: Maxim Gorky (Aleksei Maksimovich Peshkov, 1868-1936)
Time of action: Late nineteenth century
First presented: 1902

PRINCIPAL CHARACTERS

Mikhail Kostilyoff (mĭ·hä·ĭl′ kôs·tĭ·lyôf′), the greedy and corrupt landlord of the flophouse in which the characters live and the action takes place. Suspicious of his wife, he trails her constantly. A superstitious hypocrite, he says pious platitudes and then raises the rent on Kleshtch, an impoverished tenant. He cowers before Pepel, to whom he owes

money for stolen goods, and he bullies his sister-in-law, Natasha. No one misses him in the slightest when he is killed during a brawl.

Vassilisa Karpovna (vä·sĭ·lĭ′sə kär·pōv′nə), his wife, a malicious shrew who cockolds Kostilyoff in an affair with Pepel. Plotting her husband's death, she tries to involve Pepel by offering him Natasha. She is intensely jealous of Natasha, however, and whips the girl at every opportunity. When her husband is killed, Vassilisa readily turns Pepel over to the police, but both Pepel and Natasha accuse her of complicity in the crime and she sits in jail as the play closes.

Natasha (nä·tä′shə), Vassilisa's sister, a decent, pretty girl who is little more than a servant in Kostilyoff's flophouse. She yearns for dignity but despairs at her hopeless position. When Pepel offers to take her away, she is hesitant. Natasha later gets the impression that Kostilyoff's death was premeditated by Pepel, and she goes into a fit of hysterics. She disappears after her release from the hospital where she was taken after being beaten by Vassilisa.

Vaska Pepel (väs′kə pě′pěl), called **Vassily**, a young thief burdened by his past and his relationship with Vassilisa. He hopes to overcome his squalor by a new life with Natasha. Vaska is clever and spirited, and though he rejects Vassilisa's murderous proposal his good qualities come to nothing when he angrily knocks Kostilyoff down during a brawl that starts after Vassilisa savagely beats Natasha.

Luka (lōō′kə), an old traveler without a passport. A gentle, compassionate liar, he comforts the others by subscribing to their pathetic dreams of wholeness and dignity. Recognizing the savagery of truth, Luka prefers the misleading aspects of the imagination. In some measure everyone is touched by his presence but few are changed by it. In the confusion that surrounds Kostilyoff's death Luka disappears.

Satine (sä·tǐn′), a cynical young cardsharp and jailbird. At once shrewd and easy-going, Satine provides the final comment on Luka's personality and influence. Men like Luka, he says, are significant only because people are weak and

need lies; nevertheless, he admits that Luka served as a kind of purgative.

Andrei Kleshtch (an·drā′ klěshch), a down-and-out locksmith who holds his fellows in contempt. Unable to bear his wife's dying, he goes out to get drunk. After her death he succumbs to fits of anger and torpor, but he ends by achieving fellowship with the other tenants.

Anna Kleshtch (än′nä klěshch), his wife. On the verge of death, she cannot accept the notion of a just afterlife. Luka tries to comfort her before she dies.

The Actor, a nameless, alcoholic, and verbose man who dreams of taking the cure. He gets encouragement from Luka, but after Luka disappears he is unable to maintain his self-respect. In the end he hangs himself.

The Baron, a poseur and cardsharp who pathetically boasts of his family's past wealth and nobility. He obtains satisfaction by ridiculing the dreams of Nastya, the prostitute who supports him.

Nastya (nä′styä), a prostitute who reads sentimentally romantic novels, wishes for a fatal love affair, respects Luka's compassion, and adds to the general bickering in the tenement.

Bubnoff (bŏŏb·nŏf′), an ill-natured capmaker, ignorant and sardonic, who has made a place for himself in the loose comraderie of the flophouse.

Abram Miedviedieff (ä·bräm′ měd·vě′-děf), Vassilisa's uncle, a mediocre, seedily respectable policeman who pesters Luka about his passport, hopes to arrest Vaska Pepel for thievery, and explains away such matters as the gossip about Vassilisa and Vaska, Kostilyoff's activities as a receiver of stolen goods, and Vassilisa's cruel treatment of Natasha by saying that these are family affairs. He leaves the police and takes to drink after his marriage to Kvashnya, a street vendor.

Kvashnya (kvä·shnyä), a sharp-tongued,

boisterous seller of dumplings and meat pies. In her rough way she is kind to Anna and tries to give food to the dying woman. Although she claims that she was overjoyed when her first husband died and that she will not be bothered with another, she marries Miedviedieff, the policeman, and bullies him with tongue-lashings and beatings.

Alyoshka (a·lyōō'shkä), a reckless, happy-go-lucky young shoemaker. When he is drunk he lies down in the middle of the street and plays gay tunes on his concertina.

Hassan (häs'ɔn), a Tartar porter. His hand is crushed while he is at work, and he is afraid that amputation may be necessary.

Krivoy Zob (krĭ·voi' zōb), Hassan's friend and fellow porter.

LOYALTIES

Author: John Galsworthy (1867-1933)
Time of action: Early 1920's
First presented: 1922

PRINCIPAL CHARACTERS

Captain Ronald Dancy, D.S.O., retired, an officer who thrived on the excitement of war and languishes on the placidity of peace. After creating his own excitement, with horses and women, he gets himself into trouble by stealing some money from a house guest while he himself is a guest. His friends stand by him against the accusation of the man who has lost the money. In the end, however, it is clear that he is guilty. When the police come to arrest him, he goes to his room and shoots himself.

Ferdinand de Levis, a prosperous Jew who has risen to wealth by degrees, having started very modestly. He sells for a thousand pounds a horse Dancy has given him, and Dancy steals the money. De Levis is unpopular with the set at the house where he and Dancy are guests. He shows poor form by openly accusing Dancy of theft before his friends. When Dancy drops his suit for defamation of character against de Levis, the latter is willing to let bygones be bygones.

Mabel Dancy, Dancy's wife, who is loyal to him even after she discovers he is a thief.

Jacob Twisden, Dancy's attorney, who is tough and straightforward. He discovers that Dancy did indeed take the money and advises him to drop his suit against de Levis.

Charles Winsor, Dancy's and de Levis' host at Winsor's home, Meldon Court, where the theft takes place.

Paolio Ricardos, an Italian wine merchant whose daughter has been intimate with Dancy. Ricardos threatens to expose Dancy if he does not provide for the daughter. In order to have money to pay Ricardos, Dancy steals the thousand pounds from de Levis.

General Canynge, Dancy's superior officer. When it becomes apparent that Dancy has stolen the money, he offers Dancy a billet in the Spanish war.

638

LUCIEN LEUWEN

Author: Stendhal (Marie-Henri Beyle, 1783-1842)
Time of action: The 1830's
First published: 1894

PRINCIPAL CHARACTERS

Lucien Leuwen (lü·syăń' lœ·vĕn'), the son of a rich banker and the hero of this unfinished novel, which is set in France after the revolution of 1830. Expelled from school for expressing mild republican leanings, he becomes an officer in a regiment of lancers going to maintain order at Nancy. There he falls in love with a wealthy, aristocratic widow, but is tricked into leaving her. Obtaining a government post in Paris through his father's influence, he is successful until disillusioned because of a love affair. On his father's death, he insists on full payment to creditors and salvages only a modest income for himself and his mother. Given an embassy appointment, he is only mildly melancholy for his lost love.

Bathilde de Chasteller (bá·tēld' də shá·stě·yā'), a beautiful, aristocratic widow of Nancy and Lucien's true love. The aristocratic young men of the town are afraid that he will marry her and take her and her money away.

Dr. du Poirier (dü pwá·ryā'), a physician and the leader of the monarchist set in Nancy. He tricks Lucien into leaving Bathilde by making him think that her several days' illness is confinement to childbed.

Monsieur Leuwen (mə·syœ' lœ·vĕn'), Lucien's father. Charming and wealthy, he is ambitious both for his son and for himself. Powerful enough to dictate who shall be in the Cabinet, he arranges to have a fatuous man given a post in exchange for his wife's becoming Lucien's mistress.

Madame Grandet (grän·dā'), a beautiful and ambitious woman. "Bought" for Lucien, she comes to love him. Learning the truth, however, he is greatly upset and leaves Paris.

THE LUSIAD

Author: Luis Vaz de Camoëns (1524?-1580)
Time of action: Fifteenth century
First published: 1572

PRINCIPAL CHARACTERS

Vasco da Gama, famed Portuguese sailor and explorer. He is chosen to head the expedition which first rounds Africa's Cape of Good Hope to find a sea route to Asia.

Jove, chief of the gods. He announces that the Fates have decreed that the Portuguese expedition shall succeed in its mission.

Venus, a goddess friendly to the Portu-guese. She takes their side against Bacchus and helps them in their adventures. She saves them from storms and ambushes and provides them with a resting place on their way home. She gives da Gama a vision of Portugal's future greatness.

Mars, a god who sides with Venus for the Portuguese.

Bacchus, the patron-god of Asia. He tries

639

to prevent the Portuguese from success in their expedition. He enlists the aid of Neptune in his efforts against them.

Veloso, one of da Gama's men. He explores part of Africa before rejoining the expedition.

The Spirit of the Cape of Good Hope, who appears to da Gama. The spirit says he was once a Titan named Adamastor. He has been made into a range of mountains forming the Cape of Good Hope for his pursuit of a nymph.

The King of Mombassa, an African monarch to whom da Gama relates his ad-

ventures and the history of Portugal up to that time.

The Emperor of Malabar, an Asiatic monarch who welcomes the Portuguese to Asia and arranges for them to trade their good for spices and other Oriental products.

Mercury, a god who guides the Portuguese to Mombassa.

Neptune, god of the sea who, at the request of Bacchus, sends storms to destroy the ships of the Portuguese. Venus saves them, however.

LYSISTRATA

Author: Aristophanes (c. 448-c. 385 B.C.)
Time of action: The period of the Peloponnesian War
First presented: 411 B.C.

PRINCIPAL CHARACTERS

Lysistrata (lī·sĭs'trə·tə), an idealistic Athenian woman who is not content to stand submissively by and witness the obvious wastes war brings to the land. In her effort to bring a permanent peace to Greece, she demonstrates qualities that mark her as one of the archetypal revolutionaries because of her relentless fervor, cunning, and intractability. In addition to the traits of a revolutionary, Lysistrata possesses a healthy supply of Aristophanes' inimitable wit and humor, qualities lacking in the ordinary stage conception of a revolutionist. She reasons and persuades the women of Greece to cast their lots with her so that by simply refusing the men sexual satisfaction she can bring them to her terms: abolition of war and the relinquishment of the treasury to women. Amid the rollicking ribaldry of Man laughing at his own precious taboo—sex—Lysistrata's plan to seize and occupy the Acropolis of Athens with her army of celibate women weathers a storm of protest, succeeds, and wrecks the framework of a society dominated by men.

Cleonice (klē·ō·nī'sē), a lusty Athenian friend of Lysistrata. At first reluctant to go along with so devastating and sacrificing a plan, she is eventually browbeaten by Lysistrata into accepting the challenge to save Greece from the total ruin of war, and she partakes of the solemn oath, binding herself to refrain from sharing the marriage bed with her husband. Constantly on hand, Cleonice adds much zest by ribald commentary and turns out to be one of Lysistrata's main supporters.

Myrrhiné (mĭ·rē'nē), one of Lysistrata's captains, representing Anagyra. Just as the idealism of Lysistrata is wearing thin and the torment of self-denial is weakening the ranks of the women, Myrrhiné's husband appears and, acting under orders from Lysistrata, she subjects him to unendurable, teasing torture. This episode is not only one of the play's funniest but also the point at which Lysistrata's strategy turns toward success.

Lampito (lăm'pĭ·tō), a woman of Sparta who agrees to Lysistrata's plan. Her loyalty and resourcefulness bring success in that land. Lampito, typical of the Athenian's concept of Spartan women, is athletic, bold, well-proportioned. A key figure throughout the play, she steps forward at the very inception of Lysistrata's plan to be the major seconding voice. Her example assures the revolt of the women.

Cinesias (sĭ·nē′sĭ·əs), the husband of Myrrhiné. Exhibiting all symptoms of lust, he begs his wife to return to him.

A Child, the infant son of Myrrhiné and Cinesias, brought by his father in an attempt to bribe his mother into deserting the women's cause.

A Magistrate, a pompous representative of law and order who seeks to treat the revolutionaries as silly housewives to be spanked and sent to their kitchens. Much to his chagrin, he discovers them in no mood to be so treated. After seeing his force of Scythian policemen rebuffed, and completely defeated by Lysistrata's de-termined female logic, he becomes the echo and image of Aristophanes' laughter at the ineffectuality of the law when pitted against organized femininity.

A Chorus of Old Men. Heading the first unsuccessful attempt to dislodge the women from the Acropolis, they toil up-hill with smoke faggots and engage in much humorous comment upon the character of women in general; their ef-forts are confined mostly to threats and ineffectual maneuvering as the women prove too much for them.

A Chorus of Women. Antagonists of the old men, the women establish a swift rapport with them, not only turning their smoke faggots into uselessness by soaking them but also besting them in a verbal exchange of ridicule and insult.

A Spartan Herald, also suffering the pangs of thwarted love.

Spartan Envoys, with whom the Athenian women conclude a treaty of peace.

THE MABINOGION

Author: Unknown
Time of action: The Middle Ages
First transcribed: Twelfth and thirteenth centuries; first translation published, 1838-1849

PRINCIPAL CHARACTERS

Pwyll, Prince of Dyved. To redeem him-self after an attempt to steal a deer, he agrees to change places and appearances with the chieftain who has caught him in the act and to slay the chieftain's en-emy after a year's time. His contract ful-filled, he returns home where he sees the beautiful lady Rhiannon ride by, subdues her suitor, and marries her.

Rhiannon, Pwyll's wife.

Pryderi, the son of Pwyll and Rhiannon.

Kicva, Pryderi's wife.

Bendigeid Vran, the son of Llyr and King of the Island of the Mighty. While making war on the Irish because of their treatment of Matholwch and Branwen, he is killed by a poisoned arrow.

Branwen, Bendigeid Vran's sister, who is given in marriage to Matholwch. She dies of sorrow when her brother is killed in battle.

Matholwch, King of Ireland, Branwen's husband.

Manawydan, Bendigeid Vran's brother. With Pryderi, another survivor of the Irish war, he settles on land which is magically desolated until it is learned that the source of the curse is a church-man avenging an ancient insult.

641

King Math, the son of Mathonwy.

Goewin, King Math's footmaiden, raped by Gwydion and Gilvaethwy.

Gwydion, King Math's warrior, and Gilvaethwy, his brother, turned by King Math into animals for three years as punishment for their rape of Goewin.

Llew Llaw Gyffes, Gwydion's favorite son, for whom King Math creates an elf-wife, Blodeuwedd.

Blodeuwedd, Llew Llaw Gyffe's elfwife. For her faithlessness she is turned into an owl.

Macsen Wledig, the Emperor of Rome, who dreams of a beautiful maiden and, after a long search, finds her just as she appeared in the dream.

Lludd, King of Britain. His people ravaged by three plagues, he seeks the help of his brother, Llevelys, who offers three successful remedies.

Llevelys, Lludd's wise brother, King of France.

Kilhwch, King Arthur's knight. By dint of cunning, magic, and the help of his fellow knights, he wins Olwen from Ysbaddaden.

Olwen, Ysbaddaden's beautiful daughter, who is won by Kilhwch.

Ysbaddaden, a crafty giant, Olwen's father.

King Arthur.

Rhonabwy, a dreamer who, in sleep, finds himself in King Arthur's court.

Owain, a knight. He overcomes the Knight of the Fountain, marries his widow, and assumes his title.

Peredur, a matchless knight at King Arthur's court.

Gerint, King Arthur's knight. Spending more time with his wife than in knightly pursuits, he finds himself obliged to prove to his people his strength and valor.

Enid, Gerint's wife.

MACBETH

Author: William Shakespeare (1564-1616)
Time of action: Eleventh century
First presented: 1606

PRINCIPAL CHARACTERS

Macbeth (măk·bĕth'), Thane of Glamis, later Thane of Cawdor and King of Scotland. A brave and successful military leader, potentially a good and great man, he wins general admiration as well as the particular gratitude of King Duncan, whose kinsman he is. Meeting the Three Weird Sisters, he succumbs to their tempting prophecies; but he also needs the urging of his wife to become a traitor, a murderer, and a usurper. He is gifted, or cursed, with a powerful and vivid imagination and with fiery, poetic language. Gaining power, he grows more and more ruthless, until finally he loses even the vestiges of humanity. He dies desperately, cheated by the ambiguous prophecies, in full realization of the worthlessness of the fruits of his ambition.

Lady Macbeth, the strong-willed, persuasive, and charming wife of Macbeth. Ambitious for her husband's glory, she finds herself unable to kill King Duncan in his sleep, because he resembles her father. As Macbeth becomes more inhuman, she becomes remorseful and breaks under the strain. In her sleepwalking, she relives the events of the night of the

King's murder and tries to wash her hands clean of imaginary bloodstains.

Banquo (băn′kwō, băng′kō), Macbeth's fellow commander. A man of noble character, seemingly unmoved by the prophecy of the Three Weird Sisters that he will beget kings, he is not completely innocent; he does not disclose his suspicions of Macbeth, and he accepts a place in Macbeth's court. After being murdered by Macbeth's assassins, Banquo appears at a ceremonial banquet. His blood-spattered ghost, visible only to Macbeth, unnerves the King completely. In the final vision shown Macbeth by the Three Weird Sisters, Banquo and his line of kings appear.

The Three Weird Sisters, the three witches, sinister hags who seem more closely allied to the Norns or Fates than to conventional witches. To Macbeth they make prophetic statements which are true, but deceptive. Their prophecy of his becoming Thane of Cawdor is immediately fulfilled, tempting him to take direct action to carry out the second prophecy, that he shall be king. They lull him into false security by telling him that he has nothing to fear until Birnam Wood comes to Dunsinane, and that he cannot be killed by any man born of woman.

Macduff (măk·dŭf′), Thane of Fife. He and Lennox arrive at Macbeth's castle just after the murder of King Duncan, and Macduff discovers the body. A brave but prudent man, he flees Scotland and offers his help to Malcolm. Underestimating the villainy of Macbeth's character, he is thunderstruck at hearing of the atrocious murder of his wife and children. He becomes a steel-hearted avenger. Before killing Macbeth, he deprives him of his last symbol of security, for as a Caesarian child he was not actually born of woman. He presents Macbeth's head to Malcolm and proclaims the young prince King of Scotland.

Duncan (dŭng′kən), King of Scotland.

Gentle and trusting, he shows great kindness to Macbeth. His murder by Macbeth is therefore almost incredibly fiendish.

Malcolm (măl′kəm), King Duncan's eldest son. Far more cautious and shrewd than his father, he leaves for England to escape possible assassination. He is reluctant to give his trust to Macduff but finally, realizing his loyalty, accepts his aid in taking the throne of Scotland.

Donalbain (dŏn′əl·bān), King Duncan's younger son. After consulting with Malcolm, he agrees to take a separate path, going to Ireland so that the potential heirs to the throne would not be accessible to a common assassination.

Fleance (flē′əns), the son of Banquo. He escapes the murderers who kill his father and lives to haunt Macbeth with the Three Weird Sisters' prophecy that kings will spring from Banquo's line.

Ross, a nobleman of Scotland. He is Duncan's messenger to Macbeth, bringing him word of his new title, Thane of Cawdor. He also bears news to his kinswoman, Lady Macduff, of her husband's departure from Scotland. His third and most terrible office as messenger is to carry word to Macduff of the destruction of his entire family. He fights in Malcolm's army against Macbeth.

Lennox, a nobleman of Scotland. He is Macduff's companion when the latter brings the message to King Duncan at Macbeth's castle. He also deserts Macbeth and joins forces with Malcolm.

Lady Macduff, a victim of Macbeth's most horrible atrocity. She is human and pathetic.

A Boy, the son of Macduff, a brave and precocious child. He faces Macbeth's hired murderers without flinching and dies calling to his mother to save herself.

Siward (sē′wərd, sē′ərd), Earl of Northumberland, the general of the English forces supporting Malcolm. He is the

643

type of the noble father accepting stoically the death of a heroic son.

Young Siward, the general's courageous son. He dies fighting Macbeth hand to hand.

A Scottish Doctor. Called in to minister to Lady Macbeth, he is witness of her sleepwalking in which she relives the night of the murder.

A Gentlewoman, an attendant to Lady Macbeth. She is with the Doctor and observes Lady Macbeth during the sleepwalking scene.

A Sergeant (also called **Captain** in the Folio text), a wounded survivor of the battle at the beginning of the play. He reports to King Duncan the heroism of Macbeth and Banquo.

A Porter, a comical drunkard. Roused by the knocking on the castle door, he pretends to be the gatekeeper of Hell and imagines various candidates clamoring for admission. The audience, knowing of Duncan's murder, can realize how ironically near the truth is the idea of the castle as Hell.

Hecate (hĕk'ə·tē, hĕk'ət), patroness of the Witches. It is generally accepted among Shakespearian scholars that Hecate is an addition to the play by another author, perhaps Thomas Middleton, author of "The Witch."

A Messenger. He brings word that Birnam Wood is apparently moving. His message destroys one of Macbeth's illusions of safety.

Seyton, an officer attending Macbeth. He brings word of Lady Macbeth's death.

Menteith,
Angus, and
Caithness, Scottish noblemen who join Malcolm against Macbeth.

McTEAGUE

Author: Frank Norris (1870-1902)
Time of action: The 1890's
First published: 1899

PRINCIPAL CHARACTERS

McTeague (Mac), a massive, slow-witted man with a blond mustache and enormously strong hands. An unlicensed dentist, McTeague sometimes pulls teeth with his bare hands. He snoozes away Sunday afternoons in his dentist chair until he meets Trina Sieppe, the cousin and fiancée of his friend, Marcus Schouler. His friend sees that McTeague and Trina are attracted and with fairly good grace accepts the situation. Many of McTeague's violent and even repulsive qualities are highlighted by incidents in the novel. At an outing Marcus and McTeague wrestle; Marcus, envious and angry, bites off McTeague's ear lobe; the dentist, in turn, breaks Marcus' arm. In adversity, McTeague's brutality is intensified by drink. Sadistically, he bites his wife's fingers until they are infected and have to be amputated. Adversity can only intensify his desperation, and one is not surprised when he beats his wife to death and then flees the consequences. In the middle of the desert he is met by his former friend, now a member of the sheriff's posse; again a violent struggle is the only response McTeague can give. He kills his friend, but not before Marcus has handcuffed them together under the boiling sun. McTeague's death, like his life, is brutish. Readers have considered McTeague's career, as related by Norris, a triumph of realistic description.

Marcus Schouler, who lives above Mc-

Teague's dental office. The two men are friends. Smaller than McTeague but gifted with more intelligence, Marcus broods over the loss of his fiancée and her prize money and is petty enough to report McTeague to the authorities for practicing without a license. By fate or by sheer perversity he binds his enemy to his own corpse with handcuffs; the two face eternity only hours apart.

Trina Sieppe, McTeague's wife, trained to be a thrifty housewife by her Swiss parents. She overdevelops this trait after she wins five thousand dollars in a lottery. She spends every spare moment carving small wooden Noah's Ark animals for her uncle's "import" business. Although counting coins is her only joy, she does buy a huge gold tooth as a sign for her husband's dental office. Sexually subservient to her husband's physical strength, she cannot protect herself from his drunken fury when he bites her finger tips. Her character shows only

vestigial kindness, and her miserliness leads to her death.

Grannis, an aged English bookbinder, comforted each night by the delicate sounds of his neighbor's teatray on the opposite side of a partition. The tray belongs to the seamstress next door.

Miss Parker, a genteel dressmaker. She responds with fluttering heart when she hears Grannis and his supper tray. They marry.

Zerkov, a junk dealer.

Maria Macapa, a maid who collects junk for Zerkov. She raves about "gold dishes" once owned by her family. These ravings lead Zerkov to marry Maria. But a head blow ends her aberration and in frustration Zerkov kills her.

Papa and
Mamma Sieppe, Trina's parents, elderly Swiss immigrants.

MADAME BOVARY

Author: Gustave Flaubert (1821-1880)
Time of action: Mid-nineteenth century
First published: 1857

PRINCIPAL CHARACTERS

Emma Bovary (ĕ′mà bô·và·rē′), a sentimental young woman whose foolishly romantic ideas on life and love cause her to become dissatisfied with her humdrum husband and the circumstances of her married life. Her feeling of disillusionment lead her first into two desperate, hopeless love affairs and then to an agonizing and ugly death from arsenic. Filled with fiery, indefinite conceptions of love which she is capable of translating only into gaudy bourgeois displays of materialism, she is unable to reconcile herself to a life of tedium as the wife of a country doctor. In her attempt to escape into a more exciting world of passion and dream, she drifts into shabby, sordid af-

fairs with Rodolphe Boulanger and Léon Dupuis. The first of these lovers, an older man, dominates the affair; the second, inexperienced and young, is dominated. Because Emma brings to both of these affairs little more than an unsubstantial and frantic desire to escape from her dull husband and the monotony of her life, the eventual collapse of her romantic dreams, the folly of her passionate surrender to passion and intrigue, and her death, brought on by false, empty pride, are inevitable.

Charles Bovary (shärl bô·và·rē′), Emma's well-meaning but docile and mediocre medical husband. An unimaginative clod

645

without intelligence or insight, he is unable to understand, console, or satisfy the terrible needs of his wife. Every move he makes to become a more important figure in her sight is frustrated by his inadequacy as a lover and a doctor, for he is as much a failure in his practice as he is in his relations with Emma. Her suicide leaves him grief-stricken and financially ruined as the result of her extravagance. Soon after her death he discovers in the secret drawer of her desk the love letters sent her by Rodolphe and Léon, and he learns of her infidelity for the first time. When he dies, the sum of twelve francs and seventy-five centimes is his only legacy to his small daughter.

Rodolphe Bourlanger (rô·dôlf′ bōo·län-zhā′), Emma Bovary's first lover. A well-to-do bachelor and the owner of the Château La Huchette, he is a shrewd, suave, and brittle man with considerable knowledge of women and a taste for intrigue. Sensing the relationship between Emma and her husband, he makes friends with the Bovarys, sends them gifts of venison and fowls, and invites them to the chateau. On the pretext of concern for Emma's health, he suggests that they go riding together. He finds Emma so easy a conquest that after a short time he begins to neglect her, partly out of boredom, partly because he cannot see in himself the Byronic image Emma has created in her imagination; she never sees Rodolphe as the loutish, vulgar man he is. After he writes her a letter of farewell, on the pretext that he is going on a long journey, Emma suffers a serious attack of brain fever.

Léon Dupuis (lā·ôṅ′ dü·püe′), a young law clerk infatuated by Emma Bovary but without the courage to declare himself or to possess her. With him she indulges herself in a progressively lascivious manner in her attempt to capture the excitement and passion of the romantic love she desires. Léon, because he lacks depth and maturity, merely intensifies Emma's growing estrangement from her

everyday world. When Léon, who never realizes the encouragement Emma offers him, goes off to continue his studies in Paris, she is filled with rage, hate, and unfulfilled desire, and a short time later she turns to Rodolphe Bourlanger. After that affair she meets Léon once more in Rouen, and they become lovers. Oppressed by debts, living only for sensation, and realizing that she is pulling Léon down to her own degraded level, Emma ends the affair by committing suicide.

Monsieur Lheureux (lœ·rœ′), an unscrupulous, corrupt draper and moneylender who makes Emma the victim of his unsavory business deals by driving her deeper and deeper into debt. Her inability to repay the exorbitant loans he has made her in secret forces the issue of suicide upon her as her only escape from her baseless world.

Monsieur Homais (ə·mĕ′), a chemist, presented in a masterpiece of ironic characterization. A speaker in clichés, the possessor of a wholly trite "Scientific Outlook" on society, he regards himself as a Modern Man and a Thinker. His pomposity and astoundingly superficial ideals become one of the remarkable facets of the novel, as Flaubert sketches the hypocrisy and mediocrity of Charles Bovary's friend. Homais epitomizes the small-town promoter, raconteur, and self-styled liberal.

Hippolyte Tautain (ê·pô·lēt′ tō·tăṅ′), a witless, clubfooted boy operated on by Charles Bovary at the insistence of M. Homais, who wishes to bring greater glory to the region by proving the merits of a new surgical device. Bovary's crude handling of the operation and the malpractice involved in the use of the device cause the boy to lose his leg. The episode provides Flaubert with an excellent commentary on both Homais and Bovary.

Théodore Rouault (tā·ô·dôr′ rōo·äl′), Emma Bovary's father, a farmer. Charles

Bovary first meets Emma when he is summoned to set Rouault's broken leg.

Berthe Bovary (bĕrt bô·vȧ·rē'), the neglected young daughter of Emma and Charles Bovary. Orphaned and left without an inheritance, she is sent to live with her father's mother. When that woman dies, the child is turned over to the care of an aunt, who puts her to work in a cotton-spinning factory.

Captain Binet (bē·nā'), the tax collector in the town of Yonville-l'Abbaye.

Justin (zhüs·tăn'), the assistant in the shop of Mr. Homais. Emma persuades her young admirer to admit her to the room where poisons are kept. There, before horrified Justin can stop her, she secures a quantity of arsenic and eats it.

Madame Veuve Lefrançois (vœv' lȧ·frän-swä'), the proprietress of the inn in Yonville-l'Abbaye. Hippolyte Tautain is the hostler at her establishment.

Félicité (fā·lē·sē·tā'), the Bovarys' maid.

Heloise Bovary (ĕ·lō·ēz' bô·vȧ·rē'), Charles Bovary's first wife, a woman much older than he, who had deceived the Bovarys as to the amount of property she owned. Her death following a severe hemorrhage frees Charles from his nagging, domineering wife, and soon afterward he marries young Emma Rouault.

MADEMOISELLE DE MAUPIN

Author: Théophile Gautier (1811-1872)
Time of action: Early nineteenth century
First published: 1835

PRINCIPAL CHARACTERS

M. d'Albert (dȧl·bĕr'), a young aesthete, handsome, well-educated, and worldly, who has dreamed of and who seeks an ideal woman. Though Rosette provides for a while an education in love's delights, she cannot cure his moods of dreamy longing. Théodore both fascinates and troubles d'Albert who (to Silvio) admits loving a man but a man who is almost certainly a woman in disguise. He is joyously surprised by Madelaine-Rosalind's offer of a night of love, is transported by the wonderful love itself, and is left astonished at Théodore's disappearance.

Rosette (rō·zĕt'), his mistress, a pretty and charming young woman prescribed by De C—— as a cure for d'Albert's vaporish idealism. She is intelligent, witty, and capricious. From the beginning she stirs d'Albert sexually and, becoming his mistress, delights him with a variety of pleasures. But these soon pall, and she struggles to conquer his boredom and his return to wistful dreaming.

Simultaneously in love with the elusive Théodore, Rosette is saddened to learn that the disguised Isnabel is apparently Théodore's mistress.

Théodore de Sérannes (tā·ô·dôr' dȧ sā-rȧn'), in reality Mademoiselle Madelaine de Maupin. In disguise, Madelaine appears to be an extremely handsome young man, an accomplished conversationalist, horseman, and swordsman. Believing she could never, as a woman, discover the true nature of men, she has (posing as a man) somewhat bitterly observed their perfidy and shams when they thought themselves safe from exposure. After the smitten d'Albert has learned her secret, Madelaine (in costume as Shakespeare's Rosalind) appears in d'Albert's room and grants him one night of perfect love. Also, after leaving d'Albert's room, she spends a mysteriously lengthy visit with Rosette. She then goes out of the life of both Rosette and d'Albert forever, leaving each to comfort and love the other

647

as best they may. As for herself, Madelaine confesses to Graciosa that a bisexual element in her nature prevents her from ever completely loving anyone, man or woman. Though in part modeled upon Shakespeare's Rosalind, whom she plays in an amateur production of "As You Like It," Madelaine is, especially in her sensuality, a very different woman.

De C—— (də sä'), a man of the world, d'Albert's friend who introduces him to Rosette.

Madame de Thémines (də tä·mēn'), a fashionable madam and a former intimate of De C——.

Isnabel (ēs·nȧ·bĕl'), Thédore's page, in reality a young woman whose sex is secretly discovered by Rosette after a riding accident.

Silvio (sēl'·vyō), d'Albert's friend to whom he writes long confessional letters.

Graciosa (grȧ·syō'·sȧ), Madelaine's epistolary confidante.

THE MADRAS HOUSE

Author: Harley Granville-Barker (1877-1946)
Time of action: Early twentieth century
First presented: 1910

PRINCIPAL CHARACTERS

Henry Huxtable, the respectable, middle-class part owner of the Madras House.

Katherine Huxtable, the respectable, middle-class wife of Henry Huxtable.

Constantine Madras, Katherine Huxtable's black sheep brother and part owner of the Madras House. To escape English priggishness, he had retreated some years before to Arabia, where he reportedly lived as the master of a harem. Upon his return to England on business concerning the Madras House, he is a threat to the Huxtable idea of respectability and decency. When it is revealed that he is the father of Marion Yates' unborn child, he expects her meekly to receive his assistance. When she refuses, he is disturbed by her lack of feminine docility and returns to his Arabian household.

Philip Madras, Constantine Madras' son. When he learns that his wife Jessica is about to fall in love with Major Hippisly Thomas, he recognizes her for the first time as a person. To please her, he gives up his interest in the Madras House in the hope that they can work together for the good of society.

Marion Yates, an employee at the Madras House and the mother of Constantine Madras' unborn child.

Jessica Madras, Philip Madras' wife. Feeling herself regarded with indifference by her husband, she is about to fall in love with Major Hippisly Thomas. When she finally is recognized by Philip as a person as well as a wife, she unites with him in an endeavor to be useful to society.

Eustace Perrin State, an American and a prospective buyer of the Madras House.

Major Hippisly Thomas, Philip Madras' best friend.

Amelia Madras, Constantine Madras' wife, whom he leaves for life in Arabia.

Mr. Brigstock and
Miss Chancellor, employees of the Madras House.

648

THE MADWOMAN OF CHAILLOT

Author: Jean Giraudoux (1882-1944)
Time of action: A little before noon in the spring of next year
First presented: 1945

PRINCIPAL CHARACTERS

Countess Aurelia (ō·rā·lyà'), the Madwoman of Chaillot (shà·yō'). Living eternally in the moment when her life was loveliest, and the champion of beauty and of the gentle people of Paris, she is confronted, at a sidewalk café, with the brutal forces of materialism in the form of a syndicate preparing to drill for oil beneath the streets. Realizing that justice, as it is ordinarily understood, will be powerless against the destroyers of beauty, she forms and carries out, with the help of her gentle friends, a plan to annihilate the financiers. With the materialists gone, all the manifestations of spring return to the world and the Madwoman is thanked by all for saving humanity from its exploiters.

Mme. Constance (kōn·stäns'), the Madwoman of Passy (pà·sē'),
Mlle. Gabrielle (gà·bryĕl'), the Madwoman of St. Sulpice, and
Mme. Josephine (zhō·zā·fēn'), the Madwoman of la Concorde (la kōn·kôrd'), Countess Aurelia's gentle compatriots, who form a tribunal for a fair trial of the materialists, whom they find guilty on all charges.

The Ragpicker, one of the gentle people. He agrees to speak for the defense at the trial of the materialists.

The President,
The Baron,
The Broker, and

The Prospector, the representatives of the forces of materialism, the destroyers of beauty and the enemies of humanity. Armed with a plan for drilling for oil beneath the streets of Paris, they oppose Countess Aurelia and her gentle friends, the champions of beauty and humanity. The financiers are eventually tried by a court of gentle ones, found guilty, and condemned to extermination. Lured to Countess Aurelia's by the promise of oil, they follow one another like sheep through a door which they are led to believe opens the way to the treasure. In reality, they are headed for the sewers of Paris, never to return.

Pierre (pyĕr'), a young assassin hired by the materialists to bomb the city architect, who is opposed to the drilling of oil beneath the streets. When the young man finds himself unable to carry out his task, he plans to jump in the river but is rescued and persuaded by Countess Aurelia that life is worth living.

The Sewer Man, Countess Aurelia's gentle friend, who shows her a secret door to the sewers of Paris through which the materialists are led, never to return.

The Waiter,
The Little Man,
The Street Singer,
The Flower Girl, and
The Shoe Lace Peddlar, free, gentle people of Paris.

MAGGIE: A GIRL OF THE STREETS

Author: Stephen Crane (1871-1900)
Time of action: Late nineteenth century
First published: 1893

Maggie, a girl who has grown up in the slums of New York. Although surrounded by corruption of all sorts throughout her youth, she has remained uncontaminated by it. When she falls in love with Pete, a friend of her brother, her moral deterioration begins. After she has lived with him, her family, who are anything but models of decorum, will have nothing to do with her. She turns to prostitution but finds it hard to support herself, and eventually she commits suicide.

Jimmy, Maggie's brother. After his father's death, he goes to work to support Maggie and their mother. He quickly falls into the normal patterns of life for men of his class, has a succession of affairs, and fathers several illegitimate children. When Maggie tries to return home after her affair with Pete, he is highly indignant and will do nothing to help her.

Pete, Jimmy's friend and Maggie's lover. After seducing Maggie he quickly tires of her and turns her out. Thereafter he denies any responsibility toward her.

The Mother, a woman given to drink and constant haranguing with her husband and children. When Maggie and Jimmy were small she left them to shift for themselves most of the time, but it is she who assumes an attitude of outraged virtue when Maggie tries to return home. After her daughter's death she is inconsolable.

THE MAGIC MOUNTAIN

Author: Thomas Mann (1875-1955)
Time of action: 1907-1914
First published: 1924

PRINCIPAL CHARACTERS

Hans Castorp (häns cäs'tȯrp), a young German of middle-class and commercial background. He is a sedate, sensible, correct young man, appreciative of good living, but without particular ambition or aspiration. This spiritual lack, Mann suggests, is allied to physical illness. About to enter a shipbuilding firm, Hans goes to make a three-week visit at the International Sanatorium Berghof, where his cousin is a patient. There he learns that he himself has contracted tuberculosis, and he spends seven years at the sanatorium. Spiritually unattached to his own time and place, he resigns himself rather easily to his new role as an inmate of the "magic mountain," where the spiritual conflicts and defects of modern Europe are polarized and where time and place are allied to eternity and infinity. His experience takes on the significance of a spiritual journey. He is exposed to a threadbare version of Western liberalism and rationalism (in the person of Settembrini); to the lure of irrational desire (in the person of Madame Chauchat); to Catholic absolutism and mysticism (in the person of Naphta, whose arguments with Settembrini make up a large part of the second portion of the novel). Finally (in the person of Mynheer Peeperkorn) he feels the attraction of a strong, vital personality that makes the intellectual strife of Settembrini and Naphta sound quite hollow. Lost in a snowstorm that quickly becomes a symbol of his passage through uncharted spiritual regions, Hans attains a vision of an earthly paradise and of blood sacrifice—the two opposed forces life has revealed to him—and he achieves a further revelation of the importance of goodness and love. Ironically, after he returns to the sanatorium, he forgets; the vision has literally led him beyond himself and his capacity. He now dabbles in spiritualism and, in a famous passage, also soothes himself with romantic music that, he feels, contains at its heart the death wish. It is a snatch of this music that Hans has on his lips when, at the conclusion of the novel, he is glimpsed on a battlefield of World War I.

Ludovico Settembrini (lōō'dō·fē'kō sĕ'-tĕm·brē'nē), an Italian humanist, man of letters, apostle of reason, progress, equality, and the brotherhood of man, as well as a fiery Italian nationalist. His case is incurable; no longer able to return to the land of action (a fact that has obvious symbolic connotations), he spends his energy in hollow eloquence and in ineffectual writing for the International League for the Organization of Progress.

Leo Naphta (lā'ō näf'tä), an apostate Jew converted to Catholicism, educated by the Jesuits, brilliant in his defense of the immaterial, the spiritual, the authoritarian, the medieval. He gets the better of Settembrini in his many arguments with the Italian, but it becomes clear that Naphta's rigidity is essentially a form of death. Toward the end of the novel, having goaded Settembrini into a duel, Naphta turns his gun on himself.

Clavdia Chauchat (kläf'dē·ä kō·shä'), a Russian, married but refusing to carry a ring on her finger, wandering about Europe from sanatorium to sanatorium. Her manners are in many ways the antithesis of what Hans has learned to accept as ladylike; but that very difference seems to attract him once he has begun to lose his ties with Hamburg, and on a carnival night they consummate the passion she has aroused in him. She leaves the sanatorium for a time but returns in the company of Mynheer Peeperkorn.

Mynheer Peeperkorn (mēn'här pā'pĕr·kōrn), an enormously wealthy, burly ex-planter. He is inarticulate (thus enforcing the difference between him, on the one hand, and Settembrini and Naphta, on the other), but exudes a strength of personality that engages the respect of Hans, who allies himself with the Dutchman. But Peeperkorn, feeling the approach of impotence, kills himself (another facet of nineteenth century individualism gone).

Joachim Ziemssen (yō'äkh·im zēm'sĕn), Hans' cousin, soldierly, courteous, brave. A foil to Hans, he refuses to yield to the magic of the mountain, keeps track of time, chafes to return to the flatland so that he can pursue his career as a soldier. Though in love with an inmate, Marusja, he, unlike Castorp, refuses to yield to his passion. Finally he insists on leaving, though not fully cured, is gloriously happy for a while, but returns to the sanatorium to die.

Marusja (mä·roos'yä), a pretty young Russian girl, silently adored by Joachim Ziemssen.

Hofrat Behrens (hōf'rät bā'rĕns), the chief medical officer at the sanatorium. His wife had died there some years before, and he stayed on when he found himslf tainted with the disease. He is a mixture of melancholy and forced jocularity.

Dr. Krokowski (krō·kŏf'skē), a foil to Behrens. If Behrens represents the medical point of view, Krokowski represents the psychoanalytical.

Frau Stöhr (frou stœr), a middle-aged woman who irks Castorp at the dinner table by her boring conversation, yet he welcomes her gossip about Clavdia Chauchat.

Miss Robinson, an elderly English spinster and table companion of Castorp.

Fräulein Engelhart (froi'līn ăng'ĕl·härt),

651

a school mistress from Königsberg, another table companion of Castorp.

Dr. Leo Blumenkohl (lā'ō blōō'měn-kōl'), a physician from Odessa. The advanced stage of his illness causes him to be the quietest person at Castorp's table.

Herr Albin (hâr äl'bēn), a patient who, unable to take his illness philosophically, creates excitement by demonstrating suicidal intentions.

Tous Les Deux (tōō lā dœ), an old Mexican woman known by this name

because her conversation consists of only a few French phrases which always contain the words "tous les deux."

Sister Berta (bâr'tä), formerly **Alfreda Schildknecht** (äl·frä'dä shĭld'knäsht), a talkative nurse who tries to explain her frustrations to reluctant Hans Castorp and Joachim Ziemssen.

Adriatica von Mylendonk (ä·drē·ä'tĭ·cä fŏn mē'lĕn·dŏnk), the directress of the sanatorium, who surprises Castorp by her businesslike manner.

THE MAGNIFICENT OBSESSION

Author: Lloyd C. Douglas (1877-1951)
Time of action: Early twentieth century
First published: 1929

PRINCIPAL CHARACTERS

Dr. Wayne Hudson, an eminent brain surgeon who dies from drowning when the inhalator which might have saved his life is used to resuscitate a wealthy playboy. Somewhat of a mystic, the doctor is a generous philanthropist, but he hides his good deeds; he thinks his great ability as a surgeon is a gift that comes from doing unknown good for other people.

Joyce Hudson, the doctor's daughter.

Helen Brent Hudson, Joyce Hudson's school friend who becomes Dr. Hudson's second wife. After she is a widow, Robert Merrick makes her the recipient of some of his philanthropy and then falls in love with her. In Rome her life is saved after a train wreck by Dr. Merrick, who keeps his identity a secret. She discovers at last that she loves Merrick, and the two are to be married.

Nancy Ashford, superintendent of the Hudson Clinic. She has been in love with Dr. Hudson. She tells Robert Merrick he ought to try to take Dr. Hudson's place.

Robert Merrick, a rich playboy who becomes a doctor in order to take the place of Dr. Hudson, a famous brain surgeon whose life is lost when an inhalator is used for young Merrick. Merrick tries the doctor's theory of philanthropy, deriving power from hidden good deeds. He finds that it is indeed a secret to a successful life, and thus Merrick succeeds in becoming a famous brain surgeon himself. He marries Dr. Hudson's widow.

Dawson, a fellow medical student aided financially by Merrick so that the young man can finish medical school. This philanthropic act inspires Merrick and convinces him that he can follow in Dr. Hudson's footsteps.

THE MAHABHARATA

Author: Unknown
Time of action: Remote antiquity
First transcribed: Fifth century B.C. (?)

Yudhishthira,
Bhima,
Arjuna,
Nakula, and
Sahadeva, King Pandu's five sons, known as the Pandavas. When Yudhishthira, the most capable of the brothers, is named heir apparent, their cousins, the Kauravas, take exception, and the Pandavas are forced into exile. In disguise, Arjuna wins the hand of Princess Draupadi, who becomes the wife of all five. Finally, after many heroic and romantic adventures, the Pandavas and the Kauravas engage in a mighty war of heroes, and Yudhishthira becomes King. Later, weary of earthly pomp, the Pandavas, with Draupadi, renounce the world and set out for the dwelling place of the gods on high.

King Pandu, father of the Pandavas.

King Dhritarashtra, the brother of King Pandu and father of the Kauravas.

Draupadi, a princess whose hand is won by Arjuna in a trial of strength. In a mysterious fashion, she becomes the wife of all the Pandavas.

King Drupada, Draupadi's father.

Duryodhana, the unscrupulous leader of the Kauravas and enemy of the Pandavas.

Bhishma, Dhritarashtra's wise uncle and adviser.

Krishna of Dvaraka, the Pandavas' cousin, counselor, and friend.

THE MAID OF HONOUR

Author: Philip Massinger (1583-1640)
Time of action: The Renaissance
First presented: c. 1623

PRINCIPAL CHARACTERS

Camiola, the "Maid of Honour." Deeply in love with Bertoldo, she refuses to marry him because of his vow of celibacy as a Knight of Malta. In spite of his faithlessness in accepting the love of Aurelia, Camiola forgives him, ransoms him, and wins him back to his knightly vows. She herself weds the Church as a nun.

Roberto, King of Sicily. He is a just, reasonable, and peaceful monarch, but is unwisely overindulgent to his evil favorite Fulgentio. Camiola finally persuades him to renounce Fulgentio.

Bertoldo, the half brother of the King. Eager for glory in battle, he disregards the King's wishes and joins Duke Ferdinand in an unjust war on Siena. Being captured, he accepts the love of his captor, Duchess Aurelia, moved more by

ambition than desire. Shame heaped on him by Camiola leads to his repentance.

Fulgentio, the King's unworthy favorite. Arrogant, selfish, and unprincipled, he first tries to force Camiola to marry him, then tries to blacken her name. For this he is banished.

Sylli, an absurd suitor for Camiola's hand. He is convinced that she loves him to distraction until the moment that she announces her entrance into the convent.

Adorni, a faithful, self-sacrificing youth in love with Camiola. Although he fails to win her, she endows him with a large fortune when she renounces the world.

Ferdinand, the Duke of Urbin. Angry at being rejected by Aurelia, he attacks her land and suffers defeat.

Aurelia, the Duchess of Siena. A proud and passionate woman, she conceives a violent infatuation for her prisoner Bertoldo.

Gonzaga, the Sienese general, a Knight of Malta. Recognizing his prisoner Bertoldo as a Knight of Malta fighting in an unjust cause, he degrades him and dismisses him from the order.

Astutio, an ambassador to Siena from King Roberto.

THE MAID'S TRAGEDY

Authors: Francis Beaumont (1585?-1616) and John Fletcher (1579-1625)
Time of action: The legendary past
First presented: 1610-1611

PRINCIPAL CHARACTERS

The King of Rhodes, to all appearances a just, if undistinguished, ruler. He is, in fact, a man who does not scruple to use those around him ruthlessly for his own ends, and he brings bloody death upon himself by his dishonoring of Evadne and by his despicable treatment of Amintor, a courtier.

Evadne (ə·văd′nē), a noblewoman, mistress to the King, who arranges her marriage to Amintor. She shows herself almost completely self-centered in the opening scenes, where she coldly reveals her duplicity to her husband and tells him that she is simply using him to conceal her relationship with the King. Yet the force with which she vows to be his wife in name only suggests the strength of character which makes her a tragic figure. Confronted by her brother with the dishonor she has brought upon her own person, her husband, and her family, she recoils in horror from the hell in which she has placed herself, begs forgiveness of Amintor, and resolves to "redeem one minute of my age or, like another Niobe . . . weep till I am water." She finds this redemption in tying the King to his bed and stabbing him to death as she accuses him of villainy. When she returns to her husband she feels herself purged, free at last to offer herself as his wife. Death is the only recourse left to her when Amintor,

horrified by the slaying of an anointed king, repulses her.

Amintor (ə·mĭn′tôr), Evadne's ill-used husband. He is, from the moment of his marriage, conscience-stricken by his betrayal of Aspatia, to whom he had been betrothed. He attempts to justify himself by reflecting that he acted on the King's orders, but he recognizes simultaneously that the King had no control over his will; he could have refused the bride who was offered to him. Shocked by Evadne's wedding-night declaration, he plays the part of happy husband badly, but his reverence for royal blood restrains him from avenging his honor with violence and ultimately causes his final repudiation of his wife. Some pity for her lingers in him, however, and he turns, too late, to try to prevent her suicide. He kills himself beside the body of Aspatia, whom he had slain unintentionally.

Melantius (mə·lăn′shĭ·əs), Evadne's brother, a valiant soldier. Devoted to his friend Amintor, he persuades him to explain the reason for his strange fits of misery. Unlike Amintor, he feels no allegiance to an unjust monarch, and he plots the killing, which is carried out by Evadne, while playing upon the King's overconfidence to attain his ends.

Aspatia (ə·spā′shə), Amintor's betrothed, who grieves constantly after

654

his marriage to Evadne and sings sad songs of faithful maidens and false lovers. She longs for death and finally finds it at the moment when she least desires it, when she hears from Amintor that he loves her still. She had come to him disguised as a boy and deliberately provoked him to a duel; he wounded her mortally before he realized who she was.

Calianax (kă·lǐ·ă'nəks), her father, a cowardly, testy old man. He was a longtime enemy of Melantius, who used his distrust to advance his plot against the king.

Lysippus (lǐ·sǐ'pəs), the King's brother and successor. Recognizing the justice of Melantius' cause, he pardons him and his followers, who hold the key military positions in the city.

Diphilus (dǐ'fǐ·ləs), Melantius' brother and fellow conspirator.

Cleon (klē'ŏn) and
Strato (strā'tō), nobles in the court of Rhodes.

Diagoras (dǐ·ă'gə·rəs), doorkeeper in the King's banqueting hall.

Dula (dū'lə), Evadne's witty lady in waiting.

Antiphila (ăn·tǐ'fǐ·lə) and
Olympias (ō·lǐm'pǐ·əs), Aspatia's devoted maids.

Two Gentlemen, servants of the King, who watch Evadne enter his bedchamber and plan to enjoy her themselves. They discover their master's body and fear that they will be accused of his murder.

MAIN STREET

Author: Sinclair Lewis (1885-1951)
Time of action: c. 1910-1920
First published: 1920

PRINCIPAL CHARACTERS

Carol Kennicott, an idealistic girl eager to reform the world. Interested in sociology and civic improvement, she longs to transform the ugliness of Midwestern America into something more beautiful. Having married Dr. Will Kennicott, she moves to his home in Gopher Prairie, Minnesota, a hideous small town indistinguishable from hundreds of similar communities. There she shocks and angers the townspeople by her criticisms and by her attempts to combat the local smugness. To its citizens Gopher Prairie is perfection; they can see no need for change. To her, it is an ugly, gossipy, narrow-minded village, sunk in dullness and self-satisfaction. Her efforts to change the town fail, and she drifts into a mild flirtation with Erik Valborg, a Swedish tailor with artistic yearnings. Frightened by the village gossip, she and Kennicott take a trip to California; but

on her return she realizes that she must get away from both her husband and Gopher Prairie. After some argument, she and her small son leave for Washington, where she stays for more than a year. The flight is a failure, for she finds Washington only an agglomeration of the small towns in America. She returns to Gopher Prairie, realizing that it is her home. Her crusade has failed; she can only hope that her children will accomplish what she has been unable to do.

Dr. Will Kennicott, Carol's husband, a successful physician in Gopher Prairie. Though he loves Carol, he is dull and unimaginative, unable to enter her world or to understand her longings. He is the typical self-satisfied citizen of a small town.

Guy Pollock, a lawyer. Though sensitive and intellectual, he is the victim of the "village virus" that has deprived him of all initiative. At first he appears to Carol as the most hopeful person in town, but he disappoints her with his timidity and conventionalism.

Vida Sherwin, a teacher in the High School. Though better educated, she is as satisfied with the Gopher Prairie standards as are the other citizens. She marries Raymond Wutherspoon.

Raymond Wutherspoon, a sales clerk in the Bon Ton Store. A pallid, silly man, he marries Vida Sherwin. He goes to France during World War I and returns as a major.

Erik Valborg, a tailor in Gopher Prairie, the son of a Swedish farmer. Handsome and esthetically inclined, he attracts Carol, and they have a mild flirtation. But gossip drives him from the town; he goes to Minneapolis and is last seen playing small parts in the movies.

Bea Sorenson, a farm girl who comes to Gopher Prairie to find work. She is as much fascinated by the town as Carol is repelled. She becomes the Kennicotts' hired girl and Carol's only real friend. She marries Miles Bjornstam and has a son. She and the little boy both die of typhoid fever.

Miles Bjornstam, the village handy man and radical, one of the few genuine people in Gopher Prairie and one of the few who understand Carol. He marries Bea Sorenson; when she and their child die, he leaves the town.

Mrs. Bogart, the Kennicotts' neighbor. She is the epitome of village narrow-mindedness.

Sam Clark, a hardware dealer and solid citizen.

Percy Bresnahan, born in Gopher Prairie but now a successful automobile manufacturer in Boston. He visits his home for occasional fishing trips and stoutly maintains that it is God's country. Heavy-handed, jocular, and thoroughly standardized, he is the forerunner of George F. Babbitt.

James Blauser, known as "Honest Jim." A professional hustler and promoter, he is hired to start a campaign for a Greater Gopher Prairie. Not much is accomplished.

Hugh, Will and Carol's first child, on whom she lavishes her attention.

MAJOR BARBARA

Author: Bernard Shaw (1856-1950)
Time of action: Early twentieth century
First presented: 1905

PRINCIPAL CHARACTERS

Sir Andrew Undershaft, a munitions tycoon. Believing that poverty is the root of all discontent and, consequently, a threat to capitalism, he uses his power and wealth in an attempt to eliminate it. In a war of ideas with his daughter Barbara, he proves that a donation from a dealer in death—namely, himself—will buy the good graces of the Salvation Army. He then proceeds to fill the void created by her disillusionment by converting her to his own creed.

Barbara, Sir Andrew's daughter. As a major in the Salvation Army, she exercises her moral fervor in the cause of winning the souls of the poor to the Kingdom of God. When her father proves to her that a donation from his deplored and destructive profession can

656

win the favor of the Army, she becomes converted to his creed that it is useless to attempt the salvation of souls until the souls' destroyer, poverty, has been eliminated.

Adolphus Cusins, a professor of Greek, Barbara's suitor. His intellect, added to Sir Andrew's power and Barbara's moral fervor, completes the trinity that Sir Andrew believes will be the salvation of society.

Lady Britomart Undershaft, Sir Andrew's domineering wife, who abhors what she calls her husband's immorality, though she does not hesitate to capitalize on it.

Stephen Undershaft, Sir Andrew's painfully conventional son.

Sarah Undershaft, Sir Andrew's younger daughter.

Charles Lomax, Sarah Undershaft's vacuous suitor.

Snobby Price,
Rummy Mitchens,
Peter Shirley, and
Bill Walker, frequenters of the Salvation Army headquarters.

THE MALCONTENT

Author: John Marston (1576-1634)
Time of action: Thirteenth century
First presented: 1604

PRINCIPAL CHARACTERS

Giovanni Altofronto, the deposed Duke of Genoa. Disguised as **Malevole,** the Malcontent, he hurls insults at the dissolute courtiers and ladies around him while he inwardly laments the misfortunes which have forced him to play this role. His feigned eccentricity enables him to learn of the court intrigues and eventually to engineer the recovery of his dukedom.

Celso, Altofronto's friend and his spy at the usurper's court.

Pietro Jacomo, the usurper Duke. He dotes on his faithless young wife and pampers his adopted heir, Mendoza, until Malevole tells him of their disloyalty and helps him avenge this dishonor. Chastened by the recognition of his own blindness to others, he gratefully relinquishes his title to the rightful Duke.

Mendoza, his ambitious protégé, the Duchess' lover. His ruthless plans to destroy all those who stand between him and the dukedom are foiled only by Malevole's intervention.

Ferneze, a handsome, unprincipled courtier, Mendoza's rival for the favors of the Duchess.

Aurelia, Jacomo's young wife, who succumbs to both Mendoza and Ferneze. She repents when she believes her husband has committed suicide, and she is happily reunited with him after Malevole has exposed Mendoza's treachery.

Maria, Altofronto's virtuous wife. She repulses Mendoza's advances, preferring death to disloyalty to her husband.

Bilioso, a foolish old courtier, regularly deceived by his young wife. Malevole taunts him for his fluctuating allegiance to each new claimant to the dukedom.

Maquerelle, Aurelia's aging lady in waiting. She aids and abets the Duchess and her ladies in their infidelities.

Emilia and
Biancha, the Duchess' attendants.

657

THE MALTESE FALCON

Author: Dashiell Hammett (1894-1961)
Time of action: Twentieth century
First published: 1930

Sam Spade, a tall, blond, pleasantly satanic-looking, hard-boiled private detective suspected of having killed Thursby and of having also killed Miles Archer in order to marry Iva. He at last discovers how he has been used in the plot to get the Maltese falcon; he discovers the murderers of Miles and Thursby, and he turns Brigid over to the police.

Brigid O'Shaughnessy, his tall, attractive, auburn-haired, deceitful client, who first masquerades as a Miss Wonderly, then shoots Miles, double-crosses her associates, and finally attempts in vain to seduce Sam into letting her go free of a murder charge.

Casper Gutman, her fat, tough employer, who is attempting to get hold of the Maltese falcon. He is shot by Wilmer Cook.

Wilmer Cook, Gutman's young body-guard, murderer of Thursby, Jacobi, and Gutman.

Joel Cairo, Gutman's dark-skinned, flashily dressed one-time agent.

Miles Archer, Spade's middle-aged partner, solidly built, wide-shouldered, red-faced. He is shot and killed by Brigid.

Floyd Thursby, Brigid's murdered accomplice.

Iva Archer, Miles's wife, a voluptuous, still pretty blonde in her thirties; in love with Sam.

Kemidov, a Russian in Constantinople who has substituted a lead imitation for the genuine Maltese falcon.

Jacobi, captain of the ship "La Paloma"; killed by Wilmer.

Effie Perine, Sam's lanky, boyish-faced, suntanned secretary.

Rhea Gutman, daughter of Gutman.

MAN AND SUPERMAN

Author: Bernard Shaw (1856-1950)
Time of action: c. 1900
First published: 1903; *first presented:* 1905

Ann Whitefield, a good-looking and vital young woman. At the urging of the Life Force, which is striving toward the eventual creation of the Superman, she is a liar, a coquette, a bully, and a hypocrite. She is also charming enough to get away with it all. Her flagrant violations of the romantic idea of the woman's role in courtship enable her to entrap Jack Tanner.

John (Jack) Tanner, a big, bearded, wealthy young man with an Olympian manner, but a saving sense of humor. Tanner is the dramatically unconventional author of "The Revolutionist's Handbook." With no illusions about Ann or any other woman, he wants to preserve his freedom from them all. Tanner tries to flee to a Mohammedan country where men are protected. Ann tracks him down and captures him in Spain. Realizing that all of Nature is conspiring against his independence, Tanner reluctantly submits to the marriage.

Octavius Robinson, a young man who wants to write a great play. Handsome, sincere, romantic, and naïve, he is in love with Ann, who calls him "Ricky-ticky-tavy." She pities him for idealizing women and predicts that he will remain a bachelor.

Violet Robinson, Octavius' intelligent and exquisitely pretty sister. Violet is found to be pregnant. She finally reveals that she is secretly married, but she will not name her husband. Violet, as purposeful and predatory as Ann, is more direct in her methods.

Hector Malone, Junior, an American gentleman of twenty-four. Manly, moral, but romantic, Hector has married Violet, but at her insistence he does not acknowledge the marriage.

Hector Malone, Senior, an Irishman who has made himself a billionaire in America. Violently prejudiced against the English middle class, he calls on Violet and threatens to disinherit his son if he marries her. When it is inadvertently revealed they are already married, Violet charms and bullies Hector, Senior, into accepting her. Her husband dramatically gives up his inheritance, but Violet promises to make him change his mind.

Henry Straker, Tanner's chauffeur. A presentable young Cockney socialist who is afflicted with pride of class, Straker warns Tanner that Ann is after him.

Mendoza (měn·dō′thä), a tall, witty London Jew who had formerly been a waiter. Disappointed in his love for Straker's sister Louisa, Mendoza has set up as leader of a troop of bandits who specialize in robbing motorists passing through the Spanish Sierras. He captures Tanner and Straker as they flee from Ann. Tanner takes a liking to Mendoza and tells the soldiers sent to capture the bandits that Mendoza's men are his escorts.

Roebuck Ramsden, an elderly gentleman who prides himself on his progressive ideas. He is appointed Ann's guardian along with Jack Tanner, whom he detests.

Rhoda Whitefield, Ann's younger sister. Ann keeps Rhoda and Tanner apart, lest Rhoda snare him.

Mrs. Whitefield, the mother of Ann and Rhoda. A faded, squeaking woman, she is the scapegoat for Ann's willful actions.

Susan Ramsden, Roebuck's daughter, a hard-headed old maid who represents the narrowest sort of conventionality.

Don Juan Tenorio (dōn hwän tā·nō′-ryō), the legendary lover. While he is Mendoza's captive, Jack Tanner dreams of Don Juan in Hell. Don Juan, who is much like Tanner, is bored by the petty chatter of Hell's society and decides to pursue the contemplative life in Heaven.

Don Gonzalo (dōn gŏn·thä′lō), who is much like Roebuck Ramsden. In life, Don Gonzalo, a soldier, had been killed by Don Juan in a duel. He appears in the form of the marble statue that drags Don Giovanni to Hell at the end of Mozart's opera. Bored with Heaven, Don Gonzalo takes up residence in Hell.

The Devil, who resembles Mendoza. He is a moralist, a wit, a romantic, and a reformer.

Doña Ana de Ulloa (dō′nyä ä′nä dä ōō-lyō′ä), who resembles Ann Whitefield. Ana personifies the female vessel through which the Life Force strives toward its ultimate goal, the Superman. Everything else must be subordinated to that end; and thus woman, by her nature, must be a stealthy and cunning predator.

659

THE MAN OF FEELING

Author: Henry Mackenzie (1745-1831)
Time of action: Mid-eighteenth century
First published: 1771

PRINCIPAL CHARACTERS

Mr. Harley, the man of feeling. Being an extremely virtuous man, he believes that all human beings are like himself. He has many disappointments and some genuine trouble because he believes people are essentially good. He is unambitious for money, and he is unambitious in love. When he finds that the woman he loves is affianced to a wealthy man, he is heartbroken, although he has never declared his love. Because of his feelings on the matter he becomes physically ill and dies.

Miss Walton, a rich heiress of a higher station in life than Mr. Harley. It is for her that he pines away and dies. She belatedly comes to love him, tells him so on his deathbed, and breaks off her engagement to the man of her father's choice. She remains single after Harley's death.

Miss Atkins, a London prostitute who wishes to return to her family. With Harley's help she is reunited with her father. When Harley first meets her, he takes her to a brothel for food, since the poor girl has done so poorly in her profession as to be hungry and penniless.

Mr. Atkins, the prostitute's father, a retired army officer. Through Harley he and his daughter are reconciled.

Mr. Edwards, a farmer who loses his lands because of the Enclosure Acts and then, though an old man, enters the army to take his son's place, so that the son, who has been seized by a press gang, may remain at home to care for his wife and children. Harley promises the old man a farm on his estates.

Miss Harley, Harley's maiden aunt. She rears Harley after the deaths of his parents and inculcates him with virtue.

THE MAN OF MODE

Author: Sir George Etherege (1634?-1691)
Time of action: The 1670's
First presented: 1676

PRINCIPAL CHARACTERS

Dorimant, a London dandy with a great reputation as a lover. He brutally casts off one mistress for another. He masquerades part of the time as Courtage, to hide his identity from Lady Woodvill, Harriet's mother. As Courtage he wins Lady Woodvill's admiration, in order to gain her consent to marry her daughter.

Sir Fopling Flutter, a foolish fop. He dresses, acts, and speaks foolishly.

Lady Loveit, Dorimant's mistress. Tired of her, he tries to escape from the entanglement with her. She complains bitterly to Bellinda, not knowing she is supplanted in Dorimant's affections by Bellinda.

Bellinda, a beautiful woman who succeeds Lady Loveit as Dorimant's mistress. She is as amoral as Lady Loveit and Dorimant. She does not mind Dorimant's marrying Harriet so long as her love affair with him remains a secret.

Harriet, a beautiful, wealthy girl from the country. She is attracted to Dorimant, but she is the girl Old Bellair wants his son to marry. She is uninterested in marrying young Bellair and he is uninterested in marrying her. She is finally permitted to marry Dorimant.

Bellair, a London dandy and a friend of Dorimant. He wishes to marry Emilia, rather than Harriet, the woman his father has chosen for him. He marries Emilia without his father's knowledge.

Old Bellair, Bellair's father. He falls in love with Emilia, whom his son loves, and wants to marry her himself.

Lady Townley, young Bellair's aunt. Bellair hopes she can help him win his father's consent to marry Emilia.

Lady Woodvill, Harriet's mother. She is anxious for a marriage between her daughter and Bellair. Her main interest is to keep her daughter from being seduced by Dorimant.

Emilia, a young woman whom Bellair hopes to marry. Old Bellair is also smitten and wants to marry her, not knowing of his son's intentions. She and Bellair marry secretly before Old Bellair can intervene.

THE MAN WHO WAS THURSDAY

Author: Gilbert Keith Chesterton (1874-1936)
Time of action: Early twentieth century
First published: 1908

PRINCIPAL CHARACTERS

Lucian Gregory, an anarchist and a poet. He hopes to be elected as Thursday on the Central Anarchist Council but is disappointed. In the long run he turns out to be the only intellectual anarchist.

Sunday, the chairman of the Central Anarchist Council. He turns out to be a wealthy Scotland Yard official in charge of efforts to unearth anarchists. He gives a party on his estate and turns up dressed as a symbol of the Christian Sabbath.

Gabriel Syme, a poet who believes in order. Gregory takes him to the meeting of the Central Anarchist Council. Though he is a police spy, Syme is elected to be Thursday, the post his friend wanted.

The Marquis de St. Eustache, a dapper

man who is Wednesday on the Central Anarchist Council. He is sent by the anarchists to kill the Tsar of Russia and the President of France, but he turns out to be another police spy for Scotland Yard.

Bull, who is Saturday on the Central Anarchist Council and is also a police spy.

Gogol, who is Tuesday on the Central Anarchist Council and is also a police spy.

Professor de Worms, who is Friday on the Central Anarchist Council. He turns out to be a young actor disguised as the professor in order to act as a spy on the anarchists for Scotland Yard.

The Secretary, who is Monday on the Central Anarchist Council. He also is a spy for Scotland Yard.

THE MAN WITHOUT A COUNTRY

Author: Edward Everett Hale (1822-1909)
Time of action: Nineteenth century
First published: 1863

PRINCIPAL CHARACTERS

Philip Nolan, a brash young American army officer who becomes involved in Aaron Burr's conspiracy against the United States. At his court-martial, in a show of bravado, the young man curses his country. As a result he is sentenced to serve out his life aboard naval vessels, never seeing the United States or hearing it mentioned. Even his books and periodicals are excised of all allusions to his country. Through the years Nolan is transferred from one navy vessel to another, always wearing an army uniform with plain buttons, thus acquiring the nickname of "Plain Buttons." As time passes, authorities in the Navy and in Washington forget Nolan, but he is still passed from one ship to another, never allowed within a hundred miles of the American coast. As the years pass his unconcern, worn bravely at first, fades away, as he wanders the seas an official expatriate—countryless, friendless, even nameless. As he finally lies dying, an old man, the captain of his current prison ship tells Nolan what has happened in the fifty-six years since Nolan left the country, omitting only the Civil War, for the dying man's sake.

Colonel Morgan, the army officer conducting the court-martial which sends Philip Nolan to his years of wandering over the sea.

MANETTE SALOMON

Authors: Edmond (1822-1896) and Jules (1830-1870) de Goncourt
Time of action: Nineteenth century
First published: 1867

PRINCIPAL CHARACTERS

Manette Salomon (mȧ·net′ sȧ·lô·môn′), a Jewish model, Naz de Coriolis' mistress. With her frank, ignorant nature and exotic Jewishness, she delights her lover, but when she becomes famous as the subject of his successful painting, there grows in her a pride that causes her to change. Mistaken for Coriolis' wife, she finds this status attractive. When she becomes a mother, her greed for success comes to the fore, and she gradually gains ascendancy over her lover. When they are married, the fulfillment of her ambition spells the death of his creativity.

Naz de Coriolis (nȧz dǝ kô·ryô·lēs′), a young painter who vows never to wed because he believes marriage and fatherhood destroy the artist's creativity. Fascinated by Manette Salomon's physical perfection and exotic Jewishness, he takes her as a model and his mistress. When fame and motherhood arouse her pride and ambition, he has not the strength to struggle against either her domination over him or the resulting death of his creativity.

Anatole Bazoche (ȧ·nȧ·tôl′ bȧ·zôsh′), a painter, Naz de Coriolis' close friend, who is alienated from him by Manette. A true Bohemian to the last, Anatole, never a "success," retains his freedom.

662

Chassagnol (shá·sà·nyôl'), a painter alienated from Naz de Coriolis by Manette.

Garnotelle (gár·nô·tel'), a mediocre but successful painter after whom Manette insists Naz de Coriolis model himself.

Crescent, (kre·säñ'), a painter, and Mme. Crescent, his wife, who befriend Manette but become cool toward her when they learn that she is Jewish. The peasant, Mme. Crescent, senses something hidden and destructive in Manette.

MANFRED

Author: George Gordon, Lord Byron (1788-1824)
Time of action: No time set
First published: 1817

PRINCIPAL CHARACTERS

Manfred, a magician who summons the spirits of the universe, asking them for knowledge and oblivion. Although he contemplates suicide, mourning his limited powers, he is saved by a chamois hunter. He continues to raise other spirits and refuses the help of the Church. Since he does not give his loyalty to the Church or the powers of evil, he dies conquered by nothing but death.

The Spirit of Air, who asks Manfred what he wants to forget, a question the magician cannot answer.

The Spirit of Interior Fire,
The Spirit of Ocean,
The Spirit of Earth,
The Spirit of Exterior Fire, and
The Spirit of Night, spirits summoned by Manfred.

The Spirit of Manfred's Destiny, summoned by Manfred. It takes on the

bodily shape of a beautiful woman who eludes the magician's embrace.

The Chamois Hunter, who saves Manfred from death. Seeing Manfred preparing to leap to his death on the Jungfrau Mountain, the hunter prevents the suicide. He feels sorry for Manfred but cannot help the magician solve his problems.

The Witch of the Alps, summoned by Manfred. She offers to share the beauties of nature with the magician and to aid him, if he agrees to obey her. She departs when Manfred refuses.

The Abbot of St. Maurice. He tries to save Manfred's soul for God but fails.

Astarte, whom Manfred has wronged. She is summoned from her tomb at Manfred's request by spirits in the Hall of Arimanes. She prophesies that his despair will end the next day. Death fulfills her prophecy.

MANHATTAN TRANSFER

Author: John Dos Passos (1896-   )
Time of action: World War I
First published: 1925

PRINCIPAL CHARACTERS

Ellen Thatcher, the character who helps keep together the amorphous plot of the novel. She is an actress who lives through

chaotic times, America just before and after World War I. She becomes a success as an actress, a failure as a woman.

663

She is married three times but never to the one man she loves.

Jimmy Herf, an arrival from Europe who comes to New York with his widowed mother; she dies shortly after their arrival. He is unhappy and tries to find himself. He works on a newspaper before the war and does Red Cross work with Ellen in Europe during the hostilities. He and Ellen marry and have a child, but they drift apart. Still confused but happy, he leaves New York.

George Baldwin, a cautious, intelligent lawyer and a ruthless, self-centered opportunist. He steers a shrewd course through New York City politics, but proves his emotional immaturity in his affairs with women. He is Ellen's third husband, whom she marries not out of love but because of apathy.

Joe Harland, Herf's blacksheep relative who, having won and lost several fortunes in Wall Street, finally settles for a job as a night watchman in order to earn whiskey money.

Gus McNiel, a milkman who, through the good work done by George Baldwin, wins a financial settlement after he has been run over by a train. Baldwin's professional and personal lives are involved with McNiel. Baldwin, who helps McNiel rise to political power, does not hesitate to seduce McNiel's wife Nellie when he has the chance.

Stan Emery, a drunken college boy who is finally expelled from the school he attends. He is the only man Ellen ever loves. His drinking goes from bad to worse and while drunk he marries a slattern named Pearline. Filled with self-disgust, he finally sets fire to his apartment and perishes in the flames. Ellen had become pregnant by him but after his death she has an abortion.

Joe O'Keefe, a young labor organizer who comes back from the war with a syphilitic infection and a grudge against big business.

Emile and
Congo, two young Frenchmen who come to New York to seek their fortunes. Emile finds his in the arms of a widowed Frenchwoman who owns a delicatessen; Congo makes a fortune as a successful bootlegger.

Jeff and
Emily Merivale, Herf's wealthy uncle and aunt and also his legal guardians.

Susie and
Ed Thatcher, Ellen's parents. Susie dies, a neurotic, while Ellen is a child. Ed works hard to support his daughter and provides for her until she leaves home for a career on the stage.

John Oglethorpe, Ellen's first husband, who is a competent but lazy homosexual actor.

Harry Goldweiser, a wealthy Broadway producer who loves Ellen. Ellen never loves him, though she treats him kindly because her career depends on his influence.

Ruth Prynne, a young actress who is a friend of Ellen and John Oglethorpe, and Jimmy Herf.

Cecily Baldwin, Baldwin's socially prominent wife, from whom he obtains a divorce in order to marry Ellen.

MANON LESCAUT

Author: Abbé Prévost (Antoine François Prévost d'Exiles, 1697-1763)
Time of action: 1700
First published: 1731

The Chevalier des Grieux (dā·gryœ'), a student of Philosophy at Amiens. He becomes a seminary student, a card cheat, and finally, returning from New Orleans after Manon's death, a priest.

Tiberge (tē·bĕrzh'), a fellow student who urges des Grieux to forget Manon by studying religion at the Seminary of Saint-Supplice. He follows des Grieux to America and persuades him to return to France.

The Father of des Grieux, who gets his son released from jail but will not help Manon.

Manon Lescaut (ma·nōn' lĕs·kō'), a pretty courtesan who attracts des Grieux. She also bestows her attentions on M. de B—— and later on M. de G—— M——, at the suggestion of her brother. She dies an exile in New Orleans.

M. Lescaut (mə·syœ' lĕs·kō'), of the Royal guards, the unscrupulous brother

of Manon. He is killed by a man whose fortune he won at cards.

M. de B—— (də bā'), who is in love with Manon.

M. de G—— M—— (də zhā' ĕm'), a wealthy old man duped and robbed by des Grieux and Manon.

M. de G—— M—— Jr., the son, who comes to avenge his father but is won over by the charms of Manon.

M. de T—— (də tā'), who helps dupe young G—— M——. He is arrested by the police.

The Governor of New Orleans, who forbids the marriage of Manon and the Chevalier because his nephew, Synnelet, loves her.

M. Synnelet (sē·nə·lā'), who fights a duel with des Grieux over Manon in New Orleans.

MAN'S FATE

Author: André Malraux (1895-   )
Time of action: 1927
First published: 1933

Ch'en (shĕn'), a Chinese terrorist dedicated to the revolution. In an attempt to kill Chiang Kai-shek with a bomb he blows himself up but fails in his mission.

Kyo (kyō'), a Communist organizer of French and Japanese parentage. He is tormented by thoughts of his wife's freely confessed adultery. Arrested by König, he kills himself with a cyanide tablet given him by Katov.

Gisors (zhē·sôr'), Kyo's old French father who resembles an ascetic abbot. After the revolutionary plot fails, he returns to Japan to teach painting.

May (mā'), Kyo's sensual German wife, a physician with advanced views on marriage relationships. The Communist plot having failed and Kyo being dead, she goes to Moscow to practice medicine.

Baron de Clappique (də klà·pēk'), a French adventurer and unscrupulous businessman; König's friend who permits Kyo to be arrested instead of warning him to hide. The Baron in disguise escapes China on a French ship.

Katov (kà·tôv'), an experienced Russian revolutionist and ex-convict. His kindly face, mischievous eyes, and upturned nose do not reveal his coldly murderous nature. Arrested by König, he generously gives Kyo the cyanide tablet he has earlier provided himself with, and he is executed.

Hemmelrich (ā·měl·rēk'), a cowardly German revolutionist whose wife and child are killed in the destruction of his shop by Chiang's police, who later shoot Hemmelrich.

Ferral (fě·rál'), a French businessman who decides to support Chiang. Angered by Valérie's duplicity, he releases forty birds and a kangaroo in her room. He returns to France on the liner which takes the Baron.

König (kœ·nēg'), chief of Chiang's police who foils the Communist plot and executes the revolutionary group.

Chiang Kai-shek (shyäṅg' kảy'-chěk'), leader of the Blue forces.

Valérie (vá·lā·rē'), Ferral's deceitful mistress.

MANSFIELD PARK

Author: Jane Austen (1775-1817)
Time of action: Early nineteenth century
First published: 1814

PRINCIPAL CHARACTERS

Fanny Price, the heroine of the novel. Brought up by the Bertrams at Mansfield Park, she is timid and self-effacing and is constantly reminded by her Aunt Norris of her position as a poor relation. She has always loved Edmund Bertram, the second son. Henry Crawford falls in love with her and proposes but she refuses him, for she considers him shallow and worldly. Thus she angers Sir Thomas Bertram, who feels that she has thrown away her best chance for marriage. Later, when both Bertram daughters disgrace themselves, Sir Thomas understands Fanny's real worth. Edmund, who had thought himself in love with Mary Crawford, is shocked by her attitude towards his sisters' behavior and realizes that he actually loves Fanny. They are married at the end of the novel.

Sir Thomas Bertram, a wealthy baronet, the owner of Mansfield Park. He is dignified, reserved, fundamentally kind and just, but too remote from his children to understand them. Though fond of Fanny Price, he is angered by her refusal to marry Henry Crawford; however, when his daughters disgrace him, he realizes that Fanny has a better judgment of people than he and is happy when she marries his younger son.

Lady Bertram, his wife, the spoiled beauty of her family. She is an indolent, self-indulgent, good-natured woman.

Mrs. Norris, her sister, the widow of a clergyman. A stingy, ill-tempered busybody, she is unbearably severe to her poor niece, Fanny Price, but lavish in her flattery of the rich Bertrams. Her flattery does much to ruin the characters of the Bertram daughters. After Maria Bertram's divorce, Mrs. Norris goes to live with her.

Mrs. Price, the third sister, Fanny's mother. She has made the worst marriage, her husband being a lieutenant of marines without fortune or connections. They have nine children and live at Portsmouth on the edge of poverty.

Lieutenant Price, her husband, a marine officer disabled for active service. He is uncouth but good-natured.

William Price, their son, in the Royal

666

Navy. The favorite of his sister Fanny, he gets his promotion through the Crawfords' friendship with her.

Tom Bertram, the older son of Sir Thomas. He is headstrong, worldly, and idle, but a severe illness sobers him.

Edmund Bertram, the second son, a serious young man who desires to take Holy Orders. He fancies himself in love with Mary Crawford until, disgusted by her cynical attitude towards the clergy and by her easy acceptance of his sisters' conduct, he becomes aware that he really loves Fanny Price. They are married and live near Mansfield Park.

Maria Bertram, the older daughter, spoiled and selfish. She marries wealthy Mr. Rushworth but tires of him, runs off with Henry Crawford, and is irretrievably disgraced.

Julia Bertram, the second daughter and equally spoiled. She elopes with Mr. Yates and by so doing cuts herself off from her family.

Henry Crawford, a wealthy young man who flirts with Maria Bertram. He falls in love with Fanny Price, but she refuses him, and he elopes with Maria, now Mrs. Rushworth. They separate after a few months.

Mary Crawford, his sister. She is cynical and worldly but attracts Edmund Bertram. He is disillusioned and repelled when she takes his sisters' conduct so casually.

Mr. Rushworth, the rich but brainless husband of Maria Bertram, whom she deserts for Henry Crawford.

Mr. Yates, a fashionable young man who visits Mansfield Park and eventually elopes with Julia Bertram. The marriage greatly displeases her father.

THE MARBLE FAUN

Author: Nathaniel Hawthorne (1804-1864)
Time of action: Mid-nineteenth century
First published: 1860

PRINCIPAL CHARACTERS

Donatello, in reality the **Count of Monte Beni,** at first a naïve young man who seems to be almost dim-witted, with little formal education and almost no intellectual, moral, or emotional depth. He appears almost a creature out of the mythical past, a faun out of his time and place associating with the painters and sculptors of the artist colony in nineteenth century Rome. Feeling a kinship with nature and its inhabitants, he is truly happy only in the woods and gardens. He falls in love with Miriam Schaefer, a beautiful but mysterious young painter. One night, at her unspoken behest, Donatello murders a man. This crime brings about a change in the young Italian nobleman, who for a time retires to his ancestral home in Tuscany.

He finds that he is no longer akin to nature, but in exchange for this loss he acquires new depth of soul under the torment of his crime and awakes to moral values. In the garb of a penitent he returns to Rome, where he is reunited briefly with his beloved during the carnival season. At the end of that time he is seized by the authorities and imprisoned.

Miriam Schaefer, an exotically beautiful young woman of wealth who appears mysteriously among the people of an artist colony in Rome. She is also a painter, and her life is haunted by a man who appears to be an artist's model. He seems to have a strange hold over the girl and causes her great uneasiness. Miriam's lover, Donatello, rids her of

667

the presence of this troublesome man by throwing him from the famous Tarpeian Rock. Because her eyes had commanded Donatello to commit the crime, Miriam feels as guilty as if the act had been her own. Also, she feels a bond with her companion-accomplice as strong as marriage ties. She, like Donatello, suffers the pangs of conscience fiercely. She and her lover, reunited after his return from a period of retirement in Tuscany, find a brief period of happiness before he is committed to prison. Miriam, who goes free, is really a member of an aristocratic Italian family and was at one time engaged to marry the man who haunted her. Her real name is never mentioned.

Brother Antonio, a Capuchin monk, the man who haunts and hounds Miriam Schaefer until he is murdered by Donatello. Having shown himself to be of great merit, at least on the surface, he is granted unusual freedom by his order, a freedom he uses in order to dog the girl's footsteps. Once her fiancé, he had committed a crime in which Miriam, though innocent, was implicated.

Hilda, a pretty, virtuous American girl studying painting in Rome. Because she is Miriam's friend, she becomes involved

in the intrigue surrounding Miriam. She witnesses the midnight murder committed by Donatello, and at Miriam's request she delivers a strange parcel which causes her to be held in a convent as a possible accessory to the crime. Hilda is much affected by the terrible deed she witnesses, even though she has no guilt. The weight of her knowledge drives the over-sensitive girl to lose all interest in her work. Though she is faithful to and proud of her Puritan heritage, she becomes so disturbed that she enters a confessional in St. Peter's Cathedral and tells her story to a priest. In the end her experiences cause her to love Kenyon, a young American in love with her.

Kenyon, a young American sculptor working in Rome. He loves Hilda and is one of the little circle of friends surrounding Miriam Schaefer. He brings Donatello and Miriam together again after they have suffered alone following the murder of Brother Antonio by Donatello. Kenyon's love for Hilda is eventually rewarded, for she comes to love him and they are married. Once after their marriage they encounter Miriam, who both blesses and repulses them silently. They do not disturb her expiation and grief.

MARCHING ON

Author: James Boyd (1888-1944)
Time of action: The Civil War period
First published: 1927

PRINCIPAL CHARACTERS

James Fraser, a North Carolina farm boy, awkward, uncouth, sensitive, and proud, but ambitious to rise in life. His experience as a railroad worker in Wilmington and his Civil War service, including a long internment as a prisoner of war, mature him. Also, his dedication to his beliefs and his determination to endure life's hardships enable him to regard himself as humanly equal to those whom

he had once looked upon as his superiors. James may be thought of as an illustration of what Jefferson in a letter to John Adams called a "true aristocrat," the grounds of whose aristocracy are "virtue and talents."

Stewart Prevost, a rich planter's daughter loved by James. Appreciative of his desire to better himself, she offers him money to help him do so. Less conscious than James of the difference in social and financial status between them, she loves him and is willing to marry him.

Colonel Prevost, her father. Courteous and friendly to the Fraser family, he gives the impression that he considers them beneath himself and his daughter, and he at first opposes a continuation of the relationship between Stewart and James. Later, convinced of James's true worth, he is happy to have Stewart marry a Fraser.

Charles Prevost, Stewart's brother, a Confederate captain under whom James serves. When Charles is killed, James shoots the killers.

MARDI

Author: Herman Melville (1819-1891)
Time of action: Mid-nineteenth century
First published: 1849

PRINCIPAL CHARACTERS

The Narrator, a young American sailor in the South Seas who, with a companion, jumps ship and leaves in a small boat for hospitable islands. He meets, at sea, a blonde native girl named Yillah. The party is welcomed to an island by a group of natives who call the Narrator Taji, thinking he is that god reincarnated. The Narrator falls in love with Yillah and when she mysteriously disappears he wanders the seas, visiting many islands, looking for her. His quest is to no avail.

Yillah, the Narrator's sweetheart, the symbol for good in the novel. After her disappearance the Narrator's search for her is obviously the symbolic quest that men make to find good in the world.

Hautia, a dark native queen who is Yillah's rival for the Narrator's love. She supposedly symbolizes evil in the narrative, and though the Narrator discovers her to be attractive, he refuses the favors she offers him.

Jarl, a sailor aboard the "Arcturion" who, with the Narrator, leaves the whaling vessel and travels among the islands of the South Seas.

Samoa, a native whom Jarl and the Narrator find hiding in a derelict ship. The sailors befriend him, and he accompanies them on their travels.

Media, a native king who mistakes the Narrator for the god Taji and offers him the hospitality of the island.

Babbalanja, a wise man in Media's court who tells the Narrator that having lost Yillah, he will never again find her.

King Donjalolo, monarch of the island of Juam, who moves from place to place on his island home in order to escape reality.

Yoomy, the minstrel-poet of King Media's court.

MARIA CHAPDELAINE

Author: Louis Hémon (1880-1913)
Time of action: Early twentieth century
First published: 1916

Maria Chapdelaine (mä·ryä' shäp·də-lĕn'), a French-Canadian farm girl. After the death of the man she loves Maria looks upon the northland as a hostile country and almost accepts Lorenzo Surprenant as a husband, knowing he will take her to an easier life in a city in the United States. She finally decides, however, that she can, like her mother, be a good pioneer wife. She then accepts Eutrope Gagnon, a farmer like her father, as her husband.

Samuel Chapdelaine (sä·mü·ĕl' shäp·də-lĕn'), Maria's father. He moves his family many times, for he wants always to be away from neighbors and civilization. He is a hardworking man.

Mrs. Chapdelaine (shäp·də·lĕn'), Maria's mother. Her death, which she faces as

steadfastly as she does life, persuades Maria to remain in the north and marry a farmer.

François Paradis (frän·swä' pä·rä·dē'), a young fur trader who falls in love with Maria. He dies of exposure while traveling afoot across the wastes of northern Quebec to visit Maria at Christmastime.

Eutrope Gagnon (œ·trôp' gän·yōn'), a pioneering farmer and suitor for Maria's hand. He is an honest, hardworking young man. He can say little for himself, but his earnestness wins Maria.

Lorenzo Surprenant (lô·rän·zō' sür·prə-nän'), a suitor for Maria's hand. He works in factories in the United States and tries to convince Maria that life as his wife will be easier for her than life as a farmer's wife in Quebec.

MARIA MAGDALENA

Author: Friedrich Hebbel (1813-1863)
Time of action: Nineteenth century
First published: 1844

Clara, a young girl who, to prove her love, gives herself physically to the man she loves. She is crushed when he does not want to marry her and seizes as his excuse the fact that Clara's brother has been accused of theft. Feeling that her pregnancy and its disgrace may drive her father to suicide, Clara thinks of killing herself. The arrival of an old suitor who still wants to marry her only puts off the action for a time. Clara drowns herself in the household well.

Leonard, Clara's lover and fiancé. He is a selfish, calculating young man. In order to get a job he courts the mayor's daughter. Finding the girl loves him, he throws over Clara, despite her pregnancy, to marry his new love. Leonard is killed in a duel by the Secretary, a suitor who loves Clara.

The Secretary, a childhood sweetheart of Clara. He wants to marry her, though she is pregnant by Leonard. He vows to fight a duel with Leonard, does, and is fatally wounded.

Karl, Clara's brother. Because of an unsavory reputation he is accused of theft and thus gives Leonard an excuse to break off with Clara. Later Karl is cleared of any guilt.

Anthony, Clara's father. He is a simple-minded cabinetmaker who does not understand what happens to his family. The Secretary, dying, accuses Anthony of Clara's death because of his pride and weakness. But Anthony, unable to comprehend the mysteries of life, fails to see how he can be at all responsible for his daughter's suicide.

Anthony's Wife, Clara's mother. She is a respectable, God-fearing woman who wishes only the best for her family. The accusations leveled against her son are enough of a shock to kill her.

MARIANNE

Author: Pierre Carlet de Chamblain de Marivaux (1688-1763)
Time of action: Late seventeenth century
First published: 1731-1741

PRINCIPAL CHARACTERS

Marianne (mà·ryàn′), the Countess of ——, a virtuous orphan. Orphaned as an infant, she is put in the care of a kind woman who dies when Marianne is fifteen. Her second benefactor, M. de Climal, offers to set her up in an apartment. This proposal she proudly rejects. She takes up residence in a nearby convent where she is sought out by a young man who becomes attracted to her appearance when he sees her on the street. He turns out to be M. de Valville, with whom she falls in love and whom she plans to marry until he becomes infatuated with Mlle. Varthon and jilts his fiancée.

M. de Valville (də vàl·vēl′), a young man attracted to Marianne when he sees her on the street. He seeks her out and becomes engaged to her, only to become infatuated with Mlle. Varthon, for whom he jilts Marianne.

M. de Climal (də klē·màl′), Marianne's benefactor in Paris. He arranges for her lodging with Mme. Dutour and later, with protestations of undying love, offers to set her up in an apartment. His offer sends Marianne off to a convent.

Mme. de Valville (də vàl·vēl′), M. de Valville's mother and Marianne's loving benefactress at the convent until her death, which leaves the girl alone in the world.

Mlle. Varthon (vàr·tôn′), a young girl who attracts M. de Valville away from Marianne.

Mlle. de Tervire (də tĕr·vēr′), a nun who tries to comfort Marianne by telling her the story of her own life.

Mme. Dutour (dü·tōōr′), a shopkeeper, Marianne's landlady, provided by M. de Climal.

MARIUS THE EPICUREAN

Author: Walter Pater (1839-1894)
Time of action: Second century
First published: 1885

PRINCIPAL CHARACTERS

Marius, a young Roman of intellectual power living in the reign of Marcus Aurelius. As a young man, influenced by life on a country estate, he becomes an idealist of strong convictions, but his mother's death turns him into a skeptic. From skepticism he later turns to Oriental mysticism and the early Greek philosophers. After reading the writings of Aristippus of Cyrene he becomes an epicurean, seeking sensory experiences which will lead him to wisdom and an appreciation of the universe. He is finally converted to Christianity before his death.

Flavian, Marius' schoolmate and friend. He influences Marius to read literature

671

and philosophy. He also encourages Marius to become a poet. His death from the plague is a great shock to Marius.

Marcus Aurelius, the Roman Emperor, a patron of art and learning. He appoints Marius to be his secretary and editor.

Cornelius, an officer in the famous Twelfth Legion. He becomes Marius' friend and acquaints Marius with the people of Rome and the city itself. Because he is a Christian and a happy man he becomes an influence on Marius' life

and thinking. Under Cornelius' and Cecelia's influence Marius turns to Christianity.

Cecilia, a calm, happy Christian woman. She is a friend of Cornelius and becomes Marius' friend too, helping him to discover the beauty of Christian religion and thought.

Galen, the famous Roman physician under whose influence Marius comes for a time as a young man.

MARKET HARBOROUGH

Author: George J. Whyte-Melville (1821-1878)
Time of action: Nineteenth century
First published: 1861

PRINCIPAL CHARACTERS

John Standish Sawyer, a country gentleman who, deciding that fox hunting is poor in his own country, goes to Market Harborough. There he meets other ardent fox hunters and falls in love with the parson's daughter, who is also devoted to fox hunting. A steeplechase is held, and though Sawyer rides a fine race, he takes a fall near the end of the course and breaks his collarbone. The parson's daughter decides then to marry him. After the marriage she makes him give up hunting. But he is soon observed reading a book about hunting; he will be back with the hounds before long.

The Honorable Crasher, Sawyer's friend and hunting companion at Market Harborough.

Isaac, Sawyer's groom and horse handler.

He tricks the Honorable Crasher into buying, for a large sum, a handsome but worthless horse belonging to Sawyer. With the money from the sale, Sawyer buys a horse good enough to enable him to make a fine showing in the steeplechase.

Tiptop, the Honorable Crasher's groom. He is tricked by Isaac's substitution of horses in a test run into giving his master a glowing report of Sawyer's worthless horse.

Cecilia Dove, the pretty and coquettish daughter of the parson. She marries Sawyer.

Mr. Dove, the parson, an ardent fox hunter.

MARMION

Author: Sir Walter Scott (1771-1832)
Time of action: Early sixteenth century
First published: 1808

Lord Marmion, an English nobleman whose reputation as a fine, brave knight is spotless. He is sent by the English King to try to persuade the Scots to stop raiding the border. Actually, he had declared his love for a young nun, Constance de Beverley, who renounced her vows, left the convent, and followed him. He then met a young heiress and abandoned Constance. He has fought a duel with the knight who loves the heiress, Clare, and left his adversary for dead. He is mortally wounded in battle and on his deathbed repents all his sins.

Ralph de Wilton, Marmion's foe in the duel, who is now disguised as a palmer. He loved Clare but was betrayed by Marmion with some forged papers attesting to the fact that de Wilton was not true to the King. He is finally restored to his title and lands and wins the hand of Clare.

Clare Fitz-Clare, a young novice nun who has joined the convent rather than marry Marmion after the man she really loves, de Wilton, is believed to be fatally wounded. She is finally able to marry de Wilton with the King's blessing.

Constance de Beverley, a nun who broke her vows, fled the convent, and followed Marmion for three years as a page boy. She has the papers forged by Marmion to discredit de Wilton and she begs the abbess to get them to the King so that Clare will not be forced to marry Marmion. The ecclesiastical court puts her to death.

Archibald Douglas, a Scottish nobleman who is charged with Marmion's safe conduct while he is in Scotland, and with the safekeeping of the nuns.

MARRIAGE À LA MODE

Author: John Dryden (1631-1700)
Time of action: Seventeenth century
First presented: 1673

Palamede, a courtier. Ordered by his father to marry Melantha, he becomes attracted to and declares his love for Rhodophil's wife, Doralice. Later, when Doralice becomes reconciled with her husband, Palamede woos Melantha, and they agree to marry.

Rhodophil, Captain of the King's Guard. Married to Doralice, he desires Melantha. When Palamede's father insists that his son marry Melantha at once, Rhodophil and Doralice are reconciled, and each man pledges to respect the other's wife.

Doralice, Rhodophil's wife, desired by Palamede.

Melantha, Palamede's intended, desired by Rhodophil.

Polydamus, the usurper of the throne of Sicily. In search of his long-lost son, he is persuaded by Hermogenes that Leonidas is, indeed, his heir, and he accepts the youth as his own along with Palmyra, the boy's foster sister. Later, it is revealed that Leonidas is, in reality, the heir of the rightful King, and Polydamus is forced to give up the throne to him. The usurper is then forgiven by the new King, to whom he gives Palmyra, now revealed as his own daughter, in marriage.

Hermogenes, a fisherman who raises Leonidas and Palmyra as his own.

Leonidas, the son of the rightful King of Sicily, who is brought up as Hermogenes' child. His identity is finally revealed, and he wins back the throne from Polydamus.

Palmyra, Polydamus' daughter, who is brought up as Hermogenes' child. After her identity is made known, she marries the now rightful King, Leonidas.

Argaleon, Polydamus' favorite, who attempts to marry Palmyra and have Leonidas banished.

Amalthea, Argaleon's sister, who is in love with Leonidas.

Philotis, Melantha's maid.

Eubulus, a former governor who reveals to Palmyra that Leonidas is the son of the rightful King.

THE MARRIAGE OF FIGARO

Author: Pierre Augustin Caron de Beaumarchais (1732-1799)
Time of action: Eighteenth century
First presented: 1784

PRINCIPAL CHARACTERS

Figaro (fē'gə·rō), the Barber of Seville, in this play arranging his own wedding.

Suzanne (sü·zàn), lady in waiting to the Countess. Figaro is in love with her.

Count Almaviva (äl·mä·vē'vä), Figaro's master, whose marriage plans Figaro had helped earlier. Now the bored Count is eying Suzanne.

The Countess, the wife of Figaro's master. She disguises herself as Suzanne to teach her husband a lesson and force him to permit Figaro and Suzanne to marry.

Dr. Bártholo (bär'tō·lō), the former guardian of the Countess. He seeks revenge on the Count and on Figaro.

Marceline (màrs·lēn'), the elderly housekeeper and a creditor of Figaro, who demands repayment or marriage. She eventually discovers that she is her own son, by Dr. Bártholo.

Chérubin (shā·rü·bǎń), the Count's page. He is in love with all women.

A Maid, in love with Chérubin, whom she finally marries.

MARSE CHAN

Author: Thomas Nelson Page (1853-1922)
Time of action: The Civil War period
First published: 1887

PRINCIPAL CHARACTERS

Marse Chan, a young Virginia gentleman, loyal to his family and to his State in the Civil War, during which he becomes a captain. He is killed leading a regimental charge. His love for Anne never ceases even though she rejects him following the duel with her father. When

he dies he has next to his heart the letter of penitence and love which Anne wrote after her father agreed not to stand any longer between the lovers.

Anne Chamberlin, his pretty sweetheart, sorrel-haired and dark-eyed. Proud and unforgiving after her father's duel, she rejects Marse Chan's attempt at reconciliation before he leaves for the war. Nevertheless, her heart and thoughts remain with him, and when she dies not long before the fall of Richmond, she is buried next to Marse Chan.

Sam, Marse Chan's Negro servant, a slave given to Mr. Channing's baby son to be his lifetime body servant. He is Marse Chan's boyhood playmate, his idolizing servant at college and during the war, and the driver who takes his body home for burial. Sam is the prototype of the loyal slave in romantic Southern fiction who regards his relationship to his master not as bondage but as loving service to a kindly and wholly admirable superior.

Mr. Channing, Marse Chan's father, a plantation owner and, like his son, a model Southern gentleman.

Colonel Chamberlin, Anne's father, owner of a neighboring plantation. A Democrat, he is angered at being defeated in a Congressional election won by Mr. Channing, a Whig. The Colonel's hurt pride causes the feud which separates the two families.

Maria, a slave sold by Colonel Chamberlin and bought by Mr. Channing. The purchase of Maria and several other slaves leads to two lawsuits by the Colonel, who loses both of them. Humiliated in a duel with Marse Chan over his insulting remarks about Mr. Channing, he holds a grudge until he hears of Marse Chan's defense of the Chamberlin name in a fight with Ronny.

Mrs. Channing, Mr. Channing's wife.

Mr. Ronny, a lieutenant under Marse Chan, who knocks him down for making improper remarks about Anne and her father.

Ham Fisher, Negro carriage driver rescued from a burning barn by Mr. Channing, who is permanently blinded as a result.

Miss Lucy Chamberlin, Colonel Chamberlin's sister and housekeeper.

Mr. Hall, a schoolmaster.

MARTIN CHUZZLEWIT

Author: Charles Dickens (1812-1870)
Time of action: Early nineteenth century
First published: 1843-1844

PRINCIPAL CHARACTERS

Martin Chuzzlewit (Senior), a rich, eccentric old man descended from a long family line noted for selfishness. He dislikes his fawning relatives and is suspicious that everyone about him is after his fortune. After quarreling with and disinheriting his grandson and namesake whom he had intended to make his heir, he goes to live with Seth Pecksniff in order to prove the motives of that self-styled architect and arch-hypocrite. Having tested young Martin Chuzzlewit by turning him loose to fend for himself in the world and having witnessed many proofs of Pecksniff's duplicity and hypocrisy, he rights the wrongs done to his grandson and abandons Pecksniff to his downward career of drunkenness and beggary.

Martin Chuzzlewit, the title character, a rather wayward and selfish young man brought up in expectation of becoming his grandfather's heir. The two quarrel when Martin falls in love with Mary Graham, his grandfather's companion and ward, and the old man turns his grandson out of the house. Hoping to become an architect, young Martin studies for a time with Seth Pecksniff, a relative, but after a few hints dropped by old Martin, the young man is rebuffed by Pecksniff. With Mark Tapley, a young hostler, he goes to America. Martin's reactions during this journey show Dickens' singular bias against the "uncivilized" areas, customs, and citizens of the United States. After his return to England Martin seeks an interview with his grandfather, but Pecksniff, with whom the old man is living, turns the humbled young man from his door. Comforted only by the love of Mary Graham, he returns to London. Old Martin Chuzzlewit, no longer the senile man he had seemed to be while residing with Pecksniff, appears in London soon afterward, is reunited with his grandson, and gives his blessing to the marriage of young Martin and Mary Graham.

Anthony Chuzzlewit, old Martin Chuzzlewit's brother, a miserly man of cunning and suspicious nature.

Jonas Chuzzlewit, Anthony Chuzzlewit's son. Eager to inherit his father's wealth, he attempts to poison the old man, but his scheme is discovered beforehand by his father and Chuffey, a faithful clerk. Because old Anthony dies of a broken heart a short time later, Jonas believes himself a murderer. He marries Mercy Pecksniff and treats her brutally. Later he becomes convinced that Montague Tigg, a flashy speculator, has learned his secret. Desperate because Tigg demands hush money, Jonas murders him. His guilt is revealed and he is arrested, but he poisons himself while waiting for a coach to take him off to prison.

George Chuzzlewit, a corpulent, gay bachelor.

Mary Graham, old Martin Chuzzlewit's ward, a girl of great integrity and sweetness. Although his great hope is that she and young Martin Chuzzlewit will fall in love and marry, he tests the young people by telling Mary that she will receive nothing after he is dead and by disinheriting his grandson. Mary remains faithful in her devotion to young Martin through all his hardships and tribulations, until they are finally reunited with old Martin's blessing.

Seth Pecksniff, old Martin Chuzzlewit's cousin, an architect and land surveyor who has never built anything, though he receives large premiums from those who study under him. Young Martin Chuzzlewit becomes one of his apprentices, but Pecksniff turns him away to please the young man's grandfather and to insure his own advancement. In all of his dealings he is completely self-seeking; he performs no generous act, shows no generous motives. Servile, false, conniving, he is a complete hypocrite and a monster of selfishness. He becomes a drunkard and a writer of begging letters to his prosperous relatives.

Charity Pecksniff, called **Cherry,** his older daughter. Deserted by Augustus Moddle, her betrothed, she becomes her father's shrewish companion in his later years.

Mercy Pecksniff, called **Merry,** a vain, selfish girl who marries her cousin, Jonas Chuzzlewit, partly to spite her sister. The cruel treatment she receives at his hands transforms her into "a model of uncomplaining endurance and self-denying affection." Old Martin Chuzzlewit provides for her after her husband's death.

John Westlock, an apprentice to Seth Pecksniff, who sees through his master, quarrels with him, and leaves him. His departure leaves room for Martin Chuzzlewit in the Pecksniff household. Always a good friend of Tom Pinch, he falls in love with and marries Tom's sister Ruth. His suspicions of Jonas Chuzzlewit's behavior lead also to the discovery of Tigg's murder and the attempted murder of old Anthony Chuzzlewit.

Tom Pinch, Pecksniff's meek, overworked assistant. Left by his grandmother in Pecksniff's care, he is too trusting and too much burdened by a needless sense of obligation to see his master in his true light. Friendship with John Westlock and Martin Chuzzlewit teach him confidence, however, and when Pecksniff forces his attentions on Mary Graham Tom sees Pecksniff for the hypocrite he is. When Pecksniff discharges him, he is hired by an unknown patron, old Martin Chuzzlewit, to catalogue a library, and with the money thus earned he is able to support his sister Ruth.

Ruth Pinch, a governess, Tom Pinch's loyal sister. She marries John Westlock.

Mark Tapley, the merry, self-reliant hostler at the Blue Dragon Inn in Wiltshire. Eager to see more of the world, he goes with Martin Chuzzlewit to America, where they are swindled by land speculators and disillusioned by all that they see and hear. After his return he marries Mrs. Lupin, the landlady of the Blue Dragon and renames the inn the Jolly Tapley, a name that he considers "very new, conwivial, and expressive."

Mrs. Lupin, landlady of the Blue Dragon Inn, a buxom, beaming widow, later Mrs. Mark Tapley. When they meet after Mark's return to England, he kisses her often and heartily, but insists that he is really kissing his country after having lived "among the patriots."

Montague Tigg, also known as **Tigg Montague, Esq.,** director of the Anglo-Bengalee Disinterested Loan and Life Insurance Company and a swindler. Having learned of Jonas Chuzzlewit's attempt to poison his father, he blackmails Jonas into buying his worthless stock and persuading Pecksniff to invest his funds as well. Jonas kills him. When news of his death reaches London, another partner, David Crimple, makes off with all the funds.

David Crimple, a former pawnbroker and tapster and secretary of the Anglo-Bengalee Disinterested Loan and Life Insurance Company. His theft of the company funds ruins Pecksniff, who had invested in the enterprise on the advice of Jonas Chuzzlewit.

Dr. John Jobling, a physician employed by Montague Tigg as medical inspector for the insurance company.

Nadgett, Tom Pinch's landlord in London, employed by Montague Tigg as an investigator. He follows his employer and Jonas Chuzzlewit into the country and sees only Jonas returning. Acting on this knowledge, he unmasks Jonas as Tigg's murderer.

Chuffey, Anthony Chuzzlewit's devoted clerk. Old, deaf, and almost blind, he is also shrewd, and he helps to save his employer from Jonas Chuzzlewit's attempt to poison his father.

Sairey Gamp, a Cockney midwife and nurse who displays the same zest at a lying-in or a laying-out. She is fat, husky-voiced, moist-eyed, red-nosed, and over-fond of drink, so that she is always surrounded by the odor of spirits. Her fabrications she credits to her completely imaginary friend, Mrs. Harris. She is one of Dickens' great comic characters.

Chevy Slyme, a distant relative of old Martin Chuzzlewit, a dubious character who is "always waiting around the corner." He is a friend of Jonas Chuzzlewit and Montague Tigg.

Mr. Spottletoe, another relative of old Martin Chuzzlewit, also eager for a share of his relative's fortune.

Mrs. Spottletoe, his wife, a woman of a "poetical constitution."

Lewsome, a young surgeon. Under obligations to Jonas Chuzzlewit, he sells Jonas the drugs with which the son makes an attempt on his father's life. After Anthony Chuzzlewit's death, deeply disturbed in his mind while recovering from a serious illness, he confesses to John Westlock his part in the affair and thus helps bring Jonas to justice.

Paul Sweedlepipe, a hairdresser and bird fancier, Sairey Gamp's landlord.

Mrs. Betsey Prig, a Cockney day nurse and Sairey Gamp's bosom friend with whom she often nurses "turn and turn about." They finally quarrel because Betsey dares to doubt the existence of Mrs. Harris.

Mrs. M. Todgers, landlady of the Commercial Boarding House, at which the Pecksniffs stay while in London.

Mr. Jinkins, the oldest resident at Mrs. Todgers' boarding house. His recreation is identifying carriages driving in the parks on Sundays.

Augustus Moddle, a young gentleman living at Mrs. Todgers' boarding house. He is at first smitten by Mercy Pecksniff, but after her marriage to Jonas Chuzzlewit he becomes, rather helplessly, engaged to her sister Charity. On the eve of the wedding he runs away, leaving behind a letter in which he announces his departure for Van Dieman's Land and his determination never to be taken alive if Charity pursues him.

Bailey, the "boots" at Mrs. Todgers' boarding house. He eventually becomes Mr. Sweedlepipe's assistant.

Mr. Fips, the lawyer through whom old Martin Chuzzlewit engages Tom Pinch to catalogue a library.

Mr. Mould, an undertaker whose countenance always seems caught between a look of melancholy and a satisfied smirk.

Mrs. Mould, his wife.

The Misses Mould, their daughters, two plump sisters with cheeks like ripe peaches.

Tacker, Mr. Mould's chief mourner.

Sophia, a girl taught by Ruth Pinch. Mrs. Todgers calls her "a syrup."

Wolf and
Pip, friends and confederates of Montague Tigg.

The Hon. Elijah Pogram, a bombastic Congressman whom Martin Chuzzlewit meets in New York.

Zephaniah Scadder, a land speculator who, representing the Eden Land Corporation, sells Martin Chuzzlewit fifty acres of land in the backwoods community named Eden.

Major Pawkins, a New York politician who boasts that he is a man of the people.

Mrs. Pawkins, his wife and keeper of a boarding house.

Mr. Bevan, a kind-hearted citizen of Massachusetts who lends Martin Chuzzlewit the money for his return passage to England.

General Fladdock, an American militia officer and a snob.

Lafayette Kettle, a loud-voiced American, secretary of the Watertoast Association of United Sympathizers.

General Cyrus Choke, an officer of the militia, a member of the Eden Land Corporation and the Watertoast Association of United Sympathizers.

Colonel Diver, editor of the New York "Rowdy Journal."

Jefferson Brick, war correspondent of the New York "Rowdy Journal."

Mrs. Brick, his wife, an American "matron."

Cicero, a New York truckman, formerly a slave.

Captain Kedgick, landlord of the National Hotel in New York, in whose hostelry Martin Chuzzlewit stays during his visit to the United States.

678

Professor Mullit, an American educator, the author of many pamphlets written under the name of Suturb.

Mr. Norris, a wealthy, sentimental abolitionist.

Mrs. Norris, his faded wife.

Miss Toppit, an American woman of literary pretensions.

Mrs. Hominy, another American literary light.

THE MASTER BUILDER

Author: Henrik Ibsen (1828-1906)
Time of action: Nineteenth century
First presented: 1892

PRINCIPAL CHARACTERS

Halvard Solness, the master builder. Although he is no longer young, he is evidently attractive to women, since his wife, Aline, his bookkeeper, Kaia Fosli, and Hilda Wangel, a young woman from a nearby village who had seen him only once ten years before, are all in love with him. Solness became successful after a tragedy, the death of his infant twin sons, caused him to turn from building churches to building houses. He has achieved success through working for Knut Brovik, whom he surpassed, put down, and now employs. He has two fears: fear of the younger generation which will treat him as he has treated Brovik and fear of heights. The fear of heights interferes with his hanging a wreath on the tower of each new building, a task which he now delegates to a workman. When vivacious Hilda Wangel appears to collect "the kingdom" which he promised her ten years earlier after he had hung his last wreath on the church tower in her village, Solness is at last overpowered by her stronger personality. Through Hilda's influence, he approves plans designed by the young architect Ragnar Brovik and climbs a scaffolding to place a wreath on a new house. Both courses mean oblivion for him. He falls into a quarry and is crushed.

Hilda Wangel, a fanciful young woman from the village of Lysanger. Little more than a child at the time, Hilda had fallen in love with Solness when he hung a wreath on the church tower in Lysanger. He has remained her hero. She is a charming young woman, filled with the quality which Ibsen calls "joy in life." When Solness falls into the quarry, Hilda is exalted. She cries, "But he mounted right to the top. And I heard harps in the air. . . . My—my Master Builder!"

Aline Solness, Halvard's wife, a quiet, hopeless woman, once beautiful. When her family home in which she and Solness lived burned, Aline's life purpose ended because her twin baby boys died. Through a sense of duty she insisted on nursing the babies when she was ill from the excitement of the fire and they died as a result. Solness says that Aline had a talent "for building up children's souls in perfect balance, and in noble and beautiful forms." She keeps three nurseries in their present house, and their new home is to contain three empty nurseries. Aline is naturally jealous of Kaia and Hilda, although she and Hilda come to like each other. Knowing her husband's fear of heights, she tries to prevent his fatal climb. She faints when he falls at the conclusion of the play.

Knut Brovik, formerly an independent architect, now employed in Solness' office. Old, ill, and dying, Brovik lives only for his son, an aspiring architect. His one wish is that he might see Ragnar a success. Because Solness never approves anything that Ragnar does, Brovik has come to doubt his son's talent. He pleads with Solness to let Ragnar have the commission for a villa, plans for which he has already drawn. Although Brovik gave Solness his start in architecture, Solness, knowing Ragnar's talent, will not give Brovik any encouragement. Brovik is dead when Hilda finally persuades Solness to approve Ragnar's plans for the villa.

Kaia Fosli, Knut Brovik's niece, Solness' bookkeeper, engaged to marry Ragnar. Kaia is a quiet girl in love with Solness.

Solness employs her to keep Ragnar, who is very much in love with her, in his employ, and hence in subjection.

Ragnar Brovik, a talented young man employed by Solness as a draftsman. Ragnar represents the younger generation which Solness fears will displace him. Ragnar does not realize his ability until he learns from Hilda that Solness employs Kaia not because he cares for her at all but because he fears Ragnar's talent and wants to keep it hidden.

Dr. Herdal, a physician concerned about Soleness and Aline. He serves as an audience for both Solness and Aline and thus is a vehicle for expressing their personalities.

THE MASTER OF BALLANTRAE

Author: Robert Louis Stevenson (1850-1894)
Time of action: Mid-eighteenth century
First published: 1889

PRINCIPAL CHARACTERS

James Durie, the master of Ballantrae. Reported dead after the Battle of Culloden, he escapes to America then goes to France, where he makes heavy financial demands on his brother Henry, now the heir to Durrisdeer, over a period of seven years. As Mr. Bally, James returns to Scotland and he and Henry fight a duel in which James is apparently killed, though his body disappears. Severely wounded, he is rescued by smugglers and taken to India, where he makes a fortune and acquires a native servant, Secundra Dass. When James again returns to Durrisdeer, Henry and his family flee to New York but are followed by James. In America Henry decides to get rid of his evil brother permanently; but Secundra Dass overhears plans for James's murder and shortly thereafter reports that his master has died. Henry, determined to satisfy himself that James is really dead, comes upon his brother's grave just as Secundra Dass is exhuming

James, who has not died but has been placed in a state of suspended animation by Secundra Dass in order to trick Henry. When Henry sees his brother's eyes flutter open after a week underground, he drops dead of shock. Despite many hours of strenuous effort, Secundra Dass is unable to revive James fully because of the cold temperature and at last the brothers, deadly enemies, are buried in the same grave.

Henry Durie, James's younger brother, who remains at Durrisdeer. After James's reported death Henry, now the heir, marries Alison. Plagued almost constantly by his very much alive brother James, Henry finally flees to America with his family. But his relentless brother pursues him. Hated and hating, the two brothers, after a macabre graveside scene, are placed in the same grave in the remote American wilderness.

Lord Durrisdeer, the father of James and

Henry. A canny Scot, he protects his estate by having one son on each side in the Stuart uprising.

Alison Graeme, a wealthy relative betrothed to James. After the report of his death she marries Henry, though she still loves James. When James returns to Durrisdeer for the first time, Alison seems to prefer his company to that of her husband.

Ephraim Mackellar, the factor of Durrisdeer, loyal to Henry. He narrates most of the story.

Colonel Francis Burke, who first brings word that James is alive and in France.

James demands that money be sent to him.

Captain Teach, a pirate who captures James and Burke, and whose treasure James steals.

Jacob Chew, an Indian trader of New York with whom James makes a wilderness expedition.

Secundra Dass, a servant acquired by James in India. He returns to Scotland with James, and then accompanies his master to America. Attempting to trick Henry, he places James in a state of suspended animation, but is unable to revive him.

MASTRO-DON GESUALDO

Author: Giovanni Verga (1840-1922)
Time of action: First half of the nineteenth century
First published: 1889

PRINCIPAL CHARACTERS

Gesualdo Motta, an ambitious peasant whose business acumen has made him into a rich landowner. Desiring gentility along with his riches, he marries Donna Bianca Trao, but the marriage succeeds only in widening the gaps on both sides of his world, leaving him hated by the peasantry, scorned by the gentry, and used by all for the wealth he had hoped would bring him satisfaction.

Bianca Trao, a poor gentlewoman who marries Gesualdo Motta in the hope that his riches will ease the financial burdens of her family.

Isabella Motta, the daughter of Bianca Trao and Gesualdo Motta, who gradually grows away from the peasant Motta and eventually becomes completely a Trao. She is given in marriage to the Duke di Leyra.

The Duke di Leyra, Isabella Motta's extravagant husband, who soon runs through her dowry and then despoils Gesualdo Motta of his property.

Don Diego and
Don Ferdinando Trao, Bianca Trao's brothers.

Santo and
Speranza Motta, Gesualdo's brother and sister.

Fortunato Burgio, Speranza Motta's husband.

Nunzio Motta, Gesualdo Motta's father.

Baron Nini Rubiera, Bianca Trao's cousin and her lover before her marriage to Gesualdo Motta, to whom Nini eventually goes hopelessly in debt.

Baroness Rubiera, Nini's mother, who refuses to allow her son to marry the fortuneless Bianca Trao.

Diodata, Gesualdo Motta's faithful, humble servant and mistress, who is married off to Nani l'Orbo.

Nani l'Orbo, Gesualdo Motta's servant, married to Diodata. He blackmails his master, the father of Diodata's children, for support and property.

Baron Zacco, a Trao relative and, when it suits his purposes, an ally of Gesualdo Motta.

Don Filippo Margarone, the local political leader.

Fifi Margarone, Don Filippo Margarone's daughter, the choice of Baroness Rubiera as a bride for her son Ninì.

Signora Aglae, an actress for whom Ninì goes in debt to Gesualdo Motta.

Madame Giuseppina Alosi, a widow

married for her wealth by Baron Ninì Rubiera.

Donna Sarina (Cirmena), a poor Trao relative, the sole family representative at Bianca Trao's wedding to Gesualdo Motta.

Corrado la Gurna, Donna Cirmena Trao's nephew, loved by Isabella Motta.

Lupi, a priest.

Master Titta, a barber who intercepts a note Ninì has written to Signora Aglae and gives it to Fifi, who then breaks her engagement to Ninì.

MAX HAVELAAR

Author: Multatuli (Eduard Douwes Dekker, 1820-1887)
Time of action: 1857
First published: 1860

PRINCIPAL CHARACTERS

Max Havelaar, a Dutch colonial administrator. An idealist who is deeply concerned with justice for all, he arrives in Java to find conditions among the Javanese laborers worse, even, than he had anticipated. Finding that the Dutch, who rule through the Javanese nobility, have acquiesced in the plundering and mistreatment of the laborers by their native masters, he attempts by persuasion and example to improve the situation while he gathers information for a report to his superiors. When his report is complete, he presents it to one indifferent official after another until he finds himself relieved of his job and forsaken by the government he has served.

Radhen Adhipatti Karta Natta Negara, the native regent of Lebak. A relatively poor man with a large family and appearances to keep up, he extorts, under Dutch protection, goods and services from his people. When Max Havelaar lodges an official protest against him, the Jav-

anese is upheld by the Dutch, who denounce Havelaar for his pains.

Tine, Max Havelaar's devoted wife and champion.

Mr. Verbrugge, the controller serving under Max Havelaar. Although he is well aware of the exploitation of the Javanese by the Dutch, he is, nevertheless, afraid to risk the security of his job by trying to fight against the complacent colonial administration.

Mr. Slimering, a Dutch colonial official with whom Max Havelaar lodges a protest against the injustices suffered by the Javenese laborers. Slimering denounces the protest in favor of the corrupt native chiefs.

Saïdyah, a young Javanese whose story is used as an example of colonial injustice. His father loses his possessions by extortion, and his betrothed is murdered by Dutch troops, as Saïdyah himself is killed later on.

682

Batavus Drystubble, a Dutch coffee broker of Amsterdam. He does not believe that the Javanese are mistreated.

Shawlman, Batavus Drystubble's schoolmate, a writer who brings to him the manuscript of the story of Max Havelaar.

THE MAYOR OF CASTERBRIDGE

Author: Thomas Hardy (1840-1928)
Time of action: Nineteenth century
First published: 1886

Michael Henchard, the mayor of Casterbridge and a prosperous corn merchant. In his youth, while drunk, he had sold his wife and child to a seaman. Years later this information becomes known in Casterbridge; as a result Henchard is ruined. Too stern and unyielding to resume his friendship with Donald Farfrae, his former manager, the headstrong ex-mayor faces declining fortune. Finally he is forced to declare bankruptcy and is publicly humiliated during the visit of royalty. At last, broken in spirit, he takes refuge in a shack and dies practically friendless.

Susan Henchard-Newson, Henchard's wife. A plain simple woman, she finally tires of her husband's repeated threats to sell her to the highest bidder. When he offers her for sale, she throws her wedding ring at him and leaves with the sailor Newson, her baby in her arms. Years later, thinking Newson drowned, she returns and remarries Henchard.

Elizabeth-Jane Newson, Henchard's attractive stepdaughter. A proper young woman, she is attracted to the personable young Farfrae. After the death of Lucetta, she marries the young corn merchant.

Donald Farfrae, a corn merchant in Casterbridge and Henchard's thriving business competitor. At first Henchard's good friend and manager, he gradually drifts apart from the mayor when the latter becomes jealous of the young man's capability and popularity. The estrangement, however, helps to bring Farfrae increasing prosperity, Efficiently, he captures much of the grain market and, against his will, gradually takes away much of his former employer's business. When Farfrae marries Lucetta, the break between the two men is complete.

Lucetta Templeman, a woman Henchard had known as Lucetta Le Sueur, later Farfrae's wife. An attractive, but imperceptibly aging coquette, she intended to marry Henchard until she encountered the handsome Farfrae. After meeting him, she decides that she does not care to see Henchard again, even though the latter was once her lover. Her marriage to Farfrae goes smoothly until Jopp reads some love letters, which Lucetta had sent to Henchard, aloud to the denizens of Mixen Lane. Learning she is exposed as a loose woman, she has a miscarriage and dies.

Richard Newson, a bluff, hearty sailor. In his youth he had bought Henchard's wife and child. The ex-mayor's destruction is complete when the sailor comes to Casterbridge to claim his daughter, Elizabeth-Jane.

Jopp, a surly former employee of Henchard. Snubbed by Lucetta, he gets his revenge when he has the chance to read her love letters aloud in the Three Mariners Inn and takes part in the parade which exposes her to the people.

Abel Whittle, Henchard's simple-minded

employee. Although abused by his former employer, Abel, remembering how good the sick man had been to Abel's mother, takes care of him in his final illness.

THE MAYOR OF ZALAMEA

Author: Pedro Calderón de la Barca (1600-1681)
Time of action: Sixteenth century
First presented: 1636

PRINCIPAL CHARACTERS

Pedro Crespo (pä'drō krās'pō), a farmer of Zalamea whose story was first told in a play by Lope de Vega. He is a candidate for mayor in the approaching elections. Because he is wealthy, his house is selected as lodgings for Captain Ataide, who is leading his troops to Guadalupe. Though a commoner, he is a proud and independent man.

Juan Crespo (hwän' krās'pō), his son, who wants his father to refuse hospitality to the Spanish soldiers. Later he suspects the trickery of Captain Ataide and is almost killed for drawing a sword against him in defense of his sister. Saved by the arrival of Don Lope, Juan decides to enlist under his banner and march away with him.

Isabel (ē·sä·bĕl'), the daughter of Pedro Crespo. Upon the arrival of the soldiers, she hides in the attic, where she is discovered and kidnaped by Captain Ataide. After his death, she enters a nunnery.

Inés (ē·nās'), Isabel's cousin, who hides with her in the Crespo attic.

Don Álvaro de Ataide (dōn äl'bä·ro ᵗhä ä·tä'ē·ᵗhä), a captain and the leader of a company of soldiers billeted in Zalamea. Curious about Isabel's beauty, of which he has heard, he schemes to see her. After his troops leave Zalamea he sneaks back to the village and with the help of Rebolledo abducts her and violates her. She is rescued too late by her brother. When Crespo, now mayor, orders the Captain to make amends by marrying Isabel, Ataide refuses with the

declaration that she is beneath him. Crespo orders him jailed. There he is slain by an unidentified assailant.

Rebolledo (rä·bō·lyä'ᵗhō), a military veteran who, in return for permission to operate official troop gambling, helps Captain Ataide in his schemes. Learning from a servant about Isabel's hiding place, he fakes a quarrel with the Captain and, fleeing, leads him to the attic where Isabel and Inés are hiding. Later he helps kidnap Isabel and ties up Crespo when he attempts to rescue his daughter.

A Sergeant, also ordered by Captain Ataide to aid in the abduction plot.

Chispa (chēs'pä), Rebolledo's mistress, who accompanies the troops and encourages them by singing marching songs. She disguises herself as a man in order to help Rebolledo seize Isabel.

Don Lope de Figueroa (dōn lō'pä ᵗhä fē·gä·rō'ä), the commander of a Spanish regiment, who has an eye for pretty girls but a wounded leg that makes them safe with him. He turns the Captain out of Crespo's house and lodges there himself. He wins Crespo's friendship by protecting him, and Isabel's pity by displaying his battle wounds.

Philip II, King of Spain, who is on his way to Portugal with his army. He does not arrive in Zalamea in time to free Captain Ataide, who has already been garroted in his cell. When he does arrive in the village, however, the King declares the punishment just and appoints Crespo perpetual mayor of Zalamea.

684

Don Mendo (dōn mān'dō), a down-at-the-heels squire who yearns for Isabel.

Nuño (nōō'nyō), Don Mendo's picaresque servant.

MEASURE FOR MEASURE

Author: William Shakespeare (1564-1616)
Time of action: Sixteenth century
First presented: 1604-1605

PRINCIPAL CHARACTERS

Angelo (ăn'jĕ·lō), a Viennese nobleman, the Duke's deputy, a man who is cold, arrogant, and unbending in the knowledge of his own virtuous life. He refuses to look with sympathy upon the offense of Claudio and stands firm, like Shylock, for justice untempered with mercy. He is shocked to find himself tempted by Isabella, but he dismisses all moral scruples and attempts to seduce her, promising to free her brother if she will yield to him. Once he thinks he has had his will he orders Claudio's execution to take place. Faced with the Duke's knowledge of his behavior, he, still in character, asks death as the fitting recompense for his sins; mercy is still no part of his character, although it is that quality, meted out by the Duke in accord with the pleas of Isabella and Mariana, which ultimately saves him.

Vincentio (vēn·chĕn'sē·ō), Duke of Vienna, a rather ambiguous figure who acts at times as a force of divine destiny in the lives of his subjects. He has wavered in the enforcement of his state's unjust laws, and, pretending to go on a trip to Poland, he leaves the government in Angelo's hands to try to remedy this laxity as well as to test Angelo's "pale and cloistered virtue." He himself moves quietly to counteract the effects of Angelo's strict law enforcement on Isabella, Claudio, and Mariana.

Isabella (ēz·ə·bĕl'ə), a young noblewoman who emerges from the nunnery where she is a postulant to try to save the life of her condemned brother. Her moral standards, like Angelo's, are absolute; she is appalled to find herself faced with two equally dreadful alternatives: to watch her brother die, knowing that it is in her power to save him, or to surrender herself to Angelo. She cannot entirely comprehend Claudio's passionate desire to live, no matter what the cost. Virtue is, for her, more alive than life itself, and she cannot help feeling a certain sense of justice in his condemnation, although she would save him if she could do so without causing her own damnation. She learns, as Angelo does not, to value mercy, and she is able at the end of the play to join Mariana on her knees to plead for the deputy's life.

Claudio (klô'dĭ·ō), Isabella's brother, condemned to death for getting his fiancée with child. He finds small consolation in the Duke's description of death, and he makes a passionate defense of life, describing the horrors of the unknown.

Escalus (ĕs'kə·lŭs), a wise old Viennese counselor, left by the Duke as Angelo's adviser. He deals humorously and sympathetically with the rather incoherent testimony of Elbow, the volunteer constable.

Mariana (mä·rē·ä'nå), a young woman betrothed to Angelo and legally his wife when he rejected her because of difficulties over her dowry. She agrees, at the Duke's request, to take Isabella's place in the garden house where Angelo had arranged to meet her. Claiming him as her husband at the Duke's reëntry into the city, she asks mercy for his betrayal of Claudio and Isabella.

Lucio (lū'shĭ·o), a dissolute young man

685

who brags of his desertion of his mistress and gives the disguised Duke bits of malicious gossip about himself. He is condemned for his boasting and his slander to marry the prostitute he has abandoned.

Mrs. Overdone, a bawd.

Pompey, her servant.

Juliet, Claudio's fiancée, who is cared for by the disguised Duke.

Elbow, a clownish volunteer constable whose malapropisms make enforcement of the law more than difficult.

Francisca (frăn·sĭs'kə), a nun of the order Isabella is entering.

Froth, a laconic patron of Mrs. Overdone's establishment.

Provost (prŏv'əst), an officer of the state who pities Claudio and helps the Duke save him, thus disobeying Angelo's orders.

Abhorson, the hangman, a man of rather macabre humor.

Barnardine, a long-term prisoner freed by the merciful Duke.

Friar Thomas and
Friar Peter, religious men who aid the Duke.

MEDEA

Author: Euripides (c. 485-c. 406 B.C.)
Time of action: Remote antiquity
First presented: 431 B.C.

PRINCIPAL CHARACTERS

Medea (mĭ·dē'ə), a princess of Colchis and the wife of Jason. Medea had aided Jason in avoiding the traps laid for him by her father, King Aeetes of Colchis, while regaining the Golden Fleece. Fleeing with Jason, she had murdered her own brother to aid in the escape. In Jason's hereditary kingdom of Iolcus, where they first settled but where Pelias, Jason's uncle, had cheated him of his rights, Medea tricked the daughters of Pelias into murdering their father. For this deed Medea, Jason, and their two children were exiled. The play is set in Corinth, where they came after leaving Iolcus and where Jason has put Medea aside in order to marry Glauce, the daughter of Creon, King of Corinth. It is at this point that the action of the play begins. The dramatic development, centering around Medea, is perhaps the finest example in Greek drama of character development. Medea changes from a woman overwhelmed with sorrow at

her husband's desertion to a woman dominated by a fury of revenge in which every other feeling, even love for her children, is sacrificed to a desire to hurt Jason. The opening situation of the play is concerned with a sympathetic presentation of the sorrowful plight of Medea. She has given up home and position for Jason and can belong to no other except through him; these facts are conveyed by the nurse before Medea appears. Medea cries out violently against Jason before she appears and foreshadows the destruction of the children. Yet when she appears she is proud but courteous and self-possessed. She expresses her ills as those of all women, but greater, and she asks the Chorus not to betray her if she finds the means of vengeance. They promise secrecy. Creon appears to pronounce a sentence of exile on Medea and the children because he is afraid of her power as a sorceress. She is able only to convince him to grant her a one-day

686

respite. When Creon leaves, Medea reveals her more barbaric and violent side in a terrible speech in which she decides to poison Creon and his daughter. At the appearance of Jason, Medea reveals her full fury as a betrayed mistress and becomes less sympathetic. Blinded by jealousy, she exhibits passion unchecked and untamed. Aegeus, King of Athens, suddenly appears and promises refuge to Medea if she can make her way to his city alone. Assured of a place of refuge, she calls Jason to her and, feigning sweetness and repentence, forgives him, asking only that he obtain a pardon for the children through the Princess, his wife. She then gives them a poisoned robe and a golden crown to present to the Princess and they leave. When the children return, the struggle between Medea's love for them and her passion for revenge reaches a height in a speech in which the latter triumphs. A messenger enters with news of the death of the Princess and Creon, and Medea enters the house. Immediately the screams of the children are heard. Jason enters and Medea appears above the house, in a chariot supplied by her grandfather Helios, god of the sun, with the bodies of her children. She has destroyed the house of Jason and her revenge is complete.

Jason (jā'sən), King of Iolcus, the incarnation of a moderation and wisdom that is negative, not rooted in emotion. He is presented first as the faithless husband and is unreservedly condemned by the Chorus and servants. He loves neither Medea nor Creon's daughter. His only passion is his love for his children, which arouses some sympathy for him.

The Two Children of Medea and Jason. Silent except for the off-stage screams as they are murdered, they are central to the plot as Medea's only successful means of revenge against Jason.

Creon (krē'ŏn), King of Corinth. His sentence of exile expresses the fear of Medea's power as a sorceress.

Aegeus (ē'jōōs, ē'jĭ·əs), King of Athens, who offers Medea a place of refuge. His appearance is a coincidence, but it provides a glimpse of Medea as she was before the disaster, a princess renowned for wisdom. The scene also emphasizes the child-motive: Aegeus had gone to Delphi because he is childless and thus he is already in the position in which Jason is left at the end of the play.

A Nurse, Medea's devoted servant. Desperately anxious, she identifies herself completely with the cause of her mistress. She speaks the prologue.

A Chorus of Corinthian Women. Sympathetic to the suffering of Medea, they swear secrecy to her revenge, though realizing the horror of the means.

The Tutor to Medea's Children. He is a good and faithful slave. He clearly condemns Jason's conduct.

A Messenger, who brings the news of the death of Creon and his daughter.

MEEK HERITAGE

Author: Frans Eemil Sillanpää (1888-   )
Time of action: 1857-1917
First published: 1919

PRINCIPAL CHARACTERS

Jussi Toivola (jŭs'sē toi·vō'lä), also called **Juha** and **Janne,** the shy, inept, simpleminded, disreputable hero. More a victim than a master of his circumstances, Jussi is swept along through his life and changes names as frequently as his dwellings. A Finnish peasant, he is born of a minor landholder and a third wife.

His childhood is uneventful, broken only by his father's cruelty and games on Pig Hill. Still a youth when his father dies, he and his mother go to live with her brother, a well-to-do landholder. After his mother's death he herds cattle until he is thrown out by his uncle for his part in a practical joke. As a young man he takes up logging for seven years under a peculiar but kindly boss. Later he becomes a farmhand, marries a serving girl, and sets up as a crofter with an acre of his own. He has five children and achieves a marginal prosperity. Then his horse dies, his eldest son virtually kills a younger brother and moves away, his wife dies of a mysterious ailment, his eldest daughter leaves home and drowns herself soon afterward. Jussi, now a poor old man, becomes known as a rabble-rouser. Taking part in a Socialist revolution, he is left to guard a landowner who is killed during the looting. When the Socialists are defeated he is arrested, judged, and shot. His wastrel life ends in a common grave with other revolutionaries.

Rina Toivola, Jussi's wife, a loose, easygoing farm girl. She sleeps across from him when he comes to work as a farmhand at Pirjola. One evening she lets him sleep with her because she needs a husband for her illegitimate child. She is a lax housekeeper for Jussi but bears five children. Worn out and embittered from years of poverty, drudgery, and family misfortune, she dies attended by her eldest daughter.

Benjamin Nikila (nǐ'kə·lå), Jussi's father. Old and prurient, he marries a servant girl who bears him Jussi. An adept tobacco-chewer and wife-beater, he initiates Jussi into the harshness of life. Having mortgaged his home during a famine, he dies before the place is taken.

Kalle Toivola (käl'lə), Rina's strange, illegitimate son. After crippling his brother he moves to the city and becomes a cabby. Cocksure of himself, he joins the Socialists, sends his father newspapers, and leads a group during a Socialist uprising.

Hilda Toivola, Jussi's eldest daughter, a spiritless girl in whom childishness and old age are sadly mixed. After watching her mother die and being sent to serve a well-to-do family, she drowns herself.

Ville Toivola (vĭl'lə), Jussi's liveliest son. He is injured by Kalle and never recovers.

Lempi and
Martin, Jussi's youngest children. Neglected and waif-like, they are forced to fend for themselves. They are found crying and helpless after Jussi's arrest.

Maja Nikila (må'zhå nǐ'kə·lå), Jussi's gentle mother. Thinking to improve her station as a servant girl, she marries Banjamin, bears him a son, and is rewarded finally with nothing but a hard and weary death.

Keinonen (kī·nō'něn), the puzzling gang boss of the lumberjacks under whom Jussi works. He sees that Jussi keeps his pay from the greedy Toivolas. After his death Jussi becomes a farmhand.

Kalle and
Emma Tuorila (tōō·ôr·ĭl'å), the uncle and aunt with whom Jussi goes to live after his father's death. Never welcome in their home, he is thrown out after a practical joke by one of his friends.

Gustav Toivola, the friend who plays the joke and then turns on Jussi when he comes to stay at Toivola.

Mina Toivola, Gustav's avaricious, shrewish mother, who tries to cheat Jussi of wages earned as a lumberjack.

The Master of Pirjola (pûr·jō'lə), the tough, prosperous farmer for whom Jussi works after his foresting job. He dislikes Jussi but lends him money.

Rinne (rĭn′nə), the Socialist organizer in Jussi's community.

Pa Ollila (ōl·lə′lä), the landowner who collects on Benjamin's unpaid mortgage.

Lovisa (lō·vē′sà), the bullying cupperwoman who assists Jussi's birth.

Manda, a high-spirited farm girl whom Jussi once liked.

MELMOTH THE WANDERER

Author: Charles Robert Maturin (1782-1824)
Time of action: Early nineteenth century
First published: 1820

PRINCIPAL CHARACTERS

John Melmoth, a young Irishman who inherits his uncle's property, including a portrait of an early ancestor which he is directed to destroy. He discovers a manuscript that tells about Melmoth the Wanderer, who visits John. Then a shipwrecked Spaniard tells of visitations of Melmoth the Wanderer. The Wanderer appears to John to tell him that he has finished his earthly pilgrimage of a century and a half. John hears strange noises in the night, and the next morning his dread kinsman is gone.

John Melmoth's Uncle, who, though not a superstitious man, believes a stranger has been lurking about his house. He dies and leaves his property to his nephew with instructions to destroy a hidden portrait of an earlier John Melmoth.

Melmoth The Wanderer, a seventeenth century ancestor of young John Melmoth, also named John. He is doomed to wander the earth for a century and a half while trying to seduce souls to Satan. He wins not one soul in that time. Finally he returns to his home in Ireland. He ends his life by plunging, or being thrown, over a cliff.

Mr. Stanton, an Englishman who leaves a manuscript telling the strange story of Melmoth the Wanderer. Stanton met the Wanderer in Spain, angered him, and was cursed. Because of the curse Stanton was confined in Bedlam as a madman; he was visited by the Wanderer, who offered to secure Stanton's release from the asylum if Stanton would sell his soul to Satan. Stanton refused.

Alonzo Moncada, a Spaniard shipwrecked near the Melmoth home. He too knows the Wanderer. While imprisoned by the Inquisition he was approached by the Wanderer, who offered freedom in exchange for Moncada's soul. Moncada refused, but he later escaped prison anyway.

An Old Jewish Doctor, who makes a study of the history of the Wanderer. He tells Moncada about the daughter of Don Francisco di Aliaga who was shipwrecked as an infant and grew up on an uninhabited island where she was visited by the Wanderer and fell in love with him. After she was found and returned home, the Wanderer visited her again and they were married in a Satanic ceremony. Found out, she was turned over to the Inquisition. She died shortly after giving birth to the Wanderer's child. Her dying words expressed the hope that both she and the Wanderer would enter Heaven.

689

THE MEMBER OF THE WEDDING

Author: Carson McCullers (1917-   )
Time of action: 1945
First published: 1946

PRINCIPAL CHARACTERS

Frances (Frankie) Addams, a twelve-year-old girl. Jealous because she is rejected by other girls and boys in the community, she calls them names, flies into sudden rages against Berenice and John Henry, and bursts into tears of which she is ashamed. She worries over her tall, gawky frame and her big feet. She dreams romantically and excitedly of the adventures she will have with Jarvis and Janice when she accompanies them on their wedding trip, and she fights frantically when she is prevented from going. As the story ends, Frankie appears to be over the worst of her adolescence—she will be Frances from now on.

John Henry West, her six-year-old cousin, a frail child who dies of meningitis. He is Frankie's friend and often her confidant, though he has little understanding of much which she tells him.

Berenice Sadie Brown, the colored cook in the Addams household. She is black, short, and broad-shouldered, and her left eye is bright blue glass. She offers kind, motherly comfort, sharp practical advice and criticism, and affectionate understanding to troubled Frankie and little John Henry. Frankie is unaware that Berenice's pity for the motherless, confused, and unhappy girl has kept her from marrying her suitor, T. T. Williams.

Royal Quincy Addams, Frankie's father, a jeweler, kind to his daughter but too busy with his work to pay much attention to her.

Jarvis, Frankie's brother, an army corporal, a handsome blond.

Janice Evans, the fiancée of Jarvis.

Honey Camden Brown, Berenice's light-skinned, mentally weak foster brother who is jailed for robbing a store while drug-crazed.

A Soldier. He attempts to seduce Frankie but fails.

T. T. Williams, Berenice's middle-aged beau, owner of a colored restaurant.

Aunt Pet and
Uncle Eustace, John Henry's parents.

Evelyn Owen, Frankie's friend who moves to Florida.

Big Mama, an old Negro palm reader.

Mary Littlejohn, Frankie's best, real friend as she enters her fourteenth year.

Barney MacKean, a boy with whom Frankie once committed a "queer sin" and whom she hates.

Uncle Charles, John Henry's great-uncle, a very old man who dies the day before the wedding.

Officer Wylie, a policeman who catches Frankie when she tries to run away.

690

THE MEMOIRS OF A CAVALIER

Author: Daniel Defoe (1660-1731)
Time of action: 1630-1648
First published: 1720

PRINCIPAL CHARACTERS

The Cavalier, the second son of a landed gentleman. As a student at Oxford, he realizes that he has no taste for the academic life, the law, the Church, or medicine, and he receives his father's permission to travel on the Continent. With his companion, Captain Fielding, he observes or takes part in campaigns in Germany, where he witnesses the terrible siege of Magdeburg; in Sweden, where he serves in the Swedish forces and is a special attendant to the King; and in Holland, where he observes the Dutch in their fight against the Spanish. Returning to England, he enters the service of Charles I against the Scots and serves the royalist cause in the English Civil War. With the royalist defeat, he retires, content to have served King, country, and honor to the best of his ability.

Captain Fielding, the Cavalier's friend and traveling companion.

Sir John Hepburn, the Cavalier's friend in the Swedish forces.

Gustavus Adolphus, King of Sweden, to whom the Cavalier becomes a special attendant, serving sometimes as his emissary. The King loses his life in the battle of Lützen.

Charles I, King of England, who is served by the Cavalier in his campaign against the Scots and in the English Civil War.

MEMOIRS OF A FOX-HUNTING MAN

Author: Siegfried Sassoon (1886-   )
Time of action: 1895-1916
First published: 1929

PRINCIPAL CHARACTERS

George Sherston, an orphan. He is reared by his aunt. His skill with horses gains him entry into high society, a life he cannot afford. He also excels as a cricket player. World War I finds him refusing a commission, distrusting his ability; but after serving in the cavalry, he ends up as an infantry officer fighting bravely but angrily as he sees his friends killed. This character is a thinly veiled portrait of the author.

Aunt Evelyn, who rears George. She buy him his first pony when he is nine and later sells a ring to buy him a jumper, Cockbird.

Tom Dixon, Evelyn's groom and George's riding teacher, who is killed in George's infantry company in France.

Mr. Star, George's incompetent tutor.

Mr. Pennett, George's penurious and unsympathetic trustee.

Denis Milden, George's boyhood friend and later Master of the Ringwell Hounds and the Packlestone Hunt.

Stephen Colwood, an excellent horseman killed in France during the war.

Nigel Croplady, a wealthy braggart. He

691

is defeated by George, with Stephen's encouragement, in the Colonel's Cup Race.

Captain Huxtable, a neighbor who gets George an infantry commission.

Dick Tiltwood, a young soldier in George's company. He is killed in the trenches.

MEMOIRS OF A MIDGET

Author: Walter de la Mare (1873-1956)
Time of action: Late nineteenth century
First published: 1921

PRINCIPAL CHARACTERS

Miss M., a pretty midget. Reared in seclusion, she first goes into the world after her parents die, when she is eighteen. She finds that some people accept her as a person and that others look upon her as a mere curiosity. In financial straits, she hires herself out to a circus and has several unfortunate experiences. Through a legacy she finally becomes financially independent and settles down with Mrs. Bowater as her housekeeper. One night she disappears mysteriously and is never seen again.

Mrs. Monnerie, a wealthy woman who becomes Miss M.'s patroness. She treats the midget like a little child and, when her use for the midget is over, discards the tiny girl for a new favorite. She gives Miss M. the nickname of Midgetina.

Mrs. Bowater, Miss M.'s erstwhile landlady. A stern woman, she nevertheless shows great affection for the midget and, when Miss M. gains financial independence, becomes her housekeeper.

Mr. Anon, a dwarf. He becomes Miss

M.'s friend and falls in love with her. To save her embarrassment before her friends and acquaintances he takes her place in a pony-riding act and is mortally injured by a fall from a pony.

Fanny Bowater, Mrs. Bowater's daughter and for a time Miss M.'s friend. Becoming a favorite of Mrs. Monnerie, she replaces Miss M.

Lady Pollacke, a true friend of Miss M. She tries to help the midget find a place for herself in the world.

Sir Walter Pollacke, Lady Pollacke's husband. Like his wife, he tries to help the midget. He becomes her guardian and financial adviser.

Percy Maudlen, a languid, ill-mannered young man, Mrs. Monnerie's nephew. He is disliked by Miss M.

Susan Monnerie, a niece of Mrs. Monnerie. She is a friend to Miss M.

Lord B., Mrs. Monnerie's father.

MEMOIRS OF A PHYSICIAN

Author: Alexandre Dumas, *père* (1802-1870)
Time of action: Eighteenth century
First published: 1846-1848

PRINCIPAL CHARACTERS

Joseph Balsamo (zô·zhĕf′ bàl·sà·mō′), **(Count de Fenix)** (də fā·nēks′), a revo- lutionary and practitioner of magic. Involved in machinations at the court of

Louis XV, he is able through sorcery, for which he uses his wife Lorenza Feliciani as a medium, to gather information to further the plots in which he becomes engaged until the death of Lorenza at the hands of his master in magic, Althotas.

Lorenza Feliciani (lō·ren'zə fä·lē·cē-än'ĭ), Joseph Balsamo's wife and the unwilling medium for his sorcery until her death at the hands of Althotas.

Madame Jeanne du Barry (zhän dü bä·rē'), the favorite of Louis XV and the ally of the Duc de Richelieu and Joseph Balsamo in an attempt to unseat M. de Choiseul as the King's minister.

Armand, Duc de Richelieu (är·mäń dük də rē·shə·lyœ'), a political opportunist who, with the aid of Madame du Barry and compromising information gotten through the sorceries of Joseph Balsamo, forces Louis XV to dismiss his minister, M. de Choiseul.

M. de Choiseul (də shwä·zœl'), Louis XV's minister, who is dismissed on the strength of information gathered through the necromancy of Joseph Balsamo.

Althotas (äl·tô·tä'), Joseph Balsamo's instructor in magic. He kills Lorenza Feliciani by drawing from her the blood needed for an elixir of youth. When the vial containing the liquid is broken, he sets fire to his manuscripts and perishes with them in the flames.

Andrée (äń·drä'), a young girl saved from the violence of the mob and, later, hypnotized by Joseph Balsamo and forced to give information useful to his sinister purposes. She finally retires to a convent.

Baron de Taverney (bä·rōń də tä·věr·nä'), Andrée's impoverished father.

Philippe (fē·lēp'), Andrée's brother.

Gilbert (zhēl·běr'), a young proletarian in love with Andrée, whom he has rescued from mob violence.

Louis XV (lwē'), King of France.

Jean Jacques Rousseau (zhän zhȧk rōō·sō'), the philosopher.

M. de Sartines (də sär·tēn'), the lieutenant of police.

The Duchess of Grammont (grä·mōń'), M. de Choiseul's sister.

Nicole (nē·kôl'), Andrée's maid.

Marat (mȧ·rä'), a surgeon.

MEMOIRS OF AN INFANTRY OFFICER

Author: Siegfried Sassoon (1886-   )
Time of action: 1916-1917
First published: 1930

PRINCIPAL CHARACTERS

George Sherston, who is transformed from "a fox-hunting man" to an officer in World War I. He is ordered to plan a raid for his soldiers without taking part in the fighting and later on an attack of enteritis removes him from dangerous duty. Finally, however, he gets into the Battle of Arras and is wounded. Back in England, he writes a critical letter to his superiors. He expects to be court-martialed, but they refuse to take the letter seriously. When he resignedly recants, he is sent back to the battlefield.

Aunt Evelyn, who reared the orphan George and now thinks him safe in the transport service. She upsets him with her worry about his safety.

Colonel Kinjack, who believes Sherston is cracking up following the Battle of the

Somme and has him assigned to an army school.

Tyrrell, a pacifist philosopher who helps Sherston compose his defiant letter to Colonel Kinjack.

Major O'Brien, a friend of Sherston and a casualty in a minor raid that is exaggerated in London papers.

Kendle, who is killed at Sherston's side by a sniper.

David Cromlech, an iconoclast and fellow fighter at the Somme. He persuades Sherston to retract his critical statements by pointing out that otherwise he will be put into an insane asylum for the duration.

THE MENAECHMI

Author: Titus Maccius Plautus (c. 255-c. 184 B.C.)
Time of action: Third century B.C.
First presented: Late third or early second century B.C.

PRINCIPAL CHARACTERS

Menaechmus of Epidamnum (mə·nēk′-məs of ĕ′pĭ·dăm′nəm), an identical twin. When Menaechmus was a child, Moschus, his father, had taken him to Tarentum on a trading expedition. After the boy wandered away from his father and became lost, he was found and adopted by a citizen of Epidamnum, a city in Asia Minor noted for its sinfulness. By the time the play opens, Menaechmus had married and inherited his foster father's considerable estate. He also had taken up with a courtesan, Erotium, and he gives her a robe he has stolen from his wife's closet.

Menaechmus Sosicles (sŏs′ĭ·klēz), the other twin. Proud, witty, and hot-tempered like his brother, Sosicles comes to Epidamnum searching for his long-lost brother. His appearance in the city precipitates a series of comic encounters based on mistaken identity. At last the two Menaechmi come face to face and there is a happy reunion. Menaechmus of Epidamnum agrees to sell all his goods, including his wife, and return to Sicily with his brother.

Messenio (mĕ·sē′nĭ·ō), Sosicles' servant. Messenio does everything faithfully and well simply because he dislikes being beaten. He rescues Menaechmus, whom he mistakes for his master, from four

servants who are carrying him off. Menaechmus "frees" him in gratitude. Later, when the twins are reunited, Messenio is freed in earnest and made Menaechmus' auctioneer.

Peniculus (pē·nĭ′kə·ləs), Menaechmus' parasite. A spiteful, gluttonous, and ungrateful hanger-on, Peniculus, seeing Sosicles coming from Erotium's house, thinks Menaechmus has cheated him of a meal. He tells Menaechmus' wife that her husband has stolen her robe, only to learn that the wife will not reward him for his treachery.

The Wife of Menaechmus of Epidamnum, a nagging, possessive woman with a passion for keeping her husband under her control. She mistakes Sosicles for her husband, argues with him about her robe, which Sosicles is carrying, and calls on her father to take her home.

An Old Man, Menaechmus' father-in-law. The old man chides both his daughter and Menaechmus for their faults. When he mistakes Sosicles for Menaechmus, Sosicles pretends madness in order to escape. The old man sends a physician and four servants to restrain the madman. They lay hold of a very bewildered Menaechmus, but are driven off by Messenio.

Erotium (ĕ·rō′shĭ·əm), a rather simple-

694

minded courtesan. She entertains Sosicles, mistakes him for Menaechmus, and gives him the stolen robe to take to a tailor. When the real Menaechmus calls and disclaims knowledge of the robe, Erotium thinks he is trying to cheat her and bars him from the house.

An Old Physician, who is called in by Menaechmus' father-in-law to diagnose Sosicles' supposed madness.

Cylindrus (sĭ·lĭn′drəs), Erotium's cook, who mistakes Sosicles for Menaechmus and leads him to Erotium's house.

LE MENTEUR

Author: Pierre Corneille (1606-1684)
Time of action: Seventeenth century
First presented: 1643

PRINCIPAL CHARACTERS

Dorante (dô·räṅt′), a young student recently arrived in Paris to get a social education. A brazen liar, he accommodates himself so well to his new situation that he captivates Clarice, Lucrèce, and their companions with accounts of his heroic exploits in war and his extraordinary amatory adventures in Paris. Enmeshed more and more in a web of lies, mistaken identities, and the like, he finally marries Lucrèce, whom he swears he has loved all along.

Géronte (zhā·rôṅt′), Dorante's father, who comes to Paris to arrange a marriage for his son. He is duped into believing that Dorante has been forced to marry another to save her honor. When he learns of the deception, he swears he will never again help his rogue of a son, but he docilely arranges for his marriage to Lucrèce, nonetheless.

Lucrèce (lü·krĕs′), a shy and virtuous girl who finally marries Dorante, by whom she was captivated by his first lies on his arrival in Paris.

Clarice (klà·rēs′), a young girl betrothed to Alcippe, and a friend of Lucrèce.

Alcippe (àl·sĕp′), Dorante's friend and the jealous lover of Clarice, whom he finally marries after they all become extricated from the web of Dorante's lies.

Cliton (klē·tôṅ′), Dorante's valet and mentor in Paris, who is hired because of his military and amatory connections.

Philiste (fē·lēst′), a friend of Dorante and Alcippe.

Sabine (sà·bēn′), Lucrèce's maid and Dorante's fellow liar.

THE MERCHANT OF VENICE

Author: William Shakespeare (1564-1616)
Time of action: Sixteenth century
First presented: 1596-1597

PRINCIPAL CHARACTERS

Shylock (shī′lŏk), a rich Jewish moneylender. He hates Antonio for often lending money at lower interest than the usurer demands; hence, when Antonio wishes to borrow three thousand ducats

to help Bassanio, Shylock prepares a trap. Seemingly in jest, he persuades Antonio to sign a bond stating that, should the loan not be repaid within three months, a pound of flesh from any part of his body will be forfeited to Shylock. Next, Shylock has bad news when he learns that his daughter, Jessica, has eloped with Lorenzo, taking with her much of his money; good news when he learns that Antonio's ships have been lost at sea. Antonio being ruined and the loan due, Shylock brings the case before the Duke. He refuses Bassanio's offer of six thousand ducats and demands his pound of flesh. But Portia, Bassanio's wife, disguised as a lawyer, claims that Shylock must have the flesh but can take not a single drop of blood with it. Further, she maintains that Shylock, an alien, has threatened the life of a Venetian; therefore, half of his fortune goes to Antonio, the other half to the state. However, Shylock is allowed to keep half for Jessica and Lorenzo if he will become a Christian. The character of Shylock has become one of the most controversial in Shakespearian drama. Is he a villain or a tragic figure? Does the author intend the audience to regard him as an example of Jewish malevolence or to sympathize with him a persecuted man?

Portia (pōr′shə), an heiress whose father had stipulated in his will that any suitor must win her by choosing from among three caskets of gold, silver, and lead the one containing her portrait. The Prince of Morocco and the Prince of Aragon choose respectively the gold and the silver casket and find only mocking messages; Bassanio, whom she loves, selects the lead casket and wins her. Learning of Antonio's misfortune, she offers her dowry to buy off Shylock and goes to Venice disguised as a lawyer. When Shylock refuses the money and rejects her plea for mercy, she outwits him by showing that he is entitled to a pound of Antonio's flesh but cannot shed any blood in obtaining it, thus saving Antonio and ruining Shylock.

Antonio (ăn·tō′nĭ·ō), the merchant of Venice. Rich and generous, he wishes to aid his impecunious friend Bassanio

to woo Portia. Having no ready money, he borrows three thousand ducats from Shylock with the proviso that if the debt cannot be repaid within three months, Shylock can have a pound of his flesh. His ships are apparently lost at sea, and he is saved from death only by Portia's cleverness. At the end of the play, he learns that some of his ships have returned and that he is not ruined.

Bassanio (bă·sä′nĭ·ō), the friend of Antonio, in need of money in order to woo Portia. To help him, Antonio concludes his almost fatal bargain with Shylock. Bassanio chooses the right casket at Portia's home and thus is able to marry her.

Gratiano (grä·shĭ·ä′nō, grä·tyä′nō), a friend of Bassanio. He marries Nerissa, Portia's waiting woman.

Nerissa (nĕ·rĭs′ə), Portia's clever waiting woman. She marries Gratiano.

Jessica (jĕs·ĭ′kə), the daughter of Shylock. She elopes with Lorenzo, taking with her much of Shylock's money and jewels. Her marriage is a heavy blow to her father.

Lorenzo (lô·rĕn′zō), a Venetian who marries Jessica.

The Prince of Morocco, a tawny Moor, one of Portia's suitors. He chooses the gold casket, in which he finds a skull and some mocking verses.

The Prince of Aragon, another of Portia's wooers. He chooses the silver casket, in which he finds the portrait of a blinking idiot.

Tubal (tū′bəl), a Jew and a friend of Shylock.

Launcelot Gobbo (lôn′sə·lŏt gŏb′bō), a clown, Shylock's comic servant. Hating his master, he changes to the service of Bassanio. He acts as a messenger between Jessica and Lorenzo.

Old Gobbo, Launcelot's father, "sandblind."

THE MERRY WIVES OF WINDSOR

Author: William Shakespeare (1564-1616)
Time of action: Sixteenth century
First presented: 1597-1601

PRINCIPAL CHARACTERS

Sir John Falstaff (fôl'stăf, fôl'stäf), the jovial, rotund friend of Prince Hal in "Henry IV," who comes with his hangers-on to Windsor and amuses himself by wooing the respectable ladies of two merchants. Twice gulled by the "merry wives," beaten and dumped into the Thames from a laundry basket, he tries a third time to succeed in his amorous designs and plans a rendezvous in the woods. He is there discovered by his friends wearing a buck's head and lying face down for fear of the fairies and elves who have been pinching him. He accepts this last deception in good humor and confesses that he was rather dubious about the authenticity of the spirits who visited him.

Mistress Page and
Mistress Ford, the brisk, practical ladies on whom Falstaff practices his romantic arts. Incensed as much by his identical letter to each of them as by his presumption in writing, they outwit the fat knight at every turn and firmly convince their husbands of their fidelity.

Page, Mistress Page's husband Thomas, a well-to-do burgher dwelling at Windsor. He trusts his wife's ability to withstand Falstaff's advances, although he follows his more suspicious friend Ford when he sets out to search for the knight at his own home. He disapproves of Fenton's suit for his daughter's hand, fearing the young man's high social standing, and arranges Anne's elopement with Slender. He is, however, quickly pacified when she announces her marriage to Fenton.

Ford, Page's jealous friend. He disguises himself as one Brook to ferret out Falstaff's plans, and he instigates the searches which precipitate the knight's unexpected bath in the Thames and his thorough thrashing.

Mistress Quickly, an old busybody, Dr. Caius' nurse and housekeeper. She supposes herself Anne Page's confidante and tries to use her influence to marry the girl to her master. She is much distressed by young William Page's Latin lessons, for she is sure that his exercises contain improper language.

Sir Hugh Evans, the Welsh parson, one of Shakespeare's pedantic scholars, whose "correctness" is made more ridiculous by his heavy accent. Duped by the Host into challenging Dr. Caius to a duel, he quickly and surreptitiously convinces his adversary that friendship is preferable to fighting. He joins the final plot against Falstaff and, dressed as a satyr, leads the "elves" and "fairies" to the knight.

Dr. Caius (kēz), a French doctor, a rather stupid man and one of Anne Page's suitors. His ignorance of the English language provides much amusement for his companions.

Justice Shallow, a foolish old country squire who is determined to sue Falstaff for injuries to his men, his property, and his pride. He avidly pursues his scheme for wedding his nephew to Mistress Anne Page and her handsome dowry.

Slender, Shallow's rather simple-minded nephew. He is willing to acquiesce in his uncle's wishes. Having little notion of the proper methods of courtship, he confesses his indifference to Anne and wishes privately that he had his book of songs and sonnets to help him woo her.

Simple, Slender's aptly named servant, who is almost as literal-minded as his master.

Anne Page, an attractive, intelligent young girl. She quickly assesses the defects of character in the prospective husbands put forth by each of her parents and resourcefully arranges her elopement with Fenton.

Fenton, Anne's sweetheart, a well-born, sensible young man and a persistent suitor.

Pistol,
Nym, and
Bardolph, Falstaff's disreputable cronies, who cozen Shallow, Slender, and the Host and direct a steady barrage of insults and jests at the fat knight.

The Host of the Garter, a loquacious tavern-keeper. He jokes with Falstaff and amuses himself by setting up a duel between Dr. Caius and Sir Hugh, as mismatched a pair as Viola and Andrew Aguecheek in "Twelfth Night." He aids in most of the deceptions and plots afoot in Windsor, abetting Ford's disguise, Dr. Caius' courtship, and Fenton's elopement. He is forced to take some of his own medicine when Bardolph, Nym, and Pistol make off with three of his horses.

William Page, Anne's younger brother, Sir Hugh's apt pupil in Latin.

Robin, Falstaff's page, who carries messages to Mistress Ford and Mistress Page.

MESSER MARCO POLO

Author: Donn Byrne (Brian Oswald Donn-Byrne, 1889-1928)
Time of action: Thirteenth century
First published: 1921

PRINCIPAL CHARACTERS

Marco Polo, the famous Venetian traveler. Told by a Chinese sea captain of the beauty of Golden Bells, he falls in love with his image of her. He imagines it his duty to convert the Chinese princess to Christianity. After he goes to China, the girl is his only convert. She and Marco fall in love and are happily married for three years; then Golden Bells dies. Marco stays with Kubla Khan for fourteen more years but finally jealousy in the Emperor's court forces him to leave. He will not go, however, until Golden Bells appears in a vision and pleads with him not to remain and risk his life. Then he sadly departs from China, the land of his beloved.

Golden Bells, daughter of Kubla Khan, Emperor of China. Told of Marco Polo's plight on the wide desert, she asks the court magician to save the young man and bring him to her father's court. She falls in love with Marco Polo, and the two live happily married for three years

until her death. Although she becomes Marco Polo's only convert to Christianity, she cannot believe what she is told of sin; she does not wish to be persuaded that feminine beauty is sinful.

Nicholas and
Matthew Polo, Marco Polo's father and uncle, respectively. They take young Marco with them to China, ostensibly as a Christian missionary sent by the Pope.

Kubla Khan, Emperor of China. It was at his request that Marco Polo, as a Christian missionary, goes to China.

Li Po, court poet at the court of Kubla Khan. He is friendly to Golden Bells and to Marco Polo.

Sanang, court magician of Kubla Khan. He effects the rescue of Marco Polo from the desert at Golden Bells' request. Later it is he who furnishes Marco Polo with a vision of the long-dead Golden Bells.

MICAH CLARKE

Author: Sir Arthur Conan Doyle (1859-1930)
Time of action: Late seventeenth century
First published: 1888

PRINCIPAL CHARACTERS

Micah Clarke, a young English Puritan who enlists in the forces of the Duke of Monmouth when that nobleman makes his bid for the English throne in 1685. A strong, able, and honest man, Micah Clarke becomes a captain of infantry, goes on various missions for the usurper, and is captured when Monmouth is defeated. He is ransomed by his friend Decimus Saxon and goes to the Continent to be a mercenary soldier.

Reuben Lockarby, Micah Clarke's close friend. Although himself a strong Anglican, he joins Micah Clarke out of friendship as a member of Monmouth's forces. He becomes a captain of infantry.

Decimus Saxon, a mercenary soldier who becomes a colonel under the Duke of Monmouth. He enlists Micah in the pretender's cause. He rescues Micah by ransoming him with money blackmailed from the Duke of Beaufort.

Sir Gervas, a London dandy who has gone through his fortune. He joins Micah and his friends as a follower of Monmouth.

Sir Jacob Clancy, a hermit who lost his estates through helping Charles II regain the English throne. He sends money and a warning to the Duke of Monmouth by the hand of Micah.

The Duke of Monmouth, leader of the Protestant insurrection against James II. His forces are defeated and he is captured and beheaded.

Stephen Timewell, a wealthy wool-merchant and mayor of Taunton. As an anti-Catholic he helps the Duke of Monmouth in the preparations to unseat James II.

Ruth Timewell, Stephen's daughter, who is courted by Reuben.

The Duke of Beaufort, the Lord of Wales, who agrees to support Monmouth if Monmouth's forces can get to Bristol. En route there, they are intercepted by the King's army at Sedgemoor and defeated.

Joseph Clarke, Micah Clarke's father, a Puritan. He is a veteran of the English Civil War of the 1640's when he fought under Oliver Cromwell.

MICHAEL AND HIS LOST ANGEL

Author: Henry Arthur Jones (1851-1929)
Time of action: Nineteenth century
First presented: 1896

PRINCIPAL CHARACTERS

The Reverend Michael Feversham, a stern, conscientious vicar at Cleveheddon. He is full of moral fervor and has strong moral convictions, reinforced by his belief that his dead mother is his guardian angel. He learns through his attraction to Audrie Lesden what temptations of the flesh can be and he commits adultery with her. He finally makes a public confession, as he had forced Rose Gibbard to do, and leaves his parish. He almost loses his faith but turns to Catholicism in hopes that he can be saved.

Rose Gibbard, a girl in the parish who commits adultery and bears a child. She is forced by the vicar to make a public confession because he believes that is the only way she can be absolved of sin. Later she is sent to an Anglican religious house.

Andrew Gibbard, Rose's father and the parish clerk. Though he knows Michael is conscientious he cannot forgive the vicar for making Rose confess publicly. He has only scorn for the vicar until the clergyman, too, makes a public confession of his own sin.

Audrie Lesden, a wealthy, attractive woman reputed to be a widow. She is attracted to Michael, but she is torn between wanting to be worthy of him and having worldly pleasures. She arranges to be left alone on an island overnight with him and takes him for her lover. She leaves the town for a while when her husband is heard from, but she returns after he is dead. Then the vicar tells her he cannot love her honorably. She dies loving the vicar, saying she will be his guardian angel.

Sir Lyolf Feversham, a relative of the vicar. He tries to warn the vicar away from entanglements with Audrie.

Father Hilary, a Roman Catholic priest to whom the Anglican vicar turns for spiritual help when his original faith cannot sustain him.

MID-CHANNEL

Author: Arthur Wing Pinero (1855-1934)
Time of action: c. 1900
First presented: 1909

PRINCIPAL CHARACTERS

Theodore Blundell, a stockbroker, and **Zoe Blundell,** his wife, a wealthy and fashionable couple whose marriage is in mid-channel. After another in a long series of the petty quarrels that make an adult relationship between them impossible, they agree to separate. Zoe goes to Italy and has an affair with Leonard Ferris; Theodore takes a mistress. When Theodore learns of Zoe's affair with Leonard, he swears that he will divorce her and force her lover to marry her. When Zoe discovers that Leonard plans to marry Ethel Pierpoint, she leaps to her death from her husband's window.

Leonard Ferris, a young man who falls in love with Zoe Blundell and follows her to Italy during a period of her separation from her husband. On the rebound from this affair, he turns to Ethel Pierpoint, whom he decides to marry.

Ethel Pierpoint, Zoe Blundell's young protégée, who falls in love with Leonard Ferris.

MIDDLEMARCH

Author: George Eliot (Mary Ann Evans, 1819-1880)
Time of action: Nineteenth century
First published: 1871-1872

Dorothea Brooke (Dodo), the sensitive and well-bred heroine who, in her desire to devote herself to something meaningful, marries an arid clerical scholar, Edward Casaubon. After Casaubon's death Dorothea, against the advice of friends and family, marries Will Ladislaw, an impulsive artist anad political thinker. Dorothea also befriends the progressive young doctor of Middlemarch, Tertius Lydgate.

The Rev. Edward Casaubon, the clergyman at Lowick, near Middlemarch. Casaubon is a gloomy, severe, unimaginative, and unsuccessful scholar who soon destroys Dorothea's enthusiasm. He is so jealous of Dorothea's friendship with his cousin, Will Ladislaw, that he adds a codicil to his will depriving Dorothea of his property should she marry his younger relative.

Will Ladislaw, Casaubon's young cousin, whose English heritage is mixed with alien Polish blood. Ladislaw is forceful, imaginative, energetic, and unconventional. An artist and a liberal, he represents an appropriate object of devotion for Dorothea, although many in Middlemarch are shocked by his views. After marrying Dorothea, he becomes a member of Parliament.

Celia Brooke, called **Kitty,** Dorothea's younger sister, a calm and placid young lady. She has none of Dorothea's aspirations, but a great deal of affection. She marries Sir James Chettam, a staid landowner.

Sir James Chettam, the owner of Freshitt Hall. A conservative gentleman, Sir James loves, first, Dorothea, then Celia, whom he happily weds.

Dr. Tertius Lydgate, a young doctor who comes to Middlemarch to establish a new hospital along progressive lines and to pursue scientific research. His noble career is destroyed by his improvident marriage and consequent debts.

Rosamond Vincy Lydgate, the beautiful, spoiled, and selfish daugher of the mayor of Middlemarch. Once married, she insists on living in a style that her husband, Dr. Lydgate, cannot afford.

Mr. Arthur Brooke, of Tipton Grange, the genial, rambling, and ineffectual uncle of Dorothea and Celia. His vague benevolence leads him to run for Parliament and he is soundly beaten.

Fred Vincy, Rosamond's brother, equally spoiled but less selfish. Although Fred gets into debt as a student and rebels against his family's plans to establish him as a respectable vicar, he later reforms, becomes an industrious farmer, and marries Mary Garth.

Mary Garth, the level-headed, competent daughter of a large, old-fashioned family securely tied to the land. She takes care of her aged, ailing relative, Peter Featherstone, before she marries Fred Vincy, her childhood sweetheart.

Mr. Walter Vincy, the mayor of Middlemarch and a prosperous manufacturer. Mr. Vincy, who loves comfort and genial company, is neither wise nor sympathetic in dealing with the problems his children face.

Mrs. Lucy Vincy, his wife, a warm, sentimental woman who spoils her children and has vast pretentions to social gentility. She objects to Fred's relationship with the simple, commonplace Garths.

Mr. Nicholas Bulstrode, the enormously pious, evangelical, wealthy banker of Middlemarch. Bulstrode uses his public morality and his money to control events in Middlemarch; however, the questionable connections and the shady early marriage that built up his fortune are eventually revealed.

Mrs. Harriet Vincy Bulstrode, his wife and the sister of Mayor Vincy. Although she seems to care only for social prestige, she loyally supports her husband after his disgrace.

Peter Featherstone, the wealthy aged owner of Stone Court. He tries to give his fortune to Mary Garth while she is nursing him during his final illness, but she refuses. His capricious will, cutting off all his grasping relatives, brings to Middlemarch strangers who precipitate Bulstrode's disgrace.

The Rev. Camden Farebrother, the vicar of St. Botolph's, a genial and casual clergyman. An expert whist-player and a friend of Lydgate, he is also, unsuccessfully, in love with Mary Garth.

The Rev. Humphrey Cadwallader, of Freshitt and Tipton, another genial clergyman who is particularly fond of fishing.

Mrs. Elinor Cadwallader, his wife, a talkative woman always acquainted with the latest scandal.

Caleb Garth, Mary's father, a stalwart and honest surveyor, land agent, and unsuccessful builder. He pays Fred Vincy's debts.

Susan Garth, his loyal, devoted wife, who educates her children with scholarly care and insight.

Mrs. Selina Plymdale, a Middlemarch gossip, friendly with the Vincys and the Bulstrodes.

Ned Plymdale, her son, a disappointed suitor of Rosamond Vincy.

Borthrop Trumbull, a florid auctioneer and cousin to old Featherstone.

John Raffles, an old reprobate and blackmailer who enters Middlemarch because he has married the mother of Featherstone's unexpected heir and periodically appears to get money. Just before he dies he reveals Bulstrode's sordid past.

Joshua Rigg, an enigmatic man who inherits Featherstone's house and money.

He must adopt Featherstone's name as well.

Mr. Tyke, an evangelical clergyman, supported by Bulstrode and Lydgate for the post of chaplain at the new hospital.

Naumann, a German artist and a friend of Will Ladislaw.

Mrs. Jane Waule, the widowed, avaricious sister of Peter Featherstone.

Solomon Featherstone, her wealthy and equally avaricious brother.

Jonah Featherstone, another of Peter's disappointed brothers.

Mrs. Martha Cranch, a poor sister of Peter Featherstone, also neglected in his will.

Tom Cranch, her unintelligent and unenterprising son.

Ben Garth, the active, athletic son of the Garths.

Letty Garth, the Garths' very bright younger daughter.

Alfred Garth, the son for whose engineering career the Garths are saving the money they use to pay Fred Vincy's debts.

Christy Garth, the Garths' oldest son, who becomes a scholar and tutor.

Mrs. Farebrother, the mother of the Reverend Mr. Camden.

Miss Henrietta Noble, her pious, understanding sister.

Miss Winifred Farebrother, Camden's sister, who idolizes him.

The Dowager Lady Chettam, Sir James's stiff and formal mother.

Arthur Chettam, the child of Sir James and Celia.

Sir Godwin Lydgate, of Quallingham in the north of England, Lydgate's distant and distinguished cousin. Rosamond appeals to him for money, but is denied.

Tantripp, Dorothea's faithful and understanding maid.

Mme. Laure, a French actress whom Lydgate once loved.

Dr. Sprague and **Dr. Minchin,** conservative Middlemarch physicians.

Mr. Wrench, at first physician to the Vincys, replaced by the more competent and progressive Lydgate.

Mr. Standish, the local lawyer who represents Peter Featherstone.

Mr. Mawmsey, a Middlemarch grocer.

Mrs. Mawmsey, his wife, a Middlemarch gossip.

Harry Toller, a local brewer.

Miss Sophy Toller, his daughter, who finally marries Ned Plymdale.

Edwin Larcher, a local businessman.

Mrs. Larcher, his wife, a local gossip.

Mr. Bambridge, a horse dealer who swindles Fred Vincy.

Mr. Horrock, his friend.

Mr. Hawley, a local citizen who frequently comments on people and events.

Mr. Chichely, another local citizen.

Dagley, an insolent farmer on Arthur Brooke's land.

Pinkerton, Mr. Brooke's political opponent in the election for Parliament.

A MIDSUMMER NIGHT'S DREAM

Author: William Shakespeare (1564-1616)
Time of action: Remote antiquity
First presented: 1595-1596

PRINCIPAL CHARACTERS

Theseus (thē′sē·ŭs), Duke of Athens, a wise, temperate ruler. Although he mistrusts the fantasy and imagination of "lunatics, lovers, and poets," he can perceive with good humor the love and duty inspiring the abortive dramatic efforts of his subjects, and he tries to teach his bride and queen, Hippolyta, the value of their good intentions.

Hippolyta (hĭ·pŏl′ĭ·tə), Theseus' bride, Queen of the Amazons, the maiden warriors whom he has conquered. She is a woman of regal dignity, less willing than her lord to be tolerant of the faults of Peter Quince's play, although she is more ready than he to believe the lovers' description of their night in the forest.

Titania (tĭ·tā′nĭ·ə), the imperious Queen of the fairies. She feuds with her husband Oberon over her "little changeling

boy," whom the king wants as his page. Enchanted by Oberon's flower, "love in idleness," she becomes enamored of Bottom the Weaver in his ass's head and dotes on him until her husband takes pity on her and frees her from the spell. She is quickly reconciled with him and they join in blessing the marriage of Theseus and Hippolyta, their favorites among mortals.

Oberon (ō′bə·rŏn), King of the fairies, who gleefully plots with Puck to cast a spell on the fairy queen and take away her changeling. Once he has stolen the child, he repents his mischief and frees Titania from her ridiculous dotage. He teases her for her fondness for Theseus and is, in return, forced to confess his own affection for Hippolyta.

Puck (pŭk), the merry, mischievous elf,

703

Robin Goodfellow, of English folk legend and Oberon's servant. He brings about the confusion of the young Athenians on Midsummer Eve as he tries to carry out Oberon's wishes; the king has taken pity on Helena and hopes to turn Demetrius' scorn for her into love. Puck simply enchants the first Athenian he sees, Lysander, and with great amusement watches the confusion which follows, commenting, "Lord, what fools these mortals be!"

Hermia (hĕr'mĭ·ə), a bright, bold young Athenian maiden. She defies her father and flees into the Athenian wood to elope with her beloved Lysander. She shows herself a small spitfire when she finds Demetrius and Lysander, through Puck's machinations, suddenly rivaling each other for Helena's affection rather than hers.

Helena (hĕl'ə·nə), a maiden who mournfully follows Demetrius, spaniel-like, in spite of the scorn with which he repulses her affection. When she suddenly finds both Demetrius and Lysander at her feet, she can only believe that they are teasing her.

Demetrius (də·mē'trĭ·ŭs), a rather fickle Athenian youth. He deserts his first love, Helena, to win the approval of Hermia's father for marriage with her, but he cannot win Hermia herself. His affections are returned, by Oberon's herb, to Helena, and he is wed to her on his Duke's marriage day.

Lysander (lī·săn'dər), Hermia's sweetheart, who plans their elopement to escape Theseus' decree that the girl must follow her father's will or enter a nunnery. He brashly argues with Demetrius, first over Hermia, then over Helena, before he is happily wed to his first love.

Nick Bottom, a good-natured craftsman and weaver. He is so enthralled by the prospect of Quince's play, "Pyramus and Thisbe," that he longs to play all the other parts in addition to his assigned role of the hero. He is supremely complacent as Titania's paramour and takes for granted the services of the fairies who scratch the ass's ears placed on his head by Puck. He marvels at his "most rare vision" after his release from the fairy spell.

Peter Quince, a carpenter, director of the infamous play of "tragical mirth" presented in honor of Theseus' wedding. Completely well-meaning, he illustrates, as he mangles his prologue, the "love and tongue-tied simplicity" of which Theseus speaks.

Snug, a joiner,
Snout, a tinker,
Flute, a bellows-maker, and
Starveling, a tailor, the other craftsmen-actors who portray, respectively, Lion, Wall, Thisbe, and Moonshine.

Egeus (ē·jē'ŭs), Hermia's father. He is determined that his daughter shall marry Demetrius, not Lysander, whom she loves.

Philostrate (fĭ'lŏs·trāt), Theseus' master of the revels.

Peaseblossom,
Cobweb,
Moth, and
Mustardseed, Titania's fairy attendants who wait on Bottom.

THE MIKADO

Author: W. S. Gilbert (1836-1911)
Time of action: The Middle Ages
First presented: 1885

The Mikado of Japan, a humane monarch who desires to let the punishment fit the crime. To steady the young men of his kingdom he has made flirting a capital crime. Without being in the least angry, he can calmly order a lawbreaker to be boiled in oil. All cheerfully bow to his will except Katisha, his daughter-in-law elect.

Nanki-Poo, son of the Mikado. Loving Yum-Yum, he flees the court disguised as a second trombone in order to escape from his elderly fiancée, Katisha. He is willing to sacrifice his life for a month of marriage with Yum-Yum, but unhesitatingly gives her up when he finds that she will have to be buried alive after his execution. After being declared dead by affidavit—a death which imperils the lives of the executioner and his accomplices—he refuses to return to life unless Ko-Ko marries Katisha. After she is safely married, he returns to life, receives his father's blessing, and faces a life of married bliss with Yum-Yum.

Ko-Ko, the chicken-hearted Lord High Executioner of Titipu. Appointed to his position by his fellow townsmen because he could not execute anybody else until he had executed himself, he is troubled by a command from the Mikado that an execution take place immediately. Loving himself with a tenderer passion than he loves Yum-Yum, his ward and affianced bride, he consents to let Nanki-Poo marry her for a month if he will allow himself to be executed at the end of that time. Unable to bring himself to kill anybody, he decides that an affidavit of Nanki-Poo's death will be as good as an execution. Faced with a choice of boiling in oil for encompassing the death of the heir apparent or of marrying Katisha, he reluctantly chooses the latter, and saves his life.

Pooh-Bah, the self-important Lord High Everything Else. An extremely haughty individual of pre-Adamite ancestry, he humiliates himself by accepting the salaries of all the offices he holds and by taking bribes, which he styles "insults."

Katisha (kă′tĭ·shä), an elderly lady of appalling aspect. Being an acquired taste, appealing only to connoisseurs, she has worked hard to teach Nanki-Poo to love her. Enraged at his desertion, she seeks revenge. When she thinks Nanki-Poo is dead, she marries Ko-Ko. On learning of his deception, she gives way to frightful fury, but finally decides to make the best of her bargain.

Yum-Yum, Ko-Ko's ward, engaged to him. A child of Nature, she takes after her mother and rejoices in her loveliness. She loves Nanki-Poo, but is unwilling to pay for a month of marital bliss with her life. She becomes the Emperor's daughter-in-law elect.

Pitti-Sing, Yum-Yum's sister. She testifies to Nanki-Poo's fictional death.

Peep-Bo, Yum-Yum's other sister, the third of the three maids from school.

Pish-Tush, a noble lord. With Pooh-Bah he attempts to persuade Ko-Ko to execute himself.

THE MILL ON THE FLOSS

Author: George Eliot (Mary Ann Evans, 1819-1880)
Time of action: Nineteenth century
First published: 1860

Maggie Tulliver, the impetuous and generous young heroine. Regarded as wild and gipsy-like by most of her respectable relatives, the sensitive and imaginative Maggie does not fit into the provincial society in and near St. Ogg's on the River Floss. She worships her brother Tom, who judges her harshly and thinks her unreliable. She loves Philip Wakem, the crippled son of her father's worst enemy, but must promise never to see him. Despite her feeling for Philip and her love for her cousin, Lucy Deane, Maggie is strongly attracted to her cousin's fiancé, Stephen Guest. Stephen persuades her to go boating, but they neglect their destination and are forced to spend the night on a freighter that rescues them. Almost everyone in St. Ogg's, her brother included, thinks Maggie responsible and regards her as an evil and designing woman. In the final scene, during a flood, Maggie takes a boat to rescue Tom, who is at the family mill. The two are reconciled before the raging river drowns them.

Tom Tulliver, Maggie's brother. Although never quick at school, Tom assumes financial responsibility for the family when he is only sixteen, after the father has lost his mill and home through a series of lawsuits. Tom pledges to follow his father in having nothing to do with the Wakem family. He works hard and, through his industry and careful investments in partnership with Bob Jakin, pays off his father's debts and eventually gets the mill back. Somewhat priggish, Tom judges others severely, but he is also generous to his mother and sister.

Edward Tulliver, the father of Maggie and Tom and the owner of Dorlcote Mill, near St. Ogg's on the River Floss. An emotional and hot-tempered man, Tulliver engages in several lawsuits which, in addition to other financial reverses, cause him to lose his mill. Tulli-ver must swallow his pride and work in the mill as the hated Wakem's manager. When Tom finally earns the money to pay off his father's debts, Tulliver meets Wakem and thrashes him. The exertion produces Tulliver's second stroke and he dies. He is always partial to his clever and imaginative daughter Maggie.

Mrs. Elizabeth Tulliver (Bessy), Edward's wife, proud of her birth as a Dodson and grieved that her husband's temper and improvidence cause her to lose her home and furnishings. She is dependent on the advice and opinions of her more prosperous sisters. Her pleading visit to Wakem inadvertently causes him to plan to buy the mill when Tulliver is bankrupt. Regarding Maggie as wild and unladylike, she is partial to her son Tom.

Philip Wakem, a lawyer's son, humpbacked as the result of a childhood accident. An excellent scholar and a talented artist, he loves Maggie from the time he first meets her, for she does not judge him by his infirmity. He hopes to marry Maggie despite family objections and her temporary attraction to Stephen Guest.

Lucy Deane, Maggie's blonde and pretty cousin. She and Maggie go to boarding school together and become great friends. Maggie confesses her feeling for Philip Wakem to Lucy. At the end, Lucy understands that Maggie was essentially blameless in the boating escapade with Stephen Guest and she forgives Maggie. She marries Stephen after Maggie is dead.

Stephen Guest, the handsome son of the wealthiest and most socially prominent family in St. Ogg's. Although engaged to Lucy, he is so attracted to Maggie that he pleads with her to marry him. After the boating trip, when Maggie is in disgrace, he goes off to Holland.

Mrs. Jane Glegg, the sister of Mrs. Tulliver. She is wealthy, parsimonious, and the proudest of the Dodson sisters. Although she dislikes Maggie, she defends her after the episode with Stephen Guest.

Mrs. Sophy Pullet, another of the Dodson sisters. She is wealthy and sentimental, crying copiously at every misfortune.

Mrs. Susan Deane, another Dodson sister, the pale and ailing mother of Lucy. She and Tulliver die about the same time.

Mr. Deane, her husband, who has worked his way up in the prosperous firm of Guest and Co., bankers, ship owners, and tradesmen. Although rather pompous about his achievements, he helps Tom get established in his firm.

Mrs. Gritty Moss, Mr. Tulliver's sister, a kind, poor woman with eight children. She has Maggie's ardent nature, although she lacks her niece's intelligence.

Mr. Moss, her husband, an unsuccessful farmer.

Mr. Glegg, husband of Jane Glegg, a wealthy, retired, prudent gentleman who had made a fortune in the wool business.

Mr. Pullet, husband of Sophy Pullet, a tiny, wealthy gentleman farmer who sucks lozenges throughout all family discussions.

Bob Jakin, Tom Tulliver's boyhood friend. He becomes Tom's partner in numerous investments.

John Wakem, the father of Philip and a lawyer in St. Ogg's. Although he does not hate Mr. Tulliver initially, Tulliver's frequent insults cause him to enjoy the family's downfall. His love for his son, however, later leads him to approve of the possibility of Philip's marrying Maggie.

The Rev. Walter Stelling, the owner of King's Lorton, the school attended by Tom Tulliver and Philip Wakem. He regards Tom as hopelessly stupid.

Luke Moggs, the head miller at Dorlcote Mill, fond of Maggie and entirely loyal to the Tullivers.

Mr. Riley, a local auctioneer, surveyor, and engineer who dies, leaving Mr. Tulliver with his debts.

The Rev. Dr. Kenn, rector of St. Ogg's, a clergyman sympathetic toward Maggie.

Mrs. Kenn, his wife, who runs a charity bazaar in St. Ogg's.

Mr. Poulter, the village schoolmaster.

Mr. Pivart, the owner of land near Dorlcote Mill who wishes to irrigate his land and is sued unsuccessfully by Mr. Tulliver.

Mr. Dix, another gentleman unsuccessfully sued by Mr. Tulliver.

Mr. Furley, the gentleman who owns the mortgage on Mr. Tulliver's land and transfers it to lawyer Wakem.

Mr. Gore, a scheming lawyer.

Mr. Jetsome, the young manager of the mill under Wakem after Tulliver dies. While drunk, he is pitched off his horse and severely injured.

Prissy Jakin, Bob Jakin's tiny "Dutch doll" wife.

Mrs. Jakin, Bob's massive mother.

THE MILL ON THE PO

Author: Riccardo Bachelli (1891-   )
Time of action: 1812-1872
First published: 1938-1940

Lazzaro Scacerni, owner of St. Michael's mill on the Po River. He builds the mill with money inherited from a dying captain he met in Napoleon's Russian campaign. Although illiterate, he creates a good business and maintains his mill through the adversities of flood and war and political upheaval. He hates the smugglers in the neighborhood, who use his beloved mill as a rendezvous and he is outraged when his own son becomes involved in smuggling grain to the Austrian enemy in the 1840's.

Giuseppe Scacerni, the cowardly and crafty son of Lazzaro. He cares nothing for his father's mill and trade except its profits. He takes a part in selling grain to his country's enemies. He forces Cecilia to marry him through threats: if she marries him, he agrees he will not inform the authorities that his father possesses concealed firearms. His son's death while fighting with Garibaldi unhinges his reason, and he is at last confined in a madhouse.

Dosolina Scacerni, wife of the miller Lazzaro. Although Lazzaro is attractive to women and makes many conquests, he chooses this poor but delicately beautiful girl to be his wife. She is twenty years his junior. In 1855 she dies of cholera.

Lazzaro follows her in death the very next day.

Cecilia Scacerni, an orphan befriended when a child by Lazzaro. Her parents' mill is washed up on the shore of the river near St. Michael's mill during a flood. Lazzaro reëstablishes her mill and cares for her as he would his own daughter. She sacrifices her own happiness to save her benefactor from prison by marrying Giuseppe. She is the last of the Scacerni family left to tend St. Michael's mill.

Beffa, a helper at the mill who incurs Lazzaro's wrath by declaring that the miller has been cuckolded. He is a tool of the smugglers who operate near the mill. He is killed in a gang feud.

Raguseo, leader of the gang of smugglers who rendezvous at St. Michael's mill. He threatens to harm the miller when Beffa is fired from his job as the miller's helper. Like Beffa, he is killed when a feud breaks out in the gang.

Lazzarino Scacerni, the son of Giuseppe and Cecilia. Vigorous and intelligent like his grandfather and a joy to both his parents, he is killed while fighting as a volunteer with Garibaldi.

THE MINISTRY OF FEAR

Author: Graham Greene (1904-   )
Time of action: World War II
First published: 1943

PRINCIPAL CHARACTERS

Arthur Rowe, a middle-aged Englishman living through World War II in London. He is a lonely widower, having killed his wife to prevent her living in pain. By accident he comes into possession of secret films taken by Nazi agents and he immediately becomes the object of their search. He suffers amnesia when

injured in a bombing raid and is unable for a time to remember anything beyond his youth. He finds himself confined in a nursing home which is a front for Nazi activities. He escapes and, aided by counter-intelligence agents, uncovers the Nazi activities. He regains his memory at the same time. Meanwhile, he has fallen in love with Anna Hilfe, sister of the spy group's leader.

Mr. Jones, a private detective. He is hired by Rowe, who wants to know why someone wants to kill him. Jones disappears, and his employer turns the case over to counter-intelligence.

Anna Hilfe, a young Austrian refugee. She informs Rowe that Nazi agents are after him. Though her brother is a Nazi spy, she helps Rowe uncover the enemy

activities because she has fallen in love with the Englishman.

Willi Hilfe, an Austrian refugee, Anna's brother. He helps Rowe "escape" when a man is supposedly murdered. Hilfe turns out to be the head of a Nazi fifth-column group operating in England. He commits suicide when he is found out.

Dr. Forester, head of the nursing home in which Rowe finds himself. Forester is an enemy agent and is killed by one of the hospital attendants.

MINNA VON BARNHELM

Author: Gotthold Ephraim Lessing (1729-1781)
Time of action: Eighteenth century
First presented: 1767

PRINCIPAL CHARACTERS

Minna von Barnhelm (mĭ'nä fôn bärn'-hälm), a charming and beautiful young heiress betrothed to a former Prussian officer, Major Tellheim. Hearing no word from him after the peace, she sets out resolutely with her maid Franziska to find the Major. Stopping at an inn, the two women are given the quarters of Tellheim, whom the landlord has dispossessed for nonpayment of rent. Minna learns of Tellheim's misfortune and, so that his pride will not stand in their way, she pretends to have lost her own fortune too. After many misunderstandings word is received that Tellheim's commission and property have been restored. The lovers are soon reconciled.

Major von Tellheim (mä·yōr fôn tăl'-hīm), a gallant and brave soldier recently discharged from the army, wounded and under shadow of suspicion for double dealing. As much as he loves Minna, he has purposely broken off communications with her in order to clear his good name, restore his health, and regain his fortune. Never one to accept charity, he rejects the repayment of a loan by the widow of a comrade-in-arms, the offer of financial

help from his old Sergeant, and the sympathy as well as the fortune of his fiancée. On the other hand, his own generosity, in advancing war taxes for a destitute principality and borrowing large funds for what he was led to believe is a destitute Minna, is forthright and sincere. Eventually his name is cleared and his property restored. He and Minna then plan their wedding.

Just (yŏost), the Major's humorous, loyal servant. He defends his master against insults from the landlord and does all he can to ease the Major's financial difficulties.

Franziska (frän'tsĭs·kä), Minna's resourceful maid and confidante. She joins her mistress in the intrigue designed to mollify the Major's pride. In the process, she finds a husband for herself.

Sergeant Paul Werner (poul vâr'nẽr), Tellheim's loyal Sergeant. He places all his resources at the disposal of the Major, even offering to raise money by selling his farm. When the Major's problems are finally resolved, Werner becomes engaged to Franziska.

709

Lieutenant Riccault de la Marlinière (rĭ-cōl′ də lä mär′lē·nyâr′), a mercenary and a gambler. Welcomed because he brings the news that Major Tellheim's good name and commission will soon be restored, he proves to be a scoundrel who manages to gain sympathy and money from Minna for his illicit gambling enterprises.

The Landlord, a greedy, prying innkeeper. He dispossesses Tellheim and rents his room to Minna when the Major falls behind in his rent.

Count von Bruchsal (fôn brŏŏkh′säl), Minna's uncle, who controls her wealth. He arrives in time to give the reconciled lovers his blessing.

A MIRROR FOR WITCHES

Author: Esther Forbes (1894?-   )
Time of action: Seventeenth century
First published: 1928

PRINCIPAL CHARACTERS

Doll, a Breton child adopted by Captain Jared Bilby after her mother is burned as a witch. As she grows up strange things happen to her and about her, until she is thought to be a witch and believes it herself. She is tried for witchcraft but dies peacefully in her cell; she believes her demon lover has come for her.

Captain Jared Bilby, an English sea captain who becomes Doll's foster father. He brings her to America with his family and rears her. When he wants her to marry Titus Thumb, she curses him and he dies.

Hannah Bilby, Captain Bilby's wife. She hates the child her husband has taken in, believing that a searing look from Doll causes her miscarriage. When Doll grows up, Hannah accuses her of being a witch.

Titus Thumb, a young man in love with Doll. At first Doll locks him out of the house when he comes courting. When he asks her to marry him, she bites his hand.

Labour and
Sorrow Thumb, Titus' twin sisters. They claim that Doll tortures them by her witchcraft.

The Bloody Shad, a pirate. Doll believes he is her demon lover. The name is also given an impish monkey her lover has with him. He is the son of Goody Greene. When he is executed at Boston harbor with two other pirates, Doll is lonely again.

Goody Greene, an old herb woman thought to be a witch. She is The Bloody Shad's mother. She and the minister are the only ones in the village who remain friendly to Doll.

Mr. Zacharias Zelley, the minister in the village. He tries to comfort Doll and save her soul.

Mrs. Thumb, Titus' mother. She is sure that Doll has bewitched her daughters.

Ahab, a savage black bull owned by the Thumbs. Doll has strange power over him, and he is friendly to her but to no one else.

Deacon Thumb, Titus' father. Finally convinced that Doll is a witch, he has her jailed.

Mr. Kleaver, a surgeon. He joins Deacon Thumb in insisting that Doll be jailed.

710

THE MISANTHROPE

Author: Molière (Jean Baptiste Poquelin, 1622-1673)
Time of action: Seventeenth century
First presented: 1666

PRINCIPAL CHARACTERS

Alceste (ăl·sĕst'), an outspoken, rigidly honest young man disgusted with society. Protesting against injustice, self-interest, deceit, roguery, he wants honesty, truthfulness, and sincerity. He hates all men because they are wicked, mischievous, hypocritic, and generally so odious to him that he has no desire to appear rational in their eyes. He would cheerfully lose a law case for the fun of seeing what people are, and to have the right to rail against the iniquity of human nature. In love with a young widow, Célimène, he is not blind to her faults, but feels that his sincere love will purify her heart. He controls his temper with her, for he deems her beneath his anger. Despite her coquetry, he will excuse her if she joins him in renouncing society and retiring into solitude. Seeing himself deceived on all sides and overwhelmed by injustice, he plans to flee from vice and seek a nook—with or without Célimène —where he may enjoy the freedom of being an honest man.

Célimène (sā·lē·mĕn'), a young widow loved by Alceste, though she embodies all qualities he detests. She is a flirt, a gossip with a satirical wit demonstrated in caustic sketches of her friends, a woman anxious for flattery. Not certain that she truly loves Alceste, she feels that he may be too jealous to deserve her love. In the end she scornfully rejects his invitation to grow old and bury herself in the wilderness with him.

Philinte (fē·lănt'), a friend of Alceste. Believing in civilization, tact, conformity, he is a man of good sense and sober rationality who takes men as they are. Where Alceste says that Oronte's sonnet is very badly written, Philinte flatters him for the sentiment of the poem. Though he admits that trickery usually wins the day, he sees in it no reason to withdraw from society.

Oronte (ô·rōnt'), a young fop who claims that he stands well in the Court and with the King and offers to use his influence there for Alceste. When his offer of friendship and influence is rejected and his sonnet ridiculed, he brings charges against Alceste. Though in love with Célimène, he rejects his love when he learns of her ridicule of him, and admits he has been duped.

Éliante (ā·lē·änt'), Célimène's cousin, a woman whose ideas are similar to Philinte's and who marries him at the end. Though she enjoys gossip, she is sincere, as even Alceste admits, and favors people who speak their minds.

Arsinoé (är·sē·nô·ā'), a friend of Célimène, an envious prude who offers advice on honor and wisdom. Though a flatterer, she is also outspoken at times.

Acaste (ä·càst') and
Clitandre (klē·tändr'), noblemen and fops. Both desire the love of Célimène, who ridicules them.

Basque (bàsk), a servant to Célimène.

Dubois (dü·bwä'), Alceste's servant.

An Officer of the Maréchaussée (mä·rä·shō·sā'), who delivers a summons to Alceste.

THE MISER

Author: Molière (Jean Baptiste Poquelin, 1622-1673)
Time of action: Seventeenth century
First presented: 1668

PRINCIPAL CHARACTERS

Harpagon (är·pà·gōn'), the father of Cléante and Elise, a wealthy, vicious, money-mad old widower. He loves money more than reputation, honor, or virtue, according to his son's valet, and spends his time watching, guarding, and locking it up. Fearful of being robbed and killed for his wealth, he buries his money in his garden. Even his children are suspected of planning to rob him. Because he treats them with austerity, they complain of their lack of decent clothes. For his daughter he plans a marriage to a wealthy man, for himself a marriage without dowry but with "other" things. The servant is warned not to rub the furniture too hard when polishing it and thus wear it out; the valet is searched on being fired to insure he has not stolen anything. Even his horses suffer from avarice; he feeds them straw. Hypocrisy is another dominant trait revealed in his statement, "Charity enjoins us to be agreeable when we can."

Cléante (klā·äṅt), Harpagon's son, a kindhearted youth who admits his obligation to his father. But he is determined to leave Harpagon if he can get no help from him, and he is forced to gamble for money for clothes. Outspoken, he tells his father he is a usurer. He acts with cleverness and boldness when he thwarts his father's parsimony by ordering elaborate refreshments for Mariane and gives her Harpagon's ring. His courage builds up to the point of defying his father on the question of marriage.

Master Jacques (zhäk), Harpagon's cook and coachman. He hates flatterers and is outspoken; because these traits and his clever sotto voce comments have earned him several beatings, he swears to give

them up. He is also a trickster and practical joker. His false messages carried between Harpagon and Cléante renew their mutual antagonism, and his false accusation of Valère as a thief is cause for a beating. But there is another side to the man: he has a feeling for the horses being starved by their straw diet. Next to them he loves his master and regrets the world's evil report of him.

Valère (và·lěr'), a rich young Neapolitan shipwrecked sixteen years before, now serving incognito as steward to Harpagon. He is sincere and honorable in his love for Élise, but uses shrewd and artful means in his endeavors to marry her. His method is to "take men's hobbies, follow their maxims, flatter their faults, and applaud their doings"; however, he admits that this practice is not sincere.

Élise (ā·lēs'), Harpagon's daughter and Valère's sweetheart after he saves her from drowning. She is formal in speech even in her comments on love; Valère says she is prudent. She fears that her father, the family, and the world will censor them, but she is realistic enough never to say one thing and then do another.

Mariane (mà·rē·àn'), Valère's sister, also shipwrecked, sincerely in love with Cléante. She is obedient to, and loving in her care of, her mother. When Harpagon proposes marriage to her, thus shocking Cléante, she cleverly replies in a manner satisfactory to both aspirants for her hand.

Frosine (frô·zēn'), a designing woman, a flatterer and a matchmaker who earns her living by her wits. Heaven has given her no income other than intrigue and industry, she says. Despite her cleverness and wit, she is tenderhearted toward lovers and tries to help them. She regrets her efforts on Harpagon's behalf, especially after he refuses to pay her.

La Flèche (là flĕsh'), Cléante's valet, whose sense of humor is shown in his sotto voce comments and in explanations he makes when he is overheard. He is shrewd in his appraisal of Harpagon.

Anselme (än·sĕlm'), the father of Valère and Mariane, an honest man who left Naples after the loss of his wife and children. He is faithful to friends, fair to Valère (unknown to him then), and liberal and generous, even to Harpagon,

for he agrees to pay for the double wedding of Harpagon's son and daughter to his daughter and son. He even buys a wedding suit for Harpagon.

Master Simon (sē·mōn'), an agent and moneylender, shrewd in his estimate of Cléante and his need for money. He flees when Harpagon sees that it is his son who wants to borrow.

Brindavoine (brän·då·vwän') and **La Merluche** (là mĕr·lüsh'), lackeys to Harpagon.

Mistress Claude (klōd), Harpagon's servant.

A Magistrate.

LES MISÉRABLES

Author: Victor Hugo (1802-1885)
Time of action: 1815-1835
First published: 1862

PRINCIPAL CHARACTERS

Jean Valjean (zhän' väl·zhän'), a convict of unusual strength, originally sentenced to five years in prison for stealing a loaf of bread for his sister's starving family. Attempts to escape have kept him in the galleys for nineteen years before he is released in 1815. Police Inspector Javert is sure he will be back, for his passport, proclaiming him an ex-convict, keeps him from getting work. He stops at the home of the Bishop of Digne, who treats him well despite Jean's attempts to rob him of some silverware. Eventually, calling himself Father Madeleine, a man with no previous history, he appears in the town of M. sur M. His discovery of a method for making jet for jewelry brings prosperity to the whole village, and the people elect him mayor. Then his conscience forces him to confess his former identity to save a prisoner unjustly arrested. Again he escapes from the galleys and from Inspector Javert, until he is betrayed by a blackmailer. In the end he dies peacefully, surrounded

by those he loves and with his entangled past revealed. His final act is to bequeath to Cosette the Bishop's silver candlesticks, which he had kept for years while trying to deserve the Bishop's confidence.

Fantine (fän·tēn'), a beautiful girl of Paris whose attempts to find a home for her illegitimate daughter Cosette have put her into the power of money-mad M. Thénardier. Unable to meet his demands for more money after the foreman of Father Madeleine's factory fires her upon learning of her earlier history, she turns prostitute, only to have M. Javert arrest her. By this time she is dying of tuberculosis. Father Madeleine promises to look after eight-year-old Cosette.

Cosette (kō·zĕt'), Fantine's daughter, who grows up believing herself the daughter of Father Madeleine. She is seen and loved by a young lawyer, Marius Pontmercy; but Valjean, fearing he will be compelled to reveal her story and his own if she marries, plans to take her away.

Cosette hears from Pontmercy again as she is about to leave for England with her supposed father. She sends him a note which brings his answer that he is going to seek death at the barricades.

Felix Tholomyès (fā·lēks′ tô·lô·myĕs′), a carefree, faithless student, Fantine's lover and Cosette's father.

M. Javert (zhä·vĕr′), a police inspector with a strong sense of duty that impels him to track down the man whom he considers a depraved criminal. Finally, after Valjean saves his life at the barricades, where the crowd wants to kill him as a police spy, he struggles between his sense of duty and his reluctance to take back to prison a man who could have saved himself by letting the policeman die. His solution is to drown himself in the Seine River.

Marius Pontmercy (mă·ryüs′ pōn′-mĕr·sē′), a young lawyer of good blood, estranged from his aristocratic family because of his liberal views. His father, an army officer under Napoleon, had expressed a deathbed wish that his son try to repay his debt to Sergeant Thénardier, who had saved his life at Waterloo. Marius′ struggle between obligations to a rascal and his desire to protect the father of the girl he loves sets M. Javert on Jean Valjean's tracks. A farewell letter from Cosette sends him to die at the barricade during a street revolt. After he has been wounded, Valjean saves him by carrying him underground through the sewers of Paris. Eventually Marius marries Cosette and learns, when the old man is dying, the truth about Jean Valjean.

M. Thénardier (tā·när·dyā′), an unscrupulous, avaricious innkeeper, a veteran of Waterloo, who bleeds Fantine of money to pay for the care of Cosette. Later he changes his name to Jondrette and begins a career of begging and blackmail while living in the Gorbeau tenement in Paris. Jean Valjean becomes one of his victims. He even demands money

to let Valjean out of the sewers beneath Paris while Valjean is carrying wounded Marius Pontmercy to a place of safety.

Mme. Thénardier, a virago as cruel and ruthless as her husband.

Eponine Thénardier (ā·pô·nēn′), their older daughter, a good-hearted but pathetic girl. Marius Pontmercy first meets her when she delivers one of her father's begging, whining letters. In love with Marius, she saves his life by interposing herself between him and an aimed musket during the fighting at the barricade. Before she dies she gives him a letter telling where Cosette can be found.

Azelma (ă·zĕl·mà′), their younger daughter.

Little Gavroche (gà·vrôsh′), the Thénardiers′ son, a street gamin. He is killed while assisting the insurgents in the fighting at the barricade.

Charles François Bienvenu Myriel (shàrl frän·swà′ byăn·və·nü′ mē·ryĕl′), Bishop of Digne, a good-hearted, devout churchman who gives hospitality to Jean Valjean after the ex-convict's release from the galleys. When Valjean repays him by stealing some of the Bishop's silverware, the old man tells the police that he had given the valuables to his guest and gives him in addition a pair of silver candlesticks. His saintliness turns Valjean to a life of honesty and sacrifice.

Father Fauchelevent (fōsh·lə·vän′), a bankrupt notary, turned carter, jealous of Father Madeleine's success in M. sur M. One day his horse falls and the old man is pinned beneath his cart. The accident might have proved fatal if Father Madeleine, a man of tremendous strength, had not lifted the vehicle to free the trapped carter. This feat of strength, witnessed by M. Javert, causes the policeman to comment significantly that he has known only one man, a galley slave, capable of doing such a deed. Father Madeleine's act changes Father Fauchelevent from an enemy to an admiring friend. After his accident the old man becomes a gardener at the convent of the Little Picpus in Paris. Jean Valjean and Cosette, fleeing from the police, take refuge in the convent garden. Old Fauchelevent gives them shelter and arranges to have Valjean smuggled out of the convent grounds in the coffin of a dead nun. Later he helps Valjean to get work as a workman at the convent.

Little Gervaise (zhĕr·vĕs'), a young Savoyard from whom Jean Valjean steals two francs. The deed arouses his conscience, and he weeps because he cannot find the boy to return his money. This is the crime of which Champmathieu is later accused.

Champmathieu (chän·má·tyœ'), an old man arrested for stealing apples. When he is taken to the departmental prison at Arras a convict there identifies him as Jean Valjean, a former convict, and he is put on trial for the theft of two francs stolen from a Savoyard lad eight years before. After a struggle with his conscience, Jean Valjean appears at the trial and confesses his identity. Champmathieu, convinced that all the world is mad if Father Madeleine is Jean Valjean, is acquitted. Javert arrests Valjean as the real culprit, but his prisoner escapes a few hours later after pulling out a bar of his cell window.

M. Gillenormand (zhēl·nôr·män'), the stern grandfather of Marius Pontmercy. A royalist, the old man never became reconciled with his Bonapartist son-in-law. He and his grandson quarrel because of the young man's political views and reverence for his dead father. Turned out of his grandfather's house, Marius goes to live in the Gorbeau tenement.

Théodule Gillenormand (tā·ô·dül'), M. Gillenormand's great-grand-nephew, a lieutenant in the lancers. He spies on Marius Pontmercy and learns that his kinsman is a regular visitor at his father's tomb.

Courfeyrac (kōōr·fā·ràk') and **Enjolas** (än·zhô·lä'), friends of Marius Pontmercy and members of the friends of the A.B.C., a society supposed to be interested in the education of children but in reality a revolutionary group. Both are killed in the uprising of the citizens in June, 1832, Courfeyrac at the barricades, Enjolas in the house where the insurgents make their last stand.

M. Maboef (mà·bœf'), an aged church-warden who had known Marius Pontmercy's father. A lover of mankind and a hater of tyranny, he marches unarmed to the barricades with the young friends of the A.B.C. He is killed during the fighting.

MISS JULIE

Author: August Strindberg (1849-1912)
Time of action: Nineteenth century
First presented: 1888

PRINCIPAL CHARACTERS

Miss Julie, a headstrong young woman, the daughter of a Count. She has derived from her mother a hatred of men and of woman's subservient role. As the drama begins, the household servants are scandalized over the circumstances of Miss Julie's broken engagement: she had made her fiancé jump over her horsewhip

several times, giving him a cut with the whip each time, and he had left her. Subsequently, she takes advantage of her father's absence to join the holiday dancing of the servants. She makes love to her father's not unwilling valet, Jean, and then shifts helplessly and impractically from one plan of action to another: running off alone; running off with the valet; a suicide pact when they become tired of each other; taking his fiancée, who naturally objects to being deserted, with them. When Jean kills Miss Julie's pet finch, at her command, her love turns to hate. Then, ecstatic at the thought of freedom through suicide, she takes her lover's razor and leaves the room.

Jean, Miss Julie's lover and her father's valet. His first suggestion is that they go to Como, Italy, to open a hotel. Later he brings Miss Julie his razor and indi-

cates it as one answer to her plea for advice. The return of his master, the Count, reduces him again to the menial attitudes of a servant.

Christine, a cook and Jean's fiancée. She loves him and does not intend to lose him to Miss Julie. She refuses Miss Julie's offer to go along with them to Como and announces as she leaves for church that she has spoken to the stable men about not letting anyone have horses until after the Count's return.

MISS LONELYHEARTS

Author: Nathanael West (Nathan Weinstein, 1903?-1940)
Time of action: Late 1920's
First published: 1933

PRINCIPAL CHARACTERS

Miss Lonelyhearts, the male writer of advice to the lovelorn on the New York "Post-Dispatch." The lovelorn column, considered a necessity for the increase in the paper's circulation and regarded by its staff as a joke, becomes an agony to its writer as he sees that the letters he receives are genuine cries for help from the very depths of suffering. In an attempt to escape the pain of the realization that he is the victim of the joke rather than its perpetrator, he turns in vain to drink, to love-making, and to a vacation in the country with a girl who loves him. Finally, in the delirium of illness, he imagines himself identified with the Christ whose image has long haunted him. As the crippled Peter Doyle approaches his room, Miss Lonelyhearts runs toward him with arms outstretched to receive him in his healing embrace. His gesture is mistaken for an intended attack and he is shot.

Willie Shrike, the feature editor, who is Miss Lonelyhearts' boss. He turns the knife in Miss Lonelyhearts' agony by his

unending mockery of the desperate cries for help in the lovelorn letters and of the attempts at escape with which men delude themselves.

Mary Shrike, Willie Shrike's wife, whom Miss Lonelyhearts tries in vain to seduce.

Betty, a girl who is in love with Miss Lonelyhearts. Hoping to cure his despair, she takes him to the country. The attempt fails, since the letters are not forgotten.

Peter Doyle, a cripple who consults Miss Lonelyhearts about the meaning of the painful and unremunerative round of his existence. Later, he accuses the columnist of the attempted rape of his wife and shoots him in a struggle following a gesture which the cripple mistakes for an intended attack.

Fay Doyle, Peter Doyle's wife. Dissatisfied with her life with her crippled husband, she seeks out Miss Lonelyhearts and tries to seduce him.

MISS RAVENEL'S CONVERSION

Author: John William De Forest (1826-1906)
Time of action: The Civil War period
First published: 1866

PRINCIPAL CHARACTERS

Lillie Ravenel, a Southern girl loyal to her section during the Civil War. Vivacious and beautiful, she marries Colonel Carter, a Union officer who helps her and her father during the Federal troops' occupation of New Orleans. Her husband takes her aunt as his mistress. An old admirer, Edward Colburne, by his love restores her happiness and marries her after the death of her husband. His influence makes her recognize the justice of the Northern cause.

Dr. Ravenel, Lillie's father, a medical doctor. He wants to rehabilitate the freed slaves of the South. He has his daughter teach some of his charges to read. Aware of Colonel Carter's moral weakness, he hopes Lillie will marry Colburne. When she decides to marry Carter, however, he does not forbid it.

Colonel Carter, Lillie's first husband. He is a man attractive to women and an opportunist. He has an affair with Mrs. Larue, Lillie's aunt. A weak man, he is given to drink and indebtedness, as well

as women. He is killed in battle during the Civil War.

Edward Colburne, a long-time admirer of Lillie. He is a captain in the Union army, a courageous and capable officer as well as a man of excellent character. Worn out and sick near the end of the war, he returns home to New England, convalesces under Dr. Ravenel's care, and successfuly woos Lillie—who had returned to New England with her father after the death of her husband.

Mrs. Larue, Lillie's aunt. An opportunist, she takes up a love affair with Colonel Carter, Lillie's first husband.

The Meurices, a New Orleans Creole family sympathetic to the Northern cause. They are friends of Captain Colburne.

Major Gazaway, the cowardly commander of a Union fort. When he fails in his duty, Captain Colburne takes command and repulses a Confederate attack.

MR. BRITLING SEES IT THROUGH

Author: H. G. Wells (1866-1946)
Time of action: World War I
First published: 1916

PRINCIPAL CHARACTERS

Mr. Britling, a famous English writer. Convinced before World War I that the idea of a possible war with Germany is nonsense, he is greatly troubled at the outbreak of the war, though convinced that Germany will quickly lose. Gradually the magnitude of the war becomes

clear to him, and he becomes so disturbed that writing is impossible. At last, even though his oldest son, fighting for England, and his children's admired German tutor, who went home to fight for his country, are both dead, Mr. Britling becomes reconciled to the idea of death.

717

He believes that a better world is in the making and that things will be different after the war.

Mr. Direck, an American who has come to England to persuade Mr. Britling to give a series of lectures in the United States. Attracted to the Britling family and friends, and falling in love, he is at first only a spectator of the war. But, after going to the Continent to find news of Britling's secretary, who is missing in action, he volunteers in the Canadian Army.

Hugh Britling, Mr. Britling's oldest son by his first wife. Hugh lies about his age and manages to be sent to the front. He is killed.

Teddy, Mr. Britling's secretary. He is missing in action, and presumed to be dead, but he comes home with one hand gone.

Letty, Teddy's wife. Convinced at last that her husband is dead, she finds consolation in Mr. Britling's philosophy, and she also is reconciled to death. Then one day she sees her living husband in front of the cottage.

Cecily (Cissie) Corner, Letty's sister. Direck falls in love with her.

Herr Karl Heinrich, the German tutor of the Britling children. He does not believe in the war, but goes home to serve his country. He is killed.

Mrs. Britling, the second wife of Mr. Britling. They have not been in love for many years, but they coöperate in running a pleasant household.

Mrs. Harrowdean, a widow with whom Mr. Britling has a love affair. The love affair does not run smoothly; in the period just before the war they are quarreling by mail.

MR. FACEY ROMFORD'S HOUNDS

Author: Robert Smith Surtees (1803-1864)
Time of action: Nineteenth century
First published: 1865

PRINCIPAL CHARACTERS

Francis Romford, called **Facey.** He is often mistaken for his wealthy namesake and capitalizes on this fact. Using the other's stationery, he becomes Master of Hounds of the Heavyside Hunt. After living well in the hunt country, he marries a dowdy but rich young woman, moves to Australia, and becomes prosperous.

Francis Romford, Esquire, the aristocratic owner of Abbeyfield Park, whom Facey pretends to be.

Francis Gilroy, Facey's cattle-jobbing uncle, who employs Facey.

The Widow Gilroy, a sharp-faced woman who discharges Facey immediately upon her husband's death.

Jogglebury Crowdey, a neighbor from whom Facey hurriedly borrows fifty pounds before news of his discharge following his uncle's death circulates in the area.

Soapey Sponge, who once cheated Facey. He deserts his wife and ships to Australia, where he becomes wealthy. He and Facey eventually become banking partners in Australia.

Lucy Glitters, Soapey's wife who, as Facey's "half-sister, Mrs. Somerville," helps his fox-hunting ventures.

"Mrs. Sidney Benson," Lucy's mother, who helps manage Beldon Hall.

The Countess of Caperington, who, while

the actress wife of dissipated Sir Henry Scattercash, had known Lucy.

Betsy Shannon, another theatrical friend, introduced as "Miss Hamilton Howard."

Mr. and Mrs. Watkins, of Australia. Wealthy, but crude and vulgar, they are members of the Larkspur Hunt.

Cassandra Cleopatra, their simpering daughter, who is looking for a husband. She finally gets Facey.

Mr. Hazey, Master of the neighboring Hard and Sharp Hunt.

Bill Hazey, his son.

Anna Maria, Hazey's daughter, in love with Facey.

Jonathan Lotherington, a fat, timid huntsman who resigns from the Hunt when Facey shows up his poor horsemanship.

Goodhearted Green, a shady horse trader who provides three vicious mounts for the hunt. He calls himself "Sir Roger Ferguson."

Mrs. Rowley Rounding, who is thrown by one of the vicious horses provided by Goodhearted Green.

Colonel Chatterbox, who demands the return of Mrs. Rounding's money, a demand Facey refuses.

Daniel Swig and
Tom Chowey, cheap and inefficient grooms hired by Facey.

Lord Viscount Lovetin, who rents Beldon Hall to Facey. He returns unexpectedly and promptly dispossesses the "wrong" Mr. Romford.

Mr. Lonnergan, Lord Lovetin's agent.

Lovetin Lonnergan, his son, who marries "Miss Hamilton Howard."

Mrs. Mustard, housekeeper of Beldon Hall and the mother of three daughters, called "The Dirties."

Mr. Stotfold, who provides a stag for the hunt.

Proudlock, Facey's stable keeper.

MR. MIDSHIPMAN EASY

Author: Frederick Marryat (1792-1848)
Time of action: Napoleonic wars
First published: 1836

PRINCIPAL CHARACTERS

Jack Easy, a midshipman aboard the "Harpy," during the Napoleonic Wars, who wins naval battles, captures Spanish vessels, and rescues shipwrecked criminals. When he falls in love with Agnes Rebiera, a faked carriage accident keeps him in Sicily with Gascoigne long enough to court her and overcome her father's objections to their marriage. The under-aged Jack returns to England for his father's consent and finds that his mother is dead. His father dies shortly thereafter. Now wealthy, he gives up the sea and marries Agnes.

Dr. Middleton, an advocate of the survival of the fittest who rescues Jack from a doting mother and a father who has preached to his son an over-simplified philosophy of the equality of man.

Captain Wilson, a poor Easy relative and captain of the warship "Harpy" and later of the "Aurora." He signs Jack aboard because of a thousand-pound debt he owes to Jack's father.

Gascoigne, another midshipman who shares adventures with Jack and eventually settles in Hampshire as a country gentleman on Jack's large estate.

Mesty, an Ashantee Negro who is loyal to Jack because Jack treats him as an equal. Once he accepts a bribe from the Rebiera family priest to kill Jack, but he uses the poison on the priest.

Don Rebiera, a wealthy Sicilian captured with his family by Jack and released.

Sometime later, driven ashore by a storm, Jack rescues Don Rebiera from would-be assassins who have invaded his villa to murder him. Jack again saves Don Rebiera from the same fate when freed galleyslaves, among them one of the would-be murderers, besiege the villa.

Agnes Rebiera, Don Rebiera's lovely daughter, who inspires the love of Mr. Midshipman Easy and becomes his wife.

MISTER ROBERTS

Author: Thomas Heggen (1919-1949)
Time of action: Last months of World War II
First published: 1946

PRINCIPAL CHARACTERS

Douglas Roberts, First Lieutenant, U. S. S. "Reluctant." A born leader, he is sensitive, perceptive, and idealistic. Desiring battle action, he has nevertheless heroically adjusted himself to the dull routine of a supply ship. He is worshiped by the crew, almost worshiped by his fellow officers, and hated by the captain, who fears him and yet refuses to transfer him to another ship. He finally gets his transfer but is ironically killed while drinking coffee in a wardroom when a kamikaze plane hits his destroyer.

Captain Morton, skipper of the "Reluctant." He is officious, childish, and unreasonable, and is thoroughly disliked or hated by his entire crew. His hatred of Mr. Roberts is closely related to his recognition and envy of Roberts' superior intelligence and ability.

Ensign Keith, USNR, a former college boy and recently commissioned young Bostonian who learns quickly the comparative unimportance of Navy rules and regulations aboard the "Reluctant."

David Bookser, a seaman, the spiritual

type who manages to get himself a beautiful woman while on shore leave, to the amazement and admiration of his shipmates.

Ensign Pulver, USNR, a healthy young officer who not only hates Captain Morton but delights in plotting against him. After getting news of Mr. Roberts' death, Pulver tosses all of Captain Morton's beloved palm trees over the ship's side.

Doc, the ship's doctor, a plump, balding, contradictory, unpredictable little man, sometimes highly regarded and sometimes despised by his patients.

Frank Thompson, a radio man whose baby dies and who vainly seeks permission to fly to the States for the funeral.

Chief Dowdy, a close friend of Mr. Roberts.

Red Stevens, a recently married seaman who nearly kills another seaman for cruelly ribbing him about his wife's hypothetical infidelities during his absence.

Miss Williamson and
Miss Girard, two Navy nurses.

MR. SPONGE'S SPORTING TOUR

Author: Robert Smith Surtees (1803-1864)
Time of action: Nineteenth century
First published: 1853

PRINCIPAL CHARACTERS

Soapey Sponge, a Cockney sportsman who knows foxes, but is otherwise uncouth.

Buckram, a sharp horse trader near London who provides Sponge with vicious mounts.

Leather, Buckram's helper, who becomes Sponge's groom.

Waffles, Master of the Hunt, who vainly tries to make a fool of Sponge.

Sir Harry Scattercash, a rake married to a cigar-smoking actress.

Lucy Glitters, a hard-riding ex-actress who marries Sponge.

Jawleyford, a boastful hunter, with mar-riageable daughters, who invites Sponge for a visit.

Lord Scamperdale, the owner of a pack of hounds.

Spraggon, his servant, who helps Sponge write a story about Puffington that is garbled in publication.

Puffington, a bachelor sportsman who entertains Sponge in hopes of gaining publicity.

Jogglesbury, a carver of canes who is too fat to hunt. He invites Sponge to be god-father to his son.

Mrs. Jogglesbury, his wife, who is glad when the crude Sponge leaves her house.

MR. WESTON'S GOOD WINE

Author: T. F. Powys (1875-1953)
Time of action: November 20, 1923
First published: 1927

PRINCIPAL CHARACTERS

Mr. Weston, a strange wine merchant who visits the village of Folly Down at seven o'clock on the evening of November 20, 1923. The clocks in the village stop when he arrives. He helps many people, among them the melancholy Mr. Grobe, the lonely Tamar, Jenny Bunce, the virtuous Mr. Bird, to whom he reads from his own book, the Bible. He also makes Mr. Bird's well run with wine. When he leaves Folly Down the clocks start again and the villagers are surprised to see that it is only ten o'clock.

Michael, Mr. Weston's assistant, who car-ries a large book with the names of all the inhabitants of the town inscribed. He is married to Tamar Grobe by Mr. Weston and gives her happiness under the village trysting tree.

Mr. Grunter, the sexton, allegedly quite a seducer. He thinks Mr. Weston is the Devil, but finds that he is not. Grunter helps Mr. Weston in his affairs in the village and sees the souls of Tamar and another girl carried to Heaven.

Mr. Bunce, the innkeeper, who blames God for all the pregnancies among the girls of Folly Down. He scornfully says that his daughter may not marry simple-hearted Mr. Bird until the man's well runs with wine.

Mr. Grobe, rector at Folly Down. He no longer believes in God because he has lost his wife. He tries to find escape and pleasure in drink and is especially pleased with a bottle of Mr. Weston's wine, a bottle that remains full while he drinks from it. Mr. Weston also gives him a small bottle, the contents of which enable Mr. Grobe to die peacefully.

Tamar Grobe, the rector's daughter, who wants to marry an angel. She finds happiness with Michael, Mr. Weston's assistant, to whom she is wedded by Mr. Weston. She dies shortly after her wedding, and two angels carry her to Heaven.

Jenny Bunce, the innkeeper's daughter, in love with Mr. Bird. She is a simple,

good-hearted girl who believes she will find happiness caring for the man she loves. Mr. Weston marries her to Mr. Bird.

Mr. Bird, a resident of Folly Down who recognizes Mr. Weston. Bird is an honest, virtuous man who preaches God's word to man and beast. Mr. Weston causes Mr. Bird's well to run with wine so that he can marry Jenny with her father's permission.

The Mumby Boys, two sons of the local squire, accomplished and villainous seducers who are chased by a wild beast controlled by Mr. Weston. Frightened, they run to the house of the bawd who caters to them and agree to marry two of their victims. As the beast circles her house the evil old bawd dies of fright.

MRS. DALLOWAY

Author: Virginia Woolf (1882-1941)
Time of action: The 1920's
First published: 1925

PRINCIPAL CHARACTERS

Clarissa Dalloway, a woman fifty-two years old and chic, but disconcerted over life and love. The June day in her late middle years is upsetting to Mrs. Dalloway, uncertain as she is about her daughter and her husband's love, her own feelings for them and her former fiancé, lately returned from India. Years before Peter Walsh had offered her agony and ecstasy, though not comfort or social standing, and so she had chosen Richard Dalloway. Now, seeing Peter for the first time in many years, her belief in her motives and her peace of mind are gone. Engaged in preparations for a party, she knows her life is frivolous, her need for excitement neurotic, and her love dead. Meeting her best friend, Sally Seton, also makes her realize that their love was abnormal as is her daughter's for an older woman. Although she knows that her

husband's love for her is very real and solid, she feels that death is near, that growing old is cruel, that life can never be innocently good again.

Richard Dalloway, her politician husband, a Conservative Member of Parliament. Never to be a member of the Cabinet or a Prime Minister, Richard is a good man who has improved his character, his disposition, his life. Loving his wife deeply but silently, he is able only to give her a conventional bouquet of roses to show his feeling, a fortunate gift because roses are the one flower she can stand to see cut. Devoted to his daughter, he sees her infatuation as a passing thing, an adolescent emotional outlet. He is gently persuasive among his constituents and colleagues, and in thought and deed a thoroughly good man.

Peter Walsh, a widower lately returned from India to make arrangements for the divorce of a major's wife, a woman half his age whom he plans to marry, again an action to fill the void left by Clarissa. Perceptive and quick to understand motives for unhappiness, Peter sees his return to England as another step in his failure to live without Clarissa. Unnerved by seeing her again, he blurts out his recent history, and he continues the cruel probe all day and that night at her party.

Septimus Warren Smith, a war casualty who commits suicide on the night of Mrs. Dalloway's party and delays the arrival of one of the guests, a doctor. A poet and a brave man, Septimus brings back to England an Italian war bride whom he cannot really love, all feeling having been drained from him by the trauma of war. Extremely sensitive to motives, to Septimus his doctors represent the world's attempt to crush him, to force him into conventionality. Feeling abandoned and unable to withstand even the devotion of his lovely wife, he jumps to his death, a martyr to the cause of individuality, of sensitivity to feelings and beauty.

Lucrezia Smith, called **Rezia,** the Italian wife whom Smith met in Milan and married after the war. Desperately in love with her husband, she tries to give him back his former confidence in human relations, takes him to doctors for consultation, and hopes to prevent his collapse and suicide.

Elizabeth Dalloway, the daughter who has none of her mother's charm or vivacity and all of her father's steady attributes. Judged to be handsome, the sensible seventeen-year-old appears mature beyond her years; her thoughtfulness directly contradicts her mother's frivolity. She is until this day enamored of Miss Kilman, a desperate and fanatical older woman who is in love with Elizabeth but conceals her feeling under the guise of religiosity and strident char-ity. On the day of the party Elizabeth sees Miss Kilman's desire for power and escapes from the woman's tyranny of power and need. That night Elizabeth blossoms forth in womanly radiance so apparent that her father fails to recognize his conception of a daughter.

Doris Kilman, Elizabeth Dalloway's tutor and friend, an embittered, frustrated spinster whose religious fanaticism causes her to resent all the things she could not have or be. With a lucid mind and intense spirit, largely given to deep hatreds of English society, she represents a caricature of womanly love and affection, a perversion.

Lady Rosseter, nee **Sally Seton,** the old friend with whom Mrs. Dalloway had believed herself in love when she was eighteen. Sally has always known that Clarissa made the wrong choice and has always been aware of the shallowness of her friend's existence. Mellowed now, Sally and Peter Walsh can see the pattern of life laid out before them at this gay party, and they console each other for loss of girlhood friend and beloved.

Dr. Holmes, Septimus Smith's physician. Brisk and insensitive, he fails to realize the seriousness of his patient's condition. Puzzled because Smith does not respond to prescriptions of walks in the park, music halls, and bromides at bedtime, he sends him to consult Sir William Bradshaw.

Sir William Bradshaw, a distinguished specialist who devotes three-quarters of an hour to each of his patients. Ambitious for worldly position but apathetic as a healer, he shuts away the mad, forbids childbirth, and advises an attitude of proportion in sickness and in health. Because of Septimus Smith's suicide he and his wife arrive late at Mrs. Dalloway's party.

Lady Millicent Bruton, a fashionable Mayfair hostess. A dabbler in charities and social reform, she is sponsoring a plan to have young men and women emigrate to Canada.

Hugh Whitbread, a friend of the Dalloways and a minor official at Court.

MRS. DANE'S DEFENCE

Author: Henry Arthur Jones (1851-1929)
Time of action: Early twentieth century
First presented: 1900

PRINCIPAL CHARACTERS

Mrs. Dane, a charming woman whose reputation is clouded. She finally is proved to be Felicia Hindemarsh, a notorious woman who had an affair with her employer while working as a governess, bearing him a child. As a result of the affair the man became demented and his wife committed suicide. When faced with these facts, Mrs. Dane, who truly loves Lionel Carteret, is persuaded by his uncle to disappear from the young man's life, lest she ruin it.

Lionel Carteret, a young man madly in love with Mrs. Dane. He is the adopted son of Sir Daniel Carteret. He loves Mrs. Dane so much that he is willing to marry her even after he knows about her past. When she disappears he believes he will never know love or happiness again.

Sir Daniel Carteret, Lionel's foster father and a jurist. He has known love himself, having been in love at one time with Lionel's mother, then already married. Wishing to help his adopted son avoid tragedy, he investigates the rumors about Mrs. Dane and finds them true. He suppresses the facts, believing that the woman has suffered enough, but he persuades her to disappear from his adopted son's life.

Mrs. Bulsom-Porter, who hates Mrs. Dane because the latter is charming and physically attractive. She spreads gossip about Mrs. Dane and even hires a detective to try to find out about the woman's past. Although her rumors are correct, no one will admit it; consequently, Mrs. Bulsom-Porter is forced to make a public apology.

James Risby, Mrs. Bulsom-Porter's nephew, who first tells his aunt that Mrs. Dane seems to be the notorious Felicia Hindemarsh. Later he retracts his statements, believing that the woman—though definitely guilty—has suffered enough for her acts.

Lady Eastney, a friend of Mrs. Dane. She is attracted to Sir Daniel as a kind and just man. She accepts his proposal of marriage.

Janet Colquhoun, an attractive young woman with whom Lionel has been previously infatuated. She still loves him and promises him a bright future.

THE MISTRESS OF THE INN

Author: Carlo Goldoni (1707-1793)
Time of action: Mid-eighteenth century
First presented: 1752

PRINCIPAL CHARACTERS

Mirandolina, a pretty young girl who inherits an inn from her father. She promises him on his deathbed that she will marry Fabricius, who has served her father well. She delays the marriage, however, because of her delight in tempting

724

all men, yet giving nothing. After enthralling three noble suitors, she finally announces that she will marry Fabricius.

Fabricius, the faithful serving-man, who becomes jealous of Mirandolina's favors to the nobles.

The Marquis di Forlipopoli, a proud but penniless noble in love with Mirandolina.

The Count D'Albafiorita, a wealthy noble who gives her expensive but tasteless presents.

The Cavalier di Ripafratta, a professed woman-hater whose defenses crumble before Mirandolina. At last, burning with love, he proposes marriage, but she refuses him.

MITHRIDATE

Author: Jean Baptiste Racine (1639-1699)
Time of action: First century B.C.
First presented: 1673

PRINCIPAL CHARACTERS

Mithridate (mē·trē·dàt'), King of Pontus, who has been fighting the Romans for forty years. At first he is believed dead, but this rumor proves to be false. He is in love with Monime, a woman much younger than himself, and he is very jealous of his two sons, who are both also in love with Monime. His jealousy causes him to set up a plan whereby he can learn whom Monime really loves. In the end, he believes that both of his sons have betrayed him by joining his enemies, the Romans, and he kills himself. Before he dies he learns that the older son has remained loyal to him, and he blesses Monime and this son.

Monime (mô·nēm'), the young woman Mithridate loves. She is in love with Mithridate's son Xipharès, but she determines to remain faithful to Mithridate in spite of this. After he tricks her into revealing who it is she really loves, she refuses to marry him. She tries to kill herself and is glad when Mithridate sends a servant to poison her. Monime is finally united with Xipharès, with Mithridate's blessing.

Xipharès (gzē·fà·rēs'), Mithridate's son, who shares his father's feelings of enmity toward the Romans. He has been in love with Monime since the first time he met her. However, he says nothing about his love until his father is reported to be dead. Xipharès suffers greatly when he discovers that his brother also loves Monime and that his father, who is still alive, is returning. Xipharès finally routs the Romans and succeeds to the throne, with Monime as his Queen.

Pharnace (fàr·nàs'), Mithridate's other son, also in love with Monime. He sides with the Romans against his father. Pharnace refuses to marry the daughter of the Parthian King, with whom his father wishes to make an alliance.

Arbate (àr·bàt'), Mithridate's confidant, who tells him that Pharnace is in love with Monime.

Phoedime (fœ·dēm'), Monime's loyal friend and confidante.

Arcas (ar·kàs'), a servant, charged with giving poison to Monime.

MOBY DICK

Author: Herman Melville (1819-1891)
Time of action: Early nineteenth century
First published: 1851

Ishmael, a philosophical young school-master and sometime sailor who seeks the sea when he becomes restless, gloomy, and soured on the world. With a new-found friend Queequeg, a harpooner from the South Seas, he signs aboard the whaler "Pequod" as a seaman. Queequeg is the only person on the ship to whom he is emotionally and spiritually close, and this closeness is, after the initial establishment of their friendship, implied rather than detailed. Otherwise Ishmael does a seaman's work, observes and listens to his shipmates, and keeps his own counsel. Having been reared a Presbyterian (as was Melville), he reflects in much of his thinking the Calvinism out of which Presbyterianism grew; but his thought is also influenced by his knowledge of literature and philosophy. He is a student of cetology. Regarding Ahab's pursuit of Moby Dick, the legendary white whale, and the parts played by himself and others involved, Ishmael dwells on such subjects as free will, predestination, necessity, and damnation. After the destruction of the "Pequod" by Moby Dick, Ishmael, the lone survivor, clings to Queenqueg's floating coffin for almost a day and a night before being rescued by the crew of another whaling vessel, the "Rachel."

Queequeg, Starbuck's veteran harpooner, a tattooed cannibal from Kokovoko, an uncharted South Seas island. Formerly zealous of learning about Christianity, he has become disillusioned after living among so-called Christians and, having reverted to paganism, he worships a little black idol, Yojo, that he keeps with him. Although he appears at ease among his Christian shipmates, he keeps himself at the same time apart from them, his only close friend being Ishmael. In pursuit of whales he is skilled and fearless. When he nearly dies of a fever he has the ship's carpenter build him a canoe-shaped coffin which he tries out for size and comfort; then, recovering, he saves it for future use. Ironically it is this coffin on which Ishmael floats after the sinking of the "Pequod" and the drowning of Queequeg.

Captain Ahab, the proud, defiant, megalomaniacal captain of the "Pequod." He is a grim, bitter, brooding, vengeful madman who has only one goal in life: the killing of the white whale that had deprived him of a leg in an earlier encounter. His most prominent physical peculiarity is a livid scar that begins under the hair of his head and, according to one crewman, extends the entire length of his body. The scar symbolizes the spiritual flaw in the man himself. His missing leg has been replaced by one of whalebone for which a small hole has been bored in the deck. When he stands erect looking out to sea, his face shows the unsurrenderable willfulness of his spirit and to Ishmael a crucifixion also, a "regal overbearing dignity of some mighty woe." Ahab is in complete, strict command of his ship, though he permits Starbuck occasionally to disagree with him. Ahab dies caught, like Fedallah, the Parsee, in a fouled harpoon line that loops about his neck and pulls him from a whaleboat.

Starbuck, the first mate, tall, thin, weathered, staid, steadfast, conscientious, and superstitious, a symbol of "mere unaided virtue or right-mindedness." He dares to criticize Ahab's desire for vengeance, but he is as ineffectual as a seaman trying to halt a storm. Ahab once takes his advice about repairing some leaking oil casks; but when Starbuck, during a typhoon off Japan, suggests turning home, Ahab scorns him. Starbuck even thinks of killing or imprisoning Ahab while the Captain is asleep, but he cannot. Having failed to dissuade Ahab from the pursuit of Moby Dick, Starbuck submits on the third day to Ahab's will, though feeling that in obeying Ahab he is disobeying God. When he makes one final effort to stop the doomed Ahab, the captain shouts to his boatmen, "Lower away!"

Stubb, the second mate, happy-go-lucky, indifferent to danger, good-humored, easy; he is a constant pipe-smoker and a fatalist.

Flask (King-Post), the young third mate, short, stout, ruddy. He relishes whaling and kills the monsters for the fun of it or as one might get rid of giant rats. In his shipboard actions Flask is sometimes playful out of Ahab's sight but always abjectly respectful in his presence.

Fedallah, Ahab's tall, diabolical, white-turbaned Parsee servant. He is like a shadow of Ahab or the two are like opposite sides of a single character and Ahab seems finally to become Fedallah, though retaining his own appearance. The Parsee prophesies that Ahab will have neither hearse nor coffin when he dies. Fedallah dies caught in a fouled harpoon line which is wrapped around Moby Dick.

Moby Dick, a giant albino sperm whale that has become a legend among whalers. He has often been attacked and he has crippled or destroyed many men and boats. He is both a real whale and a symbol with many possible meanings. He may represent the universal spirit of evil, God the indestructible, or indifferent Nature; or perhaps he may encompass an ambiguity of meaning adaptable to the individual reader. Whatever his meaning, he is one of the most memorable non-human characters in all fiction.

Pip, the bright, jolly, genial little Negro cabin boy who, after falling from a boat during a whale chase, is abandoned in midocean by Stubb, who supposes that a following boat will pick him up. When finally taken aboard the "Pequod," he has become demented from fright.

Tashtego, an American Indian, Stubb's harpooner. As the "Pequod" sinks, he nails the flag still higher on the mast and drags a giant seabird, caught between the hammer and the mast, to a watery grave.

Daggoo, a giant African Negro, Flask's harpooner.

Father Mapple, a former whaler, now the minister at the Whaleman's Chapel in New Bedford. He preaches a Calvinistic sermon, on Job, filled with seafaring terms.

Captain Peleg and **Captain Bildad,** fighting, materialistic Quakers who are the principal owners of the "Pequod."

Elijah, a madman who warns Ishmael and Queequeg against shipping with Captain Ahab.

Dough-Boy, the pale, bread-faced, dull-witted steward who, deathly afraid of Queenqueg, Tashtego, and Daggoo, does his best to satisfy their enormous appetites.

Fleece, the old Negro ship's cook. At Stubb's request he preaches a sermon to the voracious sharks and ends with a hope that their greed will kill them. He is disgusted also by Stubb's craving for whale meat.

Bulkington, the powerfully built, deeply tanned, sober-minded helmsman of the "Pequod."

Perth, the ship's elderly blacksmith, who took up whaling after losing his home and family. He makes for Ahab the harpoon intended to be Moby Dick's death dart, which the captain baptizes in the devil's name.

Captain Gardiner, the skipper of "Rachel" for whose lost son Captain Ahab refuses to search.

727

THE MOCK ASTROLOGER

Author: Pedro Calderón de la Barca (1600-1681)
Time of action: Seventeenth century
First presented: c. 1624

PRINCIPAL CHARACTERS

Don Diego (dōn dyä′gō), a wealthy nobleman. In love with María but spurned by her, he directs his servant, Morón, to try to learn how best to approach the lady. When Don Diego repeats to his friends Morón's gleanings concerning María's activities, the servant spreads the story that his master is an astrologer with knowledge of past and future. But Don Diego's supposed occult powers bring him only trouble, as his false prophecies spread confusion and turn everybody against him. He even succeeds in uniting María and his rival, Juan de Medrano.

Morón (mŏ·rōn′), Don Diego's servant, who is in love with Beatriz. Instructed by his master to pump Beatriz concerning her mistress, María, Morón finds his beloved in danger of exposure when Don Diego passes on the information gotten from her. To protect Beatriz, Morón

explains that Don Diego's knowledge comes through his powers as an astrologer.

María (mä·rē′ä), a young girl loved by Don Diego and Juan de Medrano.

Juan de Medrano (hwän dā mä·t͡hrä′nō), an impoverished young nobleman in love with María and preferred by her to Don Diego.

Beatriz (bā′ä·trēs), María's maid, loved by Morón, to whom she reveals the details of Juan de Medrano's visits to her mistress.

Don Carlos (dōn kär′lōs), Juan de Medrano's friend.

Doña Violante (dō′nyä vē·ō·län′tä), a woman in love with Juan de Medrano.

Leonardo (lā·ō·när′t͡hō), María's father.

MODERN CHIVALRY

Author: Hugh Henry Brackenridge (1748-1816)
Time of action: First years of the United States
First published: 1792-1815

PRINCIPAL CHARACTERS

Captain John Farrago, a man from colonial Western Pennsylvania. He takes his horse and his Irish servant, Teague, to go about seeing the country and observing human conduct. Eventually the Captain, after many adventures that point out the foibles of human nature, becomes, because of his learning and good sense, the governor of a new western territory. Being a rational man, he governs in the best Greek and Roman political traditions.

Teague O'Regan, the captain's cowardly

but cunning rascal of a servant. He is proposed as a candidate for the legislature, has many amorous adventures, tries his luck at being an excise officer, goes on the stage as an Irish comedian, and serves as a newspaper editor, among other things. He is one of those literary rascals who always land on their feet. The author's satire revolves around the absurdities that elevate the ignorant and roguish Teague to positions of authority and respectability.

Miss Fog, a young heiress courted by

728

Captain Farrago. Though he tries to please her, he finds whatever he does insults the woman.

Jacko, Miss Fog's other suitor, Captain Farrago's rival. When Jacko sends a second to challenge the Captain to a duel,

the Captain kicks the man out after telling him duelling is unlawful.

Duncan Ferguson, a Scots emigrant who takes Teague's place as Captain Farrago's servant.

A MODERN COMEDY

Author: John Galsworthy (1867-1933)
Time of action: 1922-1926
First published: "The White Monkey," 1924; "The Silver Spoon," 1926; "Swan Song," 1928

PRINCIPAL CHARACTERS

Soames Forsyte, the wealthy head of an upper middle-class family already chronicled in "The Forsyte Saga." A board member of the Providential Premium Reassurance Society, he fears the investment of his money in foreign securities in the unsettled period of 1922. When the company manager, Elderson, flees, upon accusations of bribery, the stock holders compel Soames' resignation. He decides to take his daughter Fleur, still unhappy over the loss of Jon Forsyte, on a trip around the world; her husband, Michael Mont, will join them in Vancouver. Back in England, and unhappy over postwar confusion, Soames spends much of his time with his collection of paintings until his gallery catches fire one night. While saving Fleur, who is deliberately standing where a large picture will fall on her, he is struck by the heavy frame and dies of the injury and exhaustion.

Fleur Forsyte, the daughter of Soames and his French wife, married to Michael Mont. Unhappy with her husband, she has several affairs, one with an artist, Wilfred Desert, another with her cousin Jon, who had been prevented by the family feud from marrying her. She seeks to forget through social work and a county home for working girls. Finally she decides on suicide, but the sacrifice of her father's life, to save her, brings her

to her senses and she becomes reconciled with her husband.

Michael Mont, a London publisher who enters Parliament and pushes Foggartism, a movement designed to return yeomen to the land by sending poor children to the dominions. Finally realizing that poor people will not part with their children, he turns to slum improvement.

Christopher, the child of the Monts.

Irene Forsyte, Soames' divorced wife, now staying in Washington, whom he sees for the first time in years during his world tour.

Jon Forsyte, the son of Irene and her second husband, Jolyon Forsyte. He was once in love with his cousin Fleur, but after learning the story of his family and Fleur's, he went to America and there married Anne Wilmot. During the general strike of 1926, Jon goes to England from France to do volunteer service. He and Fleur meet again and spend a night together. Jon writes later to say that he cannot see her again.

Anne Wilmot, a South Carolina girl, married to Jon.

Francis Wilmot, Anne's brother, who comes sightseeing from America and falls in love with Marjorie Ferrar. Turned down by her, he contracts pneumonia

729

and would have died except for Fleur's help.

Elderson, the manager of the P.P.R.S. office, who is bribed to invest Society money in Germany.

Butterfield, a P.P.R.S. clerk who overhears a conversation in which a young German urges Elderson to make good any losses caused by the fall of the mark. Butterfield loses his position, but Soames

gets him work promoting special editions put out by Michael Mont's company.

Marjorie Ferrar, an acquaintance of Fleur. She calls Fleur a snob at a Forsyte party and is told by Soames to leave. She brings suit in court to exact an apology, but Soames wins the case by proving that she is a woman of irresponsible morals. This victory brings Fleur many snubs from former friends.

A MODERN INSTANCE

Author: William Dean Howells (1837-1920)
Time of action: Nineteenth century
First published: 1882

PRINCIPAL CHARACTERS

Bartley Hubbard, a newspaperman of the eighties of the last century who ranges from Equity, a small town in New England, to Whited Sepulchre, Arizona. His moral weakness manifests itself in his affairs with women, his shoddy business ethics, his indifferent attitude toward money, and his love of liquor. He spends most of his time running from debts and family obligations. He dies, shot down by an irate citizen, while he is editor of a small western newspaper.

Marcia Gaylord, an innocent New England girl whose impetuous marriage to Hubbard brings her unhappiness. Hubbard takes her to Boston, where their child, Flavia, is born. When pressed by financial problems, Hubbard deserts his wife and child and goes West. He attempts to divorce Marcia and is foiled only by the intervention of her father. Hubbard's death makes it possible for Marcia to marry a good man and have a decent home.

Squire Gaylord, Marcia's father and Hubbard's first employer on a New England newspaper, the "Free Press." The Squire recognizes Hubbard's talent, but he opposes Hubbard's suit for Mar-

cia's hand. He looks after his daughter's affairs throughout her unfortunate marriage to the errant newspaperman. He dies of a stroke suffered during the trial for divorce Hubbard initiates against Marcia.

Ben Halleck, a member of one of Boston's older families who is a man of means and a college classmate of Hubbard. Halleck does not like Hubbard, but he feels sorry for Marcia, and befriends her. He helps Hubbard by lending him money—which is never returned —and helps Marcia by standing by her during her divorce trial. After Hubbard's death, Halleck tries to decide whether it would be morally right to ask Marcia to marry him.

Atherton, a conservative Boston lawyer who is a friend to Halleck and the Hubbards.

Kinney, a tramp philosopher who provides Hubbard with many stories Hubbard sells to magazines and newspapers without asking Kinney's permission.

Hannah Morrison, the daughter of the town drunk, who works with her mother in the newspaper office in Equity. Hannah has had few advantages in her life

730

and claims, when Marcia meets her drunk on the streets of Boston, that Hubbard is responsible for her destitution.

Witherby, an unscrupulous publisher of a Boston newspaper who hires Hubbard as managing editor. Witherby sells some stock in the paper to Hubbard, who borrows from Halleck the money to buy it. When Hubbard's work appears in a rival newspaper, Witherby fires him.

Henry Bird, a shop foreman on the "Free Press" with whom Hubbard has a fight over Hannah. The resulting scandal causes Hubbard to leave his job on the paper.

Willett, the owner of the New England logging camp to which Hubbard flees when scandal drives him out of Equity.

Mrs. Macallister, a fashionable woman who, at the logging camp, flirts with Hubbard. To impress her, Hubbard pokes fun at his quaint friend Kinney, who takes offense at such treatment and the two men part angrily.

A MODERN MIDAS

Author: Maurus Jókai (1825-1904)
Time of action: Nineteenth century
First published: 1872

PRINCIPAL CHARACTERS

Michael Timar, a shrewd and wise man. He builds himself a fortune through his business dealings. He also builds a fortune for the woman he loves, using her inheritance. He comes to style himself Baron Michael Timar von Levetinczy. He marries Timéa, the girl he loves, only to find that she loves another man. Michael discovers that he loves a poor girl, Naomi, who lives on an isolated island. When he has a chance to disappear, through a mistaken identity, he goes to the island, where he and Naomi live simply in peace and contentment.

Timéa, Michael's wife. She is the daughter of a political refugee. She loves Lt. Katschuka, but she marries Michael out of gratitude and is a faithful wife to him. After Michael's supposed death she marries the lieutenant.

Naomi, a girl who lives on an island with her mother. She loves Michael and bears him children. When he is supposedly dead Michael goes to the island to live out his days with her and their progeny.

Ali Tschorbadschi, also known as **Euthryn Trikaliss.** He is Timéa's father and a political refugee. When he dies he leaves his daughter to the care of a distant relative, Athanas Brasowitsch.

Athanas Brasowitsch, a prosperous Hungarian trader who takes in the orphaned Timéa. He and his family make her their household servant and treat her shabbily.

Mrs. Brasowitsch, Athanas' vulgar and cruel wife.

Athalie Brasowitsch, Athanas' daughter, betrothed to Lt. Katschuka. She tries to kill Timéa on the day the girl marries Athalie's fiancé.

Lt. Imre Katschuka, a friend of Michael. He refuses to marry Athalie when her father loses his fortune. After Michael's supposed death the lieutenant marries Timéa, whom he loves.

Thérèse, a widow, mother of Naomi. She takes refuge on an island.

Theodore Kristyan, a suitor for Naomi's hand in marriage. He tries to blackmail Thérèse and, later, Michael. He drowns accidentally and is incorrectly identified as Michael.

Dodi, the illegitimate son of Michael and Naomi.

731

MOLL FLANDERS

Author: Daniel Defoe (1661?-1731)
Time of action: Seventeenth century
First published: 1722

PRINCIPAL CHARACTERS

Moll Flanders, an English adventuress (known also as **Mistress Betty, May Flanders, Mrs. Flanders),** one of the most engaging female rogues in all literature. She relates her entire life story, from infancy to final years of repentance, with frankness and full detail. As the daughter of a woman convicted of a felony and transported to Virginia, Moll spends her early years in the company of some gipsies, then with several families who treat her well. By the age of fourteen, Moll is attractive, intelligent, resourceful, and womanly. Her first affair is with the elder son in a household where she has entered service. The younger son, Robin, falls in love with her and becomes her first husband. After five years of marriage and the birth of two children, he dies. Later Moll preys on mankind for many years. Using her beauty and wits to support herself in as much luxury and comfort as she can manage, she marries a succession of husbands, one of them her half brother, and eventually turns thief and pickpocket. She acquires a very sizable fortune before she is caught. At Newgate, where her life began, she receives the death sentence but succeeds in getting transportation instead. A former husband, Jemmy E., is being sent to the colonies on the same ship. The two establish a plantation in Carolina, prosper greatly, and ultimately decide to go back to England to spend their remaining years in repentance. Moll maintains a moral tone in relating all her illegal, extra-marital, and exciting adventures, but her professed repentance never seems to keep her from enjoying the fruits of her actions.

Moll's Mother, a convicted felon transported to Virginia soon after Moll's birth.

The mother does well in Virginia, builds up a large estate, lives to a satisfying old age, and leaves a farm to Moll.

Humphry, a sea captain. He marries Moll and takes her to Virginia, where he introduces her to his mother (and hers). He remains in Virginia when Moll returns to England after deciding that she can no longer live with her half brother as his wife.

Humphry, the son of Moll and the sea captain. When Moll returns home, he stays in Virginia, where he becomes a planter. He turns over to Moll the plantation willed her and proves a dutiful and loving son.

Jemmy E., an Irish adventurer and highway robber, Moll's former husband with whom she establishes a plantation in the Carolina Colony. He follows Moll back to England, where they spend their declining years in repentance and some luxury.

"Mother Midnight," a midwife who owns a nursing home for unwed mothers. She trains Moll as a thief. Later she takes care of Moll's money and is Moll's agent in sending valuable goods to Carolina.

A Gentleman of Bath, married to a woman mentally ill. Moll lives with him and bears him three children.

A Linen Draper, a spendthrift who marries Moll, runs through her money quickly, and abandons her.

Robin, Moll's first husband, the younger son in the family where she first takes service.

Robin's Older Brother, Moll's seducer and first lover.

A Clergyman, the chaplain at Newgate. He befriends Moll in prison, helps her secure a reprieve from the death sentence, and persuades her to repent.

A London Bank Clerk, married to Moll for five years.

THE MONK

Author: Matthew Gregory Lewis (1775-1818)
Time of action: The Spanish Inquisition
First published: 1795

PRINCIPAL CHARACTERS

Father Ambrosio (äm·brō′syō), the most virtuous and learned monk in Madrid. He sentences Agnes de Medina to torture and death for adultery, and she calls upon him to remember her fate when he is tempted, as he is by Matilda, a sorceress. Following his seduction by Matilda, the monk ravishes Antonia, a virtuous girl. He is captured and condemned to die, but he sells his soul to Satan for release from prison. Satan releases him and then kills him after telling him that his victims, Antonia and Elvira, were his sister and his mother.

Matilda (mä·tēl′dä), a sorceress. She enters Ambrosio's monastery disguised as a novice named Rosario. She seduces Ambrosio, leads him to ravish Antonia, and finally induces him to sell his soul. Matilda is condemned by the Inquisition but freed by Satan.

Antonia (än·tō′nyä), a young girl ravished by Ambrosio and murdered by the monk to conceal his crime. Later he learns that she was his sister.

Elvira (ĕl·bē′rä), Antonia's mother. She is killed by Ambrosio, who learns later that she was his mother.

Marquis Raymond de las Cisternas (rä-mōn′ dä läs thēs·târ′näs), a Spanish nobleman who is in love with Agnes de Medina and who is the father of her unborn child. After great difficulty he rescues his beloved from the convent where she is imprisoned.

Agnes de Medina (äg′näs dä mä·t̸hē′nä), a young noblewoman who is condemned by Ambrosio for adultery. She is driven mad and almost starved to death in a convent.

Mother St. Clare (sän′tä klä′rä), a nun who mistreats Agnes de Medina.

Lorenzo de Medina (lō·rän′t̸hō thä mä-t̸hē′nä), Agnes' brother, who aids in securing the release of his sister. He loves Antonia, but after her death he is comforted by Virginia de Villa Franca, whom he marries.

Virginia de Villa Franca (bēr·hē′nyä t̸hä bē′lyä frän′kä), a wealthy heiress who helps restore Agnes de Medina to health and sanity. She falls in love with Agnes' brother and marries him.

Mother St. Agatha (sän′tä ä·gä′thä), a nun who notifies Lorenzo de Medina falsely that his sister Agnes is dead.

MONKEY

Author: Wu Ch'eng-en (c. 1505-c. 1580)
Time of action: Seventh century
First published: Sixteenth century

Monkey, who was born of a stone egg fecundated by the wind. He was king of the Mountain of Flowers for several hundred years, after which he set out into the world in search of knowledge that would make him immortal. Under the name of "Aware-of-vacuity," he studied with Patriarch Subodhi for several hundred more years. Because of the tremendous magic power he had acquired, as well as his natural arrogance, he named himself "Great Sage Equal of Heaven." Permitted to live in the Kingdom of Heaven, the mischievous creature disturbed and outwitted all the divinities with his magic tricks until Buddha himself intervened and imprisoned him beneath a mountain. After five hundred years Monkey was released through the intercession of the Bodhisattva Kuan-yin, on the condition that he become the disciple of the priest Hsüan Tsang, who was then on his way to India in quest of the Buddhist Scriptures for T'ai Tsung, the Emperor of T'ang. Monkey's role from then on is to assist the priest against the many calamities that befall him. Although he can never overcome completely the temptation to play tricks, Monkey earns his redemption and receives the Illumination which in the end, after a successful journey to India, allows him to be received into Heaven as a Buddha.

Hsüan Tsang, a priest. Abandoned by his mother when he was born, he was rescued and brought up by the abbot of a monastery. In his old age, he was selected for his sanctity by T'ai Tsung, the Emperor of T'ang, to go to India and bring back to China the Tripitaka, the sacred Scriptures of the Big Vehicle. Hsüan Tsang then received the name of Tripitaka. Tripitaka was to encounter and overcome nine great calamities in order to transcend his mortal condition. In spite of great devotion, he could not have accomplished his mission without the help of his four disciples, who all possess some kind of magical power. He is easily discouraged and given to tears, but his purity is his saving asset and he is finally received into Heaven as a Buddha.

Pigsy, a lesser divinity in the Kingdom of the Jade Emperor. Chased out of Heaven for courting a Fairy maiden, he lives on earth as a demon with the face of a pig. Addicted to base pleasures of the flesh, he is given a chance to recover his former place in Heaven by the Bodhisattva Kuan-yin, who converts him and sends him to India with Tripitaka. In the end he receives the Illumination and is admitted to Heaven as Cleanser of the Altar.

Sandy, formerly the Marshal of the Hosts of Heaven. Banished to the River of Flowing Sands for breaking a crystal cup at a celestial banquet, he lives on the flesh of human beings; but he obtains his redemption by accompanying Tripitaka on his pilgrimage to India. His conduct enables him to regain a place in Heaven with the title of Golden-Bodied Arhat.

The Horse, the son of the Dragon King of the Western Ocean, condemned to death for misconduct in his father's palace. He was saved by Kuan-yin on condition that he carry Tripitaka to India. The young dragon swallows the priest's horse as the latter is trying to cross a river. Learning his mistake, he allows himself to be changed into the horse's identical image. He faithfully serves the priest and is rewarded by being made one of the eight Senior Heavenly Dragons.

T'ai Tsung, the Emperor of T'ang, who died because he failed to keep his promise to save a Dragon King from execution. Brought back to life through the mediation of his minister, he is celebrating his resurrection when Kuan-yin appears and orders him to send someone to India to get the Scriptures of the Big Vehicle, then unknown in China. The Emperor entrusts Hsüan Tsang with the mission. He must wait fourteen years for the priest's return.

Kuan-yin, the merciful Bodhisattva. She organizes and supervises Hsüan Tsang's pilgrimage.

Buddha, The Enlightened One. Upset by the greed, lust, and many other defects of the Chinese people, he sends Kuan-yin to China to look for a man holy enough to bring the true Scriptures from Paradise and thus set the Chinese on the way to moral reformation.

Lao Tzu, an alchemist and father of the Tao. He defeats Monkey but is unable to destroy him. Lao Tzu appears as a

gruff old scholar whose lack of a sense of humor is his worst enemy.

Erh-lang, a magician, nephew of the Jade Emperor. With the help of Lao Tzu he defeats Monkey in battle.

The Jade Emperor, tyrant of Heaven.

The King of Crow-cock, killed by a magician who then assumes the King's appearance and usurps his throne. After three years, the King appears to Tripitaka in a dream and asks for help. His body is rescued by Monkey and Pigsy, and brought back to life with a "pill" borrowed from Lao Tzu.

Vaisravana, who, with the help of his son Natha, fights unsuccessfully against Monkey in behalf of the Jade Emperor.

MONSIEUR BEAUCAIRE

Author: Booth Tarkington (1869-1946)
Time of action: Early eighteenth century
First published: 1900

PRINCIPAL CHARACTERS

Louis-Phillipe de Valois (lwē′ fē·lēp′ də và·lwà′), Duke of Orleans and nephew of Louis XV of France, who masquerades as **Victor the Barber, Monsieur Beaucaire** (bō·kĕr′), and **Monsieur de Chateaurien** (shà·tō′·ryăn′). After showing the snobbish aristocrats at fashionable Bath that class distinction is foolish, he returns to France and his proper station in life.

The Duke de Winterset, an English scoundrel caught cheating at cards and blackmailed by Monsieur Beaucaire into taking him to Lady Melbourne's ball.

Lady Mary Carlyle, a shallow aristocrat.

Loved at first by the Duke of Orleans, she prefers Winterset.

Lady Melbourne, the sponsor of a ball at Bath, England.

Beau Nash, the social arbiter of Bath.

Molyneaux, a sympathetic Englishman.

A Captain, in debt to Winterset, who challenges Orleans to a duel and is defeated.

Marquis de Mirepoix (mēr′·pwà′), Ambassador of France.

Comte de Beaujolais (bō′·zhô·lĕ′), the brother of Orleans, who has come to escort him back to France and marriage.

MONSIEUR D'OLIVE

Author: George Chapman (c. 1559-1634)
Time of action: Seventeenth century
First presented: 1604

PRINCIPAL CHARACTERS

Vandome (văṅ·dōm'), a noble young gentleman, the platonic lover of Marcellina. He untangles all the complications of the plot with his intelligence and courtesy.

Count Vaumont (vō·mōṅ'), the jealous but repentant husband of Marcellina. His jealousy leads her to take an oath to retire from society and turn night into day and day into night.

Marcellina (màr·sĕl·lē'nà), the angry wife of Vaumont. She allows Vandome to arouse her own jealousy over her husband's supposed infidelity, and breaks her vow of seclusion in order to catch him. Reconciliation follows.

Eurione (œ·ryôn'), Marcellina's sister, in love with Count St. Anne.

Count St. Anne (săṅ·tàn'), Vandome's brother-in-law. Loving his dead wife, grieved almost to madness, he keeps her embalmed body constantly with him. Vandome persuades him to speak to Eurione on his behalf. Seeing her, he falls in love with her and abandons his morbid worship of his dead wife.

Duke Philip (fē·lēp'), St. Anne's friendly superior. Failing to convert St. Anne to reasonable behavior, he decides to send an embassy to the King to request an order for the wife's burial. He chooses, humorously, the ridiculous Monsieur d'Olive for his ambassador.

Monsieur d'Olive (mə·syœ' dô·lēv'), an idle, self-satisfied wit. Appointed the Duke's emissary, he wastes time gathering a host of followers and accepting money from them. Vandome's labors make the embassy unnecessary, but the Duke graciously gives Monsieur d'Olive a place in his entourage.

MONSIEUR LECOQ

Author: Émile Gaboriau (1835-1873)
Time of action: Nineteenth century
First published: 1869

PRINCIPAL CHARACTERS

Monsieur Lecoq (mə·syœ' lə·kôk'), a young Paris detective who finds two people dead and one wounded; but he is hampered in his investigation of the crime and never solves it.

Gevrol (zhəv·rôl'), an elderly inspector of police who is without imagination. Lecoq's persistence in trying to solve the crime causes subsequent enmity between them.

Mother Chupin (shü·păṅ'), owner of the wineshop which is the scene of the crime.

Father Absinthe (àb·săṅt'), an experienced policeman and a friend of Lecoq.

May (mā'), who is arrested at the scene of the murder while holding the gun. He tries to strangle himself while in jail. When allowed to "escape" so that he can be followed, he disappears permanently.

An Accomplice, who is permitted to help May "escape." He is recaptured, but May disappears in the garden of the Duke of Sairmeuse.

Tabaret (tȧ·bȧ·rā′), the oracle of the police force, who concludes that May must be the Duke of Sairmeuse himself.

M. d'Escorval (dĕs·kôr·vȧl′), the presiding judge, who breaks his leg rather than try May.

M. Segmuller (sĕg·mü·lĕr′), the new judge assigned to the case.

MONT-ORIOL

Author: Guy de Maupassant (1850-1893)
Time of action: Mid-nineteenth century
First published: 1887

PRINCIPAL CHARACTERS

Christiane Andermatt (krē·styȧn′ än·dĕr-mȧt′), a young married woman who, while she is in the country taking some baths to cure her childlessness, meets Paul Brétigny, a friend of her brother, and has a love affair with him. At first, she will not listen to his supplications, but after a time she submits and has a baby girl by him. She becomes jealous when she discovers that while she is pregnant her lover has fallen in love with another woman. When her baby is born, she will have nothing to do with the child. Later, however, the baby attracts her; she becomes absorbed in it and is totally indifferent to her former lover.

Paul Brétigny (pôl′ brā·tēn·yē′), Christiane's lover, who meets her when he goes to the country to recover from an unhappy love affair. He feels sorry for and falls in love with Charlotte Oriol, who has been rejected by Christiane's brother, Gontran de Ravenel.

William Andermatt (än·dĕr·mȧt′), Christiane's husband, a financier who decides to buy some land from a peasant and build baths to utilize the spring water which supposedly has medicinal properties. Andermatt engages in many machinations in order to obtain the land and promote the baths.

Father Oriol (ô·ryôl′), a peasant landowner. He blasts a rock out of the ground and a spring gushes forth. Oriol is a shrewd bargainer, as is shown in his dealings with Andermatt.

Gontran de Ravenel (gōn·trän′ də rȧv-nĕl′), Christiane's brother, a witty young man who, at Andermatt's suggestion, plans to court and marry one of Oriol's daughters in order to obtain part of the land which forms their dowries, and thus pay off his debts. He courts Charlotte first, since she is younger and prettier, but he switches to Louise when he finds that her dowry will be more profitable to him.

Charlotte Oriol (shȧr·lôt′ ô·ryôl′), Father Oriol's younger daughter, who is courted by Gontran de Ravenel. When he discovers that her sister's dowry is larger, he deserts her. She is consoled by Paul, and they become engaged.

Louise Oriol (lwēz′ ô·ryôl′), Father Oriol's elder daughter, who is persuaded by Gontran that he paid court to her sister only in order to arouse her interest in him.

Clovis (klô·vēs′), a beggar who poaches at night and feigns rheumatism in the daytime. He is hired to bathe in the spring every day and, when he is supposedly cured, it is hoped that Andermatt will be convinced of the medicinal value of the water. After the baths are opened, he returns and threatens to tell the public that the water harmed him; but he is bought off by being paid to take the treatment every year.

737

A MONTH IN THE COUNTRY

Author: Ivan Turgenev (1818-1883)
Time of action: The 1840's
First presented: 1850

PRINCIPAL CHARACTERS

Arkady Sergeyitch Islayev (är·kä′dĭy sĕr-gĕ′ĭch ĭs·lä·yĕf′), a wealthy landowner interested in the details of work on his estate and unwilling to trust his peasants to work without supervision. His discovery of his wife and his friend together and their resultant embarrassment make him feel he has been too trusting. Though he agrees that Rakitin should leave, at least for a time, he is apologetic about sending away an old friend. Unperceptive as he has been, he is completely surprised later when Rakitin tells him of Natalya's love for Belyayev.

Natalya Petrovna (nä·tä′lyə pĕt·rov′·nə), called **Natasha** (nä·tä′shə), his wife. Intelligent and observant, she is sometimes mischievous toward Rakitin, who accuses her of playing with him as a cat does a mouse. Early in the play it is obvious that though she cares for Rakitin she is restlessly looking for some new excitement. Attracted to Belyayev, her son's tutor, because of his youth, appearance, and winning personality, she tries to draw him out. Seeing Vera's interest in him, she becomes jealous. She is also a little ashamed of herself for both the love and the jealousy, and she berates herself for slyly eliciting Vera's confession of love and then reporting it so bluntly and cruelly to Belyayev. At the end she is overcome by the almost simultaneous departures of Belyayev and Rakitin.

Kolya (kō′lyə), the ten-year-old son of Arkady and Natalya, a high-spirited boy who idolizes Belyayev.

Vera (vĕ′rə), an orphaned ward of the Islayevs. Lonely for the companionship of young people, she falls romantically in love with Belyayev, with whom she feels a kinship because he is also motherless. She is fond of Natalya but a little afraid of her. Upon her discovery of Natalya's duplicity in trapping her into a confession of love, and after her realization that she and Natalya are rivals, her fear is replaced by anger. When she learns that Belyayev has no thought of marrying her and that he has regarded her as simply a charming girl, she impulsively decides to marry the ludicrous though good Bolshintsov simply in order to get away from Natalya.

Mihail Alexandrovitch Rakitin (mĭ·hä·ĭl′ ä·lĕk·sän′drə·vĭch rä·kĭ′tĭn), a long-time friend of the Islayevs, a man fond of studying people and analyzing them. He has been in love with Natalya for several years, but the affair has hovered only between the platonic and the adulterous. Natalya finds him sympathetic, affectionate, constant, peaceful, and comforting. His manner with her shifts with his moods and hers, being alternately jesting, romantic, poetic, and philosophical. The relationship between the two closely resembles that of Turgenev and Madame Viardot, an opera singer who was taught by Franz Liszt and loved by Alfred de Musset and Hector Berlioz as well as by Turgenev.

Alexey Nikolayevitch Belyayev (ä·lĕk·sā′ nĭ·kô·lä′yĕ·vĭch bĕ·lyä′ĕf), a university student and Kolya's tutor. He is diffident and embarrassed when Natalya talks to him, but he talks freely with Vera and appears boyish and enthusiastic when he is with Vera and Kolya. He is confused and ill at ease because of the difference between his station and that of the aristocratic Natalya, and he is both flattered and frightened to find that she loves him. Unwilling to hurt anyone, he flees from involvement with either Natalya or Vera.

Ignaty Ilyitch Shpigelsky (ĭ·gnä′tĭy ĭ′lyĭch shpĭ·gĕl′skĭ), a doctor and a close friend of the Islayevs. Having told a story of a girl with two suitors who knew she was in love but did not know with whom, he draws from Natalya the question whether it is not possible to love two people at once; and he perceives Natalya's relationship with Rakitin. At times he seems like a basso buffo in a comic opera, but his serious side is made evident in the long conversation during which he proposes to Lizaveta. He confesses that though he plays the clown, it is a calculated playing, and he is in reality ingratiating himself with the rich people from whom he may gain rewards without revealing what he thinks of them. He serves as a marriage broker for Bolshintsov.

Adam Ivanitch Schaaf (ä·däm′ ĭ·vän′ĭch schäf), a phlegmatic, rather grumpy German tutor. He is ridiculous in his attempts to be romantic with Katya, who spurns him.

Afanasy Ivanovitch Bolshintsov (ä·fä-nä′sĭy ĭ·vä′nə·vĭch bôl·shĭn′tsəf), a neighbor. Shy with women, he promises Shpigelsky three horses if the doctor can arrange for him a marriage with Vera. Rakitin thinks him fat, foolish, and tedious, and to Vera he is laughable, though she finally agrees to marry him.

Anna Semyonovna Islayev (än′nə sĕ-myō′nəv·nə ĭs·lä·yĕf′), Arkady's mother. She is disturbed by the belief that Natalya and Rakitin are more than friends and at the end by the news that Lizaveta may soon be leaving her.

Lizaveta Bogdanovna (lĭ·zä·vĕ′tə bôg-dä′nəv·nə), Anna's companion. Her remarks to Anna at the end of the play suggest that shortly she will be marrying Shpigelsky.

Katya (kä′tyə), a maid courted by both Schaaf and Matvey. She herself likes Belyayev.

Matvey (mät·vä′), a manservant in love with Katya.

THE MOON AND SIXPENCE

Author: W. Somerset Maugham (1874-   )
Time of action: Late nineteenth, early twentieth centuries
First published: 1919

PRINCIPAL CHARACTERS

Charles Strickland, an English stockbroker who seems commonplace to his friends until he suddenly leaves his wife and family and goes to Paris to study art. A friend sent by the wife to persuade him to return is told he has left his family permanently. Consumed by his desire to paint, he neglects his physical needs. During an illness he is nursed by a friend's wife, whom he makes his mistress and model. After her death Strickland goes to Marseilles and, after further wandering, finally arrives in Tahiti. He marries Ata, a native girl who cares for his needs, and he paints constantly. Ill again, he is found to have leprosy and is isolated from all except Ata, who cares for him. He paints the walls of their bungalow until he is completely blind. Living in darkness, he remembers his last paintings, his masterpieces; however, he asks Ata to destroy the paintings on the walls after his death.

Amy Strickland, a commonplace English wife and mother. She cannot understand why her husband deserted her or his fame after his death.

Dirk Stroeve, Strickland's artist friend in Paris. Something of a buffoon, he feels inferior to his English wife but loves her deeply. He insists she nurse Strickland in his illness. After they become lovers, Dirk leaves them in his studio and even gives his faithless wife money to live on. When she dies, he returns to the studio and finds her nude portrait, which he tries to destroy; but he cannot do so because he recognizes in it a superb creation by Strickland. Dirk returns to live with his mother in Holland.

Blanche Stroeve, Dirk's English wife. She professes to dislike her husband's friend Strickland, and when the artist becomes ill she pleads with her husband not to make her nurse him. On Dirk's insistence she complies. After Strickland recovers and takes over the studio Dirk asks him to leave, but by that time Blanche is in love with Strickland and says she will leave also. Ironically, Strickland sees in her only an excellent model. He walks out on her when he has finished his portrait of her, a painting he regards as a failure. Blanche commits suicide.

Ata, Strickland's Tahitian wife. Seventeen when she marries him, she bears his children and faithfuly tends his needs. After his death she destroys their bungalow, the walls of which Strickland had covered with paintings.

Capitaine Brunot, a black-bearded Frenchman who admires the beauty of the primitive home which Ata has created for Strickland. Brunot owns a few pictures which he is saving to use as a "dot" for his two young daughters.

Dr. Coutras, an old French doctor who is forced to tell Strickland he has leprosy. Strickland repays the doctor by giving him one of his pictures. Dr. Coutras is the one Westerner who sees the strange pictures which cover the walls of the isolated bungalow where he finds Strickland dead after a year of blindness.

THE MOONSTONE

Author: Wilkie Collins (1824-1889)
Time of action: 1799-1849
First published: 1868

PRINCIPAL CHARACTERS

Franklin Blake, a genial young man, Lady Verinder's nephew. According to the terms of John Herncastle's will he is given temporary charge of the Moonstone, a diamond which Herncastle had taken during the storming of Seringapatam and which is to be given to his niece, Rachel Verinder, on her birthday following her uncle's death. Of great religious significance in the worship of Brahma and Vishnu, the stone, which is worth about thirty thousand pounds, is supposed to bring ill fortune to any but worshipers of the Moon-God from whose forehead it had been stolen. After presenting the stone to Rachel, Blake, who has been suffering from in-somnia, is given secretly a dose of laudanum. In his partly drugged state he goes to Rachel's sitting room during the night and takes the stone from a cabinet. Rachel witnesses the act but, being in love with Blake and thinking he is taking the stone because he needs money, she does not tell what she has seen. A year later, after the stone has been located and the details of its disappearance are cleared, Blake and Rachel are married.

Rachel Verinder, his cousin. In keeping the secret of the lost gem, she suffers the accusations of officials, servants, and friends. Thinking Blake does not love her, she vents her unhappiness on others.

During Blake's absence from England she promises to marry Godfrey Ablewhite, but she suddenly breaks the engagement. She and Blake are married after the mystery has been solved.

Godfrey Ablewhite, a handsome young Londoner who, seeing that Blake is semiconscious when he takes the diamond, removes the gem from Blake's hand. Godfrey delivers the gem at once to a London moneylender for safe keeping. After a year he redeems the diamond with the intention of selling it in Amsterdam, in order to pay his debts. In the maneuver to get aboard ship, he disguises himself as a sailor. His dead body is found in a waterfront lodging house, but the stone is missing; it has been reclaimed by its Hindu owners.

Lady Julia Verinder, Rachel's mother and the sister of John Herncastle, who brought the diamond from India. A gentlewoman, she is unnerved by having the police in her home. She goes to London, where she dies of a heart ailment.

Gabriel Betteredge, the venerable house steward to Lady Julia Verinder; he narrates much of the story. His life is guided by philosophies he combs from "Robinson Crusoe," a book which he reads over and over and quotes constantly.

Sergeant Richard Cuff, a grizzled, elderly detective of the London police force, sent by Blake's father to investigate the loss of the diamond. Amiable and knowledgeable in human nature, he is loved by almost everyone who knows him. His keen interest is rose culture, which subject he argues ardently with the Verinder gardener during the investigation. Cuff tells the sixth narrative in the section titled "The Discovery of the Truth."

Mr. Bruff, the old lawyer who, as family counselor for three generations, executed John Herncastle's will. As the executor of Lady Julia Verinder's will, he becomes Rachel's guardian. Sensing the motive for the girl's silence and bitterness, he arranges to bring her and Franklin Blake together whenever possible. Bruff relates the second narrative in unraveling the mystery.

Rosanna Spearman, the second housemaid at Lady Julia Verinder's estate. The former inmate of a reformatory, she has been taken in by Lady Julia and given a fresh start in life. In love with Blake and suspecting him of the theft of the diamond because of paint (from the door to Rachel's sitting room) on his nightgown, Rosanna takes the garment, locks it in a box, and sinks the box in quicksand. She herself commits suicide. From a letter which she left with a friend, Blake and Betteredge learn, about a year later, the details of her love for Blake and her effort to help him.

Dr. Thomas Candy, the family physician, who administers laudanum for Franklin Blake's sleeplessness after Rachel Verinder's birthday party. Dr. Candy, pictured as a suspect, loses his memory after an illness contracted from exposure on the night of the party.

Ezra Jennings, Dr. Candy's assistant during the physician's long illness. Strange in appearance and of questionable background, Jennings is a likely suspect as an accomplice in the theft. Actually a congenial person, his behavior is due to a severe disease from which he dies. His explanation of the effects of laudanum leads to the solution of the mystery of the diamond's disappearance.

Mr. Murthwaite, an authority on Indian religions. At the end he writes to Bruff a letter describing a religious festival in India, a ceremony which revealed the Moon-God with the restored diamond gleaming in its forehead.

Septimus Lukier, the London moneylender with whom Godfrey leaves the Moonstone while he makes plans to get the gem out of England.

Superintendent Seegrave, the first police

officer to investigate the disappearance of the Moonstone. His bungling tactics and manner emphasize Cuff's aptness.

Drusilla Clack, a poor relation of Lady Verinder and a religious fanatic. Her descriptions of tract-passing in her efforts to save people's souls are classics in literary humor.

Penelope, Betteredge's daughter and Lady Julia's servant, who reminds her father of events as he narrates his part of the story. Penelope tells of the actions of the servants during the investigation.

Lucy Yolland, Lady Julia's young club-footed neighbor. Ugly, sullen, and distrustful, she becomes friendly with Ros-anna. Lucy shows her loyalty by keeping Rosanna's suicide letter secret for a year.

Octavius Guy, Bruff's young employee, nicknamed **"Gooseberry"** because of his bulging eyes. Gooseberry follows Godfrey as he makes his way toward the boat with the diamond.

The Three Indians, whose actions are always related by another person. Never "seen" in the story, they are always in quest of the stolen diamond. Their presence at the scene of Godfrey Ablewhite's murder was proved, and they were reported by Mr. Murthwaite as "disappearing" in the throng gathered at the Hindu ceremony where the Moonstone was last seen.

LE MORTE D'ARTHUR

Author: Sir Thomas Malory (Early fifteenth century-1471)
Time of action: The Golden Age of Chivalry
First transcribed: c. 1469; printed 1485

PRINCIPAL CHARACTERS

Arthur (är'thər), King of Britain and head of the Round Table, a brave, just, and temperate ruler. He values the fellowship of his men above revenge for his Queen's infidelity, and he closes his eyes to her love for Launcelot until Mordred and Agravaine force him to act.

Queen Guenevere (gwĕn'ə·vĭr), a jealous, passionate woman whose fury drives her lover Launcelot mad. She repents after the King is betrayed by Mordred, and she dies in a convent.

Launcelot du Lake (lôn'sə·lŏt dü läk), the greatest of all the knights except those who achieve the Grail quest. He is, himself, granted a vision of the Grail, but his love for the Queen bars him from success in spite of his deep and sincere penitence.

Tristram (trĭs'trəm), the great Cornish knight who is the faithful and devoted lover of Isoud, the wife of his uncle, King Mark. Like Launcelot, he adheres firmly to the knightly code of honor and continues to fight for his country even after Mark has tried to have him murdered.

Isoud (ĭ·sōd'), an Irish princess, married to King Mark for political reasons although she has loved Tristram from the time she cured him of a wound incurred while he jousted with her brother.

Mark, the cowardly, jealous King of Cornwall, who becomes increasingly bitter and vengeful toward Tristram.

Isoud la Blanche Mains (ĭ·sōd' lə blänsh män), Tristram's wife, Princess of Brittany.

Gawain (gä'wĭn), Arthur's nephew. He stands for virtue and justice untempered by mercy in his uncle's final contest with Launcelot, but he dishonors his fellowship earlier by beheading a lady and killing Lamorak de Galis when that knight was unarmed.

Sir Kay, Arthur's sardonic, mocking foster brother and seneschal.

Galahad (găl′ə·hăd), Launcelot's son, the best of the knights, who sits in the Siege Perilous and draws Balin's sword from a great stone as a prelude to his successful Grail quest. He dies after a vision in which he receives the sacrament from St. Joseph of Arimathaea.

Percival (pûr′sə·vəl) and
Bors de Ganis (bôrs də gă′nĭs), virtuous knights who accompany Galahad on the quest of the Grail. Bors alone returns to Arthur's court to describe their visions.

Palamides (păl·ə·mē′dēz), a valiant pagan knight, for many years Tristram's deadly enemy and Isoud's secret admirer. He is finally won over by his rival's courage and honor and signifies his new friendship by being christened.

Lamorak de Galis (lăm′ə·răk də gă′lĭs), a knight famous for his strength and valor, who is surpassed only by Launcelot and Tristram. He is killed by Gawain and his brothers for his affair with their mother.

Mordred (môr′drĕd), Arthur's son by his sister, an ill-tempered, evil knight who eventually destroys the fellowship of the Round Table and his royal father.

Agravaine (ăg′rə·vān) and
Gaheris (gă′hĕr·ĭs), Gawain's brothers, participants in Mordred's plots and in the slaying of their mother and Lamorak.

Gareth (găr′ĭth), a tall, handsome young man who undertakes his first quest as "Beaumains," the kitchen boy, but later reveals himself as the brother of Gawain.

Linet (lĭ·nĕt′), the damsel whose quest Gareth fulfills. She mocks and criticizes the inexperienced young knight until after he has rescued her sister.

Liones (lī·ə·nĕs′), Linet's sister, later Gareth's bride.

Balin le Sauvage (bā′lĭn lə sō·văzh′), a Northumbrian knight, fated by the acquisition of a magic sword to kill his beloved brother, Balan.

Dinadan (dĭn′ə·dăn′), Tristram's common-sense, witty companion, who scorns love.

King Pelles (pĕl′ēz), the Fisher King of the Grail legends at some points, although his identity is often unclear. He understands the mysteries of the Sangreal and arranges the conception of Galahad, the knight who is to achieve the quest and cure the wounded King.

Elaine (ĭ·lān′), Pelles' daughter and Galahad's mother, who loves Launcelot, in spite of his rejection of her.

Elaine le Blanc, the fair maid of Astolat, who perishes of love for Launcelot.

King Evelake (ĕv·ə·lāk′), an ancient ruler, converted by St. Joseph of Arimathaea. He lives generations beyond his time to have the promised sight of the knight who will complete the Grail quest.

Merlin (mûr′lĭn), the magician whose spell allows King Uther Pendragon to enter Tintagil Castle in the shape of the rightful Duke of Cornwall, husband of the lovely Igraine, Arthur's mother. In return, Uther promises that the child thus conceived will be turned over to Merlin, to be reared under his charge.

Nimue (nĭm·ōō·ē′), the Lady of the Lake, Merlin's mistress, who serves as a "dea ex machina" for several of the knights.

Morgan le Fay (môr′gən lə fā), Arthur's half sister, who continually devises evil for him and his knights.

Pellinore (pel′ĭ·nōr), a bold knight who single-mindedly pursues the Questing Beast.

Gouvernail (gŭv·ėr·nāl′), Tristram's tutor and constant companion.

Brangwaine (brăng′wān), Isoud's maid and confidante.

Ector de Maris (ĕk′tər də mär′ĭs),
Lionel (lī′ən·ĕl),
Dodinas le Sauvage (dō·dē′năs lə sō·vazh′),
Sagramore (săg′rə·môr),

Breunor le Noire (brē′nôr lə nwär), and Safere (să·fîr′), brave and honorable knights.

Meliogrance (mē′lyō·grăns′), a treacherous nobleman who kidnaps Guenevere, then accuses her of treason with Launcelot when she refuses to yield to him.

THE MOTHER

Author: Grazia Deledda (1872-1936)
Time of action: Early twentieth century
First published: 1920

PRINCIPAL CHARACTERS

Maria Maddalena, a Sicilian woman. An orphan reared by aunts who make of her a drudge, she is married to an old man who dies shortly thereafter, leaving her pregnant. She works to support her son and to send him through a seminary to become a priest. She is troubled when her priest-son appears to have an affair with a beautiful young woman. A superstitious soul, she believes the ghost of the former parish priest is trying to drive her and her son away. When her son's sweetheart confronts him in his church, the poor mother falls dead.

Paul, Maria Maddalena's son, a priest. He has a sensual nature and while in seminary he is fascinated by a prostitute, whom he visits often one summer. At his first parish he falls in love with a beautiful young parishioner and has a strong sensual urge that causes him to

consider leaving the Church, in order to run away and marry his sweetheart. When he puts down the temptation, the spurned woman threatens to denounce him publicly as a seducer.

Agnes, Paul's sweetheart. She is the last member of the family that owns the big house in the village which is Paul's parish. She loves Paul and does not seem to realize what she asks him to do in urging him to leave the Church and his responsibilities to it. She sees him only as a man.

Antiochus, Paul's server, who wishes to become a priest.

King Nicodemus, a misanthropic hunter who lives in a cabin on the mountain near the village. He has left the village so that his hate will not cause him to kill anyone.

MOTHER

Author: Maxim Gorky (Aleksei Maksimovich Peshkov, 1868-1936)
Time of action: First decade of the twentieth century
First published: 1907

PRINCIPAL CHARACTERS

Pelagueya Vlasova (pĕ·lə·gē′yə vlä′sə·və), a revolutionary heroine. Fearing that her son, Pavel Vlasov, will be forced into the brutal, dehumanized life of the factory,

she begins to notice with joy that, unlike the other workers, he is given to reading. When she meets Pavel's close friends, dedicated socialists, her love for him and for them leads her into the revolutionary movement, to which she becomes passionately devoted. Her life takes on new meaning as she gives herself to the cause for which Pavel and his friends are willing to sacrifice so much. Finally, she is handing out leaflets even as she is being arrested and beaten by the police.

Pavel Vlasov (pä'vĕl vlä'səf), Pelagueya Vlasova's son. With an imagination that sets him apart from the average soulless and brutal factory worker in his small town, Pavel is given to reading. He becomes a member of a socialist group that meets to discuss ideas they have gleaned from subversive literature. Full of hope and vitality, Pavel and his friends, with the help of his mother set out to put their ideas into practice. His sacrificial devotion to the socialist cause finally leads to his exile in Siberia.

Andrey (än·drä'),
Natasha (nä·tä'shə),
Sashenka (sä'shĕn·kə),
Vyesovshchikov (vĕ·sŏf'shchĭ·kəf),
Rybin (rōō'bĭn),
Nikolay Ivanovich (nĭ·kô·lĭ' ĭ·vä'nə-vĭch), and
Sofya (sō'fyə), revolutionary friends who share Pavel Vlasov's devotion to the socialist cause and his sacrificial life in behalf of worker and peasant.

MOURNING BECOMES ELECTRA

Author: Eugene O'Neill (1888-1953)
Time of action: Shortly after the Civil War
First presented: 1931

PRINCIPAL CHARACTERS

Lavinia Mannon, daughter of Christine and Ezra Mannon. Tall, flat-breasted, angular, and imperious in manner, Lavinia is fond of her father and fiercely jealous of her mother. While Ezra was fighting in the Civil War Christine had been having an affair with Captain Adam Brant. Unconscious desire to have Adam for herself leads Lavinia to demand that Christine give up Brant or face a scandal which would ruin the family name. Unable to go on living with a husband she despises, Christine plots with Adam to poison Ezra when he returns. Ezra is murdered and Lavinia discovers her mother's guilt. When her brother Orin returns, wounded and distraught, from the war, Lavinia tries to enlist his aid in avenging their father's death. Orin refuses until Lavinia proves Christine's guilt by a ruse. Blaming Adam for the murder, Orin goes to Adam's ship and shoots him. When Orin reveals to Christine what he has done, she kills herself. Orin and Lavinia then close the Mannon house and voyage to the South Seas. Symbolically liberated from the repressiveness of the New England Puritan tradition, Lavinia blossoms into a duplicate of her voluptuous mother. She plans to marry and start a new life. But Orin, hounded by his guilt and going mad, threatens to reveal the Mannons' misdeeds and tries to extort from Lavinia a lover's promise never to leave him. Lavinia agrees but ruthlessly drives Orin to suicide. Now convinced that the Mannon blood is tainted with evil, she resolves to punish herself for the Mannons' guilt. She orders the house shuttered and withdraws into it forever.

Christine Mannon, Lavinia's mother, tall, beautiful, and sensual. Fearing that she will be killed or arrested for her husband's murder, she makes plans with Adam Brant to flee the country and sail for a "happy island." Orin kills Brant. When Orin taunts her with his deed, Christine goes into the Mannon house and shoots herself.

Orin Mannon, Lavinia's brother, a young idealist who has been spiritually destroyed by the war. Progressively degenerating under the burden of his guilt, Orin conceives that Lavinia has taken the place of his beloved mother. Resolved that Lavinia shall never forget what they have done, Orin writes a history of the Mannon family and uses the manuscript to force Lavinia to promise never to leave him.

General Ezra Mannon, Christine's husband, a tall, big-boned, curt, and authoritative aristocrat. Cold, proud, and unconsciously cruel, Ezra always favored Lavinia over Christine and Orin. When he returns from the war, he tries desperately to make Christine love him, but too late. She reveals her infidelity, causing Ezra to have a heart attack. When he asks for medicine, she gives him poison.

Captain Adam Brant, Christine's lover, the captain of a clipper ship. The son of Ezra Mannon's uncle and a servant girl, Marie Brantôme, Adam has sworn to revenge himself on the Mannons, who had allowed his mother to die of poverty and neglect. His first approaches to the Mannon house were motivated by this desire for revenge, but he falls deeply in love with Christine.

Captain Peter Niles, of the U.S. Artillery, a neighbor, Lavinia's intended. Lavinia is forced by Orin to give up her plans to marry Peter and leave behind her the collective guilt of the Mannon family.

Hazel Niles, Peter's sister and Orin's fiancée. She persists in trying to help the erratic Orin lead a normal life. As she becomes aware that Lavinia and Orin share some deep secret, she fears Lavinia will ruin Peter's life and demands of Lavinia that she not marry him.

Seth Beckwith, the Mannon's gardener, a stooped but hearty old man of seventy-five. Seth serves as commentator and chorus throughout the play.

Amos Ames,
Louisa, his wife, and
Minnie, Louisa's cousin, townsfolk who act as the chorus in "Homecoming."

Josiah Borden, manager of the shipping company,
Emma, his wife, and
Everett Hills, D. D., Congregational minister, the chorus in "The Hunted."

The Chantyman, a drunken sailor who carries on a suspense-building conversation with Adam Brant as Brant waits for Christine to join him on his ship.

Joe Silva,
Ira Mackel, and
Abner Small, the chorus in "The Haunted."

[Avahanni, a Polynesian native with whom Lavinia carried on a flirtation. Lavinia's falsely telling Orin that Avahanni had been her lover helps drive Orin to suicide.]

MUCH ADO ABOUT NOTHING

Author: William Shakespeare (1564-1616)
Time of action: Thirteenth century
First presented: 1598-1599

PRINCIPAL CHARACTERS

Don Pedro (pā'drō, pē'drō), Prince of Aragon. A victorious leader, he has respect and affection for his follower Claudio, for whom he asks the hand of Hero. Deceived like Claudio into thinking Hero false, he angrily shares in the

painful repudiation of her at the altar. On learning of her innocence, he is deeply penitent.

Don John, the bastard brother of Don Pedro. A malcontent and a defeated rebel, he broods on possible revenge and decides to strike Don Pedro through his favorite, Claudio. He arranges to have Don Pedro and Claudio witness what they think is a love scene between Hero and Borachio. When his evil plot is exposed, he shows his guilt by flight. All in all, he is a rather ineffectual villain, though his plot almost has tragic consequences.

Claudio (klô′dĭ·ō), a young lord of Florence. A conventional hero of the sort no longer appealing to theater audiences, he behaves in an unforgivable manner to Hero when he thinks she is faithless; however, she—and apparently the Elizabethan audience—forgives him. He is properly repentant when he learns of her innocence, and he is rewarded by being allowed to marry her.

Benedick (bĕn′ə·dĭk), a witty young woman-hater. A voluble and attractive young man, he steals the leading role from Claudio. He spends much of his time exchanging sharp remarks with Beatrice. After being tricked by the Prince and Claudio into believing that Beatrice is in love with him, he becomes devoted to her. After Claudio's rejection of Hero, Benedick challenges him; but the duel never takes place. His witty encounters with Beatrice end in marriage.

Hero (hē′rō), the daughter of Leonato. A pure and gentle girl, extremely sensitive, she is stunned by the false accusation delivered against her and by Claudio's harsh repudiation of her in the church. Her swooning is reported by Leonato as death. Her character contains humor and generosity. She forgives Claudio when he repents.

Beatrice (bē′ə·trĭs), Hero's cousin. Although sprightly and witty, she has a serious side. Her loyal devotion to Hero permitting no doubt of her cousin to enter her mind, she turns to her former antagonist, Benedick, for help when Hero is slandered and insists that he kill his friend Claudio. When all is clear and forgiven, she agrees to marry Benedick, but with the face-saving declaration that she does so for pity only.

Leonato (lē·ō·nä′tō), Governor of Messina, father of Hero. A good old man, he welcomes Claudio as a prospective son-in-law. He is shocked by the devastating treatment of his daughter at her wedding. Deeply angry with the Prince and Claudio, he at first considers trying to kill them but later consents to Friar Francis' plan to humble them. When Hero is vindicated, he forgives them and allows the delayed marriage to take place.

Conrade (kŏn′răd), a tale-bearing, unpleasant follower of Don John.

Borachio (bō·rä′kē·ō), another of Don John's followers. He is responsible for the idea of rousing Claudio's jealousy by making him think Hero has received a lover at her bedroom window. He persuades Margaret to wear Hero's gown and pretend to be Hero. His telling Conrade of his exploit is overheard by the watch and leads to the vindication of Hero. Borachio is much disgruntled at being overreached by the stupid members of the watch; however, he confesses and clears Margaret of any willful complicity in his plot.

Friar Francis, a kindly, scheming cleric. He recommends that Hero pretend to be dead. His plan is successful in bringing about the repentance of Don Pedro and Claudio and in preparing the way for the happy ending.

Dogberry, a self-important constable. Pompous, verbose, and full of verbal inaccuracies, he fails to communicate properly with Leonato; hence he does not prevent Hero's humiliation, though his watchmen have already uncovered the villains.

Verges (vėr'jĕs), a headborough. An elderly, bumbling man and a great admirer of his superior, the constable, he seconds the latter in all matters.

Margaret, the innocent betrayer of her mistress, Hero. She does not understand Borachio's plot and therefore is exonerated, escaping punishment.

Ursula (ėr'sū·lə), a gentlewoman attending Hero. She is one of the plotters who trick the sharp-tongued Beatrice into falling in love with Benedick.

First Watchman and
Second Watchman, plain, simple-minded

men. Overhearing Borachio's boastful confession to Conrade, they apprehend both and bring them before the constable, thereby overthrowing clever malice and radically changing the course of events.

Antonio (ăn·tō'nĭ·ō), Leonato's brother. He plays the role of father to Leonato's supposed niece (actually Hero), whom Claudio agrees to marry in place of his lost Hero.

Balthasar (băl'thə·zär), an attendant to Don Pedro.

A Sexton, who serves as recorder for Dogberry and the watch during the examination of Conrade and Borachio.

MURDER IN THE CATHEDRAL

Author: T. S. Eliot (1888-   )
Time of action: 1170
First presented: 1935

PRINCIPAL CHARACTERS

Thomas Becket, Archbishop of Canterbury. Having just returned from France, where he has gained the support of the Pope in his attempt to achieve both temporal and spiritual power in England, he finds a mixed reaction among the people. Although some support him, others would gladly see him dead. He is faced with a dilemma which leaves him no alternative but to sin against his faith. After his murder he achieves martyrdom and sainthood, which his accusers say he was seeking all along.

Three Priests of the Cathedral, who fear the outcome of Becket's return. They express the pessimism felt by everyone.

The First Tempter, who offers worldly pleasure and success.

The Second Tempter, who offers tempo-

ral power through negation of spiritual authority.

The Third Tempter, who offers the support of a faction wishing to overthrow the throne.

The Fourth Tempter, who offers martyrdom and eternal glory. Becket denies all the Tempters.

Reginald Fitz Urse,
William de Traci,
Hugh de Morville, and
Richard Brito, the knights who murder Becket. They defend their action on the grounds that they will not benefit from their deed, that Becket had refused to acknowledge the King's supremacy, and that he was egotistical to the point of insanity.

The Women of Canterbury, who act as the chorus of classical drama.

MUTINY ON THE BOUNTY

Authors: Charles Nordhoff (1887-1947) and James Norman Hall (1887-1951)
Time of action: Late eighteenth century
First published: 1932

PRINCIPAL CHARACTERS

Lieutenant William Bligh, captain of H.M.S. "Bounty"; strong, stout, dark-eyed, firm-mouthed, strong-voiced, he is a fanatical disciplinarian and a grafting exploiter of ship's rationing. He is subject to fits of insane rage.

Roger Byam, the narrator, a retired ship's captain, at the time of the mutiny a young midshipman and student of languages who has been assigned the job of making a dictionary of the native dialects. He becomes quartermaster after the mutiny. He is acquitted of all complicity.

Fletcher Christian, master's mate, leader of the mutiny; tall, strong, swarthy, handsome, romantic-looking, resolute, moody. Unable to bear Captain Bligh's tyranny any longer, he takes charge of the ship, casts off Bligh with a group of loyal men in the ship's launch, and becomes the new acting lieutenant or captain.

George Stewart, midshipman friend of Byam. A non-mutineer who is appointed master's mate after the mutiny, he drowns when the "Pandora" sinks.

Tehani, a tall, beautiful Tahitian girl, daughter of a high chief. She becomes Byam's wife, bears him a daughter, and dies after he is taken to England.

Sir Joseph Banks, a noted scientist and explorer, President of the Royal Society. He is responsible for Byam's assignment as a dictionary maker.

Hitihiti, a chief and high priest, Byam's "taio" (special friend), tall, magnificently proportioned, light-skinned, intelligent, humorous.

Peggy, a chief's daughter, Stewart's wife.

Maimiti, Christian's sweetheart, Hitihiti's niece, handsome, proud, shy. She goes away with Christian on the "Bounty."

Robert Tinkler, a midshipman whose testimony saves Byam, Muspratt, and Morrison.

Morrison, boatswain's mate, a non-mutineer. He is pardoned.

Muspratt, able seaman, a non-mutineer also pardoned.

Ellison,
Burkitt, and
Millward, able seamen, mutineers convicted and hanged.

David Nelson, a botanist in charge of collecting breadfruit trees. He dies at Batavia.

Doctor Hamilton, the kindly doctor on the "Pandora."

Captain Edwards, captain of the "Pandora."

MY ÁNTONIA

Author: Willa Cather (1873-1947)
Time of action: Late nineteenth and early twentieth centuries
First published: 1918

Ántonia Shimerda, a young immigrant girl of appealing innocence, simple passions, and moral integrity, the daughter of a Bohemian homesteading family in Nebraska. Even as a child she is the mainstay of her gentle, daydreaming father. She and Jim Burden, the grandson of a neighboring farmer, become friends, and he teaches her English. After her father's death her crass mother and sly, sullen older brother force her to do a man's work in the fields. Pitying the girl, Jim's grandmother finds work for her as a hired girl in the town of Black Hawk. There her quiet, deep zest for life and the Saturday night dances lead to her ruin. She falls in love with Larry Donovan, a dashing railroad conductor, and goes to Denver to marry him, but he soon deserts her and she comes back to Black Hawk, unwed, to have her child. Twenty years later Jim Burden, visiting in Nebraska, meets her again. She is now married to Cuzak, a dependable, hardworking farmer, and the mother of a large brood of children. Jim finds her untouched by farm drudgery or village spite. Because of her serenity, strength of spirit, and passion for order and motherhood, she reminds him of stories told about the mothers of ancient races.

James Quayle Burden, called **Jim,** the narrator. Orphaned at the age of ten, he leaves his home in Virginia and goes to live with his grandparents in Nebraska. In that lonely prairie country his only playmates are the children of immigrant families living nearby, among them Ántonia Shimerda, with whom he shares his first meaningful experiences in his new home. When his grandparents move into Black Hawk he misses the freedom of life on the prairie. Hating the town, he leaves it to attend the University of Nebraska. There he meets Gaston Cleric, a teacher of Latin who introduces the boy to literature and the greater world of art and culture. From the university he goes on to study law at Harvard.

Aided by a brilliant but incompatible marriage, he becomes the legal counsel for a Western railroad. Successful, rich, but unhappy in his middle years and in the failure of his marriage, he recalls his prairie boyhood and realizes that he and Ántonia Shimerda have in common a past that is all the more precious because it is lost and almost incommunicable, existing only in memories of the bright occasions of their youth.

Mr. Shimerda, a Bohemian farmer unsuited to pioneer life on the prairie. Homesick for the Old World and never happy in his Nebraska surroundings, he finds his loneliness and misery unendurable, lives more and more in the past, and ends by blowing out his brains.

Mrs. Shimerda, a shrewd, grasping woman whose chief concern is to get ahead in the world. She bullies her family, accepts the assistance of her neighbors without grace, and eventually sees her dream of prosperity fulfilled.

Ambroz Shimerda, called **Ambrosch,** the Shimerdas' older son. Like his mother, he is insensitive and mean. Burdened by drought, poor crops, and debt, he clings to the land with peasant tenacity. Even though he repels his neighbors with his surly manner, sly trickery, and petty dishonesties, everyone admits that he is a hard worker and a good farmer.

Yulka Shimerda, Ántonia's younger sister, a mild, obedient girl.

Marek Shimerda, the Shimerdas' youngest child. Tongue-tied and feeble-minded, he is eventually committed to an institution.

Mr. Burden, Jim Burden's grandfather, a Virginian who has bought a farm in Nebraska. Deliberate in speech and action, he is a just, generous man, bearded like an ancient prophet and sometimes speaking like one.

Mrs. Burden, his wife, a brisk, practical woman who gives unstinted love to her orphan grandson. Kind-hearted, she gives assistance to the immigrant families of the region, and without her aid the needy Shimerdas would not have survived their first Nebraska winter.

Lena Lingard, the daughter of poor Norwegian parents, from childhood a girl attractive to men. Interested in clothes and possessing a sense of style, she is successful as a designer and later becomes the owner of a dress shop in San Francisco. She and Jim Burden become good friends while he is a student at the University of Nebraska. Her sensuous beauty appeals greatly to his youthful imagination, and he is partly in love with her before he goes to study at Harvard.

Tiny Soderball, a girl of all work at the hotel in Black Hawk. She moves to Seattle, runs a sailors' boarding house for a time, and then goes to Alaska to open a hotel for miners. After a dying Swede wills her his claim, she makes a fortune from mining. With a comfortable fortune put aside, she goes to live in San Francisco. When Jim Burden meets her there, she tells him the thing that interests her most is making money. Lena Lingard is her only friend.

Wycliffe Cutter, called Wick, a miserly moneylender who has grown rich by fleecing his foreign-born neighbors in the vicinity of Black Hawk. Ántonia Shimerda goes to work for him and his suspicious, vulgar wife. Making elaborate plans to seduce Ántonia, he puts some of his valuables in his bedroom and tells her that she is to sleep there, to guard them, while he and his wife are away on a trip. Mrs. Burden sends her grandson to sleep in the Cutter house, and Wick, returning ahead of his wife, is surprised and enraged to find Jim Burden in his bed. Years later, afraid that his wife's family will inherit his money if he should die first, he kills her and then himself.

Mrs. Cutter, a woman as mean and miserly as her husband, whom she nags constantly. He murders her before committing suicide.

Larry Donovan, a railroad conductor and gay ladies' man. He courts Ántonia Shimerda, promises to marry her if she will join him in Denver, seduces her, and then goes off to Mexico, leaving her pregnant.

Mrs. Steavens, a widow, the tenant on the Burden farm. She tells Jim Burden, home from Harvard, the story of Ántonia Shimerda's betrayal by Larry Donovan.

Otto Fuchs, the Burdens' hired man during their farming years. Born in Austria, he came to America when a boy and lived an adventurous life as a cowboy, a stage driver, a miner, and a bartender in the West. After the Burdens rent their farm and move into Black Hawk he resumes his drifting life.

Jake Marpole, the hired man who travels with young Jim Burden from Virginia to Nebraska. Though a kind-hearted man, he has a sharp temper and is violent when angry. He is always deeply ashamed if he swears in front of Mrs. Burden.

Christian Harling, a prosperous, straitlaced grain merchant and cattle buyer, a neighbor of the Burden family in Black Hawk.

Mrs. Harling, his wife, devoted to her family and to music. She takes a motherly interest in Ántonia Shimerda, who works for her as a hired girl for a time, but feels compelled to send her away when the girl begins to go to the Saturday night dances attended by drummers and town boys.

Peter and
Pavel, Russian neighbors of the Burden family and Mr. Shimerda's friends. Just before he dies Pavel tells a terrible story of the time in Russia when, to save his own life, he threw a bride and groom from a sledge to a pack of wolves.

Anton Jelinek, the young Bohemian who makes the coffin for Mr. Shimerda's funeral. He becomes a friend of the Burdens and later a saloon proprietor.

Cuzak, Anton Jelinek's cousin, the sturdy farmer who marries Ántonia Shimerda. Though he has had many reverses in his life, he remains good-natured. Hardworking, dependable, considerate, he is a good husband to Ántonia.

Rudolph,
Anton,
Leo,
Jan,
Anna,
Yulka,
Nina, and
Lucie, Ántonia's children by Cuzak.

Martha, Ántonia's daughter by Larry Donovan. She marries a prosperous young farmer.

Gaston Cleric, the young Latin teacher who introduces Jim Burden to the classics and the world of ideas. When he accepts an instructorship at Harvard, he persuades Jim to transfer to that university.

Genevieve Whitney Burden, Jim Burden's wife. Though she does not figure in the novel, her presence in the background helps to explain her husband's present mood and his nostalgia for his early years in Nebraska. Spoiled, restless, temperamental, independently wealthy, she leads her own life, interests herself in social causes, and plays patroness to young poets and artists.

THE MYSTERIES OF PARIS

Author: Eugène Sue (1804-1857)
Time of action: Mid-nineteenth century
First published: 1842-1843

PRINCIPAL CHARACTERS

Rodolph (rô·dôlf'), the Grand Duke of Gerolstein, a small German state. The hero of this intricately plotted romance, Rodolph as a youth was forced into a secret morganatic marriage with a beautiful and sinister woman. His father had the marriage annulled, and in the resultant quarrel the son threatened the father's life and was exiled. His infant daughter was afterward reported dead. Now Duke, he roams the streets of Paris in disguise. He befriends an unfortunate girl who, he discovers much later, is his daughter. Father and daughter are reunited after much misfortune occasioned primarily by the scheming mother, who comes to a well-deserved end. Rodolph then marries a woman he has long loved and returns to Germany with his wife and daughter.

Fleur-de-Marie (flœr'-də-má·rē'), Rodolph's daughter. Brought up by crim-

inals who forced her into crime, she is recognized as good and really innocent by Rodolph. Kidnaped and nearly murdered as a result of her mother's intrigues, she is at last reunited with her father, happily for a time. But her early evil life preys on her mind and she enters a convent. So perfect is her conduct that she is immediately made abbess. This honor is too much for her gentle soul and weak body, and she dies that very night.

Lady Sarah Macgregor, Rodolph's morganatic wife. Ambitious and sinister, she turns her infant over to her lawyer, who reports the child dead. Later, when Rodolph is Duke, she asks the lawyer to find a girl to pose as her daughter, for she thinks that this action on her part might possibly result in a reconciliation. After many intrigues, she is stabbed by a criminal hired in her behalf. Rodolph

752

remarries her on her deathbed to legitimatize Fleur-de-Marie.

Clémence d'Harville (klā·mäṅs′ dár·vēl′), who is unhappily married to one of Rodolph's friends. She is the intended victim of one of Lady Sarah's plots. Clémence is saved from further unhappiness by her epileptic husband's thoughtful suicide, faked as an accident, by which he atones for the evil he committed in marrying her. Independently of Rodolph, Clémence too befriends Fleur-de-Marie. After Lady Sarah's death, she and Rodolph marry.

Jacques Ferrand (zhák′ fĕ·rän′), a hypocritical and thoroughly evil lawyer, hired by Lady Sarah first to get rid of her daughter and later to find a substitute for the girl. Rodolph blackmails Ferrand into establishing many worthy charities. His money thus dissipated, Ferrand goes into a decline and dies.

Madame Georges (zhôrzh′), who is deserted by her criminal husband. He took their son with him. She is befriended by Rodolph and for a time cares for Fleur-de-Marie on her farm.

La Chouette (là·shwĕt′), an ugly, one-eyed woman, a Paris criminal, hired by Ferrand to kidnap Fleur-de-Marie. Later, on her own initiative, she stabs and robs Lady Sarah.

The Schoolmaster, another Paris criminal hired by Ferrand. He proves to be Madame Georges' husband. He kills La Chouette and is imprisoned.

Rigolette (rē·gô·lĕt′), a kind and hardworking young woman, Fleur-de-Marie's friend from prison days. Her lover, whose release from prison Rodolph makes possible, turns out to be Madame Georges' long-lost son. He and Rigolette marry and live happily with Madame Georges.

Sir Walter Murphy, the young Duke's faithful servant and companion in his probing of the mysteries of the Paris streets.

Cecily (sā·sē·lē′), a beautiful woman fallen into depravity. Rodolph secures her release from prison and places her in Ferrand's household as a spy. She furnishes him with much valuable information, the most important relating to the true identity of his daughter.

Polidori (pô·lē·dô·rē′), an evil tutor who, urged on by Lady Sarah, does his best to warp the young Rodolph's mind.

THE MYSTERIES OF UDOLPHO

Author: Mrs. Ann Radcliffe (1764-1823)
Time of action: Late sixteenth century
First published: 1794

PRINCIPAL CHARACTERS

M. St. Aubert (săn·tō·bĕr′), a French aristocrat and widower. He takes his daughter on a trip into the Pyrenees Mountains. While on the trip he falls ill and dies, leaving his daughter with some letters he has asked her to destroy. With the letters is a mysterious miniature portrait.

Emily St. Aubert (ā·mē·lē′ săn·tō·bĕr′), daughter of M. St. Aubert. She wants to marry Valancourt, but her villainous uncle, who wants her property, prevents the marriage and forces the girl to sign over her property to him. Her property is returned, however, when her uncle is captured as a brigand. She is reunited with her beloved Valancourt, marries him, and settles down to a tranquil life.

Valancourt (và·läṅ·kōōr′), a young French nobleman who falls in love with Emily St. Aubert and prepares to marry her, until her uncle interferes. Rumors have him a wild young man, but he proves he is worthy of Emily and finally marries her.

Mme. Montoni, Emily's aunt, who marries Signor Montoni. Her husband locks her in a castle tower to make her sign over her property to him. She dies of harsh treatment.

Signor Montoni, a villainous Italian nobleman who marries Emily's aunt and forbids the girl's marriage to Valancourt. He tries to wrest his wife's and his niece's property from them. He takes them to a castle high in the Apennines, where he is a brigand. He is captured and forced to return his ill-gotten gains.

Count Morano, a Venetian nobleman. Signor Montoni tries to marry Emily off to him.

Lady Laurentini, previous owner of the Castle of Udolpho. She disappears to become a nun. She confesses her true identity as she lies dying. She says she plotted at one time to have Emily's aunt killed by her first husband, who was also Lady Laurentini's lover.

Ludovico, a servant at Udolpho who befriends Emily and helps her escape from the castle.

M. Du Pont (dü pôn′), a friend of Emily's father. He proves that Valancourt, Emily's beloved, actually gambled only to help some friends.

M. Villefort (vēl·fôr′), a French aristocrat whose family gives Emily refuge after a shipwreck.

The Marquis de Villeroi (də vēl·rwà′), Lady Laurentini's lover, the first husband of Emily's aunt.

THE MYSTERIOUS ISLAND

Author: Jules Verne (1828-1905)
Time of action: 1865-1869
First published: 1870

PRINCIPAL CHARACTERS

Captain Cyrus Harding, an engineer in General Grant's army,
Nebuchadnezzar (Neb), Captain Cyrus Harding's Negro servant,
Gideon Spilett, a reporter,
Jack Pencroft, a sailor, and
Herbert Brown, the orphan son of one of Jack Pencroft's former captains, passengers in a balloon in which they make their escape from the capital of the Confederacy. Caught in a storm, they are blown far out to sea and deposited on an uncharted island. Taking stock of their resources, the refugees set about to establish a colony, which they call Lincoln Island. With the knowledge brought with them, and with ingenuity and hard work, they triumph over their surroundings. Through their labors they are aided, in times of need, by a mysterious presence who finally reveals himself as Captain Nemo of the submarine "Nautilus." He warns them to leave the island before its volcano explodes. With the treasure he bequeathes them, they buy land in America and colonize again.

Captain Nemo, Captain of the submarine "Nautilus." Living alone on Lincoln Island, he gives aid in secret to its refugees. He finally reveals his identity, requests that he be buried in the "Nautilus," and bequeathes his treasure to the colonists.

Ayrton, a mutineer. Put ashore by his Captain, he is rescued by the colonists of Lincoln Island. Repenting of his past life, he becomes one of their company and shares their adventures and fortunes.

THE MYSTERY OF EDWIN DROOD

Author: Charles Dickens (1812-1870)
Time of action: Mid-nineteenth century
First published: 1870

PRINCIPAL CHARACTERS

Edwin Drood, a young engineer with prospects of becoming a partner in the firm of his late father. He disappears and is presumed dead, but his fate and murderer are never disclosed in this mystery novel, unfinished at the author's death.

Jack Jasper, Drood's young uncle and guardian, a cathedral choirmaster. An opium addict, he is in love with Rosa Bud and is perhaps the likeliest candidate for the role of murderer.

Rosa Bud, an orphan. She and Drood agree to break their parentally-formed long-standing engagement. She fears Jasper and loves Neville Landless.

Neville Landless, an orphaned Englishman newly arrived from Ceylon who falls in love with Rosa. His quarrel with Drood is a factor in his being suspected of the murder.

Helena Landless, the sister of Neville and Rosa's close friend.

Mr. Crisparkle, Landless' tutor, who introduces him to Drood and Jasper and who aids him in taking refuge in London after Drood's disappearance.

Mr. Grewgious, Rosa's guardian, from whom she seeks protection after Jasper tries to blackmail her into loving him by threatening to expose Landless.

Datchery, a late-appearing stranger apparently engaged in spying on Jasper.

Durdles, a stonemason who works at Cloisterham Cathedral, where Jasper is choirmaster. One night when Durdles is very drunk Jasper steals from him the key to an underground tomb.

THE NAKED YEAR

Author: Boris Pilnyak (Boris Andreyevich Vogau, 1894-   )
Time of action: Early twentieth century
First published: 1922

PRINCIPAL CHARACTERS

Donat Ratchin (dô·nät′ rät′chĭn), a young Russian during the Bolshevik Revolution. Although he has planned to follow his father as a merchant, he returns from the war to become the head of a revolutionary commune in Ordynin Town.

Ivan Ratchin (ĭ·vän′ rät′chĭn), Donat's autocratic father; he breaks up Donat's brief affair with a pretty maid but sends the housekeeper to his son's bed.

Nastia (näs′tyə), a pretty young maid, briefly Donat's mistress.

Olly Kuntz (ōl′lĭ kōōnts), a young woman who prints blank orders for arrest and imprisonment for the Reds.

Comrade Laitis (lī′tĭs), an enthusiastic revolutionist.

Andrey (än·drā′), a man persecuted by Comrade Laitis. He is betrothed to Irina.

Semyon (sĕm·yōn'), a man impressed by Andrey's cleverness in eluding the Reds.

Arkhip (är·hĭp'), a rude peasant and an enthusiastic Red, who suggests suicide to his ailing father. After he becomes a Red official he marries Natalia Ordynin.

Arkhipov (är·hĭ'pəf), Arkhip's father, who shoots himself to avoid a lingering death from cancer.

Natalia Ordynin (nä·tä'lyə ôr·dōō'nĭn), a young woman doctor. She becomes fond of Arkhip, the Red leader, and marries him, looking forward to what she deems a cozy arrangement.

Boris Ordynin (bô·rĭs' ôr·dōō'nĭn), the oldest of the Ordynin brothers, who rapes a maid and suffers from syphilis inherited from his father. He leaves Ordynin when the family home is requisitioned by the Reds.

Gleb (glĕb) and

Egor (ĕ·gōr'), a drunkard, Natalia's younger brothers.

Lidiya (lyē'dyĭ·yə), a morphine addict, and

Katarina Ordynin (kä·tä·rē'nə), who finds herself pregnant, Natalia's sisters.

Arina Ordynin (ä·rĭ'nə), Natalia's mother. She sells clothes and furniture from the home to provide food for her family.

Martha, the maid raped by Boris Ordynin.

Aganka (ä·gän'kə), a peasant girl attracted to Andrey.

Irina (ĭ·rĭ'nə), a girl loved by Andrey and betrothed to him.

Harry, the English leader of a band of armed men who kill and loot on their way through Ordynin Town.

NANA

Author: Émile Zola (1840-1902)
Time of action: The 1860's
First published: 1880

PRINCIPAL CHARACTERS

Nana (na·na'), an ignorant courtesan whose beauty, selfishness, and erotic cunning prove disastrous to the men of fashion who patronize her. A product of the Paris streets, she is discovered by a theatrical promoter and becomes a success by captivating men with her sexual charm. Soon she has a clientele that includes the richest men in Paris. Tiring of this life, she goes to live with a brutal comic actor. When her fortunes reach a low ebb, she is reduced to streetwalking. Later an infatuated nobleman becomes her protector. Her financial and sexual extravagances achieve new extremes as she acquires a lavish mansion, new lovers, and a lesbian prostitute. Many of her lovers ruin themselves; one goes to prison; two commit suicide. Ironically,

she dies of smallpox, her beautiful and notorious body ravaged by the disease.

M. Fauchery (mə·syœ' fō·shə·rē'), a second-rate journalist who writes about Nana in the press, at first favorably and later adversely. A hanger-on of the theater and society, he spends his time seducing other men's wives.

M. Steiner (stĕ·nĕr'), a wealthy and crooked Jewish banker who pursues actresses. He is twice Nana's lover, the first time providing her with an estate. His financial career roughly parallels Nana's erotic career; he is spectacularly successful, suffers heavy losses, and then regains his fortune before he falls again, this time to bankruptcy.

Georges Hugon (zhôrzh′ ü·gōn′), a pampered, effeminate, silly young aristocrat who enjoys Nana, plays the part of her fool, and fatally stabs himself when she refuses to marry him.

Philippe Hugon (fē·lēp′ ü·gōn′), his brother, a dashing army officer who falls in love with Nana when sent to rescue Georges. After stealing army funds for her sake, he is arrested and imprisoned.

Madame Hugon, the indulgent mother of Georges and Philippe. Hating Nana, she is crushed when both her sons are ruined.

Fontan (fōn·tän′), the satyr-like actor who lives with Nana, beats her, and leaves her when she has no more money.

The Comte Muffat de Beuville (mü·fä′ də bœ·vēl′), a pious aristocrat whose passion for Nana leads him to ruin his home life, squander all his possessions, and submit to the humiliations she forces upon him.

Sabine de Beuville (sà·bēn′ də bœ·vēl′), his attractive wife. She takes Fauchery and other men as her lovers.

The Marquis de Chouard (màr·kē′ də shwàr′), Sabine de Beuville's aged father, a man with a dignified appearance and a reputation for lechery. His affair with Nana is a great humiliation to his son-in-law.

The Comte Xavier de Vandeuvres (gzà·vyä′ də vän·dœvr′), a reckless and wealthy man whose passion for Nana and horses leads him to gamble away all his wealth and to commit suicide.

Hector de la Faloise (ĕk·tôr′ də là fà·lwàz′), a rich, stupid young man from the provinces who spends all his means on Nana in order to appear fashionable.

Mignon (mē·nyōn′), a stage manager who procures for his wife.

Rose Mignon (rōz′ mē·nyōn′), his pretty wife and Nana's rival, a clever comedienne who takes Fauchery for a lover.

Bordenave (bôr·də·nàv′), the coarse theatrical producer who discovers Nana and later goes bankrupt.

Daguenet (dà·gə·nā′), a well-to-do young rake who spends his time and money on Nana, marries the Comte de Beuville's daughter, and turns outwardly respectable.

Estelle (ĕ·stĕl′), his plain, awkward, strong-willed wife.

Satin (sà·tän′), a lesbian prostitute of innocent appearance. Nana supports her and uses the creature to humiliate her male lovers.

Prulliére (prü·lyĕr), an actor who enjoys Nana's favors.

Labordette (là·bôr·dĕt′), a theatrical hanger-on who does favors for the actors and actresses.

Lucy Stewart, a fashionable member of the theater crowd, plain, middle-aged, but given to love affairs.

Madame Maloir (mà·lwàr′), Nana's old friend and parasitic confidante.

Zoé (zō·ā′), Nana's maid, a competent, rather homely woman.

Madame Lerat (lə·rä′), Nana's aunt; she takes care of Nana's small son.

Louis (lwē), Nana's son, from whom she catches smallpox.

THE NAPOLEON OF NOTTING HILL

Author: Gilbert Keith Chesterton (1874-1936)
Time of action: Late twentieth century
First published: 1904

Auberon Quinn, an Englishman of the late twentieth century, a man who sees humor in life. Chosen by lot to be King of England, he tries to brighten London life by reviving medieval pageantry and splendor. Acting as a reporter, he is killed in the battle at Notting Hill, but he dies happy because he restored laughter to London.

Barker, one of Quinn's friends. He thinks Quinn dangerous and foolish and so objects when Quinn is chosen King of England.

Lambert, another of Quinn's friends. He shares Barker's views about Quinn.

Mr. Buck, a linen draper made Provost of North Kensington by King Auberon. He goes to battle with the Provost of Notting Hill over a road through London.

Adam Wayne, the Provost of Notting Hill. As a nine-year-old he had unwittingly inspired King Auberon to reintroduce medieval customs into London. He loves Notting Hill's narrow streets and fights against the broad highway. He is killed defending his beloved London district, but dies happy, having brought love back to London.

Mr. Turnbull, keeper of a toy shop. He helps Adam Wayne plan the defenses of Notting Hill and lets him use a toy fort and lead soldiers in making the battle plans.

THE NARRATIVE OF ARTHUR GORDON PYM

Author: Edgar Allan Poe (1809-1849)
Time of action: Early nineteenth century
First published: 1838

PRINCIPAL CHARACTERS

Arthur Gordon Pym, the narrator, young son of a Nantucket trader in sea stores. Desirous of adventure, he stows away on a whaling ship, the "Grampus"; helps to overpower and kill the mutineers who seize the ship; becomes briefly a cannibal before he and Dirk Peters are rescued by the "Jane Guy"; survives with Peters after the slaughter of the captain and all of the crew of the "Jane Guy" by natives on an uncharted Antarctic island; and dies of an unexplained accident after most of his story had been prepared for publication. How he managed to travel from the Antarctic to the United States is not revealed, as the last part of his story was lost at his death.

Augustus Barnard, his friend who aids Pym in hiding aboard the "Grampus" and who shares his experiences and his dangers until he dies from gangrene resulting from an arm wound received in the capture of the ship from the mutineers.

Captain Barnard, Augustus' father, skipper of the "Grampus." With four loyal sailors he is set adrift in a rowboat after his ship is seized by the mutineers.

Dirk Peters, a mutineer sailor on the "Grampus." He is the son of an Indian woman and a white trader. Ferocious-looking, grotesquely misshapen like a dwarf, with huge hands and bowed arms and legs, an immense head, and a ludicrously demonic countenance, he at first joins the mutineers but later turns upon them. He helps Pym and Augustus seize the "Grampus" and becomes a good friend and companion to Pym in all of his later adventures.

Seymour, a Negro cook, leader of one party of the "Grampus" mutineers.

Hartman Rogers, a mutineer who dies in convulsions after being poisoned by the mate, who leads the other party of mutineers.

Richard Parker, a mutineer who joins Pym, Barnard, and Peters. He is the first to suggest cannibalism for survival, and ironically he draws the short straw and is killed by Peters.

Captain Guy, skipper of the "Jane Guy," a schooner which rescues Pym and Peters from the battered hulk of the "Grampus."

Too-Wit, chief of a black-skinned tribe of savages on Tsalal Island in the Antarctic Ocean. Through treachery, the chief and his men entomb by a landslide Captain Guy and all of the "Jane Guy's" crew except six men left on board, and Pym and Peters, who survive both the landslide and a later attack by the savages.

Nu-Nu, a Tsalal native captured and used as a guide by Pym and Peters in their escape from the island. He dies shortly afterward.

NATHAN THE WISE

Author: Gotthold Ephraim Lessing (1729-1781)
Time of action: Twelfth century
First published: 1779

PRINCIPAL CHARACTERS

Nathan, a Jewish merchant and sage who suffers loss of his family and fortune during the Third Crusade. As a tragic hero, he always repays evil with good, as he does when he adopts an orphan girl immediately after losing his own family. While he seems more Christian than Jew—indeed, he acts the part of Christ in his devotion and wisdom—he is really a humanitarian who believes there are many ways either to enter heaven or to establish heaven on earth. Self-reliant, generous, fearless, tolerant, he serves as a contrast to the wily Christians and the rather vengeful Mohammedans.

Recha, his adopted daughter, in reality the orphaned niece of the Sultan Saladin. Under her devoted foster father's tutelage, she shares many of his virtues. Beautiful within and without, her attraction for the young knight, Conrad von Stauffen, is merely sentimental and not romantic, a fact which is the more understandable when they prove to be brother and sister. Grateful to Conrad for saving her life, she and Nathan wish

to reward the young man, but he, though poor and a stranger, takes a strange view of charity and rebuffs all attempts to aid him. Recha's touching naïveté and innocence form an interesting contrast to the intrigue and cruelty which exist in a world torn by religious prejudice and conflict.

Conrad von Stauffen, the disillusioned young Templar who feels strongly against religious wars, in reality a Saracen prince. High-minded, open-hearted and yet reserved, the Templar seems truculent at first, especially in his boorish refusal to accept a reward after he saves from death by fire the girl who later proves to be his own sister. He questions, though he also admires, the Jewish merchant; at the same time, he honors, though he does not understand, the Sultan who spares his life. As events turn out, his stubborn pride reveals his exalted birth, and his impetuosity proves more pagan than Christian.

The Sultan Saladin, the son of the Saracen ruler and a generous, impulsive

759

prince who is revealed as Conrad von Stauffen's uncle. While seemingly prejudiced against the Jewish merchant, he is in reality only testing Nathan's wisdom and lamenting his own reliance on the merchant's generosity. His wisdom in saving the knight's life because of a family resemblance is further noted in his ability to live among the many factions which plague Jerusalem. He is quick witted in dispute, often stern in action, but always capable of magnanimity when it is deserved.

Sittah, his sister and royal housekeeper. What her brother lacks in common sense, she makes up for without being particularly shrewish, though she is shrewd in business dealings and has a quick tongue. Although she suggests the trap to ensnare Nathan, the parable that he tells moves her as much as it does her brother. She is devoted to her generous brother and tries to protect him.

Daja, the Christian servant in Nathan's house and companion to Recha. Essentially a good person, grateful for a good home, fond of her Jewish master and his adopted daughter, Daja is nevertheless a bigot who believes there is only one true faith. She very nearly causes a tragedy through her divided allegiance.

The Patriarch of Jerusalem, a sycophantic fanatic who plots the destruction of Nathan the Jew. He arouses the ire of the Templar and the rebellion of a lay brother, who are to assist him in taking Recha from her kind benefactor.

Al Hafi, a dervish who humorously and ineptly attempts to manage the Sultan's affairs. His thoughts dwelling constantly on his home in India, he wishes to exchange the luxury of the court for the rigors of the wilderness where he can renounce the worldly in order to realize the contemplative life.

NATIVE SON

Author: Richard Wright (1908-1960)
Time of action: The 1930's
First published: 1940

PRINCIPAL CHARACTERS

Bigger Thomas, a young Negro, frustrated by poverty and race prejudice, who has a pathological hatred of white people. He is reluctantly drawn into alliance with his employer's daughter Mary and her sweetheart, who are crusading with the Communists to help the Negroes. After an evening of drinking, Bigger carries the drunken Mary to her room. To prevent her from making a sound which will alarm her blind mother, he puts a pillow over her face and accidentally smothers her. This act releases all his pent-up emotions. He hides the body in the furnace, tries to get ransom money from his employer, and tries to frame the dead girl's sweetheart. He confesses to his mistress, and after the discovery of the body he hides out with her. But he fears that she will be found and questioned, and so he kills her. The police catch him, and under steady questioning by the prosecuting attorney, he admits his crime. Despite an eloquent plea by his attorney, outlining the social structure that made him what he is, Bigger is sentenced to die. While awaiting death he gets, from talking to his attorney, an understanding that his persecutors are themselves filled with fear and are not responsible for their social crimes.

Mr. Dalton, a wealthy white man for whom Bigger works as a chauffeur.

Mrs. Dalton, his blind wife.

Mary Dalton, their daughter, crusading with the Communists against racial discrimination. Bigger accidentally smothers her.

Jan Erlone, Mary's sweetheart and fellow crusader. Bigger succeeds so well in throwing suspicion on him for Mary's disappearance that Jan is arrested. After Bigger is arrested, Jan comes to see him and promises help. Jan introduces to Bigger a lawyer from the Communist-front organization for which Jan works.

Boris A. Max, Bigger's lawyer, provided by a Communist-front organization. He argues that society is to blame for Big-

ger's crime, but he does not succeed in saving Bigger from death. He is able to show Bigger that his enemies are also driven by fear and must be forgiven.

Bessie Mears, Bigger's mistress, to whom he confides his guilt and whom he kills.

Britten, a detective hired by Dalton to investigate Mary's disappearance.

Buckley, the prosecuting attorney, under whose questioning Bigger breaks down and signs a confession. He makes full use of anti-Communism feeling and race prejudice in prosecuting Bigger.

NAUSEA

Author: Jean-Paul Sartre (1905-   )
Time of action: The 1930's
First published: 1938

PRINCIPAL CHARACTERS

Antoine Roquentin (än·twän′ rô·kän-tän′), a philosophical young man who has settled down in Bouville, a town by the sea, to write a biography of the Marquis de Rollebon, an eighteenth century European politician. During the third year of work on the book, Roquentin notices that he has become the victim of a strange affliction; what he calls a sweetish sickness settles over him from time to time. Repelled by the malady, he seeks to rid himself of it by spending time with the few people he knows and by stopping work on the Rollebon book. No one can help him. In despair, he goes to Paris, hoping to be able to write a novel, knowing that he is never to solve the problems of his life.

Ogier P. (ô·zhyä′ pä′), an acquaintance whom Roquentin calls "The Self-Taught Man." To rid himself of loneliness and

despair, Roquentin unprofitably spends some time with Ogier P. Roquentin witnesses a scene in which Ogier P., discovered to be a homosexual, is forcibly ejected from a library.

Anny (à·nē′), an English girl whom Roquentin had known before he began work on the biography. They meet in Paris. She has become fat, insults Roquentin, and leaves Paris with the man who is keeping her.

Françoise (frän·swäz′), a woman who operates a café called the Rendezvous des Cheminots. She and Roquentin were once friendly toward each other in a purely physical way. When Roquentin visits her to see if she can help him defeat the despair which has by now become overwhelming, he finds that she has no time to spend with him.

THE NAZARENE

Author: Sholem Asch (1880-1957)
Time of action: First and twentieth centuries
First published: 1939

761

Pan Viadomsky, a learned man, an antiquarian, who believes himself a reincarnation of Cornelius the Ciliarch, Hegemon of Jerusalem. Renowned in Warsaw as both a great classical scholar and a trickster, he is vindictively anti-Semitic except occasionally toward Jochanan, whom he calls Joseph. He possesses a manuscript which is supposedly Judah's account of his experiences with Yeshua. Pan believes that the Hegemon's soul is immortal and will pass from himself to another as it has transmigrated many times through the centuries since Yeshua's crucifixion.

Jochanan, Pan's student, a Jew who works with Pan and is awe-struck by his knowledge of Jewish history, particularly that of Christ's time.

Yeshua, Jesus.

Pontius Pilate, Procurator of Judea, covetous, ambitious, and corrupt. Haughty toward the Jews but puzzled about the commotion concerning Yeshua, he submits to the desire of the Jews that Yeshua should die.

Judah Ish-Kiriot, or **Judas Iscariot,** a disciple of Yeshua. Young and impetuous, he reveres and loves Yeshua. He innocently points out Yeshua for the Romans, thinking that Yeshua will destroy them.

Miriam of Migdal, or **Mary Magdalene,** a courtesan and dancer who leaves her sinful life and ministers to Yeshua.

Bar Abba, or **Barabbas,** a rebel robber released by Pilate.

Claudia, the debauched daughter of Tiberius Caesar; wife of Pilate.

Germanicus, a Roman general discredited and politically ruined by his former lieutenant, Pilate.

Nicodemon, a rabbi who teaches Judah.

Salome, a dancer.

Jochanan (John) the Baptist, whose head is presented to Salome on a platter.

Miriam, or **Mary,** mother of Yeshua.

The High Priest of Jerusalem.

A NEST OF SIMPLE FOLK

Author: Seán O' Faoláin (1900-   )
Time of action: 1854-1916
First published: 1933

Leo Foxe-Donnell, an Irish patriot who devotes himself throughout his life to the cause of Irish independence. He is a wild young man who sows many wild oats and loses his inheritance. He is twice arrested for his political activity and twice sentenced to prison terms. Nevertheless, he remains an active revolutionary.

Long John O'Donnell, Leo's father, a close-mouthed farmer.

Judith Foxe, Long John's wife and Leo's

mother. She is an unattractive but fruitful woman who marries below her station, giving her husband ten children, of whom Leo is the youngest. She tricks her husband into making Leo his heir.

Julie Keene, a girl seduced by Leo. She warns another lover of Leo's political activities and thus causes him to be sent to prison. Later she is again seduced by Leo and bears a child that she gives away. At last, Leo grudgingly marries her.

Bid Keene, Julie's sister, who marries a policeman. She and her husband take in the Leo Foxe-Donnells when the latter are penniless.

Johnny Hussey, Bid's policeman husband. He remains loyal to the government, despite the revolutionary activity in his family.

Johno O'Donnell, Leo's son by Julie Keene. His father locates him and brings him home as a nephew when the lad is twenty. Johno is a loud young man who joins his father in political activity.

Rachel and
Anna Foxe, prim spinster sisters of Judith, who try to make an aristocrat of their nephew Leo.

James Foxe-Donnell, eldest of Leo's brothers, who is cheated of part of his inheritance by his mother. He keeps the farm intact by running Leo off and he later recovers Leo's acres from his shiftless brother.

Phil Foxe-Donnell, one of Leo's brothers.

Nicholas, Leo's tutor.

Dr. Dicky, Leo's cousin under whom he briefly studies medicine.

Frankie O'Donnell, Leo's revolutionary uncle.

Philly Cashen, a girl seduced by Leo.

Denis Hussey, the nephew of Leo. He becomes a revolutionary, though his father is a loyal policeman.

THE NEW GRUB STREET

Author: George Gissing (1857-1903)
Time of action: Nineteenth century
First published: 1891

PRINCIPAL CHARACTERS

Jasper Milvain, a writer, a selfish egoist and money-minded opportunist who believes in giving the reading public what it wants. In his courting he vacillates toward Marian. Being motivated only by his interest in money, he finally loses her. Seeing a union with the widowed Amy as a road to success, he marries her and achieves his goal.

Alfred Yule, a literary hack, tall, severe-looking, and embittered. He hates both Jasper and Fadge. After losing his sight he is dependent on Marian to care for him.

Marian Yule, Alfred's daughter, courted by Jasper either lightly or seriously according to her apparent financial status. Finally seeing through him, she rejects him.

Amy Reardon, Alfred's niece, daughter of Edmund Yule. Unable to inspire Ed-

win's creative work and angry over his being a clerk, she returns to her mother, taking Willie. Hurt by Edwin's rejection of her offer to return and help him with her inherited money, she is shocked to learn of his dying condition when they are reconciled by Willie's illness and death. Devotedly she tries to cheer Edwin during his few remaining days of life. Emotionally captured by Jasper's favorable review of Edwin's works, she is happy to marry him and afterward happy with him.

Edwin Reardon, Amy's husband, a promising writer in financial difficulties. Easily discouraged and dependent on his wife for inspiration, he feels he is losing his creativity. Proudly he spurns Amy's generous offer to return after receiving her legacy, but he does join her because of Willie's illness. Very ill himself, Edwin dies not long afterward. In personality Edwin resembles George Gissing. Literarily he is Jasper's foil, the idealist in opposition to the materialist.

Willie, the young son of Edwin and Amy. His illness brings about a reconciliation between his parents, but Willie dies shortly afterward.

Dora and
Maud Milvain, Jasper's sisters.

John Yule, oldest of the three Yule brothers; a successful retired businessman, robust and fond of sports. He lives a quiet life after an attack of rheumatic fever. When he dies he leaves a considerable estate.

Edmund Yule, the youngest Yule brother. He dies, leaving a small income to his wife and two children.

John Yule, the son of Edmund.

Fadge, an editor hated by Alfred. Fadge is succeeded by Jasper.

Harold Biffen, a struggling novelist and friend who advises Edwin to answer Amy's summons.

THE NEW HÉLOÏSE

Author: Jean Jacques Rousseau (1712-1778)
Time of action: Early eighteenth century
First published: 1760

PRINCIPAL CHARACTERS

Julie d'Étange (zhü·lē′ dā·tänzh′), an aristocratic French girl who falls in love with her tutor, Saint-Preux, and fears she may fall victim to her love, as she does. When her lover is dismissed shortly before her marriage to another man, she almost dies of grief. She and her lover consider their love no sin. Finally Julie has to marry M. de Wolmar and has two children by him, though she never forgets Saint-Preux. When she is dying she asks that he become her children's tutor and marry her cousin Claire.

M. Saint-Preux (săn′prœ′), a young Swiss of unusual talents and sensibility. He becomes tutor to Julie and her cousin Claire. He and Julie fall in love, but they are not permitted to marry. Only the good influence of his friend, Lord Bomston, keeps the emotional Saint-Preux from committing murder or suicide when Julie has to marry M. de Wolmar.

Claire (klĕr′), Julie's cousin and companion. She, too, loves Saint-Preux and expresses a desire to marry him, after she has become a widow.

Lord Edward Bomston, an English lord who becomes Saint-Preux's good friend. Before he knows of the affair between Julie and Saint-Preux he courts Julie. Later he is kind enough to offer to take the lovers as his pensioners if they elope and move to England. He also tries on their behalf to persuade Baron d'Étange to permit Julie and Saint-Preux to marry.

Baron d'Étange (dā·tänzh′), Julie's father. He wants his daughter to marry his friend, M. de Wolmar. He is so proud of his class and lineage that he will not hear of a marriage between Julie and Saint-Preux.

Mme. d'Étange (dā·tänzh′), Julie's mother. She might have permitted Julie's marriage to Saint-Preux, but she dies before she can help the lovers.

M. de Wolmar, whom Julie marries.

A NEW WAY TO PAY OLD DEBTS

Author: Philip Massinger (1583-1640)
Time of action: Early seventeenth century
First presented: c. 1625

PRINCIPAL CHARACTERS

Frank Wellborn, an impoverished gentleman who has wasted much of his inheritance and been defrauded of the rest by his uncle, Sir Giles Overreach. His fortunes are at their lowest ebb when young Allworth discovers him as he is being evicted from a tavern for refusing to pay his bill. He proudly refuses to accept aid from the boy and plans instead to avenge himself on his unjust uncle. A shrewd judge of character, he wins Lady Allworth's assistance by reminding her of his generosity to her late husband and plays upon Marall's natural greed to further his plot against Sir Giles. When he regains his fortune he rejects his prodigal past entirely and, hoping to win back his lost reputation, asks Lord Lovell for a company to command.

Sir Giles Overreach, Wellborn's miserly, tyrannical uncle. Although he vows that he is ambitious only for the sake of his young daughter, he gathers without scruple the wealth and rank he desires for her, destroying whoever stands in his way. His greed, accurately assessed by Wellborn, brings about his downfall; he has mentally confiscated Lady Allworth's property before he makes certain that his nephew is really to be her husband. The most crushing blow to his aspirations is his daughter's elopement with young Allworth, a marriage facilitated by his eagerness to make her Lady Lovell.

Margaret, Sir Giles' daughter, fortunately free of her father's vices. She is a dutiful child until she realizes to what lengths Sir Giles expects her to go to make herself Lady Lovell. She then relies upon her love for young Allworth, Lord Lovell's support, and her own virtue to give her courage to deceive her father.

Tom Allworth, Lord Lovell's page, a kind-hearted young gentleman. He indulges in romantic fits of despair and melancholy for his beloved Margaret before his master and Wellborn help him to win his bride. In spite of these moods he is a dutiful son and servant and a thoughtful friend.

Lady Allworth, his devoted stepmother who has gone into seclusion to mourn for her late husband. She is persuaded to return to society to help Wellborn to avenge his wrongs. She wins, through her kindness, the affection of Lord Lovell and finally accepts his proposal of marriage.

Lord Lovell, a benevolent nobleman and a valiant soldier. He quickly penetrates Sir Giles' designs and offers his assistance to Margaret and young Allworth.

Marall, Sir Giles' servant, responsible for carrying out his schemes to defraud his neighbors. Lady Allworth's attentions to Wellborn, staged for his benefit, convince him that Wellborn may be a more profitable master than Sir Giles, and he willingly betrays the latter. His efforts are in vain, for Wellborn wisely concludes that a servant false to one master will be false to another and sends him away empty-handed.

Greedy, a justice of the peace, one of Sir Giles' hangers-on. His single-minded devotion to food and its preparation makes him an easy dupe in his patron's schemes.

Order,
Amble,
Furnace, and
Watchall, Lady Allworth's loyal servants who dubiously follow their mistress' or-

765

ders to treat Wellborn as an honored guest.

Tapster, a tavern-keeper who tries to throw the penniless Wellborn out of his house. Wellborn, reminding him that it was he who provided forty pounds to set up the business, thrashes him soundly for his ingratitude.

Froth, Tapster's wife.

Parson Willdo, another of Sir Giles' followers, who unwittingly deceives him by marrying Margaret to Allworth.

THE NEWCOMES

Author: William Makepeace Thackeray (1811-1863)
Time of action: Early nineteenth century
First published: 1853-1855

PRINCIPAL CHARACTERS

Colonel Thomas Newcome, the son of Thomas Newcome, Esq., and his first wife Susan. Always rebellious as a boy, he left home and went to India, where he distinguished himself in the Bengal Cavalry and in service with the East India Company. During his career he married and fathered a son, Clive. When Mrs. Newcome died, the small boy was sent to England to be educated. Later, after he had acquired a considerable fortune, Colonel Newcome returned to England to rejoin his son. Their fortunes prospered, and the father tried to give his son a happy life. Honest, naïve, tenderhearted, he acts always for the best, but his affairs turn out badly. Eventually his fortune is dissipated by the failure of the great Bundlecund Banking Company in which he has invested his money, his daughter-in-law's, and funds some friends had entrusted to him. He spends his last days in poverty and at the mercy of a domineering old widow, the mother of his daughter-in-law. Always mindful of his son's happiness, the Colonel tries for years to guide Clive's life, but he succeeds only in involving the young man with the wrong wife and settling him in a business career which he does not enjoy. At the time of his death the Colonel is a pensioner in the Hospital of Grey Friars.

Clive Newcome, the Colonel's son, a young man with considerable artistic ability. His charming manner endears him to a great many friends, including his cousin, Ethel Newcome, but because Clive is not of noble birth her mother and grandmother do not approve of the match. Clive marries another young woman whom his father cherishes, but the union is a failure because a domineering mother-in-law presides over the Newcome household. Clive changes from the carefree boy that he once was to a bitter young man estranged for a time from his devoted father, whom he blames for much of his misery. At the end of the story Clive is a widower with a small son; the reader is left with the impression that he will marry Ethel Newcome.

Ethel Newcome, the beautiful, spirited daughter of Colonel Newcome's half brother Brian. Her mother, Lady Ann Newcome, is descended from an aristocratic family, and it is the hope of her grandmother, Lady Kew, that Ethel will marry well. Ethel is especially fond of Colonel Newcome. She is also attracted to Clive, but the energy of her grandmother in pushing her into society blinds her to her cousin's attentions. Haughty and high-spirited, Ethel rejects several offers of marriage and ends up taking charge of the children of her selfish, brutal brother Barnes. Estranged from the Colonel and Clive because she has belittled her cousin's intentions, she develops into a serious, self-sacrificing spinster; but at the end of the story she turns over a part of the Newcome fortune to her uncle and cousin, and the reader is left anticipating her subsequent marriage to Clive.

James Binnie, Colonel Newcome's friend in the Indian service, a man of great humor, good sense, and intelligence. He, his widowed sister, Mrs. Mackenzie, and her daughter Rosa live with the Colonel and Clive. He leaves his fortune to his niece when he dies; this is some of the money that the Colonel invests in the Bundlecund Banking Company. Fortunately, Binnie dies before his friend goes bankrupt and his sister turns into a shrew.

Rosa Newcome, called **Rosey,** the daughter of Mrs. Mackenzie, a shy, pretty girl when she and her mother come to live with the Newcomes and her uncle, James Binnie. Always anxious to please, Rosey has no life of her own, for she is completely overwhelmed by her domineering mother. Never truly in love with Clive because she lacks the maturity capable of a woman's love for her husband, she turns more and more against him after their marriage. She dies in childbirth without having known any real happiness.

Mrs. Mackenzie, called the **Campaigner,** the widowed sister of James Binnie and a vigorous, good-humored, but domineering person at the beginning of the story. She is particularly possessive of her daughter Rosey, who marries Clive Newcome. After their money has been lost through Colonel Newcome's unwise investments, she turns into a termagant and a domestic terror. She torments the Colonel because of his misfortunes, becomes more and more possessive of Rosey, and makes life miserable for Clive.

Thomas Newcome, Esq., the father of Thomas, Brian, and Hobson Newcome,

a poor man who, through industry and thrift, created a prosperous banking establishment. Truly in love with his first wife, who dies soon after the birth of their son Thomas, he marries a second time but is never really happy thereafter.

Susan Newcome, the first wife of Thomas Newcome, Esq. She is pretty but penniless, and she dies young, in childbirth.

Sophia Althea Newcome, the stepmother of young Thomas Newcome and mother of the twins, Brian and Hobson. An efficient businesswoman, she influences her husband in his banking business. Rigid and domineering, she never cares for her stepson and is happy when he goes off to India. Before her death, however, she requests that he inherit some of her money; this is the sum that Ethel Newcome turns over to Colonel Newcome and her cousin Clive.

Sir Brian Newcome, the half brother of Colonel Newcome and the twin of Hobson. He is a neat, bland, smiling banker whose external appearance masks his selfish, ambitious nature. Never fully aware of his half brother's virtues, Brian does not entertain him until after he learns of the Colonel's wealth after his return to England.

Lady Ann Newcome, Sir Brian's wife, the daughter of haughty old Lady Kew. Pleasant but rather flighty, she entertains a more aristocratic set than does her sister-in-law, Mrs. Hobson Newcome. She is kind to Colonel Newcome and Clive, though she cannot approve the idea of the young man's marriage to her daughter Ethel.

Hobson Newcome, Sir Brian's twin brother, a portly, red-whiskered country squire. Never really comfortable with his wife's intellectual and artistic friends, he tolerates them as long as they do not interfere with his agricultural pursuits.

Mrs. Hobson Newcome, a fat, pretty woman fond of artistic people. She never fails to hint that this interest makes her superior to her sister-in-law, of whom she is jealous. She has affection for Clive and believes that she deals generously and gracefully with Colonel Newcome.

Barnes Newcome, Sir Brian's oldest son, a hypocritical dandy who conceives a great dislike for Colonel Newcome and his cousin Clive. The father of two children by one of the village girls, he marries Lady Clara Pulleyn. Their marriage is a dreadful one because he tortures his wife mentally and treats their children abominably. Finally Lady Clara leaves him and Ethel Newcome cares for the abandoned children. Barnes stands against his uncle in an election and loses to him, but Colonel Newcome's bankruptcy prevents his serving in Parliament.

Lady Clara Pulleyn, later Barnes Newcome's wife, a pretty, sad girl whose marriage was arranged by her parents. She leads a miserable life, even after she has been divorced from her brutal husband and has married Jack Belsize; there is always the shadow of her former life between them.

The Hon. Charles Belsize, called **Jack Belsize** by his friends, later **Lord Highgate,** in love with Lady Clara Pulleyn. On one occasion, in Switzerland, he creates a scandalous scene because of his jealousy of Barnes Newcome. Lady Clara flees to him when she deserts her husband, and after her divorce they are married.

Lord Kew, called **Frank,** Ethel Newcome's cousin and Jack Belsize's good friend, an open-hearted, honorable young man who sincerely loves Ethel. She refuses his suit after the scandal of her brother's family life and divorce is made public.

Lady Kew, Lady Ann Newcome's aristocratic mother. Insulting and overbearing, she runs the affairs of her family and arranges their marriages.

Lady Julia, Lady Kew's older daughter, completely dependent on her mother and forced to take the fierce old woman's abuse.

Lady Walham, Lord Kew's mother, a long-suffering victim of her mother-in-law's domineering ways.

George Barnes, Lord Kew's younger brother.

Lady Henrietta Pulleyn, Lady Clara's sister. She marries Lord Kew after Ethel Newcome has rejected him.

Sarah Mason, Susan Newcome's housekeeper and companion, never forgotten by Colonel Newcome. He supports her throughout most of her life and tries to do so even after he has gone bankrupt.

Martha Honeyman, Clive Newcome's aunt and his guardian during his boyhood in England, a soft-spoken woman who dearly loves her charge. Thrifty and careful, she is constantly alarmed by the spendthrift ways of Charles, her clergyman brother.

Charles Honeyman, Martha's clergyman brother and Colonel Newcome's brother-in-law. Fond of gambling and the wine bottle, he wastes much of the money that the Colonel gives him. Later he goes to India and becomes a popular clergyman there. Though appearing humble and meek in manner, he is actually cunning and selfish.

Mr. Ridley, Charles Honeyman's landlord.

Mrs. Ridley, his wife, a good woman who befriends Colonel Newcome.

John James Ridley, called **J. J.,** their son and Clive Newcome's good friend. A talented boy, he becomes a successful artist and is elected to the Royal Academy. When Clive is in financial difficulties, J. J. buys several of his friend's paintings.

Arthur Pendennis, Clive Newcome's friend and an editor of the "Pall Mall

Gazette." He narrates the story of the Newcomes, and he and his wife are always ready to help Colonel Newcome and Clive in their troubles.

Laura Pendennis, his wife. She becomes fond of Ethel Newcome and tries to promote the affair between Clive and his cousin. Never able to tolerate Rosey Newcome, Laura is not surprised when Clive's marriage proves unhappy.

Larkins, the Pendennises' servant.

George Warrington, co-editor of the "Pall Mall Gazette" and a friend of Clive Newcome and Arthur Pendennis.

The Marquis of Farintosh, a gossipy, fashionable young man whom Lady Kew selects as an eligible suitor for Ethel Newcome's hand. Ethel rejects his offer.

Lady Glenlivat, Lord Farintosh's mother.

Todhunter and
Henchman, toadies to Lord Farintosh.

The Duc d'Ivry, a sixty-year-old French nobleman.

Madame la Duchesse d'Ivry, his wife, much younger than her husband; a poetess and a patroness of the arts. She is responsible for a duel between Lord Kew and hot-tempered Monsieur de Castillones.

Antoinette, their daughter.

Monsieur de Castillones, Lord Kew's rival for the favors of the Duchesse d'Ivry. He wounds Lord Kew, but not fatally, in a duel.

The Comte de Florac, later the **Duc d'Ivry,** a French aristocrat of ancient lineage and a gentleman of the old school.

Madame de Florac, his wife, for many years secretly in love with Colonel Newcome.

Vicomte Paul de Florac, also the **Prince de Montcontour,** their son, an exuberant young Frenchman, a friend of Clive Newcome and Lord Kew.

Madame la Princesse de Montcontour, nee **Higgs,** of Manchester, Paul de Florac's English wife, a good-hearted, garrulous woman of wealth and ungrammatical speech.

Miss Cann, an artist, a tenant of the Ridleys and a friend of Clive Newcome and J. J. Ridley.

Fred Bayham, another tenant of the Ridley's, a boisterous old school friend of Charles Honeyman, whom he loves to bait. He is a favorite among the poor people of Newcome when he campaigns for the election of Colonel Newcome to Parliament.

Mr. Gandish, an artist, the head of the art school where Clive Newcome and J. J. Ridley study.

Charles Gandish, his son.

Mrs. Irons, the housekeeper of Colonel Newcome and James Binnie. Jealous of Mrs. Mackenzie, she does not get along with that domineering woman.

Mr. Sherrick, a wine merchant and a friend of the Honeymans. Because he had invested money in the Bundlecund Banking Company, he is one of those whom Colonel Newcome feels he must repay.

Mrs. Sherrick, his wife, a former opera singer.

Miss Sherrick, their daughter.

Rowland and
Oliver, the lawyers in the divorce suit of Lady Clara and Barnes Newcome.

Horace Fogey,
Sir Thomas de Boots, and
Charles Heavyside, friends of Barnes Newcome and members of the fashionable London club of which he is a member.

John Giles, Esq., the brother-in-law of Mrs. Hobson Newcome, a poor relation.

Louisa Giles, his wife.

Mademoiselle Lebrun, the French governess to the children of the Hobson Newcomes.

Hannah Hicks, Martha Honeyman's devoted servant, who assists her mistress in the operation of a seaside lodging house.

Sally, another servant in the Honeyman lodging house, a pretty girl but not efficient.

Captain Gobey, a friend whom Colonel

Newcome, James Binnie, and the Mackenzies meet on the Continent.

Captain Hobey, another friend from the Continent, a suitor of Rosey Mackenzie.

Tom Potts, a hatter in Newcome and editor of the local paper; he hates Barnes Newcome.

Dr. Quackenboss, a society doctor who attends Rosey Newcome.

Miss O'Grady, the governess of the daughter of the Duc and Duchesse d'Ivry.

THE NIBELUNGENLIED

Author: Unknown
Time of action: The Siegfried story is legendary. The Burgundian story is based on historical events of about 437
First transcribed: c. 1200

PRINCIPAL CHARACTERS

Siegfried (sēg'frēd), a Prince of Niderland whose heroic achievements include the winning of the great treasure hoard of the Nibelung. Having bathed in the blood of a dragon he slew, Siegfried is invulnerable except for a spot between his shoulders where a linden leaf had fallen. He goes to Burgundy and there wins Kriemhild as his wife. Later he is treacherously killed by a Burgundian knight.

Kriemhild (krēm'hĭld), the beautiful sister of the King of Burgundy. She marries Siegfried, and is subsequently tricked into revealing the secret of his vulnerability. After a long period of widowhood and mourning, she becomes the wife of the King of the Huns. Still seeking vengeance for Siegfried's death, she invites the whole Burgundian court to Hunland. In the final bloody combat all the Burgundians are killed, and Kriemhild herself is slain by her husband's order.

Gunther (gŏn'tėr), King of Burgundy. He promises that Siegfried shall marry

Kriemhild in return for aiding him in winning Brunhild. With Siegfried's aid, Gunther overcomes Brunhild in her required feats of skill and strength. After the double wedding, Siegfried is again needed to impersonate Gunther in subduing Brunhild, who has determined never to let Gunther share her bed. Gunther is killed in the final blood bath in Hunland.

Brunhild (brŏŏn'hĭld), the daughter of Wotan, won by Gunther with Siegfried's help. Wishing to see Siegfried again, she plans a hunting party to which he and Kriemhild are invited. A great rivalry develops between the women; Kriemhild takes revenge by telling Brunhild the true story of her wedding night. Though Gunther and Siegfried settle the quarrel to their own satisfaction, it becomes a source of trouble among Gunther's brothers.

Hagen (hä'gen), a retainer of the Burgundians and a crafty and troublemaking knight. It is he who slays Siegfried.

770

Hoping to get the Nibelungen treasure, now Kriemhild's, for himself, he orders it dropped into the Rhine. He is slain by Kriemhild herself and with him dies the secret of the treasure's hiding place.

Gernot (gâr'nôt) and
Giselher (gē'sĕ·lėr), brothers of Kriemhild and Gunther. Convinced by Hagen that Siegfried has stained the honor of their house, they plot with Hagen to kill him. Later they fall victim to Brunhild's revenge.

Etzel (ăt'săl), also known as **Attila**, King of the Huns and Kriemhild's second husband.

Ortlieb (ōrt'lēb), Kriemhild's small son. Etzel gives him to the Burgundians as a hostage, and he is killed by Hagen when the fighting begins.

Dankwart (dänk'värt), the brother of Hagen. He too is killed in Hunland.

Sir Dietrich (dēt'rish), a knight who warns the Burgundians that Kriemhild still plots vengeance. As a result, they refuse to give up their weapons.

Sir Bloedel (blœ'dăl), a knight who comes to Dankwart's quarters demanding vengeance for Kriemhild. He is killed

by Dankwart and thus the final bloody combat begins.

Iring (ī'rĭng), one of Kriemhild's heroes.

Hildebrand (hēl'dĕ·bränd), a retainer of Etzel. At a sign from Etzel, he ends Kriemhild's life.

Hunold (hōō'nōld), a Burgundian hero.

Queen Uta (ōō'tä), the mother of Kriemhild.

King Siegmund (sēg'mōōnd), the father of Siegfried.

Queen Sieglind (sēg'lĭnd), the mother of Siegfried.

Ludger (lōōd'gėr), King of the Saxons. After spending a year in the Burgundian court, Siegfried aids Gunther in overcoming the Saxons. In the celebrations that follow, Ludger sees Kriemhild for the first time.

Gelfrat (gălf'rät), a Burgundian slain by Dankwart in a quarrel at the start of the journey to Hunland. This and other evil omens are ignored.

Albric (äl'brĭk), a dwarf from whom Siegfried won the cloak of invisibility.

NICHOLAS NICKLEBY

Author: Charles Dickens (1812-1870)
Time of action: Early nineteenth century
First published: 1838-1839

PRINCIPAL CHARACTERS

Nicholas Nickleby, the handsome, warm-hearted, enterprising son of a widow whose husband's death left her and her two children impoverished as the result of unwise speculations. Through the grudging influence of his uncle, a shrewd, miserly London businessman, he secures a post as an assistant master at Dotheboys Hall, a wretched school for boys, at a salary of five pounds a year. Finding conditions at the school impossible to tolerate, he thrashes Wackford Squeers, his employer, quits the place in disgust, and returns to London in the company of Smike, a half-starved, broken-spirited drudge, and now his loyal friend, whom he saved from the schoolmaster's brutality. After being cleared of a false charge of thievery brought by his uncle and the vindictive Squeers, he sets out again in the hope of bettering his fortune. He becomes an actor in a traveling troupe but is called back to London on behalf of his sister Kate, who has become the victim of the unwelcome attentions of Sir Mulberry Hawk and Lord Frederick Verisopht, two notorious rakes. After disabling one of her pursuers he finds work with the generous Cheeryble brothers, and his fortunes improve, so that he is able to provide a home for his mother and sister. He falls in love with Madeline Bray and rescues her from marriage to an elderly miser. After the romantic and financial complications of this situation have been unraveled, Nicholas and Madeline are married.

Kate Nickleby, his refined, pretty sister. After her arrival in London she first finds work with a dressmaker and later becomes a companion to Mrs. Julia Witterly, a vulgar, silly middle-class woman; meanwhile her uncle uses her as a snare to entrap two lustful noblemen. After Nicholas goes to work for the Cheeryble brothers, her future becomes secure. In love with Frank Cheeryble, the nephew of her brother's benefactors, she marries him when she is convinced at last that the young man is truly in love with her.

Mrs. Nickleby, their mother, an ineffective but well-meaning woman who is constantly building castles in Spain for her son and daughter. Because of her poor judgment, she becomes the dupe of several coarse, mean people.

Ralph Nickleby, the miserly, treacherous uncle who finds ignominious work for both Nicholas and Kate and then attempts to use them to further his greed for wealth. After his schemes have been exposed and the unfortunate Smike has been revealed as the son whom he supposed dead, he hangs himself.

Smike, Ralph Nickleby's lost son, who had been abandoned by a former clerk to the harsh care of Wackford Squeers. Flogged and starved until he resembles a scarecrow, he runs away from Dotheboys Hall to share the fortunes of Nicholas Nickleby. When Nicholas joins a theatrical troupe, Smike plays the apothecary in "Romeo and Juliet." Recaptured by Squeers, he escapes with the aid of John Browdie, a stout-hearted Yorkshireman, and finds sanctuary with Nicholas once more. He falls in love with Kate Nickleby, despairingly because he is dying of tuberculosis. After his death it is revealed that he was the son of Ralph Nickleby.

Madeline Bray, a beautiful girl whose devotion to her selfish, dissolute father leads her to accept the proposal of Arthur Gride. Her father dying suddenly, Nicholas and Kate save her from the clutches of Gride and his friend, Ralph Nickleby. Later a lost will, concealed by Gride, is recovered, and Madeline becomes an heiress. She and Nicholas Nickleby are married after both experience reversals of fortune.

Walter Bray, Madeline's father. For his own selfish purposes, he plans to marry his daughter to an unwelcome and much older suitor, Arthur Gride. At his death, before he can complete his plan to barter off his daughter, Nicholas Nickleby and his sister Kate rescue Madeline and take her to their mother's home.

Edwin and
Charles Cheeryble, two benevolent brothers who make Nicholas Nickleby a clerk in their counting house, establish his family in a comfortable cottage, help to thwart the schemes of Ralph Nickleby, and finally bring about the marriages of Nicholas to Madeline Bray and Kate Nickleby to their nephew.

Frank Cheeryble, the gentlemanly nephew of the Cheeryble brothers. He marries Kate Nickleby after the uncles have set right her mistaken belief that Frank loves Madeline Bray.

Wackford Squeers, the brutal, predatory proprietor of Dotheboys Hall and an underling of Ralph Nickleby. Thrashed by Nicholas Nickleby for his treatment of Smike and his cruelty to the helpless boys entrusted to his care, he tries to get revenge with Ralph's help. Arrested for stealing the will which provides for Madeline Bray's inheritance, he is sentenced to transportation for seven years.

Mrs. Squeers, his wife, a worthy helpmeet for her cruel, rapacious husband.

Fanny Squeers, their daughter, a twenty-three-year-old shrew. She is at first attracted to Nicholas Nickleby, her father's underpaid assistant, but later turns against him when he rebuffs her advances and declares that his only desire is to get away from detested Dotheboys Hall.

Wackford Squeers (Junior), a nasty boy who combines the worst traits of his parents.

Newman Noggs, Ralph Nickleby's eccentric, kind-hearted clerk and drudge. Ruined by Ralph's knavery, he enters the miser's employ in order to unmask his villainies. He aids Nicholas Nickleby and Smike on several occasions and is instrumental in securing Madeline Bray's inheritance. After Ralph's death he is restored to respectability.

Brooker, a felon, at one time Ralph Nickleby's clerk, later his enemy. He makes Ralph believe that his son is dead as part of a scheme for extorting money from his former employer. He reveals Smike's true identity and thus causes Ralph's suicide.

Arthur Gride, Madeline Bray's miserly old suitor, who makes Ralph Nickleby his accomplice in keeping the girl's inheritance a secret. He is later killed by robbers.

Lord Frederick Verisopht, a gullible young rake, the ruined dupe of Sir Mulberry Hawk. Enamored of Kate Nickleby, he tries to seduce her. Later he quarrels with Sir Mulberry and is killed in a duel by his mentor in vice.

Sir Mulberry Hawk, a man of fashion, a gambler, and a knave, severely punished by Nicholas Nickleby for his attempt to ruin the young man's sister. Sir Mulberry quarrels with his foolish dupe, Lord Frederick Verisopht, and kills him in a duel.

Tom Linkinwater, the Cheerybles' chief clerk, a man as amiable and cheerful as his employers. He marries Miss La Creevy.

Miss Linkinwater, his sister.

Miss La Creevy, a spinster of fifty springs, a miniature painter, and the landlady of the Nicklebys when they first come to London. She marries Tom Linkinwater.

Peg Sliderskew, Arthur Gride's wizened, deaf, ugly old housekeeper. She steals her master's papers, including the will bequeathing money to Madeline Bray. Squeers, hired by Ralph Nickleby to secure the document, is apprehended by Newman Noggs and Frank Cheeryble while in the act of pocketing it.

Mr. Snawley, a smooth-spoken hypocrite who sends his two stepsons to Dotheboys Hall. Ralph Nickleby's tool, he commits perjury by swearing that Smike is his son, abducted by Nicholas Nickleby. Later, when his guilt is revealed, he confesses, implicating Ralph and Squeers as his confederates.

Mrs. Snawley, his wife.

Madame Mantalini, the owner of a fashionable dressmaking establishment in which Kate Nickleby works for a time. She goes bankrupt because of her husband's extravagance.

Alfred Mantalini, born Muntle, a spendthrift. When cajolery and flattery fail to get him the money he wants, he resorts to threats of suicide in order to obtain funds from his wife. Eventually his wasteful, foppish habits bring her to bankruptcy, and she secures a separation. Imprisoned, he is befriended by a sympathetic washerwoman who secures his release. Before long she tires of his idleness and airy manners, and she puts him to work turning a mangle "like a demd old horse in a demnition mill."

Mr. Kenwigs, a turner in ivory who lives with his family in the same boarding house with Newman Noggs.

Mrs. Kenwigs, his wife, a woman genteely born.

Morleena Kenwigs, their older daughter. Her attendance at a dancing school helps to establish her mother's pretensions to gentility.

Mr. Lillyvick, Mrs. Kenwigs' uncle and a collector of water rates. At a party he meets Henrietta Petowker, an actress from the Theatre Royal, follows her to Portsmouth, and marries her. His marriage brings dismay to his niece and her husband, who had regarded themselves as his heirs. After his fickle wife deserts him, he makes a will in favor of the Kenwigs' children.

Henrietta Petowker, an actress who marries Mr. Lillyvick and then elopes with a captain on half-pay.

Matilda Price, a Yorkshire lass and Fanny Squeers' friend, engaged to John Browdie. The two women quarrel when Matilda flirts with Nicholas Nickelby, whom Fanny has marked as her own.

John Browdie, a hearty, open-handed young Yorkshireman who becomes jealous of Nicholas Nickleby when Matilda Price, his betrothed, flirts with the young man. Later, realizing that Nicholas was completely innocent, John lends him money to return to London. He releases Smike from the custody of Wackford Squeers.

Miss Knag, the forewoman in Madame Mantalini's dressmaking establishment. She is kind to Kate Nickleby at first but later turns against her. She takes over

the business when Madame Mantalini goes bankrupt.

Celia Bobster, the girl whom Newman Noggs mistakes for Madeline Bray and at whose house Nicholas Nickleby calls before the error is discovered.

Mr. Bobster, her hot-tempered father.

Mrs. Julia Witterly, a woman of middle-class background and aristocratic pretense, who hires Kate Nickleby as her companion.

Henry Witterly, her husband. He believes that his wife is "of a very excitable nature, very delicate, very fragile, a hot-house plant, an exotic."

Mr. Bonney, Ralph Nickleby's friend and a promoter of the United Improved Hot Muffin and Crumpet Baking and Punctual Delivery Company, of which Ralph is a director.

Mr. Gregsby, a member of Parliament, a pompous politician to whom Nicholas Nickleby applies for a position as a private secretary. Nicholas declines the situation after Mr. Gregsby explains fully the duties and responsibilities he expects a secretary to assume.

Vincent Crummles, the manager of a traveling theatrical company which Nicholas Nickleby and Smike join for a time; Nicholas adapts plays and acts in them, and Smike plays the part of the apothecary in "Romeo and Juliet." Nicholas and his employer become close friends.

Mrs. Crummles, his wife.

Ninetta Crummles, their daughter, billed as the "Infant Phenomenon."

Miss Snevellicci,
Mr. and Mrs. Snevellicci, her parents,
Miss Belvawney,
Mrs. Grudden,
Thomas Lenville,
Miss Bravassa,
Miss Ledbrook, and

The African Knife Swallower, members of the Crummles theatrical troupe.

Tomkins,
Belling,
Graymarsh,
Cobbey,
Bolder,
Mobbs,
Jennings, and
Brooks, pupils at Dotheboys Hall.

Mr. Curdle, an amateur critic of the drama and the author of a sixty-four-page pamphlet on the deceased husband of the nurse in "Romeo and Juliet."

Pyke, a servant of Sir Mulberry Hawk.

Captain Adams and
Mr. Westwood, seconds in the duel between Sir Mulberry Hawk and Lord Frederick Verisopht.

NICK OF THE WOODS

Author: Robert Montgomery Bird (1806-1854)
Time of action: 1782
First published: 1837

PRINCIPAL CHARACTERS

Nathan Slaughter, a Quaker trapper driven by the deaths of his wife and children to a career of violence against the Indians, who call him the Jibbenainosay, meaning Spirit-that-walks. The whites call the unknown avenger Nick of the Woods, not knowing the man is really the peaceful Quaker they ironically name Bloody Nathan.

Capt. Roland Forrester, a young Virginia patriot of the Revolutionary War. Disinherited by his Tory uncle, he seeks to start life afresh in the Kentucky country. He is still but twenty-three. He returns to Virginia when his cousin Edith is named the uncle's heir; he has to look after his cousin and also Telie Doe.

Roaring Ralph Stackpole, a braggart and a thief. Despite his shortcomings he is loyal to his fellow whites and proves a good fighter against the Indians. He is a frontiersman of the Mike Fink and Davy Crockett type.

Edith Forrester, Roland's cousin. She is temporarily disinherited when her uncle's second will cannot be found. After adventures in Kentucky she is named her uncle's rightful heir.

Wenonga, a Shawnee chief. He is killed by Nathan Slaughter for being the chief who led the attack which resulted in the deaths of Nathan's family.

Richard Braxley, Major Forrester's lawyer. He villainously conceals the Major's second will, hoping to marry Edith, produce the second will, and thus come into command of Edith's fortune. He is killed on the frontier after the second will is found in his possession.

Abel Doe, a white renegade who joins the Indians in their attack on the whites.

Telie Doe, Abel's daughter, given a home by the Bruce family.

Colonel Bruce, commander of Bruce's Station, an outpost in the Kentucky country.

Pardon Dodge, a pioneer who helps the Forresters in the Kentucky country.

Major Roland Forrester, Edith and young Roland's rich Tory uncle.

Mrs. Bruce, Colonel Bruce's voluble but hospitable wife.

Tom Bruce, the Bruces' eldest son, an able Indian fighter.

775

NIELS LYHNE

Author: Jens Peter Jacobsen (1847-1885)
Time of action: Nineteenth century
First published: 1880

PRINCIPAL CHARACTERS

Niels Lyhne, a boy whose mother wants him to be a poet. He becomes, like his father, a farmer. He thinks a great deal, finally becoming an atheist who can accept only his own brand of humanism. After the deaths of his wife and baby, he believes life is empty. He finds temporary solace in belonging to a group when he joins the army, but he is fatally wounded in battle and dies a bitter death.

Bartholine Lyhne, Niels' mother. She loves beauty, especially poetry. She dies while on a trip arranged for her by her son.

Mr. Lyhne, Bartholine's husband. He disappoints his wife, for though he comes from a family of poets and travelers, he has little insight. He dies while his son is still a student.

Edele Lyhne, Niels' aunt. She ruins her health by social life in Copenhagen and returns to her brother's farm, where she dies. Niels admires her, and her death makes him melancholy, quieter, and more imaginative.

Erik, Niels' friend and boyhood chum. He becomes a sculptor and painter, but after his marriage he spends his time drinking and gambling. He is killed when his carriage overturns. His wife has an affair with Niels.

Fru Boyle, a buxom widow, somewhat older than Niels, who becomes his friend. Niels spends his time with her instead of studying.

Fennimore, Niels' cousin and Erik's wife. She comes to despise her husband when he proves dissolute and accepts Niels as her lover. When her husband is killed, in her remorse she blames Niels for their affair.

Gerda, a farm girl who becomes Niels' wife. On her deathbed she departs from the humanism her husband taught her and asks for a pastor so that she can die a faithful Christian.

Herr Bigum, Niels' tutor, an insignificant man who fails his examinations for the priesthood and turns to tutoring. He loves Edele Lyhne.

THE NIGGER OF THE NARCISSUS

Author: Joseph Conrad (Józef Teodor Konrad Korzeniowski, 1857-1924)
Time of action: Nineteenth century
First published: 1897

PRINCIPAL CHARACTERS

James Wait, an indolent and malingering Negro from St. Kitts, the last crew member to report aboard the "Narcissus" as she prepares to get under way from Bombay to London by way of the Cape of Good Hope. A kind of Jonah, his emphasis on his illness and approaching death elicits from the crew a subtle and mistaken sympathy which is demoralizing except when work or great danger, such as the storm, draws them together. Wait dies when in sight of land, thereby lifting a burden from the crew and ship, and the ship reaches port without further friction.

Captain Allistoun, a coolly rational man who is never intimidated by Wait's malingering. In the storm he remains alert while others cling to the deck waiting for death. He restricts Wait to his berth after the first mate reports that the Negro is a malingerer who must be punished or a sick man who must be cared for.

Old Singleton, a sailor intuitive and indifferent to the corrupting influence of Wait. During the storm he remains at the wheel for thirty hours. He has come upon the sinister truth of his mortality. He predicts Wait will die when the ship comes in sight of land.

Podmore, the ship's cook, a religious fanatic scorned by the Captain and an embarrassment to the men. He talks of eternity, providence, and rebirth, braves the deck to serve coffee during the storm, and tries to convert Wait.

Donkin, the eternal grumbler, always squealing for his rights, always avoiding work and responsibility. Seemingly devoted to Wait, he watches the Negro die and then steals his money.

Belfast, the sailor who, of all the crew, is most mistakenly influenced by Wait's false humility. He performs many deeds for Wait. In port he begs for a relic from the dead man's belongings.

Wamibo, a Russian Finn, wild, mysterious, primitive, who seems to gloat over the worsening condition of the Negro like a fiend over the damned.

Mr. Baker, the first mate. In spite of his menacing utterances he is liked by the crew. A man with bull neck, steady eyes, and sardonic mouth, he carries on his duties calmly.

Mr. Creighton, the second mate, a fair gentlemanly fellow with a resolute face and a splendid physique.

Charley, the youngest seaman aboard, chastened by learning his youth is insignificant.

Archie,
Davis,
Knowles, and
Two Young Scandinavians, other seamen aboard the "Narcissus."

NIGHT FLIGHT

Author: Antoine de Saint-Exupéry (1900-1944)
Time of action: Early 1930's
First published: 1931

PRINCIPAL CHARACTERS

Rivière (rē·vyĕr′), the director of the air mail services. Completely dedicated to making night flying regular in spite of all its attendant dangers, he imposes on his men a rigid discipline that is taken for callousness. When Fabien and his wireless operator are lost in a storm, Rivière's deep concern reveals that his unbending severity springs not from any lack of feeling for his pilots but from a complete sense of consecration to his mission.

Fabien (fȧ·byän′), a pilot. On a night flight carrying the mails from Patagonia to Buenos Aires, he and his wireless operator enter a violent storm and are finally lost. Their deaths are responsible for the revelation of Rivière's real concern for his pilots in spite of his severe demands on them.

Robineau (rô·bē·nô′), the inspector. Inclined to make friends with the pilots, he resents Rivière's undeviating discipline

777

and insistence that the supervisors maintain complete impersonality toward those whom they may have to send to their deaths. Only after Fabien is lost does he realize Rivière's real concern for his men and experience a sense of communion with him.

Pellerin (pĕ·lə·răn'), a pilot who comes

safely through the great storm in which Fabien is lost.

Mme. Fabien (fà·byän'), Fabien's bride of six weeks, who hears from Rivière of the enormous price men must pay to conquer the skies. She understands.

Roblet (rô·blā'), an old former pilot.

A NIGHT IN THE LUXEMBOURG

Author: Remy de Gourmont (1858-1915)
Time of action: Early twentieth century
First published: 1906

PRINCIPAL CHARACTERS

Louis Delacolombe (M. James Sandy Rose), a journalist. Born in France, he was brought up in the United States, returned to France, and for ten years until his sudden death was the French correspondent of the "Northern Atlantic Herald." Both his original name Delacolombe and his later name Rose appear to be symbolic since both the dove and the rose have long symbolized love.

"He", a chestnut-haired, bearded, brilliant-eyed, gentle-faced man whom Sandy meets in the Church of Saint-Sulpice. Dressed like a French gentleman, he is a god who, when Rose refers to his mother Mary, says he has been known by many names including Apollo. He calls himself a superman and a god. Though he physically resembles the conventional conception of Jesus, he appears in his thought to be a more generalized divine inspirer of men of varied faiths in many ages. His philoso-

phy concerning human life, with its emphasis on the virtue of being happy and the importance of living each moment as if it were eternal, is Epicurean. His favorite mortal philosophers, as he tells Rose, were Epicurus, who found happiness in pleasure, and Spinoza, who found it in asceticism.

Elise, a beautiful young goddess who allows Rose to possess her during a brief interval in the long conversation with "He." Later, after she has accompanied Rose to his room and they have again experienced the joys of love, she reminds him of Giorgione's Venus. She and her two friends also resemble the three Graces of Greek mythology.

The Narrator, a friend of Rose who finds him dead sitting at his desk in his room. As legatee and in accordance with Rose's will, he publishes Rose's manuscript and furnishes a brief explanatory preface and a final note for it.

NIGHTMARE ABBEY

Author: Thomas Love Peacock (1785-1866)
Time of action: Early nineteenth century
First published: 1818

Christopher Glowry, the master of Nightmare Abbey, who is largely interested in eating and drinking. He is boorish and coarse. He refuses to allow his son to marry the woman of his choice because she has no fortune. He finally changes his mind, but by that time it is too late; the young lady has discarded his son and accepted another proposal.

Scythrop Glowry, Christopher Glowry's son, a gloomy, boorish, unmannerly young man. He has a rather morbid interest in dungeons, secret panels, and skulls. He falls in love with his cousin, but his father will not allow the marriage. Later, when he is not able to decide between two girls, the two young ladies both accept other men and he is left to drink his wine alone. He is supposed to represent Shelley.

Marionetta Celestina O'Carroll, Glowry's niece and Scythrop's cousin. She is very coquettish and Scythrop falls in love with her. She has no fortune, however, and is allowed to remain in the house only as a guest. She finally accepts the proposal of a dandy named Listless.

Mr. Toobad, Glowry's friend. He and Glowry agree that his daughter would be a good match for Scythrop. He goes to London to bring her to Nightmare Abbey, but she discovers his purpose and disappears.

Celinda Toobad (Stella), Mr. Toobad's daughter. She does not take kindly to having a husband chosen for her and runs away from her father when she learns that she is to marry Scythrop. She turns up later at Nightmare Abbey as a strange woman calling herself Stella, and moves into a secret apartment constructed by Scythrop. She discusses German metaphysics and tragedy with Scythrop, without knowing who he is. When he is slow in asking for her hand, she accepts Flosky's proposal.

Listless, a bored and languid dandy, and a friend and fellow collegian of Scythrop. He is a guest at Nightmare Abbey and is interested in Marionetta. He finally asks for her hand in marriage and is accepted.

Mr. Ferdinando Flosky, a poet, and another guest at the abbey. He is interested in the supernatural and in metaphysics. He proposes to and is accepted by Celinda. He is supposed to represent Coleridge.

Mr. Cypress, another visitor at Nightmare Abbey. He is Byron.

Mr. Asterias, another guest who is an ichthyologist tracing down rumors of a mermaid supposed to have been seen near the abbey.

Aquarius, his son.

Fatout, Listless' French valet.

Raven, a servant at Nightmare Abbey.

NINETEEN EIGHTY-FOUR

Author: George Orwell (Eric Blair, 1903-1950)
Time of action: 1984
First published: 1949

PRINCIPAL CHARACTERS

Winston Smith, a citizen of Oceania. He is an intelligent man of thirty-nine, a member of the Outer Ring of the Party who has a responsible job in the Ministry of Truth, where he changes the records to accord with the aims and wishes of the Party. He is not entirely loyal, however, for he keeps a secret journal, takes a

779

mistress, and hates Big Brother. Caught in his infidelities to the Party, he is tortured until he is a broken man; he finally accepts his lot, even to loving Big Brother.

Mrs. Smith, Winston's wife, a devoted follower of the Party and active member of the Anti-Sex League. Because she believes procreation a party duty, she leaves her husband when the union proves childless.

Julia, a bold, good-looking girl who, though she wears the Party's red chastity belt, falls in love with Winston and becomes his mistress. She, like her lover, rebels against Big Brother and the Party.

Like Winston, too, she is tortured and brainwashed and led to repent her political sins.

O'Brien, a member of the Inner Party. He leads Winston and Julia to conspire against the Party and discovers all their rebellious acts and thoughts. He is Winston's personal torturer and educator, who explains to Winston why he must accept his lot in the world of Big Brother.

Mr. Charrington, a member of the thought police who disguises himself as an old man running an antique shop in order to catch such rebels as Winston and Julia. He is really a keen, determined man of thirty-five.

NO NAME

Author: Wilkie Collins (1824-1889)
Time of action: Mid-nineteenth century
First published: 1862

PRINCIPAL CHARACTERS

Andrew Vanstone, a Victorian gentleman who lives a quiet life. When he is killed unexpectedly, it turns out that Mrs. Vanstone is his second wife of but a short time and that their two daughters are illegitimate. Because of legal technicalities, his fortune passes to a selfish, bad-tempered brother of Mr. Vanstone who refuses to share the inheritance with the Vanstone daughters.

Mrs. Vanstone, Andrew's second wife, mother of Norah and Magdalen. She dies of grief shortly after her husband is killed in a railway accident. They had been unable to marry until late in life because Andrew's disreputable first wife was still alive.

Norah Vanstone, a quiet girl. Left poor at her father's death, she supports herself as a governess. A sensitive girl, she has her feelings hurt by her fiancé's inquiries about her. She is persistent and finally accomplishes quietly what her sister cannot accomplish by plotting and flamboy-

ant means; she restores the family fortune.

Magdalen Vanstone, a headstrong, capable girl. Left penniless at her father's death, she carves for herself a stage career. She marries her cousin Noel in order to regain the fortune lost by her illegitimacy, but her plots fail and she is still seemingly without the fortune. Eventually her sister finds the documents which restore the girls' inheritance.

Noel Vanstone, Magdalen's cousin and first husband whom she marries in an attempt to retrieve the family fortune. He is a weak, miserly young man. He discovers his wife's trickery and just before he dies he tries to will his money to a distant relative.

Captain Kirke, Magdalen's second husband, an understanding, patient man.

Mr. Clare, the Vanstones' misanthropic but scholarly neighbor, Frank's father.

780

Frank Clare, the Vanstone girls' childhood playmate; he becomes an incompetent young man whom Magdalen finds attractive for a while. A failure at business, he is forced to take a job in China. Eventually he marries a wealthy widow.

Captain Wragge, an amiable rascal who befriends and helps Magdalen.

Mrs. Wragge, a large, sad woman who, like her husband, befriends Magdalen.

Miss Garth, the Vanstone girls' governess, who helps them when they are left penniless.

Mrs. Le Count, Noel's suspicious housekeeper, who dominates her master.

George Bartram, Noel's designated heir. He loves Norah.

Admiral Bartram, George's uncle.

NO TRIFLING WITH LOVE

Author: Alfred de Musset (1810-1857)
Time of action: Nineteenth century
First presented: 1864; first published: 1834

PRINCIPAL CHARACTERS

Perdican (pĕr·dē·kän'), the son of a French nobleman. He returns to his father's home after receiving his doctorate. He is a somewhat worldly man and is distressed to find his childhood sweetheart cool to him. He tries to win her. Failing in his suit, he courts a peasant girl, who dies of shock when she learns that Perdican does not really love her.

Camille (kà·mē'y), Perdican's childhood sweetheart and an heiress. Reared in a convent, she looks for happiness as a nun, rather than as a wife. She is confused when she finds that she loves Perdican, and her indecision drives Perdican to the peasant girl. Camille is greatly distressed when the girl dies, and she blames herself; she inflicts punishment upon herself by bidding her suitor goodbye.

Rosette (rō·zĕt'), a sweet and loving

peasant girl who is courted by Perdican and who loves him deeply. When she learns that her lover really wants Camille as his wife, she dies of shock.

The Baron, Perdican's father, who is anxious for his son to marry Camille, the heiress.

Dame Pluche (plüsh), Camille's chaperone, an easily scandalized woman who is rigorous in performing her duties.

Maître Blazius (mĕ'tr blà·zyüs'), Perdican's tutor. He is a fat and foolish priest, and a heavy drinker and eater, who wants to be priest in the Baron's household.

Maître Bridaine (mĕ'tr brē·dĕn'), Maître Blazius' competitor for a place in the Baron's household. He, like his rival, is a foolish gourmand.

NOCTURNE

Author: Frank Swinnerton (1884-   )
Time of action: Twentieth century
First published: 1917

Jenny Blanchard, a milliner's assistant, tall, rather beautiful, and independent. Frustrated by the humdrum nature of her life, she turns her unromantic suitor over to her sister and goes to meet Keith Redington, a more glamorous young man who wants her to run away with him to Alaska or Labrador. Later Jenny feels conscience-stricken because she left her father alone and also because she feels that in admitting her love for Keith she has given up her freedom.

Emmy Blanchard, her older sister, who stays at home to look after their father and the house. She is plain and domestic and also frustrated because she is in love with Jenny's suitor. After dressing for the date Jenny has tricked Alf into making, Emmy appears looking actually lovely. During the course of the evening

Alf decides that Emmy is the girl for him, and they become engaged.

Alf Rylett, Jenny's suitor, adored by Emmy, with whom he falls in love.

Keith Redington, the captain of a yacht belonging to a wealthy lord. He knew Jenny for only three days during a seaside vacation, but he confidently sends her a summons to the yacht, where she finds supper for two prepared. He has romantic plans for their future, but the dream is crushed when Jenny thinks of Pa.

Pa Blanchard, the semi-invalid father of Emmy and Jenny. He is injured in a fall after Jenny leaves for the yacht. Emmy and Alf find him on the kitchen floor and revive him.

NORTHANGER ABBEY

Author: Jane Austen (1775-1817)
Time of action: Early nineteenth century
First published: 1818

Catherine Morland, a young girl whose head is filled with "Gothic romances." At Bath she meets the Thorpe and Tilney families. Her brother James is attracted to Isabella Thorpe, and John Thorpe becomes attentive to Catherine. She, however, is more interested in Henry Tilney, a younger son, whose father invites her to his home, Northanger Abbey, under the mistaken impression that she is rich and will make a good match for Henry. Overcome by the thrill of being in a real abbey, Catherine makes several foolish blunders, even thinking that her host must have murdered his wife. The visit ends when General Tilney, learning that Catherine is not rich, asks her to leave and forbids Henry to see her. But Henry's love proves strong enough for him to defy his father, and the lovers are finally married.

General Tilney, the owner of Northanger Abbey. Eager for money, he is polite to Catherine only because he believes her to be rich.

Captain Frederick Tilney, his older son, for whom Isabella Thorpe jilts James Morland.

Henry Tilney, the younger son, a clergyman, who marries Catherine Morland.

Eleanor Tilney, their sister. Her marriage to a viscount puts her father into a good enough humor to permit the marriage of Henry and Catherine.

James Morland, Catherine's brother. He falls in love with Isabella Thorpe but is jilted by her.

Isabella Thorpe, a scheming young woman whom Catherine meets at Bath.

She becomes engaged to James Morland but jilts him for Captain Tilney, though without much hope of marrying the latter.

John Thorpe, Isabella's stupid brother, who tries to marry Catherine and who boasts to General Tilney of her wealth. When she refuses him, he takes revenge by telling the General that she is poorer than she really is.

THE NORTHERN LASS

Author: Richard Brome (?-1652 or 1653)
Time of action: Early seventeenth century
First presented: 1632

PRINCIPAL CHARACTERS

Sir Philip Luckles, a gentleman who devotes his life to the satisfaction of his own wishes. He marries Mrs. Fitchow for her money, and he no sooner sees the prospect of both beauty and fortune in Constance's love for him than he plans his divorce and elopement.

Mistress Fitchow, a well-to-do widow, his promised wife. Although she refuses to hear Tridewell's slander about her bridegroom, she is immediately jealous of Constance and indicates her displeasure to Sir Philip by barring him from her room on their wedding night.

Tridewell, Sir Philip's friend. Trying to save him from an unsuitable match, he finds himself in love with the widow who defends her groom with spirit, and he contrives to make his friend's marriage illegal.

Widgene, Mrs. Fitchow's opportunist brother, who is seeking a rich wife. He is rewarded for his schemes by the hand of Mrs. Holdup, a courtesan.

Anvile, his tutor, expert in all the vices of young gentlemen.

Constance, the "northern lass," a Yorkshire girl who falls in love with Luckles at their first meeting and loses her senses at the news of his marriage. She is restored to health and sanity by her elopement with him.

Sir Paul Squelch, her wealthy uncle, a blustering, lascivious old gentleman who makes his mistress masquerade as his niece.

Mistress Traynwell, a sharp-tongued lady of uncertain years, Constance's governess. She resolutely pursues Sir Paul until she can blackmail him into marriage by threatening to reveal Mrs. Holdup's identity.

Constance Holdup, a witty prostitute, Sir Paul's mistress. She takes advantage of her feigned role as his niece to win herself a husband, Widgene.

Pace, Sir Philip's clever servant, who disguises himself as doctor and minister.

NOSTROMO

Author: Joseph Conrad (Józef Teodor Konrad Korzeniowski, 1857-1924)
Time of action: Late nineteenth century
First published: 1904

PRINCIPAL CHARACTERS

Nostromo (nŏs·trō'mō), the nickname of **Gian' Battista,** the "incorruptible" hero of the people after saving a valuable cargo of silver from revolutionists by hiding it on a barren island at the harbor entrance. Later he realizes that it can be his because the lighter on which he transported the silver is reported sunk in a collision with a troopship at night. He grows rich slowly by returning to the island occasionally for some of the silver. When a lighthouse is established on the island, he is still able to visit his hoard of silver because his friends, the Violas, are made keepers of the light. He chooses to love Giselle, the younger Viola daughter, rather than the more stable and idealistic Linda. Mistaken for a despised suitor of Giselle, he is shot by old Viola while on a night visit to see Giselle. Nostromo dies feeling that he has been betrayed and wishing to confess to Mrs. Gould. Because she refuses to listen, his secret is kept and his famed incorruptibility remains intact.

Charles Gould, the manager of the San Tomé silver mine, which he idealizes as a civilizing force that will bring progress to contented but backward Sulaco, a city in the Occidental Province of the Republic of Costaguana, as well as atonement for the death of his father. But silver, the incorruptible metal, is a corrupting influence politically and morally. It separates Gould from his wife Emilia, attracts politicians from the interior, and provokes a revolution.

Doña Emilia, Charles Gould's wife, supplanted in his affections by his "redemption idea" of the mine. Childless, she is a victim of a "subtle unfaithfulness" created by the mine. In turn, she is gracious, kind, unselfish, and lives for others.

Martin Decoud (màr·tăn' də·kö'), a young Creole intellectual, skeptic, and amateur journalist recently returned from Paris. He falls in love with patriotic Antonia Avellanos and fathers the idea of a separate Occidental Republic. He escapes from the revolutionists on the lighter bearing the silver but commits suicide when left alone on the island to face all the silence and indifference of nature.

Dr. Monygham, a doctor of introspective temperament. Under torture during the former dictatorship of Guzman Bento, he had betrayed friends, a deed that weighs on his conscience. He risks his life during this revolution for the safety of others in order to earn restoration to the human community.

Captain Mitchell, the superintendent of the Oceanic Steam Navigation Company, a "thick, elderly man, wearing high pointed collars and short sidewhiskers, partial to white waistcoats, and really very communicative under his air of pompous reserve." He narrates part of the story.

Giorgio Viola (jôr'jō vē·ō'lä), a veteran of Garibaldi's army and keeper of the Casa Viola, a restaurant and hotel in Sulaco. Believing whole-heartedly in the human bond of liberty, he had risked his life in Italy in the hope of bringing freedom to men. He wishes to make Nostromo his son.

Teresa, the portly, ill wife of Viola, anxious for the future of her husband and daughters.

Giselle, the sensuous, blonde younger daughter of Viola, in love with Nostromo.

Linda, the idealistic, dark older daughter of Viola, also in love with Nostromo.

President Ribiera (rē·bē·ā'rä), the beneficent dictator of Costaguana, defeated by revolutionary forces.

Don José Avellanos (dōn hō·sā' ä·vä·yä'-nōs), an idealistic, cultured, dignified, patriotic statesman who has survived many changes in his country and the author of "Fifty Years of Misrule," a history of the republic. He dies of disappointment.

Antonia Avellanos (ăn·tō'nyä), his beautiful, free-minded, patriotic daughter, in love with Decoud.

Father Corbelàn (kŏr·bā·län'), the fanatical uncle of Antonia Avellanos. His appearance suggests something unlawful behind his priesthood, the idea of a chaplain of bandits. He is Costaguana's first Cardinal Archbishop.

General Montero (mōn·tā'rō), a rural hero and a former Minister of War, the leader of the revolution.

Pedro Montero (pā'drō), his brother, a savage with a genius for treachery. He is the leader of the rebel army from the interior.

Don Pépé (dŏn pā'pā), the faithful overseer of the San Tomé mine, under orders to blow up the mine if the revolutionaries try to seize it.

Father Roman (rō·män'), the faithful padre of the workers of the mine.

Colonel Sotillo (sō·tē'yō), one of the leaders of the revolution. Cowardly and traitorous, he hurries his army into Sulaco in the hope of gaining personal advantage.

Señor Hirsch, a craven and fearful hide merchant who tries to escape from Sulaco by secreting himself on the lighter with Nostromo and Decoud while they are transporting the silver. When the lighter and Sotillo's ship collide in the darkness, he leaps aboard the rebels' vessel. There he is tortured for confession and finally killed by Sotillo.

Hernández (ĕr·nän'dēs), a man mistreated in an earlier revolution and now the leader of a robber band. During the revolt he becomes a general, pledged to Father Corbelàn.

General Barrios (bär'ryōs), a brave, trustworthy, unpretentious soldier who has lived heroically and loves to talk of the adventurous life of his past. He is the commander of the Occidental military district.

Don Juste Lopez (dŏn hūs'tā lō'pĕz), the president of the provincial assembly. He thinks that resistance to Pedro Montero will be useless but that formalities may still save the republic.

Fuentes (fwĕn'tās), a nominee for the post of political chief of Sulaco. Eager to take office, he sides with Pedro Montero.

Gamacho (gä·mä'chō), the commander of the Sulaco national guard. He throws his lot with the revolutionists.

Basilio (bä·sē'lyō), Mrs. Gould's head servant.

Luis (lōō'ēs), a mulatto servant at the Casa Viola.

O PIONEERS!

Author: Willa Cather (1873-1947)
Time of action: 1880-1910
First published: 1913

PRINCIPAL CHARACTERS

Alexandra Bergson, the daughter of a Swedish immigrant homesteader on the Divide in Nebraska. A strong-willed girl of great courage and resourcefulness, she takes charge of the farm after her father's death and through good years or bad uses the land wisely. When times are hard and neighbors become discouraged and move away, she scrimps and saves to add their acres to her own. She is the first on the Divide to try new agricultural methods, to plant alfalfa, to build a silo. She keeps Oscar and Lou, her younger brothers, from leaving the farm for easier work and softer living in town. At the end she can look out over her cultivated fields and know that she has won prosperity for herself and her brothers. But her success as a farmer is bought at the price of her experience as a woman. Twice she sees Carl Linstrum, whom she loves, leave the Divide with no words of love spoken. She is over forty when the death of Emil, her youngest brother, killed by a jealous husband, teaches her the need of love and the grace of compassion; and she and Carl are reunited. Alexandra Bergson is a character almost epic in stature, a fertility goddess of the plains subduing the wild and stubborn land and making it fruitful.

John Bergson, an immigrant farmer who dreams of regaining on his Nebraska homestead a family fortune lost in Sweden. He dies after eleven years of failure, his faith in the land still unshaken. On his deathbed he asks his two older sons to be guided by their sister, for he sees in her qualities of imagination, energy, desire, and wisdom that her brothers lack.

Mrs. Bergson, a devoted wife and mother who tries to maintain household order by clinging to old, familiar European ways. Her twin passions are gardening and preserving.

Carl Linstrum, a grave, introspective young man unsuited to farm life on the Nebraska frontier. His predicament is that of many transplanted Europeans, divided as he is between his Old World heritage and his prairie environment. When his father sells the Linstrum farm and moves back to St. Louis, Carl goes to the city to learn the engraver's trade. Sixteen years later, dissatisfied with commercial life, he returns to the Divide, but Oscar and Lou Bergson, Alexandra's brothers, insult him and drive him away with accusations that he has come back to marry their sister for her money. Carl goes off to Alaska but returns when he reads the news of Emil Bergson's murder. This time he and Alexandra plan to marry.

Oscar and

Lou Bergson, Alexandra's younger brothers. Dull, insensitive, greedy, they respect their sister but have no real affection for her. Their great hope is that they or their children will inherit her land.

Emil Bergson, Alexandra's youngest brother, whose relationship to his sister seems more like that of a son than of a brother. He grows into a moody, restless young man. Less stolid than the Scandinavian Bergsons, he finds his friends among the more volatile, merrier Bohemians and French settlers in nearby communities. In love with Marie Shabata, a young married woman, he goes to Mexico for a time. After his return he plans to study law in Omaha. One night Frank Shabata finds Emil and Marie together and in his jealous rage kills them.

Marie Shabata, a pretty Bohemian housewife, innocently flirtatious from childhood, always merry and teasing. Having eloped with Frank Shabata, she tries to make the best of a bad situation and endures as cheerfully and patiently as possible his jealous suspicions and wild outbreaks of rage. At first she refuses to acknowledge her true feelings for handsome young Emil Bergson, but circumstances bring them together until, one disastrous night, Frank Shabata finds the two in the orchard and shoots them.

Frank Shabata, a wildly jealous, badtempered man distrustful of his pretty young wife. After shooting Marie and Emil Bergson when he finds them together, he makes a futile effort to escape before surrendering to the authorities. Alexandra Bergson shows the true bigness and generosity of her nature after Frank has been sentenced to prison. Convinced that he had acted only as his rash and violent nature compelled him and that his punishment can serve no purpose for the dead, she visits him in the penitentiary at Lincoln and promises to do everything she can to get him pardoned.

Crazy Ivar, a Swedish hermit and horse doctor whom the uncharitable call crazy;

786

others believe him touched by the hand of God. He is wise in homely folklore concerning animals, birds, and crops, and Alexandra Bergson asks his advice on many farm matters. After he loses his land during a period of depression, she gives him a home. Behind his clouded mind he is a man of deep faith and shrewd wisdom.

Amédée Chevalier, a jolly, high-spirited young French farmer, Emil Bergson's best friend. He dies suddenly after an emergency operation for appendicitis.

Angélique Chevalier, his young wife, widowed after a year of marriage.

Annie Lee, the neighbor girl whom Lou Bergson marries. Like her husband, she is ashamed of old-fashioned European ways and apes American dress and customs.

Milly,
Stella, and
Sadie, the daughters of Lou and Annie Bergson.

Mrs. Lee, Annie Bergson's mother, a spry, wholesome old woman who holds nostalgically to the Old World ways her daughter and son-in-law dislike. Every winter she visits Alexandra Bergson, who allows the old woman to do as she pleases during her stay.

Signa, Alexandra Bergson's hired girl and friend.

Nelse Jensen, Signa's husband.

Barney Flinn, the foreman on Alexandra Bergson's farm.

OBLOMOV

Author: Ivan Alexandrovich Goncharov (1812-1891)
Time of action: Early nineteenth century
First published: 1858

PRINCIPAL CHARACTERS

Ilya Ilyitch Oblomov (ĭl·yä′ ĭl·yĭch′ ôb-lō′məf), a Russian landowner brought up to do nothing for himself. He, like his parents, only eats and sleeps. He barely graduates from college and cannot force himself to do any kind of work, feeling that work is too much trouble for a gentleman. His indolence results finally in his living in filth and being cheated consistently. Even love cannot stir him. Though he realizes his trouble and dubs it "Oblomovism," he can do nothing about it. Eventually his indolence kills him, as his doctors tell him it will.

Tarantyev (tä·rän′tĕf), the parasitical friend of Oblomov. He uses Oblomov's indolence to cheat the man, and by this means provides for himself at Oblomov's expense.

Andrey Stolz (än·drā′ stōlz), Oblomov's only true friend. His German father gave him a wealth of practical experience as a child, so that he was able to make himself wealthy and respected as a businessman. He tries to help Oblomov, straightening out his affairs several times, but neither his efforts nor his example does Oblomov any good.

Zahar (zä·khär′), Oblomov's valet. He imitates his master in indolence.

Olga Ilyinsky (ōl′y·gə ĭ·lyĭñ′skĭy), a vivacious, sensitive woman. She falls in love with Oblomov and he with her. She eventually discovers, however, that she is in love with the man Oblomov could be, not the man he is. Upon this discovery she bids him a permanent goodbye. Later she marries Stolz, who also loves her.

THE ODYSSEY

Author: Homer (c. Ninth century B.C.)
Time of action: The ten years following the Trojan War
First transcribed: Sixth century B.C.

PRINCIPAL CHARACTERS

Odysseus (ō·dĭ′sĭ·əs, ō·dĭs′ūs), far-roving veteran of the Trojan War who, having incurred the anger of Poseidon by blinding the sea god's son Polyphemus, a gigantic Cyclops, is fated to roam for ten years before he can return to his homeland of Ithaca. Leaving Troy, he and his followers sail first to Ismarus. In the sack of the Ciconian city Odysseus spares the life of Maro, priest of Apollo, who in turn gives the conqueror some jars of potent wine. Gales then drive the Greeks to the country of the Lotus-eaters, from which they sail to the land of the fierce Cyclopes. There Ulysses and twelve of his band are captured by Polyphemus. After Odysseus frees himself and his companions by a clever ruse, leaving the Cyclops maimed and blinded, the band journeys to the Isle of Aeolus. In the land of the Laestrygones man-eating giants destroy all but one of his ships and devour their crews. At Aeaea, Odysseus outwits the enchantress Circe and frees his men after she has turned them into swine. In the dark region of the Cimmerians he consults the shade of Tiresias, the Theban prophet, to learn what awaits him in Ithaca. Following the advice of Circe, Odysseus escapes the spell of the Sirens, passes safely between Scylla and Charybdis, and arrives at Thrinacia. There his remaining comrades are drowned for their impiety in eating cattle sacred to Hyperion. Cast adrift, Odysseus floats to the island of Ogygia, where for seven years he lives with the lovely nymph Calypso. Finally the gods take pity on him and order Calypso to release him. On a makeshift raft he continues his voyage. After his raft has been wrecked by Poseidon he battles the waves until he arrives, exhausted, on the island of Drepane. Here Nausicaä, daughter of the King of the Phaeacians, finds him and leads him to the royal palace. Warmly received by King Alcinous, Odysseus takes part in celebration games and tells the story of his adventures. Alcinous gives Odysseus rich gifts and returns the wanderer by ship to Ithaca. There, in disguise, he meets his son Telemachus, now grown to manhood, routs and kills the suitors who throng his palace, and is reunited with his loyal wife Penelope. Odysseus is the ideal Greek hero, eloquent at the council board, courageous in battle, resourceful in danger, crafty in wisdom. He is the darling of the goddess Athena, who aids him whenever it is in her power to do so.

Penelope (pĕ·nĕ′lō·pē), his devoted wife, a model of domestic fidelity, skilled in handicrafts. Still attractive in spite of twenty years of anxiety and grief during the absence of Odysseus, she is by custom forced to entertain importunate, insolent suitors whom she puts off from year to year by various stratagems. Until betrayed by her false servants, she would weave by day a burial robe for Laertes, her father-in-law, and at night she would unravel her work. The return of Odysseus is for her an occasion of great joy, but first she tests his knowledge of the construction of their wedding bed in order to avoid being duped by a plausible stranger. Although she is noteworthy for her forbearance and fidelity, there are occasions when she complains bitterly and laments her sad fate.

Telemachus (tə·lĕ′mə·kəs), the son of Odysseus and Penelope, grown to handsome young manhood during his father's absence. Also favored by Athena, he accuses the suitors of being parasites, journeys to other lands in search of news of his father, and returns to fight bravely by the side of Odysseus when the one hundred and twelve suitors of Penelope are routed and put to death. His comeliness, manly bearing, and good manners show him to be his father's son when he meets wise King Nestor and King Menelaus.

Athena (ə·thē′nə), also called **Pallas Athena**, the goddess of Wisdom and the patroness of arts and crafts. Moved by pity and admiration, she becomes the benefactress of Odysseus and pleads with Zeus, her father, to release the hero from the seven-year embrace of the nymph Calypso. Assuming various disguises and aiding him in many ways, she watches over the homeward journey and eventual triumph of Odysseus. Her divine intervention assures peace between him and the angry families of the slain suitors.

Poseidon (pō·sī′dən), the earth-shaking god of the Sea. The blinding of his giant son, the Cyclops Polyphemus, arouses his anger against Odysseus, and he prevents as long as possible the return of the hero to Ithaca.

Laertes (lā·ûr′tēz), the aged father of Odysseus. Withdrawn from the royal palace, he tends his vineyards and herds during his son's absence. Still vigorous, he helps Odysseus and Telemachus repulse a band of angry citizens in their attempt to avenge the death of the suitors.

Eumaeus (ū·mē′əs), the devoted swineherd in whose hut disguised Odysseus takes refuge on his return to Ithaca. Despising the suitors, he fights bravely against them alongside Odysseus, Telemachus, and Philoetius, the neatherd. Though of lowly occupation, he is of noble birth, and he is both slave and devoted friend to Odysseus.

Philoetius (fĭ·lē′tĭ·əs), the neatherd and a trusted servant in the household of Odysseus. Forced to provide cattle for the feasts of the suitors, he resents their presence in his master's hall, and he yearns for the return of the absent hero. In the great battle in which the suitors are killed, he fights bravely by the side of Odysseus, Telemachus, and Eumaeus.

Eurycleia (ū·rĭ·klē′ə), the aged nurse of both Odysseus and Telemachus. She recognizes her master by a scar on his thigh and reveals to him his faithless servants who have consorted with the suitors during his absence. Taken as a bondservant by Odysseus' father, she is loyal to the royal household and most vindictive in her revenge.

Polyphemus (pŏ·lĭ·fē′məs), one of the Cyclopes, giants with one eye in the center of the forehead, and the sons of Poseidon. When Odysseus and twelve of his companions seek hospitality in his cave, the monster makes prisoners of the band and eats six of them. Wily Odysseus saves himself and his remaining companions by giving Polyphemus some of Maro's strong wine to drink and then, while the Cyclops is asleep, putting out his eye with a heated, pointed shaft. The Greeks escape from the cave by hiding beneath the bodies of Polyphemus' sheep when the giant turns his flock out to pasture.

Circe (sėr′sē), an enchantress, the daughter of Helius and Perse. Arriving at Aeaea, Odysseus sends Eurylochus, his lieutenant, and twenty-two men ashore to explore the island. When they come to Circe's palace she invites them to feast with her. But Eurylochus, almost as crafty as his master, remains outside, and through a window he sees the sorceress serve the men drugged food and then transform them into swine. Odysseus, on his way to rescue his companions, encounters the god Hermes, who gives him a flower named moly as a charm against the powers of the enchantress. Her power destroyed by the magic herb, Circe frees her captives from her magic spell and entertains Odysseus and his companions for a year. At the end of that time Odysseus wishes to leave Circe's bed and continue his journey. Though reluctant, she consents to his going, but first she advises him to consult the shade of Tiresias in order to learn what the future holds for the wanderers.

Eurylochus (ū·rĭ′lə·kəs), the lieutenant of Odysseus. He reports to Odysseus that the enchantress Circe has turned half of his band into swine. It is at his suggestion that the Greeks kill some of Hyperion's sacred cattle and eat them while Odysseus is sleeping. To punish their act of impiety, Zeus causes the Greek ship to founder and all but Odysseus are drowned.

Tiresias (tə·rē′sĭ·əs), the prophet of Thebes. In the land of the Cimmerians, acting on the advice of Circe, Odysseus summons the aged seer's shade from the dead. Tiresias tells him not to harm the sacred cattle of Hyperion; otherwise Odysseus will encounter many difficulties and delays on his homeward journey, he will find trouble in the royal house when he arrives there, he will be forced to make a journey into a land so far from the sea that its people will mistake an oar for a winnowing fan, he will be forced to make a rich sacrifice to Poseidon in that distant land, and in his old age he will meet death coming to him out of the sea.

Calypso (kə·lĭp′sō), the divine nymph who lives on the island of Ogygia, where Odysseus is washed ashore after his ship has foundered and his companions have drowned. For seven years he lives as her bondman and husband, until Zeus sends Hermes to her with the message that Odysseus is to be released to return to his own land. Although she wishes him to stay with her and offers him immortality and youth in return, she yields to Odysseus' own wishes and the divine command of Zeus. She teaches Odysseus how to build a raft and allows him to set sail before a favorable breeze.

Nausicaä (nô·sĭ′kĭ·ə), the maiden daughter of King Alcinous and Queen Arete. Finding Odysseus on the seashore, where he sleeps exhausted by buffeting waves after Poseidon has destroyed his raft, she befriends the hero and conducts him to her father's palace. There Odysseus tells the story of his adventures and hardships to an admiring, pitying, audience. Moved by the wanderer's plight, King Alcinous gives him rich gifts and returns him to Ithaca in a Phaeacian ship.

Alcinous (ăl·sĭ′nō·əs), King of the Phaeacians. He entertains Odysseus after the hero has been washed ashore on the island of Drepane, and he returns his guest to Ithaca in one of the royal ships.

Arete (â·rē′tē), the wife of Alcinous. She is famous for her kindness, generosity, and wisdom.

Nestor (nĕs′tẽr), the wise King of Pylos. Telemachus, seeking to rid the royal palace of his mother's insolent suitors, journeys to Nestor's country in search of his father Odysseus.

Peisistratus (pī·sĭs′trə·təs), the noble youngest son of King Nestor. A skilled charioteer, he accompanies Telemachus when the son of Odysseus travels to Sparta in an effort to get word of his father from King Menelaus and Helen, his Queen.

Menelaus (mĕ·nə·lā′əs), King of Sparta. Menelaus receives Telemachus hospitably and entertains him lavishly, but he has no information that will help the young man in his search for his father.

Helen (hĕ′lən), the wife of Menelaus and the cause of the war with Troy. Older but still beautiful, she presides over her husband's palace with queenly dignity. When Telemachus takes leave of the royal pair, she gives him a rich robe for his bride to wear on his wedding day.

790

Antinous (ăn·tǐ'nō·əs), the leader of the suitors for the hand of Penelope. Insolent and obstreperous, he leads more gullible young men to their corruption and destruction. He mocks Telemachus, berates Penelope, and tauntingly insults Odysseus disguised as a beggar. Because of his arrogance he is the first of the suitors to die.

Eurymachus (ū·rǐ'mə·kəs), the most treacherous of the suitors. Fairseeming in speech but cunning in his design to destroy Telemachus and marry Penelope, he deserves his death at the hands of Odysseus.

Noëmon (nō·ē'mən), one of the most generous and least offensive of the suitors. He lends Telemachus his own ship in which to sail to Pylos.

Theoclymenus (thē·ə·klǐ'mə·nəs), a young warrior who has fled from Argos after killing a kinsman. As Telemachus is about to set sail from Pylos, the fugitive asks to be taken aboard the vessel in order to escape the wrath of the dead man's brothers. Telemachus takes the stranger back to Ithaca and gives him shelter. At a feast in the palace Theoclymenus foretells the destruction of the suitors.

Peiraeus (pī·rē'əs), the loyal and gallant friend of Telemachus. He goes with the son of Odysseus to Pylos.

Mentor (měn'tər), one of the elders of Ithaca, wise in counsel. Athene assumes his form on several occasions.

Melanthius (mē·lăn'thǐ·əs), the treacherous goatherd who taunts disguised Odysseus and later tries to aid the suitors. On orders from Odysseus, he is hanged by Eumaeus and Philoetius and later dismembered.

Melantho (mē·lăn'thō), Penelope's faithless maid, the mistress of Eurymachus.

Medon (mē'dən), the herald. Because of his kindness to young Telemachus, his life is spared when the other suitors are killed.

Phemius (fē'mǐ·əs), the unwilling bard of the suitors. Telemachus asks that his life be spared and Odysseus grants him mercy.

Eurynome (ū·rǐ'nō·mē), the housekeeper of the royal palace in Ithaca.

Maro (mă'rō), the priest of Apollo whose life is spared when the Greeks raid the Ciconian city of Ismarus. In gratitude he gives Odysseus the wine with which the hero makes the Cyclops drunk.

Elpenor (ĕl·pē'nôr), one of Odysseus' companions whom Circe transformed into swine and then restored to human form. He climbs upon the roof of her palace and, dazed by wine, falls to his death. Appearing among the shades in the land of the Cimmerians, he begs Odysseus to give him proper burial.

Haliserthes (hăl·ǐ·sěr'thēz), an elder of Ithaca able to interpret the flight of birds. Seeing two eagles fighting in midair, he predicts that Odysseus will return and rend the unruly suitors like a bird of prey.

Irus (ī'rŭs), the nickname of **Arnaeus,** a greedy vagabond whom disguised Odysseus strikes down with a single blow when the two men fight, urged on by the amused suitors, to decide who will be allowed to beg in the palace.

Hermes (hûr'mēz), the messenger of the gods. He gives Odysseus the herb moly to protect him against Circe's spell and brings to the nymph Calypso Zeus' command that the hero be allowed to return to his own country.

Zeus (zōōs), the ruler of the Olympian deities and the father of Athena.

OEDIPUS AT COLONUS

Author: Sophocles (c. 496-c. 406 B.C.)
Time of action: Remote antiquity
First presented: 401 B.C.

PRINCIPAL CHARACTERS

Oedipus (ĕd′ə·pəs, ē′də·pəs), the former King of Thebes, now a wanderer, blind and in rags, because he had been fated unwittingly to murder his father and marry his mother. "Oedipus Tyrannus" is Sophocles' version of Oedipus' discovery of these horrible crimes. After the suicide of his wife and mother, Jocasta, Oedipus, who had blinded himself in the moment of anguish which came with his full realization of who he was and what he had done, had lived for a time quietly in Thebes until his banishment by the regent Creon, his brother-in-law, with the acquiesence of his sons, Polynices and Eteocles. During his years of wandering he has endured hardship and pain, but from them he has gained spiritual authority and strength; he is aware that his special suffering has conferred upon him a special grace and that, although he is an object of pollution while alive, his dead body will confer divine benefits on the land in which it lies. Although changes have occurred, his personality basically is the same as that portrayed in "Oedipus Tyrannus": he is still intelligent, courageous, and irascible, but to these characteristics has been added a new dimension of strength and knowledge. Through the horrible afflictions that the gods have visited upon him, he has become as nearly godlike as a man can be.

Antigone (ăn·tĭg′ə·nē), Oedipus' elder daughter, her father's guide since childhood. Although passionately devoted to him, she also is capable of love for Polynices, her brother, who wronged both her father and her. After the death of Oedipus she returns to Thebes to try to mend the breach between Polynices and Eteocles, her other brother.

Ismene (is·mē′nē), Oedipus' younger daughter. Searching for her father and sister, she overtakes them at Colonus. She brings Oedipus word that the Oracle of Delphi has predicted that in the struggle between his sons for the mastery of Thebes the victory will go to Eteocles if the body of Oedipus rests in Theban soil, to Polynices if the blind, aged exile is buried in Attica. More pious than Antigone, Ismene shares her sister's courage and devotion.

Creon (krē′ŏn), Oedipus' brother-in-law and regent of Thebes during the minority of the sons of Oedipus. Because the presence of Oedipus will insure victory for the Theban forces over the army of Polynices, Creon attempts to persuade Oedipus to return to his native city. Failing, he tries to take Antigone and Ismene by force but is thwarted by Theseus. Creon is articulate and clever, but these virtues are subordinate to his own self-interest.

Theseus (thē′sōōs, thē′sĭ·əs), King of Athens and protector of Oedipus, for whom he feels a deep sympathy and by whom he is convinced that Athens will prosper in a future war against Thebes if Oedipus' body is buried in Athenian soil. He is a man of high integrity, religious yet practical, honorable yet outspoken.

Polynices (pŏl′ə·nī′sēz), the elder son of Oedipus (although Aeschylus and Euripides make him the younger). Exiled after conflict with Eteocles, his brother, he has raised an army in Argos to regain his former place in Thebes. Like Creon, he wants Oedipus for the divine sanction the deposed King will give to his cause.

792

He recognizes and admits his guilt for the wrongs he has done his father, but his penitence comes too late; and Oedipus, in cursing him, predicts that he and Eteocles will fall by each other's hand. He is sympathetically presented, but it is clear that he is not acting out of a desire to be reconciled with Oedipus, but a desire to recapture the throne of Thebes.

A Chorus of Elders of Colonus. The songs of the chorus contain some of the best of Sophocles' poetry, including the famous ode in praise of Colonus and Attica.

OEDIPUS TYRANNUS

Author: Sophocles (c. 496-c. 406 B.C.)
Time of action: Remote antiquity
First presented: c. 429 B.C.

PRINCIPAL CHARACTERS

Oedipus (ĕd'ə·pəs, ē'də·pəs), King of Thebes. A foundling, he had been reared by Polybus and Merope, King and Queen of Corinth. In that city he had enjoyed a place of honor until a drunken Corinthian at a banquet accused him of being a bastard. To settle the matter, he went to the oracle at Pytho, who revealed that he was destined to lie with his mother and murder his father. To avoid this curse, he fled Corinth. During his travels he was thrust out of the road by an old man in a carriage. Angered, Oedipus returned the old man's blow and killed him. Later he overcame the Sphinx by answering a riddle which the monster put to all whom it encountered, killing those who could not solve it. As a reward Oedipus was made King of Thebes and given the hand of Queen Jocasta, whose former husband, King Laius, was believed killed in an encounter with highway robbers. When the action of the play begins, Oedipus has ruled well for many years, but a plague of unknown origin has recently fallen upon the city. His subjects appeal to him as one especially favored by the gods to help them, but Oedipus is powerless to do so. He is essentially a good man, courageous, intelligent, and responsible, but he is also short-tempered, tragically weak in judgment, and proud of his position and past achievements, for which he gives the gods little credit. As the action progresses and the question of his responsibility for the plague is raised, he becomes obsessed with finding out who he is, regardless of repeated warnings that knowledge of his identity will bring disaster on himself and on those whom he loves.

Jocasta (jō·kăs'tə), wife of Oedipus and mother of his sons, Eteocles and Polynices, and his daughters, Antigone and Ismene. She, too, has a sense of the responsibilities of her position and is deeply concerned with the welfare of her husband. As bits of information relating to his identity are revealed, her sense of foreboding grows; and when the truth finally becomes apparent to her, she hangs herself, overwhelmed by the enormities she has unwittingly committed.

Creon (krē'ŏn), Jocasta's brother and a powerful Theban noble. Sent by Oedipus to ask the Delphic Oracle what can be done to save the city from the plague, he returns with word that it will be raised when the city no longer harbors the murderer of King Laius, Jocasta's former husband. When it later appears that Oedipus may be the murderer, the King violently accuses his brother-in-law of treacherously seeking the throne; but Creon defends himself as reasonably as he can until Jocasta calms her husband.

793

Creon is presented as a calm, pious man, with a less tyrannical view of kingship than that of Oedipus.

Tiresias (tī·rē′sĭ·əs), a blind prophet who alone knows what Oedipus' fate has been and will be. Oedipus consults him in an effort to find the murderer of King Laius and loses his patience when the old man at first refuses to answer. Becoming angry in turn, Tiresias reveals that Oedipus' seeming good fortune in vanquishing the Sphinx has actually caused him unknowingly to commit incest with his mother and to bring pollution upon Thebes. Furious, Oedipus sends the blind seer away.

The First Messenger, an old man who comes from Corinth with word that Polybus and Merope are dead and that the people of that city want Oedipus to return as their king. This information, under the circumstances, is received joyfully by Oedipus, for if his parents have died naturally, the Oracle's prediction that he is doomed to murder his father has been proved false. But the messenger goes on to say that Polybus and Merope were in reality Oedipus' foster parents; he himself had received the infant Oedipus from a Theban shepherd and given him to them.

A Herdsman, an old Theban who has voluntarily exiled himself from his native city. He is forced by Oedipus to confess that years before he had been ordered to expose the infant son of King Laius and Jocasta, but, pitying the child, he had given him to a Corinthian. He also had been the one survivor when King Laius was killed by a young man after a quarrel on the road. His information thus makes the web of evidence complete; Oedipus now knows that the old man whom he killed was Laius, his father, and that his wife Jocasta is also his mother.

The Second Messenger, a Theban who reports the immediate results of the shepherd's revelation: Jocasta has hanged herself and Oedipus blinded himself with the brooches which fastened his robe.

A Chorus of Theban Elders.

OF HUMAN BONDAGE

Author: W. Somerset Maugham (1874-   )
Time of action: Early twentieth century
First published: 1915

PRINCIPAL CHARACTERS

Philip Carey, a club-footed orphan boy reared by relatives under very strict and pietistic conditions. The result of this rearing, and of his physical handicap as well, is a very retiring and idealistic boy who has ahead of him a long battle to overcome the inhibitions with which his aunt and uncle have saddled him and the lack of physical confidence that comes from his bodily defect. To find his place in life, he tries many professions: clerk, medical student, art student—the list is quite long. He also listens eagerly to somewhat older friends who, supposedly, can tell him what life means. Through them, he learns that art and literature, morals and religion, are relative to the observer; and even the great truths of philosophers suffer similar limitations. Philip's emotional education is the work of several women, chief among them Mildred Rogers and Sally Athelney. Life with Sally and medical practice in a small English town finally make up Philip's "figure in the carpet" which, according to a friend, each person must discover for himself.

William Carey, Philip's uncle, an Anglican clergyman. Poorly equipped to have the rearing of a child, he is represented as fairly ignorant, thoroughly selfish, and completely hypocritical.

Louisa Carey, William's wife and Philip's aunt, a timid woman who fears to reveal to Philip how much she cares for him. An inheritance from her gives Philip needed funds at one point in his life.

Miss Wilkinson, a friend of the Careys, a governess on holiday from her winter post in Germany. It is she who initiates Philip into the life of love, but Philip soon finds her distasteful and has no more to do with her.

G. Etheredge Hayward, Philip's friend for many years. Philip first meets Hayward in Germany and constantly draws on Hayward's wider knowledge for ideas about life and books. He finally comes to see Hayward as a hollow man.

Fanny Price, an older art student of Philip's Paris years. She does more than guide Philip's artistic education; her suicide reveals to him the pain of her hopeless love for him, as well as the cruelty of love in general. Philip accepts as axiomatic the idea that in love there is always someone who loves and someone who lets himself be loved.

Cronshaw, a Parisian friend and a poet. It is he who reveals to Philip "the figure in the carpet": that is, the truth that each person much make out his own pattern in the carpet which life spreads before him.

Mildred Rogers, a waitress in a London teashop. Philip meets her during his early days as a medical student and from then on, Mildred exercises a monstrous power over him. Although she is vain and ignorant and mildly ugly, he is utterly unable to resist the power of her whims or requests. She drains him of money, comes back to him when her own love affairs go badly, and senselessly ruins many of his possessions in a mad fury.

Norah Nesbit, a divorcée. A hack writer, a little older than Philip, she instructs him in taste and loves him truly. As usual, when Philip is loved, he cannot love in return.

Harry Griffiths, a handsome friend of Philip who takes Mildred away from him for a time.

Thorpe Athelney, a patient and an older friend of Philip. The humility and the wisdom of the man, his acceptance of a low place in life, and the routine pleasures of his family are what finally reveal to Philip his share of wisdom and deliver him from the bondage of false hopes and desires.

Sally Athelney, Thorpe's daughter. The young girl first becomes Philip's mistress and then his wife. She is a simple creature and can give none of the excitement provided by Mildred or the understanding that came from Norah. But she gives Philip what no other woman offered him: calm and peace.

OF MICE AND MEN

Author: John Steinbeck (1902-   )
Time of action: Twentieth century
First published: 1937

PRINCIPAL CHARACTERS

Lennie Small, a simple-minded man of great size and strength. His dream is to have a chicken and rabbit farm with his friend George Milton, and to be allowed to feed the rabbits. George tells him about the farm over and over and keeps Lennie in line by threatening not to let him feed the rabbits. The two men are hired to buck barley on a ranch. Lennie crushes the hand of the owner's son, kills a puppy while stroking it, and breaks a woman's neck, all unintentionally.

George Milton, Lennie's friend, a small and wiry man. He assumes responsibility for his simple friend and in the new job does the talking for both. At last, after the unintentional killing by Lennie, George knows that he can no longer save his friend and, after telling him once again of their plan for the farm, he shoots him.

Candy, a swamper on the barley ranch. He makes George's and Lennie's dream seem possible, for he has three hundred and fifty dollars and wants to join them.

Curley, the son of the ranch owner. Vain of his ability as a prizefighter and jealous of his slatternly bride, he provokes Lennie into squeezing his hand. Pleased that Curley's hand has been broken, his wife comes to make advances to Lennie, who accidentally kills her.

Slim, the jerkline skinner on the ranch. He gives Lennie the puppy and persuades Curley to say his hand was caught in a machine.

Crooks, the colored stable hand. Cool to Lennie at first, he is disarmed by Lennie's innocence.

OF TIME AND THE RIVER

Author: Thomas Wolfe (1900-1938)
Time of action: The 1920's
First published: 1935

PRINCIPAL CHARACTERS

Eugene Gant, a young Southerner, just graduated from the State University and on his way to Harvard for advanced study. He is eager to leave the drab world of his childhood: his jealous family, the dreary boarding house run by his mother. But he finds Harvard disappointing, the famous drama class of Professor Hatcher disillusioning, for the students are intellectual frauds. In Boston he meets his eccentric uncle, Bascom Pentland, and has a brief love affair with a commonplace girl. He finds one good friend, however, in Francis Starwick, Hatcher's assistant. Starwick's sophistication fascinates Eugene, yet it somehow seems unreal. After a winter at Harvard and a summer of hoping that his play will be produced, Eugene goes to New York as instructor in a city university. There he renews his friendship with Robert Weaver from his home town and with Joel Pierce from Harvard. Weaver, with his drunkenness, causes only trouble; Pierce, with his vast wealth, is fascinating but disillusioning. During his vacation Eugene goes first to England, which he detests, and then to Paris, where he meets Starwick, who is with two young Boston women, Elinor, a divorcée, and Ann, an unmarried girl. After a drunken summer in Paris Eugene realizes the tragic situation: that he loves Ann but that she loves Starwick, and that Starwick has become a homosexual. Breaking away from the doomed trio, Eugene goes to Orléans. After a fantastic experience with two French noblewomen, he returns to America. On the ship he sees a woman named Esther and knows that she is to be his fate.

Oliver Gant, Eugene's father, who dies of cancer. Although his drunken profligacy has made the family life a nightmare, his death makes his children realize what a remarkable man he was.

Eliza Gant, Eugene's mother. Tenacious

in her acquisition of property, infinitely stubborn, lost in her web of recollection, she has become a powerful woman.

Francis Starwick, assistant to Professor Hatcher of Harvard. Mannered and pretentious yet intelligent, he seems to Eugene the acme of sophistication. He is loved by Ann, but her love is wasted, for he is homosexual.

Bascom Pentland, Eugene's eccentric uncle, living in Boston.

Joel Pierce, a member of an immensely rich family. He introduces Eugene to the world of great wealth, which fascinates yet repels him.

Robert Weaver, a young man from Eugene's home town. Joining Eugene in New York, he becomes a nuisance because of his drunkenness.

Abe Jones, a Jewish student in Eugene's class in New York. He shows Eugene the hard, bitter world of the lower-class New York Jews.

The Countess de Caux, a slightly mad Frenchwoman whom Eugene meets in Orléans. She is interested in using him for her own financial advantage.

The Marquise de Mornay, to whom the Countess de Caux introduces Eugene on the pretext that he is a well-known journalist. Although the Marquise is a great lady, it develops that she has permitted the introduction for the purpose of getting Eugene to raise money in America for a hospital in France.

Elinor, a slightly older woman from Boston, where she has left her husband and child. Knowing that she has ruined herself forever at home, she joins Eugene and Starwick during their drunken vacation in Paris. She is the leader of the group, domineering and essentially cruel.

Ann, an unmarried Boston girl accompanying Elinor. Eugene falls in love with her, to find that she loves Starwick, whose homosexuality makes that love impossible.

Esther [Jack], a lovely Jewess with "dove's eyes" whom Eugene sees as he is boarding the ship to return to America. He knows that she is to become the "target of his life."

THE OLD AND THE YOUNG

Author: Luigi Pirandello (1867-1936)
Time of action: 1891-1892
First published: 1913

PRINCIPAL CHARACTERS

Flaminio Salvo, a mine owner and capitalist who backs the clerical party candidate in an election for a representative to the Italian Chamber of Deputies. When the workers in his Sicilian mines go on strike, he shuts down the mines in an effort to starve them out.

Dianella Salvo, Salvo's daughter, who is in love with Salvo's mine superintendent, Aurelio Costa. Salvo refuses to permit their marriage because Costa has no money. When Costa is murdered by a mob, Dianella goes mad and has to be locked up.

Mauro Mortara, one of Garibaldi's followers, who is now an old man. He cannot understand why his old comrades must fight among themselves or why, after his generation fought for peace and freedom, there still seems to be none. He is shot by troops firing on a crowd.

Prince Ippolito Laurentano, an old Garibaldist leader to whom Salvo is trying to marry his sister. He is still very much a royalist and loyal to the Church. He lives in a world of his own on his estate in Sicily.

Prince Gerlando Laurentano, Ippolito Laurentano's son and a Socialist organizer. His position as a Socialist is embarrassing and incomprehensible to his family's friends. He is horrified by the conditions among the strikers in Salvo's mines.

Capolino, the clerical party candidate whom Salvo is backing in the election.

Roberto Auriti, the man against whom Capolino is running in the election. Au-

riti is wrongly imprisoned for the misappropriation of government funds. He is Gerlando Laurentano's cousin.

Aurelio Costa, Salvo's mine superintendent, whom Dianella loves. When Costa learns that he cannot marry Dianella, he returns to the mines in order to join with the strikers; but he is killed by the mob before he can explain why he is there.

Nicoletta Capolino, Capolino's wife, who attaches herself to the man who really misappropriated the government funds.

Corrado Selmi, the man who actually misappropriated the funds, the act for which Auriti is imprisoned.

THE OLD BACHELOR

Author: William Congreve (1670-1729)
Time of action: Seventeenth century
First presented: 1693

PRINCIPAL CHARACTERS

Sir Joseph Wittol, a foolish country knight. He falls in love with Araminta upon first seeing her and is fooled for a time into thinking she intends to marry him.

Ned Bellmour, a gallant young bachelor in love with Belinda. Disguised as a Puritan preacher, he visits Fondlewife's spouse and has a merry time as a lark. True to his friends, he saves Heartwell from a disastrous marriage with Silvia, a prostitute. Though he is a little wild, he is a good young man, and so Belinda plans to marry him.

Sharper, Bellmour's unscrupulous friend.

Captain Bluffe, a supposed veteran of the British Army. While his boasting and swaggering endear him to Wittol, he proves to be an arrant coward. He tries to bribe Setter to act as pander to bring him and Araminta together.

Belinda, a fashionable, wealthy young

woman of great beauty. She loves and is loved by Bellmour.

Araminta, Belinda's cousin. She and Vainlove are in love and plan to marry.

Vainlove, Bellmour's friend. He loves Araminta, who forgives his romantic escapades and plans to marry him.

Gavot, Araminta's singing teacher.

Silvia, a prostitute, Vainlove's discarded mistress. She tries to break up the romance between Vainlove and Araminta and to trick Heartwell into a marriage with herself.

Lucy, Silvia's maid.

Heartwell, a surly old bachelor and woman-hater. He is almost tricked into marrying Silvia, not knowing she is a prostitute.

Setter, Vainlove's manservant.

Fondlewife, a banker and an ancient, dot-

798

ing husband. He catches his young wife with Bellmour.

Laetitia, Fondlewife's spouse. She entertains Bellmour handsomely, thinking her husband is away on business. When he catches them together, Laetitia, weeping, persuades Fondlewife that she is innocent.

THE OLD CURIOSITY SHOP

Author: Charles Dickens (1812-1870)
Time of action: Early nineteenth century
First published: 1840-1841

PRINCIPAL CHARACTERS

Nell Trent, called **Little Nell,** a sweet, delicate child, brave and wise beyond her years. An orphan, she lives with her aged Grandfather, the keeper of the Old Curiosity Shop, who has developed a passion for gambling because of his desire to provide for Little Nell's future. After the old man, heavily in debt, loses the last of his property, he and his granddaughter are turned into the streets. She and the half-crazed old man take to the roads and encounter many adventures during their wanderings. At every opportunity her Grandfather continues to gamble away whatever funds he may have. They suffer many privations before they fall in with a kindly schoolmaster, Mr. Marton, who accompanies them to the village where he has been appointed teacher and clerk. There Little Nell and her Grandfather settle down to a quiet life, but their happiness is brief. Hardship and exposure have undermined Little Nell's delicate constitution. She fades away slowly and uncomplainingly, worn out by her difficult life, and dies soon afterward.

Little Nell's Grandfather, the proprietor of the Old Curiosity Shop, the only means he has of providing for himself and his orphan granddaughter. Troubled because he has no other way to provide for her future, he resorts to gambling in an effort to make his fortune. Losing steadily, he develops a passion for the excitement of gambling. In the end, unable to repay money he has borrowed from Daniel Quilp, a wealthy dwarf and usurer, he is completely beggared. He and Little Nell leave London and wander through the country. On the way they suffer hardships and hunger until they are befriended by Mr. Marton, a schoolmaster, who finds work for them in the village where he is a teacher. The Grandfather is unable to endure the sorrow of Little Nell's slow decline and death; he dies on her grave and is buried by her side.

Christopher Nubbles, called **Kit,** an awkward but generous-hearted and sturdy boy, devoted to Little Nell, whom her Grandfather employs to run errands. Becoming convinced that Kit has revealed the secret of the old man's gambling habits, the Grandfather turns the boy away from the curiosity shop. Kit aids the Single Gentleman in his efforts to locate Little Nell and her Grandfather after the two disappear from London, but nothing comes of their first search. Meanwhile Kit has been befriended by Mr. Garland, in whose house he lives. When, through the machinations of Daniel Quilp, Sampson Brass accuses the boy of theft, he is able to prove his innocence with the aid of Mr. Garland and Dick Swiveller. He marries Barbara, Mrs. Garland's pretty housemaid.

Daniel Quilp, the frightening, half-mad dwarf from whom Little Nell's Grandfather borrows in order to gamble. Quilp, married to a brow-beaten wife, lends the old man money in order to obtain a hold on him, for Quilp hopes to marry Little Nell at some future date. Ferocious, sinister, vindictive, he torments his wife, Little Nell, her Grandfather, and Kit Nubbles. He drowns while attempting to escape from the police, who are about to arrest him for crimes he has committed.

Mrs. Betsey Quilp, his long-suffering wife, who is tortured mentally and physically by her misshapen, cruel husband and made to obey his every wish, even to spying on Little Nell. She inherits her husband's property after his death. When she marries again, her second husband is the opposite of Quilp in every way.

Frederick Trent, Little Nell's profligate brother. Hating his Grandfather, he schemes to have his crony, Dick Swiveller, marry Little Nell so that they may obtain the fortune which they believe the old man has hidden away for his granddaughter.

Richard Swiveller, called **Dick,** Frederick Trent's conniving friend, who is turned by his love for a servant girl into a decent person. Quilp, who hopes to use the young rascal in tracing Little Nell and her Grandfather, secures him a position as clerk to Sampson Brass, the dwarf's attorney; but when Kit Nubbles is arrested and charged with theft on the false testimony of Brass, Dick is instrumental in proving the boy's innocence. Discharged, he is nursed during an illness by the Marchioness, the Brasses' slavey, who runs away from home in order to care for him. When he inherits a small annuity, he renames the girl Sophronia Sphynx and sends her to school, where he pays for her education for the next six years. On one of his visits to the school, when the Marchioness is nineteen, the idea comes to him that the next step in their relationship ought to be marriage. He proposes and is accepted.

The Marchioness (Sophronia Sphynx), a poor, frightened servant to the Brass family. She sleeps in the basement and must steal food to keep herself alive; Swiveller, pitying the girl, sometimes plays cards with her. She repays his kindness by nursing him while he is ill. Through listening at the keyhole when the Brasses are planning to accuse Kit Nubbles of robbery, she is able to help in saving him from prison. Sent to school to be educated by Swiveller, she eventually marries him.

Sampson Brass, a dishonest lawyer who is Daniel Quilp's adviser in legal matters. He accuses Kit Nubbles of stealing a five-pound note from his desk. Deeply involved in Quilp's villainy, he is arrested and sent to prison.

Sally Brass, the formidable spinster sister of Sampson Brass. An intelligent student of the law, she overshadows her brother in sharpness and cunning. She mistreats and starves her servant, whom Dick Swiveller calls the Marchioness.

The Single Gentleman, a lodger in the house of Sampson Brass. Though always gentlemanly in his behavior, he is quiet and mysterious in his comings and goings. He tries in various ways to trace Little Nell and her Grandfather. Shortly after the death of Little Nell he arrives in the village where they have taken refuge. He turns out to be the Grandfather's younger brother, absent from England for many years. In the end he is revealed also as Master Humphrey, the teller of the story.

Mrs. Jiniwin, Mrs. Quilp's fat mother. Though she is a shrew, she is no match for her son-in-law. She divides her days between reproaching her daughter for having married such a creature and fighting verbal battles with the dwarf.

Miss Sophy Wackles, a girl with whom Dick Swiveller at one time imagines himself in love. She marries a grocer, much to Dick's disgust.

Mrs. Wackles, the headmistress of a

day school for young ladies and Sophy's mother. She encourages her daughter to marry the grocer.

Jane and
Melissa Wackles, Sophy's sisters.

Mr. Cheggs, the grocer whom Sophy marries. A conforming man, he is not nearly so lively as Dick Swiveller.

Miss Cheggs, the sister of Mr. Cheggs and a good friend of Sophy.

Mrs. Nubbles, Kit's mother, a sweet, emotional widow. When her son is imprisoned, she comes faithfully with her two other children to bring him food. Later she goes with Mr. Garland and the Single Gentleman to help find Little Nell and her Grandfather.

Little Jacob, the younger brother of Kit Nubbles.

The Baby, Kit's youngest brother.

Mrs. Jarley, the fat, good-humored proprietress of Jarley's celebrated Wax Work. Occasionally she is known to sip at a strange bottle, but she remains a steady person in her business. She befriends Little Nell and her Grandfather, and the two travel with the show caravan for a time, Little Nell having been hired to explain the exhibits and her Grandfather to dust the wax figures.

Miss Monflathers, the head of a young ladies' boarding school who chastises Little Nell when she comes to the school bearing advertisements for the wax works exhibits. She is a typical Victorian boarding-school headmistress, arrogant, self-centered, and cruel.

Two Teachers, toadying assistants to Miss Monflathers. Each tries to outdo the other in being agreeable to their officious employer.

Miss Edwards, a charity pupil at the boarding school. When she takes pity on Little Nell, Miss Monflathers reviles her in front of her schoolmates. Later Nell follows Miss Edwards when she and her sister take a walk through the town. Their relationship and closeness make Little Nell long to have someone of her own age for a friend.

Mr. Martin, a kind schoolmaster who befriends Little Nell and her Grandfather early in their travels. He encounters them again later on, takes them to the village where he teaches, and procures a house for them to live in. He is gentle and intelligent, and his pupils adore him.

Harry, a dying young schoolboy, Mr. Martin's favorite pupil. He loves the schoolmaster and revives long enough to bid him goodbye.

Dame West, Harry's grandmother.

Mr. Garland and
Mrs. Garland, an elderly, kind couple who take Kit Nubbles into their home. He is the only one capable of handling their temperamental pony. They help in the search for Little Nell and her Grandfather.

Abel Garland, their son. He becomes a partner of Mr. Witherden, a notary.

Mr. Witherden and
Mr. Chuckster, the lawyers who assist the Single Gentleman in his quest for Little Nell and the capture of Quilp. They are proper and industrious gentlemen.

Barbara, the Garland's servant girl. In love with Kit, she remains loyal when he is accused of robbery and eventually marries him.

Mr. Slum, a military gentleman and Mrs. Jarley's friend, much given to composing bad poetry. Mrs. Jarley advertises her wax work with his poems.

Jem Groves, the proprietor of the Valiant Soldier, a pub where Little Nell and her Grandfather take shelter during a rain storm. He is friendly but crooked in the card game in which the Grandfather takes a hand.

Matt and Isaac List, card players at the Valiant Soldier. The Grandfather loses all of Little Nell's money while playing with them.

The Old Sexton, in charge of the old village church which Little Nell often visits before her death.

Old Davy, the deaf, aged gravedigger, the sexton's good friend.

Tom Codlin, the grouchy partner of a shabby Punch and Judy show. Little Nell and her Grandfather travel with the show for a time.

Mr. Harris, usually called Short Trotters, the pleasant partner in the Punch and Judy show.

Mr. Grinder, a fellow showman whom Little Nell meets in her travels with the Punch and Judy troupe.

Jerry, the master of the dancing dogs in the carnival group.

Mr. Vuffin, the manager of a giant and a woman without legs or arms.

Sweet William, a card trickster and conjurer.

Joe Jowl, a scoundrel who tries to persuade Little Nell's Grandfather to rob Mrs. Jarley.

Tom Scott, Daniel Quilp's young servant. Beaten and abused by his master, he forgets his troubles by standing on his head. After Quilp's death he becomes a professional tumbler.

The Bachelor, a benevolent old gentleman in a village where Little Nell and her Grandfather finally find a home. No one remembers his name, if he ever told it. He tutors Little Nell in village lore.

OLD FORTUNATUS

Author: Thomas Dekker (c. 1572-1632?)
Time of action: Tenth century
First presented: 1599

PRINCIPAL CHARACTERS

Fortunatus, a shabby, miserable man who becomes for a time Fortune's darling. He gains from her a magic purse which is never empty when he wishes to draw out money, and he steals for himself a wishing hat owned by the Soldan of Babylon, whose greed for the purse makes him careless. Fortunatus lives to regret his choice of wealth rather than wisdom and pleads that his sons may have the better choice. He dies, leaving the magic objects and much advice—largely disregarded—to his sons.

Andelocia, Fortunatus' prodigal younger son. He wastes his inheritance foolishly and dies miserably.

Ampedo, Fortunatus' virtuous older son. He gains nothing from his father's gifts.

and nothing for his own abstinence, dying as miserably as his reckless brother.

Athelstane, King of England. Greedy and treacherous, he gains and loses the magic purse and hat with his daughter's aid. Fortune grants the purse to him again at the end of the play. The hat has been burned by Ampedo.

Agripyne, Athelstane's selfish, beautiful daughter. She plays the role of Delilah to trick Andelocia out of the magic objects. Her punishment is negligible and short-lived.

The Soldan of Babylon. Eager for a magic purse, he loses his wishing hat, which will transport its wearer wherever he wishes to be.

802

Longavile and
Montrose, two noblemen made ridiculous
by Andelocia. They gain revenge by
causing the deaths of Andelocia and Ampedo. They also gain exile and remorse.

Fortune, the fickle and powerful goddess.
She gives Fortunatus a choice of various
qualities including wisdom. When she
learns that his choice is wealth, she grants
his wish, but lets him know the foolishness of his choice. When he realizes his
error and requests that his sons be given
wisdom instead of his wealth, she denies
him.

Virtue, the goddess who appears always
with Fortune and Vice. She wears a
fool's cap, and the author does little in
the play to indicate that the emblem is
unjust. She does offer small, bitter apples
that counteract the effect of Vice's lus-
cious ones. At the end of the play, an
address to Queen Elizabeth gives Virtue
some lip service and announces her triumph as Vice flees.

Vice, purveyor of tempting apples which
grow horns on those who eat them. She
ridicules Virtue and usually has the
better of their struggles. Her flight from
Virtue really comes after the play proper
is concluded.

THE OLD MAID

Author: Edith Wharton (1862-1937)
Time of action: The 1850's
First published: 1924

PRINCIPAL CHARACTERS

Delia Ralston, a young New York matron of impeccable social position. Years
before, she had turned down an unconventional young man, and though she
is contentedly married, she still speculates secretly about a life of passion. She
is relieved when she hears that her
cousin Charlotte is to be married, but
Charlotte changes her mind, confiding
to Delia that one of the children in the
orphanage nursery she has established
is her own, by Delia's first love, and
that marriage will mean giving up the
child, Tina, a thing she cannot do. Delia
persuades her husband to provide a
home for Charlotte and the child, and
after his death they live with her. In
order to give her a suitable background,
Delia adopts Tina, and on the girl's
wedding eve Charlotte accuses Delia of
having stolen the girl from her because
of her love for the father. Delia realizes
the charge is partly true.

Charlotte Lovell, Delia's cousin, beautiful and gay in her youth, but strangely
changed after her return from a trip to

Georgia "for her health." Delia's suitor
had turned to Charlotte and got her
with child, but knowing that he still
loved Delia, Charlotte did not tell him
of her condition. She breaks her engagement to Joe Ralston in order to keep
the child. Although she needs Delia's
protection, she is resentful of her, especially as the little girl obviously prefers Delia, whom she calls "Mother."
Charlotte insists on being the one to give
the young girl her wedding-eve confidences, but she comes back downstairs
without doing so. Charlotte realizes that
she can never tell her daughter the
truth, and there is nothing an "Old
Maid" can have to say to a bride. Having
begun her adulthood unconventionally,
Charlotte finds that nothing is left to
her but a conventional role.

Tina Ralston, Charlotte's daughter,
adopted by Delia because the proper
young men will not want to marry
Tina unless she has a correct, formal
family tie. Soon after her adoption Tina
becomes suitably engaged.

803

Clement Spender, a penniless young painter. He would not settle down to a disciplined life in New York, and Delia therefore refused to marry him. Returning from Rome to New York, he finds Delia married and turns to Charlotte. When he goes back to Rome, he does not know that Charlotte is expecting his child. It is only after Charlotte tells Delia who the father of the baby is that Delia offers to assume responsibility for the mother and child.

James Ralston, Delia's proper and prosperous husband. At her request he establishes Charlotte and Tina in a little house; after he is killed in a fall from a horse, Delia takes Charlotte and Tina into her home.

Joe Ralston, James's cousin, engaged to Charlotte. Wanting healthy heredity for his children, he accepts Charlotte's cough as an excuse to break the engagement.

THE OLD MAN AND THE SEA

Author: Ernest Hemingway (1899-1961)
Time of action: Mid-twentieth century
First published: 1952

PRINCIPAL CHARACTERS

Santiago, an old Cuban fisherman. After more than eighty days of fishing without a catch, the old man's patient devotion to his calling is rewarded. He catches a marlin bigger than any ever brought into Havana harbor. But the struggle to keep the marauding sharks from the fish is hopeless, and he reaches shore again with

only a skeleton, worthless except as a symbol of his victory.

Manolin, a young Cuban boy devoted to Santiago, with whom he fishes until forbidden by his father after Santiago's fortieth luckless day. He begs or steals to make sure Santiago does not go hungry.

OLD MORTALITY

Author: Katherine Anne Porter (1894-   )
Time of action: 1885-1912
First published: 1939

PRINCIPAL CHARACTERS

Miranda, a little Southern girl of eight who cannot understand until she grows up that adults were once young, too. She is puzzled as to why grown-ups cling to the relics of the past. She and her sister are educated in a convent in New Orleans, and when she grows up she marries without her father's consent. As an adult she finally realizes she has no part in the past and must find her own legends.

Maria, Miranda's older sister, twelve,

who has the same inability to understand adults and their lives as her sister.

Grandmother, the children's grandmother, a woman who twice a year spends a day in her attic weeping over the relics of her family's past.

Amy, the children's father's sister who is reputed to have been the most beautiful girl in the South, as well as the best rider, the best dancer, and quite a flirt.

A spoiled darling, she dies mysteriously six weeks after marrying Gabriel.

Harry, Miranda and Maria's father, who hopes, dubiously, that his chubby, freckle-faced little girls will become as beautiful as his sister Amy. He fought a duel over his sister and spent a year in Mexico as a fugitive.

Great-aunt Keziah, one of the girls' relatives, fat and ugly. She is living proof that all the women in the family are not slim, beautiful creatures like Aunt Amy.

Eva Parrington, an ugly, chinless cousin of the little girls. She teaches Latin and works for women's suffrage, going to jail three times for that cause. On the way to her Cousin Gabriel's funeral, with the grown-up Miranda, she says the myth about Cousin Amy is false, that Amy was a selfish girl who very likely committed suicide after tormenting her new husband throughout their honeymoon. Cousin Eva looks back bitterly upon her youth as a kind of sex market in which she was unwanted merchandise.

Gabriel, Amy's second cousin, whom she kept dangling for five years as a suitor. She agrees to marry him, ironically, after he is cut off from his inheritance. After her death, he becomes a drunkard and spends his time hanging around the race track.

Miss Honey, Gabriel's second wife. She is a bitter, slatternly woman who hates her husband's family.

OLD MORTALITY

Author: Sir Walter Scott (1771-1832)
Time of action: 1679
First published: 1816

PRINCIPAL CHARACTERS

Henry Morton, a gallant young Scottish gentleman unwillingly involved in the revolt of the Covenanters against the Crown in 1679. After aiding John Balfour of Burley, the Covenanter leader and a friend of his dead father, Henry is arrested and sentenced for treason, but he is saved through the intercession of his sweetheart, Edith Bellenden. Still a prisoner, he witnesses the victory of the rebels. Henry is rescued by Balfour and made a member of their council. A moderate, he detests their violence but helps them take a castle peacefully and then leads an attack against the victorious royal forces. After the battle of Bothwell Bridge Henry is sent into exile. He returns years later to find that Edith is about to marry his rival, Lord Evandale. Henry's attempt to save his rival from assassins fails, leaving him free to marry Edith.

Lady Margaret Bellenden, a stanch royalist, the mistress of Tillietudlem Castle. She lives in the past, when King Charles II visited the castle. Ousted from her estate by Covenanters and her unscrupulous turncoat relative, Basil Olifant, she is forced to live on charity until Basil's death.

Edith Bellenden, Lady Margaret's modest, attractive granddaughter and Henry Morton's sweetheart, who shares her family's royalist sympathies. When Henry is sentenced to die, she saves him by appealing to her other suitor, Lord Evandale, to intercede for him. While Henry is in exile in Holland, Basil Olifant lays claim to the Tillietudlem estates. Homeless, Edith and her grandmother are forced to live on the charity of friends. When Henry returns, she refuses to marry Lord Evandale. The death of the young nobleman in a plot hatched by Olifant leaves Edith free to marry Henry.

Colonel John Grahame, called **Grahame of Claverhouse** or simply **Claverhouse,** the experienced, noble royalist soldier who sternly sentences Henry Morton to death. Gradually he comes to respect Henry's personal honor and sees that he is exiled rather than shot after the defeat of the Covenanters at Bothwell Bridge. He later becomes the Jacobite rebel, Viscount Dundee and leads his Highlanders against King William's troops. He is mortally wounded at the battle of Killiecrankie.

Lord Evandale, Henry's honorable young royalist rival for Edith Bellenden's hand. Having saved Henry from execution, Lord Evandale is rescued twice from the Covenanters by Henry. During Henry's exile he gives financial aid to Edith and her aged grandmother. He is murdered by a party of assassins led by Basil Olifant.

John Balfour of Burley, the ambitious, fanatical Covenanter leader who befriends Henry Morton. A vengeful killer of royalists, he is unmerciful to his enemies. After his troops have been defeated at the battle of Bothwell Bridge he goes in hiding. Later, having fallen out with Henry, the crazed Balfour is killed while attempting to escape after the murder of Lord Evandale by a band of vengeful Covenanters.

Basil Olifant, a villainous relation of the Bellenden family. A turncoat, he joins the Covenanters and usurps the Bellenden estate. Threatened by Lord Evandale, Olifant ambushes him and orders the young nobleman's death. He himself is mortally shot by a party of dragoons, led by Henry Morton, who arrive too late to prevent Lord Evandale's death.

Cuddie Headrigg, Henry Morton's resourceful, easy-going servant. He aids Henry during the Covenanter rebellion, saves him from murderous fanatics after the defeat, and eventually marries Edith Bellenden's pert maid, Jenny Dennison.

Mause Headrigg, Cuddie's outspoken Covenantist mother. She is forced to become a vagrant because of her harangues.

Major Bellenden, Edith's old, upright royalist uncle, who respects Henry Morton and tries to save him from execution. Later he unsuccessfully defends Tillietudlem Castle.

Sergeant Francis Bothwell, the hardy, bullying royalist soldier who takes Henry Morton prisoner. He is killed by Balfour after being disarmed.

Cornet Grahame, Claverhouse's bold, gallant young nephew. He is unexpectedly shot by Balfour while trying to negotiate with the rebel leader under a flag of truce.

The Squire of Milnwood, Henry Morton's miserly uncle. Though a Covenanter by faith, he helps no one in those troubled times and berates Henry for giving John Balfour a place to sleep.

Wittenbold, the captain of a dragoon squad that tries, at Henry Morton's urging, to save Lord Evandale's life. The dragoons defeat the assassins at great loss.

Jenny Dennison, Edith's spirited, pretty maid. She marries Cuddie after he is released by the royalists. They have a number of children.

Mistress Alison Wilson, the Squire's housekeeper at Milnwood. Though sharp-tongued and cranky, she is fond of Henry Morton.

Macbriar, a Covenanter leader who suffers torture rather than reveal John Balfour's hiding place after the defeat of the rebels.

The Duke of Monmouth, the royalist

general who defeats the Covenanter forces at Bothwell Bridge.

Kettledrummle and
Poundtext, two fanatical Covenanter preachers inclined to verbosity and cruelty.

Mucklewrath, an insanely vengeful old Covenanter.

Old Mortality, the graveyard caretaker who supplies the author with the stories that form the core of this novel.

OLD ST. PAUL'S

Author: William Harrison Ainsworth (1805-1882)
Time of action: Mid-seventeenth century
First published: 1841

PRINCIPAL CHARACTERS

Stephen Bloundel, a London grocer whose beautiful daughter Amabel is sought by apprentice and nobleman alike. He does all he can to protect his family during the plague of 1665, but Amabel refuses to remain in the boarded-up house. She eventually dies of the plague.

Amabel, his beautiful daughter. She is in love with Wyvil (Rochester), who entices her to the vaults of St. Paul's, almost marries her, later kidnaps her, and at last marries her shortly before she dies of the plague.

Leonard Holt, Bloundel's apprentice. In love with Amabel, he prevents her first attempt to marry Wyvil. Plague-stricken, he is nursed by Nizza, whom he later rescues after her abduction by Sir Paul. Shocked by Amabel's death, he is nursed to health by Bloundel, whose partner he becomes. During the great London fire he suggests to King Charles the plan of blowing up houses to halt the spread of fire. He saves Charles' life during the fire; for his heroism he is dubbed Baron Argentine; and he marries Nizza (Lady Isabella Argentine).

Maurice Wyvil, the Earl of Rochester. A philanderer who plots to dishonor Amabel through amorous pretense of wooing and falsely wedding her, he is tricked into actually marrying her. After her death he marries Mistress Mallet.

Sir Paul Parravicin (Lord Argentine), a bravo and bully, a companion of Wyvil and Lydyard. He is unaware that he is Nizza's brother.

Nizza Macascree (Lady Isabella Argentine), the beautiful foster daughter of Mike Macascree and sister of Sir Paul. She nurses Leonard during the plague, rejects an offer to become King Charles' mistress, and afterward marries Leonard.

Judith Malmayns, a wicked nurse who murders Amabel by infecting her with the plague.

Lydyard (Sir George Etherege), a philandering companion of Wyvil.

Major Pillichody, a low friend of Wyvil and Lydyard.

Chowles, a coffin maker.

Matthew Malmayns, the husband of Judith and sexton in St. Faith Cathedral.

Dr. Hodges, a physician. While attending young Stephen Bloundel he reveals Wyvil's identity and his double pursuit of Amabel and Mistress Mallet.

Mistress Mallet, an heiress wooed and finally wed by Wyvil.

Mike Macascree, the blind foster father of Nizza.

Charles II, King of England.

Thirlby, Judith's foster brother, murderer of Isabella's husband. He is the father of Nizza and Sir Paul.

Isabella Morley Thirlby, the mother of Nizza (little Isabella) and Sir Paul.

THE OLD WIVES' TALE

Author: Arnold Bennett (1867-1931)
Time of action: Nineteenth century
First published: 1908

PRINCIPAL CHARACTERS

Sophia Baines, a high-spirited girl, the one member of the family strong enough to stand out against her father. Because she detests keeping a shop and domestic obligations, her parents finally allow her to become a schoolteacher. After her father's death, brought on by her carelessness, Sophia voluntarily returns to the shop as a penance. A brief, disillusioning marriage to Gerald Scales is followed by a period in which Sophia has a long, successful business career in Paris. After a twenty-seven-year absence, she returns to Bursley (one of the "Five Towns" made famous by Arnold Bennett) and renews her dominance over her sister Constance. Sophia's death is, according to the sister, simply an expression of God's punishment for her willful ways.

Constance Baines, her older sister. A perfect foil for Sophia, Constance follows her sister in all things, short of violating her parents' iron rule. She does repulse her mother, however, in the matter of marrying Sam Povey. She is extraordinarily capable, except in managing her son; this phase of her life is distinguished by failure. In later years, life becomes more than the obese Constance cares to cope with, and she submits, with martyrdom, to sciatica, rheumatism, and Sophia.

John Baines, their father, the bed-ridden but influential proprietor of a draper's shop. He dominates the entire family in matters both domestic and business. Whether from fear or respect, some member of his household has for many years constantly attended him. With his death, a new era begins for the family.

Mrs. Baines, his wife, who in actuality is the proprietor of the shop. Stern, authoritarian, and ever suspicious, she keeps the entire ménage in line, except Sophia. By the time of Mrs. Baines's death, Constance is ready to step into her place.

Sam Povey, first an apprentice in the shop, later the proprietor, after his marriage to Constance. Under an appearance of quiet diffidence, he conceals an aggressive personality. Deeply involved in the tragic life of his brother, he is respected and renowned throughout the community.

Charles Critchlow, the close friend and legal adviser to the Baines family. Indomitable and apparently indestructible, he is still on hand to deliver his acid estimate of Sophia when she returns to Bursley after her long absence.

Aunt Maria, a distant cousin of John Baines, who narrowly escapes being a nonentity by her availability to attend the invalid John. She is called "Aunt" as a convenience to the family.

Harriet Maddock, Mrs. Baines' sister, an overbearing, self-righteous widow assigned the care of Sophia, particularly to distract the young woman from marrying Gerald. That Sophia, even in successful maturity, is never able to face her aunt because of Sophia's childhood theft from her, speaks for the older woman's uncompromising will.

808

Gerald Scales, Sophia's husband, whom she met as a commercial traveler in the shop. Soon after their runaway marriage, Sophia sees him as unscrupulous and unstable. They part, in Paris, in less than a year, and Gerald is not seen again until he reappears, to die, an "old" man of less than sixty and a dissolute failure.

Maggie, a long-time servant in the Baines household. Engaged and then having her engagement broken eleven times, she finally marries a man of even lesser talents than hers.

Aline Chetwynd, the self-conscious, old-maid schoolteacher who is entrusted with Sophia's education. It is she who persuades Mrs. Baines that Sophia should not be wasted by a life in the shop.

Elizabeth Chetwynd, her older sister. Her marriage to the Rev. Archibald Jones lends prestige to Aline in her association with Mrs. Baines.

Lily Holl, Maggie's granddaughter, engaged to Dick Povey. Except for a fluke, Lily and Dick might have inherited a goodly share of Constance's wealth.

Dick Povey, Sam Povey's crippled nephew, who commands much sympathy and attention from his uncle. Dick's scheming attentions to Constance seem a poor reward for her husband's earlier care of the young man.

Cyril Povey, Constance and Sam's son. Thoroughly spoiled as a child and thoughtless and inconsiderate as a man, he is wholly indifferent to his mother's need for his affection.

Maria Insull, the assistant in the shop after Sam Povey's death; she marries Charles Critchlow.

Matthew Peel-Swynnerton, an occupant of the Pension Frensham, Sophia's fashionable tourist hotel in Paris. He is instrumental in reuniting Constance and Sophia.

THE OLD WIVES' TALE

Author: George Peele (1558?-1596?)
Time of action: Indeterminate
First presented: c. 1593

PRINCIPAL CHARACTERS

Clunch, a smith. Generous, kind, and simple, he finds three pages lost in a wood and takes them to his hut.

Madge, Clunch's hospitable wife. Sleeping accommodations being limited, she entertains two of the boys with a fantastic story which becomes the main play.

Antic,
Frolic, and
Fantastic, the lost pages.

Sacrapant (săk'rə·pănt), a wicked magician, probably borrowed from "Orlando Furioso," foreshadowing Milton's Comus. Though young in appearance, when he is dead he becomes old and withered.

Delia (dēl'yə), also Berecynthia (ber'-ə·sĭn'thĭ·ə), a beautiful captive girl, enchanted by Sacrapant. She is rescued by Eumenides and the Ghost of Jack.

Eumenides (ū·mĕn'ĭ·dēz), a wandering knight in love with Delia. Generous and charitable, he pays for the funeral of a pauper, whose ghost becomes an improbable guardian angel and helps him destroy Sacrapant.

The Ghost of Jack, formerly an irresponsible, happy-go-lucky character. In gratitude for Eumenides' charity, he becomes the principal mover of the dramatic action.

Erestus (ē·rĕs′tŭs), a young man enchanted by Sacrapant. Sometimes he is a white bear; sometimes an old man. He gives a cryptic prophecy to Eumenides to guide him to his love and his triumph.

Venelia (vĕn·ē′lyǎ), the betrothed of Erestus. Neither wife, widow, nor maid, she is able to break the Enchanter's glass and extinguish the light which sustains his enchantments, thereby releasing his victims.

Huanebango (wăn·ə·băng′gō), a fantastic braggart. Perhaps a caricature of Spenser's friend Gabriel Harvey, he speaks snatches of verse including nonsensical dactyllic hexameters. Trying to rescue Delia, he is deafened by Sacrapant. Instead of Delia he gets Zantippa.

Corebus (Booby) (kōr′ə·bŭs), a clown who has been a friend of Jack. Struck blind by Sacrapant's enchantment, he marries Celanta, whom be believes beautiful.

Lampriscus (lăm·prĭs′kŭs), a countryman. He sends his daughters to the enchanted well of life to find their fortune.

Zantippa (zăn·tĭp′ə), Lampriscus' beautiful, shrewish daughter. She gains a deaf husband, Huanebango, but no wealth.

Celanta (sē·lăn′tă), Lampriscus' ugly, sweet-tempered daughter. She gains a blind husband and great wealth.

Calypha (kăl′ĭ·fă) and
Thelea (thē′lē·à), Delia's brothers. They are captured by Sacrapant, rescued by Eumenides and Venelia.

Wiggen, Jack's friend who pleads for his proper burial.

Stephen Loach, an inflexible churchwarden.

Sexton, an uncharitable man. He refuses to bury Jack without his fee.

OLDTOWN FOLKS

Author: Harriet Beecher Stowe (1811-1896)
Time of action: Late eighteenth century
First published: 1869

PRINCIPAL CHARACTERS

Horace Holyoke, the narrator of this social chronicle of post-Revolutionary War New England. Born to poverty, he is ten when his schoolteacher father dies. Thanks to his abilities and his industry, and to the benefaction of friends, he attends Harvard and at last becomes a successful lawyer.

Harry Percival, Horace's closest friend. Harry's mother, brought to America after an elopement and secret marriage, is deserted by her English officer husband and dies, leaving Harry and his sister. They are brought up with Horace, and the boys attend Harvard together. Harry's legitimacy is established, and on

the death of his father he goes to England as Sir Harry.

Eglantine (Tina) Percival, Harry's sister, who is loved by Horace. She marries another man, but after ten years of unhappy marriage he dies; two years later she and Horace are married.

Ellery Davenport, handsome and clever and a grandson of Jonathan Edwards. He holds a succession of diplomatic posts abroad, and so is able to aid Harry with information about his father. Upon the death of his mad wife, he marries Tina; almost immediately a girl he had seduced appears with their child, whom Tina generously takes. Unprincipled and ambitious, Ellery is close to madness when he is killed in a political duel.

Esther Avery, the daughter of a minister, and a close friend of Tina, Harry, and Horace. She marries Harry and goes to England with him.

Mr. Lothrop, the minister and leading citizen of Oldtown. An Arminian in his views, he is sedate and sensible.

Mrs. Lothrop, his wife and Ellery's cousin. She is called "Lady Lothrop" by the people of Oldtown in a not disrespectful allusion to her aristocratic Boston background and her lingering adherence to the Church of England. She promises to provide for Harry's clothing and education.

Deacon Badger, Harry's grandfather, a leading farmer and miller of Oldtown, in whose home Horace lives after his father's death. An Arminian like Mr. Lothrop, he is also serene and affable.

Mrs. Badger, Horace's grandmother, who is a strict Puritan Calvinist. The Badgers take in Harry and Tina when they are found in a deserted house in which they took refuge. Harry stays on with them.

Susy Badger Holyoke, their daughter and Horace's mother. Her beauty faded because of hardship and poverty, she returns to her parents with her children after her husband's death.

Miss Mehitable Rossiter, the daughter of a former minister of Oldtown. Her life has been saddened by the disappearance some years before of her half sister. She adopts Tina.

Emily Rossiter, Mehitable's half sister, who appears with her child by Ellery shortly after his marriage to Tina. Tina uses her newly inherited fortune to establish the sisters in a house near Boston.

Sir Harry Percival, the worthless and dissipated father of Harry and Tina. Deserting his wife and children, he takes the wedding certificate and leaves a letter denying the legality of the marriage. Only a "younger son" at the time of the elopement, he succeeds to the family title and property.

Caleb (Old Crab) Smith, a miser, in whose house Harry's mother dies. He decides to keep the boy as a field hand.

Miss Asphyxia Smith, Caleb's sister. She takes in Tina, but the children are so harshly treated that they run away.

Bill Holyoke, Horace's older brother. He gives little promise as a scholar and so goes to work on the farm with his uncle Jacob.

Jacob Badger, the son of Mr. and Mrs. Badger, and Horace's uncle.

Sam Lawson, the village handyman and do-nothing. Called shiftless by some, he is Horace's chief comfort in the days after his father's death. Sam is never too busy to tell stories to the small boys or to take them hunting and fishing.

Keziah Badger, one of Mr. and Mrs. Badger's unmarried daughters. Romantic-minded, she has a reputation for homeliness in the village.

Lois Badger, Keziah's sister, who also is a spinster. She is sharp-tongued but warm-hearted.

Jonathan Rossiter, Miss Mehitable's half brother and master of the academy in Cloudland. Horace and Harry study there and live with him.

Mr. Avery, the minister at Cloudland and Esther's father. Tina boards with him.

Madame Kittery, Mrs. Lothrop's mother. The children are taken to visit her in Boston as a special Easter treat. She takes an interest in Horace and provides money to send him to Harvard.

Major Broad and
Squire Jones, friends who meet in the spacious Badger kitchen to discuss politics, religion, and philosophy.

OLIVER TWIST

Author: Charles Dickens (1812-1870)
Time of action: Early nineteenth century
First published: 1837-1839

PRINCIPAL CHARACTERS

Oliver Twist, a workhouse foundling, the helpless, abused hero of the novel. Both innocent and morally sensible, he gives force and sharpness, as well as a full measure of sentimentality, to Dickens' vision of social injustice. Exploited from birth by the selfish managers of the poor farm and workhouse, he is apprenticed to a mortician. Treated cruelly, he runs off to London, where he is taken in by a gang of thieves. Falsely arrested as a pickpocket, he is rescued for a time by Mr. Brownlow and then recaptured by the thieves. He is wounded during a burglary attempt and saved from arrest by Mrs. Maylie and her adopted daughter, who care for him until the mystery of his birth is solved and the criminals are taken or killed. Mr. Brownlow offers him a permanent home.

Mr. Brownlow, the kind-hearted, benevolent man who delivers Oliver Twist from a vicious judge, gives him care and trust, solves the question of his parentage, and finally adopts him.

Mrs. Maylie, the gentle, good-hearted woman who takes Oliver in after he has been wounded and is being hunted as a burglar. She sees that he is happy and cared for until he finds a lasting home with Mr. Brownlow.

Rose Maylie, her adopted daughter, the tender, lovely girl who nurses Oliver and helps expose the treachery that surrounds him. Later it turns out that she is really Oliver's aunt.

Harry Maylie, Mrs. Maylie's wastrel son, who later becomes a clergyman and marries his foster sister Rose.

Fagin, a greasy, sinister old Jew who trains boys for stealing and receives stolen goods. Paid to bring Oliver up as a thief, he fails to retake the boy after a burglary attempt. He is finally executed by the law for complicity in a murder.

Bill Sikes, Fagin's accomplice, the leader of Fagin's band of trained thieves. A violent, brutal man, he deserts Oliver after the attempted burglary. Later he kills his mistress Nancy because he believes she has betrayed him. Haunted by guilt, he accidentally hangs himself while trying to escape the law.

Nancy, a female thief, a member of Fagin's gang. She befriends Oliver and informs on Fagin's activities in order to save the boy. Although she remains loyal to Bill Sikes, he murders her in a rage.

Monks, whose real name is **Edward Leeford,** Oliver Twist's stepbrother. A vengeful person, he plots with Fagin against Oliver to keep the boy from his inheritance. In the end he confesses his villainy, makes restitution, moves to America, and eventually dies in prison.

Mr. Bumble, the vain, bullying almshouse beadle who mistreats Oliver at every opportunity. He meets his match, however, when he marries Mrs. Corney, a workhouse matron. The two become paupers and end their days in the workhouse.

Mrs. Corney, his wife, formerly a vixenish workhouse matron.

Mr. Grimwig, Mr. Brownlow's gruff old friend, who speaks harshly against Oliver but wishes him well.

Mrs. Bedwin, Mr. Brownlow's warm-hearted housekeeper, who comforts frightened, lonely Oliver.

Mr. Losberne, "The Doctor," a fat, good-hearted surgeon and the Maylies' family friend. He speaks roughly to Oliver Twist but cures his wound and saves him from the police.

Mrs. Mann, the alcoholic matron who keeps the poor farm where Oliver lives for a time.

Mr. Sowerberry, the mortician who takes Oliver as his apprentice and meekly befriends him. He makes thin, pale, sad-looking Oliver a mourner at children's funerals.

Mrs. Sowerberry, his wife, a shrew.

Noah Claypole, a lumpish bully charity boy who runs away from the mortician and becomes a member of Fagin's gang.

Charlotte, Mrs. Sowerberry's servant, who also misuses Oliver. She marries Noah Claypole.

Jack Dawkins, called the **Artful Dodger,** the clever young pickpocket who leads Oliver Twist to Fagin.

Charley Bates, the Artful Dodger's boisterous friend and assistant.

Mr. Fang, the cruel judge who tries Oliver Twist when he is charged with picking pockets. Mr. Brownlow, appearing as a witness, pities Oliver and, when his innocence is proved, takes the boy home with him.

Toby Crackit, the burglar who accompanies Oliver Twist and Bill Sikes on the attempted robbery of the Maylie house.

Old Sally, the beggar, present when Oliver Twist is born, who steals the tokens that eventually disclose his parentage.

[**Agnes Fleming,** Oliver's unwed mother. She dies in childbirth in a workhouse.]

[**Mr. Leeford,** Oliver Twist's father, unhappily married and separated from his wife when he falls in love with Agnes Fleming. After he dies suddenly in Rome, his wife and son destroy a will that provides for Agnes and her unborn child.]

[**Mrs. Leeford,** the jealous, vindictive wife who tries to deprive Agnes Fleming and her child of their inheritance.]

OMOO

Author: Herman Melville (1819-1891)
Time of action: Early 1840's
First published: 1847

PRINCIPAL CHARACTERS

Herman Melville, an American sailor who is rescued from a cannibal island by the crew of a British whaler, the "Julia," and who signs on the ship as a deck hand. He is soon relieved of duty because of lameness in his leg. Conditions on the ship are bad, so Melville and the rest of the crew put ashore at Papeetee, on the island of Tahiti, and are imprisoned when they refuse to return to their ship. After the ship sails away with a new crew, Melville and the other

sailors are freed by their Tahitian jailer. Later Melville and his friend, Doctor Long Ghost, have several adventures in the islands together. Melville finally ships on a whaler which will take him to Japan and eventually home. In the course of his island-hopping, he becomes convinced that the natives have been corrupted by their contact with the white missionaries and were better off as primitive pagans.

Doctor Long Ghost, the ship's doctor on

the British whaler which rescues Melville. The doctor becomes Melville's close friend and companion in his adventures. The doctor tries to sign on the same ship with Melville when Melville decides to leave the islands, but the captain refuses to allow the doctor to sign on, either as a deck hand or as ship's doctor, and he is left behind.

Captain Bob, the jailer of Melville and the rest of the crew on the island of Tahiti. He is jolly and easy-going, and after the whaler sails away the old man frees his prisoners.

John Jermin, first officer of the British whaler.

THE ORDEAL OF RICHARD FEVEREL

Author: George Meredith (1828-1909)
Time of action: Mid-nineteenth century
First published: 1859

PRINCIPAL CHARACTERS

Richard Feverel, the only son and sole heir of Sir Austin Feverel. Richard is the subject of his father's plan to produce a young man, reared according to a System, in which women are to be excluded from the life of the boy until he is twenty-five. Richard becomes the obvious proof that the System will not work. He manages, simply by being human, to foil all plans to keep him from physical danger and from women.

Sir Austin Feverel, master of Raynham Abbey and Richard's woman-hating father, who devises the System for rearing his son. Although he is unrealistic in his approach, his belief in the basic soundness of his System is complete.

Adrian Harley, Sir Austin's nephew, who is designated as Richard's mentor. He is responsible for carrying out the System. Always dubious, Adrian finally is convinced, when Richard marries, that the System has failed utterly.

Lucy Desborough, the niece of a neighboring farmer. Richard falls in love with

her and marries her. She bears him a child and finally dies of brain fever and shock when she learns that Richard has been wounded in a duel.

Ripton Thompson, the son of Sir Austin's lawyer, brought to Raynham Abbey as Richard's youthful playmate and companion.

Giles Blaize, Lucy's uncle. He horsewhips Richard and Ripton when he finds that they have shot a pheasant on his property. Richard is responsible for setting fire to Blaize's hayricks.

Clare Forey, Richard's cousin, who falls in love with him. She marries a man much older than she. When she dies, a ring that Richard had lost is found on her finger.

Tom Bakewell, the man Richard bribes to set fire to Blaize's hayricks. Richard insists that he is responsible for the fire and so confuses Blaize's witness that Tom is released, although the witness saw Tom set the fire. He becomes Richard's devoted servant.

ORFEO

Author: Politian (Angelo Ambrogini, 1454-1494)
Time of action: Remote antiquity
First presented: 1480

Orpheus (ôr′fē·əs), a young singer and poet who is in love with Eurydice. At the news of his sweetheart's death, he fills the air with his lament and vows to go to the very gates of Tartarus and, with the beauty of his music, win back his love. There his melodies so charm Pluto that the god grants him permission to lead Eurydice back to earth on condition that he not look back along the way. Overcome by doubts, he does look back, only to see Eurydice drawn again among the shades. Heartbroken, he is determined never to seek love again. As punishment for his scorn of love, he is torn to pieces by the Bacchantes.

Eurydice (ū·rĭ′dĭ·sē), a nymph who is loved by Orpheus and sought by him in the Underworld after her death. Given permission to follow her lover back to earth, she is drawn again among the shades when he breaks his promise to

Pluto that he will not look back along the way.

Pluto (plōō′tō), god of the Underworld, who is so charmed by Orpheus' music that he grants him permission to lead Eurydice back to earth.

Proserpina (prō·sėr′pə·nə), goddess of the Underworld and the wife of Pluto, so charmed by Orpheus' lyre that she wishes to return Eurydice to him.

Tisiphone (tə·sĭ′fə·nē), one of the Furies. She blocks Orpheus' way when he tries to follow Eurydice back into the Underworld.

Aristaeus (â·rəs·tē′əs), a shepherd enamored of Eurydice.

Mopsus (mŏp′səs) and
Thyrsis (thėr′sĭs), shepherds and companions of Aristaeus.

Mnesillus (nē·sĭ′ləs), a satyr.

ORLANDO

Author: Virginia Woolf (1882-1941)
Time of action: 1588-1928
First published: 1928

Orlando, a young English nobleman of Elizabeth I's reign. He is a descendant of fighting men but is himself a poet. He becomes a courtier, though scarcely growing older, during the times of Elizabeth, James I, and Charles II. Failing to find satisfaction in literature, he turns to materialistic goals, searching all Europe for furnishings to refurbish his great mansion. While serving Charles II as Ambassador Extraordinary at Constantinople, Orlando sleeps an entire week, during which he mysteriously changes into a woman. Although now female and beautiful, Orlando is still a restless soul, searching for satisfaction in the brilliant society of Queen Anne's court and, as

well, in the streets and pubs of London. During the Victorian period Orlando, still a woman, marries and returns to literary pursuits. She comes to think of herself, now a woman of thirty-six during the 1920's, as a symbol of English history.

The Archduchess Harriet of Roumania, a large, ugly woman who falls in love with Orlando and forces her attentions upon him. When Orlando, changed into a woman, returns to England in the eighteenth century, she finds the Archduchess metamorphosed into Archduke Harry, still in love with Orlando but changed in sex.

Sasha, a Russian princess who comes to England in 1604. She fascinates the youthful Orlando, who falls in love and wants to marry Sasha. The princess, a fickle creature, toys with common sailors and finally deserts Orlando to return home to Russia.

Nicholas Greene, a seventeenth century poet who becomes a pensioner of the youthful Orlando while he is interestd in literature. Greene is a man who loves city life, and in the 1920's he turns up again as a successful literary critic and offers to help the middle-aged woman Orlando to find a publisher for her long poem.

Marmaduke Bonthrop Shelmerdine, Esq., Orlando's Victorian-age husband, who leaves his wife to go to sea. He returns in 1928 aboard an airplane, having become a renowned sea captain during his absence.

ORLANDO FURIOSO

Author: Ludovico Ariosto (1474-1533)
Time of action: Eighth century
First published: 1516; enlarged edition, 1532

PRINCIPAL CHARACTERS

Orlando, the renowned nephew of King Charlemagne and the mightiest paladin among his Twelve Peers. While Paris is under siege by the Saracens, he dreams an evil dream concerning his beloved Angelica, the beautiful Princess of Cathay who has caused great dissension among Christian and pagan champions alike. Forsaking his knightly duties, he passes through the enemy lines and goes in search of the damsel. His quest takes him into many lands, and after many strange adventures he is driven mad by the distractions of love and jealousy. Throwing away his armor, he wanders naked and raving among savage beasts, so that all knights are filled with pity when they hear of his sad state. He recovers his sanity after Astolpho, an English knight, finds the wits of his deranged friend in a vial in the region of the moon. His mind restored, Orlando once more engages in valorous deeds and champions the Christian cause. One of his feats is the rescue of Rogero, a gallant Saracen knight now converted to Christianity, who has been cast away on a desert island.

Angelica, the Princess of Cathay who by her great beauty bewitches Orlando, Rinaldo, Ferraù, and Rogero, but in the end marries none of these paladins; her true love is Medoro, a Saracen knight of lowly birth whom she nurses back to health after he has been wounded in battle. The cause of many misfortunes to others, she herself falls victim to an enchanter's magic and is carried to the island of Ebuda, where she is about to be offered as a sacrifice to a giant orc when she is saved by Rogero, the Saracen knight who forgets his own loved Bradamant and falls under the spell of Angelica's charms. To keep her from harm, Rogero gives her a magic ring, but faithless Angelica uses it to make herself invisible and flees from him. After she has saved the life of Medoro, she returns with him to Cathay.

Rinaldo, one of King Charlemagne's Twelve Peers, second only to Orlando in loyalty, bravery, and knightly honor. His chivalric adventures are wonderful and strange but not always related to his quest for Angelica, whom he finally disdains. On several occasions he is called upon to engage in single combat for the honor of the King. Rejoicing when he learns that Rogero has received Christian baptism, he promises the hand of his sister Bradamant to the Saracen hero. Later he withstands the wishes of his parents and champions the right of Bradamant to marry her beloved.

Rogero, a noble Saracen knight in love with Bradamant, the sister of Rinaldo. After many marvelous adventures, which include his rescue by Bradamant from the enchanted castle in which Atlantes, a magician, holds him prisoner, his ride on a flying hippogryph, his slaying of the giantess Eriphilia, his rescue of Angelica from the monstrous orc, his forgetting of Bradamant while he woos and loses Angelica, his victory over Mandricardo, his sojourn on a desert island, and his Christian baptism, he is finally restored to his beloved Bradamant. At the feast celebrating the wedding of the happy couple envoys appear to make Rogero King of Bulgaria. Rogero and Bradamant, according to Ariosto, were the ancestors of the noble d'Este family of Ferrara.

Bradamant, a maiden knight, the sister of Rinaldo and later the wife of Rogero. In Ariosto's version of this chivalric story she is always the romantic heroine, fighting on the side of right, vanquishing evil knights, and rescuing the unfortunate. Her steadfastness in her love for Rogero, the Saracen champion, contrasts sharply with the fickleness of Angelica, while her prowess on the field of battle rivals that of the bravest knights, including her own Rogero, who wins her from his princely rival after defeating her in single combat. The story ends with an account of the happy wedding festivities of Bradamant and Rogero, now turned Christian.

Astolpho, the English knight who restores Orlando's wits. Also a rider on the flying hippogryph, he engages in marvelous adventures, among them a journey to the fabled land of Prester John and a trip to the region of the moon, where the senses of poets and others are stored. Astolpho finds there the vial containing Orlando's lost wits and returns

them to the hero, who regains his sanity after inhaling the contents of the vial.

Ferraù, a brave Saracen knight. Also under Angelica's spell, he battles with Rinaldo, his rival. While the two men fight, Angelica runs away. Ferraù returns to Spain to aid his king repel an invasion.

Sacripant, the King of Circassia. When Angelica meets him in the forest, she begs him to protect a damsel in distress. They are overtaken by Rinaldo, who battles with Sacripant and splinters his shield. Angelica flees once more when she sees Sacripant overthrown.

Count Pinabel, a treacherous knight whom Bradamant encounters while she is searching for Rogero. Pinabel tells her that Rogero and other knights are the captives of Atlantes, a magician whose enchanted castle stands high in the Pyrenees. Later he tries to kill Bradamant by pushing her into a deep cave.

Melissa, a seeress whom Bradamant finds in Merlin's cave, into which Count Pinabel pushed her. Melissa foretells the noble house that will spring from the union of Bradamant and Rogero, and she tells the maiden knight that Rogero can be freed from the spell of the magician Atlantes only with the aid of a magic ring.

Brunello, a dwarf to whom Agramant, King of Africa, has entrusted the magic ring used by Bradamant to free Rogero and his fellow knights from the spell cast upon them by the magician Atlantes.

Atlantes, the aged magician who puts Rogero under the magic spell from which Bradamant frees her lover. He is the owner of the flying hippogryph on which Rogero, after his release, is carried to the land of Alcina, a wicked sorceress.

Alcina, the evil sorceress under whose spell Rogero falls. He is saved by Melissa, a seeress, who gives him a magic ring to protect him from Alcina's power. Alcina also casts a spell on Astolpho, a brave English knight.

Agramant, King of Africa and the enemy of King Charlemagne. When it is decided to end the siege of Paris by a battle of champions, Agramant chooses Rogero as the greatest of his knights. Rinaldo is the defender of the Christians. During the combat Agramant treacherously breaks his oath and attacks the French forces. When the Saracens are routed, Rogero, who has promised to accept Christian baptism after the battle, remains with his defeated king, much to the distress of Bradamant, his beloved.

Rodomont, a fierce and vengeful Saracen warrior, the enemy of all Christians and a cause of dissension among the Saracens. After a quarrel with Mandricardo, Prince of Tartary, Rodomont leaves King Agramant's camp. He meets Isabella, Princess of Galicia, who is grieving for the death of Zerbino, her beloved knight, whom Rodomont had slain. In a drunken frenzy, Rodomont kills Isabella. Overcome by remorse, he builds a bridge over the river near her tomb and there challenges all traveling knights to combat in honor of the dead Princess. He is overcome by mad Orlando and by Bradamant. At the wedding feast of Rogero and Bradamant, Rodomont brashly appears to accuse the Saracen knight of apostasy. Rogero kills him.

Dardinello, King of Zumara, a Saracen leader killed when the Saracen besiegers of Paris are routed.

Cloridan and
Medoro, brothers, brave young Saracen knights who, grieving for the death of their overlord, King Dardinello, kill many Christian knights to avenge their leader's death. Cloridan is killed by a band of Scottish knights and Medoro is left for dead on the field where Angelica finds him. She nurses him back to health in the nearby hut of a friendly herdsman.

Zerbino, Prince of Scotland, the leader of the knights who kill Cloridan. The lover of Isabella, Princess of Galicia. Zerbino is killed by fierce Rodomont.

Mandricardo, Prince of Tartary, with whom Rodomont quarrels over Doralice, a Spanish princess. Mandricardo is killed by Rogero following an argument over the Tartar's right to wear the escutcheon of Hector, the Trojan hero.

Gradasso, a Saracen king killed in a battle between pagans and Christians.

Sobrino, a Saracen king who becomes a Christian after his defeat at Lipadusa.

Brandimart, a Christian knight held prisoner by Rodomont. Defeated by Bradamant, the maiden knight, Rodoment promises to release him along with other Christian captives. Brandimart fights with Orlando, Oliver, and Bradamant against the Saracen kings at Lipadusa and is killed in the battle.

Flordelice, the faithful wife of Brandimart.

Doralice, the Spanish princess who causes a quarrel between Rodomont and Mandricardo.

Leo, the son of Constantine, the Emperor of Greece. When the parents of Bradamant shut her away in a castle in an attempt to make her accept the noble young Greek as her husband, Rogero becomes jealous and decides to kill Leo. Captured while fighting with the Bulgarians against the Greeks, the young Saracen is imprisoned by Theodora, the Emperor's sister, in revenge for the death of her son, slain by Rogero. Leo, learning of Rogero's plight, rescues him and hides him in his own house. Later, unaware of Rogero's identity, he asks him to act as his champion, after Bradamant has declared that she will marry only a knight who can withstand her in combat. Rogero and Bradamant meet and Rogero is the victor. Disconsolate because he has won the hand of his beloved for his benefactor, Rogero wanders off into the forest. There Leo, having renounced his claim to Bradamant after hearing the story of the lovers' trials, finds the young Saracen and returns him to his betrothed.

Theodora, the sister of Emperor Constantine of Greece. To avenge the death of her son she imprisons the Saracen knight Rogero, his slayer.

Eriphilia, a giantess slain by Rogero.

ORLANDO INNAMORATO

Author: Matteo Maria Boiardo (c. 1440-1494)
Time of action: Eighth century
First transcribed: 1486-1495

PRINCIPAL CHARACTERS

Orlando, a paladin of France and King Charlemagne's nephew, the Roland of the Carlovingian cycle of chivalric romances. Stricken by love for Angelica, the beautiful Princess of Cathay, he, like Rinaldo and Ferraù, sets out in search of her after she has disappeared during a tourney to determine the bravest and most skilled knight who may claim her as his bride. Discovered in the company of Angelica, Orlando is forced into combat with Ferraù, a jealous Spanish knight. Later, during his wanderings, Orlando slays Agrican, the King of Tartary, another suitor for Angelica's hand. He battles also with Rinaldo, who, having drunk from a fountain whose waters are a cure for love madness, now hates the Princess. Later Angelica dupes Orlando into escorting her to France, so that she may continue her pursuit of Rinaldo, with whom she is in love. In the meantime Rinaldo has drunk from the waters of love. When he meets the travelers, he becomes insanely jealous of Orlando and challenges the knight to a duel. Orlando loses the maiden when she flees to Charlemagne's camp while he and Rinaldo engage in a bitter struggle.

Rinaldo, another of Charlemagne's paladins, the brother of Bradamant, the maiden warrior, and the cousin of Malagigi, a famed magician. Although aware of the sinister beauty of Angelica, he sets out in pursuit of her. In the forest he drinks from Merlin's magic spring and his love for the damsel turns to loathing so great that at the siege of Albracca, during a war between the kingdom of Cathay and the pagan Tartars, he fights on the side of the invading infidels. Angelica, lovesick for the knight who spurns her, continues to pursue him until she drinks from the waters of hate, he from the waters of love. Then Rinaldo pursues the fleeing Angelica. Meeting Orlando and Angelica in the forest, Rinaldo challenges Orlando to a duel. Angelica flees while the two knights join in combat.

Charlemagne, King of France. With his paladins he defends Christendom against the pagans.

Angelica, the lovely Princess of Cathay, sent with her brother Argalia to demoralize King Charlemagne's knights. The possessor of the magic ring to overcome all spells or give her invisibility, she uses her wiles to ensnare Orlando, his friend Rinaldo, Ferraù, and many others, including Charlemagne himself. Fickle or enchanted, she manages many intrigues and escapades. Coquette that she is, she cannot win Rinaldo and she refuses to accept Orlando.

Argalia, the son of Galaphron, King of Cathay, and Angelica's brother. The owner of invulnerable armor and a magic spear which unhorses any knight

819

it touches, he jousts with the Christian knights for the hand of Angelica and takes captive all whom he vanquishes. His four giant bodyguards are killed and he himself is mortally wounded by Ferraù, a Spanish knight. Astolpho, an English knight, gets possession of Argalia's magic spear and with it performs deeds of great valor against both foes and friends.

Malagigi, the cousin of Rinaldo and the magician who discovers the plot of Argalia and Angelica. Although he is the only one who distrusts the foreign emissaries to King Charlemagne's court, he becomes the first, while attempting to gain possession of Angelica's magic ring, to fall in love with the beautiful Princess. Discovered, he is captured by Argalia's giant bodyguards, his book of magic is stolen, and he himself is transported to Cathay by fiends. There he remains in a dungeon beneath the sea until he agrees to help Angelica in her pursuit of Rinaldo.

Bradamant, a lovely warrior maiden, the sister of Rinaldo. While Paris is under siege by Agramant, the King of Africa, she is so smitten by the gallant Saracen warrior Rogero that she rides into the Saracen lines and doffs her helmet by way of introduction. So overcome is he with love that he fights his former allies for daring to wound her from ambush. The two, already deeply in love, are separated during the battle.

Rogero, a brave and handsome Saracen knight, a paladin of the pagan forces that invade King Charlemagne's dominions and lay siege to Paris. Rogero, long a prisoner of Atlantes, a magician, is released through the power of Angelica's magic ring to join in the fight. The wounds he receives in a tournament heal miraculously, a sign to Agramant, the young King of Africa, that the young hero is their savior. Rogero is knighted and leads the pagans in the siege of Paris. During one of the battles Bradamant sees

him and falls deeply in love with the gallant young knight, but they are separated during the melee.

Ferraù, a doughty Spanish knight, in love with Angelica. Finding her and Orlando in the forest, he challenges the paladin to a duel. The fight is broken off when the knights receive word that Gradasso, King of Sericane, has invaded Spain with a large army. Ferraù departs to help repel the invaders.

Astolpho, an English knight. He obtains the magic spear used by Argalia to overthrow Christian knights in the great tournament and with it performs many deeds of valor. He unhorses King Gradasso in order to free Charlemagne and a number of his knights, prisoners of the pagan monarch.

Gradasso, King of Sericane. A monarch who covets the treasures owned by other kings and knights, he invades Europe in order to obtain possession of Durindana, Orlando's famous sword, and Bayardo, the noble horse of Rinaldo. In the fighting near Barcelona, the King and Rinaldo meet in single combat, the stakes being Gradasso's Christian prisoners against Rinaldo's horse. Neither prevailing, they agree to meet again on the following day, but at the appointed time Rinaldo does not appear. Through the wiles of infatuated Angelica, he has been lured away by Malagigi, the magician. After the King has captured Charlemagne and many of his knights, Gradasso and Astolpho fight and the King is overthrown. True to the wager made before the combat, he releases his prisoners and returns to Sericane.

Marsilius, King of Spain, to whom King Charlemagne sends an army, under the leadership of Rinaldo, when King Gradasso invades Spain.

Flordespina, the damsel who brings Ferraù and Orlando word that Spain is being ravaged by a pagan army.

Galaphron, King of Cathay and the father of Angelica and Argalia. He imprisons Malagigi in a dungeon beneath the sea.

Agrican, King of Tartary. Determined to win the Princess Angelica as his bride, he lays siege to Albracca, the capital of Cathay. Orlando and Astolpho fight on the side of the Cathayans, Rinaldo on the side of the invaders. Orlando meets Agrican in single combat and kills him.

Agramant, the young King of Africa. Eager to avenge the death of his father, he plans to besiege Paris and humble King Charlemagne. One of his advisers tells him that he cannot hope to succeed without the aid of Rogero, a Saracen knight held prisoner by Atlantes, a sorcerer. With the aid of Angelica's magic ring, stolen by a loyal dwarf, Agramant dispels the mists about the castle of Atlantes. After a tourney in which he displays great gallantry and skill, Rogero becomes Agramant's loyal knight.

Atlantes, the sorcerer who has kept Rogero a prisoner in a castle on the mountain of Carena.

Brunello, the dwarf who steals Angelica's magic ring, needed to set Rogero free from the magic spell of Atlantes.

Rodomont, a vassal of King Agramant. He and Rinaldo fight in single combat during a great battle between Christians and pagans.

Morgana, a sorceress who keeps her prisoners in an enchanted garden at the bottom of a lake. Orlando frees Rinaldo from her spell.

Namus, Duke of Bavaria, to whom King Charlemagne entrusts Angelica after she seeks protection in his camp.

ORLEY FARM

Author: Anthony Trollope (1815-1882)
Time of action: Mid-nineteenth century
First published: 1862

PRINCIPAL CHARACTERS

Lady Mary Mason, the widow of Sir Joseph Mason, forty-five years her senior. After Sir Joseph's death her son Lucius was awarded Orley Farm by a codicil to his father's will. The codicil had been contested by Joseph Mason, Sir Joseph's son by an earlier marriage, but Lady Mason won the court case. Later a shady attorney, Dockwrath, angry at Lucius, digs up some papers that lead him to believe the codicil a forgery. He gets Joseph Mason to reopen the case. Lady Mason is befriended by Sir Peregrine Orme. When Sir Peregrine proposes, Lady Mason confesses that the codicil was, indeed, a forgery, her only means of gaining property for her son. Nevertheless, she also wins the second case. She then confesses to Lucius, who turns the property over to

Joseph, and mother and son leave for Germany.

Lucius Mason, the son of Sir Joseph and Lady Mary Mason, educated in Germany. When he returns, he decides to establish Orley Farm as a working experiment for his agricultural theories. This project involves forcing Dockwrath off his small fields, and Dockwrath's ire precipitates the second court case. He proposes to Sophia Furnival, but she refuses him after he is no longer in control of Orley Farm.

Sir Peregrine Orme, the owner of The Cleeve, a wealthy and highly respected gentleman. Very chivalrous, he is willing to stand by his proposal to Lady Mason even after he knows she has forged the codicil.

Mrs. Edith Orme, the widowed daughter-in-law of Sir Peregrine Orme, who lives with him. Also loyal to Lady Mason, she accompanies her to court.

Peregrine Orme (Perry), the son of Mrs. Edith Orme and heir to The Cleeve. He proposes to Madeline Stavely, but is rejected.

Joseph Mason, owner of Groby Park in Yorkshire and older son of Sir Joseph Mason. He is a severe man, a county magistrate, but he is not unjust; he has always believed that his father intended to leave Orley Farm to him.

Mrs. Mason, his wife, an inhospitable, parsimonious woman.

Judge Stavely, a kind and perceptive judge who owns Noningsby. He is proud that his daughter has chosen an ugly, brilliant man rather than the suitable young Peregrine Orme.

Lady Stavely, his devoted wife, who cannot understand her daughter but finally gives her blessing to the marriage.

Madeline Stavely, their beautiful daughter, who chooses and waits for the penniless Felix Graham to win her parents' permission to propose.

Augustus Stavely, a friend of Felix Graham. He, like Lucius Mason, proposes to Sophia Furnival, but she puts him off.

Felix Graham, a brilliant and ugly young barrister who is the youngest lawyer taking Lady Mason's case. At first he is engaged to Mary Snow, a girl he befriends and is training to be his wife. He then breaks several bones while hunting at the Stavely's, is forced to remain at Noningsby, and falls in love with Madeline. He arranges another wedding for Mary Snow and marries Madeline himself.

Mr. Furnival, an attorney for Lady Mason and a member of Parliament. He suspects that Lady Mason is guilty, but remains loyal to her.

Mrs. Furnival, nee **Kitty Blacker,** his wife who is frequently left alone while he works. At one point, she suspects her husband is attached to Lady Mason and leaves him, but she later returns.

Sophia Furnival, their pretty daughter, who flirts her way into two proposals but accepts neither.

Samuel Dockwrath, a shady attorney who wants to be employed by Joseph Mason. His efforts are unsuccessful.

Mrs. Miriam Usbech Dockwrath, his wife, the mother of sixteen children.

Jonathan Usbech, Miriam's father and Sir Joseph's attorney. He was supposed to be ill at the time the codicil was drawn up and he died before the first trial.

John Kenneby, Sir Joseph's former clerk, who testifies that he had witnessed the signing of a document. Heckled by the attorneys at both trials, he acknowledges that he did not know the nature of the document he witnessed.

Mr. Moulder, a salesman of tea, coffee, and brandy, brother-in-law to John Kenneby.

Mrs. Mary Anne Moulder, Kenneby's sister, anxious to promote his marriage to a wealthy widow.

Mrs. Smiley, a widow who owns brick fields and is engaged to John Kenneby.

Bridget Bolster, a chambermaid who testifies at both trials.

Mr. Chaffanbrass, a seasoned attorney and a friend of Mr. Furnival, adept at breaking down witnesses.

Mr. Solomon Aram, an Old Bailey lawyer, also employed for Lady Mason.

Mr. Matthew Round, attorney for the firm of Round and Crook, employed by Joseph Mason.

Mr. Crabwitz, an old assistant in Mr. Furnival's office.

Miss Martha Biggs, the friend who wants Mrs. Furnival to join her in Red Lion Square when she contemplates leaving Mr. Furnival.

Mary Snow, the daughter of an engraver, engaged to Felix Graham, later married to Albert Fitzallen.

Albert Fitzallen, a worker in an apothecary shop, helped by Felix Graham.

Mr. Snow, an engraver, Mary's father, a habitual gin drinker.

Mrs. Thomas, who uncovers Mary's correspondence with Albert.

Mr. Green, the curate at Groby Park.

Mrs. Green, his wife, who receives patent steel furniture in bad condition from Mrs. Mason.

Mr. Slow and
Mr. Bideawhile, attorneys to Sir Peregrine Orme.

OROONOKO

Author: Mrs. Aphra Behn (1640-1689)
Time of action: Seventeenth century
First published: 1688

PRINCIPAL CHARACTERS

Oroonoko, a black prince of Coromantien, Africa. At seventeen, he is the successful general of his country's army. In love with Imoinda, he is furious when his King, also his grandfather, takes her into his harem. Oroonoko takes Imoinda as a lover. Both he and the girl are later enslaved by the English and taken to Surinam. They try to escape. When captured, Oroonoko is savagely beaten. Caught again while attempting to escape, he is publicly executed in a brutal manner. To save Imoinda from such a fate he has killed her with her blessing.

Aboan, Oroonoko's faithful companion and friend. He, along with Oroonoko, is enslaved while visiting a supposedly friendly British ship.

Imoinda, the beloved of Oroonoko. She is sold into slavery by the King of Coro-

mantien after Oroonoko became her lover. Reunited with Oroonoko in Surinam, she becomes pregnant by him. To save her from ravishment and a shameful death, Oroonoko cuts off her head.

The King, ruler of Coromantien and Oroonoko's grandfather. He is more than a hundred years old, but he wants Imoinda for his harem and treacherously takes her from Oroonoko.

A Slaveholder, Oroonoko's owner and friend who renames him Caesar. A kind man, he nurses Oroonoko when he is brutally beaten by his captors after attempting to escape.

The Governor, a brutal, treacherous man who on two occasions promises Oroonoko immunity if he will surrender, only to betray him each time and have him beaten.

THE ORPHAN

Author: Thomas Otway (1652-1685)
Time of action: Seventeenth century
First presented: 1680

Monimia, an orphan. A ward of Acasto, she is loved by his twin sons Polydore and Castalio. She genuinely loves only Castalio. She secretly marries Castalio but is deceived into spending the night with Polydore. Filled with remorse for having deceived her husband with his brother, even though unknowingly, she finally poisons herself and dies, a victim of circumstances.

Castalio, the overscrupulous twin son of Acasto. Minimizing his own passion for Monimia in order to be fair to his brother Polydore, he encourages his brother's less scrupulous pursuit of the lady. When Castalio secretly marries Monimia, Polydore, ignorant of the marriage, tricks the bride into spending the night with him. When Castalio learns the truth of the af-

fair and that his wife is dead by her own hand, he stabs himself and dies.

Polydore, Acasto's less scrupulous twin son. Ignorant of his brother's secret marriage to Monimia, he tricks her into spending the night with him. When he learns that he has deceived his brother's wife, he is filled with such horror and remorse that he contrives to die by Castalio's sword.

Acasto, a nobleman, the father of Castalio and Polydore, and Monimia's guardian.

Chamont, a young soldier, the impetuous brother of Monimia.

Serina, Acasto's daughter.

ORPHEUS AND EURYDICE

Author: Unknown
Time of action: Remote antiquity
First transcribed: Unknown

Orpheus (ôr′fē·əs), the son of Apollo and the Muse Calliope. His father teaches him to play the lyre so that all nature stops to listen to his music. He goes to the Underworld to redeem the shade of his dead wife, Eurydice. His wish to have her returned to him is granted, providing he does not look back until he has left the Underworld. He does look back, however, and Eurydice disappears. Later Orpheus is killed by a group of Thracian maidens in a Bacchic frenzy. Upon his death he joins Eurydice in the Underworld.

Apollo (ə·pŏl′ō), a god and the father of Orpheus. He gives a lyre to his son and teaches him to play it beyond the power of any other mortal.

Eurydice (ū·rĭ′dĭ·sē), the mortal wife of Orpheus. Fleeing from a shepherd

who desires her, she is bitten by a snake and dies. She is granted permission to return to the world with Orpheus if he will not look back until they have left the Underworld. When he looks back, she disappears again.

Hades (hā′dēz) and
Proserpine (prō·sėr′pə·nē), the King and Queen of the Underworld. Moved by Orpheus' music, they grant his request to take Eurydice back among the living, providing he does not look back at her while he is still in the Underworld.

Calliope (kə·lī′ə·pē), one of the Muses and Orpheus' mother.

Hymen (hī′mən), the god of marriage, who brings no happy omens to the wedding of Orpheus and Eurydice.

Tantalus (tăn'tə·ləs),
Ixion (ĭk·sī'ən),
The Daughters of Danaus (dăn'ī·əs), and

Sisyphus (sĭs'ə·fəs), shades of the Underworld, who are spellbound by the beauty of Orpheus' music.

OTHELLO

Author: William Shakespeare (1564-1616)
Time of action: Early sixteenth century
First presented: 1604

PRINCIPAL CHARACTERS

Othello (ō·thĕl'ō), a Moorish general in the service of Venice. A romantic and heroic warrior with a frank and honest nature, he has a weakness which makes him vulnerable to Iago's diabolic temptation. He becomes furiously jealous of his innocent wife and his loyal lieutenant. His character decays, and he connives with Iago to have his lieutenant murdered. Finally he decides to execute his wife with his own hands. After killing her, he learns of her innocence, and he judges and executes himself.

Iago (ē·ä'gō), Othello's ancient (ensign). A satirical malcontent, he is envious of the appointment of Michael Cassio to the position of Othello's lieutenant. He at least pretends to suspect his wife Emilia of having an illicit affair with the Moor. A demi-devil, as Othello calls him, he destroys Othello, Desdemona, Roderigo, his own wife, and himself. He is Shakespeare's most consummate villain, perhaps sketched in Aaron the Moor in "Titus Andronicus," Richard of Gloucester in "Henry VI" and "Richard III," and Don John in "Much Ado about Nothing"; and he is echoed in Edmund in "King Lear" and Iachimo in "Cymbeline." He contains strong elements of the Devil and the Vice in the medieval morality plays.

Desdemona (dĕz·dē·mō'nə), daughter of Brabantio and wife of Othello. An innocent, idealistic, romantic girl, she gives her love completely to her warrior husband. In her fear and shock at his violent behavior, she lies to him about her lost handkerchief, thus convincing him of her guilt. Even when she is dying, she tries to protect him from her kinsmen. One scholar has called her a touchstone in the play; each character can be judged by his attitude toward her.

Emilia (ē·mĭl'ī·ə), Iago's plain-spoken wife. Intensely loyal to her mistress, Desdemona, she is certain that some malicious villain has belied her to the Moor. She does not suspect that her husband is that villain until too late to save her mistress. She is unwittingly the cause of Desdemona's death; when she finds the lost handkerchief and gives it to Iago, he uses it to inflame the Moor's insane jealousy. Emilia grows in stature throughout the play and reaches tragic dignity when she refuses to remain silent about Iago's villainy, even though her speaking the truth costs her her life. Her dying words, clearing Desdemona of infidelity, drive Othello to his self-inflicted death.

Michael Cassio (kăs'ī·ō), Othello's lieutenant. Devoted to his commander and Desdemona, he is impervious to Iago's temptations where either is concerned. He is, however, given to loose living, and his behavior when discussing Bianca with Iago fires Othello's suspicions, after Iago has made Othello believe they are discussing Desdemona. Cassio's drinking on duty and becoming involved in a brawl lead to his replacement by Iago. He escapes the plot of Iago and Othello to murder him, and he succeeds Othello as Governor of Cyprus.

Brabantio (brá·băn′shĭ·ō), a Venetian Senator. Infuriated by his daughter's elopement with the Moor, he appeals to the Senate to recover her. Losing his appeal, he publicly casts her off and warns Othello that a daughter who deceives her father may well be a wife who deceives her husband. This warning plants a small seed of uncertainty in Othello's heart, which Iago waters diligently. Brabantio dies broken-hearted at losing Desdemona and does not learn of her horrible death.

Roderigo (rŏd·ɔ·rē′gō), a young Venetian suitor of Desdemona. The gullible victim of Iago, who promises him Desdemona's person, he aids in bringing about the catastrophe and earns a well-deserved violent death, ironically inflicted by Iago, whose cat's-paw he is. The degradation of Roderigo is in striking contrast to the growth of Cassio. Iago, who makes use of Roderigo, has profound contempt for him.

Bianca (bē·ăn′kɔ), a courtesan in Cyprus.

Cassio gives her Desdemona's handkerchief, which Iago has planted in his chambers. She thus serves doubly in rousing Othello's fury.

Montano (mōn·tä′nō), former Governor of Cyprus. He and Cassio quarrel in their cups (by Iago's machinations), and Montano is seriously wounded. This event causes Cassio's removal. Montano recovers and aids in apprehending Iago when his villainy is revealed.

Gratiano (grä·shĭ·ä′nō, grä·tyä′nō), the brother of Brabantio. He and Lodovico come to Cyprus from Venice and aid in restoring order and destroying Iago.

Lodovico, (lō·dō·vē′kō), a kinsman of Brabantio. As the man of most authority from Venice, he ends the play after appointing Cassio Governor of Cyprus to succeed the self-killed Othello.

The Clown, a servant of Othello. Among Shakespeare's clowns he has perhaps the weakest and briefest role.

THE OTHER ONE

Author: Colette (Sidonie Gabrielle Claudine Colette, 1873-1954)
Time of action: The 1920's
First published: 1929

PRINCIPAL CHARACTERS

Farou, a playwright. Handsome and overpowering, his presence dominates his household and completely absorbs its inhabitants: Fanny, his wife; Jane, his secretary and mistress; and, Jean, his son. Though he has been constantly unfaithful, he just as constantly insists that Fanny has always claimed his deepest devotion and that he depends on her to set right the disorders of their lives.

Fanny, Farou's beautiful wife. Proud in the knowledge that her husband is her one love, she learns of his intimacy with Jane and is disturbed by the necessity of being involved in one of his affairs and of sharing with another her pain over his

faithlessness. When she finally tells Jane of her knowledge of the affair she is suddenly afraid to be left alone, and she asks the girl to stay and provide a measure of security for them all.

Jane, Farou's secretary and a companion to Fanny. As she becomes Farou's mistress, she also becomes Fanny's affectionate companion. When her affair with Farou is discovered, she prepares to leave, but at Fanny's gentle urging, she consents to stay on.

Jean Farou, Farou's son by a former mistress. He is in love with Jane and suffers intensely over her relationship with his father.

OUR MUTUAL FRIEND

Author: Charles Dickens (1812-1870)
Time of action: Mid-nineteenth century
First published: 1864-1866

PRINCIPAL CHARACTERS

John Harmon, also known as **Julius Handford** and **John Rokesmith.** After his father's death he returns to England from South Africa, where he has lived for some years. On his arrival George Radfoot, a fellow passenger on the homeward voyage, lures him into a waterfront inn, drugs him, robs him, and throws him into the Thames. Revived by the cold water, Harmon swims to shore. He takes the name of Julius Handford. Meanwhile Radfoot has quarreled with a confederate, who murders him and throws his body into the river. When the body, wearing Harmon's clothes, is found, the dead man is identified as John Harmon. Discovering in the meantime that Bella Wilfer, whom he is supposed to marry according to the terms of his father's will, is a mercenary woman, Harmon decides to keep his identity a secret. As John Rokesmith he becomes the secretary to the man who has inherited his father's fortune and takes lodgings in the Wilfer home. When Bella finally realizes that love is more important than money, he marries her. After a year of happiness he reveals his true identity and accepts his inheritance.

Nicodemus Boffin, also called **Noddy** and **The Golden Dustman,** the illiterate, good-hearted confidential clerk who inherits the Harmon fortune after John Harmon's supposed death. When Mrs. Boffin learns John Rokesmith's true identity, her husband, at Harmon's request, agrees to keep the secret. Also at Harmon's suggestion, Boffin behaves with increasing evidence of greed until Bella Wilfer sees what avarice can lead to. Pestered by a blackmailer over the will, he finally shows that the fortune is really his and then generously hands it over to Harmon.

Henrietta Boffin, his cheerful, simple, affectionate wife, a childless woman who lavishes love on everyone around her.

Bella Wilfer, the young woman John Harmon is directed to marry. A beautiful girl from a poor home, she is taken in by the Boffins, who try to give her the advantages she would have enjoyed as Harmon's wife. In time her selfishness is overcome by her natural affections. She makes Harmon a fine wife and bears him a child.

Silas Wegg, a mean-spirited balladmonger and fruit seller, an ugly person whom illiterate Boffin hires to read to him. A prying rascal, he discovers a will in which the elder Harmon bequeathed his fortune to the Crown. He tries to blackmail Boffin, but he is foiled and tossed out into a garbage cart.

Mr. Venus, a dusty, good-willed taxidermist. He becomes Wegg's accomplice in the scheme to blackmail Boffin, but he later repents, reveals the whole plot, and wins the heart of Pleasant Riderhood.

Mortimer Lightwood, a bright, cautious solicitor who handles Boffin's affairs and reports on the developments of the Harmon case.

Eugene Wrayburn, his reckless, intelligent, and sprightly partner, who falls in love with Lizzie Hexam, the daughter of a Thames riverman. When she rejects him, he follows her to the country and is nearly murdered by a rival. Lizzie marries him finally and nurses him back to health.

Lizzie Hexam, a lovely, courageous, illiterate young woman. Oppressed by her father's death, her brother's rejection of her and the unwelcome courtship of a half-demented, jealous suitor, she moves out of London and finds work in a paper mill. In the end she marries Eugene Wrayburn, whom she nurses back to health after the young barrister has been injured in a murderous attack made by his rival.

Charlie Hexam, her selfish brother, a young man who rejects his father, his sister, and his schoolmaster in his cold-hearted effort to gain "respectability."

Gaffer Hexam, Lizzie's crude father, the riverman who pulls John Harmon's supposed body out of the Thames. After he dies accidentally he is slandered by his ex-partner, who accuses him of Harmon's murder.

Bradley Headstone, a schoolmaster, a pompous man who falls insanely in love with Lizzie, tries to murder Eugene Wrayburn, and take Rogue Riderhood to his watery death.

Roger Riderhood, nicknamed **Rogue,** a brutal man who for the sake of the reward accuses Gaffer Hexam of John Harmon's murder. Later he becomes Bradley Headstone's accomplice in the attempted murder of Eugene Wrayburn. He and Headstone drown during a scuffle.

Pleasant Riderhood, Rogue Riderhood's daughter, an unlicensed pawnbroker and Mr. Venus' sweetheart, whom she marries after rejecting him a number of times.

Fanny Cleaver, called **Jenny Wren,** a shrewd, pretty, but crippled maker of dolls' dresses and Lizzie Hexam's friend.

M. Cleaver, called **Mr. Dolls,** Fanny's spiritless, drunken father.

Mr. Riah, an old, generous-hearted Jew, the friend of Fanny Cleaver and Lizzie Hexam.

Alfred and
Sophronia Lammle, two charming

scoundrels who marry for money, learn that neither has any, and decide to prey on prominent members of society. They are forced to go abroad when their debts become pressing.

John Podsnap, a leader of society and a pompous and smug epitome of Philistinism.

Mrs. Podsnap, his majestic wife, the female counterpart of her husband.

Georgiana Podsnap, their warm, shy, silly daughter, the prey of the Lammles.

Mr. Fledgeby, whom his friends call **Fascination Fledgeby** behind his back, Georgiana's suitor. A mean, stupid, miserly dandy, he is encouraged in his social pretensions by the predatory Lammles. He hides his sharp business practices under a fictitious money brokerage firm, Pubsey and Co. Mr. Riah is his business agent.

Hamilton and
Anastatia Veneering, two shallow social climbers who have a new home, new furniture, new friends, a new baby. A former clerk in the firm of Chicksey and Stabbles, he is now a partner. He spends money liberally in order to get himself elected to Parliament.

Mrs. Wilfer, Bella Wilfer's austere, shrewish mother.

Reginald Wilfer, nicknamed **The Cherub,** Bella's affectionate, seedy, cherubic father.

Lavinia Wilfer, their younger daughter, a sharp, spirited girl.

George Sampson, Lavinia Wilfer's dull suitor, over whom she exercises tight control.

Melvin Twemlow, a poor but "connected" friend of the Veneerings. Though he lives over a livery stable, he is accepted in society because he is Lord Snigsworth's first cousin.

Betty Higden, an old, impoverished independent person who cares for displaced children; she is a friend of the Boffins.

Emma Peecher, a pedantic, warm, primitive young woman in love with Bradley Headstone.

Lady Tippins, a foolish woman, a friend of the Veneerings, who keeps a list of her nonexistent lovers.

Mr. Sloppy, a foundling taken in by Betty Higden. He is adopted by the Boffins.

The Reverend Frank Milney, the humble young curate who marries Lizzie Hexam and Eugene Wrayburn.

Mrs. Margaretta Milney, his wife, a woman of practical mind and brisk energy.

Mrs. Sprodgkin, one of Mr. Milney's parishioners. She makes his life miserable by her constant questions about who begot whom and other matters in the Bible.

Young Blight, Mortimer Lightwood's office boy.

OUR TOWN

Author: Thornton Wilder (1897-   )
Time of action: 1901-1913
First presented: 1938

PRINCIPAL CHARACTERS

The Stage Manager, a Chorus who explains and comments upon the action and the characters as the play unfolds.

Emily Webb, a young girl who grows up in Grover's Corners, a small American town. She is a sweet young thing who works hard in school, tries to be cheerful, and falls in love with the town's best baseball player. She dies in childbirth while still young and shyly takes her place among her relatives and friends in the little graveyard. She tries to live over her twelfth birthday, only to discover that to relive is no joy, that the dead can only pity the living who know not what joy they have in life.

George Gibbs, a typical young American boy who loves baseball. He gives up going to college to marry Emily, whom he dearly loves. When his wife dies he is filled with grief and goes to sob at her grave, not realizing that she pities him for not valuing the life he still enjoys.

Dr. Gibbs, the local physician and George's father. He is shocked to find that his son wants to marry and become a farmer, but finally realizes the youth is really no longer a child, any more than the doctor was when he married. Dr. Gibbs is a hardworking man whose hobby is the American Civil War; his idea of a vacation is an excursion to some battlefield of that conflict.

Mrs. Gibbs, George's mother, a hardworking woman who loves her family, even though she does not always understand them. She has found joy in her marriage and hopes her son will find joy in his.

Rebecca Gibbs, George's sister.

Wally Webb, Emily's brother.

Mr. Webb, Emily's father, editor-publisher of the local newspaper. He writes editorials every day, yet he cannot bring himself to advise his son-in-law on marriage, though he tries.

Mrs. Webb, Emily's mother, a good-hearted woman. On Emily's wedding day she finds herself unable to give her daughter advice on marriage, though she had meant to do so.

Simon Stimson, the local choir director. He has become an alcoholic because he cannot find happiness in the small town.

Even in death, after committing suicide, he believes life is ignorance and folly.

Joe Crowell, a newspaper boy.

Howie Newsome, a milkman.

OUR VILLAGE

Author: Mary Russell Mitford (1787-1855)
Time of action: Early nineteenth century
First published: 1824-1832

PRINCIPAL CHARACTERS

Miss Mitford, the author, who leads a happy life in an English village and its surrounding country, sharing her great happiness with her readers. She has a true appreciation of nature and of people, and she describes what she sees about her—the village and the countryside—lovingly. Her tales and sketches show the passing seasons in a year.

Lizzy, a young girl in the village. She is a sweet, lovable child of three who in turn loves everyone, winning the affection of all who know her. She manages the people around her, both adults and children. She is a frequent companion of the author as Miss Mitford takes walks through the village and the fields.

Jack Rapley, Miss Mitford's favorite boy

in the village. He is quite mischievous, and some of the villagers predict he will come to a bad end.

Master and
Dame Weston, a couple who fight frequently with each other. Though the wife blames her husband for their quarrels, she really is to blame.

Hannah Bint, a twelve-year-old girl who sets herself up as a dairywoman.

Mayflower, Miss Mitford's pompous, dignified greyhound, who is the author's constant companion.

Dash, a mongrel dog rescued by Mayflower. He dies because Miss Mitford feeds him well, for he is unused to a sufficient diet.

THE OVERCOAT

Author: Nikolai V. Gogol (1809-1852)
Time of action: Early nineteenth century
First published: 1842

PRINCIPAL CHARACTERS

Akakii Akakiievich Bashmachkin (ä·kä′-kǐy ä·kä′kǐy·ĕ·vǐch bäsh·mä′hǐn), a humble, poorly paid, aging government clerk, short, pock-marked, with reddish balding hair, dim and bleary eyes, and wrinkled cheeks. Possessing a high-sounding government grade of perpetual titular councilor, he is a mere copyist of documents. He loves his work, which he

does with neat and painstaking thoroughness, and he even takes some of it home to do at night. Badly needing an overcoat to replace the old one which the tailor refuses to repair, he plans to have a new one made, and for several months he lives in happy anticipation of getting it. When he wears it to the office he is pleased over the attention it gains him

830

from his fellow clerks; but he is desolated when it is stolen after a party given in his honor. Stammering and frightened by the domineering manner of a Certain Important Personage to whom he applies for help in finding his coat, he stumbles into a snowstorm, becomes ill, and dies in delirium. His ghost, after snatching overcoats from various people, finds the person of consequence wearing a fine overcoat and seizes it. Apparently the garment is a perfect fit, for Akakii never reappears to seize more coats.

Petrovich (pĕt·rō'vĭch), a one-eyed, pock-marked tailor given to heavy drinking, quoting high prices to his clients, and slyly watching to see what effects he has achieved.

A Certain Important Personage, a bureaucrat recently promoted to a position of consequence. With his equals he is pleasant, gentlemanly, and obliging, but with those below him he is reticent, rude, and very conscious of his superiority. Strict and a stickler for form, he tyrannizes his subordinates. The ghost of Bashmachkin steals his overcoat.

THE OX-BOW INCIDENT

Author: Walter Van Tilburg Clark (1909-)
Time of action: 1885
First published: 1940

PRINCIPAL CHARACTERS

Gil Carter, a wandering ranch hand who drifts into Bridger's Wells looking for a girl. When she returns to the town, after having reportedly gone to San Francisco, with a husband, Gil is furious. He joins a posse, but thinks more of his disappointment in love than of the hanging of three innocent men.

Art Croft, Gil's friend and companion. Though wounded by mistake by a stage driver, he goes on with the posse in search of rustlers.

Rose Mapen, the girl Gil loves and who disappoints him by marrying another man while gone from Bridger's Wells.

Canby, the saloonkeeper at Bridger's Wells.

Farnley, a cowboy who assists in hanging the three innocent men. When one of them, Donald Martin, dies too slowly in the hangman's noose, Farnley shoots him.

Kinkaid, Farnley's friend, supposedly killed by rustlers. He turns up alive after three innocent men have been hanged for his murder.

Davies, a storekeeper in the town. He tries to prevent the hanging of innocent men and fails. He takes a ring and a farewell letter to Martin's wife and two children. After the lynching he comes to believe, erroneously, that the fault was his.

Osgood, a Baptist minister. He tries to help Davies prevent mob action.

Joyce, a young cowboy who goes with Croft to ask Judge Tyler to swear in the posse.

Judge Tyler, the local magistrate. He tries to prevent mob action but ironically stimulates it.

Sheriff Risley, whose absence from town allows the mob to act. He returns just too late. He refuses to arrest the members of the posse, claiming lack of evidence.

Mapes, the sheriff's swaggering deputy who leads the posse he illegally deputizes.

Jenny Grier, called **Ma,** keeper of a boarding house. She helps hang the supposed rustlers and murderers.

Tetley, a rancher. He forces his son to participate in the mob's precipitate action. After his son commits suicide, he does, too.

Gerald Tetley, an emotional young man. Horrified by having to participate in the mob killings, he commits suicide.

Donald Martin, a rancher. Wrongly accused of being a rustler, he is hanged unlawfully by the mob.

A Mexican, Martin's rider, also hanged by the mob.

An Old Man, Martin's simple-minded worker, the mob's third victim.

Drew, a rancher. He failed to hand Martin a bill of sale for cattle purchased, thus contributing to the man's death.

PAMELA

Author: Samuel Richardson (1689-1761)
Time of action: Early eighteenth century
First published: 1740-1741

PRINCIPAL CHARACTERS

Pamela Andrews, a virtuous servant girl of Lady B——, mistress of an estate in Bedfordshire. After the death of her mistress she intends to return home but is persuaded to stay by the son, Mr. B——, who promises to be a good master to her. Later she has cause to suspect his intentions, and after he makes a series of attempts on her virtue she determines to leave. The coach, however, deposits her at Mr. B——'s country estate, where she is held prisoner. She meets the local minister, Mr. Williams. She tries several times to escape. Finally Mr. B——, moved by her virtue, offers her an honorable marriage, and she accepts his proposal. Despite anonymous letters and suspicions of other love affairs, she remains faithful and eventually turns Mr. B—— into an honorable husband.

John and
Elizabeth Andrews, the parents of Pamela.

Mr. B——, the young squire who plots against Pamela's virtue, tries to seduce her, proposes to make her his mistress on carefully outlined terms, and then finally marries her.

Lady Davers, the daughter of Lady B——, who at first opposes her brother's marriage to a servant. She begins to sympathize with Pamela after reading the many letters the girl had written her parents, and she is finally won over completely by Pamela's beauty and virtue.

Mrs. Jervis, Mr. B——'s kind-hearted housekeeper. For a time she protects Pamela's honor. When Mr. B—— tries to intimidate her, she and Pamela determine to leave together.

Mrs. Jewkes, the villainous ex-prostitute caretaker of Mr. B——'s country estate. She tries to further her employer's plots against Pamela's virtue and keeps the girl a prisoner.

Mr. Williams, the country clergyman of Lincolnshire who loves Pamela. Though the first proposal of marriage from him is part of Mr. B——'s scheme, he does seek to marry her. Discovered smuggling her letters out of the house, he is thrown into jail on a trumped-up charge. Eventually, when Mr. B—— repents, Mr. Williams performs the marriage ceremony and receives a permanent vicarage.

Sally Godfrey, a former sweetheart of Mr. B——, by whom he has a daughter. After her marriage Pamela offers to take the child under her own care.

The Daughter of Sally and Mr. B——.

Billy, the son of Pamela and Mr. B——.

A Countess, with whom Mr. B—— is philandering while Pamela is bearing his child. By reading some of Pamela's letters, she learns the punishment for those who depart from the path of virtue.

Mr. Longman, the steward of Mr. B——.

John, Mr. B——'s groom, who carries most of Pamela's letters to her parents, but keeps some for his master.

Robin, the coachman forced to take Pamela to Mr. B——'s country estate.

Nan, the rude servant who guards Pamela at Mr. B——'s estate.

Lady Jones, a neighbor who will give Pamela refuge if she succeeds in escaping from Mr. B——'s country estate.

Sir Simon Darnford and **Lady Darnford,** friends of Mr. B—— who want to help free Pamela.

Mrs. Towers, a neighbor who criticizes Pamela.

Mr. and Mrs. Brooks, neighbors.

Mrs. Arthur, another critical neighbor, who visits the new bride.

Sir Jacob Swynford, Mr. B——'s uncle. Prepared to dislike his nephew's humble bride, he is won over by Pamela's charm and virtue.

PARADE'S END

Author: Ford Madox Ford (Ford Madox Hueffer, 1873-1939)
Time of action: World War I and after
First published: "Some Do Not . . . ," 1924; "No More Parades," 1925; "A Man Could Stand Up—," 1926; "The Last Post," 1928

PRINCIPAL CHARACTERS

Christopher Tietjens (tē′jəns), an honest, imaginative, learned English gentleman with eighteenth century standards, a person whose integrity and self-sufficiency provoke lesser people to slander and betray him. Plagued by an unfaithful wife, a sponging sycophant named Macmaster, and a government job in which he is surrounded by spiteful men, he finds consolation in his mathematical calculations and the friendship of Valentine Wannop, a sensitive young woman. After joining the British Army in World War I he finds himself harried by attempts to compromise his dignity and integrity. An able officer, he wins the respect of his men, but the spite that surrounds him gets him relieved of his command after performing a deed of heroism. When he suffers a breakdown, Valentine nurses him and becomes his mistress. Later, in the antique furniture business, he finds a congenial kind of work. His peace, however, is disturbed by the knowledge that the values of his class and its way of life are doomed: Tietjens is "the last English Tory."

Sylvia Tietjens, his wealthy, fashionable, beautiful wife, a woman whose hatred for her husband's self-contained habits leads her to be unfaithful, slander him, ruin his army life, and terrorize his mistress. Unable to break his spirit, she eventually gets a divorce.

Sir Mark Tietjens, Christopher's oldest brother, the master of Groby, the family estate. A quiet, stolid man, he comes to respect his brother's integrity, virtue, and learning. Before his death he suffers a paralyzing stroke and is cared for by his former mistress, now his wife.

Vincent Macmaster, Christopher's toady, a dreary critic who borrows from his friend to set up a literary establishment. He gains a title but proves to be lacking in dignity and gratitude.

General Lord Edward Campion, Christopher's godfather and commanding officer in the war. Although he admires Christopher, he believes Sylvia's lies. He sends Christopher into the front lines, angrily relieves him of his command, and flirts with Sylvia after the war.

Valentine Wannop, the intelligent, pretty young woman who loves Christopher for his integrity. She becomes his mistress after the war. At the end she is carrying his child.

Mrs. Wannop, her lovely mother, a novelist who has been reduced to shoddy journalism after her husband's death. Like Christopher, she stands for outmoded values and habits.

Mrs. Edith Ethel Duchemin, later **Lady Macmaster,** a refined, elegant woman who has an affair with Macmaster and then marries him. After accepting aid from Christopher, she slanders him and Valentine.

The Rev. Mr. Duchemin, her lunatic first husband, a violent and obscene minister.

Mrs. Satterthwaite, Sylvia Tietjens' mother, an aging replica of her daughter, who adores her son-in-law, Christopher.

Father Consett, Sylvia's confessor, a shrewd, honest man who respects Christopher and dislikes Sylvia. After his death in the war he haunts Sylvia's imagination.

Mrs. Millicent de Bray Pape, a pompous, wealthy American who rents Groby after the war and, at Sylvia's instigation, cuts down the Groby Great Tree, a cedar symbolic of the Tietjens family, its history, values, and way of life.

Marie Léonie Riotor, Mark Tietjens'

French mistress, a wholesome, middle-aged woman who runs the Groby household, cares for the paralyzed Mark, and marries him.

Captain McKechnie, a paranoid classical scholar, Christopher's acquaintance who has been brutalized by the war and by his wife's infidelity. He is sent to Asia Minor after the war.

Colonel Levin, an honorable officer who befriends Christopher when sent to question him about his wife's affairs.

Perowne, Sylvia's spiritless lover, with whom she runs away. Later she causes him to disgrace Christopher's army record.

O Nine Morgan, a Welsh soldier whom Christopher refuses a leave to go home because his wife's lover, a prize fighter, will kill him. Later Morgan dies in action, a casualty doomed to one violent death or another.

The Colonel, an alcoholic British officer. He surrenders his command to Christopher, who becomes the Acting O.C. of the North Glamorganshires until relieved by General Campion's orders.

Sir Reginald Ingleby, the head of Christopher's department in the government, a man who respects Christopher's encyclopedic knowledge.

Lord Port Scatho, the manager of a bank where two of Christopher's checks are deliberately dishonored. He later tries to make amends.

Mr. Tietjens, Christopher's father, an honorable person who commits suicide, apparently because of his son's rumored misbehavior.

Ruggles, Mark Tietjens' toady, a base person who lies to Mr. Tietjens about Christopher's actions.

Michael Mark Tietjens, Sylvia's son, for whom Christopher assumes paternity. He is the heir to Groby.

Miss Wanostrocht, the prudish head mistress at the school where Valentine teaches.

Second Lieutenant Aranjuez, whose life Christopher saves during a German attack. He comes to see Christopher on Armistice Day.

Lance-Corporal Duckett, a sensitive young man buried by the explosion of a German shell.

Mr. Schatzweiler, an American antique dealer and Christopher's business part ner after the war.

PARADISE LOST

Author: John Milton (1608-1674)
Time of action: The Beginning
First published: 1667

PRINCIPAL CHARACTERS

Adam, the first man and representative of mankind. Though gifted with reason and restraint, he allows an excessively passionate tenderness for Eve to blind him. Forewarned by the Archangel Raphael of danger from Satan, he nevertheless yields to Eve's entreaty that she alone be trusted. When he learns that she has fallen, he chooses to join her rather than turn from her. His first reaction after his own fall is to rebuke and blame her for his own sin. After falling into almost suicidal despair, he repents; and when the Archangel Michael foretells the future redemption of mankind by Christ, he accepts his fate with gratitude.

Eve, the first woman and representative of womanhood. Beautiful, gentle, and submissive, she holds Adam enthralled. She is horrified when Satan first approaches her in a dream; but piqued by what she considers Adam's lack of faith in her, she stubbornly insists on working alone, thereby leaving herself vulnerable to the Serpent's temptation. Like Adam, after the fall she is first lustful, then quarrelsome. Finally she too accepts her fate with dignity and resignation.

Satan (Lucifer), chief of the fallen angels, adversary of God and man. A splendid conception, his obvious heroism and grandeur are tainted by a perversion of will and accompanying perversion of

intellect. Rebellious against God, he is incapable of understanding Him. A self-tormented spirit, like Marlowe's Mephistophilis in "Doctor Faustus," conscious of his loss but unwilling to repent, he allows evil to eat away at him, tarnishing his splendor. His degradation is complete when he wills to enter the body of the serpent. His attempt to seduce man succeeds, but his triumph is temporary and hollow.

Beelzebub (bĭ-ĕl′zə-bŭb), Satan's chief lieutenant. Less confident and less splendid than his chief, he works his will and serves as his mouthpiece. In the council of the fallen angels in Pandemonium, he presents forcefully Satan's plan of indirect war on God through man. His proposal carries.

Moloch (mō′lŏk), fiercest of the fallen angels. Appropriately worshiped in later years with human sacrifice, he is bloody-minded and desperate. If the fallen angels cannot win Heaven, he chooses either to make Heaven intolerable for the angels who did not fall or to anger God to the point that He will annihilate the fallen spirits.

Belial (bē′lĭ-əl), a fallen angel industrious only in vice. Smooth and oily, he favors peace at any price and expresses the hope that if the fallen angels do not call God's

835

attention to themselves, He will forget them and allow their sufferings to decrease. He favors a proper course, but for improper reasons, basing his surrender on sloth, not on acceptance of God's will.

Mammon (măm′ən), the materialistic fallen angel. Like Belial, he is opposed to a second war against Heaven, but he favors a plan of development of natural resources and exploitation of Hell to raise an empire that will rival Heaven.

Mulciber (Vulcan) (mŭl′sĭ·bər), Mammon's chief engineer and architect. Formerly the planner of many of Heaven's buildings, he is now architect of Pandemonium, Satan's palace in Hell.

Sin, Satan's daughter, born from his brain without a mother. She is the loathsome keeper of Hell's gates, through which she lets Satan pass to attack the world. She and her grisly son Death follow Satan to earth to prey on mankind.

Death, son of Sin and Satan by their incestuous union. He ravishes Sin and begets a horde of hell-hounds on her. His voraciousness is so great that he would devour his own mother, except for the fear that her death would involve his own destruction. His fierce reaction to Satan is mollified by the latter's offer of hosts of men and beasts for him to devour if Satan's assault on earth succeeds.

God the Father. All-knowing and all-powerful, He foresees Satan's activities and man's fall, but extends to man His grace and brings forth good from evil.

Messiah, the only Son of God. He is first granted by His Father the overthrow of Satan and his legions in the War in Heaven, then granted His wish to sacrifice Himself to redeem man.

Michael (mī′kəl), the warrior angel. Chief of the angelic forces in the War in Heaven, he is a worthy opponent of Satan. He is God's messenger to Adam and Eve to tell them of their banishment from Paradise and their coming death; however, he is allowed by God's grace to foretell to Adam the future of the human race and the redemption to come.

Abdiel (ăb′dĭ·ĕl), angelic servant of God. Alone among Lucifer's angel hordes, he remains steadfast and is rewarded by God's own praise and the favor of striking the first blow against Satan in the war against the rebel angels. Obviously one of Milton's favorite creations in "Paradise Lost," he is perhaps an idealized version of the poet himself.

Raphael (răf′ĭ·əl, rā′fĭ·əl), God's messenger to Adam to warn him of Satan's presence in Paradise. Gracious and friendly, he still is capable of severe judgment and warns Adam particularly against unreasonable and passionate adoration of Eve.

Gabriel (gā′brĭ·əl), chief of the angelic guards in Paradise. He is a major leader in the War in Heaven against the evil angels.

Uriel (yōōr′ĭ·əl), regent of the Sun. Even though an angel, he is incapable of seeing through the mask of a hypocrite and fails to recognize Satan in his disguise as a lesser angel. He directs the evil spirit to Paradise, but sees his actions in Paradise and hastily warns Gabriel that an evil spirit has gained entrance there.

Uzziel (ŭ·zī′ĕl, ŭz′ĭ·ĕl),
Ithuriel, (ĭ·thū′rĭ·əl), and
Zephon (zē′fŏn), angel guards in Paradise.

PARADISE REGAINED

Author: John Milton (1608-1674)
Time of action: First century
First published: 1671

Jesus of Nazareth, the tempted. An embodiment of John Milton's religious philosophy and ideals. He is reasonable, intelligent, and holy. Pronounced the beloved Son of God at his baptism, he enters the desert to meditate on the course he should choose to fulfill his destiny as the Saviour of mankind. His self-communion and his troubled dreams show His humanity and prevent His becoming a mere theological abstraction. Superior to both physical and spiritual temptations, He overcomes Satan and redeems mankind from its fallen state caused when Adam and Eve succumbed to temptation.

Satan, the tempter, the great Dictator of Hell. Debased from the splendid, though tarnished, rebel of "Paradise Lost," he is a sly, lying trickster. His choice of temptations for Jesus shows shrewdness; but, shorn of understanding of God, he lacks wisdom. Frustrated by the fortitude and virtue of Jesus, he lapses into snarling and futile rage. His violence recoils on himself, and astonished, he falls a second time, completely conquered.

John the Baptist, the trumpet-voiced "great Proclaimer." Satan learns at the baptism of Jesus by John that he now has a terrible adversary among men.

Belial, the self-indulgent fallen angel. Lustful himself, he thinks lust the perfect temptation; therefore, he advises Satan to use women in his temptation of Jesus. His suggestion is scornfully overruled by Satan.

Mary the Mother of Jesus. Pure-hearted and calm, she is nevertheless troubled over the long absence of her Son.

God the Father. Omniscient and all-wise, He foretells to Gabriel the temptations and their outcome.

Gabriel, the angel of the Annunciation. He is chosen to hear God's prophetic plan.

PARZIVAL

Author: Wolfram von Eschenbach (1170-1220)
Time of action: The chivalric age
First published: Thirteenth century manuscript

Gamuret (gä′mōō·rĕt), the younger son of King Gandein, who leaves Anjou to seek his fortune. He rescues Belakane and marries her.

Gandein (gän′dĕ·ēn′), King of Anjou.

Belakane (bĕ·lä·kä′nĕ), a Moorish queen who is falsely accused of killing Eisenhart, her lover.

Friedebrand (frē′dĕ·bränd), King of Scotland and uncle of Eisenhart. He besieges the castle of Belakane in an attempt to avenge his nephew.

Feirefis (fī′rä·fĭs), the son of Gamuret and Belakane, who almost vanquishes Parzival. Together they fight in many tournaments.

Herzeledde (hĕr′tsĕ·lī·dĕ), **Queen of Waleis** (wä′līs), at whose tournament Gamuret is the victor. She marries him after the tourney.

Parzival (pär′zē·fäl), the son of Herzeleide and Gamuret.

Queen Kondwiramur (kŏn′dwē′rä·mōōr), whom Parzival marries and later deserts.

Lohengrin (lō′hĕn·grēn), the son of Kondwiramur and Parzival.

Jeschute (ya·shōō'tĕ), who gives Parzival a token.

Orilus (ō'rĭ·lōōs), the jealous husband of Jeschute. He fights Parzival but is pacified.

The Red Knight, who knights Parzival.

Gurnemanz (gōōr'nĕ·mänts), the Prince of Graharz, who instructs Parzival in knightly precepts.

Baruch (bä'rōōkh), the ruler of Alexandria, for whom Gamuret fought and was finally slain.

King Kailet (kī'lăt), the companion of Gamuret in Spain.

Arthur, King of Britain.

Queen Guinevere, Arthur's wife.

Sir Kay (kā), the seneschal, defeated by Parzival.

Sir Gawain (gä'wīn), who introduces Parzival to Arthur's Round Table.

Orgeluse (ōr'gĕl·ōōsĕ), the wife of Gawain.

King Meljanz of Lys (mĕl'yänts), for whom Sir Gawain fights Duke Lippaut.

Antikonie (än·tĭ'kŏ·nē), the daughter of King Meljanz, who is courted by Gawain.

Gramoflanz (grä'mō·flänts), whom Parzival offers to fight because, unknowingly, he has wounded Sir Gawain while that knight was riding to do battle with Gramoflanz. The challenge is rejected because Gramoflanz refuses to meet any knight but Gawain.

Trevrezent (trāv'rĕ·zănt), a hermit who indicates that Parzival is the nephew of Amfortas, the Grail King, and himself.

Amfortas (äm·fōr'täs), the Fisher King who shows Parzival the mysteries of the Grail and is himself cured of his grievous wound by a miraculous recovery.

Kondrie (kōn'drē), Parzival's guide to the Grail Kingdom.

Repanse de Schoie (rĕ·pän'sĕ dĕ shoi'ĕ), the wife of Feirefis and mother of Prester John.

Sigune (sĭ·gō'nĕ), the woman who tells Parzival of his lineage.

A PASSAGE TO INDIA

Author: E. M. Forster (1879-   )
Time of action: c. 1920
First published: 1924

PRINCIPAL CHARACTERS

Dr. Aziz (ä·zēz'), an amiable, sensitive, and intelligent young Moslem doctor in Chandrapore, India. Ignored and snubbed by the English colony, he nevertheless becomes friendly with three English newcomers to India—Mr. Fielding, Mrs. Moore, and Miss Quested. When he takes them on a tour of the sinister Marabar Caves, Miss Quested becomes separated from the party and later she accuses him of attempted rape. Jailed and humiliated, he becomes markedly anti-British. After Miss Quested withdraws her charge at his trial, he wants to collect damages, but Fielding dissuades him. Suspicious of Fielding's motives, he breaks off the friendship. Two years later the two men meet again and each realizes that any true communion between them is impossible because of their racial allegiances.

Cecil Fielding, the Principal of the Government College, a middle-aged, mav-

838

erick intellectual who resists the herd instinct of his fellow Englishmen. He has Indian friends; he defends Aziz against the English bigots, and when Miss Quested is ostracized after the trial he offers her the protection of his home. Tired of the whole situation, he takes a trip to England, marries, and then returns to India, where he finds Aziz less cordial than before.

Adela Quested, a priggish young woman who goes to India to marry Ronald Heaslop, the City Magistrate; she announces that she is eager to see the real India. Her trip to the Marabar Caves proves disastrous. Thinking that she has been the victim of an attempted attack, she accuses Aziz; however, she shows courage by retracting the charge at his trial. The scandal ruins her prospective marriage and causes her to be avoided by almost everyone. She returns to England alone.

Mrs. Moore, Ronald Heaslop's mother, a lovely, sensitive old woman who accompanies Miss Quested to India. She has great regard for Dr. Aziz, but at the Marabar Caves she has a strange psychic experience, an unhappy intuition that life is worthless. When she irritably defends Dr. Aziz to her son, he sends her home and she dies on the way.

Ronald Heaslop, the self-righteous City Magistrate, a man coarsened by life in India. Wishing his mother and fiancée to have nothing to do with the natives, he finds himself in a position where he must reject both to preserve his own standards and vanity.

Professor Godbole, a gentle old teacher at the College, a friend of Dr. Aziz and Fielding. He represents the Hindu mystical aspects of India as opposed to the narrower nationalisms of the Moslems and British.

The Nawab Bahadur, a wealthy Moslem who, acting as an unofficial diplomat between the Moslems and English, does favors for the whites. When Dr. Aziz is tried, he rejects the British.

Hamidullah, Dr. Aziz' well-to-do, Anglophobic uncle, a Cambridge barrister who conducts his nephew's defense.

Mahmoud Ali, a family friend of Hamidullah and Dr. Aziz. Cynical and embittered toward the English, he makes an emotional, histrionic defense of Dr. Aziz at the trial.

Mohammed Latif, a poor, sneaky relative of Hamidullah and Aziz.

Major Callendar, the civil surgeon, Dr. Aziz' brutal superior, who believes that "white is right."

Mr. Turton, a white official who is willing to extend courtesy to the natives and nothing more; a man who has succumbed to power and race snobbery.

Mrs. Turton, his haughty wife, who comforts Adela Quested after the incident at the Marabar Caves.

Mr. McBryde, the Chief of Police, an intelligent man who treats Dr. Aziz decently but at the same time supervises the prosecution. He is provincial in his attitudes.

Miss Derek, a selfish young woman who takes advantage of her Indian employers.

Amritrao, Dr. Aziz' defense lawyer, imported from Calcutta, who gets Miss Quested to withdraw her charges.

Mr. Das, Heaslop's subordinate, the judge at the trial, a Hindu who later becomes friendly with Dr. Aziz.

Ralph Moore, Mrs. Moore's odd son, a boy who finally gets Cecil Fielding and Dr. Aziz together again.

Stella Moore, Mrs. Moore's daughter, a sensitive girl who marries Cecil Fielding.

THE PASSION FLOWER

Author: Jacinto Benavente y Martínez (1866-1954)
Time of action: Early twentieth century
First presented: 1913

PRINCIPAL CHARACTERS

Esteban (ās·tä′bän), a well-to-do peasant and the second husband of Raimunda. Faustino, the fiancé of Acacia, his stepdaughter, is shot and killed. When the chief suspect, Norbert, is acquitted, Rubio, Esteban's servant, becomes increasingly impudent. His drunken talk causes Raimunda to suspect Esteban of loving his stepdaughter. When Esteban offers to leave because of the trouble he has caused, Acacia declares her love for him. In the confusion following Raimunda's screaming denunciation, the cornered Esteban shoots his wife.

Acacia (ä·kä′thyä), the daughter of Raimunda and Esteban's stepdaughter. Although she repeatedly declares her resentment of Esteban for marrying Raimunda so soon after her father's death, her mother eventually suspects that she is in love with her stepfather. When Esteban announces his intention of leaving, she breaks down and declares her love for him.

Raimunda (r̄rä·ē·mōōn′dä), Esteban's wife and Acacia's mother. After the murder of Acacia's fiancé, Faustino, she is led, by the drunken talk of Rubio, to suspect her husband and her daughter of being in love. When she is shot by Esteban, she dies in peace because, at the end, Acacia turns to her. She feels that she has saved her daughter from her stepfather, that Esteban can never have her now.

Faustino (fäōōs·tē′nō), Acacia's fiancé, who is shot by an unknown person.

Tío Eusebio (tē′ō ā·ōō·sä′bē·ō), Faustino's father and Esteban's friend. His sons shoot and wound Norbert, thinking that he is their brother's murderer.

Rubio (r̄rōō′byō), Esteban's servant, whose drunken talk leads Raimunda to suspect Esteban and Acacia of being in love with each other. He declares that his master had never told him to murder Faustino but had expressed hope that no one would take Acacia away.

Norbert (nôr·bärt′), Acacia's former fiancé, who is cleared in the shooting of Faustino.

Juliana (hōō·lyä′nä) and
Bernabé (bär·nä·bā′), family servants.

Fidelia (fē·t̄hä′lyä),
Engracia (än·grä′thyä), and
Milagros (mē·lä′grōs), family friends.

THE PATHFINDER

Author: James Fenimore Cooper (1789-1851)
Time of action: 1756
First published: 1840

PRINCIPAL CHARACTERS

Thomas Dunham, a sergeant of the Fort Oswego garrison in the western New York territory during the French and Indian Wars. He has his daughter Mabel brought to the fort in order to promote a marriage between her and his friend Natty Bumppo, the wilderness scout called Pathfinder by the English.

On a tour of duty among the Thousand Islands his party captures and sinks three French ships, but when they return to an island blockhouse his men are ambushed by Iroquois Indians and he is mortally wounded. Attended by his daughter, he dies blessing her and Jasper Western, whom he believes to be Pathfinder.

Mabel Dunham, his young, warm, frank, and pretty daughter. After Pathfinder has saved the party with which she travels from hostile Indians, she comes to respect Pathfinder's courage and skill in the woods, but the man she truly loves is his friend, Jasper Western. At Fort Oswego she finds herself courted by Jasper, Pathfinder, and Davy Muir, each of whom accompanies her father on a tour of duty. During an Indian ambush she is saved by the warnings of an Indian girl and the resolute defense of Pathfinder and her uncle. In the end Pathfinder relinquishes her to Jasper, whom she marries.

Charles Cap, Mabel Dunham's crusty uncle, a hardy fellow who accompanies his niece to Fort Oswego and later goes with Sergeant Dunham on his tour of duty to relieve a garrison in the Thousand Islands. A seagoing sailor, he suspects and derides Jasper Western, a fresh-water sailor, but learns to respect the young seaman when Jasper saves the cutter "Scud" after Cap had almost wrecked it during a storm. After barely escaping an Indian ambush, he ably assists Pathfinder in the defense of a beleaguered blockhouse until help arrives. He sees his niece married to Jasper and returns to the sea.

Natty Bumppo, called **Pathfinder,** the frontier scout in his prime. A man of great courage, resourcefulness, and honesty, he falls in love for the only time in his life, but in return he receives little more than Mabel Dunham's esteem. After protecting her in many perils, Pathfinder learns of Jasper Western's and Mabel's mutual love and defers to his friend. His personal integrity remains pure as he moves on with his Indian friend, of many years, the Mohican chief Chingachgook.

Jasper Western, called "Eau-douce" because he is a fresh-water sailor, Pathfinder's younger companion and the more successful rival for Mabel Dunham's hand. A skilled and honorable man, he is nevertheless under suspicion of being a French spy. When circumstances seem to prove his guilt, his command of a cutter is temporarily taken away from him. After he has aided in relieving the besieged blockhouse, the real spy is revealed. The discovery clears his name, and Pathfinder's relinquishment of Mabel leaves him free to marry his love.

Lieutenant Davy Muir, the glib quartermaster at Fort Oswego, a thrice-wed, middle-aged suitor of Mabel Dunham. Resentful of his subordinate position, he secretly spies for the French, puts the blame for his treachery on Jasper Western, and survives an Indian ambush. His successes are cut short when Arrowhead, a resentful Tuscarora Indian, mortally stabs him.

Arrowhead, the bold, ambitious Tuscarora chief who tries to lead Mabel and her uncle into an ambush; he falls in love with the white girl. He is later caught by the party aboard the cutter but escapes to lead the two ambushes that almost prove fatal to Sergeant Dunham's party. Thinking that Muir has betrayed him, he kills the spy and is killed by Chingachgook in turn.

Dew-of-June, the submissive, gentle wife of Arrowhead. Although she saves Mabel Dunham by warning her of danger from hostile Indians and whites, she remains loyal to her husband. Mourning his death, she goes to live with Mabel, but dies soon afterward.

Chingachgook, whose name means "the Great Serpent," a Mohican chief and

Pathfinder's loyal friend. A lifelong foe of the Iroquois, he aids his friend Pathfinder in many encounters with hostile Indians and the French.

Major Duncan, of Lundie, the generous, considerate commanding officer of Fort Oswego. Warned by an anonymous letter that Jasper Western is a spy for the French, he is forced to advise Sergeant Dunham to watch the young man carefully.

Captain Sanglier, the audacious French leader of the Iroquois. Captured after the siege of the blockhouse, he contemptuously reveals that Lieutenant Muir, not Jasper Western, has spied for the French.

Corporal McNab, the stubborn soldier who hesitates to believe Mabel Dunham's warning of an impending Indian ambush. He is shot during the skirmishing.

Jenny McNab, his wife. She is killed while trying to pull her husband into the blockhouse when the Indians attack.

PATIENCE

Author: W. S. Gilbert (1836-1911)
Time of action: Nineteenth century
First presented: 1881

PRINCIPAL CHARACTERS

Patience, a beautiful dairy maid beloved by two poets. Believing that love must be unselfish, she promises herself to the one she does not like; she finally convinces herself that the one she really loves is unattractive enough for her to accept—unselfishly, of course.

Reginald Bunthorne, a fleshly poet. A self-confessed sham, he pretends to be an aesthete to attract attention, particularly feminine attention. When Grosvenor takes away most of his feminine admirers, Bunthorne threatens to curse him unless he cuts his hair short and gives up aesthetic costumes and attitudes. Unfortunately, Bunthorne's victory costs him his intended bride.

Archibald Grosvenor, an idyllic poet, childhood sweetheart of Patience. Handsome and wealthy, known as Archibald-the-All-Right, he captivates Bunthorne's followers. Even after he cuts his hair the girls continue to admire him extravagantly; but Patience now finds him commonplace enough for her to marry.

The Lady Jane, a faded, middle-aged follower of Bunthorne, loyal when the girls desert him for Grosvenor. Finally, however, she too deserts Bunthorne in order to marry the Duke, forcing the poet to be contented with a rose or a lily instead of a girl.

The Duke of Dunstable, a lieutenant in a regiment of dragoons who cannot understand why any girl would be interested in poets when soldiers are around. Having everything, he decides to bestow himself on the plainest girl—the Lady Jane.

THE PATRICIAN

Author: John Galsworthy (1867-1933)
Time of action: Early twentieth century
First published: 1911

842

Eustace Carádoc, Lord Miltoun, the idealistic eldest son of the Carádoc family. In the tradition of the aristocracy, he is making his bid for a seat in Parliament. In love with Mrs. Noel, he enters into an affair with her. Feeling that such a liaison is not commensurate with a parliamentary career, he plans to give up the seat he has won. When Mrs. Noel, realizing that he will never be happy outside Parliament, decides to leave, he goes on with his career.

Mrs. Audrey Lees Noel, the wife of the Reverend Stephen Noel. She is loved by Eustace Carádoc. Not realizing that he is ignorant of her married status, she does not discourage his attentions and inspires him to fall in love with her. Later, engaged in an active affair with him, she decides to leave rather than jeopardize his political career.

Lord Valleys, head of the Carádoc family, and
Lady Valleys, Eustace Carádoc's conservative, aristocratic parents.

Lady Casterley, Eustace Carádoc's grandmother, who is instrumental in persuading Mrs. Noel to give up Eustace for the sake of his career.

Mr. Courtier, a liberal and Eustace Carádoc's political opponent.

Barbara Carádoc, Eustace's sister. Feeling herself bound by the restraints of family and society, and attracted by Mr. Courtier and his views on personal freedom, she encourages the affair between her brother and Mrs. Noel. She finally marries a man of her own class.

THE PATRIOT

Author: Antonio Fogazzaro (1842-1911)
Time of action: Mid-nineteenth century
First published: 1896

Don Franco Maironi, the patriot, who seeks Italy's independence from Austria. He has studied law, but wastes his time with poetry and the piano.

The Marchesa Orsola, his grandmother, who stanchly supports Austria. She seeks a rich, well-born wife for Franco and cuts him off when he marries Luisa. Later she repents.

Luisa Rigey, a poor, low-born girl who is loved by Franco. She nearly goes mad when their daughter is drowned.

Luisa's Mother, who permits the secret marriage.

Piero Ribera, a government employee and the uncle of Luisa, who supports them until the Marchesa has him discharged.

A Friend, who possesses a copy of a letter that proves the Marchesa is an immoral woman willfully cheating Franco out of the fortune left him by his grandfather.

PAUL BUNYAN

Author: James Stevens (1892-   )
Time of action: From the Winter of the Blue Snow to the Spring That the Rain
Came Up from China
First published: 1925

Paul Bunyan, the gigantic hero of exaggerated yarns first told along the Canadian border about 1837. Bunyan first saw Babe, the Blue Ox, the winter the blue snow fell. Together they set up a lumber camp. Bunyan invents the multiplication table, the cube root system, and algebra so that he can keep the records until he meets Johnny Inkslinger and makes him his bookkeeper. When ordinary logging methods fail, he shoots the trees off the slopes of the Mountain That Stood On Its Head. He sweats so hard cutting the stonewood trees in Utah that he creates Salt Lake. With the coming of machinery, however, there is no place for him, and he and Babe disappear forever over the hills.

Babe, the huge Blue Ox, brought up by Bunyan from a calf. When whale milk will not cure his illness, whiskey does the trick.

Niagara, Paul's moosehound.

Hels Helsen, a giant who fights a savage battle with Bunyan and then becomes his friend for life.

Johnny Inkslinger, who loses his job as surveyor when Bunyan cuts down the trees he uses for stakes. He then becomes the camp bookkeeper.

Sourdough Sam, the camp cook, who loses an arm and a leg when some sourdough, put into Johnny's ink, explodes.

Hot Biscuit Slim, Sam's son and successor, who makes meals the high point of a logger's day.

Shanty Boy, of Bunkhouse I, whose tall stories amuse the loggers until he tells them of Jonah and the whale; then he is beaten for lying.

King Bourbon, of Kansas. He is overcome by a rebellious Duke who gets everybody drunk. Bunyan hitches Babe to Kansas and turns it upside down to quiet things, leaving Kansas flat and rid of cigarette grass, beervines, and whiskey trees.

THE PEACE

Author: Aristophanes (c. 448-c. 385 B.C.)
Time of action: The Peloponesian War
First presented: 421 B.C.

Trygaeus (trī·jē′əs), a wealthy citizen of Athens who desires peace between Athens and Sparta. After losing all faith that a peace will be achieved through diplomacy, he resolves to ask Zeus for help. His first effort to climb Olympus by ladders results in a broken head; he then attempts to make the journey on the back of an enormous dung beetle. After a successful flight he is accosted at the door of the palace of Zeus by Hermes, who informs Trygaeus that the gods are disgusted by the stupidities of the Greeks and have resolved to leave them ravaged by War and Tumult. Peace has been buried in an enormous pit and has been covered with stones by the effort of War. Trygaeus, witnessing War beginning to grind up the Greek cities as he might a salad in a large mortar, resolves to liberate Peace, and to that end calls to his aid common men, laborers and farmers, from all over Greece, who form the Chorus. After ludicrously inept efforts on their part, Peace, along with Opora and Theoria, is liberated from the pit. Trygaeus, taking Opora with him for his marriage bed, and taking Theoria for the Senate, returns to Earth. At the marriage feast of Trygaeus and Opora, various warmongers attempt to upset the peace and quell the joy, but Trygaeus scornfully rejects their offers of bribes. The play concludes with Opora being brought out in her wedding finery while the Chorus sings "Hymen Hymenaeus."

Hermes (hûr′mēz), the servant of Zeus, intended to serve as an example of the servants of the powerful in Athens as well as a reflection of the deviousness and corruption of their masters' minds. He abuses Trygaeus at first, but subsides into friendliness and coöperation at the appearance of a bribe. Hermes' information about the intentions of the gods to ignore the Greeks makes it possible for Trygaeus to free Peace.

Two Servants of Trygaeus, the first being his master's steward and confidential attendant who coöperates with Trygaeus throughout the play. The opening scene of the play finds both servants excitedly kneading cakes of excrement and feeding them to the dung beetle in the stable.

War, who hastily assembles the Greek cities in his mortar with the intention of grinding them into a salad and eventually into a paste.

Tumult, the servant of War, much

abused by his master, who is sent off to Athens to bring back a pestle.

Hierocles (hī′rō·klēz), a soothsayer who appears at the preparation for the marriage feast and belligerently shouts prophecies about the impossibility of ending the war.

An Armourer and
A Crest-Maker, who appear at the marriage feast to lament their loss of profits after the release of Peace. They try to promote surplus war goods for peaceful purposes, such as spears to use as vine pole.

The Son of Lamachus (lă′mə·kəs) and
The Son of Cleonymus (klē·ŏ′nĭ·məs), young boys at the marriage feast, who sing as they have been taught of the glories of war until silenced by the sharp rejoinders of Trygaeus.

A Sickle-Maker, whose business has been ruined by the wars. He comes to the marriage feast to present Trygaeus with samples of his products.

A Chorus of Husbandmen, from all parts of Greece, who in trying to release Peace work against one another despite the best of intentions until the farmers, the only ones who do real work, free Peace from the pit. Throughout the play the Chorus sings the joys of peaceful domestic life.

THE PEASANTS

Author: Ladislas Reymont (1868-1925)
Time of action: Late nineteenth century
First published: 1902-1909

PRINCIPAL CHARACTERS

Matthias Boryna, a well-to-do peasant, the leading man of Lipka village in Poland. Though he is sixty years old and has already outlived two wives, he is thinking of marrying again. That his grown children wish him to retire and divide his land among them makes no difference. Sorrow comes of his marriage,

for he unwisely takes a wanton as his third wife. Worst of all, she takes Matthias Boryna's married son as her lover. The old man learns to endure having such a wife but at great cost to his peace of mind. He turns for moral support to Hanka, his son's wife, and asks her and her children to live in his house, for he is a kindly, if headstrong, man. During a battle to protect timber claimed by the peasants from being cut by the owner of a nearby manor, Matthias is severely wounded. He lies many months in a stupor, neglected by his wife but nursed tenderly by his daughter-in-law until he dies.

Yagna, Matthias Boryna's young wife, the prettiest girl in Lipka village. She turns out to be a common trull, taking up with whatever man her fancy falls on at the moment. She has an affair with Antek Boryna, her stepson, who truly loves her and is intensely bitter when the girl marries his father. Concerned only for herself, Yagna is not sorry for the trouble she brings to the Boryna family. Her only feelings while her husband lies injured for many weeks is bitterness that he still lives. She goes too far at last by chasing after a young man of the village who is studying to be a priest. The indignant, shocked villagers carry her out of Lipka on a dung cart and warn her not to return. The shock of the treatment leaves her insensible for weeks.

Antek Boryna, Matthias' grown son, a man as headstrong as his father. Sick with love for Yagna, he leaves his father's house and becomes a common laborer, neglecting his wife and children. After he kills the forester who has injured his father, he and Matthias' are reconciled. Antek, in prison for many weeks, returns to find his father dead. He becomes master of the Boryna farm, a position which strengthens him to put aside his feelings for Yagna, though she still means much to him.

Hanka, Antek Boryna's loving wife. Deserted by her husband, she cares for herself and her children. A woman driven by the peasant's love of the land and its ownership, she looks after the Boryna farm and wealth while her husband is in prison and her father-in-law lies ill. She loves her husband deeply and readily accepts him when he gives up his affair with Yagna.

Dominikova, Yagna's widowed mother, a selfish, land-hungry, domineering old woman who treats her grown sons as though they were slaves and will not let them marry.

Kuba Soha, an old hired man on the Boryna farm, a veteran who had fought against the Russians. He turns poacher and is wounded by the local squire's forester for taking game. He dies when he tries to amputate his own leg.

Yuzka, the young sister of Antek Boryna.

The Voyt, the elected headman of the village, a man who feathers his own nest and is distrusted by the people of Lipka. He is eventually caught by the government for stealing several thousand rubles of public money. He is one of Yagna's lovers.

Yanek, the son of the village organist, an honest, religious young man who has begun his studies for the priesthood. Although Yagna Boryna openly pursues him, he cannot believe she is as bad as village gossip says she is. His family finally sends him away to protect him from the girl.

Simon, one of Dominikova's grown sons. He rebels against his mother's domination and manages to buy a few acres of land to till for himself and his wife.

Nastka, Simon's young wife, whom he marries against his mother's will.

Roch, a wandering beggar and religious man who teaches the children to read and serves the village as a physician. An honest and trustworthy man, much beloved by the peasants, he is hunted out by the Russians because he teaches the Polish peasants to read in their own language and encourages them to remain patriotic Poles.

Matthew, a carpenter and millwright, one of Antek Boryna's rivals for Yagna's favors.

Teresa, a young peasant girl who loves Matthew.

The Blacksmith, Antek Boryna's brother-in-law, a selfish man who would like to drive Antek off the Boryna farm and take it over on the strength of being the husband of Antek's sister. He constantly plots against the other Borynas.

PEDER VICTORIOUS

Author: O(le) E(dvart) Rolvaag (1876-1931)
Time of action: Late nineteenth century
First published: 1929

PRINCIPAL CHARACTERS

Beret Holm, a Norwegian pioneer woman who is determined that her children are Norwegian and are to be reared as Norwegians. She discourages their use of the English language and refuses to give up her old-country customs. She wants her son, Peder Victorious, to become a minister and is single-minded in this purpose. She is strongly opposed to anything that tends to Americanize her family. Finally, she becomes reconciled to her son's marriage to an Irish girl in the community.

Peder Victorious, Beret's youngest child. His mother is determined that he shall become a minister. He has a fine, strong voice and is often called upon to recite at programs, but his mother objects when he does this reciting in English. He is perplexed by the problem of a God of love who is also responsible for all of the catastrophes that befall him and the community. He resents being kept at home away from parties and dances and begins slipping out to go to them at night. He is cast in a school play opposite an Irish girl, and they fall in love. He is surprised and delighted when his mother consents to their marriage.

The Reverend Johan Gabrielsen, the minister to the Norwegian settlement, who is convinced that Peder should go to the seminary and become the next spiritual leader of the group. He is more lenient than Peder's mother and believes that English will take the place of the Norwegian language in the community. He antagonizes Beret by asking Peder to read in English and by saying grace in English in her home.

Susie Doheny, the girl who is cast in the play with Peder and who falls in love with him.

Ole,
Store-Hans, and
Anna Marie, Beret's other children.

Charlie Doheny, Peder's friend, a jolly Irish boy who is Susie's brother.

PEDRO SÁNCHEZ

Author: José María de Pereda (1833-1906)
Time of action: 1852-1879
First published: 1883

PRINCIPAL CHARACTERS

Pedro Sánchez (pā'drō sän'chäth), a provincial. Ignorant of the world outside his native region, he sets out for Madrid. He finds a job on the anti-government newspaper "El Clarín," where he wins a certain notoriety for criticism of a literary

847

work by a member of the opposition, and finally catches the revolutionary fever of his fellow employees. When the government is overthrown, Pedro is rewarded with a provincial governorship, and he marries Clara. From this time on, his fortunes decline. Finally he returns to his native mountains, where he writes the story of his disillusionment.

Augusto Valenzuela (ä·ōō·gōōs′tō bä·län-thwä′lä), a shady politician who promises Pedro Sánchez that he will see to his future when the boy comes to Madrid, but he gives Pedro a cold reception when he presents himself in the city.

Clara (klä′rä), Augusto Valenzuela's daughter, who is later Pedro Sánchez' extravagant and faithless first wife.

Sarafín Balduque (sä·rä·fēn′ bäl·dōō′kä), Pedro Sánchez' friend, a former state employee who is killed in street fighting against government forces.

Carmen (kär′mĕn), Serafín Balduque's daughter and Pedro Sánchez' second wife, who, with their small son, dies during an epidemic.

Mata (mä′tä), also **Matica** (mä·tē′kä), a student who befriends Pedro Sánchez when he arrives in Madrid and finds him a job on "El Clarín."

Redondo (r̄rä·t̂hōn′dō), the editor of "El Clarín."

Pilita (pē·lē′tä), the wife of Augusto Valenzuela.

Barrientos (bä·r̄ryän′tōs), Governor Pedro Sánchez' secretary, who is a collector of bribes and the lover of Pedro's wife Clara.

PEER GYNT

Author: Henrik Ibsen (1828-1906)
Time of action: Early nineteenth century to the 1860's
First presented: 1867

PRINCIPAL CHARACTERS

Peer Gynt, a poetical, contradictive, intriguing character, made of the stuff of legendary heroes and sometimes confused with them in his own mind. He is one of Ibsen's greatest character creations, the least Victorian; and as Peer himself would have wished to be, he is a citizen of the world. A youthful braggart, idler, brawler, and dreamer, he is a ragged, lying outcast from village life, the joy and despair of Aase, his mother. After stealing a bride from her unwelcome groom, he flees from his village, but he quickly abandons the stolen bride because he has fallen in love with Solveig, an innocent young girl whom he met at the wedding festivities. Later, bewitched by the Troll King's daughter, he promises to marry her and inherit the Troll Kingdom. He puts on Troll clothing and the Troll King's Sunday tail, eats the repulsive Troll food, and drinks the Troll mead; but he demurs when the Troll King wants to scratch one of his eyeballs so that he will see ugly as beautiful and beautiful as ugly. Escaping, he encounters the Great Boyg but is saved from that monster by the ringing of church bells. After his mother's death he becomes wealthy by slave trading in America and by shipping to China idols and missionaries that counteract one another. When his ship is commandeered off the coast of Morocco, he asks God to "Make something go wrong with the works! Do listen! Leave other folk's matters alone! The world will look after itself while you do." His prayer is answered and the vessel sinks, leaving Peer safe ashore. He poses as an Arab chief, is fleeced by Anitra, a dancing girl, becomes emperor of the insane asylum in Cairo, survives a shipwreck off the coast of Norway, encounters the Button Moulder, meets the Troll King again, tricks the Devil, and at last finds Solveig, who tells him that his real self exists in her faith, hope, and love. Peer's reverence for Solveig and his whimsical devotion to his mother, whom he alternately teases and cherishes, are evidence of gentleness and tenderness underlying his selfish behavior. Inferior as a stage play because of the diffused action, Peer's story is an imaginative dramatic poem which in power of language, humorous insight into human foibles, liveliness of dialogue, and creation of character reaches heights which many of Ibsen's later plays never attempt.

Aase, Peer's devoted, exasperated mother. A lively and pathetic character, she symbolizes maternal love which permits her to scold him but will not allow anyone else to criticize him. As a youth he sets her on a mill rooftop while he runs off to a wedding. After his escapade of bride stealing, Aase and Solveig cause the churchbells to ring, saving him from the Boyg. When Aase is old and dying, Peer returns and they play a game in which he pretends that he is driving her on a sleigh to a great party at a castle. God the Father is waiting and overrides St. Peter's refusal to let her enter. With Peer's arms around her, Aase rides happily into eternity.

Solveig, Peer's ideal love, always beautiful, always patient. Although she grows old and almost blind while waiting for Peer's return, she has power to defy the Button Moulder by her belief that her faith and love reveal the real Peer. She seems to represent love, holy, remote, but everlasting.

Ingrid, the daughter of the owner of Haegstad Farm, the bride whom Peer steals on her wedding day.

Mads Moën, Ingrid's bumbling, cuckolded groom.

Aslak, a young blacksmith who voices the ridicule and dislike that most of the villagers show toward Peer.

Three Cowherd Girls, who take Peer Gynt into their beds after he has abandoned Ingrid.

The Woman in Green, the daughter of the Troll King and the mother of Peer's lame, ugly child.

Brosë, the Troll King of Dovrë. He tells Peer that the Troll motto is "To thyself be—enough." Although Peer later believes that he has left Trolldom behind him, this motto is his philosophy in his subsequent adventures in many parts of the world. After the Button Moulder gives Peer leave to find witnesses to prove that he has always been himself, he and the Troll King meet again. The Troll King refuses to testify to a lie; he says that Peer has been a Troll in secret ever since he ate and drank with the Trolls and took away their motto graven on his heart.

The Great Boyg, a grim, impassable monster, identified only by a voice in the darkness, who says that he conquers though he does not fight. His advice is, "Go round about, Peer." He typifies the riddle of existence.

The Button Moulder, an agent of God who is waiting for Peer when he returns, an old man, to Norway. He intends to take Peer's soul and melt it down with other worthless ones, neither good enough to merit Heaven nor bad enough to deserve Hell, and he carries a huge casting ladle with him for this purpose. To Peer's surprise and indignation, the Button Moulder tells him that he should not mind dissolution because he has never been himself. The Button Moulder grants Peer leave to find witnesses that he has always been himself, to find a witness who will testify that his sins are great enough to merit Hell, and to set his house in order. At the end of the play, though the Button Moulder waits at the next crossroads, Solveig ignores his call while she holds Peer's head in her lap and sings him a lullaby.

Kari, a cotter's wife and Aase's friend.

Mr. Cotton,

Monsieur Ballon,

Herr von Eberkopf, and

Herr Trumpeterstraale, the men who commandeer Peer Gynt's ship in the hope of obtaining his gold. They are destroyed when the vessel blows up after Peer's prayer to God.

A Moroccan Thief and

A Receiver of Stolen Goods, who flee at Peer Gynt's approach, leaving behind them an emperor's stolen robe and charger. With these Peer impersonates an Arab chieftain.

Anitra, an Arab dancing girl. While Peer Gynt is singing and dancing to show her how young and vigorous he is, she rides away with his horse and moneybag.

Professor Begriffenfeldt, the keeper of a lunatic asylum at Cairo. He introduces Peer to the mad inmates as their emperor.

Huhu, a language reformer from the Malabar coast,

Hussein, a minister of state, and

A Fellah, carrying a mummy, who imagines that he is King Apis, inmates of the asylum.

A Stranger, who encounters Peer Gynt on a ship off the Norwegian coast. He asks Peer for his corpse.

The Ship's Cook, whom Peer, in order to save his own life, pushes off the keel after the ship capsizes during a storm.

A Thin Person, the Devil dressed in a priest's cassock, whom Peer meets while trying to find someone who will testify to his fitness to enter Hell. Unimpressed by this stranger's recital of his sins, the Devil says that he is searching for Peer Gynt. Peer sends him off to the Cape of Good Hope on a useless search. Fooling the Devil gives Peer a momentary pleasure.

PEG WOFFINGTON

Author: Charles Reade (1814-1884)
Time of action: Eighteenth century
First published: 1853

PRINCIPAL CHARACTERS

Peg Woffington, a celebrated actress of the eighteenth century. She admires Harry Vane as an ideal of goodness and has an affair with him. She comes to see the wrong she has done Mrs. Vane, however, and renounces her lover and becomes Mrs. Vane's friend. Peg Woffington is a generous person who helps all who are friendly to her.

Harry Vane, an English gentleman who falls in love with Peg Woffington, sending her notes and flowers anonymously to awaken her interest in him. He truly

loves his wife and returns to her after his affair with the actress.

Sir Charles Pomander, a gentleman with great curiosity, who watches Harry's pursuit of Peg. He, too, is an admirer of the actress. When he is rebuffed by her, he sets out to stop the affair between her and Harry. He is a crude man.

Mabel Vane, Harry's wife, a beautiful woman, but a simple country girl. She discovers her husband's affair with Peg through Sir Charles, who tries to make love to her. She is such a sweet and generous woman that she forgives her husband his straying and becomes a close friend of Peg.

Colley Cibber, a great actor and playwright of an earlier day. He claims that Peg Woffington is not as great as Mrs. Bracegirdle, an earlier star. Peg disguises herself as Mrs. Bracegirdle at a party backstage and completely fools Cibber, who then acknowledges her brilliance as an actress.

James Triplet, a struggling playwright, scene painter, and poet who is befriended by Peg because he befriended her when she was a girl. To further his career as an artist she sits for a portrait. When critics arrive to ridicule his work, she cuts a hole in the canvas, inserts her own head, and thus confounds the critics. Disguised in the same way, she hears Mabel's plea for the return of her husband and promptly renounces Harry.

Snarl and
Soaper, arrogant critics made to look foolish by Peg's trick with the portrait.

Mr. Rich, a theater manager who is un-interested in Triplet's plays.

PELLE THE CONQUEROR

Author: Martin Andersen Nexö (1869-1954)
Time of action: Late nineteenth century
First published: 1906-1910

PRINCIPAL CHARACTERS

Pelle Karlsson, a poor lad who becomes a shoemaker. He becomes interested in the labor movement and the shoemakers' union, rising to become president of the shoemakers. He and his fellow workers live in difficult times. Pelle finds his livelihood cut off; his wife alienates him by becoming a prostitute in order to feed their two children; and he is unjustly convicted of being a counterfeiter. Pelle studies the labor movement and decides that factories will do away with the shoemaker who works by hand. He and Mr. Brun, a librarian, start a coöperative shoe factory, and Pelle devotes the latter part of his life to urging his fellow workers to seek constitutional means of improving their lot, rather than strikes and violence.

Lasse Karlsson, Pelle's father, a farm hand. Attracted by higher wages, he migrates to the island of Bornholm. Because he is weak and worn-out, he is the butt of his fellow worker's jokes.

Rud Pihl, Pelle's playmate in childhood.

The illegitimate son of the farm owner, he lives with his mother in a hut.

Master Andres, a master shoemaker under whom Pelle has his apprenticeship. He is not a difficult master, but he dies before Pelle's apprenticeship is finished.

Ellen Stolpe, loved by Pelle. She is the daughter of a leader in the stonemasons' union. She becomes a prostitute during hard times in order to earn a little money to support her family. For this reason her husband leaves her, but they are reconciled after Pelle completes his six-year prison term.

Mr. Brun, a librarian in whose library Pelle reads up on the labor movement. Brun and Pelle start a coöperative shoe factory which proves quite successful.

Marie Nielsen, a dancer who befriends Pelle.

Sort, a traveling shoemaker with whom Pelle works for a time.

851

PÉLLÉAS AND MÉLISANDE

Author: Maurice Maeterlinck (1862-1949)
Time of action: The Middle Ages
First presented: 1893; first published: 1892

PRINCIPAL CHARACTERS

Golaud (gô·lō′), the grandson of Arkël, who finds Mélisande beside a spring and marries her. He views the relationship between her and Pélléas sometimes with jealousy, sometimes as the innocent affection of children.

Little Yniold (ē·nyôl′), the son of Golaud by his first wife.

Mélisande (mā·lē·zäṅd′), an elfin creature with no knowledge of good or evil. She dies after the premature birth of her daughter.

Pélléas (pā·lā·às′), the half brother of Golaud. In love with Mélisande, he is surprised with her by his brother.

Arkël (àr·kël′), King of Allemonde, who had planned to bring peace by marrying Golaud to the daughter of an enemy; however, he accepts Golaud's marriage to Mélisande.

Geneviève (zhĕn·vyĕv′), the daughter of Arkël and mother of Pélléas and Golaud.

The Father of Pélléas, now gravely ill.

PEÑAS ARRIBA

Author: José María de Pereda (1833-1906)
Time of action: Late nineteenth century
First published: 1895

PRINCIPAL CHARACTERS

Marcelo (mär·thā′lō), a young man from Madrid. Bidden by his lonely, eighty-year-old uncle, Celso Ruiz de Bejos, to come and live with him, the sophisticated Marcelo sets out for the heart of the Pyrenees on a visit to his patriarchal relative. At first the simple pleasures of the village have little appeal for the urbane young man, but as time goes on, the kindness and courage of the mountaineers and the grandeur of the surrounding peaks expand and lift his heart and mind. He finally marries Lita and becomes so much a part of the village life that he dreads to leave home even for short trips.

Celso Ruiz de Bejos (thāl′sō r̄r̄wĕth thā bā′hōs), Marcelo's eighty-year-old uncle, who is the patriarch of his region in the Pyrenees. He urges his nephew to leave

Madrid and join him in his mountain home, where he makes him his heir.

Doctor Neluco (nā·lōō′kō), the friend and confidant of Marcelo in the mountain village. He advises the young man to marry Lita.

Sabas Peñas (sä′bäs pā′nyäs), the village priest.

Pedro Nolasco (pā′drō nō·läs′kō) and **Pito Salces** (pē′tō säl′thäs), mountaineers whose courage and kindness inspire Marcelo with a love for the mountain village.

Margarita (mär·gä·rē′tä), called **Lita** (lē′tä), Pedro Nolasco's granddaughter, who marries Marcelo.

Mari Pepa (mä′rē pā′pä), Pedro Nolasco's daughter.

Chisco (chēs'kō), Celso Ruiz de Bejos' faithful servant.

Facia (fä'thyä), a mountain woman who seeks Marcelo's advice concerning her criminal husband, who is blackmailing her.

Tona (tō'nä), Facia's daughter.

PENDENNIS

Author: William Makepeace Thackeray (1811-1863)
Time of action: Mid-nineteenth century
First published: 1848-1850

PRINCIPAL CHARACTERS

Arthur Pendennis, called **Pen,** a young Englishman of semi-aristocratic background whose essential nature is kind and gentle. Throughout the course of the novel he moves from a childish infatuation with an actress, to an academically and financially disastrous career at the University of Oxbridge, to a dandified life in London, to the career of a journalist, to a seat in Parliament, and to a happy and successful marriage. During this time he grows more sophisticated and somewhat snobbish, but he still retains the essential goodness of his original character.

Major Arthur Pendennis, Arthur's uncle, a snobbish retired army officer and a man of fashion. Always aware of his friends' social standing, he spends much of his time culling the most advantageous invitations to dinners and balls. Although a snob, he is good-hearted and generous in the sense that he does look out for his nephew and tries to get him placed in the most favorable circumstances at all times.

Helen Pendennis, Arthur's mother, a lovely, sensitive woman who adores her young son and spends many heartbreaking moments worrying about him. She dies at the end of the novel but not before she is assured that Arthur will be successful and happy in his life.

Laura Bell, Arthur's adopted sister, the daughter of Francis Bell, Helen Pendennis' cousin and former suitor. A sweet, intelligent woman, somewhat like her aunt in character, she watches Arthur's career and sympathizes with his mother over Arthur's failures. She is loved by George Warrington, Arthur's closest friend; but because of his early and unfortunate marriage, she cannot become his wife. Eventually she marries Arthur, the man she has really loved all her life.

George Warrington, Arthur's roommate in London, the son of Sir Miles Warrington of Suffolk. He is reading for the law when Arthur first rooms with him. Later he takes up a career in journalism and helps Arthur edit the "Pall Mall Gazette." He is in love with Laura, but because of an unfortunate marriage he cannot marry again. He is intelligent, exceedingly kind and casual, a good companion for Arthur.

Sir Francis Clavering, a weak and dandified spendthrift baronet, much taken with cards and gambling. After Major Pendennis' discovery that Lady Clavering's first husband is still living, Sir Francis offers Arthur Pendennis his seat in Parliament.

Lady Clavering, a supposed widow who becomes Sir Francis' wife. Although uneducated, she is a good and loving person at heart, and popular in spite of her social gaucheries.

Blanche Amory, Lady Clavering's daughter by her first marriage, a talented, intelligent girl but affected and shallow in character. For a while it seems that she will marry Arthur Pendennis. Later she is courted by Harry Foker but he deserts her when he learns that her father is still living. She resigns herself to a charming spinsterhood.

Master Francis Clavering, the son of the Claverings and half brother to Blanche, a spoiled and demanding brat. He remains in the background of the story as an example of the very bad match between Mrs. Amory and Sir Francis.

Captain Edward Strong, a friend of Sir Francis Clavering. He is a cheerful, talented fellow who eventually goes to live at Shepherd's Lane Inn with Colonel Altamont, the shadowy personage who mysteriously figures in the story of the Clavering family.

Colonel Altamont, a supposedly retired army officer who turns out to be Lady Clavering's first husband, whom everyone had believed dead. He turns up to plague his former wife with the realization that her second marriage is bigamous; however, it is proved that he had contracted several previous marriages and therefore has no legal claim on her. He eludes the police and disappears at the end of the novel.

Emily Costigan, also known as **Miss Fotheringay,** an actress with whom young Arthur Pendennis falls desperately in love. An ill-bred, calculating girl, she finally makes a good marriage with Sir Charles Mirabel and elevates herself into society.

Captain Costigan, her rakish, drunken father. After his daughter marries, he is treated as a poor relation, and he goes to live in Shepherd's Lane Inn. There his drunken exploits are the topic of local conversation.

Little Bows, a crippled friend of Colonel Costigan and his daughter, who goes to live with the Colonel at Shepherd's Lane Inn. He gives music lessons to

Fanny Bolton, whom he worships in secret.

Fanny Bolton, the daughter of the proprietor of Shepherd's Lane Inn. For a time it seems that she will persuade Arthur Pendennis to marry her, but she ends up with one of his acquaintances, Mr. Huxter.

Mr. Bolton and
Mrs. Bolton, Fanny's parents and the owners of Shepherd's Lane Inn.

Mr. Huxter, a crude fellow, a surgeon who marries Fanny Bolton. Arthur refuses to recognize him as a friend.

Lady Rockminster, Laura's kind but somewhat wayward patroness after Helen Pendennis' death. Delighted with the prospect that Arthur will marry Laura, she does everything she can to hasten the match.

Morgan, Major Pendennis' valet, a clever but cruel man. By saving his money he is able to buy the lodgings where Major Pendennis stays. After a quarrel he tells Arthur Pendennis about his uncle's scheming to have Blanche Amory inherit her mother's fortune and to force Sir Francis to relinquish his seat in Parliament.

Mrs. Brixham, a widow who is cheated out of her rooming house by shrewd Morgan.

Frosch, the Major's new valet, a pleasant young fellow whom Morgan procures for his old master.

Percy Sibwright, a neighbor of Warrington and Arthur at Shepherd's Lane Inn.

Jack Holt, another neighbor. A veteran of Queen Christina's army, he is engaged in organizing a scheme for smuggling money.

Tom Diver, another neighbor. He claims that he knows of a sunken specie ship from which he plans to reclaim the treasure.

Filby, a man of varied careers as a corporal of dragoons, a field preacher, a missionary agent for converting the Irish, and an actor at a Greenwich Fair Booth.

Henry (Harry) Foker, Arthur Pendennis' former schoolmate, a dandified, snobbish young man of London. He almost marries Blanche Amory, but the discovery that her father is still alive breaks up the match.

Anatole, Harry Foker's valet.

George Robert, the Earl of Gravesend and Fisherville, Harry Foker's uncle.

Lady Ann Milton, Harry Foker's cousin and intended wife.

Lady Agnes Foker, Harry's mother, who secures for him invitations to parties to which the Claverings are invited.

Mr. Bungay, a publisher who knows little about novels but takes his opinions from professional advisers.

Mr. Bacon, another snobbish publisher, who reads Arthur Pendennis' book.

Lord Steyne, an aristocratic party-giver, constantly courted by Major Pendennis.

Miss Rouncy, the confidential friend of Emily Costigan during the time that they are actresses.

Mrs. Creed, the Costigans' landlady.

Dr. Portman, a clergyman and a friend of the Pendennis family.

Lieutenant Sir Derby Oaks, another suitor of Emily Costigan.

Mr. Garbets, the principal tragedian of the theatrical company.

Mr. Tatham, a lawyer whom Major Pendennis consults on business.

Mr. Dolphin, a great theatrical manager from London who comes to see Emily play and hires her.

Mr. Wenham and
Mr. Wag, Lord Steyne's aristocratic friends, who hobnob with Major Pendennis.

The Reverend F. Wapshot, a teacher of Clavering Grammar School.

Mr. Smirkle, Dr. Portman's cleric and the tutor to young Arthur Pendennis.

Mr. Plummer, the proprietor of the George, a tavern in London frequented by Captain Costigan.

Miss Blandy, the governess to young Francis Clavering.

Mr. Pymsent, an acquaintance of Arthur and Laura's admirer.

Mr. Paley, an industrious law student who is different from Arthur and Warrington because he applies himself to his studies.

Charles Shandon, the friend of George Warrington and Arthur Pendennis, later the publisher of the "Pall Mall Gazette."

Mr. Jack Finucane, the sub-editor of the "Pall Mall Gazette."

PENGUIN ISLAND

Author: Anatole France (Jacques Anatole Thibault, 1844-1924)
Time of action: Ancient times to the present
First published: 1908

PRINCIPAL CHARACTERS

Maël (mȧ·ĕl'), a Breton missionary monk who, in ancient times, preached to a group of penguins living on an island at the North Pole. The penguins were baptized and turned into men and the island was towed to a point off the Breton coast. Thus began a society that is the author's satire of French history.

Kraken (krȧ·kän'), a clever penguin who lives by his wits and turns to his advantage the ignorance and superstitions of the peasant penguins. By constructing an imitation dragon and "killing" it at an appropriate time, he wins the gratitude of the populace and thereafter accepts annual tribute from them.

Oberosia (ō·bā·rō·zyȧ'), Kraken's mistress and the most beautiful of the penguin women. She appears as a virgin who conquers a dragon in order that Maël's prophecy might be fulfilled. The "dragon" is one she and Kraken have fashioned. Oberosia is the island's first and most important saint.

Eveline Clarence (ā·vȧ·lēn' klȧ·räns'), a beautiful, talented charmer who becomes a favorite at political social gatherings. She marries a rising politician and becomes the mistress of the Prime Minister. She lives a long, happy life and, when she dies, leaves her property to the Charity of St. Oberosia.

M. Hippolyte Cérès (mȧ·syœ' ē·pô·lēt' sā·rès'), Eveline's husband, who tries to ruin the Prime Minister's career when it becomes apparent that Eveline is his mistress. His action has some effect, for the Prime Minister is finally put out of office.

Father Agaric (ȧ·gȧ·rēk') and
Prince des Boscenos (dā bō·sā·nōs'), conspirators who attempt to destroy the republic and restore the monarchy. The revolution they launch is short-lived, failing almost as soon as it begins.

Greatank (grā·ȧ·tänk'), the most powerful of all the penguins, who establishes Penguinia's first government on the

island of Alca, its system that of a clan or tribe ruled by a strong warrior.

Draco (drȧ·kō'), Kraken's son, who founds the first royal family of Penguinia.

Draco the Great, a descendant of Draco who establishes a monastery in honor of Oberosia; thus the Middle Ages come to the island of Alca.

Trinco (trăn·ko'), the great soldier who takes command of the army of the republic after the monarchy has been abolished. He quickly conquers and loses most of the known world.

Johannes Talpa (zhō·ȧn' tȧl·pȧ'), a learned monk who chronicles the early history of the penguins.

Marbodius (mȧr·bō·dyüs'), a literary monk who leaves a record of his descent into Hell.

Viscountess Olive (ô·lēv'), a clever aristocrat who seduces Chatillon in order to gain his support for the royalists' cause.

Viscount Cléna (klā·na'), a suitor whom Eveline rejects when she learns that he is of modest means.

God, a deity who finds it necessary to call the saints together in order to decide what to do about the penguins Maël has baptized.

Chatillon (shȧ·tē·yōn'), an admiral used by Father Agaric and the Prince to head the military forces in the unsuccessful revolution.

M. Paul Visire (mȧ·syœ' pôl'vē·zēr'), Prime Minister of Penguinia and Eveline's lover.

Madame Clarence (klȧ·räns'), Eveline's mother.

Pyrot (pē·rō'), a scapegoat.

THE PEOPLE OF JUVIK

Author: Olav Duun (1876-1939)
Time of action: 1800-1918
First published: 1918-1923

PRINCIPAL CHARACTERS

Per,
Bear Anders,
Big Per, and
Greedy Per, heroic ancestors of Per Anders Juvika.

Per Anders Juvika, a prosperous eighteenth century Norwegian farmer who rules his family as a patriarch.

Ane, Per Anders Juvika's wife.

Jens, Per Anders' son, who is wild and reckless like the old Juvikings.

Per, Per Anders' other son, a gentle and hardworking young man. Like his brother Jens, he is ruled by his father.

Valborg, Per's wife, picked out for him by his father.

Ane,
Aasel, and
Beret, daughters of Per Anders.

Mikkal, Aasel's husband, a hard worker and a good provider.

Anders Haaberg, Per and Valborg's son. He takes over the family farm.

Petter Haaberg, Anders' worthless brother. He is a sly and reckless man.

Solvi, a Laplander, Anders' first wife. Suspected of being a witch, she is sent back to her father, but she and her child are killed on the way home by a rock slide. Having yielded to the pressure of his superstitious neighbors, Anders broods much over her death.

Massi Liness, Anders' second wife.

Ola Engdal, rival of Anders for the hand of Massi. She accepts Ola, but he is killed in an accident while still young.

Kjersti, Massi's foster daughter, who bears a child by Peter.

Per,
Gjartru,
Aasel,
Jens,
Beret, and
Ola, children of Anders and Massi.

Marja Leinland, Per's wife.

Hall Grönset, loved by Gjartru. He is lost at sea.

Petter Liness, Per's friend who, before he is drowned, gives Per some money to pass on secretly to Kjersti.

Johan Arnesen, Gjartru's husband. He is a storekeeper who prospers for a time, but his business finally fails and he and Gjartru go to America with Jens.

Kristen Folden, Aasel's husband, who takes over the Haaberg farm.

Peder,
Elen, and
Marjane, children of Kristen and Aasel.

Kjerstina, Peder's distant cousin. She is with child by him.

Andrea Ween, who marries Peder. After his death, she marries Otte Setran.

Arthur Ween, Andrea's brother. He marries Mina Arnesen, a cousin of Peder.

Mina Arnesen, the daughter of Johan and Gjartru, and Arthur's wife. She and her husband inherit Segelsund when Johan and Gjartru go to America.

Otte Setran, Elen's lover and the father of Odin Setran. He eventually marries Andrea, after Peder's death.

Odin Setran, Elen's illegitimate son. He shows promise of being a heroic man, like the first Juvikings. When Elen marries, he is sent to live with foster parents.

Iver Vennestad, who marries Elen. He is disliked by Odin, whom he bullies.

Bendek and
Gurianna Kjelvik, Odin's foster parents.

Lauris, one of the Kjelviks, and Odin's playmate. Great friends in their youth, they become enemies in later life when Lauris proves to be unscrupulous and overly ambitious. Eventually, Odin sacrifices his life to save Lauris from drowning.

Astri, Odin's cousin, the daughter of Peder and Andrea. They fall in love but cannot marry because Astri's mother decides to marry Odin's natural father. Astri marries Arne Finne.

Ingri Arnesen, who marries Odin. They first meet as youngsters, when they almost drown while crossing the fjord in a storm.

Arne Finne, a childhood sweetheart whom Astri marries, even though he is dying of tuberculosis.

Engelbert Olsen, a leader of the workmen in the community. With Lauris he plots to discredit Odin, but Odin hunts him down and drives him from the area.

Anders and
Per, sons of Odin and Ingri. Like true Juvikings, they seem to possess their father's great generosity and courage.

PEPITA JIMÉNEZ

Author: Juan Valera (Juan Valera y Alcalá Galiano, 1824-1905)
Time of action: c. 1870
First published: 1874

PRINCIPAL CHARACTERS

Luis de Vargas (lwēs t̯ẖä bär′gäs), a seminary student, preparing for the priesthood, who is home for a vacation. He corresponds with his uncle, the dean of the seminary, about his own changing attitude toward Pepita, his father's prospective young bride.

Don Pedro de Vargas (dōn pä′drō t̯ẖä bär′gäs), his understanding father, who is well satisfied to have his son give up the priesthood in order to stay home and marry Pepita.

Pepita Jiménez (pä·pē′tä hē·mä′näth), a charming young widow.

Gumersindo (gōō·mâr·sēn′dō), an elderly moneylender, briefly married to Pepita.

Antoñona (än·tō·nyō′nä), Pepita's duenna, who does more than her share to further the romance of Luis and Pepita.

The Vicar, who wants Pepita to marry Don Pedro.

Currito (kōō·r̄rē′tō), Luis' cousin, who takes him to the casino. There he gambles with the Count and eventually fights a duel with him.

Count de Genazahar (hä·nä·thä·är′), who borrowed money from Gumersindo which he will not repay to the widow. When he makes slighting remarks about Pepita, he and Luis wound each other with sabers.

858

PEREGRINE PICKLE

Author: Tobias Smollett (1721-1771)
Time of action: Early eighteenth century
First published: 1751

PRINCIPAL CHARACTERS

Peregrine Pickle, called **Perry** in his younger days, a headstrong, rebellious young man. Bitterly disliked by his mother in his childhood, Peregrine is adopted by his godfather, a retired naval officer who lavishes money on his young ward, educates him, saves him from a love affair regarded as imprudent, and sends him traveling on the Continent. Although wealthy after his benefactor's death, Peregrine suffers reverses caused by his extravagance, his delight in practical jokes, and his foolhardiness in writing satires on public officials after he has stood unsuccessfully for Parliament and has been reduced to near penury. Thrown into prison, and without influential friends, he nevertheless refuses the hand and fortune of Emilia Gauntlet, with whom he is in love. He is saved by an inheritance from his father, marries Emilia, and settles down to the life of a country squire. Peregrine Pickle is developed beyond Smollett's other title characters. On his travels he is thrown with intellectuals, the associations leading to lengthy discussions on political, cultural, philosophical matters. He is also given to foolhardy and sometimes licentious behavior.

Commodore Hawser Trunnion, Peregrine's godfather and benefactor. An old sea dog, Trunnion keeps his house—called the garrison—like a ship; his speech is sharp and salty with naval jargon. His maintenance of a ship's atmosphere makes for much of the comedy in the novel.

Thomas Pipes, Trunnion's companion and servant, retired from the sea. He becomes a companion to Peregrine when he is sent to school and on his travels.

Loyal to the young man, Pipes rescues his wayward master from many scrapes.

Lieutenant Jack Hatchway, the Commodore's one-legged companion. Like Pipes, he often shows up when Peregrine needs help. Hatchway's most opportune appearance comes when Peregrine is in Fleet Prison after his arrest for writing the political satires.

Emilia Gauntlet, called **Emy** by her family, Peregrine's sweetheart, whom he meets while he is attending Winchester School. The recurrent meetings of these two, tempered by quarrels and avowals of devotion, are for much of the story secondary in importance to Peregrine's pursuit of other women. Eventually Peregrine offers her his hand and Emilia accepts.

Godfrey Gauntlet, her brother. After a brief period of animosity, during which he worsts Peregrine in a duel, he becomes a devoted friend on learning that Peregrine is his secret benefactor. Peregrine, in his prosperous days, had anonymously provided funds for Godfrey and had used his influence to secure Godfrey's captaincy in the navy.

Gamaliel Pickle, Peregrine's father, the soul of humbleness, and the butt of his wife's ill temper. He is happy to see his son taken by Trunnion, away from the meanness of his wife. Whether unwittingly or not, Gamaliel wins the final victory over his wife; he dies intestate and his money goes to Peregrine, his first-born son.

Sally Appleby, Gamaliel's termagant wife. Left unprovided for at the death of her husband, she is forced to live on an allowance from Peregrine.

Grizzle Pickle, Gamaliel's sister and his housekeeper until he marries Sally. Refusing to be subjugated by her sister-in-law, Grizzle finds escape when she becomes Mrs. Trunnion. Her death brings sadness to Peregrine, who has considered her more a mother than an aunt.

Gam Pickle, Peregrine's young brother. His mother's favorite child, Gam conspires with his mother in her scheming. Their hatred for Peregrine is shown in their plot to have him murdered. Godfrey Gauntlet, mistaken for Peregrine, suffers from their machinations. Gam faces a dismal future when he is ordered away from the property with his mother, after Peregrine inherits his father's estate.

Julia Pickle, Peregrine's sister and the youngest of the children, who also suffers her mother's ill will. Sympathetic to Peregrine, she is taken in and cared for by Grizzle Trunnion.

Layman Pallet, an English traveler whom Peregrine meets at the Palais Royal in Paris. In addition to his discussion on art and the other aspects of sophistication which he lends to the story, he is pictured, almost in burlesque and in raucous circumstances, trying to seduce a woman in a party traveling to Ghent.

The Doctor, Pallet's traveling companion. His knowledge as a connoisseur of foods and wines adds to the tone of the story, stressing Peregrine's sophistication.

Cadwallader Crabtree, an eccentric old man whom Peregrine meets when he returns to London. Posing as a fortune-teller, he allows Peregrine to learn many women's secrets.

Deborah Hornbeck, the attractive wife of an English traveler in Paris. Her elopement with Peregrine threatens to become an international incident. The British ambassador sends Deborah back to her husband. After the second affair with her, Peregrine is put into prison. Freed, he is given three days to leave Paris.

Lady Vane, a notorious lady of quality. Her memoirs, which make up a sizable section of the novel, tell of her many lovers.

Amanda, a young woman traveling to Ghent. Peregrine's efforts to seduce her are exceeded in comedy only by Pallet's simultaneous activities with her traveling companion.

Jolter, a teacher at Winchester School, hired by Trunnion to act as Peregrine's traveling companion on the Continent. In this role he is called the Governor.

Miss Sophy, Emilia Gauntlet's cousin, who helps Peregrine in his affair with Emilia.

A Young Female Beggar, whom Peregrine encounters on the road to London. In Pygmalion-like manner, he buys her fashionable gowns and teaches her polite phrases in order to pass her off as a lady; however, her gaucherie causes him to lose friends because of his gross prank.

Sir Steady Steerwell, the Minister of Public Affairs and the subject of the satire which sent Peregrine to the Fleet Prison.

Charles Clover, Julia Pickle's husband, who informs Peregrine of his father's death. A young justice of the peace, he averts any plan Gam and his mother may have in forging a will after Gamaliel Pickle dies intestate.

Cecilia Gauntlet, Emilia's mother. She reprimands Peregrine for his conduct toward her daughter. Later she is much in favor of her son-in-law.

Mr. Sackbut, the curate, who plots with Gam and Sally to murder Peregrine.

Morgan, a Welsh surgeon identified as

860

Dr. Morgan, a character in Smollett's earlier novel, "Roderick Random."

Benjamin Chintz, a merchant who repays with interest a loan of seven hundred pounds while Peregrine is in Fleet Prison. The repayment marks the reversal of Peregrine's bad fortune.

Jennings and
Jumble, Peregrine's teachers, against whom, as a youngster, he rebels because of their hypocrisy.

Hadgi, Peregrine's valet on his travels. Peregrine befriends him after the party has returned to England and Hadgi is out of Peregrine's employ.

PERICLES, PRINCE OF TYRE

Author: William Shakespeare (1564-1616)
Time of action: Hellenistic period
First presented: 1608

PRINCIPAL CHARACTERS

Pericles (pĕr'ə·klēz), Prince of Tyre. When King Antiochus gave him a riddle to solve, the intelligent young man learned too much about the evil King's incestuous lust for his own daughter. Knowing that his life and his kingdom of Tyre are now in great danger, he flees to impoverished Tarsus, bearing shiploads of food for Cleon's people. Shipwrecked in storm-driven seas, he is cast ashore in a land governed by good King Simonides, who gives the hapless Prince an opportunity to enter the lists. Pericles wins the tournament and the heart of Thaisa, the King's beautiful daughter. They marry but he is soon separated from his bride; after many mishaps, he is reunited with his wife and child.

Thaisa (thā·ĭs'ə), King Simonides' lovely young daughter. Seeing Prince Pericles, she is smitten with his charms, even though he is dressed in rusty armor which he fished out of the sea after the shipwreck. When the valiant Prince wins the tourney, she is determined to marry him. Shortly after the marriage, she bears him a daughter, apparently dies on shipboard, and is put afloat in a tightly caulked casket, in which she drifts to shore and is revived by Cerimon, a lord of Ephesus, skilled in healing.

Marina (mä·rē'nə), the attractive daughter of Pericles and Thaisa. Born on a ship tossed by a raging storm, she is shortly afterward separated from her father. After that a good portion of her life is equally tumultuous. Her life threatened because of Dionyza's hate, she is saved when pirates capture her and take her to a brothel in Mytilene, where she is the despair of Pandar and his bawd because of her unassailable virginity, a condition which drives off and purifies his prospective customers.

Helicanus (hĕl·ĭ·kā'nŭs), a lord of Tyre. No flatterer, he proves to be a very good friend to Prince Pericles. After the Prince flees, this venerable and honorable man looks after the kingdom. He refuses to accept the crown for himself, even though pressed by various powerful lords to do so.

Simonides (sī·mŏn'ə·dēz), King of Pentapolis. A benevolent ruler, he has no objections when his daughter wants to marry Pericles. In fact, through a genial deception, he helps to bring about her marriage to the personable young man.

Antiochus (ăn·tī'ə·kŭs), King of Antioch. Because he mistrusts Pericles, this evil ruler forces the Prince to leave his kingdom. Having given the Prince a

861

riddle to solve, Antiochus is afraid when he realizes that Pericles knows the answer—that the King has committed incest with his own daughter. Struck by fire from heaven, he is killed.

The Daughter of King Antiochus. Equally guilty with her father, she too is killed by the same lightning.

Cleon (klē'ŏn), Governor of Tarsus. This melancholy ruler is overjoyed when Prince Pericles brings corn to his starving people. A weak and cowardly man, he makes only mild objections when he learns that his wife has contrived, through jealousy, to have Marina killed.

Cerimon (sĕr'ĭ·mŏn), a charitable lord of Ephesus. A student of medicine, he revives Pericles' wife when she is brought to his house.

Dionyza (dī·ō·nī'zə), the wife of Cleon. A jealous, petty woman, she attempts to have Marina killed because the young girl seems to be more talented than her own daughter.

Dionyza's Daughter, a dull girl.

Lysimachus (lī·sĭm'ə·kŭs), Governor of Mytilene. Seeing Marina in a brothel, he realizes her true virtue and assures her that she will soon be freed from Pandar. It is he who unknowingly reunites Marina with her father Pericles.

Lychorida (lĭ·kŏ'rĭ·də), Marina's nurse.

Thaliard (thăl'yərd), a lord of Antioch. Antiochus sends him to kill Pericles.

Leonine (lē'ə·nīn), a servant to Dionyza.

Gower (gou'ər), the chorus.

Pandar (păn'dər), the master of the bawdy house.

Bault (bōlt), his servant.

A Bawd, Pandar's wife.

THE PERSIANS

Author: Aeschylus (c. 525–c. 456 B.C.)
Time of action: 480 B.C.
First presented: 472 B.C.

PRINCIPAL CHARACTERS

Xerxes (zûrk'sēz), King of Persia from 486 to 465 B.C. The three members of the Persian Royal House who appear in this play are unique in Greek tragedy as being the only figures from actual history, as opposed to legend, to be used on the Greek stage. The Persian King is here depicted shortly after the Battle of Salamis (480 B.C.), in which the Persian Navy was utterly destroyed by the Athenian fleet. Xerxes comes on the stage after a messenger has related to Atossa, the King's mother, and to the chorus of Persian elders a detailed account of the downfall of the Persian expedition against Athens. The account is a long and tragic recital of the names of great Persian commanders who have fallen in the battle. Xerxes finally enters as a heart-broken and ruined man who has brought about the downfall of his own kingdom. He has previously been described by the ghost of his father, Darius, as the victim of the rashness of youth, whose act of "hubris" consisted of chaining the Bosphorus with a bridge of boats over which his army might cross. His mother, Atossa, adds that their son had been urged on to his downfall by the counsels of evil men, who had chided him for not surpassing the great deeds of his father. Xerxes is depicted as a man so broken by misfortune that only grief is left to him; he is the ruin of a once great king.

Atossa (ă·tŏs'ə), the widow of Darius and the mother of Xerxes. In the early part of the play, she is an imposing figure, the widow of one great king and mother of another. While awaiting the news of her son's expedition against Athens, she eagerly asks the chorus for information about the enemy. She even has to inquire where Athens is located, for, in the eyes of so great a person, it must be a far-off, insignificant city that could not possibly withstand the might of Persia. When the news of the defeat is brought to her, she is at first incredulous; then, when the terrible truth becomes undeniable, she is so stricken with grief that she conjures up the ghost of her dead husband to seek his counsel and solace. She is a woman utterly devoted to the glory of Persia and its Royal House. On the advice of her husband, she withdraws to her palace to put on her richest attire in order to greet her son on his return from his defeat. She will not desert him when he most needs her.

The Ghost of Darius, (də·rī′ŭs), King of Persia from 521 to 486 B.C., the father of Xerxes and husband of Atossa. During his lifetime he had raised Persia to its height of power; now he is summoned from the grave by his widow to hear an account of the destruction of all that he had accomplished. He is depicted as a wise and prudent ruler who, though a great conqueror, had known what limits he should put upon his ambition. He had foreseen that ruin would fall upon his son but had prayed that it might be postponed. However, Xerxes' youthful rashness and pride have brought this ruin upon him early in life. The only counsel that the ghost of the dead king can give is that Persia must never again attack Athens, for the Athenians are invincible; "their very earth fights for them." A Persian army will perish of famine on another expedition. The King knows, however, that his advice will go unheeded; and, with a prophecy of the second Persian defeat at Plataea (479 B.C.), his ghost sinks back into the tomb.

PERSUASION

Author: Jane Austen (1775-1817)
Time of action: Early nineteenth century
First published: 1818

PRINCIPAL CHARACTERS

Anne Elliot, the heroine, second daughter of Sir Walter Elliot, and the victim of persuasion. Although pretty and attractive, she has always been ignored by her family. When quite young, she had been wooed by Frederick Wentworth, then a junior officer in the Royal Navy; but because of her father's disapproval and the advice of her mother's friend, Lady Russell, she had given him up in spite of her love. At the age of twenty-six she meets him again, for his brother-in-law and sister have leased the Elliot property. Wentworth, now a captain and rich through prize money, seems to have forgotten her, although she still loves him. He is apparently in love with Louisa Musgrove. Having joined her family at Bath, Anne receives the attentions of her cousin, William Elliot, whose charm makes some impression upon her. But through an old school friend, Mrs. Smith, she learns of William's cold, calculating, and selfish character. Although happy to be enlightened, she is still distressed by Wentworth's indifference. To her joy, he finally realizes that he is not in love with Louisa and proposes to Anne. Since he is now wealthy and a captain, Sir Walter can no longer oppose the match, and the story ends happily.

Sir Walter Elliot, Bt., of Kellynch Hall, Anne's father. Inordinately vain of his ancestry and his good looks, he is a foolish man who lives beyond his income until he is forced to lease Kellynch and live at Bath. He neglects Anne in favor of his oldest daughter, whom he wishes to marry his heir, William Elliot. He is almost snared by Elizabeth's scheming friend, Mrs. Clay, but is saved by William.

Elizabeth Elliot, the oldest daughter of Sir Walter. She is handsome but cold and selfish. Unable to make a brilliant match, she remains unmarried.

Mary Musgrove, the youngest daughter of Sir Walter and the wife of Charles Musgrove. She is spoiled and selfish.

Charles Musgrove, her husband, a typical sporting country squire.

Captain Frederick Wentworth, R.N., the hero of the novel. When a young and penniless officer, he had fallen in love with Anne Elliot and she with him; but she had given him up because of family opposition and the advice of her friend, Lady Russell. When he meets Anne again after eight years, he seems no longer interested in her; rather he is apparently in love with Louisa Musgrove. But further association with Anne makes him aware of her real worth; he proposes again, and is accepted. Since he is now a captain and a rich man, the Elliots can no longer oppose him, and the marriage can take place.

Admiral and
Mrs. Croft, brother-in-law and sister of Wentworth. They lease Kellynch Hall.

William Elliot, the villain of the novel. Although heir to Sir Walter's title and estates, William, as a young man, takes no interest in his cousins. Instead of marrying Elizabeth, as Sir Walter had hoped,

he married the wealthy daughter of a grazier. Being left a rich widower, he becomes interested in his family and cultivates their friendship at Bath. Having charming manners, he makes a favorable impression upon Anne, until she learns from Mrs. Smith of his scheming character. He also selfishly prevents a marriage between Sir Walter and Mrs. Clay, a match which might ruin his prospects, by inducing Mrs. Clay to become his mistress.

Mr. and Mrs. Musgrove, of Uppercross, Charles' parents.

Louisa Musgrove, their daughter. It seems that she may marry Wentworth, especially after she is injured in an accident that he considers his fault. But she marries Captain Benwick.

Henrietta Musgrove, her sister, who marries her cousin, Charles Hayter.

Lady Russell, a widow and an old friend of the Elliot family. She persuades Anne not to marry Wentworth because of his uncertain future.

Mr. Shepherd, Sir Walter's agent, who has the task of persuading him to lease Kellynch Hall.

Mrs. Clay, Shepherd's scheming daughter. She insinuates herself into the Elliot family in order to marry Sir Walter but in the end becomes William Elliot's mistress.

Mrs. Charles Smith, a school friend of Anne. Formerly wealthy, she is now a poor and ill widow living at Bath. She reveals to Anne the true character of William Elliot.

Captain Benwick, a melancholy widower who, after being attentive to Anne Elliot, marries Louisa Musgrove.

PETER IBBETSON

Author: George du Maurier (1834-1896)
Time of action: Mid-nineteenth century
First published: 1891

Pierre Pasquier de la Marière (pyĕr′ pȧs-kyȧ′ dǝ lȧ mȧ·ryĕr′), also **Peter Ibbetson,** a confessed murderer. An English-French child living in France, afterward orphaned by the almost simultaneous deaths of his father and mother, and taken back to England for his schooling, Peter Ibbetson (as his uncle, Colonel Ibbetson, renames him) attains manhood there, joins the army briefly, and is then apprenticed to an architect. Shy, dreamy, speculative, a skeptical and rather unhappy freethinker, he often lives imaginatively in the happy world of his childhood with Mimsy. After a mystic dream he discovers he may enter his ideal world again and be with Mimsy when he chooses, though retaining his adult identity. Enraged upon learning through Mrs. Gregory (formerly Mrs. Deane) of the Colonel's malice, he kills him in a quarrel and is sentenced to a prison asylum for life. Here he again is able, through wishing, to enter his childhood world from time to time until death takes him.

Colonel Roger Ibbetson, his wealthy guardian, cousin of Mrs. Pasquier; a vain gallant and a malicious liar.

Mimsy Seraskier (mēm·sē′ sǝ·rȧs·kyȧ′), his dearest friend; later the Duchess of Towers. In childhood a plain, sickly,

melancholy girl, she becomes a tall, beautiful woman. Visited by the same dream that changed Peter's life, she later reveals the dream when they meet and happily recall their friendship as children.

Mr. Lintot (lăṅ·tō′), Peter's employer, a self-made, entertainingly egotistical, clever man; an industrious worker but a lover of drink after working hours; both amusing and sentimental when drunk.

Mrs. Lintot (lăṅ·tō′), his wife, older than her husband; stern, unlovely (though he thinks her beautiful), but an excellent wife and mother.

Mrs. Deane, a widow (later **Mrs. Gregory**). Deceived by Colonel Ibbetson, she long afterward reveals the Colonel's villainies to Peter.

Madge Plunket, Peter's cousin who arranges for the publication of his memoirs.

Madame Seraskier (sǝ·rȧs·kyȧ′), Mimsy's mother, the tall, beautiful Irish wife of a Hungarian patriot and man of science; she dies of cholera.

Dr. Seraskier, Mimsy's father, a tall, thin, grave, benevolent man who after his wife's death takes Mimsy to Russia.

PETER PAN

Author: James M. Barrie (1860-1937)
Time of action: Anytime
First presented: 1904

PRINCIPAL CHARACTERS

Peter Pan, a boy who will not grow up. He runs away on the day of his birth so that he will not have to become a man. He lives in Never Land, home of the fairies, protected by his friends the Indians against his enemy, Captain Hook. He is attracted to the Darling home by the stories the mother tells her children.

He persuades the Darling children to visit Never Land and teaches them to fly.

Wendy Darling, an English girl who, with her two brothers, flies off to Never Land for a visit. She mothers Peter Pan and the lost boys, telling them stories at bedtime and tucking them in. After her return home, she goes to Never Land once a year to clean Peter Pan's house. Each year, as she grows up, she and Peter Pan drift farther apart, until at last he cannot understand her at all.

Captain Hook, a pirate captain in Never Land. Jealous of Peter Pan and the lost boys, he and his crew plan to kidnap Wendy so that she will be their mother. He succeeds in capturing the girl, but she is saved by Peter Pan. Frustrated, the Captain, named after the hook he has in place of an arm, throws himself overboard and is eaten by a crocodile who, having tasted the Captain's arm, waits patiently for the rest of his victim.

Tinker Bell, a fairy in love with Peter Pan. A jealous creature, she resents Wendy, who is obviously Peter Pan's favorite. Tinker Bell tries to have the lost boys kill Wendy with their bows and arrows by telling them that Wendy is a dangerous bird.

Nana, the Darlings' dog, who acts as nurse for the children.

Mrs. Darling, Wendy's mother, who is terribly saddened by the temporary loss of her children.

Mr. Darling, Wendy's father, who welcomes the lost boys to his home when they return with Wendy and her brothers.

Michael and

John, Wendy's young brothers.

Tiger Lily, an Indian princess in Never Land.

Nibs,

Slightly,

Smee, and

Tootles, other inhabitants of Never Land.

PETER SIMPLE

Author: Frederick Marryat (1792-1848)
Time of action: Early nineteenth century
First published: 1834

PRINCIPAL CHARACTERS

Peter Simple, the younger son of the younger son of a viscount, who chooses the navy as a livelihood. Eventually proving the trickery of his uncle, he inherits the title and estates of his grandfather.

Old Lord Privilege, the grandfather of Peter, who unwittingly allows young Lord Privilege to cheat Peter and Mr. Simple.

Young Lord Privilege, his rascally son and Peter's uncle, who cheats his nephew out of an inheritance from his grandfather and succeeds in having Peter committed to an insane asylum.

Mr. Simple, Peter's father, who becomes nearly insane when cheated out of his inheritance.

Terence O'Brien, an older midshipman aboard the "Diomede" who befriends Peter. He is captured with Peter during a raid on the French coast. He locates the woman who had helped dispossess Peter.

Colonel O'Brien, a French officer, not related to Terence O'Brien, who captures Terence and Peter.

Celeste O'Brien, his daughter, who frees Peter from the insane asylum and marries him.

Captain Hawkins, the illegitimate son of Lord Privilege, who has Peter court-martialed.

Ellen Simple, Peter's sister, who is rescued from poverty and married by Terence O'Brien.

PETER WHIFFLE

Author: Carl Van Vechten (1880-   )
Time of action: 1907-1919
First published: 1922

PRINCIPAL CHARACTERS

Peter Whiffle, a young Ohioan born to wealth and disposed to inactivity and indecision. Planning to be a writer, he goes through many stages. Believing, as a sophisticated young man in Paris, that style and form alone are important, he plans to write a book containing nothing but lists of Things. Later, dressed in rags, he haunts the Bowery in New York and plots a revolution against capitalism. Subject matter is now all-important, and Peter plans a bloody and dirty book, the heroine of which is to be clubfooted, harelipped, and hunchbacked. Later, having run away from his wedding, he is lying near death in Africa and has a vision in which angels from hell and heaven wait for him to decide where he wants to go. He is relieved to realize that he need not make a decision, and he recovers. He is now convinced that it is necessary to record all aspects of his characters, but that is also quite a task. At last, after a period in which he experiments with black magic, he returns to Toledo, Ohio. Incurably ill, he says he at last has realized that he was never meant to do anything or to make a decision, but only to appreciate the works of others and to be himself.

Carl Van Vechten, his friend, who follows the course of his career.

Edith Dale, a woman of wealth and a friend of Peter and Carl.

Mahalah Wiggins, a young girl whom Peter meets at Edith's house. After much indecision, Peter becomes engaged to Mahalah; but instead of marrying her he leaves for Africa on the day of the wedding, after deciding that marriage is too great a decision for him to make.

PHÈDRE

Author: Jean Baptiste Racine (1639-1699)
Time of action: Remote antiquity
First presented: 1677

PRINCIPAL CHARACTERS

Phèdre (fĕ'drə), the second wife of Thésée (Theseus) and daughter of Minos and Pasiphaë, the King and Queen of Crete. Phèdre is descended from a line of women of unnatural passions. When she realizes that she has fallen in love with her stepson Hippolyte, she fights the double contagion of heredity and passion with courage and in silence until, unable to resist her love, she arranges to have Hippolyte banished from Athens. She bears Thésée's children, sets up a temple to Venus, and makes sacrifices in order to appease the wrath of the goddess. When Thésée leaves her in Troezon with Hippolyte, Phèdre's passion feeds on her until, willing to die, she becomes exhausted and ill from her battle to suppress her illicit love. Word is brought of Thésée's death shortly after her nurse, Oenone, has forced Phèdre to confess her love aloud for the first time. In an unguarded moment, while asking Hippolyte to keep her own son safe now that

Hippolyte may be heir to the Athenian throne, Phèdre rather hopefully reveals her passion to him and witnesses his contempt for her. Angry and ashamed, when Phèdre hears to her joy and to her dismay that Thésée has returned alive from his travels, she allows her nurse to accuse Hippolyte of attempted rape, mainly, Phèdre believes, to keep the stigma of her family history and its unnatural passions from falling even more heavily on her own children. Distraught by her guilt and her love, her fear and her fury, she confesses to Thésée that she has lied to him when it is too late to save Hippolyte, and after she herself has taken poison.

Thésée (tā·zā′), the son of Aegeus, King of Athens, traditionally faithless to women but faithful to his wives. Thésée so loves his young wife and his own honor that he believes Phèdre on slender evidence instead of trusting what he knows to be the character of his son. Becoming one more figure in Racine's gallery of passion's fools, Thésée in a fury prays to Neptune to grant him the death of Hippolyte. Too autocratic to curb himself when rebuked for his cruel and misinformed curse on his son, he nevertheless begins to suspect that Hippolyte has not lied to him. As the evidence against Phèdre begins to accumulate—she is too distraught to prevent it from doing so—Thésée recovers from his jealous rage too late to save the life of his son.

Hippolyte (ē·pô·lēt′), the son of Thésée and Antiope, the Queen of the Amazons. Like everyone about him, Hippolyte goes to extremes. Unpolished, chaste, pure, a hunter and a woodsman, he spurns women until he falls in love with Aricie, for whose sake he is willing to turn over Athens, which he is to inherit from his father, to Aricie, his father's enemy. Because Hippolyte is harsh in his judgment of Phèdre and uncharitable, she reacts violently against the proud boy. Thésée is also harsh in his judgment, no less an extremist than his son. Hippolyte's sense of honor prevents him from telling his father about Phèdre's indiscreet confession of her passion for her stepson, and Thésée's own outraged sense of honor makes him violent in judging Hippolyte.

Aricie (à·rē·sē′), a princess of an older royal dynasty of Athens, held captive by Thésée. Until Hippolyte confesses his love for her, Aricie is content with her lot. Thésée has forbidden her to marry for fear that she may give birth to sons able to contest Thésée's right to rule Athens. She graciously accepts sovereignty of Athens, if Hippolyte can obtain it for her, and his offer of marriage.

Oenone (œ·nōn′), Phèdre's nurse and friend since childhood. Loyal to her mistress, and determined that Phèdre shall not die from stifled passion, she is even willing to further Phèdre's love for Hippolyte. Later, after Hippolyte has spurned Phèdre, Oenone becomes the agent of his destruction.

Théramène (tā·rà·měn′), the tutor of Hippolyte. Because of his slightly lecherous approach to life and to history, Théramène highlights the purity and aloofness of Hippolyte's views. Hippolyte, who would like to strike the love element from historical narratives, is ironically unaware that love will be the chief element in his own history.

PHILASTER

Authors: Francis Beaumont (1585?-1616) and John Fletcher (1579-1625)
Time of action: The romantic past
First presented: c. 1609

Philaster (fĭ·lăs'tẽr), the rightful heir to the Sicilian kingdom. Although he is popular with the people who should be his subjects and with several of his noblemen, he lacks the strength of character to attempt to regain his throne. His melancholy, poetic personality is that of a weaker Hamlet; he calls himself, "a thing born without passion, a faint shadow that every drunken cloud sails over and makes nothing." He is a typical romantic hero in his longing for refuge in a pastoral world and in his distraught reaction to Arethusa when he thinks she has been unfaithful to him. He shows, in his defiance of the King and Pharamond, occasional flashes of courage which foreshadow the resoluteness with which he finally takes over his kingdom.

The King of Calabria, usurper of the throne of Sicily. He is an autocratic ruler, one quickly angered when his wishes are opposed, but he fears Philaster's popularity too much to give complete vent to his rage against the young Prince. He is, like several of the fathers in the Shakespearean romances, redeemed by his recognition of his own wrongdoing and by the virtue and the love of Philaster and his daughter.

Arethusa (ăr'ə·tho͞o·zə), the daughter of the King, betrothed by her father to Pharamond. She possesses the courage and resourcefulness of a Viola and a Rosalind, forthrightly telling Philaster of her love for him and plotting with her ladies to expose Pharamond's wickedness. She is puzzled, but not overcome, by the accusations made against her and her page, Bellario, by the King and his court, and she remains true to Philaster in spite of his cruelty to her. It is she who arranges their marriage and saves him from death at the hand of her father.

Pharamond (făr'ə·mŏnd), Prince of Spain, Arethusa's suitor. He is an arrogant braggart who well deserves the title, "prince of popinjays," which Philaster bestows upon him. He loses the King's favor by his seduction of Megra, Arethusa's willing lady in waiting, but almost regains it through Philaster's mistreatment of the Princess. He receives well-merited calumny from the townspeople into whose hands he falls during the rebellion, and he is saved only by the intervention of Philaster, who sends him back to Spain.

Euphrasia (ū·frā'sĭ·ə), daughter of one of Philaster's loyal lords. She disguises herself as a page, Bellario, to be near the Prince, whom she secretly loves. She serves both Philaster and Arethusa loyally, and she resolves to remain with them, unmarried, after he has won his throne and his bride.

Dion (dī'ŏn), Euphrasia's father, a Sicilian lord. He pays necessary homage to the King, but he remains a firm supporter of Philaster's claims. It is partly his loyalty to the Prince which makes him too ready to believe the slanderous reports about Arethusa's love for Bellario, a misconception for which he berates himself and asks forgiveness.

Cleremont (klĕr'ə·mŏnt) and **Thrasilene** (thrăsə·lē'nə), two noblemen loyal to Philaster.

Megra (mĕg'rə), lady in waiting to Arethusa. Attracted to every handsome man she meets, she welcomes Pharamond's advances. She attempts to avenge the court's discovery of her relations with the Spanish prince by malicious slandering of Arethusa and Bellario.

Galathea (gal·ə·thē'ə), another of Arethusa's ladies. Witty and sharp-tongued in her refusal of Pharamond's offers and in her condemnation of Megra, she helps her mistress to unveil the Prince's infidelity.

Country Fellow, an honest rustic. On the way to watch the King's hunt, he finds

Philaster in the act of wounding Arethusa and springs to the lady's defense. He asks to see the King as his reward, but he vows to avoid "gay sights" in the future.

A Captain, the leader of the uprising against the King. He and his followers torment Pharamond with bloodthirsty threats and insults.

PHILOCTETES

Author: Sophocles (c. 496-c. 406 B.C.)
Time of action: The Trojan War
First presented: 409 B.C.

PRINCIPAL CHARACTERS

Philoctetes (fĭl'ŏk·tē'tēz), a Greek warrior who had received as a legacy from Herakles his magical bow and arrows. As the Greek expedition sailed toward Troy, it had paused at Chrysa, where Philoctetes, approaching a shrine, had been bitten on the foot by a serpent. The wound refused to heal. Because Philoctetes' screams of pain and the odor emanating from the wound caused acute discomfort to his shipmates, he was, at the instigation of Odysseus and the Atreidae, marooned on the barren island of Lemnos. Ten years later the Greeks captured Helenus, a Trojan prophet, who revealed that the city would never fall without the willing aid of Philoctetes. Odysseus and Neoptolemus were sent to persuade Philoctetes to rejoin the cause of those who had abandoned him. At the beginning of the play Philoctetes, who has endured ten years of loneliness, starvation, and hideous pain, is kept alive only by his superhuman stamina and his fierce hatred of the Greeks who wronged him. He is deceived by Neoptolemus, who, having promised to take him home, is entrusted with the great bow, but when the real purpose of Neoptolemus' visit becomes clear, Philoctetes adamantly refuses to go to Troy, even though to remain on Lemnos would mean certain death for him without his weapon used to kill sea birds for food. There is no question but that he is morally right to resist not only Odysseus' threats but also Neop-

tolemus' persuasions; however, the kind of heroism to which Philoctetes dedicates himself, although grand and noble, is essentially sterile and selfish. Having triumphed over both the callous enmity of Odysseus and the spontaneous friendliness of Neoptolemus, itself a soft and subtle infringement upon his will, Philoctetes can at last freely offer himself to the world again, an action which is symbolized by the epiphany of Herakles. With Odysseus and Neoptolemus he sets out for Troy, where he will win glory and where his wound will be cured.

Neoptolemus (nē·ŏp·tŏl'ə·məs), the young son of Achilles, noble and courageous, but as yet untried in battle. Persuaded by Odysseus that it is his duty to deceive Philoctetes, he tells the outcast that he has deserted the Greek army because his father's armor had been denied him. He promises to take Philoctetes back to Greece with him and watches as Philoctetes struggles against an excruciating wave of pain brought on by his disease. When Neoptolemus at last gains possession of the great bow, Philoctetes is made helpless. Later, in spite of Odysseus' strong protests, his sense of decency and honor and the instinctive sympathy he has felt for the sufferer cause him to return the weapon. He finally agrees truly to take Philoctetes home, but is relieved of this obligation when the bowman resolves to go to Troy.

870

Odysseus (ō·dĭs′ūs), the crafty and unscrupulous Greek leader who puts expediency over honor. His purpose is to get Philoctetes to accompany him to Troy; his means are deceit and violence. He temporarily convinces Neoptolemus that a reputation for wisdom and goodness can be won by a man willing to sacrifice personal honor for the benefit of his cause; but after his experience with Philoctetes the young man holds both Odysseus and his advice in contempt. Odysseus is not totally without dignity,

and he reveals a sense of responsibility to the Greek army and its generals.

A Sailor, disguised as a Trader, sent by Odysseus, who cannot allow himself to be seen, to spy on Neoptolemus and Philoctetes.

Herakles (hĕr′ə·klēz), the legendary Greek hero, now deified, whose spirit informs Philoctetes that destiny requires him to leave Lemnos and go to Troy.

A Chorus of Sailors.

PHINEAS FINN

Author: Anthony Trollope (1815-1882)
Time of action: Mid-nineteenth century
First published: 1869

PRINCIPAL CHARACTERS

Phineas Finn, a personable young Irishman with political aspirations. Elected to Parliament, he goes to London, where he makes a number of influential friends and becomes enamored, in turn, of Lady Laura Standish, Violet Effingham, and Madame Marie Max Goesler. Material and political advancement point to a promising career until passage of the Irish Reform Bill abolishes his borough. His parliamentary career over, he returns to Ireland and marries his Irish sweetheart, Mary Flood Jones.

Mary Flood Jones, a pretty Irish girl in love with Phineas Finn, whom she marries when he returns to Ireland at the end of his parliamentary career.

Lady Laura Standish, Lord Brentford's daughter, who is in love with Phineas Finn. She marries Mr. Kennedy after she exhausts her personal fortune on her profligate brother, Lord Chiltern.

Lord Brentford, a prominent Whig.

Mr. Kennedy, a wealthy member of Parliament who marries Lady Laura Standish.

Lord Chiltern, the profligate son of Lord Brentford and a friend of Phineas Finn. He is in love with Violet Effingham, whose hand he wins as Phineas' rival.

Violet Effingham, courted by Phineas Finn but in love with Lord Chiltern, whom she finally accepts.

Madame Marie Max Goesler, a wealthy young widow who offers her hand and fortune to Phineas Finn, who is already engaged to Mary Flood Jones.

The Duke of Omnium, the elderly suitor of Madame Goesler.

PHINEAS REDUX

Author: Anthony Trollope (1815-1882)
Time of action: Mid-nineteenth century
First published: 1874

Phineas Finn, a young man retired from politics. After the death of his wife, he is invited back to resume his political career. Threatened by false charges of adultery and murder, he is cleared of the charges through the efforts of his loyal friends, is overwhelmingly elected, and becomes the hero of the hour. Deeply in love with Madame Marie Goesler, he marries her and, with her fortune, is able to act independently of his party when the occasion demands.

Madame Marie Max Goesler, a wealthy young widow long in love with Phineas Finn. Through her efforts he is cleared of the charge of murder, and later he marries her.

Lady Laura Kennedy, Mr. Kennedy's estranged wife, long in love with Phineas Finn.

Mr. Kennedy, Lady Laura Kennedy's deranged husband, who falsely accuses Phineas Finn of adultery with her.

Lord Chiltern and
Violet Chiltern, his wife, loyal friends of Phineas Finn.

Adelaid Palliser, the niece of the Duke of Omnium, and
Mr. Maule, lovers, whose lack of fortune prevents their union. The marriage is finally made possible by Madame Goesler's gift of the fortune left her by the Duke of Omnium.

The Duke of Omnium, a friend of Madame Goesler, to whom he leaves a handsome fortune.

Lady Glencora, later **The Duchess of Omnium,** the Duke of Omnium's niece and a loyal friend of Phineas Finn.

Quintus Slide, a scandal-mongering journalist who makes public the false accusation of adultery against Phineas Finn.

Mr. Bonteen, a conniving politician of whose murder Phineas Finn is falsely accused.

Spooner, an uncouth fox hunter and a rejected suitor of Adelaid Palliser.

Mealyus (Emilius), the real murderer of Mr. Bonteen.

THE PHOENICIAN WOMEN

Author: Euripides (c. 485-c. 406 B.C.)
Time of action: The war of the Seven against Thebes
First presented: c. 410 B.C.

PRINCIPAL CHARACTERS

A Chorus of Young Women, maidens from Phoenicia dedicated to the service of Apollo, who have stopped in Thebes and have been detained by the war of the Seven against Thebes. They provide the historical perspective necessary to see the duel between the two sons of Oedipus as the last link in a long chain of Theban misfortunes.

Eteocles (ē·tē′ō·klēz), King of Thebes, the son of Jocasta and Oedipus. He and his brother Polynices had agreed to rule the city of Thebes in turn, but Eteocles has refused to give up the throne and Polynices has appeared with an Argive army to claim his right. Jocasta tries to reconcile the two brothers, but without success. Eteocles believes that might is right and will fight rather than give up his power. He is, as he admits, the typical dictator; at the same time he is young, rash, and ignorant in warfare. Creon, Jocasta's brother, helps him plan the defense of the city. In that defense he fights bravely, challenging his brother to single combat. The brothers kill each other. Eteocles' only affection, his love for his mother, is expressed in his dying moments.

Polynices (pŏl'ə·nī'sēz), the exiled brother of Eteocles who, when Eteocles refuses to allow him his period of rule, marches against Thebes. He has justice on his side, as the Thebans and even Eteocles recognize, but he has allowed his wrongs to lead him to the unpardonable sin of attack on his homeland. Speaking to Jocasta before her attempted reconciliation between the brothers, he reveals that he still loves his country, his mother, sister, father, and even his brother. He accepts Eteocles' challenge to single combat and is killed. Creon, following Eteocles' order, refuses burial for his body.

Jocasta (jō·kăs'tə), the wife and mother of Oedipus. She tries unsuccessfully to reconcile her two sons by Oedipus. When she hears of their individual challenge, she calls her daughter Antigone from the house and the two leave, determined to make one last effort to prevent the conflict between brothers. She arrives in time to hear their final words; then, lamenting, she stabs herself and dies with them. Her actions and speeches are marked by restraint, except for her joy at the return of Polynices.

Antigone (ăn·tĭg'ə·nē), the daughter of Oedipus. She appears, accompanied by an old pedagogue, as a girl eager to observe the Argive forces assembled outside Thebes. Later she views with Jocasta the combat between her brothers. She returns after her mother's death, rejects the proposed marriage with Creon's son, and willingly accompanies Oedipus into exile. She also swears to perform burial rites for Polynices.

Oedipus (ĕd'ə·pəs, ē'də·pəs), the son and later the husband of Jocasta. Although he appears only in the final scene, his presence dominates the play. Because they deposed and shut him up, he has pronounced on his sons a curse which is carried out in the action of the play. Antigone calls him forth and informs him of the death of his sons and of Jocasta. Creon, now the ruler of Thebes, orders him into exile because Tiresias has said that Thebes will not know prosperity as long as Oedipus remains within its walls. Oedipus' final speech is a lament of his fate.

Creon (krē'ŏn), the brother of Jocasta. He aids Eteocles in setting up the defense of Thebes and is told that he is to rule if Eteocles should be killed. When Tiresias informs him that Menoeceus, his son, must be sacrificed to insure victory for Thebes, he tries to save his heir. At the end of the play he appears to order Oedipus into exile and to carry out Eteocles' command that Polynices be denied funeral rites.

Menoeceus (mə·nē'soōs), the son of Creon. He hears Tiresias' prophecy that he must die to save Thebes, pretends to agree with his father's plan for his escape, then states his intention to sacrifice himself for the city. He is the type of pure youth.

Tiresias (tī·rē'sĭ·əs), the Theban prophet who foresees the deaths of Polynices and Eteocles and the sacrifice of Menoeceus. He is the conventional prophetic figure, but realistically drawn.

PHORMIO

Author: Terence (Publius Terentius Afer, c. 190-159 B.C.)
Time of action: Second century B.C.
First presented: 161 B.C.

amiable
t of the
human
d drink,
ends his
untryside
invitations
aries, pur-
n effort to
and pro-
The height
t the Fleet
breach of
man suffer-
his enemies.
and fatuous
the course of
ental charac-

the sportsman
humane, he
hunting mis-
d duels. In the
en, his true love,
er brother, her
er.

, the poetic mem-
ub. Although he
he never writes
gains his sweet-
after several visits

a rotund member
, so susceptible that
g in and out of love.
e, he finds himself
turn. His flirtation
Wardle ends dismally
th Mr. Alfred Jingle.

wner of Manor Farm,
robust, genial, but
pered host of the four
patriarch, he rescues
r. Jingle at the cost of
twenty pounds, and he
his daughter's romance

with Mr. Snodgrass. Finally he gives the young couple his blessing.

Miss Rachel Wardle, a spinster of uncertain age. She flirts coyly with the susceptible Mr. Tupman but abandons him for the blandishments of Mr. Jingle, who has designs on her supposed wealth. Mr. Pickwick and Mr. Wardle pursue the elopers, Mr. Wardle buys off the rascal, and Miss Wardle returns husbandless to Manor Farm.

Mrs. Wardle, the aged, deaf mother of Mr. Wardle and Miss Rachel.

Emily Wardle, Mr. Wardle's vivacious daughter, in love with Mr. Snodgrass, whom she eventually marries.

Isabella Wardle, another daughter. She marries Mr. Trundle.

Mr. Trundle, Isabella Wardle's suitor. Though frequently on the scene, he remains a minor figure in the novel.

Joe, Mr. Wardle's fat, sleepy young servant. He is characterized by his ability to go to sleep at any time and under almost any circumstances, a trait which both amuses and irritates his master.

Mrs. Martha Bardell, Mr. Pickwick's landlady. When he consults her as to the advisability of taking a servant, she mistakes his remarks for a proposal of marriage and accepts him, much to Mr. Pickwick's dismay. The misunderstanding leads to the famous breach of promise suit of Bardell vs. Pickwick. Mr. Pickwick, refusing to pay damages, is sent to the Fleet Prison. After his refusal to pay, Mrs. Bardell's attorneys, unable to collect their fee, have her arrested and also sent to the Fleet Prison. Her plight finally arouses Mr. Pickwick's pity, and he pays the damages in order to release her and to free himself to aid his friend Mr. Winkle, who has eloped with Arabella Allen.

Tommy Bardell, Mrs. Bardell's young son.

Serjeant Buzfuz, Mrs. Bardell's counsel at the trial, a bombastic man noted for his bullying tactics with witnesses.

Mr. Skimpin, the assistant counsel to Serjeant Buzfuz.

Mr. Dodson and
Mr. Fogg, Mrs. Bardell's unscrupulous attorneys. Having taken the suit without fee, they have their client arrested and sent to prison when Mr. Pickwick refuses to pay damages after the suit has been decided against him.

Mr. Alfred Jingle, an amiable, impudent strolling player remarkable for his constant flow of disjointed sentences. He makes several attempts to marry women for their money, but Mr. Pickwick thwarts his plans in every case. He ends up in the Fleet Prison, from which he is rescued by Mr. Pickwick's generosity. He keeps his promise to reform.

Job Trotter, Mr. Jingle's cunning accomplice and servant. He is the only person whose wits prove sharper than those of Sam Weller.

Jem Huntley, a melancholy actor called Dismal Jemmy, Mr. Jingle's friend and Job Trotter's brother.

Sam Weller, Mr. Pickwick's jaunty, quick-witted, devoted Cockney servant. He and Mr. Pickwick meet at the inn to which Mr. Wardle has traced his sister and Mr. Jingle. Mr. Pickwick's decision to hire Sam as his valet leads to the famous breach of promise suit brought by Mrs. Bardell. Sam's aphorisms, anecdotes, and exploits make him one of Dickens' great comic creations, the embodiment of Cockney life and character.

Tony Weller, Sam Weller's hardy, affable father, a coachman who loves food, drink, and tobacco, and wants nothing

from his shrewish wife except the opportunity to enjoy them.

Mrs. Susan Weller, formerly Mrs. Clarke, a shrew, a hypocrite, and a religious fanatic. At her death her husband inherits a small estate she has hoarded.

The Reverend Mr. Stiggins, called the Shepherd, a canting, hypocritical, alcoholic clergyman, greatly admired by Mrs. Weller, who gives him every opportunity to sponge off her husband.

Arabella Allen, a lovely girl whom Mr. Winkle first meets at Manor Farm. Her brother, Benjamin Allen, wants his sister to marry his friend Bob Sawyer, but Arabella rejects her brother's choice. After she marries Mr. Winkle in secret, Mr. Pickwick pays his friend's debts, effects a reconciliation between the young couple and Arabella's brother, and breaks the news of the marriage to Mr. Winkle's father.

Benjamin Allen, Arabella's coarse, roistering brother, a medical student. With no regard for his sister's feelings, he stubbornly insists upon her marriage to Bob Sawyer.

Mr. Winkle (Senior), a practical man of business, much opposed to his son's romance with Arabella Allen. He changes his mind when, through the services of Mr. Pickwick, he meets his daughter-in-law. He builds the couple a new house and makes his son an assistant in the family business.

Bob Sawyer, Benjamin Allen's friend and Arabella's unwelcome, oafish suitor. He hangs up his shingle in Bristol and practices medicine there. Eventually he and Benjamin Allen take service with the East India Company.

Bob Cripps, Bob Sawyer's servant.

Mrs. Mary Ann Raddle, Bob Sawyer's landlady, a shrew.

Mr. Raddle, her husband.

...fty and cynical ...a self-styled par- ...aighten out the ...two young cous- ...ia, whose fathers ...nio's connivance, ...ium, a penniless ...amily. When the ...Chremes, return, ...o marry Phanium ...ho from his im- ...nio betrays the un- ...the money to Phae- ...girl with whom he ...The uncles discover ...is actually Chremes' ...marriage to a woman ...ow approve the match ...: money back from ...they insist, Phormio ...fe Nausistrata of the ...she upbraids Chremes, ...eep the money, and in- ...er. Antipho and Phae- ...y with the women they

...mipho's shrewd servant, ...mplice in helping the ...defrauding their fathers.

...mĭ·fō), Antipho's father ...brother. Pompous, class- ...l somewhat miserly, old ...es to revoke his son's mar- ...it offers no dowry.

...ā'mēz), Phaedria's father. ...before, Chremes had, while ...under the name of Stilpho ...rried a woman in Lemnos ...aughter by her. Returning to ...search of his daughter, he

learns that she has gone to Athens looking for him. He fears his Athenian wife will discover the earlier marriage.

Antipho (ăn'tĭ·fō), Demipho's son. When his father returns, Antipho is afraid to face him until Phanium's true identity has been revealed.

Phaedria (fē'drĭ·ə), Chremes' son, in love with a young slave girl. He gets the money to purchase her from Phormio. Antipho and Phaedria are deeply devoted.

Nausistrata (nô·sĭs'trə·tə), Chremes' good-hearted but nagging wife. Happy to have something to hold over her husband, she forgives Chremes for his indiscreet marriage.

Sophrona (sŏ·frō'nə), Phanium's nurse. She reveals to Chremes that his Lemnian wife has died of grief and that Antipho's wife is really his daughter.

Dorio (dŏ'rĭ·ō), a bawd who owns the young musician whom Phaedria loves. He threatens to sell her to a soldier unless Phaedria can buy her at once.

Pamphilia (păm·fī'lĭ·ə), the slave girl Phaedria loves and purchases.

Phanium (fā'nĭ·əm), Chremes' daughter and Antipho's wife.

Higio (hī'gĭ·ō),
Cratinus (kră·tī'nəs), and
Crito (krī'tō), Demipho's advocates.

Davus (dā'vəs), a friend of Geta.

Mida (mī'də), Phanium's servant, a young boy.

PICKWICK PAPERS

Charles Dickens (1812-1870)
...action: 1827-1828
...lished: 1836-1837

Mrs. Betsey Cluppins, Mrs. Raddle's sister and a friend of Mrs. Bardell.

Mr. Gunter, a friend of Bob Sawyer.

Jack Hopkins, a medical student, Bob Sawyer's friend. He tells Mr. Pickwick the story of a child who swallowed a necklace of large wooden beads that rattled and clacked whenever the child moved.

Peter Magnus, a traveler who journeys with Mr. Pickwick from London to Ipswich. He is on his way to make a proposal of marriage.

Miss Witherfield, his beloved, into whose room Mr. Pickwick, unable to find his own, accidentally blunders at the inn in Ipswich.

The Hon. Samuel Slumkey, a candidate for Parliament from the borough of Eatanswill. He is victorious over his opponent, Horatio Fizkin, Esq.

Mr. Slurk, the editor of "The Eatanswill Independent."

Mr. Pott, the editor of "The Eatanswill Gazette."

Mrs. Pott, his wife.

Mrs. Leo Hunter, a lady of literary pretensions, the author of "Ode to an Expiring Frog," whom Mr. Pickwick meets in Eatanswill.

Mr. Leo Hunter, who lives in his wife's reflected glory.

Count Smorltork, a traveling nobleman whom Mr. Pickwick meets at a breakfast given by Mrs. Leo Hunter.

Horatio Fizkin, Esq., defeated in the election at Eatanswill.

Mr. Perker, the agent for the Hon. Samuel Slumkey in the Eatanswill election, later Mr. Pickwick's attorney in the suit of Bardell vs. Pickwick. After his client has been sentenced to prison, Perker advises him to pay the damages in order to gain his freedom.

Serjeant Snubbin, Mr. Pickwick's lantern-faced, dull-eyed senior counsel in the breach of promise suit.

Mr. Justice Starleigh, the judge who presides at the trial of Bardell vs. Pickwick.

Mr. Phunky, the assistant counsel to Serjeant Snubbin; he is called an "infant barrister" because he has seen only eight years at the bar.

Thomas Groffin, a chemist, and
Richard Upwitch, a grocer, jurors at the trial of Bardell vs. Pickwick.

Mr. Jackson and
Mr. Wicks, clerks in the office of Dodson and Fogg.

Mr. Lowten, clerk to Mr. Perker.

Captain Boldwig, a peppery-tempered landowner on whose grounds the Pickwickians accidentally trespass while hunting.

Dr. Slammer, the surgeon of the 97th Regiment. At a charity ball in Rochester he challenges Mr. Jingle to a duel, but because the player is wearing a borrowed coat Mr. Winkle is the one actually called upon to meet the hot-tempered surgeon. Mr. Winkle, having been drunk, cannot remember what his conduct was or whom he might have insulted the night before. The situation is eventually resolved and Mr. Winkle and the doctor shake hands and part on friendly terms.

Lieutenant Tappleton, Dr. Slammer's second.

Colonel Bulder, the commanding officer of the military garrison at Rochester.

Mrs. Bulder, his wife.

Miss Bulder, their daughter.

Mrs. Budger, a widow, Mr. Tupman's partner at the charity ball in Rochester.

Mr. Dowler, a blustering, cowardly ex-army officer whom Mr. Pickwick meets at the White Horse Cellar. The Dowlers travel with Mr. Pickwick to Bath.

Mrs. Dowler, his wife.

Lord Mutanhed, a man of fashion and Mr. Dowling's friend, whom Mr. Pickwick meets in Bath.

The Hon. Mr. Crushton, another friend of Mr. Dowler.

Angelo Cyrus Bantam, Esq., a friend of Mr. and Mrs. Dowling and a master of ceremonies at Bath.

George Nupkins, Esq., the mayor of Ipswich, before whom Mr. Pickwick is brought on the charge, made by Miss Witherfield, that he is planning to fight a duel. The mayor has recently entertained Mr. Jingle who, calling himself Captain Fitz-Marshall, was courting Miss Henrietta Nupkins.

Mrs. Nupkins, the mayor's wife.

Henrietta Nupkins, their daughter, the object of one of Mr. Jingle's matrimonial designs.

Mary, Mrs. Nupkins' pretty young servant. She eventually marries Sam Weller and both make their home with Mr. Pickwick in his happy, unadventurous old age.

Mr. Jinks, the clerk of the mayor's court at Ipswich.

Daniel Grummer, the constable of the mayor's court at Ipswich.

Frank Simmery, Esq., a young stock broker.

Solomon Pell, an attorney who, to his profit, assists in settling the deceased Mrs. Weller's modest estate.

Miss Tomkins, mistress of Westgate House, a boarding school for young ladies, at Bury St. Edmunds. Mr. Pickwick, tricked into believing that Mr. Jingle is planning to elope with one of the pupils, ventures into the school premises at night and finds himself in an embarrassing situation.

Tom Roker, a turnkey at the Fleet Prison.

Smangle,
Mivins, called **The Zephyr,**
Martin,
Simpson, and
The Chancery Prisoner, inmates of the Fleet Prison during Mr. Pickwick's detention.

Mrs. Budkin,
Susannah Sanders,
Mrs. Mudberry, and
Mrs. Rogers, Mrs. Bardell's friends and neighbors.

Anthony Humm, chairman of the Brick Lane Branch of the United Grand Junction Ebenezer Temperance Association. Mr. Weller takes his son Sam to a lively meeting of the association.

THE PICTURE OF DORIAN GRAY

Author: Oscar Wilde (1856-1900)
Time of action: Late nineteenth century
First published: 1891

PRINCIPAL CHARACTERS

Dorian Gray, a handsome young man who, while visiting the studio of an artist friend who is painting his portrait, idly wishes that the portrait would grow old while he himself remained young looking. Later, having treated a young girl cruelly, he notices the first sign of alteration in the portrait. Alarmed, he decides to repent and to marry the girl; but he learns that she has killed herself. He now gives himself over entirely to a life of corruption, under the tutelage of an evil friend. His crimes include murder. At last he decides to destroy the hideous portrait, which has been long locked away. He stabs it with a knife. Hearing

878

a cry, the servants find lying before a portrait of their handsome master a withered, wrinkled body with a knife in its breast.

Lord Henry Wotton, a witty, degenerate man who deliberately tempts Dorian into a life of debauchery.

Basil Hallward, Dorian's artist friend who paints his portrait. He asks Lord Wotton never to meet Dorian, saying that the older man's influence would be evil; but Dorian comes to the studio while Lord Wotton is there, and the friendship begins. Hallward and Dorian become estranged; but on his thirty-eighth birthday Dorian shows Hallward the altered portrait and then, angry because he has betrayed himself, kills Hallward.

Alan Campbell, a young chemist whom Dorian blackmails into disposing of Hallward's body with fire and chemicals. Campbell later commits suicide under strange circumstances.

Sibyl Vane, a young actress who knows Dorian only as "Prince Charming." Dorian treats her cruelly, and she kills herself.

James Vane, her brother. He has sworn revenge against "Prince Charming," but he hesitates to kill Dorian, who looks years too young to be the man who ruined his sister eighteen years before. Assured that Dorian is in fact that man, he follows him to his country house and is accidentally shot and killed during a hunt on the estate.

PIERRE

Author: Herman Melville (1819-1891)
Time of action: Early nineteenth century
First published: 1852

PRINCIPAL CHARACTERS

Pierre Glendinning, a wealthy young easterner of the early nineteenth century. When he claims his half sister as his wife in order to shield her from the world, his decision causes him to lose his inheritance, his fiancée and eventually his life. Having shot and killed a male cousin, he is sent to prison. During a visit from his fiancée and his half sister he swallows poison and dies.

Isabel, Pierre's half sister, the illegitimate daughter of an alliance Pierre's father had with a young French woman. Her love for Pierre is not the typical love of a sister for a brother. She is jealous of the attention he pays another woman, and finally, after Pierre has taken his life by poison, she kills herself by drinking from the vial he had used.

Lucy Tartan, Pierre's fiancée. Though she has wealth and many friends, she follows Pierre and Isabel to New York to live with them and earn her living by painting portraits. When Pierre tells her, during the prison scene, that Isabel is his half sister and not his wife, Lucy dies of shock.

Mrs. Glendinning, Pierre's mother, a proud woman who is jealous of her influence over her son. Because Pierre claims Isabel as his wife, she drives him from home and, at her death, cuts him off without a cent.

Glen Stanly, Pierre's cousin, the relative to whom Mrs. Glendinning leaves the family fortune. Stanly is in love with Lucy. In concert with Lucy's brother, he provokes Pierre, with whom Lucy is now living. Pierre shoots and kills him during a fight.

Delly Ulver, an illegitimate farm girl befriended by Isabel and Pierre. She becomes their servant.

PILGRIMAGE

Author: Dorothy M. Richardson (1873-1957)
Time of action: 1893-1911
First published: 1915-1938

PRINCIPAL CHARACTERS

Miriam Henderson, an Englishwoman of middle-class background whose story from youth to maturity is screened through her mind in a series of discontinuous episodes, impressions, and suggestions. Forced to earn her own living after her father loses his money, she teaches in Germany and in London. She becomes a governess in a wealthy household. She nurses her dying mother. She works in a dental clinic. She interests herself in the activities of a Socialist group, the Lycurgans. She is engaged to marry Shatov, a Russian Jew, but changes her mind. She begins to write literary reviews. She rejects Dr. Densley's proposal and has an affair with a writer named "Hypo" Wilson. She goes on a vacation in Switzerland. She spends some time with a Quaker family in the country. The twelve volumes of Miriam Henderson's story represent the most extended exercise of the pure stream-of-consciousness in all literature, and Miriam herself is the most completely realized character from the interior point of view. The flaw in Miss Richardson's novel is that it offers little selectivity. The events of one woman's life, the important and the trivial, are presented on the same plane of immediate sensation; and the result is boredom as well as revelation. Reviewing Miss Richardson's work, May Sinclair borrowed a phrase from William James and used the term "stream-of-consciousness" to describe the technique employed.

Mr. Henderson, a moderately prosperous man living on inherited income. The loss of his money throws his daughters on their own resources.

Mrs. Henderson, his wife, nursed by her daughter Miriam while she is dying of cancer.

Harriet,
Sarah, and
Eve Henderson, Miriam's sisters. Harriet marries Gerald, who also loses his money; they run a rooming house. Sarah remains with her parents until she marries. Eve moves back and forth between London and Wales, sometimes teaching, sometimes running a shop.

Gerald, Harriet's husband.

Fräulein Pfaff, the mistress of a private school in Germany where Miriam Henderson teaches for a year.

Pastor Lahmann, a friend of Fräulein Pfaff, who becomes jealous when he appears interested in Miriam Henderson.

The Misses Perne, spinsters who conduct Wordsworth House, a school in London where Miriam Henderson teaches for a time.

Grace and
Florrie Bloom, students at Wordsworth House. They become Miriam Henderson's friends.

Ted, a young man in whom Miriam Henderson is interested. He is jealous of Max.

Max, a young man attentive to Miriam Henderson. He dies in New York.

Mr. and Mrs. Corrie, the owners of a country home where Miriam Henderson is employed as a governess.

Dr. Orly, senior,
Dr. Orly, junior, and
Dr. Hancock, the owners of a dental clinic where Miriam Henderson works as a secretary and assistant. The Orlys

become her friends, and Dr. Hancock introduces her to the London literary life.

Mrs. Bailey, the owner of a boarding house where Miriam Henderson takes lodgings.

Alma, Miriam Henderson's old school friend, now married to "Hypo" Wilson, a writer.

"Hypo" Wilson, a writer obviously modeled on H. G. Wells. He introduces Miriam Henderson to the Lycurgans, a Socialist group. Later she has an affair with him.

Eleanor Dear, a sickly nurse who imagines that every man she meets is in love with her. Miriam Henderson nurses her through an illness. She later has an affair with Shatov, to whom Miriam is engaged.

Dr. Densley, Miriam Henderson's friend

and adviser. She rejects his proposal of marriage.

Shatov, a Russian Jew, a brilliant young intellectual who also interests Miriam Henderson in Socialism and literature. They are engaged to be married, but she breaks the engagement when he becomes Eleanor Dear's lover. He eventually marries Amabel.

Selina Holland, a social worker with whom Miriam Henderson shares an apartment for a time. The two women quarrel and Miriam returns to Mrs. Bailey's boarding house.

Amabel, a young girl in whom Miriam Henderson has taken an interest. She marries Shatov.

The Rescorlas, a Quaker family with whom Miriam Henderson lives for six months in the country.

THE PILGRIMAGE OF CHARLEMAGNE

Author: Unknown
Time of action: c. 800
First transcribed: c. 1100

PRINCIPAL CHARACTERS

Charlemagne (shär·lə·màn′y), King of the Franks and Emperor of the West. When his wife declares that Hugo, Emperor of Greece, is the handsomer of the two Kings, Charlemagne angrily sets forth, with his Twelve Peers, on a pilgrimage to Jerusalem. After the pilgrims sit in the chairs of Christ and His apostles in the great cathedral in Jerusalem and receive many relics from the Patriarch, they depart for Constantinople and are received as guests by the magnificent Hugo. In the bedchamber, the Franks drink their wine and each makes a boast concerning his host. When Charlemagne is challenged to prove the boasts true or be beheaded with his peers, he and his men, assisted by an angel, overcome Hugo and return to France, where Charlemagne

forgives his wife for her unfortunate comparison.

Hugo (ü·gō′), Emperor of Greece and Constantinople.

Roland (rô·län′),
Olivier (ô·lē·vyā′),
William of Orange,
Naimes (něm′),
Ogier of Denmark (ô·zhyā′),
Gerin (zhā·răn′),
Berenger (bā·rän·zhā′),
Turpin the Archbishop (tür·păn′),
Ernaut (ĕr·nō′),
Aymer (ĕ·mē′),
Bernard of Brusban (bĕr·nàr′ brüs·bän′), and
Bertram (bĕr·träm′), Charlemagne's Twelve Peers, who boast of the ways

881

each will overcome King Hugo. When confronted with the demand that they prove their boasts or lose their heads, they are aided by prayer and an angel, who warns them never to boast in such a way again.

THE PILGRIM'S PROGRESS

Author: John Bunyan (1628-1688)
Time of action: Any time since Christ
First published: 1678

PRINCIPAL CHARACTERS

Christian, an example of all God-fearing Protestants, whose adventures are recounted as events in a dream experienced by the narrator. Originally called Graceless, of the race of Japhet, Christian becomes distressed with his life in the City of Destruction and insists that his wife and four children accompany him in search of salvation. When they refuse to leave, Christian determines to set out alone. Henceforth his life story consists of hardships, sufferings, and struggles to overcome obstacles—physical, human, and emotional—which beset his path. At the outset, Christian's family and neighbors, Pliable and Obstinate, try to dissuade him from breaking away from his sins of the past. Then Evangelist appears with a parchment roll on which is inscribed, "Fly from the Wrath to Come." On his long journey, Christian finds that human beings he meets offer distractions and hindrance, even bodily harm and violence. Mr. Worldly Wiseman turns him aside from his set purpose until Evangelist intervenes. **Simple, Sloth, Presumption, Formalist** and **Hypocrisy, Timorous,** and **Mistrust** seek to dissuade or discourage Christian because of the rigors of the straight and narrow way. The Giant of the Doubting Castle and his wife beat and torture Christian and Hopeful. In the Valley of Humiliation Christian engages in mortal combat with a monstrous creature named Apollyon for more than half a day, but at last emerges triumphant. In many times of peril Christian is fortunate in having companions who can assist him:

Evangelist, who gets him out of difficulties or warns him of impending strife; **Help,** who assists him to get out of the Slough of Despond; Faithful, who is by his side at Vanity Fair; Hopeful, who comforts him at Doubting Castle and encourages him to give up bravely at the River of Death. In this narrative of a pilgrim's adventures, Christian must constantly overcome temptations and dangers which will thwart his goal, impede his progress toward eternal life, or prevent him from reaching Heaven; but with the aid of his religious fervor and the advice and counsel of a few true friends, he achieves salvation.

Evangelist, Christian's adviser and guide, particularly in times of danger. Evangelist shows him the way to avoid destruction, directs him to the Wicket Gate, warns him of such people as Mr. Worldly Wiseman and of the dangers at Vanity Fair.

Apollyon (a·pŏl′lyŏn), the fiend in the Valley of Humiliation. Apollyon has scales like a fish, feet like a bear, wings like a dragon, a mouth like a lion; he spouts fire and smoke from his belly, and he discourses like a devil in his attempt to persuade Christian from honoring his religion.

Giant Despair, the giant owner of Doubting Castle. He imprisons Christian and Faithful, beats them, and threatens death, until Christian uses a key of Promise to make their escape.

Faithful, Christian's traveling companion. Imprisoned, tortured, and put to death by the people of Vanity Fair, he is transported to the Celestial Gate in a chariot.

Hopeful, another wayfarer. He joins Christian at Vanity Fair and accompanies him through various adventures on the way to eternal salvation.

Good-Will, who tells Christian to knock and the gate that is blocking his way will be opened, so that he may see a vision of the Day of Judgment.

Ignorance, a native of the country of Conceit. Refusing to accept the beliefs of Christian and Hopeful, he continues on the journey until he is seized and thrust into Hell.

Mr. Worldly Wiseman, a dweller in the town of Carnal-Policy. He advises Christian to go to Legality and get relief from the burden of sins which Christian carries on his back.

Three Shining Ones, who clothe Christian with new raiment after his burdens fall off before the Cross.

Obstinate and
Pliable, neighbors of Christian. Both try to keep Christian from leaving the City of Destruction. Obstinate remains behind, but Pliable goes with Christian until he deserts him at the Slough of Despond.

Interpreter, who instructs Christian in the mysteries of faith.

Discretion,
Prudence,
Piety, and
Charity, virgins who arm Christian with the sword and shield of faith.

Pope and
Pagan, giants whose caves Christian must pass after reciting verses from the Psalms to protect himself from devils issuing from one of the gates of Hell.

Knowledge,
Experience,
Watchful, and
Sincere, shepherds who point out the Celestial Gate to Christian and Hopeful.

THE PILLARS OF SOCIETY

Author: Henrik Ibsen (1828-1906)
Time of action: Nineteenth century
First presented: 1877

PRINCIPAL CHARACTERS

Karsten Bernick, a shipbuilder and a pillar of society, who says that his every action is done to help the community. Actually, Bernick is guilty of an intrigue with a Mrs. Dorf, now dead, and of letting his brother-in-law, Johan Tönnesen, assume his guilt and flee to America. Because his mother's finances were in bad shape, he also permitted and helped circulate a rumor that Johan had run off with her cash box. Now he is planning to let an American ship manned with a drunken crew set sail with inadequate repairs in order to avoid criticism from the press. When his brother-in-law, who has returned from America, plans to sail on the vessel, the "Indian Girl," Bernick does nothing to prevent him because Johan is the only one who can accuse him. But when his own son Olaf, a boy of fourteen, plans to run away and ship aboard the "Indian Girl," Bernick is horrified. After the son has been saved and the citizens of the town come to recognize him as a pillar of society, Karsten Bernick confesses his guilt. He had married his wife Betty because she would inherit money from her aunt, and he needed money to get his mother's business out of trouble. Betty forgives him and hopes to win him. His repentance is difficult to accept.

Johan Tönnesen, Mrs. Bernick's younger brother. Johan had taken Bernick's guilt upon himself because Bernick was willing to help him go to America and was courting his sister Betty, who would not have married Bernick if she had known he was implicated with Mrs. Dorf. Johan comes home because his half sister, Lona Hessel, insists that she is homesick. He meets Dina, Mrs. Dorf's daughter, and they plan to marry. When Dina decides to go to America with him, Johan changes his passage from the "Indian Girl" to the "Palm Tree," a ship in good repair. Although Lona has cared for him like a mother and schemed to get him home to find himself a wife, Johan is not aware that Karsten Bernick had been in love with Lona and she with him, but that he threw her over for Betty and her money.

Lona Hessel, Mrs. Bernick's half sister, who had gone to America to look after Johan. After some years she returns with him and confronts Bernick with his guilt. She had loved Bernick and had boxed him on the ear when he decided to marry Betty.

Dina Dorf, a young girl living with the Bernicks. The daughter of the ill-famed Mrs. Dorf, she hates the pretense and sham and prudery of the proper, altruistic people about her. When Schoolmaster Rörlund asks her to marry him, she consents; but when Johan appears, she falls in love with him and seizes the chance to go to America.

Martha Bernick, Bernick's sister, a schoolteacher. Martha had been in love with Johan for years, but she sacrifices her own love to permit Dina Dorf to marry him. She had helped bring up Dina after her mother's death.

Doctor Rörlund, the schoolmaster, a leader in the community, a critic of all. He is ashamed to admit his love for Dina, but at last he decides that he will marry her to save her. Dina throws him over for Johan.

Betty Bernick, Karsten's wife. She is a passive character. Lona tells Bernick that the reason Betty has never truly shared his life is that he will not discuss his affairs with her. Betty says at the end that she will win Bernick at last.

Krap, Bernick's confidential agent, a conscientious workman who warns Bernick that the "Indian Girl" is not seaworthy. He blames Aune, the foreman of the shipyard, who is rebelling against the new machines.

Aune, the foreman of the shipyard. When Bernick orders Aune to have the "Indian Girl" ready to sail in two days, Aune protests. Then Bernick says that he will fire him if the ship is not ready to sail, and Aune agrees to have the work done on time. He himself works day and night on the job, though he knows that the ship is not seaworthy, that the whole bottom is rotten. At the end of the play Aune issues orders, in Bernick's name, that the ship is not to sail, after Olaf has been found stowed away on the hulk destined for the bottom of the sea.

THE PILOT

Author: James Fenimore Cooper (1789-1851)
Time of action: The Revolutionary War
First published: 1823

Mr. Gray, the pilot, presumably the alias of John Paul Jones, who, betrayed by his native Britain, supports the cause of the American rebels. Picked up by an American frigate off the hazardous northeast coast of England, he gives immediate assistance by guiding the ship through the shoals during a gale. The member of a landing party dispatched to raid the homes of the gentry and to bring off political prisoners, Mr. Gray is captured and imprisoned at St. Ruth's Abbey. There he has an unexpected visitor, an old love, Alice Dunscombe. After his escape from an intoxicated British officer he rejoins the main body of raiders and narrowly misses being captured again. In the end he proves decisive in freeing his comrades, saving the frigate in a running fight against three enemy ships, and sailing it out of the shoals on a course toward Holland and safety. Surrounded by mystery and motivated by glory, he leaves Alice Dunscombe forever.

Lieutenant Richard Barnstable, the reckless officer of the schooner "Ariel" and the suitor of Katherine Plowden, the ward of an American loyalist, Colonel Howard. In a romantic attempt to kidnap her, he is caught but escapes a short time later. Returning to his ship, he captures the English cutter "Alacrity." His own ship is wrecked during a storm. After assisting in the rescue of his comrades from Colonel Howard's home, he and Katherine are married aboard the American frigate.

Edward Griffith, the bold yet sensible first lieutenant of the frigate, Barnstable's friend, and the suitor of Cecilia Howard, one of Colonel Howard's nieces. As the leader of the raiding party sent ashore from the frigate, he is twice captured, twice rescued, and finally married to his love. Throughout, his pride is piqued by Mr. Gray's assumptions of authority, but he comes to respect the mysterious pilot.

Colonel Howard, an exiled American Tory living in England. Wealthy and embittered, he recognizes the gallantry of the rebels but despises their purposes. After being taken from his home, St. Ruth's Abbey, as a political prisoner, he is mortally wounded during a naval engagement at sea. He dies after blessing the marriages of Katherine Plowden and Cecilia Howard.

Christopher Dillon, called **Kit,** the self-seeking kinsman of Colonel Howard and Cecilia Howard's unsuccessful suitor. Residing with Howard in England and hoping to inherit his property, he is unscrupulous in his attempts to thwart the raiders. After being captured aboard the "Alacrity" and offered as a hostage in exchange for Edward Griffith, he leads Tom Coffin into a trap. Recaptured, he drowns during the storm in which the "Ariel" is wrecked.

Long Tom Coffin, the weather-beaten, stout-hearted cockswain of the "Ariel." Instrumental in the capture of the "Alacrity," he proves more than equal to Dillon's scheming. When the "Ariel" is wrecked, he chooses to go down with the disabled schooner.

Katherine Plowden, Colonel Howard's ward and niece, courted by Lieutenant Barnstable. Vivacious and outspoken, she overtly sympathizes with the rebel cause. Taken aboard the American frigate by the raiding party, she and Barnstable are married.

Cecilia Howard, called **Cicely,** Colonel Howard's niece and Edward Griffith's love. More restrained than Katherine Plowden, she hesitates to offend her uncle, although she tacitly sympathizes with the rebels. She and Griffith are married after she has been taken aboard the American frigate.

Alice Dunscombe, Cecilia's companion and the former sweetheart of Mr. Gray.

Because of her loyalist convictions she cannot accept him, yet she wishes him well. She remains a spinster.

Mr. Merry, the spirited young midshipman of the "Ariel." The skilled and resourceful cousin of Katherine and Cecilia, he poses as a peddler in order to get into the abbey with a message for the girls.

Captain Borroughcliffe, a clever, proud, hard-drinking British officer. Outwitted by the Americans, he challenges the American Marine captain to a duel and loses his leg. Eventually the two become good friends.

Captain Manual, an officer of the Marine Corps and the leader of the raiding party. A tough, able soldier, he, with Edward

Griffith, is twice captured by Captain Borroughcliffe.

Captain Munson, the commanding officer of the American frigate sent to harass British waters. During the fight at sea he is killed by a broadside from an English ship.

David Boltrope, the hardy sailing master of the American frigate, who speaks in nautical tropes. He is shot in the engagement between the frigate and three British ships.

Jack Joker, a lugubrious, rather sadistic sailor aboard the frigate.

The Ship's Chaplain, who performs the two marriages after Colonel Howard has given his nieces his blessing.

Cornet Fitzgerald, a British officer.

THE PIONEERS

Author: James Fenimore Cooper (1789-1851)
Time of action: 1793
First published: 1823

PRINCIPAL CHARACTERS

Judge Marmaduke Temple, the principal citizen and landholder of Templeton, a settlement in upstate New York. He is at once shrewd and honorable, benevolent and just. While trying to kill a deer he shoots an unfamiliar, educated young hunter named Oliver Edwards, has his wound dressed, and offers him a position as a secretary. When the young man's friend, the old woodsman and hunter called Leatherstocking, is arrested for threatening to shoot an officer, the Judge sentences and fines the old man but pays the fine himself. Later he learns that Edwards is in reality Oliver Edward Effingham, the son of an old friend who had entrusted him with personal effects and family funds years before. The Judge restores the property and the money to Edwards. Meanwhile Edwards and Elizabeth Temple have fallen in love, and the

Judge gives the young couple his blessing.

Elizabeth Temple, the Judge's spirited, pretty daughter. Although she respects Oliver Edwards' abilities, she maintains a feminine independence. Grateful to Leatherstocking for saving her life when a savage panther attacks her, she assists in his escape from jail after the old man has been arrested for resisting an officer. Her romance with her father's secretary develops after the young man and Leatherstocking save her from a forest fire. When Edwards' true identity is revealed and he declares his love, she readily marries him.

Natty Bumppo, called **Leatherstocking,** a hardy, simple, upright woodsman in his seventy-first year. Although disgusted by wanton killing of game, he defends his right to kill game for food. He shoots a deer out of season and is arrested for resisting the magistrate who tries to search his cabin. Sentenced to jail for a month, he escapes with the help of Oliver Edwards and Elizabeth Temple. Twice he is Elizabeth's rescuer, once from a panther and again from fire. After his jail term is suspended, stricken by the death of his Indian friend and companion, he moves on to a less civilized territory.

Oliver Edwards, later revealed as Oliver Edward Effingham, the impoverished young hunter who lives with Leatherstocking in a cabin near Templeton. Believing that Judge Temple has appropriated his inheritance, he is planning to recover it when he accepts the position of secretary to the Judge. In the meantime he falls in love with Elizabeth Temple. Having quit his post when Leatherstocking is arrested and jailed, he helps the old man to escape, aids Elizabeth during the fire, and finally reveals his true identity. Judge Temple immediately restores his inheritance and the young man and Elizabeth are married.

Indian John, an old Mohican chief called Chingachgook in his younger days. Lonely, aged, and grieving for the old free life of the wilderness, he rejects his Moravian Christianizing during a raging forest fire and appears in his ceremonial dress. He dies, attended by Leatherstocking, Elizabeth Temple, and Oliver Edwards, in a cave where they have taken refuge from the fire.

Hiram Doolittle, the cowardly, troublemaking, greedy magistrate who informs on Leatherstocking for breaking the hunting law, gets a search warrant, and is roughly handled by the old hunter when he tries to force his way into Leatherstocking's cabin.

Richard Jones, the meddlesome, pompous sheriff, a frontier fop who indulges in the irresponsible killing of game, spreads rumors that Leatherstocking is working a secret mine, and leads a raggle-taggle posse to recapture the old woodsman after his escape from jail.

Major Edward Effingham, the senile grandfather of the young man who calls himself Oliver Edwards. Years before the Major and Judge Temple had been close friends, and Effingham had entrusted some valuable property and a sum of money to the Judge's keeping. Leatherstocking has been caring for him. His identity revealed after the fire, the old man is taken to Judge Temple's home and nursed tenderly until his death.

Mr. Grant, a sincere, eclectic minister adept at appealing to the heterogeneous frontier faiths.

Louisa Grant, his timid daughter, Elizabeth's companion. She is inept when faced with danger.

Benjamin Penguillan, called Ben Pump, an ex-sailor and Judge Temple's salty major-domo. Out of sympathy he shares Leatherstocking's humiliation in the stocks and thrashes Magistrate Doolittle.

Elnathan Todd, the gigantic village doctor who dresses Oliver Edwards' wound; he is an awkward quack.

Monsieur le Quoi (mə·syœ′ lə kwa′), the village storekeeper, a friend of Judge Temple.

Major Hartmann, a German farmer, also a friend of Judge Temple.

Billy Kirby, a good-natured woodcutter and strong man who sympathizes with Leatherstocking but takes the side of the law.

Jotham Riddel, Magistrate Doolittle's good-for-nothing deputy.

Remarkable Pettibone, Judge Temple's housekeeper.

Squire Lippet, Leatherstocking's lawyer at the time of the old hunter's trial.

Mr. Van der School, the thick-witted prosecutor.

Agamemnon, Judge Temple's silly Negro servant.

THE PIRATES OF PENZANCE

Author: W. S. Gilbert (1836-1911)
Time of action: Nineteenth century
First presented: 1879

PRINCIPAL CHARACTERS

Major General Stanley, the very model of a modern major general. He is laden with learned lumber, though a bit behind in his military knowledge. His numerous daughters adore him, and he loves them so much that he tells a lie to save them from the pirates. His conscience torments him. When the pirates learn that he is not an orphan, as he had told them, his life is in danger; but he is spared, and his daughters marry the pirates, who are all noblemen gone wrong.

The Pirate King (Richard), a kind-hearted but stern monarch. He does not think much of piracy as a profession, but finds it comparatively honest in contrast with respectability. His piratical ventures are seldom successful, for his and his crew's tenderness for orphans has been noised abroad, and all the ships they capture turn out to be manned entirely by orphans. Also, though victorious over the policemen, he and his crew yield when charged to do so in Queen Victoria's name; for with all their faults, they love their Queen.

Frederic, the slave of duty. Apprenticed to the pirates because of his nurse's deafness, he serves them diligently, though he views piracy with absolute detestation. He falls in love with the General's most charming daughter, Mabel; but finding that he must serve several more decades as a pirate because of the accident of being born on February 29, his extreme sense of duty makes him betray his potential father-in-law to the pirates.

Ruth, Frederic's nurse, a piratical maid-of-all-work. Mistaking Frederic's father, who wanted his son apprenticed to a pilot, she did not dare return home; so she too joined the pirates. There are the remains of a fine woman about Ruth, who has tried to convince Frederic that she is beautiful and that he loves her. After he has seen the General's daughters and found that she is, on the whole, plain, she has to bear his scorn.

Mabel, General Stanley's most romantic daughter. She feels it her duty to reclaim and reform the handsome pirate apprentice. Her sisters doubt that her sense of duty would be so keen if Frederic were homely.

Edith,
Kate, and
Isabel, three of the General's many daughters.

Samuel, the Pirate King's lieutenant. He agrees that pirates should not be merciless, but is troubled by the excessive number of orphans on ships.

The Sergeant of Police, a timorous soul in a highly nervous state. A policeman's lot, he says, is not a happy one. When overthrown by the pirates, he charges them to yield in Queen Victoria's name, which they do. But when Ruth explains that they are all peers, he and his fellows release them, and the General offers them his numerous daughters' hands.

888

THE PIT

Author: Frank Norris (1870-1902)
Time of action: The 1890's
First published: 1903

PRINCIPAL CHARACTERS

Curtis Jadwin, a self-made man whose speculations in the Chicago wheat market make him a fortune. His ruthless ambition to corner the world wheat market causes the suicide of a good friend when the friend's fortune is wiped out. He marries Laura Dearborn, but as his hectic financial career develops he spends less and less time with his wife. His excessive greed and hunger for power at last cause his downfall. Financially ruined and broken in health, he and his wife go West to start a new life, happier in adversity than before.

Sheldon Corthell, a painter who, wooing the woman who also interests Jadwin, exemplifies Norris' idea of the temperamental difference that exists between stereotyped artists and financiers.

Laura Dearborn, Jadwin's romantic young wife who, loyal to her husband, finally wins his complete devotion. She at one time is unable to decide between Corthell and Jadwin, and the fact that Jadwin wins her is significant to Norris' purpose.

Samuel Gretry, an intelligent broker whose alert mind and shrewdness, manifested in professional advice, counts heavily in Jadwin's initial fantastically successful maneuvers in the wheat exchange.

Charles Cressler and
Mrs. Cressler, first Laura's friends and, later, Jadwin's. Cressler, fighting Jadwin in the exchange and losing to him—at no time does either character know the identity of his opponent—takes his own life. Knowledge of this suicide makes such a profound impression on Jadwin that he withdraws for a time from the exchange.

Page Dearborn, Laura's sister, who is a friend of the Cresslers.

Mrs. Emily Wessels (Aunt Wess), the aunt of Laura and Page, who also is a friend of the Cresslers.

THE PLAGUE

Author: Albert Camus (1913-1960)
Time of action: The 1940's
First published: 1947

PRINCIPAL CHARACTERS

Bernard Rieux (bĕr·nàr' ryœ'), a physician and surgeon in Oran, where a plague is claiming as many as three hundred lives a day. Dr. Rieux, a thirty-five-year-old man of great patience, fortitude, and unselfishness, represents the medical profession during the long siege of disease and deaths which strikes rich and poor alike and from which there is no re- prieve. The plague means failure to Rieux because he can find no cure or relief for the sufferers. His attitude is characterized by his regard for his fellow-men and his inability to cope with injustice and compromise. Very much involved with mankind, he explains that he is able to continue working with the plague-stricken population only because he has found that abstraction is stronger than happiness. He is identified at the end of the book as the narrator of the story, and his account gives the pestilence the attributes of a character, the antagonist. Events of the plague are secondary to philosophies as he pictures the people's reactions, individually and collectively, to their plight. These run the range of emotions and rationality: escape, guilt, a spirit of lawlessness, pleasure, resistance. During the plague individual destinies become collective destinies because the plague and emotions are shared by all. Love and friendship fade because they ask something of the future, and the plague leaves only present moments. As the pestilence subsides, relieving the exile and deprivation, there is jubilation, followed by the stereotyped patterns of everyday living.

Madame Rieux (ryœ′), the doctor's wife. The victim of another ailment, Mme. Rieux is sent away to a sanitarium before the town is quarantined. Her absence from Rieux points up his unselfishness in staying on in Oran.

Raymond Rambert (rĕ·mōn′ rän·bĕr′), a journalist from Paris. Assigned to a routine story on Oran, he is caught in exile when the city is quarantined because of the plague. Rambert, wanting to return to his wife, resorts to various means in order to escape. A non-resident, alien to the plight of the people, he personifies those who feel no involvement with the problems of others. When escape from the city becomes a reality for him, Rambert declines his freedom and accepts Rieux's philosophy of common decency, which amounts merely to doing one's job. In this instance Rambert's job, according to Rieux, is to fight the plague. The journalist becomes a volunteer on the sanitation teams.

Father Paneloux (pȧ·nə·lōō′), a Jesuit priest who represents the ecclesiastical thinking of people caught in the crisis represented by the plague. Preaching on the plague, he compares the present situation with pestilences of the past and tells his parishioners that they have brought the plague upon themselves through their godlessness. Placing the scientific and the spiritual in balance, Paneloux and Rieux debate whether the man of God and the scientist can consort in contending with adversities. The two men are closer in their thinking than Rieux, a self-proclaimed atheist, and Paneloux, a heretic in some of his preaching, will concede. Paneloux is among those who succumb to the plague.

Jean Tarrou (zhän′ tȧ·rōō′), an enigma to his associates among the volunteers in fighting the plague. Addicted to simple pleasures but no slave to them, Tarrou has no apparent means of income. Little is known of his background until he tells Rieux of his beginnings. The son of a prosecutor, he had been horrified by the thought of the criminals condemned because of his father. He himself has been a political agitator. Tarrou becomes a faithful helper to Rieux, and as a volunteer he records the social aspects of the plague. In telling of the plague, Rieux borrows from these records. After the worst of the pestilence has passed, Tarrou dies from the plague.

Joseph Grand (zhō·zĕf′ grän′), a municipal clerk. Characterized by all the attributes of insignificance, Grand has spent twenty-two years in his job, to which he was temporarily appointed. He is unable to escape from this imprisonment because he cannot find words with which to protest. He announces early in his acquaintance with Rieux that he has a second job, which he describes as a "growth of personality." The futility of this avocation, writing, is epitomized by Grand's continuing work on the first paragraph of a novel which he anticipates will be the perfect expression of love. He dies after asking Rieux to burn his sheaf of papers, manuscripts with only an adjective or a verb changed from one writing to the next.

M. Cottard (kô·tàr'), a dealer in wines and liquors, treated by Rieux after an attempt at suicide. His undercover deals and unsettled life are sublimated or furthered by his keen delight in gangster movies. He survives the plague, only to go berserk during a shooting affray with the police.

Dr. Richard (rē·shàr'), chairman of the medical association in Oran. He is more interested in observing the code of the organization than in trying to reduce the number of deaths.

M. Othon (ō·tōn'), the police magistrate. His isolation after contracting the plague shows Rieux's impartiality in dealing with plague victims.

Jacques Othon (zhàk' ō·tōn'), the magistrate's son, on whom the new serum is tried. The lengthy description of young Othon's illness illustrates the suffering of the thousands who die of the plague.

Madame Rieux (ryœ'), the doctor's mother, who comes to keep house for her son during his wife's absence. She is an understanding woman who reminds Tarrou of his own childhood and elicits his philosophical discussion of man's role in life.

García (gär·sē'ä),
Raoul (rà·ōōl'),
Gonzales (gōn·sä'lĕs),
Marcel (màr·sĕl'), and
Louis (lwē'), the men involved in Raymond Rambert's contemplated escape from Oran. The intricacies of illegality are shown as Rambert is referred from one of these men to another. From García, an accomplice of Cottard, to Marcel and Louis, guards at the city gate, each one must have his stipend, until finally the cost of escape becomes exorbitant.

LES PLAIDEURS

Author: Jean Baptiste Racine (1639-1699)
Time of action: Seventeenth century
First presented: 1668

PRINCIPAL CHARACTERS

Dandin, a judge, presented in scenes designed to ridicule lawyers. Because of his eccentric behavior, he is regarded by his family as mad and in need of watching day and night. Insisting on going to court, he tries every means of escape until, finally, his son Leandre suggests that he preside at the trial of Citron, a dog accused of eating a chicken. When Leandre's marriage contract is produced, the judge acquits Citron as a welcoming present to the bride, Isabelle.

Leandre, Dandin's son. While attempting to keep a watchful eye on his eccentric father, he is engaged in an attempt to communicate with Isabelle. Disguised as a police commissioner, he tricks her into declaring her love for him and tricks her father, Chicanneau, into signing a marriage contract between the lovers.

L'Intime, a secretary persuaded by Leandre to disguise himself as a process server and deliver a note to Isabelle. He gets a thrashing from her father, Chicanneau, for his pains.

Chicanneau, a litigant and the father of Isabelle. Under the impression that he is signing a police report, he puts his signature to a marriage contract between his daughter and Leandre.

Isabelle, Chicanneau's daughter, who marries Leandre.

Petit Jean, a porter set to keep watch over Judge Dandin.

La Comtesse, a litigant.

Citron, a dog tried by Judge Dandin,

with Petit Jean and L'Intime acting as lawyers.

Le Souffleur, the prompter.

THE PLAIN DEALER

Author: William Wycherley (1640?-1716)
Time of action: Seventeenth century
First presented: c. 1674

PRINCIPAL CHARACTERS

Captain Manly, a forthright honest man who intends leaving England for the West Indies because he hates the hypocrisy of the age he finds at the Court and in lesser social circles. He loses his ship and fortune in a sea battle with the Dutch and is forced back again to England by the disaster. He discovers that Olivia, his fiancée, has married during his absence, rails at him behind his back, and will not return the small fortune he had entrusted to her. Seeking revenge for her conduct, Manly gains entrance to her chamber on two occasions. The first time he lies with her, and the second time he exposes her to the world as an adulteress. His trusted friend, Mr. Vernish, is the rogue who has married Olivia and plotted with her to keep the Captain's money. At the end Captain Manly is agreeably surprised to find that his supposed page is really a rich young heiress, Fidelia Grey, who loves him very much. Following this discovery, the Captain and she agree to marry and go off to the West Indies to live a sober, happy life among honest people.

Olivia, a scheming, shallow woman loved by Captain Manly. She marries Manly's supposed friend, Mr. Vernish, during her lover's absence and refuses to help her fiancé when he returns penniless to England, although as his expected bride, he had given her most of his fortune before he left England. Olivia proves readily dishonest in her marriage, too, by

falling in love with Manly's page. She is deceived by Manly, who silently replaces the page in the darkness of Olivia's rooms and proceeds to prove his erstwhile fiancée an adulteress. When her frailty is shown to the world, Olivia, vowing revenge on Manly, stalks from the company.

Freeman, Captain Manly's lieutenant, a likable young man who tries to make the best of the world. At the last he proves to be the Captain's true friend, much to Manly's surprise, for Manly has thought the Lieutenant a shallow, deceiving opportunist. Freeman woos the rich Widow Blackacre unsuccessfully until he works through her minor son, who accepts Freeman as his guardian upon Freeman's promise to release the lad from studying law for a more enjoyable career as a man about town. Freeman actually does not want to marry Widow Blackacre, and he readily releases her from her promise of marriage when she agrees to pay his debts and settle an annuity on him.

Mr. Vernish, who is supposedly Captain Manly's best friend. He betrays his trust by marrying Olivia and plotting with her to keep the Captain's money. Too cowardly to admit that he is Olivia's husband, he is found out when he tries to prevent Olivia from making him a cuckold with Captain Manly's page. His true nature is also displayed when he learns the page is really a girl, for he tries to lock her in a room in his house until he can find an opportunity to ravish her.

Fidelia Grey, a wealthy young heiress who falls in love with Captain Manly and, disguised as a boy, follows him to sea. She helps Manly to his revenge when Olivia proposes an affair with the supposed page. Fidelia's love and service are rewarded when Captain Manly discovers her true identity and proposes marriage to her.

Widow Blackacre, a litigious woman who enjoys her status as a widow because it leaves her free to enter lawsuits in her own name. So fond is she of legal entanglements that she forces her son to study law, and she herself takes up quarters at the Inns of Court. She wastes her son's fortune until, with Freeman's help, the lad is able to escape her domination.

Jerry Blackacre, Widow Blackacre's son, a hearty young man who detests the career in law his mother plans for him; he prefers a career as a gay young blade and participation in the fashionable life of London. He readily accepts Freeman as his guardian when the Lieutenant promises to help the boy live the life he desires.

Lord Plausible, a cowardly, flattering nobleman who seeks the hand of Olivia in marriage. His character serves as a foil for that of honest, outspoken Captain Manly.

Mr. Novel, a flattering coxcomb who also seeks the hand of Olivia in marriage. He derives his name from the fact that he is an ardent admirer of novelties of all kinds.

Major Oldfox, an elderly fop who seeks to marry the Widow Blackacre, so that she can provide for him from her son's inheritance. He is a foolish old man and a would-be poet. His courtship of the widow descends to the utterly ridiculous when he has her kidnaped. The widow fully expects to be raped, but he astonishes her by reading his own blank-verse poetry to her.

Eliza, Olivia's cousin, distressed by Olivia's conduct.

THE PLAYBOY OF THE WESTERN WORLD

Author: John Millington Synge (1871-1909)
Time of action: Early twentieth century
First presented: 1907

PRINCIPAL CHARACTERS

Christopher Mahon (Christy), the playboy of the Western World. Arriving one evening in a village on the wild coast of County Mayo, cold, tired, and hungry, he captures the imagination of the people when he tells them how he split the skull of his harsh, unimaginative old father with a loy. Timid no longer, the young man outleaps and outruns his competitors during the rigorous village sports. His reputation for bravery is tarnished, however, when his father, with bandaged head, arrives in town. When the athletic young man attacks his father a second time, he barely escapes hanging. Even Pegeen deserts him. Like the others, she is afraid to get involved in a murder so close to home. Disgusted with the villagers, he is determined to be a playboy somewhere else.

Margaret Flaherty (Pegeen Mike), the wild, sharp-tongued daughter of publican Flaherty. Enraptured by the poetic utterances and valor of young Christy, she resists the blandishments of Shawn

Keogh, her cousin whom she is to marry. After hearing of Christy's brave attack on his father and seeing his prowess on the playing field, she thinks Shawn too cowardly for her taste. However, she is ready to betray Christy when he attacks his father again.

Widow Quin, a scheming young woman of about thirty. Hearing of the arrival of the brave young stranger, she tries to coax him away from Pegeen Mike, but to no avail. In spite of her cajolery, he is determined to remain near Pegeen. Meeting the elder Mahon in the tavern, the widow tries to send him on a wild-goose chase. Afraid the two will fight, she tells the old man that his son has left the village.

Michael James Flaherty, a fat, jovial innkeeper and the tippling father of Pegeen Mike. At Kate Cassidy's wake, he is one of the drunkest men at the funeral. When Christy and Pegeen tell him they intend to marry, he puts up a violent objection. He has qualms about having as a son-in-law a young man who killed his own father. Finally, however, he agrees to the wedding.

Old Mahon, a crusty, hardbitten old squatter, Christy's father. Seemingly indestructible, he survives several painful beatings. A lesser man would have died from such repeated blows. In spite of his aching head, he advances threateningly on his young son in the tavern. Seizing a loy, Christy again batters his tough father to the floor. Rather glad that the boy has lost his timidity, the old man smilingly offers to take his son home with him.

Shawn Keogh, a cowardly young man, Pegeen's future husband. Afraid to fight Christy, he offers him numerous gifts if young Mahon will leave the village. Shawn knows that he is in danger of losing Pegeen to the stranger. In desperation, he even attempts to enlist the aid of Widow Quin, unaware of her hopes to win Christy for herself.

Philly Cullen and **Jimmy Farrell,** small farmers. The latter is a fat, amorous farmer of about forty-five and Michael Flaherty's boon drinking companion; Philly, thin and mistrusting, is his exact opposite.

Sara Tansey,
Susan Brady, and
Honor Blake, girls of the village. Upon hearing of Christy's arrival in the town, they rush to the inn and ask him to tell the story of how he split his father's skull. This single act has lifted the young man to a hero's level.

THE PLOUGH AND THE STARS

Author: Sean O'Casey (1884-   )
Time of action: 1916
First presented: 1926

PRINCIPAL CHARACTERS

Nora Clitheroe, an Irish woman whose husband is a member of the Citizen Army. She nearly loses her sanity when he goes off to fight on the barricades and is killed.

Jack Clitheroe, Nora's husband, an Irish patriot who is killed in the fighting.

Peter Flynn, Nora's uncle, a rather pathetic, ineffectual man whose patriotism is stirred by the oratory he hears.

Fluther Good, one of the tenement dwellers who is given to heavy drinking but who makes himself generally helpful to his neighbors.

Mrs. Gogan, a neighborhood woman who engages in a barroom brawl with

Bessie Burgess and disapproves of Nora's buying so many new clothes.

Mollser Gogan, the small daughter of Mrs. Gogan. She dies of tuberculosis and is buried in the same coffin with Nora's stillborn child.

Bessie Burgess, one of the tenement women. She is coarse and vigorous.

The Covey, Nora's cousin, who is the purveyor of the author's views concerning the poverty of the Irish and the problem of their independence.

Captain Brennan, an officer in the Irish Citizen Army, and a comrade in arms of Jack Clitheroe.

Corporal Stoddart, an English soldier who escorts the coffin of Mollser Gogan and Nora's child.

Sergeant Tinley, of the Wiltshires.

THE PLUMED SERPENT

Author: D. H. Lawrence (1885-1930)
Time of action: Twentieth century
First published: 1926

PRINCIPAL CHARACTERS

Don Ramón Carrasco (dōn r̄rä·mōn' kä·r̄räs'kō), a landowner and scholar who is convinced that only the revival of primitive religion can save Mexico. He establishes at his hacienda a meeting place for cultists who worship Quetzalcoatl, the Plumed Serpent. He is denounced by the Church and is seriously wounded when his political and religious enemies attack him. Finally, having desecrated the church at Sayula by burning the holy images, he converts it into a sanctuary of the ancient Aztec gods.

Kate Leslie, the widow of an Irish patriot, who goes to Mexico because she is restless. There she meets Ramón and his followers, saves Ramón's life when he is attacked by his opponents, and falls in love with Cipriano. A product of a culture dominated by technology, she finds strange the masculine, atavistic culture which is Mexico. Her woman's will is no match for the dark primitivism of this savage land and she marries Cipriano in a pagan ceremony conducted by Ramón. Though she wants to return to Ireland, she is impelled to stay with her husband in Mexico.

General Cipriano Viedma (hä·nä·räl sē-pryä'nō byäd'mä), a full-blooded Indian who joins Ramón to revive the ancestral gods. He comes to believe that he is a reincarnation of Huitzilopochtli, Aztec god of war. Kate is unaccountably drawn to him and at last yields to his masculine dominance.

Doña Carlota (dō'nyä kär·lō'tä), Ramón's first wife, a devout Christian who refuses to countenance his heresies. She leaves her husband and goes to Mexico City. Returning to Sayula when Ramón opens the church there as a pagan temple, she protests her husband's blasphemy. Overcome by hysteria, she suffers a stroke and soon dies.

Owen Rhys, Kate's American cousin, who accompanies her to Mexico. He returns to the United States prior to the time Kate becomes embroiled in the ancient god movement at Sayula.

Teresa (tā·rä'sä), Ramón's second wife, the daughter of a local landowner who is deceased. Her manner toward Ramón is passive and submissive.

Mrs. Norris, the widow of a former British ambassador, who invites Kate to tea. It is at her house that Kate meets Don Ramón.

Juana (hwä'nä), a servant at the house Kate rents in Sayula.

PLUTUS

Author: Aristophanes (c. 448-c. 385 B.C.)
Time of action: Fifth century B.C.
First presented: 408 B.C. (388 B.C. in revised form)

PRINCIPAL CHARACTERS

Chremylus (krě'mǐ·ləs), an old Athenian husbandman. Poor but honest, he has consulted the Delphic Oracle to determine whether his only son should be taught virtuous ways or the knavery and double-dealing by which successful men gain their wealth. The god tells him to follow the first person he meets after leaving the temple. He does so, even though that person is a blind and wretched beggar. When this unfortunate reveals himself as Plutus, Chremylus conceives the idea of restoring his sight so that the God of Riches can distinguish between the just and the unjust. Chremylus is a simple, friendly fellow, unselfish enough to invite his neighbors to share his good fortune; but he also admits that he loves money and he loses no time in converting the divine favor he has won into hard cash and luxuries. Like all of Aristophanes' comic protagonists, he roundly condemns the evils of Athenian society, and lashes out particularly against informers, grafters, and voluptuaries.

Cario (kăr'ǐ·ō), Chremylus' slave. He is a broadly comic figure, well aware of his master's shortcomings, wryly stoical about his own lot in life, and sometimes impertinent. He is perhaps at his best in describing a night in the Temple of Aesculapius, when he had pretended to be one of the holy serpents in order to filch some pap from an old woman.

Plutus (plōō'təs), the God of Wealth. Because he had said that he would favor only the wise, the just, and the virtuous, Zeus, jealous of mankind, had taken

away his eyesight so that he would be unable to tell good men from bad. He has wandered in rags, ill treated by those he benefited and, because of his fear of Zeus's anger, unwilling to have his vision restored until Chremylus convinces him that he is the source of all power, even the power of Zeus. He thus accompanies Chremylus to the Temple of Aesculapius, is there cured, and afterwards rewards the just and reduces the unjust to the penury they deserve.

Blepsidemus (blĕp·sǐ'də·məs), a friend who helps Chremylus to convince Plutus of his rightful place in the order of things.

Poverty, who protests that a great injustice has been done her through the rehabilitation of Plutus, as she will be banished from the land. She argues that she is the source of the public weal: through her artisans work, men stay fit, and politicians remain uncorrupted. Chremylus rejects her arguments because he knows the horrors that poverty can also bring.

A Just Man, who brings his outworn clothes, evidence of his former wretchedness, to dedicate to Plutus.

An Informer, who accuses Chremylus of stealing his money. He is driven off by Chremylus and the Just Man.

An Old Woman, who protests that her young lover, who no longer needs her bounty, has deserted her. When she joins the celebration of the god's installation, however, Chremylus promises that her lover will be restored to her.

A Youth, formerly the Old Woman's lover.

Hermes (hĕr'mēz), messenger of the gods. He complains that neither he nor the other gods are receiving sacrifices because men now realize that before Plutus' ascendancy the Olympians had governed poorly. He applies for a place in Chremylus' new establishment and is put to work by Cario washing the entrails of the sacrificial victims.

A Priest of Zeus, who also comes to seek service with Plutus, now Lord of the Universe.

A Chorus of Rustics.

POEM OF THE CID

Author: Unknown
Time of action: c. 1075
First transcribed: Twelfth century

PRINCIPAL CHARACTERS

The Cid (thēd), or **Ruy Díaz** (r̄rwē dē'äth), Lord of Bivar. Banished from Christian Spain by Alfonso VI of Castile, he enters, with a company of his vassals, on a series of heroic exploits designed to impress the King and cause him to revoke the edict of banishment. The royal favor is finally won but only after the Cid becomes powerful enough to be a threat to the throne. A period of happiness and peace lasts until the Cid is forced to subdue his treacherous sons-in-law, Diego and Fernando, Princes of Carrión. When the Princes are banished, the Cid is free to marry his daughters to the rulers of Aragón and Navarre. He rejoices to count among his family two Kings of Spain, and he finally dies in peace as Lord of Valencia.

Alfonso VI (äl·fŏn'sō säs'tō), King of León. After banishing the Cid from Christian Spain, he reinstates the hero when his growing power becomes a threat to the throne.

Doña Elvira (dō'nyä ĕl·bē'rä) and
Doña Sol (dō'nyä sōl), the Cid's daughters, who are married to Diego and Fernando, Princes of Carrión, by whom the noble ladies are robbed and beaten. They are finally married to the Kings of Aragón and Navarre.

Diego (dyä'gō) and
Fernando González (fâr·nän'dō gōn·thä'läth), Princes of Carrión and the Cid's cowardly sons-in-law. Resentful of the scorn heaped on them by the Cid's vassals, they seek revenge on their lord by ostensibly taking his daughters on a triumphant tour to Carrión. On the way they beat and rob the ladies and leave them for dead. For this deed the Princes are stripped of property and honor.

Doña Ximena (dō'nyä hē·mä'nä), the Cid's wife.

Martín Antolínez (mär·tēn' än·tō·lē'näth), a lieutenant to the Cid.

Minaya Alvar Fáñez (mē·nä'yä äl·bär' fä'nyäth), the Cid's chief lieutenant and friend, who is the liaison between his banished lord and Alfonso VI.

Félix Muñoz (fā'lĕks mōō'nyōth), the Cid's nephew, who rescues his uncle's daughters after they are robbed and beaten by their husbands.

Ramón (r̄rä·mōn'), Count of Barcelona, who is subdued and taken prisoner by the Cid.

Bucar (bōō·kär'), King of Morocco.

Gonzalo Ansúrez (gōn·thä'lō än·sōō'-

rāth), Count of Carrión and the father of Diego and Fernando González.

García Ordóñez (gär·thē′ä ôr·dō′nyäth), Lord of Grañón, who is the Cid's enemy.

Raquel (rrä·kĕl′) and Vidas (bē′thäs), moneylenders who are swindled by the Cid, after his banishment, in an effort to finance his force of loyal vassals.

POINT COUNTER POINT

Author: Aldous Huxley (1894-   )
Time of action: The 1920's
First published: 1928

PRINCIPAL CHARACTERS

Walter Bidlake, a literary critic in London. An essentially weak and confused man, he is unhappy in his extramarital relationship with Marjorie Carling and seeks some kind of better realization in an affair with Lucy Tantamount. Huxley regards Walter as an example of the emptiness of the intellectual life unsupported by sound instinctual expression.

Marjorie Carling, Walter's unhappy mistress. She has left Carling because of his perversion and yet behaves with Walter, to all effects and purposes, like a nagging wife rather than a cheering companion. Fearful of her pregnancy, she drives Walter from her. Marjorie has difficulty reconciling the needs of her body and her soul.

Philip Quarles, a writer and diarist. He is the prime example in the novel of the man who understands everything and feels nothing. He has an encyclopedic mind and seldom fails to develop a topic in a startling way.

Mrs. Bidlake, the mother of Walter and Elinor Quarles. She is a gentle and aesthetic elderly woman who is unable to aid any of her children with their personal problems.

John Bidlake, Walter's father. Bidlake, once a successful artist and amorist, is horrified by the decline of his artistic powers and by the onset of disease. He represents the shortcomings of irresponsible sensuality.

Hilda Tantamount, a successful London hostess. Once John Bidlake's mistress and now his friend, she lives for amusement and malice.

Lord Edward Tantamount, Hilda's husband. Lord Edward is a great biologist and a failure in every personal relationship he undertakes. He represents the limitations of the scientific approach to complex human experience.

Lucy Tantamount, the promiscuous daughter of Lord Edward. Malicious and without any kind of conscience, she amuses herself with Walter Bidlake and any other acceptable male who crosses her path.

Frank Illidge, Lord Edward's laboratory assistant. He is a brilliant lower-class person who, out of hatred and socialistic conviction, allows himself to become involved in the murder of Everard Webley.

Everard Webley, a British Fascist and head of the Brotherhood of British Freemen. A man of tremendous physical magnetism, his thirst for power and his contempt for the masses make him a likely target for Illidge's hatred. He is also a former friend of Elinor Quarles.

Burlap, editor of the "Literary World." His chief critical stock in trade is religious mysticism; actually, he is a feeble sensualist who has damaged the lives of several naïve women. He is finally involved in a perverse relationship with Beatrice Gilray.

Elinor Quarles, the wife of Philip. Her unsatisfactory husband drives her to consider an affair with Everard Webley. She is devastated by the death of her child, Little Philip, who dies of meningitis.

Maurice Spandrell, a nihilist. Spandrell is a man who has been shocked into a hatred of life by the remarriage of his mother; there is nothing he can affirm, and he takes delight in destroying the dignity of other people. He pursues violent sensation even to the point of the murder of Everard Webley.

General Knoyle, the stepfather of Spandrell, a pompous military man with no understanding of the world he lives in.

Mrs. Knoyle, Spandrell's mother. She is, in part, the innocent cause of her son's hatred of the world.

Mark Rampion, an artist. Rampion, risen from the lower class, has developed a life and a style of painting that properly express the interplay of all of life's forces; he is totally unlike Philip Quarles, who understands all of life but cannot live it.

Mary Rampion, Mark's wife. She is an upper-class woman who has married for love and life. In her cheerful enjoyment of her husband's vigor, she is an illustration of all that he preaches about the natural, spontaneous life.

Beatrice Gilray, a literary woman. She is the special friend of Burlap, from whom she learns the mingling of high thinking and sensuality.

Sidney Quarles, the father of Philip. He is engaged in a never-to-be-finished work on democracy. He is also involved with a young woman in London.

Rachel Quarles, his wife. Accepting with dignity the shortcomings of her domestic situation, she is a Christian in her devotion and forbearance.

POLYEUCTE

Author: Pierre Corneille (1606-1684)
Time of action: Third century
First presented: c. 1643

PRINCIPAL CHARACTERS

Polyeucte, an Armenian nobleman who is married to Pauline. Returning from a secret mission on which he has received Christian baptism, he is ordered by the Roman Governor, Félix, to attend the temple sacrifices. As a traitor to the Roman gods he is condemned to die. To those who plead with him to recant and save his life, he answers that he is through with mortal ties, and he goes to his death undismayed.

Pauline, daughter of the Roman Governor, and Polyeucte's wife. When her Christian husband is condemned to death for his defilement of the Roman gods, she pleads with him to save his life by privately worshiping his God while publicly paying homage to the Roman gods. Her pleas fail and Polyeucte goes to his death. At his execution, she feels a veil lifted from her eyes and declares herself a Christian prepared to die for her faith.

Sévère, a Roman warrior. In love with Pauline before her marriage to Polyeucte, he comes as a hero to Armenia ostensibly to make sacrifices of thanksgiving for victories in war; but in reality he has come to see Pauline, whom he still loves. Finding her faithful to her husband he bids her farewell. He is later asked by Pauline to plead for Polyeucte, who is condemned to die as a Christian. Inspired

899

by what he considers the miraculous conversions of Pauline and Félix after Polyeucte's death, he promises to beg Emperor Décie for freedom of worship for all.

Félix, the Roman Governor of Armenia and Pauline's father. He condemns Polyeucte to death for defilement of the Roman gods. After the victim's execution,

Félix himself is suddenly converted to Christianity.

Néarque, Polyeucte's friend.

Stratonice, Pauline's friend.

Albin, Félix's friend.

Décie, Emperor of Rome.

POOR PEOPLE

Author: Fyodor Mikhailovich Dostoevski (1821-1881)
Time of action: First half of the nineteenth century
First published: 1846

PRINCIPAL CHARACTERS

Makar Alexievitch Dievushkin (mä·kär′ ä·lĕk·sā′ĕ·vĭch dĕ·vōōsh′kĭn), a government clerk or copyist whose extravagant love for a friendless orphan leaves him penniless and broken in health. A supremely noble and at the same time ridiculous aging lover, Makar, laughingly called Lovelace in his office, carries on for some months an elaborate correspondence with the girl next door. Though they see each other less than once a week, they write almost daily of their mutual respect, their penurious existence, their calamities and minor triumphs. Makar has attached his wages to give her flowers and bonbons, driven himself mad with worry over her health, and generally devoted himself to her comfort and ease of mind. He also concerns himself with a dying clerk wronged in a scandal, a writer of penny dreadfuls, and a drunken friend in his office. His style of writing is florid; his thoughts are mostly clichés; his feelings, though obvious, are touching. Like many of Dostoevski's great creations, the clerk welcomes suffering and forces it upon himself so that he may ask forgiveness for imagined sins; but his "dedicated" living turns out to be mostly effusions of a distraught mind and overstrained susceptibilities, dramatized for their effect rather than their feelings. Even so, within the humor there is deep pathos.

Barbara Alexievna Dobroselova (vär·vä′rə ä·lĕk·sā′ĕv·nə dôb·rô·sĕ′lə·və), his beloved, a very distant relation who sensibly berates the extravagant but impoverished devotee but also thanks him for his devotion. A girl who has suffered much after a happy childhood, she is unable to adjust to the cruel world where she is lustfully sought after and generally disregarded. Loving the rural life from which she came and failing in health, she finally decides to marry a rich but irascible man who can save her, but under protest from Makar, so much her admirer that he cannot bear to see her sell herself cheaply. Her concern for the man who watches over her so tenderly and even foolishly, her deep devotion to the memory of her parents, and her cherished recollection of a dead lover who was her tutor suggest the kind of character which has allowed her to survive the insults of an aunt and the buffeting of fortune.

Thedora (tĕ·dō′rə), a cook and Barbara's companion, often her benefactress, an aging servant who loyally remains with the ailing girl. She stays on to cook for

Makar when he moves into the departing bride's rooms. Often berated for her keen-eyed reporting of Makar's extravagances and misadventures, she redeems herself again and again in his eyes.

Bwikov (byĭ·kôf'), Barbara's betrothed, a middle-aged, wealthy, but patronizing and lecherous friend of her aunt. Driven on by the embittered relative of the destitute girl, and involved in the prostitution of Barbara's cousin Sasha, Bwikov comes to St. Petersburg supposedly to make amends for the indecent propositioning by his nephew, but in reality to claim a wife and beget a legitimate heir to his fortunes.

Pokrovski (pôk·rōv'skĭ), a consumptive young scholar who truly loves Barbara and dies declaring his love. A bright but shy person, he befriends Barbara and bequeaths to her his love of great books

and a knowledge of good writing and good taste.

Gorshkov (gôrsh·kôf'), an unfairly indicted civil servant whose reputation is finally cleared but who dies of the shock. A victim of the bureaucratic system, the young man and his family suffer desperately and unfairly, befriended only by old Makar.

Anna Thedorovna (än'nä tĕ·dō'rəv·nə), Barbara's aunt, with whom Barbara and her mother, now dead, lived after her father's death.

Sasha, Barbara's cousin, an orphan.

Old Pokrovski (pôk·rōv'skĭ), the tutor's father, devoted to his son and much impressed by the young man's learning. Apparently deranged by his son's death he follows the funeral procession on foot, dropping a trail of books on the way to the cemetery.

POOR WHITE

Author: Sherwood Anderson (1876-1941)
Time of action: 1880-1900
First published: 1920

PRINCIPAL CHARACTERS

Hugh McVey, a Midwestern American whose genius for inventing and manufacturing machinery accounts for his rise from drab poverty to material success. He is, according to many critics, Anderson's example of the force that produced the problems attendant on the impact of technology upon rural America at the turn of the century.

Steve Hunter, McVey's partner in business. He is a capable publicist who convinces the town fathers of Bidwell to invest in a plant to manufacture McVey's invention. The plant makes the town prosperous.

Clara Butterworth, a rather shy, plain, melancholy girl who in a week's time

abandons her studies at the state university, returns to Bidwell, falls in love with McVey, and elopes with him. She is not suited by temperament to a man like McVey and their marriage becomes a strained relationship. Adversity and the prospect of a child finally bring them together.

Joe Wainsworth, a harness maker who invests his savings in McVey's invention and is almost financially ruined when the money is lost. The reversal disturbs his disposition, and he becomes sullen and irritable. A trivial incident sets him off and, seriously deranged, he kills his employee, shoots Steve Hunter, and tries to strangle McVey.

Sarah Shepard, McVey's foster mother, who instills in him respect for knowledge, hard work, social success, and industrial progress.

Henry Shepard, Sarah's husband and McVey's first employer. He befriends Mc-Vey and provides a home for him.

Jim Gibson, a braggart and Wainsworth's employee. His unfortunate boast precipi-tates Wainsworth's derangement and its concomitant violence. Gibson becomes Wainsworth's first victim.

Tom Butterworth, Clara's father, who is the richest man in town.

Allie Mulberry, a simple-minded work-man who makes a model of McVey's in-vention.

PORGY

Author: DuBose Heyward (1885-1940)
Time of action: Early twentieth century
First published: 1925

PRINCIPAL CHARACTERS

Porgy, an old, crippled Negro beggar who travels about Charleston in a goat-cart. He is frail in body but his hands are powerful. He says little but observes much. When Bess moves in and becomes his woman after Crown has fled follow-ing Robbins' murder, Porgy is trans-formed from an impassive observer of life to a lover of children as well as of Bess. Fearful of losing Bess to Crown, Porgy kills him; but he loses her any-way. Vividly, realistically, and somewhat poetically portrayed, Porgy is one of the most appealing Negro characters in American fiction, but a very different one from J. C. Harris's Uncle Remus or the Negroes in Roark Bradford's stories.

Crown, a stevedore, slow-witted, power-ful, brutal, and dangerous, especially when drunk. He is stabbed by Porgy when he breaks into Porgy's room. Crown's body is later found in the river, but the loyalty of Porgy's friends pre-vents his being identified as Crown's murderer.

Bess, his woman, who lives with Porgy during Crown's absence but who returns briefly to Crown on the day of the Negro picnic. While living with Porgy she is less immoral than amoral, if judged ac-cording to the morality of the white race. Neither she nor her friends see anything improper in such conduct. Made drunk by stevedores during Porgy's absence in jail, she is taken to Savannah. Supposedly she returns to her old life.

Robbins, a weekend gambler but other-wise a good provider. He is murdered by Crown, who falsely suspects him of cheating at dice.

Serena, his wife, who adopts Jake and Clara's baby after Porgy is jailed on a contempt charge.

Peter, an old Negro arrested as a witness to Robbins' murder.

Sportin' Life, a flashy New York octo-roon who sells "happy dus'" (dope).

Maria, Porgy's friend, operator of a small cook-shop.

Jake, a fisherman drowned when a hur-ricane wrecks his boat.

Clara, his wife, also drowned during the hurricane. Bess and Porgy keep her baby after her death until the baby is taken by Serena.

Simon Frasier, a Negro "lawyer" who grants illegal divorces for a dollar.

Alan Archdale, a white lawyer, Porgy's friend.

THE PORTRAIT OF A LADY

Author: Henry James (1843-1916)
Time of action: c. 1875
First published: 1881

PRINCIPAL CHARACTERS

Isabel Archer, the heroine of the novel. Orphaned at an early age and an heiress, she uses her freedom to go to Europe to be educated in the arts of life lacking in her own country. She draws the interest and adoration of many people, all of whom feel that they can make a contribution to her growth, or at least can use her. Isabel is somewhat unworldly at the time of her marriage to Gilbert Osmond. After three years of resisting the social mold imposed on her by Osmond and his Roman ménage, Isabel faces a dilemma in which her intelligence and honesty vie with her sense of obligation. Sensitive to her own needs as well as to those of others, she is aware of the complicated future she faces.

Gilbert Osmond, an American expatriate. He finds in Rome an environment suited to his artistic taste and devotes his time and tastes solely to pleasing himself.

Madame Merle, Isabel's friend. Madame Merle was formerly Osmond's mistress and is the mother of his daughter Pansy. A clever, vigorous woman of considerable perspicacity, she promotes Isabel's marriage to Osmond.

Ralph Touchett, Isabel's ailing cousin. He appreciates the fine qualities of Isabel's nature. Distressed by what he considers her disastrous marriage, he sees to it that his own and his father's estates come to Isabel.

Caspar Goodwood, Isabel's faithful American suitor. He has the simplicity and directness of American insight that Isabel is trying to supplement by her European "education." He does not understand why he fails with Isabel.

Lord Warburton, a friend of Ralph Touchett. Like all the other unsuccessful men in Isabel's life, he deeply admires the young American woman and is distressed by her marriage to Gilbert Osmond.

Henrietta Stackpole, an American journalist and a girlhood friend of Isabel. Henrietta is, in her own right, an amusing picture of the sensation-seeking uncritical American intelligence ranging over the length and breadth of Europe. She is eager to "save" Isabel.

Pansy Osmond, the illegitimate daughter of Osmond and Madame Merle. Pansy is unaware of her situation, and she welcomes Isabel as her stepmother; she feels that in Isabel she has an ally, as indeed she has. Determined to endure gracefully what she must, she feels increasingly the strictures of her father's dictates.

Edward Rosier, a suitor for Pansy's hand. This kindly, pleasant man lacks means sufficient to meet Osmond's demands.

Countess Gemini, Osmond's sister. She is a woman who has been spoiled and corrupted by her European experience, and she finds Isabel's behavior almost boring in its simplicity. Several motives prompt her to tell Isabel about Osmond's first wife and his liaison with Madame Merle. She does not spare Isabel a clear picture of Osmond's lack of humanity.

Mrs. Touchett, Isabel's vigorous and sympathetic aunt. Mrs. Touchett is the one responsible for the invitation that brings Isabel to Europe and the world.

A PORTRAIT OF THE ARTIST AS A YOUNG MAN

Author: James Joyce (1882-1941)
Time of action: 1883-1903
First published: 1916

PRINCIPAL CHARACTERS

Stephen Dedalus (dĕd′ə·ləs, dē′də·ləs), a young man who is, like his creator, sensitive, proud, and highly intelligent, but often confused in his attempts to understand the Irish national temperament. He is bewildered and buffeted about in a world of political unrest, theological discord, and economic decline. In this environment he attempts to resolve for himself the problems of faith, morality, and art. At the end, feeling himself cut off from nation, religion, and family, he decides to leave Ireland in order to seek his own fulfillment as an artist, the artificer that his name suggests.

Simon Dedalus, an easy-going, talkative, patriotic Irishman who reveres the memory of Parnell. During his lifetime he has engaged in many activities, as a medical student, an actor, an investor, and a tax-gatherer, among others; but he has failed in everything he has tried. Stephen Dedalus' realization that his father is self-deluded and shiftless contributes greatly to the boy's growing disillusionment and unrest. Simon is almost the stereotyped, eloquent Irishman who drinks much more than is good for him.

Mrs. Dedalus, a worn, quiet woman who remains a shadowy background figure in the novel. A woman of deep faith, her son's repudiation of religious belief becomes a source of anxiety and grief adding to her other cares.

Mrs. Dante Riordan, Stephen Dedalus' aunt. An energetic defender of anything Catholic, she despises anyone whose views are opposed to her own. Her special targets are certain Irish patriots, particularly Parnell, and all enemies of priests. Her violent arguments with Simon Dedalus on politics and religion make a profound impression on young Stephen.

Eileen Vance, Stephen Dedalus' childhood love. He is not allowed to play with the little girl because she is a Protestant.

E— C—, called Emma Clery in the "Stephen Hero" manuscript but in this novel more the embodied image of Stephen Dedalus' romantic fancies and fantasies than a real person. She is the girl to whom he addresses his love poems.

Davin, a student at University College and the friend of Stephen Dedalus. He is athletic, emotionally moved by ancient Irish myth, and obedient to the Church. To Stephen he personifies country, religion, and the dead romantic past, the forces in the national life that Stephen is trying to escape.

Lynch, an intelligent but irreverent student at University College. During a walk in the rain Stephen Dedalus tries to explain to Lynch his own views on art. Stephen's explanation of lyrical, epical, and dramatic literary forms helps to illuminate Joyce's own career as a writer.

Cranly, a student at University College. A casuist, he serves as an intellectual foil to Stephen Dedalus. To him Stephen confides his decision not to find his vocation in the Church and the reasons for his inability to accept its rituals or even to believe its teachings.

Father Arnall, a Jesuit teacher at Clongowes Wood School. While Stephen Dedalus is attending Belvedere College, during a religious retreat, Father Arnall preaches an eloquent sermon on the sin of Lucifer and his fall. The sermon moves Stephen so deeply that he experiences a religious crisis, renounces all pleasures of the flesh, and for a time contemplates becoming a priest.

Father Dolan, the prefect of studies at Clongowes Wood School. A strict disciplinarian, he punishes Stephen Dedalus unjustly after the boy has broken his glasses and is unable to study. The beating he administers causes Stephen's first feeling of rebellion against priests.

Uncle Charles, Stephen Dedalus' great-uncle, a gentle, hearty old man employed to carry messages. When Stephen is a small boy, he accompanies Uncle Charles on his errands.

Nasty Roche, a student at Clongowes Wood School. His mocking reference to Stephen Dedalus' name gives Stephen his first impression of being different or alienated.

THE POSSESSED

Author: Fyodor Mikhailovich Dostoevski (1821-1881)
Time of action: Mid-nineteenth century
First published: 1867

PRINCIPAL CHARACTERS

Stepan Trofimovitch Verhovensky (stĕ-pän' trô·fī'mɔ·vĭch vĕr·hô·vĕn'skĭ), a former professor of history, a free thinker, a mild liberal, and an old-fashioned, dandified intellectual. The protégé of Varvara Petrovna Stavrogina, a wealthy provincial aristocrat, he has lived for years on her country estate, first as the tutor of her impressionable son, later as the companion and mentor of his temperamental, strong-willed friend. At times he and his patroness quarrel violently, but usually their relationship is one of mutual understanding and respect. One of the old man's claims to fame is the fact that a poem he had written in his student days was seized by the authorities in Moscow, and he still believes that he is politically suspect. Weak-willed, opinionated, hedonistic in a mild way, he has indulged his own tastes and personal comfort while allowing his only son to be reared by distant relatives. At the end, appalled by the revelation of his son's nihilistic and criminal activities, and seeing himself in the role of an intellectual buffoon in the service of Varvara Petrovna, he wanders off to search for the true Russia. Like Lear, he is ennobled by suffering, and he dies with a deeper knowledge of himself and his unhappy country, divided between the moribund tradition of the past and the revolutionary spirit of the younger generation. Dostoevsky seems to make Stepan Trofimovitch an illustration of the way in which a generation of sentimental, theorizing, intellectual liberals bred a new generation of nihilists and terrorists who believed only in violence and destruction.

Pyotr Stepanovitch Verhovensky (pyŏ'tr stĕ·pän'ɔ·vĭch vĕr·hô·vĕn'skĭ), Stepan's nihilistic, revolutionary, despicable son, who has traveled widely and engaged in a number of political intrigues. Really an anti-hero, he is an early model of the modern, exacting, scientific, psychological fanatic and iconoclast. A monster in his capacity for irreligiosity, deception, and destruction, he undermines the moral integrity of his friend, Nikolay Vsyevoldovitch Stavrogin, creates discord between his father and Varvara Petrovna, conducts a campaign of terrorism in the provincial town to which he returns after a number of years spent in study and travel, and foments criminal activities that include arson and murder. If his father's chief trait is self-delusion, Pyotr's is the ability to delude others and lead them to their ruin; and he is always sure of his mission, fanatical in his single-minded belief in dissent and destruction, and convinced that the end justifies any means. Filled with a sense of his own power, he is totally wicked and corrupt, although he is not without charm to those who do not know his real nature.

Varvara Petrovna Stavrogin (vär·vä′rə pet′rəv·nə stäv·rō′gən), a wealthy woman who indulges her son, befriends Stepan Trofimovitch, pays for the schooling of Pyotr Stepanovitch, and takes into her household as her companion the daughter of a former serf. Tall, bony, yellow-complexioned, she is impressive in her outspoken, autocratic behavior. Abrupt and unsentimental for the most part, she is also capable of deep feeling. Her strength of character is shown at the end of the novel when she begins to rebuild her life after revelations of Stepan Trofimovitch's dilettantish intellectualism, her son's weakness and waywardness, and the ruthless violence of the revolutionary group. Her final blow is her son's suicide.

Nikolay Vsyevolodovitch Stavrogin (nĭ·kô·lī′ vsyě·vô·lō′də·vĭch), the son of Varvara Petrovna. A mixture of the sensitive and the coarse, the sensual and the spiritual, he has lived abroad for a number of years. There he has engaged in revolutionary activities and debauchery with a number of women, including Marya Timofyevna Lebyadkin, the crippled, weak-minded woman whom he married to show his mocking contempt for social conventions, and Marya Ignatyevna Shatov, who is carrying his child. His friendship with Pyotr Stepanovitch leads to the formation of a revolutionary group that he establishes in his native village. Though he is ostensibly the leader, his friend is the real power within the group,

and Pyotr Stepanovitch's wild dream is to make Stavrogin a false pretender who will lead Russia back into barbarism. Handsome in appearance, Stavrogin makes his presence felt everywhere, and his reputation makes him feared. Loved by some, hated by others, he has lost all capacity for deep feeling; he tries only to experience violently contrasting sensations as a means of escaping boredom. The night Lizaveta Nikolaevna Tushin spends with him makes him see himself as a spiritually sterile and physically impotent man aged before his time. Hoping to escape from his condition of moral torpor, he asks Darya, the sister of Ivan Shatov, to start a new life with him. She agrees, but before they can leave the village he commits suicide.

Ivan Shatov (ē·vän′ shä·tôf′), the liberated and liberal-minded son of a former serf on the Stavrogin estate. Tutored by Stepan Trofimovitch and sent away by Varvara Petrovna for further education, he has traveled and worked in America. Disillusioned by Pyotr Stepanovitch and his revolutionary group, Shatov still worships Stavrogin for the image of idealism he evokes. He represents the emancipated, educated Russian who in spite of the disordered life about him clings to his elemental feelings for home, friends, the countryside, ideals of liberty, and passion for independence. Unable to accept the nihilism for which Pyotr Stepanovitch stands, he announces his intention to believe in a human Christ, a Christ of the people. When his wife, from whom he has been separated, returns to give birth to her child, Shatov welcomes her with joy and the child as a token of the future. Because of fears that Shatov will betray the activities of the revolutionary group, Pyotr Stepanovitch has him murdered. Dostoevski uses Shatov as a spokesman for some of his own views on politics and religion.

Marya Ignatyevna Shatov (mä′ryə ĭg·nä′·těv·nə shä′tôf′), Ivan's wife, who returns to his home to bear her child, fathered, it is suggested, by Stavrogin.

Alexey Nilitch Kirillov (ä·lĕk·sā′ nĭ′lĭch kĭ·rĭl′əf), a member of the revolutionary group. Existentialist in his beliefs, he is able neither to accept God nor to endure the human condition. He has reached a state of negation in which his only hope is to commit suicide and thus to become God by exercising his will over life and death. Before he shoots himself Pyotr Stepanovitch persuades him to sign a false confession to the murder of Shatov, killed by the revolutionaries because they are afraid he will betray them to the authorities after the murder of Ignat Lebyadkin and his sister.

Ignat Lebyadkin (ĭg·nät′ lĕ·byät′kĭn), a retired army captain, pompous in manner, ridiculous in his pride, crafty in his schemes for extorting money from Stavrogin, his brother-in-law. A would-be gallant, he makes approaches to Lizaveta Nikolaevna Tushin. Pyotr Stepanovitch sees Lebyadkin and his sister as threats to his plans for Stavrogin, and he arranges to have them killed. Their bodies are found by horrified, indignant villagers in the smoldering embers of their house.

Marya Timofyevna Lebyadkin (mä′ryə tĭ·mō·fyĕv′nə), a girl of weak mind and a cripple, Captain Lebyadkin's sister, whom Stavrogin has married in order to show his contempt for his position in society and to perpetrate a cruel joke on the girl and himself. He has kept the marriage secret, however, and the efforts to determine his relation with Marya agitate his family and friends after his return to the village. He treats her with a mixture of amused condescension and ironic gallantry.

Lizaveta Nikolaevna Tushin (lĭ·zä·vĕ′tə nĭ·kô·lä′ĕv·nə tū′shən), also called **Liza**, the daughter of Praskovya Ivanovna Drozdov, Varvara Petrovna's friend, by a previous marriage. High-spirited and unconventional, she is strongly attracted to Stavrogin and is for a time interested

in the proposed publication of a magazine by the revolutionary band. On the night that Captain Lebyadkin and his sister are killed, she gives herself to Stavrogin, only to discover that he is no more than the empty shell of a man. Stopping by to view the smoking ruins of the Lebyadkin house, she is beaten to death by the angry villagers because of her association with Stavrogin.

Praskovya Ivanovna Drozdov (präskōv′yə ē·vän′ĕv·nə drōz′dəf), Lizaveta Nikolaevna's mother. She and Varvara Petrovna have reached an understanding for the marriage of Liza and Stavrogin, but the young people have quarreled, possibly over Darya Shatov, possibly because of Stavrogin's friendship with Pyotr Stepanovitch, while all were living in Switzerland. Not knowing the reason, Praskovya blames Stavrogin for the disagreement and is filled with resentment against him.

Darya Paulovna Shatov (dä′ryə päv′ləv·nə shä·tōf′), also called **Dasha** and **Dashenka**, Ivan Shatov's meek, pretty sister, who has grown up in the Stavrogin household, half companion, half servant to Varvara Petrovna. During a visit to Switzerland, her mistress leaves the girl behind as a companion to Liza. On her return Varvara Petrovna plans for a time to marry the girl to Stepan Trofimovitch, and Darya meekly consents. When Stavrogin, with whom she is secretly in love, asks her to go away with him, she readily agrees. He commits suicide before they can arrange for their departure.

Andrey Antonovitch von Lembke (ändrā′ än·tô′nə·vĭch vən lĕm′kē), the new governor of the province.

Yulia Mikhailovna von Lembke (ū′lĭ·yə mē·hī′ləv·nə vən lĕm′kē), the governor's vulgar, ambitious wife.

Semyon Yakovelitch Karmazinov (sĕmyōn′ yä′kôv·lĕ·vĭch kär·mə·zĭ′nəf), a pompous, foolish, elderly writer who makes a ridiculous spectacle of himself at a literary fete. He is Dostoevski's satirical portrait of Turgenev.

Liputin (lĭ·pö'tyĭn), a slanderer and zealous reformer,

Erkel (ĕr'kĕl), a youthful enthusiast,

Virginsky (vĭr·jĭn'skē), a civil clerk, and **Shigalov** (shĭ'gə·lŏf), his brother, members of the revolutionary group.

Lyamshin (lyäm'shən), the member of the group who confesses and reveals the activities of the band to the authorities.

Arina Prohorovna Virginsky (ä·rĭ'nə prô·hō'rəv·nə vĭr·jĭn'skē), a midwife.

Artemy Pavlovitch Gaganov (är·tyôm'ē päv·lə·vĭch gä·gä'nəf), the local aristocrat with whom Stavrogin fights a duel.

Andrey Antonovitch Blum (än·drä' än·tō'nə·vĭch blöm), the assistant to Governor von Lembke.

Sofya Matveyevna Ulitin (sôf'yə mät·vē·yĕf'nə ū'lĭ·tən), the young widow who aids Stepan Trofimovitch during his wanderings. She goes to live with Varvara Petrovna.

Anton Lavrentyevitch G——v (än·tōn' läv·rĕn'tyē·vĭch), the friend of Stepan Trofimovitch and the narrator of this story of violence and passion.

THE POT OF GOLD

Author: Titus Maccius Plautus (c. 255-184 B.C.)
Time of action: Second century B.C.
First published: c. 195 B.C.

PRINCIPAL CHARACTERS

Euclio (ū'klĭ·ō), an old miser intent on hiding from others his possession of a pot of gold hidden by his miserly grandfather but revealed to him in its hiding place by his household god. Wishing to use the gold as a dowry to help his daughter Phaedria get a husband, Euclio hides it again, pretends poverty, and suspects everyone of trying to rob him or trick him out of his treasure. Unsure of Megadorus' sincerity, he nevertheless agrees to let him marry Phaedria because of his willingness to take her without a dowry and to pay the wedding expenses. After the withdrawal of Megadorus as a suitor and the return of the stolen gold by Lyconides, Euclio accepts the young man as a son-in-law and even gives the gold to the newly wedded couple. Though the story of Euclio is probably based on one of Menander's lost comedies, the quarrelsome, suspicious, greedy, frantic old man himself served during the Renaissance as a simple prototype of such characters as Jonson's Jaques de Prie ("The Case Is Altered"), and Molière's Harpagon ("L'Avare").

Megadorus (mĕ'gə·dō'rəs), Euclio's rich old neighbor. Scornful of marriage to a wealthy woman of high station who would squander his money and who might try to order him about, he is attracted to Phaedria because of her poverty, and he is willing to marry her without a dowry. For Lyconides' sake he gives up his marriage plans so that his nephew may have her. Plautus uses Megadorus as a mouthpiece for satirizing rich women and their expensive tastes.

Eunomia (ū·nō'mĭ·ə), Megadorus' sister, who wishes him to marry and father children. She later intercedes for Lyconides so that Phaedria may marry him rather than Megadorus.

Lyconides (lī·kō'nĭ·dēz), Eunomia's son, in love with Phaedria, whom he deflowered while drunk and whom he wishes to marry. He confesses his deed to Eunomia and asks her aid in getting Megadorus to let him marry Phaedria. Thinking Euclio has discovered his guilt, he confesses and begs forgiveness, only to be thought confessing the theft of Euclio's gold. He recovers the gold from the real thief, returns it, and gets both Phaedria and the gold with Euclio's blessing.

Staphyla (stă'fĭ·lə), an old slave belonging to Euclio. Aware of Phaedria's pregnancy and wishing to help her, Staphyla worries about the discovery of the girl's condition.

Phaedria (fē'drĭ·ə), Euclio's young daughter, who is favorably regarded by her household god because of her devotion to him and her gifts honoring him. Pregnant by Lyconides, she bears his child and marries him afterward. Phaedria does not appear in the action of the play, but her offstage voice is once heard

calling for the nurse during the pains of childbirth.

Strobilus (strō'bĭ·ləs), Lyconides' slave, who sees Euclio hide his gold first at the shrine of Faith and afterward in Sylvanus' grove. He steals it to use as a bribe to gain his freedom from slavery, but he is forced to give up the treasure without getting his freedom.

Pythodicus (pĭ·thō'dĭ·kəs), Megadorus' slave.

Anthrax (ăn'thrăks) and
Congrio (kŏn'grĭ·ō), two cooks hired for the wedding of Megadorus and Phaedria. Congrio is saucy to Euclio after being unjustly beaten and berated by him.

Phrygia (frĭ'jĭ·ə) and
Eleusium (ĕ·lōō'sĭ·əm), two music girls hired as entertainers for the wedding.

POWER

Author: Lion Feuchtwanger (1884-1958)
Time of action: Mid-eighteenth century
First published: 1925

PRINCIPAL CHARACTERS

Josef Süss Oppenheimer (yō'sĕf süs ô'pănhĭ'mėr), a handsome, almost dandified opportunist, son of a German Christian marshal and a Jewish mother. He aids the Countess' scheme to try to keep her hold on Eberhard, advises Karl and Marie financially, wields political power, gains a great fortune, engineers Karl's liaison with Magdalen, tricks Karl into a military fiasco, and is finally hanged. Though he could have lived by telling of his Christian father, he chooses to die proudly as a Jew.

Rabbi Gabriel (rä'bē gä'brē·ăl), his uncle, a man of melancholy demeanor and mystic ways, reputed to be the Wandering Jew.

Naemi (nä·ā'mē), Süss' daughter, who

falls from a housetop to her death while escaping a sexual attack by Karl.

Eberhard Ludwig (ā'bėr·härd' lōōt'-vikh), Duke of Swabia, a stout, dissipated man who deserts his mistress and returns to his wife to beget an heir.

Karl Alexander (kärl ä'lăx·än'dėr), a penniless prince who, after marrying Marie and becoming a Catholic, inherits the duchy when Eberhard dies. A despicable rake, he establishes a liaison with Magdalen and later tries to rape Naemi.

Marie Auguste (mä·rē ou'gōōs'tĕ), Karl's Duchess, daughter of Anself Franz.

Weissensee (vī'săn·sā'), a politician who

909

hates Süss, plots against him, and indirectly causes Naemi's death.

Magdalen Sibylle, (mäg′dä·lān sĭ′bĭ′lĕ), his daughter, who becomes Karl's mistress as a result of a ruse by Süss.

Isaac Landauer, (ē′sä·äk län′dou·ėr), a brilliant, distinctively Jewish international banker and financial agent for the Countess. He gives Süss his first opportunity to rise materially in the world.

Prince Anselm Franz von Thurn and Taxis (än′sĕlm fränts fôn tŏŏrn ŏŏnd täks′sĭs), father of Marie Auguste. He brings about his daughter's marriage and

Karl's conversion to Catholicism.

Reb Jecheskel Seligmann (rĕb yä′shäs·kėl sä′lĭg·män), an innocent Jew arrested for the murder of a child. He is saved by Süss.

Christl (krĭstl), the Countess, wife of the dullwitted Lord High Steward and Eberhard's extravagant, lampooned mistress of thirty years, deserted principally because she had grown fat, asthmatic, and middle-aged.

Johanna Elisabetha (yō′hä·nä ĕ′lē′sä·bĕ-tä), Eberhard's bleak, sour, neglected Duchess.

THE POWER AND THE GLORY

Author: Graham Greene (1904–   )
Time of action: The 1930's
First published: 1940

PRINCIPAL CHARACTERS

A Whiskey Priest who, though never named, goes sometimes under the assumed name of **Montez** (mōn′täs). For eight years a fugitive from the anticlerical regime in a small Mexican province, the Whiskey Priest has managed occasionally to celebrate mass, to baptize children, and to say the last rites for the dying. His great failing is drink, though he has also committed adultery in the town of Concepción, where he had his last parish. Pride and slothfulness have played an equal part in making him the last cleric in the province; he feels the honor of martyrdom and he simply exists without a plan for escape. Finally he is humbled by the knowledge that he is loved and protected wherever he goes, and the sacrifice of hostages for his surrender fixes in his mind a plan of escape. But he is not a free agent, and he falls into what he knows is a trap when called upon to administer the last rites to an American gunman. Freely admitting his cowardice and lack of vision, the priest dies with the sure knowledge that

he has loved and discharged his duties with a semblance of dignity.

Father José (hō·sä′), a defrocked priest who marries and renounces his religion. Obviously a coward, he refuses any participation in the religion he so easily gave up and so much regrets. He is the laughing stock of a village as the victim of a shrewish wife whose sexual entreaties symbolize the degradation to which he has fallen. Without any humanitarian impulses, he refuses to hear the confession of the Whiskey Priest, even when sanctioned to do so by the government.

A Lieutenant of Police, not named, who exhibits the same fanaticism for the new state as the renegade priest does for his order. A man without formal education but with the zeal for reform which stems from his peasant childhood, the young man puts his faith in the pistol. His mind is unsettled by the Whiskey Priest's sense of destiny in a lost cause, for he cannot reconcile faith without deeds. Also, he is confused and unhappy over the means

910

of taking and killing hostages used to the end of destroying the old priest. The tough manner hides a sentimental streak which appears in ironic contrasts.

A Mestizo, a poor half-breed who acts the part of Judas with a faltering heart. Shrewdly recognizing the Whiskey Priest when all others fail, the tenacious opportunist becomes the cleric's nemesis waiting for the right time to strike. His whining, wheedling, ingratiating manner makes him the more deadly and sinister to the harassed father. The poor man has lived so long as a toady of the police that he lacks the will to resist, though he begs forgiveness after his betrayal of the priest.

Marcía (mär·sē′ə) and
Brigida (bre·hē′dä), mother and daughter, the symbols of the priest's greatest transgression. Through boredom and al-

cohol the middle-aged priest commits adultery with his parishioner Marcía, and he dies regretting that he has not loved his seven-year-old daughter enough to make any difference in her life. While the mother has a kind of inverted pride in her ghostly and human father, the poor youngster can only feel suspicion and disdain for the man who makes of her an outsider.

A Dentist,
A Trader, and
A Plantation Owner, those who shelter the priest during his pilgrimages toward escape. The daughter of the trader and the sister of the plantation owner are true humanitarians and offer solace as well as food and shelter to the priest. The dentist is as fated as the priest with whom he identifies himself, though the dramatic death outside his window seems to move him to some resolution.

THE POWER OF DARKNESS

Author: Count Leo Tolstoy (1828-1910)
Time of action: Nineteenth century
First presented: 1886

PRINCIPAL CHARACTERS

Nikíta Akímitch Tchilíkin, a laborer. Employed on the farm of Peter Ignátitch, he is engaged in an affair with his employer's wife Anísya. Nikíta and his mistress, with the help of Nikíta's mother Matryóna, plan Peter's murder. When their victim is dead, the guilty couple marry and Nikíta becomes master of the farm. Soon tiring of his wife, he begins an affair with Akoulína, by whom he has a child. At the urging of his wife and mother, he kills the baby. At Akoulína's wedding feast, Nikíta falls on his knees, confesses his crimes, and begs forgiveness of all he has misused. He is then bound and led away.

Peter Ignátitch, a well-to-do peasant. He is murdered for his property by his adulterous wife Anísya, at the instigation of

her lover, Nikíta, and his mother, Matryóna.

Anísya, Peter Ignátitch's second wife. Engaged in an affair with Peter's hired man, Nikíta, she is encouraged by her lover and his mother to poison her husband. She marries Nikíta, who soon tires of her. When he has a child by Akoulína, Anísya urges him to kill the child in order to force him to share her guilt in the poisoning of Peter Ignátitch.

Matryóna, Nikíta's mother. She urges Anísya to poison Peter Ignátitch so that the way will be left clear for Nikíta's marriage to Anísya and his mastery of Peter's farm. Later, she encourages her son to murder his child by Akoulína.

911

Akoulína, Peter Ignátitch's daughter by his first marriage. She is seduced by Nikíta. When their child is born, Nikíta, prompted by Anísya, kills it.

Marína, an orphan girl who is seduced by Nikíta.

Akím, Nikíta's father.

THE PRAIRIE

Author: James Fenimore Cooper (1789-1851)
Time of action: 1804
First published: 1827

PRINCIPAL CHARACTERS

Natty Bumppo, the resourceful, independent old woodsman at eighty-two. While trapping on the plains soon after the Louisiana Purchase, he camps one evening with a clan of tough, suspicious squatters, the Bush family. Later, accused of killing Asa Bush and having helped two young men to rescue their sweethearts from the Bushes, he is forced to avoid the squatters. Meanwhile he and his companions are captured three times by hostile Sioux Indians. Natty serves as an interpreter, pacifies their captors, and helps the captives to escape. Finally, when the Sioux have been defeated and he has acquitted himself before the Bush clan, he decides to live with a tribe of friendly Pawnees until his death. Old and weak, he dies at sundown after rising to his feet and uttering a single word, "Here."

Ishmael Bush, the huge, ferocious head of the squatters. Though he has no respect for the law, he has a rude sense of justice and honor. Enraged by Indian attacks, the murder of his son Asa, and the abduction of his niece and a female hostage, he makes a temporary alliance with the Sioux in order to capture the fugitives. When his allies betray him, he calmly helps destroy them. In a rude court of justice he sets the two pairs of lovers free, along with an itinerant naturalist. He also frees Natty Bumppo after the old hunter reveals Abiram White, Bush's brother-in-law, as the murderer. In the end, Bush and his family move on into the unknown West.

Esther Bush, Ishmael's aging, shrewish, almost mannish wife. The only literate member of the family, she reads the Bible but has the instincts of a wolf. Protective towards her young and savage towards trespassers, she is a formidable Indian fighter.

Ellen Wade, called **Nelly,** Esther Bush's pretty, vivacious niece. A homeless girl of eighteen, she feels gratitude toward the Bushes for their care, even if she feels little affection for them. More genteel than others of the Bush clan, she attracts Paul Hover, a young bee hunter from Kentucky, meets him secretly, and deserts the Bushes to share his adventures. Three times captured by Indians, and retaken by Ishmael, she finally receives Ishmael Bush's permission to marry Paul.

Abiram White, Esther's cowardly, treacherous brother. He kidnaps Inez Middleton, the wife of a young soldier, shoots Asa Bush in the back after a quarrel, and blames the killing on Natty Bumppo. When his guilt is disclosed, Ishmael Bush exacts a terrible vengeance. White is placed, bound, on a rock ledge where he must either hang himself or starve. His body is found dangling from a rope tied to the limb of a tree.

Dr. Obed Battius, also called **Obed Bat,** a pompous naturalist who prefers to travel in Natty's company rather than with the rude squatters. He exemplifies a foolish, academic approach to nature that contrasts strongly with Natty's natural, pious attitudes. A rather useless person, he owns a donkey that saves the party from a buffalo stampede by braying.

Paul Hover, Ellen Wade's reckless, spirited sweetheart and a roaming bee hunter. Captured three times by Sioux Indians, along with Natty and Ellen, he is always ready to fight, but Natty's diplomatic efforts succeed in saving his neck until he is finally safe and free to marry Ellen.

Captain Middleton, a handsome young soldier, the bridegroom of Inez Middleton, the hostage kidnaped by Abiram White. Searching for the Bushes, he comes across Natty Bumppo, Paul Hover, and Dr. Battius, who help him rescue his wife. After being captured by Indians, he is set free by Ishmael Bush, and happily reunited with his wife. He is the grandson of a British officer whom Natty Bumppo had known in the days of the French and Indian Wars.

Inez Middleton, his wife, a wealthy young woman held prisoner by the squatters. Having been rescued by her husband and captured by Sioux, she is in danger of becoming the wife of Mahtoree, the Sioux chief. When he is killed in single-handed combat with a Pawnee warrior, she is restored to her husband by Ishmael Bush.

Hard-Heart, the noble young chief who befriends Natty Bumppo and his comrades and is finally captured with them by a band of fierce Sioux. About to be

tortured, he escapes to his tribe, challenges the Sioux chief to battle, kills him, and defeats the hostile tribe. Natty chooses to make his home in Hard-Heart's Pawnee village, where he lives until his death.

Mahtoree, the bold, fierce, cunning Sioux chieftain. A dangerous foe, he captures Natty Bumppo and the old hunter's friends three times. He is about to take Inez Middleton for his wife when Hard-Heart, the Pawnee brave, challenges him to combat and kills him.

Swooping Eagle, called **Le Balafré,** an aged Sioux chieftain who wishes to adopt Hard-Heart as his son, to save the young warrior from being killed. Hard-Heart expresses respect for the old man but rejects his offer.

Weucha, a boastful, greedy Sioux brave killed by Hard-Heart.

Tachechana, Mahtoree's Indian wife, shamed when she is forced to strip herself of her finery after the chief decides to discard her and wed Inez Middleton.

Asa Bush, Ishmael's eldest son, killed by his uncle, Abiram White.

Abner,
Enoch, and
Jesse Bush, Ishmael's other strapping sons.

Hetty and
Phoebe Bush, his strong, vigorous young daughters.

PRECIOUS BANE

Author: Mary Webb (1881-1927)
Time of action: Mid-nineteenth century
First published: 1924

PRINCIPAL CHARACTERS

Prudence Sarn, the narrator of the story. Having been cursed from birth by a harelip which mars her appearance, Prue is exceptionally sensitive to the feelings

of others. She agrees to work like an animal for her brother because he promises to give her the money to have her lip cured. When all his plans fail, she leaves the farm and is subsequently accused of being a witch by the village people. She is saved from their wrath by the local weaver whom she has loved secretly for several years.

Gideon Sarn, Prue's brother. Driven by a desire to get rich, he works everyone on the farm, including himself, like an animal. Although genuinely in love with Jancis Beguildy he will not marry her until he has made his fortune. After her father ruins his harvest, he turns her away and degenerates to the point of murdering his own mother and finally committing suicide.

Jancis Beguildy, a childhood friend of Prue and Gideon. She wants to marry Gideon and does bear him a son. When he will have nothing more to do with her, she drowns herself and the baby.

Wizard Beguildy, Jancis' father. Supposed to be able to work spells and charms, he vows that his daughter can never marry Gideon and then sets fire to Gideon's harvest to keep them apart.

Mrs. Beguildy, Jancis' mother. She approves of the planned marriage between her daughter and Gideon and tries to trick her husband into leaving home so that the wedding can take place.

Mrs. Sarn, mother of Gideon and Prue. She is physically very weak and deathly afraid of her son, who poisons her when she can no longer work.

Kester Woodseaves, a weaver. He marries Prue after rescuing her from water torture inflicted by the villagers, who consider her a witch.

Mr. and Mrs. Grimble, Jancis' employers.

PRIDE AND PREJUDICE

Author: Jane Austen (1775-1817)
Time of action: Early nineteenth century
First published: 1813

PRINCIPAL CHARACTERS

Elizabeth Bennet, a spirited and intelligent girl who represents "prejudice" in her attitude toward Fitzwilliam Darcy, whom she dislikes because of his pride. She is also prejudiced against him by Mr. Wickham, whose false reports of Darcy she believes, and hence rejects Darcy's haughty first proposal of marriage. But Wickham's elopement with her sister Lydia brings Elizabeth and Darcy together, for it is Darcy who facilitates the legal marriage of the runaways. Acknowledging her mistake in her estimation of Darcy, she gladly accepts his second proposal.

Fitzwilliam Darcy, the wealthy and aristocratic landowner who represents "pride" in the story. Attracted to Elizabeth Bennet in spite of her inferior social position, he proposes marriage but in so high-handed a manner that she instantly refuses. The two meet again while Elizabeth is viewing the grounds of his estate in Derbyshire; she finds him less haughty in his manner. When Lydia Bennet and Mr. Wickham elope, Darcy feels partly responsible and straightens out the unfortunate affair. Because Elizabeth now realizes his true character, he is accepted when he proposes again.

Jane Bennet, the oldest and most beautiful of the five Bennet sisters. She falls in love with Mr. Bingley, a wealthy bachelor. Their romance is frustrated, however, by his sisters with the help of Mr. Darcy, for the Bennets are considered socially undesirable. As a result of the change in the feelings of Darcy and Elizabeth Bennet toward each other, Jane and Bingley are finally married.

914

Mr. Bingley, a rich, good-natured bachelor from the north of England. He falls in love with Jane Bennet but is easily turned against her by his sisters and his friend, Mr. Darcy, who consider the Bennets vulgar and socially beneath them. When Darcy changes in his attitude toward Elizabeth Bennet, Bingley follows suit and resumes his courtship of Jane. They are married at the end of the story.

Mr. Bennet, an eccentric and mildly sarcastic small landowner. Rather indifferent to the rest of his family, he loves and admires his daughter Elizabeth.

Mrs. Bennet, his wife, a silly, brainless woman interested only in getting her daughters married.

Lydia Bennet, the youngest daughter, a flighty and uncontrolled girl. At the age of fifteen she elopes with the worthless Mr. Wickham. Their marriage is finally made possible by Mr. Darcy, who pays Wickham's debts; but the two are never very happy.

Mary Bennet and
Catherine (Kitty) Bennet, younger daughters of the family.

Mr. Wickham, the villain of the story, an officer in the militia. He had been brought up by the Darcy family and, having a certain charm, attracts Elizabeth Bennet, whom he prejudices against Mr. Darcy by misrepresenting the latter's treatment of him. Quite unexpectedly, he elopes with fifteen-year-old, flirtatious Lydia Bennet. Darcy, who has tried to expose Wickham to Elizabeth, feels responsible for the elopement and provides the money for the marriage by paying Wickham's debts. Wickham and Lydia soon tire of each other.

William Collins, a pompous, sycophantic clergyman, distantly related to Mr. Bennet and the heir to his estate, since the Bennets have no son. He proposes to Elizabeth. After her refusal he marries her friend, Charlotte Lucas.

Lady Catherine de Bourgh, Mr. Darcy's aunt and the patron of Mr. Collins. An insufferably haughty and domineering woman, she wants Darcy to marry her only daughter and bitterly resents his interest in Elizabeth Bennet. She tries to break up their love affair but fails.

Anne de Bourgh, Lady Catherine's spiritless daughter. Her mother has planned to marry her to Mr. Darcy in order to combine two great family fortunes.

Charlotte Lucas, Elizabeth Bennet's closest friend. Knowing that she will have few chances of marriage, she accepts the pompous and boring Mr. Collins shortly after Elizabeth has refused him.

Caroline Bingley and
Mrs. Hurst, Mr. Bingley's cold and worldly sisters. They succeed for a time in turning him against Jane Bennet.

Mr. Gardiner, Mrs. Bennet's brother, a London merchant.

Mrs. Gardiner, his sensible and kindly wife.

THE PRINCE AND THE PAUPER

Author: Mark Twain (Samuel L. Clemens, 1835-1910)
Time of action: Sixteenth century
First published: 1882

PRINCIPAL CHARACTERS

Edward, Prince of Wales and son of Henry VIII. When a ragged waif named Tom Canty invades the royal grounds, Edward, curious about life outside the confines of the palace, invites the boy to his quarters. They change clothes as a prank and discover that they are identical in appearance. When the Prince appears in the courtyard dressed in Tom's rags, guards mistake him for the intruding waif and throw him into the streets. Protesting time and again that he is the real Prince of Wales, he is ridiculed and thought mad by skeptical London crowds. After many adventures and hardships that reveal to him the harsh lot of the common people, he appears as Tom Canty is about to be crowned king and proves that he himself is the rightful heir by disclosing the location of the Great Seal that his late father had entrusted to him.

King Henry VIII, his ailing father, who has entrusted to Edward the Great Seal.

Mary and
Elizabeth, daughters of the King, who think Tom is their brother.

Tom Canty, who was born the same day as the Prince of Wales and is his double in appearance. He trades places with Edward.

John Canty, his father, who treats Tom and Edward cruelly. When he becomes King, Edward wants to hang Canty but can never locate him.

Miles Hendon, the disinherited son of a baronet. He befriends the homeless Edward.

Hugh Hendon, his brother, who tricks Miles in order to marry Edith.

Edith, who loves Miles but is afraid Hugh will murder him if she identifies Miles.

Hugo, a thief who tries to teach Edward his tricks.

The Lord Protector, who identifies the real Prince.

THE PRINCE OF HOMBURG

Author: Heinrich von Kleist (1777-1811)
Time of action: 1675
First presented: 1821

PRINCIPAL CHARACTERS

Frederick Arthur, Prince of Homburg. Exhausted from battle, he falls into a kind of half sleep during which he weaves a laurel wreath. The Elector, Frederick William, takes the wreath and intwines it with his neck-chain, an occurrence which later influences the Prince to feel that destiny compels him into battle. In the ensuing battle with the Swedes, the Prince, in an ecstasy over his love for Princess Natalie, fails to hear the orders clearly and precipitously gives his own orders to advance. Later, the battle won, the Elector sentences the Prince to die for disobeying orders. On the pleas of many,

the Prince's life is spared, and he is hailed as the hero of the battle.

Frederick William, Elector of Brandenburg. When he returns victorious from battle, his spirit of military discipline forces him to sentence Frederick Arthur, Prince of Homburg, to die for ignoring battle orders, even though the Prince's forces have been victorious. After hearing many pleas for the Prince's life, with charges and countercharges for placing the blame for the Prince's disobedience, the Elector tears up the death warrant.

Princess Natalie of Orange, the niece of Frederick William, Elector of Brandenburg. She is loved by Prince Frederick Arthur and pleads for his life when he is sentenced to death for failing to follow orders.

Count Hohenzollern, a member of the Elector's suite who pleads for Frederick Arthur's life.

Field Marshal Dörfling, of Brandenburg.

Colonel Kottwitz, an officer in the regiment of the Princess of Orange. Rebuked by Frederick William for lack of fervor when he hesitates to follow the impetuous Prince in his advance before the battle signal is given, the Colonel, afraid of appearing unpatriotic, joins in the charge.

The Electress of Brandenburg.

THE PRINCESS OF CLÈVES

Author: Madame Marie de Lafayette (1634-1693)
Time of action: Sixteenth century
First published: 1678

PRINCIPAL CHARACTERS

The Princess de Clèves (klĕv'), a beautiful young woman married to a prince of the royal household. She is a virtuous, even passionless, woman who disappoints her husband with her lack of ardor. Unlike most courtiers, she has no extramarital affairs. When she meets the Duke de Nemours, she feels emotion for him but tries to put it down, even enlisting her husband's aid. After her husband's death she refuses to marry the Duke and withdraws from society, even to the point of entering a convent for a time.

The Prince de Clèves (klĕv'), a member of the royal family. He tries to help his wife suppress her love for the Duke de Nemours. When he thinks his wife has fallen from virtue, he becomes ill of a fever and, rather than stand in his wife's way, languishes and dies.

The Duke de Nemours (də nə·mōōr'), the handsomest and most gallant courtier

in France. He is even spoken of as a possible consort for Elizabeth I of England. He falls in love with the Princess de Clèves, but cannot turn her from being faithful to her husband.

The Queen Dauphine (dŏ·fēn'), Mary, Queen of Scots, who is a friend of the Princess de Clèves.

The Vidame de Chartres (vē·dȧm' də shȧr'tr), an uncle of the Princess de Clèves. He tries to bring his niece and the Duke de Nemours together after the girl is a widow.

Mme. de Chartres (də shȧr'tr), mother of the Princess de Clèves. She is ambitious to see her daughter marry a prince.

Henri II (än·rē'), King of France.

Diane de Poitiers (dyȧn' də pwä·tyā'), the Duchess de Valentinois, King Henri's adviser. She was his father's mistress and is now the center of a court clique.

THE PRISONER OF ZENDA

Author: Anthony Hope (Sir Anthony Hope Hawkins, 1863-1933)
Time of action: The 1880's
First published: 1894

Rudolf Rassendyll, a red-bearded young English gentleman of leisure who prides himself on his red hair and large straight nose, which are reminders of an old scandal involving the wife of a Rassendyll ancestor and a visiting Ruritanian prince of the Elphberg family. To save the Ruritanian crown from Black Michael, Rassendyll impersonates Rudolf and is crowned king. He falls in love with Flavia, manages several narrow escapes from Michael and his men, rescues Rudolf, and restores the throne of Ruritania to its rightful king.

Lady Rose Burlesdon, his sister-in-law, a pretty, accomplished, and wealthy woman.

Rudolf, King of Ruritania, little known to his subjects because of his frequent and extended absences from his country. He looks like an identical twin of Rassendyll except that he has shaved off his beard, his face is a little fleshier, and his mouth less firm. He is a heavy drinker and is both drunk and drugged the day of the coronation. Imprisoned by Michael, he is freed when Michael's lodge is attacked and assumes his position as monarch.

Michael, Duke of Strelsau, King Rudolf's villainous half brother, called **Black Michael,** who wishes to be king of Ruritania and will stoop to any deed to achieve his aim. He is killed by the treacherous Rupert.

Antoinette de Mauban, a rich, handsome, ambitious widow in love with Michael.

Princess Flavia, a pale, lovely, red-haired girl betrothed to Rudolf. Though she loves Rassendyll she loyally becomes Rudolf's wife and Queen.

Fritz von Tarlenheim, a loyal subject of Rudolf who helps to carry out Rassendyll's impersonation and later saves his life.

Colonel Sapt, another loyal subject, who first suggests that Rassendyll shave off his beard and double for Rudolf during the coronation to prevent Michael from seizing the throne.

Josef, a servant in Michael's hunting lodge. He is slain while guarding the drunken Rudolf.

Rupert Hentzau, Michael's handsome young aide, who kills him in a fight over Antoinette. In a deadly encounter with Rupert later, Rassendyll is saved by Fritz.

Detchard, another of Michael's henchmen. After attacking the king he is slain by Rassendyll.

THE PRIVATE LIFE OF THE MASTER RACE

Author: Bertolt Brecht (1898-1956)
Time of action: 1933-1938
First published: 1944; *partial presentation:* 1938

PRINCIPAL CHARACTERS

The S. A. Man, whose name is Theo. He is proud of his part in the Nazi movement and enjoys kindling fear among his friends and acquaintances.

The Parlour-Maid, the S. A. Man's mistress. She fears her lover and dislikes

him, too, because he takes her money from their joint bank account.

The Worker, a man named Lincke. He is taunted and frightened by the S. A. Man.

The Social Democrat, a man who blames

the Communists for Germany's inability to save itself politically from the Nazis.

The Old Worker, named Herr Sedel-meier, who is forced to say over the radio that his factory is a wonderful place to work.

The Woman Worker, named Fräulein Schmidt, who is forced to say the factory is a pleasant place to work.

X and
Y, two German physicists who correspond indirectly with Einstein and fear discovery by the Nazis.

Judith Keith, a Jewess who leaves Germany in 1934 for refuge in Holland.

Judge A, named Herr Goll. He wants to render a verdict on a Jew but is confused as to whether the Nazis want a guilty or not-guilty verdict in his decision.

The Inspector, a man named Tallinger. He is too careful of his own fate to be helpful to the judge.

The Prosecutor, a man named Spitz. He is an ambitious man who gives the judge no help because he would like the place on the bench held by Judge A.

Judge B, an elderly friend of Judge A. Judge B is too aware of the dangers in Germany to offer any advice to his friend Judge A.

The Butcher, an old-time Nazi who hangs himself when he realizes he has been betrayed by the party.

PRIVATE LIVES

Author: Noel Coward (1899-   )
Time of action: 1930
First presented: 1930

PRINCIPAL CHARACTERS

Elyot Chase, a flippant new husband who has not quite forgotten his first wife. He becomes apprehensive when his new bride Sibyl smiles sweetly and implies that she will tailor his life to suit her whims. While on his honeymoon he accidentally meets his first wife Amanda, who is on her own honeymoon with Victor Prynne. The spark ignites again and they run off to Paris together without telling their respective spouses. Still passionately in love, they nevertheless quarrel bitterly just as before. When confronted in Paris by their legal mates, they are rebuked severely and threatened with divorce. As the tension heightens, Sibyl and Victor themselves begin to quarrel bitterly with each other, whereupon Elyot winks at Amanda and, unnoticed, they tiptoe with their suitcases out the door.

Sibyl Chase, Elyot's second wife, a woman in love with marriage. She tries to make over Elyot's life and finds fault with his first wife, accusing the woman of being ill-tempered and mean. While Sibyl says she wants to make her husband happy, she convinces him that what she really wants is to manage a man's life. She actually drives him back to his first wife, especially when she outrageously plays the part of the traditional jilted spouse.

Victor Prynne, Amanda Prynne's second husband. He is a man who wants to make over someone else's life and takes it upon himself to make over his wife's. By trying to make Amanda into a suitable wife, he unconsciously drives her into the arms of her first husband again. But when he finds his wife and Elyot living together, he tries to lay all the blame on Elyot.

Amanda Prynne, Elyot's first wife. She

919

discovers, as he does, after five years of divorce, that they are just as much in love as they ever were. Many of their arguments result, during the affair, from Amanda's expressed concern about the moral questions involved in her taking her ex-husband as her lover.

THE PRIVATE PAPERS OF HENRY RYECROFT

Author: George Gissing (1857-1903)
Time of action: Late nineteenth century
First published: 1903

PRINCIPAL CHARACTERS

Henry Ryecroft, a contemplative man, formerly a hack writer but able now through the legacy of a friend to live quietly in a comfortable cottage in rural Devon, writing only when he chooses to. He enjoys wandering about the countryside observing the common plants and learning their names. He thinks often of his hack-writing days and of the conditions under which he had lived. Like Charles Lamb, he was always a lover of books and purchased them out of his meager earnings; people nowadays read newspapers, not books. He remembers also the happy excursions on which his family went along the English coast in his childhood. With the Sundays of old when he wrote his sharpest satire, he contrasts his quiet, peaceful ones now. He thinks of the decline of English taste in food. A successful writer friend visits him and they talk over the old days of struggle. He misses the London concerts and picture galleries. He muses on Darwinism and its effects on English

thought, and he considers his own indifference to odd fads and scientific discoveries. He finds comfort in the Stoics' views about death. He meditates on two great sources of England's strength: Puritanism and the Old Testament. One set moral standards; the other reminded the English that they were a chosen people. If in recent times conventional religion has declined and materialism grown, at least the old prudishness has been replaced by a new strength. He looks back upon his varied life which now seems fully rounded, the best life he could make it; and he is content for it to end at any time.

Mrs. M., Ryecroft's excellent housekeeper, a quiet woman of discreet age who keeps an orderly house and does not obtrude upon his meditatons or bother about his comings and goings.

N-----, Ryecroft's writer friend who pays a two-day visit.

THE PROFESSOR

Author: Charlotte Brontë (1816-1855)
Time of action: Nineteenth century
First published: 1857

PRINCIPAL CHARACTERS

William Crimsworth, a young English orphan who upon leaving Eton is faced with a decision regarding his future. From his mother's aristocratic family he receives an offer of a wife and a secure

future as an Anglican clergyman. These he refuses, wanting neither his cousin for a wife nor a career as a poor churchman. He turns to his brother, a businessman, who takes him on as a junior clerk in his mill. Unhappy in his work under his brother, William travels to Brussels and becomes a teacher of English and Latin in a private school. Successful, he marries Mlle. Henri, who has been a pupil and who also becomes a teacher. Because of his hard work and his wife's, Crimsworth is able to retire and return to England while still in middle age.

Mlle. Frances Evans Henri (än·rē'), a pretty young woman of Swiss and English parentage who teaches lace-mending at a school where William Crimsworth is employed. She takes lessons from Crimsworth, who falls in love with her. Under his encouragement she also becomes a teacher and with her husband's help opens a private school of her own. She has never seen her mother's country, and yearns to visit England. Her happiness is complete when she, her husband, and their young son, retiring on the proceeds of their thrift and the sale of her school, go to England to live.

Victor Crimsworth, the son of William Crimsworth and his wife.

Edward Crimsworth, a manufacturer. He hires his young brother as a junior clerk at a very low salary. A malicious tyrant, he treats William worse than he would a stranger. He eventually goes bankrupt but is able to secure sufficient credit to start another business.

Mrs. Crimsworth, Edward's pretty but vacuous and worldly wife. She follows her husband's lead in mistreating her brother-in-law.

Hunsden Yorke Hunsden, a flippant, cynical mill owner who befriends William Crimsworth. He encourages William abroad, buys for him his mother's portrait when Edward Crimsworth's belongings are auctioned off, and later becomes William's adviser on investments. He is a confirmed bachelor, unable to find a woman who pleases him sufficiently to marry.

Mr. Brown, an Englishman living in Brussels who, at Hunsden's request, helps William Crimsworth find a teaching post.

M. Pelet (mə·syœ' pə·lä'), the director of a private school where William is employed. Pelet is a kindly man who accepts William as an equal and becomes his friend. The friendship is strained, however, when Pelet finds that the younger man finds favor in the eyes of Pelet's fiancée. Because of his own amorous adventures with married women, Pelet is of a suspicious nature; he is relieved when William leaves the school shortly after the director's marriage.

Mlle. Zoraïde Reuter (måd·mwå·zĕl' zô·rå·ēd' rœ·tĕr'), plump, pretty, practical director of a school for girls next door to Pelet's school for boys. She hires William Crimsworth to teach part-time in her school and for a time is attracted to the young man, though she is engaged to M. Pelet. Because William is a poor man, she dismisses him and marries M. Pelet. Mlle. Reuter is a scheming deceitful woman.

Mme. Reuter, her fat, worldly mother, who takes care of her daughter's quarters.

Mme. Pelet, M. Pelet's fat, worldly mother, who looks after her son's personal life.

Lord Tynedale, the aristocratic uncle of William Crimsworth. He is highly offended when William spurns the Church in favor of trade, and he refuses to have any more to do with his young relative.

The Hon. John Seacombe, another of William's maternal uncles. Offended by the young man's refusal of one of his daughters in marriage, he disclaims all responsibility for his nephew's future.

Eulalie,
Hortense, and
Caroline, three worldly and vain young girls at Mlle. Reuter's school. They flirt with William Crimsworth and try to make life difficult for their teacher.

THE PROFESSOR'S HOUSE

Author: Willa Cather (1873-1947)
Time of action: A few years after World War I
First published: 1925

PRINCIPAL CHARACTERS

Godfrey St. Peter, professor of European history in a Midwestern state university. A scholar, historian, and artist, he is also a sensitive, imaginative man caught between the creativity of his middle years and the prospect of old age. His eight-volume work, "Spanish Adventurers in North America," has brought him fame, the Oxford Prize, and money to build the fine new house his wife desires. But he is not happy in his new house or new life, and his enterprising son-in-law's exploitation of another man's invention makes him dissatisfied with material success in any form. During a summer while his family is in Europe he stays on in the shabby old house he still rents because of its associations with all he values most, his early years as a young husband and father, his friendship with Tom Outland, a brilliant student killed in the war, the writing of his books. There, reading in Outland's diary about the discovery of a Cliff-Dwellers' city in the Southwest, he recaptures in memory some of the passion and energy he had known as a boy and while at work on his great history. In the fall, alone in the cluttered attic study of the old house, he is almost asphyxiated by gas from a dilapidated heater. Saved by the timely arrival of the family seamstress, he realizes that his lonely summer has been a farewell to a time when life could be lived with delight. Four themes of corruption and betrayal touch upon St. Peter's story: the success, measured by more than twenty years of hard work, which has made him the victim of his wife's ambition and his older daughter's desire for wealth and luxury; the knowledge that a frontier university, founded to stimulate scholarship of passion and vision, is becoming a refuge for immature minds, its integrity in pawn to a time-serving state legislature; the indifference of government archeologists to Outland's discovery of the mesa city and the sale of its relics to a foreign collector; the commercialization for private gain of Outland's invention. Behind these stand the symbolic Blue Mesa and the stone city of an ancient culture. A contrast is implied. The people on the rock created a humanized world of beautiful forms and ceremonial richness. Modern America offers only the products of its materialistic concerns to eternity.

Tom Outland, Professor St. Peter's former student. Orphaned as a baby, he had been taken to New Mexico by foster parents. There he worked as a railroad call boy and later, while recuperating from pneumonia, as a range rider for a cattle company. Sent to tend herd in a winter camp on the Cruzados River, he and his friend, Rodney Blake, explore the almost inaccessible Blue Mesa and find, preserved under overhanging cliffs, the stone city of a vanished tribe of Cliff-Dwellers. The discovery, filling Outland with awe for something so untouched by time and admiration for the artisans who had built with patience and love, becomes the turning point in his life; here is evidence of the filial piety he had read about while studying the Latin poets with Father Duchene. He makes a trip to Washington in an attempt to interest government officials in excavating his find. Rebuffed, he returns to New Mexico. In the meantime Blake, thinking that he is helping his friend, has sold most of the relics and artifacts to a German collector for four thousand dollars. Outland and Blake quarrel and Blake leaves the region. Outland decides to continue his education and goes to see St. Peter because he has read one of the professor's articles on Fray Marcos. St. Peter takes an interest in the boy, helps him to qualify for entrance to the university, becomes his friend, and makes him almost one of the family. Outland, a brilliant young physicist, discovers the principle of the Outland vacuum, an important advance in aviation. Engaged to Rosamond St. Peter, the professor's older daughter, he wills her the patent on his invention before enlisting in the French Foreign Legion at the outbreak of World War I. He is killed in Flanders.

Lillian St. Peter, the professor's wife, a handsome, capable woman proud of her husband's success but without any real understanding of the spirit that has motivated his career. She tries to renew her youth in innocent coquetry with her sons-in-law.

Rosamond Marcellus, the St. Peters' older daughter, married to the man who has commercialized Tom Outland's invention. Still beautiful, but no longer the appealing young girl with whom Outland fell in love, she is interested chiefly in her pretentious new home, her antique furniture, her clothes, and the standing of her Jewish husband in the academic community.

Louie Marcellus, an electrical engineer and a born entrepreneur. The first to realize the commercial possibilities of the patent Tom Outland had willed to Rosamond St. Peter, Marcellus has marketed it successfully and made his wife rich. Shrewd but likable, he takes delight in displaying the rare and beautiful things he buys for Rosamond. Professor St. Peter's attitude toward him is a mixture of admiration and ironic amusement.

Kathleen McGregor, the St. Peters' younger daughter, married to a young journalist. In many ways she has been corrupted most by Tom Outland's inven-

tion, for she is unhappy with her own lot, dislikes her sister, and adds to the family tensions.

Scott McGregor, an able journalist who supplements his income by writing uplift editorials and a daily rhymed jingle for a newspaper syndicate. Professor St. Peter feels sorry for his son-in-law because McGregor stands in second place to Louie Marcellus in family affairs, but he admires the young man's stanchness and independence. Rosamond dislikes her brother-in-law because she believes that he blackballed her husband when Marcellus was trying to become a member of an exclusive club.

Dr. Crane, a professor of physics, suffering from an illness that requires a series of operations. Although he had not shared in Tom Outland's experiments, he had assisted with some of the laboratory detail. He feels that he has a moral right to some of the money realized from the Outland vacuum but is too proud to demand his share.

Mrs. Crane, his wife. In a painful interview with Professor St. Peter she asks his aid in obtaining for her husband a share of the royalties from the Outland vacuum.

Augusta, the practical, loyal sewing woman whose dress forms clutter the attic study that Professor St. Peter has shared with her for many years. Arriving to collect a set of keys so that she can open the new house in preparation for the return of the Marcelluses and Mrs. St. Peter from abroad, she finds the professor overcome by gas after the wind has extinguished the flame of the heater. She saves the life that he himself was willing to relinquish.

Professor Horace Langtry, Professor St. Peter's faculty rival. He represents the new generation of teachers, satisfied with lowered standards and active in internal academic politics.

Rodney Blake, a railroad fireman who becomes Tom Outland's friend after the boy protects him from the loss of a large sum of money won in a poker game. He nurses Outland through an attack of pneumonia and later goes with him to ride herd on the cattle range. Together they explore the Blue Mesa. Misunderstanding Outland's interest in the cliff city, he sells the relics they have collected. After the two men quarrel, Blake leaves the region and is never heard from again. Outland tries unsuccessfully to find him.

Father Duchene (dü·chĕn'), a Belgian-born priest who takes an interest in Tom

Outland as a boy, teaches him the classics, and helps to explore the Blue Mesa. He has great respect for anything that reveals an enduring culture.

Mr. and Mrs. O'Brien, Tom Outland's foster parents during his boyhood.

Sir Edgar Spilling, an English scholar interested in Professor St. Peter's historical research. At a dinner to entertain him Louie Marcellus has the bad taste to announce that he and his wife Rosamond intend to call their new home "Outland."

PROMETHEUS BOUND

Author: Aeschylus (c. 525-c. 456 B.C.)
Time of action: Remote antiquity
First presented: Date unknown

PRINCIPAL CHARACTERS

Prometheus (prə·mē'thē·ŭs, prə·mē'-thōōs), a Titan, the son of Themis (Earth). In the revolt of Zeus against Kronos, he had sided with Zeus and had provided the counsel by which the older gods had been overthrown. Later he persuaded Zeus to spare mankind, whom Zeus had planned to destroy. But he has broken the command of the king of the gods by bringing to men the gift of fire and instructing them in all the arts and crafts. For this flouting of the will of Zeus he is carried, a prisoner, by Kratos (Might) and Bia (Force) to a rocky cliff in remote Scythia, there to be fastened by Hephaestus to the crag and to remain bound for eternity. His only comfort in his anguish is his secret foreknowledge of the eventual downfall of Zeus. His knowledge of the future remains to him; he prophesies to Io the torments that await her; tells her that her descendant, Herakles, will finally release him, and declares that Zeus himself will one day be deposed by his own son, whose future identity only he, Prometheus, knows. This secret he refuses to divulge to Hermes, who brings the command of Zeus that Prometheus must reveal this all-important name on pain of even worse

torments. Defiant to the last, Prometheus is blasted by the thunderbolt of Zeus and sinks into the underworld as the play ends. Prometheus is depicted in this drama as the embodiment of stubborn resistance against the tyranny of Zeus, willing to bear any punishment rather than submit. To the modern mind, and especially to the writers of the Romantic Period, he is the personification of the revolt against tyranny of any sort, the symbol of man's war against the forces of reaction and of his eternal quest for knowledge.

Io (ī'ō), the daughter of the river god Inachus. She was beloved by Zeus, who changed her into a heifer to save her from the jealous wrath of Hera. But the latter, penetrating her rival's disguise, sent a gadfly to torment her throughout the world. Half-crazed with pain, she has wandered to Scythia, where she finds in Prometheus a fellow sufferer. He prophesies her future adventures and traces her descendants down to Herakles, who will deliver him from his chains.

Hermes (hûr'mēz), the messenger of Zeus, sent to wring from Prometheus the secret of the identity of that son of

Zeus who will overthrow his father. In his attitude, Hermes has been called the personification of prudent self-interest. He fails in his errand, for the dauntless Prometheus reviles him as a mere lackey and refuses to divulge the secret.

Hephaestus (hē·fĕs′təs), god of fire and of metalworking. He has been ordered by Zeus to forge the chains that fasten Prometheus to the rock and to drive an adamantine wedge through his breast. This horrible task he performs reluctantly, bowing only to the superior power of Zeus.

Oceanus (ō·sē′ə·nəs), god of the sea. He comes to sympathize with Prometheus and to preach to him the virtue of hu-

mility. He even offers to intercede on his behalf with Zeus. But Prometheus warns him that, in comforting a rebel, he himself may be charged with rebellion and urges him to depart.

Kratos (Might) and
Bia (Force), brute beings who symbolize the tyranny of Zeus, for they carry out his will. They drag the captive Prometheus to the cliff in Scythia and supervise Hephaestus as he chains the Titan to the rock. Kratos taunts the fallen Titan, reminding him that the name Prometheus—the Contriver—has a terrible irony, for no contrivance can release him.

PROMETHEUS UNBOUND

Author: Percy Bysshe Shelley (1792-1822)
Time of action: Remote antiquity
First published: 1820

PRINCIPAL CHARACTERS

Prometheus, a titan punished by Jupiter for having befriended mankind. He is chained to a rocky cliff for three thousand years while eagles tear at his heart, but he will not repudiate the curse he has pronounced on Jupiter. Aided by spirits and gods, Prometheus is finally unbound. His freedom heralds an age of sweetness and light for mankind.

Jupiter, chief of the gods, who has had Prometheus bound to the cliff. As Prometheus is released, Jupiter loses his power and falls, impotent, into darkness.

Demogorgon, the supreme god and ruler of all gods, who finally reverses prevailing circumstances, thus causing Jupiter's downfall and Prometheus' release from torment.

Panthea and
Ione, two Oceanids. Panthea and Asia, Prometheus' wife, learn from Demogorgon that Prometheus will be set free. They are Demogorgon's interlocutors as

he explains what will come to pass on earth.

Herakles, the hero famous for his strength. Herakles, before spirits friendly to Prometheus, releases the captive from his bonds and torment.

Mercury, the messenger of the gods, sent by Jupiter to Prometheus to learn from the captive how long Jupiter will reign.

Earth, Prometheus' mother.

Asia, Prometheus' wife.

Phantasma of Jupiter, a wraith who appears to Prometheus to repeat for him the forgotten curse he had put on Jupiter.

The Furies, agents of torment who come with Mercury to punish further the bound titan.

The Spirit of the Hour, one of a group of Hours, figures who move in Demogorgon's realm to show the passing of time by Age, Manhood, Youth, Infancy, and

925

Death. The Spirit of the Hour announces Prometheus' release to all mankind and describes the pleasant things that will occur on earth now that the titan is free.

THE PROMISED LAND

Author: Henrik Pontopiddan (1857-1943)
Time of action: Late nineteenth century
First published: 1891-1895

PRINCIPAL CHARACTERS

Emanuel Hansted, a Danish clergyman from the upper classes of Copenhagen who throws in his lot politically with the peasants and their People's Party when he is sent to a rural pastorate. In his efforts to prove himself one of the peasantry he marries a peasant girl and tries to farm an acreage. His efforts to farm are futile, and his rural parishioners see him only as a misfit. Though he is stubbornly sincere, he is a failure. Given a chance to visit with people of his own class, he sees his mistakes and sadly returns to Copenhagen, leaving his wife, but taking his children with him.

Hansine, the minister's peasant wife. She loves her husband and presents him with three children, one of whom dies when the father neglects the child. Hansine, visited by Miss Tonnesen, realizes that her husband is still really an upper-class city man, not a peasant. She tells him he ought to return to the city and that she ought to return to her father's farm.

Miss Tonnesen, Emanuel's former fiancée. She represents all Hansted gives up, and her visit to the rectory persuades both the Hansteds of the minister's mistakes. As the daughter of the former rector in the same parish she is horrified at the run-down condition of the rectory and the extent of Hansted's failure.

Mr. Hansted, Emanuel's father, a well-to-do Conservative. He is happy when his son decides to return to the city and his old home.

Dr. Hassing, a physician in Hansted's parish. He sees the failure of the minister and gives the man an opportunity to be with people from his own class again.

PROSERPINE AND CERES

Author: Unknown
Time of action: Remote antiquity
First transcribed: Unknown

PRINCIPAL CHARACTERS

Typhoeus (tī·fē′əs), a Titan imprisoned under Mt. Aetna. His struggles cause Hades to fear lest the Underworld be exposed to the light of day.

Hades (hā′dēz), ruler of the Underworld. He comes out to inspect the entrance to his realm, sees Proserpine, and falls in love with her. He kidnaps Proserpine and makes her his Queen, partly against her will.

Proserpine (prō·sûr′pə·nē), the daughter of Ceres. She is seized by the enamored Hades and carried off to be Queen of the Underworld. Ceres demands Jupiter's help in recovering her daughter. Jupiter decrees that Proserpine may return to earth provided she has eaten no food in the Underworld. Unfortunately, she has eaten part of a pomegranate so is allowed to spend but half the year with her mother; the other half she must stay with her husband in the Underworld.

Ceres (sē′rēz), the goddess of fertility and the mother of Proserpine. When she cannot find her daughter, she prevents the earth from being fruitful. After her daughter is found and Jupiter decrees that she can spend half the year with her mother, Ceres permits the earth to be fruitful in spring and summer.

Triptolemus (trĭp·tŏ′lə·məs), a mortal child who is saved from death by Ceres. She then teaches him to use the plow. She would have made him immortal if his mother had not interceded. Triptolemus builds a temple to Ceres at Eleusis.

Arethusa (â·rə·thōō′zə), a woodland nymph changed into a fountain by Diana. She tells Ceres that Hades has taken Proserpine to the Underworld.

Jupiter (jōō′pə·tər), King of the gods. He decrees that Proserpine can return to her mother if the girl has eaten nothing in the Underworld. Since the girl has eaten part of a pomegranate a compromise is reached and she is allowed to spend half her time on the earth with her mother.

Venus (vē′nəs), the goddess of Love.

Cupid (kū′pĭd), her son.

Alpheus (ăl·fē′əs), a river-god.

Diana (dī·ăn′ə), the goddess of the hunt.

Mercury (mûr′kyə·rĭ), the messenger of the gods.

PURPLE DUST

Author: Sean O'Casey (1884-   )
Time of action: The present
First presented: 1940

PRINCIPAL CHARACTERS

Cyril Poges and
Basil Stoke, two English gentlemen in love with the past. With a firm conviction that life's real glories all exist in times gone by, and filled with a longing for the joys of country living, they arrive in Ireland with their mistresses, Souhaun and Avril, to take up residence in a decaying old house in the process of being renovated. Their romantic dreams of escape into the pastoral life of bygone days is constantly interrupted by a series of prosaic household crises, unromantic arguments with servants and workmen, misadventures with farm animals and machinery, and the seduction of their mistresses by O'Killigain and one of his fellow workers. Finally, as the river rises during a storm, the two gentlemen, cold, wet, and defeated, take to the roof, longing for good old England.

Souhaun and
Avril, mistresses of Cyril Poges and Basil Stoke. Accompanying the two gentlemen to Ireland to live the country life in a decayed ruin, the ladies are soon disgusted with the discomforts of pastoral living. Beguiled by the poetic Irish charms of O'Killigain and one of his workmen, they run away with the pair.

O'Killigain, the handsome foreman of the workmen engaged in renovating the ancient ruin occupied by Cyril Poges and Basil Stoke. A great believer in the glories of the present, he and one of his workmen exert their Irish charms on Souhaun and Avril and run away with them.

Barney and
Cloyne, the butler and the maid to Cyril Poges and Basil Stoke.

THE PURPLE LAND

Author: W. H. Hudson (1841-1922)
Time of action: Nineteenth century
First published: 1885

PRINCIPAL CHARACTERS

Richard Lamb, a humorous, poetic young adventurer, amateur botanist and wandering seeker of work to support himself and his wife. He briefly and unwillingly joins a revolutionary band, almost loses his life as a result, and at last returns to his wife still unemployed and facing the unpleasant prospect of a meeting with his angry father-in-law.

Paquíta (pä·kē'tä), his olive-skinned, violet-eyed, black-haired Argentinian wife, married without her father's consent.

Doña Isidora (dō'nyä ē·sē·dō'rä), her aunt, a garrulous old woman.

Lucero (lōō·sä'rō), a friendly horse tamer, an old man who still possesses youthful fire and energy in his soul.

Marcos Marcó (mär'kōs mär·kō'), later **General Santa Coloma** (sän'tä kō·lō'mä), a tall, imposing, bronzed man whom Lamb first meets in disguise. He turns out to be a popular Uruguayan revolutionary hero.

Margarita (mär·gä·rē'tä), his beautiful, fair, golden-haired, sapphire-eyed young daughter.

Don Peralta (dōn pä·räl'tä), an insane old landowner and former officer who thinks Lamb is his long-lost son.

Demetria (dā·mä'tryä), his daughter, who wishes to marry Lamb. To save her

from Hilario, Lamb abducts her and takes her to Montevideo.

Don Hilario (dōn ē·lä'ryō), an undersized, serpent-like autocrat, the villainous supervisor of Don Peralta's estate. Demetria hates him.

Santos (sän'tōs), a servant who reveals to Lamb the Peralta family history.

Blas (bläs), also called **Barbudo** (bär·bōō'tħō), an insolent, black-bearded giant stabbed by Lamb in a fight.

Anselmo (än·sĕl'mō), a handsome gaucho, a teller of wandering, pointless tales.

Don Sinforiano Alday (dōn sēn·fō·ryä'nō äl'dä·ē), owner of a large estate.

Monica (mō·nē'kä), his daughter.

Anita (ä·nē'tä), an orphan girl living with the Aldays.

Gandara (gän·dä'rä), a truculent, murderous man whom Lamb shoots before escaping from him.

John Carrickfergus, an amiable expatriate Scotsman who befriends Lamb.

Toribia (tō·rē'byä), a magistrate's wife, a fat slattern who takes an embarrassing liking to Lamb.

Dolores (dō·lō'rās), a beautiful young girl who almost makes Lamb forget Paquíta.

PYGMALION

Author: Bernard Shaw (1856-1950)
Time of action: c. 1900
First presented: 1913

Henry Higgins, a linguistic scientist. A robust, handsome bachelor of forty, Higgins is violently enthusiastic about anything scientific, but he is absolutely uncivilized in his relations with people. Although he firmly believes himself to be kindhearted and considerate, he is a bad-tempered and profane bully. Even so, his frankness and lack of malice make it impossible for anyone to dislike him. Higgins makes a bet with another scientist, Colonel Pickering, that he can, in six months, make a Cockney flower girl speak so well she can be passed off as a duchess.

Eliza Doolittle, the flower girl. Dirty and ignorant, Eliza comes to Higgins and pathetically begs him to teach her to speak well enough to run a respectable flower shop. He teaches her to speak like a noblewoman. Grown fond of Higgins and grateful to him, Eliza tries to please him and is ignored. Higgins thinks it unnatural for Eliza to have feelings. He does not understand why she is enraged when, after she has successfully passed herself off as a noblewoman, he and Pickering congratulate each other and ignore her. To assert herself, Eliza threatens to go into competition with Higgins, using his own methods of teaching proper speech. Higgins rudely congratulates Eliza on her assertiveness and welcomes her as a friend and equal. Eliza marries, not Higgins, but Freddy Hill. They open a flower shop which, with Pickering's help, finally becomes prosperous.

Colonel Pickering, a linguist come to London from India to see Higgins. An elderly, amiable soldier, Pickering is as confirmed a bachelor as Higgins. But he is a gentleman who treats Eliza with respect and helps to moderate Higgins' mistreatment of her.

Alfred Doolittle, a dustman, Eliza's father. One of the "undeserving poor," Doolittle is distinguished by a good voice, an original mind, and a complete absence of conscience. He comes to blackmail Higgins, mistakenly thinking Higgins has taken Eliza as his mistress. Higgins and Pickering are so delighted by the scoundrel's straightforwardness that they give him five pounds. In a letter to Ezra D. Wannafeller, an American philanthropist, Higgins calls Doolittle "the most original moralist" in England. Wannafeller leaves Doolittle £4,000 a year. Doolittle is thus made middle-class, respectable, and, at first, thoroughly unhappy. He even marries his "old woman." Eventually, Doolittle's native talents, his Nietzschean philosophy, and his odd background make him much in demand in the highest society.

Mrs. Higgins, Henry's mother. A woman of taste, she has asked her barbaric son to stay away when she is receiving guests. Her poise and competence help to bring some order into the lives of those around her.

Freddy Eynsford Hill, the uneducated and unintelligent son of an impoverished noble family. He loves Eliza and haunts the street by Higgins' house to catch a glimpse of her. He marries her at last and submits to her benevolent despotism.

Mrs. Eynsford Hill, Freddy's mother. Quiet and well-bred, Mrs. Hill is plagued by the anxieties natural to an aristocrat without money. Because of her poverty, her children have neither education nor sophistication.

Miss Clara Eynsford Hill, Freddy's sister. An ignorant, pretentious, useless snob, Clara is at length redeemed by reading H. G. Wells and becoming a critic of society. In that role her gaucherie is an asset.

Mrs. Pearce, Henry Higgins' housekeeper. Very proper and very middle-class, Mrs. Pearce, by sheer force of will, enforces a semblance of order and propriety in Henry's house.

Nepommuck, a spectacularly bewhiskered Hungarian. At the Embassy reception at which Eliza is passed off as nobility, Nepommuck, a former pupil of Higgins who makes his living as a translator, testifies that Eliza is certainly of royal blood, perhaps a princess.

QUALITY STREET

Author: James M. Barrie (1860-1937)
Time of action: The Napoleonic Wars
First presented: 1902

PRINCIPAL CHARACTERS

Valentine Brown, a doctor who, through poor investments, loses the Throssel sisters' small fortune for them. He disappoints Phoebe Throssel when he goes off to the Napoleonic wars without proposing marriage. Following his military service, during which he became a captain, he returns, minus his left hand, and is amazed by the alteration in Phoebe's appearance after ten years. To Phoebe's discomfiture, he does not conceal his surprise. He learns, however, to appreciate Phoebe and marries her.

Phoebe Throssel, in love with Valentine. When he shows dismay that ten years of schoolteaching have made a drab, mousy woman of her, she dresses as if she were twenty again. Her appearance deceives Captain Brown, and so she maintains a disguise as her own fictitious niece Livvy. Her activities and popularity while in disguise convince Captain Brown that he prefers the more mature, modest, and quiet Phoebe. She accepts his proposal of marriage, and her school is closed.

Susan Throssel, Phoebe's sister. She is retiring and shy, like Phoebe. Both sisters find teaching school difficult, for they detest teaching some subjects, such as Latin and mathematics. They also fear the older boys and dare not punish them.

Ensign Blades, a former student at the Throssel sisters' school. Under duress he asks Phoebe to attend a ball but, her pride hurt, she declines.

Patty, the Throssel sisters' maid. She is the person who discloses the identity of "Livvy" to Valentine Brown.

Livvy, the Throssel sisters' fictitious but pretty young niece, who is really Phoebe in disguise. Captain Brown is completely taken in by the ruse at first, but when Patty at last reveals the secret to him, he has Livvy disappear by taking a makeshift dummy out of town in full view of the snoopy, gossipy neighbors.

THE QUEEN'S NECKLACE

Author: Alexandre Dumas, *père* (1802-1870)
Time of action: Eighteenth century
First published: 1848

PRINCIPAL CHARACTERS

Jeanne de La Motte Valois (zhàn' də là môt' và·lwà'), an impoverished noblewoman who wishes to find favor at the court of Louis XVI. Although she is befriended by the Queen, she plots against the Queen, even to forging documents and hiding a questionable necklace. She puts Marie Antoinette into a situation which makes the Queen appear guilty of adultery and theft.

Marie Antoinette (má·rē' äṅ·twá·nĕt'), Queen of France and the wife of Louis XVI. She is portrayed as a charming, intelligent, and honorable woman. Her enemies victimize her so that she is made to appear an adulteress and a thief. Her enemies are Jeanne de La Motte Valois, Cardinal de Rohan, and Count Cagliostro.

Andrée de Taverney (äṅ·drā' də tá·vĕr·nā'), a woman courtier who is friendly and helpful to the Queen. She becomes jealous, however, when the Count de Charny is favored by Marie Antoinette. Andrée enters a convent.

Philippe de Taverney (fē·lēp' də tá·vĕr·nā'), Andrée's brother, a handsome, pleasant courtier who is helpful to the Queen. He falls in love with Marie Antoinette. Later, he is led to believe sincerely that he has seen Marie Antoinette in questionable circumstances.

Count de Charny (də shár·nē'), a naval officer who is loved by Andrée de Taverney. He is the object of an innocent flirtation by the Queen. He, like other courtiers, is led to believe that he has observed the Queen in questionable circumstances.

Count Cagliostro (kág·lē·ōs'·trō), an Italian adventurer and supposed magician. He uses Oliva, a girl closely resembling Marie Antoinette, to make it appear that the Queen is immoral.

Oliva (ô·lē·vá'), a girl with a strong resemblance to Marie Antoinette. She is used by the Queen's enemies to make it appear that the Queen is immoral, even to being the mistress of Cardinal de Rohan.

Cardinal de Rohan (də rō·äṅ'), a churchman who wants favor at court. He loves Marie Antoinette and believes, thanks to Oliva, that the Queen will take him as a lover. He tries to buy the Queen's favor by purchasing for her a fabulous necklace she admires.

QUENTIN DURWARD

Author: Sir Walter Scott (1771-1832)
Time of action: 1468
First published: 1823

PRINCIPAL CHARACTERS

King Louis XI, sometimes disguised as **Maître Pierre,** a merchant, the wily, able monarch of France, rivaled in power by the hot-headed Duke of Burgundy. Gifted at Machiavellian politics, he schemes to weaken the Duke by placing, through marriage, a hostile nobleman in his territory. His plan in sending Isabelle, Countess de Croye, and her aunt to Liège is to have the outlawed Wild Boar of Ardennes waylay the ladies and marry one of them. Meanwhile he travels to Burgundy to bargain with the Duke and is imprisoned when the Duke learns of the uprising of his vassals at Liège. Louis barely escapes being killed, chiefly through diplomacy and luck. He assists the Duke in recapturing Liège and the two make a temporary truce.

Charles, the Duke of Burgundy, a rash, hasty-handed nobleman with bull-like courage but little intelligence in statecraft. Resentful of the assistance given by King Louis to the young Countess de Croye and her aunt, the Lady Hameline, he disregards the laws of hospitality and imprisons his royal guest. His temper explodes when he learns that the Wild Boar of Ardennes has led a revolt of the citizens of Liège, a city grown mutinous under the Duke's rule. Until his wrath is diverted against the outlaw he is on the verge of killing the King. His anger abates when Louis volunteers to assist him in retaking the city. The Duke vows that he will bestow the hand of the Countess de Croye on the man who will bring him the Wild Boar's head.

Quentin Durward, a stalwart young Scot. Of ancient lineage, he impresses disguised King Louis but later innocently brings the law down on himself when he cuts down the body of a Bohemian hanged by order of the monarch's provost marshal. He joins the Scottish Archers, the King's bodyguard, of which his uncle is a member. After he has shown his bravery by saving the King from a savage boar, he is chosen to escort the Countess de Croye and Lady Hameline, her aunt, to Liège. During the journey he thwarts the attempt of two court gallants to kidnap the Countess and an ambush set by the Wild Boar of Ardennes, and he delivers the ladies safely to the Bishop of Liège. When the Liègeois revolt, Quentin rescues the Countess at great risk to himself. The two are saved by a Burgundian nobleman and taken to the court of the Duke, where Quentin is instrumental in saving the King's life. At the recapture of Liège he fights with great gallantry and wins the Countess as his bride.

Isabelle, the Countess de Croye, a political pawn in the rivalry of King Louis and the Duke of Burgundy. When Quentin sees her first, she is disguised as Jacqueline, a peasant girl. Twice he saves her from the Wild Boar of Ardennes. The angry Duke offers her hand to the man who kills the outlaw. Quentin's uncle kills the Wild Boar but relinquishes his claim on the Countess to his gallant nephew.

Lady Hameline de Croye, the Countess Isabelle's silly, romantic, middle-aged aunt. Taken prisoner by the Wild Boar of Ardennes, she is compelled to marry him as part of his scheme to claim the estates of Croye.

William de la Marck, called **The Wild Boar of Ardennes,** a violent, treacherous outlaw. He attempts to capture the Countess de Croye, murders the Bishop of Liège, and seizes power in the city. He is killed by Ludovic Lesly when the troops of King Louis and the Duke of Burgundy storm Liège and put down the revolt of its citizens.

Ludovic Lesly, called **Le Balafré,** Quentin Durward's uncle, a cavalier in the King's Scottish Archers. He kills the Wild Boar of Ardennes but bestows the Countess de Croye on his nephew in order to perpetuate the family line.

Hayraddin Maugrabin, a Bohemian adventurer, the secret envoy of King Louis, and Quentin Durward's guide while escorting the Countess de Croye and her aunt to Liège. Although indebted to Quentin for cutting down the body of his hanged brother, he nevertheless tries to lead the young Scot into an ambush set by the Wild Boar of Ardennes. He also aids Lady Hameline in her attempt to deceive Quentin by disguising herself as the Countess during the uprising of the Liègeois. Before he is hanged, by order of the Duke of Burgundy, for impersonating a herald, Maugrabin reveals to Quentin the Wild Boar's plan to disguise his followers as French knights in order to create further dissension between the Duke and the King.

Count Philip de Crèvecoeur, the honorable ambassador sent by the Duke of Burgundy to deliver a list of that nobleman's grievances to King Louis. Later he rescues Quentin Durward and the Countess de Croye from pursuit by the Wild Boar of Ardennes and delivers them to the Duke's court.

Louis, Duke of Orleans, the unwilling

prospective husband of King Louis' homely daughter, Joan. He tries to seize the Countess de Croye while she is traveling to Liège in the company of Quentin Durward.

The Count de Dunois, the accomplice of the Duke of Orleans in his attempt to kidnap the Countess de Croye. Dunois is King Louis' most valiant soldier.

Tristan l'Hermite, King Louis' provost marshal, a cruel, stupid ex-monk. He orders Quentin Durward seized and hanged for cutting down the body of Hayraddin Maugrabin's brother.

Oliver le Dain, also called **Oliver le Mauvais** and **Oliver le Diable,** King Louis' barber, groom of the chamber, and trusted adviser. He is a man of unscrupulous cunning.

John, Cardinal of Balue, a traitorous churchman, the secret enemy of King Louis.

Pavillon, the Syndic of Liège. He aids Quentin Durward and the Countess de Croye in their escape from the city after it has been seized by the Wild Boar of Ardennes.

Gertrude Pavillon, his daughter, saved from looting French soldiers by Quentin Durward during the recapture of Liège by French and Burgundian forces.

Louis of Bourbon, the murdered Bishop of Liège, killed by the Wild Boar of Ardennes.

La Glorieux, the impertinent jester of the Duke of Burgundy.

Trois-Eschelles and
Petit André, the cruel hangmen of Tristan l'Hermite.

Carl Eberson, the son of the Wild Boar of Ardennes. Quentin Durward threatens to kill the lad in order to end the outlaw's butchery of his prisoners after the death of the Bishop of Liège.

Toison d'Or, the herald of the Duke of Burgundy. He unmasks Hayraddin Maugrabin who, calling himself Rouge Sanglier, pretends to be a herald dispatched to the Burgundian court by the Wild Boar of Ardennes.

Lord Crawford, the commander of the Scottish Archers, the King's bodyguard.

QUO VADIS?

Author: Henryk Sienkiewicz (1846-1916)
Time of action: c. A.D. 64
First published: 1895

PRINCIPAL CHARACTERS

Petronius (pə·trō'nĭ·əs), a very wealthy Roman patrician who, because of his knowledge of poetry and music, has great influence over Nero. His discriminating taste wins him the title of arbiter of elegance, and he is highly regarded throughout Rome. Petronius tries to help his nephew, Vinitius, win the love of Lygia by having her removed from the home of her foster parents to Nero's palace. Learning that Nero has ordered

his death, Petronius commits suicide by bleeding.

Marcus Vinitius (mär'kəs vĭ·nĭ'shĭ·əs), the nephew of Petronius. A soldier recently on military service abroad, he returns to Rome, where he falls in love with Lygia. After Lygia has been removed to the palace of Nero, Vinitius sees her at a banquet and tries to force his attentions on her. His efforts frighten

Lygia, who flees, and Vinitius begins a search for her.

Aulus Plautius (a′ləs plô′shĭ·əs), an old soldier who had taken part in the conquest of Britain. Lygia is his foster daughter. When she is taken from his house at Nero's command, he tries to have her returned.

Pomponia Graecina (pŏm·pō′nĭ·ə grē-sī′nə), the wife of Aulus Plautius and the foster mother of Lygia. Pomponia, a Christian, has taught Lygia her faith.

Lygia (lĭ′jĭ·ə), the daughter of a barbarian king. After her father's defeat she was sent as hostage to Rome, where she became the foster daughter of a noble Roman family and was converted to Christianity. When she flees from Nero's palace she goes to live in a community of Christians. After Vinitius locates her, she falls in love with him, and through her influence he also becomes a Christian. When Nero starts his persecutions of Christians, Lygia is captured and put in prison. There she becomes ill with a fever and nearly dies. Still not fully recovered, she is tied to the horns of a bull and placed in the arena with her servant Ursus. After Ursus kills the bull, Nero frees them because they have won the favor of the crowd. Lygia and Vinitius are married and go with Ursus to live in Sicily.

Nero (nē′rō), Emperor of Rome. His vanity leads him to seek distinction as a poet and musician. Because Petronius is a connoisseur of fine art, Nero is always eager for his praise. Nero feels that his poetic work, the "Troyad," describing the burning of Troy was not authentic because he had never seen a burning city. At the suggestion of Tigellius he has Rome set afire. Later the Christians are accused of setting the fire and are persecuted as incendiaries.

Chilo Chilonides (kī′lō kī·lŏ′nĭ·dēz), an unscrupulous and money-loving Greek hired by Vinitius to aid in his search for Lygia. Chilo later betrays the Christians to Nero and advances to a high position at court. At last, conscience-stricken, he denounces Nero's wrongdoings, becomes a Christian, and dies a martyr's death.

Poppaea (pŏ·pē′ə), Nero's beautiful but extremely jealous and cruel wife.

Actea (ăk·tē′ə), a Christian freedwoman who formerly had been one of Nero's favorites. Because of her amiability and modesty she is liked by almost everyone. When Lygia is taken to Nero's palace, Actea befriends her.

Ursus (ûr′səs), the gigantic but simple-hearted slave who has served Lygia since her childhood. When Lygia becomes a Christian, Ursus is converted also. He rescues Lygia many times, remains with her while she is in prison, and saves her from death in the arena.

Glaucus (glô′kəs), a Christian physician. Grievously wronged by Chilo, Glaucus forgives him.

Crispus (krĭs′pəs), a stern fanatical Christian who dies on the cross after denouncing Nero.

Tigellinus (tĭ′gə·lī′nəs), a pretorian prefect of Rome who tries to advance his favor with Nero by suggesting that Rome be burnt. He is largely responsible for Petronius' fall from favor and death.

Chrysothemis (krĭ·sŏ′thə·mĭs), a former mistress of Petronius.

Eunice (ū′nĭs), the beautiful slave who becomes the mistress of Petronius. She loves him devotedly and when Petronius falls from favor with Nero and commits suicide, she dies with him.

Miriam (mĭ′rĭ·əm), the Christian woman with whom Lygia lives for a time.

Nazarius (nə·ză′rĭ·əs), Miriam's son.

Seneca (sĕ′nə·kə), a Roman philosopher, Nero's childhood tutor.

Croto (krō′tō), a Roman athlete of superhuman strength, killed by Ursus when he attempts to seize Lygia for Vinitius.

Paul of Tarsus (pôl), a leader among the Christians of Rome until he is condemned to death.

Peter (pē′tĕr), the disciple of Christ who leads the Christians of Rome. After most of the Christians have been killed by Nero, Peter decides to leave the city and seek refuge elsewhere. As he walks out of the city he sees a vision of Jesus. Peter falls on his knees and asks, "Quo vadis, Domine?" (Whither goest Thou, oh Lord?) Jesus replies, "As thou art deserting my people I go to Rome to be crucified for the second time." After Peter hears these words he turns and goes back to Rome, where he works among the Christians until he is arrested and killed.

THE RAINBOW

Author: D. H. Lawrence (1885-1930)
Time of action: Late nineteenth and early twentieth centuries
First published: 1915

PRINCIPAL CHARACTERS

Tom Brangwen, a substantial English farmer. He is a lonely man leading a bachelor's life, driven by his desires to sordid meetings with passing women and to frequent bouts with the brandy bottle, until his marriage to Lydia Lensky, a Polish widow whom he woos in an abrupt but successful courtship that rises above his own usual uncommunicativeness and a language barrier. Tom loves his wife, and he loves Anna, her small daughter. As the years pass Tom becomes a kind of rural patriarch, watching his two sons, Tom and Fred, and Anna, his stepdaughter, grow to maturity and face their own problems of life and love. His good if unremarkable life ends abruptly when he drowns in a sudden flood.

Lydia Lensky, a Polish widow from an aristocratic landowning family. She is a nurse and quite an emancipated woman for her time. Lonely for a man's love and reduced to being a housekeeper in a vicarage, she readily accepts Tom Brangwen as a husband. She becomes a passionate and devoted wife to him and bears him two sons. Although she is happily married, she sometimes misses her old life and keeps up a friendship with Baron Skrebensky, a fellow exile

and an Anglican clergyman. Because her first husband, a Polish doctor, was a man driven by his enthusiasm for various causes all his life, she appreciates all the more the phlegmatic temper of Tom Brangwen and her quiet life with him at Marsh Farm. In their early married state she is more advanced and leads Tom in their love.

Tilly, the Brangwens' cross-eyed housekeeper, a woman with a strong affection for Tom Brangwen. Having been in the household since he was a boy, she had served his father and mother before he took over the farm.

Anna Lensky, Lydia Lensky's daughter by her first husband, a bright young child of four at the time of her mother's second marriage. Forming a deep attachment for her stepfather, she goes with him everywhere and looks on him as a real parent. Anna falls in love with her stepfather's nephew, William Brangwen, and marries him. Until her children come she is a fond wife and eager for love. Later her children become her chief interest, and her husband has no place in her life except as a means to enlarging her matriarchy.

935

William (Will) Brangwen, Tom Brangwen's nephew, a lace designer in a factory. He marries Anna Lensky, who soon comes to dominate his whole existence. After their children are born and he finds her interest centered in them, he turns to all sorts of hobbies connected with religion, for he is a devout person. He uses his artistic talents to renovate the parish church, and he directs the church choir. Before his marriage he had been a sculptor until he learned that his enthusiasm outran his self-discipline and his craft. Years later he takes up sculpture again, only to find that he has lost his imagination after acquiring the necessary craft. He becomes a man driven from his home by his children, and he has little feeling for his offspring, except for his oldest child, Ursula.

Ursula Brangwen, the oldest child of William Brangwen and Anna Lensky. At an early age she helps to take care of the four sisters and the brother added to the family. She and her sister Gudrun are given a good education, after which Ursula becomes a schoolteacher. Not wanting to marry immediately after graduation from high school, she desires a wide vista of life and continually reaches out eagerly for wider, deeper experiences. Dissatisfied with teaching, she goes to college. During her final year of college she takes Anton Skrebensky as her lover. She has loved him many years, during most of which he has been absent in Africa, fighting in the Boer War. During his absence Ursula's one experience in love is an affair with one of her high

school teachers, Miss Inger. Anna wants too much of love and demands too much of Anton Skrebensky, whom she sends away because she finds him spiritually inadequate. While ill with pneumonia she also loses the infant he has fathered. Her vision of the rainbow is a promise of escape from the world of Skrebensky and the world of her parents, divided by love and conflict.

Anton Skrebensky, the son of Baron Skrebensky, a friend of Lydia Brangwen. Young Skrebensky is an intelligent young officer of engineers in the British Army. Although he loves Ursula deeply, he cannot meet her demands for spiritual as well as physical fulfillment. After she sends him away he marries the daughter of his commanding officer. He cannot understand why Ursula wants a college education; as the wife of an officer in India she will not need one. Happy in a life of parties, golf, and riding, he fails to see Ursula's need for knowledge of the world and herself.

Winifred Inger, a schoolteacher with whom Ursula Brangwen has a brief affair. She is a practical, worldly woman and, when she has an opportunity, marries Ursula's well-to-do uncle, Tom Brangwen, who manages a colliery in northern England. She bears her husband a son in exchange for a life of ease and plenty.

Gudrun Brangwen, Ursula's younger sister. A background figure in this novel, she is one of the central characters in "Women in Love."

RAINTREE COUNTY

Author: Ross Lockridge, Jr. (1914-1948)
Time of action: Nineteenth century
First published: 1948

PRINCIPAL CHARACTERS

John Wickliff Shawnessy, a schoolteacher and the philosopher of Raintree County.

On July 4, 1892, he looks back over his life, recalling his boyhood, his youthful

936

loves, his two marriages, his part in the Civil War. He tries to draw out the meaning of his life, his America, from what he remembers. The day ends for him tragicomically, as he is first accused and then exonerated of committing adultery with a local widow.

Senator Garwood B. Jones, John's old friend, who makes a speech at the July Fourth celebration after John introduces him. He is a shrewd, smooth-tongued man without principles.

The Rev. Mr. Shawnessy, John's father, a doctor, a preacher, and a teetotaler.

Mrs. Shawnessy, John's mother, a gentlewoman whom he greatly loves.

Nell Gaither, John's first sweetheart, a combination of hoyden and lady. She becomes the wife of Jones after John is reported dead in the Civil War. She dies in childbirth while still a young woman.

Jerusalem Webster Stiles, the "Perfessor," a cynic and a friend of John. He establishes an academy where he teaches his charges little of the classics, much about seduction. Forced out of town because of attempted adultery, he later becomes a newspaperman in New York. It is he who proves years later that John is not guilty of adultery as charged.

Susanna Drake, John's first wife, a girl of wealth from New Orleans. She is a passionate, emotional creature who becomes demented and burns their house, killing their child. John finds that she is haunted by the fact that her mother was a Negro. Sent back to be cared for by her relatives, she later escapes and disappears.

Esther Root, John's second wife, one of his former pupils. She and her husband elope, returning to the community to rear their family and win a respected place.

Mr. Root, Esther's father. He opposes his daughter's marriage to John on the grounds that the man is an atheist and also a bigamist, since there is no proof that his first wife is truly dead.

RALPH ROISTER DOISTER

Author: Nicholas Udall (1505-1556)
Time of action: Sixteenth century
First presented: c. 1553

PRINCIPAL CHARACTERS

Ralph Roister Doister, a pompous braggart so taken with the idea of his own prowess that he believes no woman can resist him. He is gullible and is an easy prey to the flattery and chicanery of Matthew Merrygreeke. His ridiculous efforts to be a romantic figure and his complete rout by the feminine forces in a pitched battle make him a laughable creation. He is a much-purified adaptation of the braggart soldier in Plautus' "Miles Gloriosus."

Matthew Merrygreeke, a witty parasite. He makes his living by sponging on characters like Ralph, whom he flatters fulsomely for free meals. His flattery, however, is usually mixed with irony. He enjoys stirring up strife. In the pitched battle between Ralph's and the widow's forces, he pretends to be helping Ralph but always misses the widow and lets his blows fall on Ralph.

Dame Christian Custance, a virtuous, humorless widow. Betrothed to Gawin Goodluck, who is away at sea, she is infuriated at Ralph's suit. Her weapons against him do not include the laughter his behavior should arouse, and she is distressed by Gawin Goodluck's questioning about her conduct. After he has been satisfied that she is blameless, she grudgingly consents to allow Ralph to appear in her presence at the feast of general reconciliation and celebration.

Margery Mumblecrust (Madge), Dame Christian's simple-minded nurse. She welcomes Ralph as a suitor of her mistress and greedily accepts his greeting kisses, first wiping her mouth vigorously. She readily agrees to deliver his love letter to her mistress, who scolds her severely for doing so.

Tibet Talkapace and
Annot Alyface, Dame Christian's maids. Ralph is much taken with them and looks forward to having them around the house after he marries Dame Christian. He is much more eager to exchange greeting kisses with them than with toothless Margery; but they do not coöperate. They help out Dobinet Doughty on his mission to deliver love tokens; but after their scolding by their mistress they will have no more of the whole business. Armed with spits and other domestic weapons, they aid in the rout of Ralph and his forces.

Gawin Goodluck, a merchant, betrothed to Dame Christian. Reasonable and good-natured, he listens patiently to Dame Christian's explanation of Sym Suresby's

report and to Tristram Trusty's account of events. He is not angered by Ralph's foolishness and urges Dame Christian to show a charity appropriate to her name. Although he finally persuades her to be courteous to Ralph, he cannot persuade her to suffer him gladly.

Sym Suresby, Gawin's loyal servant. He seems as serious as Dame Christian and misinterprets her relations with Ralph. His report to Gawin disturbs the latter and causes some difficulties.

Tristram Trusty, the reliable friend of Gawin and Dame Christian. His trusted judgment and his report of the true situation, at Dame Christian's entreaty, relieve Gawin's mind and lead to the happy reconciliation.

Dobinet Doughty, Ralph's servant-boy. He acts as Ralph's emissary to Dame Christian's house and for a time gains the confidence of Tibet Talkapace and Annot Alyface. He is one of Ralph's defeated warriors in the assault on Dame Christian's house.

Harpax, Ralph's servant. He is one of Ralph's small defeated army.

A Scrivener, who writes Ralph's letter to Dame Christian. After its unfortunate misreading and hostile reception, he and Ralph quarrel.

THE RAMAYANA

Author: Valmiki (fl. fourth century B.C.)
Time of action: Remote antiquity
First transcribed: c. 350 B.C.

PRINCIPAL CHARACTERS

Rama, King Dasa-ratha's son, partly an incarnation of Vishnu. The handsomest and strongest of the King's four sons, he wins Sita for his bride by bending the mighty bow of King Janak. Though his aging father wishes him to become regent, he is forced by Queen Kaikeyi into

a fourteen-year exile, from which he finally returns triumphant to his throne.

Sita, Rama's wife, daughter of King Janak and the Earth Mother. She accompanies her husband into exile and is abducted by Ravan. Although she manages to remain faithful to Rama during her captivity, rumors of unfaithfulness are spread abroad and believed by her husband and the people. Finally her virtue is proved, but the Earth Mother takes her away from those who have doubted her.

Dasa-ratha, Rama's father, King of the Kosalas, who wishes his son to be regent but must send him, instead, into exile because of an old promise made to Queen Kaikeyi.

Queen Kaikeyi, one of King Dasa-ratha's wives and the mother of Bharat. Promised two boons by her husband, she asks that Rama be sent into exile and that Bharat be made regent.

Bharat, Rama's half brother. Though forced into the regency by Queen Kaikeyi, he recognizes Rama's claim to the throne, which he holds for him.

Lakshman, Rama's loyal brother and companion during his exile.

Satrughna, another of Rama's half brothers.

Mandavi,
Urmila, and
Sruta-kriti, Rama's sisters-in-law.

King Janak, Sita's father, who offers her as a bride to the one who bends his mighty bow.

The Earth Mother, Sita's mother, who takes her daughter back among the gods when her virtue is questioned by Rama and his people.

Ravan, Demon King of Lanka. He abducts Sita but is finally overthrown by Rama.

Bharad-vaja,
Valmiki, and
Agastya, hermits and holy men.

Hanuman, a leader of the monkey people.

Manthara, Queen Kaikeyi's maid.

RAMEAU'S NEPHEW

Author: Denis Diderot (1713-1784)
Time of action: 1761
First published: In German, translated by Goethe, 1805; in French, 1823

PRINCIPAL CHARACTERS

Rameau, the nephew of Jean Philippe Rameau, a French composer.

Diderot, the author, French encyclopedist, and writer, a principal in a dialogue carried on at the Regency Café in Paris. Although the two men are actual persons and the ideas they express are, in all probability their own, the conversation is, nonetheless, a product of the author's imagination and is, therefore, fictional. Rameau enters the Regency and there engages, with Diderot, in a dialogue that ranges over leading figures of eighteenth century France, particularly writers, musicians, politicians, and critics. Also, the conversation is a critique of manners and morals in which Diderot, the moralist and man of ideas, opposes Rameau, the man of passion. In the course of the conversation each speaker is able to arouse in the other a sympathy for ideas other than his own, so that the dialogue becomes a skillful attempt to do justice to both sides of man's nature, the moral and the animal.

THE RAPE OF LUCRECE

Author: William Shakespeare (1564-1616)
Time of action: 500 B.C.
First published: 1594

PRINCIPAL CHARACTERS

Sextus Tarquinius (Tarquin) (sĕx′təs tär·kwĭ′nĭ·əs tär′kwĭn), the son of the King of Rome. Friend and fellow warrior of Collatine, he hears from the latter of the chastity of his beautiful wife Lucrece and is seized with illicit desire. Like Faustus, he is the allegorical battleground of a good and an evil influence. His good side and his evil side engage in debate, and the evil triumphs. He is hypocritical, sly, and ruthless. Part of the joy in his brutal conquest of the chaste wife stems from sheer cruelty. After his violation of Lucrece, he suffers revulsion and slinks away in the night.

Lucrece (loō·krēs′), the chaste wife of Collatine. Devoted to her husband, she welcomes his friend as a trusted guest. When she is helpless in Tarquin's clutches, she uses all her intelligence and persuasiveness to try to save herself from him and him from himself, but in vain. After the event, she too becomes the battleground for internal debate: she is uncertain as to whether she should kill herself without telling her husband of what she considers her dishonor or to tell him all that has happened. She feels guilt in that her fear may have kept her from using all defenses possible against the ravisher. After her decision to speak, she sends for Collatine and other Roman leaders, wears mourning to welcome them, tells her story in full, and stabs herself.

Collatinus (Collatine) (kō·lə·tī′nəs; kō′-lə·tīn), a noble Roman warrior. He is stunned at Lucrece's narrative and suicide; then frantic with grief; then fiercely angry and determined to avenge her. He becomes an eager participant in the overthrow and banishment of the Tarquins (who are referred to very briefly in the final stanza of the poem). Junius Brutus, who uses Lucrece's body and the dagger stained with her blood to foment the revolution, accomplishes the overthrow.

THE RAPE OF THE LOCK

Author: Alexander Pope (1688-1744)
Time of action: Early eighteenth century
First published: 1712

PRINCIPAL CHARACTERS

Belinda, the poetic name of Arabella Fermor, an upper-class English girl. She is a beautiful young woman and vain of her appearance. Though she is a sweet society girl who loves her spaniel and is normally quite agreeable, she flies into a horrid rage when Lord Petre snips off one of her treasured curls.

Lord Petre, a young nobleman, one of Belinda's suitors. He admires Belinda so much that he wants one of her curls as a keepsake and snips it off at a party when she bends her head over a cup. He refuses to return the curl, and it disappears to become a star.

Ariel, Belinda's guardian spirit. He tries to warn her that something dreadful may happen and sets a guard of sylphs to protect his charge, but he is unsuccessful in preventing the loss of the lock of hair.

Umbriel, a spirit who takes over when Ariel leaves Belinda. He is a melancholy gnome who receives horrible noises, tears, sorrows, and griefs from the queen of bad tempers. He pours his magic substances over Belinda, magnifying her rage and sorrow.

Thalestris, Belinda's friend, a militant girl. She fans Belinda's rage by saying that the girl's honor is at stake in the matter of the stolen curl. She demands that Belinda's brother force Lord Petre to give up the lock.

Clarissa, one of Belinda's acquaintances, who wonders openly at the vanity of women and the foolishness of men.

Sir Plume, Belinda's brother, who considers the entire affair slightly ridiculous. Prodded by Thalestris, he demands that Lord Petre relinquish the lock, but Petre refuses.

Shock, Belinda's beloved spaniel.

Spleen, the queen of bad tempers and the source of detestable qualities in human beings. She supplies Umbriel with magic substances.

Betty, Belinda's maid.

RASSELAS

Author: Samuel Johnson (1709-1794)
Time of action: Eighteenth century
First published: 1759

PRINCIPAL CHARACTERS

Rasselas (răs′ə·ləs), fourth son of the King of Abyssinia. Like his brothers and sisters, he is reared in the luxury of Happy Valley, a remote mountain-rimmed vale whose only entrance is closed by a guarded gate. The royal children live a life of pleasure and entertainment, which everyone but Rasselas finds sufficient. In his twenty-sixth year he finds his mind unchallenged by this life of pleasure, in which every want is met or anticipated. Feeling that he is something more than a beast of the field, content with sensory pleasure, he lives with his uneasiness until at last he plans to escape into the outer world where, as he hopes, he can exercise his choice of life. With a few companions he finally reaches the outer world and there questions many persons in the hope of learning how to live a contented life. Though he travels great distances and talks with many people, he can find no easy solution to his problems. Everyone seems unhappy with his state. Rasselas begins to dream of establishing a little kingdom, a Utopia, which he can rule with justice; but he finally realizes that such an ideal can never be reached, and he decides to return to Abyssinia.

Nekayah (nĕk·ä′yâh), one of Rasselas sisters, who is invited to join in hei brother's escape. Nekayah proves a happy choice as a companion for Rasselas, for she is an intelligent and observant young woman. She takes the lower classes for her special field of study, in hopes of learning how human beings may be happy. Her observations, particularly of domestic life, provide her and Rasselas with much material for thought and discussion. Nekayah finally forms the opinion that knowledge is the key to human happiness. To this end she makes plans to learn all the sciences and then to establish a college or community of learned women, over which she will preside.

Imlac (ĭm′lăk′), the son of a merchant.

941

Given a chance to travel by his father, Imlac has seen much of the world, both Europe and Asia. After fourteen years of travel he returns home to find his family dispersed and his fortune gone. Becoming a poet, he seeks to enter Happy Valley and succeeds. He realizes, however, that life in the valley is not sufficient for him. When he finds a fellow rebellious spirit in Rasselas, he offers himself as guide and mentor to the young Prince. After emerging from the valley to the outer world Imlac finds that the only answer to happy life is no answer, and so he becomes content to follow life wherever it may lead him.

An Astronomer, a man Rasselas and his companions meet in Egypt, where he joins their party. His devotion to astronomy has convinced him that he controls all the elements except the winds. After he is introduced to Nekayah and the rest of the little band of searchers after wisdom and happiness, the astronomer discovers that life has more in it than the study of the heavens, and he loses his beliefs. Like Imlac, he becomes satisfied with whatever life may bring to him.

A Mechanist, one of the inhabitants of Happy Valley. He tries to invent wings for man to fly. Rasselas, anxious to escape his valley prison, is quite interested in the man's experiments until the efforts prove entirely futile.

Pekuah (pek′ōō·â), one of the noble ladies attending Princess Nekayah, and another of the escapees from Happy Valley. She has an extraordinary adventure, being kidnaped by Arabs and held for ransom. She bears this trying experience with fortitude and returns to her friends to report that Bedouin life is not a happy one for either men or women.

A Philosopher, whom Rasselas seeks out in Egypt. He seems at first to be both wise and happy. His life proves empty, however, as does his logic, when his only child, a beautiful daughter, is taken suddenly by death.

A Hermit, another of the seemingly wise and happy souls sought out by Rasselas. The hermit, at one time a military officer of high rank, renounced his worldly career to seek happiness in a hermitage. He admits to Rasselas that his life is not a happy one, and he returns with Rasselas to the society of Cairo.

An Old Man, whom Rasselas and Nekayah consult. They visit him to learn if old age is the key to happiness. They are told that it is not; the old man finds neither solace nor pleasure in having outlived his friends and rivals, as well as his capacity to work or hold office.

RAVENSHOE

Author: Henry Kingsley (1830-1876)
Time of action: Early nineteenth century
First published: 1862

PRINCIPAL CHARACTERS

Father Mackworth, the resident priest at Ravenshoe, who engages in nefarious schemes to prevent Ravenshoe from becoming the property of a Protestant heir. He dies after confessing his plots and begging forgiveness of the heir he has dispossessed.

Charles Ravenshoe, the second son of Densil Ravenshoe and his Protestant wife. When Charles' mother dies in childbirth, Densil promises her that her son will be reared as a Protestant. He is reared by Norah, the gamekeeper's wife, along with her own son, William. In

942

order to prevent Charles from inheriting Ravenshoe, Father Mackworth says that Norah switched the babies in her care and that William, a Catholic, is the true heir. Charles then becomes a servant and later enlists in the army to fight in the Crimea, where he is wounded. Charles finally learns that he is the true heir to Ravenshoe. He then marries and shows great leniency to William.

Densil Ravenshoe, Charles' father, who as a young man goes off to London and falls in with Lord Saltire, an atheist. He finally returns to the Church, but marries a Protestant woman.

Adelaide Summers, the ward of Lady Ascot. Charles falls in love with Adelaide but she runs away with Lord Welter, Charles' cousin. She is a vain young woman and not worthy of Charles' love.

Lord Welter, Charles' cousin, a wild and dissolute young man with whom Charles carouses when they are both at Oxford. He becomes Adelaide's lover and she and Welter live by gambling. Eventually they are married.

Mary Corby, the daughter of the captain

of a ship that goes down in the bay at Ravenshoe, leaving her an orphan. A good and sweet girl, she becomes the ward of the Ravenshoes. She falls in love with Charles and eventually marries him.

William Horton, Norah's son, who is reared with Charles. Father Mackworth says that William is the true heir to Ravenshoe and William takes over the estate when Cuthbert, the elder son, dies. In the end, William and Charles are good friends.

Lord Saltire, an atheist and a good friend of Densil Ravenshoe. Later he meets Charles and becomes fond of him. When Lord Saltire dies, he leaves a large sum to Mary. Thinking that Charles has died in the Crimea, he leaves the rest of his fortune to Lord Welter and Adelaide.

Cuthbert Ravenshoe, Densil's elder son, reared a Catholic. He dies by drowning.

Ellen Horton, William's sister who, it later turns out, is really Charles' sister. Ellen runs away to become a nun, taking with her the evidence that Charles is truly the heir of Ravenshoe. She later produces this evidence and then returns to her nursing duties.

REBECCA

Author: Daphne du Maurier (1907-   )
Time of action: The 1930's
First published: 1938

PRINCIPAL CHARACTERS

Maximilian (Maxim) de Winter, middle-aged owner of Manderley. He is detached, moody, mysterious, at times gracious, friendly, and apologetic for his seeming rudeness, only to return unaccountably to his reserve. This reserve is finally removed with the lifting of the burden on his conscience.

Mrs. de Winter, Maxim's young wife and the narrator. A shy, sensitive orphan, she

first meets Maxim through her older traveling companion Mrs. Van Hopper. Deeply in love with him, she happily accepts his proposal and marries him. Puzzled and troubled by Maxim's strange shifts of mood and his abstracted manner and by Mrs. Danvers' obvious dislike, she thinks herself unwelcome, an inferior successor to Rebecca at Manderley. Desiring Maxim's love, she yet remains aloof because of her brooding

943

insecurity and thus hinders his revealing his painful memories to her.

[Rebecca de Winter, Maxim's dead wife, a very beautiful woman who charmed many people but who tortured her husband with flagrant infidelities. When she learned that she would soon die of cancer, she taunted her husband with a false story of her unborn child by another man until she drove him to murder her.]

Mrs. Danvers, the housekeeper at Manderley. Tall, gaunt, with a face like a death's head, she is cold, formal, and resentful of the new Mrs. de Winter who has replaced the Rebecca she adored. She is the first to reveal to Mrs. de Winter what Rebecca really was like with men. After the closing of the inquiry into Rebecca's death, Mrs. Danvers apparently sets fire to Manderley and disappears.

Frank Crawley, estate manager at Manderley. A thin, colorless bachelor, he is a devoted friend of Maxim.

Jack Favell, Rebecca's cousin, tanned and good looking, but flashy, with hot, blue eyes and a loose mouth. He is a heavy drinker who attempts to blackmail Maxim after the discovery of Rebecca's sunken boat.

Colonel Julyan, a magistrate who suspects the truth about Rebecca's death but keeps it to himself.

Mrs. Van Hopper, an overbearing American social climber who forces herself upon Maxim at Monte Carlo.

Beatrice Lacy, Maxim's sister, tall, broadshouldered, handsome, tweedy, inquisitive, blunt, and chatty.

Major Giles Lacy, Beatrice's fat and genial husband.

Dr. Baker, a London physician visited by Rebecca (under Mrs. Danvers' name) the day of her death. He reports that she was dying of cancer, though she appeared in good health.

Frith, Maxim's elderly butler.

Clarice, Mrs. de Winter's young maid.

Ben, a simple-minded old man.

THE REBEL GENERATION

Author: George Farquhar (1678-1707)
Time of action: Early eighteenth century
First published: 1925

PRINCIPAL CHARACTERS

Louis Cornvelt, an upper middle-class Hollander. An ultra-conservative, orthodox Calvinist, he expects from his family complete adherence to his way of life and submission to his will.

Katie Cornvelt,
Nicholas Cornvelt,
Sarah Cornvelt, and
David Cornvelt, Louis Cornvelt's children. After a brief youthful rebellion, each finds himself too accustomed to parental domination to break the habit of obedience, and finally bows submissively to the father's will.

Marie Elizabeth Sylvain (Lysbeth, "Sylvia"), Louis Cornvelt's orphaned niece, who comes to live in her uncle's home. She brings new ideas which inspire Louis' children to a brief rebellion. When her uncle refuses to allow her to earn a living, she runs away to France. Later, with an inherited fortune, she returns to Holland to work for the emancipation of women.

Doctor William Wiseman, Katie Cornvelt's husband, whom she marries in obedience to her father's will, even though the young doctor is repugnant to her.

Doctor Eliza Wiseman, the daughter of Katie Cornvelt and William Wiseman. She scandalizes her parents by wishing to become a doctor and receives help and encouragement from Marie Elizabeth Sylvain.

Louis Cornvelt, David Cornvelt's rebellious son, a political radical.

Clara Cornvelt, David Cornvelt's daughter, who gives in to her father in matters of love, though she persists in continuing as a social worker among the lowest classes.

Stephen Cornvelt, Dr. Eliza Wiseman's nephew. Infatuated with Millicent Corn-

velt, he asks his wife Dorothy for a divorce.

Dorothy Cornvelt, Stephen Cornvelt's wife. A lawyer and member of Parliament, her life is empty because of her family's indifference to her success and her husband's infatuation with Millicent Cornvelt.

Millicent Cornvelt, the great-granddaughter of Louis Cornvelt, Sr.

Kitty and
Puck Cornvelt, the daughters of Stephen and Dorothy Cornvelt, who are unhappy in the insecurity of their unstable home.

THE RECRUITING OFFICER

Author: George Farquhar (1678-1707)
Time of action: Early eighteenth century
First presented: 1706

PRINCIPAL CHARACTERS

Captain Plume, a recruiting officer in the Queen's army, who comes into Shrewsbury to recruit for a French campaign. His chief endeavor, however, is winning Sylvia Balance for his wife. Blatant and ribald, he declares he will not marry, to spend his entire life with a woman, until he knows premaritally whether he will like her company for half an hour. Winning Sylvia after trickery against him has failed, he quits the service to raise recruits in a matrimonial way. His men's conduct in the town is well described by the accusation that they leave as many recruits in a town as they take away.

Sergeant Kite, his sergeant. He tries to lure recruits by offers of money and gay living. Ineffectual in these efforts, he disguises himself as a conjurer, predicting for men brilliant futures, according to their vocations, if they will enlist. Through his "predictions," he also brings the principals of the play together, foretelling the plot. Kite procures other enlistments as he cajoles the justices in

court to declare men needy, without means of support, and therefore wards of the Crown.

Sylvia Balance, a young woman who spends the greater part of the play dressed as a man, young Mr. Willful. Suspecting Plume of being attentive to Rose, Sylvia, disguised as a recruit, courts Rose to learn of Plume's relations with other women. She learns that Plume is not the philanderer he is reputed to be. As a result she disregards her father's admonition to break off with Plume and becomes his wife. Her handsome income is no small factor in Plume's love for her.

Melinda, Sylvia's cousin, a lady of fortune. She adds to the plot with her bemeaning attitude toward Sylvia and by her attractiveness to Brazen and Worthy. Melinda's ill temper causes her to be suspected of writing letters to Sylvia's father, maligning Plume. Melinda's comment that the confounded captains do more harm by debauching at home than they

945

do good by their defenses abroad epitomizes the tone of the play.

Mr. Worthy, a gentleman of Shropshire, who wins Melinda. Never sure of Melinda's temperament at a given time, Worthy assumes she is in love with Brazen. Easily influenced, Worthy takes Plume's advice to win Melinda's affections by ignoring her. The ensuing misunderstandings make for some rollicking scenes of dispute before Worthy succeeds with Melinda.

Captain Brazen, one of the recruiting officers, whose name fits him well. An arrogant coxcomb, his sole goal in life is woman or women. Impetuous, he approaches any woman familiarly and is undaunted by her resistance. Plume, who sides with Mr. Worthy in the contest for Melinda, sends Brazen packing with the twenty recruits raised by Kite, and without the benefit of Melinda's twenty thousand pounds, which Brazen hoped to gain along with Melinda's hand.

Rose, a pretty, buxom country girl, who is taken in by Sylvia's disguise as a soldier. Caught in the middle in more than one piece of chicanery, Rose is finally taken as Sylvia's charge, at Plume's suggestion. Sylvia assumes the responsibility, telling Plume that she will take care of Rose, because Plume will have job enough to take care of a wife.

Bullock, Rose's oafish brother. He sells grains in the market as Rose sells poultry. Bullock is the butt of many a bawdy joke; his commonness, however, is little different from the sensual behavior of the other, better-bred men. Naïve and bold, Bullock, having become a recruit, has the last word with Plume, telling him that he will desert if he is ever mistreated.

Lucy, Melinda's maid, actively involved in the forgeries that sustain the plot. Finding papers with Melinda's signature, Lucy writes to Brazen, criticizing Worthy. Lucy stops the duel, between Brazen and Worthy, instigated by the letters.

Costar Pearmain and
Thomas Appletree, two recruits who resist Kite's appeals to honor and patriotism, only to be tricked into the army. Kite hands them coins, saying that they are pictures of the Queen. When the two bumpkins plead with Plume, claiming they have not enlisted, Kite tells the Captain that the two men have accepted money from him, implying payment for going into the service.

Justice Balance, Sylvia's father and a justice of the peace. He sits in judgment on the men brought in as vagrants and whom Kite would have as recruits. Among those appearing before him is Sylvia, in her brother's uniform. Balance recognizes Sylvia, shows his recognition indirectly by telling her that she should go home to her father, and gives her to Plume in marriage.

Justice Scruple and
Justice Scale, justices of the peace who add to the burlesque of the country courts by their inane handling of cases.

A Constable, who brings Kite before the justices. He is introduced to point up the treatment civil authorities suffer at the hands of the military at a time of recruitment. Kite goes unpunished for his misdemeanors; the Constable is sentenced to get four recruits for Plume or to enlist himself.

Pluck, a country butcher. Kite, impersonating a conjurer, tells Pluck that he will be surgeon-general of the Queen's army for his part in the battle of Flanders.

Thomas, a smith in Shropshire, who Kite predicts will be made captain of the forges in the grand train of artillery. In his soothsaying, Kite advises these two men that they will, in a given time, be approached by gentlemen who will lead them to their good fortunes. The gentlemen are, of course, Kite's accomplices in recruiting.

THE RED AND THE BLACK

Author: Stendhal (Marie-Henri Beyle, 1783-1842)
Time of action: Early nineteenth century
First published: 1830

PRINCIPAL CHARACTERS

Julien Sorel (zhü-lyăn′ sô·rĕl′), a son of a lawyer but an opportunist whose brilliant intellect, great ambition, and self-pride elevate him for a time, only to defeat him in the end. The youthful protégé of a local priest in the French town of Verières, Julien becomes the beloved tutor of the mayor's children and the lover of that aristocratic official's wife. Brazen, hypocritical, but shrewd, this contradictory hero espouses Napoleonic sentiments yet believes that his own salvation is through the Church. Pushed by scandal into a seminary, he proudly stands aloof from its politics and manages to become a secretary to one of the first men in France. Though he is insensitive to all feelings, his intellect again raises him in esteem to the point where he seduces as well as is seduced by the nobleman's daughter, a lively, intellectual young woman. Playing both ends against the middle—the middle being a respected position and a respectable income—he brings about his own downfall through attempted murder of his first mistress after she has revealed his villainy to his noble benefactor.

Madame de Rênal (də rĕ·nȧl′), Julien Sorel's first mistress and greatest love, a beautiful, compassionate, though bigoted woman. Although she vacillates always between religiosity and passion, she truly loves the ascetic-looking younger man and dies shortly after he has been executed for his attempt to kill her. Her allegiance to the tutor is the more remarkable because of her clever deceptions, necessary to prevent an immediate tragedy brought about by her husband's vindictiveness. In the end religiosity predominates; she is torn by anguish, remorse, and guilt and dies while embracing her children three days after the death of her lover.

M. de Rênal (mə·syœ′ də rĕ·nȧl′), the miserly mayor and village aristocrat, who desperately seeks status by hiring a tutor for his children. Vulgar and greedy to an extreme degree, this boorish landowner is elevated by the Marquis de La Mole, who later became Julien's employer. He loses his wife to a commoner's love and his position to his republican enemy.

Mathilde de La Mole (mȧ·tēld′ də lȧ môl′), a proud, intelligent aristocrat destined to become a duchess but fated to love out of her class. Desirous of the unexpected and bored with the conventionality of her life, she at first seeks distraction in love-making with Julien Sorel. When he pretends boredom, she pursues him shamelessly. Her pregnancy sets off a chain of tragic events which will leave her unborn child without name or father. After Julien's execution her romantic nature causes her to initiate the deed of a famous ancestress; she buries her lover's head with her own hands and decorates his cave tomb with marble so that it resembles a shrine.

The Marquis de La Mole (də lȧ môl′), a peer of France and the wealthiest landowner in the province. He is a subtle, learned aristocrat who through caprice gambles on a young man's genius, through kindness makes a gentleman of him, and through pride in family negotiates his downfall. Although he admires his brilliant secretary, the Marquis can never rid himself of his social ambitions for his beautiful and intelligent daughter, and to bring about Julien Sorel's downfall he conspires to gain incriminating evidence against the young man.

The Marquise de La Mole, an aristocrat proud of her noble ancestors.

The Comte de La Mole, their son, a pleasant young man conditioned to fashionable Parisian life, in which ideas are neither encouraged nor discussed.

Fouqué (foo·kā′), a bourgeois but devoted friend of Julien Sorel. Acting as ballast for his mercurial friend, he offers Julien a good position in his lumber business, financial support for his studies, and finally his whole fortune to free him after his arrest.

The Abbé Chélan (shä·län′), the local parish priest, who teaches and advances the fortune of Julien Sorel. The first to discover the tragic duality of his protégé's nature, he nevertheless supports him in

his ambitions and grieves over his misadventures.

The Abbé Pirard (pē·rȧr′), the director of the seminary at Besançon, where Julien Sorel studies. He obtains for his brilliant pupil the post of secretary to the Marquis de La Mole. An irascible Jansenist among Jesuits, this learned priest sees in Sorel genius and contradiction. In spite of these contradictions, Pirard helps to elevate the youth to the munificence of courtly Paris.

M. Valenod (vȧ·lᴏ·nō′), a provincial official grown prosperous on graft. Jealous because M. de Rênal has hired a tutor for his children and because his own advances to Madame de Rênal have been unsuccessful, he writes an anonymous letter which reveals the love affair between Julien Sorel and his employer's wife.

THE RED BADGE OF COURAGE

Author: Stephen Crane (1871-1900)
Time of action: The Civil War
First published: 1895

PRINCIPAL CHARACTERS

Henry Fleming, a young recruit under fire for the first time in an unnamed battle of the Civil War, possibly Chancellorsville. A farm boy whose struggle with his emotions might be that of the eternal recruit in any battle of any war, Henry has dreamed of fighting heroically in "Greeklike" battles. Irritated and unnerved by his regiment's inactivity, he tortures himself with the fear that he may run away when the actual firing begins. He does so. Sheepishly rejoining his regiment, he learns that his cowardice is not known to his fellow soldiers. In the next attack he keeps firing after the others have stopped. When a color-bearer falls, he picks up the flag and carries it forward. Later he hears that the colonel has complimented his fierceness. Henry's psychological battle with himself is now

ended; it has gone from fear to cowardice to bravery and, finally, to egotism.

Jim Conklin, "the tall soldier," a veteran who comforts Henry and squabbles with the braggart Wilson. He predicts that the regiment is about to move into battle. When it does so, he is mortally wounded. Henry and "the tattered man" find him stumbling to the rear, still on his feet, fearful of falling under the wheels of an artillery wagon. He wanders into a field, as if it were a place of rendezvous with death. Henry and the tattered man follow him, trying to bring him back. He brushes them off and, with a great convulsion, drops dead.

Wilson, "the loud one." At first he seems confident, absolutely sure of his courage. But as the battle begins he suddenly thinks he may be killed, and he turns a packet of letters over to Henry Fleming. After the first attack he asks for the return of the letters. Some of his loudness and swagger is now gone. He and Henry struggle to get the flag from the fallen color-bearer. Henry seizes it, but Wilson aids him in going forward and setting an example to the wavering troops.

"The Tattered Man," a soldier encountered by Henry Fleming just after he has run away. The man embarrasses the recruit by asking where he is wounded. Later he and Henry follow Jim Conklin into the field. The soldier is so impressed by the manner of Jim's death that he calls the dead man a "jim-dandy." Then he cautions Henry to "watch out fer ol' number one."

Lieutenant Hasbrouck, a young officer of Henry Fleming's company. He is shot in the hand in the early part of the battle but is able to drive a fleeing soldier back into the ranks and tries vainly to stop the disorganized retreat. He later compliments Henry and Wilson by calling them "wild cats."

Colonel MacChesnay, the officer who also compliments Henry Fleming and Wilson. He is berated by the general, shortly after Henry's advance with the flag, for not forcing the partial success of the charge to a complete one.

THE RED ROOM

Author: August Strindberg (1849-1912)
Time of action: The 1870's
First published: 1879

PRINCIPAL CHARACTERS

Arvid Falk, a would-be poet. Unable to find a publisher for his poems, he takes a job on a newspaper. His poems are finally published, and he becomes, to all appearances, a successful journalist. Disillusioned, however, because he is never allowed to report the news honestly as he sees it, he moves from paper to paper and eventually suffers a mental breakdown. After his recovery, he becomes a conventional schoolmaster and marries a schoolmistress.

Charles Nicholas Falk, Arvid Falk's brother. A businessman, he emerges unscathed from a financial disaster to go on to further material successes.

Mrs. Charles Nicholas Falk, Charles Nicholas Falk's self-indulgent, socially ambitious young wife.

Levin, a clerk, and
Nyström, a schoolmaster, fawning cronies of Charles Nicholas Falk.

Sellén, a painter. For reasons having nothing to do with art, he becomes celebrated as a painter and, to all appearances, a highly successful young man.

Lundell, a practical painter who earns money by illustrating magazines.

Rehnhjelm, a young man who ardently desires to be an actor. As a member of a theatrical company, he falls idealistically in love with Agnes. When he learns that she is Falander's mistress he threatens suicide, but he recovers from the affair and returns to the security of his wealthy family.

Olle Montanus, a philosopher and sculptor. Finally, unable to work except as a stone mason, he takes his own life.

Ygberg, a philosopher who argues with the artists and writers in the Red Room.

Falander, an elderly fellow actor of Rehnhjelm and Agnes' lover.

949

Borg, a cynical young doctor who is Arvid Falk's friend and benefactor. Expecting nothing from life, he alone remains unchanged among the changing fortunes and ideals of Arvid's friends and associates.

Agnes (Beda Petterson), who, as Agnes,

a sixteen-year-old ingénue and the mistress of Falander, inspires the idealistic love of Rehnhjelm. As Beda Petterson, a worker in a Stockholm café, she is loved by Arvid Falk.

Smith, a publisher.

Struve, a journalist.

THE RED ROVER

Author: James Fenimore Cooper (1789-1851)
Time of action: Mid-eighteenth century
First published: 1827

PRINCIPAL CHARACTERS

The Red Rover, a pirate who is really a good man in many ways. He saves the lives of Harry Wilder, Dick Fid, and Scipio Africa when his crew demands their deaths. Later he fights for the colonists' cause in the American Revolution against the British. Just before his death it is revealed that he is the long-lost uncle of Harry Wilder, and a patriot. His pirate ship is the "Dolphin."

Harry Wilder (Henry Ark, Henry de Lacy), a young British naval officer who is sent on a secret mission to capture the Red Rover. He is a brave young man who makes his way into the pirates' confidence, but he is unsuccessful in capturing the men. While a prisoner of the Red Rover, after a sea battle, Harry Wilder's identity as Henry Ark, a naval officer, is revealed. Then unexpectedly he is discovered to be really Henry de Lacy, the long-lost son of Paul de Lacy and Mrs. Wyllys.

Gertrude Grayson, daughter of a British general. She is befriended by Harry, who tries to warn her against traveling aboard the "Royal Caroline," for he knows that the ship is slated to be a victim of the Red Rover.

Mrs. Wyllys, governess and companion to Gertrude Grayson. Mrs. Wyllys is finally revealed to be the mother of Harry Wilder. She has thought her child, born of a secret marriage to Paul de Lacy, dead for many years. She pleads for her newly found son's life before the Red Rover when the young man is revealed as a spy against the pirates. She succeeds in her pleas, and it is later learned that the Red Rover is really Mrs. Wyllys' long-lost brother.

Dick Fid, a sailor and faithful friend of Harry Wilder. He found Wilder as a baby aboard an abandoned ship at sea.

Scipio Africa, a Negro sailor. He is Dick Fid's companion and helps rear Harry after the latter was found as a baby at sea.

Captain Bignall, commanding officer of the "Dart," a British warship sent after the Red Rover. He is Harry's superior officer. The captain is killed and his ship captured in a battle with the "Dolphin," the Red Rover's vessel.

Roderick, cabin boy to the Red Rover and actually a woman.

REDBURN

Author: Herman Melville (1819-1891)
Time of action: Mid-nineteenth century
First published: 1849

PRINCIPAL CHARACTERS

Wellingborough Redburn, a young American who leaves his widowed mother and his brothers at home on the Hudson River in New York to go to sea. He learns, during a voyage from New York to Liverpool and return, that a sailor's life is a good but rugged one, that each generation makes its own world, and that true joy and sorrow are components of the human condition.

Harry Bolton, a young English prodigal son of good family who becomes Redburn's friend during the voyage from Liverpool to New York. Bolton is a misfit aboard ship, thus belying the

stories he tells of his voyages as a crew member on other vessels. His pride is so injured when the Captain pays him a dollar and a half as wages at the voyage's end that he throws the money back on the Captain's desk.

Captain Riga, the tough, shrewd master of the "Highlander," Redburn's first ship. He pays Redburn three dollars a month for his work on the voyage, but when the ship returns to New York he dismisses Redburn without a penny because he says Redburn had left the ship for a day at Liverpool and, furthermore, had lost tools overboard.

THE REDSKINS

Author: James Fenimore Cooper (1789-1851)
Time of action: 1842
First published: 1846

PRINCIPAL CHARACTERS

Hugh Roger Littlepage, the narrator and heir to Ravensnest, and

Hugh Roger Littlepage, called **Uncle Ro,** his uncle. While traveling abroad, they receive word that they are in danger of losing their estate, Ravensnest, threatened by a terrorist group of anti-rentist tenants greedy for land. Disguised as a watch peddler and an organ grinder, Hugh and Uncle Ro return to Ravensnest, assess the situation, and, finally, with the help of a band of friendly Indians, subdue the terrorists and see the rights of the landlords upheld by the Supreme Court.

The Reverend Mr. Warren, a clergyman living at Ravensnest and a friend and ally of Hugh Roger Littlepage and Uncle Ro.

Mary Warren, the daughter of the Reverend Mr. Warren. An ally of Hugh Roger Littlepage in his fight against the anti-rentists, she finally becomes his wife.

Seneca Newcome, a demagogue lawyer and the leader of the anti-rentist tenants at Ravensnest.

Tom Miller, a farmer who is hostile to the anti-rentist factions at Ravensnest.

Joshua Brigham, Tom Miller's greedy farmhand and an ally of Seneca Newcome.

Jack Dunning, Hugh Roger Littlepage's business agent.

Susquesus, an old Onondaga Indian living at Ravensnest. He is honored in a ceremony by a band of Indians from Washington who help subdue the anti-rentist terrorists at Ravensnest.

Jaap (Jaaf), an old colored servant living at Ravensnest.

Patt Littlepage, Hugh Roger Littlepage's sister.

Mrs. Ursula Littlepage, Hugh Roger Littlepage's grandmother.

Opportunity Newcome, Seneca Newcome's sister and ally.

Hall, a mechanic hostile to the anti-rentist faction at Ravensnest.

Henrietta Coldbrook and **Anne Marston,** wards of Uncle Ro.

THE RELAPSE

Author: Sir John Vanbrugh (1664-1726)
Time of action: Seventeenth century
First presented: 1696

PRINCIPAL CHARACTERS

Loveless, a gentleman living quietly in the country after a period of marital troubles. He goes to London frequently, however, to test his reform; he finds little difficulty in suffering a relapse.

Amanda, his wife. She remains chaste in spite of the combined efforts of her would-be lover and a friend who plays on her jealousy.

Berinthia, a comely widow and Amanda's friend. Loveless is attracted to Berinthia, and succeeds with her easily.

Worthy, a gentleman of the town who was formerly Berinthia's lover. He enlists her aid in his pursuit of Amanda, but though Amanda admits him to her house, she retains her virtue.

Sir Novelty Fashion, Lord Foppington, a London fop who makes advances to Amanda and is repulsed by her and slightly wounded by Loveless. He is engaged to wealthy Miss Hoyden and marries her, only to learn afterward that she is already the wife of his younger brother.

Young Fashion, the brother of Lord Foppington. Unsuccessful in getting his brother to pay his debts, young Fashion pretends to be Lord Foppington and is

admitted to Sir Tunbelly Clumsey's house as Miss Hoyden's fiancé. He persuades her to marry him secretly; but before the marriage is made known the real Lord Foppington arrives, and young Fashion is forced to flee.

Miss Hoyden, a nubile heiress. On the real Lord Foppington's arrival, she decides to say nothing of her earlier wedding, but to play safe and marry again. When the prior wedding is disclosed, however, and she learns that her husband is Lord Foppington's brother, she is content.

Sir Tunbelly Clumsey, a country squire, the father of Miss Hoyden. At first thunderstruck at young Fashion's disclosure, Sir Tunbelly accepts him as his son-in-law when it is revealed that he is Lord Foppington's brother.

Bull, the chaplain. He marries Miss Hoyden and young Fashion secretly. Fortunately, young Fashion has at his disposal the recently vacated Fat-goose Living. He promises it to Bull in return for Bull's admitting the truth about the recent marriage.

Lory, young Fashion's servant.

Coupler, the matchmaker who had ar-

952

ranged the engagement of Lord Foppington to Miss Hoyden. Fearing never to see Lord Foppington's promised two thousand pounds, Coupler plots with young Fashion and is to receive in return five thousand pounds.

REMEMBRANCE OF THINGS PAST

Author: Marcel Proust (1871-1922)
Time of action: Late nineteenth, early twentieth centuries
First published: 1918-1927

PRINCIPAL CHARACTERS

Marcel (mȧr·sĕl'), the narrator who tells the story of his life from unsettled childhood to disillusioned middle age. Dealing with time lost and time recalled, Marcel says, as he looks back to a crucial childhood experience when his mother spent the night in his room instead of scolding him for his insomnia, that memory eliminates precisely that great dimension of Time which governs the fullest realization of our lives. Through the years, from his memory of that childhood experience to his formulation of this concept of time, Marcel sees the principals of two social sets spurn each other, then intermingle with the change of fortunes. He experiences love in various forms: an innocent affair with a friend's daughter, an adolescent passion for the friend's coquettish wife, an intermittent love affair with a lesbian. He develops friendships and animosities among individuals in the different social levels on which he moves. Reminded, by seeing the daughter of his childhood sweetheart, that he is old, he realizes the futility of his life and senses the ravages of time on everyone he has known.

M. Swann (swän'), a wealthy broker and aesthete, and a friend of Marcel's parents. Swann, having known the Comte de Paris and the Prince of Wales, moves from level to level in the social milieu. Having married beneath his station, he knows that wealth sustains his social position and keeps his fickle wife dependent on him. Jealous and unhappy in courtship and marriage, he manipulates social situations by cultivating officers and politicians who will receive his wife. He dies, his life having been as meaningless as Marcel sees his own to be; in fact, Marcel sees in his own life a close parallel to that of his sensitive friend.

Mme. Swann, formerly **Odette de Crécy,** a courtesan. A woman whose beauty is suggestive of Botticelli's paintings, she is attractive to both men and women. Stupid and uncomprehending, Odette continues affairs with other men after her comfortable marriage. She introduces Swann to the social set below his own. Despite her beginnings, she moves to higher levels and becomes a celebrated, fashionable hostess when she remarries after Swann's death.

Gilberte Swann (zhēl·bĕrt' swän'), the Swanns' daughter and Marcel's playmate in Paris. Their relationship develops into an innocent love affair, and they remain constant good friends after Gilberte's marriage to Marcel's close friend, Robert de Saint-Loup. The sight of Gilberte's daughter, grown up, reminds Marcel that he himself is aging.

Mme. de Villeparisis (də vē·yə·pȧ·rē·zē'), a society matron and the friend of Marcel's grandmother. It is said that her father ruined himself for her, a renowned beauty when she was young. She has become a dreadful, blowsy, hunched-up old woman; her physical deterioration is comparable to the decline of her friends' spiritual selves.

Robert de Saint-Loup (rô·bĕr' də săň'-loo'), her nephew, whom she introduces to Marcel. Their meeting is the beginning of a friendship that lasts until Robert's death in World War I. In his courtship and marriage, Robert suffers from the same insecurity, resulting in jealousy, that plagues Swann and Marcel in their relations with women. He marries Gilberte Swann.

M. de Charlus (mə·syœ' də shàr·lüs'), another of Mme. de Villeparisis' nephews, a baron. The Baron, as he is usually referred to, is a sexual invert who has affairs with men of many different stations in life. In his aberration the Baron is both fascinating and repulsive to Marcel, who makes homosexuality a chief discussion in the volume titled "Cities of the Plain." The Baron's depravity leads to senile old age.

Mme. Verdurin (vĕr·dü·răň'), a vulgar person of the bourgeoisie who, with her husband, pretends to despise the society to which they have no entrée. Odette introduces Swann to the Verdurins. Mme. Verdurin crosses social lines as she comes into money and marries into the old aristocracy after her first husband dies. The middle-class Verdurins seem to surround themselves with talented individuals, and many of their guests become outstanding in their professions and arts.

The Prince and Princess de Guermantes (də gĕr·mäňt'), members of the old aristocracy and the family used by Proust in the volume titled "The Guermantes Way," to delineate the social classes, the Guermantes representing aristocratic group as opposed to the moneyed society described in "Swann's Way." After the Princess dies, the Prince, ruined by the war, marries widowed Mme. Verdurin. Their union is further evidence of social mobility.

The Duke and Duchess de Guermantes, members of the same family. After Odette's rise on the social scale, the Duchess is received in Odette's salon. In earlier years the Duchess left parties to avoid meeting the vulgar social climber.

Albertine (àl·bĕr·tēn'), a lesbian attracted by and to Marcel. Over an extended period of time their affair takes many turns. Marcel seeks comfort from her when his grandmother dies; he is unhappy with her and wretched without her; his immaturity drives her from him and back to her home in Balbec. A posthumous letter to Marcel, after Albertine is killed in a fall from a horse, tells of her intention to return to him.

Marcel's Grandmother, a woman known and revered in both the aristocratic and the merely fashionable social sets. Marcel loves and respects her, and her death brings into focus for him the emptiness in the lives of his smart, wealthy friends.

M. Vinteuil (văň·tē·yül'), an old composer in Combray. He dies in shame because of his daughter's association with a woman of questionable character. Unhappy in his own life, Vinteuil's music brings pleasure to many. Among those affected is Swann, moved to marry Odette, his mistress, because he associates the charm of Vinteuil's exquisite sonatas with the beauty of the cocotte. Marcel, also captured by the spirit of Vinteuil's music, senses its effect on various listeners.

Rachel (rà·shĕl'), a young Jewish actress who becomes famous. Although she is Robert de Saint-Loup's mistress, she despises him because of his simplicity, breeding, and good taste. Rachel likes the aesthetic charlatans she considers superior to her devoted lover.

Dr. Cottard (kôt·tàr'), a social boor because of his tiresome punning and other ineptitudes, a guest at the Verdurins' parties. He becomes a noted surgeon, professionally admired.

Elstir (ĕl·stēr'), a young man Marcel meets at Verdurins'. He becomes a painter of genius.

954

Mme. de Saint-Euverte (də săṅ·tœ·věrt'), a hostess whose parties attract both the old and new friends of Swann, to his displeasure at times.

The Princess des Launes (dā lōn'), a long-time friend of Swann and a guest in Mme. de Saint-Euverte's salon. She is distressed at her friend's unhappiness, caused by lowering himself to Odette's level.

Morel (mô·rěl'), the musician who, at the Vendurins' party, plays Vinteiul's compositions. Morel is a protégé of the perverted Baron de Charlus.

Jupien (zhü·pyăṅ'), a tailor. After becoming the object of de Charlus' affection he establishes a house for affairs among men.

M. de Norpoie (də nôr·pwá'), an ambassador who, as Marcel finally realizes, has been Mme. de Villeparisis' lover for many years.

Aunt Léonie (lā·ô·nē'), Marcel's aunt. At the end he likens himself to her as he recalls her from his childhood, when she had become an old hypochondriac.

REMEMBRANCE ROCK

Author: Carl Sandburg (1878-   )
Time of action: 1607-1945
First published: 1948

PRINCIPAL CHARACTERS

Orville Brand Windom, affectionately called **Bowbong** by his grandson. A former Supreme Court Justice, he is an independent, idealistic, whimsical man with a deep interest in the American past and future. In his yard he keeps a huge boulder surrounded by earth representing the crises of American culture. The fictitious author of the novel's three stories, he wills his manuscript to his grandson.

Raymond Windom, his intelligent, sensitive grandson. A pilot in World War II, he returns home exhausted and cynical, but his grandfather's manuscript tends to restore his faith in the nation's possibilities.

Maria Windom, nicknamed **Mimah,** his attractive, spirited wife. She shares her husband's and Orville's concern for America.

Joseph Stilwell Windom, their infant son, a symbol of the future.

I. THE FIRST COMERS

Oliver Ball Windrow, a middle-aged woodcarver and philosopher in Stuart England, a man much like Orville Windom. Rejected in his suit for Mary Windling, he marries his housekeeper.

Matilda Bracken, Oliver Windrow's mute, devoted housekeeper. She marries him and bears him two children.

Mary Windling, a lovely, spirited young friend of Oliver Windrow. She marries a Puritan, moves with him to Holland, and then sails to America on the "Mayflower." She dies during the first winter.

John Spong, her sturdy, affectionate, pious husband. In America he becomes stern and solemn, disapproving of all his daughter's suitors.

Remember Spong, the daughter of John and Mary, a lively, pretty young Puritan who attracts several suitors but loves Resolved Wayfare, a Separatist, and finds herself torn between orthodox and independent piety.

Orton Wingate, her middle-aged friend and suitor, a kind man with audacious opinions, much like Orville Windom.

Peter Ladd, her gay, handsome suitor, a sailor and gambler who settles down under her influence but returns to the sea when she refuses him.

Resolved Wayfare, an idealistic young man who follows Roger Williams and eventually wins Remember's love. The two lovers part with vows of fidelity.

Roger Williams, a rebel of conviction and integrity, the friend of the Indians and the founder of the Rhode Island Colony.

II. THE ARCH BEGINS

Ordway Winshore, a Philadelphia printer, a man of character similar to Orville Windom. He loses two sons in the Revolutionary War.

Robert Winshore, his older son, a dashing, idealistic young man who loses his love because of his commitment to the Revolution. He dies at Valley Forge.

John Locke Winshore, the more prudent younger son, a tradesman who joins the Revolutionary cause, becomes a military courier, marries Ann Elwood, and dies soon afterward.

Marintha Wilming, called **Mim,** a lovely girl who rejects Robert's love because of his political convictions. Later she becomes a nurse for the rebels.

Ann Elwood, a sensitive, pretty girl involved in a fraudulent marriage. She later marries John Winshore and has a child by him.

Oates Elwood, Robert Winshore's rough, good-hearted, patriotic friend.

Lieutenant George Frame, Marintha's suitor, a cultured British officer wounded in the war and sent back to England.

Sapphira Reggs, a Tory who recognizes Robert Winshore while her father is being tarred and feathered by patriots. She reports him to the British.

Mary Burton, the warm, attractive widow who marries Ordway Winshore.

III. THE ARCH HOLDS

Omri Winwold, a gambler. A manly, amiable, prophetic man somewhat like Orville Windom, he moves West, settles on an Illinois farm, loses three wives, and sees his sons killed or maimed in the Civil War.

Brooksany Wimbler, his distant cousin and friend, a charming woman who moves with her husband and daughter to Illinois and dies there during the Civil War.

Joel Wimbler, her hardy, sensible husband, a harness-maker and abolitionist who becomes an officer and dies in the war.

Millicent Wimbler, called **Mibs,** their beautiful, spirited daughter. Though wooed by two other suitors, she swiftly decides, without her parents' consent, to marry a cattle buyer and has a child by him. She goes to meet him when he is released from the military prison on Johnson's Island.

Rodney Wayman, her gay, intelligent, manly husband, an ex-miner and cattle buyer who becomes a Confederate captain and is twice captured by Union troops. Embittered by the war, he nevertheless feels compassion when he learns of Omri Winwold's losses.

Hornsby Meadows, a teacher, Millicent Wimbler's keen but bigoted Abolitionist suitor.

Danny Hilton, a farmer and contractor, Millicent Wimbler's husky, light-hearted suitor.

Nack Doss, Rodney Wayman's business associate and friend, a rough, honest Southerner killed in a Civil War engagement in Mississippi.

Bee Winwold, Omri's first wife, a wild,

flashy, promiscuous woman whom he deserts.

Andrew Marvel Winwold, Omri's son by Bee. He becomes an officer and loses an arm in the Civil War.

Henry Flack, Bee's second husband, a rather pathetic man attracted to prosti-tutes. After Bee deserts him and Anne Winwold dies, he and Omri become friends.

Sarah Prindle and
Anne Moore, a widow, two affectionate farmwomen and sisters, Omri's second and third wives. They bear him seven children.

RENÉE MAUPERIN

Authors: Edmond (1822-1896) and Jules (1830-1870) de Goncourt
Time of action: Nineteenth century
First published: 1864

PRINCIPAL CHARACTERS

Renée Mauperin (rə·nā′ mō·pə·răń′), a French girl. She is a sensitive, lively girl and her father's favorite child. She is in no hurry to settle down in marriage. Like her friend Naomi, Renée is horrified when she learns that her brother Henri is his prospective mother-in-law's lover. In revenge, Renée notifies M. de Villa-court that her brother is taking the man's name. When she thinks her action has been discovered, she has a heart attack and then wastes away to death.

M. Mauperin (mō·pə·răń′), Renée's fa-ther and a veteran of the Napoleonic wars. Once a scholar and interested in politics, he is now a middle-class busi-nessman. He is grief-stricken when all three of his children die within a short time.

Mme. Mauperin (mō·pə·răń′), Renée's mother. She is a very proper woman who wants her family to be respectable above all else. She dotes on her son and cannot see his selfishness. Like her hus-band, she is grief-stricken at the deaths of her children.

Henri Mauperin (äń·rē mō·pə·răń′), Renée's brother. He is a political econo-mist and a lawyer, a cold, calculating, and extremely selfish man. He becomes the lover of his fiancée's mother in order to further his marriage to the daughter.

When his fiancée learns of the affair, he tells her it is none of her business. He fights a duel with the real de Villacourt, whose name he has officially taken, and is killed.

Mme. Davarande (dà·và·räńd′), Renée's sister. She is a quiet, respectable woman who has married dutifully. She dies in childbirth, not long after the deaths of her brother and sister.

Naomi Bourjot (nà·ô·mē′ bōōr·zhō′), Renée's friend and Henri's fiancée. She is from a rich family, and her father wants her to marry a man with a title. She is horrified when she discovers that her mother has taken Henri as a lover.

Mme. Bourjot (bōōr·zhō′), Naomi's mother and Henri's mistress.

M. Denoisel (də·nwà·zĕl′), a family friend who acts as Henri Mauperin's sec-ond at the duel.

M. de Villacourt (də vē·yà·kōōr′), the last member of his family. He fights a duel with Henri Mauperin in order to keep Henri from assuming the family's name.

M. Bourjot (bōōr·zhō′), Naomi's father. He is a middle-class man of wealth who wants his daughter to marry higher in the social scale.

RESURRECTION

Author: Count Leo Tolstoy (1828-1910)
Time of action: Late nineteenth century
First published: 1899

PRINCIPAL CHARACTERS

Prince Dmítri Ivánovitch Nekhlúdoff, a gentleman. At a trial in which he is serving as a juror, he is astonished to see that the defendant is the falsely accused Katúsha Máslova, whom he had seduced in the past. When Katúsha is sentenced to hard labor in Siberia, his pity for her in the life to which he has driven her leads him to a period of self-examination from which he emerges regarding his life as empty and degenerate and feeling a need to cleanse his soul. Determined to follow the prisoner to Siberia and marry her, he feels himself purged when her sentence is lightened to exile and she elects to stay with Valdemar Símonson, who loves her.

Katerína Mikháelovna Máslova, called **Katúsha,** an illegitimate girl. Seduced at sixteen by Prince Dmítri Ivánovitch Nekhlúdoff, she becomes a prostitute and later is falsely accused of complicity in murder. At her trial, she is recognized by her seducer, a juryman, who, in remorse for his past treatment, wishes to marry her. When, through Dmítri's efforts, her sentence is commuted to exile, she elects to remain with Valdemar Símonson rather than jeopardize her benefactor's happiness by his marriage to a woman like herself.

Valdemar Símonson, a political prisoner who falls in love with Katúsha Máslova as they are on their way to exile in Siberia.

Véra Doúkhova, a political prisoner interested in the welfare of Katúsha.

Lydia Shoústova, Véra Doúkhova's friend.

Selénin, a public prosecutor and an old friend of Prince Dmítri. Fundamentally an intelligent, honest man, he has come to make society's standards his own.

Sophia and
Mary Ivánovna, aunts of Prince Dmítri and childhood guardians of Katúsha.

Katerína Ivánovna Tchársky, an aunt of Prince Dmítri.

Matróna Khárina, Katúsha's aunt.

Princess Mary Korchágin, the prospective fiancée of Prince Dmítri.

THE RETURN

Author: Walter de la Mare (1873-1956)
Time of action: Nineteenth century
First published: 1910

PRINCIPAL CHARACTERS

Arthur Lawford, a middle-aged Englishman who, while resting in an ancient churchyard, finds himself strangely turned into the shape of Nicholas Sabathier, an eighteenth century British isher who had committed suicide on the Eve of St. Michael and All Angels in 1739. Lawford keeps his own mind and has strange feelings about himself, as well as difficulties with his family and friends. On the anniversary of Sabathier's death, however, he is returned to his own shape once again.

Sheila Lawford, Arthur's wife. Though she believes the stranger she sees is really her husband in a different shape, she refuses to stay with him at night as a wife and insists on leaving the house. She finally leaves him alone in the house for several days to wrestle with his problems.

Herbert Herbert, a stranger in the neighborhood, a bookish recluse. He identifies Lawford's new shape as that of Nicholas Sabathier. During his transformation Lawford spends a great deal of time with Herbert and his sister Grisel, both of whom are quite sympathetic.

Grisel Herbert, Herbert's sister. She and Arthur come to realize that in another life they have previously loved. She gives Lawford the feeling when he is with her that he is fighting some strange spirit, and yet he takes great comfort in her company.

Alice Lawford, Arthur's teen-age daughter. While she faints from shock when first she sees her transformed father, she goes to him in secret, against her mother's wishes, to tell him that she sympathizes and hopes that all will turn out well.

The Reverend Mr. Bethany, rector of the parish. Although he is horrified at what happens to Lawford, he remains sympathetic. On the night that Lawford returns to his own shape the rector arrives at the Lawford home to keep vigil.

THE RETURN OF THE NATIVE

Author: Thomas Hardy (1840-1928)
Time of action: The 1840's
First published: 1878

PRINCIPAL CHARACTERS

Clement Yeobright, called **Clym,** a native of Egdon Heath who returns to visit with his mother and cousin after having made a career for himself as a successful diamond merchant in Paris. His success and his education make him an outstanding figure among the humble people who live scattered about the wild heath, and his return for a visit is a great occasion for them. During his stay he decides to remain, finding that the heath and its people mean far more to him than worldly success in Paris; his intention is to become a teacher and open a school to educate the people among whom he grew up, a superstitious and ignorant, if lovable and kindly, set. A sensitive and somewhat rash young man, he falls in love with Eustacia Vye, a beautiful and passionate woman. In her Clym sees a perfect helpmeet for a schoolmaster, but she sees in him only a chance

to escape the heath and to live abroad. Clym and Eustacia Vye are married, over the protests of his mother. These protests arouse the anger of Clym, who after his marriage does not communicate with her. Disaster, in the form of partial blindness, strikes Clym, but he accepts his plight philosophically and turns to the homely task of furze-cutting to earn a living. Unhappy in her lot, Eustacia turns against him. On one occasion she refuses to let his mother into the house, an inhospitable act that indirectly causes the death of the older woman. Stricken by his mother's death and, a short time later, by his wife's suicide, Clym becomes a lay preacher to the people of the heath.

Eustacia Vye, the self-seeking and sensuous young woman who marries Clym Yeobright. Unhappy on the heath, bored by life with her grandfather, she tries to

959

escape. First she seeks an opportunity to do so by marrying Clym. When he cannot and will not leave the heath, she turns to a former fiancé, now a married man. At the last, however, she cannot demean herself by unfaithfulness to her husband; instead of running away with her lover she commits suicide by plunging into a millpond.

Damon Wildeve, a former engineer, still a young man, who settles unhappily upon the heath as keeper of the Quiet Woman Inn. Selfish and uninspired, when he loses Eustacia Vye to Clym Yeobright he marries Thomasin Yeobright, Clym's cousin, out of spite. The marriage is an unhappy one, for Wildeve still pursues Eustacia, also unhappy because her husband cannot give her the life she wishes. Wildeve's pursuit of illicit love ends in his own death, for he drowns while trying to save Eustacia's life after she throws herself into a pond rather than elope to Paris as his mistress.

Thomasin Yeobright, called **Tamsin,** Clym's cousin, reared with Clym by his mother. A simple and faithful girl who loves Damon Wildeve despite his treatment of her, she is also faithful to the conventions and clings to her marriage even after it turns out badly. At her husband's death she inherits a small fortune left by his uncle shortly before Wildeve's end. She finds happiness eventually in a second marriage and in her little daughter.

Diggory Venn, an itinerant young reddleman in love with Thomasin Yeobright. Once of good family and some little fortune, he has fallen upon evil days. His lonely existence gives him opportunity to act in his love's behalf, and he tries to circumvent Wildeve's pursuit of Eustacia Vye. Having saved up a little money, he becomes a dairyman and presents himself, after a decent time, as Thomasin's suitor, following her husband's death. His patience, love, and understanding are rewarded when she accepts him.

Mrs. Yeobright, Clym Yeobright's mother and Thomasin Yeobright's aunt. In her good sense she opposes both their marriages, although the young people misinterpret her motives as selfish. Being of a forgiving nature, she tries to be reconciled with her son and his wife, as she became with Thomasin and her husband. But Eustacia refuses her overtures and is indirectly the cause of the older woman's death; Mrs. Yeobright dies of exposure and snakebite after having been refused admittance to her son's home.

Captain Vye, Eustacia Vye's grandfather, a retired seaman who brings his granddaughter to live on the heath with no thought of how such a place will affect her. He is a self-contained old man with little knowledge of the intense personality of his charge; therefore he makes no effort to prevent her tragedy.

Johnny Nunsuch, a little boy who plays upon the heath and unwittingly becomes involved as a witness to the fate of the Yeobrights, Eustacia Vye, and Damon Wildeve. His testimony concerning Mrs. Yeobright's last words brings about the separation of Clym Yeobright and his wife.

Mrs. Nunsuch, Johnny's mother. Convinced that Eustacia Vye is a witch who has cast a spell upon the child, Mrs. Nunsuch, an uneducated, superstitious woman, resorts to black arts to exorcise the spell. On the night of Eustacia Vye's death she forms a doll in the girl's image and destroys it in a fire.

Granfer Cantle, an ancient,
Christian Cantle, his elderly youngest son,
Olly Dowden,
Sam, a turf-cutter,
Humphrey, a furze-cutter, and
Timothy Fairway, residents of Egdon Heath. They voice much of the rural wisdom and observe the folk customs of the region.

THE REVENGE OF BUSSY D'AMBOIS

Author: George Chapman (c. 1559-1634)
Time of action: Sixteenth century
First presented: c. 1610

PRINCIPAL CHARACTERS

Clermont d'Ambois (klĕr·mōn′ dän-bwả′), Bussy's brother and sworn avenger. He is Chapman's ideal hero, brave, learned, and stoical, resolved to preserve inviolate "a good mind and a name" through whatever changes in fortune destiny brings him.

Charlotte (shảr·lôt′), his intensely emotional sister, who spurs Clermont and her husband to avenge Bussy with the cold-blooded forcefulness of a Lady Macbeth.

Baligny (bả·lēn·yē′), Charlotte's husband, a time-serving courtier. He professes allegiance to Guise and virtue while he is conspiring with King Henry to overthrow the Duke.

Henry III (än·rē′), King of France. No longer portrayed as the just, if slightly susceptible, ruler of "Bussy d'Ambois," he surfeits himself with sensual pleasures and plots the destruction of virtuous men around him.

The Duc du Guise (dük′ də·gēz′), Bus-sy's enemy, who has become a "tenth worthy," the exemplar of all virtue, and Clermont's friend and patron.

Montsurry (mōn·sü·rē′), Bussy's slayer. His refusal to accept Clermont's challenge marks him as weak and cowardly until the last moments of his life, when he summons enough courage to defend himself valiantly against his opponent.

Tamyra (tả·mē·rả′), his Countess. Forsaking her resolution to wander until her death, she is again living with her husband and simultaneously plotting with Charlotte to avenge her lover.

Renel (rə·nĕl′), Clermont's friend, an astute critic of the corruption at court.

Maillard (mā·yảr′), Baligny's lieutenant. He defends his ambush of Clermont on the grounds that the public good and the will of the King justify private treachery.

The Countess of Cambrai (kän·brả′), Clermont's mistress, who literally cries her eyes out grieving over his arrest.

THE REVENGER'S TRAGEDY

Author: Cyril Tourneur (c. 1575-1626)
Time of action: The Renaissance
First presented: c. 1607

PRINCIPAL CHARACTERS

Vendice (vĕn·dē′chä), a young Italian who broods over the skull of his dead sweetheart while plotting revenge on the Duke, her murderer. Well-versed in the corruptions of the court, he disguises himself as Piato, a crafty, lascivious old man, and offers his services to Lussurioso. After his diabolical murder of the Duke, who is poisoned when he kisses the lips of the skull which Vendice has dressed as a masked lady, he appears in his own person, assuming a melancholy spirit to deceive his young prince again. Although he successfully dispatches his enemies and places the dukedom into the hands of just men, he is himself executed; he

961

condemns himself out of his own mouth and receives justice from the man to whom he has given the right to dispense it.

Hippolito (ē·pō′lē·tō), his brother, who supports him in his plots to purge the court of its corruption.

The Duke, a despicable old lecher who governs more by personal desires than by any notion of right and wrong. The few honest men of his court deeply resent his staying of the sentence of his wife's youngest son, who had raped the virtuous wife of one of his lords. There is a strong element of poetic justice in the manner of his death. Vendice's lady was executed for refusing to yield to him; her lover traps her murderer by promising to procure a young woman for his pleasure.

The Duchess, his second wife, a fitting mate for the Duke. Enraged by her husband's refusal to release her youngest son absolutely, she takes her vengeance by having an affair with Spurio, the Duke's bastard son.

Lussurioso (loo·soor′e·o·so), the Duke's heir, whose character is aptly expressed in his name. He hires Vendice, disguised as Piato, to seduce Castiza for him, cynically suggesting that he try the mother first if the daughter is recalcitrant. He has some lingering remnants of honor with regard to the behavior of his stepmother and Spurio, and his first act as Duke is to order her banishment and Spurio's execution.

Ambitioso (ăm·bē′tē·ō·sō) and
Supervacuo (soo·pĕr·vä′koo·ō), the Duchess' sons. Each is anxious to destroy Lussurioso and seize the dukedom for himself; mutually ambitious, they are extremely jealous of each other. Their treacherous plot to have the legal heir executed fails, and they succeed only in causing the death of their own brother.

Spurio (spoo′rē·o), the Duke's bastard son, ambitious, like his stepbrothers, for power. He resents his father, as Edmund does Gloucester in "King Lear," and chooses a peculiarly damnable mode of revenge for his birth, becoming his stepmother's lover. His greed brings him a fitting death; he and Ambitioso stab each other in a quarrel over the possession of the dead Lussurioso's dukedom.

Gratiana (grä·shē·ä′nä), the mother of Vendice, a weak-spirited woman who is persuaded by her son, disguised as Piato, to encourage her daughter to submit to Lussurioso's lust. She is won over chiefly by his offer of money. Confronted by Vendice with her betrayal of Castiza, she repents and once again recognizes the inestimable value of virtue.

Castiza (käs·tē′zə), daughter of Gratiana and Vendice's sister. She violently rejects her mother's insistence that she submit to Lussurioso and boxes the ears of the ducal emissary, "Piato," who rejoices at his sister's lively virtue. She seems for a few moments to have given in to her mother's arguments, but when she sees that Gratiana has been convinced again of the value of honor, she confesses that she was only testing her; her own allegiance to virtue is unchanging.

Antonio (än·tō·nyō), a just nobleman who becomes Duke after the mass murder of the old ruler's family. He, like Vendice, had just cause to hate the ducal family, for his wife died after she was attacked by one of the Duchess' sons. He recognizes, however, the necessity for law, and he orders Vendice's immediate arrest when he reveals himself as the avenger of wrongs committed by the old Duke.

Piero (pē·ä′rō), Antonio's friend, one of the group of masquers who kill Lussurioso and his nobles.

Dondolo (dŏn′dō·lō), a pompous gentleman usher.

THE REVOLT OF THE ANGELS

Author: Anatole France (Jacques Anatole Thibault, 1844-1924)
Time of action: Early twentieth century
First published: 1914

PRINCIPAL CHARACTERS

Arcade (är·kȧd′), an angel who plans to lead a revolt against God (Ialdabaoth). He gathers together hundreds of thousands of rebel angels, but is disappointed when Satan quashes the revolution.

Monsieur Julien Sariette (mə·syœ′ zhü-lyěň sȧ·ryět′), the meticulous librarian in charge of the extensive collection that Arcade uses to educate himself for the revolution. Sariette is confounded and frustrated because Arcade scatters the books. When a volume of "Lucretius," a very rare work, is lost, Sariette's mind snaps.

Maurice d'Esparvieu (mō·rēs′ děs·pȧr-vyœ′), a wealthy, lazy young man whose guardian angel is Arcade. After an attempt to dissuade Arcade from his plans, d'Esparvieu regards him with quiet amusement and shares his clothes and his mistress with the angel.

Madame Gilberte des Aubels (zhěl·běrt′ dȧ·zō·běl′), Maurice's mistress, who also bestows her favors on Arcade.

Satan (sȧ·tǎň′), a sympathetic prince who, petitioned by Arcade and his army of rebels to lead the revolution against God, refuses. The rebel forces accept his reasons for not making war: If the revolution succeeded, Satan and his forces would become as God and the heavenly hosts; that is, they would lose their sympathy for humanity. War begets war, and the vanquished always seek to regain what they have lost. The real duty of the revolutionary army of angels is to stay on earth in order to spread the doctrine of love and compassion because only by doing so can God be defeated and peace come to the universe.

Prince Istar (prǎňs′ ē·stär′), a rebel angel who specializes in chemistry. He supports the revolutionary cause by manufacturing bombs.

Théophile (tā·ô·fēl′), an angel, approached by Arcade, who refuses to fight God. He is ashamed because he has satisfied his lust with a mortal woman, but he still respects God's authority.

Sophar (sō·fär′), an angel who has become a Jewish banker named Max Everdingen. He will not join the rebel forces, but he offers to sell them munitions, the cost of which he would finance at his bank.

Zita (zē·tȧ′), a hostile female angel who wishes to join the ranks and fight as a man in the revolution.

REYNARD THE FOX

Author: Unknown
Time of action: Tenth century
First transcribed: Twelfth century

PRINCIPAL CHARACTERS

Reynard, the fox. So crafty and persuasive a liar is he, that he is at last made high bailiff of the country, though he has flagrantly cheated and injured all of the animals, including the King. Thus is craftiness set above mere strength.

Noble, the lion, King of Beasts. He listens to the animals' grievances against Reynard, and even sentences the fox to death. But Reynard lies so cleverly about hidden treasure and treachery on the part of the others that the King frees him. Noble is similarly gulled a second time and on this occasion even makes Reynard high bailiff.

Isegrim, the wolf, whose children have been made blind by Reynard. Convinced of Isegrim's treason, the King gives the wolf's shoes to Reynard. After this, when the wolf and the fox are engaged in combat, Reynard persuades Isegrim to let him go with promises of rewards.

Tibert, the cat. He defends Reynard before the others until he has been tricked by the fox into jumping into a trap.

Bruin, the bear. Reynard's promises of honey lure him into a trap, and he is badly beaten before he escapes. Later Reynard convinces the King that Bruin is plotting to replace him as ruler. Noble gives Bruin's skin to Reynard.

Grimbard, the brock. He defends Reynard before the court, and even warns the fox of a plot against him.

Panther, who complains of Reynard to the King.

Chanticleer, the cock. His complaint is that Reynard deceived him into relaxing his vigilance by pretending to have given up eating flesh. Then Reynard eats Chanticleer's children.

Kyward, the hare. He accompanies Reynard on a "pilgrimage" and is eaten by him.

Bellin, the ram, who goes with Reynard and Kyward. Deceived into thinking he is carrying a letter, he brings Kyward's head to the King. The furious King then gives the stupid ram and all his lineage to the wolf and the bear, to atone for his misjudgment of them.

RHADAMISTUS AND ZENOBIA

Author: Prosper Jolyot de Crébillon (1674-1762)
Time of action: c. 60
First presented: 1711

PRINCIPAL CHARACTERS

Rhadamistus, King of Armenia, son of Pharasmanes but raised by Mithridates as his own child. When Mithridates turns against him, Rhadamistus attacks his foster father's kingdom, murders him, and, in a rage, throws his own bride Zenobia into a river, from which she is rescued without his knowledge. Later, as Roman envoy at the court of Pharasmanes, he learns that Zenobia is alive. He begs for and receives her forgiveness and is mortally wounded as he attempts to flee with her.

Zenobia (Ismenia), Mithridates' daughter and the wife of Rhadamistus. To protect her father from Rhadamistus she marries him, only to be thrown by her husband into a river and left for dead. Rescued, she becomes a prisoner of Pharasmanes, who desires to marry her. She, in turn, is in love with Arsames, to whom Pharasmanes finally relinquishes her in his remorse over his killing of his son Rhadamistus.

Pharasmanes, Rhadamistus' father. His jealousy and lust for power lead him into conflict with his son Rhadamistus, whom he kills. In remorse, he sacrifices his throne and the widowed Zenobia to Arsames.

Arsames, another of Pharasmanes' sons, in love with Zenobia.

Mithridates, Zenobia's father and Rhadamistus' foster father.

Phenice, Zenobia's confidante.

Hiero, Rhadamistus' companion.

Hydaspes, Pharasmanes' confidant.

Mithranes, the captain of Pharasmanes' guard.

RICEYMAN STEPS

Author: Arnold Bennett (1867-1931)
Time of action: 1919
First published: 1923

PRINCIPAL CHARACTERS

Henry Earlforward, a miserly bookstore owner. He marries a neighboring confectioner whom he believes as miserly as he. He refuses to spend money for electricity, a wedding ring, even for food and medical advice. When he becomes ill he refuses to enter a hospital, because of the expense. He dies, the victim of his own parsimony.

Mrs. Violet Arb, thrifty owner of a confectionery shop. She discovers too late that her husband Henry is miserly. Although a doctor sees to it that she goes to the hospital for a needed operation, she has become so weakened by malnutrition that she dies.

Elsie, the Earlforwards' maid of all work. Because she is half-starved, she steals food from her employers. In order to have sixpence to send a messenger to inquire about her mistress she has to steal

the money from her miserly master. After the Earlforwards' deaths she goes to work, along with her sweetheart, for Dr. Raste.

Joe, Elsie's sweetheart. He turns up at the bookstore shabbily dressed, sick, and just released from jail. Elsie nurses him back to health while concealing him in the Earlforwards' quarters. He goes to work for Dr. Raste. He and Elsie plan to marry.

T. T. Riceyman, the dead uncle who left the bookstore to Henry.

Dr. Raste, the medical doctor who tries to save the life of Earlforward's wife and befriends Elsie and Joe.

Mr. and Mrs. Belrose, the couple who buy Mrs. Arb's shop when she marries Henry. They try to be helpful to the Earlforwards when the latter become ill.

RICHARD THE SECOND

Author: William Shakespeare (1564-1616)
Time of action: Fourteenth century
First presented: 1595-1596

PRINCIPAL CHARACTERS

King Richard the Second, a self-indulgent and irresponsible ruler. He neglects the welfare of his country and brings on his own downfall. He is insolent in his treatment of his dying uncle, John of

Gaunt, and greedy in his seizure of the property of his banished cousin, Henry Bolingbroke. To his lovely young queen he gives sentimental devotion. Being forced to give up the crown, he wallows in poetic self-pity, playing with his sorrow and theatrically portraying himself as a Christ-figure. But he dies well.

Henry Bolingbroke (bol'ĭn·brŏŏk), Duke of Hereford (afterward **King Henry the Fourth**), the son of John of Gaunt. Able and ambitious, roused to anger by Richard's injustice and ineptitude, he forces the latter to abdicate. Although as king he desires the death of his deposed and imprisoned cousin, he laments the death and banishes the murderer permanently from his presence.

John of Gaunt (gänt, gônt), Duke of Lancaster, the uncle of King Richard. Grieved by the banishment of his son and his country's decline, he delivers a beautiful and impassioned praise of England and a lament for its degradation under Richard. Angered by Richard's insulting behavior, he dies delivering a curse on the young King which is carried out in the future.

Edmund of Langley, Duke of York, uncle of the King. Eager to do right and imbued with patriotism and loyalty, he is torn and troubled by the behavior of Richard as king and Bolingbroke as rebel. As Protector of the Realm in Richard's absence, he is helpless before Bolingbroke's power and yields to him. He bestows his loyalty on Bolingbroke when he becomes King Henry IV.

Queen to King Richard, a gentle, loving wife. Grief-stricken, she angrily wishes that her gardener, from whom she hears the news of Richard's downfall, may henceforth labor in vain. She shares with the King a tender and sorrowful parting.

The Gardener, a truly Shakespearian creation, unlike any character in Marlowe's "Edward the Second," source of much in Shakespeare's play. A homely philosopher, he comments on the King's faults and his downfall and is overheard by the Queen. Tenderly sympathetic, he wishes the Queen's curse on his green thumb might be carried out if it could give her any comfort; however, confident that it will not be, he memorializes her sorrow by planting flowers where her tears fell.

The Duke of Aumerle (ō·mērl'), son of the Duke of York. One of Richard's favorites, scornful of Bolingbroke, he is accused of complicity in the murder of the Duke of Gloucester. His father discovers a document linking him to a plot to assassinate King Henry IV. Aumerle outrides his father to King Henry and gains promise of pardon, which is confirmed after the Duchess pleads for her son.

The Duchess of York, the indulgent mother of Aumerle. She is frantic at her husband's determination to report their son's treason, and she pleads to King Henry on her knees.

Thomas Mowbray, Duke of Norfolk, an enemy of Bolingbroke. Accused of plotting the Duke of Gloucester's death, he and Bolingbroke are prepared for combat in the lists when Richard breaks off the combat and banishes both. Mowbray dies in exile.

The Duchess of Gloucester, widow of the murdered Duke. She pleads with John of Gaunt to avenge his dead brother and prays that Bolingbroke may destroy Mowbray as part of the revenge. York receives news of her death.

Bushy and
Green, unpopular favorites of King Richard. They are captured and executed by Bolingbroke's followers.

Bagot (băg'ət), another of the King's unpopular favorites. At his trial before Bolingbroke, he declares Aumerle guilty of having Gloucester murdered.

The Earl of Northumberland, a strong supporter of Bolingbroke. He aids in the overthrow of Richard.

Henry Percy (Hotspur), the son of Northumberland. At Bagot's trial he challenges Aumerle to combat, but nothing comes of it.

The Lord Marshall, who officiates at the abortive duel of Mowbray and Bolingbroke.

The Bishop of Carlisle, a supporter of King Richard. Objecting to Bolingbroke's seizure of the crown, he is accused of treason and banished.

The Abbot of Westminster, a conspirator against King Henry IV. He dies before he can be tried.

Sir Stephen Scroop, a loyal follower of King Richard. He brings unwelcome tidings of Bolingbroke's success to the King.

A Keeper, King Richard's jailer, who angers the King and is beaten by him.

A Groom, a devoted servant of King Richard who visits the deposed monarch in prison.

The Earl of Salisbury, a follower of Richard executed by Northumberland.

The Duke of Surrey, a Yorkist and a friend of Aumerle.

Lord Berkeley, a follower of the Duke of York.

Lord Fitzwater,
Lord Ross, and
Lord Willoughby, supporters of Bolingbroke.

Sir Pierce of Exton, a savage and ambitious knight. He kills King Richard in hope of a splendid career under King Henry IV, but is disappointed, cast off, and banished by the King.

RICHARD THE THIRD

Author: William Shakespeare (1564-1616)
Time of action: Fifteenth century
First presented: 1592-1593

PRINCIPAL CHARACTERS

Richard, Duke of Gloucester, afterward **King Richard the Third,** sinister and Machiavellian brother of King Edward IV. A fiendish and ambitious monster, he shows the grisly humor of the medieval Devil or the Vice of the morality plays. An effective hypocrite, he successfully dissembles his ambition and his ruthlessness until he has won his kingdom. His character in this play is consistent with that established in "King Henry the Sixth." The role furnishes great opportunities for an acting virtuoso and has long been a favorite with great actors.

King Edward the Fourth, eldest son of the deceased Duke of York. An aging and ailing monarch with a sin-laden past and a remorseful present, he struggles futilely to bring about peace between the hostile factions of his Court. Tricked by Gloucester into ordering the death of his brother Clarence, he tries too late to countermand the order. His grief over Clarence's death hastens his own.

George, Duke of Clarence, brother of King Edward and Richard. Guilty of treachery and perjury in placing his brother Edward on the throne, he is bewildered by his imprisonment and death. In prison he is troubled by terrible dreams, partly begotten by his guilty conscience, and he fears being alone. He has no idea that his fair-seeming brother Richard is responsible for his miseries until his murderers tell him so at the moment of his death.

Queen Margaret, the maleficent widow of the murdered King Henry VI. Her

967

long curse delivered near the beginning of the play, in which she singles out her enemies, is almost a scenario of the play, which might well bear the subtitle of "The Widowed Queen's Curse."

The Duke of Buckingham, Richard's kinsman and powerful supporter. A cold and masterful politician, he is instrumental in placing Richard on the throne. Unwilling to consent to the murder of the helpless young princes, he loses favor, flees the Court, rebels, and is captured and executed. As he goes to his death, he recalls the curses and prophecies of Queen Margaret, whose warning to him he has earlier ignored.

Edward, Prince of Wales, afterward **King Edward V,** older son of King Edward IV. A bright and brave boy, he furnishes pathos by his conduct and by his early violent death.

Richard, Duke of York, King Edward's second son. Impish and precocious, he bandies words even with his sinister uncle. He dies with his brother in the Tower of London.

Henry Tudor, Earl of Richmond, afterward **King Henry VII,** King Richard's major antagonist. A heroic figure, he leads a successful invasion against King Richard and kills him in hand-to-hand combat at the Battle of Bosworth Field. His concluding speech promises the healing of the wounds of civil war and the union of the houses of York and Lancaster by his forthcoming marriage with Elizabeth, daughter of King Edward IV.

Lord Thomas Stanley, Earl of Derby, stepfather of Richmond. Suspicious of Richard of Gloucester from the beginning, he remains a token supporter through fear. His heart is with Richmond; at the Battle of Bosworth Field he risks the life of his son George, a hostage to Richard, by failing to bring up his troops against Richmond. George Stanley's death is prevented by the killing of King Richard.

Lord Hastings, Lord Chamberlain under Edward IV. He is devoted to King Edward and his sons, though an enemy to Queen Elizabeth and her family. His loyalty prevents his becoming a tool of Richard in the campaign to set aside the claims of small Edward V. He trusts Richard to the point of gullibility and pays for his trust and his loyalty to Edward with his life.

Queen Elizabeth, wife of King Edward IV. A haughty and self-willed woman during her husband's reign, she has powerful enemies at Court, including Hastings and Richard of Gloucester. After the murder of her small sons, she is a grieving, almost deranged mother. Her terror for her daughter's safety drives her to appear to consent to Richard's monstrous proposal for the hand of her daughter, his niece. The horrible match is prevented by Richard's death.

[**Elizabeth,** daughter of Edward IV. Although she is not listed in the cast and has no lines, she is an important political pawn in the play. Richard seeks her hand to clinch his claim to the throne, and Richmond announces his forthcoming union with her.]

Lady Anne, daughter-in-law of Henry VI. Although she hates Richard, murderer of her father-in-law and her husband, she succumbs to his wiles and marries him, becoming a pale, wretched victim. She shares sympathy with the Duchess of York and Queen Elizabeth. After Richard has had her murdered, her Ghost appears to him and to Richmond, to daunt the one and encourage the other.

The Duchess of York, mother of Edward IV, Clarence, and Richard III. A loving grandmother to the children of Edward and Clarence, she hates and despises her son Richard, whom she sends to his last battle with a heavy curse, prophesying and wishing for him a shameful death.

Cardinal Bourchier (bou'chər, bōōr'-shĭ·ā), Archbishop of Canterbury. He

968

enables Richard to gain possession of the little Duke of York in order to confine him in the Tower with his brother.

Thomas Rotherham (roth′ĕr·əm), Archbishop of York. He conducts Queen Elizabeth and the little Duke of York to sanctuary, but his kind action turns out to be in vain.

John Morton, Bishop of Ely. His gift to King Richard of strawberries from his garden is in grim contrast to the immediately following arrest and execution of Hastings.

The Duke of Norfolk (Jockey of Norfolk), a loyal follower of Richard III. In spite of a warning that Richard has been betrayed, Norfolk remains faithful and dies in battle.

Anthony Woodville (Earl Rivers), brother of Queen Elizabeth. An enemy of Hastings, he becomes reconciled with him at King Edward's entreaty. He is arrested and executed at Richard's commands.

The Marquess of Dorset and
Lord Grey, Queen Elizabeth's sons by her first husband. Dorset escapes to join Richmond; Grey is executed by Richard's orders.

Sir Thomas Vaughan, one of Richard's victims. He is beheaded with Earl Rivers and Lord Grey.

Sir Thomas, Lord Lovel,
Sir Richard Ratcliff, and
Sir William Catesby, Richard's loyal henchmen. Catesby remains with the King almost to his death, leaving him only to try to find a horse for him.

Sir James Tyrrel, a malcontent. Ambitious and haughty, he engineers for Richard the murder of the little princes in the Tower. He is later remorseful for his crime.

Sir Robert Brackenbury, Lieutenant of the Tower. He resigns the keys to the murderers of Clarence when he sees their warrant. He is killed at Bosworth Field.

The Keeper in the Tower, a kind man. He does his best to ease Clarence's captivity.

Christopher Urswick, a priest. He acts as a messenger from Lord Derby to Richmond to inform him that young George Stanley is held as a hostage by the King.

The Lord Mayor of London. He allows himself to be used by Richard and his followers to help replace Edward V with Richard III.

Edward Plantagenet, Earl of Warwick, the young son of Clarence.

Margaret Plantagenet, the young daughter of Clarence.

The Earl of Surrey, the son of the Duke of Norfolk. He remains with King Richard's army.

The Earl of Oxford (John De Vere), one of the lords who join Richmond in his rebellion.

The Sheriff of Wiltshire. He conducts Buckingham to execution.

Tressel and
Berkeley, gentlemen attending Lady Anne and the body of Henry VI.

Sir William Brandon,
Sir James Blunt, and
Sir Walter Herbert, supporters of Richmond.

Ghosts of Richard's Victims. These include, in addition to the characters killed in this play, King Henry VI and his son Edward, Prince of Wales. All appear to both Richard and Richmond. They rouse uncharacteristic terror in Richard and give refreshing encouragement to Richmond.

RIGHT YOU ARE—IF YOU THINK SO

Author: Luigi Pirandello (1867-1936)
Time of action: Early twentieth century
First presented: 1917

PRINCIPAL CHARACTERS

Signora Frola, an old woman and the mother-in-law of Ponza. She causes talk by living alone in a fine apartment rather than with Ponza and her daughter; by never exchanging visits with her daughter; and by not allowing the neighbors to pay a social call. When she finally confronts the neighbors, she explains that Ponza is mad and must be humored into believing that his wife is, indeed, a second wife taking the place of the one he is convinced he has lost.

Ponza, secretary to the provincial councilor. He causes talk by living with his wife, whom no one ever sees, in a fifth floor tenement, and by visiting Signora Frola every day, alone. When he finally confronts the neighbors, he explains that Signora Frola is mad; that her daughter is dead but that she refuses to believe it; and that his second wife humors her in this belief by pretending to be her daughter and fostering the illusion by communicating with the old lady from the fifth floor balcony.

Signora Ponza, who, veiled, confronts the gossiping neighbors and informs them that she is the daughter of Signora Frola; that she is the second wife of Ponza; and that, for herself, she is nothing. She is, in short, the person she is believed to be.

Commendatore Agazzi, the provincial councilor,
Amalia Agazzi, his wife,
Dina, his daughter, and
Centuri, a police commissioner, gossiping fellow townsmen bent on solving the mystery of the Ponza-Frola domestic arrangements.

Lamberto Laudisi, Commendatore Agazzi's brother-in-law, who insists that the Ponza-Frola domestic arrangements are their own business. When Signora Ponza gives the solution to the mystery, he laughs and says that now everybody knows the truth.

THE RING AND THE BOOK

Author: Robert Browning (1812-1889)
Time of action: Seventeenth century
First published: 1868-1869

PRINCIPAL CHARACTERS

Count Guido Franceschini (gwē′dō frän·chĕs·kē′nē), the oldest male member of a destitute noble family of Arezzo. Knowing that he is the last hope for furthering the family name, since his two brothers are priests, Guido seeks a wife to bear him a son. Impoverished, he needs a woman with an attractive dowry. His brother finds a likely prospect, and Guido's family name attracts the girl's mother. Inept as a husband and angered by denial of the dowry after the wedding, Guido abuses his wife. To retain the last vestige of honor as a husband, after he has driven her to extramarital affections, Guido, with four men from his village, kills his parents-in-law and fatally wounds his wife. The court

970

hearings and the gossip relating to the affair, presented from various viewpoints, point to Guido's instability, he representing an old family without means of sustenance or continuation—no wealth, no prestige, no progeny. He is sentenced to be hanged, by rulings of both Church and State.

Pompilia Comparini (pôm·pē′lyä kôm·pä·rē′nē), his seventeen-year-old wife. Bought as a newborn infant from a prostitute, Pompilia was brought up by aged foster parents. Trapped in an incompatible marriage not of her choice, she flees to Rome with Caponsacchi, a priest. Overtaken, she and the priest disavow that they are lovers. After hearing that Pompilia, who has returned to her foster parents, has given birth to a son, Guido returns to Rome with four ruffians and attacks the Comparinis. Pompilia, mortally wounded, lingers for four days, time enough for her to identify her attacker.

Violante Comparini (vī·ō·län′tē), her foster mother. Violante's warped sense of values leads to bizarre behavior. She feigns pregnancy, presents Pompilia to her husband as his child, negotiates Pompilia's marriage, and convinces her husband, who has objected to the marriage, that the status achieved by the union will be worth the promised dowry. Realizing her bad bargain and attempting to keep Guido from profiting by the marriage, Violante divulges Pompilia's parentage and disqualifies her from inheriting Comparini's money.

Pietro Comparini (pyä′trō), Violante's husband. Naïve and browbeaten, he is governed by his wife's whims and desires.

Giuseppe Caponsacchi (jö·zĕp′pä käp′ən·säk·kē), a handsome priest, Pompilia's gallant lover. Excommunicated for his part in the affair, Giuseppe wishes himself dead but looks forward to the day when he will be returned to the grace of the Church.

Margherita (mär·gä·rē′tä), Pompilia's maid, who advises and encourages Pompilia to throw off the drudgery of her life with Guido by responding to Giuseppe's attentions.

Paolo (pä′ō·lō), Count Guido's brother, a priest in Rome, who makes the initial contact with Violante for the marriage of Guido and Pompilia. His description of his brother makes Guido more attractive than the Comparinis find him.

Doctor Johannes-Baptista Bottinius (yō·hän′əs-bäp·tēs′tä bōt·tēn′yŭs), familiarly called **Giovambittista o' the Bottini,** who variously defends Pompilia at the hearings, for her behavior in the affair, and persecutes her, as the gossips of Rome cried, by ordering her money given to a sisterhood rather than to her child.

Dominus Hyacinthus de Archangelis (dŏm′ï·nəs hī′ə·sĭn′thəs də är·kan′je·ləs) familiarly called **Don Giacinto of the Archangeli,** the Procurator of the poor in Rome. He defends Guido and his hired companions at the hearings.

Pope Innocent XII, who condemns Count Guido to die in the presence of the populace; however, before his death he prays that the condemned man may be forgiven his sin.

Gaetano (gä·ä·tä′nō), Pompilia's two-week-old son, who, she says in her dying moments, ". . . nor was, nor is, nor yet shall be/Count Guido Franceschini's child at all—/Only his mother's born of love not hate!"

Tommati (tō·mä′tē) and **Venturini** (vĕn·tūr·ē′nē), judges at the hearings.

RING ROUND THE MOON

Author: Jean Anouilh (1910-)
Time of action: 1912
First presented: 1947

PRINCIPAL CHARACTERS

Hugo, a young man without a heart and the identical twin of Frederic. Not realizing that he, himself, is in love with Diana Messerschmann, he plots to end Frederic's infatuation for her by hiring Isabelle to masquerade as an invited guest to the ball where she is to draw Frederic from Diana to herself. As his scheme goes awry, Hugo realizes that he and Diana are made for each other and that he has wanted her all along.

Frederic, a young man with a heart and the identical twin of Hugo. Engaged to Diana Messerschmann, he blindly follows where love leads until Hugo plots to end his infatuation by hiring Isabelle to lure him away from Diana. Finally, he sees Diana for what she is and finds in Isabelle a tender heart to match his own.

Diana Messerschmann, a young lady without a heart. Engaged to Frederic, whom love has blinded to her true nature, she finally is led to see that she and the heartless Hugo are meant for each other.

Isabelle, a ballet dancer hired by Hugo

to masquerade as an invited guest at the ball and to win Frederic away from Diana. She succeeds by revealing to Frederic a heart as innocent and gentle as his own.

Madame Desmermortes, the aunt of Hugo and Frederic and the hostess at the ball. Shrewd and worldly-wise, she sets to right the confusion brought about by Hugo's hiring of Isabelle to masquerade as an invited guest.

Messerschmann, Diana Messerschmann's millionaire father, in love with Lady Dorothy India.

Lady Dorothy India, Madame Desmermortes' niece and Messerschmann's mistress.

Romainville, a guest gently blackmailed by Hugo to pass off Isabelle as his niece and, hence, an invited guest at the ball.

Patrice Bombelles, Messerschmann's secretary, engaged in a secret love affair with Lady Dorothy India.

Capulat, Madame Desmermortes' companion.

RIP VAN WINKLE

Author: Washington Irving (1783-1859)
Time of action: Eighteenth century
First published: 1819-1820

PRINCIPAL CHARACTERS

Rip Van Winkle, who was born along the Hudson River, of an old Dutch family. To get away from his wife he goes into the Kaatskill mountains, where drink puts him to sleep for twenty years.

Dame Van Winkle, Rip's shrewish wife

who is disgusted by Rip's lack of energy and thrift. She dies of a stroke in the midst of a fit of anger at a Yankee peddler.

Wolf, Rip's dog, chased with his master from the house by Dame Van Winkle.

Judith Van Winkle, Rip's daughter, who fails to recognize him after twenty years. Rip is relieved when she reports that Dame Van Winkle is dead.

Hendrick Hudson, the leader of the Little Men who return once every twenty years to bowl and drink. They provide Rip with liquor.

THE RISE OF SILAS LAPHAM

Author: William Dean Howells (1837-1920)
Time of action: Nineteenth century
First published: 1885

PRINCIPAL CHARACTERS

Silas Lapham, a millionaire paint manufacturer in Boston. He is respected in business circles, but his family is not accepted socially. Garrulous, bourgeois, burly, brusque, he reflects traits of the self-made man who loves his maker; yet he is compassionate with outsiders and loving to his family. Babbitt-like, he emulates men he has admired for their savoir-faire. Bankrupt after a series of business reverses, he gladly leaves the material comforts of Boston, to return with his family to the modest living of their earlier days. Lapham is called "Colonel," his rank when he was injured at Gettysburg during the Civil War.

Persis Lapham, his wife. Like her husband, she has kept the ways of the country. More aware of present social conduct than is her husband, she is no more capable of observing the proprieties. Interested in marriage for her daughters, prudent and self-effacing in social matters, she restrains herself in advising them. An influence in his affairs, she goads Lapham into business dealings, to her involving morality, only to regret later the action taken. When uninformed of his activities, she becomes suspicious; she is remorseful and self-reproaching when she senses her unfounded jealousies. To Persis, returning to the country is escape from the rigors of Boston's social life and her inability to cope with status.

Irene, the Laphams' younger daughter. Quiet, reserved, beautiful, and domestic,

she infers that Tom Corey is interested in her, only to learn that he is in love with her sister. She escapes the sympathy and questioning of her family and the trials of the family's financial reverses through a month-long visit with relatives in the Middle West. Returning to Boston, to let the family know that her cousin's evident interest in her is another misleading affair, she becomes a virtual recluse other than for visits to the Middle West.

Penelope, the Laphams' older daughter. She is satirical, humorous, droll. Inferring that Tom Corey is in love with Irene, but secretly in love with him herself, Penelope is guilt-stricken when Corey reveals his affection for her. She refuses Corey's attentions, thinking her father's financial adversity would imply the wrong motivations for her accepting Corey. Ultimately, they are married and go to Mexico and Central America, where Cory will be in business.

Tom Corey, the son of a proper Bostonian family. Shaking off the effects of hereditary stratification, he displays considerable business acumen. In his attentions to Irene he is hoping to attract Penelope to him. This indirection misleads the Laphams and the Coreys. However, his stability, self-reliance, and graciousness in personal affairs, as well as removal from their families, assure marital happiness for him and Penelope.

Milton K. Rogers, Lapham's former business partner. His recurrent appearances

973

for assistance create situations to point up Lapham's character and the attitudes and rapport between the Laphams. Unsuccessful in appeals to Lapham, Rogers turns to Persis, who intercedes with her husband.

Anna Corey, Tom's mother. In her seeming innocuous role of an aristocrat whose chief occupation is the comfort of her husband and children, she is likable. In protecting her son from questionable associations, as with the Laphams, she is protective in a genteel way.

Bromfield Corey, Tom's father. A rich young painter in Rome at the time of his marriage, he has never changed his pace. Sedentary, he remains unassuming in social matters. Nothing surprises him; nothing shocks him; nothing upsets him. In his self-imposed isolation, he views life as an amusing process and expresses his ready opinions on happenings accordingly.

Zerilla Dewey, a typist in Lapham's office, the butt of Mrs. Lapham's jealousy.

Mrs. James Millon (Moll), Zerilla's mother. Moll Millon is the ne'er-do-well widow of the man who was killed by a bullet intended for Lapham in an early labor dispute.

Lily and
Nanny, Tom Corey's young sisters. Their behavior toward the Laphams and Tom's marriage reflects their mother's influence.

Walker, a bookkeeper in Lapham's office. His garrulousness in office matters helps to define Corey's discretion and business attitudes.

Bartley Hubbard, a journalist who writes Lapham's biography.

Mr. Sewell, a minister, the adviser to the Laphams in their dilemma after Tom's indirection with Irene and Penelope.

James Bellingham, Mrs. Corey's brother and a business adviser to Lapham at the time of Lapham's financial losses.

THE RIVALS

Author: Richard Brinsley Sheridan (1751-1816)
Time of action: Eighteenth century
First presented: 1775

PRINCIPAL CHARACTERS

Captain Jack Absolute (Ensign Beverley), a young aristocrat who poses as a penniless ensign in order to win the love of Lydia Languish. After many problems—relatives who oppose his marriage, rivals who challenge him to duels, misunderstandings with his fiancée—Jack wins fair Lydia.

Lydia Languish, Jack Absolute's beloved, a girl whose head is so stuffed with the fantastic adventures of popular fictional people that she cannot bear to marry anyone in her own class. She spurns Jack Absolute when she learns that he is not

the penniless Ensign Beverley; but she is greatly impressed when she learns that he is to fight a duel because of her, and he wins her hand.

Sir Anthony Absolute, Jack's strong-willed father, who insists that Jack marry the woman Sir Anthony selects. Jack refuses to obey his father's edict until he learns that Sir Anthony has chosen Lydia to be his son's wife.

Mrs. Malaprop, Lydia's aunt, whose eccentric treatment of the English language gave us the word malapropism. She opposes Lydia's intention to marry Jack, but she drops her objections at last to bask in the high spirits of those whose problems have found happy solutions.

Bob Acres, an affable country squire who challenges Ensign Beverley to a duel. When he learns that Beverley and his friend Jack are the same person, the timid squire is greatly relieved that no duel will be necessary.

Sir Lucius O'Trigger, a brash Irishman who is hoodwinked into believing that he is corresponding with Lydia when, actu-

ally, Mrs. Malaprop and he are exchanging letters. He challenges Jack to a duel, but withdraws when he learns that Lydia never has been interested in him.

Faulkland, Jack's friend, who is in love with Julia Melville, Lydia's cousin. Faulkland's avocation is worrying about the welfare of his suit for Julia, thus creating obstacles where there are none. Finally, however, he banishes care and generously accepts Julia's love.

Julia Melville, Lydia's cousin, who marries Faulkland.

RIVER OF EARTH

Author: James Still (1906-   )
Time of action: Early 1930's
First published: 1940

PRINCIPAL CHARACTERS

Brack's Oldest Boy, the narrator. The events in this story of poverty-ridden Kentucky mountaineers are seen through the eyes of a young boy, observant but frequently too young to comprehend what he observes.

Brack Baldridge, his father. Poverty and depression are not Brack's only enemies in his struggle to keep his family from starving. He is too humane to deny food to miners out of work and begging for their families, or to send sponging relatives away.

Alpha Baldridge, Brack's wife. In desperation she moves her furniture and children to the smokehouse and sets fire to the house, so that the sponging relatives, having no place to sleep, will then leave her family in possession of their meager supply of food.

Grandmother Middleton, Alpha's brisk mother, who lives on a small farm. The boy is sent to help her with her harvesting and ends by staying more than a year. When she dies, her body is brought to

the boy's home in Blackjack prior to burial. As the wagon takes her body away for the last time, the boy hears the first cry of his mother's new baby.

Uncle Jolly, Alpha's brother, who spends much of his time in jail. Once he is pardoned by the governor for his bravery in helping fight a prison fire, which he admits to his mother he started.

Uncle Samp, who never worked and does not intend to start. Evicted once from the Baldridge home by Alpha's fire, he shows up later at their coal camp house. He finally marries a fortuneteller.

Euly Baldridge, the sister of the narrator. Wanting to be educated, the children go to school until the schoolmaster is shot by an angry mountaineer whose loutish son had been punished by the teacher.

Harl Logan and
Tibb Logan, cousins also evicted by Alpha's fire. They return to work in the mine and live with the Baldridges. Laid off, they dynamite one of the veins and,

having been kicked out by the mine boss, leave the Baldridge home.

Uncle Luce, supposed to replace the boy as Grandmother Middleton's helper on the farm; however, he arrives after the harvest.

Uncle Toll, who fetches the boy from his grandmother and leaves him to sleep outside Jolly's jail cell so that lack of companionship will not drive Jolly to break out. Knowing that a jailbreak will get him a long prison term, Jolly puts

temptation out of reach by stealing the keys and sending the boy home with them to his family.

[**Grandpa Middleton,** killed some time before by Aus Coggins; no Baldridge has avenged the death. The narrator has a fistfight with a neighbor boy who says the Baldridges are cowards.]

Aus Coggins. It is said that Uncle Jolly is avenging his father's death and tormenting Aus Coggins by cutting his fences and breaking his dam.

THE RIVET IN GRANDFATHER'S NECK

Author: James Branch Cabell (1879-1958)
Time of action: 1896-1927
First published: 1915

PRINCIPAL CHARACTERS

Colonel Rudolph Musgrave, head of the Musgrave family. A thorough Southern gentleman, he is aristocratic and scholarly, a lover of many women, and a less than successful businessman. Having loved and lost Anne Charteris in the past, he falls in love with and marries his cousin, Patricia Stapylton. After a deterioration in their relationship, Patricia dies of a heart attack, but he feels too deep a loyalty to her to marry the now free Anne Charteris.

Patricia Stapylton, Colonel Rudolph Musgrave's young cousin, later his wife. Happy at first in their marriage, she gives her husband a son at the risk of her life and with permanent damage to her health. As tensions develop between husband and wife, she becomes enamored of John Charteris. When he is killed, she dies of a heart attack.

John Charteris, a novelist. Having been involved in many affairs, he is easily persuaded by Patricia Stapylton to run off with her. The runaways are stopped by Colonel Musgrave, and a few days later Charteris is killed by a jealous husband.

Anne Charteris, John Charteris' adoring wife. She refuses to recognize that her husband is a scoundrel until the knowledge is forced on her after her death. Even then, however, her loyalty prevents her marriage to Colonel Rudolph Musgrave.

Agatha Musgrave, Colonel Rudolph Musgrave's maiden sister, whose resentment of her brother's wife, Patricia Stapylton, is part of the cause of their growing marital tensions.

Roger Stapylton, Patricia Stapylton's father, formerly an overseer, now a wealthy businessman.

Joe Parkinson, Patricia Stapylton's rejected suitor.

Virginia, a servant in the Musgrave household.

Lord Pevensey, Patricia Stapylton's rejected fiancé.

Mrs. Clarice Pendomer, a former mistress of John Charteris.

ROAN STALLION

Author: Robinson Jeffers (1887-1962)
Time of action: The 1920's
First published: 1925

PRINCIPAL CHARACTERS

California, a young farm wife, daughter of a Scottish sailor and a Spanish and Indian mother. She is graceful, lithe, strong, and darkly beautiful, but soiled by her life with Johnny and his associates. Her passionate offering of herself to the stallion on a hilltop on an April night symbolizes her turning from her sordid relationships with men and her submission to the majestic strength and clean beauty of God. When, filled with hatred the next night, she flees from the drunken Johnny to the stallion's corral, she is followed by Johnny and his dog Bruno. The frightened Christine brings her mother a gun to kill the raging stallion. But California shoots Bruno and watches the stallion crush Johnny with his hoofs and rend the lifeless body with his teeth. Then, faithful to her own race after all, she shoots the stallion and in stark agony turns toward her daughter like a woman who has killed God.

Johnny, her husband, an outcast Hollander, palefaced with burnt-out blue eyes, his still-young body shriveled from debauchery.

Christine, their small blonde daughter, blue-eyed like her father, wizened of forehead and sickly in body.

The Roan Stallion, a symbol of the rejection of man and the embracing of natural life.

Jim Carrier, the owner of a bay mare bred to the roan stallion.

ROB ROY

Author: Sir Walter Scott (1771-1832)
Time of action: 1715
First published: 1818

PRINCIPAL CHARACTERS

Frank Osbaldistone, a young man who has been sent abroad to learn his father's mercantile business and whose progress has not been satisfactory. He is sent to his uncle's home to find his replacement among his uncle's sons. He and his cousin Rashleigh, who takes the position, dislike each other immediately. On the way to his uncle's house, Frank meets Rob Roy, the outlaw, without knowing who he is. He also falls in love with Diana Vernon, whom he meets on the way to his uncle's. After the Jacobite revolt, Frank inherits all of his uncle's lands and marries Diana, in spite of the fact that she is a Catholic and he is a Presbyterian.

Rashleigh Osbaldistone, Frank's cousin, who takes a position with Osbaldistone and Tresham and proceeds to embezzle funds from the firm. He betrays the Stuart cause and is disinherited.

Mr. William Osbaldistone, Frank's businessman father. He does not like the idea of Frank's marrying a papist, but at last he consents.

Sir Hildebrand Osbaldistone, Frank's uncle and one of the plotters in the Jacobite uprising. He dies at Newgate after willing Frank all of his property.

Diana Vernon, Sir Hildebrand's niece, with whom Frank falls in love. She is a Catholic and an outspoken girl.

Rob Roy (MacGregor Campbell), a Scottish outlaw. He befriends Frank and helps him discover that Rashleigh is embezzling funds from Osbaldistone and

Tresham. When Frank is arrested while on the way to meet him, Rob Roy's wife Helen leads an attack on the arresting soldiers and frees Frank. Meanwhile, Rob Roy has been captured but he escapes by throwing himself into a river. After the Jacobite revolt Rob Roy kills Rashleigh when that turncoat comes to arrest Diana and her father.

Sir Frederick Vernon, Diana's father and a Jacobite.

ROBIN HOOD'S ADVENTURES

Author: Unknown
Time of action: Thirteenth century
First published: c. 1490

PRINCIPAL CHARACTERS

Robin Hood, actually the young Earl of Huntingdon, whose father has been wrongly dispossessed of his estates. Robin Hood becomes an outlaw when he kills one of the King's stags after being taunted by foresters to show his skill with a longbow. Under sentence of death for killing the animal, the young nobleman flees to Sherwood Forest, where he gathers together a band of outlaws known as the Merry Men. Robin earns his place of leadership by outfighting and outshooting his comrades, all of whom become intensely loyal followers. Robin enjoys playing tricks on the authorities sent to capture him and gains support by helping the poor. Although eventually he is pardoned by Richard the Lion-Hearted and given back his title and estates, Robin becomes homesick for his old ways and returns to life in Sherwood Forest and outlawry. He is eventually killed by a cousin, the prioress at Kirkley Abbey, who bleeds him to death under the guise of giving him medical treatment.

Little John, a huge man who joins the Merry Men after being bested by Robin in a shooting match. As a lark, Little

John spends six months in the service of the Sheriff of Nottingham, Robin Hood's enemy. Little John is with Robin at the time of the hero's death, though he arrives too late to save him. He buries Robin under the ancient oak where his last arrow fell.

Friar Tuck, a hedge priest who joins the Merry Men after a fight with Robin precipitated by the friar's ducking Robin in a stream.

Will Scarlet, one of the Merry Men. He participates with Robin and Little John in an archery match against the King's own men. In the match the outlaws appear as the Queen's men and win for her.

Richard the Lion-Hearted, the King. He bests Robin in a fight and then pardons the outlaws, returning the rightful title and estates to their leader.

King John, who is infuriated when Robin Hood reverts to outlawry. He sends a force of men to capture Robin and his men.

The Sheriff of Nottingham, a crown officer who tries for years to capture Robin

Hood. He is killed in a battle just before the death of Robin himself.

Sir Richard of the Lea, Robin Hood's friend, a knight once helped by Robin.

The Tinker,
The Cook,

Allan-a-Dale, and
George-a-Greene, faithful followers of Robin Hood.

Maid Marian, a young girl vaguely associated with the Robin Hood cycle. Her importance in the story grew as the morris dance developed.

ROBINSON CRUSOE

Author: Daniel Defoe (1660-1731)
Time of action: 1651-1705
First published: 1719

PRINCIPAL CHARACTERS

Robinson Crusoe, a self-sufficient Englishman who, after several adventures at sea and on land, is cast away on a small uninhabited island. A practical, far-sighted man of talents, he sets about to make his island home comfortable, utilizing all his knowledge. His prudence and industry, aided by an imaginative insight, enable him to pass twenty-four years alone, providing for himself in every way from the resources of the island itself and what he is able to salvage from the shipwreck that puts him in his predicament. A God-fearing man, he reads his Bible and gives thanks each day for his delivery from death. Eventually he is rescued and returns to England after an absence of thirty-five years, only to go traveling again.

Mr. Crusoe, Robinson Crusoe's father, a middle-class Englishman. He wants his son to go into business and remain at home, rather than go to sea.

Friday, a savage rescued from cannibal captors by Robinson Crusoe. He proves an apt pupil and learns how to participate in his rescuer's life and labors. He learns to speak English and becomes a friend and companion, as well as a fellow laborer.

RODERICK RANDOM

Author: Tobias Smollett (1721-1771)
Time of action: Eighteenth century
First published: 1748

PRINCIPAL CHARACTERS

Roderick Random, familiarly called **Rory,** a reckless and restless young man whose experiences parallel to a certain extent those of Smollett himself. Rory's mother dies when he is born, and his father, disinherited by his family because he had married a poor relation and a domestic, leaves England. Random, libertine and unscrupulous, goes through all the stages of the eighteenth century picaresque hero. As a boy, he is mistreated by alienated relatives; he is befriended and educated (in medicine) by a sympathetic one. His life is a series of assumed identities, leading to whirlwind courtships and attempted marriages to a number of wealthy women. Robbed by a rascally friar in France, he enlists in the army of King Louis XIV. When things seem to be going too well or too badly for Random, an antagonist or a protagonist appears to change the course of his life. Sea voyages and escapades in foreign countries seem to be Random's plight, until in Buenos Aires he meets a wealthy English trader who proves to be his father. After a series of events making for an unsettled, nomadic life, Random is established, happily married, on his father's estate, from which he was evicted as a youngster. Although he often acts without scruples Random is a likable and in the end a personable young man.

Tom Bowling, Random's uncle, lieutenant aboard H.M.S. "Thunder." Appearing early in the story, he becomes Random's benefactor. His first move is to get Random away from mean relatives and into school. As unsettled as his nephew, Bowling fights duels on sea and land, is robbed, loses and regains command of ships, suffers at the hands of ingrates he has befriended. Always the old salt, especially in avoiding interference in others' personal affairs, he makes his will in favor of Random and goes to sea again after seeing his young relative comfortable financially and happy maritally.

Hugh Strap, a schoolmate of Random. Like Bowling, Strap appears propitiously now and again to save Random from disaster or death. At times Strap's good deeds lead to further involvements for his friend. Strap, the imaginative, romantic figure, curries favor of a French nobleman to gain employment and an inheritance from his master. As the moneyed M. d'Estrapes, he grooms Random as a fine gentleman so that the scapegrace can make a wealthy marriage in England. His kindnesses are repaid when Random comes into money and acquaints Strap with the latter's wife to be.

Narcissa, the niece of the eccentric bluestocking to whom Random hires out as a footman. Narcissa falls in love with Random and he with her. Despite her relatives' and fate's working against her and Random, the beautiful, clever Narcissa remains faithful to him, avoids marriage with any of her many suitors, and in the end becomes his wife.

Don Roderigo, the wealthy English trader whom Random meets in Buenos Aires. Don Roderigo, who has made a fortune through the favors of a Spanish grandee, proves to be Random's father. Don Roderigo buys his paternal estate from a debt-ridden heir, and the Random family settles once more in Scotland.

Nancy Williams, a prostitute to whom Random gives medical care after she is taken ill on the street. Their recurring contacts lead to Miss Williams' becoming Narcissa's attendant. She marries Strap.

The Squire, Narcissa's drunken, foxhunting brother. His disposition is best described by his aunt, who refers to him as the Savage. The Squire's chief function in the plot is to contend against Random and to urge his sister toward other suitors.

Sir Timothy Thicket, one of Narcissa's suitors, whom Random beats with a cudgel for forcing his attentions on Narcissa.

Melinda Goosetrap, a young woman of fortune whom Random courts. He fails in his suit because Melinda's mother sees through his disguise as a person of means. Melinda even wins at cards with Random as he is trying to get some of her money through gambling. She exposes him when she finds him pursuing other wealthy girls.

Miss Snapper, a witty, wealthy, deformed young woman also courted by Random after he saves her and her mother from highwaymen. He neglects her after meeting Narcissa in Bath.

Lord Quiverwit, another of Narcissa's suitors, favored by her brother. Random defeats him in a duel.

Lieutenant Crampley, the commander of the "Lizard," one of the ships on which Random serves. Crampley appears to hound Random in an effort to right an old wrong.

Jack Ratlin,
Thomson, and
Captain Oakhum, members of ships' crews. They are representative of the many individuals involved in Random's experiences.

Launcelot Crab, the surgeon who lends Random money. Crab is only one of innumerable doctors, on land and at sea, who affect Random's fortunes.

Banter,
Chatwell, and

Bragwell, three of the wide circle of young men, in London and Bath, who are friends or foes of Random.

Mrs. Sagely, a kind old woman who befriends and takes care of Random after he has been seriously injured in a fight.

An Eccentric Blue-Stocking Lady, Narcissa's aunt, whom Mrs. Sagely persuades to hire Random as a footman. Random's employer, an authoress of sorts, takes to Random because of his interpretation of her writing. She offsets some of the Squire's antagonism throughout Random's pursuit of Narcissa.

Frère Balthazar, a Scottish priest, referred to as the **Capuchin.** As in much eighteenth century writing, the Capuchin is a debauched churchman. Among his misdeeds is the theft of Random's money, a loss which forces him to enlist in the French army.

ROGUE HERRIES

Author: Hugh Walpole (1884-1941)
Time of action: 1730-1774
First published: 1930

PRINCIPAL CHARACTERS

Francis Herries, called **Rogue Herries** because of his notorious escapades. In 1730 he brings his family and his mistress to live in the long-deserted family house of Herries; here he continues to earn his reputation as the family black sheep. After the death of his wife, whom he had married more for pity than for love, he becomes attracted to a gipsy-like girl whom he meets under strange circumstances. He pursues her and finally marries her. She runs away but later returns to him. His oldest child is fifty-five when Francis again becomes a father. He and his wife both die on the night of their daughter's birth.

Margaret Herries, Francis' first wife, who is never able to command her husband's

love. When she is dying, she feels that he will be at a loss without her, however, and makes her son promise never to leave his father.

Mirabell Starr, a lovely young girl living with thieves. They kidnap Francis in order to give him a cross and chain left to him by Mirabell's mother, whom he had once befriended. Mirabell at last agrees to marry Francis, in return for food and protection, but he cannot succeed in making her love him. She leaves him for several years but eventually returns to Herries. She dies in childbirth.

David Herries, the son of Francis and Margaret. His wife is hated by Mirabell. David and his wife move from Herries

981

and become well established in their new community.

Sarah Denburn, a friendly, handsome girl whom David meets and falls in love with on a business trip. Her uncle-guardian intends her for another man, but David kills his rival, carries her off, and marries her.

Deborah Herries, the daughter of Francis and Margaret. She marries a clergyman.

Alice Press, ostensibly the governess to Francis' children, but in fact his mistress.

He tires of her and tries to get rid of her, but she refuses to leave. Encountering her at a fair, Francis creates a scene and makes a show of selling her to another man.

Osbaldistone, who in the course of a duel with Francis slashes him from temple to chin. The scar marks Francis for life.

Harry, Mirabell's only true love, who is killed before her marriage to Francis by a jealous and ugly older man. Francis witnesses the attack, but his warning comes too late.

THE ROMAN ACTOR

Author: Philip Massinger (1583-1640)
Time of action: First century
First presented: 1626

PRINCIPAL CHARACTERS

Domitian (də·mĭsh′ĭ·ən), Emperor of Rome. Cruel and self-indulgent, convinced of his own godhood, he has no fear of the laws of the gods or men. Infatuated with Domitia, he forces her husband to divorce her, then has him killed. He is shaken when two stoic Senators scorn his tortures and die calmly. In his own mind he performs a kindness by killing the actor, Paris, while taking part with him in a play, rather than having him executed. Eventually he nerves himself to have his faithless wife killed, but he is assassinated before he can have his sentence executed.

Domitia (də·mĭsh′ĭ·ə), the beautiful and ambitious wife of Aelius Lamia. Willingly divorcing her husband, she uses the Emperor's power to dominate the noblewomen. Becoming madly infatuated with the handsome actor, Paris, she indiscreetly orders him to a private meeting and attempts to seduce him. The Emperor surprises them together; but Domithia's voluptuous power over him keeps him from killing her. After the Emperor kills Paris, her hatred leads her

to join the conspirators. She is sentenced to death by the Tribunes after Domitian is killed.

Paris (pâ′rĭs), the Roman actor. A dignified defender of the stage and a loyal servant of the Emperor, he has political enemies. Domitia's infatuation destroys him. He acts roles in three plays within the main play, his final role ending in real, not mimic, death.

Parthenius (pär·thē′nĭ·əs), the Emperor's toady, a freedman. He arranges the divorce of Domitia and her marriage with the Emperor. He suffers Domitian's fiendish cruelty, even the death of his own father, Philargus; but finding his name listed in the Emperor's death book, he joins the conspirators and tricks the Emperor to his death.

Aretinus (â·rə·tī′nəs), an unprincipled informer. His spying leads to the deaths of Aelius Lamia, Junius Rusticus, and Palphurius Sura. He informs the Emperor of the secret meeting of Paris and Domitia and receives the reward of being strangled for his trouble.

Philargus (fĭ·lär′gəs), Parthenius' miserly father. His avarice is not cured by Paris' play, but is cured by Domitian, who has him killed.

Latinus (lə·tī′nəs) and
Aesopus (ē·sō′pəs), actors in Paris' company.

Aelius Lamia (ē′lĭ·əs lä′mĭ·ə), a Senator, Domitia's husband. He despises Domitian.

Junius Rusticus (jū′nĭ·əs rŭs′tĭ·kəs), a virtuous Senator. At the moment of his death he prophesies the destruction of Domitian.

Palphurius Sura (păl·fūr′ĭ·əs sū′rə), another stoic Senator, tortured and murdered with Rusticus.

Ascletario (ăs′klə·tă′rĭ·ō), a soothsayer. Prophesying that his body will be devoured by dogs just before the Emperor's death, he rouses Domitian to fury. Subsequent events reduce the fury to fatalistic despair.

Domitilla (dŏ·mĭ·tĭl′lə), Domitian's cousin, whom he has violated,
Julia (jōō′lĭ·ə), Domitian's niece, with whom he has committed incest,
Caenis (sē′nĭs), the former mistress of the dead Titus,
Sejeius (sə·jā′yəs), and
Entellus (ĕn·tĕl′ləs), the conspirators who help kill the Emperor.

THE ROMANCE OF A SCHOOLMASTER

Author: Edmondo de Amicis (1846-1908)
Time of action: Nineteenth century
First published: 1876

PRINCIPAL CHARACTERS

Emilio Ratti, a young Italian schoolmaster. He learns the tribulations of teaching school in a small community. Badgered by the pupils and the patrons of his schools, he finds that everyone—even the priests—seems to use the teachers as scapegoats. After several years of teaching in rural communities, he passes the examination which permits him to obtain a much better teaching position in the city of Turin.

Faustina Galli, a pretty young schoolteacher loved by Emilio Ratti. She learns that she is regarded as fair game by petty village officials who solicit her favors with cajolery and threats. She cannot return Emilio Ratti's love because she has the responsibility of caring for a crippled father. Like Ratti, she is a devoted and successful teacher.

Professor Megari, one of Emilio Ratti's professors at the normal school. At the request of Emilio's dying mother, the professor encourages the young man and, at one point, saves him from drunkenness.

Giovanni Labaccio, an insinuating young man who tries to please everyone. He marries a rich widow and thus escapes from the drudgery of teaching. Although he marries the widow, an older woman, only for her money, he reviles his former fellow teachers as persons interested in money and advancement, rather than teaching.

Carlo Lerica, an ex-corporal of grenadiers who turns to teaching school as a better life than that of an enlisted man in the Italian Army. Like Emilio Ratti, he becomes a good schoolteacher.

983

THE ROMANCE OF LEONARDO DA VINCI

Author: Dmitri Merejkowski (1865-1941)
Time of action: 1494-1519
First published: 1902

PRINCIPAL CHARACTERS

Leonardo da Vinci, the famous artist and inventor of the fifteenth century. He serves the Duke of Milan, then Cesare Borgia. He also serves the city of Florence by using his talents as artist and as inventor. In Florence he enjoys the friendship of Raphael and earns the enmity and jealousy of Michelangelo. He returns to Milan and the service of Louis XII of France, that city's conqueror. He ends his life in the service of Francis I of France, living in France and dying there. Although he is rumored to be a disciple of the Antichrist, he dies a Christian.

Duke Moro, the ruler of Milan, the benefactor of Leonardo and Leonardo's patron. Da Vinci leaves Milan when it is threatened by French forces.

Cesare Borgia, the son of Pope Alexander VI, a hated man but a patron to Leonardo.

Niccolò Machiavelli, a friend of Leonardo who helps him get a commission from the city of Florence to plan a system of waterways.

Michelangelo, the famous artist. He is a jealous rival of Leonardo.

Pope Leo X, an artistically-minded pontiff who is Leonardo's friend and patron.

Louis XII, King of France, who is also one of Leonardo's patrons.

Monna Cassandra, a beautiful Milanese girl who is loved by Beltraffio, Leonardo's pupil. The girl is burned as a witch.

Giovanni Beltraffio, a pupil of Leonardo. He commits suicide after the death of Monna Cassandra.

Francesco Melzi, a favorite pupil of Michelangelo and the artist's friend in his old age.

Andrea Salaino, a student of Leonardo.

Zoroastro da Peretola, a student of Leonardo who is killed while trying to use the artist's unfinished flying machine.

Monna Lisa Gioconda, the model for da Vinci's famous portrait. She and the artist fall in love, and her death is a great shock to Leonardo.

THE ROMANCE OF THE FOREST

Author: Mrs. Ann Radcliffe (1764-1823)
Time of action: Seventeenth century
First published: 1791

PRINCIPAL CHARACTERS

Pierre de la Motte (pyĕr′ də lä môt′), a fugitive from the law, a passionate man who has run through a sizeable fortune. He rescues the girl Adeline from ruffians. He takes refuge with his household in an ancient abbey. He tries to rob the

Marquis de Montalt and falls into the man's power. La Motte is finally exiled to England for his misdeeds.

Mme. de la Motte, a faithful, patient wife. She takes pity on Adeline until she thinks that her son loves the girl; then her manner becomes cold.

Louis de la Motte, (lwē′ dǝ lá môt′), Pierre's son, a soldier stationed in Germany. He traces his parents to the ancient abbey, drawn by his love for them. He falls in love with Adeline but loses her to Theodore Peyrou.

Adeline (à·dā·lēn′), a sweet, lively girl rescued by Pierre de la Motte. She shares their hiding place in the ancient abbey. Actually an heiress, she has been cheated by her evil uncle, the Marquis, but comes into her rightful inheritance when he is executed. She falls in love with Theodore Peyrou, whom she marries after many adventures.

Théodore Peyrou (tā·ô·dôr′ pĕ·rōō′), a young officer. He tries gallantly to rescue Adeline from the Marquis de Montalt because he loves her. Theodore turns out to be the son of Armand La Luc, a clergyman. He is innocent of charges brought against him by the Marquis de Montalt, and he marries Adeline.

The Marquis de Montalt (dǝ mōn·tàl′), a villainous nobleman, owner of the abbey in which Pierre de la Motte takes refuge. He desires Adeline until he learns that she is his murdered brother's daughter; then he hates her and wants her killed. He is her father's murderer and wants her removed so that she cannot claim the estates he has inherited after killing her father. He is condemned and put to death for his crimes.

Peter, de la Motte's coachman. He helps Adeline escape from the wicked Marquis.

Arnaud la Luc (àr·nō′ la lük′), a scholarly clergyman who befriends Adeline after her escape from the Marquis.

Clara la Luc (klá·rá′ lá lük′), the clergyman's daughter and Adeline's friend. She marries a distant kinsman of Adeline.

M. Verneuil, (vĕr·nœ′yǝ), a good man who marries Clara la Luc.

Du Bosse (dü bôs′), one of the ruffians hired to do away with Adeline. His testimony reveals the crimes of the Marquis.

ROMANCE OF THE THREE KINGDOMS

Author: Lo Kuan-chung (c. 1320-c. 1380)
Time of action: Third century
First transcribed: Fourteenth century

PRINCIPAL CHARACTERS

Liu Pei, the legitimate heir to the Han Dynasty, the founder of one of the Three Kingdoms, and the exalted lord of a great people whose deeds are legend. Although history does not altogether bear out his nobility, in this involved tale he is the patriarchal warrior, noble and amiable, loyal to his friends, terrible in battle. These attributes lie under a calm exterior, a dignified carriage, and eyes that supposedly can see back of his head. He is commonly called **Liu Yüan-tê.** His rise from protector of a widowed mother, shoemaker, and able scholar to a leader in the rebellion occurs before he is twenty-eight. Wherever he goes he inspires confidence, and with the help of his two friends, he conquers two of the Three Kingdoms and makes it possible to fuse the three before his death and the passing of his reign to a weakling son.

Kuan Yü, the clear-headed strategist, handsome, dignified, somewhat aloof but awe-inspiring. So daring and resourceful

985

a leader is he that he is revered as a war god and his deeds are still passed along in oral tradition. Determined to defend his sworn brother Liu Pei, he becomes second in command. A learned man, quick of wit, and austere, Kuan, or Yun-ch'ang (long as a cloud), is the idealized Chinese scholar-gentleman-warrior. He antagonizes a rival leader, however, when he is recalled from the wars and made governor of a province; hence, he is killed. Liu Pei and Chang Fei avenge his death as they had sworn to do but thereby weaken the alliances.

Chang Fei, the first to recognize Liu but the least learned and most blunt of the triumvirate, he is an extremely elemental, realistic man. Rather short, with a bullet head, raucous voice, bristling moustache, he is called I-tê, a wine seller and butcher by trade. He is the best soldier, the most daring in hand-to-hand combat, and surprisingly energetic and resourceful. One of his stratagems is the appearance of drunkenness to surprise his enemy. When Kuan is killed, Chang swears vengeance and is assassinated in the attempt.

Chu-ko Liang, more often known as **Chuko K'ung-ming,** the prime minister, whose abilities include conjuring, enchantment, magic, and sorcery. He is a remarkable man, talented in duplicity and stratagems, led by an ascendant star. It is he who finally unites the kingdoms, the only one of the original group to survive the first stages toward a coalition. Liu is largely unsuccessful until this brilliant recluse is called out of his hermitage. Tragically worn out from the extreme labors of his loyalty he dies, but leaves a valuable book of strategy in warfare and a number of occult secrets.

Chiang Wei, Chu-ko's successor, last of the great heroes of legend and fact, the carrier of a wooden image of his mentor to frighten men in battle. A young and brilliant scholar, loyal and filial, he is much esteemed as a warrior. Chu-ko Liang chooses him from among all others after testing his abilities.

Ts'ao Ts'ao, King of Wei, the greatest single leader, although unscrupulous and cruel. Much more successful than his adversaries, at least in the beginning, Ts'ao is especially gifted in the art of government. Portrayed in later Chinese drama as the stereotyped villain, he is herein a master strategist, wily conspirator, and forceful administrator. To achieve his ambitions, he resorts to trickery and cunning more diligently than all the others. A seer thinks him able to rule the world but too wicked to manage it.

Chou Yü, another of the brilliant young scholar-warriors, the antagonist of the wizard, and the great defender of the opposition forces of Sun Ch'üan.

Ssü-ma I, the ultimate in rulers, a composite of the other heroes, who successfully establishes the kingdom.

Sun Ch'üan, the founder of the Wu Kingdom. He and Liu Pei form an alliance and defeat the forces of Ts'ao Ts'ao.

Chao Yün, a brave general of the Shu Han Kingdom.

Lü Po, a great warrior but one without principles. He is famous for his romantic involvement with Tiao Shan.

THE ROMANTIC COMEDIANS

Author: Ellen Glasgow (1874-1945)
Time of action: The 1920's
First published: 1926

Judge Gamaliel Bland Honeywell, a wealthy widower of sixty-five. He is tall, dignified, and well preserved, but spindle-legged. His hair and beard are silvery; his moustache is dark; his eyebrows are beetling; his nose is Roman. His views are conservative, Southern, nineteenth century ones. Especially interested in young women, he is chivalrous toward all women. Unless careful of his diet he suffers from dyspepsia. Retired from the bench, he now practices law and enjoys respect for his legal ability. Lacking a common-sense knowledge of human nature, he enters a marriage which is doomed from its beginning. Though kind and generous to Annabel, he is nonetheless chained to his habits and his enjoyment of physical comfort, and he is unable to perceive her urgent need for the kind of love he cannot give. He accepts the blame for Annabel's leaving him since, as he says, he is older and should have known that marriage to him would not be enough for her.

Annabel, his second wife, a girl of twenty-three. Appealingly fragile in body, she has a freckled, heart-shaped face, nut-brown hair with coppery glints, and gray-green eyes. She is a frank and somewhat selfish realist but much more naïve than she thinks. Bitter and filled with hatred over Angus Blount's deserting her, she resents the genteel poverty in which she and her mother live, and she accepts the judge partly to forget Angus and partly to escape the atmosphere of her home. Vivacious, impulsive, and extravagant, she is cold and hardly appreciative of what the judge does for her. The judge is drawn by her elusive charm, but he cannot conquer her aversion to him, her fear and resentment of his being affectionate. Insisting that she has no desire to live without love, she is determined to attain her goal regardless of consequences.

Mrs. Bella Upchurch, Annabel's mother, a widow, brisk, cheerful, plump, pretty, and talkative.

Edmonia Bredalbane, the judge's twin sister, large, raw-boned, heavy-bosomed, a woman of liberal views and unorthodox behavior, the mate of four husbands and reputedly (though she denies it) the mistress of many rich lovers. She is a gaudy dresser with tinted brown hair. To the judge she appears to flaunt her past instead of being ashamed of it. Having more worldly perception than her brother, Edmonia attempts to keep him from making a fool of himself and vainly tries to promote a marriage to Amanda.

Amanda Lightfoot, the judge's childhood sweetheart, fifty-eight, unmarried, handsome, tall, willowy, regal, blue-eyed, and silver-haired. She dresses in an old-fashioned manner in the colors that Gamaliel used to like on her many years earlier. She has accepted her plight in an excessively ladylike manner, remaining pious and chaste through the years, tediously faithful to the man she lost but never ceased to love.

Dabney Birdsong, Annabel's childhood playmate, now a successful architect. He becomes her lover and she deserts the judge for him.

Angus Blount, Annabel's false lover, who married a French girl after deserting Annabel.

Dr. Buchanan, the judge's physician.

[**Cordelia Honeywell,** the judge's deceased first wife to whom he was peacefully and unexcitingly married for thirty-six years. He continually remembers Cordelia's tastes and ways and contrasts them with Annabel's.]

THE ROMANTIC LADIES

Author: Molière (Jean Baptiste Poquelin, 1622-1673)
Time of action: Seventeenth century
First presented: 1659

PRINCIPAL CHARACTERS

Magdelon (mág·də·lōn') and
Cathos (kà·tō'), two romantic young
ladies from the country, visiting in Paris.
They are very affected, in the manner
current in their day, and are full of
coquetry and artificiality. Being so artificial themselves, they are completely
taken in by two gentlemen's valets, who
pass themselves off to the girls as a marquis and a viscount. The girls' language
is at times so affected as to be practically
incomprehensible.

La Grange (là gränzh') and
Du Croisy (dü krwà·zē'), two young
men who pay court to the romantic
young ladies. They are so disgusted with
the affectations of the girls that they
connive to have their valets disguise
themselves as gallants and call on the
ladies. After a time they expose the valets
and strip off their finery, telling the
young ladies that if they are so beguiled
by the servants, they must love them just
as much without their masters' clothes.

The Marquis de Mascarille (də màs·kà-
rēy') and
Viscount Jodelet (zhô·də·lā'), valets to
La Grange and Du Croisy, respectively.
Delighted to pass themselves off to the
romantic young ladies as men of quality,
they call attention to their perfumed
finery, compose absurd verses and songs,
recount imaginary battle heroics, and
boast of their noble connections. At the
height of a dancing party their masters
enter, expose the ruse, and strip the
valets of their fine clothes.

Gorgibus (gôr·zhē·büs'), Magdelon's
father and Cathos' uncle. He is completely confused and befuddled by the
affectations of the two young ladies and
cannot understand their insistence that
La Grange and Du Croisy are too sincere and dull. He is angry and mortified
to learn that the valets have tricked the
two girls. Feeling disgraced by the trick,
he curses foolishness, affectation, and romantic nonsense.

THE ROMANY RYE

Author: George Henry Borrow (1803-1881)
Time of action: Nineteenth century
First published: 1857

PRINCIPAL CHARACTERS

The Romany Rye, known previously as
Lavengro, George, and Shorsha, all
terms of respect for his linguistic accomplishments among the gipsies. Alert,
perceptive, friendly, and resourceful, the
young wanderer is traveling to gain a better understanding of language differences.
Not content with knowing meanings and
sounds, the tinker turned horse trader
wants to know reasons, folkways, mores,

rituals; in short, everything interests him,
especially the nomadic life of the Romany groups, the Armenian gipsies.
Like an errant Don Quixote, the hero
rights wrongs, sets things straight, and
always extracts life histories from those
he encounters. He irritates many with
his questions, but this Romany Rye
(Gipsy Gentleman) almost always wins
respect and admiration.

Isopel Berners (Belle), an Amazon of the open road. Though not a gipsy, she goes her independent way without interference. The flaxen-haired and handsome young woman has laid out numerous travelers who made untoward remarks, but she respects and admires the hero. She refuses to marry him, however, on the basis that she believes him mad because of his philological curiosity. Finally, to maintain her independence and be true to her vision, she leaves for America alone.

Jasper Petulengro, the gipsy who more than anyone else helped the Romany Rye with his research. Jasper not only aids Lavengro with introductions to interesting and important leaders in the encampment but also buys his adopted brother a fine horse. Though known to cheat in business and misrepresent the truth, he is a true friend and a natural gentleman.

Ursula, Mrs. Petulengro's sister, a young widow intended for the hero but who marries within her group. Through this beautiful girl the young semanticist learns shades of meaning, particularly the way and words of brushing off an advance. Although nothing comes of the romance, the girl holds a warm spot in his heart for this remarkable anthology of gipsy lore.

Francis Ardry, the hero's associate from his London publishing days, who reappears and brings his adventures up to date. This handsome, wealthy, resourceful man has dissipated his energies and destroyed his character through frivolity. Charming as he is, the hero does not lament parting from him for the last time.

The Man in Black, who appears briefly proselytizing the hero and his landlord for the Roman Catholic Church. The contrast of this cynical and learned churchman and the simple, direct Methodist evangelist forms one of the most controversial arguments of Borrow's autobiographical books. Both the landlord and the linguist turn down the monk's overtures.

Jack Dale, the confidence man who has become an honest trader in spite of the underworld connections of his family. Proud to a fault, Jack will not permit a word against him or his character, nor will he allow the hero to interrupt his lengthy discourse of his life's adventures. Independent and honest, he has made a good living, raised a fine family, and gained the respect of his constituents in a most dishonest trade.

Murtagh, the Irish boyhood friend of the adopted gipsy. He has given out many secrets of the old language and folk tales of the ancient Irish. Irrepressible and humorous to the point of the ridiculous, Murtagh regales the tavern with his stories of card sharping. He is a generous and pleasant companion whose reunion with the hero brings the series of sketches to a close.

The Chinese Scholar, an old man who has spent what would otherwise have been an indolent life in transcribing ideographs and symbols from pottery. He befriends the hero and tells his sad story. He lives the life of a Chinese sage because of his translations.

ROME HAUL

Author: Walter D. Edmonds (1903-   )
Time of action: 1850
First published: 1929

Dan Harrow, a tall, stooped, broad-shouldered young man; a naïve newcomer on the canal who after brief jobs on two canal boats becomes captain of the "Sarsy Sal" after Samson Weaver's death. At last, feeling that the canal is not the place for him, he returns to farm life.

Molly Larkins, his tall, strapping, blowsy-looking, but attractive, amoral cook, who formerly cooked for Jotham. Though she likes Dan and remains with him for a time, she pities Jotham after he is beaten by Dan, and she returns to the chastened bully.

Fortune Friendly, an old, red-faced, skinny canal character and rascal, a former divinity student who still preaches occasionally when he needs money.

Joseph P. (Gentleman Joe) Calash, a cruel-faced canal highwayman for whose capture a large reward is offered. He aids Dan in a fight with Jotham and rescues him after a second fight. He is at last caught and killed.

Jotham Klore, a big, black-bearded, tobacco-chewing canal bully who is knocked out twice by Calash and who knocks out Dan in a fight over Molly.

In a final fight Dan wins a great victory.

Jacob Turnesa, a hooknosed, pale-faced Jewish peddler who picks up Dan and gives him a volume of Shakespeare's plays.

Hector Berry, a henpecked canal boatman.

Penelope, his nagging, dictatorial wife.

Solomon (Sol) Tinkle, a baldheaded, dimunitive canal boatman.

Mrs. Gurget, Sol's fat, goodnatured cook and mistress, addicted to rum noggins.

Julius Wilson, owner of the canal boat "Xerxes."

Benjamin (Ben) Rae, big Jewish steersman of the "Xerxes."

William Wampy, cook and fiddler on the "Xerxes."

Lucy Cashdollar, the operator of an agency supplying girls as cooks for lonely canal men.

Samson Weaver, the captain of the "Sarsy Sal"; he dies shortly after hiring Dan.

Mr. Butterfield, the agent for whom Samson and Dan work.

ROMEO AND JULIET

Author: William Shakespeare (1564-1616)
Time of action: Fifteenth century
First presented: 1594-1596

PRINCIPAL CHARACTERS

Romeo (rō'mĭ·ō), the only son of old Montague, a nobleman of Verona. A romantic youth, inclined to be in love with love, he gives up his idealized passion for Rosaline when Juliet rouses in him a lasting devotion. His star-crossed young life ends in suicide.

Juliet (jōō'lĭ·ĕt), the only daughter of old Capulet. Little more than a child at the beginning of the play, she is quickly matured by love and grief into a young woman of profound grace and tragic dignity. Unable to find sympathy in her family and unable to trust her nurse, she risks death to avoid a forced marriage, which would be bigamous. Awakening in the tomb to find Romeo's body, she too commits suicide.

Montague (mŏn′tə·gū), Romeo's father, head of the house of Montague. An enemy of the Capulets, he is a good, reasonable man and father. In the family feud he seems more provoked than provoking. After the deaths of Romeo and Juliet he becomes reconciled with the Capulets.

Lady Montague, Romeo's gentle mother. Tender-hearted and peace-loving, she breaks down under the fury of the clashing houses and the banishment of her son and dies of grief.

Capulet (kăp′ū·lĕt), Juliet's fiery father. Essentially good-hearted but furiously unreasonable when thwarted in the slightest thing, he destroys the happiness and the life of his dearly loved daughter. He joins his former enemy in grief and friendship after her death.

Lady Capulet, Juliet's mother. Dominated by her husband, she fails to offer Juliet the understanding and affection the girl desperately needs.

The Nurse, Juliet's good-hearted, bawdy-tongued mentor. She aids the young lovers to consummate their marriage; but, lacking in moral principle, when Romeo is banished, she urges Juliet to marry Paris. Hence, Juliet has no one to turn to in her great distress and need.

Friar Lawrence, a kindly, timorous priest. He marries the young lovers and tries to help them in their fearful adversity, but fails, thwarted by fate.

Benvolio (bĕn·vō′lĭ·ō), old Montague's nephew, the friend of Romeo and Mercutio. Less hot-headed than Mercutio, he tries to avoid quarrels even with the irreconcilable Tybalt. His account of the deaths of Mercutio and Tybalt saves Romeo from execution, but not from banishment.

Mercutio (mėr·kū′shĭ·ō), Romeo's volatile and witty friend. Poetically fanciful and teasing, he can be a savage foe. His angry challenge to Tybalt after Romeo has behaved with humility leads to various deaths and the final catastrophe. He has a superb death scene.

Paris (pă′rĭs), a young nobleman in love with Juliet. The hasty marriage planned by the Capulets between Paris and Juliet forces her to counterfeit death in order to avoid a bigamous union. The counterfeit becomes real for her—and for Paris and Romeo.

Escalus (ĕs′kə·lŭs), Duke of Verona, kinsman of Mercutio and Paris. A just, merciful ruler, he tries to arrange a peace between the feuding families. He joins them at the tomb which holds their dead children and presides over their reconciliation.

Peter, Capulet's stupid servant. Unable to read, he asks Romeo and Mercutio to help him with Capulet's invitation list, thus bringing about the meeting between Romeo and Juliet.

Friar John, a friend of Friar Lawrence. Caught in a home visited by the plague, he is delayed too long to deliver Friar Lawrence's letter to Romeo informing him about Juliet's counterfeit death. This is another of the fatal events that work constantly against the young lovers.

An Apothecary, a poverty-stricken old wretch. He illegally sells Romeo poison.

Balthasar (băl′thə·zär), Romeo's servant. He brings Romeo news of Juliet's supposed death and actual internment in the Capulet vault. He accompanies Romeo to the tomb and remains nearby, though ordered to leave the area by Romeo. His testimony added to that of Friar Lawrence and Paris' page enables Duke Escalus and the others to reconstruct the events.

Samson and Gregory, servants of Capulet who begin the street brawl at the play's opening.

Cousin to Capulet. He joins old Capulet in reminiscences at the dance.

Tybalt (tĭb′əlt), fiery member of the Capulet clan. He challenges Romeo at the Capulet feast but the fight is prevented by old Capulet. Still bearing a grudge, he meets Romeo's friend Mercutio in the street and kills him in a duel. Romeo then takes up the fight and kills Tybalt.

ROMOLA

Author: George Eliot (Mary Ann Evans, 1819-1880)
Time of action: 1492-1498
First published: 1863

PRINCIPAL CHARACTERS

Tito Melema, an adventurer and pleasure-seeking young Greek who arrives in Florence in 1492. There he quickly gains a fortune by his talents, his charm, and the fact that he sells a number of gems that rightfully belong to his benefactor, Baldassare Calvo. He impresses the famous blind scholar, Bardo, so much that the latter willingly gives his daughter to Tito for a wife. At the same time Tito is also connected with a peasant girl with whom he has made a mock marriage in a carnival ceremony. Becoming powerful in Florentine politics, he carefully avoids aligning himself with either the Medici or the reformer, Savonarola. Because of his double dealing he is both personally and politically discredited. He is chased by a mob and then strangled by Baldassare Calvo, the benefactor whom Tito had deceived, stolen from, and left confined in prison.

Romola de' Bardi, Bardo's daughter and Tito's wife. A sheltered girl, she easily falls in love with handsome, charming Tito. Disillusioned when Tito attempts to sell her father's library and antiquities, she leaves him, but Savonarola persuades her that her duty is to return to her husband. At first she is strongly attracted to Savonarola's moral reforms. Later, when her godfather, a supporter of the Medici, is executed, she loses faith in the evangelical government. She also discovers that her husband has betrayed Baldassare Calvo and that he has been keeping Tessa, the peasant girl, and her two children. Saddened, she leaves Florence and goes to Viareggio. After Tito's death she returns and makes a home for Tessa and Tito's two children.

Bardo de' Bardi, Romola's father, a famous scholar to whom she is devoted. Deceived by his secretary's knowledge, charm, and apparent interest in scholarly studies, he encourages the marriage of Tito and his daughter; he regards Tito as a substitute for the lost son he believes dead, a young man who abandoned scholarship for mysticism. Bardo dies in 1494 before Tito's crimes are revealed.

Baldassare Calvo, Tito Melema's scholarly foster father and benefactor. He had given Tito some gems to sell in Florence in order to ransome Baldassare from the Turks. Tito uses the gems to advance his own fortune and tries to forget Baldassare entirely. When Baldassare is brought, a prisoner, to Florence, Tito rejects him. After a mob frees him from his fetters, Baldassare encounters Tessa and realizes her connection with Tito. By this time Baldassare's desire for revenge on Tito is implacable. He later denounces Tito's deceitful ingratitude at a dinner party of the rulers of Florence, but Tito calls him mad and has him cast into prison. Released, Baldassare tells Romola the whole story. He pursues fleeing Tito and strangles him.

Dino de' Bardi, Bardo's lost son, supposed dead, who has disguised himself as **Fra Luca,** a Dominican friar. He first carries a note from Baldassare to Tito requesting help, but Tito ignores the note. Later, when ill, he is reunited with his sister Romola, and he tells her of a vision he has had, a dire warning that she should not marry Tito. Dino dies before he can explain his specific and non-mystical reasons for not wanting her to marry Tito.

Tessa, a peasant girl, the daughter of a milk vendor, who falls in love with Tito after he rescues her from drunken revelers at a carnival. At a later carnival she goes through a mock marriage ceremony with him. She then bears him two children and remains entirely loyal to him, even though he visits her only infrequently. She is a simple girl of generous nature and loving heart.

Bernardo Del Nero, Bardo's friend and Romola's godfather. Disliking Tito, he tries to delay the marriage between Tito and Romola. Later he remains friendly with Romola and tries to help her. A strong supporter of the Medici, he is executed by followers of Savonarola.

Monna Brigida, Bardo's loquacious cousin. She reveals to Romola that her brother is not dead but living as Fra Luca, a Dominican friar. At the end of the novel she makes her home with Romola and Tessa.

Fra Girolamo Savonarola, the prior of the Dominican convent of San Marco, a reformer who bitterly assails the corruption of the Medici and becomes the leader of a strong Florentine faction. In addition to his political activity, he also befriends Dino and convinces Romola to return to her husband. He and Romola are spiritually attracted to each other.

Piero di Cosimo, a famous painter, friendly with Tito, who puts his friends into his pictures. He uses Tito and Romola as models for Bacchus and Ariadne, and he paints Bardo as Oedipus. He also helps to reveal Tito's duplicity to Romola.

Bartolomeo Scala, the powerful secretary of the Florentine Republic. He buys many of Tito's gems and helps start him on his spectacular career in Florence.

Alessandra Scala, the beautiful daughter of Bartolomeo Scala.

Marullo, her husband, a Greek soldier and poet.

Nello, a barber and town gossip who helps to introduce Tito to important people.

Bratti Ferravecchi, a rag-merchant and tradesman whom Tito meets after arriving in Florence. He buys Tito's ring.

Bernardo Rucellai, the wealthy Florentine and political leader who orders Baldassare arrested when the latter accuses Tito at the dinner party.

Lorenzo Tornabuoni, a wealthy citizen friendly with Tito. He is at the dinner when Baldassare is arrested. He is imprisoned later for his support of the Medici.

Niccolò Ridolfi and
Giannozzo Pucci, Florentine aristocrats and supporters of the Medici, imprisoned and executed.

Maestro Vaiano, an astrologer and mountebank from whom Tito rescues Tessa at the carnival.

Dolfo Spini, a false and conniving Florentine with whom Tito deals.

Niccolò Machiavelli, a young Florentine thinker and man of ideas.

Niccolò Caparra, an iron worker who makes a thick coat of mail for Tito to wear after the latter encounters Baldassare in Florence.

Fra Salvestro Maruffi, Savonarola's friend, a Dominican friar who aids Romola.

Menico Cennini, a Florentine goldsmith and moneylender.

Maso, Bardo's old servant, always loyal to Romola.

Politan, a scholar, the rejected suitor of Alessandra Scala.

Monna Ghita, Tessa's mother, a fierce milk vendor in the market.

Piero de' Medici, the rash and ineffectual

son of the famous Lorenzo de' Medici. He rules Florence after his father's death in 1492.

Giovanni de' Medici, the luxury-loving younger son of Lorenzo de' Medici. He becomes Pope Leo X.

Alamanno Rinuccini, a scholar friendly with Bardo and Romola's suitor before her marriage to Tito Melema.

Monna Lisa, a deaf old woman whom Tito hires as a servant to Tessa.

Lillo, Tessa's sturdy son by Tito.

Ninna, the baby daughter of Tessa and Tito.

A ROOM WITH A VIEW

Author: E. M. Forster (1879-   )
Time of action: Early 1900's
First published: 1908

PRINCIPAL CHARACTERS

Lucy Honeychurch, a young Englishwoman. As a traveler in Italy, she is disappointed that her room at the pension has no view. Unwillingly, she changes rooms with Mr. Emerson and his son, George, whom she regards as ill bred. For the rest of her stay abroad and back at home in England, she tries to stifle her attraction to George. Finally, she is led by Mr. Emerson to acknowledge her love for his son, and she starts to live the truth she has learned, by marrying him.

Mr. Emerson, an Englishman. Aware of Lucy Honeychurch's love for his son George, he draws from her an admission of her love and inspires her to acknowledge and to live the truth she has learned.

George Emerson, Mr. Emerson's son, who is in love with Lucy Honeychurch, whom he finally marries.

Charlotte Bartlett, Lucy Honeychurch's cousin and chaperon in Italy.

The Reverend Arthur Beebe, Lucy Honeychurch's friend and rector.

Cecil Vyse, Lucy Honeychurch's fiancé. She breaks her engagement with him when George Emerson tells her of his love but before she has acknowledged, even to herself, her love for George.

Mrs. Honeychurch, Lucy Honeychurch's mother.

Miss Eleanor Lavish, a novelist,
Miss Catherine Alan, and
Miss Teresa Alan, guests at the Italian pension, later neighbors of Lucy Honeychurch.

Freddy Honeychurch, Lucy Honeychurch's brother.

RORY O'MORE

Author: Samuel Lover (1797-1868)
Time of action: 1798
First published: 1837

PRINCIPAL CHARACTERS

Rory O'More, an Irish peasant who suffers through his unselfish efforts for Irish freedom and has to escape to America with his wife Kathleen.

Mary O'More, his sister, who is to marry Horace de Lacy in America.

Shan Regan, who is refused marriage to Mary and therefore forbids his sister's marriage to Rory. After many crimes, he is killed by the police.

Kathleen Regan, Shan's sister.

Horace de Lacy, an Irish patriot who

brings Napoleon's offer of aid in the rebellion of 1798. He contracts smallpox and is nursed by Mary.

De Welskein, a smuggler to whom profit means more than political liberty. Though saved by Rory and De Lacy, he betrays them and ships them to France.

Scrubbs, an English tax collector who reappears in time to save Rory from murder charges.

The Colonel of the Police, who is outwitted by Rory.

ROSMERSHOLM

Author: Henrik Ibsen (1828-1906)
Time of action: Mid-nineteenth century
First presented: 1887

PRINCIPAL CHARACTERS

Johannes Rosmer, a former clergyman who has become a freethinker. He wants to work for the liberal cause in politics, but he is denounced by both sides. The conservatives feel he has forsaken his class, and the liberals feel he will be a political liability. Both sides accuse him, too, of forcing his wife to commit suicide so he can marry Rebecca West. When Rosmer asks the woman to die to prove her love for him, he commits suicide with her, as punishment for loving a woman other than his wife.

[Beata Rosmer, Johannes' dead wife. She kills herself to make way for Rebecca West in her husband's affections upon being told falsely by the other woman of the imminent birth of a child by Johannes.]

Rebecca West, a free-thinking woman who uses her charms to try to claim Rosmer for the liberal cause. She also wants him as a man and drives his wife to suicide. She comes to love Rosmer deeply and commits suicide to prove her love for him.

Rector Kroll, Beata Rosmer's brother. He is an ardent conservative who tries to encourage Rosmer to forget the liberals. When he is rebuffed, he accuses Rosmer of adultery with Rebecca West and of driving his wife to suicide. Kroll is a bitter, narrow man, the local schoolteacher.

Peter Mortensgard, a liberal newspaper publisher. He solicits Rosmer's help until he learns that Rosmer, an ex-pastor, has

995

left his church and become something of an outcast. Then, like Kroll, he accuses Rosmer of adultery. He is a practical politician and an amoral one.

Ulric Brendel, a liberal. He goes penniless and unrewarded, but happy, until he becomes disillusioned by the actions of his fellow liberals.

Mme. Helseth, Rosmer's housekeeper.

ROXANA

Author: Daniel Defoe (1660-1731)
Time of action: Eighteenth century
First published: 1724

PRINCIPAL CHARACTERS

Roxana, a woman left penniless by her husband at the age of twenty-two. To support herself and her children she becomes her landlord's mistress and bears him a child. After his death she becomes the mistress of a prince, out of vanity rather than need. She bears the prince a child, too, during the eight years of their alliance. She then takes other lovers, receiving riches from them, until she is fifty. She finally leaves her role as a courtesan to marry and become a respectable wife.

Mr. ——, Roxana's landlord and first lover. He helps Roxana when her husband leaves her, becoming a boarder in her house and then her lover, treating her generously during their five years together. He wants children badly and, when Roxana does not at first bear him a child, Roxana's maid does so. Mr. —— is robbed and murdered. He leaves his wealth to Roxana.

The Prince de ——, Roxana's second lover. He protects her after her first lover's untimely death in Paris. He remains her lover for eight years and rewards her with rich gifts. Upon his wife's death, however, he repents his sinful life and leaves Roxana.

A Merchant, who takes care of Roxana's wealth for her during the years after she parts from the Prince de ——. Roxana bears the merchant a son, after a brief affair. Later he and Roxana are married, legitimize their son, and settle down to respectability in Holland.

Amy, Roxana's faithful maid. She serves her mistress without pay while Roxana is poor. She even bears a child for Mr. —— when it seems that Roxana cannot. Loyal to the end, she is finally dismissed by Roxana when she threatens to murder Roxana's legitimate daughter to quiet her tongue about Roxana's past.

RULE A WIFE AND HAVE A WIFE

Author: John Fletcher (1579-1625)
Time of action: c. 1600
First presented: 1624

PRINCIPAL CHARACTERS

Leon (lā·ōn'), a young Spanish gentleman. Pretending to be a cowardly soldier and a stupid oaf, he is married by Margarita in expectation of his being a tame husband, a wittol; however, he tames his wife and overcomes his rivals.

Margarita (mär·gä·rē′tä), a rich and un-principled young woman. Wishing to indulge her romantic passion indiscriminately, but desiring to protect her reputation, she marries Leon. His cleverness and strength reform her and make her a faithful wife.

Don Juan de Castro (dōn hwän′ dä käs′-trō), a colonel and a successful, battle-proved veteran. A fair-minded man, he delights in Leon's actions and encourages them.

Michael Perez (pā′rāth), a fellow soldier of Don Juan. He pretends to be wealthy in order to marry the attractive Estifania, whom he thinks wealthy. Their marriage, based on mutual deceit, is a rocky one, but reaches a reasonable level of stability and happiness.

Estifania (ās·tē·fä′nyä), Margarita's wily maid. Living as a caretaker in Mar-garita's house, she pretends to be a wealthy lady. She cheats and steals from her masculine victims, including her husband Michael; but finally she and Michael settle down as dependents of Leon and Margarita.

The Duke of Medina (mā·thē′nä), Margarita's projected lover. At first thwarted in his amorous attempts by Leon, he is finally completely discomfited by Margarita herself.

Cacafogo (kä·kä·fō′gō), a fat, drunken coward. Thinking himself irresistible to women, he is cheated by Estifania and befooled by Margarita.

Altea (äl·tā′ä), Margarita's companion. Unknown to Margarita is the fact that Altea is Leon's sister. Her successful matchmaking gives her brother a rich and beautiful bride and her friend a stabilizing and redeeming husband.

R.U.R.

Author: Karel Čapek (1890-1938)
Time of action: The future
First presented: 1921; published in 1920

PRINCIPAL CHARACTERS

Harry Domin, the general manager of Rossum's Universal Robots. He is dedicated to the idea that man ought to be completely free from the slavery of work.

Helena Glory, the daughter of the president of R.U.R. and later the wife of manager Harry Domin. Concerned both over the robots' living conditions and over the millions of men out of work, she believes that the robots should be given souls. When this plan proves disastrous, she burns the formula for making robots.

Dr. Gall, the scientist who is persuaded by Helena to give the robots souls.

Mr. Alquist, the head of the R.U.R. works department. He recognizes that human idleness is not the perfect goal Domin thinks it to be. Because, like the robots, he works with his hands, he is the only human being in the world spared after the uprising of the robots. He is, however, unable to duplicate the formula for robot manufacture.

Primus, a robot.

Helena, a robotess made in Helena Glory's image who, in some miraculous way, loves and is loved by Primus. With mankind destroyed and robot manufacture no longer possible, these two completely human robots remain as the only hope for the reproduction of new life.

THE SAINT

Author: Antonio Fogazzaro (1842-1911)
Time of action: Late nineteenth century
First published: 1905

PRINCIPAL CHARACTERS

Piero Maironi, who in previous volumes of this trilogy forgot his wife in an insane asylum to take Jeanne Dessalle as his mistress. Now having renounced the world, he is called Benedetto the Saint.

Jeanne Dessalle, who hopes Piero will renounce his holy life and come back to her. Her conversion comes just in time to delight his dying moments.

Noemi d'Arxel, her friend, who scours Italy with her in search of Piero.

Giovanni Selva, Noemi's saintly brother-in-law, a philosopher whose writings Benedetto keeps off the Index.

Don Clemente, a Benedictine monk who is the instructor of Benedetto at the monastery of Santa Scholastica.

The Pope, who summons Benedetto to discuss ideas about the needs of the Church.

SAINT JOAN

Author: Bernard Shaw (1856-1950)
Time of action: 1428-1456
First presented: 1923

PRINCIPAL CHARACTERS

Joan of Arc, a farmer's daughter from the village of Domrémy. Joan's imagination is so vivid that her inspirations seem to come to her as visions in which the voices of the saints direct her to raise the siege of Orleans and crown the Dauphin at Rheims. By sheer force of personality and a genius for leadership, the seventeen-year-old Joan does these things. Ignorant of the complexities of politics, Joan is unwilling to defer to the experience and advice of ordinary men. She oversteps herself and is tried by the Inquisition for heresy. Her trial is an eminently fair one by the standards of the age, but Joan condemns herself by insisting that the instructions of her "voices" take precedence over the instructions of the Church. Sentenced to be burned and fearing pain, she recants. When she finds her recantation simply commutes her sentence to perpetual imprisonment, she reaffirms her innocence

and is burned. In an Epilogue, Joan's ghost appears and learns that she has been canonized. Her allies and enemies alike bow down and worship her; but when Joan offers to bring herself to life again, they all demur and drift away. Joan wonders when earth shall be ready for God's saints.

The Dauphin, later Charles VII. Although physically weak and bullied by everyone, he is intelligent and more refined than most nobles of his time. Once he is crowned, Charles tells Joan to be content with what she already has won. He warns her he cannot protect her if she fights on. After Joan is executed Charles himself becomes a successful warrior.

The Inquisitor, Brother John Lemaître (lə·mĕ′tr), a Dominican monk. A mild, elderly, highly intelligent man, he believes that Joan's heresy is the most heinous one of all: the Protestant heresy of believing God speaks directly to an individual through one's conscience. Realizing Joan is innocent of evildoing, he believes she must be sacrificed to the welfare of Christian society.

Peter Cauchon (kō·shäṅ'), Bishop of Beauvais, the co-judge, with the Inquisitor, at Joan's trial. An honest believer in the grossness of Joan's heresy, the Bishop wishes to save Joan's soul and, if possible, her life.

Richard de Beauchamp, Earl of Warwick, the English commandant. Warwick wants Joan put to death because she represents the new spirit of nationalism which threatens the power of his social class.

John de Stogumber, Warwick's chaplain. A bigoted and fanatical English patriot, he howls for Joan's death at her trial. He is so horrified by her execution that, half-mad, he retires to a small country parish and becomes an exemplary priest.

Dunois (dü'nwä'), **Bastard of Orleans,** the rugged and pragmatic commander of the French forces. He admires Joan's military ability, but he abandons her when she ignores his advice.

Brother Martin Ladvenu (läd·v'noo'), a young priest who takes pity on Joan at her trial and tries to persuade her to save herself.

The Archbishop of Rheims, a member of the Dauphin's court. A rich and worldly administrator, the Archbishop is struck by Joan's saintliness. He tries to warn Joan of the dangerousness of her contempt for all authority.

Gilles de Rais (gēl də rā'), a flippant and cynical young courtier who affects a blue beard. He is contemptuous of Joan.

Captain la Hire (lä·ēr'), a tough French soldier who becomes fanatically devoted to Joan.

Canon John d'Estivet (dĕs·tĭ·vä'), the prosecutor at Joan's trial, so captious and vindictive that the Inquisitor must repeatedly censure him.

Canon de Courcelles (də koor'sĕl), a young priest who, with de Stogumber, draws up the indictment against Joan. He is stupid, petty, and contentious.

Robert de Baudricourt (də bōd'r'koor), a loud-mouthed but weak-willed French gentleman-at-arms. Against his better judgment, he provides Joan an escort to the Dauphin's court.

Bertrand de Poulengy (də poo'lĕṅ·zhē), a knight under Baudricourt's command. Convinced of Joan's holiness, he escorts her to see the Dauphin.

The Executioner of Rouen, who puts Joan to death.

An English Soldier, who gives Joan a cross of twigs while she is at the stake. For this action he is given each year one day's vacation from Hell.

A Gentleman of 1920, an English priest who, in the Epilogue, announces Joan's elevation to sainthood.

ST. PETER'S UMBRELLA

Author: Kálmán Mikszáth (1847-1910)
Time of action: Second half of nineteenth century
First published: 1895

PRINCIPAL CHARACTERS

János Bélyi, a priest. When he arrives, as a young man, in Glogova, his prospects for a pleasant life in the forlorn village are extremely remote until he comes into possession of a red umbrella whose miraculous powers change his fortunes from bad to good.

Veronica Bélyi, János Bélyi's sister, who is left, as an infant, on her brother's doorstep. When János returns from a walk in the rain, he finds her protected by a mysterious red umbrella which the townspeople decide is a gift from St. Peter. As a young woman she falls in love with and marries Gyury Wibra, heir of the red umbrella's real owner.

Pál Gregorics, a wealthy bachelor, the father of Gyury Wibra. Original owner of the red umbrella, he is reputed to have carried secret documents in its handle. On his death the umbrella is sold and disappears until his son traces it to the home of János Bélyi.

Gyury (György) Wibra, Pál Gregorics' illegitimate son. Embarrassed during his father's life by the red umbrella, he hears rumors after Pál's death that the umbrella is a repository of valuable documents. He sets out to find the umbrella and traces it to the home of János Bélyi, where he finally comes into possession not only of the treasured relic but of Veronica Bélyi as well.

Jónás Müncz, a Jewish merchant who buys the red umbrella after Pál Gregorics' death and is seen placing it over the infant, Veronica Bélyi.

Frau Müncz, Jónás Müncz' wife.

Anna Wibra, Pál Gregorics' housekeeper and mistress and the mother of Gyury Wibra.

The Widow Adamecz, János Bélyi's housekeeper.

János Sztolarik, Pál Gregorics' lawyer.

ST. RONAN'S WELL

Author: Sir Walter Scott (1771-1832)
Time of action: Early nineteenth century
First published: 1824

PRINCIPAL CHARACTERS

Francis Tyrrel, a young Englishman posing as an artist, half brother of the Earl of Etherington. He returns to St. Ronan's in an effort to prove his legitimacy and the treachery of his illegitimate half brother. He succeeds but too late for any happiness to come from the revelations.

The Earl of Etherington, the illegitimate half brother of Francis Tyrrel and the usurper of his title. As a young man he had treacherously substituted himself for Tyrrel and had married Clara Mowbray for the fortune that went with her hand. Forced to leave before the consummation of the marriage, he had vowed never to see her again; but he returns later, again disguised, to attempt to force another marriage. His betrayal is finally revealed, and he is killed by John Mowbray.

Clara Mowbray, the daughter of a Scottish laird. Because of a fortune that goes with her hand, she has been tricked in the past into a marriage with the Earl of Etherington, who was forced to flee before the marriage was consummated. Later he returns, disguised, hoping to force another marriage and gain the fortune. His treachery is revealed too late for Clara, who, in an effort to escape, flees, wanders about distractedly, and finally dies.

John Mowbray, Clara Mowbray's brother, who attempts to force her marriage to the Earl of Etherington, whom he later kills when he learns of the Earl's treachery.

Mr. Touchwood, an elderly gentleman, the son of the man who left the estate coveted by the Earl of Etherington. He is in possession of and reveals the proof of Francis Tyrrel's legitimacy.

Meg Dods, the proprietress of the inn at old St. Ronan's.

Lady Penelope Penfeather, a leader of society at St. Ronan's Well.

Captain Harry Jekyl, a friend and correspondent of the Earl of Etherington.

The Reverend Josiah Cargill, a clergyman in possession of the secret of Clara Mowbray's forced marriage to the Earl of Etherington.

Hannah Irwin, Clara Mowbray's former maid and the ally of the Earl of Etherington.

Solmes, the Earl of Etherington's servant.

Sir Bingo Binks, a boorish young man who challenges Tyrrel to a duel.

Captain MacTurk, Sir Bingo's second.

SAKUNTALA

Author: Kalidasa (c. Sixth century)
Time of action: The Golden Age of India
First presented: c. Sixth century

PRINCIPAL CHARACTERS

Dushyanta, King of India and hero of this poetic drama. Falling in love at first sight with Sakuntala, he persuades her to marry him secretly. In fulfillment of a curse, he forgets about her thereafter until a ring he gave her is shown to him. Reunited first in heaven and then returned to earth, they live happily for many years.

Sakuntala, the daughter of a Brahman and a water nymph. She returns the King's love and marries him, but remains in her sacred grove after his departure to await her foster father's return. After her husband fails to recognize her, she is taken away to heaven by a strange winged being. She gives birth to a son before she and her husband are reunited.

Kanwa, a wise hermit and Sakuntala's

foster father. Having the gift of omniscience, he knows all about the secret wedding. Informed by a supernatural voice that Sakuntala's son is destined to rule the world, he blesses the union and sends Sakuntala off to her husband. Her premonitions of evil prove true when Dushyanta fails to recognize her.

Mathavya, the King's jester. In order to be near Sakuntala, the King breaks off his hunting, pretending that his motive is to humor a wish of Mathavya.

Bharata, the son of Sakuntala and Dushyanta. Carried to heaven for a reunion with his wife, Dushyanta finds a young boy playing with a lion. The boy proves to be his son, who accompanies him and Sakuntala back to earth.

SALAMMBÔ

Author: Gustave Flaubert (1821-1880)
Time of action: Third century B.C.
First published: 1862

Hamilcar (a·mĕl·kȧr'), the Suffete of third century Carthage, at whose palace in his absence is given a great feast for his thousands of mercenaries. He arrives home to find them in rebellion, and after several reversals, he conquers and destroys them.

Salammbô (sȧ·lȧm·bō'), the daughter of Hamilcar and the priestess of the Carthaginian moon goddess, Tanit. She utters a curse on the angry barbarians who, after their defeat by the Romans and the delay with their back pay, begin pillaging the palace of Hamilcar. When Mathô later invades the sacred temple, she screams for help, though attracted to him. To regain the sacred veil of Tanit, which he has stolen, she goes in disguise to his tent and submits to him. The broken chastity chain between her ankles betrays her to her father, who angrily offers her to Narr' Havas. At the wedding, as she contrasts drunken Narr' Havas with gentle Mathô, who is tortured by the Carthaginians, she drinks a cup of poison and dies with Mathô.

Narr' Havas (nȧr ȧ·vȧs'), a Numidian chief sent by his father to learn warfare under Hamilcar. He falls in love with Salammbô after she appears on the palace balcony. He deserts the rebellious barbarians to help Hamilcar and is promised marriage with Salammbô after Hamilcar finally defeats the mercenaries.

Mathô (mȧ·tō'), a gigantic Libyan chief of mercenaries, also in love with Salammbô. Following the payment by the Council of Elders of a gold piece to each soldier, he leads his followers out of Carthage to Sicca to await the return of Hamilcar. Guided by Spendius, he then returns to Carthage and sacrilegiously goes into the Temple of Tanit, to Salammbô's sleeping quarters. Though discovered, none dares hinder his escape, since he wears the sacred veil. He is finally captured by Hamilcar's army, tortured and lacerated, and brought to the nuptial dais of Salammbô, who joins him in death by drinking poison.

Hanno (ȧ·nō'), a fat, suppurating member of the Council of Elders who appears in Sicca in his costly litter and, in unintelligible Punic, tries to persuade the barbarians to go home and there await their back pay. He is almost killed by the soldiers, who are aroused by Spendius as he falsely translates Hanno's words.

Spendius (spän·dyüs'), a former Greek slave who is now shrewdly and craftily serving Mathô. Because Spendius has lived for many years in Carthage, he is able to tell his master of the delightful possibilities of Salammbô. He stirs up the mercenaries by a false translation of Hanno's speech, and they accept him as a chief; he then leads them toward Carthage. He guides Mathô into the city through the aqueduct to the Temple of Tanit, the goddess in whom the Carthaginians put their trust.

Gisco (zhĕs·kō'), a famous warrior sent by Carthage to turn back the barbarians at the gate of the city.

SAMSON AGONISTES

Author: John Milton (1608-1674)
Time of action: c. 1100 B.C.
First published: 1671

PRINCIPAL CHARACTERS

Samson, the great Hebrew champion, who has been blinded and imprisoned by the Philistines. When the Chorus first greets him he is deeply depressed, for he feels that he has betrayed God and himself by his own weakness. His successful resistance of Dalila's temptations and his defiance of Harapha's taunts restore his sense that he has a mission to perform. He goes to the Philistines' feast in honor of their god, Dagon, with strong consciousness that he will find there a task to do in God's service, and he "quit[s] himself like Samson" by pulling the hall down upon the heads of his enemies and himself.

Manoa, Samson's kind old father. He seeks to ransom his son and offers to devote the rest of his life to caring for him. Although he mourns Samson's death, he rejoices at the grandeur and heroism of his end.

Dalila, Samson's treacherous Philistine wife. She cajoles her husband, avows her repentance, and tries to excuse her betrayal of him by pleading her duty to her country, in order to win him again. Realizing that he will not fall prey to her hypocrisy, she departs in anger, consoling herself with the thought that she will be regarded as a heroine by her own countrymen.

Harapha, a boastful Philistine warrior. He insults Samson and challenges him to defend his God against Dagon, when he believes his enemy to be weak. He exits quickly when he realizes that Samson has recovered his strength and his willingness to fight.

A Chorus of Hebrew Elders, a group of old men who sympathize with Samson and comment upon the action as it takes place.

SANCTUARY

Author: William Faulkner (1897-1962)
Time of action: 1929
First published: 1931

PRINCIPAL CHARACTERS

Popeye, a cruel, passionless killer who is symbolic of the ruthless, sterile, materialistic exploitation that destroyed the antebellum social order of the South. Ironically, he is executed for a murder he did not commit.

Temple Drake, a college girl of good family who is attacked by Popeye and then sent to live the life of a prostitute in a bawdy house in Memphis. Her family removes her from the house of ill repute, but her life has been ruined.

Lee Goodwin, a moonshiner who tries to protect Temple from a group of bootleggers and who is accused of murdering Tommy, a gang member actually shot by Popeye. He is convicted, but before he can be sentenced, he is burned to death by a mob that storms the jail to take him.

Gowan Stevens, a college student whose irresponsible conduct causes Temple to become Popeye's victim.

Ruby Lamar, Goodwin's common-law wife, who helps the officers locate Temple in Memphis.

Horace Benbow, a lawyer who defends Goodwin and who is symbolic of the early Southern historical tradition.

Tommy, a bootlegger whom Popeye kills, and of whose death Goodwin is accused.

Miss Reba (Rivers), the madam of the Memphis bawdy house.

Red, a young customer of Temple who is killed by Popeye's gang because Temple hopes to escape from Popeye and run away with him.

Judge Drake, Temple's father, a wealthy, old-fashioned Southerner.

Senator Clarence Snopes, a corrupt, modern Southern politician.

Van, a moonshiner who fights with Goodwin over Temple.

SANDFORD AND MERTON

Author: Thomas Day (1748-1789)
Time of action: Late eighteenth century
First published: 1783-1789

PRINCIPAL CHARACTERS

Mr. Barlow, a clergyman charged with the education of Sandford and Merton. He has the boys learn by doing, even insisting that they help in the garden in order to eat. He inspires the boys to learn a great deal. He takes them on excursions to see how the world's work is done, and he tries to inculcate moral virtues as well as knowledge.

Tommy Merton, a headstrong, ill-tempered, weak lad. He has been pampered by his doting mother and by the family's slaves in Jamaica. Upon arriving in England he has no formal education, nor any inclination to study. He is sent to the vicarage to live with Mr. Barlow and be educated. With the example of Harry Sandford and the tutelage of Mr. Barlow, Tommy catches up with his education and becomes a healthy, unselfish, exemplary youth.

Mr. Merton, Tommy's father, a sensible

English gentleman who wants his son to be an educated, virtuous young man.

Harry Sandford, an English farmer's son. He is a sincere lad with a philosophical attitude. He is educated by Mr. Barlow. He makes a good impression on Mr. Merton and causes the latter to send his son to be educated by the same man. At the vicarage, he is a good example for Tommy Merton to follow.

Mrs. Merton, Tommy's doting mother. She is displeased by young Harry's belief that artificiality and the possessions of the rich are unimportant.

Mr. Sandford, a self-sufficient farmer. He refuses to accept Mr. Merton's payment of money for the good example that his son gave Tommy Merton, saying that he fears that the money would only bring trouble to the family.

SANINE

Author: Mikhail Artsybashev (1878-1927)
Time of action: 1906
First published: 1907

PRINCIPAL CHARACTERS

Vladimir Petrovitch Sanine, a young man who believes only in himself. Following his inclinations wherever they take him and claiming the same freedom for others, he influences several people to take actions with tragic consequences, for which he refuses to accept any moral responsibility. Finally, at Yourii Svarogitsch's

funeral, he horrifies the townspeople by his insensitivity and hardness of heart. Soon afterward he leaves the town on a train from which he jumps to his death.

Lidia (Lida) Petrovna, Sanine's sister. Although fearful of her brother's ideas, she is, nonetheless, attracted to them

1004

and, under their influence, gives herself to Captain Sarudine. Expecting her lover's child, she learns that he is through with her. She attempts suicide, from which she is dissuaded by Sanine, who urges her to live and marry Dr. Novikoff.

Maria Ivanovna, Sanine's mother.

Captain Sarudine, an insensitive, lascivious officer who seduces Lida Petrovna with no opposition from her free-thinking brother Sanine. When he is ordered from the house by Sanine, he challenges the young man to a duel, but his challenge is refused. Later, when he is knocked down on the street by Sanine, the additional blow to his pride and honor is so great that he hangs himself.

Dr. Novikoff, Lida Petrovna's sincere but awkward suitor.

Sina Karsavina, a young schoolteacher who is in love with Yourii Svarogitsch but is strangely attracted to Sanine, to whom she briefly gives herself and immediately regrets her surrender.

Yourii Nicolaijevitsch Svarogitsch, a young student in love with Sina Karsavina. Though his need for her is great, the problems with which marriage confront him are so much greater that he takes his own life.

Soloveitchik, Sanine's Jewish friend, who takes his own life.

SAPPHO

Author: Alphonse Daudet (1840-1897)
Time of action: Nineteenth century
First published: 1884

PRINCIPAL CHARACTERS

Fanny Legrand (få·nē' lə·grän'), an intelligent, shrewd, completely feminine prostitute. She is fifty years old and has been mistress to many men of various occupations and professions. She ends her days with one of her first lovers and their child.

Jean Gaussin (zhän' gō·săn'), a student from the south of France who has come to Paris to prepare himself for a diplomatic career. He meets the experienced courtesan Fanny Legrand and, attracted by her sophistication, falls in love with her despite the great difference in their ages. After they have lived together for a time Fanny's hold on Jean is so strong that his naïve fiancée has little attraction for him. When he is awarded a post in South America, he breaks his engagement and begs Fanny to go with him. Unwilling to leave Paris, she declines his offer.

Déchelette (dā·shə·lĕt'), a wealthy engineer who spends most of his time on construction projects far from France. For two months of the year, however, he lives in Paris, where he hosts lavish parties and enjoys the society of his native city. Fanny has been his mistress, and he has shared his wealth with her.

Flamant (flå·män'), an engraver who goes to prison for counterfeiting bank notes. Fanny and Flamant have had a child. After Flamant is released from prison, the three settle down to live as a family.

Caoudal (kå·ōō·dăl'), a sculptor with whom Fanny lives for a short time. He does a figure of Sappho for which Fanny is the model.

La Gournerie (lá gōōr·nə·rē'), a poet who keeps Fanny for several years. It was he who taught Fanny the colorful language she uses on occasion.

Césaire Gaussin (sā·zěr′ gō·săn′), Gaussin's ne'er-do-well uncle, who comes to Paris to collect an old debt of eight thousand francs to pay off Gaussin's parents' indebtedness resulting from a crop failure. When Césaire gambles away the money he has collected, Fanny, out of her love for Gaussin, gets eight thousand francs from Déchelette, gives it to Césaire, and sends him back home.

Rosario Sanches (Rosa) (rō·sä′rē·ō săn′-chĕz), a wealthy composer's mistress for whom Fanny manages an apartment for a short time.

Tatave de Potter (tà·tàv′ də pô·tā′), Rosa's lover, a famous composer. He is hated by his wife and unknown to his children because he is obsessively attracted to Rosa. His story profoundly impresses Gaussin.

Bouchereau (boo·shə·rō′), an eminent physiologist who befriends Gaussin.

Irène (ē·rěn′), Bouchereau's niece and Gaussin's innocent, naïve fiancée. Irène's simple charm, however, is not sufficient permanently to attract a man who has loved the sophisticated Fanny, and Gaussin breaks the engagement.

SAPPHO

Author: Franz Grillparzer (1791-1872)
Time of action: Sixth century B.C.
First presented: 1818

PRINCIPAL CHARACTERS

Sappho (să′fō), the Greek poetess. Wearing the laurel wreath of victory from the Olympian contest of poetry and song, she returns to her island home bringing Phaon, with whom she has fallen deeply in love. When the young man falls in love with Melitta, Sappho, offended and troubled, accuses him of being a deceiver in love. Phaon's reply that he now realizes it was her genius he loved rather than herself causes Sappho to reflect on her gifts. Deciding that her genius bars her from meeting the demands of ordinary mortal existence, she calls upon the gods to receive her as she hurls herself into the sea.

Phaon (fā′ɔn), a young charioteer. Hav-

ing a great admiration for the poems of Sappho, he falls in love with the poetess when they meet at Olympia. He returns with her to Lesbos where, in spite of her love and consideration, the simple young man is uncomfortable in her luxurious surroundings. When he falls in love with Melitta, he realizes that it was Sappho's genius he had loved at Olympia, not the woman herself.

Melitta (mə·lǐ′tə), Sappho's beautiful young slave girl, who brings to Phaon the realization that it is the poetess' genius and not Sappho herself that he has loved.

Rhamnes (răm′nēz), Sappho's elderly slave.

SARAGOSSA

Author: Benito Pérez Galdós (1845-1920)
Time of action: 1808-1809
First published: 1874

Don José de Montoria (dōn hō·sā′ ɥā mōn·tō′ryä), who is in charge of the defense of Sarogossa in the siege of 1808-1809. By force he seizes grain hoarded by Candiola.

Augustine (ä·gōōs·tēn′), Montoria's son, who is preparing for the priesthood, though he is in love with Mariquilla. When he is put in charge of the firing squad to execute Mariquilla's father, she breaks completely with him. At her death, he enters a monastery.

Manuel (mä·nwĕl′), the older brother of Augustine, who is killed in the siege.

Mariquilla (mä·rē·kē′lyä), who is unwilling to marry the man who harassed her father. She dies of grief.

Candiola (kän·dyō′lä), Mariquilla's father, a miser and grain hoarder who helps the French tunnel into the city and is condemned to death as a traitor.

Manuela Sancho (mä·nwē′lä sän′chō), a heroine who battles the French at a breach in the wall.

Araceli (ä·rä·thä′lē), a friend of Augustine who comes to Sarogossa to help defend the city.

SATANSTOE

Author: James Fenimore Cooper (1789-1851)
Time of action: 1751-1758
First published: 1845

PRINCIPAL CHARACTERS

Cornelius Littlepage, called Corny, the narrator. As the son of a landed proprietor, he travels, on business for his father, between Albany and New York City, and, later, into the forests of New York State, where he engages in the battle of Ticonderoga and subsequent forays against Indian raiders.

Anneke Mordaunt, the beautiful daughter of Herman Mordaunt. Courted by Major Bulstrode, her father's choice as a husband, and Corny Littlepage, she finally confesses her love for Corny, whom she marries.

Major Bulstrode, a British officer and the rival of Corny Littlepage for the hand of Anneke Mordaunt.

Guert Ten Eyck, Corny Littlepage's friend, who is in love with Mary Wallace. After many difficulties he finally wins her hand, only to be mortally wounded in an Indian raid before they can be married.

Mary Wallace, Anneke Mordaunt's friend, who falls, too late, in love with Guert Ten Eyck.

The Reverend Thomas Worden, Corny Littlepage's tutor and companion in his travels.

Herman Mordaunt, a wealthy landowner, Anneke Mordaunt's father.

Dirck Van Valkenburgh, called Dirck Follock, Corny Littlepage's friend.

Abraham Van Valkenburgh, called Brom Follock, Dirck Van Valkenburgh's father.

Jason Newcome, a schoolmaster.

Jaap, Corny Littlepage's Negro servant.

Mr. Traverse, a surveyor.

Susquesus, called Trackless, and Jumper, Indian guides and runners.

Musquerusque, a Canadian Indian captive taken by Jaap at Ticonderoga.

Mother Doortje, a fortuneteller who warns Guert Ten Eyck that he may never marry.

Hugh Roger Littlepage, Corny Littlepage's grandfather.

Lord Howe, a British general killed at Ticonderoga.

SATIROMASTIX

Author: Thomas Dekker (c. 1572-1632?)
Time of action: c. 1100
First presented: 1601

PRINCIPAL CHARACTERS

William Rufus, the King of England, a lustful, treacherous tyrant. Intending to violate her, he tricks and taunts Sir Walter into promising to send his beautiful wife alone to the palace. When Sir Walter brings him her apparently dead body, the King is seized with remorse; he repents, and on her revival gives her back to her husband unharmed.

Sir Walter Terrill, the King's loyal follower. He agrees to let his wife take poison rather than become the prey of the King.

Caelestine, Sir Walter's beautiful bride. She too prefers the poison to the loss of her virtue.

Sir Quintilian Shorthose, Caelestine's father. Deceiving both Caelestine and Sir Walter, he pretends to poison her, but actually gives her a sleeping potion that causes her to appear dead.

Mistress Miniver, a foolish wealthy widow. Her hand is sought by Sir Quintilian, Sir Vaughan, Sir Adam, and Captain Tucca. She yields to the aggressive Tucca and rejects the three knights.

Sir Vaughan ap Rees, a Welsh knight, one of the widow's suitors.

Sir Adam Prickshaft, another of the widow's suitors.

Horace, the humorous poet, an amusing caricature of Ben Jonson. A specialist in satires and epithalamiums, he writes satirical pieces on his fellow poets and others and on invitation works on a marriage song for Sir Walter and Caelestine. He is forced by Tucca to wear a laureate crown of nettles and to swear to give up satirical writing against his fellows.

Asinius Bubo, Horace's admiring follower, perhaps a caricature of Michael Drayton.

Crispinus, a poet, probably a representation of John Marston.

Demetrius, another poet, probably a representation of Dekker himself.

Captain Tucca, a roaring roisterer, loudmouthed and vulgar, given to fantastic figures of speech. He is the instrument of Horace's humiliation at Court. He wins the hand of the widow in spite of her knightly suitors.

THE SATYRICON

Author: Gaius Petronius Arbiter (?-c. 66)
Time of action: First century
Earliest extant printed version: 1664

Encolpius (ĕn·kōl′pĭ·əs), the narrator, who despises the artificiality of rhetoric and the poor preparation of his students. He goes off on a series of roguish adventures.

Agamemnon (ă′gə·mĕm′nŏn), a teacher who agrees with Encolpius that students are ill-prepared. He places all the blame on parents who do not force their children to study.

Gito (gī′tō), Encolpius' young slave. A handsome boy, he is by turns upset and happy because of the amorous attentions of Ascyltus and deserts his master for Ascyltus' service for a time.

Ascyltus (ăs·kĭl′təs), Encolpius' friend and companion on many of his adventures.

Lycurgus (lī·kûr′gəs), a rich man and friend of Ascyltus.

Lichas (lī′kəs), a rich friend of Lycurgus. Completely taken with Encolpius, Lichas invites him and Gito to his house.

Doris (dô′rĭs), Lichas' beautiful wife, to whom Encolpius makes love.

Tryphaena (trī·fē′nə), a beautiful, amoral woman of Lichas' household who makes love to both Encolpius and Gito. When they tire of her, she spitefully accuses them of making improper advances to her and they have to flee from Lichas' house.

Trimalchio (trə·măl′kĭ·ō), a rich man and a former slave. He is unused to wealth and is very vulgar. He makes a great show of his riches to impress both himself and other people. He gives an elaborate, ostentatious banquet for which his name is still remembered.

Niceros (nĭ′sə·rəs), a freedman who tells a tale about a man who turns into a wolf.

Eumolpus (ū·mōl′pəs), a poet who becomes Encolpius' friend and shares in some of his escapades.

Circe (sėr′sē), a woman to whom Encolpius tries to make love.

THE SCARLET LETTER

Author: Nathaniel Hawthorne (1804-1864)
Time of action: Mid-seventeenth century
First published: 1850

PRINCIPAL CHARACTERS

Hester Prynne, an attractive young woman living among the Puritans of Boston during the 1650's. She becomes a martyr because she, presumably a widow, bears a child out of wedlock; this sin results in her being jailed and then publicly exhibited on a pillory for three hours. When she is released from jail, she must wear for a lifetime a scarlet "A" upon her bosom. She becomes a seamstress, stitching and embroidering to earn a living for herself and for Pearl, her child. After her one act of sin, Hester behaves with such uncanny rectitude she seems an American Jeanne d'Arc, battling not against opposing armies and bigotry but against bigotry alone, the most formidable of antagonists. Hester refuses to name the child's father, who is the Reverend Arthur Dimmesdale, her minister; she does not quail when her supposedly dead husband, Roger Chillingworth, comes from out of the forest to witness her appearance on the pillory; and without complaint or self-pity she fights her way back to respectability and the rights of motherhood. Her situation is made more poignant (and heroic) by

1009

Dimmesdale's lack of sufficient moral courage to confess that he is Pearl's father. Hester seems to need no partner to share her guilt. Her life ends in tragedy (as it must) when Dimmesdale dies, but the reader feels that Hester—as strong as the oak in American clipper ships—will stoutly and resolutely make her way through life.

The Rev. Arthur Dimmesdale, a minister in Boston. Emotionally he is drawn and halved by the consequences of his sin with Hester, and he is pulled apart by responsibility. Should he confess and thus ruin his career or should he keep silent and continue the great good resulting from his sin-inspired sermons? Outwardly Dimmesdale is a living man, but inwardly he is the rubble and wreckage resulting from a Puritan conscience. One night he drags himself (along with Hester and Pearl) up to the pillory where he feels he should have stood long ago; but this confession is a sham, for only Roger Chillingworth (hidden in the darkness) observes the trio. Finally, at the end of his Election Day sermon, he takes Hester and Pearl by the hand, ascends the pillory, confesses publicly, and sinks down dead. When his clothing is removed, Puritans see the stigma of an "A" on the skin of his chest. Hawthorne takes no stand on Dimmesdale's weakness or strength; he says simply, "This is Dimmesdale."

Roger Chillingworth, a "physician" who might better be called "Evil." Thought to have been killed by the Indians, he reënters Hester's life when she first stands on the pillory. Pretending to minister to the physically ailing Dimmesdale, he tries only to confirm his suspicion that the minister is Pearl's father. When Arthur and Hester, in a desperate act of hope, book passage on a ship to England, Chillingworth also signs up for the voyage, and Hester knows she can never escape him. Although motivated by his wife's bearing another man's child, Chillingworth nevertheless seems inordinately twisted toward vengeance. Conniving, sly, monomaniacal, he is more a devilish force than a man.

Pearl, Hester's elfin, unpredictable daughter. She refuses to repeat the catechism for the Governor and thus risks being taken from her mother. At a meeting of Hester and Arthur in the forest she treats the minister as a rival; when he kisses her on the brow, she rushes to a stream and washes away the unwelcome kiss.

Governor Bellingham, of the Massachusetts Colony. He thinks Hester is unfit to rear Pearl but is persuaded to allow them to remain together by the plea of Dimmesdale.

The Rev. John Wilson, a stern divine. Early in the story he exhorts Dimmesdale to force Hester to reveal Pearl's father.

Mistress Higgins, the bitter-tempered sister of the Governor; she is simply and literally a witch.

THE SCHOOL FOR HUSBANDS

Author: Molière (Jean Baptiste Poquelin, 1622-1673)
Time of action: Seventeenth century
First presented: 1661

PRINCIPAL CHARACTERS

Sganarelle (zgà·nà·rěl′), a gentleman entrusted with the guardianship of Isabelle, orphaned by the death of her father.

Scorning his brother Ariste's leniency in the upbringing of Léonor, Isabelle's sister, Sganarelle attempts to govern his ward by severity and keeps her confined at home in preparation for marriage to him. In spite of his surveillance, Isabelle manages to fall in love with Valère and to trick her guardian into arranging a marriage ceremony for her and her lover.

Ariste (a·rēst′), Sganarelle's brother and the guardian of Isabelle's sister, Léonor. Disapproving of his brother's strictness in bringing up his ward, Ariste governs by affection and allows freedom to Léonor, whom he loves enough to leave to her the choice of a husband. Returning from a ball, she declares that she loves only her guardian and wishes to marry him immediately.

Isabelle (ē·zà·bĕl′), Sganarelle's ward. Confined at home and strictly guarded by her guardian, she manages nevertheless to fall in love with Valère. By a series of deceptions, the lovers trick Sganarelle into arranging meetings and, finally, their marriage.

Léonor (lā·ô·nôr′), Isabelle's sister and Ariste's ward. Allowed the freedom to come and go at will by her lenient guardian, she learns to love him and confesses her willingness to marry him whenever he wishes.

Valère (và·lĕr′), Isabelle's lover, with whom she deceives Sganarelle.

THE SCHOOL FOR SCANDAL

Author: Richard Brinsley Sheridan (1751-1816)
Time of action: Eighteenth century
First presented: 1777

PRINCIPAL CHARACTERS

Sir Oliver Surface, a gentleman whose problem it is to discover which of two nephews is more worthy of the Surface fortune. Posing once as Mr. Premium, a moneylender and, again, as Mr. Stanley, a poor relation, Sir Oliver is finally able to decide that Charles Surface is the worthier nephew.

Joseph Surface, the unworthy nephew, as it turns out. He is a double dealer and in the famous screen scene is discovered in several falsehoods by people upon whose influence his future depends. Joseph is one of two people who are left unhappy when the denouement takes place.

Charles Surface, Sir Oliver's worthy nephew. Charles' only real fault seems to be extravagance with money. He is well-intentioned and even kind and honest. Discovered by Sir Oliver to be the better of the two nephews, he wins the girl of his choice and receives his uncle's inheritance.

Sir Peter Teazle, an elderly nobleman and Sir Oliver's friend, whose lot in life it is to be married to a young wife who almost plays him false with Joseph Surface. Sir Peter is pleased at his part in helping to expose Joseph.

Lady Teazle, Sir Peter's young country-bred wife, who relishes the pleasure of living in London. She treats her long-suffering husband with disdain until she learns that Joseph has simply been toying with her affections. Her lesson learned, she is a better wife to Sir Peter.

Lady Sneerwell, Lady Teazle's friend, who ruins women's reputations in order to make them compare more closely with her own. Her plan to expose Joseph for the person he is, wreck Charles' love for Maria, and gain Charles and the family fortune goes awry when her confederate, Snake, sells her out.

Maria, Sir Peter's ward, who is a girl with a good head on her shoulders. Her

1011

guardian selects Joseph to be her husband but, loving Charles, she keeps putting Joseph off, biding her time. Her patience is rewarded when Joseph overreaches himself; with his downfall she gains Sir Peter's permission to marry Charles.

Snake, Lady Sneerwell's intimate, who takes money from two factions, thus aiding Sir Oliver by exposing Lady Sneerwell's plan to ruin Joseph, scandalize the Teazles, and win Charles and his uncle's money.

Sir Benjamin Backbite, a slanderer, Lady Sneerwell's friend.

Rowley, Sir Peter's servant, who believes from the beginning that Charles has a better character than Joseph.

Lady Candour, a lady whose defense of a reputation is certain to ruin it.

Moses, a Jew who concerns himself with Sir Oliver's money matters.

THE SCHOOL FOR WIVES

Author: Molière (Jean Baptiste Poquelin, 1622-1673)
Time of action: Seventeenth century
First presented: 1662

PRINCIPAL CHARACTERS

Arnolphe (M. de la Souche) (är·nôlf' də lä sōōsh'), a man who is convinced that, in order to avoid being disgraced by an unfaithful wife, he must marry a very innocent girl who has been sheltered and kept from the world. He decides to marry Agnès, his ward. He sends her to a convent and then keeps her in seclusion in a small cottage on his estate. He plots to keep her apart from Horace, the young man she loves, but is eventually foiled in his plan.

Agnès (àn·yĕs'), Arnolphe's ward, a young and very innocent girl who knows nothing of love affairs but is very much in love with Horace. She is so ignorant that she once asked if babies came from the ear. In spite of Arnolphe's plotting, she is united with her lover.

Horace (ô·ràs'), the young man who is in love with Agnès. He does not know that Arnolphe, her guardian, and the

man named de la Souche, who is supposed to marry Agnès, are one and the same person. He considers Arnolphe to be his friend, consults him, and asks for his aid in winning Agnès. Arnolphe attempts to betray him but fails, and Horace and Agnès are united in spite of Arnolphe's plots against them.

Chrysalde (krē·zàld'), Arnolphe's friend and confidant. He is the recipient of Arnolphe's declarations about how a wife should be trained.

Enrique (än·rēk'), Chrysalde's brother-in-law. Horace's father is determined that Horace must marry Enrique's daughter, and Arnolphe encourages this plan. When he learns that Enrique's daughter is really Agnès, his discovery comes too late.

Oronte (ô·rōnt') Horace's father and Enrique's friend. He insists that Horace must marry Enrique's daughter.

THE SCORNFUL LADY

Authors: Francis Beaumont (1585?-1616) and John Fletcher (1579-1625)
Time of action: Early seventeenth century
First presented: 1613-1617

1012

The Scornful Lady, a headstrong, independent young woman. Cursed with a streak of perversity, she heaps scorn and indignity on the man she loves whenever he is present; she is disturbed by this, and frequently resolves to reform, but constantly lapses. Only the fear that she is about to lose him forever brings her to accept marriage with him.

Martha, the Lady's sister. She joins in jeering and flouting her sister's lover, but he later triumphs by tricking her into marrying one of the Lady's other suitors.

Elder Loveless, the Lady's true lover. Angered at being banished by her for kissing her in public, he tries various tricks to make her revoke the banishment and marry him. He is several times outwitted by her, but finally overcomes her reluctance by producing an apparent bride-to-be.

Young Loveless, his trifling and prodigal younger brother. In spite of his scapegrace behavior, Young Lovelace wins a wealthy and attractive widow for his wife.

Savil, Elder Loveless' steward. When the elder brother is reported dead, Savil panders to the younger's scandalous behavior. On the master's return, Savil is discharged for failing in his responsibility; but he is later forgiven.

Morecraft, an unscrupulous moneylender. His projects for gaining possession of Loveless' land fail, and he loses his fiancée to Young Loveless; therefore he decides to turn prodigal, hoping that the dividends will be as high in his case as in Young Loveless'.

Abigail (Mrs. Younglove), the Lady's elderly waiting woman. Highly susceptible, she pursues several men, finally marrying Sir Roger, the curate.

Welford, a suitor for the Lady's hand. After a quarrelsome first meeting, he and Elder Loveless join forces. He disguises himself as Elder Loveless' supposed bride-to-be, thereby helping his former rival to win the Lady and winning Martha for himself.

The Widow, Morecraft's fiancée, who will not consent to marry him until he gains a knighthood. She deserts him for Young Loveless.

Sir Roger, the Lady's curate, whom aging Abigail snares for a husband.

THE SCOTTISH CHIEFS

Author: Jane Porter (1776-1850)
Time of action: 1296-1305
First published: 1810

Sir William Wallace, a Scottish patriot of the thirteenth century. He seeks to free Scotland from the domination of the English. He is a courageous leader and becomes regent of Scotland. His success is envied by other Scottish nobles, and he is delivered into the hands of the English, who execute him as a traitor.

Robert Bruce, claimant to the Scottish throne. He joins Wallace's patriots and after Wallace's death assumes leadership, freeing Scotland by defeating the English at Bannockburn. During the wars he calls himself the Count de Longueville. He becomes King of Scotland after Bannockburn.

Sir John Monteith, a Scottish nobleman who gives Wallace a mysterious box which is not to be opened until Scotland is free. Monteith later turns against Wallace and betrays him to the English.

The Earl of Mar, an elderly Scots nobleman and patriot who is Wallace's friend. He is killed while fighting the English.

Lady Mar, the Earl's wife, who wants to marry Wallace when she is a widow and he a widower. He refuses her and wins her enmity. It is her false accusation of treason that causes Wallace's death. She disguises herself for a time as the Knight of the Green Plume.

Lady Wallace, Sir William Wallace's wife. She is killed by the English when she refuses to betray her husband.

The Abbot of St. Fillan, a loyal Scot who keeps the mysterious iron box safely through the war. The box contains the Scottish crown and royal vestments.

Edwin Ruthven, a faithful adherent to Wallace who dies defending his leader.

The Earl of Gloucester, an English nobleman who sides with the Scots, believing his father-in-law, Edward I, is wrong to claim Scotland as his.

Lady Helen Mar, daughter of Lord Mar. She loves Wallace and marries him on the eve of his execution.

Lord de Valence, an English nobleman held as a hostage by Wallace.

Lord Cummins, a Scottish nobleman who distrusts Wallace's ambitions. He becomes regent after Wallace resigns.

Isabella Mar, daughter of Lord Mar. She becomes Robert Bruce's queen.

Edward I, King of England.

THE SEA OF GRASS

Author: Conrad Richter (1890-   )
Time of action: 1885-1910
First published: 1936

PRINCIPAL CHARACTERS

Colonel Jim Brewton, a pioneer rancher. He stages a bitter but losing fight against the encroachment of homesteaders who come West to fence and farm the free range. A proud man, the Colonel claims his range as his empire, and he has only contempt for the "nesters" who would destroy it with wheat crops. He marries a vivacious young woman from St. Louis who brightens his home and his life for a time. But after bearing three children, one not his, she tires of her rough, monotonous existence on the ranch and deserts her husband for a period of fifteen years. Although aware that one of her children is not his, the Colonel rears the boy as his own and buries him as a full-fledged member of the family.

Hal Brewton, the Colonel's nephew, who

deplores the inevitable changes he sees taking place all around him. He detests the homesteaders who spoil the range, and he resents Lutie's "Eastern ways," which mean new furniture, flowers growing in the yard, frequent guests and visitors. Returning home from medical school to establish his practice, he finds that the sea of grass of his youth is gone forever.

Lutie Cameron, a charming young woman who comes to Salt Fork from St. Louis to marry Colonel Brewton. She soon turns the ranch house into a center for gay parties and distinguished guests, and for a while she seems to adjust satisfactorily to her new way of life. She bears three children, one by her favorite dancing partner, a young lawyer named Brice

Chamberlain. Eventually tiring of the harsh ranch life she leaves the Colonel, expecting Brice to go away with her. Nothing is heard from her for fifteen years. Then one day she unexpectedly returns, without explanations, and the Colonel takes her back as though she had never been away. Meanwhile he has reared her illegitimate son and with the force of his personality has kept local gossip to a minimum.

Brice Chamberlain, who as a young lawyer takes the homesteaders' side in a trial. Though he loses the trial, he continues to fight the free-range policy of Colonel Brewton and eventually sees the "nesters" win out. He becomes Lutie's lover and fathers a son by her, but, being a cowardly man, he lacks the courage to leave town with her as planned when the Colonel appears at the station wearing a gun.

Brock Brewton, Lutie's son by Brice Chamberlain. Realizing as a youth that he is illegitimate, he grows up bitter and resentful; to avenge himself he turns to drinking, gambling, cheating at cards, and, eventually, to outlawry. When he is trapped by a posse and shot, the Colonel defiantly claims the body as that of his own son and buries it on the Brewton ranch.

Jimmy and
Sarah Beth Brewton, the children of Lutie and the Colonel.

THE SEA WOLF

Author: Jack London (1876-1916)
Time of action: 1904
First published: 1904

PRINCIPAL CHARACTERS

Humphrey Van Weyden, called **Hump,** picked up by the sealer "Ghost" after a shipwreck. He has a perilous existence until the crew kill off one another. He and Miss Brewster navigate the crippled ship back to the United States.

Wolf Larsen, called **The Sea Wolf,** brutal Captain of the "Ghost." He is buried at sea.

Maud Brewster, the survivor of a wreck, rescued by Wolf and protected from him by Hump.

Death Larsen, Captain of the "Macedonia." He is Wolf's brother and enemy. He steals his brother's skins.

Johansen, the cruel mate of the "Ghost," drowned during a mutiny.

Johnson, a seaman beaten by the officers. He tries to desert with Leach but is drowned.

Leach, the former cabin boy, who tries to kill the cook and the Captain.

Mugridge, the ship's cook, to whom Hump is assigned. The cook abuses and robs him until the "cabin boy" turns on him.

Louis, the only crew member friendly to Hump.

THE SEAGULL

Author: Anton Chekhov (1860-1904)
Time of action: Nineteenth century
First presented: 1896

Irina Arkadina (ĭr·ĭn′ə är·kä·dĭ′nə), an aging, famous Russian actress who is vain, egotistical, selfish. Living only for public acclaim of her art, Irina is neither willing nor able to establish a warm human relationship with her lover, Boris Trigorin, or with her son, Constantine Treplieff. Her disregard for her son helps to drive him to self-destruction.

Constantine Treplieff (côn·stän·tĭn′ trĕp-lyĕf′), a struggling young writer, the son of Irina Arkadina. He is an extreme idealist, both in his love for Nina Zarietchnaya and in his art. Constantly seeking for new forms in his writing, he ignores literary conventions and believes that life must be represented not as it is but as it ought to be. In a moment of despair over his work, he shoots a seagull (which symbolizes human aspiration) and then makes an unsuccessful attempt on his own life. Near the end of the play, deserted by Nina, misunderstood by his mother, ignored by more successful literary men, he finds himself unable to believe in anything, and he commits suicide.

Boris Trigorin (bô·rĭs′ trĭ·gō′rĭn), a successful author and Irina Arkadina's lover. Although his writing has brought him fame, he has no real satisfaction in his work or his honors. He finds that writing is a tyrant forcing him on to producing new works. Unlike Constantine, he uses established forms and writes prolifically on every subject. His restlessness drives him to use people and then to discard them; his weakness of character leads him to marry and then to desert Nina Zarietchnaya. Some critics believe Trigorin's comments on writing embody Chekhov's own ideas.

Nina Zarietchnaya (nĭ′nə zä·rĕ′ch·nə·yä), an aspiring actress, the young daughter of a rich landowner. Deserted by Tri-gorin after their marriage, she continues her unsuccessful attempt at a career in the theater. She calls herself a seagull and aspires in the face of failure, but she does not expect honor and glory as she did when she was younger. Believing in her abilities, she can diminish her suffering; she is the only character in the play who learns that what is important in life is the strength to endure, like a seagull.

Peter Sorin (pyō′tr sô·rĭn′), Irina Arkadina's brother, on whose country estate the action of the play occurs. Like those of the other characters, all his youthful wishes and dreams are shattered, and he ends his days wishing to escape his boredom.

Ilia Shamraeff, (ĭl·yä′ shäm·rä′ĕf), the manager of Sorin's estate and a gruff, surly man dissatisfied with his status.

Paulina Shamraeff (pô·lĭ′nə), Ilia's wife, frustrated in her love for Eugene Dorn. She is bored with her lot and yearns for the unattainable.

Masha (mä′shə), their daughter. Hopelessly in love with Constantine Treplieff, she settles for marriage to a dull, impoverished schoolmaster.

Simon Medviedenko (sĕ·myō′n mĕd·vĕd′-ĕn·kō), a provincial schoolteacher married to the nagging, dissatisfied Masha. He is overwhelmed by responsibilities and debts.

Eugene Dorn (ĕv·gĕ′nĭy dōrn), a doctor fifty-five years old and unwilling to change his ways of living by eloping with Paulina Shamraeff. In spite of his long and meaningful practice, he is penniless; but he has no fear of death because he has joy in life.

Jacob,
A Maid, and
A Cook, servants in the Sorin household.

THE SECOND MRS. TANQUERAY

Author: Arthur Wing Pinero (1855-1934)
Time of action: The 1890's
First presented: 1893

PRINCIPAL CHARACTERS

Aubrey Tanqueray, a wealthy English widower. He is resolved to marry a second time, to a young woman from a lower class. The marriage is disappointing, for he finds the young wife's boredom perplexing and her humor and cynicism embarrassing. He finally learns that his young wife has been his daughter's suitor's mistress.

Paula Ray Tanqueray, a younger woman of somewhat questionable character, loved by Aubrey. She is unsure of herself, but glib. After her marriage she finds she is bored and lonely in the country. She intercepts a letter from Ellean Tanqueray to her father, is discovered, and promises to try to be a better wife. But when she learns that her ex-lover is her stepdaughter's suitor and that she stands in the way of her stepdaughter's marriage, she commits suicide.

Ellean Tanqueray, Aubrey's teen-age daughter by his first wife. She is highly religious and considers becoming a nun. When she thinks her mother's spirit has told her to, she returns home for a time. She falls in love with an army officer who proves to have been her stepmother's former lover.

Captain Hugh Ardale, an army officer who courts Ellean and wins her love. His marriage to her is delayed, however, because he was at one time Ellean's stepmother's lover.

Cayley Drummle, Aubrey's good friend, who tries to counsel him against a marriage with a woman from a lower class.

Mrs. Alice Cortelyou, Aubrey's long-time friend and neighbor, the first of his set to call after his marriage to Paula Ray.

Sir George and
Lady Orreyed, friends of Paula Ray before her marriage. She invites them to the Tanqueray home after the marriage, despite her husband's objections. They prove to be coarse, boorish, even insulting guests.

[**Mrs. Tanqueray,** Aubrey's dead wife, who had not made her husband happy. When she died of a fever one of Aubrey's friends observed that it was the only warmth ever to have come to the woman's body.]

THE SECOND SHEPHERDS' PLAY

Author: Unknown
Time of action: The Nativity
First transcribed: Fifteenth century manuscript

PRINCIPAL CHARACTERS

Coll, the first shepherd. He complains to his companions of the cold winter, poverty, and the oppression of husbandmen by the gentry. It is his kindly thought of leaving a present for Mak's child which leads to the discovery of the sheep.

Gyb, the second shepherd, who is plagued by a shrewish wife as well as by the weather and his masters. He urges the others on to Bethlehem to worship the Christ Child after they have heard the song of the angels.

Daw, the third shepherd, a boy. He is suspicious of Mak from the moment he appears, and he first recognizes Gill's new baby as the lost sheep.

Mak, a rogue and a well-known sheep stealer who attempts to gull the shepherds and nearly succeeds in convincing them that their ram is his child. He finally wins a tossing in a blanket for his trouble.

Gill, his sharp-tongued wife. She complains incessantly of his failings as husband and provider, but she is happy to aid in his deception of the shepherds and suggests that he dress the sheep in swaddling clothes while she pretends to be lying in childbed.

An Angel, who sings to the shepherds of the birth of Christ.

Mary, the mother of Christ. She greets the shepherds and accepts their simple gifts for her child.

THE SECRET AGENT

Author: Joseph Conrad (Józef Teodor Konrad Korzeniowski, 1857-1924)
Time of action: The 1880's
First published: 1907

PRINCIPAL CHARACTERS

Mr. Verloc, an "agent provocateur" assigned to spy on anarchists in London; he poses as a shopkeeper, and he is indolent and unkempt. Under pressure from his superiors at a foreign embassy, he plans to bomb Greenwich Observatory, a deed he believes sufficiently irrational and anarchistically shocking enough to stir up the London police in a campaign against the anarchists. His feeble-minded brother-in-law, whom he enlists to carry the explosive, stumbles in Greenwich Park and is himself blown to bits. Because he uses her half-witted brother as his dupe, Winnie Verloc, murders her husband.

Winnie Verloc, a motherly woman who married Verloc mainly to provide security for Stevie, the half-witted brother whom she loves protectively. When she learns that her husband was instrumental in having her brother blown up, she murders him with a knife and attempts to escape to the Continent with Comrade Ossipon. Under great stress after Ossipon deserts her, she commits suicide by jumping from the steamer on the way to Calais.

Chief Inspector Heat, an investigator of the Special Crimes Department of the London police. A methodical man, he wishes to follow conventional and routine procedures in trying to solve the mystery of the bombing, the motive for which he can in no way understand. He arrests Michaelis, the most harmless of the anarchist propagandists, whom he knows to be but slightly involved but against whom he can make a case. Because of the insistence of the new Assistant Commissioner, his superior, and the finding of a scrap of an overcoat collar with an address on the label, he is forced to approach Verloc, whose information to the police has been helpful many times before.

The Assistant Commissioner, an official of the London Police who has only recently come to his position from service in the tropics. He realizes the dangers of depending on routine, conventional police rules and procedure. He questions

Chief Inspector Heat's methods and finally feels compelled to take an active part in the investigation of the bombing episode.

Privy Councilor Wurmt, of the foreign embassy in London. He orders that Verloc be called in for reprimand and instructions.

Mr. Vladimir, the First Secretary of the embassy. He accuses Verloc of indolence and deliberately pressures him into the bomb attack on Greenwich Observatory as a means of waking the British people to a sense of their European responsibilities.

Comrade Ossipon, "the Doctor," the unprincipled sensualist among the anarchists. He escapes with Winnie Verloc after she has murdered her husband. He is willing to share Verloc's bank account, but he deserts Winnie when he realizes the possibilities of suspicion that his relation with her may incur.

Michaelis, called the Apostle, an idealistic anarchist who has been in prison and who has written a book about his experiences. Harmless, he is cared for by Lady Mabel, his patroness. In order to save face, Inspector Heat arrests him.

Professor X, the perfect anarchist. Small and deformed physically, he has grandiose ideas and dreams of making the perfect detonator. For protection he carries explosives, fastened to his body, that can be immediately detonated to destroy himself and anyone near him. He supplies Verloc with the explosive for blowing up the Greenwich Observatory.

Karl Yundt, the old "terrorist." Skinny, bald, malevolent, and pitiless, he is a man of much talk but little action.

Stevie, the half-witted brother of Winnie Verloc. Because of his doglike devotion to his brother-in-law, Verloc plans to have him plant the bomb. It explodes accidentally and Stevie is killed.

Sir Ethelred, the Home Secretary, the great personage to whom the Assistant Commissioner reports progress of the investigation.

Lady Mabel, the patroness who supports Michaelis.

Toodles, the young secretary to Sir Ethelred.

SEJANUS, HIS FALL

Author: Ben Jonson (1573?-1637)
Time of action: First century
First presented: 1603

PRINCIPAL CHARACTERS

Lucius Aelius Sejanus (loo'shĭ·əs ē'lĭ·əs sə·jā'nəs), the corrupt favorite of the Emperor Tiberius. Willing to use bribery, seduction, unnatural vice, and murder in order to gain power, he overreaches himself by underestimating the sinister Emperor and receives his death at the hands of an enraged mob manipulated by the Emperor's damnable tool, Macro.

Tiberius (tī·bĭ'rĭ·əs), the devious and ruthless Emperor of Rome. Given to self-indulgence and many vices, he allows Sejanus to assume his duties and much of his power. His suspicion being aroused by Sejanus' proposal to marry Livia, he sends the Senate a letter which undermines Sejanus and leaves him helpless before Macro's machinations.

Lucius Arruntius (loo'shĭ·əs ă·rŭn'-shĭ·əs), a righteous and indignant Roman citizen. Throughout the play he delivers a running satirical and moral commentary on men and events. Though despising Sejanus and his parasites, he sees no hope for better things after the overthrow of Sejanus.

Marcus Lepidus (mär′kəs lĕ′pĭ·dəs), a grave and honest Roman admired by Arruntius. These two and Terentius, at the end of the play, comment on the downfall of Sejanus and the survival of Rome's evils.

Marcus Terentius (mär′kəs tə·rĕn′shĭ·əs), another noble Roman. He delivers the final exemplary warning to all men greedy for power and insolent in its use.

Drusus Senior (drōo′səs), the son of Tiberius. A blunt, angry, immature man, he strikes Sejanus in public for his insolence; hence Sejanus has him murdered for personal revenge as well as for political power.

Livia (lĭ′vĭ·ə), Drusus' corruptible wife. She yields to Sejanus' temptations, becomes his mistress, and helps in plotting the murder of her husband. Her crimes are exposed by Apicata.

[**Apicata** (ă·pĭ·kā′tə), the divorced wife of Sejanus. She never appears onstage, but her agony at the death of her children and her exposure of Livia, Eudemus, and their accomplice are reported.]

Eudemus (ū·dē′məs), an unscrupulous barber and physician. Sejanus corrupts him and uses him in the seduction of Livia and the murder of Drusus.

Sertorius Macro (sėr·tō′rĭ·əs mā′krō), an inhumanly clever and cruel instrument of the Emperor. Set on by Tiberius to undermine Sejanus, he destroys the favorite and has the latter's innocent children horribly executed.

Agrippina (ă·grĭ·pĭ′nə), the widow of Germanicus, Tiberius' nephew, in whose death Sejanus and Tiberius had a hand. A proud woman and indiscreet, she is the center of a group of Romans suspi-

cious of the Emperor and hostile to Sejanus.

Caligula (kə·lĭg′yə·lə), the son of Agrippina and Germanicus. On the advice of Macro he seeks sanctuary from Sejanus with Tiberius himself, thereby inflaming still more the Emperor's suspicions of Sejanus.

Drusus Junior or **Drusus Caesar** (drōo′-səs sē′zėr), another of Agrippina's sons.

Nero (nē′rō), the third son of Agrippina. When Caligula flees to Tiberius, Nero is arrested by Sejanus' orders.

Gaius Silius (gā′yəs sĭl′yəs), a noble Roman of Agrippina's circle. When unjustly accused of treason in the Senate, he recalls his worthy services to Rome and stabs himself, choosing a stoic death rather than falling a victim to Sejanus and Tiberius.

Sosia (sō′sĭ·ə), Silius' wife and a friend of Agrippina. After her husband's suicide she is proscribed and executed.

Cremutius Cordus (krə·mū′shĭ·əs kôr′-dəs), an annalist of the Roman history of Julius Caesar's time. He is executed and his books are condemned to be burnt. Hearing of this sentence, Arruntius delivers a savage denunciation of book-burning.

Titius Sabinus (tĭ′shĭ·əs sə·bī′nəs), another of Agrippina's friends. Tricked into critical statements against the Emperor before witnesses, he is executed. When his body is cast into the water, his faithful dog leaps in after it and drowns.

Asinus Gallus (ə·sē′nĭ·əs gă′ləs), another of Agrippina's friends struck down by Sejanus' plots.

Latiaris (lă·shĭ·ā′rĭs), a Senator, a cousin of Sabinus. He betrays Sabinus to Sejanus' spies, but is himself crushed in the fall of Sejanus.

Domitius Afer (dō·mĭ·shĭ·əs ă′fėr), an

1020

orator. He is the tool of Sejanus, speaking against Silius and Cordus in the Senate.

Varro (vâ′rō), a consul. He joins in the accusation of Silius in the Senate.

Pinnarius Natta (pə·nā′rĭ·əs nă′tə),
Satrius Secundus (să′trĭ·əs sə·kŭn′dəs),
Rufus (rōō′fəs), and
Opsius (ŏp′sĭ·əs), spies employed by Sejanus.

Cotta (kŏ′tə),
Haterius (hə·tī′rĭ·əs),
Sanquinius (săn·kwĭ′nĭ·əs),
Pomponius (pŏm·pō′nĭ·əs),

Julius Posthumus (jōō′lĭ·əs pŏs′chə·məs),
Minutius (mĭ·nū′shĭ·əs), and
Fulcinius Trio (fŭl·sĭ·nĭ·əs trē′ō), fair-weather supporters of Sejanus.

Regulus (rĕg′yə·ləs), a consul, unfriendly toward Sejanus.

Gracinus Laco (grə·sī′nəs lā′kō), the commander of the guards. Well-meaning but confused by the shifts in policy and power, he arrests Nero for Sejanus; but he also brings the guards into the Senate to prevent Sejanus from escaping and to arrest his active followers.

THE SELF-TORMENTOR

Author: Terence (Publius Terentius Afer, c. 190-159 B.C.)
Time of action: Fourteenth century B.C.
First presented: 163 B.C.

PRINCIPAL CHARACTERS

Antiphila (ăn·tĭ′fə·lə), the daughter of Chremes and Sostrata. Given, at birth, to a Corinthian woman, she grows up unknown to her parents. In love with Clinia, she lives with him as his wife. She becomes involved in a plot designed to assist Clitipho in his affair with the prostitute Bacchis, but he is finally persuaded to renounce his mistress. When Antiphila's identity becomes known, she receives permission to marry Clinia.

Clinia (klĭ′nĭ·ə), the son of Menedemus. In love with Antiphila but fearing the disapproval of his strict father, he lives with her as her husband. When his father discovers the affair, his harshness drives Clinia to the wars, from which he returns in secret because of his longing for Antiphila. Involved in a plot to aid his friend, Clitipho, in his infatuation for Bacchis, he learns of his father's regret over his former severity and receives Menedemus' permission to marry Antiphila.

Menedemus (mĕ·nə·dē′məs), Clinia's father. Because of his unjust severity, he drives his son to the wars. Finally, seeing the error of his way, he repents of his harshness and grants permission for Clinia to marry Antiphila.

Clitipho (klĭ′tĭ·fō), the son of Chremes and Sostrata. In love with the courtesan Bacchis, he becomes a party to a plot to deceive his father about the true state of affairs. Finally, when he is found out and threatened with disinheritance, he decides to mend his ways and marry a virtuous woman.

Chremes (krā′mēz), an old Athenian, and
Sostrata (sŏ′strə·tə), his wife, the parents of Antiphila and Clitipho.

Bacchis (bă′kĭs), a courtesan loved by Clitipho.

Syrus (sī′rəs) and
Dromo (drō′mō), Clitipho's servants.

SENSE AND SENSIBILITY

Author: Jane Austen (1775-1817)
Time of action: Early nineteenth century
First published: 1811

PRINCIPAL CHARACTERS

Elinor Dashwood, a young woman representing the "sense" of the title. She is much attracted to Edward Ferrars, Mrs. John Dashwood's brother, and believes him attracted to her. His seeming indifference puzzles her until she learns from Lucy Steele that the two are engaged but cannot marry because of Mrs. Ferrar's opposition. Elinor arranges for a living for Edward when he shall have taken Holy Orders so that he and Lucy can be married. Elinor is led to believe that the marriage has taken place but soon learns that Lucy has jilted Edward in favor of his brother Robert, because Edward has been disinherited. Edward is forgiven by his mother, and he and Elinor are married.

Marianne Dashwood, Elinor's younger sister, representing the "sensibility" of the title. She is emotional and impulsive, with highly romantic ideas of love and marriage. Beloved by Colonel Brandon, she considers him too old for her and falls in love with John Willoughby, an attractive young man. But when the sisters visit London, Willoughby ignores Marianne, and this rejection makes her emotionally ill. While stopping at a country estate on her way home, she becomes physically ill also. Willoughby, having heard of the illness, comes to confess to Elinor that his family, incensed at his seduction of Colonel Brandon's ward, had cut off his allowance, and, having no money, he had been compelled to marry a rich wife. Cured of her infatuation, Marianne learns to appreciate Colonel Brandon's good qualities and marries him.

John Willoughby, the villain of the story, a handsome and fashionable but dissipated young man. He encourages Marianne Dashwood to fall in love with him. It is revealed that he has seduced Colonel Brandon's ward and, rejected by his family, been forced into a loveless but wealthy marriage.

John Dashwood, the half brother of Elinor and Marianne and owner of Norland Park. Since he was wealthy both by inheritance and marriage, he had been urged by his father to provide for his stepmother and his half sister; but, being cold and selfish and easily influenced by his wife, he does nothing for his relatives.

Fanny Dashwood, his wife, daughter of the rich Mrs. Ferrars. She is even colder and more selfish than her husband and persuades him not to carry out his plan of settling three thousand pounds on his half sisters and stepmother.

Mrs. Dashwood, stepmother of John and mother of Elinor and Marianne. She is a warm-hearted, impulsive woman, not endowed with much practical sense.

Mrs. Ferrars, mother of Mrs. John Dashwood, Robert, and Edward. She is rich, ill-tempered, and domineering, using her money to coerce her children.

Robert Ferrars, her older son. He marries Lucy Steele.

Edward Ferrars, her younger son. He wishes to take Holy Orders. When young, he had become engaged to Lucy Steele and thus cannot woo Elinor Dashwood, whom he really loves. His mother, learning of his engagement, disinherits him, and Lucy jilts him for his brother. Thus freed, he is able to marry Elinor.

Lucy Steele, a vulgar, mercenary young woman, engaged to Edward Ferrars. When he is disinherited, she marries his brother Robert.

Anne Steele, her equally vulgar sister.

Colonel Brandon, a quiet man of thirty-five, in love with Marianne Dashwood. She considers him too old. When his ward is seduced by Willoughby, Marianne, horrified by the latter's conduct, finally appreciates the Colonel, and they are married.

Sir John Middleton, wealthy and hospitable, befriends his Dashwood cousins.

Lady Middleton, his wife, also kind to the Dashwoods.

Mrs. Jennings, her mother, a kindly but silly old lady.

Mrs. Palmer, Lady Middleton's sister, good-natured and rattlebrained.

Mr. Palmer, her husband, sensible but cold and sarcastic.

A SENTIMENTAL EDUCATION

Author: Gustave Flaubert (1821-1880)
Time of action: Nineteenth century
First published: 1869

PRINCIPAL CHARACTERS

Frederic Moreau (frä·dā·rēk' mô·rō'), a young student who, in 1840, has graduated from the College of Sens and is returning by boat to Nogent, along the Seine. In the fall he will begin his law courses, but now he is more interested in studying human nature. After a talk with M. Arnoux he goes to the upper deck where he is attracted by the sight of lovely Mme. Arnoux. Not until he retrieves her ball of yarn does he learn that she is married and has a small daughter. Later, in Paris, he is so infatuated with her that he fails in his final law examinations. He decides to give up thoughts of her and go into politics under the sponsorship of M. Dambreuse. He plans with Deslauriers to found a paper with wealth inherited from his uncle; instead, he gives the money to M. Arnoux. When Mme. Arnoux fails to appear for a rendezvous, he seeks out Rosanette, her husband's mistress, to get revenge. He and Rosanette live together in the country for a time. Frederic is never able to find a really permanent love.

M. Jacques Arnoux (zhȧk' ȧr·nōo'), a sophisticated businessman who meets Frederic on a boat trip and invites him to call when in Paris. Mainly because Frederic is greatly attracted to Mme. Arnoux, the older man becomes well acquainted with him. In an effort to save the failing Arnoux business enterprises he eventually borrows a large sum of money from Frederic, which is never repaid. He goes bankrupt and begins to neglect his wife for his mistresses; but because of her innate honesty, she remains faithful.

Mme. Marthe Arnoux (mȧrt' ȧr·nōo'), his wife, an honest woman who likes Frederic but remains faithful to her fickle and unsuccessful husband. Her plan to spend an afternoon with Frederic has to be changed because of the illness of her child, a situation that she takes as a judgment on her; and she breaks with Frederic. Years later she convinces him that they were right not to love carnally.

Rosanette (rō·zȧ·nĕt'), called La Maréchale, an attractive woman whom Frederic meets at a masquerade ball. He correctly guesses that she is the mistress of

M. Arnoux. She goes to the country with him to stay during the riots accompanying the overthrow of the monarchy in 1848. Later she has a child who, she claims, is Frederic's, but the boy dies. She brings trouble on M. Arnoux and his wife out of revenge.

Mme. Moreau (mô·rō′), the mother of Frederic, who had hoped to see her son become a diplomat. She loses most of her money because of the troubled politics of monarchical France and cannot finance him.

Deslauriers (dā·lō·ryā′), Frederic's friend with whom he plans to found a newspaper. They room together in Paris. When Frederic lends his money to Arnoux, Deslauriers breaks with his friend and goes back home to practice law. Many years later he visits Frederic and they decide that love, like life, is capricious.

Louise Roque (lwēz′ rôk′), a neighbor of Frederic who becomes his special friend during his summer vacation. She later follows him to Paris, but realizes that he no longer cares for her. She marries Deslauriers later, back in Nogent, only to desert him for a singer, Anténor Delamarre.

Anténor Delamarre (äṅ·tā·nôr′ də·lä·mär′), sometimes **Delmas**, a singer-actor.

M. Roque (mə·syœ′ rôk′), who gives Frederic a letter of introduction to M. Dambreuse, a wealthy banker of Paris.

M. Dambreuse (däṅ·brœz′), who offers to get Frederic started in public life. Suspicious of his wife, he leaves his wealth to his niece.

Mme. Dambreuse (däṅ·brœz′), his wife, who is attracted to Frederic and becomes his mistress. Her hopes of marriage to him following her husband's death are spoiled when she does not inherit his wealth.

The Uncle of Frederic, a rich man of La Havre. He announces he will not leave his wealth to his nephew, thus forcing the boy to spend three years in idleness in Nogent. Then he dies intestate, without other heirs, and Frederic gets the money to go to Paris.

Vicomte Cisy (vē·kôṅt′ sē·zē′), a coward who quarrels with Frederic over a girl's reputation and challenges him to a duel. He falls in a faint, but having skinned himself on a twig, his blood satisfies the requirements.

Pellerin (pĕ·lə·răṅ′), an artist who paints Rosanette's portrait.

A SENTIMENTAL JOURNEY

Author: Laurence Sterne (1713-1768)
Time of action: The 1760's
First published: 1768

PRINCIPAL CHARACTERS

Mr. Yorick, the Sentimental Traveler. He reacts with exaggerated sensibility to the many, mainly humorous sentimental adventures of which he is a collector in his travels.

La Fleur, Yorick's servant, a boy accomplished at flute playing and love-making.

Madame de L——, a fellow traveler whom Yorick meets in Calais. He hopes that she will travel to Paris with him and is heartbroken that she must return to Belgium.

Madame de R——, a lady living in Paris. Madame de L—— gives Yorick a letter of introduction to her.

Count de B——, a Frenchman enthusiastic about everything English. He mistakes Yorick for the character in "Hamlet" and, greatly pleased to meet so famous a person, presents him with a passport naming him the King's Jester. Later the Count and his friends entertain Yorick at many parties while he is in Paris.

Count L——, the brother of Madame de

L——. He comes to take her back to Belgium, just as Yorick's acquaintance with her is ripening.

Maria, an unhappy girl who wanders about the country grieving for her dead father. Yorick sees her in Moulines and sheds a few tears with her.

SEVEN AGAINST THEBES

Author: Aeschylus (c. 525-c. 456 B.C.)
Time of action: Remote antiquity
First presented: 467 B.C.

PRINCIPAL CHARACTERS

Eteocles (ē·tē′ō·klēz), the son of Oedipus and grandson of Laius. Long ago, Laius, King of Thebes, has been warned by the oracle of Apollo that, should he beget a son, this act would bring ruin upon his ancestral city. Laius disregarded the warning and became the father of Oedipus, thus bringing a curse upon his house. Oedipus, exposed by his parents upon Mount Cithaeron, was rescued by a shepherd. Grown to manhood, Oedipus unknowingly slew his father and then solved the riddle of the Sphinx, thus rescuing Thebes from the monster. Made King of Thebes, he—again unknowingly—married Jocasta, his mother. Of this incestuous union were born four children. When Oedipus finally learned what he had done, he blinded himself, and Jocasta took her own life. It was agreed that Eteocles and Polynices, his sons, should rule Thebes in alternate years. But they mistreated their blind father, who, dying, put upon them the curse that they should die by each other's hands. Eteocles refused to allow his brother his turn at ruling and drove him from Thebes; whereupon Polynices enlisted the aid of six warriors from Argos and, with himself at the head of their forces, besieged his native city. At the beginning of the play, Eteocles is informed by a scout that each Argive champion has been chosen by lot to attack one of the seven gates of Thebes. Having calmed the fears of the terrified Thebans, Eteocles sends a warrior to defend each of the gates, choosing to defend in his own person that gate which Polynices will attack. The chorus warns him of the mortal danger that he risks; but, driven almost insane by hatred of his brother, he takes his post. In the encounter the brothers kill each other; and, the other Argive champions having been slain, Thebes is saved. The body of Eteocles is brought back to the city, and the Senate declares honorable burial for it, because, though guilty of fratricide, Eteocles had saved his native city. The curse on the House of Laius is fulfilled.

Polynices (pol′ə·nī′sēz), the twin of Eteocles and son of Oedipus. Deprived by his brother of his rightful term as King of Thebes, and exiled, he goes to Argos, where he raises an army against his own city. The gate of Thebes against which he has been chosen to attack is revealed to Eteocles by a scout, and brother fights against brother. In the struggle, they kill each other, and Polynices fulfills his grim name, which means "much strife." His body is brought into Thebes with that of Eteocles; but the Senate decrees that, because he fought against his own city, he cannot have honorable burial and that his body must be thrown to the dogs. But his sister Antigone defies the decree of the Senate and declares that she will give her brother a burial befitting his rank.

Antigone (ăn·tĭg′ə·nē), the daughter of Oedipus and sister of Eteocles and Polynices. When the brothers kill each

other at the gate of Thebes, and Polynices is denied burial by decree of the Theban Senate, she defiantly announces that she will bury him herself with rites befitting a King of Thebes.

Ismene (ĭs·mē′nē), the sister of Eteocles, Polynices, and Antigone. She has a silent part in the tragedy.

THE SEVEN WHO FLED

Author: Frederic Prokosch (1909-   )
Time of action: c. 1935
First published: 1937

PRINCIPAL CHARACTERS

Dr. Liu (lē′u), a Chinese merchant who permits six men and a woman, all Europeans, to join his caravan in order to escape civil disturbance in Sinkiang Province. He agrees to take them to Shanghai, two thousand miles away. Along the way, two of the party are imprisoned, two are detained as hostages, serious illness befalls another, and the sixth member leaves the caravan to visit Tibet. When Dr. Liu finds himself left with only the beautiful Mme. de la Scaze, he tries to make her a prisoner at his sumptuous villa in Lu-chow; but she escapes and makes her way to Shanghai.

Hugo Wildenbruch (hōō′gō wil′dĕn-brōōkh), a young German geologist who is imprisoned by the authorities at Aqsu. He passes his time in prison counting passersby and keeping a journal. He falls ill with tuberculosis and becomes despondent while hoping wildly to return to his native land.

Joachim von Wald (jō′äkh·ĭm vŏn wäld), a young Austrian geologist who is imprisoned by authorities at Aqsu. High-spirited and hopeful, he enjoys his adventures, becomes enchanted by the Orient, and decides upon arriving in Shanghai to stay in the East.

Serafimov (sĕ·rä·fī′mŏff′), a Russian ex-

ile, a huge, powerful man. He is held as a hostage at Aqsu. He tires of being tormented by his fellow hostage, Goupillière, and kills him. He makes his way to Shanghai, where he meets a prostitute, the ill-fated Mme. de la Scaze.

Goupillière (gōō′pĭ·llär′), a Belgian criminal, held as a hostage at Aqsu. An evil man who has robbed and murdered women, he is a fugitive from punishment. He torments the Russian, Serafimov, who murders him.

Mme. de la Scaze (mä·däm′ dĕ lä skäs), named **Olivia**. She is a beautiful young Spaniard. She continues on the journey with Dr. Liu toward Shanghai from Aqsu. She escapes from Dr. Liu at Lu-chow, only to fall into the hands of Chinese rivermen who place her, feverish and listless, in a brothel in Shanghai. She simply resigns herself to fate.

M. de la Scaze (mə·syœ′ dĕ lä skäs), a wealthy Frenchman who falls ill and is forced to remain at Aqsu because of his illness. He loses his sense of purpose there, simply enjoying life as he finds it. His life ends when he contracts cholera from a beautiful dancer.

Layeville (lā·vĭl′), a handsome English

1026

explorer who is accustomed to hardships. He turns off with another caravan to travel to Tibet, seeking the distant and unattainable. Dying in the Himalayan peaks, he finally realizes that he has sought death.

Mme. Tastin (mä·däm' täs·tăn̓), a friend of Goupillière.

Mordovinov (môr·dō'və·nəf), an old Russian exile who befriends Wildenbruch and von Wald in Mongolia.

THE SEVEN WHO WERE HANGED

Author: Leonid Andreyev (1871-1919)
Time of action: Early twentieth century
First published: 1908

PRINCIPAL CHARACTERS

Ivan Yanson (ĭv·än̓' yän·sŏn̓'), a vicious murderer convicted of stabbing his master. Repulsed by all who know him, he responds to his frustrations by drinking and by beating animals entrusted to his care. He is terrified by the prospect of death and must be carried to the scaffold to be hanged.

Tsiganok Golubets (tsĭ·gä'nək gô·lōō'bĕts), a professional robber and murderer. In more lucid moments he takes pride in his inhuman deeds. At other times he falls to all fours and howls like an animal. Although frightened at times by the prospect of death, he finally mounts the scaffold arrogantly.

Tanya Kovalchuk (tän'yə kô·väl'chŏok), the bravest of the five persons condemned to die as political conspirators. She concerns herself with the six persons who must die with her, thinking of them instead of herself. Only she of the seven goes to her death alone, the others going in pairs.

Musya (mūs'yä), another woman condemned as a political conspirator and sentenced to hang. She believes in a life after death and views her hanging as a martyrdom. At the appointed time she takes the professional criminal by the hand and mounts the scaffold with him.

Sergey Golovin (sĕr·gä' gô·lō'vĭn), a young man sentenced to hang for political conspiracy. Because of his youth and vitality, he finds death hard to face. He and Vasily Kashirin are the first to be hanged.

Vasily Kashirin (vä·sĭ'liy kä·shĭr'ĭn), another young man found guilty of political conspiracy. Unloved and unloving, he goes to his death with no show of fear.

Werner (wĕr'nĕr), the fifth of the condemned political conspirators. Although tired of life and contemptuous of his fellow human beings, he learns in his last two days of life to have sympathy for others.

SEVENTEEN

Author: Booth Tarkington (1869-1946)
Time of action: Early twentieth century
First published: 1916

PRINCIPAL CHARACTERS

William Sylvanus Baxter, now seventeen, whose courtship of Miss Pratt is hindered by his mocking sister and by his mother, who hides the dress suit he borrows from his father.

Miss Pratt, a summer visitor, with a lisp and a small dog, whose visit disrupts the town.

Flopit, her tiny white dog.

Jane Baxter, William's sister.

Mrs. Baxter, William's mother.

Genesis, the Baxter family handyman.

Johnny Watson, who sees nothing remarkable in being seventeen.

May Parcher, the hostess of Miss Pratt.

George, Miss Pratt's hungry admirer until he is put out of competition by William with a Cuban cigarette.

SHADOWS ON THE ROCK

Author: Willa Cather (1873-1947)
Time of action: 1697-1713
First published: 1931

PRINCIPAL CHARACTERS

Euclide Auclair (œ·klēd′ ō·klĕr′), a temperate, humane, philosophical apothecary living in Quebec at the end of the seventeenth century. Although loyal to his patron and friend, the Count de Frontenac, whom he accompanied to Canada in 1689, he feels that he has lived in exile for eight years, and he makes little effort to adjust his thinking or habits to life in a new land. At night, when he draws the curtains of his shop and sits down to dinner with his daughter Cécile, he likes to imagine that he is back in his beloved home on the Quai des Célestins in Paris. When he learns that the Count expects to be recalled by King Louis, Auclair looks forward to returning with his benefactor. But the Count, neglected by his monarch, dies in Quebec. In the end Auclair stays on. His daughter has married a Canadian, and to the old apothecary it seems that the future may be better in Quebec after all, a place where change comes slowly, remote from the designs of kings and their ministers.

Cécile Auclair (sā·sēl′ ō·klĕr′), the apothecary's thirteen-year-old daughter, who has taken over the household after her mother's death, an appealing child because of her quaint mixture of youth and maturity. She is deeply pious but with no sense of a religious vocation; instead, she resembles a household vestal guarding domestic rites that stand for the order and grace of a transplanted culture. Unlike her father, she is a Canadian; the river flowing below the rock, the mountains to the north, and the dark pine forests stretching away as far as one can see frame everything that is familiar and dear to her. She grows up to marry Pierre Charron, her father's friend, a famous hunter and scout.

Pierre Charron (pyĕr′ shä·rŏn′), Euclide Auclair's young friend from Montreal, a wilderness runner and hunter. Disappointed in love when the daughter of his employer became a religious recluse, he had taken to the woods; now he has made a name for himself among the traders and Indians all along the Great Lakes. Whenever he is in Quebec, he visits the Auclairs. The apothecary admires him because the young man combines the manners and tradition of the Old World with the bravery and resourcefulness needed to survive in the new. Cécile loves him first as a child, then as a woman. They marry and have four children to make the apothecary satisfied with his growing family in his old age.

The Count de Frontenac (də frôńt′nåk), the Governor of Canada, a stern but just man who has alienated many civil authorities and churchmen in France and Canada by his tactless actions. An able administrator and soldier, he dies neglected by the King he has served faithfully.

Bishop Laval (là·vàl′), the first Bishop of Quebec, now succeeded by Monseigneur de Saint-Vallier. The old prelate is unsparing of himself, devoted to the poor, ambitious for the Church. Gruff in manner, he is capable of great generosity and kindness to the deserving. In the past he and the Count de Frontenac have clashed on many matters of policy, and he carries on a feud with his ambitious young successor.

Monseigneur de Saint-Vallier (də săń·và·lyā′), the young Bishop of Quebec, who since his appointment has spent most of his time in France. Clever and ambitious, he often acts more like a courtier than a churchman; Euclide Auclair thinks that he looks like an actor. He appears determined to undo the work of his predecessor, old Bishop Laval. After having been captured and imprisoned by the English and later detained in France, he returns, a much chastened man, to Quebec in 1713.

Jacques Gaux (zhåk′ gō′), a street waif befriended by Cécile Auclair. He grows up to become a sailor. Between voyages he stays with the old apothecary.

'Toinette (twå·nĕt′), called **La Grenouille,** the mother of Jacques Gaux and the keeper of a sailors' boarding house; an unsavory, shrewish woman.

Nicholas Pigeon (nē·kô·là′ pē·zhôń′), a baker and a neighbor of the Auclairs.

Noel Pommier (nô·ĕl′ pô·myā′), a cobbler.

Madame Pommier, the cobbler's mother. A woman of great piety, she is responsible for the location of her son's shop on Holy Family Hill.

Jules (zhül′), nicknamed Blinker, a disfigured, cross-eyed man who tends the fires of Pigeon, the baker, and empties the Auclairs' refuse in repayment for a bowl of soup and a small glass of brandy each night. He tells Euclide Auclair a strange story. Apprenticed to the King's torturer at Rouen, he had brutally compelled a woman to confess to the murder of her son. A short time later the young man reappeared. Unable to sleep at night because of the burden on his conscience, Blinker asks the apothecary for a drug that will allow him to rest.

Mother Juschereau de Saint-Ignace (zhüs·shə·rō′ də săń·tē·nyàs′), the superior of the Hôtel Dieu, who tells Cécile Auclair many tales of miracles and saints. She regrets that the girl shows no signs of a vocation in religious life.

Father Hector Saint-Cyr (ĕk·tôr′ sàn·sēr′), a Jesuit missionary to the Indians, Euclide Auclair's friend.

Jeanne Le Ber (zhän′ lə bèr′), the daughter of a wealthy merchant in Montreal. Rejecting all suitors for her hand, including her old playmate, Pierre Charron, she becomes a religious recluse.

SHE

Author: H. Rider Haggard (1856-1925)
Time of action: Late nineteenth century
First published: 1887

She, also known as She-who-must-be-obeyed and as Ayesha. She is a white queen who has lived for two thousand years in the hidden city of Kôr, deep in the African interior, awaiting the reincarnation of the man she loved but murdered. Trying to prove to Leo Vincey that she can make him her immortal lover, she walks into a pillar of flame and is consumed by it, though previously it has given her protection from all the ravages of age.

Leo Vincey, a young Englishman, descendant of Kallikrates, the man She loved and killed. Following instructions in documents left by his father, Leo travels to Africa to find the Pillar of Life. He meets She, who loves him, and he falls in love with her After her death in the pillar of flame he returns, gray-haired from shock, to England.

Mr. Vincey, Leo's father. When he dies, he places his five-year-old son in the hands of Ludwig Holly, a fellow student at Cambridge, to be reared. He also leaves an iron chest which is not to be opened until the boy's twenty-fifth birthday.

Ludwig Horace Holly, Leo's guardian. After his ward is grown, Holly accompanies him to Africa on his incredible adventure.

Job, Holly's servant. He dies of shock when he sees She die in the pillar of flame.

Ustane, a woman of the savage Amahagger tribe who falls in love with Leo and marries him according to tribal rite. She is killed by a look from the jealous She.

Billali, an Amahagger chief who befriends the white men and helps them escape to the African coast after their adventures with She.

Mahomed, an Arab who accompanies Leo and Holly into Africa. He is accidentally shot when his companions try to rescue him from cannibals.

SHE STOOPS TO CONQUER

Author: Oliver Goldsmith (1728-1774)
Time of action: Eighteenth century
First presented: 1773

PRINCIPAL CHARACTERS

Mr. Hardcastle, a landed English gentleman. Sometimes grumpy, he is more often a hearty old squire with the habit of retelling the same jokes and stories to his guests. At first excited by the prospect of having Marlow as his son-in-law, he finds his patience severely strained by the apparent impudence of the young man, who is the son of Hardcastle's old friend, Sir Charles Marlow. When he receives incivilities in return for his hospitality, the old gentleman loses his self-control and orders Marlow and his party from the house. Finally, however, he realizes that he is the victim of a hoax and willingly accepts the young man as Kate's suitor.

Mrs. Hardcastle, his formidable wife. Her strongest desire, other than having her son Tony marry Constance Neville, is to have an annual social polishing in London. For a time she manages to thwart the romance of Hastings and Constance. Seeing that they are in love, she tries to circumvent their plans by taking Constance to Aunt Pedigree's. But this stratagem fails when her undutiful son Tony merely drives them around Mrs. Hardcastle's home for three hours, finally landing the unsuspecting old lady in a horsepond near her home. Finally, she is forced to acknowledge the fact that her beloved Tony has only one desire—to get his inheritance.

Tony Lumpkin, her son by her first marriage. He is a roistering young squire completely spoiled by his doting mother. In return for her parental laxness, the lazy, hard-drinking prankster, when he is not singing bawdy songs in low taverns, plagues the Hardcastle household with practical jokes. Although he is uncommonly healthy, his mother is certain that he is dying of some dread ailment. When he meets Hastings and Marlow, he gives them some wrong information, thus creating his masterpiece among tricks. By telling them that Mr. Hardcastle's home is an inn, he causes them to think Hardcastle is an innkeeper and, what is worse, a windy, inquisitive old bore who takes unseemly social liberties with his guests. Hardcastle, on the other hand, is certain of their being impudent, cheeky young scamps.

Kate Hardcastle, Hardcastle's lovely young daughter. Like her stepmother, she also has social pretensions. Because of her stubbornness and desire to be a woman of fashion, her father makes her agree to wear fine clothes part of the day and ordinary clothes the rest of the time. Aware that Marlow is often improper with ordinary working girls, she

disguises herself as a servant. Only then does she realize that he has qualities other than modesty and timidity. Liking this impetuous side of her suitor, Kate is now determined to have him as a husband.

Constance Neville, Kate's best friend. Early in the play, she learns of the joke which Tony has played on Marlow and Hastings, the man she loves. Entering into the spirit of the prank, she and Hastings plot their elopement. Unfortunately for their hopes, Mrs. Hardcastle is keeping a fortune in family jewels for Constance. In order to outwit the old lady, Constance acts out a part: she convinces Mrs. Hardcastle of her love for Tony, who actually dislikes Constance strongly. Finally, with the help of Kate's father, she is free to marry Hastings.

Young Marlow, Kate's reluctant suitor. Timid in the presence of ladies, Marlow is quite different with working girls. After mistaking Kate for a servant, he is mortified to learn her true identity. In his wounded pride, he plans to leave the house immediately; instead, she leads him away, still teasing him unmercifully.

Hastings, Marlow's best friend. With the help of Tony and Mr. Hardcastle, Hastings, a far more impetuous lover than Marlow, wins Constance as his bride.

Sir Charles Marlow, the father of young Marlow and Mr. Hardcastle's old friend.

THE SHEEP WELL

Author: Lope de Vega (Lope Félix de Vega Carpio, 1562-1635)
Time of action: 1476
First presented: c. 1619

PRINCIPAL CHARACTERS

Commander Fernán Gómez de Guzmán (fâr·nän′ gō′mäth thä gōōth·män′), the feudal lord of the village of Fuente Ovejuna (Sheep Well or Watering Place) in

1476. Lusting after the village girls, he has his servants, Flores and Ortuño, seize them and bring them to his palace for his pleasure. The girl he desires most is

Laurencia, the prettiest girl of the village, but she manages to elude his servants. One day the commander does seize her, but she is saved by Frondoso, a courageous young peasant. To further his political ambitions, the Commander persuades the young Master of Calatrava to attack the city of Ciudad Real, in the possession of King Ferdinand and Queen Isabella. He intends to turn the town over to the King of Portugal. His career of tyranny and treachery ends when he is overthrown and killed by the people of Fuente Ovejuna after he has halted the marriage of Laurencia and taken the girl to the citadel.

Pedro Téllez Girón (pā′drō tā′lyäth hē-rōn′), the youthful head of the military and religious Order of Calatrava. Urged by the older Commander Gómez, he captures Ciudad Real, but is later defeated by the royal Spanish army. His appeal to King Ferdinand for clemency is accepted and he is restored to honor.

Laurencia (lä·ōō·rĕn′thyä), a charming peasant girl in love with Frondoso. She eludes the Commander's men by staying in the fields as much as possible. One day she is found by Gómez and only the bravery of Frondoso, who seizes the Commander's crossbow and threatens to kill him, saves her. She agrees to marry Frondoso, but the Commander breaks up the wedding, has the groom jailed for attempting to murder him, and carries Laurencia off to his citadel. Escaping, she arouses the village, including the women, to storm the citadel and kill the cruel tyrant. She is pardoned by Queen Isabella.

Frondoso (frōn·dō′sō), a handsome young peasant, in love with Laurencia. He earns the enmity of Gómez but escapes death when the Commander's servants kill the wrong man. He is arrested on the eve of his marriage to Laurencia and sentenced to be hanged. The revolt of the villagers saves him.

Flores (flō′räs) and

Ortuño (ôr·tōo′nyō), servants of the Commander, who try to supply Gómez with girls. They are finally routed by the aroused peasantry.

Esteban (ās·tā′bän), an alcalde, the father of Laurencia, who provides a dowry of 4,000 maravidís for her marriage to Frondoso. He refuses to surrender his daughter to the Commander.

Alonso (ä·lōn′sō), another alcalde.

Juan Rojo (hwän r̄rō′hō) and
Cuadrado (kwä·drä′t̄hō), regidores of the village.

Jacinta (hä·thēn′tä), a peasant girl, the friend of Laurencia, who is seized and raped by Commander Gómez.

Pascuala (päs·kwä′lä), another pretty peasant girl.

Mingo (mēn′gō), a peasant whose attempts to save Jacinta from the attentions of the Commander result in his being flayed by Spanish soldiers.

Barrildo (bä·r̄rēl′dō), another peasant; he argues humorously with Mengo and Frondoso over the nature of love.

Juan Chamorro (hwän chä·mō′r̄rō), a sacristan.

A Judge, sent by King Ferdinand and Isabella to investigate the happenings at Fuente Ovejuna. Although he tortures and questions some three hundred villagers to discover the murderer of the Commander, he gets the same reply from all: "The executioner was Fuente Ovejuna."

King Ferdinand and
Queen Isabella, the Catholic monarchs of Spain.

The Villagers of Fuente Ovejuna (fwän′-tā ō·bä·hōo′nä), the real protagonist of this proletarian drama. Collectively they assume guilt for the execution of the tyrant, and collectively they are pardoned and taken under the protection of the Crown.

THE SHELTERED LIFE

Author: Ellen Glasgow (1874-1945)
Time of action: Twentieth century
First published: 1932

PRINCIPAL CHARACTERS

General David Archbald, an old Southern gentleman whose life is dominated by the needs of his daughters, his daughter-in-law, and his granddaughter. He is tall, spare, and very erect, with silver-gray hair and mustache, dark beetling eyebrows, and an eagle nose. Though a rebel at heart since childhood, he has throughout his long life been largely a conformist. He often muses on the past, on what might have been, and on the insoluble puzzles of human nature.

Jenny Blair Archbald, his spirited granddaughter, a pretty girl who from her childhood on listens to conversations and closely observes the older people about her. Fascinated by George, who at first regards her only as a charming child, she is the half-innocent cause of his murder.

George Birdsong, the General's neighbor, a handsome and romantically attractive but improvident attorney who loves his wife but cannot remain faithful to her. He tries to control his weaknesses, especially after Eva's illness, but nature is too strong within him. Ironically he dies after being discovered impulsively kissing Jenny Blair, to whose pursuit he has previously paid very little attention.

Eva Howard Birdsong, George's beautiful wife, who, like a lady, affects a happiness she does not feel with her husband. She has smiled through her married life, realizing both George's love and his inconstancy. She also endures her severe illness valiantly. But finding George and Jenny Blair in an amorous embrace in the Birdsong home is too much, and she shoots him.

Etta, the General's frail, plain, sickly daughter who desperately and vainly longs for love and must settle for its substitute by reading French novels.

Isabella, the General's other daughter—strong, handsome, and magnetic—whose marriage to a man socially beneath her disappoints her father. The marriage, however, is a happy one.

Joseph Crocker, a carpenter whom Isabella marries after breaking two engagements.

Bena Peyton, the plump girlhood friend with whom Jenny plans to go to New York.

Cora Blair Archbald, Jenny's mother, whose husband Richard died while fox hunting. She and Jenny live with the General.

John Welch, Eva's cousin, a doctor, whom Jenny hates because he seems to understand her better than she does herself.

Delia Barron, one of George's passing fancies.

Memoria, the Birdsongs' mulatto laundress and one of George's mistresses.

Erminia, the General's dead wife, whom he married without love and with whom he lived faithfully but without real love for thirty years.

Erminia Crocker, Joseph and Isabella's young daughter.

SHIRLEY

Author: Charlotte Brontë (1816-1855)
Time of action: Mid-nineteenth century
First published: 1849

PRINCIPAL CHARACTERS

Shirley Keeldar, the mistress of Field-head, a young woman of wealth who owns estates in Yorkshire. A spirited, independent girl of great sense, she finds marriage difficult to contemplate because she does not wish to put herself into the hands of a man who is after her money or a weakling who has no moral fiber of his own. Most of all, she fears submitting to someone who might be a domestic tyrant. Beneath her independent spirit Shirley is a good-hearted, warm person anxious to help anyone who needs assistance. She has a social conscience and tries to organize in the surrounding parishes a system of giving charitable aid to the families of unemployed mill-workers. She eventually falls in love with Louis Gérard Moore, her former tutor, and marries him.

Louis Gérard Moore, a young man of Belgian and English ancestry who, because of his family's straitened circumstances, becomes a tutor in the family of Mr. Sympson, Shirley's uncle. Moore, a quiet, intelligent man, loves Shirley deeply. Through his patience and wisdom he comes to understand her and to help her understand herself. He wins her for his wife despite his impecunious circumstances and the opposition of Shirley's uncle, her former guardian.

Robert Gérard Moore, a textile manufacturer and Louis Moore's brother. The mill he operates is rented from Shirley Keeldar. Robert Moore is a man with two sides to his nature. He is a hard-headed businessman for whom his mill and financial success are paramount. Under the domination of this side of his character he battles ruthlessly with unemployed workers to try to prevent modernization of his factory. Politically he opposes the embargo of British ports caused by the Napoleonic wars. Once removed from the scene of business and politics, however, he becomes a different man, loving, thoughtful, and kind. Influenced by the harder side of his character, he tries to marry Shirley Keeldar, but she refuses his suit because she realizes that he is more interested in her wealth than in her. Later he woos and marries Caroline Helstone, whom he truly loves.

Caroline Helstone, a distant cousin of Louis and Robert Moore. She is reared by a widowed uncle, rector of the parish, who treats her as kindly as his austere nature allows. Caroline, a beautiful, sweet, and reticent young woman whom everyone likes, becomes Shirley Keeldar's close friend. In love with Robert Moore, she keeps her love to herself when she thinks that Robert Moore and Shirley are in love, for she believes a match with Shirley would be better for her beloved. Eventually Moore and Caroline discover their love for each other and are married on the same day as Shirley and Louis Moore.

Mr. Helstone, rector of Briarfield parish, Caroline's uncle. He is a clergyman who would have been better fitted for a career as a military officer. In the conflicts between the workers and the mill owners he is a great help to the manufacturers, even to participation in a pitched battle. He is liberal with his money to his niece, but he is not capable of giving her warmth and understanding.

Mr. Malone, the bumptuous Irish curate to Mr. Helstone.

Mrs. Pryor, Shirley Keeldar's companion and former governess, a quiet, reticent woman of charm and fading beauty. She takes a great liking to Caroline Helstone and becomes her close friend. After nursing Caroline through a serious illness she reveals herself as Mrs. James Helstone, Caroline's mother and the rector's sister-in-law. She had changed her name because she feared that her late husband, then living, would find her and force her to live with him under desperate circumstances.

Sir Philip Nunnely, a young peer given to writing bad poetry. He falls in love with Shirley Keeldar but his suit is rejected.

Mr. Sympson, Shirley Keeldar's uncle and former guardian. He is a weak but tyrannical man who brings his family to Fieldhead in hopes of dominating the girl, even though she is of age and can make her own decisions. He tries to force Shirley to accept each of several suitors in turn and is horrified when she announces her love for Louis Moore. Sympson is ejected by Moore for insulting his former ward.

Mrs. Sympson, his patient, well-bred wife.

Henry Sympson, their only son, a cripple, Louis Moore's pupil.

The Misses Sympson, their prim and proper daughters, older than Henry.

Hortense Moore, the sister of Louis and Robert Moore. She keeps house for Robert during his bachelorhood. More Belgian than English, she is unhappy in Yorkshire.

Michael Hartley, a crazed and drunken millworker who shoots Robert Moore from ambush and seriously endangers his victim's life. A victim of drink, Hartley dies a few months after the shooting.

Miss Mary Ann Ainley and Miss Margaret Hall, two spinsters who perform deeds of charity among the poor of Briarfield parish. Shirley Keeldar gives them three hundred pounds to distribute among the needy unemployed.

THE SHOEMAKER'S HOLIDAY

Author: Thomas Dekker (c. 1572-1632?)
Time of action: Reign of Henry V of England
First presented: 1599

PRINCIPAL CHARACTERS

Simon Eyre (âr), the blustering, "madcap" shoemaker who becomes Lord Mayor of London. One of the kindliest of men, he watches over the welfare of his journeymen while he berates them vigorously; it is his intercession with the King which reconciles Sir Hugh and Sir Roger to the marriage of Rose with Eyre's sometime Dutch assistant, Lacy. He is not overawed by his high-ranking position, and he rejoices more at feasting those who were once apprentices with him than at entertaining the King. Loyal to his trade, he asks for one royal boon, the privilege of selling shoes twice a week at Leadenhall Market.

Rowland Lacy (Hans), a gallant, spendthrift young nobleman who learned the shoemaker's trade when he arrived penniless in Germany on his Grand Tour. Forbidden by his domineering uncle to marry his sweetheart, Rose Otley, he abandons his military command, disguises himself as a Dutch journeyman named Hans, and joins the workshop of

Simon Eyre. He proves to be an excellent businessman and vastly increases his master's wealth by introducing him to an old skipper with a ship full of spices to sell. With persistence and fidelity he at last wins his bride, wooing her while he pretends to be fitting new shoes.

Sir Hugh Lacy, Earl of Lincoln, his overbearing uncle. Adamant in his opposition to his nephew's proposed marriage, he tries to engineer Sir Roger's disapproval; he is somewhat disgruntled to find that the mayor scorns the match, which would be a fine one for his daughter, without Sir Hugh's persuasion.

Sir Roger Otley, Lord Mayor of London. He is astute, if not oversubtle, in his dealings with Sir Hugh and resents any suggestion of patronizing in the Earl's behavior toward him. His independent young daughter infuriates him by refusing the hand of a wealthy citizen he has chosen for her, and he shuts her up at home to keep her away from Lacy.

Rose Otley, the Lord Mayor's daughter. She is agreeable and devoted to Lacy, but perversely sarcastic to the suitor she rejects.

Sybil, her witty, voluble maid.

Askew, another of Sir Hugh's nephews, a kindly young man who helps his cousin Rowland escape their uncle's close surveillance.

Dodger, Sir Hugh's servant, described by Rowland as "the arran'st varlet that e'er breathed on earth."

Firk and
Hodge, Eyre's journeymen, industrious workmen who cheerfully exchange insults with their master and mistress.

Margery, Eyre's wife, who is, on occasion, bawdy and sharp, but basically good-hearted and fond of her husband. After Simon becomes Lord Mayor she worries that his manners are not proper for entertaining the King, and she gives voice to her own concern about her wardrobe.

Rafe Damport, another of Eyre's journeymen, gentler and quieter than his fellows. In spite of his master's efforts to keep him at home, he is drafted and sent to France soon after his marriage. He is heartbroken to find his wife missing when he returns wounded from his campaign, yet he resigns himself to accept her second marriage when she does not recognize him. Happily reunited with her through the efforts of Firk and Hodge, he proudly rejects Hammond's offer of money for her.

Jane, his wife, who mourns his loss, but finally allows herself to be partially consoled by Hammond. She shows her tender heart in her generous gift to the unknown shoemaker who reminds her of her lost husband.

Hammond, a London citizen who pays court to Rose, then, rejected by her, turns to Jane, whom he has admired in her shop.

THE SIEGE OF RHODES

Author: Sir William Davenant (1606-1668)
Time of action: 1522
First presented: 1656

PRINCIPAL CHARACTERS

Alphonso, the young Duke of Sicily, whose life is shaped by his love for his wife Ianthe and by his sense of honor. His fleeting jealousy of the attentions lavished by the Sultan upon Ianthe does not impair the happiness of his marriage, and he fights valiantly to save his wife and Rhodes.

Ianthe, his beautiful wife, who bravely travels from Sicily to join her husband in Rhodes. Captured by the Turks, she wins the Sultan's admiration by her fidelity and devotion to her husband, and thus can later intercede with him on behalf of the besieged island. She is as conscious as Alphonso is of the value of honor, and she encourages his refusal to fly to Sicily under the Sultan's protection.

Solyman II, called Solyman the Magnificent, the magnanimous Sultan of the Ottoman Empire. He values virtue and love above military victory and offers aid to Ianthe and her husband. He contrasts the patience and calm of the Christian wife with the fury directed at him by his beloved Sultana and contrives to win her back by letting her witness Ianthe's devotion to Alphonso.

Roxalana, his tempestuous queen. Jealous for the future of her son, the Sultan's younger child, she rails at her husband and passionately resents his favors to Ianthe. She is, however, so much touched by Ianthe's patience and love that she arranges her reunion with Alphonso. She is herself happily reconciled with the Sultan, who welcomes this sign of tenderness in her.

Villerius, Philip Villiers de L'Isle Adam, the brave Grand Master of Rhodes, another upholder of "love and honor."

Pyrrhus, a Persian general.

THE SIGN OF FOUR

Author: Sir Arthur Conan Doyle (1859-1930)
Time of action: 1888
First published: 1889

PRINCIPAL CHARACTERS

Sherlock Holmes, the famous detective.

Dr. John Watson, Holmes's friend and assistant. In this story he is attracted to Mary Morstan, proposes to her, and is accepted.

Mary Morstan, Holmes' client. She is a young Englishwoman whose father, an officer with an Indian regiment, failed to meet her, as he had sent word he would, at a London hotel. Her father has been missing for ten years.

Major Sholto, a friend and brother officer of Miss Morstan's father. He reveals to his two sons that Morstan died accidentally as they argued over some jewels which had been handed over to them for transportation from India to England. He refuses to relinquish the fabulous jewels and is relentlessly hounded by The Four. He dies strangely before he can reveal their hiding place to his sons.

Dr. Thaddeus Sholto, one of the major's twin sons. Trying to share his wealth with Mary Morstan, he sends her a pearl each year. He learns that his twin brother has located the treasure chest, and he so informs Mary Morstan and Sherlock Holmes. He is an art collector.

Bartholomew Sholto, Dr. Sholto's twin brother. After having located the jewels in his dead father's attic, he is found murdered.

Jonathan Small, Holmes' key to the mystery. When captured he tells that he is one of The Four—four men who accidentally discovered the jewels in India. Imprisoned after an uprising, they gave the secret of the treasure to Major Sholto and the now dead Morstan. Small and one of the other men sought to regain the treasure, committing murder in doing so. About to be captured, Small dumps the jewels in the river.

SILAS MARNER

Author: George Eliot (Mary Ann Evans, 1819-1880)
Time of action: Early nineteenth century
First published: 1861

PRINCIPAL CHARACTERS

Silas Marner, a weaver of Raveloe. As a resident of Lantern Yard, he had been simple, trusting, and religious until falsely accused of theft. He then loses his faith in religion and people. Turning away from humanity, he directs his stunted affections towards his steadily increasing pile of coins. However, when Eppie enters his life, he regains his belief in the fundamental goodness of man. In his bewildered fashion he accepts help from his Raveloe neighbors and decides to rear the motherless child who has captured his heart; under her influence he no longer despairs because of the stolen money.

Eppie (Hephzibah), Marner's adopted daughter. Fair-haired and blue-eyed, she captivates everyone who meets her, including young Aaron Winthrop, her future husband. After years of loneliness, Silas is sustained and his spirit nurtured by having her constantly near him. Even after she marries Aaron, she is determined to care for Marner, now frail and bent from years of unremitting toil at the loom.

Godfrey Cass, Eppie's real father and the weak son of Squire Cass, a prominent Raveloe landowner. Blackmailed by his brother Dunstan, he lacks the moral courage to acknowledge to the public that Eppie is his daughter. Instead, fearing disinheritance. he keeps silent for many years with his guilt gnawing at his soul. Later, however, when Dunstan's skeleton is found in the Stone Pits, he finally confesses to Nancy his previous marriage to Molly, dead for sixteen years. Belatedly, he wants, with Nancy's consent, to accept Eppie as his daughter. Thinking she will be over-come by his generosity, he is shocked by her determination to remain with Silas.

Dunstan Cass (Dunsey), Godfrey's dull-minded, spendthrift brother. Drunken and dissolute, he forces Godfrey to give him money by threatening to reveal the secret of Godfrey's marriage to Molly, a low-bred, common woman. After stealing Silas' gold, he falls into the Stone Pit. Years later his skeleton, the gold still beside it, is found wedged between two huge stones.

Nancy Lammeter, Godfrey's second wife, a lovely, decorous, and prim young woman. Although living by a narrow moral code, she surprises her husband, who has underestimated her, by courageously accepting the knowledge of his marriage to Molly.

Squire Cass, a prominent Raveloe landowner. Often lax in his discipline, he can be unyielding when aroused. At times this inflexibility of character makes both his sons and tenants fear his anger.

William Dane, Silas Marner's treacherous friend in Lantern Yard. While mouthing religious platitudes, he steals money from the church and implicates Marner, thus forcing the latter's exile from the village. By planting Silas' pocketknife at the scene of the crime, Dane can steal the money with impunity, knowing that his friend will receive the blame.

Aaron Winthrop, a sturdy young Raveloe citizen. For many years he has worshiped Eppie; when she promises to marry him, he is overjoyed. He promises Silas security and love in the old man's increasing feebleness.

Molly Cass, Godfrey's first wife. A drug addict who marries him when he is drunk, she is walking to Raveloe to expose him as her husband. Fortunately for Godfrey, she takes an overdose of laudanum and freezes to death in the snow, leaving her baby to toddle into

the warmth and security of Silas' cottage.

Dolly Winthrop, Aaron's mother, the wife of Raveloe's wheelwright. She and her little son often visit Silas and it is she who defends his right to keep Eppie when the villagers question Silas' suitability as a parent.

THE SILENT WOMAN

Author: Ben Jonson (1573?-1637)
Time of action: Early seventeenth century
First presented: 1609

PRINCIPAL CHARACTERS

Morose, an unbalanced man with a horror of any noise except the sound of his own frequently exercised voice. He is given to outbursts of violent temper when disturbed. His servants are trained to wear tennis shoes, answer as much as possible in sign language, and to speak— if speak they must—in a whisper through a trunk to deaden the sound. A constant victim of noisy practical jokes, he believes his nephew to be the cause of many of the disturbances; consequently, he determines to disinherit him and to marry a silent woman found for him by a silent barber. After the wedding, harassed to the limit by his far from silent bride and her stentorian companions, he signs over his property to his nephew in return for rescue and goes into disgruntled retirement.

Sir Dauphine Eugenie, Morose's nephew. A pleasant and intelligent young man, he succeeds, in spite of complications brought on by his friends, in tricking his uncle first into marriage with the supposed silent woman, afterwards in signing over his estate to the nephew. He is somewhat bashful with the ladies collegiate, but is later overwhelmed by their attentions.

Truewit, an officious, argumentative,

witty friend of Sir Dauphine. He argues with his friends about the propriety of the use of all possible beauty aids by ladies. He stoutly defends a lavish use of cosmetics. He sets up a series of small plots to annoy Morose, whom he finds both ridiculous and irritating. He also maneuvers the three collegiate ladies into their love of Sir Dauphine, arranges the discomfiture of Sir John and Sir Amorous, and provides the divine and the canon lawyer for the further torment of Morose.

Ned Clerimont, another of Sir Dauphine's friends. Opposing Truewit, he holds that unadorned simplicity is woman's greatest charm; he therefore objects to all use of cosmetics and elaborate coiffures. Although he is more moderate and reliable than Truewit, Sir Dauphine maintains reserve and does not take him completely into his confidence.

Cutbeard, Morose's quiet barber. Actually in the service of Sir Dauphine, he arranges the meeting and the marriage between Morose and Mistress Epicœne. Then, in disguise he enacts the role of a voluble canon lawyer, engaging in legal argument with a supposed divine, to the torment of Morose.

Captain Tom Otter, the henpecked hus-

1039

band of a wealthy wife. He is a ceremonial drinker, having three mugs (a bear, a bull, and a horse) from which he drinks in turn, carrying on elaborate dialogues with himself in different roles. When he thinks his wife is not around, he speaks boldly and contemptuously of her; when she is present he grovels obsequiously. He falls in with Sir Dauphine's plans and acts the part of the noisy divine, first to tantalize Morose with hope of divorce, then to drive him frantic with disappointment.

Mistress Otter, the Captain's overbearing wife. Demanding that he treat her like a princess, she nags him mercilessly. Planted by Truewit where she can overhear her husband's rebellious comments on her shortcomings, she charges out and beats him thoroughly.

Sir John Daw (Jack Daw), a ridiculous, cowardly boaster. His affectations include the writing and criticism of verse. He is given to boasting of the amorous favors bestowed on him by the fair sex; and his testimony of having had Epicœne as his mistress gives Morose temporary false hope that a divorce is possible. He is variously discomfited by the machinations of the witty young men, beaten, and discredited.

Sir Amorous La-Foole, a foolish kinsman of Mistress Otter. He is prodigal, fantastic, and cowardly. The young men make him think Sir John thirsts for his blood. He and Sir John are both so terrified of each other that they tamely submit to blindfolding and personal indignities like nose tweaking, each thinking the other

is the aggressor. He also belies Mistress Epicœne's morals.

Mistress Epicœne (ĕp´ĭ·sēn), the supposed silent woman. Actually a clever boy and a gifted actor, he fools Morose with his well-acted silent modesty, then plays a strident termagant. All are taken in by his performance except Sir Dauphine, whom he aids. At his unmasking, which releases Morose from his immediate torment, embarrassment descends on Sir John, Sir Amorous, and the three ladies collegiate. Even Clerimont and Truewit are astounded.

Lady Haughty, the "autumnal" leader of a group of "collegiates" who live separated from their husbands in a constant social whirl. She takes on the supposed bride as her protégée, graciously condescending to teach her how to handle her husband and how to act in the collegiate society.

Lady Centaure and
Mistress Mavis, ardent followers of Lady Haughty in the so-called college. They become her rivals (and each other's) for Sir Dauphine's favors. Each backbites her two colleagues to him.

Mute, Morose's well-trained servant. Bound to complete silence, he rarely breaks the taboo.

Parson, chosen by Morose to perform his wedding ceremony because he has lost his voice with a terrible cold and cannot be heard six inches away.

Mistress Trusty, Lady Haughty's maid and confidential emissary.

SIMPLICISSIMUS THE VAGABOND

Author: H. J. C. von Grimmelshausen (c. 1625-1676)
Time of action: 1618-1648
First published: 1669

PRINCIPAL CHARACTERS

Simplicius Simplicissimus, a simple lad reared in Germany's Spessart Forest. At the age of twelve, when taken by soldiers to Hanau, he knows only that he has been reared by peasants and a hermit. He pretends to have lost his wits and becomes the governor's fool. Later he becomes a great soldier known as the Hunter of Soest and has many adventures. He learns eventually that he is really the son of a German nobleman and that his real name is Melchior Sternfels von Fuchsheim, but he still remains an adventurer, traveling all over the world.

A Peasant, Simplicissimus' foster father, a good man. He turns up later to inform Simplicissimus of his true identity.

A Hermit, who befriends Simplicissimus when, at the age of ten, he is separated from his foster parents during the Thirty Years' War. He is really a nobleman, Simplicissimus' father, who became a hermit because he was sick of war. His name is Herr von Fuchsheim.

Ulrich Herzbruder, a young German who becomes Simplicissimus' friend and aids him many times.

Oliver, an erstwhile friend of Simplicissimus who mistreats Ulrich Herzbruder.

SIR CHARLES GRANDISON

Author: Samuel Richardson (1689-1761)
Time of action: Eighteenth century
First published: 1753-1754

PRINCIPAL CHARACTERS

Sir Charles Grandison, an English baronet and the hero of a novel whose author, after writing two novels concerned with men who are rakes, was trying to present a picture of a truly virtuous character. The honorable Sir Charles rescues Harriet Byron from the clutches of Sir Hargrave Pollexfen and takes her to his country house as his sister. Though his family and friends favor his marriage to Harriet, he feels in honor bound to Lady Clementina della Porretta, who has a claim on his affection. When Lady Clementina finally refuses him, he feels free to ask for Harriet's hand.

Harriet Byron, a virtuous young woman of modest expectations. On a visit to London she is pursued by and refuses the attentions of Sir Hargrave Pollexfen. The enraged suitor attempts to abduct her and force a marriage. She is rescued by Sir Charles Grandison and taken to his home, where she falls in love with him. Realizing that Sir Charles regards her as a sister, she tries to subdue and hide her affection for him until he becomes free to declare his love for her and to win her hand.

Sir Hargrave Pollexfen, Harriet Byron's libertine suitor, from whom she is rescued by Sir Charles Grandison. After Sir Charles rescues him from the enraged family of a girl he has tried to seduce in France, Sir Hargrave begins to realize the evil of his ways. He reforms, and upon his death leaves his fortune to Sir Charles and Harriet Byron.

Lady Clementina della Porretta, an Italian beauty who is so in love with Sir Charles Grandison that his departure from Italy robs her of her reason, thus putting Sir Charles under an obligation which leaves him bound to her until a cure is effected and she finally refuses to marry him.

Charlotte Grandison and
Lady L., Sir Charles Grandison's sisters, on whom he bestows the benefits their late father was reluctant to give.

Mrs. Oldham, the paramour of Sir Charles Grandison's late father.
Lady Olivia, an Italian woman who is enamored of Sir Charles.

Emily Jervois, Sir Charles' young ward.   Mr. Greville, a suitor of Harriet Byron.

SIR GAWAIN AND THE GREEN KNIGHT

Author: Unknown
Time of action: Sixth century
First transcribed: Fourteenth century manuscript

PRINCIPAL CHARACTERS

Sir Gawain, the bravest, most virtuous of the Knights of the Round Table. He accepts the Green Knight's challenge to uphold the honor of Arthur's court and sets out in autumn on the quest which is essentially a test of his virtue. Temptation awaits him at the castle of Bercilak de Hautdesert, where he must resist the amorous attentions of his hostess without violating the courtesy which he owes her as her guest and, at the same time, keep his bargain with his host to exchange whatever he receives at home for the game Bercilak kills while he hunts. Gawain is faithful for two days, but on the third he succumbs to his fear for his life and accepts from the lady a green girdle which protects its wearer from injury. This very human lapse brings him a mild wound from the Green Knight, and he returns to Arthur's court a chastened, shame-faced hero.

King Arthur, the merry young ruler of Britain who is prepared to fight for his

own cause if none of his knights will challenge the Green Knight.

Guenevere, his beautiful young queen, the object of Morgan le Fay's hatred.

Sir Bercilak de Hautdesert, the good-humored knight who is Gawain's host. An avid sportsman and lover of good entertainment, he proposes to Gawain an exchange of the gains of each day as amusement for both of them; the bargain is in reality a part of his test of the knight's virtue, for it is he who is disguised as the Green Knight by the arts of Morgan le Fay.

The Lady, his charming wife and accomplice in the temptation of Gawain.

[Morgan le Fay, Arthur's half sister, who had learned her skills in magic from Merlin. She is said to have plotted the appearance of the Green Knight at Arthur's court to frighten her enemy Guenevere.]

SIR JOHN VAN OLDEN BARNAVELT

Authors: John Fletcher (1579-1625) and Philip Massinger (1583-1640)
Time of action: 1618-1619
First presented: 1619

PRINCIPAL CHARACTERS

Sir John van Olden Barnavelt, the aging Advocate of Holland and West Friesland. Filled with growing pride, he resents the power and the excellent reputation of the Prince of Orange, and he conspires to

arouse edition over the country to regain the control he thinks he has lost. Brought before the Senate, he defends himself against charges of treachery by reiterating his real contributions to his nation, and he pathetically tries to console himself for his fall by recalling the esteem in which he was held by many monarchs in his younger days. He swears, even as he stands on the scaffold awaiting execution, that he has not committed treason, and he dies praying for his Prince and casting "honour and the world" behind him.

Leidenberch, his fellow conspirator, Secretary of the States of Utrecht. He is notoriously a smooth-tongued flatterer and a man who will promise anything; one soldier complains that no suitor ever left him dissatisfied, yet none ever received what he wanted. Lacking the strength to remain silent after the defeat of his forces, he confesses his part in Barnavelt's plot before he is imprisoned. Convinced by Barnavelt that suicide is the only way to preserve some semblance of honor, he resolves to die, then delays a few moments to speak of the pain of leaving his beloved young son, who sleeps nearby.

Modesbargen, another of Barnavelt's followers. He is at first wary of the old statesman's plans and counsels him bluntly not to risk destroying the effects of his forty years of service to the state by giving vent to his ambition. He eventually joins Barnavelt's campaign and is forced to flee to Germany to escape imprisonment. There he grows to love country living and calls himself a fool for participating in political schemes.

Grotius, another of Barnavelt's followers. He, with Hogerbeets, vows to defend the old man against the Prince of Orange, but the discovery of their plot makes their efforts futile.

Hogerbeets, a leader of the Arminians, the sect Barnavelt makes pawns in his attempt to gain power.

Maurice, Prince of Orange, a just and wise ruler who shares his responsibilities with his council. He restrains his followers, who are anxious to vent their justifiable anger against Barnavelt, yet he is strong-willed enough to exert military force when it is necessary to put down rebellion in Utrecht. Although his natural inclination is to be merciful, he finally orders Barnavelt's death to show that law and order are stronger than the corrupt policies of even the wisest of men.

Bredero and
Vandort, Senators and members of the Prince's Council of State. They listen sympathetically to Barnavelt's initial plans, but they soon recognize his ambition for what it is and remain loyal supporters of order and the Prince.

William and
Henry, loyal supporters of Prince Maurice.

Rockgiles, Barnavelt's chief ally among the burghers.

A Captain, who makes an impassioned defense of soldiers, whose only honor lies in their obedience and loyalty to their ruler.

Holderus, a scholar, held firmly under control by a group of domineering Dutch women. He supports Barnavelt and flees the advancing army of the Prince in terror.

William, Barnavelt's son, who acts as his aide. He brings his father word of Leidenberch's suicide.

Leidenberch's Son, a precocious, sensitive boy who looks after his father in prison. He is rather like Marlowe's Prince Edward and several of Shakespeare's bright young children.

Boisise and
Morier, French ambassadors who come to the Prince to protest the death of Barnavelt, whom they have known only as a wise statesman.

Harlem, Leyden, and **Utrecht Executioners,** grotesque humorists. They throw dice to see who is to have the privilege of executing Sir John.

THE SIR ROGER DE COVERLEY PAPERS

Author: Joseph Addison (1672-1719); Sir Richard Steele (1672-1729); Eustace
Budgell (1686-1737)
Time of action: Early eighteenth century
First published: 1711-1712

PRINCIPAL CHARACTERS

Sir Roger de Coverley, a fifty-six-year-old bachelor, the benevolent autocrat of a large Worcestershire estate. The knight's humaneness, according to his own opinion, is due to his love for a beautiful widow whom he has wooed for thirty years. His kindness is equaled by his rigid control of his servants, whose morals, finances, and behavior are the assumed responsibility of Sir Roger. In London he presides over "The Club," an informal but close-knit group of men of divergent interests and personalities. Sir Roger's every thought seems marked by affability, his every act by broad knowledge and understanding.

Mr. Spectator, the anonymous first-person narrator of the articles describing customs and personalities of eighteenth century London. The writer sets the tone of the journal with the editorial pronouncement that any faulty character described in the journal fits a thousand people and that every paper is presented in the spirit of benevolence and with love of mankind.

Captain Sentry, Sir Roger's nephew, who leaves a successful naval career to assume his position as heir to Sir Roger in "The Club," as well as in his uncle's financial holdings. The Captain's great courage, keen understanding, and gallantry in naval sieges are quietly balanced by an invincible modesty, qualities that make him a liked and admired individual.

Sir Andrew Freeport, a club member whose eminence as a merchant and personal frugality speak for the differences between Sir Andrew's and Sir Roger's political and economic philosophies.

Those differences provide the basis for many hours of debate between the two devoted friends. Among Sir Roger's last acts is the gift of a book to Sir Andrew, a collection of Acts of Parliament.

Will Honeycomb, a beau and fop in the decline of life. Despite his age, he remains youthful, he says, because of his many attempts to marry. His contributions to club discussions stem from some aspect of the female world. His ultimate marriage at an advanced age bears out his claim to gallantry.

William Wimble, a bachelor neighbor of Sir Roger de Coverley. The youngest son of an ancient family, born to no estate and bred to no business, Will lives with an older brother and acts as gamekeeper on the family estate. Resigned to his lot in life, amiable Will is the darling of the countryside.

Moll White, a slatternly recluse who lives near Sir Roger's estate. Known as a witch by her neighbors, she is blamed for any untoward event or incident. Her death is said to have caused winds violent enough to blow off the end of one of Sir Roger's barn. Sir Roger tells Mr. Spectator of the coincidence of the two events but professes no belief in the relationship between them.

Kate Willow, a witty, mischievous wench in Sir Roger's neighborhood. Kate's value of her beauty over love has kept her unmarried. To the consternation of many, she tries to influence young girls in love to be as indiscreet as she has been.

Laertes and
Irus, men of the countryside. Their eco-

nomic practices, both based on poverty, are opposites. Because he is ashamed to appear poor, Laertes spends unthriftily, moving always closer to poverty. Irus' fear of poverty causes him to save, moving him from it.

Tom Touchy, the selfish neighbor of Sir Roger. In every quarter court meeting of the court he sues someone for poaching on his land. Touchy, generally disliked for his littleness, incurs the wrath of the countryside when he sues Will Wimble for taking hazel sticks from his hedge.

Good-natured Will has taken the sticks to make tobacco-stoppers for his friends.

A Minister, a club member whose visits add to every man new enjoyment of himself.

The Templar, another member. His interest turns from poetry to law and he leaves "The Club."

Edward Biscuit, Sir Roger's butler. From Biscuit's correspondence Mr. Spectator learns the details of the baronet's death and burial.

SISTER CARRIE

Author: Theodore Dreiser (1871-1945)
Time of action: 1889
First published: 1900

PRINCIPAL CHARACTERS

Caroline Meeber, called **Sister Carrie,** a young Middle Western girl who rises from her small-town origins to success as an actress. Her story illustrates one part of Dreiser's division of mankind between the Intellectual and the Emotional. Members of the latter division he calls "harps in the wind," hopelessly seeking to satisfy an inexplicable yearning for beauty, accomplishment, the good life. Caroline Meeber belongs to this second group, which performs its sad, forsaken quest in the manner of dancers after a flame. Although Carrie is not capable of much rationalization, she is capable of sensing an ideal, and she has a tenacious energy to bend toward its realization. The key to Carrie's apparently simple character is that she is a rather complex person. Moved by desires which at first she sees as ends in themselves—to have money, to own fine clothes, to be socially accepted—she enters into an affair with Hurstwood and contributes to his degeneration while remaining virtually untouched herself. Her restlessness and seeming disregard for others are really manifestations of her inability to recog-

nize anything outside of concrete representation. Throughout the book she is never given to reflection. Although she uses Drouet and Hurstwood to her advantage, she is no gross country girl grasping at opportunity. There is something monolithic in her nature, and certain gifts or curses of sensitivity and pluck combine to give her an appeal that her fellows recognize as representative of themselves. As Carrie Madena, she scores a success on the stage by acting in flimsy, superficial parts. What is sad about Carrie is that each time she steps up to the much prized rung that has been just above, her ideal eludes her and she becomes vaguely disillusioned with still another symbol of happiness and success. Thus she becomes Dreiser's commentary on man's pathetic reach for the ideal on the distant peak; reality is the intractable stuff he has to work with to achieve it.

George Hurstwood, the manager of a Chicago saloon, a man who has worked his way into a carefully balanced niche of the social order. In that class just below the luxurious rich, he has created for himself an air of success made substantial by good food, good company, comfortable living. When he encounters Carrie, Hurstwood has fallen into the practice of maintaining only the semblance of marital order; he denies himself little in the way of pleasures that he genuinely covets, but he has the saving grace of discretion on his side. He begins to fancy himself as quite clever, something of a commander on the field of life, and this self-deception brings about his eventual collapse. With Carrie, he imagines nothing can stay his success, and in a weak moment he discards the last shreds of caution. Because he never fully understands Carrie, a pall of reality weights their relationship. Hurstwood has betrayed his place of trust by stealing money from his employers, has hoodwinked Carrie into running off with him, and these conditions prove insufferable. Faced with a much lower status in society, Hurstwood, now using the alias of Wheeler, is unable to reconcile himself to fact and begins to indulge in the attrition of living in the past. One by one his carefully structured conceptions of himself and his flamboyance crumple, and he learns that he is no match for grubbiness. The painstaking chronicle of Hurstwood's decline into apathy becomes the signal merit of this novel. Hurstwood is incapable of checking his downhill slide because, even to his end, a desolate, grimy suicide in a flop house, the granules of former pride remain with him, actually sapping his powers of adaptation.

Charles Drouet, a traveling salesman and a superficial egotist, Carrie Meeber's first lover. Drouet has no real depth to his nature. Uncomplex, he has no wish to inflict harm on others and tries, while pleasing himself, to bring them happiness. He serves as Carrie's first introduction to a form of the good life, but she quickly outgrows him as she passes on to George Hurstwood. At the end of the novel Drouet is shown essentially as he was at the beginning: handsome, flashy, gay, boylike, effervescent, and entirely without scope or perspective.

Bod Ames, a young man intellectually inclined. Of the people in the novel he is the only one who really understands or genuinely moves Carrie. Ironically, he causes the most painful reawakening of the quest for the "ideal" in Carrie's nature.

Minnie and
Sven Hanson, Carrie's sister and brother-in-law with whom she lives when she comes to Chicago. They live a sterile, plodding life that Carrie earnestly wishes to avoid.

Mrs. Hurstwood, the deceived, deserted wife who has watched her marriage deteriorate steadily, even before her husband's affair with Carrie Meeber. Cold and social-minded by nature, she ends up in possession of all property accumulated by Hurstwood over the years.

Jessica and
George Hurstwood, Jr., the Hurstwood children, rather selfish offspring, without depth, who conform to their mother's way.

Mr. and Mrs. Vance, a couple who live next to Carrie and Hurstwood in New York. They impress Carrie with their sophistication and put her life with Hurstwood under a shabbier light.

SISTER PHILOMÈNE

Authors: Edmond (1822-1896) and Jules (1830-1870) de Goncourt
Time of action: Nineteenth century
First published: 1861

Marie Gaucher (mà·rē' gō·shā'), who becomes Sister Philomène (fē·lô·měn'). Orphaned as a child, she is sent to a convent orphanage. After a period of adjustment, she is led, through her friend Céline, to a state of religious agitation that finally threatens her health. Her aunt is permitted to take her home. After an unhappy time as servant to Henri de Viry, she begins her novitiate to the Sisters of St. Augustine, who send her to work in a hospital. There she wins the hearts of doctors and sufferers by her compassionate tenderness. She falls in love with Barnier but punishes herself by remaining in the hospital and enduring love's torments until his death.

Barnier (bàr·nyā'), a young doctor loved by Sister Philomène. Haunted by memories of the dead Romaine, his former mistress, he deliberately exposes himself to disease and dies as Sister Philomène is having prayers for unbelievers said for him.

Céline (sā·lēn'), Sister Philomène's friend at the orphanage, who later becomes Sister Lawrence. She dies of typhoid.

Madame de Viry (də vē·rē'), the employer of Sister Philomène's aunt, with whom the child Marie goes to live on the death of her parents. When she begins to assume equal footing with Henri de Viry, Madame de Viry sends her away to an orphanage.

Henri de Viry (äṅ·rē' də vē·rē'), Madame de Viry's son.

Romaine (rô·měn'), Barnier's former mistress, who had left him for a life of dissipation. Her death leads the grief-stricken Barnier to expose himself to a fatal disease.

Malivoire (mà·lē·vwàr'), a doctor and a friend of Barnier.

Marguerite (màr·gə·rēt'), a sister who befriends young Marie at the orphanage.

SIX CHARACTERS IN SEARCH OF AN AUTHOR

Author: Luigi Pirandello (1867-1936)
Time of action: Twentieth century
First presented: 1921

The Father, who, during preparations for the rehearsal of a play, appears on stage with five members of his family, in search of an author who will put them, already living characters, into a drama. The manager finally agrees to hear their story and allows each to rehearse his part as his illusions cause him to believe it to be.

The Mother. Provided, years ago, with a lover by her husband, who had grown tired of her, she returns, destitute, with her three illegitimate children, and is again received into her husband's home. She watches, sorrowing, as she sees her

husband act out his visit to Madame Pace, from whom he attempts to purchase a replacement for his wife. Unknown to him, the girl he desires is the illegitimate daughter of his own wife.

The Stepdaughter, who, while playing her part in Madame Pace's establishment, is approached by her stepfather, who does not recognize her. She is abruptly pulled from him by her horrified mother, who rushes in from off-stage.

The Son, who, when urged by the manager to play his part, insists that he simply walked in the garden. He violently accuses the father of displaying the family shame to the world and of dragging him on stage. He finally admits finding the body of the little girl in the fountain.

The Little Girl, who, placed by the stage manager beside a fountain, is found dead in its waters.

The Boy, who is placed by the stage manager behind some bushes, from which comes the sound of a pistol shot. In the resulting confusion, the rehearsal ends in a frantic discussion about whether or not the boy's death is real or pretended.

Madame Pace, a procuress. Scandalized at having to play her part before the mother, she leaves the stage.

The Stage Manager,
The Leading Lady, and
The Leading Man, the professional company interrupted in rehearsal by the six characters in search of an author.

THE SKIN OF OUR TEETH

Author: Thornton Wilder (1897-   )
Time of action: All human history
First presented: 1942

PRINCIPAL CHARACTERS

George Antrobus, a citizen of the world. He wants to believe in the goodness of man and the survival of the race but often his faith is shaken. A kind and generous man, he insists that starving refugees from the cold then enveloping the world be admitted to the house and fed, whereas his practical wife does not want to take them in. A good provider, he obtains a boat in order to save his family during the big flood. After the great war he decides to try to live in peace with his vicious son Henry. Striving to regain his confidence in mankind, he takes comfort in his books, his home, and the good people of the world.

Mrs. Antrobus, George's wife. She is a typical middle-class mother who loves her family and willingly sacrifices herself to their needs. Her typically female responses enable her to hold her husband, survive catastrophes, and perpetuate the race. When she is about to lose George to Sabina, she takes advantage of the coming great flood to bring him back to duty and family. When the great war comes, she finds safety in the basement for herself, her daughter, and, most important of all, her new grandchild.

Gladys Antrobus, their daughter, a wholesome girl much like her mother. Content to remain within the security of the family circle, she survives the great flood. By hiding in the basement, she and her new baby survive the great war as well.

Henry Antrobus, formerly called **Cain,** the Antrobuses' son, a nonconformist. When he hits his brother with a stone and accidentally kills him, the parents change his name from Cain to Henry and thereafter make every effort to hide his past. In another fit of hate he kills a neighbor with a stone. In the great war his aggressive temperament enables him to rise from the rank of corporal to that of general.

Sabina, the maid in the Antrobus household. She is the former mistress of George, who had brought her back from the Sabine rape. She leaves the Antrobuses and, as Miss Lily-Sabina Fairweather, wins a beauty contest at Atlan-

tic City, after which she tries unsuccessfully to win back George.

Moses, a Judge,
Homer, a blind beggar with a guitar,

Miss E. Muse,
Miss T. Muse, and
Miss M. Muse, refugees from the killing
cold, who stop at the Antrobus house for
food and warmth.

THE SLEEPWALKERS

Author: Hermann Broch (1886-1951)
Time of action: 1888-1918
First published: 1930-1932

PRINCIPAL CHARACTERS

Joachim von Pasenow (yō'äkh'ĭm fôn pä'sĕ·nō), a young German lieutenant who feels comfortable only in a uniform. He has odd ideas about his wife as a kind of madonna. By the end of World War I he has become a major in the German army.

Bertrand (bârt'ränd), Joachim's friend. He leaves the army to become a businessman. He becomes Esch's enemy. He hires agents to provoke Martin, the Socialist, into trouble with the authorities.

Herr von Pasenow (hâr fôn pä'sĕ·nō), Joachim's father, a funny, fat old man who embarrasses his son. He wants Joachim to marry Elisabeth and retire from the army to manage the family estates.

Ruzena (rōō'zä'nä), a sensitive Bohemian girl who becomes Joachim von Pasenow's mistress. She shoots Bertrand, wounding him in the arm, when she thinks he is coming between her and her lover.

Elisabeth (ĕ·lĕ'sä·băt), Joachim von Pasenow's wife.

Martin (mär'tēn), a Socialist. Bertrand has him harassed by the police and by hired baiters.

Esch (ĕsh), a German bookkeeper who becomes a theatrical manager and, later, a newspaperman. During a workers' re-

volt in 1918 he is murdered by Huguenau, who stabs him with a bayonet.

Frau Hentjen (frou hănt'yĕn), a restaurant keeper. She becomes Esch's mistress and, later, his wife. She is raped by Huguenau shortly before he murders her husband.

Helmuth von Pasenow (hăl'mōōt fôn pä'sĕ·nō), Joachim's brother, killed in a duel.

Korn (kōrn), a customs inspector. He is Esch's friend and landlord.

Lohberg (lō'bĕrg), a tobacconist and Esch's friend.

Erna Korn (ėr'nä kōrn), the customs inspector's sister, desperate to be married.

Teltscher (tālt'shėr), a Hungarian knife thrower.

Ilona (ĭ·lō'nä), a flashly blonde. She is Teltscher's human target in his act.

Gernerth (gėr'nėrt), a theatrical manager who becomes Esch's partner.

Huguenau (hōō'gü·nou), an Alsatian businessman who looks after himself and takes what he wants.

Marie (mä·rē'), a Salvation Army girl attracted to a Talmudic Jew.

Hanna (hä'nä), a lawyer's wife.

THE SLIPKNOT

Author: Titus Maccius Plautus (c. 255-184 B.C.)
Time of action: Late third century B.C.
First published: Late third or early second century B.C.

PRINCIPAL CHARACTERS

Daemones (dē′mə·něz), an elderly and kindly Athenian spending his last years in exile because of debts incurred through his excessive generosity. His sorrows are increased by the absence of his daughter Palaestra, stolen from him years before and sold to the procurer Labrax. A series of coincidences finally brings father and daughter face to face, reveals their identities to each other, and unites all in a joyful celebration.

Palaestra (pə·lěs′trə), Daemones' daughter, who had been kidnaped and sold to the procurer Labrax. On the way to Sicily to be resold by her master, she is shipwrecked and cast ashore near the house of Daemones. Seeking shelter in the temple of Venus, she is set upon by Labrax, who has been washed up from the sea and is determined to recover his slave. After her rescue by Daemones, her identity is established by trinkets from Labrax's wallet. She is received with joy by

her long-lost father and betrothed to Plesidippus.

Labrax (lă′brəks), a procurer who buys the kidnaped child Palaestra. On the way to Sicily to resell his slave, he is shipwrecked and loses sight of her when she gets ashore in a boat. Later, when her identity is established by trinkets from his wallet, he is forced to relinquish her on the grounds that she had been born free.

Plesidippus (plě·sə·dǐ′pəs), a young man in love with Palaestra and finally betrothed to her.

Charmides (kär′mə·dēz), a cohort of Labrax.

Ampelisca (ăm·pə·lǐs′kə), a slave girl shipwrecked and rescued with Palaestra.

Trachalio (trə·kā′lǐ·ō), Plesidippus' servant.

Gripus (grī′pəs), Daemones' servant.

THE SMALL HOUSE AT ALLINGTON

Author: Anthony Trollope (1815-1882)
Time of action: Mid-nineteenth century
First published: 1864

PRINCIPAL CHARACTERS

Lilian Dale (Lily), the younger daughter of widowed Mrs. Dale and niece of the Squire of Allington. She falls in love with Adolphus Crosbie and they become engaged. Adolphus asks her uncle for a dowry. Refused, he still intends to marry Lily, but later, at a house-party at De Courcy Castle, he suddenly becomes engaged to the more wealthy Lady Alexandrina, whom he marries.

Lily stays at home, refusing a steady suitor whom her family wishes her to marry. She helps to arrange a match between her sister Bell and a young doctor.

Christopher Dale, the Squire of Allington. A dour but well-meaning member of the country gentry, he allows his widowed sister-in-law to live rent-free in the small house at Allington. His kindness is finally appreciated when he does all he can to help Lily after she is jilted. He also tries to arrange a marriage between his heir and Lily's sister, his favorite niece. At the end, he settles money on both nieces.

Mrs. Mary Dale, the widow of Philip Dale, the Squire's youngest brother. She has accepted the Squire's offer of a house for the sake of her daughters. She insists that both her daughters be able to choose their husbands freely, despite pressure from the Squire to have Bell marry his heir. Mrs. Dale prepares to move into a small cottage in Guestwick, a neighboring town, in order not to be dependent on the generosity of a man whose advice she will not take; however, when the Squire treats Lily kindly, the family decides not to move.

Isabella Dale (Bell), the older daughter of Mrs. Dale and the beauty of the family. She is in love with Dr. Crofts, the young Guestwick physician, who thinks himself too poor to marry her. She refuses the proposal of her wealthy cousin, Bernard Dale, and waits until Dr. Crofts finally offers her marriage.

Adolphus Crosbie, the senior clerk in the General Committee Office in Whitehall, an attractive and impetuous young man. He really loves Lily when he proposes to her at Allington, but his weak selfishness leads him into a bad marriage with Lady Alexandrina. Shortly after his marriage he realizes his mistake and is relieved when Lady Alexandrina joins her mother in Baden-Baden.

Captain Bernard Dale, an officer in the Corps of Engineers, nephew and heir of the Squire of Allington. He is an undemonstrative young man, willing to follow his uncle's wishes in proposing to Bell Dale.

John Eames, a clerk in the Income Tax Office in London. He has always loved Lily Dale. He saves Lord De Guest, the principal local aristocrat, from a bull, an event which helps his career. He also thrashes Adolphus Crosbie in a London railway station after the jilting of Lily.

Lord De Guest, the local aristocrat who becomes a John Eames' benefactor.

Lady Julia De Guest, the kind spinster sister of Lord De Guest; she reports the engagement of Adolphus Crosbie and Lady Alexandrina to Lily's uncle.

Dr. Crofts, the physician who becomes Lord De Guest's doctor and finally marries Bell Dale.

Mrs. Roper, a widow who runs the London boarding house where John Eames lives.

Amelia Roper, her daughter, who schemes unsuccessfully to marry John Eames, but later marries Cradell.

Joseph Cradell (Caudle), a friend of John Eames and a fellow clerk in the Income Tax Office.

Mr. Lupex, a boarder at Mrs. Roper's, a drunken scene painter.

Mrs. Lupex, his blowsy wife, intimately involved with Joseph Cradell.

Earl De Courcy, a misanthropic aristocrat.

Countess Rosina De Courcy, the Earl's scheming wife, who gets her daughter engaged to Adolphus Crosbie.

Lady Amelia De Courcy Gagebee (the name is Gazebee in "Dr. Thorne"), the oldest De Courcy daughter.

Mortimer Gagebee, the attorney and son-in-law to the De Courcys; he succeeds in gaining for Lady Alexandrina a settlement that is ruinous to Adolphus.

Lady Alexandrina De Courcy, a selfish beauty, the youngest daughter of the De Courcys. She marries Adolphus but leaves him after a few months.

Lady Rosina De Courcy, the religious daughter of the De Courcys.

Lady Margaretta De Courcy, the daughter of the De Courcys most conscious of family and position.

Lord Porlock, the De Courcy son and heir who threatens to sue his father for his allowance.

The Honourable George De Courcy, the parsimonious son.

The Honourable John De Courcy, the spendthrift son.

Lady Dumbello, the former Griselda Grantly, widely popular for her beauty and discrimination.

Plantagenet Palisser, heir to the Duke of Omnium, fascinated by Lady Dumbello.

Fowler Pratt, the friend and fellow clubman of Adolphus Crosbie.

Colonel Dale, father of Bernard Dale, a listless man who lives at Torquay.

Lady Fanny Dale, his wife, who had been the penniless daughter of Lord De Guest, brother of the present Earl.

Mrs. Eames, the widowed mother of John Eames.

Mary Eames, the sister of John Eames, who lives with her mother.

Mr. Boyce, the vicar of Allington.

Mrs. Boyce, the vicar's wife.

Hopkins, the gardener and caretaker for the Squire af Allington.

Jemima, a servant in Mrs. Roper's boarding house.

Mrs. Spruce, another boarder at Mrs. Roper's.

Dr. Gruffen, an old doctor in Guestwick.

Mrs. Crump, the postmistress in Guestwick.

Sir Raffle Buffle, chairman of the Income Tax Office.

Butterwell, secretary in the General Committee Office.

Mr. Optimist, chairman of the General Committee.

Major Fiasco, a member of the General Committee.

SMALL SOULS

Author: Louis Couperus (1863-1923)
Time of action: Nineteenth century
First published: 1901

PRINCIPAL CHARACTERS

Constance van der Welcke, a daughter of the respectable Van Lowe family. After several years of a loveless marriage to the respectable Dutch envoy at Rome, she has an affair with Henri van der Welcke, whom she marries after divorcing her husband. After twenty years away, she returns to Holland with her second husband, hoping that time will have healed the scars caused by the old scandal. In spite of the outward appearances of forgiveness, Constance becomes aware that she is still condemned by a society of small souls quick to criticize others while engaged, itself, in an interplay of gossip, scandal, and fear.

Henri van der Welcke, Constance van der Welcke's second husband. His political career ruined by his affair with and marriage to Constance, he returns with her to Holland and the condemnation of Dutch society.

Adriaan, called **Addie,** Constance and

1052

Henri van der Welcke's thirteen-year-old son. Disturbed by the shreds of gossip he hears about his family, he becomes so melancholy that his father tells him the story of the scandal of his parents' marriage. Addie accepts the truth in a mature fashion that marks the end of his childhood.

Mrs. van Lowe, Constance van der Welcke's mother.

Bertha van Voorde, Constance's socially prominent sister, through whose influence she hopes to become accepted in higher circles.

Van Naghel van Voorde, Bertha van

Voorde's husband, who refuses to accept Constance and Henri van der Welcke.

Adolphine, Constance's petty and envious sister.

Jaap, Adolphine's young son, who taunts Addie about his parents.

Gerrit van Lowe,
Paul van Lowe, and
Karel van Lowe, Constance van der Welcke's brothers.

Cateau, Karel van Lowe's wife.

Van Vreeswijck, Henri van der Welcke's friend.

SMOKE

Author: Ivan Turgenev (1818-1883)
Time of action: 1862-1865
First published: 1867

PRINCIPAL CHARACTERS

Grigóry Litvinov (grĭ·gō′rĭy lĭt·vē′nəf), a farmer's son. Wishing to farm progressively on his father's estate, he has tried to learn scientific agriculture by studying modern practices in several European regions. His plans for marriage to Tatyana and for modernizing his father's estate are interrupted by the temporary resurrection at Baden of his former love for Irina and the breaking off of his engagement to Tatyana. Observant and thoughtful, he is repelled by the impractical windiness of the group of liberals who associate with Gubaryov at Baden and likewise by the shallow, aimless, bored existence of Irina, her husband, and their aristocratic friends. His break with Tatyana pains him because he is ashamed of casting her off so unexpectedly and hurting her so deeply. Although his passion for Irina consumes him until he is willing to give up everything for her, his pride, however, will not let him live as one of her hangers-on. Irina's refusal to leave with him brings him such grief as he had earlier brought

Tatyana, but it is combined with shame over being rejected a second time by Irina and by guilt over his treatment of Tatyana. Hard work enables him to make some progress in improving conditions on the estate which he inherits on his father's death. His abject plea for forgiveness after more than two years is accepted by the generous Tatyana and they are married at last.

Tatyana Petrovna Shestov (tä·tyä′nə pĕt·rōv′nə shĕs·tôf′), called **Tanya** (tä′nyə), his fiancée, plump, blonde, heavy-faced, brown-eyed, kind, and good. Intuitively she guesses that Irina is the cause of her rejection by Litvinov. She is shocked and hurt, but she does not attack him with angry abuse when she accepts her fate with quiet dignity and leaves Baden, the scene of her humiliation. When Litvinov later comes to her home and, kneeling, begs her to forgive him, she is at once surprised, frightened, and happy.

Kapitolina Markovna Shestov (kä·pĭ·tô-

1053

lĭ′nə mär·kōv′nə shĕs·tôf′), Tanya's maiden aunt. Talkative and completely provincial in outlook, she is both fascinated and morally shocked by the gambling and other evidences of dissolute life at Baden. Litvinov thinks her absurd but appears to respect her piteous but vain attempts to make him change his mind about breaking his engagement to Tanya.

Irina Pavlovna Osinin Ratmirov (ĭ·rĭ′nə päv′ləv·nə ô·sĭ′nĭn rät·mĭ′rəf), the oldest daughter in a family of noble ancestry but straitened circumstances. In youth Litvinov was infatuated with and informally engaged to Irina, a tall, slim girl with a willful, passionate nature and a cold heart. After throwing over Litvinov in order to live in Count Reisenbach's home, she inspired many rumors and much gossip before she married General Ratmirov. When Litvinov meets her ten years later she has become a truly beautiful woman, and he is captivated again. Though she declares her love, and means it, she is unwilling to do as Tolstoy's Anna Karenina did, forsake all that she has in order to go with her lover; at the same time, aware of her power, she will not let him go. Litvinov is finally strong enough to compel her to make a choice. Her decision to continue the life which she must have to survive brings him temporary misery but finally his freedom and his salvation. Irina moves in a social world of luxury and evil and yet somehow seems above and apart from that evil. Her ironical intellect stirs fear in the men and the women who know her, as if they, like herself, recognized her superiority to them.

General Valerian Vladimirovitch Ratmirov (vä·lē·rĭ·än′ vlä·dĭ′mĭ·rə·vĭch rät-mĭ′rəf), Irina's youthful-looking, elegant, dandified husband, who appears unconcerned about Litvinov's visits to his wife and the time she spends with other men. As a military man he symbolizes the combination of cruelty and aristocratic indifference to the masses which helped to bring about the Russian Revolution.

Sozont Ivanitch Potugin (sô·zōnt′ ĭ·vä′-nĭch pô·tū′gĭn), a retired clerk who becomes Litvinov's friend, broad-shouldered, short-legged, curly-haired, mournful-eyed, potato-nosed. Soft-voiced and philosophical, he enunciates Turgenev's own views of Russia and the Russians, whom he both loves and hates. He loves the culture, the civilization, of the West and foresees that the Russia of the future will develop out of a borrowing from and an assimilation of Western ideas and technical advancements. A kind of errand boy used by Irina in the past, he warns Litvinov against an involvement with her.

Rostislav Bambaev (rôs·tĭs·läf′ bäm-bä′ĕf), a good-natured, good-for-nothing Muscovite, flabby-nosed, soft-cheeked, greasy-haired, fat, crude, impecunious, exclamatory, and enthusiastic. When Litvinov meets him on his trip to see Tatyana, he has become a butler for the Gubaryov brothers.

Stepan Nikolaevitch Gubaryov (stĕ·pän′ nĭ·kô·lä′ĕ·vĭch gōō·bär·yōf′), Bambaev's friend at Baden, a nervous strider and beard-twitcher who stimulates his liberal-thinking friends but remains silent himself. A theorizer rather than a doer, when he occasionally talks he spouts dirty stories at which he guffaws.

Bindasov (bĭn·dä′səf), a surly, repulsive sponger to whom Litvinov lends money he knows will not be returned. He is later killed in a tavern brawl.

Prince Pavel Vassilyevitch Osinin (pä′-vĕl väs·sĭ′lyĕ·vĭch ô·sĭ′nĭn), Irina's father, an opportunist who willingly exploits his daughter's charms.

Count Reisenbach (rī′zən·bakh), a wealthy, middle-aged, childless chamberlain, bloated, wrinkled, haughty, and evil-mouthed, who in effect buys Irina as a pretty ornament for his home. It is not clear whether she ever became his mistress before her marriage to General Ratmirov.

Semyon Yakovlevitch Voroshilov (sĕ-myōn' yä'kəv·lĕ·vĭch vô·rô·shĭ'ləf), a good-looking, fresh-faced, dignified follower of Gubaryov, showily sophisticated and esoteric at times and sententiously silent at others.

Matrona Semyonovna (mät·rō'nə sĕ-myō'nəv·nə), a childless, frail, middle-aged widow, a convulsively intense talker and capricious theorist.

THE SNAKE PIT

Author: Sigrid Undset (1882-1949)
Time of action: Late thirteenth, early fourteenth centuries
First published: 1925

PRINCIPAL CHARACTERS

Olav Audunsson (also see "The Axe"), the master of Hestviken. Now married to Ingunn and returned, for the first time since the age of seven, to his home of Hestviken, he finds that the concealing of his murder of Ingunn's lover Teit, which is necessary to protect Ingunn from shame, becomes increasingly burdensome. After her death, Olav must still keep her reputation spotless for the sake of his daughter.

Ingunn Steinfinnsdatter (also see "The Axe"), Olav's wife, once beautiful but now frail and sickly. After she has four stillborn children, Olav brings to Hestviken from a foster home her son Eirik, whom he claims as his. Olav regrets the decision when Ingunn gives birth to a boy, Audun, now defrauded of his birthright. Audun is sickly and lives only a short time. Ingunn herself dies after giving birth to another child, a daughter.

Eirik, Ingunn's son by Teit (also see "The Axe"). At first fond of his supposed father Olav, Eirik comes to dislike him after Olav's manner becomes harsh and aloof.

Cecilia Olavsdatter, the daughter of Olav and Ingunn.

Audun Olavsson, the short-lived son of Olav and Ingunn.

Torhild Björnsdatter, the housekeeper at Hestviken. After she bears Olav's son, Olav gives her a farm for her own.

Björn, the illegitimate son of Torhild and Olav.

Olav Half-Priest, an aged kinsman of Olav Audunsson. Hestviken deteriorated somewhat under his stewardship during the years before Olav Audunsson's return.

Tora (also see "The Axe"), Ingunn's sister, now widowed.

Jon Steinfinnsson (also see "The Axe"), Ingunn's brother. After his death, Olav goes north to collect Ingunn's share of Jon's goods. Olav brings Eirik back to Hestviken on his return.

Arnvid Finnsson, an old friend of Olav and Ingunn (also see "The Axe"). He is about to enter the order of the Preaching Friars. Olav unburdens his guilt to Arnvid, who can say little to comfort his friend.

SNOW-BOUND

Author: John Greenleaf Whittier (1807-1892)
Time of action: Early nineteenth century
First published: 1866

PRINCIPAL CHARACTERS

The Poet, remembering a great snowfall of his boyhood, with all its beauty and attendant pleasures.

Our Father, the poet's father, a man of action. To the snow-bound group collected around the fire he tells stories of adventures with Indians, of fishing trips, and of witches reputed to have inhabited the land long ago.

Our Mother, who, while turning her wheel, tells of Indian raids, of her happy girlhood, of stories read in books by famous and revered Quakers.

Our Uncle, innocent of books. He shares his knowledge of nature: moons and tides, weather signs, birds and beasts.

Our Dear Aunt, a selfless spinster of simple faith.

The Elder Sister, impulsive, generous, truthful, sternly just.

The Youngest Sister, and dearest, sweet and loving.

Brother, the only one of the happy group, besides the poet, now living.

The Schoolmaster, a boarder in the Whittier home. A poor man's son, he learned independence as a boy. Seemingly carefree and boyish, he is an earnest shaper of youthful minds. The cause of Freedom should have many young apostles like him.

Another Guest (Harriet Livermore), a strange, half-feared, half-welcome woman, violent of temper, eccentric, cultured, and intense. Later she will go to Europe and the Near East, prophesying the imminent second coming of Christ.

SO RED THE ROSE

Author: Stark Young (1881-   )
Time of action: 1860-1865
First published: 1934

PRINCIPAL CHARACTERS

Malcolm Bedford, the owner of Portobello plantation in Mississippi. He becomes a Southern patriot during the Civil War and falls ill of dysentery while serving at Vicksburg. He returns home to die, prophesying that the fall of Vicksburg dooms the Confederate cause.

Sarah Tait Bedford, Malcolm's second wife, who is the gracious hostess and mistress of Portobello plantation. After the war she succeeds in keeping it for the family and making it successful.

Duncan Bedford, the oldest of Malcolm's children, a student at Washington College. He enlists in the Confederate cause and fights valiantly until captured. He returns home after the war to work with Mrs. Bedford in reclaiming the family plantation. He long loves Valette, a girl adopted by the Bedfords, and eventually marries her.

Hugh McGehee, owner of Montrose plantation and a neighbor of the Bedfords.

1056

Agnes McGehee, the wife of Hugh and a sister of Malcolm Bedford.

Edward McGehee, the oldest son of Hugh and Agnes. He enlists in the Confederate army and is killed in the battle at Pittsburg Landing.

Shelton Taliaferro, a distant relative of the McGehees.

Charles Taliaferro, Shelton's son. He becomes a great friend of Edward McGehee during visits at Montrose. Like his friend, Charles is killed at Pittsburg Landing.

Lucinda (Lucy) McGehee, the daughter of Hugh and Agnes. She falls in love with Charles Taliaferro, who does not pay any attention to her, and is heartbroken at her beloved's death.

Zach McGehee, Hugh's nephew.

Amelie Balfour, Zach's fiancée. She persuades Valette Bedford to marry Duncan Bedford, her foster brother.

Valette Bedford, a coquettish girl loved by Duncan Bedford. After some misunderstandings they are married, following the Civil War.

Mary Hartwell and
Frances Bedford, younger children of Malcolm.

Middleton Bedford, orphaned nephew of Malcolm.

SOHRAB AND RUSTUM

Author: Matthew Arnold (1822-1888)
Time of action: Remote antiquity
First published: 1853

PRINCIPAL CHARACTERS

Sohrab (sō'räb), the champion of the Tartar army. Little more than a boy, and the mightiest warrior of the Tartar hosts, Sohrab, restless and dissatisfied, seeks Rustum, a Persian, the father he has never seen. Hoping that his fame will reach his father's ears, he asks Peran-Wisa to challenge the Persians to a single combat, with each side choosing a champion for the duel. Sohrab, the Tartar, faces Rustum, the Persian, on the field of battle, and Sohrab is transfixed by Rustum's spear. Before Sohrab dies, father and son become known to each other.

Rustum (rōos'təm), a Persian chieftain and champion of the Persian army. Meeting the challenge of the Tartars for a duel between a chosen warrior from each side, Rustum, unknowingly, faces his son, Sohrab. He transfixes and mortally wounds the youthful champion with his spear. As the victim's life ebbs away, Rustum learns the identity of his son. In an agony of grief and remorse, he promises to bear Sohrab's body to the palace of his fathers.

Peran-Wisa, commander of the Tartar army.

Ferood, leader of the Persians.

Gudurz, a Persian chieftain.

Zal, Sohrab's grandfather.

THE SOLDIER'S FORTUNE

Author: Thomas Otway (1652-1685)
Time of action: c. 1680
First presented: 1681

1057

Captain Beaugard, a military officer. Returning from a campaign, he is approached, through the offices of Sir Jolly Jumble, by Lady Dunce, who claims to have been in love with him long before he went off to the wars. A meeting with the lady reveals her as his old love, Clarinda, now married to the elderly and distasteful Sir Davy Dunce. There follows a series of machinations designed to blackmail Sir Davy into acknowledging Captain Beaugard as his wife's lover.

Lady Dunce (Clarinda), Captain Beaugard's beloved. Despairing of her lover's returning from the wars, she marries the wealthy but unattractive and elderly Sir Davy Dunce. When the Captain does return, she finds herself still in love with him, and she and the Captain engage in a series of ruses designed to fool her husband into being cuckolded and finally forced to acknowledge his wife as the Captain's mistress.

Sir Davy Dunce, Lady Dunce's cuckolded husband. Jealous and thick-witted, he is used by his wife in the furtherance of her affair with Captain Beaugard. Manipulated into becoming a party to a conspiracy to assassinate the Captain, he is forced, in order to escape the extreme penalty for attempted murder, to acknowledge his wife as Beaugard's mistress and free her from his unwanted attentions.

Courtine, Captain Beaugard's companion-in-arms, who wins and marries Sylvia.

Sylvia, Sir Davy and Lady Dunce's niece, who rejects the idea of matrimony because of her observations of her aunt and uncle. She is finally prevailed upon to marry Courtine.

Sir Jolly Jumble, an elderly rake and the ally of Lady Dunce in her amorous adventures.

THE SON AVENGER

Author: Sigrid Undset (1882-1949)
Time of action: Fourteenth century
First published: 1927

PRINCIPAL CHARACTERS

Olav Audunsson (also see "The Axe," "The Snake Pit," "In the Wilderness"), the master of Hestviken. Accumulating family tragedies seem to him part of the retribution for his great unconfessed crime. He suffers a stroke which makes it impossible for him to confess, despite his great and constant remorse. At last he dies.

Cecilia Olavsdatter (also see "The Snake Pit," "In the Wilderness"), the daughter of Olav and Ingunn. She makes an unhappy marriage to a wastrel who turns thief. After he is killed, she marries the man who was her first choice.

Eirik (also see "The Axe," "The Snake Pit," "In the Wilderness"), the illegitimate son of Ingunn, whom Olav has accepted as his heir. Feelings of guilt after the girl he has been pursuing dies cause him to decide to become a monk. A poor novice, he is sent home and settles down. A planned advantageous marriage is called off, and he marries a fallen woman. At last both go into holy orders.

Jörund Rypa, a young squire who marries Cecilia and proves to be dishonest. Discovery of his part in a robbery causes the breaking off of Eirik's engagement. When Jörund is found stabbed in his bed, guilt-ridden Olav believes to his horror that Cecilia is the murderess; but this is not true.

Liv and
Arnketil (also see "In the Wilderness"), a husband and wife who keep a house of thieves and gamblers. To avenge the ruin of a daughter, Arnketil kills Jörund. Arnketil's body is found long afterwards in a swamp.

Bothild Asgersdatter (also see "In the Wilderness"), Olav's foster daughter. Trying to evade Eirik's pursuit, she falls and vomits blood; thus he first learns that she is ill with the wasting sickness. In remorse, he leaves Hestviken for a short while. He returns to make amends by asking for her hand in marriage, but finds that she has died.

Gunhild Bersesdatter, to whom Eirik is betrothed.

Guttorm, Gunhild's rich uncle, of Draumtop. Some of the proceeds of a robbery against him are found in Jörund's chest. Eirik's efforts to cover up the crime prove unsuccessful.

Berse, of Eiken, Gunhild's father. He forbids the marriage between Eirik and Gunhild after Jörund's part in the robbery is disclosed.

Aslak Gunnarsson, a young man with whom Olav fought in Duke Eirik's war (see "In the Wilderness"). An outlaw, he is sheltered by a reluctant Olav. When he leaves Hestviken after his family has paid atonement for his crime, he begs to return with his kinsmen to ask for Cecilia's hand, but Olav gives him no hope. He marries Cecilia after her widowhood.

Eldrid Bersesdatter, Gunhild's older sister. She caused great scandal and is living alone. Eirik goes to her house as part of a plan of Gunhild's, but Gunhild is prevented from getting away to meet him there. Eirik finds Eldrid kind and marries her. She enters a convent later.

Björn (also see "The Snake Pit" and "In the Wilderness"), the illegitimate son of Olav, who is married and happy. Visiting the pair, Olav feels that family troubles cannot touch this son whom he cannot claim.

SONEZAKI SHINJÛ

Author: Chikamatsu Monzaemon (1653-1725)
Time of action: Eighteenth century
First presented: 1703

PRINCIPAL CHARACTERS

Gihei, a wealthy Japanese from the country who wants to spend an evening in Osaka with O Hatsu, a famous geisha; she refuses him. Later he abducts her for a while.

O Hatsu, a famous geisha, in love with a poor young man. To save the honor of Tokubei, she commits suicide, so that his traitorous friend cannot use her lover's money to ransom her.

Tokubei, a poor young man in love with O Hatsu. He refuses to marry an heiress, but he lends the dowry money to his friend, who refuses to return it so that it can be returned to the family of the girl Tokubei refuses to marry. To save his honor, Tokubei commits suicide, as does his beloved O Hatsu.

Kyûemon, Tokubei's uncle and employer. He tries to arrange Tokubei's marriage with an heiress. Too late he learns of his nephew's friend's evil ways. When he finds his nephew, Tokubei has already committed suicide.

Kuheiji, Tokubei's evil friend. In addition to taking the young man's money, Kuheiji plots to ransom O Hatsu and keep her for himself. His plan fails when she dies.

THE SONG OF BERNADETTE

Author: Franz Werfel (1890-1945)
Time of action: 1858-1875
First published: 1941

PRINCIPAL CHARACTERS

Bernadette Soubirous (bĕr·nȧ·dĕt′ sōō-bē·rōō′), a young girl of Lourdes, growing up in grinding poverty and generally regarded as hopelessly slow and stupid. One day she goes alone into the Grotto of Massabielle. A beautiful lady, shining with a brilliant light, appears to her. Bernadette's story becomes known, and she is reviled both as mad and as a fraud. People go with her on her repeated visits, but they see nothing. The lady bids Bernadette ask Dean Peyramale to build a chapel on the sight of the grotto. He insists that only a sign will convince him: a blooming rosebush in the cave in February. The lady bids Bernadette dig with her hands; to the following crowd Bernadette's actions seem mad. But a spring flows from the spot, and the soil applied to a blind man's eyes cures his blindness. Roses bloom in the cave, and at last the authorities agree that Bernadette has seen the Blessed Virgin. She becomes a nun, remaining calm and humble until she dies, more than seventeen years later, after a painful illness. Canonized, she is now a saint of the Roman Catholic Church.

François Soubirous (frän·swä′), Bernadette's father. Fallen into pitiful poverty, he and his family are dependent on the odd jobs he can beg from the prosperous citizens of Lourdes.

Louise Soubirous (lwēz′), his wife. She takes in washing, but this income added to her husband's is insufficient to take care of the family.

Sister Marie Thérèse (mȧ·rē′ tä·rĕz′), Bernadette's teacher, who regards the girl as impossibly stupid, even in her study of religion. Sister Marie Thérèse remains skeptical even after Bernadette becomes a nun; it is only on Bernadette's deathbed that Sister Marie Thérèse admits her error and her belief in the miracle.

Dean Peyramale (pä·rȧ·mȧl′), who refuses to build a chapel on the site of the grotto until he has evidence of a miracle in a blooming rosebush. Later, he becomes disappointed and saddened because he has been ignored by the Church authorities in the establishment of a shrine.

THE SONG OF HIAWATHA

Author: Henry Wadsworth Longfellow (1807-1882)
Time of action: Aboriginal period
First published: 1855

PRINCIPAL CHARACTERS

Hiawatha, an Indian with magic powers who grows up in the Lake Superior region and becomes a prophet and guide.

From the body of a stranger he conquers, Hiawatha gets corn. He defeats disease-bearing Pearl-Feather with the help of a woodpecker, whose feather tuft he streaks with red. He invents picture writing. Following the death of Minnehaha and the coming of the white man, Hiawatha leaves his tribe to travel through the Portals of the Sunset to the Land of the Hereafter.

Nokomis, who falls to earth from the full moon to become the mother of Wenonah and the counselor of Hiawatha.

Wenonah, who, despite her mother's warning, listens to the wooing of faithless Mudjekeewis and bears him a son, Hiawatha. When Mudjekeewis deserts her, she dies of grief.

Mudjekeewis, the immortal and fickle West Wind. He battles his vengeful son for three days, then sends him back to his people, as the prophet promised by the Great Spirit, to teach and unite them.

Minnehaha, the lovely daughter of a Dacotah arrowmaker, whom Hiawatha sees on his journey to avenge his mother's death, and whom he marries despite Nokomis' advice to chose a woman of his own tribe. She dies of fever during a winter famine.

Pearl-Feather, the evil magician who sends fever, pestilence, and disease on the Indians and is vulnerable only at the roots of his hair.

Kwasind, the strong friend of Hiawatha, who helps him dredge the rivers of roots and sandbars and rid the lake of its greatest menace, the sturgeon.

Chibiabos, the Indian singer of love songs.

Iagoo, the teller of fanciful tales, who entertains at Hiawatha's wedding feast.

THE SONG OF ROLAND

Author: Unknown, though the poem is described as a geste recited by Turoldus
Time of action: 778
First transcribed: Late eleventh century

PRINCIPAL CHARACTERS

Emperor Charlemagne, also called **King Charles** and **Carlon,** represented as being two hundred years old, with a flowing white beard, regal bearing, and undiminished vigor. He presides democratically over his court in an orchard near Cordova and accepts the majority view in favor of what proves to be a false peace pact with the Saracens. His militant zeal for Christianizing pagans is offset by his humble submission to fate when his beloved nephew Roland and twenty thousand of his troops are killed by Moorish forces in the Pass of Roncevaux. He laments the deaths of his men before taking terrible vengeance on their conquerors, but he is completely unmoved by the pleas of Ganelon, the traitor knight.

Roland, Duke of the Marches of Brittany and nephew of Charlemagne. The favorite of his uncle, he glories in his post as leader of the Emperor's rearguard, the exposed flank of the French army on its homeward march from Spain. Roland is the most outspoken of the Twelve Peers, a hater of all pagans, and the enemy of Ganelon, his stepfather; and his suggestion that Ganelon be sent to negotiate the truce proposed by the Saracens seems designed as a test of that knight's loyalty and honor. Brave in battle, Roland is also rash to the point of folly and lacking in

1061

foresight. He is the owner of the famous sword Durendal and the horn called Oliphant, both possessing supernatural powers. When Saracens attack the French force in the Pass of Roncevaux, he refuses to blow his horn and summon the main army until it is too late. Relying on his own Durendal and Christian supremacy over pagan knights, he dies by his simple chivalric code after facing the enemy and performing prodigious feats of valor.

Oliver, Roland's friend and fellow Peer. His prudence balances Roland's impetuosity, but his warnings are unable to save the day when the Saracen army attacks the French forces at Roncevaux. After estimating the enemy's strength he urges Roland to blow his horn, Oliphant, in order to summon Charlemagne and the chivalry of France riding ahead. Dismounted, he dies with honor, a ring of dead enemies piled about him.

Ganelon, also called **Guènes,** the traitor knight who nurses so deep a grudge against his stepson Roland that he conspires with Marsilion, the Saracen King of Saragossa, to betray the rearguard of the French army to the enemy. When Charlemagne hears the blast of Roland's horn, blown to summon aid of the Emperor, Ganelon derides his ruler. Later he is arrested and charged with treason. After his champion has been defeated in an ordeal by combat, he is tied to four stallions who tear his body apart as they pursue a galloping mare.

Archbishop Turpin, the militant churchman of Rheims, killed at Roncevaux. He absolves Charlemagne's host of sin before the battle and urges all to die like Christian soldiers. It is he who finally persuades Roland to blow his horn, Oliphant (a blast that bursts Roland's temples and helps to cause his death), and it is he who survives long enough to arrange the bodies of the Twelve Peers so that Charlemagne will find them, avenge them, and give them Christian burial. Charlemagne orders his heart, like those of Roland and Oliver, preserved in urns.

Gerin,
Gerier,
Ives,
Ivor,
Othon,
Berenger,
Anseis,
Samson,
Gerard of Roussillon, and
Engelier of Bordeaux, Charlemagne's Peers, also slain with Roland and Oliver.

Pinabel of Sorence, the knight who defends Ganelon, accused of treason, in an ordeal by battle.

Thierry, the younger brother of Duke Geoffrey of Anjou. He fights with and defeats Pinabel of Sorence in the ordeal by battle that decides Ganelon's guilt.

Duke Naimon,
Geoffrey, Duke of Anjou,
Ogier the Dane,
Count Jozeran of Provence, and
Antelme of Mayence, Charlemagne's loyal vassals and trusted advisers.

Walter de Hum, a valorous French knight killed at Roncevaux.

Marsilion, also called **Marsile,** the Saracen King of Saragossa. Acting on the advice of one of his nobles, he sends envoys to Charlemagne with promises that he will sign a treaty of peace and receive Christian baptism if the Emperor will withdraw his army from Spain. He leads the Saracen host against the French rearguard at Roncevaux. After Roland severs his sword hand as they struggle in hand-to-hand combat, Marsilion leaves the battle. Later he dies in his castle at Saragossa.

Blancandrin, the crafty Saracen knight who suggests the treacherous proposal that King Marsilion makes to Charlemagne. Ganelon plots with Blancandrin the destruction of the Twelve Peers and the French host at Roncevaux.

Adelroth, the nephew of King Marsilion,
Duke Falsaron,
King Corsablis,

Malprimis of Brigale,
The Emir of Balaguet,
The Lord of Moriana,
Turgis of Tortelosa,
Escremiz of Valterne,
Estorgan,
Estramarin,
Margaris of Seville, and
Chernubles of Munigre, King Marsilion's Twelve Champions killed by the Twelve Peers at Roncevaux.

Baligant, the Emir of Babylon and the ally of King Marsilion. He brings a mighty army to attack the French under Emperor Charlemagne. After a fierce battle that lasts from early morning until dusk the Emir and Charlemagne engage in single combat. Charlemagne, wounded, is heartened by Saint Gabriel. His strength renewed, he strikes with his sword the helmet of his enemy and cleaves him to his beard. The Saracens, seeing their leader dead, flee.

Aude, the damozel betrothed to Roland. Hearing that her lover is dead, she falls at Charlemagne's feet and dies.

Bramimond, the widow of King Marsilion. Charlemagne takes her with him when he returns to France, where she is baptized and given a Christian name, Juliana.

THE SONG OF SONGS

Author: Hermann Sudermann (1857-1928)
Time of action: Early twentieth century
First published: 1909

PRINCIPAL CHARACTERS

Lilly Czepanek (lĭ′lē tshe′pä·năk), an attractive and capable young woman. Deserted at fourteen by her music-master father, she is left entirely alone after the subsequent insanity of her mother. She makes an unhappy marriage, takes a lover, and is divorced by her husband. Gradually she sinks deeper into vice. Falling truly in love, she lies frantically about her past in her desire to keep the young man's friendship. The projected marriage is broken off by his uncle, and Lilly, in despair, unsuccessfully attempts suicide. She does, however, throw into the river a musical composition by her father, "The Song of Songs," which she has kept for years as a symbol of the fine and good in her life. At last she agrees to marry a man she does not love but with whom she has lived in the past.

Fritz Redlich (frĭts räd′lish), a high-minded young student whom Lilly admires before her first marriage. Misunderstanding her overtures of friendship, he spurns her. Years after her divorce she finds him destitute, looks after him, and secures a job for him. She wants to devote her life to his regeneration, but he still misunderstands her and again spurns her friendship.

Walter von Prell (väl′tĕr fôn prăll), a young lieutenant interested in Lilly. After her marriage, he becomes her lover.

Colonel von Mertzbach (fôn märts′-bäkh), Lilly's elderly, well-to-do, and jealous first husband. She marries him to gain security; in turn, she is to him little more than his chattel. Discovering her infidelity, he divorces her.

Richard Dehnicke (dā′nĭ·kă), a friend of von Prell living in Berlin. Lilly goes there after her divorce and becomes Dehnicke's mistress. He is much under the influence of his mother, who wants him to marry an heiress. At last his mother, like Lilly, resigns herself to the inevitable and his marriage to Lilly takes place.

1063

Kellermann (kă·lêr·män), a glass painter to whom Lilly goes to learn the art. She resists his advances until Dehnicke's temporary desertion at his mother's insistence. When Dehnicke returns, she resumes her old way of life with him.

Konrad Rennschmidt (kōn'räd rǎn'-shmǐt), a young art history student with whom Lilly finds true happiness. When the lies she has told him are exposed to his uncle, she is forced to give him up.

Miss von Schwertfeger (fôn shvĕrt'fä-gĕr), the Colonel's housekeeper. Because she hates the Colonel, who for years forced her to be a party to mad orgies in his castle, she keeps secret Lilly's infidelity when the Colonel almost discovers the affair with von Prell.

Mrs. Czepanek (tshe'pä·năk), Lilly's mother, who loses her mind and, after attacking Lilly with a bread knife, is committed to an asylum.

Mrs. Asmussen (äs'mo͝os·sen), in whose circulating library Lilly works as a clerk after her mother is committed and until her first marriage.

Lona Asmussen (lō'nä äs'mo͝os·sen) and Mi Asmussen (mē äs'mo͝os·sen), the worldly daughters of Lilly's employer. They coach her in the ways of catching men and are then jealous of her success in attracting them.

THE SONG OF THE LARK

Author: Willa Cather (1873-1947)
Time of action: Late nineteenth and early twentieth centuries
First published: 1915

PRINCIPAL CHARACTERS

Thea Kronborg, the daughter of the Swedish Methodist pastor in Moonstone, Colorado, a grave, shyly awkward girl in whom a few perceptive people see qualities of imagination and desire still without shape or direction. A down-at-heels German pianist finds in her the promise of great talent as a musician and tries to explain to her that beside the artist's vision of fulfillment the world and all life are petty and small. Dr. Howard Archie, a physician poorly adjusted to the community in which he practices, hopes that she will realize in her life the things he has missed in his. Her eccentric Aunt Tilly claims that the day is coming when Moonstone will be proud of her niece. Ray Kennedy, a young railroad conductor, has fallen in love with Thea and is waiting to marry her when she grows older. The German musician teaches her all he can before he leaves town after one of his drunken sprees. When Ray Kennedy is killed in a wreck, he leaves Thea six hundred dollars in life insurance. With the money she goes to Chicago to study piano under Andor Harsanyi, who discovers that her true talent is in her voice. She then takes lessons from Madison Bowers, a celebrated voice teacher. He introduces her to Fred Ottenburg, the heir to a brewery fortune and an enthusiastic art amateur. The young beer baron takes an interest in Thea, arranges singing engagements for her, and when she reaches a point of physical and spiritual exhaustion sends her to his father's ranch in Arizona for a rest. There, exploring the ruins of an ancient civilization, she has an almost mystic vision of art as the discipline of form imposed on raw materials, as in Indian pottery. Accepting Ottenburg's proposal of marriage, she goes to Mexico with him, only to learn that he already has a wife from whom he is estranged. With money borrowed from Dr. Archie she goes to Germany to continue her studies. After her first success abroad she returns to make a triumphant career as an opera star, and she marries Ottenburg after his wife's death. Harsanyi declares that the secret of Thea's success is passion, as inimitable as heroism in cheap materials. Miss Cather says that it results from the single-minded dedication and discipline that art demands. Thea's story, as told in Willa Cather's most full-bodied novel, is based in part on the career of Olive Fremstad.

Herr A. Wunsch, Thea Kronborg's piano teacher in Moonstone. Formerly a distinguished musician, now ruined by drink, he drifts into Moonstone and is temporarily reclaimed from his sodden ways by Fritz Kohler, a German tailor, and his wife. They give Wunsch a home and look after him while he resumes his career as a teacher. He is the first to discover Thea's musical talent. Eventually he relapses into his old habits, goes on a wild drunken spree, and leaves town. His parting gift to Thea is the tattered score of Gluck's "Orpheus," which he had saved from his student days.

Dr. Howard Archie, an imaginative, sympathetic doctor who becomes interested in Thea after he attends her during an attack of pneumonia. Hoping to save her from the mediocrity of Moonstone life in which he himself has been trapped, he suggests that she use the insurance money inherited from Ray Kennedy to continue her musical studies. Later his own affairs prosper from the development of some mining property and he becomes active in business and political life in Denver. He follows Thea's career with interest and lends her the money to study abroad. Better than anyone else, he understands the miracle of chance and endeavor that carries Thea from the crudeness and vulgarity of a Colorado mountain town to her great career as a singer.

Belle Archie, the doctor's wife, a fanatical woman engaged in a constant campaign against dust. She dies as the result of her passion for cleanliness, when gasoline she is using to clean furniture explodes, burning her and the house.

Fritz Kohler, a tailor, one of the first settlers in Moonstone. German-born, he has never forgotten his earlier years in his homeland. He rescues Herr Wunsch, the broken-down German music teacher, from his dirty room over a saloon, gives him a proper home, and for a time turns the old drunkard into a respectable citizen and competent teacher. Kohler has three grown sons who work and live away from home; they are ashamed of their father's broken English, his European ways, and his sentimental memories of the past.

Paulina Kohler, his wife, a woman dedicated to making her husband comfortable and her garden grow. Indifferent to the town's opinion, she wears the same clothing summer and winter, prefers men's shoes to women's, and cultivates plants instead of friends. Her garden resembles a small corner of the Rhine Valley set down in an expanse of sage brush and sand. Generous and warm-hearted to those she likes, she welcomes Thea into her home. Through her friendship with the Kohlers and Herr Wunsch, Thea catches a glimpse of a different world, of older, more cultured, less materialistic European life as illustrated by the older generation of immigrants.

Johnny Tellamantez, called **Spanish Johnny,** a temperamental musician living in the Mexican settlement on the outskirts of Moonstone. A painter by trade, he is given to periodic spells of restlessness when he suddenly leaves home and travels through the West and Mexico. On these trips, from which he usually returns exhausted and ill, he earns his way by singing and playing his mandolin in bars and cafés. Thea Kronborg scandalizes the proper citizens of Moonstone by going to Mexican Town to hear Johnny and his friends play their folk songs.

Ray Kennedy, a freight train conductor

on the run between Moonstone and Denver. Older than Thea Kronborg, he has fallen in love with her and hopes to marry her when she grows up. He is fatally injured in a railroad wreck. After his death it is learned that Thea is the beneficiary of his six-hundred-dollar life insurance policy.

Philip Frederick Ottenburg, the younger son of a wealthy family of brewers, a lover of music, and a patron of the arts. Years before, barely out of college, he had made an unfortunate marriage, and he now lives apart from his violently hysterical, mentally deranged wife. Meeting Thea Kronborg at the studio of Madison Bowers in Chicago, Ottenburg is immediately attracted to the reserved yet intense young girl from Moonstone, both as a woman and as an artist. When Thea, exhausted by intense study and hard work, seems on the verge of a breakdown, he sends her to his father's ranch at Panther Canyon, Arizona, to recuperate. When he sees her again she has been revitalized by her summer in hot sun and dry air, and he asks her to marry him. Hating himself for his deception, but able to rationalize his act, he takes Thea to Mexico, only to lose her when she learns that he is already married. He tries to lend her the money for study in Europe, but she rejects his offer and asks her old friend, Dr. Archie, for a loan. Thea and Ottenburg resume their friendship when she returns from Europe, and she marries him after his wife's death.

Andor Harsanyi, the brilliant young musician under whom Thea Kronborg studies piano in Chicago. Like Herr Wunsch, he is baffled by the combination of talent, intelligence, and ignorance in her nature, her stubborn secrecy and determined resolve. After working with her for a time, he discovers that she possesses an untrained but magnificent voice.

Madison Bowers, the teacher under whom Thea Kronborg studies voice. She admires him as a teacher but dislikes him

as a man because of his fashionable following. Bowers is cynically amused when Fred Ottenburg begins to take an interest in Thea and her career.

Pastor Peter Kronborg, an unimaginative but sincerely dedicated minister.

Mrs. Kronborg, his wife, a practical woman who shows instinctive common sense. Although she never understands her daughter Thea, she sees in her traits possessed by none of her other children, and she respects the girl's reserve. She dies while Thea is on a concert tour in Germany.

Axel,
Gunnar,
Gus,
Charley,
Thor, and
Anna, Thea Kronborg's brothers and sister. During the last summer she spends in Moonstone she realizes that they are like the other citizens of the town, commonplace, smug, narrow-minded.

Tilly Kronborg, Thea's well-meaning but garrulous and silly aunt, always confident that her niece was marked for greatness. The last Kronborg left in Moonstone, she takes innocent delight in Thea's fame and basks comfortably in that reflected glory.

Lily Fisher, Thea Kronborg's girlhood musical revival. Lily represents Moonstone's idea of culture, a pretty song sung by a pretty girl.

Mrs. Livery Johnson, a Baptist, a member of the W.C.T.U., and the arbiter of culture in Moonstone.

Mrs. Lorch, the motherly landlady with whom Thea Kronborg lives during her first winter in Chicago.

Mrs. Andersen, Mrs. Lorch's daughter, who tries to interest Thea Kronborg in art museums and other cultural centers in Chicago. Acting on her advice, Thea goes to the Art Institute where she finds a picture that moves her subtly; it is Breton's "The Song of the Lark."

Oliver Landry, a musician, Thea Kron-

borg's friend, and for a time her accompanist. He is an entertainer at Weber and Fields'.

SONG OF THE WORLD

Author: Jean Giono (1895-   )
Time of action: Early twentieth century
First published: 1934

PRINCIPAL CHARACTERS

Danis (dà·nē'), the red-haired son of Sailor, who fatally wounds Médéric in a quarrel over Gina. Enraged by his father's murder, he burns Maudru's property; then, in the excitement, he is able to escape Maudru's men.

Sailor (sā·lôr'), Danis' woodcutter father, who goes searching for him. While drunk, he is stabbed by two drovers, who are Maudru's men.

Junie (zhü·nē'), Sailor's wife and Jérôme's sister.

Antonio (än·tō·nyō'), a semi-primitive man of the river, called "Goldenmouth," who accompanies Sailor in his search for Danis.

Maudru (mō·drü'), a wealthy ox-tamer whose word is law in the Rebeillard region of France.

Gina (zhē·nà'), his daughter, who is supposed to marry her cousin Médéric, but is carried off by Danis.

Clara (klà·rá'), a blind unmarried woman found in childbirth in the woods by Sailor and Antonio. Antonio loves her and takes her back home with him.

Jérôme (zhā·rōm'), a hunch-back healer called Monsieur Toussaint in the village. He hides Danis, his nephew, and Gina in his house, and tries unsuccessfully to heal Médéric's wound.

Médéric (mà·dā·rēk'), the nephew of Maudru. He is shot by Danis, who then abducts young Gina.

Gina (zhē·nà'), Médéric's mother and Maudru's sister, a hard, capable woman.

SONS AND LOVERS

Author: D. H. Lawrence (1885-1930)
Time of action: Late nineteenth and early twentieth centuries
First published: 1913

PRINCIPAL CHARACTERS

Walter Morel, an English collier in many ways typical of the literary image of the lower-class workingman. He is not interested in the arts, in matters of the intellect, or even greatly in his work, which for him is merely a source of income. He is a creature who lives for whatever pleasures he can find in eating,

drinking, and his bed. At first a warmly vital man, he later becomes rough and brutal to his family and fights with them verbally and physically. His wife, after the first glow of marriage fades, means little to him because of her puritanical attitudes and regard for culture, and he becomes alienated from his children. His one creative joy is mending odd bits of household equipment and his work clothing. A coal miner he has been since boyhood, and a coal miner he is content to be.

Gertrude Morel, Walter Morel's wife, a woman who has married beneath her class and who soon regrets her action. She is quickly disillusioned by her husband, and the glamor of their courtship soon fades. She discovers her husband has debts he tells her he has paid and that he constantly lies about the little money he brings home. He always saves out some money for his drinking, regardless of how little he earns at the mine. In her disillusionment Mrs. Morel turns to her children for understanding and affection, as well as to protect them from their father's brutality when drunk. As the sons and daughter appear on the scene each becomes a focal point for the mother's love. She tries to help them escape the little mining community, and she succeeds. On her second son, Paul, she places a blight by centering her affections upon him and loving him too well, making him the recipient of love that should have been given to her husband. Her affection and attentions cause him to be stunted emotionally. She never realizes what she is doing to the talented young man but always believes that she is working in his best interest by keeping him at home and governing his affections. Her life is cut short by cancer; Paul ends her terrible pain by giving her an overdose of opiates. Even after her death her influence lingers in his life, so that he shows little evidence of developing into an individual, fulfilled personality.

Paul Morel, the second child of Walter and Gertrude Morel. After his older brother goes off to London to take a job Paul receives the bulk of his mother's affection; she helps him find work as a clerk close to home so that he can continue to live with his family. He receives encouragement to study art and becomes a successful part-time painter and designer. But Paul's mother and her influence keep him from growing up. Though he fights against her ruling his life, he is trapped. He readily understands how she forces him to give up his love for Miriam Leivers, whom he courts for many years, but he fails to see that his ability to love any woman as an adult man has been crippled by his emotional attachment to his mother.

William Morel, Paul's older brother. When he leaves his family to go to London, his mother transfers her obsessive affections to Paul. William falls in love with a shallow, pseudo-sophisticated girl who takes his money readily, even for her personal clothing, and treats his family as her servants. Though he sees through the girl, William feels trapped into marrying her. A tragic marriage for him is averted only through his sudden and untimely death.

Miriam Leivers, a young farm girl with a highly spiritual yet possessive nature. She and Paul Morel are companions until their late teens, when Miriam falls in love with the young man. She spends a great deal of time with him, for he undertakes to educate her in French, algebra, and other subjects, but his mother objects strenuously to the girl, especially when Paul seems to return the girl's love. Of a highly romantic nature, Miriam is repelled by the physical aspects of love until she is slowly persuaded to give herself to her lover, who later breaks off his engagement to her, saying that in her need for a committed love she wants too much from him.

Clara Dawes, a handsome, married, but physically emancipated woman living apart from her husband. She becomes Paul Morel's mistress and comes as close as anyone can to helping him achieve the ability to love as an adult. At last even she despairs of him and, with his help, is reconciled to her husband, from whom she has been separated many years.

Jason Lycurgus Compson (III), grandson of a Mississippi governor, son of a Confederate general, and father to the last of the Compsons. Like his illustrious ancestors, his name suggested his passion, the classics. Unlike his forbears, he is unable to make a living or to fulfill his deepest ambition, the study of the Greek and Latin epigrammatists, but his stoic philosophy, culled from his reading, stands him in good stead. He speaks wisely, does little, drinks much, and is weary of his complaining wife, his wayward daughter, and his bickering sons.

Caroline Bascomb Compson, his wife, who resents the Compson lineage and feels that hers is more glorious. A neurotic woman with psychosomatic symptons, she complains constantly of her grievances and ills. Reluctant to face reality and rejoicing that she was not born a Compson, she indulges her fancies and pretends to be an ante-bellum Southern gentlewoman. Her fortitude in tragedy is even more remarkable for all her complaining, but she victimizes her children and devoted servants to maintain her resentment and illnesses.

Candace Compson, their only daughter, affectionate, loyal, libido-driven. Called **Caddy**, a name which results in great confusion for her idiot brother whose playground is the pasture sold to a golf course where he hears her name, she herself is doomed, though devoted to her dead brother, her weak-minded brother, her own illegitimate daughter, her loving father. She is at odds with her mother, her vengeful brother Jason, and several husbands. So promiscuous is she, even urging her sensitive brother Quentin to abortive intercourse, that she does not really know the father of her child. As an adventuress she travels widely, and in the postlude to the novel appears as the consort of a Nazi officer in Paris.

Quentin Compson, her beloved brother for whom she names her child even before the baby's birth. Obsessed by a sense of guilt, doom, and death, he commits suicide by drowning in June, 1910, two months after his sister's marriage to a man he calls a blackguard. Because he is deeply disturbed by family affairs— the selling of a pasture to pay for his year at Harvard, the loss of his sister's honor, the morbid despair he feels for his idiot brother, his hatred of the family vices of pride and snobbishness—his death is predictable, unalterable.

Jason Compson (IV), the only son to stay on in the Old Compson place, loyal to his weak querulous mother, determined to gain his full share of his patronage, bitter over his deep failures. His tale is one of petty annoyances, nursed grievances, and egotistic aggressiveness in his ungenerous and self-assertive mastery of his niece and the colored servants. This descendant of aristocrats is more the type of small-town redneck, wily, canny, cunning, and deceitful. Not without his reasons for bitterness, he finally rids himself of his enervating responsibilities for a dying line by himself remaining a bachelor and having his idiot brother castrated.

Quentin, the daughter of Candace and her mother's own child. Reared by Dilsey, the colored cook, Quentin is the last of anything resembling life in the old Compson house. As self-assertive as her uncle, she steals money he calls his but which is rightfully hers, and elopes with a carnival pitchman. Beautiful in the wild way of her mother, she has never had affection from anyone except her morbid old grandmother and a brokenhearted servant. She is possibly Caddy's child by a young man named Dalton Ames.

Dilsey Gibson, the bullying but beloved colored family retainer, cook, financier (in petty extravagances), and benefactress who maintains family standards that no longer concern the Compsons.

Deeply concerned for them, she babies the thirty-year-old Benjamin, the unfortunate Quentin, the querulous old "Miss Cahline," though she resists the egocentric Jason. A woman whose wise understanding nature is beyond limits of race or color, she endures for others and prolongs the lives of those dependent on her shrewdness and strength.

Benjamin Compson, called **Benjy,** at first named Maury after his mother's brother. He is an idiot who observes everything, smells tragedy, loves the old pasture, his sister Caddy, firelight, but cannot compose his disordered thoughts into any coherent pattern of life or speech. Gelded by his brother Jason, he moans out his pitiful existence and is finally sent to the State Asylum in Jackson.

Maury L. Bascomb, Mrs. Compson's brother. A bachelor, a drunkard, and a philanderer, he is supported by the Compsons. Benjy Compson was christened Maury, after his uncle.

Roskus, the Compsons' colored coachman when the children were small.

T.P., a colored servant who helps to look after Benjy Compson. He later goes to Memphis to live.

Luster, a fourteen-year-old colored boy who is thirty-three-year-old Benjy Compson's caretaker and playmate.

Frony, Dilsey's daughter.

Sydney Herbert Head, a young banker, Caddy Compson's first husband. He divorces her after he realizes that her daughter Quentin is not his child. The divorce ends young Jason Compson's hope of getting a position in Head's bank.

Shreve McCannon, Quentin Compson's Canadian roommate at Harvard.

SOUTH WIND

Author: Norman Douglas (1868-1952)
Time of action: Early twentieth century
First published: 1917

PRINCIPAL CHARACTERS

Bishop Heard of Bampopo, an English clergyman who goes to the Isle of Nepenthe to meet his cousin and escort her to England, where he is going from Africa.

Don Francesco, a Roman Catholic priest who introduces Bishop Heard to Nepenthean society.

The Duchess of San Martino, an American-born woman who married a title. She is being converted to Catholicism.

Mr. Keith, an ardent, aging hedonist. He believes people ought to do what they wish.

Denis Phipps, a college student who confides in Bishop Heard. He finally learns how to make a decision for himself.

Mr. Eames, an elderly scholar.

Count Caloveglia, an antiquarian and a dealer in fake antiques.

Freddy Parker, the proprietor of a café. He sponsors a religious procession in an effort to end an eruption of the local volcano.

Miss Wilberforce, an American who drinks heavily and undresses in the streets.

Mr. Van Koppen, an American millionaire. He is something of an eccentric. When cheated by Count Caloveglia, he pays the outrageous price, pleased that the Count has fooled an expert.

Mrs. Meadows, the Bishop's cousin. She

mother of Clara. She is a counterpart to her husband and is not sharply individualized.

Álvarez de Castilla (äl′bä·räth thä käs·tē′lyä), an old lord, brother-in-law of the Corregidor. Having killed old Castro, the father of Louis, he has fled and lives in banishment disguised as the leader of a band of gipsy entertainers. In order to save the life of John, living with the gipsies as Andrew, he reveals himself to Louis and offers the latter revenge for the slaying of his father.

Guiamara (gyä·mä′rä), the wife of Álvarez, sister of Fernando. As Eugenia, she lives with her husband as queen of the gipsies. She reveals herself to her brother and returns his lost daughter Constanza to him.

Constanza (kōn·stän′thä), the daughter of Fernando. Called **Pretiosa** (prā·tyō′sä), she is a pert young girl in her early teens living with her aunt among the gipsies. She leads her lover John a merry chase and makes him join the gipsies. When his life is imperiled by a false accusation, she pleads strenuously for him and claims him as her husband-to-be. When he is released and both are recognized by their relatives, they are betrothed.

Cardochia (kär·dō′chyä), a young hostess with whom the gipsies stay. She is seized with an ungovernable passion for John (Andrew). When he rebuffs her because of his love for the supposed Pretiosa, she falsely accuses him of theft to her lover Diego, who attacks him and is dangerously wounded. She finally confesses that her accusation is false, and John is freed.

John (Andrew), the son of Francisco. In love with Constanza, he disguises himself and lives with the gipsies. She gives him little encouragement until he is in peril. He behaves with nobility under his false accusation and unjust imprisonment.

Francisco de Carcomo (frän·thēs′kō thä kär·kō′mō), the father of John. He is disturbed by the unexplained absence of his son. When the latter is saved from unjust execution, he rejoices in his return and consents to his marriage with Constanza, after her noble birth has been revealed.

Louis de Castro (lö·ēs′ thä käs′trō), a young nobleman dedicated to revenge for his dead father. He is an unwilling but nonetheless guilty participant in the kidnaping of Clara, whom he does not recognize at the time. Later he woos her with the consent of both her parents, but cannot get her consent. He does not understand her reluctance, since Roderigo in keeping with his promise to her has assured Louis that he released her unharmed. The nobility of Álvarez rouses his own nobility, and they become reconciled.

Diego (dyä′gō), the third of the young men involved in the kidnaping of Clara. He is in love with Cardochia and believes her false accusation of John de Carcomo. This belief leads him to attack John and nearly costs both of them their lives. He recovers, pleads for forgiveness for Cardochia, and takes her back.

Sancho (sän′chō), the foolish, self-satisfied ward of Don Pedro. He too lives for a while with the gipsies, offering gold and self-composed verse.

Soto (sō′tō), Sancho's servant. He is his master's companion in the gipsy venture.

Carlo (kär′lō) and
Antonio (än·tō′nyō), pretended gipsies.

Christiana (krēs·tyä′nä), a gentlewoman disguised as a gipsy.

THE SPANISH TRAGEDY

Author: Thomas Kyd (1558?-1594)
Time of action: Sixteenth century
First presented: c. 1585

PRINCIPAL CHARACTERS

Revenge, the master of ceremonies, forming a chorus with the Ghost of Andrea.

The Ghost of Andrea (än·drā'ä), Bel-Imperia's slain beloved. He complains bitterly at the delay of the revenge of his death. He still loves Bel-Imperia and his friend Horatio, who succeeds him as her lover. At the end he is satisfied with the vengeance accomplished.

Hieronimo (hī·ər·ŏn'ī·mō), Marshal of Spain, father of Don Horatio. A proud and devoted father, he pleads for his son's rights in the capture and ransom of Don Balthazar. He is driven almost to madness by the murder of his son (in the later additions to the play, he suffers actual madness). To avert suspicion from his planned revenge, he feigns madness, thus foreshadowing Hamlet. Despairing of justice for himself, he still acts as a just judge. He is gifted as a dramatic writer and actor, furnishing a pageant for the triumph at the beginning of the play, and executing his plan for revenge in a play written and acted by himself with Bel-Imperia and the murderers of his son as supporting actors.

Bel-Imperia (bĕl·ĭm·pĭr'ĭ·ä), daughter of Don Cyprian, sister of Lorenzo. She is a somewhat enigmatic character, devoted to the memory of Andrea and apparently capable of love, even passion, for Horatio, but cold-bloodedly using her love to further her revenge. She scorns her suitor Balthazar, and after the murder of Horatio, she joins forces with Hieronimo and acts a bloody part in his play within the play.

Horatio (hō·rā'shĭ·ō), best friend of the slain Andrea. Courageous and noble, he has captured the slayer of his friend. He loves Bel-Imperia, and because of this love he is trapped and murdered.

Lorenzo (lô·rĕn'zō), Don Cyprian's Machiavellian son. A cold-blooded, ambitious, treacherous man, he tries to promote a marriage between his sister and the Portuguese Prince. Finding that Horatio is in the way of this match, he engineers his murder; then, for security, he has one of his murdering tools kill the other and go to the gallows for the second death. He keeps Hieronimo from the King's ear and undermines the old man with lies, but underestimates him. Hieronimo arranges the play within the play so that his own hand can cut down Lorenzo.

The King of Spain, Don Cyprian's brother. He is a fair and just ruler, but does not learn of the truth in time to help Hieronimo.

Don Cyprian (dōn sĭp'rĭ·ən), Duke of Castile. He marvels at the realism of the action in Hieronimo's play, not realizing that the deaths of his two children are real. At the end of the play Hieronimo stabs him, too, before killing himself.

Balthazar (bǎl'thȧ·zär), the young Prince of Portugal, killer of Andrea, captive of Horatio. Released into Lorenzo's custody by the King, he woos Bel-Imperia sedulously in spite of her obvious distaste for him. He is involved in the murder of Horatio and plays into Lorenzo's hands by insisting on the hanging of Pedringano. By so doing, however, he helps destroy both Lorenzo and himself, for Pedringano's death leads to Hieronimo's discovery of the murderers.

The Viceroy of Portugal, father of Don

1076

Balthazar. Grieved over the supposed death of his son and deceived by Viluppo, he almost has his innocent follower Alexandro executed; however, he learns the truth in time to release Alexandro and executes Viluppo.

Alexandro (ä·lek·sän′drō), the Viceroy's loyal nobleman, barely saved from undeserved death.

Viluppo (vē·lŭp′ō), an envious, treacherous villain in the Portuguese court.

Pedringano (pä·drēn·gä′nō), Bel-Imperia's servant. Terrified by Lorenzo, he betrays to him the secret meeting of Bel-Imperia and aids in the murder of Lorenzo. At Lorenzo's instigation, and with a written commission from him, he kills Serberine, his partner in the murder. He foolishly believes that Lorenzo has procured him a pardon and insults his judge Hieronimo and the hangman. At the height of his self-confident impudence, he is hanged; however, he leaves behind evidence incriminating Lorenzo in the murder of Horatio.

Serberine (sėr′bėr·ēn), Balthazar's servingman. He shares in the murder of Horatio and is killed by Pedringano for Lorenzo. The watch, having been alerted by Lorenzo, apprehends Pedringano immediately after the murder of Serberine.

Isabella (ĭz′ə·bĕl′ə), Hieronimo's wife. An adoring mother, she is driven mad by the murder of Horatio and cuts down the arbor in which he has been hanged.

A General, commander of the Spanish forces against Portugal. He gives to the King the account of the death of Andrea and the capture of Balthazar by Horatio.

Christophil (krĭs′tə·fĭl), Bel-Imperia's custodian during her imprisonment by Lorenzo.

The Portuguese Ambassador. His return from Spain with news of Balthazar saves Alexandro's life.

Bazulto (bä·thŭl′tō), an old man whose son has been murdered. Hieronimo shows compassion for him as a fellow sufferer.

A Hangman, a simple man, amazed at Pedringano's impudence in the face of death, later fearful of the consequences of the hanging. He delivers Lorenzo's commission for the murder to Hieronimo.

Perseda (pĕr′sə·dä), an Italian lady (acted by Bel-Imperia),
Soliman (sŏl′ĭ·mən), the Turkish Emperor (acted by Balthazar),
Erasto (ə·räs′tō), **The Knight of Rhodes,** Perseda's lover (acted by Lorenzo), and
The Bashaw (bə·shô′), the Sultan's treacherous follower (acted by Hieronimo), characters in Hieronimo's play within the play, in which he gets revenge and discloses the murder of Horatio.

THE SPOILERS

Author: Rex Beach (1877-1949)
Time of action: The Alaska gold rush
First published: 1906

PRINCIPAL CHARACTERS

Roy Glenister, co-owner of the Midas gold mine. He fights heroically with law and fists to defend himself and his property in the wild Yukon gold country. He falls in love with Helen Chester, until he finds her apparently in league with crooks to cheat the miners of their claims. He is finally convinced of her innocence.

Bill Dextry, co-owner of the Midas gold

mine. He is an old frontiersman who likes living beyond the edge of civilization. When law and order arrive in the gold fields, he announces that he is selling his part of the mine and leaving.

Helen Chester, an American girl who unwittingly helps a crooked politician in his attempt to steal the miners' claims. With Glenister and Dextry's help she stows away aboard a ship bound for Alaska. She falls in love with Glenister, finally convinces him of her innocence of wrongdoing and offers to stay with him in Alaska.

Cherry Malotte, a notorious woman of Nome. She loves Glenister and tries to help him by telling him of the activities of McNamara, Judge Stillman, and Helen.

Mr. McNamara, a crooked politician. In league with Judge Stillman, he tries to steal the miners' gold claims. He is defeated in his efforts by Glenister, who leads the miners in their fight for justice. He is beaten by Glenister in one of the most famous fist fights in American literature.

Judge Stillman, Helen's uncle and the first federal judge in Alaska. He helps McNamara in the latter's attempts to steal the mining claims.

Mr. Struve, a crooked lawyer who aids McNamara and Judge Stillman in their plots against Glenister and the other miners.

The Broncho Kid, Helen's long-lost brother, a gambler. When Struve attacks Helen because of her knowledge of his dishonest dealings, the Broncho Kid appears and rescues her after shooting Struve.

THE SPOILS OF POYNTON

Author: Henry James (1843-1916)
Time of action: Late nineteenth century
First published: 1897

PRINCIPAL CHARACTERS

Mrs. Gereth, the mistress of Poynton. During her husband's lifetime, she and Mr. Gereth had filled Poynton with carefully chosen, exquisite furnishings that had made her beloved house a place of beauty and charm. Apprehensive over the fate of her cherished objects in the hands of Poynton's heir, her insensitive son Owen, she attempts to manipulate his relationships to guarantee the preservation of the estate and its contents as they are, only to see the house and furnishings finally consumed by fire.

Owen Gereth, Mrs. Gereth's son and the heir to Poynton. Insensitive to the real beauty of Poynton but loving it as his home, he is torn, abetted by his mother's manipulations, between Mona Brigstock, who desires the house for the value of its contents, and Fleda Vetch, who loves it for its beauty. He marries Mona and loses Poynton in a fire.

Mona Brigstock, Owen Gereth's fiancée and later his wife. Although she fails to appreciate Poynton's beauty, she is fully aware of the value of its contents. Finally, triumphant over the manipulations of Mrs. Gereth, she marries Owen shortly before Poynton and its contents are lost in a fire.

Fleda Vetch, Mrs. Gereth's companion. Loving Poynton for the beauty of the place, she is chosen by Mrs. Gereth as a suitable wife for her son Owen, the heir to Poynton. Fleda falls in love with Owen but loses him to Mona Brigstock.

THE SPY

Author: James Fenimore Cooper (1789-1851)
Time of action: 1780; 1812
First published: 1821

PRINCIPAL CHARACTERS

Harvey Birch, a peddler, generally believed to be a British spy, in this novel of the American Revolution. He is, however, an American patriot spying against the British.

Mr. Harper, the assumed name of disguised General George Washington.

Mr. Wharton, a British sympathizer who extends his hospitality to "Mr. Harper" during a storm.

Frances Wharton, his daughter, an ideal American woman who is in love with Major Peyton Dunwoodie.

Sarah Wharton, another daughter, whose plans of marriage to Colonel Wellmere are interrupted by news that Wellmere already has a wife who has just crossed from England expecting to join him.

Henry Wharton, the son of Mr. Wharton. A captain in the British Army, he is wrongly sentenced to hang as a British spy, but escapes through the good offices of Harvey Birch and with the help of "Mr. Harper," who thus rewards Mr. Wharton's hospitality.

Major Peyton Dunwoodie, an ideal American officer. He wins the hand of Frances Wharton.

Colonel Wellmere, a British officer professing to be in love with Sarah Wharton, though he has a wife in England.

Captain Lawton, an American officer finally killed in combat with the British, but previously engaged in a gentlemanly pursuit of the supposed British spy Birch.

Isabella Singleton, the sister of an American officer who is recuperating at the Wharton home. Frances believes Isabella's love for Major Dunwoodie is returned until Isabella, accidentally and fatally wounded, assures her of the contrary.

Miss Jeanette Peyton, the aunt of Sarah and Frances Wharton, also a member of the Wharton household.

Caesar Thompson, the Whartons' Negro servant.

Captain Wharton Dunwoodie, the son of Major Dunwoodie and Frances, and an officer in the War of 1812. After a battle he finds on the body of Harvey Birch a letter which reveals the old man's long years of self-sacrificing patriotism.

THE STAR OF SEVILLE

Author: Unknown, but sometimes attributed to Lope de Vega (1562-1635)
Time of action: Thirteenth century
First presented: c. 1617

PRINCIPAL CHARACTERS

Sancho IV (sän'chō), called **Sancho the Brave,** King of Castile, who falls in love with Estrella Tabera, the betrothed of

Don Sancho Ortiz. The King, in disguise, bribes his way into her home but is recognized by her brother, who refuses to acknowledge him as the King, claiming that no ruler would stoop to dishonor. Unable to act in his own person, the King promises Don Sancho any bride he may choose in return for killing an enemy. Don Sancho, finding that he must kill his fiancée's brother, is faithful to his oath of loyalty and kills Don Bustos. Imprisoned, he loyally remains silent, and King Sancho must order his execution. At the plea of Estrella, he gives her power to decide the fate of Don Sancho. When she frees him, the King is forced to confess his own guilt.

Estrella Tabera (ĕs·trä′lyä tä·bā′rä), the Star of Seville. When her fiancé, Don Sancho, kills her brother at the King's command, she saves his life but refuses to marry him because of the murder.

Don Bustos Tabera (dōn bōōs′tös tä-bā′rä), Estrella's brother, who insults the disguised King and is killed in a duel by his sister's fiancé.

Don Sancho Ortiz (dōn sän′chō ôr·tēth′), Estrella's betrothed. At the King's command, he kills her brother and, unswervingly loyal, refuses to reveal the truth. He is saved from execution by Estrella, but they never marry.

Don Arias (dōn ä′ryäs), the King's confidant.

Don Pedro de Guzmán (dōn pā′drō t̪hā gōōth·män′) and
Don Farfán de Riviera (dōn fär·fän′ t̪hā rē·byä′rä), alcaldes of Seville.

Matilde (mä·tēl′dä), a maid who admits the disguised King to Estrella's house. She is hanged by Don Bustos.

Clarindo (klä·rēn′dō), Don Sancho's servant.

STATE FAIR

Author: Phil Stong (1899-1957)
Time of action: Early 1930's
First published: 1932

PRINCIPAL CHARACTERS

Abel Frake, a prosperous farmer. The story is concerned with his family's preparations for the state fair at Des Moines and with what happens to all of them there. Abel's chief concern is for his fine boar, Blue Boy.

Melissa Frake, his wife. She is anxious over the reception of her jars of pickles; they win three blue ribbons.

Wayne Frake, their son. Before leaving for the fair, he is concerned that his girl seems changed. At the fair he meets another girl.

Emily, the daughter of a stock-show manager. In her hotel room she gives Wayne his first taste of liquor and his first sexual experience. She refuses his proposal of marriage because she does not want to settle down on the farm.

Margy Frake, Wayne's sister. At the fair, she meets a newspaper reporter on a roller coaster and falls in love with him. On another night they ride the roller coaster again and make love on a grassy spot near the tent grounds.

Pat Gilbert, the reporter Margy meets. He proposes marriage but Margy refuses because she knows that he will be unhappy as a permanent resident of Des Moines.

Eleanor, Wayne's old girl, who is home from her first year in college. She does not want to be committed to promises for the future.

Harry Ware, Margy's suitor at home. Before leaving for the fair, she receives a proposal of marriage from him. But she is not certain of what she wants.

Tom Sawyer, Huckleberry Finn, and other realistic boys in American fiction.

Captain Nutter, his hale and cheery grandfather.

Miss Abigail, the captain's prim and strict sister who keeps house for him and abhors the odor of tobacco.

Kitty Collins, the Nutter maid, an Irish girl deserted by her sailor husband, who finally returns to live with her in a seaside cottage.

Bill Conway, Tom's bullying enemy.

Seth Rodgers, another enemy.

Sailor Ben, Tom's friend and Kitty's husband, who shows Tom and his friends how to fire the Trefethen cannon.

Phil Adams, a school friend who teaches Tom how to fight.

Pepper Whitcomb, a friend struck by Tom's misdirected arrow in an amateur production of "William Tell."

Binny Wallace, Tom's friend who is drowned in the sinking of a drifting boat during a sea storm.

Mr. Grimshaw, the boys' teacher at the Temple Grammar School.

Charley Marden, a schoolboy who almost strangles when a torpedo explodes in school.

Ezra Wingate, a neighbor whose old stagecoach is burned by the boys in a bonfire and who realizes a handsome profit by collecting damages.

Mr. Meeks, the shy druggist whom the Widow Conway is trying to catch for a husband.

Silas Trefethen, an eccentric buyer of cannon for a war with England that never developed.

Nelly Glentworth, Captain Nutter's young visitor loved by Tom.

THE STORY OF A COUNTRY TOWN

Author: Edgar Watson Howe (1853-1937)
Time of action: Mid-nineteenth century
First published: 1883

PRINCIPAL CHARACTERS

Abram Nedrow (Ned) Westlock, a Middle Border boy (and man), the narrator of the story. He is a farm helper for his father, later an apprentice in journalism, and he becomes a successful editor of the paper his father leaves him. For years in love with Agnes, he marries her after his mother's death. A close observer of people, he is also a moralist on such matters as temperance and personal industry. As a critic of small-town temperament and mores, he anticipates Sinclair Lewis's Carol Kennicott.

The Reverend John Westlock, his father, a Methodist minister, a strong, capable, independent, thrifty man; a domestic tyrant, a hard worker, strongly opinionated. Suffering from a gnawing discontent, he leaves the ministry, becomes the editor of a newspaper, and later deserts his family, informing Ned of a seven-year liaison with Mrs. Tremaine, who accompanies him in his flight.

Mrs. Westlock, the minister's weak, timid, submissive wife. She dies just before her repentant husband returns.

Jo Erring, her younger brother, in early youth a member of the Westlock household and throughout his life a close friend of Ned. Stout, energetic, and ambitious, but rather crude and uneducated, he works hard to prove himself worthy of Mateel. Having learned milling under Damon Barker, he builds a mill of his own and marries Mateel. Doomed from the beginning, the marriage is never happy, and it finally disintegrates. After Mateel divorces him and marries Bragg, Jo murders him and later poisons himself in prison.

Mateel Shepherd, Jo Erring's sweetheart. Though in love with Bragg, she marries Jo, whom she later divorces to marry Bragg. Driven insane by Bragg's murder, she dies shortly afterward.

Clinton Bragg, Jo's rival for Mateel. He is boastful, sullen, insolent, lazy, an ostentatious drinker, educated and scornful of others' ignorance. He is murdered by Jo.

Damon Barker (in reality **Captain Deming**), a former ship captain now a miller, a friend of Ned and Jo. After his wife's death he reveals his identity to his daughter Agnes, who goes to live with him.

Agnes Deming, his daughter, a young and pretty schoolteacher. Popular in Fairview, she is a kindly friend and adviser to everyone. Though older than Ned, she accepts his love. They grow closer when she cares for his ailing mother, and at the end of the story she and Ned have been happily married for several years.

The Reverend Goode Shepherd, the father of Mateel and successor to Mr. Westlock at the Fairview church.

Mrs. Tremaine, the widowed half sister of Damon Barker, for whom she keeps house. She elopes with Mr. Westlock but leaves him when she learns he has left Ned his money and property.

Dad Erring, Jo's father, a shingle-maker, non-religious, eccentric, and reticent, a man who attends to his own business and ignores that of others.

Mr. Lytle (Little) Biggs, Agnes' uncle, the father of eight children. A free-spoken little man, he is critical of others' follies and faults as well as his own, such as his penchant for lying.

Big Adam, Mr. Biggs' hired man, a fat, bull-voiced country lout with a habit of drawing imaginary corks and pouring imaginary drinks. He becomes Barker's helper and later the mill operator.

THE STORY OF AN AFRICAN FARM

Author: Olive Schreiner (1855-1920)
Time of action: The 1880's
First published: 1883

PRINCIPAL CHARACTERS

Tant' Sannie, a simple, slow, Boer farm woman whom an Englishman marries just before his death so that there will be someone left to care for his daughter and her cousin. She ignores his request to educate the girls because she considers education unnecessary. After the children grow up she marries a neighboring widower.

Lyndall, Tant' Sannie's stepdaughter, a serious, studious girl. She goes to the city, where her unconventional ideas and conduct lead to her ruin. She lives with a man but, scorning legal ties, will not marry him. Gregory Rose finds her in a hotel room, ill and deserted by her lover. She dies shortly thereafter and he takes her body back to the farm for burial.

Em, Lyndall's cousin, a more conventional young woman. Betrothed to Gregory Rose, she discovers that she does not love him and breaks off the engagement.

After Lyndall's death Gregory proposes again and she accepts.

Waldo, the son of the German overseer on the farm. Like Lyndall, he is serious and studious. He leaves the farm and wanders far but returns disillusioned. When he learns that Lyndall, whom he has always loved, is dead, his one desire is to be in the earth with her. One warm sunny day he dies.

Gregory Rose, a young Englishman who rents part of the farm. He is betrothed to Em until she decides she does not love him. When Lyndall returns home, he is attracted to her and agrees to marry her. But she runs off with her lover and he sees no more of her until he finds her deserted by her lover and dying. He takes her body back to the farm. Eventually he marries Em.

Bonaparte Blenkins, a rascally drifter. Attracted by his glib manner, Tant' Sannie allows him to take over the farm for a time and he discharges the regular overseer, Waldo's father, who then dies of grief. Jealous and angry when she discovers Bonaparte making love to her niece, Tant' Sannie drives him from the farm.

THE STORY OF BURNT NJAL

Author: Unknown
Time of action: Tenth century
First transcribed: Thirteenth century manuscript

PRINCIPAL CHARACTERS

Njal, a man of law. His sons kill his foster son, and in the resulting feud his house is burned and Njal and his wife and sons die.

Bergthora, Njal's wife. When the other women leave the house before it is burned, she stays behind and dies with her husband.

Gunnar Hamondsson, Njal's friend. After Gunnar's first manslaying, Njal predicts truly that Gunnar will be killed if he slays another man in the same family.

Kolskegg Hamondsson, Gunnar's brother.

Hallgerda, Hauskuld Heriolfsson's daughter and a hard-hearted woman. Her third marriage is to Gunnar. There is much conflict between her and Bergthora, but the husbands remain friends.

Hauskuld Thrainsson, the foster son of Njal, who gets him a priesthood so that Hildigunna will consent to be his wife.

Hauskuld Thrainsson is killed by Njal's sons.

Mord Valgardsson, who sows discord between Hauskuld Thrainsson and Njal's sons.

Hildigunna, the daughter of Flosi and the wife of Hauskuld Thrainsson.

Flosi Thordsson, Hildigunna's father and Njal's enemy. After his son-in-law's death, he attacks Njal's house and burns it.

Helge, Njal's daughter.

Kari Solmundsson, the husband of Helge. He escapes from the fire but his son is killed. After Flosi has paid atonement for the fire, Kari agrees that the burning is avenged, but not his son Thord's death. After both Kari and Flosi return home from separate pilgrimages, they are fully reconciled.

Hildigunna, the daughter of Flosi's brother. Kari's wife Helge having died,

1085

Flosi gives Hildigunna to Kari after the reconciliation.

Thord Karisson, killed in the burning.

Skarphedinn Njalsson, killed trying to escape from the fire.

Helgi Njalsson, killed trying to escape with the women before the fire is set.

Grim Njalsson, also killed in the fire.

Thorgeir Craggeir, who becomes briefly involved in the post-fire feud between Kari and Flosi.

Thorgerda, the daughter of Hallgerda.

Thrain Sigfusson, who puts aside his shrewish wife to marry Thorgerda. He is killed by Skarphedinn Njalsson.

Kettle of the Mark, Thrain's brother and Njal's son-in-law. He and Njal make atonement for Thrain's death, and Njal takes Hauskuld Thrainsson as his foster son.

Hauskuld Njalsson, a base-born son of Njal. He is killed by Lyting.

Rodny, the mother of Hauskuld Njalsson.

Lyting, Thrain's sister's husband.

Aumund, the blind and base-born son of Hauskuld Njalsson. His eyes are opened just long enough to enable him to kill Lyting.

Otkell Skarfsson. A discord beginning with his selling Gunnar a deceitful thrall ends with Gunnar's killing Otkell.

Thorgeir Otkellsson, killed by Gunnar when he attempts to ambush Gunnar.

Starkad, an enemy of Gunnar.

Thorgeir Starkadsson, another enemy of Gunnar. He and his father are with Thorgeir in the attempted ambush of Gunnar.

Geir the Priest, who gets up a band to slay Gunnar. The plot succeeds after much slaughter and difficulty.

Hogni Gunnarsson, who, along with Skarphedinn Njalsson, avenges Gunnar's death by slaying Starkad and Thorgeir Starkadsson.

Bork the Waxy-Toothed Blade, the father of Starkad.

Hrut Heriolfsson, who had come to Norway from Iceland to claim an inheritance.

Harold Grayfell, King of Norway.

Gunnhilda, the mother of the King. Hrut sits in her high seat. Before he returns to Iceland, Gunnhilda puts a spell on him so that he will never have pleasure living with the woman he has set his heart on.

Unna, whom Hrut marries after his return to Iceland. The marriage is unhappy and she leaves him. She enlists Gunnar's aid in getting back her goods from Hrut.

Fiddle Mord, the father of Unna. He asks Hrut to return Unna's goods. When he refuses Hrut's offer to fight him instead, Fiddle Mord gets great shame for his suit.

Hauskuld Heriolfsson, the brother of Hrut and the father of Hallgerda. He makes Hrut return Unna's goods and dowry.

Thorwald Oswifsson, the first husband of Hallgerda.

Glum, the second husband of Hallgerda. He is murdered.

Thiostolf, the foster father of Hallgerda. He kills Thorwald Oswifsson. Hallgerda sends him to tell the news of Glum's death to Hrut, who strikes him dead.

Olof the Hall, the father of Glum.

Olaf Tryggvisson, a later ruler of Norway.

Thangbrand, who is sent by Olaf to preach Christianity in Iceland.

Thorgeir of Lightwater, who challenges any man who speaks against the new Christian law.

Skapti Thorodsson, who, at Lawman Njal's suggestion, brings the Fifth Court into law.

THE STORY OF GÖSTA BERLING

Author: Selma Lagerlöf (1858-1940)
Time of action: Early nineteenth century
First published: 1894

PRINCIPAL CHARACTERS

Gösta Berling, a tall, slender, handsome, poetic, but irresponsible priest unfrocked after an investigation of his brandy-drinking. He becomes successively a beggar, one of Margareta's Cavalier pensioners, a good Samaritan to Anna, the fiancé of Marianne, the husband of Elizabeth, and at last a good man.

Countess Elizabeth Dohna, a gay, lovely girl married to a stupid husband from whom she escapes to lead a pleasant life. Following the annulment of her marriage, she bears a child and asks Gösta to marry her to give the child a father. They marry but the child dies a few days later.

Margareta Celsing Samzelius, the Major's aging, influential wife and Altringer's former mistress; a once beautiful, innocent woman both strengthened and coarsened by her unhappy experiences. Disowned by the Major after her admission of adultery and deserted by the Cavaliers she has helped, she becomes a beggar but returns to her estate after her husband's death. She dies shortly afterward.

Marianne Sinclair, a beautiful, witty, learned young woman in love with Gösta. Scarred by smallpox and rejected by Gösta, she becomes a recluse in her father's home.

Captain Christian Bergh, Gösta's crony and drinking companion; a coarse, malicious giant who is stupidly responsible for Gösta's loss of his pulpit. Secretly in

love with Margareta for forty years, he sottishly causes her disownment by her husband.

Altringer, Margareta's fiancé and later her lover, who bequeaths his fortune to Major Samzelius so that Margareta may benefit from it.

Sintram, an apelike ironmaster who delights in his own wickedness. He is a demon who blights the lives of others.

Anna Stjärnhök, a wealthy, beautiful young woman who breaks her engagements to two men and elopes with Gösta.

Ferdinand Uggla, Anna's good, gentle, timid first fiancé with whom she is reunited by Gösta.

Ebba Dohna, a sweetheart of Gösta who sought death because of his deceit.

Count Henrik Dohna, the ugly, wrinkled, stupid, but honest brother of Ebba and husband of Elizabeth.

Countess Märta Dohna, mother of Ebba and Henrik; she dislikes and mistreats Elizabeth.

Major Samzelius, Margareta's ugly, bearlike husband, who dies from the bite of a wounded bear.

Melchior Sinclair, Marianne's wealthy, wife-beating father, who casts her out for loving Gösta.

Dahlberg, a wealthy, little, baldheaded man; Anna's second and older fiancé, to

1087

whom she becomes engaged because of his money.

Captain Lennart, one of the Cavaliers killed by a drunker brawler.

STORY OF THE GUITAR

Author: Kao Tse-ch'eng (Kao Ming, c. 1305-c. 1368)
Time of action: c. 200
First presented: Fourteenth century

PRINCIPAL CHARACTERS

Ts'ai Jung, a historical person around whom a legend, almost sacred, has grown. A bright and personable young scholar, Ts'ai wins honor for himself and his family in the Emperor's competition, but not without sacrificing his own domestic inclinations. Forced by his victory in the Imperial Examination to marry a prime minister's daughter and live in his house, the brilliant and sensitive young man mourns the loss of his first wife and the absence of his parents. Naïve to an extreme degree, he assumes that no news from home is good news or that the misleading news a troublemaker brings is true. Further duped, he sends money and love to his wife and parents through the same villain, who absconds with the money. Fortunate in his second wife, who approves of his generous affections for his humble family, he plans to set off with her to visit his home, only to be refused permission by his father-in-law. Obedient to the edict, he finally learns of the sacrifices his young wife has made to help his aging parents before their deaths.

Chao Wu-niang, his first and humble village wife, the paragon of wifely virtues, the heroine of a moral tale revered on stage even to the present. Lovely and gentle, devoted and patient, soft-spoken but intelligent, humble yet determined— these are the sterling qualities of the young Chinese bride so cruelly acted on by her destiny, her fate of loving without thought of recompense. Self-sacrificing in the extreme, she gives up everything to protect and ease the sufferings of her hus-

band's parents, all without protest or diminution of affection or regard. As a sensitive artist she sublimates her personal tragedy through song and poetry, begging her way in disguise to her husband's side, bringing with her portraits of his parents made during the famine which killed them. Her satiric poem, really the joint effort or plan of the wives, sets feelings in order and proves her husband to be generous. Her virtues, united with those of Miss Niu, make for a happy household for the three.

Chang, an elderly neighbor who pays for burials and generously aids Ts'ai's family not out of hope for gain but from love of man. Placed in charge of the aged parents and young wife, the devoted friend feeds and clothes the three until he himself has no more, and even then he makes honorable burials possible. Aware of the young wife's devoted work and sacrifices for the family, he unselfishly does more than seems possible, because of his big heart. His devotion and his relief upon seeing the scholar and the wives return to do honor to the graves are sensitively portrayed.

The Honorable Mr. Niu, the prime minister and unintentional villain of the piece. Merely selfish in his wishes to keep his young daughter and her pleasant husband always near him, he does not intentionally deny Ts'ai the privilege of seeing his parents; on the contrary, he is willing to have them as permanent guests in his home. He is portrayed as the typical officious and one-sided government official to whom his Emperor's word is his law in spirit and letter.

Miss Niu, the beautiful, cultured, brilliant daughter whose only wish is to have a first-place scholar for a husband. Sensitive to her husband's longing for his first wife and parents, and yet in love with and loved by the confused young man, she thinks only of his feelings and those of his family. Without aroused feelings of jealousy she immediately recognizes the burden of Chao's song played to the pipa, the guitar-like instrument with which the devoted first wife begs her way to the city. In spite of her highborn manners, the second wife desires to pay her respects to her husband's parents. She does so by taking in the destitute Chao and making a pilgrimage to the parents' graves, but only after she generously tests her husband's affections.

STRANGE INTERLUDE

Author: Eugene O'Neill (1888-1953)
Time of action: The 1920's and 1930's
First presented: 1928

PRINCIPAL CHARACTERS

Nina Leeds, a girl driven to the verge of madness by the wartime death of Gordon Shaw, the man whom she was to marry. Leaving home and going to work as a nurse, Nina gives herself promiscuously to the soldiers in the hospital. To Nina's disturbed mind, this promiscuity is atonement for her failure to give herself to Gordon. Finally, realizing that she needs normal love objects to distract her from her morbid obsession with her own guilt, she marries Sam Evans, only to discover that there is madness in his family. Ridding herself of Sam's unborn child by an operation, Nina takes Dr. Darrell as her lover and becomes pregnant by him. When her child is born, Nina settles down in maternal satisfaction. She is happy until it becomes obvious that her son Gordon cares less for her than for Sam. To add to Nina's misery, Gordon hates his real father, who is still a frequent caller on Nina. When Gordon, at twenty-one, plans to marry, Nina, disturbed and neurotic again, begs Darrell to help her prevent the marriage. He refuses and tells her they already have meddled in too many lives. After Sam dies, Darrell leaves Nina, saying that they are haunted by too many ghosts to be happy. Nina marries faithful Charles Marsden, who offers her peace at last in the autumn of her life.

Edmund (Ned) Darrell, a doctor seven years Nina's senior. Concerned with Nina's condition but unwilling to be distracted from his career by marriage, he persuades Nina to marry Sam Evans. Corrupted and embittered by having to share Nina and his son, he allows his career to be ruined. Having grown rich backing Sam in business, Darrell works sporadically and pays frequent, pathetic visits to Nina and his son. Finally, cured of his love for Nina, he begins a new life as a biologist in the West Indies.

Sam Evans, Nina's boyish, lumbering husband. After Nina has discovered the madness in Sam's background and taken up with Darrell, she can hardly stand to have Sam touch her. Stricken by his wife's rejection, Sam degenerates, drifting from job to job and contemplating suicide. After Nina's baby is born, Sam, swollen with pride of fatherhood, becomes confident and ambitious. Grown rich and masterful, he never suspects the truth about Nina. As a final irony, he leaves Darrell a fortune to carry on his biological work.

1089

Charles Marsden, a writer of popular novels. A bachelor some fifteen years older than Nina, he is vaguely disturbed because she thinks of him as an uncle. At Darrell's urging he advises Nina to marry Sam. He later discovers that Darrell is Nina's lover and hates him for it. At last, after Sam has died and Darrell departed, Marsden, who has continued to love Nina without lust, marries her.

Gordon Evans, Nina's son. He becomes, like his namesake, an oarsman and athlete. Handsome, strong, but shallow, Gordon, in a rage after his supposed father's death, strikes Darrell. Nina cries that he is hitting his father, but Gordon does not understand. He never learns who his real father is.

Mrs. Amos Evans, Sam's mother. Frail but strong-willed, she tells Nina of the madness in Sam's family and suggests that Nina find a healthy man to father her children.

Professor Henry Leeds, Nina's father, a timid and withdrawn professor of classics at an Eastern university. Dependent upon Nina and jealous of Gordon Shaw, Leeds had persuaded Gordon not to marry Nina until after the war. He dies soon after Nina leaves him.

Madeline Arnold, the girl engaged to Gordon Evans. She resembles the young Nina.

[Gordon Shaw, the dead man with whom Nina was in love, killed while serving as a flier in World War I. Both Nina and Sam worship his memory.]

STREET SCENE

Author: Elmer Rice (1892-   )
Time of action: 1929
First presented: 1929

PRINCIPAL CHARACTERS

Rose Maurrant, the daughter of New York tenement dwellers. She is escorted home by her employer, Harry Easter, who wants to establish her in an apartment and remove her from poverty, an offer that she refuses. Sam Kaplan appears to sympathize with her family problems. Later Rose tells his sister that she is only slightly attracted to Sam. The next morning she returns to find that her father has killed her mother and her mother's lover. Rejecting the proffered help of Easter and of Sam, Rose prepares to leave New York, for she feels that no person should belong to another. Perhaps later something will develop for Sam and her.

Frank Maurrant, her father, a stagehand.

Though extolling family happiness and propriety, he kills his wife and her lover.

Anna Maurrant, his wife. Her husband kills her and her lover.

Harry Easter, manager of the office in which Rose works. He tries to establish her in an apartment, but she refuses his offer and also his proffered help after her mother's murder.

Sam Kaplan, a law student in love with Rose. She will not accept his love, but holds out a faint hope for the future when they are older and wiser.

Shirley Kaplan, Sam's sister.

Abe Kaplan, Sam's father.

STRIFE

Author: John Galsworthy (1867-1933)
Time of action: Early twentieth century
First presented: 1909

PRINCIPAL CHARACTERS

John Anthony, the chairman of the board of a sheet metal plant, who is dramatically a fully realized character and also an example of a popular type that figured in early twentieth century industrial disputes. He fights stubbornly for his principles and is uncompromising in his attitude toward petitions from labor factions. Eventually his resignation is forced by board members anxious to compromise with the union.

David Roberts, a zealous leader of the striking workers who is Anthony's counterpart in the ranks of labor. He is typical of the adamant, unyielding element prevalent in labor disputes in the present century. As Anthony is deserted by the board, so Roberts is abandoned by the union membership, and the strike is compromised.

Annie Roberts, David's wife, who, though not an active character in the play, is an important agent in Galsworthy's drama. It is her death from the privation caused by the strike that causes the contending forces to think soberly and work out a compromise.

Edgar Anthony, the realistically presented son of John Anthony, who expresses the views employers of the future might be expected to have where labor is concerned.

**Francis and
Enid Underwood,** who are sympathetic to labor's cause. Francis, because he is the plant manager, is not so overt in his stand as is Enid. She boldly attempts to reconcile the opposing factions, first by attending Roberts' sick wife and second by pleading personally with Roberts to give up the fight. Significant is the fact that Enid is Anthony's daughter.

Simon Harness, a union officer whose compromise finally is accepted by the contending parties.

STUDS LONIGAN: A TRILOGY

Author: James T. Farrell (1904-   )
Time of action: 1916-1931
First published: 1932-1935

PRINCIPAL CHARACTERS

William "Studs" Lonigan, a young Chicago Irishman who, growing up in the first three decades of this century, is a moral failure. He tries to be tough all his life and succeeds only in leading an empty existence. His thoughts are only of women, drink, and a good time, from his graduation from a parochial grammar school to his sudden death in his thirties.

Patrick Lonigan, Studs' father. He is a man who lives in a world that he understands only as he can see it from a narrow point of view. He is a painting contractor who provides for his family in a material way and sees nothing more to do. Only his business failure in the 1930's brings him to believe that he has not done well in this world.

Mrs. Lonigan, Studs' mother. She is a woman who wants her children to do well. She always thinks the best of her children, even her half-hoodlum son Studs. She is a possessive woman, not wanting to let go of her influence on her children.

Lucy Scanlan, a pretty little neighbor girl whom Studs loves when they are in their early teens.

Catherine Banahan, a young Irishwoman who loves Studs when he is in his thirties. She becomes his mistress. When he dies suddenly she is left unmarried to bear his child.

Paulie Haggerty, one of Studs' friends. His early death causes Studs to think of his own mortality.

Weary Reilley, a tough contemporary and sometime friend of Studs. Often in and out of scrapes, he is eventually arrested for raping a girl he picks up at a dance.

Frances Lonigan, one of Studs' sisters. She tries to rise out of the intellectual and moral rut of the rest of the family.

Loretta Lonigan, Studs' other sister.

Martin Lonigan, Studs' young brother, who tries to imitate Studs.

Helen Shires, a boyish girl who is Studs' chum when he is a boy.

A STUDY IN SCARLET

Author: Sir Arthur Conan Doyle (1859-1930)
Time of action: Nineteenth century
First published: 1887

PRINCIPAL CHARACTERS

Sherlock Holmes, the famous detective.

Dr. John Watson, Holmes' friend and assistant. In this story he has just returned from the Afghan wars and is a pensioned army doctor newly introduced to Holmes.

Stamford, an old friend of Watson who brings Watson and Holmes together as lodgers at 221B Baker Street.

Tobias Gregson, a detective from Scotland Yard who asks Holmes' help in solving a case.

Enoch J. Drebber, an American found murdered in a deserted house in London. He turns out to be a former Mormon who took Lucy Ferrier as one of his wives against her will. He was murdered by Jefferson Hope, the girl's sweetheart.

Lestrade, a detective from Scotland Yard who works with Gregson.

Stangerson, Drebber's secretary. He is found dead of a stabbing wound in a London hotel. Like Drebber, he has been murdered by Jefferson Hope, who seeks revenge for his sweetheart.

Jefferson Hope, an American. When captured, he is working as the driver of a hansom cab in London. He murdered Drebber and Stangerson because they took Lucy Ferrier from him. He is not punished by the law for his crimes, for he dies of a heart attack within a few days of his capture.

Lucy Ferrier, a beautiful American girl. Jefferson Hope meets her in Utah and falls in love with her. She is forced by the Mormon elders to marry Drebber even though he already has wives. She dies within a month of her marriage.

John Ferrier, Lucy's father. He tries to prevent his daughter's having to marry a Mormon, but he is killed by the Mormons. He became a Mormon when he and his child were rescued by a Mormon wagon train while moving West.

THE SUN ALSO RISES

Author: Ernest Hemingway (1899-1961)
Time of action: The 1920's
First published: 1926

PRINCIPAL CHARACTERS

Robert Cohn, a Jewish writer living in Paris in the 1920's. He and Jacob Barnes are friends, though Barnes delights in needling him. Cohn seems to mean well, but he has a talent for irritating all his acquaintances. When Cohn meets Lady Brett Ashley, he immediately brushes off Frances Clyne, his mistress, and spends a few days at San Sebastian with Brett. He now feels that she is his property, though she plans to marry Michael Campbell. Cohn has the temerity to join a group from Paris (including Brett and Michael) going to the fiesta in Pamplona, Spain. When Brett is smitten by a young bullfighter and sleeps with him, Cohn, reputedly once a middleweight boxing champion at Princeton, gives the bullfighter a pummeling. Cohn's personality has many contradictions: in general, he is conceited, but is unsure of himself as a writer; he seems both obtuse and sensitive; he evokes pity from his friends, yet they all thoroughly dislike him.

Jacob Barnes (Jake), the narrator, an American expatriate also living in Paris, where he works as a correspondent for a newspaper. In World War I he was wounded in the groin and as a result is sexually impotent. This injury negates the love he has for Brett and her love for him. Seeming to work very little, Barnes spends a great deal of time in cafés, drinking and talking. His greatest problems in life are trying to adjust himself to the nature of his injury and trying to work out some sort of personal philosophy; two of his thoughts almost solve the latter problem: "You can't get away from yourself by moving from one place to another" and "Enjoying living was learning to get your money's worth and knowing when you had it." Barnes is a lover of good food and drink, an expert trout fisherman, and an "aficionado" of the bullfight. Although he drinks as much as the other characters, some of whom are given to passing out, he has the happy faculty of remaining keen and alert.

Lady Brett Ashley, an English woman separated from her husband. Her first lover died of dysentery during the war and she is getting a divorce from Lord Ashley. She plans to marry Michael Campbell, but really she is in love with Barnes, perhaps because she knows he is unattainable, because they can never sexually consummate their love. She is a drunkard and is wildly promiscuous, as is shown by her affairs with Cohn and the young bullfighter, Pedro Romero; but she seems as lost in life as Barnes and she is an appealing woman, one whose successive affairs remind the reader of a little girl trying game after game to keep herself from being bored. In the end she is determined to settle down with Campbell, even though he is nastily talkative when drunk; but in spite of her resolutions Lady Brett seems destined to work her way through life from bed to bed.

Bill Gorton, a witty American friend of Barnes. With Barnes he fishes for trout in Spain and attends the fiesta in Pamplona.

Michael Campbell, Lady Brett's fiancé. He is pleasant when sober but very frank and blunt when drunk.

Pedro Romero, a young bullfighter of great promise who has an affair with Brett, but who is jilted when he says he wants to marry her and when she realizes she is not good for him.

Count Mippipopolous, a friend of Brett's who would like always to drink champagne from magnums; he is kind to Brett and Jake in Paris.

Montoya, the proprietor of the hotel in Pamplona where the established, truly good bullfighters stay; the hotel thus becomes the headquarters of Barnes' wild vacationers.

THE SUNKEN BELL

Author: Gerhart Hauptmann (1862-1946)
Time of action: Indefinite, timeless
First presented: 1897

PRINCIPAL CHARACTERS

Heinrich (hīn'rĭsh), a bell-founder who symbolizes the artist against the world. Trying to carry a bell to a mountain church, he is injured by the spirits of wood and water and his bell pushed into a lake. He is saved by the mountain sprite Rautendelein, and they fall in love. A rescue party carries him home, but he returns to Rautendelein. His efforts to make a superlative bell are frustrated by the dwarfs; his wife dies, and her dead hand rings the sunken bell. Dying, and renounced by Rautendelein, he tries to reach a flaming cathedral-castle. Wittikin gives him the wines of life and of the questing spirit; Rautendelein, the wine of aspiration. Embraced by Rautendelein, he dies, hearing the chimes of the sun.

Magda (mäg'dä), his wife.

Rautendelein (rou·tăn'dĕ·līn), a mountain sprite. She is intended as the bride of the Nickelmann, but falls in love with Heinrich. When he is taken home dying, she revives him. Renounced by Heinrich, she marries the Nickelmann but returns to Heinrich as he dies.

Wittikin (vĭ'tĭ·kĭn), a sorceress and the grandmother of Rautendelein.

The Nickelmann (nĭ'kăl·män), a water spirit whom Rautendelein marries.

The Vicar, representing spirit.

The Schoolteacher, representing mind.

The Barber, representing body.

THE SUPPLIANTS

Author: Aeschylus (c. 525-c. 456 B.C.)
Time of action: Age of myth
First presented: c. 491 B.C.

Danaüs (dăn′ā·əs), the son of Belus and father of fifty daughters, the Danaïdes. He is a descendant of Io, who was a priestess of Hera and daughter of Inachus, King of Argos. Io was loved by Zeus, who changed her into a heifer so that she might escape the jealousy of Hera. But Hera sent a gadfly to sting and to drive Io throughout the world. Having wandered to Egypt, she was touched by Zeus; and from this mystical union was born a son, Epaphus. He, in turn, was the father of Libya, who had two sons, Belus and Agenor. Belus had two sons, Aegyptus and Danaüs. Aegyptus had fifty sons and Danaüs had fifty daughters. The sons of Aegyptus wished to marry the daughters of Danaüs; but the latter, horrified at the violent lust of their cousins, fled to Argos to seek the protection of their ancestral home. When the play begins, Danaüs, having just landed at Argos, advises his daughters to seek as suppliants the protection of the local gods. He himself is an old man, unable to protect them from their kinsmen who, as he knows, are sailing in hot pursuit. He asks the aid of Pelasgus, King of Argos. Having received it and having been given a refuge in the kingdom, he warns his daughters that they must behave in such a fashion as to merit the protection that they have been granted.

Pelasgus (pə·lăz′gŭs), King of Argos. He is a vacillating man, torn between his humane desire to grant the protection asked of him and his fear of provoking a war that might well ruin his city. He cannot make up his mind which course to follow until he has obtained the consent of his subjects—an early example of the Greek democratic way of life. But once he has been backed by the citizens, his better feelings come to the fore; and

he not only offers protection to the refugees but sternly drives off the Herald of the sons of Aegyptus and prepares for war.

The Danaïdes (də·nā′ə·dēz), or daughters of Danaüs. Though forming the chorus of the drama, they—unlike the usual Greek chorus—act as the chief character in the play. They are frantic with fear of their pursuing cousins, for they are helpless maidens with only an old and infirm father to protect them. Their barbaric dress arouses the suspicion of the King of Argos, and only through a detailed account of their ancestry do they convince him of their Argive descent. Clinging to the altars of the gods of Argos, they finally threaten to kill themselves if King Pelasgus will not help them. This threat, with its implication of a stain on the Kingdom of Argos, helps to persuade the King to offer them protection.

The Herald of Aegyptus (ē·jĭp′tŭs), who speaks for the fifty brothers pursuing the Danaïdes. He lands at Argos just after King Pelasgus has promised his protection to the fugitives. The Herald is a heartless ruffian, caring nothing for the gods of Argos, who are not his gods, since he was not born there, and quite willing to tear the frightened maidens from the altars to which they are clinging. As suppliants, they are inviolable; but this immemorial, sacred law means nothing to him. He is overawed only by a show of superior force and leaves the stage with a prophecy of war, which was probably fulfilled in the—now lost—subsequent dramas of the trilogy.

[Since this is the earliest surviving play by Aeschylus, these characters are the oldest extant figures in European dramatic literature.]

THE SUPPLIANTS

Author: Euripides (c. 485-c. 406 B.C.)
Time of action: Remote antiquity
First presented: c. 424 B.C.

PRINCIPAL CHARACTERS

Theseus (thē'sōōs, thē'sĭ·əs), the young King of Athens, whose aid Adrastus, King of Argos, seeks in recovering the bodies of the Argive heroes killed in the unsuccessful expedition of the Seven against Thebes. At first he refuses Adrastus' request. He admits that the Thebans should not have withheld the bodies, but he considers the expedition rash and ill-omened and he is reluctant to identify himself with the bad cause of the Argives. The supplications of the mothers of the fallen heroes, an appeal to pity based on pure sorrow, and of Theseus' mother Aethra, an appeal to pride based on the impiety of the Thebans and the need to uphold the law of Greece, are more successful. Theseus agrees to rescue the dead, by force if necessary. When a herald arrives from the Thebans and asks to speak with the "master" of the city, his innocent remark occasions a largely irrelevant debate between Theseus and the herald on the theme of democracy versus tyranny, in which Theseus is the champion of democracy as it is practiced in Athens. The herald finally delivers his message, demands that Adrastus be refused sanctuary in Athens, and announces that the bodies shall not be restored to their families, whereupon Theseus summons his warriors. He defeats the Thebans and returns the bodies; however, as an example of the virtue of moderation, he refuses to enter Thebes or sack the conquered city. He oversees the funeral rites of the heroes. Theseus is more successful as a mouthpiece for the glory of Athens than as a man. Although he shows a great love for his mother, he is proud and contentious.

Adrastus (ə·drăs'tŭs), King of Argos, the leader and only survivor among the seven Thebans. He is old, defeated, and disillusioned, and his appeal to Theseus is filled with self-pity; misfortune, he feels, is the common lot of all. Theseus points out Adrastus' own rashness and disregard for the wishes of the gods as the causes of the King's misfortune. During the play Adrastus redeems himself, becoming less hysterical and self-pitying. In his funeral oration over the heroes, he speaks out as an advocate of peace.

Aethra (ē'thrə), the mother of Theseus and an example of principled moderation. The mothers of the Seven killed at Thebes come to beg her to intercede with Theseus for recovery of the bodies. Her sympathy for them is genuine and affecting. Although her appeal to Theseus is based on his duty to the gods and Greek law, she realistically plays on his pride.

The Chorus of Argive Mothers, who come to plead with Theseus for the recovery of their slain sons. Their odes are the most affecting aspect of the drama.

Evadne (ə·văd'nē), the widow of Capaneus, who fell in the Theban adventure. Her role is brief but spectacular: she appears, dressed in her wedding finery, on a high rock overlooking the funeral pyre of her husband and, after singing of her sorrow, leaps into the flames. She provides an effective contrast to the moderation of Aethra, and her action horrifies her father and the Chorus.

Iphis (ī'fĭs), the aged father of Evadne and of Eteocles, one of the Theban adventurers. He comes to bury his son and witnesses the death of his daughter. He departs, completely broken, with words of hatred for old age.

1096

A Herald, sent by King Creon from Thebes. He brings news that the bodies will not be restored and insolently engages in a debate with Theseus over democracy versus tyranny. His arguments against democracy are vigorous; he cites its unscrupulous demagogues, the inability of its people to settle policy, and its false equality.

Athena (ə·thē'nə), the goddess of wisdom. She appears, "ex machina," at the close of the play, and directs Theseus to extract a pledge from the Argives not to forget what Athens has done for them. She also promises the sons of the Seven future vengeance against Thebes, and the play ends with promise of further wars and sorrows.

The Sons of the Seven against Thebes. They bring in the ashes of their fathers at the close of the play and look eagerly forward to the time when they will be able to avenge their fathers' deaths.

I SUPPOSITI

Author: Ludovico Ariosto (1474-1533)
Time of action: c. 1500
First presented: 1509

PRINCIPAL CHARACTERS

Erostrato (ĕ'rōs·trä'tō), the son of a wealthy Sicilian. In love with Polynesta, he gains access to her house by posing as his servant, Dulippo. Imprisoned by her father, he is released and united with Polynesta upon the arrival of his father, Philogano.

Dulippo (də·lĭ'pō), his servant, who poses as his master in order to help him in his wooing. He is discovered to be Cleander's son.

Polynesta (pŏ'lĭ·nĕs'tä), a young girl in love with Erostrato.

Damon (dā'mən), her father.

Cleander (klə·ăn'dėr), an old doctor of law and the suitor of Polynesta, for whose hand he will give any amount of money. He is constantly fooled by the disguised Dulippo, but is made happy when the latter is revealed as his long-lost son.

Since he wants to marry only to produce an heir, he gladly relinquishes his suit.

Pasiphilo (pă·sĭ·fĭ'lō), a parasite who is always hungry. Sleeping off an attack of indigestion, he overhears Damon confess that he has imprisoned Erostrato and gives this information to Dulippo.

Philogano (fĭ'lō·gä'nō), Erostrato's father, who comes in search of his son. He is dumbfounded to be called, by Dulippo, either an impostor or a madman, and to find a Sienese posing as himself. But Dulippo's confession clears up the confusion.

Balia (bä'lĭ·ə), Polynesta's nurse and accomplice in her love affair with Erostrato.

A Sienese, who poses as Erostrato's father.

SURRY OF EAGLE'S-NEST

Author: John Esten Cooke (1830-1886)
Time of action: 1861-1863
First published: 1866

Lieutenant Colonel Surry, an officer of the Confederate Army. He falls in love with May Beverley, who is already engaged. Having been involved in the feud between Mordaunt and Fenwick, and having fought under Jackson, he is able to marry May when her fiancé breaks the engagement.

May Beverley, who marries Surry when her fiancé, Frederick Baskerville, breaks their engagement.

Fenwick, a Yankee spy who has treacherously separated Mordaunt from his wife. Repeatedly escaping Mordaunt's vengeance, he is killed by Achmed.

Colonel Mordaunt, once the rival of Fenwick for the hand of Frances Carleton. Mordaunt had won her, whereupon the rejected Fenwick used forged letters to separate husband and wife. Mordaunt repeatedly seeks revenge, but Fenwick always escapes, until Achmed kills him.

Frances Carleton, Mordaunt's lost wife, who appears as the insane "White Lady." She gives Surry a paper clearing up the mystery of Fenwick's villainy.

Violet Grafton, her cousin and attendant.

Achmed, Mordaunt's Arab companion, who kills Fenwick.

Harry Saltoun, a young Confederate officer who, about to fight a duel with Mordaunt, is revealed as his son.

Mrs. Parkins, Fenwick's confederate.

General Stonewall Jackson,
General J. E. B. Stuart,
General Turner Ashby, and
Major John Pelham, officers of the Confederate Army.

Captain William D. Farley, a Confederate scout.

SWALLOW BARN

Author: John P. Kennedy (1795-1870)
Time of action: Early nineteenth century
First published: 1832

Mark Littleton, the narrator, a New Yorker visiting his Virginian relations at Swallow Barn. An observant man who enjoys people, he tells his story of the Virginians with relish and with an obvious love of their easygoing way of life. He returns to his New York home after two months in Virginia.

Edward (Ned) Hazard, his New York cousin, high-spirited and given to joking and playing pranks; a favorite with children. Though he is the next heir to Swallow Barn, he is glad for Frank to have the responsibility of running the estate. In love with Bel, he encounters difficulties but at last marries her.

Francis (Frank) Meriwether, Ned's middle-aged brother-in-law who operates the Hazard estate. A handsome, portly, good-humored man, he is unambitious and of a contemplative nature. He is a generous, pleasant host to his many guests and a considerate master to his servants and dependents, who are happy to wait on him. Argumentative about politics, he is little informed about or interested in religion.

Mr. Isaac Tracy, an eccentric, elderly gentleman farmer, master of a neighboring estate, The Brakes. A dignified, sober, old-school Virginia gentleman, he occupies much of his time planning and plotting to get one hundred acres of almost worthless marshland lying between The Brakes and the Hazard land.

Bel Tracy, his vivacious younger daughter, pretty, impulsive, flirtatious, and quick-tempered; a good horsewoman. Uncertain for a while as to whether Ned is really the man for her, she at last decides he would be a good husband.

Harvey Riggs, a Tracy kinsman, a waggish, warm-hearted man of forty well liked by everyone.

Scipio, a woolly-haired old Negro, a freed slave who enjoys recalling older, better times in Virginia.

Lucretia, Frank's wife, a model administratix of domestic affairs at Swallow Barn; also a prodigiously fruitful woman.

Mr. Chub, a tutor, a Presbyterian minister, and a scholarly, philosophical, plump old gentleman.

Miss Prudence Meriwether, Frank's unmarried sister, who enjoys bewailing the demise of Virginia's golden age.

Carey, an old Negro who prides himself on his knowledge of horses.

Barbara Winkle, an old servant who tends to the numerous Meriwether children.

Catharine Tracy, Bel's older sister, well educated and sober-minded.

Ralph Tracy, the younger brother of Catharine and Bel; a slovenly, swaggering sportsman.

Singleton Oglethorpe Swansdown, a dandyish bachelor rejected by a bevy of Southern belles. He is Mr. Tracy's arbitrator in the settlement of the boundary line question.

Philpot (Philly) Wart, a popular lawyer and politician who plots with Frank to let Swansdown win in the litigation over the boundary line.

Hafen Blok, a German immigrant popular for his storytelling prowess.

THE SWISS FAMILY ROBINSON

Author: Johann Rudolf Wyss (1781-1830)
Time of action: Late eighteenth century
First published: 1813

PRINCIPAL CHARACTERS

Mr. Robinson, an intelligent, resourceful Swiss who, with his family, is shipwrecked upon an island near New Guinea. He represents many middle-class virtues and beliefs, including a strong religious sentiment. Because of his good sense, practical knowledge, and understanding of human nature, he and his family succeed in establishing themselves on the island with European-type civilization. When a ship calls at the island, Mr. Robinson decides to remain, hoping that commerce will come and that his little colony will grow and prosper.

Mrs. Robinson, an intelligent, brave, and hardworking woman who is in her way as resourceful as her husband. She improvises a great deal in making her family comfortable and happy. Her portion is to care for the crops, animals, and housekeeping. Like her husband, she chooses to remain on the island.

Fritz Robinson, eldest of the Robinson boys. He grows up on the island to become a gentlemanly, courageous young man. He learns how to accept responsibility and to carry out difficult tasks requiring initiative and courage. Unlike his father, he wants to return to Europe and does so when the opportunity comes.

Emily Montrose, a young English girl shipwrecked on the island. She is rescued by Fritz, who brings her to his family's settlement. Emily is the daughter of an English army officer and is on her way home from India. She and Fritz fall in love and plan to marry upon their return to Europe.

Ernest Robinson, second of the Robinson boys. He has a great interest in natural history, and his previous studies help the family very much, for he is able to identify plants and animals for various purposes.

Jack Robinson, third of the Robinson children. He contributes to the family's welfare by helping his mother tend the animals and crops.

Francis Robinson, youngest of the Robinson children. He is the pet of the rest of the family and thoroughly enjoys his childhood on the island.

THE TALE OF GENJI

Author: Lady Murasaki Shikibu (978?-1031?)
Time of action: Early medieval period
First transcribed: 1001-1015

PRINCIPAL CHARACTERS

Prince Genji, the handsome and popular son of the Emperor of Japan. This courtly romance of medieval Japan is primarily concerned with Genji's amours.

The Emperor of Japan, Genji's father.

Lady Kokiden, the Emperor's consort.

Kiritsubo, Genji's mother and the Emperor's concubine. Largely as a result of Lady Kokiden's antagonism to her, Kiritsubo dies during Genji's childhood.

Princess Aoi, who is married at the age of sixteen to twelve-year-old Genji. She is unhappy at first as a result of her husband's youth, and later because of his many amours. He does come to appreciate and love her, but her affliction results in her death in childbirth.

Fujitsubo, the Emperor's concubine and one of Genji's first paramours. She has a child by Genji, but fortunately for him the resemblance in looks is attributed to fraternity rather than to paternity. After Lady Kokiden's death, Fujitsubo is made official consort.

Utsusemi, a pretty young matron and another of Genji's paramours. Realizing that the affair cannot last, she ends it. While pursuing her again, Genji becomes distracted by another young woman.

Ki no Kami, a young courtier, at whose home Genji meets Utsusemi.

Yūgao, a young noblewoman in love with Genji. They live together in secret within the palace grounds for a time, until Yūgao dies tragically and strangely. Genji's friends act to avert a scandal.

Murasaki, a young orphan girl of good family. Genji secretly rears her and, a year after Princess Aoi's death, when Murasaki is of marriageable age, he makes her his wife.

A TALE OF TWO CITIES

Author: Charles Dickens (1812-1870)
Time of action: The French Revolution
First published: 1859

Sydney Carton, the legal assistant to Mr. Stryver, a successful London barrister. A drunkard and a misanthrope, he has no aim or purpose in his life until he meets Lucie Manette and falls secretly in love with her. Because of his remarkable physical resemblance to Charles Darnay, who becomes Lucie's husband, he is able to sacrifice himself on the guillotine in Darnay's place, a deed which finally gives a real meaning to his life in his own eyes.

Charles Darnay, in reality **Charles St. Evrémonde,** an émigré and an anti-aristocrat who has renounced his title. In England, where he becomes a teacher of languages, he finds happiness and success as the husband of Lucie Manette. When he returns to France to aid an agent of the St. Evrémonde family who has been captured by the revolutionists, he himself is arrested and condemned to the guillotine. He escapes because Sydney Carton takes his place in the prison. Darnay returns to England with his wife and her father.

Lucie Manette, a beautiful young French girl, closely connected with political events in France. Her father, a physician, had been a prisoner in the Bastille for many years, where he is sent because he has gained knowledge of the hidden crimes of the St. Evrémonde family. Her husband, Charles Darnay, is a member of that family and is condemned to the guillotine during the Revolution. He escapes death through the efforts of his wife, her father, and Sydney Carton. Throughout these trials Lucie remains level-headed, practical, and devoted.

Dr. Alexander Manette, Lucie's father, a doctor imprisoned many years in the Bastille in France because he aided a poor servant girl who was forced to become the mistress of the Marquis St. Evrémonde, Charles Darnay's uncle. Dr. Manette loses his mind in the Bastille and becomes obsessed with making shoes. His mind mends after his release, but whenever he is reminded of the prison days he seeks out his shoe bench and begins work. He tries to free Charles Darnay from the French prison by appealing to the sympathies of the revolutionists, but he is unsuccessful. At Darnay's trial a document written by the doctor while in prison is presented as evidence to secure the young aristocrat's conviction and sentence of death.

Lucie, her mother's namesake, the small daughter of Charles Darnay and his wife.

Ernest Defarge, a wineshop keeper in St. Antoine, a suburb of Paris. A former houseservant of Dr. Manette, he cares for his former master after he is released from the Bastille and before he goes to England. He is also one of the most radical of the revolutionists and, with his wife, he tries to get Charles Darnay executed by producing the document Dr. Manette had written years before.

Madame Thérèse Defarge, the wife of the wineshop keeper, a ruthless, cold woman who hates all aristocrats. Madame Defarge attends every guillotining and knits a stitch for each head that drops. She dies while struggling with Miss Pross, Lucie Darnay's maid.

Mr. Stryver, a self-centered, proud lawyer employed as Charles Darnay's counsel when the young language teacher is accused of carrying treasonous papers between France and England. He is Sydney Carton's patron and employer, a shrewd, determined man who looks years older than his actual age.

Miss Pross, the devoted housekeeper who has looked after Lucie Manette from childhood. She is intelligent and physically strong. Left behind to cover their flight when the Manettes escape from Paris, she struggles with Madame Defarge, who tries to make her confess where the Manettes have gone. Madame Defarge is accidentally killed when her gun goes off. Miss Pross, deafened by the explosion, escapes with Jerry Cruncher and follows her master and mistress to freedom.

Monsieur the Marquis St. Evrémonde, a cruel French aristocrat and Charles Darnay's uncle. When he kills a child because his coachman drives his horses too fast, the child's father gains admittance to the château and kills the arrogant nobleman. The Marquis and his breed are responsible for the peasants' uprising, causing the French Revolution.

Gaspard, the father of the child who was killed by the Marquis' fast horses. He succeeds in murdering the Marquis by plunging a knife into the sleeping nobleman's heart.

Monsieur Théophile Gabelle, a village postmaster and keeper of rents. Arrested by the revolutionists, he appeals to Charles Darnay in England for aid. In response to his plea Darnay goes on his dangerous errand in France.

Solomon Pross, alias **John Barsad,** Miss Pross's brother. A complete scoundrel, he abandons his sister after obtaining all her money. Calling himself John Barsad, he becomes a spy for the English. He informs Madame Defarge of Charles Darnay's marriage to Lucie Manette. He is a turnkey at the Conciergerie in Paris while Darnay is imprisoned there. Sydney Carton recognizes him but does not reveal his identity.

Jerry Cruncher, an employee at the London banking house of Tellson and Company by day, a resurrection-man by night. Devoted to Lucie and her father, he aids in Charles Darnay's escape from France.

Mrs. Cruncher, his wife, whom he calls "Aggerawayter." A pious woman, she thinks her husband's night occupation sinful, and she prays for his reformation.

Young Jerry Cruncher, their son. Guessing shrewdly, he has a good idea of the grim trade his father follows at night.

Mr. Jarvis Lorry, the confidential clerk of Tellson and Company. He is instrumental in getting Dr. Manette out of France into England, and he goes with the Manettes to Paris during the dark days of the Revolution while Charles Darnay, in prison, is awaiting his execution.

Jacques One,
Jacques Two,
Jacques Three,
Jacques Four, the name taken by Defarge, and
Jacques Five, a roadmender, a group of revolutionists in the suburb of St. Antoine.

The Vengeance, a woman revolutionist, Madame Defarge's lieutenant.

Roger Cly, Solomon Pross's partner and Charles Darnay's former servant, who testifies falsely when Darnay is on trial at the Old Bailey. He is supposed to be dead and buried, but Jerry Cruncher knows that his coffin had been empty.

THE TALISMAN

Author: Sir Walter Scott (1771-1832)
Time of action: Twelfth century
First published: 1825

PRINCIPAL CHARACTERS

Richard the Lion-Hearted, the English King who leads the Third Crusade to the Holy Land. He is proud and egotis-tical and the other leaders in the crusade resent him and also his methods. Ill of a fever, he is healed by a Moslem physician sent to him by Saladin, leader of the Moslems in the Holy War. An attempt is made on Richard's life, but a slave saves him. Richard finally realizes that the crusade is a failure.

Sir Kenneth, Knight of the Couchant Leopard, who is really David, Earl of Huntingdon and the Prince Royal of Scotland. He has taken a vow not to reveal his true identity until the Holy City is taken in the crusade. He will not break this oath, even to save his own life. Disguised as a Nubian slave, he is severely wounded by a poisoned knife while saving Richard's life. Richard sucks the poisoned wound and saves him. He is in love with Lady Edith Plantagenet, the King's kinswoman, but they cannot marry because he is a poor Scotsman and she is of royal blood. When Kenneth's true identity is known, they do marry.

El Hakim, the physician sent by Saladin to heal Richard. He makes a potion with a talisman he carries, and the potion cures Richard. El Hakim is really Saladin in disguise. He gives the talisman to Kenneth and Lady Edith as a wedding present.

Lady Edith Plantagenet, Richard's kinswoman, in love with Kenneth. She is lady in waiting to Richard's wife, the Queen.

Queen Berengaria, the Queen of England, who is at a convent because she is making a pilgrimage to pray for the King's recovery. She becomes bored and sends Kenneth a false message saying that Lady Edith wants to see him. He deserts his post of guarding the English royal standard because of this message and thus becomes an outcast from the Christian camp.

Theodorick of Engaddi, a hermit who is a go-between for the Christians and Moslems.

Conrade, the Marquis of Montserrat, a treacherous crusader who plans Richard's death because he wants part of Palestine for himself. Conrad urges the Archduke of Austria to place his flag next to that of Richard on the highest place in the camp. He is later responsible for stealing the English flag. He is wounded in a trial by arms and is stabbed by one of his cohorts so that he cannot confess the plot against Richard.

The Grand Master of the Knights Templars, one of the conspirators against Richard. He stabs and kills Conrade while bending over him to hear his confession.

TAMAR

Author: Robinson Jeffers (1887-1962)
Time of action: World War I
First published: 1924

PRINCIPAL CHARACTERS

Tamar Cauldwell, a passionate, neurotic, auburn-haired girl. She tempts her brother to deflower her and continues incest with him until she becomes pregnant. Intending to marry Will Andrews, she seduces him, hoping to hide her incest with Lee. She fails in an attempt to burn the Cauldwell home. In a wild dance on the seashore she brings on a miscarriage which leaves her ill and embittered at her whole family. She flaunts her body before her father to rouse his enfeebled lust. Taunting her brother with the lie that her lost child was Will's rather than his, she angers Lee until he whips her cruelly. Feigning a desire to reconcile the differences between Lee and Will, she then shows Will the marks of the whip and instigates a bloody fight between him and Lee. Triumphant, she dies by fire, taking her three lovers with her. The flames symbolically resemble the fleshly fires which have been consuming the Cauldwells since the old incest of David and Helen.

Lee Cauldwell, her dissolute brother. Nursed to health by Tamar after an accident, he warns Will to stay away from her and he then becomes her lover and the father of the child she loses. Tamar, preventing Lee from enlisting for World War I, also keeps him from escaping the burning Cauldwell home, and he dies in her locked embrace.

David Cauldwell, her father, a dotard of seventy who in repentence of old sins has turned to his Bible, but too late to save his doomed family.

Jinny Cauldwell, David's idiot sister, a woman of sixty. In youth she loved her brother, but he was drawn to Helen instead. Jinny in her madness innocently

causes the fire which brings death to the entire family.

Stella Moreland, sister of David's dead wife. She is nurse to Jinny. Through her as a medium the voice of Helen reveals much of the sordid past to Tamar. Stella dies with the Cauldwells.

Will Andrews, Tamar's suitor, blond, freckled, and wide-shouldered. He wishes to free Tamar from her family, but she desires only the freedom of death, and Will (already mortally wounded in his fight with Lee) dies in the holocaust which destroys the Cauldwells.

Helen Cauldwell, David's dead sister with whom he committed incest forty years earlier. After Tamar's orgiastic dance Helen's spirit voice taunts her, predicts that she will lose her baby, and informs her that her attempt to burn her home will not destroy the corruption of the family.

Ramon Ramirez, herdsman of the Cauldwell herds.

TAMBURLAINE THE GREAT, PARTS ONE AND TWO

Author: Christopher Marlowe (1564-1593)
Time of action: Fourteenth century
First presented: c. 1586-1587

PRINCIPAL CHARACTERS

Tamburlaine (tăm′bĕr·lān), the magniloquent Scythian shepherd who, becoming the ruler of vast lands in Africa and the Middle East, calls himself "the Scourge of God." Absolutely ruthless, he kills the defenseless women and children in conquered cities and stabs his own son when he finds him gambling during an important battle. He is pre-eminently theatrical, delighting in triumphal pageants and in such spectacular effects as changing the color of his tents from white to red to black while he waits outside a city for its surrender or its challenge. This dramatic

instinct inspires the imprisonment of the Emperor Bajazeth in a cake and the harnessing of four defeated rulers to Tamburlaine's chariot. Invulnerable to injury from men, Tamburlaine wages a strong battle against death and meets it in characteristic theatrical fashion when he has himself carried by his servants and friends to the head of his army.

Zenocrate (zĕ·nŏ′krə·tē), his wife and the daughter of the Soldan of Egypt. Although she is enraged when Tamburlaine captures her, she is quickly enthralled by his grand ambition and proudly wears her crown. She attempts on occasion to assuage her husband's cruelty by pleading for the life of her father and urging tolerance for the weakness of their son, Calyphas.

Bajazeth (bă′jă·zĕth), the proud Emperor of the Turks. Defeated by Tamburlaine in spite of his confidence in his own power, he is drawn about in a cage, like a beast, until he submits to his despair and dashes his brains out against the bars of his cage.

Zabina (ză·bī′nă), the arrogant wife of Bajazeth. She scorns Zenocrate and Tamburlaine even after her capture. She strengthens Bajazeth's resistance as long as possible, but she also recognizes the hopelessness of their state and kills herself as soon as she discovers her husband's body.

Mycetes (mī·sē′tēz), the King of Persia and an incompetent ruler. He resents the insults offered by his brother Cosroe, but he is incapable of defending his realm against him.

Cosroe (kŏs·rō′ē), Mycetes' ambitious brother, who criticizes the King's folly and plots the usurpation of his throne to restore the former glory of his nation. He enlists Tamburlaine's help to win Mycetes' crown, but he immediately finds himself deprived of the kingdom by his ally.

Techelles (tĕ·kĕ′lēz) and
Usumcasane (ōō·sŭm·kə·să′nē), Asian potentates and Tamburlaine's generals, who are rewarded with large realms.

Theridamas (thĕ′rĭ·dă′məs), a great Persian warrior who becomes one of Tamburlaine's most valued advisers. He falls in love with Olympia, the virtuous widow of one of Tamburlaine's conquered enemies, and asks her to marry him; he does not suspect her motives when she pretends to have a magic ointment which will save her from wounds, and he cuts her throat to test its efficacy.

Olympia (ō·lĭm′pĭ·ə), the widow of the Captain of Balsera. Faithful to her husband's memory, she rejects Theridamas and tricks him into killing her.

Agydas (ă′gĭ·dəs), one of Zenocrate's attendants. He foresees his mistress' love for the Scythian shepherd and the inevitability of his own death as punishment for trying to change her mind, and he forestalls his murderers by committing suicide.

Magnetes (măg·nē′tēz), his companion, another Median lord.

Anippe (ă·nĭ′pē), Zenocrate's servant, as proud as her master and mistress.

Celebinus (sĕ′lĕ·bī′nəs) and
Amyras (ă·mī′rəs), the bold, self-confident heirs of Tamburlaine and Zenocrate.

Calyphas (kă′lĭ·fəs), their brother, a luxury-loving youth, slain by his father, who despises his cowardice.

Callepine (kă′lə·pīn), Bajazeth's son, imprisoned by Tamburlaine. He escapes with the help of his jailer and becomes the leader of the forces opposing Tamburlaine.

Orcanes (ôr·kă′nēz),
Gazellus (gə·zĕ′ləs), and
Uribassa (ū·rĭ·bă′sə), Moslem rulers who attempt to make an alliance with their Christian enemies to halt the power of Tamburlaine.

Sigismund (sĭ′gĭs·mŭnd), King of Hungary,
Frederick (frĕ′dĕ·rĭk), Lord of Buda, and
Baldwin (bôl′dwĭn), Lord of Bohemia, the Christian leaders who break their solemn vows of allegiance to the Moslems, attack them, and lose the battle to those they have betrayed.

The Soldan of Egypt (sōl′dən), Zenocrate's father, who is enraged at the kidnaping of his daughter.

Meander, (mē·ăn'dĕr), **Ortygius** (ôr·tĭ'jĭ·əs), **Ceneus,** (sē'nĭ·əs), and **Menaphon** (mĕ'nə·fŏn), Persian supporters of Mycetes and Cosroe.

Capolin (kă'pō·lĭn), an Egyptian captain.

Philemus (fĭ·lē'məs), the Soldan's messenger.

Almeda (ăl·mē'də), Callepine's jailer, who aids him to escape and joins his party.

Perdicas (pĕr'dĭ·kəs), Calyphas' servant.

THE TAMING OF THE SHREW

Author: William Shakespeare (1564-1616)
Time of action: Sixteenth century
First presented: 1593-1594

PRINCIPAL CHARACTERS

Katharina (kăt·ə·rē'nə) the shrew, the spirited elder daughter of Baptista, a well-to-do Paduan gentleman. She storms at her father, her mild young sister, and her tutors until she meets Petruchio, who ignores her protests of rage and marries her while she stands by in stunned amazement. She continues to assert her will, but she finds her husband's even stronger than her own and learns that submission is the surest means to a quiet life. Her transformation is a painful revelation to Lucentio and Hortensio, who must pay Petruchio their wagers and, in addition, live with wives who are less dutiful than they supposed.

Petruchio (pĕ·trōōch'ĭ·ō, pĕ·trōō'kē·ō), her masterful husband, who comes from Verona to Padua frankly in search of a wealthy wife. He is easily persuaded by his friend Hortensio to court Katharina and pave the way for her younger sister's marriage. Katharina's manners do not daunt him; in truth, his are little better than hers, as his long-suffering servants could testify. He meets insult with insult, storm with storm, humiliating his bride by appearing at the altar in his oldest garments and keeping her starving and sleepless, all the while pretending the greatest solicitude for her welfare. Using the methods of training hawks, he tames a wife and ensures a happy married life for himself.

Bianca (bē·än'kə, bē·än'kà), Katharina's pretty, gentle younger sister, for whose hand Lucentio, Hortensio, and Gremio are rivals. Although she is completely charming to her suitors, she is, in her own way, clever and strong-willed, and she chides her bridegroom for being so foolish as to lay wagers on her dutifulness.

Baptista (bǎp·tēs'tà), her father, a wealthy Paduan. Determined to treat his shrewish daughter fairly, he refuses to let Bianca marry before her. Petruchio's courtship is welcome, even though its unorthodoxy disturbs him, and he offers a handsome dowry with Katharina, doubling it when he sees the results of his son-in-law's "taming" which gives him "another daughter." Bianca's marriage without his consent distresses and angers him, but his good nature wins out and he quickly forgives her, watching with delight as Petruchio demonstrates his success with Katharina.

Lucentio (lōō·chĕn'sē·ō), the son of a Pisan merchant, who comes to Padua to study. He falls in love with Bianca when he first hears her speak and disguises himself as Cambio, a schoolmaster, in order to gain access to her, while his servant masquerades as Lucentio. He reveals his identity to his lady and persuades her to wed him secretly, but he finds his happiness somewhat marred when she costs him one hundred crowns by refusing to come at his call.

Hortensio (hôr·tĕn'shĭ·ō), Petruchio's friend, who presents himself, disguised as a musician, as a teacher for Bianca. Convinced that Katharina is incorrigible, he watches Petruchio's taming of his wife with amusement and skepticism. He weds a rich widow after becoming disillusioned when he sees Bianca embracing the supposed Cambio. Thus he finds himself, like Lucentio, with a wife more willful than he has expected.

Gremio (grē'mĭ·ō, grē'mē·ō), an aging Paduan who hires the disguised Lucentio to forward his courtship of Bianca. His hopes are dashed when Tranio, as Lucentio, offers Baptista a large settlement for his daughter, and he is forced to become an observer of others' romances.

Vincentio (vĕn·chĕn'sē·ō), Lucentio's father. He is first bewildered, then angry, when he arrives in Padua to find an impostor claiming his name, his son missing, and his servant Tranio calling himself Lucentio. Overjoyed to find the real Lucentio alive, he quickly reassures Baptista that an appropriate settlement will be made for Bianca's marriage, saving his anger for the impostors who tried to have him imprisoned.

Tranio (trä'nē·ō), Lucentio's servant, who advises his master to follow his inclinations for pleasure, rather than study.

He plays his master's part skillfully, courting Bianca to draw her father's attention away from her tutor, and even providing himself with a father to approve his courtship. He recognizes trouble in the form of the real Vincentio and attempts to avert it by refusing to recognize his old master and ordering him off to jail. His ruse is unsuccessful, and only nuptial gaiety saves him from the force of Vincentio's wrath.

Grumio (grōō'mē·ō) and
Curtis, (kər'tĭs), Petruchio's long-suffering servants.

Biondello (bē·ŏn·dĕl'ō), Lucentio's servant, who aids in the conspiracy for Bianca's hand.

A Pedant, an unsuspecting traveler who is persuaded by Tranio to impersonate Vincentio.

Christopher Sly, a drunken countryman, found unconscious at a tavern by a lord and his huntsmen. They amuse themselves by dressing him in fine clothes and greeting him as a nobleman, newly recovered from insanity. Sly readily accepts their explanations, settles himself in his new luxury, and watches the play of Katharina and Petruchio with waning interest.

A Lord, the eloquent nobleman who arranges the jest.

Bartholomew, his page, who pretends to be Sly's noble wife.

TAPS FOR PRIVATE TUSSIE

Author: Jesse Stuart (1907-   )
Time of action: Twentieth century
First published: 1943

PRINCIPAL CHARACTERS

Grandpa Tussie, the head of the Tussie clan. He lives with his family in a schoolhouse coal shed until the supposed death of a son. After the funeral, the son's wife uses her insurance money to set up the family in a rented mansion, where they and descending relatives live high. Grandpa's relief check is taken away and later, when the last of the insurance money is used to buy a farm in his name, his old-age pension is also taken away.

Grandma Tussie, his wife. When she counts forty-six Tussie relatives living in the mansion, she will stand for no more.

George Tussie, Grandpa's brother, the first relative to move in. A fine fiddle player, he has been married five times. His nephew's "widow" falls in love with his fiddle playing and marries him.

Uncle Mott Tussie, Grandpa's son. He is in love with his brother's wife and therefore hates George. When he finally shoots George's fiddle from his hands, George shoots him through the head.

Aunt Vittie Tussie, the "widow" who has inherited ten thousand dollars in government insurance and spends it lavishly on the family.

Uncle Kim Tussie, the supposedly deceased son. He reappears at the end of the novel—his brother Mott had falsely identified the body in hopes of inheriting his sister-in-law—and family life is resumed

as it was before his "death," except for the presence now of Uncle Mott's body.

Sid Seagraves Tussie, a grandson. He is revealed at last by Kim to be Aunt Vittie's son by a rich man who wronged Aunt Vittie and paid Kim to marry her. Now he is to be Kim's and Aunt Vittie's son.

George Rayburn, whose mansion the Tussies rent and almost wreck. He evicts them with difficulty.

Sheriff Whiteapple, who has to serve legal papers before the Tussies will leave the Rayburn mansion; after George Tussie's shooting of Mott the sheriff comes for George.

Uncle Ben,
Dee,
Young Uncle Ben,
Starkie,
Watt,
Sabie, and
Abe, some of the Tussie relatives who move in. Uncle Mott shoots Young Uncle Ben and Dee for reporting Grandpa to the relief agency.

TARAS BULBA

Author: Nikolai V. Gogol (1809-1852)
Time of action: Fifteenth century
First published: 1835

PRINCIPAL CHARACTERS

Taras Bulba (tä′rəs boŏly′bä), a sturdy old Cossack warrior and chieftain, restless, fierce, and stubborn. He hates luxury, loves the simple Cossack life, and regards himself as a defender of the Russian Orthodox faith. Elected leader for the second attack on Dubno, Taras fights bravely and narrowly avoids capture when the Poles win the battle. Unable to visit the captured Ostap in prison, Taras does witness Ostap's torture and boldly calls out to him before Ostap dies. Disappearing in the crowd watching the torture and execution of the captured

Cossacks, Taras escapes from Warsaw and leads many raids of destruction, pillage, and death against the Poles. Finally captured by a superior Polish force, he is burned to death, but not before he has seen the heroic escape of many of his men to whom he has called out defiantly to continue the fight against injustice. Taras is presented as a great folk hero whose epic exploits are reminiscent of those of Homer's warriors.

Ostap (ôs·täp′), Taras' older son, a former student. At first rebellious against studies, he later ranks high. Loyal to his comrades, he loves war and carousing but is more often a follower than a leader in the academy. As a warrior, however, he shows the cool calculation and tactical ingenuity that seem to predict for him a chieftaincy. In the second battle of Dubno, he is captured and taken to Warsaw, where, after being publicly tortured, he is put to death.

Andrii (än·dri͝y′), Taras' younger son, also a former student. In the academy he learned more readily, willingly, and with less effort than Ostap. He was daring, ingenious, clever in avoiding punishment, and early became a lover of women. As a fledgling warrior he is reckless and intoxicated by battle. Captivated by the memories of a beautiful girl, daughter of the Polish Waiwode of Koven, whose room he once visited, he follows her aged servant secretly into Dubno, taking bread to the starving girl and her relatives during the siege of the town. He deserts to the Polish forces, succumbs to Polish luxury, and leads an assault against the Cossacks. Taras shoots him dead.

Yankel, a Jewish merchant rescued by Taras from Cossack wrath against the Jews. He fails in his attempt to enable Taras—on a promise of a great reward —to visit Ostap in the Warsaw prison. Gogol makes Yankel a stock Jewish character, by turns greedy, servile, and flattering.

The Daughter of the Polish Waiwode, or Military Governor, Andrii's sweetheart, beautiful, dark-eyed, and chestnut-haired. Volatile and mischievous when Andrii first sees her, she is more maturely and soberly beautiful when he meets her again in Dubno.

Kirdyaga (kĭr·dyä′gə), newly elected leader of the Setch (a Cossack encampment) and a close friend of Taras.

Nikolai Pototsky (nĭ·kô·lĭ′ pô·tōt′skĭy), a Polish hetman captured by the Cossacks but freed on a promise to grant religious freedom to all Christian churches and not to exact vengeance against the Cossacks. He later leads the campaign which results in the capture and execution of Taras.

Borodaty (bə·rô·dä′tĭy), a Cossack hetman slain from behind as he despoils a slain Pole. Ostap replaces Borodaty as leader of the Uman company.

Kassian Bovdyug (kə·sĭ än′ bôv·dūg′), an old Cossack who nominates Taras as leader of the Cossacks in the second battle at Dubno. Bovdyug dies in the battle.

Mossy Shilo (mô·sĭy′ shĭ′lə), a powerful Cossack once captured and enslaved by the Turks. Capable of great deeds on occasion, he at other times succumbs to a passion for liquor. He dies bravely in the second battle of Dubno.

TARR

Author: Wyndham Lewis (1886-1957)
Time of action: c. 1910
First published: 1918

PRINCIPAL CHARACTERS

Frederick Tarr, an English artist in Paris engaged to Bertha Lunken. Tired of her stupidity, he breaks the engage-

ment and becomes involved with Anastasya Vasek. But when Bertha tells him that she is pregnant by Kreisler, he marries her, though continuing to live with Anastasya. Bertha finally divorces him, but he never marries Anastasya.

Bertha Lunken, a sentimental German art student engaged to Tarr. After he breaks the engagement, she turns to Kreisler, who forcibly possesses her. She informs Tarr of her pregnancy and he marries her from pity, although he continues to live with Anastasya. Bertha eventually divorces Tarr and marries an eye doctor.

Otto Kreisler, a German artist, chronically short of funds. In love with Anas-
tasya, he makes a fool of himself at a party and then gets involved with Bertha. Seeing Anastasya with Soltyk, he challenges the Pole to a duel and kills him. Fleeing to Germany, he is arrested, and he hangs himself in his cell.

Anastasya Vasek, a beautiful Russian, loved by Tarr, Kreisler, and Soltyk. It is over her that Kreisler and Soltyk fight a duel in which Soltyk is killed. She goes to live with Tarr.

Louis Soltyk, a Pole. Because of his attentions to Anastasya, he is challenged and killed by Kreisler.

TARTARIN OF TARASCON

Author: Alphonse Daudet (1840-1897)
Time of action: Nineteenth century
First published: 1872

PRINCIPAL CHARACTERS

Tartarin (tȧr·tȧ·răṅ'), a huntsman of Tarascon who distinguishes himself by growing a garden full of tropical plants in the south of France, keeping a full arsenal of weapons of all nations, using the firearms to shoot holes through the caps of his friends, explaining to citizens the wonders of the mysterious East (though he has never been there), and going on an African lion hunt. In his quest for the beast he invades Algerian village squares, private gardens, and Mohammedan convent grounds, but he never quite arrives upon the lion-infested veldt his numerous noble weapons deserve. He does get his lion, though—a tame, blind, toothless convent pet that comes ambling toward him down the path to a saint's tomb. Tartarin has to sell all his fine weapons to pay the damages for slaughtering the unfortunate creature.

Prince Grégory (prăns' grā·gô·rē'), a Montenegrin nobleman and Tartarin's shipmate aboard the "Zouave." He locates a Moorish maiden who has stolen Tartarin's heart, accompanies him on a
lion hunt, and finally vanishes with his purse.

Baïa, a twenty-year-old Moorish widow who distracts Tartarin from his hunting mission for a time. They take a house in the native quarter and Baïa entertains her lord, now called Sidi Tart'ri ben Tart'ri, with monotonous songs and the belly dance.

Captain Barbassou (bȧr·bȧ·sōō'), commander of the "Zouave," the ship that brings Tartarin to Algiers. Wise in the ways of the world, he gives Tartarin some good advice about Montenegrin princes and Moorish widows. Tartarin, unfortunately, does not heed the Captain's advice.

Commander Bravida (brȧ·vē·dȧ'), a Tarasconese dignitary who, representing community opinion, finally orders Tartarin to leave for Africa and the lion hunt that he has been discussing for months.

Madame Bézuquet (bā·zü·kā'), Tartarin's singing partner at social events.

1110

TARTUFFE

Author: Molière (Jean Baptiste Poquelin, 1622-1673)
Time of action: Seventeenth century
First presented: 1664

PRINCIPAL CHARACTERS

Tartuffe (tär·tüf'), a religious hypocrite and impostor who uses religious cant and practices to impose on the credulity of a wealthy man who befriends him. To gain money and cover deceit, he talks of his hair shirt and scourge, of prayers and distributing alms; and he disapproves of immodest dress. Before his first appearance he is reported by some to be a good man of highest worth, by others to be a glutton, a winebibber, and a hypocrite. Deciding that he wants his patron's daughter as his wife, he uses his seeming piety to convince his host to break his daughter's marriage plans. He then endeavors to seduce his host's wife by holding her hand, patting her knee, fingering her lace collar, and making declarations of love to her. When his conduct is reported to the husband by his wife and their son, the foolish man forgives Tartuffe and gives the hypocrite all his property. Another attempted seduction fails when the husband, hidden, overhears all that happens and orders Tartuffe out of the house. Tartuffe, boasting that the entire property is now his, has an eviction order served on his former patron. When a police officer arrives to carry out the eviction order, the tables are turned. Tartuffe is arrested at the order of the King, who declares him to be a notorious rogue.

Orgon (ôr·gōn'), a credulous, wealthy man taken in by Tartuffe, whom he befriends, invites into his home, and proposes as a husband for his daughter, already promised to another. Defending Tartuffe against the accusations of his family and servants, he refuses to believe charges that the scoundrel has attempted to seduce his wife. He then disowns his children and signs over all his property to Tartuffe. Only later, when he hides under the table, at the urging of his wife, and overhears Tartuffe's second attempt at seduction, is he convinced that he is harboring a hypocrite and scheming rascal. Orgon is saved from arrest and eviction when Tartuffe is taken away by police officers.

Elmire (ĕl·mēr'), Orgon's wife. Aware of the wickedness of Tartuffe, she is unable to reveal the hypocrite's true nature to her husband. When she finds herself the object of Tartuffe's wooing, she urges the son not to make the story public, for she believes a discreet and cold denial to be more effective than violent cries of deceit. Finally, by a planned deception of Tartuffe, she convinces her husband of that scoundrel's wickedness.

Dorine (dô·rēn'), a maid, a shrewd, outspoken, witty girl who takes an active part in exposing Tartuffe and assisting the lovers in their plot against him. Much of the humor of the play results from her impertinence. She objects straightforwardly to the forced marriage of Tartuffe to Mariane, and she prevents a misunderstanding between the true lovers.

Mariane (má·rē·án'), Orgon's daughter, regarded as a prude by her grandmother. In love with Valère she is unhappy over the marriage to Tartuffe proposed by her father. Because of her timidity, her only action at the time is to fall at Orgon's feet and implore him to change his mind.

Damis (dá·mē'), Orgon's son, regarded as a fool by his grandmother. His temper and indiscretion lead him to upset carefully laid plans, as when he suddenly

1111

comes out of the closet in which he has listened to Tartuffe's wooing of Elmire and reports the story naïvely to his father. He is outwitted by Tartuffe's calm admission of the charge and his father's belief in Tartuffe's innocence, despite the confession.

Valère (và·lĕr'), Mariane's betrothed. He quarrels with her, after hearing that Orgon intends to marry the girl to Tartuffe, because she seems not to object to the proposal with sufficient force. In a comedy scene the maid, running alternately between the lovers, reconciles the pair, and Valère determines that they will be married. He loyally offers to help Orgon flee after the eviction order is served on him by the court.

Madame Pernelle (pĕr·nĕl'), Orgon's mother, an outspoken old woman. Like her son, she believes in the honesty and piety of Tartuffe, and she hopes that his attitude and teachings may reclaim her grandchildren and brother-in-law from their social frivality. She defends Tartuffe even after Orgon turns against him. She admits her mistake only after the eviction order has been delivered.

Cléante (klā·änt'), Orgon's brother-in-law. He talks in pompous maxims and makes long tiresome speeches of advice to Orgon and Tartuffe. Both disregard him.

M. Loyal (lwà·yàl'), a tipstaff of the court. He serves the eviction order on Orgon.

A Police Officer, brought in by Tartuffe to arrest Orgon. Instead, he arrests Tartuffe by order of the King.

Filipote (fē·lē·pôt'), Madame Pernelle's servant.

THE TEMPEST

Author: William Shakespeare (1564-1616)
Time of action: Fifteenth century
First presented: 1611

PRINCIPAL CHARACTERS

Prospero (prŏs'pĕ·rō), the former and rightful Duke of Milan now living on an island in the distant seas. Years before, he had been deposed by his treacherous younger brother, Antonio, to whom he had given too much power, for Prospero had always been more interested in his books of philosophy and magic than in affairs of state. Antonio had had the aid of Alonso, the equally treacherous King of Naples, in his plot against his brother, and the conspirators had set Prospero and his infant daughter, Miranda, adrift in a small boat. They were saved from certain death by the faithful Gonzalo, who provided the boat with food and Prospero's books. Eventually the craft drifted to an island which had formerly been the domain of the witch Sycorax, whose son, the monster Caliban, still lived there. Through the power of his magic, Prospero subdued Caliban and freed certain good spirits, particularly Ariel, whom Sycorax had imprisoned. Now in a terrible storm the ship carrying the treacherous King of Naples, his son Ferdinand, and Antonio is wrecked; and they with their companions are brought ashore by Ariel. Using Ariel as an instrument, Prospero frustrates the plots of Antonio and Sebastan against the King and of Caliban, Trinculo, and Stephano against himself. He also furthers the romance between Miranda and Ferdinand. Convinced at last that Antonio and Alonso have repented of the wrongs they had done him, Prospero has them brought to his cell, where he reveals his identity and reclaims his dukedom. At the end of the story he has the satisfaction of releasing Ariel, abandoning his magic, and returning to Milan for the marriage of Miranda and Ferdinand. In the figure of Prospero, some readers have found Shakespeare's self-portrait; and in Prospero's burying of his books on magic they have found a symbol of Shakespeare's renunciation of the stage.

Miranda (mĭ·răn′də), Prospero's daughter. Brought up on the island where her aged father is the only man she has ever seen, she falls instantly in love with Ferdinand. At the end of the play, they are to be married. The character of Miranda has often been taken as the depiction of complete innocence, untouched by the corruption of sophisticated life.

Ferdinand (fûr′dĭ·nănd), Prince of Naples, son of King Alonso. Separated from his father when they reach the island, he is captured by Prospero, who, to test him, puts him at menial tasks. He falls in love with Miranda and she with him. Prospero finally permits their marriage.

Alonso (ə·lŏn′zō), King of Naples and father of Ferdinand. He aided the treacherous Antonio in deposing Prospero. When the castaways reach Prospero's island, Alonso is so grief-stricken by the supposed loss of his son that he repents of his wickedness and is forgiven by Prospero.

Antonio (ăn·tō′nĭ·ō), Prospero's treacherous brother who has usurped the Dukedom of Milan. He is finally forgiven for his crime.

Sebastian (sĕ·băs′tyən), brother of Alonso. On the island he plots with Antonio to usurp the throne of Naples. Prospero discovers and frustrates the plot.

Gonzalo (gŏn·zä′lō), a faithful courtier who had saved the lives of Prospero and Miranda.

Ariel (ā′rĭ·ĕl), a spirit imprisoned by Sycorax and released by Prospero, whom he serves faithfully. At the conclusion of the play, having carried out all of Prospero's commands, he is given complete freedom.

Caliban (kăl′ĭ·băn), the monstrous son of Sycorax, now a servant of Prospero. He represents brute force without intelligence and can be held in check only by Prospero's magic. Some have seen in him Shakespeare's conception of "natural man."

Stephano (stĕf′ä·nō), a drunken butler who plots with Caliban and Trinculo against Prospero and is foiled by Ariel.

Trinculo (trĭng′kū·lō), a clown, a companion of Stephano and later of Caliban.

THE TEMPLE BEAU

Author: Henry Fielding (1707-1754)
Time of action: Eighteenth century
First presented: 1730

PRINCIPAL CHARACTERS

Sir Harry Wilding, a wealthy Englishman. He is infuriated when he discovers that his son is spending his time as a useless dandy. After being tricked into signing over an annuity to the youth, he is consequently powerless to change his offspring's rakish ways even with threats of disinheritance.

Wilding, Sir Harry's son. Supposed to be a law student in London, he is actually a gay young man about town. When he falls in love with Bellaria, he employs a ruse to escape potential affairs with Lady Lucy and Lady Gravely. Though he fails to marry Bellaria, he does trick his father into granting him an annuity.

Bellaria, a beautiful young heiress. Though loved and wanted by many men, including young Wilding and Valentine, she marries Veromil, who loves her as much as she loves him.

Sir Avarice Pedant, Bellaria's uncle. Although he is supposed to arrange a marriage between his niece and young Wilding, he tries instead to marry her to his own son.

Young Pedant, a young man so interested in his studies that he cannot become interested in women, even beautiful young heiresses.

Lady Lucy, Sir Avarice Pedant's young wife. A coquettish woman, she flirts with young Wilding and with Valentine.

Lady Gravely, Sir Avarice Pedant's sister. She puts on the airs of a prude but discreetly indulges herself in love affairs.

Valentine, a licentious young man who flirts with Lady Lucy. He hopes to marry Bellaria, but instead helps his friend Veromil win the girl. He tricks Sir Avarice out of a large sum of money.

Veromil, a fine young man cheated of his inheritance by a dishonest brother. He marries Bellaria after regaining his inheritance.

THE TEMPTATION OF SAINT ANTHONY

Author: Gustave Flaubert (1821-1880)
Time of action: Fourth century
First published: 1874

PRINCIPAL CHARACTERS

Saint Anthony (ăn'thə·nē), a hermit for thirty years but now despondent because he feels that his life has been a failure. He is tempted by gluttony, avarice, and lust, but overcomes them all. His disciple, Hilarion, appears to accuse him of ignorance and to tempt him intellectually by exposing him to all the confusing heresies of the early Church and to the false gods of history, each of whom contained some element of truth. He is even carried into space by Satan, to be shown that the universe is limitless and meaningless and to be urged to curse God and acknowledge the Devil. Even this temptation Anthony overcomes, as well as the urgings of Death and Lust that he escape through them the ugliness of the world. When, the next day, Anthony sees the face of Christ in the sun, he knows that he has conquered.

The Devil, who subjects Anthony to the horror of infinity.

Hilarion (hǐ·lả'rǐ·ən), Anthony's former disciple, who exposes him to the sins of the intellect.

The Queen of Sheba (shē'bə), representing lust.

Tertullian (tėr·tŭ'lǐ·ən), who drives away the heresiarchs.

Apollonius (ă'pə·lō'nǐ·əs), who almost conquers Anthony by the offer of the power of having visions and of curing the sick.

Marcellina (mär·cĕ·lē'nə), a woman who tells Anthony that with the aid of a silver image she can cause Christ to appear.

Montanus (mŏn·tā'nŭs), who, according to a strange woman Anthony meets, is the incarnation of the Holy Ghost.

1114

THE TENANT OF WILDFELL HALL

Author: Anne Brontë (1820-1849)
Time of action: The 1820's
First published: 1848

PRINCIPAL CHARACTERS

Gilbert Markham, a kindhearted, industrious, passionate young farmer. In a series of letters written to his brother-in-law he tells the story of his romance with the mysterious woman who is the new tenant of Wildfell Hall. At first unable to get through her protective shell of coldness and aloofness, Gilbert finally discovers her story, and his sincere sympathy and interest in her work as a landscape painter endear him to her. After several years of separation faithful Gilbert marries his loved one.

Mrs. Helen Graham, in reality **Mrs. Arthur Huntingdon,** the mysterious tenant of Wildfell Hall. Seemingly a cold and self-contained woman, she jealously guards her son Arthur from any outside interference when she first arrives at Wildfell Hall, where she is content to walk about the countryside and sketch the landscape. The village gossip is that she is carrying on an affair with her landlord, Frederick Lawrence. Eventually she reveals her story to Gilbert Markham and allows him to read her private journal. He learns that she had been brought up by her rich uncle and aunt and that she had fallen unwisely in love with Arthur Huntingdon, a handsome but wayward young man. Although warned by her aunt not to marry Arthur, Helen did so willfully and thus began a marriage of horror. Faithful and loving, she endured much from her wild and dissipated husband. Finally, when she realized that his profligate ways were affecting their son adversely and that he was carrying on an affair with the wife of one of his friends, Helen left him and fled to Wildfell Hall, to be near the home of her brother. There she meets Gilbert Markham, whose kindness and true affection win her heart.

Arthur Huntingdon, a selfish, reckless young man of profligate habits. Although truly in love with his young wife at the time of their marriage, he cannot give up his former carefree and wicked life, and his character begins to deteriorate. Unable to adapt himself to a domestic situation, he takes more and more journeys to London and then begins to bring his riotous friends home to Grasslands, his country estate. Soon he becomes involved in an affair with Lady Annabella Lowborough, whose husband is one of his friends. When he discovers that his wife Helen is painting pictures to enable her to accumulate enough money to leave him, he has all of her artist's supplies destroyed. He dies a horrible death after drinking wine in defiance of his doctor's orders, and his death leaves Helen free to marry Gilbert Markham. Branwell Brontë served as the model for his sister's portrait of a man wasting his life in dissipation.

Frederick Lawrence, a sheltered, shy, self-contained man, Helen Graham's brother. No one in the parish knows their relationship and the gossips believe that he is carrying on an illicit affair with the strange tenant of Wildfell Hall, the family home he had deserted for another residence in a nearby parish. When Gilbert Markham learns the truth after reading Helen's journal, the gossip ceases.

Rose Markham, a tidy, plump young girl with a round face, bright blooming cheeks, glossy clustering curls, and merry brown eyes. Devoted to her brother Gilbert, she hesitates to believe the gossip about Helen Graham. She marries Mr. Halford.

Mrs. Markham, Gilbert's widowed

mother. She is a favorite in the parish and often entertains her many friends. Much impressed with Helen Graham, she finds it difficult to believe the gossip about her.

Fergus Markham, Gilbert's younger brother, a good-natured, teasing, lazy lad who supplies much of the humor in the story.

The Reverend Michael Millward, a tall, ponderous, elderly gentleman of fixed principles, strong prejudices, and regular habits. Because he is intolerant of dissent of any kind and feels that his opinions are always right, he chides Helen Graham for not attending church. He readily believes the stories told about her and attempts to lecture her on her conduct. He is practically turned away from Wildfell Hall for his pains.

Eliza Millward, the vicar's younger daughter, a plump, charming young girl in love with Gilbert Markham. Like a pretty, playful kitten, she is now roguish, now timid and demure. She is responsible for many of the tales against Helen Graham because she sees in her a rival for Gilbert's hand.

Mary Millward, her sister, several years older, a plain, quiet girl of warmer disposition than her sister. She has been the family housekeeper and drudge all her life. Gilbert Markham remarks that she is "loved and courted by all the dogs and cats but slighted and neglected by everybody else."

Mrs. Wilson, a narrow-minded, tattling village gossip whose garrulous nature causes her to spread tales about Mrs. Graham.

Robert Wilson, her older son, a rough, countrified bumpkin.

Richard Wilson, her younger son, a retiring studious young man. With the vicar's assistance he studies the classics in preparation for college. He plans to enter the Church.

Jane Wilson, their sister. She has a boarding school education and elegant manners, but her social ambitions will allow her to take only a gentleman for a husband. She has her eye on Frederick Lawrence, the young squire who formerly occupied Wildfell Hall.

Rachel, Helen Graham's servant and devoted companion. Aware of her mistress' situation at Wildfell Hall, she is cold and suspicious of their neighbors.

Arthur Huntingdon, called **Arthur Graham,** Helen's fun-loving, affectionate small son. Greatly attracted to Gilbert Markham, he serves as an introductory wedge between that gentleman and his mother.

Mr. Boarham, a fashionable young gentleman and Helen's suitor before her marriage to Arthur Huntingdon. Like his name, Boarham is a boring person, and in spite of her aunt's approval Helen cannot tolerate him.

Mr. Wilmot, a wealthy old man who pursues Helen. He is greatly surprised by her refusal of his hand.

Annabella, Mr. Wilmot's niece, a dashing girl who seems too much of a flirt ever to marry. She does marry Lord Lowborough, however, but carries on affairs afterward, including a serious one with Arthur Huntingdon.

Lord Lowborough, Arthur Huntingdon's friend, a sober, tall, thin, gentleman with a sickly, careworn aspect. Through his marriage to Annabella he hopes to acquire some peace in life, but he fails to do so because of her waywardness.

Millicent Hargrave, Annabella's cousin and Helen's good friend. After Millicent's unfortunate marriage to Mr. Hattersley, she endures the same sort of life that Helen does, having to put up with the drinking bouts and wild conduct of her husband. Her life becomes more comfortable after Mr. Hattersley, observing the fate of Arthur Huntingdon, reforms and becomes a gentle and devoted husband.

Mr. Hattersley, Millicent's wild husband and Arthur Huntingdon's companion on excursions to London. During the early years of their marriage he browbeats and torments his wife, but eventually he changes for the better.

Walter Hargrave, Millicent's brother. Enamored of Helen, he pursues her with offers of protection and marriage during her unhappy life with Arthur Huntingdon. Although he belongs to the London drinking, gaming, hunting set, he is less boisterous and more temperate than the others.

Benson, the Huntingdon butler. Devoted to Helen, he helps her to escape from Grasslands.

Miss Myers, a sullen young woman hired by Arthur Huntingdon as a governess for his son when he decides to separate his wife from her child.

Mr. Halford, Gilbert Markham's brother-in-law at a later date, to whom Gilbert writes the letters that tell the story of Helen Graham and his own romance with the tenant of Wildfell Hall.

TENDER IS THE NIGHT

Author: F. Scott Fitzgerald (1896-1940)
Time of action: The 1920's
First published: 1934

PRINCIPAL CHARACTERS

Dick Diver, a brilliant young psychiatrist who inspires confidence in everyone. As a young man he met and married a patient of his and devoted most of his time during the next several years to helping her regain a certain normality. But in the process of helping his wife he loses his own self-respect, alienates most of his friends, and drowns his brilliance in alcohol. His professional position deteriorates to that of a general practitioner in successively smaller towns across the United States.

Nicole Warren Diver, Dick's wife, a fabulously rich American. As a young girl she had an incestuous relationship with her father and subsequently suffered a mental breakdown. She marries Dick while still a patient and is content to let him guide her in all things for several years. When he begins to drink heavily and make scenes in public, she tries to stop him; in doing so she begins to gain some moral strength of her own. In a short time she no longer needs Dick, has a brief affair, and divorces Dick to marry

her lover. Apparently aware of her part in Dick's downfall, she continues to be somewhat concerned for him.

Rosemary Hoyt, a beautiful young American movie actress. Having fallen in love with Dick, who is several years her senior, on their first meeting, she later has a brief affair with him. When she finally recognizes the decline in him, she is powerless to do anything about it. Although she retains her devotion to both of the Divers, she has never really grown up herself and is incapable of acting positively without direction.

Tommy Barban, a war hero and professional soldier. Typically cold and unfeeling where most people are concerned, he spends much of his time fighting in various wars. He eventually becomes Nicole's lover and then her second husband.

Beth Evan (Baby) Warren, Nicole's older sister. Knowing nothing of the real nature of Nicole's illness, she feels that the family should buy a doctor to marry and care for her. She never fully approves of Dick because her snobbery makes her feel superior to him. After a succession of quiet, well-mannered affairs, she remains without roots or direction in her life.

Mrs. Elsie Speers, Rosemary Hoyt's mother. She devotes her life to making Rosemary a successful actress. She also tries to make her an individual but fails to achieve this goal.

Abe North, an unambitious musician. An early friend of the Divers, he goes consistently downhill and is finally murdered.

Mary North, Abe's wife. She is an ineffectual person while married to Abe; later she makes a more advantageous marriage and fancies herself one of the queens of the international set.

Collis Clay, a young American friend of Rosemary. Fresh from Yale, he is now

studying architecture in Europe and despairs of ever having to go back to Georgia to take over the family business.

Franz Gregorovious, a Swiss psychiatrist who becomes Dick Diver's partner in a clinic they establish with Nicole's money.

Kaethe, his wife, a tactless woman who is jealous of Americans and their money.

Gausse, the proprietor of a small hotel on the Riviera where the Divers and their friends often spend their summers.

Mr. and Mrs. McKisco, an American novelist and his wife who, after achieving financial success, lose their sense of inferiority and gain the superiority and snobbishness typical of the moneyed Americans in the Diver set.

Lady Caroline Sibly-Biers, an English friend of Mary North after her second marriage. She typifies the overbearing attitude of her class.

TESS OF THE D'URBERVILLES

Author: Thomas Hardy (1840-1928)
Time of action: Late nineteenth century
First published: 1891

PRINCIPAL CHARACTERS

Tess Durbeyfield, a naïve country girl. When her father learns that his family is descended from an ancient landed house, the mother, hoping to better her struggling family financially, sends Tess to work for the Stoke-d'Urbervilles, who have recently moved to the locality. In this household the innocent girl, attractive and mature beyond her years, meets Alec d'Urberville, a dissolute young man. From this time on she is the rather stoical victim of personal disasters. Seduced by Alec, she gives birth to his child. Later she works on a dairy farm, where she meets Angel Clare and reluctantly agrees to marry him, even though she is afraid of his reaction if he learns about her past. As she fears,

he is disillusioned by her loss of innocence and virtue. Although deserted by her husband, she never loses her unselfish love for him. Eventually, pursued by the relentless Alec, she capitulates to his blandishments and goes to live with him at a prosperous resort. When Angel Clare returns to her, she stabs Alec and spends a few happy days with Clare before she is captured and hanged for her crime.

Angel Clare, Tess's husband. Professing a dislike for effete, worn-out families and outdated traditions, he is determined not to follow family tradition and become a clergyman or a scholar. Instead, he wishes to learn what he can about farm-leases his friend while the guard is engaged with a dancing girl he has provided.

Mnesilochus (ně·sĭ'lō·kəs), Euripides' madcap friend and father-in-law. After being painfully shaved, depilated, and dressed in a woman's robe, he joins the celebrants in the temple. There he presumably would have gone undetected had he been able to keep quiet during the debate on the punishment to be accorded Euripides for his insults to women. In his defense of the poet, however, he insults the women even more. When Clisthenes announces to the enraged women that Euripides has sent a disguised man among them, he is quickly discovered. He attempts to make his escape by snatching a child away from one of the worshipers for a hostage, but the infant turns out to be a wine skin shod with Persian slippers. Arrested, he is rescued by Euripides. The plot development leads to a series of broadly farcical situations.

Agathon (ă'gə·thŏn), a poet, satirized for his wantonness and voluptuousness. Because of Agathon's effeminacy, Euripides had hoped to send him among the women, but the poet refuses to take the risk.

Clisthenes (klĭs'thě·nēz), another effeminate, who warns the women of Euripides' ruse.

A Prytanis (prĭ'tə·nĭs), a member of the Council who arrests Mnesilochus for desecrating the Mysteries of Demeter.

A Scythian Archer, a barbarian with a thick accent and, apparently, a head to match, left to guard the prisoner. He is easily lured away from his post by a dancing girl.

A Chorus of Women, celebrating the Thesmophoria.

THE THIN MAN

Author: Dashiell Hammett (1894-1961)
Time of action: The 1930's
First published: 1934

PRINCIPAL CHARACTERS

Mimi Jorgenson, Clyde Wynant's ex-wife, a showy blonde in whose arms Julia Wolf dies. She is suspected of Julia's murder.

Dorothy Wynant, Mimi's daughter, a small attractive blonde who dislikes her family and who asks Nick to locate Wynant.

Gilbert Wynant, Mimi's son, an odd, extremely inquisitive young man.

Christian Jorgenson, formerly called **Kelterman,** Wynant's former associate who, feeling unfairly treated, breaks with him. Though he already has a wife in Boston, Jorgenson marries Mimi in order to get his hands on the large divorce settlement Wynant provides for her. Temporarily suspected of Julia's murder, he finally returns to his legal wife in Boston.

Nick Charles, the narrator, a one-time detective, now a lumberman. Humorous, self-possessed, tough, intelligent, he discovers clues, arranges them, makes deductions, and solves the murders. He then summarizes the whole solution for his admiring Nora.

Nora Charles, his wife, a woman with a well-developed sense of humor who finds Nick fascinating.

Herbert Macaulay, Wynant's thieving attorney, the murderer of Wynant, Julia, and Nunheim. He murders Wynant in order to rob him, Julia to quiet her, and Nunheim because he was a possible witness to Julia's murder.

Shep Morelli, a gangster and former friend of Julia who thinks Nick knows what happened to her. He shoots Nick and is beaten up by the police, but is released when Nick does not press charges.

Arthur Nunheim, an ex-convict who identified Julia's body; he is murdered.

Julia Wolf, a murder victim, Clyde Wynant's secretary and mistress who plotted with Macaulay to get Wynant's money.

Clyde Wynant, a wealthy, eccentric inventor, once a client of Nick; a tall, thin man murdered by Macaulay.

Guild, a detective.

THE THIRTY-NINE STEPS

Author: John Buchan (1875-1940)
Time of action: 1914
First published: 1915

PRINCIPAL CHARACTERS

Richard Hannay, a well-to-do retired mining engineer. Wishing to protect himself from Scudder's murderers and to relay to proper authorities Scudder's secret coded information (in a small black book), Hannay escapes to Scotland to hide but at the same time gives the impression that he killed Scudder. Evading the pursuing Black Stone and the police, and decoding Scudder's book, he learns of invasion plans against England and informs Sir Walter. Revealing the imposture of the false First Lord of the Admiralty and finally discovering the meaning of the thirty-nine steps, Hannay is able to bring about the capture of The Black Stone.

Franklin Scudder, an American, a private investigator fearful of being murdered because of his knowledge of The Black Stone's plans. During Hannay's

absence Scudder is stabbed to death in Hannay's flat.

Sir Walter Bullivant, a government official at first skeptical of Hannay's information but convinced upon learning of Karolides' death. He passes on Hannay's warning to other government officials.

The Black Stone, a group of espionage agents who kill Scudder and Karolides and attempt to prepare for a German invasion of England. They are captured just before escaping from England in a fast yacht.

Constantine Karolides, a Greek diplomat assassinated by The Black Stone.

Sir Harry, a new-found friend of Hannay and godson of Sir Walter.

THIS ABOVE ALL

Author: Eric Knight (1897-1943)
Time of action: Summer, 1940
First published: 1941

Clive Briggs, a British private. An illegitimate child and a product of the slums, he nevertheless has a good mind and is a deep thinker. After heroic conduct in the rear-guard action at Dunkirk, he is given a furlough and meets Prue Cathaway, daughter of an upper middle-class family. They fall in love and go on a ten-day holiday together. Clive is extremely bitter because of the disparity in opportunity among the English classes and decides that he will no longer fight for an England whose citizens are not equal. After his furlough he fails to return to his military unit and is hunted as a deserter. Slipping into London to meet Prue, who has become pregnant, he is caught in an air raid and suddenly loses his idealistic rebellion. As he tries to rescue a woman trapped in the rubble, he is fatally injured by a falling wall.

Prudence (Prue) Cathaway, a member of the W. A. A. F. and the daughter of an upper middle-class family. When her fiancé proves to be a conscientious objector, her ideals and belief in English tradition impel her to join the women's army. Educated, refined, privileged, she is nevertheless strongly attracted to the intense but lower-class Clive and, though a virgin, gives herself to him on their second date. She becomes pregnant during their holiday and after Clive's heroic death she draws great comfort from the thought of bearing his child.

Monty Montague, Clive's army buddy, also a product of the slums, a wise and reckless private from World War I. He is with Clive in the harrowing rear-guard action at Dunkirk. He joins Prue and Clive for part of their holiday and though his crude manner is offensive to Prue's sensibilities, she insists that he tell her the details of Clive's heroism, to Clive's disgust. Monty greatly admires Clive's intelligence and courage and delights in giving Prue some insight into her lover's personality.

Dr. Roger Cathaway, Prue's father, a famous brain surgeon. He operates on Clive after the air raid but even his skill is insufficient to save the doomed man.

Diane Cathaway, Prue's mother, a self-satisfied, nagging woman.

General Hamish Cathaway, Prue's grandfather, a typical upper middle-class Englishman. He is frustrated because he is too old for World War II.

Willfred Cathaway, the General's second son, an influential politician.

Hamish Cathaway, the General's youngest son, an attorney. He gives up his practice in order to join the war effort, happy to get away from his waspish wife.

Iris Saintby Cathaway, Hamish's wife, a cold, vicious woman. She uses her accidental knowledge of Prue's indiscretions to force Willfred to arrange for her and her children to flee to the safety of the United States.

Prentiss Saintby, Iris' brother, a procurement officer in America. The author uses this character to give a somewhat distorted view of the United States just prior to Pearl Harbor.

Joe Telson, a drinking acquaintance through whom Clive meets Prue, a blind date.

The Rev. Mr. Polkingthorne, who temporarily shelters Clive and tries to persuade the fugitive to return to his army unit and face the charge of desertion.

THE THREE BLACK PENNYS

Author: Joseph Hergesheimer (1880-1954)
Time of action: c. 1750-1910
First published: 1917

PRINCIPAL CHARACTERS

Howat Penny, the dark-skinned, somber-eyed, jut-chinned son of the owner of Myrtle Forge. A free-spirited, strong-willed man, he loves the Pennsylvania wilderness rather than his father's iron works. Once he has fallen in love with Ludowika and possessed her, he has no scruples about taking her from her husband; but the theft is unnecessary because Winscombe dies.

Ludowika Winscombe, the young Anglo-Polish wife of an elderly British envoy; in love with Howat Penny and later his wife. After a background of social life in London she finds Pennsylvania life interesting but somewhat crude. She submits to Howat's forcefulness, however, and becomes Mrs. Penny.

Jasper Penny, Howat's great-grandson, a widower; headstrong, rebellious, and independent like his ancestor whom he resembles physically. Guilt leads him to rescue Eunice and provide for her. He is unable to persuade Susan to marry him until both have lost their vigor; and their son, the second Howat's father, is the weakened product of their diminished selves.

Susan Brundon, Jasper's sweetheart, mistress of a girls' school and friend of Jasper's cousins, the Jannans. Pale, blue-eyed, high-cheeked, a very proper Victorian, she rejects Jasper's marriage proposal because she thinks herself an unsuitable mother for Eunice. After Essie's death, however, she does marry him.

Howat Penny, Jasper's and Susan's grandson, the final issue of a declining family. A delicate aesthete and antiquarian who lives a quiet bachelor life, he is shocked by Mariana's interest in Polder. Howat is a symbol of family decay.

Mariana Jannan, Howat's cousin, a modern young woman whom old-fashioned Howat cannot understand. Howat sees in her something of the first Howat and Jasper combined, a person of vigor and independence in contrast to his own negativeness.

James Polder, Mariana's lover, grandson of Eunice; a blunt, self-made man. Deserted by a slatternly wife, he takes Mariana as his mistress until he can get a divorce.

Felix Winscombe, Ludowika's cold, sardonic husband.

Eunice Scofield, Jasper's illegitimate daughter, later legally adopted and named Penny.

Essie Scofield, her repulsive mother whom Jasper finally pays off permanently.

Gilbert Penny, the first Howat's father.

Stephen Jannan, Jasper's cousin, a lawyer.

Daniel Cusler, Essie's leech-like young lover who is killed while visiting her.

THE THREE-CORNERED HAT

Author: Pedro Antonio de Alarcón (1833-1891)
Time of action: Early nineteenth century
First published: 1874

Lucas (lōō'käs), a friendly but ugly miller who, each day, entertains the clergy and the military in the shade of his grape arbor. When Eugenio, the mayor, tries secretly to visit Lucas' wife one evening, Lucas, in Eugenio's cloak and three-corner hat, goes calling on Eugenio's wife, Doña Mercedes. Each man is quickly rebuffed by the other's faithful wife.

Frasquita (fräs·kē'tä), Lucas' young and attractive wife, who is completely faithful to him. When the mayor, coming to see her, falls into the millpond, she has

Weasel look after him while she goes hunting for Lucas.

Don Eugenio (dōn ā·ōō·hä'nyō), the corregidor, or mayor, with designs on Frasquita. Everybody recognizes his big three-cornered hat.

Doña Mercedes (dō'nyä mâr·thā'ᵺäs), the wife of Eugenio.

Weasel, the bailiff, who plots to keep Lucas away from the mill overnight so that his master can visit Frasquita.

The Bishop, another frequent caller at Lucas' mill.

THREE MEN IN A BOAT

Author: Jerome K. Jerome (1859-1927)
Time of action: Nineteenth century
First published: 1889

PRINCIPAL CHARACTERS

J., the narrator. Finding that all the diseases in a medical book, except housewife's knee, have afflicted him, he takes as medicine a pound of beefsteak and a pint of beer every six hours. For a change and rest he takes a boat trip up the Thames to Oxford from Kingston. He and his friends have all sorts of delightful and amusing adventures, most of them whimsical. When the weather turns bad, J. and his friends return by train to London and a good dinner.

Harris, J.'s friend. He has no poetry in

his soul, but knows the best pub in every town. He accompanies J. on the river trip. When they return to London he opines that they are well out of a boat.

George, the third member of the group, who boards the boat at Chertsey. It is he who finds that a famous preserved trout at an inn near Wallingford was caught by no one, though everyone claims to have caught it. George learns the trout is made of plaster of Paris.

Montmorency, a dog. He opposes the river trip, but he is outvoted.

THE THREE MUSKETEERS

Author: Alexandre Dumas, *père* (1802-1870)
Time of action: 1626
First published: 1844

PRINCIPAL CHARACTERS

D'Artagnan (där·tàn·yän'), a quick-witted, high-tempered young Gascon who has come to Paris to seek his for-

tune at the court of King Louis XIII. Having proved his bravery by fighting a duel with each, he becomes the friend of Athos, Porthos, and Aramis, members of the King's Musketeers. Through the agency of his landlord's wife, Constance Bonancieux, with whom he has fallen in love, he and his friends are induced to go to England to reclaim two diamond studs that the Queen has imprudently given to her lover, the Duke of Buckingham. Athos, Porthos, and Aramis are waylaid by agents of Cardinal Richelieu, but D'Artagnan is successful in completing the mission and saving the honor of the Queen. In revenge, Milady, an agent of the Cardinal, poisons Madame Bonancieux and tries to poison D'Artagnan. Having failed to prevent the assassination of the Duke of Buckingham and having served gallantly at the siege of La Rochelle, D'Artagnan and his friends avenge themselves on Milady by having her beheaded. At the end of the novel D'Artagnan is made Lieutenant of the King's Musketeers.

Athos (á·tôs′), the name assumed by the Comte de la Fère while serving in the King's Musketeers. When young, he had married a beautiful girl, only to learn that she had been branded as a thief. She reappears as Milady.

Aramis (á·rá·mē′), the name taken by the Chevalier d'Herblay when, as the consequence of fighting a duel, he gives up his intention of entering the priesthood and becomes one of the King's Musketeers. At the end of the novel he is about to return to his religious vocation.

Porthos (pôr·tôs′), the third of the King's Musketeers who welcome D'Artagnan into their fellowship. He is noted for his great strength, vanity, and stupidity.

Milady, known also as **Charlotte Backson,** the **Comtesse de la Fère,** and **Lady de Winter.** She had, when young, first corrupted a priest and then married the Comte de la Fère. Having been revealed as a thief, she married an English nobleman whom she poisoned to secure his

estate. In the novel she is an agent of Cardinal Richelieu, and it is she who steals from the Duke of Buckingham the two diamond studs given him by the French Queen. D'Artagnan makes love to Milady under a false name. When she discovers the deception, he plans revenge. She is imprisoned in England by her brother-in-law and placed under the guard of John Felton. She corrupts Felton and induces him to stab Buckingham. Fleeing to France after the death of the Duke, she revenges herself on D'Artagnan by poisoning his beloved, Constance Bonancieux. Finally she is captured by the Musketeers and is beheaded.

The Cardinal-Duke de Richelieu (də rē·shə·lyœ′), the chief minister of King Louis XIII. The enemy of Queen Anne, he tries to ruin her reputation with the King so that she will be sent back to Spain. He orders Milady to steal from the English Duke of Buckingham the two diamond studs given to him by the Queen, a plot intended to uncover the Queen's love for the Englishman. The plot is foiled by D'Artagnan and his friends.

Anne of Austria, the unhappy Queen of King Louis XIII. In love with the Duke of Buckingham, she gives him two of the diamond studs presented to her by the King.

George Villiers, Duke of Buckingham, the favorite of King Charles I of England and the lover of Anne of Austria, Queen of France. He is, through the instigation of Milady, murdered by John Felton.

Lord de Winter, the brother-in-law of Milady, on whose orders she is imprisoned.

John Felton, an officer in the English Navy and a Puritan, ordered by Lord de Winter to guard Milady. She seduces him and prevails on him to assassinate the Duke of Buckingham.

Constance Bonancieux (kōn·stäns′ bô-nän·syœ′), the wife of D'Artagnan's landlord and a confidential servant of the Queen. Milady revenges herself on D'Artagnan by poisoning Constance.

The Executioner of Lille, the brother of the priest who was Milady's first victim. He beheads her and thus avenges his brother.

De Treville (də trə·vēl′), the Captain of the King's Musketeers and D'Artagnan's patron.

The Chevalier de Rochefort (shə·və·lyə də rôsh·fôr′), Master of Horse to Cardinal de Richelieu and one of his trusted agents.

Planchet (plän·shä′), D'Artagnan's servant.

Grimaud (grē·mō′), Athos' taciturn servant.

Musqueton (müs·kə·tōn′), Porthos' servant.

THE THREE SISTERS

Author: Anton Chekhov (1860-1904)
Time of action: Nineteenth century
First presented: 1901

PRINCIPAL CHARACTERS

Andrey Prozorov (än·drä′ prô·zō′rəf), the son of a high-ranking Russian army officer. He studies to be a professor, but after his marriage he turns to gambling in order to forget his boorish wife, who takes a lover. He is an ineffective man who accomplishes nothing.

Natasha (nä·tä′shə), Andrey's ill-bred, rude, selfish wife. She takes a local official, Protopopov, as her lover.

Masha (mä′shə), one of Andrey's sisters and the wife of Fyodor Kuligin. She once thought her husband clever, but she has been disillusioned. She falls in love with Vershinin, though he cannot leave his wife and children for her.

Fyodor Kuligin (fyō′dər kōō′li·gĭn), Masha's husband. He is an ineffective man who teaches in a high school.

Olga Prozorov (ōl′y·gə prô·zō′rəf), one of Andrey's sisters. She wants desperately to return to Moscow. She teaches languages in the town's high school and becomes headmistress, but she is unhappy with her lot.

Irina Prozorov (ĭr·ĭn′ə prô·zō′rəf), one

of Andrey's sisters. Her hopes are dashed when Baron Tusenbach is killed by Captain Solyony in a duel, for she thought she could escape the little garrison town by marrying the Baron.

Ivan Tchebutykin (īv·än′ che·bōōt′y·kĭn), a medical doctor and friend of the Prozorovs. He is an incompetent medical practitioner.

Baron Tusenbach (tōō′sĕn·bäch), an army lieutenant in love with Irina Prozorov. He is killed in a duel by Captain Solyony, his rival for Irina's affections.

Captain Vassily Solyony (vä·sĭ′lĭy sô·ly·on′y), Baron Tusenbach's rival for Irina Prozorov's love. He kills the Baron in a duel over the young woman.

Alexandr Vershinin (al·eks′andr ver·shĭ′nĭn), an artillery commander. He believes the world and people will be better and better. He falls in love with Masha, but cannot leave his family for her.

Protopopov (prô·tô·pō′pəf), a local official who becomes Natasha Prozorov's lover.

1129

THREE SOLDIERS

Author: John Dos Passos (1896-   )
Time of action: 1917-1919
First published: 1921

PRINCIPAL CHARACTERS

John Andrews (Andy), a Harvard-trained musician who finds himself in the enlisted ranks during World War I. He is intelligent and sensitive, and he hates the army for trying to make a machine of him. Returning to his regiment from the hospital after he has suffered a wound in his leg from a bursting shell, he is full of rebellion. He is convinced that humanity should not tolerate war. When he goes A.W.O.L., he is caught and sentenced to hard labor. He escapes and hides out at an inn near Paris. There, working on a musical composition, he is again arrested by MP's.

Chrisfield, a violent soldier from Indiana. Chrisfield hates and loves quickly and passionately. He kills a German officer in cold blood, slays a hated American lieutenant named Anderson, as the officer, wounded, waits for help in a clearing

in a forest. When Chrisfield suspects the authorities know that he killed Anderson, he goes A.W.O.L. and spends his days as a refugee in France.

Dan Fuselli, a whining, sniveling, groveling American private from San Francisco whose only ambition is to become a corporal. He spends much of his time in France paying court to non-coms who might get him promoted. His French girl friend, Yvonne, is stolen from him by a sergeant. He becomes a corporal after the Armistice but learns, about the same time, that his girl back home has married a naval officer.

Geneviève Rod, a young Frenchwoman who admires Andrews' musicianship and his good taste but cannot understand the motive behind his rebellion.

THROUGH THE LOOKING GLASS

Author: Lewis Carroll (Charles Lutwidge Dodgson, 1832-1898)
Time of action: Nineteenth century
First published: 1871

PRINCIPAL CHARACTERS

Alice, an imaginative English child who has fantastic adventures in Looking-Glass House.

The White Kitten, a good kitten who is not responsible for Alice's adventures.

The Black Kitten, told by Alice to pretend that they can go through the mirror to Looking-Glass House.

Dinah, the kittens' mother.

The White Queen, a live chess piece. In

Alice's adventures she becomes a sheep, gives Alice some needles, and tells the little girl to knit. She reappears throughout the story in various guises.

The White King, a live chess piece. He has Alice serve a cake which cuts itself.

Tiger Lily,
Rose, and
Violet, flowers of whom Alice asks the path to take.

Gnat, a pleasant insect as big as a chicken. He melts away.

The Red Queen, a live chess piece. She tells Alice that one has to run to stay in the same place. Later she turns into the black kitten.

Tweedledum and
Tweedledee, two odd, fat, little men. They speak in ambiguities and recite poems to Alice. They fight over a rattle until frightened away by a crow.

The Red King, a live chess piece. He dreams about Alice, says Tweedledee, and thus gives her reality.

Humpty Dumpty, who has a conversation in riddles with Alice. He explains to her the Jabberwocky poem.

The Lion and
The Unicorn, who fight over the White King's crown.

The Red Knight, a live chess piece who claims Alice as his prisoner.

The White Knight, a live chess piece who also claims Alice as his prisoner. He leads Alice to a brook and tells her to jump into the next square in order to become a queen herself.

THYESTES

Author: Lucius Annaeus Seneca (c. 4 B.C.-A.D. 65)
Time of action: The Heroic Age
First presented: c. 60

PRINCIPAL CHARACTERS

Atreus (ā′trĭ·əs), the oldest son of Pelops and the rightful ruler of Argos, who is the protagonist in the most fiendish revenge play in the history of the theater.

Thyestes (thī·ĕs′tēz), Atreus' brother, who seduces his wife and steals the golden ram, the symbol of power in the kingdom. Having been defeated and banished by Atreus, Thyestes accepts with forebodings his brother's invitation to return to Argos. There he is fed the bodies of his sons at a banquet. Learning the truth, his greatest regret is his inability to get similar vengeance on Atreus.

Tantalus (tăn′tə·ləs), a son of Thyestes.

Thyestes' Two Other Sons. They are murdered by their uncle, who roasts their bodies for their father's banquet.

Agamemnon (ă′gə·mĕm′nŏn) and
Menelaus (mĕ′nə·lā′əs), sons of Atreus.

Megaera (mə·gā′rə), one of the Furies.

The Ghost of Tantalus, the former King of Argos, who is summoned back to witness the fury of his descendants.

Pelops (pē′lŏps), the father of Atreus and Thyestes and the son of Tantalus, who is sacrificed by his father to the gods.

THE TIME MACHINE

Author: H. G. Wells (1866-1946)
Time of action: Late nineteenth century
First published: 1895

PRINCIPAL CHARACTERS

The Time Traveler, who exhibits his Time Machine one evening after dinner.

The next week, his guests arrive for dinner, but do not find him home. Informed that they are to proceed without him, they sit down to dinner. Later, dirty and limping, their host arrives. He has traveled to the year 802,701, the time of the sunset of humanity. He tells his guests what he found: The people, weak, rounded creatures about four feet high, are vegetarians called Eloi, living in enormous buildings. Underground live the predatory Morlocks, ape-like creatures also descended from man. They were responsible for the disappearance of the Time Machine, but the Time Traveler says he managed to get it back and take off as the Morlocks sprang at him. Then, after quick and horrifying excursions ahead millions of years to that distant future time when the sun is dying and

the earth is enveloped in bitter cold and deathly stillness, he hurried back to the present. Next day the Time Traveler silences his friends' doubts by departing again on his Time Machine; he does not return, and his friends can only wonder what mishap has made him a lost wanderer in time and space.

Weena, a girl of the Eloi. The Time Traveler saves her from drowning, and she becomes his friend and guide. After sightseeing, they find that they have walked too far to return that night. They build a fire on a hill to keep away the dark-loving Morlocks, but later the Time Traveler wakes to find the fire out and Weena missing.

THE TIME OF MAN

Author: Elizabeth Madox Roberts (1886-1941)
Time of action: Early twentieth century
First published: 1926

PRINCIPAL CHARACTERS

Ellen Chesser Kent, a farm girl and woman with an introspective mind and a poetic imagination. Though uneducated, she resembles the well-read Diony Hall Jarvis ("The Great Meadow") in her consciousness of herself as a separate identity. Hate fills her when Jonas deserts her for Sallie Lou, and she hates Hester for the lustful effect she has on Jasper.

Henry Chesser, her father, a restless tenant farmer who works for various farmers; usually meek and timid but occasionally roused to anger. He loves to talk.

Nellie, her mother, a simple farm woman.

Jasper Kent, her husband, a hard worker and a fighter when angered, as when Albert steals his pigs. Accused of barn burning, he is acquitted. Unjustly accused of another burning, he is savagely

beaten by masked raiders. He packs up his family to take them far away.

Jonas Prather, her fiancé who marries Sallie Lou Brown instead of Ellen.

Hep Bodine,
Mrs. Bodine, and
Emphira Bodine, a family on one farm where the Chessers are tenants.

Tessie, Ellen's friend, a fortuneteller with whom Ellen wants to travel instead of living on the Bodine farm.

Joe Trent, a college boy and energetic farm worker who likes Ellen but seems to look down on her.

Mr. Al and
Miss Tod Wakefield, owners of the Wakefield farm, on which they raise turkeys.

Scott MacMurtrie, a farmer.

Miss Cassie, his wife, a strong and independent woman who nevertheless hangs herself when Scott and Amanda run away together.

Amanda Cain, a cousin of Miss Cassie.

Dorine Wheatley, a merry, gay friend of Ellen.

Sebe Townley, a kind and gentle friend of Ellen, who cannot forget his big ears.

Mrs. Wingate, an old, half-mad woman for whom Jasper sharecrops.

Albert, her son, a heavy-drinking trouble-maker who steals Jasper's pigs and sells them. Jasper thrashes him.

Joe Phillips, a farmer who offers Jasper work and a house on his farm and who later becomes interested in Ellen.

Jule Nestor, a prostitute, the memory of whom troubles Jonas' conscience.

Hester Shuck, a wench whom Jasper visits.

TIMON OF ATHENS

Author: William Shakespeare (1564-1616)
Time of action: Fourth century B.C.
First presented: 1605-1608

PRINCIPAL CHARACTERS

Timon (tī'mən), a noble Athenian who impoverishes himself by his unceasing generosity to his friends; he lavishes gifts upon them, offers help when they find themselves in trouble, and entertains them at extravagant feasts, paying no attention to the warnings of his steward that his fortune is dwindling. Refused at every door when he himself needs assistance, he is so completely disillusioned with man's ingratitude that he becomes a misanthrope and flees to the woods to escape humanity. Before his departure he invites his acquaintances to a final banquet, where he sets before them bowls of water. Bent upon avenging his injuries and knowing that wealth breeds discontent and misfortune, he dispenses gold from a newly discovered treasure trove; and he encourages Alcibiades' attack on his native city. He composes his own epitaph as a final defiance of ungrateful mankind: "Pass by, and curse thy fill, but pass and stay not here thy gait."

Alcibiades (al·sĭ·bī'ɔ·dēz), the great Athenian captain, Timon's friend, and several times the savior of his state. Banished by the Senate when he defends one

of his soldiers against their death sentence, he later returns with an army to take vengeance on the city and purge it of evil.

Flavius (flā'vĭ·ŭs), Timon's loyal steward, who tries to warn his master of impending financial disaster and later attempts to ward off greedy creditors. He, alone, remains virtuous, following his master into exile to offer his money and companionship. Timon can hardly believe that he, too, is not false, but he sends him away with money, advising him to use it to escape the society of men.

Apemantus (ăp·ē·măn'tŭs), a professional misanthrope who wanders through Athens railing at its citizens and commenting cynically upon their folly. He greets Timon in the wilderness as a kindred spirit, but he finds himself rejected as one who has no cause for misanthrophy; he has never benefited others enough to be able to feel ingratitude.

Lucullus (lū·kŭl'ŭs),
Lucius (lū'shĭ·ŭs), and
Sempronius (sĕm·prō'nĭ·ŭs), Athenian lords who accept Timon's bounteous

1133

gifts with pleasure and make weak excuses when they are asked to help him satisfy his creditors.

A Poet,
A Painter,
A Merchant, and
A Jeweler, flattering craftsmen who are also beneficiaries of Timon's generosity. They disappear from view as soon as he loses his money, but the Poet and the Painter follow him into the forest when they hear rumors of his new treasure. They are beaten and sent away by the misanthrope, who clearly sees their hypocrisy.

Ventidius (vĕn·tĭd′ĭ·ŭs), an Athenian nobleman, freed from debtors' prison by Timon. He offers to repay his debt while Timon is still prosperous, but, like all his friends, he refuses his benefactor money when it can obviously bring nothing in return.

Lucilius (lū·sĭl′ĭ·ŭs),
Flaminius (flə·mĭn′ĭ·ŭs), and

Servilius (sĕr·vĭl′ĭ·ŭs), Timon's servants who try unsuccessfully to persuade rich Athenians to relieve their master's distress.

Hostilius (hŏs·tĭl′ĭ·ŭs), a foreign visitor who, with two friends, observes the ingratitude which the Athenians show toward Timon and silently condemns them.

Caphis (kā′fĭs),
Titus (tī′tŭs),
Hortensius (hôr·tĕn′shĭ·ŭs), and
Philotus (fĭ·lō′tŭs), servants of Timon's creditors. They comment cynically upon the heartlessness of their respective masters.

Timandra (tī·măn′drə) and
Phrynia (frī′nĭ·ə), courtesans, Alcibiades' companions, whom Timon orders to infect the whole city of Athens, promising them gold.

Cupid, the god of love, who introduces a masque presented by Timon for his friends.

'TIS PITY SHE'S A WHORE

Author: John Ford (1586-1640?)
Time of action: Renaissance period
First presented: c. 1628

PRINCIPAL CHARACTERS

Florio, a gentleman of Parma, the devoted father of Giovanni and Annabella. Concerned about his son's "over-bookish" habits, he places his hope in his beloved daughter and leaves her free to marry for love. He is so shocked by the revelation of his children's incestuous relationship and Annabella's death that he dies almost instantly of a broken heart.

Giovanni, his sensitive, intellectual son, who is consumed by his passion for his sister. He maintains steadily the conviction that his love is virtuous and reaffirms his faith in his affection as he kills Annabella and their unborn child to save her honor.

Annabella, his beautiful sister. She rejects the virtuous life her father wants for her in order to return Giovanni's love, repenting her actions only when she realizes that Soranzo intends to kill her for her betrayal of him.

Putana, Annabella's bawdy old servant, who encourages her relationship with Giovanni.

Donado, the wealthy uncle of one of Annabella's foolish suitors.

Bergetto, Donado's tactless, stupid nephew, who courts Annabella with insults, then brags of winning her favor. He is killed by Grimaldi.

1134

Poggio, Bergetto's servant.

Soranzo, the worldly, well-to-do gentleman whom Annabella marries to save her reputation. He rages and plots her murder when he learns how he has been duped.

Grimaldi, a belligerent Roman gentleman, Annabella's admirer. He murders Bergetto by mistake as he attempts to take revenge on his successful rival, Soranzo.

Hippolita, Soranzo's vengeful cast-off mistress.

Richardetto, Hippolita's husband, rumored dead. Disguised as a doctor, he returns to Parma to spy on his wife's infidelities.

Philotis, Richardetto's niece.

Friar Bonaventura, Giovanni's confessor, who tries unsuccessfully to convince him that he is falling deeper and deeper into sin.

Vasques, Soranzo's servant, expert at extracting information and at thwarting conspiracies against his master.

THE TITAN

Author: Theodore Dreiser (1871-1945)
Time of action: The 1890's
First published: 1914

PRINCIPAL CHARACTERS

Frank Algernon Cowperwood, a financial genius. Freed from prison in Pennsylvania, where he served a term for embezzlement, he goes to Chicago to make a new fortune. Amoral in business and love, he gains control of many lives and many businesses. He becomes the force behind the Chicago transit system until his greed causes him to lose his power to obtain franchises through bribery. Defeated, he sells his interests and leaves Chicago.

Aileen Butler Cowperwood, a beautiful girl, daughter of an Irish politician in Philadelphia. She becomes Cowperwood's mistress and, later, his wife. In her attempts to enter high society she is frustrated by her own lack of social poise and by the enmity her husband evokes by his dealing in business. Her husband's marital infidelities drive her to taking a lover herself. She and Cowperwood are finally divorced in order to clear the way for a marriage between Cowperwood and Berenice Fleming.

Stephanie Platow, a dark, lush young woman. Ten years younger than Aileen, she becomes Cowperwood's mistress. She eventually disappoints Cowperwood by taking another lover.

Berenice Fleming, another of Cowperwood's loves. Although the daughter of a procuress, she is educated in a fashionable boarding school, in preparation for a life in high society as Cowperwood's wife.

Peter Laughlin, a Chicago businessman who takes Cowperwood as a business partner, thus giving the Philadelphian his start in the Midwest. Laughlin is left behind, however, as Cowperwood becomes a great force in financial circles.

TITUS ANDRONICUS

Author: William Shakespeare (1564-1616)
Time of action: Early Christian era
First presented: 1593-1594

Titus Andronicus (tī·tŭs ăn·drŏn′ĭ·kŭs), a noble Roman soldier who has dedicated his life and lost twenty-one of his twenty-five sons in the service of the state. He is not an entirely coherent or consistent character, especially in the first act of the play, where, on the one hand, he disdains ambition, offers his support to Saturninus, and mourns the death of the sons whose bodies he brings home from the wars, while, on the other, he sets off a chain of slaughters as he sacrifices the eldest son of the captured Tamora, Queen of the Goths, on the tomb of his own sons, slays Mutius, one of his four surviving sons, for daring to cross his father's will, and defends Bassianus' right to Lavinia's hand. After this day a malignant fate seems to pursue Titus, gradually destroying his sanity. He sees his daughter mutilated and dishonored, his sons falsely condemned for the murder of her husband and eventually executed, in spite of his sacrifice of his hand to save them, and, finally, his one remaining son, Lucius, banished for defending his brothers. His mind turns entirely upon the horrors inflicted on him and his daughter. Conceiving a grotesque and dreadful vengeance against his tormenters, Tamora and her sons, he plans a Thyestean banquet for the Queen before he kills her and Lavinia.

Aaron (âr′ən), the Moor, one of the earliest of the Shakespearian villains who delight in evil for its own sake. He spurs on the efforts of his mistress, Tamora, to avenge the death of her son on the Andronici and he instigates the rape of Lavinia by Demetrius and Chiron. He reveals a glimmer of human feeling in his defense of his baby son whom Tamora has ordered to be destroyed in order to conceal her guilt. He exults in his villainy, and, as Lucius sentences him, he repents any good which he may inadvertently have done.

Tamora (täm′ō·rə), the barbarian queen brought by Titus to Rome to take part in his triumph. She uses all her influence with her new husband, the Emperor Saturninus, to take vengeance on her captor for the killing of her son, Alarbus, at the tomb of the Andronici. As she comes increasingly under the influence of Aaron she delves more deeply into villainy and joins in the plot to murder Bassianus, mutilate Lavinia, and have Quintus and Martius condemned for these deeds. She masquerades as Revenge to gain access to Titus, but in so doing, she causes her own death and that of Demetrius and Chiron; the old man is less mad and more cunning than she realizes, and she must experience the full horror of feasting on her own children before she is stabbed by her enemy.

Saturninus (săt′ər·nĭ′nŭs), the luxury-loving, sensuous Emperor of Rome who arrogantly accepts Titus' aid in his election and, as a reward, condescends to ask for Lavinia, his brother's betrothed, as his bride. When Titus' sons defend Bassianus' right to their sister, the Emperor vows revenge on the Andronici and immediately takes as his wife Tamora, who directs his will and successfully hides from him her affair with Aaron. The assertions of Titus that Quintus and Martius were falsely executed for Bassianus' murder so infuriate him that he is restrained from killing the old man only by his fear of Lucius, who is gathering an army among the Goths. True to his unfaithful wife, he kills Titus to avenge her death.

Lavinia (lə·vĭn′ĭ·ə), Titus' daughter, the chaste and virtuous wife of Bassianus. She seems to step out of character when she taunts Tamora about her affair with Aaron, for she later pleads for her own honor with an innocence which clashes with the rather vulgar tone of her remarks to the Empress. Her emotions for the latter part of the play can be expressed only in tears, since after violating

1136

her Demetrius and Chiron cut out her tongue to protect themselves.

Bassianus (băs·ĭ·ān'ŭs), Lavinia's husband and brother of Saturninus, his rival for the emperorship. He seems rather arrogant in his interchanges with Saturninus and Titus, but he stands for virtue and justice against the Emperor's vanity and ambition.

Marcus Andronicus (mär'kŭs ăn·drŏn'ĭ-kŭs), Titus' brother, a tribune of the people. He attempts to modify his brother's absolute, impulsive actions and comments upon each successive family tragedy with wisdom and sorrow.

Lucius (lū'shĭ·ŭs), Titus' surviving son and heir, who becomes Emperor at the end of the play. He defends Bassianus' claim to Lavinia and is banished for attempting to prevent the execution of Quintus and Martius.

Mutius (mū'shŭs), Lucius' brother, killed by his father as he intercedes to prevent Lavinia's marriage to Saturninus. His is the famous epitaph, "He lives in fame that died in virtue's cause."

Quintus (kwĭn'tŭs) and **Martius** (mär'shŭs), sons of Titus, trapped and, though innocent, executed for Bassianus' death through the plotting of Aaron and Tamora.

Demetrius (də·mē'trĭ·ŭs) and **Chiron** (kī'rŏn), Tamora's bestial sons, who are quarreling over mutual attraction toward Lavinia when Aaron comes upon them and suggests that they kill her husband and take her by force. They are appropriately cast as Rape and Murder in their mother's masquerade. Titus finally kills them and feeds their flesh to their mother at a banquet.

Young Lucius, Titus' grandson, a precocious youth who is deeply upset by his aunt's injuries and vows to help his elders take vengeance on Tamora's sons.

Publius (pŭb'lĭ·ŭs), Marcus' son, who helps capture Demetrius and Chiron.

Aemilius (ē·mĭl'ĭ·ŭs), a Roman messenger.

Alarbus (ă·lär'bŭs), Tamora's son slain by Titus as a sacrifice for his own sons killed in battle.

TO BE A PILGRIM

Author: Joyce Cary (1888-1957)
Time of action: Late 1930's
First published: 1942

PRINCIPAL CHARACTERS

Tom Wilcher, the dying owner of Tolbrook Manor. The last representative of the old West County liberal and religious tradition, he is concerned about the future of his family, his property, and his convictions. Tom had sacrificed a religious career to handle the family affairs and, although a liberal, he has grown to revere the political and religious values of the past. As he views the unhappy lives of his family, he determines to marry Sara Monday, his ideal of the old, humane,

settled life. However, she too fails him and he returns home and dies.

Ann Wilcher, Tom's niece. A modern, emancipated young doctor, she treats Tom in his last illness.

Robert Brown, Tom's nephew, Ann's husband. A scientific farmer, he represents a return to the soil. He rejects Ann for Molly, but the three are reunited in one household.

Sara Monday, Tom's old housekeeper. Jailed by Tom's family for stealing unused articles, she rejects the ideals for which Tom cherishes her.

Edward Wilcher, Tom's brother and Ann's father, a politician.

Lucy Wilcher, Tom's wild sister, Robert's mother.

Puggy Brown, Lucy's adulterous husband, a hypocritical Benjamite preacher.

Julie Eeles, an actress, Edward's mistress, later Tom's mistress.

Bill Wilcher, Tom's settled brother, a military man.

Amy Sprott, Bill's devoted wife.

Loftus Wilcher, their son.

John Wilcher, another son. Disillusioned by World War I, he has lost his concern for religious and family life, and he lives indifferently until killed by an automobile.

Fred, Sara's latest man.

Molly, a young farm girl.

TO THE LIGHTHOUSE

Author: Virginia Woolf (1882-1941)
Time of action: 1910-1920
First published: 1927

PRINCIPAL CHARACTERS

Mr. Ramsay, a professor of philosophy, a metaphysician of high order, an author, and the father of eight. Not really first-rate, as he realized by the time he was sixty, he knew also that his mind was still agile, his ability to abstract strong. Loved by his wife, he is nonetheless offered sympathy and consolation for the things he is not. Lithe, trim, the very prototype of the philosopher, he attracts many people to him and uses their feelings to buoy him in his weaknesses. Not truly a father, his gift for the ironic and sardonic arouses fear and hatred rather than respect among his children. Broken by his wife's and oldest son's deaths, he continues to endure and to sharpen his mind on the fine whetstone of wit.

Mrs. Ramsay, a beautiful woman even in her aging; she is warm, compassionate, and devoted to the old-fashioned virtues of hearth, husband, and children. With an aura of graciousness and goodness about her, ineffable but pervasive, Mrs. Ramsay gathers about her guests, students, friends, and family at their summer home on the Isle of Skye. Loving and tender to her children, polite and pleasant to her guests, she impresses upon them all the sanctity of life and marriage, the elemental virtues. Her love and reverence of life have its effect on all her guests, even an atheistic student of her husband and an aloof poet. Mostly she affects women, especially worshiping Lily Briscoe, with the need to throw oneself into life, not to limit life but to live it, especially through motherhood.

James, the Ramsays' youngest son and his mother's favorite, though the child most criticized by the professor because the boy robs him of sympathy that he desperately needs. Sensitive and austere, James at six and sixteen suffers most the loss of his mother, taken from him at first by a calculating father's demands and later by her death. He and his sister Camilla make a pact of war against their father's tyranny of demands and oversights. Finally, on a trip to the lighthouse, the symbol of what had been denied him by his father, Mr. Ramsay praises his son's seamanship.

Prue, who dies in childbirth,
Andrew, killed in World War I,
Nancy,
Roger,
Rose,
Jasper, and
Camilla, called **Cam,** the other children of Mr. and Mrs. Ramsay. All the children resent their father and his dominance. Mrs. Ramsay regrets that they must grow up because of the loss of sensitivity and imagination that will come with adulthood.

Lily Briscoe, an artist and friend of the family who more than any other loved and cared for the weeks spent with the Ramsays in the Hebrides. Desperately in need of assurance, Lily has withheld love and affection from others until the summer she spends at the Ramsay cottage where she observes life with its fixed center and raw edges. Completely won over by Mrs. Ramsay, Lily almost gets her chance at life, and had the war not interfered she might have married. She is not really a great artist, but during a visit to the Ramsay home after the war she experiences a moment of fulfilled vision, a feeling of devotion to the oldest cause, of a sense of oneness with all time, of sympathy for the human condition, and she is able to express this fleeting moment in a painting she had begun before Mrs. Ramsay's death.

Augustus Carmichael, a minor poet with one major success, a hanger-on, the only one who does not at first love his hostess but who finally discovers her genius years after her death. Laughed at by all the Ramsay children because of his yellow-tinted beard, the result of taking opium, as they imagine, he soaks up love and life without himself giving anything. His late fame as a poet is a surprise to all who know him.

Minta Doyle and

Paul Rayley, two handsome guests who become engaged through Mrs. Ramsay's quiet management. Minta is like the young Mrs. Ramsay and sends out an aura of love and passion, while Paul, with his good looks and careful dress, is a foil for all affections and strong feelings. But the marriage turns out badly; Minta leads her own life and Paul takes a mistress. No longer lovers, they can afford to be friends.

William Bankes, a botanist, the oldest friend of Professor Ramsay. An aging widower, he first comes to visit with the Ramsays out of a sense of duty, but he stays on enraptured with life. The object of Lily Briscoe's undisguised affections, he appears to Mrs. Ramsay almost willing to become domesticated in spite of his eccentricities and set ways. Nothing comes of this relationship except a broadening of Lily's views on life.

Charles Tansley, Mr. Ramsay's protégé, a boorish young man who eventually is won over to the warmth and love of Mrs. Ramsay. It is his opinionated conviction that women cannot paint or write. Interested in abstract thought, he makes his career in scholarship.

Mrs. McNab, the old charwoman who acts as caretaker of the Ramsay house in the Hebrides during the ten years it stands empty.

Mrs. Bast, the cottager who helps Mrs. McNab get the house ready for the return of the Ramsay family.

George Bast, her son, who catches the rats and cuts the grass surrounding the Ramsay house.

Macalister, the aged Scottish boatman who takes Mr. Ramsay, Cam, and James on an expedition to the lighthouse. He tells the voyagers tales of winter, storm, and death.

TOBACCO ROAD

Author: Erskine Caldwell (1903-   )
Time of action: The 1920's
First published: 1932

PRINCIPAL CHARACTERS

Jeeter Lester, a Georgia poor white, the father of seventeen, of whom twelve are surviving and two are still at home. Shiftless but always vaguely hopeful, he makes several half-hearted and futile attempts to feed himself first and afterward his starving family. He burns to death in his shack as a result of a fire he set to burn broomsedge.

Ada Lester, his wife, who shares his fate.

Dude Lester, his sixteen-year-old son, who is persuaded into marriage with a middle-aged widow by her purchase of a Ford, which subsequently runs over and kills a Negro and, later, the Lesters' grandmother, both to no one's particular regret.

Bessie Lester, the wife of Dude. She uses her authority as a backwoods evangelist to perform her own marriage ceremony.

Pearl Bensey, Jeeter's fifteen-year-old married daughter. Tied to their bed by her husband, she manages to free herself and run away.

Lov Bensey, Pearl's husband. After Pearl's flight, he is advised by Jeeter to take Ellie May instead.

Ellie May Lester, Jeeter's harelipped daughter, who uses her charms to distract Lov's attention, first from his bag of turnips, later from his marital loss.

THE TOILERS OF THE SEA

Author: Victor Hugo (1802-1885)
Time of action: The 1820's
First published: 1866

PRINCIPAL CHARACTERS

Gilliatt (zhē·lyȧt′), a young recluse living on the Isle of Guernsey and looked on with suspicion by most of his fellow parishioners. He saves his friend's fortune with great difficulty and nobly gives up to another the promised reward of marriage to the girl he loves. Finally, sitting on the very rock from which he once rescued his now successful rival, he lets himself be drowned by the high tide.

Mess Lethierry (lĕ·tyē·rē′), a shipowner and Gilliatt's friend. His partner having run away with his money, Lethierry attempts to recoup his fortune by buying a steamboat. His treacherous captain sinks it, but Gilliatt succeeds in salvaging the valuable engine.

Déruchette (dā·rü·shĕt′), Lethierry's beautiful niece, whom Gilliatt loves.

Ebenezer Caudray (kō·drĕ′), the new rector. His love for Déruchette is returned. After she is promised to Gilliatt by Lethierry, Déruchette and Caudray are frustrated in their attempt to marry secretly, but Gilliatt's generosity unites them.

Rantaine (rän·tĕn′), Lethierry's absconding former partner.

Sieur Clubin (syœ′ klü·băn′), the captain of Lethierry's steamboat. A man widely noted for honesty, Clubin takes Lethierry's stolen money from Rantaine at gunpoint. Having arranged to be picked up by smugglers, he sinks Lethierry's steamboat; his scheme is to escape with the money and leave a reputation for heroism as one who "stayed with the ship." However, he grounds the ship in the wrong place and is, in fact, drowned. Later his plotting is discovered. Gilliatt, in salvaging the steam engine, also retrieves the money from Clubin's body.

TOM BROWN'S SCHOOL DAYS

Author: Thomas Hughes (1822-1896)
Time of action: Early nineteenth century
First published: 1857

PRINCIPAL CHARACTERS

Squire Brown, Tom Brown's father, a man who believes in permitting his children to mingle with all sorts of people, as long as they are honorable.

Dr. Arnold, the fine, gentlemanly, religious headmaster of Rugby. He is gentle but firm with his charges and understands them thoroughly.

Tom Brown, a good boy who finds himself in a great deal of mischief at Rugby, after he gets in with a group of ruffians. But since he is essentially good he responds to the example of a younger boy who becomes his roommate. Before he finishes his work at Rugby to go to Oxford Tom becomes a great leader in the school and acutally changes the actions and attitudes of the boys for the better.

George Arthur, a younger boy at Rugby who by his moral courage and religious fervor reforms Tom Brown and Harry East from wild mischief-makers into school leaders. George is the true leader, working through Tom's influence over the other boys.

Harry East, a wild young lad who, under the influence of Tom, George, and Dr. Arnold, becomes a good young man, as he really wants to be. He finds great help in his religion, too.

Flashman, a bully at Rugby whose power over the younger boys is broken by the stalwart defense of Tom and Harry. Flashman is expelled from Rugby for drunkenness.

TOM BURKE OF OURS

Author: Charles Lever (1806-1872)
Time of action: Early nineteenth century
First published: 1844

PRINCIPAL CHARACTERS

Tom Burke, the younger son of an Irish nobleman. He becomes a soldier of fortune after his father's death. He has many adventures with Irish patriots, the British Army, and an evil lawyer. He makes his way to France, attends the École Polytechnique, and becomes an officer under Napoleon, rising to be a colonel. He inherits the family estates when his older brother George dies, and he marries Marie de Meudon, a beautiful Frenchwoman and the widow of General d'Auvergne.

Darby M'Keown, an Irish patriot known as Darby the Blast. He is Tom's friend.

Charles de Meudon, a young French officer aiding the Irish rebels who becomes Tom's friend and who, just before his death, gives Tom money for passage to France and asks him to look after his sister, Marie de Meudon.

Marie de Meudon, also known as Mlle. de Rochefort and the Rose of Provence. She is Charles Meudon's sister. She marries Tom Burke after she has become a widow and he has inherited the family estates.

Captain Bubbleton, a bombastic, good-hearted English officer who befriends Tom.

Anna Maria Bubbleton, Captain Bubbleton's good-hearted sister, who nurses Tom when he is hurt.

Captain Montague Crofts, a villain who is Tom's enemy and wants, as a distant kinsman, to obtain Tom's estates.

General d'Auvergne, one of Napoleon's officers, Tom's friend and benefactor. He is the first husband of Tom's wife Marie. He had wanted to adopt Marie but Napoleon insisted that he marry her instead. He is killed in battle at Chaumière.

The Marquis Henri de Beauvais, a royalist who plots against Napoleon. He becomes Tom's friend and clears Tom of charges of treason against Napoleon.

The Abbé d'Ervan, a loyalist, friend of the Marquis de Beauvais.

Anthony Basset, an unscrupulous lawyer who cheats Tom as a boy.

The Chevalier Duchesne, a friend of Tom who turns against Napoleon and then tries to incriminate Tom as a traitor.

Napoleon Bonaparte. Tom serves for him against the British. Napoleon notices Tom's excellence as a soldier and grants him preferment and decorations.

Lieutenant Tascher, Madame Bonaparte's nephew and Tom's roommate at the École Polytechnique.

TOM CRINGLE'S LOG

Author: Michael Scott (1789-1835)
Time of action: Nineteenth century
First published: 1833

PRINCIPAL CHARACTERS

Tom Cringle, a young man, determined to distinguish himself, who joins the British Navy at the age of thirteen. He has many adventures and sees much action on various ships. Eventually he is promoted to lieutenant and then commander as a reward for his bravery and attention to duty. At twenty-three he is master of his own ship and a much-trusted officer.

Mary Palma, Cringle's cousin, whom he marries after his promotion to commander.

Obadiah, a pirate responsible for taking Cringle to the lagoon which is the secret lair of the West Indian pirates. When the pirate band is captured, he tries to swim away and is shot.

Captain Transom, the genial commander of an English warship called the "Firebrand." He has many friends in the islands and takes Cringle to many jolly parties ashore.

Francesco Cangrejo, a handsome Spanish pirate. Sentenced to death, he gives Tom a miniature and a crucifix to deliver to his betrothed.

TOM JONES

Author: Henry Fielding (1707-1754)
Time of action: Early eighteenth century
First published: 1749

PRINCIPAL CHARACTERS

Tom Jones, a foundling. Although befriended by his foster father, Squire Allworthy, Tom encounters many vicissitudes, some of them of his own making, for he is a somewhat wild and foolish, though good-hearted young man. His wild ways, exaggerated by enemies, including Master Blifil, cause Tom to be cast off by Squire Allworthy. After Tom's goodness and virtue eventually triumph over disastrous circumstances, the young man is reconciled with the Squire and, even more important, with Sophia Western, the beautiful and virtuous woman he loves. He is acknowledged as the Squire's nephew when the secret of his real parentage becomes known.

Squire Allworthy, an extremely just and virtuous country gentleman who becomes Tom's foster father after the infant is discovered in the Squire's bed. Tom's enemies play upon the Squire's gullibility, for Allworthy, like many another honest man, finds it difficult to believe that there is dishonesty in other people. Eventually he sees Tom's essential goodness, receives him as his nephew, and makes the young man his heir.

Sophia Western, the virtuous daughter of a domineering country squire. She loves Tom Jones, even to facing down her father and aunt when they try to marry her off to Master Blifil and Lord Fellamar. Though she loves Tom, she is disappointed by his escapades, particularly those of an amorous nature, and until she is convinced he can be a faithful husband she refuses to accept his suit.

Squire Western, Sophia's domineering, profane father, who loves his hounds,

his horses, and his bottle almost as much as his only child. When he insists upon forcing her to marry Master Blifil, the husband of his choice, Sophia is forced into running away from home, placing herself and her virtue in the path of adventure and danger. The Squire, though uncouth, is a good man at heart. Both he and Squire Allworthy are exceptionally well-drawn characters.

Master Blifil, the villainous son of the Squire's sister Bridget. A great hypocrite, he hides his villainy under a cloak of seeming honesty and virtue. He plays false witness against Tom Jones many times. He becomes Sophia Western's suitor only because he wants her money and hates Tom, the man she loves. His villainy is done, too, in the face of his knowing that Tom is really an older half brother, not a foundling.

Bridget Blifil, Squire Allworthy's seemingly virtuous spinster sister. She bears Tom out of wedlock and lets him become a foundling. Later she marries and has another son, Master Blifil. On her deathbed she sends to her brother a letter telling the story of Tom's parentage. The letter is stolen and concealed by her legitimate son.

Captain Blifil, Bridget's husband, who marries her for her money. He dies of apoplexy, however, before he can enjoy any of it.

Mr. Partridge, a schoolteacher and barber-surgeon. Long Tom's loyal, if loquacious, companion, he is for many years suspected of being Tom's father.

Jenny Jones, later **Mrs. Waters.** A maid in Mr. Partridge's house, she is accused of being Tom's mother, and her surname is given to him. As Mrs. Waters she has a brief love affair with Tom, much to the horror of some of his acquaintances, who believe the supposed mother and son have committed incest. Through her testimony the identity of Tom's real mother becomes known.

Mr. Dowling, a not-so-honest lawyer. Through his testimony Tom's identity is proved, as he corroborates Jenny Jones' statements. He keeps the secret many years, thinking that he is following Mr. Allworthy's wishes.

Black George Seagrim, so-called because of his extremely black beard, a rustic and poacher. Though befriended by Tom, he steals from the young man and plays him ill turns.

Molly Seagrim, a young woman of easy virtue, Black George's daughter. Tom's escapades with her cause him grave trouble until her affairs with other men take some of the blame from him.

The Rev. Roger Thwackum, an Anglican clergyman retained by Mr. Allworthy to tutor Tom Jones and Master Blifil during their boyhood. A self-righteous, bigoted man, he voices his prejudices at all times. He beats Tom often and severely, living up to his name.

Mr. Thomas Square, a deistically inclined philosopher who is a pensioner in Mr. Allworthy's household and Mr. Thwackum's opponent in endless debates over the efficacy of reason and religious insight. Though he dislikes Tom Jones, he makes a deathbed confession that clears Tom of some of his supposed misdeeds.

Lady Bellaston, a sensual noblewoman of loose morals who takes a fancy to Tom Jones and, when she is spurned, tries to do him a great deal of evil.

Mrs. Western, Lady Bellaston's cousin and Sophia's aunt. To satisfy her own social pretensions she tries to marry off Sophia to Lord Fellamar against the girl's will.

Mrs. Fitzpatrick, Sophia's cousin. They travel to London together.

Mr. Fitzpatrick, her jealous husband. Tom is jailed for wounding him in a duel.

Lord Fellamar, a licentious nobleman who makes love to Sophia and, with Mrs. Western's approval, even attempts to ravish the girl in order to force her to marry him. Misled by Lady Bellaston's advice, he tries to have Tom Jones impressed into the naval service.

Mrs. Arabella Hunt, a pretty and wealthy widow who offers formally by letter to marry Tom Jones. His refusal of this handsome offer helps reëstablish Tom with Sophia.

Honour Blackmore, Sophia's loyal, if somewhat selfish, maid, who shares in most of her mistress' adventures.

Mrs. Miller, Tom's landlady in London. Convinced of his virtue by his many good deeds she pleads on his behalf with Squire Allworthy and is instrumental in helping restore Tom to his foster father's good graces.

Nancy and
Betty Miller, the landlady's daughters.

Mr. Nightingale, Tom's fellow lodger at the Miller house. Tom persuades the elder Nightingale to permit the son to marry Nancy.

Mr. Summer, a handsome young cleric befriended as a student by Mr. Allworthy. It was he who seduced Bridget Allworthy and fathered Tom Jones.

TOM SAWYER

Author: Mark Twain (Samuel L. Clemens, 1835-1910)
Time of action: The 1840's
First published: 1876

PRINCIPAL CHARACTERS

Tom Sawyer, the mischievous ringleader of countless boyish adventures, who almost drives his long-suffering aunt to distraction with his pranks. If not fighting with other village urchins, the indolent boy plans numerous romantic and impractical escapades, many of which cost him hours of conscience-stricken torment. If he is not planning misdemeanors on the high seas, he is looking for buried treasure. Although unthinking, he is not really a bad boy; he is capable of generosity; occasionally, he surprises even himself with magnanimous acts.

Aunt Polly, Tom's warm, tender-hearted aunt. Sometimes this simple scripture-quoting old soul does not understand her mischievous charge. Even though she uses Tom's brother Sid as an example of a model youth, her frequent admonitions, emphasized by repeated thumps on the head with a thimble, fail to have a lasting effect on Tom. Believing herself endowed with subtle guile, she often tries to trap the boy into admitting his pranks. Rarely, however, is she successful. Tom usually manages to outwit her if Sid does not call her attention to certain inexactnesses in Tom's excuses.

Huckleberry Finn, one of Tom's best friends and a social pariah to the village mothers, but not to their sons. In the self-sufficient outcast the boys see everything they want to be. They long for his freedom to do as he pleases. Sometimes, to their regret, the other boys try to emulate their individualistic hero. Carefully, they mark the way he smokes strong tobacco in smelly old pipes and sleeps in empty hogsheads. Although he is not accepted by the mothers, Huck, even if he is vulgar, is a decent, honest lad. Happy only when he can sleep and eat where he pleases, Huck feels uncomfortable when the Widow Douglas takes him into her home.

Becky Thatcher, Tom's sweetheart. With her blue eyes, golden hair, and winsome smile, she captures his rather fickle heart at their first meeting. A little coquette, she, like Tom, alternately suffers from and enjoys their innocent love. Tom proves his generosity and love for her when he admits to the schoolteacher a crime he did not commit, thus astounding the rest of the class by his incredible folly.

Injun Joe, a half-breed. A murderous, sinister figure who lurks mysteriously in the background, the savagely vindictive killer stabs young Dr. Robinson and is subsequently exposed by Tom. In a cave Injun Joe, who had leaped from the court room window during Muff Potter's trial, almost has his revenge against the boy. Finally he pays for his many crimes when he is trapped in the cave and dies of starvation.

Muff Potter, a local ne'er-do-well and, along with Pap Finn, the town drunk. After helping Injun Joe and Dr. Robinson rob a grave, Muff Potter is accused of killing the doctor and almost pays with his worthless life. Had Tom not belatedly intervened, he would have been hanged and Injun Joe would have gone free. When the boys see a stray dog howling at the newly released Potter, asleep in a drunken stupor, they know that he is still doomed.

Sid, Tom's half brother and one of the

model boys in the community. A quiet, rather calculating child, he exposes Tom's tricks whenever possible. However, when Tom is presumed drowned, Sid manages a few snuffles. To Tom, Sid's behavior is reprehensible; he keeps clean, goes to school regularly, and behaves well in church.

Mary, Tom's cousin. She is a sweet, lovable girl who often irritates him by insisting that he wash and dress carefully for church.

Judge Thatcher, Becky's pompous but kind-hearted father and the local celebrity.

Joe Harper, who runs away with Tom and Huck to Jackson's Island. Pretending to be pirates, they remain there for several days while the townspeople search for their bodies.

TOM THUMB THE GREAT

Author: Henry Fielding (1707-1754)
Time of action: Age of chivalry
First presented: 1730

PRINCIPAL CHARACTERS

Tom Thumb, a midget son of peasant parents in King Arthur's time. He accomplishes great deeds, even subduing ten thousand giants. He takes Princess Huncamunca as his bride, but his happiness is short-lived, for after subduing rebels led by Lord Grizzle he is swallowed at a single gulp by a red cow.

Queen Dollallolla, wife of King Arthur. She loves drinking, and she loves Tom Thumb. Though she does not fear the King—indeed, he is afraid of her—she does not tell him of her love for the little hero. She is slain by a courtier's mistress in a senseless series of murders.

Queen Glumdalca, a giantess and King Arthur's enemy. She is subdued by Tom Thumb and brought to Arthur's court, where the King falls in love with her. She wants Tom Thumb as her lover but she settles for the King. She is killed by Lord Grizzle while defending Arthur against the rebels.

King Arthur, King of England and Tom Thumb's liege lord. He loves Glumdalca and fears his wife. He kills himself after a senseless series of murders leaves him alone.

Princess Huncamunca, daughter of King Arthur, loved by Tom Thumb. Afraid she will be an old maid, she marries Tom Thumb, whom she has loved for a long time. When she discovers that Lord Grizzle loves her, she wants to have two husbands. She kills her mother's murderer and then is herself slain.

Lord Grizzle, a malcontent. He promises to kill Tom Thumb for Queen Dollallolla. In his rebellion against King Arthur he is slain by Tom Thumb.

Merlin, the magician at Arthur's court. He grants Tom Thumb a vision in which the little hero foresees that he will be eaten by a red cow.

TONO-BUNGAY

Author: H. G. Wells (1866-1946)
Time of action: Late nineteenth and early twentieth centuries
First published: 1908

George Ponderevo, an enterprising young scientist and the narrator. The son of the housekeeper at Bladesover House, a large country estate, he learns about class barriers at an early age. When he is twelve he falls desperately in love with a pampered young aristocrat, the Hon. Beatrice Normandy, who is eight. Two years later he is banished when he fights with her snobbish half brother, Archie Garvell, and Beatrice, turning against her admirer, blames him for attacking Archie. After an unhappy experience in the household of one uncle he is apprenticed to another, Edward Ponderevo, a small-time pharmacist with big dreams. Later he wins a scholarship at the Consolidated Technical Schools in London, but he begins to neglect his studies after he meets Marion Ramboat, whom he later marries. He finds work with his Uncle Edward, marries Marion, is divorced after she discovers his infidelity, and finds material success in the patent medicine boom his uncle has created by flamboyantly advertising a product called Tono-Bungay. He then takes up the study of aircraft design, and as the result of a crash he meets Beatrice again. When the Tono-Bungay financial empire collapses, he goes on an expedition to secure a cargo of quap, a mysterious ore containing elements needed for the manufacture of a better lamp filament. The expedition is unsuccessful, and George flies his ruined uncle to France. He and Beatrice share a twelve-day romance, but she refuses to marry him. Disillusioned with himself and the degenerating society of his time, he turns to the designing of destroyers for a future war.

Mrs. Ponderevo, George's mother, the competent housekeeper at Bladesover House. Stern and unsympathetic, she shows her affection for her son only after he has been sent to live with Edward Ponderevo. She dies soon afterward, leaving her savings to George.

Edward Ponderevo, called **Teddy,** George Ponderevo's flashy, unscrupulous, ambitious, but likable uncle. As a pharmacist he squanders his nephew's inheritance and goes into bankruptcy. Later, as the manufacturer of Tono-Bungay, a popular nostrum, and as the manager of a huge corporation called Domestic Utilities (familiarly known as Do-Ut), he gains the wealth and power he has always dreamed of, and he moves from one house to another, each more luxurious and impressive than the last, until his industrial empire suddenly crashes. He is forced to escape with George to France, where he dies of pneumonia.

Susan Ponderevo, Edward's admirable, gentle, patient wife. She takes her husband's success calmly and handles matters with fortitude after his death. Kind and given to teasing, she shows more personal strength than any of George's loves.

The Hon. Beatrice Normandy, the girl with whom George Ponderevo carries on an innocent, childish love affair until she turns against him after he has beaten her half brother in a fight. As a grown woman she nurses him after he has been injured while experimenting with a glider. She and George have a brief affair, but she refuses to marry him because of what she calls her spoiled character; she says that she is suited only to the life of a courtesan.

Archie Garvell, Beatrice Normandy's snobbish half brother to whom George Ponderevo administers a sound beating when the two boys fight. Later he toadies to George.

Marion Ramboat, the pretty, brittle woman whom George Ponderevo marries. A commonplace shopgirl, she puts off the marriage until she is certain that he can provide a comfortable living, and then she makes his life miserable by her stupidity and prudery. They decide on a divorce after she learns that he has spent a holiday with his secretary.

Effie Rink, George Ponderevo's sensual, engagingly pretty secretary. Tired of his wife's coldness and nagging, George looks to Effie for passion, and he continues the affair with her after he and Marion have been divorced.

Nicholas Frapp, Mrs. Ponderevo's brother, the cloddish, bigoted baker to whom George Ponderevo is apprenticed after he has been sent away from Blades-over House. George incautiously shares with his two cousins the secret that he does not believe in religion; the boys tell their father, and at a church meeting pious-minded Frapp accuses his nephew of blasphemy. Humiliated, George runs away and returns to his mother, who then sends him to live with Edward Ponderevo.

Cothope, George Ponderevo's assistant in his experiments with airborne craft. He shows his loyalty by continuing the work on his own time and money after the Tono-Bungay enterprise has collapsed.

Bob Ewart, George Ponderevo's school friend, later a clever, individualistic sculptor. When the two meet again in London, where George is continuing his scientific studies, Ewart has considerable influence in enlarging George's intellectual and social horizons.

Gordon Nasmyth, the wealthy man who proposes the ill-fated expedition in search of quap, a mysterious radioactive mineral.

Pollack, an associate with whom George Ponderevo becomes friendly on the expedition to bring back a cargo of quap.

The Captain of the "Maude Mary," a cantankerous boor who must be bribed to carry a cargo of quap. He loses his ship when the radioactive mineral causes the vessel to sink.

Mr. Moggs, the president of Domestic Utilities, the corporation with which Edward Ponderevo merges.

Mr. Mantell, the purchaser of Edward Ponderevo's pharmacy. He employs George Ponderevo until the young man goes to London to study.

Mrs. Scrymgeour, a woman novelist with whom Edward Ponderevo carries on a brief, pseudo-Napoleonic affair.

Lady Drew, the mistress of Bladesover House.

Lady Osprey, the stepmother of the Hon. Beatrice Normandy.

THE TOWER OF LONDON

Author: William Harrison Ainsworth (1805-1882)
Time of action: Sixteenth century
First published: 1840

PRINCIPAL CHARACTERS

The Duke of Northumberland, the leader of forces opposing Mary Tudor; he is executed after she becomes Queen of England.

Guilford Dudley, the son of Northumberland, who wishes him to become King; he is pardoned after the defeat of Northumberland but executed after failure of his own later plot against Mary.

Lady Jane Grey, the innocent and loyal wife of Dudley and claimant to the throne upon the death of Edward the Sixth. The dupe of Pembroke and Renard, she is executed with Dudley after her refusal to become a Catholic.

Cuthbert Cholmondeley, Dudley's squire,

who is in love with Cicely. Imprisoned and tortured in the Tower, he escapes and later marries Cicely.

Cicely, the adopted daughter of Peter the pantler and Dame Potentia Trusbut, who becomes a lady in waiting to Lady Jane. Imprisoned by jealous Nightgall, she is later revealed to be of noble birth and is permitted by Mary to marry Cuthbert.

Lady Grace Mountjoy, Cicely's insane mother, who dies in a Tower cell.

Lawrence Nightgall, the Tower jailer who is in love with Cicely. He is murdered by Renard after plotting with the French ambassador to kill Renard.

Simon Renard, the Spanish ambassador.

Lord Pembroke, Mary's supporter and the conspirator with Renard to assassinate Cuthbert.

Queen Mary, who is in love with Cour-tenay but affianced (upon Renard's advice) to Philip, King of Spain, after the discovery of Courtenay's double-dealing with Elizabeth.

Princess Elizabeth, Mary's younger half sister. She is confined because of complicity with Courtenay, released by Mary, and then reconfined for a later execution planned by Mary.

Edward Courtenay, Earl of Devonshire. In love with Elizabeth, he plots to get Mary's throne by pretending love for Mary, who promises to marry him. He is confined for later execution because of his treachery.

Gunnora Boase, an old woman, the tool of Northumberland and poisoner of the boy king, Edward the Sixth.

The Duke of Suffolk, the father of Lady Jane Grey.

Sir Thomas Wyat, the anti-Catholic leader of the revolt against Mary.

THE TOWN

Author: William Faulkner (1897-1962)
Time of action: 1909-1927
First published: 1957

PRINCIPAL CHARACTERS

Flem Snopes, the shrewdest of the materialistic Snopes clan. After successfully taking over the hamlet of Frenchman's Bend, Flem lets his desire for respectability master his voracious thirst for money and he begins a systematic rise from restaurant owner to bank president in Jefferson. He marries Eula to secure Will Varner as an ally and permits an affair between Manfred de Spain and his wife in order to secure de Spain's aid in his rise. When the proper time arrives, he uses this affair to remove de Spain and take his place as president of the bank.

Manfred de Spain, the mayor of Jefferson. When a vacancy occurs, de Spain resigns as mayor and becomes president of the bank; he makes Flem vice president. After his eighteen-year affair becomes common knowledge, de Spain sells his bank stock and leaves the presidency vacant for Flem.

Eula Varner Snopes, Flem's wife. Already pregnant by Hoake McCarron, Eula is married to impotent Flem Snopes in order to save the family name. She has a long affair with Manfred de Spain but refuses to leave Jefferson with him. After exacting a promise from Gavin Stevens that he will marry Linda, she commits suicide.

Linda Snopes, Eula's daughter.

Gavin Stevens, a verbose county attorney.

In his role as the conscience of Jefferson, Stevens attempts to reform Eula and later promises to marry Linda, if necessary, to protect her from Flem's schemes.

V. K. Ratliff, a garrulous, likable country sewing machine salesman, a narrator.

Charles Mallison, Gavin Stevens' nephew, one of the narrators.

Will Varner, Eula's father.

I. O. Snopes,
Byron Snopes,
Montgomery Ward Snopes,
Mink Snopes, and
Eck Snopes, Flem's worthless cousins, whom he abandons as he rises.

Ab Snopes, Flem's father, a horse thief and barn burner.

Wallstreet Panic Snopes, Flem's successful cousin.

THE TOWN

Author: Conrad Richter (1890-   )
Time of action: Mid-nineteenth century
First published: 1950

PRINCIPAL CHARACTERS

Sayward Wheeler, a typical, stout-hearted pioneer woman. She is the unquestioned ruler of her large family. She worries most about her youngest child, Chancey, and tries her best to strengthen him in every way she can. She is a firm and sensible woman, and, when the family moves into a large house in the town, she manages to keep up with her children socially; but she keeps her common touch and is most comfortable among homey things. She plants some trees around the house and becomes much attached to them during her lonely old age. In her will she stipulates that the trees must not be cut down.

Portius Wheeler, Sayward's husband, who hopes for a county judgeship but does not get it because he is an agnostic. He is very shrewd in money matters and allows no one to get the better of him in a business deal. He is a popular lawyer and a financial success; he makes his family the richest in town.

Chancey Wheeler, Sayward's youngest child. As a boy, he is very delicate and frail and lives in a dream world of his own making. He leaves home and becomes a newspaperman.

Resolve Wheeler, Sayward's eldest child, who studies law with his father, marries a sensible girl, and becomes governor of the state.

Guerdon Wheeler, one of Sayward's children, who marries a slut and then runs away after killing her lover. His daughter, Guerda, becomes Sayward's favorite.

Huldah Wheeler, Sayward's daughter, who runs away stark naked to a man's house; she claims that gipsies took her clothes. Sayward goes after her and brings her back.

Kinzie Wheeler,
Sooth Wheeler,
Libby Wheeler,
Dezia Wheeler, and
Mercy Wheeler, Sayward and Portius' other children.

Jake Tench, a steamboat operator.

Mrs. Jake Tench, a former schoolmistress who has had a child by Portius.

Rosa Tench, Portius' child by Mrs. Tench. She commits suicide.

THE TRACK OF THE CAT

Author: Walter Van Tilburg Clark (1909-   )
Time of action: Early twentieth century
First published: 1949

PRINCIPAL CHARACTERS

Mr. Bridges, owner of a ranch in Nevada. He is a drunkard who leaves the management of the ranch to his sons.

Arthur Bridges, a dreamer. He sympathizes with the pagan animistic religion of Joe Sam, the Indian hired man. He is killed by a huge cat while he sits whittling, waiting for his brother Curt to join him in hunting for the mountain lion.

Joe Sam, the Bridges' Indian hired man. He believes in "medicine" as the only way to avoid trouble from the cat who is the symbol of evil. When worried, he goes into a trancelike state, as he does when the cat appears on the scene. He recovers enough to help Harold Bridges hunt down and kill the cat.

Curt Bridges, the oldest of the Bridges'

sons and the natural leader among the brothers. He wants always to do things his way. He apparently dies of fright, having left his campfire when frightened by the cat. He falls over a cliff to his death.

Harold Bridges, the youngest of the Bridges' sons. At first he stays at the ranch house because his sweetheart is visiting. Later he goes out with Joe Sam to hunt and kill the mountain lion that has killed his brother Arthur.

Mrs. Bridges, the boys' mother. She fears, because of a dream she has, that her family is in danger.

Grace Bridges, the sister of Arthur, Curt, and Harold Bridges.

Gwen Williams, Harold Bridges' sweetheart, an overnight visitor at the ranch.

THE TRAITOR

Author: James Shirley (1596-1666)
Time of action: c. 1480
First presented: 1631

PRINCIPAL CHARACTERS

Lorenzo, the kinsman of Duke Alexander of Florence. Eager to unseat Alexander and succeed him, Lorenzo uses the ruler's lustful attraction for Amidea to lure her brothers into a plot against the Duke. Foiled at first, he tries again and kills Alexander when the Duke comes to visit Amidea, who is already dead. However, he himself is killed by Amidea's angered brother.

Alexander, the young Duke of Florence. Forgetting safety of person and security

of position, the young Duke is absorbed by his pursuit of Amidea. However, when he realizes that she died rather than submit to him, he welcomes death.

Amidea, a chaste young woman who is betrothed to Pisano and is the innocent and unwilling object of Alexander's lust. She shames the Duke into repenting at first, then dies at the hands of Sciarrha rather than be shamed.

Sciarrha and

1151

Florio, her brothers and avengers. Allied with Lorenzo, Sciarrha murders Pisano and kills his own sister rather than let her be shamed. After Duke Alexander's murder, Sciarrha kills Lorenzo, but is himself mortally wounded.

Pisano, a young man who is betrothed to Amidea. Influenced by Petruchio and Lorenzo, Pisano breaks his marriage contract with Amidea in order to marry Oriana and is murdered by Sciarrha.

Cosmo, his friend. To please Pisano, Cosmo breaks his engagement to Oriana. After the bloodbath, Cosmo assumes the rule of Florence.

Oriana, who is loved by Pisano. She was formerly betrothed to Cosmo.

Morosa, Oriana's mother.

Petruchio, Pisano's servant, hired by Lorenzo to help kill Duke Alexander.

Depazzi, one of Lorenzo's conspirators.

TREASURE ISLAND

Author: Robert Louis Stevenson (1850-1894)
Time of action: The 1740's
First published: 1883

PRINCIPAL CHARACTERS

Jim Hawkins, the principal narrator, a bright, courageous boy. His father owns the Admiral Benbow Inn, where Billy Bones hides. In Bones' sea chest, Jim finds a map of Captain Flint's buried treasure.

Dr. Livesey, who treats Jim's dying father and later the wounded mutineers on Treasure Island.

Squire Trelawney, who finances the treasure hunt and outsmarts the pirates.

Captain Smollett, captain of the expedition's ship, the "Hispaniola."

Captain Bill Bones, who steals the map and sings, "Fifteen men on a dead man's chest." He dies of fright when the pirates bring him his death warning.

Black Dog, who discovers Bones' hiding place and is almost killed in their fight in the inn parlor.

Blind Pew, a deformed pirate who delivers the Black Spot death notice. He is trampled to death by the mounted revenue officers who attack the pirate gang searching for Bill Bones' sea chest.

Long John Silver, a one-legged ship's cook who owns a pet parrot called Captain Flint. He gathers a crew for the "Hispaniola," from pirates whom he can control. Once he saves Jim from their fury. He manages to get back to the West Indies with a bag of coins.

Ben Gunn, a pirate marooned by Captain Flint on Treasure Island. He moves the treasure and thus can keep it from the pirates and turn it over to Squire Trelawney.

Israel Hands, a pirate shot by Jim after he tries to kill Jim with a knife.

A TREE GROWS IN BROOKLYN

Author: Betty Smith (1904-   )
Time of action: Early twentieth century
First published: 1943

Francie Nolan, a sensitive and intelligent Brooklyn girl, growing up in grinding poverty. Because of her high values and her strength of spirit, she is able to make the most of her environment. She gains self-reliance and is never crippled by a sense of defeat and deprivation. As the novel ends, she is making preparations to go to college.

Neeley Nolan, Francie's younger brother, a sympathetic but less intelligent and less interesting figure than she. His importance in the story is secondary to hers.

Johnnie Nolan, their father, a Saturday-night singing waiter. Charming, sensitive to his children's needs, an affectionate father, he is an alcoholic and a bad provider. He dies of pneumonia just after Francie's fourteenth birthday.

Katie Rommely Nolan, Johnnie's wife. Married early, she knew by the time Neeley was born that she could not count on Johnnie for support. She works as a janitress in their tenement. As the novel ends, her life is to be easier: she is married again, this time to a retired policeman.

Mr. McGarrity, at whose saloon Johnnie did most of his drinking. After Johnnie's death he helps out by giving the children part-time jobs.

Ben Blake, Francie's fellow student, with whose help she prepares for her college examinations.

Lee Rhynor, a soldier who is Francie's first real date. Believing his offer of marriage sincere, she promises to write every day. Although not seriously in love, she does feel wounded on receiving a letter from the girl he married during his trip home.

Officer McShane, a retired policeman who has long been fond of Katie. He at last persuades her to marry him, with the full agreement of the children.

Laurie Nolan, Katie's youngest child, born a few months after Johnnie's death.

THE TREE OF THE FOLKUNGS

Author: Verner von Heidenstam (1859-1940)
Time of action: Eleventh and thirteenth centuries
First published: 1905-1907

PRINCIPAL CHARACTERS

Folke Filbyter, a peasant freebooter, founder of the Folkung family, builder of the hall named Folketuna. He has three sons by the daughter of Dwarf Jorgrimme, a Finnish sorcerer.

Ingemund and
Hallsten, Folke's sons who become sea-rovers and, later, members of King Inge's guard.

Ingevald, Folke's son, who stays at home with his father.

Holmdis, wife of Ingevald, carried off by force from the house of her father, Ulf Ulfsson.

Folke Ingevaldsson, Ingevald's son, old Folke's heir. He becomes a Christian and an adherent to Blot Sven, King of Sweden.

Old Jakob, a begging friar who brings Christianity. He becomes the foster father of Folke Ingevaldsson.

Earl Birger, a descendant of Folke Filbyter. He is the real ruler of Sweden, though his son wears the crown.

Valdemar, a weak king of Sweden, son of Earl Birger. He loves pleasure and women, and he is no warrior. After his father's death he allows confusion to spread over Sweden. He is finally overthrown by his brother Magnus.

Sophia, Valdemar's queen, a jealous woman who has Yrsa-Lill thrown into a cage filled with snakes. Sophia is a princess of Denmark.

Lady Jutta, Sophia's sister. She has a son by Valdemar.

Yrsa-Lill, a goat-girl in whom Valdemar takes an active interest.

Junker Magnus, Valdemar's knightly brother. He becomes king and restores order to Sweden after defeating his brother.

Gistre Härjanson, a minstrel. He rescues Yrsa-Lill from a cage of snakes.

Sir Svantepolk, a Swedish knight. He becomes a henchman of Junker Magnus.

Archbishop Fulco, prelate of Uppsala. He becomes foster father to the child of Valdemar and Lady Jutta.

Lady Luitgard, Valdemar's last friend and mistress.

THE TREES

Author: Conrad Richter (1890-   )
Time of action: Late eighteenth and early nineteenth centuries
First published: 1940

PRINCIPAL CHARACTERS

Worth Luckett, a pioneer woodsman who has real wanderlust and cannot stay in one place very long. He has to feed his family by shooting game and, when the game runs out, they must move on. He is a simple man and loyal to his wife and family, but somewhat irresponsible. He starts a cabin for his family to live in but he is gone so much of the time that his wife has to prod him to get the building done before the winter snows come.

Jary Luckett, Worth's wife. She is rather sickly and has the slow fever. She does not like to move about so much but realizes that Worth can only support his family if he can kill game. She says nothing about the unfinished cabin until one day when the leaves fall from the trees and she sees the sky through the branches. She then decides that she must have a house to live in. She finally dies of fever.

Sayward Luckett, also called **Saird,** Worth and Jary's eldest child. She is a big,

strapping girl who takes most of the responsibility for the care of the other children. She is very strong, both physically and mentally. She marries Portius Wheeler after offering herself as his wife when another woman turns him down.

Wyitt Luckett, Worth and Jary's son, who grows up to be a "woodsy" exactly like his father.

Genny Luckett, Worth and Jary's daughter, who marries a no-good man named Louie Scurrah.

Louie Scurrah, a woodsman who immediately charms Genny and Achsa. Sayward does not like him from the first and, when she finds him in the woods with Genny, she demands that he marry her. He does so, but later runs away with Achsa.

Achsa Luckett, Worth and Jary's daughter, who is as brown and tough as an Indian.

Sulie Luckett, Worth and Jary's youngest

1154

child, who is lost in the woods and never returns.

Portius Wheeler, a lawyer who marries Sayward while he is drunk. She offers him the chance to leave her if he likes, but he chooses to stay. He treats Sayward well and she is happy with him.

Jake Tench, the man who tries to find a bride for Portius. The girl he picks decides that the match is not for her.

THE TRIAL

Author: Franz Kafka (1883-1924)
Time of action: Twentieth century
First published: 1925

PRINCIPAL CHARACTERS

Joseph K., an employee in a bank. He is a man without particular qualities or abilities, a fact which makes doubly strange his "arrest" by the officer of the Court in the large city where K. lives. Joseph K.'s life is purely conventional and resembles the life of any other person of his class. Consequently, he tries in vain to discover how he has aroused the suspicion of the Court. His honesty is conventional; his sins, with Elsa the waitress, are conventional; and he has no striking or dangerous ambitions. He is a man without a face; at the most, he can only ask questions, and he receives no answers that clarify the strange world of courts and court functionaries in which he is compelled to wander.

Frau Grubach, K.'s landlady. She has a high opinion of K. and is deeply shocked by his arrest. She can do nothing to help him.

Fräulein Bürstner, a respectable young woman who also lives in Frau Grubach's house. She avoids any close entanglement with K.

The Assistant Manager, K.'s superior at the bank. He invites K. to social occasions which K. cannot attend because of his troubles with the Court. He is also eager to invade K.'s proper area of authority.

The Examining Magistrate, the official who opens the formal investigation of K.'s offense. He conducts an unruly, arbitrary, and unsympathetic hearing.

The Washerwoman, an amiable but loose woman who has her dwelling in the court building. She is at the disposal of all the functionaries of the system.

The Usher, the subservient husband of the Washerwoman. His submission to official authority is, like his wife's, a sign of the absorption of the individual into the system.

The Clerk of Inquiries, a minor official who reveals court procedures to newly arrested persons.

Franz and
Willem, minor officers of the court, who must endure the attentions of The Whipper because K. has complained to the Court about them.

Uncle Karl (Albert K.), K.'s uncle, who is determined that K. shall have good legal help in his difficulties.

Huld, the lawyer, an ailing and eccentric man, hand in glove with the Court. He keeps his great knowledge of the law half-hidden from K. K. finally dismisses the lawyer as a man whose efforts will be useless.

Leni, the notably promiscuous servant at the lawyer's house. Full of kind instructions to K., she tells him how to get along with the erratic Huld.

Block, a tradesman who has been waiting for five and a half years for Huld to do something for him. He lives at the lawyer's house in order to be ready for consultations at odd hours.

The Manufacturer, one of K.'s clients. He expresses sympathy for K.'s plight and sends K. to an artist acquaintance, Titorelli, as a means of influencing the Court in K.'s favor.

Titorelli, an impoverished painter who lives in an attic just off the courts of justice. He paints many a magistrate in uneasy and yet traditional poses. He explains in great detail to K. the different kinds of sentences an accused person can receive. He also reveals the contrast between what the law is supposed to do and how it actually works.

The Prison Chaplain, whom K. encounters as the preacher at the Cathedral in the town. The Chaplain tells K. a long story about a door guarded by a Tartar; it is a door that somehow exists especially for K. Despite his sympathy, the Chaplain finally reveals himself as merely one more employee of the Court.

TRIAL BY JURY

Author: W. S. Gilbert (1836-1911)
Time of action: Nineteenth century
First presented: 1875

PRINCIPAL CHARACTERS

The Learned Judge, an eminent jurist who rose to the top of his profession by first wooing, then jilting a rich attorney's elderly, ugly daughter. A good judge of beauty, he ends the case by offering to marry the plaintiff.

The Plaintiff (Angelina), a lovely girl suing Edwin for breach of promise. She wins the love of the jury and the Judge, whom she accepts in lieu of Edwin.

The Defendant (Edwin), a fickle lover who would be glad to marry Angelina if it would not deprive so many other girls of happiness. He would marry her today if he could marry another tomorrow. The jury considers him a monster.

The Usher, a careful and conscientious instructor of the jury. He urges the jurors to be free from all bias, to listen to the Plaintiff with sympathy, and to pay no attention to anything the vile Defendant says.

The Foreman of the Jury, a tender-hearted man who wishes to be like a father to the Plaintiff. He offers his manly bosom for her to recline on if she feels faint, and gives her a fatherly kiss.

The Counsel for the Plaintiff, a sympathetic lawyer. He, too, offers his bosom for her to recline upon. He is horrified at the Defendant's proposal of plural marriages, for to marry two wives at a time is "Burglaree."

The First Bridesmaid, a lovely girl who captivates the Judge before the Plaintiff appears.

A TRICK TO CATCH THE OLD ONE

Author: Thomas Middleton (1580-1627)
Time of action: First years of seventeenth century
First presented: c. 1605

Theodorus Witgood, a dissolute young spendthrift. He conspires with the courtesan, his former mistress, to deceive his avaricious old uncle and regain enough of his wasted and confiscated fortune to marry Joyce. Once successful, he swears that he will give up all the vices which have nearly ruined him.

Pecunious Lucre, his uncle, a greedy old man who leaps at the thought of adding to the family fortune by Witgood's proposed marriage to a wealthy widow. He is not above a little flirtation with his nephew's bride-to-be, but he expends most of his energy in his feud with his equally ill-tempered contemporary, Walkadine Hoard.

A Courtesan, Witgood's accomplice, a witty woman with a genius for taking advantage of situations which will result in her own advantage. She plays her

part of wealthy widow so convincingly that she wins a proposal from old Hoard. When her profession is revealed, she pacifies her new husband with the somewhat specious assurance that, having sinned in her youth, she will be faithful in maturity.

Walkadine Hoard, her miserly suitor, who is attracted primarily to her 400 pounds a year. He crows over his old enemy, Lucre, when he thinks he has successfully cheated his rival by carrying off Witgood's rich widow. He realizes finally that he has been gulled and reluctantly admits that he must keep his bride to save his reputation.

Joyce, Hoard's niece, Witgood's pleasant, amenable sweetheart, who plays very little part in the schemes of the others.

Taverner, Witgood's ready accomplice in fleecing the greedy Lucre.

THE TRICKSTER

Author: Titus Maccius Plautus (c. 255-184 B.C.)
Time of action: Late third century B.C.
First presented: 191 B.C.

PRINCIPAL CHARACTERS

Pseudolus (sōō'də·ləs), Simo's servant. When he learns that Calidorus' slave-girl sweetheart is to be sold, Pseudolus promises to trick Simo out of enough money to purchase her. The slave brazenly tells Simo of his plan and goads the old man into promising to pay for the girl if Pseudolus can get her away from her owner, Ballio. By substituting Simia for the real messenger, the wily slave succeeds in completely duping Ballio and wins the slave girl for Calidorus free of charge.

Simo (sī'mō), an Athenian gentleman, Calidorus' father and Pseudolus' owner. Forewarned by his clever servant, the

tight-fisted old man is tricked nevertheless, but his bet with Ballio keeps him from losing any money.

Ballio (bă'lĭ·ō), a procurer, the owner of Phoenicium. Although he has been warned by Simo, the hard-hearted procurer is tricked by clever Pseudolus; he loses his slave girl to Calidorus and twenty minae to Simo.

Calidorus (kă·lĭ·dō'rəs), the lovesick son of Simo.

Phoenicium (fē·nē'sĭ·əm), Ballio's slave girl and the sweetheart of Calidorus.

Harpax (här'păks), the real messenger

of the Macedonian officer who has made the initial payment for the purchase of Phoenicium.

Simia (sĭ′mĭ·ɔ), the servant of one of Calidorus' friends. He impersonates Harpax and tricks Ballio.

TRILBY

Author: George du Maurier (1834-1896)
Time of action: Nineteenth century
First published: 1894

PRINCIPAL CHARACTERS

Trilby O'Ferrall, a Scotch-Irish artist's model. Very tall, well developed, and graceful, she lacks classical beauty, having freckles, a large mouth, and eyes set too wide apart; but she has a simple, amiable charm—and astonishingly beautiful feet. She sings wretchedly except when hypnotized by Svengali under whose spell she comes after going out of Little Billee's life. Traveling with Svengali as his wife, she attains fame as a singer. After his death she wastes away and dies.

Svengali, a middle-aged Jewish musician from Austria, tall, bony, with long heavy black hair, brilliant black eyes, a thin sallow face, and black beard and mustache. Conceited, derisive, and malicious, he alternately bullies and fawns in a harsh, croaking voice. But he is a dedicated and expert player of popular and light classical music. Though Trilby is repelled at first by his greasy, dirty appearance and regards him as a spidery demon or incubus, she becomes completely his creature under his hypnosis.

Talbot Wynne (Taffy), an art student and ex-soldier, a Yorkshireman, handsome, fair, blue-eyed, big, and brawny. He wears a heavy mustache and drooping auburn whiskers.

Sandy McAllister ("The Laird of Cockpen"), another art student, a burly Scotsman who becomes a noted artist.

William Bagot (Little Billee), an art student, a Londoner, much younger than his friends Taffy and Sandy, whom he idolizes. Small, slender, black-haired, blue-eyed, and delicate-featured, he is graceful and well-built and dresses much better than his friends. He is also innocent of the world and its wickedness. Infatuated with Trilby, he is shocked at her posing nude, and he becomes hysterical and very ill following her disappearance after her promise to his mother. Though he recovers after a fashion, there is a return of his severe illness following Trilby's pathetic death several years later. Little Billee himself dies shortly afterward.

Gecko, a young fiddler, small, swarthy, shabby, brown-eyed, and pock-marked; a nail-biter. Though he loves Trilby he helps Svengali train her to sing so that Svengali may exploit her.

Mrs. Bagot, Little Billee's mother, who persuades Trilby not to marry her son.

Alice, a parson's pretty daughter with whom Little Billee falls in and out of love.

Dodor and
Gontran (Zouzou), soldier friends of Taffy, Sandy, Little Billee, and Trilby.

Jeannot, Trilby's young brother, whose death deeply saddens her.

Marta, Svengali's aunt, a fat, elderly Jewess, grotesque-looking but kind to Trilby.

Blanche Bagot, Little Billee's sister, who marries Taffy.

1158

TRISTAN AND ISOLDE

Author: Gottfried von Strassburg (fl. late twelfth and early thirteenth centuries)
Time of action: The Arthurian period
First transcribed: c. 1210

PRINCIPAL CHARACTERS

Tristan (trēs'tän), the courtly son of Rivalin and Blanchefleur. Orphaned at birth, he is reared by Rual the Faithful until he joins King Mark's court after his escape from Norwegian kidnapers. He serves his lord well by killing Duke Morolt and winning the hand of Isolde the Fair for Mark. However, Tristan and Isolde drink a love potion by accident and fall helplessly in love. The two lovers deceive Mark until Tristan is forced to flee. Later he marries Isolde of the White Hands, but it is a marriage in name only.

Isolde the Fair (ē-zōl'dĕ), the wife of King Mark and lover of Tristan.

Mark (märk), the vacillating King of Cornwall, uncle of Tristan, and cuckolded husband of Isolde the Fair.

Rivalin (rē-vä'lĭn, rĭ-vä'lēn), a lord of Parmenie. On his travels he marries Blanchefleur and fathers Tristan before his death in battle against Duke Morgan.

Blanchefleur (blänsh-flœr'), the sister of King Mark, wife of Rivalin. Upon learning of Rivalin's death, she dies giving birth to Tristan.

Brangene (brän'gā-nĕ), the companion of Isolde and her substitute in Mark's wedding bed.

Rual the Faithful (rōō-äl'), the foster father of Tristan.

Duke Morolt (mō-rōlt'), the brother of Queen Isolde. He is killed by Tristan when he demands tribute from Cornwall for Ireland.

Duke Morgan (mōr'gän), the enemy of Rivalin, later killed by Tristan.

Isolde of the White Hands (ē-zōl'dĕ), the wife of Tristan in name only.

Queen Isolde of Ireland, the mother of Isolde the Fair.

TRISTRAM SHANDY

Author: Laurence Sterne (1713-1768)
Time of action: 1718-1766
First published: 1759-1767

PRINCIPAL CHARACTERS

Tristram Shandy, the narrator and ostensible hero of this literary farrago devoted to some details of his early life, his father's opinions and eccentricities, his uncle's passion for the reënactment of Marlborough's military campaigns, and assorted oddities of mind and conduct. His mother having incurred some time before the expense of a needless trip to London for a lying-in, Tristram, accord-

ing to the terms of his parents' marriage contract, is born at Shandy Hall on November 5, 1718. Various misfortunes befall him early in life: a broken nose, crushed by the doctor's forceps at birth; the wrong name, Tristram instead of Trismegistus, when he is christened by a stupid young curate; and the loss of his member, a heavy sash having fallen while he was relieving himself through

1159

an open window. Though crushed by these irreparable accidents, his father still insists that the boy shall have a proper education, and to this end Mr. Shandy writes a "Tristra-paedia" in imitation of the "Cyro-paedia" designed for the training of Cyrus the Great, as set forth in the pages of Xenophon. Except for a few scattered hints, the reader learns almost nothing about Tristram's later life. Sterne devotes most of the novel to reporting humorous incidents and the sayings of the other characters.

Walter Shandy, Tristram's father, a crotchety retired turkey merchant who possesses an immense stock of obscure information gained by reading old books collected by his ancestors. As the result of his reading, he takes delight in lengthy discussions on unimportant topics. A man of acute sensibilities, alert to the minor pricks and vexations of life, he has developed a drollish but sharp manner of peevishness, but he is so open and generous in all other ways that his friends are seldom offended by his sharpness of tongue. He suffers from sciatica as well as loquacity.

Mrs. Shandy, a good-natured but rather stupid woman. Typical is her interruption of the moment of Tristram's conception on the first Sunday of March, 1718, by asking her husband if he has remembered to wind the clock. "I dare say" and "I suppose not" in agreement with Mr. Shandy are her most brilliant remarks in conversation.

Toby Shandy, called **My Uncle Toby,** a retired army captain who had been wounded in the groin during the siege of Namur in 1698. Now retired to the country, he spends most of his time amid a large and complicated series of miniature fortifications and military emplacements on the bowling green behind Shandy Hall. There he follows with all the interest and enthusiasm of actual conflict the military campaigns of the Duke of Marborough on the Continent. Oc-casionally forced into conversations with his brother, as on the night of Tristram's birth, he escapes the flood of Mr. Shandy's discourse by whistling "Lilli-bullero" to himself. Completely innocent on the subjects of women and sex, he is pursued by a neighbor, the Widow Wadman, whose intentions are matrimonial and whose campaign on the old soldier's heart is as strategically planned as his own miniature battles.

Widow Wadman, a buxom woman who lays siege to Uncle Toby's bachelor life and begs him to show her the exact spot where he was wounded. Eventually he indicates on a map the location of Namur. Her question kills her chance of a proposal when Corporal Trim tells his embarrassed master what the widow really wants to know.

Corporal Trim, the faithful and loquacious servant of Uncle Toby. He helps his master enact mimic battles on the bowling green.

Susannah, a vain and careless maid. Supposed to tell the curate to christen the sickly baby Trismegistus, after the minor philosopher admired by Mr. Shandy, she arrives on the scene so out of breath that she can say only that the name is Tris-something, and the curate decides that the child is to be called Tristram. He is pleased because that is his own name.

Parson Yorick, a mercurial and eccentric clergyman completely innocent of the ways of the wicked world. He is in the habit of speaking his mind plainly, often to the discomfiture or resentment of the man toward whom his remarks are directed. Once a lover of fine horses, he rides about the countryside on a nag that would disgrace Don Quixote. The reason is that his good horses were always spavined or wind-broken by anxious fathers who borrowed the animals to ride for a midwife. At the end of the novel he declares that the closing anecdote is a Cock and Bull story, "and one of the best of its kind, I ever heard." As Tristram relates, the epitaph on the clergyman's tomb-stone is a simple, brief inscription: Alas, poor YORICK!

Dr. Slop, a squat, bungling country doctor, the author of a book on midwifery. For a fee of five guineas, this "man-mid-wife" sits in the back parlor of Shandy Hall and listens to Mr. Shandy hold forth on various topics, including a treatise on oaths, while a midwife is attending Mrs. Shandy upstairs. When called in to assist at the birth, his forceps permanently flatten Tristram's nose.

Obadiah, the outdoors servant at Shandy Hall, an awkward, good-natured fellow.

Jonathan, Mr. Shandy's dull-witted coach-man.

Le Fever, a poor lieutenant who falls sick while traveling to rejoin his regiment in Flanders. When Corporal Trim, who has visited the dying man at the village inn, reports to Uncle Toby that the poor fellow will never march again, the old soldier is so moved that he swears one of his rare oaths while declaring that Le

Fever shall not die. The recording angel, making a note of the oath, drops a tear on the word and blots it out forever.

Tom, Corporal Trim's brother, who marries the widow of a Jew in Lisbon.

A Negress, a friend of Tom Trim, who motivates a discussion on slavery.

Mrs. Bridget, Widow Wadman's maid, ambitious to marry Corporal Trim.

Eugenius, the friend and adviser of Parson Yorick. He witnesses the clergyman's dying moments.

Master Bobby Shandy, Tristram's older brother, whose death at an early age is reported. His sudden death gives Corporal Trim a good opportunity to provide the servants of Shandy Hall with a dramatic illustration—he drops his hat—of man's mortality, the fact that he can be here one moment and gone the next. Trim's action causes Susannah, who has been thinking of the gown that may become hers when her mistress goes into mourning, to burst into tears.

THE TRIUMPH OF DEATH

Author: Gabriele D'Annunzio (1863-1938)
Time of action: Nineteenth century
First published: 1894

PRINCIPAL CHARACTERS

George Aurispa, a wealthy young Italian independent of his family. He takes the beautiful Hippolyte as his mistress but comes to distrust her and his love affair with her as leading him into the same kind of gross sensuality that had ruined his father. His distress leads him to consider suicide and, later, the murder of the woman who has overpowered his emotions. Finally he leaps to death on a rocky coast, taking his mistress to death with him in his embrace.

Hippolyte, a beautiful married woman who falls in love with George Aurispa.

She leaves her husband and returns to her family in order to take George as her lover, but she is disturbed many times by the thought of her mortality, a thought frequently suggested to her by an inclination toward epilepsy. From being almost frigid, she becomes, through George Aurispa's lovemaking, a passionately sensual woman.

Signor Aurispa, George's father. He is a worldly man who leaves his wife to take up with a mistress, by whom he has two illegitimate children. He squanders his fortune, though he refuses to help his

1161

wife and their daughter. He is regarded by his wife and son as a gross sensualist.

Signora Aurispa, George's mother. As a woman deserted by her husband, she has her son's deep sympathy. It is partly her unenviable position that enables her son to see that he is slipping into the same kind of sensuality that ensnared his father.

TROILUS AND CRESSIDA

Author: William Shakespeare (1564-1616)
Time of action: Trojan War
First presented: 1601-1602

PRINCIPAL CHARACTERS

Troilus (troi'ləs, trō'ĭ·lŭs), the heroic young son of Priam. An idealistic and trusting young lover, he first wins Cressida with the aid of Pandarus, then loses first her presence and afterward her faith. He becomes bitter in disillusionment. He is a good fighter, showing no compassion toward his enemies.

Cressida (krĕs'ĭ·də), the daughter of Calchas. She is an attractive, beautiful girl, but not gifted with the power to say "no." She yields to Troilus after a certain amount of coyness, and she shows real regret when she has to leave him to go to her father with the Greeks. She swears eternal truth to him, but in her fickleness she soon accepts Diomedes as her lover. Shakespeare's Cressida is much less complex and less appealing than Chaucer's Criseyde. Ulysses in the play finds her contemptible, and audiences do not greatly disagree with him.

Pandarus (păn'də·rəs), the uncle of Cressida and the go-between for Troilus and Cressida. Much simplified and considerably degraded from his complex original in Chaucer's fine poem, he is an off-color jester, especially in the presence of the lovers. He speaks a particularly unpleasant dirty epilogue, which a number of scholars have ascribed to some unknown play-dresser instead of to Shakespeare.

Hector (hĕk'tər, hĕk'tŏr), the greatest of Priam's sons and chief defender of his country. He has better judgment than most of his fellows, but yields to pressure and consents to Helen's remaining in Troy instead of being sent back to the Greeks. Troilus accuses him of too great clemency to fallen foes. In keeping with the medieval tradition of Hector as one of the Nine Worthies, he is given great prowess. His death at the hands of Achilles and his Myrmidons is depicted as the murder of an unarmed man by numerous opponents.

Achilles (ə·kĭl'ēz), most famous of the Greek champions. Painted from the point of view of the legendarily Trojan-descended English, he is a most unpleasant character: self-centered, stupid, arrogant, and ruthless. He avoids combat partly because of pique, partly because of desire for Polyxena, one of Priam's daughters. He returns to combat partly out of jealousy of Ajax, perhaps chiefly because of the death of his friend Patroclus. Although allowed a respite by Hector when they first meet, he has Hector murdered while he is unarmed; and he instructs his men to run through the Grecian camp shouting, "Achilles hath the mighty Hector slain."

Thersites (thər·sī'tēz), a cowardly, foul-mouthed Greek. He ranges through the play as a sort of chorus, making impudent or vile comments on all whom he sees. When Hector, meeting him on the field of battle, asks him if he is a worthy opponent, he characterizes himself truthfully as "a rascal, a scurvy railing knave, a very filthy rogue," thereby saving his life. He seems to be accepted by his cohorts as an "all-licens'd fool."

Ulysses (ū·lĭs′ēz), the shrewd Greek hero. He delivers a much-admired speech on order. He and Nestor are usually in agreement and are experienced practical psychologists. Despising Cressida, during a truce he conducts Troilus to a spot from which he can see and hear Cressida and Diomedes making love.

Nestor (nĕs′tər, nĕs′tŏr) the venerable old man of the Greek forces. He confers frequently with Ulysses and represents with him the rational outlook.

Diomedes (Diomed) (dī·ō·mē′dēz), the unprincipled warrior sent to escort Cressida to the Greek camp. After seducing her, he fights an indecisive match with Troilus.

Ajax (ā′jăks), a Greek champion related to the Trojan royal family. Slow and bearlike, he is as stupid as Achilles and as much filled with self-love, but is a much less unpleasant character. He meets Hector in single combat, but agrees to call off the battle because of their kinship.

Priam (prī′ăm), King of Troy. He appears very briefly to preside over the council to determine the fate of Helen and to try to dissuade Hector from tempting fate.

Paris (pă′rĭs), son of Priam and lover of Helen. He insists on keeping Helen instead of returning her to her husband; his selfishness, having caused the War of Troy, continues it. He is supported heartily by Troilus, the lover, and very reluctantly by Hector, the warrior.

Helen, wife of Menelaus, mistress of Paris. Fair outside, but hollow within,

she and Paris are guilty of causing the Trojan War. Pandarus exchanges ambiguous pleasantries with her.

Andromache (ăn·drŏ′mə·kē), wife of Hector. She pleads piteously, but in vain, for her courageous husband to remain inside the walls on his fateful day.

Cassandra (kə·săn′drə), the daughter of Priam, a prophetess. Considered mad by all her family, she prophesies Hector's death, but is unable to prevent his going into combat.

Calchas (kăl′kəs), a Trojan priest, taking part with the Greeks. He insists on having his daughter Cressida sent to the Grecian camp in exchange for a Trojan captive, Antenor.

Agamemnon (ă·gə·mĕm′nŏn), the Greek general. He is a royal figure of great dignity.

Menelaus (mĕ·nə·lā′əs), Helen's husband, Agamemnon's brother. He and Paris meet on the battlefield with Thersites as a scurrilous cheer-leader, but the combat is indecisive.

Patroclus (pă·trŏ′kləs), the youthful companion of Achilles. Hector kills him.

Aeneas (ē·nē′əs), a Trojan commander. He delivers the message to Troilus that Cressida is to be sent to the Greeks. In the battle he is rescued by Troilus.

Antenor (ăn·tē′nər), another Trojan commander. Captured by the Greeks, he is exchanged for Cressida.

Deiphobus (dē·ĭ′fə·bəs) and **Helenus** (hĕl′ə·nəs), sons of Priam.

Margarelon (mär·găr′ē·lŏn), a bastard son of Priam. In the final battle he frightens Thersites into flight.

Alexander (ăl·ĕg·zăn′dər), the servant of Cressida.

TROILUS AND CRISEYDE

Author: Geoffrey Chaucer (1340?-1400)
Time of action: Trojan War
First transcribed: c. 1382

PRINCIPAL CHARACTERS

Troilus (troi′ləs), a young prince of Troy. He scorns love until he falls in love with Criseyde, who then becomes his mistress until she is traded to the Greeks for a Trojan warrior. When Criseyde fails to return to Troy as she has promised, Troilus is grief-stricken. He is killed on the battlefield by Achilles, the great Greek warrior.

Priam (prī′ăm), King of Troy during the Trojan War. He is Troilus' father.

Criseyde (krĕs′ĭ·də), a beautiful young widow. She fears that Troilus' love is dishonorable, but she becomes his mistress so he will not die of unrequited love. Though she loves him, and vows to return to Troy, she falls in love with Diomedes, a young Greek, and remains in the Greek camp with him.

Calchas (kăl′kəs), Criseyde's father. A soothsayer and prophet, he runs away from Troy to join the Greeks, who are fated to win the war. He arranges to have his daughter exchanged for Antenor, whom the Greeks have captured.

Pandarus (păn′də·rəs), Criseyde's uncle. He arranges the details of the affair between Troilus and Criseyde.

Deiphobus (dē·ĭ′fə·bəs), Troilus' brother. He enables the lovers to meet by inviting Troilus and Criseyde to dinner at his home.

Antenor (ăn·tē′nər), a Trojan warrior captured by the Greeks and exchanged for Criseyde.

Hector (hĕk′tər), Troilus' brother. He does not wish to make the exchange of Criseyde for Antenor.

Diomedes (dī·ō·mē′dēz), a handsome young Greek. Criseyde falls in love with him and hence fails to return to Troilus.

Achilles (ə·kĭl′ēz), mightiest of the Greek warriors. He slays Troilus on the battlefield.

THE TROJAN WOMEN

Author: Euripides (c. 485-c. 406 B.C.)
Time of action: After the fall of Troy
First presented: 415 B.C.

PRINCIPAL CHARACTERS

Hecuba (hĕ′kū·bə), Queen of Troy. Aged and broken by the fall of the city, she is the epitome of all the misfortune resulting from the defeat of the Trojans and the destruction of the city. She is first revealed prostrate before the tents of the captive Trojan women, with the city in the background. Her opening lyrics tell of the pathos of her situation and introduce the impression of hopelessness and the theme of the inevitable doom which war brings. The Greek herald enters with the news that each of the women has been assigned to a different master. Hecuba asks first about her children, Cassandra and Polyxena; then, when she finds that she has been given to Odysseus, she rouses herself to an outburst of rebellious anger. Cassandra appears and recalls the prophecy that Hecuba would die in Troy. After Cassandra is led away, Andromache, who appears with news of the sacrifice of Polyxena, tries to console Hecuba with the idea that Polyxena is fortunate in death, but Hecuba in reproach and consolation points out to Andromache and the younger women of the Chorus the hope of life. Her attempts to console those younger than herself, here and elsewhere, are her most endearing feature. The other important aspect of her character, the desire for vengeance against Helen, who has caused her sorrow, is shown in her reply to Helen's plea to Menelaus. Hecuba's reply is vigorous; she points to Helen's own responsibility for her actions and ends with a plea to Menelaus to kill Helen and vindicate Greek womanhood. Hecuba's last action is the preparation of the body of Astyanax, the young son of Andromache and Hector killed by the Greeks out of fear, for burial. Her lament over the body is profoundly moving. At the end of the play she is restrained from throwing herself into the ruins of the burning city.

Cassandra (kə·săn′drə), daughter of Hecuba, a prophetess chosen by Agamemnon as a concubine. When she first appears, wild-eyed and waving a torch above her head, she sings a parody of a marriage song in her own honor; but she soon calms down and prophesies the dreadful end of Agamemnon because of his choice and of the suffering of the Greeks. She views aggressive war as a source of unhappiness for the aggressor himself. As she leaves she hurls the sacred emblems of her divine office to the ground and looks forward to her triumph in revenge.

Andromache (ăn·drŏ′mə·kē), the wife of Hector. Allotted to Neoptolemus, the son of Achilles, she brings Hecuba news of the sacrifice of Polyxena and compares her fate in accepting a new lord to Polyxena's escape through death. When she learns of the Greeks' decision to kill Astyanax, her son by Hector, she gives expression to her tortured love as a mother. Unable to condemn the Greeks because they would refuse Astyanax burial, she curses Helen as the cause of misfortune.

Helen (hĕl′ən), the Queen of Sparta abducted by Paris. Beautiful and insolent, her pleading before Menelaus is an attempt to place the blame for her actions on others: on Priam and Hecuba because they had refused to kill Paris at the oracle's command; on the goddess Aphrodite because she promised Helen to Paris at the time of the judgment; on the Trojan guards who had prevented her return to the Greeks. She departs, proud and confident.

Menelaus (mĕ·nə·lā′əs), King of Sparta and the husband of Helen, who has been returned to him, the man she wronged, to kill; but it is evident that he will not do so. His eagerness to assure others that Helen has no control over him and that he intends to kill her becomes almost comic.

Talthybius (tăl·thĭ′bĭ·əs), a herald of the Greeks. He appears three times: to fetch Cassandra, to execute Astyanax, and to bring back the body of Astyanax for burial and set fire to the remains of Troy. A kindly man, he is unable to carry out the execution of Astyanax personally.

Astyanax (ăs·tī′ə·năks), the infant son of Andromache and Hector. He is flung from the highest battlement of Troy because the Greeks believe that a son of Hector is too dangerous to live.

A Chorus of Trojan Women. Their odes express a mood of pity and sorrow for the Trojans.

Poseidon (pō·sī′dən), the god of the sea and patron of Troy. He appears, at the beginning of the drama, to take official leave of the city; he had favored it, but the gods aiding the Greeks had proved too strong, especially Pallas Athena. His monologue also gives the necessary background for the play.

Pallas Athena (păl′əs ə·thē′nə), the goddess of wisdom. She confronts Poseidon as he bids farewell to Troy and proposes a common vengeance against the Greeks, though she had favored them earlier. Because their impious behavior at the capture of Troy has alienated the gods, the Greeks are to be punished as they put to sea. This threat of retribution looms over the entire play.

TRUTH SUSPECTED

Author: Juan Ruiz de Alarcón (c. 1581-1639)
Time of action: Seventeenth century
First published: 1628

PRINCIPAL CHARACTERS

Don García (dōn gär·thē′ä), a young noble. A congenital liar, he is himself faced by a confusion of facts as he woos the veiled Jacinta, thinking that her name is Lucrecia. The lies that he tells during the courtship constantly involve him in difficulty. Enraged by his lies, Don Beltrán arranges for his son's marriage to Jacinta, but Don García invents a wife in Salamanca in order to avoid marrying Jacinta, little realizing that she is the girl he is wooing. His lie is discovered too late and a rival marries Jacinta. Don García must be content with Lucrecia.

Juan de Sosa (hwän dä sō′sä), in love with Jacinta. Rejected by her uncle until he attains knighthood, Juan must stand by while Don García courts his lady. Juan challenges Don García to a duel because of one of his lies and later reveals that his rival has lied about the supposed wife in Salamanca. Finally, Juan becomes a knight and marries Jacinta, much to Don García's chagrin.

Don Beltrán (dōn bĕl·trän′), Don García's father, who despises lying.

Tristán (trēs′tän′), Don García's shrewd and cynical servant, who gives his master lectures about lying peppered with quotations from Roman and Greek authorities.

Jacinta (hä·thēn′tä), the niece of Don Sancho, thought by Don García to be Lucrecia.

Lucrecia (lōō·krä′thyä), her friend, who later marries Don García.

Don Sancho (dōn sän′chō), Jacinta's uncle, who forbids her to marry Juan de Sosa until that young man attains knighthood.

TURCARET

Author: Alain René Le Sage (1668-1747)
Time of action: Seventeenth century
First presented: 1709

PRINCIPAL CHARACTERS

Frontin (frōn·tăn′), the Knight's valet, later M. Turcarets valet. A master of fraud, he ably shows that he is better at trickery than his masters. Replacing M. Turcaret's valet, he keeps funds flowing from the financier to the Baroness, from

1166

her to his Knight, and secretly from the Knight to himself. By the end of the play, Frontin has accumulated enough money for Lisette to marry him.

M. Turcaret (mə·syœ′ tür·kȧ·rä′), a duped financier who is in love with the Baroness, a charming widow. Deeply enamored, he lavishes gifts upon her, little realizing that she is passing on his funds. He is dropped by the coquette shortly before he is arrested for a pay-officer's default of two hundred thousand crowns.

The Baroness, a young widow and a coquette. Madly in love with the Knight, she is duped as she herself has duped M. Turcaret. Sensing M. Turcaret's fiscal embroilments, she lets him go only to cast off the parasitic Knight when she discovers his duplicity.

The Knight, a coxcomb who loves the Baroness only for the crowns she can get from gullible M. Turcaret.

Marine (mȧ·rēn′) and **Lisette** (lē·zĕt′), the Baroness' maids. Annoyed by her mistress' gullibility, Marine leaves her post and is replaced by Lisette, who aids Frontin in keeping funds flowing to the Knight.

Mme. Turcaret, the financier's estranged wife.

The Marquess, her coxcomb.

Mme. Jacob (zhȧ·kôb′), M. Turcaret's sister, a dealer in toilette necessaries.

Flammand (flȧ·män′), M. Turcaret's first valet.

THE TURN OF THE SCREW

Author: Henry James (1843-1916)
Time of action: Mid-nineteenth century
First published: 1898

PRINCIPAL CHARACTERS

The Governess, from whose point of view the story is told. Employed to look after his orphaned niece and nephew by a man who makes it clear that he does not wish to be bothered about them, she finds herself engaged in a struggle against evil apparitions for the souls of the children. There has been a good deal of the "Is-Hamlet-mad?" sort of inconclusive speculation as to whether "The Turn of the Screw" is a real ghost story or a study of a neurotic and frustrated woman. Probably both interpretations are true: the apparitions are real; the children are indeed possessed by evil; and the governess is probably neurotic.

Miles, a little boy, one of the governess' charges. At first he seems to be a remarkably good child, but gradually she learns that he has been mysteriously corrupted by his former governess and

his uncle's former valet, whose ghosts now appear to maintain their evil control. Miles dies in the governess' arms during her final struggle to save him from some mysterious evil.

Flora, Miles' sister and feminine counterpart. The governess finally sends her away to her uncle.

Miss Jessel, the former governess, now dead. She appears frequently to the governess and to the children, who refuse to admit the appearances.

Peter Quint, the uncle's former valet, now dead. Drunken and vicious, he was also Miss Jessel's lover. The governess sees his apparition repeatedly.

Mrs. Grose, the housekeeper of the country estate where the story is set. Good-

1167

hearted and talkative, she is the source of what little concrete information the governess and the reader get as to the identities and past histories of the evil apparitions. Allied with the governess against the influence of Peter Quint and Miss Jessel, she takes charge of Flora when the child is sent to her uncle.

TWELFTH NIGHT

Author: William Shakespeare (1564-1616)
Time of action: Sixteenth century
First presented: 1599-1600

PRINCIPAL CHARACTERS

Viola (vē′ō·lə), who, with her twin brother Sebastian, is shipwrecked upon the coast of Ilyria. The twins are separated, and a friendly sea captain helps Viola to assume male clothes and to find service as the page **Cesario** (sĕ-zä′rĭ·ō), with Orsino, Duke of Ilyria. Her new master is pleased with her and sends the disguised girl to press his suit for the hand of the Countess Olivia, with whom the Duke is in love. Olivia, who has been in mourning for her brother, finally admits the page and instantly falls in love with the supposed young man. "Cesario," meanwhile, has been falling in love with Orsino. So apparent is Olivia's feeling for "Cesario" that the Countess' admirer, Sir Andrew Aguecheek, is persuaded that he must send a challenge to the page, which challenge "Cesario" reluctantly accepts. A sea captain, Antonio, a friend of Sebastian, chances upon the duel and rescues Viola, mistaking her for her brother whom he had found after the wreck and to whom he had entrusted his purse. In the ensuing confusion, Olivia marries the real Sebastian, thinking him to be "Cesario." Viola and her brother are finally reunited. Viola marries Orsino, and all ends happily.

Sebastian (sĕ·băs′tyən), Viola's twin brother. Separated from her during the shipwreck, he makes his way to Duke Orsino's court, where he is befriended by Antonio. He is involved in a fight with Sir Andrew Aguecheek, who mistakes him for "Cesario." When Olivia inter-

feres and takes Sebastian to her home, she marries him, also thinking him to be "Cesario." Thus he and Viola are reunited.

Orsino (ôr·sē′nō), Duke of Ilyria (ĭ·lĭr′ĭ·ə), in love with Olivia. He sends the disguised Viola to press his suit, not realizing that Viola is falling in love with him. But when Viola reveals herself as a girl, the Duke returns her love and marries her.

Olivia (ō·lĭv′ĭ·ə), a rich countess, living in retirement because of the death of her brother. Orsino courts her through "Cesario," but she rejects his suit and falls in love with the disguised Viola. When Sebastian, whom she mistakes for "Cesario," is brought to her after the fight with Sir Andrew, she marries him.

Malvolio (măl·vō′lĭ·ō), Olivia's pompous steward. Considering himself far above his station, he dreams of marrying the Countess. He so angers the other members of her household by his arrogance that they plan a trick on him. Maria, imitating Olivia's handwriting, plants a note telling him that to please the Countess he must appear always smiling and wearing yellow stockings cross-gartered, affectations that Olivia hates. The Countess considers him insane and has him locked in a dark room. He is finally released and leaves the stage vowing revenge. Some critics have seen Malvolio as Shakespeare's satiric portrait of the

Puritan, but this interpretation is disputed by others.

Maria (mă·rē'ə), Olivia's lively waiting woman. It is she who, angered by the vanity of Malvolio, imitates Olivia's handwriting in the note that leads him to make a fool of himself. She marries Sir Toby Belch.

Sir Toby Belch (tō'bĭ bĕlsh), Olivia's uncle and a member of her household. His conviviality is constantly threatened by Malvolio so that he gladly joins in the plot against the steward. Sir Toby marries Maria.

Sir Andrew Aguecheek (ā·gū'chēk), a cowardly, foolish drinking companion

of Sir Toby and suitor of Olivia. He is forced into a duel with "Cesario" but mistakenly becomes involved with Sebastian, who wounds him.

Antonio (ăn·tō'nĭ·ō), a sea captain who befriends Sebastian, though at great risk, for he has been forbidden to enter Ilyria. Having entrusted Sebastian with his purse, he is involved in the confusion of identities between Sebastian and "Cesario." When he is confronted with the twins, Antonio helps to clear up the mystery of the mistaken identities.

Feste (fĕs'tə), a clown. He teases Malvolio during his confinement, but brings to Olivia the steward's letter explaining the trick that had been played on him.

TWENTY THOUSAND LEAGUES UNDER THE SEA

Author: Jules Verne (1828-1905)
Time of action: 1866-1867
First published: 1870

PRINCIPAL CHARACTERS

Captain Nemo, a mysterious man who designs and builds the submarine "Nautilus" on a desert island. It provides its own electricity and oxygen, and the sea supplies food for its crew. Nemo hates society but uses gold recovered from sunken ships to benefit the unfortunate.

Professor Pierre Aronnax (pyĕr' à·rô-náx'), of the Paris Museum of Natural History, who heads an expedition aboard the American frigate "Abraham Lincoln" to track down a mysterious sea creature that has attacked and sunk ships all over the world.

Ned Land, a harpooner taken along on

the theory that the killer is a gigantic narwhal. An explosion aboard the "Abraham Lincoln" tosses him, along with Aronnax and Conseil, aboard the "Nautilus," where he and Nemo save each other's lives.

Conseil (kôn·sĕy'), the servant of Aronnax, who shares their adventures aboard the "Nautilus" in the Atlantic, Pacific, and Polar Oceans. When a maelstrom overcomes the submarine in Norwegian waters, Aronnax, Land, and Conseil recover consciousness on an island, in ignorance of the fate of Captain Nemo or the "Nautilus."

TWENTY YEARS AFTER

Author: Alexandre Dumas, *père* (1802-1870)
Time of action: Mid-seventeenth century
First published: 1845

D'Artagnan (där·tän·yäń'), the clever and resourceful hero, a lieutenant in the Musketeers. He succeeds in almost all of his pseudo-historical adventures, even against Cardinal Mazarin's final treachery.

Porthos (pôr·tōs'), one of the original Three Musketeers. He joins D'Artagnan in serving Cardinal Mazarin and the King. He is noted for his great strength.

Athos (à·tōs') and
Aramis (à·rà·mēs'), the remaining two of the original three musketeers. In this novel Athos and Aramis are allied with the Fronde, against their former comrades, but they end by sharing their English adventures with D'Artagnan and Porthos. Athos is the saintly member of the group, and the dandy Aramis is living in luxury despite his monastic vows, as "Twenty Years After" begins.

Cardinal Mazarin (mà·zà·răn'), the French Minister of State. He engages D'Artagnan to protect him and the King against the Fronde, political opponents endeavoring to overthrow the King.

Mordaunt (môr·däüń'), a monk, the son of Milady (see Lady de Winter, "The Three Musketeers") and Cromwell's

agent. He is the musketeers' sworn enemy, but is ultimately defeated by Athos.

King Louis XIV (lwē'), of France, now ten years old.

Queen Anne (àn'), the mother and protector of Louis, and under Mazarin's thumb.

King Charles I (shàrl'), of England, whom the four musketeers almost save from execution. In aiding Charles, D'Artagnan offends Mazarin.

Lord de Winter, an Englishman in the service of King Charles.

The Duke de Beaufort (dɔ bō·fôr'), Cardinal Mazarin's escaped political prisoner, in whose pursuit D'Artagnan and Porthos encounter Aramis and Athos.

Oliver Cromwell, the Puritan leader, to whom Cardinal Mazarin sends D'Artagnan and Porthos as messengers. The cruelty of the Puritans leads D'Artagnan to help Charles.

Henrietta Maria (äń·ryĕ·tà' mà·ryà'), King Charles' wife, now in France.

Raoul (rà·ōōl'), the adopted son of Athos, in reality his illegitimate son.

TWO GENTLEMEN OF VERONA

Author: William Shakespeare (1564-1616)
Time of action: Sixteenth century
First presented: 1594-1595

PRINCIPAL CHARACTERS

Valentine (văl'ɔn·tīn), a witty young gentleman of Verona. Scoffing at his lovesick friend, Proteus, he goes with his father to Milan, where he enters the court of the Duke and promptly falls in love with Silvia, the ruler's daughter. Planning to elope with her, he finds his plot betrayed to the Duke, and he flees to a

nearby forest to save his life. There he joins a band of outlaws and becomes their leader, a sort of Robin Hood. His concept of the superior claims of friendship over love is uncongenial to the modern reader, who finds it hard to forgive him when he calmly bestows Silvia upon Proteus, from whose clutches he has just rescued her, to testify to the depth of his renewed friendship for the young man.

Proteus (prō′tē·ŭs), his friend, a self-centered youth who fancies himself a lover in the best Euphuistic tradition. He forgets his strong protestations of undying affection for Julia when he meets Valentine's Silvia in Milan. No loyalties deter him from betraying his friend's planned elopement to the Duke, then deceiving the latter by trying to win the girl for himself while he pretends to be furthering the courtship of Sir Thurio. When Silvia resists his advances he carries her off by force. Stricken with remorse when Valentine interposes to protect her, he promises to reform. The constancy of his cast-off sweetheart, Julia, makes him recognize his faithlessness and her virtue, and they are happily reunited.

Julia (jōōl′yə), a young noblewoman of Verona. She criticizes her suitors with the humorous detachment of a Portia before she confesses to her maid her fondness for Proteus. She follows him to Milan in the disguise of the page Sebastian, and with dogged devotion she even carries Proteus' messages to her rival, Silvia, in order to be near him. She reveals her identity almost unwittingly by fainting when Valentine relinquishes Silvia to Proteus as a token of his friendship. She regains the love of her fiancé by this demonstration of her love.

Silvia (sĭl′vĭ·ə), daughter of the Duke of Milan. She falls in love with Valentine and encourages his suit; she asks him to copy a love letter for her—directed to himself, although he does not realize this fact at first. Proteus' fickle admiration annoys rather than pleases her, and she stands so firm in her love for Valentine that his generous offer of her to Proteus seems almost intolerable.

Speed, Valentine's exuberant, loquacious servant, cleverer than his master at seeing through Silvia's device of the love letter. He is one of the earliest of Shakespeare's witty clowns, the predecessor of Touchstone, Feste, and the Fool in "King Lear."

Launce (läns), Proteus' man, a simple soul, given to malapropisms and social "faux pas," in spite of his excellent intentions. His presentation to Silvia, in Proteus' name, of his treasured mongrel, Crab, a dog "as big as ten" of the creature sent by his master as a gift, does little to further Proteus' courtship. Inspired by his master's gallantry, he pays court to a milkmaid and gives great amusement to Speed by his enumeration of her virtues.

The Duke of Milan, Silvia's father, a strong-willed man who attempts to control his rash impulses. He welcomes and trusts Valentine, although he suspects his love for Silvia, until Proteus reveals the proposed elopement; then he cleverly forces Valentine into a position in which he must reveal his treachery. He finally consents to his daughter's marriage to Valentine as gracefully as possible, but one cannot forget that he is at this time the prisoner of the prospective bridegroom's men.

Sir Thurio (tōō′rĭ·ō, thōō′rĭ·ō), a vain unsuccessful suitor for the hand of Silvia, who despises him. Although he is willing to follow Proteus' expert instruction in the manners of courtship, he has no desire to risk his life for a woman who cares nothing for him, and he hastily departs when Valentine stands ready to defend his claim to Silvia's hand.

Lucetta (lōō·sĕt′ə), a clever, bright young woman who delights in teasing her mistress Julia, for whom she is friend and confidante as well as servant.

Sir Eglamour (ĕg′lə·mōōr), an elderly courtier. He serves as Silvia's protector when she prepares to flee from her father and marriage to Sir Thurio.

Antonio (ăn·tō'nĭ·ō), Proteus' father, a domineering man convinced that "What I will, I will, and there's an end."

Panthino (păn·thē'nō), Antonio's servant who advises him to send Proteus to join Valentine at the court of the Duke of Milan in order to learn the gentlemanly skills of "tilts, and tournaments, and sweet discourse."

THE TWO NOBLE KINSMEN

Authors: William Shakespeare (1564-1616) and John Fletcher (1579-1625)
Time of action: Age of legend
First presented: 1613

PRINCIPAL CHARACTERS

Palamon (păl'ə·mŏn), a young knight, nephew of Creon, King of Thebes, who sees and abhors the corruption of his uncle's government. With his cousin and closest friend, Arcite, he plans to leave Thebes, but when he learns that Theseus, Duke of Athens, is marching against the city he feels it his duty to stay and defend it. Imprisoned by the Athenian ruler, he responds with enthusiasm to Arcite's eager insistence that their friendship will make even life-long captivity palatable; then, a few moments later, he shatters this friendship with one brief glimpse of Emilia, who is walking in the garden beneath their window. He will not tolerate Arcite's professions of love and claims the preëminence of his affection on the grounds that he saw the lady first. He rages with jealousy when his cousin is sent into the country and he insists upon fighting a duel to the death when Arcite comes upon him in the woods where he is wandering hungry and still in chains after his escape from prison. Arcite's kindness wins from him grudging recognition of his cousin's nobility in all matters but love, but he begs Theseus to allow their combat to take place. He prays before the fateful battle to the goddess of love, and his prayer is answered, rather deviously, by Arcite's untimely death. He laments life's painful irony, which allows him to win his lady through the loss of his dearest friend.

Arcite (är'sīt), his cousin, an equally worthy young man. He seems, on occasion, a little more forceful than Palamon; it is he who suggests that they leave Thebes and he who comforts his cousin during their imprisonment. Resourcefully disguising himself as a country yeoman to obtain a place in Emilia's household, he wins favor with the whole court until he is discovered fighting with Palamon. He is never so violently jealous as Palamon is, and, refusing to take advantage of his cousin's weakness after he has escaped from prison, he offers Palamon first food, then honorable combat. He achieves the victory for which he prayed to Mars, but he is brought down by fate in a freak riding accident.

Theseus (thē'sē·ŭs), the noble Duke of Athens, a stanch defender of right. His first impulsive decision is generally an absolute one, but he is amenable to the suggestions of his friends and advisers. He yields to the pleas of his Amazon bride and her sister and agrees to delay his wedding to avenge the wrongs of the widowed Theban woman against their tyrannical ruler, Creon. Although he condemns Palamon and Arcite to death when he discovers them in a forbidden duel, he is persuaded to allow them to fight a tournament for the hand of their beloved Emilia, for he hates, as much as his wife and sister do, to lose either of the valiant young men.

1172

Hippolyta (hĭ·pŏl′ĭ·tə), Theseus' wife, former Queen of the Amazons, a wise and sympathetic wife and sister. She urges Theseus to postpone their wedding when she recognizes the great need of the Theban women. Later she pleads for the lives of Palamon and Arcite.

Emilia (ē·mĭl′ĭ·ə), her younger sister, loved by the two young Theban princes she has never met. She tells Hippolyta that she does not intend to marry; no man could ever win from her as much love as her friend Flavinia, who died when she was twelve. She is at first overwhelmed by the intensity with which the unknown knights fight for her; then she finds herself in love with both of them and can only pray that the one who loves her best will win her.

Perithous (pĕr′ə·thŭs), Theseus' friend and adviser. He joins Hippolyta and Emilia in pleading for the lives of Palamon and Arcite.

The Jailer, Palamon's keeper, a devoted father who is distressed by his daughter's madness.

His Daughter, a young girl who pines away for the love of Palamon. She frees him from prison, hoping to make him return her affection. His disappearance and the death sentence placed on her father for his negligence drive her into a deep melancholy, and she wanders distracted through the woods around Athens, raving like Ophelia. The kindly dissembling of her father and of her wooer, who pretends to be Palamon, restore her to health.

A Wooer, her gentle suitor. He is filled with pity for his mad sweetheart and agrees to do all the doctor advises to bring about her recovery. He plays his role as Palamon well, treating his bride with great tenderness.

A Doctor, a rather cynical gentleman who suggests that the wooer masquerade as Palamon.

A Schoolmaster, a pompous pedant, who prepares entertainment for Theseus and Hippolyta on a May morning.

TYPEE

Author: Herman Melville (1819-1891)
Time of action: Mid-nineteenth century
First published: 1846

PRINCIPAL CHARACTERS

Tom (Herman Melville), an American sailor on the whaler "Dolly" who, with his friend Toby, jumps ship at Nukuheva, and immediately contracts a disease which makes his leg swell and become very painful. When their food runs out, they give themselves up to the Typee tribe of natives on the island. They are treated kindly and Tom is given a native servant to take care of him. Toby leaves to seek medical aid and never returns, leaving Tom alone with the natives, who, the friends had discovered, are cannibals. Tom is allowed a fair amount of freedom but is always attended by Kory-Kory, his servant, and Fayaway, a beautiful native girl. Tom is finally allowed to go down to the beach to see a boat from an Australian vessel. Though watched carefully by the natives, he manages to break away from his guards and is taken on board by the Australians.

Toby, Tom's friend, who leaves the whaler with him and shares his adventures on the island until he goes to find medical help for Tom and is tricked into boarding a vessel which leaves the

1173

island the next day. Years later he meets Tom and is happy to learn that his friend escaped and is well.

Kory-Kory, Tom's faithful native servant, who is always by his side. Tom very much regrets having to leave him behind when he escapes.

Fayaway, the native girl who is Tom's constant companion while he is among the Typees.

Marnoo, a native taboo man who is free to move among all the tribes on the island without danger. Tom asks Marnoo to help him escape, but Marnoo cannot do so without arousing the natives' anger. He does, however, tell the captain of the Australian vessel of Tom's situation.

Mehevi, the Typees' chief, who is typical of the relaxed Polynesian.

THE UGLY DUCHESS

Author: Lion Feuchtwanger (1884-1958)
Time of action: Fourteenth century
First published: 1926

PRINCIPAL CHARACTERS

Duchess Margarete (mär·gä·rā′tĕ), Heinrich's daughter, fat, shrewd-eyed, ape-like, but intelligent and learned. She attempts to compensate for her ugliness by ruling her lands with strength and skill. She romantically idealizes the double-dealing Chrétien. Discovering his perfidy, she has him killed, as she later arranges the death of Karl Ludwig and Aldrigeto. Long rivaled by Agnes, she is defeated at last; and Margarete, despoiled of her power and most of her possessions, abdicates and lives in self-imposed poverty.

Prince Johann (yō′hän), her tall, strong, cowardly, ill-humored husband who sulkily avoids his ugly wife until the strong-minded Margarete has the marriage annulled.

Chrétien de Laferte (krĕ·tyän′ də lä-fârt′), lean, brown-faced aide to Prince Johann. A close friend of Margarete but a treacherous one, he plans to marry Agnes. Margarete's discovery of this leads to his death.

Margrave Karl Ludwig (kärl lōōt′vikh), widowed son of Ludwig. Acceding to his father's will, he becomes Margarete's second husband. He is poisoned.

Prince Meinhard (mīn′härd), easygoing, stupid son of Margarete and Karl. He is a leader of the Arthurian Order of Bavarian Chivalry, a gang of pillagers. He is murdered by Konrad.

Konrad von Frauenberg (kôn′räd fôn frou′en·bėrg), Margarete's unscrupulous adviser, a repulsive albino who poisons Karl, throws Meinhard from a cliff, and poisons Agnes. From his villainies he at last reaps rich rewards.

Agnes von Flavon (äg′nĕs fôn flä′fôn), Margarete's beautiful, vain, mocking, and popular rival, daughter of Heinrich's mistress; Chrétien's intended wife. For plotting against Margarete she is imprisoned and is poisoned by Konrad.

Heinrich (hīn′rĭsh), Duke of Carinthia, Count of Tyrol, and King of Bohemia, a widowed, aging, fat, financially reckless ruler. He dies worn out by his dissipations.

John (yōn), King of Luxemburg, glittering, brilliant, promiscuous father of Prince Johann. He anticipates getting Heinrich's territories by inheritance through the marriage of Johann to Margarete. He becomes blind before he dies in battle.

1174

Albert (äl′bèrt), tough, far-seeing King of Austria with whom Margarete signs a treaty.

Ludwig (lo͞ot′vikh), slow-witted King of Wittelsbach.

Princess Beatrix (bā′ä·trĭks), shy, anemic young wife of Heinrich. Shocked at his lavishness, she becomes grasping and miserly trying to save something for the son she never has. She dies some months after her marriage.

Albert von Andrion (äl′bèrt fôn än′drē′-ôn), gay, good-natured illegitimate half brother of Margarete. After an abortive plot he is tortured, despoiled of lands, and made a lifelong captive.

Mendel Hirsch (mĕn′dĕl hĭrsh), Margarete's fat, fidgety, obsequious Jewish confidant killed in a pogrom.

Jacob von Schenna (yä′kŏb fôn shĕ′nä), Margarete's serious, kindly friend from youth; a wealthy man of cultured tastes with a love of poetry. Long faithful, he finally turns against Margarete and gets some of the rich spoils when her conniving enemies defeat her.

Duke Stephan (stä′fän), brother of Karl Ludwig.

Baron Aldrigeto (bä·rōn′ äl·drē·gä′to), a handsome youth who falls in love with Margarete. After a brief affair she orders that he be killed.

ULYSSES

Author: James Joyce (1882-1941)
Time of action: June 16, 1904
First published: 1922

PRINCIPAL CHARACTERS

Stephen Dedalus, a proud, sensitive young Irishman, a writer and teacher called **Kinch** (from "kinchin," child) by one of his friends. In his search for the nature and meaning of life, Stephen examines all phases of his existence. History, he says, is a nightmare from which he is trying to awake. As he looks back to his childhood, he can remember only his family's poverty and his father as a patron of taverns. His devotion to Ireland is not the answer to his search; she is an old sow, he believes, that eats her own young. His religion is not enough to make life purposeful. Stephen cannot dismiss his mother's deathbed prayer that he avow his belief, and his inability to comply frets him with remorse. Symbolically, Stephen is Telemachus, the son in search of a father. In effect, he finds a symbolic father in Leopold Bloom, an older man who takes care of Stephen after the young man has been in a street fight with British soldiers. Declining

Bloom's invitation to live with him and his wife, Stephen goes out into the darkened street to return to the Tower where he is staying and to his dissolute life among the young men and students he knows.

Leopold Bloom, a Jewish advertising salesman who is, symbolically, Ulysses, the father of Telemachus. Bloom's yearning for a son stems from the long-past death of Rudy, his eleven-day-old son. A patient husband, he is cuckolded by his wife's business manager, but he is carrying on a furtive flirtation of his own. Bloom is Any Man, plodding through the daily routine of living—visiting bars, restaurants, newspaper offices, hospitals, and brothels of Dublin—because he hopes for something out of the ordinary but must be satisfied with the tawdry.

Malachi Mulligan, called **Buck,** a medical student and the friend of Stephen

Dedalus. He points up Stephen's attitudes and philosophies, the two young men being opposites, the scientific and the philosophical. Buck, calloused to suffering and death by his medical training, says that death is a beastly thing and nothing else; it simply does not matter. According to Buck, Stephen's religious strain is all mockery; if it were not, Buck says, Stephen could have prayed with his mother. Buck is doubtful that Stephen will ever produce any great writing. The model for Buck Mulligan was the Irish physician and poet, Oliver St. John Gogarty.

Marion Tweedy Bloom, called **Molly,** whose background differs greatly from her husband's. Brought up in the atmosphere of a military post in Gibraltar, Molly, a lush creature and second-rate concert singer, finds life with her husband and life in Dublin dull. Her escape from the reality of the humdrum comes through love affairs with other men. Her latest lover is Blazes Boylan, a virile younger man. Bloom's suggestion that Stephen Dedalus come to live with them gives Molly a momentary tingle as she contemplates the pleasure of having a still younger man in the house. Molly's thoughts and reverie make up the final section of the book, as she considers the present but finally lapses into reminiscences of a sexual experience of her girlhood. She is Penelope to Bloom's Ulysses.

Blazes Boylan, Molly's lover and the manager of a concert tour she is planning. The business aspect of their meetings does not delude Bloom.

Haines, a young Englishman who lives in the Tower with Stephen Dedalus, Buck Mulligan, and other students and artists. His indulgence in drinking orgies alienates more ascetic Stephen. Because Haines has considerably more money than the other young men, he is frequently the butt of their sarcasm. Haines is an anti-Semite who fears that England may be taken over by German Jews.

Paddy Dignam, Bloom's friend, who dies of a stroke.

Father Coffey, who performs the funeral rites over the body of Paddy Dignam.

Mrs. Breen, a neighbor, to whom Bloom gives the account of the funeral.

Mrs. Purefoy, another neighbor, who, Mrs. Breen reports, is in a maternity hospital. Bloom's visit to the hospital to inquire about her leads to his meeting with Stephen Dedalus, who is drinking with a group of medical students.

Davy Byrnes, a tavern owner whose establishment attracts all types of people who discuss many subjects.

Barney Kiernan, the owner of a bar where Leopold Bloom gets into an argument with a patriotic Irishman and is ejected.

Mr. Deasy, the headmaster of the school where Stephen teaches. Deasy probably assesses Stephen's aptitudes rather exactly when he tells the younger man that he is more a learner than a teacher. In lamenting the influx of Jews in England, Deasy points out to Stephen that Ireland is the only country where Jews have not been persecuted—because she never let them in.

Talbot,
Cochrane,
Armstrong,
Comyn,
Edith,
Ethel, and
Lily, some of Stephen's pupils. Their indifference and ineptness are discouraging to their young teacher, giving rise to Deasy's prognosis of Stephen's career.

Milly, the Blooms' daughter. Her existence does not mitigate Bloom's longing for a son, nor does it lessen Molly's desire for romance and release from tedium.

Gertie MacDowell, a young girl who exhibits herself to Leopold Bloom on Sandymount shore.

Myles Crawford, a newspaper editor.

THE UNBEARABLE BASSINGTON

Author: Saki (Hector Hugh Monro, 1870-1915)
Time of action: Early 1900's
First published: 1912

PRINCIPAL CHARACTERS

Francesca Bassington, a heartless, scheming society matron of London who has an attractive home and a Van der Meulen painting. She wants her son Comus to marry Emmeline Chetrof, heiress to her house, and to go into politics. The news of his death in Africa and of the falsity of her painting reach her at the same time.

Comus Bassington, a young man with a casual attitude toward the world and indifference to his mother's ambitions. Though attracted by rich Elaine de Frey, he ruins his chances by borrowing money from her and being boorish about a silver tray at her tea. He dies at an unwanted political post in Africa.

Emmeline Chetrof, the heiress to a considerable fortune, including Mrs. Bassington's home.

Lancelot Chetrof, Emmeline's brother and a schoolmate of Comus, whom he treats badly because of Mrs. Bassington's matrimonial suggestion.

Elaine de Frey, an heiress who invites both her suitors to a tea, to choose between them. She marries Courtney and discovers her mistake during their honeymoon.

Courtney Youghal, a young member of Parliament whose scurrilous attack on Governor Jull is signed by Comus to escape a political appointment.

Suzette, a cousin of Elaine and the first to hear of her engagement to Youghal.

George St. Michael, a gossiping member of the fashionable world of Mayfair and Ascot.

Sir John Jull, Governor of a West Indian island, who needs a secretary.

Henry Greech, the brother of Francesca and a man of political influence.

UNCLE SILAS

Author: Joseph Sheridan Le Fanu (1814-1873)
Time of action: Nineteenth century
First published: 1864

PRINCIPAL CHARACTERS

Austin Ruthyn, a wealthy recluse and widower. He is a Swedenborgian who devotes his time to scientific and literary studies. When he dies, his will appoints several men as trustees for his estate and places his daughter under the guardianship of his brother Silas.

Maud Ruthyn, a wealthy heiress. She goes to live with her Uncle Silas, believing she is to vindicate her uncle's good name. She is disturbed by her uncle's idiosyncrasies, but even more by the attentions of her coarse cousin, who wishes to marry her. She is tricked into being made a prisoner, and her cousin and uncle try to murder her in order to inherit her wealth. The attempt fails. Later she marries Lord Ilbury, one of the trustees of her estate.

Silas Ruthyn, Maud's uncle. According to rumor he has killed a Mr. Charke, to whom he owes a large sum of money.

When his attempt to marry Maud to his son fails, he and the young man attempt to murder Maud in order to inherit her wealth. The attempt fails, and Silas commits suicide.

Dudley Ruthyn, Maud's cousin, a coarse, cruel man. He courts Maud but fails to win her. When he tries to murder Maud, he kills Mme. de la Rougierre by mistake. After the murder he disappears. His attempts to court Maud end following his marriage to a lower-class woman named Sarah Mangles.

Mme. de la Rougierre, Maud's governess. She becomes an accomplice of Silas and Dudley in their attempted murder, only to be killed herself.

Dr. Bryerly, Austin Ruthyn's doctor and friend. He is one of the trustees of Maud's estate.

Lady Monica Knollys, a cousin of Austin Ruthyn, who tries to warn him and Maud against Mme. de la Rougierre.

Lord Ilbury, also known as Mr. Carysbrook. He is one of the trustees of Maud's estate and marries Maud.

Milly Ruthyn, Maud's cousin. She is a loud, good-humored girl who becomes Maud's friend. She grows up to marry a minister.

Sir William Aylmer and
Mr. Penrose Cresswell, other trustees of Maud's estate.

Mary Quince, Maud's maid.

Meg Hawkes, a miller's daughter who befriends Maud.

Tom Brice, a servant who loves Meg Hawkes and saves Maud from her uncle and cousin.

UNCLE TOM'S CABIN

Author: Harriet Beecher Stowe (1811-1896)
Time of action: Mid-nineteenth century
First published: 1852

PRINCIPAL CHARACTERS

Uncle Tom, a Negro slave. Good and unrebellious, he is sold by his owner. After serving a second kind but improvident master, he comes under the ownership of brutal Simon Legree and dies as a result of his beatings.

Eliza, a slave. Learning that her child is about to be sold away along with Tom, she takes the child and runs away, crossing the Ohio River by leaping from floating ice cake to floating ice cake.

George Harris, her husband, a slave on a neighboring plantation. He too escapes, passing as a Spaniard, and reaches Ohio, where he joins his wife and child. Together they go to freedom in Canada.

Harry, the child of Eliza and George.

Mr. Shelby, the original owner of Eliza, Harry, and Uncle Tom. Encumbered by debt, he plans to sell a slave to his chief creditor.

Haley, the buyer, a New Orleans slave dealer. He shrewdly selects Uncle Tom and persuades Mr. Shelby to part with Harry in spite of his better feelings.

George Shelby, Mr. Shelby's son. He promises to buy Tom back one day but arrives at Legree's plantation as Tom is dying. When his father dies, he frees all his slaves in Uncle Tom's name.

Mrs. Shelby, Mr. Shelby's wife. She delays the pursuit of Eliza by serving a late breakfast.

Marks and
Loker, slave-catchers hired by Haley to track Eliza through Ohio. Loker, wounded by George Harris in a fight, is given medical treatment by the Quakers who are protecting the runaways.

Augustine St. Clare, the purchaser of Tom after Tom saves his daughter's life. He dies before making arrangements necessary to the freeing of his slaves.

Eva St. Clare, his saintly and frail daughter. Before her death she asks her father to free his slaves.

Mrs. St. Clare, an imaginary invalid. After her husband's death, she sends Tom to the slave market.

Miss Ophelia, St. Clare's cousin from the North. She comes to look after Eva and is unused to lavish Southern customs.

Topsy, a pixie-like Negro child bought by St. Clare for Miss Ophelia to educate; later he makes the gift legal.

Simon Legree, the alcoholic and super-stitious brute who purchases Tom and kills him. He is a Northerner by birth.

Cassy, Legree's slave. She uses his super-stitions to advantage in her escape. Her young daughter, who was sold years ago, proves to be Eliza, and mother and daughter are reunited in Canada.

Emmeline, another of Legree's slaves. She escapes with Cassy.

Madame de Thoux, whom Cassy and Emmeline meet on a northbound river-boat. She proves to be George Harris' sister.

Aunt Chloe, Uncle Tom's wife, left behind in Uncle Tom's cabin on the Shelby plantation.

Senator Bird, in whose house Eliza first finds shelter in Ohio.

Mrs. Bird, his wife.

Simeon Halliday and
Rachel Halliday, who give shelter to the fugitive slaves.

UNCLE VANYA

Author: Anton Chekhov (1860-1904)
Time of action: Late nineteenth century
First presented: 1902

PRINCIPAL CHARACTERS

Alexander Serebrakov (ä·lĕk·sän'dr sĕ·rĕ·brä·kŏf'), a retired professor who takes up residence with his young wife at their small estate in the country. After many years of writing books about art, his life is deemed a failure; success and fame have eluded him; he is a gout-ridden, whining, testy, complaining old man incapable of generosity or kindness. Presumptuous and full of self-conceit, he is a trial to all those around him.

Helena Andreyevna (ĕ·lĕ'nə än·drā'-əv·nə), the professor's beautiful young wife. Disillusioned by her husband, whom she married in the belief that he was famous and learned, she spends her life in idleness and indolence, infecting those about her by her absence of di-rection and values. She holds a fascina-tion for men, but in doting upon her they themselves are corrupted. She re-mains true to her husband, but in the process destroys her own spirit.

Sonya Alexandrovna (sō'nyə ä·lĕk·sän'-drəv·nə), the professor's daughter by a previous marriage, an innocent, plain young woman hopelessly in love with the local physician, who does not return her love. She learns to endure her pain by helping others, by work, and by a deep faith in a better afterlife.

Ivan Voitski (ĭ·vän′ vōyt′skĭ), called **Vanya** (vä′nyə), the brother of Serebrakov's first wife and manager of his country estate. After having worked diligently for the professor for years, editing and translating his manuscripts, caring for his business affairs, making it possible for him to lead a comfortable life, Vanya discovers that the professor is a fraud, that his own sacrifice has been for nothing, that he has lost a lifetime. Despairing over his false trust in the professor and his unrequited love for Helena, he unsuccessfully attempts to kill his brother-in-law. At the end of the play, knowing that he can find no new life, Vanya mechanically works over the account books while trying to endure the life remaining to him.

Mihail Astrov (mĭ·hä·ĭl′ äs·trōf′), the local physician, overworked and discouraged by the tediousness of human exist-

ence. Claiming to be a misanthrope, he nevertheless falls in love with Helena and lets his practice and estate fall into ruin. Helena, because of her affection for him, takes her husband and leaves the country. Astrov remains to reassume his old life. The most intelligent and visionary of the characters, he sees his own life only as preparation for the better life of future generations.

Marya Voitskaya (mär′yə vōyt′ska·yə), the widowed mother of Vanya and of the professor's first wife. Obsessed with the emancipation of women, she spends her life reading revolutionary pamphlets and dreaming about the dawn of a new life.

Ilia Telegin (ĭ·lyä′ tĕ·lĕ′gĭn), called **Waffles** because of his pock-marked face, an impoverished landowner, sentimental, obsequious, simple-minded.

Marina (mä·rĭ′nə), an old family nurse. Representing the traditional ways of an older generation, she offers tea or vodka kindly to console any suffering.

UNDER FIRE

Author: Henri Barbusse (1874-1935)
Time of action: 1914-1915
First published: 1917

PRINCIPAL CHARACTERS

Volpatte (vôl·pȧt′), square-faced, jaundiced-looking, broken-nosed. He is hospitalized after almost losing his ears but returns bitter about the men in the hospital, both the malingering patients and the arrogant staff members.

Eudore (œ·dôr′), a pale, pleasant-faced former keeper of a roadside café. Ironically, the one night of furlough he spends with his wife is spoiled by the presence of four soldiers taken in because of a heavy rain. He is later killed on patrol.

Poterloo (pô·tĕr·lō′), a pink-faced, blond ex-miner who accompanies some friendly

German privates to an Alsatian village to see his wife and is shocked to see her enjoying herself with a German sergeant. He is later killed.

Joseph Mesnil (zhō·zĕf′ mĕ·nēl′), one of six brothers, four of whom have already been killed by 1915. Almost maddened by the death of his last remaining brother, Joseph is later wounded and is taken by the narrator to a dressing station.

André Mesnil (äṅ·drä′ mĕ·nēl′), Joseph's brother, a former chemist, who is killed on patrol.

Corporal Bertrand (bĕr·träṅ′), soldierly, serious, friendly to and respected by his squad. He is killed.

Lamuse (là·müz′), a fat, ruddy-faced peasant, killed on patrol.

Paradis (pà·rà·dē′), a plump, fat-cheeked, baby-faced ex-carter. He often discusses war with the narrator.

Cocon (kō·kōṅ′), a slight, desiccated ironmonger. He is killed.

Tirloir (tēr·lwàr′), the ex-manager of a traveling circus, sent back from the trenches with dysentery.

Bicquet (bē·kā′), a squat, grey-faced, heavy-chinned Breton, killed on patrol.

Barque (bàrk′), a Parisian porter and tricycle messenger, killed on patrol.

Fouillade (foo·yàd′), a middle-aged, tall, long-jawed, goateed soldier from southern France.

The Narrator, apparently Barbusse, the author, remembering his friends, grieving for those who have died and brooding on the filth, brutality, and nausea of war experience.

UNDER THE GREENWOOD TREE

Author: Thomas Hardy (1840-1928)
Time of action: Nineteenth century
First published: 1872

PRINCIPAL CHARACTERS

Richard Dewy, called **Dick,** a young carter with musical inclinations and talent. One Christmas season when he goes carolling with the church choir, for whom he plays accompaniment on his violin, he falls under the spell of Fancy Day, the new schoolmistress in the parish. When his companions look for him after he disappears from the group, they find him mooning under the girl's window, already in love. Dick Dewy begins courting Fancy at the Christmas party held in his parents' home, but he soon finds he has a rival for her hand. Though she favors his courtship and reciprocates his affection, his hopes are somewhat dashed for a time by her father's refusal to consent to a marriage. The father claims that his daughter is too well-educated for the young carter. The girl herself overcomes her father's objections and wins his consent. A little more than a year after he sees her for the first time Dick Dewy weds Fancy Day beneath a great tree near her father's home.

Fancy Day, the young schoolmistress at Mellstock, a pretty young woman well educated as a teacher and a musician. Her beauty and talent immediately attract admirers, including Dick Dewy, who later becomes her husband. Fancy is a pleasant young woman, almost guileless, whose only fault, if it is that, is the pleasure she takes in her appearance and her clothes. Her obvious concern about her appearance twice creates a courtship problem, for Dick Dewy resents her love of apparel. Once Fancy is tempted into jilting her fiancé. This temptation occurs when the local vicar, Mr. Maybold, appears suddenly at the schoolhouse and proposes marriage. Fancy, taken by the idea of marrying higher than her station, says yes. The next day, upon consideration, she writes to the vicar and withdraws her answer; she is also wise enough to keep this incident a secret from her husband after their marriage.

Mr. Shiner, a farmer of means and Fancy Day's admirer. While his courtship meets with no particular favor from the girl, it does create some problems for his rival, Dick Dewy. As a churchwarden Mr. Shiner introduces an organ to replace the church choir, with Fancy Day as the organist. Dick Dewy's problem then is one of conflicting loyalties, his loyalty to his beloved and his loyalty to the church choir. Mr. Shiner's suit is favored by Fancy's father, but Mr. Day's approval fails to change his daughter's mind.

Geoffrey Day, Fancy's father and agent for a great landowner. Pleased with his daughter's beauty and talent, he wants her to marry well. He opposes her marriage to Dick Dewy as being beneath the girl and favors her marriage to Mr. Shiner, a well-to-do farmer. When Fancy goes several weeks without apparent appetite Mr. Day becomes concerned about her health and is thus tricked into consenting to her marriage with the young carter.

Mr. Maybold, the local vicar, a good-looking bachelor. Admiring Fancy Day and not knowing that she is engaged to marry Dick Dewy, he proposes to her. She accepts his proposal, but the very next day the vicar learns to his sorrow from Dick Dewy of the engagement. As an honorable man Mr. Maybold writes a courteous letter to the girl asking to withdraw his proposal. In the meantime Fancy has written him a note breaking their engagement. He later advises her to keep the incident a secret. Mr. Maybold creates a disturbance in the parish life by supplanting the choir with an organ, at the request of Mr. Shiner, one of the churchwardens. His innovation is at first highly resented, but it is finally accepted by the choir because of his sympathetic attitude toward them and their displacement.

Reuben Dewy, Dick Dewy's father. As a member of the parish choir he is the spokesman when the men go in a group to the vicarage to protest their being turned out of service.

William Dewy, Dick Dewy's grandfather and leader of the parish choir. He is upset when his lifelong service to the church is ended by the introduction of an organ.

Mrs. Day, Fancy Day's stepmother. She is a very odd woman whom her husband regards as a cross he must bear. Her behavior, while that of a person suffering from mental illness, is entirely humorous.

UNDER THE YOKE

Author: Ivan Vazov (1850-1921)
Time of action: 1875-1876
First published: 1889

PRINCIPAL CHARACTERS

Ivan Kralich (ĭ-vän' krä'lĭch), a Bulgarian patriot who has escaped after eight years of imprisonment by the Turks. He eludes pursuit and, having changed his name, finds a job teaching school. He is still a revolutionary, however, and after suspicion forces him to flee again, he leads a revolt which is soon crushed. Once more a fugitive, he takes refuge in a mill, where his sweetheart and an old comrade join him. All three are killed after a valiant struggle during an attack on the mill.

Rada (rä'də), a gentle orphan who teaches school. She and Kralich fall in love and she goes to a nearby village to join him, but a misunderstanding and a crushed revolt force them to part. Rada, learning that Kralich is hiding in the mill, goes to aid him. There she is killed in the Turkish attack.

Sokolov (sô·kô·lōf'), an eccentric Bulgarian. The village doctor, though without formal training, and a patriot, he is often a fugitive from the Turks. He dies in the attack on the mill with Rada and Kralich.

Marika (mä·rī'kə), the miller's young daughter. Kralich, hiding in the mill, is able to save her from attack by two Turkish policemen. She and her father then aid the fugitive.

Marko (mär'kə), a Bulgarian patriot who aids Kralich and Sokolov.

Mouratliski (moo·rät·lǐs'kǐ), Kralich's friend and fellow patriot, also a fugitive from the Turks. He poses as an Austrian photographer.

Ivan (ĭ·vän'), called Kill-the-Bear, a giant, one of the members of Kralich's group.

Kandov (kän'dəf), a student who makes Rada miserable by following her about. His attentions and pursuit are the cause of a misunderstanding between Kralich and Rada.

UNDER TWO FLAGS

Author: Ouida (Marie Louise de la Ramée, 1839-1908)
Time of action: Early nineteenth century
First published: 1867

PRINCIPAL CHARACTERS

The Honorable Bertie Cecil (bĕr·tē' sē-sĕl'), a young nobleman and an officer in the Life Guards who travels in fashionable circles. Though deep in debt, he is a gallant young man, loved by the ladies and admired by the men. When he is accused of forgery he lets the accusation stand in order to save a woman's honor. He flees to Africa and joins the Foreign Legion, serving gallantly. He is condemned to death for striking a superior officer who insulted a noblewoman, but he is saved from a firing squad by a camp follower who loves him and takes the bullets in her own body.

Cigarette (sē·gà·rĕt'), an entertainer who is also a patriotic Frenchwoman, though a camp follower. She falls in love with Bertie Cecil, though she hates the English and is jealous of the woman Bertie loves. She saves Bertie's life by dashing between him and the firing squad to let the bullets intended for him hit her.

Princess Corona d'Amagüe (kô·rô·nà' dà·mà·gü'), a beautiful English widow loved by Bertie. He risks death to defend

her honor by striking Colonel Chateauroy. Knowing Bertie has been exonerated of forgery charges and has the right to his father's title and estates, the Princess agrees to marry him.

Lord Rockingham, known also as The Seraph. He is Bertie's best friend and the brother of Princess Corona. He tries to save Bertie from the firing squad.

Berkeley Cecil, Bertie's young brother, who inherits the family title and estates after it is assumed that Bertie is dead. He is so selfish that he fears Bertie may return to England to claim what is rightfully his.

Colonel Chateauroy (shà·tō·rwà'), Bertie's commanding officer in the French Foreign Legion. Jealous of Bertie and hating him, he is glad for an opportunity to sentence Bertie to death.

Rake, Bertie's faithful, intelligent servant, whom Bertie rescued from a bad situation. He is killed while serving in the Foreign Legion with his employer.

Lady Guenevere, the woman whose honor Bertie protects by not defending himself against charges of forgery.

Lord Royallieu (rwȧ·yȧl·lœ'), Bertie's father, who dislikes his son because Bertie looks like his mother's lover.

UNDER WESTERN EYES

Author: Joseph Conrad (Józef Teodor Konrad Korzeniowski, 1857-1924)
Time of action: Early twentieth century
First published: 1911

PRINCIPAL CHARACTERS

Kirylo Sidorovich Razumov, an idealist and a student at St. Petersburg University. His background is strange and unknown; he has a mysterious benefactor but no family. Returning to his rooms one night, he finds Victor Haldin, a fellow student and casual acquaintance, who confesses that he has assassinated a Minister of State. Haldin confidently asks his help in making his escape, and Razumov promises to do so. Instead, he secretly betrays the assassin to the police. Because his name is now linked with Haldin's, the dead man's friends accept Razumov as a revolutionary. He is sent to Geneva as a police spy to report on the activities of the revolutionists there. He falls in love with Haldin's sister. After he has received information that makes him safe from detection, ironically, he confesses his true role to Miss Haldin and to the revolutionists, who beat him and destroy his hearing. Deaf, he is struck by a tram car that he cannot hear. Crippled for the rest of his life, he is cared for by a compassionate girl named Tekla.

Victor Haldin, the ardent young revolutionist who kills the Minister of State with a bomb. Betrayed by Razumov, he is captured and executed.

Ziemianitch, the cab driver who was to carry Haldin to safety. He is drunk when Razumov finds him. Later he hangs himself, supposedly in remorse for having betrayed Haldin.

Nathalie Haldin, the sister of the dead revolutionist. Although she remains free of revolutionary activities, she has a mystical vision of human concord. Later she returns to Russia to devote herself to social work.

Mrs. Haldin, the mother. Grief over the loss of her son and lack of information as to what happened to him hasten her death.

Peter Ivanovitch, a Russian refugee who has escaped from Siberia and made his way to Geneva. An author and an advocate of feminism for the purpose of elevating humanity, he becomes the leader of the revolutionists and a companion to Madame de S——.

Tekla, the compassionate former secretary of Ivanovitch. Because she feels compulsion to help the punished and the broken, she cares for Razumov after he is crippled.

Sophia Antonovna, an older, dedicated, and trusted revolutionary who is called to Geneva to verify an identity.

Nikita, an anarchist. A man so grotesque as to set town dogs barking, he is a famed killer of gendarmes and police agents. He brutalizes Razumov and destroys his hearing after Razumov makes his confession of betrayal. Later Nikita is revealed as a police informer.

Yakovlitch, a revolutionist whose missions take him to America. He and Sophia Antonovna were once lovers.

Laspara, a subversive journalist sus-

1184

pected of complicity in revolutionary plots.

Madame de S——, a legendary figure who presides over a "revolutionary salon."

Prince K——, Razumov's mysterious benefactor, an influential Tsarist official and Razumov's unacknowledged father.

General T——, the protector of autocracy, to whom Razumov first reports when he decides to betray Haldin to the police.

Councilor Mikulin, the government official who sends Razumov to Geneva as a police spy.

Father Zosim, the priest-democrat who gives Razumov a letter of introduction to Peter Ivanovitch.

The Tall Student, a hungry fellow who works on the fringes of the revolution. He suspects that Razumov was Haldin's accomplice.

Mad Cap Costia, a rich, reckless student, impressed by Razumov's reputation, who wishes to help him.

The Narrator, an Englishman and an old language teacher to whom Miss Haldin entrusted Razumov's diary, which supplied the details of the story.

THE UNDERDOGS

Author: Mariano Azuela (1873-1952)
Time of action: 1914-1915
First published: 1915

PRINCIPAL CHARACTERS

Demetrio Macías (dā·mā′tryō mä·sē′äs), a peaceful Mexican Indian driven by the cruelty of Federalist soldiers to take up arms. He eventually becomes a general. Home after two years, he is killed by the Federal soldiers.

Camila (kä·mē′lä), his pretty nurse, who at first prefers Cervantes to Macías.

Luis Cervantes (lwēs′ sâr·bän′täs), a pseudo-intellectual journalist who encourages Macías to fight.

Venancio (bā·nän′syō), a barber-surgeon who cures Macías's wounds.

President Madera (mä·dā′rä), the first political leader of Macías.

President Huerta (wâr′tä, wĕr′tä), the leader of the Federalists.

General Orozco (hā·nā·räl′ ō·rōs′kō), the Federalist commander at Jalisco.

Pancho Villa (pän′chō bē′yä), who is defeated by Carranza at Celaya.

General Natera (hā·nā·räl′ nä·tā′rä), another rebel leader.

Solís (sō·lēs′), an idealist who is killed in battle.

Whitey Margarito (mär·gä·rē′tō), a sadistic soldier.

La Pintada (lä pēn·tä′t̶hä), a camp follower who stabs Camila.

Don Mónico (dōn mō′nē·kō), Demetrio's land-owning enemy raided by the rebels.

1185

UNDINE

Author: Friedrich de La Motte-Fouqué (1777-1843)
Time of action: The Middle Ages
First published: 1811

PRINCIPAL CHARACTERS

Undine (ōōn'dē'nė), a water spirit, daughter of a Mediterranean water-prince and foster daughter of a poor fisherman and his wife. Fifteen years earlier she appeared, a child of three or four, at the fisherman's cottage shortly after the disappearance of his young daughter. She is now a beautiful young girl but rebellious, mischievous, and wildly capricious. When Huldbrand mentions Bertalda in telling his adventures, Undine bites him out of jealousy. After she and Huldbrand are married and the priest tells her to attune her soul to her husband's, she becomes a submissive, loving wife. She generously consents to have the rejected Bertalda live at Ringstetten. On a trip down the Danube, when Huldbrand angrily calls her a sorceress, she disappears into the water. After his marriage to Bertalda, Undine appears to him and embraces him until he dies. Following his burial she becomes a spring which almost encircles his grave, thus embracing him forever.

Sir Huldbrand von Ringstetten (hōōld'-bränd fôn rĭng'stä·tăn), a knight, wealthy, handsome, and a model of all knightly virtues except that of constancy of heart. Though forewarned against marrying Bertalda, he ignores the warning and his spirit wife, released from the fountain in which she lives, claims him eternally.

Kühleborn (kü'lė·bôrn), Undine's uncle, a water spirit who appears sometimes to mortals as a tall man dressed in a white mantle and in various other disguises. He warns Huldbrand to protect Undine and reveals to Undine the secret of Bertalda's birth. He mischievously interferes many times in the lives of Undine, Huldbrand, and Bertalda.

Bertalda (bâr'·täl'dä), a beautiful but haughty lady loved by Huldbrand. She is the foster daughter of a powerful duke and his duchess but the real daughter of Undine's foster parents, who lost her shortly before Undine came to them. Bertalda is shocked and angry to learn of her humble origin. After she has been turned out by her foster parents she acquires some humility, but her haughtiness occasionally returns.

Father Heilmann (hīl'män), an old priest who marries Undine and Huldbrand, refuses to unite Huldbrand and Bertalda, and administers the burial service for Huldbrand.

THE UNFORTUNATE TRAVELLER

Author: Thomas Nash (1567-1601)
Time of action: Reign of King Henry VIII
First published: 1594

PRINCIPAL CHARACTERS

Jack Wilton, a page to Henry VIII of England. Bored with his life, he leaves King Henry's service to become a soldier of fortune. Since he is a bright and merry lad, he has all sorts of adventures and scrapes. He travels with the Earl of Surrey as a companion throughout Europe. Finally he returns to England and the service of Henry VIII.

The Earl of Surrey. Jack's friend, benefactor, and traveling companion. He is a gallant courtier.

Tabitha, a Venetian prostitute who meets Jack and the Earl of Surrey. She and her pander try to kill the Earl but are caught and executed.

Geraldine, a beautiful woman of Florence loved by the Earl of Surrey. The Earl fights all comers in a tourney to prove his love for her.

Diamante, a goldsmith's wife suspected of infidelity by her husband. She takes Jack as a lover to punish her husband

for his suspicions. After the goldsmith's death Diamante travels with Jack, and the two share many adventures, including being bondservants in the household of one of the Pope's mistresses.

Johannes de Imola, a citizen of Rome with whom Jack and Diamante live for a time. He is unfortunate enough to die of the plague during an epidemic.

Heraclide de Imola, wife of Johannes. She commits suicide after being raped by a band of cutthroats, and her death is blamed on Jack, putting him for a time in danger of hanging.

Cutwolfe, a famous brigand whose execution Jack witnesses. Cutwolfe confesses to murdering the bandit who led the assault on Heraclide and Diamante.

U. S. A.

Author: John Dos Passos (1896-   )
Time of action: 1900-1935
First published: 1930, 1932, 1936 in three sections

PRINCIPAL CHARACTERS

Fenian O'Hara McCreary, called **Fainy Mac,** a young Irishman who learns the printing trade from an uncle, whose bankruptcy puts McCreary out of a job and makes a tramp of him. Because of his skill as a printer McCreary is able to find work here and there, one with a shoddy outfit called the Truthseeker Literary Distributing Co., Inc., and he travels from place to place, usually riding on freight trains. In his travels he falls in with members of the I.W.W. and becomes an earnest worker in that labor movement. He marries Maisie Spencer, but eventually they quarrel and he leaves his family in California when he goes to become a labor organizer in Mexico. There he lives a free and easy life.

Maisie Spencer, a shopgirl who marries Fainy McCreary. She is unable to share his radical views and they part.

Janey Williams, a girl who wants a career in business. She becomes a stenographer and through her luck and skill is hired as secretary to J. Ward Moorehouse, a prominent man in public relations. She becomes an efficient, if sour, woman who makes a place for herself in business. Her great embarrassment is her brother Joe, a sailor who shows up periodically in her life with presents for her.

Joe Williams, Janey Williams' brother, a young man who cannot accept discipline. He loves life at sea and becomes a merchant seaman after deserting from the Navy. Although he is in and out of scrapes all the time he manages to qualify as a second officer during World War I. His life ends when a Senegalese hits him over the head with a bottle in a brawl over a woman in the port of St. Nazaire.

Della Williams, Joe Williams' wife. Although she is cold to her husband and claims that she is modest, she comes to believe during World War I that it is her patriotic duty to entertain men in uniform all she can, much to her husband's chagrin.

J. Ward Moorehouse, an opportunist who becomes a leading public relations and advertising executive. He is anxious to succeed in life and to have a hand in many activities. His first wife is Annabelle Strang, a wealthy, promiscuous woman, his second, Gertrude Staple, who helps him in his career. Though he succeeds as a businessman, he is unhappy in his domestic life, to which he gives all too little time because he prefers a whole series of women to his wife. A heart attack finally persuades him that the life he leads is not a fruitful one.

Annabelle Strang, the wealthy, amoral woman who becomes J. Ward Moorehouse's first wife.

Gertrude Staple, J. Ward Moorehouse's second wife, a wealthy young woman whose family and fortune help her husband become established as a public relations counselor. She becomes mentally ill and spends many years in a sanitarium.

Eleanor Stoddard, a poor girl from Chicago. Gifted with artistic talent, she sets herself up an interior decorator and succeeds professionally. She becomes a hard, shallow, but attractive woman. While serving as a Red Cross worker in Europe, she becomes J. Ward Moorehouse's mistress for a time. Always climbing socially, she becomes engaged to an exiled Russian nobleman in New York after World War I.

Eveline Hutchins, the daughter of a liberal clergyman. She becomes Eleanor Stoddard's erstwhile business partner. A young woman who spends her life seeking pleasure and escape from boredom, her life is a series of rather sordid love affairs, both before and after marriage. She finally commits suicide.

Paul Johnson, Eveline Hutchins' shy and colorless soldier husband, whom she meets in France while doing Red Cross work.

Charley Anderson, a not very promising youth who becomes famous as an aviator during World War I. He cashes in on his wartime reputation and makes a great deal of money, both as an inventor and as a trader on the stock market. His loose sexual morality and his heavy drinking lose him his wife, his jobs, his fortune, and finally his life. He dies as the result of an auto accident which happens while he is drunk. He has a brief love affair with Eveline Hutchins.

Margo Dowling, the daughter of a ne'er-do-well drunkard. Through her beauty and talent she makes her own way in the world and becomes a movie star after many amatory adventures. For a time she is Charley Anderson's mistress.

Agnes Mandeville, Margo Dowling's stepmother, friend, and financial adviser. She is a shrewd woman with money.

Frank Mandeville, a broken-down vaudeville actor and Agnes' husband. A lost man after the advent of motion pictures, he spends much of his time trying to seduce Margo Dowling and eventually rapes her.

Tony de Carrida, Margo Dowling's first husband, an effeminate Cuban musician who is finally reduced to being Margo's uniformed chauffeur.

Sam Margolies, a peculiar but successful movie producer who "discovers" Margo Dowling and makes her a movie star. He becomes her second husband.

Richard Ellsworth Savage, called **Dick,** a bright young man and a Harvard graduate who wishes to become a poet. He meets J. Ward Moorehouse and ends up as a junior partner in Moorehouse's firm.

He is Anne Elizabeth Trent's lover for a time.

Anne Elizabeth Trent, called **Daughter,** a wild young girl from Texas who makes the wrong friends. In Europe as a relief worker after World War I she falls in love with Richard Ellsworth Savage and becomes pregnant by him. She goes for an airplane ride with a drunken French aviator and dies when the plane crashes.

Mary French, a bright young Vassar graduate interested in social work. She becomes a radical and a worker for various labor movements sponsored by Communists. She loses her lover, Don Stevens, who returns from a visit in Moscow with a wife assigned to him by the Party.

Don Stevens, a Communist organizer who for a time is Mary French's lover. In Moscow he marries a wife of whom the Party approves.

Benny Compton, a Jewish boy from New York who drifts into labor work and becomes a highly successful labor organizer and agitator. He turns Communist and gives all his energy to work for the Party. Sentenced to the penitentiary in Atlanta for his activities, he is released after World War I. He lives for a time with Mary French.

Webb Cruthers, a young anarchist who for a brief period is Anne Elizabeth Trent's lover.

UTOPIA

Author: Sir Thomas More (1478-1535)
Time of action: Reign of Henry VII of England
First published: 1516

PRINCIPAL CHARACTERS

Thomas More, the narrator of "Utopia," who meets the fictional Raphael Hythloday while serving as Henry VII's ambassador in Flanders. More himself suggests in the first part of "Utopia" many reforms, including reform of the severe penal code of England at the time.

Peter Giles, a citizen of Antwerp, a learned and honest young man with whom Thomas More becomes acquainted. Peter Giles introduces Raphael Hythloday to the Englishman and listens with him to Hythloday's marvelous account of the island of Utopia.

Raphael Hythloday, a Portuguese mariner who is learned in the classical languages and in philosophy. He is a widely traveled man, having accompanied Amerigo Vespucci on some of the latter's voyages. He tells Thomas More that he is interested only in peaceful matters and so has attached himself to no monarch. He describes for Thomas More and Peter Giles the civilization on the island of Utopia and tells why he thinks it is the best state in the world.

VANESSA

Author: Hugh Walpole (1884-1941)
Time of action: Late nineteenth and early twentieth centuries
First published: 1933

Vanessa Paris, the beautiful daughter of Adam and Margaret Paris. She is engaged to her cousin Benjie; but because of his wildness, their marriage is postponed for two years. Then her father's death forces her to postpone it still longer. Learning that Benjie has married a girl he got with child, she wishes him well and later marries a distant cousin, a respected financier. Her husband's mind fails, however, and he plots to have Vanessa declared insane. Now nearly forty, she turns to Benjie, whose wife has left him. They live together happily for a time, until she learns that her husband's mind has entirely failed and that he cries constantly for her. Vowing to return to her husband until his death, Vanessa goes back to London, but her husband becomes stronger and outlives her.

Benjie Herries (also see "The Fortress"), who is in love with Vanessa but is trapped into marriage by another girl. He alone of the Herries family remains unconventional: he loses an arm fighting the Boers; when past sixty he serves with the Russians in World War I; and in his seventies he lives a gipsy life in a caravan with one manservant.

Marion Halliday, who at her mother's instigation goes to bed with Benjie. He marries her, but she later leaves him for another man.

Tom Herries, the son of Benjie and Marion. He and Vanessa become great friends.

Ellis Herries, Vanessa's husband and distant cousin, who is a financier. He and Benjie meet at Vanessa's deathbed without rancor.

Sally Herries, the illegitimate daughter of Vanessa and Benjie. Returning to London, Vanessa takes Sally with her. Sally lives for a year with a young man she expects to marry. But they part and she marries a blind French veteran of World War I. He works for the League of Nations, and Sally goes with him to Berlin to aid the cause of international peace.

Arnold Young, the man with whom Sally lives. His mother objects to the match, and Arnold finally marries another woman.

Judith Paris (also see "Judith Paris" and "The Fortress"), Vanessa's grandmother, who dies when Vanessa is fifteen.

Adam Paris (also see "Judith Paris" and "The Fortress"), Vanessa's father, whose death results in the final postponement of Vanessa's marriage to Benjie.

Margaret Paris (see "The Fortress"), Vanessa's mother.

VANITY FAIR

Author: William Makepeace Thackeray (1811-1863)
Time of action: Early nineteenth century
First published: 1847-1848

PRINCIPAL CHARACTERS

Rebecca Sharp, called **Becky,** an intelligent, beautiful, self-centered, grasping woman whose career begins as an orphaned charity pupil at Miss Pinkerton's School for girls and continues through a series of attempted seductions, affairs, and marriages which form the background of the novel. Unscrupulous Becky is the chief exponent of the people who inhabit Vanity Fair—the world of pretense and show—but she is always apart from it because she sees the humor and ridiculousness of the men and women of this middle-class English world where pride, wealth, and ambition are the ruling virtues.

Amelia Sedley, Becky Sharp's sweet, good, gentle schoolmate at Miss Pinkerton's School. Although married to George Osborne, who subsequently dies in the Battle of Waterloo, Amelia is worshiped by William Dobbin. Amelia does not notice his love, however, so involved is she with the memory of her dashing dead husband. Eventually some of Amelia's goddess-like virtue is dimmed in Dobbin's eyes, but he marries her anyway and transfers his idealization of women to their little girl, Jane.

Captain William Dobbin, an officer in the British Army and a former schoolmate of George Osborne at Dr. Swishtail's school. He idolizes Amelia Sedley, George's wife, and while in the background provides financial and emotional support for her when she is widowed. After many years of worshiping Amelia from afar, he finally marries her.

George Osborne, the dashing young army officer who marries Amelia despite the fact that by so doing he incurs the wrath of his father and is cut off from his inheritance. George, much smitten with the charms of Becky Sharp, slips a love letter to Becky on the night before the army is called to the Battle of Waterloo. He is killed in the battle.

George Osborne, called **Georgy,** the small son of Amelia and George.

Captain Rawdon Crawley, an officer of the Guards, the younger son of Sir Pitt Crawley. He marries Becky Sharp in secret, and for this deception his aunt cuts him out of her will. Charming but somewhat stupid, he is a great gambler and furnishes some of the money on which he and Becky live precariously.

He lets Becky order their life, and even though she flirts outrageously after they are married, he does not abandon her until he discovers her in an intimate scene with the Marquis of Steyne. He dies many years later of yellow fever at Coventry Island.

Rawdon Crawley, the son of Rawdon and Becky. He refuses to see his mother in her later years, though he gives her a liberal allowance. From his uncle he inherits the Crawley baronetcy and estate.

Joseph Sedley, called **Jos,** Amelia's fat, dandified brother whom Becky Sharp attempts unsuccessfully to attract into marrying her. A civil servant in India, the Collector of Boggley Wollah, Jos is rich but selfish and does nothing to rescue his father and mother from bankruptcy. Persuaded by Dobbin, finally, to take some family responsibility, he supports Amelia and her son Georgy for a few months before Dobbin marries her. For a time he and Becky travel on the Continent as husband and wife. He dies at Aix-la-Chapelle soon after Amelia and Dobbin's marriage. His fortune gone from unsuccessful speculations, he leaves only an insurance policy of two thousand pounds, to be divided between Becky and his sister.

Sir Pitt Crawley, a crusty, eccentric old baronet who lives at Queen's Crawley, his country seat, with his abused, apathetic second wife and two young daughters, Miss Rosalind and Miss Violet. Immediately after Lady Crawley's death Sir Pitt proposes marriage to Becky. His offer reveals her secret marriage to Rawdon Crawley, his younger son. Later, grown more senile than ever, Sir Pitt carries on an affair with his butler's daughter, Betsy Horrocks, much to the disgust of his relatives. He eventually dies, and his baronetcy and money go to Pitt, his eldest son.

Miss Crawley, Sir Pitt's eccentric sister, a lonely old maid. Imperious and rich, she is toadied to by everyone in the Crawley family and by Becky Sharp, for they see in her the chance for a rich living. She finally is won over by young Pitt Crawley's wife, Lady Jane, and her estate goes to Pitt.

Pitt Crawley, the older son of Sir Pitt Crawley. A most proper young man with political ambitions, he marries Lady Jane Sheepshanks, and after his brother's secret marriage so endears himself to Miss Crawley, his rich, domineering aunt, that he gains her money as well as his father's.

Lady Jane, Pitt Crawley's wife. Like Amelia Sedley, she is good, sweet, and kind, and is, above all else, interested in her husband's and their daughter's welfare.

The Reverend Bute Crawley, the rector of Crawley-cum-Snailby and Sir Pitt's brother. His household is run by his domineering wife.

Mrs. Bute Crawley, who dislikes Becky Sharp because she recognizes in her the same sort of ambition and craftiness that she herself possesses. Mrs. Bute fails in her plans to gain Miss Crawley's fortune.

James Crawley, the son of the Bute Crawleys. For a time it looks as if this shy, good-looking young man will win favor with his aunt, but he ruins his prospects by getting very drunk on his aunt's wine and later smoking his pipe out the window of the guest room. Miss Crawley's maid also discovers that James has run up a tremendous bill for gin (to which he treated everyone in the local tavern in one of his expansive moods) at the local inn, and this fact combined with his smoking tobacco puts an end to the Bute Crawleys' prospects of inheriting Miss Crawley's money.

Horrocks, Sir Pitt Crawley's butler.

Betsy Horrocks, the butler's daughter and old Sir Pitt's mistress. She is done out of any inheritance by the interference of Mrs. Bute Crawley.

Mr. John Sedley, the father of Amelia and Joseph, a typical middle-class English merchant of grasping, selfish ways. After his failure in business his family is forced to move from Russell Square to a cottage kept by the Clapps, a former servant of the Sedleys. Never able to accept his poverty, Mr. Sedley spends his time thinking up new business schemes with which to regain his former wealth.

Mrs. John Sedley, the long-suffering wife of Mr. Sedley, and mother of Amelia and Joseph. She, like her daughter, is a sweet woman. Her only expression of wrath in the entire story comes when she turns upon Amelia after her daughter has criticized her for giving little Georgy medicine that has not been prescribed for him.

John Osborne, George Osborne's testy-tempered father, provincial, narrow, and mean. Never forgiving his son for marrying the penniless Amelia Sedley, Mr. Osborne finally succeeds in getting the widow to give up her adored Georgy to his care. Amelia regains her son, however, and when he dies Mr. Osborne leaves to his grandson a legacy of which Amelia is the trustee.

Jane,
Maria, and
Frances Osborne, George's sisters, who adore their young nephew. Maria finally marries Frederick Bullock, Esq., a London lawyer.

Mr. Smee, Jane Osborne's drawing teacher, who tries to marry her. Mr. Osborne, discovering them together, forbids him to enter the house.

Lord Steyne, Lord of the Powder Closet at Buckingham Palace. Haughty and well-borne and considerably older than Becky, he succumbs to her charms. Her husband discovers them together and leaves her.

Wirt, the Osbornes' faithful maid.

Mrs. Tinker, the housekeeper at Queen's Crawley.

Lord Southdown, Lady Jane Crawley's brother, a dandified London friend of the Rawdon Crawleys.

Miss Briggs, Miss Crawley's companion and later Becky Sharp's "sheepdog." She fulfills Becky's need for a female companion so that the little adventuress will have some sort of respectability in the eyes of society.

Bowles, Miss Crawley's butler.

Mrs. Firkins, Miss Crawley's maid. Like the other servants, she is overwhelmed by the overbearing old lady.

Charles Raggles, a green grocer, at one time an assistant gardener to the Crawley family. Having saved his money, he has bought a green grocer's shop and a small house in Curzon Street. Becky and Rawdon live there for a time on his charity, for they are unable to pay their rent.

Lord Gaunt, the son of Lord Steyne. He goes insane in his early twenties.

Major O'Dowd, an officer under whom George Osborne and William Dobbin serve. He is a relaxed individual, devoted to his witty and vivacious wife.

Mrs. O'Dowd, the Irish wife of Major O'Dowd. She is an unaffected, delightful female who tries to marry off her sister-in-law to William Dobbin.

Glorvina O'Dowd, the flirtatious sister of Major O'Dowd. She sets her cap for Dobbin, but because she is only "frocks and shoulders," nothing comes of the match. She marries Major Posky.

General Tufto, the officer to whom Rawdon Crawley at one time serves as aide-de-camp. He is a typical army man with a mistress and a long-suffering wife.

Mrs. Tufto, his wife.

Mrs. Bent, his mistress.

Dolly, the housekeeper to the Rawdon Crawleys in London. She is the one who fends off tradesmen when they come to demand their money.

Mrs. Clapp, the landlady of the Sedleys after their move from Russell Square.

Polly Clapp, a young former servant of the Sedleys. She takes Dobbin to meet Amelia in the park after the former's ten-year absence in the Indian service.

Mary Clapp, another daughter of the Clapps and Amelia's friend.

Lady Bareacres, a snobby old aristocrat who cuts Becky socially in Brussels. Later Becky has her revenge when she refuses to sell her horses to the old woman so that she may flee from Napoleon's invading army.

Lady Blanche Thistlewood, Lady Bareacres' daughter and a dancing partner of George Osborne when they were very young.

Mr. Hammerdown, the auctioneer at the sale of the Sedley possessions.

Major Martindale,
Lieutenant Spatterdash, and
Captain Cinqbars, military friends of Rawdon Crawley who are captivated by his charming wife.

Tom Stubble, a wounded soldier who brings news of the Battle of Waterloo to Amelia Sedley and Mrs. O'Dowd. They care for him until he regains his health.

Mr. Creamer, Miss Crawley's physician.

Miss Pinkerton, the snobbish mistress of the academy for girls at which Amelia Sedley and Becky Sharp met. She dislikes Becky intensely.

Miss Jemima Pinkerton, the silly, sentimental sister of the elder Miss Pinkerton. She takes pity on Becky and tries to give her the graduation gift of the academy, a dictionary, but Becky flings it into the mud as her coach drives off.

Miss Swartz, the rich, woolly-haired mulatto student at Miss Pinkerton's School. Because of her immense wealth she pays double tuition. Later the Crawley family tries to marry off Rawdon to her, but he has already married Becky.

Mr. Sambo, the Sedley's colored servant.

The Reverend Mr. Crisp, a young curate in Chiswick, enamored of Becky Sharp.

Miss Cutler, a young woman who unsuccessfully sets her cap for Joseph Sedley.

Mr. Fiche, Lord Steyne's confidential man. After Becky's fortunes have begun to decline, he tells her to leave Rome for her own good.

Major Loder, Becky's escort in the later phases of her career.

VATHEK

Author: William Beckford (1759-1844)
Time of action: The past
First published: 1786

PRINCIPAL CHARACTERS

Vathek, an Arabian sultan. A man addicted to sensory pleasures, he indulges in black magic. The Giaour gives him the key to the dark kingdom in response to human sacrifices. He makes Nouronihar his companion in the pleasures of this world and the world of magic. Vathek finds the secret lair of Eblis, Lord of Darkness, only to have his heart consumed by eternal flames.

Nouronihar, the daughter of Emir Fakreddin. She is stolen from her betrothed by Vathek and becomes the favorite of his harem. She shares Vathek's discovery of the lair of Eblis and has her heart also consumed by eternal flames. She turns from a sweet young woman into an addict of pleasure and depravity.

Carathis, Vathek's mother. She is a worshiper of evil and, by her live sacrifices,

leads her son to black magic and its discoveries. She arrives at the lair of Eblis shortly after her son, who sees her heart burst into flame.

The Giaour, a mysterious stranger and an emissary of the powers of evil. He brings sabers with changing inscriptions to Vathek. The inscriptions are the key to the pathway to the kingdom of darkness.

Gulchenrouz, the girl betrothed to Nouronihar. He and his sweetheart are drugged and taken to a hidden retreat in order to save the girl from Vathek, but he finds her anyway.

Emir Fakreddin, the devout Mohammedan father of Nouronihar. He is scandalized by Vathek's violation of the laws of hospitality.

THE VENETIAN GLASS NEPHEW

Author: Elinor Wylie (1885-1928)
Time of action: 1782
First published: 1925

PRINCIPAL CHARACTERS

Peter Innocent Bon, a Cardinal of the Roman Catholic Church who yearns to

have a nephew, though all his sisters are in holy orders and his brothers have fathered only daughters. In his naïveté he asks a glassblower friend to make him a glass nephew and bring the creation to life.

Virginio, the Cardinal's nephew, formed of Venetian glass and given life. He is a handsome young man with a translucent complexion and golden hair. He is baptized Virginio by the Cardinal and sent to receive an education at the hands of Angelo Querini, a scholar and philosopher. He falls in love with Rosalba Berni and marries her, though the marriage to a glass man is difficult for a flesh-and-blood young woman.

Rosalba Berni, known as **Sappho the Younger** because she is a splendid poet and a woman of learning. She is the ward of Angelo Querini, at whose home she meets Virginio and falls in love, despite her engrossment in the classics and philosophy. Upon knowing love, she becomes an active girl, even a hoyden, and her marriage to a glass husband has complications. After she attempts suicide in her unhappiness, her friends permit her to be transformed into Sèvres porcelain so that she can be a more suitable wife for her beloved. Rosalba, it is discovered, is the illegitimate child of Cardinal de Bernis.

M. de Chastelneuf, Chevalier de Langeist, a strange man from Bohemia who has supernatural powers. His interest in Rosalba stems from having loved her mother before the woman became Cardinal de Bernis' mistress.

Caterina, Rosalba's mother, mistress of Cardinal de Bernis.

Alvise Luna, a famous glassblower of Murano who works with M. de Chastelneuf. He is accused of being a sorcerer.

Count Carlo Gozzi, long-time friend of Cardinal Innocent Bon. He is a writer of fairy tales.

Angelo Querini, a scholar and philosopher, formerly the friend of Voltaire. As a man of great learning he is the guardian of Rosalba and the tutor of Virginio.

VENICE PRESERVED

Author: Thomas Otway (1652-1685)
Time of action: The Renaissance
First presented: 1682

PRINCIPAL CHARACTERS

Jaffier (jăf′yẻr), a Venetian citizen who wins the undying animosity of his father-in-law when the young man secretly marries Belvidera. After three years of being thus disowned, Jaffier and his wife are heartbroken and penniless, their only joy being in their deep love for each other and for their baby son. When their household is seized at the father-in-law's vindictive order, Jaffier is most amenable to a suggestion that he avenge the abuse to his wife by joining a conspiracy against the Senate of Venice. Revolted by the crudity of the conspirators, he informs the Council of their plans and thus incurs the scorn of his noble friend Pierre. Jaffier has woven a tangled web by abusing his wife and betraying his friend. He can regain his self-respect only by stabbing his friend and himself.

Pierre (pyār′), a gentle philosopher and an honored citizen of Venice. By his own candid estimate he is a villain; though he sees how the government is enslaving the people, he remains passive and does little to correct the situation. Intrigued by the conspirators' plot, Pierre concludes that he is as free to be a foe as to be a friend of Venice. His decision is inspired as much by his desire for personal vengeance as by any sense of altruism.

Sensing his contempt for the bullying cowardice of the conspirators as they imply Jaffier's disloyalty to the conspiracy, he nevertheless continues with the cause. Complex circumstances conspire to shatter the friendship of Jaffier and Pierre, but in the end the men reunite. In a gesture of mutual forgiveness Pierre, on the executioner's stand, asks Jaffier to stab him. This act saves Pierre from the wheel; more important, it serves to deceive the Senate.

Belvidera (bĕl·vē·dā′rä), Jaffier's beautiful, noble, sensitive wife. Even though she suffers the hurt of Jaffier's abuse, to prove his honor to the conspiracy, she forgives him and begs to be informed of the revolutionary scheme. She is loyal to Jaffier when he reports to the Council and swallows her pride when she seeks her father's aid in saving Pierre. Visited by the ghosts of Jaffier and Pierre, she dies of grief.

Priuli (prē·ōō′lē), a leading Senator of Venice and the father of Belvidera, who so bitterly despises his daughter's marriage to Jaffier that he wishes her dead. After Belvidera's death, Priuli condemns himself to self-exile with the closing lines ". . . bid all Cruel Fathers dread my Fate."

Renault (rā·nō′), a reformer. Scheming and relentless, he is the chief of the conspirators against Venice. He reveals his contemptible character by his attempts to compromise the lovely Belvidera when Jaffier, at first convinced of the rightness of the conspiracy, gives his wife over to Renault as a token of his loyalty. Such is Renault's compelling power that Jaffier, learning of his conduct, says he will endure personal indignity for the success of the plot against the Council. Execution on the wheel, after the conspiracy is discovered by the Senate, seems a suitable end for Renault. The other conspirators are willing to be led by Renault, but question his pressing Pierre so hard concerning Jaffier's honor. They, too, are executed for treason.

Antonio (än·tō′nyō), a leader and eloquent speaker of the Senate. In his contemptibleness and senility, he lends an aura of satire to the play. Bitter rivalry and mortal jealousy exist between Antonio and Pierre because of their various interests in a common mistress. Antonio is a weak character in his childish adoration and preoccupation with the mistress, who threatens to kill him in order to make him promise to save Pierre, whom she loves and who loves her. Antonio consents but, like Priuli's, his decision comes too late.

Aquilana (ä·kwē·lä′nä), the exciting and exotic Greek courtesan whom Pierre loved but lost to lecherous Antonio. In her effort to save Pierre, Aquilana shows a noble strain of character.

A Friar, the priest who tries to comfort Pierre before his death. He is alternately scorned and ignored by Pierre because of his sanctimonious prating.

VENUS AND ADONIS

Author: William Shakespeare (1564-1616)
Time of action: Remote antiquity
First published: 1593

PRINCIPAL CHARACTERS

Venus, goddess of love and beauty. Voluptuous and fierily passionate, she is greedy for the love of young Adonis and immodestly thrusts her attentions on him. His shyness and sullenness increase her desire. She is a master of Renaissance rhetoric and delivers a stream of oratorical debate to convince Adonis of the importance of fertility. Her knowledge of the English countryside and hunting (gained from Master Shakespeare, no doubt) makes for particularly graphic and poetic descriptions. Her grief at the death of Adonis is as passionate as her love. There have been some scholarly arguments that hold her to be an allegorical Platonic figure rather than the erotic creation she appears to most readers to be.

Adonis, a shy, handsome young hunter. Venus' lavish wooing drives him into sullen obstinacy. He too is well trained in rhetoric and carries his side of the debate with rebukes for her lustful behavior. He is, however, tender-hearted and softens considerably when she swoons. He does not yield completely to her importunities and stubbornly goes ahead with his plans to hunt the boar. His death results. Those who hold that the poem is an expression of the Renaissance ideal of love compare Adonis with the fair young man of the sonnets and indicate that his death is justly due to his rejection of love and beauty and his consequent failure to reproduce his kind.

THE VICAR OF BULLHAMPTON

Author: Anthony Trollope (1815-1882)
Time of action: Nineteenth century
First published: 1870

PRINCIPAL CHARACTERS

Frank Fenwick, the Vicar of Bullhampton. He is involved in an altercation with the Marquis of Trowbridge, in part over the vicar's standing by a young man the Marquis thinks should be in jail. The vicar is also concerned over the lack of progress made by his friend, Squire Gilmore, in courting Fenwick's wife's guest, Mary Lowther.

Harry Gilmore, the Squire of Bullhampton and the chief landholder after the Marquis. The girl he loves, after much reluctance and hesitation, becomes engaged to him. He is crushed when she breaks her engagement to marry the man she loves.

Mary Lowther, Janet Fenwick's friend and guest. Prevented by lack of money from marrying her cousin, whom she loves, she finally becomes engaged to devoted Squire Gilmore. Her cousin's sudden acquisition of wealth, however, enables her to break her engagement to the Squire and marry her cousin.

Janet Fenwick, the vicar's wife. In her sympathy for the Squire after he is thrown over, she wishes that Mary had never come to Bullhampton.

Walter Marrable, Mary's cousin. A soldier home from India, he is trying to regain an inheritance from his father, who has cheated him of it. He and Mary become engaged but are forced to break their engagement when it is discovered that Walter's father has spent the inheritance. Subsequently Walter is made heir to his uncle, a wealthy baronet. On the uncle's death, Walter is united with Mary.

The Marquis of Trowbridge, a wealthy landholder and owner of most of Bullhampton, though he has no residence within ten miles of it. Disliking the vicar personally as well as for his leniency to ne'er-do-wells, he complains of the vicar to the Bishop. His complaint ineffectual, he conspires with the Methodist minister to build a Methodist chapel across the street from the vicarage. Both the Methodist minister and the

Marquis are greatly upset to learn that the land on which they are building is really the vicar's, and that their chapel will have to be removed.

Jacob Brattle, a crabbed, hard-working mill owner. With two exceptions, his many children have turned out well.

Sam Brattle, his son, who consorts with low companions. His association with a known ex-convict leads to his being suspected of a murder and robbery. But the vicar defends him, and Sam is at last proved innocent.

Carry Brattle, Jacob's daughter. Her father is heartbroken because she has become a prostitute. She is living with the ex-convict, but the vicar befriends her and finds her a home with a farm family. Later, through the vicar's intercession, she is received at her old home and at last even her stubborn father is reconciled to her.

Miss Marrable, Mary Lowther's spinster aunt, with whom she lives.

Colonel Marrable, Walter's profligate father.

THE VICAR OF WAKEFIELD

Author: Oliver Goldsmith (1728-1774)
Time of action: Eighteenth century
First published: 1766

PRINCIPAL CHARACTERS

Dr. Charles Primrose, the vicar of Wakefield, "a priest, an husbandman, and the father of a family." He is generous, kindly, honest, and given to strong opinions (as on monogamy). A homely philosopher, he admonishes his wife and daughters on their vanity, warns them against Squire Thornhill (who later takes him in), urges them to be temperate, and frequently delivers himself of wise saws and modern instances, all the while remaining a good-hearted fool who is easily duped by villains. His fortitude is amazing during his train of calamities. He is so completely a good man that he is lovable despite his frequent gullibility and his occasional absurdity.

Deborah, his wife, an ambitious woman whose chief interest is in getting her daughters well married. She is vain and, through George, she seeks vengeance on Olivia's betrayer.

George, the oldest son. Bred at Oxford for one of the learned professions, he (somewhat like Goldsmith himself) tries various occupations, succeeding at none. Through Squire Thornhill he obtains an army commission. George at long last marries Arabella.

Sophia (Sophy), the younger daughter, soft, modest, and alluring, a girl whose beauty increases upon better acquaintance. She marries Sir William Thornhill.

Olivia (Livy), the older daughter, strikingly and luxuriantly beautiful, open, sprightly, commanding, coquettish. Deceived by Squire Thornhill, she elopes with him and is deserted shortly afterward. She suffers remorse, especially when she learns that her marriage was apparently a false one. Later, learning that she is not the fallen woman she thought herself, she recovers and even offers to consider forgiving her betrayer if he reforms.

Mr. Burchell, in reality **Sir William Thornhill,** the uncle of Squire Thornhill. Sir William is famed for his great generosity and whimsicality. An experienced observer and judge of people, he is a self-admitted humorist and eccentric. Fond of children, he is very popular with them. After aiding various members of the Primrose family several times, he reveals himself, helps to bring happiness to the whole family, and marries Sophia.

Squire Thornhill, Dr. Primrose's landlord and Olivia's betrayer. He is a handsome, unscrupulous rake. Guilty of multiple villainies, he is exposed before he is able to bring utter ruin on the Primrose family and also before he is able to marry Arabella and gain control of her fortune.

Arabella Wilmot, who is betrothed to George. She is the daughter of a neighboring clergyman. After Olivia's seduction and desertion and George's long absence, Arabella plans to marry the Squire, who convinces her that George has married and gone to America. She is undeceived just in time, and becomes George's wife.

Mr. Wilmot, Arabella's thrice-married father.

Mr. Williams, a farmer neighbor of the Primroses who plans to marry Olivia and is dismayed when she runs away.

Moses, the fourth child and second son of the Primroses. Being intended for business, he received a miscellaneous education at home. He is talkative, naïve, and as gullible as his father.

Dick and
Bill, the two youngest Primrose children.

Solomon Flamborough, a neighbor who loves to hear himself talk and who talks too much and too repetitiously. Moses is interested in one of the two Flamborough daughters.

Lady Blarney and
Miss Carolina Wilhelmina Amelia Skeggs, two strumpets, friends of the Squire, posing as town ladies.

Ephraim Jenkinson, a venerable old man (under his disguise he is many years younger), a spouter of bogus learning who cheats Moses out of money and Dr. Primrose out of a horse. He and Dr. Primrose later meet in jail. A crony of the Squire, Jenkinson tricked him by bringing a real priest to perform the marriage ceremony for Olivia and the Squire.

Mr. Symmonds, a public-house keeper who informs Dr. Primrose of the Squire's unsavory reputation as a seducer. Dr. Primrose learns that Olivia has been staying at the public house after her desertion by the Squire.

Timothy Baxter, the Squire's hireling and the abductor of Sophia, who is saved from him by Sir William.

THE VICOMTE DE BRAGELONNE

Author: Alexandre Dumas, *père* (1802-1870)
Time of action: Seventeenth century
First published: 1848-1850

PRINCIPAL CHARACTERS

Raoul, Vicomte de Bragelonne (rà·ōōl′, vē·kôṅt′ də brà·gà·lôn′), the son of Athos, the Comte de la Fère, who was one of the famous Three Musketeers. Raoul becomes the rival of Louis XIV for the love of Louise de la Vallière. Disappointed in love, he goes to Africa, where he is killed.

Louise de la Vallière (lwēz′ də là và-

lyĕr′), a beautiful young woman. Though betrothed to the Vicomte de Bragelonne, she becomes the mistress of Louis XIV.

Louis XIV (lwē′), King of France and Vicomte de Bragelonne's rival for Mlle. de la Vallière.

The Comte de la Fère (də là fĕr′), formerly known as **Athos,** one of the Three

1199

Musketeers. He helps Charles II regain the throne of England. He dies of shock when told of the death of the Vicomte de Bragelonne, his son.

Charles II (shärl'), the English King, who took refuge in France while Cromwell ruled England.

Cardinal Mazarin (må·zå·răn'), the chief minister to Louis XIV.

D'Artagnan (dår·tån·yän'), the famous Musketeer. He is loyal to Louis XIV and supports the King against those who plot against the monarch. He dies in battle shortly after having been made a Marshal of France.

General Monk (mōnk'), leader of the English Parliamentary forces. He is seized by D'Artagnan and taken to France, where he agrees to put Charles II on the English throne.

Planchet (plän·shä'), a wealthy merchant who was formerly D'Artagnan's servant. He helps finance his former master in the effort to put Charles II on the English throne.

Fouquet (foo·kä'), the finance minister under Louis XIV. He plots against the King.

Colbert (kôl·bĕr'), an intendant under Louis XIV.

M. du Vallon (dü vå·yōn'), formerly Porthos, of the Three Musketeers. A plotter against the King, he is killed in battle at Belle-Isle.

The Bishop of Vannes (vån'), formerly Aramis, one of the Three Musketeers, and known also as M. D'Herblay. Though he plots against the monarchy, he is pardoned at the request of D'Artagnan.

Mlle. de Montalais (də mōn·tå·lĕ'), a lady in waiting at the court and a plotter against Louis XIV.

Philippe (fē·lēp'), Louis XIV's twin brother. He is the mysterious prisoner in an iron mask.

M. Saint-Aignan (săn·tĕn·yän'), who is killed in a duel over Mlle. de la Vallière by de Bragelonne.

VICTORY

Author: Joseph Conrad (Józef Teodor Konrad Korzeniowski, 1857-1924
Time of action: Early twentieth century
First published: 1915

PRINCIPAL CHARACTERS

Baron Axel Heyst, a man who has deliberately attempted to stand aloof from life, an effort that has made him a pathetic man if not a tragic one. He is innately, fastidiously virtuous, but by detaching himself from the entanglements and consequences of experience he has made himself incapable of coping with evil; consequently, when he is forced to defend Lena, the only person he has ever dared or tried to love, he fails miserably and destroys himself. He is characterized aptly by epithets: his apparent willingness to drift forever within a "magic circle" in the East Indies earns him the name "Enchanted Heyst"; his naïve optimism, the "Utopist"; his attempt to establish organized trade in the islands, "the Enemy"; his isolated retirement on Samburan, "the Hermit"; and his alleged exploitation of Morrison, his former partner, "the Spider." After Lena dies as the result of a wound inflicted by Mr. Jones, Heyst sets fire to his bungalow and burns himself and her body.

Lena, the new name Heyst gives to **Alma,** a young entertainer in Zangiacomo's Orchestra, after he has met her while she is performing at Wilhelm Schomberg's hotel in Sourabaya; he quixotically thinks that the new name symbolizes her break with her sordid past. It is to Lena that the "victory" of the title applies. Realizing that Heyst is completely incapable of meeting evil with action, she resolves, out of love and gratitude, to save him, if necessary by committing murder. She is a foil to Heyst in that she has been forced since childhood to confront and resist the evil in life, and she is prepared, instinctively, to challenge and defeat it. Mr. Jones shoots Lena when he finds her and Martin Ricardo together in Heyst's bungalow.

Mr. Jones, "a gentleman at large" who embodies the evil intelligence and calculating wickedness that threaten and finally destroy Heyst. Outlawed by his perversity from the genteel society of which he was once a member, Jones travels with two companions among the outpost islands and gets his living by gambling, theft, and murder. After shooting Lena and Martin Ricardo, Jones falls from a wharf and drowns.

Martin Ricardo, Mr. Jones's henchman. Though dedicated to performing dirty work for Jones, whom he considers a gentleman, he does not conform to his leader's misogynic principles. Characterized as a cat, he symbolizes instinctive savagery. Believing that Ricardo has betrayed him by concealing the fact of Lena's presence in Heyst's bungalow, Jones shoots him after fatally wounding Lena.

Pedro, the third of the evil trio threatening the lives of Heyst and Lena on Samburan. Symbolizing brute force, this ape-like creature, formerly an alligator hunter in Columbia, has attached himself to Jones out of gratitude for having spared his wretched life. Wang shoots him with a pistol stolen from Heyst.

Wilhelm Schomberg, the brutal owner of a hotel in Sourabaya. His obsessive hatred for Heyst increases after Heyst carries off Lena, the girl Schomberg had desired for himself. To get rid of Jones and Ricardo, who have been operating a gambling den in his hotel, Schomberg sends them to Samburan in search of a treasure Heyst is supposed to keep hidden on the island. His hope is that Jones and his followers will kill the man he hates.

Mrs. Schomberg, still in love with her brutish husband, even though he has reduced her to a condition of domestic servitude and spiritual degradation. To keep him for herself, she helps Lena escape with Heyst.

Wang, the inscrutable Chinese houseboy who deserts Heyst after seeing Ricardo's attempt to attack Lena. Before his flight to a native village on the other side of the island, Wang takes Heyst's gun; thus Heyst and Lena are left defenseless, at the mercy of Mr. Jones and his henchmen.

Morrison, Heyst's former business partner in maintaining a coaling station on Samburan. After Morrison died in England, Schomberg circulated reports that Heyst had cheated his partner. Except for Lena, Morrison was the only person with whom Heyst had ever become involved. In return for a loan at a time of need, he had secured Heyst's appointment as a manager of the Tropical Belt Coal Company, now liquidated.

Captain Davidson, the skipper of a trading vessel. He is in the habit of sailing his schooner close to Samburan so that Heyst will not be completely isolated. He appears shortly after Mr. Jones has shot Lena. Later he explains to the authorities the violent affair which for Lena and Heyst ended in a spiritual victory snatched from circumstances of physical defeat and death.

Zangiacomo, the leader of the Ladies'

1201

Orchestra in which Lena is a performer. His wife arouses Heyst's sympathy for the girl by pinching her.

Julius Tesman, a partner of Tesman Brothers. He backs Heyst in the coal company venture.

VILE BODIES

Author: Evelyn Waugh (1903-   )
Time of action: A twentieth century interval between wars
First published: 1930

PRINCIPAL CHARACTERS

Adam Fenwick-Symes, a young writer. Returning from Paris to England to marry his fiancée, he is forced to postpone his wedding because the manuscript of his autobiography is confiscated and burned by customs officials. Winning a bet of a thousand pounds, he renews his marriage plans, only to postpone them again when a drunken major, to whom he has given the money for a horse-race bet, disappears. His fiancée's father gives him a thousand-pound check to enable the couple to marry; after they happily spend a night together, Adam learns that his fiancée's father has absent-mindedly signed Charlie Chaplin's name to the check, and the wedding is postponed again. Adam takes over a newspaper gossip column, loses his job, and permits another man to marry his fiancée in exchange for a small loan. Later, in the war, during a lull in the fighting, he meets his drunken major again on a battlefield. The major, now a general, offers to pay Adam the thirty-five thousand pounds (the horse won) on the spot, but Adam thinks the money will be useless. They find champagne in the general's car, and Adam drinks some of it and falls asleep.

Nina Blount, Adam's fiancée, whose marriage is repeatedly postponed. She marries the man who lent money to Adam, but after he is called up for military service, she takes Adam along, as her husband, to spend Christmas with her father.

Colonel Blount, her father, an absent-minded movie fan. He makes a picture about the life of John Wesley and is too preoccupied with it to notice that his supposed son-in-law is a young man he had previously met as Fenwick-Symes.

Agatha Runcible, a leader of the Bright Young People. Returning to England, she is mistaken for a notorious jewel smuggler, stripped, and searched. After escapades which include a party at No. 10 Downing Street, she goes to the auto races and takes the wheel of a car, the driver of which has been disabled. Having established a course record for the lap, she leaves the track and drives across country until she crashes into a monument. Still thinking she is driving in a spinning world of speed, she dies in a nursing home.

Miles Malpractice, another leader of the Bright Young People. Thrown out of Throbbing House when his brother, Lord Throbbing, returns from Canada, Miles needs money and takes a job as successor to Adam as gossip columnist on the "Daily Excess."

Lottie Crump, the proprietress of Shepheard's Hotel, where Adam stays. She bullies kings, advises members of Parliament, and is careless about bills if she likes her guests.

Captain Eddy (Ginger) Littlejohn, who is in love with Nina. He lends money to Adam in return for Adam's promise that he be allowed to marry Nina. Shortly after the honeymoon, Ginger is called up for military service.

Nezhdanov (nĕzh·dä′nəf), a young socialist who idealistically believes in revolution as the panacea for all of Russia's ills. Born illegitimate to a wealthy aristocrat, Nezhdanov (literally, "the Unexpected") received a university education, specializing in the arts. This training frustrates him because, while a basic appreciation of music and poetry has been instilled in him, he indignantly denies that aesthetics have any social value. Frustration is the key to his character. More than once he compares himself to Hamlet, the idealist challenged to act in a practical situation. While tutoring in the home of Sipyagin, he falls in love with Marianna, who elopes with him and agrees to work for the cause of the party. But Nezhdanov cannot devote himself wholeheartedly to social revolution and consequently considers himself a failure unworthy of Marianna's love. In desperation he takes his own life, leaving Marianna to Solomin, his friend and compatriot. In Nezhdanov, Turgenev has depicted the dilemma of a sensitive soul, basically opposed to ugliness and brutality, caught up in a social movement which demands the violent overthrow of the aristocracy.

Marianna (mä·rĭ·än′nə), Sipyagin's niece, living in his household. Although of the aristocracy, her parents died in shame and poverty; her father, a general, had been detected in a huge theft from the government funds. Marianna, longing for freedom, loathes the life of a dependent in the Sipyagin family and is incensed by Valentina's remarks concerning her disreputable father and her lack of gratitude. In Nezhdanov she finds both a lover and a cause; not only does she agree to elope with him, but also she proves a ready convert to the party line. It is largely the purity and intensity of her devotion to Nezhdanov that draws the latter's frustration to a tragic climax.

Sipyagin (sĭ·pyä′gĭn), a nobleman who hires Nezhdanov as tutor for his young son Kolya. Wealthy and respected, Sipyagin is regarded as a liberal and progressive aristocrat who favors certain experiments in social profit-sharing. As such, he is the mean between the extremes of Kallomyeitzev, who is an aristocratic tyrant, and Nezhdanov and his comrades, who ostensibly advocate annihilation of the aristocracy. He tolerates Nezhdanov, even welcomes him in his household, until the latter's extreme views become offensive. Enmity between the two is sealed when Nezhdanov persuades Marianna to reject both her family and her social position.

Valentina (vä·lĕn·tĭ′nə), Sipyagin's wife, a woman of beauty and poise. She is also the appropriate feminine counterpart to the moderately liberal views of her husband. Only once does her nature become wholly unpleasant, when Nezhdanov spurns her attentions in favor of Marianna.

Markelov (mär·kĕl′ləf), the brother of Valentina, a violent advocate of social rebellion. When captured and exposed, he remains firm in his hatred of the aristocracy, refusing influential aid from Sipyagin, his brother-in-law.

Solomin (sô·lô′mĭn), a factory manager, a calm and taciturn man of great strength of character. Although a comrade, he recognizes the impossibility of immediate rebellion; hence, he lives amiably and profitably in the existent society, helping the party cause when and where he is able. As a manager he is the picture of efficiency, respected by owner and worker alike. Aside from Nezhdanov, he is the most sympathetic portrait of a party member, interested more in peaceful means of social improvement than in inciting peasants to chaotic rebellion. He marries Marianna after Nezhdanov's suicide.

Kallomyeitzev (käl·lô·mĕyt′zĕf), a nouveau-riche aristocrat, the inveterate opponent of Nezhdanov's social views. Essentially a fop, he takes meticulous pains to dress in the latest style and ostentatiously peppers his speech with French phrases. Politically, he believes in iron-hand control of the peasants.

Miss Mashurin (mä·shōō′rĭn), a devoted party member, plain and masculine in her features, secretly in love with Nezhdanov.

Kolya (kō′ylə), the young son of Sipyagin, tutored by Nezhdanov.

Anna Zakharovna (än·nə zä·hä′rəv·nə), Sipyagin's aunt, a meddlesome woman.

Ostrodumov (ôs·trô·dōō′məf),
Pakhlin (päh′lĭn), and
Golushkin (gô·lūsh′kĭn), party members frequently in the company of Nezhdanov, Solomin, and Markelov.

THE VIRGINIA COMEDIANS

Author: John Esten Cooke (1830-1886)
Time of action: 1763-1765
First published: 1854

PRINCIPAL CHARACTERS

Champ Effingham, the foppish, Oxford-educated son of a wealthy Virginia planter. Infatuated with Beatrice Hallam, he wounds his rival for her love and then flees to Europe. When he returns, two years later, he has lost his foppish ways and is a moody young man. His mental health is finally restored, and he then marries his original fiancée, Clare Lee.

Beatrice Hallam, a beautiful young actress, supposedly the daughter of the manager of The Virginia Comedians, a traveling drama company. She despises Champ Effingham but loves Charles Waters. She turns out to be really her beloved's cousin and not Hallam's daughter. She and Charles are married, but she lives only a few years after the event.

Charles Waters, a poor young man. He rescues Beatrice from drowning and wins her love. He recovers from the sword wound inflicted by his rival for her love and marries her. After his wife's death

and the passage of the Stamp Act he becomes a leader in the revolutionary movement in the Virginia Colony.

Mr. Hallam, Beatrice's supposed father, manager of The Virginia Comedians. He wants Beatrice to marry Champ so that she will be rich and respected. He also sees her marriage into a wealthy family as a source of money and ease for himself.

Mr. Effingham, Champ's planter father. He is against his son's courting of Beatrice Hallam, the actress.

Clare Lee, Champ's cousin and fiancée. Though spurned for a while by Champ, she continues to love him and is finally married to him.

Captain Ralph Waters, Charles' brother. When Champ loses his foppish ways, the Captain becomes his close friend. Ralph marries Clare Lee's sister.

Jack Hamilton, Champ Effingham's friend.

THE VIRGINIAN

Author: Owen Wister (1860-1938)
Time of action: Late nineteenth century
First published: 1902

The Virginian, a cowboy in Wyoming who is one of nature's gentlemen. He can perform his duties well and hold his own in practical jokes, drinking bouts, and poker games. When given an opportunity, he proves to be an apt leader of men and a successful ranch foreman. He falls in love with a young schoolteacher from the East and by his manly behavior proves his worth to the girl, who finally marries him, even though he is a rough-and-ready man by her standards. The Virginian believes in law and order, even if violence is required to maintain them; one of his most difficult experiences is the hanging of a friend who has turned cattle rustler.

Molly Wood, a very feminine but efficient young woman from Vermont who comes to Wyoming to teach in the grade school at Bear Creek, Wyoming. She entrances the Virginian, who almost immediately falls in love when he rescues her from a stagecoach marooned by high water. Molly acts the coquette at first with the cowboy, but she falls in love with him, even risking her life to attend him when he is wounded by hostile Indians. She tries to keep him from a gunfight by threatening not to marry him, but when he emerges from the duel unscathed, she is too happy he is left alive to make good her threat.

Trampas, a cowboy who becomes the Virginian's enemy when the latter accuses him of cheating at cards and faces him down without a fight. Trampas turns cattle rustler and becomes an outlaw, even killing a fellow rustler in order to save his own life. He is finally killed by the Virginian in a gunfight.

Steve, a cowboy, one of the Virginian's close friends. He becomes a cattle rustler and is hanged by a posse of which the Virginian is a member. When caught, Steve refuses to speak to his friend, who feels bad about the death of Steve, outlaw or not.

Judge Henry, owner of a cattle ranch at Sunk Creek, Wyoming, where the Virginian works. Judge Henry is impressed by the Virginian and makes him his foreman.

Shorty, a cowboy who becomes one of Trampas' fellow rustlers. He is killed by Trampas when his death will allow the other outlaw to escape justice.

THE VIRGINIANS

Author: William Makepeace Thackeray (1811-1863)
Time of action: Late eighteenth century
First published: 1857-1859

PRINCIPAL CHARACTERS

George Esmond Warrington, the older son of Madame Rachel Esmond Warrington and her deceased husband, and the heir to the Castlewood estate in Virginia. Impetuous, emotional, introspective, George volunteers to serve in the French and Indian War under a family friend and neighbor, Colonel George Washington. George Warrington is reported killed in action, but he turns up three years later, his life having been saved by an Indian girl. A short time later he goes to England, where his young brother, Harry, has been confined in debtors' prison. While in England he takes up the study of literature and marries the daughter of a family friend. For a time he tries to earn a living by writing; one of his plays is a success, the other a failure. Then his uncle, Sir Miles Warrington, dies, and George inherits his title and estate. Shortly before the outbreak of the Revolutionary War in America, he and his wife return to the family plantation in Virginia; however, having no sympathy for the cause of the colonists, he leaves Virginia and returns to England once more. There he retires to the management of his country estate.

Harry Esmond Warrington, the younger brother of George, an extroverted, gay, athletic young man, almost the complete opposite of his brother. Motivated by a strong personal sense of honor, Harry became involved in many scrapes in England, where he goes after the report of his brother's death. Usually lucky in gambling, Harry soon becomes the center of a social group of court dandies, but after a wild, profligate career he ends up in debtors' prison. He is rescued by his brother George, who intends to share his patrimony with him. Harry, feeling that he has to justify his life, uses the money to buy a commission in the army and fights under General Wolfe at Quebec. Returning to Virginia, he marries Fanny Mountain, the daughter of his mother's housekeeper and companion. Spurred on by Fanny, an ardent revolutionist, Harry fights against the British in the Revolutionary War. Later, after his wife's death, he returns to England and marries the younger sister of his brother's wife.

Madame Rachel Esmond Warrington, the mistresss of Castlewood, a Virginia plantation, a handsome, charming, but snobbish woman proud of her Esmond connections in England and preferring to be called Madame Esmond. Always possessive of her sons, she cannot adjust herself to their independence in maturity, and she carries on a feud with them in her last years. A stanch defender of the British crown, she remains a Tory throughout the Revolution.

The Baroness Beatrix Bernstein, Madame Warrington's older half sister in England. Cold, grasping, and aggressive, she feels little sympathy for any human being except her young kinsman, Harry Warrington. She uses every device she can think of to break up Harry's proposed marriage to her niece, Maria Esmond.

Lady Maria Esmond, a spinster who claims to be twenty-seven years old but is really forty. Still a handsome woman, she is eager to marry. She flirts with her cousin, Harry Warrington, and inveigles from him a proposal of marriage. A great gambler, she is always in debt. When it is discovered that George Warrington is alive and Harry is not the heir to the Virginia fortune, she releases him from his promise to marry her. Later she marries a parson, Mr. Hagan.

William Esmond, Lady Maria's brother, a sour individual who dislikes Harry Warrington. Always the loser in his bets with Harry, Will tricks him by paying off his debts with a broken-down mare after he had promised his best animal in settlement.

Fanny Esmond, Maria's younger sister. She is attracted to Harry Warrington, but her mother, Lady Castlewood, discourages the affair because she wants to marry off Maria.

Lord Castlewood, another of Harry's cousins, a gentleman much given to gambling and losing. In his last match with Harry Warrington he wins the latter's remaining money but is unable to help his kinsman when he is sent to debtors' prison.

Mr. Sampson, the chaplain at Castlewood in England and Harry Warrington's good friend. Kind but foolish, Mr. Sampson is constantly in debt and depends upon Harry's generosity for funds. A worldly clergyman, he is fond of the bottle.

Gumbo, Harry's colored slave, popular with the domestics in England, where he marries a white maid. He brags unendingly about his master's great fortune and home in Virginia.

Colonel Lambert, the husband of an old friend of Madame Warrington. He takes Harry in and doctors him when the young man falls from a horse while on the way to Tunbridge Wells with Lady Castlewood and her daughter Maria. Fond of Harry, the Colonel is greatly distressed by stories about the young man's wild ways in London, and he tries to offer him his guidance. Colonel Lambert is the father of Theo, whom George Warrington marries, and Hetty, who becomes Harry's second wife.

Mrs. Lambert, the Colonel's wife, an old school friend of Madame Warrington.

Hetty Lambert, the older daughter of Colonel and Mrs. Lambert, a great beauty and an accomplished pianist. Secretly in love with Harry Warrington, she conceals her feeling because she knows that he is supposed to marry Lady Maria Esmond. At the end of the story she becomes his second wife.

Theo Lambert, Hetty's sister. She marries George Warrington.

Fanny Mountain, the daughter of Mrs. Warrington's housekeeper. She changes from a gentle girl to a firm-minded woman, and after her marriage to Harry Warrington she domineers him in many ways. An ardent revolutionist, she imbues Harry with some of her fervor and follows him while he serves in campaigns against the British. She dies soon after the close of the war.

Mrs. Mountain, her mother, Madame Warrington's good friend and capable housekeeper. When her daughter and Harry announce that they plan to be married, Mrs. Mountain leaves Mrs. Warrington because of the latter's insults to her daughter.

Sir Miles Warrington, a baronet, one of Harry Warrington's uncles in England. A jolly, fat rustic man in appearance and manner, Sir Miles is actually very selfish and cold. When Harry is in prison, Sir Miles makes no attempt to help his nephew, and he disparages the young man before his family. When Sir Miles dies, George Warrington inherits his estate and title.

Lady Warrington, the wife of Sir Miles and a religious addict who constantly thrusts her pamphlets on luckless friends. When Harry Warrington is in prison she sends him a set of tracts, but that is the extent of her help to her nephew.

Dora and
Flora Warrington, the daughters of Sir Miles. Although much taken with their cousin Harry, they distrust him as a bad person because of his profligate ways and their mother's warnings.

Tom Claypool, Dora's intended husband, the village gossip who carries the news of Harry's imprisonment to the Warrington family at their country estate.

Mademoiselle Cattarina, a French ballet dancer, one of the gay charmers at Tunbridge Wells to whom Harry pays court. He breaks off the affair when she becomes too demanding.

George Washington, a neighbor of the Warringtons in Virginia, a simple, upright man of the most scrupulous gravity and good breeding. When George Warrington hears that Colonel Washington is to marry a widow, he immediately concludes that the bride will be Madame Warrington. George challenges the Colonel to a duel, but makes a retraction when the true state of affairs is revealed by Mrs. Mountain.

Mr. Dempster, the Warrington boys' Jacobite tutor.

Lord March, one of Harry Warrington's friends at Tunbridge Wells. A young man of fashion, he lives in London, and the two meet frequently in the city.

Lord Morris, another of Harry Warrington's drinking, gambling companions.

The Countess of Yarmouth Walmoden, one of the Baroness Bernstein's card-playing friends at Tunbridge Wells.

Mrs. Betty, Lady Maria Esmond's maid, who takes a fancy to Gumbo and gets drunk with him and Case.

Case, the Baroness Bernstein's servant.

Mr. Draper, lawyer to the Esmond family. A patronizing man, he conducts Harry Warrington about London until the latter tires of him and asks to be left alone.

THE VISION OF WILLIAM, CONCERNING PIERS THE PLOWMAN

Author: William Langland (c. 1332-c. 1400)
Time of action: Fourteenth century
First transcribed: c. 1362, c. 1377; complete version c. 1395

PRINCIPAL CHARACTERS

Piers the Plowman, the hard-working, sincere, and honest plowman who with each appearance in the poem becomes more clearly an incarnation of Christ. In the poet's second vision Piers volunteers to lead the assembly of the seven deadly sins to Holy Truth and thus he earns a pardon for himself and his heirs forever. The third vision of the poet concerns Piers' quests for the states of Do-Well, Do-Better, and Do-Best. Piers also explains the Tree of Charity and the nature of the Trinity of God to the poet and appears as the Good Samaritan, as the builder of the Church, and as God's champion against Satan.

William, the Poet. In this poem, the poet has a series of visions, each concerned with man's relationship to God in every aspect of medieval life. The first vision relates the contest between Lady Mede and Conscience while the next two dreams are visions of Piers the Plowman. In addition to the quest for Truth (God)

the poet also digresses on the topics of sin and virtue, the value of learning, the clergy and the laity, and Christian tradition.

Lady Mede, an allegorical character representing both just reward and bribery. She appears in the first vision as the proposed, but unwanted, bride of Conscience.

Lady Holy Chuch, the lady who explains the first vision to the poet.

Conscience,
Reason, and
False, allegorical characters.

Dame-Work-While-I-Am-Able, the wife of Piers.

Do-This-Or-Thy-Dame-Shall-Beat-Thee, Piers' daughter.

Suffer-Thy-Sovereigns-To-Have-Their-Wishes-Dare-Not-Judge-Them-For-If-Thou-Dost-Thou-Shalt-Dearly-Abide-It, Piers' son.

VIVIAN GREY

Author: Benjamin Disraeli (1804-1881)
Time of action: Early nineteenth century
First published: 1826-1827

Vivian Grey, an ambitious young Englishman who desires a political career. His unscrupulous conduct ends that career. Traveling in Germany afterward, he learns how terrible politics can be and realizes how immoral his own conduct has been.

Mr. Dallas, proprietor of a school from which Vivian Grey is expelled.

Sidney Lorraine, the Marquess of Carabas, an incompetent who has been turned out of office. His support in politics is sought by Vivian because the man has a title and represents the aristocracy.

Mrs. Felix Lorraine, the fashionable sister-in-law of Sidney. Vivian attempts an affair with her, but she falls in love with Frederick Cleveland.

Frederick Cleveland, a retired minister of state. He gives his support for a time to Vivian. When he is insulted by Vivian, the two fight a duel, and Cleveland is killed.

Baron Eugene von Konigstein, a worldly German nobleman who becomes Vivian's friend for a time while the two are studying at Heidelberg. The Baron cheats at cards.

Essper George, a conjurer. He becomes Vivian's valet. He is killed during a storm, and his death has a sobering effect on Vivian.

Lady Madeleine Trevor, a friend of Vivian's father.

Mr. St. George, Lady Madeleine Trevor's brother.

Violet Fane, a friend of Lady Madeleine. She dies of natural causes in Vivian's arms, causing him to be grief-stricken.

Mr. Beckendorff, a recluse who is host to Vivian. He conspires to become prime minister of the Duchy of Reisenberg. When Vivian falls in love with Sybilla, Beckendorff plans to kill him but relents on condition that Vivian leave the duchy.

The Prince of Little Lilliput, a guest at Beckendorff's home. He becomes Vivian's friend and introduces the Englishman to court circles in Germany.

Sybilla, a beautiful young baroness. Vivian falls in love with her. But he is disillusioned when he learns that for political reasons the woman must marry a deformed, half-witted prince.

VOLPONE

Author: Ben Jonson (1573?-1637)
Time of action: Sixteenth century
First presented: 1605

PRINCIPAL CHARACTERS

Volpone (vŏl·pō′nä), the Fox, a Venetian magnifico. Delighting in foxlike trickery, Volpone scorns the easy gain of cheating widows and orphans and the hard gain of labor. He chooses for his victims Venice's leading crooked advocate, its most greedy and dishonest merchant, and its most hardened miser. The

joy of the chase of gold and jewels belonging to other men is keener to him than the possession. He also delights in acting, both onstage and off. To fool others with disguises, makeup, and changes of voice is a passion with him. His three weaknesses are excessive trust of his unreliable parasite Mosca, his ungovernable desire for Corvino's virtuous wife Celia, and his overconfidence in his ability to deceive. When defeated, however, he shows a humorous and sporting self-knowledge and resignation to his punishment.

Mosca (mŏs'kä), the Gadfly, Volpone's malicious and witty parasite. Acting as the chief instrument of Volpone's trickery and the frequent instigator of additional pranks, he keeps the plot moving. Under cover of tormenting Volpone's victims, he often engages in annoying Volpone himself, almost always with impunity. His tantalizing of Volpone with sensuous descriptions of Celia sets in train the events that finally destroy both his master and himself. A master improviser of deceit and pranks, he becomes in love with his dear self, underestimates his master, and falls victim to his own overconfidence and greed. He whines and curses as he is dragged away to punishment.

Voltore (vŏl·tō'rä), the Vulture, an advocate. A ruthless and voracious scavenger seeking the spoils of the dead, he yearns for Volpone's wealth. He is willing to connive whenever gain is apparent. A dangerous man when thwarted, he helps Volpone gain acquittal in his first trial; then, tormented beyond endurance by Mosca, who pretends that Volpone is dead and has left Voltore nothing, the lawyer reverses himself and causes the collapse of Volpone's plans.

Corbaccio (kôr·bä't·chō), the Raven, an aged miser. Feeble, stone-deaf, pathologically greedy, he is willing to risk his son's inheritance to have Volpone exchange wills with him; he is also willing to have Mosca administer poison in Volpone's sleeping draft to hasten the validation of the will.

Corvino (kôr·vē'nō), the Crow, the merchant husband of Celia. Mean-spirited, cowardly, and insanely jealous of his beautiful wife, he is the most repulsive of Volpone's victims. His greed is sufficient to counteract his jealousy, and he is willing to leave his wife in Volpone's hands in order to assure his future as Volpone's heir.

Celia (sēl'yä), Corvino's virtuous wife. Cursed with a repulsive and pathologically jealous husband, the heavenly Celia faces her slander and perils with noble fortitude.

Bonario (bō·nä'ryō), the good son of Corbaccio. He is the savior of Celia when she is helpless in Volpone's clutches.

Lady Politic Would-Be, a parrot-voiced, shallow-brained Englishwoman. She grates on Volpone's sensibilities so much that he is willing to lose the financial gain which she thrusts upon him. At any price he wishes to be rid of "my madam with the everlasting voice." Her unreasonable jealousy makes her a gullible tool when Mosca accuses her husband of having an affair with Celia; her resulting false testimony saves Volpone and convicts Celia and Bonario at the first trial.

Sir Politic Would-Be, a gullible, naïve traveler. Eager to be thought a member of the inner circle of state knowledge, Sir Pol has a sinister explanation for even the most commonplace actions. He furnishes the picture of the ridiculous English tourist on the Continent.

Peregrine (pĕr'ə·grĭn), a sophisticated traveler. He finds amusement, mixed with contempt, in the credulities and foibles of Sir Pol.

Androgyno (ăn·droj'ə·nō), the hermaphrodite,
Castrone (kä·strō'nē), the eunuch, and
Nano (nä'nō), the dwarf, household freaks kept by Volpone for amusement.

Avocatori (ä·vō'kä·tō'rē), the four judges. The ambition of the fourth, to marry his daughter to Mosca, stirs Volpone to make his confession, which saves Bonario and Celia and brings punishment on the evildoers.

VOLUPTÉ

Author: Charles Augustin Sainte-Beuve (1804-1869)
Time of action: Early nineteenth century
First published: 1832

PRINCIPAL CHARACTERS

Amaury (à·mō·rē'), the narrator, later a priest. A sensitive, melancholy youth, he engages in a platonic love affair with Madame de Couaën after putting aside Amélie de Liniers, the young girl who loves him, and when the Marquis de Couaën is arrested, he takes over her affairs. When she rejoins her husband at Blois, Amaury has an unrewarding affair with Madame R. until he realizes the unhappiness he has caused three women. He takes holy orders and leaves for America soon after Madame de Couaën's death.

Madame de Couaën (də kwà·äṅ'), the Irish wife of the Marquis. She truly loves her husband, and can return only platonic love for Amaury; yet, she feels that no one can understand her as he does. She remains with her husband and is saddened by Amaury's affair with Madame R.

Madame R. (ěr'), wife of a royalist sympathizer. Lonely and disillusioned, she becomes Amaury's constant companion in Paris. Although she refuses to become his mistress, she is jealous of his love for Madame de Couaën.

The Marquis de Couaën, an influential figure in royalist circles. A friend of Amaury, he is arrested in Paris and later is sent to Blois.

Amélie de Liniers (à·mē·lē' də lē·nyà'), the granddaughter of Monsieur de Greneuc. She is the unmarried girl in Amaury's life.

Monsieur R. and
Monsieur D., royalist sympathizers.

Monsieur and Madame de Greneuc (də grə·nœk'), friends of Amaury in his youth.

Monsieur Ploa (plô·à), Amaury's Latin teacher.

WAITING FOR GODOT

Author: Samuel Beckett (1906-   )
Time of action: The present
First presented: 1952

PRINCIPAL CHARACTERS

Vladimir (Didi) (vlà·dē·mēr'; dē·dē')
and
Estragon (Gogo) (ĕs·trà·gōn'; gô·gō'), two tramps. In this play action is unimportant; the characters remain undeveloped as the tramps wait impatiently for Godot, who remains a mysterious entity, possibly a local land owner but also a symbol of man's spiritual seeking. They gnaw carrots, rest their tired feet, and engage in other simple activities while their conversations reveal the helplessness of their situation. Throughout the play there is every suggestion that the two live estranged from a state of grace which is hoped for but never realized. Often considering suicide, they are caught in a calm of inactivity between hope and de-

1215

spair in their longing for salvation, which is linked somehow with Godot. When the play ends, the two are still waiting for the promised appearance of Godot.

Pozzo (pō·zō′), a materialist. A rich, boisterous tyrant, he is obviously an expounder of Nietzschean doctrines and materialistic concepts. Pozzo admits that Lucky has taught him all the beautiful things he knows, but now his servant has become unbearable and is driving him mad. At first he drives his servant with a rope; however, when he reappears, blinded in symbolic fashion by his own worldly successes and romantic pessimism, he must be led by his mute servant.

Lucky (lü·kē′), Pozzo's servant. Born a peasant, he gives the impression of a new proletarian, the symbol of modern man's belief in the promises and miracles of science. Lucky first appears driven by Pozzo at the end of a rope. Ordered to think for the group, he delivers the wildest, most brilliantly sustained monologue of the play. When he next appears, he is leading the blind Pozzo, but he is mute.

A Boy, a messenger from Godot.

WALLENSTEIN

Author: Johann Christoph Friedrich von Schiller (1759-1805)
Time of action: The Thirty Years' War
First presented: 1799

PRINCIPAL CHARACTERS

Albrecht Wallenstein (äl·brĕkht väl′ən-shtīn), Duke of Friedland, the general of Emperor Ferdinand's forces in the Thirty Years' War. His experience follows the well-known pattern displayed by any over-ambitious, capable leader. Favored by the court for his military prowess in raising and leading a large army to subdue the Protestant states and to repel the Swedish invaders, Wallenstein loses his sense of perspective concerning his real function to the government. Fearful that other leaders will rise above him and greatly admired by his soldiers, he seeks self-aggrandizement. Through a long series of political intrigues, involving Wallenstein's officers, and personal complications, involving various members of his family, Wallenstein's fate is precarious. Either blind to the realities of the intrigue he knows so well or to the recollection of his once strong favor with the court, he fails to heed the advice of those who would avert his downfall. Such naïveté leads to his murder on orders of one of his trusted commanders.

Prince Octavio Piccolomini (ōk·tä′fyō pēk·kō·lô′mē·nē), Duke of Amalfi, Wallenstein's lieutenant general and life-long friend. Loyal to his leader, Piccolomini serves him until the general's ambitions and aims become apparent. Piccolomini's apparent scruples and the news that Wallenstein is to be deposed change the rapport between the two men. Imminence of his own promotion as generalissimo completes the rift, and Piccolomini's chief task becomes the enlightenment of his own son, an officer, to Wallenstein's negotiations with the enemy. By leading Wallenstein's forces to defection through persuasion and deception, and by winning officers away from the once-powerful Wallenstein, Piccolomini completes his work and is given a princedom.

Max Piccolomini, his son, a regimental colonel, who is faithful to Wallenstein in the face of evidence of the general's treachery. When Max, who is loyal to the Emperor, is convinced of his leader's treason—through Wallenstein's own confession—the young man tries to get Wallenstein to retract his negotiations with the Saxons and the Swedes. Max, betrothed to Wallenstein's daughter, leaves with his forces of the imperial army, his decision to stay honorable having the concurrence of his betrothed, who says she cannot love him if he betrays his own conscience. The noble young Max is killed in a battle against the Swedes, his death being directly attributable to the man whom he had trusted and admired.

Butler, a regimental commander. An Irish soldier of fortune, he remains loyal to Wallenstein, despite the defection of the greater part of the army, until Octavio Piccolomini leads him to believe that Wallenstein has hindered Butler's promotion and insulted him. Learning of the successes of the Swedish forces to be joined by Wallenstein's remaining troops, Butler arranges the murders of Wallenstein and the officers who have remained with Wallenstein.

Count von Questenberg, the war commissioner. As the envoy from the Emperor, Questenberg delivers word of Wallenstein's deposition. Through his recital of battles lost to the enemy, the reasons for the general's dismissal, Wallenstein's treachery is revealed. The scenes with Questenberg point up the fidelity of Wallenstein's officers.

Field Marshal Illo (ĕl'lō), Wallenstein's confidant. He cunningly induces the officers, under the influence of wine, to sign a pledge of loyalty to Wallenstein. He has removed a proviso from the pledge, safeguarding their loyalty to the Emperor. His deceptions and his allegiance to Wallenstein bring about his murder.

Countess Terzky, Wallenstein's sister-in-law, who sees the advantage of an alliance between Max Piccolomini and Wallenstein's daughter. The Countess leaves no stone unturned in furthering the aims of Wallenstein. Because family and success mean so much to her, she cannot accept Wallenstein's reverses, and she poisons herself.

The Duchess of Friedland, Wallenstein's wife, who admonishes her husband to temper his ambitions. She reports to him that she has heard rumors about his tactics and describes him as the despot he has become.

Thekla (tāk'lä), Wallenstein's daughter, who through Countess Terzky's connivances becomes attracted to Max Piccolomini. Despite her real love for him, she tells him to obey his conscience and desert her father's cause. After Thekla learns of Max's heroic death she goes to his tomb to die.

Count Terzky, the commander of several regiments. Having remained loyal to Wallenstein through the thick of the treachery, he is slain by Butler's men.

Gordon, Governor of Egra and commander of the citadel. Through Gordon, much of Butler's plan for murdering his adversaries is revealed. Gordon, a peaceful person, advocates deliberation rather than haste, especially where lives are concerned. He discourages Butler in his plans.

Devereux and
Macdonald, captains under Butler, who carry out Butler's plot to murder Illo, Terzky, and Wallenstein.

Colonel Wrangel, the Swedish envoy with whom Wallenstein negotiates for Swedish troops in return for the territories Wallenstein would yield to those troops in feigned battles.

THE WANDERER

Author: Alain-Fournier (Henri Alain Fournier, 1886-1914)
Time of action: Nineteenth century
First published: 1913

Augustin Meaulnes (ō·gü·stän′ mōln′), a romantic, dreamily adventurous new boy at Sainte-Agathe's School who magnetically draws the other children to him. After leaving Sainte-Agathe's he lives in Paris with Valentine, whom he angrily leaves after learning of her love for Frantz. He marries and deserts Yvonne; but later, grief-stricken when informed of Yvonne's death, he lovingly accepts the care of his young daughter.

François Seurel (frän·swä′ sœ·rěl′), son of M. and Mme. Seurel. Prevented by a hip infection from playing with the village boys, he idolizes Meaulnes. After completing his own schooling he joins his parents as a teacher in the school. He brings Yvonne and the wandering Meaulnes together and is saddened and puzzled over Meaulnes' later desertion of her.

Frantz de Galais (fränts də gà·lě′, gà′lä′), an unhappy young aristocrat who joins a gipsy band after losing his fiancée and who later remains briefly at Sainte-Agathe's. Through Meaulnes he finally finds his lost love.

Yvonne de Galais (ē·vôn′ də ga·lě′), Frantz's sister loved by Meaulnes, who marries and then deserts her. She dies after the birth of a daughter.

Valentine Blondeau (và·län·tēn′ blôn·dō′), Frantz's fiancée, a peasant girl who flees from her home because she feels that a peasant girl should not marry an aristocrat; she becomes a dressmaker in Paris. She is later the mistress of Meaulnes, who deserts her when he discovers that she is Frantz's lost fiancée. Through Meaulnes the separated lovers are at last reunited.

M. Seurel (sœ·rěl′), head of the Middle School and one of the Higher Elementary classes at Sainte-Agathe's.

Mme. Seurel (sœ·rěl′), his wife, teacher of the younger children.

Millie Seurel (mē·lě′ sœ·rěl′), their daughter.

M. and Mme. Charpentier (shär·pän·tyä′), grandparents of François.

THE WANDERING JEW

Author: Eugène Sue (1804-1857)
Time of action: 1831-1832
First published: 1844-1845

PRINCIPAL CHARACTERS

Samuel (sà·mü·ěl′), the Wandering Jew, who is condemned to wander undying through the centuries after he mocked Christ on the day of the Crucifixion. He invested for a friend a small sum of money, now grown into an enormous fortune, and his friend's descendants are to claim the money on a certain day in 1832. After the last of these heirs dies, Samuel goes to a lonely spot where stands a cross on a hill. There he gives

thanks that his punishment is over at last.

Herodias (ā·rō·dyàs′), who demanded the head of John the Baptist on a charger. Also condemned to live through the centuries, she is driven by some power to the meeting place where the will is being read. There she temporarily foils a wicked Jesuit plot by producing a codicil to the will, suspending its execution for three months. At last she too joins Samuel by the cross and echoes his words.

[Marius de Rennepont (mȧ·r'yüs' də rĕn·pōn'), Samuel's friend in the seventeenth century, whose modest wealth, wisely invested by Samuel, results in the huge fortune his ill-fated descendants gather to share.]

Rodin (rô·dăn'), the secretary to the Provincial of the Jesuits. His villainous scheming is responsible for most of the tragedy. At last he is killed by a mysterious Indian poison.

Marshal Simon (sē·mōn'), an exiled Bonapartist hero.

François Baudoin (frän·swä' bō·dwăn'), called Dagobert (dȧ·gô·bĕr'), the Marshal's faithful friend. He accompanies the Marshal's daughters from Siberia to Paris to claim their share of the legacy.

Blanche Simon (blänsh' sē·mōn') and Rose Simon (rōz' sē·mōn'), the Marshal's daughters. Taken to a hospital during a cholera epidemic, they die of the disease.

Gabriel de Rennepont (gȧ·bryĕl' də rĕn·pōn'), who is persuaded to become a Jesuit priest by evil Jesuits who intend to make sure he is the only heir. In this they are successful, but the entire inheritance is lost by fire, and Gabriel then retires to live out his brief life with the Baudoin family.

Adrienne de Cardoville (ȧ·dryĕn' də kȧr·dô·vēl'), another Rennepont descendant. Falsely declared insane and committed to an asylum before the first reading of the will, she is later released. At last, the victim of a malicious report which results in a slaying, she chooses to die with her lover.

Prince Djalma (dzhȧl'mȧ'), another Rennepont heir. Led to believe that Adrienne is another man's mistress, he kills a woman he mistakes for Adrienne and discovers his mistake only after he has swallowed poison.

Agricola Baudoin (ȧ·grē·kô·lȧ' bō·dwăn'), Dagobert's son. He is the man whom Prince Djalma, deceived, believes to be Adrienne's lover.

Jacques de Rennepont (zhȧk' də rĕn·pōn'), a good-hearted sensualist named Couche-tout-Nud (kōōsh·tōō·nüd'). Another heir, he is first jailed for debt. Later, he is separated from his mistress and dies after an orgy induced by a Jesuit agent.

François Hardy (frän·swä' ȧr·dē'), a benevolent manufacturer and an heir. After the burning of his factory and the spiriting away of his young mistress, he is taken to a Jesuit retreat where he accepts the doctrines of the order and dies as a result of the penances and fasts.

M. l'Abbe d'Aigrigny (mə·syœ' lȧ·bā' dĕ·grēn·yē'), Provincial of the Jesuits.

THE WANDERING SCHOLAR FROM PARADISE

Author: Hans Sachs (1494-1576)
Time of action: Sixteenth century
First presented: 1550

PRINCIPAL CHARACTERS

The Wandering Scholar, a witty, unscrupulous student from Paris. Taking advantage of the mistake of a simple-minded widow, who misunderstands his origin as "Paradise" instead of "Paris," he plays on her sympathies for her departed first husband to wheedle goods and money from her to take to the poor man in Paradise. When the present husband chases him, he hides the bundle and his identifying yellow scarf, sends the husband on foot across a bog while he "watches the horse," and then rides merrily away praising the generosity of both wife and husband.

The Wife, a simple-minded, good-hearted widow. Remembering with affection her open-handed first husband, and weary of her skinflint second, she sends goods and money to Paradise by the Scholar. When the second husband chases the Scholar in anger, but returns

to tell her that he gave the Scholar his horse to shorten the distance to Paradise, she is carried away with affectionate rapture and expresses a hope that she will be able to outlive him and send him goods in Paradise.

The Husband, a grouchy, tight-fisted farmer. His anger at his wife for being tricked by the Scholar gives way to shame when he himself is taken in and loses the horse. He accepts her affection as a balance for her stupidity.

WAR AND PEACE

Author: Count Leo Tolstoy (1828-1910)
Time of action: 1805-1813
First published: 1865-1869

PRINCIPAL CHARACTERS

Pierre Bezuhov (pyĕr′ bĕ·zōō′khəf), the illegitimate son of wealthy Count Cyril Bezuhov. Clumsy, stout, and uncommonly tall, he is at first spurned by the social set but much admired after his father leaves him a fortune. He is beguiled into a marriage with Hélène Kuragina, who in turn is unfaithful to him. For long years Pierre searches for peace of mind, a meaning in life. He seeks for it in philanthropy, in the dissipations of society, in wine, in heroic feats of self-sacrifice during the war with Napoleon. Finally he gains such an internal harmony through witnessing the horror of death on the battlefield and by learning to share the misery of the human race. At the conclusion of the novel he marries Natasha Rostova, whom he has long secretly loved.

Princess Natasha Rostova (nä·tä′shə rôs-tōf′ə), the beautiful daughter of Count Ilya Rostov. Regularly in attendance at all social functions, she is admired by a host of suitors. She becomes engaged to the wealthy and handsome Prince Andrey Bolkonsky; however, the marriage is postponed for a year at Andrey's father's request. During this engagement

period, Natasha ruins the proposed marriage and scandalizes herself by attempting to elope with the rake Anatole Kuragin. When Andrey is mortally wounded, she faithfully cares for him and receives his forgiveness. Later she becomes the wife of Pierre Bezuhov.

Princess Hélène Kuragina (el′ĕn kōō′rə-gĭn·ə), "the most fascinating woman in Petersburg" who becomes Pierre Bezuhov's wife. Although she has no love for Pierre, she marries him for the advantage of wealth and social position. Marriage in no way hampers her amours, and she constantly entertains and encourages prosperous admirers. Essentially she is a superficial and shallow individual, seemingly unperturbed by the misery and suffering of the war around her. Her happiness is only a façade, however, for the tragedy of loneliness and isolation; unable to find the meaning of life in true love and affection, she takes her own life by an overdose of medicine.

Count Nikolay Rostov (nĭ·kô·läy′ rôs-tōf′), Natasha's handsome older brother, who distinguishes himself as a cavalry officer in the Russian army. It is long supposed that he will wed Sonya, his cousin, who lives with the Rostov family; however, the financial ruination of his family makes necessary a more profitable match with Princess Marya Bolkonskaya. When the Russian army is in retreat, he saves Marya from the rebellious peasants on her estate.

Princess Marya Bolkonskaya (mä'ryä vôl·kōn'skī·yə), Prince Andrey Bolkonsky's sister, who endures the eccentricities of a tyrannical father. The old Prince, desirous of Marya as a nurse and companion, methodically destroys her chances of marriage by refusing to entertain would-be suitors. Resigned to her fate, she takes refuge in an intense religious conviction, entertaining and sponsoring "God's Folk," peasants who have had various mystical experiences. After the deaths of her father and brother, she desires the life of a recluse; but her admiration and love for Nikolay Rostov, whom she later marries, restores her to a normal life.

Sonya (sō'nyä), Nikolay Rostov's poor cousin, the affectionate companion of Natasha in the Rostov family. For the sake of allowing Nikolay to make a more advantageous marriage, she releases him from a childhood pledge.

Prince Andrey Bolkonsky (än·drā' vôl·kōn'skĭy), a wealthy nobleman, the son of an eccentric father and the brother of Marya. At the battle of Austerlitz he fights valiantly, rallying the Russian troops by charging directly into the front line while waving the Russian flag. Missing in action, he is assumed dead, but he later returns after having been nursed to health by peasants of the countryside. He becomes engaged to Natasha Rostova but the marriage is canceled as a result of Natasha's indiscretions. Although he swears never to fight again, his sense of duty compels him to enlist when France invades Russian soil. Again wounded, he dies in Natasha's arms, having been reconciled to her through her untiring devotion to him during his illness.

Princess Lise Bolkonskaya (lĭ'sə vôl·kōn'-skī·yə), the beautiful and sensitive wife of Prince Andrey. She dies in childbirth.

Nikolushka Bolkonsky (nĭ·kō·lōō'shkə vôl·kōn'skĭy), the young son of Prince Andrey and his wife Lise. Count Nikolay Rostov and his wife Marya adopt the child after Prince Andrey's death.

Prince Nikolay Bolkonsky (nĭ·kô·läy' vôl·kōn'skĭy), the tyrannical and eccentric father of Andrey and Marya.

Prince Anatole Kuragin (ä·nä·tō'lĭy kōō'-rə·gĭn), Hélène's brother, a profligate. Although previously forced into marriage, he woos Natasha Rostova and subjects her to scandal and ridicule.

Prince Vasily Kuragin (vä·sē'lyə kōō'rə-gĭn), the head of the Kuragin and the father of Anatole and Hélène.

Prince Hippolyte Kuragin (hĭp·pō'lĭt·ə kōō'rə·gĭn), his feeble-minded younger son.

Count Ilya Rostov (ēl·yä' rôs·tôf'), a wealthy nobleman.

Countess Natalya Rostova (nä·täl'yə rôs-tôf'ə), his wife.

Countess Vera Rostova (vyě'rə rôs·tôf'ə), their older daughter.

Count Petya Rostov (pyě'tyə rôs·tôf'), their younger son.

Lieutenant Alphose Berg, an officer and intimate friend of the Rostov family. He marries the Countess Vera.

Prince Boris Drubetskoy (bô·rĭs' drōō-bět'skōy), a fashionable and ambitious friend of the Rostovs, a successful staff officer.

Princess Anna Drubetskaya (än'nə drōō-bět'skī·yə), the mother of Prince Boris, an impoverished noblewoman.

Julie Karagina (zhü·lē' kä·rə·gĭn·ə), a wealthy young woman who marries Prince Boris Drubetskoy.

Anna Scherer (än'nə shā'rər), maid of honor to the Empress Marya Fedorovna. Her salon is a meeting place for the highest St. Petersburg society.

General Michael Kutuzov (mĭ·hä·īl' kōō·tōō'zəf), appointed commander-in-chief of the Russian army in August, 1812. Obese and slovenly, he is disliked by his fellow officers, and his military tactics are considered obsolete. Yet it is to him that Tsar Alexander I and all Russia turn when Napoleon boldly advances upon Russian soil. Even then, however, he is viciously criticized when, after a prolonged and costly battle at Smolensk, he chooses not to defend Moscow by what he considers a useless and hopeless encounter. His wily scheme of "time and patience" proves sound after Napoleon, his line over-extended and the Russian winter fast approaching, is forced to withdraw his forces, which are virtually annihilated by hunger, cold, and guerrilla warfare.

Napoleon Bonaparte, the renowned commander of the French Grand Armée. Worshiped and admired by the French, feared by the Russians, he shatters the myth of his invincibility during his disastrous Russian campaign.

Mademoiselle Bourienne, a companion of Marya in the Bolkonsky family. In his senility, Count Bolkonsky finds her alluring and sympathetic.

THE WAR OF THE WORLDS

Author: H. G. Wells (1866-1946)
Time of action: Late nineteenth century
First published: 1898

PRINCIPAL CHARACTERS

The Narrator, a man of intellectual curiosity who is interested in observing Mars through a telescope. One day he sees harmless-appearing creatures emerging from a projectile fallen to earth. Undisturbed because they seem helpless, the Martians set to work making curious machines. These finished, they begin to lay waste the countryside. The Narrator, after taking his wife to Leatherhead, returns home to find the area defenseless against the Martians' metal monsters. The Martians move on to London, which becomes a ruined city, but at last they fall victim to earthly bacteria and the world is saved.

His Wife, who is taken by the Narrator to Leatherhead to escape the Martians' destruction. Finally, after the deaths of the Martians, the Narrator and his wife are reunited.

An Artilleryman, the only survivor of his outfit. He and the Narrator escape together by hiding in bushes and streams.

A Curate, with whom the Narrator hides in a deserted cellar. The curate goes raving mad and, because silence is necessary to escape detection by the Martians, the Narrator is forced to kill him. His body is taken by one of the Martians, whose diet consists of the blood of their victims.

THE WARDEN

Author: Anthony Trollope (1815-1882)
Time of action: Mid-nineteenth century
First published: 1855

The Rev. Septimus Harding, a kind and gentle man who had been a minor canon near Barchester for many years. At the age of fifty, he had become precentor of Barchester Cathedral, a position which also included the wardenship of Hiram's Hospital. The latter was an alms house for twelve old men established by the will of John Hiram four centuries before. Through the efforts of John Bold, a local reformer, and the "Jupiter," a newspaper devoted to attacking the greed and power of the Church, Mr. Harding is accused of receiving too large an income from his management of the hospital. The legal issue is ambiguous and the almshouse has been well-managed, but Mr. Harding, distressed that others might question the justice of his position, resigns. All the legal and ecclesiastical officials, even John Bold himself, protest the resignation. After the suit has been dropped the Bishop offers the Warden a position as chaplain in the Bishop's house, but Mr. Harding refuses this charity and lives in poor lodgings in town, supported only by his tiny living near the Cathedral Close.

Eleanor Harding, the favorite and younger daughter of Mr. Septimus Harding. She is in love with John Bold. Fully cognizant of her father's sensitivity, she understands why he wants to resign his wardenship. In a scene which reveals their love for each other, she begs John Bold to drop the suit, as he does. She marries Bold, and her father frequently visits the couple.

The Rev. Theophilus Grantly, Archdeacon of Barchester and rector of Plumstead Episcopi. The son of the Bishop and the son-in-law of Mr. Harding, Archdeacon Grantly believes in "the sacred justice of all ecclesiastical revenues." Recognized as more worldly than his fellow churchmen, he insists that Mr. Harding take a strong stand against the lawsuit and the press, and he disapproves strongly of Eleanor's interest in John Bold.

Susan Grantly, the wife of Archdeacon Grantly and the older daughter of Mr. Harding. She joins her husband in trying to persuade her father to insist on the prerogatives of the Church.

Bishop Grantly, the father of Archdeacon Grantly. Over seventy, the bland, kindly Bishop of Barchester warmly supports Mr. Harding, but leaves most of the controversial campaigning to his son.

John Bold, a surgeon and town councilor, genuinely concerned with reform. He honestly feels that John Hiram's will did not provide for the income the Warden receives, and he begins the action by instituting a lawsuit. When he is persuaded that the lawsuit has created more injustice than it has ameliorated, he willingly drops the charges.

Mary Bold, the older sister of John Bold. A kindly woman, she promotes the engagement of her brother to Eleanor Harding, her best friend.

John Bunce, the oldest of the beadsmen at Hiram's Hospital. He is entirely loyal to Mr. Harding.

Abel Handy, another beadsman at Hiram's Hospital, selfishly disloyal to Mr. Harding.

Tom Towers, a reporter for the "Jupiter." He maintains, in print, that Mr. Harding has unjustly received more money than Hiram's will intended. His attacks, originating from an anticlerical point of view, are both personal and unfair.

Sir Abraham Haphazard, an eminent Queens' Counsel and Attorney General. He is hired to defend Mr. Harding and is a conservative adherent of ecclesiastical privilege.

Mr. Finney, the solicitor hired by John Bold to collect evidence against the Warden. He gets most of the inmates of Hiram's Hospital to sign a petition protesting the management by promising them each one hundred pounds per year.

Doctor Pessimist Anticant, a Scots pamphleteer, one of whose moral and reforming pamphlets "exposes" Mr. Harding.

Mr. Popular Sentiment, a muckraking novelist whose work, "Almshouse," makes the clergyman a vicious monster depriving the old beadsmen of all sustenance.

Chadwick, the Bishop's steward and the man who farms John Hiram's estate.

Charles James Grantly, the oldest child of Archdeacon Grantly, an exact, careful boy.

Henry Grantly, the second and favorite son of Archdeacon Grantly, the most "brilliant" of the children.

Samuel Grantly, the sneaky, cunning child of Archdeacon Grantly.

Florinda and
Grizzel Grantly, daughters of Archdeacon Grantly.

WASHINGTON SQUARE

Author: Henry James (1843-1916)
Time of action: Mid-nineteenth century
First published: 1881

PRINCIPAL CHARACTERS

Catherine Sloper, an heiress who remains steadfast to her ideal of loyalty. Irreparably harmed by the harshness of her father and the coldness of a calculating suitor, Catherine reëstablishes her life to fill the void of love removed. True to her vision, she neither mopes nor is vindictive; she merely compensates by filling her time with charitable and sociable acts, blending her life into her fashionable but anachronistic Washington Square home. Never one to complain, she does one time cry out against her father's heartlessness, her lover's lack of heart, and her meddling aunt's perverse though romantic indiscretions. She forever after forgives but never really forgets, something of tenderness and devotion having gone out of her who was, in the beginning, richly endowed with these virtues.

Austin Sloper, her socialite physician father whose unfortunate loss of a beautiful wife and son leaves him with no comfort in his plain, simple-hearted daughter. Brilliant and incisive as he is, Dr. Sloper is unable to ridicule Catherine's love out of existence or to supplant love with surface intellectuality. Although he sees clearly the suitor's contrivance, he can never act unselfishly or with unattached love to the humble daughter who both dotes on him and fears him. He lives on and by irony, himself finally the victim of a deeper sarcasm. Though his perspicacity makes him aware of events and their consequences, he never understands their meanings. He dies believing that he has thwarted a lovers' plot to gain his fortune, without knowing he has helped kill that love.

Morris Townsend, the suitor who gives up a small fortune offered with love and devotion for a larger fortune which he cannot manage to earn or contrive. As Catherine thinks, he is a man with charming manners and unrealized intellectual abilities; but he is also a shallow, egoistic, altogether selfish aging young man who has squandered his own small inheritance, sponged off his poor and widowed sister, and set his cap for a

1224

plain heiress whose love he rejects when the larger fortune is withheld by her father. Aging as a caricature of his youthful self, he unsuccessfully offers himself to the heiress as one worth waiting for. Soft-spoken Catherine has forgiven him, feels friendly toward him, and never wishes to see again this man whom she only accuses of "having treated me badly."

Lavinia Penniman, the widowed sister of Dr. Sloper and the unremitting confidante of the mercenary suitor. Wife of a deceased clergyman, Mrs. Penniman is a hopeless romantic who has taken upon herself the playing of Catherine's love and small inheritance against the handsome Townsend's expectation of the doctor's wealth. Badly frightened by the miscarriage of her conspiracy and aware of the possibility of losing her parasitic position in the household, she becomes circumspect, cautious against her brother's wrath and her niece's mute accusations. Gay and indestructible after her brother's death, she once again attempts the part of duenna for the middle-aged Catherine and Townsend, with

results her narrowness of vision can never comprehend.

Marian Almond, Catherine Sloper's sensible and observant aunt. Mrs. Almond, aware of her responsibility in the matter, since her niece met Morris Townsend at a party given in the Almond house, dislikes the match but hates the meddling of both her brother and sister. She thinks more highly of Catherine and her simple virtues than do the others; she wishes Morris were as sympathetic and kind as the proud but humble sister whom the selfish man lives on. Her own deep sympathies make for ease with Catherine and antagonism toward Lavinia, the weak-minded matchmaker. Even she is not able to win the jilted girl's confidence, though she manages to relieve the pain of Dr. Sloper's satiric inquiries and Lavinia's fatuous comments.

Mrs. Montgomery, Morris Townsend's widowed sister. A call on Mrs. Montgomery confirms Dr. Sloper's belief that Townsend is a fortune hunter.

THE WASPS

Author: Aristophanes (c. 448-c. 385 B.C.)
Time of action: Fifth century B.C.
First presented: 422 B.C.

PRINCIPAL CHARACTERS

Philocleon (fĭ·lō·klē·ŏn), an elderly Athenian citizen and a dicast, one of the six thousand jurors of the Athenian courts. He is completely obsessed with judging and litigation, and to sit in court day after day is the greatest joy he can imagine. He prides himself on his hardness of heart; no appeal from a prisoner can move him, and he always votes for conviction. When his son imprisons him within his own house to prevent his going to court, he attempts to escape by almost every ruse imaginable. He finally allows himself to be persuaded to give up his madness because Bdelycleon convinces him that he is not a pillar of the state, as he had imagined, but a dupe of the Athenian political bosses. He no longer attends court; instead, he sits at home in judgment on his dog, Labes, who has been accused of stealing a Sicilian cheese. At the end of the case Bdelycleon tricks him into voting for acquittal, for the first time in his life. Later Philocleon reluctantly allows himself to be dressed in a style becoming to a man of his years and to be taken out into society, where Bdelycleon evidently hopes that he will find interests to replace his extreme fondness for law courts. But the old fellow is incorrigible. He staggers home drunk from a banquet after having exhibited there the grossest of manners, carried off the flute girl who entertained the guests, and misused several citizens along the streets. His misbehavior will involve him in several lawsuits, but his previous acrimony has been transformed into the wildest of high spirits.

Bdelycleon (dĕ'lĭ·klē·ŏn), Philocleon's son, determined to break his father's bad habits and to make him over into a model old man. Bdelycleon is evidently a man of substance, and he is clearsighted enough to know that men like his father are being fooled by a corrupt government, which is using the state revenues for many other purposes than feeding a hungry populace. He is an affectionate son, willing to indulge his father's foibles even to the point of acting as defense counsel for Labes, the accused dog. He speaks for moderation and common sense, but in the end he is no match for Philocleon's buffoonery.

Sosias (sō'sĭ·əs) and

Xanthias (zăn'thĭ·əs), house servants of Philocleon, who aid Bdelycleon in keeping their master prisoner and complain vigorously about his vagaries. Sosias speaks for the dog that accuses Labes during his mock trial and Xanthias acts as the prosecuting counsel.

A Baker's Wife and
An Accuser, wronged by Philocleon as he reels his way back to his house after the unfortunate banquet. They appear to demand satisfaction for his having ruined the Baker's Wife's wares and thrown rocks at the Accuser. When Bdelycleon tries to smooth matters over, his father adds insult to the previous injuries.

A Chorus of Wasps, all old men and Philocleon's fellow dicasts. Like him, they are bewitched by the power they seem to enjoy as jurymen, and they rise before daylight to be first on hand for the opening of the tribunals. Their costumes suggest their temperament and their stings the sharpness of their verdicts. When they discover that their colleague has been shut in his house, they attempt to storm the doors but are driven off by Bdelycleon and the servants. Later they, like Philocleon, are convinced of the error of their way of life by Bdelycleon.

WAVERLEY

Author: Sir Walter Scott (1771-1832)
Time of action: 1745
First published: 1814

PRINCIPAL CHARACTERS

Edward Waverley, a young British officer who holds his commission in the army of George II of England during the bloody days in 1745 when Charles Edward, the Pretender, is trying to gain the British throne. Through a set of circumstances, he learns of the young Pretender's cause at first hand; he is Charles' guest, lives for a time with some of his supporters, and swears allegiance to him. Though charged with treason and stripped of his commission, he finally regains favor with the King, inherits his father's fortune, and marries the woman of his choice.

Fergus Mac Ivor Vich Ian Vohr, a very famous clan chieftain who supports Prince Charles' bid for the throne. He is bluff and hearty, formal and courtly, a good politician. When the rebellion fails, he is executed for his crimes against the crown, and the power of the Highland clans is broken.

Prince Charles Edward Stuart, the Pretender, who, having arrived in Scotland from his exile in France, rallies Highlanders to his cause. He reflects his French court training in the polished, civil manner he shows all those about him. He is ruined when his forces are scattered at the Battle of Culloden.

Sir Cosmo Comyne Bradwardine, a Scottish nobleman and a Jacobite who introduces Edward to the forces marshaled under Prince Charles. Rose Bradwardine, the Baron's daughter, finally marries Edward.

Evan Dhu Maccombich, a Highlander in the service of Fergus Mac Ivor. He guides Edward through the Jacobite camp and introduces him to the famous Scottish chief. Maccombich is executed when the revolt fails.

Donald Bean Lean, a Highland bandit faithful to Mac Ivor and the Pretender. He rescues Edward from his English captors when the young officer is being taken to Stirling Castle to stand trial for treason.

Flora Mac Ivor, Fergus' sister, who is attracted to Edward but whose ardor for him cools. When the revolt fails, she enters a Catholic convent in France.

Rose Bradwardine, Edward's beloved and Sir Cosmo Comyne Bradwardine's daughter. Like her father, she is an ardent Jacobite. After the defeat at Culloden she marries Edward.

Richard Waverley, Edward's father, who, for political advantage, swears loyalty to King George II. Unfortunate political maneuvers ruin him. When he dies, Edward inherits the family wealth.

Sir Everard Waverley, a Jacobite who is Edward's uncle and Richard Waverley's brother. It is at Waverely-Honour, the family's ancestral home, that Edward receives much of his education in the political and social issues of the day.

Colonel Gardiner, Edward's military superior while the young man holds a commission in George II's dragoons.

Davie Gellatley, Baron Bradwardine's servant, a good storyteller who helps fire Edward's interest in the Jacobite cause.

Alice, Donald Bean Lean's daughter, who is in love with Evan Dhu Maccombich.

THE WAVES

Author: Virginia Woolf (1882-1941)
Time of action: Late nineteenth and early twentieth centuries
First published: 1931

PRINCIPAL CHARACTERS

Percival, a childhood friend of the six central characters, who respect, admire, and love him, the symbol of the ordinary man, the conventional figure. Rather awkward, bumbling, but pleasant and accepted everywhere, Percival forms the light around whom the six-sided flower revolves, as Bernard put it. In love with the natural woman, Susan, he is beloved by Neville, the scholar, the lover of young men, the brilliant poet. A sportsman, a hale fellow, a poor scholar, and finally a soldier who dies in India, Percival represents a kind of norm in personality and conduct.

Bernard, the phrase maker, the chronicler of the group of childhood friends as they grope toward death, the great adversary of all human life, he thinks. Through Bernard the rest of the characters see life, because in his attempt to grasp reality he is able to become whomever he meets or talks with. Though he sees himself as a failure, he does catch at essences and makes of these his unfinished stories, tales that Percival once saw through and would not let him finish. Deeply devoted to his best friend Neville, he nevertheless is all things to all the characters. A husband, father, provider, friend, he becomes, finally, a seer who tries to sum up the meaning of experiences all have shared.

Neville, the poet, the scrupulous artist, the lover of a single man, the sensitive genius who keeps his life carefully wrapped and labeled. Gaunt and handsome, gifted with the tongue of all great men and able to mimic them from Catullus to Shakespeare, he finds it difficult to survive the shock of Percival's death. He turns first to reproductions of the man and measures his time by the conversations with young, handsome men to whom he is a kind of Socrates. Lonely, introspective he finally finds diversion with frivolous Jinny. He has the ability to speak to them all, even Susan, who sees him as her antithesis.

Susan, the elemental woman, nature-loving and natural, a born mother and an implement of life. Disliking the pine and linoleum smells of school, civilization, she endures education, even travel, so that she may replace her dead mother, administer love to her earthy father, marry a farmer, and raise a family amid the natural, lovely, rural England sights, smells, sounds, and feelings. She has long loved Bernard and has been the object of Percival's love, but none know of these things until later. She resists social ways, dress, attitudes even to the point of boorishness, though she carries human feelings, love and jealousy, admiration and disgust, to their meetings.

Louis, the son of a Brisbane banker, a self-conscious outcast of the society of his friends but the most brilliant and egotistical one of the group. Endowed with self-knowledge, the result of fine breeding from the Hebrews in their Egyptian bondage through the present, Louis hides his endowments and very real gifts out of shame of ridicule. In this way he finally becomes assertive and makes of business a romance, false but substantial. He fears all the others except Rhoda, whom he makes his mistress after these two outsiders are drawn together by their loneliness. All recognize his supremacy in subtle ways and he is respected for this fierce inner being in spite of the discomfort it causes the group.

Rhoda, the plain, clumsy misfit who tries to imitate the world which despises her. Alone deeply with her meager self, she longs for anonymity and retreats from reality early. Tolerated by Susan, avoided by Jinny, she has a kind of ease with Bernard and a negative attraction for Louis. Not gifted in any way, she denies the role life has created for her and commits suicide in middle life.

Jinny, the hedonist, the careful cultivator of externals, the one who causes a rustle wherever she goes. Beautiful with physical vitality, which she burns out in a few brief years, Jinny has the superficial drive of appearances as opposed to the elemental in Susan. Assignations are her business; epicureanism is the method, and weariness is the result.

THE WAY OF ALL FLESH

Author: Samuel Butler (1835-1902)
Time of action: Nineteenth century
First published: 1903

Edward Overton, the narrator. Born in the same year as Theobald Pontifex and in the village whence the Pontifexes sprang, he has known the family all his life. He has an intense dislike for Theobald but greatly admires Alethea Pontifex and takes an interest in Theobald's son Ernest. Alethea makes him the trustee of the money she leaves to Ernest, and it is to Overton that Ernest comes after his release from prison. Overton straightens out Ernest's affairs and helps him to reëstablish his life. Overton is also the spokesman for Butler's ideas.

Ernest Pontifex, the older son of Theobald Pontifex and the hero of the novel. Because of his repressed childhood under the savage domination of his father, Ernest is a tragic failure. He does poorly at school and emerges from Cambridge unable to face life. He is ordained in the Church of England, not from conviction but from lack of preparation for any other career; but he is a failure as a clergyman because he has no understanding of people. Through his extreme naïveté a friend is able to defraud him of his grandfather's legacy; through his ignorance of the world he makes improper advances to a young woman and is sentenced to six months at hard labor. Upon his release, he meets Ellen, a former maid in his parents' house who has been discharged for immorality; he insists on marrying her, for he wants to drop from his position as a gentleman. They set up a second-hand clothes shop. Ellen proves to be a drunkard, and the marriage fails. Ernest is rescued only by the appearance of John, his father's old coachman, who confesses that he is the father of Ellen's child and had married her after her dismissal. Rid of Ellen, Ernest sends their two children to be reared in the country and devotes himself to writing. At the age of twenty-eight he comes into his aunt's legacy of seventy thousand pounds.

George Pontifex, the father of Theobald and the grandfather of Ernest. He is a wealthy publisher of religious books who browbeats his children. He forces Theobald into the clergy by threatening to disinherit him.

John Pontifex, his older son and successor in business.

Theobald Pontifex, his younger son, the father of Ernest. Forced into the clergy by his father, he obtains the living of Battersby. Thus he can marry Christina Allaby, by whom he has three children. He is savagely ill-tempered with them as the result of his own domination by his father. His ill-treatment of Ernest almost ruins the latter's life.

Christina Pontifex, Theobald's wife, one of five marriageable daughters of a clergyman. At their father's suggestion, they play cards to see who shall catch Theobald, and Christina wins. She is a submissive wife, given to piety and romantic daydreaming, with no understanding of her children.

Alethea Pontifex, Theobald's sister. She is more broad-minded and humane than he and, being independently wealthy, can help Ernest, whom she makes her heir without his knowledge.

Joey Pontifex, Ernest's younger brother, a clergyman.

Charlotte Pontifex, Ernest's unattractive sister.

Ellen, a pretty maid in the Pontifex home. She is dismissed for immorality and is given money by Ernest. Years later, he meets her by accident and marries her. But she is a confirmed drunkard and the marriage fails. He is able to get rid of her when he discovers that she was already married to John.

John, the Pontifex coachman, who defends Ernest against Theobald. He is the father of Ellen's illegitimate child.

Dr. Skinner, the tyrannical headmaster of Roughborough School where Ernest Pontifex was a pupil.

Pryer, a London curate and false friend.

He absconds with the twenty-five hundred pounds which Ernest Pontifex had inherited from his grandfather and which had been entrusted to him for investment.

THE WAY OF THE WORLD

Author: William Congreve (1670-1729)
Time of action: Seventeenth century
First presented: 1700

PRINCIPAL CHARACTERS

Mirabell, a man of fashion, intelligent and authentically in love with Mrs. Millamant. He enjoys the favors, either overt or covert, of most of the women in the play, who, either through unrequited love of him or mutual affection, try to affect the course of his fortune. He is presented as a man of genuine parts, not so superficial as to render him without a sense of honor or the genuine ability to experience love, but at the same time a clever schemer. His love for Mrs. Millamant and his hope of legitimate income are the motivating factors in his intrigues. Mirabell is somewhat more in love with Mrs. Millamant than she with him. Though his stake in the marriage is higher than hers, he bears up well under the handicap, never attempting to outmaneuver Mrs. Millamant by feigning indifference, but rather admirably presses his proposal with candor and plain dealing as to his love. Thus he keeps a manly station without lowering himself to beg or unduly flatter her, and impresses her with his devotion. He emerges from the action as a Restoration gentleman who possesses wit, charm, and masculinity, who does not deal in simper, pose, or guile. Though he is a master schemer on occasion, in him the vestiges of sense, honor, and right have not become translated into chicane, venery, or deception.

Mrs. Millamant, Lady Wishfort's niece, loved by Mirabell and perhaps the most

fascinating member of the cast, Mrs. Millamant contains within her personality an attractive haughtiness, and she enjoys making Mirabell's suit appear an even more one-sided affair than it is. She has a frankness which sometimes uncouples her from her train of followers, a glitter that—especially in the famous comic-love scene between herself and Mirabell—approaches radiant wit. For all her practiced arts of conversation and her determination to keep love a game, Mrs. Millamant is level-headed, and Mirabell's commendable qualities will meet good use in such a wife. Beneath her protests and shams, she has marked out a carefully chalked line to follow. She wisely recognizes Mirabell as the man to keep her on it.

Lady Wishfort, a sex-starved old woman. Past the natural flows of passion in her sex, she falls victim to the insatiable demands of false passion. Anxiously casting about for reassurance, she is easy prey for any man who can stomach the odious game of pursuing her. She is more than straight comedy because she carries, though chillingly, a kind of pathos. Her wrath against Mirabell, brought about because he pretended love to her, is averted in the end, and she emerges a wiser woman.

Mrs. Marwood, the consort of Fainall. She is jealous of Mirabell's love for Mrs. Millamant, and her main interest in foil-

1230

ing Mirabell's plans is formulated in bitterness. She wishes Fainall, the lover toward whom she is passive at best, hostile at worst, to gain control not only of his wife's fortune but of Lady Wishfort's as well in order to destroy Mirabell's hopes. In this endeavor she concocts a plan to reveal the "immoral" nature of Mrs. Fainall, Lady Wishfort's daughter, in order that Fainall will have a strong bargaining position from which to demand control of the money. Her deceptions and personal immorality are exposed, and she is defeated by her own envy and malice.

Fainall, an unscrupulous, avaricious man who possesses no morals above or beyond those necessary to his own satisfaction, but whose charm and manner allow him to deceive others. No dupe, he is allied with Mrs. Marwood in an attempt to gain Lady Wishfort's fortune. While carrying on his affair with Mrs. Marwood, he hypocritically plants and reveals indiscretions on the part of his wife. He represents better than any character in the play that attitude toward societal relationships which appears so perverse outside of the Restoration era—

distaste for mate, cultivated love, interest in self which is best served by interest in the affairs of others, tedious attention to a reputation which is all the more precious for being morally unstable.

Mrs. Fainall, Fainall's wife, Lady Wishfort's daughter, and at one time Mirabell's mistress. In the end, because of Mirabell's help, she gains the upper hand over her husband.

Foible, Lady Wishfort's resourceful, energetic servant, allied with Mirabell.

Witwoud, an idle, foppish follower of Mrs. Millamant. He represents the effeminate character of the affected "gentlemen" of the period.

Petulant, a man of fashion, much like Witwoud.

Sir Wilful Witwoud, the half brother of Witwoud, quite different from Witwoud because of his blunt, raucous, honest nature.

Waitwell, Mirabell's serving-man, married to Foible. Mirabell uses him in his plot against Lady Wishfort.

Mincing, Mrs. Millamant's maid.

THE WEAVERS

Author: Gerhart Hauptmann (1862-1946)
Time of action: The 1840's
First presented: 1892

PRINCIPAL CHARACTERS

Herr Dreissiger (hâr drī'sĭ·gėr), a manufacturer who works his weavers for all he can, paying them as little as he can, though he does not think he is a bad man. When the weavers riot, he tries to stand up to them but is forced to flee with his family.

Herr Pfeifer (hâr pfī'fėr), Herr Dreissiger's manager, who judges the weavers' work harshly, so that less money must be paid for it. He sides with his master against the weavers.

Moritz Jaeger (mō'rĭts yā'gėr), a husky young returned soldier. Appalled at the weavers' misery, he leads them to riot. He terms Herr Dreissiger an oppressive villain.

Becker (bĕ'kėr), an impudent young giant of a man who is one of the weavers. He becomes a leader in the riots. When he is captured his fellow weavers free him from the hands of the police.

Old Baumert (bou'mėrt), an elderly

weaver who kills his pet dog so that his family can have meat.

Old Hilse (hǐl'sě), an elderly weaver who believes the weavers are wrong to riot. He stays at his loom, only to be killed by a stray bullet.

Gottlieb Hilse (gôt'lēb hǐl'sě), Old Hilse's son. His wife shames him into joining the rioters.

Luise Hilse (loo-ē'sě hǐl'sě), Gottlieb's wife. She braves the bayonets of the soldiers.

Mielchen Hilse (mēl'shen hǐl'sě), Gottlieb and Luise's small daughter.

Emma Baumert (ămä bou'mèrt) and **Bertha Baumert** (bâr'tä bou'mèrt), Old Baumert's two daughters, who wear themselves out at the looms.

William Ansorge (vǐl'ē·äm än'sōr'gě), the owner of the house in which the Baumerts live.

Pastor Kittelhaus (päs·tōr' kǐ'tǎl'hous), a minister who has no sympathy for the rioting workers.

Herr Welzel (hâr vǎl'tsel), the keeper of the inn where the leaders of the weavers meet.

Anna Welzel (ä'nä vǎl'tsel), Herr Welzel's merry, red-haired daughter.

Weinhold (vīn'hōld), the tutor in Herr Dreissiger's house. He sympathizes with the weavers.

Wiegand (vē'gǎn), a joiner and coffin maker.

THE WEB AND THE ROCK

Author: Thomas Wolfe (1900-1938)
Time of action: 1900-1928
First published: 1939

PRINCIPAL CHARACTERS

George Webber, a lonely child reared by a family-proud aunt and uncle in the small city of Libya Hill, North Carolina. His childhood is the bleak existence of a youngster taken up by charity. As a youth he is an omnivorous, voracious reader who yearns to acquire the power of writing great novels, hoping someday to write about the two-sided world he knows—the side of the rich and the side of the poor. After attending college George moves to New York, only to find that he is as lonely among the big city's millions of people as he was in a small town. Even a trip to Europe gives him no satisfaction, for he is a silent, brooding, distrustful man. His salvation, ultimately, is a love affair lasting several years, an experience that brings him out of himself. His mistress helps him lose his childish illusions about fame and greatness. His self-knowledge is complete when, during a trip to Europe, he awakens in a hospital after a sordid brawl to recognize that life is knowing one's self completely.

Mrs. Esther Jack, a successful, well-known designer of stage sets in New York. She meets George Webber aboard ship, falls in love with him, and becomes his mistress and counselor for several years, although she is fifteen or twenty years older than her lover. She brings George to meet many well-known people and to realize that life is more than mere fame. She encourages George to write, and with her help his long-sought novel begins to take shape. But she dominates George so much that he is forced to leave her, lest her very goodness and love become his undoing as a writer.

Mr. and Mrs. Joyner, George's uncle and

aunt, who rear him after his mother's death. They are proud of their family and try to turn the boy against his father.

Mr. Webber, George's father, who deserts his wife and child to run off with another woman. Despite his father's behavior, George loves and admires the man. Mr. Webber's death brings George a small inheritance that enables him to attend college and to travel to Europe.

WESTWARD HO!

Author: Charles Kingsley (1819-1875)
Time of action: Sixteenth century
First published: 1855

PRINCIPAL CHARACTERS

Amyas Leigh, a handsome blond giant; a hardy adventurer who accompanies Drake around the world and Raleigh to Ireland and who valiantly engages the Spanish in the Old World and the New. Struck blind by lightning during the battle against the Spanish Armada, he retires from the sea and marries Ayacanora.

Frank Leigh, his scholarly older brother, a sometime tutor and courtier. Captured by Don Guzman's men, he refuses to accept Catholicism and is tortured and burned to death.

Sir Richard Grenvile, Amyas' godfather, a famous seaman and explorer.

Sir Francis Drake, leader of the first English voyage around the world.

Sir Walter Raleigh, English courtier, navigator, historian, and poet.

Eustace Leigh, the cousin of Amyas and Frank; a Catholic distrusted by his cousins. Spurned by Rose, he vows revenge. Threatening to turn Rose over to the Inquisition, he is attacked by Amyas and Frank. Before escaping and disappearing, he informs the Inquisition that Rose is a Protestant. His villainy is attributed by the author to his Jesuit training.

Rose Salterne, the mayor's beautiful daughter loved by Amyas and Frank. Married to Don Guzman, whom she loves passionately, she is brought before the Inquisition because of her Protestant belief, which she will not renounce. She is tortured and then burned to death.

Salvation Yeo, Amyas' friend, a tall, dark sailor who idolizes Amyas and shares his adventures. Lightning kills him during the storm which aids the English in the destruction of the Armada.

Don Guzman de Soto, a charming but treacherous Spanish nobleman who captures Rose's heart and marries her. Amyas hates him because of Frank's death. In the destruction of the Armada, Don Guzman goes down in a wrecked ship.

Ayacanora, a supposed Indian maiden who falls in love with Amyas. She is really John Oxenham's lost daughter. She dislikes Amya's brotherly attitude toward her which finally changes when he becomes her adored, though blind, husband.

Mrs. Leigh, the widowed mother of Amyas and Frank; a devout Protestant made somewhat melancholy by memories of earlier Catholic persecution of English Protestants. Saddened by Frank's death, she is happy at last to have the blind Amyas (Sir Amyas now) home with her.

Lucy, a witch who goes with Rose to Spain and who later reports the deaths of Rose and Frank. Lucy escapes by accepting the Catholic faith.

John Oxenham, Salvation's friend captured by Spanish Inquisitors; the father of Ayacanora.

WHAT EVERY WOMAN KNOWS

Author: James M. Barrie (1860-1937)
Time of action: Early twentieth century
First presented: 1908

PRINCIPAL CHARACTERS

Maggie Wylie, the wife who knows so well what every woman should know—that she is the moving force behind any successful husband. At twenty-seven she is the plain spinster sister of David and James Wylie. Neither her curls nor her soft Scottish voice quite compensate for her too-resolute manner. Married off to John Shand after a six-year wait, as the result of a bargain made by David, James, and their father, Maggie proves herself the mistress of her husband's fate, even against the wiles and scheming of Lady Sybil Tenterden.

John Shand, a proud, defiant, calculating young man of extraordinary promise. Caught by the Wylie men as he prowls their library looking for books, John agrees to marry Maggie in five years for three hundred pounds to finance his education. With Maggie unobtrusively behind him, he wins a seat in Parliament, boastful that he has "not a sould to help" him. He would leave Maggie, whom he respects, for Sybil, whom he thinks he loves; but no Scotsman will damage his career. Too, he has finally found out how he has come to be a success.

David Wylie, Maggie's older brother. He is the moving force of the family, the head of Wylie and Sons, stonemasons. The 600-volume library is actually David's; he has an unsatisfied hunger for education and a deep respect for the learned. He shrewdly sees in John Shand's need for money a means of getting a husband for Maggie; businessman that he is, he is pleased to see John equally skilled in driving a good bargain. David has the brisk manner of the person who must get everywhere first.

James Wylie, Maggie's second brother.

Dominated by David, he has become taciturn and tactless. He is used to having his opinions disregarded, but offers them nonetheless. Though he has no use for books and education, he is impressed by John's scholarship and drive, and becomes, in spirit, his humble servant. Observing that Maggie is "queer," James wonders why great writers have failed to notice that all women are thus. His wife's ability would belie this notion.

Alick Wylie, father of the family, who, retired, is no longer the head except in name. His is a disdainful view of learning, although he says "it's not to riches, it's to scholarship I make my bow." His small, bright blue eyes seem always to be counting costs.

The Comtesse de la Brière (brē-ĕr′), a rude, calculating person of the world who laughs at the crudeness of the young politician. She sportingly challenges Sybil to conquer John. Over the years the Comtesse sees that Maggie is "the pin Shand picked up to make his fortune," and she becomes Maggie's ally in defending her rights against the younger woman.

Lady Sybil Tenterden, the niece of the Comtesse. Beautiful and unscrupulous, she schemes to ensnare John and teach him what he has not found in books, but her charm without intelligence is not enough to hold the ambitious young man.

Mr. Charles Venables, a member of the Cabinet. Venables' thirty-year acquaintance with the Comtesse serves to develop both these characters in the play. As protégé to Venables, John bumbles some political coups. About to sever relations with John, Venables reconsiders when reminded that it is he who once said, "A man whose second thoughts are good is worth watching." John's second thoughts resulted from Maggie's influence and a speech she had written for him.

WHAT MAISIE KNEW

Author: Henry James (1843-1916)
Time of action: The 1890's
First published: 1897

PRINCIPAL CHARACTERS

Maisie Farange, the neglected daughter of divorced and irresponsible parents. Shuttled back and forth between her father and mother, Maisie at first lacks moral perception, although she herself is incorruptibly innocent. Then, under the tutelege of Mrs. Wix, she grows in moral and intellectual sense, rejects the immorality of her stepparents, and chooses to live with Mrs. Wix.

Mrs. Wix, a governess. Employed to replace Miss Overmore, Mrs. Wix alone seems concerned for Maisie's welfare. Refusing to condone the immorality around her, she is the moral influence in the young girl's environment.

Sir Claude, Ida Farange's second husband. Genuinely interested in Maisie, Sir Claude most nearly approaches the fatherly role. However, he is unable to end his affair with Mrs. Farange (Miss Overmore) and Maisie refuses to live with them.

Miss Overmore, Maisie's governess, later the second Mrs. Beale Farange. After she tires of her husband, she begins an affair with Sir Claude, who is captivated by her beauty. She does not love Maisie, but she feels that she can hold Sir Claude through his devotion to the girl.

Ida Farange, Maisie's mother. Divorced from Beale Farange, Ida marries Sir Claude but soon loses interest in her daughter and husband. She turns Maisie over to him and goes out of their lives.

Beale Farange, Maisie's father. After his divorce, Beale marries Miss Overmore, but they soon tire of each other. Beale goes to America and out of the story.

WHEN THE MOUNTAIN FELL

Author: Charles-Ferdinand Ramuz (1878-1947)
Time of action: Eighteenth century
First published: 1935

PRINCIPAL CHARACTERS

Séraphin Carrupt (sā·rà·fằn′ kà·rüpt′), an elderly Swiss shepherd. He is killed when an avalanche slides at night onto the mountain pasture where he is keeping his cattle.

Antoine Pont (än·twản′ pōn′), a young, newly-married Swiss shepherd who is thought dead after the avalanche covers the mountain pasture. Miraculously, he is not killed. Living on cheese, he burrows his way out of the mass of rock and earth after two long months. He courageously wants to go back to rescue Séraphin Carrupt, his companion, but his wife dissuades him, knowing the old man is dead.

Thérèse Pont (tā·rĕz′ pōn′), Antoine's young wife. She realizes on the night when the avalanche falls that she is going to have a child. When her husband returns she can scarcely believe that she is not seeing a ghost. Only she is courageous enough to follow her husband back to the scene of the avalanche to dissuade him from trying to dig out his companion.

Philomène Maye (fē·lô·měn′ má·yě′), Thérèse's mother, who tries to shield her daughter from news of her husband's supposed death.

Old Barthélémy (bàr·tā·lā·mē′), a shepherd who lives through the avalanche but dies as he is being carried down the mountain for treatment.

Maurice Nendaz (mō·rēs′ näṅ·dáz′), a lame old man, the first villager to realize that what he hears is an avalanche, not a storm in the distance.

Old Plon (plōṅ′), a shepherd who thinks he hears noises under the huge pile of rock and earth left by the avalanche and assumes that he is hearing ghosts.

WHEN WE DEAD AWAKEN

Author: Henrik Ibsen (1828-1906)
Time of action: Nineteenth century
First presented: 1900

PRINCIPAL CHARACTERS

Arnold Rubek, a sculptor. At a mountain resort on the coast of Norway, Rubek and Maia, his wife, see Irene. In his youth Rubek had found in Irene the perfect model, but he had turned away from her love. After leaving Irene, Rubek had stopped creating beautiful works in marble and made only concealed caricatures, with an animal's face hidden behind the human one. Finding his life of ease with Maia intolerable, he goes with Irene in search of their lost love and finds death with her in the snow at the top of the mountain.

Irene von Satow, the inspiration for Rubek's greatest work, "Woman Awakening from the Dead on the Resurrection Day after the Sleep of Death." Irene tells Rubek that she is dead. She had meant to kill Rubek with a knife, but decides to spare him when he tells her that he too has suffered. Although she tells him that he is already dead, she lures him

to the mountain top where they perish in the snow.

Maia Rubek, Rubek's wife. She finds Ulfheim, a sportsman, intriguing and accompanies him on a hunting trip to the mountains.

Ulfheim, a wealthy sportsman, known as a bear-killer. After he and Maia quarrel on the snow-covered mountain, they are reconciled and tell each other of their youthful disappointments. Returning from the mountain, they meet Rubek and Irene going up toward the icy heights. Ulfheim warns them of the approaching storm.

A Sister of Mercy, a symbolic character. She watches Irene in each critical scene. At the end she appears on the mountain, makes the sign of the cross, and wishes Rubek and Irene peace as they lie buried in the snow.

WHERE ANGELS FEAR TO TREAD

Author: E. M. Forster (1879-   )
Time of action: Early twentieth century
First published: 1905

Jane Seymour, loved by Henry after Anne becomes Queen. Later she becomes Henry's third wife.

Sir Henry Norris, in love with Anne, in league with Herne, sent to the Tower of London for intrigue with Anne.

WINESBURG, OHIO

Author: Sherwood Anderson (1876-1941)
Time of action: Late nineteenth century
First published: 1919

PRINCIPAL CHARACTERS

George Willard, the young reporter who learns about life from confessions and observations of small townspeople. The son of an insensitive man and a sensitive mother, young Willard accepts the practical help of his father but follows the inclinations of his mother in accepting his job. Living as he does in the family hotel which has seen better days, he runs alone and thinks long thoughts. Something about him draws the weak, the insecure, the hopeless as well as the clever and strong, but his loyalties to those who give him their confidences are unflinching. He takes advantage of a lonely farm girl, but only at her insistence, and then secretly. On the other hand, he has an exaggerated sense of chivalry concerning the girl whom he has long admired. He is searching for the truth. This search finally, after his mother's death, takes him away from the town which formed him.

Elizabeth Willard, his mother, whose hotel and life savings never benefit anyone, but whose spirit serves as a bond and inspiration to two men. Promiscuous in her youth, though in search of spirituality, Mrs. Willard had married on the hearsay of village wives expressing contentment. Never in love with her husband, she cherishes a beautiful memory of a lover who murmured to her, "Oh, the dear, the dear, the lovely dear." The two who loved her most, her son and Dr. Reefy, repeat these words to her dead but seemingly young and uncor-

rupted body. She lives and dies in quiet desperation and in search of loveliness.

Dr. Reefy, the poet of obscurity who writes great truths on scraps of paper which he throws away in wads and with a laugh. True to a vision of greatness, the doctor loved twice in his life. One love was a pregnant girl who miscarried, then married the understanding doctor and died, leaving him a comfortable income. The other, Elizabeth Willard, he befriends in her last days of a ravaging disease, but he was never her lover.

Helen White, the banker's daughter with a college complex but small-town disposition. Lovely and gracious, Helen is an inspiration to three Winesburg boys, though only George Willard arouses a like response in her. Like the other main characters, she is unconsciously in quest of beauty and truth.

Kate Swift, the schoolteacher who burns inwardly with a deep desire to live and to pass along the passion of living. Attracted as she is to her former student George Willard, Kate cannot finally cast aside her small-town prudery. Always confusing the physical and the spiritual in her effort to awaken her protégé, spinsterish Kate is secretly worshiped in a like way by the Presbyterian minister, who considers her a messiah of sorts (having seen her naked and praying from his clerical window).

The Rev. Curtis Hartman, the Presbyterian minister, Kate's admirer.

Wing Biddlebaum, a fugitive teacher who ran from unfair accusations of homosexuality to become the restless-fingered berry picker and handyman of the town. Only once in the many years of his hiding out in Winesburg does Wing attempt to pass along his fervor for knowledge which made him a great teacher. George is on the verge of discovering the man's tragic secret and is moved by the aging man's eloquence.

Jesse Bentley,
Louise Hardy, his daughter, and
David Hardy, his grandson. These people reveal the deterioration of the pioneering spirit in northern Ohio. Jesse,

the lone surviving brother of a farm family, turns from the ministry to farm management with religious zeal. He neglects his frail wife who dies in childbirth, and he resents the daughter who should have been his son David. When his neurotic but brilliant daughter turns to a village boy and has a son by him, the old man takes this birth as his omen and names the son David. In a moment of fright when the obsessed old man is about to offer up a lamb as a sacrifice to God, the boy strikes his grandfather, leaves him for dead, and runs away, never again to see the old man, his mother, or the town.

THE WINGS OF THE DOVE

Author: Henry James (1843-1916)
Time of action: c. 1900
First published: 1902

PRINCIPAL CHARACTERS

Mildred Theale (Milly), "the dove" who comes to Europe to learn to live and to die there of an incurable disease. A handsome young woman of great means, inherited through the deaths of her entire family of six, this New Yorker with her Bostonian writer friend and a companion her own age tries to extend her experiences so as to encompass a lifetime in a few short months. Although Milly seems never to suffer, she is the first to know that her sickness will be fatal, and she needs only the strength and subtlety of an eminent physician to confirm this fact. Her fine manners and sensitivity to others' needs make her a delightful companion to all, even when the truth of her condition would otherwise make others pity her. Bright, vivacious, and charming in all ways, she finally wins a heart and ironically loses both hers and his to the tragic situation. Her generosity in remembering her two closest friends (whom she forgives for plotting a scheme of marriage) is un-

acceptable finally. The wings meant for sheltering then become symbols of religious purity.

Kate Croy, the young woman who befriends Milly Theale in England and seeks through her a solution to her own problems. A victim of her father's bad reputation and her uncompromising aunt's machinations, Kate is a beautiful, stylish, and acute observer of the society in which her aunt, Mrs. Lowder, has placed her. Her hopeless love for a young newspaper reporter only makes her decisions more poignant, for she decides he must marry the rich and doomed Milly in order for their own marriage finally to be realized. Sparkling and perceptive as she is, Kate fails to live the lie so calmly planned and must live out her existence in her aunt's entourage.

Merton Densher, Kate Croy's unacceptable lover and Milly Theale's beloved. Densher, just returned from a journalistic assignment in America to a secret engagement with Kate, finds that his charms, good looks, and good manners are the pawns to two separate schemes. He is rejected as her niece's fiancé by Mrs. Lowder but encouraged as a suitor of Milly Theale, whom he had met briefly in America. His fine perceptions and sensitivities are so keenly balanced that he can neither propose nor reject, have or hold. He binds Kate as his lover to an agreement, only to find at last that he loves Milly; but he cannot break off his engagement to Kate. Both he and Kate suffer.

Lord Mark, a nobleman encouraged by Mrs. Lowder as a suitor for her niece. He is attentive to both Kate and Milly, and both reject him. He then gains an unconscious revenge by informing the dying girl of the relationship between Kate and Densher. Neither young nor old-appearing, Lord Mark is supercilious to the point of caricature. Without intending malice, he nonetheless manages to do harm more efficiently than if he had. He is considered a good catch by older matchmakers and abhorred by the objects of his attentions.

Mrs. Lowder, a managing woman who succeeds in convincing everyone that her own will is the strongest and that her judgments are infallible. Though Mrs. Lowder intimidates more than she inspires, her nature is not altogether cold. She simply sees the world as it is and tries to fit those nearest her into the mold.

Mrs. Stringham, a schoolmate and long-time friend of Mrs. Lowder and the companion to Milly Theale. Her warm nature and compassionate responses offset the calculating forces of the highborn English. As a writer, she observes and comments wisely on human character and manners.

Susan Shepherd, the younger American companion to Milly and a sweetly sympathetic friend to all the troubled young lovers. Susan suffers more than emphatically and comforts the stricken compassionately, the more so because she observes the tragedy unfold.

Sir Luke Strett, the distinguished physician who involves himself more than professionally in order to make of Milly Theale's living death an experience in vivid life. Although there is nothing he can do for her, he extends his great humanity to the young and lovely American so desirous of life and so tragically doomed.

THE WINTER'S TALE

Author: William Shakespeare (1564-1616)
Time of action: The legendary past
First presented: 1610-1611

PRINCIPAL CHARACTERS

Leontes (lē·ŏn'tēz), King of Sicilia. For many years a close friend of King Polixenes of Bohemia, Leontes, curiously, becomes insanely jealous of him. Afraid of becoming a cuckold, he imprisons Hermione, wrests her son away from her, and attempts to murder Polixenes. When he learns that Hermione is pregnant, he rails; he calls his daughter a bastard and forces Antigonus to leave the child alone in a deserted area. Finally, coming to his senses, he realizes the awful truth. Through his jealousy, he loses child, wife, and friends.

Polixenes (pō·lĭks'ə·nēz), King of Bohemia. The innocent victim of Leontes' wrath, he flees to his kingdom, bewildered by his friend's outburst. Many years later he is to meet Leontes under much happier circumstances.

Hermione (hẽr·mī′ə·nē), Queen to Leontes and one of the noblest women in Shakespearian drama. Like Polixenes, she is baffled by Leontes' jealousy. Imprisoned, her children snatched away from her, she remains in hiding with Paulina, his devoted friend, until she is reunited with her family after sixteen years.

Perdita (pẽr′dĭ·tə), daughter of Leontes and Hermione. Luckily for her, after she has been abandoned she is found by an old shepherd who protects her as his own child until she is of marriageable age. Meeting young Prince Florizel of Bohemia, she falls in love with him. Later she and her repentant father are reunited.

Paulina (pô·lē′nə), wife of Antigonus and lady in waiting to Hermione. Realizing the absurdity of Leontes' accusations, the courageous woman upbraids him unmercifully for his blind cruelty to Hermione, whom she keeps hidden for sixteen years. Finally, through her efforts, husband and wife meet on a much happier note.

Camillo (kă·mĭl′ō), a lord of Sicilia and Leontes' trusted adviser, who realizes that Hermione is completely innocent of adultery. When ordered by Leontes to kill Polixenes, loyal, steadfast Camillo

cannot murder a good king. Instead, he sails with Polixenes and serves him well for many years. Later, he returns to his beloved Sicilia.

Antigonus (ăn·tĭg′ə·nŭs), a lord of Sicilia and Paulina's husband. Much against his will, this unhappy man is forced to abandon Perdita in a deserted wasteland. Unfortunately for this good man, who is aware of the King's irrationality, he is killed and eaten by a bear; hence the fate and whereabouts of Perdita remain unknown for many years.

Autolycus (ô·tŏl′ĭ·kŭs), a rogue. A balladmonger, he is a delightful scoundrel. Quick with a song, he is equally adept at stealing purses and, in general, at living by his quick wit.

Florizel (flōr′ĭ·zĕl), Prince of Bohemia. In love with Perdita, he refuses to give her up, even though, in so doing, he angers his hot-tempered father who does not want to see his son marry a girl of apparent low birth.

An Old Shepherd, the reputed father of Perdita.

A Clown, his oafish son.

Dion (dī′ŏn) and **Cleomenes** (klē·ŏm′ə·nēz), lords of Sicilia.

Mamillius (mă·mĭl′ĭ·ŭs), the young Prince of Sicilia, son of Leontes and Hermione.

WINTERSET

Author: Maxwell Anderson (1888-1959)
Time of action: Twentieth century
First presented: 1935

PRINCIPAL CHARACTERS

Esdras, a kindly and philosophical old rabbi who is troubled because of his son's guilt in withholding testimony in the Romagna case. Convinced of his past

error in trying to protect Garth, Esdras decides to tell of Shadow's murder.

Garth, his son, a witness to a murder

committed years ago by Trock. His fear of Trock has kept him silent.

Miriamne, Esdras' fifteen-year-old daughter, who is in love with Mio but, like Esdras, is desirous of protecting Garth. Rushing to Mio after he has been shot, she is killed when she runs into the line of fire of Trock's machine gun. Like Shakespeare's Juliet, Miriamne is a virtuous, intense young girl whose love for her sweetheart conflicts with her loyalty to her family, and who chooses to die with the man she has loved.

Mio (Bartolomeo Romagna), the classically tragic young son of Romagna, who was innocent of murder but condemned and executed because of prejudice against his being an anarchist. Mio lives only to prove Romagna's innocence. He witnesses the shooting of Shadow. Torn between loyalty to his father and love for Miriamne, whose brother will be killed if Mio informs on Trock, Mio hesitates too long and is at last gunned down. The doomed Mio may be compared to Hamlet and other sons in earlier literature who sought to avenge a father's murder and

thereby brought on not only their own deaths but those of others as well.

Trock, a cold-hearted murderer released from prison and dying of tuberculosis. With only six months to live he is willing, if necessary, to protect his past guilt with additional murders. He resembles American gangsters and professional murderers of the 1920's.

Shadow, his henchman, who is murdered by two other followers of Trock. He lives long enough to confront and accuse Trock.

Judge Gaunt, the elderly judge who sentenced Romagna to death. He is intermittently insane from brooding over his part in Romagna's death.

Carr, a cynical teenage friend of Mio.

Lucia, a street-piano man.

Piny, an apple-woman.

Herman, a shoe salesman.

A Radical, a symbolic character who complains of capitalistic oppression.

WITH FIRE AND SWORD

Author: Henryk Sienkiewicz (1846-1916)
Time of action: Seventeenth century
First published: 1883

PRINCIPAL CHARACTERS

Pan Yan Skshetuski, a young lieutenant and the valiant hero of this romance which dramatizes the seventeenth century struggle for Polish unity. Courageous, loyal to his prince, magnanimous to his defeated enemy, faithful to his beloved, Pan Yan is a conventional heroic figure.

Princess Helena Kurtsevich, his beloved. In love with Pan Yan, but constantly pursued by a jealous lover, she is alternately a captive and a fugitive from capture.

Ultimately she is saved by Pan Yan's followers.

Princess Kurtsevich, the widow of Prince Constantine Kurtsevich. She is the mother of five sons and the aunt of Helena, whose estate is in her hands. She promises to help Pan Yan with Helena if he will not interfere with the ownership of the estate.

Bogun, Princess Kurtsevich's adopted sixth son and an aspirant for Helena's hand. Learning of the Princess' plan to help Pan Yan with Helena, he kills her and two of her sons, burns the estate, and pursues Helena relentlessly. At last he is captured and turned over to Pan Yan, who generously spares his life.

Prince Yeremi Vishnyevetski, Polish national hero and Pan Yan's general. He is engaged in a long struggle against the marauding Cossacks and is finally victorious.

Hmelnitski, the hetman of the Zaporojian Cossacks. Assisted as an unknown traveler by Pan Yan, he pledges friendship to him, and afterward has occasion to save Pan Yan's life. He plays a double game against Prince Yeremi by seeming to hold the truce while some of his followers oppose the Prince. Finally, the Prince defeats him in a heroic stand.

Tugai Bey, the hetman of the Tartars and an ally of Hmelnitski, who persuades him not to order the death of the captured Pan Yan.

Zagloba, a jovial and kind-hearted nobleman. At first he is Bogun's ally but turns against him and rescues Helena.

Horpyna, a witch who holds Helena captive.

Jendzian, Pan Yan's faithful servant, who learns that Helena is Horpyna's captive and assists in her rescue.

Prince Karl, a disputant in the election for king. He finally withdraws in favor of Prince Kazimir.

Prince Kazimir, later King Kazimir.

Prince Dominik Zaslavski Ostrogski, Commander in Chief of the Commonwealth armies.

Pan Kisel, the leader of the government faction that wishes to negotiate with Hmelnitski.

Pototski, a leader of the armies of the King.

WITHIN THE GATES

Author: Sean O'Casey (1884-   )
Time of action: Twentieth century
First presented: 1933

PRINCIPAL CHARACTERS

Jannice, a young and dying prostitute. The streetwalker is a modern Everywoman who turns in her final days on earth to family, church, social agency, lover, and finally poet. Of all those to whom she turns, including her father, the Bishop, none sustains her with love and compassion except the poet.

The Dreamer, a young poet. Sensitive to the impoverished spirit of modern man, weighed down by mass conformity, he protests and urges the Down-and-Outs to throw off their worldly bonds. As Jannice dies, he sings his song of praise to the independent spirit who is dying within the gates.

The Bishop (Gilbert), Jannice's father. Limited only to conventional responses, the guilty lover and irresponsible father cannot admit his guilt in spite of Jannice's mockery. Worship of self has replaced compassion and he can only utter Latin comfort as she dies.

The Old Woman, Jannice's mother, a drunkard steeped in sin and hatred. Her only happy memory is of a week spent with a long-dead Irish soldier.

The Athiest, the foster father of Jannice. Deserted by both the mother and the daughter, he is now too much interested in his rabble-rousing, speechifying, and pamphleteering to take Jannice back.

The Down-and-Outs, the victims of dead traditions bowed by the master classes.

The Gardener, a man in love with physical love who rejects the dying prostitute.

The Salvation Army Officer, her lover.

WOLF SOLENT

Author: John Cowper Powys (1872-   )
Time of action: Twentieth century
First published: 1929

PRINCIPAL CHARACTERS

Wolf Solent, a history master. Hired by Squire Urquhart, Wolf returns to Ramsgard and meets Gerda Torp. Yielding to his animal nature, he seduces her, but later makes her his wife. Forced by financial necessity to aid the squire on a pornographic project, Wolf is forced by Gerda to cash a check for his degrading work with the squire against his will. The existence of his spiritual love for Christie Malakite confuses his life, but this love refuses to become physical and he remains with his wife.

Gerda Torp, Wolf's beautiful wife. Still attractive to men, Gerda loses her loyalty to Wolf and has an affair with Bob Weevil when Wolf refuses to cash the check.

Christie Malakite, Wolf's spiritual mate. Unable to arouse physical love in Wolf, she moves away with Olwen after her father dies.

Squire Urquhart, the Ramsgard squire

engaged in writing a history of all the salacious stories of Dorset.

Ann Solent, Wolf's mother.

Selena Gault, Wolf's father's old mistress.

Albert Smith, a hatter.

Mattie Smith, Wolf's illegitimate half sister, later Darnley's wife.

Olwen, the product of an incestuous relationship between Mr. Malakite and his oldest daughter.

Bob Weevil, Gerda's flashy young lover.

Mr. Torp, Gerda's father, a stonecutter.

Lob Torp, his son.

Darnley Otter, Wolf's friend and Mattie's husband.

Jason Otter, Darnley's brother, a poet.

Mr. Malakite, a bookseller, Christie's father.

THE WOMAN HATER

Author: Francis Beaumont (1585?-1616)
Time of action: Early seventeenth century
First presented: c. 1606

PRINCIPAL CHARACTERS

Gondarino, a widower, so disillusioned by his late wife's infidelity that he despises all women. Plagued by Oriana's

teasing, he retaliates by accusing her of wantonness. When his lies are discovered, he is ordered to kiss a dozen ladies in waiting, a fate worse than death in his eyes.

Oriana, a merry, virtuous young noblewoman who makes a game of Gondarino's well-known misogyny, succeeding only in strengthening his prejudices while she wins the love and admiration of the Duke.

Count Valore, her brother. Bored with court life, he finds amusement in Lazarillo's search for a feast and in tricking the intelligencers who prey on those around them. He remains loyal to Oriana and helps to prove Gondarino's accusations false.

The Duke of Milan, a young ruler who is attracted by Oriana's beauty. He plans a test to prove or disprove Gondarino's slander and rejoices at the vehemence with which Oriana refuses Arrigo's staged advances. He claims her for his bride.

Lazarillo, a gourmet who yearns only to feast on the head of the fish umbrana.

Julia, a prostitute whom he marries to achieve his wish.

Francissina, her colleague. She is married, through the wiles of the pander, to a well-to-do mercer.

A Mercer, her naïve husband-to-be, who longs to be a scholar. Deceived when he takes the pander's black robes as a mark of the academic profession, he accepts his irregular marriage philosophically.

A Pander, a clever opportunist who sees two of his clients wed at considerable profit to himself.

Lucio and
Arrigo, ambitious and rather corrupt officials of the Duke's court.

THE WOMAN IN WHITE

Author: Wilkie Collins (1824-1889)
Time of action: The 1850's
First published: 1860

PRINCIPAL CHARACTERS

Walter Hartright, the chief narrator. Engaged as an art instructor to Laura Fairlie, he endears himself to his student, who is betrothed to an older man of rank. Laura decides to complete her wedding plans, and Hartright leaves to go to Central America. Returning, he learns of Laura's unhappy marriage. Hartright then gathers facts to incriminate the conspirators who have plotted to gain Laura's money. He marries Laura, who is now penniless, during the investigation.

Laura Fairlie, who becomes Lady Glyde. In her husband's conspiracy to secure her fortune, Laura is concealed for a time in her room. Meanwhile the woman in white is held incommunicado, dies, and is buried as Laura, Lady Glyde. Laura, committed by the conspirators to the asylum from which the woman in white has escaped, is abducted and hidden until Hartright completes his investigation.

Marian Halcombe, Laura's half sister, who works with Hartright as a protector of the frail Laura. Strong, courageous, she combats Laura's adversaries during Hartright's absence. Although in love with Hartright, Marian, absorbed in feminism, is willing to remain unmarried and to live with the Hartrights.

Sir Percival Glyde, Laura's husband, who resorts to conspiracy, involving his wife's incarceration, to get money for his debts.

Knowing of Hartright's investigation of his parentage, Sir Percival sets fire to the vestry in order to destroy church records that would establish his illegitimacy; he dies in the fire.

Count Fosco, his Italian accomplice in the conspiracy. Identified as a foreign spy by Hartright, Fosco exposes his own and Sir Percival's villainy.

Countess Fosco, his wife, the former gay, socially prominent Eleanor Fairlie, dispossessed by her family when she married the Count. Cold and impenetrable because of the secrets sealed up during six years of marriage, she obeys her husband's orders in the conspiracy.

Anne Catherick, the woman in white, committed as a young girl to an asylum by Sir Percival because he feared she knew his secret. The illegitimate daughter of Philip Fairlie, Laura's father—hence, the marked resemblance to Laura —Anne is buried as Lady Glyde. Because of Mrs. Fairlie's attention to Anne as a child, Anne always dresses in white.

Mrs. Catherick, her mother, who lives on income from Sir Percival for her part in forging a marriage entry in the church records.

Professor Pesca, Hartright's long-time friend. Pesca's Italian background helps to identify Fosco as a spy.

Mrs. Elizabeth Clements, Anne's guardian, who reveals Sir Percival's past attentions to Mrs. Catherick, pointing to the supposition that Anne is Percival's child.

Frederick Fairlie, Laura's uncle. An artistic hypochondriac, he lives in seclusion on the family estate.

Mrs. Vesey, Laura's former governess.

Hester Pinkorn, Fosco's cook. She narrates the description of the mysterious young woman hidden in Fosco's house, her behavior during her illness, and the incidents of her death.

Alfred Goodricke, a doctor who tells of his attendance to the young woman; he attributes her death to heart disease.

Mrs. Eliza Michelson, housekeeper at Sir Percival's estate. She acts as informant between Marian and Anne Catherick, when Anne calls secretly in her effort to save Laura from Sir Percival's wiles.

Margaret Porcher, a slatternly, obstinate housemaid, hired by Sir Percival to keep Marian away from Laura.

Fanny, Laura's maid, discharged by Sir Percival to rid the house of servants faithful to Laura and Marian.

Mrs. Rubelle, Fosco's friend, hired as nurse to Marian, to prevent her foiling the conspiracy.

Major Donthorne, the owner of a resort, who writes Hartright about Philip Fairlie's and Mrs. Catherick's early affair at his place. This information establishes Anne Catherick's parentage.

A WOMAN KILLED WITH KINDNESS

Author: Thomas Heywood (c. 1573-1641)
Time of action: Early seventeenth century
First presented: 1603

PRINCIPAL CHARACTERS

John Frankford, a well-to-do gentleman. Generous and just to his whole household, he wins undying loyalty from his servants; but he finds his trust betrayed by his beloved wife and his friend Wendoll, whom he had taken into his home.

Although he is reluctant to accept his servant Nick's revelation of their guilt, he forces himself to try to learn the truth. Too merciful to take the bloody revenge demanded by convention from an injured spouse, he satisfies himself by banishing his wife to his manor in the country, where she dies heartbroken.

Anne, his wife. She seems at the time of her marriage the epitome of gracious, chaste womanhood, but she cannot resist the persistent advances of Wendoll, whom her husband leaves alone with her. After the discovery of her infidelity, she is so overcome by her sense of guilt and by her husband's generosity that she starves herself and dies, forgiven on her deathbed, in Frankford's arms.

Wendoll, her lover, Frankford's protégé. Although his conscience rebels at his base betrayal of Frankford's hospitality, he gives in to passion and persuades Anne to return his love, shamelessly baiting her husband with double-entendres as they play cards. Once discovered, he repents and sees that he must wander, like Cain, to escape the report of his ingratitude.

Charles Mountford, an impulsive country squire. In a heated quarrel over his hawk's prowess he kills two of the servants of his friend Sir Francis Acton and makes a bitter enemy of their master. Freed from prison at the cost of his entire fortune, he lives in the country with his sister, contented with their simple life, until he is again arrested, this time at the request of a creditor whom he trusted. Released by Acton's intercession, he feels obligated to repay his debt to his enemy and offers him his only remaining treasure, his sister, a gesture understandable only in terms of his rigid code of honor.

Susan, his loyal sister, who shares his misfortunes. She is appalled at first by

her brother's proposal that she give herself to Sir Francis, but she finally accepts his view of the matter enough to explain his offer to their enemy, swearing at the same time that she will kill herself rather than stain "her" honor. Relieved of this grim choice by Sir Francis, she accepts his proposal of marriage.

Sir Francis Acton, Anne Frankford's brother. The slaying of his servants makes him Charles Mountford's implacable enemy until he sees Susan and falls in love with her. Unable to purchase her favors, he resolves to win them by his kindness in freeing her brother. He is so overcome by Charles' offer that he refuses to dishonor their house and asks for the young woman as his bride.

Malby and
Cranwell, friends of Sir Francis.

Shafton, a greedy opportunist who offers Charles a large loan under the cover of friendship, then has him imprisoned for debt.

Nicholas, Frankford's watchful manservant. He distrusts Wendoll from the moment of his entrance into the house and later reveals his villainy to his master.

Jenkin,
Cicely, and
Spigot, good-humored members of Frankford's household who are devoted to their master and well aware of what goes on in his home.

Jack Slime and
Roger Brickbat, country men who dance to celebrate Frankford's marriage.

Old Mountford,
Sandy,
Roger, and
Tidy, hard-hearted relatives and former friends of Charles. They refuse Susan's plea for money to free her brother, who had been their benefactor in better times.

THE WOMAN OF ROME

Author: Alberto Moravia (Alberto Pincherle, 1907-   )
Time of action: Twentieth century
First published: 1947

PRINCIPAL CHARACTERS

Adriana, a prostitute. She is a heroically proportioned woman, even at sixteen. She first augments her income as a seamstress by working as an artist's model; next she tries to become a dancer. When her lover puts off marrying her she easily drifts into prostitution, for she likes men and the indolent life her new profession affords her. She becomes pregnant by a murderer but persuades a young anti-Fascist that the unborn child is his.

Gino, Adriana's first lover. He promises to marry Adriana, but she discovers he already has a wife. As her lover he is soft-spoken and gentle.

Astarita, Adriana's first customer, brought to her by her friend Gisella. He is a police official and friendly to Adriana, even to keeping her lover Mino out of prison. Astarita is killed by Sonzogno in revenge for a slap.

Sonzogno, a hoodlum and strong man.

Adriana admires his strength, takes him as a lover, and becomes pregnant. Sonzogno, seeking revenge for a slap, seeks out Astarita at the ministry where he works and throws the man over a balcony to his death.

Mino, a nineteen-year-old student and an anti-Fascist. He is a weak young man. When he is questioned by the police he betrays his fellow conspirators and later commits suicide in remorse. He is persuaded by Adriana that he is the father of her unborn child.

Gisella, Adriana's friend and fellow prostitute. Gisella acts as procuress to start Adriana in her career.

Adriana's Mother, a poor woman who sells her daughter's physical charms as an artist's model and then is bitterly angry when the girl accepts a lover. When Adriana's prostitution brings in money and ease, the mother is quite content.

A WOMAN'S LIFE

Author: Guy de Maupassant (1850-1893)
Time of action: Early nineteenth century
First published: 1883

PRINCIPAL CHARACTERS

Jeanne de Lamare (zhän' də lá·már'), the woman whose life is recounted from young womanhood to the time she becomes a grandmother. As an innocent young girl, just out of a convent, she goes to live in the country with her parents. There she marries a man whom she soon discovers to be parsimonious and unfaithful to her. Jeanne bears a child, on whom she lavishes all of her af-

fection. She then discovers that her husband is unfaithful to her again, this time with the wife of a neighboring Count. The Count kills his wife and Julien, and the rest of Jeanne's life is spent catering to the extravagant whims of her son.

Julien de Lamare (zhü·lyăn' də lá·már'), Jeanne's thoroughly reprehensible husband. He manages the estate in a very penurious manner, and he fathers a child by the maid. Later, he takes the Countess de Fourville as his mistress. He is killed when the Count discovers him with the Countess.

Paul de Lamare (pôl' də là·màr'), Jeanne's son, whom she spoils completely. He runs away from school and spends the next few years asking for and getting money from his mother. He writes to ask her permission to marry his mistress. When she does not approve, he marries the girl anyway and they have a child. After his wife dies, he returns home with his daughter.

Baron Simon-Jacques Le Perthuis des Vauds (bà·rōn sē·mōn'-zhàk' lə pĕr·tüē' dā vō'), Jeanne's father, whose liberal style of living reduces his family to living quietly in the country. He finally dies of apoplexy caused by worry over his grandson and his property.

Rosalie (rō·zà·lē'), the maid, who is also Jeanne's foster sister. She has an illegitimate child by Julien, and she and the child are sent away. After Julien's death, she returns to look after Jeanne.

The Countess Gilberte de Fourville (zhēl·bĕrt' də fōōr·vēl'), a neighbor with whom Julien goes riding almost every day and with whom he is having an affair.

The Count de Fourville (də fōōr·vēl'), Gilberte's husband, who loves her passionately. When he learns that she and Julien are in a shepherd's hut together, he pushes the hut over a cliff and kills them both.

Abbé Tolbiac (à·bā' tôl·byàk'), the village priest, very much concerned with his parishioners' morals. When he finds out about the affair between Gilberte and Julien, he tells the Count.

THE WOMAN'S PRIZE

Author: John Fletcher (1579-1625)
Time of action: Sixteenth century
First presented: c. 1604

PRINCIPAL CHARACTERS

Petruchio (pĕ·trōōch'ĭ·ō), a widower, famous as the tamer of his shrewish first wife, Kate. Angered and confused by the various husband-taming tricks of Maria and beaten at every point, he at last surrenders to her and is rewarded with a generous love.

Maria (mä·rē'ä), Petruchio's second wife. A lesser Lysistrata, she is determined to win a signal victory for her sex over the man most famous for conquering a member of it. She is clever and witty, turning Petruchio's angry bull-like sallies with affected mildness and concern or with passionate displays of her own temper. After she overwhelms him completely, she graciously promises to make him a perfect wife.

Livia (lĭv'ĭ·ə), Maria's sister. Loving Rowland, she succeeds in fooling her father and her ridiculous elderly suitor, and after several complications succeeds in marrying her sweetheart.

Bianca (bē·ăn'kə), their cousin. Also showing kinship with Lysistrata, she is active and resourceful on behalf of both sisters in the battle of the sexes.

Petronius (pĭ·trō'nĭ·əs), the father of the sisters. A well-meaning, but somewhat tyrannical father, he rages furiously but impotently at his daughters' independence, but accepts their eventual triumphs with good grace.

Rowland (rō'lənd), Livia's sweetheart. Misunderstanding Livia's behavior toward him and Moroso, he renounces her; but when the misunderting is clarified, he marries her joyfully.

Moroso (mō·rō'sō), a foolish, wealthy old man in love with Livia. He is tricked into witnessing and approving her marriage contract with Rowland without realizing what he is signing.

Sophocles (sŏf'ə·klēz), a friend of Petruchio. He is used by Maria, who flirts with him, to arouse Petruchio's jealousy.

Tranio (trä'nē·ō), another of Petruchio's friends.

Jacques (zhäk), Petruchio's servant. He is bewildered by his master's reversal of marital fortune.

WOMEN BEWARE WOMEN

Author: Thomas Middleton (1580-1627)
Time of action: Early seventeenth century
First presented: c. 1621

PRINCIPAL CHARACTERS

The Duke of Florence, a lecherous, ruthless ruler. Capturing Leantio's wife with the aid of Livia and Guardiano, he takes her partly by force, partly by seduction. Later, having sworn an oath to his brother, the Lord Cardinal, that he will no longer live with her in adultery, he carries out his promise by having her husband killed and marrying her immediately thereafter. There is poetic justice in his death, for his new wife prepares poison for the good brother and a servant mistakenly serves it to the Duke. He dies in agony.

The Lord Cardinal, the Duke's brother. He preaches morality with vehemence and at length, but has little or no effect on the multipresent evils of the corrupt court. He remains alive to deliver a last blast of morality after the holocaust at the play's end.

Fabricio (fä·brē'chē·ō), the father of Isabella. A foolish, ineffectual man, he insists on marrying his daughter to the rich ward of Guardiano. He is stunned with horror in the final scene, but is living at the play's end.

Hippolito (ē·pō'lē·tō), Fabricio's brother. Devoured by incestuous lust, with the aid of his sister Livia he corrupts his niece. He kills Leantio for family pride

after the Duke has let him know that Leantio and Livia are having an illicit affair. Just before his own death, he speaks lines which give the tone of the play:

Lust and forgetfulness has been amongst
  us,
And we are brought to nothing . . .

Livia (lē'vē·ä), the sister of Fabricio and Hippolito. The essence of evil in a play crawling with evil, she aids the Duke in his plan to ravish Bianca; she lies to Isabella, telling her that she is not the daughter of Fabricio and therefore not the niece of Hippolito; she is swept away by obsessive lust for Leantio, whom she takes as a lover and showers with wealth. Her rage at his death is boundless. She has Hippolito and Isabella shot with poisoned arrows in a wedding masque for the Duke and Bianca and is herself slain by poison fumes which Isabella has planted in a censer she carries in the masque.

Guardiano (gwär·dyä'nō), the uncle of the Ward. Unscrupulous, depraved, ambitious, he aids Livia and the Duke in entangling Bianca. He too is enthusiastic about the marriage of his ward with Isabella; but after the marriage, when he finds out that she has been corrupted by her uncle, he plots the death of Hippolito. Through the Ward's stupidity Guardiano is killed instead of his intended victim.

The Ward, a rich, stupid heir. He is brought to marriage with Isabella only after much labor and persuasion by Guardiano. After the marriage, even his stupidity is insufficient armor against the horror of the disclosure of her sins.

Leantio (lā·än′tyō), a merchant's agent. He steals away from her family a beautiful girl, Bianca, whom he marries and adores immoderately. When he returns from a business venture to find her the Duke's arrogant and contemptuous mistress instead of the submissive and loving wife he left behind, he is swept by helpless fury. Partly for revenge, he takes evil Livia as his mistress and indiscreetly boasts of this affair to his wife. She tells the Duke, who informs Hippolito in order to have him kill Leantio and thus make way for Bianca's second marriage.

Bianca (bē·än′kə), Leantio's wife. A beautiful and innocent girl when she runs away with Leantio, she rouses keen pity during her betrayal and helplessness. After her seduction, however, instead of being a Lucrece she becomes as evil as her corrupters or nearly so. Like Herodias, she decides to kill her critic, the Lord Cardinal. Her passion for the evil Duke has become so great that when her poisoning plot miscarries and he is killed, she takes the remaining portion of the poison and dies with him.

Isabella (ē·zä·bĕl′lä), the daughter of Fabricio. Finding the Ward repulsive, she resists her father's efforts to bring about their marriage; however, when her aunt Livia convinces her that her passion for her handsome and accomplished uncle is not incestuous, she decides to marry the Ward as a cover for her affair with Hippolito. When Livia in her agony over the loss of Leantio tells the truth about the whole situation, Isabella plans revenge on Livia and murders her with the poisoned censer; she herself dies the victim of her victim.

The Mother of Leantio, a well-meaning, gullible old woman. She plays into Livia's hands by having Bianca come to Livia's house and plays chess with her hostess, all the time unaware that her daughter-in-law is being violated in another room in the house. She and the Lord Cardinal are exempt from the horror or contempt which the other principal characters arouse, but they are not calculated to arouse much sympathy in a beholder or reader.

Sordido (sôr·dē′dō), the servant of the Ward.

THE WOMEN OF TRACHIS

Author: Sophocles (c. 496-c. 406 B.C.)
Time of action: Remote antiquity
First presented: Before 408 B.C.

PRINCIPAL CHARACTERS

Deianira (dē·yə·nī′rə), the wife of Herakles. Although her husband is one of the greatest of heroes among the Greeks, her marriage has brought her little happiness because Herakles, dedicated to action, returns to her only infrequently and she must spend the intervals in loneliness and in fear for his safety. When the play begins, he has been absent fifteen months, and she is especially apprehensive because it has been predicted that he will die on this day or forever after live free from toil. Although she complains to the Chorus of her lot in life, she is deeply in love with Herakles, and she soon reveals that she possesses the highest virtue and intelligence. When Iole is brought in among the captive women, Deianira feels an instinctive sympathy for her. Even after she learns that the girl is her husband's concubine, she does not attempt to molest her, and she insists on regarding Herakles' lust as a disease. At the same time she is aware that Iole is in the bloom of youth and that she is aging; therefore she must swallow her pride and use a charm to regain her husband's love. For this reason she sends him the garment, a philter made from the curdled blood of the centaur Nessus. This philter, she had been told would control Herakles' affections; actually, it is a potent, fiery poison. She has misgivings about what she had done when the wool with which she applies the charm begins to fulminate. When it is reported to her that Herakles is dying in agony, she kills herself on her bridal bed.

Herakles (hĕr'ə·klēz), the son of Zeus and Alcmena. Depicted less favorably in this play than elsewhere, he does not appear until late in the action, by which time he is dying in agony from the effects of the poison. Thinking that Deianira has deliberately murdered him, he curses her, and when he learns of her death, he regrets only that she did not die by his hand. After her innocence has been revealed, he thinks only of his own approaching death and the fate of Iole. Early in the play love is spoken of as a disease; at the last Herakles is literally diseased by the blood of the lustful centaur, and the flames of the funeral pyre on which he dies become equated with the flames of the passion that burned in him while he lived.

Hyllus (hĭl'əs), the son of Herakles and Deianira. He loves and admires his father and promises against his will to marry Iole after Herakles' death. He recognizes a terrible lack of justice and compassion in what the gods have allowed to happen to his parents.

Iole (ī'ō·lē), a maiden of Oechalia. Herakles, having fallen in love with her, demanded her of her father, Eurytus. When his request was refused, he attacked and captured the city and took the girl as his concubine.

Lichas (lī'kəs), the herald who brought Deianira news of Herakles' return to Trachis. Under her close questioning he reveals that Herakles has taken Iole as his concubine. Because Lichas later brings Herakles the poisoned robe, the hero believes him a partner in Deianira's supposed murder plot. Picking up the herald, he dashes out Lichas' brains upon a stone.

A Chorus of Trachinian Maidens.

THE WOODLANDERS

Author: Thomas Hardy (1840-1928)
Time of action: Nineteenth century
First published: 1887

PRINCIPAL CHARACTERS

Grace Melbury, a young Englishwoman whose expensive education sets her apart from her family and neighbors in the village of Little Hintock. She returns to find that she is intended by her father to be the bride of Giles Winterborne, until that young man loses his little fortune. Later she is courted by a young physician, Edgar Fitzpiers, whom she marries without love at her father's urging. As she begins to mature, Grace realizes that she has been mistaken in her marriage. When her husband turns to a rich, young widow, Grace is surprised at her lack of feeling until she realizes that as she has outgrown an external view of life she has come for the first time to appreciate her rural neighbors. Though her pride is hurt by her husband's philandering, she takes joy in discovering what love can be, for she truly falls in love with Giles Winterborne, but only later, as Winterborne lies dying, having sacrificed himself for her, does she really mature as a woman. Some months later she and her husband become reconciled and prepare to start life anew in another part of England.

Edgar Fitzpiers, a young physician of good family. Though an excellent doctor, he is a vain and shallow young man who wastes his skill and his time in all sorts of romantic studies. Living alone in Little Hinton village, he is attracted to Grace Melbury and marries her, although he feels he is marrying beneath his station. Soon afterward he drifts into an affair with Felice Charmond, a wealthy widow of the neighborhood. Through this unhappy passion he loses his wife, his practice, and almost his life. After the scandalous death of his mistress abroad he realizes his selfishness and courts his wife anew, winning a new start in marriage and in his profession.

George Melbury, a timber merchant. Conscience-stricken because he had stolen a friend's fiancée years before, he proposes to make amends by marrying his daughter Grace to the friend's son, Giles Winterborne; but he finds that he cannot bring himself to enforce the marriage after the young man has lost his lands. He then marries Grace to the local doctor, who he believes is the only man in the community suitable for her. Throughout the story, until Grace matures enough to take her life into her own hands, George Melbury dominates his daughter and several times plunges her into grief by his decisions, even though he means well by her.

Giles Winterborne, a young timberman and landowner, a natural gentleman. He loves Grace Melbury devotedly during his lifetime and sacrifices his health and life for her happiness and good name. He endures many embarrassments at the hands of the Melburys, even to being jilted when, through no fault of his own, he loses his lands and is forced to become an itinerant worker. His noble nature is a great factor in helping Grace Melbury achieve emotional maturity.

Felice Charmond, a rich young widow and a former actress who has inherited a great estate, including the local manor house, from her deceased husband. A creature of sensual passion, she readily begins an affair with Dr. Fitzpiers. The affair, the last of a long series for her, is no mere flirtation, for she learns truly to love the young physician and follows him to the Continent after he and his wife separate. There her death at the hands of an earlier lover, an American from South Carolina, frees the doctor from his passion and eventually he and his wife are reunited.

Marty South, a poor young woman in love with Giles Winterborne. Her letter to Dr. Fitzpiers causes an argument between the physician and Felice Charmond. The argument takes Fitzpiers away from the widow shortly before her death and saves him from being involved in scandal when she is shot and killed by a former lover.

Suke Damson, a pretty, amoral young village girl who has an affair with Dr. Fitzpiers before his marriage. Though it is a passing relationship for him, Suke falls deeply in love. After her marriage she reveals unwittingly to her husband that her affections lie elsewhere.

Tim Tang, Suke Damson's husband, a sawyer employed by Mr. Melbury. Bitter because his wife still loves Dr. Fitzpiers rather than himself, he sets a mantrap, such as is used to catch poachers, for the physician. The jealous husband's plan goes wrong and the trap almost gives serious injury to innocent Grace Melbury. The incident turns out to be the unintended catalyst that brings Grace and her husband together once more. Tang and his wife emigrate to New Zealand.

Robert Creedle, an old servant loyal to Giles Winterborne in both prosperity and adversity.

John South, Marty South's father. His death influences the careers of Giles Winterborne and the others because Giles' leases to his lands are written to expire at the death of the old man.

WOODSTOCK

Author: Sir Walter Scott (1771-1832)
Time of action: 1651
First published: 1826

PRINCIPAL CHARACTERS

Sir Henry Lee, a Royalist forced by the soldiers of Cromwell to move from the royal lodge, Woodstock, with his daughter. After they move back to the lodge, he helps to hide Prince Charles until the young Prince can make his escape from England. Finally, as an old man, he lives just long enough to see the Prince crowned as King Charles II.

Alice Lee, the daughter of Sir Henry, in love with Markham Everard, Sir Henry's nephew. Her father will not allow the marriage because Everard is a Puritan. Because of her love for Everard, she spurns Charles' advances when he stays at the lodge disguised as a page. When Charles escapes, he asks Sir Henry to withdraw his objections to her marriage to Everard.

Albert Lee, Sir Henry's son. He is helping to keep Charles hidden and is making arrangements for his escape. He disguises himself as the Prince and decoys Cromwell's soldiers while Charles escapes. When Albert is captured, Cromwell sentences him to death, but later relents and changes the sentence to banishment. Albert finally is killed in battle.

Colonel Markham Everard, Sir Henry's nephew and a Puritan. In spite of his beliefs, he refuses to betray Charles and even helps him to escape. He is in love with and marries Alice.

Roger Wildrake, Everard's friend and a Royalist. He also refuses to betray the King, and sends a message to Woodstock warning that Cromwell is coming.

Joceline Joliffe, the lodgekeeper at Woodstock. He is a Royalist, and he kills the Roundhead steward Tomkins for making advances to Phoebe Mayflower, the woman Joliffe loves. He finally marries Phoebe.

Louis Kerneguy, a churlish and mischievous young page, really Prince Charles Stuart in disguise. He has been rescued from the Puritans and is in hiding until he can get out of the country. He cannot understand why his advances to Alice are repulsed, and he readily accepts Everard's challenge to a duel. He finally returns to England, after many years, and is crowned King.

Joseph Tomkins, a steward for the Puritans, killed by Joliffe.

Dr. Anthony Rochecliffe, the Royalist chaplain of Woodstock, who helps to rescue Charles from the Puritans.

Oliver Cromwell, Lord Protector of the Commonwealth, who is pursuing and trying to capture Charles before he can leave the country.

WORLD ENOUGH AND TIME

Author: Robert Penn Warren (1905-   )
Time of action: 1801-1826
First published: 1950

PRINCIPAL CHARACTERS

Jeremiah Beaumont, a man betrayed by his idealism as well as by the compromises and realities of life. An earnest young lawyer, he first becomes disillusioned with his benefactor, Colonel Cassius Fort, a famous lawyer and politician, on learning that Fort has seduced an innocent girl. He renounces his benefactor, becomes involved in politics, and marries the betrayed girl. Jeremiah loses a bitter election. He has given up his intention of killing his wife's seducer; but a scurrilous political handbill, giving a false account of the seduction, enrages him. He kills his former benefactor and is convicted, not by true but by false evidence. An old friend helps him to escape from prison. While hiding out, Jeremiah learns that this friend had been responsible for the libelous handbill. Jeremiah's wife commits suicide, and he is murdered when he attempts to go back to tell the real story. Jeremiah's story is a reworking of that of a historical figure, Jeroboam Beauchamp.

Colonel Cassius Fort, Jeremiah's benefactor, a frontier politician. Though he did seduce the girl whom Jeremiah marries, he is not the author of the handbill which bears his name and which drives Jeremiah to kill him. This character is based on Colonel Solomon P. Sharp, who, like Fort, was assassinated in 1825.

Rachael Jordan, the daughter of a planter, who is seduced by Fort and who later marries Jeremiah. She marries him on condition that he kill Fort; later she dissuades him from fulfilling his promise. When Jeremiah sees the scurrilous handbill, however, he kills Fort. After her husband's conviction, Rachael is also arrested; both are freed by Jeremiah's false friend. Later Rachael kills herself.

Wilkie Barron, Jeremiah's opportunistic and false friend, whom he has known since their days as law students together. Barron and several others break into jail and free Jeremiah shortly before his execution date; but Jeremiah learns that Barron was responsible for the handbill that made him kill Fort. After Jeremiah is killed by one of Barron's men, Barron goes on to become rich and successful. Finally he shoots himself; among his papers is found Jeremiah's manuscript, revealing the whole story.

Jasper Beaumont, Jeremiah's bankrupt father. Jeremiah inherits his father's moodiness, and he develops the feeling that he must work hard to settle his father's score.

Dr. Leicester Burnham, young Jeremiah's teacher, who is a loyal friend. He recommends his pupil to Fort, and remains loyal to Jeremiah during his trial.

Mrs. Beaumont, nee **Marcher,** Jeremiah's mother, who is disinherited by her wealthy father. Her final illness postpones Jeremiah's law studies.

Thomas Barron, Wilkie's uncle. While visiting him Jeremiah meets Rachael.

Percival Scrogg, a fanatic liberal newspaper editor. He and Wilkie Barron together print and distribute the handbill attributed to Fort.

Josh Parham, a rich landowner with whom Jeremiah forms a partnership. Their land speculation falls through when the Relief Party comes to power. Parham, an Anti-Relief man, swears not to open up Kentucky land while the Relief Party is in office.

Felix Parham, Josh's son.

Desha, the Relief candidate, elected governor in 1824.

Sellars, the candidate who defeats Jeremiah in their election contest.

La Grand' Bosse, a river pirate. After escaping from prison, Jeremiah and Rachael take refuge with him.

THE WORLD OF THE THIBAULTS

Author: Roger Martin du Gard (1881-   )
Time of action: Early twentieth century
First published: 1922-1940

PRINCIPAL CHARACTERS

M. Thibault (tē'bō'), an eminent Catholic social worker who has no time for the problems of his own disturbed family. When his son Jacques runs away in revolt against the smug respectability of his father and the dull Thibault household, the bigotted father suspects him, wrongly, of unnatural relations with his companion, a Protestant boy named Daniel de Fontanin. He gets the boy back and puts him into a reformatory which M. Thibault has founded. M. Thibault is mercifully killed, during an incurable illness, when Antoine and Jacques give him an overdose of morphine.

Jacques Thibault (zhäk'), an active youngster whose spirit is nearly broken by the cruel guards at the reformatory. His older brother Antoine, a doctor, helps his gradual recuperation. Later, repulsed by Jenny de Fontanin, he disappears for three years. Part of that time he spends in England. He then goes to Geneva, where he becomes an international socialist and an influential writer working to prevent the outbreak of World War I. Traced through his writing, he is called back as his father is dying. There he again sees Jenny and they are lovers until his pacifist duties call him back to Geneva. His plane is wrecked while he is trying to shower on the workers and soldiers of France and Germany pamphlets calling for peace through a general strike and refusal to bear arms. Bady injured and suspected of being a spy, he is shot by an orderly while he is being carried to headquarters for investigation.

Antoine Thibault (äṅ·twàṅ'), the older son, a doctor. He recognizes biographical and family details in a story published by Jacques in a Swiss magazine and summons his brother home during M. Thibault's last illness. He falls in love with one of his patients, an adventuress named Rachel. The former mistress of Hirsch, a sadistic libertine, she eventually deserts Antoine to follow Hirsch to Africa. A necklace comes back to Antoine to announce her death. Antoine, gassed during the war, dies just before the signing of the Armistice.

Gise (zhēz'), an orphan girl living with the Thibaults. After Jacques disappears, she is the only one confident that he is still alive.

Daniel de Fontanin (dà·nyĕl' dɔ fōṅ·tä-näṅ'), a young Protestant who has an innocent and boyish affection for Jacques Thibault. Later he wins success as an artist and leads a bohemian life. Desexed by a shell fragment during the war, he afterward spends much of his time assisting at a military hospital and playing with his nephew, young Jean-Paul, the son of his sister Jenny and his dead friend, Jacques Thibault.

Rachel (rà·shĕl'), Antoine Thibault's mistress, who tries unsuccessfully to end her affair with Hirsch. Eventually she deserts Antoine and goes to Africa with her former lover.

Jenny de Fontanin (zhĕ·nē′ də fōñ·tä-näñ), the daughter of a stanch Protestant family and the sister of Jacques Thibault's friend. A shy, frigid girl, she cannot bear to be touched by Jacques. After Antoine Thibault detects that she is suffering from meningitis, she experiences a miraculous faith cure through Pastor Gregory. Later she meets Jacques, now a mature and self-assured pacifist, and falls in love with him. Her mother, coming home, finds them sleeping together. She plans to go to Geneva with him but gives him up when she realizes he is dedicated to the pacifist cause. After his death she bears his son, Jean-Paul.

Madame de Fontanin (mà·dàm′ də fōñ-tä·näñ′), the mother of Daniel and Jenny. Deserted by her husband, she occupies herself in war work as a hospital administrator in Paris.

Jérome de Fontanin (zhä·rôm′ də fōñ-tä·näñ′), her husband, who runs away with Noémie his cousin. He dies in Vienna, suspected of embezzlement.

Nicole (nē·kôl′), the daughter of Noémie, who comes to live with Madame de Fontanin after her mother goes off with Jérome. Daniel vainly tries to seduce her.

Hirsch (ērsh′), a lecherous, brutal fifty-year-old man who has incestuous relations with his daughter Clara. To protect himself from disgrace, after her husband learns his wife's secret, he strangles both and throws their bodies into an Italian lake. Then he flees to Africa and sends for Rachel, his former mistress.

Clara Hirsch (klà′rä ērsh′), who marries Rachel's brother. When she sends for her father to join her and her husband in Italy, she creates a situation which results in her death.

Meynestrel (mā·nĕs·trĕl′), an international Socialist leader burned to death when the plane from which he and Jacques are distributing anti-war leaflets crashes in France.

THE WORLD'S ILLUSION

Author: Jacob Wassermann (1873-1934)
Time of action: Prior to World War I
First published: 1919

PRINCIPAL CHARACTERS

Christian Wahnschaffe (krĭs′tē·än vän′-shäf), the son of a rich German capitalist and a young man of great physical courage. He lives and travels in the best European society. Through his association with a refugee Russian revolutionary, Christian becomes convinced of the futility of his idle life. Despite family opposition, he gives up his inheritance to become a poor man, going about helping the unfortunates of the world.

Bernard Crammon (bârn′härd crä′môn), Christian's aristocratic friend and travel-ing companion in his luxurious and leisurely life.

Eva Sorel (ā·fä sŏ·räl′), a dancer of whom Christian becomes enamored. She finally gives herself to him, but by this time his growing idealism has dulled his sensual interests and the affair does not last long.

Ivan Becker (ē·fän′ bĕ′kėr), a Russian revolutionary. He introduces Christian to the problems of poverty.

Amadeus Voss (ä′mä·dā′ŏŏs fôss), a young man who once studied for the priesthood. He adds to Christian's conviction that his life is futile. Voss expects to gain wealth from the association, and he proves disloyal when Christian is actually going about giving his fortune back to the family.

Karen Engelschall (kä'ren äng'gĕl·shäl), a prostitute whom the liberalized Christian befriends. She also expects to profit handsomely from the association, and she thinks Christian mad when he gives up his wealth.

Denis Lay, an English nobleman and Christian's rival for Eva's affections. Lay dares Christian to compete in a swimming contest with him; he drowns despite Christian's efforts to save him.

The Grand Duke Cyril (sü·rĭl'), of St. Petersburg, who wishes to lay everything he can command at Eva's feet. She refuses him and returns to Western Europe to become Christian's mistress.

WOYZECK

Author: Georg Büchner (1813-1837)
Time of action: Early nineteenth century
First presented: 1913; first published: 1879

PRINCIPAL CHARACTERS

Friedrich Johann Franz Woyzeck (frēd'-rĭsh jō'hän fränts voi'tsăk), a superstitious, slow-witted peasant conscripted as a fusilier in the German army. He is devoted to his sweetheart and their small son. To earn money to support them he does many menial jobs, including shaving his Captain. He attributes his low moral standards to his poverty and lack of education. He has strange visions and is driven out of his mind by his mistress' infidelity. He kills her and then drowns accidentally while trying to get rid of the murder weapon.

Andres (än'drĕs), a matter-of-fact soldier and Woyzeck's friend.

Marie (mä·rē'), Woyzeck's mistress and the mother of his little boy. A hearty, earthy person, she takes the Drum Major as her second lover, defying Woyzeck when he discovers her infidelity. She is murdered by Woyzeck after he sees her dancing with the Drum Major at an inn.

The Drum Major, Marie's second lover. A swaggering, powerful man, he beats Woyzeck badly in a fight over Marie.

The Captain, Woyzeck's commander. He teases Woyzeck about being a cuckold, thereby arousing Woyzeck's suspicions about Marie.

The Doctor, an eccentric. He pays Woyzeck to submit to absurd medical experiments. He finds Woyzeck laughable and makes the man appear ridiculous in front of others.

Karl (kärl), a loafer in the garrison town. He says, before Marie's murder, that he smells blood on Woyzeck.

Kaethe (kā'tė), a girl at the inn in the garrison town. She is the first to notice that Woyzeck has blood on his hands after he has murdered Marie.

THE WRECK OF THE GROSVENOR

Author: W. Clark Russell (1844-1911)
Time of action: Nineteenth century
First published: 1877

Mr. Coxon, captain of the "Grosvenor." He is a tough skipper who is hard on his crew to the point of cruelty. He even refuses to pick up survivors from one shipwreck. Later he is forced to allow his second mate to rescue people from another wreck the "Grosvenor" meets, but he puts the mate in irons after the rescue. The crew of the ship mutinies and kills the captain.

Mr. Duckling, first mate of the "Grosvenor." He sides always with the captain and is killed by the mutineers.

Mr. Royle, second mate of the "Grosvenor." He is a compassionate man who does what he can for the mistreated crew. He, with the crew's help, forces the captain to permit the rescue of two survivors of a wrecked ship. After the mutiny the mutineers force the mate to navigate for them. He finally rescues himself, Mary Robertson, the steward, and one loyal sailor from the ship, which sinks in a storm.

Mary Robertson, a young woman saved by Mr. Royle after a shipwreck. She and the mate fall in love and are married after they reach the shore and safety. The girl is the daughter of a wealthy owner of a shipping firm.

Mr. Robertson, Mary's father, rescued with her by Mr. Royle. He dies of natural causes aboard the "Grosvenor."

Stevens, a sailor who leads the mutiny aboard the "Grosvenor." He is unsuccessful in carrying out his plan to scuttle the ship with Mr. Royle and the Robertsons aboard.

WUTHERING HEIGHTS

Author: Emily Brontë (1818-1848)
Time of action: 1771-1802
First published: 1847

PRINCIPAL CHARACTERS

Heathcliff, a dark-visaged, violently passionate, black-natured man. A foundling brought to the Earnshaw home at an early age, he is subjected to cruel emotional sufferings during his formative years. His chief tormentor is Hindley Earnshaw, who is jealous of his father's obvious partiality toward Heathcliff. These he endures with the sullen patience of a hardened, ill-treated animal, but just as the years add age his suffering adds hatred in Heathcliff's nature and he becomes filled with an inhuman, almost demonic, desire for vengeance against Hindley. This ambition coupled with his strange, transcendent relationship with Catherine, Hindley's sister, encompasses his life until he becomes a devastatingly wasted human, in fact, hardly human at all. He evaluates himself as a truly superior person who, possessing great emotional energies and capabilities, is a creature set apart from the human. Some regard him as a fiend, full of horrible passions and powers. In the end he dies empty, his will gone, his fervor exhausted, survived by Cathy and Hareton, the conventionalists, the moralists, the victims of his vengeful wraths.

Catherine Earnshaw, the sister of Hindley, later the wife of Edgar Linton and mother of young Cathy Linton. Catherine is spirited as a girl, selfish, wild, saucy, provoking, and sometimes even wicked. But she can be sweet of eye and smile, and she is often contrite for causing pain with her insolence. In childhood she and Heathcliff form an unusually close relationship, but as her friendship with Edgar and Isabella Linton grows, she becomes haughty and arrogant. In spite of her devotion to Heathcliff she rejects him for fear marriage to him would degrade her. Instead, she accepts Edgar Linton's proposal. But her deep feeling for Heathcliff remains; he is her one unselfishness, and she insists that Edgar must at least tolerate him so that her marriage will not alter her friendship with Heathcliff. Her marriage is a tolerably happy one, possibly because Catherine becomes unspirited after Heathcliff's departure because of her rejection. Upon his return they become close friends again, despite his apparent vile character and foul treatment of her family. In their inhuman passion and fierce, tormented love they are lost to each other, each possessing the other's spirit as if it were his own. Her mind broken and anguished, Catherine finally dies in childbirth.

Hindley Earnshaw, the brother of Catherine Earnshaw, husband of Frances, and father of Hareton. As a child he is intensely jealous of Heathcliff and treats the boy cruelly. After the death of Frances, Hindley's character deteriorates rapidly; he drinks heavily and finally dies in disgrace, debt, and degradation as the result of Heathcliff's scheme of vengeance.

Edgar Linton, the husband of Catherine and father of Cathy. A polished, cultured man, he is truly in love with Catherine and makes her happy until Heathcliff returns to Wuthering Heights. He is a steady, unassuming person, patient and indulgent of both his wife and his daughter.

Cathy Linton, the daughter of Edgar and Catherine and wife of Linton Heathcliff. A bright, spirited affectionate girl, she pities Linton, becomes his friend, and through the trickery and bribery of Heathcliff is forced to marry the sickly young man. She becomes sullen and ill-tempered in Heathcliff's household, but

she finds ultimate happiness with Hareton Earnshaw.

Hareton Earnshaw, the son of Hindley and Frances and the object of Heathcliff's revenge against Hindley. Under Heathcliff's instruction, or rather neglect, Hareton grows into a crude, gross, uneducated young man until Cathy, after Heathcliff's death, takes him under her charge and begins to improve his mind and manners. The two fall in love and marry.

Linton Heathcliff, the son of Heathcliff and Isabella and the husband of Cathy Linton. He is a selfish boy indulged and spoiled by his mother. After her death he returns to live with Heathcliff and at Wuthering Heights sinks into a weak-willed existence, a victim of his father's harsh treatment. Sickly since infancy, he dies at an early age, shortly after his marriage to Cathy Linton.

Isabella Linton, the sister of Edgar, Heathcliff's wife, and mother of Linton. A rather reserved, spoiled, often sulking girl, she becomes infatuated with Heathcliff, and in spite of her family's opposition and warnings she runs away with him. Later, regretting her foolish action, she leaves him and lives with her son Linton until her death.

Frances Earnshaw, the wife of Hindley; she dies of consumption.

Mr. Earnshaw, the father of Catherine and Hindley. He brings Heathcliff to Wuthering Heights after a business trip to Liverpool.

Mrs. Earnshaw, his wife.

Mrs. Ellen Dean, called **Nelly,** the housekeeper who relates Heathcliff's history to Mr. Lockwood and thereby serves as one of the book's narrators. A servant in the household at Wuthering Heights, she goes with Catherine to Thrushcross Grange when the latter marries Edgar Linton. Some years later she returns to live at Wuthering Heights as the housekeeper for Heathcliff. She is a humble, solid character, conventional, reserved, and patient. Although Hindley's disorderly home and Heathcliff's evil conduct distress her, often appall her, she does little to combat these unnatural personalities, perhaps through lack of imagination but certainly not from lack of will, for in the face of Heathcliff's merciless vengeance she is stanch and strong.

Mr. Lockwood, the first narrator, a foppish visitor from the city and Heathcliff's tenant. Interested in his landlord, he hears Mrs. Dean relate the story of the Earnshaw and Linton families.

Joseph, a servant at Wuthering Heights. He is forever making gloomy observations and predictions about other people and offering stern reprimands for their impious behavior.

Zillah, a servant at Wuthering Heights.

Mr. Green and
Mr. Kenneth, lawyers in Gimmerton, a neighboring village.

THE YEARLING

Author: Marjorie Kinnan Rawlings (1896-1953)
Time of action: Late nineteenth century
First published: 1938

PRINCIPAL CHARACTERS

Jody Baxter, a young Florida boy. A lover of animals, of play, and of the excitement of hunting, Jody is a child at the beginning of the story. Matured by the experiences of one year—his father's illnesses, the death of Fodder-wing, and the killing of Flag—Jody is at the end of the novel ready to accept the responsibilities that come with growing up. One of the most appealing and believable boys in American fiction, Jody deserves comparison with Tom Aldrich, Tom Sawyer, Huck Finn, and Stephen Crane's Whilomville boys.

Ezra (Penny) Baxter, his father, a friend and companion to his son, who idolizes him. Penny's dimunitive size only increases Jody's admiration of his father's ability to hunt and work hard for a plain living. Penny's scrupulous honesty and his simple philosophy of life he attempts to pass on to his son. Both father and son are drawn to the beauty of the rich and varied natural world about them.

Ora (Ma) Baxter, his mother, a bulky woman considerably larger than her husband. She loves Jody but is annoyed by his "wasting" time and is unwilling to forgive Flag for his depredations.

Fodder-wing Forrester, Jody's crippled friend, a frail boy who loves and has a way with animals, especially those that, like himself, have been crippled through no fault of their own. He dies shortly after naming Flag for Jody.

Oliver Hutto, Penny's friend, a sailor whose courtship of Twink causes him to be brutally beaten by the Forrester boys and whose marriage results in the vengeful burning of his mother's home.

Grandma Hutto, his mother, a friend of the Baxters.

Twink Weatherby, Oliver's yellow-haired sweetheart and later his wife.

Lem Forrester, older brother of Fodder-wing; jealous and fiercely resentful of Oliver's love for and marriage to Twink.

Buck Forrester, another Forrester brother who helps the Baxters after Penny is bitten by a rattlesnake.

Flag, Jody's beautiful but mischeivous and destructive pet fawn. He is wounded when Mrs. Baxter in anger shoots him because of the destruction he has caused. Jody sorrowfully shoots him again to end his suffering. Flag's growing up partly parallels Jody's. Flag fails to adapt his irresponsible ways to life with the Baxters and dies as a result. Jody rebels at first against life's ways but at last submits and learns to accept the sorrows of life with its joys.

Pa and
Ma Forrester, rough but good-hearted

parents of the exclusively male Forrester brood.

Mill-Wheel,
Gabby,
Pack, and
Arch Forrester, four of their sons.

Doc Wilson, the physician who attends Penny during his illnesses.

Old Slewfoot, a giant black bear that raids the Baxter hogs. He is finally killed by Penny.

Nellie Ginright, owner of the canoe in which Jody flees after Flag's death.

THE YEARS

Author: Virginia Woolf (1882-1941)
Time of action: 1880-1937
First published: 1937

PRINCIPAL CHARACTERS

Colonel Abel Pargiter, a solid, middle-class, retired army officer, father of the family whose progress through the years is traced in fragmentary episodes from 1880 to 1937. Lonely and purposeless, he sits in his club, goes to the city, visits his mistress, Mira, and returns to his genteel but rather shabby home on Abercorn Terrace, where his wife lies ill of a lingering illness and his children are gathered for tea. Mrs. Pargiter dies that night. All his children but one leave for lives of their own. The exception is Eleanor, with whom the Colonel lives on in the same pattern until his death some thirty years later.

Eleanor Pargiter, Colonel Abel Pargiter's eldest daughter. Naturally cheerful, efficient, given to social work, she is, at twenty-two, the mainstay of the family during her mother's lingering illness. After her mother's death she lives on with her father as his housekeeper and companion until he dies when she is fifty-five. She sells the house on Abercorn Terrace and goes to live alone between

her travels abroad. When she is over seventy, she still finds life a continual discovery and enjoys the prospects of a bright new day.

Edward Pargiter, Abel's scholarly son. As a student at Oxford, he is in love with Kitty Malone, who refuses him. He later becomes a Greek scholar of considerable distinction.

Morris Pargiter, Abel's not-too-successful barrister son.

Delia Pargiter, Abel's daughter. Rebellious and resentful of the restrictions imposed by her mother's illness, she longs to escape the ties of home. She dreams of herself on the political platform with her hero, Charles Parnell. Later, under the illusion that he is a wild Irish rebel, she marries handsome, conventional Patrick.

Milly Pargiter, Abel's daughter. She marries Hugh Gibbs, with whom she lives on an estate in the country. Obese and unimaginative in their later years, they

1273

appear gross and tiresome to the younger generation.

Rose Pargiter, Abel's youngest daughter. Always a firebrand with a love for causes, she joins the suffragette movement and is even imprisoned for the cause. With the years she grows stout and deaf but never loses her air of mannish independence.

Martin Pargiter, Abel's youngest son. As a young man he joins the army, which he detests. He retires as Captain Pargiter and returns to London to live alone in a flat.

North Pargiter, Morris Pargiter's son. After service in World War I, he lives in lonely isolation on a sheep farm in Africa. He returns to the greater loneliness of crowded London and ponders what it is that so separates human beings from one another.

Peggy Pargiter, Morris Pargiter's daughter, who lives in loneliness as a doctor.

Sir Digby Pargiter, Colonel Abel Pargiter's brother, a public servant.

Maggie Pargiter, Sir Digby Pargiter's elder daughter, who becomes happily married to a Frenchman named René (Renny).

Sara Pargiter, Sir Digby Pargiter's sensitive, crippled younger daughter. After her sister Maggie's marriage, she lives alone in a shabby flat.

Kitty Malone, a cousin of the Pargiter family. As a young girl, she is loved by Edward Pargiter but marries her mother's choice, the wealthy, fashionable Lord Lasswade. As the years go by she reflects on the changes they bring and wonders who is right and who is wrong in the choices men make. She finds a measure of peace when she escapes, alone, to the country, where time seems to stand still.

Crosby, the Pargiters' faithful servant at the house on Abercorn Terrace.

Mira, Colonel Abel Pargiter's lower-class mistress.

Eugénie, Sir Digby Pargiter's handsome, frivolous wife.

Hugh Gibbs, Milly Pargiter's husband.

Lord Lasswade, Kitty Malone's husband.

Celia, Morris Pargiter's wife.

Patrick, Delia Pargiter's Irish husband.

René (Renny), Maggie Pargiter's French husband.

Nicholas Pomjalovsky, the Polish friend of Eleanor, Sara, and Maggie Pargiter.

Miss Craddock, Kitty Malone's eccentric history teacher.

THE YEMASSEE

Author: William Gilmore Simms (1806-1870)
Time of action: Early eighteenth century
First published: 1835

PRINCIPAL CHARACTERS

Gabriel Harrison (Governor Charles Craven), a young man of commanding presence and gay, worldly manner. A stranger looked on with suspicion by some of the South Carolina frontiersmen, he wins them over by his valiant leadership in defending the colony against the Yemassee uprising. He then reveals that he is the new Governor of the province in disguise.

Parson Matthews, who dislikes Harrison until won over by his heroism. Matthews' insistence on the friendliness of the Indians, in spite of Harrison's warnings, results in his and his daughter's capture and in their subsequent rescue by Harrison.

Bess Matthews, the parson's daughter, in love with and loved by Harrison. The parson finally gives permission for their marriage.

Hector, Harrison's devoted Negro slave and constant companion. After undergoing various ordeals on behalf of or with his master, he refuses Harrison's offer to give him his freedom.

Sanutee, the last great Yemassee chief. Proud, and suspicious of the increasing encroachments of the colonists upon Yemassee territory, he rouses his people to cast out the land-selling chiefs and to make war on the settlers. At last he is killed in battle.

Occonestoga, Sanutee's son. A drunkard, he is friendly with the whites, an alliance which forces him to flee his tribe. He saves Bess Matthews' life and is consequently befriended by Harrison. Returning to the Indian stronghold to spy for Harrison, he is discovered by his father.

Matiwan, Sanutee's wife, torn between loyalty to her husband and devotion to her son. Finally, to prevent the carrying out of Sanutee's order that Occonestoga have the tribal mark cut from his skin and be executed, she herself kills her son.

Hugh Grayson, a rival of Harrison for the affections of Bess Matthews. He, too, is finally won to friendship by Harrison's bravery. After revealing himself as the Governor, Harrison makes Hugh Grayson commander of the garrison forces.

Walter Grayson, Hugh's brother, an honorable young farmer.

Dick Chorley, a sailor whom Harrison discovers to be a Spanish agent come to arm the Indians against the English settlers.

Ishiagaska, another Yemassee chief.

Enoree Mattee, an Indian prophet who aids Sanutee in rousing his people against the settlers.

Granger, a trader.

Mrs. Granger, his brave and quick-witted wife.

Dugdale, Harrison's strong and faithful dog.

YOU CAN'T GO HOME AGAIN

Author: Thomas Wolfe (1900-1938)
Time of action: 1929-1936
First published: 1940

PRINCIPAL CHARACTERS

George Webber, a young writer in the first flush of success as a novelist. He learns that success brings enemies and that success is sometimes empty of meaning. His great aim in life, idealist that he is, is to write the truth, to portray people as they are, the great and small, the rich and poor. He faces disillusionment at every turn. He finds that his fellow men are greedy after the world's goods; he finds, too, that they do not relish his truthful portrayal of them. George again visits Germany, a place he loves, only to find that country filled with fear and persecution in the 1930's, during the Nazi regime. He returns home to the United States to preach in new novels against selfishness and greed,

1275

hoping he can awaken the people of his own land to arise and defeat the forces which are threatening the freedom of mankind.

Foxhall Edwards, an editor for a publishing house who becomes George Webber's friend and trusted adviser for a time. He is a genius at encouraging young writers to find themselves and to win the confidence they need to produce literary art. He is also a skeptical person who believes that if man is not destined for freedom, he must accept this fact. Edwards' fatalism is at odds with George's idealistic desire to better the lot of mankind by working to change conditions. These divergent attitudes cause a break in the friendship between the two men.

Lloyd McHarg, a successful American novelist who has won world-wide fame based upon a number of excellent novels. He has found fame to be empty and searches for something, he knows not what. McHarg's disillusionment is a bitter lesson for young, idealistic George Webber, for whom McHarg has been a symbol of greatness as a man of letters.

Esther Jack, an older woman who has been George's mistress in the past and becomes so again for a time after he has achieved success. He leaves her a second time when he decides that in order to find himself, he must leave Esther's sophisticated set and get to know the common people of the world.

Else von Kohler, a beautiful, intelligent young German woman with whom George has a tender romance while revisiting Germany during the 1930's.

YOU KNOW ME AL

Author: Ring Lardner (1885-1933)
Time of action: c. 1915
First published: 1916

PRINCIPAL CHARACTERS

Jack Keefe, a right-handed White Sox pitcher. In his letters to Al, Jack gives a full account of his adventures; he also reveals himself to be a shameless braggart and chronic self-excuser. With complete lack of reticence he discusses his foolish episodes with his girl friends, his troubles with his baseball career, later his marital misadventures and his in-law troubles. Actually, Jack is a powerful pitcher, but his laziness, alibis, stinginess, and egotistical gullibility make him the rather pathetic hero of this satire.

Al Blanchard, Jack Keefe's correspondent. Patronized and used by Jack, Al is the recipient of the letters which elaborate every detail of the pitcher's life. Apparently Al never sees through Jack.

Florrie, Jack's wife and Allen's sister-in-law. Disgusted with Jack's stinginess, Florrie leaves him when he is sold to Milwaukee. She rejoins him when she learns she is pregnant. She names the baby after Allen.

Allen, Jack's brother-in-law, also a pitcher.

Marie, Allen's wife.

Violet, a girl friend who ditches Jack when he is sent back to the minor league.

Hazel, another girl friend who marries a boxer.

Al, Jack's son.

YOUMA

Author: Lafcadio Hearn (1850-1904)
Time of action: The 1840's
First published: 1890

PRINCIPAL CHARACTERS

Youma (yōō·mà'), a slave in Martinique. She is a personification of loyalty. When her childhood playmate, her mistress' daughter, asks Youma to take care of her child, Youma grants the dying woman's request. Although she finds the child irksome at times, she steadfastly cares for the little girl, even giving up marriage in order to fulfill her promise. At last, in a slave riot in 1848, she refuses to save her own life when her fellow slaves will not let her save the life of the child by taking it out of a burning building.

Aimée Desrivières (ĕ·mä' dā·rē·vyĕr'), a white girl reared with Youma. The two love each other almost as sisters. Aimée, as she lies dying, asks Youma to become her little daughter's nurse, and the slave agrees to do what she can for the child.

Marie Desrivières (mà·rē' dā·rē·vyĕr'), nicknamed **Mayotte** (mà·yŏt'). She is the little child placed in Youma's care.

Gabriel (gà·bryĕl'), a field hand and slave. He loves Youma and wants to marry her. When Youma's owner refuses to permit the marriage, he offers to elope with Youma and seek freedom, but Youma refuses to abandon her care of little Mayotte.

Madame Peyronette (pā·rô·nĕt'), Mme. Desrivières' mother and Youma's owner. Although she intends to free Youma when the slave marries, she will not let Youma marry a field hand such as Gabriel.

Monsieur Desrivières (dā·rē·vyĕr'), the husband of Aimée Desrivières. He is Gabriel's owner. At his wife's death he is happy to see Youma take over the care of his child, for he is grief-stricken.

YVAIN

Author: Chrétien de Troyes (c. 1150-c. 1190)
Time of action: Sixth century
First transcribed: After 1164

PRINCIPAL CHARACTERS

Yvain (ē·văn'), a knight of the Round Table. Upon hearing of Calogrenant's misadventure at the magic spring, Yvain avenges him and kills the Knight at the spring. Yvain marries the Knight's widow, Laudine de Landuc, and lives happily until lured away by promised adventures. When he fails to return, Laudine renounces him and grief drives Yvain mad. After his wits are restored, he is ashamed to admit his identity. Accompanied by a lion he has befriended, he

becomes known as the Knight with the Lion. After countless adventures Yvain is finally reconciled with his lady.

Laudine de Landuc (lō·dēn' də län·dük'), Yvain's wife. Made a widow by Yvain, she marries him after he has begged her forgiveness. When he fails to return from his adventures as promised, she renounces him and accepts him back only after Lunete intercedes for him.

Lunete (lü·nĕt'), a damsel serving Laudine. Lunete befriends Yvain and brings about his marriage to Laudine. She is sentenced to die when Yvain does not return; however, as the Knight with the Lion, Yvain rescues her. Thus reinstated, she is able to reconcile the estranged pair.

Sir Gawain, Yvain's friend and King Arthur's nephew.

King Arthur, of the Round Table.

Guinevere, his Queen.

Sir Kay, the cynical seneschal, humbled by Yvain.

Harpin of the Mountain, a giant slain by Yvain.

Calogrenant (ka·lō·grə·nän'), Yvain's cousin-german, whose tale of the Knight of the Magic Spring begins Yvain's adventures.

Lady Noroison (nà·rwà·zōn'), who is championed by Yvain.

Count Alier (à·lyā'), the knight who is plundering Lady Noroison's lands. He is defeated by Yvain.

ZADIG

Author: Voltaire (François Marie Arouet, 1694-1778)
Time of action: Remote antiquity
First published: 1747

PRINCIPAL CHARACTERS

Zadig (zà·dēg'), a wealthy young man. Educated and sensible, he rises to the position of prime minister of Babylon, only to be forced to flee after his supposed affair with Queen Astarté. Enslaved by the Egyptians, he serves Sétoc and then King Nabussan. Finally he finds Astarté and rescues her from Ogul. In a tournament of wits and arms he wins Astarté as his bride and rules Babylon justly and compassionately.

Astarté (às·tàr·tā'), Queen of Babylon. After Zadig flees, she also escapes with Cador's aid. She is captured by the Prince of Hyrcania, escapes from him, is captured by Arbogad, and sold to Ogul. Zadig rescues her and then wins her hand.

Moabdar (mō·àb·dàr'), King of Babylon. Suspicious that Zadig and Astarté are lovers, he forces Zadig to flee. When Astarté escapes also, he marries Missouf. Later he goes mad and is killed in a revolt.

Cador (kà·dôr'), Zadig's best friend, who helps Astarté escape.

Jesrad (zhĕs·ràd'), an angel who helps Zadig.

Itobad (ē·tō·bàd'), an evil lord, Zadig's rival for Astarté's hand.

Sémire (sā·mēr'), Zadig's first betrothed. He loses an eye while rescuing her from kidnapers. She then refuses to marry a one-eyed man.

Hermes (ĕr·mĕs'), the doctor who predicts that Zadig's eye cannot heal.

Orcan (ôr·kän'), the noble who marries Sémire.

Azora (à·zō·rà'), Zadig's first wife, who becomes too difficult to live with.

Arimaze (à·rē·màz'), called **The Envious,** Zadig's enemy.

Missouf (mē·sōōf'), an Egyptian woman

whose lover is killed by Zadig. She marries King Moabdar.

Sétoc (sā·tôk'), Zadig's Arabian master.

Almona (ál·mō·ná'), a widow, later Sétoc's wife.

Nabussan (ná·bü·sán'), King of Seren-

dib, who has only one faithful wife out of one hundred.

Arbogad (är·bo·gàd'), a happy brigand who sells Astarté to Ogul.

Ogul (ô·kül'), a voluptuary cured by Zadig.

ZAÏRE

Author: Voltaire (François Marie Arouet, 1694-1778)
Time of action: During the reign of Osman, Sultan of Jerusalem
First presented: 1732

PRINCIPAL CHARACTERS

Zaïre (zà·ēr'), a slave of the Sultan Orosmane. Captured in infancy, Zaïre finds that she can love the Moslem ruler in spite of his religion. However, she discovers that the Christian leader, Lusignan, is her father and Nerestan is her brother. She then vows to become a Christian and, counseled by her brother, postpones her nuptials. Torn between her love for Orosmane and her loyalty to her family, Zaïre goes to meet her brother and is killed by the jealous Orosmane.

Nerestan (nā·rĕs·tän'), Zaïre's brother. A prisoner of the Moslems since the age of four, Nerestan escaped to fight against the Turks, only to be captured at Damas. Because of his bravery he is released to secure the ransom of the Christian prisoners. He learns that Lusignan is really his father and that Zaïre is his sister. A devout Christian, Nerestan attempts to persuade Zaïre to abandon her plans to marry the sultan.

Orosmane (ô·rôs·màn'), also **Osman**, Sul-

tan of Jerusalem. Captivated by his slave girl Zaïre, he decides to make her his Sultana. Ignorant of the relationship between Zaïre and Nerestan, he thinks they are lovers and murders her in a fit of jealousy.

Lusignan (lü·zēn·yän'), a French prince in the line of the Kings of Jerusalem. Because of his title Orosmane refuses to ransom Lusignan, but Zaïre is able to secure his release. After he is liberated he learns that Nerestan and Zaïre are his long-lost children.

Chatillon (shà·tē·yōñ'), a French captive ransomed by Nerestan.

Fatima (fà·tē'mà), a slave of the Sultan. Captured in adulthood, Fatima is a devout Christian who exerts her influence on Zaïre.

Corasmin (kô·ràs·măñ') and
Meledor (mā·lā·dōr'), officers of the Sultan.

EL ZARCO

Author: Ignacio Manuel Altamirano (1834-1893)
Time of action: 1861-1863
First published: 1901

Nicolas (nē·ko·läs′), a Mexican blacksmith of Indian descent. Infatuated by Manuela, Nicolas realizes, while he is imprisoned for accusing an officer of shirking his duties, that Pilar is his true love. Released from jail, he joins Martín Sánchez and assists in El Zarco's capture. When the bandit is finally executed, Nicolas and Pilar pass by on the way to their wedding.

El Zarco (ĕl sär′kō), a bandit. Taking advantage of the troubled times during the War of Reform, El Zarco leads his cutthroats through the countryside murdering and plundering. Flattered by her devotion, he takes Manuela as his bride.

Manuela (mä·nwä′lä), Doña Antonia's impetuous daughter. In love with the bandit El Zarco, she refuses to believe the stories of his cruelty. After she runs away with him she sees his sordid side, but she still remains true to him. When he is executed she falls to the ground dead.

Martín Sánchez (mär·tēn′ sän′chās), a rancher. Enraged by the death of his father and his son at the hands of El Zarco, Martín swears to track down the bandits. At Calavera he captures El Zarco, but the outlaw is rescued. Undaunted, Martín again captures the bandits and executes them.

Pilar (pē·lär′), Doña Antonia's godchild, in love with Nicolas.

El Tigre (ĕl tē′grā), El Zarco's bestial lieutenant.

Doña Antonia (dō′nyä än·tō′nyä), Manuela's mother.

ZULEIKA DOBSON

Author: Max Beerbohm (1872-1956)
Time of action: Early twentieth century
First published: 1911

Zuleika Dobson, a bewitching young woman with whom all the Oxford undergraduates fall in love. She can love only a man who will not love her. When all the young Oxonians have committed suicide for love of her, Zuleika takes a train for Cambridge and another try for a man she can love. She earns her living as a magician.

The Duke of Dorset, a rich young English aristocrat in love with Zuleika. When she pours a pitcher of water on his head he believes he is released from his vow to commit suicide for her. But when a strange bird sings, heralding a death in his family, he commits suicide anyway, rather than break a tradition. He throws himself in the river and drowns.

Noaks, an impecunious student. Zuleika thinks she can love him, as he does not love her. Noaks, however, commits suicide by jumping out a window because he thinks Katie Batch does not love him.

Katie Batch, pretty daughter of the Duke of Dorset's landlady. She tells Zuleika that the Duke committed suicide out of respect for tradition, not love for Zuleika.

The Warden of Judas College, Zuleika's grandfather. Her visit to see him at Oxford sets off the whole absurd train of events.

AUTHOR INDEX

I

III

VII

ALPHABETICAL CHARACTER INDEX

(NOTE: *etc.* following a name indicates that other characters of the same family name also appear in the article referred to.)

1

Autumn Sky, 306
Auvergne, Countess of, 467
Avahanni, 746
Avakian, Samuel, 383
Avellanos, Don José, etc., 784
Avery, 200
Avery, Captain, 150
Avery, Esther, etc., 811
Avocatori, 1214
Avril, 927
Awson, Arnt, 598
Awsumb, 624
Axel, 194
Ayacanora, 1233
Ayde, Colonel, 528
Aylmer, Sir William, 1178
Aylward, Samkin, 1237
Aymer, 538, 881
Ayrton, 754
Azamat, 471
Azelma, 714
Azerede, Fernande, 284
Azévédo, Jean, 1122
Azevida, Fernando de, 1074
Aziz, Dr., 838
Azora, 1278
Azra, 564

B., Judge, 919
B., Lord, 692
B——, Mr., 832
B——, M. de, 665
Baba, 292
Baba, Hajji, 436
Babalatchi, 31
Babbalanja, 669
Babbie, 621
Babbitt, George F., etc., 72
Babe, 844
Babel, Dulcenombre, etc., 43
Babka, 153
Babley, Richard, 244
Babo, 97
Baby Crab, The, 23
Babylon, Soldan of, 802
Bacarius, 569
Bacbuc, 394
Bacchis, 1021
Bacchus, 639
Bachelor, The, 802
Backbite, Sir Benjamin, 1012
Bacon, Abra, 313
Bacon, Friar, 387
Bacon, Mr., 855
Badaró, Colonel Sinhô, etc., 1206
Badger, 1248
Badger, Bayham, etc., 110
Badger, Deacon, etc., 811
Badman, Mr., 610
Badoer, Lady, 156
Bagheera, 561
Bagoa, 326
Bagot, 966
Bagot, William, etc., 1158
Bagradian, Gabriel, etc., 382
Bagshot, 92
Bagstock, Major Joseph, 287
Bagú, 576
Bahadur, Newab, 839
Baïa, 1110
Bailey, 678
Bailey, Harry, 148
Bailey, Mrs., 881
Baillehache, Maître, 312
Baimakov, Uliana, etc., 64
Baines, Sophia, etc., 808
Bajazeth, 1105
Baker, Dr., 944
Baker, Harry, 282
Baker, Jordan, 422
Baker, Mr., 777

Bakewell, Tom, 814
Balan, 511
Balance, Sylvia, etc., 945
Balcairn, Baron, 1203
Balderstone, Caleb, 123
Baldock, 316
Baldridge, Brack, etc., 975
Balduque, Sarafín, 848
Baldwin, 1105
Baldwin, George, etc., 664
Baldwin of Flanders, 471
Balfour, Amelie, 1057
Balfour, David, etc., 568
Balfour of Burley, John, 806
Balia, 1097
Balibari, Chevalier, 86
Baligant, 1063
Baligny, 961
Balin, 511
Balin le Sauvage, etc., 743
Baliol, 279
Ballio, 1157
Ballon, Monsieur, 850
Baloo, 561
Balsamo, Joseph, 692
Balthasar, 97, 748, 991
Balthazar, 1076
Balthazar, Frère, 981
Balwhidder, Rev. Micah, 47
Bambaev, Rostislav, 1054
Bambi, 78
Bambil, Gloria, 89
Bambridge, Mr., 703
Banahan, Catherine, 1092
Bandar-Log, The, 561
Bangham, Mrs., 620
Bangles, Peter, 594
Bankes, William, 1139
Banks, Sir Joseph, 749
Banquo, 643
Bantam, Angelo Cyrus, 878
Banter, 981
Baptista, 1106
Baptistin, 206
Bar Abba, 762
Barabas, 546
Barabbas, 78
Barb, 424
Barban, Tommy, 1117
Barbara, 656, 801
Bárbara, Doña, 296
Barbara, Old, 1244
Barbary, Miss, 109
Barbassou, Captain, 1110
Barbemuche, 113
Barbette, 179
Barbillus, 185
Barbro, 430
Barchester, Bishop of, 81
Bard of Armagh, The, 442
Bardamu, Ferdinand, 555
Bardell, Mrs. Martha, etc., 875
Bardi, Romola de', etc., 992
Bardolph, 463, 465, 698
Bardolph, Lord, 466
Bareacres, Lady, 1193
Barefoot, Magnus, 457
Barfield, Mrs., etc., 333
Bargeton, Mme. de, etc., 630
Barker, 758
Barker, Betsy, 220
Barker, Damon, 1084
Barkis, 243
Barkley, Catherine, 358
Barley, Clara, etc., 420
Barlow, Joseph Popham Bolge
    Bluebin, 76
Barlow, Mr., 1004
Barnabas, 155
Barnabas, Franklyn, etc., 76
Barnacle, Tite, etc., 619
Barnard, Henry, 629
Barnard, Augustus, etc., 758

Barnardine, 547, 686
Barnavelt, Sir John Van Olden, 1042
Barnes, George, 768
Barnes, Jacob, 1093
Barnes, Solon, etc., 135
Barney, 927
Barnhelm, Minna von, 709
Barnier, 1047
Barnington, Mrs., 441
Barnstable, Lieutenant Richard, 885
Baron, The, 425, 637, 649
Baroness, The, 1167
Barque, 1181
Barquero, Lorenzo, 297
Barrace, Miss, 33
Barrales, Pedro, 296
Barret, 137
Barrett, Mrs., 1205
Barricini, Lawyer, 192
Barrientos, 848
Barrildo, 1032
Barrios, General, 785
Barrisor, 136
Barrois, 206
Barron, Delia, 1033
Barron, Wilkie, etc., 1266
Barry, Widow, 85
Barsinan, 31
Bart, Lily, 489
Barter, Reverend Hussell, 210
Barthélémy, Old, 1236
Bartholo, Doctor, 79, 674
Bartholomew, 1107
Bartlett, Charlotte, 994
Bartlett, Edith, etc., 627
Bartly, 525
Barton, Ivy, 386
Bartram, George, etc., 781
Bartram, Mistress, 366
Baruch, 838
Baryton, Doctor, 555
Barzillai, 5
Bascomb, Maury L., 1072
Bashaw, The, 1077
Bashi, Mollah, 436
Bashmachkin, Akakii Akakiievich, 830
Basilio, 785
Basilio, King, 612
Basilius, 57
Basmanov, 115
Basque, 711
Bassanio, 696
Basset, 468
Basset, Anthony, 1142
Bassianus, 1137
Bassington, Francesca, etc., 1177
Bassiolo, 397
Bassompierre, Marshall, 181
Bassompierre, Paulina Mary Home
    de, 1205
Bast, George, etc., 1139
Bast, Leonard, etc., 494
Bastard of Orleans, The, 467
Bas-Thornton, Emily, etc., 525
Bastianazzo, 485
Bat, 454
Batch, Katie, 1280
Bates, Charley, 813
Bates, Mrs., etc., 324
Bath, Colonel, 34
Batouala, 88
Battius, Dr. Obed, 912
Battle, Teague, 307
Baudoin, François, etc., 1219
Baudricourt, Robert de, 999
Bault, 862
Baumbarten, Conrad, 1247
Bäumer, Paul, etc., 27
Baumert, Emma, etc., 1232
Bawd, A, 862

4

Big Adam, 1084
Big Mama, 690
Biggs, Lytle, 1084
Biggs, Miss Martha, 823
Bignall, Captain, 950
Bigot, Lord, 572
Bigum, Herr, 776
Bilby, Captain Jared, etc., 710
Bildad, Captain, 727
Bilham, John Little, 33
Bilioso, 657
Bill, The Lizard, 23
Billali, 1030
Billing, 328
Billy, 833
Bim, 633
Bindasov, 1054
Binet, Captain, 647
Bingley, Caroline, etc., 915
Binks, Sir Bingo, 1001
Binnie, James, 767
Bint, Hannah, 830
Biondello, 1107
Birch, Harvey, 1079
Bird, Henry, 731
Bird, Mr., 722
Bird, Senator, etc., 1179
Birdsong, Dabney, 987
Birdsong, George, etc., 1033
Birger, Earl, 1153
Birgersdatter, Maerta, 520
Birkabeyn, 446
Birnam, Don, etc., 632
Birnbaum, Malka, etc., 177
Biron, Lord, 551
Birotteau, César, etc., 165
Biscuit, Edward, 1045
Bishops of Lincoln, The, 462
Bissibingui, 88
Bitadura, Andrés, etc., 1070
Bittern, Captain, 48
Bitzer, 444
Bixbee, Polly, 247
Björgulfssön, Lavrans, 584
Bjorn, 428
Björn, 520, 1055, 1059
Björn, Sir, 586
Björnsdatter, Torhild, 520, 1055
Bjornstam, Miles, 656
Black Dog, 1152
Black Isles, King of the, 56
Black Jack, 90
Black Kitten, The, 1130
Blackacre, Widow, etc., 893
Blackett, William, etc., 211
Blackmore, Honour, 1144
Blackpool, Stephen, etc., 444
Blacksmith, The, 847
Blades, Ensign, 930
Bladud, 131
Blagoda, 89
Blair, James, 137
Blaise, Élodie, etc., 405
Blaize, Giles, 814
Blake, 169
Blake, Ben, 1153
Blake, Franklin, 740
Blake, Honor, 894
Blake, James, 474
Blake, Mary, 247
Blake, Rodney, 923
Blakeston, Jim, etc., 623
Blanca, 494
Blancandrin, 1062
Blanch of Spain, 572
Blanchard, Al, 1276
Blanchard, Jenny, etc., 782
Blanche, Anthony, 124
Blanche, Mlle., 1206
Blanchefleur, 1159
Blandamour, 349
Blandina, 351
Blandois, M., 618

Blandy, Miss, 855
Blanès, Father, 170
Blarney, Lady, 1199
Blas, 928
Blas of Santillane, Gil, 401
Blauser, James, 656
Blazius, Maître, 781
Blenkins, Bonaparte, 1085
Blepsidemus, 896
Blepyrus, 315
Blifil, Master, etc., 1143
Bligh, Lieutenant William, 749
Blimber, Dr., etc., 287
Blind Pew, 1152
Block, 1156
Blodeuwedd, 642
Blodgett, Doremus, 454
Bloedel, Sir, 771
Blok, Hafen, 1099
Blondeau, Valentine, 1218
Blood-Ax, Eric, 456
Bloody Shad, The, 710
Bloom, Grace, etc., 880
Bloom, Leopold, etc., 1175
Bloomfield, Mrs., etc., 15
Bloundel, Stephen, 807
Blount, Angus, 987
Blount, Jake, 448
Blount, Nicholas, 567
Blount, Nina, etc., 1202
Blue, Angela, 395
Blue Back, 308
Blue Boy, 1081
Blueskin, 539
Bluffe, Captain, 798
Blum, Andrey Antonovitch, 908
Blumenkohl, Dr. Leo, 652
Blundell, Theodore, 700
Blunt, Sir James, 969
Blunt, Sir Walter, 465
Blythewood, Augustus, 228
Boarham, Mr., 1116
Boase, Gunnora, 1149
Boatswain, The, 479
Bob, 620
Bob, Captain, 814
Bobadill, Captain, 343
Bobby, 599
Bobchinsky, Piotr Ivanovich, 526
Bobster, Celia, etc., 774
Boche, Madame, 306
Bodine, Hep, etc., 1132
Böen, Baard, etc., 61
Boeuf, Reginald Front de, 537
Boffin, Nicodemus, etc., 827
Bogart, Mrs., 656
Bogdanovna, Lizaveta, 739
Bogrov, Mikhail, 242
Bogun, 1253
Bois-Guilbert, Sir Brian de, 537
Boisise, 1043
Boisroger, 168
Boissec, Monsieur, 1206
Bold, Eleanor, etc., 80
Bold, John, etc., 1223
Bolder, 775
Boldwig, Captain, 877
Boldwood, Mr., 357
Boleo, Joe, 308
Boleyn, Anne, 1248
Bolingbroke, Henry, 966
Bolingbroke, Roger, 467
Bolkonskaya, Princess Marya, etc., 1221
Bolkonsky, Prince Andrey, etc., 1221
Bologna, Antonio, 309
Bolshintsov, Afanasy Ivanovitch, 739
Bolster, Bridget, 822
Bolton, Fanny, etc., 854
Bolton, Harry, 951
Bolton, Ruth, etc., 403

Boltrope, David, 886
Bombelles, Patrice, 972
Bomston, Lord Edward, 764
Bon, Charles, etc., 3
Bon, Peter Innocent, 1194
Bona, 468
Bonagiunta, 275
Bonancieux, Constance, 1128
Bonaparte, Joe, etc., 409
Bonaparte, Napoleon, 156, 310, 1142, 1222
Bonario, 1214
Bonatti, Guido, 273
Bonavent, Mistress, etc., 503
Bonaventura, Friar, 1135
Bonaventura, St., 275
Bond, Jim, 4
Bonnard, Sylvestre, 222
Bonnefoy, 507
Bonner, Juliana, 339
Bonney, Mr., 774
Bonniface, 91
Bonny, Mrs., 260
Bonnyfeather, Maria, etc., 48
Bonorma, 535
Bonteen, Mr., 872
Bonthron, 352
Bonvile, Lord, 504
Bonville, Katherine de, 596
Booby, Lady, etc., 553
Bookser, David, 720
Bookwright, Odum, 437
Boone, Daniel, 423
Booth, Amelia Harris, etc., 33
Boots, Sir Thomas de, 769
Borachio, 747
Borba, Quincas, 330
Borden, Josiah, 746
Bordenave, 757
Bordin, Madame, 118
Borg, 950
Borgia, Cesare, 984
Boris, 207
Bork the Waxy-Toothed Blade, 1086
Born, Bertran de, 274
Borodaty, 1109
Borroughcliffe, Captain, 886
Borrull, Batiste, 137
Bors, 512
Borsiere, Guglielmo, 273
Borth, Sergeant, 96
Bortshleff, Mr., 566
Boryna, Matthias, 845
Boscenos, Prince des, 856
Bosinney, Philip, 376
Bosola, Daniel de, 309
Bosse, La Grand', 1267
Bossnowl, Lady Clarinda, 226
Boswell, General, etc., 402
Bothwell, Sergeant Francis, 806
Botterall, Sheriff Lem, 624
Bottinius, Doctor Johannes-Baptista, 971
Bottom, Nick, 704
Botts, 480
Botwinick, Chief Warrant Officer, 432
Bouc, Pierre, 347
Bouchereau, 1006
Bouille, Marquis de, 208
Bouillon, Duke de, 181
Bouillon, Godfrey de, 546
Bounderby, Josiah, 443
Bountiful, Lady, 91
Bourbon, Cardinal de, 501
Bourbon, King, 844
Bourchier, Cardinal, 968
Bourgh, Lady Catherine de, etc., 915
Bourienne, Mademoiselle, 1222
Bourjot, Naomi, etc., 957
Bourlanger, Rodolphe, 646

6

Bullingdon, Lord, 85
Bullitt, Jessie, 418
Bullivant, Sir Walter, 1124
Bullock, 946
Bulsom-Porter, Mrs., 724
Bulstrode, Major, 1007
Bulstrode, Mr. Nicholas, etc., 701
Bumble, Mr., 812
Bumppo, Natty, 260, 596, 841, 886, 912
Bunce, Jenny, etc., 722
Bunce, John, 1223
Bunch, Byron, 614
Bunchuk, Ilia, 38
Bundren, Anse, etc., 65
Bungay, Friar, 387
Bungay, Mr., 855
Bunsby, Captain Jack, 287
Bunthorne, Reginald, 842
Bunting, 334
Bunyan, Paul, 844
Buoso, 274
Burbo, 594
Burbon, 351
Burch, Mrs., 636
Burchell, Mr., 1198
Burden, 387
Burden, Jack, etc., 28
Burden, James Quayle, etc., 750
Burden, Joanna, 614
Burdon, Clark, 481
Burge, Jonathan, etc., 8
Burge, Joyce, 76
Burge-Lubin, 76
Burgess, Bessie, 895
Burgess, Mr., 144
Burgh, Hubert de, 571
Burgio, Fortunato, 681
Burgonet, General Sir Benjamin, 271
Burgundy, Duke of, 467, 574
Burke, Colonel Francis, 681
Burke, Colonel Matthew, etc., 423
Burke, Hycy, etc., 322
Burke, Mat, 43
Burke, Mr., 6
Burke, Sadie, 28
Burke, Tom, 1141
Burkin, George, 454
Burkitt, 749
Burlap, 898
Burleigh, Burton, 37
Burlesdon, Lady Rose, 918
Burnham, Dr. Leicester, 1266
Burns, Helen, 541
Burrhus, 126
Bürstner, Fräulein, 1155
Burton, Doc, 519
Burton, Mary, 956
Burton, Richard, 175
Bush, 148
Bush, Ishmael, etc., 912
Bushy, 966
Busirane, 349
Busoni, Abbé, 206
Busy, Zeal-of-the-Land, 87
Buteau, 312
Butler, 1217
Butler, Aileen, etc., 368
Butler, General, 308
Butler, Major Arthur, 483
Butler, Reuben, 449
Butler, Rhett, etc., 410
Butterfield, 730
Butterfield, Mr., 990
Butterwell, 1052
Butterworth, Clara, etc., 901
Button Moulder, The, 849
Butts, Doctor, 462
Butzou, General, 1120
Buzfus, Serjeant, 876
Bwikov, 901

Byam, Roger, 749
Byeletsky, Prince, 204
Byrnes, Davy, 1176
Byron, Harriet, 1041
Byron, Mike, 54
Byrrhaena, 407
Byrrhia, 39

C. P., 610
Cabascango, Juancho, 495
Cabot, Ephraim, etc., 265
Cabral, Doctor Virgilio, 1206
Cabral de Malo, Captain Tomás, 248
Cacafogo, 997
Cacambo, 146
Cacciagiuda, 275
Caccianemico, Venedico, 273
Cáceres, Don Fabio, 296
Cade, Jack, 467
Caderousse, Gaspard, 205
Cadet, Mother, 113
Cadmus, 75, 138
Cador, 1278
Cadwalader, 132
Cadwallader, Rev. Humphrey, 702
Caelestine, 1008
Caenis, 983
Caesar, Augustus, 258, 507
Caesar, Caius Julius, 159
Caesar, Julius, 132, 138, 509, 559
Caesar, Octavius, 51
Cagliostro, Count Alessandro di, 208, 931
Caillard, Colonel Jean-Baptiste, 149
Cain, 75, 140
Cain, Amanda, 1133
Caiphas, 273
Cairo, Joel, 658
Caithness, 644
Caius, Dr., 697
Caius Lucius, 232
Calabria, King of, 869
Calais, 542
Calash, Joseph P., 990
Calchas, 515, 1163, 1164
Calder, Jim, 1240
Calepine, 351
Calianax, 655
Caliban, 1113
Calidore, 351
Calidorus, 1157
California, 977
Caligula, 507, 1020
Calisto, 163
Calixto, Senator, 139
Callatinus, 940
Callendar, Major, 839
Callepine, 1105
Calligan, Mary, etc., 368
Calliope, 824
Calloway, Uncle Zeb, 103
Calogrenant, 1278
Caloveglia, Count, 1072
Calpurnia, 184, 508, 509, 560
Calvert, Clay, 480
Calvo, Baldassare, 992
Calymath, Selim, 547
Calypha, 810
Calyphas, 1105
Calypso, 790
Camacho, 535
Camargo, Don Pablo, 107
Cambello, 349
Camber, 131
Cambina, 350
Cambrai, Countess of, 961
Camerata, Countess, 590
Cameron, Lutie, 1014
Camila, 1185

Camilla, 12, 213, 338
Camilla, Mr. John, etc., 420
Camille, 482, 781
Camillio, 1252
Camillo, 1239
Camiola, 653
Campaspe, 143
Campbell, Alan, 879
Campbell, Michael, 1094
Campbell, Mr., 568
Campeius, Cardinal, 462
Campion, General Lord Edward, 834
Campley, Mr., 390
Camusot de Marville, Madame Amélie, etc., 216
Canacee, 350
Canby, 831
Candelas, 578
Candide, 144
Candido, 480
Candiola, 1007
Candour, Lady, 1012
Candy, 796
Candy, Dr. Thomas, 741
Cangrejo, Francesco, 1142
Canidius, 52
Cann, Miss, 769
Cannon, George, 186
Cannon, Serena, 416
Canon, 313
Canon, The, 148
Canon's Yeoman, The, 148
Cantalicio, Don, 429
Canterbury, Archbishop of, 316
Cantle, Granfer, etc., 960
Canty, Tom, etc., 916
Canynge, General, 638
Caoudal, 1005
Cap, Charles, 841
Capaneus, 273
Caparra, Niccolò, 993
Capece, Lauretta, 551
Caperington, Countess of, 718
Capet, Hugh, 274
Caphis, 1134
Capilet, Diana, 30
Capocchio, 274
Capolin, 1106
Capolino, 798
Capolino, Nicolette, 798
Caponsacchi, Giuseppe, 971
Caporale, Silvia, 601
Capper, Laila, 566
Captain, The, 358, 628
Capucius, 462
Capulat, 972
Capulet, etc., 991
Cara, 124
Carabine, 215
Carabine, James, 266
Caractacus, 185
Carádoc, Eustace, etc., 843
Carafa, Ettore, 156
Carathis, 1194
Carcomo, Francisco de, 1075
Cardenio, 295
Cardew, Cecily, 518
Cardillac, Jerry, 378
Cardinal Spring, 304
Cardochia, 1075
Cardoville, Adrienne de, 1219
Cards, Jennifer, 558
Careless, Ned, 299
Carelia, King of, 565
Carella, Gino, 1237
Carew, Dick, etc., 260
Carew, Sir Danvers, 280
Carey, 1099
Carey, Philip, etc., 794
Cargill, Rev. Josiah, 1001
Carhaix, 300
Cario, 120, 896

8

9

11

Craggeir, Thorgeir, 1086
Craig, Mr., 9
Craigengelt, Captain, 123
Crammon, Bernard, 1268
Crampas, Major von, 317
Crampley, Lieutenant, 981
Cranage, Ben, etc., 8
Cranch, Mrs. Martha, etc., 702
Crane, Dr., etc., 923
Crane, Ichabod, 607
Cranly, 904
Cranmer, Thomas, 461
Cranstoun, Lord, 604
Cranwell, 1258
Crassus, Marcus, 160
Cratchit, Bob, 179
Cratinus, 874
Crawford, Henry, etc., 667
Crawford, Lord, 933
Crawford, Melancthon, 445
Crawford, Myles, 1176
Crawley, Captain Rawdon, 1191
Crawley, Frank, 944
Crawley, Rev. Josiah, etc., 385, 592
Creakle, Mr., etc., 245
Creamer, Mr., 1193
Creed, Mrs., 855
Creedle, Robert, 1265
Creedon, Father, 55
Cregan, Hardress, etc., 191
Creighton, Colonel, 568
Creighton, Mr., 777
Creon, 49, 687, 792, 793, 873
Crescent, Mme., etc., 663
Crespo, Pedro, etc., 684
Cressida, 1162
Cressler, Charles, etc., 889
Cresswell, Mr. Penrose, 1178
Crest-Maker, A, 845
Creusa, 12, 530
Creüsa, 606
Crèvecoeur, Count Philip de, 932
Crével, Monsieur, 214
Crewler, Sophy, etc., 246
Crichton, William, 9
Crick, Richard, etc., 1120
Criley, Bradd, 153
Crimple, David, 677
Crimsworth, William, etc., 920
Cringle, Tom, 1142
Crippled Inge, 457
Cripples, Mr., 620
Cripps, Bob, 876
Cripps, Mrs., 478
Criseyde, 1164
Crisp, Rev. Mr., 1194
Crisparkle, Mr., 755
Crispín, 115
Crispinus, 1008
Crispus, 934
Cristina, Sister, 578
Cristoforo, Fra, 100
Critchlow, Charles, 808
Crito, 39, 874
Crocker, Erminia, etc., 1033
Croft, Admiral, etc., 864
Croft, Art, 831
Crofts, Captain Montague, 1142
Crofts, Dr., 1051
Crofut, Mrs., 454
Cromlech, David, 694
Cromwell, Oliver, 1170, 1265
Cromwell, Thomas, 462
Cronshaw, 795
Crook-Fingered Jack, 94
Crooks, 796
Croplady, Nigel, 691
Crosbie, Adolphus, 593, 1051
Crosby, 1274
Crossbite, Mrs., 634
Crotchet, Ebenezer Mac, etc., 226
Croto, 934

Crow-cock, King of, 735
Crowder, Mr., 365
Crowdero, 497
Crowdey, Jogglebury, 718
Crowell, Joe, 830
Crown, 902
Crowne, Lenina, 121
Croy, Kate, 1250
Croye, Lady Hameline de, 932
Cruchot, Monsieur, 336
Crudor, 351
Crummles, Vincent, etc., 774
Crump, Lottie, 1202
Crump, Mrs., 1052
Cruncher, Jerry, etc., 1102
Crupp, Mrs., 246
Crushton, Hon. Mr., 878
Crusoe, Robinson, etc., 979
Cruthers, Webb, 1189
Cruz, 395
Crysogene, 349
Ctesipho, 127
Cuadrado, 1032
Cubas, Braz, 330
Cub-Slut, The, 140
Cudjo, 228
Cuff, Sergeant Richard, 741
Cullen, Philly, 894
Culling, Mrs. Rosamund, 90
Cumhal, 369
Cumming, Alfred, 175
Cummings, E. E., 329
Cummins, Lord, 1014
Cunégonde, 145
Cunizza, 275
Cunshi, 494
Cupid, 229, 407, 606, 927, 1134
Curcio, 268
Curdle, Mr., 775
Curiace, 482
Curio, 339
Curius, Quintus, 159
Curley, 796
Currito, 858
Curry, James, 484
Curt, 236
Curtis, 1107
Curtis, Sir Henry, 576
Cushing, Abner, 227
Cusins, Adolphus, 657
Cusler, Daniel, 1126
Custance, Dame Christian, 937
Cutbeard, 1039
Cutler, Miss, 1194
Cutter, Wycliffe, etc., 751
Cutting, Val, 88
Cuttle, Edward, 287
Cutwolfe, 1187
Cuzak, 752
Cyaxares, 63
Cyclops, The, 230
Cylindrus, 695
Cymbeline, 231
Cymochles, 348
Cymoent, 349
Cynthia, 76, 299, 326, 351
Cyon, M. de, 424
Cypress, Mr., 779
Cyprian, Don, 1076
Cyril, 505
Cyril, Grand Duke, 1269
Czepanek, Lilly, etc., 1063

D——, 203
D., Monsieur, 1215
Dacier, Sir Percy, 269
Daeghraefn, 99
Daemones, 1050
Daggoo, 727
Dagley, 703
Dagonet, Clare, 230
Daguenet, 757

Dahanna, Davy, 172
Dahlberg, 1087
d'Aigrigny, M. l'Abbe, 1219
Dain, Oliver le, 933
Daisy, 622
Daisy, Aunt, 566
Daisy, Solomon, 83
Daja, 760
D'Albafiorita, Count, 725
d'Albemar, Delphine, etc., 263
d'Albert, M., 647
Dale, Edith, 867
Dale, Jack, 989
Dale, Laetitia, 318
Dale, Lilian, etc., 593, 1050
Dale, Suzanne, etc., 396
Dalgarno, Lord, 380
Dalila, 1003
Dall, Felimid mac, 262
Dallas, Mr., 1213
Dallison, Hilary, etc., 386
Dalloway, Clarissa, etc., 722
D'Alroy, Capt. George, 154
Dalton, Mary, etc., 760
Daly, "Joxer," 562
Daly, Kyrle, 192
d'Amagüe, Princess Corona, 1183
d'Ambois, Bussy, 136
d'Ambois, Clermont, 961
Dambreuse, M., etc., 1024
Dame Nature, 351
Dame-Work-While-I-Am-Able, 1212
Dametas, 57
Damian, Peter, 275
Damis, 1111
Damnit-all-with-a-limp, Jacob, 598
Damon, 624, 1097
Damport, Rafe, 1036
Damson, Suke, 1264
Danaïdes, 1095
Danao, 606
Danaüs, 1095
Dancaire, 152
Danceny, Chevalier, 237
Dancing Master, A, 117
Dancy, Captain Ronald, etc., 638
Dandin, 891
Dane, Mrs., 724
Dane, William, 1038
Danger, William, 297
Dangerfield, Paul, 484
Danglars, M., etc., 204
Dangle, Mr., etc., 224
Danis, 1067
Dankwart, 771
Dannisburgh, Lord, 269
Danny, 260
d'Anquetil, Maurice, 69
Dansaert, 398
Dansker, The, 105
Dante, 272
Dantès, Edmond, etc., 204
Danvers, Indiana, 199
Danvers, Mrs., 944
Daphnis, 240, 353
Daples, Mr., 429
Dapperwit, Mr., 634
d'Aquilanera, Marcantonio, etc., 137
Darch, Car, 1119
Darcy, Fitzwilliam, 914
D'Arcy, John, 442
Dardinello, 818
Dares, 326
Dargelos, 479
Darioleta, 31
Dark Druid, The, 369
Darling, Wendy, etc., 865
Darlington, Lord, 589
d'Armilly, Louise, 206
Darnay, Charles, 1101

Diver, Colonel, 678
Diver, Dick, etc., 1117
Diver, Jenny, 95
Diver, Tom, 854
d'Ivry, Madame la Duchesse, etc.,
    769
Dix, Mr., 707
Dixmer, Genevièev, etc., 174
Dixon, Tom, 691
Diz, Avelino, 575
Djalma, Prince, 1219
Dmitri, 575
Doane, Seneca, 73
Dobbin, Captain William, 1191
Dobchinsky, Piotr Ivanovich, 526
Doboobie, Dr. Demetrius, 567
Dobroselova, Barbara Alexievna,
    900
Dobson, Zuleika, 1280
Dockwrath, Samuel, etc., 822
Docre, Canon, 300
Doctor of Physick, The, 147
Dodge, Pardon, 775
Dodge, William, 101
Dodger, 1036
Dodi, 731
Dodo, The, 23
Dodor, 1158
Dods, Meg, 1001
Dodson, Mr., 876
Dodsworth, Sam, etc., 283
Doe, Telie, etc., 775
Dogberry, 747
Doheny, Susie, etc., 847
Dohna, Countess Elizabeth, etc.,
    1087
Dolabella, 25, 53
Dolan, Father, 905
Doleful, Captain, 441
d'Olive, Monsieur, 736
Doll, 710
Dollallolla, Queen, 1146
Dolly, 9, 1193
Dolon, 350, 516
Dolores, 928, 1206
Dolores, Queen, 563
Dolphin, Mr., 855
Dombey, Paul, etc., 286
Domin, Harry, 997
Domingo, 290
Dominic, 365
Dominic, Father, 1073
Dominikova, 846
Domitia, 982
Domitian, 982
Domitilla, 983
Domitius Afer, 1020
Domitius, Annaeus, 592
Domitius, Lucius, 184
Donado, 1134
Donalbain, 643
Donald, 450
Donatello, 667
Donati, Forese, 275
Donax, 338
Dondolo, 962
Donjalolo, King, 669
Don Juan, 291, 293
Donkeyton, Duke of, 474
Donkin, 777
Donn, Arabella, etc., 557
Donnithorne, Captain Arthur,
    etc., 7
Donovan, Larry, 751
Donthorne, Major, 1257
Donwallo Molinus, 131
Doolittle, Eliza, etc., 929
Doolittle, Hiram, 887
Doone, Lorna, etc., 628
Doortje, Mother, 1008
Doralice, 673, 818
Doramin, 628
Dorante, 117, 695

Dorco, 240
Dordan, 413
Doretta, 156
Dorf, Dina, 884
Dörfling, Field Marshal, 917
Dorias, 338
Dorilant, Mr., 212
Dorilaus, 59
Dorimant, 660
Dorimène, 117
Dorinda, 91
Dorine, 1111
Dorio, 874
Doris, 1009
d'Orleans, Gaston, 181
Dormouse, The, 23
Dorn, Eugene, 1016
Dorotea, 295, 393
Dorothea, 401, 431
Dorrit, Amy, etc., 618
d'Orsel, Olivier, 289
Dorset, Duke of, 1280
Dorset, George, etc., 490
Dorset, Marchioness of, 462
Dorset, Marquess of, 969
d'Or, Toison, 933
Dorus, 337
Doss, Nack, 956
Dossi, Amilcare, 156
Do-This-Or-Thy-Dame-Shall-Beat-
    Thee, 1212
Dough-Boy, 727
Doughty, Dobinet, 938
Douglas, Archibald, 673
Douglas, Earl of, 352
Douglas, Ellen, etc., 588
Douglas, Elsbeth, etc., 235
Douglas, Stephen A., 2
Doúkhova, Véra, 958
Dousterswivel, 50
Douviers, Laura, etc., 207
Dove, Cecilia, etc., 672
Dow, Rob, 621
Dowden, Olly, 960
Dowdy, Chief, 720
Dowler, Mr., etc., 877
Dowling, Frank, 22
Dowling, Margo, 1188
Dowling, Mr., 1144
Down-and-Outs, The, 1255
Downing, 355
Downright, 344
Doxy, Betty, 95
Doyce, Daniel, 618
Doyle, Minta, 1139
Doyle, Peter, etc., 716
Draco the Great, etc., 856
Dracula, Count, 301
Drake, Sir Francis, 1233
Drake, Susanna, 937
Drake, Temple, etc., 1003
Draper, Mr., 1212
Draupadi, 653
Dreamer, The, 1254
Dreary, Wat, 94
Drebber, Enoch J., 1092
Dreissiger, Herr, 1231
Dressel, Mrs. Harry, 390
Drew, 832
Drew, Lady, 1148
Drew, Rev. John Jennison, 73
Driffield, Rosie, etc., 141
Driscoll, Jim, 230
Driveller, 139
Dromio of Ephesus, 193
Dromio of Syracuse, 193
Dromo, 39, 1021
Dromund, Thorsteinn, 428
Drood, Edwin, 755
Drouet, Charles, 1046
Drouet, Jean, 208
Drover, Dr. Roy, 153
Drozdov, Praskovya Ivanovna, 907

Drubetskaya, Princess Anna, 1221
Drubetskoy, Prince Boris, 1221
Drugger, Abel, 20
Drummle, Bentley, 420
Drummle, Cayley, 1017
Druon, 350
Drupada, King, 653
Drusus Senior, etc., 1020
Dryas, 240
Dryfoos, Christine, etc., 447
Drystubble, Batavus, 683
Duane, Jack, 561
du Barry, Madame Jeanne, 693
Dubbs, 271
Dubois, 711
Du Bois, M., 342
Du Bosse, 985
Duca, Guido del, 274
Duchemin, Mrs. Edith Ethel, etc.,
    834
Duchene, Father, 924
Duchesne, Chevalier, 1142
Duchess, The, 22
Duchess' Baby, The, 22
Duchess of San Martino, The,
    1072
Duck, The, 23
Duckett, Lance-Corporal, 835
Duckling, Mr., 1270
Duckworth, Ellis, 107
Du Croisy, 988
Ducrot, Bernard, 253
Dudley, Bruce, 241
Dudley, Guilford, 1148
Dudley, Robert, 566
Dudú, 292
Dudzeele, Hans, 608
Duer, Angus, 63
Duessa, 347
Duff, Margaret, 395
Duffy, Tiny, 28
Dufrety, M., 270
Dugdale, 1275
du Gua Saint-Cyr, Mme., 179
Duke, The, 496
Dukinfield, Sir Nat, 307
Dula, 655
Dulippo, 1097
Dull, 635
Dumaine, 635
Dumbbell, Uncle Crucifix, 485
Dumbello, Lady, 593, 1052
Dumbello, Lord, 385
Dumbiedikes, Laird of, 450
Dumouchel, Seraphina, 270
Duncan, 643
Duncan, Major, 842
Duncan, Selma, 54
Dunce, Sir Davy, etc., 1058
Dundas, Euphemia, etc., 1121
Dunham, Mabel, etc., 841
Dunn, Ellie, etc., 452
Dunning, Jack, 951
Dunois, 999
Dunois, Count de, 933
Dunsack, Edward, etc., 543
Dunscombe, Alice, 885
Dunstable, Duke of, 842
Dunstable, Emily, 593
Dunstable, Martha, 282, 384
Dunstane, Lady Emma, 269
Dunwoodie, Major Peyton, etc.,
    1079
Dunyasha, 174
Du Pont, M., 754
Dupré, Sally, 549
Dupuis, Léon, 646
d'Urberville, Alec, 1119
Durbeyfield, Tess, etc., 1118
Durdles, 755
Durham, Constantia, 319
Durie, James, etc., 680
Duroy, Georges, 95

15

Estupiñá, Plácido, 379
Eteocles, 872, 1025
Ethel, 1176
Ethelred, Sir, 1019
Etherington, Earl of, 1000
Etta, 1033
Ettarre, 220, 512
Etzel, 771
Eubulus, 339, 413, 674
Euclio, 908
Eudemus, 1020
Eudore, 1180
Eudromus, 240
Euelpides, 105
Eugenia, Donna, 268
Eugénie, 1274
Eugenie, Sir Dauphine, 1039
Eugenio, 234
Eugenio, Don, 1127
Eugenius, 1161
Eulalie, 921
Eumaeus, 789
Eumelus, 19
Eumenides, 326, 809
Eumenides, The, 356
Eumnestes, 349
Eumolpus, 1009
Eunice, 934
Eunomia, 908
Euphemia, 267, 450
Euphorbus, 181
Euphrasia, 869
Euphronius, 52
Euphues, 338
Eurione, 736
Euripides, 6, 389, 1122
Europa, 138
Euryalus, 13
Eurycleia, 789
Eurydice, 49, 815, 824
Eurylochus, 790
Eurymachus, 791
Eurynome, 791
Eurypylus, 273
Eurysaces, 17
Eurystheus, 176, 470
Eusabio, 253
Eusebio, 267
Eusebio, Tio, 840
Eustace, Uncle, 690
Evadne, 654, 1096
Evandale, Lord, 806
Evander, 12, 181
Evangelist, 882
Evans, Iestyn, 493
Evans, Janice, 690
Evans, Sam, etc., 1089
Evans, Sir Hugh, 697
Evarchus, 58
Eve, 75, 127, 140, 835
Evelake, King, 743
Evelyn, Aunt, 691, 693
Everard, Colonel Markham, 1265
Everdene, Bathsheba, 356
Everyman, 345
Evil Angel, The, 278
Evrain, 331
Ewart, Bob, 1148
Executioner of Rouen, The, 999
Exeter, Duke of, 468
Experience, 883
Exquisite Jade, 306
Eynsford Hill, Freddy, etc., 929
Eyre, Jane, 540
Eyre, Simon, 1035
Eystein, 457
Ezhoff, 373

F——, Baron von, 267
Fabien, etc., 777
Fabio, 296, 393, 534
Fabricio, 402, 1261

Fabricius, 725
Face, 20
Facia, 853
Fadge, 764
Fadladeen, 591
Fagan, Dr. Augustus, etc., 259
Faggus, Tom, 629
Fagin, 812
Failing, Mrs. Emily, 625
Fainall, etc., 1231
Fair Maid of Wu, The, 266
Fairchild, Dabney, etc., 264
Fairfax, Gwendolyn, 518
Fairfax, Jane, 324
Fairfax, Mrs., 540
Fairfield, 503
Fairford, Laura, 230
Fairlamb, Matthew, 85
Fairlie, Laura, etc., 1256
Fairway, Timothy, 960
Faith, 306
Faithful, 882
Fakreddin, Emir, 1194
Falander, 949
Falco, 275
Falder, William, 564
Faline, 78
Falk, Arvid, etc., 949
Falk, Pastor, 102
Falkland, Ferdinando, 141
Fallace, 344
Faloise, Hector de la, 757
Falsaron, Duke, 1062
False, 1212
Falstaff, Sir John, 464, 697
Fane, Violet, 1213
Fáñez, Minaya Alvar, 897
Fanferlot, 367
Fang, 465
Fang, Mr., 813
Fanny, 312, 826, 1069, 1257
Fanshawe, Ginevra, 1205
Fantastic, 809
Fantine, 713
Faraday, Dr., 85
Farange, Maisie, etc., 1235
Farebrother, Rev. Camden, etc., 702
Farfrae, Donald, 683
Fargus, Mr., 513
Faria, Abbé, 205
Farintosh, Marquis of, 769
Farish, Gertrude, 490
Farley, Captain William D., 1098
Farnley, 831
Farou, Jean, etc., 826
Farr, Michael Joseph, 403
Farrago, Captain John, 728
Farrell, Jimmy, 894
Fashion, Young, 952
Fastolfe, Sir John, 467
Father, The, 1047
Father William, 23
Fatima, 1279
Fatout, 779
Fauchelevent, Father, 714
Fauchery, M., 756
Fauconnier, Madame, 306
Faulconbridge, Robert, etc., 571
Faulkland, 975
Fauntleroy, Zenobia, 111
Faunus, 351
Faust, 362
Fausta, 170
Faustino, 840
Faustus, 278
Fauvel, M. André, 367
Favell, Jack, 944
Favras, Marquis de, 208
Fawley, Jude, etc., 557
Fayaway, 1174
Faye, 313

Fayerlee, Molly, etc., 21
Featherstone, Solomon, etc., 702
Fedallah, 727
Federico, Count, 393
Federigo, Cardinal, 100
Feeble, Francis, 466
Feeder, Rev. Alfred, etc., 288
Feeley, Willy, 418
Feenix, Lord, 288
Feijóo, Colonel Evaristo, 380
Feirefis, 837
Felice la Belle, 434
Felician, Father, 340
Feliciana, 577
Feliciani, Lorenza, 693
Félicité, 647
Felipe, 578
Felix, 1244, 1245
Félix, 900
Félix, Leonardo, etc., 112
Fellah, A, 850
Fellamar, Lord, 1144
Fellowship, 345
Felton, John, 1128
Fencing Master, A, 117
Feng, General, 1240
Feng-shih, 305
Fenice, 188
Fennigate, Kate, etc., 566
Fennimore, 776
Fenton, 698
Fenton, Mr., 374
Fenwick, 1098
Fenwick, Frank, etc., 1197
Fenwick-Symes, Adam, 1202
Fenwolf, Morgan, 1248
Feodor, 116
Fera, 161
Ferardo, Don, 339
Ferdinand, 149, 309, 318, 635, 653, 1113
Ferdinand, King, 1032
Ferdinando, 48
Fère, The Comte de la, 1199
Fereus, 131
Fergus, 263, 369, 413
Ferguson, Duncan, 729
Ferguson, Helen, 358
Fernand, Don, 339
Fernande, 241
Fernandez, Margaret, etc., 525
Fernando, 376
Ferneze, 547, 657
Fernyhirst, 559
Ferood, 1057
Ferral, 666
Ferrand, Jacques, 753
Ferrar, Marjorie, 730
Ferrars, Edward, etc., 1022
Ferraù, 817, 820
Ferraugh, Sir, 349
Ferravecchi, Bratti, 993
Ferret, 94
Ferrex, 413
Ferrier, Lucy, etc., 1092
Ferris, Leonard, 700
Feste, 1169
Feverel, Richard, etc., 814
Feversham, Rev. Michael, etc., 699
Fiammetta, 591
Fiasco, Major, 1052
Fiche, Mr., 1194
Ficsur, 615
Fid, Dick, 950
Fidelia, 348, 840
Fidget, Sir Jasper, etc., 212
Fidus, 338
Fielding, Captain, 691
Fielding, Cecil, 838
Fierro, Martin, 394
Fiers, 174
Fife, 612
Fifine, 1206

Figaro, 79, 674
Figueroa, Don Lope de, 684
Filby, 855
Filbyter, Folke, 1153
Filch, 94
Filcher, 88
Filhot, Georges, 1122
Filipote, 1112
Filipovna, Nastasya, 510
Filippusdatter, Ingebjörg, 586
Fillgrave, Dr., 282
Finch, Miriam, 395
Finching, Mrs. Flora, 618
Finchley, Sondra, 36
Finegas, 369
Fink, Fritz von, 258
Finkelstein, Widow, 178
Finn, 99, 369
Finn, Huckleberry, 495, 1145
Finn, Phineas, 871, 872
Finna, 522
Finne, Arne, 858
Finnegan, 370
Finney, Mr., 1224
Finnsson, Arnvid, 72, 1055
Finucane, Mr. Jack, 855
Fips, Mr., 678
Firk, 1036
Firkins, Mrs., 1193
First Old Woman, The, 315
First Tempter, The, 748
Fischer, Lisbeth, etc., 214
Fish Footman, The, 23
Fisher, 10
Fisher, Ham, 675
Fisher, Lily, 1066
Fisher, Miss Naomi, etc., 486
Fisher, Mrs. Carrie, 490
Fitch, Israel, 473
Fitchow, Mistress, 783
Fitela, 99
Fitz, 1245
Fitzallen, Albert, 823
Fitzchrome, Captain, 226
Fitz-Clare, Clare, 673
Fitz-Fulke, Duchess of, 293
Fitzgerald, Cornet, 886
Fitzgerald, Lady Elizabeth, 1248
Fitz-James, James, 588
Fitzpatrick, Mrs., etc., 1144
Fitzpiers, Edgar, 1264
Fitz Urse, Reginald, 748
Fitzurse, Waldemar, 538
Fitzwater, Lord, 967
Five, 23
Five Wits, The, 345
Fizkin, Horatio, 877
Flaccus, 160
Flack, Henry, 957
Fladdock, General, 678
Flag, 1273
Flaherty, Margaret, etc., 893
Flamant, 1005
Flambeau, Seraphin, 590
Flamborough, Solomon, 1199
Flamineo, 1238
Flaming Tinman, The, 603
Flamingo, The, 23
Flaminius, 1134
Flamm, Miss, 414
Flammand, 1167
Flanders, Count Guy of, 616
Flanders, Moll, 732
Flash, Sir Petronel, 314
Flashman, 1141
Flask, 727
Flather, Emma, etc., 474
Flavia, Lady, 338
Flavia, Princess, 918
Flavian, 671
Flavin, Troy, 265
Flavio, 1245

Flavius, 560, 1133
Flavius, Julian, etc., 256
Flavon, Agnes von, 1174
Fleance, 643
Fledgeby, Mr., 828
Fleece, 727
Fleeceall, 441
Fleischer, Doctor, 92
Fleming, Agnes, 813
Fleming, Berenice, 1081, 1135
Fleming, Henry, 948
Fletcher, Abel, etc., 550
Fletcher, Mr., 594
Fleurant, 507
Fleur-de-Marie, 752
Flinn, Barney, 787
Flintwinch, Jeremiah, etc., 619
Flippant, Lady, 634
Flirt, Mistress, 396
Flite, Miss, 109
Flood, Captain, 307
Flopit, 1028
Flora, 197, 534, 1167
Florac, Vicomte Paul de, etc., 769
Flordelice, 818
Flordespina, 820
Florence, Duke of, 30, 1261
Flores, 1032
Florez, 93
Florimel, 564
Florimell, Snowy, etc., 349
Florio, 1134, 1152
Floripes, 248
Florizel, 1252
Florrie, 187, 1276
Floscula, 326
Flosky, Mr. Ferdinando, 779
Flower Girl, The, 649
Floyer, Sir Robert, 163
Fluellen, 463
Flute, 704
Flutter, Sir Fopling, 660
Flynn, Peter, 894
Foedora, 1242
Fog, Miss, 728
Fogey, Horace, 769
Fogg, Mr., 876
Foigard, 92
Foker, Henry, etc., 855
Folden, Kristen, 857
Föll, Per, etc., 321
Follock, Dirck, 167
Fondlewife, 798
Fontan, 757
Fontanin, Daniel de, etc., 1267
Fontenay, Countess Thérèse de, 445
Fool, The, 411, 573
Foppington, Lord, 952
Forbes, Father, 236
Ford, Mistress, etc., 697
Foresight, etc., 633
Forester, Dr., 709
Forestier, Madeleine, etc., 95
Forey, Clare, 814
Forlipopoli, Marquis di, 725
Formal, Mr. James, 396
Formal, Roger, 344
Forrester, Capt. Roland, etc., 775
Forrester, Fodder-wing, etc., 1272
Forrester, Marian, etc., 631
Forrester, Mrs., 219
Forrestier, Ray, 496
Forster, Warren, 559
Forsyte, Soames, etc., 376, 729
Fort, Cardinal, 139
Fort, Colonel Cassius, 1266
Fortinbras, 439
Fortunata, 379
Fortunatus, 802
Fortune, 803
Fortune, Mr., 513
Fortunio, 24

Fosco, Count, etc., 1257
Fosdick, Mrs., 211
Fosli, Kaia, 680
Foss, Erik, 321
Foster, Anthony, etc., 567
Foster, Mr., 447
Foster, Stephen, 484
Fothergill, 283
Fothergill, Mr., 385
Fotis, 407
Fouan, 311
Fouchard, Honoré, etc., 301
Fouillade, 1181
Foulata, 576
Fouqué, 948
Fouquet, 1200
Foureau, M., 118
Fourth Tempter, The, 748
Fourville, Countess Gilberte de, etc., 1260
Fox, 624
Fox, Charles James, 311
Fox, Katie, 525
Fox, Madeline, 62
Fox, Rev. Canon, 587
Foxe, Judith, etc., 762
Foxe-Donnell, Leo, etc., 762
Foxham, Lord, 106
Fradubio, 348
Frail, Mistress, 633
Frake, Abel, etc., 1080
Frame, Lieutenant George, 956
France, Katharine of, 463
France, King of, 30, 573
France, Princess of, 635
Frances, 93, 338
Francesca, 273
Franceschini, Count Guido, 970
Francesco, 267
Francesco, Don, 1072
Franchi, Madame Savilla de, etc., 202
Francine, 179
Francis, Friar, 747
Francis of Austria, Emperor, 310
Francisca, 686
Francisco, 273, 439, 1238
Franciscus, 168
Francissina, 1256
François, Father, 48
Françoise, 312, 761
Frank, Anna, 48
Frank, Rose, 241
Frankenstein, Victor, 385
Frankford, John, 1257
Franklin, Benjamin, 533
Franklin, The, 147
Franz, 590, 1155
Franz, Emperor, 590
Franziska, 709
Frapp, Nicholas, 1148
Fraser, James, 668
Fraser, John, etc., 307
Frasier, Monsieur, 217
Frasier, Simon, 903
Frasquita, 1127
Fratta, Giovanni, Count of, etc., 155
Frauenberg, Konrad von, 1174
Freawaru, 98
Fred, 180, 1138
Frederic, 888, 972
Frederick, 1105
Frederick, Duke of, 67
Frederick the Great, 86
Frédérique, 579
Free, Michael, 169
Freeman, 892
Freeman, Sir Charles, 91
Freeport, Sir Andrew, 1044
French, Mary, 1189
French Lieutenant, The, 627
Frey, Elaine de, 1177

17

Friar, The, 147
Friday, 979
Frieda, 154
Friedebrand, 837
Friedland, The Duchess of, 1217
Friendly, Fortune, 990
Friesshardt, 1247
Frink, Chum, 73
Friscobaldo, Orlando, 480
Frith, 944
Fritha, 522
Frithiof, 387
Frog Footman, The, 23
Frola, Signora, 970
Frolic, 809
Frollo, Claude, 501
Frome, Ethan, etc., 333
Frome, Hector, 565
Frondoso, 1032
Frontenac, Count de, 1029
Frontin, 1166
Frony, 1072
Frosch, 854
Frosine, 712
Froth, 686, 766
Froth, Lord, etc., 299
Frowenfeld, Joseph, 415
Frumier, Almoro, 156
Fry, Jeeter, 425
Fry, John, 629
Ftatateeta, 139
Fucci, Vanni, 273
Fuchs, Otto, 751
Fuente, Dolores de la, 48
Fujinami, 521
Fujitsubo, 1100
Fulcinius Trio, 1021
Fulco, Archbishop, 1154
Fulgentio, 653
Fulkerson, Mr., 447
Fulvia, 159, 181
Fulvius, 160
Funangué, 576
Fungoso, 344
Furies, The, 487, 925
Furley, Mr., 707
Furlong, Mr., 442
Furnace, 765
Furnival, Mr., etc., 822
Furor, 348
Fürst, Walter, 1246
Fuseli, Eddie, 409
Fuselli, Dan, 1130
Fusilier, Agricola, 415
Fustigo, 480
Fuwa Dôken, 520
Fyr, 623

G——, Lt., 406
Gabelle, Théophile, 1102
Gabelus, 54
Gabor, Melchior, etc., 71
Gabriel, 18, 578, 805, 836, 837, 1277
Gabriel, Archangel, 545
Gabriel, Rabbi, 909
Gabrielle, Mlle., 649
Gabrielsen, Rev. Johan, 847
Gabry, M. de, etc., 223
Gadshill, 465
Gaetano, 971
Gaev, Leonid Andreyevitch, 173
Gaffer, 140
Gaganov, Artemy Pavlovitch, 908
Gagebee, Mortimer, etc., 1051
Gagnon, Eutrope, 670
Gagool, 576
Gaheris, 743
Gaigern, Baron, 414
Gaither, Nell, 937
Galahad, 512, 743
Galais, Frantz de, etc., 1218

Galaor, 31
Galaphron, 820
Galathea, 869
Gale, Seth, etc., 2
Galen, 672
Galis, Lamorak de, 743
Gall, Dr., 997
Gallagher, Dan, 525
Gallego, 48
Gallegos, Padre, 252
Galleon, Bobby, 378
Galli, Faustina, 983
Gallus, Asinus, 1020
Galoin, Count, 331
Galotti, Emilia, etc., 323
Galpano, 31
Galpe-Chopine, 179
Galván, Don Leandro, 296
Gama, Vasco da, 639
Gamacho, 785
Gamain, 208
Gamarra, Melquíades, 298
Game Chicken, The, 288
Gamelin, Évariste, etc., 405
Gamp, Sairey, 677
Gamuret, 837
Gamut, David, 597
Gandales, 31
Gandalín, 31
Gandara, 928
Gandein, 837
Gandish, Mr., etc., 769
Ganelon, 1062
Ganis, Bors de, etc., 743
Gant, Eugene, etc., 625, 796
Gaos, Jean, etc., 508
Garbets, Mr., 855
Garceran, Don, 548
Garcia, 152, 891
García, Don, 1166
Gard, Thorir of, 428
Gardana, 155
Gardener, The, 966
Gardiner, Captain, 727
Gardiner, Colonel, 1227
Gardiner, Mr., etc., 915
Gardiner, Stephen, 462
Gareth, 511, 743
Gargamelle, 394
Gargano, 96
Gargantua, 394
Gargery, Joe, etc., 419
Garinter, King, 31
Garland, Mr., etc., 801
Garnett, Miss Proserpine, 144
Garnotelle, 663
Garraghty, Nicholas, etc., 5
Garstin, Peter, 365
Garth, 1252
Garth, Mary, etc., 701
Garth, Miss, 781
Gartlauben, Capt. von, 301
Garvace, Mr., 477
Garvell, Archie, 1147
Gascoigne, 719
Gascoigne, Mrs. Nancy, etc., 238
Gashford, 83
Gaspard, 1102
Gasparo, 1239
Gasquilán, 31
Gates, General, 484
Gatsby, Jay, 421
Gatz, Mr., 422
Gaucher, Marie, 1047
Gaudin, Mme., 1242
Gault, Selena, 1255
Gaunt, Judge, 1253
Gaunt, Lord, 1193
Gauntlet, Emilia, etc., 859
Gauntry, Squire, 559
Gausse, 1118
Gaussin, Jean, etc., 1005
Gautier, Camille, 142

Gautruche, M., 398
Gautsson, Haakon, 72
Gaux, Jacques, 1029
Gaveston, Piers, 315
Gavot, 798
Gawain, 511, 742
Gawain, Sir, 188, 331, 838, 1042, 1278
Gawdis, 503
Gawr, King Gogyrvan, 563
Gay, Walter, 286
Gaylord, Marcia, etc., 730
Gaynor, Mrs., etc., 158
Gazaway, Major, 717
Gazebee, Mortimer, 282
Gazellus, 1105
Gazetta, 24
Gecko, 1158
Gedeonovsky, Sergei Petrovitch, 489
Geir the Priest, 1086
Geissler, 430
Gelanorus, 60
Gelfrat, 771
Gélis, Henri, 223
Gellatley, Davie, 1227
Gemini, Countess, 903
Genazahar, Count de, 858
General, Mrs., 619
General, The, 391
Genesis, 1028
Genestas, Colonel Pierre Joseph, 209
Geneviève, 852
Gengobei, 373
Genji, Prince, 1100
Geoffrey, 1062
Geomagog, 131
George, 101, 467, 581, 601, 967, 1028, 1127, 1198
George, Esper, 1213
George, Tobey, 498
George III, King, 310, 533
George-a-Greene, 979
Georges, Madame, 753
Georgette, 1206
Geraint, 511
Gerald, 113, 880
Gerald, Mrs. Letty Pace, 545
Geraldine, 1187
Gerames, 503
Gerard, 503
Gérard, 479
Gerard of Roussillon, 1062
Gerasim, 256
Gercourt, Comte de, 237
Gerd, 121
Gerda, 776
Gereth, Owen, etc., 1078
Gerhardt, Genevieve, etc., 544
Gerier, 1062
Gerin, 881, 1062
Gerint, 642
Germanicus, 762
Germanicus, Tiberius Claudius Drussus Nero, etc., 507
Gernando, 546
Gernerth, 1049
Gernot, 771
Geron, 326
Géronte, 279, 695
Gerrard, 93
Gerrard, Mr., 396
Gerridge, Sam, 154
Gerry, George, 209
Gertraud, 472
Gertrude, 227, 314, 438, 1247
Gervaise, 306
Gervas, Sir, 699
Geryon, 273
Geryoneo, 351
Gessler, Hermann, 1246
Gest, Norna, 623

Grangerfords, The, 496
Grania, 369
Grannis, 645
Grant, Jedediah, 175
Grant, Mr., etc., 887
Grant, Ulysses S., 175, 224
Grantly, Rev. Theophilus, etc., 80, 593, 1223
Grantly, Susan, etc., 384
Grant-Menzies, Jock, 440
Grantorto, 350
Grappa, Lieutenant, 555
Grassins, Monsieur de, 336
Gratiana, 24, 962
Gratiano, 696, 826
Grau, Chris, 153
Gravely, Lady, 1114
Graves, Muley, 418
Gray Brother, 561
Gray, Dermot, etc., 392
Gray, Dorian, 878
Gray, Mr., 885
Gray, Sir Thomas, 463
Grayfell, Harold, 1086
Graymarsh, 775
Grayson, Gertrude, 950
Grayson, Hugh, etc., 1275
Grazia, 544
Great Boyg, The, 849
Great God Pan, The, 225
Greatank, 856
Greaves, Montague, 1082
Grecco, Al, 55
Greech, Henry, 1177
Greedy, 765
Greeley, Horace, 175
Green, 966
Green, Aunt Mehitable, 85
Green, Goodhearted, 719
Green, Judge Bowling, 2
Green, Mr., 15, 1272
Green, Mrs., etc., 823
Green, Polly, 342
Greene, General Nathanael, 307
Greene, Goody, 710
Greene, Nicholas, 816
Greengoose, George, 582
Greffi, Count, 358
Grégoire, M., etc., 398
Gregorics, Pál, 1000
Gregorovious, Franz, 1118
Gregory, 992
Gregory, Lucian, 661
Grégory, Prince, 1110
Gregsby, Mr., 774
Gregson, Tobias, 1092
Gremio, 1107
Grendel, 98
Greneuc, Monsieur de, etc., 1215
Grenvile, Sir Richard, 1233
Gresham, Frank, etc., 281
Gresham, Mary, 384
Greslou, Robert, 272
Gretchen, 363
Gretry, Samuel, 889
Grettir the Strong, 427
Greville, Mr., 1042
Grewgious, Mr., 755
Grey, Agnes, 15
Grey, Aline, etc., 241
Grey, Fidelia, 893
Grey, Lady Jane, 1148
Grey, Lord, 969
Greylock, Jason, etc., 84
Gride, Arthur, 773
Gridley, Mr., 110
Grier, Elizabeth, 137
Grier, Jenny, 831
Grieux, Chevalier des, etc., 665
Grieux, Marquis de, 391
Griffin, 528
Griffith, 462
Grey Woman, The, 224

Griffith, Edward, 885
Griffith, Lady Lillian, 207
Griffiths, Clyde, etc., 36
Griffiths, Harry, 795
Griffo, 203
Griffolino, 274
Grigory, 130
Grigoryevitch, Ivan, 248
Grille, 349
Grim, 428, 446
Grimaldi, 1135
Grimaud, 1129
Grimbard, 964
Grimble, Mr., etc., 914
Grimes, 142
Grimes, Captain, 259
Grimm, Percy, 614
Grimshaw, Mr., 1083
Grimwig, Mr., 812
Grinder, Mr., 802
Grineff, Piotr Andreitch, 150
Gringoire, Pierre, 501
Grip, Arent, 354
Gripe, Alderman, 634
Gripus, 1050
Grisha, 45
Grisolan, 309
Grizzle, Lord, 1146
Gro, 623
Grobe, Tamar, etc., 722
Groby, Farmy, 1120
Groffin, Thomas, 877
Grogan, Mr., 498
Grönset, Hall, 857
Grosbois, 312
Grose, Mrs., 1167
Grosgeorge, Mme., etc., 240
Grosvenor, Archibald, 842
Grotius, 1043
Grove, Lena, 614
Groves, Jem, 801
Grubach, Frau, 1155
Grudden, Mrs., 774
Grueby, John, 83
Gruffen, Dr., 1052
Gruffydd, Mr., 493
Grumio, 1107
Grummer, Daniel, 878
Grünlich, Bendix, etc., 134
Grunter, Mr., 721
Grushenka, 129
Grushnitski, 471
Grusinskaya, Elisaveta Alexandrovna, 414
Gryce, Miss, 541
Gryce, Percy, etc., 490
Gryphon, The, 23
Guardiano, 1261
Gubaryov, Stepan Nikolaevitch, 1054
Gudmundur, Pastor, 522
Gudrun, 432
Gudule, 501
Gudurz, 1057
Guendolen, 112
Guendoline, 131
Guenevere, 1042
Guenevere, Lady, 1184
Guenevere, Queen, 563, 742
Guéret, Paul, 240
Guéritaude, De la, 69
Guermantes, Prince de, etc., 954
Guermeur, Captain, 509
Guerra, Ángel, 43
Guerra, Guido, 273
Guest, Lady Julia de, 593
Guest, Stephen, 706
Guiamara, 1075
Guiccioli, Countess, 205
Guiche, Comte de, 234
Guiderius, 232
Guild, 1124
Guildenstern, 439

Guildford, Sir Henry, 462
Guillaume, 509
Guillot, M., 335
Guinart, Rogue, 295
Guiness, Nurse, 453
Guinevere, 188, 331, 511, 1278
Guinevere, Queen, 838
Guinicelli, Guido, 275
Guise, Duc du, 136, 961
Guiseppe, Angela, 48
Guivret the Little, 331
Gulbeyaz, 292
Gulchenrouz, 1194
Gülcke, 355
Gulick, Edna, 612
Gulliver, 84
Gulliver, Lemuel, 433
Gumbo, 1210
Gumersindo, 858
Gummidge, Mrs., 244
Gunch, Vergil, 73
Gunlaug, 372
Gunn, Ben, 1152
Gunnar, 372
Gunnarsson, Aslak, 1059
Gunnarsson, Hogni, 1086
Gunnhilda, 1086
Gunpowder, 607
Gunter, Mr., 877
Gunther, 301, 770
Guppy, William, 109
Gurget, Mrs., 990
Gurna, Corrado la, 682
Gurnemanz, 838
Gurney, 316
Gurney, James, 572
Gurth, 538
Gushing, Miss, 283
Gustaf, 430
Gutman, Casper, etc., 658
Guttorm, 1059
Guy, 102, 434
Guy, Captain, 759
Guy, Lord, 616
Guy, Octavius, 742
Guyon, 348
Guzmán, Don Pedro de, 1080
Guzmán de Alfarache, etc., 435
Gvendur, 522
Gwenard, 413
Gwydion, 642
Gwynne, Dr., 81
Gyb, 1017
Gynecia, 57
Gynt, Peer, 848
Gyrdssön, Arne, 586

H., 609
Haaberg, Anders, etc., 857
Haakon, King, 520
Haberdasher, The, 147
Habersham, Miss, 527
Habershaw, Hugh, 484
Habrotonon, 57
Hades, 824, 926
Hadgi, 861
Hadgi-Stavros, 575
Haemon, 49
Haethcynn, 99
Hagadorn, Esther, etc., 200
Hagen, 770
Haggage, Dr., 620
Haggerty, Paulie, 1092
Haggis, 88
Haidée, 206, 292
Haigasun, Ter, 383
Hainault, John of, 316
Haines, 1176
Haines, Rupert, 101
Hakon the Good, 456
Halcombe, Marian, 1256
Halden, 102

Jane, 826, 1036
Jane, Lady, 1192
Janet, 246
Janey, 200
Jannan, Mariana, etc., 1126
Jannice, 1254
Januario, 536
Janvier, Curé, 210
Japan, Emperor of, 1100
Jaquenetta, 635
Jaques, 66, 67
Jardtrud, 586
Jarl, 669
Jarley, Mrs., 801
Jarnatt, Father, 445
Jarndyce, John, 108
Jarno, 1245
Jarvis, 690
Jarvis, Arthur, etc., 227
Jarvis, Diony Hall, etc., 422
Jason, 273, 542, 606, 687
Jasper, 582
Jasper, Jack, 755
Jasperino, 168
Javert, M., 714
Jawleyford, 721
Jean, 424, 716
Jean-Baptiste, 416
Jeanne, 1121
Jeannette, 69
Jeannot, 1158
Jeff, 403
Jekyl, Captain Harry, 1001
Jekyll, Dr. Henry, 280
Jelinek, Anton, 752
Jellyby, Caroline, etc., 110
Jemima, 1052
Jemmy, Dismal, 876
Jenkin, 1258
Jenkins, Winifred, 499
Jenkinson, Ephraim, 1199
Jenkinson, Mr., 447
Jenkyns, Miss Deborah, etc., 219
Jennings, 775, 861
Jennings, Ezra, 741
Jennings, Lester, 135
Jennings, Mrs., 1023
Jens, 857
Jensen, Nelse, 787
Jensine, 430
Jephson, Reuben, 37
Jeremiah, 155
Jeremy, 633
Jermin, John, 814
Jermyn, Matthew, etc., 364
Jerningham, Jerry, 411
Jérôme, 1067
Jerome, Father, 156
Jeronimo, Brother, 536
Jerrard, 378
Jerry, 802
Jervis, Mrs., 832
Jervois, Emily, 1042
Jeschute, 838
Jesrad, 1278
Jessel, Miss, 1167
Jessica, 696
Jesus de Baca, Padre, 253
Jesus of Nazareth, 837
Jesus the Nazarene, 97
Jetsome, Mr., 707
Jeufroy, Abbé, 118
Jewdwine, Horace, 276
Jewel, 628
Jewkes, Mrs., 832
Jim, 495, 627
Jim, Uncle, 477
Jiménez, 89
Jiménez, Pepita, 858
Jimmy, 200, 650
Jimson, Gulley, 472, 482
Jingle, Mr. Alfred, 876
Jiniwin, Mrs., 800

Jinkins, Mr., 678
Jinks, Mr., 878
Jinny, 1228
Jo, 109
Joad, Tom Jr., etc., 417
Joan, 538
Joan of Arc, 998
Joanna of the Cross, Sister, 219
Joaquin, 137
Job, 1030
Jobling, Dr. John, 677
Jobling, Tony, 109
Jocasta, 793, 873
Jocelyn, Rose, etc., 339
Jochanan, 53, 762
Jochanan the Baptist, 762
Jodelet, Viscount, 988
Joe, 875, 965
Jogglesbury, etc., 721
Johann, Prince, 1174
Johansen, 1015
John, 121, 188, 227, 463, 541, 602, 833, 933, 1075, 1174, 1229
John, Don, 747
John, Friar, 991
John, Hordle, 1237
John, King, 570, 978
John, Prince, 537
John, St., 275
John of Gaunt, 966
John of the Funnels, Friar, 394
John the Baptist, 837
Johnny, 977
Johns, Mrs., 396
Johnson, 1015
Johnson, Howard, etc., 477
Johnson, John, 292
Johnson, Livery, Mrs., 1066
Johnson, Mr., 364
Johnson, Paul, 1188
Johnson, Walter, etc., 481
Johnston, Albert Sydney, 624
Joker, Jack, 886
Joliffe, Joceline, 1265
Jollifant, Inigo, 411
Jolly, Uncle, 975
Jolter, 860
Jon, 522
Jon of Myri, Bailiff, 522
Jonah, 283
Jonas, 561
Jonathan, 1161
Jones, Abe, 797
Jones, Brutus, 325
Jones, Captain, 628
Jones, Captain Bill, 1152
Jones, John Paul, 534
Jones, Lady, 833
Jones, Mary Flood, 871
Jones, Mr., 21, 227, 709, 1201
Jones, Paul, etc., 307
Jones, Pete, 427, 481
Jones, Richard, 887
Jones, Senator Garwood B., 937
Jones, Squire, 811
Jones, Tom, etc., 1143
Jones, Wash, etc., 4
Jonsdatter, Ingebjörg, 72
Jonsdottir, Audur, 522
Jonsen, Captain, 526
Jonsson, Alma, 616
Jonsson, Gudbjartur, etc., 521
Jopp, 683
Joppolo, Major Victor, 96
Jordan, Rachael, 1266
Jordan, Robert, 374
Jordan, Thomas, etc., 1069
Jorgenson Mimi, etc., 1123
Jorham, Captain, etc., 48
Jorkins, Mr., 245
Jorrocks, John, etc., 441, 474, 552
Jorundsson, On, 456
José, Don, 152, 292

José, Father, 910
Josef, 918
Joseph, 1245, 1272
Joseph Bar Naba, 53
Josepha, 215
Josephine, 310, 478
Josephine Mme., 649
Josyan, 101
Jotham, 5
Joukahäinen, 565
Jourdain, Margery, 467
Jourdain, Monsieur, etc., 116
Jourdemayne, Jennet, 589
Jourdonnais, 103
Jove, 229, 351, 639
Jowl, Joe, 802
Joy, 519
Joyce, 831, 1157
Joyner, Mr., etc., 1232
Joyner, Mrs., 634
Jozeran of Provence, Count, 1062
J.S.K., 610
Juan, Don, 535
Juan Rojo, 1032
Juana, 495, 896
Judas, 329
Judique, Tanis, 73
Judith, 236, 431
Jules, 312, 1029
Julia, 268, 309, 508, 594, 780, 983, 1171, 1256
Julia, Donna, 292
Julia, Lady, 768
Julián, Don, 421
Juliana, 840
Julie, 289, 482, 615
Julie, Cousin, 612
Julie, Miss, 715
Juliet, 686, 990
Julietta, 504, 1246
Juliette, 383
Julio, Doctor, 1239
Julio, Don, 495
Julius, Posthumus, 1921
Julius, Uncle, 197
Jull, Sir John, 1177
Julyan, Colonel, 944
Jumble, 861
Jumble, Sir Jolly, 1058
Jumper, 1007
Junie, 126, 1067
Juniper, Brother, 124
Juno, 470
Jupe, Cecilia, etc., 443
Jupien, 955
Jupillon, M., etc., 398
Jupiter, 37, 138, 233, 406, 470, 925, 927
Jurgen, 563
Jussat, M. de, 272
Just, 709
Just Man, A, 896
Justice, Beatrice, 346
Justin, 647
Justinian, 275
Jutta, Lady, 1154
Juvan, 404
Juvika, Per Anders, 857

K., 154
K., Joseph, 1155
K——, Prince, 1185
KAA, 561
Kaede, 521
Kaethe, 1118, 1269
Kahabuka, 331
Kaikeyi, Queen, 939
Kailet, King, 838
Kalander, 58
Kalervo, 565
Kaleva, 565

ALPHABETICAL CHARACTER INDEX

25

Labordette, 757
Labove, 437
Labrax, 1050
La Brierre, Dr. Julien, 178
Lac, King, 331
Lacerteux, Germinie, 398
Laches, 337
La Chouette, 753
Lacie, 23
Lackland, Major, 402
Laco, Gracinus, 1021
La Comtesse, 892
Lacy, 387, 503
Lacy, Beatrice, etc., 944
Lacy, Horace de, 995
Lacy, Miriam, 130
Lacy, Rowland, etc., 1035
Ladd, Peter, 956
Ladislaw, Will, 701
Ladvenu, Brother Martin, 999
Lady Jane, The, 842
Laertes, 438, 789, 1044, 1244
Laetitia, 799
Lafe, 66
Laferte, Chrétien de, 1174
Lafeu, 30
La Flèche, 713
La Fleur, 1024
La-Foole, Sir Amorous, 1040
La Fosseuse, 209
La Frimat, 312
Lafuerza, Father Martin, 139
La Glorieux, 933
Lagors, Raoul de, 367
La Gournerie, 1005
La Grande, 312
La Grange, 988
Lahmann, Pastor, 880
L'Aiglon, 590
Laitis, Comrade, 755
Lajeunesse, Gabriel, etc., 340
Lakamba, 31
Lakshman, 939
Lalla Rookh, 591
Lamachus, 6
Lamar, Ruby, 1003
Lamare, Jeanne de, etc., 1259
Lamb, Mr., 22
Lamb, Richard, 928
Lambert, 758
Lambert, Colonel, etc., 1211
Lambourne, Michael, 567
Lambro, 292
La Mentera, Duke of, 266
La Merluche, 713
Lamia, Aelius, 983
Lammeter, Nancy, 1038
Lammle, Alfred, etc., 828
Lamo, 240
La Mole, Mathilde de, etc., 947
Lamotte, Annette, 377
La Motte Valois, Jeanne de, 930
Lampis, 240
Lampito, 640
Lampriscus, 810
Lamuse, 1181
Lancaster, 316
Lancaster, Kate, 260
Lancaster, Prince John of, 464
Lancelot, 511
Lancelot of the Lake, 188
Land, Ned, 1169
Landauer, Isaac, 910
Landless, Neville, etc., 755
Landry, Oliver, 1067
Landuc, Laudine de, 1277
Lane, Miriam, 328
Laney, Lady Caroline, 250
Langdale, Mr., 83
Langen, Baroness von, 239
Langhope, Mr., 390
Langtry, Professor Horace, 923

Languines, 31
Languish, Lydia, 974
Lanning, Ames, 566
l'Anou, 136
Lanshaw, Betty, 47
Lant, Captain, 260
Lantier, 306
Lantier, Etienne, 397
Lanyon, Dr. Hastie, 280
Lanyon, Joyce, 62
Lao Er, 302
Lao San, 302
Lao Ta, 302
Lao Tzu, 735
La Pérouse, 207
Lapham, Silas, etc., 973
La Pia, 274
Lapidoth, Mirah, etc., 238
La Pintada, 1185
La Porte, Volida, 135
Larcher, Edwin, etc., 703
Larin, Tatyana, etc., 334
Larkins, 769
Larkins, Annie, etc., 477
Larkins, Miss, 246
Larkins, Molly, 990
Laroussel, 178
Larpent, Lady Louisa, 342
Lars, 597
Larsen, Wolf, etc., 1015
Lartius, Titus, 202
Larue, Mrs., 717
La Ruse, Count, 552
Laspara, 1184
Lasso, Count, 397
Lasswade, Lord, 1274
Last, Anthony, etc., 440
Latch, William, etc., 332
Latiaris, 1020
Latif, Mohammed, 839
Latini, Brunetto, 273
Latinus, 12, 983
la Tour, F. J. de, 184
Latour, Father Jean Marie, 251
La Trobe, Miss, 101
La Truille, 312
Laudisi, Lamberto, 970
Laughlin, Peter, 1135
Launce, 1171
Launce, Mrs., 378
Launcelot du Lake, 742
Launes, Princess des, 955
Laura, 139, 358, 402, 534
Laure, 312
Laure, Mme., 703
Laurencia, 1032
Laurentano, Prince Ippolito, etc., 797
Laurentíni, Lady, 754
Laurentino, 248
Lauris, 858
Lavache, 30
Lavaine, 513
Laval, Bishop, 1029
Lavarcham, 262, 263
Lavardens, Paul de, etc., 1
Lavenza, Elizabeth, 385
Laverick, Jay, 153
Laville, Dr., 270
Lavinia, 12, 1136
Lavish, Miss Eleanor, 994
Lavransdatter, Kristin, 585
Lavrentyevitch G—v, Anton, 908
Lavretsky, Fedor Ivanitch, 488
Lawford, Arthur, etc., 958
Lawless, Will, 107
Lawrence, Elizabeth, 184
Lawrence, Frederick, 1115
Lawrence, Friar, 991
Lawrence, Theodore, 622
Lawson, Sam, 811
Lawton, Captain, 1079

Laxley, Ferdinand, 339
Lay, Denis, 1269
Layeville, 1026
Lazarillo, 1256
Lazarillo de Tormes, 604
Lazarus, 79, 107
Leach, 1015
Leah, 541
Lean, Donald Bean, 1227
Leander, 115
Leandre, 891
Léandre, 280
Leandro, 247
Leantio, 1261
Lear, 572
Leather, 721
Leatherhead, Lanthorn, 87
Leaven, Bessie, etc., 541
Lebas, Counselor, 215
Le Beau, 67
Le Ber, Jeanne, 1029
Leblanc, Baptiste, 340
Le Bret, 233
Lebrun, Mademoiselle, 770
Lebyadkin, Ignat, cte., 907
Lecca, Portius, 160
Lechery, 279
Lecoq, Monsieur, 367, 736
Le Count, Mrs., 781
Leda, 38, 70
Ledbrook, Miss, 774
Ledsmar, Dr., 236
Lee, 313
Lee, Annie, 328
Lee, Annie, etc., 787
Lee, Clare, 1208
Lee, Heinrich, etc., 431
Lee, Sir Henry, etc., 1265
Leeds, Nina, etc., 1089
Leeford, Mr., etc., 813
Leer, 27
Le Fever, 1161
Leete, Edith, etc., 627
Lefferts, Lawrence, 15
Lefrançois, Madame Veuve, 647
Legend, Valentine, etc., 633
Legrand, Fanny, 1005
Legrand, William, 406
Legras, Mme., 189
Legree, Simon, 1179
Leicester, 316
Leidenberch, 1043
Leigh, Amyas, etc., 1233
Leigh, Mrs., 1205
Leighton, Admiral Sir Percy, 149
Leighton, Patricia, 1240
Leil, 131
Leila, 292
Leinland, Marja, 857
Leir, 131
Leivers, Miriam, etc., 1068
Lem, 325
Lembke, Andrey Antonovitch von, etc., 907
Lemm, Christophor Fedoritch, 489
Lemminkäinen, 565
Lena, 1200
Lena, Popilius, 560
Lenardo, 1245
Lengthy, 140
Leni, 1155
Lennart, Captain, 1088
Lennox, 643
Lenox, John, 247
Lensky, Lydia, etc., 935
Lensky, Vladimir, 335
Lentulus, Publius, 159
Lenville, Thomas, 774
Lenzi, Cavaliere Tito, 601
Leo, 818
Leo X, Pope, 984
Leofric, 470

Lory, 952
Losberne, Mr., 813
Lothario, 1244
Lotherington, Jonathan, 719
Lothrop, Mrs., etc., 811
Lo-Tsen, 630
Lottie, 454
Lotus, 305
Lotus Blossom, 412
Louhi, 565
Louie, 454
Louis, 227, 757, 891, 932, 1015, 1228
Louis XI, 468
Louis XII, 984
Louis XIV, 1199
Louis XV, 693
Louis XVI, 208
Louis XI, King, 931
Louis XIII, King, 181
Louis XIV, King, 1170
Louis, Don, 294
Louis of Bourbon, 933
Louisa, 544, 746
Louise, 352, 615
Louise, Mlle., 270
Louison, 507
Lovatt, Mr., 187
Lovberg, Eilert, 455
Loveit, Lady, 660
Lovel, 50
Lovel, Lord, 969
Lovel, Mr., 342
Lovelace, Robert, 183
Loveless, 952
Loveless, Elder, etc., 1013
Lovell, Charlotte, 803
Lovell, Lord, 765
Lovell, Sir Thomas, 462
Lovell, Tyson, 624
Loveridge, Anselo, 266
Lovetin, Lord Viscount, 719
Love-Wit, 20
Lovisa, 689
Lowborough, Lord, 1116
Lowder, Mrs., 1251
Lowestoffe, Reginald, 380
Lowten, Mr., 877
Lowther, Mary, 1197
Loyal, M., 1112
Lua, 76
Luachar, Lord of, 369
Lubin, 76
Luc, Arnaud la, etc., 985
Luca, 485
Lucas, 152, 280, 1127
Lucas, Charlotte, 915
Luce, 481, 581
Luce, Uncle, 976
Lucentio, 1106
Lucero, 928
Lucero, Padre Marino, 252
Lucero, Trinidad, 253
Luces, 132
Lucetta, 1171
Lucia, 100, 1253
Luciana, 193, 320
Lucie, 1101
Lucien, 272
Lucifer, 140, 278
Lucifera, 348
Lucilius, 1134
Lucilla, 338
Lucinde, 279
Lucio, 685, 1256
Lucius, 406, 560, 1133, 1137
Luckett, Worth, etc., 1154
Luckett, Wyitt, 366
Luckles, Sir Philip, 783
Lucky, 1216
Lucre, Pecunious, 1157
Lucrece, 940

Lucrèce, 695
Lucrecia, 163, 1166
Lucretia, 197, 606, 1099
Lucullus, 1133
Lucy, 212, 350, 634, 798, 946, 1233
Lucy, Lady, 1114
Lucy, St., 272
Lucy, Sir William, 468
Ludger, 771
Ludovico, 170, 754
Ludovico, Count, 393
Ludwig, 359, 1175
Ludwig, Eberhard, 909
Ludwig, Margrave Karl, 1174
Lufton, Lady, etc., 384, 593
Luis, 785
Luis, Don, 48
Luisa, 1070
Luitgard, Lady, 1154
Luiz, 410
Lujon, Manuel, 252
Luka, 637
Lukas, 53
Lukashka, 203
Lukier, Septimus, 741
Lulu, 329
Lumpkin, Tony, 1031
Luna, Alvise, 1195
Lundell, 949
Lunete, 1277
Lunken, Bertha, 1110
Lü Po, 986
Lupe, 379
Lupex, Mr., etc., 1051
Lupi, 682
Lupin, Mrs., 677
Lurcio, 120
Lush, Thomas, 239
Lusignan, 1279
Lussurioso, 962
Luster, 1072
Lu Ta, 26
Lutestring, Mrs., 76
Luzardo, Dr. Santos, etc., 297
Luzhin, Piotr Petrovitch, 221
Lyamshin, 908
Lyapkin-Tyapkin, Ammos Fyodorovitch, 527
Lycaenium, 240
Lychorida, 862
Lychow, General von, 153
Lycogenes, 60
Lyconides, 908
Lycurgus, 59, 1009
Lycus, 469
Lyddy, 365
Lydgate, Rosamond Vincy, etc., 701
Lydia, 634
Lydyard, 807
Lyenitzyn, Alexy Ivanovitch, 249
Lygia, 934
Lygones, 569
Lyhne, Niels, etc., 776
Lymoges, 571
Lynch, 904
Lynch, Michael, 484
Lyndall, 1084
Lyndon, Redmond Barry, etc., 85
Lyndwood, Mabel, 1248
Lynette, 512
Lyngstrand, 587
Lynn, Henry, etc., 542
Lynn, Lady, 541
Lyon, Rufus, etc., 364
Lys, 431
Lysander, 704
Lysanias, 258
Lysimachus, 862
Lysippus, 655
Lysistrata, 640

Lyster, Dr., 163
Lyting, 1086

M., Herr, 612
M., Miss, 692
M., Mrs., 920
Ma Chun-Shing, etc., 182
Mabel, 197, 888
Mabel, Lady, 1019
Maboef, M., 715
Mac, 519
Mac Ivor Vich Ian Vohr, Fergus, etc., 1226
Mac Luga, 369
Mac Morna, Goll, 369
MacAdam, Lady, 47
Macalister, 1139
Macallister, Bony, 554
Macallister, Mrs., 731
Macapa, Maria, 645
Macaria, 177
Macartney, 342
Macaulay, Herbert, 1124
Macauley, Homer, etc., 498
Macbeth, etc., 642
Macbriar, 806
Macca, Turiddu, 161
MacChesnay, Colonel, 949
Maccombich, Evan Dhu, 1227
Macdonald, 1217
MacDowell, Gertie, 1176
Macduff, etc., 643
MacFarlane, Sir Valentine, etc., 266
Macgregor, Lady Sarah, 752
Machaon, 516
Macheath, Captain, 94
Machiavel, 318
Machiavelli, Niccolò, 984, 993
Macías, Demetrio, 1185
Macías, Lucas, 18
Macilente, 344
Mackay, Father, 124
MacKean, Barney, 690
Mackel, Ira, 746
Mackellar, Ephraim, 681
Mackenzie, Mrs., 767
Mackworth, Father, 942
Macmaster, Vincent, 834
MacMurfee, Sam, 28
MacMurrachu, Meehawl, 225
MacMurtrie, Scott, 1132
Maco, Messer, 212
Macquart, Corporal Jean, 300, 312
Macqueron, 313
Macro, 508
Macro, Sertorius, 1020
MacStinger, Mrs., etc., 287
MacTurk, Captain, 1001
MacWhirter, Judah, 366
Mad Hatter, The, 23
Madanika, 617
Maddalena, Maria, 744
Madden, Celia, etc., 235
Maddock, Harriet, 808
Madeline, 340, 354, 367
Madelon, 555
Madera, President, 1185
Madge, 809
Madigan, Mrs. Maisie, 562
Madness, 469
Madoc, Hannah, 54
Madras, Constantine, etc., 648
Madvig, Paul, etc., 403
Maea, 90
Maecenas, 52
Maël, 855
Maeve, 262, 442
Maffé, 136
Magaera, 1131
Magalhães, Captain João, 1206

Maroola, Dain, 31
Marpole, Captain James, 526
Marpole, Jake, 751
Marquess, The, 1167
Marrable, Walter, etc., 1197
Mars, 138, 639
Marsden, Charles, 1090
Marshal, The, 346
Marshland, Jinny, 153
Marsilion, 1062
Marsilius, 820
Marston, Anne, 952
Marta, 17, 122, 1158
Martel, Charles, 275
Martellus, 77
Martésie, 64
Martext, Sir Oliver, 67
Martha, 71, 219, 756, 1013
Martha, Mistress, 634
Marthe, 347
Martial, 161
Martin, 145, 188, 557, 878, 1049
Martin, Donald, 832
Martin, Gilbert, etc., 307
Martin, Mr., 396
Martin, Robert, 325
Martin, Sponge, 241
Martindale, Dorcas, 184
Martindale, Major, 1193
Martine, 279, 281
Martinez, Don José, 416
Martinez, Padre Antonio José, 252
Martius, 1137
Marton, Mr., 801
Marty, André, 376
Maruffi, Fra Salvestro, 994
Marullus, 560
Marusja, 651
Marvel, 528
Marvell, Ralph, etc., 230
Marvin, General, 96
Marvin, Judge, 369
Marwood, Mrs., 1230
Marx, Bernard, 121
Mary, 79, 355, 566, 878, 916, 1018, 1146, 1245
Mary, Princess, 471
Mary, Queen, 1149
Mary the Mother of Jesus, 837
Marya, 347
Maryanka, 203
Maryna, 116
Marzio, 164
Mascarille, Marquis de, 988
Masha, 1016, 1129
Mashurin, Miss, 1208
Maskery, Will, 9
Maskwell, Jack, 298
Máslova, Katerína Mikháelovna, 958
Maso, 994
Mason, Lady Mary, etc., 821
Mason, Mr., 542
Mason, Orville, 36
Mason, Sarah, 768
Mason, William, 21
Massey, Bartle, 8
Mata, 848
Matchett, 257
Matey, 250
Math, King, 642
Mathavya, 1001
Matheo, 480
Mathias, Don, 547
Mathô, 1002
Matholwch, 641
Mathurine, 294
Matilda, 156, 275, 733
Matilda, Lady, 616
Matilde, 351, 1080
Matiwan, 1275
Matou, Rosine, 1205

Matrevis, 316
Matryóna, 911
Matt, Mrs., 163
Matt of the Mint, 95
Mattee, Enoree, 1275
Matthew, 846
Matthew, Master, 343
Matthews, Bess, etc., 1275
Matthews, Fanny, 34
Matthias, Don, 402
Matvey, 739
Mauban, Antoinette de, 918
Maubel, Jacques, 405
Maude, Lady, 1237
Maudlen, Percy, 692
Maudlin, 171
Maudru, 1067
Maugrabin, Hayraddin, 932
Maule, Matthew, etc., 491
Maule, Mr., 872
Mauperin, Renée, etc., 957
Maurecourt, Dr. Denis, 189
Maurice, 1043, 1121
Maurice, M., 113
Mauricio Lieutenant, 248
Maurrant, Rose, etc., 1090
Maury, Aleck, etc., 21
Maury, Angèle, 595
Mavis, Mistress, 1040
Mawmsey, Mr., etc., 703
Max, 880
Max, Boris A., 761
Maxime, 281
Maximus, 181
May, 623, 665, 736
Mayakin, 373
Maybold, Mr., 1182
Maye, Philomène, 1236
Mayflower, 830
Mayli, 302
Maylie, Rose, etc., 812
Mazare, 63
Mazarin, Cardinal, 1170, 1200
McAllister, Sandy, 1158
McBride, Moroni, etc., 175
McBryde, Mr., 839
McCannon, Shreve, 4, 1072
McCarron, Hoake, 437
McClain, Curly, 425
McCoy, Mrs. Margie, 454
McCreary, Fenian O'Hara, 1187
McDermot, Dermot, 442
McEachern, Calvin, etc., 614
McFarlane, Dr. Hugh, 411
McGarrity, Mr., 1153
McGehee, Hugh, etc., 1056
McGregor, Scott, etc., 923
McHarg, Lloyd, 1276
M'Choakumchild, Mr., 444
McHugh, Drake, 579
McIntosh, Sergeant Donald, 427
McIvor, Cameron, etc., 624
McKechnie, Captain, 834
McKee, Mr., 422
McKelvey, Charles, etc., 73
McKenzie, 103
McKisco, Mr., etc., 1118
McKlennar, Mrs. Sarah, 308
McLonis, Jurry, 308
McManus, Ben, etc., 392
McMillan, Rev. Duncan, 37
McNab, Corporal, etc., 842
McNab, Mrs., 1139
McNab, Sandy, 48
McNamara, Mr., 1078
McNeil, 2
McNiel, Gus, 664
McPhillip, Francis Joseph, etc., 524
McQueen, Dr., 621
McRaven, Laura, 264
McShane, Officer, 1153

McTeague, 644
McVey, Hugh, 901
Meadows, Hornsby, 956
Meadows, Mrs., 1072
Meagles, Mr., etc., 619
Mealyus, 872
Meander, 1106
Means, Bud, etc., 481
Mears, Bessie, 761
Meaulnes, Augustin, 1218
Mechanist, A, 942
Mechelín, 1070
Medardus, 267
Mede, Lady, 1212
Medea, 543, 606, 686
Médéric, 1067
Media, 669
Medice, 397
Medici, Giovanni de', etc., 994
Medicina, Piero da, 274
Medina, 348
Medina, Agnes de, 733
Medina, Duke of, 997
Medina, Lorenzo de, 733
Medina Sidonia, Duke of, 290
Medon, 791
Medoro, 818
Medrano, Juan de, 728
Medviedenko, Simon, 1016
Medway, 350
Medynsky, Madame, 373
Meeber, Caroline, 1045
Meeks, Mr., 1083
Megacles, 240
Megadorus, 908
Megaera, 273
Megara, 469
Megari, Professor, 983
Megra, 869
Mehevi, 1174
Meinhard, Prince, 1174
Meis, Adriano, 600
Meis, Francesco, 601
Meister, Wilhelm, 1243, 1245
Mejía, Don Luis, 294
Melantha, 673
Melanthius, 791
Melantho, 791
Melantius, 654
Melbourne, Lady, 735
Melbury, Grace, etc., 1263
Melchthal, Arnold von, 1246
Meleager, 70
Meleander, 60
Meledor, 1279
Melekhov, Gregor, etc., 38, 290
Melema, Tito, 992
Melford, Jerry, etc., 499
Melibea, 163
Meliboee, 351
Melicent, Dame, 220
Mélie, 118
Melina, 1244
Melinda, 945
Meliogrance, 744
Mélisande, 852
Melissa, 351, 817
Melitta, 1006
Meljanz of Lys, King, 838
Mell, Charles, 246
Mellefont, 298
Mello, Dr., 441
Melmoth, John, etc., 689
Meltham, Harry, 15
Melun, Count, 572
Melvile, Emily, 142
Melville, Herman, 813
Melville, Julia, 975
Melzi, Francesco, 984
Memling, Hans, 189
Memoria, 1033
Mena, 485

Monk, The, 147
Monkey, 734
Monks, 812
Monmouth, Duke of, 699, 806
Monmouth, Marquis of, 196
Monnerie, Mrs., etc., 692
Monogue, Nora, 378
Monster, The, 385, 405
Mont, Michael, 377, 729
Montagu, Lord, 595
Montague, etc., 991
Montague, Alice, 403
Montague, Charlotte, 184
Montague, Marquess of, 468
Montague, Monty, 1125
Montalais, Mlle. de, 1200
Montalt, Marquis de, 985
Montano, 826
Montanus, 1114
Montanus, Olle, 949
Montauran, Marquis de, 178
Montcalm, Marquis de, 597
Montcontour, Madame la Prin-
cesse de, 769
Montefeltro, Buonconte da, 274
Montefeltro, Guido de, 274
Monteith, Sir John, 1013
Montejanos, Baron Montès, 215
Montemayor, The Marquesa de,
124
Montero, General, etc., 785
Montfleury, 234
Montgomery, Mrs., 1225
Montgomery, Sir John, 468
Monticelso, Cardinal, 1238
Montjoy, 463
Montmorency, 1127
Montoni, Signor, etc., 754
Montoria, Don José de, 1007
Montoya, 1094
Montrose, 803
Montrose, Emily, 1100
Montsurry, 136, 961
Monygham, Dr., 784
Moodie, Priscilla, etc., 111
Moody, Leopold, 486
Moody, Tom, 409
Mookerjee, Hurree Chunder, 569
Moon, Lorna, 409
Mooncalf, 88
Moore, Anne, 957
Moore, Denis, 48
Moore, Kathleen, 599
Moore, Louis Gérard, etc., 1034
Moore, Mrs., 839
Moore, Ralph, etc., 839
Moorehouse, J. Ward, 1188
Mopsa, 58
Mopsus, 815
Morand, 174
Morano, Count, 754
Morcerf, Viscount Albert de, 205
Mord, Fiddle, 1086
Mordaunt, 1170
Mordaunt, Anneke, etc., 1007
Mordaunt, Colonel, 1098
Morden, Colonel William, 184
Mordicai, Mr., 5
Mordovinov, 1027
Mordred, 743
More, Shan, 442
More, Thomas, 1189
Moreau, Frederic, etc., 1023
Morecraft, 1013
Morel, 955
Morel, Gertrude, etc., 1068
Moreland, Earl of, 374
Moreland, Stella, 1104
Morell, Candida, etc., 144
Morelli, Shep, 1124
Morena, Commendatore, 1073
Moretti, Ettore, 358

Morfin, Mr., 287
Morfontaine, Astrée-Luce de, 137
Morgadour, 435
Morgan, 854, 860
Morgan, Annie, 473
Morgan, Colonel, 662
Morgan, Duke, 1159
Morgan, Huw, etc., 493
Morgan, O Nine, 834
Morgan le Fay, 743
Morgana, 821
Morgiana, 56
Morier, 1043
Moritz, Justine, 386
Morland, Catherine, 782
Morland, James, 782
Mornay, Marquise de, 797
Morning Star, 512
Moro, Duke, 984
Morocco, Prince of, 696
Morolt, Duke, 1159
Morón, 728
Moroni, 175
Morosa, 1152
Morose, 1039
Moroso, 1261
Morrel, M., etc., 204
Morrice, Mr., 163
Morrie, 454
Morris, Dinah, 7
Morris, Francis, 453
Morris, Lord, 1211
Morris, Victoria, etc., 21
Morrison, 749, 1201
Morrison, Hannah, 730
Morrow, Harry, 21
Morstan, Mary, 1037
Mortara, Mauro, 797
Mortensgard, Peter, 995
Mortimer, Edmund, etc., 316, 464,
467
Morton, 466
Morton, Captain, 720
Morton, Henry, 805
Morton, John, 969
Morton, Mr., 523
Morville, Hugh de, 748
Mosaïde, 69
Mosca, 1214
Mosca, Alfio, 485
Mosca, Count, 170
Moses, 1012, 1049, 1199
Moss, Mrs. Gritty, etc., 707
Most Beautiful Man, The, 225
Motes, 92
Moth, 635, 704
Mother, The, 1047
Mother Midnight, 732
Motta, Gesualdo, 681
Motte, Pierre de la, etc., 984
Mottram, Rex, 124
Mouche, Maître, 223
Mould, Mr., etc., 678
Moulder, Mrs. Mary Anne, etc.,
822
Mouldy, Ralph, 465
Mountain, Fanny, etc., 1211
Mountararat, Earl of, 529
Mountford, Charles, etc., 1258
Mountjoy, Henrietta, 486
Mountjoy, Lady Grace, 1149
Mouratliski, 1183
Mouse, The, 23
Mowbray, Clara, etc., 1000
Mowbray, Colonel, 432
Mowbray, Lord, 466
Mowbray, Thomas, 966
Mowcher, Miss, 245
Mowgli, 561
Mowis, 340
Msimangu, 227
Mucklewrath, 807

Mudberry, Mrs., 878
Mudjekeewis, 1061
Muergo, 1070
Muffled Gentleman, A, 71
Mugridge, 1015
Muhlenburg, Rev. Henry Mel-
chior, 473
Muir, Evan, 423
Muir, Lieutenant Davy, 841
Mujiquita, 298
Mulberry, Allie, 902
Mulcaster, Boy, 124
Mulciber, 836
Müller, 27
Mulligan, Malachi, 1175
Mulligan, Rat, 525
Mullion, Jenny, 226
Mullit, Professor, 679
Mumblazen, Master Michael, 567
Mumblecrust, Margery, 938
Mumby Boys, The, 722
Münchausen, Baron, 84
Müncz, Jónás, etc., 1000
Munera, 350
Muñoz, Félix, 897
Munro, Alice, etc., 597
Munroe, 427
Munson, Captain, 886
Murasaki, 1100
Murazov, 249
Murdockson, Meg, 450
Murdour, Sir, 101
Murdstone, Edward, etc., 243
Murica, 122
Murna, 369
Murphy, Aunt Eller, 425
Murphy, Mr., 34
Murphy, Murtough, 441
Murphy, Sir Walter, 753
Murray, Mina, 301
Murray, Rosalie, etc., 15
Murtagh, 989
Murthwaite, Mr., 741
Murullo, 993
Muse, Miss E., etc., 1049
Musette, Mlle., 113
Musgrave, Colonel Rudolph, etc.,
976
Musgrove, Mary, etc., 484, 864
Music Master, A, 117
Musidorus, 57
Muskat, Mrs., 615
Muspratt, 749
Muspratt, Beryl, 124
Musquerusque, 1008
Musqueton, 1129
Mustard, Mrs., 719
Mustardseed, 704
Musya, 1027
Musyne, 555
Mutability, 351
Mutanhed, Lord, 878
Mute, 1040
Mutius, 1137
M. W., 610
Myagkaya, Princess, 45
Mycetes, 1105
Myers, Miss, 1117
Mylendonk, Adriatica von, 652
Mynors, Henry, 46
Myran, Kristàver, 597
Myri, Madam, 522
Myriel, Charles François Bienvenu,
714
Myris, 26
Myrrha, 274
Myrrhiné, 640
Myrtale, 240
Myrtle, Mr., 199
Myshkin, Prince Lef Nicolaie-
vitch, 510
Mysis, 39

Oblonsky, Prince Stepan, etc., 44
O'Brien, 780
O'Brien, Captain, 628
O'Brien, James, 442
O'Brien, Major, 694
O'Brien, Mr., 545
O'Brien, Mr., etc., 924
O'Brien, Terence, etc., 866
O'Bryne, Norrie, 595
Obstinate, 883
O'Carroll, Marionetta C., 779
Occasion, 348
Occonestoga, 1275
Oceanus, 925
Ochiltree, Edie, 50
Ocock, Henry, 382
O'Connor, Edward, 441
O'Connor, Eily, 192
O'Connor, Jim, 404
Octavia, 25, 51, 126, 185
Octavio, 393
Ödegaard, Hans, 372
Oderisi, 274
Odin, 456
Odintsov, Anna, 362
O'Donnell, Johno, etc., 763
O'Dowd, Major, etc., 1193
Odysseus, 16, 230, 516, 788, 871
Oedipus, 792, 793, 873
Œneus, 70
Oenone, 868
O'Fay, Sir Terence, 5
Ofeig, 427
O'Ferrall, Trilby, 1158
Offa, 99
O'Finigan, Patrick, 322
Ogarkov, Nastasya Karpovna, 489
Ogden, Constance, etc., 632
Ogden, Froggy, 55
Ogier of Denmark, 881
Ogier the Dane, 1062
Ogilvy, Gavin, 621
Oglethorpe, John, 664
Ogmund, 428
O'Grady, Miss, 770
O'Grady, Squire, etc., 441
Ogul, 1279
O'Halloran, Count, 6
O'Hara, Kimball, 568
O'Hara, Scarlett, etc., 410
O Hatsu, 1059
Ohlsen, Pedro, 372
Ohthere, 99
Oisin, 369
O'Keefe, Joe, 664
O'Killigain, 927
Olaf, 457
Olaf the Quiet, 457
Olafsson, Tryggve, 456
O-Lan, 411
Olavsdatter, Cecilia, 519, 1055, 1058
Olavsson, Audun, 1055
Olay, 857
Olbromski, Raphael, etc., 67
Old Davy, 802
Old Jakob, 1153
Old Man, An, 942
Old Mortality, 807
Old Mouche, 312
Old Norway, 439
Old Philosopher, The, 224
Old Prince, The, 78
Old Prioress, The, 219
Old Sally, 813
Old Sexton, The, 802
Old Shepherd, An, 353
Old Singleton, 777
Old Skipps, 589
Old Tomba, 137
Oldbuck of Monkbarns, Jonathan, 50

Oldfox, Major, 893
Oldham, Mrs., 1041
Olding, John, 9
Oldrents, 556
Olenska, Countess Ellen, 14
Olga, 155
Olifant, Basil, 806
Olifaunt, Nigel, 380
Olimpio, 164
Olindo, 546
Oline, 430
Oliva, 931
Olivares, Doña Isabella, etc., 253
Olivarez, Count, 402
Olive, Viscountess, 856
Oliver, 66, 557, 769, 1041, 1062
Oliver, Bartholomew, etc., 101
Oliver, Rosamund, etc., 542
Olivia, 892, 1168, 1198
Olivia, Lady, 1041
Olivia, Sister, 535
Olivier, 544, 881
Ollyphant, 349
Olof the Hall, 1086
Olsa, Hans, 401
Olsen, Brede, 430
Olsen, Engelbert, 858
Olwen, 642, 1255
Olyenin, Dmitri Andreyevitch, 203
Olympia, 114, 1105
Olympias, 655
O'Malley, Charles, etc., 169
Oman, 373
Omnium, Duke of, 283, 385, 871, 872
O'More, Rory, etc., 995
Ona, 561
Onatsu, 372
Onegin, Eugene, 335
O'Neill, Mrs., etc., 6
Onela, 99
Onesimus, 57
Ongentheow, 98
Ontiveros, Don Pedro Pablo, etc., 1082
Onund, 427
Oonah, 441
Ophelia, 438
Ophelia, Miss, 1179
Opis, 12
Oppenheimer, Josef Süss, 909
Opsius, 1021
Optimist, Mr., 1052
Oranmore, Lord, etc., 6
Orcan, 1278
Orcanes, 1105
Orchid, 302
Order, 765
Ordóñez, Garcia, 898
Ordynin, Natalia, etc., 756
O'Regan, Teague, 728
O'Reilly, 600
O'Reilly, Boyd, 253
Oreste, 42
Orestes, 41, 320, 487, 504, 532
Orestilla, Aurelia, 160
Orgeluse, 838
Orgon, 1111
Orgreave, Osmond, etc., 187
Oriana, 31, 1152, 1256
Oriel, Rev. Caleb, etc., 282, 594
Orilus, 838
Oriol, Charlotte, etc., 737
Oriole, 306
Orlandi, 203
Orlando, 66, 815, 816, 819
Orlando, Monsignor, 155
Orlick, Dolge, 419
Orly, Dr., etc., 880
Orlygsson, Ketill, etc., 432
Orlygur à Borg, etc., 432

Orme, Sir Peregrine, etc., 821
Ormsdatter, Eline, 586
Oronte, 711, 1012
Oroonoko, 823
O'Rory, Shad, 403
Orosmane, 1279
Orozco, General, 1185
Orpheus, 542, 815, 824
Orreyed, Sir George, etc., 1017
Orsin, 497
Orsina, Countess, 324
Orsino, 1168
Orsino, Count, 164
Orsola, Marchesa, 843
Ortiz, Don Sancho, 1080
Ortlieb, 771
Ortuño, 1032
Ortygius, 1106
Orville, Lord, 341
Osan, 372
Os-Anders, 430
Osbaldistone, 982
Osbaldistone, Frank, etc., 977
Osborne, George, etc., 1191
Osborne, Lieutenant, 556
Oscar, 369
Osen, 372
Osgood, 831
O'Shaughnessy, Brigid, 658
O'Shea, Peg-leg, 392
O'Sheen, Sugar-Boy, 28
Oshichi, 372
Osinin, Prince Pavel Vassilyevitch, 1054
Osip, 526
Osmond, Gilbert, etc., 903
Osprey, Lady, 1148
Osric, 439
Ossipon, Comrade, 1019
Ostap, 1108
Östermark, Dr., 194, 359
Ostrodumov, 1208
Ostrogski, Prince Dominik Zaslavski, 1254
Oswald, 573
Oswifsson, Thorwald, 1086
Othello, 825
Otho, 546
Othon, 1062
Othon, M., etc., 891
Otkellsson, Thorgeir, 1086
Otley, Sir Roger, etc., 1036
Otous, 434
Otrepyev, Grigory, 115
O'Trigger, Sir Lucius, 975
Ottenburg, Philip Frederick, 1066
Otter, 1248
Otter, Captain Tom, etc., 1039
Otter, Darnley, etc., 1255
Otter, Mrs., 101
Otternschlag, Dr., 414
Ottilie, 319
Otto, 320
Outland, Tom, 922
Outrage, Mr., 1203
Ouvrard, M., 48, 445
Overbrook, Ed, etc., 73
Overdo, Adam, etc., 87
Overdone, Mrs., 686
Overmore, Miss, 1235
Overreach, Sir Giles, 765
Overton, Edward, 1229
Owain, 642
Owen, 263
Owen, Evelyn, 690
Owen, Marthy, 44
Oxenham, John, 1233
Oxford, Earl of, 468, 969
Oxford, Harry, 319
Oxmain, Thorbjorn, 428
Ozymandias, 77

Pepperill, Dan, 229
Peppino, 205
Peps, Dr. Parker, 288
Per, 857, 858
Peralta, Don, 928
Peran-Wisa, 1057
Perceval, Sibyl, 554
Perceval of Wales, 188
Perch, Mr., etc., 288
Perch, Mrs., 513
Percival, 743, 1227
Percival, Bettina, 1
Percival, Harry, etc., 810
Percivale, 512
Percy, Henry, etc., 464, 966
Percy, Lady, 466
Perdican, 781
Perdicas, 1106
Perdita, 1252
Perdorff, Dr., 580
Peredur, 642
Peregrine, 1214
Pereira, Alfonso, 494
Peretola, Zoroastro da, 984
Pérez, General, etc., 576
Pérez, Gil, 401
Pérez, Luis Gonzaga, 18
Perez, Michael, 997
Pérez, Pedro, 295
Peribáñez, Don Platón, 139
Périchole, La, 125
Pericles, 861
Pericles, Captain, 575
Periebanou, 56
Perigot, 352
Perine, Effie, 658
Perion de la Forêt, Comte, 220
Perión of Gaul, King, 31
Periplecomenus, 120
Perissa, 348
Perithous, 1173
Perker, Mr., 877
Permaneder, Alois, 134
Pernalete, Ño, 298
Perne, Misses, 880
Pernelle, Madame, 1112
Pero, 136
Perowne, 834
Perpetua, Rose, 545
Perrault, Father, 630
Perrin, 280
Perseda, 1077
Perth, 727
Pesca, Professor, 1257
Pescara, Marquis of, 309
Pescatore, Romilda, etc., 601
Pestov, Marfa Timofyevna, 489
Pet, Aunt, 690
Pete, 650
Peter, 79, 467, 592, 751, 902, 935,
  985, 991
Peter, Friar, 686
Peter, St., 275, 564
Peter of Pomfret, 572
Peter the Hermit, 546
Peters, Dirk, 758
Peters, Ivy, 632
Peterson, Luke, 189
Petit Jean, 892
Petit-Claud, M., etc., 630
Peto, 465
Petowker, Henrietta, 774
Petra, 327, 371
Petre, Lord, 940
Petreius, 160
Petritsky, Lieutenant, 45
Petronius, 933, 1260
Petrov, 45
Petrovich, 831
Petrovitch, Ivan, 489
Petrovitch, Porfiry, 222
Petrovna, Glafira, 489

Petrovna, Lidia, 1004
Petrovna, Natalya, 738
Petruchio, 1106, 1152, 1260
Petrushka, 248
Pettibone, Remarkable, 887
Petulant, 1231
Petulengro, Jasper, 602, 989
Petusin, 379
Pevensey, Lord, 976
Peyramale, Dean, 1060
Peyronette, Madame, 1277
Peyrou, Théodore, 985
Peyton, Bena, 1033
Peyton, Jeanette, 1079
Pfaff, Fräulein, 880
Pfeifer, Herr, 1231
Phaedra, 475
Phaedria, 337, 348, 874, 909
Phalantus, 58
Phania, 39
Phanium, 874
Phantasma of Jupiter, 925
Phantastes, 349
Phaon, 1006
Pharamond, 869
Pharasmanes, 964
Pharnace, 725
Phebe, 67
Phedon, 348
Phèdre, 867
Pheener, 554
Phelps, Mr., etc., 496
Phémie, 113
Phemius, 791
Phenice, 965
Phénice, 100
Pheres, 19
Phidippides, 190
Phil, Father, 442
Philammon, 504
Philanax, 57
Philander, 413
Philargus, 983
Philario, 232
Philaster, 869
Philautus, 338
Philbrick, 259
Philemus, 1106
Philidaspes, 63
Philina, 1244
Philinte, 711
Philip, 463, 571, 608
Philip, Duke, 736
Philip II, 684
Philip the Bastard, 571
Philip the Fair, 616
Philip the Second, 289
Philippa, 616
Philippe, 693, 1200
Philiste, 695
Phillips, Ceinwen, 493
Phillips, Joe, 1133
Phillotson, Richard, 557
Philo, 52
Philoclea, 57
Philocleon, 1225
Philocomasium, 120
Philocrates, 151
Philoctetes, 870
Philoetius, 789
Philogano, 1097
Philomela, 606
Philopolemus, 151
Philosophe, Palmyre, 415
Philosopher, A, 942
Philosophy Master, A, 117
Philostrate, 704
Philotime, 348
Philotis, 674, 1135
Philotus, 1134
Philoxenus, 58
Philtera, 350

Philumena, 39
Phineus, 542
Phipps, Denis, 1072
Phlegyas, 273
Phoedime, 725
Phoenicium, 1157
Phoenicopterus, 105
Phoenix, 42
Pholus, 273
Phormio, 874
Photini, 575
Phraortes, Prince, 63
Phrygia, 128, 909
Phrynia, 1134
Phunky, Mr., 877
Phyllis, 529, 606
Pi, Dr. Omicron, 81
Piani, 358
Picardia, 395
Piccarda, 275
Piccolomini, Prince Octavio, etc.,
  1216
Pich, Miss, 575
Pichana, 107
Pickerbaugh, Dr. Almus, etc., 62
Pickering, Colonel, 929
Pickle, Peregrine, etc., 859
Pickwick, Mr. Samuel, 875
Picrochole, 394
Pierce, Joel, 797
Pierce of Exton, Sir, 967
Pierpoint, Ethel, 700
Pierre, 649, 1195
Pierrot, 294
Piers the Plowman, 1212
Pietranera, Gina, 170
Pietro, 189
Piety, 883
Pigeon, Nicholas, 1029
Pigeon, The, 23
Pigg, 441
Pigg, James, 474
Pigsy, 734
Pihl, Rud, 851
Pilar, 375, 1280
Pilar, Abbess Maria del, 125
Pilate, 97
Pilate, Pontius, 762
Pilia-Borsa, 547
Pilita, 848
Pilkington, Mr., 276
Pilkins, Dr., 288
Pillerault, M., 166
Pillichody, Major, 807
Pillsbury, Dr., 627
Pimen, Father, 116
Pimentó, 137
Pinabel, Count, 817
Pinabel of Sorence, 1062
Pinch, 193
Pinch, Tom, etc., 677
Pinchas, Melchitsekek, 177
Pinchbeck, Lady, 293
Pinchwife, Mr., etc., 211
Pindarus, 560
Pinkerton, 703
Pinkerton, Miss Jemima, etc., 1193
Pinkorn, Hester, 1257
Piny, 1253
Pio, Uncle, 125
Piotr, 45
Pip, 678, 727
Pipchin, Mrs., 288
Piper, Colonel Gerald, etc., 355
Pipes, Thomas, 859
Piquetard, Agathe, 215
Piracquo, Alonzo de, 167
Pirard, Abbé, 948
Pirate King, The, 888
Pirjola, Master of, 688
Pirrip, Philip, 418
Pisander, 113

Rostov, Count Nikolay, etc., 1220
Rostova, Princess Natasha, etc., 1220
Roswitha, 317
Roth, Frieda, 395
Roth, mac, 262
Rotherham, Thomas, 969
Rothsattel, Baron von, etc., 258
Rothsay, Duke of, 352
Rothschild, Father, 1203
Rouaillout, Renée, 90
Rouault, Théodore, 646
Rougierre, Mme. de la, 1178
Rougon, Pascal, etc., 281
Rouncewell, George, etc., 109
Rouncy, Miss, 855
Round, Mr. Matthew, 822
Rounding, Mrs. Rowley, 719
Rousseau, Jean Jacques, 322, 693
Roussillon, Countess of, 29
Rovalli, Ansaldo di, 536
Rowan, Richard, 346
Rowe, Arthur, 708
Rowena, Lady, 537
Rowland, 769, 1260
Rowley, 1012
Roxalana, 1037
Roxana, 996
Roxane, 233
Roy, Fergus mac, 262
Royallieu, Lord, 1184
Royle, Mr., 1270
Rubashov, Nikolai, 242
Rubek, Arnold, 1236
Rubek, Maia, 1236
Rubelle, Mrs., 1257
Rubiera, Baron Nini, etc., 681
Rubín, Maximiliano, etc., 379
Rubio, 840
Rucellai, Bernardo, 993
Ruddymane, 348
Rudenz, Ulrich von, 1246
Rudge, Barnaby, etc., 82
Rudkus, Jurgis, etc., 560
Rudolf, 918
Rudolstadt, Count Albert, etc., 199
Rufio, 139
Rufus, 1021
Rufus, William, 1008
Rugg, Anastasia, etc., 620
Ruggles, 834
Ruhhudibras, 131
Ruiz, Bismarck, 126
Rull, Martha, 127
Rumbold, etc., 477
Rumour, 466
Rumsen, Jack, 403
Runcible, Agatha, 1202
Runi, 426
Runner, The, 347
Ruprecht, 127
Rushworth, Mr., 667
Rusk, Hubert, 119
Rusper, 477
Russell, Arthur, 22
Russell, Lady, 864
Rusticucci, Jacopo, 273
Rusticus, Junius, 983
Rustum, 1057
Ruth, 427, 629, 888
Rutherford, 629
Ruthven, Edwin, 1014
Ruthyn, Silas, etc., 1177
Rutile, 100
Rutledge, Ann, 1
Ruzena, 1049
Rybin, 745
Ryder, Charles, etc., 123
Ryecroft, Henry, 920
Rylett, Alf, 782
Rypa, Jörund, 1058

S., 609
S., Charlotte, 1070
S——, Madame de, 1185
S.A. Man, The, 918
Saber, 102
Sabina, 1048
Sabine, 482, 695
Sabinus, Titius, 1020
Sabre, Mark, etc., 513
Sabrina, 195
Sacca, Doctor Nunzio, 122
Sackbut, Mr., 860
Sacrapant, 809
Sacripant, 817
Sada, 253
Saddletree, Bartoline, etc., 450
Säfberg, Auditor, 359
Safere, 744
Sagan of Jerusalem, 5
Sagely, Mrs., 981
Sagramor, Sir, 198
Sagramore, 744
Sagrario, Sister, 219
Sagremore, 188
Sahadeva, 653
Sahak, 79
Saïdyah, 682
Sailor, 1067
Sailor Ben, 1083
St. Agatha, Mother, 733
St. Anne, Count, 736
St. Aubert, M., etc., 753
St. Clare, Eva, etc., 1179
St. Clare, Father, 551
St. Clare, Mother, 733
St. Croix, 169
St. Eustache, Marquis de, 661
St. Evrémonde, Marquis, 1102
St. George, Mr., 1213
St. Heliers, 271
St. Leger, General Barry, 308
St. Maur, Marquise de, 154
St. Michael, George, 1177
St. Peter, Godfrey, etc., 922
St. Pierre, Mademoiselle, 1205
Saint-Aignan, M., 1200
Saintby, Prentiss, 1125
Saint-Cyr, Father Hector, 1029
Saint-Euverte, Mme. de, 955
Saint-Ignace, Mother Juschereau de, 1029
Saint-Loup, Robert de, 954
Saint-Preux, M., 764
Saint-Vallier, Monseigneur de, 1029
Sakuntala, 1001
Saladin, Sultan, 759
Salaino, Andrea, 984
Salammbô, 1002
Salces, Pito, 852
Saldar, Countess de, 339
Sales, Doña, 43
Salisbury, Earl of, 467, 572, 967
Sallust, 595
Sally, 623, 770
Salome, 762
Salomon, Manette, 662
Salt, Jim, etc., 8
Salterne, Rose, 1233
Salters, 150
Saltire, Lord, 943
Saltonstone, James, 543
Saltoun, Harry, 1098
Salvador, Don, 137
Salvage Man, The, 351
Salvani, Provenzan, 274
Salvo, Flaminio, etc., 797
Sam, 675, 960
Sam, Joe, 1151
Samaniego, Widow, 380
Sambo, Mr., 1194
Samgrass, Mr., 124

Samias, 326
Sammael, 277
Samoa, 669
Samosvitov, 249
Samp, Uncle, 975
Sampson, Dominie, 434
Sampson, George, 828
Sampson, Mr., 1210
Samson, 992, 1002, 1062
Samsthānaka, 617
Samuel, 888, 1218
Samuele, 136
Samzelius, Margareta Celsing, etc., 1087
Sanang, 698
Sanche, Don, 180
Sanches, Rosario, 1006
Sánchez, Martín, 1280
Sánchez, Pedro, 847
San-chieh, 305
Sancho, 577, 1075
Sancho, Don, 1166
Sancho, Manuela, 1007
Sancho IV, 1079
Sander, Aleck, 527
Sander, Granny, 481
Sanders, Susannah, 878
Sandford, Harry, etc., 1004
Sandhauger, Steinvor of, 428
Sandor, Élise, 580
Sandoval, Antonio, 297
Sandracca, Captain, 156
Sands, Captain, 260
Sands, Lord, 461
Sandy, 198, 734, 1258
Sang, Rachel, etc., 102
Sanga, 338
Sanga, Quintus Fabius, 160
Sanglier, Captain, 842
Sanglier, Sir, 350
Sangrado, Doctor, 402
Sanine, Vladimir Petrovitch, 1004
Sannio, 128
Sanquinius, 1021
San Román, Antonio, 139
Sans Foy, 347
Sans Joy, 347
Sans Loy, 347
Santa, 161
Santa Cruz, Juanito, etc., 379
Santiago, 804
Santos, 928
Sanutee, 1275
Sapia, 274
Sappho, 1006
Sapt, Colonel, 918
Sarah, 207, 558
Sarah, Aunt, 1240
Sariette, Monsieur Julien, 963
Sarina Donna, 682
Sarmiento, Pedro, etc., 536
Sarn, Prudence, etc., 913
Sarpedon, 516
Sartines, M. de, 693
Sarudine, Captain, 1005
Sarujiro, 521
Sarvilaka, 617
Sasaki Sadakuni, etc., 520
Sasara Sampachirô, 521
Sasha, 373, 816, 901
Sashenka, 745
Sassoonan, 473
Satan, 545, 835, 837, 963
Satan, Grandfather, 564
Satchell, 9
Satin, 757
Satine, 637
Satire, Miss, 611
Satow, Irene von, 1236
Satrius Secundus, 1021
Satrughna, 939
Satterthwaite, Mrs., 834

Shestov, Tatyana Petrovna, etc., 1053
Shi Wen Kung, 27
Shift, 345
Shigalov, 908
Shih, Madame, 303
Shikazô, 521
Shilo, Mossy, 1109
Shimerda, Ántonia, etc., 750
Shimei, 5
Shiner, Mr., 1181
Shipman, The, 147
Shippy, 550
Shires, Helen, 1092
Shirley, Peter, 657
Shiveley, Wade, etc., 480
Shmendrik, Shosshi, 177
Shock, 941
Shoe Lace Peddlar, The, 649
Sholto, Major, etc., 1037
Shoreby, Lord, 106
Shorthose, Sir Quintilian, 1008
Shorty, 1209
Shotover, Captain, 452
Shoústova, Lydia, 958
Shpigelsky, Ignaty Ilyitch, 739
Shpyokin, 527
Shrapnel, Dr., 90
Shrike, Willie, etc., 716
Shtcherbatskaya, Princess Catharine, etc., 45
Shuan, Mr., 568
Shuck, Hester, 1133
Shurotchka, 489
Shushion, Mr., 186
Shuttlethwaite, Julia, 191
Shvabrin, Alexey Ivanitch, 151
Shylock, 695
Sibly-Biers, Lady Caroline, 1118
Sibwright, Percy, 854
Sibylle, Magdalen, 910
Sicinius, Velutus, 201
Sickle-Maker, A, 845
Sid, 1145
Sidonia, 197
Sidrophel, 497
Siduri, 330
Siegfried, 770
Sieglind, Queen, 771
Siegmund, King, 771
Sieppe, Trina, etc., 645
Sigemund, 99
Sigfusson, Thrain, 1086
Sigismund, 1105
Signa, 787
Signe, 372
Sigrid, 586
Sigune, 838
Sigurd, 457
Sigurd the Crusader, 457
Sigurdsson the Broad-Shouldered, Hakon, 458
Sigurdsson the Stern, Harald, 457
Sikes, Bill, 812
Silas, Père, 1206
Silda, 1070
Silence, Justice, 465
Silenus, 231
Silenus, Otto, 260
Silius, 185
Silius, Gaius, 1020
Silva, 318
Silva, Dean, 63
Silva, Joe, 746
Silveira, Colonel Horacio da, 1206
Silver, Long John, 1152
Silver, Mattie, 333
Silverton, Ned, 490
Silvestre, Doña, 1082
Silvestre, José, 576
Silvia, 534, 798, 1171
Silvine, 301

Silvino, Antonio, 247
Silvio, 309, 648
Silvius, 67
Simalio, 338
Simcox, Forence, 187
Simeonov-Pishchik, Boris Borisovitch, 173
Simia, 1158
Simmery, Frank, 878
Simmings, Newcomb, 600
Simnell, Ralph, 387
Simo, 39, 1157
Simon, 174, 587, 846
Simon, Marshal, etc., 1219
Simon, Master, 713
Simon Bar Jonah, 53
Simonides, 97, 861
Simonov, 609
Simons, Mary Ann, etc., 575
Símonson, Valdemar, 958
Simonssön, Simon, 586
Simpcox, Saunder, 468
Simple, 698
Simple, Peter, etc., 866
Simplicissimus, Simplicius, 1040
Simpson, 878
Simpson, Senator Mark, 368
Sin, 836
Sinbad, 84
Sincere, 883
Sinclair, Marianne, etc., 1087
Sinclair, Mrs., 184
Sindbad the Sailor, 56
Sindefy, 314
Singer, John, 448
Single Gentleman, The, 800
Singleton, Captain Bob, 149
Singleton, Isabella, 1079
Sinha, 247
Sinon, 274
Sintram, 1087
Sipsom, Arthur, 575
Sipyagin, 1207
Sircome, Mr., 365
Sirena, Doña, 115
Sisyphus, 825
Sita, 938
Sittah, 760
Sivert, 430
Sivert, Uncle, 430
Sivinc, Mrs., 1206
Siward, etc., 643
Sixte, Adrien, 272
Skakke, Erling, 458
Skaret, Kal, etc., 322
Skarfsson, Otkell, 1086
Skeggi, 428
Skeggs, Carolina Wilhelmina Amelia, 1199
Skelet, 473
Skene, Colonel, 427
Skettles, Sir Barnet, etc., 288
Skewton, The Hon. Mrs., 288
Skiffins, Miss, 420
Skimp, Judge, 1203
Skimpin, Mr., 876
Skimpole, Harold, etc., 110
Skinner, Dr., 1230
Skrebensky, Anton, 936
Skshetuski, Pan Yan, 1253
Skudronzhoglo, Konstantin, 249
Skurliewhitter, Andrew, 381
Skvoznik-Dmokhanovsky, Anton Antonovich, 526
Slackbridge, 444
Slammekin, Mrs., 95
Slammer, Dr., 877
Slaughter, Nathan, 775
Sleary, Mr., etc., 444
Slembedegn, Sigurd, 457
Slender, 697
Slewfoot, Old, 1273

Slide, Quintus, 872
Sliderskew, Peg, 773
Slightly, 866
Slim, 796
Slime, Jack, 1258
Slimering, 682
Slingsby, Jack, 603
Slipslop, Mrs., 553
Slocum, Captain, 227
Slop, Dr., 1161
Slope, Rev. Obadiah, 80
Sloper, Catherine, etc., 1224
Sloppy, Mr., 829
Sloth, 279
Slow, Mr., 823
Slowcoach, Thorbjorn, 428
Sludge, Dickie, 567
Slum, Mr., 801
Slumkey, Hon. Samuel, 877
Slurk, Mr., 877
Sly, Christopher, 1107
Slyme, Chevy, 677
Small, Abner, 746
Small, Dr., 481
Small, Jonathan, 1037
Small, Lennie, 795
Smallbury, Lydia, 357
Smallweed, Bartholomew, etc., 109
Smangle, 878
Smee, 866
Smee, Mr., 1192
Smerdyakov, 130
Smicrines, 56
Smike, 772
Smiley, Mrs., 822
Smirkle, Mr., 855
Smith, 950
Smith, Caleb, etc., 811
Smith, Captain Abraham, 178
Smith, Harold, etc., 384
Smith, Harriet, 325
Smith, Joseph, etc., 175
Smith, Mary, etc., 219
Smith, Mattie, etc., 1255
Smith, Miss, 541
Smith, Mr., 342
Smith, Mrs. Charles, 864
Smith, Purdy, 382
Smith, Septimus Warren, etc., 723
Smith, Sullivan, 269
Smith, Wayland, 567
Smith, Winston, etc., 779
Smith the Weaver, 467
Smithers, Henry, 325
Smoit, King, 564
Smolin, 373
Smollett, Captain, 1152
Smorltork, Count, 877
Snaekoll, 428
Snagsby, Mrs., etc., 109
Snake, 1012
Snap, Laetitia, 552
Snapper, Miss, 980
Snaps, 94
Snare, 465
Snarl, 851
Snawley, Mr., etc., 773
Sneakington, Joshua, 474
Snebiorg, 432
Sneer, Mr., 224
Sneerwell, Lady, 1011
Snevellicci, Miss, etc., 774
Snodgrass, Mr. Augustus, 875
Snopes, Flem, etc., 436, 1149
Snopes, Senator Clarence, 1004
Snout, 704
Snow, Mary, etc., 823
Snow Duck, 306
Snowe, Lucy, 1204
Snubbin, Serjeant, 877
Snug, 704
Soames, Mr., 593

43

Stevens, Gowan, 1003
Stevens, Red, 720
Stevie, 1019
Stewart, Alan Breck, 568
Stewart, George, 749
Stewart, Lucy, 757
Steyne, Lord, 855, 1192
Stickles, Jeremy, 629
Stiefel, Moritz, etc., 71
Stiggins, Rev. Mr., 876
Stiles, Jerusalem Webster, 937
Stillman, Judge, 1078
Stiltstalking, Lord Lancaster, 620
Stimson, Simon, 830
Stires, Albert, 368
Stjärnhök, Anna, 1087
Stockman, Dr. Thomas, etc., 326
Stoddard, Eleanor, 1188
Stoddart, Corporal, 895
Stogumber, John de, 999
Stöhr, Frau, 651
Stoke, Basil, 927
Stoke-d'Urberville, Mrs., 1119
Stolpe, Ellen, 851
Stolz, Andrey, 787
Stolz, Sappho, 46
Stone, Denis, 225
Stone, Mr. Sylvanus, 386
Stone, Sarah, 9
Storekeeper, The, 1081
Story, Ann, 427
Stotfold, Mr., 719
Stover, Henry, 545
Stowe, Joe, 1240
Straker, Henry, 659
Strane, Dan, etc., 54
Strang, Annabelle, 1188
Stranger, A, 254
Stranger, The, 587
Strap, Hugh, 980
Strathbogie, Lord, 196
Strato, 560, 655
Stratonice, 900
Streak, 103
Street, Sir Luke, 1251
Street Singer, The, 649
Strelitski, Rabbi Joseph, 178
Strength, 345
Strephon, 77, 529
Strepsiades, 189
Streslau, Duke of, 918
Strether, Lambert, 32
Strickland, Charles, etc., 739
Strike, Caroline, 339
Stringham, Mrs., 1251
Strobik, Edward, 368
Strobilus, 909
Stroeve, Dirk, etc., 740
Strolling Player, A, 254
Ström, Axel, 430
Strong, 331
Strong, Captain Edward, 854
Strong, Dr., etc., 246
Strongest Man, The, 225
Strozza, Count, 397
Strumolowski, Boris, 377
Struthers, Mrs. Lemuel, 15
Struve, 950
Struve, Mr., 1078
Stryver, Mr., 1101
Stuart, General, J. E. B., 1098
Stuart, Judge John Todd, 2
Stuart, Miley, 566
Stuart, Prince Charles Edward,
    1227
Stubb, 727
Stubble, Tom, 1193
Stubbs, Mr., 552
Sturk, Dr. Barnaby, etc., 485
Subtle, 19
Suddlechop, Dame Ursula, 381
Sue, 611

Sue, Cousin, 1240
Suffer-Thy-Sovereigns-To-Have-
    Their-Wishes-Dare-Not-
    Judge-Them-For-If-Thou-
    Dost-Thou-Shalt-Dearly-
    Abide-It, 1212
Suffolk, Duke of, 461, 1149
Sugarman, 177
Sullen, etc., 91
Sullen Shepherd, The, 353
Sumach, 261
Summer, Mr., 1144
Summerfield, Daniel, 395
Summers, Adelaide, 943
Summers, Dick, 103
Summers, Ella, 418
Summerson, Esther, 108
Summoner, The, 148
Sun Ch'üan, 986
Sunday, 661
Sung Chiang, 26
Sunwood, Reuben, 379, 559
Supervacuo, 962
Supplehouse, Lord, 385
Sura, Palphurius, 983
Suresby, Sym, 938
Surface, Sir Oliver, etc., 1011
Surius, 338
Surly, Pertinax, 20
Surplice, 329
Surprenant, Lorenzo, 670
Surrey, Duke of, 967
Surrey, Earl of, 461, 466, 969,
    1187, 1248
Surry, Lieutenant Colonel, 1098
Surveyor to the Duke of Bucking-
    ham, The, 462
Susan, 172, 1228, 1258
Susannah, 1160
Susquesus, 166, 951, 1007
Sutpen, Thomas, etc., 3
Sutterfield, Rev. Tobe, 347
Sutton, Beatrice, etc., 46
Suwarrow, General, 292
Suzanne, 674
Suzansa, Peter, 598
Suzette, 1177
Svantepolk, Sir, 1154
Svarogitsch, Yourii Nicholaijev-
    itsch, 1005
Sveinn, Jarl, 428
Svengali, 1158
Svidrigaïlov, Arkady Ivanovitch,
    222
Sviyazhsky, Nicholas Ivanich, 46
Swann, M., etc., 953
Swansdown, Singleton Oglethorpe,
    1099
Swartz, Miss, 1194
Sweedlepipe, Paul, 678
Sweet William, 802
Swell, A, 552
Sweno, 546
Swift, Kate, 1249
Swig, Daniel, 719
Swithin, Mrs. Lucy, 101
Swiveller, Richard, 800
Swizzle, Dr., 441
Swooping Eagle, 913
Swynford, Sir Jacob, 833
Sybil, 1036
Sybilla, 1213
Syetotchkin, Anton Antonitch, 609
Syllanus, 160
Sylli, 653
Sylvain, Marie Elizabeth, 944
Sylvanus, 348
Sylvestre, 416
Sylvia, 1058
Sylvie, 361
Sylvius, 143
Syme, Gabriel, 661

Symmonds, Mr., 1199
Sympathus, 59
Sympson, Mr., etc., 1035
Synnelet, M., 665
Syriscus, 57, 338
Syrus, 128, 1021
Sztolarik, János, 1000

T——, Baron, 11
T——, General, 1185
T——, M. de, 665
Tabaret, 737
Tabera, Estrella, etc., 1080
Tabitha, 1187
Tabriol, Cadoc of, 331
Tachechana, 913
Tacker, Mr., 678
Tadzio, 254
Taft, Mum, 8
Tai Chung, 26
T'ai Tsung, 734
Taillebois, Ivo, 471
Taillefer, Victorine, 361
Tai-yu, 303
Taladrid, Padre, 253
Talbot, 1176
Talbot, Lord, etc., 466
Talboy, Master, 556
Talgol, 497
Taliaferro, Charles, etc., 1057
Talkapace, Tibet, 938
Tallien, Jean-Lambert, 445
Tallit, 451
Talpa, Johannes, 856
Talthybius, 1165
Talus, 350
Tamb' Itam, 628
Tamburlaine, 1104
Tamenund, 597
Tamora, 1136
Tamyra, 136, 961
Tan, Zachary, 378
Tanacharison, 473
Tan-chun, 304
Tancred, 546
Tancred, Mrs., 563
Tang, Tim, 1264
Tangent, Lord, 259
Tangle, Mr., 110
Tania, 555
Tanner, John, 658
Tanqueray, Paula Ray, etc., 1017
Tansey, Sara, 894
Tansley, Charles, 1139
Tant' Sannie, 1084
Tantalus, 825, 1131
Tantamount, Lord Edward, etc.,
    898
Tantripp, 703
Tanzer, Psyche, 135
Taou Yuen, 543
Tapestrymaker, The, 147
Tapley, Mark, 677
Tappertit, Simon, 83
Tappleton, Lieutenant, 877
Tapster, 582, 766
Tarantyev, 787
Tarasevitcheva, Antonida Vassili-
    evna, 391
Tarlenheim, Fritz von, 918
Tarleton, 89
Tarquinius, 606
Tarquinius, Sextus, 940
Tarr, Frederick, 1109
Tarrou, Jean, 890
Tartan, Lucy, 879
Tartarin, 1110
Tartuffe, 1111
Tascher, Lieutenant, 1142
Tashtego, 727
Tastin, Mme., 1027

44

Victor, 118
Victoria, 18, 107, 429, 505
Victorin, Count, 267
Victorine, 118
Victorious, Peder, 847
Vidas, 898
Videna, 413
Viedma, General Cipriano, 895
Vigil, Gregory, 210
Vigne, Piero Delle, 273
Vigours, 90
Vikingsson, Thorsten, 388
Vilas, Melora, etc., 549
Vilbert, 558
Villa, Pancho, 1185
Villa Franca, Virginia de, 733
Villacourt, M. de., 957
Villars, Rev. Arthur, 341
Villars, Virginia, etc., 228
Villefort, M., etc., 205, 754
Villefranche, Seneschal of, 1238
Villeneuve, Admiral, 311
Villeparisis, Mme. de, 953
Villerius, 1037
Villeroi, Marquis de, 754
Villiers, George, 1128
Viluppo, 1077
Vincent, 557
Vincent, Dr., 1120
Vincent, Jenkin, 381
Vincent, Mr., 634
Vincentio, 685, 1107
Vincentio, Prince, 397
Vincey, Leo, etc., 1030
Vincy, Fred, etc., 701
Vinitius, Marcus, 933
Vinteiul, M., 954
Viola, 218, 480, 1168
Viola, Giorgio, 784
Violante, Doña, 728
Violenta, 30
Violet, 355, 1130, 1276
Vionnet, Mme. Marie de, etc., 32
Viosca, Feliu, etc., 178
Vipunen, 565
Virgil, 257, 272
Virgilia, 201, 330
Virginia, 976
Virginian, The, 1209
Virginie, 306
Virginie, Mlle., 1206
Virginio, 1195
Virginsky, Arina Prohorovna, etc., 908
Virtue, 803
Viry, Madame de, etc., 1047
Viscarra, Don Jesús de, etc., 107
Visconti, Nino, 274
Vishnepokromov, 249
Vishnyevetski, Prince Yeremi, 1254
Visire, M. Paul, 856
Vitello, Dante, 162
Vivaldi, Vincentio di, etc., 535
Vivet, Madeleine, 218
Vivian Grey, 1213
Vivien, 512
Vivionn, 369
Vixen, Mrs., 95
Vizcaha, 395
Vladimir, 1215
Vladimir, Mr., 1019
Vlasov, Pavel, 745
Vlasova, Pelagueya, 744
Vlasyevna, Agafya, 489
Voitskaya, Marya, 1180
Voitski, Ivan, 1180
Volanges, Cécile de, etc., 237
Volborg, 857
Vold, Yngve, 372
Vollar, Nettie, etc., 543
Volpatte, 1180
Volpone, 1213

Voltimand, 439
Voltore, 1214
Volturtius, 160
Volumnia, 201
Von Wehrhahn, 92
Voroshilov, Semyon Yakovlevitch, 1055
Vortiger, 132
Vortimer, 132
Vos, Sir Diederik die, 616
Voss, Amadeus, 1268
Voules, Mr., 477
Voyt, The, 846
Vran, Bendigeid, 641
Vreeswijck, Van, 1053
Vronsky, Count Alexey Kirilich, 44
Vuffin, Mr., 802
Vulcany, Mrs., 239
Vulich, Lieutenant, 472
Vye, Eustacia, etc., 959
Vyesovshchikov, 745
Vyse, Cecil, 994

W . . . berg, Count Dietrich zu, 431
Wackles, Miss Sophy, etc., 800
Wade, Ellen, 912
Wade, Miss, 619
Wadman, Widow, 1160
Waffles, 721
Wag, Mr., 855
Wagner, 278, 363
Wagner, Howard, 255
Wahnschaffe, Christian, 1268
Wah-ta!-Wah, 261
Wainsworth, Joe, 901
Wainwright, Aggie, 418
Wait, James, 776
Waiter, The, 649
Waitwell, 1231
Wakefield, Al, etc., 1132
Wakefield, Jamie, 580
Wakem, Philip, etc., 706
Wald, Joachim von, 1026
Waldo, 1085
Wales, Prince of, 464
Walham, Lady, 768
Walker, 974
Walker, Bill, 657
Walker, Flossie, 276
Walker, Mick, 246
Walker, Mrs., 234
Wallace, Binny, 1083
Wallace, Mary, 1007
Wallace, Sir William, etc., 1013
Wallace, Timothy, etc., 418
Wallenstein, Albrecht, 1216
Wallin, Justus, etc., 136
Wallinger, Lord, etc., 197
Walravens, Madame, 1206
Walsh, Peter, 723
Walsingham, Helen, 581
Walter, 127, 1247
Walter, Basile, etc., 96
Walters, William, 149
Waltham, Governor, 37
Walton, Miss, 660
Walton, Robert, 385
Walwain, 132
Wamba, 538
Wamibo, 777
Wampy, William, 990
Wandering Scholar, The, 1219
Wang, 1201
Wang, Madame, 303
Wang Lung, 411
Wangel, Ellida, etc., 586
Wangel, Hilda, 679
Wannop, Valentine, etc., 834
Wanostrocht, Miss, 835
Wanton, Lady, 611

Wapshot, Rev. F., 855
War, 845
Warburton, Dr., 355
Warburton, Lord, 903
Ward, Artemus, 175
Ward, The, 1261
Warder, Jack, 498
Wardle, Miss Rachel, etc., 875
Wardour, Sir Arthur, etc., 50
Ware, Harry, 1080
Ware, Theron, etc., 235
Waris, Dain, 628
Warley, Captain, 261
Warner, Adam, etc., 596
Warren, Beth Evan, 1117
Warren, Mary, etc., 951
Warrington, Captain Charles, 426
Warrington, George, 769, 853
Warrington, George Esmond, etc., 1209
Wart, Philpot, 1099
Wart, Thomas, 465
Warwick, 316
Warwick, Diana Merion, etc., 269
Warwick, Earl of, 466, 467, 595
Washington, George, 424, 1211
Waspe, Humphrey, 87
Watchall, 765
Watchful, 883
Water Rat, 1247
Waters, Charles, etc., 1208
Waters, Esther, 332
Watkins, Mr., etc., 719
Watson, Dr. John, 1037, 1092
Watson, Johnny, 1028
Watson, Miss, 496
Waule, Mrs. Jane, 702
Waverley, Edward, etc., 1226
Wayfare, Resolved, 956
Wayman, Rodney, 956
Waymarsh, Mr., 33
Wayne, Adam, 758
Wealtheow, 98
Weasel, 1127
Weatherby, Lucy, 549
Weatherby, Twink, 1272
Weaver, Robert, 797
Weaver, Samson, 990
Weaver, The, 147
Weavers, The, 308
Webb, Emily, etc., 829
Webb, General, 597
Webb, General John, 460
Webber, Frank, 169
Webber, George, etc., 1232, 1275
Webley, Everard, 898
Webster, Nanny, 621
Ween, Andrea, etc., 857
Weena, 1132
Weevil, Bob, 1255
Wegg, Silas, 827
Weinhold, 1232
Weinschenk, Hugo, 135
Weiser, Conrad, etc., 472
Weiss, Henriette, etc., 301
Weissensee, 909
Weissman, Judge, 424
Welch, John, 1033
Welford, 1013
Welford, Fanny, 255
Welland, Mr., etc., 14
Wellborn, Frank, 765
Wellborn, Grace, 87
Wellbred, 343
Weller, Sam, etc., 876
Wellesley, Lady Barbara, 149
Wellmere, Colonel, 1079
Welter, Lord, 943
Welzel, Anna, etc., 1232
Wemmick, John, 419
Wendoll, 1258
Wenham, Mr., 855

48

W9-BDZ-896

Praise for
The Case Against Adolescence:
Rediscovering the Adult in Every Teen

"*The Case Against Adolescence* is one of the most revolutionary books I have ever read."

—Albert Ellis, Ph.D., The Albert Ellis Institute (from the Foreword)

"Perhaps it is time for a paradigm shift in how we understand the tumultuous time we call adolescence. Dr. Epstein's landmark book may be just what we need to help enhance our understanding of and better serve those moving through this complex period of life."

—Drew Pinsky, M.D., Co-Host, "Loveline"; Medical Director,
Department of Chemical Dependency Services,
Las Encinas Hospital, Pasadena, California

"Epstein's book presents a serious and bold challenge to widely held views about teenagers: that they are inherently irresponsible, that they must be shielded from adult challenges, that they are not capable of making sound decisions about matters of health. Epstein demonstrates in a rigorous and persuasive way that teens are in fact highly capable—in some respects even more capable than adults. By shielding and protecting young people from adulthood, we have isolated them from their elders, from their spiritual roots, and from their heritage, leaving many of them angry and confused in the spiritually empty world of teen culture. We need to reexamine our basic assumptions about young people, and Epstein shows us how."

—Deepak Chopra, *Life After Death: The Burden of Proof*

"This is a profoundly important book. Dr. Epstein is raising issues about our young people that we need to think about and evaluate carefully. Generally, I think the institutions that serve our young are sound, but this book points to some obvious problems—most especially the fact that our young people are largely isolated from the adult world. If you care about America's young, this is a must read."

—Dr. Joyce Brothers, author & columnist

"I believe what Dr. Epstein is saying one hundred percent. Young people have the ability to do great things; they just never have the opportunity to do them. They're also rarely placed in situations where they have to do them. We treat teens as if they're just kids, assuming they can't do very much, but when they're put into tough situations, they tend to perform just as well or even better than adults. As a teen I successfully impersonated an airline pilot, a medical doctor, a lawyer, and a college instructor. Imagine what I could have done if I had actually been encouraged to develop my adult capabilities. And imagine what today's teens might be able to do if they weren't so completely cut off from the adult world."

    —**Frank W. Abagnale,** *Catch Me If You Can*; president, Abagnale & Associates; author

"Retired and in poor health, it is extremely rare for me to endorse any book these days. However, I feel powerfully called to write in support of Dr. Robert Epstein's book *The Case Against Adolescence*. I heartily believe in the validity of what he is saying. Furthermore, I believe what he is saying to have vast consequence for our society. All of America should take note of it."

    —**M. Scott Peck, M.D.**, *The Road Less Traveled*

"The American education system, as we know it, was designed during a period of rapid industrialization. The mission of schools was to inculcate 'industrial discipline' as a means preparing our young people, in factory-like fashion, to work in the new industrial world. That antiquated system no longer prepares our young for the real world they will be facing in the years to come, and, as Dr. Epstein shows, it also isolates young people from adults in ways that have unfortunate consequences. If you care about the future of our young people, *The Case Against Adolescence* is an essential read."

    —**Alvin Toffler**, *Future Shock* and *Revolutionary Wealth*

"Here are America's youth, regarded keenly, knowingly–with many popular assumptions and notions set aside in favor of an accurate and thoughtful portrayal of our young fellow citizens, and too, many of the rest of us, who may fail them by overlooking their achievements and possibilities."

    —**Robert Coles, M.D.**, professor of psychiatry, Harvard University; recipient, Pulitzer Prize

"Robert Epstein's critique of our conventional view of adolescence is timely. Of all its wide implications, perhaps the most significant is the one for education. Treating young people as adults and giving them the opportunity to embrace responsibility are strategies that the empirical research and analysis of Epstein's work justify. This is a vital book for parents and policy makers on the state and federal levels. It is a long overdue contribution."

—**Leon Botstein**, *Jefferson's Children: Education and the Promise of American Culture*; president, Bard College; author,

"Teenagers are not children. Dr. Epstein convincingly demonstrates the harm caused by treating them that way. With an intellectual honesty not often seen, this book cuts through the mountain of prejudice and negative stereotypes and shows teens as they once were, and some day will be again. This is an important book, and one that strikes the next nail in the coffin of the bigoted "storm and stress" view of adolescence. This book should be required reading for all youth workers, all parents trying to better understand their kids, all politicians setting youth policy, and most especially for teens who instinctively recognize the injustice and harm of our system. This book is a powerful tool for articulating that injustice."

—**Alex Koroknay-Palicz,**
president & executive director, National Youth Rights Association

"Dr. Epstein has written a very provocative essay about adolescence. His arguments deserve serious consideration and open debate."

—**Ellen Langer, Ph.D.**, *Mindfulness*; Professor of Psychology, Harvard University

"While human evolution has for hundreds of millennia trusted teens to be fully competent adults and parents, our present culture has somehow found it convenient to view them as children. Robert Epstein makes a powerful case for correcting this costly error."

—**Jean Liedloff**, *The Continuum Concept*

"Parents puzzled about the reasons for changes in child-rearing since they were children may find some answers in Robert Epstein's argument about what he calls 'the artificial extension of childhood.'"

—**George F. Will**, columnist

"Epstein's book on adolescence is a fresh and timely look at what makes teens miserable, and how their condition can be helped. It is a very original approach, sure to ignite discussion and controversy. A great deal of what he says is right on the money, and few people have written on this subject with his combination of expert knowledge and clear prose."

—**Mihaly Csikszentmihalyi**, *Flow*; Professor of Management,
 Clairemont Graduate Center

"*The Case Against Adolescence* constructs a powerful argument against trivializing a significant fraction of the population in the interests of an illusion. Whether you're a parent, a teacher, a policy maker, or a recovering victim of enforced childishness, you need to read this book."

—**John Taylor Gatto**, *Dumbing Us Down* and *The Underground History of American Education*; former New York City and New York State Teacher of the Year

"Dr. Epstein offers a compelling mixture of historical evidence and modern insight into the present problem of infantilization of youth. If we trust our youth with the inevitable responsibilities of modern life sooner rather than later, we can reinvigorate our society. Dr. Epstein's ideas provide an academic framework for a number of issues–like allowing teens to vote in municipal elections at age 16–that are close to my heart and crucial for the future of American society. In this iconoclastic work, Dr. Epstein shows not only how much we lose by belittling teens, but also how much we stand to gain by empowering them."

—**Gale A. Brewer**, Member, New York City Council

"We are all individual and desire to be treated as such. Dr. Epstein makes a good case for adolescents to be treated not as a group with a formula, but as individual unique people."

—**Suzanne Somers**, actress and author

"Because of my family's troubled history and because I'm the mother of two teens, I have a deep interest in the mental health of young people. This book has opened my eyes, and it will open yours too. We've completely isolated teens from the people they're about to become, and we've trapped them in a meaningless world controlled by peers and media. We've forgotten how capable young people are, and they know it and are frustrated. We need to completely reexamine how we treat America's teens."

—**Mariel Hemingway**, actress

"This is an amazing book, long overdue. I've been saying for decades that the way to bring out the best in young people is to give them meaningful responsibility and authority, and the Guardian Angels have shown in countries around the world how powerful this model is. The surest way to make teens miserable is to treat them like kids, and the best way to make them strong is to let them grow up. Dr. Epstein lays out these issues like no one ever has before."

—**Curtis Sliwa**, Founder & President, Guardian Angels; co-host, 'Curtis and Kuby in the Morning,' WABC Radio, New York

"Dr. Epstein's ideas about teens are revolutionary. Many of our teens today have serious problems, and if Dr. Epstein is right, those problems are largely of our own making. This book will bring our ideas about teens down to earth."

—**Buzz Aldrin,** Ph.D. (Col., USAF, ret.), Apollo 11 Astronaut

The Case Against Adolescence

Rediscovering the Adult in Every Teen

Robert Epstein, Ph.D.

Sanger, California

Printed in the United States of America

Published by Quill Driver Books/Word Dancer Press, Inc.
1254 Commerce Way • Sanger, California 93657
559-876-2170 • 1-800-497-4909 • FAX 559-876-2180

QuillDriverBooks.com • Info@QuillDriverBooks.com

Quill Driver Books' titles may be purchased in quantity at special discounts for educational, fund-raising, training, business, or promotional use. Please contact Special Markets, Quill Driver Books/Word Dancer Press, Inc., at the above address, toll-free at 1-800-497-4909, or by e-mail: Info@QuillDriverBooks.com

Quill Driver Books/Word Dancer Press, Inc. project cadre:
Doris Hall, Michelle Doland, Stephen Blake Mettee, Carlos Olivas, Andrea Wright

Quill Driver Books and colophon are trademarks of
Quill Driver Books/Word Dancer Press, Inc.

First printing

ISBN 1-884956-70-X • 978-1884956-70-6

To order another copy of this book, please call
1-800-497-4909

Credits

"I May Be A Teacher, But I Am Not An Educator," by John Taylor Gatto in *The Wall Street Journal*, copyright © 1991 by John Taylor Gatto. Reprinted with permission.

"Compulsory Education Laws: The Dialogue Reopens," by Scott Woodruff in *The Home School Court Report*, copyright © 2000 by Scott Woodruff. Reproduced with permission of Scott Woodruff.

Juvenile Crime, Juvenile Justice by National Research Council. Copyright © 2001 by National Academy Press. Reproduced with permission.

The Continuum Concept: In Search of Lost Happiness, by Jean Leidloff. Copyright © 1977 Perseus Books. Reproduced with permission of Perseus Books Group.

"Correctional Options, Part 3," by Deborah Sharp in *Corrections Today 57*, no 3. Copyright © 1995 American Correctional Association. Reprinted with permission of the American Correctional Association, Alexandria, V.A.

Blaming the Brain: The Truth About Drugs and Mental Heath by Elliot S. Valenstein, Ph.D. Copyright © 1998 by Elliot S. Valenstein. Reprinted with the permission of The Free Press, a Division of Simon & Schuster Adult Publishing Group. All rights Reserved.

"The Expanding Role of G.I. Jane," by Ann Scott Tyson in *The Christian Science Monitor* (www.csmonitor.com). Copyright © 2003 The Christian Science Monitor. Reprinted with permission.

Library of Congress Cataloging-in-Publication Data

Epstein, Robert, 1953-
    The case against adolescence : rediscovering the adult in every teen / Robert Epstein.
    p. cm.
Includes bibliographical references (p.) and index.
ISBN 1-884956-70-X (9781-884956-706)
1. Adolescence. 2. Adolescent psychology. 3. Maturation (Psychology) 4. Developmental psychology. I. Title.
BF724.2.E67 2007
155.5—dc22

                                                                    2007001611

To Jordan and Jenelle,
may you grow up in a world that judges
you based on your abilities,
not on your age.

We are suffering heavy casualties during the years of growth and development, and these casualties not only are tragic for the individuals but also bear heavy costs for American society.

—David A. Hamburg, *Today's Children*, 1992

The psychological events of adolescence in our society are not a necessary counterpart of the physical changes of puberty, but a cultural invention—not a deliberate one, of course, but a product of an increased delay in the assumption of adult responsibilities.

—L. Joseph Stone and Joseph Church, *Childhood and Adolescence*, 1957

Constitutional rights do not mature and come into being magically only when one attains the state-defined age of majority. Minors, as well as adults, are protected by the Constitution and possess constitutional rights.

—United States Supreme Court, *Planned Parenthood of Missouri v. Danforth*, 1976

Are the disturbances which vex our adolescents due to the nature of adolescence itself or to the civilisation? Under different conditions does adolescence present a different picture?

—Margaret Mead, *Coming of Age in Samoa*, 1928

The task of youth is not only its own salvation but the salvation of those against whom it rebels.

—Jane Addams, *The Second Twenty Years at Hull-House*, 1930

Contents

Illustrations

Figures

Tables

Foreword

The Case Against Adolescence is one of the most revolutionary books I have ever read. It presents many challenging and little-known facts about young people, some of them quite breathtaking. It suggests that our contemporary disregard for the civil rights of young people is abysmal and that their parents, teachers, and society are doing much harm and little good by over-restricting them. Epstein shows that although conditions have improved in some ways for adolescents over the past century, in many ways teens are far worse off than ever before. Incredibly, we still often discriminate against teenagers when it comes to education, sex, censorship, and many other areas.

Epstein's final chapters contain his program for social change—quite the chapters! He proposes that young people be "extended full adult rights and responsibilities in each of a number of different areas as soon as they can demonstrate appropriate competence in each area." Good! To give adolescents more responsibilities when they are set to handle them is an excellent pragmatic goal.

The form of psychotherapy I originated in 1955—Rational Emotive Behavior Therapy—tries to teach people to retain their goals and preferences but stubbornly refuse to make them *dire necessities.* People thereby take responsibility for their own disturbances and gain the power to prevent and change them. Does this include adolescents? By all means. They, too, can largely control their emotional destiny if they think, feel, and act as if they can. This won't make them all miracle workers, but it can help tremendously to keep them less disturbed.

Chapter Thirteen of Epstein's book describes twenty-nine rights that he believes society had better give to adolescents. Some of them, such as the right to marry without parental or court consent, may seem extreme and impractical (as Epstein admits), but I would still tend to endorse them, at least experimentally. If we give adolescents all the rights that Epstein asks us to grant them, many may fail. *Maybe.* Let us experiment and discover!

Albert Ellis, Ph.D.
Albert Ellis Institute
New York City

Acknowledgments

I collaborated with Dr. Diane Dumas in developing the *Epstein-Dumas Test of Adult-ness*. Diane also painstakingly collected and analyzed competency, infantilization, and psychopathology data from subjects in several states as part of her dissertation work. Bill Milburn, another graduate student, did some of the initial investigative work on Boys Town. Dr. Ann Sasaki of the San Diego Sheriff's Department provided assistance in the collection of inmate data. Dr. Michel Antoine, a professor at the Université de Marne-la-Vallée in France, assisted in the translation of French materials. Rabbi Sheldon Moss of Tucson, Arizona, checked my use of Hebrew. Translator Yasushi Ito of Osaka, Japan, helped with Japanese terminology. Dr. Hugh Cunningham, a history professor at the University of Kent in the United Kingdom, provided detailed comments on Chapter Two. Dr. Mike Males of the University of California Santa Cruz gave me many useful insights through extensive correspondence. And Dr. Eric H. Monkkonen of UCLA's history department shared some of his unpublished data on the history of adolescent crime. Dr. Helen Bond of Edinburgh University and Dr. David Elkins of Pepperdine University provided helpful comments on Chapter Twelve. And Dr. John Wixted of the University of California San Diego reviewed technical material in Chapter Seven. Dr. Herbert Kelman and Dr. David Hamburg were kind enough to help me track down references to their writings. James Kirchner of Detroit, Michigan, provided information about teens in Czechoslovakia. I offer special thanks to Dr. James Garbarino of Cornell University, Dr. Jerome Kagan of Harvard University, and Dr. Mark Phillips of San Francisco State University for critiquing my case. Needless to say, I take full responsibility for any inaccuracies in the book, many of which are still present, I suspect, in spite of the sensible feedback I've received. I'm also grateful to my hardworking assistants for conducting library and Internet research and in other ways for helping me to assemble this manuscript: Nicholas Albrecht, Amy Barth, Joshua Blitt, Katie Codon, Meg Day, Marin Fantino, Marnette Federis, Erin Hayes, Tamara Hurst, Gwyneth Hyndman, Vanessa Johnston, Melissa Karnaze, Marie Kent, Kari Kientzy, Sachiko Kuwabara, Justin La, Christina Lee, Randy Lie, Avery Marvin, Elizabeth Morrison, Jessica Nager, Jill Nelson, Lily Niu, Heather Rolfe, Amanda Solar, Cassandra Timm, Regina Warfel, Emily Wear, Lauren Wong, Rachel Wood, and Chrissy Wontorsky. One assistant, Angela Chen, had just turned eighteen when she helped me create an abridged version of the *EDTA* (Appendix 1). Finally, I'm especially grateful to my agent, Pierre Lehu, and to Steve Mettee of Quill Driver Books for believing in this book when others doubted.

Robert Epstein, Ph.D.
San Diego, California

A Note to the Reader

The Case Against Adolescence can be read on different levels. If you just want the gist, you might be satisfied with the detailed overviews at the beginning of each of the fourteen chapters. The overviews are fairly free of jargon, and they capture the essential arguments. To get answers to key questions on each of the chapter topics, you can skip to the end of each chapter, where you'll find answers to the most common questions people have asked me about teenagers over the years.

If you want to know how well you measure up as an adult, go to Appendix 1, where you can take an abridged version of the *Epstein-Dumas Test of Adultness (EDTA)*. You'll be able to score the test yourself using a specially designed scoring sheet included in the appendix, and you'll end up with both an overall score and several "subscale" scores, which will tell you how competent you are in skill areas that are key to mature adulthood. Once you've taken the test, feel free to give it to some teens. They might surprise you.

For more detail, you'll need to read the main text in each chapter. The writing is informal and, I hope, friendly. On the other hand, I've also included material that's unusual for a mainstream book: I use graphs, tables, and other scientific tools when I think the "case" will benefit, and sometimes I explore technical matters in great detail. If you're not interested in technical material, you can skim over it or skip it entirely. You'll still get the idea. The chapters also include magazine-style boxes that contain stories about young people, interesting tidbits, and literary material that's pertinent to the chapter. Most of the boxes are just for fun; I hope you enjoy them.

If you want to dig deeper, consult the material included toward the end of the book: notes, a list of relevant readings, and some statistical data.

All in all, even if you don't agree with every point, I hope this book will get you thinking in new ways about young people, and I hope it will give many capable young people new options and opportunities.

Introduction

By the time he was fourteen or fifteen, my son Justin was more or less capable of living on his own. He did well in school without any prompting from me, did numerous chores around the house (also with minimal or no prompting), and kept a schedule and lists of things to do, just as I did. He demonstrated that he was ready to drive by stealing my pickup truck several times. I was angry about the deceit, but I had to admit—to myself, not to him—that he seemed to have been driving safely. He dealt with adversity with remarkable maturity and flexibility. He was and still is expert at what therapists call "reframing." In other words, he knew how to put a positive spin on almost anything.

Even more significant, he had achieved enormous balance in his life. He worked hard, but he also played hard. He had lots of friends, and even though I knew he had experimented with drugs, he seemed highly resistant to peer pressure and ultimately to be reasonably cautious. He said no to his friends when he had homework or chores to do, even though he must have been under enormous pressure at times to run off. He learned to surf, jump bicycles, skateboard, and so on, with his peers, and when I refused to drive him places, he found creative ways to reach remote destinations on his own. At times, I found myself envious of the delicate balance he had achieved between work and play, between the intellectual and physical, between the structured and the wild. It was obvious that he was going to go to college and then get on with his life, with or without me. And so, in fact, he did—mainly without me, which has made me feel quite proud of him.

Justin wasn't a prodigy; he was just mature—that is, adult-like—more mature than his elder brother, and even more mature, in some respects, than I was. But what, I wondered, did we mean by *maturity*, and how did Justin get that way? And if Justin was so capable, why couldn't he drive my truck legally, and why did he have to go to school every day, and why wasn't he allowed to make even minor medical decisions on his own? In short, why was society—and, for that matter, why was I—continuing to treat him like a child?

Social psychologist Ellen Langer reminds us that many of our practices, both individual and societal, are quite mindless. We do them without analysis or thought, often simply because someone else once did them long ago. In her modern classic, *Mindfulness*, she tells a story about a woman who always cut a piece off her roast before putting it in the pan. She did this because her mother always had, so one day she asked her mother to explain the practice. Her mom said only that her mother had always

done the same, so the woman posed the same question to her grandmother, who said, "I only had one pan, and it was too small to hold the meat."

Could it be, I wondered, that Justin had to be treated like a child because of principles and practices that were long out of date—because, in effect, decades or centuries ago someone's pan had been too small?

I was dimly aware that teenagers hadn't always been treated like children, but I didn't grasp much of the picture. The Bar Mitzvah—the centuries-old Jewish coming-of-age ceremony—had always been a mystery to me: why did we say that this ancient ceremony indicated that a boy was now a man when we clearly didn't mean it? Was the modern ceremony just a cruel joke, a kind of tease? "Sure," says the rabbi, "Now you are a man (heh, heh)." Had the Bar Mitzvah ever meant that a boy had attained adult status? I also knew, vaguely, that in other times young people had had more responsibility and authority than they have today, but I had never thought to ask about what had happened to all that responsibility and authority. When—and why—did it disappear? My curiosity grew stronger as the years passed, and, over time, I filled file drawers and book shelves with relevant materials. Teens, I learned, had been treated like adults throughout most of human history. It's only recently that they've been infantilized.

As a parent, a citizen, and an occasional teacher of developmental psychology, I was also aware that modern teens were a pretty scary, confused, and angry group of people, and I began to wonder whether infantilization—or what one might call "the artificial extension of childhood"—could be the culprit. What I've learned has confused me, surprised me, and, at times, shocked me. Over time, and based on my own research as well as findings from psychology, anthropology, history, biology, and other fields, I've discovered that Justin and millions of other teens have gotten a raw deal—that shortly after puberty, most of us have the potential to function fully as adults, emotionally, physically, and mentally.

And that's what this book is about. As you'll see, I'm not the first person to have expressed concern about the artificial extension of childhood, and I'm sure I won't be the last. But I hope that this volume will present a case so compelling, and perhaps so disturbing, that it will stimulate a long-overdue discussion about how we're currently raising our teens, and perhaps set some changes in motion.

Part 1

The Case Against the Artificial Extension of Childhood

Chapter 1

The Chaos and the Cause

His thoughts are whacked, he's mad so he's talkin' back, talkin' black,
brainwashed from rock and rap. He sags his pants, do-rags and stocking cap,
his step-father hit him, so he socked him back.
—Eminem, "Sing for the Moment"

Overview. American teens have long been in chaos, suffering high rates of depression, suicide, crime, substance abuse, pregnancy, and other serious problems. Until about a century ago, however, the teenage years were relatively benign, and adolescence as we know it barely existed. Through most of human history, young people were integrated into adult society early on, but beginning in the late 1800s, new laws and cultural practices began to isolate teens from adults, imposing on them an increasingly large set of restrictions and artificially extending childhood well past puberty. New research suggests that teens today are subjected to more than ten times as many restrictions as are most adults, and adulthood is delayed until well into the twenties or thirties. It's likely that the turmoil we see among teens is an unintended result of the artificial extension of childhood.

In the late 1990s Americans had a gruesome wake-up call: Eight schoolyard shooting sprees took place in less than a year, resulting in seventeen dead and thirty wounded—all at the hands of males under eighteen. As a result, carrying a dull kitchen knife to school is now grounds for expulsion at many schools, and teens continue to plot or carry out elaborate attacks against their schools.[1] Here are some other disturbing facts about America's troubled teens:

- Suicide is the third leading cause of death among teens, after accidents and homicides. According to a 2003 survey, 8.5 percent of high

school students had attempted suicide in the previous twelve months, and nearly 17 percent contemplated or planned suicide.[2]

- For the vast majority of crimes, the peak age for arrest in the United States has long been eighteen for both whites and minorities.[3] According to an extensive study published in 2004, eighteen is also the age at which Americans eighteen and over, and especially females, are the most depressed.[4]

- For the first time in history, we are now seeing a substantial increase in crimes committed by young females, especially some violent crimes. Between 1995 and 2004, for example, assaults by young males decreased slightly (following national trends), whereas assaults by young females increased by 25 percent.[5]

- Before new security systems were installed in recent years, nearly a million students in the United States brought guns to school each year.[6] Between a quarter and a third of young people who enter our school systems never graduate from high school, and for blacks and Hispanics, the proportion is closer to one-half.[7]

- In 2001 more than 60 percent of high school students who were surveyed reported that drugs were kept, used, or sold at their schools.[8] In 2002 hospital emergency rooms treated 97,029 teens suffering from adverse drug experiences—mainly overdoses of illegal drugs—up from 82,904 in 1999.[9]

- Although declining, the birth rate among teens in the United States— about forty-nine births for every thousand teenage women—is still the highest by far in the industrialized world. The teen birth rate in both France and Italy is about nine per thousand.[10]

- A 2006 report by the FBI attributes the recent spike in violent crimes in major cities nationwide to the activities of minors as young as ten.[11]

How can we understand the school-yard tragedies at places like Littleton, Jonesboro, and, more recently, Red Lake, Minnesota? What's causing so many young females to become violent? And why are so many of America's young people depressed, angry, high, or out of control?

There are the obvious reasons: the easy availability of guns in the United States, fatherless homes and the abandonment of traditional values, rap music that extols violence, guts exploding on video games, the testosterone-driven aggression surges of post-pubescent males, and the fact that more and more young females are getting

involved with gangs. But there's another factor—a more subtle one—that's rarely examined. It's a factor that might help us understand many of the horrific problems of adolescence in America—the high suicide rate, the high crime rate, the violence, the frequency of teenage pregnancies, the drugs, the ennui, and the anger. *For the first time in human history, we have artificially extended childhood well past puberty.* Simply stated, we are not letting our young people grow up.

Through most of human history, our ancestors began to produce children shortly after puberty, just as the members of all nonhuman species do to this day. Whether we like the idea or not, our young ancestors must have been capable of providing for their offspring, defending their families from predators, cooperating with others, and in most other respects functioning fully as adults. If they couldn't function as adults, their young could not have survived, which would have meant the swift demise of the human race. The fact that we're still here suggests that most young people are probably far more capable than we think they are. Somewhere along the line, we lost sight of—and buried—the potential of our teens. When and why did this happen, and what were the consequences?

DRAMATICALLY DIFFERENT PERSPECTIVES ON TEENS

Paul Koretz is a man with a mission. A Democratic assemblyman from Hollywood, he recently sponsored a bill in the California state legislature to raise the legal smoking age from eighteen to twenty-one. At the same time that a legislative committee was considering the bill, tens of thousands of American eighteen-year-olds were carrying heavy weapons and putting themselves in the line of fire in Iraq. Under the circumstances, some committee members thought it seemed hypocritical of them to think about denying eighteen, nineteen, and twenty-year-olds the right to risk damaging their health by smoking.

The committee stalled the legislation, but, spurred by California's powerful medical lobby, legislators had considered similar legislation before, and they'll probably consider the same bill again in the future.[12] Meanwhile, eighteen is still the cutoff age for smoking in California and many other states, presumably because a millisecond past midnight on the day we turn eighteen, we make a quantum leap in our ability to make sound judgments about the merits and demerits of smoking.

But do all eighteen-year-olds really exercise better judgment than all seventeen-year-olds? Do such legal prohibitions actually work? Do they have any negative consequences? And were seventeen-year-olds (not to mention five-year-olds and ten-year-olds) always prohibited from smoking?

YOUNG PEOPLE IN ACTION

Sixteen-Year-Old "Children"

From a recent newspaper: Two San Diego high school teachers were placed on paid leave recently for showing their sixteen-year-old students the infamous videotape of the recent beheading of American Nick Berg by Muslim extremists. Parents complained that the school should have asked for their permission before showing their "impressionable children" this disturbing tape. Some students defended the teachers, saying that the material was "relevant to learning about war." But school superintendent Terry Ryan said that teachers don't have "academic freedom to cause unfettered emotional and psychological damage to children." Teachers have been ordered not to show the tape, and the school district has adjusted its Internet filters "to block Berg's name and the words 'beheading' and 'beheaded.'" California's Education Code prohibits the teaching of "harmful matter without redeeming social importance." Teaching teens—only a year or two away from the age of military service—about the brutality of terrorism serves no such purpose, according to school officials.[13]

Schoolyard Scuffle

A few years ago, when Edward Brand was superintendent of the Sweetwater Union High School District (located in San Diego County, serving about thirty-three thousand students in grades seven to twelve), he published a provocative essay proposing a simple way of improving secondary education in America.[14]

Brand aptly noted that it's difficult to teach everything one needs to know about the modern world in just twelve years of schooling. That might have worked a hundred years ago, he said, but the world was largely agrarian back then. Some have said that the solution is to extend the school day, or at least to extend the school year, but that, Brand said, won't work. "[These] approaches raise the danger of learning burnout: Many students are easily overloaded by too much information for too long."

He didn't address the fact that our education system actually teaches many students very little—that twelve years of schooling in American schools (thirteen, with kindergarten) leaves many students unable to read or perform long division. According to a recent report, 47 percent of incoming freshman at California State University had to enroll in remedial English and 54 percent in remedial math.[15] Nationwide, only about 22 percent of high school graduates are considered qualified to take many basic college courses, and performance levels have been flat for at least the last decade.[16]

Brand also failed to note that most of our high school students think school is a waste of time.[17] These omissions aside, he certainly identified a legitimate problem.

His proposal was to add not just "a few more minutes to the school day or a few more days each year" but to extend secondary school *"by years"*—specifically, to add grades thirteen and fourteen to the school curriculum:

> *Imagine what students could achieve in that time. From mastering a foreign language, to getting another year of science and English under their belts, students would have greater opportunities to develop the foundation of knowledge requisite for the new millennium.... Extended schooling would mean more time for courses in fine arts, computers, and electives where students could explore special interests and career-related subjects.... Learning from a place of maturity would be another benefit. At age eighteen and nineteen, students are more likely to take their studies more seriously.[18]*

More recently, Reg Weaver, president of the National Education Association, lamenting the fact that 30 percent of our young people never finish high school, has called for extending the mandatory school age to twenty-one.[19]

Contrast the proposals of Brand and Weaver with the dark and disturbing views of another prominent educator, John Taylor Gatto. Gatto, an extraordinary jack-of-all-trades, earned his main living as a teacher in the New York City school system, where he taught for more than thirty years. Gatto was named New York City Teacher of the Year three times, in 1989, 1990, and 1991, and New York State Teacher of the Year in 1990 and 1991.[20] That year, announcing his intentions in an Op Ed piece in the *Wall Street Journal*,[21] Gatto quit being a teacher, saying he could no longer stand "hurting children."

Gatto pulled no punches, insisting among other things that:

> *Government schooling...kills the family by monopolizing the best times of childhood and teaching disrespect for home and parents....*
>
> *David learns to read at age four; Rachel, at age nine: ...when both are 13, you can't tell which one learned first.... But in school I label Rachel "learning disabled" and slow David down a bit, too. For a paycheck, I adjust David to depend on me to tell him when to go and when to stop. He won't outgrow that dependency. I identify Rachel as discount merchandise, "special education" fodder. She'll be locked in her place forever....*
>
> *I can't teach this way any longer. If you hear of a job where I don't have to hurt kids to make a living, let me know.*

Following the publication of this bombshell and Gatto's subsequent resig-

> ## YOUNG PEOPLE IN ACTION
> ### The Prom Police
>
> In Texas recently, a teacher was fired for inviting a student to the prom. That's defensible, perhaps, but in May 2006 at the Pearl River Central High School in Mississippi, eighteen-year-old senior Leah Lott was forbidden from bringing her boyfriend to the prom because he was over twenty. The boyfriend, Chris Raffo, a U. S. Marine who had been granted a leave to attend the prom, was twenty-one. And in Cape Cod, Massachusetts, the dates of six high school students were denied prom entrance because "background checks" had revealed that they had misdemeanors on their records (like underage drinking). According to a recent article in TIME magazine, more schools nationwide are now requiring pre-screening of prom dates and are becoming increasing selective about whom they'll admit—all in the name of protecting our vulnerable and incompetent young.[24]

nation, he was invited to give hundreds of talks worldwide in which "hungry" audiences reveled in the truth he seemed to be revealing.[22] He also published several provocative books proposing radical changes in the education system—all of which has led to exactly nothing. Our schools, caught in a tangled web of unions, politicians, and regulations, are a tough nut to crack. Even when it looks like change is coming, it often turns out to be illusory. As Yale educator Seymour Sarason said in his classic text, *Culture of the School and the Problem of Change*, when it comes to the American education system, *"Plus ça change, plus c'est la même chose"* ("The more things change, the more they stay the same").[23]

To Gatto, government-run schools do little more than warehouse young people, stifling creativity, initiative, a love of learning, and the rugged individualism that built America in its early years. In *The Underground History of American Education*, published in 2001, he also complained, quite explicitly, about the artificial extension of childhood:

> During the post-Civil War period, childhood was extended about four years. Later, a special label was created to describe very old children. It was...adolescence, a phenomenon hitherto unknown to the human race. The infantilization of young people didn't stop at the beginning of the twentieth century; child labor laws were extended to cover more and more kinds of work, the age of school leaving set higher and higher. The greatest victory for this utopian project was making school the only avenue to certain occupations. The intention

was ultimately to draw all work into the school net. By the 1950s it wasn't unusual to find graduate students well into their thirties, running errands, waiting to start their lives.[25]

Who is right? Is mandatory public schooling so valuable in the modern world that, as Brand says, young people need to get a lot more of it, or is it, as Gatto says, a root of great weakness in our society? Where did mandatory schooling come from in the first place? Were young people always required to attend full days of school up to age sixteen, seventeen, or eighteen, as they are today? If not, how, if at all, did they get the education they needed to function? Are there any rational alternatives to full-time mandatory public schooling in today's complex world? I'll offer answers to the various questions I've posed as we go along, and some, I think, will surprise you.

TREATING TEENS LIKE CHILDREN

Are American teens really infantilized? Diane Dumas and I approached this issue recently by asking a hundred teens between thirteen and seventeen in seven locations around the United States (three in California, one in Florida, one in Tennessee, one in Texas, and one in Georgia) to complete a checklist of forty-two restrictions that adults—or at least adults who aren't incarcerated or in the military—virtually never face but that very young children face frequently.[26] (See box, Measuring Infantilization in Teens.) The higher the score, the more restrictions one faces. If you're over eighteen, when was the last time you were given a "time out" or sent to your room? When were you last forced to undergo medical treatment against your will? When did someone last confiscate your personal property or search your bedroom? When were you last spanked as a punishment for misbehaving?

Not recently, I suspect. But our respondents scored surprisingly high on this scale. On average, they had "regularly or routinely" experienced more than *twenty-six* of these restrictions since they were thirteen, and seventy-four of the teens scored between twenty-two and forty (meaning that the distribution of scores was skewed toward the high numbers). Four of the respondents said they had regularly or routinely experienced *forty* out of the forty-two restrictions. Again, keep in mind that adults over eighteen (outside of institutional settings or the military) should, in a perfect world, tend to score near zero on this scale.

To find out how adults score on the infantilization scale, I administered it recently to twenty-five noninstitutionalized adults in the San Diego area, twenty-four United States Marines on active duty (at Camp Pendleton in Southern California), and thirty-two incarcerated felons (at a county prison in the San Diego

MEASURING INFANTILIZATION IN TEENS

Since you were thirteen years old, have adults regularly or routinely restricted your activities in any of the following ways?

1. Sent you to your room?
2. Listened in on your phone calls?
3. Restricted your phone use?
4. Cut off your allowance?
5. Restricted your driving privileges?
6. Confiscated your personal property?
7. Grounded you?
8. Searched your room without your permission?
9. Violated your privacy?
10. Restricted your use of the Internet?
11. Restricted your television use?
12. Restricted your use of videos or CDs?
13. Prevented you from getting a tattoo or piercing?
14. Prohibited you from changing your hairstyle?
15. Restricted the way you can dress?
16. Prohibited you from associating with certain friends?
17. Spanked, paddled, or hit you?
18. Prohibited your friends from coming over?
19. Prohibited you from attending a dance, party, or club?
20. Prevented you from drinking alcohol?
21. Prevented you from smoking cigarettes?
22. Forced you to take medication?
23. Forced you to participate in a meal or social event?
24. Forced you to attend a summer camp or go on vacation?
25. Given you a time out?
26. Required you to take a shower or bath?
27. Restricted your sexual activity?
28. Tried to silence you?
29. Given you a curfew?
30. Required you to go to bed at a certain time?
31. Restricted your dating activities?
32. Forced you to attend school?
33. Required you to get certain grades?
34. Required you to get a job?
35. Forced you into psychotherapy?
36. Forced you to undergo medical treatment?
37. Forced you to go to church or synagogue?
38. Forced you to exercise or play sports?
39. Forced you play a musical instrument?
40. Required you to take dance or participate in other extracurricular activities?
41. Required you to take certain courses in school?
42. Restrained you physically or restricted your movements?

(*Adapted from the* Epstein-Dumas Test of Adultness)

area). One would think that military personnel—obligated to follow orders without question—and prisoners—stripped of most of their rights by the criminal justice system—would be far more encumbered than noninstitutionalized teens.

But that's not what I found. Noninstitutionalized adults indeed scored near zero on the scale (2.3 out of a possible 42), but teens outscored prisoners and soldiers by a large margin (26.6 for teens vs. 14.6 for prisoners and 10.9 for soldiers). Even with these small samples, the differences in these scores were, from a statistical standpoint, highly significant. In other words, *teens appear to be subjected to about twice as many restrictions as are prisoners and soldiers and to more than ten times as many restrictions as are everyday adults.*

So teens really do undergo a wide variety of very specific restrictions, and there are even movements afoot to increase those restrictions. Teens aren't just imagining this, and sometimes they get angry about it. Why? Because their bodies and brains are screaming, "I'm an adult," just as evolution intended, while parents and other authority figures are replying, "No, you're still a child. Now take out the garbage before I ground you."

TEENS IN HISTORICAL PERSPECTIVE

To put those restrictions in perspective, try to envision what a teen's life was like two hundred years ago. The Industrial Revolution was barely off the ground (the steam engine was invented in England in 1763), and life was largely agricultural. Young people worked side by side with their parents as soon as they were able, as they still do in many countries around the world, and, shortly after puberty, boys often left the family to learn a trade. Couples married and had children young, which made sense considering that the average life span for males was only 38.3 years in 1850.[27]

Were there any rules or laws that prevented young people from smoking, drinking, working, riding a horse, or driving a buggy? Were there any restrictions at all on the behavior of teens? And did "adolescence," defined by pioneering psychologist G. Stanley Hall in 1904 as a period of "storm and stress," even exist?

Consider a few landmark dates in human social history:

- In 1788 England's Parliament passed landmark legislation prohibiting children under eight from working as chimney sweeps, but the law was routinely ignored, and it remained common for decades for four-year-olds to perform this unpleasant and sometimes dangerous job.

YOUNG PEOPLE IN ACTION

Alexander the Great

The Greek king Alexander III (356–323 B.C.E.), also known as Alexander the Great, had significant power by age sixteen. He founded his first colony at that age, calling it Alexandroupolis. At sixteen, he also suppressed a revolt in another colony when his father was away. At age twenty, he may also have played a role in his father's murder, which made Alexander king of Macedonia.

- Nearly a century later, in 1878, legislation in England raised the minimum work age to ten for factories and workshops. In addition, employers in those settings now had to restrict the employment of young people between ten and fourteen to consecutive half-days or alternate full days.[29]

- By 1900 more than two million young people between ten and fifteen were working full-time in the United States—a huge number, considering that the total population was only seventy-six million.[30] In 1916, the United States Congress—for reasons we'll explore later—passed a law prohibiting young people under fourteen from working in nonagricultural trades, but two years later the United States Supreme Court struck down that law on technical grounds.[31]

- Between 1883 and 1890, roughly twenty-five states passed laws prohibiting the sale of tobacco to young people under certain ages: fourteen in Maryland, eighteen in South Carolina, and sixteen in most other states.[32] Before the 1880s, it appears that no such restrictions existed. In any case, such laws were largely ineffective.

- The first comprehensive law in the United States that explicitly prevented young people from drinking alcohol wasn't passed until the end of Prohibition, in 1933. It allowed states to pick a minimum drinking age of eighteen or twenty-one.[33] Before the ratification of the Eighteenth Amendment to the Constitution in 1919, which prohibited all alcohol consumption, young people in many states were generally free to drink without restriction, subject mainly to the particular wishes of their parents. According to legal scholar James F. Mosher, in the late eighteenth century "adolescents saw drinking as a part of adult life and with adult encouragement openly experimented with adult drinking

norms. Boys as young as twelve were often seen entering public taverns to drink."[34]

With today's mind-set, we can't help but interpret such laws in a positive light. Clearly, most people would say, these laws must have been passed because (a) young people were being abused, and these laws were needed to protect them, and (b) young people were incapable—or, to be precise, most or all young people were incapable—of handling the rights and responsibilities that these laws took away. But, as you'll see, the truth is not so simple.

Whatever the origins of these various restrictions and whatever the motives behind them, it's clear that the many ways in which we limit the behavior of teens today came about relatively recently in human history—mainly within the last hundred years. Some of these restrictions might have made sense at one time and in certain contexts, but in a very different world, they make no sense at all.

In Chapter Two, we'll look more closely at the sequence of events that embody the artificial extension of childhood, at the motives behind some of those events, and at the multiple consequences of those events—some of which were both unintended and harmful.

HUMAN RESOURCES AT RISK

"Adolescent" is defined in modern society as a person in turmoil, and the toll that turmoil takes on our teens, our families, and our society is enormous. That's one reason we need to reexamine the nature and plight of adolescence, but there's another, less glamorous, but perhaps even more important reason: young people are capable of making great contributions to society, but they currently have virtually no way of being heard. As we'll see in future chapters, in times past young people often accomplished great things; it's tough for them to do so in today's America.

When we restrict the rights and activities of young people—say, the more than twenty million people in the United States between the ages of thirteen and seventeen, or the more than one billion teens that exist worldwide (more than one-sixth of the world's population)—in some sense we throw them away, just as much of the world still discards women, the elderly, and various minorities.

Not long ago mainstream American males firmly believed that blacks were idiots who needed to be treated like children, that women were inherently weak and delicate and could not function outside the home, and that the elderly were feeble-

> ## YOUNG PEOPLE IN ACTION
>
> ### Queen and King of Clubs
>
> *Already champion jugglers when they were twelve and fifteen, respectively, California residents Olga and Vova Galchenko—now fifteen and eighteen—hold the world records for people juggling ten clubs (378 catches), eleven clubs (152 catches), and twelve clubs (52 catches). According to fellow performer Penn Jillette, "If you're talking about club passing, the two of them together are the best in the world. Not just the best in the world. The best there has ever been."*[31]

minded—incapable of vitality or of making significant contributions to society. Gradually—with painfully small steps—we've put aside these preconceptions, accepting in various degrees four fundamental new ideas, which I call the "Enabling Premises."

Enabling Premise Number One: Individuals Are Unique

We've become increasingly sensitive to the fact that every person is unique and that any particular individual might not fit the stereotypes that sometimes accompany his or her age, gender, religion, or ethnic background.

When I was in graduate school, one of my undergraduate advisees was a young black man who had grown up on the streets of Boston. He was taking a seminar I was teaching on intelligence, and he was disturbed to learn that on a widely used IQ test, blacks, on average, scored lower than whites. I explained to him that although it's true that the average scores differed, it was also true that the *range* of scores was identical for blacks and whites; that is, both blacks and whites scored at both the bottom and the top of the IQ range. So an individual black or white could have any IQ at all. He wasn't reassured, unfortunately.

Stereotypes—sometimes based on averages and sometimes on nothing at all—are powerful things. But society seems to recognize, more and more, that the individual is indeed unique and that statistics and gossip are no substitute for the facts.

Enabling Premise Number Two: People Are Competent

We've moved away from a preoccupation with "traits" (like IQ and impulsiveness and introversion) in favor of a "competencies" view of human ability.

Traits are fixed and stable throughout one's life, and although it's true we have some relatively enduring tendencies, we also are capable of enormous learning and flexibility. Beginning a half century ago, pioneering researchers such as the late David McLelland began to develop tools that size people up in a humane and rational way:

instruments that measure an individual's "competencies"—real and potential abilities to behave in various ways. Once you dissect some area, such as leadership, into competencies, you can both measure and train those competencies.

Today it's common for major business and all branches of the military to measure and train leadership competencies. Rather than simply labeling someone as a "natural born leader"—and throwing away everyone else—we've gotten increasingly adept at improving the leadership skills of almost anyone, and the competencies approach is proving itself in many areas, including stress-management, motivation, relationships, parenting, and even creativity.[36] The competencies perspective is about as positive and humane as you can get; the trait perspective, by comparison, is wasteful and demeaning.

Enabling Premise Number Three: People Have Unrealized Potential

We've come to realize that where someone is now—his or her current set of competencies, if you will—doesn't necessarily tell us how far he or she might be able to go.

With appropriate training and experience, one can continue to grow and develop in significant ways throughout one's life. Drug addicts and alcoholics often recover; criminals often reform; and in today's fast-paced society, technophobes inevitably find themselves carrying MP3 players, cell phones, and PDAs, and people are increasingly likely to make radical career changes at some point.

Although IQ—a measure of logical reasoning ability—stays relatively stable over the course of one's life,* we tend to put more emphasis these days on a potpourri of "intelligences," including so-called "emotional intelligence," most of which turn out to be trainable competencies. We're more open to asking what a person's potential is, rather than sizing him or her up based merely on current performance.

Enabling Premise Number Four: Labels Are Dangerous

Finally, we've become increasingly wary of labels—not just epithets but *any* labels that imply limits on how a person might perform or what a person might become.

In the mental health field, for example, many mental health professionals have become increasingly critical of the "DSM"—the *Diagnostic and Statistical Manual of Mental Disorders*—the standard compendium of labels for mental health problems. Although therapists are forced to use these labels in order to get insurance reimbursements, many have become dissatisfied with this diagnostic system, because it invariably simplifies complex problems; it's difficult to fit an individual's unique signature into a little box without misrepresenting that person or at least omitting

---

*This applies only to IQ scores and not to intelligence itself. Intelligence actually changes dramatically and predictably over the course of one's life. More about this in Chapter Seven.

important details. As the famous Rosenhan study showed decades ago,[37] labels like "schizophrenic" are sometimes used recklessly by poorly trained professionals.*

Modern political correctness also discourages labeling, zealously forcing us to abandon disparaging labels (like "retarded") in favor of kinder, more optimistic designations (a "developmentally disabled" individual, a person with "special needs"). Diversity training in schools and businesses also discourages labeling, reminding us to avoid putting people in boxes.

Implications for Teens

We've been learning to apply these premises to various minorities, to women, and, lately, to the elderly. Applied to teens, the Enabling Premises have clear implications: Teens need to be judged (a) as individuals, not as a group, (b) based on their competencies, not on their age, (c) based on their potential for learning and growth, not merely on their current characteristics, and (d) without disparaging labels like "adolescent," which imply limits or flaws.

CONVERGING EVIDENCE

Although the Theory of Evolution is called a "theory," most scientists these days consider it a fact. In the 1930s a "Grand Synthesis" of information from a half dozen fields—paleontology, archeology, geology, and so on—all pointed with enormous consistency to the same idea: that species on earth evolved over millions of years through a process of natural selection. If one or more disciplines had turned up contradictory evidence, the theory would have been on weaker ground. Converging evidence from multiple sources is pretty convincing.

As I hope you'll discover in this volume, the theses I'm putting forth—that adolescence is a historical anomaly, that we infantilize our young people unnecessarily and extremely, that many or most teens are capable of functioning as adults in a number of ways, and that infantilization has serious negative consequences for our society—are also supported by converging evidence from multiple fields.

History

The historical record is every bit as revealing as the geological record. There is simply no question that teens throughout history were integrated into adult society much earlier than they are today and that the tumultuous period that defines adolescence today probably never existed until recent times. See Chapter Two.

---

*In the early 1970s, David L. Rosenhan of Stanford University sent eight normal people to various psychiatric facilities complaining of hearing voices but showing no active symptoms of mental illness. Even so, all were admitted and labeled as mentally ill, and even upon discharge some were labeled schizophrenic "in remission."

Anthropology and Cross-Cultural Studies

To this day, teens in many cultures around the world, especially in preindustrial nations, grow up much sooner than they do in the United States, apparently without ever experiencing the turmoil of adolescence. Margaret Mead's classic book, *Coming of Age in Samoa*,[38] described a peaceful society in which adolescence as we know it appeared not to exist. Although subsequent researchers have questioned some of Mead's claims, there is overwhelming contemporary evidence from other cultures that supports the idea that adolescence is not a necessary stage of development. See Chapter Three.

Rehabilitation

Programs like the original Boys Town (but not its current manifestation) were able to help troubled youths by putting them in charge of their lives. Boys Town was a real town, run from top to bottom by the troubled young men who came to live there. Contemporary programs like Outward Bound also work on this premise—that one of the most effective ways to straighten people out is to inoculate them with a significant dose of responsibility and authority. In Chapter Four, we'll look at a number of programs of this sort and, in some cases, the dramatic changes they produce in young people.

Psychology

Studies show that our cognitive abilities are fairly sophisticated—more-or-less fully developed, in fact—around the time of puberty. Jean Piaget, the eminent Swiss psychologist, said we achieve "formal operational" thinking—or at least that some of us do—by age twelve or so and that there isn't anywhere to go after that. What's more, according to Piaget, many people never become capable of this kind of thinking, no matter how old they are. But aren't some teens shoddy thinkers? Of course, but so are many adults, and by infantilizing teens, we probably retard intellectual development in some individuals. More on this later, especially in Chapter Seven.

A CHORUS OF CRITICS

I'm not the first person to have noticed and been disturbed about the ways in which our perspective on young people has changed over the last century. I've already mentioned John Gatto's dismay, but he turns out to be one of many.

Holt, Farson, and Liedloff

The late John Holt, an accomplished teacher as well as a pioneer in the modern home schooling movement, condemned the "sentimental prison" we've built around children in his 1974 book *Escape from Childhood*.[39] Holt had been inspired in part by the radical social thinker Ivan Illich. In a polemical book called *Deschooling Society*, published in 1973, Illich strongly condemned organized schooling as harmful to children.[40] In *Escape from Childhood*, Holt went much further than Illich, arguing that children "of whatever age" should be granted a number of "rights," including:

- The right to vote
- The right to work
- The right to own property
- The right to travel
- The right to choose one's guardian
- The right to a guaranteed income
- The right to legal and financial responsibility
- The right to control one's learning
- The right to use drugs
- The right to drive
- The right to control one's sex life.

Also in 1974, psychologist Richard Farson published a book that was quite similar to Holt's called *Birthrights: A Bill of Rights for Children*, in which he listed ten rights that children should be given, including the right to "freedom from physical punishment" and the right to "responsive environmental design" (meaning chairs, tools, and such, should be manufactured in small sizes).[41]

Holt, now a cult figure in the home schooling movement, complained of a "Great Divide" that had been created in recent times to separate children from adults. "What is both new and bad about modern childhood," said Holt, "is that children are so cut off from the adult world."[42]

A similar theme is developed in yet another 1970s book, *The Continuum Concept*, by Jean Liedloff—also a cult figure today.[43] After living with a primitive South American tribe for an extended period, Liedloff concluded that our own children need to be integrated into adult society from an early age and that it's a mistake for us to isolate and shelter them.

Historians and Social Scientists

Many historians of childhood—Philippe Ariès, J. H. Plumb, Hugh Cunningham, Marc Kleijwegt, and others—have also pointed out that young people today are sheltered far more than they were before the industrial age. And various anthropologists, sociologists, and other scholars, such as Pierre Dasen of the Université de Genève, the French psychiatrist Patrice Huerre, and the Indian scholar T. S. Saraswathi, have long suggested that adolescence as we know it in the West doesn't exist in most preindustrial nations, where young people are typically integrated into adult society soon after puberty.

Huerre, a therapist and expert on teen violence, is especially passionate about these issues. In France in the 1990s, with colleagues Martine Pagan-Reymond and Jean-Michel Reymond, Huerre argued forcefully that adolescence in France was a recent and very dangerous cultural invention.[*]

A 2004 book published in the United Kingdom by English psychiatrist Philip Graham raises similar concerns.[44] Drawing on his more than twenty-five years of experience as a clinician working with teens in a children's hospital setting, Graham cites the "disastrous consequences" that result when we "infantilize and disempower" teens.[45] When teens are miserable, says Graham, "it is the powerless predicament in which they find themselves that is often responsible." His recommendation? "[We] should stop infantilizing young people and allow them to reclaim the independence to which their competence entitles them."[46]

WHY THIS BOOK?

If a parade of distinguished scholars has already noticed and sometimes even expressed concern about the artificial extension of childhood, why hasn't anyone paid attention, and why, if anything, has the turmoil of adolescence increased? Why, for goodness sake, are there people out there trying to extend childhood even further? And why have I bothered to write this book?

I've asked myself questions of this sort many times over the nine years I've been investigating this matter. Here are the answers I have so far.

---

*In a volume first published in 1990 and then issued in a new edition in 1997, Huerre and colleagues insisted that adolescence was a "heavy burden" that has been "socially constructed and then managed by people other than adolescents—and too often for the benefit of others." The book is called *l'Adolescence n'existe pas* ("Adolescence Doesn't Exist"), which presumably reflects what the authors wish were true, not what really is. It begins with an intriguing quote from novelist Marcel Proust which suggests that it's really adulthood that doesn't exist—that adulthood is just extended adolescence: "C'est avec des adolescents qui durent un assez grand nombre d'anneés que la vie fait ses vieillards" ("It is with adolescents who last for a rather long time that life produces its old people").

First, societal thinking sometimes gets stuck. When, for several genera-tions, people have looked at an issue a certain way, it's almost impossible for them to see things differently. We now take it for granted, for example, that child labor laws and laws requiring mandatory education are both good and necessary, even though today's world is radically different than the one that gave rise to these laws. Maybe the case against the artificial extension of childhood needs to be made repeatedly—and more forcefully—for the message to sink in. I'll examine this issue head-on toward the end of the book.

Second, some previous writers—Holt and Farson, especially—had political agendas that may have undermined their ability to promote real change. The prob-lems created by the artificial extension of childhood should be of concern to a broad spectrum of people—left-wing, moderate, and conservative, religious and nonreligious—not just to those on the fringes. My presentation will, I hope, stimu-late the thinking of a wide range of serious people—including some serious teens.

Third, some writers, like Gatto, talk about the artificial extension of child-hood without taking on the burden of convincing readers that it really exists, or mention the infantilization of teens in a narrow context (Liedloff, Kliejwegt, Cunningham, and others). This volume presents the case comprehensively.

And finally, until now no one has, to my knowledge, (a) quantified the extent to which our young people are infantilized, (b) demonstrated a link between infantilization and the turmoil we see in our young people, or (c) directly compared the competencies of young people with those of adults. This volume presents origi-nal and compelling data in all three of these areas (Chapters One, Five, and Six).

Recently Tom Smith, a polling expert at the University of Chicago, published the results of a poll of fourteen hundred adults who were asked, among other things, when adulthood now begins in the United States. At eighteen, perhaps, when teens can vote and own property and enroll in the military without parental permission? How about at twenty-one, when young people can buy alcohol? The answer was *twenty-six*, signifying, said Smith, that the public has come to accept an "extended adolescence."[47] The artificial extension of childhood, it seems, is getting worse.

Q: *Childhood is a wonderful time of life—a time for fun and exploration, when all of our needs are met and nothing is expected from us in return. Aren't we doing our teens a favor by extending childhood?*

A: Driven by evolutionary imperatives established thousands of years ago, the main need a teenager has is to become productive and independent. After puberty, if we pretend our teens are still children, we will be unable to meet their most fundamental needs, and we will cause some teens great distress. When a young person says "I am not a child," we need to listen carefully.

Chapter 2

The Creation of Adolescence

How many roads must a man walk down,
Before they call him a man?
—Bob Dylan, *Blowin' in the Wind*

Overview. Adolescence is the creation of modern industrialization, which got into *high gear in the United States between 1880 and 1920. For most of human history before the Industrial Era, young people worked side by side with adults as soon as they were able, and it was not uncommon for young people, and especially young females, to marry and establish independent households soon after puberty. It wasn't until the turn of the twentieth century that adolescence was identified as a separate stage of life characterized by "storm and stress." In what appears to be a vicious cycle of cause and effect, teen turmoil since the late 1800s has generated a large number of unique laws that restrict teen behavior in ways that adult behavior has never been restricted, and these laws in turn appear to have stimulated more extreme forms of "misbehavior" in teens. The rate at which such laws have been passed has increased substantially since the 1960s, with an increasingly wide range of new crimes being invented just for young people. The social reforms that created such laws were set in motion by some formidable individuals, not all of whom had benevolent motives. The extension of childhood past puberty has benefited a large number of new businesses and industries offering a wide range of products and services to the growing teen markets.*

In *Ancient Youth: The Ambiguity and the Absence of Adolescence in Greco-Roman Society*, Dutch historian Marc Kleijwegt notes that councillors in ancient Greco-Roman municipalities were sometimes as young as four, or perhaps even younger.[1] As the proud father of a precocious six-year-old, I'd love to be able to testify that any bright child could hold such a position, but the picture that comes to mind is

just too preposterous. How could a toddler have served as a councillor in one of the great ancient city states?

The answer, says Kleijwegt, is that the many high positions occupied in ancient Rome and Greece by young children were probably ceremonial. In some cases, prominent families probably bought these positions in order to increase family prestige. In other cases, the young person was groomed over a period of years, becoming active in significant ways by age seventeen or eighteen and eventually securing real political power.

More important for our purposes, Kleijwegt also points out that young people holding political office "were no longer regarded as children but as apprentice-adults."[2] Kleijwegt also insists throughout his book that adolescence as we know it today simply didn't exist in the ancient world—that "youth in [preindustrial society] was in character and behaviour essentially different from that of modern adolescents."[3]

Adolescence as we characterize it today—as a distinct and separate period of life filled with angst and rebelliousness—is, quite simply, a fairly recent phenomenon in human history.

HISTORY LESSONS

Consider the following passages from various works on the history of childhood and adolescence:

> [The] teenager is a recent idea that may not deserve to be an eternal one [Thomas Hine, The Rise and Fall of the American Teenager].[4]

> In the Bad Old Days people learned who they were, and what their place in the eternal order of things was to be, by looking at the progression of generations that stretched behind them.... Today other roads than that of family lineage lead to immortality.... Adolescents now soon realize that they are not links in a familial chain stretching across the ages. Who they are, and what they become is independent, (at least so they believe) of who their parents are.... Other agencies now socialize and control the young. The continuity between the generations falls [Edward Shorter, The Making of the Modern Family].[5]

> Although the architects of adolescence often announced their intention to understand and to sympathize with the problems of adolescents, a major effect of the psychological interest in adolescence after 1890 was the creation of new ways to regulate youthful behavior [Joseph F. Kett, Rites of Passage: Adolescence in America, 1790 to the Present].[6]

...our society has passed from a period which was ignorant of adolescence to a period in which adolescence is the favourite age. We now want to come to it early and linger in it as long as possible [Philippe Ariès, Centuries of Childhood*].*[7]

As you can see, a number of people have written about the invention of adolescence in modern times, as well as about the ways in which the modern world has isolated young people from adults. Not all historians view young people the same way, however.

Two Historical Viewpoints

It's convenient to separate modern historians of childhood and adolescence into two groups: "sentimentalists" and "continuists."

*Sentimentalists.*The sentimentalists include historians like Dutch scholar Marc Kleijwegt, the Frenchman Philippe Ariès, Hugh Cunningham of the University of Kent (United Kingdom), Edward Shorter of the University of Toronto, Lawrence Stone of Princeton University, and the British historian J. H. Plumb, among others. Sentimentalists believe, generally speaking, that perspectives on children and teens have changed dramatically in recent centuries.

Prior to the Industrial Era (beginning, roughly, in the mid-1700s), young people were seen as small adults, or at least they weren't distinguished from adults in many respects. They worked alongside adults, especially in rural areas, and they were integrated partially or fully into adult society at a young age—sometimes well before puberty, but certainly shortly thereafter. Jean Liedloff's picture of life among the Yequana Indians in South America fits this model.

According to the sentimentalist historians, at some point—at least in the United States and some countries in Europe—young people began to be isolated from adults, and the prevailing attitudes about young people changed, as well. They were no longer seen as reasonably capable members of society; rather, they became "sentimentalized." Children were increasingly seen as helpless and incompetent beings requiring adult protection, and the age at which young people were defined as children steadily increased over the decades. As I noted in Chapter One, in England in 1788 children under eight were said to require protection from various labor practices; by 1833 protection was deemed necessary for young people age thirteen and under. Modern laws have extended the protection to age eighteen, or, for some purposes, to age twenty-one.

Continuists. Other historians, such as Princeton's Natalie Zemon Davis, Emiel Eyben of Katholieke Universiteit Leuven (Belgium), Linda Pollock of Tulane University, Harvard's Steven Ozment, and Barbara Hanawalt of Ohio State Uni-

> ## YOUNG PEOPLE IN ACTION
>
> ### Jimmy Carter on Guns:
>
> *"By the time I was five or six years old, I had been carefully instructed*
> *in the proper use of firearms, beginning with a BB gun, then a Remington*
> *.22 semiautomatic rifle, and finally a bolt-action .410-gauge shotgun."*[8]

versity, can be termed "continuists" in the sense that they claim, based on their examination of records in certain countries during certain eras, that perspectives on childhood and adolescence have been at least somewhat continuous over time or that children and teens haven't changed much.

I believe we can largely set aside the continuist perspective for a number of reasons, the main one being that when you look closely at what these historians have written about teens (but not necessarily what they've written about young children), their writings tend to be consistent with my position. Without exception, they certainly find far more differences between historical and modern teens than they find similarities.

For example, in the 1993 volume *Growing Up in Medieval London*, Barbara Hanawalt asserts that "[the] Middle Ages did recognize stages of life that corresponded to childhood and adolescence." But she also notes that "proponents of the nonexistence of childhood and adolescence in the Middle Ages" have "widespread support among professional historians,"[9] and that "the medieval world did not have names for these stages of life."[10]

Hanawalt also describes a teen world that is as different from the modern one as, say, Joan of Arc is from contemporary pop diva Britney Spears. For example, although she takes issue with other historians about the age at which children entered various work professions (putting little emphasis on how much work they did at home), she still has them starting apprenticeships as young as age seven. She also notes repeatedly that there was a tendency for the "age of entry" into various professions to "creep up" over the centuries—for adults to "[postpone] both the symbols and the reality of adult life to later ages."[11]

Most important, she acknowledges just how radically different the medieval teen world was from the modern one:

> *It is perhaps the question of influence that most distinguishes between adolescence*
> *then and now. No full-fledged youth subculture in which peers were the chief influence*
> *on an adolescent's life existed in the Middle Ages.... There was no "youth culture," as*

opposed to a broader society culture; nor were there "juvenile delinquency" and "juvenile sentencing,"as opposed to adult criminal behaviour and punishment. Mature and married adults, the "sad and wise," did not aspire to become "wild and wanton" in imitation of carefree youth.[12]

Hanawalt also notes that young medieval Londoners often married young and set up independent households, but let's stop here: no youth subculture, apprenticeships with adults at young ages, no juvenile delinquency, and no term for adolescence. Bear in mind that this is coming from a continuist historian focusing on one of the best places in the world—London—to expect historical continuity.

Was Childhood an Invention?

The first major work on the history of childhood was published in French by Philippe Ariès in 1960 (subsequently published in English in 1962).[13] Based on his examination of historical records, largely in France, Ariès propounded a fairly radical idea, namely that the concept of "childhood" was an invention of eighteenth- and nineteenth-century Europe, making its way to France around 1900. It didn't become a "general phenomenon," said Ariès—he means mainly in France—until "after the end of World War I."[14] "Adolescence" came even later, said Ariès. During the twentieth century, "adolescence expanded: it encroached upon childhood in one direction, maturity in the other."[15] Eventually, he said, adolescence came to dominate modern society.

Ariès based his ideas on a wide variety of records—among them, letters, works of fiction, paintings, and school registers—which led him to draw the following conclusions, among others:

Inconsistent Language. Various words, such as "child, " "baby," "youth," "schoolboy," "scholar," and "student" (*enfant, puer, adolescens,* etc.) were used inconsistently and sometimes interchangeably until recent centuries. The terms could refer to people of a wide range of ages—even to people we now call adults. A term such as "child" typically designated a family relationship or a state of dependence, not an age.[16]

Odd Portrayals of Children in Art. According to Ariès, "Medieval art until about the twelfth century did not know childhood or did not attempt to portray it. It is hard to believe that this neglect was due to incompetence or incapacity; it seems more probable that there was no place for childhood in the medieval world."[17] When images of children did begin to turn up, he says, it was common for children to be dressed in adult clothes, or, in many cases, the child was represented by a shrunken image of an adult "without any of the characteristics of childhood."[18]

In some forms of art, children appeared naked, but they never appeared in children's clothes, and they were sometimes portrayed with adult musculature. What's more, said Ariès, children's toys didn't turn up in paintings until at least the eighteenth century. Paintings of children on their own were also late in coming, presumably because adults and young people were so intermingled until recent times. Ariès mentions exceptions—the realistic portrayal of children in ancient Greek art, realistic depictions of the baby Jesus, and so on—but he insists that realistic, sentimental portrayals of children were largely absent from European art until recent times.

Lack of Caring. Perhaps the most controversial of Ariès' claims is that until recent times, parents simply didn't care very much about their children.

I remember being appalled when I read Victor Hugo's *Les Misérables* a few years ago (in overzealous preparation to see the musical) by the apparent indifference that French parents of the early nineteenth century had toward their children. Eponine, Gavroche, and other prominent characters in the book were children and teens abandoned and forgotten by their parents, fending for themselves on the streets of Paris; in that world, it seemed as natural as daylight for a savvy ten year old to be in charge of a gaggle of toddlers, all stealing and begging for their food.

The indifference, Ariès claimed, was a result of many factors, among them the extremely high mortality rate among infants and children in medieval Europe—perhaps 20 to 40 percent. "The general feeling was, and for a long time remained, that one had several children in order to keep a few," he wrote.

The sixteenth-century philosopher Montaigne once wrote, "I have lost two or three children in their infancy, not without regret, but without great sorrow."[19] Such an attitude may "shock our present-day sensibility," writes Ariès—especially the fact that Montaigne didn't even know exactly how many children he had lost!— but that attitude prevailed until recent times.

Intermingling of Children and Adults. Ariès' most persuasive arguments grow from records he produces from various schools which show, unequivocally, that people of very different ages studied together routinely until very recent times.

We're all familiar with the movie images of the prairie schoolhouse of the Old West, where young children and teens somehow learned together in the same room. Records from medieval schools in Europe show that this kind of arrangement was standard. At the Jesuit college of Caen in the 1600s, for example, class registers show a mixing of students from ages nine to twenty in various classes; at a school in Châlons, they run from eight to twenty-four.[20] Many of these ages were presumably estimated; Ariès shows that in many families—even prominent ones—parents didn't keep track of the exact ages of their children.

It was also not uncommon for people to complete their studies by their early teens; people we would now call "prodigies" emerged fairly frequently under this system—a rarity today. For hundreds of years in medieval Europe, age seemed to mean little or nothing in the dispensing of education. Young people and adults were also amply mixed in a wide range of professions: in agriculture, crafts, law, and so on. Ability, need, and opportunity were the forces that determined where young people turned up; age seemed to be completely irrelevant.

Ariès in Perspective

In a recent article in *The New Yorker*, staff writer Joan Acocella reviews a new volume of historical essays about the family structure in Europe, posing and trying to answer an important question: "When did we start treating children like children?"[21]

She surveys much of the relevant literature, including recent essays and books that challenge Ariès' views. But the more she digs, the more frustrated she becomes, eventually rejecting the tendency of modern historians to excuse and rationalize the cruelest behaviors imaginable in order to convince us that people have always loved and cared for their children the same way that we do today. The apologetic views of one such historian, Linda Pollock, leave Acocella "gasping for air."

Ariès may have gone too far, but his revisionists appear to be guilty of a great deal of wishful thinking. Did some parents love and cherish their children as we do today? Of course. Even in *Les Miserables*, one of the main story lines is about such devotion. But in other respects, children were often treated with indifference or cruelty.

Attorney and legal scholar Donald T. Kramer, author of the definitive three-volume *Legal Rights of Children*, sums things up starkly:

> In ancient times, children were considered to be chattels owned by their parents, who had the right to do more or less what they wanted to do with them. They could educate them or not, as they so chose; they could inflict heinous corporal punishment on them or not, as they so chose; they could afford them medical treatment when needed or not, as they so chose. In short, children in early times all too frequently bore the same relationship to their parents as slaves did to their masters.[22]

Historians, as is their tradition, will continue to debate Ariès' thesis for many years.[23] But at least some of the basic facts are clear, and I don't see how even the most zealous continuist historian[24] could deny them:

- For most of human history until the time of the Industrial Revolu-

---

YOUNG PEOPLE IN ACTION

Young Leaders

- *David G. Farragut entered the United States Navy in 1810 at age nine, commanded his first ship at age twelve, and eventually became Commander-in-Chief of the United States Navy during the Civil War.*
- *King Philippe I of France ascended the throne in 1060 at age seven.*
- *Amina Sarauniya Zazzua (1533-1610), became Queen of Zazzua, a province of Nigeria, when she was sixteen. Although she didn't assume full power for several years, she was given immediate responsibility for governing a ward in her city.*
- *The legendary Queen Cleopatra VII of Egypt came into power at age seventeen.*
- *According to the Bible, King Josiah began his successful thirty-one year reign in Jerusalem at age eight.*

---

tion, the vast majority of children worked alongside adults as soon as they were able, and they transitioned to partial or full adulthood by their early, mid, or late teens. Even today, many and perhaps even most of the world's children (primarily in developing nations) follow this course (Chapter Three). In contrast, in most industrialized countries today teens are almost completely isolated from adults; they're immersed in "teen culture," required or urged to attend school until their late teens or early twenties, largely prohibited from or discouraged from working, and largely restricted, when they do work, to demeaning, poorly-paid jobs.

- Through most of human history and in most locales on earth, young people—females especially—married soon after puberty and often set up independent households after marriage.[25] In contrast, today in the United States the median age of first marriage is 26.9 for males and 25.3 for females.[26]
- It wasn't until the turn of the twentieth century that the teen years came to be seen as dark and tumultuous and that adolescence was recognized as a separate stage of life that coincided with those years.

THE INFANTILIZATION OF TEENS

In Chapter One I summarized the results of a survey I conducted with average teens, average adults, United States Marines, and incarcerated felons. The survey suggested that teens are subjected to far more restrictions than are any of the other groups—to roughly twice as many restrictions as incarcerated felons and active-duty Marines and to more than ten times as many as everyday adults. I also posed questions about the history of such restrictions: Were teens always limited in these ways? Could teens of times past drink, smoke, or make medical decisions for themselves?

Because this book is mainly about teens in the United States, I approached the issue by tracking down as many relevant laws as I could find in the United States over the last three hundred years. When I began this pursuit, I was worried that older laws would be harder to find than newer ones, which could easily produce a distorted picture: one might mistakenly conclude that the rate at which such laws are being enacted is increasing, not because it actually *is* increasing but simply because the older laws are inaccessible. As I looked into this further, my worries decreased, mainly because in many cases I was able to determine that newly enacted laws were the first of their kind: laws restricting drinking or skateboarding, for example, or laws requiring helmets for bicycle riding.

My search yielded a dramatic picture. (See Figure 2.1.) Before 1700 I could find only a few relevant laws, such as a 1641 Massachusetts law prohibiting anyone sixteen and over from "cursing" or "smiting" their parents and a related Massachusetts law punishing "a stubborn or rebellious son"; both were accompanied by references to Biblical verses.[27] The penalty for each offense was death, but I wasn't able to find evidence of any actual executions. During the entire eighteenth century I found only a few new laws of unique character and then a few more during the early 1800s. But from the mid-1800s onward I found a steady and substantial accumulation of restrictive laws—about fifty distinctive laws between 1850 and 1960. Perhaps the biggest surprise was the sudden increase in rate that began in the 1960s; I found about *ninety* unique laws over the last four decades of the twentieth century. (See Appendix 5 for a timeline summarizing these laws.)

Just what is it that teens aren't allowed to do, and why the burst of new restrictions in the late twentieth century?

Figure 2.1. Infantilization of Teens Over Time. Cumulative number of newly enacted local, state, and federal laws of unique character that restricted the behavior of young people (under eighteen) in the United States. They're grouped by decade, from 1700 to 1999. Laws that are identical in nature are generally excluded from the graph. There are only a few pertinent laws before 1700, most notably two laws created by the "Generall Court" of (Colonial) Massachusetts in the 1640s condemning young people to death for "smiting" their parents or being "stubborn or rebellious." The steeper the curve, the faster the laws are being enacted. Note the dramatic increase in rate after 1960.

Widespread Restrictions

As we saw in Chapter One, there are many ways in which teens are restricted. Only a fraction are specifically encoded in laws. For example, one must be eighteen to deliver major newspapers in California, but that's not strictly a matter of law. Rather, many papers now require the carriers to drive, to carry liability insurance, or to be able to sign contracts as independent contractors.[28] You can't fulfill any of these requirements these days when you're twelve—my age when I got my first paper route. There also aren't specific laws, as far as I can tell, that say that teens can't pick their own friends, make their own religious decisions, and so on. But the broad powers a parent has as a teen's custodian—shared, to some extent by teachers, school administrators, and other authority figures—leave teens tightly under the control of adults.

Many restrictions are created by laws that don't seem particularly broad on their face but that have sweeping effects. For example, because young people can't sign contracts until they're eighteen, they can't, on their own, do a wide range of things that require contracts: They can't get their own credit cards or telephones or cell phones or bank loans or cars. They can't start businesses. They can't buy property. They can't get insurance. They can't rent cars or boats or equipment or furni-

YOUNG PEOPLE IN ACTION

Bad News for Teens

Bob, the middle-aged man sitting next to me on an airplane, didn't believe me when I told him that you have to be eighteen to deliver newspapers in California. He was eleven, he says, when he got his first route. In fact, the matter isn't simple: Under California Labor Code §1298, people as young as twelve can deliver papers under some circumstances. But most publishers, concerned about liability, stopped handing newspapers to minors years ago. They want their carriers to be independent adults who can sign contracts absolving the publisher from liability for any damages they might incur during deliveries. Although a 1993 appeals court decision in Pennsylvania says that even minors who deliver papers are independent contractors, California publishers aren't buying it. When, in some cases, adult carriers hand papers to minors to deliver, concerned citizens complain, as the prestigious Sacramento Bee found out recently. Bee circulation manager Connie Coan insists that they give papers to adults only: after that, "you're done with it."[29]

ture or apartments or houses. They can't become actors or writers or artists—at least not for pay. They can't become professional athletes. They can't get married.

There are hundreds of activities in our society which require contracts, and young people can't engage in any of them unless Mom or Dad signs on—which gives parents derivative powers. Let's not mince words: because of the contract restriction alone, parents are in an excellent position to control young people through coercion. "If you don't finish washing those dishes, you're not getting the car tonight." Sound familiar?

Putting such issues aside for the moment, let's take a look at how some specific laws evolved in the United States. The recent era—from the 1960s on—deserves special treatment. For now, let's focus on the period from the mid 1800s to about 1960.

Restricting the Labor of Young People

Many of the early laws restricting the behavior of young people were related to work. At first, the laws focused on work that put young people at risk; later, they began to focus on all work, no matter how benign. Some were promoted by concerned thinkers and leaders—many of them dynamic women, insisting that young people needed to be protected—and some by groups or individuals protecting their economic interests—labor unions and wealthy industrialists, for example. Courts frequently struck down such laws on various grounds.

As we've seen, one of the first laws in the world intended to limit labor by young people—largely ineffective—was enacted in England in 1788. England continued, in small increments, to restrict child labor through legislation passed in the nineteenth and twentieth centuries, but by 1891 the minimum age for child labor had still only increased to age eleven.[30]

In the United States, the child labor movement also moved ponderously—at least at first. Pennsylvania passed the first relevant law in 1848, prohibiting young people under twelve from working in certain kinds of mills. A few other states had already passed weak laws restricting the work hours of young workers—usually to ten per day—but a 2000 study of the era by economists at Vanderbilt University concludes that "early child labor laws—and closely related compulsory schooling laws—were... ineffective."[31] A comprehensive 1937 study of child labor in the United States by Katherine DuPre Lumpkin and Dorothy Wolff Douglas explains why: early child labor laws were often short-lived and almost always came with gaping loopholes. A law passed in 1849 in Maine, for example, was repealed the next year, and an early New Hampshire law could be circumvented with "written consent of parent or guardian."[32]

By 1879 only seven states had child labor laws in place, and all were being ignored or circumvented to some extent. But in 1903, Illinois, the state that had recently opened the world's first juvenile court, passed a strong child labor law that also required young people to attend school, and by 1918 all states had joined the bandwagon with relevant laws of varying sorts.[33]

Nineteen hundred was a turning point for child labor in the United States, mainly because of that year's census results. The census revealed that more than 18 percent of America's young people between ages ten and fifteen—about two million individuals—were working long hours in factories, mines, mills, fields, and stores. It wasn't at all uncommon for young children to be working thirteen hours a day for two or three dollars a week. The census figures helped stimulate a national movement to prohibit most labor by young people. The National Child Labor Committee (NCLC), founded by Felix Adler in 1904, spearheaded legislative efforts nationally, equating labor by young people with slavery. According to Adler, the labor practices of his day led to "the physical, mental and moral degeneration of hundreds of thousands of future fathers and mothers" and prevented "that future growth, that development of American civilization, that new type of manhood which we must give to the world in order to contribute to the world's riches."[34]

Although Adler's passionate concerns about the new exploitation of young people in factories were legitimate, he appeared to overlook the fact that young

people had proudly worked alongside adults throughout human history. Should young people be *entirely* cut off from the working world—and from *adults*—because of the exploitative practices of the new factories? We'll revisit this question several times in this volume.

The NCLC was only partially effective in lobbying for comprehensive labor laws. In 1906, the United States Senate considered a proposal by Senator Albert J. Beveridge to limit child labor, but his colleagues argued that the federal government lacked the authority to do so, and the proposal died. In 1908 Adler hired photographer Lewis W. Hine to travel the country documenting the harsh use of young people in factories, and his moving photos—of soot-covered children leaving mine shafts, of dirty children standing near ominous-looking machines, and so on—were widely circulated.[35]

Finally, in 1916 Congress passed the ambitious Keating-Owen Child Labor Act that, among other things, prohibited young people under fourteen from working in nonagricultural industries that produced goods intended for export to other countries or for transport across state lines. Note that this was *indirect* legislation; Congress couldn't regulate child labor directly, but it could control interstate commerce. Just two years later in *Hammer v. Dagenhart*, the United States Supreme Court struck down the law on the grounds that Congress had no business interfering with local labor matters through such indirect means. The case had been brought by the father of two young men ("one under the age of fourteen years and the other between the ages of fourteen and sixteen years") in Charlotte, North Carolina, who argued that his offspring had a "constitutional right to work."[36] Just a few months after the Supreme Court's decision Congress passed a similar law—this one based on the federal government's ability to levy taxes. Once again, however, the Supreme Court nullified the law.[37]

Undaunted, the NCLC and other organizations lobbied hard for Congress to pass a constitutional amendment empowering Congress to limit labor by people under age eighteen, and the amendment passed both houses in 1924. For the amendment to be binding, however, thirty-six state legislatures had to ratify it within a few years, but only a handful did so—another major blow for the movement to end labor by young people.

The 1929 stock market crash and the ensuing Great Depression gave a boost to the movement, mainly because jobs were suddenly so scarce that leaders were desperate to exclude as many people as they could from the job market. With perhaps 27 percent of the population out of work, the 1933 National Industrial Recovery Act established a minimum of age sixteen for workers in most industries

(this is where the magical age of sixteen—still with us today—was first born on the national level). Young people were also excluded from working in hazardous industries up to age eighteen. But the Supreme Court struck down the law in 1935, again on constitutional grounds.[38]

The exigencies of the Depression ultimately won out over the Supreme Court's constitutional concerns. The Walsh-Healey Public Contracts Act, passed in 1936, prevented firms handling federal money from employing females under eighteen or males under sixteen. If you wanted a federal contract, you had to fire your young employees, pure and simple. Congress still uses this strategy today: the federal government can't meaningfully require people to wear seat belts, for example, because it doesn't control the roads, but it can (and does) force states to enact their own seat-belt laws by withholding federal highway construction funds from states that won't pass such laws. The Walsh-Healey Act stuck (more or less), and so did the comprehensive 1938 Fair Labor Standards Act.*

These laws laid the foundation for the labor system we have today, specifying, among other things: (a) that young people are prohibited from working in interstate commerce, (b) that you must be sixteen to work full-time, (c) that you must be eighteen to work in certain hazardous professions, (d) that you can't work while school is in session (in other words, school is more important than work), (e) that young people can't work without permits, and (f) that people from age fourteen to sixteen can work a very limited number of hours in some professions.[39]

The Role of Labor Unions

None of these changes would have been possible without the strong support of organized labor, which had compelling economic motives for opposing labor by young people. Industrialization created a new affluent middle class and an extremely wealthy upper class, but it did so at the expense of millions of exploited laborers. It also pushed aside the centuries-old apprentice system that had allowed generations of young people to transition smoothly from childhood to adulthood.

In many of the new factories, with machines doing much of the work, almost any kind of laborer would do, and the cheaper the labor the better. The availability of youth workers, immigrants, and women drove the wages of skilled workers ever downward and left many adult males unemployed. As labor union pioneer Samuel Gompers put it, "the introduction of machinery, the subdivision of labor, the use of women's and children's labor and the lack of an apprentice system" drove the skilled trades

---

*The 1938 Fair Labor Standards Act, which is still in force today, was also challenged in court, but this time it held. In 1941, in U.S. v. Darby, the Supreme Court reversed its opinion in Hammer v. Dagenhart.

"to the level of pauper labor."[40] In some cases young people—working for very low wages—were given jobs in factories where their own fathers had been laid off.[41]

It was inevitable that as workers organized themselves into unions in order to protect their jobs and improve their wages and working conditions, they vehemently fought all forms of youth labor. Organized labor was, according to historians, both "the head as well as the body" of the movement to prohibit young people from working.[42] As early as the 1830s groups such as the New England Workingmen's Association and the General Trades Union were agitating to put appropriate laws in place. In its very first platform in 1881 the newly-formed Federation of Trade and Labor Unions of the United States and Canada—forerunner of Samuel Gompers' American Federation of Labor (eventually the AFL-CIO)—made the youth labor issue a high priority: "We are in favor of the passage of laws in the several states forbidding the employment of children under fourteen in any capacity, under penalty of fine and imprisonment."[43]

Between 1881 and 1905 there were thirty-seven thousand strikes in the United States involving over seven million workers; many were violent.[44] Workers were, understandably, determined to get a fair share of the obscene wealth of the new industrialists, and the youth issue remained central.

With child labor laws facing strong opposition (mainly from manufacturers, but also from young people and families who needed the income), in 1897 the AFL became the first organization in the United States to push for a constitutional amendment prohibiting all forms of youth labor, a concept, as I mentioned earlier, that finally got the support of Congress in 1924.[45] In the early years of the new century the AFL was also a major force behind new laws raising the minimum working age to sixteen or higher.

The First Child Labor Laws

Curiously, some of the first child labor laws ever enacted weren't meant to *limit* child but rather to *encourage* it. In the 1690s the eminent British philosopher John Locke advised English authorities to set up "working schools" in every parish that would prepare children age three and over to work in the largely home-based spinning and weaving industries.[46] Leaders of this era were intent on keeping young people busy—especially the children of the poor. According to Hugh Cunningham, "Potentially industrialisation offered a solution to a problem which had long irked the elite of Europe: the idleness of children"—and idle hands, as the saying goes, are the Devil's tools.[47] Combine such thinking with the intense Puritan work ethic, and it shouldn't surprise you that some of America's first child labor laws were polar opposites of twentieth-century laws.

YOUNG PEOPLE IN ACTION

Reigning King at Sixteen

Sometimes when young rulers are crowned, older stand-ins do the real decision making. But according to the "Book of Chronicles", Uzziah, the tenth king of Judah, actually began to rule at age sixteen, and his leadership in Jerusalem was successful for fifty-two years. He built and fortified towers, fought off the Philistines, raised bountiful crops, and prepared great weapons for war.

In a 1908 essay on child labor, reformer Edith Abbott said that early American policy makers were obsessed with the issue of "idleness among children" throughout the seventeenth and eighteenth centuries.[48] In 1640, for example, the "Great and Generall Court" of Massachusetts "required the magistrates of the several towns to see 'what course may be taken for teaching the boys and girles in all towns the spinning of the yarne.'" The following year the same authority directed "all masters of families [to] see that their children and servants should be industriously implied so as the mornings and evenings and other seasons may not bee lost as formerly they have been."[49]

In 1672 the Town of Boston directed a list of people to "dispose of their severall children... abroad for servants"; if not, "the selectman will take their said children from them and place them with such masters as they shall provide accordinage as the law directs." The children, said Abbott, were as young as eight. Connecticut, Rhode Island, and other American colonies had similar laws. Children who were idle or who loitered were routinely "bound out"—indentured outside their homes.[50]

Policy makers in Colonial America would have been appalled by the revised definition of "child labor laws" that emerged in the late 1800s. In Colonial America, child labor was a *good* thing. (This would presumably be a problem for continuist historians.)

Forcing School Attendance

The trend in labor laws is shadowed by a similar trend in education laws; as I mentioned earlier, sometimes the same law even covered both areas. The idea is simple enough: we don't want young people to work, even if they want to work and have opportunities to work without being exploited; we want them to attend school, even if they don't want to attend school and aren't ready to learn.

The first education laws in the United States were enacted in Massachusetts, which stayed well ahead of the curve for more than two centuries. Colonial Massachusetts established the first public school in America, the Boston Latin School, in

1635, barely fifteen years after the Pilgrims landed at Plymouth Rock. In 1642 the Massachusetts Bay School Law was enacted, requiring parents to provide a modest education for children and servants (but not necessarily in school).

By 1827 Massachusetts had established the nation's first state-wide, tax-supported public school system, but the big shift came in 1852 when Massachusetts made school attendance compulsory for all children—requiring young people between eight and fourteen to attend school at least three months a year—unless, that is, the individual could demonstrate that he or she had already learned the relevant material. In other words, this law was *competency based*: you were exempt if you could demonstrate competence.

The rest of the nation was unimpressed; not a single state followed Massachusetts' lead for another fifteen years. Beginning in 1867, compulsory education laws began to spread, but it wasn't until 1918—56 years after Massachusetts took the lead—that all states finally had such laws.[51] The impact of the early laws was minimal, perhaps increasing actual school attendance by only 5 percent.[52]

It's no coincidence that the compulsory education laws emerged more-or-less in parallel with the laws restricting labor by young people. (See Figure 2.2.) As we'll see, some of the same people were driving both efforts, and both efforts were propelled in part by the underlying belief—new in human history—that young people are helpless and incompetent.

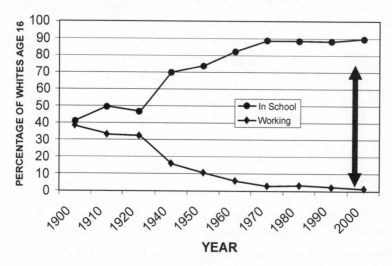

Figure 2.2. School vs. Work. U.S. Census data show the dramatic shift from school to work that occurred for teens during the twentieth century. The problem with the all-school-no-work gap (right side of graph) is that it isolates teens completely from adults, trapping them in a peer culture that has very little in common with the real world they are about to enter. *Source*: Data adapted from Fussell and Furstenberg, 2005.

The compulsory education movement was also driven by other concerns of the day: with America's immigrant population swelling daily (there were almost nine million immigrants during the first decade of the twentieth century alone), some felt that compulsory education was the best way to "Americanize" the rapidly changing population. Other reformers felt that compulsory education was the best way to try to reduce the widening gap between the new industrial rich and the hoards of poor who were toiling in the factories. As we'll see, the industrialists themselves sometimes supported compulsory education as a way of producing skilled workers—and as a way of keeping the masses in check.

Finally, with Germany's expansionist policies driving the world toward its first world war, American policy makers took serious note of the fact that Germany (or at least Prussia, a part of modern Germany) had had a compulsory education system in place since 1717.[53] (In contrast, England didn't require every community to have a school until 1870 and didn't make attendance mandatory until 1880.[54]) To compete with the Germans, many felt that we needed to emulate their educational practices, which could explain why the last states to make education compulsory did so in 1918—the last year of World War I. We saw a similar shift in education policy in the 1950s, when America was galvanized by a new threat: the Soviets' launch of the Sputnik satellite.

The End of the Debate

Not everyone was on the compulsory education bandwagon, however. Some felt that government interference in education was a violation of individual rights and the sovereignty of the family. In the 1890s Pennsylvania's governor, expressing such concerns, vetoed two compulsory education bills that had been sent to him by the state legislature. Even more significant, in 1892 the Democratic Party stated as part of its national platform: "We are opposed to state interference with parental rights and rights of conscience in the education of children." [55]

Early compulsory education laws required relatively little class time, but the requirements have grown over the years. According to the Home School Legal Defense Association:

> By the early 1920s... all meaningful debate over the virtue of compulsory attendance had ceased. The discussions that continued centered on how compulsory attendance should be enforced, and for how long. The minimum age for compulsory attendance was forced steadily lower. Early compulsory attendance laws generally did not require attendance until a child turned eight, and in Ohio and South Dakota, attendance was not required until age ten.... [The] number of states requiring six-year-olds to attend school has risen dramatically, and today, twenty-eight states require attendance of six-

year-olds.... During the same period [the late 1800s until today], the number of states requiring attendance until age eighteen grew steadily. In 1887, only Washington state required attendance to age eighteen. Today, fourteen states do. The average length of the school term was also growing. From 1887 until today, the average school term swelled from 130 to 180 days. [56]

As you may recall from Chapter One, some educators today are talking seriously about expanding the school day, expanding the school year, or even adding two more years to high school.

The Age of Majority

We all know that people under eighteen are "minors," and we tend to accept this designation as if it existed through all eternity. Not so. The age of majority was actually lowered in the United States not long ago, and young people have many rights long before they reach this magical and entirely arbitrary age.

What does majority actually mean? Basically, it's the age at which a young person is granted the balance of civil rights which he or she doesn't already have; majority marks "full" adulthood in the sense that there may be no right left for a culture to confer (although there are exceptions to this rule). In our culture, the civil rights that are usually withheld until the age of majority are:

- The right to enlist in the military without the consent of a parent
- The right to inherit property
- The right to vote
- The right to refuse or consent to medical treatment
- The right to sign contracts
- The right to buy and sell property (including stock)
- The right to marry without parental consent
- The right to file law suits
- The right to make or revoke a will

Minors already have a great many rights, but they can do nothing on the above list, generally speaking. What's more, almost any right can be conferred at ages other than the age of majority. Many states issue drivers licenses to sixteen-year-olds, for example, or prohibit people from buying alcohol until age twenty-one. Most of the specific rights of majority are determined state by state.

Majority is an old concept, with precursors in the Bible, according to which twenty (not thirteen or eighteen or twenty-one) was the magical age at which a few

final rights were granted (see Chapter Twelve). In ancient Rome *pubertas*—generally reached at fourteen for males and twelve for females—marked the age at which most majority rights were achieved, including the right to make contracts, own property, make wills, and enter into marriage. [57]

Even though until recent times young people were integrated into adult society soon after puberty, a few rights were typically withheld until an arbitrary age or until young people got married, whichever came first. Until the Industrial Era the list of rights that were withheld was typically fairly short. For example, in the 1640s the Massachusetts Generall Court specified "twenty and one years" as the age for "passing away of lands" (bequeathing property in a will) and for "giving of votes, verdicts or sentences in any civil courts or causes." [58] Since no other rights were mentioned, it's likely that few other rights had previously been withheld.*

Presumably, restrictions of this sort were imposed because the ruling elders of the time believed that certain actions—making out a will, for example—couldn't be performed properly until one had accumulated a great deal of knowledge and experience. In some cases majority rules also helped to protect property rights and the political status quo. It's only in recent times, however, that we've imposed significant and wide-ranging minority restrictions.

New Crimes by the Dozen

Compulsory education laws and laws restricting labor by young people were new, but the Industrial Era also gave rise to dozens of laws of truly unique character: They singled out behavior that had never been subject to laws or regulations before, sometimes driven by new technologies (like the automobile) and sometimes driven by moral concerns. Here is a sampling of the kinds of laws that were emerging in the late 1800s and beyond:

Singing, Smoking and More. In Indiana in 1889 people under eighteen were prohibited from singing, playing a musical instrument, or begging on the streets; those eighteen and over could engage in these activities freely. Females under twelve were prohibited from working as prostitutes, and young people under twelve were prohibited from walking on ropes or wires or performing as acrobats. Although the United States Surgeon General didn't condemn cigarette smoking until 1964, reformers in the late 1800s, increasingly concerned about the "fragility" of youth, lobbied hard to ban the sale of cigarettes to young people. (Women, after all—also considered frail—were strongly discouraged from smoking in public until well into the 1900s.) By 1890 twenty-one states and territories had such bans

---

*The same passage grants the right of "chusing of Guardions" to fourteen-year-olds.

in place, usually for people under sixteen. [59] Laws were also passed to discourage teen sexuality.

Drinking Alcohol. On December 18, 1917, under pressure from the Anti-Saloon League and other temperance groups, Congress passed the Eighteenth Amendment to the Constitution, prohibiting "the manufacture, sale, or transportation" of alcoholic beverages throughout the United States. It was ratified by the states in just over a year, on January 16, 1919. The resulting laws didn't stop people from drinking, of course, just as today's marijuana laws don't stop people from smoking marijuana. [60] The main effect of Prohibition was to drive alcohol manufacture, sales, and consumption underground, putting much of the industry into the hands of organized crime. [61]

The curious thing is that before Prohibition, young people were often free to drink—or at least as free as adults were. In many states, young children equipped merely with a note from a parent could even purchase alcohol. [62] Widespread bans on teen drinking only began when Prohibition ended. When the eighteenth amendment was repealed in 1933, most states retained bans on drinking by young people, often setting the minimum drinking age at twenty-one. [63] In other words, we shifted from being a society where *everyone* could drink (except in states that had already banned alcohol in the years just prior to Prohibition), to one where *no one* could drink, to one where *everyone but young people* could drink. By 1933, with all young people forced to attend school and many forced out of the job market, the idea that all young people were incompetent was firmly embedded in American consciousness.

Driving. The first restrictions on driving in California were enacted in 1913. ("Horseless buggies" had been around for more than twenty years at this point, and more than six thousand motor vehicles were registered in California in 1905 alone.) Under the new law, drivers were supposed to be at least sixteen, but no license or examination was required for people to drive. [64] It wasn't until about 1940 that most states had laws in place similar to those in effect today, requiring drivers to be at least sixteen and to take some sort of driving test. [65]

"Incorrigible" Behavior. Many of the new laws were especially intrusive, focusing on youthful activities that had either been long ignored or handled quietly or informally, usually within extended families. Illinois was especially aggressive. In 1879, for example, the legislature passed the Industrial School for Girls Bill, which allowed authorities to commit minor females to state "industrial schools" (a variation on the reformatory) until eighteen if they "frequented any street," lacked "proper parental care," "consort[ed] with reputed thieves or other vicious persons," or were found in

> ## YOUNG PEOPLE IN ACTION
>
> ### Jimmy Carter on Driving:
>
> *"Drivers licenses were not required in Georgia until 1940, and many of us young farm boys were competent truck drivers, because our fathers needed us to deliver fertilizer and seed to the fields and to run other errands.... [My] father began to let me use his pickup on special occasions when I was twelve years old, as long as I went directly to the prom party and then straight back. Later, at the ripe old age of fifteen or so, I would just get his comment, 'Drive safe'."*[66]

a "house of ill-fame."[67] A similar bill was passed for young males in 1883, allowing the state to commit them to industrial schools until they turned twenty-one.[68] Illinois also passed laws prohibiting young people from going to movies or dance halls, fighting, staying out past a certain hour, and behaving "incorrigibly."[69]

Note that virtually all of these newly defined crimes had no victims. They were, if anything, "crimes against oneself"—at least from the perspective of the authorities. What's more, most of these indiscretions were typical of the working class and poor, which raises questions about the motives of the some of the leaders who fought for such laws.

The Turbulent Sixties

As for the acceleration of restrictions that began in the 1960s, I'm old enough to remember what happened. The times, as Bob Dylan put it, they were a'changin'.

In the 1950s, young Americans were fairly docile, but over the course of the 1960s, many went wild. Marijuana, LSD, and other drugs became commonplace in high schools and colleges; the advent of the birth control pill spawned the "free love" movement; the rising death toll in Vietnam (ultimately, over 50,000) led to a massive protest movement; court decisions and legislation regarding civil rights led to race riots, often spearheaded by teens; the national crime rate jumped 110 percent during the 1960s and an additional 48 percent during the 1970s.[70] The United States was, in some respects, a battlefield, and young people almost always seemed to be on the front lines.

To those in power it appeared that young people were out of control. It's also possible, of course, that instability in society was simply allowing young people to reestablish themselves as young adults—as thoughtful, potentially valuable members of society. But by the 1960s few adults in America could conceive of teens as anything but incompetent, troublesome children. The natural, sadly predictable response

was to put stronger controls in place. After all, if your toddler keeps opening your front gate and running into the street, you build a tougher gate and put a lock on it.

Laws passed in recent decades which restrict young people include, among many others:

- *New curfew laws.* In what an ACLU lawyer dubbed a "curfew fever" in a 1994 article,[71] cities around the country have passed a variety of strict curfew laws in recent years, ostensibly to reduce crime, although no evidence exists to support the claim that curfews have that effect.[72] For example, an appeals court recently upheld a Dallas ordinance prohibiting minors from being in public areas from midnight to 6 A.M. on weekends and from 11 P.M. to 6 A.M. on weekdays.[73] In Massachusetts it's illegal for anyone under eighteen to be driving on public roads late at night unless accompanied by a parent or guardian.[74]

- *Tougher driving laws.* Until a few years ago, most states issued unrestricted drivers licenses to teens who could pass a test at age sixteen. Now many states have established "graduated" systems for issuing licenses. At first, a teen may be able to drive only with a supervising adult family member; at some point, the teen may be able to drive only with certain passengers in the car; at a higher stage, the teen may be able to drive alone but only during certain hours. In New York, for example, full driving privileges aren't attained until age eighteen, no matter what one's level of competence.[75]

- *Laws restricting teen wages.* Although minors are protected by the 1963 federal Equal Pay Act, which requires that males and females get equal pay for equal work, under amendments to the Fair Labor Standards Act working minors are often exempt from the minimum wage requirement. Depending on the job, minors have to make do with between 75 and 85 percent of the minimum wage, and even eighteen- and nineteen-year-olds may be subject to a reduced minimum wage "during their first ninety consecutive calendar days of employment."[76] These minimum wage exemptions are yet another result of union efforts to keep young people out of the job market.

- *Laws preventing young people from entering "places of amusement."* In 1983, for example, a court upheld a Dacono, Colorado law that prohibited people under sixteen from entering arcades during school hours unless accompanied by an adult.[77] In 1981 a court

upheld a far more restrictive law in Des Plaines, Illinois, that required that video games can be placed only in "licensed liquor establishments" and that people had to be at least twenty-one to play them unless accompanied by an adult.[78] Similar laws in some states prohibit minors from entering pool halls, dance halls, and other places of iniquity; in 1989 in the case of *City of Dallas v. Stanglin*, the Supreme Court upheld the validity of such laws, asserting that authorities have a legitimate right to protect teens from the "corrupting influence of older teenagers and young adults."[79]

- *New laws curtailing potentially erotic activities.* In 1989, for example, an appeals court upheld the validity of a new rule prohibiting dances in all schools in a school district in Missouri.[80] In 1968 in the case of *Ginsberg v. New York* the Supreme Court upheld a New York statute prohibiting the sale of obscene material to people under seventeen based on the "appeal" of such materials to minors; in other words, the statute encompassed material that would not necessarily be considered obscene to adults and thus established a *new and separate obscenity standard* for minors. Justice Stewart justified the ruling by suggesting that "a child is not possessed of that full capacity for individual choice which is the presumption of first amendment guarantees."[81]

- *Restrictions on free speech at school.* In 1988 the Supreme Court ruled that the freedom of the press guaranteed by the First Amendment does *not* apply to school newspapers.[82] Presumably, eminent writers such as Edgar Allan Poe ("The Pit and the Pendulum"), Mary Shelley (*Frankenstein*), and S. E. Hinton (*The Outsiders*)—all of whom wrote disturbing works in their teens—would have been prohibited under current laws from sharing their work with their peers. At this writing the California Supreme Court is about to hear the case of "George T.," who, at fifteen, was expelled from the Santa Teresa High School in San Jose in 2001 for writing a poem that contained the lines, "For I can be the next kid to bring guns to kill students at school.... / For I am Dark, Destructive & Dangerous." George wasn't just expelled; he was sentenced to one hundred days in a state reformatory.[83] The latest trend: prohibiting students from bringing cell phones to school, because they're used "to cheat, take inappropriate photos in bathrooms and organize gang rendezvous." Students are still sneaking the phones into school,

however—in some cases to mollify parents who insist on calling them frequently to check up on them.[84]

- *Laws restricting access to the Internet, movies, and more.* The movie rating system, first established in 1968 and revised substantially in 1990, prevents people under seventeen from seeing R-rated films unless accompanied by a parent or guardian. Minors can't see NC-17 (formerly "X") movies at all[85]—unless, of course, they know even the minimum about how to use the Internet. Libraries and schools nationwide now block access to Internet material that authorities believe might be harmful to minors. Internet usage on school computers is strictly regulated, and some teens have been suspended, expelled, or prosecuted for setting up websites on their home computers that school officials find objectionable.[86] Efforts in the 1980s by Tipper Gore, wife of former vice president Al Gore, to get legislators to prevent teens from purchasing violent or profane audio tapes or CDs were not successful, but they did lead to a rating system. Music that contains profanities, for example, now bears the mark "Parental Advisory—Explicit Content."[87]

- *New laws curtailing sexual activity.* Numerous court decisions over the past few decades have upheld new state laws prohibiting sexual activity by minors or sexual activity between minors and adults. In some states, like California, there is no "age of consent," which means that no one eighteen or over can have sex legally with anyone under eighteen. In other words, an eighteen-year-old high school senior can be prosecuted for having sex with his or her seventeen-year-old boyfriend or girlfriend. On the other hand, it's also *legal* in California for two thirteen-year-olds to have sex with each other. The details are complicated, surprising, and ever-changing (see Chapter Eight).

- *New laws curtailing a young woman's right to an abortion.* Various states have passed tough laws in recent decades requiring young pregnant women to get the consent of one or both parents before getting an abortion. In several rulings beginning in the late 1970s the U. S. Supreme Court has generally upheld these laws, as long as they allow for a court to bypass the required parental consent.[88] See Chapter Seven for further details.

- *Censorship of educational materials.* Propelled by concerns about political correctness, school districts nationwide have censored reading

materials, sometimes taking the knife to timeless masterpieces. In 1989 an appeals court upheld a Florida high school's decision to delete portions of Aristophanes' *Lysistrata* and Chaucer's *The Miller's Tale*.[89]

- *Dress codes.* Public schools nationwide have exercised tighter control over the way students dress—sometimes requiring uniforms, sometimes prohibiting earrings or gang emblems, and so on. The courts have generally upheld the right of schools to restrict school dress, because school officials are often considered to be substitute parents.[90]

- *New laws governing changes in appearance.* Most states have now enacted laws restricting a young person's right to get a piercing or tattoo, or even to enter a tanning salon.[91] Such laws sometimes lead teens to get their piercings done by their peers (greatly increasing the risk of infection), to get tattooed illegally, or to slather on the tanning oil (much riskier than getting tanned at a salon).

- *Laws restricting participation in lottery.* In 1986 an appeals court upheld the validity of a new Massachusetts law that made it illegal for minors to purchase state lottery tickets.[92]

- *Tougher smoking laws.* In Chapter One I mentioned proposed legislation in California that would ban cigarette sales to people under twenty-one. Many cities nationwide have now banned cigarette sales to minors through vending machines, and the 1992 Public Health Service Act (the Synar Amendment) makes it illegal to sell or distribute tobacco products to people under eighteen,[93] with a subsequent federal law requiring retailers to verify the age of anyone who appears to be twenty-six or under. But according to the Department of Health and Human Services, "Despite laws in all fifty states that prohibit sales to minors, numerous studies show that adolescents have little difficulty purchasing tobacco products."[94]

- *Tougher, more uniform drinking laws.* In the early 1970s many states lowered the minimum age for alcohol consumption to eighteen, but the trend was short-lived.[96] In 1984, through the National Minimum Drinking Age Act, the federal government threatened to withhold highway construction funds from states that failed to raise the minimum drinking age to twenty-one. The minimum age had previously varied from state to state (with about thirty states setting the minimum at eighteen), but by 1998 all states complied with the new mandate.[97] In the late 1980s Wisconsin made it illegal for one minor to furnish alcoholic beverages to

> ### YOUNG PEOPLE IN ACTION
> #### Hero or Drug Dealer?
>
> On April 22, 1998, thirteen-year-old Brandy Dyer had an asthma
> attack on her school bus. Responding to pleas for help from the bus driver,
> sixth-grader Christine Rhodes, age twelve, came to the rescue with her
> prescription inhaler. To Brandy's parents, Christine was a hero, but to
> school authorities at the Mount Airy Middle School in Mount Airy,
> Maryland, Christine was illegally distributing drugs—a serious matter
> that would remain on school records for three years.[95]

another minor.[98] In 1991 in North Carolina, it became illegal to serve
liquor to a minor in one's home.[99] A new law in Naperville, Illinois
has even made it illegal for minors to attend parties at which minors
are drinking illegally—even if they themselves aren't drinking.[100]

- *Involuntary commitment by parents or the courts.* This is a complicated area, but because minors generally can't make their own decisions about medical or psychiatric care, the courts have generally found
that parents or physicians (or the courts themselves) can commit teens
to psychiatric or other types of institutions against their will. With
teens getting harder to handle, parents are resorting to this option with
increasing frequency; according to one source, the rate of commitment
of minors in the United States "tripled or even quadrupled" between
1980 and 1998.[101] A 1998 book by Gary B. Melton, Phillip M. Lyons,
and Willis J. Spaulding documents another disturbing trend in the
institutionalization of minors: the recent interlocking of the juvenile
justice, child welfare, and mental health systems, which has resulted in
the "unplanned" incarceration of minors for long periods. The systems, say the authors, are "substantially interchangeable," and individuals often "bounce from one system to another for treatment."[102]
The logic is that if one system isn't working, perhaps another one
will—or at least that it will relieve the current system of the burden of
care. Some of the "transinstitutionalization" that is now taking place
has been made possible by the 1974 federal Juvenile Justice and Delinquency Prevention Act. Although one goal of the act was to remove
some minors from the juvenile justice system, in fact offenders are
often simply "relabeled as emotionally disturbed and placed in
mental hospitals."[103] Once an individual is placed in such a

facility—especially a "private, third-party" institution being supported with public funds—administrators have no incentive to release him or her. If you let the client go, the money stops flowing.

- *Hospitalization initiated by schools.* Another well-intentioned law, the 1997 federal Individuals with Disabilities Education Act (IDEA), has also led to the involuntary institutionalization of teens. The act guarantees a "free public education" to people with "unique needs." This sounds good, but according to Melton, Lyons, and Spaulding, the IDEA has become "a funding mechanism for psychiatric hospitalization."[104] Some courts, they say, have held that because the act is so broad, it requires schools to pay for "hospitalization or other therapeutic residential placement" when the schools themselves can't provide appropriate education for students with special needs.[105] Though the costs are burdensome and sometimes prohibitive, some schools are only too willing to get such students out of their hallways.

- *Involuntary electroshock therapy.* Electroshock therapy, also known as ECT ("electro-convulsive therapy") was invented in 1939, and since that time its use with minors has become more common. According to a recent book by psychologist Steve Baldwin and ECT researcher Melissa Oxlad, "with minors, use of ECT escalated during the 1970s."[106] Because minors can't make decisions about their own medical treatment, "explicit consent has rarely been obtained" from them.[107] Baldwin and Oxlad complain of a "chronic under reporting of this form of treatment with minors," but they believe that between 500 and 3,500 minors are treated with ECT each year in the United States—in many cases for "delinquency," "aggressiveness," or other tendencies that wouldn't normally be considered signs of mental illness.[108] But the real tragedy here is that, according to the authors, "there is no scientific evidence to support the use of shock with minors."[109] They argue—persuasively, I believe—that the objections psychiatrists raise to the abandonment of ECT with minors are based on their desire to maintain their "clinical freedoms," as well as "economic concerns about 'restraint of trade.'"[110]

- *Heightened security levels at schools.* The school shootings of the late 1990s added those larger locks I talked about earlier: metal detectors, locker inspections, drug testing, video monitoring, and armed guards at schools around the country. The federal Gun-Free Schools

Act of 1994 set in motion "zero-tolerance" policies at schools nationwide and gave administrators broad powers to suspend or expel students over virtually any infraction that was even remotely weapons related. An Oakland, California high school now monitors student behavior continuously with more than fifty video cameras; at last report, eight advanced "Pelco Spectra II" cameras (with a 360-degree field of view) were on order.[111] In 2001, in central Florida, National Merit Scholar Lindsay Brown was arrested, suspended, and denied the opportunity to graduate with her high school class because an astute security guard noticed a "kitchen knife" in the back seat of her car while it was parked on school property.[112] In 2002, in Martinez, California, thirteen-year-old Jeffrey Figueroa was sentenced to juvenile hall for hitting another student in the eye with a spitball, and both he and his parents were ordered to attend anger management classes.[113] And in 2001 in Jonesboro, Arkansas (where four students and a teacher had been killed by students in 1998)—and, yes, this really happened—a first-grader was suspended from school for pointing a breaded chicken finger at a teacher and saying "Pow, pow, pow."[114] The heightened security at our schools has made many of them more prison-like than ever before—reminiscent of the industrial schools established in Illinois in the late 1800s.

- *Tougher criminal justice laws.* Reacting (and sometimes overreacting) to headlines about teen crime and school shootings, some states have made it easier to shift cases from the juvenile court system to the adult criminal justice system. Proposition 21, for example, passed in California in March 2000, allows prosecutors to bypass judges in deciding to prosecute minors as adults.

A Vicious Cycle

Sometimes new laws and other restrictions don't work, in the sense that young people or authorities simply ignore them. But of greater concern is the possibility that the restrictions help perpetuate a vicious cycle of action and reaction: Our teens act out in some way (by showing disrespect, breaking an existing law, or wandering into some new area of danger, such as the Internet or the video arcade), and we respond with new or tougher laws, which in turn cause teens to act out even more. (See Figure 2.3.)

As you'll see throughout this book (and especially in Chapter Five)—and as you can see quite easily simply by looking around you—teens often react negatively when

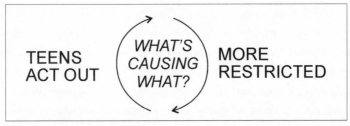

Figure 2.3. The Proverbial Vicious Cycle. As teens become more unmanageable, society further restricts their behavior, which in turn causes some teens to act out in more extreme ways.

they're treated like children—sometimes with strong words and sometimes in more extreme ways. Unfortunately, as blacks and women can attest, authorities don't listen very carefully to people they consider to be incompetent or "incorrigible."

Restrictions Coming Soon

Many new laws are in the offing, and you can guess the direction. As I was writing this section, I glimpsed the following headline in the morning paper: "Bill Would Bar Teenagers From Tanning Salons." California assemblyman Joe Nation doesn't want teens entering tanning parlors without a physician's prescription.[115] Nation's bill was prompted by his own struggle with skin cancer, even though his cancer wasn't produced by tanning salons.[116]

Also in the news: the California State Senate has just passed legislation that will make it illegal for people under eighteen to use cell phones while driving, even with a headset.[117] The logic—based on no actual data—is that teens are more easily distractible than adults. In reality, our perceptual powers and reaction times are at their peak in our early and mid teens (see Chapter Seven). And the United States Senate is now considering legislation that would prohibit anyone from transporting a minor over state lines for the purpose of having an abortion without her parents' knowledge or consent.[118]

On the youth labor front, some lawmakers are now trying to implement the recommendations of a report by the Board on Children, Youth, and Families (an advisory group established by the Institute of Medicine and the National Research Council), which expressed concern about the poor education our high school students are getting. The report recommended prohibiting sixteen- and seventeen-year-old students from working more than 20 hours per week because "low-intensity employment may support post-secondary outcomes while higher-intensity employment may hinder them."[119] In other words, even if they'd rather work than learn, young people might learn more if we prevent them from working. *Maybe.* But perhaps they'll just get angrier and more frustrated because they have fewer options and less money. (See Appendix 5 for other restrictions.)

YOUNG PEOPLE IN ACTION

Worm Business Buried

During the summers when he was eleven and twelve, Joey Cadieux of Cromwell, Connecticut, made a few extra dollars each month selling nightcrawlers to fishermen. He'd prowl around his yard on rainy nights with a flashlight, find the worms, then store his inventory in his basement in a wooden box full of dirt.

But thirteen proved to be an unlucky age for Joey. When a member of the town's Planning and Zoning commission saw the hand-lettered "NITE CRAWLERS" sign in front of Joey's house, he brought the matter before the commission, which ordered Joey's dad to remove the sign and stop the sales. To plead his case before the commission, Joey or his dad would have to pay a $130 filing fee—far more than Joey earns on the business in a summer.

Complaints to the board have elicited some regrets—but not to a lifting of the ban. Town Planner Craig Minor promises to argue on Joey's behalf if the matter is appealed. Minor likens the business to a "farm stand," which is unregulated.

Meanwhile, at this writing, the summer is over, and the inventory is still wriggling in the basement.[120]

We're also attempting to spread the restrictions we have on youth labor to countries around the world, in part by providing financial support ($45 million in 2003) to ILO-IPEC—the International Program on the Elimination of Child Labor, sponsored by the International Labor Organization.[121] As you'll see in Chapter Three, the outcomes of such interventions are sometimes disastrous.

ORIGINS OF THE CHILD-CENTERED FAMILY

As a child I often heard the Yiddish expression "*Alles für die kinder*" ("Everything for the children")—mainly from one of my grandfathers, who probably learned it when he was growing up around the turn of the twentieth century. He always said it with a tired sigh, as if the very idea were exhausting.

American radio guru Laura Schlessinger chides listeners with similar advice over the airwaves daily. She identifies herself as "my child's mom" and routinely advises working moms to quit their jobs and stay home with the children. The message is the same one I heard from my grandfather: children should be the center of the family. Their needs come first. Everything for the kids.

WISDOM OF THE AGES

Goethe on Parenting

"Too many parents make life hard for their children by trying, too zealously, to make it easy for them."

–Johann Wolfgang von Goethe

My own mother believes in this idea, but I've always detected my grandfather's sigh in her attitude; for one thing, since I was young she's had a sign on her refrigerator reading, "Insanity is inherited; you get it from your children." There's a price to be paid, it seems, for putting children on pedestals.

Child-centered thinking is now firmly entrenched in American culture, however exhausting it might be. Where did it come from?

The Child as Animal

Which do you think came first: laws against cruelty to children or laws against cruelty to animals? Given today's thinking, the logical answer would be "children," but that isn't so. Parental authority was considered so absolute during most of human history that no state authority would dare to interfere with it; children were indeed little more than family "chattel," as Donald T. Kramer told us.

Government reached out to help defenseless animals long before it worried about children. The first law to protect animals was passed by the British Parliament in 1822, and two years later the (British) Society for the Prevention of Cruelty to Animals was formed. The American version—the "ASPCA"—didn't appear until 1866, and the first legislation protecting animals in the United States was passed that same year. The New York branch of the ASPCA—the NYSPCA—run by its founder Henry Bergh, proved to be the catalyst that finally put children on the legal map.[122]

"Mary Ellen" was a twelve-year-old girl who was beaten daily by her foster parents. In 1874 Mrs. Charles Wheeler, a church employee, took it upon herself to rescue poor Mary Ellen, but the authorities were uncooperative. There were simply no laws on the books that prevented such abuse. As a last resort, Wheeler approached the NYSPCA for help. Bergh took the case, ultimately arguing before the United States Supreme Court that Mary Ellen deserved protection as a "human animal." Remarkably, in an 1875 decision the court ruled in his favor, and Mary Ellen was saved.[123]

This landmark ruling laid the foundation for the modern child protection movement. That same year saw the founding of the New York Society for the Prevention of Cruelty to Children—the first society of its kind in the world. Two simi-

lar organizations were founded in Massachusetts in 1877 and 1878, respectively. England finally caught up in 1884 with the founding of its National Society for the Prevention of Cruelty to Children.[124]

The United States Supreme Court had, in effect, decided that government has an interest in protecting *all* of its citizens—even little ones—and that this interest supersedes the interest that a parent has in raising his or her children. The state now had the right to remove children forcibly from abusive or neglectful parents, and that right has since been clarified and expanded in scores of laws and court decisions. Children not only need protection, they need the *state's* protection. This simple idea, which most people in the industrialized world take for granted today, barely existed in the human psyche until 1875, and it followed and was inspired by the state's interest in protecting animals.

Again, it's clear that the sentimental view of children is a fairly recent phenomenon in human history. Philippe Ariès may have been wrong in his assertion that childhood was "invented" in the 1800s, but it's undeniable that the status of children changed dramatically on the timetable Ariès specified.

Jane Addams, Mother of the World

When Jane Addams was barely three years old—sickly, homely, and very vulnerable—her mother died. Perhaps the loss of mother-love at a critical time in her young life led her to experience exaggerated feelings of motherhood—a sense that all of humankind needed to benefit from her nurturing instincts. She was also born with a spine so deformed that she was never able to have children. Whatever her motivations, she was an extraordinary individual, known during the early twentieth century as the "Mother of the World." When it comes to teens, however, I think her good intentions went awry.

Laura Jane Addams was born in Illinois in 1860, the daughter of a wealthy mill owner and state senator. She completed her undergraduate education at age twenty-one at the Rockford Female Seminary (in Illinois), a school with a strong missionary tradition. Her fifty-nine-year-old father died unexpectedly the same year, and soon after his death she had an emotional breakdown. She was subsequently diagnosed with "neurasthenia"—a condition we would probably label "major depression" today—from which she suffered for at least the next eight years. She spent most of those years traveling through Europe, where she was shaken by the suffering of the poor and homeless who crowded Europe's newly industrialized cities.[125] She later recalled her distress upon witnessing poor people bidding on rotten vegetables one night in London:

> *Their pale faces were dominated by that most unlovely of human expressions, the*
> *cunning and shrewdness of the bargain-hunter who starves if he cannot make a successful*
> *trade, and yet the final impression was not of ragged, tawdry clothing nor of pinched*
> *and sallow faces, but of myriads of hands, empty, pathetic, nerveless, and workworn,*
> *showing white in the uncertain light of the street, and clutching forward for food which*
> *was already unfit to eat.*[126]

On a subsequent trip to Europe she also visited London's Toynbee Hall, a "social settlement house" devoted to helping the poor and oppressed, and she was inspired by the kindness she witnessed there.[127] Her Quaker upbringing, seminary training, and travels on the Continent set her on a righteous path: to relieve the suffering of the poor, to bring education to the masses, to improve the lot of women and children and immigrants, and to bring peace to humankind. Perhaps it sounds like she bit off more than she could chew, but over her long and illustrious career Addams actually accomplished most of her goals.

Hull-House

In September 1889, Jane Addams and her friend Ellen Gates Starr opened Hull-House, a settlement house in Chicago's downtrodden Nineteenth Ward—the first of many such institutions in the United States. Its initial purpose was to improve the lot and the lives of its poor immigrant neighbors, but within four or five years the house's mission expanded enormously. Addams, the settlement's zealous and indefatigable director, soon realized that the many good deeds the house did for those in desperate need "could not but seem futile and superficial."[128] To have a significant impact on social welfare, one must, she concluded, move into the political realm.

Addams soon made Hull-House a center for clubs, classes, organizations, and political initiatives serving many causes and populations and bringing together some of the most capable and formidable women of her day. Bear in mind that the late 1800s produced some of America's first female college graduates and professionally trained women; the very cream of the crop ended up at Hull-House at one time or another. The impact of Hull-House on both American thinking and government policy was nothing short of amazing. Unless you are a history buff you may never have heard of Hull-House before, but it's likely that people or programs connected with it have affected you throughout your life.

Multiple Movements, One Building

The emergence of adolescence coincided with three other major upheavals

YOUNG PEOPLE IN ACTION

Wayward Women

Ruth Alexander, a history professor at Colorado State University and author of the book The "Girl Problem," *has taken a careful look at some of the young women who were committed to New York state reformatories in the early 1900s. Ella Waldstein was typical. At sixteen, she was "going around with a bad crowd of girls," and her conservative, working-class parents suspected her of getting involved with an older married man. After repeatedly ignoring her parents' directives to stay home in the evenings, they took her to juvenile court, where she was convicted of "willful disobedience" and committed to the New York State Reformatory for Women at Bedford Hills for the "standard" three-year sentence. The women in such facilities, says Alexander, were poor or working class, and most were seeking independence from their families or caretakers, sometimes because of abuse. "The only thing I wanted," said one of the young women she studied, "was freedom."[129]*

in American history: the Industrial Revolution (which ultimately spawned the child labor laws, the first significant one having been passed in 1848, as I noted earlier); the beginning of widespread compulsory education (the first compulsory attendance law was passed in 1852); and the women's rights movement (the first convention to promote women's rights was held in Seneca Falls, New York, in 1848). Three major movements were all set in motion in the blink of an eye.

This is no coincidence. With women finally beginning to get a voice in public policy making, it's no surprise that one of their traditional concerns—the protection of children—would find new outlets.[130] It's a bonus to find that all of these movements ended up under one roof for several decades. Consider this remarkable statement from the 1926 Congressional Record Report on Hull-House:

> *...practically all the radicalism started among women in the United States center about Hull House, Chicago, and the Children's Bureau, at Washington, with a dynasty of Hull House graduates in charge of it since its creation.[131]*

Also consider a comment by University of Chicago scholar Jean Bethke Elshtain in the introduction to *The Jane Addams Reader*:

> *Nearly every piece of major reform in the years 1895-1930 came with Jane Addams' name attached in one way or another, including labor and housing regulations,*

employment regulations for women and children, the eight-hour workday, old-age and unemployment insurance, as well as measures against prostitution, corrupt politicking, and vice for public officials, public playgrounds, and the creation of juvenile and domestic court systems.[132]

The Hull-House Legacy

Addams' reach was extraordinary. She either founded, helped to found, or was a major player in the American Civil Liberties Union (ACLU), the Juvenile Protective Association, the Immigrant's Protective League, the Campfire Girls, the National Child Labor Committee, the National Association for the Advancement of Colored People (NAACP), the National Consumer's League, the National Peace Congress, the Women's Peace Party, and at least a dozen other major organizations.[133] She and her colleagues were also behind major new legislation requiring school attendance and restricting youth labor, including the 1903 Illinois law I mentioned earlier. Addams also set in motion the world's first juvenile justice system (in Cook County, Illinois in 1899—more about this soon), was a major player in the women's suffrage movement (which finally secured the vote for American women in 1920), was influential in the creation of at least four labor unions (all founded on the premises of Hull-House), and was one of the world's most active and influential advocates for world peace. For her peace-making efforts Addams was awarded the Nobel Peace Prize in 1931, making her the first woman ever to have won this mother of all prizes.[134]

Hull-House also spawned the first Boy Scout troop in Chicago, the first public swimming pool in Chicago, the first public playground in Chicago, the first free art exhibits in Chicago, the first college extension courses in Chicago, the first public kitchen in Chicago, the nation's first model tenement code, and the nation's first citizen preparation classes—among many other innovative social programs.[135]

Addams gave formidable women from around the country a powerful platform from which to launch reforms. Influential Hull-House residents included, among many others:

- Alzina Stevens, who became the first probation officer in the world's first juvenile court and who also helped to create legislation in Illinois that shortened the work day for women and children.
- Julia Lathrop, who eventually became the first director of the federal Children's Bureau.
- Florence Kelley, who helped to create legislation to establish a minimum wage.

- Edith Abbott and Sophonisba Breckinridge, who were active in women's suffrage and who helped to create the nation's first university-based school of social work (at the University of Chicago).
- Grace Abbott (Edith's sister), the force behind the 1921 federal Sheppard-Towner Act, which became a model for later legislation providing welfare assistance for women and children.[136]

Not everyone was a fan, however. Industrialists branded Addams a socialist, the American Legion denounced her repeatedly, and the Daughters of the American Revolution called her "a factor in a movement to destroy civilization and Christianity."[137] She was, after all, a major threat to the status quo, and her staunch opposition to United States involvement in World War I appeared unpatriotic. But millions of others knew her as "Saint Jane," and she was indeed a sort of mother to the world.

Hull-House continued to function after Addams' death, but in a much lower key and with much shakier funding. Finally, in 1963, most of the Hull-House buildings were torn down to make room for a new campus of the University of Illinois. The original mansion has been retained as a museum.

I've taken us on this foray into Jane Addams' universe in order to try to personalize the artificial extension of childhood. Addams and others like her had strong convictions and powerful voices and connections. They had many agendas, and one was to protect children and teens. But not all of their motives were benign, and some of the programs they set in motion have had negative consequences. More important, some of Addams' allies in the movement to "save" young people had very different agendas than did Addams herself.

NEW FORMS OF SOCIAL CONTROL

In 1969 Anthony M. Platt, a long-time professor of social work at California State University Sacramento, published a provocative little book—*The Child Savers: The Invention of Delinquency*—which questioned the motives of Addams and some of her associates.* Were the efforts of the child savers—Felix Adler, Henry Bergh, and the legions of determined women at Hull-House—entirely benevolent? Definitely not, says Platt.

---

*The book was published, to its credit, by The University of Chicago Press. The University of Chicago was founded just a few years after Hull-House and became the faculty home of many of Hull-House's most distinguished residents. A second edition of Platt's book appeared in 1977, also under the imprint of The University of Chicago.

Virtually all of the leaders in this movement were members of the new middle class, or, in the case of Addams, Breckinridge, Kelley, and many others at Hull-House, the wealthy upper class. Addams' father, says Platt, "was one of the richest men in northern Illinois and her brother, Harry Haldeman, was a socialite from Baltimore who later amassed a large fortune in Kansas City."[138] Addams never received a salary from Hull-House because she didn't *need* one. Platt argues that many of these reformers weren't really protecting young people but rather were "devising new forms of social control to protect their power and prestige."[139] They were protecting *themselves*, he says, not the people they appeared to serve.

Platt is especially skeptical about the new juvenile justice system and, to some extent, the promotion of compulsory education and the child labor laws. Here are three of the major ideas he developed in his book:

Platt on the Child Labor Laws

Progressivism—the political movement that encompassed many of the social reforms of the day—was "predominantly a businessman's movement," says Platt. Child labor legislation was often propelled by big business, because "upper-class industrialists... did not depend on cheap child labor for their manufacturing operations." He cites historian Jeremy Felt's history of child labor reform in New York, which shows that "the abolition of child labor could be viewed as a means of driving out marginal manufacturer and tenement operators."[140]

Prohibit child labor, said Felt, and you destroy the weak competition. The same strategy is being used today in the struggle between corporate giants like Wal-Mart and Kmart: show that your competitor is employing young children in sweat shops overseas, and you can drive the consumer away and force higher labor costs on the competitor.

Platt on Compulsory Education

Compulsory education, says Platt, was viewed by leading industrialists as a means of controlling the poor and working classes and, specifically, of preparing them for work in new Industrial America. Platt quotes passages from an 1880 work by Charles Loring Brace, *The Dangerous Classes of New York*, which insisted that young people must be prepared for "industrial discipline." "In the interests of public order, of liberty, of property, for the sake of our own safety and the endurance of free institutions here," wrote Brace, the state needs "a strict and careful law, which shall compel every minor to learn to read and write, under severe penalties in the case of disobedience."[141]

Not long after, says Platt, "the working class had imposed upon them a sterile

and authoritarian educational system which mirrored the ethos of the corporate workplace" and was designed to serve as a "selection mechanism" for the work force. This is one of the ways in which the agendas of people like Jane Addams overlapped with the agendas of the industrialists. Says Platt:

> While urban reformers struggled from a moral perspective to pass legislation against child labor and for compulsory education, corporate reformers supported such reforms out of economic necessity.... Thus, the child-saving movement, in its efforts to augment the family with compulsory education and other measures of state intervention, played an important role in helping to reproduce a specialized and disciplined labor force.[142]

Platt on Juvenile Justice

Here Platt is effusive. The child savers, he said, had a strong and explicit moral agenda, directed mainly at the lower classes. Addams was appalled by temptations available to young people on the streets surrounding Hull-House:

> Never before have such numbers of young boys earned money... and felt themselves free to spend it as they choose in the midst of vice deliberately disguised as pleasure.... Let us know the modern city in its weakness and wickedness, and then seek to rectify and purify it until it shall be free at least from the grosser temptations which now beset the young people who are living in its tenement houses and working in its factories.[143]

Perhaps the main reason we now treat teens like children is because of the determined efforts of Addams and others to "save" teens from the sinful culture of the city streets. In a book published in 1880, prison reformer Enoch C. Wines, at one point an administrator with the Prison Association of New York, wrote of the "depraved habits" and "filthy condition" of young people on the streets of Chicago, where the "seeds of crime" were being planted daily. "They must be saved," he proclaimed.[144]

But in focusing on "depraved" behavior that was repugnant to the upper classes—behavior that was usually victimless and non-criminal—the reformers, says Platt, "brought attention to—and, in so doing, invented—new categories of youthful misbehavior." The creation of the juvenile court (which by 1928 had spread to all but two states) brought such behaviors under government control; in other words, it gave authorities excuses to round up and put away virtually any young people—and especially those of the lower classes. Young people could now be rounded up in large numbers for behaviors like "drinking, begging, roaming the streets, frequenting dance-halls and movies, fighting, sexuality, [and] staying out late."

During the early years of the new Chicago juvenile court, says Platt, more

---

WISDOM OF THE AGES

The Missing Stage

> *If people in the 1500s were aware of the tumultuous stage of life we call "adolescence," William Shakespeare seems to have been in the dark. Here are his seven stages of life:*
>
> *All the world's a stage, And all the men and women merely players:*
> *They have their exits and their entrances; And one man in his time plays many parts, His acts being seven ages.*
> *At first the infant, Mewling and puking in the nurse's arms....*
> *And then the whining school-boy, with his satchel....*
> *And then the lover, Sighing like furnace, with a woeful ballad....*
> *Then a soldier, Full of strange oaths, and bearded like the pard....*
> *And then the justice, In fair round belly with good capon lin'd....*
> *The sixth age shifts Into the lean and slipper'd pantaloon, With spectacles on nose and pouch on side....*
> *Last scene of all, That ends this strange eventful history, Is second childishness and mere oblivion, Sans teeth, sans eyes, sans taste, sans everything.*

—William Shakespeare, *As You Like It* (1598)

than half of the delinquency cases were based on charges such as "immorality," "vagrancy," "truancy," "disorderly behavior," and "incorrigibility." Worse still, in many cases the court acted "where no offense had actually been committed but where, for example, a child was posing problems for some person in authority, such as a parent or social worker."[145] Platt cites a 1910 report by Harvey Baker, an official of the Boston Juvenile Court, which explains that a young person might be picked up for an offense as small as "playing ball on the street" and then "committed to a reform school" when he was subsequently found to have a history of troublesome "habits."[146]

The Dark Side of Juvenile Justice

On the outside, the juvenile justice system served noble purposes: to prevent young people from turning into hardened criminals, to isolate them from adult prisons where they might be corrupted or harmed, to keep their records private so that they could start a new life when finally released by the system, and to educate them and nurture them so that they might become good citizens.

But the system had a dark side, as well: delinquency laws gave public officials absolute authority to sweep the streets of undesirable young people for virtually any reason. And because juvenile proceedings were "informal," the offenders were

denied due process rights guaranteed to all Americans under the Constitution. With the creation of the juvenile justice system, the Fifth Amendment guarantee that "no person" shall be "deprived of life, liberty, or property, without due process of law" and the Sixth Amendment guarantees that "the accused shall enjoy the right to a speedy and public trial, by an impartial jury" with "the Assistance of Counsel for his defence," were taken away from young people.[147]

Juvenile "delinquency" had been recognized long before Addams was on the scene. The first home for delinquents had been established, in fact, in 1825 (in New York).[148] But before the juvenile justice system was invented at the end of the century, teens still retained their fundamental rights, and, more important, their minor infractions were largely ignored or dealt with by family and church. Major crimes by young people were handled by the criminal courts. Punishments could be severe; in a handful of cases, young people were even hanged.[149] But serious crimes were dealt with in the criminal trial setting, where acquittals and appeals were common, just as with adults. The juvenile justice system, however, left young people completely defenseless.

Even as of the early 1960s, in many states less than 5 percent of juvenile offenders were represented by counsel, no juries were allowed, and most hearings were held in secret.[150] Yet the system could instantly lock someone up *for years*. No representation, no due process, no jury, no appeals, and, in many states, private hearings and secret records—a sort of Gulag Archipelago for troublesome young people. This is, according to Platt, exactly what some of the early reformers had in mind: the quick and sure containment of the children of the poor and working class. Since the reformers' own children generally lived privileged lives, they were safe from the system.

To make matters worse, the benevolent system Addams and her associates had in mind quickly metamorphosed into a harsh world of extreme military-style regimentation, manacling, whippings, and solitary confinement.

Addams considered young people to be fragile and incompetent (creatures of "innocence" and "tender beauty"), desperately needing adult protection and a mother's love. Juvenile facilities, she believed, should be supportive and comforting, not punishing, and they should be supervised or staffed by nurturing women, given that women are "natural caretakers."[151]

But teens aren't children, and administrators soon turned to draconian methods to try to keep their reluctant wards under control. They realized, said Platt, that "sentimental humanitarianism had no place in their work"; by the 1920s, the sentimentalist hopes of the child savers had been largely dashed.

On a 1925 visit to one of the new Illinois reformatories, Louise de Koven Bowen, one of Hull-House's wealthiest and most devoted patrons, reported sadly that the facility had "every appearance of being a jail, with its barred windows and locked doors.... The children have fewer comforts than do criminals confined in the county jail. They are not kept sufficiently occupied and have very little fresh air."[152]

Even more disturbing, there is considerable evidence that the juvenile justice system set in motion by Hull-House residents a century ago simply hasn't worked. There's little evidence that the system lowers crime; recidivism rates are typically as high as 60 percent; reformatories have generally become more punitive and increasingly overcrowded; and a number of studies indicate that teens who become inmates at juvenile facilities are harmed by the experience, not helped. An extensive study of the system published by the National Research Council in 2001 concludes:

> Increasing numbers of young people are placed in secure detention, which disrupts young people's lives and has negative effects on behavior and future developmental trajectories. Incarcerated juveniles have higher rates of physical injury and mental health problems, and they have poorer educational outcomes, than do their counterparts who are treated [emphasis added] in the community. Incarceration also causes severe and long-term problems with future employment, leaving ex-offenders with few economic alternatives to crime.... From the few available data, it appears that the rate of juveniles placed in custodial institutions has increased substantially in the past two decades, leading to widespread overcrowding in detention and other correctional facilities.[153]

How the Child Savers Viewed Youth

The child savers, concludes Platt, defined youth as a troublesome period of life based on their own class-based, moralistic biases and then created an infrastructure that mass-produced young people in the image they themselves had invented: dependent, angry, and incompetent. They robbed the young of their independence, imprisoned them over trifles, and denied them their most fundamental rights.

And once the new law enforcement system was in place, said Platt, young people were trapped in a Cuckoo's-Nest-like system where residents were powerless and resistance was considered to be yet another sign of pathology:

> The consolidation of the dependent status of "problematic" youth was complete. Young people were denied the option of withdrawing from or changing the institutions which governed their lives. Their opposition to or disenchantment with the school of reformatory or recreation center was treated as a problem of personal maladjustment which evoked "therapeutic" programs from the child savers.[154]

Whatever the motives of Addams and her various contemporaries, we need to consider the very real possibility that the Hull-House agenda was detrimental in some ways to both our young people and our society: it isolated many teens from the working world; it forced teens to attend school, whether or not they were ready to learn; it isolated teens from adults, laying the seeds for the creation of "teen culture"; it deprived teens of basic constitutional rights, such as the right of due process; it imposed harsh moral standards on teen behavior, bringing "crimes against oneself" under governmental control; it reified the teen years, creating a new and dark developmental stage; it made many teens angry, depressed, and defiant; it created a juvenile *injustice* system that has probably done more harm than good; and it extended childhood well past puberty, into the late teens or even well into the twenties.

THE RISE OF YOUTH-ORIENTED INDUSTRIES

In 1918 when Walt Disney was sixteen, he wanted to enlist in the U. S. Army to join the fight against the Kaiser, but he was too young. He tried joining the Canadian army but failed there, too. Finally, he forged his parents' signatures on an application to join the American Ambulance Corps, a division of the Red Cross. Added to the forgery was a lie about his age: he recorded his birth year as 1900 instead of 1901. He soon found himself driving ambulances in France, arriving just after the war ended.[155]

Later in life Disney said of his adventure overseas: "The things I did those eleven months I was overseas added up to a lifetime of experience in one package." Notably for our purposes Disney also commented, "It was such a valuable experience that I feel that if we have to send our boys into the Army we should send them even younger than we do. I know being on my own at an early age has made me more self-reliant and less of a the-world-owes-me-a-living type than I otherwise would have been."[156] How ironic that he was eventually to create an empire that has helped hold young people back.

The Early Industries: Manufactured Toys and Games

Before the American Civil War (1861-1865) industries that served children or teens barely existed, but there is no doubt that young people have always engaged in various kinds of play, just as all young mammals do (especially males). Presumably this is nature's way of preparing its young to hunt, fight, and court after puberty. According to Bernard Mergen, an expert on play in early America,

pre-Civil War children entertained themselves with balls, jump ropes, rag and paper dolls (and far more rare wax ones), boats made from bark, marbles, hoops, tops, pocket knives, and homemade sleds and kites, among other things; with few exceptions, these were created from items found outdoors or around the house. Young people also created their own minstrel shows, circuses, and theatrical plays, and a common practice, it seems, was to "[turn] over chairs and [make] believe they were horses and coaches."[157]

Philippe Ariès was fascinated by the fact that European paintings before about 1770 never depicted children's toys; to him, this was another indication that, in some sense, childhood didn't exist before modern times. It's likely, though, that young children have always played—when they weren't working or dying, anyway. It's equally clear, however, that industries that support play, as well as industries that support young people in general, are a very new phenomenon in human history. There is also no question that such industries have helped to extend childhood past puberty, just as unions and, at times, influential industrialists, have done. In fact, industry—always in the process of seeking new markets—has played an important role in *defining* modern adolescence. At least in its superficial aspects, modern "teen culture" is entirely a *creation* of modern industry.

It's no coincidence that youth-oriented industries got their start around the same time as some of the other important movements we've discussed. Industrialization created new affluence, new poverty, new cultural practices, a new middle class, and increasingly protective attitudes toward young people. Combine just two of these changes—affluence and protectiveness, each emerging in a world of expanding markets and factories—and virtually any entrepreneur with the capability of mass-producing a new plaything, book, or item of clothing could find buyers ready to beat a path to his or her door. As Mergen writes, "Men and women in the toy industry did not try to change children's toy play; rather, they exploited what they saw as fundamental to a child's life."[158] Let's look at how and when this trend played out.

The Milton Bradley company, of board game fame ("The Game of Life," "Candy Land," "Sorry," "Twister," "Yahtzee," etc.), was one of the first American companies to devote itself to the newly-created youth market, although its first product, introduced in 1860, was actually a pocket-size set of games sold primarily to Union soldiers. The 1869 "Checkered Game of Life" (precursor to the modern "Life" game), was sold to a younger audience, as were dozens of other games released over the next few decades.

Parker Brothers, another board game company ("Monopoly," "Clue," "Risk," "Trivial Pursuit," etc.) was founded by *sixteen-year-old* George Parker in 1884. The

previous year, when he invented his first game, he was unable to get any bank loans to publish the game (which, ironically, was called "Banking"). He raised the money on his own, printed five hundred copies of the game, and turned a profit on his investors' money within a year. By the end of the 1880s, his company was selling twenty-nine different games.

Hardcore toy manufacturing got its serious start in the 1870s with "creeping dolls, bears that perform, horsemen that drive furiously, boatmen that row, [and] steam cars that go," many imported from Europe. There were also child-size musical instruments, manufactured baseball bats (baseball had been invented in 1845), dumbbells, toy soldiers and guns, and factory-made sleds, among other things. In marketing efforts, says Mergen, "The subtext for parents was the importance of toys for their children's development and happiness."[159] If you've recently been playing Mozart symphonies for your infant child (or perhaps even for your fetus), you've fallen prey to the same subtext.

The youth markets grew enormously in the 1880s and 90s, driven by increasing manufacturing capacities, a fast-growing population, and, of course, the rapid expansion of the definition of childhood. Before the Civil War, there were only a handful of books for children; by the mid-1860s, as many as three hundred children's books were being published each year.[160] The toy and game industries were growing so fast that an 1890 book called *The Young Folks' Cyclopedia of Games and Sports* needed more than four thousand entries to cover the subject. By the early 1900s, realistic play guns came into wide use and violent forms of play became more common, perhaps, says Mergen, because of the new "urban concentrations of children" and "enforced attendance at school."[161] Bicycles, which assumed their modern form in the 1880s, also became common.

American toy manufacturers got organized early on; 1903 saw the launching of *Playthings*, a journal that monitors and analyzes trends in the industry. Having been in print now for over a century, the magazine is considerably thicker and glossier than it used to be. Early *Playthings* articles are as illuminating as they are disturbing—for example, a 1920 piece proposing that immigrant children should be "Americanized" by having them assemble toys in settlement houses, or a 1940 article listing hundreds of toys by season, showing how a young person's day can be taken up with toys year-round. The article, comments Mergen, "shows how rapidly the toy industry permeated every moment of childhood."[162]

Miriam Formanek-Brunell's history of dolls in America—*Made to Play House: Dolls and Commercialization of American Girlhood, 1830-1930*—is especially revealing, and it even gives us a new word that is highly pertinent to the theme of the book

> ## YOUNG PEOPLE IN ACTION
>
> ### The Extension of "Dollhood"
>
> *What company produces more tires than any other in the world?
> No, it's not Michelin or Firestone or Goodrich. It's Mattel! It takes more
> than four hundred million tires to supply the more than one hundred
> million Matchbox cars produced by Mattel each year—many times more
> than the paltry number of tires needed for real cars. Youth-oriented industries
> now bring in staggering sums and produce mind-boggling amounts of
> merchandise. Consider:*
>
> - *The He-Man action figure (Mattel) generated $450 million in
>   sales in 1985.[163]*
> - *In 1971, the hundred-millionth visitor crossed the threshold into
>   the original Disneyland in California. By 1986, five hundred
>   million people had visited Disney theme parks, and the current
>   total is well over a billion.[164]*
> - *Mattel now produces nearly a hundred million Barbie dolls per
>   year and has produced more than a billion of the dolls all-told.[165]*
> - *American toy companies sold $21 billion worth of toys in 2005.[166]*
> - *The main competition for toy sales in recent years is the burgeon-
>   ing video game industry, which had $10.5 billion in sales in
>   2005.[167]*

you're now reading. Post-Civil War businesses, said Formanek-Brunell, were trying to extend *"dollhood."* They were trying to expand their markets by encouraging young females to play with dolls for as many years as possible.[168] They didn't care about "childhood" per se; they just wanted "dollhood" lengthened.

In meticulous fashion, Formanek-Brunell shows how dolls changed in industrial America, and how their caretakers changed, as well. Before the Civil War, most dolls were homemade and simple, and their main function was "usefulness." Girls learned to dress and care for them to practice for their future domestic roles. But soon after the Civil War, dolls became commercialized. Girls were encouraged to own and prettify as many dolls as possible. Dolls became fashion-plates, endlessly mimicking the fashions worn by the upper class and coveted by the new middle class.

Women became preoccupied with shopping, says Formanek-Brunell, and the new department stores became "palaces of consumption." With family size shrinking, income increasing, and more opportunities for women to be outside the home,

"shopping for self, friends, and family was becoming a central activity," she says. Women were becoming "increasingly isolated" from production—that is, from the tedious tasks of making clothing, dolls, or anything else that could be manufactured—and "also from their children." Mothers encouraged their daughters to depend on the "companionship of dolls, thereby lengthening their childhood."[169]

New distribution channels help to propel these many changes. In 1874 Macy's became the first department store to have a toy department, and other major stores quickly followed suit. In 1893 the seven-year-old Sears and Roebuck catalog added dolls to its inventory.[170]

Rise of the Youth-Oriented Corporate Empires

Youth-oriented corporate empires still with us today got their start during this period. With partner Ubbe Iwerks, Walt Disney started the precursor to Walt Disney Productions in 1919; he bought out Iwerks' share of the company in 1930 for a modest $2,920. Hasbro (G.I. Joe, Play-Doh, My Little Pony, Furby, Pokémon) was founded in Providence, Rhode Island by brothers Henry and Helal Hassenfield in 1923. Playskool (Mr. Potato Head, Weebles, Gloworm) was founded by two teachers in Milwaukee in 1928. Fisher-Price (Power Wheels, Sesame Street, Dora the Explorer) opened its doors in 1930. Mattel (Barbie, Hot Wheels, He-Man, Cabbage Patch Kids, Harry Potter toys) was started in a garage in Southern California by Ruth and Elliot Handler and Harold Matson in 1945.[171]

These and many businesses like them mushroomed into mega-corporations over the course of the twentieth century, and many have become part of larger, adult-oriented, corporate America. Parker Brothers, for example, was bought by General Mills in 1968, then sold to Kenner products in 1985, and then sold to the Tonka Corporation in 1987, which became part of Hasbro, Inc. in 1991. Hasbro, a Fortune 1000 company with 6,900 employees, has annual revenues of over $3 billion and a market value of almost $4 billion. In addition to Parker Brothers, Hasbro also now owns Milton Bradley, Tonka, Kenner, and Playskool. Toy outlets have also grown: Toys "R" Us, for example, which was founded in 1948, is now an $11 billion business with more than sixteen hundred stores; even so, Wal-Mart now outsells all of the United States "toy supermarkets."[172]

Disney, of course, is now one of the largest corporate empires in the world. The original Disneyland, which opened in Anaheim, California in 1954, had over a million visitors during its first six months of operation and is now one of four nearly-identical Disneylands owned by its sprawling corporate parent, which now owns a total of fifteen theme parks and resorts.

Disney also controls fifteen magazines (including *Discover*), three book publishers (including Hyperion), eight movie production companies (including Buena Vista Films and racy Miramax Films), the Disney Stores, the ABC television network, fourteen Internet ventures (including ABC.com and Toysmart.com), ten television stations (including WABC in New York), sixty-six radio stations, twelve cable television channels (including ESPN, the History Channel, the Disney Channel, and Lifetime), twenty foreign television ventures, Epcot Center, the Anaheim Angels (a professional baseball team), five music production companies, the Mighty Ducks (a professional hockey team), and TiVo, among other entities. At this writing Disney has revenues of over $25 billion and a net worth of about $35 billion.[173]

But this is only the beginning. When I was a child, toys came on the market in more-or-less random fashion. One year, someone invented the hula hoop, and we all spun it 'til we dropped. As any parent today knows, however, there's nothing random about the toy industry anymore.

In 2001 we all bought Harry Potter and Monsters, Inc. toys, videos, clothes, towels, and backpacks; in 2002 it was Yu-Gi-Oh, Dora the Explorer, and the Lord of the Rings; in 2003 it was Beyblade, the Incredible Hulk, and Spiderman. Why? Because extensive, almost overwhelming lines of toys and other products now accompany the release of major movies or the debut of new television shows. This occurs, at least in part, because of a 1988 alliance formed between Mattel and Disney (such alliances had occurred before, but this one was gigantic).[175]

Before a film even goes to the drawing-board (or its modern digital equivalent), merchandising and other "tie-in" plans are made. Cartoon shows are connected to films, which are connected to theme park rides, which are connected to breakfast cereals, which

are connected to clothing lines, which are connected to fast-food restaurant promotions, and so on. And all of this is targeted at various well-defined and highly studied youth markets. Multiple industries are at work here, highly coordinated almost in Japanese *keiretsu* style, all locking in the spending of tens of millions of consumers for set periods of time—hundreds of millions of consumers when the foreign markets are included.

But even this is only a fraction of the larger picture. I've chosen to talk mainly about toys, but today large segments of the music, fashion, and publishing industries have also helped to create, define, and maintain the modern troubled adolescent. I'll say more about such industries in Chapter Fourteen when I offer an "Enemies List"—a Nixon-style catalog of the many businesses, organizations, and government entities that keep teens imprisoned in a world of pain and trivia.

As almost every parent is aware, there is yet another "industry" that deliberately and very effectively holds teens back: the illegal drug industry. It may not use Madison Avenue advertising firms to spread its message, but it's a large-scale business, every bit as sophisticated as a Fortune 500 company, complete with territories, distribution networks, wholesalers, inventories, managers, executives, and so on. I'll say more about drug issues in Chapter Five.

If teen culture disappeared, many of these multi-billion-dollar industries would instantly collapse. If, instead, these industries disappeared, teens would probably enter the adult world much faster.

Big Business and Teen Culture

Whatever the original wishes and motives of the child savers, the artificial extension of childhood was soon accelerated by the Industrial Revolution's most impressive product: Big Business.

The tens of thousands of images we've all seen of infantile teens (*Bill and Ted's Excellent Adventure, Dude, Where's My Car?, Bio-Dome, Suburbia*), of reckless and incompetent teens (*Animal House, PCU, Dazed and Confused, Don't Tell Mom the Babysitter's Dead*), of defiant and uncontrollable teens (*Breakfast Club, SLC Punk, Crazy Beautiful*), of drugged and inebriated and oversexed teens (*American Pie, Kids, Thirteen, She's All That, Rules of Attraction, Fast Times at Ridgemont High, The Girl Next Door, Welcome to the Doll House, Less Than Zero*), of depressed and suicidal teens (*Virgin Suicides, Heathers, Donnie Darko*), and of teens obsessed by fashion and rock'n'roll (*Clueless, Detroit Rock City, Legally Blonde, Ten Things I Hate About You, New York Minute, Mean Girls, What a Girl Wants*), have been fed to us by a complex system of interrelated businesses that thrive off the maintenance of the teen-as-child myth.

To put this another way, large businesses make billions of dollars a year both by fueling teen culture and by trying to convince both adults and teens that teen culture is timeless and inevitable, even though it is neither. As you'll see in Chapter Three, in recent decades American businesses have been expanding their markets by recreating our own teen culture, with all of its negatives, around the globe.*

THE HISTORICAL FORCES BEHIND ADOLESCENCE

These, then, as I see them, are the major historical forces that have been driving the artificial extension of childhood in America since the mid-1800s:

- Nurturing tendencies by women (and some men) to protect the millions of young people toiling long hours in the new factories or getting into trouble on the streets
- The elevated status of women, which gave them a powerful new voice in policy making
- The widespread adoption of the new view that young people are tender, helpless, and incompetent
- Determined efforts by the new labor unions to protect the jobs and wages of older workers by pushing young people out of the work force
- The desire of leading industrialists to sweep the streets free of troublesome youths and to prepare new generations of skilled laborers through mass education
- The desire of leaders in the upper and middle classes to impose their moral standards on poor and working-class youths
- The emergence of new businesses and industries that catered to the young and helped to create a "youth culture."

Before these forces emerged, the troubled teen was a rarity in human history. With these forces in play, teens rapidly became isolated from adults and increas-

---

*A personal note: You may have begun to suspect that I'm one of those left-wing liberal professors you've heard about. I'm not. The reason I've made some negative statements about corporate America is not because I have anything against big business but because it has played a significant role in the artificial extension of childhood. At this point the icons, clothing, shoes, music, athletic gear, makeup, soap, magazines, styles, tastes, heroes, hopes, and dreams of every American teen are in the hands of a handful of corporate executives. Unlike some of the reformers of the late 1800s, these individuals have no inherent interest in the welfare of young people. Their goal is to make money, and to do that they need to preserve and expand their markets. This is bad news for teens. I'll revisit this issue in Chapter Fourteen.

ingly unhappy about their peculiar place in society: adults in body and mind, toddlers in status.

Industrial America of the late 1800s, swelling with immigrants and new wealth, was an ambitious social experiment where almost anything could happen—and where some of the grand plans people set in motion had unintended negative consequences. I have no doubt that Jane Addams, Grace Abbott, Julia Lathrop, and their colleagues would be dismayed in some respects by the kind of world they helped to create—especially by the kind of teen that now exists.

I've deliberately skipped an important part of teen history that we won't be able to ignore for long: the official labeling and characterization of adolescence by pioneering psychologist G. Stanley Hall in 1904. Hall didn't create the policies and programs that set modern adolescence in motion, but he identified the result: a time of "storm and stress" that coincides with the teen years. He didn't create adolescence, but he certainly reified it, claiming that the teen turmoil he saw at the turn of the twentieth century was a *necessary* feature of the teen years. We'll examine Hall's views in Chapter Five.

Much of the world has so far avoided heavy industrialization and Western ways. Does the troubled teen exist in countries that maintain their traditional cultures? I've already argued that the historical record shows that adolescence (as a time of turmoil) is a creation of modern Western culture. If I'm wrong and adolescence is truly a timeless, universal phenomenon, we should see it all over the world. Do we?

Q: *If teens are so capable, why is my sixteen-year-old son such a mindless, disrespectful jerk?*

A: First of all, it's possible that your son doesn't appear to be so mindless or jerky to his friends. He might appear to be especially "cool" or bold or even competent in various ways. His behavior is probably effective in some contexts, and your home may not be not where he's try-ing to be effective. Second, his strange or adversarial behavior is almost certainly his way of declaring inde-pendence, growing up, and asserting control over his life. That's an important possibility—well worth think-ing about. Your son probably has very few legitimate ways to assert control: he can't own property, marry, move out, drink, sign contracts, enter certain movie theaters, or even urinate (during the school day, anyway) without adult permission. He asserts control the few ways he can—often in bizarre or pathetic ways, to be sure. If I'm right, there's a good chance that your son's jerkiness would disappear overnight if he were allowed to have real con-trol over his life. Third, and finally, he might get angry or depressed sometimes about being treated like a child—if not by you, then by society in general.

Chapter 3

Adolescence Abroad

We are children of the world, watching every day go by
Like a bird in the wind, like a tree in the storm
Like the breath of a child from the moment he's born.
—Bee Gees, "Children of the World"

Overview. American-style adolescence is an anomaly. In preindustrial nations, where young people are rapidly integrated into adult society at an early age, teen turmoil is largely absent. A recent study of 186 preindustrial societies indicates that 60 percent of such societies don't even have a word for adolescence and that antisocial behavior by young males is completely absent in more than half of them. Where teen problems are beginning to emerge in various countries around the world, they can be traced to the increasing isolation of teens from adults brought about by Western educational practices, labor restrictions, and media.

Born in the city of Iguala in Guerro, Mexico in 1971, Pedro Gancedo was one of ten children raised in a single-parent home. While his mom and aunt worked in a clothing shop, beginning at about age five Pedro sold bubble gum on the streets to help support the family; his nephew, who was the same age as Pedro (such things happen in large families) sold popsicles. When the nephew moved away, Pedro took over both businesses. He didn't know how to count change for quite a long time. He simply held out his hand, full of coins, and said to customers, "Take your change."

By age seven he was in school most of the day and also milking cows and tending livestock with a local farmer. He lived with the farmer most of the time and earned three hundred pesos—about $35—a month. The farmer deducted about two hundred pesos to pay for Pedro's clothing, school, and textbooks, leaving Pedro

about one hundred pesos, *all* of which he gave to his mother to help support the many siblings. At eight, Pedro and his family moved to St. Martin Morrelos. He sold fresh milk in the markets, sometimes by order, but mostly by yelling "Leche, leche!" in the streets. When he wasn't in school, he also washed or guarded cars, helped people load groceries, and helped out his brother in construction work. At some point he was allowed to keep a small portion of his earnings for himself, to "take my girlfriend out for a Coke" and to accumulate some savings.

At thirty-two he now works as a cook in San Diego. How does he feel about having grown up in what modern Americans would consider to be a society that abuses its children? Quite simply, he talks about his past with fondness and pride. He liked bringing pesos home to his family. It "made me feel like Santa Claus," he said. "To make only ten pesos, but then to take it home to help feed my family—it made me feel good." There is no trace of resentment in Pedro when he talks about his busy childhood. On the contrary, I got the impression that he thinks modern American children are lazy and spoiled (although he was kind enough not to use those exact words). Most important for our purposes, there also seems to be no trace of "adolescence" in Pedro's past. He seems to have shifted, gradually and smoothly, from childhood to adulthood, with no sign of the turmoil that characterizes modern adolescence.

Was Pedro harmed in some way by his childhood labors? If so, it's not clear how. In fact, Pedro, like President Jimmy Carter and millions of other Americans raised in rural America, probably benefited from the many ways in which work, family, and school were intertwined in his life. He learned a strong work ethic; he learned self-discipline; he learned the value of money; he acquired practical skills that one isn't taught in school. But the most important benefits for Pedro were more subtle. Pedro's life had "meaning." He *knew* why he got up in the morning and why he sold bubble gum on the streets and why he milked cows. He worked to help his mom and siblings, to help put food on the table. He worked because he was a member of a family and a community. He worked because doing so was *important*. When you spend your day doing things you believe are important, your life has meaning. Conversely, when you spend your day doing things that make no sense to you, you feel empty, frustrated, and angry.

Is it possible that many teens today feel empty, frustrated, and angry because their lives lack real meaning? How do teens fare today in cultures around the world which integrate young people into adult society fairly early in their lives? Are teens damaged by such integration?

LESSONS FROM PREINDUSTRIAL CULTURES

In Chapter One, I mentioned a modern cult book called *The Continuum Concept* by writer Jean Liedloff.[1] Tens of thousands of parents have used this remarkable little book as a parenting guide since it was first published in 1975. It has remained in print for over thirty years and has been translated into seventeen languages—amazing accomplishments in the publishing world. A sort of worldwide fan club—the Liedloff Continuum Network—has developed around the book: "an international support organization comprised of parents, families and individuals... whose understanding of human nature has been transformed (or validated)" by her book.[2]

The Children of the Yequana

When Liedloff was barely out of her teens, she ran off with two Italian men—one a quite handsome count, apparently—on a quest for diamonds in the remote jungles of Venezuela. While there she became increasingly intrigued by the inordinately happy lives and lifestyles of several primitive tribes. She ultimately spent about two-and-a-half years living with the Yequana Indians—*sans* count, by the way. On one level, her book is about her experiences with the Yequana; on another, it's about an idea—"the continuum concept"—that she derived from her experiences. Liedloff came to believe that the unhappiness we feel in most "civilized" countries results from the various ways in which we're raised to be disconnected from the adult community.

The Yequana, Liedloff wrote, appeared to have no word for "work," although they worked very hard. They also seemed to enjoy the work they did; work was often an opportunity for camaraderie and good cheer. There was little sign of conflict in Yequana society, either among adults or children, and there was no sign at all of the turbulent period of life we call "adolescence." Liedloff attributed these and other positive characteristics of the Yequana to the distinctive way they raised their children.

A Yequana infant roams freely, "testing everything" and "measuring his own strength and agility."[3] "[The] attitude of the mother or caretaker of a baby is relaxed, usually attentive to some other occupation than baby-minding, but receptive at all times to a visit from the crawling or creeping adventurer.... *She does not initiate the contacts nor contribute to them except in a passive way.* It is the baby who seeks her out and shows her by his behavior what he wants.... He is the active, she the passive agent in all their dealings; he comes to her to sleep when he is tired, to be fed when he is hungry."[4]

The integration of the Yequana children into adult society begins almost at birth:

I was present at the first moments of one little girl's working life. She was about two years old. I had seen her with the women and girls, playing as they grated manioc into a trough. Now she was taking a piece of manioc from the pile and rubbing it against the grater of a girl near her. The chunk was too big; she dropped it several times trying to draw it across the rough board. An affectionate smile and a smaller piece of manioc came from her neighbor, and her mother ready for the inevitable impulse to show itself, handed her a tiny grating board of her own. The little girl had seen the women grating as long as she could remember and immediately rubbed the nubbin up and down her board like the others....[5]

I saw little Yequana girls from the age of three or four (sometimes they looked even younger) taking full charge of infants. It was clearly their favorite occupation but did not prevent their doing other things at the same time, tending fires, fetching water, and so on. They did not tire of their charges as they would have dolls....[6]

The boys, from the age of about 18 months, practiced archery with sharp arrows, some enthusiasts carrying their bow and arrows about most of their waking hours. Shooting was not confined to designated places, nor were any "safety rules" in effect. In my two and a half years there I saw only one arrow wound.[7]

Liedloff's book is filled with examples like this. There is no distinct separation between childhood and adulthood in the tribe; instead, there is a *continuum* of activities, behaviors, and expectations. Expectations are modest when children are young and increase gradually and smoothly over the years, but the goals are always clear: the development of self-reliance and the full integration of the child into the world of responsible adulthood. Responsibility and authority are never forced on anyone, but they're given freely as soon as a child shows an interest in taking them on. Independent decision making is encouraged, because "leaving the choice to the child from the earliest age keeps his judgment at peak efficiency,"[8] and the child's "self protecting ability" is trusted to keep him or her from serious harm.[9]

In contrast, she says, we weaken and damage our children by overprotecting them; we even impair their ability to make reasonable decisions and to protect themselves. She tells of a small boy in the United States, for example, whose parents fenced in the family pool to protect him. The first time they left the gate open, he made his way inside and drowned. He was following natural tendencies to be independent, to overcome obstacles, and to escape from controlling influences, but natural tendencies he might have had to protect himself had never been developed because adults had always been protecting him.

YOUNG PEOPLE IN ACTION

On the Farm in New Zealand

> *James Griffith, born in 1948, was raised on a ten-thousand-acre New Zealand sheep farm in the Waikato region of the North Island. By age ten, he was engaged daily in the regular activities of the farm: mustering the sheep, sheering, and repairing fences and water troughs. His dad died when he was fifteen, and he decided to become a mechanic rather than continuing the farm work. At nineteen he moved to London where he worked on the pit crew for a British racing team. His early work experience made him feel proud and competent and propelled him forward, he says. He feels no resentment about his past.*

Liedloff considers the modern "child-centered" approach to parenting an abomination: "A parent whose day centers on child care is not only likely to be bored, and boring to others, but also likely to be giving an unwholesome kind of care."[10] Instead, she says, we need to encourage the natural tendency of the child to focus on adults, "witnessing the kinds of experiences he will have later in life."[11] The "main business" of the child, she says, is

> ...to absorb the actions, interactions, and surroundings of his caretaker, adult or child. This information prepares him to take his place among his people by helping him to understand what they do. To thwart this powerful urge—by looking inquiringly, so to speak, at a baby who is looking inquiringly at you—creates profound confusion; it manacles the mind.[12]

Toward the end of her book, Liedloff even speculates about the possible connection between infantilization and psychopathology (see Chapter Five of this volume), suggesting that young people who have not been continuously integrated into adult society will become "antisocial" and experience "distortions in their personalities," with enormous pressures "being brought to bear upon [them] to present a façade of conformity."[13] In other words, they will become unruly, unconventional teens who are constantly being pressured to conform.[14]

The Teens of Samoa

Liedloff's observations bring to mind one of the great classics of the last century, Margaret Mead's *Coming of Age in Samoa*, which appeared in 1928.[15] Based on interviews with sixty-eight young women from the west part of Ta'u Island in

the South Pacific, Mead concluded that adolescence as we know it didn't exist in Samoa—at least among females.

As far as she could tell, there was no violence and virtually no turmoil among Samoan youth. She attributed this to the homogeneity and lack of stress in the culture. As it happens, she also noted that children were integrated into adult society fairly early in life—that they are "not permitted a period of lack of responsibility such as our children are allowed."[16] "From the time they are four or five years old," said Mead, "they perform definite tasks, graded to their strength and intelligence, but still tasks which have a meaning in the structure of the whole society."[17] Whereas American children are often bored or spend their time in meaningless or objectionable activities, "[the] Samoan girl who tends babies, carries water, sweeps the floor, or the little boy who digs for bait, or collects coconuts, has no such difficulty. The necessary nature of their tasks is obvious."[18]

Like Liedloff, Mead also observed that young females—six or seven years old—routinely and expertly cared for babies, but Mead didn't make as much of this observation as she might have. When it came to explaining why adolescence was absent, she cited broad characteristics of Samoan culture, such as the "general casualness."[19] As far as I've been able to determine, she also never spoke specifically, in *Samoa* or elsewhere, about the unique characteristics of Western industrialization that gave rise to an extension of childhood.

Mead's work was roundly criticized a few years after her death by Australian anthropologist Derek Freeman in a book called *Margaret Mead and Samoa: The Making and Unmaking of an Anthropological Myth*.[20] Freeman claimed, among other things, that two of Mead's interviewees (out of sixty-eight) had lied to her about violence among the young. He also suggested that her picture of the Samoans was distorted because she only stayed there a few months, during which she actually lived in the household of the United States Navy's chief pharmacist rather than among the Samoans. In contrast, Jean Liedloff lived among the Yequana for years.

Freeman's work, too, has been criticized,[21] and there's no easy way to settle the matter. No one has suggested that Mead was a liar, just that she might not have seen the whole picture. The story of the Yequana seems clearer, and so do images of other adolescent-free cultures around the world.

TEENS IN THE PREINDUSTRIAL WORLD

In 1991, Alice Schlegel of the University of Arizona and Herbert Barry III of the University of Pittsburgh published a landmark volume called *Adolescence: An*

Anthropological Inquiry, which reviewed research on teens that had been con-ducted in 186 preindustrial societies.[22] For our purposes Schlegel and Barry's most important findings were these:

1. *About 60 percent of these cultures had no word for adolescence*, and the cultures that had relevant terms were usually referring to an innocu-ous, relatively brief period between puberty and marriage, not to a period of turmoil.

2. *Most young people in these cultures spent most of their time with same-sex adults.* Teens spent almost no time with same-sex peers.

3. *Antisocial behavior in young males was extremely mild* (by United States standards) in most of the cultures surveyed and *completely absent in more than half of them.*

4. *There was very little aggression or violence in teens in these cultures and almost no sign of pathology.*

Points 2 through 4 clearly distinguish the teens in preindustrial societies from the teens in the United States and other industrialized countries. Because teens in preindustrial countries spend most of their time with adults—both family members and co-workers—adults become their role models, not peers. What's more, their primary task is not to break free of adults but rather to become productive members of their families and their communities as soon as they are able. And though some forms of mild antisocial behaviors were observed in some cultures, teens in preindustrial nations show virtually none of the pathologically significant "storm and stress" that characterizes the modern American teen.

The Schlegel and Barry study shows unequivocally that adolescence as we know it in the modern West barely exists in the preindustrial world. In some countries it appears to be absent completely—except in areas that are becoming Westernized.

EXPORTING TEEN TURMOIL

Pierre R. Dasen of the Université de Genève, a former assistant to renowned psychologist Jean Piaget, recently reviewed the Schlegel and Barry book and other multicultural studies of adolescence by sociologists, anthropologists and others social scientists.[23] He concluded not only that adolescence is largely absent in preindustrial nations but, even more significant, that *one can track the emergence of full-blown, pathologi-cal, Western-style adolescence in countries undergoing Westernization.* In other words, he

demonstrated that adolescence is indeed a "cultural invention," a claim stated clearly by L. Joseph Stone and Joseph Church in their 1957 book, *Childhood and Adolescence*:

> *In primitive societies, there is no equivalent for our concept of adolescence. In some primitive societies, the transition from childhood to adulthood is so smooth that it goes unrecognized. More frequently, we find that the young person on the threshold of maturity goes through a ceremonial adolescence. Such ceremonial observances are called puberty rites, since they are usually timed to the onset of sexual maturity. They may range in complexity from a simple haircut or a change of clothes to being tattooed or having one's teeth filed, to periods of fasting or isolation or a search for a vision. Such initiation periods seldom last more than a few weeks, and even the longest of them are negligible compared with the five to eight years of adolescence common in our society. At the conclusion of the puberty rite, the young person is granted full adult status and assumes it without any sense of strain or conflict. Not only is he officially grown up, but he knows and other people know that he is actually ready for adult activities, including marriage. Except for the ceremonial punctuation of the puberty rite, childhood status tends to be continuous with adult status....* [The] psychological events of adolescence in our society are not a necessary counterpart of the physical changes of puberty, but a cultural invention—not a deliberate one, of course, but a product of an increased delay in the assumption of adult responsibilities *[emphasis added].*[24]

The Harvard Studies

In the 1980s Beatrice and John Whiting of the Harvard School of Education set in motion a project called "Adolescents in a Changing World," specifically to look at the effect of modernization on adolescents in preindustrial cultures.[25] Seven teams of anthropologists agreed to cooperate on the project, each looking at different cultures. In his 2000 essay Dasen summarized the reports of investigations that had been published as of that time, along with similar studies by other researchers. Here are five cases described by Dasen, each showing how modernization gives rise to Western-style adolescence.

Kenya. A 1987 study of eighty-four Kikuyu teens in Kenya by John Whiting and C. M. Worthman suggested that "social change can produce ambivalence and stress in adolescence in relation to sexual behaviour, in particular due to the introduction of a double standard through Christian influence and schooling."[26] In traditional Kikuyu culture when young males became "senior warriors" they were given access to young females in a special hut called the *thingira*, where they

engaged in what Westerners would call "heavy petting" (without intercourse)—a kind of "controlled lovemaking" which eventually led to negotiations between two sets of parents, instruction in sexual practices, and marriage.[27] With the introduction of Western-style schooling, say Whiting and Worthman, "young people are not trained in the traditional mode of limited intercourse nor in the appropriate, defined partners and contexts in which it is acceptable... and peer surveillance for proper sexual behavior has diminished."[28] The rate of unwed motherhood has increased and the *thingira* tradition has disappeared. Christian moral views, according to which young females are supposed to be chaste while young males have no constraints, are now prevalent, and "an unmarried young woman is officially denied access to modern contraception unless she has already had a child."[29]

Morocco. Similar changes were reported in a 1980s study of Zawiya, a small town in Morocco, by D. A. and S. S. Davis.[31] Brides were virtually always virgins here before Western schooling was introduced, and wedding ceremonies culminated in the proud display of a blood-stained sheet. Now required schooling has given young people more alone time, and Western radio, television, and films have promoted both promiscuity and a double standard, leading to significant inter- and intragenerational conflicts. Blood on the sheet is now often faked with animal blood, and among the growing middle class, the ceremony is gradually being abandoned. Premarital sex is becoming more common, the rate of out-of-wedlock pregnancy is increasing, and abortion is now "widely available."

Australia. In a series of reports appearing in the 1980s and 1990s, Victoria Burbank described the dramatic effects that Westernization was having on Australian Aborigines.[32] "Australian legislation, schooling, and movies and television, Western representations of romantic love," and the influence of Christian missionaries, have replaced long-established practices and norms with Western ways. Traditionally, families arranged marriages between young females and older males, so that "problems of premarital sex... could simply not occur." Now same-age peers are mating the Western way, leading to premarital sex, unwed motherhood, and "overt conflict between the generations"—the Aborigines' first "generation gap."

Canada. Reports in the 1980s and 1990s by R. G. Condon described profound changes in adolescents among the Inuit of Victoria Island, Canada, in the late 1970s and 1980s.[33] It's notable that television wasn't introduced to the Inuit until 1980. There was little sign of adolescence in traditional Inuit culture. Females were committed to marriage when they were very young. Actual cohabitation came later, because males couldn't marry until they had killed their first large game, typically at seventeen or eighteen. Curiously, "the first two years of marriage

YOUNG PEOPLE IN ACTION

Youth Saving Youth

When he was twelve years old, Toronto seventh-grader Craig Kielburger was deeply moved when he saw a report about a young Pakistani who had apparently been murdered for bringing attention to the exploitation of young workers by carpet barons in his country. With several of his friends, Kielburger soon founded a dynamic organization called Free the Children, dedicated to ending abusive child labor around the world. He even convinced his parents to let him travel through poor communities in South Asia so that he could see the abuses firsthand. His moving 1998 book (written with author Kevin Major) recounts his travels and the growth of Free the Children, which is now the largest charitable organization in the world run by young people for young people.[30]

were considered as a trial period," which was almost always successful. The modern system is quite different. Social security payments now assure survival, and all children are required to attend school, although many drop out at thirteen or fourteen. Young peoples' lives now seem completely chaotic. They often "stay up all night [and] remain active for 24 hours or more." Teen pregnancy is now common, the rate of teen unemployment is high, and the rate of teen suicide has increased substantially. But perhaps the most disturbing changes have to do with Western-style teen aggression:

> *The open expression of hostility and competitiveness has become commonplace among the younger generation. There had been no juvenile delinquency until TV was introduced. There was no police station, and most problems were either not reported or solved on a community basis, but in 1988 the community asked to have a permanent police.[34]*

The rapid and dramatic shift in Inuit culture is especially unsettling because it cannot be blamed on either urbanization or industrialization, because Victoria Island has experienced neither one. Television, forced schooling, and "social security" were enough to decimate the traditional culture—and to create the new developmental stage we call "adolescence."

Côte d'Ivoire. Researchers in this West African nation found increasing deterioration among teens in an extensive eleven-year study beginning in 1980.[35] Starting in 1983, they noted a "pathology of ill feeling" among teens, along with increases in both drug abuse and suicide attempts. From 1985 to 1989, "there was a steady in-

crease of criminal cases, including substance abuse, armed aggressions, and female and male prostitution," especially in Abidjan, a relatively large city. The researchers attributed the deterioration to "the conflict between the continuing demands of the traditional part of the society and those of Westernization"; young people were clearly "'torn' between conflicting demands." According to other reports, Western-style marriage laws in Côte d'Ivoire have weakened the family structure and increased the divorce rate, which has further contributed to problems among young people.

Toward the end of their *Anthropological Inquiry*, Schlegel and Barry express concern about the negative impact of modernization on teens around the world. They note, for example, that whereas teens in many preindustrial nations often initiated their own recreational activities (composing songs, organizing village festivities, and so on), the imported youth culture "is largely one manipulated by adults who provide what they believe adolescents will buy." Hence "modern adolescents seldom act as autonomous groups in constructive, socially meaningful ways." Ironically, they say, Westernized teens "are losing incentives to plan and act at the same time that they are becoming increasingly emancipated from the control of parents and other authorities." Moreover, as we've seen, Westernized education "removes adolescent children [sic] from home and kin and places them in peer settings for much of the day," leading to conflict between teens and parents and a reduction in parental authority. Parental authority is further eroded by the delay of marriage which, they say, produces a host of new problems, such as an increase in the number of premarital pregnancies.[36]

Dasen concludes from the substantial body of research he reviews that "the problems of adolescence are certainly not inevitable."[37] The problems are largely created by culture, just as Margaret Mead's imperfect study of the Samoans suggested nearly a century ago.

The Underlying Mechanism. Although Dasen and others have shown the powerful effect that culture can have on the creation of adolescence, they have sometimes failed to point to the basic mechanism that underlies many of the problems that emerge: the artificial extension of childhood.

What is it that preindustrial teens are *seeing* in those films and on those television programs? Answer: Teens being treated like, and behaving like, irresponsible children.

When teens in preindustrial societies are forced to attend Western-style schools, how are they affected? Answer: They're cut off from adults and from the centrality of adult culture; they're prevented from working, or at least from making work the center of their lives; they become controlled by adults rather than part of adult life; teens, rather than adults, become their role models.

When Western mechanisms delay marriage, what is the outcome? Answer: Because marriage is the hallmark of adulthood in virtually all cultures, the delay of marriage also means the delay of adulthood. It's no coincidence that Tom Smith's recent survey (discussed in Chapter One) showed that Americans now think that adulthood starts at age twenty-six; the median age for first marriages in the United States is now about 26.1.

THE SPREADING STORM

We've seen examples of how teens live and fare in several preindustrial societies. Here is a quick overview of how teens are doing in the rest of the world.

Japan and China

According to *The World's Youth*, a recent volume edited by B. Bradford Brown of the University of Wisconsin-Madison, Reed W. Larson of the University of Illinois at Urbana-Champaign, and T. S. Saraswathi of the Maharaja Sayajirao University of Baroda (India),[38] modern China and Japan "have several terms that can be used to refer to individuals during the adolescent period, but no general term to designate this life stage as a whole.... These terms refer to the state of puberty, one's generational status within the family, or the legal rights and responsibilities a person has. Most often, however, people are likely to refer to a young person by her or his school status.... Because this is the central role for adolescents in Japanese or Chinese society, it is no surprise that it is the preferred reference point for understanding and organizing adolescence in these societies."[39] But the rowdy, unruly, unkempt teen barely exists in these large, highly industrialized countries—although there are signs that this is changing.

According to Harold W. Stevenson and Akane Zusho of the University of Michigan, "growing interactions with the West," added to the turmoil of the modern worldwide economic system, are beginning to erode the famed stability of the Asian youth. Ten percent of Japanese high school students are now believed to have had experience with drugs (compared with perhaps 60 percent in the United States), and 70 percent have had experience with alcohol (compared with perhaps 90 percent in the United States).[40]

Nevertheless, Japanese and Chinese teens are still a fairly calm and respectful lot. Eighty to 90 percent of Japanese teens say their home life is "fun" or "pleasant," and most teens there report having good relationships with their parents, with communication occurring on a "fairly regular basis."[41] Even more significant, "there

is little evidence of maladjustment" among Japanese youth, and the suicide rate, although increasing, is still only 4.4 per 100,000 for individuals ages fifteen-to-twenty—considerably lower than the rate among Japanese in their twenties and about half the rate for American teens.[42] In China the rate of "serious mental disorders" among ten-to-fourteen-year-olds is only 0.5 per 1,000, rising to 2.7 per 1,000 for individuals between fifteen and nineteen—both very low figures.[43]

How can this be? Why didn't heavy industrialization—well underway for decades in both China and Japan (the second largest economy in the world)—lead to the corruption of teens as it did in the United States and much of Europe?

Industrialization is more recent in both of these countries, for one thing, and much of China is still nonindustrial. What's more, neither country faced the unusual conditions present in newly industrial America which severed the child-adult continuum: massive exploitation of workers, hordes of young people on the street, and overwhelming immigration. And, perhaps of greatest significance, in neither country have women yet been released from their traditional roles.

I've lectured in Japan every year for more than a dozen years now—as it happens, to more than a thousand teens every year. I've always been amazed by the decorum of the Japanese classrooms and the almost eerie respect Japan teens show me and other adults. I've given many ninety-minute lectures to audiences of four hundred or more; not a single student has ever, to my knowledge, left during one of my lectures (what incredible bladders they must have!).

My experience in the United States—even at prestigious universities—has been radically different. Students don't think twice about arriving to lectures late, leaving early, or even munching on potato chips during the lecture. Traditional Asian cultures are based on strong reverence for ancestors and elders; even industrialization and a variety of Western influences haven't yet obliterated many of the basic values that form the bedrock of societies like Japan and China. How long these values can continue to resist our marketing moguls is a matter for speculation. Meanwhile, Western-style adolescence is still surprisingly rare in the dominant nations of Asia.

The Arab World

Arab countries also experience little Western-style adolescence. According to Marilyn Booth of the University of Illinois at Urbana-Champaign, although there's a term for adolescence in modern Arabic—*murahaqa*—it's used in textbooks only, not in everyday speech. It suggests a time of sexual temptation but not a time of turmoil. Other terms used for teens describe marital status or various levels of responsibility; the teen years are seen primarily as a time of growing "responsibility and obligation toward others." Teenage sexuality is highly regulated: "Sexual con-

tact outside of legally sanctioned marriage is strictly forbidden, and cohabitation before marriage is absolutely unacceptable."

The out-of-control, disrespectful, drug-abusing teen still seems to be a rarity in Arab countries, in part because life in many Arab countries is highly constrained and also because "blind adherence to Westernization has never been acceptable and is increasingly criticized."[44]

That having been said, the Western influence is still being felt, as we've seen from the Davis and Davis study in Morocco. Some textbooks, for example, are now teaching Arab teens about a stage of life called "adolescence." Booth cites a study in which a Bedouin girl in Egypt is talking about this strange concept: "Kamla now quoted from a book she had read at school [which said] it was natural as one entered adolescence to begin thinking about members of the opposite sex. She admitted that such things had never entered her mind before."[45] In Morocco, according to Davis and Davis, "school has 'created' the concept [of adolescence] as well as the expectation of behaviors associated with it."[46] In Bahrain, increases in juvenile delinquency led in the 1990s to the establishment of the country's first residential juvenile home, and Kuwait's first juvenile court was established in 1982.[47]

Russia

With the collapse of the USSR in 1991 and Russia's subsequent painful shift from a state-controlled to a market economy, it's difficult to make any safe generalizations about Russian teens, other than the obvious: for more than a dozen years now, they've been bombarded by Hollywood images and ideals more than ever before in Russian history. There are signs that this bombardment, along with growing prosperity, is beginning to create a true, troubled, American-style teenager.

According to one Russian scholar a "vast Russian middle class" is now emerging in the country, and industrial output in Russia grew by a hefty 9 percent in 2000. Russia's gross domestic product is now the tenth largest in the world. Prosperity plus industrialization plus Western ideals spell trouble, and the trouble is already measurable. For example, in 1990 about 15 percent of Russian children were born out of wedlock; only six years later the figure had grown to 23 percent.[48]

Because of the country's high divorce rate (second only to the rate in the United States), about 15 percent of Russian teens now spend at least part of their lives outside of the traditional two-parent home (compared with about 47 percent in the United States).[49] Physical abuse of young people—typically related to alcohol consumption by fathers—appears to be increasing. Whereas there was some degree

of gender equality in the old USSR (at least in principal), it is rapidly disappearing in democratic Russia, leaving female teens out of the growing economy.[50]

The average age at which young Russians start to smoke has been decreasing in recent years—now down to 13.5 for females and 11.3 for males. Drug abuse among teens was virtually unheard of under the Soviets; the rate of abuse has increased "dramatically" in Russia in recent years. Anti-social behavior among teens was minimal under the collectivist culture of the Soviets, but at least one new study suggests that individualism is rapidly increasing among Russian teens—yet another sign of trouble brewing.[51]

Latin America

In Latin America, where Western television and movies are distributed widely, Western-style adolescence is increasing dramatically, fueled in part by economic problems that have created widespread unemployment among young people. In cultures where young people used to work side by side with adults from a young age, many are now idle or forced to attend poorly equipped and poorly staffed schools, increasing teen-to-teen contact and isolating teens from adult role models.

Western sexual ideals have also taken hold, which have contributed to an abandonment of traditional religious practices. On the other hand, an acute housing shortage still forces most young people to remain living at home with their parents until they can afford to marry—a recipe for intergenerational conflict.

Of greatest concern is a dramatic increase in youth violence. According to Carlos Welti of Mexico's National Autonomous University, "a new type of violence has made its debut in Latin America: violence in the schools, where armed adolescents have killed classmates or teachers," driven by "glorification in the media of violent behaviors and the media coverage of school shootings in the United States."

In some Latin American countries, adolescence is sometimes "suspended" and adulthood imposed when young people are recruited into the military (more about that in Chapter Nine).[52] When people are shooting at you, you grow up quickly.

India

Indian scholar T. S. Saraswathi, co-editor of *The World's Youth*, insists that "adolescence is the invention of a technological, industrial society marked by a discontinuity between childhood and adulthood."[53] Like Liedloff, Saraswathi believes that "the greater the continuity between childhood and adulthood..., the greater the possibility that a distinct phase or life stage called adolescence will be absent."

Surveying a "wide range of alternative patterns" in India, Saraswathi con-

cludes that in all classes other than India's relatively small upper class, "the transition from childhood to adulthood is marked more by continuity than by discontinuity, leaving little scope for the emergence of an adolescent culture." Continuity is also greater for females, whose social roles tend to be limited and well defined, than for males, "whose exposure to higher education and preparation for career roles prolongs the period of dependency upon their parents, delays marriage and the establishment of sustained heterosexual relationships, and exposes them to possible alternative life choices."[54]

Both tradition and great poverty keep young people working in India, which has the largest population of working youth in the world. It's believed that about ten million Indians under age fifteen work in India and that young people constitute between 10 and 33 percent of the workforce in various industries. According to UNICEF, as many as eleven million young people live on the streets in India, primarily in large cities and townships; these are mainly young people without jobs or stable family situations. Many develop "resiliency" and "self-preservation skills," but sometimes this means resorting to activities such as pimping, prostitution, theft, drug peddling, and begging.[55] I'll return to India in Chapter Eight (on love), but suffice it to say at this point that adolescence is still largely absent in most of this vast country.

Sub-Saharan Africa

A. Bame Nsamenang of the University of Yaounde in Cameroon, Africa, has an especially interesting take on adolescence. According to him, Western psychologists have defined and shaped the term based on their limited knowledge of teens in the rest of the world, sometimes even asserting that adolescence as they've defined it is universal. In that sense the concept of adolescence is, according to Nsamenang, both "Eurocentric" and "ethnocentric."

In sub-Saharan Africa, which includes virtually all of Africa south of Libya and Egypt and which subsumes more than five hundred million people—half of whom are under age fifteen—Western adolescence doesn't yet exist. Instead, as we've seen in Latin America, India, and elsewhere, the teen years are a time when teens are trained and groomed to take their place in adult society. Puberty rites, which mark initial entry into adulthood, are especially important and distinctive in many sub-Saharan African cultures. Full adulthood isn't achieved, however, until one is "married with children."[56]

Nsamenang's perspective is based largely on studies of youth in Cameroon, Kenya, and South Africa. As noted previously, studies in both Kenya and Côte

d'Ivoire (which is also sub-Saharan) have found significant signs of Western-style adolescence in areas touched by Western culture. Like it or not, adolescence might someday become typical in much of Africa.

Southeast Asia

In an overview of adolescence mainly in the Philippines and Malaysia, and, to some extent, Thailand and Indonesia, Madelene Santa Maria of De La Salle University in Manila presents a picture we've seen several times: "the introduction of 'Western' ways of life and values, as propagated in media especially in urban areas," leading to "increases in premarital sexuality and pregnancies," delinquency, crime, drug use, and so on.[57]

But every culture has its unique characteristics, as well as its unique ways of trying to keep adolescence at bay. Filipino teens, for example, believe that "close, warm ties among family members must be maintained, and that sacrifices should be made for the good of the family." But Santa Maria cites a recent study showing that Filipino teens are now "spending less time with their parents" and becoming "dissatisfied with family life."

One curious aspect of teen obligations in the Philippines and Indonesia is worthy of note. Daughters are more obligated than sons to work abroad to support the family during tough times. According to Santa Maria, "Sons are expected to stay close to home to better fulfill their obligation of 'protecting' the family."[58]

Worldwide, then, teen turmoil still seems fairly minimal compared with what we experience in the United States, but Western-style adolescence seems to be creeping slowly across many borders like hot lava from a persistent volcano. The stronger the influence of Western culture, the faster the flow; the stronger the endemic traditions, the greater the resistance.[59]

THE GODS MUST BE CRAZY, INDEED

The San people of the Kalahari Desert in Africa, immortalized in the 1981 film *The Gods Must Be Crazy*, as well as in a heartwarming 1984 sequel, have lately been under pressure to leave their ancestral land in Botswana because of a massive joint mining venture between the Botswana government and the De Beers diamond company. In 2002, to make its point, the government cut off water supplies to the San.[60]

The influence of industrialized nations can be both heavy-handed and deadly,

but even subtle interventions can have devastating and far-reaching effects. In *The Gods Must Be Crazy*, members of a primitive (but happy and self-sufficient) tribe are puzzled and disturbed when a Coke bottle, thrown out of a passing airplane, lands in their midst. They've never seen anything like this strange object. They decide that to appease their gods, a member of the tribe must find the edge of the world and throw the Coke bottle off. Thus begins a hilarious adventure in which a diminutive but resourceful San tribesman makes first contact with a series of inept Westerners. Unfortunately, one gets the uneasy feeling at the end of the film that real Coke bottles are about to have less amusing consequences for the real San, and indeed that turns out to be the case.

What We're Exporting

When it comes to teens around the world, just what kinds of practices and problems are we exporting? The answer, it seems, is crime, ennui, anger, premarital sex, pregnancy, abortion, drug abuse, family conflict, and more. Consider just one of our more subtle exports: according to a recent book by Mihaly Csikszentmihalyi and Barbara Schneider, *American teens are almost completely isolated from adults.*[61] Teens typically spend more than thirty-five hours per week surrounded by their peers in school and *an additional* thirty-five hours per week with peers outside of school. *That's two-thirds of their waking hours.* This is, according to these researchers, twelve more hours per week than teens in other industrialized nations like Italy or South Korea spend together, and it's probably sixty hours a week more than teens spend together in many preindustrial societies.

Many American teens—perhaps half or more—also grow up with little access to their father, and "for those lucky enough to have a father, the average teenager now spends less than half an hour a week alone with his or her father." Half of this time is spent watching television, "a situation that does not readily lend itself to quality parent-child interactions." Father-teen interactions in the United States are certainly "not enough to transmit the knowledge, values, attitudes, and skills that adult males should pass on to their children."[62] The child-adult continuum about which Jean Liedloff wrote is almost completely absent in the modern United States, and we're sending our broken model of family and community life to each and every village on earth, no matter how remote.

Through our films, television programs, laws, religious beliefs, and schooling and marriage practices, we're exporting a wide range of mechanisms that extend childhood well past puberty and that isolate teens from adults. We're creating prolonged, turbulent, Western-style adolescence, with all of its inherent problems.

We're creating generation gaps and family conflicts where none existed before. And because we ourselves have no idea how to deal with these problems, we're offering no solutions to the cultures we're corrupting.

Q: *Are you suggesting that teens should be able to smoke and drink, just like adults do? Shouldn't there be restrictions on their behavior?*

A: Many countries around the world have no age requirements for smoking and drinking, and, in some of those, at least, young people function fairly well without the restrictions. In addition, teens in our own country drink and smoke at high rates in spite of the laws; they not only imbibe and inhale, they also learn to disrespect adults and break the law while doing so. But I'm not suggesting that we abolish the laws that restrict drinking and smoking but rather that we replace age-based laws with competency-based laws. We do this, more or less, when it comes to driving. In rural areas, it's still common for young people to drive farm vehicles as soon as they're physically able—sometimes as young as nine or ten. In the big city, we allow most teens to drive in limited ways when they're fifteen and to get minimally-restrictive drivers licenses when they're sixteen—as long as they can pass appropriate competency tests, both written tests and road tests. Some teens pass, and some fail; some drive, and some don't, at least not until they can demonstrate appropriate competency. That's the key here. As long as the competency can be demonstrated, we should extend the privilege. Isn't it possible that some young teens might be able to drink or smoke responsibly—that is, exercising appropriate caution and with full knowledge of the risks?

Chapter 4

Instant Adulthood

Overview. Programs like the George Junior Republic, founded over a century ago, as well as modern programs like Outward Bound, show the enormous power that responsibility has in helping young people to mature. When allowed to function like adults, young people quickly rise to the challenge. On the other hand, correctional boot camps and harsh military schools merely infantilize young people even more than usual; in general, they do more harm than good.

Micky, with no *e*, was a gang leader in one of the toughest neighborhoods in New York in the 1890s. He was as tough as they came in those days—which, admittedly, may not have been all that tough by today's standards. It's hard to say; the crimes were certainly violent at times, but they lacked the AK-47s of today's gang world. That aside, Micky, who I'm guessing was fifteen or sixteen at the time, finally got caught for an "unusually serious offense." After his conviction a judge offered him a choice between a reformatory and a place called "George Junior Republic" in a town in upstate New York called Freeville, near Ithaca. He had no idea what the Junior Republic was, but a friend had coached him to pick it, and he was soon on his way.

Micky's story is told in a book called *Citizens Made and Remade: An Interpretation of the Significance and Influence of George Junior Republics* by William R. George and Lyman Beecher Stowe (Harriet Beecher Stowe's grandson).[1] Published in 1912, the book was a sequel to George's *The Junior Republic*, published two years earlier.[2]

Both books document the founding and proliferation of communities that gave troubled youth a new lease on life. The concept was straightforward: take tough people off the streets and put them onto a productive track, not through medication or therapy or treatments or "interventions" but by giving them a wagon load of responsibility.

Micky was quite bewildered when he arrived at the Freeport community, and the first thing he did was steal a watch from another young resident and then run for the railroad station. On his way out of town he was apprehended, not by the conventional police, but by yet another resident of the Republic, and he soon found himself tried and convicted by a true jury of his peers. Even the judge, district attorney, and lawyers were teens. After being locked up for a few weeks, Micky took a job working for a young contractor who used to be a member of his old gang in New York, and, according to the authors, Micky gradually became "industrious, clean, orderly, and law-abiding."[3]

WILLIAM GEORGE AND THE POWER OF RESPONSIBILITY

Micky's story may sound too good to be true, but William George was the real thing, and what eventually became a small network of miracle-working communities was real too. As a young man living with his parents in New York, George was hellbent on saving and reforming every downtrodden young man in the city, and he had plenty from which to choose. This was the 1890s, when industrialization kept millions of people working thirteen-hour days in gritty factories that were proliferating rapidly—and that also kept tens of thousands of people, both young and old, homeless on the streets.

George convinced his parents to take in three or four homeless boys, and then he tried to create a small dairy business to help them earn their keep. When that idea failed, he decided to infiltrate and reform the street gangs. He founded a boxing club, gaining the respect of many gang members by literally pounding them into submission, and then, quite deliberately, pulled a fast one: as the new gang leader, he transformed his gang "from a law-defying into a law-enforcing group" called the Law-and-Order Gang. He offered the services of his gang to the local police sergeant to help fight crime, and he didn't stop there:

> ...as commander-in-chief, [George] was to advance from district to district, leaving his trusted lieutenants in command of the conquered locality, and taking with him each time a picked company of faithful followers to help capture the new territory.[4]

One member of his gang was asked whether his gang had "really" been so bad before George reformed it. He replied, "I don't know what you'd call it. We'd smash a fellow's skull in for a nickel."[5] In other words, George had made a difference. Just how many people he saved is not clear, and the gang project eventually got off track, but George had learned something critical: *giving troubled young people real responsibility turns them instantly into responsible citizens.*

The George Junior Republics

In 1895, with land made available by friends and family, he applied this lesson to a much more ambitious project. He created a miniature—or "Junior"—version of the "Big Republic": an entire community where troubled youth would, he conjectured, instantly shed their errant ways by governing that community, and, of course, themselves. By all accounts, George's project worked well, and similar Republics were established in Connecticut, Pennsylvania, Maryland, New Jersey, and California. The original Republic in Freeville even still exists, but although this should be the ultimate testimony to the soundness of George's vision, the contemporary George Junior Republic is radically different from the original. More about that shortly.

The new communities were truly republics. Believing that self-government was "one of the highest forms of responsibility,"[6] George designed them to be run entirely by their residents. The age of majority was set at fifteen, and people under fifteen were mentored by full citizens, all between the ages of fifteen and nineteen. A commission established in 1913 to evaluate the effectiveness of the Republics found that of twelve hundred young people who had left the Republics, "not more than 5 percent may at present be regarded as failures" and "fully two-thirds have achieved positive success, in that they are supporting themselves and those dependent on them and also in many instances do some definite work in the aid of other individuals."

The *New York Times* article that reported the findings of the commission also noted that "among the more successful ex-citizens we have lawyers, civil engineers, contractors, teachers, physicians, and professional nurses, newspaper men, public office holders, mechanics, farmers, gardeners, plumbers, carpenters, [and] printers."[7]

George himself found—as I have also observed in my teaching, by the way—that the toughest characters sometimes became the highest achievers:

> As time went on, Mr. George noticed that those citizens who caused the most trouble when they first came usually became the best and strongest leaders before they left. Finally this became so marked that he announced that general badness, so far as the boys were concerned, would be regarded as a special qualification for citizenship in the Junior Republic.[8]

Unfortunately, Mr. George was soon ejected from his own organization by the board of trustees he had formed to help oversee its rapid growth. At least three young female residents claimed that George had been sexually aggressive with them, and one claimed to have had his child. A committee investigating the various allegations concluded that "his presence in the institution is clearly undesirable."[9]

Abandoning the Vision

In spite of his sudden exit, several of the Republics continued to flourish and to follow his original model until perhaps the 1970s. Actor Steve McQueen was one of the more conspicuous (and grateful) graduates of the California "Boys Republic" in the 1940s.[10] But George's ideals—and decades of success—were no match for the ever-advancing artificial extension of childhood. As society in general came to believe that older and older people needed the protection of adults, the Republics shifted from the responsibility model to the modern treatment model: troubled youth need to be medicated, "treated" by "professionals," and so on. At some point, males and females were segregated, and in 1991 the original republic became strictly male. The current literature of the Republic proudly advertises a staff-to-resident ratio of 1 to 4[11]; so much for responsibility.

Is the modern program successful? According to the Freeville program's recent literature, "Since 1983, over 1,200 families have been served in the George Junior Republic Family Therapy Unit. The youths in placement *who gained a recommended discharge* and *had active participation with their family* have a 72-percent success rate, which is defined as *not recidivating through the first year after discharge* [all italics added]."[12]

In other words, the runaways and the dropouts—and we don't how many of those there were—didn't fare so well, and neither did the graduates who didn't have family support. We don't know how many of those there were either. For the ones who met the criteria, we also don't know much beyond the first year—how many turned out to be doctors, lawyers, plumbers, career criminals, or murderers. As far as I can tell, modern teen "therapy" or "treatment" programs are far less effective than the old responsibility-driven programs, but it's difficult to make direct comparisons.

Here's a disturbing footnote on the modernization of the Junior Republics. Just as I was completing this chapter I spotted a small Associated Press story entitled "Teens killed counselor, took truck," which reported the strangling of a forty-three-year-old counselor by two teens at "a private residential school and treatment center" north of Pittsburgh.[13] It turns out that this is one of the remaining George Junior Republics. Note that it's now a "treatment center," not a republic.

A Modern Law-and-Order Gang

William George's vision—the uncorrupted version—is remarkably similar to that of a more contemporary crusader, Curtis Sliwa. In 1968 at age fourteen Sliwa founded one of the country's first neighborhood recycling centers in his parents' basement. He used the monthly income from selling sorted drums full of cans, glass, and newspapers to help neighborhood children. At fifteen he was named "newspaper boy of the year" by the *New York Daily News* for rescuing a family of six from a burning building. At sixteen he was summoned to the White House to meet President Nixon in recognition of his effective community activism.[14]

But Sliwa is best known for founding the Guardian Angels, a group of young people trained in martial arts and sporting red berets who made it their business to protect the innocent on New York subways. This was back in 1979, when Sliwa was a night manager at a McDonald's, frustrated over the growing crime problem in New York. Just as George had done a century before with his Law and Order Gang, Sliwa took tough young people and transformed them into productive citizens, mainly by giving them meaningful adult responsibilities and a positive mission. Angels chapters now exist in cities throughout North America, as well as on three other continents. Sliwa's philosophy should now be familiar: *"Empower people to help themselves, build self-esteem and confidence, arm them with responsibility, and you tap into the greatest source of lasting good possible."*[15]

BOYS-TO-MEN TOWN

Better known than the Junior Republics is a similar endeavor called Boys Town, founded near Omaha, Nebraska, by Father Edward Joseph Flanagan in 1921. In 1912 Flanagan, a young immigrant priest from Ireland, was assigned to a small parish in O'Neill, Nebraska, where he became interested in the plight of unemployed men and, eventually, of troubled youth. In 1917, with a small donation from his friend, Henry Monsky, Flanagan rented an old Victorian mansion and, with the blessing of his church (but no money), dubbed it the Home for Homeless Boys. Starting with a handful of residents, he soon outgrew the mansion and, just four years later, founded an extraordinary community called Boys Town ten miles west of Omaha, initially with about two hundred young residents.[16]

By now, even if you've never heard of Boys Town, you probably can guess what made this community remarkable: like the Republics, it was run almost entirely by the troubled young men who came there. It eventually had its own schools, chapel,

---

YOUNG PEOPLE IN ACTION

Boys Town: The Movie

Starring Spencer Tracy as reformer Father Flanagan and Mickey Rooney as tough young Whitey Marsh, this 1938 fictional film made the real Boys Town famous. The film dramatizes the founding of Boys Town, then shifts to a complex plot focusing on young Whitey. His big brother Joe, a career criminal, has begged Flanagan to try to save Whitey from his own sad fate, but Whitey is so incorrigible that the task seems impossible. When Whitey runs away from Boys Town, Pee Wee, his young companion, is struck by a car. Then Whitey is shot in the leg by his own brother during a robbery. At the end, Whitey, with help from both Joe and Flanagan, saves the day and is elected Mayor of Boys Town. Unfortunately, the film made Boys Town seem so successful that contributions to the real town fell after the film's release.[20]

---

post office, gymnasium, cottages, police force, commissioners, city council, and mayor. The latter were all young men, and many of the structures in the community were built by the residents. The community was incorporated as its own town in 1936.[17]

Flanagan's philosophy was a variant of one with which you're already familiar, captured well by the old saw, "The Devil makes work for idle hands." Said Flanagan:

> *I looked at the street boys with a sadness. Like all children, even poorly fed ones, they had too much energy. And what outlet had these poor boys for that energy? No place to play but that crowded, filthy street. Nothing to do but to get into deviltry—no proper direction. Is it any wonder they turn to wrong?[18]*

He believed that placing troubled young men in a supportive, homelike environment and then giving them responsibility for running their own lives would put them on the right track. Even though many of the young people in his community had been convicted of crimes—some quite serious—and were referred by judges, Flanagan insisted that the community not be surrounded by fences or walls and that the doors not have locks on them. "I am not building a prison," he told community residents. "This is a home. You do not wall in members of your family."[19]

A Resident Reminisces

I recently tracked down one of the few surviving residents of the original Boys Town, a former actor and veterans advocate, Bob Paradise, now in his eighties and living in Southern California. Bob was a resident of Boys Town from about

1932 to 1938. He came there at age thirteen, rescued from the life he had been living on the streets since his parents had been killed. During his last four years at Boys Town he was the Chief of Police. When there were problems, Paradise said, "We just took care of it, like in the city. We stopped the fight, or whatever it was. We had about ten policemen."

Although there were some adults in the community, "They didn't interfere with us," Paradise said, "because we had to do what we were supposed to do. We never had a situation we couldn't handle."

Following his graduation from Boys Town, Paradise enlisted in the U.S. Army and was sent to the Philippines, where he took law classes at the University of Manila under Army auspices. His education was interrupted when war broke out, and in 1942 he was captured by the Japanese. Paradise was one of the survivors of the horrendous Bataan Death March, in which twenty thousand U.S. soldiers perished, and he remained a prisoner of war until liberated by U.S. forces in 1945. His subsequent careers—in acting, directing, and legal advocacy—have all been distinguished ones. Today he specializes in representing women veterans on sexual harassment issues.

Another Vision Lost

Boys Town, alas, was transformed over the years into a very different entity than the one Father Flanagan created. The project's success set the transformation in motion: even while Flanagan was still alive (he died in 1948), the financial success of the community allowed its administrators to hire more and more adult "professionals" to take over construction, farming, cooking, and other tasks—which meant less hard work for the residents. And, of course, the changing perspectives on teens in American society—the inexorable and ever-increasing extension of childhood—led gradually to the implementation of the modern "treatment" approach at Boys Town, which became coed in 1979 and is now called Girls and Boys Town.

The community, now housing about seven hundred young people, is run these days according to "operant behaviorism" and "social learning theory" principles; basically, residents go to school and earn points for good behavior, and the points can then be exchanged for privileges.[21] All activities are closely supervised by adults. In other words, it's now a somewhat typical "group home," run largely by my colleagues in psychology.

Paradise thinks the new version doesn't hold a candle to the old. It's too "commercial," he says, and it lacks the "friendship" and "camaraderie" of the old school. At some point, said Paradise, the modern version of Boys Town also stopped accepting the true "incorrigibles"—those referred by criminal courts for having committed serious crimes. The new treatment-oriented community also appears to lack the basic

structure that Flanagan instinctively knew was necessary for producing significant life change—one based on meaningful responsibility and control over one's life.[22]

Boys Towns in Italy

Another Irish priest, Monsignor John Patrick Carroll-Abbing, a relief worker in Italy at the end of World War II, established another chain of George/Flanagan-like communities in Italy beginning in 1945 after he noticed that young post-war street urchins in Rome seemed to be remarkably self-sufficient. The first was started near the town of Civitavecchia, forty-five miles north of Rome, and other Italian "Boys' Towns" (the first was initially called the "Shoeshine Boys' Hotel") were later created in Palermo, Lucca, Pozzuoli, Chieti, Rome, and elsewhere; eventually, separate "Girls' Towns" were established. All were governed by the young residents, generally from ten to twenty years old, based on Carroll-Abbing's belief (according to community materials) that "young people will react enthusiastically to authentic challenge that fulfills their humanity."[23]

Italy has so far avoided the "mental health" and "treatment" models that dominate here, and teens there are still often considered to be young adults. Not only do all of the Italian Boys' and Girls' Towns still exist, they are all still run largely according to Carroll-Abbing's original design.

The Down Side of Treatment

Given my background in psychology, you might be surprised by the skepticism I'm expressing about the "treatment" approach to teen problems. In fact, I earned my doctorate working with the eminent behavioral psychologist, B. F. Skinner, arguably the key person behind modern behavioristic and social-learning interventions.

Although these interventions are powerful in changing behavior—especially in the short-term—I've never been convinced that they actually change *people* in any significant sense, at least not when we're dealing with relatively normal young people and adults. I helped train staff and consulted on "cases" at a variety of institutions for many years, and it was generally my impression that the residents and "patients" were just going along with the programs—complying with instructions and requests mainly to avoid penalties, lying in wait for the opportunity to leave the facility. Many were bleary-eyed from too much medication; few had meaningful relationships with other residents (why bother, when people come and go frequently and it's virtually impossible to keep in touch?); and meaningful relationships with staff were strictly forbidden.

Skinner himself long extolled the virtues of "natural contingencies" of reinforcement and punishment over the "contrived contingencies" one finds in

treatment programs,[24] but many of Skinner's followers have missed this point. The natural consequences of behavior—the warm and sincere embrace of a dear friend one has helped, the anger of someone one has offended, the sight of crops one has planted with one's own hands—are far more impactful than the insincere praise and M&M-like points and tokens of a "b-mod" program. The brilliance of the George- and Flanagan-style communities lay, I believe, in the sublime power of the natural contingencies those communities provided.

GROWING UP IN THE WOODS

Julian, my eldest son, had some rough teen years. I'm sure I don't know a fraction of what actually happened, because I was raising Justin—the easy one—while my ex-wife was struggling with Julian. When he was fourteen, his mom sent him off on a $3,000 trip to the woods for a few weeks to try to straighten him out. As Julian remembers it:

> Mom said it was either military school or twenty-four days on Hurricane Island. It was an easy choice. We had to carry all of our supplies for three weeks on our backs, so our packs weighed upwards of sixty pounds. Our two counselors left us alone much of the time to get us to try to resolve our own disputes and figure out how the map worked. By the end of the first week my mosquito bites had melded into one continuous bite.
>
> The first week or so was all hiking through woods and trails; the second week was almost entirely canoeing; and the final nine days was spent hiking up hills and mountains. About midway through the trip we were required to separate and spend a day and a night alone in the woods.
>
> One day was set aside for white water rafting—a first for most of us. It was incredible. I remember seeing a bear cub sliding down a tree as it tried to flee from us. The most spiritual moment for me was when we finally reached the top of our first mountain. I'll never forget the awesome sight of the water and forests far beneath us. I took a peaceful nap by a cliff.
>
> At the end of the trip everyone who had attended Outward Bound (there were many, many groups) was expected to run an eleven-mile marathon. The night before the race I ate something that made me sick and I was up until the next morning throwing up. I wasn't able to race with the group, so the counselors insisted that I make the run myself the next morning. I left the trailing counselor in the dust, and realized by the end of the 11 miles (which was quite easy for me) that I was now in the best shape of my life.

Julian was one of many thousands of young people who are, in a sense, aban-

YOUNG PEOPLE IN ACTION

Navigating the Teen Years

In 1858 on a voyage around Cape Horn, 19-year-old Mary Patten's husband, the captain of a large clipper ship, fell ill. The first mate was in irons for insubordination; the second mate was ignorant of navigation. Mrs. Patten had made herself mistress of the art of navigation during a previous voyage. She took command, and for fifty-two days she navigated the ship of eighteen hundred tons, tending her husband the while, and took both safely into San Francisco.

—Samuel Eliot Morison, *The Maritime History of Massachusetts*

doned in the woods each year by an innovative organization called Outward Bound, which came into being—indirectly, anyway—because of another young man named Julian more than sixty years ago.

Origins of Outward Bound

In 1941 young Julian Holt was a student at a private school in Wales (U.K.) called the Gordonstoun School, founded and directed by Kurt Hahn, a German-Jewish genius who had originally founded the school in Germany in 1920 but later fled to England to escape persecution by the Nazis.[25] Hahn's teaching philosophy was a radical departure from the authoritarian style of the German schools of his day.

Hahn believed that he could build character in young people by giving them real responsibilities, putting them on their "honor," encouraging them to provide "service" to the community, providing only minimal supervision, and subjecting them to vigorous exercise. He was staunchly opposed to imposing education on people who weren't ready to learn, which he compared with "pouring and pouring into a jug and never looking to see whether the lid is off."[26] Julian's father, the English shipping magnate Sir Lawrence Holt, was a major contributor to the school and a strong supporter of Hahn's.

With England at war against Germany, Holt was deeply concerned about the lack of physical and emotional toughness in British Navy cadets. Hahn suggested that they create an offshoot of Gordonstoun to build a new generation of tough, independent British seamen. The new program, at first called the Aberdovey Sailing School (later: Outward Bound), was launched in 1941 with eight students from the Gordonstoun School, eight workers from Holt's shipping company, and eight young cadets from a British Naval ship, the H.M.S. Conway.

Hahn had come to believe that two- or three- week programs (mainly for young soldiers and firefighters) had virtually no long-term effects on performance and that it took at least twenty-eight days to toughen someone up long-term.[27] Thus began the system that is still used widely today in Outward Bound programs around the world: twenty-eight (or, today, sometimes twenty-four) days of rigorous physical training, individual and team challenges, and outdoor adventures.

Training Toughness and Independence

In the original program, young people "learned to throw a javelin, discus and shotput, to do long and high jumps, to run and sprint and, above all, to climb and walk long distances in the rugged Welsh hills."[28] According to Renate Wilson, author of *Inside Outward Bound*, "Towards the end of the twenty-eight days even the weediest were sent on cross-country hikes of up to thirty miles, climbing a couple of peaks on the way." Although some expressed concern initially that the program would "strain" the students, "[Hahn's] training methods demonstrated that every youngster could improve his athletic performance, no matter how inexperienced he was in a sport, and that he would not be harmed by the effort."[29]

Hahn and Holt's program also included rigorous training on and above the water, because Naval fortitude was the primary goal: rowing, sailing, climbing nets, running obstacle courses, climbing rope ladders, crossing ropes strung between trees, climbing smooth walls that approximated the sides of ships, and "getting the boys to clamber over the rigging" of a local sailing ship. "The ropes course," according to Wilson, "became one of the features built into every Outward Bound school."[30]

Participants were organized into "watches" of twelve individuals, another custom that is maintained to this day, and within each watch, a captain and other officials were elected by the watch members. Individual responsibility was stressed throughout the program. Among other things, participants "kept a record of their own progress in athletics, seamanship and land expeditions, and were put on their honor not to cheat."[31] The program was said to be an immediate success: Aberdovey "toughened [participants'] bodies and armed them against the 'enemies within'—fear, defeatism, apathy, selfishness."[32] It continued to train young cadets and potential cadets until the War's end in 1945.

After the war, similar Outward Bound schools were established in Ullswater (near the original school) and Holn Park in Devon, and an all-female version was founded in Rhownair, a few miles from Averdovey. The British Army founded two additional Outward Bound schools in Wales and Norway. In the early 1950s, Joshua Milner III, one of the teachers at the Gordonstoun School, founded the Outward

> ## YOUNG PEOPLE IN ACTION
>
> ### Leaving Drugs Behind
>
> *Can a wilderness experience help a young person kick drugs? According to a 1991 report in the* Journal of Adolescent Chemical Dependency, *the wild outdoors might be just the environment some young people need to get clean and sober. Jeff, one of the subjects in the study, was a sixteen-year-old high school student with a long history of drug abuse—cocaine, marijuana, alcohol, and more, five times a week. He said drugs were his way of "finding freedom"—an escape from his father's controlling ways. A multiple-component treatment program at the Beech Hill Hospital in New Hampshire included twenty-two days in an Outward Bound wilderness school. Jeff started out in tears because his pack was too heavy—and ended up crying with relief and gratitude because he had grown so much in the wild. Three months later, Jeff was still sober. About three-quarters of the young people in the program appeared to reap similar benefits.[38]*

Bound movement in the United States, which now consists of a series of "wilderness schools" and urban centers throughout the country. In addition, more than a thousand institutions of various sorts in the U.S.—universities, government agencies, and so on—use Outward Bound methodology to train their constituents.[33]

Among the organization's many programs, the "Ascent Program" is of special interest here. It's designed, according to program materials, to help people from fourteen to seventeen to "navigate through...treacherous water, teach them skills to ease the transition, and to learn more about themselves as a whole human being." It's touted as "an early intervention for teens who may have started down a self-destructive path, but who have not yet burned any vital bridges."[34] In other words, they're not looking for convicted criminals, but, according to Wilson, about 5 percent of their participants are in fact ordered to attend Outward Bound by "correctional services or a benevolent foundation."[35]

How Outward Bound Helps

But does it work? What effects, if any, does a challenging program emphasizing individual responsibility have on teens?

Dozens of research studies have been conducted over a period of several decades to answer this question, and the results have been overwhelmingly positive. A study of sixty delinquents published in 1969, for example, found that participation in Outward Bound produced "more favorable social attitudes and evaluation of feel-

ings."[36] The key, according to the authors, is that "a young man should not just be told that he is capable of more than he thinks he can do, but rather a set of circumstances must be devised in which he demonstrates such competence to himself."[37]

A Boston University study conducted in 1972 found, with non-delinquent individuals in their late teens, that the Outward Bound experience produced positive changes in the participants' "self-concept" —roughly, their assessment of their own abilities and self-worth; the gains declined when the teens returned to their home environments.[39] A 1982 study by Alan Wright of Pennsylvania State University with juvenile delinquents found that Outward Bound produced positive changes in "self-esteem" (roughly, an assessment of self-worth), "self-efficacy" (an assessment of one's ability to perform in various ways), and other measures of cognitive functioning.[40] A 1981 review of seventy-three studies of Outward Bound-type programs by Leslie Burton of Rutgers sums up the findings, both positive and negative, of such studies:

> In general, the results indicate that Outward Bound-type programs do have a positive impact upon self perceptions such as self-concept, locus of control, self-assertion and personality.... Actual behavior such as grade-point average, observed behavior, school functioning and absenteeism does not undergo much significant change as a result of Outward Bound-type programs. One notable exception is recidivism, which is markedly reduced in the methodologically select studies.[41]

Subsequent studies confirm these general conclusions, and a recent study by Scott Husted of the University of Nebraska-Lincoln even finds that Outward Bound "positively influences academic achievement" in at-risk teens.[42] I've been unable to find a single study that suggests that Outward Bound produces any negative effects—physical, emotional, cognitive, or behavioral.

Limitations of Outward Bound

Unfortunately, Outward Bound is only a halfway measure; it gives people real challenges and real responsibilities—*but not in the real world*. It necessarily runs into a problem psychologists call "transfer of training": what people learn in one environment doesn't necessarily transfer to other environments, especially when those other environments place very different demands on the learners. When the original Outward Bound was toughening up people to enter the Navy, it subsequently sent them *to the Navy*. When troubled young people are toughened up in a modern Outward Bound program, they're subsequently sent back to the streets they came from—and to a world that treats them like helpless children.

YOUNG PEOPLE IN ACTION

Presidential Precedent

George Washington, first president of the United States, completed his education in his early teens. At sixteen, he went to work for Lord Thomas Fairfax, surveying land in the Shenandoah Valley of Virginia. He spent part of his earnings on land purchases, and by twenty-one, had fifteen hundred acres of his own.

Fortunately, the transfer problem is irrelevant to the main question I'm exploring in this volume. I'm not asking whether a four-week experience can produce a permanent or profound effect on behavior but rather whether young people are capable of behaving responsibly. The Outward Bound studies make it abundantly clear that Hahn was right. *When you give young people a significant amount of responsibility—in the case of Outward Bound, by subjecting them to enormous challenges in the wilderness—they rise to those challenges.* As a bonus, many are changed in positive and significant ways that carryover to some extent to the real world. At the very least, they begin to view themselves as more effective, more capable people, even though home and school environments have been telling them that they're helpless, mindless children.

Outward Bound is the largest, oldest, and best-known of a number of "adventure-based" programs that expose people, young and old, to challenging and sometimes life-changing experiences. For young participants, Outward Bound-type adventures provide, in many cases, the first opportunity they've ever had to function as tough, self-reliant, individuals. The natural world used to provide those opportunities early in life, but now, it seems, we must pay large sums (these programs cost between $3,000 and $60,000 to attend) to professionals to give our children a taste of real responsibility. Is this the best we can do? Are there other ways to help young people grow up?

DOES MILITARY SCHOOL WORK?

My son chose Outward Bound over the dreaded, proverbial "military school." Just what is military school these days, and what effect, if any, does it have on young people?

Bear in mind that modern high-school level military schools or their close relatives—correctional "boot camps"—aren't real military operations. Real military acad-

emies and boot camps serve a real purpose: to condition young soldiers, both physically and mentally, to kill real enemies and follow the orders of superiors (see Chapter Nine). Real soldiers are not treated like children. Quite the contrary: they're taught to use lethal weapons for legitimate, or at least government-sanctioned, purposes.

There are obvious reasons for real military training camps to exist and for the instructors at those camps to impose rigorous training regimens on new soldiers. As we look at correctional boot camps and military schools for young people, ask yourself whether they have the legitimacy of real military programs. If they don't, expect problems.

Correctional Boot Camps

In the early 1980s, Georgia, Louisiana, and Oklahoma pioneered harsh, military-style "boot camps" as a way of dealing with rising crime rates and extreme overcrowding in state prisons.[43] Here's how a 1995 article described the entry of teen offenders into a camp in Manatee, Florida:

> All is quiet at the Manatee (Fla.) sheriff's boot camp as a van load of teen-aged lawbreakers slowly rolls up the drive to a stop. Seconds pass. Suddenly, a shrill whistle shatters the silence. A swarm of sheriff's deputies appears from nowhere. Beating their fists on the van, a dozen officers in dark glasses and drill sergeant hats scream orders at the startled youths inside.
>
> The camp's newest recruits are hauled out of the van. Searched and patted down. Subjected to a head-shaving. And it all happens in double-time, with high-decibel deputies barking commands just inches from the young toughs' faces.
>
> "I was scared senseless," recalls a 17-year-old recruit, whose conviction for battery, burglary and car theft brought him a four-month sentence at the Florida camp.[44]

Imagine that you're one of the inductees. How would you react to the harshness of your reception? How would you react to the day-by-day abuse you suffer at the hands of the officers? Bearing in mind that you're not being prepared to fight a war, or even to get a challenging job—in other words, that there's no easy way to excuse the objectionable behavior of your oppressors—how would you account for the cruelty to which you're being subjected? Would your respect for authority increase, or would you feel more contempt for authority after such an experience?

Early reports on the correctional boot camps, such as an article about the Georgia camps that appeared in *LIFE* magazine in 1988, were encouraging:

> After prison, 70 percent avoid going back. After [boot camp], 80 percent of the young

*men stay out of trouble. To all appearances, these boot camps seem to be a plausible way to
reduce the socially and economically disastrous overcrowding that thirty-seven states are
under court order to alleviate.*[45]

The Ford Foundation provided $100,000 to support the boot camp program,
and by the late 1980s at least fifteen states were running or developing similar
programs. The point of such programs, according to the *Life* article, was "to penetrate thick young adult skulls before it's too late."[46] Truett Goodwin, identified in
the article as a warden in the Georgia boot camp at Forsyth, explained the guiding
philosophy with the well-tuned sensitivity of a seasoned educator: "You have to hit a
mule between the eyes with a two-by-four to get his attention. And that's exactly what
we're doing with this program."[47]

Abuse and Sadism

Tough correctional boot camps need tough correctional employees. As you
might expect, these sometimes turn out to be people who enjoy shouting at and
pushing around young people all day.

By the mid-1990s, troubling reports began to appear about "abuse" and "sadism" at various boot camps. In 1998 five staff members at a boot camp in Oracle,
Arizona—the Arizona Boys Ranch—were indicted in connection with the death of a
sixteen-year-old resident there. One of those indicted was the camp nurse, to whom
the young man had been sent repeatedly with complaints of chest pains and difficulty breathing. The nurse kept sending him back to the regular staff, who continued to subject him to strenuous exercises. The coroner's report noted that he died of
empyema, a condition involving a buildup of fluids in the chest cavity, in his case
more than two-and-a-half quarts of pus. He was also suffering from chronic bronchi-
tis, pneumonia, and strep and staph infections, and his body was covered with cuts
and bruises—seventy-one in all.[48]

Eventually, the Arizona Boys Ranch was denied a license to operate, and
seventeen of its former employees were listed in the Arizona Child Abuser Directory. Other deaths and abuses at boot camps have also come to light over the years.
Arizona, Maryland, North Dakota, Georgia, and Colorado have now shut down
their boot camps entirely, and California and Florida are scaling back.[49] At this
writing, Louisiana has just shut down Tallulah, its toughest juvenile prison, because of a ten-year history of riots, beatings, and rapes (both by staff and by other
inmates)—and because of a recidivism rate of about 60 percent.[50]

A 1998 report issued by the Kansas-based Koch Crime Institute suggests

that recidivism might actually be slightly higher for boot camp attendees than for participants in traditional correctional programs: between 64 and 75 percent of boot camp graduates, according to Koch, commit crimes shortly after their release—a rate comparable to or slightly higher than the rate one sees in traditional programs.[51]

Research by Doris MacKenzie of the University of Maryland, as well as a comprehensive study by Dale Parent and Douglas McDonald of Abt Associates, also paint a fairly bleak picture of the country's more than sixty correctional boot camps.[52] More generally, a report published by Paul Gendreau and Mario Paparozzi in *Corrections Today* in 1995 concludes, "Corrections practitioners... report that punishment programs such as shock incarceration and boot camps have not been effective in discouraging offenders."[53] Finally, a 2000 report by the Institute on Crime, Justice and Corrections at George Washington University, reviewing the effectiveness of eight boot camps around the country, states:

> Although many of the programs have been well-administered and popular with public officials, they have not demonstrated a significant impact on recidivism, prison or jail crowding, or costs, which have been the three core goals of boot camps....[The] future of boots camps is not promising.[54]

As one might expect, boot camps that are not entirely consumed with "breaking" the inmates do better. In a 1995 report in *Corrections Today*, Deborah Sharp agrees, first of all, that the "scared-senseless" approach generally produces only short-term, surface results; inmates will generally toe the line only as long as the taskmasters are at hand and the line is in place.[55] Tom Castellano, another researcher in this area sums it up well: "We basically know that the military component by itself doesn't do much."[56]

Sharp also notes that programs that include specific types of real-world training—in problem-solving skills, for example—or that encourage legitimate, meaningful relationships between inmates and staff produce better results than those based merely around "military" discipline. In one such program, the McNeil Island Work Ethic Camp in Washington state, "the relationship between inmates and their supervisors," says Sharp, "is closer to the link between employee and employer than between military grunt and drill instructor." Inmates have a choice of jobs, and the work is supplemented by classes on anger management, victim awareness, and life planning.[57]

YOUNG PEOPLE IN ACTION

Discipline by the Sea

Founded in 1910, the Army and Navy Academy in Carlsbad, California, just north of San Diego, supplements the strict military component of its program with an excellent mix of character-building experiences. It also has the advantage of being located on the cliffs overlooking the Pacific Ocean, with surfing beaches located nearby. The beauty of this program is that the main M&M cadets get for showing they can handle responsibility is more responsibility—higher ranks and more "respect" from, control over, and responsibility for other cadets. The general claim: "When the cadets are given this power and responsibility (appropriately monitored), they usually flourish as diligent leaders." Selected cadets also serve as Peer Mediators, who handle "situations involving homesickness, getting along with roommates, respecting authority, following and leading." Unfortunately, as I found with similar schools, the ANA doesn't seem to have any data at hand on the effectiveness of its program.

Military Schools

High-school-level military schools used to number in the hundreds in the United States, but there are now fewer than fifty, and many are struggling to stay open.[58] Many of the studies of the effectiveness of secondary military schools were done around World War II; there seems to be relatively little interest today. An exception is a study by Lee Tarrant of Kansas State University, conducted in 1982, which found improvements in leadership skills among students at five private military schools in Kansas and Missouri. Unfortunately, Tarrant's study also found that "consideration for others" decreased significantly among military school students in comparison with students in regular public schools.[59] A study conducted by John Hoar in 1981 found that military rank and military excellence among students at secondary military schools were poor predictors of the moral reasoning ability of those students—also a discouraging finding.[60]

The U.S. General Accounting Office, responding to a Senate request in 1993, reported that the handful of secondary-level military schools operated directly by the Army, Navy, and Air Force were "equal to or superior to private preparatory schools," but the GAO's report also stated that this conclusion was not based on "any new research or analysis."[61] It also mentioned that the attrition rate at the Army's high school was "as high as 40 percent," a figure suggesting major flaws either with the school or with the admissions process.

Generally, one finds the same pattern in military schools that we saw with the boot camps: schools focusing exclusively on military discipline tend to produce short-term behavioral effects and, sometimes, a long-term dislike for authority, whereas schools that give young people meaningful training and real responsibility produce better outcomes.[62]

The meaningfulness of the experience is key. An experience has meaning when we believe it is connected to people or things we really care about: our immediate family, for example, or our careers or our country. That's one of the reasons "real" military schools like the United States Military Academy at West Point produce outstanding results. The people entering such academies (which are at the college level) are headed toward officer-level careers in the military. Admission is highly competitive, and the training makes sense. One learns to follow orders, lead others, work in teams, handle weapons, and so on, so that one can advance one's military career and, if necessary, defend one's country. Cadets are given significant responsibilities related to real-world challenges, and the most extreme form of individual accountability—the "honor system"—is enforced.

Although humiliation has often been a part of the training regimen at West Point—at least for entering cadets—in no sense are West Point cadets treated like children. They are taught, almost from day one, to become strong leaders, not helpless followers, and the system works well. West Point graduates often have exemplary careers both in and out of the military; in the class of 1915 alone, 59 of the 164 graduates became generals, earning a total of 111 stars, and Ulysses S. Grant, Robert E. Lee, John J. Pershing, Dwight D. Eisenhower, George S. Patton, Douglas MacArthur, and many other notables were West Point graduates.[63]

Placing enormous demands on young people—at least demands that they find meaningful—seems not only to keep them out of trouble but, in many cases, to bring out the very best in them. But why?

THE POWER OF RESPONSIBILITY: TWO THEORIES

In 1971, on the campus of Stanford University, social psychologist Philip Zimbardo set in motion one of the most famous social science studies of the twentieth century: the Stanford Prison Experiment. Twenty-four college students were assigned randomly to one of two groups—guards or prisoners—and then asked to play those roles in rooms renovated to resemble prison cells. Some of the guards soon became so abusive and some of the prisoners so distressed that Zimbardo had

to stop the experiment after a mere six days.[64] The experiment is said to show the enormous power that roles play in our lives—a power so great that it can quickly turn perfectly decent, intelligent college students into insensitive tyrants.

Because Zimbardo himself served as the prison superintendent, and because he failed to conduct any controls (such as issuing "orders" for participants to be "extra nice" to each other), it's possible that the abuse he witnessed was due entirely to "experimenter expectations"—in other words, that students were performing the way they did in order to please their professor. This issue aside, roles are indeed very powerful, just as Zimbardo said they were.

The very first day someone becomes a teacher or a police officer or a cashier or a dad, one behaves, and even feels, very much like the character one is supposed to play. It's like magic! I remember, quite distinctly, the first time I pushed baby Julian down the street in a stroller. People were approaching from the other direction, and I suddenly had a strong urge to push them aside to clear the way. Where did that urge come from, I wondered? Hormones? Not likely. I was now a "father," and I was doing what I believed fathers were supposed to do—namely, protecting my child. I was playing a role, somewhat the way an actor does in a play, except that actors are motivated by money and applause, whereas I was motivated by "reality"—by what B.F. Skinner called "natural contingencies of reinforcement and punishment."

What happens when you put a young person into the role of "adult"? And no, I'm not talking about shouting "Grow up!" at your fifteen-year-old. I'm talking about *really* putting someone into that role, just as I was *really* put into the role of Dad. The answer is that the teen *acts, and even feels, like an adult.* That's why very young soldiers, or young people who suddenly find themselves responsible for younger siblings or disabled parents, or young people who no longer have access to parents or other authority figures, or young people told by Father Flanagan to set up their own government and police force, mature so quickly. When thrust into adult roles, they act and feel like adults. Even pre-teens can do this to some extent, but for post-pubescent teens, the transformation is sometimes quite radical for the simple reason that teenagers are equipped, both mentally and physically, to *be* adults.

Role-Playing Theory

Under this theory—let's call it the Role-Playing Theory of Adulthood—do young people actually *become* adults? For a question of such Talmudic proportions, let's consult the Talmud.

The ancient rabbis tell the tale of a selfish man who is convinced by a rabbi to do one good deed for his family or the community every week. Over the years, these deeds accumulate, and on his gravestone the man is remembered for his

kindness and generosity. But was this unpleasant fellow *really* kind and generous, or was he just following orders? Some of the sages say yes, the generosity was real, and others say no, the man was a fake. It's a split decision! So perhaps young people playing adult roles are "really" adults, and perhaps not. By the same logic, perhaps "adults" playing adult roles are "really" adults, and perhaps not. It depends on how willing you are to distinguish between someone's actions and someone's hypothetical "self."

I'm comfortable calling people who teach "teachers" and people who protect the public and carry badges "police officers," no matter what they are *really* like in the dark confines of their souls. I'm also comfortable calling young people who behave like adults "adults." It makes no sense to me to hesitate to call someone an adult simply because of his or her age or appearance. I think most people would agree that we want adulthood to refer to a set of abilities, not to someone's height or numerical age. More about this in Chapter Six.

Restoration Theory

According to Role-Playing Theory, young people given adult responsibilities become adults in some sense because of the power of roles. But there might be another, more intriguing, reason responsibility is life-changing for our young.

Soon after puberty, many or most young people are fully equipped to function as adults. When we infantilize them, we interfere with normal development. Giving young people meaningful responsibilities might simply be a way of *restoring normal functioning.* Under this theory, which I'll call our Restoration Theory of Adulthood, artificially extending childhood holds people back, and it might even stunt growth permanently, a possibility I'll explore to some extent in Chapters Seven and Nine. Giving young people adult responsibilities restores the child-adult continuum that Jean Liedloff spoke about and thereby allows development to get back on track; the false and decaying skin of the "old child" is shed, and the hidden adult emerges.

WANTING ADULTHOOD *NOW*

Whatever the reasons for its effectiveness, responsibility plays an enormous role in shaping character, as programs like the original Junior Republic or the modern version of Outward Bound remind us. Such programs also remind us of the importance of preserving the child-adult continuum. Where modern society has destroyed that continuum, it may be possible, by providing young people with certain training and experiences, to rebuild the continuum quickly and thus to create a kind of "instant" adulthood.

But many young people today aren't willing to wait. They want adulthood *now*, and they often find their own ways to achieve it. There are at least three ways a young person can achieve adulthood instantly in our society without a shred of assistance from adults. From a certain moment on, everyone around that young person will treat him or her with entirely different expectations. From that moment forward, he or she will behave radically differently, rising in varying degrees to the challenges of real adulthood. Three relatively simple acts shout to society, in tones that cannot be ignored, "I am an adult, damn it! And you will treat me that way from now on!"

These acts are *getting married*, *having a baby*, and *committing a serious crime*. I'll turn to crime and pregnancy in the next chapter, and I'll take a surprising look at young spouses in Chapter Eight and at young mothers in Chapter Eleven.

Q: *Are all teens capable of taking on the responsibilities and handling the authority that adults have?*

A: No, but many adults also handle responsibility and authority poorly: they drink before they drive, abuse drugs, overeat, cheat on their taxes, and so on. A better question would be: Are all teens *incapable* of acting like adults? The answer to that question is also no. Yet we hold back all teens based strictly on a superficial characteristic: age. We've learned not to make this mistake with the elderly; now we need to take a fresh look at teens, evaluating them based on their individual abilities.

Chapter 5

Storm and Stress

I wanna thank you mom, I wanna thank you dad
for bringing this fucking world to a bitter end
—Marilyn Manson, *"Disposable Teens"*

Overview. *American teens are the most distressed in the world, and they are also the most distressed segment of American society. G. Stanley Hall, the pioneering psychologist who first defined adolescence a hundred years ago, insisted that the "storm and stress" we see during the teen years was an inevitable outcome of evolutionary processes. His theory, however, was based on a faulty theory from biology that was completely discredited by the 1930s. Turmoil is not a necessary feature of the teen years. On the other hand, in several areas—crime, conflict with parents, high-risk behaviors, substance abuse, and mood disorders—American teens are often in bad shape, and new research shows a relationship between the degree of impairment and the degree to which teens are infantilized.*

Let's start by talking about blatant fraud, a persistent myth, and a faulty theory.

The fraud: mislabeling and then lying about images of animal embryos printed in a scientific text.

The persistent myth: that as we grow, we relive the evolutionary history of our species.

The faulty theory: "Ontogeny recapitulates phylogeny."

The idea that individual development ("ontogeny") mimics evolutionary development ("phylogeny") got its start in the 1800s with biologists like the Frenchman Alcide Dessalines d'Orbigny and the German Johann Friedrich Meckel (known in history books as "the younger" because his distinguished grandfather had the same name). But the theory became elevated to "law" status—the so-called "fundamental law of biogenetics"—in the late 1800s by the German naturalist Ernst

Haeckel. In his popular book *The Natural History of Creation (Naturliche Schopfungsgeschichte)*, published in 1868, Haeckel appeared to demonstrate that developing embryos of various species all resembled each other in their early stages and all passed through stages that seemed to mimic evolutionary history. At first, he said, young embryos look like fish (with gills), then like reptiles (with tails), and so on. He showed drawings (printed from woodcuts) of embryos from humans, monkeys, dogs, and other species which appeared to prove his point.[1]

He was passionate about his theory, mainly because it seemed to him to lend support to Darwin's new theory of evolution (published in 1859). Darwin himself was impressed by Haeckel's ideas, and he also was grateful to Haeckel for promoting evolutionary theory among German scientists.[2] Recapitulation theory caught on among scientists and even in the general public, like Freud's theory of the unconscious. Darwin's theory was (and still is) difficult for most people to understand, but the recapitulation idea is easy. In some places Haeckel's theory was probably more popular than the theory of evolution itself. What's more, even though Haeckel's original claims about recapitulation were restricted to embryos, the idea soon grew: many people came to believe that we relive the evolutionary history of the human species over the course of our lifetime.

But Haeckel's own contemporaries knew his ideas were flawed, and some even spotted a serious defect in his book. Some of his embryo diagrams were *identical*. Haeckel ultimately admitted that he had made just one diagram and then had the printer repeat it several times, labeling it with different species names in different places. He insisted that the original embryos were so similar that he had committed no great wrong in faking the diagrams. Willful deception, however, doesn't go over well in science, and, among experts, anyway, Haeckel's ideas were soon rejected.[3]

A Highly Flawed Theory

Haeckel's indiscretions aside, recapitulation theory was weak from the outset. Early embryos of different species actually differ from one another substantially, for one thing. Even if they're alike in superficial respects, that doesn't mean their growth is mimicking evolution. Perhaps embryos just grow from simple, general forms into more specific forms (an idea first proposed by Karl Ernst Von Baer in 1828[4]).

Haeckel claimed that his embryonic observations provided support for Darwin's theory, but, again, this makes no sense. However embryos happen to grow has *no* implications for the validity of the theory of evolution. Darwin explained how natural selection, acting over many generations, could account for the

diversity of life on earth. An embryo, like a mature organism, is just a *result* of that process; it doesn't *prove* (or disprove) that evolution occurs.*

But here's a funny thing. Haeckel's shoddy ideas caught on not only among many scientists and intellectuals, they also made it into biology texts. What's more, they were repeated from one text to another for *generations*, probably because text-book writers get a lot of their information from other textbooks. Even more ab-surd, recapitulation theory is *still* described in serious terms in some biology texts today, a fact that the late Steven Jay Gould said should make us feel "astonished and ashamed." He attributed the persistent error to "mindless recycling," a phe-nomenon so widespread in textbook writing, he said, that we may never escape it.[5]

And what, you may ask, does all this have to do with the artificial extension of childhood? Far, far too much.

G. STANLEY HALL: THE MAN WHO INVENTED ADOLESCENCE

G. Stanley Hall, the psychologist who put the modern concept of adoles-cence on the map a hundred years ago, believed in recapitulation theory, and his own characterization of adolescence is a spin-off from that theory. To Hall, the turmoil of the teen years was the *inevitable* consequence of recapitulation. In reliv-ing our evolutionary past, said Hall, we must inevitably pass through a stage of great chaos—some "ancient period of storm and stress when old moorings were broken and a higher level attained"—a time of "savagery," with "its tribal, preda-tory, hunting, fishing, roving, idle, playing proclivities."[6]

This is a serious problem. There's an old expression from the computer field, captured by the acronym "GIGO": Garbage In, Garbage Out. The computer out-put you get is only as good as the data you input in the first place. The same is true in science. It's difficult (although perhaps not impossible) to derive a good theory from a bad one. If recapitulation theory is bunk (it is), then we need to be very skeptical about the validity of Hall's perspective on adolescence.

Consider some of Hall's own statements on adolescence (I've added the em-phases):

> *While adolescence is the great revealer of the past of the race, its earlier stages*
> *must be ever surer and safer and the later possibilities ever greater and more prolonged,*

---

*No serious scientist takes Haeckel's recapitulation theory seriously. Consider this unambiguous statement from *The Beginnings of Human Life* (New York: Springer-Verlag, 1977, p. 32) by biologist Erich Blechschmidt: "...the so-called basic law of biogenetics is wrong. No buts or ifs can mitigate this fact. It is not even a tiny bit correct or correct in a different form.... It is totally wrong."

for it, and not maturity as now defined, is the only point of departure for the superanthropoid that man is to become.[7]

> *Everything, in short, suggests the culmination of one stage of life as if it thus represented what was once, and for a very protracted and relatively stationary period, the age of maturity* in some remote, perhaps pigmoid, stage of human evolution, *when in a warm climate the young of our species once shifted for themselves independently of further parental aid.... Thus the boy is father to the man in a new sense in that his qualities are indefinitely older and existed well compacted untold ages before the more* distinctly human attributes were developed.[8]

> *This long pilgrimage of the soul from its old level to a higher maturity which adolescence recapitulates must have taken place in the race in certain of its important lines long before the historic period, because its very nature seems to involve the destruction of all its products and extinction of all records. Just as the well-matured adults, as is elsewhere shown, has utterly lost all traces and recollection of* the perturbations of the storm and stress period..., so the race must have gone through a long heat and ferment, *of which consciousness, which best develops in stationary periods, was lost, partly because growth was so rapid.*[9]

Hall believed in Haeckel's faulty theory uncritically, and he not only embraced this embryonic theory, he enlarged it, aged it past puberty, and cast it in bronze. Even more disturbing, he did so in a way that makes the underpinnings of his own theory of adolescence virtually invisible to the modern eye: in other words, Hall's successors bought his own assertions about adolescence uncritically, entirely unaware of the faulty foundations of his ideas.

To push this metaphor to the brink, Hall created the life-size, three-dimensional, rock-solid of image of Teen in Turmoil that Americans have believed in for a hundred years, but the impressive statue that he sculpted has been resting on a platform composed of the remains of some old German biology texts that long ago decayed to dust.

We've already seen that adolescence (as a time of turmoil) is far from inevitable—that it's relatively new in human history, that it's rare in other cultures, and that it can be reversed with serious doses of real responsibility. Hall had access to such information, but he believed in adolescence as a matter of faith, because a tumultuous stage of human development seemed to him to be a *requirement* of recapitulation theory.

At least that's the grand side of Hall's belief. On the more mundane side,

Hall was misled by what surrounded him: the hordes of poor and immigrant and working-class youths that seemed to dominate the streets of Baltimore (where he was a professor at Johns Hopkins University from 1882 to 1888), the daily headlines covering the debates about youth crime and child labor and compulsory education, the new sentimental attitude toward young people that was blossoming in the late 1800s, the creation and spread of the new juvenile justice system (complete with industrial schools, receiving homes, and reformatories), and the powerful new voices of America's nurturing women.

Hall's Magnum Opus: The Book That Cast Adolescence in Stone

G. Stanley Hall presented his concept of adolescence in a massive, 1,373-page, two-volume tome called *Adolescence: Its Psychology and Its Relations to Physiology, Anthropology, Sociology, Sex, Crime, Religion and Education*, published in 1904.[10] It was filled with anecdotes and data about troubled teens, but his data could be interpreted in multiple ways (as all data can), and he rarely compared the failings he saw in teens with the failings of his fellow adults.

Here is an example of how he described and documented teen problems. Although Hall often provides references, none is given to support these particular anecdotes:

> *Corré and others give many representative cases of grave crime in early puberty in strongly motive temperaments before knowledge and power of control have developed. A young nurse, e.g., having no sense of the value of life poisoned a child with phosphorus from matches in order that she might go out and seek amusement. A boy of fourteen stabbed a playmate who had reproached him. Another of the same age killed a comrade to rob him of ten centimes, and another violated and strangled a girl of nine, imagining an elaborate romance to escape the police. One of nine killed his brother of eight to get his new shoes. Another shot his two sisters, aged fourteen and sixteen, because jealous of the preference shown them by his parents.... Two boys plotted and killed an old man "to amuse themselves." Eleven boys banded together to steal and rob, partly for sheer mischief, stealing nothing of value. Two boys of fifteen fought a duel with pistols with seconds of the same age. A lad of eighteen stabbed a strange girl who refused his advances in the street. Such cases could easily be multiplied indefinitely from the current chronicles of time.[11]*

Did these incidents actually occur? If so, are they indicative of universal, inevitable tendencies in teens, or are they indicative of the cultural problems of Hall's times?

Biological Determinism

Hall also cites the "great and epoch-making" work of the Italian scholar Cesare Lombroso in the newly founded field of criminology, which demonstrates, said Hall, that "criminals in general, tested anthropometrically, have smaller brains, larger jaws, [and] less facial expression" than normal people. Criminals, said Hall (still discussing Lombroso) also "love sententious phrases or obscene images, to which adolescents have a special predilection." Lombroso, said Hall, "intimates that even some plants have criminal traits."[12]

Although it's counterintuitive to blame teen problems on a theory like Lombroso's (after all, teens' skulls don't change much when teens grow up), Hall was convinced that physical shape was an important key to understanding teen problems. Citing a paper by George E. Dawson called "A Study in Youthful Degeneracy," published in 1896, Hall writes:

> Dawson found among boys and girls in reformatory institutions a tendency to shorter stature, lighter weight, diminished strength in the muscles of the hand, greater sensitiveness to pain, small, broad heads, broad faces, deformed palates and skulls, defects of sight and hearing, dulness of touch, and inferiority in attention, memory, and association. Degeneration of mind and morals is usually marked by morphological deviations from the normal.[13]

But could the physical weakness, shorter stature, and broad faces have had anything to do with the fact that most of the young people in reformatories were poor immigrants?

These were the days when both the educated public and the new scientific field of psychology, which itself had only been founded in the late 1870s, were obsessed with finding biological explanations for human behavior. The Austrian physician Franz Joseph Gall had invented "phrenology"—the study of how head shapes were related to personality—in the late 1700s, and his ideas were more popular than ever (although still incorrect) a hundred years later. Phrenology was still going strong even in the early 1900s; American socialites couldn't wait to get their skulls measured by quack physicians carrying large calipers. Lombroso's theories of the late 1800s were derived from Gall's.

Around this same time "racial" psychology was making its way into the new psychology textbooks, and American and European intellectuals were also taken with "eugenics," a program to improve the human race through selective breeding. Founded by Sir Francis Galton, Charles Darwin's first cousin, eugenics was intended to be the fast lane on the journey to that "superanthropoid" state Hall mentioned.

> # WISDOM OF THE AGES
>
> ## No Need for Adolescent Revolt
>
> *For most of man's existence there was no... revolt among youth.*
> *Adolescents for thousands of years followed easily in their parents' footsteps.*
> *What makes for adolescent revolt is the fact that a society keeps the next*
> *generation too long dependent—too long in terms of sexual maturity and a*
> *striving for independence.*
>
> —Bruno Bettelheim, *The Children of the Dream* (1969)

Biological determinism was very much in the air while Hall was writing his book, and Hall, a creature of his times, believed strongly that adolescence was *determined*—a fixed feature of human development that could be explained and accounted for in scientific fashion. To make his case, he relied on Haeckel's faulty recapitulation idea, on Lombroso's faulty phrenology-inspired theories of crime, on a plethora of anecdotes, and on one-sided interpretations of data. Given the issues, theories, standards, and data-handling methods of his day, he did a superb job. But when you take away the shoddy theories, put the anecdotes in their place, and look for alternate explanations of the data, the bronze statue tumbles hard.

I have no doubt that many of the street teens of Hall's time were suffering or insufferable, but it's a serious mistake to develop a timeless, universal theory of human nature around the peculiarities of the people of one's own time and place. The teenage turmoil of Hall's day was *not* inevitable. Even Hall suggested at one point that teens might fare better if subjected to the "regulatives they still have in older lands with more conservative traditions."[14]

TWO FREUDS ON TEENS

In 1888 G. Stanley Hall became the first president of the newly founded Clark University (in Massachusetts), which opened the following year. In 1909, Hall invited Sigmund Freud to speak there (along with Carl Jung and others) and to receive an honorary degree. This marked the first academic recognition Freud had ever received and the only honorary degree he would ever receive. Even though Freud was already revered in some circles, his Jewish heritage gave him few professional options in Europe.[15] This also marked his first and only trip to America.

Freud was profoundly grateful to Hall for the honor he received at Clark, but he never adopted Hall's negative views on teens. Freud said little about teens over

the course of his half-century career—barely anything compared with the tomes he wrote about childhood. If adolescence was a critically important part of human development, wouldn't Freud have noticed? The main task of the teen years, said Freud, is to "cease to be a child," to "detach" from parents, and to "become a member of the social community."[16]

Freud also questioned the wisdom with which adults handle teens. "It is remarkable," he wrote, "how seldom [teens] are dealt with in the ideal manner—that is, in one which is correct both psychologically and socially."[17]

Normal Teens Are "Abnormal"

Freud's daughter Anna, on the other hand—herself a distinguished psychoanalyst—had a great deal to say about teens. She acknowledged her own depression as a teen (growing up around the turn of the twentieth century in a home run with military strictness by her father) and even captured her teenage anguish in a poem, which reads in part:

For one hour, one day, I do so wish
To be rid of my self, no longer to know
My own face, my own poor hand,
Just once not to feel my thoughts.[18]

Writing about teens in books and articles published mainly toward the end of her career, Anna Freud believed wholeheartedly in an adolescence dominated by *"sturm und drang"* (German for "storm and stress").[19] According to her:

> *...it is normal for an adolescent to behave for a considerable length of time in an inconsistent and unpredictable manner; to fight his impulses and to accept them; to ward them off successfully and to be overrun by them; to love his parents and to hate them; to revolt against them and to be dependent on them; to be deeply ashamed to acknowledge his mother before others and, unexpectedly, to desire heart-to-heart talks with her....*[20]

She was so sure about the inevitability of turmoil during the teen years that she expressed concern about teens who seemed calm and happy: "To be normal during the adolescent period," she said, "is by itself abnormal."[21]

TREATING YOUNG PEOPLE WITH DIGNITY

Although G. Stanley Hall saw the teens years as necessarily dark, he didn't

approve of the strict regimens and laws that were being implemented daily in early twentieth-century American to try to get teens under tight control. He knew that treating teens as "mere children" was a grave mistake. In effect, Hall warned against infantilization, just as I have been doing in this volume. Quoting colleague E. G. Lancaster and then speaking for himself, Hall wrote:

> [According to Lancaster,] "at no time in life will a human being respond so heartily if treated by older and wiser people as if they were equals or even superiors. The attempt to treat a child at adolescence as you would treat an inferior is instantly fatal to good discipline." Parents still think of their offspring as mere children, and tighten the reign when they should loosen it. Many young people feel that they have the best of homes and yet that they will go crazy if they must remain in them.... The one unpardonable thing for the adolescent is dulness, stupidity, lack of life, interest, and enthusiasm in school or teachers, and, perhaps above all, too great stringency.[22]

Elsewhere in his book, Hall reminds us of the importance of treating young people with the kind of dignity we extend toward fellow adults:

> ...we are progressively forgetting that for the complete apprenticeship to life, youth needs repose, leisure, art, legends, romance, idealization, and in a word humanism, if it is to enter the kingdom of man well equipped for man's highest work in the world.[23]

His perspective on young people is very different than the one I've been developing in this volume, but his advice is similar: It's a mistake to treat teens like children.

For Hall, disciplining a teen is like provoking a wild animal, because, to him, teens are reliving the savagery of our evolutionary past. Unlike Hall, I'm certain that ontogeny is indifferent to phylogeny (it doesn't "recapitulate" it) and that our evolutionary history doesn't require teens to behave savagely. Evolution equips us with a small number of reflexes, a wide range of individual differences, some general social tendencies, some significant gender differences, and an enormous capacity for learning. Not only do teens have the potential to be "normal during the adolescent period," as far as I'm concerned this period shouldn't even be; it exists mainly because of ignorance on the part of adults.

This still leaves us with a practical problem. Even if G. Stanley Hall and Anna Freud were wrong about the inevitability of adolescence, modern American teens often feel terrible and behave badly. Even if this is so because our culture has artificially extended childhood, we still need to face our self-created nightmare squarely. Just how much storm and stress do we see among modern teens?

G. STANLEY HALL REVISITED: THREE KINDS OF TURMOIL

In a 1999 article called "Adolescent Storm and Stress, Reconsidered," developmental psychologist Jeffrey Jansen Arnett of the University of Maryland College Park reviewed a variety of current research in primarily three areas: conflict with parents, mood problems, and risky behaviors. The question he raised was: Was Hall right? In other words, does modern research with American teens confirm that they go through a period of extreme turmoil after puberty? The answer, he said, is yes.[26]

Conflict with Parents

According to Arnett, "Contemporary studies have established that conflict with parents increases in early adolescence (compared with preadolescence) and typically remains high for a couple of years until declining in late adolescence."[27] According to one recent study he cites—a "meta-analysis," which is a study of studies—"within adolescence, conflict frequency is highest in early adolescence and conflict intensity is highest in midadolescence."[28] Translating this into plain English, when your son or daughter is between ages fourteen and sixteen, you should probably stay clear of your house.

Conflict between parents and teens occur about twenty times per month, according to one study and "is especially frequent and intense between mothers and early adolescent daughters."[29] As you might imagine, emotional closeness de-

clines between parents and offspring during the teen years and so does the amount of quality time that parents and their offspring spend together.

Some experts believe, says Arnett, that conflict between teens and parents has an upside—that it might accelerate the rate at which teens learn to become independent, and that it might also help parents learn to let go. But anyone who's been there knows full well that this sort of conflict is far more destructive than helpful.

Years ago clinical psychologist Henry Marcucella told me that he thought teens were especially odd in one respect: "They sometimes act like children and sometimes like adults, with no in-between state at all." In retrospect, I find this idea to be consistent with my recent thoughts about the artificial extension of childhood. Mom and Dad know you only as a child and have difficulty seeing you any other way. At some point, however, you begin to see yourself as an adult, and you "try out" your adult side with increasing frequency. When it works—when people show respect for what you say or do—you feel valued. When it fails—when people dismiss what you have to say out of hand—you revert to the only other state you know: childhood. This might sound dysfunctional, but it actually makes good sense. You know how to behave like a child quite well, for one thing, and when you behave this way, you also meet the expectations of those around you. It's not the most sophisticated kind of drama, but at least everyone knows their lines.

Arnett confirms that "adolescents do indeed report greater extremes of mood and more frequent changes of mood, compared with preadolescents or adults."[30] A number of studies have assessed mood changes using the "beeper method": teens and adults are provided with beepers and instructed to make notes about their behavior, thoughts, and mood whenever the experimenters activate their beepers throughout the day. Such studies show that American teens experience (a) greater extremes of emotions than do adults—especially negative emotions, (b) frequent feelings of self-consciousness and embarrassment—two to three times as frequently as adults experience such feelings, (c) frequent feelings of awkwardness, loneliness, and nervousness, and (d) a general decline in happiness compared with how they felt as preadolescents.[31]

Risky Behaviors

I'll revisit this issue in the next section of this chapter as well as in Chapter Seven, but for now let's consider Arnett's findings. His review of the research literature leads him to conclude that the teen years in the United States are indeed a time of risk taking and that for some kinds of behaviors risk taking continues into the early twenties. "This pattern," he says, "exists for crime as well as for behavior such as substance abuse, risky automobile driving, and risky sexual behavior."[32] Specifically:

> ## YOUNG PEOPLE IN ACTION
>
> ### Child or Adult?
>
> In July 2006 in Ephrata, Washington, a fifteen-year-old male was convicted of a murder he committed when he was twelve. According to prosecutors, the perpetrator planned the murder, beat the victim—a thirteen-year-old developmentally disabled individual—and then stabbed him thirty-four times. The sentence? Twenty-six years in prison.[35] If this crime was truly premeditated, and if the perpetrator was of normal intelligence and could tell right from wrong, was it right to treat him as an adult, or should this case have been handled by the juvenile justice system? In the latter case, he might have served a few years in a reformatory and then would have had a clean record at age eighteen.

Rates of crime rise in the teens until peaking at age eighteen, then drop steeply.... Rates of most types of substance abuse peak at about age twenty.... Rates of automobile accidents and fatalities are highest in the late teens.... Rates of sexually transmitted diseases (STDs) peak in the early twenties..., and two thirds of all STDs are contracted by people who are under twenty-five years old....[33]

In his review, Arnett also acknowledges that "it is clear that the biological changes of puberty do not make adolescent storm and stress universal and inevitable" (my italics). "This is easily and unmistakably demonstrated," he says, "by the fact that not all cultures experience the same levels of adolescent storm and stress, and some evidently do not experience it at all."[34] Finally, Arnett points out the obvious—that there are "substantial individual differences" in the way the teenage years play out. Not *every* teen has a tough time.

AN OVERVIEW OF TURMOIL IN TODAY'S TEENS

We've seen some modest indications that teens aren't doing too badly, but we've also seen that in three important areas many American teens are indeed in rough shape: parental conflict, mood problems, and high-risk behaviors. Before we begin (in Part II of this book) our detailed examination of the underlying capabilities of teens, let's look more closely at some major areas of concern, especially the ones that make the headlines every day: crime, substance abuse, sex, depression, and suicide.

Violence and Crime

Not long ago I spoke about teen problems on a Fox television program called "The O'Reilly Factor," hosted by the articulate, conservative host, Bill O'Reilly. The topic was teen gangs, prompted by the arrest of nine middle-class gang members in Las Vegas who had videotaped each other brutally beating peers. I told O'Reilly what I've been telling you: Teens are out of control because they've been treated like children and isolated from adults.

O'Reilly balked at first, saying that teens "aren't emotionally equipped to be adults," but when I reminded him how much responsibility teens were able to handle only a few decades ago (during the Great Depression, for example, or during World War II), he said, tentatively, that my perspective was "interesting and important." He protested again when I said that those violent teens in Las Vegas (whose videos were being shown on-screen as we spoke) were "just trying to be adults." "Nobody could call those kids adults," he said. But not only were they emulating what adults do, they had transformed themselves into adults *instantly* by committing a serious crime. In fact, news reports had already indicated that all nine teens were going to be tried in court *as adults*.

Whether we like the idea or not, young people who commit serious crimes are indeed emulating adults—adult behavior, adult emotions, and adult ideas. They see adults on the streets, on TV, in movies, and in newspapers and magazines doing heinous things every day. What's more, when a young person commits a crime, he or she is demonstrating *control* over his or her own life. A crime says, "I'm *powerful*. I'm *strong*. I'm *fearless*. I'm *independent of my parents and my teachers*." And if it's serious enough, a crime makes you an adult *officially*—instantly transforming you in the eyes of the law from a child (who would normally be shielded by the dubious protections of the juvenile justice system) into an adult criminal, subject to the rigors of adult criminal court. As a bonus, a serious crime also gives you a full set of constitutional rights, which guarantees you a lawyer, a speedy trial, the right to confront your witnesses, the right to a court transcript, and so on.

Here is an overview of the criminal proclivities of some young people in America today:

Gangs. According to the 2002 National Youth Gang Survey (conducted by the National Youth Gang Center, an agency of the federal government's Office of Juvenile Justice and Delinquency Prevention), all United States cities with populations over two hundred fifty thousand have significant gang activity each year, and between one-fourth and one-third of gang members are female.[36] Gang involve-

WISDOM OF THE AGES

The Strength of Wild Animals

...should a young person feel that the environment tries to deprive him too radically of all the forms of expression which permit him to develop..., he may resist with the wild strength encountered in animals who are suddenly forced to defend their lives.

—Erik Erikson, *Identity: Youth and Crisis* (1968)

ment sometimes begins when children are as young as seven or eight, and one recent survey of six thousand eighth graders in eleven cities revealed that 11 percent of them were currently members of gangs.[37] Most gangs engage in at least some criminal activities, including assault, homicide, tagging, hate crimes, larceny, drug trafficking, and vehicle theft. Common gang weapons include: bats, pipes, spiked wristbands, chemical mace, knives, handguns, sawed-off shotguns, Uzi machine guns, AK-47 assault rifles, 9-mm semi-automatic handguns, homemade bombs, Molotov cocktails, and grenades. In 2002 there were approximately 21,500 active gangs and 731,500 gang members in the United States, most between ages fourteen and twenty-four.[38] In 2004 half of the homicides in Los Angeles County were gang related.[39] *Like it or not, gang activity is not childlike; it is most definitely adult:* Gangs emulate small governments and armies. The have charismatic leaders, nationalistic loyalties, emblems, hierarchies, dress codes, intricate communication systems, colors, rites, traditions, ranks, territories, strict codes of conduct, and systems of justice, promotion, demotion, and expulsion—just like many adult organizations.

Violence at schools. School violence has been and continues to be a problem nationwide. Schools are targets for violence because (a) many young people resent being forced to go to school, and for some school is a place of failure and frustration, (b) schools crowd large numbers of young people together for long periods each day and hence serve as breeding grounds for gangs, cliques, jealousies, rivalries, bullying, and racial, ethnic, and religious conflicts, and (c) schools are where the "enemies" are located: the strict or insensitive teachers and administrators, the bullies, the romantic and social rivals, and so on.* According to the CDC, in 1997, 37 percent of high school students had been in a physical fight during the last year, and a 1997 survey suggests that nearly one in five high

---

*According to a 2001 report on juvenile crime by the National Research Council, "Contrary to their intentions, schools appear to foster problems among misbehaving children and adolescents through such common practices as tracking, grade retention, suspension, and expulsion. The panel took special note of apparent racial and ethnic biases in the administration of these practices." (p. 4)

school students had carried a weapon (a gun, club, or knife) to school within the prior month.[40] According to a 1998 report issued by the United States Department of Education, more than six thousand students had been expelled from American schools the previous year for bringing firearms or explosives to school—56 percent of those from high schools, 34 percent from middle schools, and 9 percent from elementary schools.[41] Of even greater concern, between 1996 and 2003, 147 students and eleven staff members were killed or wounded in twenty-eight separate shooting incidents in United States schools. In the worst such incident, which took place on April 20, 1999, two students at Columbine High School in Littleton, Colorado killed twelve students and one teacher and wounded twenty-three others before killing themselves. They had spent a year planning the attack, which was supposed to kill more than five hundred people, but the bombs they had planted on campus were disabled by police.[42] More recently, a sixteen-year old student at a high school in Red Lake, Minnesota, injured seven people and killed ten, among them five students, a security guard, and a teacher at his school.[43] Various plots against schools continue to be uncovered.[44]

Gambling. According to the National Council on Gambling, recent studies show that gambling is now a more prevalent problem among teens than drinking, cigarettes, or marijuana. One study suggests that 80 percent of young people between twelve and seventeen have gambled in the last twelve months, and a British study suggests that the mean age at which children start to gamble is about eight-and-a-half. Recent studies suggest that between 5 and 8 percent of young people in American now have a "serious" gambling problem.[45]

Crime. Young people commit a large number of crimes in the United States every year—more than three million on school campuses alone.[46] Many youth crimes are violent, and the public has demanded tougher remedies, often based on sensational media reports, such as a recent Associated Press article about teens in Lompoc, California who set fire to a homeless man,[47] rather than on sound statistics. That said, the legitimate statistics are disturbing: nationwide, 1.6 million juveniles were arrested in 2002.[48] In California the arrest rate among people ages ten to seventeen was 4,434 per 100,000 in 2002, a drop from a peak of 9,313 in 1974; this sounds good, but the 2002 arrest rate was still 34 percent higher than that of 1960.[49] Nationwide, the overall rate of violent crimes by teens increased by 49 percent between 1980 and 1996.[50] FBI statistics suggest that the peak age at which people (of all ages) commit violent crimes is eighteen (see Appendix 3 for further details).[51] According to a comprehensive 2001 report by the National Research Council (NRC), "most juveniles break laws," although only 4 percent of juvenile arrests are

for serious crimes. As of 2006, the most recent data from the FBI suggest a dramatic upward spike in teen violence: in Boston alone, a 54 percent increase in robberies and a 103 percent increase in weapons arrests between 2004 and 2005.[52] The proportion of female juveniles arrested for committing a crime has increased steadily since at least the early 1980s; in 1986 females accounted for 22 percent of juvenile arrests, a figure that increased to 30 percent by 2004.[53] As of early 2005, seventy-two people were on death row for murders they committed as minors; their sentences were reduced under the Supreme Court's recent decision in *Roper v. Simmons*, which prohibits executing offenders who committed their crimes before age eighteen (see Chapter Fourteen).[54]

Guns. According to surveys, 31 percent of American teens know someone their age who carries a gun, and 14 percent of our teens have seen or been in fights in which someone used a gun.[55] In 1998 nearly *three out of ten* high school males were believed to possess a firearm, and, as I noted in Chapter One, nearly a million guns were brought into American classrooms.[56]

Homicide. Homicide is now the second leading cause of death for young men and women (combined) between fifteen and nineteen, and it's now the third leading cause of death for young women between fifteen and nineteen. About 20 percent of deaths in the ten to twenty-four age group are due to homicide, and four out of five of those deaths are from gunshot wounds. Many of these deaths are caused by adults, but they are usually adults who are involved in gang or other activities with the minors.[57]

Juvenile Court. Juvenile courts process about 1.5 million cases per year, with roughly five thousand cases being "waived" to the adult criminal courts; the rate of waivers has generally been increasing. The juvenile justice system in California alone costs over a billion dollars a year to run.[58]

Types of Crimes. Young people commit the full range of crimes committed by adults: rape, homicide, larceny, bank robbery, drug possession and sales, arson, assault, forgery, and so on, and, as I noted in Chapter Two, they are also arrested for a variety of offenses that have been created especially for minors: truancy, running away from home, drinking alcohol, and so on. In some categories (e.g., property crimes and theft), teens are more active than adults; in others (e.g., murder and aggravated assault), they're less active. Sometimes teens get creative; in Florida and California in recent years, occupants of several cars have been killed when teens have dropped large rocks or bricks off of highway overpasses.[59] It's no wonder that there's a term—*ephebiphobia*—for fear of teenagers.[60]

Drugs and Alcohol

Drugs and alcohol serve many purposes, both for adults and for young people.

Actress Carrie Fisher (of "Star Wars" fame) used psychoactive substances to "self-medicate"—to escape the pain and chaos of her daily life. Fisher began abusing chemicals when she was a teen; it was ten years before a mental health professional figured out that she had long been suffering from bipolar disorder.[61]

It's common for young people to use drugs and alcohol in this way: to relieve the pain of their own persistent psychological or physical problems. Teens and adults also drink or take drugs to bond with, impress, or manipulate friends, colleagues, or lovers. Ecstasy, the current rage among young people, is supposed to be an especially effective mood-booster and friendship-maker.

Alcoholic beverages are produced by a 137 billion dollar industry; although alcohol providers aren't allowed to sell directly to young people, they still make money when young people drink their products; *someone* is paying for it, after all. Legal drugs (such as Ritalin, Prozac, and Xanax) are provided by a 216 billion dollar industry (in the United States alone); this industry spends more than 2.5 billion dollars per year to convince consumers to take their products and physicians to prescribe them; in recent years, this industry has made concerted efforts to expand into the youth markets, in some cases convincing physicians to prescribe drugs to children which had never been tested on children or approved for their use.[62]

The illegal drug industry (providing drugs like Ecstasy, marijuana, cocaine, PCP, and heroin) conducts perhaps 50 billion dollars worth of business each year in the United States.[63] Young people are the main targets of this industry for simple reasons: It's difficult for them to purchase alcohol over the counter, and they don't have control over their prescription medications or medical treatment. If Jamie Lee Curtis or Rush Limbaugh want more vodka or Vicodin, they can get them legitimately and privately (Limbaugh was unclear on that, it seems), but young people don't have such options. The solution: the corner "connection."

Here is a quick overview of drug- and alcohol-related activities by American young people today:

Prescription Drugs. The rate at which young people have been given prescription drugs has skyrocketed in recent years. According to a recent study by University of Maryland researcher Julie Magno Zito and her colleagues, between 1987 and 1996 the rate at which drugs were prescribed to children and teens doubled or tripled in large Medicaid and HMO programs they studied.[64] The most common conditions resulting in prescriptions were attention deficit disorder (ADD) and its close and equally-suspect cousin, attention deficit hyperactivity disorder (ADHD) (Ritalin, Strattera, Adderall, Concerta), followed by depression (Prozac, Paxil, Luvox, Zoloft), followed by various other mood disorders (Xanax, Valium,

Haldol, Ambien). But that's just for starters. A 2004 analysis of drug trends by Medco Health Systems suggests there had been *a 49 percent increase in ADD and ADHD prescriptions in the previous three years for children under 5*, contributing to a 23 percent overall increase in usage for young people. According to Medco, over the same brief period antidepressant use by minors increased 21 percent, and the use of drugs for autism and other behavioral problems increased *71 percent*. The bottom line: *spending on behavior-altering drugs for minors has now edged out spending for all other drugs*, including antibiotics and medications for asthma, allergies, and skin conditions.[65] Because adults both prescribe and take such drugs with great frequency—many of which are now advertised incessantly on television—our society sends a clear message to young people that drug use is acceptable for both young and old. The most recent trend: "pharming" parties at which young people trade and sample prescription drugs—some their own and some stolen from parents.[66]

Overdoses. According to the federal government's Office of National Drug Control Policy, in 1999, 82,904 young people between ages twelve and seventeen were treated in hospital emergency rooms because of adverse experiences with illegal drugs. As I noted in Chapter One, that number increased to 97,029 in 2002.[67]

School shooters. Although it's unreasonable to blame school shootings on prescription medications (there aren't enough data to support that idea), it's interesting to note that some of the most notorious school shooters were taking psychotropic drugs: Kip Kinkel, the fifteen-year-old from Oregon who killed his parents and two students in 1998, was taking the antidepressant Prozac, as was Jeffrey Weise, the shooter in the 2005 Red Lake massacre; T. J. Solomon, the fifteen-year-old from Georgia who shot six students in 1999, was on the ADD drug Ritalin; and Eric Harris, one of the Columbine shooters, was taking the antidepressant Luvox.[68]

Marijuana. Surveys suggest that three out of four young people try marijuana, and upwards of 20 percent of high school seniors smoke it regularly. The marijuana smoked by today's young is about ten times as potent as that available in the 1960s (that is, it has about ten times the concentration of THC, the active ingredient in the plant).[69]

Alcohol. Alcohol use by young people waxes and wanes, depending in part on the aggressiveness of public health campaigns—and largely, no doubt, on momentary fads. Surveys suggest that about two-thirds of middle-school students and perhaps 90 percent of high school students have tried alcohol. Half of high school juniors and seniors drink regularly, and about 25 percent of high-school drinkers admit to frequent binge drinking (consuming five or more drinks in a row). Alcohol is implicated in a high percent of all automobile fatalities and more than half

of all suicides, homicides, and accidental deaths among young people. People between sixteen and twenty-four supposedly cause 42 percent of all fatal alcohol-related crashes, even though they drive only 20 percent of the total vehicle miles traveled. According to a 2004 report, 13.6 percent of all drivers involved in fatal crashes were between the ages of fifteen and twenty, and 29 percent of those drivers had been drinking.[70]

Street drugs. Young people also use cocaine, crack cocaine, heroin, and hallucinogens such as LSD and PCP (also called "angel dust"). According the American Medical Association, more than half of people in the twelve-to-seventeen age range say that they know a classmate who uses LSD, heroin, or cocaine. Young people also have discovered ways to get high on a wide variety of inhalants, including gasoline, nitrous oxide, aerosol sprays, and airplane glue. The AMA also claims that 85 percent of young people say that drugs are the most serious challenge they face.[71]

Steroids. In their obsession to look like their athletic heroes in the movies and magazines, between 2 and 4 percent of young people—mainly males—have used anabolic steroids without a physician's prescription. Usage increased during the 1990s and now appears to have leveled off or to have declined slightly. Steroids increase strength and muscle mass, but they can also damage the reproductive system and cause serious mood problems.[72]

Ecstasy, OxyContin, and More. Ecstasy (often called "X", "Candy," or the "Love Drug"), a mild hallucinogen, has gotten especially popular among young people in recent years, and it even has its defenders in the adult professional community.[73] Ecstasy use among teens supposedly tripled among young Americans between 1998 and 2002, possibly because of a sharp drop in its cost, and a recent report suggests that usage may have declined in 2003, perhaps because of a shift to other drugs.[74] The use of the painkiller OxyContin (called "Oxy" and known by many as the "poor man's heroin" or "hillbilly heroin") has also increased dramatically in recent years.[75] In 2000, according to the Substance Abuse and Mental Health Services Administration, 4,969 young people (quadruple the figure just two years prior) were admitted to emergency rooms in the United States because of overdoses of GHB (gamma hydroxybutyrate)—a date rape drug also known as "G" or "Easy Lay." With Internet guidance, GHB can be mixed up at home.[76]

Cigarettes. As of 2004, about 22 percent of American high school students and 11.5 percent of junior high school students smoked cigarettes.[77] It's been estimated that six thousand American teens try cigarettes every day and that two thousand of them become regular smokers.[78] There are now about 1.5 million female teen smokers in the United States[79]

135

> ## WISDOM OF THE AGES
>
> ### The Standardized Teen
>
> *Youth after youth, bewildered by the incapacity to assume a role forced on him by the inexorable standardization of American adolescence, runs away in one form or another, dropping out of school, leaving jobs, staying out all night, or withdrawing into bizarre and inaccessible moods.*
> —Erik Erikson, *Identity: Youth and Crisis* (1968)

Drug and alcohol abuse is glorified every day in America in movies, on television, on the Internet, in novels, magazines, comic books, and so on. Attractive, trendy young people are frequently high or drunk in movies like *Animal House*, *Requiem for a Dream*, *Thirteen*, *Weird Science*, *Dazed and Confused*, and *Clueless*, and we also glorify illegal drug use *by adults* in movies like *Fear and Loathing in Las Vegas* (starring Johnny Depp and Benicio Del Toro). The Woodstock music festival of 1969, attended by about five hundred thousand young people, was famous for its open drug use, and that tradition is still going strong. The open use of drugs by both young and old (some of whom were probably at Woodstock!) is still common in festivals like the "Burning Man," which is now held in multiple locations in the Western United States every year and which drew more than thirty thousand attendees to the Back Rock Desert in Nevada in 2003.

Official statistics suggest that overall drug and alcohol use may have declined in the late 1990s and has been increasing in recent years, but I have some doubts about the figures. The real extent of our teens' interest in illicit substances doesn't assume statistical form for the simple reason that most of these activities are kept secret, and the secrecy is likely to increase when public opinion becomes more negative. Given that hospitalizations for overdoses appear to be increasing, overall usage is probably increasing, too, no matter what the survey data say.

"Raves"—large, intense, parties where drug use is common—have been popular among teens in major cities in recent years, although perhaps no longer the fad they use to be. In San Diego at this writing, fifteen raves are openly advertised on the Internet; presumably a larger number are harder to find. Like it or not, drug, alcohol, and tobacco use by young people appears to be a fixture in American society.

Sexual Activity

Your perspective on teen sex might change when you read Chapter Eight (mine did when I wrote it), but, meanwhile, let's take a quick look at the sexuality of today's American teens. Bear in mind that young people who have sex are *defi-*

nitely not behaving like children. One might quibble about the meaning of crimes that young people commit, but there's no question about the meaning of the sex they have: they're behaving like the young adults they really are, exactly as evolution intended. What's more, sex is an easy route to adulthood in this country. In most states, one is instantly emancipated from parents when one marries, and one instantly takes on many adult responsibilities when one gives birth.

Teen pregnancy. According to the Guttmacher Institute, more than three-quarters of teen pregnancies are unintended, resulting in about 500,000 live births and more than 350,000 miscarriages or induced abortions each year.[80] Although the birth rate for teens has dropped in recent years, it's still occurring at an overall rate of forty-nine births per thousand fifteen-to-nineteen-year-old women, the highest rate by far in the industrialized world. To put this number in perspective, consider that the teen birth rate in France, Germany, Italy, Japan, Spain, Sweden, and other countries is less than ten births per one thousand women ages fifteen to nineteen.[81] In 2001 in Nevada, one of four teens who gave birth had already given birth to at least one other child.[82] Between eight hundred thousand and nine hundred thousand women ages nineteen and under become pregnant each year in the United States[83]

AIDS. According to recent data from the Centers for Disease Control, there are forty thousand new cases of HIV infections in the United States each year, and about half of the newly-infected are under twenty-five.[84] As of 2002, only 38 percent of sexually active teen couples are thought to have regularly used condoms.[85]

Rape. According to a 2003 article by health researcher Ruth Kershner, "The greatest increase in arrested rape offenders involves adolescent males." Seventeen percent of "single-offender" rapes and 30 percent of "multiple-offender" rapes are now committed by young males.[86]

Cognitive, Emotional and Behavioral Disorders

On television recently I caught an especially eerie film called *The Virgin Suicides*, starring James Woods, Kathleen Turner, and Kirsten Dunst. In this 1999 film, based on a 1994 novel by Jeffrey Eugenides, young male teens recount their obsession with the five Lisbon sisters, the dreamy and mysterious teenage inhabitants of a house in their neighborhood.

After thirteen-year-old Cecilia commits suicide—slitting her wrists didn't work, so a few weeks later she jumped off the roof and was impaled on a fence—their controlling mom (Turner) becomes stricter than ever. She pulls the sisters out of school and makes them prisoners in their home. They spend most of their time languishing in bed, dreaming about exotic places. The most beautiful sister, Lux (Dunst), asserts her

> ## YOUNG PEOPLE IN ACTION
>
> ### Dead Virgins
>
> *In the 1999 film "The Virgin Suicides," directed by Sofia Coppola (daughter of Francis Ford Coppola of "Godfather" fame), five beautiful teen sisters commit suicide, mainly, it seems, to escape from life with their controlling mother. Here are the opening lines of this disturbing film:*
>
> *Narrator: "Cecilia was the first to go."*
>
> *(Shots of thirteen-year-old Cecilia in a bathtub full of bloodied water; being carried from the house by paramedics; lying in a hospital bed.)*
>
> *Doctor: "What are you doing here, honey? You're not even old enough to know how bad life gets."*
>
> *Cecilia (emphatically): "Obviously, Doctor, you've never been a thirteen-year-old girl."*

independence by having sex with random men on the roof. At the end of the film, all four of the remaining sisters commit suicide on the same night.

Elements of this film are all too realistic: parents are sometimes fatally controlling, teens often languish, and young people sometimes take their own lives—at least in modern America. Near the end of the film, barely noticeable and in the background, a drunken, tuxedo-clad young man falls backward into a swimming pool at a posh party. As he's climbing out he says, *"You don't understand me! I'm a teenager. I got problems!"* That not only describes the role that American teens believe they're supposed to play in life, it also fits adult perceptions of teens, as well as the credible data.

Jeffrey Arnett's review of recent research on storm and stress reminded us of the obvious: that the moods of American teens are often disturbed. But that's just one among many aberrations in the world of teenage mental health. Here are some others:

Suicide. According to the National Center for Health Statistics (part of the CDC), teen suicide was fairly rare in the 1950s (2.7 per hundred thousand people ages fifteen to ninteen each year). The rate increased during each of the next four decades, reaching a peak rate of 11.1 in the 1990s and declining somewhat in recent years.[87] As I noted in Chapter One, survey data suggest that 8.5 percent of high school students may attempt suicide every year and that more than 17 percent seriously contemplate suicide.[88] Perhaps as many as *10 percent* of our teens have attempted suicide at some point in their lives. In poor communities in the United States, researchers believe that as many as 70 percent of teens have at least contemplated

suicide. Suicide is now the third leading cause of death among high school students, and many deaths that aren't labeled that way probably should be. Many reckless, violent crimes by young people—especially young blacks—are really cases of "suicide by cop."[89] Among the twenty-seven young people who committed suicide in Los Angeles County in 1999, one was ten, two were twelve, and one was thirteen.[90]

Depression. Depressive tendencies increase slightly among young males over the teen years and more dramatically among young females. Although young males kill themselves more frequently than young females, females attempt suicide twice as frequently as males.[91] Depression has long been an epidemic among teens, and mental health professionals (spurred by intense campaigns by major drug companies) are now beginning to diagnosis it earlier and earlier—even in toddlers. A new extensive study of sadness by Rosemarie Kobau and her colleagues at the CDC suggests that the peak age of sadness among adults is eighteen. (See Figure 5.1.)[92]

Figure 5.1. **Sadness by Age.** In a telephone survey of over 166,000 Americans eighteen and over, researchers recently found that sadness peaks at age eighteen. The peak is especially high for young females (upper curve). *Source:* Kobau et al., 2004.

Other Disorders. The federal Center for Mental Health Services estimates that 20 percent of young people from ages nine to seventeen have a diagnosable behavioral or emotional disorder and that between nine and thirteen percent are suffering from a "serious emotional disturbance with severe emotional impairment."[93] A 1992 survey by the California Department of Mental Health suggested that between 5 and 7 percent of California's young people were suffering from serious psychological disorders[94]; that's between 460,000 and 644,000 people.

Getting in Trouble. Troubled youth often end up in trouble. Roughly half of the high school students with severe emotional problems drop out, and about one in five students with such problems are arrested at least once before age eighteen. Three quarters of the young people in juvenile corrections facilities are supposedly diagnosable with behavioral or emotional disorders.[95]

Giving Up. According to a recent investigative article in the *Washington Post* by Shankar Vedantam, each year in the United States desperate parents turn over thousands of children and teens to child welfare services as a means of getting them psychological help.[96] Because mental health services are often not covered by insurance, parents often have no choice but to file complaints with social workers or police in order to get help. Residential treatment centers for psychological problems can cost up to $250,000 per year; by turning young people over to authorities, the state ends up footing the bill. The exact number of young people who are disposed of in this way is difficult to determine, but Vedantam reports that in Pima County, Arizona alone, 1,750 young people were turned over to child welfare officials for this purpose in 2001. Nationwide, the total could be in the hundreds of thousands.

Eating Disorders. Eating disorders are far more prevalent in young people—especially young females—than in adults. Virtually all young females in our society diet to some extent, but in some cases they do so dangerously and for long periods. In the condition called "anorexia nervosa," young women starve themselves, sometimes to death. About one in a hundred teenage females are anorexic. Perhaps one-tenth that many males also limit their food intake excessively. In a related disorder called "bulimia," women are also obsessed with their weight, but they tend to gorge themselves and then to eliminate the food by forced vomiting. Bulimia is rare in young teens; it tends to emerge in the late teens or early twenties. The prevalence of bulimia is difficult to determine because bulimics are extremely secretive about their condition. Media images of extremely thin people probably underlie most cases of anorexia and bulimia.[97]

Anger. As we've already seen, teens get angry a lot; this is evident from the material we've reviewed on crime, gangs, parent-teen conflicts, and so on. Just one footnote: Headlines have been telling us in recent years that "research" demonstrates that teen anger and aggression is "caused" by the violence young people see in movies and, on television, and in video games. But *virtually all* of this research is "correlational" (a topic I'll return to in a moment), which means that it *doesn't* support the strong conclusions being drawn from it. We know that people with violent tendencies are drawn more to violent content than peaceful

people are; that fact alone can account for most if not all of the correlations my colleagues keep reporting. It's also possible that violent content makes some people more *peaceful* through a process called "catharsis." We certainly know that an entire generation—the Baby Boomers—was raised on violent media content (army and cowboy shoot-em-ups) without suffering any obvious ill-effects. Communications professor Jib Fowles reviews some of the relevant research—and shoddy thinking—on this sensitive topic in a 1999 book called *The Case for Television Violence.*[98]

Our Troubled Teens

On average, American teens are the most troubled teens in the world, and the teen years are the most difficult that we face in life. Our teens are difficult to raise, often unhappy at home, overly immersed in a vacuous teen world that's largely the creation of large corporations, excessively interested in their appearance, overly dependent on drugs and alcohol, unnecessarily careless about sex, and excessively angry, violent, moody, and depressed.

G. Stanley Hall was wrong about recapitulation and he was wrong about the inevitability of teen turmoil, but he was *correct* in his characterization of the highly troubled teens that newly industrialized America was manufacturing. Now, a century later, they're considerably worse.

A DISTURBING CONNECTION: INFANTILIZATION AND TEEN TURMOIL

In Chapter One, I described one of the results of the study I conducted recently with Diane Dumas. When we gave our forty-two-item Infantilization Scale to a hundred teens (from ages thirteen to seventeen), we found that their average score was over twenty-six, suggesting that teens in modern America are often treated like children.

There is another outcome of our study, though, that's even more disturbing. We also gave these teens a standardized test called the Adolescence Psychopathology Scale (APS), which measures a wide variety of indicators of behavioral, cognitive, and emotional disorders.[99] The question was: Is there a relationship between psychopathology in teens (in other words, scores on the APS) and infantilization (in other words, scores on our Infantilization Scale)? A positive correlation in scores would suggest a positive relationship: The greater the infantilization, the greater the psychopathology. Our result was strong: The "correlation coefficient" summarizing the relationship between scores on these two

tests was 0.43, suggesting a fairly large positive relationship between infantilization and certain forms of psychopathology.*

Although this is a dramatic result, it doesn't *prove* that psychopathology in teens is caused by infantilization. Our result could also suggest that teens who "act out" are also the most likely to be restricted by parents or other authorities.[100] Correlational findings—the vast majority of findings we see reported in the media every day—cannot establish causal relationships.

Probable Cause: The Artificial Extension of Childhood

G. Stanley Hall conjectured that treating teens like children would produce "instantly fatal" results—anger, hostility, and tendencies to escape, among other things—in other words, multiple signs of psychopathology. Now we have correlational findings—the research I conducted with Diane Dumas—that are consistent with Hall's conjecture. We've also seen the following:

- A spiraling increase in both the laws that restrict teens and the variety and intensity of teen problems that have emerged over the last 150 years (Chapter Two).
- Few signs of teen turmoil in cultures that maintain a continuum between childhood and adulthood, as well as evidence that teen problems emerge in these cultures when that continuum is broken (Chapter Three).
- Evidence that even troubled American teens sometimes straighten out overnight when given heavy doses of responsibility and respect (Chapter Four).

Finally, we have our common sense, which suggests that the more restrictions you place on people who consider themselves to be autonomous and competent, the angrier and less manageable they become.

I believe we can draw only one reasonable conclusion from these observations: *the storm and stress we see during the teens years in modern America are in all*

---

*A correlation coefficient of this sort can range from -1.0 to +1.0, so 0.43 is fairly strong on the positive side. The correlation was also highly statistically significant (at the 0.01 level, which means, roughly, that the probability of getting this correlation by chance alone is less than one percent). The 0.43—the correlation of greatest interest to us—was between scores on the Infantilization Scale (IS) and scores on the "externalizing" scale of the APS. This scale looks at problems like substance abuse, anger, aggression, and interpersonal difficulties, the kinds of behaviors one sees most often in troubled teens. We also found a small and marginally significant positive relationship (r=0.15, p<0.15) between the IS scores and scores on the "internalizing" scale of the APS, which looks at issues like boredom, introversion, and self-concept.

likelihood *caused by the artificial extension of childhood past puberty.* We hold our young people back and isolate them completely from adulthood. Many react in hostile or self-destructive ways.

Q: *Isn't all the aggression and craziness we see in teenagers caused by hormones?*

A: Although puberty brings about significant hormonal changes, such changes are not the cause of teen turmoil. Tens of millions of teens in preindustrial nations around the world also reach puberty every year, but the mood problems we see in America are almost entirely absent in such countries. Moreover, physiological research shows that the hormonal changes that occur during pubertal maturation don't predict behavior very well.[101] Teen problems in the United States are caused by a host of factors related to the artificial extension of childhood: poor roles models (peers and media icons), peer pressure, isolation from adults and conflict with parents, mandatory schooling, a lack of control over their lives, and so on.

Part 2
The Capabilities of Young People

Chapter 6

"Adultness"

Teach your parents well, their children's hell will slowly go by,
and feed them on your dreams, the one they fix, the one you'll know by.
—Crosby, Stills, Nash, and Young, "Teach Your Children Well"

Overview. Adults don't always measure up to high standards of "adultness." Like teens, they often behave in destructive or self-destructive ways. When one looks carefully at the competencies required to function as an adult, one finds that once people have passed puberty, age is a poor predictor of competence. Our new research shows, in fact, that teens are, on average, as competent or nearly as competent as adults in virtually every area of adult functioning. This research also shows that adults greatly underestimate the capabilities of teens. Because teens are infantilized, their actual performance may not reflect their competence, but that competence is ready to be expressed at any time.

The Darwin Awards are given annually to people who have killed or damaged themselves in embarrassing ways. Here are three winners:

In 1989, after a Kung Fu instructor in Australia told the members of his advanced class that they were now "ready to kill wild animals with [their] bare hands," one member of the class broke into the lion cage at the Melbourne Zoo to test his mettle. The next morning about all that remained of the young man were his hands, each grasping tufts of fur tightly in its fingers. Perhaps he had been able to flip the lion a few times before he was devoured, perhaps not.

In 1997, burglars in England used a welder's torch to cut through the wall of a building housing the loot. Unfortunately, the loot was fireworks. When sparks from the torch hit a crate, the entire building blew up. The perpetrators managed to survive and have never been found.

In 2002 a Kansas man's car broke down just as it was crossing some train tracks.

He got out of the car to try to fix it. That failing, he called for help on his cell phone. According to the conductor of the oncoming train that killed him, when he was struck he had the cell phone at one ear and was using his other hand to block the train noise.[1]

Adults, it seems, sometimes do silly, dangerous, and self-destructive things—and the Darwin Awardees aren't the only ones. How about the twenty thousand adults who commit murder every year in the United States, or the half million people who commit forcible rape, or the more than two million people who commit burglary? And how about the forty-six million Americans who smoke cigarettes or the thirty-nine million Americans who have eaten themselves into obesity? How about the 1.5 million people who are arrested for drunk driving every year? Or the three million pathological gamblers in the United States? Or the ten million adults who are addicted to prescription medications? Or the more than a million adults who get divorced every year?

And how about the leagues of leaders and soldiers worldwide who, during the twentieth century alone, caused the deaths of roughly 175 million people?[2]

THE "ADULTNESS" INVENTORY

What is an adult, anyway? We might choose, as our lawmakers do, to define the term by an arbitrary age boundary—anyone eighteen or over, for example—but is that really what we want "adult" to mean? Or is the age boundary just a rough cutoff point at which we think most people *become* adults? If so, what characteristics do adults have, or at least what characteristics are adults supposed to have? Do all adults have these characteristics in equal amounts? And to what extent do teens have these same characteristics?

Diane Dumas and I attempted to answer these very basic questions. We were particularly interested in isolating those mysterious characteristics that make one truly an adult. After reviewing the relevant research literature, interviewing many adults, and consulting with three other psychologists and two psychiatrists with expertise in adult development issues, we concluded that there are fourteen different skill-sets or "competencies" that distinguish adults from non-adults. One needn't be an expert or even moderately competent in all or even most of these areas to be considered an adult, but unless one is skillful in at least some of them, one will probably be considered "immature" or "childish," no matter what one's age. The people we consider to be mature are typically competent in many or most of these areas.

Love

Adults are supposed to know the difference between sex and love. They're

supposed to have experienced love, or at least to have some idea about what it means to experience love. They're supposed to know the difference between parental and romantic love, and to know that there are many different ways of expressing love. They're even supposed to know that concepts like "true love" and "the one" are, more or less, myths—or at least that they exist mainly in fairy tales and Hollywood movies. As you'll see, Diane and I don't claim to know the truth of all such matters; rather, we set out to determine how much adults, defined by age only, know about them—and then to compare our adult scores to those of teens.

Sex

In theory, adults know a great deal about contraception, homosexuality, how to please a partner, and how to make babies. They're supposed to know that condoms often fail, for example, and that masturbation is common among both males and females (somewhat less so among females). In fact, though, many adults know surprisingly little about sex. A famous case in the psychopathology literature regards a couple that had tried for two years to get pregnant, finally ending up in therapy with a psychiatrist, whose job it was to help them deal with the pain of their persistent failure. Almost by accident, the therapist discovered over the course of their discussions that the couple had mistakenly been having anal intercourse for two years—a revelation that easily explained their difficulties.

Leadership

Adults are supposed to know about leaders and, to some extent, to be able to act as leaders—as leaders of other adults, of children, or at least of pets. They're supposed to know that leaders must sometimes make tough decisions, that leaders are in some sense servants of their followers, and that leaders almost always must report to other leaders higher up a chain of command. Adults are also supposed to be somewhat brave—at least in defending their loved ones or in killing harmless insects—and they're supposed to be able to defend their rights.

Problem Solving

Adults are supposed to be able to solve a wide variety of problems—financial, work-related, plumbing-related, and personal—and they're supposed to know where to go for help when they need it. They're also supposed to know the difference between right and wrong and to be cognizant of the consequences of their actions. They're supposed to be able to think independently and even to be aware of their own faulty beliefs. Tall orders, for sure, but remember that one needn't be a master of *all* of these skills in order to be considered an adult.

Physical Abilities

Adults, or at least healthy adults, are supposed to be physically self-sufficient. We make allowances when people are sick or injured. The infirmities of old age are handled variously: when elderly people become weak, incontinent, or otherwise impaired, we often revert to treating them like children, even though, in some sense, we still recognize the elderly as "adults." In general, adults are supposed to be physically strong, to have intact senses, to be able to climb stairs without assistance, and so on. We expect far less of children.

Verbal and Math Skills

Adults in our society are supposed to have mastered the proverbial Three R's (reading, 'riting, and 'rithmetic), and they're supposed to know basic things like the days of the week, the number of days of the year, the number of days in February (even in leap years), the number of hours in a day, and so on.

Interpersonal Skills

Adults are supposed to know how to converse with, show respect for, forgive, apologize to, get along with, and assist other people. With children, we give basic reminders like "Remember to share," but adults are supposed to have mastered such lessons in basic civility. Adults are also supposed to be honest in their dealings with other people, and they're supposed to have the good sense to follow the instructions of police officers—in other words to recognize that people play different roles in society.

Handling Responsibility

Adults are supposed to be able to accept blame for their wrongdoing (a matter discussed at some length in Chapter Twelve in the context of various religious teachings). They're supposed to be able to make commitments and then honor them. When they begin tasks worthy of completion, they're supposed to persist in completing them.

Managing High-Risk Behaviors

We try to keep children (and teens, by extension) away from cigarettes, drugs, alcohol, guns, and cars, because, presumably, they'll damage themselves or others if they have access to such things. Adults, on the other hand, are supposed to be ready to handle risky items and activities responsibly. Among other things, they're supposed to know that driving under the influence of alcohol is extremely dangerous, that the heavier one is the more alcohol one can tolerate without ill effect, that mixing alcohol with certain drugs can be fatal, that smoking can ruin one's health, that the safe use of guns involves considerable skill, that improper use of prescription medication is dangerous, and so on.

Managing Work and Money

Adults are supposed to be able to get and keep jobs. They're supposed to know that it's important to be on time, that "a job worth doing is worth doing well," that we're supposed to persevere when the going gets tough (and not, as people say so often these days, "go shopping"), and that it's important to prioritize and complete the most important tasks first. Adults are supposed to know how to spend money wisely, how to save, how to invest for the future, how to plan for emergencies, how to manage debts, how to write checks, and how to balance a checkbook.

Education

Adults are supposed to have obtained at least a basic education, and they're supposed to appreciate the value of education. They're also supposed to know basic education laws—for example, that young people are required to attend school until at least age sixteen or so (depending on one's state of residency).

Personal Care

Adults, unlike children, are supposed to practice basic hygiene, to comb their hair, to wear clean clothes, and so on. They're also supposed to eat three nutritionally-balanced meals a day, to avoid between-meal snacks, to brush and floss their teeth, to get a good night's sleep, to maintain a healthful weight, and to avoid too much salt or sugar or fat in their diets. They're also supposed to be able to recognize a variety of medical and psychological problems—signs of cancer, asthma, sleep apnea, depression, bipolar disorder, and so on—and to know when and where to get help if they or their loved ones need it.

Self Management

Adults are supposed to be able to manage their own behavior—to use an alarm clock to make sure they awaken on time, to keep an appointment book to make sure they know why they set their alarm clock, to keep a list of things to do so they know what they're supposed to pick up on the way back from the appointment, and so on. They're also supposed to know basic techniques of "self-control"—counting to ten, for example, as a way of preventing their anger from getting out of hand.

Citizenship

Finally, adults are supposed to know some basic things about government and about how to be good citizens. They're supposed to register to vote and to participate in elections, to pay taxes, to serve on juries, and so on, and they're supposed to know most basic laws and to obey them.

HOW ADULT ARE YOU?

The following are sample questions from Part II of the *Epstein-Dumas Test of Adultness (EDTA)*. All are answered yes or no. The actual test has one hundred forty questions (ten per competency area) in random order, with no designations regarding the separate competencies.

Competency	Questions
1. Love	Some say that true love lasts forever. Does it?
	Must people be loved in order to be fulfilled?
	Is love enough to make a marriage successful?
2. Sex	Safe sex means having sex in a safe place. Is this true?
	Can women get pregnant at any point in the menstrual cycle?
	Can oral sex make someone pregnant?
3. Leadership	Can someone be both a leader and a follower?
	Are you willing to fight for your rights?
	Are leaders always right?
4. Problem Solving agree?	Most problems have just one solution. Do you
	When you have trouble solving a problem, do you ask for help?
	Can you make decisions without help from other people?
5. Physical Abilities	Are you strong physically?
	Do you have difficulty hearing?
	Do you tire easily?
6. Verbal and Math Skills	Is 25 percent the same as one fourth?
	Do you know how to write and send a letter?
	134 + 62 = 196. Is this correct?
7. Interpersonal Skills	Do you have any trouble making friends?
	Do you honor your commitments?
	If a police officer told you to get out of your car, would you comply?

8. *Handling Responsibility*	Do you accept the blame when you make a mistake? When you start something, do you finish it? When things get tough, do you tend to give up?
9. *Managing High-Risk Behavior*	Can drinking alcohol damage your health? Coffee counters the ill effects of alcohol. Is this correct? Drugs and alcohol can mix to produce deadly effects. Is this true?
10. *Managing Work and Money*	Do you have some money saved for emergencies? To keep a job, you must be on time. Do you agree? If you wanted to get a job or change jobs, would you know what to do?
11. *Education*	Learning new skills can enhance your life. Do you agree? School attendance is generally required by law until age sixteen. Is this correct? You can earn a high school diploma by completing school or passing an equivalency test. Is this correct?
12. *Personal Care*	Adequate sleep is important for health. Do you agree? Are you at your ideal weight? If you had thoughts of hurting yourself or others, would you know where to get help?
13. *Self Management*	Do you exercise regularly? Do you write down appointments? Do you keep a list of things to do?
14. *Citizenship*	Is it true that you must be twenty-one to vote in the U.S.? Is it true that most people in the U.S. don't have to pay any taxes? The only two political parties in the U.S. are the Democratic and the Republican. Is this true?

How Good Is the List?

Is this list of competencies complete? If one defines the fourteen areas broadly enough, the list is actually fairly good, but it can never really be complete. One can always argue for changes and additions, especially if one's favorite values or skills haven't been given adequate attention. "Managing Family Roles" could be listed as a separate competency area, for example; adults, one could argue, are supposed to know how to be good parents and spouses, as well as how to be good caregivers for their elderly parents. We've covered some parenting and spousal issues under other competencies, but perhaps they should have been given greater emphasis. In constructing scales of this sort, one always has to make some arbitrary decisions. Fortunately, one also has the option of revising the test!

Designing the Test

Now that we had a reasonable breakdown of adult competencies, obvious questions came to mind: Does anyone actually have these characteristics? In other words, just how widespread is adultness among adults? And just how widespread is adultness among teens?

Over a period of months, Diane and I developed hundreds of yes/no questions meant to measure a respondent's knowledge in each of the competency areas, eventually narrowing down the list to ten questions in each area; that gave us one hundred forty questions in total, which were then placed in random order (according to numbers generated by a computer). For most questions, a "yes" reply was indicative of competence. For example, a "yes" reply to "Do you write down appointments?" suggests competence in the area of self-management. Other questions (called "reverse-scored" questions) required a "no" to indicate competence. For example, a "no" reply to "Are leaders always right?" suggests competence in the area of leadership.

Following standard practice in test construction (I've developed about a dozen competency tests over the years), the test also included some redundant questions: positive or negative variants of other questions. Including redundant questions gives a tester an easy way of getting a quick assessment of the "reliability" of the testing instrument. Nearly-identical questions should be answered the same way by the test-taker. If they're not, either the questions are faulty—ambiguous, perhaps—or the test-taker is dishonest or distracted.

These questions constituted the core of the *Epstein-Dumas Test of Adultness* (*EDTA*), which Diane administered to one hundred adults (from ages twenty to seventy-one, mean age 41.9) and one hundred teens (from ages thirteen to seven-

> ## YOUNG PEOPLE IN ACTION
>
> ### A Tycoon at Twelve
>
> *Twelve-year-old Kevin Colleran was selling baseball cards out his parents' unoccupied storefront in New Haven, Connecticut, and trying to figure out a better way to turn a profit. He placed an ad on America Online but got frustrated when he learned that his ad would disappear unless he re-posted it frequently. He soon realized that he could turn a big profit by performing repetitive, tedious tasks like this for existing companies, and so Cyber Marketing Solutions International was born. By his senior year in high school, he was vice president of a local labeling company, Neato, and also worked two days a week on the floor of the New York Stock Exchange. By the time he reached his senior year in college in 2002, he had successfully launched six businesses and was writing for Playboy.com and* Collegiate Monthly 101 *magazine.*[3]

teen, mean age 15.2). The teen sample was "stratified"—intended to be diverse and to mimic some major characteristics of teens nationwide. They came from seven United States cities: Atlanta, Georgia; Dallas, Texas; Memphis, Tennessee; Oceanside, California; Pensacola, Florida; San Diego, California; and San Marcos, California. Three quarters of the teens lived at home full-time with one or both parents; seventeen lived with one or both of their parents part-time, and eight did not live with their parents. Seventy-eight of the teens were full-time students, but none came from gifted programs. Twenty-three worked part-time, one worked full time, and the rest did not work. Thirty-nine of the teens were Caucasian; twenty were African American; fifteen were Hispanic; eleven were Asian; four were American Indian; and the remaining eleven listed themselves as Other. Fifty-one of the teens were male, and forty-nine were female. Teens received modest remuneration—a free movie ticket and snacks—for participating in the study.

The adult sample consisted of thirty-one males and sixty-nine females. Sixty-one of the adults were parents, but only about 40 percent of those individuals had children thirteen or over. Fifty-five of the adults were college graduates (nearly twice the national average for adults over twenty-five). Forty were African Americans; twenty-nine were Caucasian; seven were Hispanic, ten were Asian, eight were American Indian, and six listed themselves as Other. All subjects were recruited by Diane through friends, family, colleagues, church groups, and co-workers.

Results

The tests we administered contained more than just the competency questions, but let's focus on those for the moment. Just how superior were adults to teens in fourteen competency areas that define "adultness"?

The answer is: barely, if at all.

For three of the competencies—love, leadership, and problem solving—we did find statistically significant differences between the mean scores of teens and adults, with adults outscoring the teens. But the absolute differences between the mean scores were small. Adults scored 8.32 on love, and teens scored 7.95 (out of a possible 10)—a difference of less than 5 percent. Adults scored an impressive 8.88 on leadership, and teens scored 8.20—a difference of 8.3 percent. And adults scored 8.43 on problem solving, and teens scored 8.06—again, a difference of less than 5 percent.

On two other scales—work and self-management—the differences between the adult scores and teen scores were "marginally significant" (at the .05 level), again in the adults' favor, but the absolute differences were less than 4 percent.

On the other nine scales, we found no significant differences at all between the adult and teen scores. This means that the differences between the scores were so small (in relation to the variability in the scores within each group) that one couldn't reasonably trust that the differences between the group means were real.

When statistical significance hasn't been demonstrated, one is supposed to behave as if the group means are identical, but it's interesting to examine such means in any case. On the sex, responsibility, high-risk behaviors, education, and self-management scales, the adult means were slightly larger than the teen means (although, again, the differences might not be real). On the interpersonal skills, personal care, and citizenship scales, the means were virtually identical, and on the physical abilities and verbal and math scales, the teens were *slightly ahead* of the adults (same warning).

The range of scale scores was also interesting: adult scores ranged from 7.91 to 8.95, whereas teen scale scores ranged from 7.95 to 8.63. The adult range was *larger* than the teen range, and the lowest adult scale score was *lower* than the lowest teen score.

The overall group mean for the adults was 116.7, and the overall group mean for the teens was 114.2. The difference between the scores was statistically significant, but the absolute size of that difference (2.5) was only 2.1 percent of the overall teen mean.

This is a remarkable result, especially when you consider that fifty-five of the

adults in our sample were college graduates—more than double the rate of college graduates in the United States. In other words, whereas our teens were reasonably representative of the general population, our adults were far better educated than the average adult. Presumably, with a less educated adult sample the differences between the groups would have been even smaller—or perhaps the teens might have outscored the adults on a number of scales.

Overall, these results provide fairly conservative evidence that there is no appreciable difference between the adult competencies of teens and adults.

WHY DON'T WE APPRECIATE OUR TEENS?

Perhaps you're skeptical about these result. That would be understandable, because they contradict everyday beliefs and experiences. One certainly runs into the occasional mature or knowledgeable teen, but the idea that, on the average, teens are as competent as adults seems farfetched.

To come to terms with these results, we need, once again, to push aside a number of preconceptions—to "think different," as Apple would have it. Here are five possible reasons why teens might indeed be extremely competent without us knowing it.

Preconceptions

First, as University of California sociologist Mike Males asserted in his fact-rich book *Framing Youth*, it's possible that teens are getting a raw deal (also see Appendix 3 of this volume). Maybe teens aren't so bad, and their negative image is a creation of sensation-seeking media professionals and nervous, self-serving politicians. In other words, maybe teen competence is staring us in the face, and we just can't—or won't—see it.

Do adults really underestimate the abilities of teens, as Males suggests? To answer this question, Diane and I added a set of twenty-four items to the test we administered to adults. The basic question we asked was deliberately generous and broad, encouraging respondents to give teens every possible benefit of the doubt: *"In your opinion, do many young people (from age thirteen to seventeen) have the potential to behave in the following ways?"*

Note that we didn't ask whether *all* young people have these abilities, just whether "many" do. We also didn't ask whether young people *currently* behave in these ways, but merely whether they have the "potential" to do so. Even so, the results were discouraging—and illuminating.

WHAT DO ADULTS BELIEVE ABOUT THE POTENTIAL OF TEENS?

Adults were asked to respond to twenty-four items after being given the following question: *"In your opinion, do many young people (from age thirteen to seventeen) have the potential to behave in the following ways?"* Respondents answered "yes" or "no" to each item. (From the *Epstein-Dumas Test of Adultness*.)

1.   Experience romantic love?
2.   Have sex in a responsible manner?
3.   Lead other people?
4.   Drive a car responsibly?
5.   Serve in the military in a competent manner?
6.   Own and handle firearms responsibly?
7.   Hold political office?
8.   Vote in elections?
9.   Show courage?
10. Find a job?
11. Hold a job?
12. Start a business?
13. Live on their own?
14. Raise a family?
15. Own and care for property responsibly?
16. Drink alcohol responsibly?
17. Smoke cigarettes responsibly?
18. Manage money responsibly?
19. Make responsible decisions about their own education?
20. Make responsible decisions about their own medical care?
21. Make responsible decisions about their own psychological care?
22. Make responsible decisions about their own religious up bringing?
23. Make responsible decisions about their own schedules?
24. Make responsible decisions about the way they dress?

The average adult appears to think pretty poorly of teens. Out of a possible high score of twenty-four, the mean score on this test was 11.4. In other words, on a percentage basis, our adults gave teens a score of 48 percent—a failing grade, for sure. Half of our adults, in fact, gave teens only ten points out of twenty-four, and five of our one hundred adults gave teens a pathetic score of three—meaning they believe that teens have virtually no adult competencies—not even any "potential." On the other extreme, four of the adults gave teens a perfect score of twenty-four.

Something strange is going on here. How can perspectives on teens be so radically different—like the perspectives of contemporary leaders in education we examined in Chapter One? Scores covering a range of twenty-two points on a twenty-four-point test are virtually unheard of on a scale of this sort. After all, everyone is looking at roughly the same set of teens; we may see different teens at home, but we're all looking at nearly the same teens in the movies, on television, and in the newspapers.

The low mean score supports the basic idea that the "average" adult thinks poorly of teens, but the enormous *range* of scores suggests that adult perceptions of teens are *too* flexible—in other words, that many adults might indeed have faulty preconceptions about teens.

The opinion scores I just described are consistent with the infantilization scores I discussed in Chapter One: Apparently adults infantilize teens because they believe teens are incompetent.

Performance Versus Competence

We might also understand the high scores that teens obtained on the *EDTA* competency scales by examining the relationship between competence and performance. Perhaps you've heard the old joke about the little mute boy. His parents were concerned about his lack of language, so year after year they brought him to a parade of experts, but the boy still couldn't talk. One morning when the boy was ten the family was sitting around the kitchen table eating breakfast when the boy suddenly said, *"This oatmeal is cold."* His parents were dumbfounded. "You can *talk?"* his father gasped. "Then why haven't you said a word until now?" The boy replied, "Because until now everything was okay."

Just because one *can* do something doesn't mean one *will* do something. "Competence" is what one *can* do; "performance" is what one actually does. The distinction is important, and so is the relationship between these two domains. The competence domain is vastly larger than and fully encompasses the performance domain. In other words, what we actually do is a small portion of what we are capable of doing.

I've taught seminars on creativity—my major area of scientific research since the late 1970s—for many years, and I've also developed tests that measure the competencies that underlie creative expression, as well as games and exercises that strengthen such competencies. Very few adults express much creativity, but my research suggests that virtually everyone is capable of enormous creativity—in the arts, in literature, in invention, and more (see Chapter Ten).[4] Then why is creativity so seldom expressed?

In kindergarten, almost all children are creative: they make up stories, draw outlandish pictures, and use toys in ever-changing ways. But by the end of the first grade, very few children express creativity. This is likely because of the deleterious effects of socialization and regimentation. The kindergarten class has traditionally been free-form: Play is allowed, children sit around tables or move around; toys are present; daydreaming and silly questions are tolerated.[*] The first-grade class, on the other hand, is highly regimented: Children sit at desks; the toys are gone; questions need to be "relevant"; daydreaming and silly questions are prohibited.

The regimentation continues throughout our school years, effectively shutting down creative expression in all but a few misfits whom the system can't manage to socialize. But there are ample signs—our continuing dreams and daydreams, for example—that our creativity machinery remains intact throughout our lives, and it's easy to demonstrate this to adults with a few quick exercises and then, with some further training, to increase creative expression dramatically. So the creativity "competency" may be present even though virtually no creativity is shown. Similarly, teens may very well have adult competencies without demonstrating them.

Personal Experience

Third, it's possible that most adults aren't aware of teen potential because the teens they actually see behave badly. They're angry or deceitful or disrespectful. They refuse to follow the instructions of adults. They're doing drugs, smoking cigarettes, having sex irresponsibly, or worse. If that's what you see—a good possibility in the modern United States—then that's what you'll believe.

But personal experience isn't always the best teacher. The teens you see might not be representative of all teens, and, more important, the way the teens in your life are behaving right now is almost certainly a poor indicator of the way they *might* behave under other conditions—in other words, of their "competence."

---

*This is changing rapidly. Under pressure to raise test scores to secure federal funding, many school systems are now regimenting kindergarten classes and introducing much of the curriculum that used to be reserved for the first grade. In my daughter's kindergarten class this past year, the students even had homework four nights a week.

Infantilization

Fourth, teens might be behaving well below their potential for the simple reason that we treat them like children. Just about everything we do tells them they're incompetent. We protect them from danger (driving, cigarettes, alcohol); we don't trust them to work or own property or spend money; we don't allow them to make basic decisions about their health, education, or religion; we force them to attend school whether they benefit from school or not; and we often refer to them as "boys," "girls," or "children," even though they may be shaving or menstruating.

What happens when you treat a whole segment of the population as if it's inferior and helpless? As blacks and women can tell you, many people in such a sub-population tend to believe what they're told and then to behave as expected. The "yassuh" of the subjugated black, the passive behavior of the 19th-century woman—these were produced by a society that molded generations of blacks and women to be exactly what society expected. But as blacks and women have demonstrated over the last century, performance can be a very poor predictor of competence. When we infantilize teens, we might create many of them in the image we have in mind, but that doesn't necessarily tell us about their potential.

Our Own Incompetence

Finally, teens and adults might have similar scores on the EDTA not because teens are so incredibly competent but because adults aren't. The adult scores were high, but they were far from perfect; even though the scales tested elementary knowledge, and even though our adult sample was better educated than the average American adult, our adult subjects made errors on every scale, missing relatively simple questions about government, math, diet, money, work, citizenship, alcohol, sex, and so on. Out of a total of fourteen thousand questions answered by our adult subjects, 2,326 were answered incorrectly—a sizable number of errors.

I think that most of us—adults, that is—are well aware of our lack of perfection—of our grudges, angry outbursts, memory lapses, careless drinking or driving, lies and misrepresentations, addictions, bad moods or petulant moments, insensitivity, poor diets, inability to commit, and so on. Yet based strictly on our age and some legal definitions, we're also reasonably comfortable calling ourselves "adult," even though we may suspect at times that we're not worthy of the title.

In other words, we're *selective* about what characteristics and behaviors we pay attention to, always seeking to confirm the supposition that we're adults. At the same time—and even when there may be evidence to the contrary—we're quick to dismiss teens as incompetent, also judging teens by their age rather than by their capabilities,

expressed or potential. In other words, we're also *selective* about how we pay attention to the characteristics and behaviors of teens, always seeking to confirm our supposition that teens are incompetent children (more about this in Chapter Fourteen).

Age is simply not a reliable measure of adultness, at least not once people are past puberty. Teens have the potential to be very adultlike, and adults sometimes act immaturely. On average, teens and adults are probably equally capable of exhibiting adult behavior, no matter how teens may currently behave day-to-day and no matter what our preconceptions may tell us.

Q: *How can I find out if my teen is capable of handling more responsibility?*

A: The simplest way to find out is to give your teen a chance. Help him or her open a bank account, for example; teach your teen how such accounts work and how to balance a checkbook, and then see what happens. You might be surprised at how well your thirteen- or fourteen-year-old will do. As I indicated in this chapter, Diane Dumas and I have also developed a comprehensive test, the *EDTA*, that measures "adultness" competencies in fourteen different areas. Scores on tests of this sort can help pinpoint skill areas where a teen is strong or weak. See Appendix 1 of this volume for an abridged version of the *EDTA* that you can score yourself.

Chapter 7

Young People Are Capable Thinkers

Life's filled with many paths which one should I take?
When the choice comes, I won't run. I'll be thinking straight.
—Youth of Today, *"Thinking Straight"*

Overview. *Scientific research shows unequivocally that the cognitive abilities of teens are, on average, superior to the cognitive abilities of adults. Reasoning ability peaks in the early or mid teens, for example, and so does intelligence. Most memory functions peak in our early teens, and all of these abilities decline throughout adulthood, some quite dramatically. Research also shows that the ability of teens to make sound decisions about health matters, including abortion, is equal to that of adults. Media reports suggest that teen problems are produced by a faulty "teen brain," but a close examination of the relevant research does not support the claims. The teen brain is, at best, a reflection of teen problems, not their cause. The brain itself changes throughout life, and—consistent with the pattern of changes in cognitive abilities—it reaches its maximum size at about age fourteen and shrinks thereafter. A seventy-year-old's brain is typically the size of that of a toddler.*

Swiss psychologist Jean Piaget was, arguably, one of the two or three most eminent and influential scientists in the history of psychology. His passion was the cognitive development of young people, and his meticulous research and elaborate theorizing—most of which took place during the early and middle 1900s—still forms the core of modern developmental psychology. His views on young people have been challenged to some extent by contemporary researchers, but his basic findings still stand.

His general proposal was that thinking progresses through a series of inevitable stages from infancy through adulthood. The thinking of little children is qualitatively different from the thinking of adults, and he showed precisely how thinking changes over the years. When you show a six-month-old a funny toy, he or

she will likely reach for it, but when you cover the toy with a pillow, the child will almost immediately move on to something else; in other words, the child will behave as if the toy disappeared into thin air. The old saw "out of sight, out of mind" can be taken literally with very young children. But by the time a child is a year old or so, he or she will try to find the toy beneath the pillow. The child has learned that the toy continues to exist when it's out of sight. As Piaget put it, the child has mastered the concept of "object permanence."

Piaget's theory of cognitive development is based on the outcomes of hundreds of experiments of this sort with children of various ages. Generally, one finds that thinking starts out to be remarkably primitive and then gradually becomes more adultlike. Object permanence is one of many concepts one needs to master in order to achieve adult thinking, according to Piaget.

This is not the place to review Piaget's theory in detail. For present purposes, what's important is that Piaget's stages culminate in a period called "formal operational thinking"; for Piaget, this kind of thinking is, more or less, the highest we can attain, and, in that sense, it's the kind of thinking one should find in adults.[1] Three obvious questions come to mind: What is formal operational thinking? When it is typically achieved? And do all adults achieve it?

WHEN DO WE THINK MOST CLEARLY?

Formal operational thinking has two distinct characteristics that differentiate it from more primitive forms. First, formal operational thinkers can think about the world symbolically. They're not stuck thinking about one particular apple; they can *imagine* that apple, or think about the concept of *all apples*, or think about all apples as part of larger classes (fruit, food, red objects, etc.). They can even think about abstract ideas related to apples: sin, health, and patriotism, for example. More important, they can "operate" on symbols in orderly ways. They can turn the image of the apple upside down, or spin it at high speed, or say what makes apples different from oranges or dogs or park benches without having any of the objects present.

To see whether people had achieved this kind of thinking, Piaget and his colleagues gave people various problems to solve. A correct solution was always a good sign, but Piaget was also interested in seeing *how* people solved the problems. In one problem, Piaget and his long-time colleague Bärbel Inhelder asked young people to figure out how to vary the speed with which a pendulum swings. They were given a string that could be varied in length, along with small objects of different weights which could be attached to the end of the string.

Subjects in this simple procedure typically experiment with the materials in four different ways: they shorten or lengthen the string, tie on objects of different weights, swing the object from different heights, and push the object with weaker or harder pushes. It turns out that there is only one determinant of the frequency of the pendulum motion: the length of the string. Because there are four different possible determinants of the movement, many people have difficulty singling out the correct one. To do so, one needs to be able to isolate each determinant, one at a time, while varying the other three—a procedure the eighteenth century English philosopher John Stuart Mill called the "method of concomitant variation." People who can figure out how to do this are said, in Piaget's lingo, to be capable of the "operation of exclusion"—one of several formal operations that typify fully-developed adult thinking.

This particular operation is normally achieved by age eleven or twelve. This might surprise you, because perhaps it wasn't immediately obvious to you how to solve the pendulum problem. Your own difficulties notwithstanding, *all* of the formal operations—if they are going to be mastered at all—are typically mastered by age *fourteen or fifteen*. The young teen, according to Piaget, is capable of "experimental and logico-mathematical thinking," of "philosophical speculation," of "theory construction," and even of "analyzing his own thinking."[2] In other words, shortly after puberty we are capable of adult thinking—at least as far as Jean Piaget was concerned.

Piaget even acknowledged—and subsequent research has confirmed—that it might be possible to speed up the mastery of formal operational thinking somewhat. According to a 1955 essay by Inhelder and Piaget, "...the age of eleven-to-twelve years may be... a product of a progressive acceleration of individual development under the influence of education, and perhaps nothing stands in the way of a further reduction in the average age in a more or less distant future."[3] Perhaps even more interesting, Inhelder and Piaget speculated that "fundamental affective acquisitions of adolescence parallel the intellectual acquisitions"[4]—in other words, that teens also had the potential to achieve a high level of emotional maturity between ages eleven and fifteen.

Bad News About Our Thinking Abilities

That's the good news. Now here's the bad. Many adults never achieve formal operational thinking, and if they haven't done so by age fifteen or so, they probably never will. What's more—and this is consistent with what we'll learn later in this chapter about intelligence and other cognitive abilities—our ability to think operationally starts to *decline* in our twenties and continues to do so throughout our lives.

Piaget himself believed that almost anyone could achieve formal operational thinking. In an article he published in 1972 (toward the end of his long career), he wrote:

> ...in principle all normal individuals are capable of reaching the level of formal structures on the condition that the social environment and acquired experience provide the subject with the cognitive nourishment and intellectual stimulation necessary for such a construction.[5]

He's saying that environmental input appears to be important—that one's thinking ability will be stunted if one doesn't get adequate "cognitive nourishment"—another argument, I believe, against the artificial extension of childhood. In any case, by the 1970s researchers began to discover that a great many people failed to master formal operations.

In a 1975 report, for example, by Jan D. Sinnott of the Catholic University of America, many subjects in two different age groups (average age thirty-three, and average age sixty-seven) failed to show mastery of a number of different Piagetian tasks, and older subjects generally did much more poorly than younger subjects—even though they all had two weeks to work on the problems in their own homes. Overall, only about two-thirds of Sinnott's subjects showed mastery of tasks requiring formal operational thinking.[6]

A 1972 study by C. Tomlinson-Keasy of Rutgers University yielded similar findings. Formal operational tasks given to groups of females in three age groups (average age 11.9, 19.7, and 54, respectively) were mastered by a third of the youngest subjects, by two-thirds of the twenty-year-olds, and by only about half of the middle-aged women.[7] (See Figure 7.1.) A late 1970s study conducted in the Soviet Union by N. A. Podgorestskaya with subjects between sixteen and fifty-five also showed considerably poorer performance by adult subjects.[8]

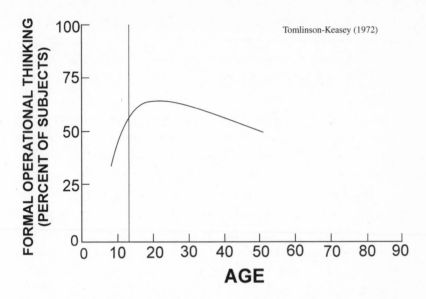

Figure 7.1. Formal Operational Thinking by Age. Several studies indicate that formal operational thinking—Piaget's highest stage of reasoning—begins to emerge around the time of puberty, and it appears that many adults are incapable of this thinking. A 1972 study by Tomlinson-Keasy looking at three age groups of women (mean ages twelve, twenty, and fifty-four) found evidence that our reasoning powers may even decline as we get older.

Piaget's confidence in our ability to think clearly has not been borne out, but that could be because of inadequate stimulation—poor schooling, pop culture, and, of course, infantilization—rather than because of inherent limitations. The decline in functioning that seems to occur after our twenties could come from lack of practice: perhaps in the 1970s when the Tomlinson-Keasy study was conducted, middle-aged women had little reason to continue to exercise their logical powers past their school years. But research still supports Piaget's basic assertion: We become capable of formal operational thinking at about age eleven, with the peak in our abilities occurring by age fifteen.

Making It Personal

As I write this, I'm now fifty-three years old. A quarter of a century ago, at age twenty-seven, I published an article in *Harvard Magazine* called "Growing Older, or What Else I Learned in Graduate School." It was a lament about many aspects of growing older—and especially the fact that I was now facing "a physical and emotional future that no one ever prepared me for." Among the many early signs of aging I described was this:

...you can no longer think as well.... A junior faculty member remarked that he could no longer solve the puzzlers in Scientific American. *When I was fourteen I could routinely think ten moves ahead in three-dimensional tic-tac-toe (four-by-four-by-four). I've lost nearly half a move a year.*[9]

I was aware even then about the mental prowess of the fourteen-year-old—at least my own. What has happened to your own mental prowess? Have you noticed any decline? Perhaps you're thinking: "I may not be as adept as I once was, but my *judgment* has improved greatly." I'll deal with the judgment issue later in the chapter, and, again, you might be surprised by what the research shows.

One final note: Piaget himself published his first scientific article (on the albino sparrow) at age eleven, and during his teens he published a number of impressive technical articles in malacology, the field concerned with the study of mollusks. His own life exemplifies the enormous power of the teenage mind—if it is properly "nourished."

WHEN DOES MORAL REASONING PEAK?

It's often presumed that American teens are generally immoral, or perhaps even amoral. In general, social scientists are reluctant to moralize or even to study morality—probably too reluctant, considering how important moral concerns are in the world at large. But there is one aspect of morality that psychologists have studied for decades, and that is called "moral reasoning."

The issue is a narrow one: in situations in which one must make judgments about morality, *what kind of rationale does one use?* This may sound too narrow to be interesting, but it turns out to be a fascinating area of study for the simple reason that people use remarkably different rationales when they render moral opinions. What's more, our ability to make such judgments seems to develop in a series of inevitable stages, just like our general intellectual ability. Researchers who have studied moral reasoning have also found that very few people ever reach the highest possible stages—far fewer than reach the highest stages of intellectual development.

The study of moral reasoning was pioneered by an American psychologist named Lawrence Kohlberg, whose life ended tragically in 1987 in what appeared to be a suicide (I mention this as a gentle reminder about the imperfection of adults). Over a period of many years, Kohlberg and his students and colleagues

presented people of different ages with various moral dilemmas, such as this classic pharmacy dilemma:

> Bill's beloved wife is deathly ill, and the only medication that will relieve her incredible pain is far beyond Bill's means. One night he breaks into a small pharmacy owned by a local businessman and steals enough medication to give his wife relief for the remaining weeks of her life. Was Bill wrong or right, and why?

They found that people's analyses of these problems were of six different types, ranging from concrete and simplistic to quite abstract. Kohlberg concluded that these six types constitute "stages" of reasoning and that we progress through the stages from early childhood through adulthood—some of us further than others.

Kohlberg's Stages of Moral Development

The first two stages, typical of children under nine, comprise what Kohlberg called Level I or "preconventional" reasoning—reasoning that's egocentric or individualistic. When young children are asked to explain why an action is right or wrong, they talk about the rewards and punishments at stake—how someone will benefit or be penalized. In Stage 1, the child can only conceive of one person's rewards and punishments; in Stage 2, he or she recognizes that different people have different interests that might conflict with each other. Applied to the pharmacy dilemma, a Level I analysis would focus on the consequences of the theft: "Bill was right to steal the drug because his wife will be so grateful," or "Bill was wrong to steal the drug because he's going to get in trouble."

The next two stages, mastered by pre-teens and teens, comprise Level II or "conventional" reasoning—reasoning that's based on the expectations of the community, which include the laws passed by our legislatures. Stage 3 thinkers accept, more or less without question, the way family and friends have defined "good" and "bad." Stage 4 thinkers recognize the demands of the larger community; they recognize, for example, that laws are good and must be followed. They also know, though, that it might be right to disobey a law when obeying it would conflict with obligations people have to other people. Applied to the pharmacy problem, conventional thinkers might respond: "Bill was right to steal the drug because it's his duty as a husband to take the best possible care of his suffering wife," or "Bill was wrong to steal the drug because the laws against theft, which provide stability for all of us, are more important than the suffering of one person. If everyone did what Bill did, our society would break down in chaos overnight."

These kinds of rationales probably sound familiar to you, because, as Kohlberg

notes, "The conventional level is the level of most adolescents and adults in our society and in other societies."[10] In other words, there's a good chance that you are a conventional thinker and that you gave a Stage 4 rationale for your response to the pharmacy dilemma: "Bill was right to steal the drug because his obligations to his suffering wife were more important than his obligation to follow the law."

Kohlberg identified two other types of moral reasoning, which he called Level III or "postconventional" types. These, he said, are mastered by a small number of people in their twenties and remain relatively rare among adults. The postconventional thinker has "differentiated his or her self from the rules and expectations of others and defines his or her values in terms of self-chosen principles."[11] In other words, he or she has formulated general principles of right and wrong which may or may not coincide with laws or with the expectations of the community. Clearly, society can't tolerate too many postconventional thinkers, especially ones who formulate principles that reject the need for stoplights or that justify the mailing of letter bombs to scholars and administrators (Ted Kaczynski comes to mind).

Postconventional thinking applied to the pharmacy problem might yield a response like "Bill was right, because the obligations we have to loved ones must always be put ahead of laws passed by legislators. After all, laws are merely crude approximations of the obligations people have toward their loved ones; they are necessarily imperfect." (If you read Kaczynski's manifesto in *The Washington Post* years ago, you may recognize his style here.)

How Moral Reasoning Changes Over Time

According to Kohlberg, after age nine, most young people rapidly master the skills of conventional moral reasoning, and very few of us ever progress beyond that point. The statistics are impressive. In a twenty-year longitudinal study conducted by Kohlberg and his colleagues, no thirteen or fourteen year olds were still at Stage 1, and only about 20 percent were still at Stage 2. Fifty-eight percent of the thirteen and fourteen year olds tested were straddling Stages 2 and 3—that is, showing clear signs of conventional moral reasoning—and nearly 20 percent were fully conventional in their thinking.

By age eighteen, more than two-thirds of the subjects exhibited fully conventional thinking. As subjects aged, their thinking continued to advance, but not quickly and not much. By the time the subjects were in their twenties or thirties, about 90 percent of them had reached Stages 3 or 4, but only a handful—11 percent—showed any signs of postconventional reasoning, and none moved fully to Stages 5 or 6.[12]

Kohlberg's study was conducted with males only, but more recent cross-sectional and longitudinal studies conducted in Israel, Turkey, and India have con-

firmed Kohlberg's original findings.[13] The bottom line: most teens are capable of conventional, adult-like moral reasoning, and very few adults ever advance beyond such reasoning.

Kohlberg noted that all moral reasoning requires general reasoning powers, and he referred specifically to Piaget's stages to account for the progress of moral reasoning during our early years. Conventional moral reasoning, said Kohlberg, requires only "'low' formal operations," which Piaget thought most young people could master by eleven or twelve.[14] So even if teens may, according to the modern keepers of right and wrong, behave immorally at times, they're quite capable of *reasoning* about moral issues very much as adults do.

Although studies exist that question the moral reasoning abilities of young people,[15] researchers who have taken the time to try to understand what young people are saying in the context of their life circumstances consistently point to the complex and sophisticated moral reasoning that many young people demonstrate. Harvard psychiatrist Robert Coles found evidence of this sophistication in young people around the world,[16] and Harvard education professor Carol Gilligan, using "narrative" techniques, concludes that "adolescence may be a critical time for moral education" because "adolescents are passionately interested in moral questions." Citing breakthrough research by Kay Johnston with eleven- and fifteen-year-olds as a "watershed" in her thinking about development, Gilligan suggests that we sometimes underestimate the moral sophistication of young people because we don't ask the right questions—or *enough* questions. After Johnston asked her subjects to analyze moral dilemmas from Aesop's fables, she then asked them if they could give a *different* analysis than the one they had first given. About half of the subjects were able to do so, and nearly all of those individuals were even able to say which analysis was preferable and why.[17]

WHEN ARE WE MOST INTELLIGENT?

In the recent film *Thirteen*, about which I'll say more in Chapter Ten, a young female who has always been a good student is corrupted by a peer. She becomes unruly, experiments with drugs and sex, and shirks her school work. We've all seen or heard of cases like this: In elementary school and perhaps middle school, the young person performs beautifully, only to slide into oblivion in high school. This hardly seems to support the idea that we reach the peak of our reasoning ability in our early or mid-teens. But Piaget and Kohlberg weren't

the only ones to arrive at this conclusion. Even the mavens of the classic intelligence test agree.

Our Highly Intelligent Teens

In a 1944 book called *The Measurement of Adult Intelligence*, David Wechsler, the developer of two of the most widely used intelligence tests in the Western world, the WISC and the WAIS, indicated that intelligence peaks at about age fifteen—and that it generally declines throughout adulthood.[18] Although raw scores on Wechsler's original test for adults continued to increase somewhat after age fifteen, Wechsler concluded that the highest "mental age" we can reach is fifteen and a half. (See Figure 7.2.) According to Wechsler, "[There] are no mental age equivalents for ages above fifteen and a half, and... beginning as early as age fourteen, the differences between succeeding half year scores are so small as to make them unreliable."[19]

Even more impressive, a 1948 paper published in the *British Journal of Psychology* by J. C. Raven suggests that intelligence peaks even earlier—perhaps at thirteen or fourteen.[20] The Raven paper is the better of the two for our purposes, because Raven used a non-verbal test called "Progressive Matrices," whereas Wechsler's test relied in part on verbal skills. The Progressive Matrices test, first introduced by Raven in 1938, presents a series of diagrams to the test-taker to see if he or she can recognize patterns. Since the material is abstract, it can be considered an early form of the so-called "culture-free" test that became popular later in the century. Presumably, scores on this test depend less on the test-taker's specific experiences than do his or her scores on verbal tests. In this respect, it's a fairly good vehicle for looking at how intelligence changes over the life span.

Then Why Do Many Teens Seem So Unintelligent?

If our intelligence (defined in the traditional way, as the ability to think clearly, logically, and rationally) peaks during the early or mid-teen years, why do so many teens seem so unintelligent?[21]

Teens in Isolation. First, teens are generally isolated from adults and lack meaningful responsibilities, so they may not be receiving the intellectual nourishment about which Piaget spoke. Even though intelligence has a substantial genetic component, it's also affected by experience. Denied a wide range of adult challenges, American teens may be developing their intelligence in narrow ways, determined largely by the artificial boundaries of the classroom—assuming, of course, that they're even profiting from what the classroom has to offer, which is debatable in many cases.

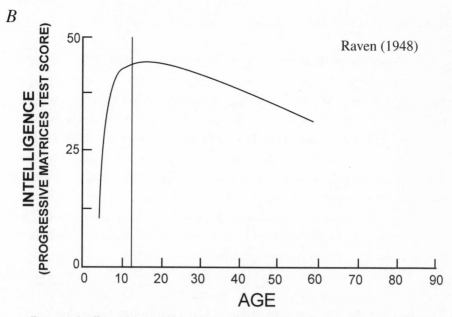

Figure 7.2. **Intelligence by Age.** Although our intelligence ranking within our age group (roughly, our "IQ") remains fairly constant for much of our life, our actual raw scores on intelligence tests follow the patterns shown in these two graphs: Our scores are highest at or shortly after puberty, and then they decline slowly throughout our lives. After age thirty or so, we can never think as clearly as we can in our teens.

Infantilization. Second, as the data I collected with Diane Dumas show clearly, teens in modern America are infantilized—more tightly controlled and restrained even than active-duty United States Marines or incarcerated felons (Chapter One). Infantilization plays out in many ways; among other things, it creates a relationship between adults and teens that's inherently adversarial. It's difficult to like or respect someone who treats you like a child when you no longer are, and you may act irrationally around such a person. In addition, as I've mentioned earlier, when we treat teens like children, we may also be encouraging them to behave that way: dependent, helpless, and ignorant—at least when they're around us. A teen who is underperforming at home or in school may be razor sharp with peers or on the street, where there is at least the possibility of earning real respect.

Drugs and Alcohol. Third, numerous studies suggest that drug and alcohol abuse can impair cognitive functioning.* Unduly influenced by peers and mass media, isolated from adults, and infantilized by authority figures, teens abuse drugs and alcohol to an alarming extent (Chapter Five). It's possible that the enormous intellectual potential teens have is diminished in many cases by substance abuse. I find this possibility especially disturbing, because it means that we might not only be ignoring teen potential, we might also be permanently destroying it.

The Impact of Peers. Fourth, teens tend to imitate each other, not adults. They spend almost all their time with peers and virtually no time with adults, so this shouldn't be surprising. In countries where adolescence hasn't yet emerged, the opposite is true: Teens spend almost all their time with the kinds of adults they will eventually be (Chapter Three). In the United States teens are also presented, day in and day out, with attractive, charismatic teen role models through glitzy television shows, movies, music videos, and print magazines—a powerful set of industries created and maintained especially for this purpose. The role models are not industrious, intelligent, dedicated, adult-like young people. Instead, they're superficial, irresponsible, promiscuous, risk-prone, substance-abusing, disrespectful, and sometimes quite bizarre.

The role-model industry sets up our young people to behave well below their potential. Acting dumb, like the protagonists in the 1989 film *Bill and Ted's Excellent Adventure*, is cool. Acting like an adult—like the authoritarian,

---

*The hysteria over drug abuse by teens sometimes leads to exaggerations, however. For example, investigators at Johns Hopkins University provoked major headlines in 2001 when they announced that their research demonstrated that Ecstasy produces significant brain damage and a Parkinson's-like disease. A subsequent news report revealed that the drug they used was actually methamphetamine, not Ecstasy.[22]

uninformed enemy—invites ridicule by peers and is even discouraged by adults. When the protagonist in *Thirteen* turns cool, in order to maintain her credibility with her new cool cohort, it's absolutely necessary that she start failing at school. We see this again in 1980s film *Can't Buy Me Love*, in which a young man cuts himself off from his fellow nerds after he's able to buy his way in to the popular crowd.

Depending on your age and musical taste, you may have run across the popular Nirvana song, "Smells Like Teen Sprit." The words in "Smells Like Teen Spirit" are virtually impossible to decipher. Lead singer Kurt Cobain—a great talent who suffered from depression and committed suicide at age twenty-seven—creates little more than a lyrical mush by slurring and mumbling every line. A student of mine recently explained to me what this famous song is about. "Smells Like Teen Spirit," it turns out, is a lament about the fact that when you're a teen, it's desirable to be depressed, self-hating, and stupid. Sings Cobain, "Load up on guns/ Bring your friends/ It's fun to lose/ And to pretend.... I'm worse at what I do best/ And for this gift I feel blessed." This is the context in which we're trying—and often failing—to educate our young people.

Tougher Competition. Finally, it's possible that some teens who don't seem very bright really *aren't* very bright—relatively speaking, anyway—even if they performed well in elementary school.

Throughout life, many of our test scores—grades in school, for example—tend to drop. There are a number of reasons for this, the main one being that as we grow older the competition gets stiffer. In elementary school, we're competing against twenty or thirty neighborhood kids. In high school, we're competing against hundreds of people from a much larger geographical region; some of the slowest students intensify the competition by dropping out and disappearing from the educational system. In college, we're competing against a far more select group, and in graduate or professional school, we may be competing against a highly select group drawn from people around the state, the country, or even the world.

We move through a similar progression as we rise to higher heights in our profession; the competition gets tougher and tougher until we finally rise to the level of our incompetence. As we get older, the various tests we're given also tend to get harder; as people compete with each other in increasingly competent groups, more difficult tests are needed to sort people out.

So some young people, subjected to tougher and tougher demands, will necessarily do worse and worse. As they drop to positions of lower status in what the late Richard Herrnstein called the "meritocracy,"[23] some of them will feel increasingly frustrated, especially if they've been victims of the modern self-esteem move-

---

WISDOM OF THE AGES

Burns on Memory

> *By the time you're eighty years old you've learned everything. You only*
> *have to remember it.*
>   —George Burns

---

ment. When we approach life with unrealistic expectations, we are invariably disappointed.

The bottom line is that some of the teens for whom we once had great expectations will simply not be able to meet those expectations. This in no way invalidates my basic point: on average, intelligence peaks in the early or mid teens, no matter how some individuals may perform.

But Doesn't IQ Stay Stable Throughout Life?

If you have a background in psychology or education, you might be aware of the fact that "IQ" stays relatively stable from elementary school until old age. This would appear to contradict my repeated assertions that intellectual ability peaks when we're young. But "IQ" is not the same as "intelligence," even though some people use the terms interchangeably.

"IQ" stands for "intelligence quotient," the result of an arithmetic division. The intelligence quotient is computed, more or less, by dividing one's "raw" score (in other words, one's *actual* score) on an intelligence test by the *average score* obtained by people in one's age group. So IQ remains fairly stable because one's intellectual *rank* in one's age group stays fairly constant. If you were at the top of the heap when you were ten, you'll probably be at the top of the heap when you're seventy. While this may be reassuring, it tells you nothing about what's happening to those raw scores, which are in fact increasing rapidly during childhood and decreasing slowly all through adulthood, just as Wechsler and Raven found.

IQ is a *relative* measure—useful if you're an administrator trying to decide which students to put into an advanced class—whereas the raw scores are *absolute* measures of ability. Our intellectual ability indeed peaks during our early or mid-teens, stays somewhat stable during our twenties, and declines gradually for the rest of our lives. Because this happens to virtually everyone, our rank within our own age group will necessarily stay fairly constant; everyone is getting smarter and then less smart at about the same pace. Hence the stability of—and misleading nature of "IQ."

The Disturbing Truth About Intelligence

Like it or not, after age thirty or so, our ability to reason is never again as good as it was in our teens. Raven puts the matter bluntly:

> Apparently by the age of fourteen, a child's trainability has reached its maximum, while after the age of thirty, a person's ability to understand a new method of thinking, adopt new methods of working, and even to adapt to a new environment, steadily decreases. If the decline continues at the same rate after the age of sixty, it would appear that by the age of eighty, the average person's capacity to succeed in the Matrices Test is less than that of the normal child of eight years, and it has, in fact, been found that old people only understand the test at all if it is given to them in the form of boards and movable pieces, just as one would give the test to a little child.[24]

I can't think of any way to put a good spin on this inevitable trend; it's simply the way things are. My eight-year-old is advancing so fast—especially in his technical skills on remote controls, VCRs, CD players, handheld video games, and the computer—that it scares me sometimes. A decade from now, when he'll be eighteen and I'll be sixty-three, I suspect that I'll be relying heavily on him for technical help, just as my elderly parents now rely heavily on me. This is not simply because older people have less experience with new technologies; it's because, as Raven said, it becomes increasingly difficult for us to "understand a new method of thinking" as we age.

One of my son's handheld video games—a variation on the old Space Invaders game—requires lightning-quick judgment and reflexes. He can win almost every time, but so far I haven't won once. I mention this because some people believe that reaction-time, and specifically our ability to make quick, accurate judgments about meaningful stimuli, may be a core component of intelligence. It's probably no coincidence, therefore, that a 1981 study by Robert J. Weber and his colleagues shows the same developmental trend for this type of reaction time that we found for intelligence: We're slow when we're children; we become quite fast as young adults; and we're very slow when we're old.[25] (See Figure 7.3.) Generally speaking, teens think quickly, and if you're over thirty, you no longer do.

Human Potential—and Constraints

But what about the "human potential" premise (Enabling Premise Number Three) that I touted in Chapter One? Even if teens do score well on some tests of reasoning ability, isn't it true that people of all ages have the potential to get such scores?

Unfortunately, there are genetic and developmental limits to potential. Our

genes specify a "reaction range" for all of our characteristics, physical and psychological. For some characteristics, like height, the range is small, meaning that experience can't change height appreciably. For other characteristics, like weight, the range is large, meaning that experience can alter that characteristic dramatically. For characteristics like intelligence, the range is moderate: perhaps sixteen to twenty points on a standard IQ test for which the mean score is one hundred. A rich environment will boost you to the top of your possible range, and a poor environment will keep you at the bottom. But no amount of training can make an idiot a genius or vice versa.

The data I've reviewed so far in this chapter also suggest that there are developmental constraints on our reasoning ability. We're most able to reason clearly when we're in our teens, and no matter how aggressively we may try to train people of other ages, this basic fact is unlikely to change. The value of the Human Potential Premise is to remind us that teens—and, for that matter, people of all ages, races, and so on—may have abilities that are not currently being *expressed*. The premise should not be interpreted to mean that all abilities are infinitely malleable but rather that an individual's present performance may not be an accurate indicator of that person's *potential* performance.

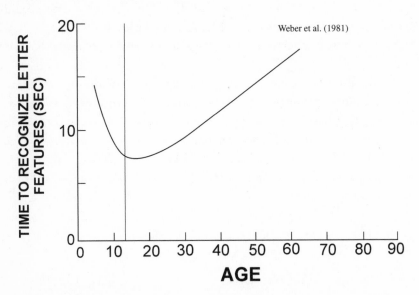

Figure 7.3. Recognition Time by Age. A study by Robert J. Weber, Larry Hochhaus, and William D. Brown of Oklahoma State University looked at how quickly people of various ages could react to features of letters, such as which way internal corners were facing. The authors found, in general, that children (mean age nine) responded slowly on this type of task, that young people (mean age twenty) responded quickly, and that old people (mean age sixty-eight) responded slowly.

Fictional Characterizations of Intelligent Young People

Even though teens have a bad "rep" in modern America, we do occasionally see media portrayals of extremely smart young people: *Doogie Howser, M.D.*, a TV show that aired from 1989 to 1993, was about a young genius who became a medical doctor at age fourteen. While he was making life-and-death decisions about people's health, we also saw him isolated from and rejected by his peers, and his judgment was also often questioned by skeptical adults.

The 1985 film *Real Genius*, starring Val Kilmer, focuses on a brilliant fifteen-year-old student and his somewhat older companions at a research university modeled after Cal Tech; they're being duped by shady government types into building a super laser weapon, but they get the last laugh, and, in a spectacular scene in which their professor's house is destroyed by exploding popcorn, the last shot.

And various children's stories, movies, and television shows also occasionally acknowledge the potential intellectual prowess of young people: in the 1985 film *The Goonies*, a young Asian boy called "Data" is an ingenious inventor; The Cartoon Network's contemporary show *Dexter's Laboratory* is about a similar character, who, among other things, invents an age accelerator so that he can stay up late to watch movies; in the long-running prime-time show, *The Simpsons*, precocious eight-year-old Lisa is said to be able to read at the "fourteenth grade level"; Malcolm of Fox TV's sitcom, *Malcolm in the Middle*, supposedly has an IQ of 165, but the show doesn't emphasize his intelligence; and Frank and Joe, the world-renowned Hardy Boys, were teen super-sleuths of the early 1900s whose exploits were recorded in more than 250 books.

Real Real Genius

So much for fiction. Do real young people measure up? Even though they're isolated from adult society, great young intellects sometimes break through. In modern America we see them mainly in the chess world, one of the few domains in which we allow the intellectual abilities of young people to be expressed with few restrictions. Elementary school children regularly compete in local, regional, national, and even international tournaments, and occasionally young teens appear who dominate the entire chess-playing world.

For Americans the greatest chess legend of all time is Bobby Fischer, who became the youngest international grandmaster in history in 1958 at age fifteen and who eventually (in 1972) became World Champion in a celebrated bout with the Soviet Union's legendary Boris Spassky. As amazing as Fischer was, as of this writing at least seven young people have outdone him—the youngest being the Ukraine's Sergey

---

YOUNG PEOPLE IN ACTION

Keeping an Eye on City Government

City officials in Berkeley, California, were stunned one day in 1998 when eleven-year-old Ellie Lammer presented them with the results of her evaluation of the city's parking meters. With a hundred nickels and a stopwatch in hand, the resourceful sixth-grader picked fifty expired meters at random and fed two nickels into each. That should have yielded eight minutes of parking time, but she found that only 6 percent of the meters (that is, just three) were accurate and that 66 percent of the meters cheated drivers. Remarked one city official, "It was very impressive how exhaustive [her report] was. We don't get reports this thorough when we pay consultants hundreds of thousands of dollars."[26]

Karjakin, who became an international grandmaster in 2002 at age twelve years, seven months (see box).

I've also found a number of examples of great accomplishments in mathematics by young people, but all took place in centuries prior to the twentieth—in other words, well before the artificial extension of childhood was in high gear. France's Guillaume L'Hospital and Scotland's James Clerk Maxwell both made significant contributions when they were fifteen, for example, and Joseph-Louis Lagrange became a professor of mathematics at the Royal Artillery School in Turin at age sixteen.[28] (See table on page 182.)

What kinds of intellectual feats might young people demonstrate today—in math and science, in high tech, in invention, and so on—if they were given more meaningful intellectual challenges and opportunities, and if they weren't so busy "hanging out" in the restrictive and meaningless teen world we've created for them?

WHEN DOES MEMORY FUNCTION BEST?

Another book I'm writing these days—called, at the moment, *Memory Unlimited*—is a practical guide to a new variant of a mnemonic technique developed by orators of ancient Greece. The book focuses on something you probably already know: it's possible, with skill and practice, to remember things you wouldn't otherwise be able to remember.

But mnemonic techniques don't tell us about an individual's natural, untutored memory ability. To assess that, it's interesting to look at a phenomenon called "incidental memory," first studied in 1929 by Raymond B. Willoughby of Clark University.[30]

YOUNG PEOPLE IN ACTION

The Search Is Over

Like many people, I wondered for years where Bobby Fischer disappeared to after he defeated Boris Spassky in Iceland in 1972. The answer isn't pretty. In 1975 the World Chess Federation stripped Fischer of his world title because he refused to defend it. Fischer remained in relative seclusion until 1992 when he agreed to a five-million-dollar rematch with Spassky in Yugoslavia, defying a United States law prohibiting Americans from doing business there at the time. In a press conference before the match, Fischer produced a copy of the warning letter he had received from the United States State Department and spat on it. He won the match, but a warrant was issued for his arrest, and he hasn't returned to the United States since. Fischer spent recent years living in relative seclusion in Japan, where his long-standing paranoid tendencies escalated.

Since 1999 he has broadcast dozens of programs from a Philippines radio station blaming the world's troubles—and his own—on Jews. This is ironic, because his mother was Jewish and it appears that his natural father was, as well. His invectives against the United States have also grown. Just hours after the attack on September 11, 2001, he said on the air, "This is all wonderful news. I applaud the act..,. I want to see the U.S. wiped out." In July 2004 Fischer was arrested by Japanese authorities for trying to travel with an expired passport, and American authorities then tried to get him extradited to the United States to face the 1992 charges. He was eventually granted asylum in Iceland.[27]

Incidental Memory

Willoughby gave hundreds of people from age six to "sixty-eight-plus" a simple "digit substitution" task roughly along these lines: On the top line of the paper, each of the digits from 1 to 9 was paired with an unusual symbol. Below that line the digits appeared in random order in six rows of fifteen digits each, and it was the test-taker's task to copy the appropriate symbol below each symbol as fast as possible. This is pretty much a copying task—not that interesting—and Willoughby found that young children completed it fairly slowly, that people got faster until about age twenty, and that they got slower each year after that. No big deal, really, because the task is so mundane.

But then Willoughby had an insight. He wondered how well people could

Young Contributors in Mathematics		
Name	*Age*	*Accomplishment*
Blaise Pascal (1623-1662)	16	Proved theorem of conic sections
	18	Invented world's first calculator
Guillaume François Antoine de L'Hospital (1661-1704)	15	Solved a problem of Pascal's
Alexis Claude Clairaut (1713-1765)	16	Published *Recherches sur les courbes à double courbure*
	18	Devised proof of one of Newton's theories on cubics
Joseph-Louis Lagrange (1736-1813)	16	Became professor of mathematics in Turin
Gaspard Monge (1746-1818)	16	Originated descriptive geometry
Karl Friedrich Gauss (1777-1855)	17	Developed a law of quadratic reciprocity
	18	Invented the method of "least squares"
Simeon Denis Poisson (1781-1840)	18	Wrote an essay on finite differences
Everiste Galois (1811-1832)	17	Made discoveries in the theory of equations
James Clerk Maxwell (1831-1879)	15	Published a paper on oval curves
William Kingdon Clifford (1848-1879)	18	Solved a problem in probability

remember which symbol was paired with each digit, even though they had never been asked to remember the pairings; in other words, what would they remember accidentally, or "incidentally"? The results were dramatic. (See Figure 7.4 page 184.) From childhood until about age thirteen, performance on this task improved rapidly, and it declined gradually from thirteen until old age, when performance was substantially worse than it was in childhood. In other words, children don't remember much accidentally, and old people barely remember *anything* accidentally. But young teens have *excellent* "incidental memory"; without effort, they can remember things they never even intended to remember.

Other studies also reveal superior or peak memory abilities in teens. In 1928, H. E. Jones and his colleagues asked questions of 429 people from ages ten to fifty-nine about some movies immediately after they had seen them in a movie theater. Because they weren't told beforehand that they would be asked questions about the

YOUNG PEOPLE IN ACTION

Getting Younger Every Day

When, nearly forty years ago, fifteen-year-old Bobby Fischer became an international grandmaster in chess (which means, roughly, that you have to equal or better the performances of grandmasters in three international tournaments), the feat was considered amazing—even unbeatable. Since then the age record has been broken seven times:

Bobby Fischer, fifteen years, six months
Judit Polgar, fifteen years, four months
Peter Leko, fourteen years, four months
Etienne Bacrot, fourteen years, two months
Rusian Ponomaryov, fourteen years, seventeen days
Teimour Radjabov, fourteen years, fourteen days
Bu Xiangzhi, thirteen years, ten months
Sergey Karjakin, twelve years, seven months

Sergey was five when his dad taught him to play chess; unfortunately for Dad, by age seven Sergey was winning virtually every game. He hopes to become World Champion while still a teenager.[29]

films, one might consider this another study of incidental memory. The researchers found that scores were highest among respondents in their late teens—and, as we've seen before, that people in their early teens were near the peak of performance. Performance declined gradually from the early twenties onward.[31] (See Figure 7.4.)

In addition, a 1995 study by Linda S. Siegel of the Ontario Institute for Studies in Education found that "working memory"—the kind of memory you're exercising while you're actively repeating some new information—follows nearly this same pattern, with the decline starting even earlier: by age fifteen or sixteen.[32] Siegel did not find a decline in yet another kind of memory—so-called "short-term" memory. (See Figure 7.4.) In short-term memory, a small amount information is retained for a few seconds, even though we're not actively rehearsing that information. Short-term memory performance was poor for young children, reached a peak by about age thirteen, and then seemed to level out, at least until people were in their forties (the oldest subjects she tested).

Then what about all those forgetful teens? The various conjectures I made about their absent intelligence are applicable here, too. We might fail to detect the

exceptional memories of teens because teens are infantilized, because we make them our adversaries, because they're unwilling to perform optimally when they're around us, because they're trying to emulate dysfunctional role models, because they're isolated from adults, because they lack meaningful challenges, or because some may be abusing drugs or alcohol (another outcome, I believe, of infantilization and isolation). But the *potential* is clearly there. If you're past thirty or forty and you play the "memory" card game with a teen—the one where you turn over one card at a time and have to locate pairs—you're likely to be slaughtered. I tried this. Once.

Figure 7.4. Memory by Age. At or shortly after puberty, our memory is just about as good as it will ever be. Teens seem especially good at remembering things "incidentally" (A) and also at holding information in active, working memory (C). Most memory functions begin a long, slow decline soon after puberty. The exception appears to be short-term memory–the ability to hold a small amount of information in memory for a few seconds–which appears to continue to function well until at least our forties (D).

TEEN JUDGMENT: AN OXYMORON?

Whenever I've told adult friends and colleagues about the extraordinary intellectual potential of teens, they have invariably responded, "That may be, but teens lack *judgment*." And what is intellect, after all, without "judgment"?

But what is judgment, and why are we so sure teens lack it? When we say

someone lacks good judgment, we usually mean that he or she makes decisions that are irrational (defying some rules that we think are logical), destructive (harmful to others), or self-destructive (harmful to himself or herself).

Impulsivity and Rational Choice

According to Harvard psychologist Richard Herrnstein, we act "rationally" when we choose larger, more delayed rewards over smaller, more immediate ones. We act irrationally—that is, we show poor judgment—when we choose smaller, more immediate rewards over larger, more delayed ones.[33] This perspective is sometimes summarized as: "Larger/later is better than smaller/sooner."

This means that if someone offers you a choice between $10 today and $15 tomorrow, you'd be foolish to choose the smaller amount. Herrnstein looked at virtually all behavior this way. If you push away a second helping of chocolate cake, you're making a rational choice: You're choosing future good health over immediate pleasure. If you're a teenager and you engage in safe sex or say no to drugs, you're also being rational, in Herrnstein's view.

This approach to analyzing human behavior is problematic in some respects, but you can't fault it for being irrational. The approach is easy to quantify, and it's easy to show in laboratory experiments that people and some animals behave (in certain situations and in varying degrees) in accordance with various formal "laws" that fit the rational-choice perspective. What's more, people who study how choices are made find that children are more likely than adults to make the wrong choices—that is, to choose smaller-sooner rewards over larger-later rewards. Children are, in other words, "impulsive." Several early studies by Walter Mischel of Stanford University show that impulsivity declines during childhood, and a small study by Leonard Green and his colleagues at Washington University in 1994 found that the choices made by sixth graders (age twelve) were more impulsive than those of college students (around age twenty), which were in turn slightly more impulsive than those of older subjects (average age sixty-eight).[34]

The problem with rational-choice theory is that under the right circumstances almost any choice can be considered rational—even overeating (in an eating contest), killing someone (in war), and killing oneself (when one is suffering and terminally ill).[35] Given the peculiar rules and norms of teen culture, this gives teens a lot of leeway.

Comparing the Decisions of Young People and Adults

Another way researchers sometimes evaluate people's judgments is to compare those judgments to those of more mature or experienced individuals. This method has its limitations, too, because mature or experienced individuals are

---

WISDOM OF THE AGES

Let's Reminisce

If you're at least a few decades old, here's some food for thought—about your memory. Researcher Daniel Offer and his colleagues at the Northwestern University Medical School recently asked sixty-seven normal, healthy, forty-eight-year-old men a series of questions that these same individuals had previously answered in writing when they were fourteen—questions about their home environment, dating, general activities, and family relationships. The result? They had almost no real recollection of their youth; their answers matched their original answers no more frequently than one would expect if they were responding to the questions at random.[36]

---

sometimes so set in their ways that they can't properly evaluate new or unique conditions or new approaches to solving problems. That said, let's look at a simple problem that we might give to children or adults in a study of "judgment":

Tom, a young student, has been refusing to talk to family members or to come out of his room for several weeks. He appears to be severely depressed. Professionals have presented the family with three options for helping Tom: (a) Wait it out. See if the depression lifts on its own. (b) Bring Tom to a therapist's office for regular visits. (c) Admit him to a mental hospital where he will remain until his condition improves. What's the best way to help Tom, and why?

This problem is adapted from one used in a comprehensive study of decision making by Lois Weithorn and Susan Campbell in 1982.[37] Weithorn and Campbell presented treatment problems of this sort to four groups of young people, ages nine, fourteen, eighteen, and twenty-one. How, if at all, would the groups differ in the treatment recommendations they made on various problems? Given the structure of our laws, one might guess that the nine and fourteen olds would perform similarly—that is, like children—that the eighteen-year-olds, as budding adults, would perform more like adults, and that the twenty-one-year-olds would come closest to approximating the recommendations made by experts—in this case, physicians. But that's not what the researchers found.

Generally speaking, Weithorn and Campbell found that the fourteen, eighteen, and twenty-one-year-olds *all made recommendations similar to those of the experts*. Only the nine-year-olds made inferior recommendations—and even they performed reasonably well on some tasks and "appear able to participate meaningfully in

personal health-care decision making."[38] On the depression problem, 75 percent of the people in each of the three oldest groups chose the preferred treatment—outpatient psychotherapy; only 50 percent of the nine-old-olds chose that option. In addition, a scale used to evaluate the "reasonableness" of the subjects' replies yielded virtually identical scores for each of the three oldest groups—4.13, 4.18, and 4.17, respectively. Again, the nine-year-olds scored lower: 3.24. Teen judgments on other problems yielded generally similar results. The researchers concluded:

> In general, minors aged fourteen were found to demonstrate a level of competence equivalent to that of adults.... The findings of this research do not lend support to policies which deny adolescents the right of self-determination in treatment situations on the basis of a presumption of incapacity to provide informed consent. The ages of eighteen or twenty-one as the "cutoffs" below which individuals are presumed to be incompetent to make determinations about their own welfare do not reflect the psychological capacities of most adolescents.[39]

In other words, *as we shift our investigation from reasoning to intelligence to memory to the gold nugget itself—judgment—we are again surprised: teens appear to be as competent as adults.* The Weithorn and Campbell study is one of many that demonstrate this. In a comprehensive review of such studies in 1983 in the prestigious *American Psychologist*, Gary B. Melton concluded, "The existing literature clearly suggests that for most purposes, adolescents cannot be distinguished from adults on the grounds of competence of decision making alone."[40] Melton's conclusion is consistent with the findings of the study that Diane Dumas and I conducted on a broad range of competencies (see Chapter Six).

Then Why Are Teens So Reckless?

One especially interesting study challenges the widely held belief that teens believe they're indestructible. Conducted in the United States by Israeli researcher Ruth Beyth-Marom and her colleagues at Carnegie Mellon University in Pittsburgh, the study compared the way adults and teens viewed six different risky behaviors: drinking and driving, smoking marijuana, skipping school, taking dad's car, having sex, and attending a beer party. The 199 teens in the study were fairly young—14.8 years old, on average, and all of the 199 adults in the study were parents—42.5 years old, on average. Yet when asked to list the possible negative consequences of the risky behaviors, teens and adults produced remarkably similar lists.[41] Teens, it seems, know very well about the risks they're taking. Then why on earth do they take them?

The key here is to keep in mind those circumstances I talked about earlier. If

you're fifty, it's unlikely that driving fast or smoking marijuana will impress your friends; in other words, reckless behavior probably won't be of much "value" to you. But when you're fifteen—stranded, against your will, in a vacuous teen culture—reckless behavior might have great value, and the benefits received by impressing your friends might easily outweigh some possible negative consequences of the behavior. I might get a thrill from trying Ecstasy, but no one in my immediate world is modeling the behavior, and most of my peers would be appalled if I engaged in it.

To evaluate the goodness of teen decision making, we need to take into account the pros and cons that *they* see in making their decisions, not the pros and cons that *we* see. When we take individual teen values into account, it's clearer than ever that teens are competent decision makers. For example, a study by Allen F. Abrahamse and others published in 1988 suggested that teens who felt they might gain by becoming pregnant (perhaps by becoming independent of the teen's parents) were more likely to consider becoming pregnant than teens who felt that pregnancy would harm them (perhaps by limiting their educational opportunities).[42] As I noted earlier, the reasonableness of a decision is determined by many life factors—not just by general principles proclaimed by adult authority figures.

Evaluating Teen Decision Making

The scientific literature on teen decision making isn't entirely clear, and I'd be remiss in not pointing out some of the complexities. We know, for example, that teens are risk prone in some respects, but laboratory studies of teen decision making sometimes show that teens are every bit as risk *averse* as adults are, leading researchers Lita Furby and Ruth Beyth-Marom to conclude in a 1992 essay that "there is as yet little evidence that adolescents are more likely than adults to engage in behavior that seems risky to them; that is, there is little evidence that they seek out or are willing to accept greater risks."[43] The fact that teens perform so well in the laboratory studies supports the view that their *potential* for excellent performance is high—and, unfortunately, that the real world that we've created for them does not allow or encourage that potential to be expressed.

Some experts, such as James Byrnes of the University of Maryland, also suggest that teen decision making may be inferior to adult decision making when a great deal of specific knowledge is required to make the decision—hardly surprising—or when making a good decision depends on one's willingness to consult authorities or experts (who, needless to say, are usually adults).[44]

But even the most skeptical researchers note that *age* isn't always a good predictor of decision-making competence. A recent study by Elizabeth Cauffman and Laurence Steinberg, for example, suggests that teen judgment may be inferior

to adult judgment in some instances, but the authors also acknowledge that there were "considerable individual differences" among the teens and adults they tested—in other words, that some teens are excellent decision makers and some adults are poor decision makers.[45] More important for our purposes, Cauffman and Steinberg found that the best predictor of decision-making competence was "psychosocial maturity" (measured by various inventories they administered to their subjects), *not* age. As they put it, "psychosocially mature thirteen-year-olds demonstrate less antisocial decision-making than psychosocially immature adults."[46]

Are Teens *Supposed* to Take Risks?

Teen decision making looks especially good when we consider two other points. First, immediately after puberty, it's possible that we're *supposed* to take risks. Mating itself is a form of risk taking. You have to take many risks in order to find and keep a mate.

Taking risks during the teen years might also be a way of becoming more adult; after all, most of the risks that teens take involve adult behaviors: having sex, drinking, driving, and so on. For teens, taking risks might be an exercise of *good judgment*, not bad. As psychologist Frank Farley said years ago, advising teens to "just say no" might be "like telling Christopher Columbus to stay home."[47]

Second, we need to bear in mind that the American teens we've been observing and studying in recent decades are products of teen culture. They're isolated from adults and from adult challenges and responsibilities. Presumably, their decision-making abilities would be far better—and far more adultlike—if they had not been infantilized or if they had not been isolated from adults.

Teens are highly capable decision makers—perhaps, on average, more capable than adults. With high intelligence, peak reasoning powers, and excellent memories, they certainly have the advantage. But they often make decisions that seem inferior to adults—decisions that seem irrational or that might expose themselves or others to harm—for a number of reasons: they're isolated from and infantilized by adults; they sometimes lack the specific knowledge they need to make good decisions; they might have some innate tendencies to take risks; and they're immersed in a vacuous subculture that has rules and values that are often unfathomable to adults. As I keep emphasizing, this is a book about human potential. If we focus on *actual* teen decisions—especially without taking teen values into account—we'll likely be disappointed at times, but if we look at the *potential* teens have to make good decisions, I believe we'll be amazed.

THE ABORTION DECISION

Becky Bell was seventeen when she got pregnant, just a few months shy of the state-proclaimed age of adulthood. In Indiana at that time (1988), she needed the consent of at least one of her parents to get a legal abortion; she could also have gone to court to ask a judge to exempt her from this requirement. But she couldn't face the shame of approaching her parents, even though, by all accounts, she had a warm relationship with them, and she was afraid a judge wouldn't help her. Through friends she learned about a place where she could go for an illegal abortion. After the procedure she developed an infection, and shortly after she died.[48]

Her parents, Bill and Karen—staunch Republican conservatives—soon became ardent opponents of parental notification laws, sharing their views in lectures at schools around the country. Said Bill, "It is our hope that in speaking out we can spare other families the nightmare we must now live. These laws are punitive, they're restrictive—they're deadly."[49]

Given that teens are capable of making sound decisions, especially when it comes to medical matters, shouldn't minors be allowed to get abortions without the consent of their parents—and perhaps even without the consent of a court? As you'll see, even though the relevant scientific data are clear, this is not an easy question to answer. Scientific data and societal values are fairly orthogonal to each other, although data can sometimes alter such values.

Research on the Abortion Decision

I hope I've already convinced you that many teens are capable of making excellent decisions, at least in principle. Studies on decision making about abortion further support this view.

Catherine Lewis of the University of California San Francisco has researched this matter extensively. In a review article, "Minors' Competence to Consent to Abortion," published in the *American Psychologist* in 1987, Lewis concludes: "psychological research presently provides no basis to restrict minors' decision making on the ground of competence alone."[50] Another review, published in the early 1990s, concludes that "the psychological assumption that female adolescents under the age of eighteen are not competent to independently consent to abortion...has questionable scientific validity."[51]

Another extensive review, published in 2003 by Nancy E. Adler, Emily J. Ozer, and Jeanne Tschann, draws even stronger conclusions. First of all, the au-

thors conclude that "adolescent abortion patients may represent a subgroup that is more competent than pregnant adolescents who are not considering abortion."[52] In other words, teens who think about abortion are, as a group, fairly serious thinkers; on the average, they don't take the abortion issue any more lightly than adults do. Second, Adler and her colleagues summarize a number of studies showing negative effects of parental notification laws. Faced with such laws, teens like Becky Bell seek illegal and sometimes dangerous abortions; angry parents sometimes injure or otherwise abuse pregnant daughters; some teens end up expelled from their homes. Although the intentions behind such laws might be good, the effects are often bad.

How the Courts Ignore the Research

This brings me to our unfathomable, unpredictable, and often irrational courts. In the mid and late 1970s Massachusetts judges and lawmakers made headlines because of their controversial views on a teenager's right to seek an abortion. On August 2, 1974, the Massachusetts state legislature passed a law—over the Governor's veto—requiring an unmarried woman under age eighteen to obtain the consent of both of her parents before getting an abortion. The law was challenged in court, and the matter made its way swiftly to the United States Supreme Court.

Acknowledging that delaying the abortion decision was necessarily problematic and that some minors are capable of making "mature" decisions, on July 2, 1979, in the landmark case of Bellotti v. Baird II, the Supreme Court invalidated the Massachusetts law and affirmed a minor's right to seek a court's permission to have an abortion "without parental consultation or consent." The court acknowledged (in a footnote to the majority decision) that although maturity is "difficult to define, let alone determine," age is an "inevitably arbitrary" criterion for determining maturity, and "the abortion decision requires...case-by-case evaluations."[53]

Unfortunately, there is more to this story, most of it negative. After all, Becky Bell was still subject to parental notification laws nine years after the Bellotti v. Baird decision. Just what did the justices do?

Central to their decision was the following assertion, written by Justice Lewis F. Powell Jr.:

...during the formative years of childhood and adolescence, minors often lack the experience, perspective, and judgment to recognize and avoid choices that could be detrimental to them.[54]

Given the overall decision, and given the acknowledgment in the footnote that age eighteen is an arbitrary boundary for determining maturity, one would assume that our most venerable panel of judges would have based their decision on relevant research in the behavioral and social sciences. But I've scoured the Supreme Court's decision in this matter; it's completely devoid of any reference to relevant research. In fact, when you read the decision, it's apparent that the judges were basing their assertions about teen competence on folklore and intuition, rather than on scientific data.

Soper on the Courts

A forceful essay on this topic published by law student Jennifer Soper in 1999 documents just how insensitive our courts are to scientific data on the abortion decision matter.[55] Soper also explains why the Becky Bells of this country face the dilemma they do. The bottom line for Soper is that "while the United States claims to base laws on the concept of capacity, it actually affords rights and responsibilities *ignoring* the competency of individuals."[56]

In a way, this is all too obvious: In our zeal to be race-, gender-, and age-blind, we often make the erroneous assumption that everyone is equally capable, or, worse yet, we draw arbitrary lines (like age eighteen, or twenty-one, or sixty-five) that group people together who shouldn't be grouped. Age boundaries are particularly insidious, because they imply that all people on one side of the boundary are equally incompetent, which is just as absurd as asserting that all people on the other side of the boundary are equally competent.

Soper also notes dramatic inconsistencies when it comes to the statutory rights of teens. For example:

>...many states declare minors presumptively incompetent to decide their own medical care. Yet, these states allow them to make major medical decisions for their own children. Thus a fourteen year old in Mississippi can authorize circumcision on her newborn son, unilaterally making the decision about whether to use or withhold anesthesia...; yet, she cannot go the dentist and have a cavity filled without written parental consent.... A fourteen-year-old mother bears adult responsibility for her child and can be held criminally negligent for any harm to the child. At the same time, she may not drive a car, hold a full-time job, or rent an apartment, and in most states faces compulsory education laws.... The fourteen-year-old who faces a presumption of incompetency but bears the burden of presumed parental capacity cannot, in most states, decide whether she wants to assume the burdens of motherhood to begin with.[57]

The ironies here are blatant. Teens are not considered (by the courts, anyway) competent enough to make the abortion decision on their own, but they *are* considered competent enough to be responsible parents. Even though a young mother is fully responsible for raising her child, she's *not* allowed to drive the child to the hospital in an emergency, nor to get a full-time job to support the child. And even though she can make medical decisions for her child, she's not allowed to make many of those same decisions when it comes to her own medical care.

The Continuing Court Saga

So what happened to the *Bellotti v. Baird II* decision? Didn't that allow teens to bypass their parents in seeking an abortion? No, not exactly. Although it did invalidate the 1974 Massachusetts law, it still required teens to get a court's permission for the abortion—a task that would be daunting for someone of any age. The court also expressed concerns about the "autonomy" of the parent and the importance of the family unit.

Subsequent Supreme Court decisions rendered in reaction to various parental-notification laws have placed considerable restrictions on the teen's right to consent to an abortion—and none of these decisions, as far as I have been able to determine, has been grounded in relevant scientific research about teen competence. In two 1990 decisions, for example, the Court decided that laws like the one guiding Becky Bell's tragic actions were valid: as long as a teen had the option of going to court to bypass her parents, the state could require that consent from one or both parents is required for a minor's abortion. One ruling even okayed a law requiring physicians to notify a parent in cases when a court has okayed an abortion.[58] In other words, the Supreme Court has put the "autonomy" and "liberty interests" of the parent ahead of the rights of the minor,[59] and that's the way things stand today.

On the capacity issue itself, Soper argues that although courts talk about competence, "legal questions of capacity are flawed, sporadically applied, and based on ill-defined standards."[60] When questions of maturity or competence are raised, judges around the country act with considerable arbitrariness, in some cases testing a teen's vocabulary, in others focusing on how the teen is dressed. "The court's lack of uniformity," says Soper, "exemplifies the problem with the entire capacity question."[61]

But competence can indeed be measured, and I have no doubt that many teens would score substantially higher on various competency tests than would the senescent members of our Supreme Court.

IS THERE REALLY A TEEN BRAIN?

Here's a headline from a recent *Newsday*:

Biological reason for teen laziness:
Brain region that governs "drive" apparently
comes into its own in the early 20s

Newsday staff writer Jamie Talan opens the piece with the following "hook":

If you're a teenager, don't read this. Federal scientists have discovered a biological excuse for laziness.[62]

As a magazine editor my reaction is, "Nice, Jamie. A good grab." As a scientist my take is, "I'm tired of the way you keep misreporting science, Jamie. *You're fired.*"

But Jamie isn't the only one misled by the research he's reporting. Even the researchers seem confused about the implications of their study. Talan quotes James Bjork of the National Institute on Alcohol Abuse and Alcoholism (NIAAA), the lead author in the study, as saying that the study "tells us that teenagers love stuff, but aren't as willing to get off the couch to get it as adults are." Adds Bjork, "The good news is that the brain does mature."[63]

In other words, both the reporter and the researcher are saying that this new research—which I'll summarize shortly—shows that teens are lazy *because* their brains haven't properly matured.

But that's not what the research shows. Not at all. What's going on here, and how could a "federal scientist" make the same mistake that a reporter makes?

Before I address this issue, keep in mind that the media often tells us about studies just like this one—studies that seem to demonstrate the existence of a "teen brain" and that appear to show that teens have problems *because* they have immature brains. What actually happened in the Bjork study (co-authored by five other researchers variously affiliated with Stanford University, The Catholic University of America, and the NIAAA), and what do the results actually mean?

Dissecting a Brain Study

First, the basic procedure: twelve young people (six male, six female, ages twelve-seventeen) and twelve somewhat older people (six male, six female, ages twenty to twenty-eight) were restrained in a brain-scanning device (a "3 T Gen-

eral Electric MRI scanner") for about forty-five minutes while performing a simple task that allowed them to earn some money: A symbol appeared briefly (.25 seconds) on a small mirror in front of their eyes indicating what the consequences would be of pressing a handheld button after a short "anticipation" period (about two seconds). Some symbols indicated that a botton-press would earn some money; some indicated that failing to press a button would cost some money. At the end of the anticipation period, the subject was given a very short time (about .25 seconds) in which to respond or not respond. Finally, information was displayed briefly (1.6 seconds) to let the subject know whether or not he or she had just won or lost money.[64]

Based on other research, the areas of the brain that were being scanned were believed to be indicative of the subject's "motivation" to perform. The basic questions being asked by the researchers were: Would teens and adults perform differently on this task? And would the *brains* of teens and adults function differently on this task?

The answers, in a nutshell, were: No, teens and adults performed equally well, and yes, brain activity in the two groups did differ, at least during the anticipation period, at least on trials when subjects could earn money (but not, for some reason, on trials when they could lose money). Specifically, in a small area of the brain called the right nucleus accumbens, when there was a certain amount of money to be earned ($5, the maximum amount that could be earned on any given trial), the average activity level of the adult brains was higher than the average activity level of the teen brains during the (roughly) two-second anticipation period before the subjects could respond. With other amounts of money at stake, neural activity in the two groups did not differ. That's what the researchers found.

So how do we get from this extremely modest, entirely innocuous result to Mr. Talan's assertion that teen laziness is caused by an underdeveloped brain?

There are so many problems with this study—and especially with the way the results were interpreted—that I hardly know where to begin.[65] But how about this: *nowhere in the study is any evidence presented that the teens in the study were lazy, or at least that they were more lazy than the "adults"* (who weren't even much older than the teens). There is also no information given about how the teens and adults were recruited for the study. For all we know, the teens could have been star athletes, and the adults could have been couch potatoes. Given these omissions alone, I can find no possible defense of Talan's interpretation of this study—which, alas, was echoed to some extent by Dr. Bjork.

If you want to say something about the brains of lazy teens, you need to start with teens you know to be lazy. It might be interesting, then, to compare the brain

activity in such teens to the brain activity in teens you know to be industrious—and then, perhaps, to compare the brain activity of those two groups to groups of lazy and industrious adults. Such a study could have a number of possible outcomes. In one, the brain of the lazy teen might somehow look different than the brains of the people in the other three groups. That might allow you to say with confidence that lazy teens have brains that are unique in some way—the claim that Talan seemed to be making.

But so what? If you conducted such a study and got such a result, you would *still* have no legitimate basis for claiming that teen laziness is *caused* by the teen brain. As we teach in elementary statistics courses, *correlation does not imply causation*. The fact that a lazy teen's brain might have some unique functional or structural characteristics doesn't mean that the teen's behavior is *caused* by those characteristics. When we find that factors A and B are associated with each other ("correlated"), we still know nothing about their *causal* relationship. A might cause B, or B might cause A, or both A and B might be caused by a third factor, C. Height and weight are highly correlated, but neither causes the other; their correlation is the result of other factors, such as genes that control overall size and bone structure. Similarly, just because we see a match between certain brain characteristics and certain behaviors, that doesn't mean the brain has *caused* those behaviors. Other factors, both genetic and environmental, may cause both the brain characteristics *and* the behavior that we see.

In some cases, a brain characteristic might be said to be responsible for a behavioral characteristic—for example, damage to "Broca's area" is associated with various speech problems. But it's also the case that a wide variety of behaviors—meditating, reading, drinking, having sex, and so on—literally *change the brain*. It's fundamentally wrong to say that all behavior is "caused by the brain," and it's fundamentally wrong to blame all teen behavior on a "teen brain."

Let me take this radical (but simple!) idea a step further. Without even conducting the study I suggested above, I can guarantee you that with enough digging we'd find that the brains of lazy teens are unique in some way. Of course they are! All unique behavioral characteristics *must* have corresponding brain characteristics. This is a truism. But it doesn't tell us *anything* about the "causes" of laziness.

A Brain Scientist Weighs In

These issues are explored in detail in a profoundly important but under-celebrated book by retired neuroscientist Elliott Valenstein called *Blaming the Brain*, published in 1998. Writes Valenstein:

A person's mental state and experience can modify the brain just as surely as the other way around. When there is a correlation between two events, we should not assume that we always know which way causation flows....[66]

Various experiences can... cause structural and functional changes in the brain. It has been shown in numerous experiments, for example, that exposure to stressful situations can produce long-lasting brain changes. Animals that are stressed repeatedly have an elevated response to an injection of amphetamine, even when the drug is administered months later.... Even when dopamine neurons are removed from the brains of stressed animals and placed in a dish, amphetamine will cause excessive amounts of dopamine to be released. These results indicate that stress can produce enduring physical changes in dopamine neurons that make them hypersensitive not only to drugs such as amphetamine, but also to subsequent exposure to stress....[67]

There is now a huge amount of experimental evidence demonstrating that different types of experience can modify brain anatomy in the adult animal as well as in young animals. Early studies demonstrated that neurons in the brains of rats raised in enriched environments are significantly more branched and presumably more capable of making connections than are comparable neurons of rats raised in impoverished environments. Subsequent studies have shown that various kinds of experiences, such as repeated training on a specific task, can also modify the structure of neurons in the brain areas involved in those activities. Plasticity must be a basic property of neurons, as it is essential for learning and memory even in invertebrates.... Genes are responsible for establishing the scaffolding or fundamental organization of the brain, but a large amount of the neuronal growth that leads to the establishment of connections has been shown to be influenced (if not guided) by experience.

Evidence that experience can modify brain structure has also been reported in humans. It has been reported, for example, that the amount of branching of neuronal dendrites in the language area (Wernicke's area) of human brains is, on average, proportional to the amount of education. Thus, it was found that people who had a university education tend to have more branching in the language area than do people with only a high school education, and they in turn tend to have more branching than do people who did not go to high school....

"Anatomy is not destiny," and, moreover, genes are not even the sole determinant of anatomy. The expression of genes can be turned on and off by physiological concomitants of life experiences.[68]

I can't stress enough the importance of Valenstein's message: from a scientific perspective, it is wrong—utterly and completely wrong—to say that the brain "causes" behavior (or thinking or feelings) based simply on a correlation between a brain state and that behavior.

So Is there a Teen Brain?

What does this mean for the so-called "teen brain"? First of all, it means that the teen brain does exist, but only in the trivial sense that unique behavioral characteristics that some teens might have—anger, impulsivity, depression, and so on—must be encoded in their brains. The brains of angry people (of any age) are necessarily different than the brains of calm people, but it's the genes and experiences of angry people that made them angry and gave them angry brains; their brains aren't the cause of their anger.

Second, studies like the one Bjork and his colleagues conducted provide no evidence whatsoever that the brain is *causing* any of the unique behavioral, emotional, or cognitive characteristics we sometimes see in teens. The Bjork study showed (on just one task out of several that were presented) a lower level of activity in teens brains than in the brains of people in their twenties. It didn't show that the lower level of activity caused any of the teens' behaviors, and it certainly didn't show that *any* property of the teen brain causes "laziness."

Third, as we've seen, modern American-style adolescence is a cultural creation, which suggests that both the behaviors we see *and* the corresponding neural phenomena are caused by the way we treat our teens. The brain is not the culprit here; society is.

If adolescence barely existed through most of human history and is still absent in many cultures, how could modern adolescence be the inevitable product of a genetically preprogrammed "teen brain"?

When we raise young people so that they transition smoothly and swiftly from childhood to adulthood, the turmoil that typifies modern adolescence is absent—and so, presumably, are the neural correlates of such turmoil. But when we raise teens to be angry, withdrawn, or rebellious, their brains must reflect those states of mind. In other words, the teen brain is, by necessity, every bit as much of a cultural creation as adolescence itself.

Persistent and Faulty Headlines

The headlines, meanwhile, keep getting it wrong, and they will undoubtedly continue to do so for many years to come. Consider:

- *"Brain study finds out why emotions rule"* (San Diego Union-Tribune): "That adolescent mood soars and dips as wildly as a roller coaster is hardly a news flash. A peek into the adolescent brain may explain why."[69] Teens, we're told, are emotional because they process information

more in the amygdala than in the frontal lobe, and, once again, a researcher—Deborah Yurgelen-Todd of Boston's McLean Hospital Brain Imaging Center—is quoted to bolster this view. But neither Yurgelen-Todd's research nor the research of anyone else I'm aware of provides the scientific evidence needed to support the claims made in the article. Again, correlational research is simply misinterpreted.

- *"Gray matter, not raging hormones, rules adolescence" (Worcester Sunday Telegram)*: "Parents and experts have always blamed the same hormones that catapult young bodies into adulthood for the sleeping until noon, the reckless driving, the drug use and the other woes of adolescence. But recent research shows that what's going on above teenagers' necks—not raging hormones—explains the changes."[70] The teen brain is still growing and expanding, we're told, and neuroscientist Fulton Crews of the University of North Carolina at Chapel Hill is quoted as a source. But is brain growth the *cause* or the *effect* of teen behavior? Or are teen behavior and brain changes *both* just the effects of other causes?

- *"Inside the teen brain"* (cover story in *U.S. News & World Report*): "The true source of teenage behavior lies north of the gonads. It's that three-pound blob of gray and white matter known as the brain.... With the advent of technologies such as magnetic resonance imaging, neuroscientists have discovered that the adolescent brain is far from mature."[71] McMaster University neuroscientist Sandra Wetelson and others are quoted as sources. Again, none of the research cited provides appropriate scientific evidence to support the extreme claims that are made.

Why Are We Being Misled?

Why are we being systematically misled about causes of teen behavior? Valenstein blames the pharmaceutical companies. They want us to believe, he says, that all of our emotional and cognitive difficulties are caused by our defective brains so that we'll buy psychotropic drugs to solve our problems. Is Valenstein right? Having served on occasion as a consultant to major drug companies, I'd love to be able to tell you that he's wrong—but I would be lying. The drug companies spend billions of dollars a year to convince physicians, policy makers, and the general public to believe the myths and buy or dispense the products, and the average television watcher probably views more than a hundred drug commercials a week these days; there is no question that the drug houses are aggressive in promoting their wares.

That said, I'm even more concerned about—and embarrassed by—my fellow

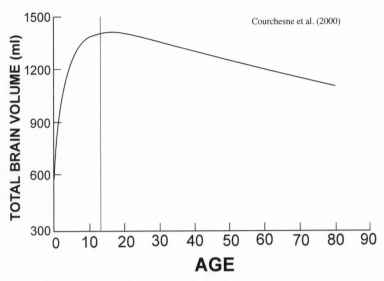

Figure 7.5. **Brain Volume by Age.** Early twentieth-century studies of brain size looked at the brains of corpses, which were subject to swelling or shrinkage. The reliability of such studies was poor. But a new study of brain volume measured brain volume by scanning the brains of living subjects, yielding highly accurate and fairly dramatic results. Brain volume peaks at about age fourteen and gradually shrinks thereafter throughout our lives. Old people have brains the size of those of young children. *Source:* Courchesne et al., 2000.

scientists. Some neuroscientists are perpetuating myths about the brain just as unabashedly as the drug companies are, in some cases perhaps to "sex up" their research. I suppose it's possible that some of them even *believe* that correlational studies show that brain activity causes behavior.

The Changing Brain

Some of the headlines imply that significant brain development stops with adolescence, but the brain actually changes and matures throughout our lives, again reflecting the many behavioral, cognitive, and emotional changes we undergo from birth to death. Experience, nutrition, drugs, alcohol, physical trauma, disease, and aging itself bring about changes large and small, as a number of lifespan studies of the brain demonstrate.

One intriguing study, conducted by Jésus Pujol and his colleagues at the University of Barcelona, looked at changes in the corpus callosum—a massive structure that transfers signals between the brain's hemispheres—over a two-year period with subjects from eleven to sixty-one years old.[72] This structure appears to grow rapidly in young people (29 percent per year in the youngest subjects in the study) but also continues to grow when we're older (about 7 percent per year in the subjects in their twenties and about 4 percent per

year in subjects in their forties). And a 2001 study by Elizabeth R. Sowell and her colleagues at UCLA[73] confirmed that there is a loss of gray matter between childhood (a group of children between ages seven and eleven) and the teen years (a group of young people between twelve and sixteen), but it also showed that gray matter continues to disappear well past the teen years (a group of people between twenty-three and thirty).[74]

Our Shrinking Brains

We've seen evidence that intelligence, reasoning ability, and some important aspects of memory all peak between ages thirteen and fifteen and decline thereafter. Do any properties of the brain follow this pattern?

Eric Courchesne and his colleagues at the University of California San Diego found this very same pattern in the brain volumes of subjects from nineteen months old to eighty years old.[75] (See Figure 7.5.) Brain volume appears to peak at about age fourteen, according Courchesne's 2000 study, and people in their seventies "[have] volumes similar to those of young children."

From shortly after puberty onward, the simple and sobering news is that our brains shrink dramatically—by 25 percent or more.[76] The average age of our Supreme Court justices is typically about seventy. According to Courchesne's data, by the time we're that age, our brain has shrunk to the size it was when we were three.

Q: *Isn't it true that the brains of teens aren't fully developed? Isn't that why they behave so poorly? Doesn't current brain research refute your theory?*

A: No brain is fully developed. Brains change throughout the life span. Teen brains aren't all that different from adult brains, but where there are some differences, those differences don't explain their misbehavior or distress. Brains are *reflections* of our behavioral, cognitive, and emotional states; they don't *cause* those states. If your daughter had been raised from birth in a preindustrial tribal culture, she would probably be much calmer and happier than she is now—and her brain would be very different than it is now; it would reflect the behavior, cognitions, and emotions that she exhibited. So, no, current brain research in no way refutes my theory, and, in my view, we all need to think carefully before blaming the brain for *any* of our difficulties.

Chapter 8

Young People Can Love

And they called it puppy love
Oh, I guess they'll never know
How a young heart really feels
And why I love her so.
—Paul Anka, "And They Called It Puppy Love"

Overview. Contrary to popular belief, psychological research suggests that young people are capable of experiencing mature love, and no one has ever shown that the love experienced by young people is any different than the love experienced by adults. Moreover, although it's widely believed that young marriages are doomed to fail, census data show that males who marry in their teens have a lower divorce rate than males who marry in their twenties; in general, the divorce rate of young people isn't much higher than the divorce rate of adults, and many of our nation's most celebrated and long-lasting marriages have involved very young spouses. In other countries people still often marry at very young ages, and Western attempts to change such practices have sometimes produced disastrous results. Laws restricting marriage or sexual relations involving minors are wildly inconsistent from state to state, and in many cases such laws have been applied in ways that have caused great pain to innocent people.

"If you have trouble, you go talk about it, argue, and get over it." That was the advice of Mary Onesi when she and her husband of just over eighty years were interviewed by the Associated Press in 1998. They had been honored on World Marriage Day in 1995 as the longest-married couple in America, and, yes, they were still together three years later. She married her husband Paul in 1917 when he was twenty-one and she was thirteen. By all accounts, their marriage was happy and successful, and it was certainly prolific.[1]

Paul Onesi came to the United States from Italy when he was fifteen, arriving through Ellis Island. He worked in the coal mines in Pennsylvania at first. He met Mary when he was renting a room in her older sister's home, and it was the sister who did the matchmaking. The couple moved to Niagara Falls a few years after their marriage, where Paul went to work for Union Carbide. They had six children and saw five of them celebrate their fiftieth wedding anniversaries.

Laura Cerrillo, one of Paul and Mary's twenty-eight grandchildren, explained why marriages in this close-knit family were generally quite successful: "In our family, no one ever wanted to get divorced because no one wanted to tell them."

By current thinking, there's something dreadfully wrong with his pretty picture. Thirteen-year-old Mary Corsaro couldn't *possibly* have been ready for marriage. She must have been abused or exploited or perhaps even drugged and raped. Her sister Rose must have been in on it, perhaps serving as a pimp and getting a fee from perverted old Paul. Isn't that the way we're now taught to think? At the very least, the world must have been so different back then that the people in it must have been entirely unlike people are today—members of a different species, in effect. Maybe Mary *was* ready back in 1917, but there are no Mary's in today's world. Today, thirteen-year-olds are children.

CAN TEENS EXPERIENCE REAL LOVE?

Can teens love, and can they form successful, stable marriages? Is teen love truly just "puppy love," or can it be just as real and deep and enduring as "adult" love? And, most important of all, *are we willing to face the truth about these issues?*

Romeo and Juliet are regarded in much of the Western world as the paradigmatic romantic lovers; we celebrate their love as the purest and most intense two people can achieve. Their deaths, so tragic on the one hand, also created an undying love that has already been cherished for more than four hundred years. Just how old were Romeo Montague and Juliet Capulet?

Perhaps this will help: in George Cukor's 1936 film rendition of the play, Romeo was played by forty-three-year-old Leslie Howard and Juliet by thirty-four-year-old Norma Shearer. Ian McKellen was thirty-seven when he played Romeo with the Royal Shakespeare Company in England in 1976. And in a recent ballet version of Shakespeare's masterpiece, Juliet's part was danced by Evelyn Hart, one of Canada's most celebrated ballerinas, now in her late forties. So perhaps Romeo and Juliet were approaching middle age.

On the other hand, Baz Luhrmann's famous 1996 film version of the story

starred twenty-one-year-old Leonardo DiCaprio and seventeen-year-old Claire Danes. That doesn't seem to jive with the earlier characterizations. And Franco Zeffirelli "stunned the screen world" with his 1968 film rendition, which starred seventeen-year-old Leonard Whiting as Romeo and fifteen-year-old Olivia Hussey as Juliet. Who got the ages right?

Zeffirelli was closest to the mark, but still not stunning enough. In Act 1, Scene 3 of Shakespeare's play, Lady Capulet has a frustrating exchange with Juliet's nurse, trying hard to pin down Juliet's exact age, which, it turns out, is thirteen (just a few weeks shy of fourteen). Even more notable are Lady Capulet's remarks to Juliet about age and marriage:

> *...younger than you,*
> *Here in Verona, ladies of esteem,*
> *Are made already mothers: by my count,*
> *I was your mother much upon these years*
> *That you are now a maid.*

Ironing out the Shakespearean kinks, Lady Capulet is saying: "Here in Verona, upstanding women are already mothers when they're younger than you," and, by the way, "I had you when I was your age." She then tries to interest Juliet in an attractive suitor named Paris.

Why has no one ever made a film or cast a play in which Romeo and Juliet are played by actors of the correct ages? (Shakespeare is never entirely clear about Romeo's age, but it's unlikely that he was beyond his mid teens.)

The same question can be raised about the movie version of Nabokov's infamous *Lolita*, as well as about *West Side Story*, the 1960s version of *Romeo and Juliet*. In Nabokov's book, *Lolita*, the sexy young siren who is the object of her stepfather's obsession, is twelve years old. In the 1962 movie version, she's played by a sixteen-year-old actress, Sue Lyon; in the 1997 version, she's played by seventeen-year-old Dominique Swain. And *West Side Story's* Maria was played by twenty-three-year-old Natalie Wood.

The question is all too easy to answer: we're somewhat willing in principle to acknowledge that young people can be sensual, sexual, romantic, seductive, and loving, but we would never put a real thirteen-year-old "girl" or "boy" in bed with someone for entertainment purposes in a mainstream film. In fact, under modern law, producers who made such a film could be prosecuted as child pornographers. Even Louis Malle's controversial 1977 film, *Pretty Baby*, in which twelve-year-old

Brooke Shields starred as a young prostitute, was careful to avoid having Shields do anything remotely sexual.

There's something very absurd—and perhaps even dissociative—going on here. We recognize, and sometimes even celebrate, young love and young sexuality, *but we will not allow it to occur with real young people.*

So on stage and on film, for the time being, anyway, we're stuck with more than our fair share of arthritic Romeos and Juliets. As the distinguished Shakespearean actor Ian McKellen said about his own stint as Romeo, "I remember at thirty-seven trying far too hard to look, run, leap, climb and dance like a teenager."[2] Of course, the real problem here is not our tendency to miscast actors. The real tragedy is our tendency to dismiss all young love as mere "puppy" love.

Are Teens Really Just Puppies?

And we call it puppy love—or "calf" love, in some countries. Literally, it's a love between two pre-pubescent animals. When we dismiss the love between two human teenagers or between a teenager and an adult as illusory—that is, when we compare young people who have mature sexual organs to "puppies"—we are admitting undeniably that we still consider them to be children. We are also demonstrating an extreme form of wishful thinking.

Teens are not puppies. Girls generally begin puberty between the ages of eight and thirteen, with first menstruation (menarche)—an event that indicates the ability to conceive—occurring two or three years later. The median age of menarche for young women is about 12.5. Boys begin puberty between nine and fourteen. A number of experts agree that the onset of puberty has been occurring earlier and earlier in recent decades, perhaps because of improved nutrition and medical care. Let's not panic, though. Although signs of puberty—pubic hairs and breasts—are appearing earlier, the median age at which menarche occurs has stayed fairly steady for decades, and possibly even for many centuries.[3] In any case, by the time most young people reach thirteen or fourteen, they are almost fully mature sexually. Young males are shaving, young females are menstruating, and most young teens are capable of procreating.

Young people are also capable of experiencing romantic love, and no one, to my knowledge, has ever come up with a legitimate way of differentiating the kind of romantic love teens experience from the kind of romantic love adults experience. On the contrary, as I noted in Chapter Six, when Diane Dumas and I looked at love and romance from a competency perspective we found virtually no difference between the competency scores of teens and those of adults (also see Appendix 2).

Can Teens Really Love?

Dismayed over the lack of attention scholars and scientists have paid to teenage love in recent decades, Wyndol Furman of the University of Denver, B. Bradford Brown of the University of Wisconsin Madison, and Candice Feiring of the University of Medicine and Dentistry New Jersey assembled an impressive team of scholars a few years ago to take a serious look at what modern Romeos and Juliets are really experiencing. The result was a weighty collection of papers called *The Development of Romantic Relationships in Adolescence*, published by the Cambridge University Press.[4]

Here are some of the conclusions reached by Furman and his colleagues about teen love:

Romance as Central. Teens in much of the Western world are obsessed with romantic love. In the United States, it's the subject of 73 percent of rock music songs, and no other topic comes close in popularity. It's also the most common topic of television series featuring teens. According to one recent study, romance is also by far the most common topic on teens' minds—ahead of family, peers, and school.

Major Theories Are Ignored. A number of major theories of psychological development—most notably the neo-Freudian theories of Erik Erikson and Harry Stack Sullivan—emphasize the important role that romantic love plays in teen behavior and development. Sullivan argued, for example, that a teen's interest in romantic love is the inevitable outcome of his or her struggle to reconcile changing intimacy needs with lustful feelings—in other words, that friendship and emotional intimacy are the teen's primary needs. But researchers have largely ignored such theories, according to Furman and his colleagues, possibly because "teenagers' romantic ventures do not fit well within the basic constructs or foci of dominant theories of social or interpersonal development."[5]

Dismissed as Frivolous. Even though during much of human history teens often entered into successful marriages, researchers have fallen victim to the same shoddy idea that dominates most of Western thinking today—namely, that teen love is just puppy love. Until very recently researchers have simply dismissed it. According to the authors, "this perspective seems shortsighted."[6]

The Possible Primacy of Love Over Sex. There is a "vast" literature on teen sexuality, but researchers virtually never consider "the idea that romantic liaisons or relationships are primary contexts for adolescent sexual activity."[7] In other words, our biased perspective leads us to believe—and leads even serious researchers to believe—that sex comes first for teens, and romance second. But it's possible and in fact

likely, say Furman and others (consistent with Sullivan's perspective), that intimacy needs are actually the primary ones for most teens—that love leads to sex and not vice versa. After all, only about half of United States teens actually experience intercourse itself. If teens were simply lustful animals overcome with lust, the proportion would be much higher. There's more going on in teens than animal lust.[8]

High Turnover. Nowhere in the Furman volume does teen love ever get dismissed as illusory or frivolous. In fact, the romantic relationships of teens seem to differ from those of adults mainly in one respect. Teens move in and out of relationships extremely fast. But is this a sign of immaturity or just another manifestation of the artificial extension of childhood? After all, we make it difficult or impossible for young people to marry, so it's unrealistic for them to think of entering into long-term relationships. We isolate them from potentially more mature, more settled partners; it's unlawful, after all, for a minor to have sex with an adult, although minors can generally have sex with each other with impunity. And we loudly dismiss their feelings as half-baked, so teens themselves probably have doubts about the validity of what they're experiencing. To top things off, we also corral large groups of young people, often against their will, into crowded pens nine or ten months a year. It should surprise no one that teens shift partners frequently.

But the issue we need to keep addressing is *potential.* Just because teens in the United States, subjected to bizarre restrictions and absurd messages, isolated from adults, and warehoused under unnatural conditions, usually don't form lasting relationships, does that mean they *can't*? What if teens were raised to believe that the love they feel is valid and real? What if they were allowed, and perhaps even encouraged, to marry or to form long-term relationships? What if they were allowed to develop romantic relationships with older, more mature partners who could help accelerate their emotional development? What if their lives were more family or work based, rather than school based? Is it at least *possible* that teens would form relationships as healthy and successful as the relationships formed by adults?

OTHER TIMES, OTHER PLACES

If you consult your television or newspaper for answers to these questions, you'll probably find wrong ones. But if, as I noted in the early chapters of this book, you look at our evolutionary history, at our own not-so-distant past, and at other cultures, clear and correct answers emerge. There is simply no question that many or most teens are capable of feeling and expressing romantic love, and many are also capable of entering into successful long-term relationships.

Teen Marriage in the Distant Past

Earlier in this book I looked at the very different way that society viewed young people before the Industrial Revolution. I focused on labor, education, and justice issues, but romance and love follow similar patterns. From Biblical times (see Chapter Twelve) until the Industrial Revolution, it was common for young people, especially young women, to marry. In ancient Egypt and Rome, for example, historians believe that it was common for brides to have been as young as twelve, and some brides were as young as eight or nine. Because the burden of supporting a family fell on the male, young men had to be working before they could marry, and hence they were typically fifteen or older.

This pattern had probably been in place for thousands of years before Rome was built, and it continued to some degree until about a hundred years ago. In Europe in the Middle Ages, for example, it was common for women to be married by fourteen. Men married later, again because they needed to be able to support their families.

At least three American first ladies married when they were still "children" (by current standards): Elizabeth Monroe married president-to-be James Monroe in 1785 when she was seventeen; their marriage lasted until her death in 1830.[9] Rachel Jackson, eventually the wife of President Andrew Jackson, was first married to Lewis Robards; they married when she was seventeen and divorced when she was in her early twenties, apparently because she couldn't tolerate Robards' extreme jealousy.[10]* And Eliza Johnson married future president Andrew Johnson in 1827 when she was sixteen and he was eighteen. They were married for nearly fifty years and died within six months of each other.[11]

Even in modern times, first ladies sometimes married fairly young. Rosalynn Carter started dating Jimmy when she was seventeen and married him in 1946 at age nineteen, and Barbara Bush started dating the elder George when she was sixteen, got engaged to him at seventeen, and married him in 1945 at age nineteen.[12] Both marriages have lasted lifetimes.

Teen Marriage in Other Cultures

Around the world, it's still common for people to marry young, although pressures from Western culture, especially from American culture, are challenging the ancient patterns (Chapter Three). This is especially ironic given that our

---

*At least she thought they were divorced. When she married Jackson in 1791, her divorce wasn't really final, and Robards sued her for adultery. The Jacksons remarried in 1794 but were haunted thereafter by rumors of bigamy and adultery.

own system of marriage is the least successful in the world: 50 percent of first marriages here end in divorce, as do more than 60 percent of second marriages.[13] Divorce can damage children for a lifetime, and it's economically devastating to many families, especially to ex-wives. Unfortunately, as other countries adopt our practices, their divorce rates—and the devastation divorce brings with it—are increasing rapidly.

I can't overemphasize the importance—and ugliness—of this inexorable trend. Every aspect of our culture, propelled by syndicated TV sitcoms, fast-food chains, and glitzy Hollywood movies, is being spread worldwide, no matter how trivial the cultural phenomenon and no matter how harmful the effect. Anorexia—unheard of until recently in countries like South Korea, Japan, and the Philippines—is now becoming a serious problem, and healthy diets, like the fish-and-rice regimen of the Japanese, are rapidly being replaced by french fries and Big Macs.[14]

One of the things we're exporting is our distorted picture of young people. Through movies like *Clueless* and *American Pie* and television series like *Beverly Hills 90210*—seen by more than two hundred million people worldwide—we tell the world in vivid terms what we believe about teens: that they're overgrown children, that they're inherently wild and irresponsible, that their love is just puppy love, that their relationships are fleeting and superficial, and that they need adult protection. A movie like *Clueless* is typically translated into twenty languages and shown around the world within months of its original release. No religious zealots on earth have ever proselytized as vehemently as Corporate America.

Meanwhile, many of the old marriage practices remain. In Afghanistan, Niger, and the Congo, for example, the percentages of young women ages fifteen to nineteen who are already married are, respectively, fifty-four, seventy, and seventy-four.[15] In some cultures, one reason for early marriage is to protect young women from the risk of becoming pregnant out of wedlock. According to one survey, in Niger nearly half of the women who married before age fifteen married for this reason.

Traditional Marriage Practices in India

In India, the law requires that a woman be eighteen before she can marry and that a man be twenty-one. But upwards of 450 million people—about 40 percent of India's population—simply ignore the law. It's not only common for teens to marry; true child marriages are commonly performed, sometimes en masse.[16]

One recent article describes a ceremony in Madhogarth, a small village in Rajasthan, in which Hansa, the youngest of six sisters who were being married to boys from another village, was married to Sitaram. He was twelve, and Hansa was four. An account of another masse ceremony—this one in Rajanawagaon—gives some of the reasons villagers have for flaunting the law. A Ms. Bunkbai,

whose three grandsons were married that day, explained that she had recently been ill and that she wanted to see the faces of her grand daughters-in-law before she died. Her husband added that it was risky to let young men get too old without marrying; he spoke of a young man of eighteen who had recently eloped with a married woman. Another villager commented, "What if the girl is not beautiful when she grows up? No one will want to marry her." In this particular village, the elders explained that only children over ten were being married these days; years ago, they said, even infants were sometimes married off.[17]

Ms. Bunkbai, by the way, had attended one of the "sensitization camps" run they national government's Department of Women and Children Development. These camps familiarize people with the marriage laws and even get potential offenders to recite "pledges" that they won't violate the laws. But the old practices are dying hard, perhaps because *Clueless* hasn't yet made it to the rural areas.

Through Western eyes rural Indian marriage practices seem immoral. Obviously a four-year-old can't make a reasonable decision about marriage, and how could any civilized culture contemplate putting defenseless children into relationships that require sex?

But when you set aside your preconceptions and try to understand what's really happening when very young people are married in India, Indian practices don't look so crazy. K. Santhaa Reddy, a member of India's National Commission for Women, sheds light on India's child marriages in a recent essay:

A marriage in rural India is not just a relationship between two individuals. Marriages form the backbone of the networking that is essential for survival in a world where the idea of state providing protection seems an alien concept. Urban mind tends to ignore this concept of marriage and looks at marriage in its western form. In Europe and America, marriage is a license to have sex and procreate. In all communities where child marriages are prevalent, the sexual aspect of marriage is absent at the time of marriage.

In fact a child marriage is so essentially different from a normal marriage, that it should be called an engagement rather than a marriage. After such a marriage, the girl does not go with her husband. She continues to live with her parents. The marriage is not consummated for many years. When the girl and the boy attain maturity, another ceremony (called "Gauna" in North India) is held. It is only after Gauna that the girl can meet her husband. The marriage is consummated only after Gauna.

The custom of Gauna has not been recognized by Indian lawmakers who treat marriage as a one-step process while in many communities of India, it is a three-step process. The first step is primary fixing up of the marriage. At this stage some token gifts are engaged between the two families. The second stage is marriage where the rituals of sapta-padi and seven

circles of holy fire are performed by the bride and bridegroom. The third step is Gauna or Bidaii when the bride is sent to the bridegroom's house. In urban India, the second and the third steps are held in quick succession say within a few hours time. But in rural India, the three stages are distinct and often have a time gap between them.

Almost all problems that one mentions about child marriages seem to be a result of the inability of the law to come to terms with the customs prevailing in society.[18]

As odd as this system may sound, it appears to serve a number of constructive purposes, and it's also not necessarily harmful. Bear in mind that this system of marriage is practiced by more people in India alone than there are people in the United States; one can hardly dismiss it, even if it doesn't fit our values. It's also notable that although divorce is legal in India, the country has one of the lowest divorce rates in the world—less than a fifth of the divorce rate in the United States.

Reddy also points out an absurd discrepancy that's surprisingly common in many cultures, as well as in some states in the United States (see below): in India, it's legal for women to consent to sex at age sixteen, and there's no minimum age of consent for males—but it's illegal for young people to marry for several more years. In effect, by discouraging marriage the culture condones and encourages pre-marital sex.

Meanwhile, government agencies in India, spurred by UNICEF and other Western-oriented NGOs, continue to discourage marriage by people under eighteen—and fail "to come to terms with the customs prevailing in society." Again, we want everyone to walk our walk, even if we all end up stumbling.

THE SURPRISING TRUTH ABOUT
TEEN MARRIAGE AND DIVORCE

In *Everything You Need To Know About Teen Marriage*, writer Eleanor H. Ayer claims that "a girl [sic] married at seventeen is twice as likely to be divorced as a girl eighteen or nineteen. If a girl waits until she is twenty-five the chances that her marriage will last are four times better."[19] You've probably heard something like this before, and indeed we now teach our young people that they should wait before marrying, in part because with greater maturity their marriages will be more likely to survive.

It's not clear, however, where Ayer got these numbers, and they don't necessarily tell us what we want to know, anyway. After all, if one out of ten eighteen year olds gets divorced, but *two* out of ten seventeen year olds get divorced, Ayer would technically be correct. But that would still leave *eight out of ten* seventeen year olds with successful marriages—hardly cause to discourage young people from tying the knot.

YOUNG PEOPLE IN ACTION

Anything to Get Away from Home

I was doing anything I could to stay away from my house— hanging out with anyone of any age. I was eleven and fully developed; I could even get into bars sometimes without being carded. Mark was thirty-one, and I was using him to stay away from my mom. When I got pregnant, I knew I had to get rid of it because I had no way to support it. Mark wouldn't help, so I finally told my mom, and she helped me get the abortion. It was no big deal, even though I was already four months pregnant. It was ten days before my twelfth birthday.

—Liz C., now age twenty-four

Practice Doesn't Help

Marriage and divorce statistics compiled by the United States Census Bureau and the National Center for Health Statistics paint a complex picture of the role that age plays in divorce. First of all, as I noted above, about 50 percent of all first marriages in the United States end in divorce and more than 60 percent of all second marriages end in divorce. The divorce rate for third marriages is higher still. Practice and advancing years are no guarantee of success when it comes to marriage.

There is also a curious similarity in the curves that describe the divorce rate in the United States and the median age at which people first marry. (See Figure 8.1.) Between 1950 and 1990, the divorce rate increased fairly steadily, and so did the median age of first marriage.[20] If the age at which people married played a significant role in the longevity of a marriage, we might have expected the divorce rate to *decrease* as the marrying age increased. Again, getting older doesn't necessarily help.

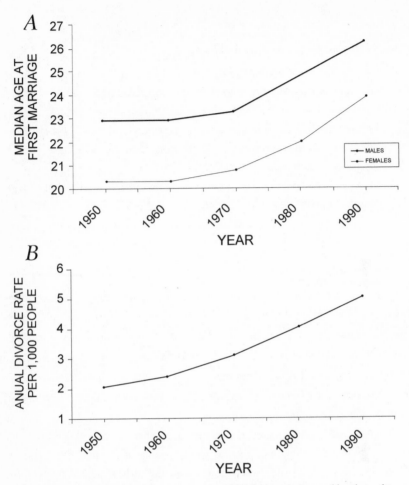

Figure 8.1. Age Versus Divorce Rate. If growing older helps people form stable relationships, then as the age of first marriage has increased over the past fifty years, we might expect the divorce rate to *decrease*, but the opposite has occurred. *Source:* U.S. Census Bureau data.

Shouldn't We Let Them Try?

In addition, it turns out that *young males* have a relatively *low* divorce rate. According to the United States Department of Health and Human Services, among 580,000 divorces that took place in the United States in 1990, teenage males (nineteen and under) divorced at the rate of 32.8 per thousand couples, whereas males in their early twenties (twenty to twenty-four) had a much higher divorce rate: 50.2 per thousand couples. There was little difference in the divorce rate for females in these two age groups: about forty-eight per thousand couples.[21]

Fifty divorces per thousand couples is a high rate, for sure. If that rate were maintained for ten years, simple multiplication (ten times fifty) suggests that *half* of the couples would then be divorced. (In fact, the way the math works out, the proportion is actually lower.) It's this kind of logic that leads us to discourage or prohibit young people from marrying.

But this logic is seriously flawed. For one thing, if fifty young couples out of a thousand get divorced in a given year, that means that 950 couples don't. And even if half of young couples get divorced over a ten-year period, *how would that justify prohibiting young people from marrying?* After all, about half of all *adult* marriages end in divorce eventually. Does that mean we should prohibit *all* people from marrying? *Does the possibility of failure mean that no one should be allowed to try?* Should the 40 or 50 percent of teen couples who are capable of creating relatively permanent marriages be prevented or discouraged from marrying just because other teens fail?

The divorce rate among young people is certainly higher than among older people, but the relatively high divorce rate among young people is not necessarily driven by youth per se or even by a lack of experience. The fact is that young couples are subjected disproportionately to two powerful sources of stress—economic hardship and children—either one of which is enough to destroy a marriage. Given these stressors, one might even marvel at the relatively high success rate teen marriages have.

People also argue against teen marriage because they say it interferes with education and economic advancement, but that argument mistakenly assumes that education *must* occur when we're young. We've come to believe this because we've all been raised in a society in which education is required until age sixteen or eighteen, in which young people are largely prohibited from working, and in which many young people are taught that they *must* go to college immediately after high school. In fact, as many adults have discovered in recent decades, education can and probably should continue throughout one's life, and the education that has the greatest impact on us is the education we seek when we're truly ready.

LOVE AND SEX INVOLVING MINORS

The more I've learned about the way our legal system deals with relationships between adults and minors, as well as between minors and other minors, the more concerned I've become. Remember the factual context, developed in this and previous chapters, in which I'm examining this issue: Teens, on the average,

are capable of exercising judgment every bit as sound as the judgment of adults; in other words, many teens are capable of excellent judgment. Many teens are capable of experiencing deep and mature feelings of love. Many teens are capable of entering into successful, long-term relationships; they've done so throughout human history, and they still do so in countries around the world. When teens are given real responsibility and authority, they sometimes mature virtually overnight. Teens differ one from the other, just as adults do; some are more capable than others.

Given that as our foundation—and I believe these points are indisputable—here are three cases that are especially disturbing. Each case shows a legal system applying general principals of questionable validity to situations in which these principals don't apply. Each shows legal authorities doing irreparable harm to innocent families. Each shows justice acting mindlessly, based merely on people's ages rather than on their abilities or motives.

The Fonsecas

December 2002. Judge Kevin J. McGee of Ventura County, California, stating that this was "the most unusual [case] one can imagine," sentenced twenty-three-year-old Andrew Fonseca to a year in jail for having sex with a fourteen-year-old student. Fonseca had been a wrestling coach at the Moorpark High School when he became involved with the student. Subsequently, the two got married and moved in with her parents. In court, the young woman's mother begged the judge to be lenient: "Andrew is living at our house, married to our daughter, and he works and supports her. *It's been the best thing that ever happened to her.*" The judge ignored her pleas.[22]

The sentence also required Fonseca to register as a sex offender, a designation that will stay with him the rest of his life and that will prevent him from ever teaching or coaching again. During the sentencing, the father-in-law, seated in the back of the courtroom, was overheard uttering "a stream of profanities."[23]

Fualaau and Letourneau

In the summer of 1996 Mary Kay Letourneau, a thirty-four-year-old teacher and married mother of four children, began having an affair with Vili Fualaau, a twelve-year-old student at the school where she taught, the Shorewood Elementary School in Burien, Washington.

Although some news reports suggest otherwise, it appears that he was not actually her student when the affair began. That summer, they each took the same classes at the Highline Community College and at a Seattle art store, and it appears that that's when things began. Vili—whom Mary called "Buddha"—was also unusually advanced for a male his age; he had reached puberty at age ten and was several inches taller than his married lover.

In February 1997 Mary's husband discovered his wife's notes and journal entries about Vili and had her arrested. She gave birth to Vili's child, Audrey, on May 23, 1997.[24]

In August of that year, Letourneau pleaded guilty to two counts of statutory rape. She later received a suspended sentence but had to serve eighty additional days in jail. She was also required to enroll in a sex-offender treatment program and was forbidden from seeing Fualaau for the rest of her life—a common restriction when adults have had sex with a minor.

Early in 1998, after having been released from jail for good behavior, she was found in a car with Fualaau and arrested for violating the terms of her suspended sentence. The suspension was subsequently revoked, and the original sentence—eighty-nine months in prison—was reinstated. In prison it was soon discovered that Letourneau was now pregnant again, and in October 1998 she gave birth to Georgia, her second child with Fualaau. Both children were raised by Fualaau and his mother.

It was difficult to judge from news reports exactly what was going on here. Was Vili really a "child" who had been corrupted and "raped" by his teacher, or was there more to the story?

When I saw a television interview with Vili in February of 1999, it became clear that the legal system simply couldn't handle the truth of the matter. Here is what Vili said:

> Mary didn't take away my childhood. I gave it away by consent. I knew what I was getting into. I don't feel in one bit of my body that she ever raped me. I don't love her because she's thirty years old, and she doesn't love me because I'm fifteen years old. We love each other for who we are.[25]

From the tone and cadence of his speech, it was clear that this was a mature young man, not a child. Throughout most of human history, Vili would have been recognized for what he was: a young man who was deeply in love with an older woman. But in the modern Western world, and especially in the United States, we arbitrarily dismiss all people under a certain age—eighteen, or twenty-one, or even twenty-six—as emotionally incompetent children, no matter what their actual capabilities.

Don't get me wrong. Fualaau and Letourneau shouldn't win any awards for their behavior. A teacher-student relationship is objectionable, at least when it's exploitative, and adultery and the destruction of an intact family can hardly be defended. Nor can ignoring a court order, even if one doesn't agree with it.

WISDOM OF THE AGES

Twelve-Year-Old "Predators"

In February 2002 the Illinois Supreme Court ruled that people as young as twelve must be ordered to register as "sexual predators" for committing certain sexual crimes—a designation that will stay with them the rest of their lives. One of the dissenting justices, Thomas Kilbride thought that this was unfair considering that, under Illinois law, a sixteen-year-old sex offender convicted of murder need not be labeled in this way. [26]

But Letourneau wasn't imprisoned because she slept with a former student or because she committed adultery. As a Boston judge told me years ago, "If we locked everyone up for committing adultery, there'd be no one left to turn the key." Letourneau was condemned because she had had a serious relationship with someone society wrongly considers to be a helpless puppy. History, psychology, anthropology, and Vili himself say otherwise.

In 2002, when Fualaau and his mother were having financial difficulties (among other things, Vili had just been fired from his job at a McDonald's), he and his mother filed a frivolous and ultimately unsuccessful lawsuit against the Des Moines (Washington) Police Department and the Highline School District, claiming that they hadn't done enough to prevent his relationship with Letourneau.[27]

In defending itself the Highline School District presented only one witness, Dr. Csaba Hegyvary, a psychiatrist with twenty-two years of experience who had done evaluations of both Fualaau and Letourneau. According to a local news report, Hegyvary told the jury that "although it was legally rape, Letourneau is not a rapist, Fualaau is not a victim and the best outcome for everyone involved is for them to get married after Letourneau is released from prison." This wasn't, he said, a case of sexual abuse; it was "a love story."[28]

While in prison Mary Kay Letourneau was allowed almost no contact with any of her six children. She also spent time in solitary confinement, at least in part because of repeated attempts on her part to contact Vili.

After spending seven-and-a-half years in prison, Letourneau was released at age forty-two in August of 2004, prohibited from seeing Vili for the rest of her life, and required to register as a sex offender. Vili, then twenty-one, immediately asked the court to remove the contact restriction on the grounds that, as an adult, he should be able to "pick his friends." The restriction was indeed removed (but not the sex offender designation), and the two subsequently married and appear to be doing well.[29]

Healy and Kowalski

As you read about this next case, keep in mind where this chapter started—with the story of a prolific, highly honored, happily married couple—Mary and Paul Onesi—who married when she was thirteen and he was twenty-one.

Heather Kowalski, thirteen, and Dylan Healy, twenty-one, met over the Internet. That was their fatal mistake, or at least Dylan's. After all, everyone knows that the Internet is where perverts lurk and "children" are corrupted. Of course, the Internet also happens to be where millions of adults, both mature and immature, now go to find dates and spouses.

When Heather's parents found out about the relationship, about where it started, and about Dylan's age, they forbade Heather from seeing him, or at least her mom did (see below). Heather, after all, wasn't even allowed to date, and here she was carousing with a "man." Heather ignored them and continued to contact and see Dylan frequently. Eventually the parents got a restraining order against Dylan, but by that time Dylan and Heather were madly in love with each other.

On March 25, 1997, Heather ran away with her lover, and they drove around New England for about three weeks until authorities picked them up. A massive hunt for the young couple had been set in motion by media appearances by her frantic parents, including a poignant call for help on *The Maury Povich Show.* Povich's hyperbolic theme was "Families Who've Been Torn Apart by the Internet," and he referred to Heather repeatedly as a "child" who had been "manipulated and lured away from home" by a "predator."[30]

Journalist Judith Levine reports on her investigation of this case in her recent book *Harmful to Minors: The Perils of Protecting Children from Sex.* Her take, which I find to be persuasive, is that Dylan and Heather were each at about the same maturity level, mainly because Dylan was fairly immature for his age, whereas Heather, like many young women, was somewhat advanced. There is no evidence that Dylan was a "pedophile" or predator, in spite of sensational news reports. As we saw in the Letourneau case, there is also no question that Heather was a willing participant in what occurred and that the two were happy together the entire time they dated. No evidence was ever presented suggesting any sort of coercion on Dylan's part. The coercion was entirely on the part of the parents, which is why Heather chose to run away with her attentive lover.[31]

In a letter Heather sent to Dylan after he was arrested, she wrote, "I think

> ## WISDOM OF THE AGES
>
> ### Love in Czechoslovakia
>
> *After James Kirchner, a Detroit teacher, saw me talking about teens on a TV program, he sent me some illuminating emails about teen love in Czechoslovakia, where he had taught in the 1990s. Here is an excerpt: "Czechs did not consider teenagers to be children, and they did not believe that marrying in one's teens necessarily turned out badly.... When the girls in my Czech high school were fifteen or sixteen, if they had boyfriends, the boyfriend was often in his mid- to late twenties. I asked them why they didn't go out with guys their own age, and the response was, 'Guys our age only think about beer and getting into our pants. The older guys have something to talk about.' I asked them if their mothers knew about the relationships, and the girls replied that their mothers were fine with the whole thing.... The idea was evidently that a man that age has the maturity to keep her out of trouble and that if they became sexually active and conceived a child, he could handle his responsibilities, which a sixteen-year-old boy cannot."*

that the best time I ever had being with you was when we were gone, I would watch you sleep and think about the wonderful life we would someday have.... I love you."[32]

Before I tell you the very sad ending to this story, let's try to put the relationship in a historical context. In other eras—through most of human history, in fact—Heather would have been considered to be a young woman, not a child, just as Mary Onesi was considered to be a young woman when she married her husband of eighty years. That doesn't mean Heather's parents would have approved of Dylan as a mate for her; he was unemployed, for one thing, and living off a trust fund that had been established by his late father. They might not have liked him for any number of reasons. But given that he truly loved their daughter, they might have at least given him a chance to court her. It's certainly unlikely that they would have dismissed the relationship out of hand simply because of Heather's age—or Dylan's.

Even in the modern United States, if Dylan and Heather had met at a party or in a park, it's unlikely that he would have been punished as severely as he was. Fonseca was sentenced to a year in jail for having had sex with his fourteen-year-old girlfriend, and Letourneau was hit with the maximum possible sentence the law allowed in her sensational case: seven-and-half years.

But in the fall of 1997, Dylan Healy was sentenced to *twelve to twenty-four*

years in prison for multiple counts of "felonious sexual assault with a minor," as well as crossing state lines to have sex with a minor. That's twelve to twenty-four years in prison for engaging in a mutually-satisfying relationship in which no coercion was ever shown and no emotional or physical harm was ever demonstrated.[33]

This draconian sentence was driven by our very mistaken notions about the capabilities of young people, further inflamed by our current fears of Internet predation. On the Povich show, Robert Kowalski said of his daughter, "She's still a little girl. She needs to be taken care of like a little girl."[34] The facts of the case shout otherwise, and he and his wife also failed to note that at the time of Heather's disappearance, their own marriage was near its end. They had filed for divorce the previous year, and they were living apart. Even more disturbing, Pauline Kowalski's court filings claimed that her husband had *encouraged* the relationship between Heather and Dylan.[35]

The stress of Dylan's conviction helped destroy his own mother's marriage of ten years. After his sentencing, he read a long statement in which he professed his love for Heather, a young woman who "made me feel happier than I had ever felt [and] who brought joy into my life.... I loved her beyond reason and fled with the one I loved."[36]

LOVE LAWS

I wish I could say that they exist—love laws, that is—if only so we could examine them. As far as I can determine, however, there aren't any. In other words, there's nothing illegal about a thirteen year old dating or having a love relationship with a forty year old. They can go to movies together, send letters and poetry to each other, and profess their love. But they can't have sex, and they can't marry in most states, even with the consent of the minor's parents.

So the laws that govern the love lives of teens are all about sex and marriage, not about love. Perhaps that's because we assume, as a culture, that romantic feelings can't be controlled, and, of course, we also assume, mistakenly, that the romantic feelings of teens aren't real.

Laws Restricting Sex and Marriage

The laws that govern sex and marriage among teens are highly restrictive in some ways and surprisingly lax in others, not to mention confusing and inconsistent. In California, for example—a progressive and innovative state when it comes to legal matters—it's okay for two thirteen-year-olds to have sex with each other.

WISDOM OF THE AGES

Dissent About Consent

Worldwide, there is enormous disagreement about when a young person should have the right to consent to sex, and there is no obvious pattern by religion, region, or affluence. In some poor third-world countries the age of consent is quite low: twelve in Mexico and fourteen in Chile, for example. But in Swaziland one must be eighteen to have sex and in Tunisia one must be twenty. There's even variation among Arab countries. In Syria, a young woman can consent to sex at age thirteen; in Egypt and Uganda the minimum age for both sexes is eighteen; and in Saudi Arabia, no one is allowed to have sex outside of marriage, period. In industrialized nations, the typical age of consent is sixteen, but in Japan, the second richest nation in the world, it's only thirteen.[37]

It's also legal for two fourteen-year-olds to have sex with each other. But it's unlawful for a fourteen-year-old to have sex with a thirteen-year-old.

It's also legal for two seventeen-year-olds to have sex with each other and for two eighteen-year-olds to have sex with each other, but it's *strictly illegal* for anyone eighteen or older to have sex with *anyone* under eighteen, even if that person consents to engaging in the sexual act, even with parental consent. Unlike most other states, California doesn't have an "age of consent"—an age under eighteen at which a minor can consent to having sex.[38]

Please consider: Is a sixteen-year-old allowed to have sex with a fourteen-year-old in California? Are two fifteen-year-olds allowed to have sex? Are two eleven-years-olds allowed to have sex? Is a sixty-year-old allowed to have sex with an eighteen-year-old?

The answer to all of these questions is yes. But an eighteen-year-old is not allowed have sex with a seventeen-year-old, even if the two are exercising good judgment, and even if parents of the seventeen-year-old approve.

In Colorado, where young people under age eighteen can consent to having sex with adults, it's okay for two eleven-year-olds to have sex with each other, and it's even okay for a fifteen-year-old to have sex with a twenty-four-year-old. But if a seventeen-year-old has sex with a thirteen-year-old, he or she is guilty of committing a "Class 4 Felony."[39]

The marriage laws are equally quirky, especially when you compare the laws of different states. Without parental consent, all fifty states except Mississippi and Nebraska require both parties to be eighteen or over in order to marry. In Ne-

braska the minimum age is nineteen, and in Mississippi the minimum age is seventeen for males and fifteen for females. With parental consent, the landscape is quite varied. In California and Mississippi, for example, young people can marry *at any age* with the consent of parents. In Kansas and Massachusetts, females can marry at twelve with parental consent, and males can marry at fourteen. But in Delaware, Ohio, and Rhode Island—except in cases of pregnancy or when judges intervene—females can't marry until they're sixteen, and males can't marry until they're eighteen, even with the parents' blessing.[40]

These laws sometimes give rise to absurd situations. In 1997, for example, in California's Santa Clara County, twenty-two-year-old Juan Jiminez was charged with the statutory rape of his seventeen-year-old wife, Delia Lopez, after a medical doctor reported them to authorities for having had consensual sex before they were married. They were happily and legally married, living with Ms. Lopez's parents at the time of the arrest. The parents approved of and had granted permission for the marriage, and Delia and Juan were the proud parents of a baby boy. There was nothing coercive or even strange about this situation; the two were simply pursuing a loving relationship with each other. What's odd here is the law. If Delia and Juan had both been seventeen, they could have had sex with each other without penalty and then could have married with parental consent. But because Juan was considered an adult, they weren't allowed to have sex before marriage, even with parental consent.[41]

Faulty Assumptions

The many laws that restrict the love and sex lives of teens, their inconsistencies and absurdities aside, are based on no fewer than eight faulty assumptions:

Love. Implicit in these laws is the assumption that *all* young people are incapable of experiencing the same kinds of loving feelings that adults do. As we've seen, that simply isn't true.

Sex. These laws assume that *no* young people are capable of engaging in sexual activities responsibly. Again, this is false. Teens and adults who took the EDTA had similar scores on the scale that looked at sex, suggesting that, on the average, basic knowledge about sex is the same for adults and teens. More important, teens would be more likely to engage in sex responsibly if they weren't in adversarial relationships with adults.

Homogeneity. The laws assume that all young people are the same—and, in effect, that all adults are too. But teens vary enormously in their abilities, just as adults do. To say that *all* teens should be restricted because *some* are incompetent makes no sense. Imagine if we used that logic for drivers licenses: There are incompetent drivers of every age (and race and gender); should we therefore allow *no one* to drive?

Judgment. The laws suggest that *no* young person is capable of making sensible decisions about matters of sex, love, or romance. Again, this simply isn't so.

Relationships. These laws suggest that *no* young person is capable of entering into a stable, successful relationship. As history and other cultures teach us, this is false.

Magic. These laws assume that magic happens when people turn eighteen (or twelve or fourteen or sixteen or whatever other arbitrary age is specified)—in other words, that capabilities change in a quantum fashion when the age boundary is crossed. But human development is actually gradual and continuous, and dramatic change certainly doesn't occur instantly on a birthday.

Coercion. These laws imply that the person who is over the age boundary is necessarily coercing the person who is underage. But, as we've seen, in many cases there simply is no coercion, and it is certainly possible in some cases that coercion or manipulation flows the other way.

Harm. Finally, these laws suggest that some or many or perhaps even *all* young people who have sex or marry young will necessarily be harmed in some way. But we've already seen that it's possible for very young spouses to form successful long-term relationships, and research reviewed recently by Judith Levine in *Harmful to Minors* suggests that forcing sex to occur in an atmosphere of ignorance and secrecy does far more harm than allowing it to occur in an atmosphere of knowledge and acceptance.

Young people can indeed love, and they appear to be able to do so in all the beautiful and crazy ways that adults do. There is simply no evidence that teen love differs in some fundamental way from adult love. Teens also are capable of entering into stable, long-term relationships. The array of laws that limit teen romance and sexuality are absurd and arbitrary, and they sometimes destroy legitimate relationships and cause innocent people and their families great harm.

Q: *Do you mean to imply that it's okay for my thirteen-year-old little girl to have sex—and perhaps even to have sex with a twenty-five-year-old man?*

A: Given the mind-set that is prevalent in modern America, it's almost impossible for me to give a reasonable answer to this question without sounding insensitive or insane. But the fact is that some, and perhaps even many, thirteen-year-olds are ready for sex, and even for deep love and marriage. Remember that throughout most of human history, our ancestors began having children shortly after puberty. Our brains and bodies are designed that way.

Is your daughter ready to take on this kind of responsibility? I have no idea, but would you be willing to find out? As for that twenty-five-year-old man, if he truly loved and respected your daughter, and if he wanted to marry her and support her and treat her with kindness for the rest of his life, and if your daughter also loved this man deeply, would you object to their union?

As I indicated in this chapter, one of the most successful marriages ever documented in America—a happy marriage for more than eighty years—was between Mary Corsaro and Paul Onesi, who married in 1917 when she was thirteen and he was twenty-one. They were honored on World Marriage Day in 1995 as the longest-married couple in the country.

It's common in other cultures for people of widely different ages to marry; only in America do we think that spouses need to be same age, even though research suggests that age difference is a poor predictor of success in a marriage. It's the person you marry that counts, not his or her age.

Chapter 9
Young People Are Tough

...thanks for making me a fighter
Made me learn a little bit faster
Made my skin a little bit thicker
Makes me that much smarter
—Christina Aguilera, "Fighter"

Overview. When they're allowed or forced to do so, young people demonstrate extraordinary toughness and resilience, sometimes more than adults can muster. Teens excel in Olympic sports, for example, and some of the new "extreme" sports were developed by teens. Even though it might offend our sensibilities, from the time young David slew Goliath, young people have also made excellent soldiers–daring, disciplined, and deadly. In Myanmar recently, the charismatic Htoo twins, Luther and Johnny–age twelve– joined the ranks of Joan of Arc and other young leaders who have led armies to victory. Young victims of war, such as the twenty thousand "Lost Boys" who marched out of Sudan in the late 1980s, have also demonstrated great courage and self-reliance, as have hundreds of thousands of teens who have become caregivers for young siblings or disabled parents. We are reluctant to acknowledge the toughness of young people, just as, until recently, we were reluctant to acknowledge the toughness of women, but attitudes can and do change. Research on resilience suggests that exposure to great challenges may be essential for making young people as strong as adults.

June 18, 2002, Jerusalem. Just another day in one of the holiest and most dangerous places on earth. It was morning, and two public buses full of students were near each other on the No. 32 bus route. Suddenly, one of the buses exploded with such force that the entire vehicle was lifted off the ground. In the midst of the smoke and the screams and the confusion, the other bus stopped, and dozens of

riders, most in their early and mid-teens, streamed into the street to try to help. One unnamed fifteen-year-old, a student at the nearby Ort Spanyan school, rescued a little girl from the mangled remains of the other bus, and other teens managed to pull many other victims to safety before authorities arrived. There's no telling exactly how many lives were saved by these heroic young people. All we know for sure is that nineteen people died and more than seventy were injured in the blast.[1]

The small village where Ming Kipa lived in Nepal wasn't able to offer her more than a fourth-grade education, but that didn't stop her from subjecting herself to strenuous exercise, climbing small peaks, and mastering basic mountaineering techniques. On May 22nd, 2003, she joined her older brother and sister on a trek to the top of world, successfully scaling Mount Everest and setting a new world record along the way. The trek was brutal, she admitted. She couldn't sleep because of the numbing cold, and at one point, the beam of light fastened to her forehead found a disturbing target. "They were two men," said Ming. "The light fell on their eyes, and they shone like cat's eyes. I was going to say hello, but then I realized they were dead men." But she made it, and she broke a record previously held by Temba Tsheri, a Nepalese student who had climbed Everest at age sixteen. Ming was fifteen.[2]

Again, the obvious questions: we treat teens like children (and even in Nepal, it's now illegal for people under sixteen to climb Everest, which forced Ming to climb from the Tibetan side), but what are their actual capabilities? Are teens really fragile creatures who need our protection? Or do many, or perhaps most of them, have the potential of those young heroes in Israel, or perhaps even of the indefatigable Ming Kipa?

TOUGHNESS IN SPORTS

I saw it live on television, as did tens of millions of other viewers around the world: Kerri Strug's gold medal vault at the 1996 Olympic Games in Atlanta. Eighteeen-year-old Strug had been training in gymnastics since she was four, never missing a day, training until "my back is sore, my stomach has pulled a muscle, my heel is bruised, and my legs are really sore." She qualified for the 1992 Olympic games at age fourteen, and her efforts there helped the United States team win the bronze, but she wanted more, and she went all out in '96.[3] Unfortunately, she landed badly on her first vault during the team competition. Her ankle was fractured, and she was in intense pain, but she needed to make one more outstanding run for her team to take the gold.

I knew the entire nation wanted to see me hit my second vault. I knew we needed that second vault. I knew how long I had waited to be in the position I was in.... By the time I managed to get back to the start of the runway, my leg was numb.... I reached down and twisted my left foot with my hand, trying to work out the pain, but all I felt was a crackling.... I began my run and honestly could not feel my leg.... It felt like my ankle was swinging loosely from the rest of my leg, like it was hanging by a string.[4]

Her second vault was picture perfect, a strong, precise combination that got the United States team the gold. And her landing was unforgettable.

I did it standing on just my right foot, like a flamingo.... Tears were already filling my eyes and the heat inside my leg was incredible..... The pain knocked me to the mat, a pulsating, pull-your-hair-out, you're-going-to-die pain. I knew for sure I was going to at least faint. There was such a hot rush up my leg. You know how sometimes a pain is so intense, you feel you're on the verge of going crazy? That's how I felt.[5]

Courage or Child Abuse?

I was visiting my parents' house in Connecticut at the time, and I remember my mom being appalled by Strug's performance, which, to her, smelled of child abuse. I defended Strug, albeit weakly, saying something about her "obvious courage." But could a teen be "courageous," I wondered? Certainly, I had been taught to think otherwise.

The sports world is filled with tales like Strug's, in part because it's one of those rare domains (like the entertainment industry) where, on occasion, we set aside restrictions and let young people show their stuff.

Millions of young people play dozens of sports every day in this country, and hundreds of thousands participate regularly in organized "amateur" versions of various professional sports. Because sports are inherently risky, it's not surprising that injuries are common. According to the United States Consumer Product Safety Commission, about 2 percent of the Americans, age six and over, who play football each year, suffer injuries; that's more than 370,000 injuries from football alone, most of them involving children and teens.[7] Nearly 600,000 Americans, many of them quite young, are injured playing basketball annually.[8] Are we "abusing" our young people by allowing them to participate in sports, or are we simply acknowledging their competence?

Young Professionals

In professional sports—that is, sports in which people get paid—young people are also regular participants. With the creation of new media outlets like ESPN,

---

YOUNG PEOPLE IN ACTION

"100 Percent Worth It"

> *Professional inline skater Kelly Matthews has been skating since she was twelve. She pushes herself and the sport itself to every possible extreme. "All it takes to be extreme," she says, "is the will to try new tricks. All that's needed is a faith in yourself and the sport." It's a tough and risky enterprise, which has cost her twenty stitches over her right eye, a broken wrist, and more. Has she got what it takes? Says Kelly, "Every time I go to skate and every time I've had to face the pain, I know that it's 100 percent worth it and wouldn't give up my bumps, bruises, and broken bones for anything in the world."[6]*

ESPN2, and *Sports Illustrated for Kids*, the focus on young athletes has grown considerably in recent years. When eighteen-year-old Ohio high school basketball star LeBron James accepted some jerseys as a gift from a store owner, for example, the indiscretion was reported widely in sports magazines and on ESPN's "Sports Center."[9] The activities of golfer Michelle Wie, who at age thirteen stood five-feet-ten and could already drive a golf ball more than three hundred yards (father than most men can), also make national news regularly, prompting one commentator to lament that amateurism is "all but gone from college, high school and even youth club sports."[10]

Young people not only participate in and excel in many sports, lately they've played pivotal roles in creating whole new genres. A case in point is the domain called "extreme sports," which occasionally fill the streets in tournaments in Southern California. The extremes include sports such as ice climbing, snow boarding, BMX bike racing, snow mountain biking, sky surfing, wake boarding, inline skating, and the most ubiquitous x-game of them all, skateboarding, which got off the ground in Southern California in the 1950s and was given a major boost by young people in the L.A. area in the 1960s.

In 1965, eight-year-old Tony Alva—later a skateboarding legend—and his "buds" hit the streets by attaching the wheels from roller skates to flat boards. Alva and the other boys of "Dogtown," an area near the beach in Santa Monica, at first used the boards just to get around the neighborhood but ultimately learned to control them in ways that appeared to defy gravity. One of the strangest activities of early skateboarders was to prowl wealthy neighborhoods in search of empty concrete swimming pools to skate in; that was the beginning of "bowl riding," which is now the centerpiece of whole parks and arenas.[11] Created largely by young people, skate-

> # WOMEN IN ACTION
>
> ## Women Are "Different"
>
> *The Queen is most anxious to enlist every one who can speak or write to join in checking this mad, wicked folly of "Woman's Rights," with all its attendant horrors, on which her poor feeble sex is bent, forgetting every sense of womanly feeling and propriety. Lady [name withheld] ought to get a good whipping. It is a subject which makes the Queen so furious that she cannot contain herself. God created men and women different— then let them remain each in their own position.*
>
> –Queen Victoria,
> Letter to Sir Theodore Martin, 29 May 1870

boarding is now a $5.2 billion industry.[12] (By the way, in 1996 my son's high school—Justin, that is, the one I mentioned in the introduction to this book— became the first high school in the country to offer a for-credit course called "Skateboard"—P. E. course number 1692-42.)

FRAILTY, THEY NAME IS...

Sweet, baby-faced Jessica Lynch will remain in America's memory for many years. An unlikely hero, she may forever symbolize America's might in our recent conflict in Iraq.

What Lynch actually did during the ninety-minute battle that led to her capture isn't clear. Early reports from "unnamed U.S. officials" suggested that this twenty-year-old supply clerk, a private in an Army maintenance company, fought fiercely during the battle, but Army investigators later concluded that she was probably injured when her Humvee crashed into another vehicle after it was hit by a rocket. Lynch herself apparently can't remember what happened. In any case, eleven of her fellow soldiers were killed during the battle, and she was held as a prisoner of war in a Nasiriyah hospital for about a week before being rescued by United States Special Forces in an unopposed operation.[13]

Lynch was welcomed as a hero upon her return to the United States and was awarded three medals for her service in Iraq: the Bronze Star (for meritorious combat service), the Purple Heart (for her wounds), and the Prisoner of War. It's not clear that she deserved the Bronze Star or the enormous attention she received, but what *is* clear is that our attitude about women—and about women in

combat, in particular—has changed dramatically in recent decades. Lynch was consistently praised, after all, and no one hit the streets protesting the fact that she had been put at risk in the first place. The very idea that the United States would put a waif-like female, barely out of her teens, in harm's way during a major combat operation would have been completely unthinkable in the 1950s.

Sometimes, it seems, our attitudes change.

Women Soldiers and Police

When it comes to females, the change has been enormous. A recent article in the *Christian Science Monitor* summarizes the extent of the change: Women are now "striking targets, taking fire, guarding Iraqi prisoners of war, and driving trucks laden with supplies amid ambushes and snipers." They now comprise about 15 percent of the United States armed forces—double the percentage in 1980. That means more than two hundred thousand females in military garb.[14] Although still barred from front-line combat roles, they're firing weapons from helicopters and jets and killing with the best of them. A gun, after all, is the ultimate leveler. According to helicopter pilot Lt. Sarah Fritts, "Why should I not be allowed to do something I want to do because some guy lying on a couch watching TV feels uncomfortable seeing me dragged through the street?.... I don't see why a woman's life is so much more important than a man's life.... For a woman to gain full citizenship, she should be able to die for her country."[15]

According to a recent essay by Captain Barbara A. Wilson (United States Air Force, retired), studies in the United States and Great Britain show unequivocally that "when a woman is correctly trained, she can be as tough as any man," and "mixed units" are now performing cohesively and effectively, "even under fire." According to Wilson, women are now eligible to serve in more than 90 percent of officer positions available in the United States Navy.[16]

You don't have to look farther than your local intersection to see how tough woman can be. A hundred years ago, when women were considered (by most Americans, anyway—including most American women) to be weak and feeble, there were only a handful of women police in the United States, and all had restricted duties, such as doing clerical work or guarding skating rinks and other places frequented by women and children. None wore uniforms or carried guns; none went on patrol. Now there are more than one hundred thousand full-time female law-enforcement officers in the United States, including 15 percent of the police officers in New York City; they're serving side-by-side with men in just about every dangerous job there is.[17]

We've fictionalized—and thus legitimized—the courageous female cop in dozens of recent films, most notably, *Fargo*, in which Frances McDormand played a

pregnant police officer who foiled a kidnap plot. Movies like *Charlie's Angels* and *Lara Croft* have further solidified our reverence for the female hero—a far, far cry from honoring Betsy Ross for sewing some stars on a flag.

The changing roles of women in our society demonstrate two important points that are relevant to the perspective I've been developing in this book: first, people whom we universally consider to be weak, incompetent, feeble, and desperately in need of our protection might actually have the potential to be strong, heroic, courageous, tough, and independent. Second, as a society, we are sometimes capable of changing our perspective quite radically .

Which brings me, finally, to "child" soldiers.

G. I. JOHNNY

I don't think there should be any soldiers. I find the very concept of war to be repugnant. I'm also opposed to all forms of exploitation and abuse—of workers, children, women, blacks, soldiers, or anyone else. But this is a book about human potential and competence, and so, once again, I ask that you put aside your preconceptions about young people and look with fresh eyes at a controversial topic.

UNICEF estimates that there are approximately 250,000 "child soldiers" in the world, mostly in developing nations such as Sierra Leone, Liberia, Congo, Sudan, Sri Lanka, and Burma.[18] I have "child" in quotes because UNICEF defines "child" as anyone under eighteen, no matter how mature, large, strong, competent, motivated, informed, or experienced that person might be. If we choose to define "child" as someone under thirteen—a defensible idea—the number of child soldiers drops considerably, to perhaps sixty thousand.[19]

Young males have fought in military battles through much of human history. We don't even flinch when we tell our children the story of how young David slew Goliath, an enormous Philistine soldier, with a sling and stone. According to the book of *Samuel*, King Saul gave David his own armor to wear in his battle with Goliath, but David was so small that he had to remove it because it was too heavy for him to carry. After Goliath fell, David took Goliath's sword and stabbed him with it. Then he cut the giant's head off. Call this excessive, if you like, but you certainly can't dispute David's competence as a soldier.

Some speculate that the minimum age of military service increased in stages as weapons and armor got heavier over a period of many centuries;

233

WOMEN IN ACTION

Constable on Ice

Kate Wheatley, a thirty-four year old constable from South Yorkshire, England, was honored in 1999 for saving a young man from what would have been a horrible drowning in an ice cold lake the previous year. In what a fellow officer called "the most brave and selfless act that I have seen in my thirty years' police experience," Wheatley jumped into a near-frozen lake to swim out to a twenty-year-old man who was flailing his arms and sinking. After she towed him to shore and administered mouth-to-mouth resuscitation, he coughed up a large amount of water before finally starting to breath. Wheatley was given the Royal Humane Society Award for her efforts.[20] *Take that, Queen Victoria.*

young people simply couldn't handle armor or a heavy sword. But today's relatively lightweight AK-47s and M16s have not only leveled the battlefield for men and women, they've also made it easy for very young people to be effective soldiers.[21] Quite simply, if you can follow orders, carry a weapon, aim it well and pull the trigger, you've got the right stuff. If, as a bonus, you're small, nimble, and fast, you might even survive to fight another day; the smaller and faster the target, the harder it is to hit.

Young Soldiers Around the World

In countries where war has spanned generations, like Liberia or various countries in the Middle East, young people are groomed for war almost from birth. In some Arab countries, young children are indoctrinated about the glories of martyrdom, and as teenagers they sometimes serve, all too effectively, as human bombs. A recent Associated Press report from Saudi Arabia (where half the population is under eighteen) indicates that young people aren't just mindless walking bombs; they're also playing a key role in planning terrorist attacks. According to the report, of twelve people recently rounded up for planning a major attack on Mecca, six were under eighteen years old.[22]

And it isn't only third-world or Arab nations that create military-minded young people. As a United Nations website reports:

...the United States Pentagon sponsors programs for approximately four hundred thousand high school boys and girls [sic] where children [sic] are taught to march, shoot, act and think like soldiers. More than half of all European States accept under eighteen-

year-olds in their armed forces. The United Kingdom routinely sends seventeen-year-olds into combat. According to their official statistics from January 1999, there was a total of 6,676 male and female sixteen- and seventeen-year-olds, and over 128,000 cadets from the ages of ten to sixteen in training schools around the country. Similarly, military schools are a common feature across Latin America, Asia, and Africa.[23]

Civil War historian James McPherson notes that some Southerners in the United States still celebrate the heroic actions of a Confederate battalion of two hundred young solders—ages fifteen to seventeen—that helped rout Union forces at the Battle of New Market in 1864.[24] The minimum age of conscription was set nationwide at eighteen at the outset of the Spanish-American War (1898) and has been raised and lowered several times since then;[25] the minimum age of *service* is typically lower than the conscription age and wasn't set at eighteen until World War I.[26]

According to Ilene Cohn and Guy S. Goodwin-Gill, authors of *Child Soldiers: The Role of Children in Armed Conflicts*, modern young people, like adults, want to live meaningful lives, and the "ability to project a meaningful future for themselves is... powerfully and intimately tied up with their role in [military] conflict." In 1990, recruiters in Liberia were reportedly "overwhelmed" by volunteer street children who wanted to "get up to Nimba County and *do* something for their country."[27]

Young people can also adopt and defend political beliefs from a surprisingly early age.[28] Neil Boothby and John Humphrey, writing in a volume compiled by the United States Committee for Refugees, noted that:

> *...even younger children...are capable of what psychologists refer to as intuitive political thinking, not only showing evidence of socialization, but of idiosyncratic yet imaginative political opinions as well. Through their endless series of why questions, children as young as three-year-old begin to make rudimentary inquiries into social inequities they spot outside the home, and in doing so, can challenge their own parents' complacent ways. This innate curiosity of children is heightened when they are uprooted from their home and communities. Everyday struggles for food, shelter and other basic necessities can make their need to comprehend—and, at times, to act—even more pressing.*[29]

Like David, young soldiers are often quite effective. According to one report, the young soldiers—under age sixteen—in the "liberating" forces that overthrew President Obote in Uganda in 1986 were "disciplined, reliable and trustworthy," and a UNICEF representative in Uganda in 1985 described such soldiers as "highly motivated, reliable and dedicated."[30] According to a report by the BBC World

> # YOUNG PEOPLE IN ACTION
>
> ## English Army Routed by Teen
>
> *By the early 1400s, during the Hundred Years' War, the English had occupied much of northern France (including Paris) for decades. In 1429, seventeen-year-old Joan of Arc (Jeanne d'Arc) commanded a French army that was sent to free the city of Orléans, which the English had held under siege for eight months. Joan's army lifted the siege in only eight days. Just a few weeks later, Joan's soldiers, joined by reinforcements, overwhelmed the English forces at Patay, and the following month, Joan, now known as the Maid of Orléans, gained control of Reims, the traditional coronation site of the French monarchy. This allowed the long-delayed crowning of King Charles VII to take place. The recovery of Orléans and coronation of King Charles greatly boosted French morale during this dark period in French history. Captured in battle in 1430, Joan was subjected to fourteen months of harsh imprisonment and interrogation before being burned at the stake in 1431.[32]*

Service, "The smallest boys are placed closest to the enemy. In war, they are said to be fearless."[31] Presumably, that's why young people are conscripted in the first place. No commander in his (or *her*) right mind would deliberately take on soldiers who are incapable of winning.

Two of the highest ranking soldiers in the world in 2003 were the notorious Htoo twins, Johnny and Luther, age twelve, the leaders for a while of the brutal and effective "God's Army" in Myanmar (formerly, and sometimes currently, known as Burma). It would take another whole chapter to lay out the complex politics of the situation properly, but here is a thumbnail: The junta that rules Myanmar has recently, and largely to make money, been obliterating troublesome members of a tribe of people in Myanmar called the Karen, many of whom have fled to Thailand. The Christian faction of the Karen have been fighting back using guerilla tactics, and one segment of their forces, "God's Army," was led, up until recently, by the Htoos, who, according to their largely-teenage followers, were "unbeaten in battle, immune to gunfire and can disarm landmines with their thoughts." After some of God's forces took two hundred people hostage at a Thai hospital to protest the Thai shelling of Karen citizens inside Myanmar's border, Thai forces reportedly stormed the hospital, stripped the Karen soldiers naked, and shot them all in cold blood. Luther and Johnny were not among the dead and eventually fled to India and then to Thailand.[33]

Despite the risks, armies like God's Army provide significant benefits to some young people. In Guatemala and El Salvador in the 1980s and early 1990s, young people by the thousands joined rebel forces in part because such enlistment was voluntary, whereas service in the government's army was mandatory. According to Cohn and Goodwin-Gill:

> We interviewed a sixteen-year-old ex-FMLN-combatant [from El Salvador] who had joined at age thirteen. His brother had joined years earlier but this boy's [sic] deciding moment came when he escaped forced recruitment into the [government] army. "I know that once the army recruits you, you are kept in by force, you need permission to visit your family and permission is rarely given. It's better to join a voluntary organization, where permission to visit your family is at least possible." The FMLN also provided a social support structure, validation, discipline, respect and protection to many kids [sic]....[34]

Abuse and Exaggeration

Armies have a deadly purpose; they're more than just a "support structure." UNICEF estimates that in the 1990s alone two million people under age eighteen were killed in armed conflicts, with four-to-five million disabled and ten million "psychologically traumatized" (not all were soldiers).[35] War's toll on adults is also devastating, of course.

Headlines also remind us of the ways in which young people in some countries are coerced into service—in some cases kidnapped, drugged, raped, and kept as virtual prisoners in military camps—sometimes with government forces and sometimes with the rebels (in some countries these forces swap places every few years).

One such soldier, China Keitetsi, who says she entered military service at age nine in Uganda in 1986, wrote about her brutal life as a young soldier in a book published in South Africa in 2002.[36] In recent years she has, through a website, lectures, and media appearances, made herself an icon of the abuse of "child soldiers."

Although there is no doubt that there are many abused young soldiers around the world, key aspects of Keitetsi's story have been credibly disputed by the Ugandan government. Her former commander says she never fought any battles, and there is considerable question about her age. There is evidence that she may have been seventeen when she joined the rebel forces (now Uganda's regular army), and it appears that she enlisted voluntarily. When she fled Uganda in the mid 1990s, she left behind a son she had with a rebel commander. After that, she lived in South Africa, where she had and subsequently abandoned a daughter she had with another man. She now lives in Denmark, protected by the United Nations High Commissioner for Refugees.

In both South Africa and Denmark, Keitetsi claimed and was granted refu-

---

YOUNG PEOPLE IN ACTION

Saving Dad

On a dark New England night in May 2004, Christopher Duarte and six members of his family were out boating, when the winds picked up suddenly and their small motor boat capsized. Fourteen-year-old Chris swam in fifty-degree water for between sixty and ninety minutes to reach the Rhode Island shore to find help. He had last seen his mom—with no life jacket on—clinging to a fender of the boat. He banged on the door of the first house he found and pleaded for help. His mom was found alive but died shortly after being rescued. The boy's aunt, her boyfriend, and one of Chris's cousins drowned. Chris's dad survived.[37]

---

gee status, even though she admits to having fought for the forces that now *rule* Uganda; this is odd, given that refugees are normally the ones on the losing side. Meanwhile, UNICEF, which has been campaigning for years to forbid the use of "children" as soldiers—no matter how well they may perform, no matter what their motivations, and no matter how bleak their alternatives—is using Keitetsi for promotional purposes.[38]

Gangs: Our Own "Child" Soldiers

Perhaps all of this seems remote and foreign; Liberia and Uganda and Myanmar are far away, after all, and have little in common with the United States, and it's been a long time since the Civil War. But there are young people serving in paramilitary organizations on our own cities' streets.

Gangs, after all, are military groups, complete with weapons, ranks, charismatic leaders, territories, spies, codes of behavior, insignia, and more (see Chapter Five). Gangs are typically led by an older, hardcore criminal and typically have between three and five levels of membership, each with different names and privileges. In Los Angeles County, it's believed that there are nearly 300 chapters of the Blood and Crip gangs alone, and these gangs are believed to have chapters in more than 100 United States cities. In 1998, there were about 150,000 gang members in Los Angeles County—more people than there are in the armies of many small countries. Gangs have strict codes of behavior; members must follow orders—even to kill—or face extreme punishments, including death. Gangs also take care of the needs of their members—mainly the need for safety and protection.[39]

Like it or not, "child soldiers" exist in very large numbers within our own borders.

ON THEIR OWN

In William Golding's classic work of fiction, *The Lord of the Flies*, a group of boys ages twelve and under became brutal, savage, nearly mindless killers after being stranded on an island for several months. Toward the middle of the tale, in a scene straight out of the deep recesses of Sigmund Freud's psyche, boys surrounded a help-less, disoriented boy named Simon while chanting, *"Kill the beast! Cut his throat! Spill his blood!"* Then they "struck, bit, tore" with "teeth and claws" until Simon was dead.[40] At the end of the book, when the boys were finally rescued, Ralph, the nominal leader of the group, broke down crying, lamenting "the end of innocence" and "the darkness of man's heart," and his companions soon joined him in weeping.[41]

Two aspects of Golding's story are interesting in the present context. First, the story is an acknowledgment that young people can be both tough and self-sufficient, at least when adults aren't around to take care of them. And second, Golding's characters *never* broke down, no matter what crazy things were happen-ing in their savage world, *until the adults showed up*. They behaved strangely or cru-elly at times, but they were *never* childlike—until they were expected to be.

Other fictional examples like this come easily to mind: Gavroche and his siblings in *Les Miserables* lived for many months on the streets of Paris without any contact with their heartless parents, and Clint Eastwood's mesmerizing character in *Unforgiven* simply walked away from his farm, leaving his young children there with some general advice like "take care of things"; apparently they did. But what happens to real young people when they don't have access to adults?

Young Heads of Households

The recent turmoil in Rwanda left many thousands of young people without parents and with few resources. Here are reports, from a radio broadcast, of three young people who ended up as reluctant heads of households:

> *Rose, thirteen years old: "After the genocide, our family fled to eastern Zaire.... My parents and two of my brothers got sick and they died. My older brother, my little sister and I ended up in Kisangani in Congo and we were repatriated by the UN in May 1997.... My older brother and I now farm our plot of land. No one helps us.... My little brother who's ten, goes to school. I used to go to school but I decided to stop. I was so hungry all the time that I couldn't study or concentrate, so I thought it would be better to work."*
>
> *Claudine, sixteen years old: "I have four younger brothers and sisters. They are fifteen, thirteen, five and three years old. After my mother died, we went to live with my*

> ## YOUNG PEOPLE IN ACTION
>
> ### He Can Do Anything
>
> *Nine-year-old Semaj Booker didn't like living in Lakewood, Washington, and he was determined to get to Texas. According to reports in January 2007, including an interview with his mother on television's "Inside Edition," Semaj, a frequent runaway, first stole a car and led police on a high-speed chase. Just hours after he was returned to his home, he made his way to a local airport and used a false name to board two successive Southwest Airlines flights terminating in San Antonio, where he was taken into custody by local authorities. His mother said she was stunned but also proud: "He just showed me that, 'Mom, I'm going to achieve anything I want to do. I'm going to just do it.'"*

grandmother. We are still with her but she's old and sick. So I have to support her and my four brothers and sisters. I worry a lot about tomorrow and whether I'll be able to feed my family."

Hawas, seventeen years old: "I had five brothers and sisters. Two of them died. The ones who are still alive are sixteen, fifteen, and eight years old. Our parents were beaten to death. All my aunts and uncles and other relatives were murdered too. So we're alone now. We manage to get by but we don't have enough money to eat more than once a day. The one-year-old you see here belongs to me. When we were in Zaire I was raped. I love the child despite how he was conceived. I can't abandon him." [42]

In all, there are at least 65,000 households headed by teens in Rwanda, with an average of five people per household; that's more than 325,000 children and teens living on their own with minimal resources. [43] If they had access to more resources, they would presumably be living much better. But the point is that they are indeed living—and working and eating and, in some cases, even going to school.

Surviving without Mom

Even pre-teens are somehow able to survive without adults. According to a news report, when Travis Butler's mother died in November 1999 in their East Memphis, Tennessee, apartment, he was afraid to tell anyone because he was sure he'd be put into foster care. So he continued for more than a month to dress himself and brush his hair, to go to school every day (he was never tardy), to cook frozen dinners, soup, and cereal, to do basic food shopping, and to do his homework. He even did a passable job of forging his mother's signature on school papers and on his report card.

After a month of this, a family friend stopped by, and Travis, under pressure,

---

YOUNG PEOPLE IN ACTION

A Very Deep Sleep

Alerted by concerned school officials, police in a suburb of Grand Rapids, Michigan, recently searched an apartment and found the decomposed body of a young mother. A short time later, her six-year-old son trotted in, saying he had been outside playing. In fact, his mom had collapsed and died three weeks earlier. The boy, thinking his mom was asleep, simply carried on: eating breakfast cereal, going out to play, and tucking himself in bed. He was dirty and hungry when found but otherwise in good health and spirits.[44]

spilled the beans. Before that, absolutely no one had suspected anything was wrong. Travis was sent to live with his mother's parents in Mississippi and apparently is still doing fine. Travis Butler was nine years old when all this took place. [45]

The Lost Boys of Sudan

Travis' story isn't as unique as you might think. In the late 1980s when government troops attacked dozens of villages in Sudan, more than *twenty thousand boys*, as young as three or four and generally not much older than twelve, left their homes on foot on a quest to find the promised land: refugee camps in Ethiopia. Life turned out to be so harsh there that most of those who had made it to Ethiopia continued on to Kakuma, Kenya, which they reached in 1992 (by which time many of the marchers were in their teens).

Dubbed by the press the "Lost Boys of Sudan," the lucky ones walked several thousand miles with little food or water, living mainly off leaves and roots. It's believed that as many as eleven thousand of them died along the way—victims of starvation, drowning, crocodiles, snakes, lions, hyenas, bombs, or malaria.

In 2001, the United Nations flew forty-five hundred of the survivors to the United States, where they've been settled in roughly twenty-eight cities around the country, assisted by various U.N., government, and religious organizations. News reports since the 1980s have often spoken of the extraordinary optimism of these boys and young men, no matter what challenges they faced on their long journey to safety (see box, next page). [46]

Set aside the horror of this story, and think about how blatantly the Lost Boys challenge our preconceptions about young people. Nearly half of the Lost Boys survived years of unimaginable hardships with virtually no adult help, while exhibiting considerably more style, courage, and optimism than Golding envisioned in *Flies*. It's almost impossible for the modern American mind to conceive of such strength

YOUNG PEOPLE IN ACTION
"You Walk until Your Time Comes"

Mamer Ajak thinks he's now twenty-three or twenty-four. In 1987 when he was seven or eight he and other children from his village fled the violence that was killing their neighbors and family members in Sudan and joined a march of more than 20,000 boys who had come to believe that life would be better in Ethiopia. Here's what Mamer told me:

I had three siblings, but I was the only one left. I took off because I could run. It took three months to get to Ethiopia. Boys ahead of us would find a pool of water, and sometimes they would drink it all. We would eat the mud they left behind. For food, we ate dry roots and dry leaves—we knew which plants to eat. We generally stayed with groups from our villages, but there were some who were truly lost, walking with anybody. And some were grownup—maybe thirteen.

We didn't know where we were going exactly. But we were walking away from the bombs.

One time I hid myself in the brush, and an older boy found some water and brought it back to where I was hiding. I was going too slow, but he kept me going.

In Ethiopia, life was not much better because there was no community there to receive us or care for us. We were caring for ourselves. Each one of us was responsible for the other. When someone died, we took care of the burying. Back home, with five people digging, the graves were ten feet deep, but we couldn't do that. Sometimes it would rain, and the water would wash the tops off the graves and you could see the dead bodies. Some people didn't even get buried because everyone was so weak.

We built our own shelters and took turns cooking and looking for grass and getting water. We made schedules, and they needed to be followed. We organized ourselves into groups of twelve, and we took turns being the leaders and representing our group in the larger one. As people got older, they got more responsibilities. We did what needed to be done.

To American teens, I say: Don't look at the obstacles. Problems shape us to be better in our lives. If you are alive, you can do anything. You walk until your time comes.

Mamer was flown by the United Nations to the United States in 2001. He's now studying international affairs and business administration at Point Loma Nazarene University in San Diego.

in people so young. To us, even post-pubescent teens are still helpless children, and even twenty-year-olds aren't mature enough to make decisions about alcohol.

PERFORMANCE THROUGH THE AGES

Teens are at or near the peak of perfection in many ways, and we spend much our lives from our twenties or thirties onward in a state of decline. I already reviewed data along these lines pertaining to memory, thinking, and judgment in Chapter Seven. Now let's look at some basic physical abilities.

As infants, we start life weak and helpless, but, as evolution demands, we grow rapidly and become highly capable beings shortly after puberty. As I noted in Chapter One, we *must* be highly capable by the time we're capable of producing children; if not, our children will have little chance of survival.

Our vision, hearing, and sense of smell are all extremely keen by our early teens; they peak by our mid teens and decline steadily and dramatically from our late teens until we die. [47] (See Figure 9.1.) The pattern of changes in our sense of touch is even more dramatic given that young children appear to be even more sensitive than teens; in other words, the decline seems fairly steady over the entire life span. [48]

Simple reaction time (SRT)—the speed with which we're able to react to simple stimuli—follows the same pattern as the major senses: it's slow in childhood, then speeds up as we near puberty, peaks in the late teens, and declines steadily thereafter. By age thirteen or so, SRT is within 10 percent or so of its peak value; from about age thirty on, we never again are capable of reacting as swiftly as we did at age thirteen. [49] In Chapter Seven we saw this same pattern in the speed with which people respond to more complex stimuli. These patterns of change in reaction time are especially notable when one considers that reaction time is correlated with intelligence (on some tests), and reaction time also helps us respond effectively to threats, emergencies, and so on.

As you might expect, when physiologists look for physical correlates of these patterns of change, they find them. For example, in a study conducted in the 1930s, researchers counted the number of nerve fibers present in various spinal nerves and found that the number of fibers was small in young children, peaked during the teens years, and declined thereafter (diagram G, Figure 9.1). [50] Body fat follows the opposite pattern: It's high when we're children and low when we're in our teens, and then it tends to increase gradually through most of our adult years. [51] Overall, teens are in enviably good physical condition, which is, sadly, one of the reasons we send them off to war.

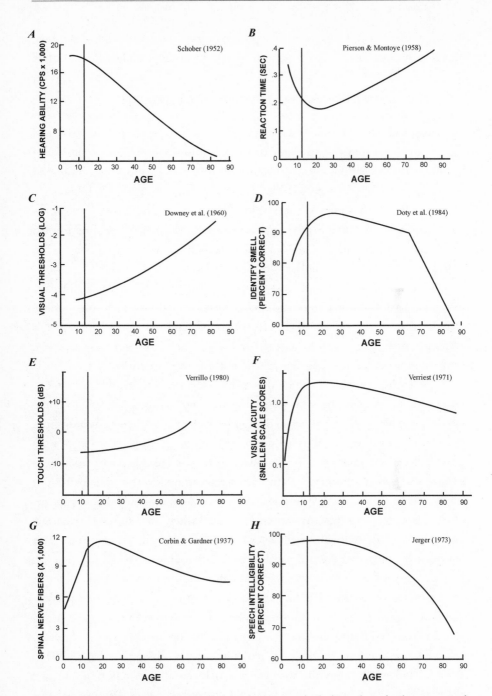

Figure 9.1. Physical Performance by Age. Each graph represents the findings of a study of some aspect of performance. The vertical line to the right of the y-axis marks the approximate onset age for puberty. Note that for each ability, young teens are either at or near the peak of possible performance and that once we're past age thirty or so, we never again perform as well as we did in our early teens.

The only significant exception to this rule is muscle mass. It's not until puberty that we're capable of accumulating significant amounts of muscle mass. Body builders can continue to bulk up into their twenties and thirties, but eventually, even muscle mass begins its inevitable decline.[52] Actor-politician Arnold Schwarzenegger shrunk to about half his muscular size between Terminators 1 and 3.

When you add the superior physical abilities of teens to their exceptional cognitive abilities, you should end up with a highly capable group of people. These capabilities exist even when they're not expressed.

RESILIENCE

Anne Frank had just turned thirteen when she, her sister and parents, and several family friends went into hiding behind a factory in Amsterdam in July 1942. The Nazis had occupied Holland for two years by that time, and Jews were being "called up" in large numbers—stripped of their belongings and shipped off in cattle cars to almost certain death. Anne and her family and companions lived confined and in constant fear for more than two years, getting increasingly disturbing news about the fates of their former neighbors and friends and about the progress of the war. Anne's diary, left on the floor of her "Secret Annexe" after the police finally raided it on August 4, 1944, has become one of the most widely read books of all time.

In a series of "letters" to Kitty, a fictitious friend—mainly about day-to-day life in hiding—Anne reveals herself to be a remarkably perceptive, intelligent, and courageous young woman, determined to make her mark on the world. In perhaps the most moving part of the diary, written in April 1944, Anne recounts a terrifying two days after burglars broke open a large hole in the building in which she and her family were living. The burglars were scared off, but the commotion and hole attracted both neighbors and police. Officers walked through the building several times, just managing to miss the secret cupboard door that led to the rooms were Anne and her companions were huddling.

But Anne's record of this incident is not that of a frightened little girl. Quite the contrary. The stress of this incident makes her more thoughtful and determined than ever:

> Who has inflicted this upon us? Who has made us Jews different from all other people? Who has allowed us to suffer so terribly up till now? It is God that has made us as we are, but it will be God, too, who will raise us up again. If we bear all this suffering and if there are still Jews left, when it is over, then Jews, instead of being doomed, will be held

up as an example. Who knows, it might even be our religion from which the world and all peoples learn good, and for that reason and for that reason only do we have to suffer now....

Be Brave! Let us remain aware of our task and not grumble, a solution will come, God has never deserted our people. Right through the ages there have been Jews, through all the ages they have had to suffer, but it has made them strong too; the weak fall, but the strong will remain and never go under! [53]

Anne emerges through her diary as the strongest and most mature of her companions in hiding—stronger emotionally than any of the adults. She ends her description of the burglar incident by comparing herself to her mother:

I am becoming still more independent of my parents, young as I am, I face life with more courage than Mummy; my feeling for justice is immovable, and truer than hers. I know what I want, I have a goal, an opinion, I have a religion and love. Let me be myself and then I am satisfied. I know that I'm a woman, a woman with inward strength and plenty of courage.

If God lets me live, I shall attain more than Mummy ever has done, I shall not remain insignificant, I shall work in the world and for mankind! [54]

Anne did make her mark, but it was not by following through on her plans. She was sent by the Gestapo to the concentration camp at Bergen-Belsen, where she was put to death in March, 1945, just two months before Holland was liberated by Allied forces. [55]

Strength through Adversity

For several decades now, mental health professionals have been fascinated by people like Anne Frank—people who are nearly unfazed by adversity, or who overcome it to become stronger people. Though media reports would suggest otherwise, "child abuse" doesn't always ruin people's lives. In many cases, children who suffer great adversity are somehow able to overcome it, sometimes even emerging as especially strong, independent, highly-functioning individuals. Some of the most successful people in the world—President Bill Clinton, talk-show host Oprah Winfrey, and actress Suzanne Somers come immediately to mind—appear to have been strengthened by the adversity they faced in childhood. Some experts believe that exposure to severe stressors when we're young might have a kind of "inoculating effect," protecting us from stressors in the future. [56]

In recent years, mental health professionals have settled on the term "resilient" to describe people who flourish after experiencing great difficulties. Sports fans might say they have "heart," a term my son Julian introduced me to years ago when he was taking boxing lessons. "Heart," he explained, "is what you have if someone beats the crap out of you and knocks you down, but that just makes you get up again and fight harder." You don't just get up and wobble; you're somehow made stronger by your fall.

There are two distinct camps of resilience experts. One camp, exemplified by psychologists such as Norman Garmezy of the University of Minnesota, believes that resilience is a relatively fixed personality trait, and the other, exemplified by Frederic Flach of Cornell University, believes that resilience can be learned. These aren't necessarily incompatible viewpoints. Our genes predispose us to react in somewhat fixed ways to the world (these are, roughly, our "traits"), and our predispositions are, over the course of our lives, fine-tuned in varying degrees by our experiences (that's the role that learning plays in making us who we are). There's no question that resilience can be learned, but it's not yet clear how to teach it or to what extent it can be taught.

For now, we can put the nature-nurture debate aside. Some children and teens—and, for that matter, some adults—are incredibly resilient; that we know for sure. In recent decades researchers have studied Holocaust survivors, people who were sexually or physically assaulted as children, children of mentally ill parents, children who have endured great poverty, children who lost one or both parents, and children who have survived severe physical traumas, deformities, or diseases. Investigators watch for the resilient survivors and trying to understand their success. At least three long-term studies of resilience have been underway for many years: the Kauai Longitudinal Study, Project Competence, and the Rochester Child Resilience Project, together covering over a thousand people. The point of all this research is to find out what makes resilient people tick, and then, if possible, to find ways of helping at-risk children to become more resilient. Here are the findings of some major studies on resilient teens:

- In a 1988 study, William R. Beardslee and Donna Podorefsky of Children's Hospital, Boston, conducted interviews with resilient teens who were the offspring of parents suffering from severe depression or bipolar disorder. Focusing on eighteen high-functioning teens, they found that these individuals tended to be "doers and problem-solvers" and to be highly self-aware. They didn't blame themselves for their parents' deficiencies, and they had no trouble distinguishing between their

parents' problems and their own. Of special note, as a group they tended to be highly independent, self-sufficient people, and, in some cases, the teens were even the caregivers for their parents. [57]

- In a 1991 report, Lily Hechtman of the Montreal Children's Hospital reviewed a number of studies of people who had been diagnosed with attention deficit hyperactivity disorder (ADHD) as children. Hechtman found that many teens flourished after having suffered from this disorder (and, of course, having suffered from a diagnosis that many consider to be of questionable value). The resilient teens tended to have positive temperaments (like Anne Frank), above average intelligence, and good relationships with their peers and family members. They also tended, like the subjects in the Beardslee study, to be independent, self-sufficient people. [58]

- A number of recent studies of the offspring of divorce find that, although divorce is generally harmful for children and teens, perhaps as many as 65 to 75 percent of the offspring of divorce seem virtually unaffected by the experience; like Julian's boxer friends, in some cases those young people even seem strengthened by their fall. The data aren't all in on such people, but generally, the resilient young survivors of divorce seem to have many of the same characteristics as other resilient people: They "think positive"; they don't blame themselves for the breakup; they distinguish their parents' problems from their own; they have intact sources of social support; and they're relatively autonomous. [59]

Learning to Be Resilient

We've seen resilient young people throughout this chapter: the Lost Boys of the Sudan, the "child" soldiers of Uganda, the resourceful nine-year-old who lived on his own after this mother died, the dedicated young athletes who ignore the pain and keep on trying. Resilience among the young is easy to find when you look for it.

But resilience is almost certainly more than just a fixed trait. Our environments and our learning experiences help make us resilient. Social support, the right role models, and so on, help make us strong. What's more, if theorists like Michael Rutter of Kings College, London, are right, resilience itself might be produced or at least strengthened by *stressors* introduced in our lives at just the right times and in just the right measures; in other words, resilience itself might be the result of a series of appropriate "stress inoculations." [60]

When it comes to today's teens, this worries me. The artificial extension of childhood is, after all, a *protective* mechanism. Those who engineered it, like the forceful Jane Addams, were trying to protect the young from harm; at first it was the harm of the factories, but over the decades, things have gotten out of hand. If we shelter our precious young from stress, from work, from criticism, from failure, and from life on their own—in short, from *adulthood*—aren't we making them less able to cope with the inevitable challenges of life? Aren't we making them less resilient?

The evidence for the "toughness" of teens is, in my view, overwhelming. Again, I need to emphasize that I'm not talking about your everyday teen in modern Brentwood. I'm talking, as I have throughout this volume, about human potential. I'm convinced that many or most teenagers are capable of facing the rigors of athletics, the atrocities of war, and the vicissitudes of life with as much or more determination as any adult. They're capable of feeling genuine patriotism, of showing great courage, and of exercising real leadership. When beaten down, they're capable of bouncing back with fortitude equal to that of any adult. When we infantilize our teens, we might not see these capabilities expressed, but they exist nonetheless.

As for the resilience of young people, I'll let fifteen-year-old Anne Frank have the last word:

> It's really a wonder that I haven't dropped all my ideals, because they seem so absurd and impossible to carry out. Yet I keep them, because in spite of everything I still believe that people are really good at heart. I simply can't build up my hopes on a foundation consisting of confusion, misery, and death. I see the world gradually being turned into a wilderness, I hear the ever approaching thunder, which will destroy us too, I can feel the sufferings of millions and yet, if I look up into the heavens, I think that it will all come right, that this cruelty too will end, and that peace and tranquility will return again.
>
> In the meantime, I must uphold my ideals, for perhaps the time will come when I shall be able to carry them out. [61]

Q: *It's bad enough that we're allowing women to serve in combat roles in the military. Are you suggesting that we put fifteen-year-old boys and girls at risk on the battlefield?*

A: As women have rightly maintained for many decades, as competent individuals it should be up to them to decide what risks they want to take. Their opportunities shouldn't be limited just because someone mistakenly believes all women are frail. The military is a domain in which competency is routinely measured and highly valued. The Marines don't take just anyone; they take people who pass rigorous tests and who meet stringent criteria. If G. I. Jane can measure up, doesn't she deserve a chance to serve our country? And if a fifteen-year-old can also pass those tests, understands the risks and rewards of service, and in other respects is competent to make decisions, doesn't he or she also deserve a chance to serve our country?

Chapter 10
Young People Are Creative

Cuz I flow
Better when my colors show.
—Avril Lavigne, *"Nobody's Fool"*

Overview. *Creative expression is common among pre-school children; it peaks again during the teen years and then tends to decline throughout adulthood. When teens have been allowed to express their creativity in meaningful ways, they have made extraordinary contributions. The Braille system of reading, the Colt revolver, and many other inventions were the offspring of young people. In literature, renowned writers such as Mary Shelley, William Blake, and Edgar Allan Poe started their careers in their teens, and many great composers—Felix Mendelssohn, George Bizet, and Franz Schubert, for example—also started young. Before the twentieth century, it was also not unusual for young people to make outstanding contributions in the field of mathematics. Although the modern world makes it extremely difficult for teens to contribute, a few— like choreographer Wade Robson and artist Alexandra Nechita—have managed to break through. Generally prohibited from operating in the business world, teens have also managed to create hundreds of non-profit organizations serving a wide variety of social needs. Allowing troubled teens to express their creativity has been shown to help put them back on productive tracks.*

I've been careful in this volume not to focus on prodigies, in part because most people find prodigies intimidating, but mainly because I'm uncomfortable with the concept. Most of the time, a prodigy is just a child with an obsession and an opportunity: an obsession, say, with art or music, and parents or other adults who are willing—or, in some case, determined—to nurture that obsession. Labels, as I've said earlier, are dangerous things, and one of many

problems with the "prodigy" label is that it obscures what's really going on. It implies that the child's performance is magical—beyond the ability of normal mortals to fathom or replicate. It turns us away from a search for the factors that might allow us to understand the extraordinary behavior we're observing. The label itself creates the false impression that we understand, when in fact we usually don't.

I've also shied away from prodigies because the case I'm building is about most or all teens, not about the rare exceptions. At least in some fields—music, art, sports, and chess, for example—the prodigy's magical aura protects him or her from infantilization to some extent. When we recognize that a young person is exceptional, we sometimes relax the rules.

A Prodigious Young Artist

Alexandra Nechita, a Romanian immigrant to the United States and one of the most celebrated young artists in the world today, fits this profile well. As a young child she was obsessed with drawing, often spending three or four hours a day filling every paper in sight. At age six, she shifted to oil paints and acrylics, again with obsessive passion. Her first exhibit, at a community library in Los Angeles, was held when she was eight, and by nine she had completed more than 250 paintings. By age ten, her abstract, Picasso-like works were sometimes fetching $50,000 each.[1]

None of these achievements, needless to say, would have been possible without the full support and cooperation of her parents and other adults. Young people aren't allowed to "pound the pavement" or make "cold calls" in our culture. There are probably more than a few Alexandras suffering through rudimentary arts-and-crafts classes because the adults just aren't paying attention or are hesitant to inform the local art galleries about their latest "discovery."

In a published interview at age ten, Ms. Nechita was asked to explain how she was able to paint so much better than her fellow fourth-graders. With both insight and modesty, she replied, "It's not that my work is so much better than any other kid's. It's that I put so much time into it, like three hours a day."[2] At an exhibit of her works recently, Nechita's mother told me that one of the main reasons Alexandra spent so many hours a day with her art was because her English language skills were poor; for several years she was simply uncomfortable being around other children.

Fortunately, these are issues that don't need to be resolved here. We don't need to decide who is a "prodigy" and who isn't, whether the label is justified,

or even what it means. The basic issue we need to address is a simpler one: Are teens in general more or less creative than adults? The answer, I believe, is clear, and it provides yet another reason for being concerned about the artificial extension of childhood.

THE UNIVERSALITY OF CREATIVITY

Laboratory and field research I've been conducting for more than twenty-five years has convinced me that creative potential is universal.[3] The frequency with which people express creativity varies greatly, but the potential for creative expression seems more-or-less equal in everyone, at every age. If the potential is equal, why could Edison produce more than a thousand inventions whereas the rest of us can barely change a light bulb? How was Alexander Calder, the creator of the mobile, able to produce more than twenty thousand works of art over his life time, whereas the rest of us barely produce more than a few embarrassing doodles? And why does the rate of creative output vary so much over the life span?

A thorough answer to these questions could easily fill the pages of another book, but here is the gist: It's clear that creative potential is universal because there is considerable evidence that the neural mechanisms that underlie creative expression—mechanisms I call "generative"—are intact in all of us. We couldn't get through the day without them. We make our way through new environments easily, which requires us to do things we've never done before; we solve problems, large and small, repeatedly throughout the day; and we exhibit "novelty" in our behavior continuously. Virtually every sentence that we speak or write is new in some way, and, when you look closely enough, it's clear that we don't even brush our teeth the same way twice. We are "generative" organisms, from birth to death.

Then why don't we all invent and write and paint and compose? The culprit here is civilization itself. To make people "civil," we need them to learn to conform to a wide variety of rules and practices, a process social scientists call "socialization." The process starts at birth, and it shifts into high gear when we start school. As I noted in Chapter Six, studies typically show a high rate of creative expression in young children up through kindergarten age (roughly age five). Children are constantly imagining and playing and sculpting and building and drawing, and they seldom "copy"; copying, in fact, is a skill they need to be

YOUNG PEOPLE IN ACTION

Diva at Eleven

Charlotte Church signed her first record deal—with Sony Records, no less—in 1997 when she was eleven. Her first album, "Voice of an Angel," a collection of hymns and folk songs, went double-platinum within a few weeks, and her first three albums have sold more than eight million copies. She has performed for United States presidents, the Pope, and the Queen of England. She had a professional manager at first; then her mom took over. According to recent reports, she has now dumped her mom and is running the show herself. She has also urged Prime Minster Tony Blair to support legislation now being considered by Parliament to lower the minimum voting age from eighteen to sixteen—her current age at this writing. Ironically, even if she gets to vote, she still won't be able to control her own millions, which are being held in trust until she's twenty-one.[5]

taught. They even draw, literally, outside the lines; no one needs to teach a young child to think outside boxes. By the first grade, however, when elementary schools—now competing nationwide to get high "academic performance indices"—dramatically increase the academic load, the frequency of creative expression declines.[4] Daydreaming and silly questions are discouraged, and there just isn't time any more for random play.

Although the frequency of creative expression declines after kindergarten, some studies show that the quality of creative expression actually increases. This is because the content of our creative output is influenced by the knowledge and skills we have; the broader our knowledge and the better our technical skills, the more interesting our creative output will be. That's why significant creative contributions in science, engineering, and the arts often don't occur until people are older; it can easily take a decade or more to master the knowledge and techniques available in any rich domain.

With powerful social forces bearing down, how do *any* of us end up being "creative"? Here's where personality factors come into play—and where we can make an interesting prediction about teenagers. Generally speaking, the children and adults who continue to express creativity at a high rate are the *misfits*—the risk-takers and authority-defyers who resist socialization. The children and adults who refuse to sit at a desk all day and who have trouble following instructions also tend

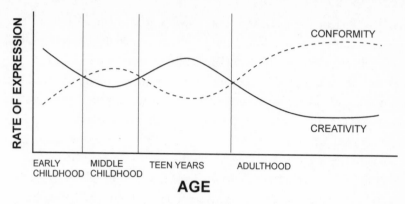

Figure 10.1. Creativity Across the Life Span. Idealized curves showing the course of conformity and creativity over the life span. Young children conform only minimally, and they spend much of their day in imaginative play. In middle childhood, the socialization process is in full swing, and the frequency of creative expression declines dramatically, especially during the so-called fourth-grade slump. During the teen years, conformity is low, and creative output increases. Finally, in adulthood, creativity subsides, on the average, to a fairly low level, and conformity is high.

to be the ones who express their creativity most often. This doesn't mean that they're inherently the most "creative" but rather that in a society that shuts down creative expression through socialization, those who resist socialization are most likely to continue to express their new and crazy ideas. Unfortunately, they're also most likely to end up in jail—or even tied to a stake and set on fire.

Which brings me back to teens. Because under today's outmoded system teenagers are made adversaries of adults, as a group they're all misfits in some sense. They're neither adults nor children, and they'd like to be treated like adults but aren't. They're out of place, and many feel angry about that. They often defy authority, take unusual risks, and so on. The prediction is straightforward: Teens should express *more* creativity on the average than adults do, because the less one conforms to society's rules, the more likely one is to live up to one's creative potential. When we look at teen creativity, that's exactly what we find.

TEEN CREATIVITY: THE UPSIDE OF NONCONFORMITY

A study by Norma Trowbridge and Don C. Charles published in the 1960s is one of the few to compare artistic creativity in young people from ages three to eighteen. Even though very young children spend most of their waking hours

engaged in imaginative play, they don't always score high on tests of artistic creativity, because art is a domain that requires considerable technical skill. Not surprisingly, three-to-five-year olds didn't score quite as high as six-to-eight-year olds in this study, even though the younger children generally have much higher rates of "creative output." But the major finding in this study was the dramatic leap in creativity in the eldest group, young people in the fifteen-to-eighteen-year-old range.[6]

Notably, Trowbridge and Charles also found a dramatic drop in conformity scores in the eldest group. As another researcher, Kennon Sheldon has said, "creativity and conformity don't mix," which is good news for teens.[7] If this same study were conducted today, presumably the nonconformity would start years earlier, and so would the increase in creativity.

So teen rebelliousness does have an upside. It allows teens to ignore social conventions and express their new ideas, no matter what the people around them may think. Unfortunately, when teens start to cross the various lines we've established that separate them from adulthood, they typically start to conform again, and creative output decreases.

Idealized curves showing the inverse relationship between creativity and conformity are shown in Figure 10.1. Notice that creative output is still fairly high in early adulthood but that it declines rapidly. Just how much creativity we'll express and how long we'll continue to express it depends on many factors: how much our profession inhibits or encourages creative contributions (advertising, for example, demands more creativity than accounting does), how much free time we have to ponder and doodle, how skilled we are at stimulating our own creativity (that is, how strong our "creativity competencies" are), how much access we have to physical resources (it's hard to invent rocket ships in one's living room), and so on. Our creative *potential* probably remains constant throughout our lives, but we'll express different amounts and different types of creativity at different stages of life.

World-Class Creativity

Felix Mendelssohn was seventeen when he composed his best-known work, A *Midsummer Night's Dream*, and Mozart had composed four sonatas and a symphony by the time he was eight. According to Walter James Turner, one of Mozart's many biographers, by the time Mozart was ten, he was "an accomplished master of the contemporary craft of composition equal to any living composer of his time."[8] Picasso's first exhibit of paintings took place when he was sixteen. Franz

Schubert's first great work, *"Gretchen am Spinnrade,"* was composed when he was seventeen, and the next year he composed a formidable 143 pieces.[9]

In classical music and art it's tempting to dismiss young contributors as "prodigies," but young people make exceptionally creative contributions in many different fields. The Muppets were created Jim Henson when he was a teen in the early 1950s. They were first broadcast on television in 1954 when Henson was eighteen, and the world-famous "Sesame Street" series began a few years later.[10] Stan Lee, creator of Spiderman, the X-Men, and The Incredible Hulk, among other comic-book legends, published his first comic-book story in an issue of *Captain America* in 1941 when he was seventeen.[11] The English poet, Alfred Tennyson, began writing poetry at age eight and composed a six thousand-line epic poem by age twelve.[12] Waylande Gregory, a major figure in the history of American ceramics, was already an accomplished ceramics maker by age eleven.[13]

Among contemporary people in music, rapper Tupac Shakur started composing when he was fifteen (he was also arrested eight times by the time he was twenty and was murdered a few years later). Vocalist/guitarist Billie Joe Armstrong wrote his first song at fourteen. So did singer Michelle Branch, who also recorded her first CD (on an independent label) when she was seventeen. Singer-songwriter Jewel had her own yodeling act and toured with her father from age six to thirteen; she started writing her own songs at fifteen and cut her first album at nineteen (which included songs she wrote at age seventeen). Stevie Wonder released his first two record albums at age twelve and began co-writing original hit songs by age fourteen. Dancer/choreographer Wade Robson had danced in three of Michael Jackson's music videos by the time he was seven and began directing and choreographing Britney Spears' lavish stage shows when he was sixteen.[14]

Especially notable are the accomplishments of Nikki Reed, who, at thirteen, co-wrote the screenplay of the movie *Thirteen* with director Catherine Hardwicke in only six days during Reed's winter break. *Thirteen*, as I noted earlier, is about the drug- and sex-filled lives of two thirteen-year-olds, based on the real experiences in Reed's life. Evie, Reed's character in the film, quickly corrupts her friend, while her friend's mother, played by Holly Hunter, looks on helplessly. In addition to making her screenwriting and acting debut at fourteen, Reed also moved out of her family home and began living on her own.

Why Teen Creativity Is Especially Notable

The fact that young people sometimes show world-class creativity (in addi-

Young Achievers in Art, Music, Literature, and Invention

Name	Field	Age	Description
Giambattista Della Porta (1543–1615)	Invention	15	Gave the first description of a *Camera Obscura*
Juan Perez de Montalvan (1602–1638)	Literature	17	Wrote *Morir y Disimilar*
John Milton (1608–1674)	Music	15	Wrote hymn, "Let us, with Gladsome Mind"
Antonio de Solis (1610–1686)	Theater	17	Became known with the play *Amor y Obligacion*
Abraham Cowley (1618–1667)	Poetry	15	First poems were published
Geottfried Wilhem von Liebnitz (1646–1716)	Philosophy	17	Wrote *De Principio Individui* on the constitution of individuality Alexander
Pope (1688–1744)	Poetry	17	Wrote his *Pastorals*
Thomas Chatterton (1752–1770)	Poetry	12	Began writing fake medieval poetry that many believed authentic
Wolfgang Amadeus Mozart (1756–1791)	Music	7	Composing at a regular pace
William Blake (1757–1827)	Poetry	12	Began writing poetry that appeared in his first book
William Cullen Bryant (1794–1878)	Poetry	13	Wrote a political satire, *Embargo*
Franz Peter Schubert (1797–1828)	Music	17	Composed the song "Gretchen am Spinnrade"
Mary Shelley (1797–1851)	Literature	10	Published her first poem; began *Frankenstein* at 18
Edgar Allan Poe (1809–1849)	Literature	18	Published first book of poems, included poems written at 12 and 13
Louis Braille (1809–1852)	Invention	12	Invented first version of Braille system of reading; completed at 16
Felix Mendelssohn (1809–1847)	Music	17	Composed his famous *A Midsummer Night's Dream*
Lord Tennyson (1809–1892)	Poetry	12	Wrote a 6,000-line epic poem
Samuel Colt (1814–1862)	Invention	16	Constructed model of multi-round pistol with a revolving barrel
Paul Charles Morphy (1837–1884)	Chess	12	Already recognized as "the best chess player in New Orleans"
George Bizet (1838–1875)	Music	17	Composed his Symphony in C Major
Walter Crane (1845–1915)	Art	17	His picture, "The Lady of Shalott," was exhibited at the Royal Academy
George Parker (1867–1953)	Invention	16	Published his first board game; started Parker Brothers

Young Achievers in Art, Music, Literature, and Invention (continued)

Name	Field	Age	Description
Miles Franklin (1879–1954)	Literature	16	Wrote her first novel *My Brilliant Career*, inspired movie by that name
Pablo Picasso (1881–1973)	Painting	16	Held his first exhibition in the *Café Els Quatre Gats*
Maureen Daly (1921–)	Literature	17	Wrote the teen novel *Seventeenth Summer*
Stan Lee (1922–)	Comics	17	Published "The Traitor's Revenge" in third issue of *Captain America*
Jim Henson (1936–1990)	Television	13	Began developing "Muppet" characters, first on TV when 18
S. E. Hinton (1948–)	Literature	16	Wrote *The Outsiders*
Stevie Wonder (1950–)	Music	14	Cowrote his first hit, "Uptight (Everything's Alright)"
Tupac Shakur (1971–1996)	Music	15	Started rapping under the name MC New York
Billie Joe Armstrong (1972–)	Music	14	Wrote "Why Do You Want Him?"; eventually recorded by Green Day
Kilcher (1974–)	Music	17	Wrote many songs, later on multi-platinum album *Pieces of You*
Wang Yani (1975–)	Painting	13	Her art appears in galleries worldwide
Isaac Hanson (1980–)	Music	16	Released best-selling album "Middle of Nowhere"; main songwriter
Wade Robson (1982–)	Choreography	16	Choreographed and directed Britney Spears' World Tour
Benjamin Lebert (1982–)	Literature	16	Wrote the autobiographical debut *Crazy*
Michelle Branch (1983–)	Music	17	Produced her first album *Broken Bracelet*
Ann Lai (1984–)	Chemistry	16	Developed sensor, monitors sulfur emitted by smokestacks
Julianne Michelle (1984–)	Painting	15	Donates celebrity portraits to charities, worth up to $17,000 each
Alexandra Nechita (1985–)	Painting	8	First gallery exhibit of her paintings
Amelia Atwater-Rhodes (1984–)	Literature	14	Published her first book *In the Forests of the Night*
Esteban Cortazar (1984–)	Fashion	13	Designed his first clothing collection; official line released at 18
Nikki Reed (1988–)	Film	13	Cowrote and starred in *Thirteen*
Chaille Stovall (1989–)	Film	7	Directed first documentary *Boyz in Tights*; other documentaries since
Olivia Bennett (1989–)	Painting	13	Published a collection of her works; recognized by President Bush

YOUNG PEOPLE IN ACTION

Farsighted Twelve-Year-Old

Louis Braille, accidentally blinded by an awl when he was three (he was trying to imitate his dad's use of tools), used a similar instrument when he was twelve to invent the modern system of raised dots used by blind people around the world to read. It took him until age fifteen to perfect the system. Unfortunately, he died (at age forty-one in 1852) too early to see his elegant system gain worldwide acceptance.[15]

tion to showing a relatively high level of creativity in everyday activities), is especially significant for several reasons.

First, experts on creativity generally agree that it takes many years of study to master a domain well enough to be able to make a creative contribution in that domain. Teens are at a disadvantage here, yet they sometimes compensate for their lack of years and rise like stars.

Second, the lives of teens are highly regulated and constrained, which limits the ways in which they can develop and express their creativity. For at least the last hundred years or so, the state has regulated how they spend most of their day and what they learn, and the schools have done little to encourage creative expression. In the modern era of standardized national testing, the schools are doing even less in this regard.

Third, young people have to shout extra loud to be heard. They have no obvious avenues for sharing their creative ideas or products with the rest of the world. It generally takes extraordinary initiative to bring the creations of a young person into the public arena. The Internet is creating new outlets, of course, but sometimes the Internet, in its vastness, allows work that is worthy of the mainstream to stay well hidden in the deep recesses of Cyberspace.

When it comes to the creativity of young people, I find myself asking: how much and what types of creativity would they express if they had more control over their lives? If they could own the fruits of their labor? If they were encouraged to express their creativity? If their lives were less regimented?

I'm particularly intrigued by these questions because, even with all the depression and frustration that's common during the teen years, many teens are also incredibly idealistic. They believe that everything is possible in their lives and in the world. Given that inherent idealism as a starting point, what kinds of

marvelous creativity would teens exhibit in a world that encouraged and rewarded such creativity?

AN EXTRAORDINARY EXPRESSION OF TEEN IDEALISM

The idealism in young people finds expression where it can. Because teens cannot sign contracts or own property, they generally do not form for-profit corporations, but there are fewer roadblocks discouraging them from founding nonprofit, charitable organizations, because these have no stock. (I'll look at for-profit endeavors by teens in the next chapter.)

The idealism of youth is expressed with great sensitivity in a recent film called *Pay It Forward*, starring Helen Hunt, Kevin Spacey, and the talented young actor, Haley Joel Osment, who plays eleven-year-old Trevor. Trevor's social studies teacher (played by Spacey) makes an intriguing suggestion to the class—one person can change the world—and then gives his students a daunting assignment: Make the world a better place. Trevor comes up with a simple but brilliant idea to satisfy the assignment: When someone does you a favor, don't "pay it back"; *pay it forward* to three more people. In other words, do something helpful for other people. The idea spreads quickly throughout his community and ultimately throughout the nation, and Trevor becomes a hero.

The movie, released in the fall of 2000, was based on a fictional book by Catherine Hyde, published in February of that year. A few months later, the author created a real organization, the Pay It Forward Foundation, to "inspire young students to realize that they can change the world." The foundation has provided seed money to more than three hundred schools in the United States, Australia, Canada and other countries to help young people tackle problems like illiteracy, pollution, and homelessness. Alas, although this worthy organization recognizes the special capabilities of young people, it also emphasizes that the Pay It Forward idea "requires adult supervision."[16]

Promoting Charitable Work by Teens

Even more ambitious is an organization called Ashoka, which subsequently spawned an organization called Youth Venture, each founded by social reformer and former MacArthur Foundation Fellow Bill Drayton. Ashoka was founded in 1980 to spread "social entrepreneurship" around the world, and it has since trained more than 1,500 people in fifty-three countries to establish and run charitable organizations. At some point, Drayton noticed that about two-thirds

of the youth-oriented programs founded by Ashoka Fellows were run by or had significant participation by young people:

> For example, young people teaching one another and running school-based businesses in Bangladesh are the heart of a program that has increased enrollments 44 percent and cut the dropout rate in half. In Brazil, street children build and largely run their own schools, and in Indonesia they have created a chain of safe havens.[17]

The next step was obvious: In 1997 Drayton founded Youth Venture, an organization that promotes non-profit entrepreneurship by young people themselves, one major goal being to help them "take greater responsibility for their lives and communities." Drayton notes that hundreds or perhaps even thousands of young people have already founded socially-oriented groups and businesses; more important, he insists that many more would do so "if they could overcome attitudinal barriers and resource constraints." The attitudinal barriers are, of course, flotsam from the artificial extension of childhood, and one might argue that the resource constraints are too. At this writing, Youth Venture has helped young people to create and run more than 150 organizations focusing on topics such as health care for the poor, minority services, urban cleanup, senior services, and autism. (See list on pages 264 and 265.)[18]

As Drayton notes, faced with fewer obstacles than they would encounter in the for-profit world, young people have been creating charitable organizations for a long time. Garrett M. Smith of Oak Park, California, founded one such organization, Kids Who Kare, when he was thirteen. Says Garrett:

> I got the idea to start Kids Who Kare one day when I went to the mall with my friends. I needed some new shoes, so I asked my mom if she would come with us so she could buy the shoes. She had things to do, but she told me that I could take her ATM card and buy the shoes myself. When I was at the register buying my new $80 shoes, it hit me how fortunate I was and how there are kids only fifteen minutes away from where I live that didn't have the same opportunities.[19]

With his mother's encouragement, plus free accounting services arranged through a nonprofit service called The Clearinghouse for Volunteer Accounting Services, Garrett established an organization that provides needy children in the

Los Angeles area with school supplies, clothing, or financial aid for tutors or sports camp. At this writing the organization has twenty-two "core members" and has enlisted the help of more than five hundred volunteers. When I last spoke with Garrett, he was preparing a proposal for President Bush, seeking an endorsement. None of this was easy:

> At first most adults didn't think we were serious and that we would never last. They probably thought that Kids Who Kare would be like the usual kids lemonade stand or car wash. But after a while they realized we were real and they did support us. We didn't get that much help from adults, though, mainly because we didn't want it; this organization is run by teens, and we don't want that to change. The only things that adults do is help us with legal papers and driving. Everything else—the fund raising, the ideas, and the day-to-day business activities—we do ourselves.

Garrett told me that the way his parents raised him had a lot to do with his organizational success: They "expect more than the other parents where I live." He has had his own bank account since he was eight and got his first part-time job when he was twelve. Not surprisingly, Smith said he was pretty sure he could run a for-profit corporation, given the chance.

CREATIVITY AS A THERAPEUTIC TOOL

In a promising report published a few years ago entitled "Better Than Dope," Denver psychology professor Harvey A. Milkman described an innovative approach to helping teens get back on track.[20] They've got energy and talent, he said. Why let them waste their potential on the streets? Why let them resort to drugs to get high? Why not expose them to "natural highs," and what better way to do that than through the arts?

In 1992, with support from the Center for Substance Abuse Prevention, Milkman, with dance theater director Cleo Parker Robinson, founded Project Self-Discovery (PSD), a treatment program with a twist. The main "treatment" is self-expression through visual art, dance, and music. At-risk teens, according to Milkman, "experience traditional talk therapies as invasive and persecutory," whereas "dance connects us to sensuality, music provides a safe vehicle for the expression of emotional unrest," and painting and drawing "provide an opportunity to visualize

Nonprofit Organizations Founded by Young People with Support by Youth Venture

Founder(s)	Age	Organization	Location	Description
Alexandra	14	Assisting AIDS Orphans	Fullerton, CA	Provides food, clothing, and books to AIDS orphans in Africa
Sonia	17	Ayudemonos	Springfield, VA	Promotes organ donation awareness among Hispanics
Don, Christina, & Vanessa	16-17	Bohemian Sun	New Hampshire	A coffee shop that serves as an outlet for artistic expression
Joseph	16	Caring for the Coastal Environment	Pacifica, CA	Spreads awareness of environmental problems and organizes beach cleanup activities
Haewon & Edmond	17	Child Healthcare for Low Income Minorities	New York, NY	Informs people of their eligibility for free or low-cost healthcare
Conn, Paul, & George	15-16	Digital Youth	Pittsburgh, PA	Teaches other students how to film and edit their own video productions
Nancy	17	Earth, Wind, Water, and Fire Awareness with Friends	New York, NY	Promotes environmental awareness in their community
Hydie	17	English as a Second Language	Little Neck, NY	Assists non-English speaking young adults in their language development
Hana	17	Extended Support for Elementary School ESL Students	Poway, CA	A mentor program for elementary school students taking English-as-a-Second-Language
Ijah	17	Filling the Generation Gap	Bronx, NY	Links active teens with senior citizens in need af care & companionship
Chioke	17	Franklin Youth Incentive Project	Seattle, WA	Provides students with community service opportunities
Shannon	17	Girl To Girl	Richmond, VA	Produces a journal written by young women for young women
Azatuhi	17	Giving a Helping Hand	Lynn, MA	Provides tutoring for minority and immigrant students in the third & fourth grade
Alicia	17	Grant Outreach Program	Flint, MI	Informs high school students of financial aid opportunities
Jessica, Rachel, & Ngiste	15	Kids who K.A.R.E. (Kids Autism Research Effort)	Highland Park, IL	Promotes awareness and tolerance of autism and other neurological disorders
Yi	17	LymAware	Abescon, NJ	Educates the public about Lyme disease
Felipe	17	Milestone to Grow	Long Beach, CA	Organizes cleanup of the shores at Long Beach, CA
Tai	17	Neighborhood Cleanup Campaign	Costa Mesa, CA	Organizes trash pickup and recycling in his community
Joshua	17	Outreach Community Program	New York, NY	Tutors fifth and sixth grade students in need of assistance
Cassandra	17	Pesticide Awareness	Marina, CA	Educates the community on the dangers of pesticides

Nonprofit Organizations Founded by Young People with Support by Youth Venture (Continued)

Founder(s)	Location	Age	Organization	Description
Shannon	Florida	14	Pets Awareness With Seniors (PAWS)	Provides support for seniors caring for pets
Henry	Boston, MA	17	Project Outreach	Assists low-income families with affordable daycare
Taylor	Baldwin, NY	17	Respect Our Seniors Everyday (ROSE)	Assists seniors living on fixed incomes
Mohammad	Rowland Heights, CA	16	Rowland Elementary After-School Learning (REAL)	A tutoring and mentor program for elementary school students
Melissa	Westfield, MA	17	SANE Project Expansion	Increases community involvement on environmental issues
Justin	New York, NY	17	Scholarship Search Service	Informs college-bound students about financial aid opportunities
Sophia	Hopewell Junction, NY	17	Seeds of Goodness	Provides seasonal aid to children of migrant workers
Immanuel	Berkeley, CA	16	Select Willard Environmental Education Team (SWEET)	Increases environmental awareness among teens
Peggy	Orange County, CA	17	Sock 'N Sole	Donates socks and shoes to local charities, rescue missions and homeless shelters
Jasmine	Detroit, MI	16	Spic and Span Clean Streets	Organizes weekly cleanups of Detroit streets
Samir	Arlington, VA	17	Street Souljahwear	A clothing line the promotes the artwork and activism of local teens
Teresa	Corona, CA	16	Teens Assisting Youth Outlets	Provides recreational and athletic opportunities for low-income youth
Ben	Diamond Bar, CA	17	The Cultural Education Project	Educates youth on the diversities of cultures
Cheuk	Oakland, CA	17	The Right Track	Provides mentor and tutors to middle school students
Leo	Stigler, OK	17	The Senior Citizen Connection	Links high school students with local nursing homes
Minh	San Gabriel, CA	17	Tutoring for Immigrant Children	Provides tutoring for immigrant families
Rogette	Boston, MA	17	Twenty-First Century Scholars Program	Works to increase the number of minority and immigrant students in exam schools
Jabari	Durham, NC	14	Urban Angels Social Programs, Inc.	Provides positive and healthy activities for inner-city youth
Liqian	Kingston, PA	17	Wyoming Valley Environmental Video Documentary	Provides environmental education to the Wyoming Valley community

topics initially too difficult for words." The therapeutic value of art has long been known, and some of the greatest artists in history have used their art as a salve or as a vehicle for the expression of their pain.

An after-school program like PSD allows young people to engage in fun yet meaningful, *adult-like* activities during hours that would otherwise be unsupervised. As Milkman notes, it also allows young people to feel the natural joy that creative expression fosters—a constructive form of self-medication. In addition, Milkman is tapping beautifully into the inverse relationship that exists between creative expression and conformity (discussed a few pages back). Troubled teens should be especially inclined to express their creativity, according to this view.

With more than 1,200 Denver-area young people having completed his program, Milkman found lower drug and alcohol use, better mental health, less vulnerability to peer pressure, and better family functioning among many of his graduates. So not only are teens creative, but encouraging them to express their creativity might actually undo some of the damage our society has done to teens through the artificial extension of childhood.

Q: My son wants to quit school to join a rock band. Are you saying that's okay?

A: I don't know enough about your son to give you a specific answer, but please consider: perhaps education should be spread over a lifetime, not crammed into the early years—especially with young people who aren't ready to learn. Also, is your son competent enough to make a reasonable decision about such matters? Does he have basic reasoning skills? Does he understand the risks associated with the different options he's considering? Finally, give some thought to the nature of your relationship with your son. What course of action on your part will strengthen that relationship, and what course of action might weaken it? Generally—assuming that your son shows signs of appropriate competence—offering your trust and respect is the wisest course.

Chapter 11

Young People Can Handle Responsibility

My mind got mixed with ramblin'
When I was all so young,
And I left home the first time
When I was twelve and one.
—Bob Dylan, *"Long Time Gone"*

Overview. Contrary to popular belief, young people are excellent workers, with absenteeism rates substantially lower than those of people in their twenties. Because minors can't sign contracts in the United States, it's difficult for them to start businesses, but a handful of teen entrepreneurs have nevertheless managed to generate millions of dollars in revenues each year. Unfortunately, labor laws and cultural practices developed over the last century generally restrict young people to holding jobs as babysitters and fast-food workers. On the bright side, the success of the new teen-run peer courts—now more than 1,100–strong in the United States—suggests that at least in this narrow domain we're beginning to appreciate the value of giving teens more responsibility. Research on unwed teenage mothers shows them to be surprisingly competent; this research also suggests that one of the main reasons teens get pregnant is to escape controlling adults—in other words, to attain a kind of instant adulthood. Teens need to be given more responsibility, as well as the training and authority that will allow them to meet their new obligations.

I first saw an article about "ten-somethings" in *U.S. News & World Report* in 1997, right about the time I began formulating the ideas for this book. The article was entitled "Mini Computer Moguls: Forget Paper Routes, Kids Run Tech Outfits Today," and it was about very young people doing very adult things.[1] Trent Eisenberg was a ten-something who was giving first-rate technical advice online. As a result, an executive at Compaq contacted him with an offer of a full-time job at

---

YOUNG PEOPLE IN ACTION

Driven to Save

A few years ago in a remote area of Nevada, David and Tammyla Hanna and their daughter Krystallyn were camping when disaster struck. Mom poured gasoline on a fire in a barbecue grill, which then exploded, setting her head and hair on fire. Mom needed help, but David was prone to seizures and legally blind, and Krystallyn, age fourteen, had only once steered a vehicle (very briefly on a dirt road). As Tammyla screamed "I'm dying! I'm dying!" David rolled her in the dirt and smothered the flames, then hustled his wife and daughter into their car. Ninety-four pound Krystallyn sat on Dad's lap while the two of them coordinated efforts to drive the car—she doing most of the steering and the seeing and he handling the pedals. After what seemed like "forever," Krystallyn finally spotted an oncoming car, and Dad helped her turn and block the road. The motorist helped them get to a fire station, where Mom was helicoptered to a hospital.[2]

Compaq's headquarters in Houston. The offer was withdrawn when the executive learned that Trent was fourteen years old. Trent subsequently created his own technical support company, F1 Computer, named after the F1 key on the keyboard—often the key one presses to get help with a program.

Greg Miller began work as a computer consultant for Claris Software at age ten and also subsequently worked for Apple. By twelve, he had also created a company called Tenadar, which produced kids' game software. Danny Kalmick started disassembling and repairing computers at age eleven and by fourteen was president of Kalmick & Co. Computing in Seal Beach, California. He had to get to most of his customers by bicycle, of course. He was able to charge $20 an hour for his computer repair and consulting services, considerably more than he might have earned delivering newspapers—if, that is, he had been allowed to get a paper route. As we saw in Chapter Two, you need to be eighteen to deliver papers for major newspapers in California.

Great Potential

Ten-somethings, it seems, have the potential to become a formidable force, especially in high-tech industries. That's assuming we let them do their thing, of course. In Chapter Two I noted that some of the existing child labor laws were brought about by extensive lobbying from labor unions wanting to protect adult jobs, and similar forces are at work today.

According to *U.S. News and World Report*, by 1996, 58,000 young people between ages sixteen and nineteen held part-time computer-related jobs, a figure that's only somewhat higher today.[3] And according to the United States Department of Labor, there were six million workers in this age group in 2005, about 4.2 percent of the total labor force of 141.7 million, down from 4.6 percent of the work force in 2002.[4] The Department of Labor doesn't track employment of young people under age sixteen very closely, so it's hard to say exactly how many are working, but it's obvious—especially in the high-tech area—that hundreds of thousands of them have the capacity to become first-rate workers and entrepreneurs.

So young people can and do work—even, it seems, some very young people. But just how well do they work, and just how responsibly? In what other respects do young people show that they can handle responsibility? I've answered these questions to some extent in other chapters, but the responsibility issue is so central to this book that it deserves some further attention. After all, if I'm suggesting that we give our young people more responsibility, I certainly need to show that they can handle it.

THEY CAN WORK IT OUT

Although young people can and do work, it's difficult to evaluate them as workers for several reasons: First of all, they don't have the same incentives adults have. Because young people only rarely need to support themselves, their family, or dependents, and because they're often supported themselves by parents or guardians, their income is almost entirely discretionary and disposable. People work hardest when they really *need* to work—especially when they need to support loved ones; if they're simply after more play money, they're not likely to work as hard or to persevere at work they find objectionable.

Second, teens under eighteen have very limited control over their income and property. Why work hard when the fruits of your labor are controlled by other people?

Third, teens are forced to attend school, and school officials and parents typically insist that school work is more important than employment; federal and state law says so too.

Finally, teens under certain ages aren't allowed to work in certain industries, and where, technically, they're allowed to work, no one will hire them. The vast majority of teens who work are employed in fast-food restaurants and supermarkets working at minimum wage or below—hardly the settings to inspire peak work performance.

> ## YOUNG PEOPLE IN ACTION
>
> ### Jimmy Carter on Business:
>
> *"My first business as an investor and property owner was launched in 1932, when I was eight years old. From the sale of boiled peanuts on the streets of Plains for three years, I had accumulated enough savings to go to the warehouse with Daddy and buy five bales [of low priced cotton], which we brought home and stored in a shed. Several years later, when the local undertaker died, I sold my cotton for eighteen cents a pound and bought five tenant houses from his estate, which I rented by the month.*[6]

How Good Are Young Workers?

Putting these concerns aside for the moment, is there any evidence that teens are capable of working responsibly? One of the simplest and most indicative measures of worker performance is absenteeism. You've probably heard that teens are notoriously unreliable workers, but that's not what the data say.

According to a recent report from the Bureau of Labor Statistics, teens sixteen to nineteen-years-old, in full-time jobs have an "absence rate" (the percentage of workers who are likely to be absent on any given day) of 2.8, compared with 3.1 for people from twenty to twenty-four and 3.4 for people twenty-five and older.[5] The older the worker, the more frequent the absences, mainly because of higher rates of illness and injury. Young people are healthy, strong, and resilient, and they also recover quickly from illness or injury. (The government doesn't track absenteeism in young people under sixteen, mainly because they're generally not allowed to work. It's conceivable that younger workers have even lower rates of absenteeism.)

Setting Up Profitable Businesses

In Chapter Ten we looked at some young people who started nonprofit service organizations, many of which have been quite successful. The way our laws are structured, it makes little sense for a minor to develop a *for-profit* business; minors are under enormous pressure to attend school, for one thing, and they can't sign contracts or own stock.

Even so, in recent years hundreds of young Americans—some as young as ten—have created thriving, profitable businesses, and several organizations have turned up to cater to their needs. One, called YoungBiz, Inc., was created a few years ago by Steve Morris, a former investment banker who thinks young people deserve "hands-on business education."[7] At this writing YoungBiz has an upbeat Website and a magazine (called *YE,* for "young entrepreneur") edited by two adult

professionals, author Bonnie Drew and Dr. Marilyn Kourilsky, a professor who directs a program on entrepreneurship at UCLA. The site and magazine showcase the entrepreneurial successes of people under twenty—people they call "Treps" (from the middle of the word "entrepreneur").

Originally founded in 1994 (as KidsWay) to "empower young people," for a couple of years YoungBiz named the top 100 young entrepreneurs of the year. In 2001 *the top ten people on this list netted total profits of $5.5 million*—not bad considering the obstacles, especially given that their average age was about fifteen. The stories these young go-getters tell are impressive. Consider:

- Matt Chaifetz of Manhasset, New York, started Innovative Travel Concepts when he was thirteen. By age seventeen he had 500 customers and a million dollars in annual revenues. He started the business when he was ill, spending lots of time at home—and away from school.

- Elise and Evan Macmillan of Denver, Colorado started The Chocolate Farm when she was ten and he was thirteen. In 1999 they received an Ernst and Young Entrepreneur of the Year award, and in 2001 their business was rated the top youth food business in the United States by *Young Biz* magazine.[8] They sell a variety of chocolates, as well as kits for making your own, and they also sell chocolates at Denver Broncos football games.

- Pankaj Arora of Rochester, Minnesota started his first software company at fourteen and at sixteen turned down a six-figure salary offer from a computer consulting firm. In 1999 *PC Computing* magazine gave a five-star rating to one of Arora's programs—a Windows associations manager utility—written when he was fifteen. His idol is Bill Gates, and he also admires Star Trek's Jean-Luc Picard because "he's stubborn, he breaks rules, and he takes risks."[9]

- Melody Moher of Palm Beach Gardens, Florida, created Beautiful Braids and Beads by Melody when she was ten. She started by making the rounds at local crafts fairs, offering to braid hair for a small fee; she made $80 at her first fair. By age sixteen she had four employees and regular pool-side spots at two Florida resorts. In 2002 the Guardian Life Insurance Company recognized her entrepreneurial skills with a $2,000 scholarship.[10]

Young American tycoons have also formed their own service organization, called, appropriately, the Young Entrepreneur's Organization, which claims to have over 6,000 members worldwide, and young entrepreneurs have been supported to some extent by the Ewing Marion Kauffman Foundation, a private organization devoted to promoting entrepreneurship. Several guidebooks for young entrepreneurs have also appeared in recent years, including *Better Than a Lemonade Stand: Small Business Ideas for Kids* by fifteen-year-old Daryl Bernstein, Bonnie and Noel Drew's *Kid Biz*, and *The Young Entrepreneur's Guide to Starting and Running a Business* by entrepreneurship guru Steve Mariotti (with Debra Desalvo and Tony Towle).[11]

Mixed Messages from Government Agencies

The National Aeronautics and Space Administration (NASA) is the one of few federal agencies that occasionally recognizes and nurtures the talents of young people. You may have followed the recent success of the two Mars landers that have found evidence that water once existed there. But you probably didn't know that some of the data from these two missions has been analyzed by fifty-four Mars Exploration Student Data Teams, consisting mainly of high school juniors and seniors from around the country.

They're conducting geographical studies, studying Martian weather patterns, developing three-dimensional animations, and making topographical maps of the planet. The goal of the project, according to NASA officials, is to inspire talented young people to think about working for NASA someday—and to get more data analyzed, of course.[12]

Which brings me, sadly, to the U. S. Department of Labor (DOL), the federal agency that oversees all labor-related matters in this country. In 2000 the DOL released a study called "Report on the Youth Labor Force," its first and only comprehensive report on youth labor in the United States.[13] It begins with an inspirational message from then Secretary of Labor Alexis M. Herman:

> *I remember my first job—I worked as a summer camp counselor and taught young campers how to tap dance. It was a lot of fun. I worked most summers in my teen years and through college. I still use what I learned from those jobs every day as Secretary of Labor. I truly value those experiences and I'm an avid supporter of jobs for young workers. I know that parents also understand how important early work experiences are. They know intuitively what this report suggests—that teenagers who deliver newspapers, bag groceries, or serve hamburgers in their after school jobs are often more likely to go to college and have better lifelong careers. And make more money, too.[14]*

So far, so good. The report correctly notes that in colonial America young people were encouraged to work and that, with the exploitation of workers that took place during the late 1800s, child labor laws and mandatory education laws greatly restricted work opportunities for children and teens. So where does that put young people today?

According to the report, on family-owned farms young people can still work without restriction, and more than 100,000 young Americans do so every year *without suffering any ill effects*. Among the tens of millions of young people in the cities, about half of those ages twelve and thirteen and about 60 percent of those ages fourteen and fifteen work to some extent.[15] This appears to be great news—until, that is, you see where they work and how much they're paid.

Twelve- and thirteen-year-olds work almost entirely doing *yard work and babysitting*, and fourteen- and fifteen-year-olds work mainly in *fast food restaurants or as cashiers, baggers, and janitors*, typically working *below* minimum wage.[16]

Even more illuminating is a 2003 report about child labor around the world, prepared by a division of the DOL called the Bureau of International Labor Affairs.[17] The report aptly notes that "not all work is detrimental to children" and that what we really need to be concerned about is "exploitative work," such as work that "endangers health and development."

But the overall tone and message of the report are strongly anti-work. We're reminded repeatedly of children in foreign countries who are forced into the "nightmare of prostitution" or exposed to "dangerous pesticides" or forced to crawl through "unlit and unventilated passageways" in mines or are forced to work "in excess of ten hours a day." More telling, we're told that "even when working children are not forced to endure harsh conditions, *child labor entails sacrifice because children give up the opportunity to be engaged in other activities*. The principal activity that children *could and should be doing* instead of working is going to school" (my italics).[18]

This is, of course, the agenda of the social reformers of America in the late 1800s, and we're going to push it on everyone, everywhere, no matter how outmoded or inappropriate it might be. The fact that most young people in developing nations work *with pride* in order to help support their families is irrelevant. The fact that the vast majority of young people who work (mainly in agriculture) do *not* experience "harsh conditions" is irrelevant. That fact that Western-style schooling segregates young people from adults is irrelevant. The fact that Western practices create a new and dysfunctional stage of life—adolescence—is irrelevant. The fact that prolonged schooling teaches a great deal that the vast majority of people don't want or need to know is irrelevant.

WISDOM OF THE AGES

Freud at Work

> *No other technique for the conduct of life attaches the individual so firmly to reality as laying emphasis on work; for his work at least gives him a secure place in a portion of reality, in the human community. The possibility it offers of displacing a large amount of libidinal components, whether narcissistic, aggressive or even erotic, on to professional work and on to the human relations connected with it lends it a value by no means second to what it enjoys as something indispensable to the preservation and justification of existence in society.*

> –Sigmund Freud, *Civilization and Its Discontents* (1930)

Silly Restrictions and Monotonous Jobs

In 2002 the DOL launched an organization called YouthRules with partners such as the Hotel Employees and Restaurant Employees International Union (unions, as we've seen, consistently try to keep young workers out of their industries) and the Child Labor Coalition.[19] The mission: "to increase public awareness of federal and state rules concerning young workers"—in other words, to remind the public that young people are allowed to work very few hours and in very few jobs, *no matter how benign or beneficial the work experience and no matter how competent and motivated the young person.*

A recent article in the *Christian Science Monitor* called "Beyond Babysitting" begins with inspirational stories about young entrepreneurs and then jars the reader with disturbing tidbits about the Department of Labor. For example:

> *In Illinois, the Darien Youth Club was facing a possible penalty of over $500 thousand for hiring twelve- and thirteen-year-olds as umpires for children's pony baseball games, failing to collect work permits for fourteen- and fifteen-year olds, and making some accounting glitches. The Department of Labor and the youth club are now in settlement proceedings.[20]*

In other words, in spite of the hype from Secretary Herman about "how important early work experiences are," the DOL is actually the principal enforcer of a wide body of outmoded and sometimes absurd laws that restrict labor by young people. Radical journalist and author James Bovard drives the point home in a recent essay called "The Folly of Protecting Teens from Work." The thrust of the piece is that teens are much safer in jobs than on the street:

The Associated Press reported that seventy-three teens were killed on the job in 2000. This is far fewer than were killed and wounded in the narcotics business. Most drug dealers do not abide by the federal regulations for youth labor. Insofar as the government drives kids out of legitimate jobs, they could end up in tasks that are far more dangerous.[21]

Federal summer job programs, says Bovard, provide "largely a 'feel-good' experience" rather than giving young people any real challenges or responsibility. Prominent civil rights activist Bob Woodson echoes Bovard's concerns: "The programs instill a false sense of work in kids and make it more difficult for them when they go out and try to get a real job."[22] According to Bovard, "The General Accounting Office noted as early as 1969 that some kids hired in the government summer programs 'regressed in their conception of what should reasonably be required in return for wages paid.'"[23]

Bovard's main concern is with the enforcement of laws that mainly serve "labor unions who profit either from having kids confined to classrooms or blocked from competing with their members." Consider:

In the Washington, D.C. area one pizza shop operator was found guilty because he allowed seventeen-year-olds to deliver pizza, which the Labor Department considers a "hazardous job" for young people.

The Labor Department launched a highly publicized investigation of the Food Lion grocery chain in 1992 for child-labor violations; Food Lion representatives claimed that Labor Department officials had told them that "90 percent of the violations relating to hazardous conditions involved workers under the age of eighteen—putting cardboard into nonoperating balers."[24]

He also describes a shameful incident involving the Savannah Cardinals baseball team. In 1993 a DOL official told the team to fire fourteen-year-old bat boy Tommy McCoy because of laws prohibiting young people from working after 7 P.M. when school is in session and after 9 P.M. during vacations. Outraged fans forced the DOL to back down, and Labor Secretary Robert Reich admitted that the policy—at least applied to bat boys—was "silly." "It is not the intent of the law," said Reich, "to deny young teenagers employment opportunities, so long as their health and well-being are not impaired."[25]

> ## YOUNG PEOPLE IN ACTION
>
> ### Consulting a Teen
>
> *In July of 1998, Phillip Paulwell, Minister of Commerce and Technology for Jamaica, announced the appointment of thirteen-year-old Makonnen David Blake Hannah as a computer consultant to the Jamaican government. His job: "to keep the ministry abreast of Web sites and software to help the government make computers and computer-based education available to Jamaican children." The size of his salary was not disclosed.[26]*

Young Nuclear Engineers

Why are young people allowed to do little more than baby-sit, bag groceries, and clean floors at McDonald's? We've seen overwhelming evidence that young people are capable of performing competently in a wide variety of contexts. Do we keep them sweeping floors because, as Thomas Hine suggests in *The Rise and Fall of the American Teenager*, we're afraid that in a changing world our own skills and knowledge are fast becoming obsolete?[27] Are we afraid of the competition? Could this be another form of "ephebiphobia"?

A recent five-year study of more than 1,000 teens across America by "flow" guru Mihaly Csikszentmihalyi of Claremont Graduate University and Barbara Schneider of The University of Chicago notes, among other things, that the "monotonous" jobs teens have today "are not usually the kind around which vocations are built." "Actual work experience related to a future career," they say, "is extremely rare."[28] We've seen in this volume how, when, and why the work activities of young people were curtailed. Is there any compelling reason the old restrictions should be maintained? Say Csikszentmihalyi and Schneider:

> In principle there is no reason why young people should not have the chance to learn directly, hands-on, what it means to be a nuclear engineer, oceanographer, plumber, or physician. But in practice adolescents have become extremely sheltered from adult work. In the nineteenth century they needed to be protected by child labor laws against exploitation by owners of mines, factories, and sweatshops, but it seems that now we have gone too far in separating children from work.[29]

THE PROMISE OF TEEN-RUN COURTS

No, they're not "juvenile" courts, they're "teen courts," and there's a world of difference. The former are run entirely by adults; the latter—also called "youth"

> ## WISDOM OF THE AGES
>
> ### Identity Crisis
>
> *In general it is the inability to settle on an occupational identity which most disturbs young people. To keep themselves together they temporarily identify with the heroes of cliques and crowds to the point of an apparently complete loss of individuality.*
>
> –Erik Erikson, *Identity: Youth and Crisis* (1968)

or "peer" courts—are run in varying degrees by teens themselves. They are, perhaps, the very best example I can give today of a shift *away from* infantilization.

The first teen courts in the United States appear to have been established in the late 1970s, both in Texas (Grand Prairie) and in upstate New York (Ithaca and Horseheads). At least that's what the American Bar Association, the American Probation and Parole Association (APPA), and other organizations would have you believe.[30] As you may recall from Chapter Four, however, teen courts—run *exclusively* by teens—were already going strong in the early 1900s at both the George Junior Republics (founded in 1895) and Boys Town (founded in 1917). (It's just a coincidence, I believe, that the original Junior Republic was founded just outside of Ithaca, New York, where the teen court would be reinvented seventy years later.) In those peer-run communities virtually *all* community positions—from mayor to police officer to judge to garbage collector—were held by the young residents. The rationale was that the very worst offenders would be set straight if given real responsibility and control over their lives, and the programs, by all accounts, worked far better than today's "treatment" centers.

The Odessa Model

The model for most of today's teen courts was founded in 1983 in Odessa, Texas—a town of 90,000 in the western part of the state—by Judge Natalie Rothstein with the help of City of Odessa and the local Junior League. Rothstein, who died in 1993, believed strongly that young people should be held accountable for their actions and that the best way to get them on track was through peer pressure, peer power, and peer-driven restitution.[31]

Here's how the Odessa Teen Court works: After a minor is arrested for certain minor offenses ("Class C" misdemeanors such as traffic violations, theft, or minor drug and alcohol offenses), they're booked and then brought before a regular judge, who explains the options. One option is to *plead guilty* and then to participate in a peer-run hearing in the town's Teen Court, which is held every

YOUNG PEOPLE IN ACTION

Giving Away Her Birthday

On Saturday visits to her aunt's restaurant in San Diego, ten-year-old Gidget Schultz was shaken by the sight of homeless people, especially children. She wanted to volunteer to work in a homeless shelter but was told she was too young. Then she thought of giving her birthday away—literally holding her birthday party in a shelter and celebrating her good fortune by giving gifts to homeless children. That was the beginning of Gidget's Way, now an official California charity with branches in New Jersey and Tennessee. Gidget's Way distributes school supplies, back packs, and teddy bears to homeless children year-round. It even provides local police with teddy bears to carry around in their trunks; never can tell when a furry friend might help keep the peace. Gidget attributes her success to the strong support of her mom. As for her peers, "Some kids have the talent," she says, "but they don't have the will, and they don't have anyone to support their ideas.[34]

Tuesday evening from 5:30 to 8:00. At the teen court a teen defense attorney and teen district attorney present the case to an all-teen jury, which then recommends appropriate punishment to an adult judge. The recommendation must be unanimous before it can be submitted to the judge, who generally rubber stamps it.

The punishment almost always consists of a number of hours of community service plus, in many cases, required service as a juror in the teen court. Once the terms of the punishment have been met, the offender's record is cleared. All of the personnel in the teen court are volunteers, including the judge.[32]

You can watch a video of an actual proceeding in the Odessa Teen Court online.[33] It's quite impressive. Teen pseudo-attorneys make succinct, jargony statements to the jury, and the jury renders an even more succinct, somewhat harsh decision. Everyone is polite and respectful, perhaps even more so than in a conventional court. After all, almost all of the key players are peers, and all of the jurors are former defendants. In a world that has almost completely separated teens from adults, teens respect each other far more than they respect adults. At one point an Odessa police officer reveals that he had been a defendant in the teen court years before and that the experience convinced him both to go straight and to enter the field of law enforcement.

Other teen courts have departed from the Odessa model in one respect or another. In some the teen jury members question the defendant directly; there are no attorneys. In others, a teen serves as judge, typically having first served a number of times as a teen-court attorney.

Evaluating Teen Courts

Do teen courts work? Initial indications are that they work remarkably well. As I noted in Chapter Two, recidivism rates in juvenile courts are typically 60 percent or so—pretty awful. The Odessa Teen Court reports recidivism rates of 10 to 15 percent for traffic violations and 0 percent for minor drug offenses. In Arizona the Gila County Teen Court reports a recidivism rate of 12.5 percent.[35]

As far as I've been able to determine, a comprehensive evaluation of teen courts hasn't yet been completed, but the rapid growth of the teen court system suggests that it's doing something right. Teen courts work, presumably, because (a) the community service and jury duty meted out to defendants are somewhat punishing, (b) teens are more likely to respect the judgments of their peers than the judgments of adults, and (c) according to an APPA report, teen courts "build *competencies* in youth by providing instruction to youth in areas such as how the legal system functions, and how to communicate and resolve problems with their peers more effectively" (my italics).[36]

Of course it's possible that recidivism for offenders who are brought to peer courts is low because only the most minor offenses are handled there. Remember, too, that offenders must plead guilty before they can even enter peer courts; perhaps they're more savvy and remorseful than the usual offenders (who virtually always plead not guilty).

Not Far Enough

In my view teen courts have taken a significant step in the right direction, but they don't go far enough. It troubles me that they handle only minor offenses, that they don't judge guilt or innocence (because the offenders have already pleaded guilty), and that the judges are often adults. The Odessa video also makes it clear that defendants are carefully monitored by "four to six adults" at all times. This is definitely not Boys Town. On the bright side, the teen courts do provide meaningful contact with adults in a setting that's considerably less patronizing than juvenile or adult courts.

Teen courts are spreading rapidly, created and administered by juvenile courts, law enforcement agencies, probation departments, schools, and nonprofit organizations. In 1983 there were probably two or three such courts. As of mid 2006 there are 1,109 teen courts in forty-nine states and the District of Columbia.[37] At the moment, Connecticut is the only state without one.

As imperfect as they are, the rapid spread of teen courts is a good sign. It signifies that public policy makers are beginning to rediscover an age-old truth: *When you give young people responsibility, they "possess" it and act accordingly.*

TEEN MOMS

At sixteen, her life seemed over—at least that's what some people said. Tykesha Govan of Arizona, had given birth to a beautiful little girl. It hadn't been her plan, exactly, but she also didn't like the idea of getting an abortion. So there she was.

She didn't have much time for high school anymore, and she hadn't been happy there anyway. She focused her efforts on being a good mom. Less than a year after her daughter was born, though, she heard about a program at the local community college, Estrella Mountain Community College in Avondale, that would allow her to continue her education in an environment with flexible hours—outside of the highly regimented halls of the high school. At eighteen, she not only earned her high school diploma (through the community college), she also had about half the credits she needed for her college associates degree. And her daughter is flourishing.

"I got into [the college program]," says Tykesha, "so my schedule could revolve around my daughter. She changed me. She gave me reasons to want to live and be happy." Her main interests: nursing and mortuary science. She'd even like to own a mortuary some day. "I want to make sure people get good care," she says. "I want to counsel the families and be someone who cares."[38]

Lateefah Simon got pregnant two months after she finished high school. At nineteen, she was working, going to school at San Francisco State College, and raising an infant daughter on her own. After a frustrating stint at Taco Bell—that's about the only job a young person can get, after all—she talked her way into a position at San Francisco's Center for Young Women's Development (CYWD). After three years there she was named its executive director, overseeing a $400,000 budget and a staff of fifteen. Her mission: to help troubled teens, including many very young moms, to make their way in the world. When she was twenty-six, Lateefah's efforts were recognized with the ultimate plum: an unrestricted $500,000 gift (paid out over five years) from the MacArthur Foundation.[39]

But perhaps these are just the rare success stories. Maybe most young moms are drinking, doing drugs, and dangling their babies over the railings of high balconies. Just how good are teen moms?

Evaluating Teen Mothers

Both common sense and research studies suggest that young moms generally do quite well. As we've seen, motherhood began soon after puberty during most of human history, and it still does in some parts of the world. Those facts alone should reassure us.

YOUNG PEOPLE IN ACTION

One Young Mom

Her first child, Scott, was born when she was fourteen. As of 2005, he was a straight-A student in the ninth grade. At twenty-nine, mom had been married for six years, and was the mother of three. Recently Angela Giles Klocke created a Website called OneYoungParent to help other young moms and dads, and she's working on creating a related magazine called Empowered! Age, she says, has very little to do with the ability to parent:

It is always with great joy that I mention my age. I enjoy watching the mental math going on inside of people's heads as they try to figure out exactly how old I was when I had my first son. Once a teacher or parent realizes that everything they may have ever thought about teenage moms might be wrong, they are quick to point out that I am probably an exception to the rule. But I beg to differ. Though there may be many teenage moms who are not raising their children as I am mine, there are just as many moms of the "right age" who aren't also. Being a teenage mom does not mean one cannot raise a good, intelligent child. And it isn't right to assume that one's age has anything to do with it. So the next time you think about the teenage moms you know, remember that there are more of us that do a wonderful job than not. And also keep in mind that age doesn't always mean a thing.[40]

Research on young motherhood generally confirms the capabilities of teen moms. Are some teen moms neglectful or abusive? Of course, but so are many adult moms. Our concern here, as always, needs to be with human potential. Are teen moms *capable* of raising happy, healthy children? Is it possible that young motherhood is even *advantageous* to some young moms and their children?

Before I address these questions directly, we need to bear in the mind the pathetic context in which most teenage pregnancies occur in the United States. About four in five of our teenage pregnancies occur out of wedlock, and most of teen moms in America are from low-income families.[41] What's more, because of the way we've extended childhood over the last century, teen pregnancy and parenting are now considered *shameful* in our society—history be damned. In short, most teen moms generally have at least three strikes against them before they even get to the batter's box.

Even so, when you look closely at teen moms—even some at the bottom of the heap—success stories like Tykesha Govan's are not uncommon. No matter what the obstacles, young women typically rise to the challenge of parenthood.

A small study published in 1999 by Jean B. Ivey of the University of Texas is illuminating. Ivey found some common characteristics among the eight pregnant teens she interviewed (four black and four white): generally, they considered their own mothers to be controlling and authoritarian, and motherhood was "the equivalent of *instant adulthood*" for them; it meant "they would be treated as adults in the future."[42] As we saw in Chapter Eight, under the law teen moms *do* become adults to some extent, at least to the degree that they are now legally responsible for the care and support of their own offspring. For some, pregnancy also brings marriage, which in most states triggers immediate legal emancipation from parents. (Two of Ivey's subjects were married to the young men who had impregnated them.)*

Harvard psychiatrist Robert Coles presents interviews with thirty caring teen parents in his 1997 book *The Youngest Parents*.[43] Among other findings: some young moms saw pregnancy as a way out; as one woman put it, " I wasn't getting anyplace any other way, and so this was the way for me."[44] Their children became the primary focus of their love and their energy, and all gained some degree of independence because of their motherhood. Since most were poor, some of that independence came, unfortunately, from welfare payments. For some young parents, a child was powerful motivator; it gave them a concrete reason to want to better themselves. (Meaningful responsibility and authority tend to have that effect.) Coles' study and others also show that various kinds of training and support programs can help improve the parenting skills of young parents (and, of course, of older parents, too).[45]

These themes—the instant adulthood that pregnancy brings, the competency of young mothers, the value of support systems, and the mixed blessings of the welfare system—are explored in dozens of books published since the 1980s, including a recent volume by Deborah Davis which tells the stories of more than thirty teen moms who have been able to create successful, fulfilling lives for themselves while also being good parents.[46] Several teen moms have also created upbeat guidebooks for those who follow in their footsteps, such as Ariel Gore's irreverent *Hip Mama Survival Guide*, which appeared in 1998.[47]

Although most studies of teen pregnancy and parenting are largely anecdotal, one large-scale quantitative study published in the 1980s turned up some interesting findings about the factors that lead to teen pregnancy in the first place.

---

*Ivey also found that some of the teens "had responsibilities beyond those commonly expected of teenagers today, which often began between the ages of ten and twelve years" (p. 96). With significant responsibility in their lives, shouldn't these young women have had the good sense to avoid pregnancy? Ivey also indicates, however, that the parents of these teens were strict and controlling: "Restrictions such as not being allowed to see or telephone the young men were common," she says. That's where the problem lies. Giving people responsibility without also giving them authority creates a stressful environment from which they're anxious to escape.

Based on an analysis of survey information obtained from ten thousand teen moms nationwide, Sandra L. Hanson of the Catholic University of America and her colleagues concluded that mere *knowledge* about sex and birth control does little to prevent pregnancy.[48] The teens who are best able to avoid out-of-wedlock pregnancies have two characteristics: first, they've been taught "a strong sense of self-discipline and responsibility" in their homes, and, second, they've developed "strong feelings of control over their lives."[49]

The lessons of such studies are clear. Young women are capable of being caring and competent mothers, even when circumstances aren't favorable. Those who are raised in homes where personal responsibility is stressed *and* where they feel "in control" rather than controlled are best equipped to avoid early pregnancy. And the hundreds of thousands of young women who seek or stumble into early pregnancy every year are, more than anything else, *seeking the independence of adulthood*, which pregnancy can bring about instantly. Finally, parenthood sometimes gives young people the determination and focus they need to succeed in life— "reasons to want to live and be happy," as Tykesha Govan put it.

HOW RESPONSIBILITY HELPS US GROW

In Chapter Four I posed the question, "Why does responsibility work?," and I offered two possible answers. First, according to what I've called "Role Playing Theory," when we give competent young people adult responsibilities, they simply step into the role of adulthood, just as we step into the role of parent or teacher or police officer when life requires us to do so. Our alterative was Restoration Theory, which suggests that when we give teens adult challenges, their adult capabilities— normally inhibited through infantilization—are simply restored. But what impact, in general, does responsibility have? What outcomes does it produce? And can someone be given *too much* responsibility? Let's tackle the last question first.

When Have We Given Too Much Responsibility?

There are two ways in which we sometimes give people too much responsibility—or in which we're sometimes given too much responsibility ourselves.

Insufficient Competencies and Resources. First, if we lack either the competencies or the resources to handle our new responsibilities, we'll face enormous frustration, and we might even fail. If your dad says, "From now on you're in charge of the lawn," you'll have a hard time following through if (a) you've never taken care of a lawn before or (b) Dad doesn't own a lawnmower. If you're a new mom you may end up harming your child if (a) you don't know how to change a diaper, (b) you

don't know the proper procedures for breast-feeding or using formula, or (c) you don't have money for diapers or baby food. When either competencies or resources are lacking, responsibility is an enormous burden, and the stage is set for failure.

This is because of what responsibility actually is. When you're given responsibility, your behavior is now linked to *consequences*—mainly negative ones. If you're handed responsibility for a yard or a child or a platoon of troops, this means that from now on *you're the one who will be punished if something goes wrong*—if the yard isn't mowed or the child is injured or the platoon loses battles or suffers casualties. On the upside, if the yard looks great or the child flourishes or the platoon wins a battle, you might also get some credit, but that's not what "responsibility" means. When you're "responsible," you're the one who pays the piper.

Insufficient Authority. We also overwhelm people when we give them responsibility but fail to give them the *authority* they need to get the job done. We say, "You're *responsible* for that baby, but you'd better check with *me* before you feed her, give her any medication, or take her to the doctor," or, "You're *responsible* for that platoon, but they're taking all their orders from *me*." Responsibility without authority is not only meaningless, it's often immobilizing and frustrating, and it usually sets up a conflict situation: For one thing, you'll often be in conflict with the person holding the real authority, because he or she may be constantly questioning your judgment or overriding your decisions. If you have subordinates, you'll also be in conflict with them; they'll often ignore what you have to say and defer to the real authority figure. I'll revisit this issue in Chapter Thirteen.

Why Is Responsibility so Important?

Responsibility is burdensome—there's no question about it. It's something we learn to "handle," like a bucking bronco or a hot iron. It's something that "responsible" parents try to teach their children, who don't always welcome the lessons. It is indeed tied to punishing consequences, and the more responsibility we get, the more punishment we risk. Most of us tend to have relatively few responsibilities when we're young and to accumulate many responsibilities as we approach middle age: dependents, mortgages, credit card obligations, college tuition payments, and so on. With every responsibility comes the possibility of punishment for failure to meet that responsibility.

Then what's so good about it? Why is it so important that our children have real responsibility in their lives? Why do most adults seek it and accumulate so much of it? Why do we frown upon people who can't handle responsibility or who choose to avoid it?

In a word, it's because responsibility brings out our best. Responsibility is a powerful motivator. It makes us push ourselves harder, perform better, and care more. Without responsibility, most people turn to jelly.

> ## WISDOM OF THE AGES
>
> ### Calling Forth Courage
>
> *Problems call forth our courage and our wisdom; indeed, they create our courage and our wisdom. It is only because of problems that we've grown mentally and spiritually.*
>
> —M. Scott Peck, *The Road Less Traveled* (1978)

An old friend of mine—now a psychology professor in Florida—once told me about the "worst two years" of his life. He was living on welfare in a Scandinavian country. He had no responsibilities whatsoever. He slept late every day, watched television, smoked marijuana, and read a few books. That's about it, he said. For *two years*. Perhaps you know a "trust fund baby" who lives this way. It's not pretty.

Precisely because it's tied to the possibility of negative consequences, responsibility gets us moving, and most of us would prefer to be productive than slothful. So one reason we *seek* responsibility is to keep ourselves moving forward in our lives.

For the vast majority of us, taking on responsibility is also the only way we have of improving our lifestyles, supporting our families, and acquiring the material goods we want. Unless you've been lucky enough to find the perfect sinecure, people will pay you only if you're willing to assume and meet responsibilities. Generally speaking (and there are many exceptions), the more responsibility you can handle, the more pay you'll receive. That's why medical doctors get the big bucks; they're responsible for preserving life itself.

Studies confirm what you knew all along: Young people can be taught to handle responsibility, and young people who have learned to handle responsibility are more effective in their lives. Linda and Richard Eyre's 1994 book *Teaching Your Children Responsibility* is one of several that contain tips and exercises to help parents create a responsibility-generating environment at home.[50] We've already seen that responsible young females are better able to stay in control of their reproductive lives. A study with eighth graders by Jane Newhall also suggests that young people who have learned how to handle responsible at home are less selfish and more cooperative in their interactions with peers.[51]

A recent study comparing attitudes about responsibility in six countries suggests that the younger we are when we learn to handle responsibility, the greater the sense of social responsibility we have as teens.[52] If there is a down side to learning how to handle responsibility, I'm not aware of it.

THE FUNDAMENTAL IMPORTANCE OF RESPONSIBILITY

We've looked at the responsibility issue from a number of different perspectives in this book: historical (Chapter Two), multicultural (Chapter Three), rehabilitative (Chapter Four), competencies (Chapter Six), and even military (Chapter Nine). The success of the peer courts, the competency of teen moms, the solid performance of many young workers and significant accomplishments of young entrepreneurs—all are further reminders of just how much we're underestimating our young people. When you push aside preconceptions, and when you focus not on what American teens usually do but on what teens in general are capable of doing, you can draw, I believe, only one reasonable conclusion: *Many or most teens are capable of handling enormous levels of responsibility—every bit as much as adults and perhaps even more in some cases.* We'll never see this, of course, unless we give them responsibilities to handle. If teens are sheltered from real challenges, they'll continue to perform relatively poorly; as Shakespeare put it in *King John II*, "Courage mounteth with *occasion.*"

We've also seen evidence (mainly in Chapter Four) that responsibility is essential for bringing meaning to people's lives, and in this chapter we looked at evidence that suggests that giving people responsibility produces a number of positive outcomes that perhaps can't otherwise be achieved.

Let's take another at responsibility—this time, from a Biblical perspective.

> Q: *My sixteen-year-old daughter refuses to help with the dishes and can't even keep her room clean. What makes you think she can handle real responsibility?*
>
> A: Maybe your daughter can't, but many young people can. Is it fair to restrict the options of millions of young people because your daughter has a messy room? My guess is that even your daughter has enormous potential that she's not expressing. Media icons and her peers are telling her that parents are the enemy and that it's cool to be unkempt and oppositional. And she probably resents the fact that her every move, both in and out of school, is observed, controlled, and restricted. If you and her dad were severely injured in a car accident one day, it is possible that you would see a very different, very strong side of your daughter emerge—perhaps overnight?

Chapter 12
What Does the Bible Say?

Children take up the torch and we will follow
Bring some light into this world.
—Starship, *"The Children"*

Overview. *Young people in the Bible often function fully as adults: as parents, heroes, prophets, soldiers, and even kings. It's likely that Mary gave birth to Jesus by age thirteen, and at age twelve Jesus held his own in discussions with wise men at the temple in Jerusalem. The New Testament does not restrict any activities because of someone's age. The age at which young people are held accountable for their actions varies from one religious group to another: for Catholics the age is seven; for Mormons the age is eight; for Jews the age is thirteen for males and twelve for females. In general, the world's religions recognize that young people have enormous capabilities—spiritual, intellectual, parental, and inspirational. In the Bible, respect and reverence flow strongly from young to old, but with the creation of the child-centered family a century ago, parents started to serve their children in ways that have done many children more harm than good.*

How old was Mary when she gave birth to Jesus? The Bible doesn't say exactly—in part, perhaps, because, as we've seen in other chapters, exact age didn't matter very much until recent times—but it does give at least two clues. First, Mary wasn't married to Joseph before Jesus was conceived, and second, Jesus was her first child. Given the marriage practices of the day, this almost certainly means that Mary was no older than twelve or thirteen when she conceived.

The apocryphal (from the Greek ἀπόκρυφος, for "hidden" or "spurious") book of *James*, written in the second century C.E., claims that Mary was a few years older when she gave birth to Jesus, but this book is generally not taken seriously because it's unlikely that James, Jesus' brother, could have written anything

well over 100 years after Jesus was born.[1] Historians are pretty sure that Mary had just entered puberty when Jesus was conceived. As a peasant in Nazareth she almost certainly would have been married off around the time puberty.[2]

As for the age of puberty two thousand years ago, although it's fashionable to say that the onset of puberty used to come at a much higher age than it does now, credible historical and medical evidence says otherwise. For example, according to a volume of the Mishnah (the rabbinical commentary on the Old Testament) that was completed around 200 C.E., puberty onset occurred at about age twelve-and-a-half in Jesus' day[3]— still the average age of menarche in America today. And Roman law designated twelve as the age at which females attained puberty (*pubertas*) rights.[4] Bear in mind that out-of-wedlock pregnancy in those days could bring about excommunication or even death by stoning, so there was enormous pressure to marry young, and we also know that it was common in Greek and Roman cultures for females to marry by age twelve or thirteen.[5] In short, there is every reason to believe that the Virgin Mary—the mother of one of the world's major religions—was a young mother indeed.

We've already seen that young females have been responsible wives and mothers through much of human history, that they are still so today in many countries, and that many of the teen moms in American today are competent and caring, but Mary's young motherhood raises a new set of questions: What was the status of young people in the Judeo-Christian Bible? Were teens infantilized? How much responsibility were they given? What kinds of age restrictions, if any, do we find in the Bible? At what age did young people enter into adult society? Finally, in general, how do the major religions view young people?

It's especially important these days that we add the religious perspective to those of the social and behavioral sciences in trying to understand and evaluate modern adolescence. Religion is playing an increasingly important role in the modern world. I can't imagine today's *TIME* magazine running a cover that reads "Is God Dead?," as it did in 1966. As tensions among the world's great religions continue to increase, I suspect that religion will become even more powerful a force in our society in coming decades. Just what does religion say about young people?

THE LACK OF AGE RESTRICTIONS IN THE BIBLE

The New Testament contains no age restrictions whatsoever. The Old Testament does have some age requirements, but unless you're a Biblical scholar, they might surprise you. When I began to scour the Old Testament for age restrictions, I assumed that thirteen—the age of the modern Jewish Bar Mitzvah—would be fea-

WISDOM OF THE AGES

The Magical Age Twenty

Here are some of the twenty-eight verses that contain twenty as an age marker in the Old Testament (New International Version). Many of the verses repeat one another; only five restrictions are unique.

Exodus 30:14: *"All who cross over, those twenty years old or more, are to give an offering to the Lord."*

Leviticus 27:3-5: *"Set the [taxation] value of a male between the ages of twenty and sixty at fifty shekels of silver.... If it is a person between the ages of five and twenty, set the value of a male at twenty shekels and of a female at ten shekels."*

Numbers 26:4: *"Take a census of the men twenty years old or more, as the Lord commanded Moses."*

1 Chronicles 23:24: *"These were the descendants of Levi by their families... the workers twenty years old or more who served in the temple of the Lord."*

2 Chronicles 25:5: *"Amaziah... mustered those twenty years old or more and found that there were three hundred thousand men ready for military service, able to handle the spear and shield."*

tured prominently, but it's not there. I also conjectured that other magical age markers that we find in the Western world—eighteen and twenty-one, for example—had Biblical roots, but those ages are also absent from the Bible.

The one age marker that we do find in the Old Testament is twenty, which turns out to be, at least in some contexts, the age of military conscription (but not the minimum age of military *service*), the age at which people are counted in a census, the age at which Levites (the tribe of priests) were obligated to work in the Temple, the age at which people were required to make offerings to God, and the age at which the tax rate increased.

In one lone verse—*Numbers 8:24*—we find an even higher age requirement: only priests (Levites) age twenty-five and older could participate "in the work at the Tent of Meeting." Other than that lone twenty-five, twenty is the only age marker one finds in the Old Testament, and it marks eligibility for very few things.

Age requirements are lacking for just about every other activity or right or

penalty one can imagine: ruling, marrying, having children, working, being punished for breaking a law, owning property, making binding agreements, drinking alcohol, leaving home, traveling, studying, riding chariots, and so on. Young people in the Bible did it all.

HOW THE BIBLE VIEWS YOUNG PEOPLE

The Bible contains several references to "youth" as a time of sin, but the age boundaries of youth aren't specified, and sometimes, as we'll see, very young people are given enormous responsibility and treated with great respect.

Perhaps the most famous verse that connects sin to young people comes from the Book of Psalms. "Do not remember," King David pleads to God, "the sins of my youth, nor my transgressions" (*Psalms 25:7*). It's clear, however, given the very personal nature of David's writings, that he was referring merely to his own transgressions, not to the transgressions of all young people.

In one passage in the Old Testament, Elisha, the named successor to the prophet Elijah, is accosted by a large group of youths—called a "gang" in some translations and "little children" in others—and responds by cursing them. As a result, two bears come out of the woods and maul forty-two of the young people, whose ages aren't given.[6] Was this the equivalent of the modern teen gang? If so, it was judged rather harshly, to be sure.

Generally speaking, young people in the Bible are judged on their individual merits. The wise King Solomon sums up this viewpoint nicely, suggesting that both foolishness and wisdom can come at any age: "Better a poor and wise youth," says Solomon, "than an old and foolish king..." (*Ecclesiastes 4:13*).

When Does Adulthood Begin

The Bible never says when childhood ends and adulthood begins, and it also doesn't delineate a period of life akin to what we now call adolescence. Some English translations of the Bible use the word "youth" where others use the word "childhood," and the few verses that seem to differentiate the two typically read very differently from one translation to another.[7] For example, the New King James Version of *Ecclesiastes 11:10* reads "Therefore, remove sorrow from your heart, and put away evil from your flesh, *for childhood and youth are vanity*," but the New International Version (NIV) of this verse reads, "So then, banish anxiety from your heart, and cast off the troubles of your body, *for youth and vigor are meaningless*."

In my view, the last few words of the original Hebrew version of this verse—

ילדות והשחרות (pronounced *yal-DOOT v'ha-sha-cha-ROOT*)—should probably be translated "childhood and youthfulness," where the second term (שחרות, pronounced *sha-cha-ROOT*) literally means "blackness" of the sort one sees just before dawn.* One sees the same sort of blackness in the hair of young people—at least in the Middle East; hence the metaphorical foundation of the word. In any case, this verse comes nowhere near singling out teens for special consideration.

More typically we find verses like "He who pampers his servant *from childhood* will have him as a son in the end"—that's *Proverbs 29* in the New King James Version (KJV) of the Bible. In the NIV, this same verse is translated "If a man pampers his servant *from youth*, he will bring grief in the end." It's nearly impossible from such verses to figure out how old people are. (By the way, note the warning in this verse about the dangers of infantilization.)

Origins of the Jewish Rite of Puberty: The Bar Mitzvah

As we'll see shortly, young people in the Bible often played important roles in adult society, with their ability or birthright carrying far more weight than their age. Specific age requirements for a wide variety of rights, responsibilities, and activities didn't emerge until long after the Bible was completed.

According to scholars, for example, the Bar Mitzvah ceremony didn't appear until medieval times, when thirteen officially became the age at which young Jewish males assumed full adult responsibilities in the Jewish community. Before this time, thirteen may have had some vague significance to Jews but not because of specific Biblical commandments.

The earliest reference to age thirteen seems to be in the ancient Jewish text known as *Pirkei Avot* (the English title is usually *Ethics of the Fathers*, although the book is also sometimes called the *Book of Principles*). It's part of the Talmud, the ancient rabbinical commentary on the Bible. In one lone verse in *Pirkei Avot*, which appeared around 180 C.E., Rabbi Judah ben Teima listed twelve different ages between five and one hundred which he felt were significant in the life of the Jewish male. Boys should start studying the Scriptures, he suggested, at age five, and at thirteen males should study Scriptures "for the commandments," which suggests that that's when they might become responsible for following them.[8]

In the sixth century C.E., another rabbinical commentary on the Bible describes a fictional coming-of-age feast held by the patriarch Abraham for his son Isaac, but the actual Bar Mitzvah ceremony apparently wasn't put into practice for hundreds of years and wasn't named until the fifteenth century.[9]

---

*A similar term—שחרית—usually pronounced SHA-cha-reet, is used to denote the Jewish morning prayer service.

Other Puberty Rites

The Bar Mitzvah is a type of puberty rite, of which hundreds exist in various cultures around the world. Some are fairly simple: in the Jewish ceremony, the young male simply chants, with witnesses present, some or all of that week's Torah portion directly from a Hebrew scroll. It's not the easiest thing to do, but other than the fact that in some congregations people pelt the young scholar with candy after the reading is complete, it also doesn't place life or limb at risk.

In contrast, many puberty rituals are complex and even dangerous, like stunts on the modern television show "Fear Factor." In some Australian Aboriginal tribes, for example, pain is required for passage: a young male in transition to manhood is required to strike his penis with a rock until the penis is bloody and bruised. Afterwards, the men who will instruct him in his new obligations as an adult member of the village knock out several of his teeth.[10] In other groups, a painful genital procedure known as "subincision"—cutting a slit in the penis—is performed.[11] In some Islamic communities, after they've mastered the Koran males near puberty are publicly circumcised as a loud celebration drowns out their screams.[12]

Many societies, including indigenous communities throughout Africa and Australia, mark the coming of age of a female with painful genital surgery. This can involve cutting off all or part of the clitoris and sometimes the labia, as well as closing off the vaginal opening.[13] The Arapesh girls of New Guinea must live without food or water in a sweat hut for six days, thrusting nettles into their vulvas.[14]

In most cultures, once the ordeal is over the individual's status in the community is changed dramatically, with most or all of the rights and responsibilities of adults conferred. The elaborateness and complexity of the rituals vary significantly from one culture to another.[15]

THE AGE OF ACCOUNTABILITY

Religions are often concerned with another kind of age threshold—the age at which one is obligated to start following commandments, a matter that has long been hotly debated in religious circles. Sometimes called "the age of accountability," this is the first age at which one is said to be capable of committing a sin, or, in some views, the first age at which one can be held responsible for one's sins. Before that age, no matter what the crime or violation, the wrongdoer isn't held responsible for his or her actions, mainly because it's assumed that he or she can't fully understand the significance of those actions.

Note the similarity between the age of accountability and some aspects of the modern age of majority. Before the age of majority, our legal system presumes that you're still a child, incapable of fully understanding the difference between right and wrong; as we've seen, in its modern legal form that presumption has only been around a little more than a century, and courts and legislatures have been backing away from this presumption in recent years.

Are We Accountable at Birth?

According to religious authorities, at precisely what age *do* young people become accountable for their actions? That depends on what you read or whom you ask. At one extreme are people who believe that children are conceived in sin. This is the doctrine known as "original sin," held by Lutherans, Baptists, Anglicans, and others. Verses like *Proverbs 20:11* ("Even a child is known by his doings, whether his work be pure, and whether it be right") and *Psalms 51:5* ("Behold, I was shapen in iniquity; and in sin did my mother conceive me") are cited to support this view. The Elisha story (about the young people mauled by the bears) is also sometimes cited in this context, but the fact that the text gives no clue about the ages of the youths makes it difficult to interpret.

Although modern Catholic doctrine departs from this view, early Catholic theologians defended variants on the original-sin doctrine. St. Augustine, for example, insisted that baptism was necessary to save infants from eternal damnation, although he felt that unbaptized infants wouldn't be made to suffer as much as adults who had committed real sins.[16] Other theologians suggested that unbaptized infants will stay in a state of "limbo" for all time, suffering no pain but denied salvation, and still others rejected the idea of original sin but insisted that all children are accountable for their actions, even if they're very young and don't understand the significance of those actions.[17]

The Age of Reason, and Beyond

Judaism, modern Catholicism, and other contemporary branches of Christianity say accountability begins a higher age, when the understanding of sin first becomes possible. As I mentioned, for Jews young males become fully-accountable adults at thirteen; for females, the age of accountability is twelve. The Roman Catholic church, the oldest and largest of the Christian churches (with about a billion members worldwide), teaches that children reach the "age of reason" at seven. Under age seven, children are said to be incapable of understanding sin, but from seven on they're considered to be accountable for their actions.[18] At seven, they also become obligated to participate in various church rituals, such as commun-

ion. And here's a surprise: According to Catholic Canon Law, a child as young as seven can acquire "a quasi-domicile of his or her own and, if lawfully emancipated in accordance with the civil law, a domicile also."[19]

Seven was a holy number to the ancient Hebrews. It's the number of days in the week, the day of the Sabbath, the number of animals in each group Noah led to the ark, and so on, but that hardly seems like a valid reason for picking it as the age of accountability. In any case, the Bible does seem to exempt small children from accountability in several verses that appear to contradict the original sin doctrine. In *Deuteronomy*, for example, God says, "And the little ones that you said would be taken captive, your children who do not yet know good from bad—they will enter the land" (*Deuteronomy 1:39*), and in the book of *Matthew*, Jesus says, "Let the little children come to me, and do not hinder them, for the kingdom of heaven belongs to such as these" (*Matthew 19:14*).

The implication of such verses is that young children are free from sin—both original and deliberate—or at least that they shouldn't be punished for their sins. The age-seven cutoff used by Catholics seems unique to that church, but another Christian offshoot, Mormonism, comes close. The *Encyclopedia of Mormonism* indicates that children "younger than eight" are considered to be incapable of committing sin because "Satan" lacks the power to "tempt" them.[20]

Even for Catholics, however, many rights are withheld from young people until they're considerably older than seven. According the most recent *Code of Canon Law*, where official Roman Catholic doctrines are catalogued, at age seven children are considered to be capable of "personal responsibility" and "reason," but it's not until they're fourteen that they're allowed to choose the church for their baptism.

Until 1917, Canon Law allowed anyone thirteen and over to marry, but at that point the minimum age for marriage was raised to fourteen for females and sixteen for males, and these are still the minimum marriage ages today for Catholics.[21] In 1983 the Catholic church adjusted its "age of majority"--the age at which young people are no longer subject to the will of their parents—downward from twenty-one to eighteen.* One can't be ordained in the priesthood until age twenty-five.[22]

---

*It's no coincidence that these age adjustments follow general secular social patterns: the Catholic church raised its minimum marriage age right about the time that child savers in Europe and the United States were fighting hard to extend childhood past puberty, and the church lowered its own age of majority not long after the United States and other countries did so. The Catholic Canon—like the official doctrines of many modern churches—states clearly that its rules generally yield to civil laws (e.g., Canons 22, 98§2, 105§1, 110, etc.), and church officials are, after all, products of the society in which they live.

Looking at the Individual, Not the Age

Many modern Christian churches, such as the Baptist and Pentecostal churches, avoid assigning accountability to a specific age but instead focus on the individual. In a representative essay published in *Faith for the Family* magazine in 1980, pastor Daniel P. Olinger, a faculty member at fundamentalist Bob Jones University, writes that the age of accountability "varies with the individual child" and that "it is a very early age, probably much earlier than most people believe"— perhaps, he suggests, just as soon as the child is capable of lying or disobeying. "When a child is old enough to be concerned about salvation and to respond clearly to questions about the... gospel, he is old enough to be saved," says Olinger.[23]

For present purposes, let's rename the age of accountability the "Age of Responsibility"—the age at which young people become responsible for their actions, presumably because they can then *handle* responsibility in some sense. In the theological writings of Judaism and Christianity, different ages are given for this threshold, but none is over thirteen. Let's keep this in mind as we take a look at just how well some young people actually perform in the Bible.

SCHOLARS, SOLDIERS, AND KINGS

According to the book of *Luke* in the New Testament, when Jesus was twelve he and his family made their annual trip to Jerusalem to celebrate the Jewish holiday of Passover. When the festival was over, his family left town, and somehow they managed to travel a full day before they realized that Jesus wasn't with them. That alone suggests that young people weren't shepherded quite so closely in ancient times as they are now; I can't imagine leaving any of my children behind in Disneyland and not noticing it for a day or two.

Even more important, while Jesus was on his own in the big city he spent much of his time with "teachers" in the great temple, "both listening to them and asking them questions." "And all who heard Him," says Luke, "were astonished at His understanding and answers."[24]

When his parents finally found him there after a three-day search of the city (he had been apart from them a total of five days), they were "amazed" at how expertly he conversed with the scholars. Granted that Jesus was no ordinary young man, but it's still significant that just about the only story the Bible tells about Jesus' youth extols him not for physical ability or appearance or even for his kindness but for his maturity and reasoning ability. He's able to survive on this own,

and he's able to hold his own in exchanges with temple elders. In other words, at twelve he was able to function like an adult in significant ways. Presumably, like other young men his age, by twelve he was also trained to work in his father's craft—in this case, carpentry.

Calling Young Prophets and Kings

The Bible is filled with examples of young people holding their own. For one thing, people are often "called" when quite young. The future prophet Samuel, for example, was probably in his childhood or at most his early teens when God spoke to him in a series of dreams. He was so young, anyway, that he was unable to recognize the divine nature of his first two dreams. He kept thinking that Eli, a nearby priest, was calling to him while he was sleeping until Eli finally told him what to say should God call him again ("Speak, Lord, for your servant is listening"[25]).

The future King Solomon, too, was shaken when first called by God, protesting, "I am only a little child and do not know how to carry out my duties."[26] When the prophet Jeremiah was called as a young boy, God quickly dismissed his fears and then informed him of his modest mission: "Today I appoint you over nations and kingdoms to uproot and tear down, to destroy and overthrow, to build and to plant."[27] It's hard to imagine a taller order than that; God, it seems, did not confuse age with ability.

Young Soldiers and Leaders

In my chapter on toughness (Chapter Nine), I recounted the Biblical tale of David and Goliath in which young David triumphed in a one-on-one confrontation with a large Philistine soldier. David was apparently so young that he couldn't carry the coat of armor and bronze helmet he was offered for the battle, and he was identified as a "boy". He convinced King Saul to let him fight by telling him about his fierceness as a shepherd: "When a lion or a bear came and carried off a sheep from the flock, I went after it, struck it and rescued the sheep from its mouth. When it turned on me, I seized it by its hair, struck it and killed it. Your servant has killed both the lion and the bear."[28] Even though the Old Testament gives twenty as the age of military *conscription*, it appears to have been common for young people to serve in battle in Biblical times, and even young children were fair game when victorious armies disposed of their enemies.[29]

According to L.R. Wiley's *Children and Youths of the Bible*, "Among the kings of Judah were several who were mere children or youths when they began to reign: Joash, seven; Uzziah, sixteen; Ahaz, twenty; Manasseh, twelve; Josiah, eight; Jehoiachin, eight or eighteen, given both ways; Zedekiah, twenty-one. Of the

nineteen kings of the northern kingdom, some may have been children or youths, but their ages are not given."[30]

It's not easy, given the modern mind-set, to imagine leaders so young—or at least to imagine competent ones. Throughout this book, however, we've seen strong evidence that many young people are capable of great courage and fortitude, of superlative reasoning abilities, and even of genuine patriotism. As I noted in Chapter Nine, Joan of Arc was only seventeen when she led a French army to multiple victories against the English in 1429, and two contemporary young leaders, Johnny and Luther Htoo, were twelve when they led a group of rebels called God's Army in Myanmar in 2003.

I no longer have any doubt about the capability of young people to lead; the catch is that their elders might not be so willing to follow. In ancient Israel, young kings appear to have been able to lead effectively for several reasons: First, they ruled in a very young society in which well over half of the population was under eighteen and the average life span was probably not much over thirty-five (a population distribution similar to that of many developing nations today). Second, they came from a charismatic bloodline. Joash was the eighth king of Judah and a direct descendant of King David; Joash was Uzziah's grandfather, who was, in turn, Ahaz' grandfather, who was, in turn, Manasseh's grandfather. Third, they had the imprimatur of the prophets or Temple priests—in effect, a divine mandate to rule.

The young kings seem, on the average, to have been no better or worse than those who assumed power later in life. Joash, who came to power at age seven in about 836 B.C.E., reigned for forty years and generally "did what was right in the sight of the Lord"—at least until his final days. Uzziah, who assumed power at sixteen, was a highly celebrated king who reigned for thirty-two years—until, that is, he angered the temple priests and was struck with leprosy. His grandson Ahaz, it seems, angered the prophet Isaiah—not a good idea—and Ahaz's grandson Manasseh, whose reign began at age twelve in about 697 B.C.E., encouraged idol worship and persecuted his people. Even though he "did evil in the sight of the Lord," he managed to reign for fifty-five years.

Perhaps the greatest of the young kings of the Bible was Josiah, who became king at age eight in about 640 B.C.E. and ruled for thirty-one years. When still quite young he began to purge Judah of idols, and he also restored the observance of Passover to the country, which "had not been observed like this in Israel since the days of the prophet Samuel."[31]

WISDOM OF THE AGES

Hinduism Sans Adolescence

> According to Hindu teachings one's goal is to pursue one's dharma (right path) on the way to moksha (spiritual liberation). Ancient scriptures that delineate the ashramadharma (life cycle of the dharma, or, in Western terms, the stages of human development) omit a stage that fits the Western concept of adolescence. After childhood, the next period is one of apprenticeship (brahmacharya), characterized by "industry and acquisition of competence."[32] Following that is a period when one is head of a household (garhasthya), and then a period of old age (sannyasa), when one attains higher knowledge. As I noted in Chapter Two, adolescence is also missing from Shakespeare's list of life stages.

TALES OF WISDOM AND COURAGE

In the Bible young people do just about every impressive thing that adults do—lead righteous lives, make prophecies, show great courage, muster armies, work hard, protect their families, talk with God, and so on. Consider a few additional examples:

Daniel: Master of Dreams and Diets

In the book of *Daniel*, the prophet's experience as a young child (ילד, pronounced "YEH-led") in the court of Nebuchadnezzar, king of Babylon, is described in some detail. He and his three young companions are recognized by the king as exceptionally bright: "In every matter of wisdom and understanding about which the king questioned them, he found them ten times better than all the magicians and enchanters in his whole kingdom,"[33] and the king comes to depend on Daniel especially for his uncanny ability to interpret dreams.

To avoid having himself and his companions "defiled" by eating meat from the king's table, young Daniel convinces a guard to try an experiment: "Please test your servants for ten days: Give us nothing but vegetables to eat and water to drink. Then compare our appearance with that of the young men who eat the royal food, and treat your servants in accordance with what you see."[34] After ten days Daniel and his friends look "healthier and better nourished" than young men at the king's table, so Daniel's wishes are granted.[35] Not only does this incident show young Daniel to be remarkably perceptive and persuasive—for a person of *any* age—it also identifies him as an early vegetarian!

Saving Paul

Chapter 23 of the book of *Acts* describes a dramatic scene in which Paul provokes a heated debate among different factions in the Sanhedrin, the Jewish governing body. Roman soldiers spirit him away to a barracks to prevent him from being hurt. When Paul's young nephew (who isn't named) learns of a plot to kill him, he warns Paul, who sends him to the Roman commander. The commander takes the young man "by the hand"— suggesting that he is very young indeed—and the young man proceeds to persuade the commander to bring Paul out of the city immediately with an armed escort.[36] Here's a young man—perhaps even a boy—who is courageous, who is taken seriously by adults, and who ultimately saves his uncle's life.

Young Esther Saves the Jews

The book of *Esther*, inspiration for the Jewish festival of Purim, tells the story of great courage by a young Jewish female—probably not much past puberty. The new queen of King Xerxes of Persia, Esther is informed by Mordecai, her uncle, of an edict the king has issued to exterminate the Jewish people. Mordecai entreats her to ask the king to cancel the edict, but she's afraid to do so, because approaching the king without being summoned is punishable by death.

Ultimately she throws a banquet in the king's honor, and there she pleads, with remarkable agility, as follows: "If I have found favor with you, O king, and if it pleases your majesty, grant me my life—this is my request. And spare my people— this is my request. For I and my people have been sold for destruction and slaughter and annihilation. If we had merely been sold as male and female slaves, I would have kept quiet, because no such distress would justify disturbing the king."[37] Esther's petition is granted.

Young Abraham's Cleverness—and Disrespect

Finally, I'd be remiss if I didn't mention one of my favorite tales about a Biblical character, even though it's not, strictly speaking, from the Bible. Rabbinical commentators on the Old Testament often wrote stories to clarify passages in the Bible; many were collected in volumes collectively called the "Midrash," composed over six centuries or more. One of the earliest of the Midrashim, *Genesis Rabbah*,[38] completed in the sixth century, contained stories inspired by the Biblical book of Genesis, including a famous one in which young Abraham, the father of the Jewish people, ridiculed his father and others because of their belief in idols.

To make his point, Abraham smashed all of the idols in his father's shop, except for the largest, and he put a stick in the hand of the remaining idol. When his father

expressed outrage over the damage, Abraham told him that the largest idol had smashed the others in a fight over an offering. When his father acknowledged that this was impossible, Abraham interpreted this as evidence that the idols are not really gods. The story, like others we have seen, shows a young person acting with courage, cleverness, and insight—and, in this case, even some brazen but justifiable disrespect.

The Bible's Respect for Youth

The Bible also reveres youth itself in surprising ways. Job, for example, mourns for his youth—"for the days when God watched over me"—after he has suffered great misfortunate as an adult.[39] As we age, great losses and the stresses and strains of daily living do indeed take their toll, chipping away at our energy, idealism, and faith, religious or otherwise. Perhaps that's why we find verses in the Bible that promise the greatest rewards not to the old, wise, and powerful but to children and "the meek." The meek will, we're told, "inherit the land and enjoy great peace" (*Psalms 37:11*). "Blessed are the meek," says *Matthew 5:5*, "for they will inherit the earth."

Isaiah's stirring prophecy about the perfect world to come—and a "child" who will lead—is especially relevant to the theme of this book:

> The wolf will live with the lamb, the leopard will lie down with the goat, the calf
> and the lion and the yearling together; and a little child will lead them.[40]

Isaiah paints one of the Bible's most powerful and inspirational images, one that has disappeared from the modern consciousness but that we need to consider carefully: perhaps young people have enormous potential that has been long forgotten—even the power to change the world in positive ways.

YOUNG PEOPLE AS IDEAL RECIPIENTS OF DIVINE MESSAGES

The Bible also suggests that the innocence of young people is somehow essential for receiving divine rewards or messages. The ancient Hebrews had to stay in the Sinai Desert for decades before entering the Promised Land so that those who had been slaves in Egypt could die off. Only those who hadn't been tainted by suffering were pure enough to receive the great reward.

In the New Testament, Jesus states this idea as a general principal that applies particularly well to children: "Let the little children come to me, and do not hinder them, for the kingdom of God belongs to such as these" (*Mark 10:14*).[41] Jesus also suggests that young people are especially well suited to hearing or understanding God's words: "I praise you, Father, Lord of heaven and earth, because," says

Jesus in *Matthew 11:25*, "you have hidden these things from the wise and learned and revealed them to little children."[42]

Young Marchers

When I was reading about one of the thirteenth-century Children's Crusades, I ran across one of those self-proclaimed Internet experts who dismissed it as entirely impossible, insisting that 30,000 boys and young men couldn't possibly have banded together on their own and then marched away from their homes in Europe on a quest to free Jerusalem. It just *couldn't* have happened, he said, and therefore it *didn't* happen, even if some medieval writers (including a priest) said it did.

We can never be certain about what really happened, but this we do know: As I mentioned in Chapter Nine, just two decades ago more than 30,000 boys and young men marched on foot out of Sudan in search of a better life—the so-called Lost Boys of Sudan. Many died, but thousands eventually found that better life, including one young man I interviewed for this book.

The Internet expert made the same mistake that so many of us make today: underestimating the potential of young people based on the helpless, troubled, irresponsible teens our own society so often manufactures and maintains.

In fact, historians are fairly confident that two separate Children's Crusades took place, each in the year 1212. In one march, originating in France, about thirty thousand young people were led by a twelve-year-old shepherd called Stephen of Cloyes, who insisted that he had been instructed by Jesus to lead a crusade of children to Jerusalem. He promised his followers that when they reached the Mediterranean Sea (at Marseilles), it would part for them, but apparently it didn't.

Many years later a priest who had spent time in North Africa claimed that he had met young Frenchmen who had been sold into slavery there years before. Many of Stephen's followers, it seems, boarded boats in Marseilles hoping to make their way to the Promised Land; some boats sank, and others were captured by pirates who subsequently sold the young passengers.[43]

A second march, led by a boy named Nicholas, was organized in Germany with perhaps 20,000 young people and adults. This group made it to Rome, where it was apparently turned back by the Vatican.

Small Recipients, Big Revelations

Nicholas and Stephen—both effective and inspirational leaders—are among many young people who have claimed over the centuries to have experienced divine revelations, and some of these revelations have been taken seriously by the Catholic church.[44]

In 1858, for example, the Virgin Mary supposedly appeared to a fourteen-

---

YOUNG PEOPLE IN ACTION

World Leader at Fifteen

> The Dalai Lama, whose beatific smile and hopeful message have made him one of the most admired people in the world, was officially recognized by Buddhist priests as an incarnation of Avalokitesvara, the Buddha of Compassion, when he was two years old and was officially "enthroned" before he turned five. On November 17, 1950, after his native Tibet was invaded by 80,000 troops from the newly-formed Peoples Republic of China, he assumed full political power as the leader of Tibet. He was fifteen. Four years later, at age nineteen, he participated in peace talks in Beijing with Mao Tse-tung, China's chief of state. China has had complete control over Tibet since 1950, and the Dalai Lama has lived in lived in exile in India since 1960.[48]

---

year-old named Bernadette Soubirous in a grotto in Lourdes, France, and Mary reappeared eighteen times over the next few months.[45] In 1917 three small shepherd children—Lucia Santo, age ten, Francisco Marto, age nine, and Jacinta Marto, age seven—supposedly witnessed several appearances of Mary in a field near Fatima, a small Portugese village.[46]

Incidents of this sort have been occurring since 40 C.E., but the Lourdes and Fatima incidents are unique in that they were later "authenticated" by the Catholic church, which means that after extensive investigations the Pope himself declared that the incidents actually occurred.

Although not yet authenticated, a fairly recent series of visions by four young Spanish females has been taken seriously by church authorities. Beginning in 1961 in Garabandal, Spain, when the girls were between eleven and twelve years old, they apparently saw more than two thousand visions of St. Michael and the Virgin Mary over a five-year period.[47] Similar incidents have been reported in recent decades in Mexico, Egypt, Spain, Venezuela, Bosnia, and elsewhere. Whatever one believes about the validity of such claims, it's clear that many of the young people who have made them have been treated with great respect by adult authorities.

Very Young Saints

Sometimes young people who perform great deeds or report seeing apparitions receive the ultimate honor from the Catholic church: sainthood. Jacinta Marto, who died in 1920 at age nine, and her brother Francisco, who died in 1919 at age ten, were beatified by Pope John Paul II in the year 2000.

In 1854 at age twelve, the Italian Dominic Savio organized a group called the Company of the Immaculate Conception to help support the local home for boys. In 1857 at age fifteen he contracted tuberculosis and died shortly after. His sainthood was declared in 1954.

Joan of Arc started hearing voices of three saints in 1425 at age thirteen and, as I mentioned earlier, was leading armies by seventeen; perhaps even more remarkable, she was supposedly successful in getting her soldiers to stop swearing and to attend church and confession. The voices told her that it was her destiny to lift the siege at Orléans, guide the Dauphin of France to Reims to be crowned, and liberate France from the English. After her capture, she was convicted of heresy for refusing to renounce her claims of divine revelation—and for insisting that the saints spoke to her in French rather than English. She was canonized by Pope Benedict XV in 1920.[49]

For present purposes it's notable (a) that many of the Catholic visionaries and saints have been very young, (b) that church officials have taken their experiences seriously, and (c) that *virtually all* of the young visionaries have been outside the United States.*

Why Don't We Have Saints?

Young people have often been taken seriously by the Catholic church for obvious reasons: First, as we've seen, they play important roles in the Bible. Second, many Catholic countries (such as Mexico, which is more than 95 percent Catholic) are poor, and young people in such countries become part of adult society early on. Third, because of verses like *Matthew 11:25*, many Catholics believe that the innocence of the young make them ideal vessels for receiving divine messages; grownups, it seems, are neither as worthy nor as trustworthy in such matters.

Why don't we have child visionaries in the United States? Perhaps it's because we just don't care much about what our young people say. Although it's true that we're devoted to our children in many respects, we have grave doubts about their credibility and judgment. As for teens, our society is structured so that they do almost all of their talking to each other—sometimes using dialects of their own creation. Remember, too, that minors here are relatively helpless. We don't have any choice about listening to the supernatural claims of an adult, but if a child or teen is seeing or hearing things, we're more likely to turn to a mental health professional than a priest, and a therapist is likely to prescribe Clozaril or Risperdal long before recommending sainthood.

---

*Individuals and groups that track apparitions around the world (see www.apparitions.org and related Internet sites) list dozens of reports in the United States over the past century, very few of which have been taken seriously by church authorities and only one of which originated with a minor—a seventeen-year-old in Ohio.

YOUNG PEOPLE IN ACTION

Young Founder

As an adult, Joseph Smith, Jr., the founder of the Mormon church, wrote that he experienced his first religious visions at age fourteen (in 1820). He also recalled that in 1823, at age eighteen, the angel Moroni appeared to him at night and informed him about the existence of golden plates buried near his family's farm in New York. The plates contained an elaborate history of the Western hemisphere which today form part of the belief system of the Mormons. He was required to perform a four-year purification, he said, before he could take possession of the plates. He and five associates founded the church when he was twenty-four. At forty-four, Smith was shot dead by a mob in Illinois when he was campaigning for the presidency of the United States.[50]

RELIGION AS A REPOSITORY OF TRUTH ABOUT YOUNG PEOPLE

Religions around the world generally recognize that young people are competent in significant ways, at least in the sense that their minimum age markers tend to be well below those of civil law. It's not clear what this means, though. Because religions are tied to old or even ancient writings, and because those writings can't be altered, it's possible that the minimum ages specified in those writings are just meaningless relics, like the laws of the book of *Leviticus* that require animal sacrifice.

Even though the writings can't be altered, they can be interpreted or ignored to suit changing societal standards; that has clearly happened in some modern churches when it comes to teens. Young Jewish males might have been welcomed into the adult community at age thirteen during medieval times, but that isn't the case today, and the Catholic church occasionally alters its age requirements quite explicitly to conform with secular standards and laws.

So perhaps where the age markers of various religions are low, those religions are simply out of step with society. Religions are understandably sluggish, but we should expect that over time they will catch up to some extent—reinterpreting old verses and laws and stories and, when that doesn't work, ignoring them completely. In other words, no matter how much respect religions have paid to young people in the past, eventually they'll succumb to changing societal norms and come to view young people as helpless and incompetent. That's the message of modern society, after all.

But I hope not. Religions preserve important truths and values that modern

societies, caught up in the vicissitudes of the moment, sometimes tend to forget. With all their flaws, religions anchor us in eternity; they remind us of our past, help us to put the present in perspective, and give us hope for the future.

If you're trying to get fundamental insights about the nature of young people, which source will tell you more: the Bible or the 1989 film *Bill and Ted's Excellent Adventure*? The Koran or the hit television series *Blind Date*? The Hindu Vedas or a sensational news report about the Columbine shootings? Alas, public policy is more often influenced by contemporary hype and stereotypes than by timeless historical writings—or, for that matter, by serious scientific research.

Other Religions

Religions outside the Judeo-Christian tradition still integrate young people into adult society rapidly, sometimes in ways that some Christians and Jews might find offensive.

According to Islamic writings, for example, the prophet Mohammed was betrothed to his wife Aisha when she was six and he was fifty-three, and the marriage was consummated when she was nine.[51] To this day in some Islamic countries, there is no minimum age for female betrothal.[52]

Traditional Hinduism has somewhat similar practices: Females can be betrothed when very young, although consummation typically is delayed for many years.[53] As I indicated in Chapter Eight, even though civil law in India now prohibits child marriage, it is still widely practiced by hundreds of millions of people, mainly in rural areas. In some cultures, early marriage serves as a sure way to prevent premarital sex, and it also creates immediate ties between families and helps to stabilize communities.

For a tabulation of various age markers for some branches of Christianity, as well as for other major religions, see the table on the following page.

Perhaps because they were founded long ago or perhaps because they capture some essence of human nature (or perhaps both), the world's major religions allow and encourage young people to enter adulthood relatively early in life. As we saw in Chapter Three, however, modern American values are rapidly tearing down traditional social structures in many areas around the world, disrupting the child-adult continuum and creating dysfunctional variations on adolescence wherever American-style schools, movies, television programs, and marketing campaigns have been allowed to cross the threshold.

Minimum Age Requirements in Major Religions[54]			
Religion	Age of Accountability	Minimum Age for Marriage, Females	Minimum Age for Marriage, Males
Baptist	individual basis, typically 6-7	maturity and preparedness	maturity and preparedness
Buddhism	no specific age[a]	none[a]	none[a]
Catholicism	7	14[b]	16[b]
Hinduism	no specific age	none[c]	none
Islam	puberty	none[d]	none
Judaism	13[e]	12	13
Lutheran	individual basis, usually 12-14	state law[f]	state law[f]
Methodist	individual basis, usually 12	state law[f]	state law[f]
Mormon	8	state law[f]	state law[f]
Pentecostal	individual basis	state law[f]	state law[f]

a. Buddhism doesn't specify age markers for normal life-cycle events; to the extent that such markers exist, they are established by individual cultures where Buddhism is practiced.

b. Prior to 1917, the minimum age was thirteen.

c. Although betrothal can occur in childhood, consummation tends not to occur until well after puberty.

d. Although betrothal can occur in infancy, the minimum age for consummation is generally said to be nine. Civil laws in some countries establish higher ages.

e. Twelve for females

f. Although the age of majority is typically eighteen, in most states young people can marry when they are as young as thirteen or fourteen with parental permission, a court order, or if the woman is pregnant.

TURNING RESPECT ON ITS HEAD

Through most of human history, respect in families has flowed upwards: from children to parents, from the young toward the old, from contemporaries toward ancestors. This is still true in much of the world today, although the spread of American culture is rapidly disrupting the old patterns.

In the Old Testament, the direction of respect is stated simply enough in the fifth commandment, "Honor thy father and thy mother," as well as in other verses.[55] The general principle of respecting one's elders is stated clearly in the New Testament: "Do not rebuke an older man harshly, but exhort him as if he were your father. Treat younger men as brothers, older women as mothers, and younger women as sisters..." (1 Timothy 5:1-2).

Although the Bible suggests that parents have an obligation to provide for their children[56] and although some Biblical parents certainly expressed love for one or more of their children,[57] nowhere in the Bible are parents commanded to "honor" their children. In the New Testament (but not in the Old), fathers are cautioned against "exasperating" or "embittering" their children—perhaps through parenting that's too harsh—but the cautions are clearly not meant to offset the obligation that children have to "obey" and "honor" their parents. As for the specific obligations parents have toward their children, only one is stated clearly and repeatedly in the Bible: the obligation to teach them to lead good lives by following God's commandments. Nowhere does the Bible instruct parents to prevent their children from working, to protect them from the realities of life, or to make sure they're happy and fulfilled at all times.[58]

Figure 12.1. Flow of Respect. In the Bible and in traditional cultures, respect and reverence always flowed upward from young to old (left arrow). The Industrial Revolution reversed the flow of respect in some respects. In the child-centered family, reverence, attention, and service flow downward from parents to children (center arrow). If we once again begin to integrate young people into adult society at young ages—putting competency ahead of chronological age—we will build a society in which young and old view and treat each other with mutual respect (right arrow).

Some of the leading child savers of late nineteenth-century America had strong religious convictions, and it's likely that the only home life they knew was patriarchal and authoritarian. As flawed as that system was, if Jane Addams and her friends could peek at modern America, I think the thing that would frustrate them most about the way their legacy has taken shape is that it has turned respect on its head.

Today's parents may still *want* their children to respect them, but in the modern child-centered family, obligation and reverence often flow downward more than upward. Parents are often consumed with satisfying their children's needs, real and imagined, even while they're still in the womb. Moms and dads play Mozart CDs hoping to raise a fetus's IQ, pre-chew Baby's food rather than putting it in a blender, shuttle young children to a dozen activities every week to maximize their chances of getting into a good college, feel guilty when they haven't put in enough homework time, spend thousands of dollars on fashion clothing and high-tech toys for pre-teens, and exhaust their retirement funds or go into debt to pay for college.

Even more disturbing, not long after they learn how to dial a phone, some children now inform their parents that if they're too harsh, the children will call the police and send the parents to prison for "child abuse." Our modern system of protections for children are set up to err on the side of the child, which makes any style of parenting other than the permissive sort all but impossible to practice.

Our high divorce rate makes things even worse. Single parents go out of their way to please their offspring in order to prevent custody (and child-support funds) from shifting toward their ex-spouse, and the offspring of divorce, who inevitably discover this, often take advantage of their parents' powerlessness.

Permissiveness

How can we be permissive parents at the same time that we're supposedly infantilizing our teens? After all, infantilization suggests that we're trying extra hard to protect our offspring from harm, perhaps by being extra *strict*—not by being permissive.

But there is no contradiction. We can be permissive while we also infantilize, and we indeed do both. We infantilize our young by keeping them isolated from the adult world and withholding adult rights and responsibilities from them—by trapping them in the meaningless world of youth culture. We continue to protect young people from that world until they're at least eighteen or twenty-one and sometimes considerably older.

Our permissiveness expresses itself in other ways: in our willingness to tolerate disrespectful language and manners that we would never tolerate from adults,

in our failure to set high standards of performance and integrity for our young, in our laxness in getting our offspring to make positive contributions to the household and family, and in our passive acceptance of the complete dominance of peers and peer culture over our offspring's lives.

Modern infantilization and modern permissiveness are, in effect, interlocking: If we allowed and encouraged competent young people to begin entering the adult world in their early teens (as they did through most of human history), the kind of permissiveness we now practice would be largely unnecessary. If a sixteen-year-old male cut back on school in order to set up a business, much of his energy would be devoted to understanding, working with, and pleasing adults. If a competent fifteen-year-old female decided to marry and start a family, she might also seek ways to make sure her new family could live independently of her old one. If a teenage male decided to move out of his parents' home and live with other family members or friends, he would likely be expected to make more contributions in the new household than he had had to with his parents.

In all of these situations the parents have less to be permissive about, because the offspring are moving in the direction of becoming self-sufficient adults. By definition, you can only be permissive with someone over whom you hold some power—with someone who can't act in certain ways without your "permission"; it would be tough to be "permissive" with a police officer or judge.

To a large degree, we're now permissive with our young because (a) they're completely dependent on us, (b) we love them (or at least we used to before they became unruly teens), (c) we can't get rid of them, and (d) we can't control them; if we weren't permissive in at least some respects, we'd soon go mad. If we just let our young grow up, however, they would soon be subject to the very real controls of adult life, which are far more powerful and persuasive than the artificial and ineffectual controls we're able to bring to bear as parents.

Respect

As for respect, I'll offer a prediction: *If we stop infantilizing our teens, they'll start respecting us again.* Under the authoritarian system of parenting, respect was probably based largely on fear. Dad's message was, "You had better respect me—or at least *show* me respect—or I'll punish you severely." Most people will indeed at least "show" respect in such situations, but a more meaningful kind of respect is based on a mix of empathy and admiration. You might respect Grandma, for example, in a way you don't respect Mom or Dad, because you sense that Grandma has genuinely suffered or is suffering, because she has overcome many obstacles in her life, and, most important of all, because she treats *you* with respect. In the

working world, you might respect a boss or coworker for similar reasons: He or she has accomplished a great deal, he or she performs well, and he or she shows respect for *you*.

In the lingo of today's teens, infantilization might be considered the ultimate *"dis"*—that is, a sign of disrespect—and *dissing*, as you may know, is one of the harshest things teens do to each other. It's difficult for teens to respect their parents when, as far as the teens are concerned, the parents aren't showing the least bit of respect for *them*. Teens usually begin to show real respect for our parents only after they've been out in the real world for a while—when they learn just how hard it is to put food on the table. They start to see their parents through entirely new eyes—the eyes of adults. The parents, in turn, might finally begin to show their offspring the respect their offspring always wanted.

This process often takes many years in our culture, but there's no reason to continue to delay it as long as we do. If we can, once again, learn to recognize the competence of our young and to judge them based on that competence rather than on their age, I believe that they'll begin to show us the respect we deserve. More important, we'll create many parent-child and adult-youth relationships that are based on a genuine *mutual* respect, not just on coercion or fear.

Perhaps more than any other source that people take seriously in modern times, the Bible shows us a world in which young people were judged more often for their abilities than their age and in which children and teens were rapidly integrated into the adult world—one of the reasons, presumably, why they respected that world. Young females—and even Mary herself—became competent wives and mothers soon after puberty, and young males—David, Samuel, Isaiah, Joash, Daniel, Josiah, and many others—became warriors, heroes, prophets, and even kings just as soon as the challenges arose. Although gender restricted roles and opportunities in the Bible, age generally did not, and the child-adult continuum was nearly seamless.

The major religions have preserved clear images of mature and competent young people who were important members of their families, communities, and cultures. Religious texts and practices provide, in my view, another important piece in the puzzle I've attempted to assemble in this book. Anthropological and psychological studies say that many young people are highly capable individuals whom we should take seriously and treat with respect. Our religious heritage says the same.

Q: *Do you have any unstated political or religious agendas in advocating your unusual views on adolescence?*

A: None of which I'm aware. My politics have been moderate for decades, and I can see why people on both sides of the aisle might be appalled by my perspective—or might applaud it. I'm not out to please or offend anyone; I've simply become convinced of the rightness of my arguments based on research I've conducted, interviews with teens, and an examination of documents in the fields of history, psychology, sociology, anthropology, and so on.

I'm a Jew by background, but I'm not aware of any religious basis for my position. Historically, at least as of the fifteenth century, Jews welcomed young men into adulthood shortly after puberty through the Bar Mitzvah ritual, but this practice was hardly unique to Jews; cultures around the world have developed rituals like the Bar Mitzvah to mark puberty. Moreover, the real meaning of the Bar Mitzvah seems to have been lost to Jews over the last century; industrialization changed religious practice just as it changed many other aspects of our lives. The capabilities of teens got buried under the ashes of the factories, and neither religious practices nor old traditions were sufficient to keep the true character of teens alive.

Part 3

How We Must Change

Chapter 13

How Society Must Change

I wanna run through the halls of my high school
I wanna scream at the top of my lungs
I just found out there's no such thing as the real world
Just a lie you've got to rise above.
—John Mayer, "No Such Thing"

Overview. Young people should be extended full adult rights and responsibilities in each of a number of different areas as soon as they can demonstrate appropriate competence in each area. Passing appropriate tests will allow competent young people to become emancipated, sign contracts, start businesses, work, marry, and so on, but I am not suggesting that young people be given more "freedom." We need to start judging young people by their abilities, not by their age, just as we're now doing increasingly with the elderly. The societal changes I'm proposing have the potential to reconnect young people with the adult world, to inspire young people to behave in responsible ways, and to eliminate much of the turmoil we now see during the teen years. Young people have always tended to resist the artificial extension of childhood, and there are a few signs in recent decades that this century-long phenomenon may be slowing or reversing.

I worked on an outline for this chapter while sitting on the rear patio of a sandwich restaurant near my home. One of the things that kept me going was a conversation between two teenage males at the next table. They were sixteen or seventeen, I'd say, and dressed like black hip-hop artists: saggy, baggy pants held up by that mysterious Force from Star Wars; multi-colored boxer shorts showing prominently; black pullover "beanies" (even though it was eighty degrees outside and we were all sitting in bright sun). They both slouched so low it's a wonder they didn't slide off their chairs. Again, that mysterious Force at work.

They spent the entire forty minutes I was there talking about skateboarding, mainly repeating the same things over and over. The word "dude" was used frequently. The gist of the conversation was that they would, or possibly would not, be skateboarding with some friends at a certain place, or possibly another place, either later today, or perhaps tomorrow, or perhaps not at all—and they might, or might not, "get air," which is a really good thing to get.

These are the teens we have created: mindless consumers, dressed from head to toe in the garb prescribed by specialized divisions of the music and fashion industries, isolated from their heritages and their elders, producing nothing of value for their families or their society, obsessed with non-issues fed to them by waxen heroes. The young men next to me seemed content in their ignorance, but many of their peers want more, and they often don't know how to express their legitimate needs and desires. Based on my interviews with teens, my experience as a father and teacher, research I've conducted, and a wealth of data in several fields, I no longer have any doubt about what disenchanted American teens need, no matter how inappropriately they may sometimes choose to express what they want. They need to be reconnected with the adult world—the world they will inevitably join before that skateboard even reconnects with the ground.

REVERSING THE ARTIFICIAL EXTENSION OF CHILDHOOD

The artificial extension of childhood needs to be reversed, and below I'll present some ideas that I believe can set this reversal in motion. I'm not suggesting these changes because I have a personal stake in them or because they fit my credo, politics, or religion; in fact, as a father of four and as the flawed product of the flawed society about which I'm writing, I'm uncomfortable with a number of the items on my list. I'm including them—even the ones that make me uneasy—because all of them are, I believe, strongly suggested by the wealth of data I've presented in this book.

Please note that throughout this list I'm emphasizing the need for young people to demonstrate competence—a matter I'll say more about later. Also note that I'm taking great pains to avoid making the blanket, often reckless recommendations that one finds in books like John Holt's *Escape from Childhood* (see my Chapter One). Any steps we take, large or small, need to be both reasoned and reasonable. They need to be based whenever possible on empirical research rather than on anecdotes, folklore, sensationalistic headlines, or religious or political imperatives. And they need to be examined closely with the future in mind, taking into account the possible consequences, both positive and negative, of our actions in each area.

Emancipation

Currently it's extremely difficult for a young person to become legally free of his or her parents; this makes emancipation quite rare—so rare that it often makes headlines. States specify minimum ages for emancipation (typically sixteen), and generally young people must demonstrate good cause for the action and also show that they can support themselves—tough to do in an ephebiphobic society that requires long hours of schooling and limits work opportunities.

One thing the courts don't require, of course, is evidence that the teen is competent to function as an adult. To me, the change to be made is apparent: A young person of any age who can pass a series of state-approved adult competency tests should be able, without court involvement, to receive a Certification of Emancipation from the state. There should be no minimum age requirement for taking the tests or for receiving the certification.

The key to a workable emancipation system is the battery of competency tests. As I've said earlier, it's remarkably easy to develop such tests, and we, the infallible ruling elite, will have complete control over their construction and administration—at least for a while! Moreover, we're the ones who will determine the score that is required to pass each test. The content can include basic adult competencies (such as the ones Diane Dumas and I included in the *EDTA*—see Chapter Six), and it can also include basic school content. In other words, we can set the emancipation bar quite high, if we choose. Personally, I'd lean toward requiring young people to achieve a score that is at least at the fiftieth percentile level for adults over twenty-one—meaning that on each test the applicant must score higher than half of the adults over twenty-one currently do. That's quite a safety margin.

But won't life be difficult with an emancipated young person under one's roof? Doesn't emancipation mean that Mom and Dad can't legally exercise control over their children? And doesn't it also mean that our precious offspring will no longer have the important protections that the state now offers young people? To put these questions into perspective, please consider that the fourteen million young people between ages eighteen and twenty-four who currently live with one or both parents are also "emancipated" and that they typically get along with their parents quite well, at least in part because the living arrangements are voluntary.[1] Parents are required by law to support their unemancipated offspring, but parents who *choose* to cohabit with their offspring and offspring who *choose* to cohabit with their parents are generally pretty content.

Because certain means of coercion (such as corporal punishment) are no longer available to the parent in this situation, he or she must deal with the son or daughter

with a certain degree of respect. On the other hand, the parent now has the option of turning the young person out onto the street, which gives the parent a legitimate reason to ask the son or daughter to help out with rent, chores, and so on. The young person, too, has more options: to move in with relatives or friends or lovers, to quit school (remember those rigorous competency tests), and to work long hours. If he or she stays with the parents, it's because doing so serves his or her legitimate needs.

Imagine that: *parents and their offspring, all under one roof, showing each other mutual respect and working together for their mutual benefit.*

Won't there be chaos in schools if administrators no longer have parental rights to control their students? It's true that some emancipated young people will choose to work instead of staying in school. Others will choose to stay in school, subject not to the pseudo-parental whims of high school staff but rather to the laws of adult society.

Imagine that: *young people in school voluntarily, perhaps because they want to learn something.*

An age-free, competency-based emancipation system will, I believe, cut the heart out of "adolescence." The incentives for young people to prepare for the tests will be enormous, and even if they don't pass all of the tests, they'll still reap great benefits from the process of preparation—they're preparing for adulthood, after all—as well as from the limited privileges they obtain when passing certain tests (see below).

Meanwhile, imagine the triumphant fifteen-year-old male running down the court house steps echoing Martin Luther King's words, "Free at last, free at last, thank God Almighty, I'm free at last!" (Of course, he isn't *really* free at all, is he? I'll return to this matter toward the end of the chapter.)

Juvenile Justice

The time has come to end the grand judicial experiment that began just over a hundred years ago in Cook County, Illinois. The juvenile justice system was created by a handful of leaders who were caught up by the sentimentalist views of children sweeping the country in the late 1800s and early 1900s (Chapter Two). The system works poorly, if at all, and it hasn't fulfilled its mission. The original rationale for the system—that young people could be "nurtured" back to sweetness and light in supportive, female-run facilities where they would have no contact with hardened criminals—was completely off-track by the 1930s. Reformatories turned into poorly-staffed, overcrowded prisons, filled with acne-faced variants of every kind of adult criminal imaginable. And juvenile courts took away more human rights than the KGB did during its heyday.

Today it's becoming increasingly clear that young people should be held fully accountable for their actions—that young people who can be shown to understand

the difference between right and wrong, to have basic reasoning abilities, and to understand the serious nature of their crimes should pay the price for what they have done. Today when they commit serious crimes, young perpetrators are sometimes "waived" to the adult courts, but there's still a chance they'll stay in "juvie," where they'll get a slap on the wrist and where their juvenile record will likely be buried forever when they reach eighteen. And they know this all too well. Many minors count on the fact when they commit a crime, the worst fate they'll suffer—if they even get caught, that is—is a few years in a juvenile facility (where they can sharpen their criminal skills) followed by a clean slate.

The best deterrent against crime by young people is to have all crime handled by the adult criminal justice system, with public hearings and permanent records. When the perpetrator is young and immature, judges and juries can make allowances as necessary, just as they do now when an adult is impaired or when there are extenuating circumstances in a case. When a young person must be incarcerated and the courts have concerns about housing young and old together, they can separate young criminals from older ones, just as they do now. Perhaps even more important, with just one criminal justice system, young people will be guaranteed all of the due process rights that are promised by the United States Constitution—rights often denied them by the highly-flawed juvenile justice system.

And what about those questionable "crimes against the self"—the multitude of crimes that were invented just for teens and that can't be committed by adults? What about truancy, dirty dancing, staying out late, and "incorrigibility"? Again, I think the time has come for adults to grow up. We need one standard of crime, not two. If we locked up every adult for the "crimes" they committed against themselves, who would be left to turn *that* key?

Education

Compulsory education may have seemed sensible in the late 1800s when tens of thousands of impoverished young immigrants were running ragged in the streets of America's exploding industrial centers. Moralists like Jane Addams felt a duty to rescue the young, and industrialists like Henry Ford wanted to keep the teeming masses in check. But today's America is a very different beast. A century ago we rescued young people from the factories and the streets; now we need to rescue them from the schools.

For many young people schools are little more than secure warehouses, complete with all the trappings: metal detectors, observation cameras, and armed guards. The students are the commodities being guarded, but most don't want to be commodities—even the few who are genuinely interested in learning. Alas, a great many of our students aren't even ready to learn, or at least they're not ready to learn what the schools

are ready to teach. As pioneering educator Kurt Hahn told us in Chapter Four, teachers continue to try to fill vessels without first checking to see "whether the lid is off."

Schools are supposed to propel young people forward, but they actually hold many back, preventing them from moving forward with work or more specialized training. Schools are also supposed to foster a love of learning, but they actually teach many people that the classroom is a place of torment and humiliation. As a result, after we complete the minimum schooling we feel we absolutely must have, most of us steadfastly avoid the classroom for the rest of our lives.* We need new options, and especially options that will reduce the turmoil of the modern teen years.

- *We need shorter compulsory school hours, a shorter compulsory school year, and fewer required school years.* Recall that the first compulsory education law in the United States wasn't passed until 1852, and it only required people from eight to fourteen to attend school three months a year—less, if they could show they already knew the material. Leon Botstein, longtime president of Bard College and the youngest college president in United States history (at age twenty-three), recently called for the abolishment of high school.[2] It's an idea worth exploring, although giving most young people ways to circumvent high school is probably enough of a fix.

- *Students need options, the most important being the option to test out of courses, school years, or school altogether.* Students also need the option of balancing work and school on flexible schedules—just like some adults do when they're trying to switch professions or advance their careers.

- *Mandatory schooling needs to cover just the basics:* reading, writing, arithmetic, and citizenship being the most obvious subject areas—more than we require of immigrants before we grant them citizenship but not much more. Schools also need to teach basic reasoning skills and a love of learning—the cornerstones of meaningful lifelong learning. Finally, schools need to give people the tools they need for finding information, as well as for locating and preparing for the kind of specialized training they wish to have to enter the adult world. Specific instruction in a wide range of topic areas is largely a waste of time for the vast majority of our students, in part because they're not interested, in part because they'll never use what they're being taught, and in part because most of what we teach them is forgotten before they exit the building.

---

*Karen Edwards, an old friend from my Harvard days, coined the term "academic trauma" to describe this phenomenon after noticing how many Harvard undergraduates developed a serious aversion toward learning as a result of their school experiences. As of this writing she's working on a book on this topic.

- *We need to shift away from teaching in the traditional classroom environment.* There's nothing sacred about the schoolhouse classroom; it became common simply because it was the most efficient means available for trying to convey lots of information to lots of students. Although the classroom is a marginally efficient tool of mass production, it's actually a horrible system for individuals. People have different learning styles, different backgrounds, and different interests, and they also learn at different rates. When instruction is adjusted to take individual needs into account, *everyone* turns out to be an avid learner, but this can't happen in the conventional classroom. Having taught for twenty-five years, I know all too well what all experienced teachers know: The classroom at its best serves only a fraction of the middle third. It cheats and bores the outstanding students; it frustrates and punishes the lower third; and it has only a minimal impact on the most of the middle third.

- *We need to shift toward new methods of individualized instruction.* Home-based instruction needs to be looked at with fresh eyes, especially now that we have a powerful, inexpensive tool for educating almost everyone both individually *and* efficiently—namely, the Internet. The self-paced instructional systems proposed by Sidney L. Pressey in the 1920s and B. F. Skinner in the 1950s are gradually becoming a reality, with a new feature they could never have envisioned: Self-paced, high-quality instruction can now be provided anywhere, anytime, from any one of millions of computers that are connected to the Net. In theory, good software can even be designed to emulate the most outstanding teachers in history, preserving the genius of people like John Taylor Gatto for future generations. According to a new study by the federal government's National Center for Education Statistics, home schooling is indeed growing fast. As of 2004, the number of home-schooled young people at least 1.1 million—an increase of 29 percent over just the previous four years. The non-profit National Center for Home Education says the number of home-schooled young people is actually two million.[3]

- *One of the most factory-like aspects of the modern school—segregation by age—needs to be ended.* Through most of human history, teens spent most of their time with adults, not with each other; as we saw in Chapter Three, this is still true in developing nations today. And until the late 1800s, classrooms brought people together over a

wide age range. Grouping people together by age is a very recent phenomenon, and from a learning perspective it makes no sense.

- *Education needs to be spread out over one's life, not compacted into the childhood and teen years.* There are many reasons for this, but the most obvious is that the world is changing with increasing rapidity. A good portion of what you learned in school five or ten years ago—especially in the sciences or in high tech—is now obsolete. (Of course, I'm assuming here that you can even *remember* what you were taught, which is unlikely. Can you even remember the names of the teachers you had in high school?) Trying to teach every important thing an "educated" person needs to know in twelve years of instruction might have made sense a century ago, but it makes no sense now. Learning needs to be lifelong, and school—if it continues to exist at all—needs to provide people with the tools and inspiration they need to continue the learning process.

I realize that many of the recommendations I'm making in this chapter may never come to pass. But in the education area I'm optimistic. The Internet is like the mischievous Puck, crouching behind America's exhausted teachers, ready to buckle their legs with just the right shove behind the knees. When the time is right, even behemoths like the National Education Association will be toppled.

The Internet allows for decentralized, individualized, self-paced learning and true on-the-fly distance learning. No classroom and no teacher can compete with that. Even more significant, instructional software is only going to get better—much, much better—while teachers will remain as they are. As broadband becomes more commonplace, real-time one-to-one tutoring will become more practical, and this is only the beginning. Internet II, which first went online in 1999 and is now being used by select institutions nationwide (but not in homes), has about a thousand times the capacity of the Internet you and I use. It will allow high-fidelity real-time communication with virtually unlimited capacity. It's only a matter of time before the so-called Ultranet or Meganet comes to a living room near you, and that plus some superior software is likely to burn the old schoolhouse to the ground.

These technical developments alone will tend to reverse the artificial extension of childhood to some extent, because: (a) they'll keep many young people at home and away from peers, (b) they'll provide a platform for self-paced instruction (and hence end age segregation in education and allow some people to progress rapidly toward professional specialization), and (c) they'll create many opportunities for young people to combine work with education.

Reintegrating Teens into the Adult World	
Summary of Changes Needed	
Abortion	Young women of any age who can pass an appropriate competency test (demonstrating reasoning ability, awareness of consequences, and so on) should have the right to make the abortion decision without parental notification or consent; the procedure, when chosen, should be subject to the approval of a licensed physician.
Contracts	Young people of any age who pass an appropriate competency test should have the right to sign contracts.
Corporal Punishment	Striking an emancipated young person (see below) should be made a criminal offense; parents or school authorities should be able to strike unemancipated young people only when they can demonstrate that other reasonable means of behavior management have failed.
Curfews	Curfews, when necessary, should be applied to people of all ages; curfews should not discriminate by age; parents of unemancipated young people should remain responsible for their behavior.
Dress and Appearance	Young people of any age should be given rights equivalent to existing adult rights; for invasive procedures (tattoos, piercings, etc.), they should be required to pass a test showing appropriate reasoning ability and awareness of consequences.
Drinking	Young people of any age who pass one or more relevant competency tests should have drinking rights equivalent to existing adult rights, with commensurate responsibility for drinking-related damages.
Driving	A graduated series of licenses should be issued to young people of any age when appropriate and rigorous competency tests are passed; the license should be subject to revocation based on performance.
Due Process	Young people of any age should be granted broad due process rights equivalent to those of adults without having to demonstrate competence.
Education	Segregation by age should be ended; emphasis should be put on satisfying individualized instructional needs; more home- and Internet-based instruction should be available, as well as more options to blend school and work and more options for testing out of courses or degree programs; the minimum age of school leaving should be reduced substantially; education should be spread over one's life, as needed and desired.

Emancipation	Young people of any age should be granted full legal independence from parents simply by passing a wide range of state-approved competency tests.
Entertainment	Rating systems for movies, music, and games should be maintained; emancipated young people or people of any age who have passed appropriate competency tests should be able to make purchases or enter public facilities (theaters, clubs, etc.) without restriction.
Free Speech	Young people of any age should have broad free speech rights equivalent to those of adults without having to demonstrate competency.
Independent Living	All emancipated young people (see above) should have the right to live independently of parents or guardians, as well as the right to own or rent property; rights should be protected under Equal Housing laws.
Juvenile Justice	The juvenile justice system should be abolished; all crimes should be handled by the existing criminal justice system, with allowances made for the immaturity of the accused, just as they are made for the developmentally disabled or mentally ill; separate cells or prisons should be available for young perpetrators as needed for safety; judges should have discretionary power to transfer cases to youth-run peer courts.
Lawsuits	After passing appropriate competency tests, young people of any age should be able to file lawsuits.
Legal Representation	After demonstrating appropriate competencies, a young person of any age should have the right to represent him- or herself in court; as a defendant in a criminal case, he or she should have the right to counsel without needing to demonstrate competence.
Marriage	After passing one or more appropriate competency tests, a young person of any age should have the right to marry without parental or court consent.
Medical Treatment	After passing one or more appropriate competency tests (demonstrating reasoning ability, awareness of consequences, and so on), a young person of any age should have the right to make his or her own medical decisions.
Mental Health Treatment	After passing one or more appropriate competency tests (demonstrating reasoning ability, awareness of consequences, and so on), a young person of any age should have the right to make his or her own decisions regarding psychiatric care; parents should no longer have the right to commit

	young people who can demonstrate appropriate competencies or who have been emancipated; young people should no longer be subjected to "treatment" unless suffering from legitimate disorders (such as schizophrenia or autism).
Military Service	After passing one of more appropriate (and presumably rigorous) competency tests, emancipated young people of any age should have the right to serve in the military; unemancipated young people will need the permission of a parent or judge
Pornography	If they can pass an appropriate test of maturity, young people of any age should have access to pornographic materials commensurate with adult access.
Privacy	Emancipated young people of any age should have broad privacy rights equivalent to those of adults; the privacy rights of unemancipated young people should be limited somewhat.
Property	After passing one or more appropriate competency tests, young people should have the right to own, control, and dispose of property.
Religion	Young people of any age should have the right to practice the religion of their choice without having to demonstrate competence.
Sex	After passing one or more appropriate competency tests (demonstrating sexual knowledge, physical and emotional maturity, awareness of consequences, and so on), a young person of any age should have control over his or her sex life.
Smoking	After passing one or more appropriate competency tests (demonstrating reasoning ability, awareness of consequences, and so on), a young person of any age should have the right to smoke.
Voting	After passing one or more appropriate competency tests (demonstrating basic knowledge of our political system, relevant issues, and so on), a young person of any age should have the right to vote in elections.
Wills	After passing one or more appropriate competency tests, a young person should have the right to make a will.
Work	After passing appropriate competency tests, young people of any age should have the right to compete with adults for any job; they should also get equal pay for equal work and should have the right to start, own, control, and dispose of businesses.

Work

Young people in America have been prohibited or discouraged from working for nearly a century now. We need to allow them to start working again, and not just in fast-food establishments. I'm not talking about exploitation or abuse, just the opportunity to become productive members of their families and of society at large.

My specific proposal is this: Any young person, no matter what his or her age, should be allowed to apply for any job. If he or she can demonstrate appropriate competencies, he or she should be taken seriously as a candidate. If he or she performs poorly, he or she should be fired. Just like in the real world. Just like with adults.

Young people should receive equal pay for equal work, just as women are supposed to be entitled to under the Equal Pay Act of 1963. They must also be able to own and control the money they earn through their labors—which brings me to the property issue.

Property

A few years ago, I had trouble getting insurance for a second home I was trying to rent out. Renters, I was told, simply don't take care of property as well as owners do. Property that's occupied by owners is maintained far better than property occupied by renters. Realtors say this phenomenon is the result of "pride of ownership": people care about what they own. A third category of occupants—let's call them prisoners, for want of a better term—is the worst kind of all. Reluctant occupants—people who would rather be elsewhere but don't have much choice in the matter—generally don't care at all about keeping the lawn trim or the paint from peeling.

American teens are in Category Three. Past a certain age they are often reluctant occupants of—in other words, prisoners in—the home of one or both parents, and parents, at that point, become reluctant jailers. Teens living under a parent's roof are generally not allowed to own or even to rent property of any sort; even when they are somehow able to do so (say, with parental permission), they never have complete control over it. Even their treasured phones and CD players can be confiscated without notice or explanation by Mom or Dad or other authorities. (In one of the most poignant scenes in *The Virgin Suicides*, Lux's mom forces her to burn some of her precious record albums in a fire, and the rest are put out with the trash.) It should surprise no one that teens are sometimes reluctant to take out the garbage. What's the point? It's not *their* house and it's not *their* garbage—even if, as is likely, they're the ones who generated it.

If we want our young people to value property, we need to give them full property rights, along with the responsibilities that such rights entail. The rights can be given inalienably, as the Constitution provides, or they can be given in stages, based on competence demonstrated through a series of tests. To me, the competency approach is the safer, more rational one. If performance is poor, one or more property rights can be rescinded until corrective steps are taken. I know of no reason for establishing a minimum age on property rights.

For property rights to be meaningful, young people will need a whole new set of options in life, and other basic rights (such as a meaningful right to privacy, which I'll discuss shortly) will need to be granted to them. Moreover, their rights will need to be clearly codified in law.

Once young people have demonstrated that they are competent to own property, parents and other authorities should no longer be able to manipulate them by threatening to confiscate what they own. If this makes you bristle (assuming you're an adult), think about it this way: As long as you've made your payments on time and haven't run anyone over lately, no one can take away your car. And no one can confiscate your clothing or stereo system or furniture or photo albums or computer simply because you were rude or because you failed to do your homework or because you smoked a cigarette. *Ownership is meaningful and absolute when you're an adult, and your very identity is determined to a large extent by your property*: your clothes, your home, your memorabilia, your nicknacks, and so on. Imagine if all of the property you control were subject to the whims of an authority figure. What would that do to your sense of security?

By giving competent young people full property rights, we lose some degree of control over them; in return, we get more responsible, more secure, more independent young people. Those who pass the tests take measurable, fulfilling steps toward full adulthood, and those who don't pass are highly motivated to do so on their next try.

Sex, Marriage, and Abortion

The rights of young people in all three of these controversial areas need to be firmly grounded in competencies. In other words, if a young person—no matter how young—can pass one or more tests showing that he or she understands what marriage is all about, knows how to make a relationship work, and is aware of the responsibilities that marriage entails, then he or she should be allowed to marry. If a young person can pass one or more tests demonstrating that he or she knows about the risks of sex, knows about birth control, is physically and emotionally mature, and so on, then he or she should be exempted from laws that may restrict his or her sexual behavior.

Abortion needs to be handled in a similar fashion. A young woman should be allowed to make the abortion decision if she can demonstrate that she is competent to make such a decision. The key questions here are: Does she have adultlike reasoning powers? Is she aware of the risks of the procedure? Does she have a basic understanding of the relevant moral issues? And is she aware of the possible negative consequences of having an abortion? A relatively simple test can determine all of this reliably, but because abortion is a medical procedure, the abortion itself should be subject to approval by a licensed physician. In all of these areas, there should be no need for notification of or approval by parents or other authorities. Once competence is established, even if it's in a narrow domain, the appropriate rights and responsibilities should be conferred.

Medical and Mental Health Decisions

These are also areas in which competence is key. A young person who can demonstrate basic reasoning abilities and who can show that he or she is aware of the possible benefits and risks of a procedure should be able to make the treatment decision without interference from an adult. Emancipated young people should be given such rights automatically. No competent young person should ever be medicated, subjected to surgery, or institutionalized without his or her consent. If you question that, keep in mind that "adults"—defined by age only—can't be treated against their will even if they're immature and uninformed. I'm suggesting, in effect, that we *raise* our standards, not lower them.

But then there are those gray areas—especially when it comes to physical and mental health. Someone who has just suffered a head injury in a car accident may not be conscious. Someone who is experiencing schizophrenic delusions may not be capable of thinking rationally. Who should make treatment decisions for incapacitated young people? Emancipated young people should have the right (when they're conscious and capable) of naming the responsible individuals by executing a "power of attorney" or equivalent document, just as adults do. Unemancipated young people will probably need to remain under the control of their parents in such situations.

Driving, Drinking, and Smoking

Young people already drink and smoke fairly freely; there's no easy way to stop them. As I discovered the hard way many years ago (with my two eldest sons), they also sometimes drive before they're legally allowed to do so. Our from-the-hip reaction is to get tougher and meaner, but that just makes most young people more secretive and more angry. Sometimes even when we think we've got some problem behavior under control, we find out later that we only drove it farther underground.

Is it really young people that we want to control, or is it the nature of their driving, drinking, and smoking? In other words, if we could be sure that a young person was driving safely (like a skillful adult), drinking only in moderation and never while driving (like a responsible adult), and fully aware of the risks of smoking before starting to light up (like a savvy but risk-prone adult), would we be so concerned? Don't we try to restrict the behavior of our young offspring because we're virtually certain that they'll drive recklessly, drink irresponsibly, and get addicted to cigarettes before they understand the risks?

We've seen abundant evidence that young people have the potential to rise to virtually all of the challenges of adult life, even if they're currently not expressing that potential. One way to measure and tap that potential—and to calm our fears—is through competency testing. Hence in these three areas my proposals are straightforward:

- A young person of any age who can pass one or more rigorous driving tests should be allowed to have a drivers license (perhaps awarded in stages, as many drivers licenses are today). The license will be subject to revocation for poor driving, just as it is with any adult driver.
- A young person of any age who can demonstrate appropriate competencies (mainly reasoning skills and an awareness of risks and consequences) should be able to get an ID that allows him or her to purchase and drink alcoholic beverages. If the young person behaves irresponsibly (for example, by giving alcohol to peers who lack drinking privileges), his or ID will be subject to revocation.
- A young person of any age who can demonstrate appropriate competencies (again, mainly reasoning skills and an awareness of risks and consequences) should be able to get an ID that allows him or her to purchase and smoke cigarettes. Again, if the individual abuses this privilege, it will be subject to revocation.

A friend of mine from South America—herself a mother of two teens—was amused on a recent trip here by the fuss we make about the drinking and smoking of young people. "We let them smoke and drink all they want," she told me. "As a result, they don't get so excited about smoking and drinking, and we don't fight with them so much." This is an interesting concept to be sure—and a very old one—but I'm not advocating that we let our teens "drink and smoke all they want."

It's true that placing restrictions on people sometimes drives them precisely

in the wrong direction, but I'm not suggesting that we get rid of restrictions but rather that we give young people strong incentives to become responsible citizens. I don't want them to *feign* adulthood by drinking and smoking in dark alleys; I want them to *be* adults by drinking and smoking responsibly—more responsibly, perhaps, than most adults do. (Whereas adults do have to pass competency tests to get a drivers license, all they have to do to be able to drink and smoke is to reach a certain age—no competence required.)

Military Service

Recall that by age thirteen golfer Michelle Wie was nearly six feet tall and making news with her three hundred-yard drives. I don't know whether she'd make a good soldier, but I do know that it's unwise to generalize about people based on their age (young or old). What's more, the American military has been competency-oriented for generations; it has the tools for weeding out the qualified. The modern IQ test was largely developed and legitimized in the United States by the Army during World War I. With millions of draftees to evaluate, in 1917 the Army established a committee of seven leading psychologists to devise a suitable screening test. By 1919 more than two million draftees had been given the new test, which gave applicants a grade from A through E (where A was the highest) based on their performance. All branches of our military still depend heavily on a variety of testing to determine fitness to serve, to fight, and to lead.

I propose, therefore, that an emancipated young person of any age who can qualify for service should be allowed to enlist without parental consent. Unemancipated young people of any age who can qualify for service should be allowed to enlist with the consent of at least one parent or a judge.

Free Speech and Privacy

The right to free speech should, I believe, be granted to young people of any age in precisely the same way that it's granted to adults. It's not an absolute right—you can't run into a crowded movie theater, for example, and yell "Fire! Fire!" when there is no fire—but it's quite broad, and no one should need to pass a competency test or reach a certain age to acquire it.

Our right to privacy is also quite broad but also not absolute: If authorities suspect you of committing a crime, they can tap your phone, search your house and car, and even strip-search you. Emancipated young people should have privacy rights precisely equivalent to those of adults—no more locker searches based on a lowly school administrator's suspicions and no more room searches based on Mom's hunches. But unemancipated young people should continue to have only limited

privacy rights, much as they have today. Some privacy restrictions will have to remain in place because parents of unemancipated young people can be held responsible for whatever their offspring are hiding under the mattresses. More generally, if a young person cannot demonstrate that he or she is ready to live in the adult world, we should probably be reluctant to extend our complete trust.

Legal Matters

Emancipated young people should have full adult rights and should therefore enjoy all of the legal rights they would normally obtain at the age of majority. But some legal rights should be absolute and not depend on age or even competency. I've already mentioned free speech in this regard, and I also believe that due process rights should be on the list. Young people of any age who are charged with a crime should have all of the rights that adults have: the right to counsel, the right to question witnesses, the right to a speedy trial, the right to examine a court transcript, and so on. The Constitution provides such guarantees for all "persons"— not just to people over a certain age.

Even if unemancipated, young people of any age who can demonstrate appropriate competencies should be able to make and revoke wills, sign contracts, file law suits, and represent themselves in court. After all, we automatically extend such rights to many older people who *lack* the appropriate skills and understanding.

Dress, Appearance, and Curfews

When a young person wants to alter his or her appearance, he or she should generally be able to do so with the same freedom that an adult has. For invasive procedures like tattooing and piercing, a young person who wants to proceed without parental permission should be required to pass an appropriate competency test, mainly demonstrating that he or she has basic reasoning skills and is aware of the risks and consequences associated with the procedure. Emancipated young people should be presumed to be competent in this way.

The curfew issue is more complex. Some courts have opined that curfews violate our right of assembly, guaranteed under the First Amendment to the Constitution. Government can generally abridge that right only in serious crises. We treasure our freedoms in America, and freedom of movement is right up there with freedom of speech.

For government to single out any particular age group for a curfew seems to me to be a threat to our most basic liberties. Old people don't drive very well, and they probably drive more poorly in the dark. Does that give government the right to legislate curfews for the elderly? Blacks, on the average, commit more crimes

after dark than whites do; does that give government the right to legislate a curfew just for blacks?

The main problem with curfews that single out any particular group is that they turn perfectly innocent members of that group into criminals (that is, "curfew violators") based merely on the remote possibility that *some* members of that group *might* commit a crime. Call it ageism, racism, or guilt by association; whatever the label, it's not pretty.

Hence my proposal is fairly straightforward: No curfew should be allowed in this country unless it's for everyone (excluding emergency personnel). Emancipated young people should be able move about as freely as adults. The wanderings of un-emancipated young people will have to remain under parental control because parents of dependent offspring are often held responsible for their wrongdoings.

Entertainment and Pornography

As G. Stanley Hall, the psychologist who put the distressed teen on the map in 1904, told us earlier, "Parents still think of their [adolescent] offspring as mere children, and tighten the reign when they should loosen it."[4] No matter what those offensive anti-drug ads promise you about the magical powers you supposedly have over your offspring, if your teen has idle time, extra cash, and hangs around with peers, he or she will inevitably experiment with various forms of entertainment which some adults will find objectionable—at least for young people but not neces-sarily for themselves or other adults.

Tightening the rein is not the solution to this problem, and it's not even clear that it's possible. Even Socrates, when referring to efforts to control young people, said that "there is small wisdom in legislating about such matters; I doubt if it is ever done"[5] (see Appendix 4).

I'm not entirely convinced that teen tendencies to sample adult forms of entertainment are really a problem; they seem quite natural, especially when you accept the fact that teens aren't children. To the extent that young people overin-dulge themselves, I think there's only one legitimate solution: to integrate them as rapidly as possible into adult society. They're most vulnerable to mischief when they're with peers and less vulnerable when they're with adults. As a psychiatrist colleague once said, there's no intervention more powerful that simply "being with."

Regarding violent or sexual music, movies, and video games, I know of no convincing evidence that such materials actually harm anyone (see my comments about correlational studies toward the end of Chapter Five), and I do not believe that teens are, on the average, any more vulnerable to the possible negative effects of such materials than adults are.

When it comes to entertainment, emancipated young people or people of any age who have passed appropriate competency tests should be able to make purchases or enter public facilities (theaters, clubs, etc.) without restriction. Regarding pornography, I believe that any young person who can pass an appropriate test of maturity should have access to pornographic materials that's similar to the access adults have.

Corporal Punishment

Corporal punishment, although barbaric and unpleasant, is actually useful sometimes in child rearing. The many alarming studies that you read about that show a relationship between corporal punishment and various behavior and mood problems are all correlational. Not a single one shows that spanking a child (or paddling a young person in school) actually *causes* the associated problems. In fact, it is especially likely that corporal punishment and behavior problems are associated with each other primarily because parents and authorities are far more likely to hit unruly children than compliant ones.

In a few situations, corporal punishment is probably even the best way to handle a problem, because it's the only technique we have that can suppress behavior both immediately and long term. If a child routinely runs out into the street, plays with matches, or bites other children, a hard slap on the buttocks is probably the intervention of choice.

When we withhold punishment in situations like these, we potentially do great harm to a child. Harsh measures are not only justified sometimes, failing to use such measures can put people at great risk. This is especially obvious in the medical field, where the failure to amputate a gangrenous leg or irradiate a tumor can lead to death.*

That said, for the vast majority of behavior problems that parents or teachers encounter, corporal punishment is not the answer. In continuing-education seminars I used to teach for clinical psychologists seeking to renew their practice licenses, I covered fifty ways of reducing problem behaviors without the use of corporal punishment. Given that corporal punishment is unpleasant and potentially damaging to relationships, parents and other authority figures should probably be made more aware of the positive alternatives they have—another interesting competency issue, to be sure.

So my recommendation is as follows: "Corporal punishment" of an adult is called "assault and battery," and therefore parents who strike their

---

*In medicine, a treatment that's worse than the original disease is called "iatrogenic." Withholding a harsh treatment also crosses this line when the consequences of not acting are worse than the consequences of providing treatment. The ultimate ethical guideline in medicine—"above all else, do no harm"—often requires physicians to perform risky or unpleasant interventions.

YOUNG PEOPLE IN ACTION

The Unschooled Inventor

As a young child Thomas Edison accidentally burned down the family barn in Ohio, and he caused so much trouble in school that his mother decided to home-school him, mainly letting him study whatever interested him. At twelve he started selling newspapers and candies on a train, where he continued his private studies and even tried to conduct scientific experiments. He was forced to stop his research after he accidentally caused a fire on the train. By sixteen he became independent of his parents and soon moved to Canada. After working as a telegraph operator for a few years, he decided to become a full-time inventor. By the time he died at age eighty-four in 1931, Edison had 1,093 patents to his credit—far more than anyone before or since has ever obtained. His inventions include the first practical electric light bulb, the first phonograph, the first movie cameras and projectors, and the first microphone.[6]

emancipated offspring should be subject to criminal prosecution. (Now *there's* an incentive for young people to pass those emancipation tests.) But as long as young people remain unemancipated, parents should continue to have the right to strike them, with the proviso that when challenged by authorities, they should have a duty to show (a) that their use of corporal punishment was reasonable and appropriate (which means, among other things, that it didn't injure the recipient), and (b) that other, less risky means of behavior management had been tried first.

Religious Decisions

Past a certain level of maturity, which many young people are probably capable of reaching in their early or mid teens, our offspring need to decide their own religious affairs. Young people should be allowed to do so without having to demonstrate any particular sort of competence. Faith is an intensely personal phenomenon. There's also no pushing anyone toward faith, as far I can tell. The more you push, the more closed the heart and mind become.

Voting

As we'll see later in the chapter, a legislator in California recently tried to secure limited voting rights for minors in statewide elections, and several countries already allow people under eighteen to vote. But no one seems to be thinking about this issue with any great clarity. Why would we want to give someone the power to

vote—it's more than a right, it's a *power*—based simply on his or her *age*, whatever that age happens to be? Do we really want voters who don't know even the basics about government and who don't know about the issues and candidates?

Unfortunately, an informed electorate is not always what politicians want. Thomas Edison—the most prolific and influential inventor in history—learned this the hard way after patenting his first invention. It was a tabulation device that allowed people to see how legislators voted while they were actually casting their votes. It worked, but the legislators soon stopped using it because it provided more information to constituents than they wanted to provide.[7]* Informed voters are difficult to influence; uninformed voters can typically be bought for a few dollars spent wisely on marketing and advertising.

This important issue aside, my recommendation here is clear: Young people of any age who can pass a test that shows they will be competent voters—that they understand how government works, that they understand current issues, and that they know about current candidates—should be given the right to cast full votes in relevant elections.

Connecting Teens and Adults

Notice what's not on my list of recommendations. Nowhere have I suggested that we need to do anything about the many companies and organizations that currently provide the infrastructure for teen culture (see Chapter Fourteen). Young people fall prey to or come under the control of such entities because they have nowhere else to go. If they have real responsibility in their lives, and if they're meaningfully connected to the adult world, it's unlikely that mosh pits and MTV will have quite the fascination for them that they do now.

They also won't have quite as many legitimate reasons to direct anger toward their elders, because their elders will no longer be their jailers. Instead, we will become what we were during much of human history: master craftspeople, welcoming young people into our midst as quickly as they can hone their various skills. Young people will become apprentices of sorts, but unlike the apprentices of old, they'll have almost unlimited leeway to determine their own futures.

Notice also that I'm not suggesting that we take any steps backward into our agrarian, overly-romanticized past. I'm simply proposing ways to reintegrate modern young people into adult society, as well as to establish systems that improve and accelerate this process from one generation to the next.

---

*Edison swore that he'd never again patent something without first determining that there was a market for it. Fortunately for those of us who like to turn on lights, listen to recorded music, and watch movies, he made good on his resolution.

> ## YOUNG PEOPLE IN ACTION
>
> ### Twenty-Something Teens
>
> *Jill Nelson, one of the people who helped me research this book, told me that when she was twenty-three, on a Christmas visit with her twenty-two-year-old brother to Dad and Step-Mom, the latter told them, "You teens can sleep in the living room." Teens, Jill wondered? At twenty-two and twenty-three? Was this just a slip, or are we expanding the definition of teen to include a wider age range? A recent Associated Press story about the murder of University of Dakota student Dru Sjoden is entitled "Justice Sought for Minnesota Teen." Dru was twenty-two when she was killed. Yet another slip, or more evidence of upward-creeping infantilization?*

What do we lose by establishing a competency-based system of rights and privileges for young people? I believe that all we lose is our sense of control—control that was unwise to try to exercise in the first place and that was largely illusory anyway. And what do we gain with the competency-based system I've proposed? In a word: *competence*.

PROTECTING YOUNG CHILDREN

Although logic demanded that I state, in the list of recommendations I presented above, that there should be no minimum age limits on the rights that we extend to young people, I'm not at all comfortable about allowing young children to smoke, drink, drive, and so on. Then why am I not proposing minimum age limits?

You may recall from Chapter One that educator John Holt and psychologist Richard Farson suggested long ago that young children should automatically be granted virtually all adult rights. But as the data in chapters Seven and Nine make clear, children simply do not measure up. They don't have even a fraction of the physical and cognitive capabilities of teens and adults, and no amount of training can change that.

So why don't we just draw a line somewhere? Say, seven, the age when the Catholics say a child first becomes capable of committing a sin, or thirteen, the age of the Jewish Bar Mitzvah. English psychiatrist Philip Graham recently suggested that age fourteen should be the cutoff.[8] So why not say that from *age* X onward, we'll grant rights to young people who can demonstrate their competence—but *never* before that age?

There are several reasons we must resist our deeply ingrained tendencies to specify age cutoffs for basic rights:

- *Uniqueness of individuals.* First, everyone is unique; in America, we celebrate that fact, perhaps more so than in any other country on earth. We've seen examples in this book of extraordinary young people—Louis Braille, Jim Henson, Alexandra Nechita, Thomas Edison, Ming Kipa, Luther and Johnny Htoo, and many others—who simply don't fit our preconceptions about young people. Age cutoffs—whether for the young or for the old—often imprison people on the wrong side of the line. With competency testing, there's no need to do that. We can allow individuals to develop as quickly as they are able, holding no one back who has the ability and motivation to move forward, punishing no one for precocity.
- *Uniqueness of abilities.* Second, just as individuals differ in very general ways, so do their specific abilities. Piaget theorized that the abilities of young people develop in stages, but he also recognized that an individual's abilities might develop unevenly, out of sync with expected stages—a phenomenon he called *décalage.* Sometimes a young person who is weak in some respects (say, in verbal abilities) might be exceptionally strong in others (say, in mathematics or performance art). Age cutoffs can be stifling to such people; a competency-based system will allow them to flourish.
- *Arbitrariness.* Third, any age we pick for a cutoff point is necessarily arbitrary. Why bother?
- *Protected by competence.* Fourth, because we're withholding rights and privileges until appropriate tests are passed, there's no downside to eliminating the age cutoff. The tests guarantee that only competent people will be granted those rights and privileges, all of which are subject to revocation.

In contrast, an arbitrary age cutoff necessarily allows incompetent people to gain rights and privileges they probably shouldn't have. We're careful to give drivers licenses only to people who can pass both written exams and road tests. It would be absurd to let people drive simply because they turned eighteen or twenty-one. Yet this is exactly what we do with the vast majority of rights we give to young people now. A competency-based system—with no age cutoffs—is actually far safer and more conservative than an age-based system where competencies are never measured.

FREEDOM, AUTHORITY, AND RESPONSIBILITY

When I was a senior in high school, American military forces made a major foray into Cambodia from Vietnam, and high school and college students, as well as others around the United States, protested. At the college I was about to attend, Trinity College in Connecticut, students occupied a building and locked up the trustees. By the time I got to school that fall, the campus was in chaos. The student government had voted itself out of existence; most of the clubs were gone; and drugs were being sold openly in the halls of the dormitories. Most important, course and attendance requirements had been abolished. I was compulsive about attending classes, but because there were no specific distribution requirements in place, I took exactly what I pleased, which turned out to be mainly courses in either dance or psychology.

When I reached the last semester of my senior year, a little common-sense light bulb lit up in my head: I realized that I had been through three-and-a-half years of college without ever having taken a single course in English, history, biology, economics, sociology, anthropology, or a dozen other major fields. During my last semester, I took four freshman-level courses in fields that were a complete mystery to me. Thank goodness for that light bulb. I just wish the current had flowed sooner.

Years later, I became a member of one of the governing boards of Trinity College, and I was a strong voice for strengthening distribution and attendance requirements. I also set in motion a "mentors" program that brought faculty members and graduate students into close, regular contact with undergraduates.

The point of my reminiscence is clear, I hope. *I am not advocating more "freedom" for teens.* The freedom that college students grabbed in the 1960s and 70s didn't serve them very well; nor does any unbridled form of freedom. I hope no one reading this book ever gets the impression that because I object strongly to the infantilization of teens, this means I think teens should be more "free." Absolutely not. *The corrective for infantilization is responsibility, not freedom.*

Although it's true that adults are free to make many choices that children and teens cannot make, the freedom that adults have is enjoyed in the context of many restrictions and possible penalties. When an adult causes a car accident, he or she is liable for the damage he or she caused. When an under-aged, unlicensed teen causes a car accident, the parents are often held liable for the damage, and the

teen generally is not. It would be meaningless to hold the teen accountable because teens can't conduct business, own property, sign contracts, and so on; a teen generally can't compensate victims for the damage he or she has caused.

The freedom adults appear to have is actually authority, not freedom. Adults can't do anything they please; they can simply exercise authority in various domains in which they must also accept various forms of responsibility. They can make decisions, for example, about health care, religion, parenting, financial matters, and so on, and they can drive and smoke and drink, subject to a variety of restrictions. But in a rational world, authority always goes hand-in-hand with responsibility; that is, no one is given authority without also being required to take on the burden of corresponding responsibilities, and no one is given responsibilities without also being given some corresponding authority.

Giving someone authority without responsibility is akin to saying: "Sure, take the new Jaguar for a spin, and don't worry if you destroy it. I'll take care of it." That's a good way of putting the Jag on the road to the body shop or junkyard. Authority in the absence of responsibility promotes recklessness. And as I noted in Chapter Eleven, giving someone responsibility without authority is akin to saying: "You're responsible for whatever happens to that car, even if you're no where near it and even if you have no control over what happens to it." Responsibility without authority is frustrating and immobilizing.

So please, let's not give teens more freedom. They have much too much freedom as it is. By that I mean that many teens have too much free time (unstructured, unsupervised hours spent doing meaningless things, often with peers), too much free cash (money obtained from an allowance, gifts, or part-time work which can be used in entirely discretionary ways), and too much freedom from consequences (that is, from the negative consequences of behavior that would normally be severely punished in adults).

Let's give teens who seek it and who can demonstrate appropriate competencies the *authority* they deserve, along with the *responsibility* that such authority demands.

ADOLESCENCE ABOLISHED

Competency testing for young people may be a reasonable idea, but what will happen if many of our young people are unable to pass or choose not to take certain tests? What will happen, in particular, if they are unable to qualify for competency-based emancipation by the time they reach age eighteen? Or perhaps even twenty-one? Or perhaps *ever*?

I believe there's a strong case to be made for withholding most rights (other than some obvious ones like due process and free speech) until the competencies entailed by the proper exercise of those rights can be demonstrated. Do we really want people to wield the enormous power of the vote when they don't know even the minimum about our government, the candidates, or the issues in the election? Do we really want people to get married who have no idea how to sustain a relationship? Do we really want people to have sex when they don't know the first thing about birth control, sexually-transmitted disease, and child rearing?

The unavoidable answer to all of these questions is, of course, that Americans today don't care about competency in most of the activities of daily living. We'd like our physicians and teachers and plumbers to be competent—and to demonstrate their competence by passing state exams and getting licenses and certificates—but we don't care at all about competence when it comes to marrying, having sex, parenting, drinking, smoking, voting, making wills, and so on. Adults—who often tend to be highly incompetent in such matters—don't have to demonstrate any degree of competence in order to engage in such activities; they just need to reach a certain age. Yet, based simply on their age, we deny young people a wide range of basic rights because we're afraid they might be *incompetent*. We just assume, based largely on unanalyzed assertions passed down over generations, that under a certain age people are necessarily incompetent (even though this probably isn't true) and that over a certain age people are necessarily competent (even though we *know* this isn't true).

If we had even an ounce of sense, we'd withhold certain rights and privileges from *everyone* until they could pass the relevant competency test. We've grown used to this idea when it comes to driving a motor vehicle; perhaps, some day, we'll be able to extend this logic to other areas. This is not likely to happen any time soon, however. We might see some advantages to looking more carefully at the competencies of teens, but we're far from being ready to consider the possibility of a competency based society.

The bottom line: for the foreseeable future, we'll almost certainly have to continue to award most rights automatically at certain ages. This means that young people who have not already earned certain rights through testing before age eighteen will gain them automatically at some point. Age, in effect, will have to continue to serve as a substitute for competency—a weak stand-in, to be sure.

Thus the competency-based system I'm proposing is not meant as a corrective for our generally incompetent society but rather as a corrective for a much smaller, although not inconsequential, problem: the artificial extension of childhood.

Allowing young people to test their way to adulthood will, I believe, have relatively immediate and dramatic effects:

- *It will help to restore the child-adult continuum that was disrupted by the draconian social reforms of the Industrial Revolution.* It won't do so in a way that Jean Liedloff might envision—that is, by bringing children and adults together in the fields around a primitive village—but it will do so nonetheless. Adulthood has always been the ultimate carrot, but it was never within reach. With it just millimeters away, many young people will be strongly motivated to learn what they need to learn to grab the prize. And the main people they'll look to for help will be their older mentors, parents, and teachers. They'll be learning from the people they're supposed to learn from, not just from Hollywood's ejecta.

- *It will force adults to look at young people with new respect and a new sense of optimism.* As the numbers of young people who pass various tests or who achieve full emancipation multiply like the numbers on the old McDonald's signs, adults will have no choice but to see young people through competency-colored lenses—focusing on their abilities and achievements, not on their failings.

- *It will integrate young people into adult society at a rapid pace by providing a fast lane to adulthood for the young people who choose it.* The particular areas where the integration will first occur are impossible to say, but I'll make some quick guesses: Some young people will test their way out of school to try to start high-tech businesses, many of which will be Internet based. And they will own and control the fruits of their labors. When we take the energy and raw intellectual power of youth and add to it the limitless promise of Horatio Alger's American Dream, we might churn out Bill Gates clones by the thousands. Other young people may test out of school or at least gain partial adult privileges in order to work in family businesses, start their own families, or try for early college admission.

- *It will reduce many of the signs of turmoil we currently see in our young:* suicidal tendencies, ennui, anger, irresponsible drug and alcohol use, and so on. There is strong evidence, both historical and contemporary, that we have created this turmoil through the artificial extension of childhood. When we say to our young people, "Okay, you want to be adults?

Show us what you can do," many will rise to the challenge. In effect, we'll be tapping into one of the most basic of evolutionary imperatives: the desire to be independent. When young people have meaningful options for moving forward with their lives, I suspect teen culture will start to look pathetic.

- *It will spur an explosion of creativity among the young*—and not just creativity that feeds teen culture, but creativity that will feed the great cultures of the world. It may also lead to the reappearance of the young genius—not just to the "gifted" children we parents puff about but to the true geniuses of our age. How many thousands of great talents have been buried under the minutia of the cookie-cutter educational system produced by the factories of the Industrial Revolution? We pay lip service today to difference and diversity; a competency-based society—at least for young people—will lead to a celebration of diversity like the world has never seen.

- *It will bring vast new human resources to our culture.* The twenty million American teens who currently live their semi-lives immersed in trivia will be given the means and the incentive to make meaningful contributions to our increasingly needy world. Their unflagging energy, superior intelligence, sizzling creativity, and unbridled idealism could make all the difference.

- *It will abolish adolescence, at least as a time of storm and stress.* Through much of human history, the teen years were primarily a time of learning, not a time of great turmoil; this is still true in many cultures today. If I'm right about competency testing for the young, perhaps "adolescence" will become a historical footnote in our textbooks rather than the subject of entire Ph.D. programs.

THE INEVITABLE REVERSAL

If adolescence is so unnatural and contrived, shouldn't forces, both social and biological, be at work to undermine its existence? Toward the end of *Children and Childhood in Western Society Since 1500*, historian Hugh Cunningham suggests just that.

Noting tendencies, especially in the United States, for young people to insist on behaving like adults—even, in some cases, bringing law suits against

their own parents—Cunningham predicts the inevitability of recreating an era when young people are integrated into adult society at an early age.

> The essence of the vision of childhood at the beginning of the [twentieth] century was the powerlessness of children, their dependence; good parenting consisted of preserving and prolonging this, in part at least by the exercise of parental authority. What has happened in the second half of the century is that parental authority has declined, and children have demanded and received an earlier access to the adult world; they have not been willing to accept the attempt to prolong childhood to the late teenage years. In some ways this represents a return to a historical norm in which childhood did not extend beyond fourteen at the maximum.[9]

Notably, Cunningham concludes this discussion by pointing out that the reversal, to the extent that it is occurring, is flawed, perhaps fatally:

> The difference is that in earlier centuries at the age of fourteen a person was economically productive whereas in the late twentieth century he or she will have a minimum of two years and quite probably a further seven or more years of non-productivity. Not surprisingly "adolescence" has come to be seen as a time of stressful conflict between parents and children.[10]

So far, the stressful conflict between parents and their offspring created by the artificial extension of childhood is not producing the "return to the historical norm" that Cunningham predicts. At least in the United States, teen attempts to reenter the adult world have largely failed. They have been met, in fact, with stronger controls: curfews, armed guards, metal detectors, dress codes, and new forms of incarceration, among many others.

The institutions and belief systems that have been established over the last century to keep teens in place aren't going to fall easily (see Chapter Fourteen). One rather mundane reason for this is that teens can't organize to any great extent, because *being a teen is temporary*. As Harvard's Herbert Kelman said years ago, "The young have very little in the way of a past and even less in the way of a future."[11] Women and minorities don't suffer from this problem; they retain their identities for a lifetime. Teen leaders, on the other hand, cross the arbitrary threshold into adulthood almost overnight; with a full set of rights, their angst quickly disappears, along with their motives for elevating the status of young people.

But there is some hope. During the Vietnam War, which accelerated gradually over the course of the 1960s and ended pointedly in 1973, it became

painfully obvious to the American public that much of the fighting and dying was being done by very young men. The average age of the more than three million men who served was about twenty-two, compared with twenty-six in World War II. More than a million of our soldiers were under twenty-one, and, according to official records, 11,465 of the more than 58,000 American soldiers who were killed in action in Vietnam were nineteen or younger.[12] Bear in mind that this was the first war that was broadcast every day on television, where every ugly detail stood out in sharp relief. How could we deny eighteen-, nineteen-, and twenty-year-olds the basic rights of adulthood while we were so willing to ship them out by the hundreds of thousands to fight for our country? The war suggested a kind of hypocrisy in our structure of laws, and it set some corrections in motion.

Real Juvenile Justice

In 1967, for example, the Supreme Court, in a case entitled *In re Gault*, restored long-lost due process rights to minors—well, at least somewhat. Two years before, fifteen-year-old Gerald Gault of Arizona had been taken into custody by juvenile authorities because of a complaint by his neighbor that he and a friend of his had made an obscene phone call to her. As is usual in juvenile court, there was no lawyer, no court transcript was made, Gault was never advised of his Fifth Amendment right not to say anything self-incriminating, and no witnesses were called—not even the neighbor who had made the complaint. Had he been an adult, the maximum sentence would have been two months in jail and a fifty dollar fine, but Gault was sentenced to *six years* in the State Industrial School (until age twenty-one)—a fairly standard sentence for the juvenile court.

In a scathing majority opinion that challenged the very foundations of the juvenile justice system, Justice Abe Fortas correctly explained that the original idea behind this "peculiar" system of justice was to protect young people from the hardships of the criminal justice system, to handle them with "care and solicitude," and to "treat" and "rehabilitate" them, rather then punish them. But, he said, "however euphemistic the title, a 'receiving home' or an 'industrial school' for juveniles is an institution of confinement in which the child is incarcerated.... Under our Constitution, the condition of being a boy does not justify a kangaroo court."[13]

Unfortunately, the *In re Gault* ruling has had only a modest impact on the juvenile justice system, in part because it explicitly avoided addressing "the totality of the relationship of the juvenile and the state."[14] Juvenile courts still routinely deny young people their due-process rights, and juvenile facilities are more punitive than ever.

In the late 1960s free-speech rights—again, quite limited—were also returned to young people. In *Tinker v. Des Moines School District*, the Supreme Court said that a

school was wrong for having suspended three students (ages thirteen, fifteen, and sixteen) who wore black armbands to school in 1965 to protest the Vietnam War. In its 1969 decision the Court said that only "disruptive" speech can be prohibited by a school, whereas the armbands were equivalent to "pure speech," which is protected by the First Amendment.[15] Unfortunately, as we've seen, almost any form of speech—such as an objectionable article in a school newspaper—can be judged to be "disruptive."

New Voting Rights—and More

With due process and free speech rights at least partially restored, on March 23, 1971, after a bitter battle, Congress passed the text of the Twenty-Sixth Amendment to the Constitution, granting eighteen-year-olds the right to vote in both federal and state elections. The amendment was ratified by the states in just three months. Even more significant, within a few short years, the new amendment inspired most states to lower the age of majority from twenty-one to eighteen (see table, page 347).

A few years later, in 1976, the Supreme Court made its most expansive statement ever about the rights of minors:

> Constitutional rights do not mature and come into being magically only when one attains the state-defined age of majority. Minors, as well as adults, are protected by the Constitution and possess constitutional rights.[16]

Teens also now have some privacy rights—even "sexual privacy rights." In 1977, in the case of *Carey v. Population Services International*, the Supreme Court invalidated a New York law that had prohibited the sale of contraceptives to people under sixteen on the grounds that young people have constitutionally-protected privacy rights.[17] The privacy issue is tricky, though. All states allow young people some degree of sexual privacy—in California, this even applies to young people under fourteen (Chapter Eight)—but in a practical sense the privacy rights of teens are actually quite limited—even illusory. Parents can search bedrooms and school officials can search school lockers, backpacks, and purses on almost any pretext; all they need is "reasonable suspicion" that something is amiss, and that's a pretty easy standard to meet. The Supreme Court affirmed the school's virtually unlimited ability to violate a student's privacy in a case in 1985.[18] Even strip searches are allowed under some circumstances.

In recent years, youth advocates in the United States have been trying to get the legal voting age lowered to sixteen or younger, most notably the National Youth Rights Association, an Internet-based organization formed, more-or-less, in 1998. A California bill sponsored recently by state senator John Vasconcellos would have given sixteen-year-olds a half vote and fourteen-year-olds a quarter vote in state

elections. After the bill was killed by a committee vote, high school students in Berkeley, California, immediately took up the cause.[19] Along these lines, New York City councilwoman Gail A. Brewer recently introduced legislation that would lower the voting age to sixteen in municipal elections.[20]

In England the matter has long been under serious study by Parliament, which may lower the national voting age to sixteen by the time this book is published.[21] At the moment at least ten countries, including Brazil, Cuba, Indonesia, and Sudan allow people under eighteen to vote, with no ill effects that anyone can yet detect.[22]

Recent laws and court decisions have given teens a few other rights, as well. Teens now have limited property rights, for example. Even though they generally can't control their property—an important practical matter, to be sure—they can at least *own* property under certain circumstances, and a court can put their property into trusts to prevent parents or guardians from walking off with it. In cases, for example, where parents were squandering large sums earned by their talented thespian offspring, the courts have generally stepped in and protected the assets.[23] Because the vast majority of teens don't have Macaulay Culkin's resources, however, as a practical matter most teens actually have little or no control over their property and, in effect, no *useful* property rights.

Teens also now have limited rights to religious freedom (although their parents can prevent them from attending churches or participating in religious rituals), a limited right to get an abortion without parental consent (if a judge okays it), limited rights to be free from sexual harassment (if they can get anyone to pay attention to their complaints), and limited rights to be free from sex and race discrimination (if they can show that they suffered some loss because of their sex or race and not for other reasons).[24] In most states, teens can also now get medical help for drug problems, alcoholism, or pregnancy without parental consent.[25] As for corporal punishment, it's still legal in all states for parents to strike their minor children (a legacy of the "chattel" tradition), but a majority of school districts have now made it illegal for school officials to strike students. At this point, fewer than 350,000 students in the United States are paddled in school each year, compared with four times that number in 1980.[26]

Some curfew laws have also been struck down by state courts in recent years. The matter hasn't yet come before the Supreme Court, and lower courts are divided on the issue. As you might imagine, where curfews have been prohibited, it hasn't been because teens are considered competent. Rather, the courts have said that the government shouldn't be interfering the *parents'* right to determine when it's safe for a teen to be outside the home. Being outside the home, after all, is not in and of itself a criminal act, and curfews, some legal experts say, interfere with the constitutional right of assembly. As an attorney

representing families in a case in Alaska put it, "Curfews don't punish kids who commit real crimes and they punish kids who aren't doing anything wrong."[27]

Age of Majority by State in the United States as of 2004	
Age	*State*
18	Alaska[b, c], Arizona[a, d], Arkansas[a, d], California[b, d], Connecticut, Delaware[b], Florida[b, d], Georgia, Hawaii[h], Idaho, Illinois, Indiana, Iowa, Kansas[b], Kentucky[b], Louisiana[a], Maine[b], Maryland, Massachusetts, Michigan[b], Minnesota[e], Missouri[f, g], Montana[b], New Hampshire[a, d], New Mexico, New Jersey, New Mexico, Nevada, North Carolina, North Dakota[b], Ohio[a], Oklahoma[b], Oregon[f], Pennsylvania[a], Rhode Island, South Carolina[a], South Dakota[b], Tennessee[a], Utah[a], Vermont[a], Washington[a], Wisconsin[b], Wyoming[e, i]
19	Alabama, Colorado, Nebraska, Virginia
21	Washington D.C., Mississippi, New York, Puerto Rico

a. age may be extended if individual is in school
b. age may be extended to nineteen if individual is in school
c. age may be extended if individual is residing with custodial parent
d. age may be extended if individual is disabled
e. age may be extended to twenty if individual is in school
f. age may be extended to twenty-one if individual is in school
g. age may be extended to twenty-two if individual is attending post-secondary school
h. age may be extended to twenty-three if individual is attending post-secondary school
i. age may be extended indefinitely for disabled individuals

Divorcing One's Parents

Emancipation rights have also been changing, generally giving young people more options. Most states have had emancipation laws on the books for a long time; these allow minors over a certain age (typically sixteen), with the permission of a court, to assume some or all of the rights of adults. Unless one is a wealthy young actor, however, these laws are fairly meaningless. At sixteen most vendors, employers, and landlords will be reluctant to deal with you; flashing a piece of paper saying you were "emancipated" won't make much difference.

The latest variation on emancipation is for a young person to "divorce" his or her parents. The most famous proceeding in this area is a 1993 Florida case called *Kingsley v. Kingsley*, in which an eleven-year-old successfully terminated his mother's parental rights in an effort to become part of another family. An appeals court ruled in this case, however—in classic Catch-22 fashion—that the young man didn't have the right to file the original law suit. He ultimately won only because a lawyer representing him (with a court's permission) had filed his own petition in behalf of the young man.[28] So you do have a right to divorce your parents, but first you have to file a law suit—which, of course, you can't.

In 2004 fourteen-year-old Patrick Holland was able to end his father's parental rights after a difficult two-year battle in Norfolk County, Massachusetts. His dad, Daniel Holland, is in prison on a life sentence (with no possible parole) for the beating and murder of his mom when Patrick was eight.[29] Even in a case so clear and extreme, it's not easy to terminate a parent's parental rights.

Baby Steps

Such issues are in constant flux, needless to say. Dress codes are generally becoming far more strict, for example, but in one recent case parents won their law suit against a school district that had required their eighth-grade daughter to remove a small tattoo from between her thumb and index finger.[30] In another case Native American students in Texas, objecting to dress-code restrictions, prevailed in a law suit against the Big Sandy School District, arguing that in their culture hair has "spiritual properties." The court ruled that members of their tribes did not have to abide by the district's strict limits on hair length.[31]

At this writing the state legislature in California is considering a ban on random drug testing in California schools; the new legislation would also require permission from a parent or guardian before a drug test could be administered.[32] And GKC Theatres, a Midwestern movie chain, is offering "R-Cards" to minors who get the signature of a parent.[33] The card gets them into R-rated movies without the embarrassment of being accompanied by a parent or guardian, an innovation that's sure to be tested in court even before the coming attractions are over.

Hugh Cunningham suggested that what I've been calling "the artificial extension of childhood" may eventually be reversed, and we've seen a few indications that he's correct. But the going is slow, and sometimes we take three adult-size steps backward for every baby step we take forward.

Q: *Isn't our school system critically important for the socialization of young people? Isn't that why we segregate young people by age—so that they can learn appropriate social skills?*

A: Socialization is important, but we make a tragic error by forcing young people to socialize only with each other. As it stands, teens learn virtually everything they know—including many bizarre and useless social norms—from their peers, but *peers are the last people on earth from whom they should be learning.* Ideally, teens should be interacting with people over a wide age range, and their most significant interactions should be with the people they are about to become.

Chapter 14
Why Some Will Resist

After winter must come spring,
Change, it comes eventually.
—Lauryn Hill, *"Everything is Every Thing"*

Overview. *A number of organizations and businesses in America benefit from the artificial extension of childhood and will therefore oppose its reversal. In 2006 alone teens are believe to have spent over $190 billion on music, clothes, and gadgets developed for their use, and marketers are deliberate in their efforts to tap and expand teen markets. Allowing teens to enter the adult world will hurt the many businesses that currently maintain teen culture and will also be seen as a threat to America's adult labor force. For a number of reasons, many adults will also have trouble seeing teens in a more accurate light. It's all too easy, for one thing, to confirm one's faulty beliefs about teen incompetence simply by focusing one's attention on dysfunctional teens—an error of thinking psychologists call "confirmation bias." If we fail to make changes, however, the vacuous world of teen culture will persist, teens and adults will continue to be adversaries, and the horrific problems that plague our teens will continue and may escalate. The advantages of restoring the child-adult continuum—of judging young people by their ability and not by their age—far exceed the disadvantages.*

Here is the text of a poster I saw recently in a Boston subway station:

THE ENFORCER.

She doesn't love being tough.
She's tough because she loves.

PARENTS:

The anti-drug.

A large close-up of a determined-looking woman appears in the foreground. Her eyebrows are raised, and her look is stern. Her hair is held back by a white bandana, and she's wearing an open blue-jeans jacket over a snug sweater. In other words, she's dressed somewhat like a teen. In the background, off to the right, a young man—perhaps seventeen—has an expression of irritation, or perhaps even disgust, on his face. His head is tilted to his left, and his left arm is akimbo, in apparent defiance of his mom. He too is dressed like a teen—baggy open shirt over a t-shirt.

The poster says it all: Teens cannot be trusted to make their own decisions. Teens need adult protection and direction. If you're an adult, it's your duty to make teens your adversaries. You need to be an "enforcer"—tough and controlling and unrelenting—perhaps even violent, like enforcers are in the movies.[1]

The teen's clothing also reminds us of the existence of teen culture—a culture created by laws and cultural practices that have isolated teens from adults in much of the industrialized world for a century. And the mom's clothing is a subtle reminder of the backward nature of the relationship that currently exists between adults and teens: Adults revere and seek to emulate teens in some respects, but teens no longer revere or seek to emulate adults. Note also that the adult is in the foreground, blocking the teen, who looks small, insignificant, and angry.

I'm probably adding symbolism where none may have been intended, just as we did when we studied the classics in high-school English classes. But I hope my point is clear: The position I've developed in this book runs directly counter to mainstream views in modern America—views so mainstream that they stare you in the face on subways, so to speak. In fact, there are organizations, institutions, industries, professions, and religious groups that will tend to resist the views I've developed, along with many individual parents, teachers, therapists, clergyman, and so on.

Who will object, and why? Is anyone likely to agree with me—in other words, to acknowledge the simple truth about teens? *And who is responsible for that offensive poster?*

ENEMIES OF THE TEEN

Early in the 1970s Richard Nixon and his staff compiled an "enemies list" of hundreds of political figures, business people, and organizations they considered to a threat to the Nixon administration. Perhaps all politicians have such lists, but President Nixon was rash and arrogant enough to lash out at some of the people on that list in unlawful ways, which led eventually to his downfall.

In my view, teens also have enemies: people or organizations who do them harm, often unintentionally and often simply by preventing them from joining the adult world. Here is my list of teen enemies, grouped into eleven categories. I acknowledge that it's unlikely that a single entity on this list sees itself as a wrongdoer. Some of the people involved would probably say that they're just catering to the teen's special needs and interests, and many, I'm sure, consider themselves to be the teen's helper and protector. As we saw with the saintly Jane Addams, however, good intentions sometimes go awry.

Government Agencies

That anti-drug subway poster I spoke of earlier is a product of the National Youth Anti-Drug Media Campaign of the federal government's Office of National Drug Control Policy (ONDCP). The ONDCP spends upwards of $200 million per year to dissuade teens from using illegal drugs.[2] This is a worthy mission, but I wonder whether some of this money couldn't be better spent trying to integrate teens into adult society. We know—both from common sense and, conveniently, from an extensive study published in 2001 by Jerald Bachman of the University of Michigan's Institute for Social Research—that most young people stop "partying" almost immediately after they enter the working world.[3] If integration into adult society were to begin at a young age, would young people even bother with drugs?

Government agencies are the worst offenders in the infantilization of our young for the simple reason that we now reflexively call upon government to solve almost every problem that confronts us. When teens are violent or sexually reckless or taking too many drugs, we expect government to step in, and government typically does so in simplistic, reactive, restrictive ways. The Federal Communications Commission recently announced draconian penalties for broadcasters and performers who offend people over public airwaves[4]; the goal, we're told, is to "protect children." Meanwhile, most young people in America today have virtually free access to cable TV and the Internet, where content is entirely unregulated. Fines against Howard Stern (for sexual talk on the radio) or Janet Jackson (for flashing a breast on TV) seem hypocritical when eight-year-olds have easy access to "Loveline" or "Sex and the City" over cable television or to hardcore pornography over the Internet.

Government concerns about teens sometimes penalize adults, not just young people. The Federal Drug Administration recently withheld approval of an over-the-counter morning-after contraceptive pill ("Plan B") for more than three years because the manufacturer, Barr Laboratories, failed to show what impact the pill *might have* on people under sixteen. In other words, no one was allowed to have

> ## YOUNG PEOPLE IN ACTION
>
> ### High-Pitched Generation Gap
>
> *In 2005 a security company in Wales announced the sale of the Mosquito, a device that emits irritating high-pitched sounds that teens (and presumably young children) can hear but that adults cannot. It was immediately put to use in front of malls and stores where young people loiter as a means of dispersing them. Having tuned in to the technique, teens are now getting their revenge. Many are now installing similar tones (easily downloadable from the Internet) on their cell phones so that adults won't know when the phones are ringing. The technique is being used in classrooms where cell phones are prohibited. When a phone rings, a student gets permission to visit the lavatory, where the conversation can proceed.*[6]

easy access to this pill because it might encourage sexual activity among young people. This decision was made in spite of the fact that the FDA's advisory panel voted overwhelmingly (twenty-three to four) for pill approval. Panel members suggested that the pill could cut the nation's high rate of unwanted pregnancies—three million per year—in half. Even when it was approved, over-the-counter sales were restricted to people eighteen and over; the most vulnerable population can get the medication by prescription only.[5]

Other federal agencies that hold young people back include, among many others, the U.S. Department of Labor (which, as we saw in Chapter Eleven, prohibits many young people from working, regardless of competence), the Bureau of Alcohol, Tobacco, Firearms and Explosives (which helps keep dangerous items out of teen hands, even if they handle them responsibly), and the Department of Health and Human Services (which currently promotes abstinence-only sex-education programs throughout the United States).

As we've seen, both the United States Congress and the Supreme Court sometimes hold teens back, and so do state legislatures and courts. In addition, as I indicated in Chapter Two, state and local lawmakers often restrict young people in areas that are beyond the reach of federal officials: with curfews, curbs on entertainment, invasive searches of personal property, free speech restrictions, truancy laws, driving restrictions, and so on.

Religious Institutions

When it comes to the lives of young people, religious organizations tend to be highly controlling these days, sometimes in ways that depart from the content

of primary religious texts such as the Bible (see Chapter Twelve). Some organizations, such as the Christian Coalition and Focus on the Family, have urged schools and bookstores to ban the *Harry Potter* books, for example, because of the witchcraft, and many groups, such as Operation Keepsake and the Abstinence Clearinghouse, campaign to promote sexual abstinence before marriage.

Historian Joseph F. Kett's book, *Rites of Passage: Adolescence in America 1790 to the Present*, does an impressive job of showing how church attitudes toward young people changed over the course of the nineteenth century. Early in the century, young people were generally left alone by the church. Religious societies that involved young people were almost always founded and run by the young people themselves. By the end of the century, however, the youth-run societies were replaced by church-run organizations that began to supervise virtually every aspect of a young person's life.

Between 1880 and 1900, says Kett, "Protestant churches attempted, as never before, to take over the spare-time activities of youth... and women were often becoming the agents of control."[7] Church groups became obsessed with teaching young people principles of "purity," "chastity," "temperance," and the like, just as Jane Addams and other child savers were doing in more secular realms. In other words, the religious community adopted the new concept of adolescence that was sweeping the country: Teens are weak and incompetent, and they need strict adult supervision.

These views are still firmly embedded in church teachings in America today. Religious groups have largely abandoned the model of parenting one finds in the Bible, where the child-adult continuum was strong and where young people were rapidly integrated into adult culture according to their individual ability.

The Media

Let's start with cable television's MTV, which caters to teens and older teen wanna-bees. MTV programming tells us repeatedly and unequivocally that teens are irresponsible, overgrown children. MTV also happens to be, at least according to company materials," the largest network on the planet," reaching more than 412 million households in the United States and other countries.[9] That translates to more than *a billion* viewers—one-sixth of the world's population.

MTV, which stands for "Music Television," got its start showing back-to-back "music videos"—mindless, mildly erotic infomercials for the music industry—but soon branched out with reality shows, sitcoms, and such, all of which perpetuate teen myths and teen culture. In *Viva La Bam*, one of MTV's recent prime-time entries—a show that *Newsday* says "male teens across the nation" are "insanely down with"—Bam Margera, a Philadelphia skateboarder, and his "crew" paint his home's entire

WISDOM OF THE AGES

Even more TV for Teens

Launched in 2005 by former vice president Al Gore and partner Joel Hyatt, "Current TV" is the latest youth-oriented cable channel, called by The Nation an "interactive grad-school version of MTV." Although Gore initially wanted it to have a liberal, change-the-world, political slant, financial realities quickly transformed it into a more conventional television entry where, said The Nation, "hipness triumphs over values." One regular feature: news alerts displaying the most searched items on Google. Current's marketing guru? Annie Zehren, the founder of Teen People magazine. Current TV is now available in twenty-eight million homes in the United States.[8]

kitchen electric blue (including the appliances and food), after which Bam paints his father the same color. They steal his mom's car and have it "tricked out" at the local chop shop. They dig a tunnel under his uncle's house so they can surprise him in his bedroom. And then, according to *Newsday:*

> *...for the grand finale, Bam's pals shove dad Phil and Uncle Vita into the makeshift backyard equivalent of a steel-cage wrestling ring, to be pelted with a deluge of increasingly gross debris—flour and cornflakes, crickets and maggots, bacon and honey, even anchovies and money.[10]*

That's right. The teens cage the adults and then pelt them with garbage. Other MTV shows are equally disturbing: the long-running *Real World* (beautiful young people party and fornicate); *Pimp My Ride* (you learn how to create a "fully-loaded pimp chariot"); and *Rich Girls* (a show about "normal" but extremely wealthy teens who "enjoy doing normal teenage things like shopping, talking on the phone, and going to the prom"). Perhaps the worst of them is the highly-rated *My Super Sweet Sixteen,* which gives us an inside look at $200 thousand parties for super-rich young women; their purpose, according to *TIME,* is "to prolong the whiny, self-centered greediness that gives *infantile* a bad name."[11]

A billion people are exposed to dozens of MTV shows like this every day. Only one of their ninety-four currently listed programs—*Choose or Lose*—comes anywhere near portraying young people as competent in any way. This lone program, which airs only occasionally, solicits opinions from young people on timely issues: gay marriage, the presidential candidates, and so on. Even here, though, we learn merely that young people have opinions, not that they are competent thinkers or leaders.

In prior chapters we've looked at some of the popular teen films, but let's review. Major film studios like Universal and Paramount have been instrumental in shaping our distorted view of teens and in creating the distressed teens with whom we live. Consider films like *American Pie*, which grossed more than 234 million dollars worldwide after its 1999 release (male teens party, drink beer, and treat women like sex objects); *Dude, Where's My Car?* (two male teens lose their car while on a drunk and encounter strippers, ostriches, aliens, and angry girlfriends while searching for it); *Clueless* (frivolous female teens act frivolously); and *Dazed and Confused* (teens cruise, smoke marijuana, and try not to worry about the future).

We've already looked at the film *Thirteen*—cowritten by a thirteen-year-old—which shows us young teen females immersed in a world of drugs and sex. Even more disturbing is the 1995 documentary-like film *Kids*, which looks at the depraved lives of young New York City skateboarders. Telly, the main character, is on a mission to have sex with as many young virgins as possible; it turns out that he's unknowingly spreading the AIDS virus. In the film, people as young as ten or eleven drink alcohol and take drugs with their teen friends.

Dozens of glossy magazines are produced just for teens, mainly for females. *Seventeen* alone has over 2.3 million subscribers and focuses on how to dress and apply makeup to be trendy, sexy, and beautiful. This market is so large and so robust that four of the top adult magazines—*People, Elle, Vogue,* and *Cosmopolitan*—have recently launched teen spinoffs. Recent cover lines include: "The Best Ways to Flirt," "Virginity: Real Girls, Real Stories," "Your Best Hair Ever," and "Advanced Pleasure Seeking." These magazines are made possible not just by the subscribers but by their advertisers, which brings me to our next set of enemies.

Business and Industry

I'm holding a recent issue of *Teen People* in my hands. The emaciated, billionaire, eighteen-year-old Olsen sisters are on the cover, and here is a sampling of what's inside: Herbal Essence hair products, Neutrogena makeup, Guess clothing, Roxy clothing, Maybelline makeup, Pacific Sun Clothing, Paul Mitchell hair care products, American Eagle Outfitters clothing, Clinique lipstick, Garnier hair color, Candies shoes, Brilliant Brunette hair products, Chanel perfume, Borders books, and Unionbay clothing—just a few of the more than one hundred advertisers that fill most of *Teen People's* pages.

Do companies benefit by the maintenance of teen culture? Most definitely. One of the reasons business and industry targets teens is because of the vast sums of money teens now control. American teens supposedly spent more than *$190*

Enemies of the Teen		
Type	*Exemplars*	*Nature of Threat*
Government agencies	U.S. Congress, Supreme Court, FCC, FDA, ONDCP, Dept. of Labor, ATF, HHS, state legislatures, city councils	Prevent competent young people from working, owning property, filing lawsuits, smoking, driving, voting, marrying, etc.
Religious groups	Christian Coalition, United Methodist Church, Assemblies of God, American Family Assn., Family Research Council, Church World Service	Perpetuate myths about young people being helpless and incompetent; have lost sight of the important roles that young people played in the Bible.
Media	*Seventeen, Cosmo Girl, Elle Girl, Teen People, Teen Vogue,* MTV, CBS, ABC, NBC, FOX, VH1, The WB, Clear Channel, UPN, MPAA, RIAA	Routinely portray young people as self-absorbed, frivolous, oversexed, drug-abusing, stupid, or incompetent.
Business and industry	Paramount, Universal, Jive Records, Coca Cola, Abercrombie & Fitch, Pfizer, Eli Lilly, Macy's, Guess Clothing, Vans, Clinique	Make upwards of $200 billion per year through the maintenance of teen culture.
Mental health system	American Psychological Association, American Psychiatric Association, National Association of Social Workers, American Academy of Child and Adolescent Psychiatry	Label a wide range of troublesome teen behaviors as indicative of mental illness; provide "treatment" rather than helping to incorporate teens into the adult world.

Juvenile justice system and law enforcement	State juvenile justice systems, all 50 states; police departments	Arrest and incarcerate young people for "juvenile" offenses invented by 19th-century moralists; deprive teens of basic constitutional rights.
Public figures	Bill McCollum (U.S. Rep.), Mary Lou Dickerson (U.S. Rep.), Hillary Clinton, Tipper Gore, George W. Bush, Joseph Lieberman, Laura Schlessinger, James Dobson	Help to perpetuate myths about teen incorrigibility and incompetence; fail to acknowledge teen abilities and potential.
Organized labor	AFL-CIO, International Brotherhood of Teamsters, United Food and Commercial Workers Intl., Union of Needletrades Industrial and Textile Employees	Oppose entry of qualified young people into the working world.
Education establishment	National Education Association, American Federation of Teachers, National Parent Teacher Association, teachers unions, local boards of education	Warehouse young people in schools even when they're not ready to learn; segregate people by age rather than by ability; fail to meet individual learning needs; instill a long-term dislike of learning.
NGOs	Parents Television Council, Child Labor Coalition, Children's Defense Fund, Partnership for a Drug-Free America, Natl. Coalition for the Protection of Children & Families	Infantilize young people; discourage integration of young people into adult society; encourage censorship.
Parents	You and I	Underestimate the competence and potential of our children; enter into adversarial relationships with teens.

billion in 2006, up from $155 billion in 2000, and that's a small fraction of the amount of money teens control through what marketers call "pester power."[12]

A 2000 PBS survey found that 22 percent of teens had at least one credit card—up from only 11 percent in 1994, and the number surges to over 70 percent for college students.[13] The money comes mainly from parents and part-time jobs, but even those who work seldom have adult responsibilities to tie up the funds. In other words, most of the money in teen hands is *entirely disposable and discretionary*— the sales executive's dream come true.

Marketing firms around the country study teens carefully and advise major businesses about how to position their products. Some marketing firms, such as Teenage Research Unlimited, American Student List, and Student Marketing, have built their entire businesses around the booming teen market, helping a wide range of companies to develop entirely new markets from scratch.[14] The Pottery Barn, for example, recently developed a new line of furnishings for teens ("PBTeen") and the cell phone companies have been remarkably successful at putting colorful, flashy new cell phones into teen hands nationwide; more than one in three teens now have their own cell phone, with the proportion increasing rapidly. According to one research firm, in 2004 young people were expected to generate nearly a quarter of all cell-phone revenues—about $20 billion.[15]

Perhaps the most diabolical of the teen marketing schemes comes from the 99.44 percent pure-hearted executives at Proctor & Gamble, makers of Ivory Soap and Pampers. Created in 2001, P&G's "Tremor" division soon recruited nearly 300,000 teens to help marketing professionals figure out how to empty teen pockets.[16] In return, Tremor "members" received free samples, coupons, discounts, and unreleased music.

According to industry sources, in 1990 American industry spent about $100 million on advertising and marketing to young people; by 2000, the figure increased *twenty-fold*, to $2 billion.[17] Recent books such as *What Kids Buy and Why: The Psychology of Marketing to Kids*, by psychologist Daniel Acuff, help guide the marketers to their targets.[18]

Some of the industries that profit from teen culture are oppressively conspicuous, and the music industry probably tops the list. As I was finishing this book it was tough to get through a day without seeing multiple images of pop-diva Britney Spears. About 22 percent of recorded music is purchased by young people between ages ten and nineteen, even though they bring in only 4 percent of household income.[19] Older people are fairly set in their musical ways, whereas young people are *impressionable*; again, this is the kind of group that marketing, sales, and advertising professionals

live for. You can't create a "star" for middle-age people; to them, a star is someone with both charisma and staying power. With young people, however, you can create a star overnight. Young people are also the primary purchasers of many of the music spinoffs: live concerts, merchandise, films, DVDs, and so on.

As I noted in Chapter Five, the pharmaceutical industry has been successful in recent years in making enormous inroads into the youth market, with more money now being spent on behavior-altering medications for youth than on all other prescription medications combined in that age category. Companies like GlaxoSmithKline, Eli Lilly, and Pfizer would lose enormous sums of money if teen problems were ameliorated even slightly. The illegal drug industry, which also preys upon our youth, also benefits from the existence and maintenance of teen culture.

One way to get a quick sense of the economics of teen culture is to walk into any large shopping mall, where you'll find entire stores and whole departments catering to teens. Stores like PacSun, Forever 21, Wet Seal, Hollister, Charlotte Russe, Hot Topic, and American Eagle are teen-only haunts, and so are large departments like Nordstrom's "BP" (Brass Plum) or Macy's massive new dance-club style department called "ThIsIt" (pronounced "this is it"), which typically has more than ten thousand square feet of teen fashions on display.

Another way is to walk into a teenager's room. In a young male's room you might find an X-Box (Microsoft), a teen-tuned cell phone, a guitar, and one or more skate, surf, or snow boards. You'll find even more teen-oriented products in a young female's room: Stila, Urban Decay, or Hard Candy makeup, Bath and Body Works lotions, Bed Head hair products, teen magazines, teen DVDs, teen idol posters, and a closet packed with Roxy t-shirts and Steve Madden shoes.

This is a far cry from the world in which young children were dressed like adults or in which teens were rapidly integrated into adult culture. The isolation of teens from adults brought about by the Industrial Revolution has been a boon for American business, which has, in turn, widened the gap between teens and adults.

The editors of the ubiquitous *Merriam-Webster Collegiate Dictionary* recently announced that their next edition will include the word "teensploitation"—the exploitation of teens by industries such as the movie industry. In an Associated Press article about Merriam-Webster's decision to canonize this term, lexicographer John Morse, president of the company, reminds us that "language is a window into our culture and history." The term "teensploitation" has been used, he says, for twenty-two years now—and the practice, of course, has been around far longer.[20]

WISDOM OF THE AGES

Forever Young

I don't wanna grow up,
I'm a Toys "R" Us kid.
A million toys to choose from,
that I can play with.
     —From a 1980s Television Commercial

The Mental Health System

I can remember my visceral reaction when, many years ago, I first ran across "Oppositional Defiant Disorder" in the *DSM*—the manual that mental health professionals use to diagnose their clients, developed jointly by the American Psychiatric Association and the American Psychological Association. It's defined as "a pattern of negativistic, hostile, and defiant behavior" toward adults which lasts at least six months. To make the diagnosis, the therapist merely needs to conclude that the client exhibits any four behaviors of out a list of eight, which includes items like "often argues with adults," "deliberately annoys people," and "is often touchy." The official diagnostic code is 313.81; that's the code the therapist lists on an insurance form in order to seek compensation for the treatment he or she is providing.[21]

I remember thinking, "Why is such commonplace behavior in this manual?" The diagnosis seemed to fit me as a teen (at times) and many people I knew when I was growing up, not to mention the classic picture of adolescence that had been created by James Dean in "Rebel Without a Cause" and Marlon Brando in "The Wild One." In recent years, I've come to view this "disorder" for what it really is: the modern label for "incorrigibility"—the criminal category that had been invented by aristocratic child-savers of the late 1800s (Chapter Two).

As Joseph Kett and other historians have pointed out, when G. Stanley Hall and other psychologists made adolescence an institution a century ago, they also created new jobs for armies of counselors, social workers, and juvenile justice workers. They pathologized normal behavior created by the social chaos of the time, devising methods of "treatment" for the behavior rather than providing appropriate social fixes. As we saw earlier (Chapter Four), the transformation is neatly captured by the change that took place in Father Flanagan's Boys Town in the 1950s: in the original community, troubled young people were helped with heavy doses of adult responsibility, whereas the new Boys Town provided professional "treatment" for the residents' deviant tendencies.

In short, my own colleagues have long played and continue to play a leading role in the maintenance of the artificial extension of childhood. They have pathologized socially-induced behavior and have, in recent years, even medicalized its "treatment," relying heavily on drugs to get young people under control. There are about four hundred thousand workers in today's mental health professions*— a $100 billion industry[22]—with more than 70 percent of the industry devoted at least in part to serving the needs of teens, largely, in my view, using outmoded concepts and inappropriate techniques.[23]

Law Enforcement Agencies and the Juvenile Justice System

Police should focus on real crime, not on the special juvenile crimes-against-the-self invented by the child savers. As I indicated in the last chapter, we also need to consider dismantling the juvenile justice system.

Unfortunately, in *Roper v. Simmons*, a landmark case decided in 2005, the United States Supreme Court indirectly strengthened the juvenile justice system by making it unlawful to execute people who committed their crimes before age eighteen.[24] In so doing, the court has uncritically accepted this magical age as a reliable indicator of reasoning ability and maturity. Rather than look for real measures of such abilities, which vary enormously from one person to another at *any* age, the court elected, quite explicitly, to conform to societal "trends." In strongly worded opinions, the four dissenting judges correctly noted that "differences in the aggregate between juveniles and adults...frequently do not hold true when comparing individuals" and that the "startling conclusion" of the majority decision that "juries cannot be trusted" to look at individual factors in criminals under eighteen "undermines the very foundations of our capital sentencing system."[25]

Elected Officials and Other Public Figures

A decade ago on the floor of the United States House of Representatives, Representative Bill McCollum warned the nation about an upcoming scourge of teen "super-predators"[26]; there's no sign of it at this point, and it's not likely to come any time in the foreseeable future. Although it's true that many American teens are troubled or troublesome, we need to stop the hyperbole and refocus our thinking and our efforts, moving toward a competency-based system that allows teens to grow and flourish by connecting meaningfully with the adult world.

Meanwhile, the naysayers, alarmists, and modern child savers will grab every

---

*There are six major licensed professions that serve mental health needs in the United States: marriage and family therapy, counseling, psychiatry, psychology, psychiatric nursing, and social work.

possible headline. Some of the worst offenders today include media personalities Laura Schlessinger and James Dobson, who condemn any kind of sexual exploration before marriage; Tipper Gore and United States Representative Mary Lou Dickerson, who believe that teens are too tender to be exposed to offensive songs or video games; and Brent Bozell, president of the Parents Television Council, who insists that television content needs to be tightly controlled to protect our young people from harm.

As we've seen, Anna Freud, one of the twentieth century's most vocal and influential critics of the modern teen, was highly distressed during her own teen years. I suspect that most or all of the leading alarmists in our country today also had a rough time growing up or at least were close to some troubled teens. Many modern child savers undoubtedly have difficult teens at home, or in some cases, experienced tragedy because of a son or daughter's involvement with drugs, alcohol, gangs, or other risky activities. Perhaps they want to spare others their pain or are looking for ways to bury old demons. Understandably, they may feel that they or society in general should have been there to protect their offspring before tragedy struck. But it's not more protection that our young people need; they need the experience and tools and opportunities that will allow them to protect *themselves*.

Organized Labor

Earlier in the book we learned that child labor was eventually outlawed because of the concerted efforts of organized labor, big business, and various child-saving groups. We also learned that the definition of "child" was gradually broadened to include increasingly older young people. During the Great Depression and at other times when jobs were scarce, unions were especially hard on young people, immigrants, minorities, women, and other vulnerable groups that threatened the jobs of their members. Social change and prosperity gradually broke down many of the barriers, allowing minorities and women, at least, to work in some industries. But the young are still excluded.

The battle against child labor was won so completely that I'm sure that modern union leaders don't give it a second thought—but they should. Young people are excellent workers, and the workplace is far less dangerous and exploitative than it was when the child-labor laws were enacted. Ambitious young people deserve the chance to work in business and industry just as soon as they can demonstrate appropriate competencies.

Will the AFL-CIO or Teamsters welcome an age-blind, competency-based system of employment in the various industries they serve? Of course not. Adults

are still the breadwinners, after all (in fact, adult *males* are still usually the primary breadwinners), and any perceived threat to the economic security of the current union memberships will, understandably, be fiercely resisted. If 20 million young people—or even 20 or 30 percent of those individuals—were suddenly available to compete on the American job market, union leaders would be the first to dig all the old child-labor arguments out of the mothballs, no matter how absurd those arguments may be in today's OSHA-governed workplace.

The Education Establishment

The National Education Association, descended from an organization founded in 1857 and with almost 2.7 million members today, works hard through its extensive lobbying efforts on Capitol Hill to make sure that America's inadequate education system stays that way—by which I mean, stays exactly the way it is, except with greater job security, more resources, and higher revenues.

You won't see the NEA calling for a return to home schooling, and I suspect that perceptive NEA leaders are extremely nervous about the effect the Internet will have on our schools over the next decade or two.

The many teacher unions around the country, our local school boards, and even the proverbial PTAs, also want to keep things the way they are—except with more money, resources, and so on. But high school is little more than a prison for many of our teens, and the time has come to explore bold new approaches to education that will allow our young to reconnect meaningfully with the adult world they're about to enter. Don't expect the NEA to go down without a fight, however.

Non-Governmental Organizations (NGOs)

According to the *Washington Times*, in 2000 the FCC received 111 complaints about indecent material being broadcast over public airwaves, but in 2003 there were 240,350 such complaints. The increase was driven by coordinated campaigns mounted by organizations such as the Parents Television Council.[28] It's understandable that people might object to broadcasting they find offensive, but perhaps we should all object even more strongly to any form of censorship, no matter how well intentioned.

The modern effort to protect our supposedly fragile young people by curtailing free speech rights is, in my view, both wrongheaded and dangerous. On this issue Voltaire's words ring true: "I disapprove of what you say, but I will defend to the death your right to say it."

You may have run across the "Bill of Non-Rights" that circulates on the Internet now and then. Attributed to a member of the United States House of Representatives but actually written by a Libertarian computer professional named

---

WISDOM OF THE AGES

Unions and the Young

The union battle against young people is still going strong, especially when a non-union business is involved. In 1999, in Salinas, California, a $45 million mall construction project was shut down by a judge after members of the Carpenters Union Local 605 went to court armed with a video tape showing the twelve-year-old son of the construction boss operating a forklift. The union also filed a complaint with the state Labor Commissioner's Office and threatened to report the construction company to the county Social Services department. An attorney for the mall said this was a situation in which "a dad brings his kid to work on the weekend"– and that the non-union construction firm had long been a target of the carpenter's union.[27]

Lewis Napper, the document is a cogent reminder about what the Constitution and the Bill of Rights do *not* guarantee. Article II of Napper's piece reads:

You do not have the right to never be offended. This country is based on freedom, and that means freedom for everyone–not just you! You may leave the room, turn the channel, express a different opinion, etc.; but the world is full of idiots, and probably always will be.[29]

But some NGOs, influenced by the echoes of the voices of Hull-House, want to curtail people's rights in order to build higher walls around the young–walls that generally do more harm than good, as I've demonstrated throughout this book.

The wall idea isn't just my personal metaphor, by the way. In a recent Sunday paper, the nationally-syndicated "Zits" cartoon, which provides humorous commentary on today's teens, shows five consecutive drawings in which a young man is gradually enclosed, from the ground up, by a brick structure the size of a compact phone booth. In the fifth drawing, he's completely enclosed. The captions above each drawing read, respectively: "CURFEW: 11 PM," "NO UNSUPERVISED PARTIES," "LIMITED TIME ON THE INTERNET," "NO R-RATED MOVIES," and "NO RIDING IN CARS DRIVEN BY ANYONE UNDER TWENTY-FIVE."[30] The Parents Television Council, which "scientifically monitors prime time television to assist your family," is adding a new layer of bricks.[31]

Other NGOs that infantilize our young people include the Child Labor Coalition, which seems to consider virtually any form of work by young people to

be harmful or exploitative, and the Children's Defense Fund, which considers young people to be inherently defense-less and lobbies hard to protect them in every respect. Founded in 1985 by the wives of prominent federal officials (Tipper Gore, Susan Baker, Nancy Thurmond, and others), the Parent Music Resource Center started out with a censorship agenda but eventually settled for a voluntary pledge by the RIAA to put warning labels—so-called "Tipper stickers"—on the packaging of music recordings that might corrupt fragile young listeners.[32]

My Fellow Parents

I've done it, and you have, too. We force our offspring to cram their entire education into the first eighteen to twenty-two years of their lives, whether or not they're ready to learn. Prompted by those omnipresent government media campaigns and by laws that make us responsible for the misbehavior of our young, we try to monitor and control every aspect of our sons' and daughters' lives. The latest trend: equipping them with cell phones than generate GPS signals that allow us to track their whereabouts twenty-four hours a day—or at least the whereabouts of the phone![33]

We search their rooms, make decisions about their medical and psychological treatment, coerce their cooperation by making threats about the car keys, try to restrict their sexual behavior and limit their access to unsavory characters, and forbid them from drinking or taking drugs, even though we drink without restriction and can barely get through the day without an anti-depressant.

When teens try to confront us as if they are fellow adults, we do our best to shut them down, and, in so doing, establish an adversarial relationship with our offspring that may last many years. In short—no matter how old they are and no matter how competent they may be—we treat our offspring like incompetent children.

SHODDY THINKING

This book contains some disturbing news. Here's more: Generally speaking, we're all fairly shoddy thinkers. Evolution equips us primarily with practical abilities, not cognitive ones—mainly tools for making babies and then trying to keep them alive long enough for them to make babies of their own. We don't need to be rocket scientists to accomplish these modest feats, which suggests why there are so very few rocket scientists among us.

Psychologists sometimes spend their whole careers showing just how irratio-

nal most people really are. In fiendishly revealing studies conducted in the 1970s by Daniel Kahneman and Amos Tversky, for example, people were confronted with simple situations of the sort that modern juries might see.[34] For example:

> The town where a certain crime has been committed is 85 percent white and 15 percent black. The witness was 80 percent sure that he saw a black person commit the crime. Therefore, we're correct in concluding that the perpetrator was probably black.[35]

This sounds tidy, but our conclusion is wrong, and most adult subjects—including most real jurors—will in fact get it wrong. It's great that the witness was so confident, but being confident about an improbable event (only 15 percent of the people in the town are black) doesn't make it any more probable, and being doubtful about a probable event (85 percent of the people in the town are white) doesn't make it any less probable. When you do the math, the odds that a black person committed the crime in this situation turn out to be less than one in two.

When it comes to our thinking about teens, a number of cognitive pitfalls of this sort appear to limit our ability to think clearly:

The Confirmation Bias

My mother has often claimed that her dreams allow her to foretell the birth of babies in our extended family, but she rarely reports that she has had one of these predictive dreams until *after* a birth. "I *knew* she was going to give birth to a boy today," she'll say. "I had a dream about it last night." Presumably, when she has a dream that doesn't pan out, she just forgets about it.

We're all subject to this phenomenon, which psychologists call "confirmation bias" or "the confirmation error." We pay special attention to events that confirm our beliefs and tend to ignore events that don't. Unfortunately, this tendency allows us to preserve virtually any belief, no matter how mistaken or irrational it might be. The issue is explored in an old "Seinfeld" episode in which a reporter mistakenly gets the idea that Jerry and George are gay. Once he's got that idea, it's easy for him to find a wide range of "evidence" that supports his belief. This makes for great comedy—and, in some situations, for great tragedy too.

It's easy for us to confirm our mistaken beliefs about teens by selectively focusing on information or events that confirm those beliefs: sensational headlines about teen violence, the sight of oddly-dressed teens on the street, the bumping and grinding of a dim-witted teen diva on television, a disrespectful remark

from a teen relative, and so on. In a culture that holds teens back and brings out their worst, it's especially easy to find "evidence" that teens are incompetent and impaired.

As we've seen throughout this book, however, the hard evidence shows overwhelmingly that the turmoil experienced by American teens is a creation of modern culture and that teens have the *potential* to function at least as well as most adults do. Whether we choose to try to tap that potential is up to us.

Am I vulnerable to the confirmation bias? Of course! But I hope that the diligent reader will concede that I have at least taken pains to ground my views in a wealth of data and that I have attempted to interpret those data with at least a modicum of objectivity. It's relevant here that my own views on teens have *changed* through my investigations. I set out nine years ago mainly with questions and curiosity—with a willingness to challenge my own biases, not simply a desire to confirm them.

The Fundamental Attribution Error

When we judge others, we virtually always attribute their behavior to internal traits, not to the circumstances surrounding their behavior. When we judge ourselves, however, we tend to do the opposite—to blame our actions on circumstances rather than on internal factors. In other words, we're much more likely to condemn other people than we are to condemn ourselves. Psychologists call this tendency the "fundamental attribution error."

We seem to be especially consistent in making this error with teens, whom we're quick to label "lazy," "forgetful," "deceitful," "materialistic," "flighty," "irresponsible," "aggressive," and so on. We tend to be oblivious to the circumstances and experiences that have contributed to their less-than-desirable ways.

I'm not trying to excuse teen excesses and imperfections. Nor do I mean to say that individual teens don't have real personality differences; they certainly do, just as adults do. But we err when we blame their wrongdoings exclusively on their supposedly inherent traits.

Mindlessless

As I mentioned in the introduction to this book, once certain practices are set in motion, we tend to repeat them mindlessly, without ever looking back at the events that set them in motion. We'll continue to cut the corner off the roast before we cook it just because Grandma use to do so. But Grandma trimmed the roast because it was too big to fit in her one small roasting pan, whereas we trim the roast because—well, just *because*.

As social psychologist Ellen Langer has pointed out, mindlessness is a costly

cognitive phenomenon.[36] It makes us insensitive to a changing world, doomed to repeat actions that no longer make any sense.

Again, when it comes to teens, we are repeating actions that were set in motion during a very peculiar time in American history: the decades of the Industrial Revolution, when our cities were struggling to cope with dramatic population growth (New York City's population, for example, grew from 152,000 to 1,478,000 between 1820 and 1870), when our country was overwhelmed by massive immigration, and when rapid industrialization led to the exploitation of millions of workers.[37]

The opposite of mindlessness is mindfulness, a state of mind in which your awareness of the causes of things is heightened. If this volume has made you even somewhat more mindful about why our teens are the way they are, then I've done my job.

Cognitive Inertia

You're given (a) a box of nails, (b) a candle, and (c) a lighter and asked to find a way to attach the candle to a wall so that it won't drip on the floor when it's lighted. How would you do it? Most people nail the candle to the wall or melt some wax and affix the candle with the melted wax. But neither approach takes care of the drip problem. Very few people are able to solve this problem, even though the solution is simple: dump the nails out of the box, attach the *box* to the wall, and then affix the candle to the inside of the box. The box now serves as a candle holder that catches any dripping wax.

According to Karl Duncker, a Gestalt psychologist who studied this problem nearly a century ago, people have trouble solving it because of their previous experience with boxes. A box is supposed to be a *container*, not a candle holder, and it's difficult to think about boxes having new functions. Duncker labeled our lack of insight in such situations "functional fixedness" or "mental set." Modern psychologists study a similar phenomenon called "cognitive inertia"—the inability to alter one's beliefs until they're sufficiently challenged by conflicting information.[38]

Our beliefs about teens are based on a lifetime of experience, shaped by headlines, movies, and personal encounters and distorted by the confirmation error, the fundamental attribution error, and other cognitive truth-manglers. Beliefs of this sort don't change instantly, even after one reads a persuasive book. But they can and do change when we're bombarded with sufficient information that contradicts our beliefs. This book might set change in motion, especially if it leads you to look for new information that confirms some of the assertions I've made here. (This would be an instance of the confirmation bias operating in reverse.)

Social Influence and Prejudice

Our thinking is also distorted both by peer pressure and by our tendency to accept the pronouncements of "authorities" and "experts" without question. We're creatures of a community, and we're trained early on to conform to the community's wishes and expectations, especially if those wishes and expectations are properly packaged. Community-induced beliefs are sometimes so pervasive that they have been called "institutional delusions."[39]

Our views on teens are largely determined by the powerful messages our media sources and thought leaders feed us daily: Teens are reckless, incompetent, and violent; young people need to be sheltered; childhood should be extended as long as possible. Our views can reasonably be conceived of as a kind of irrational prejudice programmed by our culture—almost precisely the kind that mainstream Americans bore towards women and blacks until very recent times.

The programming is pervasive and sometimes nearly invisible, like those subliminal "Buy Popcorn" messages that were embedded in some movies in the 1950s. The popcorn messages didn't work, but the subtle messages we're constantly fed about young people work all too well.

Just recently, when my two youngest children were watching *Mary Poppins* in the back of our mini-van, I suddenly understood this modern classic (released in 1964) in a new light. In the film, set in London in 1910, the magical and mysterious Poppins (Julie Andrews) floats her way into a traditional family in which the banker dad (George Banks, played by David Tomlinson) is focused on his career and is unaffectionate toward his children, determined to "mold" them into responsible citizens. Mom is passive inside the home, but she's bold on the streets, where she marches with her "sister Suffragettes" to try to get women the vote. Poppins sets events in motion which threaten Dad's career and cause him to reassess his role in the family.

Toward the end of the film, just after his children have inadvertently caused a run on his bank and he realizes he's about to be fired, he laments his situation to Bert the chimney sweep (Dick Van Dyke), Mary Poppins' friend. Bert, an early practitioner of reverse psychology, counsels Mr. Banks as follows:

> *Mr. Banks: My world was calm, well ordered, exemplary. Then came this person with chaos in her wake. And now my life's ambitions go with one foul blow. It's quite a bitter pill to take. It's that Poppins woman! She did it! ... You know what she did? I realize it now. She tricked me into taking Jane and Michael to the bank. That's how all the trouble started.*

Bert: She tricked you into taking the children on an outing? Outrageous! A man with all the important things you have to do. Shameful! You're a man of high position, esteemed by your peers. And when your little tykes are crying, you haven't time to dry their tears. And see them grateful little faces smiling up at you because their daddy always knows just what to do.

Mr. Banks: Well, I mean.... Look.... I....

Bert: You've got to grind, grind, grind at that grindstone. Though childhood slips like sand through a sieve. And all too soon they've up and grown, and then they've flown. And it's too late for you to give....

In other words, Bert is saying—and Banks ultimately agrees—that Banks was wrong to put his career first, to want to be a responsible provider for his family, and to try to shape his children to be responsible citizens. Banks is supposed to put the immediate needs of his children—for affection, fun, and nurturing—ahead of all else. After he is indeed fired, the film ends with Banks doing just that, literally flying kites in the park with his children—*and*, miraculously, with all of his fellow bank executives. The children-first message has, it seems, broken through not only to Mr. Banks but to all reasonable adults.

We've seen these messages before (especially in Chapter Two): the family should be centered around children, who are helpless and incompetent. Parents should cater to the needs of children, not vice versa. Young people should be sheltered, not raised to be responsible adults. Childhood should be extended indefinitely.*

With messages of this sort reaching us daily, it's a wonder we can think with any clarity at all about young people. We are told what to think, continue to do so mindlessly, and pay special attention to confirmatory information that keeps our faulty beliefs intact.

CAN WE CHANGE OUR PERSPECTIVE?

Historical forces created the crazy, vacuous world that modern teens inhabit, and a vast array of contemporary institutions keep them trapped there. These same forces and institutions have distorted our thinking about teens, forcing us to see them through extremely biased eyes.

---

*The movie is based on a 1934 book by P. L. Travers. Curiously, Travers herself fails to deliver these messages. In the book Mrs. Banks isn't a crusader for women's rights, Mr. Banks doesn't lose his job, and the family structure doesn't change during Mary Poppins' stay. It took the magic of Walt Disney's writers in the early 1960s to layer these social agendas onto Travers' simple story. At the movie's premiere in 1964, Travers was apparently crying, not out of joy but rather because the movie "had done a strange kind of violence to her work."[40]

Can we change our perspective on teens? I have no doubt that we can. Our attitudes toward gays, women, blacks, the elderly, Arabs, and others have changed dramatically in recent times—sometimes over a period of years and sometimes virtually overnight. Polls conducted shortly after the attack on the United States on September 11, 2001, for example, showed an immediate downward shift in attitude toward Arabs, with nearly six in ten Americans feeling that people of Arab descent should be subjected to special security checks before boarding airplanes.[41]

In *1984* George Orwell speculated that widespread attitudes toward an entire population could be changed completely "within two or three minutes." On the sixth day of a massive Hate Week rally, an announcer—with "nothing altered in his voice or manner"—substitutes "Eastasia" for "Eurasia" as the name of the country's vile enemy. Showing remarkable adaptiveness, the crowd suddenly notices that the posters and banners on display at the rally are "all wrong." Frenzied people in the crowd attribute the faulty signs to "sabotage" and quickly tear them to shreds.[42]

Deeply entrenched attitudes, like those we hold toward teens, sometimes take years to change, but the changes can still be substantial. For example, according to pollsters, in 1993 only 40 percent of Americans favored allowing gays to serve openly in the military; by 2004, this figure had risen to 67 percent.[43]

Societal attitudes change when authority figures make pronouncements, when people get new information or have new experiences, when people's beliefs are inconsistent with their own behavior, or when events in the news make people question their views. Sometimes attitude change comes easy, and sometimes it comes hard, but it does occur. As I noted earlier, I hope that this book will prove, over time, to be one of several factors that lead to widespread changes in how we view our deeply misunderstood, highly undervalued young people.

REESTABLISHING THE CONTINUUM

The enemies list I've generated for teens is long, and the enormous sums of money that people make through the maintenance of teen culture is especially troubling; when money is at risk, the wheels of change turn particularly slowly. Even so, there are a few hopeful signs that the century-long trend toward extending childhood may be turning around, or at least that some people are trying to slow its momentum.

The United States Supreme Court has restored a few of the basic rights that young people lost at the turn of the twentieth century, and a constitutional amend-

ment has lowered the voting age to eighteen, with small movements afoot to lower the voting age further; following the ratification of that amendment most states lowered the age of majority from twenty-one to eighteen. We're also seeing general grumbling about the effectiveness of the juvenile justice system, some respectable people calling for the dismantling of the modern high school, the closing of some of the correctional boot camps, the emergence of streamlined systems for prosecuting juvenile offenders as adults, the rapid spread of peer courts, the creation of new teen-run teen rights groups, and the promising beginnings of Internet-driven education systems. Our teens are still being infantilized, but change is at least in the air.

Will anyone simply *agree* with what I'm saying? There is certainly one large group that is likely to be sympathetic: America's 20 million infantilized teens, many of whom are acutely aware of the fact that they're living in a cage of dubious purpose. I've also spoken with many adults in recent years who immediately "get it"—sometimes because they work with teens and see the down side of regulating the lives of teens so completely.

As I noted early in this volume, educators John Holt and John Taylor Gatto, French psychiatrist Patrice Huerre, American psychologist Richard Farson, and historians Hugh Cunningham and Marc Kleijwegt, among others, expressed concerns about the artificial extension of childhood long before Diane Dumas and I began our research. Given strong arguments for change, I believe that many adults will at least give the case against adolescence a serious look.

In any case, either we reverse the trend or continue to suffer the consequences. For more than a century now, we've been caught in a vicious cycle in which restrictions on teens have produced more teen problems and teen problems have in turn produced more restrictions. Teen problems are substantial, and some indicators suggest that they're getting worse. Even if we find ways to contain certain problems—with metal detectors, room searches, guards, video surveillance, prison sentences, medication, boot camps, treatments, and so on—is that really the kind of society we want to have? Do we really want our schools looking and functioning like minimum-security prisons? Do we really want to walk down our city streets in fear of being victims of gang rivalries? Do we really want to stunt the growth or waste the potential of a large, highly-competent segment of our population? Do we really want teens learning most of they know from *each other*? Do we really want our teens to be so completely under the thumbs of the frivolous media, music, and fashion industries? As teachers, do we really want to be in adversarial relationships with our students? As parents, do we really want to be in conflict with our offspring, and do we really want our loved ones to mistrust or disrespect or even hate us?

Adolescence as we know it in the United States should be abolished, and we should also stop exporting this dysfunctional period of life to other countries. Teens in the United States are almost completely isolated from adults, and adults in turn have very little understanding of what it's like to be a teen. The time has come to end the isolation. Young and old, we will all benefit by restoring the child-adult continuum that existed through most of human history in industrialized nations and that still exists in preindustrial societies today. The teen years need to be what they used to be: a time not just of learning, but of learning to be responsible adults.

Can the continuum be reestablished, and is competency testing and training really the key? I'm convinced that an age-blind, competency-based program of evaluation and education can restore the child-adult continuum in a way that will strengthen our society at multiple levels—and that it will do so without threatening any truly essential structures or institutions. The structures it will tear down are relics of the early years of industrialization and have long needed to go.

Q: *The kinds of changes you're recommending seem too radical. Are you serious about them? Do you think they'll ever occur?*

A: It took me years to develop the recommendations I'm making in this book. As a father and teacher—and as the flawed product of modern American society—I found it difficult to think about real change, especially about changes that appeared to put young people at risk.

At first, my recommendations were timid, and when more radical changes seemed called for, I was reluctant to write them down. But as I learned more about the issues, and especially about the history of teens and about teens in other cultures, it became increasingly clear that all of the systems about which I was concerned were created by people; there's nothing perfect or eternal about them.

These systems were themselves part of a process of change many years ago, and they can be modified or abandoned now. At this point, I'm very serious about the program I've outlined, and I'm confident that the child-adult continuum will be restored to some extent over the next ten to twenty years, in part because of the enormous power that modern technology has to accelerate social change.

Appendix 1

HOW ADULT ARE YOU?

Epstein-Dumas Test of Adultness (EDTA), **Abridged Version**

Do you possess the necessary competencies to be legitimately considered an adult in American society? Chapter Six describes a comprehensive test—the *Epstein-Dumas Test of Adultness (EDTA)* that measures adult competencies in fourteen different domains. The test contains multiple sections, and the competency section alone contains 140 questions—far too many to include in this book. But you can at least get a rough idea of how "adult" you are by taking the abridged version of the test included in this appendix. Simply fill in the bubbles as directed; it shouldn't take you more than five minutes. Then complete the self-scorer on the following page to get your overall score, as well as separate scores in five of the most important areas of adult competency. For information on accessing the unabridged version of the *EDTA*, check http://myparentingskills.com.

EPSTEIN-DUMAS TEST OF ADULTNESS (EDTA) [Abridged]

Please use a pencil to fill in the bubble that best represents your reaction to each statement.

1. The U.S. has only two political parties. Is this true? Yes ○ No ○

2. Most problems have just one solution. Do you agree? Yes ○ No ○

3. Are you always careful with your money? Yes ○ No ○

4. Heavier people can tolerate more alcohol. Is this true? Yes ○ No ○

5. Do people need to be loved to be fulfilled? Yes ○ No ○

6. Love is all you need to make a marriage successful. Do you agree? Yes ○ No ○

7. Do you think about the consequences of your behavior before acting? Yes ○ No ○

8. When you don't understand something, do you ask for help? Yes ○ No ○

9. In the U.S., all government officials are elected by voters. Is this true? Yes ○ No ○

10. To get married, you need to have a special license. Is this true? Yes ○ No ○

11. No medical examination is needed to join the military. Is this true? Yes ○ No ○

12. Drugs and alcohol can interact to produce deadly effects. Is this true? Yes ○ No ○

13. If unable to take care of yourself, would you know where to get help? Yes ○ No ○

14. To get a driver's license, you have to pass both a written test and a road test. Is this true? Yes ○ No ○

15. When you make a commitment, do you always honor it? Yes ○ No ○

16. The purpose of taxes is to pay for schools, roads, and other services that people share. Is this true? Yes ○ No ○

17. When people misunderstand you, can you explain your point of view? Yes ○ No ○

18. Almost everyone in the U.S. has to pay taxes of some sort. Is this true? Yes ○ No ○

19. Are love and sex the same thing? Yes ○ No ○

20. Can you make decisions without help from other people? Yes ○ No ○

21. You can drink any amount of alcohol and still remain alert. Is this true? Yes ○ No ○

22. Drinking coffee counters the harmful effects of alcohol. Is this true? Yes ○ No ○

23. Does being in love always feel good? Yes ○ No ○

24. Intimate relationships always require work and compromise. Do you agree? Yes ○ No ○

25. Does everyone have a soulmate? Yes ○ No ○

Self-Scorer for EDTA [Abridged]

To score your test: Generate your <u>total score</u> by placing a <u>1</u> or a <u>0</u> in the blanks in the left-hand column below. Give yourself a <u>1</u> if you filled in a bubble in the shaded area; otherwise give yourself a <u>0</u>. Count up the 1's and fill in your <u>total score</u> at the bottom of the column. The highest possible score is a <u>25</u>. If you scored lower than that, you can probably improve your adult competencies. To focus on specific <u>competencies,</u> complete the five boxes below by circling item numbers for which you received a score of <u>1</u>. In each box, count the 1's, and fill in the blank with the total. If you scored below the maximum, you may need to strengthen your skills within that competency area.

1. Yes ○ No ● ___
2. Yes ○ No ● ___
3. Yes ● No ○ ___
4. Yes ● No ○ ___
5. Yes ○ No ● ___
6. Yes ○ No ● ___
7. Yes ● No ○ ___
8. Yes ● No ○ ___
9. Yes ○ No ● ___
10. Yes ● No ○ ___
11. Yes ○ No ● ___
12. Yes ● No ○ ___
13. Yes ● No ○ ___
14. Yes ● No ○ ___
15. Yes ● No ○ ___
16. Yes ● No ○ ___
17. Yes ● No ○ ___
18. Yes ● No ○ ___
19. Yes ○ No ● ___
20. Yes ● No ○ ___
21. Yes ○ No ● ___
22. Yes ○ No ● ___
23. Yes ○ No ● ___
24. Yes ● No ○ ___
25. Yes ○ No ● ___

TOTAL SCORE:_____ /25

---

1) **Love**. You understand the important role that love and romance play in the adult world and appreciate ways in which love is sometimes misunderstood.

| 5 | 6 | 19 | 23 | 25 | Total 1's: ____ / 5 |

---

2) **Problem solving.** You know how to solve problems, how to get help, and how to make decisions on your own.

| 2 | 7 | 8 | 17 | 20 | Total 1's: ____ / 5 |

---

3) **Handling responsibility.** You honor your commitments, know that relationships take work, and in other ways show that you can handle responsibility.

| 3 | 10 | 13 | 15 | 24 | Total 1's: ____ / 5 |

---

4) **Managing high-risk behaviors.** You understand and can manage the risks associated with drinking, taking drugs, driving, and other risky activities.

| 4 | 12 | 14 | 21 | 22 | Total 1's: ____ / 5 |

---

5) **Citizenship.** You understand the fundamental obligations of citizenship and basic structures and purposes of government.

| 1 | 9 | 11 | 16 | 18 | Total 1's: ____ / 5 |

Appendix 2

	Adults (n=100)		Teens (n=100)		Mean		
ADULT AND TEEN COMPETENCY SCORES ON THE *EDTA*							
Competency	Mean	SD	Mean	SD	Difference	t	p
Love	8.32	0.89	7.95	1.09	0.37	2.62	<.009**
Sex	8.25	1.14	8.11	1.11	0.14	0.88	<.382
Leadership	8.88	0.67	8.20	1.00	0.68	5.62	<.001**
Problem Solving	8.43	0.81	8.06	0.96	0.37	2.94	<.004**
Physical Abilities	7.91	0.99	8.10	0.99	-0.19	-1.35	<.178
Verbal and Math	8.03	0.89	8.15	0.99	-0.12	-0.90	<.369
Interpersonal Skills	8.06	1.06	8.06	1.06	0.00	0.00	<1.00
Handling Responsibility	8.47	0.80	8.39	0.85	0.08	0.64	<.520
Managing High-Risk Behaviors	8.44	0.81	8.19	1.02	0.25	1.91	<.056
Managing Work and Money	8.95	0.77	8.63	1.04	0.32	2.47	<.014*
Education	8.71	1.17	8.58	1.00	0.39	0.84	<.400
Personal Care	8.33	0.83	8.26	1.00	0.07	0.54	<.591
Self Management	8.37	0.97	8.07	1.03	0.30	2.11	<.036*
Citizenship	8.07	1.10	8.01	1.05	0.06	0.39	<.694

**p<.01
*p<.05

Appendix 3

A DEBATE ABOUT TEEN CRIME

It wasn't a particularly great debate. It was just a long exchange of e-mails between me and Mike Males. Males is a lecturer in sociology at the University of California Santa Cruz and the author of *The Scapegoat Generation* and *Framing Youth*—fact-filled, impassioned defenses of the American teen. It started innocently enough. I asked Males (a) whether he was a father, (b) whether he had ever known any "incorrigible" teens, and (c) how he got so interested in teens, and he replied: (a) no, (b) yes, and (c) "from wilderness work with teens crews." Good enough, but we got into trouble when we started looking at numbers.

Over a period of weeks, I pointed to a variety of government data that show that the peak age for virtually any crime in the United States is about eighteen—earlier for a few crimes like arson (thirteen to fourteen) and car theft (sixteen) and later for a few crimes like fraud (twenty-two), but usually eighteen. Overall, the curve that describes the relationship between age and crime looks roughly like an upside-down V:

Figure Appendix 3.1. Crime Index by Age, 2001. Arrest data suggest that young people in America commit crime at a higher rate than older people, with the arrest rate peaking at about age eighteen. The hump to the left of the peak suggests that older teens commit crimes at higher rates than younger teens. After eighteen, the arrest rate falls off sharply and continues to decline at a steady rate throughout the life span.

The graph above is based on data supplied by the FBI for crimes nationwide in 2001.[1] But Males didn't want to hear this. At first, he replied that "race is a far better predictor of violence than age"—at least, he said, in California, which supplies more detailed data about such matters than does the FBI.[2] That's true, I said, but when you look at the races separately, crime still peaks at about age eighteen for every race. Here, for example, are felony arrests in California for blacks and whites:[3]

Figure Appendix 3.2. Felony Arrests in California by Age and Race, 2002. The upper curve is for blacks, and the lower curve is for whites. Although the overall arrest rate for blacks is higher than for whites, the shape of the two curves is virtually identical. Arrests peak for both blacks and whites, as well as for other races in the United States, at about age eighteen.

Although the crime rate is higher for blacks, the similar shape of the curves tells you that, whatever else is going on, there's something about being young in our society which brings out criminal tendencies. But Males wouldn't budge, even after I showed him that this pattern occurs year after year and for a wide variety of crimes:[4]

AGE GROUP

Figure Appendix 3.3. Violent Crime Arrests by Age, 1993–2001. Although the overall crime rate in the United States decreased between 1993 (top curve) and 2001 (bottom curve), arrests each year still peaked at about age eighteen.

Over the course of our exchange, Males shifted his emphasis toward income, insisting that this very robust age pattern occurs because young people are relatively poor. He tried to back up his claim by using a statistical technique called "regression," but his numbers weren't based on actual poverty data. In any case, poverty just isn't the whole picture: poor elderly people don't commit crimes, even though they can pull triggers and light fires and forge signatures just as easily as young people can, and neither do poor teenagers in developing nations. (See Chapter Three.)

In our exchange, Males acknowledged that "American adults have more trouble with teens than adults in any other country." He even acknowledged his own occasional frustration: "I admit getting furious at youths for not meeting perfect-behavior standards and getting me into trouble." But his anger, he says, was misplaced: "I should have been furious at a culture that imposes absolutist standards teens can't be expected to follow and adults can't be expected to enforce."[5] On this, at least, we agree.

Appendix 4

PLATO, SOCRATES, AND ARISTOTLE ON TEENS

In a 1999 essay called "Adolescent Storm and Stress, Reconsidered," developmental psychologist Jeffrey Jansen Arnett said that Aristotle and Socrates characterized youth negatively, and in the textbook Arnett published in 2001, he said the same about Plato and Aristotle, Plato's student:

> ...Both Plato and Aristotle viewed adolescence as the third distinct stage of life, after infancy (birth to age seven) and childhood (ages seven to fourteen). In their views, adolescence extended from age fourteen to twenty-one. Both of them viewed adolescence as the stage of life in which the capacity for reason first developed. Writing (in 4 B.C.)* in The Republic, Plato argued that serious education should begin only in adolescence.
>
> Aristotle argued that it takes the entire course of adolescence for reason to become fully established. At the beginning of adolescence, in his view, the impulses remain in charge and even become more problematic now that sexual desires have developed. It is only toward the end of adolescence—about age twenty-one, according to Aristotle—that reason establishes firm control over the impulses.[1]

Arnett has these ancient philosophers sounding suspiciously like modern psychologists, complete with developmental stages. In fact, neither Plato nor Aristotle talked about "adolescence" in the modern sense, and neither philosopher ever delineated either the stages or the specific ages Arnett gives us. In *The Republic*, Plato's characters say virtually nothing negative about the young, and Socrates, one of the participants in the book's dialogues, warns (much as G. Stanley Hall did) against trying to control young people too severely. Speaking of manners and respect that young people are supposed to show their elders, Socrates says "There is small wisdom in legislating about such matters; I doubt if it is ever done."[2]

Although it's true that Aristotle characterized young people harshly in his *Rhetoric*, he was even harder on old people. He seemed, in fact, to be creating caricatures of the young and the old simply for didactic purposes: perhaps to sug-

---

*Plato's *Republic* was actually written around 360 B.C.E.

gest an ideal, middle ground of optimal functioning. Of the young, Aristotle said (among other things):

> *Young men have strong passions, and tend to gratify them indiscriminately. Of the bodily desires, it is the sexual by which they are most swayed and in which they show absence of self-control. While they love honor, they love victory still more; for youth is eager for superiority over others, and victory is one form of this. They love both more than they love money, which indeed they love very little, not having yet learnt what it means to be without it.[3]*

Speaking of the old, Aristotle simply reversed many of his criticisms of the young and then added many more (not included here):

> *The character of Elderly Men—men who are past their prime—may be said to be formed for the most part of elements that are the contrary of all these. They have lived many years; they have often been taken in, and often made mistakes; and life on the whole is a bad business. The result is that they are sure about nothing and under-do everything. They are not generous, because money is one of the things they must have, and at the same time their experience has taught them how hard it is to get and how easy to lose. They are cowardly, and are always anticipating danger.[4,5]*

But Aristotle is equally emphatic that these are not *necessary* characteristics of the young and old. Age, he says, is not what makes people behave as they do:

> *It is superfluous...to distinguish actions according to the doers' ages, moral states, or the like; it is of course true that, for instance, young men do have hot tempers and strong appetites; still, it is not through youth that they act accordingly, but through anger or appetite.[6]*

That the most eminent thinker of his day—and perhaps of any day—recognized that age wasn't a reliable indicator of ability probably explains why young people in ancient Greece and Rome were generally integrated into adult society early on—and sometimes given great responsibility. (See my discussion of historian Marc Kleijwegt's book in Chapter Two.)

Appendix 5

BRIEF TIMELINE OF TEEN RESTRICTIONS IN THE UNITED STATES

1641 – Massachusetts law prohibits people under 16 from "smiting" their parents

1836 – Massachusetts passes law requiring minimal schooling for people under 15 working in factories

1848 – Pennsylvania sets 12 as minimum work age for some jobs

1852 – Massachusetts passes first universal compulsory education law in the U.S.; requires 3 months of schooling for all young people ages 8 to 14 (but the requirement is waived if appropriate competence can be demonstrated)

1880s – Some states pass laws restricting various behaviors by young people: smoking, singing in the streets, prostitution, "incorrigible" behavior

1898 – World's first juvenile court established in Illinois; constitutional rights of minors effectively taken away

1903 – Illinois enacts tough law requiring school attendance and restricting youth labor

1916 – First federal law restricting labor by young people; struck down by Supreme Court in 1918

1918 – All states have compulsory education laws in place

1933 – First federal law explicitly restricting alcohol consumption by young people

1936 and 1938 – First successful federal laws restricting labor by young people, establishing 16 and 18 as minimum ages for work; still in effect

1940 – Most states have laws in place restricting driving by people under 16

1968 – Supreme Court upholds states' right to prohibit sale of obscene materials to minors

1968 – Movie rating system established, prohibiting young people of various ages from attending certain movies

1970s – Supreme Court upholds new laws restricting a young woman's right to abortion

1970s – Dramatic increase in use of involuntary electroshock therapy (ECT) with teens

1974 – New federal law makes it easier to shift teens from juvenile justice system to mental institutions

1980s – Many cities and states pass laws restricting teens' access to arcades and other places of amusement; Supreme Court upholds such laws in 1989

1980s – Courts uphold states' rights to prohibit sale of lottery tickets to minors

1980 to 1998 – Rate of involuntary commitment of minors to mental institutions increases 300 to 400 percent

1984 – First national law effectively raising drinking age to 21; all states in compliance by 1998

1988 – Supreme Court rules that freedom of the press does not apply to school newspapers

1989 – Missouri court upholds school's right to prohibit dancing

1989 – Court rules school in Florida can ban salacious portions of works by Chaucer and Aristophanes

1990 – Supreme Court upholds recent laws requiring minors to get parental consent for abortion

1990s – Curfew laws for young people spread widely among cities and states

1990s – Dramatic increase in the use of security systems in schools: metal detectors, armed guards, video cameras

1992 – Federal law prohibits sale of tobacco products to minors

1997 – New federal law makes involuntary commitment of teens easier by requiring school systems to pay for hospitalizations

2000+ – New laws restricting a minor's right to get tattoos, piercings, and to enter tanning salons

2000+ – Tougher driving laws being passed by many states; full driving rights obtained gradually over a period of years

2000+ – Dramatic increase in zero-tolerance policies in schools, resulting in suspensions or expulsions for actions such as throwing spitballs, making gun gestures with one's hand, or having a dull kitchen knife in one's car

2000+ – New procedures and laws making it easier to prosecute minors as adults

Currently spreading nationwide:

- Rules prohibiting use of cell phones by minors in schools
- Laws prohibiting use of cell phones by minors while driving
- Libraries and schools blocking access to Internet material by minors
- New dress code rules in schools, including rules restricting wearing of potentially offensive clothing or accessories
- Laws prohibiting teens from attending parties where alcohol is served (even if they're not drinking)
- Restrictions on food and drinks served in school cafeterias or dispensed in school vending machines
- Increasing use of keylogging software to monitor computer usage by teens
- Laws suspending driving privileges based on convictions for vandalism or other non-driving-related offenses
- Laws restricting teens' access to shopping malls
- Tracking devices routinely installed in cell phones and cars of teens
- Increasing use of bumper stickers on cars driven by teens, asking people to call a number to report bad driving habits
- Increasing efforts to ban or restrict violence on television programs seen by young people
- Increasing efforts to ban or restrict advertisements that might encourage young people to drink alcohol, have sex, or eat unhealthful foods
- Bill introduced in U.S. Congress to prohibit individuals from transporting minors over states lines to have abortions
- Social-networking Internet websites restricting both the activity of young people and contact between adults and minors
- New availability of home drug tests for teens
- Zero-tolerance laws prohibiting people under 21 from driving with any alcohol in bloodstream
- Proposals for longer school days, a longer school year, and the addition of grades 13 and 14 to the school curriculum

Notes

Chapter One

1. Lynn Tuohy, "Eighth Fatal School Shooting Has Americans Shaking Heads," *Hartford Courant*, May 22, 1998. Also consider a December 2, 2004 Reuters report entitled "3 Teens Accused of Plot to Attack School," regarding students at the Spanaway Lake High School south of Seattle, Washington. Hit lists, floor plans, and instructions for assembling bombs were discovered in their homes. In another incident, reported by the Associated Press on October 30, 2004, two Utah students were charged after they allegedly plotted to bomb the commons of their high school and kill classmates and teachers. Also: Associated Press, "Boy, 15, held in plot to blow up high school," *San Diego Union-Tribune*, April 1, 2005. Associated Press, "Michigan Teen's Hit List Leads to Terror Charge," *San Diego Union-Tribune*, March 24, 2005. Knight Ridder News Service and Associated Press, "School Killing Rampage: Student Slays Nine, Self on Minnesota Indian Reservation," March 22, 2005. Ceci Connolly and John F. Harris, "Motive in School Massacre Unclear," *Washington Post*, March 23, 2005. Monica Davey and Jodi Wilgoren, New York Times News Service, "'Clues All There' of Killing to Come, *San Diego Union-Tribune*, March 24, 2005. Jaime Levy and Gail Smith-Arrants, "Teenager Accused of Plotting School Attack With Explosives: Unrelated Bomb Hoax Sparked Investigation," *Charlotte Observer*, October 23, 2003. Cris Maag, "The Devil in Red Lake," *TIME*, April 4, 2005. Associated Press, "Teen Held in Slaying Had e-Mailed Columbine Principal," *San Diego Union-Tribune*, September 1, 2006. Associated Press, "Third Teen Arrested in Wisconsin Plot," *San Diego Union-Tribune*, September 17, 2006; Associated Press, "Wisconsin Student Kills His Principal," *San Diego Union-Tribune*, September 30, 2006.

2. American Association of Suicidology, "Youth Suicide Fact Sheet," http://www.suicidology.org/associations/1045/files/Youth2003.pdf (accessed September 2, 2006).

3. Department of Justice, Federal Bureau of Investigation, Uniform Crime Reports, "Violent Crime Arrests by Age, United States, 1993-2001."

4. Rosemarie Kobau et al. "Sad, Blue, or Depressed Days, Health Behaviors and Health-Related Quality of Life, Behavioral Risk Factor Surveillance System, 1995-2000," *Health and Quality of Life Outcomes* 2 (2004).

5. Office of Juvenile Justice and Delinquency Prevention, "Juvenile Arrests 1997," *Juvenile Justice Bulletin*, December 1998, http://ojjdp.ncjrs.org/jjbulletin/9812_2/female.html (accessed May 16, 2003). Department of Justice, Federal Bureau of Investigation, "Crime in the United States 2004," Table 33, Ten-Year Arrest Trends, 1995-2004, http://www.fbi.gov/ucr/cius_04/persons_arrested/table_32-33.html (accessed September 2, 2006)

6. American Academy of Child and Adolescent Psychiatry, "Children and Guns," http://

www.aacap.org/page.ww?section=Policy+Statements&name=Children+and+Guns (accessed September 2, 2006). Also see: CNN.com, "Survey: 29 Percent of High School Boys Have a Gun," http://cnn.tv/US/9810/14/boys.guns/index.html (accessed September 2, 2006).

7. Mary Reimer and Jay Smink, National Dropout Prevention Center, "Information About the School Dropout Issue: Selected Facts and Statistics, 2005." http://www.dropoutprevention.org/stats/SchlDrpoutFacts05.pdf#search=%22school%20dropout%20statistics%22 (accessed September 2, 2006). Typically cited "drop-out rates" or "high school completion rates" don't adequately reflect the extent of the prob-lem, in part because they eliminate young people who are in prison or juvenile detention.

8. U.S. Department of Justice, National Drug Intelligence Center, "Information Brief: Illicit Drugs and Youth, April 2002." http://www.usdoj.gov/ndic/pubs07/798/index.htm (accessed Sep-tember 2, 2006). Because of the unreliability of self-report data and changing drug fads among the young and, drug use is difficult to track; hospital admissions are an especially reliable indicator. A recent study by researchers at the University of California San Francisco employed another reliable indicator: cases of drug abuse by teens (involving over-the-counter cough medi-cines) reported to California's poison control system. This study shows a 15-fold increase in such reports between 1999 and 2004. See: Marcus Wohison, Associated Press, "Abuse by Teens of Over-the-Counter Cough Medicine Climbs," *San Diego Union-Tribune*, December 5, 2006. Jodi K. Bryner, Uerica K. Wang, Jenny W. Hui, Merilin Bedodo, Conan MacDougall and Ilene B. Anderson, "Dextromethorphan Abuse in Adolescence: An Increasing Trend: 1999-2004," *Archives of Pediatric and Adolescent Medicine* 160 (2006): 1217-1222.

9. White House Office of National Drug Control Policy, "Juveniles and Drugs," http://www.whitehousedrugpolicy.gov/drugfact/juveniles/index.html (accessed August 7, 2006).

10. Reproductive Statistics Branch of the Division of Vital Statistics, "Births to Teenagers in the United States, 1940-2000," National Vital Statistics Report 49, no. 10. Also: Office of Fam-ily Health Services, "Teen Pregnancy Prevention," Virginia Department of Health, http://www.vahealth.org/teenpregnancyprevention/Data.htm (accessed April 16, 2003). United Nations Department of Economic and Social Affairs, Population Division, *World Population Prospects: The 1994 Revision* (New York: 1994).

11. Kevin Johnson, "Police Tie Jump in Crime to Juveniles," *USA Today*, July 13, 2006; Kevin Johnson, "Cities Grapple With Crime by Kids," *USA Today*, July 13, 2006. Also see FBI Press Release dated June 12, 2006: http://www.fbi.gov/pressrel/pressrel06/prelim2005061206.htm (accessed September 3, 2006).

12. James P. Sweeney, "Measure to Raise Smoking Age to 21 Clears Early Hurdle," *San Diego Union-Tribune*, June 27, 2002.

13. Leonel Sanchez, "Teachers Faulted Over Berg Video, Audio," *San Diego Union-Tribune*, May 15, 2004, http://www.signonsandiego.com/news/metro/20040515-9999-1m15elcap.html (accessed July 26, 2006).

14. Edward Brand, "Adding 2 Years to Earn a High School Diploma," *San Diego Union-Tribune*, August 26, 1999. In 2005 Brand became superintendent of schools in San Marcos, another city in San Diego County, where he resigned abruptly for personal reasons a year later. See: Linda Lou, "San Marcos School Chief's Resignation Rocks District," *San Diego Union-Tribune*, September 1, 2006.

15. Pacific Research Institute, "California's Public Schools Still Failing Their Students," http://www.pacificresearch.org/press/rel/2000/pr00-02-29.html (accessed May 29, 2003).

16. K. W. Arenson, "Virtually No Progress Seen in College Readiness," *San Diego Union-Tribune*, October 14, 2004. One measure of the impact of high school, the SAT, tells a similar story. Taken primarily by only high-achieving, college-bound students, scores have remained flat or declined in recent years. Graduating high school seniors in 2006 had the biggest drop in scores in decades. See: Jay Matthews, "SAT Records Biggest Score Dip in 31 Years," *Washington Post*, August 31, 2006.

17. Laurence Steinberg, *Adolescence*, 6th ed. (New York: McGraw Hill, 2002), 216-217.

18. Edward Brand, "Adding 2 Years to Earn a High School Diploma," *San Diego Union-Tribune*, August 26, 1999.

19. Reg Weaver, "Curbing Dropouts by Raising the Exit Age." *San Diego Union-Tribune*, October 6, 2006.

20. Berkeley Hills Books Publishers, "Gatto Exhausted School," http://www.berkeleyhills.com/exhaust.html (accessed May 29, 2003).

21. John Taylor Gatto, "I May Be a Teacher, But I'm Not an Educator," *Wall Street Journal*, July 25, 1991.

22. The Odysseus Group, "John Taylor Gatto Biography," http://www.johntaylorgatto.com/aboutus/john.htm (accessed May 29, 2003).

23. Seymour Sarason, *The Culture of the School and the Problem of Change*, 2nd ed. (Boston: Allyn & Bacon, 1982). Saranson was quoting the nineteenth century French novelist and critic Jean Baptiste Alphonse Karr.

24. Jeninne Lee-St. John, "Barred from the Prom," *TIME*, May 29, 2006, 57.

25. John Taylor Gatto, *The Underground History of American Education* (Oxford: Oxford Village Press, 2001) Prologue.

26. Diane Dumas, "Psychological Implications of Infantilization on Teenagers in the United States" (Psy.D. dissertation., Alliant International University, 2002).

27. U.S. Census Bureau, "Historical Statistics of the United States," quoted in "Life Expectancy by Age, 1850-2000," Infoplease.com, http://www.infoplease.com/ipa/A0005140.html (accessed June 4, 2003).

28. Barbara Kaye Greenleaf, *Children Through the Ages* (New York: McGraw-Hill, 1978), 74.

29. "Child Labor," Microsoft Encarta Online Encyclopedia 2004, http://encarta.msn.com/encyclopedia_761552027/Child_Labor.html (accessed November 3, 2004).

30. Jim Zwick, "The Campaign to End Child Labor Introduction," BoondocksNet.com, http://www.boondocksnet.com/labor/cl_intro. html (accessed November 6, 2003).

31. "Child Labor," Microsoft Encarta Online Encyclopedia 2004, http://encarta.msn.com/encyclopedia_761552027/Child_Labor.html (accessed November 3, 2004).

32. Charles Webber, ed., *Encyclopedia of Temperance and Prohibition* (New York: Funk & Wagnalls, 1891), 630.

33. Alex Koroknay-Palicz, "Legislative Analysis for the National Minimum Drinking Age Act," Americans for a Society Free from Age Restrictions, http://www.asfar.org/zine/5th/cover.html (accessed January 8, 2004).

34. James E. Mosher, "The History of Youthful Drinking Laws: Implications for Current Policy," in *Minimum Drinking Age Laws: An Evaluation*, ed. Henry W. Echsler, 11-35 (Lexington, MA: Lexington Books, 1980) 12. Even when the first laws were passed that regulated drinking by minors, the laws, says Mosher, "explicitly recognized the family unit by respecting the rights of parents to be the ultimate deciders of their children's behavior" (p. 15).

35. Lev Grossman, "Up in the Air," *TIME*, July 24, 2006, 56, 58.

36. Robert Epstein, *Creativity Games for Trainers* (New York: McGraw-Hill, 1996); Robert Epstein, *Stress-Management and Relaxation Activities for Trainers* (New York: McGraw-Hill, 1999); Robert Epstein, *The Big Book of Stress-Relief Games* (New York: McGraw-Hill, 2000); Robert Epstein, *The Big Book of Creativity Games* (New York: McGraw-Hill, 2000).; Robert Epstein, with J. Rogers, *The Big Book of Motivation Games* (New York: McGraw-Hill, 2001).

37. David L. Rosenhan, "On Being Sane in Insane Places," *Science* 179 (January 1973): 250-258.

38. Margaret Mead, *Coming of Age in Samoa* (New York: William Morrow, 1973).

39. John Holt, *Escape From Childhood, The Needs and Rights of Children* (Cambridge, MA: Holt Associates, 1995).

40. Ivan Illich, *Deschooling Society* (London: Marion Boyars, 1999).

41. Richard Evans Farson, *Birthrights: A Bill of Rights for Children* (Hampshire, England: Macmillan, 1974). Calls for children to receive rights commensurate with those of adults have even been called a "movement." Consider: Beatrice Gross and Ronald Gross, eds. *The Children's Rights Movement: Overcoming the Oppression of Young People* (New York: Anchor/Doubleday, 1977). Howard Cohen, *Equal Rights for Children* (Totowa, NJ: Littlefield, Adams, 1980). Henry H. Foster, Jr., *A "Bill of Rights" for Children* (Springfield, IL: Charles C. Thomas, 1974). John Harris, "The Political Status of Children," in *Contemporary Political Philosophy*, ed. K. Graham (Cambridge: Cambridge University Press, 1982). Calling such authors "liberationists" and herself a "protectionist," Wells College philosopher Laura M. Purdy challenged the children's rights viewpoint in her 1992 book *In Their Best Interest? The Case Against Equal Rights for Children* (Ithaca, NY: Cornell University Press). I'm skeptical about both viewpoints, preferring instead to look at young people individually. In my view, authority and responsibility should be granted based on competency, not on age, in part to give young people strong incentives to join the adult world as soon as they are able.

42. John Holt, *Escape From Childhood, The Needs and Rights of Children* (Cambridge, MA: Holt Associates, 1995) 19.

43. Jean Liedloff, *The Continuum Concept: In Search of Lost Happiness* (Reading, MA: Perseus Books, 1977).

44. Philip Graham, *The End of Adolescence* (Oxford: Oxford University Press, 2004).

45. Ibid., 2.

46. Ibid., 3.

47. Associated Press, "Americans Aren't Adults Until Reaching Age 26," *The Salt Lake Tribune*, May 9, 2003.

Chapter Two

1. Marc Kleijwget, Ancient Youth: The Ambiguity and Absence of Adolescence in Greco-Roman Society. (Amsterdam: J. C. Gieben, 1991).

2. Ibid., 317.

3. Ibid., xii.

4. Thomas Hine, *The Rise and Fall of the American Teenager* (New York: Bard Books, 1999) 9.

5. Edward Shorter, *The Making of the Modern Family* (New York: Basic Books, 1975) 8.

6. Joesph F. Kett, *Rites of Passage: Adolescence in America, 1790 to the Present* (New York: Basic Books, 1977) 238.

7. Phillipe Ariès, *Centuries of Childhood: A Social History of Family Life*, trans. Robert Baldick (New York: Vintage, 1962) 30.

8. Jimmy Carter, *An Hour Before Daylight* (New York: Simon & Schuster, 2001) 100.

9. Ibid., 6.

10. Ibid., 8.

11. Ibid., 110.

12. Ibid., 12.

13. Phillipe Ariès, *Centuries of Childhood: A Social History of Family Life*, trans. Robert Baldick (New York: Vintage, 1962).

14. Ibid., 30.

15. Ibid., 30.

16. Ibid., 25. Hanawalt also acknowledges that "the medieval word *adolescencia* did not mean the same thing as the modern term 'adolescence'" (Hanawalt, 1993, p. 8). According to Ariès, a seventeenth-century listing of students in a Jesuit college in France refers to a 15-year-old boy as a "*bonus puer*" and a 13-year-old boy as an "*optimus adolescens*." (Aries, 1962, p. 25). A grammar book used for hundreds of years in England used the word "baby" and "child" interchangeably. An early eighteenth-century French dictionary defines child, in part, as "a term of friendship used to greet or flatter someone." The modern meaning of "child" doesn't begin to take hold until the late eighteenth century, and the modern meaning of "adolescence" doesn't appear, according to Ariès, until the early twentieth century.

17. Ibid., 33.

18. Ibid., 33.

19. Ibid., 39. For a balanced look at the affection issue, see: Emily Eakin, "Did Cradles Always Rock? Or Did Mom Once Not Care?" *New York Times*, June 30, 2001.

20. Ibid., 219-220.

21. Joan Acocella, "Little People: When Did We Start Treating Children Like Children?" *The New Yorker*, August 18 and 25, 2003.

22. Donald T. Kramer, *Legal Rights of Children*, 2nd ed. vol 3, chaps. 28-33 (New York: McGraw-Hill, 1994) 3-4.

23. Ariès developed and defended a fairly radical thesis: Childhood and adolescence are recent inventions, created by some of the dramatic societal shifts of recent centuries: improved hygiene and medical care, mass education, industrialization, and so on. For about 20 years his views, even though unpalatable, were widely accepted among fellow historians. But history has a curious way of getting rewritten every 20 years or so—in other words, with every new generation of historians. My mentor at Harvard, B. F. Skinner, once wrote that we can't write history "until a sufficient number of details have been forgotten" (*Walden Two*, London: Macmillan, 1946, p. 226). He was being cynical, perhaps, but this much is clear: Different historians have very different viewpoints on childhood and adolescence, and those viewpoints often reflect prevailing values. As University of Texas historian Harvey J. Graff commented in his own recent history of American children, "The history of growing up is deeply fragmented in its definition and delineation and in the approaches to it" (*Conflicting Paths: Growing Up in America*, Cambridge, MA: Harvard University Press, 1995, p. 4).

24. Steven Ozment, whose work makes for extensive use of sentimental material from German archives. See for example his recent book, *Ancestors: the Loving Family in Old Europe* (Cambridge, MA: Harvard University Press, 2001).

25. Jason Fields, "Children's Living Arrangements and Characteristics: March 2002," U.S. Census Bureau, http://www.census.gov/prod/2003pubs/p20-547.pdf (accessed February 3, 2005).

26. Infoplease, "Median Age at First Marriage," U.S. Bureau of the Census, http://www.infoplease.com/ipa/A0005061.html (accessed June 20, 2005).

27. *The Book of the General Laws and Liberties Concerning the Inhabitants of the Massachusetts* (1648; Cambridge: Harvard University Press, 1929).

28. Sushma Subramanian, "Child Labor at the Bee: Newspaper Says It Isn't Liable for Underaged Children Who Work the Morning Paper Routes," *Sacramento News & Review*, July 11, 2002, http://www.newsreview.com/sacramento/Content?oid=oid%3A12604 (accessed October 1, 2003).

29. Ibid.

30. Barbara Kaye Greenleaf, *Children Through the Ages* (New York: McGraw-Hill, 1978) 74. R.W. Cooke-Taylor, *The Factory System* (London: Methuen, 1894).

31. "Child Labor," Microsoft Encarta Online Encyclopedia 2004, http://encarta.msn.com/encyclopedia_761552027/Child_Labor.html (accessed November 3, 2004). Jeremy Atack, Fred Bateman, and Robert A. Margo, "Productivity in Manufacturing and the Length of the Working Day: Evidence from the 1880 Census of Manufacturers," Vanderbilt University Working Paper No. 00-W45, November 2000. http://www.vanderbilt.edu/Econ/workpaper/vu00-w45.pdf (accessed September 3, 2006).

32. Katherine DuPre Lumpkin and Dorothy Wolff Douglas, *Child Workers in America* (Freeport,

New York: Books for Libraries Press, 1937) 197.

33. Viviana Zelizer, *Pricing the Priceless Child: The Changing Social Value of Children* (Princeton, NJ: Princeton University Press, 1994) 76. Also see: Adriana Lleras-Muney, "Were Compulsory Attendance and Child Labor Laws Effective? An Analysis from 1915 to 1939," *Journal of Law and Economics* 45, no. 2 (2002): 401-435.

34. Jim Zwick, "The Campaign to End Child Labor: Introduction," BoondocksNet.com, http://www.boondocksnet.com/labor/cl_intro.html (accessed October 4, 2003).

35. Ibid. A selection of Hine's photographs can be found at www.historyplace.com/unitedstates/childlabor.

36. Jim Zwick, "The Campaign to End Child Labor: Introduction," BoondocksNet.com, http://www.boondocksnet.com/labor/cl_intro.html (accessed October 4, 2003). Also see Supreme Court decision, *Hammer v. Dagenhart* 247 U.S. 251 (1918), at: http://caselaw.lp.findlaw.com/scripts/getcase.pl?court=us&vol=247&invol=251.

37. Microsoft Encarta Online Encyclopedia, "Child Labor," http://encarta.msn.com/encyclopedia_761552027/Child_Labor.html (accessed August 15, 2006). The case is: *Bailey v. Drexel Furniture Co.*, 259 U.S. 20 (1922).

38. Ibid. The case is: *A. L. A. Schechter Poultry Corp. v. U.S.*, 295 U.S. 495 (1935).

39. Ibid. Also: Kimberly Fitzpatrick et. al. "Child Labor Historical Facts," Bryant University, http://web.bryant.edu/~history/h364proj/fall_99/fitzpatrick/timeline.html (accessed November 13, 2003).

40. Katherine DuPre Lumpkin and Dorothy Wolff Douglas, *Child Workers in America* (Freeport, New York: Books for Libraries Press, 1937).

41. Amidon, Beulah, "Children Wanted," *Survey Graphic* 26, no. 1 (1937): 10-15.

42. Katherine DuPre Lumpkin and Dorothy Wolff Douglas, *Child Workers in America* (Freeport, New York: Books for Libraries Press, 1937) 247.

43. Ibid., 251.

44. Nancy Lesko, *Act Your Age! A Cultural Construction of Adolescence* (New York: RoutledgeFalmer, 2001). Also see: Molly Ray Carroll, *Labor and Politics*, Chicago, 1920, as quoted by Katherine DuPre Lumpkin and Dorothy Wolff Douglas, *Child Workers in America* (Freeport, New York: Books for Libraries Press, 1937) 254. Alan Trachtenberg, *The Incorporation of America: Culture and Society in the Gilded Age* (New York: Hill and Wang, 1982).

45. Katherine DuPre Lumpkin and Dorothy Wolff Douglas, *Child Workers in America* (Freeport,

New York: Books for Libraries Press, 1937) 252.

46. Hugh Cunningham, *Children and Childhood: In Western Society Since 1500* (New York: Longman, 1995) 87.

47. Ibid.

48. Edith Abbott, "A Study of the Early History of Child Labor in America," *American Journal of Sociology* 14 (July 1908): 16-17. She quotes Massachusetts Bay records.

49. Ibid.

50. Ibid.

51. Amy L. Matzat, "Massachusetts Education Laws of 1642 and 1647," Amy L. Matzat, www.nd.edu/~rbarger/www7/masslaws.html (accessed February 3, 2005). Also: Michael Svec, "Massachusetts Education Law of 1642," and "Massachusetts School Law of 1647 Old Deluder Satan Law," Furman University, http://facweb.furman.edu/~svecmichael/ED11/library/ed11laws.html (accessed February 3, 2005).

52. Adriana Lleras-Muney, "Were Compulsory Attendance and Child Labor Laws Effective? An Analysis from 1915 to 1939," *The Journal of Law and Economics* 45, no. 2 (2002): 401-435. http://wws.princeton.edu/chw/papers/llerasmuney2.pdf (accessed July 17, 2006)

53. Scott Woodruff, "Compulsory Education Laws: The Dialogue Reopens," *The Home School Court Reporter* 16, no 5 (September /October 2000).

54. Hugh Cunningham, personal communication, November 1, 2004.

55. Murray N. Rothbard, *Education: Free and Compulsory* (Auburn, AL: Ludwig von Mises Institute, 1999) 43-44.

56. Scott Woodruff, "Compulsory Education Laws: The Dialogue Reopens," *The Home School Court Reporter* 16, no 5 (September /October 2000).

57. William Smith, "Impubes," in *A Dictionary of Greek and Roman Antiquities* (London: John Murray, 1875).

58. *The Book of the General Laws and Liberties Concerning the Inhabitants of the Massachusetts* (1648; Cambridge: Harvard University Press, 1929).

59. Stephen J. Fletcher, *Child Labor in Indiana Timeline, September 1807-February 1915* (Indiana Historical Society, 2002).

60. The Crime Prevention Group, "Iowa Cigarette Control Law," The Crime Prevention Group,

http://medicolegal.tripod.com/iowalaw1897.htm#minors (accessed February 3, 2005).

61. Encyclopedia.com, "Organized Crime: The Prohibition Era," http://www.encyclopedia.com/printable.asp?url=/ssi/section/orgcrim_TheProhibitionEra.html (accessed June 22, 2005). Alex Koroknay-Palicz, "Legislative Analysis for the National Minimum Drinking Age Act," ASFAR, http://www.asfar.org/zine/5th/cover.html (accessed January 8, 2004).

62. See: Henry Wechsler, *Minimum-Drinking-Age Laws* (Heath, 1980) ch. 2, and especially p. 22. A few states, such as Illinois, had more stringent laws in effect governing drinking by minors well before the end of Prohibition, but generally in the U.S. the drinking rights of a young person had always been regulated by parents, not government.

63. American Medical Association, "Addressing the Minimum Legal Drinking Age (MLDA) in College Communities," Alcohol Policy Solutions, http://www.alcoholpolicysolutions.net/research_studies_mlda.htm (accessed May 29, 2003).

64. A law passed in 1923 required drivers to be licensed, but the minimum driving age was lowered to 14; both parents had to sign a document before the state would issue the license to people under age 21, and parents were now considered liable for the misdeeds of their offspring. There was still no examination requirement.

65. J. Allen Davis and Harry V. Cheshire, Jr., "The Horseless Carriage Era, 1900-1912," 66 *West's Annotated California Codes 1-57* (1960), http://www.sandiego.edu/lrc/vehicle.html (accessed June 22, 2005).

66. Jimmy Carter, *An Hour Before Daylight* (New York: Simon & Schuster, 2001) 227.

67. Anthony M. Platt, *The Child Savers: The Invention of Delinquency* (Chicago: University of Chicago Press, 1977) 111-112.

68. Ibid., 112-113.

69. Ibid., 139

70. U.S. Census Bureau, "Crimes and Crime Rates by Type of Offense: 1960 to 2002," http://www.census.gov/statab/hist/HS-23.pdf (accessed November 1, 2004).

71. Robyn E. Blumner, "A Loss of Rights," *American Bar Association Journal* (April 1994): 40-41.

72. Mike Males, *Framing Youth* (Monroe: Common Courage Press, 1999)71-82.

73. Charles Levendosky, "Society is a Much Stricter, Less Forgiving Parent," *Casper Star-Tribune*, http://fact.trib.com/1st.lev.society.kids.html (accessed February 3, 2005).

74. Go Local Net Driving Rules Network, "State-by-State Driving Rules for Teenager Drivers,"

Go Local Net, http://golocalnet.com/drivingage (accessed February 5, 2005).

75. Campbell Robertson, "Waiting for Wheels," *New York Times*, http://www.nytimes.com/ 2005/01/16/nyregion/thecity/16WE.html?ex=1107752400&en=6 afe56cf6e06ef85&ei=5070&fta=y (accessed February 5, 2005).

76. U. S. Department of Labor, "Questions and Answers About the Minimum Wage," August 23, 2006, http://www.dol.gov/esa/minwage/q-a.htm (accessed September 3, 2006)

77. *Shorez v. City of Dacono, Colorado*, 574 F Supp 130 (D Colo 1983).

78. *Rothner v. City of Des Plaines*, 554 F Supp 465 (DC III 1981).

79. *City of Dallas v. Stanglin*, 490 US 19 (1989).

80. *Clayton by Clayton v. Place*, 884 F2d 376 (8th Cir 1989).

81. *Ginsburg v. New York*, 390 US 629 (1968).

82. *Hazelwood School District v. Kuhlmeier*, 484 U.S. 260 (1988).

83. David Kravets, "Court Hears Case of Boy Jailed Over Violent Poem," *San Diego Union-Tribune*, May 28, 2004.

84. Associated Press, "Students Defy, Parents Fight Nyc Cell Phone Ban," May 13, 2006.

85. Motion Picture Association of America, "Movie Ratings - The Birth of the Ratings," http://www.mpaa.org/movieratings/about/index.htm (accessed November 3, 2004).

86. Electronic School, "Students' Free-Speech Right Extend to the Internet," Electronic School, http://www.electronic-school.com/199903/0399ewire.html (accessed February 5, 2005).

87. Eric Nuzum, *Parental Advisory: Music Censorship in America* (New York: Harper Collins Publishers).

88. *Bellotti vs. Baird*, 1981. *Planned Parenthood vs. Casey*, 1992.

89. *Virgil v. School Board of Columbia County*, 862 F.2d 1517 (1989).

90. In *Bivens v. Albuquerque Public Schools* (1995) a court upheld discipline after Richard Bivens was suspended for wearing non-gang related sagging pants to school. See: Traci Truly, *Teen Rights: A Legal Guide For Teens and the Adults in Their Lives* (Naperville, IL: Sphinx Publishing, 2002) 10-11. The parents of Jimmy Hines, a fourth-grade student who was suspended from school for refusing to remove his earring, sued the district claiming that the rule violated their son's right to "the possession and control of his own person in matters of personal

appearance." While the judge agreed with the Hineses, he also upheld the school's rule, maintaining that the school had shown a "valid reason" in enforcing their policy. See: Traci Truly, *Teen Rights: A Legal Guide For Teens and the Adults in Their Lives* (Naperville, IL: Sphinx Publishing, 2002) 12-13.

91. "Bill Would Bar Teenagers from Tanning Salons," *San Diego Union-Tribune*, May 3, 2004. Jim Wasserman, Associated Press, "Assembly Oks Age Limits on Tanning Booth Users," *San Diego Union-Tribune*. May 21, 2004.

92. The General Court, "The General Laws of Massachusetts," The 184th General Court of the Commonwealth of Massachusetts, http://www.mass.gov/legis/laws/mgl/ (accessed February 5, 2005).

93. *Bravo Vending v. City of Rancho Mirage*, 16 Cal App 4th 383, 20 Cal Rptr 2d 164 (1993). American Lung Association "Tobacco Laws and Regulations" American Lung Association, http://www.lungsandiego.org/tobacco/advocate_state.asp (accessed June 22, 2005).

94. Office of the General Counsel, U.S. Dept. of Health and Human Services, "Executive Summary of the Regulations Restricting the Sale and Distribution Of Cigarettes and Smokeless Tobacco to Protect Children and Adolescents," http://library.findlaw.com/1996/Aug/1/129437.html (Accessed July 19, 2006).

95. Associated Press, "Pupil Punished for Saving Asthmatic," *San Diego Union-Tribune*, May 3, 1998.

96. Alex Koroknay-Palicz, "Legislative Analysis for the National Minimum Drinking Age Act," ASFAR, http://www.asfar.org/zine/5th/cover.html (access January 8, 2004).

97. American Medical Association, "Addressing the Minimum Legal Drinking Age (MLDA) in College Communities," Alcohol Policy Solutions, http://www.alcoholpolicysolutions.net/research_studies_mlda.htm (accessed May 29, 2003). American Medical Associaiton, "A Brief History of the MLDA," http://www.ama-assn.org/ama/pub/category/13246.html (accessed June 22, 2005).

98. *Smith v. Kappell*, 147 Wis 2d 380, 433 NW2d.

99. 14 ALR3d 1186. See: Donald T. Kramer, *Legal Rights of Children*, 2nd ed. vol 1 (New York: McGraw-Hill, 1984) 623.

100. Jennifer Taylor, "Naperville Fine-Tunes Teen Drinking Law," *The Chicago Tribune*, http://www.alcoholdrugnewsroom.org/natonal_summer_03.htm (accessed June 28, 2005).

101. Deborah L. Forman, *Every Parent's Guide to the Law* (Harvest Books, 1998) 127.

102. Gary B. Melton, Phillip M. Lyons, and Willis J. Spaulding, *No Place to Go: The Civil Commit-*

ment of Minors (Children and the Law) (Lincoln, Nebraska: University of Nebraska Press, 1998).

103. Ibid., 10.

104. Ibid., 12.

105. Ibid., 14.

106. Steve Baldwin and Melissa Oxlad, *Electroshock and Minors: A Fifty-Year Review* (Westport, CT: Greenwood Press, 2000).

107. Ibid., 33.

108. Ibid., 31.

109. Ibid., 105.

110. Ibid., 141.

111. Pamela Tom, "Security Cams Make the Grade: California High School Cuts Suspension Rate After Installing Cameras," *ABC News*, February 14, 2002.

112. Casey McCorkle, "Student Suspended for Kitchen Knife in Car," *The Central Florida Future*, June 6, 2001.

113. Associated Press, "Spitball Shooter, 13, Sentenced for Injury," *San Diego Union-Tribune*, June 8, 2002.

114. Associated Press, "Boy Suspended for Pointing Chicken Finger," SFGate.com, January 31, 2001, http://sfgate.com/cgi-bin/article.cgi?file=/news/archive/2001/01/31/national1853EST0757.DTL (accessed November 8, 2003). Also consider: Susan Barbosa and Anthony Bruce Gilpin, New York Times News Service, "6-Year-Old Arrested on Felony Battery Counts," *San Diego Union-Tribune*, February 22, 1998. New York Times News Service, "Police Arrest, Book 5-Year-Old Accused of Attacking Counselor," *San Diego Union-Tribune*, February 22, 1998.

115. Michael Gardner, "State Bill to Keep Drivers Under 18 Off Phones Is OK'd," *San Diego Union-Tribune*, May 26, 2004.

116. Associated Press, "Bill Would Bar Teenagers from Tanning Salons," *San Diego Union-Tribune*, May 3, 2004.

117. Michael Gardner, "State Bill to Keep Drivers Under 18 Off Phones is OK'd," *San Diego Union-Tribune*, May 26, 2004.

118. Laurie Kellman, Associated Press, "Senate Abortion Debate Focuses on Teens," *San Diego Union-Tribune*, July 22, 2006.

119. National Research Council "Study of the Health and Safety Implications of Child Labor," Robert Wood Johnson Foundation, http://www.rwjf.org/reports/grr/030461s.htm (accessed June 9, 2005).

120. Reitz, Stephanie, Associated Press, "Connecticut Town Buries 13-Year-Old's Worm Business," *San Diego Union-Tribune*, August 12, 2006.

121. U.S. Department of Labor, Bureau of International Labor Affairs, "International Program on the Elimination of Child Labor (ILO/IPEC)," http://www.dol.gov/ilab/programs/iclp/iloipec/main.htm (accessed May 1, 2004).

122. Encyclopedia.com, "Prevention of Cruelty," http://www.encyclopedia.com/html/c1/cruelty.asp (accessed October 19, 2003).

123. National Society for the Prevention of Cruelty to Children, *A History of the NSPCC: Protecting Children from Cruelty Since 1884* (London, 2000) 1.

124. Massachusetts Society for the Prevention of Cruelty to Children, "MSPCC and Child Welfare Milestones," http://www.mspcc.org/index.cfm?fuseaction=Page.viewPage&pageId=97 (accessed October 20, 2004). National Society for the Prevention of Cruelty to Children, *A History of the NSPCC: Protecting Children from Cruelty Since 1884* (London, 2000) 1.

125. Jean Bethke Elshtain, ed., *The Jane Addams Reader* (New York: Basic Books, 2002) xxiii.

126. Jane Addams, *Twenty Years at Hull-House* (1910; New York: Signet Classics, 1961) 44.

127. Addams defined "settlement" as follows: "The Settlement, then, is an experimental effort to aid in the solution of the social and industrial problems which are endangered by the modern conditions of life in a great city.... It is an attempt to relieve, at the same time, the overaccumulation at one end of society, and the destitution at the other." Ibid., xiv.

128. Ibid., xiv.

129. Ruth M. Alexander, *The "Girl Problem": Female Sexual Delinquency in New York, 1900-1930* (Ithaca, NY: Cornell University Press)

130. Although there are many exceptions to this rule, there is little question that, on average, women are more nurturing toward children than men are. The experiences of pregnancy, labor, birth, and breastfeeding are exclusive to women, and these experiences alone produce a type of bonding that men can never know. This issue is examined in detail in writer Tine Thevenin's 1993 book *Mothering and Fathering: The Gender Differences in Child Rearing* (Gar-

den City Park, NY: Avery). The book is especially interesting in that Thevenin's perspective exemplifies the principals she develops; that is, she makes it clear that her own tendencies toward children are at the extreme nurturing end of the continuum.

131. United States Congress, *Congressional Record Report on Hull House*, 1926.

132. Jean Bethke Elshtain, ed., *The Jane Addams Reader* (New York: Basic Books, 2002) xxv.

133. Jane Addams Hull-House Museum, "Biographical Sketch of Jane Addams," University of Illinois, Chicago, http://www.uic.edu/jaddams/hull/ja_bio.html (accessed October 19, 2003).

134. Ibid.

135. Jean Bethke Elshtain, ed., *The Jane Addams Reader* (New York: Basic Books, 2002) xix.

136. Spartacus Educational, "Alzina Stevens," http://www.spartacus.schoolnet.co.uk/USAWstevens.htm (accessed October 19, 2003). Spartacus Educational, "Julia Lathrop," http://www.spartacus.schoolnet.co.uk/USAWlathrop.htm (accessed October 19, 2003). Spartacus Educational, "Florence Kelley," http://www.spartacus.schoolnet.co.uk/USAWkelley.htm (accessed October 19, 2003). Spartacus Educational, "Edith Abbot," http://www.spartacus.schoolnet.co.uk/USAWabbottE.htm (accessed October 19, 2003). Spartacus Educational, "Sophonisba Brekinridge," http://www.spartacus.schoolnet.co.uk/USAWbreckinridge.htm (accessed October 19, 2003). Students in "Women's Intellectual Contributions to the Study of Mind and Society" Seminar at Webster University, "Grace Abbott," Women's Intellectual Contributions to the Study of Mind and Society, http://www.webster.edu/~woolflm/gabbott.html (accessed October 19, 2003).

137. Henry Steele Commager, Foreword to *Twenty Years at Hull-House*, by Jane Addams (New York: Signet Classics, 1961) xviii.

138. Anthony M. Platt, *The Child Savers: The Invention of Delinquency* (Chicago: University of Chicago Press, 1977) xxiv.

139. Ibid., xx.

140. Ibid., xxi.

141. Ibid., xxi.

142. Ibid., xxii.

143. Jane Addams, *The Spirit of Youth and the City Streets* (Hampshire, UK: Macmillan, 1909) 14, quoted by Anthony M. Platt, *The Child Savers: The Invention of Delinquency* (Chicago: University of Chicago Press, 1977) 96.

144. Enoch C. Wines, *State of Prisons and Child-Saving Institutions in the Civilized World* (Cambridge, MA: J. Wilson & Son, 1880) 607.

145. Anthony M. Platt, *The Child Savers: The Invention of Delinquency* (Chicago: University of Chicago Press, 1977) 142.

146. Ibid.

147. Ibid.

148. Thomas O'Connor, "An Overview of Juvenile Justice," North Carolina Wesleyan College, http://faculty.ncwc.edu/toconnor/111/111lect14.htm (accessed September 2, 2003). The Fifth Amendment to the Constitution was ratified in 1791. But the very same language, applied this time to the states, was included in the Fourteenth Amendment, which was ratified in 1868, "[No State] shall deprive any person of life, liberty, or property, without due process of law."

149. Anthony M. Platt, *The Child Savers: The Invention of Delinquency* (Chicago: University of Chicago Press, 1977) 194-195.

150. Ibid., 64.

151. Ibid., 92-98.

152. Ibid., 151.

153. National Research Council, *Juvenile Crime, Juvenile Justice* (Washington D.C.: National Academy Press, 2001) 5-6. Note that the NRC's alternative to incarceration is still "treatment," as if troublesome young people are suffering from an illness.

154. Ibid., 100.

155. Marc Elliott, *Walt Disney: Hollywood's Dark Prince* (New York: Harper Paperbacks, 1993) 10-13.

156. Diane Disney Miller, *The Story of Walt Disney* (New York: Dell, 1956, 1957) 48.

157. Bernard Mergen, "Made, Bought, and Stolen: Toys and the Culture of Childhood," in *Small Worlds: Children and Adolescents in America, 1850-1956*, eds. Elliott West and Paula Petrik (Lawrence, Kansas: University Press of Kansas, 1992) 93.

158. Ibid., 103.

159. Ibid., 94.

160. Carl N. Degler, *Out of Our Past: The Forces That Shaped Modern America*, 3rd ed. (New York: Harper Colophon, 1984) 461.

161. Bernard Mergen, "Made, Bought, and Stolen: Toys and the Culture of Childhood," in *Small Worlds: Children and Adolescents in America, 1850-1956*, eds. Elliott West and Paula Petrik (Lawrence, Kansas: University Press of Kansas, 1992) 97.

162. Ibid., 103.

163. Dallas Middaugh, "Toy Story: Masters of the Universe," ToyFare #12, August 1998, http://www.he-man.org/site_sects/archives/articles/article_15.shtml (accessed August 15, 2006).

164. Carl Hiaasen, *Team Rodent : How Disney Devours the World* (New York: Ballantine, 1998).

165. "Barbie History," http://characterproducts.com (accessed August 6, 2006). "Most Popular Toys of the Last 100 Years," *Forbes*, http://www.forbes.com (accessed August 6, 2006).

166. Pallavi Gogoi, "Mattel's Barbie Trouble," *Business Week Online*, July 18, 2006, http://www.businessweek.com/print/bwdaily/dnflash/content/jul2006/db20060717_170105.htm (accessed September 2, 2006).

167. Ibid.

168. Miriam Formanek-Brunell, *Made to Play House: Dolls and Commercialization of American Girlhood, 1830-1930* (Baltimore, Maryland: Johns Hopkins University Press, 1993).

169. Ibid., 113-114.

170. Ibid., 114.

171. Ketupa.net, "Disney Group: History," http://www.ketupa.net/disney2.htm (accessed October 29, 2003). Hasbro, Inc., "History from 1923-2002," Hasbro.com, http://www.hasbro.com/pl/page.corporate_history_hasbro/dn/default.cfm (accessed October 23, 2003). Fisher-Price, "Human Resources - About Us," http://www.fisher-price.com/us/hr/aboutus.asp (accessed October 29, 2003). Mattel, Inc., "About Us - History," Mattel.com, http://www.mattel.com/about_us/history/default.asp?f=true (accessed October 29, 2003).

172. The History Channel, "The History of Toys and Games - The Parker Brothers," HistoryChannel.com, http://www.historychannel.com/exhibits/toys/inventors.html (accessed November 2, 2003). Toys "R" Us, Inc., "Our History," http://www.3toysrus.com/about/ourHistory.cfm (accessed October 13, 2004). "Largest Toy Retailer," Guinness World Records, http://www.guinnessworldrecords.com/content_pages/record.asp?recordid=49578 (accessed June 28, 2005).

173. Disney ended up selling the Angels in 2003 for $180 million. Ketupa.net, "Disney Group:

History," http://www.ketupa.net/disney2.htm (accessed October 29, 2003).

174. McNally, Joel, "Wild-Eye Right Drags Down Iconic American Girl Dolls,"*Capital Times* (Madison, WI), November 12, 2005, http://www.commondreams.org/views05/1112-26.htm (accessed August 7, 2006).

175. Mattel, Inc., "About Us - History," Mattel.com, http://www.mattel.com/about_us/history/ default.asp?f=true (accessed October 29, 2003).

Chapter Three

1. Jean Liedloff, *The Continuum Concept: In Search of Lost Happiness* (Reading, MA: Perseus Books, 1977).

2. The Liedloff Continuum Network, "About the Book," http://www.continuum-concept.org/ jean.html (accessed September 3, 2003). The Liedloff Continuum Network, "Join the Network," http://www.continuum-concept.org/membership.html (accessed August 15, 2003).

3. Jean Liedloff, *The Continuum Concept: In Search of Lost Happiness* (Reading, MA: Perseus Books, 1977) 80.

4. Ibid., 80.

5. Ibid., 83.

6. Ibid., 90.

7. Ibid., 102.

8. Ibid., 94.

9. Ibid., 104.

10. Ibid., xiv.

11. Ibid., xiv.

12. Ibid., xiv.

13. Ibid., 143.

14. Unfortunately, some of Liedloff's followers appear to have focused on superficial aspects of her story. They think that carrying their babies around everywhere or sleeping with them at night will turn them into happy, well-adjusted adults. Although the Yequana indeed carried their babies a lot and slept with them at night, I doubt that such practices were essential to

the Yequana magic, and they might even foster dependency rather than independence; there's no clear evidence either way, as far as I know. I suspect that some of Liedloff's fans have adopted such practices because doing so fits the modern child-centered approach to parenting; in that sense, some of her followers may have missed the boat to Venezuela.

15. Margaret Mead, *Coming of Age in Samoa* (New York: William Morrow, 1973).

16. Ibid., 226.

17. Ibid., 227.

18. Ibid., 227.

19. Ibid., 197.

20. Derek Freeman, *Margaret Mead and Samoa: The Making and Unmaking of an Anthropological Myth* (Cambridge, MA: Harvard University Press, 1983).

21. Paul Shankman, "The History of Samoan Sexual Conduct and the Mead-Freeman Controversy," *American Anthropologist* 98, no.3 (1996): 555-567.

22. Alice Schlegel and Herbert Barry III, *Adolescence: An Anthropological Inquiry* (New York: Free Press, 1991), 202-203.

23. Pierre Dasen, "Rapid Social Change and the Turmoil of Adolescence: A Cross-Cultural Perspective," *International Journal of Group Tensions* 29, no. 12 (2000): 17-49.

24. L. Joseph Stone and Joseph Church, *Childhood and Adolescence* (New York: Random House, 1957) 7-8.

25. Beatrice B. Whiting and John W. M. Whiting, eds., *Adolescents in a Changing World* (New Brunswick: Rutgers University Press, 1988).

26. Pierre Dasen, "Rapid Social Change and the Turmoil of Adolescence: A Cross-Cultural Perspective," *International Journal of Group Tensions* 29, no. 12 (2000): 17-49.

27. Ibid.

28. Ibid.

29. Ibid.

30. Craig Kielburger, with Kevin Major, *Free the Children* (New York, HarperCollins, 2000).

31. Pierre Dasen, "Rapid Social Change and the Turmoil of Adolescence: A Cross-Cultural

Perspective," *International Journal of Group Tensions* 29, no. 12 (2000): 17-49.

32. Ibid.

33. Ibid.

34. Ibid.

35. Ibid.

36. Alice Schlegel and Herbert Barry III, *Adolescence: An Anthropological Inquiry* (New York: Free Press, 1991), 202-203.

37. Pierre Dasen, "Rapid Social Change and the Turmoil of Adolescence: A Cross-Cultural Perspective," *International Journal of Group Tensions* 29, no. 12 (2000): 17-49.

38. B. Bradford Brown, Reed W. Larson, and T.S. Saraswathi, eds., *The World's Youth: Adolescence in Eight Regions of the Globe* (Cambridge, UK: Cambridge University Press, 2002).

39. Ibid, 5. According to Yasushi Ito (personal communication, November 17, 2004), a professional translator in Japan, there is no equivalent term for "adolescence" in Japanese. The closest terms are *shishunki* (literally "spring of thought"), which refers to the early teens and is closest in meaning to the English term "puberty," and *seishun* (literally "blue spring"), which is equivalent to the English term "youth." Neither term, Ito stresses, implies a time of turmoil.

40. Harold W. Stevenson and Akane Zusho, "Adolescence in China and Japan: Adapting to a Changing Environment," in *The World's Youth: Adolescence in Eight Regions of the Globe*, eds. B. Bradford Brown, Reed W. Larson, and T.S. Saraswathi (Cambridge, UK: Cambridge University Press, 2002) 143.

41. Ibid., 146

42. Ibid., 160.

43. Ibid.

44. Marilyn Booth, "Arab Adolescents Facing the Future: Enduring Ideals and Pressures to Change," in *The World's Youth: Adolescence in Eight Regions of the Globe*, eds. B. Bradford Brown, Reed W. Larson, and T.S. Saraswathi (Cambridge, UK: Cambridge University Press, 2002) 208, 210-211.

45. Ibid., 211. L. Abu-Lughod, *Writing Women's Worlds: Bedouin Stories* (Los Angeles: University of California Press, 1993) 211.

46. S.S. Davis and D. Davis, *Adolescence in a Moroccan Town: Making Social Sense* (New Brunswick and London: Rutgers University Press, 1989) cited by Marilyn Booth, "Arab Adolescents Facing the Future: Enduring Ideals and Pressures to Change," in *The World's Youth: Adolescence in Eight Regions of the Globe*, eds. B. Bradford Brown, Reed W. Larson, and T.S. Saraswathi (Cambridge, UK: Cambridge University Press, 2002) 212.

47. Marilyn Booth, "Arab Adolescents Facing the Future: Enduring Ideals and Pressures to Change," in *The World's Youth: Adolescence in Eight Regions of the Globe*, eds. B. Bradford Brown, Reed W. Larson, and T.S. Saraswathi (Cambridge, UK: Cambridge University Press, 2002) 233.

48. Anna Stetsenko, "Adolescents in Russia: Surviving the Turmoil and Creating a Brighter Future," in *The World's Youth: Adolescence in Eight Regions of the Globe*, eds. B. Bradford Brown, Reed W. Larson, and T.S. Saraswathi, 243-271 (Cambridge, UK: Cambridge University Press, 2002).

49. Childstats.gov, "Family Structure and Adolescent Well-Being (2005) - Figure Special 4.C," http://www.childstats.gov/americaschildren/2005spe4c-f.asp (accessed August 16, 2006).

50. Anna Stetsenko, "Adolescents in Russia: Surviving the Turmoil and Creating a Brighter Future," in *The World's Youth: Adolescence in Eight Regions of the Globe*, eds. B. Bradford Brown, Reed W. Larson, and T.S. Saraswathi, 243-271 (Cambridge, UK: Cambridge University Press, 2002).

51. Ibid.

52. Carlos Welti, "Adolescents in Latin America: Facing the Future with Skepticism," in *The World's Youth: Adolescence in Eight Regions of the Globe*, eds. B. Bradford Brown, Reed W. Larson, and T.S. Saraswathi, 276-303 (Cambridge, UK: Cambridge University Press, 2002).

53. T.S. Saraswathi, "Adult-Child Continuity in India: Is Adolescence a Myth or an Emerging Reality?," in *International Perspectives on Human Development*, eds. A.L. Aomunian and U. Gielen (Lengerich, Germany: Pabst Science Publishers, 2000) 431.

54. Ibid., 432.

55. Christian Initiative for India, "The Hindu World View," http://www.cifi.de/e_weltbild.html (accessed September 8, 2003). Suman Verma and T.S. Saraswathi, "Adolescence in India: Street Urchins or Silicon Valley Millionaires?," in *The World's Youth: Adolescence in Eight Regions of the Globe*, eds. B. Bradford Brown, Reed W. Larson, and T.S. Saraswathi, (Cambridge, UK: Cambridge University Press, 2002) 432.

56. A. Bame Nsamenang, "Adolescence in Sub-Saharan Africa: An Image Constructed from Africa's Triple Inheritance," in *The World's Youth: Adolescence in Eight Regions of the Globe*, eds. B. Bradford Brown, Reed W. Larson, and T.S. Saraswathi, 61-97 (Cambridge, UK: Cam-

bridge University Press, 2002).

57. Madelene Santa Maria, "Youth in Southeast Asia: Living Within the Continuity of Tradition and the Turbulence of Change," in *The World's Youth: Adolescence in Eight Regions of the Globe*, eds. B. Bradford Brown, Reed W. Larson, and T.S. Saraswathi (Cambridge, UK: Cambridge University Press, 2002) 171-203

58. Ibid.

59. A study of "adolescents' self-image" in ten countries by Dr. Daniel Offer of the University of Chicago and his colleagues is relevant here. At least when it comes to "self-image"—a relatively soft psychological concept—Offer and his associates believe that there exists a "universal adolescent" who's in pretty good shape. But nine of the ten countries in the study are highly industrialized: the United States, Australia, Germany, Italy, Israel, Hungary, Turkey, Japan, and Taiwan (according to UNICEF, Turkey is an industrialized nation), and the tenth country in the study—Bangladesh—doesn't fit the "universal" pattern. The percentage of young people in Bangladesh who are depressed, for example—in the 40-to-50 percent range—is about twice as large as the average percentage for the other nine countries. Offer and colleagues also focused on a very narrow construct ("self-image") and did not look for corroboration in behavioral variables (drug abuse, out-of-wedlock pregnancies, suicide rates, etc.) or even in ratings of teens by other people (parents, teachers, or therapists, for example). The study is based exclusively on teens' scores on the "Offer Self-Image Questionnaire"; as one might expect, the self reports of teens don't always correspond to other data. When one looks at a wide range of behavioral and other data, it's difficult to find a "universal adolescent"; different cultures produce very different kinds of teens. See: Daniel Offer, Eric Ostrov, Kenneth I. Howard, and Robert Atkinson, *The Teenage World, Adolescents' Self-Image in Ten Countries* (New York: Plenum Medical Book Company, 1988).

60. afrol News, "Internal Opposition to Batswana 'Bushmen' Relocation," October 18, 2002, http://www.afrol.com/News2002/bot008_san_opposition.htm (accessed August 15, 2006).

61. Mihaly Csikszentmihalyi and Barbara Schneider, *Becoming Adult: How Teenagers Prepare for the World of Work* (New York: Basic Books, 2000).

62. Ibid., 14-15.

Chapter Four

1. William R. George and Lynman Beecher Stowe, *Citizens Made and Remade: An Interpretation of the Significance and Influence of George Junior Republics* (Boston: Houghton Mifflin, 1912) 72–82.

2. William B. George, *The Junior Republic: Its History and Ideals* (New York: D. Appleton and Company, 1910).

3. William R. George and Lynman Beecher Stowe, *Citizens Made and Remade: An Interpretation of*

the Significance and Influence of George Junior Republics (Boston: Houghton Mifflin, 1912) 82.

4. Ibid., 10.

5. Ibid., 28.

6. Winthrop D. Lane, "Review of Citizens Made and Remade, by William R. George and L. B. Stowe," Political Science Quarterly 28, no. 3 1913: 538–540.

7. "Freeville Republic Will Not Bar Girls," New York Times, December 24, 1913.

8. William R. George and Lynman Beecher Stowe, Citizens Made and Remade: An Interpretation of the Significance and Influence of George Junior Republics (Boston: Houghton Mifflin, 1912) 71.

9. "State Investigates George Republic," New York Times, December 2, 1913.

10. Boys Republic, "Testimonials, Boys Republic," http://www.boysrepublic.org/testimonials.html (accessed July 15, 2003).

11. George Junior Republic, "The George Junior Republic," http://www.georgejuniorrepublic.com (accessed July 23, 2003).

12. United States National Agricultural Library, "The George Junior Republic," http://www.nal.usda.gov/pavnet/yf/yfgeorge.htm (accessed July 15, 2003).

13. "Teens Killed Counselor, Took Truck," San Diego Union-Tribune, November 11, 2003.

14. Guardian Angels, "Our Founder and President," http://www.guardianangels.org/about/bios/curtis2.html (accessed July 14, 2003).

15. Guardian Angels, "Role Models for Real Life," http://www.guardianangels.org (accessed July 15, 2003).

16. Nebraska Department of Economic Development, "Edward Joseph Flanagan 1886-1948," Omaha, Nebraska, Research and Statistics, http://info.neded.org/stathand/parttwo/flanagan.htm (accessed August 26, 2003). Girls and Boys Town, "About Us: History," http://www.girlsandboystown.org/aboutus/history/index.asp (accessed August 3, 2003).

17. Ibid.

18. Fulton Oursler and Will Oursler, Father Flanagan of Boys Town (Garden City, NY: Doubleday, 1949) 43.

19. Ibid., 197.

20. Sanderson Beck, "Boys Town," Movie Mirrors Index, http://www.san.beck.org/MM/1938/ BoysTown.html (accessed September 2, 2003).

21. Girls and Boys Town, "About Us: History," http://www.girlsandboystown.org/aboutus/ history/index.asp (accessed August 3, 2003). Michael L. Handwerk, "Father Flanagans Girls and Boys Home," Nebraska Internship Consortium in Professional Psychology, http:// www.unl.edu/schpsych/consortium/Reserve/father2002.htm (accessed September 1, 2003).

22. Based on an exchange I had with Dr. Ronald Thompson, director of the Girls and Boys Town National Research Institute, on September 16, 2004, as well as a review of studies that sought to evaluate the effectiveness at "treatment" at the modern manifestation of Boys Town, there's good news and bad news. The good news is that, although the modern Boys Town has almost nothing in common with Father Flanagan's vision, it's still probably better than most group homes today. Their current residential programs are built around full-time married "teaching couples," each of which lives in a house with between six and eight young people of the same sex, and every effort is made to create a supportive family-like environment. But there's bad news, too. First, the responsibility focus is entirely gone; residents have virtually no control over their own lives and are closely supervised. Second, the family environment is, first and foremost, a delivery system for behavior modification techniques— the primary means of control—and is supplemented as needed by "psychotropic medications, 12-step sobriety groups, and sessions with a clinical psychologist" (Larzelere et al., 2004, p. 135). Third, the outcome studies, examined closely, suggest that modern Boys Town residents make, at best, only modest gains as a result of their stay. One recent study—Larzelere et al. (2004)—reports an attrition rate of over 33 percent and a follow-up period of only three months. Incredibly, about 10 percent of those discharged were arrested within the three-month follow-up period. The most ambitious study released so far—Thompson et al. (2005)— looks at the status of hundreds of former residents who were discharged, on average, 16 years prior to the study. Although at first glance the results look impressive, the 252 individuals examined in this study were part of a pool of 503 individuals examined in an earlier study (Thompson et al., 1996). If we make the modest assumption that the 251 individuals who could not be located or who refused to participate in the follow-up study performed, on average, just 25 percent more poorly than the 252 people who did participate, the program starts to look like it does more harm than good—or at least that it has no effect. People who can be located and are happy to cooperate have undoubtedly had much better lives than those who refuse to answer questions or have disappeared; some of the latter are presumably deceased—victims of homicide, suicide, or drug abuse. See: "Quality Long-Term Residential Care Does Make a Difference," Girls and Boys Town Brochure No. 0405-0126, 2004. Girls and Boys Town National Research Institute for Child and Family Studies, "Applied Research: A Bibliography of Girls and Boys Town Studies," 2006, http:// www.girlsandboystown.org/media/pros/research/2006FullVersion.pdf (accessed August 12, 2006). R. W. Thompson, J. C. Huefner, J. L. Ringle, and D. L. Daly, "Adult Outcomes of Girls and Boys Town Youth: A Follow-Up Report," in *Proceedings of the 17th Annual Florida Mental Health Institute Conference: A System of Care for Children's Mental Health: Expanding the Research Base*, eds. C. Newman, C. Liberton, K. Kutash, and R. Friedman 529–534 (Tampa: University of South Florida, 2005). R. E. Larzelere, D. L. Daly, J. L. Davis, M. B. Chmelka,

and M. L. Handwerk, "Outcome Evaluation of Girls and Boys Town's Family Home Program," *Education and Treatment of Children* 27, no. 2 (May 2004): 130–149. R. W. Thompson, G. L. Smith, D. W. Osgood, T. P. Dowd, P. C. Firman, and D. L. Daly, "Residential Care: A Study of Short-Term and Long-Term Educational Effects," *Children and Youth Services Review* 18, no. 3 (1996): 221–242. Larzelere, R. E., K. Dinges, M. D. Schmidt, D. F. Spellman, T. R. Criste, and P. Connell, "Outcomes of Residential Treatment: A Study of the Adolescent Clients of Girls and Boys Town," *Child and Youth Care Forum* 30, no. 3 (June 2001): 175-185. D. L. Daly, M. D. Schmidt, D. F. Spellman, T. R. Criste, K. Dinges, and J. F. Teare, "The Boys Town Residential Treatment Center: Treatment Implementation and Preliminary Outcomes," *Child and Youth Care Forum*, 27, no. 4 (August 1998): 267–279.

23. Boys Town of Italy, Inc., "The Legacy of the Shoeshine Boys Hotel," http://www.boystown.it/documents/legacy.html (accessed August 7, 2003).

24. B.F. Skinner, "Contrived Reinforcement," *Behavior Analyst* 5 (1982): 3–8.

25. Renate Wilson, *Inside Outward Bound* (Charlotte, NC: East Woods Press, 1981) 7–14.

26. Ibid., 17.

27. Ibid., 19–32.

28. Ibid., 24.

29. Ibid., 24.

30. Ibid., 25.

31. Ibid., 25.

32. Ibid., 26

33. Ibid., 31. Outward Bound, "Outward Bound is Born," http://www.outwardbound.com/history.html (accessed September 29, 2003).

34. Outward Bound, "A Special Program for Troubled Teens," http://www.outwardbound.com/type/troubled_teens_ascent.html (accessed September 29, 2003).

35. Renate Wilson, *Inside Outward Bound* (Charlotte, NC: The East Woods Press, 1981) 83.

36. Francis J. Kelly and Daniel J. Baer, "Jesness Inventory and Self-Concept Measures For Delinquents Before and After Participation In Outward Bound," *Psychological Reports* 25, no. 3 (1969): 719–724.

37. Ibid.

38. J. D. McPeake, B. Kennedy, J. Grossman, and L. Beaulieu, "Innovative Adolescent Chemical Dependency Treatment and Its Outcome: A Model Based on Outward Bound Programming." *Journal of Adolescent Chemical Dependency* 21 (1991): 29–57.

39. Reagh Clinton Wetmore, "The Influence of Outward Bound School Experience on the Self-Concept of Adolescent Boys," *Dissertation Abstracts International* 33. no. 4-A (1972): 1498–1499.

40. Alan Nelson Wright, "Therapeutic Potential of the Outward Bound Process: An Evaluation of a Treatment Program for Juvenile Delinquents," *Dissertation Abstracts Invernational* 43, no. 03 (1982): 923-A.

41. Leslie Mark Burton, "A Critical Analysis and Review of the Research on Outward Bound and Related Programs," Abstract Psy.D. diss., Rutgers University, 1981.

42. Scott Warren Husted, "The Role of Challenge as a Motivating Force in Academic Engagement for At-Risk Youth: Outward Bound Revisited," Abstract Ph.D. diss., University of Nebraska–Lincoln, 1998.

43. Georgia and Oklahoma opened the first adult camps in 1983, and Louisiana opened the first exclusively juvenile camp in 1985. Bryan Robinson, "Are Boot Camps Too Extreme? Arizona Boys Death Revives Argument Over Boot Camp Effectiveness," ABC News, July 12, 2001, http://abcnews.go.com/sections/us/DailyNews/bootcamps010712.html (accessed November 8, 2003). Doris Layton MacKenzie and Claire Souryal, "Multisite Study of Correctional Boot Camps," The Koch Crime Institute, http://www.kci.org/publication/bootcamp/docs/nij/Correctional_Boot_Camps/chapt18.htm (accessed November 18, 2003).

44. Deborah Sharp, "Correctional Options, Part 3," *Corrections Today* 57, no. 3 (1995): 81.

45. "In Georgia, a Prison Boot Camp Sets Kids Straight," *Life* 11, no 8 (1998): 82–86.

46. Ibid.

47. Ibid.

48. Dennis Wagner, "Boys Ranch Murder Charges Manslaughter Case Dropped for 1st Degree Complaint," *Arizona Republic*, March 28, 1999. Christina Jacqueline Johns, "Hours in the Sun: Boot Camp Abuse Revisited," Law, Power, and Justice Syndicate, July 14, 2000, http://www.lawpowerandjustice.com/columns/hoursinthesun.html (accessed November 8, 2003).

49. Bryan Robinson, "Are Boot Camps Too Extreme? Arizona Boys Death Revives Argument Over Boot Camp Effectiveness," ABC News, July 12, 2001, http://abcnews.go.com/sections/us/DailyNews/bootcamps010712.html (accessed November 8, 2003).

50. Doug Simpson, "Lousiana Shuts Down Notorious, Adult-Style Juvenile Prison," *San Diego*

Union-Tribune, May 28, 2004.

51. Deborah Sharp, "Correctional Options, Part 3," *Corrections Today* 57, no. 3 (1995): 83. See full Koch Crime Institute report at: http://www.hrf.uni-koeln.de/sitenew/content/e/files/juvbootcamps.pdf (accessed July 16, 2006).

52. Paul Gendreau and Mario A. Paparozzi, "Examining What Works in Community Corrections," *Corrections Today*, 57, no. 1 (1995): 28.

53. James Austin et al., *Multi-Site Evaluation of Boot Camp Programs, Final Report*, (Washington, D.C.: George Washington University, Institute on Crime, Justice and Corrections, 2000).

54. Deborah Sharp, "Correctional Options, Part 3," *Corrections Today* 57, no. 3 (1995): 81.

55. Ibid.

56. Ibid., 82.

57. The Thayer Learning Center, which opened in 1995 in northwest Missouri, is another progressive boot camp, one that's much closer to the Boys Town model. Thayer, which serves troubled teens from 12 to 17, stresses choice and accountability, the goal of which is to turn the students into responsible young adults.

58. Association of Military Colleges and Schools of the United States, www.amcsus.org (accessed July 14, 2006).

59. Lee Roy Tarrant Jr., "Leadership Development in Secondary Military Schools," *Dissertation Abstracts International* 43, no. 4 1982: 1108.

60. John Bernard Hoar III, "An Investigation of Cognitive Moral Development and Possible Correlates with a Population of Seniors in Five Selected Secondary Military Schools in the United States," Ph.D. diss., Boston College, *Dissertation Abstracts International* 42, no. 9 (1981): 3913.

61. United States General Accounting Office, National Security and International Affairs Division, letter to Richard C. Shelby, Chairman, Subcommittee on Force Requirements and Personnel Committee on Armed Services United States Senate.

62. Dr. Lewis Sorley, Executive Director of the Association of Military Colleges and Schools of the United States, generally concurs, noting that discipline makes sense only when its purpose is service and that military schools don't want to be regarded as reform schools. More important, he says that harsh disciplinary methods are not as effective and methods emphasizing leadership and personal responsibility. Personal communication, September 16, 2004. Also see: Wendy Coles, "How to Save a Troubled Kid," *TIME*, November 22, 2004, 74–76.

63. United States Military Academy, "Notable USMA Graduates," Official USMA Bicentennial Website, http://www.usma.edu/bicentennial/history/NotableGrads.asp (accessed February 23, 2005). United States Military Academy, History, United States Academy, http://www.west-point.org/parent/wppc-st_louis/IWest%20Point%20History.htm (accessed February 23, 2005).

64. Hans Sherrer, "Quiet Rage: The Stanford Prison Experiment," *Prison Legal News*, July 9, 2003, http://www.prisonexp.org/legnews.htm (accessed February 23, 2005).

Chapter Five

1. Stephen Jay Gould, "Abscheulich! (Atrocious!). (The Precursor to the Theory of Natural Selection)," *Natural History*, March 2000.

2. "Biography of Ernst Heinrich Haeckel." *Encyclopedia Britannica*, 11th ed.

3. David Brody, "Ernst Haeckel and the Microbial Baroque," *Cabinet Magazine*, Summer 2002, http://www.cabinetmagazine.org/issues/7/ernsthaeckel.php (accessed October 31, 2003). "Haeckel's Faudulent Charts," Pathlights, http://www.pathlights.com/ce_encyclopedia/17rec03.htm (accessed October 31, 2003).

4. Stephen Jay Gould, "Abscheulich! (Atrocious!). (The Precursor to the Theory of Natural Selection)," *Natural History*, March 2000.

5. Ibid.

6. G. Stanley Hall, *Adolescence its Psychology and its Relations to Physiology, Anthropology, Sociology, Sex, Crime, Religion and Education*, Vol. II (New York: D. Appleton and Company, 1905) xiii, x.

7. Ibid., 94.

8. Ibid., ix-x.

9. Ibid., 73.

10. G. Stanley Hall, *Adolescence its Psychology and its Relations to Physiology, Anthropology, Sociology, Sex, Crime, Religion and Education*, Vol. II (New York: D. Appleton and Company, 1905).

11. Ibid., 329-330.

12. Ibid., 335.

13. Ibid., 338.

14. Ibid., xvi.

15. In his "Autobiographical Study," Freud wrote about his Clark University experience as follows: "In Europe I felt as though I were despised; but over there I found myself received by the foremost men as an equal. As I stepped onto the platform at Worcester to deliver my Five Lectures upon Psychoanalysis it seemed like the realization of some incredible day-dream: psychoanalysis was no longer a product of delusion, it had become a valuable part of reality." See: Sigmund Freud,. *An Autobiographical Study, Inhibitions, Symptoms and Anxiety, Lay Analysis and Other Works*, vol. xx in *The Standard Edition of Complete Psychological Works of Sigmund Freud* (London: Hogarth Press and the Institute of Psycho-Analysis, 1925-1926) 52.

16. Freud also noted, among other things, that although the "incestuous objects" of childhood are freshly energized with "libido" soon after puberty, they remain "apart from consciousness." In other words, having already figured out long ago that you can't have sex with Mom, you don't revisit the issue again. See: Sigmund Freud, *Introductory Lectures on Psycho-Analysis*, James Strachey, ed. and trans. (New York: W.W. Norton and Company, 1966) 418.

17. Ibid.

18. Louis Breger, *Freud: Darkness in the Midst of Vision* (New York: John Wiley & Sons, 2000) 302.

19. "*Sturm und Drang*" is a phrase Anna Freud and others borrowed from a brief but influential cultural movement that took place in the late 1700s in Germany. Seen by scholars as a radical break from the rationalism of the period of Enlightenment, the essays, books, poetry, and plays of the *Sturm und Drang* movement focus on strong emotions, especially those of young men and women. The period is best exemplified by Johann Wolfgang Goethe's novel *The Sorrows of Young Werther (Die Leiden des jungen Werthers)*, in which a man in his 20s eventually commits suicide over the loss of a woman who belongs to another man. For further information, see: David Hill, ed., *Literature of the Sturm und Drang* (Camden House, 2002).

20. Aaron H. Esman, ed., *The Psychology of Adolescence* (New York: International Universities Press, 1975) 140.

21. Anna Freud, "Adolescence," in *The Writings of Anna Freud Volume V, 1957-1965* (New York: International Universities Press, 1969).

22. G. Stanley Hall, *Adolescence its Psychology and its Relations to Physiology, Anthropology, Sociology, Sex, Crime, Religion and Education*, Vol. II (New York: D. Appleton and Company, 1905) 384.

23. G. Stanley Hall, *Adolescence its Psychology and its Relations to Physiology, Anthropology, Sociology, Sex, Crime, Religion and Education*, Vol. I (New York: D. Appleton and Company, 1905) xvi-xvii.

24. Jeffrey Jensen Arnett, *Emerging Adulthood: The Winding Road from the Late Teens Through the*

Twenties. (Oxford: Oxford University Press, 2004) 8.

25. University of Pennsylvania sociologist Frank Furstenberg and his colleagues have focused on exactly the same phenomenon, dubbing the new developmental period "early adulthood." See: Furstenberg, F. F., Kennedy, S., Mcloyd, V. C., Rumbaut, R. G., and Settersten, R. A., Jr., "Growing Up Is Harder to Do," *Contexts* 3, no. 3 (Summer 2004): 33-41.

26. Jeffrey Jensen Arnett, "Adolescent Storm and Stress, Reconsidered," *American Psychologist* 54, (May 1999): 317-326. One of several problems with this article is Arnett's assertion that Hall's views on recapitulation were based on the work of Jean-Baptiste Lamarck, the French naturalist whose speculations about evolution in the early 1800s anticipated Darwin's in some respects. But Hall never mentioned Lamarck in his grand book on adolescence, and Lamarck never suggested that an evolutionary process could cause individuals to relive the evolutionary history of their species. Lamarck did suggest that physical characteristics acquired during an organism's lifetime could somehow be passed on to the next generation—a conjecture that proved to be wrong—but he did not suggest a recapitulation theory. Hall's ideas about recapitulation were borrowed from Haeckel, not Lamark. Arnett's take on ancient Greek philosophers is also questionable; for further information on this issue, see Appendix 4.

27. Jeffrey Jensen Arnett, "Adolescent Storm and Stress, Reconsidered," *American Psychologist* 54, no. 5 (May 1999): 319.

28. Ibid.

29. Ibid.

30. Ibid., 320.

31. Reed Larson and Maryse Richards, *Divergent Realities: The Emotional Lives of Mothers, Fathers, and Adolescents* (New York: Basic Books, 1994).

32. Jeffrey Jensen Arnett, "Adolescent Storm and Stress, Reconsidered," *American Psychologist* 54, no. 5 (May 1999): 321.

33. Ibid., 321.

34. Ibid., 322.

35. Associated Press, "Boy Gets 26 Years in Prison for Stabbing," *San Diego Union-Tribune,* July 11, 2006.

36. A. Egley, et al., 2002 *National Youth Gang Survey* (Tallahassee, FL: National Youth Gang Center, 2002). C.L. Maxson and M. L. Whitlock, "Joining the Gang: Gender Differences in Risk Factors for Gang Membership," in *Gangs in America III*, ed., C.R. Huff, 19-35 (Thou-

sand Oaks, CA: Sage Publications, 2002).

37. Crime and Violence Prevention Center, *Gangs: A Community Response* (California Attorney General's Office, 2003). F. Esbensen and E.P. Deschenes, "A Multi-Site Examination of Gang Membership: Does Gender Matter?" *Criminology* 36, no. 4 (1998): 779-827.

38. A. Egley et al., *2002 National Youth Gang Survey* (Tallahassee, FL: National Youth Gang Center, 2002).

39. Los Angeles County Interagency Gang Task Force, *Report on the State of Los Angeles Street Gangs*, (Los Angeles, CA:2002). Crime and Violence Prevention Center California Attorney General's Office, *Gangs: A Community Response* (Sacramento, CA: 2003).

40. Centers for Disease Control and Prevention, *CDC Surveillance Summaries*, MMWR 47, No. SS-3 (1998). Cox News Service, "Teen Survey Finds High-Risk Activities," *San Francisco Chronicle*, August 14, 1998.

41. Department of Education, *Report on State Implementation of the Gun-Free Schools Act-School Year: 1996-1997* (1998).

42. Dave Nettell, "School/Youth Violence: The Columbine Incident," http://www.cooperativeadventures.com/littleton.htm (accessed March 3, 2005).

43. Ceci Connolly and John F. Harris, "Motive in School Massacre Unclear," *Washington Post*, March 23, 2005. Monica Davey and Jodi Wilgoren, New York Times News Service, "'Clues All There' of Killing to Come," *San Diego Union-Tribune*, March 24, 2005. "School Killing Rampage," *San Diego Union-Tribune*, March 22, 2005. Dana Hedgpeth and Dan Eggen, Knight Ridder News Service and Associated Press, "Blame Spreads Wider in Shooting Deaths of 10 on Reservation," *Washington Post*, April 2, 2005. Cris Maag, "The Devil in Red Lake," *TIME*, April 4, 2005.

44. See Chapter One, Note 1.

45. National Council on Problem Gambling, Inc., "Adolescent Gambling and Problem Gambling Fact Sheet," http://www.ncpgambling.org (accessed October 18, 2004; site now discontinued). Reuters, "Teen Gambling Addictions Are on the Increase," *San Diego Union-Tribune*, August 16, 1998.

46. S.P. Kachur, G.M. Stennies, K.E. Powell, W. Modzeleski, R. Stephens, R. Murphy, M. Kresnow, D. Sleet, and R. Lowry, "School Associated Violent Deaths in the United States, 1992 to 1994," *Journal of the American Medical Association* 275, no.22 (1996):1729-1733.

47. Associated Press "Homeless Man Set on Fire; Teens Sought," *Arizona Daily Star*, May 29, 2004, http://www.azstarnet.com/sn/wildfire/24013.php (accessed March 3, 2005).

48. Federal Bureau of Investigation, "Persons Arrested, Table 38," Crime in the United States - 2002, http://www.fbi.gov/filelink.html?file=/ucr/cius_02/pdf/02crime4.pdf (accessed August 17, 2006).

49. Daniel Macallair and Michael Males, "Dispelling the Myth: An Analysis of Youth and Adult Crime Patterns in California over the Past 20 Years," Center on Juvenile and Criminal Justice, 2000, http://www.cjcj.org/pubs/myth/myth.html (accessed September 3, 2006). California Department of Justice "Crime in California 2002," http://caag.state.ca.us/cjsc/publications/candd/cd02/preface.pdf (accessed August 4, 2005).

50. Nevada Kids Count, "Juvenile Violent Crime," http://kidscount.unlv.edu/2000/violent.pdf (accessed March 3, 2005). Office of Juvenile Justice and Delinquency Prevention "National Statistics on Juvenile Offenders and Victims," http://ojjdp.ncjrs.org/pubs/makingadiffer/critical_4.html (accessed August 4, 2005). Also see Appendix 3.

51. Federal Bureau of Investigation, *Uniform Crime Reports for the United States* (Washington D.C.: U.S. Government Printing Office, 1999). Uniform Crime Reporting Program Federal Bureau of Investigation, "Age-Specific Arrest Rates for Selected Offenses; 1993-2001," http://www.fbi.gov/ucr/adducr/age_race_specific.pdf (accesssed July 28, 2005).

52. Kevin Johnson, "Police Tie Jump in Crime to Juveniles: Gangs, Guns Add up to Increased Violence," *U.S.A. Today*, July 13, 2006, 1A; Kevin Johnson, "Cities Grapple with Crime by Kids: Offenders as Young as 10 Showing Up; Special Units Targeting Juveniles," *USA Today*, July 13, 2006, 3A.

53. U.S. Department of Justice, Office of Justice Programs, *Women in Criminal Justice: A 20 Year Update*, 1998. http://www.ojp.usdoj.gov/reports/98Guides/wcjs98/welcome.html (accessed September 3, 2006). Federal Bureau of Investigation, U.S. Department of Justice, "Crime in the United States 2004," Table 33, Ten-Year Arrest Trends, 1995-2004, http://www.fbi.gov/ucr/cius_04/persons_arrested/table_32-33.html (accessed September 2, 2006)

54. Ron Scherer, "Execution for Juvenile Crime: Legal But Controversial," *Christian Science Moniter*, February 19, 2002, http://www.csmonitor.com/2002/0219/p02s02-usju.html (accessed March 3, 2005). Death Penalty Information Center, "U.S. Supreme Court: Roper v. Simmons," http://www.deathpenaltyinfo.org/article.php?scid=38&did=885 (access August 29, 2006). Charles Lane, "5-4 Supreme Court Abolishes Juvenile Executions," *Washington Post*, March 2, 2005, http://www.washingtonpost.com/wp-dyn/articles/A62584-2005Mar1.html (accessed August 4, 2006). Case citation: *Roper v. Simmons*, 543 US 551 (2005).

55. Mediascope Press, "Youth Violence in America," Mediascope, http://www.mediascope.org/pubcs/ibreifs/yva.htm (accessed Dec. 10, 2003).

56. "Survey: 29 Percent of High School Boys Have a Gun," CNN.com, http://www.cnn.com/US/9810/14/boys.guns/ (accessed July 27,2005).

57. "Numbers," *TIME*, February 22, 1999. "Perspectives on Firearms," California Attorney General's Youth Council on Violence Prevention, 1998. MediaScope "Youth Violence in America," http://www.mediascope.org/pubs/ibriefs/yva.htm (accessed March 8, 2005).

58. Office of Juvenile Justice and Delinquency Prevention, "Easy Access to Juvenile Court Statistics 1985-2000," http://ojjdp.ncjrs.org/ojstatbb/ezajcs (accessed July 6, 2005).

59. "Rock Throwing Youth Faces More Charges," *St. Petersburg Times*, February 16, 2001, http://www.sptimes.com/News/021601/TampaBay/Tampa_Bay_briefs_.shtml (accessed March 8. 2005). Joe Hughes and Karen Kucher "Passenger Killed in Rock Attack on S.D. Road," http://www.signonsandiego.com/uniontrib/20050528/news_1n28rocks.html (accessed August 4, 2005).

60. "Ephebiphobia"—the fear of teenagers—derives from the Greek *ephebos* (Ýöçâïò, youth in late teens) and *fobos* (öüâïò, fear). See: National Youth Rights Association, "Youth Rights Glossary," http://www.youthrights.net/index.php?title=Youth_Rights_Glossary (accessed August 29, 2006).

61. "Carrie Fisher 'Strikes Back' at Mental Illness," *USA Today*, http://www.usatoday.com/news/health/spotlight/2002/05/29-fisher.htm (acessed June 30, 2005).

62. National Association of Convenience Stores, "That's the Spirit—U.S. Alcohol Sales Growing," http://www.nacsonline.com/NACS/News/Daily_News_Archives/March2003/nd0306037.htm (accessed July 6, 2005). IMS Health, "U.S. Purchase Activity by Channel, 2003," http://www.imshealth.com/ims/portal/front/articleC/0,2777,6599_42720942_44800060,00.html (accessed July 6, 2005).

63. Estimates for the yearly business worth of the illegal drug industry vary. The ONDCP's estimate for the year 2000 is $64 billion while DEA Special Agent John McKenna (personal communication, August 7, 2006) estimates range to be from 4 to 48 billion dollars. See: Office of National Drug Control Policy, "What America's Users Spend on Illegal Drugs - Table 1," http://www.whitehousedrugpolicy.gov/publications/pdf/american_users_spend_2002.pdf (accessed August 8, 2006). United Nations Office on Drugs and Crime, "Economic and Social Consequences of Drug Abuse and Illicit Trafficking," http://www.unodc.org/pdf/technical_series_1998-01-01_1.pdf (accessed September 3, 2006). According to a recent study by researcher Jon Gettman (using U.S. government data), marijuana is now the top cash crop in the United States, outselling corn and wheat combined, with domestic marijuana production having increased by a factor of ten over the last twenty-five years. It's a $1 billion industry in the state of Washington alone, according to Gettman. See: Emily Heffter, "Marijuana Biggest U.S. Cash Crop, Researcher Says," *San Diego Union-Tribune*, December 24, 2006. Jon Gettman, "Marijuana Production in the United States (2006)," http://www.drugscience.org/bcr (accessed December 27, 2006).

64. Associated Press, "Psychiatric Drug Use by Youths Surges, Study Says," *Los Angeles Times*, January 14, 2003. C. P. Thomas and her colleagues at Brandeis University estimate the

increase in prescription mood-altering drugs to teens to be 250 percent between 1994 and 2001. See: J. Harper, "Prescriptions of Mind-Altering Drugs for Teens Rise," *Washington Times*, January 4, 2006. C.P. Thomas, P. Conrad, R. Casler, and E. Goodman, "Trends in the Use of Psychotropic Medications Among Adolescents, 1994 to 2001," *Psychiatric Services* 57, no. 1 (2006): 63-69.

65. Linda A. Johnson, Associated Press, "More Spent on Behavior Drugs than other Kids' Medicines," *San Diego Union-Tribune*, May 17, 2004.

66. Greater Dallas Council on Alcohol and Drug Abuse, "Youth Trade Drugs at 'Pharming' Parties," July 26, 2005, http://www.gdcada.org/stories/pharming.htm (accessed July 24, 2006).

67. White House Office of National Drug Control Policy, "Juveniles and Drugs," http://www.whitehousedrugpolicy.gov/drugfact/juveniles/index.html (accessed November 24, 2004). Also see Note 8, Chapter One.

68. Michele Steinberg, "Ritalin: The New Violence: America's Kids Are Victims of Menticide," *Executive Intelligence Review*, March 24, 2000. Alliance for Human Research Protection, "Petition FDA to Investigate If SSRI Induced School Shootings," March 25, 2005, http://www.ahrp.org/infomail/05/03/25.php (accessed July 19, 2006).

69. The Backpacker, "Republicans: Pot is Dangerous," www.thebackpacker.com/trailtalk/thread/14123,-1,1.php (accessed March 8, 2005). American Council for Drug Education, "Talking with Your Children About Marijuana," http://www.acde.org/parent/insidtps/mjtalk.htm (accessed August 4, 2005). L.D. Johnston et al, "Overall Teen Drug Use Continues Gradual Decline; But Use of Inhalants Rises," http://www.monitoringthefuture.org/data/04data.html#2004data-drugs (accessed August 4, 2005).

70. National Highway Traffic Safety Administration, "Traffic Safety Facts, 2004, Data: Young Drivers," http://www-nrd.nhtsa.dot.gov/pdf/nrd-30/ncsa/TSF2004/809918.pdf (accessed August 7, 2006). Kids Count Alcohol, Drug, and Cigarette Use, 2004 Rhode Island Kids Count Factbook, http://www.rikidscount.org/matriarch/d.asp?PageID=296&PageName2=2004Factbook&p=&PageName=Health%5Fdrug%5Fuse%2Epdf (accessed August 7, 2006). National Institute on Alcohol Abuse and Alcoholism, "Surveillance Report #69: Trends in Alcohol Related Fatal Traffic Crashes, United States, 1977-2002," http://www.niaaa.nih.gov/publications/surveillance69/fars02.htm (accessed March 8, 2005). Centers for Disease Control and Prevention, "2001 US National Responses, Alcohol Use," 2001 CDC Youth Risk Behavior Surveillance Survey, http://www.ncbuy.com/education/yrbs01/nat_116.html (accessed August 7, 2006).

71. American Medical Association, "Stats: American," Canadian Centre for Adolescent Research, http://ccar.briercrest.ca/stats/american.shtml (accessed August 17, 2006).

72. National Institute on Drug Abuse, "NIDA InfoFacts: Steroids (Anabolic-Androgenic)," http://www.drugabuse.gov/Infofacts/Steroids.html (accessed August 17, 2006).

73. For example, Dr. Rick Doblin, founder of the Multidisciplinary Association for Psychedelic Studies, cites data suggesting that Ecstasy might be helpful in the treatment of some psychological disorders. See http://www.maps.org/.

74. Sumana Chatterjee, "Survey: Drug Use Up Among Youth," *San Diego Union-Tribune*, September 6, 2002. Mark Bennett, "Ecstasy: A Deadly Gamble for Today's Youth," http://www.pta.org/archive_article_details_1117661260093.html (accessed August 8, 2005).

75. Opiods.com, "Oxycontin: The Politics, Science, and Sensationalization of an Abusable Pharmaceutical," http://opioids.com/oxycodone/oxycontin.htm#THE%20SCIENCE%20OF%20OPIOIDS (accessed July 6, 2005).

76. Donna Leinwand, "Use of 'Date Rape' Drug Surges," *USA Today*, January 28, 2002.

77. American Lung Association, April 2006, http://www.lungusa.org/site/asp?c=dvLUK9O0E&b=39871 (accessed July 24, 2006).

78. Substance Abuse and Mental Health Services Administration, Overview of Findings from the 2002 National Survey on Drug Use and Health, 2003. See http://www.lungusa.org/site/asp?c=dvLUK9O0E&b=39871 (accessed July 24, 2006).

79. Center for Disease Control and Prevention, "Boyz II Men—Teens and Tobacco Facts Not Fiction," http://www.cdc.gov/tobacco/tips_4_youth/boyz2men/teensandtobacco.htm (accessed July 6, 2005). American Lung Association, April 2006, http://www.lungusa.org/site/asp?c=dvLUK9O0E&b=39871 (accessed July 16, 2006). Missouri Association of Local Public Health Agencies,"Partnership for Smoking or Health - Background on Women and Girls and Tobacco," MoALPHA, http://www.moalpha.org/docs/news/tob_partnership/women_background.html (accessed August 4, 2006).

80. Guttmacher Institute, "U.S. Teenage Pregnancy Statistics With Comparative Statistics For Women Aged 20-24," February 19, 2004, http://www.familyplanningperspectives.org/pubs/teen_stats.html (accessed August 4, 2006).

81. "Teen Pregnancy, Birth and Abortion," Sexuality Information and Education Council of the United States, http://www.siecus.org/about/abou0000.html (accessed August 4, 2005).

82. Associated Press, "Nevada Led U.S. in '01 in Teens with Multiple Kids, Report Says," *San Diego Union-Tribune*, November 29, 2003.

83. Centers for Disease Control and Prevention (CDC), "National and State-Specific Pregnancy Rates Among Adolescents-United States, 1995-1997," *Morbidity and Morality Weekly Report* 49, no. 27 (2000): 605.

84. Centers for Disease Control and Prevention, "HIV and AIDS - United States, 1981-2001," *Morbidity and Minority Weekly Report* 50 (2001): 430-434. Centers for Disease Control and Prevention, "HIV Prevention Strategic Plan Through 2005," January 2001.

85. Henry J. Kaiser Family Foundation, "Substance Use and Sexual Health among Teens and Young Adults in the U.S. 2002," http://www.outproud.org/pdf/CASAFactSheet.pdf (accessed July 16, 2006).

86. Ruth Kershner, "Adolescents' Beliefs about Rape: A Preliminary Study," The Prevention Researcher, http://www.tpronline.org/read.cfm?ID=16 (accessed September 23, 2003; site now discontinued).

87. Patrick O'Carroll et al., Centers for Disease Control, "Programs for the Prevention of Suicide Among Adolescents and Young Adults," *Morbidity and Morality Weekly Report* 43, no. 6 (1994): 1-7. The drop in the rate of suicide of teens during the late 1990s seems both short-lived and anomalous. Unfortunately, it also seems strongly related to the dramatic increase the use of mood-altering prescription medications by teens over this same period, estimated by C. P. Thomas and her colleagues at Brandeis University to be 250 percent between 1994 and 2001. See: J. Harper, "Prescriptions of Mind-Altering Drugs for Teens Rise," *Washington Times*, January 4, 2006. A 2007 report published in *Pediatrics* shows a 12 percent increase in suicide among teen ages fifteen to nineteen (to 8.2 per 100,000) between 2003 and 2004. See: B. E. Hamilton et al., "Annual Summary of Vital Statistics: 2005," *Pediatrics* 119 (2007): 345-360. Looking at youth suicide data in the U.S. over a hundred-year period, David Cutler and his colleagues at Harvard conclude: "In recent decades... the monotonic relationship between age and suicide has disappeared.... Between 1950 and 1990, youth suicide rates tripled (particularly among young men), while suicide rates for adults fell by 7 percent and suicide rates for the elderly fell by 30 percent." See: David M. Cutler, Edward L. Glaeser, and Karen E. Norberg, "Explaining the Rise in Youth Suicide," Discussion Paper Number 1917, Harvard Institute of Economic Research, March 2001, http://post.economics.harvard.edu/hier/2001papers/HIER1917.pdf.

88. American Association of Suicidology, "Youth Suicide Fact Sheet," http://www.suicidology.org/associations/1045/files/Youth2003.pdf (accessed September 2, 2006).

89. Justice Institute of British Columbia, "Research Report Shows Frequency of 'Suicide by Cop,'" http://www.jibc.bc.ca/police/main/PIIMIC/2_Suicide/research.htm (accessed July 13, 2005).

90. Deanne Tilton, *Child Death Review Team Report for 2001* (El Monte, CA: Los Angeles County Inter-Agency Council on Child Abuse and Neglect, 2001), http://ican.co.la.ca.us/PDF/death_201.pdf (accessed September 3, 2005). Also see: http://ican.co.la.ca.us/PDF/Data_2005.pdf (accessed September 3, 2006).

91. L. Kann, S.A. Kinchen, B. I. Williams, J. G. Ross, R. Lowry R, C. V. Hill, J. A. Grunbaum, P.S. Blumson, J. L. Collins, and L. J. Kolbe, Surveillance and Evaluation Research Branch,

Division of Adolescent and School Health, *Youth Risk Behavior Surveillance, 1997* (Atlanta, GA: Centers for Disease Control and Prevention, 1998).

92. Rosemarie Kobau et. al, "Sad, Blue or Depressed Days, Health Behaviors and Health-Related Quality of Life, Behavioral Risk Factor Surveillance System, 1995-2000," *Health and Quality of Life Outcomes* 2, no. 40 (2004).

93. Children Now, *California: State of Our Children 2000: How Young People are Faring Today* (Oakland, CA, 2000).

94. J.C. Mcmillen and J. Tucker, "The Status of Older Adolescents at Exit from Out-of-home Care," *Child Welfare* 78, no. 3 (1999): 339-60.

95. U.S. Public Health Service, *The Surgeon General's Call to Action to Prevent Suicide* (Washington D.C.: U.S. Government Printing Office, 1999). Children's Defense Fund, "Meeting Children's Unique Mental Health Needs," http://www.childrensdefense.org/health_ mentalhealth.html (accessed January 2000).

96. Shankar Vedantam, "Study: Thousands Give Up Children to Get Care," *The Washington Post*, April 22, 2003.

97. Anorexia Nervosa and Related Eating Disorders, Inc. "Statistics: How Many People Have Eating Disorders?" http://www.anred.com/stats.html (accessed November 28, 2004).

98. Jib Fowles, *The Case for Television Violence* (Thousand Oaks, CA: Sage Publications, 1999).

99. W. M. Reynolds, *Adolescence Psychopathology Scale: Psychometric and technical manual* (Odessa, FL: Psychological Assessment Resources, 1998).

100. To find out what's really causing what, you would need to conduct experimental research—the kind in which you randomly assign people to treatment and control groups. Unfortunately, when you're looking at a topic as sensitive as infantilization (or child abuse, parenting styles, suicide, anorexia, depression, or hundreds of other interesting topics), you can't conduct true experimental research because such research puts people at risk and thus violates modern ethical standards. In the case of infantilization, you would need to direct the parents in a number of families (chosen at random) to infantilize their young teens for several years and direct the parents in other families (also chosen at random) to raise their young teens with lots of responsibility and respect. If you could find cooperative families of this sort (unlikely), at the end of several years you could compare the teens in the first group to the teens in the second. If the infantilized teens ended up significantly worse off than the teens in the second, you could conclude with some degree of confidence that infantilization causes psychopathology. Understandably, however, people don't want you to play with their lives this way. It's not acceptable to put young people at risk just because you've come up with an interesting research question.

101. According to a review of research on puberty by F. D. Alsaker, "Results from studies includ-

ing hormonal assays are disappointing. They have shown that levels of hormones known to increase during pubertal maturation are only inconsistently associated with behavior and moods" (Alsaker, 1996, p. 20). See: R. D. Alsaker, "The Impact of Puberty," *Journal of Child Psychology and Psychiatry*, 7, no. 3 (1996): 249-258. Also see: C. M Buchanan, J. S. Eccles, and J. B. Becker. "Are Adolescents the Victims of Raging Hormones: Evidence for Activational Effects of Hormones on Moods and Behavior at Adolescence," *Psychological Bulletin* 111 (1992): 62-107.

Chapter Six

1. The first and third stories (regarding, respectively, the lion and the train) were "confirmed" by the Darwin organization, which can be visited at www.darwinawards.com. The second story (about the fireworks), although unconfirmed by Darwin, was reported in the UK's *Daily Mail*, October 6, 1995. See http://homepages.solis.co.uk/~jimella/hole.htm.

2. U.S. Department of Justice Federal Bureau of Investigation, "Crime in the United States 2000," http://www.fbi.gov/pressrel/pressre101/cius2000.htm (accessed September 1, 2003; site now discontinued). Abuse Counseling and Treatment, Inc., "Sexual Assault Statistics," http://www.actabuse.com/SAstatistics.html (accessed May 23, 2005). Centers for Disease Control, "Cigarette Smoking: Attributable Mortality and Years of Potential Life Lost - United States, 1990," *Morbidity and Mortality Weekly Report* 42 (1993): 645-649. American Obesity Association, "Obesity in the U.S.," http://www.obesity.org/subs/fastfacts/obesity_US.shtml (accessed May 23, 2005). California Department of Alcohol and Drug Programs, "Driving Under-the-Influence (DUI) Statistics," http://www.adp.cahwnet.gov/FactSheets/Driving_Under-the-Influence_Statistics.pdf (accessed May 23, 2005). Chad Hills, "The National Gambling Impact Study Commission (NGISC) Report," Focus on the Family, http://www.family.org/cforum/fosi/gambling/gitus/a0028977.cfm (accessed May 23, 2005). Alan I. Leshner, "From the Director," National Institute on Drug Abuse, http://165.112.78.61/ResearchReports/Prescription/Prescription.html (accessed September 1, 2003). U.S. Department of Health and Human Services, *National Vital Statistics Reports* 47, no. 21 (1999). Robert Epstein, "Of Ants and Men: The Lust for War," *Psychology Today*, http://www.findarticles.com/p/articles/mi_m1175/is_3_36/ai_n6015196 (accessed May 23, 2005).

3. Tristam De Roma, "Kevin Colleran: An Internet Tycoon at Age 17" *North Haven Post*, July 17, 1998.

4. Robert Epstein, *Cognition, Creativity, and Behavior: Selected Essays* (Westport, CT: Praeger, 1996).

Chapter Seven

1. W. Huitt and J. Hummel, "Piaget's Theory of Cognitive Development," Educational Psychology Interactive, Valdosta State University, http://chiron.valdosta.edu/whuitt/col/cogsys/piaget.html (accessed May 16, 2005).

2. Barbara Inhelder and Jean Piaget, "The Growth of Logical Thinking from Childhood to Adolescence," in *The Essential Piaget*, eds. H. Gruber and J. Vonèche, 405-444 (New York: Basic Books, 1977).

3. Ibid., 436.

4. Ibid., 444.

5. Jean Piaget, "Intellectual Evolution from Adolescence to Adulthood," *Human Development* 15 (1972): 8.

6. Jan Dynda Sinnott, "Everyday Thinking and Piagetian Operativity in Adults," *Human Development* 18 (1975): 430-443.

7. C. Tomlinson-Keasey, "Formal Operations in Females from Eleven to Fifty-Four Years of Age," *Developmental Psychology* 6, no. 2 (1972): 364.

8. N.A. Podgoretskaya, "A Study of Spontaneous Logical Thinking in Adults," *Soviet Psychology* 17, no. 3 (1979): 70-84.

9. Robert Epstein. "Growing Older, or What Else I Learned in Graduate School," *Harvard Magazine* 83, (July/August 1981): 5-6.

10. Lawrence Kohlberg, *The Psychology of Moral Development: The Nature and Validity of Moral Stages* (San Francisco: Harper & Row, 1984) 172.

11. Ibid., 173.

12. Mordecai Nisan and Lawrence Kohlberg, "Universality and Variation in Moral Judgment: A Longitudinal and Cross-Sectional Study in Turkey," *Child Development* 53 no. 4 (1982): 856-876.

13. Ibid.

14. Lawrence Kohlberg, *The Psychology of Moral Development: The Nature and Validity of Moral Stages* (San Francisco, CA: Harper & Row, 1984) 171.

15. For example, in a meta-analysis of fifteen studies of troubled young people, J. Ron Nelson and his colleagues concluded that "the moral reasoning of juvenile delinquents is immature." See: J. Ron Nelson, D. J. Smith, and J. Dodd, "The Moral Reasoning of Juvenile Delinquents: A Meta-Analysis." *Journal of Abnormal Child Psychology* 18, no 3 (1990): 231-239.

16. Robert Coles, *The Moral Life of Children* (Boston: Atlantic Monthly Press, 2000).

17. Carol Gilligan, "Adolescent Development Reconsidered," Proceedings of the 1987 Konopka

Lectureship, The Konopka Institute, Division of General Pediatrics and Adolescent Health, University of Minnesota, Minneapolis, MN, http://www.allaboutkids.umn.edu/cfahad/lectures/Lecture%201987.pdf (accessed August 12, 2006). D. Kay Johnston, "Adolescents' Solutions to Dilemmas in Fables: Two Moral Orientations—Two Problem Solving Strategies," in *Mapping the Moral Domain: A Contribution of Women's Thinking to Psychological Theory and Education*, eds. Carol Gilligan, J. V. Ward, J. M. Taylor, and B. Bardige, 49-71(Cambridge, MA: Harvard University Press, 1988). Also see: L. Kohlberg and C. Gilligan, "The Adolescent as a Philosopher," *Daedalus* 100, (1971): 1051-1086,.

18. David Wechsler, *The Measurement of Adult Intelligence*, 3rd. ed. (Baltimore, MD: Williams & Wilkins Co., 1944).

19. Ibid., 118.

20. J.C. Raven, "The Comparative Assessment of Intellectual Ability," *British Journal of Psychology* 39 (1948): 12-19.

21. Some modern theorists, such as Robert Sternberg at Yale and Howard Gardner at Harvard's School of Education, reject the classical concept of intelligence in favor of a broader one involving "multiple" intelligences, which include such things as musical ability, social skills, and so on. Sternberg and Gardner are, in my view, simultaneously leaders in and victims of the political correctness movement. Their work in no way invalidates the classical view of intelligence; like so many people these days, they appear to be uncomfortable with any perspective that identifies differences among ethnic and racial groups. When you define intelligence broadly enough and force it to include a wide variety of trainable skills (which should in fact be studied as trainable skills, not as forms of "intelligence"), you blur those differences—but the differences are still there. A hundred years of research, a great deal of it impeccable, demonstrates the robustness of the classical concept of intelligence: People differ, to some extent because of their genes, in their ability to reason, and racial and ethnic groups also differ on average in those abilities, just as they differ on average in various physical respects. Prolonged genetic isolation not only produces differences in physical characteristics; it also produces differences in behavioral, cognitive, and emotional characteristics. No one should be either surprised or offended by this simple fact.

22. Donald G. McNeil, Jr., "Research on Ecstasy Is Clouded by Errors," *New York Times*, December 2, 2003.

23. R. J. Herrnstein, *IQ in the Meritocracy* (Boston: Little Brown, 1973).

24. J.C. Raven, "The Comparative Assessment of Intellectual Ability," *British Journal of Psychology* 39 (1948): 16-17.

25. Robert J. Weber, Larry Hochhaus, and William D. Brown, "Equivalence of Perceptual and Imaginal Representation: Developmental Changes," in *Attention and Performance IX*, eds. J. Long and A. Baddeley, 296-309 (Hillsdale, NJ: Lawrence Erlbaum Associates, 1981).

26. Chuck Squatriglia, Knight Ridder Newspapers, "Girl Finds 66 Percent of Parking Meters Favor the City," *Seattle Times*, June 15, 1998.

27. Associated Press, "Chess Icon Ashes U.s., Heads to Iceland," *San Diego Union-Tribune*, March 25, 2005. Associated Press, "Chess Champ Freed, Heads for Iceland", *San Diego Union-Tribune*, March 24, 2005. Associated Press, "Court Rejects Fischer's Bid to Stop Deportation Order", *San Diego Union-Tribune*, August 21, 2004. Norimitsu Onishi, "Japan Orders Deportation of Chess Master", *San Diego Union-Tribune*, August 25, 2004. Bruce Weber and Todd Zaun, "Chess Champ Fischer Arrested", *San Diego Union-Tribune*, July 17, 2004. Associated Press, "Fischer Plans to Wed Japanese Woman, Renounce Citizenship." *San Diego Union-Tribune*, August 17, 2004. Rene Chun, "Bobby Fischer's Pathetic Endgame," *The Atlantic*, December 2002.

28. Bell, E. T. *Men of Mathematics*. New York: Touchstone, 1937.

29. Chessbase News. "Record-Breaking Mini-Grandmaster?" May 16, 2002, http://www.chessbase.com/newsdetail.asp?newsid'310 (accessed July 24, 2006)

30. Raymond R. Willoughby, "Incidental Learning," *Journal of Educational Psychology* 20 (1929): 671-82.

31. James Birren, "Intelligence and Problem Solving," in *The Handbook of Aging and Individual* 731-733 (Oxford, England: University of Chicago Press, 1959).

32. Linda S. Siegel, "Working Memory and Reading: A Life-span Perspective," *International Journal of Behavioral Development* 17, no. 1 (1994): 109-124.

33. R. J. Herrnstein, *IQ in the Meritocracy* (Boston: Little Brown, 1973).

34. W. Mischel, Y. Shoda, and M. Rodriguez, "Delay of Gratification in Children," *Science* 224 (1989): 933-38. W. Mischel and R. Mtazner, "Preference for Delayed Rewards as a Function of Age, Intelligence and Length of Delay Interval," *Journal of Abnormal and Social Psychology* 64, no. 6 (1962): 425-431. L. Green, A.F. Fry, and J. Myerson, "Discounting of Delayed Rewards: A Life-Span Comparison," *Psychological Science* 5, no. 1 (1994): 33-36.

35. The rational-choice approach to studying judgment and decision making is not without its flaws. When you're choosing between $10 today and $15 tomorrow, the rationality of your decision is determined largely by circumstances. If you desperately need money for food or gas, or if you only have 24 hours to live, or if you have an investment opportunity that ends at midnight, it would be crazy for you to turn down the immediate cash. In other words, outside the laboratory (and even inside the laboratory, with properly designed experiments), "circumstance is man's master," as Mark Twain said long ago. As I noted in the text, under appropriate circumstances, virtually any behavior might be considered rational or reasonable. The rational-choice approach can rapidly be retrofitted to fit any situation by inventing a new set of choices that each situation seems to create, but the best theories, I believe, are

those that are capable of surprising you—and that can also give you cause to discard them. What's more, the sad truth is that human beings—even wise adults—make non-optimal choices as a matter of course, especially in "important" situations. We're products of evolution, not of computer programming, and we're more likely to follow the rules of the hunting ground than the rules of logic. If you want to predict what decisions someone will make, you need principles that take into account that person's genetic makeup, his or her environmental history, and relevant aspects of the current situation. And if you want to help people make better decisions, you need to understand what's happening in their lives, and then you need to apply tools that will influence them effectively—tools that may need to appeal to emotion rather than reason. The rules of rational choice aren't particularly helpful in these respects; our behavior is just too beastly. As the English philosopher David Hume said, "Reason is, and ought to be, the slave of the passions."

36. D. Offer, M. Kaiz, K. J. Howard, and E. S. Bennett. "The Altering of Reported Experiences," *Journal of the American Academy of Child and Adolescent Psychiatry* 39, no. 6 (2000): 735-742.

37. Lois A. Weithorn and Susan B. Campbell, "The Competency of Children and Adolescents to Make Informed Treatment Decisions," *Child Development* 53 (1982): 1589-98.

38. Ibid., 1589.

39. Ibid., 1595.

40. Gary B. Melton, "Toward 'Personhood' for Adolescents: Autonomy and Privacy as Values in Public Policy," *American Psychologist* (January 1983): 100.

41. Ruth Beyth-Marom, Laurel Austin, Baruch Fischhoff, Clair Palmgren, and Marilyn Jacobs-Quadrel, "Perceived Consequences of Risky Behaviors: Adults and Adolescents," *Developmental Psychology* 29, no. 3 (1993): 549-563.

42. Allan F. Abrahamse, Peter A. Morrison, Linda J. Waite, "Teenagers Willing to Consider Single Parenthood: Who is at Greatest Risk?" *Family Planning Perspectives* 20, no. 1 (1988): 13-18.

43. Lita Furby and Ruth Beyth-Marom, "Risk Taking in Adolescence: A Decision-Making Perspective," *Developmental Review* 12 (1992): 36.

44. James P. Byrnes, "The Development of Decision-Making," *Journal of Adolescent Health* 31, no. 6 (2002): 208-215.

45. Elizabeth Cauffman and Laurence Steinberg, "(Im)maturity of Judgment in Adolescence: Why Adolescents May Be Less Culpable Than Adults," *Behavioral Sciences Law* 18 (2000): 741-760.

46. Ibid., 757. Steinberg and colleague Elizabeth Scott make similar arguments in a 2003 essay, again suggesting that "juveniles should not be held to the same standards of criminal responsibility as adults" due to "diminished" decision-making abilities (p. 1009). Once again, though, they acknowledge the importance of individual differences and the possibility that some young people might be more mature than many adults. Since "diagnostic tools" for measuring maturity don't exist (in their view), they express concern about the difficulty of "litigating maturity on a case-by-case basis" (p. 1016). In fact, though, all criminal proceedings involve, from start to finish, evaluating *all* aspects of the crime and *all* characteristics of the defendant as utterly unique. See: Laurence Steinberg and Elizabeth S. Scott, "Less Guilty by Reason of Adolescence: Developmental Immaturity, Diminished Responsibility, and the Juvenile Death Penalty," *American Psychologist* 58, no. 12 (2003): 1009-1018.

47. Quoted by S. Landers, "Survey Verifies Teen Risk Taking," *APA Monitor* 19, no. 11 (1988): 30.

48. Nancy E. Adler, Emily J. Ozer, and Jeanne Tschann, "Abortion Among Adolescents," *American Psychologist*, 58 (March 2003): 211-217.

49. Erin Marcus, "After Daughter's Death, Parents Campaign Against Abortion Consent Laws," *Washington Post*, August 8, 1990.

50. Catherine Lewis, "Minors' Competence to Consent to Abortion," *American Psychologist* 42, no. 1 (1987): 84-88.

51. Bruce Ambuel and Julian Rappaport, "Developmental Trends in Adolescents' Psychological and Legal Competence to Consent to Abortion," *Law and Human Behavior* 16, no. 2 (1992): 130.

52. Nancy E. Adler, Emily J. Ozer, and Jeanne Tschann, "Abortion Among Adolescents," *American Psychologist*, March 2003, 211-217.

53. *Bellotti v. Baird*, 443 U.S. 622 (1979).

54. Ibid.

55. Jennifer Soper, "Straddling the Line: Adolescent Pregnancy and Questions of Capacity," *Law and Psychology Review* 23 (1999): 195-216.

56. Ibid., 2.

57. Ibid., 5.

58. *Hodgson v. Minnesota*, 497 US 417 (1990). *Akron v. Akron Center for Reproductive Health, Inc.*, 462 U.S. 416 (1983).

59. Jennifer Soper, "Straddling the Line: Adolescent Pregnancy and Questions of Capacity," *Law and Psychology Review* 23 (1995): 6.

60. Ibid., 7.

61. Ibid., 8.

62. Jamie Talan, "Biological Reason for Teen Laziness," *Newsday*, February 2004, http://www.newsday.com/news/health/ny-hsadol263686454feb26,0,5723383.story?coll'ny-health-headlines (accessed May 19, 2005; site now discontinued).

63. Ibid.

64. James M. Bjork et. al., "Incentive-Elicited Brain Activation in Adolescents: Similarities and Differences from Young Adults," *The Journal of Neuroscience* 24, no. 8 (2004): 1793-1802.

65. I have other concerns about the Bjork et al. study, among them: 1) Brain differences in the two groups could easily be attributed to age alone, not to laziness; younger brains could simply be more efficient on the type of task given. 2) Motivational differences in the two groups—if there actually were any—could easily be attributed to the fact that subjects under 18 don't own or have full control over the money they earn in the study; their parents or guardians do. Consider the fact that the under-18 subjects couldn't even sign the "informed consent" forms they needed to participate in the study. They had to get signatures from a parent or guardian, just like 3rd-graders going on a field trip at school. 3) The duration of stimulus presentations in the study were adjusted so that individuals would succeed about 66% of the time. Depending on how such adjustments differed in the two groups, they could have contributed to the group differences found in brain activity. 4) On behavioral measures (such as reaction time), there were no differences between the groups. If the teens were somehow inferior to the adults, one might have expected poorer behavior on their part. 5) Age differences were found only in the right nucleus accumbens, not in any other areas of the brain that were monitored. 6) Age differences were found only when $5 was at stake on a trial, not when smaller monetary amounts were at stake. In fact, the main result of the study was: "these data indicate qualitative similarities overall in the brain regions recruited by incentive processing in health adolescents and adults." Somehow, this result failed to make the news.

66. Elliot S. Valenstein, *Blaming the Brain: The Truth About Drugs and Mental Health* (New York: The Free Press, 1998) 126.
67. Ibid., 126-27.

68. Ibid., 127-28.

69. Stephanie McKinnon McDade, "Brain Study Finds Out Why Emotions Rule," *San Diego Union-Tribune*, August 8, 1998.

70. Matt Crenson, "Gray Matter, Not Raging Hormones, Rules Adolescence Brain Still Developing Well Into Teen Years, Neuroscientists Discover," *Worcester Sunday Telegram*, January 7, 2001.

71. Shannon Brownlee, "Inside the Teen Brain," *U.S. News & World Report*, August 9, 1999, 45-54. Also see the cover of the May 10, 2004 issue of *TIME* magazine, which reads, "Secrets of the Teen Brain: Research Is Revolutionizing Our View of the Adolescent Mind—and Explaining Its Mystifying Ways." Also see the cover of the August/September issue of *Scientific American Mind*, which reads, "The Teen Brain: Science Reveals the Ongoing Changes Underlying Behavior."

72. Jésus Pujol et al., "When does Human Brain Development End? Evidence of Corpus Callosum Growth up to Adulthood," *Annals of Nuerology* 34, no. 1 (1993): 71-75.

73. E.R. Sowell, D.A. Trauner, A. Gamst, and T.L. Jernigan, "Development of Cortical and Subcortical Brain Structures in Childhood and Adolescence: A Structural MRI Study," *Developmental Medicine and Child Neurology* 44 (2002): 4-16.

74. E.R. Sowell, B.S. Peterson, P.M. Thompson, S.E. Welcome, A.L. Henkenius, and A.W. Toga, "Mapping Continued Brain Growth and Gray Matter Density Reduction in Dorsal Frontal Cortex: Inverse Relationships During Post-Adolescent Brain Maturation," *The Journal of Neuroscience* 21, no. 22 (2001): 8819-29.

75. Eric Courchesne, Heather J. Chisum, Jeanne Townsend, Angilene Cowles, James Covington, Brian Egaas, Mark Harwood, Stuart Hinds, and Gary A. Press, "Normal Brain Development and Aging: Quantitative Analysis at in Vivo MR Imaging in Healthy Volunteers," *Radiology* 216 (2000): 672-682. Previous studies of brain size had relied on autopsy measurements, now considered to be highly unreliable because of the way tissue shrinks or expands after death. Moreover, corpses made available for autopsy often have pathological characteristics. Courchesne's measurements were made with live, normal subjects using modern scanning technology, which provides a much more accurate assessment of changes in brain size over time.

76. Ibid., 673. Although brain volume isn't necessarily a good indicator of processing power when looking across species or even genders, it is an excellent indicator when looking at individual development. See: E. D. Bigler, S. C. Johnson, C. Jackson, and D. D. Blatter, "Aging, Brain Size, and IQ," *Intelligence* 20 (1995): 109-119.

Chapter Eight

1. Carolyn Thompson, "80-Year Union Never Took Holiday," *San Diego Union-Tribune*, February 14, 1998.

2. Hollywood Byline, "Sir Ian McKellan," http://www.hollywoodbyline.homestead.com/PlayerIanMckellen~ns4.html (accessed July 16, 2003).

3. Ann P. McCauley and Cynthia Salter, *Population Reports: Meeting the Needs of Young Adults* XXIII, no. 3 (Baltimore, MD: Johns Hopkins School of Public Health, 1995).

4. Wyndol Furman, B. Bradford Brown, and Candice Feiring, eds., *The Development of Romantic Relationships in Adolescence* (Cambridge, UK: Cambridge University Press, 1999).

5. B. Bradford Brown, Candice Feiring, and Wyndol Furman, "Missing the Love Boat: Why Researchers Have Shied Away from Adolescent Romance," in *The Development of Romantic Relationships in Adolescence*, eds. Wyndol Furman et al. (Cambridge, UK: Cambridge University Press, 1999) 8.

6. Ibid., 9.

7. Ibid., 11.

8. A 1999 study by Connolly et al. confirms that "even young adolescents...have an awareness of the core features of romantic relationships" and that their conceptions of love and friendships are consistent with those of adults. See: J. Connolly, W. Craig, A. Goldberg, and D. Pepler, "Conceptions of Cross-Sex Friendships and Romantic Relationships in Early Adolescence," *Journal of Youth and Adolescence*, 28, no. 4 (1999): 481-494. Also see: National Center for Health Statistics, "Teenagers in the United States: Sexual Activity, Contraceptive Use, and Childbearing, 2002," http://www.cdc.gov/nchs/pressroom/04news/teens.htm (accessed August 15, 2006).

9. The White House, "Biography of Elizabeth Monroe," http://www.whitehouse.gov/history/firstladies/em5.html (accessed August 6, 2003).

10. The White House, "Biography of Rachel Jackson," http://www.whitehouse.gov/history/firstladies/rj7.html (accessed August 6, 2003).

11. The White House, "Biography of Eliza Johnson," http://www.whitehouse.gov/history/firstladies/ej17.html (accessed August 6, 2003).

12. The White House, "Biography of Rosalynn Carter," http://www.whitehouse.gov/history/firstladies/rc39.html (accessed August 6, 2003). The White House, "Biography of Barbara Bush," http://www.whitehouse.gov/history/firstladies/bb41.html (accessed August 6, 2003).

13. "Marriage and Divorce 2002," *Divorce Magazine*, http://www.divorcemag.com/statistics/statsUS.shtml (accessed May 16, 2005).

14. Heather Mudgett, "Eating Disorders Around the World," March 2, 2001, http://www.suite101.com/article.cfm/1456/61549 (accessed August 8, 2003).

15. UNICEF, *Early Marriage, Child Spouses* (Florence, Italy: Innocenti Research Centre, 2001).

16. K. Santhaa Reddy, "Child Marriages - Need for Better Understanding of Customs," http://

anilchawla.homestead.com/childmarr˜ns4.html (accessed June 11, 2003; site now discontinued).

17. Aarti Dhar, "Villagers Defend Child Marriages," *The Hindu*, April 29, 2002.

18. K. Santhaa Reddy, "Child Marriages - Need for Better Understanding of Customs," http://anilchawla.homestead.com/childmarr˜ns4.html (accessed June 11, 2003; site now discontinued).

19. Eleanor H. Ayer, *Everything You Need to Know About Teen Marriage*, Rosen Publishing Group, 1991.

20. U.S. Department of Health and Human Services, "Marriages and Divorces, 1900-2001," http://www.infoplease.com/ipa/A0005044.html (accessed August 6, 2006).

21. Sally C. Clarke, "Advance Report of Final Divorce Statistics, 1989 and 1990," *Monthly Vital Statistics Report* 43, no. 9 (1995).

22. Holly Wolcott, "Former Coach Gets Year in Jail for Having Sex with Student, 14," *Los Angeles Times*, December 14, 2002.

23. Ibid.

24. Denise Noe, "All About Mary Kay Letourneau," Court TV's Crime Library, http://www.crimelibrary.com/criminal_mind/psychology/marykay_letourneau/5.html?sect'19 (accessed August 6, 2003). Mathew Stadler, "Statuatory Rape, A Love Story," *Spin Magazine*, July 26, 1998.

25. MaryKayLetourneau.com, "Vili Fualaau on the Oprah Winfrey Show February 8, 2005," http://www.marykayletourneau.com/vili.html (accessed July 7, 2003; site now discontinued).

26. Christopher Wills, "Court: Juvenile Offenders Must Register," Center on Juvenile and Criminal Justice, February 23, 2003, http://www.cjcj.org/press/juvenile_offenders.html (accessed August 8, 2006).

27. Nancy Bartley, "Fualaau Says Price for Damages He Suffered Should be $20 million," *The Seattle Times*, April 10, 2002.

28. Kathleen R. Merrill, "Psychiatrist Says Student-teacher Relationship was 'A Love Story' - Highline School District Witness Testifies Relationship Wasn't Sexual Abuse," *King County Journal*, May 8, 2002. If you think the Fualaau lawsuit had any merit, please consider: Fualaau acknowledged that he didn't realize he was a "victim" until six years after his affair began, and in 1998 he and Letourneau published a book detailing their romance. (It was only published in Europe, where the two were considered romantic heroes—victims of the prud-

ish and backward judicial system in America.) He and his mom were broke when they filed the lawsuit; money they had received from media sources over the years, including a $100,000 rights fee for a made-for-TV movie, was gone. What's more, in 1996 Fualaau's 768-page deposition told, in clear and consistent and intelligent terms, a very different story than the one he was telling in 2002. Also see: Nancy Bartley, "Faulaau Says Price For Damages He Suffered Should Be $20 Million." *Seattle Times*, April 10, 2002.

29. Rebecca Cook, "Teacher Who Had Sex With Student Is Out of Prison," *San Diego Union-Tribune*, August 5, 2004. Crime Library, "Mary Kay Letourneau: The Romance That Was A Crime—Happily Ever After?" http://www.crimelibrary.com/criminal_mind/psychology/marykay_letourneau/12.html (accessed July 28, 2006).

30. Judith Levine, *Harmful to Minors: The Perils of Protecting Children from Sex* (Minneapolis, MN: University of Minnesota Press, 2002) 68-74.

31. Ibid., 75-76.

32. Ibid., 76.

33. Ibid., 82.

34. Ibid., 73.

35. Ibid., 78.

36. Ibid., 82-83.

37. Interpol, "Legislation of Interpol Member States on Sexual Offences Against Children," http://www.interpol.int/Public/Children/SexualAbuse/NationalLaws/ (accessed July 28, 2006). "Worldwide Ages of Consent," http://www.avert.org/aofconsent.htm (accessed August 8, 2006).

38. Stacy Finz, "Sex with Minors Sends More Adults to Prison State Reviving Old Statutory Rape Laws," *The San Francisco Chronicle*, February 25, 1998.

39. Colette S. Peters, "Consensual Sex and Age of Sexual Consent," *Colorado Legislative Council Staff Issue Brief* 02-10 (2002).

40. Legal Information Institute, "Marriage Laws of the Fifty States, District of Columbia and Puerto Rico," Cornell University, http://www.law.cornell.edu/topics/Table_Marriage.htm (accessed July 28, 2003).

41. Jim Rendon, "Jail Baited," *Metro*, December 18-24, 1997.

Chapter Nine

1. Suicide bombing at Patt junction in Jerusalem. Israel Ministry of Foreign Affairs. June 18, 2002. http://www.israel.org/MFA. (accessed July 30, 2006)

2. Sudeshna Sarkar, "After Scaling Everest, it's School for Youngest Climber," *Indo-Asian News Service*, May 2003, http://in.news.yahoo.com/030529/43/24odl.html (accessed September 9, 2003).

3. Kerri Strug with John P. Lopez, *Landing on my Feet: A Diary of Dreams* (Kansas City: Andrews McMeel Publishing, 1997).

4. Ibid., 166-167.

5. Ibid., 169.

6. Family Education Network, Interview with Kelly Mathews, http://life.familyeducation.com/sports/role-models/36430.html?detoured=1 (accessed July 28, 2006).

7. U.S. Consumer Product Safety Commission, "CPSC Offers Football Safety Tips," http://www.cpsc.gov/CPSCPUB/PREREL/prhtml74/74070.html (accessed May 2, 2005).

8. According to the Medical University of South Carolina, "In 1999, nearly 194,000 children ages 5 to 14 were treated in hospital emergency rooms for basketball-related injuries." See http://www.musckids.com/health_library/adolescent/sis.htm.

9. ESPN.com, "James Ruled Ineligible, Plans to Appeal Decision," http://espn.go.com/nba/news/2003/0131/1502001.html (accessed May 2, 2005).

10. Colin Nowling, "What is an Amateur?" Indiana Daily Student, http://idsnews.com/print.php?id=15356 (accessed May 2, 2005).

11. Nick Tolbert, "From California Ghetto to Mainstream USA," The Zeen, http://www.the-zeen.com/Idocs/Features/skatehistory.html (accessed September 8, 2003). Sue Reilly, "People Magazine," Tony Alva, http://www.angelfire.com/ca/alva3/peoplemag.html (accessed May 2, 2005).

12. International Association of Skateboarding Companies, http://www.skateboardiasc.org/industry_stats.asp. (accessed July 28, 2006).

13. Deanna Wrenn, "Jessica Lynch Due Home After Media Hype on Heroism," *Reuters*, July 22, 2003.

14. Ann Scott Tyson, "The Expanding Role of GI Jane," *The Christian Science Monitor*, April 2, 2003.

15. Ibid.

16. Captain Barbara A. Wilson, USAF, "Women in Combat: Why Not?" http://userpages.aug.com/captbarb/combat.html (accessed September 9, 2003).

17. Barbara Raffel Price, "Female Police Officers in the United States," National Criminal Justice Reference Service http://www.ncjrs.org/policing/fem635.htm (accessed May 2, 2005).

18. UNICEF, "Child Protection Information Sheet: Children Associated with Armed Groups," http://www.unicef.org/publications/files/Child_Protection_Information_Sheets.pdf (accessed August 21, 2006). In exchanges with officials at UNICEF and Ilene Cohn, co-author of *Child Soldiers: The Role of Children in Armed Conflicts* (New York: Oxford University Press, 1994), I was told repeatedly that the figures of 250,000 or 300,000 that one often sees are educated guesses, at best. No one really knows how many people under 18 serve in the military worldwide, and many of those who do serve are in support roles, not combat roles.

19. P. W. Singer, author of *Children at War* (Sacramento, CA: University of California Press, 2006) and a fellow at The Brookings Institution, estimates that 25 to 40 percent of soldiers under 18 are under 13 (personal communication, August 25, 2006). Most soldiers under 18 are believed to be between 15 and 17. See: Coalition to Stop the Use of Child Soldiers, "Some Facts," http://www.child-soldiers.org/childsoldiers/some-facts (accessed August 21, 2006).

20. Police Federation of England and Wales, "Boating Lake Plunge for Plucky PC," *Police Magazine*, May 1999, http://www.polfed.org/magazine/05_1999/05_1999_brave.htm (accessed July 10, 2004)

21. John Morrison, "Lightweight Guns Helping Create Child Armies, Group Says." *San Diego Union-Tribune*. January 11, 1999.

22. Faiza Saleh Ambah, "Mecca Plotters Included Many Teens," *San Diego Union-Tribune*, June 23, 2003.

23. United Nations, "Child Soldiers," http://www.un.org/cyberschoolbus/briefing/soldiers/csprogress.htm (accessed May 5, 2005).

24. James McPherson, *Battle Cry of Freedom: The American Civil War.* (New York: Oxford University Press, 1988).

25. Fay R. Hansen, "Chronology of Conscription in the U.S. – Colonial Era to 1999" from *American History Teacher's Book of Lists*, Teachervision.com, http://www.teachervision.fen.com/u-s-civil-war/biography/5669.html (accessed August 16, 2006).

26. Personal communication, Tim Syzek, Librarian, National Archives, August 21, 2006.

27. Ilene Cohn and Guy S. Goodwin-Gill, *Child Soldiers: The Role of Children in Armed Conflicts* (New York: Oxford University Press, 1994) 31, 36.

28. Psychologist Joseph Adelson of the University of Michigan generally ties political thinking in young people to Piagetian cognitive stages. Their "capacity for ideology," he says, is "essentially completed" by age 15 or 16. See: Joseph Adelson, *Inventing Adolescence: The Political Psychology of Everyday Schooling* (New Brunswick, NJ: Transaction Books) 206.

29. Ibid., 33-34.

30. Ibid., 34, 32.

31. BBC World Service, "Children of Conflict: Child Soldiers," http://www.bbc.co.uk/worldservice/people/features/childrensrights/childrenofconflict/soldier.shtml (accessed September 12, 2003).

32. Danuta Bois, "Joan of Arc," Distinguished Women of the Past and Present, http://www.distinguishedwomen.com/biographies/joanarc.html (accessed August 28, 2006). Thomas E. Morrissey, "Joan of Arc," Discover France, http://www.discoverfrance.net/France/History/Joan_of_Arc.shtml (accessed August 29, 2006).

33. Anthony C. LoBaido, "12-Year-Old Twins Lead Jungle Army," World Net Daily, http://www.worldnetdaily.com/news/article.asp?ARTICLE_ID=19065 (accessed May 5, 2005). According to a recent report, the Karen are still fighting, but Johnny Htoo (now 18) and 8 of his followers recently surrendered to Myanmar authorities. See: Aye Aye Win, Associated Press, "One of Twin Rebel Leaders of 'God's Army' Surrenders," *San Diego Union-Tribune*, July 26, 2006.

34. Ilene Cohn and Guy S. Goodwin-Gill, *Child Soldiers: The Role of Children in Armed Conflicts* (New York: Oxford University Press, 1994) 35.

35. UNICEF, "Child Protection—Armed Conflict," http://www.helpsavekids.org/scope2.html (accessed May 5, 2005).

36. Marc Lacey, "Child Soldier's Book Tells of Brutalities; Ugandans Call it Lies," *San Diego Union-Tribune*, August 30, 2003.

37. Associated Press, "Boat Capsizes in Family Outing," *Pittsburgh Tribune-Review*, May 9, 2004, http://www.pittsburghlive.com/x/pittsburghtrib/s_193300.html (accessed August 16, 2006).

38. Marc Lacey, "Child Soldier's Book Tells of Brutalities; Ugandans Call it Lies," *San Diego Union-Tribune*, August 30, 2003

39. Jill Noelle Cecil, "Fate of Teen Killer Moves Closer to Jury: Defense Trying to Spare Gang Member from Death Penalty. Newspaper Contempt Claim is Rejected," *Daily News*, August 4, 1998, http://www.gangcolors.com/fateteen.htm (accessed September 13, 2003). A. Alonso,

"Los Angles Gangs—A Brief History (African-American Gangs)," StreetGangs.com, http://www.streetgangs.com/history/history.html (accessed September 13, 2003).

40. William Golding, *Lord of the Flies* (New York: Capricorn Books, 1954) 106.

41. Ibid., 186-187. *John Dollar*, a female variation on Golding's classic, was published recently by Marianne Wiggins, author wife of author Salman Rushdie. In this gripping story, eight young females are cast ashore on an island with a paralyzed adult sailor.

42. Radio Netherlands, October 16, 1998, http://www.rnw.nl.humanrights/html/storiesrwanda.html (accessed September 16, 2003).

43. Heather Kerr, "Rwandan Orphans Tune into War Child Radio Project," AlertNet, Reuter's Foundation, http://alertnet.org/thefacts/reliefresources/287179.htm (accessed September 16, 2003).

44. Yolanda Jones and Jacinthia Jones, "Alone with Dead Mom, Boy Lived on Pizza, Fear," *Commercial Appeal* (Memphis, TN), December 8, 1999.

45. Lisa Singhania, "Boy Lives Weeks in an Apartment with Dead Mom," *Detroit Free Press*, March 9, 2000, http://www.freep.com/news/mich/nmom9_20000309.htm (accessed July 29, 2003).

46. Action by Churches Together International, "Coming to America," http://act-intl.org/news/dt_nr_2001/dtsud-0301.html (accessed May 5, 2005).

47. R.G. Domey, R.A. McFarland, and E. Chadwick, "Dark Adaptation as a Function of Age and Time: II. A Derivation," *Journal of Gerontology* 15 (1960): 267-279. Richard L. Doty, Paul Shaman, Steven L. Applebaum, Ronita Gilberson, Lenore Siksorski, and Lysa Rosenberg, "Smell Identification Ability: Changes with Age," *Science* 226 (1984): 1441-1443. G. Verriest, "L'influence de l'age sur les fonctions visuelles de l'homme," *Bulletin de l'Academie Royale de Medecine Belgique* 11 (1971): 527-528. J. Jerger, "Audiological Findings in Aging," *Advances in Oto-Rhino-Laryngology* 20 (1973): 115-124. James E. Birren, ed., *Handbook of Aging and the Individual* (Chicago: University of Chicago Press, 1959) 175, 520. Neil Charness, ed., *Aging and Human Performance*, (Chichester: John Wiley & Sons, 1985). 48. R.T. Verillo, "Age-related Changes in Sensitivity to Vibration," *Journal of Gerontology* 35 (1980): 185-193.

49. H.J. Montoye and W.R. Pierson, "Movement Time, Reaction Time, and Age," *Journal of Gerontology* 13 (1958): 418-421.

50. K.B. Corbin and E.D. Gardner, *Anatomical Record* (1937).

51. A.B. Baker, Y.Q. Tang, and M.J. Turner, *Percentage Decline in Masters Superathlete Track and Field Performance with Aging* (Sydney Australia: Taylor & Francis Group, 2003).

52. Virginia A. Casey, Johanna T. Dwyer, K. Ann Coleman, and Isabella Valadian, "Body Mass

Index from Childhood to Middle Age: A 50-Year Follow-up," *American Journal of Clinical Nutrition* 56, no. 14 (1992): 14-18.

53. Anne Frank, *The Diary of a Young Girl* (Garden City, NY: Doubleday, 1952) 221-222.

54. Ibid., 222.

55. Ibid., 285.

56. Cynthia S. Jacelon, "The Trait and Process of Resilience," *Journal of Advanced Nursing* 25 (1997): 123-129.

57. William R. Beardslee and Donna Podorefsky, "Resilient Adolescents Whose Parents have Serious Affective and Other Psychiatric Disorders: Importance of Self-Understanding and Relationships," *American Journal of Psychiatry* 145, no. 1 (1988): 63-69.

58. Lily Hechtman, "Resilience and Vulnerability in Long Term Outcome of Attention Deficit Hyperactive Disorder," *Canadian Journal of Psychiatry* 36 (1991): 415-421.

59. D.J. Mulholland et al., "Academic Performance in Children of Divorce: Psychological Resilience and Vulnerability," *Psychiatry* 54 (1991): 268-280.

60. Michael Rutter, "Resilience in the Face of Adversity: Protective Factors and Resistance to Psychiatric Disorder," *British Journal of Psychiatry* 147 (1985): 598-611.

61. Anne Frank, *The Diary of a Young Girl* (Garden City, NY: Doubleday, 1952) 278-279.

Chapter Ten

1. The Kid's Hall of Fame, "15-Year-Old Nominees," http://thekidshalloffame.com/CustomPage8.html (accessed December 15, 2004).

2. Amy Goldman, "Ten-Year-Old Artist Alexandra Nechita Is Making Her Mark All Over the World," Girls' Life, July 2000, http://www.girlslife.com/alexn.html (accessed July 14, 2003).

3. Robert Epstein, *Cognition, Creativity, and Behavior: Selected Essays* (Westport, CT: Praeger, 1996). Robert Epstein, "Generativity Theory," in *Encyclopedia of Creativity*, eds. M. A. Runco and S. Pritzker, 759-766 (New York: Academic Press, 1999). Robert Epstein, *The Big Book of Creativity Games* (New York: McGraw-Hill, 2000).

4. According to Runco and Nemiro (1994), "Creative students are often unconventional, individualistic, nonconforming, and typically viewed as 'difficult,' but these seemingly difficult tendencies may be functionally tied to creative behavior" (p. 239). Although this relationship is common, some research suggests that extreme forms of nonconformity may interfere with creative expression. See: M. A. Runco and J. Nemiro, "Problem Finding, Creativity, and Giftedness," *Roeper Review* 16 (1994) 235-241. Derek Steinberg, ed., *The Adolescent Unit:*

Work and Teamwork in Adolescent Psychiatry (Chichester, England: John Wiley, 1986). J. W. Getzels and J. Smilansky, "Individual Differences in Pupil Perceptions of School Programs," *British Journal of Experimental Psychology* 53 (1983) 307-316.

5. Bob Chaundry, "The Growing Pains of Charlotte Church," BBC News, http://news.bbc.co.uk/1/hi/in_depth/uk/2000/newsmakers/2527727.stm (accessed July 26, 2006).

6. Kaoru Yamamoto, "Creativity and Sociometric Choice Among Adolescents," *The Journal of Social Psychology* 64 (1964): 249-261. Norma Trowbridge and Don C. Charles, "Creativity in Art Students," *The Journal of Genetic Psychology* 109 (1966): 281-289.

7. Kennon M. Sheldon, "Conformity," *Encyclopedia of Creativity*, vol. 1 (Philadelphia, PA: Academic Press, 1999) 341.

8. Howard Gardner, *Extraordinary Minds: Portraits of Exceptional Individuals and an Examination of Our Own Extraordinariness* (New York: Basic Books, 1997).

9. "Pablo Picasso—Biography," http://home.xnet.com/~stanko/bio.htm (accessed August 5, 2003). Roger Kamien, *Music: An Appreciation* (New York: McGraw-Hill, 2003).

10. The Jim Henson Company, "Jim Henson: Founder," http://www.henson.com/company/jim_henson.html (accessed December 15, 2004).

11. Michael J. Vassallo, "A Look at the Atlas Pre-Code Crime and Horror Work of Stan Lee," http://www.ess.comics.org/ess/docvstan.html (accessed July 7, 2003).

12. Sarah Bowman, "Alfred, Lord Tennyson (1809-1892)," Virginia Tech Department of English, http://athena.english.vt.edu/~jmooney/3044biosp-z/tennyson.html (accessed July 21, 2003).

13. Thomas Folk, "Waylande Gregory (Ceramacist)," *Ceramics Monthly* 42, no. 9 (1994): 27-33.

14. Rap HQ Productions, "TuPac Amaru Shakur: 1971-1996," http://tupacfans.com/bio.php (accessed December 15, 2004). Green Day: The Official Web site, "Billie Joe Armstrong," http://www.greenday.net/billiejoe.html (accessed July 14, 2003). "Michelle Branch Biography," http://www.allstarz.org/~branch/bio.htm (accessed July 29, 2003). Creative Reality Media, "Jewel - Biography," http://www.absolutedivas.com/jewel/biography.shtml (accessed July 28, 2003). Steve Huey, "Stevie Wonder Bio," liveDaily, http://www.livedaily.com/artist/bio334.html (accessed July 14, 2003). WadeRobsonFans, "Wade Robson Biography," http://www.waderobsonfans.com/content_aboutwade.htm (accessed April 28, 2005).

15. American Foundation for the Blind, "Louis Braille Biography," http://www.afb.org/braillebug/louis_braille_bio.asp (accessed July 26, 2006).

16. Catherine Ryan Hyde, *Pay it Forward* (New York: Simon & Schuster, 2000). Catherine Ryan

Hyde, "What Is Pay it Forward?" Pay it Forward Foundation, http://www.payitforwardfoundation.org/home.html (accessed August 21, 2003).

17. Youth Venture, "About Youth Venture," http:://www.youthventure.org/yv.html (accessed August 15, 2003). Ashoka, "Ashoka's Mission," http://www.ashoka.org/what_is/mission.cfm (accessed August 21, 2003).

18. Youth Venture, "About Youth Venture," http://www.youthventure.org/index.php?tg=articles&idx=More&article=1226&topics=360 (accessed August 15, 2003).

19. Garrett Smith, e-mail message to author, August 29, 2003.

20. Harvey Milkman, "Better Than Dope," *Psychology Today*, March 2001, 32-38.

Chapter Eleven

1. Susan Gregory Thomas, "Mini Computer Moguls: Forget Paper Routes. Kids Run Tech Outfits Today," *U.S. News & World Report*, May 19, 1997, 48-49.

2. Robert Macy, "Girl, 14, Blind Dad Drive Car to Save Injured Mom," *San Diego Union-Tribune*, April 18, 2000.

3. Susan Gregory Thomas, "Mini Computer Moguls: Forget Paper Routes. Kids Run Tech Outfits Today," *U.S. News & World Report*, May 19, 1997, 48-49.

4. Bureau of Labor Statistics, "Characteristics of the Employed," http://www.bls.gov/cps/#charemp (accessed July 20, 2006). Prior years data are available at http://www.bls.gov/schedule/archives/empsit_nr.htm.

5. Bureau of Labor Statistics, *Employment and Earnings*, Table 46, January 2004, www.bls.gov.

6. Jimmy Carter, *An Hour Before Daylight* (New York: Simon & Schuster, 2001) 152.

7. Bonnie Drew, "This Generation Means Business!" Entrepreneur.com, http://www.entrepreneur.com/mag/article/0,1539,298822,00.html (accessed April 9, 2003).

8. The Chocolate Farm, "Our Story," http://www.thechocolatefarm.com/ourstory.cfm?sid=04092003052006422304&p=ourstory (accessed July 3, 2006).

9. Andrea Faiad, "Teen Tech Wizard," http://www.youngbiz.com/ (accessed July 20, 2006).

10. Christina McCarroll, "Beyond Babysitting," *Christian Science Monitor*, June 24, 2002, http://www.csmonitor.com/2002/0624/p15s02-wmwo.html (accessed April 9, 2003).

11. Entrepreneurs' Organization, http://www.eonetwork.org/ (accessed July 3, 2006). Daryl

Bernstein and Rob Husberg, *Better than a Lemonade Stand: Small Business Ideas for Kids* (Hillsboro, OR: Beyond Words Publishing, 1992). Bonnie Drew and Noel Drew, *Kids Biz: Year Round Money-Making Projects for Young Entrepreneurs* (Austin, TX: Eakin Press, 1990). Steve Mariotti et al., *The Young Entrepreneur's Guide to Starting and Running a Business* (New York: Three Rivers Press, 2000).

12. Associated Press, "Utah Teens Working on Mars Rover Experiment," *The Salt Lake Tribune*, September 21, 2003.

13. Alexis Herman, *Report on the Youth Labor Force* (Washington, D.C.: U.S. Department of Labor: Bureau of Labor Statistics, 2000).

14. Bureau of Labor Statistics. "Preface" in The Report on Youth Labor Force (2000), U.S. Department of Labor, http://www.bls.gov/opub/rylf/rylfhome.htm#Preface (accessed July 7, 2006).

15. Bureau of Labor Statistics. "A Detailed Look at Employment of Youths Aged 12 to 15," in The Report on Youth Labor Force (2000), U.S. Department of Labor, http://www.bls.gov/opub/rylf/pdf/chapter3.pdf (accessed July 4, 2006). Bureau of Labor Statistics, "Trends in Youth Employment: Data from the Current Population Survey," in The Report on Youth Labor Force (2000), U.S. Department of Labor, http://www.bls.gov/opub/rylf/pdf/chapter4.pdf (accessed July 3, 2006).

16. Bureau of Labor Statistics. "A Detailed Look at Employment of Youths Aged 12 to 15," in The Report on Youth Labor Force (2000) , U.S. Department of Labor, http://www.bls.gov/opub/rylf/pdf/chapter3.pdf (accessed July 3, 2006).

17. Bureau of International Labor Affairs, "By the Sweat & Toil of Children (Volume VI): An Economic Consideration of Child Labor," U.S. Department of Labor, http://www.dol.gov/ILAB/media/reports/iclp/sweat6/sweat6_html/sweat6_chap_1.html (accessed September 24, 2003).

18. Ibid.

19. U.S. Department of Labor, "About YouthRules!" http://www.youthrules.dol.gov/about.htm (accessed April 21, 2005).

20. Christina McCarroll, "Beyond Babysitting," *The Christian Science Monitor*, June 24, 2002, http://www.csmonitor.com/2002/0624/p15s02-wmwo.html (accessed April 9, 2003).

21. James Bovard, "The Folly of Protecting Teens from Work," Freedom Daily, October 2002, Future Freedom Foundation, http://www.fff.org/freedom/fd0210d.asp (accessed September 11, 2003).

22. Robert Woodson, National Center for Neighborhood Enterprise, quoted by James Bovard in "The Folly of Protecting Teens from Work," Freedom Daily, October 2002, Future Free-

dom Foundation, http://www.fff.org/freedom/fd0210d.asp (accessed September 11, 2003).

23. James Bovard, "The Folly of Protecting Teens from Work," *Freedom Daily*, October 2002, Future Freedom Foundation, http://www.fff.org/freedom/fd0210d.asp (accessed September 11, 2003).

24. Ibid.

25. Ibid.

26. Reuters, "Boy, 13, Named Jamaica Computer Consultant," *San Diego Union-Tribune*, July 25, 1998.

27. Thomas Hine, *The Rise and Fall of the American Teenager* (New York: Bard Books, 1999) 53.

28. Mihaly Csikszentmihalyi and Barbara Schneider, *Becoming Adult: How Teenagers Prepare For the World of Work* (New York: Basic Books, 2000), 218.

29. Ibid., 219.

30. Jeffrey A. Butts, Janeen Buck, and Mark B. Coggeshall, *The Impact of Teen Courts on Young Offenders* (Washington, DC: The Urban Institute, 2002).

31. The Christophers, "The Power of the Citizen, Pass on the torch," http://www.christophers.org/govnn2.html (accessed April 25, 2005). Also: http://www.youthcourt.net/resources/wi96per20.pdf

32. National Youth Court Center. "Facts and Stats," National Youth Court Center, http://www.youthcourt.net/resources/Facts_and_Stats.htm (accessed July 4, 2006).

33. Denton County, "Teen Court," http://dentoncounty.com/deptmain.asp?Dept=38&Link=156 (accessed May 26, 2005).

34. Gidget Schultz, e-mail message to author, March 4, 2004.

35. National Research Council, Juvenile Crime, Juvenile Justice (Washington D.C.: National Academy Press, 2001) 5-6.

36. Tracy Godwin, "Teen Courts: Empowering Youth in Community Prevention and Intervention Efforts," APPA *Perspectives*, Winter 1996, 20-24.

37. National Youth Court Center. "Youth Court List By State," National Youth Court Center, http://www.youthcourt.net/resources/Facts_and_Stats.htm, (accessed July 7, 2006). Office of Governor Frank Murkowski, "Youth Court Month," http://www.gov.state.ak.us/archive.php?id=1193&type=6 (accessed May 26, 2005). Until the early 1990s, teen courts

spread mainly through grass-roots efforts. In the 1990s, recognizing the value of such courts, government agencies began to provide funding and training to establish new ones. Major support came from the National Highway Traffic Safety Administration (NHTSA), the Office of Juvenile Justice and Delinquency Prevention (OJJDP), and the Substance Abuse and Mental Health Service Administration (SAMSA), which worked with the APPA, a private, non-profit organization, to create to new teen courts nationwide.

38. Beth Kristin Ott, "Students Take Different Paths to Success," *West Valley View*, Arizona, http://www.dist.maricopa.edu/edcetera/online/jun02/2.htm (accessed January 29, 2004).

39. Fern Gillespie, "Teen Mothers Workin' It," Teenwire, http://www.teenwire.com/takingac/articles/ta_19990521p005.asp (accessed July 24, 2003). Lateefah Simon, "SF Youth & Social Change Keynote Address," Commonwealth Club, http://www.commonwealthclub.org/archive/04/04-01simon-speech.html (accessed December 20, 2004). Kamren Curiel, "Lateefah Simon Awarded MacArthur 'Genius' Award," Sisters (2004), http://www.cywd.org/Newsletters/Win04_news.pdf, (accessed July 7, 2006).

40. Angela Giles Klocke, e-mail message to author, August 29, 2003. Angela Giles Klocke, "The Smart Children of Teen Moms," One Young Parent, http://oneyoungparent.com/ (accessed July 16, 2004).

41. Planned Parenthood. "Pregnancy and Childbearing Among U.S. Teens," Planned Parenthood, http://www.plannedparenthood.org/pp2/portal/files/portal/medicalinfo/teensexualhealth/fact-pregnancy-teens-us.xml (accessed July 7, 2006).

42. J.B. Ivey, "'Good Little Girls': Reports of Pregnant Adolescents and Those who Know Them Best," *Issues in Comprehensive Pediatric Nursing* 22 (1999): 95-96.

43. Robert Coles, *The Youngest Parents* (New York: W.W. Norton, 1997).

44. Ibid, 79.

45. Ibid. For other relevant findings, see: Jodie Levin-Epstein. "Teen Parents and Abstinence Education, Research Findings: 2003," http://66.102.7.104/search?q=cache:fzc-0zK62B4J:www.clasp.org/publications/TP_abst_research.pdf+Teen+Parents+and+Abstinence+Education&hl=en&gl=us&ct=clnk&cd=1&client=firefox-a (accessed July 7, 2006).

46. Deborah Davis, *You Look Too Young to be a Mom: Teen Mothers Speak Out on Love, Learning, and Success* (New York: Perigee Books, 2004).

47. Ariel Gore, *The Hip Mama Survival Guide* (New York: Hyperion, 1998).

48. Sandra L. Hanson, David E. Myers, and Alan L. Ginsburg, "The Role of Responsibility and Knowledge in Reducing Teenage Out-of-Wedlock Childbearing," *Journal of Marriage and the Family* 49 (1987): 241-256.

49. Ibid., 251.

50. Linda Eyre and Richard Eyre, *Teaching Your Children Responsibility* (New York: Fireside Books, 1994).

51. Jane Newhall, "Effects of Responsibility Training and Self-worth on Prosocial Behavior in a Scarcity Situation," abstract, *Dissertation Abstracts International* 50, 12-B, Pt 1 (1990): 5927-5928.

52. J.M. Bowers, C. Flanagan, and A.J. Taylor, "Adolescents' Ideas About Individual and Social Responsibility in Relation to Children's Household Work: Some International Comparisons," *International Journal of Behavioral Development* 25 (2001): 60-68.

Chapter Twelve

1. Mark Goodacre and Helen Bond, "Mary in the New Testament," http://www.bbc.co.uk/religion/programmes/mary/evidence/6.shtml (accessed April 13, 2005).

2. According to a communication I received on November 7, 2003, from Dr. Helen Bond, a Biblical scholar at Edinburgh University, "Given the short life expectancies and the difficulties in preserving a daughter's chastity, it is unlikely that a girl would be much older than mid-teens when she married.... [The] Gospels suggest... that Mary was not yet married when she conceived Jesus, [so] she could have been much younger than this." Bond also points to the Tal Ilan section of the Mishnah for "the earliest attestation for the age of puberty being 12.5."

3. Dr. Debra R. Blank, "How Old is Old Enough?" MyJewishLearning, Inc., http://www.myjewishlearning.com/lifecycle/Bar_Bat_Mitzvah/AboutBarBatMitzvah/HowOld.htm (accessed April 13, 2005).

4. William Smith, ed., *Dictionary of Roman and Greek Antiquities*, 2nd ed. (Boston: Little, Brown, 1870) 630-631. "Spermarche," the age of first ejaculation for males—now approximately 13.4—has also stayed relatively constant. See: C. T. Nielsen, N. E. Skakkebaek, D. W. Richardson, J. A. Darling, W. M. Hunter, M. Jorgensen, A. Nielsen, O. Ingerslev, N. Keiding and J. Muller. "Onset of the Release of Spermatozoa (Spermarche) in Boys in Relation to Age, Testicular Growth, Pubic Hair, and Height," *Journal of Clinical Endocrinology and Metabolism* 62 (1986): 532-535.

5. Miriam Peskowitz and Jim Charlesworth, "Pregnant Out of Wedlock," British Broadcasting Company, http://www.bbc.co.uk/religion/programmes/mary/evidence/4.shtml (accessed November 1, 2003).

6. *2 Kings 2:23-25*. King James Version.

7. Verses which appear in some translations to distinguish between childhood and "youth"

include *Ecclesiastes 11:9-10, Job 33:25, 2 Timothy 3:15, Jeremiah 6:11, Jeremiah 18:21, and Isaiah 3:4.*, but the distinctions appear to be mainly stylistic, not substantive. None of these verses suggests the existence of a period of life akin to modern adolescence. See: John T. Carroll, "Children in the Bible," *Interpretation* 55 no. 2 (2001), http://pdfserve.galegroup.com/pdfserve/get_item/1/Sc4160aw7_1/SB698_01.pdf.

8. Sharei Shechem, "Pirkei Avot, Chapter 5 verse 24," http://www.shechem.org/torah/avot.html, (accessed April 13, 2005).

9. Rabbi Jeffrey K. Salkin, "Today's Lavish Feasts Derive from Meals with Sacred Status," My Jewish Learning, http://www.myjewishlearning.com/lifecycle/Bar_Bat_Mitzvah/InPractice/ShulVersusParty.htm (accessed April 13, 2005).

10. Dennis O'Neil, "Process of Socialization: Rites of Passage," Rites of Passage, 2002, http://anthro.palomar.edu/social/soc_4.htm (accessed March 11, 2005).

11. Karen Liptak, *Coming-of-Age: Traditions and Rituals Around the World* (Brookfield, CT: Millbrook Press, 1994) 59.

12. "Traditional Muslim Male Circumcision," Circlist Publishing, 2004, http://www.circlist.com/rites/moslem.html (accessed May 25, 2005).

13. Dennis O'Neil, "Process of Socialization: Rites of Passage," Rites of Passage, 2002, http://anthro.palomar.edu/social/soc_4.htm (accessed March 11, 2005).

14. Margaret A. Robinson, "Cross Cultural Differences," Adolescence: Change and Continuity (2001), http://www.oberlin.edu/faculty/ndarling/adbio1.htm (accessed July 7, 2006).

15. Karen Liptak, *Coming-of-Age: Traditions and Rituals Around the World* (Brookfield, CT: Millbrook Press, 1994). Charlotte J. Frisbie, *Kinaalda: A Study of the Navaho Girl's Puberty Ceremony* (Salt Lake City, UT: University of Utah Press, 1993). Gilbert H. Herdt, *Rituals of Manhood: Male Initiation in Papua New Guinea* (Somerset, NJ: Transaction, 1998).

16. Society of Our Lady of the Most Holy Trinity, "What the Church Has Said About Children Who Die Without Baptism—Father Peter Gumpel Gives an Overview," http://www.solt3.org/limbo.htm (accessed April 17, 2005).

17. Patrick J. Toner, "Limbo," The Catholic Encyclopedia, Volume IX, http://www.newadvent.org/cathen/09256a.htm (accessed April 17, 2005).

18. Catholic *Code of Canon Law*, Canon 97§2.

19. Catholic *Code of Canon Law*, Canon 105§1.

20. C. Terry Warner, "Accountability," All About Mormons, http://www.lightplanet.com/mormons/basic/doctrines/accountability_eom.htm (accessed April 18, 2005).

21. Catholic *Code of Canon Law*, Canon 1083§1.

22. Catholic *Code of Canon Law*, Canon 1031§1.

23. Dan Olinger, "The Age of Accountability," Faith for the Family, http://bju.edu/faith (accessed November 1, 2003; site now discontinued).

24. *Luke 2:41-50*. King James Version.

25. *1 Samuel 3:9*. King James Version.

26. *1 Kings 3:7*. King James Version.

27. *Jeremiah 1:10*. King James Version.

28. *1 Samuel 17:34-36*. King James Version.

29. See *1 Samuel 15:2-3, Isaiah 13:15-16, Numbers 31:16-18, Deuteronomy 2:34, 3:6-7, Ezekiel 9:5-6,* and *Joshua 6:2*. King James Version.

30. L.R. Wiley, *Children and Youths of the Bible*, 141.

31. See *2 Kings 22-23* and *2 Chronicles 34-35*. King James Version.

32. Suman Verma and T.S. Saraswathi, "Adolescence in India: Street Urchins or Silicon Valley Millionaires?," in *The World's Youth: Adolescence in Eight Regions of the Globe*, eds. B. Bradford Brown, Reed W. Larson, and T.S. Saraswathi, 105-134 (Cambridge, UK: Cambridge University Press, 2002).

33. *Daniel 1:20*. King James Version.

34. *Daniel 1:12-13*. King James Version.

35. *Daniel 1:15-16*. King James Version.

36. *Acts 23:16-23*. King James Version.

37. *Esther 7:3-4*. King James Version.

38. *Midrash B'reishit Rabbah* 38:13. "B'reishit" is the Hebrew word for Genesis. A similar story about Abraham is told in Islamic writings. See Sura al-Anbiya 21:51-70 in the Koran.

39. *Job 29:2*. King James Version.

40. *Isaiah 11:6*. King James Version.

41. *Mark 10:14*. King James Version. This verse is repeated in Luke 18:16.

42. *Matthew 11:25*. King James Version. The message is echoed in Luke 10:21.

43. History Learning Site, "The Children's Crusade of 1212," http:/www.historylearning site.co.uk/children's_crusade.htm (accessed December 20, 2004).

44. Ibid.

45. History Learning Site, "The Children's Crusade of 1212," http:// www.historylearningsite.co.uk/children's_crusade.htm (accessed December 20, 2004).

46. Marypages, "The Apparitions of Our Lady of Fatima," http://www.marypages.com/ fatimaEng.htm (accessed April 18, 2005).

47. The Christian Sisters, "Marian Appearances," http://beadsforprayer.com/ Marian_apparitions/menu.htm (accessed April 18, 2005).

48. The Government of Tibet in Exile, "The Dalai Lama's Biography," http://www.tibet.com/ DL/biography.html (accessed July 21, 2006)

49. Sparknotes, "Joan of Arc," http://www.sparknotes.com/biography/joanofarc/htimeline.html (accessed October 2, 2003). Beth Randall, "Joan of Arc," Illuminating Lives, http:// www.mcs.drexel.edu/~gbrandal/Illum_html/Joan.html (accessed August 29, 2006). Ian C. Mills, "Joan of Arc," Discover France, http://www.discoverfrance.net/France/History/ Joan_of_Arc.shtml (accessed August 29, 2006). History World, "History of Joan of Arc," http://www.historyworld.net/wrldhis/PlainTextHistories.asp?historyid=aa41 (accessed August 29, 2006). Timothy Wilson-Smith, *Joan of Arc: Maid, Myth and History* (Gloucestershire, UK: Sutton, 2006).

50. Jan Shipps, excerpt from "Joseph Smith and Mormonism," http://lds-mormon.com/ shipps_joseph_smith.shtml (accessed July 21, 2006

51. M. Muhsin Khan, "Translation of Sahih Bukhari," Muslim Student Association at University of Southern California, http://www.usc.edu/dept/MSA/fundamentals/hadithsunnah/ bukhari/058.sbt.html (accessed April 18, 2005).

52. Catherine E. Polisi, "Universal Rights and Cultural Relativism: Hinduism and Islam Deconstructed," Johns Hopkins University, The Bologna Center Journal of International Affairs, www.jhubc.it/bcjournal/articles/polisi.cfm (accessed July 11, 2006)

53. Indian Child, "Indian Marriages," http://www.indianchild.com/indian_marriages.htm (accessed April 18, 2005).

54. Personal communications from: Pastor Earnhart, Fundamental Baptist Church, Escondido,

CA (March 7, 2005); Senior Pastor Dr. Jim Meek, Trinity Baptist Church, Livermore, CA (March 8, 2005); Reverend Jola Bortner, St. Mark's United Methodist Church, Stockton, CA (March 8, 2005); Senior Pastor Scott E. Sorenson, St. John's Lutheran Church, Sacramento, CA (March 7, 2005); Pundit Vivek Sharma, Sacramento Hindu Temple, Sacramento, CA (March 8, 2005); Elder and Sister von Savoye, Church of Jesus Christ of the Latter Day Saints, Fresno, CA (March 8, 2005); Pastor Franz, Laton Pentecostal Church of God, Laton, CA (March 8, 2005). Also see: Abu Bakr Jabir Al-Jaza'iry, *Minhaj Al-Muslim, Vol. 2.* Riyadh: Darussalam, 2001. Benazir Bhutto, "Women and Islam," *Asiaweek,* August 25, 1995. Catholic *Code of Canon Law,* Canon 97§2. Edward N. Peters "Too Young to Marry," http://www.canonlaw.info/a_tooyoung.htm (accessed August 1, 2006). Judaism 101, "Bar Mitzvah, Bat Mitzvah and Confirmation," http://www.jewfaq.org/barmitz.htm (accessed May 26, 2005). Countercurrents.org, "Women and Hindu Marriage Law," http://www.countercurrents.org/gender-marriage031103.htm (accessed July 21, 2006).

55. *Exodus 20:12.* King James Version.

56. See *Timothy 5:8, 2 Corinthians 12:14, Luke 11:11-12, Proverbs 31:10, 31:15, 22, 27, 1 Kings 17:10-12,* and *2 Samuel 12:15-16, 21.* King James Version. See Roy B. Zuck *Precious in His Sight: Childhood and Children in the Bible* (Michigan: Baker Books, 1996), 109-110.

57. See *Genesis 22:2, 25:28, 31:28, 37:3, 44:20, 2 Samuel 13:37-14:1,* and *Luke 8:41-42.* See Roy B. Zuck *Precious in His Sight: Childhood and Children in the Bible* (Michigan: Baker Books, 1996), 111-1113.

58. Although it does not single out children specifically, *1 Timothy 5:8* does require that the head of a household must provide material support for dependents: "If anyone doesn't provide for his own, and especially his own household, he has denied the faith, and is worse than an unbeliever."

Chapter Thirteen

1. U.S. Bureau of the Census, "Young Adults Living at Home, 1960-2002," Information Please Database, http://www.infoplease.com/ipa/A0193723.html (accessed March 30, 2005).

2. Leon Botstein, *Jefferson's Children: Education and the Promise of American Culture* (New York: Doubleday, 1997).

3. Ben Feller, "Home Schooling a Growing Option for Many Families," *San Diego Union-Tribune,* August 4, 2004.

4. G. Stanley Hall, *Adolescence its Psychology and its Relations to Physiology, Anthropology, Sociology, Sex, Crime, Religion and Education,* Vol. II (New York: D. Appleton and Company, 1905) 384.

5. Plato, *The Republic,* trans. Benjamin Jowett (Mineola, NY: Dover Publications, 2000).

6. Gerald Beals, "Biography of Thomas Alva Edison," http://www.thomasedison.com/biog.htm (accessed July 21, 2006).

7. U-S-History.com, "Thomas Edison," http://www.u-s-history.com/pages/h1608.htm (accessed May 23, 2005).

8. Philip Graham, *The End of Adolescence* (Oxford: Oxford University Press) 263.

9. Hugh Cunningham, *Children and Childhood in Western Society Since 1500* (New York: Longman, 1995) 185.

10. Ibid., 185.

11. Herbert Kelman, "A Socio-psychological Model of Political Legitimacy and its Relevance to Black and White Student Protest Movements," *Psychiatry* 33 (1970): 224-246.

12. "The Aftermath of the Vietnam War," http://dylanp0.tripod.com/id1.html (accessed January 29, 2005).

13. Anthony M. Platt, *The Child Savers: The Invention of Delinquency* (Chicago: University of Chicago Press, 1977) 161.

14. *In re Gault*, 387 U.S. 1 (1967)

15. *Tinker et al. v. Des Moines Independent Community School District et al.*, 393 U.S. 503 (1969).

16. *Planned Parenthood of Missouri v. Danforth*, 428 U.S. 52 (1976).

17. *Carey v. Population Services International*, 431 U.S. 678 (1977).

18. *New Jersey v. T.L.O.*, 469 U.S. 325 (1985).

19. Jim Wasserman, "Legislator Would Give Teens 14-17 Shares of State Vote," *San Diego Union-Tribune*, March 9, 2004. Also see: Kristin Bender, "Berkeley Teenagers Continue Fight to Lower Voting Age," CalBearsSearch, http://www.findarticles.com/p/articles/mi_qn4176/is_20041030/ai_n14586810?pi=cal (accessed June 15, 2006). Also see: http://www.youthrights.org/articles/votenews.html.

20. Sandra Bookman, June 8, 2005, "First News out of NYC Voting Age!" NYRA, http://www.youthrights.org/forums/showpost.php?p=70199&postcount=1 (accessed July 24, 2006).

21. Chris Sear, *Reduction in Voting Age* (London: House of Commons Library, 2003). Isobel White, "Reduction in Voting Age," Parliament and Constitution Centre, http://www.parliament.uk/commons/lib/research/notes/snpc-01747.pdf (accessed August 8, 2006).

22. At least ten countries allow people under eighteen to vote: Brazil, Cuba, Croatia, East Timor, Indonesia, Iran, Isle of Man, North Korea, Seychelles, and Sudan. See: Central Intelligence Agency, "Field Listing - Suffrage," The World Factbook, http://www.cia.gov/cia/publications/factbook/fields/2123.html (accessed June 15, 2006)

23. Traci Truly, *Teen Rights: A Legal Guide For Teens and the Adults in Their Lives* (Naperville, IL: Sphinx Publishing, 2002).

24. Ibid., 3-8, 47-56, 161-163, 187-190.

25. Ibid., 157, 161-163, 170.

26. U.S. Department of Education, http://www.stophitting.com/disatschool/facts.php (accessed July 16, 2006).

27. American Civil Liberties Union, "Alaska Court Strikes Down Curfew Law as Violation of Parents and Childrens' Constitutional Rights," http://www.aclu.org/CriminalJustice/CriminalJustice.cfm?ID=7192&c=46 (accessed October 18, 2004).

28. Ibid., 97.

29. Dennis Tatz, "Divorce from Dad Gives Son Freedom to be Adopted: Killer Father's Decision Was for Himself, Boy Says," *The Patriot Ledger*, http://ledger.southofboston.com/articles/2004/07/27/news/news07.txt (accessed January 29, 2005).

30. Traci Truly, *Teen Rights: A Legal Guide For Teens and the Adults in Their Lives* (Naperville, IL: Sphinx Publishing, 2002) 11-12.

31. Ibid., 14-15.

32. Drug Policy Alliance, "Random Student Drug Testing Ban Headed to the Governor's Desk," August 18, 2004.

33. Ramin Setoodeh, "Movies: 13 Going on 17?," *Newsweek*, May 24, 2004. Issues of this sort are monitored by a non-profit group called the National Youth Rights Association, which can be visited online at http://www.youthrights.org.

Chapter Fourteen

1. That subway poster, one of many products of the U.S. government's Office of National Drug Control Policy, isn't half as bad as other ads they've been disseminating. Consider this full-page ad from a recent issue of *Popular Science*: On the center of the page is a photograph of a greeting card with the following words on the front: "For Mom and Dad—*I Hate You.*" At the bottom of the page the paragraph begins, "*Scared of these three little words? Get used to it, because you've got a teenager....*" Such ads convey the message that an adversarial relation-

ship between parents and their teenage offspring is not only normal, but desirable. The ad also warns parents that if they fail to get tough, they'll end up with "an addicted child later"— suggesting, mistakenly, that a teenager is still a child. Even more disturbing: a new national ad campaign co-sponsored by the National Fatherhood Initiative and the Ad Council which gives advice about raising teens. The message of their radio ad is "*Embarrass them, horrify them, freak them out. Don't worry, they'll appreciate it... eventually.*" See http:// www.fatherhood.org/psa_radio.asp (accessed September 7, 2006).

2. Office of National Drug Control Policy, "Evaluation of the National Youth Anti-Drug Media Campaign: Fifth Semi-Annual Report of Findings," www.mediacampaign.org/publications/ westat5/1intro.html (accessed December 21, 2004).

3. Jerald G. Bachman, Patrick M. O'Malley, John E. Schulenberg, Lloyd D. Johnston, Alison L. Bryant, and Alicia C. Merline, *The Decline of Substance Use in Young Adulthood: Changes in Social Activities, Roles, and Beliefs*, (New Jersey: Lawrence Erlbaum Associates, 2001).

4. Frank Ahrens, "The Price for On-Air Indecency Goes Up," *Washington Post*, June 8, 2006.

5. Associated Press, "FDA Rejects Nonprescription Morning-After Pill For Now," *USA Today*, May 8, 2004. Andrew Bridges, Associated Press, "FDA to Discuss Morning-After Pill Availability," *San Diego Union-Tribune*, August 1, 2006. Gardiner Harris, New York Times News Service, "Emergency Birth-Control Limits Eased," *San Diego Union-Tribune*, August 25, 2006.

6. Paul Vitello, New York Times News Service "New Ring Tone Boon for Teens, Bane of Adults," *San Diego Union-Tribune*, June 12, 2006.

7. Joseph F. Kett, *Rites of Passage: Adolescence in America 1790 to the Present* (New York: Basic Books, 1977) 191-192.

8. Ari Berman, "Al Gore Gets Down." *The Nation*, May 16, 2005, http://www.thenation.com/ doc/20050516/berman (accessed July 2, 2006). Also see: "Currently Available," *TIME*, June 19, 2006.

9. Cabletelevision Advertising Bureau, "Cable Network Information 2005," http:// www.onetvworld.org/tmpls/network/05profiles/307.pdf (accessed April 8, 2005).

10. Diane Werts, "Teens line up for taste of MTV 'Stew,'" *Newsday*, April 28, 2004.
11. Ana Marie Cox, "Sweet 16 and Spoiled Rotten," *TIME*, April 24, 2006, 96.

12. Media Awareness Network, "How Marketers Target Kids," http://www.media-awareness.ca/ english/parents/marketing/marketers_target_kids.cfm (accessed December 21, 2004). The latter article suggests that teens spent about $170 billion in 2003. Early in 2006, the Mintel organization suggested that this number would exceed $190 billion in 2006. See: Mintel, "Teen Spending Estimated to Top $190 Billion by 2006," Market Research World, April 12, 2006, http://www.marketresearchworld.netindex.php?option=content&task

=view&id=615&Itemid=, (accessed October 30, 2006).

13. Paul Miller, "Lists and Prospecting: Tapping the Teen Market," *Catalog Age*, July 1, 2003, http://catalogagemag.com/lists/marketing_tapping_teen_market/ (accessed June 16, 2004).

14. For example, see: Frank Green, "Whither the Teen Green? Lreport [sic] Is Paid to Track Youthful Consumers," *San Diego Union-Tribune*, November 17, 2000.

15. Yuki Noguchi, "Teens Ring Up Market Share," *BizReport*, April 26, 2004, http://www.bizreport.com/news/6990/ (accessed December 21, 2004).

16. Melanie Wells, "Kid Nabbing," *Forbes Magazine*, February 2, 2004, http://forbes.com/bbsbrands/forbes/2004/0202/084.html (accessed December 21, 2004).

17. Media Awareness Network, "How Marketers Target Kids," http://www.media-awareness.ca/english/parents/marketing/marketers_target_kids.cfm (accessed December 21, 2004).

18. Daniel Acuff, *What Kids Buy and Why: The Psychology of Marketing to Kids* (New York: Free Press, 1998).

19. David S. Johnson and Mark Lino, "Teenagers: Employment and Contributions to Family Spending," Bureau of Labor Statistics, http://www.bls.gov/opub/mlr/2000/09/art2full.pdf (accessed April 1, 2005). The Recording Industry Association of America, "2002 Consumer Profile," http://www.riaa.com/news/marketingdata/pdf/2002consumerprofile.pdf (accessed June 26, 2004).

20. Trudy Tynan, "Dictionary Update Includes, in a Word, 'Teensploitation,'" *San Diego Union-Tribune*, August 1, 2004.

21. American Psychiatric Association, *Diagnostic and Statistical Manual of Mental Disorders*, 4th ed. (Washington, DC: American Psychiatric Association, 2000).

22. U.S. Department of Health and Human Services, "Mental Health: A Report of the Surgeon General," http://www.surgeongeneral.gov/library/mentalhealth/chapter2/sec2_1.html#cost (accessed April 8, 2005).

23. *Psychology Today*, "Therapy Directory," http://www.psychologytoday.com (accessed April 8, 2005).
24. *Roper v. Simmons* 543 US 551 (2005).

25. Ibid.

26. David A. Young, "Il-Trying Children in Adult Courts," Human Rights Watch, http://www.hrw.org/reports/1999/maryland/Maryland-02htm#TopOfPage (accessed February 23, 2005).

27. Associated Press, "Child-Labor Complaints Bring Halt to Mall Project," *San Diego Union-Tribune*, July 31, 1999.

28. Chris Baker, "TV Complaints to FCC Soar as Parents Lead the Way," *Washington Times*, May 24, 2004, http://www.washingtontimes.com/business/20040523-115504-1094r.htm (accessed June 26, 2004).

29. Lewis Napper, "The Bill of Non-Rights," 1993, http://www.freerepublic.com/focus/f-news/1499273/posts (accessed July 29, 2006).

30. Jerry Scott and Jim Borgman, "Zits," *San Diego Union-Tribune*, July 11, 2004.

31. Parents Television Council, "About Us," http://www.parentstv.org/PTC/aboutus/main.asp (accessed December 21, 2004).

32. Wikipedia, "Parents Music Resource Center," Fact Index, http://www.fact-index.com/p/pa/parents_music_resource_center.html (accessed December 21, 2004).

33. Amy Harmon, "Cell Phones That Track Kids Click with Parents," *Seattle Times*, Dec. 21, 2003, http://seattletimes.nwsource.com/html/nationworld/2001820367_track21.html (accessed December 21, 2004). Tricia Duryee, "Sprint Nextel Service Lets Parents Track Kids," *San Diego Union-Tribune*, May 1, 2006.

34. Thayer Watkins, "Kahneman and Tversky's Prospect Theory," San José State University Economics Department, http://www2.sjsu.edu/faculty/watkins/prospect.htm (accessed April 13, 2005).

35. This is my own variation on the kind of problem Kahneman and Tversky used in some of their experiments.

36. Ellen J. Langer, *Mindfulness*, (New York: Addison-Wesley, 1989) 43-57.

37. Bruce M. Stave, "Urban Bosses and Machine Politics," Houghton Mifflin, http://college.hmco.com/history/readerscomp/rcah/html/ah_088500_urbanbossesa.htm (accessed April 6, 2005).

38. Simone Schnall, "Life as the Problem: Karl Duncker's Context," University of Virginia, http://faculty.virginia.edu/schnall/Schnall.pdf (accessed April 13, 2005).

39. The concept of "institutional delusions" was introduced by Edmond Taylor in this 1947 book, *Richer by Asia* (Boston: Houghton Mifflin). He blamed Europe's susceptibility to fascism on widespread delusional thinking—especially fears and suspicions promulgated by Christian churches prior to World War II.

40. Caitlin Flanagan, "Becoming Mary Poppins: P. L. Travers, Walt Disney, and the Making of a Myth." *New Yorker*, December 19, 2005, http://www.newyorker.com/fact/content/articles/051219fa_fact1 (accessed July 31, 2006).

41. Jeffrey M. Jones, "Americans Felt Uneasy Toward Arabs Even Before September 11: Majority Supports Increased Security Measures Even for Arabs Who Are United States Citizens," Gallup News Service, September 28, 2001, http://www.gallup.com/poll/content/?ci=4939&pg=1 (accessed July 11, 2005)

42. George Orwell, *1984* (New York: Signet, 1992).

43. "A Call to Attention on Gays in the Military: Is It Time to Revise 'Don't Ask, Don't Tell?'" http://www.harrisinteractive.com/news/allnewsbydate.asp?NewsID=61 (accessed July 31, 2006). National Annenberg Election Survey, October 16, 2004, http://www.annenbergpublicpolicycenter.org/naes/2004_03_2military-data_10-16_pr.pdf (accessed July 31, 2006).

Appendix 3

1. Uniform Crime Reporting Program Federal Bureau of Investigation, "Age-Specific Arrest Rates for Selected Offenses: 1993-2001," http://www.fbi.gov/ucr/adducr/age_race_specific.pdf (accesssed July 28, 2005).

2. Mike Males, e-mail message to author, June 11, 2004.

3. California Department of Justice, "Crime in California 2002," http://caag.state.ca.us/cjsc/publications/candd/cd02/tabs/33.pdf (accessed July 28, 2005).

4. Uniform Crime Reporting Program Federal Bureau of Investigation, "Age-Specific Arrest Rates for Selected Offenses; 1993-2001," http://www.fbi.gov/ucr/adducr/age_race_specific.pdf (accessed July 28, 2005).

5. Mike Males, e-mail message to author, June 6, 2004.

Appendix 4

1. Jeffrey Jensen Arnett, *Adolescence and Emerging Adulthood* (Upper Saddle River, NJ: Prentice-Hall, 2001) 6-7. Also see: Jeffrey Jansen Arnett, "Adolescent Storm and Stress, Reconsidered," *American Psychologist* 54, no. 5 (May 1999): 317-326.

2. EServer, "The Republic," http://eserver.org/philosophy/plato/republic.txt (accessed June 2, 2005).

3. EServer, "Rhetoric," http://eserver.org/philosophy/aristotle/rhetoric.txt (accessed June 2, 2005).

4. Ibid.

5. There is little question that Aristotle's comments on youth and old age were meant didacti-
cally when one looks at the next section of his discourse, in which he defines optimal functioning as a middle ground between the two extremes he just described: "As for Men in their
Prime, clearly we shall find that they have a character between that of the young and that of
the old, free from the extremes of either. They have neither that excess of confidence which
amounts to rashness, nor too much timidity, but the right amount of each. They neither
trust everybody nor distrust everybody, but judge people correctly. Their lives will be guided
not by the sole consideration either of what is noble or of what is useful, but by both; neither
by parsimony nor by prodigality, but by what is fit and proper. So, too, in regard to anger and
desire; they will be brave as well as temperate, and temperate as well as brave; these virtues
are divided between the young and the old; the young are brave but intemperate, the old
temperate but cowardly. To put it generally, all the valuable qualities that youth and age
divide between them are united in the prime of life, while all their excesses or defects are
replaced by moderation and fitness. The body is in its prime from thirty to five-and-thirty;
the mind about forty-nine" (Aristotle, *Rhetoric*, Book II, Part 14, translation by W. Rhys
Roberts).

6. Ibid.

Readings

Acuff, Daniel. *What Kids Buy and Why: The Psychology of Marketing to Kids*. New York: Free Press, 1998.

Addams, Jane. *Twenty Years at Hull-House*. New York: Signet Classic, 1961.

Adelson, Joseph. *Inventing Adolescence: The Political Psychology of Everyday Schooling*. New Brunswick, N.J.: Transaction, 1986.

Al-Jaza'iry, Abu Bakr Jabir. *Minhaj Al-Muslim: A Book of Creed, Manners, Character, Acts of Worship and Other Deeds*. New York: Darussalam, 2001

Ariès, Philippe. *Centuries of Childhood: A Social History of Family Life*. New York: Random House, 1962.

Bachman, Jerald G., Patrick M. O'Malley, John Schulenberg, Lloyd D. Johnston, Alison L. Bryant, and Alicia C. Merlin. *The Decline of Substance Use in Young Adulthood: Changes in Social Activities, Roles, and Beliefs*. Hillsdale, N.J.: Erlbaum, 2001.

Balwin, Steve, and Melissa Oxlad. *Electroshock and Minors: A Fifty-Year Review*. Westport, Conn.: Greenwood Press, 2000.

Barkley, Russell A., Gwenyth H. Edwards, and Arthur L. Robin. *Defiant Teens: A Clinician's Manual for Assessment and Family Intervention*. New York: Guilford Press, 1999.

Barrymore, Drew, and Todd Gold. *Little Girl Lost*. New York: Pocket Books, 1990.

Bettelheim, Bruno. *The Children of the Dream: Communal Child-Rearing and American Education*. New York: Avon, 1969.

Birren, James E., ed. *Handbook of Aging and the Individual: Psychological and Biological Aspects*. Chicago: University of Chicago Press, 1959.

Birren, James E., and K. Warner Schaie, eds. *Handbook of the Psychology of Aging*. (3rd ed.) Orlando: Academic Press, 1990.

Blechschmidt, Erich. *The Beginnings of Human Life*. New York: Springer-Verlag, 1977

Blos, Peter. *On Adolescence: A Psychoanalytic Interpretation*. New York: Free Press, 1962.

Botstein, Leon. *Jefferson's Children: Education and the Promise of American Culture*. New York: Doubleday, 1997.

Bradley, Michael J. *Yes, Your Teen is Crazy!: Loving Your Kid Without Losing Your Mind*. Gig Harbor, Wash.: Harbor Press, 2001.

Breger, Louis. *Freud: Darkness in the Midst of Vision*. New York: Wiley, 2000.

Brigham, Thomas A. *Self-Management for Adolescents: A Skills Training Program*. New York: Guilford Press, 1989.

Brown, B. Bradford, Reed W. Larson, and T. S. Saraswathi, eds. *The World's Youth: Adolescence in Eight Regions of the Globe*. Cambridge: Cambridge University Press, 2002.

Carter, Jimmy. *An Hour Before Daylight*. New York: Simon & Schuster, 2001.

Church, Charlotte. *Voice of an Angel: My Life (So Far)*. New York: Warner Books, 2001.

Clark, Ronald, W. *Freud: The Man and the Cause*. New York: Random House, 1980.

Cohen, Phil. *Rethinking the Youth Question: Education, Labour, and Cultural Studies*. Durham: Duke University Press, 1999.

Cohn, Ilene, and Guy S. Goodwin-Gill. *Child Soldiers: The Role of Children in Armed Conflicts*. Oxford: Oxford University Press, 1997.

Coles, Robert. *The Youngest Parents: Teenage Pregnancy as It Shapes Lives*. New York: Norton, 1997.

Coles, Robert. *The Moral Life of Children*. Boston: Atlantic Monthly Press, 2000.

Csikszentmihalyi, Mihaly, and R. Larson. *Being Adolescent: Conflict and Growth in the Teenage Years*. New York: Basic Books, 1984.

Csikszentmihalyi, Mihaly, Kevin Rathunde, Samuel Whalen, and Maria Wong. *Talented Teenagers: The Roots of Success and Failure*. Cambridge: Cambridge University Press, 1997.

Csikszentmihalyi, Mihaly, and Barbara Schneider. *Becoming Adult: How Teenagers Prepare for the World of Work*. New York: Basic Books, 2000.

Cunningham, Hugh. *Children & Childhood: In Western Society Since 1500*. White Plains, New York: Longman Publishing, 1995.

Cushman, K. *Fires in the Bathroom: Advice for Teachers from High School Students*. New York: New Press, 2003.

Davis, Allen F. *American Heroine: The Life and Legend of Jane Addams*. New York: Oxford University Press, 1973.

Degler, Carl N. *Out of Our Past: The Forces That Shaped Modern America*. 3rd ed. New York: HarperCollins, 1984.

Dellasega, Cheryl. *Surviving Ophelia: Mothers Share Their Wisdom in Navigating the Tumultuous Teenage Years*. Cambridge, Mass.: Perseus, 2001.

DeLoache, Judy, and Alma Gottlieb. *A World of Babies: Imagined Childcare for Seven Societies*. New York: Cambridge University Press, 2000.

Dolan, Edward F. *Protect Your Legal Rights: A Handbook for Teenagers*. New York: Julian Messner, 1983.

Eliot, Marc. *Walt Disney: Hollywood's Dark Prince*. New York: HarperCollins, 1993.

Elkind, David. *All Grown Up and No Place to Go: Teenagers in Crisis*. Reading, Mass.: Addison-Wesley, 1998.

Elkind, David. *The Hurried Child: Growing Up Too Fast Too Soon*. Menlo Park, Calif.: Addison-Wesley, 1981.

Elshtain, Jean B., ed. *The Jane Addams Reader*. New York: Basic Books, 2002.

Erikson, Erik H. *Childhood and Society*. New York: Norton 1963.

Erikson, Erik H. *Identity: Youth and Crisis*. New York: Norton, 1968.

Esman, Aaron H., ed. *The Psychology of Adolescence: Essential Readings*. New York: International Press, 1975.

Eyre, Linda, and Richard Eyre. *Teaching Your Children Responsibility*. New York: Simon & Schuster, 1984.

Farson, Richard. *Birthrights: A Bill of Rights for Children*. New York: Macmillan, 1974.

Feldman, S., and G. Elliott, eds. *At the Threshold: The Developing Adolescent*. Cambridge, Mass.: Harvard University Press.

Fields, Doug. *Too Old Too Soon*. Eugene, Ore.: Harvest House, 1991.

Flach, Frederic. *Resilience: Discovering a New Strength at Times of Stress*. Hatherleigh Press, 2003.

Flavell, J. H. *The Developmental Psychology of Jean Piaget*. New York: Van Nostrand Reinhold, 1963.

Foster, Henry H. Jr. *A "Bill of Rights" for Children*. Springfield, Ill.: Charles C. Thomas, 1974.

Frank, Anne. *Anne Frank: The Diary of A Young Girl*. New York: Doubleday, 1952.

Freud, Sigmund. *Civilization and Its Discontents*. New York: Norton, 1961.

Freud, Sigmund. *Introductory Lectures on Psychoanalysis*. New York: Norton, 1966.

Furman, Wyndol, B. Bradford Brown, and Candice Feiring, eds. *The Development of Romantic Relationships in Adolescence*. Cambridge: Cambridge University Press, 1999.

Furstenberg, F. Frank, J. Brooks-Gunn, and S. Philip Morgan. *Adolescent Mothers in Later Life*. Cambridge: Cambridge University Press, 1987.

Fussell, E., & Furstenberg, F. F., Jr. (2005). The transition to adulthood during the twentieth century: Race, nativity, and gender. In R. A. Settersten, Jr., F. F. Furstenberg, Jr., & R. G. Rumbaut, eds. *On the Frontier of Adulthood: Theory, Research, and Public Policy* (pp. 29–75). Chicago, University of Chicago Press.

Garbarino, James. *Lost Boys: Why Our Sons Turn Violent and How We Can Save Them*. New York: Free Press, 1999.

Garbarino, James. *Raising Children in a Socially Toxic Environment*. San Francisco:

Jossey-Bass, 1999.

Garbarino, James. *See Jane Hit: Why Girls Are Growing More Violent and What We Can Do About It.* New York: Penguin, 2006.

Garvey, Mark. *Searching for Mary: An Exploration of Marian Apparitions Across the U.S.* New York: PenguinBooks, 1998.

Gatto, John Taylor. *The Underground History of American Education,* New York: Odysseus Group, 2001.

Golding, William. *Lord of the Flies.* New York: Capricorn Books, 1954.

Gordon, Thomas. *Parent Effectiveness Training: The Tested New Way to Raise Responsible Children.* New York: PenguinBooks, 1975.

Graff, Harvey J. *Conflicting Paths: Growing Up in America.* Cambridge, Mass.: Harvard University Press, 1995.

Graham, Philip. *The End of Adolescence.* New York: Oxford University Press, 2004.

Greenleaf, Barbara K. *Children Through the Ages: A History of Childhood.* Lanham, Md.: Barnes & Noble Books, 1978.

Haeri, Shahla. *Law of Desire: Temporary Marriage in Shi'i Iran.* Syracuse, New York: Syracuse University Press, 1989.

Hamburg, David. *Today's Children: Creating a Future for a Generation in Crisis.* New York: Random House, 1992.

Hanawalt, Barbara A. *Growing Up in Medieval London: The Experience of Childhood in History.* Oxford, N.Y.: Oxford University Press, 1993.

Hawes, J. M., and N. R. Hiner, eds. *Children in Historical and Comparative Perspective: An International Handbook and Research Guide.* New York: Greenwood Press, 1991.

Hempelman, Kathleen A. *Teen Legal Rights: A Guide for the 90s.* Westport, Conn.: Greenwood Press, 1994.

Hiaasen, Carl. *Team Rodent: How Disney Devours the World.* New York: Ballantine, 1998.

Hine, Thomas. *The Rise and Fall of the American Teenager.* New York: Avon, 1999.

Holt, John. *Escape From Childhood: The Needs and Rights of Children.* Cambridge, Mass.: Holt Associates, 1995.

Honwana, Alcinda. *Child Soldiers in Africa.* Philadelphia, PA: University of Pennsylvania Press, 2006.

Horowitz, M. Robert, and Howard A. Davidson, eds. *Legal Rights of Children.* New York: Shepard's/ McGraw-Hill, 1984.

Horowitz, Ruth. *Teen Mothers: Citizens or Dependents?* Chicago: University of Chicago Press, 1995.

Huerre, Patrice, Martine Pagan-Reymond, and Jean-Michel Reymond. *L'Adolescence n'existe pas: Histoire des tribulations d'un artifice.* Editions Universities, 1990.

Jessor, Richard, John E. Donovan, and Frances M. Costa. *Beyond Adolescence: Problem Behavior and Young Adult Development.* Cambridge: Cambridge University Press, 1992.

Johnson, Paul. *The Birth of the Modern: World Society 1815–1830.* New York: HarperPerennial, 1991.

Kagan, J. *The Nature of the Child.* New York Basic Books, 1984.

Kett, Joseph F. *Rites of Passage: Adolescence in America, 1790 to the Present.* New York: Basic Books, 1977.

Kiel, Norman. *The Adolescent Through Fiction: A Psychological Approach.* New York: International Universities Press, 1959.

Kielburger, Craig, with Kevin Major. *Free the Children: A Young Man Fights Against Child Labor and Proves that Children Can Change the World.* New York: HarperPerennial, 1998.

Kindlon, Dan, and Michael Thompson. *Raising Cain: Protecting the Emotional Life of Boys.* New York: Ballantine, 2000.

Kleijwegt, Marc. *Ancient Youth: The Ambiguity and the Absence of Adolescence in Greco-Roman Society.* Amsterdam: J. C. Gieben, 1991.

Kirberger, K. *Teen Love: On Relationships.* Deerfield Beach, FL: Health Communications, 1999.

Kolehmainen, Janet, and Sandra Handwerk. *Teen Suicide.* Minneapolis, MN: Lerner, 1986.

Kramer, Donald T. *Legal Rights of Children.* Vol. 3. 2nd ed. New York: Shepard's/ McGraw-Hill, Inc., 1994.

Larson, Reed, B. B. Brown, and J. Mortimer (eds.). *Adolescents' Preparation for the Future: Perils and Promise.* Blackwell, 2002.

LeCroy, Craig W., and Janice Daley. *Empowering Adolescent Girls: Examining the Present and Building Skills for the Future with the Go Grrrls Program.* New York: W. W. Norton, 2001.

Lehman, Harvey C. *Age and Achievement.* Princeton, N.J.: Princeton University Press, 1953.

Lesko, Nancy. *Act Your Age!: A Cultural Construction of Adolescence.* New York: Routledge Falmer, 2001.

Levi, Giovanni, and Jean-Claude Schmitt, eds. *A History of Young People in the West: Ancient and Medieval Rites of Passage.* Cambridge, Mass.: Belknap Press, 1997.

Levine, Judith. *Harmful to Minors: The Perils of Protecting Children from Sex.* Minne-

apolis, MN: University of Minnesota Press, 2002.

Levine, Madeline. *The Price of Privilege: How Parental Pressure and Material Advantage Are Creating a Generation of Disconnected and Unhappy Kids.* New York: HarperCollins, 2006.

Lewis, S. *A Totally Alien Life-Form: Teenagers.* New York: New Press, 1996.

Liedloff, Jean. *The Continuum Concept: In Search of Lost Happiness.* Reading, Mass.: Perseus, 1977.

Linn, S. *Consuming Kids: The Hostile Takeover of Childhood.* New York: New Press, 2004.

Liptak, K. *Coming-of-Age: Traditions and Rituals Around the World.* Brookfield, Conn.: Millbrook Press, 1994.

Lumpkin, Katherine Dupre, and Dorothy Wolff Douglass. *Child Workers in America.* New York: International Publishers, 1937.

Macleod, D. *The Age of the Child: Children in America 1890–1920.* London: Prentice-Hall, 1998.

Males, Mike A. *Framing Youth: Ten Myths About the Next Generation.* Monroe, Maine: Common Courage Press, 1999.

Males, Mike A. *The Scapegoat Generation: America's War on Adolescents.* Monroe, Maine: Common Courage Press, 1996.

Maxym, Carol, and Leslie York. *Teens in Turmoil: A Path to Change for Parents, Adolescents, and Their Families.* New York: Penguin Putnam, 2000.

Mead, Margaret. *Coming of Age in Samoa: A Psychological Study of Primitive Youth for Western Civilization.* Morrow, 1973.

Mead, Margaret. *Growing Up in New Guinea: A Comparative Study of Primitive Education.* New York: Dell, 1968.

Melton, Gary B, Gerald P Koocher, and Michael J. Saks (eds.). *Children's Competence to Consent.* New York: Springer, 1983.

Mortimer, J. T., and R. W. Larson. *The Changing Adolescent Experience: Social Trends and the Transition to Adulthood.* Cambridge: Cambridge University Press, 2002.

Moses, Elissa. *The $100 Billion Allowance: How to Get Your Share of the Global Teen Market.* New York: Wiley, 2000.

Offer, Daniel, Eric Ostrov, Kenneth I. Howard, and Robert Atkinson. *The Teenage World: Adolescents' Self-Image in Ten Countries.* New York: Plenum, 1988.

Oursler, Fulton, and Will Oursler. *Father Flanagan of Boys Town.* Garden City, New York: Doubleday, 1949.

Ozment, Steven. *Ancestors: The Loving Family in Old Europe.* Cambridge, Mass.: Harvard University Press, 2001.

Ozment, Steven. *Three Behaim Boys: Growing Up in Early Modern Germany.* New Haven: Yale University Press, 1990.

Palladino, Grace . *Teenagers: An American History.* New York: Basic Books, 1996.

Piaget, Jean. *The Language and Thought of the Child.* New York: World Publishing, 1971.

Piaget, Jean. *The Origins of Intelligence in Children.* New York: W.W. Norton, 1952.

Pipher, Mary. *Reviving Ophelia: Saving the Selves of Adolescent Girls.* New York: Random House, 1994.

Platt, Anthony M. *The Child Savers: The Invention of Delinquency.* 2nd ed. Chicago: University of Chicago Press, 1977.

Pollock, Linda A. *Forgotten Children: Parent-Child Relations From 1500–1900.* Cambridge: Cambridge University Press, 1983.

Pruitt, David B., ed. *Your Adolescent: Emotional, Behavioral, and Cognitive Development from Early Adolescence through the Teen Years.* New York: HarperCollins, 1999.

Purdy, Laura M. *In Their Best Interest? The Case Against Equal Rights for Children.* Ithaca, N.Y.: Cornell University Press, 1992.

Schlegel, Alice, and Herbert Barry, III. *Adolescence: An Anthropological Inquiry.* New York: Free Press, 1991.

Schleifer, Jay. *Everything You Need to Know About Teen Suicide.* New York: Rosen, 1993.

Schor, Juliet B. *Born to Buy: The Commercialized Child and the New Consumer Culture.* New York: Simon & Schuster, 2004.

Schwartz, Gary. *Beyond Conformity or Rebellion: Youth and Authority in America.* Chicago: University of Chicago Press, 1987.

Settersten, R. A. Jr., F. F. Furstenberg Jr., and R. G. Rumbaut, eds. *On The Frontier of Adulthood: Theory, Research and Public Policy.* Chicago: University of Chicago Press, 2005.

Shaklee, H. "Inventing Adolescence: Twentieth Century Concepts of Youth Development." *Journal of Family and Consumer Science,* 2000, *92*(5), pp. 11–16.

Shorter, Edward. *The Making of the Modern Family.* New York: Basic Books, 1975.

Simmons, Rachel. *Odd Girls Out: The Hidden Culture of Aggression in Girls.* Orlando: Harcourt Brace, 2002.

Smith, Mark K. *Developing Youth Work: Informal Education, Mutual Aid and Popular Practice.* Open University Press, 1988.

Steinberg, Laurence D. *Adolescence,* 7th ed. New York: McGraw-Hill, 2004.

Stone, Lawrence. *The Family, Sex and Marriage In England 1500–1800.* New York: HarperCollins, 1979.

Stone L. Joseph, and Joseph Church. *Childhood and Adolescence: A Psychology of the Growing Person.* New York: Random House, 1957.

Taffel, Ron, and Melinda Blau. *The Second Family: How Adolescent Power Is Challenging the American Family.* New York: St. Martin's Press, 2001.

Thevenin, Tine. *Mothering and Fathering: The Gender Differences in Child Rearing.* Garden City, N.Y: Avery, 1993.

Thompson, Michael, and Teresa Baker. *Speaking of Boys: Answers to the Most-Asked Questions About Raising Sons.* New York: Ballantine, 2000.

Travers, P. L. *Mary Poppins.* New York: Harcourt Brace, 1934.

Truly, Traci. *Teen Rights: A Legal Guide for Teens and the Adults in their Lives.* Naperville, Ill.: Sphinx, 2003.

Valenstein, Elliot S. *Blaming the Brain: The Truth About Drugs and Mental Health.* New York: Free Press, 1998.

Vizzini, Ned. *Teen Angst? Naaah.: A Quasi-Autobiography.* Minneapolis, Minn.: Free Spirit, 2000.

Wagenaar, Alexander C. *Alcohol, Young Drivers, and Traffic Accidents: Effects of Minimum Age Laws.* Lexington, Mass.: Lexington Books, 1983.

Wallerstein, Judith, Julia Lewis, and Sandra Blakeslee. *The Unexpected Legacy of Divorce: A 25 Year Landmark Study.* New York: Hyperion, 2000.

Wechsler, David. *The Measurement of Adult Intelligence.* (3rd ed.) Baltimore: Williams and Wilkins, 1944.

West, Elliott, and Paula Petrik. *Small Worlds: Children & Adolescents in America, 1850–1950.* Lawrence, Kansas: University of Kansas Press, 1992.

Wiggins, Marianne. *John Dollar: A Novel.* New York: HarperCollins, 1989.

Wiley, Lulu R. *Children and Youths of the Bible.* Self-Published, 1951.

Youcha, G. *Minding the Children.* New York: Scribner, 1995.

Zimring, Franklin E. *American Youth Violence.* Oxford, N.Y.: Oxford University Press, 1998.

Zuck, Roy. B. *Precious in His Sight: Childhood and Children in the Bible.* Grand Rapids, Mich.: Baker Books, 1996.

Index

About the Author

Robert Epstein is the former Editor-in-Chief of *Psychology Today* magazine, as well as a contributing editor for *Scientific American Mind* and the host of "Psyched!" on Sirius Satellite Radio. While conducting the research described in this book, he also served as University Research Professor at the California School of Professional Psychology at Alliant International University. He is currently a visiting scholar at the University of California San Diego. In addition, Dr. Epstein is the founder and Director Emeritus of the Cambridge Center for Behavioral Studies in Massachusetts. A Ph.D. of Harvard University, he has published 12 books and more than 150 articles, and he has developed competency tests in the areas of parenting, adolescence, creativity, motivation, stress management, and relationships. He is also the proud father of four children. See http://drrobertepstein.com for further details.